# GENEALOGICAL DICTIONARY

## of

## MAINE and NEW HAMPSHIRE

BY

### SYBIL NOYES
### CHARLES THORNTON LIBBY
### WALTER GOODWIN DAVIS

GENEALOGICAL PUBLISHING CO., INC.
BALTIMORE                                    1972

Originally Published in Five Parts
Portland, 1928-1939

Reprinted
Genealogical Publishing Co., Inc.
Baltimore, 1972

*F18
.N68
1972

*Library of Congress Cataloging in Publication Data*

Noyes, Sybil, comp.
   Genealogical dictionary of Maine and New Hampshire.
   Reprint of the 1928-39 ed., which was originally published in five parts.
   1. Maine—Genealogy. 2. New Hampshire—Genealogy. I. Libby, Charles
Thornton, 1861-1948. II. Davis, Walter Goodwin, 1885-1966. III. Title.
F18.N68 1972          929.1'03          79-88099
ISBN 0-8063-0502-9

*Made in the United States of America*

# PREFACE

Nearly twenty years have elapsed since the idea of the Genealogical Dictionary of Maine and New Hampshire, to be prepared and written by Charles Thornton Libby and financed by me, took shape. Certainly no one, except perhaps some particularly gregarious contemporary, has been more familiar with the personalities, activities and life of seventeenth-century Maine than Mr. Libby. That this great store of knowledge should never become available to others, or would have to be reacquired by later students of local history and genealogy, seemed a sad waste. After seven years, much of which time was devoted to the gathering of material from original sources and which Mr. Libby felt could have been extended indefinitely with profit, I felt it wise, if my object of publication was to materialize, to call a halt to the collection of *data*, doubtless far short of perfection, and in 1928 the first part of the work appeared. The second part, in the preparation of which Miss Sybil Noyes, a very able Maine genealogist, assisted Mr. Libby, appeared in 1933, and the three succeeding parts in 1936, 1938 and 1939 respectively. It is with mingled feelings of relief and triumph that the work is brought to a conclusion with the issue of these final sheets.

Although that title is spread across the top of twenty-eight pages, it will be most unfair to Miss Noyes, and in a less degree to me, to cite the book as "Libby's Genealogical Dictionary." After the publication of Part II, ending with the family of Frye, Mr. Libby abandoned the task, and its completion, involving patient collation of scattered and often inadequate material, genealogical judgment, intensive library work and some original research, fell to Miss Noyes with such aid as I could give her. Mr. Libby wrote the account of certain families (Gorges, Hutchinson, Jordan, Libby and portions of others) in Part III, and acted as a consultant in problems in which he was known to have a personal interest, but his deep-seated conviction that the book should not be published at all did not make for an entirely happy situation. Certainly he should not be considered responsible for any genealogical conclusions reached after the time of his withdrawal.

To professional and experienced genealogists dilation on the possibility of error is unnecessary. The dictionary contains hundreds of thousands of statements of fact as well as of judgment. Needless to say, some of them are erroneous. We do wish to emphasize, however, that in our opinion the last word has not been said on any of the families herein treated. The deep mine of original and public records was far from exhausted. In some cases, in fact, it was admittedly subjected to a mere surface spading, and concentrated work on one instead of a thousand families may yet produce rich rewards.

Thanks are due to many for aid and encouragement. To the late Col. Charles E. Banks, who at the outset turned over his two great manuscript volumes of Maine genealogies, now in the Bangor Public Library. To the late Rev. Everett S. Stackpole, the historian of Kittery. To Charles H. Batchelder, whose knowledge of early New Hampshire genealogy and topography has been invaluable. To the late M. A. C. Shackford, who should have been the historian of Dover. In addition to those who have given valuable aid with their own ancestry, gratitude for more general assistance goes to Mary Lovering Holman, Elizabeth French Bartlett, Donald L. Jacobus, Samuel B.

Shackford, Charles W. Tibbetts, Wilbur D. Spencer, George A. Moriarty, Jr., and Clarence A. Torrey. That the dictionary may be of use to genealogists of their calibre is the highest hope that we have for it.

Walter Goodwin Davis

Portland, Maine
August 18, 1939.

# EXTRACTS FROM MR. LIBBY'S PREFACES

I hope that the time-consuming work on the Lists has not been misspent. Certainly this method saves much space and broadens the vision, acting as an antidote for the narrowing affect of ancestor hunting as sometimes pursued. There is a special reason for this method in Maine. By far the greater part of those who came here removed elsewhere, all the way from Massachusetts to Carolina and the West Indies, and the same was to a large extent true of New Hampshire. I have thought it important to distinguish real men of unfamiliar names, even a name that occurs in our records but once, from mere "shadow men" who never existed except by such errors as misreading obsolete or faded handwriting. First and last much historical work has been done by people whose eyesight had failed or who were unfamiliar with ancient records and documents. Even experts blunder in deciphering blind writing of unknown names. If my work results eventually in identifying some of our short-time residents in their future homes, the general course of colonization will become better understood, and, to the point, it may lead to the discovery of now unknown wives and mothers. The resort to citing and indexing, instead of reprinting, more than quadrupled the number of lists practical to use, but this method was confined strictly to books found in all historical libraries. It was intended to print civil and military lists for each town unless this had been done in a town history, but the limit of space prevented, after the Saco list was in type.

The limit of 1692 set for Savage's Genealogical Dictionary of New England is here extended seven years to 1699, and as Vermont was then unsettled the present work amounts to a "Savage" for Northern New England. Beyond this I try to give the marriages and deaths of the third generation, instead of only the births. In rare instances, where it has been necessary to solve problems in the fourth generation in order to keep the earlier generations straight, the results are printed, but in general only a count of noses can be given of the children of parents married shortly before or after the year 1699.

Doubtless the large number of surnames appearing, even for a day, among so small populations as New Hampshire and Maine had in the seventeenth century will surprise many. Of these not a few have been handed down in distant parts, but of English surnames that have once existed, it is probable that a large majority are extinct. Those still existing could by easy invention be multiplied a hundred fold. To one who has not slept with the variant pronunciations and spellings (and misreadings) of English surnames in former days, one extraordinary variation seems as likely as another, with the result that quite impossible notions are commonly seen in print, whereas an almost incredible divergence may be in strict accord with well established trends. Instances will be found in these pages.

# EXPLANATIONS

The arrangement is mainly the same as in Savage's Genealogical Dictionary of New England except that each head of a family is given a paragraph and numbered.

Under each surname the heads of families are arranged alphabetically, regardless of generations, and the figure following a name refers the reader to the paragraph treating of that person's parentage, not always fully proven.

Through each paragraph the names of the children are distinguished by bold face type. A question mark against the number of children does not imply doubt whether the person had children, but how many—usually more.

Modern spellings prevailing in New England are used for surnames that have been perpetuated. Such as have become extinct are modernized according to the general trend of similar names, whenever it is clear what sound the ancient spelling stood for; otherwise the obsolete spelling is followed, usually with no attempt at cross references.

Dates have been modernized when safe to do so. But some dates taken from print do not disclose whether modernized or not, and are copied as found; where important, resort to the original records is necessary in some cases. Quaker records of months, many of them improvised a half-century afterwards, are treacherous.

The figures for the relative frequency of New England surnames are reckoned from the 1790 census, after the infusion of Scotch-Irish names but before the more recent multiplication from other countries.

The symbols used in "Savage" and in Farmer's Register are used from page 73 onward:

§, Governor or President.    †, Deputy Governor.    ‡, Assistant or Councillor.    *, Representative.    ‖, member of the Ancient & Honorable Artillery Company.

There is no cross index, partly because the book itself is an index, partly to encourage initiative among beginners in genealogy, who should be made to realize that there were many persons of the same name in old days as now. The place of a cross index is imperfectly supplied by the cross references.

# TOPOGRAPHY

Space has not been taken up for clarifying each reference to a locality, rather assuming a degree of familiarity with New England topography on the reader's part. The following table will partly supply deficiencies on either side, but the cutting up of large into small townships, with changes of names and governments, sometimes involving duplication, makes it necessary to watch one's step, especially because of the course here followed, stating what modern town a man lived in if known, otherwise the ancient town now cut up into many.

**Acadia,** once French name for Nova Scotia, including most of Maine.

**Agamenticus,** see York.

**Alna,** see Sheepscot.

**Amoriscoggin River,** the Androscoggin.

**Andrews' Island,** now Cushing's, Casco Bay.

**Arrowsic Island,** Newtown under Gov. Andros, set off from Georgetown as Arrowsic in 1841.

**Arundel, Kennebunkport,** see Cape Porpus.

**Back Cove,** see Deering.

**Back River,** the tide water west of Dover Neck; regional name for Madbury.

**Bagaduce,** now Castine, Me.

**Ball Island,** now Rutherford's, South Bristol.

**Bath,** see Georgetown.

**Berwick,** Newichawannock, Unity Parish. See Kittery.

**Biddeford,** Saco so named in 1718, after Bideford, co. Devon, England.

**Black Point,** (Prout's Neck), Stratton's Island, early regional names for the country between Spurwink and Winter Harbor. See Scarborough.

**Bloody Point,** a tax district of Dover, primarily the point in Newington opposite Dover Point, became the chief part of Newington.

**Blue Point,** see Scarborough.

**Boiling Rock,** Portsmouth, Kittery.

**Braveboat Harbor,** see Kittery.

**Brentwood,** see Exeter.

**Bride Hill,** Hampton, the nearest neighborhood to Exeter, Stratham and Greenland.

**Bristol.** Sundry attempts were made to name a town for Bristol, England. Dover Neck is marked Bristol on an early map. Mr. Maverick called York Bristol. The earliest to endure is Bristol on the Massachusetts-Rhode Island frontier. Pemaquid was incorporated as Bristol in 1765.

**Broad Bay,** the head of the Muscongus River.

**Brunswick,** Pejepscot and Maquoit, incorporated in 1715 and 1788.

**Cape Bonawagon,** Cape Newagen, a fishing station by 1624, appar. the outer point of Southport. In the Kennebec Purchase map, 1765, the whole length of Southport is marked "Cape-naiggen Island."

**Cape Elizabeth,** first a landmark, then a region, then a township including Spurwink, Richmond Island and Purpooduck. See Falmouth, South Portland.

**Cape Neddick,** a small settlement which Massachusetts included within York township.

**Cape Newagen,** see Cape Bonawagon.

**Cape Porpus,** a small settlement in early times somewhat tributary to Saco (Winter Harbor) or to Wells. Renamed Arundel in 1717, Kennebunkport in 1821; yet made two towns in 1915.

**Cape Porpus River,** now the Mousam, in Kennebunk, but rarely applied to a small stream in Cape Porpus.

**Capisic,** Falmouth, later in Westbrook, later Deering, now Portland.

**Casco Bay,** see Portland and Wescustogo.

**Casco River,** the Presumpscot, or by some claimed to be Portland Harbor.

**Cathance,** a settlement on Merrymeeting Bay, now in Bowdoinham.

**Cochecho,** the present town (city) of Dover.

**Cochecho Point,** the tip of Dover on Rollinsford side.

**Cold Harbor,** Eliot, see Kittery.

**Concord, N. H.,** altered from Rumford, settled as part of Massachusetts at Penacook.

**Corbin's Sound,** the sound east or south of Ocean Point, Boothbay.

**Cornwall,** Sagadahoc. See p. 2.

**Crooked Lane,** see Kittery.

**Cumberland,** see North Yarmouth.

**Cumberland Mills,** Ammoncongin, see Westbrook.

**Damariscove,** Damarell's Cove, see List 8.

**Deering,** included Back Cove, Stroudwater, Woodford's, Morrill's, set off from Westbrook and later annexed to Portland.

**Devonshire,** a name for Sagadahoc contemplated by Mass. just before New York took possession.

**Dover,** had been called Hilton's Point, Upper Piscataqua, Bristol, Northam, before it was incorporated as Dover in 1640. It included Durham, Newington, Somersworth, Rollinsford, Madbury and Lee.

**Dover Neck,** site of the pioneer town of Dover, now a farming district.

**Dover Point,** Hilton Point.

**Dunstan,** west Scarborough, named for a hamlet in Yealmpton, co. Devon.

**Durham,** Oyster River, see Dover.

**Eliot,** set off in 1810. See Kittery.

**Eppeford,** Merryland (now in Wells), Great Plains, Mousam (now in Kennebunk), names designating the interior of ancient Wells, from the bounds of York eastward.

**Epping,** see Exeter.

**Exeter,** besides Stratham, was divided into Newfields, Newmarket, Brentwood, Epping and Fremont.

**Falmouth, Me.,** "in Casco Bay," lost Cape Elizabeth, Portland, Westbrook, leaving only that part east of Presumpscot River.

**Falmouth Foreside,** New Casco, the frontage on Casco Bay of modern Falmouth.

**Fore River,** Portland Harbor.

**Fore River,** the tide water east of Dover Neck, including the lower Cochecho.

**Freeport,** see North Yarmouth.

**Fresh Creek,** above Cochecho Point.

**Fresh River,** Exeter.

**Georgetown,** as incorporated in 1716, included a new settlement on Arrowsic Island, with the unoccupied territory now Bath, Woolwich, Phipsburg, and the present Georgetown, or Parker's Island.

**Gorgeana,** a city, see York.

**Gosport,** New Hampshire's part of the Isles of Shoals from 1715 until annexed to Rye.

**Great Cove,** see Kittery.

**Great Island,** New Castle, for years the commercial and political center of New Hampshire. Early a tax district of Portsmouth; later included north part of the present Rye; incorporated in 1693.

**Greenland,** the name that Capt. Champernowne gave his farm, later a tax district of Portsmouth, later made a town.

**Harpswell,** see North Yarmouth.

**Harraseeket,** and River, Freeport.

**Hawke,** now Danville, set off from Exeter.

**Hilton's Point,** Dover Point, the tip of Dover Neck.

**Hog Island,** Appledore, Isles of Shoals.

**Holmes' Island,** appar. Ball, now Rutherford's, South Bristol.

**Hypocris,** now Fisherman's Island, Boothbay.

**Isles of Shoals** (Appledore), chiefly in Maine (Hog, Smuttynose, Cedar, Duck); three in New Hampshire, incorporated as Gosport (Star, White, Lunging).

**Jamestown,** Pemaquid, List 124.

**Jeremisquam Island,** now Westport.

**Jeremisquam Neck,** the easternmost point of Woolwich.

**John's Bay,** west of Pemaquid Point.

**Kennebunk,** set off in 1820 from the easterly end of Wells. See Mousam.

**Kennebunk River,** the ancient bounds between Cape Porpus and Wells.

**Kennebunkport,** see Cape Porpus.

**Kittery,** at first the neighborhood opposite Dover Point. The Maine side of the Piscataqua River was early called Piscataqua below, Newichawannock above; later the whole was included in Kittery township, over 25 miles long by the river. Localities along this stretch were distinguished (* indicates regional names used for both sides of the river) as Braveboat Harbor, River's Mouth or The Point, Spruce Creek, Crooked Lane, Great Cove (Eliot line, nearly opposite Newington line), *Boiling Rock, *Long Reach, Kittery, Cold Harbor, Sturgeon Creek, *Thompson's Point (South Berwick line), *Newichawannock, *Quamphegan, *Salmon Falls (on the Berwick line opposite Rollinsford), *Great Falls (Berwick and Somersworth).

**Laconia Plantation,** List 41.

**Lamprey River,** formerly the bounds between Durham and Newmarket, now wholly in Newmarket.

**Lee,** set off from Durham. See Dover.

**Little Harbor,** primarily a harbor, the regional name for the bank of the Piscataqua west of Great Island.

**Long Reach,** see Kittery.

**Lubberland,** the region in Durham north of the Lamprey River.

**Lygonia,** Plow Patent. See p. 4.

**Madbury,** Back River, see Dover.

**Maquoit,** the head of Casco Bay, now in Brunswick. See Wescustogo.

**Matinicus Island,** outside Penobscot Bay, claimed by the Penobscot Indians until the fall of Quebec.

**Merryland,** see Wells, Eppeford.

**Merrymeeting Bay,** where the Androscoggin meets the Kennebec, bordered by Bath, Bowdoinham and Woolwich.

**Mousam,** Kennebunk. See Cape Porpus River, Eppeford.

**Muscongus,** see Pemaquid.

**New Castle,** see Great Island.

**Newfields,** South Newmarket, see Exeter.

**New Harbor,** a small harbor about two miles across the peninsula from Pemaquid Harbor, so called in a forged document 33 years before first mentioned in a genuine paper.

**Newichawannock,** see Kittery.

**Newington,** Bloody Point, Long Reach, incorporated in 1714. See Dover, Kittery.

**Newmarket,** see Exeter, Newfields.

**Newmeadows,** early name of the settlement on both sides of that river, between Harpswell and Georgetown.

**New Somersetshire,** earlier name for Gorges's Maine.

**Newtown, Me.** See List 19.

**Newtown, N. H.,** Wheelwright's Pond, Lee.

**Nonsuch,** an Indian locality east of Oak Hill, Scarborough, which gave name to the river there and to Nonsuch Point in Portland Harbor.

**Northam,** Dover. List 351a.

**North Yarmouth,** now Yarmouth, having lost Harpswell, Freeport (which included Pownal), Cumberland and—

**North Yarmouth,** modern, the late-settled lands back of the original town, which lost both name and records.

**Ogunquit,** a small separate settlement which Massachusetts included within Wells township.

**Old Orchard,** the ocean front of Saco, set off in 1883.

**Oyster River,** Durham, a tax district and parish of Dover set off in 1732.

**Parker's Island,** now the town of Georgetown.

**Pejepscot,** originally the falls at Brunswick, later a regional name, now strayed away upriver.

**Pemaquid,** anciently included New Harbor and Muscongus, named Jamestown under Gov. Andros, now Bristol.

**Penacook,** see Concord.

**Pepperellboro,** see Saco.

**Phipsburg,** site of the Popham Colony. See Georgetown, Winnegance.

**Piscataqua.** The pioneers recognized two settlements, Upper and Lower, each taking in the settlers on both sides of the river. Among mariners the name long persisted for the whole river. See Portsmouth, Kittery, Dover.

**Plymouth,** in early Me. and N. H. papers, often meant Plymouth, Eng.

**Popham Colony,** Phipsburg. List 6.

**Portland,** first applied by mariners to Portland Head, Sound, Passage, Island, in Cape Elizabeth, at the entrance of the southerly passage to Portland harbor; selected in 1786 as the name for town, three miles distant, when Falmouth Neck was set off from Falmouth.

**Portsmouth,** grew into a city at Strawberry Bank, originally included New Castle, that part of Rye north of Locke's Neck (Straw's Point), Greenland and part of Newington.

**Pownal,** set off from Freeport.

**Pownalborough,** now Dresden, formerly included Wiscasset and Alna.

**Pownal Fort,** Fort Point, Stockton.

**Prouts Neck,** the original Black Point.

**Purpooduck,** Pooduck, South Portland.

**Quamphegan,** South Berwick, see Kittery.

**Rascohegan,** Parker's Island, Georgetown.

**Richmond Island,** the oldest regional name between Winter Harbor and Sagadahoc. See Cape Elizabeth.

**Rollinsford,** Quamphegan and Salmon Falls, set off from Somersworth.

**Round Pond,** so called by 1641, Broad Bay.

**Rye,** the name selected in 1726 when all the mainland of New Castle was set off except seven estates (added in 1791) ; additions from Hampton in 1730 and 1738.

**Saccarappa,** now Westbrook.

**Saco,** Winter Harbor, early regional names. Massachusetts incorporated both sides of the river as Saco, and even after the south side had become Biddeford and the north side Pepperelboro, the name Saco long persisted for the region about the falls. Pepperellboro, so named when set off from Biddeford (1762) was later renamed Saco. Old Orchard was set off from Saco.

**Sagadahoc,** see p. 2, List 101.

**Sagadahoc Island,** now Stage, the early Sagadahoc fishing station outside Georgetown.

**Sagamore Creek,** lower Portsmouth, partly in Rye.

**Salmon Falls,** Rollinsford, see Kittery.

**Sandy Beach,** see Rye.

**Scarborough,** township created by Massachusetts from Black Point, Blue Point, Dunstan, and the western edge of Spurwink.

**Sheepscot,** later New Dartmouth, now the parts of Newcastle and Alna on the Sheepscot River.

**Shrewsbury Patent,** Stratham, List 386.

**Smuttynose,** see Isles of Shoals.

**Somersworth,** Great Falls, see Dover.

**South Portland**, Purpooduck, a city set off from the town of Cape Elizabeth, which was set off from Falmouth.

**Spruce Creek**, see Kittery.

**Spurwink**, an early regional name. See Cape Elizabeth, Scarborough.

**Squamscot**, see Stratham.

**St. George's River**, see Sagadahoc, p. 2.

**Star Island**, Isles of Shoals, Gosport.

**Stevens River**, the higher part of Newmeadows River, separating Cumberland and Sagadahoc Counties.

**Stratham**, set off from Exeter in 1716, includes most of the Squamscot patent, part of which went to Exeter, part to Portsmouth (Greenland), and a little probably to Hampton. See Dow's Hampton, p. 63.

**Stratton Island**, between Prout's Neck and Old Orchard, an early regional name for Scarborough.

**Strawberry Bank**, a neck between creeks which grew into the town (city) of Portsmouth.

**Stroudwater**, set off from Falmouth with Westbrook and annexed to Portland with Deering.

**Sturgeon Creek**, Eliot, see Kittery.

**Swan Island**, in the Kennebec, once in Pownalboro, from 1847 to 1917 the town of Perkins.

**Tatnick**, a neighborhood at the head-line of South Berwick, adjoining Wells and land taken from York.

**Thompson's Point**, the lower point at the mouth of the Cochecho River; a regional name for that stretch of the Piscataqua. See Kittery. Also a point in Dover; see Landmarks of Ancient Dover, 2d edition, p. 251.

**Two Beacon Marsh** was up Damariscotta River; Two Beacon Gut appar. north of Rutherford's Island, South Bristol.

**Wells**, planted as a town on the Webhannet River; made a township by Massachusetts to include Ogunquit and Kennebunk. See Eppeford.

**Wescustogo**, North Yarmouth, sometimes called Casco Bay.

**Westbrook**, set off from Falmouth, includes Saccarappa and Cumberland Mills. See Deering.

**Widgins** (Hubbard's Ind. Wars and Hist. of Boothbay), presum. -Widger's-, settlement of James Widger (poss. Jeremisquam Neck?)

**Winnegance**, now East Boothbay, the vicinity of the Indian carrying place between Winnegance or Linekin's Bay and the Damariscotta River.

**Winnegance**, now the town line between Bath and Phipsburg, the Indian carrying place between the Sagadahoc and Casco Bay.

**Winter Harbor**, Biddeford Pool, where Richard Vines proved that white men can endure New England winters. See Saco.

**Wiscasset**, formerly East Pownalborough, earlier seaboard Sheepscot.

**Wiscasset (Whichcasset) Bay**, in 1765 the bay next inland from the upper end of Southport.

**Woolwich**, Nequasset, Tuessic, see Georgetown.

**Yarmouth, Me.**, the present name of the original North Yarmouth.

**York**, called Agamenticus by Indians, mariners and merchants, Bristol by Mr. Maverick, Gorgeana by Sir F. Gorges; later was called East York and for many years Old York, so long as New York was known among mariners as York.

# ABBREVIATIONS

± more or less, about
*a. acre
ab. about
aband. abandon
abs. absent
abut. abutting, abuttor
acc. account, accused
access. accessible, accessory
accid. accident
accom. accommodate
accred. accredit
acct. account
accus. accusation
ack. acknowledge
acq. acquaint, acquire, acquit
adj. adjacent, adjoin
adm. administer, -trator, admit
adm. c.t.a. administrator cum testamento annexo
adm. d.b.n. administrator de bonis non
advan. advantage
aft. after
afterw. afterward
ag. against, aged
agreem. agreement
al. alleg. allegiance
anc. ancient
ano. another
ans. answer
antic. anticipate
app. appear, appoint
appar. apparent
appr. appraise, apprentice
appt. appointment
arr. arrive
assess. assessor
assignm. assignment
asso., assoc. associate
atten. attention
attrib. attribute
aut. autograph
author. authority
b. born
bap., bp. baptized
bast. bastard
bec. because
bef. before
beh. behalf
bel. belong
benef. benefit, beneficiary
beq. bequest
bes. besides
bet., betw. between
biog. biographer
bookk. bookkeeper
bot bought
br., bro. brother
brot brought
bur. buried
bus. business
c. circa
carp. carpenter
capt. captain, captive, captivity
cert. certain
ch. child, -ren, church
char., -ac. character
childh. childhood
chron. chronology
cit. citizen
co. company, county
cod. codicil
coll. collect, college
collat. collateral
com. command, commission, committee
comb., -in. combination
comp. company
compen. compensation
compl. complain
com. t.e.s.c. commissioner to end small causes

conc. concern
concub. concubine
cond. condition
conf., -id. confidence
conn., -ec. connection
conserv. conservator
consis. consistent
const. constable, constant
cont., -in. continue, continual
contemp. contemplate, contemporary
contr. contract
conv. convey, convention
cor.j. coroner's jury
cous. cousin
covt. covenant
cr., cred. creditor
critic. criticising
crim. criminal
ct. court
c.t.a. cum testamento annexo
d. day, death, died
d.s.p. died sine prole (without issue)
d.y. died young
dau. daughter
dea., -c. deacon
dec. decease
decl. decline, declining, declaration
defend., deft. defendant
degen. degenerate
dep. deputy
dep., -os. depose, deposition
desc. descendant
devel. develop, -ment
diff. different, difficult
diffic. difficult
disal. disallow
disapp. disappear, disappoint
discl. disclosed
disconc. disconcert
dishon. dishonored
dism. dismiss
disord. disorder
dist. distant, distinguish, distribute
div. divide, division
domin. dominant, dominate
dwg. dwelling
effic. efficient
elab. elaborate
eld. elder, eldest
elsew. elsewhere
emigr. emigrant, emigrate
emin. eminent
empl. employ, employer
ent. enter, entire
entert. entertain
enum. enumerate, enumeration
esc. escape
espec. especial
est. estate
estab. establish
ev., evid. evident, evidence
event. eventual
exc. except
excel. excellent
exch. exchange
excl. exclude
exec. execute, execution, executor
exp. expense
exped., expdn. expedition
expl. explain
explic. explicit
extr. extreme
extric. extricate
exub. exuberance
f., fa. father
fam. family
fav. favor
fig. figure

| | | | |
|---|---|---|---|
| flour. | flourish | lieut. | lieutenant |
| fol., foll. | follow | lightn. | lightning |
| foreg. | foregoing | litig. | litigant, litigation, litigious |
| forem. | foreman | liv. | lived, living |
| forf. | forfeit | lux. | luxurious |
| form. | former | m. | married, mile, more, mother |
| furn. | furniture | main., -t. | maintain, maintenance |
| garri. | garrison | manif. | manifest |
| gdn. | guardian | matric. | matriculate |
| gen. | general, generation | med. | medicine |
| geneal. | genealogy | meet. | meeting |
| gent. | gentleman | mem. | memory |
| goodm. | goodman | mem., -b. | member |
| goodw. | goodwife | ment. | mention |
| gov., -t. | governor, government | merch., -t. | merchant |
| gr. | grand, great, grant | mid. | middle |
| grandp. | grandparent | milit. | militant, military, militia |
| grch. | grandchild, -ren | min. | minister |
| grd. | granddaughter | misc., -l. | miscellaneous |
| grfa. | grandfather | misdem. | misdemeanor |
| gr.j. | grand jury | mispl. | misspelling |
| grmo. | grandmother | misrep. | misrepresent |
| grs. | grandson | misr. | misreading |
| gr. st. | gravestone | mo. | month, mother |
| handwr. | handwriting | mortg., mtg. | mortgage |
| harb. | harbor | murd. | murder, murderous |
| hers. | herself | nar. | narrative |
| hims. | himself | nat. | natural |
| hist. | history | navig. | navigate |
| ho. | house | negot. | negotiate |
| h.h. | household | neigh. | neighbor, neighborhood |
| honor. | honorable | neph. | nephew |
| housek. | housekeeping | n.c.m. | non compos mentis |
| housewr. | housewright | nunc. | nuncupative |
| husb. | husband | oblig. | obligation |
| illeg. | illegal, illegible, illegitimate | obscur. | obscurity |
| illegit. | illegitimate | obv. | obvious |
| imag. | imagination, imaginary | o. c. | owned covenant |
| immed. | immediate | occa. | occasion |
| imp., -oss. | impossible | occu., -p. | occupy, occupant, occupational |
| impart. | impartial | off., offic. | office, official |
| implic. | implication | oppo. | opposite |
| import. | important | oppor. | opportunity |
| impris. | imprison, imprisonment | ord. | order, ordain |
| impuls. | impulsive | ordin. | ordination |
| inc., -l. | include, inclusive | organ. | organize, organization |
| incid. | incident, incidental | orig. | original |
| inconseq. | inconsequential | otherw. | otherwise |
| incorp. | incorporate | outl. | outlive |
| incumb. | incumbent | overthr. | overthrow |
| indebt. | indebtedness | p. a. | power of attorney |
| indel. | indelibly | par. | parent, parish |
| indent. | indenture | part., -n. | partner, partnership |
| indic. | indicate, indicative | partic. | participate, particular |
| indictm. | indictment | pecul. | peculiar |
| inf. | infant | perh. | perhaps |
| infant. | infanticide | perm. | permission, permanent |
| infl. | influence | pet., ptn. | petition |
| inform. | information | phonet. | phonetic |
| inhab. | inhabitant | pl., plaint. | plaintiff |
| inher. | inherit, inheritance | plaus. | plausible |
| inq. | inquest | polit. | political |
| ins., insolv. | insolvent | poss. | possible |
| insubserv. | insubserviency | possib. | possibility |
| int. | interest, intend, intention, intestate | post. | posterity |
| intest. | intestate | posth. | posthumous |
| interp. | interpret, interpretation | pract. | practice, practically |
| interpol. | interpolated | predec. | predecessor |
| intox. | intoxication | premat. | prematurely |
| inv., invent. | inventory | prepar. | preparatory |
| invar. | invariable | pres. | present |
| invit. | invitation | presum. | presumably |
| irresp. | irresponsible | prev. | previous |
| isl. | island | primogen. | primogeniture |
| iss. | issue | prin. | principal |
| item. | itemized | priv. | privilege |
| j. | jury | prob. | probable, probate |
| judgm. | judgment | prof. | professional |
| judic. | judicial | prog. | progeny, progress |
| k. | killed | progen. | progenitor |
| kn. | known | prom. | prominent, promissory |
| leav. | leaving | prop. | property, proprietor |
| leg. | legatee | propr. | proprietor |
| lic. | license | prosec. | prosecute, prosecution |

prov.  proved, provide, province, provisional
prtd.  printed
pub.  public, publish
purch.  purchase
pursu.  pursuant
q.c.  quitclaim
quest.  questionable
rec.  record, receive
recog.  recognition
recom.  recommend
reconc.  reconcile
recur.  recurrent
r. e.  real estate
reg.  register
rel.  relative, release
relat.  relation, relative, relationship
rem.  remain, remove
remem., -b.  remember
rep.  represent, representative
req.  request, require
res.  reside, resident
resid.  resident, residuary
ret.  retire, return
riv.  river
s.  son
s. and h.  son and heir
selectm.  selectman
serv.  servant, service
sev.  several
sett.  settled, settler
sh.  share
sher.  sheriff
shipwr.  shipwright
simul.  simultaneous
sis.  sister
sold.  soldier
solic.  solicit
spec., -ul.  speculator, speculation
statem.  statement
stipul.  stipulation
subcon.  subconscious
subm.  submit, submission
subp.  subpoena
subscr.  subscribe
subseq.  subsequent
succ.  successful, successive, successor
sud.  sudden
suff.  sufficient
sum.  summons
super.  superintendent
supp.  support, suppose
surm.  surmise
surn.  surname
surpr.  surprise
surv.  survive, survivor
susp.  suspect, suspicion
sw.  sworn
tav.  tavern
temp., -o.  temporary
test.  testify, testimony
townsh.  township
trad.  tradition
trans.  transfer, transient, transit, translate
trav.  travel
unag.  unaggressive
unasc.  unascertain
unbrid.  unbridled
uncond.  unconditional
unconn.  unconnected
unders.  understanding
undeter.  undetermined
undisc.  undisclosed, undiscovered
undiv.  undivided
unfort.  unfortunate
unkn.  unknown
unm.  unmarried
unnec.  unnecessary
unobtr.  unobtrusive
unrel.  unrelated
uns.  unsolved
untang.  untangled
unus.  unusual
valua.  valuable, valuation
var.  varied, variant, various

verd.  verdict
verif.  verify, verification
vicin.  vicinity
vict.  victuals, victualers
vols.  volunteers
volun.  voluntary
vs.  versus
w.  wife
war., -r.  warrant
wh.  which
whereab.  whereabouts
wid.  widow, -ed, -er
wit.  witness
wk.  week
wo.  woman
Art. Co.  Ancient and Honorable Artillery Co.
Assist.  Assistant
Asp.  Notarial Records of William Aspinwall, 1644-1651. Record Commissioners Reports, vol. 32 (Boston), 1903.
Amesb.  Amesbury
Asso.(c.)  Associate
Barb.  Barbadoes
Barr.  Barrington
Berw.  Berwick
Bid.  Biddeford
Bodge  George M. Bodge's Soldiers in King Philip's War, 3d Ed. (Boston), 1906
Camb.  Cambridge
Cape Eliz.  Cape Elizabeth
Cath.  Catholic
Damaris.  Damariscotta, Damariscove
Doc. Hist.  Documentary History of the State of Maine, vols. I-XXIV, edited by William Willis, Charles Deane, Mary Frances Farnham and James P. Baxter (Maine Historical Society, Portland), 1869-1916.
East. Cl.  Eastern Claims
En. Brit.  Encyclopedia Brittanica
Episc.  Episcopal
Essex Antiq.  Essex Antiquarian
Essex Q. Ct. Rec.  Essex Quarterly Court Records
Falm.  Falmouth
F. O.  Freeman's Oath
Folsom  George Folsom's History of Saco and Biddeford
F. & I. War  French and Indian War
Gay's Transc.  Gay's Transcripts
Glouc.  Gloucester
Gt. Isl.  Great Island
Hamp.  Hampton
Harps.  Harpswell
Harv. Cat.  Harvard University Catalogue
H. C.  Harvard College
Hoyt  Old Families of Salisbury and Amesbury, David W. Hoyt, 1897-1919
Ind.  Indian
Ipsw.  Ipswich
Ken.  Kennebec
Ken'port.  Kennebunkport
Kit.  Kittery
Lech.  Thomas Lechford's Note Book, 1638-1641
Little Comp.  Little Compton
Marb., Marbleh.  Marblehead
Mass. Arch.  The manuscript archives of the Commonwealth of Massachusetts in the office of the Secretary, including 326 volumes of scrapbooked files.
Mass. Col. Rec.  Records of the Governor and Company of the Massachusetts Bay in New England, Nathaniel B. Shurtleff, editor (Boston), 1853-1854.
Mather's Mag.  Cotton Mather's Magnalia
Me. Hist. Soc.  Collections of the Maine Historical Society
Me. H. & G. Rec.  Maine Historical and Genealogical Recorder
Me. P. & C. Rec.  Province & Court Records of Maine
Narraga.  Narragansett
N. E. Reg.  New England Historical & Genealogical Register.
Newc.  New Castle

N. H. Prob.  New Hampshire Probate
N. Y. Gen. & Biog. Rec.  New York Genealogical
   & Biographical Register
Norf.  Norfolk
North Yar.  North Yarmouth
O. A.  Oath Allegiance
O. F.  Oath Fidelity
Pisc.  Piscataqua
Port.  Portland
Ports.  Portsmouth
Portug.  Portuguese
Prov. Marshal  Provost Marshal
Roch.  Rochester
Sag. Creek  Sagamore Creek
Sals., Salis.  Salisbury
Sav.  Savage's Genealogical Dictionary
Scarb.  Scarboro
Scit.  Scituate
**Spur.  Spurwink**

Stackp.  Rev. Dr. E. S. Stackpole
Str. Bk.  Strawberry Bank
Suff.  Suffolk
Trel.  Trelawny Papers
Trel. Plant.  Trelawny Plantation
Watert.  Watertown
Weym.  Weymouth
Willis Mss.  Manuscript collections of Hon. William Willis of Portland, in the custody of the Maine Historical Society
Winth.  Governor Winthrop's Journal or History of New England, edited by James Savage, (Boston), 1853.
Wint. Harb.  Winter Harbor
Y. D.  York Deeds (York County, Mass., now Maine), Books I-XVIII (Books I-XI published by the Maine Historical Society), (Portland, Bethel), 1887-1910.

## THE LISTS are numbered by hundreds in four sets:

### General Lists

### By Towns or Localities

#### MAINE

#### NEW HAMPSHIRE

☞ The region of Nashua, N. H., was genealogically part of Massachusetts until after the Scotch-Irish came to Londonderry; likewise the whole southern tier of the present New Hampshire towns until 1741.

# GENEALOGICAL DICTIONARY

## *of* MAINE *and* NEW HAMPSHIRE

# LISTS

**Acadia** was French almost all the time, and the Penobscot Indians an un-conquered race, until the English took Quebec (1759).    Lists 1-5.

**1** Penobscot Trading House, 1630.
The trading station set up by Edward Ashley, or Aslley, under the Muscongus patent, was on the Penobscot river, was the same that fell to the Plymouth Colony after Ashley was shipped home, the same taken from them by the French — apparently in Castine, although Ashley took oath that his dwelling was about sixty miles distant from the English.    The witnesses against him were:

| | |
|---|---|
| John Deacon | Olivir Gallow |
| Henry Sampson | Thomas Willett |
| George Watson | William Phips |

who took oath, July 1631, before:
Capt. Walter Neale    Capt. Henry Keye

**2** English on the Penobscot, 1666.
— Doc. Hist. vi. 20 (Mass. Arch. lxvii. 53a)

**3** The best view of this region just before Philip's War may be had in Doc. Hist. vi. 42-88, 131. — Mass. Arch. lxi. 63-98.
Alter Isaac Chippien to Trippier, p. 46.
Alter John Farmer to Fa(r?)mer, p. 46.
Alter Peter Grout to Grant, p. 50.
Richard Suiet -sic- (for Swett?), p. 62.
Add Robert Wills±40, 1675, aboard of John Munnings' vessel when Skipper Uring's vessel was taken. Arch. lxi. 98.
Thomas Mitchell's bondsmen were:
John Lux of Boston.
John Dallen of Monhegan. Arch. lxi. 73.

**4** An Indian Slave Ship.
— Suff. Court Files 1592.

| | |
|---|---|
| Thomas Weber | sworn 27 Aug. 1676 |
| Thomas Odger or Agger | before Thomas Gardner |
| Henery Pamer | Richard Oliver |
| Richard Glase or Glass | Commissioners for the County of Devon. |

Being at Mt. Desert met with Mounsier Margoow frenchman who told them the Ketch Endevor John Horton master, with John Lauerdore aboard, did carry 9 Indians away from Michias and more from Cape Sables.
The Ketch Endever was chartered from Simon Lynde of Boston by Hen. Lawton and John Loverdure.
William Waldron was merchant aboard.
Thos. Gardner wrote from Piscataway 12 Sept. 1676:
I was informed by John Cole they had shackles aboard, wherefore I wrote a letter to the master and company at Monhegan warning them not to take any Indians east side of Kenibek river because we had made peace with them. He and his son-in-law John Erthy pestered by the Indians charging breach of covenant.
Petition of Priscilla Leverdure widow of Peter Leverdure. She English, he French, John their son, also another son that lives in these parts.
Henry Lawton broke prison;
the master fined;
Waldron and
Glover tried and discharged.

**5** Names of Inhabitants between the Rivers Penobscot and St. Croix 11 May 1688.
— 3 Mass. Hist. Coll. i. 82.
**At Penobscot**
St. Castin and Renne his servant.
**At Agemogin Reach**
Charles St. Robin's son.
La Flower and wife. St. Robin's daughter.
**Pettit Plesance by Mount Desart**
Lowrey, wife and child.
Hind's wife and four children — English.
**In Winscheage Bay, on the eastern side of Mount Desart**
Cadolic and wife.
**At Machias**
Martell, who pretends grant for the river from Quebeck. His servants:
John Bretoon, wife and child, of Jersey.
Latin, wife and three children — English.
**At Pessimaquody, near St. Croix**
St. Robin, wife and son, with like grant from Quebeck.
Letrell, Jno. Minns' wife and four children — Lambert and Jolly Cure his servants.
**At St. Croix**
Zorzy, and Lena his servant. Grant from Quebeck.

**Sagadahoc** may signify the country from the Kennebec to St. Georges, only described, never named, until called Devonshire by Mass. in 1674; renamed Cornwall by New York in 1683. In the Charter of 1691 it was termed "the territory lying between the River of Sagadahoc and Nova Scotia," which was its official designation down to the Revolution, although it had been made juridicially part of York County in 1716, and set off in a separate county (Lincoln) in 1760.     Lists 6-16.

**6      The Popham Colony in 1607.**
This list of the primeval period is only printed because of newly discovered names contributed by Col. Banks. These six names, with 11 known before, make about one-tenth of the colony. Cf. Thayer's The Sagadahoc Colony (Gorges Soc.) 1892; 1 Me. Hist. Coll. iii 279; Mass. Hist. Soc. Proc. xviii 82.
Mr. Fosque.
John Havercombe, master of the Gift of God.
Lancelot Booker, Rotherham, York, born 1576.
John Diaman, Stoke Gabriel, born 1553.
Timothy Savage, St. Brigid, London, born 1563.
John Fletcher, Stepney, born 1581.
(John Elliott, Newland, Essex, was born 1584.)

**7      The master's list of the crew of one of**
Capt. John Smith's ships, on his first voyage, 1614. — Neill's Eng. Colonization of Am.
Master,    Edward Brawnde
Mates    John Bennett
           Briane Tocker
Owner    William Treedel
Merchant    John Edwards
Bosone    John Hille
Mate,    John Downe
Gunner and pilot    William Gayneye
Mate,    James Farre
Quarter Masters    Nicholas Collins
                  Thomas Weber
                  John Barrens
                  Hennerye Batteshill
Steward    John Brimelcome
Cooks    Nicholas Head
          John Hutton
Some of the sailors:
John Wiles       Philip Wiles       Thomas Tobbe
Thomas Roberts    John Hept

**8      Damariscove, 'Canada,' 1622-1626.**
John Povy's Letter and the Minutes of the Virginia Council show a plantation at Damrills Cove frequented by vessels from Virginia. Among the names mentioned:
Mr. Vengham, a man of experience in those parts,
——— Corbin    Luke Edan    Henry Hewet
Capt. John Martyn       Mr. Humphrey Rastell
Wm. Holland    John Crookdeack    John Smith
Tho: Scott, a Quartermaster, Sackford Wetherell
Nicolas Roe    Jeffrey Cornish, (his brother hung)
Thomas Crispe, gent.             Arthur Avelinge
Edward Nevill (disfranchised) Mr. Robert Newman
Edward Barker    Wm. Foster     John Walton
John Oldame, merchant        Capt. John Stone

**9      A Monhegan Plantation in 1624.**
              — Putnam's Gen. Mag., Dec. 1916.
Thomas Piddock of London in 1628, aged 27, deposed:
Edmund Dockett, Wm. Pomfret and himself
in June-July, 1624, being at Menhegan as factors for
Abraham and Ambrose Jennings and Wm. Cross merchants of Plymouth and London did lade fish of The Jacob of (Nore)kham in Freezeland, Tho: Neeson Mr.
The Prosperous, Robert Bennett master
The Golden Catt, John Corbett(also Corbyn)master
Wm. Vengam, 'who was planted upon that island.'

**10      Accounts between Mr. Francis Knight**
and Mr. John Holland, 1647-1648.
              — Suff. Deeds. iii. 100-101.

**11      Plymouth Government on the Kenne-**
bec. June 20, 1654.
              — Plymouth Col. Records iii. 58.
Cites orders issued by 'the Council of State of England to govern those living upon or near adjoining unto the river commonly called Kenibec.' Records return of Mr. Thomas Prence who by authority had, 15 May 1654, ordered the marshal of New Plymouth to summons a meeting at the house of Thomas Ashly at Merry Meeting on 23 Apr. 1654, where and when the following took the oath of fidelity:
Tho: Purchase gent.       John Browne
John Stone                William Davis
Thomas Ashly              Thomas Weber
John Richards             Thomas Atkins
James Smith               James Coale
William James             John Parker
Thomas Parker             Emanuell Hughes
John White                Alexander Thawyt
Officers chosen: Mr. Thomas Purchase Assistant to the Government in this part of the Jurisdiction of New Plymouth.
Leeft. Tho. Southworth Assistant now residing at Cushenage (and such other as shall be sent thither from time to time to have the government of that family.)
Thos. Ashly Constable and licensed as innkeeper.

**12      Persons who took the Oath of Alle-**
giance to the King 5 Sept. 1665.
              — Me. Prov. & Court Rec. i. 245.

**13      Petition of Inhabitants of the East-**
ern Parts 18 May 1672 to be taken under Massachusetts government. The original petition is a fair copy, subject to errors in deciphering autographs.            — 1 Me. Hist. Coll. v. 240.
-Kenebec,· read Hammon, Denice, Davys, Thomas Cock, John Cock.
-Cape Bonawagon,· read Gammon, Pride, Arthers, Calton, Hoalfe, Skinner.
-Damoras Coave·, read John Allen, Alter, Symon Newcombe, Oband.
-Ships Cott,· read Dwinthim, Mercer, Corbinson, Collcott, Gympe [Gent?].
-Pemaquid,· read Gardiner, and add John . . .
-Monhegan,· read Celle, Worring, Fluen, Wills, Whittell, Lackrow, Hockridg, Widger.

**14      Englishmen Trading within French**
Bounds. Waldron v. Smith.
              — Suff. Court Files 1194.
Went to St. Johns trading. On the return were blown off and not knowing where they were went aground on making land.
Sander the Scotchman(Alex: Waugh±34, 1672) went ashore upon Addiwocket Bay withinside of Winskeage Island. They hired three Indian squaws to guide them to the English precincts. The sails were sold to 'one Mrs. Philips, widow, at a place Hippocriss.' Part of the cargo was left at Musquash Cove with Oliver Duncomb, at the Eastward. Thomas Wilcot±30.
Alexander Waugh — being off Mt. Desert Hills for the safety of our lives we run the vessel ashore.
William Waldron — his cousin Lidget's bond. Put furs aboard in Nova Scotia. Came from Corbin Sound to Boston by water in about two weeks voyage in a shallop belonging to Mrs. Phillips of Ippocrists.

Job Tookie±22 Boston witness in 1673, heard of Oliver Duncomb's death.

John Hincks±23, 21 Jan. 1672[3. After Christopher Smith was castaway in 1671 I heard Silvanus Davis offer Mr. Smith his passage & goods to Boston for what he had, and it should cost the said Smith nothing; and Mrs. Philips asked Smith to leave her boat and accept said Davis's offer.

Roger Rose±37, Jan. 1672[3, was last fall at the house of Andrew Neale having some discourse with the son of Mrs. Phillips of Hypocriss.

George Manning±28.

Peter Woodhouse±25, Jan. 1672[3, heard **Sylvanus** Davis's offer.

George Buckland±42, Jan. 1672[3 'going up a river to Corbin Sound;' Smith lodged at his house all the time he was at Corbin Sound; paid two mooseskins, owes him 17 shillings.

Richard Shute±39      }    they met at a place
Edward Naylor±38      }    called Muspeeky in
Thaddeus Makarty±33 }    March, 1671[2, became partners — first sailed for Machias where we heard the news of Oliver Duncomb's death, from thence hastened to Musquash Cove.

John Wrieford.

In Waldron's account:

To provisions at Round Pond.

Paid Mr. Shippy of Strawberry Bank for warehouse room.

Paid for carpenter work on the ship Mr. Henderson built for me:

| | |
|---|---|
| Roger Deering | Joseph Hasey |
| Edward Carter | Elihu Gunnison |
| Philip Cromwell | and others |

**15**   Courts in Sagadahoc set up by Massachusetts, July 22, 1674. Doc. Hist. iv. 343-348 (Arch. iii. 307).

345 William Walters is Waters in Mass. Records v. 17.

John Uerrine is Verrine in original.

Nicholas Denning is Deming in Mass. Rec. v. 17.

346 John Stover is S×over in original.

**16**   'Cornwall' under New York Rule. Magistrates commissioned 1680-1686.
     — 1 Me. Hist. Coll. v. 38, 102, 113.

**17**   Petition for Forts and against Mr. Patteshall, between 22 Nov. 1683 and 21 Apr. 1684. As the original was burnt in the Albany fire, the print can only be corrected by conjecture.
     — 1 Me. Hist. Coll. v. 88.

Justes ——— read Justice of the Peace.

Phi = Parson read Justice of the Peace.

Christopher Ryer read Dyer.

William Lowering read Lovering.

Robert Cook read Scott?

Affte Nele read Arthur.

Goury Gray read Georg?

John Lange read   ?

Elius Trucke read Elias Trick.

**18**   Petition to the King praising Gov. Andros, dated 25 Jan. 1689-90, by 'the present & late inhabitants of the Province of Maine & County of Cornwall.' A contemporary copy by a stranger is printed in Doc. Hist. v. 34. The original is abstracted in Sainsbury, No. 740, with different readings:—

[Vines] for ——— Ellacott.

Lawrence Downes for Jones.

William Dennis for Dines.

John Wreford for Wrifard.

John Doll[on] for Dolton.

John Shierley (?) for ———.

James Law for Francis Lord.

**19**   Sir Edmund Andros's Unofficial Report of the Eastern Defences and what happened to them after he was deported, made on his arrival in England. Cf. Doc. Hist. v. 120 for Mass. reply to his statements.

| | |
|---|---|
| Pemaquid (Bristol) | 156 men under Capt. Anthony Brockholes, Lieut. James Weems, Capt. Tyng, Capt. George Minot. |
| New Dartmouth. (Newcastle) | 84 men under Lieut. John Jordan, Capt. Withington. |
| Damariscotta River. (East Boothbay) | A redoubt (at the Pass) on Damariscotta River relieved every week from New Dartmouth. |
| Sagadahoc (Stage Island) Newtown (Arrowsic) Fort Anne (Woolwich) Pejepscot (Topsham) | 180 men. These several forts on the Kennebec commanded by Lieut. Col. Mackgregory and Major Thomas Savage with Capt. Manning's company. |
| Falmouth (Portland) | 60 men. Capt. Geo. Lockhart. |
| Saco River. (Biddeford) | 88 men. Capt. John Lloyd, his own company and a detachment from Maj. Henchman and Capt. Bull. |
| Kennebunk (Kennebunkport) | 'Fort' commanded by Lieut. Puddington, to be relieved from Saco. |
| Wells | 'Small fort to be relieved from Saco.' |

**Maine** at the time of its largest extent included all from the Piscataqua to the Sagadahoc or Kennebec, its minimum under Gov. Godfrey but two towns. The brief rule of Lygonia comes under Maine. Although the Isles of Shoals are partly in Maine, their lists are kept together under New Hampshire.　　Lists 21-39.

**21　Calendar of the Trelawny Plantation,** Richmond Island and Spurwink (afterwards Falmouth and now Cape Elizabeth, Maine). Collected from the Trelawny Papers, published as Volume III of the Documentary Series of the Maine Hist. Society. Done rather hastily, errors may be disclosed by concentrating on single names, but all statements contradictory of the Editor's footnotes are believed to be dependable.

Full List of Supply Ships:

| Year | Name | Master Out | Sailed | Arrived | Master Back | Sailed | Arrived |
|---|---|---|---|---|---|---|---|
| 1631-2 | (Sinnamon?) | John Winter | Ab. 17 Apr. 1632 | | John Winter | Aft. 30 July 1632 | |
| 1632-3 | Welcome | John Winter | Bef. 10 Jan. 1632-3 | | —— Gill | Ab. 15 July 1633 | |
| | | | | 2 Mar. 1632-3 | | | (captured) |
| 1633-4 | Hunter | Owen Pomeroy | | 2 Feb. 1633-4 | Owen Pomeroy | 3 July 1634 | |
| | | | | | | | 7 Aug. 1634 |
| | James | (Tristram?) Bowes | 29 Aug. 1634 | | —— Bowes | Ab. Oct. 1634 (lost) | |
| 1634-5 | Speedwell | Narias Hawkins | 26 Apr. 1635 | | John Winter | Ab. 28 June 1635 | |
| 1635-6 | Agnes | John Winter | Aft. 26 Mar. 1636 | | —— Bowes | Ab. 27 June 1636 | |
| | | | | 24 May 1636 | | | |
| 1636-7 | Hercules | Wm. Chappel | Ab. 30 Nov. 1636 | | William Chappel | 8 July 1637 | |
| | | | | 13 Feb. 1636-7 | | | |
| | The Bark | built here, launched 10 June 1637 | | | for England | | |
| | Richmond | sailed for the Bay 26 July 1637 | | | Stephen Nichols | 20 July 1639 | |
| | | | | | | | 31 Aug. 1639 |
| 1637-8 | Fortune | James Holman | 10 May 1638 | | James Holman | Ab. 11 June 1638 | |
| | | | | | | | 30 July 1638 |
| | Samuel | William Perrum | Ab. June 1638 | | William Perrum | 19 July 1638 | |
| | | | | | | | 24 Sept. 1638 |
| 1638-9 | Hercules(?) | Wm. Hingston | Ab. 20 Sept. 1638 | | William Hingston | 17 July 1639 | |
| | | | | 30 Jan. 1638-9 | | | |
| | Samuel(?) | | 17 Nov. 1639 | | | 14 Dec. 1639 for Virginia | |
| '39-40 | Star | Narias Hawkins | 4 June 1640 | | Ab. 27 June 1640, 10 Sept. 1640 | | |

(Name changed to The Friendship? Hawkins was back. master of The Friendship 10 Sept. 1640.)

| 1640-1 | The Ship | built here, launched 15 June 1641 | | | Stephen Sargent | Ab. 2 Aug. 1641 | |
| | Richmond | | | | | | |
| 1642-3 | Margery | Hugh Ball | Aft. 22 Nov. 1642 | | Ambrose Boaden | | |

[The Hercules, William Hingston Mr., made other fishing voyages in 1641-2 and 1643-4.]

**1631.　Dec. 1.** Patent to Robert Trelawny and Moses Goodyear.

**1631-2.　Jan. 18.** Power of attorney to John Winter and Thomas Pomery (the latter did not come over) to take possession.

**July 21.** John Winter secured livery of seisin of Richmond Island from Richard Vines. Witnesses: Thomas Ca[mmock], Isaac Aller[ton], Richard [——, not Bonython], Thomas [Allgar].

**July 30.** John Winter secured livery of seisin of the main land from Richard Vines. Witnesses: Isaac Allerton, William Hingston, Thomas Allgar.

**1637.　June 30.** John Winter secured livery of seisin of 2,000 acres [Nonsuch], from Richard Vines. Witnesses: Thomas Purches, Edward Trelawny, William Chappell, Henry Abley, George Newman, Arthur Browne, Arthur Macworth.

**1642.　Oct. 17.** Robert Trelawny was imprisoned as a Royalist Member of Parliament.

**1643.　Apr. 8.** Mrs. Trelawny died.

**1644.　Nov. 19.** Mr. Trelawny died.

**1645.　May 20.** John Winter turned over his authority to his son-in-law, Rev. Robert Jordan.

**1648.** Mr. Jordan had three boats at sea on account of the Plantation.

| In Casco Bay before the Patent | Left by Mr. Winter in 1632 to keep possession | Harry ——, Wife of the Towne | Came in The Speedwell 1635 | Gibson |
|---|---|---|---|---|
| Mr. John Winter | Thomas Alger | **Came in** | Mr. Narias Hawkins | Arthur Gill |
| Mr. Henry Russell | John Baddiver | **The Hunter** | Mr. Edward | Peter Gullett |
| Mr. Joseph Russell | Andrew Alger | **1634** | Trelawny | Andrew Heifer |
| Mr. William Lash | **Came in** | Mr. Owen Pomeroy | George Rogers | Reignold Jenkins |
| Mr.　　Guyer | **The Welcome** | A fishing company | Richard Cummings | John Lopes |
| William Gibbins* | **1633** | including apparently: | Roger Willing | Tobias Short |
| * Possibly one of | Mr. John Winter | Richard Downing | Alexander Freethy | (three |
| the 20 men left by | Thomas Dustin | Richard Corber | William Freethy | boat's crews) |
| Christopher Levett | Matthew Cammage | Robert Waymouth | Roger Bucknall | **Came in** |
| in 1624 | Henry Townesend | Jos: Crase | Peter Hill | **The Hercules** |
| John Mills | Arthur Heard | William Helborne | John Lander | **1636-7** |
| Peter Garland | Peter Hill | Tho: Arrowsmith | William Ham | Mr. William |
| John Cosens | Charles Hatch | William Tucker | John Billin | Chappell |
| Ambrose Boaden | John Hoskin | John Sanders | Oliver Clark | Mrs. Joan Winter |
| John Taylor | Rowland Ok*r*s | Ship's carpenter, | John Symons | Sarah Winter |
| Bennett Wills | Thomas Kin.,. | Thos: Treleage | John Vivion | John Winter Jr. |
| Thomas Alger | John Mills | **Came in** | Peter Cobb | Tristram Alger |
| **A servant of** | John Wilkinson | **The James** | **Came in** | John Libby |
| **Mr. George Cleaves** | Richard Pynne | **1634** | **The Agnes** | Nicholas White |
| **in 1633, afterwards** | Edward Fishcock | Mr. (Tristram?) | **1636** | William Freethy |
| **employed by** | Henry Roberts, | Bowes | Mr. John Winter | Benjamin Stevens |
| **Mr. Winter** | the Baker | George Dearing | Rev. Richard | Thomas Shepherd |
| Oliver Weeks | | | | Priscilla Bickford |
| | | | | The old Bickford |

| | | **Came in** | **Removed from** | Thomas Vennion |
|---|---|---|---|---|
| Edward Mylls | George Bunt | **The Hercules** | **Brunswick** | William Crimpe |
| Richard Martin | and his son | **1638-9** | **1641** | boatswain |
| Stephen Lapthorne | Anthony Clark | Arthur Gill's wife | Rev. Robert Jordan | Walter Penwill |
| John Hole | Pentecost Hayman | John Burrage | **Hired Here** | son of Clement |
| Nicholas Edgecomb | William Hearle | Robert Saunders | **1641-2** | Richard Moursell |
| Nicholas Matthew | Richard Field | Sampson Jupe | Nicholas Hewit | or Marsill |
| John Amory | William Lucas | (— boat's crews) | Edward Wodley | John Morgin |
| Richard Niles | William Allen | **Came in** | John Sanders | George Weimoth |
| Thomas Bone | Mark Gaude | **The Samuel** | **Hired Here** | gunner |
| John Hempson | Henry Edmonds | **1639** | **1642-3** | John White |
| Charles Hatch | Edward Best | ? ? | Jonas Beyly | Thomas Greneslade |
| Philip Hatch | Henry Hancock | **Resorted** | John Libby | Ralfe Welch |
| Roger Saturly | Richard Joy | **to the Plantation** | Nicholas Edgecomb | Richard Nyles |
| Anthony Chapple | and his boy | **1640** | **Came in** | Nicholas Bonsale |
| The maid Tomson | Edward Treby | Mr. Francis Martin | **The Margery** | Richard Creber |
| (Ellis Curkeitt?) | Jonas Beele | and two daughters | **1642-3** | carpenter |
| (two boat's crews) | Thomas Lissen | **Came in** | Mr. Hugh Ball | Robin Hatch |
| **Hired here** | Philip Hingston | **The Star** | Edmond Andrews | **Came in** |
| **1637** | Thomas Hammecke | **1640** | Robert Saunders | **The Hercules** |
| John Roberts | William Mellin | ? ? | Benj Stephens | **1643-4** |
| **Came in** | John Garland | **Hired Here(?)** | John Burrage | Paul Mitchell |
| **The Fortune** | (four boat's crews) | **June-July** | and wife Annis | **Hired Here** |
| **1638** | **Came in** | **1641** | **The Crew** | **1648** |
| Mr. James Holman | **The Samuel** | Michael Maddiver | Mr.Ambrose Bouden | Roger Satturly |
| Mr. Stephen Sargent | **1638** | John Lakesley | Master back | Jeremiah |
| and two servants | Mr.William Perrum | William Guich | Clement Penwill | Humphreys |
| Paul Mitchell | Wilmot Randall | | | |

**22** Paper backed in contemporary hand:
The Coppy off Mr. Cleeves petition
read in parliament.

| | | |
|---|---|---|
| Richard Tucker | George Frost | Thomas Page |
| Michaell Mitton | John Bonython | Ambrose Berry |
| *Arthure | *John West | George |
| Mackworth | Willm Coale | Puddington |
| Willm Ryall | *John Smith | John Baker |
| Arnold Allen | *John Wadley | Edward Johnson |
| *Henry Watts | Willm Smith | Henry Lynne |
| Henry Boade | *John | John Alcock |
| *Andrew Alger | Wilkinson | |
| *Willm | †Anthony | |
| Haymonde | Newlands | |
| †Tho: Raynolds | *Fran: Robinson | |
| Henry Sympson | Joseph Jenkes | Avowed by me |
| †Richard Barnard | *Peter Weare | George Cleeve |

* Repudiated their names on the petition in York
court in 1645.
† As Mr. Cleeve signed these names in London
without authority, he probably misstated these
for ·William· Reynolds and ·Bartholomew· Barnard. The ·N· in Newlands was apparently
partly altered to ·M·.

**23** Edward Rigby's Letter to his Councillors, 19 July 1652, suspending their authority and declaring their acts void since his father's
death. — York Deeds i. 64.

**24** Petition to the Lord Protector, 1657.
Hutchinson printed this petition without the
signatures (Papers, p. 314): the document in
Mass. Arch. (iii. 242) is a copy. This copy is
correctly printed in Doc. Hist. iv. 140, but obvious
errors may be corrected:
For Walter Neuuell read Pennell.
For Nathaniel Load read Nathan Lord.
For Humph Shadbore read Chadborne.
For Sampson Auger read Anger.

**25** Petition from Maine, except Saco and
Scarborough, for Mass. to use force, not
merely declarative acts, to protect the inhabitants
against a pretended power of Esq. Gorges's commissioners, [Fall of 1662] — Mass. Arch. 3: 269.
Me. Prov. and Court Records i. 199.

**26** Petition to the King, (1666?).
Doc. Hist. iv. 148 (Folsom Orig. Doc., p. 78;
Sainsbury no. 1752).
For John Budstarte read Budsarte.
For John Dauas read Daves.

**27** Refugees at Salem in Jan. 1675-6.
The following persons from Maine were granted
a temporary residence by the Selectmen.
— Essex Inst. Coll. xlviii. 20, 21, 25,
(From Falmouth) (From Saco)
Mr. Francis Neale [Edward Sheaner?]
Geo. Ingarson John Elson
[John Mungy] Walter Meur
Samuel Pike Arthur Wormsted
Goodwife Stanford William Frost
John Ingerson Arthur Hewes
John Wallis Goodman [Silley]
Geo. Ingerson Jr. Syman Bouth
John Skillin Walter Penewill
(Cape Porpus) Gyles Ebbens
(Matthew) Barton Elizabeth Wakefield
Humphrey Cace

**28** Yorkshire Petition, 5 July 1676, that
Maj. Richard Waldron be restored to his former Magistratical authoritie over this county — granted 10 Aug. 1676.

| | | |
|---|---|---|
| Ezekiel | Francis | John Wincoll |
| Knights Sr. | Littlefeild | John Daves |
| Willyam | Brian Pendleton | Charles Frost |
| Sheldon | John Broughton | Geo: Broughton |
| Henery **6** | Sam Austin | John Littlefeild |
| Browne | Humphrey | Jos. Bolles |
| Tho. **1** Doubtie | Chadbourne | Danl: **3** Gooddin |
| James **1** Oarr | Benjamin | William Spencer |
| John Wells | Bernard | Wm. **2** Moore |
| Thomas Baston | William | Niven **3** Agnew |
| Joseph Storer | Playsted | James **6** Smith |
| | Abra: Preble | Richard Foxwell |
| | Will Hammonds | William **5** Love |
| | Jos: Hammond | Abra: **2** Conley |
| | William **7** Ashly | Joseph **6** |
| | John Thomson | Littlefeild |
| | Tho: **2** Litlefeld | Thomas Mills |
| | Gowen Willson | Peter **6** Clayes |
| | | Jonathan |
| | | Hammond |

**29** Petition of General Assembly to the
King [June?] 1680. Major Brian Pendleton
officiated as Deputy President at the Court of
Pleas 30 June 1680, although Major John Davis
had been appointed to that office at the General
Court. — Doc. Hist. iv. 396; from copy in Mass.
Arch. iii. 343.
Samuel Davis [·sic·] error for John.
James Emery [·sic·] is probably correct although
the original Maine Court Records record his name
Anthony.

**30** Major Shapleigh's Petition, printed in 1 Me. Hist. Coll. i. 302 as of 1680 and in Doc. Hist. iv. 309 as of 1668, was read in Council in London, 30 Sept. 1680. The prayer was to be reinstated under Royal authority, although Mass. had bought the Gorges patent. The original petition must have remained in the hands of Maj. Shapleigh, who had two fair copies made, signed in person by himself, John Hole, William Scriven and a few others. One of these copies was intercepted by Mass. and is now in the N. Y. Public Library. A copy of this copy is in Mass. Arch. iii. 288, printed in Doc. Hist. iv. 309. Major Shapleigh's other copy, which reached London, is C. O. 1. 46. No. 14. What is printed in Me. Hist. Coll., with 19 fewer names, may possibly be from the original. The Mass. copy was made by passing a ruler down the petition and taking off the names crosswise the page as reached, thus destroying local associations, besides misreading many names. The original petition must have been started in Kittery, headed in four columns by Nicholas Shapleigh, John Hole, Enoch Hutchins and Richard White. The three columns below reproduce to some extent the original local groupings, but without transferring single names of men apparently away from home when they signed.

| | | |
|---|---|---|
| Nic: Shapleigh | John Miller | Nathan Bedford |
| John Hole | John Batson | Geo: Ingerson |
| Enoch Huchins | John Pudington | Anthony Bracket |
| Richard White | Sampson Anger | Thadeus Clarke |
| Roger Dearing | Thomas Mussey | John Davies |
| John Twisden | —— | Laurence Davies |
| James Wiggin Sr. | | Wm. [Reener?] |
| Digery Jeffrey | | [Pearce?] |
| Stephen Jenkins | | William Rogers |
| Tho: Furnall | | John Welden |
| Tho: Hanscom | | John Skilling |
| Rich: Miller | | Joseph Ingerson |
| Rich: Green | | George Ingerson |
| Edmund Hamon | | Joseph Hodsden |
| Tho: Rice | | Tho: Stanford |
| Rich: Nason | | Robert Stanford |
| Rich: King | | John Wallis |
| Gabriell Tetherly | | Nathl. Wallis |
| Christian | | Sampson Penlee |
|    Remuick | | Philip Lewes |
| Peter Dixon | | John Holman |
| Elihu Gunison | | Steph: Latherbe |
| Joshua Downing | Continuation | Robert Haines |
| Richard Gowell |   of Col. 1. | William Haines |
| John Morill | John Trickey | Richard Bray |
| Jabez Jenking | Francis Trickey | Josiah White |
| John White | William Hilton | Rich: Cawley |
| John Greene | John Billing | Tho: Bickford |
| George Buren | Sampson White | Henry Libbe |
| Adrian Fry | Rice Thomas | Xtopher |
| Richard Banks | John Bale |   Edgecomb |
| John Key | Lewis Tucker | John Jordan |
| Rowland Young | Nicho: Tucker | Samuel Jordan |
| Jeremiah Sheres | Humphrey | Domin: Jordan |
| Joseph Daniell |   Churchwell | Jeremiah Jordan |
| Thomas Trafton | Paul Williams | Wm. Mansfield |
| Nathl. Raines | Thomas Patten | John Flee |
| John Bran | John Dymond | Ambrose Boden |
| Arthur Baiel | Jonathan Nason | Peter Shaw |
| Jasper Pulman | John Taylor | Christo: Spurrell |
| Nathl. Daniell | Wm. Furbush | John Tinny |
| Will: More | John Granger | James Randle |
| Clement Short | Benj. Nason | John Mackerel |
| Alex: Cooper | Nathan Lord Jr. | John Simpson |
| John Card | Abram Lord | Anthony Roe |
| Thomas Curtis | James Stacpole | Philip Foxwell |
| Tho: Littlefeild | John Nason |   Weymouth |
| Tho: Bragden | Xpher Batt |      Bickton |
| James Wiggin Jr. | Andra Serle Sr. | Henry Elkins |
| John Mogridge | John Serle | Tho: [Mosse?] |
| John Amerideth | John Neale | John Baret |
|      Sr. | Peter Grant | Robert Edge |
| John Amerideth | | John Hill |
|      Jr. | | William Scriven |
| Wm. Tetherly | | Richard Rogers |

**31** Protest delivered by John Hole to President Danforth, 18 March 1679-80, signed largely by the same persons as **30**. As printed in Doc. Hist. iv. 391, errors are reproduced from what is only a copy, Mass. Arch. iii. 341. The following names correct such errors, and also include those not found in **30**.

| | |
|---|---|
| John Murrel | John Banks |
| Arthur Beale | John Batson |
| Gabriel Tetherly | Daniel Dill |
| Christian Ramuck | John Persons |
| Richard Green | William Ashley |
| Geo. Burren | |

**32** President Danforth's Town Trustees. These trust deeds were to transfer from the Lord Proprietor to the inhabitants in each town the vacant lands in each town, subject to quitrents. The deeds for Saco, Wells and Kittery are missing, but those we know of survived precariously, and there is no reason to doubt that they were given to all of the towns. They were all executed in Boston 26 July 1684.

**North Yarmouth**

| | |
|---|---|
| Jeremiah Dummer | John Royal |
| Walter Gendall | John York |

    — York Deeds xvii. 97.
(An earlier unacknowledged deed, 28 June 1684, has John Harris in place of Mr. Dummer. — Proprietors' Records.)

**Falmouth**

| | |
|---|---|
| Capt. Edward Tyng | Capt. Anthony Bracket |
| Capt. Silvanus Davis | Mr. Dominicus Jordan |
| Mr. Walter Gendall | Mr. George Brimhall |
| Mr. Thadeus Clark | Mr. Robert Lawrence |

    — York Deeds xiv. 226.

**Scarborough**

| | |
|---|---|
| Capt. Joshua Scottow | Andrew Brown |
| Mr. Walter Gendall | Ambrose Boaden |
| Rickard Honeywell | John Tenney |
| William Burridge | |

    — 1 Me. Hist. Coll. iii. 232.

**Cape Porpus**

| | |
|---|---|
| John Barrett Sr. | John Badson |
| John Purrington | |

    — York Deeds xiv. 209.

**York**

| | |
|---|---|
| Major John Davis | Capt. Job Alcock |
| Edward Rishworth, Esq. | Lieut. Abraham Preble |

    — York Town Records, p. 500.

**33** Remonstrance against Removing the Records to Scarborough, 6 July 1686. — Doc. Hist. vi. 213-215 (Mass. Arch. cxxvi. 22).
York:   Alter Nicarm Mark— to Micam Macheyntvre.
        Alter Henry Lampell to Lamprell.
Saco:   Alter Thomas Mose Jr. to Hale [Haley].
        Alter Stuen berthbe to [? rthbe].
        Alter William Diser to Dicer.
Wells:   Alter Nathl. M—— to Masters.
        Alter John Barrel to Barret.
Berwick: Alter Wm. Blaisteed to Plaisteed.
        Alter William Loue to Love.
        Alter Anthonie Fotham to Fothano.
        Alter Tho: Gooding to Gooding [-win].
York:   Alter Mark Richard Bancks -duplicate-
        Alter John —— to Wanttworth.
        Alter J—— Grant to James Grant.

**34** Land Warrants under Andros in 1687-1688, excellently well printed in Col. Soc. of Mass., xxi. 292. The original in Mass. Arch. has plainly (79) 'John' Ockman, but the recorder must have misread Tobias. 'Arriscott' must be Harraseeket, now Freeport. Thomas Shippard (32) appears altered from Sheppard. Daniel Hogg (58) must be Fogg. All the land warrants in Maine are cited.

**35** Councils of War, Scarborough and Falmouth, Nov. 11-13, 1689. — Doc. Hist. v. 3-4.

**36** Garrisons East of the Piscataqua April 30, 1690. Doc. Hist. v. 91 (Mass. Arch.) John Honiwell [-sic-] intended Richard.

**37** Casualty List of Expedition Eastward, 7 Aug. 1691. — Doc. Hist. v. 281-282.

**38** Garrisons Reviewed by the Governor in Nov. 1711. — Me. H. & G. Register ii. 113. The whereabouts of this document, at that time in the hands of S. P. Mayberry, is at present unknown. Corrected by conjecture:
Read Jo Littlefield   Joseph.
Read Deken? Littlefield   Deliv(erence).
Read 10 Jona Littlefield   Josiah.
Read Mr. Daniels   Mr. Donnell's.
Read Mr. Blake   Mr. Black.
Read Peter Newell   Peter Nowell.
Read Mr. Pentons   Mr. Norton's.
Read Mr. Rames   Mr. Raines.
Read Mr. Walkers   [Mr. James Warren's?].
Read Mr. Neeson   Mr. Nason.

**39** Casualty List, killed, wounded and taken, 10 August 1703.
The burning memory of this treacherous day cost many hundred Indians their lives, women and children included.

**Wells**

| | | |
|---|---|---|
| Joseph Hill's two children killed, himself and wife wounded | 2 | 2 |
| William Parsons and three children killed and his wife taken | 4 |   1 |
| Jeremiah Story, one child killed and two taken captive | 1 |   2 |
| Samuel Hill, his wife and seven of his family taken | |   9 |
| Benjamin Curtis killed | 1 | |
| Joseph Sawyer, his wife and her sister killed and one taken | 3 |   1 |
| James Adams, his wife and three children taken | |   5 |
| Thomas Wells, his wife and four children killed | 6 | |
| Moses Littlefield's wife and three children taken | |   4 |
| | 17   2 | 22 |

**Cape Porpus**

| | | |
|---|---|---|
| Philip Dudy's wife and four children taken | | 5 |
| William Letherby's wife taken and two children killed | 2 | 1 |
| John Turbett's wife taken | 1 | 1 |
| John Sanders killed | 1 | |
| John Davis taken | | 1 |
| John Batson's wife, her sister, and four children taken | | 6 |
| | 3 | 14 |

**Winter Harbor and Saco**

| | | |
|---|---|---|
| John Sargent and his son Joseph killed | 2 | |
| Benj. Sargent's wife killed and three children taken | 1 | 3 |
| Joshua Pilsbury killed | 1 | |
| Ebenezer Hill and his wife and two of Capt. Wheelwright's children taken | | 4 |

| | | |
|---|---|---|
| Daniel Smith, his wife and one child taken | | 3 |
| Nathan Taylor killed | 1 | |
| Lt. More and Samuel Smith taken | 1 | 2 |
| John Hibard killed | 1 | |
| Robert Edgecomb's son taken | | 1 |
| John Benighton and his wife and four children taken | | 6 |
| Henry Smith killed | 1 | |
| Humphrey Scammond and two children taken | | 3 |
| Thomas Harvey killed | 1 | |
| Joseph Cole and his son killed, his wife and one child taken | 2 | 2 |
| | 10 | 24 |

**Blackpoint**

| | | |
|---|---|---|
| John Simpson and two of his family taken | | 3 |
| Mary Ellson taken | | 1 |
| | | 4 |

**Spurwink**

| | | |
|---|---|---|
| Dominicus Jordan killed, his wife and children taken | 1 | 6 |
| Jeremiah Jordan's wife and seven children taken, one of which killed three days after | 1 | 7 |
| John Jordan and four of his family killed | 5 | |
| | 7 | 13 |

**Purpooduck**

| | | |
|---|---|---|
| Thomas Lovett and his wife and four children taken | | 6 |
| Joseph Matteford killed and his wife taken | 1 | 1 |
| Henry Thrasher killed | 1 | |
| Benjamin Wallis's wife and three children killed | 4 | |
| Joseph Wallis's wife killed | 1 | |
| Joseph Morgan's wife and two children killed | 3 | |
| Josiah Wallis's wife and three children killed | 4 | |
| Michael Webber's wife and six children killed | 7 | |
| Leonard Slow, his wife and three children killed | 5 | |
| | 26 | 7 |

**Casco**

| | | |
|---|---|---|
| Lewis Tucker's wife and daughter killed | 2 | |
| Philip Lawless and his wife and five children taken | | 7 |
| Hugh Mackenny and William Strobbs' wife killed | 2 | |
| Thomas Southard and his wife taken | | 2 |
| Rose Thomas's wife taken | | 1 |
| William [K or V]enney and John Jones killed | 2 | |
| Mr. David Phippeny and son John killed | 2 | |
| Mr. John Kent and Stephen Lucas killed | 2 | |
| | 10 | 10 |
| Total | 73   2 | 94 |

**New Hampshire's** four towns first came together as a separate government when taken away from Massachusetts in 1679-80, reviving the name by which Capt. Mason called his patent. Hampton had always been part of Massachusetts; the upper and lower Piscataqua combinations did not unite before yielding to that government; Exeter yielded last of all. Lists 41-69.

**41** **Calendar of the Laconia and Mason Plantations,** now Rye, Newcastle, Portsmouth and Berwick. Collated from papers saved by Mr. Ambrose Gibbins and in the British Archives supplemented from Winthrop's History and Fleet's Journal. (Six forged documents now kept with the Gibbins papers are disregarded.)　　Full List of Supply Ships:

| Year | Name | Master Out | Sailed | Arrived | Master Back | Sailed | Arrived |
|------|------|-----------|--------|---------|-------------|--------|---------|
| 1630 | Bark Warwick | Wetherell | March 27 | June 1 | | Aug. 14 | |
| 1631 | Pied Cow | Capt. Henry Keyes | March | June | [Brought trade goods, three wives and some Frenchmen to make salt.] | | |

[Mr. Bright and Mr. Lewis were also mentioned]

| | Bark Warwick(2) | John Dunton | July 4 | Sept. 9 | Remained several years in Virginia. |
|---|---|---|---|---|---|
| | | Capt. Henry Fleet | [Brought a soldier for exploring (Thomas Wannerton?), and a factor(Mr. Herbert?)to take charge of trade goods. | | |
| 1631-2 | Pied Cow(2) | Wm. Stephenson | Nov. 17 | John Raymond, purser. |

[Brought goods to be delivered to Capt. Neale what he had cash beaver to buy with, the balance to be sold outside.]

| | Lion's Whelp | John Gibbs | Jan. | [A trading and fishing voyage into which ten 'adventurers' put £485. In London in 1638 Mr. Gibbs had recovered a judgment against the Laconia partners, and also against Capt. Neale for a bill drawn on them 6 Aug. 1632 for spices and sugar. |
|---|---|---|---|---|
| | Ship John | | April 18 | [George Vaughan, factor. Consignment of trade goods to be disposed of for cash beaver.] |

These were the last goods sent over by the Laconia Company. The next voyage of Pied Cow was Gorges and Mason's own venture. Whether Capt. Mason by himself sent a ship is uncertain, as Mr. Jocelyn's papers are lacking.

| 1634 | Pied Cow (3) | | May 5 | July 8 | Aug. 6 | was on point of sailing for Saco to load clapboards and staves. |
|---|---|---|---|---|---|---|

[Brought Mr. Jocelyn to take charge, mills for Berwick and York, and three partners under contract to set up Capt. Mason's mills and run them on shares.]

1622, Aug. 10. Patent of the 'Province of Maine' to Sir Ferdinando Gorges and Capt. John Mason.

1629, Nov. 17. Patent to the Laconia Company (Sir Ferdinando Gorges, Capt. John Mason and partners.) Attorney to make livery of seisin Edward Godfrey.

March 6. License issued to Capt. Henry Keyes to transport from Portsmouth, Eng., to Pascataway 30 quarters of meal and 20 quarters of pease for the relief of the Planters there, who through want of such supplies are not able to proceed to a further discovery there.

1631, Nov. 1. ( Captain Walter Neale, Henry Jocelyn lieutenant and Richard Vines
Dec. 1. ( gentleman, attorneys of the President and Council of New England to make livery of seisin in the Cammock and Trelawny patents.

Nov. 3. Confirmation to the partners of the Laconia Company by name. Attorneys to make livery of seisin Capt. Thomas Cammock, Henry Jocelyn or any of the officers.

1632, Dec. 5. Capt. Neale recalled and the servants ordered dismissed.

1633, June 17. Servants dismissed.

July 15. The Governor departed from the plantation.

Aug. 15. Capt. Walter Neale and some eight of his company sailed from Boston.
　　— Winthrop.

Dec. 6. Division of land and 32 hogs among the partners.

1634, May 5. Henry Jocelyn sent back to take

charge of Capt. Mason's separate share. July 20. Mr. Jocelyn took charge.

1634-5, Feb. 3. Allotment of New Hampshire and northern Massachusetts to Capt. John Mason.

Apr. 22. Patent of same. Attorneys to make livery of seisin Henry Jocelyn, Esq., Ambrose Gibbins, gentleman.

Aug. 19. King's patent to Capt. John Mason.

Dec. Capt. John Mason died.

1635-6,——. Mr. Jocelyn gave over his charge to Mr. Gibbins and removed to Maine.

1638, May 6. Mrs. Ann Mason gave power of attorney to Capt. Francis Norton of Charlestown, Mass., to recover her husband's estate.

1638-9, Feb. Robert Houghton, citizen and brewer of London, brother-in-law of Capt. Norton, took a 5-year lease, being already in possession by his agents.

Feb. 28. Suit against Sir Ferdinando Gorges for non-payment of stock subscription, June, 1632; plaintiffs recovered.

1640, May 14. Capt. Norton back in London testifying as a witness in litigation.

1650-1, March 3. Mrs. Ann Mason gave power of attorney to Joseph Mason to recover her husband's estate. He accused the following servants of embezzling it: Mr. Roger Knight, Mr. Ambrose Gibbons, one Chadburne and his sons, Wall, Goddard and others, although those turned off in 1633 without their wages were promised deeds of land.

| The Laconia Company of London, otherwise called by their own secretary 'merchant adventurers beyond the seas' consisted of: Sir Ferdinando Gorges | Capt. John Mason John Cotton William Cotton (Gorges and Mason after the latter bought out the two Cottons held a half interest. The other four shares | were from time to time held by:) Henry Gardner George Griffeth Thos. Wannerton Edwin Guy or Gayer Richard Pulford | Capt. Neale's Beaver-Cash Acct. This abstract includes all names (and corrects errors) occurring in the fully printed document in Prov. Papers I 71, showing disbursements after 1 Apr. 1633. Presumably the men dealt with did not belong to the plantation, but may have come |
|---|---|---|---|

Thomas Eyre
Elyanor Eyre
Eliezer Eyre
William Gyles
July 4, 1664, George Griffeth, Henry Gardner and Eleazer Eyres sold a quarter interest to Capt. John Littlebury.

**Inclusive List of People Sent Over**

Capt. Walter Neale
Mr. Edward Godfrey
Mr. Ambrose Gibbins and wife
Lieut. Henry Jocelyn
Capt. Thomas Cammock
Mr. Thomas Wannerton
Mr. —— Herbert
Mr. John Raymond
Mr. George Vaughan
Roger Knight and wife
Charles Knill
William Cooper
Ralph Gee
Wm. [Dermit*]
Thomas Feverill
A boy [drowned]

Thomas Blacke or Blake
Stephen Kedder
Thomas Crockett
Sidrach Miller his two servants
Adrian Tucker
Henry Langstaff
James Wall
Wm. Chadbourn
John Goddard
Thomas Spencer
John Wilcox
Mr. Card (minister)
Mr. John Reynolds 'the old Doctor'
John Heard
Francis Matthews
William Berry
Michael Chatterton
Thomas Withers

For the foregoing, by land holdings or otherwise, there is some contemporary evidence. The following, early on the river, may have been sent over to this plantation, or possibly some of these may have come with Mr. Thomson.

Ould Father Peach
John Bennett
John Grear or Goder
—— Petfree
Lawrence Ellins
John Wotton
William Jones
Dr. Renald Fernald
Anthony Brackett
John Wall
Robt. Puddington
Henry Taylor
John Jones
Nicholas Row
Matthew Coe
William Palmer

Eighteen of these names are found in the fraudulent list fabricated about the year 1705.

with Mr. Thomson.
Pd the Smith for work.
Pd Mr. Bole for aq. vitae.
Pd Mr. Luxon for vinegar.
Pd Mr. Luxon for butter.
To the Taylor for mending.
For 14 fathom of wamp.
For 1 fathom of black wamp.
To the fishermen for carrying me into the Bay.
For Labrisset and Charles, their charge £1.
Pd to Capt. Mason for 1½ hogs. of mault.
More to Capt. Mason for 5½ lb. of sugar.
More to Capt. Mason for 8 gals. of sack.
John Pickering amunition breeches.
Steephen [not carried out].
To John Goder (?) for three booshels of corne.
For Phillip Swadden for 9 booshels of corne.

*Not 'Dermit;' prolonged study will be necessary to decipher this name.

†This must have been phonetic for Ambrose, the L standing for the obsolete gutteral l which was exiled from the English tongue under the stigma of lambdacismus.

**42** Fined for felling trees wastefully (1643). — N. H. Deeds i. 17.
Philip Swadden
Tho: Johnson
Andrew Harwood
Tho: Furson

**43** Sworn as Freemen, 1644, 1657. — N. E. Register viii. 77.
In the heading cancel Exeter. (In 1854 the records now at Concord were kept at Exeter.)
[Sworn 17 Apr. 1644, four Exeter men.]
[Sworn 14 July 1657, 19 Portsmouth men.]
Robert, anglicized from Hujbrecht, Mattoone.
Question William [Movis?]

**44** Petition to Mass. of the Inhabitants in Piscataqua and the Isles of Shoals' to fortify the river, 18 May 1653.—Mass. Arch. iii. 212.

Strawberry Bank
Kittery
Isles of Shoals
Dover

Brian Pendleton
Richard Cutt
Tho. Withers
Nic: Shapleigh
Rice Cadogin
Philip Babb
Richard Waldron
Hatevill Nutter

**45** Petition 18 May 1659 for twelve miles square at Pennecooke, signed also by other Essex County men:
Richard Walderne
Val: Hill
Peter Coffin
John 3 Hird
William Furber
Roger Plaisteed
Benj. Swett
Nathaniel Weare

**46** Commissioners in 1660 to end all differences regarding town boundaries:

Portsmouth
Mr. Thomas Broughton
Capt. Brian Pendleton
Mr. Elias Stileman

Dover
Capt. Walderne
Elder Wentworth
Leut. [Ralph] Hall
Sergt. Will. Furber
Richard Ottis

Oyster River
Mr. [Valentine] Hill
Ensign John Davis
Will. Roberts
Will. Williams Sen.
Robert Burnum

**47** Mr. Corbett's Petition [26 July 1665] for which the Bostoners jailed him has been printed three times, (Folsom, Jenness), most accessibly in N. H. Prov. Papers xvii. 512, where it may be corrected, partly by Folsom:
For Hancking, Hu-
Blake, prob. Black
Lea, prob. Dea
Geo. Iraf, in Folsom
Drap, prob. Drake
Frances, change to Francis thrice
James (Harben?)
Termly to Twamly
Necoth to Newtt
Robert (Heden?)

**48** Sir William Warren's list named for Councillors of New Hampshire, 7 July 1679, among whom he had dealt with Messrs: Sheafe, Waldron, Coffin and Cutt. Those marked (*) were approved on the same day, although only nine of them were named in the charter.

In Exeter
*Mr. John Gilman
*Mr. John Foulsam

In Portsmouth
Mr. Sampson Sheafe
*Mr. Elias Stileman
*Mr. John Cutt
*Capt. Thomas Daniel
*Mr. Richard Martin
*Capt. Nathaniel Fryer
*Mr. William Vaughan

In Dover
*Maj. Richard Waldren
*Mr. Peter Coffin
*Mr. John Gerrish
*Mr. Anthony Nutter

In Hampton
*Mr. Saml. Dolton Sen.
*Capt. Christopher Hussey
*Mr. John Samburn
Mr. Nath. Wyer

**49** Province Voting List, 16 Feb. 1679-80, for electing deputies for the General Assembly. — N. H. Prov. Papers xix. 659.

**50** Military Commissions 25 March 1680 — N. H. Prov. Papers xix. 667.
Alter Capt. Thomas Dainel to Daniel.

**51** Owners of Shipping, August 1681. Corrected by conjecture. — Prov. Papers xviii. 922-923.
Alter Matthew Eslis to Estes.
Question Thomas Conell.

**52** 1683-1686. This List consolidates four lists preserved in Concord or London, all four general for the whole of New Hampshire.

(1) Tax lists of 1684 sent to London, of which the N. H. Hist. Soc. have copies.
— London Transcripts iv. 89-113
(2) Secretary Chamberlain's list of householders from which jurymen were drawn for the Mason suits. — Prov. Papers ii. 554
(3) A compiled list of the Mason suits, perhaps incomplete.
(4) Petition against Gov. Cranfield taken to London by Nathaniel Weare, agent for the petitioners.
(2) and (3) were entirely different sets of men. Those not posted to (1) or (4) are as follows:
(2), total number 33

Benj. Matthews            William Hilton
John Rand                 Francis Lyford
Henry Roby                Edward Sewall
Nathl. Boulter            Charles Hilton
Christopher Palmer        Humphrey Spencer
John Lock

(3), total number **74**

**Great Island**           **Oyster River**
Sampson Sheafe            Robert Burnum
John Rawlins             John Hill Sr.
                         Samuel Hill
**Hampton**
Benj. Brown               **Kittery**
Samuel Sherburn          (islands in Piscat-
                          aqua River)
**Exeter**               Thomas Furnell
William More              William Furnell
William Ardell            Thomas Withers

(4) The original petitions in London bear 321 signatures, as against 213 in the copy printed in Prov. Papers i. 559. The following names are not found in (1):

Ralph Hall [Dover]        Samuel Blagdon
Joseph Beard          3   Jacob Lavers
Thomas Tibbets
John Duglis               Daniel Lamprey
James Nutt Jr.               Hampton  3
John Woodman              John Leavett
John Hayes                Morris Hobbs Jr.
John [Dam Sr.?]           John Smith
Thomas Chesle             James Marston
William Tascat
Nathaniel Hill            John Berry Jr.
    Oyster River   3      John Foss Jr.
Jonathan Woodman          John Seavey      2
John Nutter
Benj. Bickford            Christopher Kenniston
George Brawn
Thomas Rawlins            Will Holdridge
William Vaughan
Richard Waldron Jr.       James Prescott
Samuel Wentworth   2      John Clifford Sen.
John Partridge Jr.        John Clifford Jr.  3
Thos. Deverson            Thomas Ward
——an White                Moses Swett
William Cate              Henry Lamprey
Richard Monson            Seth Fogg
Thomas Cotton             Samuel Palmer
Robert Almery             Thomas Marston   2
Samuel Rand               Francis Page
Silvanus Wentworth        Samuel Marston
Thomas Cram               Samuel Dow
James Derry               Humphrey Perkins
Jeremiah Burnham          Philemon Dalton
Joseph Stevenson          Philip Towle Jr.
James Davis               Joshua Towle
Thomas Bickford           Nathan[iel] Seavey
Joseph Meader             Jonathan Perkins
                          Richard Sanborn
Thomas Crosby             Theophilus Dudley
William Fifield (Jr.)     James Sinkler
                          William Perkinson
Thomas Graffort           Daniel Bean
Alexander Dennett         Alexander Magoon
Splan Lovell              Nicholas Gordon
Thomas Pickering          Philip X. Huntun
Thomas Lucy               Samuel Bean

Nicholas Smith            John Sherburn
Philip Moody              Henry Sherburn
Simon Wiggin              Thomas Edmonds
George Walker             Anthony Stanyan
Tobias Langdon            John Plaisted
John Sloper               John Pickering Jr.
John (Clark?)             Samuel Neal
John (Folsom?)            John Banfield

(1) New Hampshire tax lists, P. R. O.  C. O. 54, no. 25 I-VIII. Intended only for those refusing to pay taxes to Gov. Cranfield, many willing to pay were included, while some, especially a large part of the congested population of Strawberry Bank, were omitted. Apparently the complete lists for Greenland and Sandy Beach were sent.

**Portsmouth and Strawberry Bank**
Sworn by John Pickering, Constable
(In this list those not refusing to pay were omitted).

John Denick           4   William Walker        4
George Hunt[ress]     4   Daniel Wescott        4
John Hunkin           4   Ephrim Lyn
William Ham               John Baker         3, 4
Richard Jackson       4   John Cavileare        4
William Earll      3, 4   Nicho: Walden         4
Richard Martin     3, 4   James Lovett          4
John Saward               Mrs. Daniel           3
Samuel Case (Keais)   3   Richard Shortridg     2
Obediah Morse      3, 4   Robert Pudington      4
Ed. Melcher        3, 4   Hugh Leare            4
John Tucker           4   Daniel Duggins        4
Mathew Nelson         4   James Jones
Jane Joce             3   William Cotton        4
Richard Waterhouse    4   Nehemiah Partridg     4
John Parteridg        4   Richard Webber        2
George Fabins             John Fletcher         4
John Bartlett             Sam: Clarke        2, 4
John Shipway       3, 4   Timothy Davis         4
William Williams          William Pitman        4
Thomas Wakeham            John Wakeham
John Serll                Lewis Williams        4
William Mason             Henry Kerk
Henry Savage          4   Edward Skat [Cate]    4
William Brooken       4   John Cotton           4

**Great Island**
Sworn by Daniel Ushaw, Constable, 25 Aug. 1684.
Richard Abbott            James Robinson        2
Elias Stileman        4   Joseph Read the Smith
Pheasant Eastwick         Nicholas Heskins
Thomas Parker             Joseph Rayne
Edward Randle             John Amaseen          3
William Row               Joseph Mussett
Daniel Ushaw &c.          Widow Jones
Joseph Purmett        2   Samuel Roby
David Kemball             George Walton
Henry Crowne              John Clarke & Man
Mathew Estes              Thomas Jones
John Lewis            2   Widow Johnson
Thomas Cobbet             Arthur Head
Capt. Barefoot            James Leach           2
Francis Tucker             & 2 Sons             2
Jeremy Hodgsdon           John Cross
Widow Lux                 Aron Ferris
Andrew Cranch             James Payne
Mr. Hincks                Edward Carter         2
Mr. Eliott & Tho. Joce    Jeremy Walford
Edw. Beale

A fragment of the Strawberry Bank list, 4 Sept. 1684, is in N. H. Court Files. viii. 181.
Frances Jons             Mr. Severit
Richard Monson           Rub: Hull             4
Nathan Whit              Tom: Gubtaill
John Boman               Rech: Watts
Jethroo Furbord       3  Will: Petmans
Will Racklee—wiff         Richard Dore
George Snell—wiff     4   Philip Tucker—wiff
Mr. Haroll—wiff           Mark Hunkins—wiff
Mr. Cutt, mariner         Ladowick Fouler
        —wiff                    —will pay

**62** Address of New Hampshire Inhabitants, 10 Aug. 1692, asking equal privileges with Massachusetts. 'Whereas your Majesties have been graciously pleased to settle the government of the Province of the Massachusetts wherein x x x we always hoped to have been included, but finding it otherwise x x x we are but four poor towns daily exposed from French and Indian enemies.' This petition was circulated outside before reaching Portsmouth, and did not reach Newcastle or Rye at all. The four columns were signed up as follows:

Right-hand, started at Hampton, then at Greenland and Portsmouth.
Second, started at Exeter, then at Stratham and Portsmouth.
Third, started at Dover Neck, then at Cochecho, Durham, Portsmouth.
Left-hand, started at Durham, then at Newington, Greenland, Portsmouth.

The petition has survived only in a copy attested by W. Bridgeman, (P.R.O. C.O.1. 5:924), most clearly written, but by a clerk who did not know the inhabitants and could not read all of their signatures, so that the document contains many imaginary persons. In replacing such names by the real signers so far as possible, I have had the help of B. F. Stevens's copy made for the N. H. Hist. Soc. and of Hon. Charles H. Batchelder. The names placed in brackets are probably mere misreadings.

John Woodman Sen.
John Woodman Jun.
Jonathan Woodman
Robert Huckins
Stephen Jones
Jeremiah Burnum
Edwardes Wakeham
Joseph Pitman
Ezekiel Pitman
William Jackson
Edward Lethers
Philip Chesley
George Chesley
Samuel Chesley
Thomas Chesley
James Davise
Thomas Bickford
Stephen Jenkins
John Derry
Francis Pitman
Thomas Edgerly
Barnard Squire
Thomas Edgerly Jun.
Thomas [Dison]
Zachariah Egerly
John Dam Sen.
John Bickford
Thomas Row
John Pinder
Nathaniel Hill
Thomas Laighton
William Furber
Henery Langstaff
George Brawne
Henery Langstaff
John Hill
Robert Goss
Luke Malone
John Johnson
Leonard Weeks
Samuel Weeks
William Philbrock
Richard Andrews
Nathaniel Huggins
Edward Peave
Thomas Avery
Robert Briant
Mathias Haines
John Johnson Sen.
Sam: Whidden
William Vaughan
Richard Waldron
John Partridge
John Hunking
Nicholas Bennett
Edward Melcher
William Furber Sen.
Samuel Banks
John Clark
John Fletcher
Matthew Nelson
Henry Crown
Tho: Deverson
John Gerrish
John Barsham

Job Clements
John Tuttle
Robert Evens Sen.
Robert Evans
Marke Giells
John Thomly
John Church
Richard Scammon
John Winget
John Eles
Trustrum Herd
Ezekiel Wentworth
Thomas Downs
John Ham
Gershom Wintworth
John Cooke
Benjamin Herd
Samuel Herd
John Horn
Timothy Wintworth
Ralph Hall
John Hays
Jenkin Jones
George Record
Mat: Record
William Horn
Nathaniel Herd
Thomas Young
John Roberts
Thomas Roberts
Zachariah Field
Nathaniel Roberts
Joseph Roberts
Sam: Tibbets
John Hall
Henry Hobbs
Richard Randall
William Damm
Nathaniel Hall
Tho: Whitehouse Sen.
John Tutle Jun.
Charles Adams Sen.
Henry Marsh
Charles Adams Jun.
John Williams
John Edgerly
Richard [blank]
John Meader Sen.
John Meader Jun.
Charles Allen Jun.
Richard Martin
Sam: Penhallow
Obediah Morse
William Hunking
John Tucker
Tho: Harvey
William Partridge
Benj: Cotton
Tho: Pickering
John Bennet
Splan Lovell
Saml: Shuckford
Richard Gerrish
*John Dockam
James Levitt

Andrew Wiggin
John Gilman Sen.
Moses Gilman Sen.
John Foullsam
Kinsley Hall
James Sinkler
Edward Sewell
Samuel [Lenard]
David Larans
Benjamin B. I. Jones
James M. Kid
Bily Dudley
Richard Morgan Sen.
George Peirson
John Sinckler Sen.
Theophilus Dudley
Jeremiah Gilman
Moses Gilman Jun.
John Gilman Jun.
John Ficket
William Wentworth
Jonathan Thing
John Bene Sen.
Christian Dolhaf
John Bene Jun.
Jeremiah Connar
Nicholas Gourdin
James Bene
Alexander Magoon
Nicholas Smith
Stephen Dudley
John Sleeper
Humphrey Wilson
Peter Folsom
John Young
Ephraim Foulsham
Robert Wadley Jun.
Philip Duery
Clement Mody
Phill: Hontone
Robert Young
John Young Jun.
John Wilson
Rich Glidon
Daniel Beane
Sam: Thing
William More
Tho: Veasy
Geo: Veasy
Jonathan Wadly
Simon Wiggins
Andrew Wiggins Jun.
Mark Hunking
Thomas Wacums
Mark Ayers
Elisha Briard
John Dam Jun.
John Pickerin Sen.
Edward Ayers
Geo: Snell
Clement Micervey
Timothy Davis
Sam: Keais
Philip Lewis
John Sherbourne

Nich: Follett
Thomas Philbrick Sen.
Benjamin Fifeld
Peter Weare
Joseph Berry
Nathaniel Berry
Sam: Philbrick
John Moulton
Nath: Bacheler Sen.
Nath: Bacheler Jun.
Francis Page
Moris Hobs Sen.
Benjamin Moulton
William Fifields
John Sambourn Sen.
John Sambourn Jun.
John Tucke
Thomas Derbourn
John Smith
Isaac Godfrey
Tho: Webster
Daniel Moulton
James Johnson
Daniel Tilton
Benj: Shaw
Jonathan Sanburn
Abraham Drake Jun.
Tho: Philbrock Jun.
Sam: Neal
John Cate
Robert Hinkson
James Johnson
Sam: Haines
Joshua Brackett
John Davies
John Scrivener
Nat: Folsom
John Widgwood
Bradstreet Wiggins
James Godfry
Isaac Cole
Thomas Reed
Nath: Wright
Philip Cromwell
John Cromwell
Moses Garnsby
Abraham Lewis
Christopher Keniston
George Keniston
*John Dockham
Wm. Davies
Edward Fox
Charles Allin Sen.
William Pitman
Thomas Kirkes
William Williams
John Snell
John Chevallier
Sam: Rawlings
Rich: Jose
Nathaniel Ayers
Richard Jackson
Jacob Lavers
John Hill Sen.
John Plaisted

**63**   New Hampshire Militia [about June 1700] — London Transcripts x. 145.

William Vaughan, Major      William Cotton, Field Marshal

| | Captain | Lieut. | Ensigne | Soldiers |
|---|---|---|---|---|
| Hampton | Henry Dow | John Moulton | Samuel Maston | 130 |
| | Jacob Green | Joseph Sweat | John Gove | 70 |
| Dover | John Tuttle | Nathaniel Hill | Hatevill Roberts | 116 |
| | John Woodman | James Davis | Stephen Jones | 80 |
| Portsmouth | John Pickerin | John Snell | Nath: Ayers | 86 |
| | Tobias Langdon | Aaron Moses | John Sherborn | 65 |
| Exeter | Peter Coffin | Simon Wiggens | Nicholas Gillman | 150 |
| New Castle | John Hinckes | Theodore Atkinson | | 53 |

**64**   Civil Lists 25 Aug. 1699.
— N. H. Prov. Papers ii. 321.

**65**   Province Treasurer's Account for 1694.
— N. H. Prov. Papers xvii. 628-629.

**66**   War Disbursements in 1694-1695.
— N. H. Prov. Papers xvii. 644-648.

**67**   Military Services in 1695-1696.
— N. H. Prov. Papers xvii. 654-656, ii. 179, xi. 642-644.

**68**   War Disbursements in 1697.
— N. H. Prov. Papers xvii. 667-669.
669 Alter John Norce to Vorce.
Alter Tho: Dolce to Dotee.

**69**   Commissioners to Settle all Town Bounds; Dec. 3, 1701.

| | |
|---|---|
| Portsmouth | Major William Vaughan |
| | Capt. Mark Hunkins |
| | Capt. John Pickiring |
| Hampton | Nathl. Weare Esq. |
| | Capt. Henry Dow |
| | Ephraim Marston |
| Dover | Capt. John Tuttle |
| | Lefft. James Davis |
| | Lefft. William Furber |
| Exeter | Mr. Jonathan Wadley |
| | Ensign Nicholas Gillman |
| | John Foulshem |
| New Castle | Mr. James Rendell |
| | James Leach |
| | William Berry |

---

## Merchants' Accounts and other documents taking in more than one province.

**71**   Probate Accounts of Stephen Crawford's Estate, 1641-1647.
— Me. Prov. & Court Rec. 120-122.

**72**   Isaac Grosse, Will and Book Accounts May 29 - June 5, 1649. — N. E. Reg. vii. 228.
Alter Olive Ellen to [Wm. Ellingham?]
William Welster the Brewer [-John- Webster, Strawberry Bank?]

**73**   Book Accounts of John Mills, 22 Oct. 1651. Executors: Samuel Maverick, Robert Knight, Paul White. Partly indexed.
— N. E. Reg. iv. 285.
Alter Robert Nauney to Nanney.
Alter Capt. Francis Champrowne to Champernoune.

**74**   Passenger List of Scotch Prisoners 8 Nov. 1651. Almost unindexed.
— Suff. Deeds i. 5-6.

**75a**   Book Accounts of Capt. Bozoan Allen, 22 Sept. 1652. Partly indexed.
— N. E. Register viii. 60-62.

**75b**   Book Accounts of Mr. Robert Button, 10 March 1652-3. Unverified and partly indexed. — N. E. Reg. viii. 59.

**76**   Piscataqua and Isles of Shoals Petition, 18 May 1653. Two signers for each settlement. — Doc. Hist. iv. 52.

**77a**   Doubtful Debts due the Estate of George Munnings, Boston, 8 Jan. 1658[9.
— N. E. Reg. viii. 354.

**77b**   Accounts of Capt. Thomas Thornhill 4 May 1660. Partly indexed.
— N. E. Register x. 175.
[Alter Henry Lamperry to Lamprill?]

**78**   Debts due to Mr. John Mitchell's Estate 1666. — Me. Prov. & Court Rec. i. 252-3.

**79**   Debtors and Creditors to William Scadlock's estate, 1667. — Me. Prov. & Court Rec. i. 338.

**80**   Debts due to Mr. John Croad's Estate, 1671. Partly indexed.
— Essex Quarterly Courts iv. 401.

**81**   John Wincoll's list of unpaid bills of the Salmon Falls mills 6 Dec. 1662-6 Apr. 1671 1671.

| | |
|---|---|
| Town of Dover for rent | £50 |
| Major Waldron | 8 |
| Mr. Peter Coffin | 34 |
| Nyvan Agnew of Kittery | 40 |
| John Key of Kittery | 3 |
| Mycome Micatere of York | 28 |
| Major Shapleigh | 30 |
| John Greene Senior | 5 |
| John Taylor | 5 |
| Mr. John Cutt | 80 |
| Capt. James Pendleton | 18 |
| Capt. Elias Stileman | 7 |
| Richard Thorla and Thomas Thorla | 40 |
| (and others in Boston) | |

**82**   Agreement Regarding a Ship, 2 Sept. 1670. Henry Greenland, Walter Barefoote, Robert Marshall, with George Norton of Kittery shipwright for finishing the hull of a vessel he was then building near the head of the great bay in the river of Piscataqua, each to own ¼.

Wit:
Jeremiah Hubbard
Edward Chambers
Tho: Watkins

Summons 22 Feb. 1671[2 Walter Barefoote v. Robert Marshall
Issued by John Hall.
Return of John Robearts (aut) marshal that he had arrested the body, and delivered him to keeper of Dover jail as he refused to give bail.
The arrest was in the evening at the house of Francis Morgan at Kittery (±28) 28 Feb. 1671[2 and Marshal Roberts proposed to take him up river that night to the jail in another county.
The Marshal of York offered to take him to York jail, in the county where arrested, and was entrusted with the prisoner that night at Mr. Bray's house.
The Marshall Roberts ordered Walter Barefoot and Edward Colcut to assist in the arrest.
John Wiborne testified that Francis Morgan offered to be his bondsman with his house and six head of cattle. The Marshall was serving three writs: Wentworth, Walter Barefoot, Henry Greenland.
24 Oct. 1671 Robert Marshall's instructions to "my only mate" John Bennett to stay aboard the

Pincke Lenham and let nobody aboard, but to take and stow away any goods put aboard by Doctor Greenland, Capt. Barefoote or George Norton.
Wit: Peter Bragg
    John Ameredith, constable
Accounts show supplies, etc., furnished by:
    Capt. James Pendleton
    Capt. Lockwood
    Tho: Beard
Three carpenters taken to Exeter by John Scarlet to help build the vessel.
Supplies sent by Paul Hall.
Mr. Bartholomew Stratton and his son and Thomas Snowe and Jacob Browne for rigging her.
John Beadle wages.
John Clarke for going three times to Charlestown to fetch the men.
Andrew Newcomb for the men's passage.
Robert Emens for wages.
Jacob Brown    "
Diet for men at Mr. Ameredeth.
    "    "    "    " Mr.Morgans.
    "    "    "    " Mr. Brays.
    "    "    "    " Saml. Windfers.
    "    "    "    " Saml. Windford.
Cask of rum delivered to John Bragg sent by Paul Hall.
John Roberts, Marshal, dep. that Robert Marshall said he should not need the assistance of Mr. Greenland and Capt. Barfoot and Geo. Norton so long as his unkle Thatcher's bags and Mr. Hull s mint holds out.
John Roberts master of the } Dep. 1 Jan. 1671[2
    Pincke Lenham } before Elias Stile-
Gabragan Bonnithon±20 } man Commissioner
that Robert Marshall and others came aboard and took away the rigging when partly laden and men shipped.
Robert Couch } heard Capt. Barefoote several
Isaac Woodde } times say.
Mr. Henry Kemble had furnished the iron work.
Robert Lauis received 6 gallons of rum from Thomas Beard of Dover for the use of Robert Marshall by order of Walter Barefoot. 22 July 1672.
Capt. Richard Lockwood±40 } July 1672
Mr. Arthur Clapham±50 }
Capt. Lockwood del. a barrel of tar at Walter Barefoot's order.
John Hole constable of Kit. 27 Feb. 1671[2.
Jacob Browne±32 sworn before Richard Parker 4 Sept. 1672, often heard Walter Barefoote say.
Saml. Browne±32 same as last.
20 Oct. 1671 warrant issued by Elias Stileman Comr. to John Hole constable of Kittery to aid the marshal's deputy or appear before Mr. Richard Cutt to answer for the same.
John Hole's return: went in a boat alongside the vessel Geo. Norton built, Geo. Norton and others being aboard, would not let the marshal come aboard but pushed him so that he fell into the water. Their names John Roberts, Joseph Carre.
Samuel Brown, deputy marshal, made complaint 25 Oct. 1671 before Edward Rishworth:
Having arrested Robert Marshall, attempt to rescue him, supported by Doctor Barefoot, was made by Doctor Greenland, who seized the staff from Constable John Hole, which he thrust with and used oaths and curses "which made my flesh tremble to hear," and believed we would have been murdered by him had not the constable recovered his staff and commanded peace, and Mrs. Morgan, Ephraim Lenn, John Pickeren and John Shapley persuaded to peace.
Mrs. Lockwood testified.
Jacob Brown testified: "George Norton told me I should not come on board alive," and John Roberts and Joseph Cary also resisted.

**83**  Roster of Militia during, or before or after, King Philip's War.
A compilation.  — Bodge 475-476.
John Gattinsley read Gattinsby.

**84**  Aged First-Comers Gave Depositions
25 Aug. 1676. — N. H. Prov. Papers xvii. 521-523.
Alter Henry Dowell to Donnell.

**85**  Oath of Fidelity taken in Essex County, 1677-1678. Partly indexed.
    — Essex Quarterly Courts vi. 398-402.

**86**  Falmouth and 'East York.'
Last court, [Wells] before 16 July 1672 "one Anthony a black man," Anthonious Lamy, a portyngayle, for giving physic suspected to have caused the death of John Gouch.
Hannah Averell wife of Thomas. Lamy wanted to take him to Henry Donnell's but he said he could neither walk nor go on a horse, and his wife said he could not go.
Walter Barefoote } depose in court the unguent
Henry Greenland } produced in court they never
Francis Morgan } thought proper to be given
    } inwardly in any case whatsoever.
Lydia Gooch wife of John Gooch late dec. After my husband's death Anthony Lambe demanded £40 of me or £25 in silver or myself.
Thomas Averill±36, 5 July 1672, John Gooch's mother gave John a little liquor, they went to Goodwife Baker for directions, which the Portuguese hearing of at York was much displeased.
Ruth Gooch±67 }
Lideah   "   ±28 } 3 July 1672
**Testimonial for the Doctor**
Top of the sheet headed Cascey Bay 20 Aug. 1672
John Munjoy          Thomas Brackett
Henry **8** Daniels   Pheneas Rider
John Cox             John **2** Lewis
Richard **3** Bray    Ellener **6** Lewis
Anthonie Brackett    John Clays
Joseph **2** Reding   Thomas Clayes
George Ingersoll     Peter Houssown
    Samson Penley
    **East York**
    Edmond Cock
    Samuell Dunell
    Benjamin Whitney
    John **6** Card Seniour
    John Card Juniour
    Thomas Start

**87**  John Stydson's Inventory, July 1673, in York Court Records.

| Debts Desperate | Debts hopefull |
|---|---|
| John Parsons | Good: Tomson |
| Thos. Donnell | Mr. Dereing |
| John G[row]th | Robort Junkine |
| John Pirkine | Edw. Chambers |
| Ric Rich | James Grant |
| Benj Johnson | Alex: Maxell |
| Jere Moulton | John Hoy |
| Hene Sayward | Mr. Neale |
| Mr. Francis Hooke | Mr. Lane |
| David Kymball | Mr. Corbet |
| John —— | |
| Cursung —— [possibly Cursonwhitt] | |
| Job Everest | |
| Fran: Smale | |
| Fran: Rider | |
| Dan: Moore | |
| Phyneas Rider | |
| Goodman Ingerson | |

**88**  Royalist Review of Public Men, (1676?). This anonymous paper, Mass. Arch. iii. 300, may be a copy. It treats as living men who died in 1674 and 1676 and terms deceased one living on Great Island in 1679. The writer had not heard of the misplacements of Philip's War; it was certainly written before Mass. bought Maine, probably in England. As printed Doc. Hist. iv. 314:

Alter Mr. Mahone to Vahone [Vaughan].
Mr. James Whelewright [sic] meant Samuel.
Henry Sawyer [sic] a spelling of Sayword.

**89** List of debts & credits of Mr. Lidget's
estate made 31 Mar. 1683 by Henry Dering,
who used once a year to draw up for Mrs. Eliza-
beth Saffin, 'as I was her bookkeeper.'
        [Only a few selected]
Tho. Daniell & Henry Dering          Boston
Richard Waldron Senior               Dover
Peter Coffin                         Dover
Richard Pattishall                   Boston
Edward Cowell                        Boston
John Woodmancy & Mary Tappet         Boston
Thomas Holmes & John Brecke
Isaac Waldron
Joseph Cowell                        Boston
Tho Daniel & Wm. Vaughan             Portsmouth
Reuben Hull                          Portsmouth
Richard Waldron Senior & Junior      Dover
        **Bad & Desperate Debts**
Oliver Purchase                      Lynn
David Campbell                       Portsmouth
Peter Twisden                        Isle Shoals
William Bickham          Portsmouth or Kittery

**90** Account of Robert Elliot against John
Hinckes, 1680 to 1700.
        **Debtor**
1680  Money to Mr. Samuel Wentworth
      Fish as money to Mr. Ellic Nichols
1682  Paid Mr. Philip Fall in corn
      4 bbl mackerel delv. John More
      4 cords wood by John Ball
      4 qtls. fish by Capt Francis Hook
      Paid Capt Peeck
1683  4 cords wood to Capt. Cock by John Ball
      60 quintills mercht. fish to pay Hubord
      Lent you in money by John Sherborn
      78 quintils codfish to pay Mr. Elic Nichols
      By Capt. Wareham you promised to pay
1684  32 gal rum 2 doz cod hooks to Edw. Woo-
      ton
      2 hhd Molasses delivered Humphrey
      Eliot to himself May 18
      Lent you to pay Daniel Maine
1685  Paid Richard Oliver for bringing fish
      Sugar & turnips to Mary Tomson
      Paid John Booden for you
1687  Paid Capt Clay for you
      225 lbs iron to Essex the Smith
      To sundries to Capt. Daniel Hutson
      By Peter Shaw      money
      By money Mr. John Pilgram
1689  12 hhd. salt to Edw. Wooten
      "   "   "   " Thos Embling
      Money paid John Pette for you
      (Feb. 18, 1689-90) 3 doz codhooks to Wai-
      mouth Bicton
      2 nets delv. Robert Jordan
      2 cords wood by Weeks
1693  Paid Daniel Littlefield for you
      Paid Mr. John Waldron Marblehead
      Wheat delivered you by Mr. Geo. Jaffry
      1 hhd. molasses Mr. Pepper by order
1695  Wheat Mr. Hasleton 56 lbs
1697  6 bbl salt from Mr. Harris Boston
      To my house & Stage you bought of me at
      Spurwink in Oct 1685
        **Creditor**
1680  By Buttons & silk to Mr. Thos Roberts
      By Mr. John Brock 1681
      By Job Bishop
      By Treferin
      By Ben Berry
      to Mr. Ph. Hatch      £4-12-00
      5 Qnt mch. fish to Mr. Dearing
      By money paid Mr. Simeon Stoddard £50
      By ditto by Mr. Foxwell              5
      Edward Woten
      1½ hhd salt to Wm. Moregould

4  hhd salt to Wm. Row
5   "   "   "  Wm. Mansfield
4   "   "   "  Waymo. Lydston
4   "   "   "  Richard Oliver
7   "   "   "  Lydston
6   "   "   "  Robert Haines
3   "   "   "  John Abbot
6   "   "   "  Robert Jordan
5   "   "   "  Lains
1 quint fish by Webber
refuse fish to complete Collins bill
By James Randal
6 Qt. Codfish towards Shaw's debt
1689  1 gal rum to John Knight
      1 hwt. bread to Mr. Pepperrell
      Bread to Hollicome
      ¾ bread to Gammon & Brown
      Bread to Thomas Wise & Pulman
      "   "  John Ham
      "   "  Wm. Oliver
      Bread & corn to Bette Finix
      Paid by John Row
      By Mr. Penhallow                    £10
      By Mr. Geo. Vaughan                   6

**91** Creditors of the Estate of Nathan
        Bedford, 25 Sept. 1683.
Mr. Nathaniel Fryer    John Walden, net maker
Thomas Baker           Thomas Parker
Mr. Blackman           Mr. John Hinkes
Silvester Harbert      John Lewis
Mr. William Stoughton  for a widow's interest
Mr. Robert Eliott      Mr. Watts
Mr. Francis Tucker     James English
John Jacob             Richard Cally

**92** Accounts in Thomas Ladbrook's Es-
        tate, Portsmouth, 30 Sept. 1684.
Goody Brucken          Mr. Ottes Cochecho
Rob. Brains            Xtefer Nobell
John Cook              Goodman Dam
Mr. John Cut Presedent Mr. Pall
Mr. Clemmons           Will Perkins
Capt. Daves            Mr. Fenix
Sam. Clark             John Homs
Goodman Downs          Will Shuckford
Mr. John Cut Jun       Robert Smart
Jo Curtis              Charles Gleden
Will Folet             John Fabins
Mr. French             Mager Shapligh
Mr. Edgerly            Frank Trickey
Mr. Ellot              John Tucker
Mr. Hull               Mr. Turtherly
Ed Hilton              Tom Trickey
Will Hilton            Moses Gillman
Rech Gren              John Davenport
Mr. Hunkins                   by noot
Mr. Grenland           John Lee by noot
Mr. Huch [possibly     John Hadlee
      Huck]                   by noot
Mr. Crown              Omfree Spencer
Mr. Levet Exsester     Jerimy Sheers
Nex Hares              Weber
Mr. Holl               Rob. Wadlee
Will Haskins           John Walden
Eli Guneson            James Wigens
      Keneston         Mr. Wier of York
Steven Jons            John Westbruck
Will Johnson, York     Mr. Wegens
Rech Jackson           Tom Willee
Rob. Lang              Mr. Wenford
Mr. Moody              Mr. Wethers
Mr. Meriday

**93** Debtors to George Munjoy's Estate,
        1685. — York Deeds v. 37.
?Elias Redding recorder's error by Eleanor?

**94** Capt. John Gerrish's Account Book,
        Aug. 9, 1686, to March 5, 1687-8. N. E. H.
& G. Register, xxxvi. 73.
        Checking up by the original shows the following

misreadings:
Mr. Lord for Mr. Love.
John Wodget for Wedget [Wedgwood].
Peter Noys for Nap [Knapp].
Mr. Godyer for Weyer [Weare].
Jefrye Jenkings for Josep[h].
Richard Tomson for Robert
Guttensby for Gattensby.
Daniel Furbyr for Furbess.
Richard Hilton is surcharged Edward.
John Wood senior and junior are abbreviations
  for Woodman of Oyster River, but possibly
  there was also one John Wood at Dover.
Harry Merry and Meridy must be one man [Hen-
  ry Merrow].
Apparently four Evanses are named, Capt. Evens,
  Robert Evens, Sen., Robert Evens, Jr., Ed
  Evens.
Joseph Barnot for Barnet(?) [Barnard].
James Hugings looks more like Hagings.
Will Arington is also written Urington and Yer-
  ton.
Names or designations overlooked:
John Wod[man] Jr        Cafferly
Jonathan Wood[man]      Davy Davis
John Wood[man] Sen      John Derry
———— Magune           Deny Deny [Dennis]
John Winget Jr          Other names in loose
Jeremy Gillman and         papers belonging with
  his father              the book:
Mr. Hilton 6 oxen       James Smith
Good. Edgerly           Scammon
Mr. Coffin              Tom

**95**  Henry Maine's Estate, List of Debts
  Paid, 1687.
  —Doc. Hist. vi. 338 (Mass. Arch. cxxix. 94).
Edward Undery [-sic-] read Vickery.

**96**  Journal of Rev. John Pike
  1678-1709. Massachusetts names are not indexed. — N. H. Gen. Records iii. 77, 97, 145.

**97**  Abstract of Militia in New England
  —Board of Trade N. E. Vol. 5, No. 91.
Received May 13, 1690 (from Gov. Andros.)
[Some counties commanded by colonels, some by
  majors.
Boston, 8 companies, 954 men.
Essex County, 10 companies, including Salisbury,
  Amesbury and Haverhill.
County of Dukes County, no returns]
        **Province of New Hampshire**
            Col. Robert Mason
Officers' Names     Towns            No. of Men
            Portsmouth 1st Co.
            Portsmouth 2d Co.
            Hampton
            Exeter
            Dover 1st Co.
            Oyster River 1st Co.
        **Province of Maine**
            Col. Robert Mason
            Upper Kittery
            Lower Kittery
            York
            Wells
            Cape Porpus
Capt. Blakman       Saco
Capt. Tho. Scottow  Scarboro
Capt. Edw. Ting     Falmouth 1st Co.  ⎫
Capt. Silvanus Davis Falmouth 2d Co.  ⎬ 115
Capt. Gendall       North Yarmouth    029
            Harwich
        **County of Cornwall**
Capt. Rowden        Newtowne and
                      Sacodehocke     094
Capt. Nicho. Manning New Dartmouth    047
Capt. Wallen        James Towne and
                      New Harbour     060
            Monhegin and other
              fishing islands

**98**  Names in accounts between Hutchinson, Boston, and Wm. Partridge, Portsmouth, 1689-1696—Suffolk Court Files, 3394,
6413.

    1689                Thos. Wacom
Obediah Morse          H. Major
Wm. Devesen            Mr. Penhallow
Ben. Backway           Math Carlton
Capt. Bant             Mr. Geo. Jaffrys
Dr. Cooke              Charls Story
    1693                Sm. Lockwood
Capt. Thos. Corbett    Sm. Thing
Capt. William Fernald  Jonathan Thing
Richard & Winthrop          1695
  Hilton, masts        William Partridge Esq.
James, Thos. & Saml.   Mr. Joseph Hammond
  Chesley, masts       David Jeffries
Richard Manson         Samuel Wentworth
Elizabeth West         Capt. William Fernald
Thos. Dymond             acct. Ship Partridge
Abraham Haseltone      Capt. John Gerrish & Co.
Samuel Smith           Elizabeth West
Robert Tufton            Henderson
Thos. Holland            Harvey
Thos. Packer           George Long
John Knight               1695-1696
Henry Penny            Samuel Thing
Richard Gerrish        Cotton & Company
    1694                  Waterhouse
William Ardol             Rogers
Jonathan Plummer
Edward Ayres              1699
  Arnold               Capt. Foy
Mr. Joshua Moody       Mr. Moody
Mr. Cook               Philip White
William Owins          Harvey & sloop hire

**99**  Six Lists printed in Chap. IV, Vol.
  1 of Coleman's New England Captives Carried
to Canada. 1925.
The names in these lists are indexed by standard
  spellings, or not indexed.
 74 Matthew Cary's list Oct. 1695.
                  — Mass. Arch. 38. 1-4.
 77 Col. John Phillip's list 24 Jan. 1698/9.
                  — Mass. Arch. 70. 398.
 91 Gov. Dudley's list 5 March 1710/11.
                  — Mass. Arch. 71. 765.
123 Louis XIV's bounty list 11 Nov. 1702.
                  — Parkman MS., Mass. Hist. Soc.
125 French naturalization May 1710.
                  — Canadian Arch.
128 French naturalization June 1713.
                  — Canadian Arch.
 75 Alter Richard to Hickbut Short.
    Alter John Shiply to Shisly [Chesley].
 78 Alter Mary Hatter to Catter [-K- altered
    to -C-].
    Abiall Masterson altered from Snell.
 91 The Deerfield item was entered later at the
    foot of the page.
 92 Alter Jabeth to Jabesh Simpson.
127 Magdelaine Cout [Coul? = Cole?].

# Sagadahoc Settlements, from the Kennebec to St. Georges. Lists 101-191.

## St. Georges. List 101.

**101** Silvanus Davis's Recollections of English occupancy east of the Sagadahoc or Kennebec river (written in March 1701) have been misunderstood, bungled in print, and made the scapegoat for a brood of historical misstatements. He tried to include every one who ever lived anywhere there at any time, from 25(?) years before he came there himself down to 1690. As printed in the N. E. Reg. xxi. 356:

The words 'at St. Georges' refers only to Mr. Foxwell and Philip Swadden. [Foxwell of Scarborough and Swadden of Piscataqua.]

The figures '84' and '84 families' are estimated totals of what precedes — all the fishermen and farmers near the coast.

The words 'within land' belong with 'Between Kennebec and George's River 12.'

Under the heads of 'Fishermen,' 'Farmers,' 'Farmers withinland' and 'Inland between Kenebec and George's River,' his memory traveled from West to East four times, naming personally only the two ancient Indian traders at St. George's long before his own day. Between the French and the English, St. George's was a no-man's land.

## Monhegan. Lists 111-114.

**111** Trial 2 Jan. 1655[6. Rev. Robert Jordan vs. John Ridgway who in 1651 had been partners in a fishing voyage to Monhegan. Defendant appealed;

Gregory Jefferies and Tho. Warner, his bondsmen.

**Depositions**

John Heyman±40, sworn before Mr. Duncan; acted for Mr. Jordan at Monhegan.

Samuel Mavericke, (autograph).

George Bickford, sworn in 1652.

Matthew Abdy±28, 17 May 1654; the fish were taken in to Charlestown and delivered to Capt. Breden for John Ridgway and to Robert Corben for Mr. Jordan.

Tho. Mitchell±25, 8 Feb. 1655[6, saw the boats at Spurwink.

John Lauranc±35, 7 Jan. 1655[6; mentioned Nicholas Lauranc.

*Samuel Okeman±25.

*Roger Seward, went to Monhegan.

**\*Fishermen, as also**

| | |
|---|---|
| Samuel Coaker | Henry Carter |
| John Brookin | Peter Way |

**Commissioners Taking Depositions**

Edward Rishworth, Recorder
Nathaniel Duncan, Commissioner

| | |
|---|---|
| Henry Jocelyn | Robert Booth |
| Henry Watts | Richard Hitchcock |

**112** Murder on Monhegan. The return of a Boston jury, 4 Dec. 1654, ''being called to veue the body of Mathew Kehnige;'' finding Death caused by a wound on the head.

Thomas Michell±26, 28 July 1657; being at Munhiging and coming into the house of Mathew Cunnig, saw him bleeding; asked the young man that struck him why he lifted up his hand against an old man. Said Grigrey answered: It was done and could not be undun.

Nathaniel Gallop, Samuell Gallop±26, 7 Dec. 1654; Being at Monhiggin about middle of Oct. last past and hearing the report on the Island that Mathew Camage had received a blow by Gregory Castle upon the head by a hammer, these deponents say that they heard the said Mathew Cannidge say that he had bled about two quarts, and further heard the said Cennidge say that if he had the said Castle in a place where ther was any government he would trouble him for it. He came aboard their bark in the evening, his senses gone

from him, went into his cabin very sick, and so continued until they came to Boston where he died.

## Pemaquid and Muscongus. 121-126.

**121** At Muscongus 1653-1667.

Capt. Summersett
to Richard Fulfort.

| Witnesses | Richard **1** Fulfard |
|---|---|
| Philip Swaddan | to Humphrey Horrell |
| Thomas Cole | Witnesses |
| John **1** Brown | John **1** Brown |
| John **1** Hayman | Alexander Goul |
| Richard Pearce | — York Deeds. xii. 323. |

**122** Cleared, New York for Pemaquid, 1681-1686. — 1 Me. Hist. Coll. v. 135-136.

**123** Two Depositions sworn in Boston 16 Jan. 1683-4. Wm. Pow±37 that last Oct. he paid Dr. George Jackson £5 in fish on Robert Hughes's account in part pay for his cure of said Hughes at Pemaquid.

James Provoe±45 (Frenchman, interpreted by his countryman Michael Bodrot, who speaketh good English), in Nov. 1682 being at the fort at Pemaquid in company with Capt. Skinner and others, heard Mr. Philip Parsons say that Mr. St. Aubin was no more indebted to him than the £10 for which he had given an order to Sergt. Phillips.

**124** Pemaquid Valuation (Jamestown). (by mistake endorsed Newtown in the hand of John Usher, Province Treasurer), taken 14 Oct. 1687. — N. E. Reg. xxxii. 312.

By the courtesy of Mr. William A. Jeffries, the present possessor of the original, the print was verified by a photostat of it.

Alter Thomas Ley to Vey (for Way?).

**125** Petition Favoring Lieut. James Weems, 11 May 1689. — Doc. Hist. vi. 479 (Arch. cvii. 34).

Alter John Williams to John Walker (Jun?).

Alter A K Woodrop to Al: Wooddrop.

**126** A List of the men under the command of Lieut. James Weems when the enemy attacked the garrison at Pemaquid in August 1689. — Mass. Arch. 70: 500.

| | |
|---|---|
| Roger Sparkes gunner | William Jones |
| Paul Myham Sargt. | Mat. Taylor |
| Jones Marreday Corp. | Fredck Burnet |
| Robert Smith Drummer | Robert Baxter |
| Rulord Clay | John Banels |
| John Peterson | Thomas Shaffs |
| William Gullington | John Allen |
| Brugan Org | Rodger Heden |
| Richard [Dicurows?] | Joseph Mason |
| Thomas Mappulton | John Herdin |
| Richard Clifford | Benj. Stanton |
| John Beirnes | Robert Laurence |
| Thomas Barbor | Thomas Baker |
| Henry Walton | Owel James |
| Robert Jackson | Ralph Praston |

**127** Surrender of Pemaquid Fort as Reported by the Garrison Soldiers to Gov. Stoughton, Aug. 1696. On the 4th instant arrived two French men-of-war, etc.

Came ashore under flag of truce:
The Lieut. General.
Mr. Boadwine, a Frenchman belonging to this town.

Others Mentioned
Capt. Chub
Sergt. John Gutch
Thomas Farrand

— Suff. Court Files 3353

| Signed | |
|---|---|
| James Bushnell | |
| James **2** Lyon | |
| David **1** Frances | |
| Ebenezer Ingoldsby | |
| Mark **6** Rounds | |
| Robert Hilton | |
| John **6** Sweeting | |
| Richard **6** Bryer | |
| Richard **2** Brown | |
| John Downing | |
| John **1** Shind | |

## Damariscotta. Winnegance, Damariscove, Cape Newagen.

**141** From the evidence in Savage & wife v Patteshall the following names of residents on Damariscove Island:

-Before and after,-
John Sillman
Hunnewell
Soward

-After Philip's War-
Elias Trick*
Richard Reading*
Richard Paddishall
———— Douning(?)*

*Householders

**142** April 1677. Thomas Norman, atty for William Waldron sued James Skinner of Marblehead for not turning over his goods which he brought from Damaris Cove when they fled from the Indians. Skinner willing to turn them over if paid for his trouble. Judgment for deft.
Wm. Hobby : went with Wm. Waldron to James John Silman: Skinner's house at Marblehead to demand his goods.
Abigail Waters±23 25 Apr. 1677, Wm. Waldron was at my husband William Waters' house last summer and hired a chamber where he left goods when he went to Boston. My husband ordered James Skinner not to meddle with Wm. Waldron's goods but to lock the door and give the key to some of John Selman's family.
Thomasin Gover±37; were at James Skinner's at Marblehead.
Richard Skinner aged 16:
Elizabeth Arthers±61, 25 Apr. 1677; was at William Waters house at Damariscove.
Abraham Welman±30: were at Damariscove in John Roe±35 : August last.
when the boats were hastening away and all had gone but James Skinner; said Skinner risked his life to go to some of his friends or relations that were at William Waters's house, and none durst go to the house a second time.

## Sheepscot. Lists 161-165.

**161** Giles Evidences of Title.
— York Deeds ix. 238-239.

**162** Agreement of Sheepscot Men in Boston 19 Aug. 1682 to resettle on equal terms before 29 Sept. 1683.
— 1 Me. Hist. Coll. v. 48-57.
Corrections by the original at Albany, N. Y.
p. 49 Alter Jewtt's Neck to Jentt's.
55 Alter W. Phillips Jenier to Senier.
56 Supply the year, xxxiiii.
57 Alter Thomas Gent to Jent.
Thomas Mener to Mercer.
Wm. Lowering to Lovering.
Daniel Gentt to Danill Jentt.
Elizabeth Phyps to Phips.
Henry Towlyn to Jocelyn.
William Short to Sturt.
Henry Towlyn to Jouslyn.
William Loueridge to Lovering.
Thomas Gent to Jent.
Bath Anderson' to both overseers.
Christo Dye to Dyer.

**163** Protest against Landlords on Sheepscot Neck, 21 Apr. 1684.
— 1 Me. Hist. Col. v. 95.
By the original at Albany,
Alter Foot to Robert 6 Scoot.
Lovering wrote his name
Caleb Ray 'insing.'
Jent, Lovering and Scott 'overseers.

**164** Sheepscot Petition to Gov. Andros, 2 May 1688. — Doc. Hist. vi. 399 (Arch. cxxviii. 213).
Alter Thomas Clapp to Clay.
Alter John W—— to [-almost certainly- White].

## Kennebec. Lists 181-191.

**181** Mr. John Tedd vs. Inhabitants of the Kennebec, he of Charlestown, writ dated 18 June 1657, for seizing his vessel near Agossent and keeping his merchandize for trading up their river, especially on Sunday and selling liquor to the natives. Verdict for the defendants.
Middlesex Court Files.
Mr. Richard Collicott a defendant.
John King±57, 23 June 1657, was with Mr. Richard Collicott in Kennebec River in May, 1656, being master & owner of the vessel. Mr. Collicut was 20 miles away from the place where Mr. Tead's vessel was taken. Four days later Mr. Collicut was at Alexander Thoit's house. None of the goods came aboard Mr. Collicutt's vessel. 'John Richards of Kennebec or resident thereabouts' one of the abettors.
(Mr.) George Munnings±58, 23 June 1657: Joshua Tead's vessel was taken by some of the inhabitants of the Kennebec (John Richards was called their captain) and carried up to the place where this deponent lived, they acting under advice of Mr. Collicott, whom they hoped to consult at Capanagassett as regards the Plymouth government. This deponent, Mr. Collicut and Thomas Holland, went aboard with Mr. Tead and paid the £50 to give up the vessel and part of his furs.
Joanna Munnings±46, 23 June 1657; Her husband being at Kennebec when Joshua Tead's bark was taken by John Richards and others, he asked said Richard and William Cocke whether they had a commission from the Governor of Plymouth. Wm. Cock and old Richards both wished they had never meddled with it.
Matthew Clark±30, 6 June 1657: Mr. Collicott of Dorchester, being at Alexander Thoit's house on Kennebec River, went aboard Joshua Tead's vessel, the Swallow. Deponent heard James Smith and his wife say that Mr. Collicott advised taking Joshua Tead, and that he would like to worry the coasters out of the river.
John Lawrence±35, 20 March 1656-7:
Thomas Holland±22, in May 1656: he beig at the house of Alexander Thoyts in Kennebec River, the inhabitants of said river surprised a vessel of Mr. Joshua Tead. Mr. Collicott was 20 miles distant from the place when it was enacted.

**182** Persons on the Western Side of Kennebec River who took the oath of allegiance to the King 8 Sept. 1665. — Me. Prov. & Court Rec. i. 243.

**183** John Cock's Deposition, 1 Apr. 1740. Late of Kennebec River, but now of Dorchester, aged 82, ('a hearty man of a sound mind and good understanding').—York Deeds xxi. 218.
Born at Tuessic in Kennebec River near Arrowsic Island. Lived there and at a place called Small Point, on the left as we go up Kennebec, between Winnegance Creek and the Sea, 'which lands were possessed by the several persons hereafter named:'
Mr. John Leighton possessed next Winnegance Creek, over against Arrowsic Mills.
Mr. Thomas Webber lived one mile below Mr. Leighton.
Mr. William Baker lived.
Mr. Sylvanus Davis's land.
Mr. John Parker lived there, house about a mile from Mr. Davis house.
Thomas Humphreys, only a small creek parting his house from Mr. Parker's.
Mr. Ichabod Wiswell, the minister of the place.
Mr. John Vearing. A high land called Vering's Head was on his land.
Mr. Simon Newcomb.

Mr. Wm. Cock. A high head was on his land, called Cock's Head.

Mr. John Cock, my father, lived near, on part of the said William Cock's land. They two married sisters, but were related only by marriage. I lived with my father. Went fishing with old Mr. John Parker.

Mr. Thomas Atkins, an ancient settler who followed farming wholly. Against his land was a bay called Atkins Bay.

Ambrose Hunnewell.

Henry Emms. Had a brother killed there by the Indians.

Old Mr. Parker only claimed the land where he lived.

**184**   Report on Kennebec River Defense
23 April 1677. Left by the army at the mercy of the Indians. — Doc. Hist. vi. 164 (Mass. Arch. lxix. 117).

Alter ——— Shaw, Jr., to (Andrew Johnson) Sergeant.

Alter Jeremiah Hidsdan to Hodsden.

**185**   Hammond v. Phips, Suff. Court Files
1682. The widow Elizabeth Hammond had sued the future governor William Phips, for a quantity of dried beef, writ dated 25 Oct. 1677. John White±22, at work at Sheepscot River with Wm. Phips.

Samuel Smith, son of Mrs. Hammond, said he had the beef from Roushick garrison.

Margaret Loverell±22:   had been staying
Joane Goage±21:         at Rowsick garrison.

**186**   Arrowsic under James II.
Suff. Court Files 2428. An unsigned copy, complete, with a fragment of the original (stray papers), of the grant by John Palmer, Esq. of the Council in New York, etc., of 900 acres on the Southerly end of Arrowsic Island to:

Lawrence Dennis          John Tillman
John Buttery             James Widger
Samuel Bowles            John Moulton
John Ryford              Thomas Ashley
John Spencer

**187**   Grants on Arrowsic by Governor
Andros, Sept. 6, 1679. — Doc. Hist. iv. 386, from copy in Mass. Arch. iii. 336.

**188**   A Letter to Thomas Lake of London
from Mrs. Mehitable Warren and Elisha Hutchinson at Boston 29 June 1687, states that Sir Edmond Andros soon after the war gave permission to about 20 families to settle on the lower end of Arrowsic Island, but without ownership, and that certain of these had now been given patents at Nequasset, (Woolwich), by Gov. Dongan of New York: — Suffolk Court Files 139154.

Will Slack,         100 acres
William Stevens,    100    "
James Denis,        200    "
Arthur Neal,        100    "
John Rely,          100    "

**189**   'List of Militia on Kennebeck River
under Capt. John Rowden May 1688.'
— Mass. Arch. 128: 196.

As printed in Doc. Hist. vi. 362,
Five names, Davis to Horsley, belong in a different paper.

Add Sen. to Lawrence Dennis.
Alter John Tollman to Tellman.
Alter James Williams to Millians.
Alter Richard J. to Richard Lang.
Alter Thomas Felman to Helman.
(Following James Dennis, Will Denis.)
(Following Matthew Salter, Larence Bickford.)

**190**   Sagadahoc Guides wanted in 1689.
John Paine           John Hornebroke
Wm. Dennis           John Parker
                     — Doc. Hist. iv. 465.

**191**   Account of the Eastern Parts and of the several Settlements that have ever been made on the Lands formerly purchased by Mr. Wharton and now bought by Eight of Us:
— Pejepscot Mss.

The narrow carrying place that parts Casco Bay from Merrymeeting Bay, settled by Stevens, who has a son now at New Haven married to Parker's daughter.

**Settlements on the eastern side of small point neck.**

Next to abovesaid Stevens, at the upper Whigby or Wiskege, by Lawson, owned by Ephraim Savage.

William Rogers about 2 leagues lower.

Thomas Watkins about a mile lower.

Mr. Gooch the minister about a mile lower down the river.

John Filman about a mile lower.

Capt. Reynolds about a mile lower.

John Layton at the neck just above Winegance.

Mary Webber about 2 mile lower — her son goes now with Capt. Bracket.

William Baker about a mile lower.

Sylvanus Davis, now suppose Nelson.

John Parker.

Thomas Humphreys.

Ichabod Wiswall.

John Verin.

Samuel Newcomb.

William Cock and John Cock within half a mile.

Robert Edmunds, said to be claimed now by Sir Charles Hobby.

James Mudge within a quarter of a mile.

Thomas Atkins, said to have bought the whole neck down to Small Point of Indians and to have sold their interest to the other inhabitants. Some of his heirs supposed to be now living at Roxbury or Dorchester.

Ambrose Hunniwell the lowest settlement on that side, about four mile short of Small Point. Hunniwell that works for Capt. Belcher one of that family.

**On the western side of that neck**
only Drake, who settled at Small Point harbour— lived there but a little while.

**On Merriconeg Neck only two settlements**
Richard Potts who lived at the lower end.

John Damarel about 3 miles above him.

**But one settlement at Mair Point**
by John Phippany.

**But one settlement at Maquoit**
by Robert Haines.

**Settlements between Pejepscot and Swan Island on the north side of Merrymeeting Bay.**

Samuel York about 4 or 5 mile down from the Falls on the eastern side. Living now at Squam, Cape Ann, he supposed the likeliest man to inform how far Merriconege Neck or Shapley's Island have been possessed or improved.

James Thomas half a mile below. He and his heirs supposed to be wholly extinct.

Williams half a mile farther — only a man and his wife — had no children — supposed to be extinct.

James Giles about four miles up Muddy River.

Thomas Giles at point on south side of Muddy River mouth. Of these families Gyles of Winnisemet Ferry, and Giles the Interpreter now lives at Salisbury.

Thomas Watkins at Shildrake Point, between Muddy River and Cathance.

Alexander Browne east side of mouth of Cathance River.

Dependence Collicut claims that point — no settlement between said Collicut & Swan Island.

One settlement at Swan Island by Collicut, Alexander Brown and Humphrey Davies by turns.

## The Province of Maine by Towns. Lists 201-299.

### Pejepscot and Maquoit.

Nothing amounting to a List has been found for this region. The patentee, Mr. Thomas Purchase, was the earliest to 'submit' to Massachusetts government, and afterwards acted with every government within reach. A settler at Maquoit called himself of Wescustogo (North Yarmouth).

### North Yarmouth. Lists 211-214.

**211** Mr. Francis Neale's Credentials in the Massachusetts General Court. 2 April. [1666]. Doc. Hist. iv. 316. By the original, Arch. iii. 294:
Alter John Ryains to Maine.
Add to the date Wescustogo.

**212** Grant of Plantation at the Bottom of Casco Bay at a river called Swegustagoe, by Act of General Court 19 May 1680, in response to petition of [Suff. Court Files 139599].

| | |
|---|---|
| Joseph Phippen | Francis Neale Sr. |
| George Ingersoll | John Pickering |
| Robert Nicholls | John Marston |
| John Ingersoll | John Wales |
| Francis Neal Jr. | Nathl. Wales |
| John Johnson | Jonathan Putnam |
| John Royal | |

**213** Petition of the Illutherians (1686). Doc. Hist. vi. 238, 224 (Mass. Arch. cxxvi. 387a, 200).

| | |
|---|---|
| Nicolas Davis | John Alberry |
| Nath: Sanders | Daniell Sanders |

**214** Account of North Yarmouth.written for Sullivan's Hist. of Maine (p. 185), names 15 inhabitants in 1685, apparently a traditional list. As Sullivan misread Blashfield 'Bearkfield,' other unknown names (*) may be but blunders for known people.

| | |
|---|---|
| Walter Gendall | Amos Stevens |
| John Royall | John Provender |
| Thomas Bearkfield | John Shove* |
| [Blashfield] | Samuel Lime* |
| Henry Combes | Joseph Harris |
| William Ashfell | John Acton* |
| William Larrabee | John Shepherd |
| Samuel Larrabee | Peter Blackman |

The town grants laid out by Capt. Anthony Brackett and Mr. Thomas Bayly about 1685 include also:

| | |
|---|---|
| Isaac Lareby | John Harris Sr. |
| Benjamin Lareby | Roger Edwards |

Still other names in the Proprietors' records are: Mr. George Pearson, Recorder of the Town. John Maine, John Holman (former residents) John York.

A copy of the printed report of the Boston committee on resettling the town, 29 Jan. 1733-4, with errors corrected in writing, is in Suff. Court Files 37124; but all the errors are not corrected. Apparently 36 is the true number of old settlers recognized but indistinguishably mingled with 64 newcomers in the lot-drawing in 1728. Shares 104-106 were later allotted in the rights of:

| | |
|---|---|
| John Phillips | or | Nathaniel Wallis |
| John Royal | | Thomas Mains |

The following inclusive list recorded from the 100 (net) names may yet omit some other settlers back of the abandonment of the town in 1688:

| | |
|---|---|
| Thomas Daggett | Samuel York |
| Samuel White | Tobias Oakman |
| (Richard Bray) | John Harris |
| Stephen Larrabee | Joseph Maylem |
| Thomas Larrabee | Margery Stevens |
| Edward Shove | John Batten |
| George Felt | Robert Stanford |
| John Atwell | Joseph York |
| Joshua Nichols | Samuel Brown |

Among the early landholders, the Committee

thought it prudent to allow a few ancient titles to specific lands:
[Thomas Stevens's Indian deed.]

| | |
|---|---|
| John Royal | Walter Gendall |
| George Felt | Mr. Richard Dummer |
| Thomas Shepherd | John Shepherd |
| Bridget Wallis | (Ann Stevens?) |
| Arnold Allen | — Redding |

### Falmouth (and Cape Elizabeth).

**221** Jordan Muniments of Title, 1642-1660, recorded 7 Nov. 1717. — York Deeds viii. 244-245.

**222a** Back Cove Petition against Landlords Jordan and Cleeve. May 30, 1660. — Doc. Hist. iv. 160 (Mass. Arch. iii. 248). For Thomas Cellen (·sic· in orig.) read Skillin.

**222b** Petition against Mr. Cleeve and Others. (Spring of 1663).—Doc. Hist. iv. 308. By the original, Mass. Arch. iii. 287:
Alter Benj. Halwell to Hatwell [Atwell].
Alter Samson Perli to Penli.
Alter Edw. Macering to Manering.

**222c** Petition 1 Aug. 1665 praising Mass. and reciting their refusal to sign the petition against both Gorges and Mass., printed in Willis's Portland, p. 164, from Hutch. Coll. 396, (all but two Falmouth), requires obvious corrections:
Alter Ambrose Bounds to Bowden.
Francis Neate to Neale.
Phineas Hidar to Rider.
Benj. Hatewell to Atwell.
John Marklie to Wacklie.

**222d** Petition to Mass. to Appoint the Judges, June 10, 1671. Doc. Hist. iv. 325. By the original, Arch. iii. 314:
Alter Phenthas inum to Pheinhas Rider.

**223a** Withdrawals from Falmouth and Scarborough (1675?). Doc. Hist. iv. 349
Alter Hen: to Junkin Williams.
Alter Gerom Black to **From Black Point.**

**223b** Petition for Change in Commanders, 2 Feb. 1675-6. — Doc. Hist. iv. 353 (Arch. iii 312).
Alter Lavance Davis to Laraunce.
Alter Denis Movoah to Moroah.
[?Bartho Wallis, read Nartha?].
Alter Humphrey Rorham to Dorham.
Alter Thomas hues to Lewis.
Alter Timothy Sparill to Spurill.

**224** Original petition of refugees from Casco on an island praying to send a vessel to fetch off the people, not over a dozen men with many women and children — the men and women can work, the orphaned children, offspring of Christians, ought to be rescued and put out to service. Written by Francis Neale, who also signed Thomas Purchas's name. (Aug. 1676.)
— Suff. Court Files 26061.

| | |
|---|---|
| Thomas **6** Skillings | Thomas Purchas |
| | Francis Neale |
| | Abraham Addams |
| | Jonathan **7** Addams |
| | Elizabeth **6** Harvie |
| | Edward **2** Barton |
| | Dorcas **2** Andrews |
| | William Phillipps |

**225a** President Danforth's Plan to plant a strongly defended town on the site of Portland, 23 Sept. 1680. — York Deeds xiii. 122-129

**225b** Portland House Lots, 26 March 1688. — Doc. Hist. vi. 385 (Mass. Arch.

After Welding insert: -John Harris house lot-canceled.

**226** 'A List of the Inhabitants of Spurwink, Richman's Isl. & Cape Elizabeth in the Town of Falmouth Oct. 15, 1683,' This purports to be an attested copy out of the Falmouth town records by Anthony Brackett, town clerk; but the existing paper (Willis Mss. R. 31) is but a copy, most clearly written except when imitating names the copyist could not read, thus throwing suspicion on other names.

| | |
|---|---|
| Mr. Nathaniel Frier | 0:16:8 |
| *Mr. Gendal | 1: 9:4 |
| Mr. Eliot | 0:13:6 |
| Mr. John Jordon | 1: 0:8 |
| Mrs. Jordon (Jer's mother) | 0:18:7 |
| Dom Jordon | 1: 0:8 |
| Jed: Jordon | 1: 0:8 |
| Peter Shaw | 1: 0:8 |
| Wm. Lucus | 0:12:9 |
| *Tho. Page | 0:12:9 |
| Robert Jordon | 0:11:3 |
| *Robert Parrot | 0:11:3 |
| *Tobias Page | 0:12:9 |

'Poll money as underwritten' [paying 1s, 8d each]

| | |
|---|---|
| Gendall | Richard Short |
| John Jordon | Wm. Mansfield |
| Dom. Jordon | John Swind |
| Jedediah Jordon | Peter Rendal |
| Peter Shaw | Henly |
| Wm. Lucas | Patten |
| Tho: Page | James Rendal |
| Robert Hayns | John Rendal |
| Robert Jordon | Henry Libby |
| Henry Longman | Mr. Hardy |
| Edward Vickery | Mr. Rowland |
| Rober Kennells | Thos. Backer |
| Clem Swett | Wa. Bestord |
| John Parrot | Andrew Cranch |
| Tho. Page | Jo. Flee |
| Rich Webb | [Simon Hinkson?] |
| Hew Glandfeld | John Frefell |
| Jeremiah Jordon | John Windsland |
| John Clark | Shadract Bell |
| Richard Calley | Richard Pope |
| Tho. Edwards | Richard Bason |
| Peter Callens | Francis Breck |
| John Hance | Michael Webber |
| Waymond Lissen | Saml. Sligins |
| Benjamin Turbell | |

*All in this list appear also in the rate made 24 Nov. 1684 except those starred, with the following additional names:

| | |
|---|---|
| Samuel Jordan [with Mrs. Sarah] | |
| John Parrot | 4:11 |
| Sam. Sweet | 2: 6 |
| Mr. John Clark | 2: 6 |
| John Hame | 2: 6 |

This latter rate was to be turned over, one-half each, to Mr. Henry Harwood and Capt. Anthony Brackett.

On the back appear the town charges to be met:

| | £ s |
|---|---|
| Lt. George, John and Geo. Jr. Ingersoll for locating the bounds of Clark's Point | 00:18 |
| Peter Morrel for work on the fort | 00:03 |
| 'Hadden and Clark' going deputies to York | 00:15 |
| Richard Pousland, money lent to the town to go for Mr. Burroughs | 01:10 |
| [Antho?] Warden, to pay part of Mr. Burrough's Passage | 00:05 |
| Mr. Harwood for paying the rest of ditto & for boards and nails for the minister's house & paying the workmen | 05:05 |
| John & Geo. Ingercoll for 1 m. of boards to floor the Meeting House | 01:10 |
| Wolves | 01:10 |

**227** Memorandum by Phineas Jones about 1733 of an intended journey to obtain depositions that the following persons were settlers under President Danforth:
— Willis MSS. Book N. 158.

| **Purpooduck** | **Old Casco** |
|---|---|
| Dennis Moroh | Jonathan Oras |
| Samson Pendley | William Perce |
| Lenard Slew | Sylvanus Davis |
| Joel Madefer | Bartholomew Gidney |
| Samuel Jordan | ——— Phillips |
| Jedediah Jordan | and ——— English |
| John or Wm. Graves | **Back Cove** |
| Philip Britton | John Whelden |
| **New Casco** | John Rider |
| Lewis Tucker | John Smith |
| Elisha Andrews | Zachariah White |
| **Stroudwater** | Philip Lewis |
| George [Bruens?] [Burrine?] | |

**228b** Testimonial Exonerating Captain George Lockhart, 26 April 1689. — Doc. Hist. vi. 478 (Arch. cvii. 3).
Alter Saddaus to Thaddaus Clark, Left.
Alter George ——— to Bramhall.
Alter Joseph ——— to Joseph Cous, Sergt.
Alter Thomas ——— to Thomas Claies, Clerk.

**228c** Petition of the Inhabitants against their Officers, May 24, 1689.
— Doc. Hist. vi. 482 (Arch. cvii. 55).
Alter George ——— to [Gray?].
Alter Francis ——— to Nicolle.
Alter Henry Crosby to [Cressy?].
Alter Samuel ——— to Sligings.
Alter Robert Sharey to Shares.

**228d** Casualty List for Battle of Sept. 21, 1689. — Doc. Hist. iv. 454. Cf. Willis, Portland 279.
Another report is in 4 Mass. Hist. Coll. v. 214. By the original, Mass. Arch. xxxv. 14:
Thomas Burton appears altered from Barton.
Edward Evens was altered from Greene.
After Evens insert Thomas Shafte (-Thaxter- in ms. copy made for Wm. Willis. — Bk. N, p. 222).
Alter Thomas Berry to Bary.
Read Giles Row belonging to the fort.
Alter James Freese second to senior.

**229** Three Petitions Including Old Proprietors' Rights, 1717, 1718, 1728, are treated as one, but not verified and only partially indexed. — Willis, Portland, 889, 890, 893.

## Scarborough.    Lists 231-239.

**231** Mr. George Cleeve's Credentials from Scarborough to the Mass. General Court [1653-1657]. — Doc. Hist. iv. 46 (Arch. iii. 210).

**232** Submission of Scarborough and Falmouth in a joint meeting at Mr. Jordan's house at Spurwink, which was made part of Falmouth, 13 July 1658. — York Deeds i. 78.
Correctly printed from the record, in Edw. Rishworth's hand. The original is gone (Mass. Arch. iii. 246 is a copy) but:
Arthur Augur Jujor must be Lieut.
Abraham Follen (Fellew in Doc. Hist. iv. 157 and Mass. Records ir. 358) must be Joslen.

**233** Petition against Mr. John Thorpe, the Minister, (May 22, 1661). — Doc. Hist. iv. 169 (Arch. x. 94).

**234a** Fishermen in Boston Courts, 1667. John Lux v. Edmund Downe for false imprisonment; 'being a stranger and far from home, could get no bail; was kept 8 weeks from fishing, which spoiled the whole year. Lux also sued Edward Cock and Edward Pike.
John Mare±25, July 1667. Made 221 kentals of fish this winter & spring. John Lux's goods were carried some one place and some another

by reason of his absence.

Elias Oakeman±23. Same as last.

Christopher Elkins±25, 1667, Edward Cock & Edward Pike told him they were shipped by John Lux as boatmasters beginning last winter. Nathaniel Beadford±28. The latter end of Feb. John Lux and his two boatmasters Cock & Pike were at my house, [Spurwink] going to fish at Damarels Cove.

**234b** Scottoway Hill Farm, Scarborough.

Eliza **1** Bason±73 in 1728. Formerly lived near Dunstan; knew three tenants under Mr. Scottow on his farm formerly Mr. Abraham Josling's.

Nicholas Wilmot. Went to school to
John Howell John Howell's wife.
Richard Barows — Prout v. Graffam, '1728.'

**235** Foxwell v. Alger, an appealed case affecting title to marsh between Dunstan and Blue Point, writ dated 28 Nov. 1668. The existing papers are copies made by Edward Rishworth in great haste, and clerical errors must be guarded against. The General Court of Mass. sustained a verbal grant by Thomas Gorges before 1658 as against a later town grant. The following were on this marsh in August, 1668:
[Suff. Court Files 1046.]

Mr. Richard Foxwell Andrew Alger
Daniel Kaly, his servant His son John
Philip Foxwell Matthew: youngest
Nicholas Edgecomb Andrew: sons
Christopher Edgecomb Arthur Alger
Jacob Rabskine John Palmer

Mr. Richard Foxwell being at the house of An-
Mr. John Smyth drew Alger at Dunstan,
George Barlow he being the first inhab-
John West itant there, 'these men

Agnes Auger±48, [26 Nov. 1668] : ab. 15 years ago made an agreement to take up every man his lot and to live at Dunstan together,' with forfeiture to the others if not built on within a year and a day.

Henry Watts, 24 Mar. [1638?], for over 20 years Mr. R. F. has held 500 acres reaching up the river.±67 [14 July 1669] 'Andrew Auger & Barlow' mowed there before Mr. Foxwell did.

Thomas Elkins±64: 4 Oct. [a little before] Mr. George Taylor±60: Thomas Gorges went back he ordered Elkins to go to the inhabitants of Blue Point and require them to pay their rents to Capt. Bonighton.

Richard Bonython's deed, 24 May 1642, to his daus.

Elizabeth Bonython: to compensate legacies from Susanah Foxwell: their grandmother in England; witnesses: Wm. Smyth, Jonas Baly, Nicholas Edgcomb.

Mr. Henry Jocelyn, 16 Feb. 1658 [9 before Robert Jordan, Associate: 13 or 14 years ago Mr. Thos. Gorges, Dep. Gov., gave orders to put Geo. Dearinge in possession of 200 acres of land at the place where Jonas Balie, who m. the widow of Geo. Dearinge, now liveth.

John Foxwell±30, 14 July 1669: at his first mowing there no one dwelt at Dunstan, 'not of the English.'

Arthur [Alger] ±45, 7 June 1670; Andrew was in quiet possession 14 years untroubled until the King's Commissioners came hither.

Andrew Alger, 19 Aug. 1670: 'at least 16 years agone' Mr. Foxwell yielded up any rights he had to the inhabitants of Dunstone for their encouragement to settle there.

John Howell±37, June 1669: was servant to Andrew Alger 13 or 14 years ago; about 15 years ago the inhabitants that sat down at Dunstan had a meeting.

Mr. John Smyth±77, 26 Nov. 1668: about 12 years since, living at Dunstan.

Nicholas Edgecome of Saco± [76?] 22 June 1670:

about 1656 Mr. John Smyth and Geo. Page mowing this marsh were warned.

Scarborough town grant, 22 Sept. 1669, signed by selectmen and clerk.

John Rule±25, 16 June 1670: made survey, 'being a stranger.'

John Auger±30, 6 July 1670: for his father Andrew.

John Palmer±30 June 1670.

John Libby Jr. aged [24?] 25 June 1669: mowed there for Alger about 6 years ago.

George Page±28, 14 June 1669.

Philip Foxwell±17, 26 Nov. 1668.

Christopher Edgcomb±25, 26 Nov. 1668.

Daniel Kaly±25, 26 Nov. 1668.

John Sygus, aged 28 years, 30 June 1670.

Robert Ellett, 7 July 1670: the house John Jackson hath built.

[Other depositions, missing from the files but printed in Me. H. & G. Rec. iv. 137-138:

Lucretia Foxwell±24, 26 Nov. 1668.

John Ashton±30, 26 Nov. 1668.

John Jackson summonsed by H. Williams, clk.

John Jackson, P.A. 28 Aug. 1671 'to my loving father in law Giles Bardg.'

John Bonighton Sen. bondsman for R. F. 19 Aug. 1670.

James Gibbines Sen. mentioned 1670.

Edward Colcord, attorney, reasons of appeal.

**Officials:**

Peter Weare, Recorder.

Edward Rishworth, Recorder.

Francis Neale, Associate, and clerk of the writs.

Henry Williams, clerk of the writs.

Arthur Alger, commissioner to end small causes.

Richard Hitchcock, com. to end small causes.

**236** Capt. Joshua Scottow's Lawsuits 1676-1680 about the soldiers sent from Boston and their pay. — Suff. Court Files 1526, 1781, 1828, 162190.

Cf. Bodge 326-337, Doc. Hist: vi. 102, 139-143, 145, 148, 157, 196-200, 202-3.

Letter dated 12 July 1676 To
 Winter Harbor Mr. Edward Rishworth
Brian Pendleton Maj. Nicho: Shapleigh
George Munjoy Mr. Saml: Wheelwright

We had no hand in sending for the soldiers to secure Mr. Scottow's interest at Black Point; the charges ought to be levied upon the person or place benefitted.

Ra: Allison :
Jos: Oliver :    28 July 1676
Wm. Sheldon : Protest against the town's
John Tynny : paying the soldiers, as Mr.
Rich: Foxwell : Scottow was enabled to keep
Gyles Barge : his fishermen at sea the whole
John Cocke : season, move his barn, etc.

Accounts from the book at Black Point kept partly by Mr. Scottow, partly by Nathaniel Willett:

Craft bought of Anthony Roe
Fishing craft " " Peter Hinxen
Fishing craft " " Thomas Westgat
Lines " " Jo: Slades
Nets " " John Starts
Shallop " " Antho: Roe & Tho: Bigford

John Tinney±40, 4 Oct. 1676.

Mr. Warren, Walter Gendall and others, and later Wm. Sheldon, brought a paper which he signed. Twelve of the Boston soldiers were quartered, 2 at his house, 5 at Samuel Oakman's, 5 at Walter Gendall's.

Humphrey Warren, merchant of Boston, 20 July 1676 coming in from Kennibec in Nov. 1675 was with Mr. Walter Gendall, Mr. Robert Jordan Jr., and Mr. Nathan Bedford. I sent for Stephen Sargent who I was told was at Black Point, and he told me that Major Pendleton and Mr. Fletcher had twice sent to Mr. Scottow for help and been refused. I went to Black Point and found Mr. Scottow urging 30 or 40 men to roll his barn to

the top of the hill. I ordered Stephen Sargent to stay with his barges to await Mr. Scottow's positive decision.
Capt. Peter Rodrygo, a Dutchman,±32, 24 July 1676. The day Liby's houses were burnt within two miles of Mr. Scottow's house, I wanted him to give me 40 men to go fight them off. He would not, nor go himself. Stayed at Mr. Foxwell's garrison all the winter.
Anthony Row±40, 2 Nov. 1676. There were men enough there to hold the place if under proper command.
Ellner Barge aged [16?] relative to the first attack of the Indians "Lord's day in the Evening."
Patrick Denmarke, concerning widow Temple after her husband was killed.

Other Deponents in 1676

| | |
|---|---|
| Margt. Jackson±30 | Tho: Bigford±36 |
| Henry Brookins±35 | Wm. Sheldon±58 |
| Ralph Manson | Nicho: Frost±28 |
| [Allison]±54 | |
| Joseph Oliver | Edward Small±22 |
| Rich: Honewell±31 | Walter Gendall±35 |

[Missing from the files but printed in Me. H. & G. Rec. iv. 137  Emanuel Davis±21]
Letter dated Piscataqua 29 Jan. 1677[8
Richard Waldron Sergt. Major
                    to Capt. Josh: Scottow
The General Court orders 6 soldiers to be sent you; am now sending two by Benj. Trustram:

| | |
|---|---|
| William Bray | Augustin Parker |

'Sir it is very difficult to gett men to serve you, such an odium is on your name here that men openly professe they had rather be hanged then serve under your command. Please to order so that the men I now & shall send may contradict and make false that report.'
Order signed John Hull, Treas. 9 July 1679 'To the Constables and Selectmen of York × × pay £100 to Capt. Joshua Scottow out of your five and thirty country rates × × by him assigned to his son Samuel Walker.'
Writ 26 Nov. 1679, Joshua Scottow of Boston against Mr. Nicholas Shapleigh, Mr. Edward Rishworth and Mr. Samuel Wheelwright, damages £400, for defamation in a signed paper exhibited in the General Court by said Rishworth in 1676, the great damage arising from his garrison being surrendered while he was in Boston to answer their complaints. Rishworth's defence was that they were only asking for instructions whether to pay Capt. Scottow's bill against York County.
Mary Oakman±45, 27 Nov. 1679. She and her husband were in Mr. Scottow's garrison when Mog the Indian gave them till next day to get away with their goods.
Edward Hownsell±26, 1 Dec. 1679. We had 11 Province soldiers, 40 or 50 inhabitants and near a barrel of powder. The house would not have been given up had Mr. Scottow been there.
John Vicars deposed the same.
John Purrinton±44, 16 Jan. 1679[80. Was at Saco 3 weeks after Capt. Wincoll had 9 English killed on Saco sands. Soldiers at Mr. Scottow's garrison told me he would not let them go to help. Thomas Cousens±30, 16 Jan. 1679[80. Was with Capt. Wincoll. Five men came from Mr. Foxwell's, leaving but two in garrison, no nearer than Mr. Scottow's.
John Tenny±40, 19 Jan. 1679[80. He and S. Wheeler 'being in the garrison with Walter Gendall' in 1675, went to Scottow for soldiers and were refused.
Ebenezer Ingoldsby and Wm. Darby, Boston, soldiers sent to Black Point. When we came there we were all quartered out to the different garrisons, and some to Mr. Gendals on the other side of the river, namely John Lowell, Ezech Hamlin and two or three more. We two were quartered at Saml. Oakman's, near John Tinney's.
Andrew Augur±26, 28 Jan. 1679[80. In the year

1675 eleven were killed and one carried away at Saco sands, he being at Black Point when the first guns were heard.
Henry Williams±43, 28 Jan. 1679[80. Wounded 10 Oct. 1675 and brought for cure to Black Point by water on the 13th. This was a week before any soldiers came from Boston. A company under Ralph Allanson who started to relieve our friends told me on their return that on account of two rivers to cross and the tide three parts in, they could not reach them.

**237a** 'A List of Names of the Inhabitants of Blackpoint Garison Octo: 12th, 1676.' Endorsed: 'Handed in by Mr. Jocelyn Oct. 1676.' — Original in N. E. H.-G. S. Some names obviously interlined for lack of room are here placed at the end of each list.

**In the Garison**
John Tenney
Henry Brookin
Nathaniell Willett
Charles Browne
Edward Hounsell
Daniell Moore
Francis Sholet
Hampton and Salsbery
                    Soldiers

**In the hutts** without the Garison but joyning to it.
Anthony Roe
Thomas Bickford
Robert Tydey
James Lybbey
John Lybbey
Anthony Lybbey
Samuell Lybbey
George Taylor
Dunken Chessom
William Sheldon
John Vickers
Richard Basson
Robert Eliott
Francis White
John Howell
Richard Moore
James Oglebey
Richard Hunnewell

**Living muskett shot** from the garison.
Ralph Allison
Mathew Aleyson
Joseph Oliver
Christopher Edgecome
John Edgecome
Micaell Edgecome
Robert Edgecome

**Living three muskett shot** from garison.
Henry Elkins
John Ashdon
John Warrick
Goodman Luscome
Tymothy Collins
Andrew Browne Senier
Andrew Browne
John Browne
Joseph Browne
William Burrage
Ambrose Bouden
                    Constable
Tho: Cumming
John Hermon
Samuell Okerman Sen.
Samuel Okeman
John Elson
Peter Hincson
Symond Hincson
Richard Willin
John Symson
Tno: Cleaverly
John Cocke
Richard Burrough

A list of the names of those of the Inhabitants aforesaid that were prest by vertue of Capt. Hauthornes order to be for the service of the Garison.
Edward Hounslow
James Oglebey
John Cocke
Daniell Moore
Dunken Chessom
Richard Burrough
William Burrage
Francis Shealett

**237b** Soldiers under Captain Scottow, Jan. 1675-6 - Mar. 1677-8. A compilation. Partly indexed.          — Bodge 338-339.

**237c** Petition (winter of 1675-1676), being the frontier, do intend we a man of us to leave our station. — Doc. Hist. vi. 106 (Mass. Arch. lxix. 79).
Alter Henry Berkins to Brookins.

**237d** Testimonial Exonerating Capt. Scottow, 15 July 1676. — Doc. Hist. vi. 116 (Mass. Arch. lxix. 28).
Alter Richard Wilkins to Willing.

**237e** Address to the Massachusetts Government, 1676, defending Capt. Scottow. Bodge, p. 334. The signers are in five columns, the first including Esq. Jocelyn and the selectmen, Bouden, Libby Sen., Oakman, Libby Jr., and the other four headed by Row, Cleverly, Moore and Wasgate.
For 'Teshmond' read Jeshmond [Chessemore].

**238a** Scarborough Tax List 28 Nov. 1681.
— Town Book, p. 7.

| | | | | | | | |
|---|---|---|---|---|---|---|---|
| Mr. Philip Fox- | | | | Sheppia | . | 7 | 6 |
| well | 1 | 4 | . | Wm. Shelten | . | 7 | 6 |
| James Robin- | | | | Henry Brouck- | | | |
| son | . | 6 | 6 | ins | . | 4 | . |
| Giles Bardge | . | 9 | 6 | Mr. Walker | 0 | 7 | . |
| John Jackson | . | 3 | 8 | Andrew Algur | . | 7 | 6 |
| Richard Calley | 1 | 2 | . | Capt. Scotto- | | | |
| John Moulton | . | 3 | 6 | way | 3 | 11 | 4 |
| Andrew | | | | Nich. Willmat | . | 5 | . |
| Browne | 1 | 6 | . | John Palmer | . | 3 | . |
| John Libby Jun. | | 3 | 10 | John Astone | . | 2 | 6 |
| John Libby Sen. | 7 | | . | Elias Okmans | . | 2 | 6 |
| Henry Libby | . | 3 | . | Rodger Vickers | 2 | | 6 |
| Anto: Libby | . | 3 | 3 | Rich. Basson | . | 2 | 6 |
| Anto: Row | . | 3 | 9 | Dunkin Stew- | | | |
| Peter Hinxson | . | 4 | 9 | ard | . | 7 | 6 |
| Richard Honi- | | | | Mr. Jordons | . | 10 | 6 |
| well | . | 12 | 6 | John Figitt | . | 2 | . |
| John Sampson | . | 9 | 6 | Simon Hinx- | | | |
| Robert Eliot | . | 3 | 9 | son | . | 2 | . |
| Georg Taylor | . | 4 | 6 | Robert Tidy | . | 2 | . |
| John & James | | | | Rich. Willing | . | 2 | 6 |
| Mils | 1 | 6 | 6 | Edw. Bennet | . | 2 | 6 |
| Joseph Winick | . | 5 | 9 | John Elson | . | 2 | 6 |
| Mr. Watts | 1 | 6 | . | Hen. Elkins | . | 2 | . |
| William Bur- | | | | Tho: Cleverly | . | 2 | . |
| idge | . | 6 | . | Geo: Broks | . | 2 | . |
| John Macrell | . | 4 | . | Fra: Shallet | . | 2 | . |
| [McKenney] | | | | Fra: White | . | 2 | . |
| Josias Okmans | . | 4 | . | John Starke | | | |
| John Simson | . | 3 | 6 | [Start] | . | 2 | . |
| Ambrose Bow- | | | | John Warrek | | | |
| dens | . | 10 | . | [Warwick] | . | 2 | . |
| John Tenny | . | 7 | . | Benjaman | | | |
| Andrew John- | | | | Peckring | . | 2 | . |
| son | . | 5 | 6 | John Howell | . | 2 | . |
| Tho: Backer | . | 4 | 6 | Andrew Brown | . | 2 | . |
| Waymon Beck- | | | | John Brown | . | 2 | . |
| ton | . | 5 | . | Mark Rounds | . | 2 | . |
| John Skillin | . | 12 | . | Tho: Bickford | . | 2 | . |
| Mr. Edward | | | | Joseph Brown | . | 2 | . |

The following names found in a list of the in-habitants dated 22 Sept. 1681 (Town Book, p. 29) do not appear in the tax list:

| | |
|---|---|
| Ambrose | William Punchin Rich: Huniwell |
| Bowden Sen. | Daniel Fogg    Hugh Glanfield |
| John Bowden | Dav: Libby    James Wiggins |
| Thomas Scottow | Mat: Libby    Sam: Vicars |

Town grants were made in 1682-1686 to still others:

| | |
|---|---|
| 1682　May 17 | Mar. 15 Nic: Durall |
| Robert Tidy | June 18 |
| May 23 | Thomas Litherby |
| Simon Hinxon | 1685　June 1 |
| May 26 | John Osborn |
| John Samson | Henry Kerby |
| Aug. 28 | Oct. 17 John Samson |
| John Slaughter | 1686　Apr. 1 |
| 1683　Jan. 13 | Mary Becteon |
| James Robinson | William Green |

**238b** Vickers v. Walker, 1685.

Indenture for 9 years from 1 Feb. 1675-6 apprenticing Joseph, son of Roger Vickers of Scarboro, to Samuel Walker of Boston, merchant, (mariner in writ). Witnesses: Roger 6 Vickers, John Hayward [Boston]. The father sued for his son's wages.
Mary Vickers, aged 50. Her son Joseph was 21 15 Aug. 1685.
Matthew Augure aged 28, Boston, 29 June 1685. Was on the Brigantine The Samuel, S. Walker owner and master.
Peter Dennis, aged 15 or 16. French boy.
John Rule±42, 5 Aug. 1685. Master of coaster.
Francis Shulet±35, 1 July 1685, sworn at Black Point.
John Start±52, 30 June 1685, in service of S. Walker. — Suff. Court Files 2346.

**239a** Tenants on the Cammock Patent.

List of leases made or promised by Henry Jocelyn, Esq., and Capt. Joshua Scottow, compared 16 July 1688 by Edward Tyng and Silvanus Davis. The document was taken to the magistrates in Portland, who inserted 'with others promised by Scottow' and added their certificate. The crosses in the margin were made by them. — Me. H. & G. Recorder i. 194 (original in Suff. Court Files 2497).

Insert after Libby 213 acres, extend the brace to include Burridge and against it enter -4- families.
Alter Eli to Elnior Jackson and 'his' to -her-.
Alter Peter Hindson to Hinkson.
Alter Christopher Busset to Picket.
Alter Richard Myllyn to Wyllyn.
Alter Henry Ebbings to Elkins.
Alter old Maddiner to [Michael] Maddiver.
Alter John Firkett to Fickett.
Alter July 16, 1668 to 1688.

**239b** Proprietors 22 June 1720.

| | |
|---|---|
| John Wornthworth Esq. | Jobe Burnum |
| George Vaughane Esq. | Hezekiah Phillips |
| Richard Wybert Esq. | Philip Duly |
| Elisha Plaistead Esq. | Thomas Harris |
| Mr. William Cotton | Thomas Seavy |
| Mr. John Emerson | Ebenezer Seavey |
| Samuel Penhallow Esq. | William Newbry |
| Henry Libby | Edmond Ward |
| Roger Deering | Ambrous Boden |
| Thomas Laraby | Thomas Mason |
| Roger Hunnewell's widow | Tobias Oakeman |
| William Libby | Joseph Beard |
| Samuel Libby | William Fernald |
| James Libby Henry's son | James Libby, Portsm'th |
| John Laraby | James Libby 3d |
| Benjamin Laraby | Daniell Libby's Heirs |
| William Michell | Humphrey Scammon |
| Roger Perrey | Thomas Cotton |
| John Booden | John Tydy |
| Samuel Oakeman | Stephen Greenleafe |
| John Libby | John Bigford |
| John Libby the 3d. | Added 22 June 1721 |
| Joseph Calfe | Andrew Brown |
| Daniel Foog | Henry Bigford |
| Robert Mackeny | John Hardison |
| John Millikin | John Fogg |
| Nathan Knight | |

## Saco (and Biddeford). Lists 241-249.

**241** The Lewis and Bonython Patent.

Livery of seisin made 28 June 1631 by Edward Hilton gent. to Tho: Lewis gent.
Witnesses: Thomas Wiggin　Henry Watts
James Parker　George Vaughan

**242** 7 Sept. 1636. The booke of rates for the minister to be paid quarterly the first payment to begin at Michaelmas next:

| | £ s d |
|---|---|
| Capt. Rich Bonython | 03:00:00 |
| Rich. Vines | 03:00:00 |
| Tho. Lewis | 03:00:00 |
| Henry Boade | 01:10:00 |
| John Wadlow | 01:00:00 |
| Tho. Williams | 02:00:00 |
| Robt. Sankey | 01:10:00 |
| Theop. Davies | 01:10:00 |
| Geo. Frost | 01:10:00 |
| Clement Greeneway | 01:00:00 |
| John Parker | 01:00:00 |
| John Smith | 01:00:00 |
| Samuell Andrewes | 01:00:00 |
| Will. Scadlock | 01:00:00 |
| Robt. Morgan | 00:15:00 |
| Henry Warrick | 01:00:00 |
| Rich. Hitchcock | 00:10:00 |
| Tho. Page | 01:00:00 |
| Ambrose Berry | 01:00:00 |
| Henry Watts | 01:10:00 |
| Rich. Foxwell | 01:10:00 |

**243a** List of inhabitants obtained by the Massachusetts Commissioners in advance of the meeting to demand submission, 5 July 1653. Doc. Hist. iv. 86 (Mass. Arch. iii. 230, 224, 229).

'West Saco'
Mr. Thomas Williams
Mr. Richard Hitchcox
Mr. John West
*Mr. John Smith
Robert Booth
William Scadlock
Ralph Tristrum
*John Layton
Peter Hill
*John Hollicum
*John Sparks
Christopher Hobs

*Nicholas Bulle
Thomas Hale
Philip Hinkson
Richard Cummins
*Roger Hunniwell

'East Saco'
*Mr. John Bonithon
James Gibbins
Henry Waddock
Thomas Reading
George Barlo
Thomas Rogers

*The seven starred did not submit; nor the following whose names appear in the town records the same year:
Andrew Alger
Roger Hill
Edward Andrews
William Scadlock Jun.
Walter Penuell

**243b** List of Saco Voters.
Saco town book contains a memorandum in Robert Booth's hand 'A record of such as were made freemen of Saco in the year 1653.' Besides the names in Mass. Arch. iii. 224, (correctly printed in Doc. Hist. iv. 80) are these:
John Lighton Sr.
Edward Andrews
Wm. Scadlock Jr.
Roger Hill
Mr. John Smith

**244a** Inquest, Mary Haile, 27 Dec. 1653.
Coroner's Jury. — Saco Town Book.
Capt. Rogger Spencer
Mr. Tho. Williams
Mordecai Cravitt
Ralph Trustrum
Peter Hill
John Hallsone
Walt Mare
Jeremie Umfrees
Rogger Hill
John Bouden

**244b** Fishing catastrophe, in court 4 July 1654. — York County Records.
John Hollicum adminis-
Roger Hunnewell tration
Paul Mitchell granted
John Rowland to:
Robert Booth
Richard Hitchcock
Henry Waddock
Wm. Scadlock
The administrators to satisfy John Sparke and Christopher Hobbs 'for their disbursements upon their fishing voyage.'
William Foster, adm. granted to his brother-in-law Christopher Hobbs.
Charles Hatch, adm. granted to his brother Philip

**244c** Inquest, Sydrick Luscome, Sept. 1, 1660. Jury's verdict, accidentally drowned. — Saco Town Book.
Leut. Wm. Phillips
*[Mr. John Smith]
Mr. John Gra[.. ant*]
Mr. John Alldein
Richard Hichkox
James Gibbins
John Lighton
Thomas Roggers
Edward Andrews
*[Nickolas Egcome]
Georg Page
Robert Booth
Robert Feeld
Henry Waddocke
*Stricken out

**244d** Inquest, Richard Raser, 17 May 1661.
Verdict, accidentally drowned.
— Saco Town Book.
Leut. Wm. Phillips
Mr. Richard Hichkox
Ralph Trustrum
Mr. Wm. Tharall
Gregory Jefery
Thomas Mills
Richard More
John Rice
Richard Randall
Nickolas Buly Jr.
[    ]ms Ward
John Helson
Arthur Wormstall
Jacob Wormwood

**244e** Inquest, Thomas Lattimer, 24 June 1661, which lived with John Chater of Wells & ran away from him this month & was found drowned in Saco River. — Saco Town Book.
Coroner's Jury
Mr. Thomas Williams    Henry Waddocke

James Gibbines
William Scadlock
John Sparke
Ralph Trustrum
John Bouden
Freegrace Norton
Nickolas Buly
William Kirkeet
Edward Andrews
Nicholas Egcome
Edward Clarke
Jacob Wormwood

**244f** 'We indict the freemen of Saco' for not attending the orders of the Massachusetts court. — York County Records, 7 July 1663.
Mr. Williams
Rich: Hitchcock
Ralph Trustram
Hene: Waddocke
James Gibbines
Nicho: Edgecomb
Edw: Sanders
John Smyth
Rich: Cummins
Tho: Rogers
Mr. John Bonython
Roger Hill

**245** A Tax List of (1664-1668) recorded in the town book lists the names downstream the river, skipping from side to side; then from the mouth of the river to Winter Harbor; then along Old Orchard beach.

West Bank
Brian Pendleton

John Davis
William Luscom

Christopher Hobbs
Michael Naziter

Nicholas Buly
Nicholas Buly Jr.
John Carter

Roger Hill
John Bouden
Robert Temple
John Anderson
[Henderson]
Walter Mare
?[Sargent]*
Richard Hitchcock
Arthur Wormstall
John Helson
Mr. Williams
Ralph Trustrum
J. Sargent
W. Penuel
John Lighton

East Bank

John Bonython

Arthur Hewes
John Smith

James Gibbins

Nicholas Edgecomb
Henry Waddock

Old Orchard
Richard Coman
Thomas Rogers

Personal
James Harmon
Thomas Haile

*The entry here was ——, Scots, stricken out and 'Sargent' written above. The original name or names will be hard to make out.

**246** Women's Seats in Saco Meetinghouse Sept. 22, 1666, given in tabular form in the town records, Seat 1 entitled 'Mis,' the other seats 'Goodis.'
Seat 1. *Maverick, *Phillips, Pendleton, *Hooke, *Bonithon, *Williams, Trustrum.
Seat 2. Wadock, Coman, Gibbins, Booth, Buly, Hickox.
Seat 3. Penuel, Kirkeet, Rogers, Bouden, Hill, Helson.
Seat 4. Sily, *Hobs, *Luscom, Mare, Wormstall, *Scadlock.
Seat 5. *Davis, *Randall, Sargent, Harman, *Nazeter.
Seat 6. Chilson, Egcome, Henderson, Wakfeeld, Booth, Lighton.
Seat 7. Hewes, Page, Frost.
*Gone at the re-seating 9 Dec. 1674, when only one 'Mis' (Pendleton) remained. To fill vacancies in front, promotions were made mainly from the seat behind. New names appearing are:
Seat 2. Goody Temple.
Seat 4. Cartter, Gibbins Jr., Rule, Sharp.
Seat 5. Peard, Presbere, Case, Harmon Jr., Read, Henderson Jr.
Seat 7. Warrin, Charchwell, Harvey, (Frie?).

**247** Thos. Williams in deeding half of the land he then lived on named his neighbors, 14 June 1662. — York Deeds ii. 125. Arthur Wormstall's house.

Richard Hitchcock's cornfield.
The lot which was John Layton's.
The house built by John Elson.
Walter Mare's brook and cornfield.
Walsingham Chelson's house.
Mr. William Phillips 'who now inhabiteth the Neck of Land by Winter Harbor.'
Witnesses: Seth Fletcher.
John Spur [Elson?]

**248a** Saco Fort Soldiers. Undated order for discharging men from Saco Fort:
Jonathan Whitney    Samuel Smith
Samuel Pitcher      John [Stevenson?]
Isaac Cleaveland    — Hill MSS.

**248b** Saco Fort Soldiers 16 Dec. 1696.
Original order signed Anthony Brackett, Captain, detailing the following men to serve under Capt. John Hill.

| | |
|---|---|
| James Tufts | James Smith |
| Thomas Southeron | [canceled] |
| Umphrey Dearing | Jonathan Morss |
| Abel Pilsbury | Jonathan Stimson |
| George Wittey | Samuel Shorey |
| John Crocker | Lodwick Dowes |
| Edward Evenes | Isaac Holding |
| [crossed out] | Samuel Smith |
| Jonathan Whittney | Ephraem Craftte |
| | Experance Poope |

## 249 Civil, Military and Clergy Lists.

**Representatives**
1659 Robert Booth
1660 Richard Hitchcock
1662 Lt. William Phillips
1664 Lt. William Phillips
1667 Capt. Brian Pendleton
1668 Robert Booth (to Casco)
1680 John Harmon
1681 John Harmon
1682 John Davies [rejected]
1683 Mr. Benj. Blackman also 1684
1684 Mr. John Sargent
1685 Mr. Geo. Turfrey
1686 Humphrey Scammon
1688 Edward Sargent

**Commissioners to End Small Causes**
1653 Robert Booth Richard Hitchcock Henry Warwicke
1654 H., Wad. & B.
1655 Mr. Thos. Williams B. & Wad.
1656 Mr. Thos. Williams AmbroseBerry Robert Booth
1657 H., B., & Wad.
1658 Wad., T. & B.
1659 B., H., & Wad.
1660 B., Wad. & T.
1661 Left. Wm. Phillips Wad. & B.
1662 Wad. T. & B.
1663 (app. by Mass.) 'same as last year' (chosen at Saco) Lt. Wm. Phillips Mr. Hooke James Gibbines
1664 (app. by Mass. P., Wad. & B.) (chosen at Saco) Mr. Francis Hooke James Gibbines Henry Waddock with Maj. Phillips to assist
1667 Capt. Pendleton T. & Wad.

1668 G., T. & B.
1669 Major Brian Pendleton B., G. & T.
1670 T., G. & B.
1673 P., T. and Thomas Rogers

**Selectmen**
1655 Robert Booth 16 yrs to 1671
Henry Waddock 14 yrs to 1672
Richard Hitchcock 9 yrs to 1668
Ralph Tristram 10 yrs to 1675
James Gibbins 14 yrs to 1674
?4 more to 1683
1656 Mr. Thomas Williams

**Clerk of the Writs Town Clerk**
1656 Robert Booth until death except 1664
1664 Francis Hooke (Mass. app. Booth)
1672 Humphrey Case 4 years
1680 John Abbot 3 yrs. to 1683
1681 John Davies (Edw. Sargent app.)
1684 Pendleton Fletcher 2 yrs. to 1686
1688 Wm. Geale (or Heale) Thomas Doughty

**Town Treasurer**
1656 Mr. Tho. Williams

**Road Surveyor**
1666 Richard Hitchcock
1667 Ralph Tristram
1671 John Henderson and again 1674
1672 Simeon Booth
1680 Richard Peard
1681 John Layton John Bonython
1682 Walter Penwell
1683 John Sargent Francis Backus

**Lot Layers**
1681 Mr. Blackman John Harman John Abbot

**Fence Viewers**
1674 Ralph Tristram Roger Hill

**Master of Magazine**
1667 James Gibbins

**Constables**
1653 John Leighton
1655 James Gibbines
1656 Ralph Tristram Williams Commings
1657 Mr. Tho. Williams
1658 Richard Commings
1659 Tho: Rogers
1660 Ambrose Berry
1661 Roger Hill
1662 John Bouden
1663 Walter Mayer
1664 Nicholas Bouly
1665 Robert Booth [Thomas Rogers app.] John Henderson deputy
1666 Arthur Wormstall
1666-7 George Page deputy
1667 Simon Booth
1668 John Sargent
1669 Robert Temple Abraham Radver deputy
1670 John Presbury
1671 John Helson [Robert Temple app.]
1672 Christopher Hobbs
1673 Richard Peard [Humphrey Case app.]
1674 Richard Commins
1675 John Carter
1676 James Gibbines
1680 Phineas Hull
1681 Pendleton Fletcher
1682 Francis Backhouse
1683 Thomas Haley Daggett
1684 William Daggett
1685 John Abbot
1686 William Dysar
1688 Richard Peard

**Grand Jurymen**
1653 Wm. Scadlock

1654 William Scadlock and 1657, 1671, James Gibbines and 1657, 1671,
1655 John West
1656 Thomas Rogers (Henry Waddock app.)
1657 James Gibbins also 1662, 1668
1658 Richard Hitchcock also 1660, 1668
1659 Henry Waddock
1661 Richard Commins
1662 Robert Booth also 1664
1662 Freegrace Norton
1663 Ralph Tristram
1668 Roger Hill also 1669, 1683, 1687, 1690
1672 Humphrey Case
1673 Humphrey Case
1674 John Henderson
1675 John Sharpe
1676 John Presbury
1678 Francis Backus
1682 John Harmon
1684 Phinea Hull
1685 Humphrey Scammon
Philip Foxwell
1686 Francis Backus
1688 Pendleton Fletcher
1689 John Bonython Robert Edgecomb John Sargent

**Petty Jurymen**
1656 Richard Hitchcock
1659 Edward Clark
1660 Richard Hitchcock
1663 William Luscome
1664 Robert Booth
1666 William Luscome
1668 John Sharpe and 1674
1669 Robert Booth James Gibbins Jr.

1670 James Gibbins Sr.
1671 Humphrey Case
1672 Mr. John Bonython
1673 John Henderson
1674 John Sharpe
1675 John Presbury
1676 John Harmon
1680 John Edgecomb
1682 Roger Hill
1683 Phinias Hull
1684 Humphrey Scammon
1685 Francis Backus
1686 George Page
1687 Edward Sargent
1688 Roger Hill
1689 (?John Pratt)

**Military**
Cf. Me. P. & C. Rec.; Bodge 475; Doc. Hist. vi. 267; Lists . . .
1659 Mr. John Bonython, Lt. [not confirmed]
1663 Richard Hitchcock, Lt.
Capt. Wm. Phillips
Sergeant Major 1668
Capt. Brian Pendleton
Sergeant Major 1680
John Sargent, Lt.
John Abbot, Ensign

**Preachers**
1636 Richard Gibson
1641 Thomas Jenner
1653 [George Barlow]
1658 [Robert Booth]
1659 Mr. —— Dunham
1659 John Hale
1661 [Francis Hooke]
1662 Seth Fletcher
1665 Barnabas Chauncy
1669 Seth Fletcher
1685 William Milburne

## Cape Porpus (Kennebunkport).

**251** 'The Names of the Inhabitants of Capt Porpus.' This list was posted to 'My loving friend Morgan Whowell at Cape Porpus,' under Mr. John Cutt's seal.

Griffin Montague          Ambros Berrie
*Edward Clark             *John Elsin
John Cole                 Stephen Batson
William Reinolds          Christopher Spurwell
Peter Turbutt             Morgan Howell
Gregorie Jefferi          Simon Trott
Thomas Warner             *Rich: Moore
*Aurther Wormstall

*Except the four starred, they all submitted to the Mass. Commissioners 5 July 1653; also John Baker.                    — Doc. Hist. iv. 88.

**252** Submission to Massachusetts, 5 July 1653.                  — Doc. Hist. iv. 86, 84.

**253** Fishing Voyage in 1660, financed by Capt. Brian Pendleton.—York Deeds i. 91.

Thomas Warner             Thomas Mills
(drowned)                 Geo. Phippeny
Wm. Smalledge             Wm. Battine

**254** Agreement about Lands naming 12 in-inhabitants in 1663. — York Deeds i. 145.

**255** Petition in favor of government by Mass. 28 Apr. 1668. Two copies circulated (?) signed mostly in duplicate, 16 to each, 22(?) in all. Only one original has been found, (Mass. Arch. iii. 275) which varies from what is printed in Doc. Hist. iv. 217 as follows:*
For Richard Moore, Richard Hix.
'' Richard Brian, Richard Bran.
'' Edmond ———, Edward Berton.
'' Simon trote, Simon Busey.
'' Stephen Batson, Charles Potem
'' Thomas Warner, Thomas Musell
'' John Cole, John Beret.
'' John Elsin, John Sandears.
(John Gooch striken out.)
*As the original is blind and the 'marks' re-produced in the print seem identical with those in the original, it is suspected that the printed names were improvised.

**256** Town Grants naming inhabitants. March-June 1681. York Deeds ix. 120, x. 32. Alter Millard to Miller, [Alison to Alger?].

**258** Quarrel in house of Philip Eades Cape Porpus. — York Court Records vi. 124, 296, and files. Depositions backed Jan. T. 1702-3.
Downing Homan             Joseph Bailey
Isaac Annis               x  x  Coombs

**259** Cape Porpus Town Records, as now preserved at Kennebunkport, are a copy cer-tified by Secretary Willard, before the fire in the Boston Court House 9 Dec. 1747, and subject to clerical misreadings. Bradbury (Hist. of Kenne-bunkport, p. 61) named 27 men as 'the only names found on what remains of the old Cape Porpus records.' These names are all to be found in the ten pages now extant, and as revised by Harold Clarke Durrell are:
John Barrett Sr.          Samuel York
Humphrey Scammon          John Downing
John Batson               John Davis
John Sanders              Immanuel Haynes
William Frost             Jacob Wormwood
Joseph Littlefield        Nicholas Moorey
Edmund Littlefield        John Rennals
John Miller               John Loring
John Miller Jr.           Richard Blanchet
William Thomas            Simon Cundey [Bussey?]
William Barton            Emanuel Davis
Richard Randall           John Purinton Sr.
Thomas Mussey             Lieut. John Purinton Jr.
              Isaac Cole

## Wells (and Kennebunk).  261-269.

**261** 'Wells Mens Names.' This list is a memo. on Sherman & Ince's orig-inal return of the bounds, 19 Oct. 1652. — Mass. Arch. iii. 6. For their submission see Doc. Hist. iv. 74, 75, 85, Mass. Arch. iii. 221, 229.

Mr. Henry Bond
*Mr. John Gouge
  *Ezekiel Knight
  Wm. Hamon
  John Barrett Jun.
  John Wakefeild.
  Tho. Milles
  John Wadleigh
*Mr. Joseph Emerson
  *Jonathan Thing
  Robert Wadleigh
  William Wardell
  †John Crosse
  Samuell Austine
  Anthony Littlefeild
  Francis Littlefeild
  John Saunders
  *John Barrett Sen.
  John Littlefeild
*Mr. Joseph Bowles
  Ould Goodman Littlefeild
  Nicholas Coole
  †John Baker
  (added in another hand)
  John Bushe
  John White
*Submitted 4 July 1653.
†Did not submit.
Did submit but not in the list:
  Thomas Littlefield
  Francis Littlefield Jun.
  William Cole
(The last name was added by Secretary Rawson)

**262** First Laying Out of Wells. 'Present inhabitants 15 June 1658.' The second column is a contemporary list cop-ied from the original into the present town book, pp. 109-110. The first column is a compilation. The contemporary list gave the names in order of the houses on the single road constituting the town, from North to South, only two south of Webhannet river. The Barrett Jr. lot was the center of the massacre 10 Aug. 1703; the John Littlefield lot became the site of the Storer gar-rison, the most northerly permanent stand of the English.

                          John Sanders Sen.
(Little River and Branch River intervene)
                          John Barit Jr.
(A long stretch of unoccupied land of Rev. John Wheelwright, Robert Nanny, William Cole, Wil-liam Symonds)
                          Samuel Austin
                          Thomas Mills
John Wadleigh             Goodman Wadley Sen.
('The Gore' and the Town Lot intervene)
                          John West
                          William Hammond
                          Mr. Flecher
William Wardell           Goodman Cross Sen.
William Wentworth         Nicholas Cole
Edward Rishworth          John Barrett Sen.
George Haborne            John Littlefield
Joseph Bolles             Joseph Bowles
Ezekiel Knights           Mr. Knight
(Francis Littlefield Senior's original grant intervenes)
                          Edm. Littlefield
(Webhannet River intervenes)
                          Francis Littlefield Jr.
Samuel Austin             Francis Littlefield Sen.
Robert Hethersy           William Ashley

**263** Submission to Massachusetts, July 4-5, 1653. In two lists, Doc. Hist. iv. 72-75 (Arch. iii. 218, 221).
Alter Thomas Mittes to Milles.

**264** Petition Favoring Mr. Seth Fletcher, the Minister, May 17, 1661. — Doc. Hist. iv. 172 (Arch. x. 97).

**265** Powers of Selectmen 18 June 1670, all the powers of a town meeting except granting lands.

| Selectmen | |
|---|---|
| Mr. Saml. Wheelwright | John Gooch |
| Wm. Hammond | Wm. Ashleigh |
| John Littlefield | Tho: Littlefield |
| Samuel Austin | Ezekiel Knights |
| James Gooch | Nathl. Masters |
| Names Signed | Tho: Baston |
| to Agreement | Peter Cloyes |
| Abram Tilton | Jonathan Hammond |
| John Barret | Francis Backhouse |

**266** Soldiers' charges down to Sept. 1, 1677. — Doc. Hist. vi. 194 (Mass. Arch. lxx. 409).
Cancel ·To· before & Jo: Gough Estate.
Alter Peter B——— to [Peter Busse?].

**267a** Cry for Help, 22 May 1690. Doc. Hist. v. 103 (Mass. Arch. xxxvi. 75).
Alter ——— Huet to Nicoles Huet.
Alter Nat Ellen to Ellens.
Alter John Hobart to Hurburt.
Alter Joseph Stover to Storer.

**267b** 'A list of souldiers under the Command of John Hill.'
[Nov. 8, 1693 — 23 Feb. 1693-4]

| men's names | whare belong |
|---|---|
| Capt. John Hill | Wells |
| Joseph Storer Leut. | — — |
| Jos. Hill Sergt. | — — |
| Jos. Boston | — — |
| Ja. Denmark | — — |
| John Hartshorn, Clark | Haverhill |
| Abraham Whitacer | — — |
| Tho. Davis | — — |
| Saml. Person | — — |
| Gilbart Warren | — — |
| John Emerson Sargt. | Newbury |
| Jonathan Plumer | — — |
| Steven bolton | — — |
| Will Faning | — — |
| Moses oden | — — |
| Franses breten | — — |
| Jos. Chandler | — — |
| Tho. Williams | — — |
| Henry Chanler sargt. | Andever |
| Nath. Abot | — — |
| Will Blunt | — — |
| John Russ | — — |
| Tho. Averhill | Topsfield |
| Richard Crocker | — — |
| Will Hobs | — — |
| Richard Waters Corp. | Salem |
| Obediah Bridges | — — |
| Jos. English | — — |
| Judah Rogers | — — |
| Ephraim Sheldon | — — |
| Richard Tozer Sargt. | Watertown |
| Andrah White | — — |
| Saml. Ball, [or Bull] | Marblehead |
| Will Dagget Corp. | — — |
| Tho. Welman | Lenn |
| John Dean | — — |
| John Driver | — — |
| Will Barber | — — |
| Caleb Townsend | — — |
| men's names | whare belong |
| Robert Kimball | Bradford |
| John Gage | — — |
| John Willams | Beverly |

| | |
|---|---|
| Nath [blank] | — — |
| Saml. Masters | Manchester |
| Ezekiell Nolton | — — |
| Mark Pitman | — — |
| Will Watels [made over] | Milton |
| John Burrill | Cambridge |
| Eliezer Ward | — — |
| Will Brown | Dedham |
| Danel Wright | — — |
| Danel Magrigery | — — |
| Jonas Wakeham | — — |
| Cornelas Durlen | Medfield |
| John Fisher | — — |
| John Stone | Malden |
| John Carter | — — |
| Tho. Grover | — — |
| David Wilamson | Hingham |
| Jos. Pluckfoul | — — |
| Adam Blackman | Dotchester |
| Enoch Cleveland | Woburn |
| John Hakens | — — |
| Ben Norton | Salburey |
| John Sias | Epswich |
| Gorg Greely | Epswich |
| Will Hamand | Cap An |
| Peter Ginks | Wenham |
| Archebel [M or N]aquerey | Mude River |
| James Craford | Hamton |

**268a** Inquest, John Mc Kenney April 15, 1697. — York Court Files.
Coroner's Jury / Names on the back of the warrant

| | |
|---|---|
| Jonathan Hammond | David Littlefield |
| John Wheelwright | Constable |
| Josiah Littlefield | John Cloys |
| Eliab Littlefield | Nathaniel Cloys |
| Antony Coomes | William Frost |
| Marke Rounds | Ezekiel Knight |
| Samuel Jones | Jonathan Littlefield |
| James Ros | Nathaniel Clark |
| Nathaniel Frost | Joseph Wheelwright |
| John Drisco | |
| James Denmarke | |
| John Rodgers | |

**268b** A fragment of a probate account in York Court Files shows dealings with:

| | |
|---|---|
| Mr. James Gooch | Lev. Joseph Storer |
| Lev. Wheelwright | Jane Littlefield |
| Abraham Masters | Joseph Taylor |
| Zekel Knite | David Littlefield |
| Mr. Ommery [Emery] | Joseph Smith |
| Benjamin Mare | Peter Littlefield |
| Jacob Wormwood | Samuel Hill |

for shoes, &c. for the children
to money paid out for adm.
to nursing two children

**269a** Proprietors of Common Lands March 27, 1715/16, voted 'that the right and propriety of all the common and undivided lands within the said township doth belong unto:' — Town Records, p. 22.

| | |
|---|---|
| Col. John Wheelwright | Mr. John Butland |
| Mr. Samuel Emery | Mr. George Butland |
| Mr. Jonat. Hamond | Mr. Samuel Stewart |
| Mr. Joseph Storer | Mr. James Baston |
| Capt. Joseph Hill | Mr. Nathaniel Cloyse |
| Mr. Jonat Littlefield | the heirs of the estate |
| Mr. Daniel Littlefield | of John Cloyse dec. |
| Mr. William Sayer | Mr. John Harmon |
| Mr. Dependance | Mr. Stephen Harding |
| Littlefield | Mr. Zachariah Goodale |
| Mr. Samuel Hatch | Mr. Moses Stephens |
| Mr. Nicholas Cole | the heirs of the estate |
| Mr. Francis Sayer | of Benjamin Gooch |
| Mr. Daniel Littlefield | deceased. |
| Mr. Joseph Littlefield | Ditto Daniell Sayer dec. |
| Mr. Ezekiel Knite | Ditto Thos. Baston dec. |
| Mr. John Wells | Ditto Wm. Persons dec. |
| Mr. Nathaniel Clerk | Mr. Thomas Wells |
| Mr. Joseph | Mr. Jeremiah Storer |
| Wheelwright | Mr. Samuel Hill |

## 269b   Wells Town Grants, an incomplete compilation.

Wells town and proprietors' records have suffered woefully; this list of grants (including some abuttors) is supplemented from Bourne's and Remick's Histories and York deeds and court files — very subject to error.

1649
July 20. William Hammond
& John Bush
1651
Nov.25. Mr.Wheelwright's farm
165—
—— Robert Booth
1654
—— Robert Wadleigh 200
1657
June 3. John Gooch.
165—
—— John Sanders 100
—— John Sanders 50
—— Fr. Littlefield Jr. 200
—— Mr. Jos. Emerson
—— Mr. Seth Fletcher
—— John Cross
1659
Dec.7. Francis Lit. Sr. 200
Joseph Bolles 200
June 10. Thomas Mussell 200
1660
Nov.20. Jonathan Thing 110
Wm. Hammond 110
John Bush 110
Nicholas Cole 110
—— John Littlefield 100
—— Harlakenden Symonds &
Nicholas Cole 300
1661
June 1. John Gooch &
Wm. Symonds &
Wm. Hammond 500
1666
Oct.2. John Reede 100
Thos. Littlefield 100
—— Nathaniel Masters 100
—— (John Rhodes 100)
1668
Apr.20. Francis Backhouse 150
—— Joseph Cross 150
1669
—— Nathaniel Masters 50
1670
Jan. 4. Henry Sayword 300
James Johnson
Thomas Paty 100
June 24. Benj. Storer 100
—— John-Gooch 50
1673
Apr.15. John Manning

167—
—— Nicholas Cole Sr.
& Edmond Lit.
& Samuel Lit. 30
—— Jonathan Hammond
—— (Stephen Batson)
—— John Trott
—— Charity Webb
—— Isaac Cousins
—— Robert Hilton
—— (John Wentworth)
1675
May 4. Thomas Baston 100
Mr. John Buss 200
Jeremiah Storer 110
Samuel Storer
John Bates 110
June 20. John Richardson
—— John Wells
John Drisco 50
Nathl. Cloyes 160
1677
Oct.4. John Harmon
Gilbert Endicott
—— Peter Bass
1678
Jan.31. Thos. Averill 200
Abraham Tilton 10
1679
Aug.14. Mrs. Eliz. Locke
Henry Brown
Eleazer Hathorne 300
1680
Mar.16. Samuel Littlefield 100
Edmund Littlefield 100
Nicholas Cole 100
July 20. Nathan Littlefield 100
1681
July 11. John Cloyes 150
—— William Frost
John Masters
Dec.6. Abraham Masters 100
1682
—— William Frost &
Jonathan Hammond
1683
June 18. Jonathan Lit. 200
July 23. John Woodin 110
—— James Ross 100
Samuel Averill 110
John Littlefield Jr. 100
Joseph Storer 50
1684 Apr. 29. Thos. Cousins

Thos. Cole
Aug.25. Benj. Curtis 110
—— John Barrett Jr. 100
Nicholas Morey 100
Henry Brown
& James Orr 4½
1685
May 25. William Taylor
Ralph Andrews 100
—— William Sawyer
1686
Apr.29. Nicholas Cole Jr. 110
1688
May 21. Wm. Frost Sr. 50
—— Wm. Frost Jr. 50
1693
Dec.23. Thomas Cole
Joseph Taylor 110
Moses Littlefield 50
Jeremiah Storer 100
(James Guttridge)
David Littlefield
& Saml. Hatch
& Wm. Frost
1694
Mar.14. John Harmon (90)
James Wakefield 100
James Denmark
Nathl. Clark 50
Apr.10. Joseph Crediford 100
Daniel Littlefield 10
1695
—— Samuel Littlefield &
Jonathan Hammond
& Eliab Littlefield
& John Butland
1698
Joseph Littlefield 10
1699
Nov.22. Daniel Low
Alex. McMillan 100
—— William Vinney 100
Joseph Taylor 100
Thos. Baston Jr. 100
James Baston 100
Samuel Stewart 100
Lt. Joseph Storer 100
James Adams 50
William Frost
& Saml. Hatch 100
Henry Scates 100
Nicholas Cole 100
John Harmon 50

## 269c   List of Proprietors 9 May 1734, with their number of shares. — Prop. Rec. p. 85.

| Name | Shares | Name | Shares | Name | Shares | Name | Shares |
|---|---|---|---|---|---|---|---|
| Col. John Wheelwright | 12 | William Low | 1 | John Stuart | 1 | Peter Rich | 1 |
| John Littlefield | 6 | John Butland | 4 | Peletial Littlefield | 7 | John Wells Jr. | 1 |
| Peter Littlefield | 4 | Caleb Kimball | 5 | Jos. Stewart's heirs | 1 | David Littlefield | 5 |
| George Jacobs | 5 | Zach. Goodale | 3 | Samuel Wheelwright | 6 | David Littlefield Jr. | 1 |
| Mallichi Edwards | 2 | John Stevens | 1 | Nathl. Wheelwright | 6 | Henry Maddock | 1 |
| heirs of Josiah Winn | 5 | Joseph Gachell | 2 | Thomas Wells | 10 | Jeremiah Storer | 1 |
| John Winn | 1 | Benj. Hatch | 3 | Nicholas Cole | 6 | Nathaniel Wells | 1 |
| Gersham Maxwell | 2 | Charles Annis | 2 | Francis Sayer | 14 | Nathaniel Hill | 2 |
| John Cussens | 5 | Benj. Credfore | 1 | Daniel Morson | 2 | Elezer Clark | 4 |
| Samuel Stewart | 6 | Thos. Peney Jr. | 1 | John Stevens | 1 | Joseph Sayer | 1 |
| James Baston | 6 | Samuel Hatch Jr. | 1 | Depend'ce Littlefield | 5 | William Sayer | 6 |
| Francis Littlefield | 14 | Philip Hatch | 1 | Joseph Hill | 14 | Wm. Taylor | 1 |
| Enoch Davis | 6 | Arcalos Huit | 1 | John Storer | 16 | Richard Boothby | 1 |
| Samuel Treadwell | 6 | Thomas Peney | 2 | Nathaniel Clark | 6 | Samuel Hatch | 4 |
| Moses Stevens | 4 | Isaac Littlefield | 1 | James Samson | 3 | John Eldrig | 4 |
| Jonathan Littlefield | 6 | Nehemiah Littlefield | 1 | John Wells | 8 | William Eaton | 4 |
| Joseph Wheelwright | 8 | Zach. Goodale Jr. | 2 | Samuel Clark | 4 | Joseph Littlefield | 10 |
| James Littlefield | 4 | Moses Stevens Jr. | 1 | Ichabod Cousins | 2 | Stephen Harding | 2 |
| George Butland | 4 | Jacob Perkins | 4 | Stephen Laraby | 2 | David Lawson | 2 |
| Samuel Littlefield Jr. | 2 | Daniel Chaney | 3 | James Wakefield | 1 | Abiel Merriel | 2 |
| Job Low | 2 | | | John Wakefield | 1 | John Webber | 2 |
| | | | | Nathanl Wakefield | 1 | Samuel Emery | 4 |
| | | | | Thomas Wormwood | 2 | Henry Boothby | 1 |
| | | | | John Gilpatrick | 1 | Samuel Littlefield | 2 |

| | | | |
|---|---|---|---|
| John Gouch | 4 | John Bourn | 1 |
| James Gilpatrick | 1 | John Freese | 1 |
| Joseph Day | 1 | Thad Watson alias | |
| John Look | 2 | Thomas | 1 |
| Nathaniel Kimball | 2 | Joshua Wells | 4 |
| Richard Kimball | 1 | Mr. Saml. Jeffords | 8 |
| Nathan Littlefield | 1 | Mrs. Emry widow | |
| Samuel Emmons | 1 | of Rev. Emry | 4 |
| Jeremiah Littlefield | 1 | Heirs of Wm. Person | 4 |

But seven months later the Proprietors voted:
'all the men in said town of Wells that hath a
house & land within the same shall be a proprietor.' — P. 68.

## York.    Lists 271-279.

**271** Patentees of 24,000 acres recited in
Arthur Bragdon's deed, 11 June 1637.
— York Deeds xxvii. 83.
Ferdinando Gorges, son & heir of John Gorges of
London, Esq.
Walter Norton, Lieut. Col.
Seth Bull, citizen & skinner of London.
Samuel Maverick Esq.
Thomas Graves, gent. engineer.
Ralph Glover, merchant.
William Jeffries gent.
John Busley
Dixey Bull.
Robert Norton Esquire.
Richard Norton, gent. of Sharpenhoe.
Matthew Bradley of London, gent.
John Bull, son of said Seth Bull.

| Witnesses | To |
|---|---|
| J × × × yyell | Samuel Maverick |
| Wm. Ruiske | grantor |
| Edward Fountayne | Wm. Jefferies |
| Will: Pyrie | grantor |

To be laid out by William Hooke.

**272** Twenty-Seven Owners of the Patent
— 2 Me. Hist. Coll. ii. 323-325.

**273** Grants Made by Mr. Godfrey
probably prior to 1640. — Mass. Arch. 3:
238, better printed in 1 Me. Hist. Soc. ix, 378.
For Phillop Adams & More -read- &c., more.

**274** Probate Record of the City of Gorgeana 3 July 1648. — Me. Prov. & Court
Rec. i. 126-129.

**275** An Imperfect List of the Inhabit-
ants of York, made up in advance of their
submission to Mass. — Mass. Arch. iii. 193.
As printed in Doc. Hist. iv. 34:
Alter Ould Goodman Lovis to [John] Lavis.
Alter Mr. Ed: Gousone to Jonsone.
Cancel apostrophe in Will: Garnesey.
Alter Thomas Courfous to Curtous.
Alter Cap. Nuttache to Cape Neddick.
Read Philip Admas [Adams].
Read Gorges Brances [submitted Brancen, prob.
Geo. Bronson].
Read Thomas Denell [Donnell].

**276** Submission to Massachusetts
Nov. 1652. The original report of the Com-
missions (Arch. iii. 199) has the names in four
columns headed by:
Mr. Francis Raines, Tho: Crockett, John Al-
cocke, etc.
Mr. Edward Godfry, [John Lovis] Robert Edge,
etc.
Mr. William Hilton, William Moore, Henry Don-
ell, etc.
Mr. Edward Rishworth, John Harker, Niccolas
Davis, etc.
As printed in Doc. Hist. iv. 62:
Alter Georg Beanten to Brancen [Bronson?].
Alter John to Wm: Ellingham.
Read ——— Lewis [John Lavis].

**277** Protest by the Inhabitants against
the decision of the Mass. commissioners
in favor of Mr. Godfrey, presented 21 Oct. 1654.
— Mass. Arch. 3: 237, better printed in 1 Me.
Hist. Soc. ix, 381.
They signed in three cols. headed by:
John Alcocke      Joseph Emerson Ed: Rishwooth
Nicholas Davis    Francis Raynes Abra: Preble
Henry 8 Dunnell Peter Weare      Edward Johnson
For Thomas Car his [mark] read Curtis.

**278** Billeting Account in 1694.
— Doc. Hist. v. 397.

**279** The final division of lands in York
consisted of:
1. June 20, 1732, chief division from 1 to 8
   shares each.
2. Sept. 25, 1732, those omitted or aggrieved,
   about 100 in this list, most of them added
   shares to the number of shares in the first list.
3. Sept. 25, 1732, 'Granted to such young men
   as were born in this town, are more than
   Twenty one years of age; now live in the
   town & have paid rates in it, and have no
   share granted them before — each two shares
   apiece.'
4. To John Thompson, lame man, 40 acres.
5. To Mr. Joseph Sayward, one of the elders,
   land to compound his debts.
But many other grants had been made to new
comers not named in these lists, in full of their
just claims, or forfeited.
Names found in both lists are printed but once,
the additional shares being added in the first list.
Only the laying out of the two-share grants would
disclose the unnamed 'young men.'

| | | | |
|---|---|---|---|
| Edward Bale | 8 | Abiel Goodwin | 6 |
| Joseph Bragdon | 6+2 | John Stover | 8 |
| Mr. Joseph Banks | 8 | George Stover | 6+2 |
| Job Curtis | 8 | Heirs of Depend- | |
| John Donnell | 6+2 | ence Stover 2d | 8 |
| Nathl Donnel Sen. | 8 | Mr. Samuel Moody | 8 |
| Samuel Donnell | 4+2 | Joseph Weare | 8 |
| Nathl Donnell Jr. | 6+2 | Elias Weare | 6 |
| Col. Johnson Har- | | John Woodbridge | 8 |
| mon | 8 | Joseph Young Jr. | 8 |
| Mr. John Harmon | 8 | Rowland Young | 6 |
| Mr. Richard Mil- | | Joseph Austin | 8 |
| berry | 8 | Thomas Baker | 6 |
| John Moor | 8 | Mr. Jonathan Bane | 7+1 |
| Samuel Moor | 4 | Mr. Arthur Bragdon | 8 |
| Maj. Jeremiah | | William Bracey | 8 |
| Moulton | 8 | Josiah Bridges | 6 |
| Mr. Caleb Preble | 8 | Samuel Came Esq. | 8 |
| Capt. Edward | | Thomas Card | 8 |
| Preble | 8 | Joseph Freethy | 8 |
| The Heirs of Jo- | | Robert Gray | 6 |
| seph Preble | 8 | Andrew Grover | 6 |
| Samuel Preble | 5 | Matthew Grover | 6 |
| Stephen Preble | 8 | Job Banks | 6 |
| Francis Raynes | 8 | Aaron Banks | 6 |
| Nathan Raynes | 8 | Josiah Black | 6 |
| Nathan Raynes Jr. | 8 | Mr. John Carlise | 5+1 |
| John Preble | 7 | John Curtis | 4 |
| Hezekiah Adams | 6 | Ralph Farnum | 5+1 |
| Thomas Adams Jr. | 6 | Daniel Farnum | 5 |
| Heirs of Elisha | | James Grant | 8 |
| Allen | 4 | Daniel McIntire | 5 |
| Samuel Averill | 5 | James Grant Jr. | 5 |
| Job Averill | 5 | Aquila Haynes | 5 |
| Manwaring Bale | 4 | Joseph Henney | 2 |
| Samuel Banks | 5 | Benj Johnson Jr. | 4 |
| Abraham Bowden | 6 | Joseph Kingsbury | 4 |
| Caleb Boynton | 6 | Nathaniel Lewis | 2 |
| Henry Brookin | 4 | Alexander Junkins | 8 |
| Nicholas Came | 6 | Daniel Junkins | 6+2 |
| Ebenezer Coburn | 6 | John McIntire | 8 |
| James Donnell | 4+2 | Micom McIntire | 7+1 |
| Nathaniel Freman | 6 | Josiah Main | 7 |
| Mr. Joseph Say- | | Joseph Moulton | 8 |
| ward | 8 | J. Junkins | |

| | | | | | | |
|---|---|---|---|---|---|---|
| Joseph Junkins | 4+1 | John Nowel | 5 | Samuel Came Esq. | 1 | Noah Moulton if |
| Capt. Peter Nowel | 8 | Jedediah Preble | 6 | The sons of Maj. | | he settle in this |
| Constant Rankin | 8 | Joseph Cole | 4+2 | Moulton among | | town 2 |
| Mr. John Sayward | 8 | Peter Nowel Jr. | 5 | them, as he shall | | Use of Grammar |
| William Shaw | 7 | James Hill | 2 | order and dispose | 8 | School 8 |
| Dr. Daniel Simpson | 8 | Zebulon Preble | 6 | Samuel Black | 6 | John Baker 4 |
| Charles Trafton | 8 | John Rackleff | 4 | Col. William Pep- | | Children of John |
| Zaccheus Trafton | 6+2 | Nathaniel Rams- | | perell Jr. | 8 | Kingsbery Dec. 4 |
| Philip Welch | 6 | dal | 5+1 | John McIntire Jr. | 3 | Abraham and Na- |
| Mr. Joseph Young | 8 | John Sedgley | 4 | Norton Wood- | | thaniel Burrill, |
| Moses Banks | 8 | Samuel Simpson | 6 | bridge | 1 | 2 each 4 |
| Heirs of Elihu | | Henry Simpson | 5+1 | Samuel and each | | Jonathan Philbrook 2 |
| Parsons | 8 | Henry Simpson Jr. | 5+1 | Joseph Baker | 2 | Philip Pike, if he |
| Samuel Webber | 6 | John Smith | 6 | Ebenezer Bane | 2 | shall settle in |
| Samuel Adams | 8 | Joseph Smith | 5 | Thomas Card Jr. | 2 | this town 2 |
| James Allen | 7 | Benj. Thompson | 5 | Mr. John Say- | | James Freethy 2 |
| Matthews Young | 7 | Andrew Toothaker | 4 | ward's sons | 4 | Jonadab Lord 8 |
| Philip Adams | 8 | John Thompson | 4 | Zaccheus Trafton | 2 | Samuel Webber Jr. 2 |
| Wymond Bradbury | | Benj. Webber | 5 | Ebenezer Young | 4 | Samuel Adams Jr. 2 |
| Jr. | 8 | Charles White | 3 | Dr. Alex Bulman | 8 | Edward Bale Jr. 2 |
| First Parish in York | 8 | Andrew Wittum | 2 | Dr. Bennet, if he | | Josiah Bale 2 |
| Second Parish in | | Jonathan Young | 6 | settle in this | | Ichabod Linscot 2 |
| York | 8 | Benaiah Young | 5 | town | 8 | Elisha son of |
| James Carr | 4 | Nicholas Bale | 4 | Sons of Hopewell | | James Allen 2 |
| Samuel Clark | 5 | William Dunning | 5 | Weare dec. | | Joseph Bragdon Jr. 2 |
| John Davis Jr. | 1 | Daniel Dill | 3 | 2 shares each | 4 | Josiah Bridges Jr. 2 |
| John Davis | 1 | Nathan Adams | 4 | Christopher Pottle | 3 | Peter Grant 2 |
| John Fowall | 1 | John Letton | 2 | Samuel Ingraham | | John Oliver 2 |
| William Harris | 1 | Samuel Shaw | 4 | if he settle in | | Samuel Bale 2 |
| John Higgins | 1+1 | Joseph Moody | 8 | this town | 2 | |
| Hugh Holman | 1 | Zebulon Young Jr. | 8 | | | |
| Joseph Holt Jr. | 2 | Ephraim Aires | 2 | | | |

Mr. Richard Jaques 2
Joseph Milberry 4+1
Nathaniel Leman 2
Wiat Moor 4
William Grow 4
Benjamin Harmon 4
Johnson HarmonJr. 4
Joseph Holt 6
Samuel Johnson 6
Thomas Payne 4
William Pierce 2
Diamond Sargent 4
William Sellers 3
Samuel Sewall 6
Nicholas Sewall 5
John Spencer 6
Mr. Benjamin
  Stone 5+1
Isaac Stover 4
Joseph Stover 3
Joseph Swett 6
Eliakim Wardwell 6
Peter Weare 6
Joseph Weare Jr. 5
John Webber 6
Waitstill Webber 4
Joseph Webber 8
Nathaniel Whitney 6
Job Young Jr. 5
Mr. Joseph Bane 8
William Bale 5
William Bale Jr. 4
Lewis Bane 6
John Bane 5+1
Jabez Blackledge 4
Ebenezer Blasdel 5
John Booker 5
John Bradbury 4
Mr. Thomas
  Bragdon 6+2
Samuel Bragdon 8
John Card 4
Heirs of William
  Card 4
John Linscot 4
Joseph Linscot 5
Joseph Leavitt 3
Alexander McIn-
  tire 4+2
Abel Moulton 5+1

Col. William Pep-
  perell 8
William Moore 5+1
Walter Murch 3
George Rodick 1
John Wells 1
Barsham Allen 3+1
Joseph Brasey 2
John Bridges 1+1
John Stover Jr. 2
Thomas Cook 1
Henry Beedle 1
Amos Goudy 1+1
George Gray 1
John Grover 2+1
Joseph Kilgore 1
Edmund Black 1+1
Joseph Simpson 3
Ebenezer Nowell 2
James Oliver 1
Robert Oliver 2+1
Samuel Thompson 2+2
Daniel SimpsonJr. 2+1
Samuel Milberry 5+1
Moses Ingraham 1+1
Joseph Main 3
Jeremiah Bragdon 3
John McLucas 1
John Milberry 3+1
Joseph Plaisted 6+2
Josiah Linscot 3+1
Daniel Bragdon 2
Matthias Young 2
Alexander Junkins
  Jr. 1+2
Jeremiah Moulton
  Jr. 4
John Cane 1
Ebenezer Moulton 1+1
Samuel Bragdon Jr. 5

**Additional List**

Nathl Raynes Sen. 8
Thos. Adams Sen. 8
Job Young Sen. 8
Ebenezer Young 4
Benjamin Johnson 3
William Mogridge 1
Richard Braon 1
Samuel Came son of

## Kittery and Berwick. Lists 281-299.

**281** Inhabitants who did, and those who did not, attend Saco court 25 June 1640 — Me. Prov. & Court Rec. i. 42.

**282** Submission to Massachusetts Nov. 1652. Three lists of names, one made up beforehand (Mass. Arch. iii. 203), the original paper signed by most of those who submitted (-idem- 203), and the list given in the Report of the Commissioners (-idem- 194), are printed in Doc. Hist. iv. 25, 22, 41. A facsimile of the second is in Stack. Kit. 143-144. The third was recorded and is printed in Mass. Records iv.(i) 124; a copy of it was also recorded in the York County records and is now missing, but certified copies of that record are in York Court Files about 1700 and in Suff. Court Files 153.
Mr. Richard Leader did not submit.
John Bursley was omitted in the report.
Gowen Wilson was not in the preliminary list.
Alter Mary Bayly to Bachiller.

**283** Petition against Richard Leader Dec. 1652. As printed in Doc. Hist. iv. 45 (Mass. Arch. iii. 208).
Alter Christian Ramay to Ramax [Remich].
Alter Daniell Downing to Danell [Dennis].
Alter Renolds Jinckins to Renolde.
Supply Henary Bla x all [Blackappe?].

**284** Lawsuit over Land in 1654. Judgment giving plaintiffs 30 acres of swamp and meadow. — York Court Records.

| Plaintiffs | Defendants |
|---|---|
| Daniel Paul | Goodman Greine |
| John Symons | Robert Waymouth |
| George Rogers | James Emery |
| Mrs. Batcheller | |

**285** Creditors of Robert Weymouth's estate, 1663. — York Court Records.

| | |
|---|---|
| Mr. Wm. Leighton | Ewen Edwards |
| Left. Charles Frost | Mr. John Cutt |
| John.Lovering | Hene: Donnell |
| Left. Edward Hayes | Will: Ellingham |
| John Cocke | John Downing |
| Richard Greene | Rich: White |
| Dennis Downing | Abra: Conley |
| Thomas Turner | |

**286** Inquest, Robing Williams, 23 Feb. 1674-5. Found dead in the cellar of John Fabing's house in Spruce Creek. Jury:

| John Brey | John Marten |
| Goyen Wilson | Francis Trigey |
| Roger Durent | Joseph Peirce |
| Thomas Padon | Henry Beck |
| Digory Jeffery | Samuel Collings |
| Jeremiah Goddrig | |

John Ameredy — James Gavensey

**287** Inquest, John Cox, 18 Aug. 1675. The little canoe filled. Jury:

| George Lytton | Peter Coleworthy |
| foreman | Joseph Crockett |
| Francis Trickey | Daniel King |
| Stephen Grafton | Humphrey Churchwood |
| Ephraim Crockett | Jeremiah Love |
| Edward Chambers | Samuel Knight |
| John Morgaridg | |

**288** Petition ±1679 for direct government. Recites purchase of Maine but complains that Mass. is suppressing freedom of religion. Signers all but two of Kittery. — P.R.O. C.O.1. 50, 124 I.

Peter Grant, George Gray, James Grant, John Nason, John Key, John Searle, Clement Short, John Neale, Niven Agnew, Wm. Furbish, Nathan Lord Sr. Christopher Batt, Miles Thomson *Nathan, Rich: Nason Bedford, Jonathan Nason *Walter Rendel, Nicho: Hodsden (or Kendel), John Greene Sr. Will: Rogers, Nathaniel Lord Will: Scriven, Bennoni Rich: Cutts, Hodsden Diggerie Jeffrey, John Taylor James Wiggons, James Waren Senior, Alexander James Wiggons, Cooper Junior, Andrew Sarle Rice Thomas, Nic: Shapleigh Dennis, Downing Sr. Joshua Downing, Jeamis Tobee Thomas, Hancome, Richard Whitt, Fran: Champernowne, Fran: Morgan

**289** Kittery Garrisons in (1704?) — Boston Public Library MSS. G. 3340. *Inhabitant enlisted April 12. †Inhabitant enlisted April 1.

Capt. Pleested's Garrison
Sergt. Ebenezar Coburn, Boyall Hambleton; Sergt. Benj. Palmer, Selvanus Wintworth; Corpl. John Flint, Ebenezar Wintworth; Joseph Fuller, Thomas Chick; Daniel Lowe, Abram Mace; Daniel Hooker, *Nicolas Tubett; Jonathan Hobbs

Capt. Abbott's Garrison
Thomas Butler, Moses Spencer; Josiah Gooderdge, Solomon Smith; †Isaac Spencer, James Geffords

Capt. Hill's Garrison
Benony Boington, †Richard Nason; John Hains, †John Tomson; John Ford, †John Hearll; Ebenezer Perkins, *Robert Greay; Alexander Greay

James Warren's Garrison
Edward Dolen (Joseph Sefhens? canceled)

James Emery's Garrison
†Thomas Abbot, Simon Emss

John Key's Garrison
Joseph Standege, John Pugsly

Liutt. Frostt's Garrison
Sergt. Israel Hoytt, John Horenbrook; Cornelus Cosenwhit

Mr. Walden's at Cochecho
Wm. Stockwell, Isaac Burton; Seth Dorman, James Severett

Mr. Peperill's Garrison
Dimond Sargent, Jams Chadwick; David Redleff, Methias Cavele; Richard Hidder

**290** Sufferers from the Indians in the Second War. Three times printed. Stackpole's Kit., p. 175, copied the print in Mass. Acts and Resolves viii. 574, which made errors and omitted James Thomson. — Doc. Hist. ix. 174 is from the original return, Mass. Arch. Alter Tho: Thurcom to Huncom. Alter Aaron Phores to Phares. Alter Henry Be(neent) to Bencent. Samuel Shores -sic- for Shorey.

**291** Garrisons in the Three Years War. Sept. 17, 1722. Better printed in Me. H. & G. Recorder iii. 160 than in Stackpole's Kit. 179. Read:
11. —— Daniel Fogg and Daniel Fogg Jr.
23. —— John Manson.
24. —— James Brideen, James Brideen Jr.
28. Samuel Hutchins.
30. Ebenezer More.
31. —— Alex: Macginnery? or Macquinery?.
32. —— Ebenezer Emons.

**292** Petition of landowners at Broad boate Harbor against surveying and granting their lands to Walter Barefoote, dated 15 Aug. 1688.
John Bray, John Billing; Digery Jeffery, Eprem Crocket; John Andrews, Joseph Couch; Saraigh Michell widow

**293** Petition against Capt. Walter Barefoot, (1687). — Doc. Hist. vi. 351, 278 (Mass. Arch. cxxix. 246; cxxvii. 307). Alter John Holess to Hole. Alter Joseph Wilton to Wilston. Alter Nathaniel Sene to Kene.

**294** Coroner's Inquest, Jan. 1697-8. Man found in the river.
Enoch Hutchins, Richard Carter; Nicholas Tucker, John Foorde; Joseph Crockett, Andrew [Athyle]; Rowland Williams, Elisha Ingerson; John Bonitam, Wm. La x x; Richard Braye, Thomas Fau . . ur

**295** Inquest, William Munsey, 11 June 1698, of Dover, cooper, drowned. Coroner's Jury (Kittery).
William Godsoe, Richard Rogers; John Ingerson Sr., James Bredeen; Thomas Rice, Richard Endle; Rowland Williams, Henry Benson; Joseph Wilson, Elisha Ingerson; John Woodman, Georg Crucey

**296** Landowners in 1712. This committee report, which laid the foundation for proprietors' rights in the undivided lands, is printed in Stackpole's Kit. from the town records. The following amendments are from an attested copy by Tobias Leighton, Town Clerk, about 1735: — Stack. Kittery 149-151.
For Mr. Moore, John More.
For Widow Hooke, Madam Hooke.
For John Ferris, John Fenix.
For Tho: Rice Jr., Tho: Rice.
For R. Rogers, Richard Bryers.
For Thos. Muzett, Thos. Muzzeet.
After John Nason insert:
Nicholas Jellison 8.
For John Wadlin read Wadley.
For Christo: Bots, Batts.

**297** Final Division of the Common Lands, 11 Feb. 1744-5. Some of the names are those of living owners, but for the most part of men long dead whose rights in 1745 were owned by William Pepperell, etc.
— Me. H. & G. Recorder vii. 122-129.
Alter the two Pasuages to Parsonages.
Alter Richard Crockel to Crocket.

**298**   **Land Grants in Kittery, and to Whom Laid Out.**
This list is abridged from a ledger account made for the Proprietors in 1764. Locations are generally omitted, also almost all grants after 1699; and where a man had several grants laid out to himself, some of them are usually omitted. — Original Me. Hist. Soc.

1652. John Andrew, before his house at Brave Boat Harbor.
1653. To same; 1701, John Andrew at Scotch Neck.
1659. Richard Abbott, 13; 1659.
1673. To same, 50; 1712, Bial Hamilton; 1671, Richard Abbott.
1659. Joseph Alcock, 20; 1659, self.
1669. To same, 20; 1669, self.
1669. Thos. Abbott; self.
1671. To same, 50; 1720, self; 1729, Nathaniel Gubtail.
1669. Nivan Agnew, 1720, Deliverance Goodwin; 1741/2, John Goodwin.
1671. Walter Allen; 1680.
1699. To same; self.
1671. Robert Allen and Adrian Fry; 1671, both behind Henry Pownald's land.
1699. Robert Allen; Rev. John Newmarch.
1694. Jos: Axwell; 1694, Axwells.
1694. Jos: Abbot; 1709, self; 1730, Thos. Abbott Jr.
1699. Francis Allen; 1702, 1705, 1732, 1741, Robert Allen.
1699. Thos. Abbott Jr.; 1727, Thos. Butler Jr.; 1736, Joseph Hart; 1747, John Wentworth.
1699. Walter Abbott; 1705, self; 1709, self and Joseph Abbott;
1699. John Adams; 1709, self.
1699. Edw. Ayers; 1703, self.
1699. John Abbott; 1700, self; 1736, Jonathan Abbott; 1738, Jos. Wodsom; 1738, Minister Mosses; 1754, Aaron Abbott; 1754, Samuel Abbott; 1754, John Wodsom.
1680. Christopher Adams; 1682, self; 1736, Nathaniel Guptill; 1748, Wm. Waterhouse; 1738, Wm. Grant; 1760, Ephraim Joy; 1755, James Plaisted.
1682. John Ameredeth; 1738, John Ameredeth Junior.
—— Robert Andrew; 1711, Joseph Mitchell.
1650. Thos. Broughton; 1650, self; 1736, Thos. Butler; 1741, Moses Butler; 1729, Elisha Cooke Esq.
1653. Mrs. Bachelor; Behind her house.
1662. James Barry, stated by Micom Macintire.
1673. To same. Addition laid out by Philip Hubbard, 20 Dec. 1707.
1667. John Bray; 1699, self.
1669. Christopher Beedle; 1679, self, "head of his father's lot in the Long Reach."
1671. Isaac Bootts; 1715, Samuel Brackett; 1748, Samuel Brackett Jr.
1671. John Broughton; John Croad.
1671. Geo. Broughton; 1750, Samuel Walton.
1671. Jos: Barnard.
1671. Eliz.bth Broughton; 1672, self, adjoining her brother John; 1728, Nathan Lord Jr.

1671. Geo. & John Broughton.
1671. John Ball, at head of his land at Spruce Creek; 1693, self.
1680. To same; 1736, Franc. Pedegrow.
1694. To same; 1713, Benj. Hutchens.
1678/9. Chr. Bampfield; 1699, self.
1673. John Brady; 1674, self; 1729, Uriah Page.
1694. Henry Brooking; 1698, self.
1694. Henry Barns; 1696, self.
1694. Richard Barns.
1694. Henry Benson; 1700, 1720, self; 1737, Joseph Chadborn & D. Robinson.
1694. John Brooks; 1696, self; 1718, Wm. Godsoe.
1699. Thos. Butler; 1702, Nicholas Gowen; 1728, Thos. Butler; 1736, Patrick Gowen.
1699. James Burdeon; 1700, Peter Lewis Jr.
1699. Henry Barter; 1712, self.
1703. John Belcher; 1709, Charles Frost 2d; 1729, Charles Frost 3d.
1682. Henry Bodge; 1682, self; 1735/6, John Morrill Jr.
1678. John Billing, 20; Stated, by Crockett's land.
1703. Thos. Ball, 30; Francis Pedegrow.
1685. Elias Brodred, 30; not laid out?
1721-2. Samuel Brackett laid out by grant he says to the heirs of Stephen Jenkins.
1651. Humphrey Chadbourn, 30; stated.
1652. To same, 200; 1718, grandson Humphrey; 1714, son Humphrey.
1671 Wm. Chadbourn.
1651. Abra. Conley, 40; 1740, John Lord 3d; 1723, Martha Lord Senior.
1652. To same and John Heard, stated, by their homesteads at the cedars.
1653. To said Conley, 50; 1699, Conley 40 at Sturgeon Creek; 1683, Nathan Lord Senior.
1669. To same; 1706, William Lord; By addition to Nicholas Frost's lot 25; 1744, David Clark; 1734, Nathaniel Gerrish.
1653. Thos. Crockett, stated, marsh he improves at Brave Boat Harbor.
1656. To same, stated 40 at Crockett's Neck.
1671. Alex. Cooper, 60; 1672, self.
1680. To same, 18.
1666. Robert Cutt, 20.
1699. To same, 40.
1671. Henry Child; 1674, self; 1714, Wm. Child; 1750, Wm. Child.
1671. James Chadbourn; 1701, his widow; 1726, Bial Hamilton; 1728, Nathaniel Gerrish.
1673. John Craford, addition; 1670, 60a Dirty Swamp.
1694. Wm. Crafts; 1736, Bray Dearing.
1694. Jos: Couch; 1694, Roger

Dearing; 1701, said Couch.
1699. To same; 1729, Peter Grant; 1736, Joseph Gould.
1673. To same; 1694, self and Dearing; 1701, said Couch.
1694. John Cooper; 1702, self.
1694. Jos: Curtis Senior; 1699-1724, self.
1682. To same, 20, no grant; 1682, at Spruce Creek.
1694. Jos: Crockett; 1694, self, by Dearing's land.
1699. To same; 1701, self; 1718, Joseph Crockett Jr., by York path.
1684. To same; 1694, self.
—— To same, no grant, 10; 1679.
1699. Hugh Crockett; 1699, self.
1699. Richard Crockett, 30; 1712, Henry Barter.
1670. Ephraim Crockett, stated; to self, adjoining John Shapleigh's land.
—— To same, no grant, 40; 1679, by his own land.
1699. Thomas Chick; 1713, Bial Hamilton.
1699. Dodavah Curtis; 1720, self.
1699. Elisha Clark, 30; 1701, John Sheperd Senior.
1699. Joseph Crockett Jr.; 1709, Pepperrell.
1699. Robert Cutt Jr.; 1700, self; 1709, Wm. Sentinall; 1720, Godsoe self.
1699. Richard Cutt, 30; 1700, Robert Cutt.
1699. Richard Chick, 40; 1700, self.
1699. Joseph Curtis Jr., 30; 1699, self.
1666. Francis Champernoon, 500; stated, by Lockwood's land.
1668. To same, 300; stated by Crockett's land.
—— To same, no grant, 65; 1697, Nicholas Tucker, near Crockett's Neck.
—— Joshua Crockett, no grant, 40; 1679, "James Fernald lives upon, 1734, By Allen & Gray's land."
1652. Dennis Downing, 10; stated at Downing's Point.
1694. Dennis Downing Jr., 40; 1709, Joshua Downing Sr.
1694. Roger Dearing, 40; 1727, self; 1694, self; 1719, Robert Mitchell.
1699. Roger Dearing Jr., 30; 1701, self; 1726, self; 1719, Ebenezer More.
1694. Thos. Dearing; 1724, John Frost on Hogg Island on the Isle of Shoals.
1699. To same; 1722, Rev. Jeremiah Wise.
1694. John Dearing; 1755, Moses Hodsdon; 1703, self.
1699. To same; 1701, self.
1694. Alex. Dennet; 1700, self; 1730, John Fernald; 1736, John Worster.
1694. Walter Dinever; 1700, Robert Cutt.
1699. Joshua Downing; 1709, self; no grant, 1679, self;

no grant, 1682, self.
1699. Jos. Dearing; 1699, self.
1703. To same; 1736, B. Dearing & Roger Mitchell.
1699. John Downing; 1699, said Downing; 40, 1700, Joseph Hill; no grant, 1674, John Demant.
1699. Peter Dixson; 1700, self; 1700, self.
—— To same, no grant, 30; 1679, self, by Tetherly.
—— To same, no grant, 10; 1679, self, by Spinney.
1654. Thos. Dustin, 20; 1733, Timothy Dustin and John Watts in Crooked Lane.
1703. Joshua Downing Jr., 60; 1709, Joshua Downing Senior.
—— Richard Davis, 15; 1698, self.
1650. Anthony Emery, stated head of Mast Creek.
1651. To same, stated at the Third Hill path.
1651. To same and Nicholas Frost, 200, stated S. side of Sturgeon Creek; 131, 1672, Philip Benmore; 10, 1736, John Morrill Senior.
1652. James Emery, 50, stated at the Fowling Marsh.
1669. To same, stated by York Pond, 50; 1685, Richard Davis; 1732/3, Daniel & Simon Emery, 75 — for their grandfather James Emery's addition; 1752, to B. Stacy & Josh. Emery.
1654. Wm. Ellingham, 60; stated near Thomson's Point.
1656. To same, 40, stated by hors la down mills.
1659. Thos. Etherington and James Heard, 69; 1702, Wm. Heard, By Catherine Treworthy.
1671. Mary Etherington; 1672, self.
1671. Patience Etherington, 50; 1718, James & Thos. Heard.
1671. Wm. Evirit, 10; stated.
1678. Robert Easmond; 1678, self.
1685. Zachariah Emery, 50; 1685, self.
1685. Noah Emery, 50; 1685, self.
1694. Job Emery, 20; 1727, Robert Love.
1699. To same; 1704, Gabriel Hamilton.
1694. Daniel Emery; 1712, Elihu Gunnison; 1748, Joshua Emery.
1699. James Emery Sr., 50; 1712, son James Emery.
1699. Hezekiah Elwell, 30; 1701, 1709 and 1719, to Pepperrell.
1699. Richard Endell; 1701, Pepperrell; 1724, Pepperell.
1684. To same, 20; 1688, self.
1669. Elizabeth Edwards, 5; stated by Bedel's land.
1683. Rev. John Emerson, 50.
1651. Nicholas Frost, stated Long Marsh with upland.
1651. To same, & Anthony Emery, 200; 1672, Frost & Benmore.
1652. To same, 200; stated at Sturgeon Creek.
1652. To same, 100; stated at

Thomson's Point.
1668. Wm. Furbush, stated, 10; 1736, Daniel Furbush.
1673. To same, 50; 1694, Enoch Hutchins; 1749, Wm. Hooper & John Worster; 1742, Trustrum Fall where he lives.
1668. Adrian Fry, 10; stated by Crauley's land.
—— To same, without grant, 10; 1679, self.
—— To same, without grant, 10; 1666.
1682. To same, 20; 1699, John Brooks; 1709, self.
1671. Jabez Fox; 1674, self.
1671. John Fernald; 1674, self.
1699. To same; 1708, self.
1699. John Fernald Jr., no grant, 20; 1680, self; 1714, self.
1699. James Fernald; 1716, Nicho. Morrell.
1674. Samuel Fernald; 1678, self.
1699. To same; 1700, Robert Cutt.
1673. Wm. Fernald; 1674, self.
1694. Alexander Ferguson; 1706, self; 1735, Eleazer Ferguson; 1740, Moses Hodsdon; 1714, Black Will negro; 1750, Wm. Clark Jr.
1694. Wm. Fry; 1700, self; 1703, self.
1694. Thos. Fernald; 1709, John Robinson.
1694. Daniel Furbush; 1720, Nathaniel Gubtail.
1703. Confirmation of all the land his father possessed; 1730. John Furbush; 1735, Daniel Furbush Jr.; 1730, Wm. son of Daniel Furbush.
1694. Left Wm. Fernald; 1736, Samuel Wingate.
1699. Aaron Ferris, 20; 1700, Rev. Mr. Newmarch.
1699. John Fenix; 1701, Pepperrell.
—— To same, no grant; 1679, self.
1699. Benj. Foster, 20; 1719, Samuel Shorey.
1699. Nathaniel Fernald; 1709, Nicholas Morrell.
1703. John Follett; 1713, Diamond Sergant.
1679. John Ferguson, 40, stated.
—— James Frost, no grant; 1720, James Frost.
1652. Daniel Goodwin, stated, by Fowling Marsh.
1656. To same; 1733, Ichabod Goodwin.
1673. To same; 1751, Thos. Goodwin; 1678, self.
1673. To same; 1759, Aaron Goodwin.
1652. Hugh Gunnison; 1696, Elihu Gunnison.
1653. To same, stated, Island.
1653, Nov. 24. John Green, stated, 8; by Simond's Marsh.
1654, Oct. 13. To same, stated, 50; by Barnard Squire's lot.
1669, Dec. 13. To same, addition stated, 60; by the side of the marsh he bought of Daniel Goodwin.
1685. Aug. 21. To same. 10.
1678-9, Mch. 20. To John Green Jr., 20; 1685, Aug. 25, self; Bolt Hills by Thomson's Land.

1678-9, July 28. To same, 10; 1679, self; Bolt Hills.
1662. James Grant, 50; stated by John Keay's land.
1671. To same, 60; 1672, self.
1669. To same, addition to his house lot; 1735, Capt. John Grant, 60; 1756, John Hamilton.
1666. Wm. Gowen, 20; 1669. self.
1669. Peter Grant, 100; stated at York Pond.
1669. To same, addition; 1729, Peter Grant Jr.
1671. To same, 50; 1712, Wm. Grant.
1669. Richard Green; self.
1671. Geo. Gray, 60; 1672, self.
1671. Nicholas Gellison, 50; 1674, self.
1666. John Gatensby, on condition not complied with.
1673. To same, confirmation 60 to each of above; 1734, Daniel Wadlin; John & Moses 120.
1694. Thos. Goodwin; 1701, self; 1706, self.
1694. Wm. Grant, 20; 1725, Alexr. & Charles Grant; 1703, Peter Grant; 1737, by this and Francis Harlow to Peter Grant.
1699. To same; 1701, self; 1707, self & Joy.
1694. James Grant, 20; 1701, Said Grant.
1694. Daniel Goodwin Jr.; 1706, self.
1694. John Geer; 1702, John Follett; 1712, Andrew Haley.
1694. Moses Goodwin; 1700, Abraham Lord; 1743, Benj. Lord Jr.; 1735, Moses Goodwin Jr.; 1736, Aaron Goodwin.
1699. To same; 1704, Gabriel Hamilton.
1698. Wm. Godsoe.
1694. Elihu Gunnison; 1696, self.
1703. To same; 1711 Richard Foy, 1744 James Foy.
1699. Robert Gray; 1700, self.
1699. Daniel Green; 1700, Joseph Hill.
1699. Richard Gowell; 1710, John Thomson of the Reach.
—— To same, no grant; 1679, 30 by Tetherly's land.
—— To same, no grant; 1679, 30.
1703. Alexr. Grant; 1709, self; 1718, Stephen Hardison.
1685. Nicholas Gowen; 1699, self; 1742, Samuel Lord; 1702, self.
1694. To same; 1736, Patrick Gowen; 1736, Wm. Stanley; 1734, Hugh Ross.
1703. John Gowen; 1709, self.
—— To same, no grant; 1694, at Black Will's.
1685. Wm. Gowen Jr.; 1694, John Gowen; 1735, Hugh Ross; 1735, Joshua Emery; 1735, Lemuel Gowen; 1735, Margaret Emery; 1742, Benj. Horsom.
1694. John Gelding; 1700, self.
1694. Wm. Goodwin; 1709, self; 1726, Wm. Libbey.
1694. James Goodwin; 1708, 1709, 1728, Richard Lord.
1656. Nich. Hodsdon, stated by Miles Thomson's lands.
1673. To same, 100; 1721, John

Morrell; 1721, John Hodsdon; 1727, Joseph Holt; 1728, Geo. Clark; 1736, I. Shorey and B. Hodsdon.
1659. Tristram Harridon, 40.
1673. To same.
1662. John Heard.
1661. Wm. Hilton, stated, in the Great Cove.
1668. James Heard.
1673. To same.
1669. John Hole, 150; 1669, self.
1671. Israel Hodsdon, stated, 12; 1702, Daniel Emery.
1671. Phineas Hull; 1674, self; 1714, to Wm. Childs by Thos. Newberry's.
1671. Robert Harrison, 50; 1671, self.
1671. Benoni Hodsdon; 1713, self.
1694. To same; 1734, Thos. Hodsdon.
1703. To same; 1735, Joseph Hodsdon; 1736, Patrick Gowen; 1736, John Hodsdon Sen.; 1754, Samuel Ferguson; 1755, Wm. Dowt—
1673. Andrew Haley; 1699, self.
—— Edward Hays, no grant, 1674.
1679. Thos. Hanscom, no grant, 1682.
1694. To same; 1698, Samuel Spinney.
1694. Dennes Hix; 1694, Roger Dearing.
1694. Thos. Hooper, 20; 1700, Robert Cutt.
1694. Andrew Haley Jr.; 1696, self.
1694. John Hanscom, 20; 1735, Job Hanscom.
1694. Philip Hubbard; 1706, self.
1694. Wm. Hays, 20; 1710, Andrew Pepperrell.
1694. David Hutchens.
1699. To same; 1701, self.
—— Enoch Hutchins, no grant, 60; 1672, Eastern Creek.
—— Enoch Hutchins Jr., no grant; 1703.
1694. To same; 1736, Grindle Knight; 1739, John Eaul Jr.; 1742, Samuel Lord.
May 16, 1694. Edmund Hammond, 10; 1719, Benj. Hammond, where he now dwells.
—— Same, no grant found, 20; 24 Oct. 1682, said Hammond at Puden Hole.
—— To same, 10; 24 Oct. 1682, said Hammond at Puden Hole.
1699. Wm. Haley; 1699, self.
1699. John Heard, 50; 1699, self.
1702. To same, confirmation all that land granted to his grandfather and Abraham Conley.
1699. John Hoyt, 50; 1700, self.
1699. Francis Harlow, 20; 1700, self.
1703. To same, 30; 1730, Abraham Lord; 1734, Peter Grant; 1731, Gabriel Hamilton; 1733, Samuel Lord.
1699. Samuel Hutchins; 1699, self.
1699. Benj. Hutchens; 1699, 1712, self.
1699, Joseph Hills; 1700, self.

1699. Samuel Hills; 1710, self; 1729, John & Elisha Hill.
1699. Moses Hanscom; 1703, Enoch Hutchins.
1699. Joseph Hammond Senior; 1701, self.
1699. Joseph Hammond Jr., 30; 1702, Thos. Rhodes.
1703. Capt. John Hills, 100; 1709, self; 1721, Mary Hills; 1748, Peter Morrell; 1729, John Hill Jr.
1679. John Hearl, 50; 1742, Wm. Clark Jr.; 1738, Etherington Hearl.
—— To same and Patience Etherington; 1748, Moses Hodsdon; 1740, Miles Thomson & Jonathan Stone.
—— Wm. Hight claims by Richard Matune's grant, not found, 9; 1748.
—— John Hunking of Portsmouth. By grant he says to Mary Leighton, 1679; 1694, self.
—— Jeremiah Hodsdon, Berwick Record, no grant found, 20; 1 Mar. 1671/2, land Israel Hodsdon's house stands on.
—— Edward Hays, Berwick Rec., no grant found; 1741, Samuel Lord.
1653, Feb. 21. Thomas Jones, 40; 21 Feb. 1653, where he formerly improved at the heathy meadow; 1720, John Leighton.
1694. John Ingersoll, 30; 1696, self, by Gunnison's land.
1694. Ephraim Joy.
1699. To same; 1709, Hubbard & Tozer.
1703. 1712, Bial Hamilton; 1715, James Frost; 1729, James Frost; 1726, Bial Hamilton.
1679. Jabez Jenkins; 1679, self.
1653. Renold Jenkins, stated, 40.
20 Dec. 1668. Confirmations to said Jenkins, by Israel Hodsdon.
1699. Reynold Jenkins Jr.; 1710, self.
1699. Samuel Johnson, 30; 1703, Thos. Rhodes; 1720, Samuel Shorey; 1751, Nicholas Morrill.
1699. James Johnson; 1699, self; 1719, Samuel Johnson; 1735, Samuel Johnson Jr.
1682. Cornelius Jones, Entailed; 1700, 1720, Henry Benson.
1683. To same, stated; 1736, 1743, John Hamilton.
1682. Digory Jeffrey, no grant, 30; by York line.
1662. John Keay, 50; By Clement Short's land.
1671. To same; 1700.
1685. John Keay Jr., stated, 50.
1703. To same; 1712, self and Wm. Grant.
1665. Richard King, stated, 1669, self.
1679. To same; 1679, 1694, self.
1694. To same; 1702, self.
1699. Nathaniel Keene; 1705, 1719, self; 1735, John Lord; 1730, Francis Allen.
1699. Daniel King, 30; 1700, self, Burnt Hill; 1702, his father Richard King at north side of his father's 12 acres.
1674. Wm. King, addition to

Wm. Palmer's house lot.
—— Joseph Kilgore, two grants purchased of Joshua Waymouth.
1652. Nathan Lord, stated; 1683, self.
1671. To same; 1708, 1710, Benj. Lord.
1673. To same and Alexander Cooper.
1679. 1714, James Frost; 1743, Abraham Lord.
1694. 1709, self; 1727, Benj. Lord.
1654. Richard Leader; stated, at Great Works.
1653. To same, stated, at Saco Pond.
1654. To same, stated, 300, South side Great Works.
1654. Richard & Geo. Leader, stated, North side Great Works.
1654. George Leader, 20, By White's Marsh; 1674, Wm. Hutchinson; 1731, John & Elisha Hill.
—— To same, addition, 100; 1735, Robert Evins & Sarah his wife.
1655. John Lamb; 1662, Peter Grant and Wm. Piles by Love's Brook.
1656. To same, By John Green's lot.
1659. Wm. Love, stated, 60; self.
1659. Wm. Leighton, 13, Laid out by Selectmen, By Richard Abbot at Crooked Lane.
1671. Elizabeth Leighton, 50, Long marsh.
1668. Catherine Leighton, stated, 12.
1671. To same, 50; 1672, self.
1694. John Lydston; 1710, Joseph Hill.
1694. Peter Lewis Senior; 1696, self.
1682. To same, no grant; 1746, Jonathan Moore.
1694. Peter Lewis Jr.; 1700, self.
1694. Andrew Lewis; 1700, self.
1685. John Leighton; 1694, self.
1699. Wm. Landell; 1700, self, "at the head of his father Lewis' land."
1681. Weymouth Lydston, 20; 1682, self; 1735, John Lydston.
1703. Morgan Lewis; 1726, Nathaniel Lewis.
1703. Wm. Lewis; 1710, Wm. Wilson; 1713, Geo. Ferris; 1713, A. Lewis; 1718, Wm. Wilson; 1719, Joseph Wilson; 1736, Joseph Hearl & Jonathan Hamilton; 1735, Samuel Wingate.
1651. Robert Mendum, stated, 50, at Ashen Swamp.
1652. To same, stated, at Turkey Point.
1654. Antipas Maverick, 10.
1663. Confirmation of all the land between the two creeks.
1656. Alex: Maxwell, stated, on North by James Warren's.
1662. Micom McIntire, stated, 50, by James Barrow's land, the last of the seven grants.
1668. John Morrell; 1678, N. Lord Jr.; 1722, his son John Morrell.
1669. Same; 1678, N. Lord Jr.

1668. Tos ame; 1678, N. Lord Jr.
1679. Richard Miller; 1679, self.
1694. Christopher Mitchell;
1694, self, by his father's land.
1699. To same; 1701, self, by
his own land; 1701, Joseph
Mitchell.
1673. To same; 1736, Samuel
Mitchell; 1674, Christ. Mitchell, by his house; 1758, Jonathan and James Clark.
1694. Robert Mitchell, 20;
1694, Roger Deering.
1694. Richard Mitchell.
1694. Joseph Mitchell; 1699,
self, Braveboat Harbor; 1721,
self.
1694. Nicholas Morrell; 1701,
self, by his father's; 1709, self.
1699. John Morrill; 1722, self.
1699. Jonathan Mendum; 1699,
self.
1699. John Moore; 1719, N.
Keene; 1735, Benj. Libby.
1694. John Mogaridge; 1698, self.
1694. Samuel Miller, 10; 1694,
self, Kittery.
1694. Wm. Munsey, 20; 1709,
Nicholas Morrell.
1699. Ebenezer Moore, 30;
1700, self; 1701 James Foy,
1719 self.
—— Richard Matune; 1736,
Tobias Leighton.
—— To same, no grant found;
1748, Wm. Hight.
1655. Richard Nason; 1654, a
neck of land by the river;
1750, B. & Samuel Nason;
1732, Thos. Wallinford.
1654. To same, Neck of land
between Quamphegon & Sal-
mon Falls.
1669. To same, stated, 100;
By or near Cox's Pond.
1671. Jonathan & John Nason;
1672, themselves.
1665. To same, themselves, two
points of land.
—— To same, addition; 1740,
Samuel Shorey; 1742, James
Frost Jr.; 1735, Thos. Abbott
& R. Nason; 1735, Job Em-
ery.
1671. John Neal; 1703, Andrew Neal son of grantee.
1671. Thos. Newberry; 1672,
self; 1729, John Holmes.
1679. Sylvanus Nock; 1709,
Thos. Nock; 1734, Thos. and
Ichabod Goodwin; 1742, Zachariah Nock.
1694. John Nason; 1709, Wm.
Lord Jr.; 1740, Benj. Lord Jr.
1694. Andrew Neal; 1699, self;
1699, 1700, P. Wittum on N.
side of Sturgeon Creek near
Leonard Drown's house.
1699. To same; 1745, Joseph
Knock; 1702, self.
1694. John Nelson; 1723, Ebenezer Downs.
1699. To same; 1742, Thos.
Thomson.
1694. Benj. Nason; 1703, self,
By his father's land; 1709,
self; 1735, Benj. Nason.
1694. Baker Nason; 1703, self,
By his father's land.
1694. James Neal, 20 (? not
laid out).
1669. Charles Nelson, 20; 1672,
self.

1651. Henry Powning, stated,
6, at his home lot.
1683. James Plaisted, 60; 1735,
Ichabod and James Goodwin.
1685. To same; 1743, Roger
Plaisted.
1653. Daniel Paul, stated, Behind his house.
1665. To same, stated, 20; 1671,
son Stephen.
1659. Roger Plaisted. Love's
Bridge.
1671. Roger Plaisted Jr.; 1718,
Daniel Simpson; 1730, Samuel Plaisted.
1683. Wm. Plaisted; 1743, Roger Plaisted.
1694. Ichabod Plaisted; 1701,
self; 1716, Samuel Plaisted.
1665. Stephen Paul.
1694. Wm. Pepperell.
1699. Andrew Pepperell.
1703. Thos. Penny; 1710, Chas.
Frost.
1669. Wm. Piles, 60, by Love's
lot; 1751, John Smith Jr.
1653. Thaddeus Reding, 60, For
the use of Leader's saw mill;
1737, J. & E. Hill; 1737, Robert Evans.
1665. John Ross, stated, 20, by
Etherington.
1661. Christian Remick, stated,
1, in the Great Cove.
1673. John Read, 50; 1718,
John Smith.
1699. To same, 30; 1713, Henry Barter.
1694. Joshua Remick; 1699, self.
1699. To same; 1714, 'John
Thomson in Kittery;' 1748,
Nathaniel Libby; 1709, John
Morrell Jr.
1694. Isaac Remick; 1694, self.
1682. To same, 20; 1693, self.
1694. Wm. Rogers; 1753, Moses
Ricker, Daniel Emery; 1735,
to his son William.
1694. Richard Rogers of the
Reach; 1702, self.
1694. Thos. Rice; 1698, self.
1682. To same, no grant, self,
by Shepherd; 1720, H. Benson; 1736, Nathaniel Keene.
1685. Abraham Remick, 30;
1685, self.
1699. Wm. Roberts; 1710, Wm.
Pepperell.
1703. Wm. Roberts Jr., 50,
never laid out?
1699. Richard Rogers Jr.; 1700,
self, By Crockett; 1736, Patrick Gowen.
1694. Jacob Remich, 10.
1703. Richard Randall; 1712,
R. Tozer.
1684. Wm. Racklief; 1685, self.
—— Richard Roe, no grant,
40; 1682, by York line.
1703. Richard Rice, 40; 1710,
Wm. Tetherly; 1716, Benj.
Libby.
1651. Thos. Spencer, stated, 10;
Saco Pond.
1652. To same, stated, 200, by
Bazel Parker's land.
1669. To same, 100; 1671, by
his brother William; 1737, D.
Wadlin by Cox's Pond; 1743,
Moses Spencer.
1651. Jere Shears, stated, 100;
1674, Christopher Adams.
1669. John Shapleigh; 1749,

Nathaniel Keene.
1652. Wm. Spencer, stated;
1671, self.
1653. Nicholas Shapleigh, stated, the home patent by Averill house.
1653. The same, stated, 6, by
Frank's Fort.
1654. John Simons, stated, by
Daniel Paul.
1659. Thos. Spinney; 1736,
Grindle Knight.
1662. Clement Short, stated, 50,
next to Geo. Veasey.
1665. Andrew Searl; 1736-1755,
Bial and Gabriel Hamilton,
Jonathan Clark, Zachariah
Nock, John Sullivan.
1667. Wm. Searl, stated and
laid out at Spruce Creek.
1669. John Shepard, 10, on
condition.
1671. To same, 10, self.
1671. Daniel Stone, 60; 1672,
self; 1714, Jonathan Stone.
1671. James Smith, by his
house lot.
1673. To same; 1712, John
Smith.
1671. Francis Small, 100; 1674,
self, by John Gatensbys.
1671. Humphrey Spencer, stated, upland by his father's,
1674.
1682. James Spinney; 1683, self.
1694. Samuel Small; 1700, self,
By Sturgeon Creek.
1694. Abraham Spiller, 10, never laid out?
1694. Samuel Spinney; 1699,
self.
—— To same, no grant; 1679,
self.
1671. Moses Spencer, 50; 1718,
son Moses Spencer; 1702, Daniel Goodwin.
1671. Peter Staple; 1679, self,
by his wife's land.
1694. John Spinney; 1708, self;
1731, his heirs; 1737, John
Lord; 1713, N. Morrell; 1735,
Wm. Tetherly.
1694. Wm. Stacy; 1700, self,
by Dover river.
1699. To same; 1729, Uriah
Page.
1694. Jonathan Stone; 1710, self.
1694. Alex: Shapleigh, 1713, N.
Shapleigh.
1699. Thos. Spinney Jr.; 1713,
Samuel Spinney; 1734, Thos.
Spinney Jr.; Grindell Knight;
1720, John Shepard.
1699. Peter Staple Jr.; 1702,
1719, self.
1699. Wm. Stone, 30, never
laid out?
1699. John Shepard; 1701,
1720, self.
1699. Wm. Smith; 1700, self.
1703. To same; 1715, John Le-
gro and Joseph Pray; 1764,
Heirs of said Smith, Beaver
Dam; 1754, Philip Yeaton.
1699. Jacob Smith; 1700, Robert Cutt.
1679. John Sharp, condition
forfeited, 40; 1709, Nicholas
Morrell.
1685. Clement Short Jr., on
condition; 1738, Charles Short.
1685. Clement Short Senior, on
condition; 1738, Charles Short;

1706, Thos. Short.
1687. James Tobey, lot confirmed.
1682. John Trickey, 20; 1736, Peter Morrell.
1650. Katharine Treworgy, at the Heathy Marsh.
1653. To same, 20.
1655. John Taylor, stated, by John Lamb's lot, 50; 1729, Moses Goodwin Jr.; 1750, Stephen Hardison; 1726, Wm. Libby; 1741, Wm. Goodwin; 1738, Deliverance Goodwin.
1656. Miles Thomson, stated, by Thomson's Point Brook.
1669. To same, addition; James Frost & Moses Goodwin.
1671. To same, 100; 1674, self, by Nason's land.
—— To same, Berwick Record, 15 Jan. 1734-5, to his grandson John, 45.
1671. To same, 50; 1711, Wm. Goodwin.
1669. Richard Tozier, 60, stated, above Salmon Falls.
1671. To same; 1712, self.
1694. To same; 1709, Philip Hubbard & self; 1740, Paul Wentworth.
1661. Francis Tricky, 20, stated, Crooked Lane.
1694. Stephen Toby, self.
—— By order of James Toby, 4; 1696, Stephen Toby.
1694. Bartholomew Thomson; 1701, self; 1728, Elisha Andrews.
1708. To same; 1723, Jonathan Stone Jr.
1694. Thos. Thomson; 1702, Thos. Rhodes.
1694. Nicholas Tucker; 1719, Samuel Hutchins; 1725, H. Scammon, Thomas Mannering, on Smuttynose; 1735, Nathan Lord.
1694. Alex: Thompson; 1698, self.
1694. John Toby; 1710, Stephen Toby.
1694-1699. James Toby; 1702-1710, Stephen Toby.
1694. James Thompson; 1702, self; 1734, Francis Allen; 1734, Francis Allen Jr.
—— Gabriel Tetherly, 20; 1669, self, Great Cove.
1694. To same, 20; 1679, self, by King's.
1694. Thos. Rogers; 1698, self; 1702, B. Hutchins.
1699. To same.
1699. John Thompson; 1700, Robert Cutt; 1731, John Thomson.
1678. Wm. Tetherly, conditional, 30; 1679, self.
1708. Benedictus Tarr, 50; 1710, self.
1703. John Thomson of the Reach; 1710, self.
—— John Thomson Scotchman, 10; 1679, self, Head of Stephen Paul & Gabriel Tetherly.
—— To same, 30; 1679, self, 10; 25 Sept. 1679, self, at Bolt Hill.
1662. Geo. Veasey, stated, 50, by John Wincoll.
1699. Moses Voden, 30; 1700,

self, by Sturgeon Creek.
1651. John White, stated, by Sturgeon Creek way.
1654. To same, 20, self, at Crooked Lane.
1652. Thos. Withers, 800, stated Spruce Creek.
1671. Henry Wright, 50; 1712, Ichabod Plaisted.
1652, Dec. 16. John Wincoll, stated, by Birchen Point.
1653, Aug. 24. To same, 60, on condition of paying £12 per year.
1652, Dec. 11. To same, stated, by Toziers.
1671, Apr. 13. To same, Joins Searls at the Little River; 1742, John Shorey; 1748, Joseph Rickard.
1671. To same, addition, 100, by his former 100, never laid out?
1653. Robert Waymouth, 6, self. By land granted to James Emery.
1656. To same, behind his house.
1656 to 1671. James Warren; 1741, John Warren; 1745, Samuel Wentworth; 1711, self; 1707, Moses Spencer; 1737, B. Waymouth & Tho. Hobbs; 1796, James Evans; 1735, James Warren.
1658. Gowen Wilson.
1665. Peter Wittum; 1728, Joseph Small.
1671. Nicholas Weeks.
1671. Edw. Waymouth; 1710, Timothy Waymouth.
1694. To same; 1715, Timothy Waymouth.
1671. Thos. Wills for Thos. Chick's family, 60; 1720, Richard Chick; 1719, Tho. Chick Jr.; 1719, John Holman; 1719, Thos. Weed.
—— Thos. Wills, 100; 1714, Richard Cutts.
1673. Joseph Wilson.
1673. John Wilson; 1678, self.
1694. John Woodman; 1696, Samuel Spinney.
1694. Rowland Williams; 1694, self; 1694, David Hutchins.
1694. Wm. Wadley; 1702, self; 1728, Wm. Clark Jr.
1694. James Warren Jr.; 1700, self; 1707, Moses Spencer; 1720, Stephen Hardison.
1694. Peter Wittum Jr.; 10; 1700, self.
1699. To same, 30, self.
1694. Joseph Weeks; 1700, Elihu Gunnison.
1694. Gilbert Warren; 1702, James Stackpole; 1736, John Thomson.
1699. To same; 1708, self; 1703, Wm. Rogers; 1739, Samuel Falls.
Emery.
1699. Paul Williams; 1715, Robert Cutt.
1699. Thos. Worster; 1710, Francis Allen.
1699. Rev. John Wade; 1701, self; 1741, John Lord Jr.; 1714, Elizabeth Wade; 1755, Joshua Emery.
Hardison.
1685. Moses Worster; 1713, Thos. Worster.

1703. Black William; 1714, his son Will by Long Bridge; 1718, his son Will by his own land.
1681, June 24. James Wiggin Jr.; 1735, Tobias Leighton; 1736, Peter Morrell.
1678-9. James Wiggin Sr., 50; 1735, John Morrell Jr.; 1736, John Hooper Jr.; 1737, John Lord; 1751, Nathaniel Keen; 1735, Jeremiah Frost Senior.
1735, James Frost Sr.; 1739, John Faul Jr.
1681, June 24. Samson White, 40; 1736, John Pierce; 1736, Tobias Leighton; 1736, Coolly McAlley; 1736, Stephen Hardison.
1679. Richard White; 1736, John Morrell Jr.
1740-1749. Samuel Wentworth had laid out, addition to his house lot, addition to Thos. Thomson's house lot, grant to John Thomson, 20 Mar. 1698-9.

## Others Taking Land by Grants Not Found.

Jonathan Hamilton by William Hearl's grant.
Nathaniel Joy by Patience Etherington & John Hearl.
Joseph Ricker by Samuel Treworthy.
Joseph Ricker by James Wiggin Sr., and William Rogers.
Jonathan Ricker by Richard Cutt, 1693.
John Shorey and Benjamin Hodsdon by Samuel Shorey's addition.
Joseph Hearl in 1735 by his father, John Hearl's addition.
William Spencer and Mary Etherington in 1674 laid out an addition.

## Additional Notes from the Records.

1744. David Clark had land laid out by Nicholas Frost's addition.
1654. William Ellingham had land laid out near Thomson's Point, between Treworthy and Philip (Frost?).
1682. John Bray had land laid out as adv. estate of Philip Gunison.
1654. The neck of land where William Palmer now dwells was laid out in 1674 to himself and William King.
1651. Henry Powning given the land at his house at Cold Harbor.
1659. Grant to Timothy Prout, John Wincoll and William Osborn, adjoining Richard Tozier, forfeited.
1655. Rice Thomas given a neck of land behind Mr. Gunnison's house.
1714. John Thompson Jr. had land laid out, part of the grant to his father John Thompson, 20 Mar. 1678-9.
—— land laid out to Anthony Emery and Robert Waymouth in partnership.
—— land laid out assigned by John White to William Thomson adjoining Goodman Benmore.

## The Province of New Hampshire by Towns. Lists 301-400.

### Isles of Shoals (partly Maine).

**301** Inhabitants of Isles of Shoals
May 18, 1653, petition Mass. to establish a court
there. . 20 signers. Granted.
— Mass. Arch. iii. 214; Doc. Hist.
iv. 53; facs. Edw. Small and Allied Families.

**302a** Fishermen's Troubles in 1660.
Stephen Ford  :   owned their stages
Richard Endell  :   in common
Mr. Edmund Packard trespassed on them.
Witnesses:
Edward Ball±30, servant of Ford.
Elias Bickford          Thomas Snelling
Chris: Christophers±26, Benedict Oliver±31.

**302b** Witnesses at Isles of Shoals to a
bill of sale dated 21 June 1661, Stephen Ford
to Richard Endle. — York Deeds i. 109.
Arthur Clapporne        Michael Endle
Robert Taprill          John Davis
Fortunatus Home         John Redman

**303** Administration on William Urin's
Estate granted to four merchants in 1664
was declared illegal.
Mr. Jonathan Wade  :              Oliver Fox
Capt. Brian Pendleton  :  vs.    George Kelly
Mr. Richard Cutt  :              Tho: Garman
Nathaniel Fryer  :               Edward Kock
                                 James Payne
for taking away                  Simon Newcom
fish belonging to                John Hoskins
the estate

**304** Roger Kelly's Account in Mr. Stile-
man's books, 1668-9. Hogg Island.
Court Files ii. 141.
Goods delivered by
John Brown      John Bugg      John Knott
Goods for Richard Cauley.
Paid Jeremiah Guttridg by order.
Two pairs of children's shoes.

**305a** Isles of Shoals Court Cases. Will
Urin±20 deposed in June 1673. William
Oliver, his master at the Shoals. W. O.'s wife
had liberty to milk the cow of Philip Odihorne
wherever he could find her. Edward Holland
came out to us among
William Sealey's  :   fish flakes while we were
Andrew Diamond's  :   seeking the cow; found her
Michael Endell's  :   near Mr. Belcher's house.
Roger Kelly in 1674 brought suit against Lewis
Tucker for reporting that
Mark Row        :   were drinking and lay
Edward Holland  :   drunk at his house in
John Badston    :   his cabins.
Peter Twisden issued the writ.
Michael Endell, constable, served it.
Nicholas Tucker went bail.

**305b** Absent from their wives. Esq. John
Fabes's list 29 Sept. 1673.
Richard Tomes        Isay Odihorne
Stephen Harwell      Peter Evans
Richard Bois         Edward Holland Sr.

**305c** Inquest, Walter Wakeham
Aug. 2, 1674. Verdict: Went into the water
of his own free will, and was drowned.
— N. H. Court Files iii. 85.
John Hunkings        Edward 6 Vittery
Walter Mathews       Richard Endell
Roger Kelly          John More
Henery Meane         Christopher Jose
Michaell Endell      Lewis Tucker
Hugh Allward         John Light

**306a** Mooring Rights at Isles of Shoals.
Mr. Roger Kelly had had William Hilton
jailed for assaulting James Neale. The deposi-
tions were taken 20 Dec. 1677, before Peter Twis-
den, Commissioner. — N. H. Court Files 15971.
Depositions
Nich. Bickford±22   Roger Kelly's boat, moored
.Nathan Quick        in Smuttynose Cove, shortly
James Neele          afterwards was cast adrift.
Soon after this John Andrews, Samson White and
William Hilton, 'coming home along to the said
Kelly's dore of his house, and threatening his men
to come out' and fight — which they did not —
'but the said Hilton, Andrews and White' being
charged with casting her off, Samson White took
hold of John Ashe by his neckcloth as he stood
at said Kelly's door.
Robert Andros±25     Friday night Dec. 14, being
Sampson White        in the house of Mr. Reuben
John Andros          Hull and hearing an outcry,
John Flea            went out to the end of the
house and did see Henry Harvey, James Nealle
and John Ash have holt of William Hilton by the
collar, and several of Mr. Roger Kelly's men sur-
rounding said Hilton.
Nathan Quicke±35     saw Wm. Hilton violently
strike Roger Kelly's servant James Neele with
an oar.
Henry Harvey±28      saw William Hilton run at
James Neele and strike him down with an oar
or a boat's foremast, and strike him several blows
after he was down.
Elisha Barton±22.    Wm. Hilton passing by Mr.
Kelly's door, Henry Harvey called him lubber
and logerhead.  Said Hilton told said Harvey if
he had anything to say to him he should come to
him.  Then said Harvey with James Neele and
John Ash went out and he did run into Mr. Hull's
yard and took up a small canno ower to defend
himself, but whether he did strike one of them
I know not.'
John Ash±22     saw John Andrews and Wm. Hilton
cast off the moorings of Mr. Kelly's boat,
Clement Hardy encouraging them. When I got
home John Andrews, Sampson White and Wm.
Hilton were challenging Mr. Kelly's family to
come out and fight, and saying we should not
make fast on Mallago side.

**306b** Isles of Shoals Government. Walter
Randall admitted he was in the combination
at the Shoals, and had signed it, and that Wm.
Chinicke wrote the names of 'those that could not
write.'  (The combination was 'of a high nature.'
— Court Files 13647.
John Purington  :   Signed as bondsmen, bond
Wm. Chinicke    :   dated 22 December 1677.
John Clarke     :   Witness: Nich: Heskins.

**306c** Inquest, Wm. Taylor, 31 Dec. 1677.
Struck with a broom handle 25 Dec.,
died 30 Dec. Roger [Dari]±23, passing the house
of Mr. John Hunkins, went up in the chamber
and brought down John Winsland, who was not
accused by the coroner's jury nor indicted by the
(Suffolk) grand jury. Suff. Court Files 1686.
Other witnesses:
William Puggy±46     Michell Endell
Thomas Luckes±24     James Blackden
Lazerus Peverle±20   William Olliver
Richard Ambrose±35   Peter Lewes
Commissioners        Philip Odiorne
Mr. Peter Twisden    William Diamond
Mr. John Febens      John Oliver
Mr. John Hunkins     Henry Meane
Jury                 Edward Gould
James Gibbens        Robert Tomms
Edward Vettery

**306d** Administration granted to Roger Kelly, 25 June 1678, on the estates of:
— N. H. Deeds v. 24.

Gabrell Grubb :
Nathan Quick :
Robert Goodwin :

lost at sea in a storm the last winter. Inventories taken 25 Feb. 1677-8 by

John Hunking :
John Fabes :
John More :

Frances the widow of Gabriel Grubb consents.

**307a** Inquest 3 July 1687, Henry Mains Sr., fisherman, drowned. John Fabes, Esq. J. P. Phesant Eastwick, Esq., coroner.

Matthew Atkins foreman
Robert Parker
William 6 Lakeman
Walter Randall
Hugh 6 Allured
Richard 6 Oliver

Philip Odihorne
William 6 Mitchell
Philip 7 Hach
Edward Gold
Robert Tomms·
Henery Veasey
Richard 6 Tucker

**307b** Estate of Wm. Button, Jersey Merchant. Inventory sworn 15 Sept. 1687 before Mr. John Fabes by Claude Champion, adm. Mr. Twisden and Nicholas Goold appraisers; Robert Elliot, Esq. bondsman. — N. H. Probate Files 117. Cf. Prov. Papers xxxi. 387.

Debtor to
John Yousring
Henry Putt
Richard Roslings
Henry Mayne

Creditor from
George Meager
Richard Tospe
Peter Wales
Mary Luex
Margaret Barter
Roger Dasvis
Henry Gouslde
John Yousring

Ellener Welcom
Elizabeth Osdeyhorne
Henry Mayne

Others named
Widow Wallis
John Cross
Thomas Hobart
Richard Escot
Mr. Andrew Disment
Mr. Tho. Disment
Mr. Samuel Belshow
Mr. Blackden
Edward Lesrier

**308a** Three Petitions, 12 March 1691-2, 19 March 1691-2, 26 Jan. 1692-3. — Doc. Hist. v. 365, 369, 312 (Mass. Arch. 37: 314, 252). 252).

**308b** Star Island, Jan. 1693-4. Names in a warrant directed to Edward Gould, constable.

*John Dambrell
*Hugh Galloway
* and wife Anne
Francis Merrifield

Thomas Wise
and wife Elizabeth
*Hannah Yeaton
*crossed out.

**309** The Inhabitants of Star Island in 1702 petition York Court regarding a saints' bell now in the secret custody of Mr. Roger Kelly, given formerly by the master of a ship that used to trade at the Shoals, and was in the church on Smuttynose Island, but that church was allowed to decay and fall, and the materials have been carried off for secular uses. Now Star Island, having 'purchased God an house,' petitions the Court to deliver the bell to Mr. Thomas Diamond and Mr. Richard. Goss the selectmen.
— Autographs, York Files.

James Blackdon
Thomas Dimond
Richard Goss
Edward Goold
John [Muchemore]
*John Frost
*Richard Eaton

Richard Gumer
William Waymouth
*John Carter
*John Barter
Samuel Eburne
Minister of Star Isl.
*By order.

**Newcastle (Great Island).** 311-319.

**311a** Inquest 12 Jan. 16[61-2]. Joshua Kendrick and Thomas Wilson burnt to death in their house.
Coroner's Jury
Mr. Nathl. Fryer
Mr. Edward Loyde
Mr. John Forde
George Wolten
Wm. Howard
Robert Taprill
Robert Mussell

Charles Frost
William Lucks
Barnard Squire·
Joseph [Bastens]
William Ash
[Wolter Knight crossed out]

**311b** Corbet's Petition to the Royal Commissioners, July 1665. — N. H. Prov. Papers xvii. 511-512.

**311c** Declaration for Massachusetts Government, 10 Oct. 1665. — N. H. Prov. Papers i. 284. (Also Mass. Arch. cvi. 160). Alter William Laiton to Lajton. (Copy in Weare Papers renders it Lasters).
Alter John Clarke to Town Clarke [clerk].

**312a** ·Inquest, Hercules Taylor, 18 May 1669. Seaman on The Grace of Bristol, drunk in a canoe, upset and drowned.
Coroner's Jury
Edward West
John Lewis
Joseph Mors
Thomas Parker
John Light
Alex. Jones

David Camble
Stephen Graffum
Tho. Follensby
Samuel Robey
Daniel Moore
John Kettle

**312b** Inquest. Taken up 29 Dec. 1670, thought to be a servant of Mr. Fryer missing at least a month named Nicholas Bouey. Jury:
Robert Ellett
Edward West
Robert Couch
Paul Hall
John Wesley
Richard Hayward

John Kettle
Joseph Nesfield
Ambros Benett
James Pendleton Jr.
John Skorck
David Camble

**312c** Tax payers of Great Isl. and Sandy Beach in 1671. The document is missing from N. H. Court Files, I, 599, but the following names are found in the index.

| | | |
|---|---|---|
| Amazeane, John | Hunkins, Mark | Seavey, Thos. |
| Allex, Jones | Hunkins, Widow | Seavey, Wm. |
| Beck, Henry | Johnson, James | Sherborne, |
| Berry, James | Jones [Alex] | Henry |
| '' John | '' George | Sherborne, |
| Bickham, Wm. | '' Thomas | John Jr. |
| Brackett, | Kemball, David | Sherborne, |
| [Arthur] | Kettle, John | Samuel |
| Broad, William | Lamb, Bial | Sherborne, Mr. |
| Brooking, Wm. | Lear, Tobias | Sharpe, James |
| Carter, Edward | '' Hugh | Shortridge, |
| Cranch, Andrew | Leach, James | Richard |
| Clarke, John | Lewis, John | Sloper, John |
| Colins, Roger | Lock, John | '' Richard |
| Creber, Thos. | Lux, William | Squire, Barnard |
| Dering, Henry | Marden, John | Stileman, |
| Drake Nathaniel | Moss, Joseph | Richard |
| Dormand, Usher | Moses, John | Stileman, Elias |
| Fabin, John | Odiorne [James] | Terry, John |
| Ferguson, | Onion, Thos. | Tucker, Richard |
| Gilbert | [Oshaw, | Treworgye, |
| Foss, John | Dormand] | Samuel |
| Fryer, Nathaniel | Parker, Thos. | Walton, George |
| Graffan, Stephen | Pendleton, | Walford, Old |
| Graves, Wm. | James | Walker, Joseph |
| Harris, Samuel | Peverly, Widow | Wallis, George |
| Harvey, Joakim | Purington, | Wayte [White?] |
| Harbutt, | Robert | Richard |
| Sylvester | Rand, Francis | West, Edw. |
| Haskins, | Randall, Edward | Wilcomb, |
| Nicholas | '' James | Richard |
| Hoff, Ferdinando | Roby, Samuel | |
| Holmes, John | Russell, Philip | |

**312d** Inquest 10 Nov. 1672. Two men and a woman washed ashore at Rye Beach from a wreck. — Court Files ii. 445.

| Coroner's Jury | William Berry |
| Nath. Drake | Abiel Lamb |
| Foreman | John Lock |
| John Kettel | John Mardin |
| Joseph Berry | John Foss |
| John Berry | Philip Russell |
| James Berry | Hugh Ford |

**312e** Mr. Henry Dering, Constable, having been thrown down and nearly choked in arresting Capt. Walter Barefoot, prosecuted him, Charles Hilton, and the latter's man, George Sweete. Summons dated 23 Dec. 1672 to Witnesses:

| John Lewis | Jeremiah Tibbetts |
| Joseph Permet±22 | Jonathan Mendam |
| Gilbert Ferguson | Henry Beck |
| Simon Hinkson±19 ('my master John Lewis's shop) |
| John Groth | Mark Ridley |
| Mary Wentworth | Roger Rose |
| Ann Green±19 | Abel Porter |
| Samuel Wentworth | James Burgis±18 |

**312f** Capt. Davis's Night at Great Island.
Capt. John Davis of York, afterwards Deputy President of Maine, being at Great Island of an evening, and hearing that Dutch warships were outside. — (1673).

| Capt. John Davis | : |
| 'My son John | |
| Peniwell' | : cautiously visited the |
| Francis Tucker | : fort at midnight and |
| 'now resident' | : found nobody on |
| Gilbert Furguson | : guard. |
| a cooper±28 | : |
| Nicholas Haskins±36 | : |

Furguson and others had previously been playing leapfrog on Sergt. John Lewis's hill, and had gone to Sergt. West's for a quart of sack.

| Some of them, | : Ensign Joakim |
| including | Harvey±42 |
| Richard Harvey±22 | : Joseph Moss the |
| (Mr. Hugh(?) Tucker | : Smith |
| went the rounds of | : Mr. Russell |
| the houses to arouse | : Mr. Fryer |
| the island, among | : Mr. Kettle |
| them | : Sam: Robye |
| | John Clark |

Hannah Moulton was at John Lewis's when the pounding came at their door. Her sister was at prayer and her brother was upon his knees. William Lux±53 testified. Capt. Davis next day apologized and was fined.

**312g** A Missing Cask of Wine, 1673. — N. H. Court Files ii. 433.
Sanco Pamco±19 testified that

| Henry Davis | : stole a cask of |
| Richard Bedworth | : wine belonging to |
| Mr. Richard Gibbs | from |
| Mr. Fryer's | basement |

**312h** Inquest, Thomas Dalbey, 10 May 1674. Accidentally drowned. Jury:

| George Wallis | John Kettle |
| James Johnson | Edward Randle |
| John Lewis | Joseph Morse |
| Nicholas Haskins | William Lux |
| Saml. Wentworth | William Seavy Jr. |
| Alex. Walden | Abel Porter |

**313a** Great Island, Sandy Beach and Sagamore Creek Tax for the Portsmouth minister for the year 1677, with delinquent list dated 26 Feb. 1678-9. Corrected by conjecture: — Prov. Papers xviii. 918-920.
Gabriyer Boniton, read Gabrigan Bonython.
Alter Stephen Grassam to Graffam.
Dan Dornion [Dunyan?], read Duggin?
Old Dormer, read Dorman Oshaw.

Mr. Edw. Cawner, read Carter.
Ru: Rogers, read Ric: (Richard).
Josh: Berry, read Joseph?
Thomas Crehor read Thomas Creber.
Tho Moses read John.
Alter Ferdina Hooss to Hooff.
Alter William Brabin to Brokin.
Hugh Towne read [Leare?].
Question Jas. Brackett.
Alter John Bonman to Bouman.

**313b** Inquest, Antipas Maverick, 22 July 1678. Fell out of canoe, body found at Samuel Fernald's island. Jury:

| John Lewis | [John Diamond crossed out] |
| Walter Barefoot | Saml. Wentworth |
| Andrew Cranch | Stephen Grafton |
| Nicholas Heskins | John Lock |
| Mathew Atkins | Thomas Parker |
| Richard Rogers | Samuel Severn |
| [Tho. Furnel crossed out] | Henry Trevethen |

**313c** Inquest, Stephen Reed, 7 June 1679. Accidentally drowned. Jury:

| Henry Russell | Joseph Couch |
| William Lux | James Robinson |
| George Davis | Nehemiah Partridge |
| George Harris | Henry Trevethan |
| Andrew Cranch | John Kettle |
| Richard Williams | Joseph Berry | James Randle |

**313d** 'Account of those that be dead & the poore Eastern people that is gone.' Collector's rebates about 1680. — Court Files v. 105.

| George Walton the younger | Francis Sholot |
| Antony Brackit the younger | Wamon Bictin |
| [John Reecks, canceled] | William Rann |
| Richard Lake | Mrs. Harbut son |
| John Luis refused to pay for his man |
| Marks Baker that I never knew. |

**313e** Inquest, Esaias Odihorne, 4 July 1681. — N. H. Hist. Coll. viii. 66.
Alter Samuel Roberts to Robey.

**313f** Inquest, Silvester Harbert, 22 Aug. 1683. — N. H. Hist. Coll. viii. 144.
John Lewis's mark **6**.
Alter John Davis to Davies [Doctor].
Alter James Billings to Phillips.
William Haskins's mark **8**.

**313g** Subpoena dated 5 September 1683. Court Files vii. 455. Signed by Nathaniel Fryer, Deputy Governor.

| William Haskins | Joseph Pormutt |
| Thomas Potts | and his wife |
| Philip the Jassem | John Crowder |
| (or markem?) | James Robson |
| Mis Monday | |

**314** Four Shipping Lists, 1684-1685.

| Ketch Diligence | Ketch America |
| about 1684 | Dec. 30, 1684 |
| Nicholas Baker, master | John Jackson Sr., |
| George Tucker | master |
| of Great Island | John Jackson Jr., mate |
| Joseph Friend | Joshua [C changed to] |
| James Washford | Gruche |
| Elias Loud | Jo: Markham |
| George Corrine | Philip Cook |
| **Ship Success** | Jo: Orchard |
| Jan. 15, 1684[5 | **Ketch Richard** |
| Matthew Estes, master | of Great Island |
| Jo: Hatch | May 16, 1685 |
| Phil: Fall | Thomas Cobbet, master |
| Ja: Skeat | Saml. Snell, mate |
| Will: Davis | Jo: Jackson |
| Ja: Mountes | Beriah Higgins |
| 2d. column | Joshua Jackson |
| Andr: Brock | Jeremy Holmes |
| Geo: Tucker | Richard Archer |
| Will: Procise | Saml. Belcher |
| Sim: Mountes | |

**315a** Two Petitions for Separate Township, 1692-3. Originals, bound up interleaved with the Council Records.
— Prov. Papers ii. 95-6, 94-5.
96 Alter Henry Roby to Keerck [Kirke].
Alter Steven to Jerrem Walford.
Alter Thomas Lane to Lang.
94 Read William Forbes Furbush.
John Fenicks, alter [?] to [·sic·].
Alter Ezerya Elwell to Ezeceya [Hezekiah].
Alter Jn. Church to Irl Chur——
Daniel Oshaw, alter [?] to [·sic·].

**315b** Four loose tax lists, 1698-1700, in a trunk in the Newcastle Selectmen's office, three for Great Island, 1698, one for Sandy Beach.

| Great Island 1698 | Mrs. Swain† |
|---|---|
| Selected names only | Mr. John Batson |
| Jeffrey Currier | Mr. James Leach† |
| Henry Tryferin | Mr. John Leach† |
| Mr. Wm. Hinderson | Daniel Oshaw† |
| Mr. Thos. Holland | Mr. John Card† |
| Mr. Saml. Winkley | John Searl sr.† |
| Mrs. Wilcom | John Searl jr.† |
| Mr. John Swain | William Jones* |
| Richard Hales | Nathan White† |
| Will Hinderson | Edward Beal† |
| John Fayrfeld | Eliz. Tryworthy |
| John Crowder | Fr. Child |
| Grace Tomlin | Mr. [John] Holden† |
| Mr. Saml. Alcock | James Filpot |
| Mrs. Eliz. Wears | Saml. Frost |
| [Joshua Fryer | Jedediah Jordan* |
| striken out] | Mr. Edw. Cary |
| Jeremiah Jordan | Widow Horn† |
| Hanah [Matershed] | Joseph Moseet |
| David Campbel | Mr. Saml. Markland |
| **Great Island 1699** | Mathew Rumny |
| *In all three years | Kenny Langmaid |
| †In 1699 and 1700 | Shadrach Bell† |
| Capt. Nathaniel Fryer† | Mr. Nath. Fryer |
| Robert Eliot† | John Martyn |
| John Hincks Esq.† | [or Marlyn]† |
| Capt. Walton† | **Great Island 1700** |
| Mr. Sampson Sheafe† | New names |
| Mr. Richard Maundy† | Mrs. Estwick |
| Mrs. Lucy Stileman* | Mrs. Tufton |
| Mr. Phesant Estwick | Edward Hales |
| Theodore Atkinson† | Joshua Fryer |
| Mr. William Kelly† | Joseph Jackson |
| Mr. Thomas Payne† | Francis Shalote |
| Mr. James Waymouth† | Samuel Allen Esq. |
| Capt. Thomas Cobbett† | **Sandy Beach 1698** |
| Mr. John Clark† | John Bickford |
| Mr. Jacob Clarke† | Tobias Leer |
| Thomas Jones* | Robert Palmer |
| Richard Tucker† | Mr. Wm. Sevy |
| John Amazeen† | Nich. Hodg |
| Jere Walford* | John Sevy |
| Foster Tryferin† | Tho. Sevy |
| James Robinson† | Benj. Sevy |
| George Trundee† | John Mardin |
| Mr. John Hurst† | John Shute |
| Wm. Mansfield† | Tho. Ran |
| Andrew Cranch† | Saml. Ran |
| Thomas Martiel† | Mr. John Brakit |
| Samuel Jordan† | John Berry sr. |
| Mr. Fr. Tucker† | Wm. Berry |
| Mrs. Sarah Hopkins† | James Berry & Son |
| Joseph Reed† | John Foss & Son |
| Mr. John Holicorne† | James Mardin |
| Mr. Saml. Comfort† | Samuel Douse |
| Mr. Richard Buckly* | Wm. Wallis |
| Mr. Jacob Randall† | Mr. Odiorne |
| Mrs. Fabes† | George x x |
| Mr. John Lewis† | Mr. James x x |
| Mr. Thos. Parker | Samuel Sevy |
| Mr. Richard Taurlton† | Joshua Bracket |
| Mrs. Purmett† | John Walker |
| Robert Jordan† | Edward Bartlet |
| Edward Randall† | James Berry |
| John Mardin† | |

**315c** The Inhabitants of Newcastle sworn July 1696. Great Island. As printed in Prov. Papers ii. 89, correct order and a few misreadings:

| | | |
|---|---|---|
| John Hinks | Thomas Holland | Samuel Moudy |
| Thomas Cobbett | John Samson | Phes. Estwick |
| James Rendle | Benj. Sevie | Jos. Measzeat |
| Richard Buckly | Jotham Odiorn | Foster Traferin |
| Samuel Winkly | Will Ainup | x x x |
| Samuel Accutt | [or Arnup] | Henry Traferin |
| Samuel Comfort | x x x | x x x |
| Theodore | Georg Harris | Jeff Currier |
| Atkinson | James Philpot | Will Mansfield |
| x x x | x x x | Jos. A[t]well |
| Richard Hales | Saml. Dowse | John Marting |
| Edward Hales | x x x | John Clark |
| Jeremiah | Richard Taulton | x x x |
| Walford | x x x | Will Tucker |
| x x x | Thomas Horne | |
| Samuel Foss | | |

**316** Newcastle 1708 Tax Rate on which the division of common lands was based.

| To Be Collected by John Searles | £ s d | For Constable Goss to Collect | £ s d |
|---|---|---|---|
| Robert Elliott Esq. | 3 10 . | Mr. Sherborn | 1 8 0 |
| Mrs. Hincks | 1 . . | Tobias Lear | 1 8 0 |
| Maj. Walton | 2 15 . | Nich Hodge | . 17 . |
| Mr. Sampson Sheafe | 2 . . | Mr. Wm. Seavey | 3 10 0 |
| Mrs. Waymouth | 1 . . | Benj. Seavey | 1 10 0 |
| Mrs. Beazer | 1 . . | Mr. John Brackett | 2 10 0 |
| Mrs. Kelly | . 6 . | Saml. Brackett | 0 8 0 |
| Theodore Atkinson | 2 15 . | Tho. Rand | 1 8 0 |
| Mrs. Clerk | . 10 . | Wm. Webster | 1 4 0 |
| Thos. Jones | 0 8 . | Nehemiah Berry | |
| Jacob Clerk | 1 10 . | | 0 16 0 |
| John Stevens | 1 2 . | Jude Berry & | |
| Christo Amaseen | 2 5 . | Son | 0 10 0 |
| Thos. Marshall | 0 12 . | Mr. John Foss | 0 15 0 |
| Jereh. Walford | 1 5 . | Joshua Foss | 0 12 0 |
| Foster Tryferine | 0 12 . | James Marden | 1 2 0 |
| Andrew Cranch | 0 8 . | Mr. Wm. Wallis & Son | 2 12 0 |
| John Cranch | 0 12 . | Saml. Wallis | 0 8 0 |
| Mrs. Tucker | 0 8 . | Widow Odiorne | 0 10 0 |
| Lt. Reed | 2 5 . | John Odiorne | . 16 . |
| Capt. Hollicome | 2 0 . | Mr. James Randell | 1 16 . |
| Mrs. Fabees | 0 8 . | Geo. Wallis | 1 6 . |
| John Holden | 1 0 0 | Richard Goss | . 14 . |
| Robt. Jordan | 0 12 . | Samll. Dowse & Son | 1 2 . |
| John Salter | 0 18 . | Saml. Berry | 0 8 . |
| John Leach | 1 0 . | James Berry & Son | 1 10 . |
| Edw. Randell | 0 12 . | William Mardon | 0 17 . |
| John Card | 0 18 . | Joseph Seavey | 0 10 . |
| James Leach | 1 5 . | Wm. Seavey Jr. | 0 8 0 |
| John Mardon | 0 12 . | Tho. Barnes | 0 8 0 |
| Widow OShaw | 0 8 . | Nathl. Rand | 0 9 0 |
| John Cross | 0 10 . | Rowland Jenkins | 0 8 0 |
| James Phillips | 0 10 . | Wm. Caverly | 0 9 0 |
| Henry Payne | 0 10 . | Stephen Noble | 0 8 0 |
| John Searls | 1 0 . | **Marshes** | |
| William Jones | 1 0 . | Saml. Seavey | 0 2 6 |
| Edward Martin | 0 12 . | Geo. Walker | . 10 . |
| Nathan White | 1 . . | Capt. Pickrin | 0 9 0 |
| Shadrach Bell | 0 12 . | Mrs. Josses | 0 8 0 |
| Joseph Jackson | 1 4 . | Capt. Hunkins | 0 4 0 |
| Jotham Odiorne | 2 2 . | John Lock | 0 3 0 |
| Francis Shalott | 0 10 . | Mr. John Dennett | 3 0 . |
| Saml. Frost | 1 0 0 | Peter Ball | 0 1 6 |
| Joseph Simpson | 1 12 . | Tho. Jackson | 0 1 6 |
| Benj. Parker | 2 . . | Capt. Langdon | 0 6 0 |
| John Russell | . 15 . | John Jackson | 0 1 6 |
| John Frost | 2 . . | Sauthridge | 0 3 0 |
| Andrew Pepperell | 2 . . | | |

| | | | | George Walton | . 18 . |
|---|---|---|---|---|---|
| James Chadwick | 1 | . | . | Zach Foss | . 10 . |
| Georg Perkins | . | 10 | . | Joseph Feild | . 10 . |
| James Allard | . | 10 | . | Henry Tryvethan | . 12 . |
| Thos. Payne | 1 | 5 | . | Matthew Williams | . 10 . |
| George Gowdy | 0 | 10 | . | Tho. Barnes Jr. | . 10 . |
| Francis Carman | 0 | 10 | . | Daniell Grindall | . 10 . |
| Christo Federick | 0 | 12 | . | James Langly | . 10 . |
| Henry Langmaid | 0 | 10 | . | James Stilson | 0 15 . |
| John Yeaton | 0 | 10 | . | Peter Matthews | . 10 . |
| Richard Yeaton | 0 | 10 | . | Sampson Sheafe Jr. | . 18 . |
| Edward West | . | 15 | . | Barneby Crusey | . 10 . |
| John Abbot | . | 10 | . | Widow Head | . 6 . |
| Samuel Perry [torn] | . | 15 | . | | |

**317** Inquest, Christopher Lux, 26 Aug. 1680. — N. H. Hist. Coll. viii. 50.
Alter Henry Cround to Crowne.
William Haskins striken out.
Alter Jeremiah Herdsden to Hodsden.

**318a** Inquest, 20 Oct. 1693. Drowning of Mr. William Button, Jerseyman.

| Witnesses | Philip Muddle |
|---|---|
| Robert Harrison | John Amosen Sr. |
| Edward Potter chirurgeon | William Jones |
| | Jeremiah Jordan |
| John Lamprill was in the boat | Thomas Jones |
| Jury | James Sharpe |
| Richard Oliver foreman | James Robinson |
| Daniel Ushaw | John Russell |
| James Leech Jr. | Samuel Comford |
| John Bickford | Also Summonsed |
| | Daniel Jones |
| | Robert Wetherick |

| James Phillips | Andrew Crance |
|---|---|
| John Hust | Matthew Ham |
| Joseph Elwell | Nicholas Haskins |
| Ezekiah Elwell | Jacob Randell |
| Thomas Pain | Richard Stileman |

**318b** Inquest, John Row, 25 Oct. 1693.
Verdict: drowned. Coroner, Wm. Redford.
Witnesses: Peter Mason, Daniel Jacobs.
Constable, John Leech. Jury:

| James Roberson | John West |
|---|---|
| James Leech Jr. | Foster Trefethen |
| Daniel OShaw | John Amoseen |
| James Booth | Thomas Jones |
| Joseph Alcock | Jacob Randell |
| Thomas Parker | Nathan White |
| David Cambal | Samuel Eastman |
| John Hust | Thomas Pain |
| Edward Wilson | Mr. Kerk |
| Wm. Denick | Andrew Crance |
| John Churchwell | Matthew Ham |
| Arthur Head | John Crowder |

**318c** Inquest 27 Feb. 1695-6. William Grills and Georg Major driven ashore by stress of weather and drowned. Constable Samuel Rand. Inquest held at the house of Mr. John Odiorne. — Court Files x. 256.
Jury:

| John Bracket | William Berrey |
|---|---|
| Benj. Seavey | William Wallas |
| James Berrey Sr. | Thomas Seavey |
| James Berriey Jr. | John Seavey |
| John Berriey | John Shute |
| Saml. Douse | Samuel Seavey |
| Tho. Mardeyn | Wm. Seavey |
| Richard Goss | John Bickford |
| John Foss | Robert Palmer |
| James Mardeyn | James Rendle |

**319** Petition of Great Island Inhabitants to the King, 15 May 1690, asking for a general governor and military supplies.

| John Hinckes | Nath Fryer Sen. | Robert Elliot | Tho. Cobbett |
|---|---|---|---|
| John 6 Lewess | Nathaniel Fryer Jr. | Peter Eason | Shadrach Walton |
| John West | James Leach Jr. | James 6 Leech Sen. | Thomas Yackham |
| Thomas Paine | James Roberttson | Richard 6 Abbot Sen. | Edward Carter |
| Edward 6 Rendle | Richard Cade | | John Cross |
| Jeremia 6 Walford | John Diment | | James Paine |
| James Casowah | Ephraim 6 Amicene | | Nathan White |
| Henry Trevthan | Benjamin Islington | | Wm. Godsoe |
| Thomas 6 Jones | Dermont 2 Oshaw | | Abraham Clark |
| John 6 Amicene | Edward 1 Beale | | Francis Tucker |
| Richard 6 Oliver | Aaron Ferris | | Daniel Moulton |
| Richard 6 Hoult | William Jones | | Noah Parker |
| Nicholas Heskins | Isaac Wharf | | Jacob Rendle |
| John Hopkins | James Phillips | | William Rennalds |
| John Tufton | John Crowder | | Phesant Eastwicke |
| Wm. Bickham | Samuel Martyn | | William Roe |
| Jos: Rayn | John Russell | | Andrew Brown Sen. |
| Robert Tufton | Robert Jordan | | Henry Smyth |

**Portsmouth** before it was divided included (now Rye) the second oldest permanent English settlement north of Virginia.

## Portsmouth and Greenland. 321-339.

**321** Grant of the Glebe by Inhabitants of the Lower End of Pascataquack, 25 May 1640. Most of the signers lived on the west side of the river. By the original record, Portsmouth Town Book, p. 99, the last four names in the right-hand column read: — Prov. Papers. i. 113.
John Wotton     Matthew Coe
Nicholas Row     William Palmer

**322** Original Sagamore Creek Lots, as told by Capt. John Pickering c. 1718. — Portsmouth Town Papers.
Goodman Moses was the first in Sagamore Creek.
Andrew Haiffer next, where Toby Langdon lives.
Mr. Gibson where Slopper lives.
Mr. Lane boote Haiffer and Gibson.

Mr. Sherborn boote booth of Mr. Lane and Mr. Langdon, and Mr. Slopper had it of Mr. Sherborn.
All the above were 8-acre lots, viz:
Mooses, Haiffer, Gibson and Walford, which were all these on that side of the creek.

**323** F. W. Hackett's -Portsmouth Town Records- has been found very well done by the original book, except some misplacement of the leaves. The folio numbers in a hand perhaps 200 years old were ignored in binding, so that folios 11 and 13 were bound in as folios 2 and 3. For the current records, which started 5 April 1652, read pp. [1, 2, 7, 9-24, 27-35]. . For the transcripts from 'the old book' read pp. [8, 3, 4, 25, 5]; also one item on page [21]. Corrections: P. 20, for John Hart(?) read John Hum[pkins?]

'for Ro. Kn.' (Roger Knight) is a later marginal note.

P. 21, bottom, insert Thomas Walford.

P. 23, for Brockins read Bruckins.

P. 27, for houbert Mattean read Heubert Mattun.

Pp. 29, 76, The date in Samuel Haines's grant is 12 Sept. 1653 — apparently an error, being a transcript from the old book.

P. 31, transfer 'the younger' from Webster to Pickering.

P. 34, John Webster wrote the names of Thomas Walford and James Johnson.

P. 37, middle, make it ·John· & Richard Cut; at bottom, for Commes read Commins.

P. 38, for Jacksons read John Jackson Sen.

P. 39, for Grassum read Graffum; for Wallis read Wollis; for Shores read Shares, 4 dayes; insert before Phil Nick, Phil Russell 3 days' work.

P. 48, The 'old doctor' was Mr. John Renals.

**324** Town Clerks and Selectmen.
— N. H. Gen. Records ii. 97-101, Hackett's Portsmouth 13-37.

**325** Inquest, Geo. Walton's child, 5 May 1657. Accidentally drowned. Jury:

John Pickering foreman
John Webster
Richard Comins
Tho. Furson
Robert Mattoone
[not autograph]
Roger Knight
Wm. Brookin
Robert Mussell
Wm. Cotton
Edward Barton
Tho. Peverly
Francis Trickie

**326a** Subscribers for the Minister's Support, 14 Feb. 1658-9. Well printed in N. H. Gen. Records i. 9.

**326b** New Subscribers for the Minister's Support, 8 March 1665-6. Well printed in N. H. Gen. Records i. 10-11.

**326c** Subscribers for the Minister's Support Begun to be taken 17 March 1670-1. — N. H. Gen. Rec. i. 11.

12 Alter Sam: Cate to Case.

**327a** Inquest, 6 July 1663, Robert Marshall and Jer: Dolley, in a canoe drunk, both 'drowned last night.' Jury:

Mr. Abraham Corbett
Wm. Seavey
James 6 Johnson
Francis 6 Drake
Peter 1 Wallis
John Odyorne
Richard 1 Tope
John 1 Haskell
Robert 6 Sheares
Wm. 1 Pasmore
Edward 8 Beale
James 6 Cate

**327b** Inquest, 10 July 1671, Alexander Keniston with his horse crossing above John Pickering's milldam was drowned.

Coroner's Jury

Tho. Ladbrook
Samuel Case
John Tucker
Obadiah Morse
Thomas Wakam
John Brown
Richard Samson
Wm. Richards
John Thomson
Richard Door
George Jones
John Pickering

**327c** Robert Clemants, 4 July 1673. Accidentally drowned. A Jury:

John Tucker
Tho. Ladbrook
John Shipway
Barnard Squire
Lodowick Fowler
John Goffe
Robert Burnam
Dodovah Hull
Benjamin Starr
Israel Phillips
Thomas Carter
Walter Luckraft

**327d** Inquest, John Ellis, 13 Sept. 1673.
John Ellis. James Skate, George Ford, Walter Luckraft, Edward Skate and Hanca, a Negro, were nere the house of Caleb Beck. James Skate and his son were taking leave of the rest, who had been drinking flip (a quart of rum mixed with water or beer), and Lodowick Fowler had been drinking with them but now 'being of the

watch came up the lane after them.' Fowler's gun went off, shooting Ellis in the leg so that he died. Fowler was indicted and convicted in Boston. Evidence sworn before Richard Cutt.

Coroner's Jury

John Shipway
John Cutt Jr.
John Tucker
Tho. Ladbrook
Richard Jackson
John Goff
Thomas Carter
Israel Phillips
Georg Lavis
Samuel Kees
Tho. Crafford
Edward Beale

**328** Mr. Richard Cutt's Servants, 26 Jan. 1669[70

Mary the maid had given things to Wm. Walker and Alice [his wife], including two gallons of rum 'against he came from Mr. Rayner's buriall,' and money.

In William Walker's box were found things he said David Goodin gave him and Humphrey Yard. Mary owned up to all the things found in her box, and George's in the second box.

Daniel Daly acknowledged he had taken the things in his box because he saw the others taking.

Florence owned that she spoke to Mr. Tasker's carpenter to carry the two boxes to Barbadoes.

Mary said she had the whisk of William Cutt, and gave Philip Fall 6 sh. for a gold ring.

Alice said Mary said she had her money from Old England.

Wm. Walker & Alice said that Mary Wacom made the handkercher, and she said she did not.

David Gooding±22, 1 July 1670, said: while I kept my master's shop in his house Alice [     ] and William Walker took things from the shelves while my master was at meals.

Mary Nott deposed against Alice. Mary spoke to Florence to speak to the carpenter to carry the box for England. She took things which George told her Harry carried down upon a horse to John Locks. William wanted stockings the color of Reuben's, Mr. John Cutt's man.

John Lock said that Henry Brookin brought the box to his house.

Geo. Hunt, aged 24, said: In 1669 John Tompson and himself being at dinner at the creek house, Alice White, late servant to my master Capt. Richard Cutt, came to us weeping. She said that Jone Clement had been with her mistress and told her of things in her box. The next week himself and Florence Driscoll going to look for missing cattle, asking at Goodman Ham's if he had seen them, the aforesaid Jone Clements told us that she being at Mr. Mattoones, Alice White called her up to her chamber and showed her her things. Jone told her she wondered how she could get so much and brought so little with her, for I brought more and could carry away nothing; also Florence Driscoll told him that he received several things from Mary Knat which he carried down to Great Island to his box at Dorman Osea. Henry Brookin (not one of the servants)±27 in 1670, carted away goods for them.

Daniel Moulton, constable, served the search warrants, aided by Mr. William Antropas, John Harker and a young man Manuel.

Dermon executed the sentences of whipping.

**329** Tax List, Strawberry Bank, 24 Sept. 1681. — N. H. Hist. Coll. viii. 61, Prov. Papers i. 428 (Court Files v. —).

George Hunt [-sic-] for Huntress
Alter Mr. Otsella to Mrs. Ursilla Cutt.
Alter John Hurdy to Huddy.
Alter George Loveis to Lavis.
Alter Henry Kerch to Keirk.
Alter Anthony Ellm's estate to Ellin's.
Tho: Gill [-sic-].
Alter Wakan to Wakam twice.
Alter Philip Founds to ———.
Alter Robert Almonie to Almorie.
Alter John Brown to Boman.
Alter Anthony Furber to Jethro.

**330a** Land Grants and Inhabitants, from the Town Book.
For other land grants see Lists 323, 330b. Also cf. N. H. Gen. Rec. i. 1, ii. 22, 59.

1655, July 10. For Rye marsh see N. H. Gen. Rec. ii. 59.
1656, Oct. 7. Hannah Jones — her father T. Walford.
1656-7. John Locke 8 a. betw. Jackson and Cotton.
Jan. 1. William Morris 8 a. by the freshet; James Scott 1 a. on Great Island.
Jan. 29. Henry Sherburn 60 a. Nathaniel Drake 1 a. on Great Island.
Leonard Weeks 8 a.
Thomas Peverly 8 a.
Mar. 20. [Nathl. Drake 4 a. at Sandy Beach.
[Francis Rand 4 a. at Sandy Beach.
[Oliver Trimmings 4 a. at Sandy Beach.
1657, Sept. 7. Mr. Brian Pendleton 1 a. adj. his house lately bought of Francis Trickey adj. Geo: Walton's wharf.
William Urin 40 ft. sq. on Gt. Isl. [and put up a frame].
Henry Sherburne 1 a. adj. lot granted to Joseph Pendleton.
Tobias Langdon 1 a. adj. the one-acre promised to Mr. Batcheler by the town.
Mr. John Cutt 1 a. on Gt. Isl.
1657-8, Jan. 4. John Harte 8 a. and rec. inhab. [Tho: Inioun having bought Robert Davis's 8 a. at Sagamore Creek].
Jan. 11. Robert Davis 4 a. betw. Tho. Inion and John Hart.
William Brockens — a. betw. his own and Henry Savidge.
Feb. 24. Tho: Longlee 1 a. on Gt. Isl.
[No more than 8a. to be granted to strangers, and then only to such as are tradesmen, and at that to have no rights in the commons.
1658, May 13. John Jones 8 a. betw. Wm. Cotton and John Jackson.
Oct. 13. 20 a. to Richard Comins and Wm. Cotton in behalf of the neighbors on the neck of land they live on.
William Morris 8 a. in a rocky plain beyond John Jones.
1658-9, Feb. 21. Tho: Walford 10 a. at the head of Sagamore Creek northward.
Joshua Rogers 1 a.
1659, May 2. Robert Matoone 3 a. of marsh formerly Henry Taylor's adj. John Jackson.
Oct. 19. Robert Ellett 1 a.
Edward Clarke 1 a. adj. last.
James Drew 1 a. and rec. inhabitant.
[Mr. Lampree & wife warned out of town.
[21 Jan. 1666-77. Bernard Squire had an unrecorded grant several years ago.
Dec. 16. [Isacke Cussens is entertained as a tradesman.

1660-1. [See List 330b.]

Jan. 13. Grants on Great Island.
James Johnson 1 a. near the house that was Mr. Batcheler's.
John Hunkins 1 a. near James Leach.
John Fabins 1 a. next John Hunkins.
Widow Marie Walford 1 a.
John Lewes 1 a.
Mr. Elias Stileman 1 a.
Mr. James Pendleton 1 a.
Mr. Caleb Pendleton 1 a.
John Johnson 1 a.
John Odihorne 1 a.
Mr. Taprell 1 a.
Denis Occormacke 1 a.
Richard Jackson 8 a. at the Boiling Rock.
James Leach 8a.
Tho: Jackson 8 a.
John Hunkins 8 a. below the Boiling Rock.
Capt. Pendleton 8 a.
Elias Stileman 8 a.
Philip Lewis 50 a.
             to pay to the
Robert Ellett  : town £10 each
John Lewes  : for town lands
Mr. Frier  : they have appropriated and
Goodm. Mussell : built on.
[Laid out 1 a. to Alexander Jones.
[    1 a. to Mr. Paine.
['Laid out next unto the old Docter's Land which Capt. Pendleton bought one acre of land given Joseph Pendleton of fouer rod broad by the water side.'
['Corner of the house set up by Lamprey.'
[Laid out 1 a. to John Webster.
Jan. 22. James Cate's grant increased to 8 a.
Robert Elliot's grant increased to 8 a.
Marke Hunkins : 'the whole
Christopher    neck of land
[Sowton?]  : on which they
(interlined)    now live unto
Richard      John Jack-
Shortridge  : son's fence.'
Otho Tuckerman:
Joseph Walker  : 1 a. each and
Richard Sea-   received in-
ward Jr.    : habitants as
Silvester Herbert: new comers.
Feb. 4. Mr. Nathaniel Fryer 1 a. Great Island.
Mr. Edward Lyde 1 a. Great Island.
Mr. Richard Stileman 1 a. Great Island.
Feb. 5. Voted that 'The Old Planters should have 600 acres of land distributed among them.' — not exclusively to them but to include others who stand in need.
[No date: Laid out on Great Island.
[Thomas Walford.
[William Lux 1 a.
[Mr. Robert Taprill.
[Francis Gray 1 a.

[Laid out to George Jones which he bought of Jonas Clay's wife in Sagamore Creek, adj. Tho: Onion.
[Thomas Onion 8 a.
[John Lock 8 a.
[John Jones 8 a.
[James Drew 8 a.
[8 a. to Wm. Morris below Robert Elliot's house.
[Laid out to John Harte near to Jos: Rogers's house.
[Tho: Hinckson 28 a. together with 10 a. granted to Tho: Walford.
            laid out in
[John Jones 40a.: one piece
[James Drew  adj. Wm.
13 a.     : Brookins,
[Francis Jones  John Locke
13 a.     : and Wm.
            Morris.
[Sarah Firnald 13 a. laid out.
[Robert Puddington 13 a. laid out.
[Joshua Rogers's house at Sagamore Creek.
[Mary Walford's acre of land.
[25 Sept. 1662 Mr. Abra: Corbet.
[Matthew Ham's house.
1662, May 12. [John Odiorne 20 a. near Mr. Cutt's ditch.
1664-5, Jan. 31. [Henry Beck 60 a. of dividend lands at Sagamore Creek.
[Mr. West 1 a. of his dividend land at Gt. Isl.
[Mr. Richard Coming ditto.
Feb. 16. Widow Jones 1 a. on Great Island formerly left unrecorded by the clerk.
March 6. Joseph Moss 1 a. Great Island.
Thomas Jones 1 a. Great Island.
[Laid out to Dermont Usher.
[Laid out to Richard Perce 1 a.
['Allen Lyde's marsh.'
Nov. 6. [John Kettle admitted inhabitant.
[Laid out to John Odiorne.
23 a. of dividend land.
10 a. due to O. Trimming's old grant.
8 a. which James Johnson gave him.
1665-66, March 6. [Laid out Charles Allen 25 a.
1666, Apr. 16. [Walter Abbot his 30 a. grant 1652 together with 13 a. of Peter Abbot's.
[Samuel Fernald. 50 a. granted to his father and 13 a. granted John Partridge.
[Wm. Seavy 101 a. dividend land.
8 a. he bought of Gee.
['Laid out to Wm. Seavy for Mark Hunking 20 a. of land granted to Edm. Barton in '52.
June 19. Edmund Green a piece of land on Gt. Isl. to build a house on.
John Marden 1 a. on Gt. Isl. adj. J. Moss.

[Laid out to Geo. Wollis 37 a. adj. J. Odiorne.

[John Westbrook's formerly Tho. Hinckson's.

[Laid out to Mr. Moodey at Harrood's Creek his 80 a. grant and 55 a. bought from Anthony Ellings.

1667, Apr. 22. [Nehemiah Partridge admitted inhabitant.

May 21. Philip Russell 1 a. on Gt. Isl. provided he build.

Francis Jennings ditto.

John Johnson 'Long Point' near his house.

John Lewis 1 a. on Great Isl.

John Fabins 1 a. on Great Isl.

Thomas Parker 1 a. on Gt. Isl.

John Amenseen 1 a. on Great Island.

Steven Graffam 1 a. on Great Island.

[John Rann stopped from fencing land near Richard Sloper's.

Aug. 19. Tho: Follinsby 1 a. Gt. Isl. provided he build.

John Tanner 1 a. Gt. Isl. provided he build.

Mr. Tho: Daniell 1 a. Gt. Isl. provided he build.

Mr. Wm. Vaughan 1 a. Gt. Isl. provided he build.

Mr. Jenkin Harvy 1 a. Gt. Isl. provided he build.

Sam Drew 1 a. Gt. Isl. provided he build.

John Kettle 1 a. Gt. Isl. provided he build.

Sept. 9. Ens. John Davis allowed to fence his marsh against the town commons.

20 acres granted to Philip Lewis, Charles Allen, Wm. Daviss, Leonard Weeks.

Oct. 1. [Mr. Dearing to keep public house.

Dec. 9. [Laid out in the Long Reach to Mr. Richard Cutt 10 a. granted to Mr. Charterton in 1652, together with 45 a. granted to the Great House for Mr. John Cutt, and 10 a. granted Mr. Campion in '52.

1667-8, Jan. 14. Edward Randall 1 a. Gt. Isl. if he build.

Sam: Roobey 1 a. Gt. Isl. if he build.

1668, Apr. 9. William Cotton's son John ditto.

1668-9, Feb. 3. Mr. Edward West 1 a. on Great Island.

John Clarke 1 a. on Great Isl.

Daniel Moulton 1 a. on Gt. Isl.

Jer: Jones 1 a. on Great Isl.

Edw: Carter 1 a. on Great Isl.

Wm. Lux 1 a. on Great Island in consideration of a highway through his field.

[Clark and Carter's laid out in partnership.]

March 8. James Pendleton Jr. 1 a. Great Island.

Jeffrey Currier 1 a. Gt. Isl.

Elias Stileman Jr. 1 a. Gt. Isl.

1669, May 12. John Brewster, 5 or 6 a. adj. his homestead.

1670-1, Jan. 2. Mr. John Shepway 1 a. Gt. Isl.

Feb. 24. Sam: Treworthie provided he comes & inhabits.

[Samuel Drew having died with his house half built, it is confirmed to his heirs.

Mr. Robert Elliot 1 a. on Gt. Island.

John Terry 1 a. on Great Isl.

Edward West 1 a. on Gt. Isl.

Mr. Henry Dering 1 a. on Great Island.

Thomas Gubtell 1 a. on Great Island.

[Laid out to John Kenniston 13 a. bought of John Johnson.

March 3. Samuel Sherburne 1 a. Great Island.

Mr. John Fletcher 1 a. on Great Island.

March 13. Mr. Hubricht Muttoone 7 or 8 a. at the head of his house lot.

March 17. Mr. Richard Tucker 20 a. next to Mark Hunking on the other side of the creek beyond Goodm. Seavy's.

1671, May 24. Goodm. John Kenniston adj. what he bought of John Johnson.

Mr. John Jackson, mariner, 1 a. Great Island.

Joseph Walker 13 a.

One acre for a burying place (Greenland).

Oct. 26. [Mr. Henry Russell warned to leave town.

Dec. 21. Mr. John Stilsone admitted inhabitant.

1672, Aug. 15. Wm. Haskins, joiner, inhabitant.

1672-3, March 6. [Laid out to Jeremiah Jones 1 a. on Great Island adj. Samuel Robey.

March 13, Mr. Shipway 60a.

John Holmes 20 a. to recompence highway.

1673. [Laid out to John Berry 13 a. at Greenland.

1673-4, March 16. [Laid out to John Peverly son of Thomas Peverly deceased 67 a.

1674, May 18. [Laid out to Caleb Beck his 13 a. of dividend land, adj. his father.

[Laid out Nicholas Row's 50 a. grant 1652, which his son William Row saw measured, adj. land James Randall bought of Mr. Fryer.

1679, Oct. 24. [Laid out 13 a. to Richard Jackson for the use of his father Richard Seaward.

1686, July 20. [John Kelley, wife, and two children, ordered back to Boston.

[Peter Harvey warned for entertaining his sister and two children.

[John Reed and Mis Stocker: both to have 'the like' notice as Kelley and Harvey. Reed to bind himself out or the Selectmen will. John Rooe and Wm. Seavey Jr. bondsmen.

July 30. [Warrant to warn out of town Thomas French alias York.

Wife of Philip Chasely.

William Godso.

Wife of Nicho: Hodgdon.

Aug. 24. [Francis Brock to be placed under family government.

**330ᵇ** Distribution of Common Lands, Jan. 22, 1660 [1, as of the year 1657, including sons 21 (or under 21 if married) and daughters 18 whether married or not. — Town Book, p. 69 (ancient p. 36).

As printed, Rambles i. 27:
Alter Thomas Ornyon to Onnyon.
Francis Drake follows Philip Lewis.
Francis Jones follows Joseph Atkeson.
Alter Henry Seavey to Savidg.

The second column of figures represents 600 acres of additions to be distributed in the discression of the selectmen to rectify the allotment.

In a second table showing the acres already in possession and the acres due, the following names are omitted:

Thomas Seavy     Christopher Jose     George Row

**330ᶜ** A list of grants claimed, with John Pickering's notes regarding them about 1710.
— N. H. Hist. Soc.

*Moses
*Becke
*Geo. Walker

*Capt. Langdon     *Henry Sherborn
*Richard Sloper
*Phanan alias Pickerin
Randall farm Sherborn & Fryer
Will Roo   ·Nicholas
John Peverly   ·Thomas
Nelson's alias Walford
Westbrook & Holms   ·none
Henry Sherborn Jr.
James Johnson ½
Rich Cuming ½
Walter Abbot ½ Ales Westbrook
Mr. Joshua Moody
Hains
Lewes
Keneston alias Johnson   ·none
Sam Wheding
John Johnson   ·Francis Drake
Left. Neall
Philip Lewis alias Jotham Lewes
Philbrick ½   ·noone
*Jos. Berry   *·John Berry
Weeks   *·John Fose
Hinkson ½   ·noone

— Continued on Page 48 —

**330d** A true copy of the town rate made in the year 1698 by virtue whereof all the town lands to be divided in equal proportion according thereto.'

Major Vaughan
Mr. Richard Waldron
Mr. Penhallow
Mr. Saml. Cutt
Mark Ayers
John Hatch
Michael Wedden
Mrs. Harvey
Edward Kennard
Mrs. Cutt.
Mary Cutt
Widow Drew
Mr. Jaffrey
John Tuck
Widow Hopley
Mrs. Grafford
George Snell
Nathl. Jackson
Timothy Davis
Spleen Lovell
Elisha Bryard
John Shackford
Ichabod Plaisted
Saml. Keais
Widow White
Wm. Williams
Widow Redford
Jacob Lavers
Mr. Bullard
Nathl. Mellcher
Thomas Wacomb
Saml. Shackford
John Huncking
Thos. Laraby
Richard Jose
Coll. Packer

John Oliver
Mr. Rymes
Mrs. Eburne
John Knight
Wm. Partridge
John Snell
Edward Ayres
Joshua Peirce
Capt. Allcock
John Partridge
John Plaisted
Henry Keirke
Capt. Pickring
Wm. Rackley
John Libby
John Cotton
John Bartelet
Mathew Libby
Widow Nicolls
Mathew Nellson
Thos. Greeley
John Downing
George Vaughan
John Cowell
John Miller
John Dennet
John Gillden
John Ham
Dennet Alex.
Richard Elliot
Edward Toogood
Richard Webber
Wm. Pittman
Thos. Daverson
James Lovet
Wm. Hunckings
Benj. Sergent

Nathl. Ayers
Samuel Hartt
Daniel Fogg
Anna Clerk
Jonas Waukefield
Samuel Moor
Robt. Allmerry
John Fabens
John Abbot
John Preston
William Cotton
Richard Manson
John Manson
Thomas Barnes
Edward Polley
John Jackson
John Jackson Junior
Samuel Jackson
John Seward
Marke Huncking
Richard Shortridge
Mary Sherburne
Thos. Main
Richard Dore
Widow Carr
Robert Langg
James Howard
John Savage
Edward Cate
Thos. Ash
Obediah Morse
Deborah Morse
Richard Sanders

Edward Wells
Francis Jones
John Leighton
John Cross
Abraham Bartelet
Hugh Banfield
Thos. Wedden
James Norway
Richard Tree
John Clark
Edw. Randall
Thomas Rouse
James Booth
Solomon Hughs
Richard Waterhouse
Capt. Samuel Hill
Elisha Ensly
Widow Fabens
Mrs. Beck Carwithey
Widow Allkins
Anthony Roe
James Allen
Capt. John Wentworth
Henry Seward
Samuel Libby
James Libby
Thos. Perkins
Joseph Jackson
Doctor Baxter
Mr. Fletcher Abraham Remech
Philip Lambeth
Wm. Bickham
Joseph Hull
Roger Swain

Wm. Parker
James George
Andrew Brock
Joshua Brown
Widow Richards
Capt. Richard Garresh
Mr. Fol'etts house Jun.
Daniel Jackson
David Libby
Henry Sherburn mariner
Josiah Clark
Thomas Abbot
William White Ruporte
Mattoon
Daniel Libby
Peter Abbot
John Lang
John Pickering Jun.

**Greenland**
Tobias Langdon
Aaron Moses
Jos: Berry
Saml. Whidden
John Foss
Saml. Hains
Widow Mary Lewis
John Johnson Jr. and his father's lands
Thomas Beck
John Philbrook
Nathl. Huggins
Thos. Pickering

Christopher Kenniston
Nathl. Berry
John Cate
Benj. Cotton
Nathan Knight for Edmunds est.
Thomas Westbrook
Elias Percher
Peter Bab for Edmunds est.
Robert Hickson
Daniel Allen, self and father's est.
John Urin
John Bruester
Mary Hains
Robert Goss
Samuel Snell
John Holmes
John Hill
Capt. Neall
Wm. Philbrook
Samuel King
Leonard Weaks self & sons
John Johnson Senior & his sons
Henry Sherburn
Richard Sloper
George Walker Clement
Meshervey
John Peverly
Joseph Fanning
John Sherburn
Benj. Skilling

**330e** A list of those Rated in 1698, which were accounted not freeholders when the vote passed for a division of the commons.
— Mdm. those which are ·crossed· are allowed since this draft was drawn.
[Those names in brackets were stricken out.]

[John Hatch]
Mary Cutt
Widdo Drew
[Elisha Bryer]
[John Shackford]
[Wm. Williams]
[Widdo Redford]
[Samuel Shackford]x
Thos. Letherby x
John Oliver
John Libby x
John Bartlett
Matthew Libby
Widdo Niccols
Thomas Greely x
John Downing
John Couell
John Miller
Ben Sargent
Samuel Harte x
Daniel Foog
Jonas Wigfues
Samuel Moore x
Robert Almory x
John Monson
John Jackson Jun. x
Samuel Jackson x
Thos. Maine x
Thos. Aish
Debora Mors
Richard Sandors
John Laiton Jr.
Samuel Crose x
Thos. Whitten

James Norway
Richard Tree
John Clarke
Edw. Randle
Solomon Hewes x
Richard Waterhouse x
Samuel Hill x
Elisha Eugsly
Widoe Fabes x
Mrs. Corwiththy
James Allen
Henry Seward x
Samuel Libby x
James Libby x
Thos. Perkins x
Jos. Jackson
Doctor Bagster
Abraham Ramatch
Philip Lambeth x
Richard Biccom
Joseph Hull x
Roger Swaine x
James George
Joshua Browne x
Widoe Richards x
Nicholas Follett x
Daniel Jackson x
David Libby
Josiah Clark
Tho. Abbett
Rupert Mattone
Daniel Libby x
Peter Abbett x
Widdo Mary Lewes x

Xpher Kenestone x
Elias Percher x
Peter Babbe x
Robert Gose
Samuel Snell
Samuel Knight
Jos. Fanning x
Benj. Skeillin x
Mrs. Grafforte

**330f** A list of those not freeholders and where they lived in 1698.
John Hatch in Shipway's house
Michael Whidden in Major Vaughan's
Widow Drew in Natt Ayre's
Mr. Jeffreys house
Widow Hoply in Fletcher's
Elisha Bryand in Mr. Lovell's
John Shackford in John Jackson
Wm. Williams in the shop
Widow Redford house
Samuel Shackford in Obed Morse
John Oliver in Mr. Snell or Hull
John Libby 3, mill Vaughan
Matthew Libby, Cutt's farm
Widow Nichole in Natt Ayres'
Matthew Nelson Tanyard, Vaughan
Thos. Greely in Mr. Kaise
John Downin in Geo. Vaughan farm
ole Miller in Mr. Waldron's farm
Benj. Sergent in Sam Cutt's farm
Daniell Fogg in Mrs. Swain
Samuel Moore in Aron Moses
Robert Almory ship
Thom. Ash Henry Sherborn
Elisha Eusly in Morse's house
Anthony Row in Lyght house
James Allen in Light
John Wentworth ship
Joshua Brown in Jose's
Widow Richards in Jose's
David Libby in Solomon Cotton
Mrs. Swain, own rate for Daniel Fogg

— Continued from Page 46, List 330c —
Drake & Wm. Berry
John Hoomes ·20 a. grant not laid out
Samuel Sherborn
Mr. Fryer
Mr. Randall's farm
Samuel Sherborn
Joseph Berry,   ·Can find no return of any
                      laid out to him.
Robert Hinkson  ·No grant at all.
Philbrick  ·No grant at all.
Samuel Sherborn  ·60 a. grant  No return
*Anthony Brackett

**331a** Town Treasurer's Accounts, 1669-76.
— N. E. Register xxxviii. 58-59.

**331b** Tythingmen's Lists, 3 June 1678.
— Brewster's Rambles i. 60.
Alter Hen. Herke to Kerke.

**331c** North Church Records, 1671-1699.
— N. H. Gen. Records iii. 49.

**332a** Inquest, Thomas Evans, 18 Oct. 1687
— N. H. Hist. Coll. viii. 289.
Alter Tho. Starboard to —— bird.
Alter Robert Elkins to Alkins.
Alter Jacob Levers to Lavers.
Alter John Sewer to Sewar.

**332b** Rye and Greenland Tax List
Dec. 1688. — Brewster's Rambles i. 61.
Alter Christopher Kempstons to Kenisston.
Alter Sadwick to Ludwick Fowler.
Question William Keat.
Read John Vrine Urine.

**333a** Inquest, John Bruce, 14 March
1689-90, a Frenchman, struck in the back by
Joshua Hubbard, mate, died. Depositions taken
before Wm. Vaughan, Richard Martyn and Na-
thaniel Fryer.
Henry Jacobs±22.
Thomas Galloway aged 22.
Samuel Comfort aged 24: 'my cabin' aboard ship
America, Capt. John Holmes master.
Peter Johnson±22, aboard The America.
                        Coroner's Jury
Obadiah Morse          Timothy Davis
John Pickering Jr.     Richard Webber
William Cotton         Elisha Plaisted
Jacob Lavers           Mathew Nelson
Nehemiah Partridge     James Levet
Thomas Abbot           Mark Ayres
Samuel Rawlings

**333b**     Clearings and Entries.
Port of Portsmouth, in 1692. — N. H. Prov.
Papers ii. 77-84.

**334a** Fined for Not Turning Out to
Musters, 18 May 1693.—Prov. Papers ii. 106.
Alter Ferdinando Husse to Huffe.
Insert: Samuel Rymes crossed off.
Insert: Thomas Walker crossed off.
Insert: John Serjeant crossed off [followed by
J. (for Jr.?) started and blurred].
Alter: Samuel Babb to Sampson Babb.
After John Ham, J (for Jr.?) started and blurred.
Insert: Richard Shortridge crossed off.

**334b** A Londoner drowned at Portsmouth.
Inquest 25 Oct. 1695.
   Taken up by            Jury
Capt. John Long       William Jarvis
William Goodwin       Alex. Campbell
Robert Young          Tho. Deverson
Joseph Kerby          Joseph Edwards
James Lite            Robert Clarence
                      Nicholas Oliver
   Witness            Xpher Watson
John Titterson        Wm. Heptworth

William Joye          Tho. Willcock
Court Worme .         William Baker

**335a** Seating of the Meeting House,
13 Mar. 1693-4. — N. H. Gen. Rec. iii. 172.
174 Alter Mr. Bufam to Basam.
Alter John Vrin to Urin.
Alter Peter Mills to Wells.
Alter Edward Pevey to Pavey.
175 Alter John Beverly's wife to Peverly.
176 Alter James Kenist's wife to Keniston.

**335b** Price of a Stolen Feast, Dec. 1694
The following young men, some of them
doubtless merchants' apprentices, were ordered
whipped in the dooryard of John Pickering Jr.
for stealing a turkey, cidar, etc.
Daniel Gilman         Samuel Seward
Daniel More           Moses Wingett
James Booth           William Barton
Samuel Kenny          Joseph Mason

**336b** Military Service, Apr. to Nov. 1696.
— Prov. Papers xiii. 237, ii. 181-182.
Doubtful names not confirmed or indexed.
[Question Peter] Fogg.

**336c** Province Creditors, 9 Nov. 1699
— N. H. Prov. Papers iii. 90-92.
Read Splan Lovett Lovell.

**337** Proprietors of Common Lands based
on the Tax List of 1698, holding in 1711,
April 2, some of them in their own right, others
by heirship, assignment, attorneyship, or as administrators. — N. E. Reg. li. 44-46.
45 Alter Henry Sawer to Seward.
46 Alter Nickles Felcher to Fletcher.

**338a**     Greenland Parish Rate,
5 Feb. 1711-12.   Corrected by conjecture.
— N. E. Reg. 22. 451.
John Sockum read Dockum.
Jeaml Whitten read [Samuel?].
Ben. Meereas read Mecreas.
— Junr read [Robert Briant Jr.?].
Josih Brackett [presumably John].

**338b** Greenland church Members,
before 1712. — N. E. Register xxviii. 252.

**338c** Greenland Petition to Establish
Newington bounds, 1714.—Prov. Papers xii. 65.

**338d** Petition of Residents on the Pattin
adjacent to Greenland to be annexed, 17 June
1716[7. — Prov. Papers ix. 321.
Alter John Eveny to Every [Avery].
Thomas Letherby [·sic·] for Larrabee.

**339** Original Proprietors of Barrington
granted to Portsmouth in 1722.
— N. H. Prov. Papers ix. 41-45.

# Newington (Bloody Point). 341-343.

**341** Inquest, Bloody Point, 27 June 1660
—— —— found dead. Coroner's Jury:
Mr. Clements         John Bery
Goodman Osten        Goodman Brecket
Goodman Daves        Goodman Ran
Matthew Williams     x x x x
Goodman Meady        John Hill
Joseph Atkins        x x x x
Robert Elet          x x x x
x x x x

**342** Bloody Point Petition after 1663
— Newington Town Book.
to be taxed with Dover, not with Strawberry
Bank. Mass. Arch. iii. 442. As printed Prov.
Papers i. 176, alter:
John Fayes to John Tayer.

Wm. Frayser? to Wm. [Feayats?].
Radaric? to Andrew **6** Harad.

**343**    Parish Meeting 21 Jan. 1712-13.

| Pledges for the | *List of those desir- |
|---|---|
| Minister's Salery | ing pews 25 Oct. 1714 |
| *Lt. John Downing £1 | and also |
| *John Downing Jr. 15s | Capt. John Knight |
| *Ens. John Fabyan 15s | Mr. Geo. Huntress |
| *William Furber 16s | Sergt. John Bickford |
| *John Nutter 18s | Thomas Leighton |
| *Hatevil Nutter 14s | Ens. John Knight |
| *Clemet Meserve 10s | Samuel Thomson |
| Alex. Hosden 10s | Others named as town |
| Moses Dam 15s | officers to 1716: |
| Thomas Row 15s | Capt. Richard Gerrish |
| Eleazer Coalman 10s | William Shackford |
| Benj. Richards 06s | John Trickey |
| *Richard Downing 10s | Twenty-five accounts |
| Benj. Bickford 10s | for building meeting- |
| Richard Pumery 05s | house includes: |
| *John Dam 18s | John Quent |
| William Whittam 05s | Thomas Bickford |
| Benj. Bickford Jr. 03s | James Pickering |
| *Jethro Bickford 10s | Abel Pevey |
| Henery Nutter 10s | Edward Pevey |
| Nathl. Pevey 03s | Samuel Huntris |
| Joshua Crockett 08s | |

**Dover.    Lists 351-359.**

**351a**    Petition dated, 'Northam,
4, 1 Moneth' [1640] against coming under the
government of Massachusetts before the patentees
should be heard from. The original petition is
signed in three columns headed by Richard Walderne (Edward Colcord, Robert Huckins); William Waldern (John Tuttle, Henry Beck, Edmund Starbuck); Thomas Larkham (William
Jones, John Follett).
As printed in Prov. Papers i. 128,
Alter Robert Varney to Nanney.

**351b**    The Combination, dated 22 October
1640, printed four times in Prov. Papers,
best in x. 701. This document only exists in a
copy made by strangers 40 years afterwards, and
contains names found nowhere else, some young
Englishman pretending to make out all the signatures in obsolete writing perfectly.

| Alleged signers | Known names |
| unheard-of | missing |
|---|---|
| Henry Lahorn | Henry Langstaff |
| Edward Starr | Edward Starbuck |
| Richard Laham | Richard Rogers |
| | Richard York |

The original London copy is signed in three col-
umns, headed by:
Champernowne, Knowles, Colcord, Lahorn, Starr,
etc.
Larkin, two Walderns, Storer, Furber, etc.
Follett, Nanney, Jones, Swadden, etc.

**352**    The 20-acre lots laid out in
1642 on the west side of Back River, 40 x 80
rods, numbered from South to North, with later
owners in parentheses.
Lot 24 Richard Pinkom.
   23 Name not given.
   22 John Westell (Richard Pinkham, Thom-
      as P.).
   21 Henry Becke* (Thos. Leighton, John L.).
   20 Hatevil Nutter* (Moses Wingate, Israel
      Hodgdon).
   19 John Hall* (of Greenland, Moses Win-
      gate, Israel Hodgdon).
   18 Thomas Layton (John Drew).
   17 John Croose (John Dam, Wm. Pomfret,
      Thos. Whitehouse, John Drew).
   16 Robert Huggins* (John Drew).
   15 Samuel Haynes (John Hill, Wm. Follett,
      John Drew).
   14 Edward Starbuck (John Drew).

13 William Hilton (Joseph Tibbetts).
12 William Pomfret (Will Dam).
11 John Damm (Will Dam).
10 John Ugrove* (James Nute).
 9 Bartholomew Smith (James Nute).
 8 William Storey (Philip Cromwell, Richard Pinkham).
 7 John Tuttle.
 6 George Webe (Nathl. Hall, Ralph Hall).
 5 Edward Colcord.
 4 Mr. Larkham (John Goddard).
 3 Henry Tibbetts.
 2 Richard Rogers (Ambrose Gibbins, Thos.
   Layton Jr.).
 1 Thomas Roberts (Zachariah Field).
   *Also shared in the 6-acre grants of Coch-
echo marsh in 1648, with Anthony Emery,
Mr. Bellow, Geo. Walton, John Heard, William Waldron, Henry Langstaff, John God-
deres, James Nute, James Rallenes, Wm. Fur-
burre, Richard Waldern, John Backer.

**353**    Representatives and Town Officers
          — Hist. Mem. 1-10.
8 Insert William Furber, Deputy in 1648.

**354a**    Tax List made 19 December 1648.
   Well printed in N. H. Gen. Rec. i. 177.
Alter John Turtle to Tuttle.

**354b**    Tax List made 8 December 1649.
   Printed in full in Hist. Mem. 353.
Alter date from 1639 to 1649.
Alter Elder to Old Nickles Hickman.
Alter James Orderway to Ordeway.
Read John laues Lavis.

**354c**    Tax List made in December 1650.
   Well printed in Hist. Mem. 349.
After Radford insert:
Canceled: Edward Coettell — 10 —
Alter James to Janaes (Jonas) Bines.
After Goodie Feilld insert:
Canceled: James Bankerd.

**355a**    Dover Voters.    A list headed
'These are Fremen' in the town records is
well printed in N. E. Reg. iv. 247. Elder Star-
hooke is checked off in later ink. After Mr.
Gibons the name of John Hall is twice entered
and crossed out. At the foot Mr. Clemons was
added in later ink. It is not dated but is followed by dated entries:
Henry Tebetes, constable, 5 Apr. 1653.
Mr. Valtin Hill, Debety, 27 Mar. 1654.
Mr. Hill to set with the Magestrates in Cort.
Capt. Wallden, Mr. Hill, Wm. Pomfrett chosen
to end small Cases.
   The list headed ' x x x taken the oath of
fidelity' is well printed down to Wm. Willyums
Jr. Thus far occupies the left-hand of a page,
evidently all entered at one writing, and with
much room left in the column.
   Yet on the right-hand is another column, as
follows:

| John Bucksan | John Robertes |
| Mr. Gibons | Petter Coffen |
| John Hird | Antoney Nutter |
| Wm. Willyams | [The following in la- |
| John Olt | ter ink, etc.] |
| Joseph Austin | John Martaine |
| Tho: Beard | Tho: Roberts |
| Rafe Hall | John Hilton |
| Richard Cater | [The following in la- |
| [The following in later | ter ink, etc.] |
| ink, etc.] | John Bickford |
| These chosen the 24th | (crossed out) |
| 10mo., 55 (24 January | Richard Ottes |
| 1655-6). | (checked Refewsd) |
| John Hall Deacon | Tho: Nocke |

**355b**    Dover Petition against the Patentees (1654?). Poorly printed in Prov.
Papers i. 212. The original is signed in two col-

umns, the right-hand headed by Richard Wal-
derne, Nutter, Gibbins, Starbuck, Furber.
— Mass. Arch. iii. 446.
Insert John Hill after James Bunker.
Insert Oliver **2** Kent after John Bickford.
Alter John Dande to Dame.
Alter Ralph Hill to Hall.
Alter Thomas Wells to Wellie.
Alter John W—— to Robbardes.
John Heard's mark a carpenter's square.
Alter Thomas Northe to Nocke.
Alter Matthew Billes to Gilles.

**356a**    Tax List made 21 July 1657.
Well printed in Hist. Mem. 355.
Alter Nathell Wise to [Wi'fe?].
Read: Patrick the socskett [Scott?].
   After R. Carell insert:
Ed 8l ⨯ ⨯ for his head.
Read: Mr. Pitman his head.
   [This last an added name].

**356b**    Tax List made 10 November 1657.
Well printed in Hist. Mem. 356.
Alter John Carter to Curttes.
Alter John Louring to Lovering.

**356c**    Tax Rate made 12 October 1658.
Well printed in Hist. Mem. 362.
Alter William Hoket to Hakett.

**356d**    Ten Men Received as Inhabitants
together, 10 Feb. 1658[9. — Hist. Mem. 340.
Alter Walter Packson to Jackson.
Alter James Air to Orr.

**356e**    Tax Rate made 22 November 1659.
Printed in full in Hist. Mem. 364.
Alter Edward to Mr. Edmund Bushnall.
Read John Stathom.
Read Welsh James Grant.
   Before Samewell Wentworth
Insert: Elder Wentworth 1: 10: 4.
Alter Tredick to Thomas Treick.
Read Niven the Scot.
   Insert, last name, crossed out:
John Otis his man 0: 5: 0.

**356f**   Inhabitants of Dover Neck having
rights in the Oxe Pasture, list taken 13 June
1661. — Hist. Mem. 365.

**356g**    Tax List made 19 November 1662.
Printed in Notable Events 55 — correctly
copied from the Dover Enquirer (original gone).

**356h**    Tax List made 7 December 1663.
Printed in Notable Events 58 — correctly
copied from the Dover Enquirer (original gone).
The tax list made 16 Oct. 1664, as printed in
the Dover Enquirer before the original disappeared, shows the following changes:

| Gone | New | | | |
|---|---|---|---|---|
| Capt. Barffoott | Job Clements | 2 | 9 | 6 |
| Petter Glanfield | James Newtt Jr. | 0 | 18 | 9 |
| Saraie Astin | John Tuttle | 0 | 7 | 6 |
| Humfrey Varney | John Wingett | 0 | 15 | 0 |
| Christafer Batt | Elexander & | | | |
| Richard Rooe | Wm. Walden | 0 | 15 | 0 |
| Cochecho | Philip Cromwell | 2 | 12 | 6 |
| John Kiniston | Richard Pink- | | | |
| Richard Seaman | ham | | | |
| Thomas Rallins | Cochecho | | | |
| Clement Rafe | Mr. Payne | | | |
| Antoney Page | Samewell | | | |
| John Sharpe | Robins | 0 | 7 | 6 |
| Philep Cromwell | Tho: Hanson Jr. | 0 | 11 | 3 |
| Abraham Folet's man | William Kemp | 0 | 7 | 6 |
| Wm. Follet at Belli | Micom the | | | |
| bank | Scotchman | 0 | 7 | 6 |
| Capt. Wiggin at tollend | | | | |
| Mr. Nathl. Frier | | | | |

**356j**   Lost Dover and Durham Tax Lists.
New names noticed in the tax lists year by

year from 1665 to 1672 were printed in the N. E.
Reg. iv. 249-250 before the book containing them
disappeared.
Jeremie Hosson probably Hodsdon.
George Gore probably Gove and Goe.
Richard Boles probably Ball.
William Kemp probably Kim.

**356k**    Tax List made 2 December 1666.
Printed in Notable Events 67 — correctly
copied from the Dover Enquirer (original gone).
Alter Clarke Gilles to Marke Gilles.
Alter John Scriven to Scriver.

**356l**   Declaration for Massachusetts Gov-
ernment, 9 Oct. 1665. — N. H. Prov. Papers
i. 285. (Mass. Arch. cvi. 157).
Alter John Brewster to Bruester.
Alter Richard Goss [Jose] to Richard Goss.
Alter Anthony Ellery to Ellens.
Stephen Grassam [-sic-] for Graffam.

**356m**   Received as Inhabitants 1665-1669
but with no share in the commons, except
pasturage.     — N. E. Reg. iv. 249-250.

**357a**   Liquor Selling and the Dickinson
Case at Concord in 1668. — N. H. Hist. Coll.
iii. 214-224.

**357b**    Inquest, Samuel Roberts,
March 29, 1669. Accidentally drowned. Jury:
1669. Accidentally drowned. Jury:

| | |
|---|---|
| Hatevil Nutter | John Tuttell |
| Thomas Layton | James Nute |
| Job Clements | John Anger |
| John Robberts | John Pincham |
| Philip Cromwill | *Wm. Roberts |
| Patrick Jemason | Job Clements Jr. |

      *Refused to take oath

**357c**    Oath of Fidelity
taken 21 June 1669.—Hist. Memoranda 116.

**357d**    Inquest, Thomas Homsly,
Aug. 23, 1670. Accidentally drowned. Jury:

| | |
|---|---|
| John Scrivener | Joseph Sanders |
|    Foreman | Nathl. Stevens |
| John Stone | Lawserous Purmet |
| Thomas Payne | Thomas Downes |
| John Smith | David Larkings |
| John Church | Nich: Frost |
| James Coffin | |

**357e**    Inquest, Hannah Stokes,
Sept. 21, 1674. A child drowned. Jury:

| | |
|---|---|
| Philip Benmor | Jeremiah Tibbetts Jr. |
| Thomas Roberts | Ralph [Welx]. |
| John Tuttell | Richard Penkum |
| John Hall | John [Emson] |
| Tho. Whitehouse | John Robrds |
| Jeremiah Tibbetts Sr. | Philip Cromell |

**358a**    Inquest, Charles Le brittoon,
July 10, 1695. Accidentally drowned. Jury:

| | |
|---|---|
| Samuel Tibbetts | Richard Hussey |
|    Foreman | Peter Varney |
| Joseph Tibbetts | Thomas Ash |
| Joseph Roberts | Nathaniel Hall |
| Jeremiah Tibbetts | Ephraim Tibbetts |
| John Twomble | Timothy Robbson |
| John Bunker | |

**358b**   Sham Land Grants Surreptitiously
antedated in the Town Book as of 1659-1701.
Legislative investigation reported 30 April 1731.
Partly indexed. — Prov. Papers ix. 163-167.
164 Jeremiah Barnum read Burnum.
     Nathaniel Landers read Lamos.
     Alter Roger Vose to Rose.
165 Bryant Higgins read Beriah.

**358c**   Account of Pretenders to Lands at
Cochecho Point.—N. H. Prov. Papers ix. 155.
Alter Lt. Hatevil Roby to Roberts.

Alter ——— to Pots, 'had for his wife's portion.
This memo. had to do with Richard Waldron's
suit, in court 1719-1728, which dispossessed a
dozen people.

Defendants in the Original Writ:
Benjamin Mason, shoemaker.
Elisha Clark, ferryman. William Blackstone.
William Stiles, blacksmith.
Howard Henderson, mastliner.
Peter Cook, husbandman.
Richard Hamock, husbandman. Samuel Cosen.
James Wilmet, cooper.
Joseph Canney, husbandman.
John Foy. Samuel Alley.

**358d** Distances from Old and New Meeting House, 1715. — N. H. Prov. Papers xi.
508-509.

**359a** Dover Tax List 23 July 1677.
Now first printed. The next earlier list, 14
Feb. 1675-6, was poorly printed in the Dover Enquirer and reprinted without corrections. Both
that list and this have corners gone; as printed
below, the names in brackets are taken from the
1675-6 list to replace names lost from the 1677
list. — Dover Town Records 'No. 5.'

**Dover Neck and Cochecho**

| | | |
|---|---|---|
| Mr. Nutter | 03 | 08 |
| Deacon Hall | 06 | 10 |
| Deacon Dam | 09 | 02 |
| Joseph Canie | 09 | 08 |
| Widow Canie | 05 | 00 |
| Widow Benmore | 04 | 00 |
| Silvanus Nock | 04 | 0) |
| John Pnkham | 06 | 01 |
| Widow Tibet and her son Jeremie | 07 | 01 |

[The above five names in 1675 [6 were:
Thomas Canie
Henry Tibit
Philip Benmore
John Pinckham
Jeremi Tibbetts]

| | | |
|---|---|---|
| Thomas Beard | 09 | 11 |
| Thomas Pirkins | 03 | 00 |

[Isaack Stockes]

| | | |
|---|---|---|
| Tho. Roberts | 08 | 00 |
| Phillip Cromell | 05 | 02 |

[Richard Pinkham]
Thomas White-

| | | |
|---|---|---|
| house | 08 | 06 |
| John Roberts | 18 | 01 |

[John Tuttle]
Leiftenant Pom-

| | | |
|---|---|---|
| frie | 02 | 09 |
| James Newt Jr. | 06 | 00 |

[Mr. Clements]
[Jonathan Watson]
[Thomas Leighton]
[James Nute Sen.]
[Abraham Nute]
[John Hall Jr.]
R[ichard Rich]
John [Dereie]
Thom [Teare]
[Capt. Barfoote]
Ralf [Welch]
Zache[rie Feild]
Nathaniel [Steephens]
Ginkin Joanes

| | | |
|---|---|---|
| John Ham | 05 | 00 |
| William Horn | 05 | 00 |
| Tho. Hamett | 04 | 10 |
| John Elis | 01 | 08 |

[Humphrey Varney]

| | | |
|---|---|---|
| Henery Hobs | 05 | 06 |
| John Windiet | 08 | 06 |
| John Foss | 03 | 09 |
| Petter Coffen | 01 | 08 | 03 |
| John Masson | 01 | 04 |

**Benjemen Masson**

| | | |
|---|---|---|
| son | 01 | 08 |
| Joseph Sanders | 01 | 08 |
| Tho. Yong | 01 | 05 |

[David Larking]

| | | |
|---|---|---|
| Tho. Austen | 01 | 05 |
| Tho. Homes | 05 | 08 |

Capt. Wal-

| | | |
|---|---|---|
| dern | 01 | 08 | 10 |
| George Ricer | 04 | 04 |

and brother

| | | |
|---|---|---|
| Tho. Paine | 08 | 06 |
| Richard Otis | 18 | 01 |
| John Gerrish | 01 | 08 | 05 |
| John Evens | 01 | 05 |
| John Heard | 06 | 06 |
| Thomas Hanson | 04 | 08 |

Mr. George Wal-

| | | |
|---|---|---|
| dern | 02 | 11 |
| Robert Evens | 04 | 04 |
| Ralf Twomlie | 05 | 00 |

Gershom Wnt-

| | | |
|---|---|---|
| worth | 02 | 05 |

Ezekiel Went-

| | | |
|---|---|---|
| worth | 02 | 07 |

[James Coffin]
[William Taskett]
[Tho. Downes]
[Widow Hanson]
[Tobias Hanson]
[Elder Wentworth]
[John Church]
[Mark Giles]
[Benjamin Heard]
**Bloody Poynt**
[Sargant Hall] 02 04
[Hen]ery

| | | |
|---|---|---|
| [La]ngather | 03 | 11 |
| William Furber | 10 | 10 |

William Fur-

| | | |
|---|---|---|
| ber Jnior | 01 | 10 |
| Richard Catter | 10 | 05 |
| Richard Roe | 06 | 02 |

John Bickford

| | | |
|---|---|---|
| No. 2 | 02 | 00 |
| Edward Allin | 01 | 03 |
| James Raulins | 05 | 08 |
| Wm. Shackford | 04 | 04 |

Zachariah

| | | |
|---|---|---|
| Trickie | 02 | 04 |
| x x x x x x | 06 | 10 |
| x x x x x x | 04 | 06 |
| x x x x x x | 05 | 05 |
| x x x x x x | 01 | 10 |
| x x Bickford or | 01 | 10 |
| Anthony Nutter | 14 | 00 |

[Francis Huckts]

| | | |
|---|---|---|
| Isack Trickie | 04 | 00 |

Mr. William

| | | |
|---|---|---|
| Henderso·· | 07 | 00 |

Elihu Gulison

| | | |
|---|---|---|
| and 8 men | 05 | 00 |
| Richard Scamon | 01 | 08 |
| James Green | 01 | 08 |
| William Kim | 01 | 08 |
| Steephin Howel | 01 | 06 |
| Steephin Seavie | 01 | 08 |
| John Michill | 01 | 06 |

[In the 1676 Bloody
Point list next be-
fore Anthony Nutter
is: x x el W x x]
**Oyster River**

| | | |
|---|---|---|
| Ensigne Davis | 07 | 01 |

[——— Beard]

| | | |
|---|---|---|
| James Hukins | 03 | 11 |
| Tho. Edgerly | 06 | 11 |
| John Alt | 07 | 11 |
| John Hill | 04 | 03 |
| John Bickford | 07 | 09 |

[Joseph Bickford]

| | | |
|---|---|---|
| Tho. Wilie | 03 | 09 |
| John Meader | 06 | 03 |
| Joseph Smith | 07 | 00 |

William Wil-

| | | |
|---|---|---|
| liams Jr. | 04 | 05 |

Philip Chesly

| | | |
|---|---|---|
| Sen. | 06 | 10 |
| Robert Watson | 08 | 04 |

[Walter Jackson]

| | | |
|---|---|---|
| Steephen Joans | 08 | 11 |
| Edward Leathers | 04 | 00 |
| John Davis Jr. | 01 | 06 |
| James Smith | 08 | 06 |
| William Hill | 04 | 00 |

Tho. & Philip

| | | |
|---|---|---|
| Chesly | 04 | 00 |

[Philip Cromett]

| | | |
|---|---|---|
| John Godard | 11 | 01 |
| John York | 04 | 02 |
| Benjemen York | 02 | 00 |
| Nickolas Dow | 05 | 05 |
| Samuel Willi | 01 | 09 |
| Charles Adams | 04 | 03 |
| Nickelas Haris | 02 | 11 |
| Joseph Stinson | 04 | 05 |

[Thomas Stimson]

| | | |
|---|---|---|
| Steephin Willie | 01 | 05 |
| John Drew | 03 | 00 |
| Joseph Feild | 08 | 04 |
| William Durgen | 25 | 08 |
| Thomas Moris | 04 | 10 |

[Teague Reall]

| | | |
|---|---|---|
| Nickolas Follett | 04 | 08 |
| John Woodman | 08 | 04 |
| Robert Burnam | 09 | 00 |

William Wil-

| | | |
|---|---|---|
| liams Senior | 06 | 08 |
| Mr. John Cutts | 01 | 07 |

Nathaniel Lu-

| | | |
|---|---|---|
| mack | 01 | 07 |
| Salathiel Denbo | 01 | 00 |
| Davie Daniel | 03 | 02 |

Benjemen Ma-

| | | |
|---|---|---|
| thws | 06 | 08 |
| Francis Drew | 03 | 11 |
| William Picklson | 05 | 06 |
| William Pittman | 08 | 09 |
| George Goe | 01 | 03 |
| William Follett | 05 | 11 |

[new names added]

| | | |
|---|---|---|
| John Michamore | 02 | 00 |
| William Borden | 01 | 03 |
| Abrham Clerk | 01 | 06 |

[John Mihel was taxed
in the 1675-6 list
next after Edward
Leathers]
[The following names
in the 1675-6 list
have the word 'Noth-
ing' entered against
them; these were
dropped that year:
Isaac Stockes
Richard Pinkham
John Tuttle
Capt. Barfoote
Humphrey Varney
David Larking
Francis Huckts
——— Beard
Joseph Bickford
Walter Jackson
Philip Cromett
Thomas Stimson
Teague Reall
Elder Wentworth
John Migel]
[Alongside of the 1675-
6 List, with corner
gone, is found the
following memoran-
dum:
W x x x x x x x x
Ell x x x x x x x x
Richa x x x x x x x
Stephen x x x x x x
Samll·Rand x x x x
Jams Greene x x x
Ephraim Severn 01 00
Benj. Nason 01 00
Willam Kim 01 00
Stephen Horrill 01 06
Joha Michell 01 08
John Michmore 02 00
Willam Boydan 01 08]

**359b** Tax List, (1680?)
— N. H. Hist. Coll. viii. 60, Prov. Papers i.
427 (Court Files v. 129).

Alter Saml Wentworth to Pall.
Alter Humprey Barney to Varney.
Alter Thomas North to Nocth.
Alter John Frost to Fost.
Alter Harvey to Henrey Hobbs.
Alter Richard Seamon to Scammon.
Alter John Windicot to Windiet.
Alter Will Gifford to [Hafford?].
Alter Phillips to Phillip Chesley.
Add ·minor· to James Hawkins.
John Cox ·sic·
Alter Wildram to William Dam.
Abraham Nutt ·sic·
Alter Phillips Cromwell to Phillip.
Alter Iecobad Rawlins to Iccabad.
Alter Michall Brown to Brawn.

## Durham (Oyster River). 361-369.

**361a** Oyster River Tax List 22 Nov. 1659.
Corrected by original. Notable Events 47.

| | |
|---|---|
| Thomas the Stiller, | John Hillton |
| with ·Umfre· in margin | John Dinill |
| Einsin John Davis | William Risbey |
| William Williams, | Thomas Giun |
| with ·Juner· in margin | Stephen the Westirman |

**361b** Inquest, James Mooray, 2 Nov. 1659.
Killed by falling limb. Hist. Durham i. 83.

**362a** Protest of Oyster River against
Unfair Treatment by Dover Neck, 1660.
— Hist. Mem. 53.

**362b** Inquest, Thos. Canada, 26 Dec. 1660.
Found with a tree fallen across him near the
house of Thomas Humfrees.

| Coroner's Jury | Charles Adams |
|---|---|
| John Beckford | Thomas Willy |
| John Davis | William Smith |
| Mathew Gyles | Patrick Gimison |
| Wm. Williams | James Middleton |
| John Meader | Joseph Feild |
| Tho. Stevenson | Stephen Joanes |

**363a** Tax List made in 1661 or 1662.
Printed in Notable Events 51 — correctly
copied from the Dover Enquirer (original gone).

**363b** Tax List made 19 November 1662.
Well printed in Notable Events 57 — copied
from the Dover Enquirer (original gone).
Alter John Woed to John Woed × × .

**363c** Tax List made 7 December 1663.
Well printed in Notable Events 60 — correctly copied from the Dover Enquirer (original
gone).
The tax list made 16 Oct. 1664, as printed in
the Dover Enquirer before the original disappeared, shows the following changes:

| Gone | New | | | |
|---|---|---|---|---|
| Thomas Morrise | James Huggins | 0 | 10 | 0 |
| John Hillton | Edwin Erwin | 1 | 12 | 0 |
| Alex. McDonald's | (Henry Browne) | | | |
| estate | & James Oer | 2 | 2 | 6 |
| (Henry Browne) | Sackrey Filld | 0 | 12 | 6 |
| and Company | Thomas Rallines | 0 | 10 | 0 |
| Thomas Humfries | Joseph Smith | 0 | 19 | 9 |
| James Bonker | John Smith | 0 | 7 | 6 |
| ———— Smith | Ens. John Davis | 1 | 7 | 6 |
| ———— Davis | | | | |
| Matthew Williams | | | | |
| Robord Chapman | | | | |

**364** Estate of Alexander Macdannel,
Scotchman, drowned 'between York and Dover' 16 Jan. 1663-4. Adm. granted in County
Court at Boston 26 Jan. to John Roy of Charlestown. — Suff. Court Files 632.

Bondsman    Solomon Phipps
Appraisers

| John Tod | Walter Jackson |
|---|---|
| John Alt | Henry Browne |

Depositions
Philip Cheasly ± 46    2 Feb. 1663 [4
talked with him 10 days before he was
drowned.
The following deposed before Richard Russell that they had heard him call John Roy
his only kinsman in this country.

| John Bennit ± 33 | Sarah Bennit ± 22 |
|---|---|
| John Edmanster ± 26 | Hannah Edmanster ± 22 |
| William Manus ± 20 | |
| Anguish Make Farshon ± 30 | |

Inventory besides a horse and cattle
showed: Debts due from
Edward During    Wm. Furbush

| Capt. Pendleton | Peter Coffin |
|---|---|
| Mr. John Payne | |
| | Debts due to |
| Walter Jackson | Goodman Abbut |
| Philip Chesly | David Daniell |
| Tho: Douty | Goodman Beard |
| Patrick Danmarke | Eleazer Fild |
| John Bickford | |

**365** Tax List made 2 December 1666.
Printed in Notable Events 68 — correctly
copied from the Dover Enquirer (original gone).

**366** Petition for Separate Township,
May 25, 1669. — Stackpole's Durham i. 171.
In the original, Mass. Arch. 10, 104, the four col-
umns are headed by: John Bicford, Richard York,
John Davis, etc.; John Woodman, John Meader,
Thomas Willey, etc.; Joseph Field, Zacharias
Field, John Goddard, etc.; Joseph Stimson, John
Smith, James Smith, James Huckins, etc., and
Barnard Pope's name is at the foot of the sheet.

**367a** Inquest, Elizabeth Jenkins,
Sept. 3, 1687. — N. H. Hist. Coll. viii. 288.

**367b** Inquest, a stillborn infant. Coroner's jury sworn before John Woodman,
J. P., Dec. 1692.

| Tho: Egerly, foreman | Tho: Egarly Jr. |
|---|---|
| John Davis | [Joseph Keent |
| Edward Lethers | canceled] |
| Stevin Ginks | Thomas Drew |
| Samuell Addames | Ezekel Pitman |
| Charles Addames | Goody (Sary) Bunker |
| [Edw: Roe, canceled] | midwife |
| Joseph Meder | Goody (Ann) Ginkings |
| John Wille | Goody (Abigail) Rose |
| Benj. Mathes | Goody (Susan) Davis |

**368a** Petition for Separate Township,
1695. — Stackpole's Durham 14.
Alter ———— Davis to David Davis.
Alter Henry Vines (?) to Henry Rines.

**368b** Five Petitions regarding a Separate
Parish, 1715-1717. — Stackpole's Durham,
pp. 174, 176, 178, 180, 182.
178 Alter David Lyntard to Kyncard.
182 Alter Joseph Nudder to Medder.

**369** Final Division of Common Lands,
18 March 1733-4.
— Stackpole's Durham 19-21.

## Exeter and Stratham. Lists 371-389.

**371** Indian Deeds dated 3 April 1638.
and confirmed 10 April 1638 contain the following names: — N. H. Hist. Coll. i. 147-148.

| Grantees | Witnesses |
|---|---|
| John Wheelwright | James 1 Cornall |
| of Piscataqua | William 6 Cole |
| Samuel Hutchinson | Lawrence 1 Cowpland |
| of Boston | Edward Colcord |
| Augustine Storr | Nicholas Needham |
| of Boston | William Furbur |
| Edward Colcard | John Underhill |
| of Piscataqua | Darby 1 Feild |
| Darby Field | |
| of Piscataqua | |
| John Compton | |
| of Roxbury | |
| Nicholas Needome | |
| of Mt.Wollaston | |

**372** Original Unrecorded Indenture
1 [April or May] 1639 between Thomas Wiggin and the Rulers of Exeter.

| John Wheelwright | Richard Moris |
|---|---|
| George Smythe | Nicholas Needham |
| [later clerk of court] | Isaac Grosse |
| Lenoard Morres | Rulers of Exeter |
| Witnesses | — N. H. Court Files 17795. |

**373** The Exeter Combination or agreement for self-government, which straightway enacted by-laws for capital punishment based on biblical interpretations, was dated 5 June 1639. It was signed by 35 men, nearly half of them by their marks, whose names were written out by Augustine Storre and Edward Rishworth. At least five of the signers were Wheelwright family connections. The signers presently scattered themselves, from the Kennebec to Rhode Island or farther, only three remaining at Exeter. Five accompanied Mr. Wheelwright to Wells, of whom one remained there. Farmer's Belknap i. 20; Prov. Papers i. 131. A hand-engraved facsimile is the frontispiece of Bell's Exeter, printed at p. 17. A copy made in 1683 by Edward Smith, town clerk, is in Court Files 17795, in which he rendered names which are doubtful in the present condition of the original:

| | |
|---|---|
| Thomas Crawley | Samuel Walker |
| Robert Smith | Robert Read |
| Robert Soward | George Rawbone |

**374a** Petition to Massachusetts, May, 1643.
According to Bell, this was the petition peremptorily rejected. Of 17 signers, 11 had signed the Combination. The original shows the upper right-hand corner torn off, which may have had four more signers, one of them Robert ————.
— Bell's Exeter 44, Mass. Arch. cxii. 9.

**374c** Petition, 29 May 1645, in John Legat's hand.
— Prov. Papers i. 178 (Mass. Arch. cxii. 14).
Alter Richard Carter to Carver.

**375a** Petition against Dover, Hampton and Capt. Wiggin, May 12, 1646. — N. H. Prov. Papers i. 170 (Mass. Arch. cxii. 8). Wrongly treated as of 1643 in Bell's Exeter. See Mass. Records iii. 64.
Alter Richard Carter to Carver.
Alter William M—— to Mooer.
Alter Ballthazar Willis to Willix.

**375b** Buying the Minister's House.
Agreement with Hilton and King about buying Mr. Wheelwright's house for Mr. [Nathaniel] Norcrosse, dated 25 May 1646 and signed on the Town Book by:

| | |
|---|---|
| Thomas **2** Jones | Francis **7** Swaine |
| Robert Hithersay | Anthony Stanyan |
| Humphery Willson | Saml. Grenefeld |
| Abraham Drak | John **3** Smart |
| Nichol **6** Swaine | James Wall |
| Robert **6** Smith | Henry Roby |
| John **6** Cram | Nath: Boulter |
| Tho: Pettit | John Legat |

All except Nicholas Swain and Smart are in a list of men entered in the margin who had done their part towards Mr. Nutter's fence, 6 May 1645: also the following:

| | |
|---|---|
| William Mauer | ———— Read |
| Ralph Hall | ——ichard Carver |
| ——ho: Biggs | John Bursly |
| ——frey Dearborn | Bellshazzar Willix |
| ——eorg Barlo | Tho: Weight |

**376a** Town Records from Dec. 1639 to 17 June 1644. — Bell's Exeter 435-447, N. H. Prov. Papers i. 137-145.

**376b** Town Grants 1644-1740.
Partly indexed. — Bell's Exeter 130-146. See also List 376a.

**377** Representatives and Town Officers.
Mass. Records for 1669 give Hampton two deputies, one of whom, Josh. Gilman, must have been John Gilman for Exeter. — Bell's Exeter 148-151.

**378** Edw. Gilman Jr's schedule of lands, Oct. 10, 1651, mortgaged one-half of to his father Richard Smith:
Town grant to Christop Lawson 30 acres on the Neck.
Town grant to Edward Gilman, the rest not formerly granted on the Neck.
Town grant to John Busly 10 acres on the Neck.
Town grant to Saml. Greenfeild 10 acres on the Neck.
Town grant to Wm. Winborn 10 acres on the Neck.
Town grant Dearborn third-part of 6 acres of meadow.
Town grant Edward Gillman liberty for sawmills and masts.
Thomas Jones 20 acres of upland by Robert Smith.
Mr. Gillman 100 acres upland by the common field.
Christor Lawson 100 acres upland " " "
6 lots of 20 acres apeece in the common field.
Mr. Stanion's house and lot of 2½ acres.
27 acres not improved in his great lot.
8 acres of meadow.
1 acre of meadow for Cumptons.
30 acres of upland for Comptons.
10 acres of upland for Comptons.
2 acres of meadow for Comptons.
10 acres of upland for Reads.
3 quarters acre of meadow for Reads.
20 acres by the falls Mr. Stanyan.
Mr. Stanian farm 300 acres upland and 80 acres meadow.
6 acres upland by Dearborns.
Greenfeilds 20 acres neare Mr. Hilton's.
3 acres of meadow at stone brooke.
3 quarters acre of Wits [?Willex?].
6 acres of upland neare ston brooke.
70 acres of land in the woods.
Bursle house which was Boulter's.
2 house lots 5 acres.
10 acres without the fence.
a house lot that was Teds.
2 house lots that was Littlefeilds.
20 acres near Stone brooke.
house lot that was Montagues.
8 acres at the lots ends.
3 quarters of meadow of Ted's.
3 quarters of meadow of Mr. Purmets.
1½ acres of meadow of Littlefeilds.
Dearborn's house and two house lots.
four acres of land at the fence end.
a great lot 10 acres.
3 quarters of meadow.
a great lot Joaneses.
3 quarters meadow.
Smith's house lot.
Boulter's two acres.
¾ parts of the saw mill.

**379** Signed consent to Gen. Court grant of mile sq. to Mr. Saml. Symonds, 25 May 1659.

| | | |
|---|---|---|
| Moses Gilman | Nicholas Smith | Saml. Dudley |
| Robert Smart | Wm. Taylor | Edw. Hilton |
| Ralf Hale | Jonathan Thing | Wm. More |
| John Bean | Nicolas Lissen | John Gilman |
| Tho: Biggs | John Warren | |

**380** Robert Wadleigh's account of disbursements about the sawmill at Lamprill River, 15 Jan. 1664[5 to Oct. 1668.
— Court Files i. 249.

| | |
|---|---|
| John Woolcot wages | £40 |
| 5 days time of 12 oxen and 2 men | 05 |
| Wm. Rogers & Mr. Robt. Gardner and Rowland Flansell wages & dyet | 06 |
| Wm. Graves wages & dyet | 09 |
| Henry Browne for halling of timber and dyet | 11 |
| Digory Jeffrey 4 mos. | |
| Philip Gullison 9 mos. | |
| Mr. Robert Gardner 9 mos. | |
| Arthur Stranguidge wages & dyet | 16 |

Isaac Cole 4 mos.
Mr. Robert Bellgrove wages & dyet          22
Robert Allen    do                         11
Joseph Smith    do                         04
James Godfrey 8 days with self & 8 oxen
My own time 8 years                       150
To 3 years dyet                            54
John Palmer wages & dyet                   05
Hen Magoone wages & dyet                    1
Jonathan Robinson
Goodman Lissen 1½ years

**381**   Soldiers' Assignments of Pay to the
Town Oct. 24, 1676. — Bodge 449.

**382**   Shares and Rents in Exeter Mills.
— N. H. Court Files ix. 189.
This memorandum was apparently never com-
pleted.

| | | | |
|---|---|---|---|
| Jonathan Thing | 7 yrs. | ¼ mill | 40 m. boards yearly |
| Jonathan Robinson | 10 yrs. | ¼ | £8 per annum |
| Eleaz Elkins | 8 yrs. | ¼ | £2·10s |
| Moses Levet | 2 yrs. | ¼ | |
| David Robinson | 8 yrs. | ¼ | |
| Phillip Carte | 6 yrs. | ¼ | |
| Ephraim Foulsham | 1 yr. | ¼ | |
| John Foulsham | 20 yrs. | ¼ mill | |
| Christopher Dolhof | 12 yrs. | ¼ | |
| Ralf Hall | 20 yrs. | ¼ mill | 40 m. boards yearly |
| Kingsly Hall | 6 yrs. | ¼ mill | |
| Rich: Morgan | 12 yrs. | | |
| Nath: Foulsham | 4 yrs. | ⅛ mill | |
| Thomas Chesley | 12 yrs. | | £4·10s |
| Philip Chesley | 12 yrs. | | £4·10s |
| Zachary Field | 6 yrs. | | £3 |
| William Tasket | 8 yrs. | | 80s |
| James Huckins | 12 yrs. | | 40s |
| Sampson Sheaf | | | |

**383**   Tax List, 20 April 1680.
— N. H. Hist. Coll. viii. 59, Prov. Papers i. 426.
Alter Imp. Gov. to Imprimis, Mr.
Alter Jeremy Canaught to Conaught.
Robert Stewart was an inserted name.
Alter Mr. Bartholomew Pipping to Tipping.
Thomas Tidman [·sic·] for Stedman.
The end names (on back side): Taylor, Goff,
Gledon, Thomas.

**384a**   Inquest, Thos. Stidman, Jan. 1693-4.
Fell through in Mr. Hilton's sawmill.

| Coroner's Jury | Jonathan Plummer |
|---|---|
| David Larkin | James Godfrey |
| Tho. Wiggin Jr. | Samuel Peas |
| Simon Wiggin | Benjamin York |
| Jeremiah Gilman | Francis Willett |
| Andrew Wiggin | Constable |
| Saml. Hilton | Nathl. Wright |
| John N ✕ ✕ | Witnesses |
| Wm. N ✕ ✕ | Jabez Colman±22 |
| Edward Woodman | Ezekiel Woodward±25 |
| | Nathl. Giddens±18 |

**384b**   Inquest, Capt. Jonathan Thing, Oct.
1694. Shot by his own gun in falling from
horseback.

| Coroner's Jury | Tho. Rollins Sr. |
|---|---|
| Mr. Wm. Ardill | Benjamin Gons |
| David Larins | Thomas Dudley |
| Thomas Spede | Richard Morgin Sr. |
| Nick Noris | Nathl. Foulsom |
| Philip Dudey | Constable |
| John Snikler Jr. | James Sinkler |
| Robert Young | Witnesses |
| Ephraim Foulsom | Samuel Thing |
| James Kid | Peter Foulsham |
| David Robeson | |

**385**   Church Seatings 3 Feb. 1697-8. [·sic·]
— Bell's Exeter 173-174.

## STRATHAM

**386**   The Shrewsbury Men.
This English list is printed rather than disregard Pope's Me. & N. H. Pioneers. They were
the owners of 'the Shrewsbury patent' in Stratham. The source is Mass. Arch. iii. 440, well
printed in N. H. Prov. Papers i. 162-164. (Alter
Brewer to Bruen). They did not sign as witnesses, but as partners consenting to receive
Obadiah Bruen as a partner. Richard, not Nicholas, Scammon, signed the copies of the early
papers in 1666. Richard Hunt did not sign the
Dover Combination in 1640 nor witness Mr.
Larkham's deed in 1642, (Bartholomew Hunt
signed the Combination.) No original owner in
the Shrewsbury patent left England. There is
no evidence that Mr. Bruen even visited Dover;
he came to Plymouth, tried Gloucester and settled in Connecticut.

| | |
|---|---|
| Richard Hunt | In 1685 R. P. sold to |
| Thomas Wingfield | Obediah Bruen. |
| Thomas Knight | In 1640 O. B. sold to |
| Thomas Hunt | Rev. Tho: Larkham. |
| William Rowley | In 1642 T. L. sold to |
| Richard Percival | William Waldron. |

Nicholas Hickman had custody of the key to
the barn on the patent.
About 1663 Richard Scammon married Mr.
Waldron's daughter.

**387**   Inquest, 'Scowmscutt,' 5 Apr. 1699.
Elisha Draper drowned in trying to recover
his trout line at Mr. Wiggin's mill pond 'this
morning.'
Samuel Sayer±24 a witness.

| Coroner's Jury | John Parkings |
|---|---|
| Theophilus Dudley | George Trunde |
| foreman | Howard Henderson |
| Moses Leavett | Brodstreet Wiggin |
| Robert Smart | Hance Woolford |
| William Parkings | William Frinch |
| John Wedgwood | James Godfrey |

**388**   Stratham. Five petitions are pre-
served from the Quamscot region of Exeter,
three for and two against separation.
Petition in 1704 or earlier.
— Prov. Papers ix. 777.
Alter Richard Downes? to Bounds.
Alter Thomas ——— to Pouel.
Alter Richard Monger sr. to Morgen.
Alter Edmund Gramon to Wm. Scamon.
— heading the second column.
Alter Thomas Spild sr. to Speed.
Alter Richard Mongen to Morgen.
Proponents 2 Dec. 1709.
— Prov. Papers iii. 406-407.
Protest dated 5 Dec. 1709.
— Prov. Papers iii. 407, xii. 113.
Proponents 10 Jan. 1715-6.—Prov. Papers ix. 779.
Signed in four columns headed by Simon Wiggin,
William Powell, Thomas Rollings, Samuel Piper
Alter Edw. Maservy to Messery.
Alter John Mason to Nason.
Alter John Searll to Satchell.
Alter John Satchell to Leare.
Alter Wm. Seaman to Scammon.
Alter James Dorety to Douty.
Protest of inhabitants of 'that tract of land
called the patent,' signed by 17, besides 8 who
had signed the petition and now retract.
— Prov. Papers ix. 780.

## Hampton and Kingston. 391-400.

**391a** The First-Comers to Hampton.

A memorandum in the handwriting of Edward Colcord, with two names interpolated by another contemporary hand.
— Norfolk Court Files (Salem), p. 124.

A note of the Families in Hampton the First summer Mr. Batcheller came to Hampton.

[John Browne*]
Mr. Husiah
Goodman Johnson
Goodman Tucke
Thomas Jones
Good. Sandersin
Good. Daves
Good. Swaine
Good. Grenfild
Abraham Perkins
Isak Perkins
Francis Pebody
Good. Cool

**Young men that had lots**
Willyam Wakfild
Willyam Fifild
Moses Coxe
Thomas Kinge
Anthony Taylor
Tho. Ward
Gilles Fuler

**Married Men**
Good. Daulton
John Hugins
Good. Mingy
Tho. Moulton
[John Moulton*]
*Interpolated names

Willyam Palmer
Good. Maston
Good. Esto
Leutenent Houerd
Robt. Casell
Good. Cros
Will. Sargent
Author Clark

**The second summer**
Good. Page
Good. Maston
Good. Auston
Good. Smith
Good. Fillbroc
Good. Sanders
Daniel Hindrake
John Wegod
Tho. Chaes
Good. Fuller
Good. Inglish
Good. Rooper
Good. Ambros
Widdou Parker

**391b** Petition against William Haward, March 7, 1642-3. — N. H. Prov. Papers i. 165 (Mass. Arch. lxvii. 33).

**392a** Early Town Grants.

The list in Dow's Hampton, pp. 18-19, is a compilation, but mainly taken from a summary on pp. 41-45 of the Town Book dated 30 June 1640. Dow omits from that list:
Timothy Dwight   (one illegible).
———— Jennery [Chenery?] if he come.
Dow rearranged the list alphabetically and inserted:
Ambrose, Bristow, Carpenter, Carre, Knight, Legat, Roper, Sleeper, Wainwright.
Special minutes entered in the Town Book list:
John Ward came not here.
Tim. Dalton Jr. — his father's.
William Inglish if he come.
Barnabas Horton if he come.
Ed Palmer adjoining to his father's.
Daniel Hendricke that was for Richard Carre.
Timothy Dwight, since W. Ropes.
Robert Tuck's name is among the first sixteen given farms.
Quite a number never came, or only stayed long enough to perform conditions. Some others who early held lands were:
Richard Cole      Benj. Wieth      Robert Knight
John Gager      William Hunton (Huntington?)
A valuation list of about 1645 includes:
Henry Green      Edward Colcord   Jonathan Thing
John Merean      John Wooding     Samuel Getchell
Edward Tuck      John Clifford    Henry Sayward
Thomas Waldo     John Bursley    (Harry Sawyer)
'Nathaniel Howard's services.'

**392b** Table of Town Officers.
— Dow's Hampton i. 563-571.

**392c** List of Witnesses Summonsed in the Eunice Cole witchcraft case (1656).
— Suff. Court Files 26203.

Bridget Hugins and dau. Susannah.
Abraham Drake      Tho: Philbrick.
Ann Colcott   Johannah Sleeper.
Sobriety Moulton.
Abraham Perkins and son.
Xpher Palmer and wife Susan.
Rich: Ormsby      Left. Hussey.
John Redman      Anthony Taylor.
John Godfrey.
Jeffrey Mingay and wife.

**393a** Seating the Meeting-House.
March 4, 1649-50. — Town Book, pp. 28-29.

**Men's Seats**
At the table: Rodger Shaw, Cristofar Husse, John Moulton, Philemon Dolton, Robert Page, William Easto, William Fuller, Robert Tuck.
On the south side against the desk:

| First Seat | Second Seat | Third Seat |
|---|---|---|
| Wm. Maraton | Edward Colcord | Thomas Maraton |
| Fran. Peabody | John Samborn | Manewill Hillyard |
| Richard Swaine | Wm. Samborn | Gesper Blak |
| Thomas Filbrik | Thomas Chaah | Moyses Cox |
| John Swaine | Wm. Moulton | John Cliffer |
| Abraham Perkines | Isak Perkinges | Antony Tailer |

At the west end of the table:

| First Seat | Second Seat | Third Seat |
|---|---|---|
| Jefere Mingo | Hen Grene | Hen Efkin |
| Antony Stanyen | Hene Dou | John Redman |
| Thomas Word | Steu Samborn | John Wedgwod |
| Edmon Johnson | Tho Levit | Giles Fuller |
| Thomas Moulton | Wi. Fifeld | Tho Sleper |
| Wm. Godfre | John Merean | William Cole |
| Fourth Seat | Fifth Seat | |
| Godfre Derborn | John Hugines | |
| Nat Bouler | John Felrik | |
| Ed Tuck | John Woding | |
| John Cask | Thomas Nudd | |
| Mo Hobes | | |
| Francea ———— | | |
| ———— Smith | | |

**Women's Seats**
in the east end of the south side

| First Seat | Second Seat | Third Seat |
|---|---|---|
| Rodger Shaw | Goody Mingo | Goody Levit |
| for a wife | Tho: Moulton's | Goody Grene |
| John Moulton's | wife | Goody Fifele |
| wife | Goody Johnson | Goody Merean |
| Goody Maraton | Goody Word | Young Goody |
| Goody Tuck | Goody Godfre | Swaine |
| Goody Dolton | Goody Chaes | Goody Swaine |
| Goody Page | Goodman Erato | the younger |
| Goody Fuller | for a wife | Goody Hilyer |

The ferst seett next Mistris Whelewrit: Ould Mistris Husse, her dafter Husse, Goody Swaine, Goo: Felbrik, Goody Pebody, Goody Brown, Mistris Stanyen, Mary Perkinges.

| Second Seat | Third Seat | Fourth Seat |
|---|---|---|
| Goody Colcord | Goody Dou | Edward Tuck's |
| John Samborne's | Goody Blake | wife |
| wife | Steven Samborn's | Goody Cask |
| Will Samborne's | wife | Young Goody |
| wife | Goody T———— | Foll———— |
| Susan Perkinges | Goody Cliffer | Goody Smith |
| Margit Moulton | Goody Cox | Goody Bouler |
| Christofar Palmer | | Goody Derborn |
| for a wife | | Goody Elkin |

Goodman Raborn, Giles Fuller, Francis Swaine in this [Fourth] seat for wives appointed.
The fore sett of the est sid of the est dore that is to be mead leving a sufisent space for a par of staires for an intended gallere:
Goody Wedgwod   Goody Sleper   Goody Redman
Goody Hobbes      Goody Cole

**393b** Cow Common Rights 23 Feb. 1645-6 and 23 March 1663. — Dow's Hampton i. 33, 62 (Town Book ii. 120-124).

**394** Church Members 18 September 1671.
— Dow's Hampton i. 357-358.
Goodwife Lewis must have been Hannah (Philbrick) Lewis of Greenland.

**395** Soldiers' Assignments of Pay to the Town. Aug. 24, 1676.          — Bodge 370.

**396** Tax List 8 May 1680.
— N. H. Hist. Coll. viii. 57, Prov. Papers i. 424 (Court Files v. 111).
Jon. wherever in this paper means John.
Alter Phillips to Phillip Towle.

**397a** Inquest, John Godfrey's child, July 13, 1680. — N. H. Hist. Coll. viii. 45.

**397b** Inquest, Nathl. Smith, 31 July 1680.
— N. H. Hist. Coll. viii. 49.
Alter Heat Lovet to Areat.

**398** Aged Men's Petition, 2 Mar. 1683-4.
— N. H. Prov. Papers i. 457.
Alter John Drown to John Brown.
Alter Isaiah to Isaack Perkins.
Alter Anthony Tabor to Anthony Talor.

**399a** Military Service, 1694-1696.
Arrests for Rioting — throwing down fences in town bounds dispute. Warrant served by Aaron Moses on ten men, and bail taken:          [N. H. Prov. Papers xii. 102-109.
John Redman for his son John Redman.
Jacob Wedgewood for John Levet.
Abraham Cole for David Wedgewood.
Isaac Marston for Caleb Marston.
Thomas Roby for James Perkins.
James Perkins for Thomas Roby.
John Lefet for Jacob Brown.
Jonathan Prescott for himself.
          Samuel Telton "cled."
          John Magoon held.

## KINGSTON

**400** The settlement of Kingston proceeded in an unusual degree on paper. If actually settled in the midst of the Second Indian War, it was ·twice· abandoned; surely once, in 1703.
The charter, dated 6 Aug. 1694, was to:

| | |
|---|---|
| *James Prescutt Sen. | Jacob Garland |
| Isaac Godfree | John Mason |
| *Thomas Philbrick | *Ebenezer Webster |
| Junior | Nathaniel Sanborn |
| *Gersham Elkens | Benjamin Sanborn |
| *Samuel Colcord | John Moulton |
| *Thomas Webster | Daniel Moulton |
| Samuel Darbon | Francis Towle |
| William Godfree | |

*Received grants 19 Dec. 1700.
Organization was effected 2 Mar. 1695, prob-

ably outside of Kingston, as follows:

| Selectmen | Constables |
|---|---|
| James Prescott Sen. | [Samuel Dearborn] |
| Isaac Godfrey | John Mason |
| Gershom Elkins | Ebenezer Webster |
| **Town Clerk** | |
| Nathaniel Sanborn | |

Frequent town meetings were held 1700-1703. Dec. 19, 1700, grants were voted to six of the patentees and six new names:

| | |
|---|---|
| Aaron Sleeper | Jabez Colman |
| Moses Elkins | Jonathan Sanborn |
| Ichabod Robey | Peter Johnson |

Early in 1701 home lots and the near-by meadows were divided to eight men 'as the first settlers:'

| | |
|---|---|
| Ebenezer Webster | Aaron Sleeper |
| Moses Elkins | Thomas Webster |
| Jonathan Sanborn | Thomas Philbrick |
| Ichabod Robey | Jabez Colman |

[All crossed out on the town book]
But in the same summer these meadows were re-divided to include five others:

| | |
|---|---|
| Samuel Colcord | ?Joseph Fifield |
| James Prescott | ?Nathaniel French |
| Edward Fifield | ?Gershom Elkins |

A grant to 17 men, 17 Mar. 1701-2 included:

| | |
|---|---|
| Jacob Gilman | Peter Johnson |
| Samuel Colcord Jun. | Jeremiah Philbrick |
| Gershom Elkins | Moses Sleeper |

10 July 1702, 16 lots laid out included:

| | |
|---|---|
| Thomas Scribner | Philip Huntoon |
| Nathan Taylor | James Bean |

A bond dated 30 Apr. 1705, binding the signers to re-settle the town 'about the first of September next' was signed by:

| | |
|---|---|
| Cornelius Clough | Samuel Fellows |
| Caleb Clough | †John Webster |
| William Long | Joseph Clifford |
| †Henry Wadleigh | Francis Mason |
| Samuel Judkins | Joseph Young |
| Thomas Sleeper | Simon French |
| †Jonathan Colcord | Stephen Gilman |
| Tristram Sanborn | †Jeremiah Clough |

†Included in a list of 35 men who by town vote 5 March 1714-5 had forfeited their rights.
8 Apr. 1707 - 22 Oct. 1707, the following had deserted and were living in or near Exeter:

| | |
|---|---|
| Edward Fifield | Philip Huntoon |
| Samuel Calcott | Daniel Beane |
| Jonathan Calcott | Jabez Colman |
| James Beane | |

---

**WHY the 'Lists.'** The method of lists has been adopted to save space, for one reason, while at the same time affording a better perspective. Instead of a very brief mention of a petition or tax-list repeated for each man whose name appears in it, a fuller account can be printed with all the names in their relative association and each man referred to it by number. This affords a wider atmosphere and is less likely to impart unreal ideas of our early New England conditions, besides often showing proximity of neighbors.

Most of the more important lists have already been printed in books to be found in all historical libraries; these are not reprinted if printed correctly or if requiring few corrections. But reference is made to every name in all of them, just as if they were all reprinted here. Thus this dictionary serves as a general index.

In printing-office exigencies many printed petitions are mangled beyond recognition, so that the citizens who headed them are lost from view and inconsequential people shuffled to the heads of columns. It has been deemed worth while to avoid this fault. The historical view has been kept as much in the foreground as possible. History rests on genealogy but should not be distorted by it.

Some of these 'lists' are plainly not contemporary papers, but compilations from documents too long to print. While not carrying the authority of an unedited reproduction of an original, it is believed that these constructed lists will convey no false impressions to the general inquirer, rather the contrary. Although dead some time, our forefathers were quite human while they lived. On the other hand we must never be so clownishly unjust as to judge the doings of a former century from the viewpoint of our own. The human eye sees in, not through, its environment.

# GENEALOGICAL DICTIONARY

## of MAINE and NEW HAMPSHIRE

**Abb(e)y** Thomas, misreading of Henry Abley.

**ABBOTT**, a general English surname.

1 **CAPT. JOHN**(5) aged ±64 in 1713, 72 in Dec.1721, trifurcated in the Abbott Gen., will dated 19 Mar., proved 5 May 1722, names wife Mary, who was Mary Hepworth, formerly of Ireland, m. at Newington 30 July 1718. He lived at Portsmouth except about ten years between the wars at Saco, where he was prominent. Lists 331b, 313a, 90, 33, 249, 335a, 330d, 316. As a coaster he served the country well in three wars. Ch. in will: **John**, eldest, b. 1676, fisherman, Portsmouth; perhaps m. 1st a dau. of Richard Webber, surely m. 11 Dec. 1715 Elizabeth Darling; will 22 June 1764, mentions seven ch., besides children of late grandson John. He d. 5 Feb. 1768. (Lists? 67, 339.) His son John, cordwainer, m. 21 Nov. 1723 Joanna Gear, dau. of John and Sarah (Wills). **James**, accused by Hannah Guptil 5 Mar. 1699-1700, m. by 1708 Susannah (Lear), widow of Philip Lambeth; was drowned in millpond, inquisition 15 July 1721, and the widow m. Samuel Adams and left will, 19 June 1750, 26 Dec. 1753; 3 sons. **Abigail**, m. 28 Feb. 1708-9 William Loud of Portsmouth who left her a widow with ch., will 23 Mar. - 27 Apr. 1743. **Walter**, given his grandfather's Great Island lot, taxed there 1720. The blacksmith John who in 1715 was in Boston, farrier, with wife Mercy (Leach), and deceased in Portsmouth in 1735, was perhaps his son and Richard Webber's grandson. **Reuben**, will 20 Mar. - 27 Nov. 1745, 7 ch. and wife Susannah; m. 9 Oct. 1715 Susannah Shortridge dau. of Richard and Alice(Creber), who m. 2d one Pitman. List 339. **Sarah**, m. 13 June 1717 Robert Pickering from Barnstable, Eng. **Ruth**, m. Sept. 1714 William Spriggs of Portsmouth. **Anna**, m. 31 May 1716 William Bradden, son of John and Prudence (Mitchell).

2 **PETER**(5) adult in 1660, List 330a, carpenter, presum. the soldier in Saco fort reported drowned 8 April 1695, as Peter was his sole heir in 1707, ±50 in 1725, in 1756 still living in Portsmouth with 4 or more ch. Lists 330d, 330e, 337, 339.

3 **RICHARD**, obviously some relation to(5), adult 1658, lived at Kittery, later at Great Island; a blacksmith, he became armorer and gunner at the fort, and later Province jailer, the prison being in the fort. While in Maine he was grand juror, 1664, and was bondsman for Capt. John Davis in 1668. He was attorney for John Turner of London in contesting Tristram Harris's estate. No ch. by two wives, Elizabeth in 1676 and Mary, widow of Stephen Graffam, who was again a widow in 1712. Lists 298, 326a, 25, 80, 313a, 331b, 317, 52.

4 **ENS. THOMAS**(5) blacksmith, d. in Berwick 8 Mar. 1712-3. As a youth he apparently lived at(3); m. Elizabeth Green, dau. of John and Julian; held lands on both sides of Quamphegan falls. Lists 33, 36, 289, 296, 298. Will 20 May 1707 names 9 ch.: **Thomas**, b. 7 Sept. 1664, named in grandfather's will, lived single, illiterate. (Lists? 37, 330d, 330e, 333a, 298.) In 1727 deeded father's land for life support to his brother Joseph's son Thomas, b. ab. 1693, called junior in 1732, who m. Elizabeth, widow of Isaac[3] Spencer and James[4] Emery. **Joseph**, m. Alice Nason, dau. of Jonathan and Sarah (Jenkins). She and son Thomas took admin. 4 Oct. 1726. 8 ch. Lists 290, 298. **Moses**, living in 1707. **John**, weaver, m. 1st 3 Jan. 1694 Abigail Nason, another dau. of Jonathan and Sarah (Jenkins), 2d, 22 Jan. 1716, Martha (Lord) Littlefield, q.v., who took admin. 25 May 1719 and m. 18 Aug. 1720 Alexander Taylor. 9 ch. Lists 290, 296, 298. **Walter**, b. 24 June 1673, d. 22 Dec. 1740, m. 3 Jan. 1694, Elizabeth Key, dau. of John, who lived long. 7 ch. Lists 290, 296. **Elizabeth**, m. Thomas[1] Butler, who came as a soldier. **Patience**, m. William Lord in 1705. **Mary**, m. Josiah Goodrich of Berwick. **Hannah**, m. 6 Nov. 1712 Humphrey[4] Chadbourne.

5 **WALTER**, vintner and innholder, at Portsmouth by 1645. Will 16 May, 26 June 1667, named two sons of Thomas, and ch. Lists 43, 323, 326a, 330a, 330c, 47. His wife Sarah, 64 in 1681, mistress of a Portsmouth tavern with two husbands and none, was otherwise in the public eye. She m. 2d Mr. Henry Sherbourne. Ch.: **Peter**, b. by 1639.

**Sarah,** m. Mr. Thomas Wills. **Thomas,** b. 1643. **William. Walter,** d. at Jamaica, admin. granted to his brother Thomas 29 June 1675. **John,** 1649. **Mary,** b. ab. 1652, by two husbands was founder of two well-known families, m. 1st Thomas[1] Guptill, 2d William[1] Caverly. **Elizabeth,** m. Leonard[1] Drown.

**ABDY,** Matthew, Monhegan fisherman keeping his family in Boston. Lists 75b, 111. Came in The Abigail, 1635; ±28 in 1654, ±48 in 1669; m. 1st Tabitha, dau. of Robert Reynolds, 2d 24 May 1662 Alice Cox, prob. from Maine. Ch. **Mary,** 1648. **Tabitha,** 1652. **Matthew,** in old age bed maker and sweeper at Harvard College, d. Dec. 1731, and another son, m. in 1687, living in New Haven in 1732, if we believe the humorous verse by Rev. John Seccombe, grandson of our Maine Seacomb.

**ABINGTON,** William, possibly the brother of Mr. John of Maryland. In Piscataqua court in 1642 he was sued "for letting a prisoner go," also won a suit against Joseph Jenks.

**ABLEY,** Henry, shipmaster and factor of Bristol, Eng., coming here 1637-1651.

**Aborn,** or Rabone, George. See Haborne.

**ACCABY,** Thomas, Portsmo. 1671. List 326c.

**Accutt,** Samuel. List 315c. See Alcock.

**Ackerman,** see Akerman.

**Ackermucke,** Dennis, see McCormick.

**ACTON,** (Batten?), John, N. Yarmouth. List 214.

**ADAMS,** the 57th commonest English and Welch surname, and became the 11th commonest in New England.

**1 ABEL,** servant to Dame Hunkins, Portsmouth, aged 40 in 1660. List 326c.

**2 ABRAHAM,** b. 16 Jan. 1641-2, son of Nathaniel of Weymouth and Boston, came early to Falmouth Foreside for a short time (List 224), later an innkeeper in Boston, m. 1st by 1665 Sarah Mackworth, dau. of Mr. Arthur and Mrs. Jane; 2d Abigail Wilmot, dau. of Nicholas, who in Oct. 1694 stripped the house and was taken by John Frizell to Phila.; yet was named ex. in husband's will 6 Apr. - 18 Apr., 1700, and lived till c. 1716. Ch. **Sarah,** m. 1st one Scarlet; 2d, 25 July 1694, Peter Grant, of Boston, mariner. **Abraham,** b. in Boston 11 Nov. 1667. **Jane,** b. 22 Feb. 1669, m. John Snelling of Boston, blockmaker, who named her and "children" in his will 16 Feb. - 14 Mar. 1699-1700. She next m. 25 June 1705 John Chamberlain. 1? ch. **Mackworth,** b. 17 Apr. 1672. **Isaac,** b. 10 Nov. 1674. **Zachariah,** mariner, d. 16 May 1703, by wife Dinah Lord, m. 3 July 1701, had an only dau., and his wid. m. 24 Oct. 1706 William Hayden of Boston. Only two Mackworth ch. named in will. By 2d wife, **Abigail,** b. 25 Jan. 1687, d. 20 Nov. 1702. **Mary,**

b. 11 June 1690, was the widow Ellicott in 1718, app. m. 1st Vines Ellicott Jr., 2d, 15 Jan. 1724, Ebenezer Allen. **Samuel,** b. 11 Feb. 1691-2. **Abraham,** b. 14, d. 16 July 1693. **Elizabeth,** of Charlestown, 3 May 1715 when she m. Francis Gilbert of Boston, slater.

**3 CHARLES,** b. ±1621, bot of John Ault in Durham 10 Apr. 1645; about 1655 built and fenced where he lived until killed in 1694. Constable in 1662. Lists 354abc, 356a, 361a, 362b, 363b, 311c, 365-6, 357c, 359a, 54, 49, 52, 94, 367a, 57, 62, 367b. m. Rebecca Smith. Ch. **Deliverance,** accused James Wiggin Jr. in 1679. **Charles** 1668. **Mary,** m. Wm. Tasker. **Sarah,** 1671, m. 10 Jan. 1691-2 Henry Nock, 2d Eleazer Wyer. **Samuel,** lot layer and juryman in 1694. Killed with w. and ch. 1694. List 367b. **Mercy** or **Ursula** 13 Mar. 1674, taken 19 July 1694; m. in Canada Charles Brisebois, and d. bef. 1732 leaving ch. List 99. — Samuel Adams, List 368b, is unexp.; one Samuel m. at Portsm. Susannah (Lear) Lambeth-Abbott.

**4 CHARLES**(3), adm. father's est. 9 Jan. 1694-5. His own inv. was taken 9 Nov. 1695. List 62. Wife Temperance Benmore, dau. of Philip and Rebecca (Tibbetts). Ch. **Rebecca,** m. Joseph Durrell. **Esther** m. aft. 1716 Thos. Bickford.

**5 CHRISTOPHER,** the earliest of his name in N. E., first appeared, "mariner," of Portsm. in 1668, buying his Kittery homestead, which fell to Hon. Mark Dennett, who wrote "by tradition from Wales." Lists 296-8. Will 13 June 1686, 21 Sep. 1687, names 4 ch., "cousin" Isaac Goodridge, wife Margaret. List 331c. She was dau. of Mark Hunking and d. c. 9 Dec. 1722, leaving will. Goodridge called her "My aunt Mrs. Margaret Adams." Ch. **Anne,** m. 1st Joseph Couch Jr., 2d David Hill, 3d Nicholas Weeks. **John,** 1674, shipwright. Lists 291, 297-8. Will 2-15 June 1737 names wife Amy (Dennett) and 6 ch. **Mary,** (List 331c), m. 1st Alexander Shapleigh, 2d John Dennett. **Mark,** d. 1706-1722 s.p.

**6 DAVID,** bro. of(2), in 1667 wit. his brother's deed from Mrs. Mackworth. Of 8 ch. by two wives recorded in Boston, only one survived his death in 1705, as stated in petn. of dau. **Sarah,** b. 7 Mar. 1664, m. Elihu Wardwell (of Boston, carpenter, living 1710).

**7 DERRICK,** ±36 in 1678, boatswain of The Primrose, N. H.

**8 FRANCIS,** in 1651 sued (N. H.) Mr. Clement Campion for 9 mos. wages.

**9 GEORGE,** witness at Scarboro 1685-1688. List 228c.

**10 JAMES,** b. 29 Mar. 1668, son of James (Scotch prisoner) and Priscilla (Ramsden) Adams of Concord. Witnessed S. Wheelwright's will 30 Jan. 1699-1700. Original

memb. of Wells church 29 Oct. 1701. Lists 269b, 39, 99. Alive in Montreal 2 June 1706 he may have d. bef. reaching Boston. His heirs in 1729 were two bros. and a sister. Wife Catherine Ford, m. in Charlestown **5** Jan. 1696-7, m. 2d 14 Oct. 1706 William Larrabee. Ch. wiped out by the Indians: **Catherine**, b. at Charlestown 11 Sep. 1697. **Mary**, b. in Wells 19 Mar., 1699-1700. **James**, b. 2 Nov. 1701. **Infant**, b. Aug. 1703. **Clement**, b. and d. at Montreal Nov. 1704. **Clement**, b. Nov. 1705, soon d.

11 **JOHN**, in 1662 aut. **1** as wit. to deed, Bailey to Endell, of the Isles of Shoals.

12 **JOHN**, in 1665 was haying with T. Perkins for Major Waldron. Lists 356ghk.

13 **JONATHAN**, bro. of (2), blockmaker, Boston, d. 7 Apr. 1707 aged 64. Will **1** Apr. names wife Rebecca (Andrews), dau. of James and Dorcas (Mitton), and ch. (out of 11 recorded in B.): Samuel (eldest son), Jonathan, Nathaniel, James, Rebecca, Dorcas, Mary, Lydia.

14 **NATHANIEL**(16). List 99. Wife, **Magdalen**, dau. of Mainwaring and Mary (Moulton) Hilton, m. 2d 1696 Elias Weare. Ch. **Nathaniel**, b. 24 Sept. 1693, blacksmith and fisherman on Star Isl., m. Mary who m. 2d 1737-8 Wm. Robinson. 4 ch. rec.

15 **PETER**, d. 1 Nov. 1671, adm. 26 Mar. 1672 to Thos. Jackson, Portsmo., under bond to secure the heirs.

16 **PHILIP**(18), selectman of York 1665 grand jury 1666, 1671, 1672. Adm. to son Thomas 8 Mar. 1691[2. Lists 273, 275, 276. His widow Elizabeth (dau. of Thomas Turpin) in will 6 June - 18 Oct. 1710 named dau. Sarah Black, grandch. Daniel and Elizabeth Black, Nathaniel Adams, Samuel Johnson. Ch. **Thomas**, 1648. **Elizabeth**, m. Samuel Johnson. **Sarah**, m. Daniel Black. **Nathaniel**. **James**, a degenerate, banished in 1679; adm. to Thomas Donnell in 1693.

17 **RICHARD**, merchant, petitioned for land at Sheepscot, c. 1687.

18 **SAMUEL**, d. early at York. Ch. **Philip**, b. ±1632, and perh. John Parker's wife. Land granted to Philip adjoined land "sometime his father's, now John Parker's." List 273.

19 **THOMAS**(16), York. List 38. M. Hannah, dau. of John Parker. Will 18 Apr. 1726 - 24 June 1737. Ch. (List 279): **Hannah**, b. Aug. 1676, m. 5 May 1698 Thomas Baker. **Philip**, b. Aug. 1678, d. 14 Apr. 1747, m. his cousin, Elizabeth Roanes, dau. of Wm. and Mary (Parker). 1 dau. **Samuel**, b. Feb. 1680-1, m. Lydia Gowell, dau. of Richard. Will 6 Apr. - 15 May 1753. 13 ch. **Hezekiah**, b. 1686, m. Mary Weare, dau. of Joseph and Hannah (Penwell). 8 ch. **Esther**, b. 1686, m. John Booker. 8 ch.

**Nathan**, b. 1688, m. Hannah, widow of Thomas Palmer and dau. of Joshua and Ann (Lancaster) Remick. 10 ch. **Elizabeth**, 1691, m. 17 Jan. 1713-4 John Sedgley. 7 ch. **Thomas**, b.1694, m.4 Apr.1723 Sarah Mitchell, dau. of Richard and Sarah (Couch). 6 children.

20 **WALTER**, Scarborough, 1689; had m. Mary (Boaden) widow of Samuel Oakman, dau. of Ambrose Boaden.

21 **WILLIAM**, a runaway apprentice brought from England by Mr. Thomas Withers and 20 Nov. 1672 apprenticed to himself for 7 years. By 1683 he had sold 4 a. of land given to him by Mr. Withers. One William m. 23 Oct. 1718 Mary Lang, dau. of John and Grace (Brookins) and the same year bought land; d. 1752. 3 sons.

**ADGER**, Thomas. Lists 15, 4, and possibly (Alger) 13. Thos. Ager, a child, drowned off the wharf (in Salem?) 23 May 1675.

**AGAWAM**, William, aged 18, 8 Dec. 1677, (of Ipswich Indian blood?); caught in the plundering voyage to Cape Porpus.

**AGNEW**, Nivan, "Niven the Scott." In 1676 he adm. the est. of James Barrow or Barry, (having presum. m. his childless widow), and lived on his land in Berwick. Lists 356e, 361b, 81, 28, 288, 298.

**AINUP** or **Arnup**, Will, Newcastle, 1696. List 315c.

**AKERMAN**, a West of England surname.

1 husband of **SARAH**, of Portsmouth, "sister-in-law" of Edward Melcher. In the 1693 church seatings she was "Goody," not widow, and in the same year William Williams, butcher, q.v., admitted to lodging with her nine years. List 335a. In 1719, "widow," she deeded her land to her dau. **Mary**, wife of Henry Tibbetts, who in 1713 was Mary Samson.

2 **BENJAMIN**, Portsmouth, butcher, doorkeeper to the court, m. 1st in 1708 Elizabeth Hodge, 2d Mary Bradden, dau. of John and Prudence (Mitchell). His will, 31 Dec. 1757-25 Jan. 1758, provides for wife Mary, and gives to son Benjamin (the tanyard at Islington that was Kirke's) and seven other children. List 339.

**AKERS**, Samuel, Exeter. List 376b.

**ALBERRY**, John, Illutherian at North Yarmouth 1686. List 213.

**ALCOCK**, Olcott, a typical English surname.

1 **JOHN**, called "farmer," prob. as rent-collector for Sir F. Gorges at York. There by 1639. Alderman in city board. Selectman and grand juryman repeatedly, 1653-1674, except under the King's Commissioners. Com. t.e.s.c. Referee. Ensign 1659. Lists 22, 24, 25, 273-277. Adm. 6 July 1675 to sons

Joseph, Job, S. Dummer, R. Banks. Wife Elizabeth in 1650 and survived. **Samuel,** grants in 1652, 1653; witness in 1652; sued for cutting timber in 1653. Lists 275, 276. **Mary,** b. 1632, m. Peter Twisden. **Joseph,** b. 1634. **John,** wit. deed in 1650. **Job,** b. 1638, shipwright and magistrate; filled continuously all the offices held by his father; also lieut. and captain, assemblyman in 1680, councillor named in Royal Charter. After the York massacre "a hundred souls" in his house had their sole dependence on him for food. He was a judge of the Court of Common Pleas (Chief Justice in 1693) until his removal to Portsmouth in 1696, where he was promptly made a justice there. Lists 83, 29, 32, 33, 36, 335a, 331c, 330d, 337. Wife Dorothy Reyner, dau. of Rev. John and Frances (Clark), predec. him. Lists 331c, 335a. Will, 2 Dec. 1712 — 27 Jan. 1716-7, remembers many relatives and makes his chief heir his wife's neice Abigail (Broughton), wife of Robert Walker. **Elizabeth,** m. Richard Banks. **Hannah,** m. Capt. Geo. Snell. **Sarah,** m. 1st John Giddings of Ipswich, (10 ch.), 2d Henry Herrick of Beverly; d. in Gloucester 29 Dec. 1711. **Lydia,** m. Rev. Shubael Dummer.

2 **JOHN**(3), shipwright, Kittery. List 36. Nunc. will proved 25 Aug. 1693 names only wife, who d. within three months, Joanna Ameredith, dau. of John and Joanna (Treworgye). Ch. named in Grandfather Ameredith's will 26 Jan. 1690-1, **Joanna,** m. 2 Aug. 1706 at Kittery Wm. Sentle. 1 son. **Abigail. Mary. Joseph,** master mariner, Portsmouth. List 339. In 1754 among the Ameridith heirs were Alcock Stevens, cooper, Joanna and John Martin, mariner, Anna Harvey, widow, all of Newcastle. Adm. 26 Feb. 1745-6 to widow Keturah (m. 9 Apr. 1712 Keturah Rawlins, dau. of Capt. Benj. and Eunice of Boston; her will 5 — 30 Oct. 1754). 5? ch.

3 **JOSEPH**(1), carpenter, Kittery. Sergeant 1659. Lot layer 1671, 1674. Grand jury 1676. Died in 1677. In 1662 both with wife Abigail, dau. of Daniel and Elizabeth (Lever), sold "my house and land" in Eliot. Lists 275, 276, 298. Doc. Hist. vi. 275. She was "Widow Alcock Junior" in Oct. 1678, but soon m. Robert Rowsley, mariner, of Portsmouth, where she took lodgers and was living in 1708. Ch. **John. Samuel,** b. March 1665. **Mary,** m. David Vaughan of Boston. 8? ch. Joseph, List 318b.

4 **CAPT. SAMUEL** (3), master mariner, Portsmouth. Juryman 1696. Lists 315bc, 96. Died 13 Oct. 1708. Will, 17 May 1704, names other relatives besides son and wife, who was Elizabeth Chadbourne, dau. of Humphrey and Lucy (Treworgye). In 1691

she was appar. at a dafice at a York tavern when the party were captured by the Indians. List 331c. The widow in partnership with her cousin Elizabeth (Treworgye) Field-Cross, kept a dry goods shop (sometime "John Field & Co.") Her will, 4 July 1743 — 28 Mar. 1744, untangles the snarl of the probates of her husband and her son as printed. Only child, **Samuel.** List 339. Married, 11 Oct. 1722, Elizabeth Wheelwright, dau. of Col. John and Mary (Snell), who m. 2d 29 May 1726 John Newmarch. Adm. 21 Oct. 1723 to mother Elizabeth. Samuel[5] only grandchild, bap. at Wells 5 June 1726, boatbuilder, Portsmo., died in 1747.

**ALDEN,** Mr. John, ±42 1679-80; m. dau. of Maj. Wm. Phillips. List 244c.

**ALDRICH,** 1 John, ±40 Dec. 1669, carpenter of the ship Adventure, Capt. Marchartt, Great Island.

2 **JOHN,** New Hamp. 1686, may have been living at Groton in 1691. — Savage.

3 **WILLIAM,** in 1662 confessed judgment in N. H. court in favor of John Penwell, Mr. John Howell, Richard Allison.

**ALDWORTH,** Matthew, wit. for Francis Knight in 1649, presum. member of the eminent Bristol family which came not but sent many. See Elbridge, Knight, Shurt.

**ALEXANDER,** a general English and Scotch surname, the 59th commonest in Scotland.

1 **JAMES,** Jerseyman, Casco? List 99.

2 **JOSEPH,** not unlik. related to (3), penman, ±39 in 1693, flourished on both sides of the Piscataqua 1681-1694, chiefly in Portsmouth. In 1693 he was nursing Mr. John Alcock and urgent to draft his will. Possibly the same ±42 in 16.. working in Edward Gouge's tanyard in Boston. Lists 57, 335a.

3 **RICHARD,** spendthrift merchant taken in by Major Shapleigh, and kept his books. Thanked God for easy existence yet one day in 1673 "Major Shapleigh's man" got drunk. Corresponded with John Wingfield, Barbadoes merchant. John Shapleigh made use of the back side of the draft of a cultured and colorful letter reviewing his life addressed to "Mr. Johnson." Here 1665, living 1676.

4 **THOMAS,** ±27 in 1688, wit. to S. Windsor's will at the Shoals.

**ALGER,** spoken Auger, a West of England surname.

1 **ANDREW,** b. 1610. The Alger brothers named their Indian purchase in Scarborough Dunstan for Dunstone in the parish of Yealmpton, Devon. Andrew came with Winter and after his time was out became a fishing master himself, having his house on Prout's Neck. Cleeve in 1643

called him "of Stratton's Island," a name for Scarborough. He had a grant in Saco before Mass. came in, but led a company to withdraw to Dunstan. Juryman 1640, constable 1661, selectman, surveyor. Lists 21, 22, 239a, 243a, 231, 235, 236, 83, 238a. He was killed about 10 Oct. 1675. His will, made 23 Mar. 1669-70, was proved at Salem 30 June 1676, by his widow, Agnes, who was b. 1621. List 235. Ch. **John**, b. 1640-1. **Daughter**, m. John Ashton and quickly d. s.p. **Elizabeth**, b. 1644, m. John Palmer. **Joanna**, b. 1650, m. 1st Elias Oakman, 2d John Mills; living in 1727. **Andrew. Matthew.**

2 **ANDREW**, at Sheepscot in 1665, was prob. the same at Cape Porpus in 1670. Lists 12, 256. Andrew on the Salem water front in 1678 was prob.(3). The Cape Porpus man and his wife were refugees at Newbury, when he died, Aug. 1694.

3 **ANDREW**(1), shipmaster, killed in Falmouth battle 21 Sept. 1689. He m. at Falmouth c. 1684 Jane Andrews, dau. of James and Dorcas (Mitton), who m. 2d 19 Feb. 1692 Robert Davis of Boston. In 1690 Jane Algur was up for selling without license. Ch. **Dorcas**, m. 24 Oct. 1706 Matthew Collins of Boston. 3 ? ch.

4 **LIEUT. ARTHUR**, brother of (1), ±45 in 1670, prob. the same bap. in Yealmpton, Devon, 29 Aug. 1622, s. of John. John Algar of Dunstone in Yealmpton was buried in 1630, Agnes wife of John Algar Sen. of Dunstone in 1634. Algers were many in that parish, several Andrews, only one Arthur. The will of Richard Alger of Yealmpton, 25 Apr. 1616 — 30 May 1626, names son John the elder, son John the younger, wife Margaret. One Richard was of Dunstone. Constable 1658, grand jury 1661, 1665-8, 1671-4, attorney for the town 1665, sergeant 1665, lieut. commanding 1668, 1675, deputy to Gen. Court 1671-2. Lists 231, 232, 235, 88. Wounded at Dunstan when his brother was killed, he died at Wm. Sheldon's house 14 Oct. 1675. His widow Anne, (dau. of Godfrey and Alice (Frost) Sheldon), was taken to Marblehead, and proved his nunc. will 30 June 1676. They brought up three sons of Giles Roberts. She m. 2d the Woburn innkeeper, Samuel Walker, 1617-1686, was the schooldame after his death, and d. 21 Mar. 1716. She had two Walker ch. Isaac, b. 1 Nov. 1677, settled in Concord, N. H., (where a confused tradition handed down made her name Ann Bruce), 9 ch. and Ezekiel Walker, b. 5 Mar. 1679, lived in Boston, 9 ch.

5 **JOHN**, signed Allger as wit. 1664 to will of Mary Lux, who had lived at Cape Porpus, but was prob. at Damariscove when her will was made. Cf. John (6), Andrew (2).

6 **JOHN**(1), Boston, innholder; m. **Mary** Wilmot, dau. of Nicholas. He prob. d. early, as his children were with their aunt Adams at Charlestown: **John**, carpenter, lost in the Canada Expedition, 1690. Will 4 Apr. 1690. **Elizabeth**, m. John Milliken of Boston. They settled on the Alger lands at Dunstan in Scarb., where he d. in 1749, she 9 Feb. 1754. 10 ch. rec. at Boston 1691-1711.

7 **MATTHEW**(1), mariner. Lists 223a, 238b. Went master of a transport in the Phips Expedition, 1690, and died of fleet fever. Married in 1680 Martha, widow of Robert Carver, Boston, boatman. Ch. **Mary**, b. 9 Jan. 1680-1. **Hannah**, b. 22 May 1686; d. at Gloucester in 1696. His widow lived at Gloucester and m. 9 Nov. 1700 Jeffrey Massey of Salem, who d. at Glouc. 10 Mar. 1715-6, she 13 Aug. 1718, ±62.

8 **THOMAS**, from Newton Ferrers, 3 miles from Dunstone. List 21.

9 **THOMAS**, Damariscove, 1672; possibly Adger.

10 **TRISTRAM**, came with Winter, wife in Eng. List 21. At Brixton, an hour's walk from Dunstone, one Tristram m. in 1613 and had a dau. b. 1618.

**ALGOOD**, John, sued Nathan Bedford in Wells court 1673.

**ALKINS**, Robert, in 1684 master of the Ketch Supply (Great Isl.); m. 9 Nov. 1686 Patience (Fernald), wid. of Ebenezer Evans, dau. of Thomas and Temperance (Hunkins) Fernald. As Widow Alkins she was taxed, 1690, 1698. Lists 332a, 335a, 330d, 336c, 337. Only child **Elizabeth**, b. 10 Jan. 1687-8, m. 8 Aug. 1706 John Kennard.

**ALLARD**, (Hollard?), an uncommon English surname.

1 **HUGH**, ±35 in 1674; m. at Isles of Shoals Grace, widow of William Tucker, and cont. his fishing trade. She was about 12 years his senior, with many children, and became the midwife at the Shoals. In 1671 he mortgaged his house and fish plant on Smuttinose to Mr. Wainwright to secure delivery of fish, and in 1686 still owned them. Lists 305c, 307a. Appar. only child, **James**.

2 **JAMES**(1), taxed at Sandy Beach 1691, was fisherman at the Shoals. Lists 332b, 316. His widow Oner was cited to adm. 19 June 1722. Ch. appar. **James**, living with Wm. Wallis in 1695, in 1702 had quit the service of Mr. James Randall. Constable of Gosport in 1723; living in 1738 when James Jr. m. Sarah Down. **Grace**, m. Elias Parcher 12 Aug. 1708. **Mary**, in trouble in 1710, presum. m. Roger Thomas 6 July 1717.

**ALLEN**, the 38th commonest English surname, 53d Scotch (Allan), became 6th in New England.

1 **ARNOLD**, at Casco Bay 1640, from London; juror, appraiser. Wife Mary was app. sister of Richard Tucker's wife. Only child was apprenticed by Mr. Tucker to Thomas Dexter of Lynn bef. 1645. His lands in some way passed to the Moshers, Mosher's Island had been called Arnold's Island.

2 **CHARLES**, Greenland, 1657, b. by dep. 1623-1631, living 28 Aug. 1706; m. 2d 1667, Susannah Huggins, dau. of John and Bridget. Lists 335a, 331c. In 1705 he deeded his farm for life support to son Daniel. Lists 330a, 326ac, 52, 332b, 57, 62, 335a. Ch. by first wife: **Mary**, m. 1st Edward Fox, 2d 18 Oct. 1716 Hance Wolford; living in Greenland in 1740. By second wife: **Daniel**, b. 1669; d. 22 Jan. 1745-6; m. in 1699 Hannah Berry. Lists 335a, 330d, 337, 338ac. 2? sons. **Charles**, b. 1670. Lists 62, 335a. Of Wells in 1747. **Susannah**. **Martha**, in 1741 was wife of John Bickford of Dover Neck. **John**, m. Mary Burnham, dau. of Samuel of Durham, where he settled; Rochester 1734-1743. Lists 338abc. 6 ch. bap. in Durham. **Jude**, d. 16 June 1738. His wife Deborah Locke, m. bef. 1710, left will 17 - 23 Sep. 1753. List 338b. 7? ch. In 1744 the estate of Charles (2) had descended in sevenths.

3 **EDWARD** (Alleyn) witnessed deeds, Thos. Atkins to Robert Edmunds, Kennebec, 1664, 1669, 1673. Poss. a Boston trader and the same named overseer in Mr. Purchase's will. Edward Alleyn of Boston, tailor, m. 7 May 1652 Martha Way, dau. of George and ―― (Purchase), and had 7 ch. recorded in Boston.

4 **EDWARD**, received from his father, Hope Allen (wife Rachel), of Boston, a large part of Portland, bot from Mr. Cleeve, and sold it to George Bramhall and Henry Kirke. App. came first to Berwick, and was fined in York Court, July 1673, for abs. from meeting, but soon settled on Dover Neck below Thompson's Point. Prison keeper 1678, prob. bookkeeper for Maj. Waldron. In 1703-1704 he visited Lynn, to assist the widow about his bro. Capt. Benjamin's estate. Lists 359ab, 55a, 52, 57. His wife, Sarah, died about 1720. Ch. 3 sons and "several" daus.: **Edward**, b. c. 1670, (perh. the same rec. at Boston 11 July 1671); m. Ann Coleman dau. of Joseph. 10 ch. rec. at Nantucket 1693-1718. **Jacob**, cordwainer, lived west of Back River, Dover. Will 8 July 1752 - 31 Jan. 1753. He m. 1st 5 Feb. 1701-2 Martha Dam, dau. of William and Martha (Nute); 2d Mary (Spencer) Jones, wid. of Joseph, dau. of Moses and Elizabeth Spencer; living in 1761. 6 ch. by each wife. **Son**, "went to sea." **Rachel**, m. 3 Oct. 1692 John Twambly. **Sarah**, m. Benj. Wentworth of Somersworth.

Prob. also: **Leah**, m. 1 Dec. 1699 Thomas Canney, and **Elizabeth**, m. 2 Dec. 1700 Thomas Pinkham.

5 **JOHN** (Alleyn), came to Sheepscot as second husband of Mary (Jent) Mason, widow of John, dau. of John and Elizabeth Jent. Was early around Sagadahoc but undisting. from John (6) as wit. 1657 at Pemaquid, or at Damariscotta 1672. John (5) was J. P. and prob. sheriff 1686. As late as 1699 he bot a dwelling and fishing plant on Damariscove. Self and wife appeared before the Eastern Claims Committee. One Mary Alleyn died at Marblehead Jan. 1726-7. Lists 16, 17, 162, 163.

6 **JOHN**. See John (5) and Lists 13, 85. Wife Rebecca Reynolds, dau. of Nicholas, Esq., and Dorothy. They lived on the Reynolds land on the w. side of the Kennebec, and were refugees at Marblehead, where they died. Ch. **Nicholas**. **John**, b. at Kennebec, m. Hannah Moses. 4 daus. **Miriam**, bp. at Marb. 21 June 1685; m. 24 Feb. 1707-8 John Bird. 2 ch. **Abraham**, bap. 15 Dec. 1689. Made trip to the Reynolds lands with bro. John and Capt. Michael Hodge in 1736. **Ebenezer**, bap. 1 Jan. 1692-3.

7 **JOHN**. Pemaquid soldier 1689. List 126.

8 **JOSEPH**. Witness at N. Yarm. 1674. Y. D. ii. 190.

9 **LEWIS**, blacksmith, bot in Wells 1685 house and shipping, built mill; in 1704 he had removed to Annapolis Royal and the French governor sent him to the English to exchange prisoners. In 1720 he and wife Margaret were still there. As late as 1733 he visited Wells.

10 **PETER**. In York Court Oct. 1660 he and John Bayden paid John Clark's fine. Four years later one of the name perished in the woods near Andover.

11 **ROBERT**, Sagadahoc wit. 1651, Pemaquid wit. 1658. Poss. the Allen of "Allen's Falls," Sheepscot. He dep. in Bristol, Eng., 21 Feb. 1658-9, that he had known John Brown from ab. 1641 to June 1658. One Robert Allen and Margaret Seale were before the Boston Court of Asso. 6 June 1637. At Marblehead in 1642 Sarah wife of Ro. Allen and John Devereaux were witnesses. Poss. John (6) was a son.

12 **ROBERT**, Kittery, 1666. A descendant wrote about 1830 that two brothers came from England, one settling in Kittery, the other further south. Lists 380, 78, 298, 358b. He m. Hannah White, dau. of John, and lived on her land. Adm. to son Francis 21 Apr. 1701. Known ch. **Francis**, Quaker, bot out Wm. Thompson's heirs in 1708. Wife Hannah Jenkins, dau. of Jabez and Hannah (Curtis). In 1708 Wm. Frye called him "cousin." Will 8 Mar. 1744-5 - 17 Oct. 1749.

11 ch. **Robert,** b. c. 1680; living in 1722; m. in 1700 Sarah (Litten), widow of John Lary, dau. of Geo. and Sarah Litten. 1? ch. **Elizabeth,** m. 23 Sept. 1700 John Cole. [Stack. adds **Anna,** m. 10 Sep. 1702 Nathaniel Fernald.]

13 **GOV. SAMUEL,** Esq., a London merchant whose ambition led him to buy the Mason patent (by a conveyance eventually held to be illegal), lived here about 7 years, died 5 May 1705, in his 70th year, and was buried in the fort at Newcastle. Before coming he had been represented by lieutenant governors. His wife, Elizabeth Dowse, was an heiress. See Farmer's Belknap and Wentworth Gen. Ch. **Thomas,** came with his father but returned; d. in 1715. 3 ch. **Elizabeth,** second wife of John Usher, Esq. 4 ch. **Jane,** m. 2 July 1708 Thomas Steel of Boston. 7 ch. **Frances,** m. in 1702 George Walton. **Ann,** m. 5 June 1723 in Boston Thos. Locklin.

14 **THOMAS.** List 368b. Elizabeth, "aged wife of Thos. Allen," was bap. in Durham 26 June 1726. She was Elizabeth (Roberts), widow of Nicholas Dunn, dau. of Wm. Roberts, and presum. brought her second husband back to Durham with her. She was living in 1746. Her son Nicholas Dunn and one Thomas Allen, who m. Elizabeth Tucker 30 Feb. 1723-4, were shipwrights at Kittery.

15 **WALTER,** b. 1643-1646, deposed that he came in 1660. Lists 298, 290. First wife prob. the Elizabeth Allen insulted by Thos. Newberry in 1671, and a Berwick wit. in 1676; m. 2d by 1694 Mary Holmes, dau. of Thomas and Joanna (Freathy). Both were bp. 22 Apr. 1725. Only 4 known ch. **James,** living in 1734. Lists 330 def, 279, 38. After living in Portsmouth, where he m. Dorothy Barsham, dau. of Mr. John and Mehitable Barsham, he settled in York. 8? ch. **Abigail,** m. in 1708 Jonathan Stimpson; widow, with a son, in 1736. **Samuel,** m. 19 June 1717 Jane Cook. **Joseph,** m. Elizabeth Triggs. 3? ch. Of the following possible ch. the two last are improbable. [**John,** m. perh. two wives: at York Elizabeth Thompson, dau. of Alexander. 1 ch.; 14 Feb. 1721-2 Elizabeth Shears, dau. of Tamson (Gowell) Shears-Hanscom.] [Elisha, York, ferryman, drowned on trip to Isles of Shoales 1 July 1624. Lists 279, 38. Wife, Elizabeth Beal, dau. of Arthur and Anne (Hilton), lived to old age on Stage Neck, lately dec. in 1762. 10 ch.] [Thomas, shipwright and innkeeper, m. 1st in Portsmo. 24 Aug. 1712 Mary Couch, dau. of Joseph and Joanna (Dearing); 2d, 30 Feb. 1723-4, Elizabeth Tucker. Removed to Newbury. See Thomas (14).]

16 **WILLIAM.** Trelawny Plant. List 21.

17 **WILLIAM,** Newcastle, accused 27 May 1702 by Elizabeth Cranch.

**ALLERTON,** Isaac, Mayflower passenger and aggressive merchant, perh. the most widely known, personally, of all New England planters, in 1633 set up a trading station at Machias, promptly sacked by the French. See Vines, Savage, Small and Allied Families, pp. 596-669.

**ALLISET,** John. Falm. wit. 1672. Dep. in Boston 6 May 1731 ±80, well knew Mr. George Cleeve; lived 8 years with Mr. Geo. Munjoy and Mary his wife. Overseer of cordwood, Boston, 1689, 1691. Wife Grace Dyer, dau. of Christopher. 9? ch. See Small and Allied Families p. 1175.

**ALLISON,** Allanson, common in the North of England.

**ANDREW** "Alison," List 256, misreading of Alger?

1 **MATTHEW,** witnessed deed to (2) in 1673. List 237a.

2 **RALPH,** ±54 in 1676. Evid. new arrivals in Scarborough, the Court 7 Nov. 1665 dealt with absence from meeting of "Mis Dixon, sister to Mr. Hene: Watts" and "Mr. Ralph Allison & his wife," and his children. Appar. Mrs. Dixon was his own or his wife's mother, more likely his, as the grandfather was Ralph Watts of Cockford in Yorkshire. Clerk of the writs 1674, grand jury 1675. Lists 26, 236, 237ac. Besides the surviving heirs were appar. son Matthew and dau. wife of Joseph Oliver, unless he was first husband of **Jane,** m. (1st prob. Sergt. Joseph Oliver), 2d Peter Shaw, 3d Robert Leach of Manchester, was widow in Beverly in 1734. **Anne,** m. Andrew Brown.

3 **RICHARD,** ±29 in 1662, ordered to fetch his wife or go to her. Signed joint note with Rachel Webster. Accused 27 June 1665 by Frances Lashly of Dover. In 1710 Susannah Elison lived in Portsmouth.

**ALMARY,** Robert, 27 June 1676 member of crew attaching the Black Cock, from Barbadoes, for wages; ordered back to England. Jury 1696, innkeeper 1714. Lists 52, 329, 330def, 334e, 335a, 337. Will 20 Feb. 1711-2 - 8 June 1716. Wife Hannah Partridge, dau. of John and Mary (Fernald), d. c. 1733. Lists 331c, 335a, 339. Ch. **John.** List 339. Appar. d. s.p. and Capt. John who m. Love Cutt in 1733 was a grandson. **Hannah,** m. John Hill. **Bartholomew. George,** bap. 21 Jan. 1693-4, m. 4 Aug. 1713 Martha Hardin. 2 ch. **Robert,** bap. 15 Sept. 1695, m. 15 Nov. 1716 Mary Hart. 4 ch. **Rachel,** m. John Robinson of Boston.

**ALSOB,** Alsup, Thomas. Danvers soldier killed at Falmouth 1690. He had deserted(?) from Sagadahoc the year before.

See Savage, and ch. records; also Doc. Hist. vi. 489, 498.

**ALSTON**, or Austin, George, m. 25 Oct. 1714 Rebecca (Brookings) Rowse. Abraham Austin, fisherman, 1716, is unexp.

**ALTER**, Leonard, Damariscove 1672. List 13.

**AMAZEEN**, John, Newcastle 1659. In 1662 "John Ammisoone the Greek" (Mr. Rishworth) sued Mr. Edward Lyde. He m. Mary, widow of Jeremiah Walford, and brought up her ch. Lists 326bc, 312c, 330a, 331b, 313e, 52, 319, 318ab, 315abc, 68. Constable 1682. Will 13 Aug. 1700 - 6 Feb. 1705-6. Ch. **Christopher**, in 1707 was joint owner with Joseph Jackson of the sloop Adventure. List 316. Will 25 Mar. 1752 - 27 Apr. 1756, names only son Joseph and his sons. **Ephraim**, seen only in List 319, poss. misr. of Christopher. **John**, b. 1663, taxed 1690, living in 1700.

**AMBLER**, John. Lists 96, 99, 368b. See Stackp. Durham.

**AMBROSE**, a not uncommon English surname.

1 **ALICE**, one of the "vagabond Quakers" whipped at the cart's tail out of N. H. towns in 1662.

2 **HENRY**, b. ±1613, house carpenter, Hampton, and moved with his work. Grant 1640, freeman 18 May 1642. He sold his house to Mr. Wheelwright 20 Oct. 1647, but presum. built himself another, as he was still in Hampton in 1649. In Salisbury 1650, Boston 1654, Charlestown 1656, but of Boston at death. Grand jury 1649, jury 1650. Lists 391a, 392a, 393b. Adm. 19 Nov. 1658 to widow Susannah, who m. 2 Oct. 1663 John Severance of Salisbury and in 1692 had lived 10 years his widow. Ch. **Ebenezer**, b. c. 1640, in court 1669. **Samuel**, bap. 25 July 1641, in 1670 had bot a boat. Mrs. Hope Ambrose in petition for divorce 3 Sept. 1678 recited that Mr. Samuel Ambrose over 4 years ago abandoned self and ch. without maintenance, and keeps another woman in Jamaica. Two ch. recorded in Salisb. **Henry**, b. June 1649, Salisb., weaver; m. Oct. 1672 Susannah widow of Timothy Worcester. Lived in "Salisbury alias Hampton;" both joined the church 16 Oct. 1715. 3 ch. rec. **Abigail**, b. 28 Dec. 1654, m. Oct. 1672 Wm. Osgood.

3 **RICHARD**, Isles of Shoals, in court in 1676 for fighting. Had house on Star Isl. 1693. Lists 306c, 308a.

**AMEE**, a French name translated Friend.

1 **JOHN**, Kittery. Lists 290, 296, 297. In court 1700, 1702. Mar. Sarah, dau. of Philip and Mary Gullison, and lived on their place on the north side of Braveboat Har-

bor creek; she deeded it to Stephen in 1753. Ch. (besides others who may have been only grandch.): **John**, b. 11 July 1695. **John**, b. 27 Dec. 1699. **Lawrence**, b. 28 Feb. 1702; pub. to Rachel Dolbe 16 Dec. 1724; she m. Jacob Clinton 13 Dec. 1735. Ch. **Elizabeth**, m. 5 Jan. 1731 Thomas Pillar. **George**, accused by "Clear," servant of T. Gerrish, Apr. 1732. **Stephen**, pub. to Mehitable Hodsdon 29 Mar. 1740. He was bondsman for Elizabeth and George.

2 **PHILIP** (Freind), 21 in 1694, dep. at Portsmo.

**AMERIDETH**, John, cooper, Kittery. The parish records of Townstall and Dartmouth, Devon, have the baptisms of six ch. 1615-1624 of John and Jane (Whiting) Amerideth, m. 7 Jan. 1614. John, bap. 26 Nov. 1615, was here by 1647. Jury 1669. Grand jury 1670. Lists 82, 286, 30, 297. Will 26 Jan. - 16 June 1691. Wife Joanna Treworgye, dau. of James and Catherine (Shapleigh), was a licensed retailer after her husband's death. Ch. **John**, d.s.p. Lists 30, 298. **Joanna**, m. John Alcock.

**AMES**, Wm. York or Wells wit. 1712. Daniel, Exeter. List 376b.

**AMORY**. 1 **Henry**, of Bideford, Eng., heir of Abraham Hayman in the Vines patent.

2 **JOHN**, Trel. Plant. List 21.

3 **AMORY** in R. I. desc. from Anthony Emery.

**AMOS**, William, Portsmouth. List 339. He m. 1st Esther Savage, dau. of John; 2d 17 Oct. 1727 Mary Wall, who m. 12 Nov. 1732 Abraham Bartlett. Ch. **Mary**, bp. 1720.

**ANDERSON**. 1 **Alexander**, Scotch prisoner. List 74.

2 **CORNELIUS** (Andreson), Flanderkin, privateer captain, 1675. List 3.

3 **DAVID**, Scotch prisoner. List 74.

4 **JOHN** [See Henderson], apprentice to Wm. Scadlock for two years, 17 Sept. 1661, had 16 mos. to serve and get £10.

5 **JOHN** (Pepperell spelt Androsen), 21 in 1695, at Kittery, had recently come out of captivity with Elisha Ingersoll.

6 **JOHN**, Scotch prisoner. List 74.

**ANDREWS**, a general English surname, and became the 33d commonest in New England.

1 **CAPT. AMOS** (Andros), appointed by Gov. Andros 27 Aug. 1687 commander of Pemaquid fort.

2 **SIR EDMUND** (Andros). Lists 34, 225a, 188, 97, 19. Despised and somewhat misrep. administrator under James II. See The Andros Tracts: 1868, vol. i, pp. v-liv. Dict. Natl. Biog.

3 **EDWARD** or Edmund, presum. the man told of by John Josselyn, was buried in Saco 16 Apr. 1668. He had held 40 acres

under the Lewis & Bonython patent. Lists 21, 243ab, 244cc.

**4 EDWARD**, weaver, (wrote), was in Berwick by 1704, assoc. with others including perh. **Norah**, near him in 1706 tax list; **Elisha** (List 298) m. Rebecca Weymouth 23 May 1712; **Mary**, m. Thos. Everett 14 July 1724; **Nicholas**, sued by John Frost 1713; **Joanna**, in trouble Jan. 1706-7. In 1707 Edward was joint grantor with Daniel Furbish of land willed to Anne (Heard) Hanson-Evans. Aug. 11, 1709, m. Sarah Churchill, dau. of Arthur and Eleanor (Bonython); both living 1726; she surviving 1731.

**5 LIEUT. ELISHA**(6), mariner. Lists 227, 35. For his dist. military career see Doc. Hist. v and vi, passim. Adm. 29 Aug. 1702 to Nath. Holmes. Wife Eleanor Brackett, dau. of Capt. Anthony and Anna (Mitton), m. 2d 6 Dec. 1705 Richard Pulling of Boston, who d. 6 Feb. 1721-2; she was licensed as a retailer and was living in 1733. Ch. **Abigail**, m.14 Feb.1711-2 John Kent. **Elisha** b. in Boston 13 Dec. 1698, land owner in Falm. in 1719. **Josiah**, b. 23 Mar. 1700-1; d. 21 Sep. 1702.

**6 JAMES**(16), yeoman and mariner, long the leading citizen of Falmouth Foreside, whose farm was the site of the Casco Bay fort 1700-1716. Jury 1666, 1674; grand jury 1675. Lists 221, 222bd, 223a, 34. Doc. Hist. vi, 471. Will 4 Jan. 1698-9, d. 5 May 1704 aged 79. Wife Dorcas Mitton (List 224), dau. of Michael and Elizabeth(Cleeve), he m. 2d, int. Boston 6 Aug. 1696, Margaret (Phips) Halsey, dau. of James and Mary Phips, who surv. Ch. **James. Samuel.** List 223a. **Elisha. Josiah.** Doc. Hist. vi, 406. List 34. Adm. Suff. 1691. **Rebecca**, m. Jonathan Adams. **Dorcas**, b. 1663, m. Ebenezer Davenport. **Jane**, m. 1st 1684 Andrew Alger, 2d, 19 Feb. 1692, Robert Davis of Boston.

**7 JAMES**(6). Lists 223a, 228b. Ch. **Jemima**, b. 1675, cared for by her grandfather; m. in Boston 29 Jan. 1694 Benj. Snelling, s. of Jane (Adams); d. 9 Dec. 1707.

**8 JEDEDIAH**, housewright, in 1659 bot land on Dover Neck which he sold in 1669 after moving to Salisbury, where he d. 12 July 1673. Lists 356aefghk. His wife, Mary Pike, dau. of Major Robert and Sarah (Sanders), who m. 2d 24 Aug. 1674 John Allen. Ch. **Joseph**, b. 10 Mar. 1669-70, in 1692 quitclaimed to his father-in-law; in 1700 not recently heard from.

**9 JOHN**, b. 1600, Kittery, 1640, farmer. Lived in Eliot until 1649 when he sold and became the first settler at the head of Braveboat Harbor. Jury 1651; grand jury under Mass. 1663-1664. Lists 281-283, 298. He paid many fines for his strenuous wife

Joane, b. 1621, and himself was in court for threatening to beat Gov. Godfrey and Mr. Withers. July 4, 1671, she was granted adm. on the estate of her husband, "who by a common fame is deceased," and within a few months m. Philip Atwell, but soon put him out and called herself Andrews. In 1688 Edmund Gatch beat the aged woman. Ch. **daughter**, m. by 1665 Robert Winchester. **Robert**, by two dep. b. 1652, d. s.p. aft. 1678. List 306a. **John**, by dep. app. twin with Robert. **Sarah**, b. 1653, m. Christopher Mitchell. **Joane**, perh. m. John Searle, fisherman, brother-in-law of Christopher Mitchell. **Anne**, m. by 1671 John Billing.

**10 JOHN**(9), fisherman. Lists 292, 306a. Wife was Margaret by 1672. Adm. 3 Apr. 1694 to(only)son **Robert**, whose widow Susannah was granted adm. 7 Oct. 1718, and was still single 1723. 3 ch.

**11 JOHN**, Newmarket, lived on Capt. Richard Hilton's mill grant before 1694.

**12 LUCAS** (Andries), master mariner. List 122.

**13 OLIVER.** Warrant to bring before court at Newcastle 22 Nov. 1699.

**14 RALPH.** Lists 13, 269b. Two men?

**15 RICHARD**, in 1655 witnessed deed of the Great House at Strawberry Bank. In 1682 was in Hampton jail for calling himself married to widow Jane Avery of Greenland, although he had a wife in Rhode Island, not seen in 4 years and m. to another man. Lists 332b, 62.

**16 SAMUEL**, called citizen of London by George Cleeve, came in The Increase, 14 Apr. 1635, aged 37, with wife Jane 30 and ch. Jane and Elizabeth, 3 and 2, and servant Elen Lougie, 20. He quickly went to Biddeford, (List 242), built a house, and died. His widow soon m. Mr. Arthur Mackworth. Her will, refugee at Boston, 20 May - 24 Oct. 1676. Ch. **James**, b. 1625. **Jane**, b. 1632, m. Francis Neale. **Elizabeth**, b. 1633, m. 1st Richard Pike, 2d Mr. Thomas Purchase, 3rd John Blaney Sen. **Philippe**, m. George Felt.

**17 MR. THOMAS**, sued John Stratton and Henry Watts in Saco Court 25 Mar. 1636.

**18 THOMAS**, in 1681, with Anthony Farley and John Winslow Jr., bot John Moore's dwelling and fishing plant on Star Isl.

**ANGELL**, Philip, Pemaquid. Lists 85, 124. Philip and

Pierce Angell, with other eastern men, took O. A. at Marblehead 18 Dec. 1677. In 1676 Pierce ack. debt payable in fish to John Dallin.

**ANGIER**, Anger, an uncommon English surname.

**1 JOHN**, "at present of Kittery," gave duebill to Roger Plaisted 15 Oct. 1655. List 357b.

2 **SAMPSON**, fisherman, in York by 1648, was app. the same bap. at Lezant, Cornwall, 20 Oct. 1624, son of Sampson and Anne (Bate). Whether son or father came on a fishing voyage in 1640 may be questioned. (Lech. 265.) Juryman 1649, 1650, 1655. Constable 1655. Lists 275, 276, 72, 24, 30. App. he went home to prove his father's will, and came again after m. 17 July 1666 Susannah Isaacke. His wife was Susannah in 1668, but by 1672 he had infalic. m. one Sarah, who was idling her time at the taverns and in 1681 had her bare bottom spanked by Margaret Bond. Yet his will, 13 May 1691 - 10 Jan. 1693-4, made her sole benef. He d. s.p., prob. in the York massacre. She m. 2d Arthur Hewes and bef. Jan. 1693-4 was living in Portsmouth.

**ANNAY**, John, with Wm. Wright, witn. 1681 against Joseph Weeding for selling liquor. — York Court.

**ANNIS**. 1 **Charles**, Newbury, b. 1638, m. 15 May 1666 Sarah Chase, dau. of Aquilla.

2 **ISAAC**, Cape Porpus, 1703. List 258. Presum. son of (1). See Newbury Records.

**ANTHONY**, John, m. 24 Feb. 1699 at Hampton Jane Rundlett, dau. of Charles and Mary (Shatswell). List 99. One Jane Anthony m. in Boston 4 July 1711 John Newton.

**ANTROBUS**, Wm., perh. related to Mr. Richard Martyn's wife, whose mother was Joan (Antrobus) Lawrence-Tuttle, was about Portsmo. 1667-1672, appar. an apprentice to Richard Stileman. List 328. Later he was in the employ of Mr. Peter Lidget in Boston, where he died. Inv. 22 Apr. 1675.

**ARCHDALE**, Col. John, brother-in-law of Ferd. Gorges Jr. See Maine Prov. & Court Records i. xxxix.

**ARCHER**, 1 **Benjamin**, took O. A. in York town meeting 16 Mar. 16[79]80; taxed at Cochecho in 1681-2.

2 **RICHARD**, of Portsmo, m. 16 July 1688 Mary West, presum. the dau. of Edward and Elizabeth (Walton). List 314.

**ARDELL**, Wm., appar. young Englishman operating from Boston, was sued in Me. courts in 1682; in 1683 had not paid for a horse bot in York. In 1684 he was "late of Exeter," in 1689 "late of Boston." In Apr. 1687 in Suff. Sup. Court he was acquitted of counterfeiting silver coin. Sheriff of N. H. 1696-1699. He died in his lumber camp in Newmarket in 1709 and was buried by Richard Hilton, who had taken his inventory June 9. Sewall noticed the death of "Mrs. Mary Ardell." 20 Oct. 1711, whose only child, Abia wife of John Barrell, was by her first husband, Joseph Sanderson (mar. contract with W. A. dated 27 Feb. 1681-2). Her sister Frances Thompson came later from the North of England. Lists 52, 57, 98, 376b, 384b.

**ARDEN**, William, surgeon under Major Church and at Casco Fort, 1689-1690.

**ARIN**, William, -sic- in orig., known only by Mr. Pike's list of those killed at Cochecho 28 June 1689—— poss. short for the next man, or, if Mr. Pike got this list in a letter, a misreading of Kim (Kemp).

**ARINGTON**, William, (Urington), see Yarington.

**ARLOT**, Benedictus. Signed and ack. deed of Agnes Bickford, minor, June 1705-1706, ratifying deed of her mother Jane (Bickford) Dockum.

**Armiger**, Wm. York, 1724. Y.D. xi. 160, 175.

**Armitage**, Joseph, for presentment at Dover Court fined at Ipswich Court Sept. 1647.

**ARMSTRONG**, Robert, Londoner, boasted himself bred an attorney; disciplined in 1700 for insolence in the provincial court. In Newcastle 1698, prob. came with Gov. Allen. Naval Officer and Collector, and Deputy Surveyor of His Majesty's Woods. In 1726 with wife Elizabeth he sold land in Londonderry, N. H. List 339. Doc. Hist. x. passim.

**ARNUP** or **Ainup**, Will, Newcastle, 1696. List 315c.

**Aronson**, Jurian, Dutch privateer 1676. List 3.

**ARROWSMITH**. 1 **Edward**, Pemaquid or Winnegance, 1665. List 12.

2 **THOMAS**, Trel. Plant. List 21.

**ARTHUR**, John, Lieut., Isles of Shoals 1653. List 301. Perhap. same as John (Arthers), Cape Newagen 1672. List 13. Wife Elizabeth ±61 in 1677. List 142.

**Arthy**, see Earthy.

**Arwin**, Edwin, see Edward Erwin.

**ASH**, Ashe, a usual English surname.

1 **JOHN**, Dover, 1659. List 356e. Perh. moved to Amesbury.

2 **JOHN**, Isles of Shoals, ±22 in 1677. List 306a.

3 **THOMAS**, Durham and Dover; lived at Portsmouth during Indian troubles. Lists 57, 330def, 358ad. Will 14 Jan. - 3 June 1718. Wives, 1st, Hannah Chesley, dau. of Philip and Elizabeth; 2d, bef. 1700, Mary, the mother of James Rawlins, mariner, of Portsmouth, dec. Ch. **Hannah**, m. 30 May 1714 Benj. Pierce. 6 ch. **Thomas**, wife Eleanor. Sold out at Cocheco Point in 1743. 4 ch. bap. 26 Mar. 1736. **Judith**, bap. with her mother 28 Sept. 1718. "Other daughters" named in will.

4 **WILLIAM**, about Kit. and Berw. from 1671. In court July 1675 for living from his wife. Died 5 Oct. 1675; inv. showed a heifer and corn.

**Ashcraft**, John, soldier at Wells in 1691.

**ASHFIELD**, William, No. Yarmouth, 1682; refugeed at Malden, but bef. his death moved to Lynn, where his widow d. 17 June 1695. List 214. She was Jane Larrabee, dau. of Stephen. Ch. **Sarah**, m. Isaac Willey, Lyme, Conn. **(Hannah?)**. **Mary**, b. in Malden 20 Dec. 1691; m. at Boston 29 May 1712 Samuel Proctor. **Jane**, m. at Boston 11 May 1715 William Goodwin, both living at Marblehead in 1754. 5 ch. rec. **Miriam**, m. at Boston 19 July 1716 Jeremiah Hart.

**ASHLEY**, the name of seven English parishes.

1 **EDWARD** (Astley), the earliest known Indian trader on the Penobscot, virtual grantee of the Muscongus patent, whose unbrid. strenuous. was fortuitously cut off with mixed, if any, genealogy. Bradford's Hist. (1912) ii. 83, 109, 107, 78-133 passim. Proc. Mass. Hist. Soc. xlv. 493-498. Winth. ii. 126. List 1.

2 **THOMAS**, Kennebec, one of prob. two, poss. three of the name. The one who lost his wife Joanna in Boston 27 Dec. 1661 and m. the widow Hannah Browme 31 Jan. 1661-2 was prob. not the Kennebec fisherman, to whom the earlier records may plausibly attach: Of Charlestown ±26, 19 July 1639, with Abraham Hawkins ±28, servants now and before leaving England of Mr. Tho. Rucke, came in The Castle of London; 1640-1642 carried on fishing with various partners until in the latter year his house was in the sheriff's hands. Our Thomas in 1661 bot land of the Kennebec Indians, which he sold after they drove him back to Boston, 1675 and 1678, partly to his son. Lists 10, 11, 186. Newtown overseer in 1681. His wife in 1678 was Rebecca. Ch. **Thomas**.

3 **THOMAS**(2), Boston, by wife Mary, prob. she that d. 17 Apr. 1692, had ch. **Mary**, b. 1 Sep. 1681, m. John Spikes of Boston and perh. 2d 7 Sept. 1727 Gamaliel Clark. 1¶ ch. **Anne**, b. 3 Dec. 1682; m. Capt. Isaac Mansfield of Marblehead; d. 24 Aug. 1749. 4 ch. rec. **Thomas**, b. 17 Sep. 1684, had removed to North Carolina by 1715.

4 **WILLIAM**, Wells, Providence. York 1651. Constable, Wells, 1659. Lists 262, 264, 25, 265, 266, 28, 31. In 1693 he was stopping with Abraham Harding and recited in petn. that he was moved to Boston and that himself, wife, and daughter had gone overland to Providence, where his wife had friends. He m. one or two of Stephen Batson's daus., certainly Elizabeth, who was childless in 1674. Sarah Ashley, in S. B.'s will, may be variously exp., likelier as a Trott m. to Ashley's son by a previous wife. John Ashley, who m. at Wells 1 Nov. 1720 Hannah Baston, dau. of Thomas, is unexp. He d. bef. 23 Dec. 1723.

**ASHTON**, the name of 16 English parishes.

**JOHN**, Scarborough, b. c. 1638; refugee at Newcastle in 1676, at Marblehead in 1690; living 1714. Lists 235, 237a, 238a. Three wives, 1st a dau. of Andrew Alger, who d. s.p.; 2d Susannah Foxwell, dau. of Mr. Richard and Susannah (Bonython) Foxwell, mother of all the ch. and d. at Newcastle; 3d, 30 July 1691, Mary (Edgecomb), widow of George Page, dau. of Nicholas and Wilmot (Randall) Edgecomb, who joined the Marblehead church in 1728 and deposed aged ±83 in 1730. Ch. **Susannah**, m. at Marblehead 14 Oct. 1684 Robert Codner; d.s.p. **Mary**, m. at Scarb. 23 Feb. 1687 Daniel Libby. **Samuel**, fisherman, m. 15 July 1686 Mary Sandin. 6 ch. **Elizabeth**, bap. 11 Dec. 1687, m. Nicholas Merritt, who d. at Marblehead in 1736. 10 ch. **Philip**, shoreman, m. 20 Nov. 1701 Sarah Hendly. 2 ch. Philip Jr. in 1725 printed Ashton's Memorial, Strange Adventures of Philip Ashton, Taken by Pirates. This narrative mentions (his cousins) Joseph Libbee, who saved him from drowning, and Benj. Ashton. **Joseph**, b. 1678, d. 22 Aug. 1725. (Gravestone at Marbl.); m. 1st 4 Aug. 1700 Mary Page, 2d 25 Jan. 1713-4 Mary (Dutch) Page, widow prob. of Christopher, dau. of Hezekiah Dutch, who surv. him. 5+4 ch.

Atherton, Jonathan, mariner, ±41 in 1678, Great Island witness.

**(Athyle?)**, Andrew, Kittery, 1698. List 294.

**ATKINS**, a familiar English surname; "Tommy Atkins" means an English soldier.

1 **HATTON**, wit. with John Freke at Newcastle 1661.

2 **JOSEPH**. List 341. See Atkinson.

3 **MATTHEW**, Isles of Shoals. Lists 313b, 307a.

4 **ROBERT**. See Alkins.

5 **THOMAS**, Kennebec, farmer. Bot of Indians by 1656 in Phipsburg; returned after Philip's War and died there, bef. 10 Nov. 1686. Lists 10, 11, 183, 191. Wife Elizabeth. Ch. no sons, 10 daus. **Elizabeth**, b. 1645, lived at Kennebec about 12 years till she m.; was Widow Davis of Beverly 1709-1716. One Elizabeth Davis m. one Samuel Clark at Marblehead, 25 Jan. 1720. **Mary**, m. by 1666 Wm. Hackett. **Rebecca**, m. one Hall, living in 1716 at Tarpolin Cove, Elizabeth Islands. **Susannah**, m. one Green. **Rachel**, m. 1st John Drake of Kennebec, 2d James Barry of Boston. **Anne**, m. Samuel Clark, blacksmith of Marblehead. 3 ch. rec. **Sarah**, m. Samuel Gurney of Little Compton, R. I. **Esther**, m. Geo. Pike of Mendon, and was a widow in 1716. **Abigail**, m. Thomas

Washburn, Bridgewater. **Ruth,** m. John Haskins, Scituate.

**ATKINSON,** a general English surname.
1 **JOHN,** ±28 in 1666, was acting for "my uncle" Theodore Atkinson of Boston. Settled in Newbury. Grandf. of Sergeant Joseph Atkinson killed at Wells 1 Aug. 1706. List 96.

2 **JOHN**(3), sold his father's 13 a. grant. List 67. In 1706 John Tufton wounded him in the head with a narrow axe. In 1707 his child was bound out for 21 years to Col. Thomas Packer.

3 **JOSEPH,** Portsmouth, b. c. 1634. In 1652, around Sagamore Creek, sued Mary Clay for slander. In 1657 was bondsman for Gowen Wilson in York Court. Settled in Greenland. Lists 43, 330b, 326ac, 311b, 47, 331a. Adm. 24 Sep. 1678 to town officers; "children" mentioned. Roger Sarchwell, who expected to marry the widow Ann, instead rendered bill for money, salt, dry goods and 2 mos. work. Ch. **John** (poss. took name Satchell, of Greenland, with wife Eleanor, in 1713, spelt Sachel in his will, of Stratham, proved 8 Feb. 1725-6; and prob. **Jane,** who accused Daniel Allen in 1694.

4 **THEODORE,** Boston, cousin of (1) and step-son of Mary (Wheelwright) Lyde, ±19 in 1664 was acting for his father. Killed in the Narragansett fight 19 Dec. 1675, his widow Elizabeth (Mitchelson) m. Mr. Henry Dering. 4 ch. incl. **Theodore,** b. 3 Oct. 1669. **Abigail,** b. 13 Dec. 1672, m. John Winslow, James Oborn and Samuel Penhallow, Esq.

5 **THEODORE**(4), eminent citizen of Newcastle 1693-1719, Indian captive and envoy, captain, justice, sheriff, assemblyman, councillor. Lists 399a, 315cb, 68, 63, 336c, 316. Died 6 May 1719. Wife Mary surv., called cousin in Ruth Tarleton's will. She was a member of the church in Boston. Ch. **Elizabeth,** b. Bost. 28 Nov. 1692; m. 22 May 1711 Dr. Robert Pike; d. 5 Feb. 1719-20. Ch. **Mary,** b. Newcastle 6 June 1695; m. 11 June 1713 Rev. Wm. Shurtleff; d.s.p. aft. 1760. **Theodore,** b. 30 Dec. 1697, m. 4 Sept. 1732 Hannah (Wentworth), widow of Samuel Plaisted, dau. of Lt. Gov. John and Sarah (Hunking) Wentworth; d. 22 Sep. 1779. Eminent magistrate and diplomat. Scratched a useful record of deaths on the bottom of his silver platter. List 358b. His wife d. 12 Dec. 1769. 2 ch.

**ATWELL,** a typical English surname, especially North of England.
1 **BENJAMIN,** known only for selling 95 ducks at the Trelawny plantation in 1639-40. Presum. his widow Dorothy m. Richard Martin. She was mother of **Benjamin** Atwell and **Lydia,** appar. Atwell, wife of Robert Corben, to whom in 1673 she deeded her estate for life support.

2 **BENJAMIN**(1), m. in 1668 Alice Lewis, dau. of George. Lists 222bc. Killed by Indians 11 Aug. 1676. Ch., besides one who d.y., **Joseph,** b. 1671, who at 14 chose William Scriven of Kittery guardian. Mr. Scriven claimed for him the entire estates of his father, grandfather Martin and uncle Corben. Lists 298, 315c.

3 **JOHN,** N. Yarm., according to trad. written by Amos Atwell, b. 1730, came from England with John Mains, whose dau. he m. He is mentioned at Lynn in 1650, but came with Mains to N. Yarm., where "Atwell's Creek" is on the south side of Royal's River below the cemetery. Under Danforth John York got his land. In Philip's War he fled to York, where he built and fenced at Cape Neck. From York in 1690 he fled to Lynn, where two Johns lived in 1695 and his son John with wife Margaret were living in 1727. He raised a family in N. Yarm., four ch. were named by the grandson of one of them, not including Andrew, bap. at Charlestown 20(1) 1692. Ch. **John,** removed from Lynn to Killingly, Conn.; m. in Wenham 12 Dec. 1693 Margaret Max. 3 ch. rec. **Richard,** m. (int. 11 Sept. 1703) his cousin Lydia Felt, dau. of Moses and Hannah (Mains). They were parents of Richard of Attleboro. **Joseph. Sarah,** m. Joseph Townsend of Malden.

4 **PHILIP,** lived in Kittery and vicinity over 20 years, employed in the fisheries. He m. the widow of John Andrews by 1672 but soon had a falling out and 26 Mar. 1673 had taken his chest out into the bushes. He was questioned in 1695 for absence from meeting.

**Atwood,** John, called himself of Sheepscot in petition for land, 1688.

**Augustine,** John, Falmouth, see Gustin.

**Aullwers,** John, Falmouth, see Oliver.

**AULT,** John, Durham, b. by deps. 1601-1605. Constable 1650. Grand jury 1650, 1660. In 1657 he and Richard York adm. est. of Geo. Bronson. Lists 354abc, 355ab, 356a, 361a, 363abc, 364, 365, 359a, 49. He m. Remembrance Tibbetts, who came aged 28 in 1635 with Henry. They deeded lands to their three daus. in 1669, 1672 and 1674. Ch. **Rebecca,** b. 1641, m. 1st, in 1660, Henry Hallowell, 2d 28 Sep. 1665 Tho. Edgerly. **Elizabeth,** m. William Perkins. **Remembrance,** m. John Rand.

**AUSTIN,** (Augustine), a general English surname, common in the middle counties.
1 **FRANCIS.** His lot at Dedham had passed to Francis Chickering bef. 1640. Land grants in Hampton, to himself 30 June 1640, to his widow 13 July 1642. She was Isabel

Bland, dau. of Mr. John and Isabel Smith alias Bland of Martha's Vinyard. Cf. Banks M. V. ii. He quickly d. and she m. Thomas Leavitt. Known ch. **Isabella**, b. c. 1633, m. Philip Towle. **Jemaima**, bp. with Keziah, m. John Knowles. **Keziah**, bp. 24 Jan. 1641, called Tucker in wills of step-father and mother, living at a distance, poss. mother of Samuel of Chatham.

2 **GEORGE**, see Alston.

3 **JOHN**, see Ashton.

4 **JOSEPH**, b. ±1616, Matthew, b. ±1620, and Samuel, but little younger than Benj. Bosworth b. ±1615, all had to do with Dover. Matthew named a dau. Isabel. Samuel was an early friend and [church?] brother of Capt. Benj. Bosworth, from the region of Dedham, whence Francis Austin came to Hampton. The relations of these men to each other, to the Austins of Charlestown, and to Annis (Austin) Littlefield, have not been exam. Joseph was a wit. in Eliot in 1648. By Oct. 1649 he had m. Sarah Starbuck of Dover, dau. of Edward and Catharine (Reynolds) Starbuck. Const. 1656-7, grand jury 1651, × ×, 1660. Lists 354abc, 355a, 356abcefg, 341. Will 25-29 Jan. 1662-3. "Sarah Austin," was taxed in 1663. (List 356h.) She m. 2d, 2 Mar. 1664-5, Humphrey Varney. Ch. **Thomas**. **Benjamin**, Nantucket. His est. was divided in 1681 among four bros. and sist. **Nathaniel**, Nantucket. **Deborah**, m. 1668 John Coffin, 1647-1711; d. on Nantucket 4 Feb. 1718. 9 ch. **Mary**, m. 17 May 1674 Capt. Richard Gardner of Nantucket, 1653-1728, Judge of Probate; d. 1 June 1721. 10 ch.

5 **MATTHEW**, York, weaver. See (4). Serg. 1659; selectman 1665, 1669-73, 1683-6; Jury 1662. Grand jury 1663, 1674, 1676, 1679, 1681, 1686. Lists 25, 33. Will 19 Nov. 1684 - 1 Mar. 1685-6. He m. 1st a dau. of Tho. Canney; 2d Mary (Davis) Dodd, widow of George Dodd, dau. of Nicholas Davis, who m. 3d after 1669 (William of Boston?) Wright, and was living in York in 1713. Ch. by first wife, **Matthew**, b. ±1658; by 2d wife, **Mary**, m. 1st, bef. 6 June 1686, Jonathan Saywood, 2d, Lewis Beane. **Sarah**, b. bf. 1667, m. 1st Joseph Preble, 2d Job Young. **Isabella**, b. aft. 1667, m. Samuel Bragdon.

6 **CAPT. MATTHEW**(5), innholder, many years juryman, foreman 1711, 1712, prominent in county affairs. Adm. 6 Jan. 1718-9 to James Grant. Wife Mary Littlefield, dau. of Capt. John. Ch. **Matthew**, "only son," killed by Indians 11 Aug. 1704. List 96. **Mary**, taken by Indians bef. 1695; m. 3 Jan. 1710 Etienne Gibau of Montreal, carpenter; d. 4 Oct. 1755. List 99. 9 ch. **Patience**, m. James Grant of York, gent.

Ch. b. 1709-1723. **Elizabeth**, m. 25 Dec. 1712 Ralph Farnham. 10 ch. **Ichabod**, accused by Sarah Moore, dau. of John and Martha (Walford) Moore (her son "Ichabod" b. 12 Aug. 1712, perh. called himself Benoni, possibly that Ichabod drowned at Gloucester 17 Mar. 1734-5); m. in 1717 Susannah Young, dau. of Matthews and Eleanor (Haines). He d. 19 Sep. 1718 and his widow m. Magnus Redlon. Her ch. by both husbands were recorded together: Ichabod, b. 29 Mar. 1717-8, four by Redlon. **Joseph**, had the homestead, m. 19 Apr. 1725 Sarah Grant, dau. of James and Mary (Nason) Grant of Berwick; d. 4 Feb. 1799. List 279. 3 ch. rec. **Benjamin**, of Berwick, laborer, in 1746.

7 **SAMUEL**, Wells, innholder. See (4). Of Dover 1649, const. 1650, sold his house 1650. Const. of Wells 1655, com. t.e.s.c. 1663-4, 1669, 1678, grand jury 1665-1667, 1679, 1681, 1683 (foreman 1666, 1688), assemblyman 1682. Refugee at Charlestown. Lists 354b, 261-263, 24, 25, 265, 266, 28, 33. He m. 1st Elizabeth Gooch, dau. of Mr. John and Ruth; 2d, by 1661, Sarah, widow of William Storer of Dover, and brought up her children recorded 1640-1651. Only ch. **Elizabeth**, by 1st wife, m. Samuel Hill of Biddeford, Wells and Charlestown, who made a home for his aged parents.

8 **THOMAS**(4), Dover, house carpenter and wheelwright. Juryman 1679. Lists 359ab, 49, 52, 57. Had the homestead. He m. Ann Otis, dau. of Richard and Rose (Stoughton). Ch. **Rose**, b. 3 Apr. 1678, m. Ephraim Tibbetts. **Sarah**, b. 1 Mar. 1682, m. 22 Dec. 1712 John Canney. **Nathaniel**, b. 2 Mar. 1687, d. 1749; m. Catherine Neal, dau. of Andrew and Catherine (Furbish). 12 ch. **Thomas**, b. 5 June 1689, d. 10 Nov. 1706. List 96. **Joseph**, b. 30 June 1692; d. 20 June 1776; m. Sarah. 8 ch., including Rose and Stoten. **Nicholas**, b. 20 Aug. 1695, of Dover 1720, settled in Abington, Pa.; wife Jane. 13 ch. **Anne**, twin. **Samuel**, b. 2 Oct. 1698, d. bef. 1776; m. 23 Nov. 1727 Abigail Pinkham, dau. of Solomon and Mary (Field). 7 ch. **Benjamin**, b. 31 July 1704, d. 1782; m. 19 Sep. 1729 Sarah Pinkham, dau. of Thomas. 9 ch. b. in Somersworth.

**AVANT**, Francis, yeoman, Kittery, 1693-1696. Bot at Spruce Creek.

**Aveling**, Arthur. Damariscove 1622-1626. List 8.

**AVERILL**, Avery, Every, Everell, oftener Avery in England.

1 **JOHN**, perh. two men; (Everell) Wells wit. 1660; (Averill) sued two Portsmo. men 1665-1666.

2 **JOHN**(6) (Avery); in 1703 bot a half interest in a sawmill on Winnecut River. Lists 57, 338bd. He m. Elizabeth (Hill),

widow of Wm. Davis, dau. of John and Elizabeth Hill. List 338b. He was living in 1728, she surviving in 1731 and prob. d., "John Avery's mother," 14 Dec. 1747. Son **John**, m. 18 Mar. 1724-5 Bridget Huggins, granddau. of Nathaniel and Sarah. Ch.

3 **LAWRENCE** and **JOHN** (Avery), dealt with the Cutts in 1650-51. See Wm. Follett. See(9).

4 **PAUL** (Averell), Berw. wit. 1695. Y. D. vi. 160.

5 **ROBERT**(6) (Avery), Greenland. In 1726 and 1729 he deeded his homestead in halves to his sons **Robert** (m. Sarah Pett 5 Nov. 1724) and **Edward**. Both sons had children.

6 **THOMAS** (Avery), Greenland, b. ±1631, was in Portsmo. (proprietor) by 1657. In 1671 he was app. public executioner. Lists 326ab, 311b, 47. Inv. Sep. 1681 showed an old house and a new one. His widow Joan prob. m. Richard Andrews. Ch. **Thomas**, b. 1657. **John. Robert.** Also prob. others, as **Elizabeth**, in court 1692.

7 **THOMAS** (Averill), Wells and York, bp. 7 Jan. 1630 at Chipping Norton, Oxfordshire, son of Wm. and Abigail (Hinton), who came to Topsfield. He came to Wells bef. 1671 and settled far inland, near the headline of South Berwick, in a region afterw. dist. by the ruins of his chimney, "Averill's Back." At the approach of the 2d War he withdrew to Cape Neddick, and thence to Chebacco, in Ipswich. In 1672 his wife was Hannah. List 86. His and his wife's last years were spent in York, on the shore east of Cape Neddick, where his oldest son had his land and was granted adm. of his estate 7 Apr. 1714. Lists 298, 33, 86, 267b, 269b. His surv. ch. were **Sarah**, m. Ebenezer Lufkin. **Job**, 1671-1726, York; m. Mary Preble dau. of Joseph and Sarah (Austin). His sons lived in York. List 279. **Benjamin**, of Gloucester, mariner; m. at Boston 24 July 1702 Mary "Chambet" or Chamblet, an heir of Henry Champnois. See Averell Gen. 1926: pp. 98, 103, passim. The Averills of Kennebunkport, called by Bradbury four brothers, were grand-nephews of (7). Of the four, Job, of Middleton and Sheepscot, was a cousin, but B.'s authority for Samuel's being a brother must be accounted good.

8 **THOMAS**(6) (Avery), Greenland; m. 8 Oct. 1697 Abigail Coombs, widow. "Old Thomas Avery" died 6 Sep. 1744. Lists 332b, 47, 57, 62, 67, 335a, 338a. Prob. had daus.

9 **WILLIAM** (Every) had son **Ebenezer**, aged 11 in 1668, bound to Richard Cutt, who had taken him an infant. See(3).

**Averta**, Susannah, "a Jersey maid at Mr. Martyn's," in 1672 lay sick at his house.

John Thompson brought Dr. Morgan, and agreed to pay her bills.

**Avery**, see Averill.

**AXALL**, Humphrey, in 1682 was sued by the Est. of Samuel Biss; in 1685 deposed in Portsmo.; in 1687 was bound over in York Court; about 1692 m. Mary (Jenkins) widow of John Green, dau. of Reynold and Ann Jenkins, occupied her late husband's place on Eliot Neck, and was highway surveyor. Having joined the Baptists, they removed to South Carolina.

**AYERS**, a West of England surname. See Eyre, for Thomas, Eleanor, Eleazer, of London; also for Simon, John, Benj., of Boston.

1 **EDWARD**, Portsmouth, blacksmith, one of four or five bros. concerned in the Piscataqua, sons of Capt. John, of Ipswich and Brookfield, killed by the Indians 2 Aug. 1675. See Hist. B. p. 180. Lists 62, 67, 335a, 330d, 337, all name most of them. Edward was of Kit. 1686, serving as appraiser with Hammond. In Portsmo. he was grand juryman, selectman. Lists 359b, 296-298, 98, 60, 336c. His broken grst. reads: 30 day . . . 172[3] in 65th year. The next stone: Alice wife of Edw. Ayers d. 9 Feb. 1717-8, aged 53. His next wife, Hannah (Martyn), widow of Richard Jose, dau. of Richard and Sarah (Tuttle) Martyn, m. 2 Oct. 1718, d. 12 Jan. 1718-9. He then m. 23 Feb. 1719-20 Margaret Williams, who was of Ipswich in 1734. Ch. **Elizabeth**, m. 1st 30 Oct. 1701 Dr. Caleb Griffeth (4 ch.); 2d, Nov. 1709, Lieut. Henry Lyon of York, later of Roxbury; 3d, 23 Feb. 1720-1, Moses Ingraham of Portsmo., tailor, later of York (1 ch.). **Edward**, had grant in Brookfield, d.s.p. **Susannah**, m. 20 Sep. 1715 John Cutt, cooper. **Abigail**, m. 25 Nov. 1709 Joseph Moulton. **Mary**, m. 10 Apr. 1710 John Foster of Boston, and was his widow in 1763. 10 ch. **Hannah**, m. 16 July 1724 Nathaniel Fellows, cooper. **Phebe**, m. 15 Feb. 1721-2 Joseph Sherburne, mariner. **John**, bp. with three older, July 1708; m. 6 Jan. 1722-3 Mary Hunking, who d. 17 July 1754 in 50th year; his fam. Bible has not his death. 13 ch.

2 **EPHRAIM**, York. List 279.

3 **JAMES**, see Orr. List 356d.

4 **JOHN** (Aires), see (9).

5 **MARK**, bro. of (1), Portsmouth, cordwainer. Lists 57, 333a, and under (1). Foreman of jury 1698, grand jury 1699. Was of Newington in 1721, yet the gravestone in Portsmo. is app. for his wife: Sarah, d. 12 Jan. 1727[8, aged 66; she had been ch. mem. in Ipswich. Ch. **George**, cordwainer; m. 10 Dec. 1712 Abigail Perkins, dau. of Jonathan and Sarah; both living in 1747. List 339. Ch. **Thomas**, bp. Portsmo.

10 Dec. 1693, clothier, Newington; m. Hannah. Ch. (Also perh. Rebecca and Mary, joined the Newington church 1726-1728.)

6 **NATHANIEL**, bro. of (1), Portsmouth, blacksmith, b. June 1670; d. at Boston 4 Dec. 1737. Foreman of jury 1692, 1697, sergeant, justice. Joined Portsmouth church 22 June 1693. Lists 57, 62-64, 68, 330b, 331c, and under (1). He m. Amy (Cowell) widow of Jethro Furber, dau. of Edward and Agnes, who was living at Boston in 1740. List 331c. Ch. **Nathaniel**, Boston, 4 ch. **Amy**, m. 16 Jan. 1710-11 Samuel Swasey. 1? son. **Elnathan**, Boston, ch. **Edward**, Boston, 2+5 ch. See Ayres Gen. 1870: p. 21.

7 **THOMAS**, bro. of (1), Ipswich and Portsmouth, farmer. Lists under (1). He m. 21 Mar. 1677-8 Hannah Errington, and prob. 2d Elizabeth ———, who was dism. from the Rowley to the Portsmo. church 5 May 1700. Adm. 5 Dec. 1722 to sons Abraham and Thomas. Ch. rec. in Newbury and Ipswich: **Thomas**, b. 25 Jan. 1678-9, prob. d.y. **Hannah**, b. 2 Aug. 1680; m. 16 Oct. 1711 Edward Toogood. **Rebecca**, b. 27 May 1682. **Susannah** (prob. that dau. b. June 1686), m. 19 May 1707 Wm. Scales of Rowley, Ipswich, Portsmouth, Falmouth, and finally, where he was killed by the Indians 24 Apr. 1725, North Yarmouth, (6 ch.); 2d Capt. Cornelius Soule. **Abraham**, b. 18 June 1688; m. 18 Oct. 1716 Mary Jackson, dau. of Samuel and Mary (Melcher), who m. 2d Jacob Lavers. 4 ch. **Sarah**, b. 29 Aug. 1690. **Thomas**, leased the Hall-Peirce farm at Greenland. He m. 13 Aug. 1713 Ruth Sherburne, dau. of John and Mary (Jackson). Will 3 June - 25 July 1764. 9 ch. **Mehitable**, b. 5 Apr. 1697, prob. m. 29 Apr. 1718 Abraham Senter, from Ipswich.

8 **WILLIAM**, Portsmouth, sadler, perh. that son of Samuel of Ipswich b. 26 Jan. 1681, another bro. of (1). Adm. 28 Sep. 1716 to widow Mary (Hopley), dau. of Robert and Elizabeth (Tucker), m. 24 Oct. 1706. She m. 2d, 4 Oct. 1716, Sampson Doe and 3d, one Stevens, her name in 1765 when she made her will. Ch. **Hopley**, m. 4 Oct. 1730 Mary Frost of Newcastle. **William**, bp. 20 June 1714.

9 **ZACHARIAH** (Eaires), with John Aires ±23, were witnesses at Durham in the Chesley cattle case, 1672. See Hoyt's Sals. p. 37. Zachariah m. 27 June 1678 Elizabeth Chase, dau. of Aquila.

**AYNEL**, William, of Portsmouth, mariner, in 1684 sued Mr. John Hunkins, merchant, for wages.

**BABB**, a West of England surname, and Philip occurs near Dartmouth.

1 **PETER**(2) was appr. 27 June 1676 to Joseph Hall of Greenland, who had kept him 2 years. In 1696 he leased the Hall farm, but a year later was living in John Westbrook's house near the great swamp. Lists 57, 334a, 335a, 330de, 337. In 1713 he was taxed in Greenland, in 1714 "Widow Babb and son." She was Sarah Cate, dau. of James and Alice. List 338b. Ch. **Philip**, had homestead; m. 1st 29 May 1718 Rachel Lewis, prob. dau. of Abraham, 2d 11 Nov. 1736 Fredrika (Berry), widow of Samuel Huggins, dau. of Wm. and Judith Berry. List 339. Will 1758-1782 names wife Fredrica and 8 ch. **Priscilla**, m. 26 Nov. 1724 Nathaniel Knight. **James**, cordwainer, removed to Scarb. ab. 1728, later settled in Westbrook; d. Apr. 1748, leaving widow Hannah. 5 ch. **John**, removed to Scarb. ab. 1728; m. 25 May 1731 Sarah (Bennett), widow of Wallis Fenderson and dau. of Henry and Margaret Bennett. She was buried 9 Dec. 1765, he 19 Feb. 1773. 4? ch. **Mary**, bap. 1713, prob. m. 17 May 1727-8 Elisha Berry of Scarb. Prob. other ch., as Isaiah, bp. Oct. 1710. Sarah, m. Walter Foss 13 Sep. 1726.

2 **PHILIP**, prominent fishing master at Isles of Shoals (Hog) from 1652 or earlier until his death. Local magistrate. In 1668 Roger Kelly was bonded for abusive carriages towards Mr. Babb and his wife; in 1671 Lawrence Carpenter for cruel usage of Mary Babb's servant. Lists 282, 301, 76, 25. Inv. was taken 31 Mar. 1671, and his widow soon died. Prob. other ch. besides: **William**. The books of Philip English, Salem merchant, have a charge against William Babb & Co. [Tho. Babb] "To goods sold them to carry to the Southward." The acct. runs to 1684. Adm. to widow Deborah 30 June (inv. 20 Feb.) 1690-1, Essex Co., Mass. **Thomas**. Indentured in Apr. 1675 to Henry Greene of Hampton "a child that now lives with him." Thomas Babb's acct. with Mr. English runs to July 1685. He m. Bathsheba Hussey, dau. of John and Rebecca (Perkins) of Hampton and Delaware. Will 1748-1751, Delaware, names ch. Peter, Thomas, Philip, Mary, Rebecca, Lydia. The names Peter and Philip occur among the Babbs of Va. and N. C. **Philip**. **Sampson**. **Peter**, b. 29 Sep. 1671.

3 **PHILIP**(2), m. in 1692 Lydia Bragdon, dau. of Arthur and Lydia (Twisden), who m. 2d Samuel Norton, a soldier from Amesbury, where they were living in 1723. Ch. Joshua, of Portsmouth, glazier, 1721-1757; m. 12 Dec. 1720 Deborah Bickford, dau. of Benj. and Sarah of Newington. Ch.

4 **SAMPSON**(2), Portsmouth. Lists 334a, 335a, 339. Will 1736-1739. Perh. m. 3 wives: 1st "Elizabeth," in list of church

members bef. 1708, likelier the minister's error for Sarah (wife of (2); Sarah, named as mother of Esther; Grace, named as mother of Benjamin and in will, prob. Grace (Taprill), widow of Israel Hoit, dau. of Robert and Abishag (Walton) Taprill. Ch. **Sampson,** m. Dorothy Hoit, dau. of Israel and Grace (Taprill). **Richard,** settled in Barrington; m. in Greenland 14 Nov. 1735 Margaret Filgar, dau. of Charles. **William,** m. 7 Dec. 1732 Dorcas Haines, dau. of Aquila and Mehitable (Freethy). 5 ch. **Mary,** m. 16 Apr. 1721 Jeremiah Hodsdon. **Elizabeth,** m. John Alltimes, later of Kennebunkport. Will 12 Oct. - 10 Nov. 1750. 4? ch. **Alice,** received into covenant 9 Feb. 1729. **Sarah,** m. one Johnson. **Susannah,** m. 19 June 1734 Wm. Johnson. **Esther,** bp. 26 Feb. 1720-1, m. 6 May 1741 Wm. Cotton. **Benjamin,** bp. 10 Mar. 1722-3.

5 **THOMAS,** English shipmaster and factor; brought many passengers; dealt with Edward Trelawny and others. He kept his family at Wapping, his wife Eleanor dau. of George Rolfe; Barbara Rolfe was her relation.

**BACEY,** 1 John, Senior, aged ±65 in 1703, knew Casco Bay bef. Philip's War.

2 **RICHARD,** ±27 in 1679, fisherman for Roger Kelly. In 1681 was sued by Mr. Wainwright for advances in a fishing voyage.

**Bachiler,** see Batchelder.

**BACKUS,** or -house, Francis, appeared at Ogunquit, Wells, in 1668, where he sold out in 1671. Settled in Wells village, moved to Saco about 1681, escaped to Plymouth Colony. Lists 269b, 265, 266, 249, 33. He m. 1st 1672 Rebecca Cross, dau. of John; 2d Dorcas (Seeley), widow of James Gibbins, dau. app. of Richard Seeley. He was a witness in Plymouth Court in 1697, but "of Saco" again in 1702, and his wife still living, in the interim of peace. The younger ch. were by the 2d wife. **Elizabeth,** in 1697 was "late of Duxberry," m. 22 Feb. 1699 Ebenezer Wing of Sandwich. **Nathaniel,** of Sandwich. Will 2 Oct. 1727 named wife Remember and 7 ch. **Joshua,** d.s.p.; adm. 1706 to Nathaniel. **Hannah,** m. 23 Feb. 1699 Benj. Nye of Falmouth, Barnstable Co. 7 ch. **Daniel,** b. 1691, living in Dartmouth in 1719. [One Samuel was a fort soldier in Maine in 1696.]

**Backway,** Benjamin, see Bagworth.

**BACON,** William. In 1674 he and Tho. Kennedy (John Redman, atty) sued the town of Hampton for ejecting them from a house they had built on the commons. In 1674 he collected £1 for killing a wolf. In 1678, living in Rye, he got drunk. Wm. **Baker** (Bacor) is misprinted Bacon in 1 Me.

Hist. Soc. v. 63.

**BADCOCK,** Nicholas, accused by Ann Cole 8 Oct. 1686, married by Justice Barefoote. Male child. Taxed 1690.

**Badiver,** John. Richmond Island. List 21.

**Badreck** (Bothwick?), Robert, Cochecho wit. 1669.

**Badson,** see Batson.

**BAGLEY,** James, Falmouth, 1690. List 225a. Doc. Hist. vi. 489, 498. See Hoyt's Salisb. p. 612.

**BAGNALL,** Walter, came as a servant to Mass., perh. by 1623; at Richmond or Richmans Island by 1628. By unscrup. dealings with the Indians he had accumulated wealth when he and John (Bray?) were murdered by them, (about Oct. 3, 1631), two months before the Island was granted to him by the Council for New Eng. "Black Will" was later hung for it by Capt. Neale. A pot of gold and silver coin supposed to have been Bagnall's was ploughed up 11 May 1855.

**Bagster,** see Baxter.

**BAGWORTH** (Backway), Benjamin, fell off the deck of his ship at Newcastle (Piscataqua), "where he always traded," in July 1698 — body not found. Here from 1686. He kept his wife Jane, childless, who called John Endicott, cooper, "brother-in-law," in Boston. Heirs lived in Southwark, Surrey.

**BAILEY,** Bayliff, the 53d commonest English surname, and became the 40th commonest in New England.

1 **ELTHIN** (Bailiff), see Hilkiah(3).

2 **HENRY,** Falmouth; refugee at Dorchester, where he died 12 Nov. 1717. List 228c. Will 1716-1717. He m. Mary Penley, dau. of Sampson and Rachel, who was still his widow, of Stoughton, in 1734. Ch. **Edward,** of Dorchester. **Elizabeth,** m. John Wentworth. See Wentworth Gen. i. 193.

3 **HILKIAH,** Scarb. 1645. Evid. misread "Elthin" (Bailiff) in Y. D. ii. 53. Hilkiah was sued by Capt. Cammock at the same time as Richard Foxwell, "Elthin" was tenant of Mr. Foxwell on land adj.(6).

4 **JAMES,** Bidd. wit. 1671. Y. D. ii. 97.

5 **JOHN,** fisherman at Isles of Shoals, 1659-1667. Ch. **Willmot,** m. Michael Endell, to whom her father deeded his house, 1662.

6 **JONAS** (Bully?), Scarb., b. 1607. This man's will called Nicholas Bully his brother, yet his own name was only spelt Bayly, Baly, Beyley, Beyly, Balie, Baile, Beill, Bcell. Perh. the two were brothers-in-law. Jonas came to Richmond Isl., thence to Blue Point, where he m. 1st Elizabeth, widow of George Dearing, and had his land; 2d, Eleanor, widow of John Jackson, who m. 3d Giles Barge. Lists 21, 23, 232, 233,

235. Will 11 Nov. 1663–9 Feb. 1663-4. No children.

7 **JOSEPH**, Newbury, b. 4 Apr. 1648, bot Maine lands in the Indian country in 1692 and persevered in settling them until killed. Oct. 1723. Of Arundel 1700, Casco Fort Feb. 1702-3, Arundel, 'late of Newbury' 1703. List 258. Wife Priscilla Putnam. 10 ch. rec.

8 **THOMAS** (Bayly), surveyor at North Yar. 1685. List 214. Falm. 1687. Perh. the bro. of Rev. John, who came to Watertown from Eng. via Ireland.

**BAKER**, Backer, the 32d commonest English surname and became the 24th commonest in New England.

1 **ABRAHAM**, alleged alias of Mr. Abraham Corbett — York Court.

2 *****JOHN**, executed in London. The records of John Baker in Boston, York, Cape Porpus and London evid. refer to one man, and appar. also in Dover 1647-50. Plausible address, soon disappointing, appeared everywhere. An early church mem. in Boston, he fled to York, thence conscience stricken back to Boston, where he was reädmitted 26 Mar. 1642; again dismissed to church at York 6 Sep. 1646. At York he was so greatly trusted that Mr. Hooke got judgment for £500 against him, but gave the cattle back to his wife (List 86) and children, who poss. include some of the name not traced. Lists 22, 261, 252. At Dover John Baker was lieut. and deputy to the General Court, but quickly vanished. Lists 352, 353, 354ab, 53.

3 **JOHN**, Portsm., currier. About 1680 he m. Sarah (Wall), wid. of Tho. Dew, and later stated in petn. that he was supporting her many ch. and his one. Lists 329, 332a, 52, 57. Adm. c.t.a. was granted 30 Nov. 1697 to his only son, the widow having d. without proving the will. She had been a licensed innholder after his death. List 335a. Ch: Benjamin, b. 1680, was appr. to a Kittery shipwright; in 1701 sold his father's house; in 1712 his sister was adm. his estate. Bethula, bp. 13 June 1708, m. same year Benj. Gatchell, shipwright.

4 **JOHN**, witnessed James Grant's will at York, 1693.

5 **JOSEPH**, b. ab. 1646; in 1659 received deed of a house lot on Great Island from Robert Mussell; d. at Peter Twisden's house at Isles of Shoals 16 Oct. 1672, leaving an unfinished house and garden plot on Great Island. Adm. to creditors.

6 **MARK**, Hampton, 1678. Arrested in Gove's Rebellion, his petition stated he was born in England, had been many years here, and was Gove's servant. Lists 396, 313d.

7 **NICHOLAS**, List 314. Poss. the same of Marblehead 14 July 1696, int. m. Eliza-

beth Bartlett of Boston, dau. of George of Spurwink.

8 **ROBERT**, Cape Newagen, 1672. List 13.

9 **THOMAS**, Scarborough and Falmouth. If but one man, he moved back and forth. See Doc. Hist. vi. Lists 238a, 91, 226, 34, 228c. His son Thomas, who was of Taunton in 1721 when he sold the land granted by Scarb. in 1682, was app. the Indian prisoner. List 99 (i. 76).

10 **THOMAS**, Pemaquid soldier, List 126, prob. was not (9) or (11), but perh. was the prisoner recovered by Church. List 99 (ii. 24).

11 **THOMAS**, York, yeoman, b. 1674; m. 5 May 1698 Hannah Adams (18); adm. 18 Feb. 1745-6 to her and son Issacher. 8 ch. rec. 1699-1718, including with himself in List 279 John, Joseph and Samuel.

12 **WALTER**, 1642, appar. a local creditor of John Phillips of Dover.

13 **WILLIAM**, Kennebec, house carpenter, b. 1649, wit. a Parker deed 1669. Lists 13, 183, 184, 187, 191. Messenger, 1684 (not Bacon, as pr. 1 Me. Hist. Soc. v. 63); killed by Indians 20 July 1689. He m. Sarah Parker, dau. of John and Margaret, who gave him land. Adm. 16 Sep. 1701 in Suff. Co. to son John, of Boston, house carpenter. John was of Charlestown 9 Mar. 1695-6 when he m. Tabitha Pickman of Salem, who m. 23 Sep. 1718 Edward Drinker of Boston, joiner. Her son Joseph Baker, joiner, m. Hannah Barnes 7 Sep. 1727.

14 **WILLIAM**, Portsmouth, 1695. List 334b. Balch. 1 Freeborn, s. of John, Salem, aged 23, dep. 19 Aug. 1657 about Henry Thorner of Wapping, Eng.

2 **Joan**, Portsm., a town charge 1726, bur. 1728.

**Bale**, see Beale.

**BALKWELL**, William, appr. with Joseph Hammond on S. Wheelwright's est. 1700.

**BALL**, a general English surname.

1 **BONADVENTURE** (wrote), wit. at Portsmouth or Rye 1664.

2 **EDWARD**, ±30 18 June 1660, fishing for Stephen Ford. In York Court, July 1661, questioned for living from his wife, he promised to go or bring her; was here in 1666. In 1667 he and [Robert] Winchester were joint creditors of Wm. Scadlock. Lists 302a, 79. Cf. Edward Ball, fisherman, Block Island, N. Y.

3 **HUGH**, English shipmaster. List 21.

4 **JOHN**, York, partner of Way, Stover and Powell 3 July 1649. Juryman. Lists 72, 75b. He is the more likely father of (5) and bro. of (8).

5 **JOHN**, b. ab. 1635, Kittery, bot on Spruce Creek in 1667. See (4) and (8). Lists 90, 290, 296-298. Wife Joanna was ±70 in

1716. His petition to Gov. Andros claims a 'numerous family,' but as they deeded their estate to dau. Elizabeth for life support we lack proofs of the others: **William**, adm. 29 Oct. 1696 to widow Mary, app. dau. or sist. of Wm. Roberts. Inventory lists 'his voyage' £29. Tho. and Wm., fishermen of Kittery in 1721, were their sons (Lists 291, 298); also poss. John who m. Anne Allen 9 Dec. 1717, or this may have been the grandfather, or poss. the uncle. **John**, ±18 in 1693, sailor about the Piscataqua. John Jr. had land laid out in Kit. in 1698. **Elizabeth**, m. 1st, 20 Oct. 1700, Edward Hammons; 2d Francis Pettegrew. **Joanna**, m. 1702 Benj. Hutchins. **Mary**, m. 12 Oct. 1700 Joseph Crockett Jr. **Thomas**, Kit. grant 1703; accused in 1705 by Elizabeth Thompson dau. of John and Sarah (Emery), and presum. father of Joanna Ball of Berwick who m. 3 May 1720 Edward Hopkins. List 298.

6 **JOHN**, from Concord, soldier at Scarborough in Philip's War.

7 **PETER**, b. 1645, fisherman, in 1672 bot house and 20 a. in lower Portsmo. Lists 331b, 329, 57, 66, 67, 316, 337, 339. In 1713 both Sen. and Jr. subsc. to build meeting house. Will 1719-23 Feb. 1725-6. Ch: **Peter**, m. Amy ——— 17 Dec. 1712. Will 4 May 1752–24 June 1753, 6 ch. **Christian**, wife of Philip Paine in 1730. **Sarah**, m. 11 Nov. 1713 Robert Ward, later of Boston, mariner. **Mary**, m. 1st one Jackson; 2d, 15 Nov. 1716, Wm. White. **Susannah**, m. bef. 1715 John Fickett; widow in 1730. **Elizabeth**, m. 3 Dec. 1719 John Roe; widow in 1730. **Margaret**, of Kittery, spinster in 1730.

8 **RICHARD**, fisherman, app. a rover: Salisbury in 1650, Cape Porpus 1653-1655, Dover 1668. List 356j. Adm. 1702 to nephew John (5), who in 1711 sold his Salisbury grant.

9 **SAMUEL** (Ball or Bull), Marblehead, soldier at Wells 1693-4. List 267b.

**BALLARD.** 1 **Augustine**, shipmaster, see Bullard.

2 **JOHN**, Portsmouth, 1693, in 1694 bot house lot near the Great House, which was sold in 1709 for his dau. **Hannah**. His widow Hannah (Snell), dau. of Capt. George and Hannah (Alcock), m. 2d Dependence Littlefield. Lists 335a, 336b, 337.

**Banals**, John, Pemaquid 1689. List 126.
**Bancroft**, see Barcroft.
**Bane**, see Beane.

**BANFIELD**, a typical English surname.
1 **CHRISTOPHER**, b. ab. 1636, was about Newington 1661-1663; juryman for Dover 1664; sergeant Kittery 1700; lot layer, appraiser. In 1667 Rowland Flansell and he were partners. In 1672 and 1675 he was in York Court for living away from his wife. He m. 2d Grace widow of Richard Miller (and bought in the Miller heirs); 3d Sarah (Libby), widow of Richard Rogers of Eliot. Died 5 May 1707; his widow was living in 1729.

2 **JOHN**, Portsmouth, fisherman and mariner, b. 1642. He bot land of John Moses in 1667. Lists 331ab, 326c, 329, 52, 335a. Died at Barbadoes while his younger ch. were small. Wife Mary Pickering, dau. of John, was granted adm. 4 Nov. 1707, and was living in 1711. List 335a. Ch: **Hugh**, b. 1673, lived on the homestead. Lists 67, 334a, 336b, 330d, 337, 339. He m. 1st in 1698 Abigail Jones dau. of Francis and Susannah (Willix); 2d 9 Aug. 1722 Hannah (Bartlett) widow of Edward Wells jr., dau. of Abraham and Elizabeth Bartlett. Adm. 12 Dec. 1727 to his bro. Samuel. Widow m. one Monson and was his widow in 1755. 6+3 ch. His son John was 'Senior' in 1743, when John jr. was Charles's son. **Mary**, m. Thomas Perkins jr., later of Arundel. **Agnes**, m. 1st by 1696 Nicholas Fletcher, 2d 9 June 1713 Richard Parsley, tailor, and settled in Barrington. Ch: **Samuel**, b. 1678, Capt. List 339. Adm. 26 Jan. 1742-3 to Joseph Langdon. He m. 1st Mary Seavey, dau. of William and Hannah (Jackson), who d. 9 July 1724; 2d 4 Mar. 1724-5 Keziah True. 1 dau. by each w. **Charles**, bot land in 1708; m. Jan. 1715-6 Elizabeth Rice, dau. of Thomas and Mary (Withers), who m. 2d 25 Oct. 1724 Stephen Lang. 2 ch. **George**, living 1760; m. 1st 1710 Miriam Shortridge, dau. of Richard and Alice (Creber); 2d 25 May 1727 Mary Locke, sister of Deborah (Locke) Allen. 4+2 ch. **Abigail**, m. 8 Dec. 1715 Tho. More, of Boston, carver; dec. by 1755. Ch. **Sarah**, rec. into covenant 2 Jan. 1714-5.

3 **NICHOLAS** ([Ban?]feild), wit. against Wm. Furbish in York Court, May 1682.

**BANISTER**, Capt. **William** of Barbadoes, now (1696) resident in Piscataqua, sells a quarter of his sloop.

**BANKS**, a general English surname, once common in Kent.

1 **JOHN**(3), town grants 1678-1696, perh. liv. some yrs. in southern N. E. undisting. from the Fairfield family; selectman 1693, often gr.j. 1687-1714. Will 1724—1726. Ch. by unkn. 1st w: **John**, York gr. 1702, d.s.p. bef. 1719. **Elizabeth**, m. Nehemiah Closson of Little Compton, R. I. Both liv. in Lebanon, Conn., 1738. 5 ch. bp. 1718, b. 1710-1718 in Little Comp., 4 in Lebanon 1720-1727. By 2d w. Elizabeth Turbet (her will 1737—1738): **Moses**, Lieut., mar. 1713 Ruth Weare. List 279. 11 ch. **Mary**, liv. 1737. **Aaron**, coaster, d. 1763 at York, m. (int. 12

Feb. 1725-6) Mary Haines. List 279. Ch. **Hannah**, liv. 1737.

2 **LT. JOSEPH**(3), active in Ind. war, repeat. gr. j., selectm. List 279. D. ab. 1744, m. 28 Feb. 1694-5 Elizabeth Harmon. Ch: **Job**, b. 24 Feb. 1695-6. Will 1770—1772. M. Elizabeth Card (6), d. 17 Mar. 1731-2. 7 ch. **Samuel**, b. 25 June 1697. List 279. Settled in Saco ab. 1735. M. (int. 21 Sep. 1728) Sarah Webster (Stephen of Newbury). 4 ch. **Tabitha**, b. 12 Feb. 1702-3, m. Samuel Bragdon(6). **Lydia**, b. 28 Jan. 1705-6, m. 22 Nov. 1730 John Card, bro. of Elizabeth supra. **Mary**, b. 12 Oct. 1708, m. Daniel Bragdon (6). **Joseph**, b. 12 Sep. 1711. **Elizabeth**, d. 30 Aug. 1720, ag. 6. **Richard**, d. 27 Mar. 1720, ag. 2.

3 ‡**RICHARD**, of 'Scituate Row,' York, (see Preble), he and Thomas Curtis sharing the lot of Thomas Chambers; he had taken the freeman's oath at Scituate, Mass., in same list with Preble. York wit. Mar. 1642-3. Godfrey's Council 1651-2. Prom. in town, church and probate business, often selectm. 1653-1680, Com.t.e.s.c. under Mass. 1669, 72, 79, repeat. gr. j., overseer of county prison 1673. Appar. vict. of York massacre, adm. 28 Nov. 1693 to s. Joseph. Lists 24, 25, 33, 273-7. M. 1st ab. 1644 Elizabeth Curtis, bp. Aug. 1624 in Ash, Kent, d. of Tho. and Richardine, and stepdau. of Thomas Chambers (2); 2d Elizabeth Alcock (1), liv. 1698. Ch: by 1st w: **Elizabeth**, m. at Scituate, 1st 17 July 1666 Wm. Blackmer, who d. 21 Apr. 1676; 2d 24 Jan. 1676-7 Jacob Bumpas; removed to Rochester. 7 ch. 1667-1687. By 2d w: **John**, b. ab. 1657. **Job**, fined for cursing 1684, d. s.p. **Joseph**, b. 1667.

4 **SAMUEL**, presum. relat. to (3); brothers John, Richard, Samuel, bap. St. Vedast, Foster Lane, London, 1608, 1611, 1616, untraced. Shipwright, sold. in Philip's War, sued in Suff. Ct. 1680 on joint note with Samuel Donnell of York dated 15 Apr. 1679. At York 1681, town gr. at Cape Neddick, York, 1689 (sold by his grs. Peter Bours, Esq., of Newport, R. I. in 1731). Gr.j. 1687-88. In 1692 was building a ship at Portsm. (aut. Suff. Ct. files 2549), recently dec. 25 Feb. 1692-3, wid. Mrs. Sarah (perh. Donnell, or Stover) Banks lodging in the Great House in the summer of 1693. She m. 2d John Lancaster, shipwright (see Hoyt's Salis.), who d. at Newport 13 Dec. 1717, ag. 47 yrs. 6 mo., by whom Mary (Lancaster), b. 15 Apr. 1703, d. inf., Sarah (Lancaster), m. 23 Jan. 1717 Thomas Coggeshall. Her will names grs. Peter Bours, Esq., and Coggeshall grch. Ch: **Samuel**, (perh. by earlier w.), adm. 1710 to sis. Bathsheba Bours. 2 ch. **Bathsheba**, disting. by having her min. record simul. on town book her four marriages and death, to Peter Bourse 6 Jan.

1704-5, John Hart 27 Feb. 1711-2, Franklin Morton 3 June 1717, Jacob Dehane, 27 Feb. 1721-2; d. Jan. 1722-3. 1 son.

**Baple** (Beaple), Mr. John, made a fishing voyage to Isles of Shoals 1637. Me. P. & C. i. 8, 52.

**BARBER**, occup. surname, commoner in Mid. Eng.

1 **JAMES**. In 1830 James Means wrote of the Falmouth family: John and James Barbour, brothers, came from Ireland. Willis MSS. N 241.

2 **JAMES**, soldier under Scottow. List 237b.

3 **JOHN**, taxed Oyster River 1659, ch. seating Amesbury 1667, Newfields wit. 1675, rec. inhab. 1678. Lists 361a, 363a, 381. Wife Sisly. Kn. ch: **John**, ±67, 23 May 1737. **Robert**, b. Amesbury 4 Mar. 1669-70.

4 **JOHN**(3), Newfields, scouting co. 1710. List 376b. Liv. 1744. M. Anna Smart, ±83 in 1759. Kn. ch: **John**. List 376b. M. Jane Davis (37) 19 Jan. 1726-7; wife Ann in 1768. **Joseph**, Crown Point 1744. **Anne**, acc. John Perkins jr. 5 May 1723.

5 **ROBERT**(3). List 376b. K. by Ind. in Newfields 1 July 1706. Ch: **Daniel**, mariner Gloucester, d. in Antigua 8 Nov. 1735, ag. 29; wid. Anna m. one Plummer. 3 daus. **Robert**, b. 1699. List 376b. Had homestead. M. (Eunice Hall?), Sarah Bean, b. 1707. 7 ch. **Mary**, m. 18 May 1727 Nathan Taylor. **Abigail**, unm. 1731.

6 **THOMAS**, gr. j. York Co. 1703; Daniel Kenniston his apprent. He was app. the coastwise trader who had 5 ch. rec. Boston 1704-1714 and d. 10 Mar. 1718-9, ag. 46, adm. to wid. Eliz., Jeremiah Storer bondsman. Lt. Josiah Littlefield in 1710 wrote to Cousin Thomas Barber, Boston. (Storer? Masters? Wardwell?). See Lists 237b, 126.

7 **WILL**, soldier under Hill. List 267b.

**BARCLEY**, Barclay, Berkeley.

1 **HENRY** (Barkeley, Berkelott, Berkett), came over in 1658-9 as adm. of est. of his f. Wm. Berkeley, former alderman of London. Staying here ab. two yrs. at Maj. Shapleigh's, he acted as atty. for (and was sued by) Walter Barefoot. Est. in the hands of Lt. Edw. Hayes Sep. 1671. Mass. Arch. 39.423.

2 **JAMES** (Barkley) bound himself 6 Sep. 1659 for 4 yrs. to John Johnson, Portsm.

3 **WILLIAM** (Barcley), Esq., of London, took blanket mtg. of Nicholas Shapleigh 1648. Father of (1).

**BARCROFT**, John, and w. Jane, came in -The James- 1632, with Henry Sherburne. Bot goods from John Raymond, Laconia Co. factor. By 12 Sep. 1633 his wife was putting him to trouble in Boston, Samuel Maverick his bondsman for her. Winth. 1, 132, Col. Rec. i. 108. See conflict. accts. Essex

Ant. ii. 94, N. E. Reg. 56.84. Likelier John and Jane Barcroft carried to Isle of Wight Co., Va., 1637.

**BAREFOOT,** an ancient burgher fam. in Basingstoke; also a name for foundlings.

†‡**WALTER,** surgeon, Capt., app. had held letter of marque. First appeared May or June 1657 shaving navy men's tickets, app. at York. 1658 Kittery, 1663 Boston mercht. Later at Dover, Stratham, Newfields, Newcastle; unm. here, accu. of abandoning wife and ch. in England. Oppressive litigant, repeat. in jail. In 1686 he procured from Andros a warrant for 1000 a. at Spruce Creek and was met by a remonstrance of 16 families living on it against whom he had never made claims. Doc. Hist. vi. 350. Deputy coll. of customs under Randolph, Counc. under Cranfield and Deputy Gov. Justice under Dudley. Lists 34, 292-3, 312e, 313b, 356ghk, 359a. Will 3—8 Oct. 1688 gave his house on Great Isl. with cert. lands to the fam. of John Clark, ment. sis. Sarah, w. of Thomas Wiggin, and cous. John Lee. 1672, called Ichabod Rollins cousin.

**Barfield,** Nicholas, app. B. written over D. (cert. Nic: ---a---feild), wit. 1682 with Eliot men against Wm. Furbush.

**BARGE.** One Giles B. was in Lytton Cheney and Compton Abbas. co. Dorset 1621-5.

1 ***GYLES,** landowner Gloucester 1653, Scarb. See Coe. Appar. kept company with the Jacksons over 30 yrs. In 1658 he and John Jackson subs. for the ministry at Glouc.; in 1660 they brought a joint suit against Thomas Harvey for defamation; in 1662 he was wit. to papers for John Briers and John Jackson jr.; presently they were all in Scarb., where he m. by 1673 the wid. Eleanor Bailey. Lists 236, 238a. Selectm. 1609, 70, 71, gr. j. 1671-2, Assemblyman 1682, 83. In Philip's War rem. to Dorchester where he d. 25 Sep. 1691 (a church collection taken for him), and she 15 Dec. 1691. In 1683 'now of Dorchester' she deeded her Scarb. lands to her grs. John Jackson on cond. that he live dutifully with his grfr.

2 **THOMAS,** his house lot on Dover Neck sold by Mrs. Anne Godfrey to Edw. Colcord.

**Barger,** Philip, Falmouth. List 229. Willis thought he came with Peter Bowdoin.

**BARKER.** 1 **Edward,** Damariscove 162---. List 8

2 **ENOCH,** Greenland. List 338b. Church memb. bef. 1712. Adm. 1727 to wid. Bridget (Cate 1), who m. Daniel Donovan. 5 ch.

3 **ESTHER,** 1722, signed with Peter Peve and Edw. Wilmot, deeding land willed to them by Thomas Robie. N. H. Deeds 19.246.

4 **NOAH,** bro. of (2), from Rowley, Ipsw. 1717, Stratham 1724. Will 1748 names w. Martha, 9 ch.

5 **THOMAS,** wit. 1663.

**Barkecley,** see Berkeley.

**Barkwell,** William, 1700, Y. D. vi. 77. Mr. B. taxed Str. Bank 1707.

**BARLOW, George,** bef. coming to Exeter with Wheelwright had been whipped 19 Sep. 1637 for idleness, presum. studying theology. Freeman's oath 1648. Withdrew 1652 to Saco, thence on the Mass. advance, to Scarb., where bef. 1665 he d. Litigious and prosec. for preaching. Lists 373, 375b, 376ab, 235, 243ab, 249, 252, 263. Wid. Cicely m. Henry Watts who improved his farm and 20 May 1670 sold it. The Quaker missionaries, prosec. by Geo. Barlow of Sandwich, receptive to tales ab. our Geo., misapplied them.

**Barnaby,** Ruth, in 1764, called 100, was made to depose conc. John Brown (15). She d. 12 Feb. 1765.

**BARNARD,** common English name, one place in North of England.

1 **BARTHOLOMEW,** carpenter, from St. Margaret's, Westminster. At York 1636, on delegation to Saco court 1640, alderman 1641, judgment vs. Sir Ferdinando Gorges 1647, jury same yr. and rem. aft. 1647 to Boston where he and Thomas Joy built the Town House. List 22. Tavern lic. 1675. He m. 13 Aug. 1626 Alice Weedon; 2d at Boston ab. 1664 Jane Laxton, who had tavern lic. 1678 and d. 13 May 1698. Ch: **Bartholomew,** bp. 27 Mar. 1627, poss. m. at Hartford 25 Oct. 1647 Sarah Burchard. 7 ch., of whom Thomas in 1691 was gdn. of Christopher Hobbs from Saco. **Ralph,** bp. 27 Mar. 1627. **Matthew,** bp. 7 Sep. 1628, carpenter, left ch. in Boston. See Nicholas Davis (41). **Anne,** bp. 1 Nov. 1630. **Richard,** b. ab. 1637, m. 2 Mar. 1659 Elizabeth Negus, d. Dec. 1706. Ch.

2 **BENJAMIN,** s. of John and Phebe of Watertown, ±26 in 1676. Betw. Apr. 1675 and June 1676 he was running the Broughton mill at Salmon Falls by the thousand. Ret. to Watertown during Philip's War, was of Watert. 20 Dec. 1675, when he bot land in Kit. of Humphrey Spencer, and of Dover 24 Aug. 1687. Lists 28, 94. M. Sarah Wentworth. In the 2nd war his w. was taken by the Ind. and he ret. to Watert. where he d. 12 Sep. 1694, leaving wid. (who m. 2d Samuel Winch of Framingham by whom 2 ch.) and two ch. for whom their uncle Paul Wentworth was app. gdn. See Wentworth Gen. p. 109-110. Ch: **Sarah,** b. 1692. **Benjamin,** b. 24 Aug. 1693, m. Elizabeth Parris, dau. of Rev. Samuel of Sudbury, 2d 18 Dec. 1726 Mary Wellington of Hopkinton.

3 **GEORGE**, owed George Munjoy's estate 1685. List 93.

4 **JAMES**, br. to (2), 'of Watertown' 1662, bot land in Wells 1662, m. 8 Oct. 1666 Abigail Phillips.

5 **JOSEPH**, br. to (2), b. 12 Nov. 1642, had land in Kit. 1670, was 'of Watertown' 20 Oct. 1676, moved to Berwick ab. 1678. In 1686 he sued Gilbert Endicott for debt. Lists 94, 298. App. d.s.p. bef. 1708. Y. D. 7.115.

6 **ROBERT**, a York wit. 1708. Y. D. 7.98.

**BARNES**, name of a parish in Surrey.

1 **BONAVENTURE**. In Me. Ct. 27 Oct. 1668 Mr. Barnes gave bonds to go to his wife in Eng. bef. 15 Oct. 1669.

2 **HENRY**, Spruce Creek, adm. to Gowen Wilson 1669. App. m. Rebecca Wilson, who m. 2d Henry Bodge who was k. by Ind. 20 Aug. 1694. List 96, p. 82. Ch: **Henry**. See Richard, Isaac, Joanna.

3 **HENRY**(2), shipwright, liv. on the Bodge homestead. Lists 298, 96 p. 104. K. by Ind. 4 May 1705; m. by 1698 Abishag Beale (1), who m. Francis Carman by 1719 and was liv. 1728. Kn. ch: **Benjamin**, of York 1727.

4 **ISAAC**, m. 6 Dec. 1694 in Berwick, Sarah Goodwin.

5 **JAMES**, son of Widow Barnes, in 1714 presented writings to Com. on Eastern Claims, (land at Long Creek in So. Port.), and later got them back. Me. H. & G. Rec. v. 35.

6 **JOANNA**, Kittery, York Ct., Jan. 1710-11, black bastard.

(7 **JOHN**, Merriconeag 1670. See Burns.)

8 **JOSHUA**, rated to New Meeting House, Portsm. 1717.

9 **RICHARD**. List 298. Kittery grant same day as Henry.

10 **SAMUEL**, ±35 in 1699, liv. with Thos. Pickering, Newington.

11 **SARAH**, from Wells, m. Francis Usselton of Topsfield ab. 1656.

12 **THOMAS**, of Hog Island, fisherman, owned house, flake room, etc., 1672, later of Rye and taxed Portsm. 1698. Lists 57, 68, 313a, 316, 330d, 332b. Liv. 1732. He m. 1st by 1689 Mary Rand, dau. of Francis; 2d by 1696 Joan, wid. of Thomas Stevens and mother of John Stevens, adult 1697. Ch: **Thomas**, Portsm. Lists 316, 339. W. Hannah and 5 or more ch. 1710-1728 (incl. Bridget). Adm. 1764 to s. Samuel. **Dau.**, m. Stephen Noble. **Elizabeth**, m. 4 Dec. 1707 Joshua Shackford of Dover. **Abraham**. Taxed Str. Bank 1707. Rated to Old Meet. Ho. List 339. M. 17 Aug. 1711 Anne Wallis, dau. of George, who was dec. 1724-5. Ano. Elizabeth m. John Jordan, North Ch., 18 Sep. 1712, Mary was a domestic in Wibird family 1730-1740.

13 **WILLIAM**. Rated to Old Meet. Ho. 1717. List 339. Of Winborn, co. Dorset, m. 1st 3 Dec. 1719 Rebecca Dodge of Beverly; 2d 9 Apr. 1732 Elizabeth Roe. Will July—Aug. 1738. 2 ch.

**Barnett**, see Burnett.

**BARNWELL**. 1 John, taxed Str. Bank 1713.

2 **MARY**, Portsm., licensed 1694, and selling without license 1696. List 335a.

**Barrell**, see Burrell.

**BARRETT**, ancient forename, general except in North of England.

1 **JOHN**, at York 1637, in 1641 with Leonard Hunter was in poss. of land lately fenced on York River; rem. to Wells, where he first liv. on Mr. Wheelwright's Ogunquit farm, but soon bot from Mr. Rishworth his farm next No. of the Storer Garrison. Jury 1655-56, const. 1657. Lists 24, 25, 261-263. Wife Mary, b. ab. 1617, named with s. John in his will 17 Apr. 1662—4 July 1664, was still his wid. when she deeded homestead and goods to her son, 14 Sep. 1670, appar. prepar. to m. Thomas Ladbrook of Portsm. Son: **John**.

2 *LT. **JOHN**, of Wells 1658, and in 1660, when he sold to Nathl. Boulter land in Hampton bot of George Barlow. Evid. is wanting when or why he came to Wells, or how relat. to John (1); his purch. and sale of Barlow's land was app. a speculation. Savage says he was of Malden 1653. Aft. exchang. his farm now in the northern part of Wells for the Anthony Littlefield farm at Great Hill, Kennebunk, he liv. there 7 or 8 yrs., but in June 1666 he is descr. as 'late of Wells but now at Cape Porpus.' Ensign Wells 1659, Lieut. Cape Porpus 1670, gr. j. 1660, 69, 73, 79, 84, 86, 89, jury 1667, 1672, selectm. Cape Porpus, Deputy Cape Porpus 1681. Lists 261-264, 252, 255, 266, 256, 259, 32. He and two sons k. by Ind. in fall of 1688. Inv. 12 Feb. 1689-90 as John Barrett sr. of Cape Porpus. He m. Mary Littlefield, liv. 1703. Ch: **Mary**, m. William Thomas. **Two sons** killed in 1688. **John**, k. by Ind. Apr. 1689.

3 **JOHN**(1), only ch., was given by will 150 a. at Stony brook, which he sold aft. his mo. gave him the homestead, where he spent his life. Constable 1668, 1670, selectm. 1689, gr. j. 1684. Lists 265, 266, 269b, 33. M. at Charlestown 6 June 1664 Elizabeth Cousins (2). Adm. 2 Jan. 1693-4 to dau. Elizabeth Littlefield. Ch: **Elizabeth**, m. 1st Nathan Littlefield; 2d James Denmark (1). She with her 2d husb. sold her grfr's homestead. See Ancestry of Lydia Harmon, pp. 49-50, Hoyt's Salis. 565-6.

4 **JOHN**, Pemaquid 1687. List 124.

5 **RICHARD**, soldier at Black Point. Lists 237be.

6 **ROBERT**, the Frenchman. Me. Prov. & Ct. i. 104, 111.

7 **SAMUEL**, Portsm. (Cutt's) wit. 1661.

8 **SUSANNAH**. 'Ould Susannah Barrett' d. Hampton 5 Apr. 1675. See (2).

**BARROW, Barry**, 1 **James**, Berwick. He had grants in Kit. 1662, 1673. Lists 25, 298. Wm. Gowen had James Barrow at his house and cured him of scurvy. K. by Ind. 16 Oct. 1675. Adm. 4 Apr. 1676 to Niven Agnew, who mar. his wid. and liv. on his farm, next north of those shown in Stackp. Kittery, p. 133. No ch. Agnew's will, calling him 'my predecessor,' devised his lands.

2 **RICHARD** (Barrows, Barows), a Scottow's Hill, Scarb., tenant. List 234b.

**Barry**, see Barrow and Berry.

**BARSHAM, John**, b. 8 Dec. 1635, son of William and Annabel (Bland) of Watertown. See Austin (1). Harvard 1658; schoolmaster 1661-62 in Hampton (where his uncle Thos. Leavitt lived), and had to sue for his salary; Hampton wit. Apr. 1667, Exeter 1669, taxed in Portsm. 1673, where in 1693 he was schoolmaster, and d. 1698. Lists 326c, 331a, 335a. Many existing orig. deeds and probate papers are in his handwriting. His w. Mehitable app. d. 1678. List 331c. Ch: **Annabel**, b. 31 May 1670. **Mary**, b. 26 Feb. 1671-2. **Dorothy**, b. 23 Feb. 1673-4, m. James Allen (15). **Sarah**, b. 11 Aug. 167--; by trad. m. 1st Benj. Bickford (5), 2d Hon. Jotham Odiorne. **William**, b. 25 Apr. 1678.

**Barson**, see Basson.

**Barstow** (Bas-), John, Isl. of Shoals, ±33 1674.

**BARTER**, uncommon English surname.

1 **HENRY**. Bradbury in 1837 was told that he was Welsh and came over in same vessel with the first Pepperell. Selectm. 1709. Gr. j. 1711. Deacon 1720. Lists 296-298, 291. He m. Sarah Crockett (2), 2d 1730, Jane (Jackson) Frink (3). His will Oct. 1746—May 1747 names all 7 ch: **Elizabeth**, m. one Jones, liv. a wid. 1751. **Sarah**, b. 26 Mar. 1693, m. 3 May 1716 James Grindle. **Eleanor**, b. 12 Aug. 1695, m. 25 Oct. 1724 Joseph Creesey of Rowley. **Henry**, mariner, b. 29 Jan. 1697, m. 1 July 1722 Mary Heard, dau. of Capt. John. His will 1765—1779. 6 ch. **Richard**, b. 7 Sep. 1700, was supported by William. **William**, mariner, b. 29 Aug. 1703, m. (int. 22 Aug. 1730) Mary Jones. Settled in Ken'port. 8 ch. **Martha**, m. (int. 8 Feb. 1729) Samuel Jones; wid. 1751.

2 **JOHN**, Mr., taxed Portsm. 1672, small.

3 **JOHN**. List 309. Likely had wife (or mother) Margaret (List 307b), and s. **John**, from the Shoals, at Portsm. poor ho. betw. 1781 and 1785, ag. 79. See Peter (4).

4 **PETER**, a mariner going to Eng. 1670; bot house on Star Isl. 1686. Margaret, List 307b, likely his wife. See John (3). In 167--, ±35, she was recently from Plymouth,

Eng. See Evans (11). In 1749 a Peter Barter of Gosport bot house and land of Nathl. Adams, Peter jr. a wit.

**Bartholme**, Thomas, Piscat. 1650. Me. P. & C. i. 143.

**BARTLETT**, common in S. W. of England.

1 **ABRAHAM**, b. 1666, fisherman of Portsm., m. by 1686 Elizabeth Jones, wid. of James. Prob. she was the Elizabeth bap. privately 24 Aug. 1718. In 1691 John Sherburn willed him a mare colt. Lists 330d, 335a. Ch: **Hannah**, m. 1st 9 Nov. 1713 Edward Wells, 2d 9 Aug. 1722 Hugh Banfield (2). **Abraham**, b. 1692, d. Portsm. Mar. 1785, ag. 93; m. 1st 13 Nov. 1718 Deborah Savage (John), who was liv. 1722-3, but likely had d. by 1729-30 when he had as housekeeper Elizabeth Lear; m. 2d 12 Nov. 1732 Mary (Wall) Amos, wid. of William. 3+6 ch. bp.

2 **EDWARD**, at Sandy Beach 1698. List 315b.

3 **GEORGE**, early fisherman in Casco Bay, sold ¼ of the old house and House Island. Later, by 1663, took from Henry Jocelyn a lease of 50 a. at Spurwink adj. John Jackson and Samuel Oakman, where he d. List 239a. Wife Mary. Inv. 14 Feb. 1674-5, incl. plantation and 8 kine; adm. July 1675 to Walter Gendall. Ch. ment. of whom app. only one surv.: **Elizabeth**, m. (int. Boston 14 July 1696) Nicholas Baker of Marblehead.

4 **JOHN**, of Portsm. 1681, soldier 1695-96. Taxed 1698. Lists 329 (1681), 57, 67, 335a, 336b, 330de. In 1694 he swept the meeting house; in 1713, 'very aged and feeble,' became a town charge.

5 **NICHOLAS**, b. ±1620, fisherman, escaped to Maine after serving Charles I eight years, the last three on Prince Charles's guard without pay. When Charles was restored he went back, but came again in -The Nathaniel- of Dartmouth in 1662. He (and Damaris Searle-Phippen) had liv. in Totnes, Devon, 'next neighbor' to Christopher Babbidge. Over him courted George Cleeve, who in 1651 deeded him 100 a. now in the business district of Portland. From Ken'-port he presum. rem. to Portland, was in Boston with Cleeve in 1660. After his 2d coming he liv. in Salem and for yrs. fished for Philip English. Liv. 1706. Wife ment. 1672, 1682-5.

6 **THOMAS**, appraiser Isles of Shoals, 1671.

7 **WILLIAM**, a wit. in Maine Ct., July 1663. In Sep. 1671 Richard Potts, John Batten, Will Bartlett and John White were prosec. for letting Francis Morgan out of prison at Falmouth.

**Bartley**, William. Doc. Hist. iv. 9. misr. of Barclay.

**BARTOE**. 1 **Abraham**, taxed Gt. Isl. 1720.

2 **NICHOLAS**, from Amesbury, grant at

Arundel laid out in 1720 next N. E. of wid. Mary Cole. K. by Ind. 1723. Wid. m. in Amesb. 24 July 1729 Daniel Hoyt. 6 ch. rec. in Amesb.

**BARTON,** name of 37 parishes, townsh., etc. all over Eng. exc. S. W. In the west, manors or large farms often so named.

1 **BENJAMIN,** at Kennebec 1672. List 13.
Ruth Berry claimed land at New Harbor, 'acre and a halfe at Witch Barton on ye Westward Side.' See Edward (3).

2 **EDWARD,** landowner, Marblehead 1643, living there ±4 yrs., prev. of Salem, deft. 1640; soon moved to Portsmouth, owning land above Sagamore Creek, afterw. the Wentworth est., till c. 1659. Plf. in Me. Ct. 1650, and in court next year for beating wife. Jury St. Bk. 1650, gr. j. 1656. He bot from Anthony Littlefield 300 a. at Cape Porpus with a little old house, and built a new one, occu. 20 odd yrs. by hims. or fam. until driven away by Ind. Lists 323, 325, 326a, 330a, 43, 255. Inv. 16 June 1671, adm. next mo. to wid. Elizabeth. Ch: **Dau.** app. m. John Purington. **William,** with br. Matthew wrongly travelled on Sunday, 1672. **Matthew. Elisha,** b. ab. 1655, wit. William's deed 1672. List 306a. M. Mary Crockett (6), both liv. Kittery 1688. Also likely other ch., inc. **John,** runaway apprent. of Wm. Ellingham 1659; **Job** or **George,** see N. H. Ct. Files, inquest 29 June 1669; **James,** apprent. himself for 4 yrs. to Mary Hilliard, Salem, in 1671.

3 **EDWARD,** (one Edw. ag. 33 in 1680), fisherman Pemáquid, 1672. Of Cape Newagen 1674, sued in Boston Ct., perh. the Pemaquid abuttor. Jailed in Boston 3 Sep. 1680 for resisting draft for Me. expdn; sued there in 1682. Lists 13, 15, 224.

4 **MATTHEW**(2), b. ab. 1640, shoreman, Salem 1671, accts. with Philip English 1687. In Salem, gave dep. about early Cape Porpus as late as 1729, in which yr. he and w. Elizabeth q.c. his father's 300 a. there. Three wives, 1st Martha, 2d Sarah bef. 1680, m. 3d 20 Dec. 1694, Wid. Elizabeth Dickinson, dau. of John and Elizabeth Tapley. Ch. by 1st w: **Jonathan,** wit. with Matthew at Salem 1679. **Samuel,** b. ab. 1664. List 94. M. ab. 1690 Hannah Bridges, dau. of Edmond and Sarah (Towne); liv. Framingham and Oxford, Mass., dying in latter 13 Mar. 1727. 8 ch. See N. E. Reg. 84.404. **Mary,** bp. 27 Apr. 1678, d. Jan. 1758. By 2d w: **Susanna,** b. 10 May 1680. **Matthew,** b. 6 Nov. 1682. **Sarah,** b. 1 Apr. 1685, m. 10 June 1708 Daniel Rawlins of Newbury. **Elizabeth,** b. 20 Apr. 1687. By 3d w: **John,** b. 6 Dec. 1695. **Patience,** bp. 8 Aug. 1697, m. 7 Nov. 1721 James Mascoll. **Susanna,** bp. 29 Mar. 1702. **Susanna,** bp. 31 Oct. 1703, m. 29 June 1723 Nathaniel Knight, son of

Lawrence and Elizabeth (Ingersoll). 3 ch. **Martha,** bp. 3 Mar. 1707. **Benjamin,** bp. 10 Oct. 1708.

5 **WILLIAM**(2), prior to 22 Nov. 1672 bot 100 a. at Cape Porpus from bro.-in-law John Purington; lot layer there. Lists 33, 259. His abs. from meeting brot him before the court in York Co. July 1674; in Essex Ct. 1680, an execution for debt was levied on him, to serve John Cromwell 4 yrs. or until execu. paid. His name not seen aft. 1686, when his w. and Walter Penwell were cautioned, who m. 15 Apr. 1700 at Newbury. In 1722 liv. in Ken'port, they deeded William's homestead for life supp. to son-in-law Solomon Holman, who deeded it to his son in 1730. Ch: **Mary,** b. ab. 1673, m. Solomon Holman of West Newbury, ship carpenter; d. there 18 Oct. 1736, ag. 63. 12 ch. 1694-1717. **Ebenezer,** mariner, Newbury and Ken'port; cast away and drowned at Newbury Bar 6 May 1721. M. Newbury 5 May 1710 Esther Flood. 5 ch. rec. there, inc. Penuel. **John,** in 1724, of Arundel, sold ½ his father's 100 a. gr.; soldier under Lt. Brown, k. 25 Dec. 1724. Perh. m. Hannah, wid. of Nathaniel Parker (his adm. 10 May 1711). 3 ch. **Susanna,** m. Solomon Smith of Biddeford. Their dau. Rebecca, b. 28 Mar. 1723.

6 **WILLIAM.** List 335b. Portsm. 1694, besides others about the Piscataqua not long after.

**BASFORD,** name of 3 places in Salop-Notts.

**JACOB,** Hampton Falls, 'alias Corretuck' with Joseph Perkins, 1685, put Governor Cranfield's rent gatherer Thos. Thurton beyond the Province line; the alias presum. because he had liv. in Carolina. He m. Elizabeth Clifford, and recd. deed 1686 of app. whole est. of her f. John Clifford, sr., to maintain him and wife thru life. She joined Hampton Ch. 9 May 1697 and her 4 ch. were bap. He m. 2d 27 Mar. 1708 Sarah Cram. Propr. Chester 1722, and res. there by Aug. 1731 until his death, the town supporting his wid. in old age. Ch: **James,** apprent. of Benj. Batchelder 1705, taxed in Hampt. Falls 1708, bound himself in 1710 to Jos. Curtis of Kit. for one yr. Of Dover 1715, Oyster River or Dover until 1729, from Hampton to Chester 1730. In 1746 he was defending his Chester grants in the courts. Wife Mary Davis(37). Ch. **Mary,** b. 28 Aug. 1687, m. 26 Jan. 1709 Jeremiah Folsom. **Elizabeth,** b. 7 May 1692, m. 2 Aug. 1711 Capt. John Davis, s. of John(23). **Margaret,** b. 20 June 1695, m. 9 Dec. 1718 William Willey. **Hephzibah,** b. 28 June 1699, m. Richard Clifford(2). In 1721 Jacob and his w. had a ch. Lydia Clough bap., having taken her as their own.

**BASS**, uncommon surname, old in Mid. Eng.

1 **EDWARD**, plf. in York Ct. 1670 against Roger Kelly. Shoals wit. 1672.

2 **PETER**, Wells, 1677. List 124. O. A. York, Mar. 1679-80. With Saml. Harmon appr. John Foxwell's est. 1680, prison keeper 1682. M. dau. or stepdau. of George Parker, perh. dau. of Wm. Johnson. In 1683 Parker and w. Hannah deeded est. to son-in-law Peter Bass for life supp. and to bring up Eleazer Johnson as his own ch. D. bef. 25 June 1684 when court restored land to Parker, £5 to be secured to young Peter Bass at 21. Ch: **Peter**, under age 1684. **Jonathan**, who, instead of Peter, recd. the £5 from Saml. Johnson, 'successor to George Parker,' and ack. receipt in Boston 1701.

3 **PETER**, taxed Pemaquid 1687, personal. List 269b. May have been s. of (2).

4 **RICHARD**, a tall thin-faced fellow pocks-rotten, ran away with a shallop of John Dalton of Monhegan, with a serv. of the owner, and ano. fellow, 1682.

**Bassey**, Richard, see J. Oswell. See also Bacey.

**BASSON, Richard**, b. 1625, d. Boston 8 Nov. 1716, 'aged 91.' Fined for drunkenness (Barsum) at Portsm. 1659, John Sherborne bondsman; Scarb., abs. from meet. in 1667, liv. near Dunstan; Falmouth 1683-4. Lists 237e, 238a, 226. Wife Elizabeth, ±73 in Aug. 1728, knew Dunstan early. List 234b. Ch: **Gershom**, seaman, Boston, adm. gr. to his f. 1699. **Samuel**, b. 1677, d. Boston 20 Mar. 1705, m. 25 June 1700 Mary Pickworth. Ch: Samuel, Richard, Mary, b. 1701-5. One Mary m. (int. 16 July 1722) John Eakins of Carolina. **Katherine**, d. 14 Feb. 1702. **John**, b. Boston 30 Dec. 1691.

**Bastens** (?), Joseph, Gt. Isl. 166--. List 311a.

**BASTER** (Bastard), **Walter**, fisherman for Peter Lewis, sued by Henry Dering 1673; Cape Eliz. 1683; N. H. 1695. Lists 226, 66.

**BASTON**, a parish in Lincolnshire, Bastin pecul. to Devon.

1 **DANIEL**(7), was deeded 150 a. by his brothers and sisters 1713, and sold out to bro. Saml. Stewart 1721-2. He was implicated in escape of John Tracy, forger, 1714. Jury 1715. One of those under Capt. Moulton in Col. Westbrook's command listed as dead 25 Dec. 1724 - 24 Apr. 1725. M. Prudence Stimson in Wells, 20 Dec. 1715. Ch: **Prudence**, b. 15 May 1719. **Sarah**, b. 23 Sep. 1722. Both bap. 30 Apr. 1727 at Ipswich, where a Wid. Boston d. 10 May 1745.

2 **GERSHOM** (7), joiner, with sev. residences, Scarb., late of Wells, 1728; York 1733, Killingly, Conn., 1736, after a stay at Woodstock, during which he recovered against John Morrill of Scarb.; retd. to Maine and in 1742 James Baston and James

jr. q.c. to him 150 a. He and 3 of his sons went against Louisburg. With w. Elizabeth he joined the ch. 1756; she liv. 1760 and he 1764. Ch: **Elijah. Elizabeth**, b. 1718. **Mary**, b. 1720. **Joseph**, b. 1722. **Shubael**, bp. 1724. **Thomas**, b. Scarb. 22 Dec. 1728. **Wentworth**, m. Hannah Weare of No. Yarm. **Daniel**, youngest son.

3 **JAMES** (7), gr. j. 1703, bondsman for Francis Sayer 1704, joined ch. 1705. Lists 269abc. With bro. Daniel and two Bucklins, one the constable, contrived escape of John Tracy, forger, 1714. M. Elizabeth Royal, dau. of John. D. bef. 1769. Ch: **James**, bp. 1712, called by f. 'my only son and child,' 1748. After being pub. to Mary Freeman 6 Oct. 1733, he m. 1st 10 May 1739 Eleanor Morrison, who joined the church the same year; 2d 2 Dec. 1743 Sarah (Storer) wid. of Uriah Nason, dau. of Jeremiah. 1+5 ch., incl. John Royal, bp. 30 Mar. 1740, bur. at Cape Ann 1776, s.p.

4 **JOHN**, Sheepscot, 1664. Y. D. ii. 8.

5 **JOHN**, ±32 in 1673, with Henry Light ±30, set Edward Holland from the Island to Piscataqua, after Elizabeth Oliver's baby was born.

6 **JOSEPH** (Boston), soldier, 1693-4. List 267b.

7 **THOMAS**, housewright, a Wells wit. 1674. Retired to Essex Co. twice during Ind. Wars; 18 Feb. 1678-9 he was formerly of Wells now of Ipswich; Salem 1680-1685, and there a 2nd time after May 1690; also lived at Charlestown where adm. inhab. Gr. j. 1674, 1702; jury 1691, 1701. Lists 265, 266, 267a, 269b. Either he or s. Tho. orig. mem. Wells Ch. 29 Oct. 1701. W. Hannah, ag. 28, in Ipswich ct. 30 Mar. 1680, one of many who bot stolen goods from Samuel Dutch's wife. He d. bef. 3 May 1713. Adm. ab. 1730 to son James, who had buried his mother. Ch: **Mary**, m. Benjamin Preble. **James. Thomas. Dorcas**, schoolmistress, m. 30 Jan. 1700-1 Samuel Stewart. **Abigail**, bap. 5 Aug. 1683 at Salem, m. 18 Oct. 1706 Stephen Wellman of Lynn. **Daniel**, bap. 2 Aug. 1685 at Salem. **Hannah**, m. 1 Nov. 1720 John Ashley, who d. 1723. **Sarah**, bap. 15 Oct. 1693 at Salem, m. (int. 4 Sep. 1714) Benj. Nurse of Salem. **Gershom**, b. 2 Mar. 1695-6.

8 **THOMAS**(7). List 269b. M. 24 June 1703 Mary Cloyes (2) who m. 2d 25 Nov. 1708 George Butland(1). Ch: **Mary**, b. 2 June 1704, d.y. **Abigail**, bp. 1706.

**BATCHELDER**, Bachiler, common in Hants, Bucks, Herts.

1 **ALEXANDER**, a Portsm. merchant. In 1652 ferryman. Gr. j. 1657, 59. 4 Aug. 1658 A.B., Henry Donnell and Richard Tucker were arbitrators bet. Edw. Shaw and **Mr.**

Abraham Jocelyn. Lists 43, 323, 326a, 330a. Adm. gr. 26 June 1660 to wid. Ann whose own will 5 Nov. 1660—26 June 1661 names s. John, with small sums and clothing to James Leech, his wife and 4 ch., Jane Fursen, Wid. Mary Walford and 4 ch., servants Richard Pierce and Tho. Paine. Ch: **John**, m. and had ch. in 1661.

2 **BENJAMIN** (3), Hampton Falls, b. 19 Sep. 1673, d. 12 Jan. 1718. In the Ind. wars he served as scout and messenger. M. 25 Dec. 1696 Susanna Page, dau. of Francis, who m. 2d 13 Jan. 1730 John Cram. 12 ch., one **Susannah**, m. 20 July 1738 Ebenezer Webster and was grmr. of Daniel, who, contrary to the Enc. Brit., which derives his talents from his mother, Eastman, himself, in a letter to his son, credits them to his grmr. Batchelder.

3 **NATHANIEL**, ±70 in 1700, grson of (5), s. of Nathaniel and Hester (Mercer) who did not come, lived in Hampton. Deed from his grfr. in 1647. In 1653 N. B. and Nathl. Drake wit. John Redman to Saml. Fogg. Const. 1683, 9 yrs. selectman. gr. j. 1683, 92, 94, 95, 98, 99. Lists 49, 52, 54, 55a, 57, 62, 392b, 393b, 396. He m. 1st 10 Dec. 1656 Deborah Smith, dau. of John and Deborah (Parkhurst), d. 8 Mar. 1675-6; 2d 31 Oct. 1676 Mary (Carter) Wyman, wid. of John of Woburn, d. 1688; 3d 23 Oct. 1689 Elizabeth, wid. of John Knill. He d. 17 Dec. 1710. Ch. by 1st w: **Deborah**, b. 12 Oct. 1657, m. 25 Jan. 1677 Joseph Palmer. **Nathaniel**, b. 24 Dec. 1659. **Ruth**, b. 9 May 1662, m. 8 July 1684 Dea. James Blake of Dorchester; he d. 22 Oct. 1732, she 11 Jan. 1752. Ch. **Hester**, b. 22 Feb. 1664-5, m. Dea. Samuel Shaw. **Abigail**, b. 28 Dec. 1667, m. Dea. John Dearborn (4). **Jane**, b. 22 Jan. 1670-1, m. 10 Nov. 1687 Benjamin Lamprey. **Stephen**, b. 31 July, d. 7 Dec. 1672. **Benjamin**, b. 19 Sep. 1673. **Stephen**, b. 8 Mar. 1675-6, m. 25 Aug. 1698 Mary Dearborn (3). He d. 19 Sep. 1748. List 399a. 7 ch. By 2d w: **Mercy**, b. 11 Dec. 1677, m. Samuel Dearborn (2). **Mary**, b. 18 Sep. 1679, d.y. **Samuel**, b. 10 Dec. 1680, m. 1 Apr. 1706 Elizabeth Davis (69?) of Newbury. Liv. No. Hampton. 12 ch. **Jonathan**, b. 1683, m. 2 Dec. 1708 Sarah Blake (2). Liv. Hampton. 1 ch. rec. **Theodate**, b. 1684, m. 18 Nov. 1703 Morris Hobbs. **Thomas**, b. 1685, m. 1st 14 Mar. 1712 Mary Moulton, dau. of Benj., d. 22 May 1716; 2d 16 Jan. 1718 Sarah Tuck, dau. of Dea. John, d. 15 Feb. 1764. He liv. on father's homestead; d. 10 Feb. 1774. 9 ch. by 2d w. **Joseph**, b. 9 Aug. 1687, m. Mehitable Marston. **Mary**, b. 17 Oct. 1688, d.y.

4 **NATHANIEL**(3), b. 24 Dec. 1659, m. ab. 1685 Elizabeth Foss (1). He was dea., assessor 1719-20, selectm. 1722, orig. propr. of Chester, d. 1745. Lists 57, 62, 392b. Ch:

**Deborah**, b. 9 Apr. 1686, m. 1st David Tilton, 2d 14 June 1733 Dea. Jonathan Fellows of Ipsw. **Nathaniel**, b. 19 Feb. 1690, m. 24 Feb. 1717 Sarah Robie, dau. of Samuel. Liv. Kensington. Will 1 Oct. 1723—3 June 1724. 4 ch. rec. **John**, b. 28 July 1692, m. 30 Dec. 1714 Abigail Cram, d. 16 Mar. 1753. 12 ch. **Josiah**, Dea., b. 1 July 1695, m. in 1722 Sarah Page, dau. of Francis. He d. Charleston, N. H., 9 Oct. 1759, she d. May 1781. 6 ch. **Jethro**, b. 2 Jan. 1698, m. 15 May 1721 Dorothy Sanborn, dau. of Dea. Benjamin. Liv. Hampton Falls and Exeter. Adm. gr. to her 5 June 1723. She m. 2d 13 Oct. 1736 Abraham Moulton. 2 ch. **Elizabeth**, b. 1694, m. Richard Sanborn. **Nathan**, b. 2 July 1700, m. 25 Feb. 1724 Mary Tilton, dau. of Capt. Joseph. Liv. East Kingston, deacon, d. 17 Mar. 1755. 8 ch. Capt. **Phineas**, b. 1 Nov. 1701, m. Elizabeth Gilman, b. 22 Mar. 1709, d. 27 May 1773. Liv. East Kingston, d. 16 Jan. 1793. 11 ch. ***Ebenezer**, b. 10 Dec. 1710, wife Dorothy. Liv. East Kingston, deacon, rep. 1774. 10 ch.

5 **REV. STEPHEN**, b. 1561, matric. St. John's Coll., Oxford, 17 Nov. 1581, B.A. 3 Feb. 1586-7, vicar at Wherwell, Hants, 17 July 1587 until then deposed in 1605, but liv. there in 1614. Of So. Stoneham, co. Hants, in 1631, he was lic. to visit his children in Holland, but having taken up with the company of merchant adventurers called the Plough Company, he came to N. E., arriving at Cambridge in the William and Francis- 5 June 1632, ag. 71. He preached at Lynn the first yr. and was made freeman there 1635; of Ipswich in 1636 and Yarmouth 1637, failing settlement at both; Newbury 1638. In 1638-39 he was the leader in the settlement of Hampton and is said to have named the town; excommunicated there but restored. In 1641 he was 'umpire' in an important reference case in Me. In 1644 he was called to Exeter but was prohib. from preaching there by the Genl. Ct. Apr. 20, 1647, he was 'late of Hampton now of Strawberry Bank.' Lists 391a, 392a, 393b. His 1st wife may have been a Bate, a rel. to Rev. John Bate, vicar at Wherwell, who called Stephen jr. 'cousin'; he m. 2d at Abbots-Ann 2 Mar. 1623-4 Christian Weare, wid.; 3d at Abbots-Ann 26 Mar. 1627 Helena Mason, wid., ±48 in 1631, who d. bef. 3 May 1647, when Portsm., as he wrote, assigned 'an honest neighbor (a widow)' to help care for his fam.; 4th unhappily the widow, Mary Beedle (4) of Kittery, with whom in 1650 he was ordered to live. The same yr. he was charged with marrying without bans. Oct. 16, 1651, she and George Rogers were convicted; 14 Oct. 1652 she was presented for entertaining idle people on the Sabbath. She asked for divorce 18 Oct. 1656, alleg. he had gone to England

many yrs. since and mar. again, herself and two invalid ch. destitute on her hands. Lists 282, 284, 298. The date of his return to Eng. is unkn., his P.A. to Christopher Hussey was approv. by Hampton Ct. in Nov. 1654. He d. at Hackney near London ab. 1660. Ch. by 1st w: **Theodate**, b. 1588, m. Christopher Hussey. **Nathaniel**, b. 1590, merchant of Southampton, Eng., d. 1645. By w. Hester (Mercer) had 5 kn. ch: Stephen, Anna, Francis, Nathaniel (3), Benjamin. **Deborah**, b. 1592, m. Rev. John Wing. **Stephen**, b. 1594, liv. with f. at Wherwell in 1614, having been expelled from Magdalen Coll. as the author of libellous verses. **Samuel**, b. 1597, a minister, late of Gorcum, Holland, in 1640. **Ann**, b. 1600, m. 1st one Sanborn, 2d bef. 1640 Henry Atkinson of London. **Mary** Batchelder, ch. of his 4th w., 21 in 1671, had m. by 26 Mar. 1673 William Richards, whom the court on his petn., after delib., app. adm. of S. B.'s est.

**BATEMAN**, presumably occup., tanner's helper.

1 **EDWARD**, with John Brown, both lately of Pemaquid, bot land at Nequasset from the Ind. 1 Nov. 1639. E. B. bot out Brown's int. in 1646 and sold to James Coole in 1654. List 10. Pemaquid wit. 1657; wit. deed Damariscotta Indians to Sylvanus Davis 1659.

2 **JOHN**, brought foreclosure suit against Thos. Greenslade, Casco Ct., 1667. Likely of Boston and Hingham, 2 s. and 4 dau. named in will 1690.

**BATES**, 87th commonest name in N. E.

1 **GEORGE**, thatcher, adm. to Boston Ch. 24 Jan. 1636, dism. to Exeter 6 Jan. 1639, recd. back into Boston Ch. 31 May 1640.

2 **JOHN**, sued by Nathl. Fryer July 1673, sold house and farm in Wells to Fryer Apr. 1674, and that summer with w. Martha was abs. from meeting in Wells. List 269b.

3 **WILLIAM**, Newcastle, bot land there from Elizabeth Fabes, exec., 1704; d. bef. 1731. Ch: **Mary**, m. Jotham Berry 11 Nov. 1731. **Judith**, m. James Marden.

**BATSON**, patronym., Bartholomew.

1 *JOHN(3), Cape Porpus, selectm. 1679, const. 1680, assemblyman 1682, 84. Lists 32, 256, 259, 305a. He was gr. mill priv. with Isaac Cole and Saml. York in 1681, owned half the sawmill and was found drowned under the mill wheel, inquest 3 Apr. 1685. Adm. gr. in May 1685 to wid. Elizabeth (Sanders, m. June 166--), Richard Randall her bondsman, and again in 1729-30 to grs. John Batson. Wid. Elizabeth m. 2d one Walden, adm. to Cambridge Ch. 26 May 1697 as Wid. Batson alias Goody Walden; 3d 2 Dec. 1700 John Gove of Cambridge (bro. of Edward), who d. 24 Dec.

1704, ag. ±77. She was liv. in Camb. 1725. Ch: **John**. **Nathaniel**, bp. adult Camb. 30 Jan. 1697-8, app. d. s.p. **Elizabeth**, m. 1st in Boston 18 Apr. 1693 John Fairfield of Ipswich, 2d in Boston 5 Dec. 1718 Dependence Littlefield of Wells. **Mary**, b. ab. 1676, d. in Camb. 2 Mar. 1760, ag. 83 (grst.). She m. 1st in Camb. 6 Nov. 1701 Thomas Prentice who d. 7 Dec. 1709; 6 ch. incl. Rev. Thomas Prentice of Ken'port; 2d bef. 1720 Nathaniel Robbins; 3d 24 Nov. 1742 Samuel Lyon of Roxbury. **Sarah**, b. ab. 1685, bp. adult Camb. 28 Feb. 1696-7, m. 12 Aug. 1714 James Reade of Camb., d. 25 Nov. 1721. 1 son who d.y.

2 **LT. JOHN**(1), ship carpenter, Me. jury 1687, was of Newcastle in 1693, N. H. jury 1697, but returned to Cape Porpus by 1698 and liv. on his father's land. With Saml. Hill of Charlestown he built a sawmill in 1699; later they took Joseph Storer as partn. Tavern 1700-1701. Lists 60, 68, 315bc, 96. K. in fight with Ind. at Black Point in Oct. 1703 (Pike), two mos. aft. his w. Anna (Odiorne), and their ch. were carried capt. to Canada. There she was bp. in the Catholic ch. 14 Mar. 1705. She m. 2d bef. 15 Dec. 1705 a fellow captive, James Stilson; liv. Newcastle 1721. Ch: **Mary**, b. Newcastle 5 Feb. 1697, bp. in Canada 24 June 1704, m. Thomas Parsons; 2d Richard Tarlton. Liv. Newcastle. **John**, b. Newcastle 16 May 1699, bp. in Canada 18 Jan. 1705, m. Love Clark (14). He was a coaster of Newc. Ch. **Clement**, b. in Canada 25 Nov. 1703, bp. same day, d.y.

3 **STEPHEN**, of Saco in 1637 with w. Elizabeth bound dau. Margery to Capt. Bonython. He was of Wells by 1639 or 41, but soon at Cape Porpus, a small river there still bearing his name. His last yrs. were spent in Wells. In 1649 he wit. Wadleigh's Ind. deed; in 1662 sold 300 a. land and outfit on Stag Isl. to Peter Oliver, mercht. of Boston. Lists 251, 252, 255, 269b. 'Honest Stephen Batson and his wife' Elizabeth sheltered the Quaker Edward Wharton. She was forced to retract her accus. against her husb. and her dau. Clay in 1660; the next yr. she was holding two swine that belonged to James Harmon. He d. in Wells 30 June 1676, his will 8 Mar. 1673-4 specifying son, 3 daus., grch. John Trott, and also app. grch. Sarah Ashley and Mary Trott. Ch: **John**. **Dau.**, the mother of John Trott. (?Dau., mother of Sarah Ashley?). **Margery**, apprent. to 3 masters 1637-8 (app. m. 1st William Kendall), 2d Richard Young, 3d Robert Elliot (5). **Mary**, m. 1st Jonas Clay (1), 2d William Brockus. **Elizabeth**, app. helped her parents and was given the home; m. late William Ashley (4).

**BATT**, Christopher, bp. 24 Sep. 1633 at St.

Martin's in Salisbury, son of Christopher and Anne (Baynton) of Salisbury, Salis., N. E., and Boston; rem. to Dover by 1662, but soon settled on land up the Salmon Falls river beyond Stackpole's farthest limit. His f. had an orchard of apple, pear and plum trees on Washington St. in the heart of Boston (and was himself fatally shot by his own son in his orchard shooting at a target), and the s. set out an apple orchard in the wilderness, his bro. Paul with him at times. Coroner's jury 1668. Lists 356gh, 288, 296. He d. s.p., perh. one of the nameless victims of the Indians; adm. gr. to his nephew Rev. Christopher Toppan 12 Jan. 1712-13.

**Battely,** Mr., West India gent. hired the old Cutts warehouse.

**BATTEN,** Batting. One J. B. m. Margaret Butson at Uffculme, Devon, 29 Apr. 1633. See Creber.

1 **ARTHUR,** of Marblehead 1654, Cape Porpus wit. 1662, m. Abigail Spurwell 1664.

2 **ELIAS** (Battene), struck by a spar and k. 29 Apr. 1682 at a launching in John Diamond's shipyard.

3 **JOHN** (poss. father of 1), fisherman, at Isles of Shoals 1647. In court 16 Oct. 1647, for trying to collect pay from John Seeley which he had already recd.

4 **JOHN,** with three others, was in Court for letting Francis Morgan out of Falmouth jail 1671 (see Will. Bartlett). He owned land in No. Yarmouth, lived there and in Lynn; m. Sarah Main, dau. of John and Elizabeth. List 214. Ch: John b. Lynn 1 Sep. 1671. In 1679 his mother 'of York' bound him 'aged about 8' to Joseph Couch, shipwright of Piscataqua. A scout under Col. John Wheelwright. **Abraham,** ag. ±70 Apr. 1749, husbandman of York, liv. in Norton's garrison, d. Aug. 1751. He m. bef. July 1702 Mary Young, dau. of Robert, d. 30 Nov. 1726; 2d Sarah Wright, dau. of Henry and Sarah (Start). 8 ch.

5 **WILLIAM,** fisherman, of Saco 1655-1660, Scarb. 1665, occupying there half of a house owned by Christopher Elkins jr., with whom his wife was suspected in 1667, with James Muchemore under susp. in 1668. She was Joan Moore, dau. of Richard and Bridget of Scarb.

**BATTERSBY.** 1 **Christopher,** Berw. wit. 1683. Y. D. iii. 136.

2 **JOHN,** m. Boston 28 Feb. 1711 Sarah Phelps; 'annulled,' she in Kinsale, Ire., 12 Mar. 1716-7; m. 23 July 1724 Sarah Bryant. Will 1725-1726.

**Battle,** Hannah, 1659, see Quinch Smith.

**Bauden,** William, Isl. of Shoals 164--. Me. P. & C. i. 120.

**Bawlden** (Baldwin?), Isabella, 1675. See Case (1).

**BAXTER,** old (feminine) form of baker in North of England.

1 **DR. JOHN,** Portsmouth, prev. in several scrapes in Suffolk Co., called Sarah, wife of Peter Golding, a liar; in 1684 convicted of beating Sarah Burgess and Sarah Barrett. He was of York, retailing rum in 1687; the next yr. hired a room for 6 yrs. from William Richards of Portsm., practicing there and suing John Pickering jr. for medical services in Apr. 1700. Lists 330de. In 1696 he was acc. of having 2 bastards by 'Nositer.' Some time later he m. Rebecca (Mayer) Nossiter, wid. of Peter of Salem and Boston, and was liv. with her in Charlestown 28 Mar. 1701 when she filed bond to settle her 1st husband's est. Ch: John and Rebecca, d. Feb. 15 and 21, 1697-8, ag. 1 yr. 3 mo. John.

2 **JOHN**(1), housewright of Ken'port, sold father's common rights in Portsm. 1730. M. Sarah Durrell (2). His will 1742.

3 **JOSEPH,** cordwainer of Mendon, sold land and bldgs. at Hampt. Falls, 1732.

4 **ROBERT,** Pemaquid 1689. List 126.

**Bayden** (see also Boyden), John, Kit. with Davis (36), up for swearing dreadfully 1662. List 78. See Allen (10).

**BEALE,** -s, Bale. Common English name.

1 **ABISHAG,** sister of (8), b. 1662, m. 1st by 1698 Henry Barnes(3), 2d Francis Carman; both liv. in 1717 on part of her bro.'s homestead, she liv. 1728.

2 **ARTHUR,** witness 1663 against Richard White. Isles of Shoals fisherman, keeping fam. in York, liv. next the ocean fronting no. on York Riv., having built on Hilton land by 1667. In 1678 he was letting out a serv., Hannah Wakeley. Often in court unnec. In 1684 was infringing Moore's ferry privilege, lic. ferryman in 1698, tav. keeper 1699, retailer 1700. Gr. j. 1691, jury 1702. Lists 30, 31, 33. Will 1699—1711; left 1 s., 4 daus. and wife who d. ab. 1715. Ch: **Nicholas;** town grant, List 279, sold by sisters in 1733. **Edward. Elizabeth,** m. 1704 Elisha Allen. **Mary,** m. 1702 William Pearce, d. 1 Apr. 1730. **Sarah,** m. 1st Joshua Knapp; 2d John Busher, calker; both liv. 1735; she a wid. 1743, in 1747 deeding to son Ebenezer Knapp of York. **Anne,** m. one Hornsbee, liv. at a distance.

3 **CALEB,** drunk in 1662, lawsuit in 1671, fighting with James Robinson in 1672. Dec. in 1675, his dau. ag. 5 then bound to Walter Gendall. In 1730 one Caleb Beal was app. adm. est. of Moses Durell, Boston, mariner.

4 **EDWARD,** Isles of Shoals fisherman, family at Newcastle. It is imposs. that one man was husb. of Sarah Cotton, of 'Ann Beal, wife of Edward Beal' (who in 1684

had Frances Russell whipped for calling her names, her ch. bastards, her f. and mo. beggars, who would have starved but for Goodman Abbott) and of Frances Beal (abs. from meet. in 1670, on whose body an inquest and autopsy was held in 1673, the charge to be borne half by the town of Portsm., half by her husb.); but it was quite poss. for a quiet fisherman at the Shoals, keeping out of debt, out of mischief, liv. in a hired house or his employer's, to live and die outside the records, leaving ch. These records may refer to an earlier Edward, in 1669 fisherman for James Blagdon; in 1670 John Moore fined for striking him; in 1672 at the Shoals he had left money for safe keeping in the hands of Edward Cater, dec. 'Arthur Sen.' in York Deeds ii. 160 was prob. subconscious from John Frost. The Edward we know m. Sarah Cotton (6), William Cotton his bondsman in 1672, minister's rate 1677, taxed 1680-81. Lists 52, 313a, 315ab, 319, 327ad, 331b. Will Sep. 1706—Jan. 1706-7. Ch: **John**, of Portsmouth 1707, of Boston, mariner, 1730. Lists 315c, 336b. M. 23 Sep. 1708 Elizabeth Skipall. 6 ch. rec. at Boston. **Sarah**, m. at Boston 5 Aug. 1703 William Waine; wid. in 1730. **Elizabeth**, presum. mo. of Sarah Moore of Boston, single woman, one of the grch. in 1730. **Martha**, youngest, mar. 4 June 1716 Ralph Burne of Shadwell, co. Middlesex; wid. in Portsm. 1730.

5 **EDWARD**(2), called 'my only son' in 1711; m. 1694 Elizabeth Littlefield. Lists 38, 279. He deeded the homestead to his s. Josiah in 1736; wid. liv. 1747. Ch: **Mannering**, b. 1 Jan. 1697-8. List 279. M. Sarah Mitchell, d. York 20 Nov. 1781. 4 ch. rec. **Nicholas**, b. 30 Apr. 1702, mariner, m. Bethula Young. 1 dau. rec. **Joanna**, b. 19 July 1706, m. 31 Mar. 1726 Johnson Lunt of Newbury, d. 1 Sep. 1791. **Edward**, b. 10 July 1708. List 279. **Josiah**, b. 17 Apr. 1710. List 279. M. 1st (int. 8 Jan. 1736) Esther Sayword; 2d Mercy Webber. Ch. **Elizabeth**, b. 16 Jan. 1711-12, pub. 1 Mar. 1734-5 to Nathaniel Crediford (forbid by her); m. 30 Nov. 1738 Josiah Littlefield. **Zachariah**, b. 17 Jan. 1711-12, m. 11 Mar. 1735-6 Ruth Stickney of Newbury. **Catherine**, b. 23 Nov. 1713, m. 5 June 1734 Benjamin Harmon. **Benjamin**, b. 11 Jan. 1718-9, m. Mary —— Drew, Moore or Jones.

6 **RICHARD**, admonished in Me. court in 1693.

7 **ROGER**, fined at Spurwink in 1658 for disturb. public worship.

8 **WILLIAM**, app. relat. to (2), b. 1664, brot up with his sis. by Mr. John Hole. In 1695 he was Mr. Henry Dering's tenant on land formerly Richard White's. In 1698 on scout duty was seriously injured, aft.

which was fined for selling without lic. and later licensed; ferryman at York 1707-8. List 279. He m. Jane Trafton, both liv. 1757, he 1760. Ch: **Zaccheus**, presum., and prob. others, not rec. in York, but in Kit. 1719. Will, Bowdoinham, 1768—1772, names w. Mary, 6 ch. **Richard**, b. in York, d. early. **Obadiah**, b. 11 June 1695, fisherman, Ipswich, m. (int. 2 June 1716) Mary Wood, dau. of Mary (Davis 9), his wid. in 1737. 6 ch. bp. **William**, b. 1 Apr. 1698, weaver. List 279. M. 6 Dec. 1719 Elizabeth Benson. 12 ch. **Joanna**, b. in York, k. by Ind. 27 May 1712. **Mary**, b. 5 Mar. 1704-5, m. 6 Mar. 1727 Samuel Fitts. **Samuel**, b. 1 July 1707, had the homestead. List 279. His w. Joanna (Jeffreys) d. 6 Jan., he 9 Mar. 1789. **Simeon**, b. 3 June 1711. **Comfort**, b. 31 Aug. 1715, pub. to Abraham Pugsley of Kit. 23 Apr. 1743. **Benjamin**, b. 6 Feb. 1719, m. Mary —— Drew, Moore or Jones.

**BEAMAN**, **Thomas**, ±26 in 1678, poss. Philip's War. Wells 1682. List 33. M. 1684 Deborah ——. Ch.

**BEAN**, Bane, No. of Eng. and Scotland.

1 **DANIEL**(2), Exeter, soldier 1695-96, jury 1695. Lists 52, 57, 62, 67, 376b, 400. Adm. gr. to s. Daniel 7 May 1718. Wife Mary. Ch: **Daniel**, m. Ann (Sanborn?). 4 ch. **John**, m. Martha Sinclair (James). 2 ch. **Samuel**, m. one Sarah, who d. 1750; he d. 9 Apr. 1737. 7 ch. **Mary**, m. John Quimby.

2 **JOHN**, b. ab. 1634, was a Scotch prisoner brot to N. E. in 1651; liv. in Exeter, where he d. betw. 24 Jan. and 8 Feb. 1718. Lists 74, 379, 376b, 381, 383, 52, 57, 62, 67. He m. 1st Hannah Lissen, dau. of Nicholas, whose deed he wit. 1654; 2d one Margaret. Ch. by 1st w: **Mary**, b. 18 June 1655, m. 1st 25 June 1674 Joel Judkins; 2d David Robinson of Stratham. **Henry**, b. ab. 1657, d. 5 Mar. 1662-3. **Hannah**, b. ab. 1659, m. Apr. 1682 Abraham Whittacre, who was k. by Ind. 18 July 1692. 4 ch. By 2d w: **John**, b. 15 Aug. 1661, d. 18 May 1666. **Daniel**, b. 23 Mar. 1662-3. **Samuel**, b. 23 Mar. 1665-6, d. 1778, m. Mary Severance of Amesbury. Lists 52, 57, 67, 376b. 4 ch. **John**, b. 13 Oct. 1668, d. 1719. Lists 62, 67, 376b, 400. Wife was Sarah, who m. 2d one Robinson. 6 surv. ch. **Margaret**, b. 17 Oct. 1670, m. William Taylor. **James**, b. 17 Dec. 1672, d. 6 Jan. 1753. Lists 62, 67, 376b, 400. 2 ch. by unkn. 1st w.; m. 2d Dec. 1697 Sarah Bradley, 6 ch.; 3d 2 Nov. 1738 Mary (Prescott) (Coleman) Crosby, wid. succ. of Jabez Coleman (3) and Thomas Crosby(3). **Jeremiah**, b. 20 Apr. 1675, d. 1727. List 67. Wife Ruth, 7 ch. **Elizabeth**, b. 24 Sep. 1678, m. John Sinclair jr. 5 ch. **Catherine**, b. ab. 1680, m. 1700 Richard Dolloff. 10 ch.

3 **LEWIS**, Mr., of York, by family tradi-

tion Scotch. A wit. 21 Nov. 1668, he had land gr. 5 Mar. 1668-9. M. ab. 1668 Mary Mills (?dau. of Robert, stepdau. of John Harker). An Ind. victim 7 Apr. 1677, adm. was gr. to the wid. 11 Sep. 1677, and again to s. Lewis 8 May 1695. Wid. m. 2d Charles Brisson. Land formerly granted to Mr. Lewis Bean was laid out to 'Mrs. Brissom' 9 June 1689. Ch: **Lewis**, b. 28 Apr. 1671. **Elizabeth**, m. Joseph Carlile. **Ebenezer**, and likely others, k. by Ind. 25 Jan. 1691-2. **Joseph**, Capt., b. ab. 1676, captured by Ind. 25 Jan. 1692, released ab. 1699. In 1702 he entered military service, was interpreter and Lieut., and was granted pension and exempted from poll tax after 3 fingers and thumb shot off. Lists 99 p. 78, 161, 358d. M. 1703 Joanna Freethy (4). 10 ch. **James**, taken by Ind. 25 Jan. 1692, d. bef. 1721.

4 **LT.** and **CAPT.** *LEWIS(3), in active military service, and prom. in civil life; selectm. 1698 and often gr.j. 1693, 97, 98, foreman 1701. Dep. 1703-18, J. P. many years. List 279. His wife was Mary (Austin 5) Sayward. He d. 25 June 1721 and she 25 Mar. 1723. His sons were granted 300 a. on their petn. to Genl. Ct. 1743, their father had raised several companies of vols. without compens. and partic. in killing nigh 50 Ind. Ch: **Jonathan**, b. 14 Dec. 1692, d. 6 Dec. 1777, m. Sarah Nowell, dau. of Capt. Peter. 12 ch. **Mary**, b. 7 Jan. 1695-6, m. 31 Jan. 1713 John Sayward. **Lewis**, b. 16 June 1697, d. 30 May 1770, m. Abigail Moulton, dau. of Lt. Joseph. 7 ch. **John**, b. 18 July 1700, d. 17 May 1740, m. 18 Nov. 1726 Mary Hubbard, dau. of Philip of Berwick. 5 ch. **Elinor**, b. 28 Dec. 1702, m. Abel Moulton. **Mehitable**, b. 21 Sep. 1705, m. (int. 13 Nov. 1725) Samuel Young. **Ebenezer**, b. 31 Dec. 1707, d. 7 Jan. 1736 unm.

**Beanter**, see Branson. List 276.

**Beaple**, see Baple.

**BEARD**, a common Eng. name, one hamlet in Derbyshire.

1 **AARON**, Cape Bonawagon petitioner 1672, ch. rec. Boston 1681. Lists 13, 15, 189.

2 **JOHN**, Star Isl. 1661, abs. from wife.

3 **JOSEPH**(4), ±21 in Sep. 1678, a Dover tavern keeper 1683, 86. Lists 49, 52, 55ab, 359b, 239b. In 1692 he was jailed at Hampt. for hitting his wife in the head with a stave and threatening her life. She was Esther Philbrook, who was gr. adm. 9 Feb. 1703-4, and m. 2d 12 Nov. 1705 Sylvanus Nock. Kn. ch: Ensign **Joseph**, m. 24 Mar. 1700-1 Elizabeth Waldron. Ch. He called Ralph Hall 'uncle' 1713; was Scarb. propr. 1720, d. bef. 4 Dec. 1723. See Dolloff, Samuel. **Esther**, m. 3 Nov. 1707 Joseph Hall. **Ann**, m. bef. 1715 William Wittum of York, d. 9 July 1726. 4 ch. Presum. also **Mary**, m.

17 Dec. 1711 John Hearl of Kit. 6 ch. In 1766 William Dyer of Newmarket and w. Elizabeth, and Joanna Stevens, single, of Newm., were his or his son's grch.

4 **THOMAS**, ±70 in 1678, carpenter of Dover, one-time serv. of Mr. Treworgy; party to lawsuit 1641, coroner's jury 1646 or 7. He bot house and land at Dover 1644, with Valentine Hill was gr. the falls of Oyster Riv. for a sawmill 1649, bot land at Scarb. 1659, wit. William Beard's deed 1675. Lists 354abc, 355b, 356abcefghk, 359a, 353, 82, 54. His will 16 Dec. 1678—25 Mar. 1679 names w. Marie (Mary), 2 sons, 3 daus. She m. 2d one Williams. Ch: **Martha**, m. bef. Dec. 1678 George Bramhall. **Joseph**, b. ab. 1657. **Elizabeth**, m. bef. Dec. 1678 Jonathan Watson. **Thomas**. **William**, b. 12 May 1664, d. 17 May 1664 or 5. **Hannah**, b. 24 Oct. 1666, not in will. **Mary**, m. 25 July 1689 John Hudson.

5 **WILLIAM**, evid. related to (4), owned land at Oyster Riv. bef. 1640, party to lawsuit 1641, taxed 1648. Lists 71, 354ac, 355ab, 356a, 359a, 361a, 362a, 363abc, 364-366, 353, 311c (Dover). In 1675 he and w. Elizabeth gave joint deed of dwg. ho. and land to James Huckins, with very strong warranty, by, thru or under either of them, Tho. Beard a wit. He was k. by Ind. ab. 1 Nov. 1675; adm. gr. to wid. Elizabeth 27 June 1676, the prop. to be divided betw. her and Edward Leathers.

**BEARE** (Beer). 1 **Eleazer** (Beeres), Berw. wit. 1674. Y. D. ii. 188.

2 **THOMAS**, Eastern Claims ab. 1715, 100 a. at Cape Porpus adj. Wm. Kendall, deed from Wm. Barton 22 Nov. 1672. Me. H. & G. Rec. iv. 105.

**BEAZER** (Bezar), **Richard**, merchant, m. aft. 1700 Mrs. Elizabeth, wid. of Thomas Paine of Newc., and soon d. List 316. She of Newc. 1720, gone 1723, perh. to York. N. H. Deeds 14.240.

**BECK**, ancient in East of England.

1 **CALEB**(2), of age or m. by 1661, householder in 1677. Lists 326c,.327d, 330ab, 331b. Widow Beck taxed 1690. Adm. gr. 11 Mar. 1694-5 to wid. Hannah (Bowles 3). List 335a, p. 176. In 1696 she was liv. in her husband's house in the heart of Portsm.; m. 2d bef. 1702 Nathl. Wright. One Caleb Beck had ch. 1712-15 in Schenectady, N. Y. See N. Y. Gen. and Biog. Rec. 38.98.

2 **HENRY**, Portsm., came on -The Blessing- in 1635, ag. 18, or another of the name. See (4). His grs. Henry (Thomas) recorded that he was born in (Guy Warwick) in Warwickshire. Reg. 60.299. He was at Dover 1640-48. In 1652 he was assigned 10 a. in the 'out lots' in Portsm. and was liv. at Sagamore Creek 28 June 1657, when he sold his

Dover land. Jury 1652. Lists 351ab, 352, 354a, 49, 52, 312c, 313a, 323, 326ac, 330abc, 331ac, 335a. His w. Anna wit. John Partridge's deed 16 Sep. 1669. With w. Ann he deeded prop. to s. Thomas for their life supp. 6 Jan. 1679. Last ment. in list of church memb. 1699. Kn. ch: **Caleb. Henry. Thomas.**

3 **HENRY**(2), mariner, Great Isl. In 1673 ag. ±19 he was an apprent. of Mr. John Lewis. (Yet his f. called 'Sen' in 1664?). He or his f. taxed in Portsm. in 1681-2. Lists 286, 312e. Adm. gr. 26 Apr. 1686 to wid. Elizabeth, who m. 2d 23 June 1687 Richard Estes (2).

4 **THOMAS**(2), b. ab. 1657, farmer, Portsm. Jury 1693, 95, 96, gr. j. 1694, const. 1697. selectm. 1703. Lists 52, 57, 324, 330d, 332b, 335a, 337, 339. Wife Mary (†Frost). List 335a. 29 Mar. 1725 he deeded his dwg. and land to s. Samuel for life supp. of self and w., Samuel to make cert. payments to his sisters. 14 Apr. 1731, ±74, he dep. ab. roads in Portsm. for 60 yrs. past. His death 7 Nov. 1734, ag. 77, and that of his widow -Anna- 25 Feb. 1753, ag. 94, were interpol. in the Newbury town records, by Joshua Coffin from 'an old manuscript,' which said that his father came in -The Angel Gabriel- from Hertfordshire, was cast away at Pemaquid, lived to 110, m. 'Ann Frost of Piscataqua, N. H.,' and had ch., otherwise unk., Joshua and Mary who m. Dea. White— presum. wafted back a generation from Dea. Joshua White of Kittery Point. Ch: **Thomas,** b. 1683, shipwright, Portsm., d. 1 Jan. 1774, ag. 91. List 339. He m. Elizabeth Deverson(1), d. 7 —— 1746, ag. 62 (grst.); 2d Dorothy Mattoon, dau. of Richard. 8 or m. ch. Thomas tertius was taxed in 1726. **Joshua,** Newbury, m. 20 Apr. 1716 Abigail Daniels. 18? ch. **Abigail,** m. 10 Mar. 1716-7 John Jackson, shipwright of Little Harbor, both liv. 1771. **Henry,** b. 14 Nov. 1695, cordwainer, m. 18 Dec. 1718 Hannah Walden, 2d at Greenland 25 Oct. 1733 Jane Cate (3). List 339. Ab. 1765 he moved to Rumford (Concord) near the Louden line. Ch. 4+3. **Mary,** m. 19 May 1728 Joshua White of Newcastle, cooper, who bot at Kit. Point in 1735 and became deacon of the Ch. **Samuel,** b. 1699, husbandman, Portsm., m. 30 July 1718 Mary Partridge, d. of Wm. She d. June 1784 and he Jan. 1786, ag. 87. 12 ch. rec. Portsm. **Hannah,** m. May 1724 Nathl. Lang.

**BEDDEN.** 1 **John,** m. Portsm. 9 Nov. 1727 Mary Akerman.

2 **WALTER,** Isl. of Shoals creditor 1687. List 95.

**BEDFORD,** county, city, one other place. One Nathan B., s. of John and Isabel, bp. 26 July 1640 at Totnes, Devon. Nich-

olas Bedford late of Stoke Gabriel, Devon, Suff. Prob. 1684.

1 *****NATHAN,** ±28 in 1667, ±37 in 1676, is first found in Scarb. 15 June 1660, buying marsh from Henry Watts, from whom he bot 100 a. of land in 1680; tav. keeper 1675-76 he was at Newcastle, and aft. return. to Scarb. was assoc. with Mr. Robert Eliot of Newc. in fishing and trading. In court, he sued John Mare 1667, with w. Ann abs. from meet. 1672, defaulted bond at Wells 1678. Jury 1667, 76, 80, assemblyman 1681. Lists 234a, 236, 239a, 288, 30, 91. Found bruised and drowned after a search, his death occa. consid. inquiry; the inquest found 24 Aug. 1681 that the bruises were not fatal without drowning, and the Court accepted the verd. without having suspicion of any person, so clearing Capt. Scottow, evidently under susp., who had lost a case against him that yr. He m. Anne Munden, to whom adm. was gr. 27 Sep. 1681 with Mr. Robert Elliot; inventories taken at Richmond Isl. incl. fishing station and trading goods at Spurwink River and Blue Point. She m. 2d by 1682 Richard Kelly or Calley and liv. on the Boaden farm in Scarb. which her 1st husb. bot in 1679; liv. 1704. Ch: **Nathan. Deborah,** m. 14 Aug. 1686 Michael Webber. **William?** Portsm. wit. 1693.

2 **NATHAN** (1), was a joint wit. 4 June 1684 with Deborah Munden (Munday), a Newcastle boarding ho. mistress; evid. studied med. with Capt. Barefoote, who rememb. him in his will 1688; taxed at Newcastle 1690. He was surgeon of the ship -Providence- 7 July 1693, and d. of small pox, prob. unm., his mo. Anne Cawley receipting to Capt. Knowles's wid. in 1704 in full for N. B.'s services as his doctor, part already paid to her dau. Deborah Webber.

3 **NICHOLAS,** Black Point 1676-77, relat. to (1) and with him exam. in a case against Walter Gendall. He was on Black Point Neck with Wm. Lucas.

**Bedworth,** Richard, Great Isl. 1663. List 312g.

**BEEDLE,** Beadle, occup., attendant.

1 **CHRISTOPHER**(4), Kittery. Adm. 13 Sep. 1708 to Peter Staples jr. Inv. incl. land only. Ch: **Christopher,** had town grant 1679. M. 1686 Sarah Lockwood, who (says Banks) m. 2d Thomas Phinney of Barnstable. **Susannah,** m. Joseph Hill.

2 **HENRY,** York, m. Elizabeth (Fost) Dill, wid. of Daniel. List 279. Both liv. 1738. Ch: **Sarah,** b. 24 Apr. 1714, m. by 1735 Edmund Bridges. 7 ch. **Elizabeth,** b. 6 Sep. 1715. **Ithamar,** b. 2 July 1719, m. 1st Priscilla Day(3), 2d Mary Thurber, dau. of Richard. Ch. 2+4. **Eleazer,** b. 21 May 1722. **Martha,** b. 14 Nov. 1724.

3 **JOHN**, List 82. See Bidwell.

4 **ROBERT**, Kittery, had grant adj. John Simmons from Tho. Gorges in 1641. List 298. Wid. Mary m. Rev. Stephen Batchelder(5). Ch: **Christopher. Elizabeth**, mar. Stephen Edwards, 2d Peter Staples. See Hoyt's Salis. 879, 61.

5 **THOMAS**, in Me. Ct. for swearing 1653. Soldier in Philip's War.

**Beex & Co.** of London, (John Beex, Richard Hutchinson, Col. Wm. Beale, Capt. Thos. Alderne), concerned in Richard Leader's enterprises in Lynn and Berw. Y. D. i. 74, 82.

**Beggar**, Francis. Cape Porpus? Brad. 62, 94.

**BELCHER,** rare except in Berks, Bucks, Oxford.

1 **JOHN**, joiner, b. 1 Sep. 1661, eldest s. of Josiah and Ranis (Rainsford) of Boston, liv. at Mr. Charles Frost's ho. in Kit. ab. 40 yrs. and was comfortably supported by Mr. Frost, his f. and grf., so states his will 17 Feb. 1729-30—9 Apr. 1731. List 298.

2 **REV. SAMUEL**, b. ab. 1641, son of Jeremy of Ipswich, Harvard 1659, was ment. as min. of Kittery in Robert Mussell's will 1663; later settled at the Shoals, and was ord. min. at Newbury, 10 Nov. 1698. At the Shoals, he was a Star Isl. wit. 4 July 1670, appraiser 1675, Capt. Lockwood's bondsman 1677, a wit. with Jeremiah senior 1678, and overseer of Walter Matthews's est. that yr. Lists 305a, 307b, 95. Mary Belcher was a Star Isl. wit. 1673 and signed (aut.) a paper 1676, but a Shoals deed was wit. by Samuel and Mercy in Jan. 1686-7 and sworn to by them at Newbury in 1707, and he left a wid. Mercy when he d. at Ipswich 10 Mar. 1715. She d. there 14 Nov. 1723.

3 **SAMUEL**, sailor 1685. List 314.

**Belgrave**, Mr. Robert, Lamprill Riv. 166—. List 380.

**Belgrove**, John, with Wm. Tremells, sued Andrew Patten in Me. Ct. 1666.

**BELL,** common in Mid. and No. of Eng., 32d commonest in Scotland.

1 **JOHN**, Newcastle 1696, in court for oaths.

2 **REBECCA**, Newcastle. In 1700 the town paid her for keeping Thomas Hardy.

3 **SHADRACH**, Newcastle, first ment. at Cape Eliz. 1683. Taxed Newcastle 1691. Lists 226, 315bc, 316, 66, 68. His wid. Rachel and three younger sons deeded common rights in 1722; 16 Sep. 1723 adm. was gr. to the wid. and son Shadrach. Ch: **Shadrach**, b. 3 July 1685. **Elizabeth**, b. 19 Mar. 1687-8. **Meshach**, b. 29 Jan. 1689-90; 7 Mar. 1709-10 he was serv. of Robt. Elliott, Esq., tempted away and detained several days by his mother. **Benjamin**, b. 5 Aug. 1695. **Thomas**, b. 12 Mar. 1699-1700.

**BELLEW, William,** Dover, wit. Rev. Thomas Larkham's deed 1642. Concerned with

Edward and Wm. Paine. Partner with Wm. Waldron, in 1647, he headed the petition of his creditors. Sold house and 20 a. 1645. Arbiter 1647. Taxed 1648. See Ballou Gen.

**Bemis** (Beames), Joseph, Piscat. wit. 1676. Y. D. iii. 22.

**BENDALL, Philip**, serv. of Richard Cutt in 1660, wit. an Ind. deed at the Eastward in 1664, and sold land up the Sheepscot River in 1665. List 13. In Philip's War he escaped to Scituate, aband. 16 head of cattle besides swine and crops.

**BENJAMIN.** 1 **John**, m. Elizabeth (Rogers) Carter, Foxwell heir.

2 **SAMUEL**, drunk in court time 1661. Philip Chesley undertook his fine.

**BENMORE.** 1 **Charles**, of the Shoals, seaman, but called -Pinmar- in his own deed. 10 May 1659 he bot a lot next to James Pendleton's ho. on Gt. Isl. and built a house; in 1674 he and w. Elizabeth, liv. at the Shoals, sold this and soon rem. to Boston. List 326c. In 1707 she wit. in Boston the will of John Palmer of Dunstan. Ch. rec. at Boston: **Lydia**, b. 27 Feb. 1677. **Stephen**, b. 25 May 1678. **Martha**, b. 4 Aug. 1686. Also app. **Charles** who in 1685 had been apprent. to Cornelius White, decd.; and **John**, who had w. Elizabeth and s. John, b. 3 Feb. 1692, and m. 2d in Boston, 16 Nov. 1693 Mary Richards.

2 **PHILIP**, in 1664 with John Brewster of Portsm. bot land at Kennebec from John Parker and Mary Webber, which they sold to Collicott in 1667. He rem. to Dover and m. there 28 Sep. 1669 Rebecca (Tibbetts) Nock, wid. of Thomas. List 359a. Dover wit. 1671, land gr. there 1673, gr.j. 1673. Lists 323, 326b, 356d, 357e, 359a, 298. Will 22 May—27 June 1676, names wife, 2 ch. and cous. Mr. John Evans. She d. 30 Mar. 1680, adm. 1 June to William Willey. Ch: **Temperance**, m. Charles Adams(4). **Esther**, liv. 1680.

**BENNETT,** Bennick, short for Benedict.

1 **LT. ABRAHAM**(3), ag. 59 in Mar. 1733-4, ± 62 in 1737-8, mariner in 1700, d. aft. 3 Jan. 1753-4. He had gr. at Oyster River 19 Mar. 1693-4. Jury and gr.j. 1698, selectm. 1717, Lt. commanding vols. at Oyster River 1724. In 1713 he dep. (aut.) ab. mills at Hiltons. Lists 358b, 368b, 369. He, wife Sarah (Chesley 5) and all their ch. but Martha were bap. by Rev. Hugh Adams 17 Feb. 1716-7. One A. B. was living in Durham in 1773, ag. ab. 97. Ch: **Sarah**, m. James Marston. **Ruth. Abraham**, b. 14 Feb. 1703-4, m. Abigail Wedgwood. **Benjamin**, m. Mary Gilman. **Eleazer. Martha**, unm. 1740.

2 **AMBROSE**, 1670. List 312b.

3 **ARTHUR**, ±30 in 1672, ±40 in 1679, was taxed at Oyster River 1666-7. In 1672 he gave a joint note with Francis Thorne.

Lists 356d, 365. He d. 20 Jan. 1682-3, adm. 11 Apr. 1683 to wid. Mary (Goddard), who m. 2d Joseph Field(6). Mary Bennicke was a wit. at Exeter 16 June 1678, Antipas Maverick to Major Shapleigh. Ch: **John. Abraham,** b. ab. 1675. **Ruth,** m. 23 Feb. 1691-2 Francis Matthews.

4 **EDWARD,** with John Winsland bot land at Spruce Creek in 1668 and sold to John Moore. He was of Scarb. appr. est. of Saml. Oakman 28 June 1676, and had m. Oakman's dau. Susannah and recd. part of his Spurwink lands bef. 1689-90. Pet. Andros 18 Jan. 1687-8, had poss. ab. 30 a. at Scarb. for several yrs. past. Lists 34, 238a. His fam. was in Marblehead by 1692; wid. m. there 12 Aug. 1723 Peter King, who d. 1726, ag. 70; she liv. 1737, ag. 77. 4 ch. of Susannah Bennett bp. in Marb.: **Constance,** 12 Mar. 1692-3, m. 25 Nov. 1700 John Hine. **Edward,** 16 Apr. 1693, m. 30 Nov. 1713 Sarah Macally. **Oakman,** 16 Feb. 1695-6. One Oakman m. in Marb. 26 Nov. 1740 Hannah Spikman. **Mary,** 27 July 1701. One Mary m. in Marb. 5 Jan. 1718-9 Edmund Ford.

5 **HENRY,** b. ±1664, s. of Henry and Lydia (Perkins) of Ipsw., m. there 20 May 1685 Frances Burr, dau. of John and Mary (Smith), m. 2d one Margaret, the mo. of his surv. ch. He was liv. in Newington 1716. Will, of Portsmouth, 23 Apr.—30 May 1739 named 3 mar. daus., son-in-law Wm. Lang exec., grd. Sarah Fenlayson, grs. Nathl. Fenlayson. Ch. rec. in Ipsw., by 1st w: **Mary,** b. 3 Mar. 1685[6-8.] By 2d w: **Frances,** b. 8 Sep. 1694; of Portsm. m. Nov. 1715 Wallis Finlason, 2d John Babb(1). **Margaret,** b. 22 Mar. 1697. **Joanna,** b. 7 Oct. 1701, m. 1 Jan. 1722-3 Daniel Jackson. **Lucy,** b. 29 Nov. 1703, m. 19 Dec. 1731 Wm. Lang.

6 **JOHN,** Capt. John Smith's mate 1614. List 7.

7 **JOHN,** later of Marblehead, came in 1630, accord. to John Peach, in the same ship. List 41. Wife Margaret, ag. 64 in 1670, came later. Adm. to her June 1663, liv. 1674. Ch: **Mary,** b. ab. 1638, m. 1st Christopher Codner, by whom ch: Joane (-Mary-in Court's order), b. 1655, m. Joseph Bubier, Christopher, b. Sep. 1657, appr. 1674 to Joseph Emmons; 2d in 1661 Elias White, annulled 1663; 3d by 1665 Richard Downing. Ch.

8 **JOHN,** and Sarah, 1664. List 364.

9 **JOHN**(3), named in uncle John Goddard's will. List 62. Lubberland petn. 1694. Of Exeter (Lamprill River) but living away in 1702. Presum. ch: **Benjamin,** fisherman, m. at Glouc. 16 Dec. 1714 Penelope Cook. Drowned 18 July 1723, aged 36, his wid. came to Durham, liv. 1751. 4 ch., of whom Benj. and Wm. d. in Newport, R. I. ab. 1747. **Arthur,** cordwainer, Newmarket.

K. by Ind., adm. to Thomas Rawlins 6 June 1722. He m. Dorcas Rawlins, who m. 2d Joseph Glidden. 4 or m. ch. **Mary,** m. in Greenland 9 Jan. 1718-9 Isaac Libby, and named a grch. Arthur Bennick.

10 **JOHN,** mariner 1670. List 82, 124. See 11 **JOHN,** Pemaquid 1687. John Oswell.

12 **MOSES,** had 10 a. gr. at Saco 8 Dec. 1681. Betw. the wars he and Richard Tarr ran Blackman's mill at Blue Point.

13 **NICHOLAS,** Portsm., tailor. With Richard Seward he was a wit. Mrs. Margaret Adams to Wm. Fernald in 1689. Clerk of the train band 1695, gr.j. 1693, jury 1695. In Feb. 1695-6 he sued his bro.-in-law Nicholas Fletcher. Wid. Mary (Fletcher 4) was living Portsm. 16 Nov. 1696, and then had servant James Staples. List 335a. Ch: **Mary,** named in her grfr's will.

14 **ROBERT,** 1624. List 9.

15 **WILLIAM.** In 1677 he was one of several who had bot liquor from Richard Welcome's wife; in 1679 had been abs. from his wife 4 or 5 yrs. ±31 29 Feb. 1687-8, he dep. ab. nunc. will of Samuel Windsor at Edward Martin's, Smuttynose.

**BENNING. Harry,** b. ±1661, mariner, s. of Ralph of Boston, stepson of Henry Dering(4), was a servant of Mr. Wm. Vaughan 1678-1681, a Berw. wit. 1684, bot and sold land in Portsm. 1687; taxed in Boston 1688, named next to one George Vaughan. He m. a dau. of Anstiss (Gold) Bissett, stepdau. of John Wilkins of Boston, and d. bef. 19 Nov. 1688. Poss. s. **John,** Boston, merchant, adm. 15 Mar. 1731-2 to s.-in-law Jeremiah Green, distiller.

**BENSON.** 1 **Henry,** first app. at Spruce Creek, Kit., as wit. of Enoch Hutchins' will 1693, grant 1694. He m. Mary Waters, d. of John, and liv. on her land. During Ind. troubles app. hired a farm in Portsm., 'Henry Benson & Farm' taxed Str. Bk. 1713. They sold their homestead in 1743 to son Henry. Lists 290, 295-298. Ch. may include: **Mary,** aek. covt. Portsm. 1714, mar. Wm. Nicholson 1 Jan. 1721-2. **Mercy,** aek. covt. Portsmouth 1714, m. Nathl. Brown. **James,** taxed Portsm. 1720, m. 1st 20 Mar. 1718-9 Deborah Rollins; 2d 8 Apr. 1725 Susannah Rowe, heir of Edw. Liv. in Newington. Ch. **Jemima,** m. 7 Oct. 1716 John Alexander. **Elizabeth,** m. 6 Dec. 1719 Wm. Beal. **John,** m. June 1724 Hannah Brown (not Crown); liv. at Spruce Creek. **Henry,** bp. Portsm. No. Ch. 19 Sep. 1714, q.c. land above Spruce Creek 1727, m. 4 Apr. 1736 Mary Quint. Ch. liv. at Ken'port and Biddeford. **Parthenia,** m. 31 Mar. 1726 Nathaniel Presbury. **Abigail,** m. (int. 2 Jan. 1730-1) Ebenezer Wittum. **Joanna,** m. 23 Sep. 1736 Giles Jeffrey.

2 **Thomas,** Arundel wit. 1725.

Bentley, George, Piscat., 1683. List 313f.
See Syl. Herbert.

Benton, George, 1652.

Berrisford, Henry, Philip's War. List 237b.
One H. B. came 1635, ag. 32.

BERRY, a parish in Devon, Barrow 2 in Somerset-Worcester.

1 AMBROSE, trader, an early settler at Saco on west side of river, now Biddeford. Taxed 7 Sep. 1636, lawsuits with Robert Sankey 7 May 1637 and John Smith 25 June 1640, juror 1640. Thomas Cammock and Ambrose Berry were sued by Thomas Crockett in 1640. He bot 100 a. near Smith's Brook, 20 Apr. 1642. Lists 22, 75b, 242, 249, 251, 252. He was listed with inhab. of Cape Porpus 5 July 1653, when he took O. A. to Mass.; or, perh. he d. c. 1642-44, and it was his son Ambrose, and not he, who took O. A., and his s., and not he, who m. Ann Bully(2) in July 1652 and was buried 3 May 1661. Adm. gr. to wid. Ann in July 1661. Bef. 7 Nov. 1665, she was the w. of William Scadlock, and m. 3d John Carter(4); liv. in Boston 1680. Ch: Ambrose.

2 AMBROSE(1), or perh. grs. of (1), mariner of Boston, deeded flowage rights in Bully's Creek to John Hill, 18 Sep. 1686. He was master of the sloop -Friendship- in 1695, and was cast away nnd drowned on Cape Ann, 25 Sep. 1697, only two saved; wid. was Hannah. As a young man he had been wounded in Ind. fights at Black Point 1676-77. Ch: Ambrose, m. 1st at Newb. 10 Jan. 1716-7 Hannah Kingsbury; 2d, 3 June 1728 Sarah Emery. Son John. Hannah, b. 30 July 1686, m. at Newb. 29 Oct. 1710 Isaac Chase, d. in Sutton, Mass. May 1771. Joseph, b. 11 July, d. 16 July 1693. Benjamin, twin, b. 11 July, d. 24 July 1693. John, b. 3 Aug. 1697.

3 BENJAMIN, son or br. of (10), m. 27 Nov. 1689 Elizabeth Withers, dau. of Thomas of Kit. He d. bef. 1698; wid. m. 2d Dodovah Curtis. List 90. Ch: Benjamin, d. unm. *Withers, d. unm. 11 Dec. 1732. His will made mo. Elizabeth sole benefic. Rep. to the Gen. Court, crossing by the Charles River ferry, he was thrown overboard and was so long in the icy water that he died.

4 GYLES, ag. 45 in Dec. 1674, sued Daniel Salmon for debt in Essex Co. 28 Nov. 1654. He was gr. the lot betw. Richard White and Goodm. Frost in York, 23 Dec. 1665, and 'of York' deeded it 20 July 1669 to Isaac Walker. In July, 1669, he was indicted for not going home to his wife for several yrs. and in Oct. was given 2 mos. to depart the Province; he went to Star Island and in N. H. Ct. 1673 was presented for abs. from wife. In 1681, living on Smuttynose, he was sued by Hugh Allard and by Francis Johnson.

5 JAMES(12), of Newcastle in 1718, sold to s. James of Greenland 10 a. east of Breakfast Hill. Lists 52, 312c, 312d, 313a, 315b, 316c, 318c, 326c, 332b. Wife Eleanor Wallis, dau. of George. Ch: George, b. 1674, of Newc. 1702, m. in Hampt. 1 Jan. 1702 Deliverance Haley (Andrew) of Kittery, he then of Sandy Beach; settled in Kit. 5 ch. James, b. 1676, of Greenland, m. 4 July 1700 Eleanor Jenness, dau. of Francis; both liv. 1762. Lists 315b, 326a, 338acd. 7 ch. Samuel, m. Abigail (Webster) Marden, wid. of James; she d. 19 June 1750 in 75th yr. 4 ch. Ebenezer, mar. 1st, 17 Sep. 1714 Keziah Knowles, 2d, 14 Nov. 1727 Mary Kingman, widow. Ch: 6+5. Rachel, m. 1st Richard Goss of Rye, 2d Job Chapman(6); d. 19 Feb. 1798, ag. 97.

6 JAMES (Barry), Boston, mariner, mar. Rachel (Atkins) Drake, wid. of John(4) of Small Point, dau. of Thomas Atkins(5); both liv. in Boston 1716. (?List 122). Ch. b. at Boston: James, 8 Jan. 1688. James, 12 July 1690. John, 12 Oct. 1695. Rachel, 14 July 1698.

7 JOHN(12), b. 1637, was living at Sandy Beach in 1703, d. bef. 1717. Wife Susanna living in 1680. He had land grants 1683, 93, 98; gr.j. 1673-1678. Lists 52, 54, 57, 311b, 312cd, 313a, 315bc, 318c, 326a, 330abc, 332b, 338a, 341. Ch: John, b. 14 Jan. 1659 (1660?). William, b. 1663. Hannah, m. 1699 Daniel Allen(2).

8 JOHN(7), m. Mary Souther (John of Hampt.), both living in 1729, of Greenland, when they sold (mtge?) house and 13 a. granted to John Berry and laid out 15 Nov. 1673. Lists 52, 57, 399a. Ch: Nehemiah, m. 14 Mar. 1705 Alice Locke, 2d, perh. 22 Oct. 1724 Sarah Rand. ?Jonathan, b. 15 Jan. 1693. Ithamar, b. 5 Mar. 1698, m. 19 June 1722 Anne Philbrick, settled in Chester. 8 ch.

9 JOSEPH(12), b. ab. 1639, d. bef. 1717. His house at Sagamore Creek bot from George Jones sr. 16 Feb. 1673-4, he sold in 1697, then of Greenland, where he lived in 1682. His 13 a. grant of 1661 was laid out in 1710, his house then standing on the adj. land, which was Nathl. Drake's old grant. Gr.j. 1675, 1682, 83, 1696. Lists 52, 62, 68, 312d, 313a, 330bcd, 332b. Ch. by w. Rachel: Nathaniel, with his br. Joseph sold ⅛ of the orig. homestead; m. 2 July 1691 Elizabeth Philbrick. He was taxed in Greenland 1698 and mov. to Mansfield, Conn., ab. 1717. Lists 62, 330d, 335a, 337, 338abc. Rachel, m. Abraham Lewis. Jane, m. 5 Jan. 1692-3 Robert Goss. ?Deliverance, m. 14 Feb. 1697-8 Richard Pomeroy. Joseph, a soldier at Ft. William and Mary in 1708; rem. to Scarb. and was Penhallow's tenant there prior to July 1717. By w. Mary 7 ch. incl.: Elisha who

m. in 1728, Capt. Joseph, adult in 1733, liv. 1783, and Thomas, b. 29 Aug. 1717, d. 10 Apr. 1755. (grst. at Newmeadows.)

10 **JOSEPH**, Piscataqua, mariner, mate of -The Joanna- in 1686. (Master of -The Elizabeth- reg. in N. H., clearing Boston for Antigua in 1715? Poss. his will, Boston, 1719-1722, naming wife Elizabeth, who m. 2d one Dows of Choptauk, Md.) He wit. deed to Benjamin in Kit. 12 Apr. 1675, and bot land there from Thomas Withers 9 Jan. 1683-4. Ch: ?Benjamin. ?Joseph, Portsm., mariner, a Barr. propr., dep. in 1758, ag. 72, ab. Richard Cutt's warehouse when he was a child. In 1739 his w. was Lydia, and Elizabeth Berry (wrote) wit. their deed. J. B. of Portsm., fisherman, in that year was occu. part of the house of Edward Cater dec.

11 **THOMAS**, killed in Ind. fight at Falm. 21 Sep. 1689. List 228d.

12 **WILLIAM** was at Strawberry Bank bef. 1636; in 1645 his land adj. Turpin and Cummings; of Str. Bk. 10 July 1648, he sold to Anthony Ellins. Land at Sandy Beach was gr. him 31 Jan. 1648, and 40 a. more in 1652, over which his ch. and grch. scattered, undiv. until 1719. Selectman 1646, const. for lower part of Str. Bk. 1650, gr.j. 1650. Lists 41, 321, 323, 324, 330c. Adm. gr. 28 June 1654 to wid. Jane, who dep. in 1686, ag. 67, that she and her husb. liv. here bef. Mr. (Francis) Williams came. She m. 2d Nathaniel Drake(5). Ch: **John**, b. 1637. **Joseph. Elizabeth**, m. ab. 1652 John Locke. **Mary**, m. John Foss(1). **James. Rachel**, m. John Marden. **William**. Most of the grdaus. are unkn. Sarah, who m. Samuel Dowse(2) 1 Mar. 1688-9, was evid. one, likelier(7).

13 **WILLIAM**(12), taxed in 1682, gr.j. 1695, comr. to settle all town bounds 3 Dec. 1701. Lists 69, 312d, 313a, 52, 332b, 318c, 315b. He was liv. 1704, but d. bef. 1708; wid. Judah, whom he m. 8 July 1678, List 316, m. 2d in 1708 Nathaniel Huggins. Ch: **Elizabeth**, b. 15 Oct. 1686, m. 24 July 1705 Christopher Palmer. **Nathaniel**, b. 13 Feb. 1688-9, mar. Esther Wallis. **Stephen**, b. 18 Jan. 1690-1, m. 4 Jan. 1716 Anna Philbrook (Thomas). 6 ch. **William**, b. 18 Nov. 1693, d. 8 Oct. 1786, m. 21 Dec. 1721 Sarah Lane (William of Hampton); she d. 3 Jan. 1776. 2 ch. **Jeremiah**, b. 8 Mar. 1695-6, k. by fall from tree, 8 May 1719. **Frederica**, b. 15 Jan. 1697-8, m. 1st Samuel Huggins, 2d Philip Babb jr.(1). **Abigail**, b. 15 Mar. 1699-1700. **Jane**, b. 26 Jan. 1701-2.

14 **WILLIAM**(7), b. ab. 1663, m. 19 Dec. 1689, Sabina Lock, 'born on the Ocean,' who m. 2d 8 Dec. 1710 Abraham Lewis and 3d 7 Mar. 1716-7 John Philbrick; and d. in 1761, ag. 95. Ch: **Thomas**, b. 8 Oct. 1690. In 1701 he was apprent. to Samuel and Alice Haines to learn dish turning; served under Capt. Waldron in the Canada expedn. He d. 28 June 1760 'aged 72;' wife Mehitable, m. by 1715, d. 1 Aug. 1758 ag. 61. 4 ch. **Joshua**, m. 13 Dec. 1716 Abiah Philbrook was called 'son' in John Philbrook's will, 1737. J. B. of Epsom in 1757 sold there; J. B. of Greenl. in 1762 sold in Epsom.

**BEST.** 1 Capt. ——, Popham, 1607. List 6.

2 **EDWARD**, came to Richmond Isl. 1638 and ran away. List 21.

**BESTONE** (Beson), **Thomas**, around Kit. Point or Portsm. 1647-1663, wit. Indian deed at Wells 1650, the same deed recorded Y. D. i. and iii, Suff. D. xi, as Beeson, Baston, Bestone. Ab. 1645 or 46 he was cutting wood with Tho. Crockett, wit. a will in 1663, prob. rem. bef. 1665. In 1687 his land was regranted to Rishworth who was in possess. in 1674.

**Bettenham**, John, Portsm., mariner, m. Mary King (Geo.).

**Beverly**, Lenox, Pemaquid soldier 1688. See Doc. Hist. ix. 31.

**Bevill**, John, Shoals fisherman with Henry Brookings. Joane his wid. 1657.

**Bewers**, John, Shoals fisherman 1673.

**Bezoon**, John, Philip's War. List 237b. See Marblehead.

**BICKFORD**, common in Devon. Beckford, a parish in Glouc.

1 'Old' Bickford, at Richmond Isl. 1637, to be sent home as unfit for a fisherman here. Priscilla, the fat maid, was presum. his relation. List 21. Doc. Hist. iii.

2 **ANDREW**, Arrowsic 1679. List 187.

3 **BENJAMIN**, Isl. of Shoals 1653. List 301.

4 **BENJAMIN**(13), in 1680 wit. a deed at Bloody Point, where he liv. Constable. Lists 52, 94, 343, 369. Will 4 Apr. 1724—2 June 1725. Ch: **Mary**, m. 8 Dec. 1707 Joshua Crockett(5). **Benjamin**, m. 22 Oct. 1718 Deborah (?Baur). 9 ch. **Thomas**, d. bef. 22 Feb. 1775, m. in Greenland Sarah Simpson. 8 ch. **Abigail**, m. 16 Aug. 1716 Zebulon Dam(4). **Elizabeth**, m. 20 Feb. 1718 John Dam(4). **Deborah**, m. 12 Dec. 1720 Joshua Babb(3). **John**, Rochester, mar. 23 Feb. 1725 Sarah Hodgdon. 4 ch. **Joseph**, d. bef. 15 Nov. 1754. Wife Margery. 3 ch.

5 **BENJAMIN**(12), b. 20 Oct. 1672, liv. 2 Nov. 1697. (Coroner's jury 1694, constable 1696.) He m. Sarah Barsham, who m. 2d Hon. Jotham Odiorne. Only ch: **Temperance**, mar. by 1718 John Underwood; 2d George Walton.

6 **BENJAMIN** (Beckford), Wells 1690. List 267a.

7 **EDWARD**, Portsm., bot house at Sagamore Creek 1660, tax abated 1680. Tavern lic. 1685-86. Lists 356l, 326c, 313a, 331b, 52. His wife and ch. were examined, without result, in death of Henry Sherborne

1680-1, found dead soon aft. complaining against Edward for harming his cattle and his ch. for stealing. Wife was Mary, if Nicholas was his son. Ch: **Edward**, fisherman, d. Boston 9 July 1713. Nunc. will, not allowed, gave estate to kinswoman Sarah Leach, his sisters and brother's son having enough. **Mary**, m. Joseph Hilliard of Boston 1713. **Margaret**, m. 1st at Boston 24 May 1701 George Wright, 2d John Davis (26 jr.). Also, likely **John**(18), and perh. **Nicholas**, taxed in 1689, or **Benjamin**, taxed with Edward at Little Harbor in 1689, one or another likely father of a son living in 1713. One Edward had his tax abated in Portsm. in 1718.

8 **ELIAS**, Isles of Shoals 1660. List 302a.

9 **GEORGE**, Monhegan 1672. Doc. Hist. vi. 119. App. the one at Salem 1666 with wife Christian ag. 17. Lists (111), 80, 13, 15. Of Marbleh., adm. to Christian 28 June 1678. Ch: **Priscilla**, m. in Marb. 30 Oct. 1689 Nicholas Tucker. **John**, fisherman, yeoman, m. in Marb. 8 Feb. 1697-8 Rebecca Pinson of Salem; liv. Reading 1757. 10 ch. rec. Salem.

10 **HENRY**(22), recd. 80 a. gr. at Scarb. 1720; weaver, at one time mariner; bot in Portsm. 1704. Lists 239b, 339. Joined the South Ch. 7 Nov. 1756. In 1760 he deeded his home to Titus Salter, his son-in-law. Wife Sarah, liv. 1737. Ch. bap: **Thomas**, b. 1704, schoolmaster, will 9 Sep. 1768, d. 18 Dec. 1772 ag. 68 (grst. Portsm.) He m. 4 Oct. 1727 Elizabeth Furber (Jethro 3). 8 ch., 6 named in will. **Sarah**, bp. with last 26 Sep. 1708. **Twin daus**., bp. 17 Oct. 1708. **Rachel**, bp. 16 Aug. 1711. **Hannah**, bp 1 Nov. 1713, m. 15 Jan. 1737-8 Capt. Arthur Waterhouse. **Mary**, bp. 27 May 1716. **Aaron**, bp. 25 Oct. 1718; wife Mary d. 3 Oct. 1752 ae. 26 (grst.). **Abigail**, bp. 2 Oct. 1720. **Elizabeth**, bp. 6 May 1722, m. 11 July 1745 Capt. Titus Salter.

11 **JOHN**, fisherman, Isles of Shoals, sold fish to Winter at Richmond Island July 1641—June 1642. List 301. Of Shoals, adm. 24 June 1662 to Philip Tucker.

12 **JOHN**, ±60 30 Mar. 1669, of Oyster River, where he bot land from Darby Field 16 July 1645. Gr.j. 1650, 59, 1683; lic. victualler 1657. Freed from training at Dover 26 June 1671. Lists 354abc, 355ab, 356abce, 361ab, 362ab, 363abc, 364, 365, 311c, 366, 359a, 353, 54, 49, 52. Will 12 Feb. 1685. He m. Temperance Hull, b. 1626, dau. of Rev. Joseph. Ch: **Elizabeth**, mar. Joseph Smith. **Joseph**. In 1676 his tax list next his father, not heard of after, except Hubbard p. 186. List 359a. **Lydia**, m. Francis Drew(2). **Mary**, m. Nicholas Harrison. **John**. **Thomas**, b. ab. 1660. **Hannah**, b. 5 Nov. 1665. **Temperance**, m. Jeremiah Burnham(2). **Joanna**, b. 1669, m. 12 Nov. 1696 John Redman jr., 2d Sam-

uel Healey. **Benjamin**, b. 20 Oct. 1672.

13 **JOHN**, Bloody Point, m. Elizabeth Cater(2). Gr.j. 1664, 'John Bickford Jr.' Lists 356ghjk, 359ab, 54, 52. He must have been Goodfather Bickford living in fall of 1685. Ch: **John**. **Benjamin**. See also Thomas(22).

14 **JOHN**(13), presented for drunkenness 24 June 1673, 'John Bickford Jr. of Bloody Point.' Lists 52, 359ab. Wife Jane, who was a memb. of Portsm. church when she m. 2d John Dockum(1). List 331c. Kn. ch: **Mary**, a cripple, d. unm. bef. 1705. **Agnes**, a minor 14 June 1705, m. Samuel Lary.

15 **SERGT. JOHN**(12), Long Point, Newington. Lists 62, 343. Constable. 1693, 1694. Adm. gr. 5 Sep. 1715 to wid. Susannah (Furber 2) and their son Jethro. Her will 8 Nov. 1731—13 Nov. 1732. Ch: **Bridget**, b. 30 July 1685, m. 1st Roger Couch(2); 2d Roger Mitchell. **Jethro**, b. 15 Nov. 1689. List 343. M. Hannah Downing(2). 10 ch. **John**, b. 16 Mar. 1691-2, d.s.p. bef. 1732. **Mary**, b. 13 Aug. 1693, m. John Walker. **Joseph**, b. 13 July 1695, mariner of Bristol, Eng., 1740. **Anna**, b. 18 Sep. 1698, m. Samuel Walker. **Pierce**, b. 9 Mar. 1701-2, m. 23 Feb. 1725 Hannah Miller; 2d Martha Chick (Richard). **Lemuel**, b. 6 Mar. 1703-4, m. Temperance Downing(4); d. before 25 Sep. 1745. 2 ch. **Eliakim**, twin of Lemuel, d. at Ken'port 22 Mar. 1748. Wife Mary. **Dodovah**, b. 20 Aug. 1709, m. (int. 13 Oct. 1730) Winnifred Chick (Richard). 1 ch.

16 **JOHN**, Kennebec. List 189.

17 **JOHN**(22), came from Scarb. to Dover Neck. He m. 1st, 1 Dec. 1692 Elizabeth Tibbetts, dau. of Jeremiah, who d. aft. 7 Nov. 1732; 2d Martha Allen(2). List 358d. His will 23 May 1744—27 Apr. 1757. Ch: **Martha**, b. 23 July 1692 or 93, m. Nathl. Hanson. **Thomas**, b. 18 May 1694, m. 10 Mar. 1717 Esther Adams(4), 2d wife Joanna. He d. before 1765. 9 ch. **John**, b. 10 Mar. 1698, d. bef. 1762, m. Judith Tibbetts, dau. of Joseph and Elizabeth, d. Mar. 1782. 4 ch. **Henry**, b. 1 Jan. 1702-3; wife Elizabeth. **Joseph**, b. 8 Mar. 1705-6, d. 11 Feb. 1776. 1st wife Elizabeth, 2d Deborah. 5 ch.

18 **JOHN** (see 7). In 1697 he was ferrying men to Great Isl. fort and piloting them to John Sherburne's in the Plains. Newcastle ferryman 1704-1706. Left a widow. Lists 318ac, 315bc, 68. One John B. of Portsmouth m. 15 Sep. 1719 Elizabeth Britten. See Hist. Durham ii. 29.

19 **LAWRENCE**, had gr. on Arrowsic 6 Sep. 1679. Lists 187, 189.

20 **NICHOLAS** (see 7, also 21). In June 1676 in court for stealing at Strawberry Bank, and his mother Mary for receiving the goods stolen.

21 **NICHOLAS**, poss. s. of (11), or same as

(20), ±22 in 1677. List 306a. Isles of Shoals fisherman, Roger Kelly's crew; good aut. 1677-1681.

22 **THOMAS**, Scarb., ±36 in 1676. Lists 239a, 236, 237ade, 238a, 30, 34. His end myster., presum. went with ch. to N. H. and deeded unrec. to son John. Perh. on coroner's jury in Breakfast Hill region (with bro.-in-law Larrabee?) in Mar. 1693-4. See N. H. Ct. files 15187: Note for a cow payable in boards by T. B., Ephraim Trickey and Benj. Rawlins, dated 22 Sep. 1682, on which Trickey's est. was sued in 1701. Poss. the Thomas who joined Portsm. So. Ch. 6 Sep. 1713. He m. Joanna Libby. Kn. ch: **Deborah**, m. 10 Mar. 1685-6 Jeremiah Jordan, 2d by 1714 Wm. Jones of Newcastle; she was liv. in Falm. in June 1752, ag. bet. 80 and 90. **John. Henry.**

23 **THOMAS**(12), born 1660. His garrison house at Durham Point withstood an Ind. attack 1694. Lists 52, 57, 61, 62, 66, 353, 368a. Will 13 Oct. 1706—4 Mar. 1707. He m. Bridget Furber(2). Ch: **Joanna. John**, b. 1690. Lists 368b, 369. Wife Deborah. 6 ch. **Eleazer**, d. bef. 2 July 1751. Lists 368b, 369. M. at Greenland 28 Dec. 1721 Sarah Johnson. 5 ch. **Joseph**, b. 1696, of Durham 1767. Lists 368b, 369. M. Alice Edgerly (John). 4 ch. **Thomas**, shipwright, Durham. Will 8 Apr. 1786—22 Aug. 1787 names w. Bethia and kinsman John Footman jr. s. of Francis deceased.

24 **WILLIAM**, fisherman, in 1661 sold John Brown's leasehold est. at Pemaquid. Kennebec 1672, had gr. at Arrowsic 1679. Wm. B., Tho. Ashley sr. and Ralph Curtis were overseers (selectmen) of Newtown, Arrowsic, 1681, and as overseer he was one of the signers of deed from inhabts. of Newtown and Sagadahoc to Capt. Sylvanus Davis 1681. Lists 13, 15, 187, 189. One William Biggford was in Marblehead 1677.

**BICKHAM**. Two parishes Beckham in Norf.

1 **RICHARD**, taxed 1698. List 330c. See (3).

2 **WILLIAM**, b. ±1632, brother of Richard Bickham, mercht. of Bristol, Eng., and uncle of Francis Knight and of Ephraim Lynn or his wife, was at Kit. Point in 1672, taking a mortg. jointly with Maj. Shapleigh; called mercht. 4 Mar. 1674-5 when Vickers, Bickham & Co. gave P. A. to Francis Tucker to sue him. He was overseer of Rev. Robert Jordan's will in 1678, wit. Geo. Walton's will 1685-6, appr. Henry Beck's estate 1686, Spruce Creek wit. 1688. Lists 312c, 89. App. dead by 1689 when Major John Davis sold ½ his dwg. at Kit. Point, built by Dr. H. Greenland, with spec. warranty against heirs of Greenland and Mr. Wm. Bickham. See N. E. Reg. 70:283.

3 **WILLIAM**, as Doctor Bickum was surety for Rachel Mitchel in 1693. House 'where

Mr. Bickham now liveth' ment. in 1694, presum. owned by Richard Bickham of Eng., unless Richard taxed in 1698 (List 330c) is an error for Wm. Lists 319, 330d. His w. Mary Webber, dau. of Richard, was joint wit. with Lydia Webber in 1699; both liv. 1710. Either she or her dau. ack. covt. in So. Ch. 1716. Ch: **Mary**, named as grdau. in Richard Webber's will 1720; of Portsm. 20 Nov. 1723 she m. Stephen Wyatt of Newbury.

4 **WILLIAM**, one of crew of -The Katherine- 1701; common rights 1721-2.

5 **WILLIAM** (Bickum), of Dolis in Devon, and Hannah Hepworth m. at Portsm., 22 Oct. 1723. One Wm. -Beckman- was rated to the Old Meet. Ho. in 1717. William Bickham had his tax abated in 1718, an added name in 1723.

**Bicknell**, Richard, see Bucknell.
**Bicknell**, Richard, see Bucknell.

**BICKTON, Wymond**, was sued in Portsm. 28 Jan. 1669-70 as Waymon Beckton. He had been at Mr. Richard Cutt's house and until he went away Wm. Earle's wife washed his clothes. At Black Point in Apr. 1675, Andrew Alger complained of Waymouth Bicketon for stealing iron work from his mill; the same yr. his w. Mary and Francis Shallet were in Court, altho in 1679 she wit. against Shallet for stealing. Aft. a few yrs. in N. H. they were at Black Point again by 1680, where he deeded land 1683, was bondsman for John Tenney 1684, and had a public house 1688. Lists 313a, 331b, 30, 313d, 238a, 90. She had 30 a. gr. adj. Tidy in Apr. 1686. List 238a.

**Bidwell**, John, Damariscove 1672. List 13. See also Beedle.

**BIGGS, Thomas**, perh. came ag. 13 in -The Blessing- to Boston in July 1635. He was in Exeter by 1643, engaged in a lawsuit there in 1644, sued John Smart and w. Margaret in 1647 for slandering hims. and w. Esther, and in 1651 was fined for refus. to appear when sum. by the marshal. Hampt. jury 1662. His holdings incl. a gr. for a sawmill on Pisc. River and lands on Lamprill River, which he sold to John Gilman in 1652, and land which he and Esther sold in 1663. As Hester she was an Exeter wit. 1645. Lists 374a, 375b, 376ab, 377, 379. He rem. to Brookhaven, L. I., where he was prom. and was living as late as 1697. Ch: **Thomas. John.**

**BILLINGS**. Place name in East and North of England.

1 **JOHN**, came in 1635 to the Trelawny plant., ran away and settled on Kittery Point, fisherman; was an equal partner with John Lander and with him sold 8 a. they had cleared next Spruce Creek to Joseph Miles last of Feb. 1639. He lived on 'the

further point of all—from Braveboat Harbor. He sued John Winter in 1640 and d. bef. July 1646 when his wid. Elizabeth sued Robert Mendam. Lists 21, 321. She m. 2d Rice Thomas, who in Dec. 1647 bot from Thomas Crockett the land her 1st husb. had sold to Miles. Ch: John.

2 JOHN(1), b. by 1640. Aug. 12 1661 he deeded land and cattle to his mo. Elizabeth Thomas for life, to revert to him, and confirmed the deed 23 June 1680; successfully sued his stepf. for meadow in 1664. Lived at Braveboat Harbor. Lists 298, 30, 292. He m. by 1671 Anne Andrews(9), who was liv. 1689. Inv. 3 Dec. 1690, Capt. Hooke adm. Anne, his wife, had been whipped in 1684 for slandering Mrs. Hooke. Ch: Elizabeth, ment. in 1687. John, d.s.p. 1740. Joseph, appren. to Capt. Gerrish in Dover. As plf. in a suit 1744 he named self and br. John as the only surv. ch., of whom John had d.s.p. Lists 291, 296, 297. He m. 29 Nov. 1716 Hannah Wilson. Will 1748—1764. 7 ch.

BINNS, Jonas, Dover 1648-1659. Lists 354a, 354bc, 361b.

Birch, John, 1656, wit. for Joseph Mason. See Brich.

Birkhead, John, 1661, thrice wit. with Antipas Maverick, Kit. Y. D. i. 114, 116, 117.

Bisco, Nathaniel (fine aut. Suff. Ct. files 309), Eliot wit. 1651. List 80.

BISH. 1 John, was liv. at Tuessic (Woolwich) in 1688, owning land with Lawrence Dennis, and had previously been a landowner at Pemaquid, selling out there to Thomas Sharpe. List 189. He and his fam. were captured by Ind. bef. 4 Sep. 1688, when he was found prisoner of 5 Ind. in his own house. Heirs ment. in deed 1722, but only kn. ch: John.

2 JOHN(1), Casco Bay, mariner, 27 Dec. 1721, when he sold land at Tuessic, but ack. deed 18 Dec. 1724 in Boston, where he m. (int. 2 Feb. 1721) Ann Cox. Ch: John, b. at Boston 31 Jan. 1722.

BISHOP. 1 John. Arrowsic grant 1679. List 187.

2 JOHN, m. at Kit. 8 Jan. 1712-3 Eleanor (Frye), wid. of John Brooks(4). In 1716 they were in Kingston.

3 NICHOLAS, from 'St. James, Great Brit.,' m. 11 Aug. 1715 Mary Bradden(2), who m. 2d by 1729 Benj. Akerman. 'Mr.' B. rated to the New Meeting Ho. 1717. Barrington Prop. 1722. List 339. Presum. son: James, mariner, adm. 26 Jan. 1742-3 gr. to (his half-blood uncle?) John Tapley of Kit., mariner.

BISS, Samuel, by verdict of coroner's jury hung himself, appar. a travelling tailor. No known relatives. Adm. 6 Apr. 1680 to the York Clerk of the Writs, John Twisden, who sued Humphrey Axall.

Bissell, John, Sagadahoc 1674. J. Bis- or Bar-sell of Litchfield, Conn., sold in Pemaquid 1736. Y. D. 18.63. Lists 15, (83?).

Bixby, George, of Topsfield, deeded in 1732, w. Mary consenting, the 100 a. lot in Ken'port granted 25 June 1681 to Andrew Alger(2), later John Purington's? Y. D. xv. 217. Dea. G. B. d. Topsfield 3 May 1783, ae. 92. W. Mary d. 8 Feb 1767, very aged.

BLACK, the 46th commonest Scotch name.

1 DANIEL. Lists 74, 47. Likely Daniel of Boxford and f. of (2) and (3).

2 DANIEL(1), b. 24 Aug. 1667, weaver, came from Topsfield as early as 1695, and in 1696 bot a house in York, where he appr. est. of John Preble 6 Jan. 1695-6. Sergt. 1696-7, selectm. 1699, jury 1699-1700-1-3, retailer 1703, tavern keeper 1700-8. See Benj. Donnell. His 1st w. Mary Cummings of Topsfield d.s.p.; he m. 2d at Topsfield 19 July 1695 Sarah Adams(16); both living 24 Aug. 1709, she a wid. 12 Aug. 1712, and gr. adm. 15 May 1718. She d. 28 July 1727. Ch: Sarah, b. 20 July 1697, m. Joseph Weare. Samuel, b. 29 May 1699, only son in 1727; mariner. List 279. His wife Dorcas (Bragdon 6) was gr. adm. 14 Jan. 1745-6. 8 ch. Elizabeth, b. 5 Nov. 1701, m. (int. 8 Sep. 1733) Noah Moulton. Daniel, b. 17 Mar. 1703-4, d. bef. 1727. Mehitable, b. 27 Oct. 1706, in Nov. 1730 forbid pub. to Michael Dalton of Newbury, m. 9 Nov. 1731 Pelatiah Littlefield of Wells.

3 JOSIAH(1), b. 1676, came to York and was a tenant of George Norton early. He sold his own grants, and in 1719 the Scituate owners deeded to him and w. Mary, then to their ch., the land where his house stood. List 279. Both deeded homestead to s. Josiah Tertius, in 1744. Ch: John, b. 13 Apr. 1697. Mehitable, b. 1 Aug. 1699. Deborah, b. 25 Nov. 1702, m. 28 May 1724-5 John Davis(32). Hepsibeth, b. 30 Jan. 1708-9, m. (int. 16 Jan. 1728) her cousin, Edmund Black, s. of James of Boxford. List 279. Josiah, b. 23 June 1712, m. bef. 1737 Esther Bean (Joseph 3). Ch. Mary, b. 23 Apr. 1715, m. Josiah Black, whose gdn. 2 Jan. 1726-7 was Mary's father; he was bro. of Edmund. Ch. Priscilla, b. 23 Nov. 1717.

4 THOMAS (or Blake). List 41.

5 WILLIAM, otherwise 'Black Will,' a slave of Maj. Shapleigh, manumitted by John Shapleigh in 1701, acquired 100 a. in 1696. In 1708 he bound his land to protect the town on Charles Frost's freeing Tony, and allowed him to build on his land. Lists 290, 298. He had a ch. by Alice Hanscom in 1691, and presum. ano. by Elizabeth Brooks in 1712, and his will, proved 1 Jan. 1727-8, provides that his wife Sarah be supported by his two sons. It gives to s. Wm. the

money -Anthony Freeman- owes for the 2 a. his house stands on. Ch: **William**, alias Black Will jr., kept house with Elizabeth Turbet jr. His ch. Elizabeth and William are named in their grfr's will. In 1739 Black Will, a mulatto man, was in poss. of New Cape Newagen Isl., Harpswell, and in 1760 Wm. Black of Harpswell sold his half of the 100 a. formerly of his grfr. William Black. **Joshua**, had 12 ch. rec. by w. Mary, the 2 eldest named in their grfr's will and 8 in his own will 19 Jan. 1753—5 Apr. 1756.

**Blackappe**, Henry, Kittery 1648. Y. D. i. 3. List 283.

**BLACKLEDGE, Nathaniel**, b. Camb. 12 Oct. 1666, stepson of Hugh March. Soldier and irresp. List 399a. He m. by 1695 Mary (Milbury) Freethy, wid. of James, dau. of Henry Milbury of York; his wid. in 1726, she d. 28 May 1735. Ch: **Jabez**, bot in York 1716. List 279. Wife Sarah, 7 ch. 1717-1736.

**BLACKMAN**, Blakeman, pecul. to Hants. 1 **ADAM**, Dorchester. List 267b.

2 *****REV. BENJAMIN**, H. C. 1663, s. of Rev. Adam of Stratford, Conn., was himself min. at Saco and Scarb., but more prom. in other ways, and a large landowner through purch. and his m. to Rebecca Scottow, dau. of Capt. Joshua of Bost. and Scarb. 10 Apr. 1680 he was of Black Point buying in Saco, owned a sawmill on Saco Riv. in 1681, and soon bot a large tract from the Lewis & Bonython heirs, later selling ⅔ to Samuel Walker and Sampson Sheaf of Boston. With Walker petitioned Andros in 1688. Deputy 1682, Fort Loyal com. 1684, Capt. 1687, J. P. 1688. Rem. to Bost. and d. when dau. not over 3 or 4. Wife Rebecca d. 20 Mar. 1715, her grst. still at Copp's Hill. **Rebecca**, only ch. in 1742, m. at Boston 21 July 1710 Thomas Goodwill; sold rem. ⅓ of tract in Saco to William Pepperell jr., 1717. 3 or more daus.

3 **PETER**, North Yarm. 1685, where a lot was allowed his heirs. List 214. In 168— Moses Felt was bound to the peace towards P. B. and his family. Sullivan named him among those who still had posterity there. One Peter was in Suffolk Ct. Oct. 1681, one on Cape Cod.

**BLACKSTONE**, a rare Eng. surname. 1 **PETER**, 'old' in 1719. In that year a young man known as Thomas Blackstone was receiving plank for old Peter B., Captain of a ship then in the Piscataqua River. N. H. Ct. files 18430. Whether this was the Thomas taxed in Dover in 1716, and some relat. to either Peter or (2) is unasc. In 1716 Capt. Peter was sued for 30 weeks' shaving at Newcastle. In 1717 Pepperell sued him for 4 gal. of rum in 1714, and for a debt of Tho. Potts charged over by P. B.'s

order in 1715. Potts was neighbor of (2).

2 **WILLIAM**, Dover Point, planter, had gr. of 40 a. on Fresh Creek Neck in 1693-4, and with w. Abigail sold land in 1696 deeded them that yr., by her parents, Humphrey and Sarah Varney. Jury 1695. List 358c. Living 1 Apr. 1724, he was dead by 1727; his wid. was liv. in 1729, when she with other settlers there from 30 to 40 yrs. bef. signed a Cocheco Point petn. Deeds in 1754 of the int. of three ch. in a grant in Rochester he owned with Richard Hammock and James Hanson, indicate seven ch., of whom only four are cert. kn.: **Abigail**, a Berw. wit. in 1714, m. Ambrose Claridge of Portsm. **Elizabeth**, m. George How of Portsm.; wid. 1754. **Benjamin**, elder son 1754, m. at Ipswich, 7 Nov. 1724, Mehitable Hunt, dau. of William and Sarah (Newman), and settled in Falm. His will made 30 Apr. 1759; d. bef. 19 Dec. 1763. 10 ch. **William**, b. 1718, m. and settled in Newcastle, Me. Ch. Wives of two other early settlers at Newcastle, Lydia, w. of Samuel Hall, and Patience, w. of Josiah Clark(37), are by trad. claimed as Blackstone daus. by desc., while one or more of the foll. perh. have better claims: Thomas, Dover tax list 1716, added name in Portsm. same year; Mary, of Dover, m. at Portsm. 14 Jan. 1730-1 Thomas Blackle of Staverton, Devon.; Sarah, a Portsm. wit. in 1715; or even Hannah, m. at Marblehead 11 Feb. 1710-1 Benj. White. Several of these may have d.s.p. before 1754.

**BLACKWELL, Jeremiah**, came on -The Truelove- 1635, ag. 18. Exeter 1639. List 376a.

**BLAGDON**, flour. in Tiverton, Devon. Name of 3 places Somerset-Northumb. 1 **GEORGE**(2), a Star Island wit. 1707, m. Jane Paine (Thomas of Newcastle) and d. early without lawful issue. See Paine. Adm. on his estate was renounced 12 May 1721 by Daniel and Elizabeth Grindle in favor of their sis. Kelly; real est. sold for debts.

2 **LT. JAMES**, b. ab. 1638, bot at the Shoals in 1668, and was long prom. at Star Isl., tav. keeper, justice, and freq. admr. and appr. to 1714. Gr.j. 1672, selectman 1679, const. 1686. Lists 306c, 307b, 308a, 309, 95, 59. The 1st of two wives was Martha, the 2d Joan, m. by 25 Apr. 1693 and who had been wid. of William Diamond(5) and Edward Carter(2). Adm. to s. George 17 Mar. 1715-6, and again to s.-in-law William Kelly 5 Mar. 1721-2. Kn. ch: **George. Lydia**, m. William Kelly of Newcastle. **Elizabeth**, m. Daniel Grindle.

3 **DR. SAMUEL**, surgeon of Portsm. by 1686, by 1688 had m. Mary (Seward), wid. of Dodavah Hull, dau. of Richard. In 1696

they were liv. in Boston. Lists 52, 57. She was again a wid. in Portsm. in 1713, and in 1715 was liv. with her dau. Hannah in the home of her s.-in-law Nicholas Follett. List 331e. She d. 11 Dec. 1735 ag. 75 (grst.) Ch: **Samuel**, d. in Boston 9 June 1696. **Hannah**, of Portsmouth, single, in 1748; adm. gr. to Samuel Dalling, mariner, 15 Mar. 1756.

**BLAISDELL**, Bleasdale. The names Ralph and Henry occur thru the region so. of Bleasdale Forest and B. Moors in Lancashire bef. 1630.

**RALPH** (aut. Bleasdale), tailor, came in -The Angel Gabriel- 1635; at York until 1640. Wit. deeds with Hooke; both rem. to Salis. In 1640 he was on commit. to draft declar. to new prov. gov. He had gr. in Salis. in 1640, and in 1642, 'of Salisbury' sold out in York. Innholder 1645-47. Jury 1647, 48. List 72. In Dec. 1649 'of Lynn' he was app. int. a voyage. Adm. gr. June 1651 to wid. Elizabeth, who d. Aug. 1667, adm. to Joseph Stowers. Ch: **Henry**, b. about 1632, tailor. As a boy at York he tended Mr. Hooke's goats on Cape Neddick Neck. Pioneer at Amesbury. Wife Mary Haddon d. 12 Dec. 1691, and he m. a 2d w. Elizabeth. D. 1702-1705. 11 ch., of whom Ebenezer, 1657-1710, was f. of Ebenezer (Blacy, in John Ingersoll's will, whose dau. Abigail he mar.), who rem. to York, (List 279), of Ralph who rem. to Kingston, and of John 1668-1733, f. of Ralph who rem. to East Kingston. **Mary**, b. 5 Mar. 1641-2, m. 1st Joseph Stowers, 2d, 19 Dec. 1676 Wm. Sterling, d. 29 May 1681. 3+5 ch. **Ralph**, b. 1643, d. 1666 or 7. **Martha**, m. 1st Richard Bowden(9), 2d (Thomas?) Selley, 3d, 15 Jan. 1686 John Clough; liv. 1707. 1+1 ch. **Sarah**, d. 17 Jan. 1646-7.

**BLAKE**. South of Eng. A line of Jasper Blakes owning lands in Wimbotsham, Norfolk, goes back 5 generations.

1 **JASPER**, Hampton, seaman and fisherman, origin unkn., but either he or his wife (Dow says his wife) related to both Daltons, and he had deed of gift from Rev. Timothy Dalton 10 Oct. 1657. First appear. 1647 wit. a Timothy Dalton deed. Lists 393ab. He d. 5 Jan. 1673-4; will 18 July 1673 names Deborah, 4 sons, oldest dau., 'small children,' and 'cossen Mr. Samll. Dalton.' She d. 20 Dec. 1678. List 393a. Ch: **Timothy**, b. 16 Oct. 1649. **Deborah**, b. 15 Jan. 1651-2, m. aft. Oct. 1671 Eleazer Elkins(3). **Israel**, not rec., but named in father's will. **John**, b. 31 Oct. 1656. **Sarah**, b. 14 Feb. 1658-9, d. 29 Sep. 1660. **Sarah**, b. 30 June 1661, m. Alexander Magoon. **Jasper**, b. 16 Nov. 1663. **Samuel**, b. 6 June 1666, inquest filed 27 June 1666. **Dorothy**, b. 17 Sep. 1668, m. Nathl. Locke. **Phile-**

mon, b. 23 May 1671, m. 20 Jan. 1698 Sarah Dearborn(2). Will, of Hampt. Falls, proved 28 Apr. 1741, names wife and 6 ch., incl. Elisha. List 399a. **Maria**, b. 1 Mar. 1672-3. Besides Tim., Deborah and John, there were five other ch. liv. 10 Nov. 1679.

2 **JOHN**(1), jury 1692, gr.j. 1698. Lists 396, 52. In his will 22 Mar. 1715-6—14 May 1716 he names w. Frances and all his ch. exc. Abigail. Ch: **Dorothy**, b. 8 Apr. 1686, in court Feb. 1711-2, m. Thomas Crockett(7). **Sarah**, m. 2 Dec. 1708 Jonathan Batchelder(3). **John**, b. 2 Sep. 1689, List 338b, m. Mary Dearborn, d. of Samuel(2). List 338b. 8 ch. **Samuel**, b. 13 Dec. 1690, in 1757 rem. from Hampt. Falls to Epping, d. 1762. Son Stephen. **Jasper**, b. 4 Dec. 1693, m. Susannah Brackett(2), moved to Falm. **Jonathan**, b. 15 Nov. 1697, in 1721 was of Newbury, ship carpenter. **Mehitable**, b. 3 Aug. 1701, m. 1st Jonathan Godfrey, 2d Enoch Sanborn. **Nathan**, b. 4 June 1705, m. Judith Batchelder; d. 5 Mar. 1783. Had the homestead. 8 ch. **Abigail**, bp. 11 May 1707.

3 **THOMAS** (or Black), serv. at Newichawannock 1633-4. List 41.

4 **THOMAS**, ±29 in 1674, Portsm. wit. Tax abated 1675.

5 **TIMOTHY**(1), List 397b, m. 20 Dec. 1677 Naomi Sleeper, naming her and all his ch. in his will 26 Oct. 1715. He d. 5 Jan. 1717-8. Ch: **Deborah**, b. 27 June 1679, m. John Morgan. **Moses**, m. 25 Dec. 1701 Abigail Smith. Will, Kensington 1747—1752 names w. and 7 ch., not Tim. **Israel**, b. 1 Jan. 1683, set. in Nottingham, and d. Apr. 1753. Wife Leah. Will 1753—1753 names 7 ch. **Timothy**, b. 1 Feb. 1685, liv. at Hampt. Falls; m. at Kit. 25 Mar. 1716 Joanna Mitchell, d. of Christopher. Ch. **Aaron**, b. 27 June 1688, m. one Martha. **Naomi**, b. 4 Sep. 1690, m. Richard Foye. **Ruth**, b. 3 Nov. 1693, m. 6 June 1717 Oliver Smith of Exeter. **Samuel**, b. 3 Nov. 1696, m. 8 Jan. 1719 Ann 'Sylle,' (?dau. of Thomas and Ann (Stanyan).

6 **WILLIAM**, drunken sailor in N. H. Ct. 28 June 1664, belonging to the pinke of which Mr. Clements was master.

**BLANCHARD**, Richard (Blanchet), Cape Porpus ab. 1685. List 259. Taxed Portsmouth, vicin. Little Harbor 1693, 1695 tax abated. M. 12 July 1686 Elizabeth Hussey, who m. 2d 10 Apr. 1705 Richard Randall. Presum. son: **Richard**, of Durham (1731) and Dover and ab. 1733 to Canterbury, where he d. bef. 19 Oct. 1750, likely the one, reported as Richard or Benjamin, scalped by Ind. there 1746. Wife Sarah 'Head,' m. at Oyster River 3 Sep. 1719, was niece of John Reynolds. Benjamin and 'old Sergt.' Richard of Canterbury and Northfield perh. their sons.

**BLAND**, Mr. John, alias Smith, was living

at Edgartown, on Martha's Vineyard, in 1646, undoubtedly the John Smith assoc. with the Mayhews in the first movement from Watertown to the Island, where he was always -Bland-. In Watert. liv. his mother Adrian, 2d w. of Jeremiah Norcross, and there is recorded 'Isabel, w. of John Smith, bur. 12 July 1639, ag. 60.' The Hampt. Drakes test. that they knew his dau. Isabel Bland from childhood, that her f. John Bland lived in Colchester, and that his ancestry was Bland, not Smith. App. his stepf. was Smith. His will made 2 Nov. 1663 names w. Joanna and 'all the children that are alive that I owne': Isabel, m. 1st Francis Austin(1), 2d Thomas Leavitt. Annabel, m. William Barsham of Watert.; eldest s. John(1).

Blandfield, John, Portsm., drunk 1670. See N. E. Reg. ii. 104.

Blaney (Blanne), John, Lynn, coastwise trader, ±63 in 1693. See Thomas Purchase, Richard Pike, Thaddeus Riddan.

BLASHFIELD One T. B. of 'Langtondine' sailed from Liverpool for Barbadoes 1654-1663.

1 THOMAS, aft. serv. in King Philip's War and marrying at Beverly 28 Mar. 1676 Abigail Hibbert, dau. of Robert and Joan, rem. to No. Yarmouth ab. 1680, liv. on 60 a. at Broad Cove he had possess. ab. 7 yrs. when he pet. Andros. A wit. there in 1683. In 1686 gr. adm. est. of Roger Edwards. Lists 85, 214. He ret. to Bev. and in 1706 sold his No. Yarmouth home to John Watts of Salem, at other times selling 50 acres at Back Cove and land and marsh at North Yarm. He d. at Bev. 25 Oct. 1714; widow Abigail d. there 27 Feb. 1725 ag. ±75. Ch: Thomas. Abigail, m. at Bev. 20 June 1704 Jonathan Wheeler. Henry, b. Bev. 19 Nov. 1692, m. 1st 29 Dec. 1720 Mary Morgan, dau. of Joseph and Sarah (Hill), d. 14 Nov. 1740 ag. 44, 2d (int. Bev. 1 Mar. 1740-1) Lydia Lovitt. He was bur. 15 Apr. 1778 ag. 86. 10 ch. Luke, bp. at Bev. 27 June 1703, m. there 1 Dec. 1720 Rose Trenance.

2 THOMAS(1). In Mar. 1696 he belonged to the crew of a Salem galley com. against the French. Always a mariner and later of Portsm. There he m. wid. Hannah (Graves) Stephens bef. 10 Dec. 1716 when they exch. with Tho. Hammett for a Portsm. lot half a dwg. her mother Amy (Onion) Graves, widow (of Francis), had deeded to her for life supp. in 1715. In Aug. 1728 they deeded their dwg. to Benj. Akerman. A wid. by 1733, she was liv. in 1751, then sued on a note she had given to Walter Logan of Boston in 1749. By her 1st husb. she had a dau. Mary Stephens bp. 14 Feb. 1713-4, who m. 1st 26 Dec. 1732 Geo. Church of Romford, Essex, Eng.; 2d in June 1747 Daniel Robin-

son. In Nov. 1719 she had 2 ch. bap. in the No. Ch., both presum. Blashfields, of whom Hannah m. 14 July 1737 Joseph Thresher, born at Salem, 2d one Peirce. Thomas, bp. in Berwick 3 June 1722, had been apprent. to Thomas Hammett, sailmaker, ab. 2 yrs. in 1733, when his mother asked that he be discharged.

Blasser (Blazo, Blazier?), Daniel, 1672, arrested Nathan Bedford and did not enter writ.

Blatchford, Francis, abuttor in Kit. town grants 1683. Y. D. iv. 24, vi. 43.

Bleach, Hercules, (aut. Whipple MSS.), Pendleton wit., Saco, 1670.

BLUNT. 1 Samuel of Marblehead, see Churchill(1).

2 WILLIAM, Andover, soldier under Hill 1693-4. List 267b. Father of Rev.

John, H. C. 1727, minister at Newcastle.

BLY, Blyth. Blyth name of 3 places in North of England.

1 JOHN, ±45 in 1709, age agreeing with John b. in Salem 27 Jan. 1665, s. of John and Rebecca. List 67 (List 80 his father). 31 Jan. 1689-90 he and Roger Deering appr. John Bray's est.; in 1695-6 as John Blyth wit. a Whidden deed. In 1705 he was a butcher in Portsmouth, owning a slaughter house in 1709. J. B. taxed Str. Bank 1713. Possibly Priscilla Bly 'formerly Jerman' in 1690 was his 1st wife. In 1715 his widow Martha (m. as early as 1709) was one of three victims of extortion for letting people have liquor, and with a child to main., also a dau. old enough to tell them they could have no rum. She was liv., 'Mother Bly,' in 1722. Older children may have been: John, Portsm., m. 28 Oct. 1718 Grace Lewis, presum. same who m. 2d Nathl. Boulter(1), and 3d in Scarb. 17 Sep. 1744 Henry Dresser. Elizabeth, bastardy Me. Ct. 1718, the father a negro.

2 THOMAS, ±31 in 1653. One Thomas Bligh in Boston tax list 1687, next to Ambrose Hunnewell.

3 WILLIAM, cordwainer, likely br. of (1), b. 17 Sep. 1676 (or 78). A Portsm. wit. in 1702, he was surveying in Kit. in 1705; rem. to Ipws., selling his Portsm. dwg. in 1710. Of Portsm. he m. (int. Ipsw. 30 Jan. 1702) Susanna Wood, who d. his wid. 1 Feb. 1727. One Wm. Blyth m. in Greenland 22 Dec. 1729 Hannah Pickering. Ch. rec. Ipsw. and likely several older: Susannah, bp. 2 Aug. 1713. Hannah, bp. 11 Mar. 1715. John, bp. 16 Mar. 1718.

BOADE, Mr. Henry, gent., a dist. rel. of Gov. Winthrop and of unkn. rel. to Rev. Timothy Dalton. Plaint. in Saco Ct. 1636-7, gr.j. 1640. With Mr. William Cole he was bondsman for Wm. Colfex in Sep. 1640 and

may have been res. in Wells then, altho his 100 a. at Winter Harbor were not sold until Aug. 1642. Trustee of Wells in 1643, selectm. 1647, Com.t.e.s.c. Lists 242, 252, 261, 263, 22, 24, 71. On 12 June 1655, liv. at William Hammond's in Wells, he sold ho. and land to H. and W. Symonds for life supp. of hims. and wife. Will 8 Jan. 1654-5—16 July 1657, wife Anne ex. She m. 2d (contract 6 Oct. 1657) Samuel Wensley of Salis., and with him released to the two Symonds 16 Dec. 1657.

**BOADEN**, Bowden, Cornwall-Devon.

1 **ABRAHAM** (Booden), York. See Boody.

2 **AMBROSE**, from Holberton, Devon, (whence also John Winter, Peter Hinkson and Geo. Taylor), b. ± 1589, m. 28 Jan. 1624-5 Marie Lethebridge. He was a mariner, apprent. to John Winter who m. Johane Boaden; as master of ·The Margery· brot over Thomas Cammock and reed. in payment a gr. at Higgins Beach, Scarb., but was still making voyages and keeping his family in Holberton as late as 1643. Selectman with Wm. Smith, coroner 1646, gr.j. 1667. Lists 21, 239a, 222c, 232. He became blind ab. 1670, d. Oct. 1675; inv. taken 8 Feb. 1675-6, adm. to Samuel Oakman 5 July 1676. Ch: **Ambrose. Agnes**, bur. 28 Nov. 1637. **Grace**, bur. 12 Sep. 1638. **John**, bp. 2 May 1630. **Mary**, bp. 27 Oct. 1634, m. 1st Samuel Oakman, b. 1630, 2d Walter Adams(20)● **Agnes**, bp. 3 Nov. 1639, m. John Tenney. **Abraham**, bp. 11 Sep., bur. 19 Dec. 1641.

3 **AMBROSE**(2), fisherman 1679. Ab. 1653 he bot 200 a. up the Spurwink River of Robert Jordan, and 26 a. of Joshua Scottow, adj. Saml. Oakman, in 1668. His petn. to Andros 1686 stated he had settled three families on this land. Gr.j. 1670, 71, 76; selectman 1676, 1683, 84, 86. Lists 30, 32, 232, 237ac, 238a, 239a. He was driven off by the Ind., d. 1704. Wife Mary and ch: **Damaris**, b. ab. 1652, dep. in 1752 ag. 100; m. Richard Webber. **Susanna**, m. John Edgecomb(1). **Rebecca**, m. John Brown(20). **John**, b. ab. 1665. **Ambrose**, b. ab. 1666. **Jonathan**, b. ab. 1670, m. by 1697, was f. of Tabitha Ball. **Tabitha**, m. in Marbleh. 31 Oct. 1700 John Rhodes 3rd, d. 4 Mar. 1719. 2 ch.

4 **AMBROSE**, b. ab. 1640, of no relat. to the Scarb. fam., unless, not imposs., it came through 'Mr. Jocelyn's negro' slanderously recorded by Mr. Cleeve. He was ab. lower Kittery 1672-1687, if not bef. and aft., with no suggest. of fam.

5 **AMBROSE**(3), b. in Scarb. ab. 1666, m. in Salem 14 Dec. 1693 Lydia Sheldon, d. in Marbleh. 1 June 1728; she d. 31 Mar. 1746 ag. 80. List 239b. Ch: **Elizabeth**, b. 9 Dec. 1695, m. 31 Dec. 1713 David Furnace of Marb. 8 ch. **Benjamin**, b. 1699, m. 1st 27

Nov. 1721 Elizabeth Ambrose of Boston, d. 11 Oct. 1766; 2d 5 Jan. 1769 Tabitha (Smithurst) Calley, who d. 17 Nov. 1776 ag. 75; he d. 9 June 1777. 3 ch. **Lydia**, b. 1701, m. 26 Mar. 1719 Ebenezer Stacey of Marb., d. 5 Sep. 1761. 8 ch. **Mary**, m. 1st 29 July 1728 Nathaniel Stacey, 2d Nathaniel Homan. **Ambrose**, m. 8 Mar. 1732 Mary Russell. 4 ch.

6 **JOHN**, 'of Black Point,' who in 1640 sold at the Trelawny plantation a seventh as many wild ducks and geese as Mr. Mitton did, could not be the 10-year-old son of (2), unless poss. he was a boy liv. with Capt. Cammock, who by trad. was brot over by (2).

7 **JOHN**, who first app. in Saco in 1653, gave evid. ab. early matters on the Spurwink River, and is accredited the John(2), bp. at Holberton 2 May 1630. He was liv. in Saco 1653, bot 200 a. of Joseph Bowles 1659, dep. 1660 ab. Jordan giving Ambrose his choice of lands, const. 1662. Of Saco 9 Apr. 1675, he was gr. adm. of est. of Robert Ford in hands of Ralph Tristram; selectman Saco 1684, and living there 26 July 1687. Lists 244ae, 245, 249. He m. 1656 Grace Bully(2), List 246, and d. in Boston 4 Apr. 1697. She d. there 10 Jan. 1710 ag. 74. Ch: **Hannah**, b. 9 July 1658, m. Daniel Weare of Boston, from York; d. 4 May 1697. 3 ch. **Lucy**, b. 25 June 1660, unm., tempor. at Saco 1679. **John**, b. 15 July 1671. **Nicholas**, b. 19 Jan. 1673-4. **Mary**, m. 7 May 1703 William Carley of Boston. **Margaret**, mar. Nathaniel Foxwell(3). **Ruth**, unm. 1726 Boston. **Ann**, m. 17 Feb. 1708 John Mullins of Boston.

8 **JOHN**(3), b. ab. 1655 in Scarb. Lists 238a, 239a. The 1st of his five wives was a Simpson: he m. 2d (int. Boston 26 May 1713) Rebecca Fowle; 3d (int. Kit. 3 Oct. 1719) Joanna Ingersoll, he then of Scarb.; 4th in Marblehead Joanna Colman, both of Dartmouth; 5th in Marbleh. 1 June 1732 Sarah Oakman. Will 4 Nov. 1737—29 Mar. 1743. Ch: **Samuel**, m. 21 Feb. 1704-5 Mary Webber. **Mary**, mar. 14 Feb. 1712-3 Richard Horton. **Hannah**, m. 6 Dec. 1716 Samuel Hitchens. **Benjamin**, m. 3 Dec. 1729 Grace Forster. 3 ch. **Simpson**, b. ab. 1699, m. 1st 27 Dec. 1720 Charity Tucker; 2d 20 June 1737 Mary Kelley, wid. of Thos. 9 ch. **Jonathan**, m. 29 Jan. 1730 Eleanor Majory. 6 ch. **Abijah**, m. 8 Jan. 1734 Mary Tucker. **Rebecca. Susanna**, bp. 15 Sep. 1723 (dau. of John and Joanna).

9 **RICHARD**, Isles of Shoals. In 1652 Hercules Hunkins sued Wm. Pitt, Thos. Hamlin and Richard Boden for assault. Perh. the same who wit. the Ind. deed of Swan Isl. to Lawson in 1667, and the same who m. Martha Blaisdell and kept his fam. in Boston. His wid. m. 2d (Thomas? John?) Selley; 3d John Clough of Salisb. Ch: **Elizabeth**, b. at Boston 18 May 1661, m. John Davis(23), and

named a son Ichabod Bowden. Sarah Bowden, who m. Benj. Towle of Hampton, in Amesb. 7 Nov. 1693, may have been relat. to Richard and the same b. in Boston 28 Jan. 1669 or 70, dau. of John and Agnes. Her death record agrees, 22 June 1759 ag. 88, and she named a dau. Martha.

10 **WALTER**, Isles of Shoals, fisherman; will 18 Sep. 1676—7 May 1690, being by chance at George Litten's house, gave his est. to his friends, George Litten and Sarah his wife.

11 **WILLIAM**, signed Dover Comb. 1640, lawsuit 1642. List 351b.

12 **WILLIAM** (Boden) at Lamprill River, drunk, 1679.

**BOARDMAN**. 1 **Thomas**, Cape Porpus gr. 8 May 1688, of Ipsw. ab. 1715. Eastern Claims, Me. H. & G. Rec. iv. 105.

2 **WILLIAM**, m. Elizabeth Parsons (Mark), of Boston about 1715. Eastern Claims, Me. H. & G. Rec. viii. 82-3.

**BODGE**. One H. B. was of Alvington, Devon, 1642. See Creber.

**HENRY**, Spruce Creek, Kit., by 1669. Lists 293, 298. K. by Ind. (stepf., not f. of Henry Barnes) 20 Aug. 1694. 1st w. Elizabeth, 2d Rebecca (Wilson), wid. of Henry Barnes. Ch: **Henry**, shipwright, early at Charlestown, living 1732. Ab. 1687 was an appr. of Gabriel Tetherly. M. by 1702 Hannah Swain. 8 ch. **Edward**, shipwright, had returned to Kit. 1728. An older Edward Bodge, serv. of Thos. Moulds, was drowned at Salem 2 May 1678. **Benjamin**, settled in Durham by 1715; did not receive gr. in 1734. Shipwr. of Dover, 1732. List 368b. M. by Mar. 1709-10 Sarah, 'lately called Sarah Williams.' 5 ch. bp. **Priscilla**, m. in Lynn 5 Jan. 1692-3 James (Braiden of Boston) Bradeen(1). **Elizabeth**, Y. D. vi. 117, 1701, d.s.p.

**Bodret**, Michael, 1684. Frenchman. List 123.

**Boffin** (Buffin?), John. Kennebec 1664. Y.D. x. 152.

**Bogardus**, Jonas, Kennebec 1688-9. Lists 125, 189.

**Bole**, Mr., List 41. Poss. same as Mr. John Boles. See Bowles(2).

**Bollward**, Jacob, see Bullard.

**Bolt**, John, Shoals fisherman, sued J. Seeley 1647.

**BOLTWOOD**, **Ebenezer**, s. of Samuel killed in the Deerfield massacre 29 Feb. 1703-4, came to Berw. aft. 1713, m. Mary Turner, d. of John and Elizabeth (Grant). 4 ch. bp. incl. **John Turner** Boltwood. Wm. and Elizabeth Heard in 1730 called E. B. 'our trusty son.' Ct. files.

**BOND**, general over England, espec. Devon-Somerset.

1 **MARGARET**, b. ab. 1631, York 1680. See Angier(2). Memb. of Portsm. Ch. 1696.

List 331c. Widow Bond was a Portsm. town charge 1701, 1715.

2 **NICHOLAS**, b. ab. 1619, of York, where his land adj. John Parker. Jury 1651, wit. with Nicholas Davison to Pemaquid lease 1661, fishing for Mr. John Cutt in Nov. 1679. Lists 275, 276, (331b). Wife Jane (Norton) Simpson, wid. of Henry, dau. of Col. Walter Norton, was liv. 16 June 1688, maint. 14 or 15 yrs. by son Henry Simpson and expect. to be in future. Yet her husb. in 1680 was likely the N. B. appointed in Portsm. to look aft. the behaviour of the boys during Sunday services.

3 **NICHOLAS**, killed by Ind. Salis. 17 Aug. 1703. List 96. He m. 5 Dec. 1684 Sarah Rowlandson, who m. (int. 15 Aug. 1713) Dea. Abraham Merrill of Newbury, and in 1716 as heir to Joseph Rowlandson conv. to John Brown land in Hampton in the right of Dea. Richard Wells. Ch: **Thomas**. **William**. **Joseph**.

4 **ROBERT**, from St. Mary Ottery, Devon, m. Mercy Ham of Portsm. 14 Dec. 1722. 'Bond the fisherman' was taxed in 1719, Mill Dam.

5 **THOMAS**, wit. Lawson to Lake, Kennebec, 1650.

6 **WILLIAM**, Portsm. 1690. List 57.

**Bone**, Thomas, see Boone.

**Bonsale**, Nicholas, Richmond Island 1642-3. List 21. Doc. Hist. iii. 361.

**BONYTHON**, a manor in Cury, Cornwall. 1 **JOHN**(3), much written of, liv. on his father's patent from 1653 until the Ind. war. With his f. on the bench, under the Gorges govt., an edict of outlawry was pronounced against him. Under Mass. author. he was, for like cause, ordered arrested, alive or dead, and was imprisoned in Boston. With the domin. traits of the Cornish gentry, he had none of his father's virtues. Our poet Whittier dubbed him 'Sagamore of Saco,' and rhymed the euphonic abiding place of his soul. Jury 1640, gr.j. 1667. Elected Lt. and rejected by the court, 1659. In 1667 Mr. Munjoy called him Capt. Lists 22, 232, 235, 243a, 244f, 245, 249. In Philip's War he escaped first across the river and then to Marbleh., where his nunc. will, written 17 Feb. 1676[7, was sworn to 17 Sep. 1680. This was 'deposited in the County Registers of York' (C. E. Banks in N. E. Reg. 34:99). The wid. Agnes, 25 Mar. 1684, and her s. John, were ordered to bring in an inv. and settle the est. acc. to law. List 246. Nearly 50 yrs. later, 1732, adm. was gr. to Sarah Andrews and Robert Edgecomb (3 jr.), court ordering notice to heirs in Reading, Lynn and Marbleh. Ch: **Thomas**, d.s.p., was lying sick at Marbleh. when his father made his will, 1677. **John**, b. 1647. **Eleanor**,

in court 1667, mar. Arthur Churchwell(1). **Gabrigan**, b. Aug. 1652, apprent. to Geo. Norton as shipwr. Lists 82, 313a. Drowned by a boat sinking between Piscataqua and Cape Porpus; adm. to bro. Mr. John, 28 June 1682. **Winnifred**, m. 1674 Robert Nicholson.

2 **JOHN**(1), called eldest son in father's nunc. will. He sold his lands about Saco Falls to develop the town. 1681 road surveyor, 1685 selectm., 1689 gr.j. Lists 249, 294, 39. In 1694 at Kit., 'late of Saco,' he gave a deed, and in 1700 was still there. In the false peace, 10 Aug. 1703, he with his w. and four ch. at Saco were reported carried off, the last heard of the parents. Peter Weare understood from Richard that his father was k. Perh. 7 ch. incl: **Patience**, a wit. with Mrs. Hooke in Kit. in 1696, m. (Benighton) at Lynn 21 May 1717 Joseph Collins of Marbleh., cordwainer. **Mary**, b. 1681, m. 1st at Lynn 9 Sep. 1707 Samuel Mansfield who d. 6 Dec. 1719; 6 ch. rec.; 2d 19 Dec. 1724 Dea. John Bancroft jr.; d. 25 Feb. 1763 (grst. Lynnfield). **Richard**, of age by 16 Nov. 1713, formerly apprent. to James Weymouth of Newcastle, cordwainer, sold Saco lands for a mare and a gun and money in hand. By later deeds he sold to Peter Weare and Wm. Nick. He m. at Marbleh. 6 Dec. 1716 Mary Martin; 2d 29 Nov. 1722 Abigail Cooke, to whom adm. was gr. 20 May 1730. Adm. in Maine day gr. June 1734 to Col. Edmund Goff of Marbleh. The parentage of Mary Bonython, m. in Boston 11 years later, is unasc., poss. his stepd. She m. (Benighton, int. 26 Sep. 1729) John Getchell. 7 ch. rec. in Boston 1733-1748. **Samuel**, reported captive in Canada in 1711. List 99.

3 ‡**CAPT. RICHARD**, patentee of what is now Saco and Old Orchard, s. of John Bonython and Elinor, d. of Wm. Myleinton. Although his father inherited the manor of Bonython in the parish of Cury, almost at Land's End, Richard was b. at the maternal est. in St. Columb Major on the Cornish north coast, bp. 3 Apr. 1580. As a younger son he was trained to arms and commanded a company in the wars with France. The Lewis and Bonython patent, 4 x 8 miles, was like several others except that it was taken more seriously. Mr. Lewis had been over before it was granted, came over with it and remained in charge here, while Capt. Bonython remained behind to send over the 50 people whom they were to send within seven yrs. Nothing indicates his earlier arrival here except that his house was ready for the first court held in the Province, 25 Mar. 1636, when William Gorges appar. gave place to him in the center of bench. See Doc. Hist. iii. 92, 96. P. & C. i. passim. Folsom's 'Saco' does full credit to his character and conduct under difficult circumstances. He

sat in the court held 6 July 1646 after Mr. Vines left the country, and 14 July 1647 he exch. lands with Dr. Robert Child for a lot for his dau. Elizabeth on the other side of the river. He may not have d. here, and may have taken John with him, but cert. he was dead or away by 1654, when John was pulling down the buildings of his brothers-in-law. His grs., a child, Thomas Cummings, is termed 'executor to Capt. Richard Bonython,' but the will has not been found. Lists 235, 241, 242, 281. He m. Lucretia Leigh, d. of Wm. and Phillippa (Prest) of St. Thomas-by-Launceston. Living 1647. The bap. of their ch. are rec. in the parish of St. Breage: **Grace**, bp. Apr. 1610. **Elizabeth**, bp. Sep. 161—. List 235. M. ab. 1647 Richard Cummings(3). **Susannah**, bp. Feb. 1614, m. Richard Foxwell(5). **John**.

4 **WILLIAM**, presum. illeg. s. of (1) by his father's servant Ann. In 1667 he mortg. his 6-ton shallop to Mr. Munjoy, and the same yr. John Davis and he were fined for taking one of Roger Hill's swine. In 1670 he served on a Saco coroner's jury, and with Judith Gibbins wit. a deed. In 1675 he was sued for debt by Mr. Fryer.

**BOODY**, Bowdey, Bowden, Voden, a Channel Isl. name variantly anglicised. See also Boaden.

1 **ABRAHAM** (Booden, Bowden), bot land in York 29 Sep. 1705. List 279. M. (July Court 1706) Martha Wormwood, daughter of William. Will July—Aug. 1751. 9 ch.

2 **MOSES** (Bowdy, Boudey, Bouden, Voden), mason, Kittery. Same man as Moses Boden of Newbury 1695, sick soldier? Lists 290, 298. M. 29 Nov. 1697 at Dover Ruth Wittum. Ch. (not named in nunc. will, 18 Dec. 1714): Abigail, b. 27 Oct. 1699 in Kit., m. York 7 May 1727 Samuel Shaw. 8 ch. **Ruth**, b. 22 June 1702, m. York Dec. 1728 John Bennett of Kittery. **Moses** (Bowdy), blacksmith, m. at Amesbury 2 June 1730 Phebe Weed. In ct. (counterf. money) 1745. 5 ch. rec. 1731-39. Besides likely: **Mary**, m. York 22 Nov. 1733 Josiah Bridges. **Sarah**, 'of Dover,' in ct. 1735. Wit.: Rose Tibbetts, Sarah Kenney.

3 **ZACHARIAH** (Boody, Boodey), b. ab. 1677; by trad. deserted a French ship in Boston harbor; in Sep. 1707 had wife Elizabeth at Oyster River, later of Madbury; d. ab. 1755. Of 5 ch. bp., 4, with 3 others, joined in heirship deed 1758.

**BOOKER.** 1 **John**, by trad. from Eng. with a bro., York 1707, m. Esther Adams(19). List 279. 8 ch. rec. 1713-1728.

2 **LAUNCELOT**, Popham Colony 1607. List 6. **Booletey** (-tey, -key), Abigail, see Bowles (1). N. H. Ct. Files i. 423.

**BOONE.** 1 **John**, Isles of Shoals. Adm. 12

Oct. 1680 granted to Peter Twisden. See also Bourne.

2 **RICHARD**, Monhegan 1672. List 13.

3 **THOMAS** (Bone), from Saltash, came in -The Hercules- to Richmond Isl. and ran away.

4 **SAMUEL**, Kingston, R. I., and No. Yarm., 1720-1733. Y. D. x. 29, xvi. 44.

**BOOTH**, a common Eng. name, long flour. in Cheshire. A hamlet in Yorkshire.

1 **HUMPHREY**, wit. Ind. deed to Lawson, Spencer and Lake, Kennebec, 1653.

2 **JAMES**, tailor, Portsm., b. ab. 1663. He was taxed at Great Isl. in 1688, const. 1692-93, wit. 1688 to 1712. Lists 335b, 61, 315a, 318b, 330d, 337. Wife Mary bef. 4 Mar. 1696-7. List 331c. Widow Booth, taxed Str. Bank 1713, may have m. 2d 13 Jan. 1714[5 Samuel Hart. Charles Story's will gave Barbara Booth 5s.

3 *****ROBERT**, b. ab. 1602, was first of Exeter, a land measurer there in 1644. He rem. to Wells, Cape Porpus, and finally to Saco, where in 1654 he was on a commission to build the prison for Saco, Cape Porpus, Wells and York, and in 1655 on comm. for assess. the towns. Jury 1647, 64, 67, gr.j. 1665. Lists 374c, 376ab, 263, 269b, 252, 23, 24, 111, 243ab, 244bc, 249. He m. bef. 1650 a 2d w. Deborah, (List 246), named in his nunc. will, made 4 days before his death 18 Mar. 1672-3, with four daus. (incl. d.-in-law Rebecca), and two sons, the sons to divide the mill. Wid. m. 2d Thos. Ladbrook of Portsm., d. bef. 26 May 1684. Ch. rec. Saco: **Mary**, b. 30 Sep. 1627, m. Walter Pennell. **Ellen**, b. Feb. 1634, m. 1st July 1652 Nicholas Bully(3); 2d 26 Dec. 1664 John Henderson. **Simeon**, b. 10 May 1641. **Martha**, b. 12 Apr. 1645, m. 2 Oct. 1663 John Leighton. By 2d w: **Robert**, b. 24 July 1655. With bro.-in-law John Leighton he was with the Davis-Agawam band from Portsm. 8 Dec. 1677.

4 **SIMEON**(3), weaver, in Philip's War fled to Salem. He sold his home farm in Saco to Major Pendleton 8 Oct. 1675. Lists 249, 27. He was recd. into Salem Ch. 10 Mar. 1679, freeman 19 May 1680. 'Of Massachusetts' in 1682, by will of wife's f., and prob. in 1684, he soon moved to Enfield, Conn.; there constab. and selectm. Nunc. will made five days before his death, 28 Feb. 1702-3, in Hartford. He m. 5 Jan. 1663 Rebecca Frost, dau. of Daniel of Fairfield, Conn., d. Enfield 25 Dec. 1688; 2d 8 Dec. 1693 Elizabeth, wid. of Samuel Elmer, d. Hartford 26 Jan. 1727. Ch., all but Wm. bp. in Salem: **William**, d. ab. 1664, d. Aug. 1753, m. in Enfield 30 Aug. 1693 Hannah Burroughs. 4 ch. **Zachariah**, b. ab. 1666, with three sis. foll. bp. Salem 19 May 1678; d. 28 May 1741; m. 1st 15 July 1691 Mary Warriner; 2d 26 May 1696 Mary

Harmon. 10 ch. **Elizabeth**, b. ab. 1668, m. 11 Oct. 1693 Jonathan Pease, d. 8 Jan. 1722-3. **Bridget**, b. ab. 1668, m. 3 May 1694 John Allen, d. Enfield 5 Sep. 1714. **Rebecca**, accid. k. by a gun in the hands of a boy in John Henderson's ho. in Salem, 29 Oct. 1684. **Mary**, bp. Salem 16 Dec. 1678, m. 28 Feb. 1699 Ebenezer Spencer, d. 3 Sep. 1724. By 2d wife: **Sarah**, b. 11 Dec. 1695, m. Daniel Perry. **Phebe**, b. 1697, d. unm. 1756.

5 **THOMAS**, Mr., Kittery, took mortg. for £520 on Antipas Maverick's ho. and land 5 Aug. 1661, cancelled 2 Jan. 1663[4; deft. in ct. 1663; former judgm. against Walter Barefoot confirmed 18 July 1665. A d. or stepd. m. (mar. settlement 7 Dec. 1663) Wm. Ellingham.

**Boswell**, see Buswell.

**BOTTS**, pecul. to Staffordshire (Bott).

**ISAAC**, Berwick, grant 1671; in Mar. 1674-5 bot above Salmon Falls where he built, and was k. by Ind. 16 Oct. 1675. List 298. Wid. Elizabeth, appar. Freethy(5), m. Moses Spencer bef. July 1679. Only ch: **Elizabeth**, b. 1673, m. 20 Nov. 1694 Samuel Brackett(5).

**Boule**, Mr. Abraham, 'the French doctor,' rated to New Meet. Ho., Portsm., 1717. Adm. 29 May 1723 to Daniel Greenough. M. Hannah Gwinn of Boston, who m. 2d 24 July 1729 James Fosdick.

**BOULTER**, presum. occup., (arrow maker or meal bolter), yet a chapelry in Durham.

1 **JOHN**(2). Adm. 14 Dec. 1703 to Philip and Martha Door. He m. Martha Jackson, dau. of John, who m. 2d Bryan Door(2). She joined Hampton Ch. 1701. Ch: **Nathaniel**, b. 20 July 1700, housewright, m. 23 July 1723 Grace Bly (see 1), poss. Grace (Lewis), wid. of John. In 1730 they sold their homestead at Hampt. Falls and rem. to Scarb. Will 3 Mar.—26 Aug. 1739-40. App. his wid. m. 17 Sep. 1744 Henry Dresser. Ch: **John**, b. 7 Feb. 1702, rem. to Falm., m. Mary Jordan, dau. of Jedediah. **Lydia**, b. 27 Oct. 1703, m. 20 Jan. 1697-8 Philemon Blake, s. of Philemon(1).

2 **NATHANIEL**, b. ab. 1625, pipestave maker, Hampt., (sometimes at Exeter). A dilig. litig., was hims. juryman 1663-1666, and twice was atty. in ct. for others. Lists 374ac, 375ab, 376ab, 378, 393ab, 396, 49, 52, 55b. D. 14 Mar. 1694-5. He m. Grace Swain. List 393a. Ch: **Mary**, b. 15 May 1648, m. James Prescott. **Temperance**, b. 8 Jan. 1651, liv. 1670. **Nathaniel**, b. 4 Mar. 1653-4. **Joshua. Joshua. Rebecca. Grace**, these four d.y. **Hannah**, b. 27 June 1667, liv. 1703. Portsm. carried one Hannah Boulter to Hampton in 1723. **Elizabeth**, b. 23 Feb. 1668-9, m. Joseph Fanning(1). **John**, b. 2 Dec. 1672.

3 **NATHANIEL**(2), List 396. Died 1 June 1689; mar. Mary Drake(1), who mar. 2d Richard Sanborn. Ch: **Mary**, m. Jonathan Dearborn(5). **Elizabeth**, b. 8 Sep. 1688, both bp. 19 Nov. 1699.

**BOUNDS, Richard**, tailor, soldier under Matthew Austin. N. H. Prov. Pap. xiv. 1. Exeter 1705. Taxed Portsmouth 1707, 1713. Lists 376b, 388. At No. Ch., Portsm. 31 Oct. 1714 Abigail Bounds ack. covt. and had 2 s. and 2 daus. bap.

**BOURNE**, name of 7 places from Hants to Durham.
  **JOHN**, Portsmouth, taxed 1707, 1712. M. Joanna (Dore), wid. of David Cane. In 1707 Joanna -Boarn- was paid by the town for keeping Roger Andros. She ack. covt. in the So. Ch. 19 June 1715 and her five ch. were bap. She m. 3d 25 Feb. 1716-7 Stephen Knowles (Nole) from 'Lahant' (Lelant or Lezant?), Cornwall. Ch: **Mary**, owned covt. 19 June 1715, m. 3 Nov. 1715 John Gardner from Gloucestershire. **John**. See Bourne's 'Wells.' Judge Bourne knew by the record of his mar. int. that he came there from Kit., and by trad. that he was born on Smuttinose Isl. See Boone(1). D. 17 July 1788, ag. 80. **Benjamin. William. Elizabeth.**

**BOUTINEAU, Stephen**, came to Falmouth with Peter Bowdoin and with him rem. to Boston, where he m. his dau. Mary 22 Aug. 1708. In 1748 he was the only surv. elder of the French Ch. there. List 229. 10 ch.

**Bovey**, Nicholas, drowned, body taken up at Great Isl. 29 Dec. 1670. List 312b.

**BOWDE, Mr. Isaac**, (beaut. aut. -Boude-Prob. 432), Great Isl. 1682, formerly of London, merchant. Jury 1682. In 1683 he was boarding with Mr. Elliot and using 'Mr. Faben's house' (Fabes) for a warehouse. In 1684 shipmaster to Barbadoes. In 1688 his est. was suing Humphrey Chadbourne's est.

**BOWDOIN**
  **PETER** (Pierre Baudouin), French Huguenot, came from La Rochelle by way of Ireland, bringing from Wexford in his own vessel, acc. to his petn. to Andros in French, six persons with four little ch. Arriving in Portland in 1686, he withdrew to Boston on the first outbreak of Ind. troubles, where in a few yrs. he d., Sep. 1706, having firmly estab. his house. His widow Elizabeth d. 18 Aug. 1720, ag. 77. Lists 34, 127. 4 ch: **John**, wit. 1686, who left desc. in Northampton co., Va. Hon. **James**, 1676-1747, List 229. **Elizabeth**, m. Thos. Robbins, liv. 1749. Ch. **Mary**, m. 22 Aug. 1708 Stephen Boutineau.
  **Bowen**, William, of Cambridge, innholder, adm. issued 22 Oct. 1735 to wid. Martha of Portsm.

**BOWES. 1 Thomas, Mr.**, came from Eng. in 1697 to adm. est. of his uncle Henry Watts of Scarb., and prob. returned. 'Thomas Bowes and Sarah Bowes' were mar. in Boston 21 June 1697.

2 **TRISTRAM**, mariner, at Richmond Isl. List 21.

**Bowey**, John, wit. Waddock to Scammon, 1681. Y. D. iii. 103.

**BOWLES**, Bolles, E. of Eng., ancient in Lincolnshire.

1 **ABIGAIL** (Boales), young servant of Alex. Jones, Great Isl., insulted by David Campbell 1670.

2 **JOHN** (Boles), Mr., wit. against Winter 1640; poss. clerk's error for Joseph.

3 ‡**JOSEPH** (Bolles), gent., bp. Worksop, co. Notts, 19 Feb. 1608, s. of Thomas, Esq. and Elizabeth (Perkins) of Osberton Manor; apprent. at Kingston-on-Hull. First located here at Winter Harbor, court wit. 1640; later of Wells. There selectm., gr.j. 1657, 1673, jury 1665, 1672, clerk of the writs, com.t.e.s.c., one of Gorges's comrs. 1664, councillor 1665, election comr. 1676, interspersed with two visits home 1655-6, 1663. Several records of drunkenness. Lists 261-264, 266, 269b, 28. Will 18 Sep.—29 Nov. 1678 names w. Mary, 3 sons, 5 daus. Thereaft. widow's home in Portsm., where both had been members of the ch. List 331c. Liv. 25 Feb. 1690-1. She and her ch. benef. under will of Morgan Howell 1666. Ch. rec. Wells: **Mary**, b. 7 Aug. 1641, mar. Major Charles Frost(2). **Thomas**, b. 1 Dec. 1644. **Samuel**, b. 12 Mar. 1646. **Hannah**, b. 25 Nov. 1649, m. Caleb Beck(1). **Elizabeth**, b. 15 Jan. 1652, m. 1st appar. Philip Locke; 2d William Pitman. List 331c. **Joseph**, b. 15 Mar. 1654. **Sarah**, b. 20 Jan. 1657, m. Humphrey Chadbourne (2). **Mercy**, b. 11 Aug. 1661, liv. 1678.

4 **JOSEPH**(3), Mr., carpenter at Ipswich 1677, living on homestead aft. father's death. Jury 1680, gr.j. 1683. Died 25 Sep. 1683, 'by some convulsion fits;' adm. to wid. Mary (Call), dau. of Philip of Ipsw. She m. 2d at Ipsw. 31 Dec. 1685 Nathl. Lord, d. there 4 Oct. 1737. Ch: **Hannah**, b. ab 1674, m. Joseph Hill. **Joseph**, carpenter, Ipsw., m. there (int. 29 Mar. 1707) Lucretia Derby. With his mo. sold his grf.'s whole farm in Wells to Joseph Hill in 1707.

5 **RICHARD**, Dover 1666 (Sav.). List 357a (Bowl).

6 **SAMUEL** (3), husbandman, as a youth wit. an Ind. deed in 1661. Lists 186, 125. He m. Mary Dyer(8), and was liv. on Dyer's Neck, Sheepscot, during Ind. attacks 1689; escaping to Mass., he was of Braintree several yrs., perh. temp. of Middleboro where one Saml. was liv. in 1705, and of Roches-

ter when he sold his Sheepscot and Wells lands 1712-1713. In 1714 he deeded homestead in Roch. to three sons with reserv. for self and w.; both liv. Bridgewater 5 Sep. 1723. Ch., all but Joanna and Deliverance, bap. First Ch., Braintree, the parents named in error as John (not Samuel) and Mary Bowl: **Mary**, bp. and owned covt. 4 Sep. 1692. **Joanna**, owned covt. 1st Ch., Braintr. 4 Sep. 1692 (rec. as Susanna); m. 1st 23 Jan. 1701-2 Joseph Tilden of Marshfield, d. bet. 4 Apr.-29 Sep. 1712; 2d 1716 Charles Turner of Scituate. She d. in Boston 1756. Desc. m. Moultons of York. **Bethiah**, bp. 4 Sep. 1692, m. Plymouth 20 Feb. 1702-3 Helkiah Bosworth. **Experience**, bp. same day, mar. Taunton 17 Jan. 1703-4 Edward Hammett, who d. at Tisbury, Martha's Vineyard, 20 Mar. 1745, she surv. **Joseph**, bp. same day. W. Mary, m. bef. 1715. Ch. b. at Rochester. **Samuel**, bp. same day, d. at Roch. aft. 3 Oct. 1764, m. bef. 1715 Lydia Balch, dau. of Benj. and Grace of Beverly. **Jonathan**, bp. same day, d. at Roch. bef. 7 June 1773, leav. wid. Mary, m. bef. 1721. **William**, bp. 11 Nov. 1694, prob. d.y. **Deliverance**, bp. 27 June 1699, First Ch., Marshfield, m. Pembroke 24 May 1733 Daniel Hayford, who d. there 11 Dec. 1764; she surv., prob. d. bef. 1770.

7 **THOMAS**(3), New London, Conn., settling there by invit. of Winthrop; d. 26 May 1727. Aft. the murder of his 1st w. Zipporah Wheeler (m. 13 July 1671) and their ch. Mary and Joseph, in 1678, he m. 2d Rebecca Waller of New London, d. 10 Feb. 1711-12; 3d Hopestill Chappell, wid. of Nathl. Ch: **Mary**, bp. 27 July 1673. **Joseph**, bp. 25 Apr. 1675. **John**, bp. 5 Mar. 1677-8; upon mother's death placed in care of Aunt Bennett, afterw. at Norwich. M. 1st 3 July 1699 Sarah Edgecomb (10 ch.); 2d Elizabeth Wood.

8 **THOMAS**, fisherman, Sagadahoc 1672, List 13. Of Kennebec, had d. bef. Dec. 1676, David Oliver admr.

**Bowman** (Boman), John, Portsm. fisherman in 1672 was liv. in one half of one of Mr. John Hunking's houses. In 167— recently from Plymouth, Eng. See Evans(11). In 1674, 'late of Isles of Shoals' he bot house from Joseph Berry, still called J. B.'s abuttor at Sag. Creek in 1697, but 'widow Bowman' owned there in 1696. Both were given church seatings in 1694. Lists 52, 313a, 329, 331ab, 335a. In 1676 they took Abigail Pomeroy (Joseph) to bring up, and to have £12. **Bowne**, William, Kennebec militia 1688. List 189.

**BOYCE** (Boies). 1 **Antipas**, Boston merchant, headed the Kennebec purchase from the Plymouth Colony; m. 24 Jan. 1660 Hannah Hill (Valentine), who soon d. Will,

July—Aug. 1669, names only ch: **Antipas**, b. 8 Feb. 1661, who d.s.p. in Barbadoes in 1706, as by adv. in Boston News Letter 3 Aug. 1719, when Capt. Nathaniel Hill claimed to be his bro.-in-law's heir. See Boyse, Maine Wills 628, N. E. Reg. 19.308, 41.92.

2 **RICHARD** (Boyes), in court 1674 for not going home to his wife. List 305b. Lost at sea 30 Jan. 1677[8. See Broad(4).

**BOYDEN**. 1 John, 1662. See Bayden.

2 **WILLIAM** (also Borden), 1676 Oyster River, added name stricken out. List 359a.

**BOYNTON**. 1 **Benoni**, Kit. soldier (1704?). List 289. Won suit in Me. Ct. 1712. Same killed in Lovewell's fight?

2 **CALEB**, York, List 279. M. Christian Parsons (John). 8 ch. rec. 1712-1731.

3 **JOSEPH**, Great Isl. wit. 1691. Y. D. vii. 235.

**Boysey**, John, wit. Sanborn to Cutts 1650.

**BRABROOK** (see also Broadbrook), **John**, Hampton grant 1640, perh. never came. List 392a. See Bond's Watertown, pp. 92, 705. Adm. Nov. 1654. Wid. Elizabeth was taken from Woburn to Watertown in 1663. Ch: **Elizabeth**, b. 4 Nov. 1640, m. David Cummings. **John**, b. 12 Apr. 1642, will, Newbury, 27 June 1662, names uncle Henry Short, gives int. in house and land to br. Thomas after mother's death, and all estate in Eng. equally to mother, bros. Samuel and Joseph and 4 sist. **Thomas**, b. 4 May 1643, Watertown. **Samuel**, liv. 1667. **Rebecca**, m. in Concord 15 Sep. 1666 Adam Draper, turned 21 in Sep. 1669, Newbury. **Sarah**. **Rachel**, (last 3 minors in 1668), m. 19 Mar. 1677 John Fuller(2).

**BRACKETT**, rare Eng. surname, in Norfolk 1574.

1 **ANTHONY**, ±47 in 1660, was early at Portsm., where he sold his house in 1650 and had a 30 a. gr. in 1652; taxed at Sandy Beach 1671. Jury 1650, 1667, gr.j. often, selectm. 1655, 56, 1668. Lists 41, 321, 330bc, 323, 324, 341, 43, 47, 49, 52, 54, 57, 326ac, 311b, 312c, 313a, 332b. His Sandy Beach homestead he deeded in 1686 to s. John for life supp. of self and wife. In Ind. attack 28 Sep. 1691, there were 16 killed or carried away, chiefly 'old Goodman Brackett's and Goodman Rand's families.' Will 11 Sep. 1691—11 July 1692 named s. John exec. Ch: **Anthony**. **Thomas**. **Eleanor**, List 330b; m. 26 Dec. 1661 John Johnson. **Jane**, m. 1st 19 Apr. 1667 Mathias Haines; 2d Isaac Marston. **John**.

2 *****CAPT. ANTHONY**(1), b. ab. 1636, was at Falmouth in 1660, selectm. 1680, 81, assemblyman 1681, 82. He and his whole fam. were capt. by Ind. 11 Aug. 1676, but escaped. Ensign 1676, and in Philip's War

helped build a garrison at Kennebec River; Lieut. 1680. Lists 223b, 330b, 25, 86, 184, 313ad, 30, 32, 93, 214, 225a, 226, 228bd. K. by Ind. at Falm. 21 Sep. 1689, adm. to s. Anthony 4 Mar. 1689-90. He mar. 1st Anne Mitton, who d. at Sandy Beach ab. 1677; 2d 19 Nov. 1678 Susanna Drake(1), d. Nov. 1719. Ch. by 1st w: **Anthony. Seth**, k. by Ind. near the fort in Falm. May 1690. List 228c. **Zachariah**, d.y. **Mary**, m. 1st Joseph Ring; 2d June 1710, Nathaniel Whittier of Salis. **Eleanor**, mar. 1st Philip Foxwell(4), 2d her cousin Elisha Andrews(5), 3d Capt. Richard Pullen. **Keziah**, m. 1st John Patterson of Boston, shipmaster, adm. 31 Jan. 1709-10; 2d 11 Oct. 1711 in Boston Joseph Maylem, brickmaker, who d. 29 Jan. 1732 ag. 75. Her will proves that she was Anthony's dau., not John's. As regards being taken captive at Rye Beach, there is nothing to show that John had any dau. but Abigail, and it is plaus. that this Keziah, instead of liv. with her stepmo., was liv. with her grandp. when they were k. Her grf.'s will left his granddau. Keziah a large legacy. She was redeemed by Matthew Carey in 1695. Her will 3—20 Mar. 1732-3 names relatives on her mother's side, incl. her aunt Elizabeth Clark and Abigail (Andrews) Kent, besides nearer kin; no ch. By 2d w: **Jane**, b. 7 Feb. 1679, d.y. **Zipporah**, b. 28 Sep. 1680, m. Apr. 1698 Caleb Towle. **Zachariah**, b. 20 Jan. 1682, farmer. In 1719, Aug. 7, he sold his homestead in Hampt. and rem. to his father's homestead in Deering, which he and Anthony divided in 1731. In 1735 he dep. that he had liv. there ab. 16 yrs. last past. After his 2d m. he removed to Ipsw., adm. Oct. 1755. He m. 1st at Newbury 1 Dec. 1707 Hannah Rolfe, liv. 1736; 2d (int. 16 Feb. 1741) Mary Ross from Ireland; her est. adm. 1793. 11 ch. **Anne**, b. 18 June 1686, m. James Leavitt. **Susannah**, b. 29 Aug. 1689, m. Jasper Blake(2). In Dec. 1757 she dep. that her f. had 6 ch. by each w., of whom one of the 1st fam., two of the 2d, d.y.

**3 LT. ANTHONY**(2), b. ab. 1669. In 1690 a captive up the Androscoggin, he escaped to the army at Maquoit. 1695 Lt. of the Mass. co. scouting the Maine frontier. Later followed coasting, keeping his family in Boston. Lists 228c, 191, 248b. His wid. Mary was a Falm. propr. (List 229-1717), and m. Richard Peirce 8 July 1718. Ch. rec. Boston: **Mary**, b. 13, d. 30 Jan. 1702. **Mary**, b. 8 May 1704, m. 25 Sep. 1723 Edward Hall, wid. in 1733. **Anthony**, b. 25 Jan. 1708, adm. Suff. 1764, m. 1 Jan. 1729 Alithea Drown, d. of Simeon(1); 2d 27 Nov. 1735 Elizabeth, wid. of his step-cousin Mark Maylem of Newport, R. I.

**4 JOHN**(1), 'farmer,' b. in Portsmouth ab.

1650. Highway surveyor 1677, 1692, 94, 1700; assessor 1698; selectm. 1699. Gr.j. 1684, 92, 95, 97, 1700. He recd. the homestead for life supp. of his parents. Liv. 1716. Adm., after citation, 6 Dec. 1726 to s. Samuel. Lists 313a, 331a, 52, 55b, 318c, 332b, 315bc, 316, 338c. He m. 1st Martha Philbrick, dau. of John; 2d 24 Nov. 1698 Dinah (Sanborn) wid. of James Marston. Ch: **Abigail**, captured by Ind. 1691, bp. in Canada 17 Dec. 1698, ag. 16, m. Pierre Roi alias le Veille 16 Dec. 1715; bur. in Notre-Dame of Quebec 3 Dec. 1743, ag. 57. List 99, pp. 75, 213-4. In 1727 Peter King alias Roi of Greenland and w. Abigail q.c. to bro. Samuel. 'Frenchman Brackett' was taxed that yr. **Samuel**, had the homestead; selectman; d. 25 Oct. 1766. He m. 23 Jan. 1712-3 his stepsis. Lydia Marston. 6 ch.

**5 SAMUEL**, turner, Berwick, b. in Billerica 4 Mar. 1672-3, s. of John and Hannah (French), m. in Braintree 6 Sep. 1661. Contemp. accts. ment. only 3 ch. of (6) and Wm. Willis excludes Samuel, of whom nothing appears here back of his m. record. Mr. Willis in 1827 had Nathaniel Adams see a sis., ag. 87, of Dr. Joshua Brackett, who said that four Brackett brothers came to this country, one to Boston, one to Casco and two to Greenland, one of whom rem. to Portland. Of greater weight, would Anthony(1) in his will give a heifer to grs. Samuel without saying which one if he had two? James H. Brackett, author of the Brackett Gen., must have asked his old folk leading questions. Lists 290, 298. He m. 25 Nov. 1694 Elizabeth Botts, and was called 80 at death, 27 Apr. 1752. Wid. d. 21 Apr. 1753. Kn. ch: **Samuel**, b. 6 Sep. 1695, will prov. 1786. List 298. He m. 1st Sarah Emery (Job 2), d. 20 Dec. 1742, 11 ch.; 2d 13 Sep. 1743 Abigail (Banfield d. of Hugh 2), wid. of Thos. Coss(2), 3 ch. **Mary**, owned covt. 20 Dec. 1719, m. Thos. Tuttle, d. 28 Feb. 1773. **Elizabeth**, owned covt. 20 Dec. 1719; July Ct. 1723 accus. Barsham Allen; m. by 1730 Samuel Abbott, s. of John(4). **Bathsheba**, bp. 24 Dec. 1719, m. Jonathan Abbott, son of John(4); d. 21 Feb. 1802. **Hannah**, bp. 24 Dec. 1719, owned covt.; m. (int. 11 Nov. 1730) Samuel Thompson of York. Their father had sisters Bathsheba, Elizabeth, Hannah.

**6 THOMAS**(1), with John Johnson bot Francis Drake's homestead in Greenland 5 Aug. 1668. Moved to Falm. and occupied there the house formerly Michael Mitton's. Selectm. 1672. Of Greenland, planter, he gave bond 2 June 1671 to supp. his mother-in-law, Elizabeth Harvey, who the same day deeded him prop. Lists 326c, 331a, 86, 223b, 93. He was k. by Ind. 11 Aug. 1676, wife and 3 ch. carried to Canada. His w. Mary

(Mitton), d. in captivity. See Y. D. xii. 319. The ch. were ransomed by their grandfather(1). Ch: **Sarah,** m. John Hill of Greenland. **Joshua,** Lieut., by sev. dep. b. 1674, but taxed 1693, d. 19 June 1749 ag. 77 (grst. on homestead in Greenland). Lived some yrs. in Exeter (Newmarket) bef. settling in G. Lists 62, 229, 315b. He m. 1st 13 Oct. 1726 Mary Weeks; 2d Mary Haines, living 1748. List 338b. Ch. **Mary,** m. Christopher Mitchell.

**BRACY,** Bressey, an ancient landed family in Cheshire, poss. of Norman origin.
1 **JOHN,** b. ab. 1640, bp. 5 Sep. 1647 in New Haven, son of Mr. Thomas and Phebe (Bisby) from London and Maulden, county Beds.; d. 19 Jan. 1708-9 in Wethersfield. See -The Ancestry of Sarah Stone-: 1930. Tailor by trade and an irresp. drifter, liv. discred. in York about 25 yrs.; m. ab. 1677 Anne (Pearce) Carmichael. Only ch: **William,** b. ab. 1678.
2 **WILLIAM,** weaver, constable 1714, jury 1709, 13, 19; gr.j. 1716, 17; com. to lay out county roads 1715, 19. List 279. In 1732 he sold out in York and bot in Bid. Will 1755-1757. Ch. by 2 of 3 wives: Mary Marston, m. in Hampton 30 Oct. 1699, Penelope (Trafton) Day (d. 6 Nov. 1728), and as her 4th husb., 23 Oct. 1729 Mary (Cole 24) Rylance. Ch: **Joseph,** b. 2 Feb. 1702-3, weaver, List 279, soldier in Dummer's War; m. 13 Feb. 1728-9 Mary Durgin (d. of Francis 4); 10 ch. **Abigail,** b. 26 Jan. 1704-5, m. 4 Dec. 1725 in York, Jacob Curtis from Boxford, later of Arundel, d. 21 Aug. 1801 ag. 95. 10 ch. **Mary,** b. 26 June 1707, m. 9 Apr. 1731 John Treworgy of Arundel; 2d 26 June 1753 John Davis (s. of John jr. 23). Ch. **Phebe,** b. 18 Dec. 1709, m. Jonathan Emery (Job 2). 5 ch. bp. By 2d w: **Dorothy,** b. 25 Mar. 1716, m. Gideon Conner (John 2). 7 ch. rec. Salis. **Sarah,** b. 26 June 1718, m. 8 Apr. 1736 Henry Boothby of Wells, s. of Thomas from Ulster. 4 ch. **Prudence,** b. 24 Dec. 1721, m. 9 Nov. 1749 Nathaniel Abbot of York, d. bef. 1751. 1 s. **Patience,** b. 17 June 1724, m. Richard Downes (Gershom 6), later of Waterboro. 6 ch. **Benjamin,** 1728-1731.

**BRADBURY,** a township in Durham.
1 *****CAPT. THOMAS,** of an anc. landed fam. of Essex, bap. last of Feb. 1610-11 at Wicken-Bonhunt, s. of Wymond Bradbury, lord of the manor, by Elizabeth, d. of Wm. Whitgift and Margaret (Bell), sis. of one w. of Sir Ferd. Gorges, who sent him over as agent. In London 1 May 1634, here 5 May 1636 or earlier, he dep. that he was liv. in York when two of Wm. Hooke's sons were born, and presum. his own b. 1 Apr. 1637, 2 Oct. 1638. His wife suckled Wm.

Hooke. 'Starved for spiritual food' at York 13 Sep. 1637 (see Rev. Wm. Tompson), by 1640 he had rem. to Salisbury. Freeman May 1640. First ment. in county rec. as 'John,' constable, 1641. Later clerk of courts and highly honored, capt., rep. 7 yrs., assoc. justice. Will 14 Feb. 1694, d. 16 Mar. 1694-5. He m. Mary Perkins, whose virtues are commemor. incid. to sav. her life in the witchcraft murders; d. 20 Dec. 1700. Of 11 ch: **Wymond,** b. (Ipswich?) 1 Apr. 1637. **Judith,** b. in York 2 Oct. 1638, m. 1665 Caleb Moody, bro. of Rev. Joshua. **Thomas,** b. Salis. 28 Jan. 1740-1, last ment. 1665. **Mary,** b. 17 Mar. 1642-3, m. 17 Dec. 1663 John Stanyan. **Jane,** b. 11 May 1645, m. 15 Mar. 1668 Capt. Henry True. **Jacob,** b. 17 June 1647, d. 12 Mar. 1669 at Barbadoes, unm. **William,** b. 15 Sep. 1649. **Elizabeth,** b. 7 Nov. 1651, m. 12 May 1673 Rev. John Buss(1).
2 **WILLIAM**(1), merchant, Salis., d. 4 Dec. 1678. He m. 12 Mar. 1671-2 Rebecca (Wheelwright) Maverick, who d. 20 Dec. 1679. Ch: **William,** b. 16 Oct. 1672, Salis., deacon, d. 20 Apr. 1756. Wife Sarah (Cotton sis. of 5) d. 21 Feb. 1733. 13 ch., incl. Sarah, mar. Ambrose Downes(4), Crisp of York, m. 22 Dec. 1737 Mary Paine. **Thomas,** b. 24 Dec. 1674, m. 30 Oct. 1700 his cousin Jemima True (d. 5 weeks later); 2d (int. 24 Oct. 1702) Mary Hilton (Edward), who d. 15 June 1723 ag. 45. 2 ch. **Jacob,** b. 1 Sep. 1677, Salis., d. 4 May 1718. He m. 6 July 1698 Elizabeth Stockman, who m. 2d 6 July 1720 John Stevens, and rem. with her younger ch. to No. Yarm. 9 ch., incl. Dorothy, m. Rev. Ammi Ruhamah Cutter.
3 **WYMOND**(1), in 1668 master of the ketch -Geo. and Samuel- in the Barbadoes trade; d. at Nevis 7 Apr. 1669. He m. 7 May 1661 Sarah Pike, who mar. 10 May 1671 John Stockman. Ch: **Sarah,** b. 26 Feb. 1661-2, m. Abraham Morrill, d. 5 Mar. 1708-9. 2 ch. **Ann,** b. 21 Nov. 1666, m. Jeremiah Allen, d. 26 Jan. 1732-3. No ch. **Wymond,** b. 13 May 1669, cooper, rem. to York ab. 1718, d. 17 Apr. 1734. Wid. Maria (Cotton, sis. of 5) m. 2d Capt. John Heard. 9 ch., incl. Jabez, b. 26 Jan. 1692-3, milit. officer and Ind. agent in Me., d. at Boston 13 Jan. 1781, unm. Wymond, Brunswick, m. Phebe Young, Mary Donnell. John, York, mar. Abigail Young. Rowland. **Ann,** b. Mar. 1701-2, m. Jabez Fox of Falm. Theophilus, Newbury. List 279.
**Bradcock,** Stephen, Saco wit. 1659. Y. D. i. 139.

**BRADDEN,** see also Bretton. A large variety of Br- a, e, or i- d or t- n surnames are grouped under these two. English place names count: Bradden 1, Bratton 4, Bredon 1, Bretton 2, Brotton 1. See Creber.

1 **JAMES** (Bredeen, Bradeen), Kittery, ±36 in 1699, s. of Bryant Bradeen (Berreden, Burden), ± 28 in 1671, of Chelsea, by Eliz., d. of John Lewis of Malden, named in will (Briant Bradeen) 1720. By 1698 he was liv. neigh. to Paul Williams and mowed for him, and worked for Saml. Spinney. Lists 295, 290, 291, 298. He m. at Lynn (Braiden of Boston), Jan. 5, 1692-3 Priscilla Bodge(1), liv. 1731. In 1739 he was to 'live in the house he now lives in as long as he lives;' d. 1741. Besides the 3 rec., his ch. may incl. others: **Elizabeth**, Spruce Creek wit. 1715, m. James Davis(16). **James**, b. 18 Apr. 1703, m. 11 Feb. 1727-8 Mary Oliver (Robert) of York. List 291. 9 ch. rec. York. **Mary**, b. 8 Feb. 1705, m. 7 Aug. 1727 James Oliver of York. **Bryant**, b. 11 Feb. 1707, m. 27 Dec. 1733 Hannah Fernald (Nathl. 3); 2d 9 Apr. 1761 wid. Elizabeth Cate. 9 ch. rec. Kit. **Sarah**, mar. (int. 23 Apr. 1724) Nathaniel Hooper. **Peter**, mar. 1 Jan. 1729 Elizabeth Muzeet. **Martha**, Eliot wit. 1728, m. (int. 3 Oct. 1730) Thomas Chick (Richard). **Lucy**, mar. (int. 30 July 1737) Richard Roberts. **John**, in 1737 wit. family deed. Y. D. xix. 85.

2 **JOHN** (Bradden), Star Island wit. 1700, same yr. bot land at Sagamore Creek. He d. bef. 1706; adm. 4 June that yr. to wid. Prudence (Mitchell) who was then wife of Robert Tapley. By 1726 she was Prudence Spoor; will 9 Dec. 1729—5 May 1730. Ch: **William**, fisherman, redeemed his mother's house 1714, m. 31 May 1716 Anna or Agnes Abbott(1). List 339. 7 or m. ch. **Mary**, m. 11 Aug. 1715 Nicholas Bishop of St. James, Gt. Brit.; 2d bef. 9 Dec. 1729 Benj. Akerman(2). **Sarah**, named as Sarah Roberts in mother's will; m. 1st 29 May 1716 Nathaniel Robinson, alias Roberts; 2d 10 May 1731 John Norris, liv. 1762. 3 ch. **Noah**, apprent. to Capt. John and Joanna Hollicome; m. 19 Nov. 1721 Abigail Partridge, who m. 2d 28 Oct. 1725 Edw. Chapman(4). 1 dau. rec. **Elizabeth**, m. Nov. 1720 David Horney from Galway, Ireland. **John**, bp. 18 Nov. 1716, mariner, living 1739. Widow Mary 'late of Portsm. now of Boston' 1747. Ch. bp. 1723, 1729.

**BRADDOCK.** 1 **Nicholas**, Piscataqua 1664-67, bringing tobacco from Virginia.

2 **ROBERT** (Bradrock), sued by John Wentworth 1673. Adm. 3 Oct. 1677 to Dr. John Fletcher, Israel Phillips. Inv. personal effects only.

**BRADLEY.** 1 **Abraham**, Eliot wit. 1703. Y. D. vii. 25.

2 **JOHN**, recd. inhab. Dover 1665-69. List 356m.

3 **MATTHEW**, of London, gent. York patentee. Lists 271-2.

4 **RICHARD**, at John Partridge's, Portsm. 1675.

**BRADFORD.** 1 **John**, from London, m. 10 Dec. 1718 Dorcas (Miller), wid. of Samuel Hudson, dau. of Alexander, b. Boston 29 May 1695, d. Portsm. 27 June 1769. List 339.

2 **MATTHEW**, of Portsm., merchant, mar. Hannah (Redford), wid. of John Wainwright, dau. of Wm. and Sarah (Frost 2).

**BRADSHAW**, **Richard**, Spurwink, appar. staked a claim there, or poss. had leave of Capt. Neale, and sold his improv. there to Richard Tucker, accord. to Cleeve. Going back for a patent, he was given one up the Androscoggin River, on the same day Black Point was patented to Capt. Commock. Spurwink was patented to Trelawny. Aut. in Brit. Admir. Dep. 4 Mass. Hist. Col. vii.

**BRADY** 1 **Elizabeth**, sued for slander by Rev. Geo. Burdett in 1640.

2 **JOHN**, tanner, Kittery, wit. deed to Job Clements 1665; in 1677 had been given some goods of Tristram Harris, decd.; d. 9 Oct. 1681. Will 30 Aug. 1681, Job Clements sr. a wit., ment. tan yard and bark mill. Wid. Sarah m. 2d James Treworgy.

**BRAGDON.** The names Arthur, Thomas, occur in a B. family in Stratford-upon-Avon.

1 **ARTHUR**, b. 1597, York 1637. Constab. 1640, 48, 57, alderman 1641, Prov. Marshal, Lt. 1652, 58, 9 yrs. gr.j. 1649-1669, selectm. 1653, 55. Lists 271, 275-277, 25. Wife Mary in 1661. Deed to s. Thomas for life sup. of self and w. is dated 20 May 1678; adm. gr. 2 Oct. 1678 to same. Known ch: **Thomas**. **Arthur**, b. 1645. **Samuel**.

2 **ARTHUR**(1), ensign 1668, 78, gr.j. 1673, 83, 88, Prov. Marshal 1689. Lists 25, 33, 83. Lt. Arthur, Daniel and Thomas Bragdon, with James Freethy and Wm. Wormwood, were all dead and their inv. taken on the same day, 14 Oct. 1690, appar. the 'five out of nine' surpr. while loading a vessel at Cape Neddick, ment. by Niles. He m. Lydia Twisden. Ch: **Arthur**, b. 1670, Capt., gr.j., rem. to Scarb. in 1728 where he was an orig. memb. of the first ch. In 1742, A. B., gent., in jail, sued his creditor for beating him so that his life was despaired of. Liv. 5 Nov. 1746. He m. 1st Lydia Masterson, who by contemp. hist. was k. with their five ch. 13 Oct. 1703. By fam. trad. in Scarb. he left her baking and found her and their four ch. scalped on his return. But a dau. Abial was carried capt., and was still liv. in 1711. Lists 96, 99. The mo. had been a capt. bef. He m. 2d in Hampton 3 Nov. 1704 Mehitable Marston. His 2d fam., 6 ch. rec., incl. Solomon, b. 18 Nov. 1709, who m. a Jordan and was attorney for the incorpor. Jordan heirs. **Lydia**, m. 1st 1692 Philip Babb; 2d Samuel Norton.

**3 ARTHUR**(7), b. 1666, Deacon, but prev. Ensign; weaver, had a mill at the foot of Cape Neddick pond. Gr.j. 1693-8, 1701. Lists 38, 278-9. Will 15 Mar. 1736-7 ment. wife Sarah (Came 2), their 7 ch. and Farnham grch. Ch: **Sarah,** b. 10 Dec. 1692, in ct. Jan. 1713-4, m. at Portsm. 6 Sep. 1720 Benj. Johnston. **Martha,** b. 3 Jan. 1694-5, m. 1713 Jonadab Lord. **Hannah,** b. 25 May 1697, m. Daniel Farnham, d. 27 Nov. 1729. 4 ch. **Tabitha,** b. 21 Aug. 1699, m. John Linscott. **Thomas,** b. 20 Feb. 1702-3, Ensign, m. 23 Mar. 1726-7 his double cous. Mary Came(3), d. York 28 June 1774. List 279. 9 ch. **Bethia,** b. 20 June 1704, m. (int. 20 May 1727) Joseph Leavitt. 7 ch. Mercy, b. 1 Apr. 1707. **Love,** b. 19 May 1709, m. 25 Apr. 1734 Wm. Sawyer of Wells.

**4 BENONI.** Altho liv. appar. in Kit. and Berw., Benoni Bragdon had gr. in York 17 May 1702, 'if he settle it.' Attrib. to (2) and Hannah Mains. In 1725 joined the ch. at Berwick and in 1742 was sexton. He m. (Jan. Term 1701-2) Joanna Allen, both bap. in Berw. 3 Jan. 1719-20. Of those here listed, Hannah, Jethro, Arthur, John and Benj. were certainly their ch: **Hannah,** b. 25 Dec. 1701, m. Joseph Linscott. 7 ch. York 1720-1732. **Jethro** (Bragenton), b. 28 Mar. 1704, m. 1727 Elizabeth Tucker, dau. of Lewis; k. in Wm. Frye's windmill in Kit. 13 Sep. 1733. **Arthur,** bp. Berw. 9 Apr. 1727, mar. Hannah Wittum (Daniel of York). 5 ch. **Thomas** (Braginton), Berw. wit. 1724, bp. 30 Apr. 1727. 4 ch. bp. Berw. **Benjamin,** Berw. gr. 1729. **Elizabeth,** int. 16 Nov. 1734 with Cornelius Lary, both of Kittery; bp. Berw. 1741; of Portsm. 3 Sep. 1753 acc. Wm. Melally of Portsm., mariner. **Samuel,** m. at Wells 1 Nov. 1744 Mary Spriggs. **Abigail,** of Berw., acc. Joshua Smith Apr. 1743. **John,** bp. 1 May 1726 (infant?). One John Bragdon m. Sarah Abbot Nov. 1750. **Joanna,** bp. adult Portsm. 1 Mar. 1746-7. Quite unplaced are Mary, York, in ct. Oct. 1720. Sarah, of Kit. acc. Francis Littlefield Jan. 1720-1. Daniel, Boston Ct. Rec. xvii. 113-4.

**5 SAMUEL**(1), liv. on father's homestead. Lists 33, 279. Gr.j. 1690, 91, 93, 94. Will 10 May 1709—6 Jan. 1712-3 ment. wife, 2 sons, 'my four daus.' Magdalin [Hilton], Patience, Sarah, Ruth. He m. Mary (Moulton) Hilton, liv. 1725. Ch: **Samuel,** b. 31 July 1673. **Mary,** b. 24 Nov. 1675, m. Abraham Preble (Nathl). **Patience,** b. 17 Apr. 1678, mar. Samuel Came(3). **Sarah,** b. 20 Mar. 1680-1, mar. Daniel Paul. **Jeremiah,** b. 17 Mar. 1683-4, not in will. **Ruth,** b. 9 Apr. 1691, m. Eliakim Wardwell. **Joseph,** b. 19 Sep. 1694, Lieut. In 1727 he was living on homestead of Arthur(1), 30 a. on N. E. side of York River. Will, of York, gent., 30 May 1759—17 Apr. 1766 ment. wife Sarah (Stick-ney, m. in Newbury 26 Nov. 1719) and 5 ch., besides sev. d.y.

**6 SAMUEL**(5), coaster. In 1727 he was liv. on his grf.'s land on S. W. side of York River, 45 a., bot from Arthur(3). He and all of his sons had town grants, List 279. D. 3 Mar. 1746[7 ag. 73, 3 mos. (grst.). He m. 25 Dec. 1694 Isabella Austin(5), d. 2 June 1722 ag. 48 (grst.); 2d Lydia (Young), ag. 85. Ch: **Dorcas,** b. 7 Sep. 1695, m. Samuel Black(2). **Mary,** b. 7 Apr. 1698, m. (int. 1737) Wm. Ball of Kit. **Samuel,** b. 6 Apr. 1700. Will 1764—1769 ment. wife Mercy, 7 ch., King grch. M. 1st Tabitha Banks(2), d. 28 Dec. 1745; 2d Mercy Mains. 5+4 ch. From two daus. by 1st w. came the poet Longfellow and the statesman Rufus King. **Isabella,** b. 13 Aug. 1702, m. Joseph Mitchell. **Jeremiah,** b. 30 Mar. 1704, Deacon and patron of Rev. 'Handkerchief' Moody. By local trad. unm., but pub. 13 Nov. 1738 to Elizabeth Sargent. Will 1763, 1767—1767 ment. 3 bros., 4 sis. **Daniel,** b. 7 June 1707, m. 12 Dec. 1733 Mary Banks(2). 6 ch. rec. **Joseph,** b. 7 Mar. 1709-10, York, gent., m. Mary Sewall (Capt. Samuel). 6 ch. rec. and named in will. **Mehitable,** b. 19 Sep. 1712, m. 25 Feb. 1736-7 Benj. Mitchell of Newbury, d. 5 Jan. 1803.

**7 THOMAS**(1), gr.j. 1665-66, 75, 78, 85, 98-90; selectm. 1679-81. Lists 25, 30, 33, 279. K. by Ind. See (2). Adm. 3 Dec. 1690 to s. Arthur sr. Ch: **Arthur,** b. 1666. **Daniel,** k. with father. **Martha,** m. ab. 1693 James Smith. **Elizabeth,** m. ab. 1704 Josiah Bridges. 7 ch. **Bethia,** m. Thos. Kimball, ch. 1710-13; 2d Charles White, ch. 1717-23.

**BRAGG,** pecul. to Devon, old there.

**1 JOHN,** son of Timothy of Ipsw., ±50 in 1746, ±68 in 1757, m. Ipsw. 28 May 1711 Mary Bennett. He was at Edward Polly's house, Portsm. 1711-12. Taxed there 1713. In 1757, sworn in Boston, dep. that he liv. in Scarb. 1717-1754. Tenant under Vaughan. He and w. Mary joined church there 1728. He and his bro. Ebenezer had grants there 1720. Ebenezer of Shrewsbury in 1728 deeded his grant to bro. Nathaniel of Wenham, both housewrights. Nathaniel in 1731 sold to (1). Ch. bap: **Mary,** in Portsm. 19 Apr. 1717, m. Nov. 1735 John Stewart. **Timothy,** same day, d. Scarb. 15 Mar. 1725. Two **Elizabeths,** d. Scarb. 1722, 1725. See Davis(8).

**2 PETER,** Piscataqua 1670. List 82. One Peter of Isles of Shoals m. (int. Dec. 1722) Anne Ball of Kittery. Wid. A. B. at Shoals 1734 m. Richard Nock.

**Braines,** Robert, see Bryant.

**BRAMHALL,** Bromhall, the former a township in Cheshire. One George, London, 1637.

BRAMHALL 107 BRAY

1 **GEORGE**, Dover, Boston, Portsm., Falm. Altho first appear. at Dover, taxed 1670, it is not unlik. that he came first to Boston from the W. I. with Ann Bromehall, Boston midwife, who depos. bef. Dudley 16 Oct. 1677, ±55, ab. matters when she liv. at St. Christophers; that he was put to the tanner's trade with Job Clements, then back to Bost. as super. of the Houchin tannery, back to marry a Dover girl, started bus. for hims. at Portsm., where the tanners and shoemakers had him fined for using two trades, then to Falm. in the project which gave his name to a large part of the best resid. section of Portland, but cost him his life. Lists 356j, 331b, 49, 225a, 329, 32, 34, 228bd. He m. Martha Beard(4). List 331c. Fatally wounded by the Ind. the day before, he d. 21 Sep. 1689. The wid. fled to Plymouth, later liv. in Hingham, where she m. 9 Dec. 1698 Gershom Hall of Harwich. Ch: **Joseph**, b. ab. 1676, wine cooper, Boston, d. July 1716, m. in Boston 25 Aug. 1714 Grace Record, sole benef. in his will 22 Apr. 1715 —20 Aug. 1716; she mar. 2d 21 Mar. 1721 Philip Marshall. **George**, tanner, Hingham, m. 14 July 1711 Anna Baker of Barnstable. Will 1749 (Brimhorn) names wife, 2 sons, 3 daus. **Hannah**, m. app. her stepbro., Jonathan Hall of Harwich. **Joshua**, clothier, Plym., m. 20 Nov. 1709 Sarah Rider of Taunton. Went to Portland to claim father's land, but returned leaving son Sylvanus in Port. Will 2 June 1762—27 Apr. 1763 names w. Sarah, 3 sons, 2 of them decd., 2 daus. and grsons.
2 **THOMAS** (Bromhall), mariner, master's mate, Boston, Ct. of Asst. 1677, perh. br. or father of (1).
**BRAND.** 1 **Richard** (Bran), Cape Porpus 1668. List 255. See also Brawn.
2 **THADDEUS**, Lynn, killed in Black Point battle 29 June 1677. See Davis: 'Ancestry of Lt. Amos Towne.'
**Branford**, John, Falm. 1689. List 228c.
**Branscomb**, Deborah, of Portsm., ±59 in 1711, dep. conc. the parents in Swansea, So. Wales, of Hopkins Davis's wife. Elizabeth B. was called dau. in Nathan White's will 1747, and E. B. was called 'cousin' in Margaret Reed's will, wid. of Hugh, in 1760. Capt. William B. (d. 16 May 1788, ag 78 y. 9 m.), and Charles B. moved into Hampton 1764.
**BRANSON**, George (also Braunson), b. ab. 1610, first of Dover, party to lawsuit in 1647, then at York, and finally at Oyster River, where k. by his own bull, inq. 2 July 1657. Lists 354abc, 275, 276.
**BRAWN.** In region of Northants 3 Brawnstons, in Devon, parish of Braunton.
1 **EDWARD** (Brawnde), Master 1614. List 7.
2 **GEORGE**(5), Newington and Eliot. Lists

50 p. 10, 54, 57, 62, 290, 296, 297. In 1702 he exchanged the Bloody Point homestead for a place on Sturgeon Creek, Kit. Living 1718. He m. 1st Mary, 2d Sarah (Wittum), wid. of Wm. Sanders. In 1750 his ch. sold eighths, showing 7 ch. liv. or with liv. issue. Poss. the missing one is disguised in what seems a subconscious tangle, York Ct. Jan. 1697-8: 'George Spencer & Brawn his now wife.' Kn. ch: George, called eldest s., fisherman. Poss. the subconscious tangle should read George -Brawn- & . . . . . Spencer. He m. 9 Feb. 1710-1 Mary Tidy. In 1710 John Wittum and G. B. were joint defendants. Leonard Drown brought ejectment against him in 1715. See Y. D. xii. 293. Adm. Jan. 1731-2 to wid. Mary, who mar. 2d 17 Aug. 1732 Thos. Penny of Wells. 5 ch. rec. or bap. Left 4 under 7. **Michael**, b. Dover 1 June 1679. Marriages in that name: 8 Jan. 1722 to Abigail Wittum, 21 June 1750 to Hannah Smith. **Eleanor**, mar. 7 Sep. 1704 Jacob Rhodes. **Elizabeth**, m. 28 Jan. 1705-6 David Thomas. **Richard**, ag. 77, of York, June 1770. List 279. He m. (int. 18 Sep. 1725) Eunice Wittum (Peter). 9 ch. 1726-1745. **Peter**, m. 1 Jan. 1729 Elizabeth Muzeet. Liv. 1752. 2 ch. rec. (**John**, wit. 1714, Y. D. viii. 147; 1745 Louisburg Exp.; poss. the 7th ch.).
3 **JOHN**, owned land in York on Alcock's Neck by 1641; perh. liv. in 1669. Wife d. of Wm. Dixon. Kn. ch: **Richard. John**, b. ab. 1647, liv. unm. on father's land, by court rec. indic. a degen. See Y. D. viii. 172. List 30. O. A. 22 Mar. 1680-1. Will 8 Oct. 1703—29 May 1704, favored his Moore cousins.
4 **JOHN**(6), accu. of slander in 1684, m. (Ct. Jan. 1694-5) Anna Langley. They sold their house at Kit. Point in 1698, and in Ind. attack at Spruce Creek 4 May 1705 he was killed.
5 **MICHAEL**, 30 June 1651, bot John Lavis's land at Bloody Point, and in 1675 had a gr. there. Wit. for Mass. in Kit. Nov. 1652. Michael, ±30 in 1672, liv. 1675, was presum. his s., and it was likelier the surv. f. taxed at Bloody Point down to 1684. Lists 355a, 356ceghk, 359b, 52. One of them was fined in 1669 for cursing the N. H. court. App. only ch: **Michael. George.**
6 **RICHARD**(3), York. In 1666 his w. Mary escaped whipping for stealing by being with ch. Neither heard of after. Kn. ch: **Susannah**, in ct. 1683, 86. **John**, 'jr' in 1684.

**BRAY**, called Norman. A manor in St. Just, Cornwall. With comb., 8 over all England. See Creber.
1 **JOHN?** See Walter Bagnall.
2 **JOHN**, shipwright, Kittery, ±50 in 1670, came from Plymouth, Devon, where one John, s. of John, was bp. in St. Andrews 24

Oct. 1624. He was sued by Digory Jeffries in Mar. 1663-4. Jury 1665, gr.j. 1666, 68, 70, 71, 81, 86, lot layer 1669, selectm. 1671, 1683, tav. and ferry lic. 1672-79. Lists 331c, 82, 33, 286, 292, 298. Will 22 Jan. 1688-9—15 July 1690. Wife Joan b. ab. 1630; adm. 11 Jan. 1693-4. Ch: John, gr.j. 15 July 1690; (grant 1699? List 298). Joan, m. 1678-9 Clement Deering(1). Margery, b. 1660, m. Col. William Pepperell. Mary, mar. Joseph Deering(6).

3 JOHN(4), husbandman. His f. 24 Dec. 1669 deeded him land, with reversion to bro. Nathl. and his heirs. With Nathl. he took O. A. at Glouc., app. aft. Dec. 1677. Poss. one of the two bros. k. by Indians on Cousins Isl., he had d.s.p. and unm. bef. Dec. 1678, although he had lived with Ann Lane (James) without his father's consent and had a dau. by her.

4 RICHARD, North Yarmouth, by 1649 or earlier, in 1651 bot half of Cousins Isl., and lived there some time. In Philip's War he fled first to York, and with John Mains was an appr. at Cape Neddick 25 Oct. 1676, although two of his sons (Hannah Hazelton's brothers) remained on or returned to Cousins Isl. and were k. by Ind. while looking after their cattle. Of Boston, tailor, in Jan. 1678-9, he was at York, selling land in No. Yarm. in 1685. Lists 211, 214, 86, 30. His wife, m. bef. Feb. 1650-1, is found as Rebecca, Rebella, Sabella, Isabella. Ch: John. Nathaniel, app. d.s.p. bef. Jan. 1678-9. See John(3). Samuel, tailor, poss. one of the two k. by Ind., his widow Jane, 'formerly of Casco Bay now in Boston,' 8 Jan. 1678-9. Richard. William. Hannah, ±68 3 April 1728, m. 1st John Freethy(4); 2d Robert Hazeltine of Rowley.

5 RICHARD, prop. Exeter 1657, on jury and coroner's jury same year; jury 1663. Lists 356a, 361a, 376b. See 'Hist. Durham,' Vol. I. D. at Lynn Oct. 1665. See Essex Qtly. Cts. iii. 297-8. Adm. Apr. 1666 to wid. Mary, who was Mary Whitlock in 1689. Ch: John, under 21 in 1666; of Middletown, Monmouth Co., East Jersey, sold Exeter land in 1689. Mary, under 18 in 1666.

6 RICHARD(4) (aut. 1691, ancient hand), was bef. York court for fighting 3 Feb. 1685-6. Likely the gunner's mate at the Fort, Boston, in 1687. Of York, shoemaker, 1691; cordwainer al. fisherman ab. 1700. Gr.j. York 1693, 1694. List 294. He m. by Oct. 1691 Mary (Sayward), wid. of Robert Young; d. in Arrowsic, 'old Mr. Bray,' 6 Jan. 1717-8. Ch: Samuel.

7 SAMUEL(6), m. (Ct. Apr. 1714) Mary Preble, dau. of Abraham, Esq. He removed to Arrowsic, d. there 30 Dec. 1717, 'a hopeful young man.' Widow mar. 2d Wm. Craige, 3d Joseph Plaisted. 2 sons.

8 THOMAS, Dover, fined 27 June 1676. A wit. 1674-1680.

9 WILLIAM(4), first seen at York. List 236. O. A. at York Mar. 1679-80; York gr. 1686, but app. never laid out. In 1684 he was prison keeper, discharged from the place 31 Mar. 1685; prison keeper again 1690, his last appear.; he may have been killed in the massacre.

Bready, see Brady.

BRECK, see also Brick and Brock.

1 FRANCIS, Cape Eliz. 1683. List 226.

2 JOHN, Arrowsic, 1679. List 187.

BREME, John, in 1661 bot ¼ of House Isl. in Portland Harbor from Nich. White, which he sold to George Munjoy — unrec. deed (Willis MSS. R. 17), 'fisherman, of Casco sometime of Spurwink Island,' his mark an anchor. In 1665 drunk and disord., 1666 wit. Ind. deed to Munjoy, 1679 at Arrowsic. Lists 25, 187.

Bretnell, John, Isl. of Shoals 1653. List 301.

Bretoon, John, Frenchman, mariner, Machias. In 1683 in Boston court ack. debt to John Alden. Wife and ch. 1688. List 5.

BRETTON, see also Bradden.

1 FRANCIS (Britton, Breten), soldier from Newbury. Lists 37, 267b.

2 JOHN (Bretoon, Brittoon), see Bradden (2) and Bretoon.

3 JOSEPH (Britten, Breden), Portsm. wit. 1709, 1713. In 1722 shoreman making Col. Mark Hunkins' fish on Ferry Island. One Elizabeth Britten m. at Portsm. 15 Sep. 1719 John Bickford of Portsm. (See 18.)

4 MARY (Brittaine), ±34 m. June 1705, wit. for John Frost on Smuttinose. One Mary of Portsm. m. William Warren from Devonshire 8 Jan. 1715-6.

5 PHILIP (le Bretton). Lists 227, 229.

6 PHILIP (Breading), Capt., of Boston, mariner, residing in Portsm. 1733.

7 THOMAS (Breeden), Capt., an Eng. exploiter at large. Lists 2, 111. P. & C. i. 182, 186, 191. See Savage.

8 WILLIAM, Mr. (Brettun, Britton), called by 'Britton Ancestry' son of James and Jane of Charlestown, was in Saco, a wit., 6 June 1674; m. Mary Pendleton, who was brought up by her grandf. Major Brian P., and mar. 2d Joseph Cross(7); 3d Nicholas Morey. Ch: William, mariner, Taunton, m. there 26 Oct. 1698 Lydia Leonard, his admx. 17 Mar. 1725-6, liv. 1752. 10 ch. incl. Pendleton Brettun.

BREWER. 1 James, York, by wife Mary Averill (Job 7), 2 ch. 1727-30.

2 NATHANIEL, North Yarm. prop. Y. D. 18.260.

3 SARAH, Mary, see Tho. Webster, Wm. Lane.

**BREWSTER,** Bruster, occup. surname, female brewer, No. of Eng. and Scotch for brewer.

1 **SERGT. JOHN,** not in Portsm. by 1658 or he would have shared in div. of commons 22 Jan. 1660-1. List 330b. (Also Roger Knight had no dau. or she would.) In 1662 he received a deed from John Sherburne on the Plains, which was the homestead of many generations of his desc. They spelt the name -Bruster-, rewritten in ink -Brew- wherever Dr. G. G. Brewster found it in the original town or province records. He and Philip Benmore bot at Kennebec (Parker's Isl.) in 1664, and sold in 1667. Freeman 15 May 1672. Jury 1666; gr.j. 1671, 1683, 1687 (forem.); road surveyor. Lists 356b (Portsmouth), 323, 326c, 330a, 331ab, 332b, 49, 52, 54, 55b, 57. The deed from John Sherburne, part of his homestead, with proviso that grantee or his w. or ch. cannot sell without first giving the grantor an oppor. to buy, (Deeds iii. 92a), is consis. with the wife being his dau., yet the father's will in 1691 treats his dau. Mary 'Sherburne' as if unm. Aside from this, no orig. record untampered with suggests a connection bet. the Brusters and any other fam., until aft. the s. John had m. Mary Sloper, grdau. of Henry Sherburne. In 1694 the son and Aaron Moses were wit. together, and later in a suit for trespass brought by a person of high influence, the son's bondsman was the John Knight (signed 'Chevallir'). The name 'John Brewster' inserted in a modern hand bet. the names of Roger Knight and Anne Knight is one of Dr. Brewster's forgeries (Deeds i. 95). The will of the first Bruster, 16 Dec. 1691, names w. Mary, who is called widow in the tax list of 24 Apr. 1693 and in List 335a, (tax abated Mar. 1694-5), and ch: **Sarah,** m. 26 Sep. 1679 Robert Hinkson. **Elizabeth. Martha. John,** b. 1667. **Mary. Jane. Rachel.**

2 **JOHN**(1), ag. 53 in July 1720, taxed 1688, carpenter, liv. on the homestead entailed on his s. John. Innholder 1709-1715, in 1718 had a bowling alley much frequented by sailors. Const. 1693, jury 1693, gr.j. 1694, 1697, 1698. Selectm. 1721. Lists 332b, 330d, 335a, 337, 339. Adm. 8 Aug. 1726 to wid. Mary (Sloper) and s. John, she liv. 17 Feb. 1743[4. List 335a. Ch: **John,** b. 1 Jan. 1690, tailor. Will 28 Oct. 1743—25 Apr. 1744 names only his 3 bros. and Sister White. **Samuel,** b. 30 Apr. 1692, housewright. Adm. 21 Nov. 1754 to wid. Margaret (Waterhouse), his second cous. 10 or 11 ch. List 339. **Abigail,** b. 18 Oct. 1694, m. Samuel White, joiner; wid. by 1748. **Joshua,** b. 21 Apr. 1696, blacksmith, m. June 1720 Sarah Jose; 2d 12 Sep. 1722 Margaret Thompson from Coleraine, Ire. Conflict of dates as if his 1st was liv. when he m. 2d is uninvest. **Joseph,** cord-

wainer, b. 21 Oct. 1701, m. 6 Feb. 1723-4 Phebe Noble. They d. (grst.) 4 Dec. 1766, 16 Aug. 1767, she ae. 67. Ch.

3 **WRESTLING,** alias Doctor George Gaines Brewster, 1797-1872, graduate dentist, trial justice, memb. N. E. Hist.-Gen. Soc. See N. E. Reg. xxx. 475. On four early pages of the oldest N. H. court book the name Wrestling Brewster is inserted in modern handwriting as plaintiff or defendant, in one entry with the original name erased by scratching clear through the leaf, so that the name Wrestling Brewster is written partly on the following leaf. He descended from Mary (Sherburne) Sloper, who made a list of the dates she could learn, incl. the deaths of her grandparents Gibbins, no name of Brewster or Bruster in it. This list had been rearranged on parchment by an accomplished penman, and was printed -verb. et lit.- by his truthful brother (Rambles II. 51), when it was in danger of being destroyed. A pretended copy with fictitious alterations was printed in the Register in 1863 (N. E. Reg. xvii. 252), and still another with further fict. alt. in 1907 (N. E. Reg. lxi. 82). Hon. John Wentworth, of the Went. Gen., a successful lawyer, and Rev. Ashbel Steele, author of -Life and Times of Elder Brewster-, were among those deceived, despite the honest brother, who yet was deceived by a forged funeral ring (Rambles I. 71), not allowing for Old Style in reckoning the age of their ancestress, as well as misrep. her social status.

**BRIAR,** Briard, Briers.

1 **ELISHA** (Briard), blockmaker, Portsm., d. 27 May 1718, ag. 57 (grst.) First app. as wit. with Mr. Richard Paine, Nov. 1686. Wit. two wills with Edw. Melcher 1689-91. In 1695 the town paid him for 'old (Richard) Lewis's coffin. In 1698 he was in attendance on the Council and Assembly. Jury 1694, 1695, 1699. Constable 1700. Lists 57, 62, 66, 330def, 335a, 336c, 337, 339. Adm. 3 Sep. 1718 to wid. Abigail (Drew 11, m. 4 Oct. 1689). Lists 331c, 335a. Liv. with her son-in-law in Greenland 1741. Rec. ch. all surv.: **Margaret,** b. 30 Nov. 1693, m. James Cate(1). **Abigail,** b. 11 Dec. 1695, m. 2 Jan. 1715-6 Wm. Cross of Bideford, Devon. **Samuel,** b. 18 Sep. 1697, blockmaker, adm. 10 Dec. 1723 to wid. Lucy (Lewis, of Kit., m. 16 Apr. 1719), who m. 25 June 1724 Sylvanus Tripe. 2 or m. ch. **Sarah,** b. 2 Feb. 1700-1, m. 1st Tho. Manwaring; 2d one Watson; liv. 1756. **Mary,** b. 21 Aug. 1702.

2 **GILES** (Brier), taxed in Exeter (Stratham) 1714. List 388. One widow Mary Bryar with s. Francis from Stratham was adm. to Hampton Falls Ch. 1722. Ch. rec: Mary, 1713. **Charles,** 1717.

3 **JOHN** (Briers), Glouc. fisherman in partn. with John Jackson. See Coe. Rem. to Spurwink, then to Blue Point, Scarb. List 85. Escaped from Indians to Marblehead, where in Feb. 1677-8 he was bound servant to Erasmus James for 7 yrs. for debts. He m. at Glouc. 25 Mar. 1651-2 Elizabeth 'Jackson,' dau. of Eleanor, perh. bef. her m. to John Jackson. She d. in Beverly 2 Aug. 1722, ag. 93 (±30 in 1664). Ch.rec. in Glouc: **Grace**, b. 28 Nov. 1655, m. Wm. Chilson(2). **John**, b. 29 May 1658, d.s.p. **Benjamin**, b. 15, d. 27 Jan. 1660. **Mary**, b. and d. 11 Jan. 1661. **Mary**, m. at Marbleh. 28 Oct. 1701 Moses Fluent, who claimed land at Spurwink by deed from Mr. Jocelyn dated 20 May 1664. See List 239a.

4 **CAPT. JOHN** (Briard), Portsm., ± 69 in 1771. See Libby.

5 *\***LT. RICHARD** (Briar), b. in Newbury 10 Feb. 1665-6, one of five or more stepbros. and sisters who came to Kittery: Richard, William and Edith or Ada Briar, John and George Frink. Richard Briar of Newbury and Ipswich by his 1st w. Eleanor Wright, who d. 29 Aug. 1672, was f. of the Briars, and for his 2d w. m. the mo. of the Frinks, Mary (Wood, dau. of Obadiah), by her 1st husband John Frink. Ada Briar m. Joseph Weeks. Richard Briar was Lieut. from 1690; repeat. grandj.; Rep. 1702. Lists 296, 297, (127?). On Oct. 7, 1701 Mr. Charles Story and Lt. Richard Bryar were adm. attorneys-at-law within York County. He m. Mary (Cutt 7), wid. of Humphrey Churchwood. They app. left town in 1704 (for Carolina?), in 1709 he was 'living out of this Province,' and in 1742 his lands were deeded by his bro.-in-law Richard Cutt to his s. Thomas who had long been in poss.

6 **THOMAS** (Brier). Quamscot by 1734, bot from Simon Wiggin in 1712. Taxed Exeter (Stratham) 1714. List 388. Living in Epping 1763. 3 wives: 1st Abigail; 2d 14 Oct. 1719 Mercy Mason, who d. 10 June 1723; 3d 23 Jan. 1723-4 Elizabeth Godfrey, liv. 1746. Kn. ch: **Peter**, b. 2 Jan. 1711-2, mariner, of Epping, w. Rachel. **Judith**, b. 18 July 1720. **Thomas**, b. 30 Sep. 1724, adm. 1752 to wife Rachel. 4 ch. bapt.

7 **WILLIAM**, bro. of (5), in Kit. by 1699. Lists 296, 297. In 1710 he took a 10 yr. lease of Woodman's ferry, and was innholder. Will 15 Apr. 1718, d. 5 May 1718. He had recently exch. farms with Diamond Sargent and rem. to York. He m. ab. 1702 Sarah Esmond(1), who m. 2d 19 Oct. 1722 Benj. Hammons. Ch: **William**, b. 20 Dec. 1702, shipwright, m. 11 May 1728 Elizabeth Weeks. 6 ch. rec. **Mary**, b. (9 Jan.) 1705, mar. Andrew Haley. **Rebecca**, b. (9 Jan.) 1708, m. William Tapley. **Sarah**, b. 12 Jan. 1709, in court 1725, m. 19 Mar. 1726-7 Caleb

Hutchins. **Edah**, b. 4 July 1712 (-Eady- in father's will, -Eadith- in court 1731 for selling spirits), m. 1732 Wm. Wilson jr. **Elizabeth**, bp. 1 May 1715, m. Joseph Hutchins. **Richard**, weaver, liv. 1738. **Margaret**, mar. John Haley.

**Brich**, John, wit. 1653 Ind. deed to Lake. Phillips' Rec. p. 19. Mass. Arch. 16, 33. See Birch.

**Brick**, Arnold, Greenland. In 1694 William Richards gave bond for A. B. and his w. coming into town, and in 1695 taxes abated. Lists 67, 68, 96, 336b, 338a. W. Hannah, List 338b. He m. 2d 18 Feb. 1730-1 Eleanor (Smart) Fox, wid. of Benj.(1). Presum dau: **Sarah**, m. 28 Feb. 1728-9 Robert Elliot.

**Brickell**, James, sold ¼ of est. of Thomas Cloyes(6). Y. D. 14.191.

**BRIDGES. 1** Edmund, 1682, atty. for John Reynolds sued by Francis Tucker.

2 **JOSIAH** and sons, York. List 279. M. Elizabeth Bragdon(7). 7 ch. rec. 1705-1734.

3 **MATTHEW**, of Cambridge, in 1682 referee at York.

4 **OBADIAH**, soldier at Wells 1693-4. List 267b.

**BRIDGHAM, William**, m. Boston 13 Nov. 1709 Tabitha Sloper (Richard, -Slocum- in rec.) 'Mr. Bridgman' rated to New Meet. Ho., Portsm. 1717. Lists 62, 339. Liv. 1732. Wid. liv. 1735. Ch: **William**, b. Boston 16 June 1712. **Henry**, bp. 1 Mar. 1718-9, d.y. **Jacob**, bp. 11 Dec. 1720. **Elizabeth**. In 1765 his land was owned ¾ by John Elliot, glazier, ¼ by Jonathan Ayers, cordwainer.

**Briggs**, Rebecca and Wm. See Dyer(1).

**Brigham**, John, 1651.

**BRIGHT. 1** ——— Mr. 1631. List 41.

2 **HENRY**, Hampton grant 1640. Appar. came not. List 392a. See Dow, Savage, Bond's Watertown.

**Brimblecome**, John, 1614. List 7.

**Brines**, Brian, see Bryant.

**Brinley**, Lawrence, York patentee. List 272. See Waters' Gleanings 13-16.

**Brinsmead**, William, plf. in Me. Ct. 1683.

**BRISCOE. 1** Robert, from Beverly, mariner, m. Eliz. (Leavitt), widow of James Dudley(1). Inter. will N. H. Prob. ii. 350. Wid. m. 3d 22 Sep. 1730 Rev. John Odlin.

2 **WILLIAM**. In S. G. Drake's collated list of Sagadahoc inhab. Hub. Ind.Wars ii. 199.

**BRISSON**, Charles (also Brissom, Bissum, Breisson), of York by Sep. 1680, then suing John Card and wife; in 1685 was sued by John Wentworth for damage done by his turkeys; drunk and striking his w. in 1686. He m. Mary, wid. of Lewis Bean(3), and had the Bean lands in his hands Mar. 1689-90. See Carlisle. Adm. gr. to Matthew Austin 5 Jan. 1698-9.

Bristow (Bristoe), ——, wid. of ——, early grantee at Hampton. Herself appar. ment. 1640, 1646, 1652; her lot 1663, 1664, 1676. Her lot, with its cow common right, passed to John Brown.
Briton, etc., see Bretton.

**BROAD**, pecul. to Cornwall. With comb., 23 places all in the So. of Eng. See Creber.

1 **GEORGE**, master of ship for Barbadoes 30 June 1668.

2 **THOMAS**, of Portsm., mariner, 1722, 2d mate under Mr. Henry Sloper.

3 **WILLIAM**, Portsm., perh. the wit. with Richard Tucker in 1659 to deed of Robert Mussell to Joseph Baker; or the wit. in 1664 of Robert Ellet(5) to Abraham Corbett. Adm. 27 June 1665 to s. **William**.

4 **WILLIAM**(3), fisherman, Isles of Shoals and Great Isl. In 1666 he bot a house on Star Isl. which in 1670 he sold to Henry Brooking. In 1669 he bot house and 100 a. which next yr. he sold to Dygory Jeffrey. He was one of ten Shoals fishermen drowned in the great storm of 30 Jan. 1677-8. His inv. was larger than the total of the other nine:

| | | | |
|---|---|---|---|
| Richard Hill | £ 5 | Adm. | R. Welcome |
| Noah Gresham | £ 6 | " | " " |
| Richard Boyce | £ 8 | " | " " |
| Henry Light | £ 11 | " | Henry Mains |
| Edw. Perryman | £ 13 | " | " " |
| Nathan Quick | £ 2 | " | Roger Kelly |
| Robert Goodwin | £ 2 | " | " " |
| Gabriel Grubb | £ 21 | " | " " |

at his widow's request
Roger Holland £ 57 Adm. bro. Edw. Holland
Wm. Broad £ 161 " wid. Judith Broad
See List 306d. The appraisers included James Blagdon, Edw. Gould, John Hunking, John Fabes, John Moore.
Lists 312c, 313a, 326c. He m. 1st Abigail Glanfield, liv. 9 June 1670; 2d Judith, who m. 2d in Haverhill 26 May 1678 Stephen Webster, tailor. Ch: **Abigail**, ±13 in 1677. **William**, ±9 in 1677, app. was apprent. to Hon. Robert Elliot. Both ch. app. d.s.p. and Richard Tucker, will 15 June 1694, was in some way the heir. N. H. Probate I, 393.

**BROADBENT, Joshua**, hornbreaker, Boston, 1684-86, later gent. Of Boston, merchant, 5 Nov. 1685, he was arrested for slandering the N. H. gr.j.; next yr. appointed N. H. Provost Marshal. In 1690, in prison in Boston, he pet. the King to release him. M. in Woburn 6 Apr. 1685 Sarah Osborn. Rec. ch: **Sarah**, b. Boston 14 June 1687.

**BROADBROOK** (see also Bradbrook), **Beriah**. Insolvent, 1 Nov. 1710, no house or home, with w. and 5 small ch., awaits a vessel to take him to Delaware Bay. (Joseph Severance f.-in-law?) Suff. Ct. Files 8142.
Berriah, Brodbrooks jr., Harwich wit. 1730.

In 1759 B. B. dep. how Edward Small and fam., driven by the Ind., were first at Truro, some yrs. later at Chatham, and he over 50 yrs. ago was drowned. Suff. Ct. Files 137037.

**BROADHEAD, Elias.** In 1684 'one Broadhead that lives at Cochecho' helped Elizabeth Tibbetts to break jail. In 1686 in Me. Ct. E. B. ack. judgment to Reuben Hull. Lists 33, 298.

**BROADRIDGE** (-rick, Broderage), **Richard**, grantee at Falmouth bef. 1690. W. Constant Withington of Dorchester, b. 16 Nov. 1661; both liv. 1718. N. E. Reg. 75.145. His Falm. rights were sold in 1729 by her niece Hannah (Hall) and husb. Pelatiah Rawson of Milton. Y. D. 13.14.

**Broadway** (Bradaway), **Richard**, Sagadahoc 1674. List 15.

**BROCK** and comb., 17 places all over Eng.

1 **ANDREW**, mariner, Portsm., bot land from William Partridge 6 Dec. 1697, shared in town commons 1711, dead by 1715. Lists 314, 330d. Wid. Anna m. James Jaffrey bef. 1720. As Anna Brock she was a wit. 1698. Ch: **William**, Portsm. merchant. 1720, living 1736. (List 99? p. 124.)

2 **FRANCIS**, Portsm. 1686, wit. with Saml. Keais 1694. List 330a.

3 **REV. JOHN**, son of Henry of Dedham, H. C. 1646, minister at Isles of Shoals, a wit. there 1651, but perh. not perm. settled until aft. 1652. One of com. on Godfrey's land grants in York 1654-55. List 90. Ordained min. at Reading 13 Nov. 1662, and m. same day Sarah (Symmes) wid. of Rev. Saml. Haugh, who d. 15 Apr. 1681; he 18 June 1688.

**BROCKHOLES, §Anthony**, Pemaquid, ±55 in 1694, Capt., Major, J. P., Gov. of New York. When Gov. Andros was overthrown, Major B. was Commander in Chief at the East, and was ordered dismissed and sent to Boston—one of the accu. that he was a Roman Cath. He went to N. Y. List 19. N. E. Reg. x. 26.82.

**BROCKUS** (Brookehouse), **William**, mar. Mary (Batson), wid. of Jonas Clay. Both living Barbadoes, when they gave P. A. to Richard Tucker to sell 8 a. at Sagamore Creek (Jonas Clay's land), by which Mr. Tucker deeded it to George Jones 1670.

**Broderage**, see Broadridge.

**Broderick**, Robert, 1672, accu. of stealing pipe staves in Dover.

**Bromfield**, William, Exeter 1664. List 376b.

**BRONSDON.** 1 **Joseph**. Piscat. wit. 1688. Y. D. v. 48.

2 **ROBERT**, Boston merchant, d. 22 Nov. 1701, ag. 63. See Y. D. 12.213.

**Brookhaven**, John, Pemaquid 1689. Doc. Hist. v. 45.

**Brookhouse**, see Brockus.

BROOKINGS 112 BROSSY

## BROOKINGS

**BROOKINGS.** Brooking, eminent in So. Devon. Henrys in Plympton and Yealmpton, Devon.

1 **GODFREY**(2?), Isles of Shoals, was sued by Thomas Donnell 1674. Drowned 10 Dec. 1681, he left wid. Hannah (Drew 17), who m. 2d Nicholas Follett(6), and 4 small ch. Kn. ch: **William**, of Dover in 1704 sold Oyster River land given him by his grandmo. Thomasine, wid. of Francis Matthews.

2 **HENRY,** Isles of Shoals. In 1657 Richard Sealy receipted to him for debt due Jone, late wife of John Bevill. Presented in June 1661 for liv. from his wife. Poss. f. of: **William,** b. ab. 1629. **Henry,** b. ab. 1641. **Godfrey,** b. ab. 1649.

3 **HENRY**(2?), servant of John Pickering sr. in 1667. He bot Wm. Broad's house on Star Isl. in 1670, but by 1672 had mar., likely as 2d wife, Eleanor, wid. of George Knight of Scarb., and was liv. there. With a young w. Sarah he was of Spruce Creek in 1686; Kittery grants 1694-1696. Lists 328, 236, 237acde, 238a, 293, 298. She m. 2d bef. 1712 John Linscott, 3d John Donnell(2). Adm. on his est. gr. 1729-30 to s. Henry of York, in order to claim his Scarb. lands. Francis Raynes, for reasons unk., joined other heirs in consenting to this adm. Ch. rec. in Kittery: **Samuel,** b. 11 June 1687, carpenter, soldier in Dummer's War, taxed Str. Bank 1713, rem. to Arrowsic. Mar. 21 Sep. 1712 Mary Kirke, who m. 2d (int. 3 Feb. 1727-8) Matthew Grover. Ch. **Henry,** b. 19 Mar. 1688-9, had gr. in York in 1713 cond. on settl. there. Gr.j. 1716. List 279. In 1707 and in 1716 he was working for Raynes. In 1737 with w. Sarah, dau. of Dea. Rowland Young, sold home in York; rem. to Georgetown. 5 ch. rec. York 1717-1724. **Mary,** b. 8 Mar. 1690; acc. of bastardy in 1708, child black. **Mercy,** b. 17 Jan. 1695. In 1712 her mo. acc. Wm. Jones of Portsm. in her behalf; m. Sep. 1713 John Davis(31). **Deliverance,** b. 17 Jan. 1695, mar. 24 Jan. 1716-17 Francis Locke. **Sarah,** b. 20 Nov. 1702, acc. Enoch Dill, had son Enoch b. in York 19 June 1732.

4 **JOHN,** fisherman, Monhegan, 1651. List 111.

5 **WILLIAM**(2?), husbandman and fisherman, Portsm., where he had gr. 1652. Gr.j. 1655, 1660, 1667-8, coroner's jury 1657. In 1667 he sold land at Gt. Isl. and dep. there in 1680, ag. ±51. Several times drunk. Lists 325, 330ab, 323, 312c, 313a, 326ac, 329, 331b, 52. Adm. 26 Nov. 1694 to wid. Mary (Walford), who m. 2d Wm. Walker; liv. 20 Jan. 1702-3, when heirs agreed to div. Lists 92, 315a. Ch: **Rebecca,** mar. 1st by 1679 Thomas Pomeroy, 2d Clement Rummerill, 3d Thos. Rouse, 4th George Alston. **Sarah,** m. Jacob Brown(11). **Martha,** b. ab. 1669, m.

1st John Wakeham, 2d John Lewis, 3d Joseph Randall. **Mary,** m. Thomas Lucy. **Grace,** m. 1695 John Lang.

## BROOKS

**BROOKS,** general Eng. name except far North. Became 82d commonest in N. E.

1 **EDWARD** of Ramsgate, par. of St. Lawrence, Gt. Brit., m. Catherine Toby of Portsm. 17 Apr. 1735.

2 **ELIZABETH,** and others unconnected. In 1712 had a child by Black Will. In 1717 was 'living then at Cape Neddick' with Thomas Reed, who had aban. w. and ch. in Braintree, was given 25 stripes, and said he would marry the wench if the baby proved white; m. 4 Aug. 1716 at Portsm. Thomas Reed, calling himself of London, Eng., and Elizabeth Brooks of Portsm.

3 **GEORGE,** wit. to original deed of Rascohegan Isl. 1672. Lists 238a, 239a.

4 **JOHN,** ±28 in 1696, had Kit. gr. 1694, sold 1696. Lists 290, 298. He m. by 1692 Eleanor Frye(1), who was gr. adm. 26 Nov. 1712. She m. 2d 8 Jan. 1712-3 John Bishop and by 1716 had removed to Kingston. Ch: **Elizabeth,** b. 24 Jan. 1695, m. Ebenezer Fellows(1). **Robert,** b. 1 Nov. 1698, Scarb. 1724, Biddeford 1734, Buxton. M. Sarah Sawyer, d. of John and Rebecca (Stanford). Wid. in 1760, of Biddeford, 1773 of Cape Eliz. 4 or more ch. incl. John, Hannah, Sarah and Isaiah. **Sarah,** b. 11 Oct. 1699. **Hester,** b. 22 Nov. 1702. (Int. Biddeford 14 Oct. 1731 Saml. Cole, Esther Brooks.) **John,** b. 27 Feb. 1703-4, of Kingston 1725, of Biddeford in 1726, sold out in Kingston in 1729. Living in Kit. in 1786, ag. 82. He m., presum. 2d, by Aug. 1740, Eleanor (Meader) Libby of Bid., who in 1748 was a wit. at Kit. Point.

5 ‡**THOMAS,** alias Basil Parker, why the double name unkn. One Basil Parker was adm. to comp. of haberdashers, London, 4 May 1610, who was likely the same B. P., haberda., of St. Gregory's by St. Paul's m. 2 Feb. 1610-11 to Anne Saville. One Basil Brooks came over on the same ship with one Henry Dunnell in 1635. The Me. man came to N. E. for the Shrewsbury merchts., who were sued for his wages by Edw. Colcord in 1649. As Thomas Brooks he first app. at Saco ct. 25 June 1640, but as Basil Parker wit. deeds 1643-1646. Recorder 1647 to death, Councillor 1650-51. Owned land in common with Peter Weare. List 281. He appar. d. at Gunnison's tavern, leaving records in Gunnison's trust; adm. 18 Oct. 1651 to Mr. John Alcock, with whom and his wife he was several times a wit.

6 **THOMAS,** mariner, 1686. List 122.

7 **WILLIAM,** shipwright, Kit. Lists 291, 296, 297. He mar. 11 Aug. 1709 Mary Fogg(1). 5 ch. See Stack. Kit.

**Brossy,** Mary, see Crucy(8).

**BROUGHTON**, the name of 25 parishes, chapelries and townships in No. Mid. and East Eng.

1 *‡**CAPT. GEORGE.** In 1662 app. was apprent. to Samuel Hall, the Salisbury lawyer. In 1670 bot a wharf in Charlestown. Gr.j. 1676, foreman 1683. Cornet 1680, Capt. 1681, 1682. Assemblyman Me. 1680, 1681, 1682. Lists 28, 29, 298. Liv. 1687, last ment. 24 Aug. 1687. He m. Perne Rawson, b. May 1646, d. of Edw., Secy. of the Province. In 1696 his wid. pet. for a liquor lic. reciting: driven from home by the Ind. and their est. lost, her hus. dead, her s. John her only support, since dead. Ch: **John**, b. 22 Jan. 1667. **Rachel**, b. 1 Sep. 1670, wife in 1701 of Thos. Rew of Boston, mariner. Mar. int. forbid. Boston 7 Jan. 1696-7 Thos. Rue and Rachel Hill. **Mary**, b. 10 Aug. 1672, of Boston unm. 1701. **Edward**, b. 12 Oct. 1673. **Perne**, b. 15 June 1677, all at Boston. **Sarah**, mar. one Johnson of Boston 1701. Wm. and -Mary-Johnson had s. Broughton b. in Boston 6 May 1706. **Rebecca**, m. at Boston 10 Apr. 1707 Edw. Cowell, cooper; both liv. Truro 1737.

2 **CAPT. JOHN**(4). Gr.j. 1679, 1687. Lists 28, 33, 298. He was shot down by the Ind. on his way to Berwick 29 June 1689, the day after the Cochecho massacre. Inv. sworn in Boston by Mrs. Abigail Broughton, wid., 13 Feb. 1690-1. He mar. Abigail Reyner, who m. 2d 30 Mar. 1696 Thos. Kendall of Woburn, and d. 31 Dec. 1716. Ch: **Thomas**, gunsmith, d.s.p. Boston 4 Dec. 1702, adm. to Timothy Wadsworth. He had recently been 'armourer at her Majesty's Fort at Casco Bay' 46 weeks. **Elizabeth**, b. 22 Sep. 1677, Boston, d. 22 Mar. 1703-4, unm. **Nathaniel**, in Salem 1707; of Boston 1710. **Mary**, mar. in Woburn 3 Nov. 1701 Jacob Fowle. **Abigail**, unm. in Portsm. 1710, heir to her uncle Job Alcock(1), mar. Robert Walker, mariner, his will 17 Nov. 1714—27 Jan. 1716-7; 2d 16 May 1722 Richard James; liv. 1737. Her only ch. Sarah, bp. 31 Mar. 1715 was w. of Wm. Farrow in 1737, his wid. 3 Aug 1750 and w. of Benj. Stanton 18 Dec. 1751. Meantime either she or another grandau. of (2) was Sarah Celleghan or Callyhan of Portsm., spinster, 27 Nov. and 30 Jan. 1750-1. N. H. Deeds 42.371, Y. D. 29.44.

3 **JOHN** (see Bradden), late desc. in Portsm. call their name Broughton, speaking it like -thought-, not -though-.

4 **THOMAS**, Mr., ±54 in Dec. 1667, ±63 in July 1676, d. in Boston 12 Nov. 1700, ag. 87, int. and no prob. Wealthy by inher. and mar., and with rich connections in London (bro. Wm. and cous. Peter Cole), he was too honorable and fair to plunge successf. into trade. In 1670 he assigned for benefit of creditors, yet in 1671 was placed at the head of an important commiss. for laying out inter-province roads, without results. His elder sons struggled to redeem the fam. fortune, but with increasing diffic. due to Ind. wars. In 1651 began his campaign to monop. lumber milling on the Pisc., soon exhaust. his own capital. In 1657 he was acting under P. A. of Richard Leader, partn. with Wm. Paddy and Val. Hill to build a dam and mill on Lamprill River. In 1673 he was living in his own house, with a 'foreroom,' ab. 20 m. by water and land from Henry Dering's house (Portsmouth). Hired house, Boston, 1701. Lists 356abce, 323, 326a, 46, 80, 296, 298. He m. Mary Biscoe, d. of Nathaniel. Ch: **George**. **John**, b. ab. 1644. **Child**, d. ag. 7 d. **Elizabeth**, b. Watertown 15 Jan. 1646, m. Obadiah Reed, who in 1720 deeded her Kit. gr. of 1671. List 298. **Mary**, b. Boston 5 July 1651. **Thomas**, b. 26 May 1653, d.y. **Nathaniel**, b. 5 Dec. 1654, in 1672 was a wit. with his uncle Wm. Bond; taxed 1674; commander of ketch -Friendship-; master of barque -Exchange- in 1688. **Thomas**, b. 23 Dec. 1656, has been confused with his nephew. **Hannah**, b. 28 Dec. 1658. **Sarah**, b. 9 June 1660. These two adm. memb. of Boston 2d Ch. 11 Aug. 1706; the latter liv. Boston unmar. 1727? **Patience**, b. 14 Apr. 1663, d. Boston 28 Dec. 1705.

**BROWN**, 6th commonest name in Eng. and Wales (almost unkn. in Wales), 6th in Scotland, became 2d in N. E.

1 **ALEXANDER**, Kennebec 1665-1669, in 1667 was in charge of John Winslow's trading station at 'Kedumkock,' 3 m. below Cobbossecontee. He settled at Merrymeeting Bay, and also had a plantation 'Brown's Farm,' 5 or 6 m. above Richmond Fort. Me. H. & G. Rec., vii. 191.

2 **ANDREW**, in 1651, with William Smith, received from the Lygonia govt. a 500 a. gr., now in Scarb., east of Dunstan, 'now & forever hereafter to be called' Burlescombe. When the adj. 500 a. of Mr. Henry Watts, later the famous Vaughan or Storer farm, had come to Andrew Brown jr., the f. and s. owned 1000 a. Each petitioned Andros for 500 a. Jury 1665; gr.j. 1667; const. 1670; committee to get a min. 1682; selectm. 1682, 1686, 1687. Lists 232, 233, 237abd, 32, 319. Refugee first at Portsm. where in 1694 he mortg. his farm : in 1696 was in Boston, liv. with s. William. In 1663 Jonas Bailey's will remembered 'Andrew Brown's five suns.' In Boston during Philip's War, in his petn. for the release of his sons Andrew and John from garrison duty at Scarb., the scrivener had him plead for 'his wife and seven smale children.' The following Browns were all at Scarb., of whom Andrew, John, William and Elizabeth are explicitly proven ch: **Joseph**,

**Charles**, Lists 237a, 339. **Andrew**, b. about 1658. **John. Joshua**, b. ab. 1662. Dep. in 1715 that he was b. in Scarb. and liv. there ab. 30 yrs. **William. Samuel**. William and Samuel wit. deed Watts to Brown 1687. **Elizabeth**, m. Matthew Libby.

3 **LT. ANDREW**(2), b. ab. 1658, d. 4 July 1723, ag. 66 (grst.). Selectman in three towns. Was given Mr. Watts' farm for life support. Refugee in York, where his house was a garrison, and he had a pew in the meetingho. In Arundel with Joseph Storer he built a mill. Ensign 1687. Selectm. 1684, 1687, 1688; gr.j. 1698, 1699, 1704, 1705. Lists 237a, 239b, 38. M. Anne Allison(2); 2d 23 Jan. 1709-10 Sarah (Hill), wid. of William Priest. She d. in 1726. Ch: **Elizabeth**, m. John Stackpole. **Mary**, mar. Samuel Carr. **Catherine**, b. ab. 1689, m. Joshua Lassell. 6? ch. **Andrew**, b. 1691, d. 14 Mar. 1722, ag. 31 (grst.); m. in Boston 12 Dec. 1718 Mary Kneeland, who in 1754 was Mary Turner, Boston. 1 dau. **Matthew**, liv. 1720; soon d.s.p. *****Allison**, Lieut., b. 1697, d. 16 Apr. 1728, ag. 31 (grst.) Sarah (Smith) Stackpole dep. that her grandmo. d. soon aft. her uncle Allison's birth, and he was suckled by his aunt Libby. The first deputy from Arundel to the General Court, 1723. Interest. will 29 Mar. 1728. M. Hannah Scammon (Humphrey), who mar. 2d by 28 Mar. 1729 John Treworgy. 2 ch.

4 **ARTHUR**, Mr., by his own evid. was bred a merchant and liv. 'at Casco' from ab. 1634. In 1637 Mr. Arthur Browne and Mr. Arthur Macworth were both living access. to John Cousins, and later were partners in trade. In 1640 he was att. for Abraham Shurt, and when last ment., 1641, he had rem. eastward to Winneganee, near Pemaquid.

5 *****BENJAMIN**(14), was settled by his father in Seabrook. Selectman 1696, 1705, 1710, 1711. Lists 392b, 52, 396. Deeded to his sons in 1723, and d. ab. 1736. Rep. 1697. His w. Sarah was in 1851 called dau. of William Brown of Salis. by Asa W. Brown, who in 1868 said 'the m. of Benjamin is tradition solely, no record can be found to prove or disprove.' He said she d. ab. 1730 ag. nearly 90, but that Sarah Brown was b. 12 Apr. 1658. Ch: **William**, b. 5 June 1680, d. Sep. 1725. Will 1725–1726; m. 9 June 1701 Ann Heath, dau. of John and Sarah (Partridge), his wid. in 1764, Kensington. 11 ch. **Sarah**, b. 11 Sep. 1681, d. 30 Oct. 1684. **Benjamin**, b. 20 Dec. 1683, d. 9 Feb. 1766, So. Hampt., m. 7 Jan. 1718 Sarah Gove. 7 ch. **Elizabeth**, b. 16 July 1686, m. Benj. Green; liv. in Hampt. Falls; d. 14 Mar. 1748. **John**, b. 18 Mar. 1688, d. 14 Mar. 1748, Seabrook; m. 21 Jan. 1715 Abigail Johnson. 6 ch. **Jacob**, b. Mar. 1691; d. 23 Apr. 1762; m. 1st Mary Green; 2d Oct. 1737 Jemima

(Chandler) Rowell, wid. of Moses Rowell of Kingston. In 1715 his f. gave him land in 'a place called Shrewsbury patent,' but he settled in Hampt. Falls. 5 ch. **Stephen**, b. 17 July 1693, d. 1 Dec. 1723, m. 21 May 1722 Martha Heath. Lived in Kingston. 1 son. **Mary**, b. 1696, m. Thomas Cram jr. **Thomas**, b. 21 May 1699, d. Nov. 1765, Seabrook, m. 2 May 1729 Mehitable Towle (Joseph). 5 ch. **Jeremiah**, b. 20 Nov. 1701, d. June 1758, Seabrook; m. 3 Dec. 1728 Mary Weare. 4 ch.

6 **BENJAMIN**. Stratham. List 388.

7 **HENRY** Brown, James Orr and Edward Urine, Oyster River, Scotchmen, presum. some of Mr. V. Hill's 7 Scots, were adm. inhab. of Dover 1658. In 1662 they bot from Tho. Withers a 'farm' at Braveboat Harbor, lower Kit., and 50 a. of land northwest of it. With Tho. Doughty, another of them, they rem. to upper Kit. and to Saco Falls, perh. operating at both places 1667-1668. B. & O. sold out at Oyster River 1667-1669. Doughty having m. at Saco, B. & O. by 1675 had left him for Wells, where at first they got out logs for the Sayward mill, later for their own, at Mousam, now Kennebunk village, rememb. as late as 1738 as the Scotchmen's mill. Bourne's Wells has two pp. of entert. hist. of their wifeless lives in the howling wilderness, B., O. and Robert Stewart, bound by contract under seal (not found) to hang together till death and the last survivor to have what the others left, all vanishing together by 1690. But R. S. did not come from York to Wells until 1686 and liv. at Boston 1690-1715, while J. O., of Wells, logger and sawyer, sold his and H. B.'s gr. 8 Sep. 1692. Lists 356d, 361a, 363ac, 364, 365, 380, 28, 33, 266, 269b (1679, 1683). In 1686 H. B. and J. O. sued Mr. John Bray for defamation of the title of their Braveboat Harbor purchase. The descent of this title has not been traced, but the next lot southwest names the abuttors on a half-mile bound in 1715 Henry Brown & James Oare; in 1722 at the beginning of the description, 'Henry -Brooking- and James Oare;' at the end of the same desc., 'Mary Deering's bounds;' in 1728 'Col. Wm. Pep., Bray Deering, & Ebenezer Mores or Will Deerings.' York Deeds viii. 84; xi. 43; xiii. 151.

8 **HENRY**, N. H. Probate i. 419. See Crown.

9 **HENRY**, rated to Old Meet. Ho., Portsm., 1717; m. aft. 1715 Deborah Wills (Edw.), who by 1723 had gone (run?) away. By 1739 she was dead leaving only ch. **John**.

10 **JACOB**, ±32 in 1672, memb. of sheriff's force from Boston, compl. of Dr. Greenland for rescuing a prisoner, David (Campbill). List 82.

11 **JACOB**(14), liv. on the homestead; d. 13 Feb. 1740, ag. 87. Jury 1684, 1696; coroner's 1694; gr. 1695, 1698. Lists 52, 396,

399a. In 1739 he settled his est. on his ch. and d. in Rye 13 Feb. 1740; adm. gr. to Samuel of Hampton 26 Mar. 1740. M. Sarah Brookings(5). Ch: **John**, b. ab. 1684, d. Apr. 1747 Hampt. Falls; m. 15 Nov. 1706 Ruth Kelley. Will names wife, 4 ch. and dec. son's 4 ch. **Samuel**, b. 4 Nov. 1686, liv. on his grf.'s homestead, d. 14 Jan. 1772; m. Elizabeth Maloon. 7 ch. **Abraham**, d. 15 Feb. 1769 Hampt. Falls; m. Argentine Cram 6 Feb. 1717-8. 6 ch. **Joshua**, b. 1 Apr. 1691, d. 10 Dec. 1783 North Hampt.; m. 1st Rachel Sanborn; 2d Sarah Leavitt. 4 ch. **Sarah**, b. 21 Dec. 1721 Philip Griffin; d. in Chester. **Jacob**, b. 22 Dec. 1695, d. bef. his f.; m. 16 Nov. 1721 Joanna Jones. 2 daus. **Abigail**, b. 3 Mar. 1698, m. 1st 27 Mar. 1718 John Dowst; 2d 16 Dec. 1724 Amos Knowles. **Jonathan**, b. 24 Feb. 1700, d. 10 July 1766 Kensington; m. 27 Feb. 1725 Joanna Abba; 2d aft. 1753 Joanna, wid. of Joshua Brown, trader, of Kingston. 10 ch. **Jeremiah**, bp. 28 June 1702; d. ab. 1780 Saco; m. Elizabeth Moody. 8(?) ch.

12 **REV. JAMES**, perh. the youth of 17, s. of Joseph of Southampton, who came in -The James- 1635, perh. same apprent. to Rev. Richard Mather, is said to have preached at Portsm. from 1654 or earlier to 1656. That town in 1656 voted to engage Rev. Samuel Dudley. The town voted to distrain for Mr. Brown's pay 10 July 1655, and again 14 Apr. 1656, when Richard Sherburne agreed to entertain him. List 323. In 1656 of Newbury he is called 'late teacher' at Portsm.; in 1674 he was still at Newb.

13 **JAMES**, traveling glazier, from Ipsw. List 331a.

14 **JOHN**, b. 1589? An original planter of Hampton, Oct. 1638, he was among the half dozen dignitaries granted a 'farm,' and in 1653 paid the third largest tax. Savage discredited his age at d., 28 Feb. 1687, ag. 98 yrs., but thinks he may have come on -The Elizabeth- from London 17 Apr. 1635, ag. 40, discussing the matter under three Johns. Selectm. 1651, 1656; jury 1663, 1666; grandj. 1665; tythingman 1664; freed from training in 1662. Lists 291ab, 392ab, 49, 54, 398. W. Sarah d. 6 July (Hampton Falls says June) 1672. List 393a. Ch: **Sarah**, m. 13 Mar. 1661 John Poor. **John**, ±38 in 1682; given land by his f. in 1666; in 1669 was lying sick at his sister's house at Charlestown under Dr. Chickering's hands. Served long in Philip's War. List 395. D. 29 Aug. 1683. **Benjamin. Elizabeth**, m. 23 Oct. 1669 Isaac Marston. **Jacob**, b. ab. 1653. **Mary**, b. 13 Sep. 1655. **Thomas**, b. 14 July 1657. **Stephen**, killed in the Black Point battle 29 June 1677; adm. gr. in Middlesex to br. John Poor of Charlestown.

15 **JOHN**, Pemaquid, smith, whose name is a thousand times in print, chiefly because of a forged Ind. deed antedated nearly a century. His earliest contemp. ment. is (not 1625 but) 1 Nov. 1639, the date of the Ind. deed of the lower part of Woolwich to Edw. Bateman and 'John Brown sometime of Pemaquid.' In 1664, selling out to Bateman, he was again 'of Pemaquid.' His s. John, b. ab. 1636, dep. in 1721 that he liv. at New Harbor, Pemaquid, until ab. 30, when he went back 8 miles to live on land his bro.-in-law Pierce had bot of the Indians (1642). One lease to his father, by Mr. Shurt and Robert Knight, had been assigned to William Bickford(24) by 1661. Mr. Knight came over at the expiration of Mr. Shurt's 5-yr. contract in 1640. We may conj. how long bef. 1639 John Brown came. Robert Allen(11), back in England in 1658, dep. that he had kn. one John Brown of Newharbour in New Eng. 17 yrs. (the earliest contemp. ment. of New Harbor), and had often been told by him that his father was -Richard- Brown of Barton Regis, co. Glouc., and that he married with Margaret, d. of Francis Hayward of Bristol, wayte player. The occa. of this dep. has not been ascert. Allen calls him a mason but he is called smith in deeds here. The hundred of Barton Regis, containing four parishes, one of them Margotsfield, makes the northerly suburbs of Bristol. John Brown, s. of -Thomas- Browne of Margotsfield, was appr. 20 Nov. 1611 to Robert North, blacksm., and was duly made citizen of Bristol 12 Feb. 1624[5. James Phippes, s. of Wm. Phippes, b. in Margotsfield, was apprent. 1 Mar. 1625-6 to John Brown of Bristol, blacksm. and -Joan-, his wife, for 8 yrs. Discrep. have not been reconc., but the father of Sir Wm. Phips, James of Woolwich, was a gunsmith. See Cox(33). In Philip's War the Browns escaped to Boston, where the f. liv. with his eldest son. Conflict. untrust. dep. leave us uncert. whether he or his wife came back. Lists 11, 13, 121. Ch: **Elizabeth**, m. Richard Pierce. **Margaret**, mar. Alexander Gould, Morris Chamblet. **John**, b. 1635. **Francis**, wit. Ind. deed 1666, sold land at New Harbor, last ment. 1674, List 15. **Mary**, m. Richard Redding. **Emme** or Nem, b. 1645, m. Nicholas Dennen.

16 **JOHN**, Scotchman, b. ab. 1631, m. in Boston 24 Apr. 1655 Esther, d. of Thomas Makepeace, whose will 30 June 1666 rememb. them and their 5 ch. He rem. from Cambridge ab. 1663 to Marlboro, where he sold out in 1678 and rem. to East Deering, Falmouth. Gr.j. 1683, selectman 1687. Lists (74?), 34, 225a, (228b), 228c. In the second war he esc. to Watertown. Will 20 Nov. 1697 names 4 sons and 5 sons-in-law, incl. John Adams, Tho. Darley or Darby, and John Hartshorn. Wid. Esther in 1699 deed-

ed to s. Joseph. Ch: **Joseph**, b. Cambridge 8 Feb. 1655-6, k. by a cart 24 Sep. 1671. **Elizabeth**, b. 26 Mar. 1657, m. 10 Jan. 1677 John Gustin. **Sarah**, b. 18 July 1661. **Mary** b. 19 Dec. 1662. **John**, b. Marlboro 27 Nov. 1664; wit. Falm. 1681, Y. D. xiii. 228; Falm. petn. 1689. List 228c; liv. 1697. Poss. (23) or John of Marshfield, shipwright, who bot and sold the neighb. Andrews farm 1712-1718, wit. Thomas Brown. **Hester**, b. and d. 1667. **Thomas**, b. 1669, Falm. petn. 1689. Lists 228cd; liv. 1697. See John. **Daniel**, b. 1671, liv. 1697. **Deborah**, b. 1673, m. Jeremiah Meacham of Salem. **Abigail**, b. 9 Mar. 1675. **Joseph**, b. 1677, Dea. in Watertown. See Bond 145, 731.

17 **JOHN**(15), ±85 in Feb. 1720-1. Ab. 1665 he rem. from New Harbor and made a settlement on the east bank of the Damaris. River on land bot of the Ind. by his bro.-in-law Pierce. As honest as his only son was not, he took oath in 1721 that he had never heard of Margaret Hilton's deed until lately and that his f. never claimed the back country, and in his deed to his s. John he partic. excluded it. This was shortly bef. his death at Framingham. In Philip's War he escaped to Boston, but soon went back. Lists 162, 164. In the next war he again fled to Boston and was one of the wit. against Lt. John Jordan. Ch: **John**, called only s. by his father, sisters unk. Drowned in Broad Bay in 1746, ag. 70, by one dep. in 1766. Undist. from other J. B.'s until his m. in Boston 16 Mar. 1703 to Ann Dorrell. Folsom says that in Dummer's War he had a garrison at Saco Falls on the east bank; by deeds he was there 1700-1729, altho drifting about raising small sums by warranty deeds of vast tracts. In 1729-30 his w. was Sarah, 'alias Sarah Joy,' app. Sarah (Nock), wid. of Ephraim. In 1730 he was of 'Damariscotta near Pemaquid.' He 'stayed on his father's land until nearly perished for food and then came over' to Dr. Winslow's house on the so. side of the river, later at Mr. Wm. Vaughan's. In Jan. 1733-4, of New Harbor, he deeded to his 'kinsman & nephew' (app. on his 1st wife's side) Joseph Morse, from Boston, baker, 14,000 a. of the John Brown claim for life support.

18 **JOHN**, Isles of Shoals, ±36 in 1673. List 304 (1668-9). One Brown mar. Martha (Matthews) Snell.

19 **JOHN**, Portsm. cor. jury 1671. List 327b.

20 **JOHN**(2), soldier in 1676, taxed in 1681, dec. in 1696, leaving sons **John** and **Samuel**. Lists 237ab, 238a. M. Rebecca Boaden(3). Fisherman having his house at Marblehead, on the 'Lookout.' His last fishing voyage was under Joseph Hallett, himself and Ambrose Boaden sr. shoremen. Adm. gr. to wid. 17 Sep. 1695. Adm. on her est.

gr. 17 Nov. 1725. Ch: **John**, fisherman Marbleh., m. 6 Nov. 1718 Rebecca Frost of Salem. Est. adm. 1726. 2 sons rec. **Elizabeth**, m. 27 Nov. 1712 John Neal s. of Francis from Me., wid. 1747. **Rebecca**, m. James Andrews of Marbleh., shoreman, by 1725; both liv. 1739. **Samuel**, shoreman, m. 18 Oct. 1726 Deborah Main. Will 1730—1740. One dau. Mary or Mercy. **Sarah**, m. 5 Dec. 1715 Wm. Dagworthy; both liv. 1739. **Benjamin**, coaster, Marbleh., m. 17 Nov. 1719 Sarah Dennis; both liv. 1744.

21 **JOHN**. Saco witness 1662. York Deeds xvi. 70.

22 **JOHN**, in Wells ct. 25 May 1686 complainant against Edw. Doyle for stealing silver from his chest. Maj. John Davis paid Doyle's fine to be repaid in work. Selectman of York 1696. Jury 1683, 1685; gr.j. 1686. See (16, 20).

23 **JOHN**, ag. 64 in Oct. 1730, poss.(?) s. of (16), b. 27 Nov. 1664. Both men bot parts of the Tho. Wise - Nathl. Wallis 200 a. farm on the south bank of the Presumpscot River, Falm. This man, liv. in Glouc. ab. 1716, sent his deed to be shown to the Com. on Eastern Claims, dated 20 Mar. 1681, from Tho. Blashfield, 50 a. fronting the ocean, and in 1719, of Glouc., yeoman, w. Elizabeth, sold it. In the interim he had come down to Falm. to secure his right as a settler under Danforth. In 1730 he made several dep. conc. Falm. Foreside and the Ingersolls. Lists (228b?), 229. His wife, mo. of Sarah, was d. of John Ingersoll. Heirship deeds 1750-54 indic. 9 ch. incl: **Sarah**, m. John Wotton of Glouc., fisherman, both liv. 1731; dau. Sarah, liv. 1750. **John**, eldest son, shipwright, of Glouc. in 1722 bot of Thomas Sanders the Anthony Libby - John Corney 60 a. at Barberry Creek, So. Portland, which with his father's gr. included Brown's Hill, Lygonia. He deeded 1749-1759 to sons John, mariner, and Elisha. **William**, of Glouc., fisherman. **Elisha**, of Glouc., coaster.

24 **JOHN**, Exeter. List 376b (1725). In 1753 John of Brentwood had lost his s. John leaving widow Anna and infant Mary. In 1732 Elizabeth B. was Clement Moody's dau.

25 **JOSEPH**, York wit. 1713. Y. D.

26 **JOSEPH** and Elizabeth, Portsm., had **Mary**, b. 1736.

27 **JOSHUA**(2), remained at Portsm. among his wife's relations. Lists 330def, 334a, 337. Bot land there in 1705. M. Rebecca Libby who was wid. in 1722 and liv. in 1732. Ch: **Andrew**, farmer. When the Eliot ch. was formed, 22 June 1721, the first record of baptism is 'Andrew Brown and his children.' Had had Scarb. grants in 1720. Original memb. of Scarb. ch., organized 26 June 1728. M. Susanna. Will 6 Dec. 1737—3 Mar.

1740-1. 6 ch. **Charles,** Portsm. List 339. Liv. 1756. M. 14 Nov. 1711 Mary Mitchell. 6(?) ch. **Samuel,** weaver. List 339. Had Scarb. gr. in 1720 and later liv. there. M. 9 Sep. 1716 Bethia Libby, who joined Scarb. ch. in 1743. 5(?) ch., some of whom settled at Bath. **Mary. Hannah,** m. 18 June 1724 John Benson. **Sarah,** m. 11 Nov. 1722 Wm. Libby. **Ephraim.**

28 **MR. NICHOLAS,** mariner, in N. H. ct. 1647 sued Joseph Austin for not delivering plank. In Me. the same and fol. yr. he was twice sued for debt. See Asp. 47. Adm. 10 May 1648 to his partner Mr. John Seeley. Inv. £223.01.08 (⅓ his partner's). Appr: F. Matthews, N. Shepleigh, Wm. Seavey, Humphrey Lux John Rayes.

29 **NICHOLAS,** constable Isles of Shoals 1681; gr.j. 1694, 1695; bondsman 1705. One Nicholas m. Portsm. No. Church 4 Oct. 1708 Elizabeth Sampson. Rated to Old Meet. Ho. 1717.

30 **RICHARD,** Pemaquid surrender. List 127.

31 **SAMUEL,** ±32 in 1672, with (10) and sheriff from Boston. List 82. Wit. for Robert Marshall 1671, 1672.

32 **SAMUEL,** No. Yarm. List 214.

33 **THOMAS**(14), d. 29 June 1744, Hampton; m. Abial Shaw who d. 21 Dec. 1739, ag. 77. Gr.j. 1693. Lists 395, 396. Ch: **Thomas,** b. 14 Dec. 1686, d. 7 June 1766; m. Dorcas Fanning, 5 ch., only 2 in will. **Joseph,** b. 30 Jan. 1689, d. 19 Mar. 1759, Rye; m. Elizabeth Moulton. 7 or 8 ch. **Sarah,** b. 3 Apr. 1691; m. Joshua Towle. **Elizabeth,** b. 21 Apr. 1694, m. 31 Jan. 1723 Solomon Dowst. **Ebenezer,** d. 20 Oct. 1780, Kensington; m. 1st 27 Feb. 1724 Sobriety Moulton; 2d Mary Flanders. 14 ch. **Josiah,** b. 15 Feb. 1701, d. 4 Dec. 1790, Kensington; m. 1st 1 Jan. 1724 Elizabeth Towle; 2d 5 Dec. 1744 Mary Bradbury. 10 ch.

34 **THOMAS,** Newcastle, mariner. He mar. Sarah (Jordan) Conner, widow of Samuel(4), and in 1742 was one of the Jordan heirs suing Joshua Moody. His wid., liv. in Rye in 1759, gave a warranty deed with her sis. Cleare, w. of John Martin of Newcastle.

35 **WILLIAM**(2), mariner, app. keeping his fam. in Boston bef. Scarb. was depopulated in 1690. Prob. his widow was Mary Brown who dep. in Boston in June 1741, ag. ab. 82, that she was born in Scarb., knew the Algers, was there when Robert Nichols was killed, but was rem. to Boston bef. the Algers were killed. His ch. perhaps were: **Mary. William,** b. 30 Dec. 1688. Wm. Brown, cordwainer, of Boston sold the equity in his grfr.'s farm to the mortgagee. **Samuel,** b. 3 Dec. 1691. **Rebecca,** b. 5 Apr. 1700. **Jeremiah,** b. 20 May 1703.

36 **WILL,** Dedham soldier. List 267b.

**Browsen,** Henry, York wit. 1714. Y. D. 8.175.

**BRUCE.** 1 **James,** Hampton 1660 (drunk), 1667 with Peter Johnson wit. Boulter-Souter, Hampton. O. A. Haverhill 28 Nov. 1677.

2 **JOHN,** Portsm., Frenchman, struck in the back by the mate of -The America-, died. Inquest 14 Mar. 1689-90. List 333a.

3 **(MICHAEL),** misr. of -Brand- (Brawn). P. & C. ii. 5.

**BRUEN,** *Obadiah, bap. 25 Dec. 1606 in Tarvin, east of Chester, bought into the Shrewsbury patent. List 386. Sprung from an old landed family, there was printed the year after he came over a tiny book on his father, -The Very Singular Life of John Bruen Esq. of Bruen Stapleford, Cheshire-. Bruen-Stapleford is a township in Tarvin. The book says that Obadiah and his sister Mary have gone to America. He came first to Plymouth, 1640, Gloucester by 1642, New London, Conn. 1651-1667, then to Newark, N. J. with his son. Rep. often both in Mass. and Conn. In Mass. he was on the committee to compare the printed law book with the original laws. See N. E. Reg. xix. 107, -Ancestry of John Barber White-, p. 203.

**Bruens**(?) (Burrine? Brewer?), George. List 227.

**Brundread,** Henry, Piscataqua, ±19 in 1702.

**BRYANT,** common So. of Eng. name.

1 ——— (Bryant), m. Hannah Stover (Sylvester), Scit.

2 ——— (Bryant), hus. 1721-5 of Elizabeth (Barnell or Moore) Cutts(9) who in 1747 was wife of John Saville jr., Boston, feltmaker.

3 ——— (Bryant), m. Eleanor Hill (Jos.), Greenland.

4 **DAVID** (Bryant), cond.Ind. gr. Scarb. 1720.

5 **DENNIS** (Brian), ±22 in 1679 was at Oyster River helping John Drew and Zachariah Field. Taxed 1681.

6 **GEORGE** (Bryant) and Jemima Jewell m. Portsm., 19 Feb. 1729-30. Jemima, single woman, of Newcastle, in ct. 1763.

7 **JAMES** (Bryant), in 1704, shipped under Capt. Richard Waterhouse for England, taken by a Spanish privateer; he was in jail 24 mos. in Bilboa as a pledge for the ship's ransom. In 1712 his w. Honor was going out scrubbing. In 1718, James, Newcastle fisherman, bot a house. In 1764, still of Newcastle, she q.c. to her son Walter Bryant, Esq., the estates of her hus. James and her s. James, 'for his care of me the last 30 years.' Kn. ch: **Walter,** housewright, became a noted surveyor, selectm. of Durham 1736, Newmarket 1738-1764. He m. Elizabeth Folsom. Ch. **James,** Portsm. sailor 1755, d.s.p.

8 **JOHN** (Bryant 10), Scarb. Lists 338bc. Will 1759-1760 ment. w. Mary, ch. Elea-

nor Watson, Temperance Harford, grandch. Flye (ch. of d. Mary, who m. John Flye 2 Jan. 1736-7) and ch. of son John, dec. (will Aug.–Oct. 1750), incl. Samuel Davis Bryant.

9 **JOHN** (Bryant), the forger, Sc., Saco, Bid., app. from Plym. Co., m. 1st Hannah Sands, d. of Patience (Gibbins); 2d 1 Aug. 1748 Mary (Cole 17), wid. of John McLucas from York. Ch. by both wives.

10 **ROBERT** (Braines), b. ab. 1654, in 1681 was an apprent. of Nehemiah Partridge, but had left him for Chris. Kenniston. Lists 62, 67, 68, 332b, 335a, 336b, 338ab. Wife Mary, Lists 335a, 338b. D. on homestead 1741. Ch: **Robert** (Bryant), apprent. to Wm. Philbrook, adult 1707, in 1742 was of Durham, cooper. Lists 338ac. W. Sarah, List 338b. Ch. **John**, adult 1707. **Abraham**, Greenl. 1742. **Elisha**, b. ab. 1692, m. 31 July 1717 Armon Davis, 2d 16 Apr. 1725 Abigail Morgan. **Mary. Rebecca. Charity.** These three presum. the same m. in Greenland, Mary to Daniel Davis 4 Dec. 1711, Rebecca to Wm. Davis 19 July 1717, Charity to Edward Hopkins, 23 Jan., 1718-9, 2d 23 June 1726 Moses Clough. **Hannah**, wife of Philip Harry of Newmarket in 1742. **Abigail**, m. Benj. Kenniston. **Deborah**, acc. Nathl. Watson jr. in 1735, wife of John Brazel in 1742.

11 **THOMAS** (Bryan) 'and his partners,' fishermen, bef. 1666 had bot land at Cape Porpus. Y. D. ii. 146.

**Bryce**, Patrick, traveller, wit. to Alexander Cooper's will 1683-4.

**Brye**, Philip, Sagadahoc 1674. List 15.

**Buckland**, see Butland and Bucknell.

**BUCKLEY, Richard**, appar. came from Boston as Commissary in Second War. Doc. Hist. v. 263, 299, (vi. 452). The will of Sarah Binding of Chartsey, Surrey, widow, will 1687, gives £100 to dau. Sarah, w. of Mr. Richard Buckley of Boston. In Newcastle or Portsm. he kept a dry goods store. O. A. Great Isl. 1696. Lists 68, 315ab. Of Portsm., adm. gr. 7 Jan. 1706-7 to wid. Sarah. 'Mrs. Buckley & house' taxed Portsm. 170—. By 1708 she was of Boston, suing eastern debts. S. B. and William Graham m. 5 Feb. 1711, ch. 1714, 1721. Will 1740 unexam.

**BUCKNELL**, pecul. to Devon. Four, -nell, -nall, -nill, in Mid. England.

1 **GEORGE**, ag. (42?) in Jan. 1672-3, ag. 56 in 1676, a farmer on the inside of Ball or Rutherford's Isl. (appar. called Holmes's by Silvanus Davis), and appar. kn. by fishermen as Geo. Buck of Corbin's Sound. His name occurs: Buck-nell, -land, -head. In 1672 Chris. Smith, a coaster, ack. in court a debt 'to Geo. Bucknall but Geo. Buckland I never knew.' He wrote -Bucknell-. About Pemaquid by 1647. In 1651 he was voyaging with Mr. Elbridge as far as Casco Bay. Lists 10,

12, 14, 15, 80. Wife Elizabeth. List 10. Ch. unkn. exc. presum: **Richard**. List 15. Dep. ag. 20 at same time with father.

2 **ROGER, Richmond** Island 1635. List 21. Wages paid to wife in Eng.

3 **WILLIAM**, m. in Greenland 9 Apr. 1717 Sarah Whidden.

**BUCKNER, Charles**, apothecary, Dover 1657. Savage says schoolmaster. Clerk of the Writs (aut.). Lists 356bcefg. By 1668 he was of Boston, with w. Mary, selling out in Dover. In Boston during sessions of the General Court he wit. documents with Isaac Addington. Adm. to wid. Mary 25 Aug. 1684. She was presum. Mary (Hunting), dau. of Elder John of Dedham, who m. in 1653 Wm. Jay of Boston and was called Buckner in her mother's will 1676. Israel Wight of Boston in 1664 deeded to Christopher Palmer a ho. and 2 a. of Charles Buckner's in Dover.

**Bucksan**, John, Dover, 165—. List 355a.

**BUDEZERT, John**, Mr. (also found in print Budesert, Budisect, Budefoot), of Scarb. in 1664 suing John Mayer for slander, and still there in 1669. List 26. In Oct. 1668 he succ. Richard Foxwell and Chris. Pickett as adm. estate of Philip Griffin of Scarb. and Salis., whose wid. Agnes (Ann) he m. A gr. at Edgartown, Martha's Vineyard, was made to him 15 Dec. 1671, but he soon d.; adm. gr. in Suff. Co. 27 Aug. 1672 to wid. Agnes of Salis., where she d. 29 Nov. 1682.

**BUGG, John**, Isles of Shoals, Portsm. 1669, Wells 1685. In 1672 tax list J. B. follows John Partridge and Edw. Clark; Clark's estate sued joint note of John Smith and J. B. 1673 of Shoals. Wells innholder 1686-87. Lists 304, 33.

**BULGAR, Richard**, b. ab. 1608, bricklayer, early at Boston and Roxbury, was dism. to the church at Exeter 6 Jan. 1638-9; in N. H. lived prin. at Exeter, but of Dover, planter, 1640. Lieut. 1641. Lists 373, 374a, 376ab, 377. In 1642 he wit. deed from Ralph Blaisdell of Salis. to Robt. Knight of York, and in 1646-7, of Boston, was acting at York for Henry Walton of Portsmouth, R. I. He rem. to Portsm., R. I., by 1650, was solicitor genl. for that colony in 1656, liv. there 1679. Wife Lettice (Underhill), dau. of John and Leonora (Pawley), stepdau. of Richard Morris. Ch: **John**, bp. Boston 20 Apr. 1634.

**BULL**, common Mid. Eng. surname.

1 **DIXY**, York patentee. Lists 271, 272. Presum. the same that tried piracy about Pemaquid in 1632. See -Pirates of the N. E. Coast-, pp. 20-43.

2 **JOHN**(3). Lists 271, 272.

3 **SETH**, London. York patentee. Lists 271, 272.

4 **THOMAS**. List 237b. App. error for Ball.

**BULLARD,** a rare English surname.
1 **AUGUSTINE,** Portsm., shipmaster, taxed 1690, retailer's lic. 1693. Lists 335a, 330d, 96. He m. 12 Oct. 1693 Hannah (Riddan), wid. of Henry Dyer(3). Will 24 Oct. 1706—8 Sep. 1709 gave his est. to his w. to bring up his son, except the real est. to his son Benj. and steps. Henry Dyer. 5 s. each to bros. Benj. and Jasper of Barbadoes. Wid. here in 1711. Ch: **Benjamin,** in 1729 was of Bridgetown, Barb., merchant.
2 **JACOB** (Bollward), in 1668 brot suit in Me. Ct. for services. Likely Bullard of Watertown, an aged blind person in 1710, 'unhappily sent from another province' back to his native town, where he was buried 21 Nov. 1715. His land gr. for Narragansett service was claimed by a nephew Joseph Ball.
**BULLIVANT, Benjamin,** physician, Attorney General under Andros, in Me. Ct. 1686 wit. against a York common drunk.
**Bullock,** John, Pemaquid const. Lists 124, 125. Appar. same of Salem, injured in Philip's War.

**BULLY,** common in So. Devon, Nicholas recurrent. Bulley, a chapelry in Glouc. See also Bailey (6, 3, 4).
1 **JOHN**(2), adm. in Suff. Co. 7 Feb. 1678-9 to wid. Rebecca. Ch: **Sarah,** b. Boston 26 July 1677.
2 **NICHOLAS,** fisherman, early at Saco, see Bailey(6). Bot house 1650. Lists 243a, 24, 244e, 245, 249. Will Suff. 7 Sep.—1 Nov. 1678. Goody Buly. List 246. Ch: **Nicholas. Anne,** m. 1653 Ambrose Berry(1), William Scadlock, John Carter(4). **Grace,** b. ab. 1636, m. John Boaden(7). **Tamsen,** bur. 30 July 1661. **Elizabeth,** m. 24 Jan. 1669-70 Tho. Doughty. **John.**
3 **NICHOLAS**(2), town gr. Saco 1653. Lists 24, 244d, 245. Adm. to wid. 5 July 1664. James Harmon, who had been liv. on his land under bond, surrend. it to J. Henderson in 1667. M. July 1652 Ellen Booth(3), who m. 2d 29 June 1664 John Henderson. Ch. unk. exc: **Abigail,** b. 1 Feb. 1654-5, m. Peter Henderson. **Nicholas,** b. 1 Feb. 1661-2.

**BUNKER,** rare Eng. name, Bucks, Devon.
1 **JAMES,** coroner's jury, Kit., 1647, ±50 in 1678. Worked for Mrs. Treworgy 1648-9. In Dover tax list (cancelled) 1650. Wit. with Wm. Follett 1652, joint gr. together 1653. Gr.j. 1657, 1659. Lists 354c, 355ab, 356a, 361ab, 363ac, 47, 49, 57, 94, 368a. His garrison withstood the Ind. in 1694. Will 14 Oct. 1697—24 June 1698 names wife Sarah (Nute), List 367b, and part of his ch: **James. Joseph. John. Mary,** m. Tho. Drew(14).
2 **JAMES**(1), was his father's exec. and had the homestead. Const. 1698, 1699. Lists 66, 368ab, 369. D. 1722, adm. 5 May 1724 to

sons James and Joseph. He mar. 1st Anne Thomas; 2d Martha Downs(6), who m. by Dec. 1725 John Mackelroy and was bap. on a sick bed in Dover 1744; both liv. 1750. Ch: **James,** cordwainer, will 14 May 1759 names w. Sarah (Giles). 7 ch. **Benjamin,** m. Abigail. Both liv. in Brunswick 1740, in Dover 1741. **Clement,** m. 24 Mar. 1738-9 Rebecca Drew(6). Liv. in Durham 1765. **Patience,** m. John Drew(6 jr.). **Love,** m. Tho. Millet, d. 3 Nov. 1763. Of 13 ch. 7 d. of (diphtheria?). **Joseph,** will 9 Sep. 1778, bur. 18 July 1784. List 369. M. 1st Ann Giles, 2d, named in will, Elizabeth. 5 ch. By 2d w: **Elijah,** weaver, m. Judith who bore 11 ch., the youngest at 53. She joined Dover ch. in 1756 and was dism. to Sanford in 1791.
3 **JOHN**(1), k. by Ind. 8 July 1707; adm. to s. Zachariah 27 Apr. 1737. M. Dorcas Field(12), his wid. in 1718. Lists 57, 96, 358a. Ch: **John,** b. 16 July 1696, m. 5 Feb. 1720-1 Hannah Drew(14), who m. 2d Joseph Jackson. 2 ch. rec. but app. d.y. **Sarah,** b. 20 Oct. 1699, m. Tho. Pinkham. In 1755 her grantees sued for ⅕ of her father's land. **Daniel,** b. 22 Oct. 1702, m. Elizabeth; liv. Dover 1752. **Zachariah,** b. 25 Feb. 1707-8, m. Deborah Varney. Adm. to son Dodavah in 1757. 7 or m. ch. **Elizabeth,** twin with last; app. she or a sis. m. a cous. Daniel Jacobs. At his house the Dover min. 13 Nov. 1744 bap. 2 of his ch., 5 of Zachariah Bunker's, 3 of Tho. Pinkham's.
4 **JOSEPH**(1), d. early, adm. 29 July 1717 to son-in-law Joshua Davis. His widow Mary m. in 1705 Richard Denbo, and became the Quaker preacher. List 368a. The homestead fell to 5 ch., birth dates by the trad. Friends' rec: **Esther,** b. Apr. 1693, m. Joshua Davis(40); appar. her name in 1748 was misread -Dam. **Mary,** b. June 1697 by the Friends' rec., 24 June 1698 by her own fam. rec.; m. 20 May 1718 Clement Drew(14). **Lydia,** b. Oct. 1699, unm. 1748. **Sarah,** b. Dec. 1702, m. John Clements(4). **Relief,** b. 6 July 1725 James Burnham(2).
**Bunt,** George, boatswain, Richmond Island. List 21. **Son** mentioned.

**BURDETT.** 1 **Edward,** living at the Shapleigh house, Kit., bef. 1645. See Messant.
2 **GEORGE,** Rev., b. ab. 1602, bred at Trinity Coll., Dublin, and grad. 1624 at Sidney Sussex Coll., Cambridge, he had been preaching at Great Yarmouth, Norfolk, when, under discipline, he aband. wife and ch. and came to N. E. After two years at Salem, preaching or 'working with his hands,' he came to Dover 1637 and success. intrigued there until discov., then at York until Mr. Tho. Gorges arrived, then back via Pemaquid. A desc. in this country traced a prom. Irish fam. from him. Anne Messant, presum. some rel. to him, as otherwise, living

with him her reput. would have collap., m. Edw. Godfrey. A talented exponent of free love, under cover of antinomianism, his ch. are naturally unkn. Wife Susan, by whom **George**, bp. at Great Yarmouth 1 May 1634, and other ch. supported by the corporation. By Mary Purington, York, (disclaimed in her husband's will) **Sarah**, b. 1641, became the heir of her stepfather. Maj. John Davis(18), and m. John Penwell.

**Burdis**, Ann, ±22 in 1672, wit. against Tho. Parker.

**BURGESS**, common surname in Mid. and So. Eng.

1 **ANN** (Burgis), b. ab. 1650, servant of Samuel Wentworth 1671.

2 **BENJAMIN** (Birdges), wit. will of James Smith, Berwick, 1687.

3 **JAMES**, b. ab. 1654, Newcastle wit. 1672. O. A. Newc. 1696. Lists 312e, 315c.

4 **JOHN**, of Westly (Westerleigh, county Glouc.?), made his will at Richmond Isl. on a fishing voyage, 11 Apr. 1627, w. Joanna exec., sons **Robert, John, William**. Wit: John Witheridge, James Forde, Edward Nott. Proved 24 May 1628 by Joanna Burgess alias Bray.

5 **RICHARD**, York 1643 or earlier, there liv. away from his wife 1653; servant of Lt. Davis 1659. By grants and purch. owned land in various parts of the town to 1673, he and partners proprs. 1665. List 273.

**BURKES**. 1 **Henry** (Berke), b. ab. 1655, dealing with Henry Kirke in 1678 (N.H.).

2 **WALTER** (also Burcks), tanner, York, was completing his indent. with George Broughton, Kittery, in 1680; that yr. got judgm. vs. Benj. Barnard, most of it to be pd. to James Smith. Of York by 1685, liv. 16 Apr. 1706; had placed his prop., incl. tanyard, in hands of Sergt. Arthur Bragdon and Rev. Mr. Moody with instructions what to do. No wife or ch. kn.

**BURLEIGH**, James, b. 10 Feb. 1659 in Ipsw., bot land in Exeter (now 'Bayside' Newfields) in 1694. He m. 25 May 1685 Rebecca Stacey who predec. him. His sons by agreem. settled his est. 20 Feb. 1723-4. Five of them had grants in 1725. Ch: **William**, b. 27 Feb. 1692-3, m. Eleanor Johnson, d. of Ens. John and Hannah (Haines). D. in Stratham 11 May 1769. Lists 368b, 376b. Ch. **Joseph**, b. 6 Apr. 1695, m. Mary Stevens, d. of Edw. and Mary (Lawrence). Adm. Mar. 1761. Ch. **Thomas**, b. 5 Apr. 1697, making 3 b. in Ipsw.; m. 26 Dec. 1720 Dorothy Lyford. Settled in Nottingham. **James**, b. in Exeter. **Josiah**, m. Greenland 25 Feb. 1724-5 Hannah Lewis. Will 3—25 Feb. 1756. 4 ch. **Giles**, m. 9 Dec. 1727 Elizabeth Joy of Salis. Will proved in 1761. 5 ch.

**BURNELL**. 1 **Samuel**, Monhegan 1689. See Dollen.

2 **TOBIAS**, Mr. John Pennell's mate, drowned. Was engaged to Bysha Lux. Adm. 16 Jan. 1674-5 to John Clark, Wm. Lux and Edward Carter; bef. 29 June 1675 to Abel Porter in Suff. Co.; 4 Mar. 1675-6 to John Clark and Edward Carter; 31 Oct. 1677 to Humphrey Wills who brought P. A. from a sister Agnes Burnell of Alphington, Devon.

**BURNETT**. 1 **Deborah**, Boston, ±70 in Sep. 1737. Kept house at Sheepscot for John Mason's wid. who m. Allen; James Mason waited on deponent at her marriage; knew Elizabeth Gent and son Thomas and their house. One Joanna Burnet m. Wm. Sentall, Boston, 21 June 1708.

2 **FREDERICK**, Pemaquid gar. 1689. List 126.

3 **GEORGE**, drunk at Geo. Walton's inn, 1657.

4 **JOHN**, Boston, m. Deborah Rogers(Wm.), the Kennebec deponent, she ag. 56 (sic) in 1734, liv. 1738. He liv. 1724. 5 ch. rec. Boston 1696-1707, and most of their mar. Suff. Prob. 1729, 1738, unexam.

**BURNHAM**, name of 11 places Norfolk to Somerset.

1 **JAMES**, 'late soldier at Wells,' acc. Oct. Term 1710 by Elizabeth Denmark as father of James Burnham of Arundel, who m. Grace Dalzell, and was stepson of Peter Rich. See Denmark(1), Maine Wills, N. E. Reg. lxxv. 115, 48-9, 108-9.

2 **LT. JEREMIAH**(5), gr.j. 1692, 95, 97, 99. Lists 52, 57, 62, 94, 353, 358b, 367a, 368ab. Adm. 5 June 1718 to s. John. He m. Temperance Bickford(12); 2d Mary (Diamond 4) Spinney, who returned to Kit., her will 4 Dec. 1733—12 Mar. 1734-5. Ch: **John**, Lists 368b, 369; widower 9 Jan. 1717-8 when he m. Lydia Chesley(3). Adm. 30 May 1749 to s. John. 5 ch. **Hannah**, b. 13 May 1690, m. Col. Samuel Smith. **James**, m. 1st 27 Dec. 1713 Sarah Rogers; 2d 6 July 1725 Relief Bunker(4). In 1748 James and Relief q.c. her father Joseph Bunker's est. 1 son bap. **Robert**, Lists 368b, 369; m. 14 May 1714 Elizabeth Smith (Capt. John); d. 1759, leaving wid. and 5 ch., adm. 30 July 1760 to s. Winthrop. She d. 1783. **Sarah**, m. 23 June 1717-8 Jonathan Thompson. **Temperance**, bp. with last 30 June 1717, adult, unm. 1720. **Elizabeth**, mortally wounded by Indians 24 May 1724, lived 4 d. By 2d w: **Jeremiah**, b. 17 Aug. 1714, shipwright of Kit. 1735. Wife Anne in 1745; 2 ch. Will 23 Oct. 1793 names w. Sarah, who d. 16 June 1798, ag. 74. He d. 13 Apr. 1799.

3 **JOB**, Deacon, grandneph. of (5), and of Hon. Job Clements(3), uncle of (4), b. ab. 1676 in Ipsw., s. of Thomas and Lydia (Pingree), wit. with John Plaisted at Berwick 1696. In 1705 he was evicted by Ruth Haskins from house and lands in Ipswich.

Taxed Hampton Falls 1709. In 1714 he was renting a farm in Greenland. He dep. 18 Mar. 1734[5, ±59, that he had lived at Blue Point, Scarb., over 16 years. During Dummer's War, when most of the inhab. withdrew, he served as moderator, first selectm. and gr.j. List 239b. Will 1 Apr. 1756, disall.; d. 2 June 1756. He m. Abigail Harris of Ipsw., b. 5 Mar. 1675, d. Aug. 1755. Kn. ch: **Job**, b. Ipsw. 4 Dec. 1698, joiner, Scarb. 1756, liv. 1774; m. in Marbl. 29 Sep. 1719 Hannah Martyn. 5 ch. b. Marbl., 2 b. Scarb. 1742-45. **Daniel**, b. 19 Sep. 1700, d. bef. f.; m. [1723] Rebecca McKenney. 8 ch. For Hannah, d. of one Job, m. one Leavitt, liv. 1756, see Suff. Ct. files 75662.

4 **MOSES**, neph. of (3), b. 9 Mar. 1705 in Ipsw., s. of Moses and Anne, m. in Scarb. 13 Nov. 1729 Mercy Harmon. Buried 16 Dec. 1777. 9 ch.

5 **ROBERT**, carpenter, ±55 30 Sep. 1679, youngest of 3 bros., John, Thos., Robt., called kinsmen in will of Robert Andrews of Ipsw. Fol. his trade in Boston and elsew. bef. and aft. coming to Oyster River, 1654. Clerk of Dover train band 1662. Selectm. 1660, 1672, gr.j. 1671, 76, jury 1683. Lists 356a, 361a, 362a, 363abc, 365, 366, 327c, 331a, 353, 359a, 46, 47, 49, 52, 57. See Corbett. Nunc. will 11 June 1691 at Chebacco, Ipsw., d. next day. Ch: **Robert**, b. Boston 25 Sep. 1647, d. Oyster Riv. 25 Feb. 1663[4. **Elizabeth**, b. Boston 27 Nov. 1651, m. John Davis(24). **Sarah**, b. ab. 1654, m. James Huckins, 2d Capt. John Woodman. **Samuel. Jeremiah. Robert**, b. 21 Aug. 1664, liv. 1683.

6 **SAMUEL**(5), first taxed 1681, d. 1695-96. Lists 52, 57. Wife Mary liv. in 1685. Ch: **James**, living 1742, m. 1st Temperance Harrison, who d. 23 ——— 1713; 2d Mary Hill, d. by 1742 when her f. Nathl. beq. to her four sons. **Mary**, m. John Allen(2). **Frances**, m. John Bartlett, both liv. Amesbury 1721.

**BURNS.** 1 **John**, Merriconeag (1670?). See Barnes.

2 **JOHN** (Beirnes), Pemaquid 1689. List 126.

**BURRAGE**, a rare So. of Eng. surname.
1 **BENJAMIN** (Burrage?), 1640. P. & C. i. 72.

2 **JOHN**, husbandman, from Thorncombe, Devon, came to Richmond Isl. in 1639 and again with w. Avis or Agnes in 1642. Settled at Libby's River, Scarb. Lists 21, 239a. Adm. gr. Sep. 1663; by 1664 his wid. had m. Thomas Hammett. With two husb. or none, she liv. here 30 or 40 yrs. without getting into the ct. records either as accus. or wit., and by lack of town and ch. rec. her name does not appear at all. Only kn. ch: **William**, b. ab. 1648.

3 *WILLIAM(2), Scarb., had 50 a. gr. 1682, selectm. 1681, 82, 84, 85, 87, 88, comm.

1685, assemblyman 1684, town clerk 1685, 87. Lists 32, 34, 225a, 237abc, 238a. Liv. at Newton aft. 1690, liv. 1739. Wife Sarah in 1686. 'Old widow Burrage' d. in Newton 30 Aug. 1745. Ch. rec. in Boston: **Elizabeth**, b. 10 June 1691. **John**, b. 11 Feb. 1693. **Sarah**, b. 24 Sep. 1695.

**BURREN**, appar. a Channel Isl. name.
1 **GEORGE** (or Bussy), first app. 1665 success. defend. suit for debt by Robert Wadleigh, later again by Nathl. Fryer. Recorder Rishworth spelt his name sometimes Burren, sometimes Bussy, once altered it Burren to Bussy, and once wrote it 'George Burren or Bussy.' Occas. drunk 1667-1681. July 1674 Geo. Burrine and w. Sarah pres. for abs. from meet. (at York), said they attended at the point (Kittery); lived at lower Kit. or on York side of Braveboat Harb. May have rem. to Falmouth. Lists 30, 31, 227. See Corrine. List 314. Not impos. parents of **Mary** (Burren), m. in Hampton 9 Jan. 1695 James Fogg(2).

2 **JOHN**, Y. D. iv. 40, error for Burrage.

3 **WILLIAM** (Burrage?) appr., Scarb. 1682.

**BURRILL**, a general Eng. surname. Borel an ancient forename.
1 **JOHN**, North Yarm. 1666, sold to James Lane 20 May 1673. List 211.

2 **JOHN**, likely same as (1), app. at Sagadahoc in 1674; of Chelsea, w. Anne, 1686. Y. D. iv. 36, vi. 17.

3 **JOHN**, poss. s. of or same as (1 or 2), m. 28 Sep. 1694 Hannah (Preble), wid. of Wm. Milbury of York, dec. by May 1727, adm. to cred. 21 Apr. 1729, wid. Hannah renounc. She was his widow still in Aug. 1748, ±75. Ch: **Hannah**, b. 27 June 1695, pub. to John Wilkinson 1729, m. 2 Nov. 1732 Remick Cole. **Sarah**, b. 24 Dec. 1697, acc. Edw. Preble Oct. 1721, m. by 1725 Samuel Johnson jr. of York. **Mary**, b. 12 Jan. 1702-3. **Anna**, m. 19 Nov. 1727 John Fowall, fisherman. **Abraham**, b. 22 Sep. 1711. List 279. **Nathaniel**, b. 22 Dec. 1713. List 279. **Humility**, b. 28 Oct. 1716, d. 23 June 1676. Likely others, esp. **Rachel**, York wit. 1732.

4 **JOHN**, Cambridge, soldier under John Hill 1693-4. List 267b.

5 **JOHN** (Barrill), John Brawn's boy, in 1703, likely s. of (3) by an earlier wife, poss. s. of (2); likely liv. with Wheelwright in 1723. Y. D. xi. 102.

**BURRINGTON.** 1 **Bartholomew**, Isles of Shoals, likely the same s. of John and Audrey, bap. 25 Oct. 1635 at West Teignmouth, Devon, in 1666 got verdict against Mark Rowe for calling him thief; 1670 absent several years from his wife, ordered home; 1668 fined for threatening to break the constable's neck on the rocks.

2 **THOMAS**, master of coaster 1692. List 333b. T. and Lydia rec. ch. Boston 1687-.

**BURROUGHS**, Burrow-s, a common English name. Two parishes in Cambs.-Leicester.

1 **REV. GEORGE**, H. C. 1670, first ment. as a student there. Wm. Burrough of Staple Inn, London, in 1685, gent., was his own cousin. Altho rememb. in two Eng. wills by his f., Nathaniel, of Limehouse in Stepney, Middlesex, merchant, 13 Dec. 1681, and his uncle, John Style, of Stepney, 26 Oct. 1685, yet his antec. are not clear. It can hardly be quest. that his mo. was Mrs. Rebecca, who joined the ch. in Roxbury 19 July 1657, having been converted by the N. E. missionaries in Virginia; perh. his father was not, or perh. he was a travelling merchant until late in life, and when he settled down in Limehouse she went to him. She was given letters by the Roxbury ch. 29 Nov. 1674, 'going for England.' On leaving college he may have gone to Eng. and there m. Apr. 12, 1674 he joined the ch. and had a ch. bap. He named his first dau. Rebecca, two sons for himself, and none (unless he d.y.) Nathaniel. He was soon preaching at Portland, where his spirit of service, -sans- avarice, is of record. In Philip's War he went to Salis., was preaching there in May 1680, and from Nov. 1680 to Mar. 1683 preached in Danvers. By June 1683 he was back in Portland, preaching also in Scarb. In 1686 'Mr. Burrows minister at Black Point' was notified to preach before the General Assembly at York. List 226. York Deeds xi. 248. Doc. Hist. iv. 456, v. 275, 294, 316. In 1690, when the Eng. frontier was forced back to Wells, there he held, doing a hero's work until arrested for witchcraft, taken to Salem, tried and hanged. May 28, 1692, there was no chaplain in Wells. Doc. Hist. v. 342. One of nature's noblemen, standing head and shoulders above the spiritual leaders (Indian medicine men in white garb) of the benumbed, ghost-stricken mob, off and on the bench, who had this crime to answer to high Heaven for, he was the only real man then in evidence. Judge Sewall, a pitiful object on the bench that sentenced him, knew him well. 'Nov. 18, 1685 Mr. G. Boroughs dined with us.' 'Jan. 21, 1690-1. Sermon by Mr. Burroughs on the Beatitudes.' 'Aug. 19, 1692. George Burrough executed at Salem. Mr. Burrough by his Speech, Prayer, protestation of his Innocence, did much move unthinking persons, which occasions their speaking hardly concerning his being executed.' Possibly his physical fitness turned the scales against him. Like all professional men kept in condition by horseback travel, his ministry in the straggling eastern settlements may have devel. unbeliev. strength. The name of his first wife occurs only as the mo., Hannah, of his child born in Salisbury. She d. in Danvers in Sep. 1681. He m. 2d by 1683 Sarah (Ruck, b. 12 Aug. 1656), wid. of Capt. Wm. Hathorne, d. of John and Hannah (Spooner), who m. 3d in Boston 21 Apr. 1698 Mr. John Brown of Salem, as Sewall commented. Ch: **Rebecca**, bp. Roxbury 12 Feb. 1673-4, m. 1st 1698 Isaac Fowle, 2d 18 Oct. 1716 Ebenezer Tolman. **George**, bp. Roxbury 25 Nov. 1675, d.y. **Hannah**, b. Salis. 27 Apr. 1680, m. at Boston 8 Mar. 1705 Jabez Fox (2 jr.). **Elizabeth**, bp. Salem 4 June 1682, m. at Boston 2 Nov. 1704 Peter Thomas. By 2d w: **Charles**, bp. at Salem with Jeremiah and Josiah June 1693; m. 1st at Salem 3 Oct. 1706 Elizabeth Marston, who d. May 1711; 2d in Marlboro 11 Mar. 1711-2 Rebecca Townsend. 2+7 ch. **George**, bp. Salem Apr. 1691, m. at Ipsw. (int. 27 Feb. 1713-4) Sarah Scales, whose bros. came to Me. 3 ch. bp. In 1732 had rem. with w. and fam. to Glouc. **Jeremiah**. One Jeremy d. at Ipsw. Mar. 1752. **Josiah**, d. at 15 at his uncle Samuel Ruck's house. **Mary**, at Attleboro in 1713, m. by 1735 Joseph Tiffany of Norton. For the heirs in 1735 see Y. D. xvii. 311. Phineas Jones's list of them, ab. 1730, calls Jeremiah distracted, 'Widow Hannah Fox near Bantom Point,' 'Rebecca Tolman near the drawer bridge,' 'Peter Thomas, m. one, merchant by the swing bridge,' 'Mary married at Attleboro.' In 1713 the Province granted money to the father's ch., and as late as 1750 the next gen. was asking for more.

2 **RICHARD** (Burros), tenant on the Scottow's Hill farm, Scarb., aft. John Howell. His w. was a sister of Hannah (Cloyes) Hallam—her dep. 1728. List 237a.

**BURSLEY**, Busley, Burslin. A parish in Staffordshire named Burslem.

1 **HUGH**, Mr., York patentee. List 272. Presum. related to (2).

2 *__**JOHN**, Mr., 'old planter' at Weymouth, freeman 1631, York patentee 1637. At Weymouth 1634, 1638. Rep. 1636. His end unkn. unless same man as (3). The Court of Assist. in 1638 sitting at Cambridge fined 'Richard Collicot & John Buslin' for neglect of jury duty, and in 1641 referred 'Mr. John Burslin' to Salem Ct. Lists 271, 272.

3 **JOHN**, Mr., m. at Sandwich ab. 28 Nov. 1639 Joanna Hull (Rev. Joseph). Inv. Plymouth Col. 21 Aug. 1660. Wid. m. Dolor Davis. 8? ch., 5 bap. at Sandwich.

4 **JOHN** (Bursley), taxed Hampton 1645, Exeter same year. By 1649, aft. much controv. at Exeter, he had left town, and mortg. to Edward Gilman jr. several houses with lands prev. owned by Mr. Isaac Gross, Mr. Philemon Pormort, Belshazzar Willix. John Tedd, John Legett, Henry Robie, Goodman Littlefield, Griffin Montague. In Eliot

Maj. Shapleigh in 1649 set out to him the farm he later sold to Humphrey Chadbourne. Lists 392a, 374c, 375ab, 376ab, 378, 354b, 282. Last ment. 1653. In 1655 his w., who was Susannah Wyeth, stepd. of Samuel Greenfield, was liv. on N. H. side when Richard Carle in ct. promised not to sleep in her ho. unless another woman was abed with her. Only kn. ch: **Sarah**, ag. 13 in 1667, liv. with her aunt Abigail Chadwell, was raped by a degenerate.

**BURT.** 1 **Henry**, ±21 in Feb. 1663-4. 'My man' in Jonas Bailey's will 1663.

2 **JOHN**, Sheepscot landowner. Y. D. 29.269.

**BURTON, Henry**, Salem, m. (int. 2 Aug. 1715) Sarah Clark (43).

2 **ISAAC**, Kit. Garrison 170—. List 289.

3 **JACOB**, ±25 15 Feb. 1682-3, 'my master Robert Mason Esq.'

4 **JOHN**, wit. Pickering will 1715.

5 **RICHARD** (Bourton), appr. of Chr. Page's fishing tackle on Stratton's Isl., Scarb. 1667.

6 **THOMAS**, petn. of Wm. Waldron's creditors 1647.

7 **THOMAS** (Barton? Benton?), Falm. casualty list 21 Sep. 1689. List 228d.

8 **VINCENT**, appr. est. John Tucker, Portsm. fisherman 1670. Wit. Marbl. will 1684.

**BUSH, John**, Cape Porpus, leased 400 a. near Little River from Cleeve 20 Sep. 1647; with John Sanders and Peter Turbet early purch. a large tract from the Ind. Sosowen, selling his int. to H. Symonds in 1660. Liv. on land of Major Pendleton in 1663, in consid. of having it rent free during life of self and w. Grace, he deeded to Pendleton land on other side of Batson's River. Const. 1654, selectm. Wells 1654, gr.j. 1654-55, Com.t.e.s.c. 1656. Lay preacher 1662, public worship sometimes held in his house. Lists 75b, 252, 261, 263, 269b, 254. See Y. D. xii. 213. He d. betw. Apr. and Aug. 1670. Widow Grace (Sanders) dau. of John, mar. 2d Richard Palmer, who was acc. in ct. 4 Apr. 1671 of having ano. wife in England. No kn. ch.

**Bushby, Robert**, sailor, m. in Boston 7 Sep. 1710 Christian Egbeer, b. there 30 June 1690. Came to Portsm. in 1722 with 5 ch. and many debts. 2 bp. 1726. Wid. m. 18 Oct. 1725 Edward Clark (9) and 18 Aug. 1728 Joseph Miller.

**Bushell** (Brackett?), Anthony, wit. in Wells Ct. 1684 with Wm. Stacy in a Sturgeon Creek case.

**BUSHNELL.** 1 **Edmund** (-nall), Mr., Dover, 1659. List 356e.

2 **JAMES**, at Pemaquid surrender. List 127.

3 **JOHN**, Boston, m. Sarah, app. (Lovering, sis. of Wm.), wid. of John Place. Rec. ch: **John**, b. 4 Aug. 1687. J. B. m. Boston 27 June 1710 Mary Gustin.

**BUSS**, pecul. to Kent. Attrib. to Barnabas.

1 **REV. JOHN**, b. ab. 1640, app. the Cousin John Buss rememb. in the will of Dea. Robert Merriam of Concord (1681), was presum. rel. to Mr. Wm. Buss, altho unment. until 1673. Preacher and doctor in the two provinces ab. 45 yrs., his unus. char. may be judged by the Ct. order, Nov. 1677, req. Maj. Waldron, Rev. Mr. Joshua Moodey and Mr. Shubael Dummer to go to Wells and try to prevent Mr. Buss's intended removal, and from his own pet., 1718, N. H. Prov. Pap. xvii. 736. Belknap noticed the burning of his valuable library in 1694. First ment. 1673, wit. a Bradbury deed and m. Elizabeth Bradbury. Pursu. to vote of Mass. General Court, 27 May 1674, calling him of Concord, he was sworn freeman at Wells 7 July 1674, where he struggled through Philip's War. Foll. 1718 his prolong. life was spent in silence till his death in March 1736, and his childless wid. was helped by the town until bur. in 1768. Lists 266, 269b, 57, 368b, 369. He m. 1st 12 May 1673 in Salis. Elizabeth Bradbury (1); 2d Mary Hill (Valentine), d. 1716; 3d Elizabeth. Ch. by 1st w: **John**, b. ab. 1676. Elizabeth, m. John Smith (James). By 2d w: **Hannah**, m. Joseph Chesley (5). **Joseph**, joiner, Portms., m. 25 Oct. 1711 Lydia Davis (Timothy). Adm. 28 Jan. 1756 to s. Joseph, joiner, whose wid. Mary by 1762 had m. Wm. Pearne. Widow Lydia's will 1758—1759. 3 ch.

2 **JOHN** (1), ag. 77 in Jan. 1753, in 1712 signed a receipt in Henry True's acct. book for 'my own and my sister Elizabeth Smith's full part' in est. of 'my Grandmother Elizabeth Bradbury.' Lists 368b, 369. His w. Alice, liv. 1722, was niece of John Reynolds; w. Sarah, liv. 1743, was dau. of Edward Wakeham. Ch. poss. incl: **Stephen**, bp. 14 July 1717, wit. with Caleb Wakeham in 1732. **Mary**, -niece- in will of Lydia (Davis) Bass. **Joseph** (Dr. Stackp.) **Samuel. William.**

3 **JOSEPH** and **WILLIAM**, killed in the Cochecho massacre 28 June 1689, if sons of (1), either were boys or sons of an earlier wife. List 96.

4 **PETER** (Bosse or Busse). List 266. Printed -Busse- in Acts & Resolves, if correct presum. rel. to (1).

5 **WILLIAM**, killed 28 June 1689. See (3).

**BUSSY**, Bussell, presum. a Channel Island name.

1 **GEORGE**, see Burren.

2 **JOHN** (3), gr. 40 a. in Oyster River in 1694. He and his sons were shut out of Oyster River parish when the south part became Durham. Will 24 Nov. 1737—28 Feb. 1738-9 ment. w. Sarah and 12 ch: **Martha**, m. one Brown. **Elizabeth**, m. 9 May 1718 Benj. Bell. **Sarah**, m. one Williams by 1723;

2d by 1737 John Roberts of Madbury, b. 6 Dec. 1694, d. 23 Jan. 1771. She d. Dec. 1770, ag. 72 y. 11 d. (grst. on Bussy farm). **Margaret,** b. 5 July 1698, m. John Demeritt. **John,** b. 11 Feb. 1703, m. 4 Jan. 1724-5 Sarah Wibird. Will 1770—1774 names 10 ch. **Wid.** d. in New Durham 25 Sep. 1788. **William,** m. 28 Nov. 1729 Sarah Pitman. 7 ch. bap. **Henry,** had the homestead but rem. to Barrington. He m. 1st Abigail Daniels(4); 2d Judith Horn. Will 1764—1767. 2+7 ch. **James** (Buzze), m. 15 Nov. 1733 his cous. Rachel Credeford. Liv. in Rochester 1749. **Isaac,** m. Izett Hudson, b. 1715, d. of Samuel and Dorcas (Miller). Their dau. Ann m. 17 Jan. 1753 Joseph Stevenson. **Mary,** bp. adult 19 June 1726, m. Job Demeritt jr. **Hannah,** bp. a young girl, 23 June 1723, m. James Leighton. **Ann,** bp. 'young dau.' 3 Apr. 1727, unm. in 1737.

3 **SIMON,** m. 1658 Margaret Wormwood. Cape Porpus wit. 1668, 1671, 1672. Lists 255, 256, (259). Ch: **John. Rachel,** m. by 1692 Joseph Credeford. **Dorcas,** m. by 1700 Edw. Evans(3). **William. Mary,** m. Renald McDonald. Also poss., as the father's death is unk., Simon, on a Cape Porpus coroner's jury in 1685. Like uncertainty envelops the Bussy family cut off by the Ind. 'at Kennebunk near Winter Harbor.' Numerous hist. writers all app. trace back to Mather's Mag. ii. 509, vaguely tacked on the end of what happened in No. Yarm. in 1688. Also the hus. of 'Widow Buzy,' among the Cape Porpus refugees at Piscataqua in 1694, paid for keeping Goodwife Taylor.

4 **SIMON.** Sep. 17, 1667, an Oyster River coroner's jury returned their verdict on the 'untimely death of Simon Buzie,' not ment. in his lifetime. If the truth were kn., he might be f. of (3), or his s. by an earlier w. (in which case there were not three Simon B.'s), or a nephew, or fifth cousin.

5 **WILLIAM**(3), only once ment. (Y. D. 24, .174), presum. f. of 'Cousin Mary Bussell,' who was grantee, 1726-1730, from three aunts or uncles. Her aut. -Busey- in Me. Ct. files 1722.

**BUSTION,** John, whence Bustin's Isl., Casco Bay, d. bef. Philip's War. Some yrs. prior he had deeded to Wm. Haines, Pine Point, in Freeport, and Bustin's Isl., to close an acct. for supplies, and went to live with Thomas Redding, where he liv. till he died. Y. D. x. 31.

**BUSWELL,** an uncommon Mid. Eng. surname.

1 **ISAAC,** drill master at Hampton 1645, liv. at Salis. Of his ch., **Isaac,** m. 2d Susannah Perkins (Isaac) (who m. 2d Wm. Fuller 6), and had Sarah, m. Wm. Foss(7). See Hoyt.

2 **SARAH.** In 1677 Sarah Taylor was ordered by the court to keep away from one Sarah Buswell.

**Butcher,** Samuel, summonsed into court, Great Isl. 22 Nov. 1699.

**BUTLAND,** phonet. var. from Buckland, latter the name of 20 places in So. of Eng.

1 **JOHN**(2), in ct. (for swearing) in 1659 in connection with (2). Lists 33, 269b. Gr.j. 1688. In 1687 he exch. his 600 a. farm at the mouth of the Kennebunk River for James Littlefield's farm in lower Wells. Adm. 1 Nov. 1704 to sons. His w. Sarah, m. by 1670, was appar. d. of Elizabeth (Norton) Stover, called Lancaster in her mother's will at Scituate, 7 Dec. 1714, and Longstaff in m. at Pembroke, 24 Oct. 1717, to John Roan. But see Lancaster. Ch: **Margaret,** in court 1692. **John,** seaman, later farmer, Wells. List 269ac. Jury 1702, 1715, gr.j. 1709. He m. 11 June 1705 Bethia Hatch (Samuel), ment. in father's will 1742. 6 ch. bap. **George,** millman, Wells. Lists 269ac. Jury 1709, '11, '12. Constable 1714. He m. 25 Nov. 1708 Mary (Cloyes 2), wid. of Thos. Baston(8), liv. 1750, ag. 67. Both memb. of Wells ch. 3 ch. bap. **Sarah,** m. at Newport, R. I., Jan. 1704 (————Clark family————Butland) Cornelius Crick. 26 Oct. 1704, she was in Wells, 'of Newport, widow of Cornelius Crick, dec.,' quitcl. to bros. John and Geo. **Elizabeth,** m. 16 Nov. 1703 Moses Stevens. **Hannah,** m. in Wells 16 July 1706 James Willett, who had gr. there 1713. Son James, 'adopt. s. of Dea. Storer,' bp. 1714, sold his father's grant in 1734.

2 **WILLIAM,** perh. the same (Butland) who adm. est. of s. **Thomas,** seaman, in Suff. Co., Nov. 1655. First app. in Wells in 1658, ordered home to his wife, having been away from her 6 or 7 yrs.; he may have gone to her, as he last appears here 1666. List 264. His lands, title unrec., fell to **John.**

**BUTLER,** occup. surname, keeper of the master's wine cellar.

1 **JAMES,** Saco wit. 1687. See Andrew Rankin.

2 **THOMAS,** b. ab. 1674, who 'came as a soldier,' was by fam. trad. the immigrant. How he, or his son, was 'cousin' to Susannah (Seward) Simpson, (her will 1738), or her hus., is unasc. He soon became a valu. citizen of Berwick, schoolmaster, much in town bus. Lists 289, 290, 298. He m. Elizabeth Abbott(4), who d. 2 Dec. 1728 (grst.). He d. in 1747 leaving 4 ch: **Thomas,** b. 6 Mar. 1698, m. Mehitable Goodwin (Thomas), who d. 1761. List 298. Will Feb.—Apr. 1759. 7 ch. **Elizabeth,** b. 22 Sep. 1699, mar. Thos. Goodwin. \***Moses,** b. 13 July 1702, Capt. at Louisburg. List 298. He m. Mercy Wentworth, named in will 10 Sep. 1756—2 Jan.

1757. 10 or 11 ch. **Love**, b. 10 July 1713, m. Wm. Frost(5).

**BUTTERY**, John, Arrowsic, 1673. Lists 186, 187, 189. In 1685 he commanded the foot company. One John was of Reading 1665, his wife ±25 ab. 1660, and ch. John and Elizabeth. Likely father of **John**, militia, 1688. List 189.

**BUTTON**. 1 **Robert**, of Salem and Boston, merchant. Lists 10, 75b. Will 1651.

2 **MR. WILLIAM**, merchant, Jerseyman, altho he had a family on Guernsey Isl. Great bus. on Piscat. River stopped by drowning, 19 Oct. 1693, ag. 37 (grst.). Lists 318a, 307b. Accts. mention a brother here (Thomas).

**Buxton**, John jr., Salem, see Chick. Y. D. 13.82.

**BYNNS**, Jonas, Oyster River, 1648-1657. Lists 354ac, 355b, 361ab. Wrote Ambrose Gibbins's will. Left no fam., but 'Jonas Bines his creek' (1707), 'Jonas's Point' (1774).

**Byram**, Nicholas, wit. Kennebec Indian deed to John Richards, 1654. Y. D. 35, 46.

**CADE**, see Cady.

**CADILLAC, Antoine De La Mothe**, Mount Desert, at times officially connected with the government at Quebec. List 5. See 1 Me. Hist. Soc. vi. 273-7.

**CADOGAN, Rice**, fisherman, at York and Isles of Shoals, where he was a leading cit. (Doc. Hist. iv. 50), first app. as plaint. vs. a York def. 'for killing his hogs' in 1648. Constable at Star Island 1650; O. A. 1652. Lists 44, 72, 76, 275, 276, 301. His land was sold for him by Bryan Pendleton 30 June 1659, and as 'Ri: Cadogan, an indigent person,' he d. in Charlestown 5 Nov. 1695, ag. 60 or (much) more.

**CADY**. 1 **Gilbert** (Cadee), 1676, sued by Roger Kelly.

2 **RICHARD** (Cade), Great Isl., 1690. List 319.

**CAHAN, Charles**, in Boston 23 Oct. 1678 wit. an overseas charter party, in 1686 was given innholder's license in Berw. Adm. 13 June 1688 to wid. Catherine (Taylor). also granted innholder's license. Ch. unkn. See Cane.

**CALEF** (Calfe), 1 **Jeremiah**, Portsm. Lists 339, 376b. M. Lucy Chadbourne (3). Both liv. 1729.

2 **JOSEPH**, of Boston, tanner, m. (int. 23 Oct. 1718) Hannah Jordan, and built on the Jordan lands in Scarb. List 239b. Doc. Hist. iii. 426, 433. See Suff. Ct. Files 139914.

**CALL**, repeatedly misreading of -Ball-.

**PHILIP**, b. Ips. 17 Jan. 1659, bro.-in-law of Joseph Bowles(4), d. at Portsm. Jan. 1690.

**Callens** (Collins?), Peter, Cape Eliz. 1683. List 226.

**CALLEY**, see also Kelly.

1 **RICHARD**, ±24 in 1674, Kit. wit. 1666, in 1672 was in Roger Kelly's fishing crew. In 1678 he was a boat master for Mr. Kelly, who sued him for shifting to Nathan Bedford at Spurwink. By 1682 he had m. Bedford's wid. Anne (Munden), and liv. on the orig. Boaden farm, now Higgins' Beach. Lists 30, 91, 226, 238a, 304. He d. early and in 1704 his wid. liv. in Boston, her signature wit. by Anne Ibrook.

2 **RICHARD**, carpenter, bot. in Stratham 1702. List 388. Adm. 26 Oct. 1737, to s. Richard. Aft. a 1st wife mo. of most of his ch., he m. 2d abt. 1724 Catherine (Gilman), wid. of Peter Folsom(8), and 3d one Mary (Mercy?) who in 1739 sued John and Stephen Gilman and Humphrey Wilson on their notes. Ch: **Richard**, joiner, Stratham, m. at Newbury 15 July 1728 Sarah Palmer of Bradford, d. 28 Mar. 1776. **Elizabeth**, m. 25 July 1732 Benj. Abbott of Portsm. **William**. **Mary**, m. by 1736 Tufton Wiggin (Thomas). **John**. **Thomas**. **Abia**, under 14 in 1738, when Jonathan Clark was her gdn.; m. bef. 1743 Israel Merrill of Falm. **Nicholas**, under 14 in 1738, when James Folsom, glazier (his half-bro.), was his gdn.; was a glazier; d.s.p. 1743 leaving 12 Calley and Folsom brs. and sis.

3 **WILLIAM**, in 1664 sold a house on Smuttynose Isl. formerly occupied by his tenant.

**Callow** (misp. -Gal.- in List 1), Oliver, Watertown and Boston, at Penobscot 1630.

**Calton** (Kelton?), Thomas, Cape Bonawagon 1672. List 13.

**CAME**, a Devon-Glouc. name. One Arthur C. m. Marian King in Plymstock, Devon, 30 Nov. 1633.

1 **ARTHUR** (Cham), land grant in Exeter 1664, likely same as

2 **ARTHUR**, York, blacksmith, had built a house by 1669 and had grants in 1670 and 1686. Jury 1676, 1688, 1693, 1696; coroner's j. 1685; gr.j. 1687, 1690, 1691, 1693, 1696, 1697; O. A. Mar. 1679-80. Lists 376b, 33. On 9 Oct. 1710 he and w. Violet, who was liv., a wid., in 1725 deeded their prop. to their s. Samuel for support. **Samuel**. **Elizabeth**, m. bef. 1694 Philip Welch. **Sarah**, m. Arthur Bragdon(3). **Eleanor**, m. Daniel Junkins. Also, presum., **Mary**, m. 14 Mar. 1699-1700 William Larrabee.

3 ‡*****CAPT. SAMUEL**, York, millwright, ±27 in 1702, m. 1st 22 Nov. 1699 Patience Bragdon(5), who d. 13 Nov. 1753, ae. 77; 2d 18 Mar. 1753-4 Elizabeth (Young) wid. of George Stover, who d. 8 July 1778. Lists 38, 279. After a disting. pub. career, d. 26 Dec. 1768 in 95th yr. Will, 28 June 1764— 2 Jan. 1769, a mine of geneal. material. Ch: **Abigail**, b. 18 Sep. 1700, m. Jonathan

Young. **Patience**, b. 30 Aug. 1702, m. Joseph Kingsbury. **Mary**, b. 15 Jan. 1704-5, m. Thomas Bragdon(3). **Tabitha**, b. 14 Apr. 1707, m. 1st John Nowell, 2d John Frost. **Hepsibah**, b. 24 Dec. 1709, m. 1 Apr. 1731 Josiah Linscott. **Joseph**, b. 25 Apr. 1715, m. Keziah McIntire, who was his widow in 1764, when their ch., Patience Young, Keziah Paul, Jane, Mary, Joseph and Arthur Came were legatees of their grf. **Sarah**, b. 30 Nov. 1716, m. Samuel McIntire. **Hannah**, b. 10 Mar. 1719, m. Silas Nowell. **Dorcas**, b. 7 Nov. 1723, m. Samuel Milbury.

**CAMER.** 1. **Edward** (Keemer), ±70 in Apr. 1696, bot. Purchase's Isl. at Kennebec ab. 1661, and with w. Mary sold it in 1677 aft. fleeing to Boston.

2 **THOMAS**, List 354b, error for Canney. Cammel (Campbell?), Edward, 'lived at Winnegance 1679.' Me. H. & G. Rec. ix. 134.

**CAMMOCK**, pecul. to Lincolnshire, giving 4 mayors to Boston.

**CAPT. THOMAS**, bap. 18 Feb. 1592[3 in All Saints, Maldon, Essex, son of Thomas by Frances (Rich), dau. of the 2d Baron Rich; m. Margaret; came over sev. times, 1630 with Neale, 1632, 1638 with John Josselyn, and perh. was on his way in 1643. On report that he had d. in W. Ind., his inv. was taken 14 Oct. 1643, leaving his wid. free to m. Mr. Jocelyn. In London in 1641 one Thomas Phillips had been committed to the Fleet prison for causing the arrest of Thomas Cammock, the Earl of Warwick's servant, and Mr. Trelawny was intending to do the same. Gorges named him one of his Council in 1636; juryman 1640. His 500-a. grant in Eliot became half of 'Kittery House.' Lists 41, 21. The romance of this man's birth, high opportun., brief and colorless life, childless mar., unkn. end, with his relations to Jocelyn, have made him much written of. His cousin, the powerful Earl of Warwick, must have handed him a captain's commission of a letter of marque, and the same must have handed him his Scarb. patent, issued 1 Nov. 1631, (Doc. Hist. iii. 10), which he left idle several yrs. while nims. idled at Piscataqua. See Doc. Hist. iii. 2, 10, 18, 61, 138, 140, 262, 274; vi. 1, 390. Prov. & Ct. i. 1, 44, 45, 64, 72. Y. D. ii. 85. 1 Me. Hist. Soc. Coll. iii. 12.

**CAMMOND**, Abel, signer of Dover combination in 1640 (List 351b), sued in N. H. in 1642 and in York in 1650, was a wit. in Exeter in 1648, prob. associated with Christopher Lawson, whose deed from the Ind. he wit. (Abel Cannon) in 1667.

**CAMPBELL** (Camble, Campell), 1 **Alexander**, Portsm. 1695. List 334b.

2 **DAVID** (aut. Cambell), Great Isl., ±26 1671. Shoals wit. 1668. In court 1669. Lists 326c, 52, 89, 312ab, 313a, 315b, 318b.

3 **WILL** (Campbell), Wells, 1690. List 267a.

**CAMPION.** 1 **Clement**, ±34 in 1632, mariner, sailed from London for Virginia in his ship -Constance- in 1635 with passengers and cargo, and remained in America trading bet. N. E., Va. and Barbadoes, Tho. Joy and (John) Shaw of Boston being his partners in 1647. At Strawberry Bank, where he owned a house sold to Tho. Burton of London bef. 1650, he is variously recorded bet. 1641 and 1651. Lists 71, 323, 330a. He also owned a house at Charlestown, sold in 1647. Richard Waite of Boston, his adm., conv. remaining Portsm. land to Richard Cutt in 1659.

2 **ROBERT**, see Champion. Campny, Henry, see Champnoise. Canade, see Kennedy.

**CANE**, see also Keene.

1 **DAVID** (Cane = Keene?), Portsmouth, m. 1691 Joanna Dore(2), who m. 2d John Bourne, 3d Stephen Knowles.

2 **NICHOLAS**, York, not unlik. s. of Charles Cahan, b. ab. 1682, an apprent. of Capt. Abraham Preble, whose wife he called 'my mother Preble.' He m. 1st Mary Parsons (John) and 2d 11 Jan. 1753 Sarah (Gray) wid. of Joseph Jellison. List 279. In 1755 he had rem. to Sanford. D. bef. 1758. See Benj. Donnell. Ch: **John**, b. 1706, m. one Judith and was prob. that J. C. of York who m. Mary Favour 28 Nov. 1735 in Kittery. Ch. **Abigail**, m. 27 Nov. 1727 Christopher Pottle. **Mary**, m. Abel Whitney. **Joshua**. **Mercy**, m. Samuel Staples. **Samuel**. **Elizabeth**, b. 1724, int. 13 Mar. 1746-7 James Gypson.

3 **RICHARD** (Cain = Keene?), wit. a Fernald family deed in 1689.

**CANNAGE** (Cammage), **Matthew**, came to Richmond Isl. 1633, fisherman at Monhegan, murderously assaulted by Gregory Cassell, d. in Boston 1654. Lists 21, 112. Court of Asst. iii. 59-63.

**CANNEY**, see also Kenney, Cane.

1 **JOSEPH** (3), was given a house and land east of Huckleberry Hill, Dover Neck, in 1673, and added the Stokes lot. Gr.j. 1676, jury often. Lists 359ab, 49, 52, 54, 55ab, 57. Adm. 17 Nov. 1690 to wid. Mary. He m. by 1669 one Mary, who app. d.s.p.; 2d 25 Dec. 1670 Mary Clements(3), 3d ab. 1673 Mary Dam (2), who m. 2d 22 Nov. 1701 William Harford. Ch: **Jane**, b. 15 Dec. 1671. **Joseph**, b. 14 Oct. 1674. List 358c. In 1707 he sold to John his part of the homestead; settled at Cochecho Point, and aft. the Waldron suit near Campion's Rocks. Liv. 1735. He m. 1 Dec. 1699 Leah Allen

(4). 2 or m. ch. **Mary**, b. 25 Feb. 1678-9,
m. 3 June 1702 Samuel Willey, d.s.p. 2 June
1703. **Thomas**, had his stepf.'s homestead.
Will 10 Apr. 1758—30 June 1762. He m.
Rose (Pinkham), wid. of James Tuttle. 10
ch., 1712-1731 in Friends' rec. **John**, lived
on homestead, d. 1747. Adm. 1751 to dau.
Sarah. He m. 22 Dec. 1712 Sarah Austin
(8). 2 daus. **Elizabeth**, m. 19 May 1712
Reynold Jenkins.
2 **RICHARD** (Kenney), placed under Canney because the desc. bear that name.
First app. (Kenny) in Eliot, a lumber hand
of Joshua Downing in Oct. 1681, and in 1687
m. a granddau. of Rollins, just across the
river. List 94. Liv. 1697. He m. 15 Aug.
1687 Deborah Stokes, presum. the same bp.
at Dover 18 Feb. 1727-8. Cert. 2 and presum. more ch: **James** (Cenney), Somersworth, m. Mary Tuttle, dau. of John and
Judith; adm. 1769 to John Canney. **Richard**, unprov., but aut. Kene and Keene seem
to disclaim Canney; d. 26 Mar. 1770. He
m. Rebecca Otis, dau. of Richard. 3 ch. rec.
**Ichabod**, b. 26 June 1705, weaver, called s.
of Richard, dec., in mar. rec. 19 Oct. 1729
to Susannah Stanyan. Madbury, will May—
July 1774. 6 ch.
3 **THOMAS**. Constable 1648, gr.j. 1643,
1656, petty j. 1651. Lists 351b, (353),
354ac, 355ab, 356abfghk, 342, (357c), 311c
(Dover), 54. Bef. 1656 he had bot 'Thompson's Point,' and was then granted 16 a. adj.
'the outmost point turning up to Cochecho.'
In 1652 he adm. Henry Plympton's est. In
1653 his eyesight had become impaired, reputation later. In 1671 he had rem. to York,
but went back to Dover, last ment. in ct.
for intox. June 1681. In 1723 his right in
the ox pasture, 1-25th of Dover Point, was
sold by John (and wife Esther) Hall. Kn.
ch: Dau., m. Matthew Austin(5). **Mary**, m.
1655 Jeremy Tibbetts. **Thomas**. **Hannah**,
b. 1641, m. Henry Hobbs. **Joseph**.
4 **THOMAS** (3), lived at Thompson's Point,
Dover Neck, at the mouth of Cochecho
River. Lists 356j, (353), (357c), 359a. He
d. 15 May 1677, his wid. taxed that yr. List
359a. Inv. attested 25 June 1678 by Sarah
and John Wingate. Wife Sarah Taylor
(Anthony), who m. 2d John Wingate, 3d
Richard Paine. His family bible marked
'Thomas Canny his Book god Giv him grace
therin to Looke,' and 'Sarah Pain,' came
down in the Wingate family and is now in
the writer's poss. 6 ch. **Sarah**, b. 3 Aug.
1667, m. by 1687 Tho. Roberts jr. **Martha**,
b. 5 Feb. 1669-70, m. Benj. Nason. **Mary**,
b. 17 Jan. 1671-2, m. John Twombly. **Lydia**,
b. 26 Aug. 1673, m. Tobias Hanson. **Thomas**, b. 1 Nov. 1675, m. by 1696 one Grace. In
1705 he deeded 45 a. adjac. to Thompson's
Pt. to his br. Samuel; d.s.p. 1707. **Samuel**,

b. 24 May 1677, blacksm. Bap. 26 June
1724. Lists 335b, 358d. His uncle Wm. Love
willed him 1½ a. at Chalky Point bot of
Henry Hobbs, which he sold to Ichabod
Plaisted. Will 25 July—1 Sep. 1735 names
w. and 8 ch. He m. 15 Mar. 1698-9 Sarah
(Hackett), wid. of Joseph Rankin. Their
s. Love in 1740 sold the homestead to Capt.
John Gage. Their half-sis. Abigail Wingate
m. in Boston 16 Nov. 1704 Samuel Kenny
or Kanney, trunkmaker, bro. of Nathaniel.
**Canton**, Peter, Portsm. tax abated 1695.
**Cape**, Harry or Hen:, in Me. Ct. for drink-
ing 1670-72.
**Carade** (Canade?) Thomas, wit. Jordan-
Madiver 1657.
**Carary**, Nick, Sagadahoc 1674. List 15.
**Caraway**, Anthony, Dover, 1657. List 356b.

**CARD**, an uncommon Eng. surname. Middlesex, Dorset, Durham.
1 ——, Mr., Episc. minister 1630. List 41.
2 **FRANCIS**. Liv. up Kennebec River, he
and his fam. were taken capt. 14 Aug.
1676; he escaped. Doc. Hist. vi. 149, 153.
3 **JOHN**, by Dover Ct. in 1653 ordered home
to his wife; appar. went. Likely same
as (4).
4 **JOHN**, cooper, app. in Kit. 1664, in 1666
sold his leasehold est. in Lower Gabwell,
Combe-in-Teignhead, Devon, and bot and
settled in York. Jury 1666, 1668. Const.
1673. Cor. ju. 1685. Lists 86, 30. Wife
Mary in 1669; m. 2d 16 Jan. 1683[4 Elizabeth, wid. of Robert Winchester, see Manwaring. App. killed in massacre. Will 1691-
—21 Feb. 1692[3 names w. Elizabeth, 4 ch.,
2 gr.ch. Elizabeth Card d. in York 17 Mar.
1731. Ch: John, b. ab. 1643. Agnes, m. by
1680 Edward Cox(2), 2d one Calley or Kelly.
Mary, liv. 1691. William, b. ab. 1662. Thomas, b. 1668.
5 **JOHN** (4), ±21 in 1664, with his f. 1664-
1673. In 1664 he sued Roger Kelly for
9 mos. wages. List 86. Last ment. 1674.
Ch. named in grf.'s will: John, master mariner, Newcastle, 1699. Lists 315b, 316. He
m. Anne Randall (Edw.), both liv. 1755. 3
or m. ch. Mary.
6 **THOMAS** (4), York. List 279. Will 28,
d. 30, Sep. 1746, names w. Martha (Winchester, m. 26 July 1694, liv. 1756), 2 s., 1
dau., 4 ch. of s. Wm. dec. Ch: **William**,
Ens., b. 4 Feb. 1696[7, mariner, d. 12 Mar.
1731; m. 9 Feb. 1723-4 Patience Hubbard
(Philip) who m. 2d 21 Aug. 1733 Daniel
Farnham. **Elizabeth**, b. 19 Nov. 1699, m.
Job Banks (2), named in will. **John**, Capt.,
b. 26 Jan. 1701-2, d. 24 Dec. 1746, m. 22 Nov.
1730 Lydia Banks (Joseph), liv. 1747. List
279. **Mary**, b. 3 Mar. 1703-4, d. 10 July 1724.
**Miriam**, b. 14 Sep. 1706, m. 18 Feb. 1728-9
Amos Goudy. **Thomas**, b. 27 Jan. 1708-9, d.

s.p. List 279. **Winchester**, b. 7 July 1710, rem. to Woolwich; m. Elizabeth Grow. **Joseph**, b. 23 July 1714, d. 19 Aug. 1724.

7 **WILLIAM** (4), master mariner. In 1686 he belonged to Mr. Severett's crew; 1691 master of brigantine -Beginning- of York; 1699 master and half-owner of brigantine -Increase-. He m. 10 Jan. 1692-3 wid. Hannah (Ellery) Coit of Glouc., where he afterw. liv., and d. 7 July 1736. Ch: **William**, lost near Cape Sable Apr. 1722. He m. 1717 Rebecca Wallis. 3 ch: **Hannah**. **John**. **Benjamin**, b. 1710, d. of fever at Canso, 1738. He m. Rachel York (Joseph). 3 ch. **Cardea**, Gilbert. See Currier.

**CARDER**, Samuel, Newcastle, 1732. In 1757 Elizabeth Carder deeded to Joseph Newmarch the house and land in Newc. 'that was owned by my parents Wm. & Mary Mansfield.'

**CAREY** (Cary), 1 Mr. **Edward**, Newcastle, shipwright, 1699. Lists 315bc.

2 **HANNAH**, m. 15 Aug. 1688 John Thurston of Kittery.

3 **JONATHAN**, wit. a Kennebec deed. Ab. 1715, Eastern Claims hearings, he claimed Ken. lands for himself in right of w. Margaret and other heirs of John Parker.

4 **JOSEPH** (or Carre), 1672, in crew of the -Pinke Lenham-, Pisc. River. List 82.

5 **MATTHEW**, Boston shipmaster, brought captives from Canada. List 99. Bur. Boston 18 Dec. 1706, w. Mary bur. 24 Jan. 1707.

**CARIGAN**, Daniel, servant to Gov. Samuel Allen, sold elephants' teeth to a sailor at Portsm.

**CARKEET**, K-er, -ir, -ur, ite, eitt. See Creber.

1 **ELLIS** (Curkeitt), 1639. List 21 (p. 182).

2 **STEPHEN**, in 1688 bot a vessel from Hon. Robert Elliot.

3 **WILLIAM**, in 1654, already liv. on it, bot Tho. Redding's plantation in Saco. His m. rec: 'William Kirkeet was married the 25 of the 9 mo 1655.' In 1659 James Gibbins, under the patent, bounded Henry Waddock's and W. C.'s lands together, 'which the said H. W. doth take in full satisfaction for himself and Wm. Curkeete.' Whether his unnamed w. was Margaret Waddock, who may plausibly have had one or two (Wallis?) hus. bef. 1693 when she was John Tonney's wife, in uninvest. In 1700 John and Margaret Tenney sold 400 a. which incl. Carkeet's land. He was bur. 20 Mar. 1661-2. His inv. lists 17 head of cattle. Lists 24, 244e. Goody Kirkeet, 1666, List 246. App. only ch.

4 **WILLIAM** (3), mariner, m. in Salem 10 May 1686 Lydia Glanfield, dau. of Robert and Lydia (Ward). In 1689 Glanfield

was master and Curkeet mate of the ketch -Friendship-. In 1705 he gave a blanket deed to his wife. In 1712 he was master of the -Sloop Endeavor-, ent. Boston from Virginia. In 1714 she was a Salem proprietor. In 1720 Lydia Kerkite, wid., sold the Saco lands of (3) to Humphrey Scammon jr., whose f. had app. been in poss. 40 yrs. since. Y. D. iii. 103, vi. 80, x. 245, 246. Rec. ch: **Lydia**, b. 31 Aug. 1686. **William**, b. 18 Apr. 1689. **Robert**, b. 11 Nov. 1697. **Benjamin**, b. 13 Oct. 1706.

**CARLE**, forename, from Carolus.

1 **RICHARD**. One Richard partook in an eloping party in 1650, see Geo. Way. In Dover in 1655 R. C. had occasion to promise not to sleep in the house of John Bursley's wife, Susannah (Wyeth), unless another woman slept with her. If Em = Amie, he perh. m. her sister Em Wyeth, stepdau. of Samuel Greenfield. His wife was Amie in 1682, with a d. Amie m. to Samuel Knight. Taxed in Dover 1657. Lists 356ab. Liv. in Spruce Creek, Kit., bef. 1662, later on 15 a. gr. in Great Bay, Eliot, which he sold off, 1676, 1682, 1693. ±70 in 1697.

2 **TIMOTHY**, carpenter, ±19 in 1678, ±28 in 1686, was around Wm. Haskins, Great Isl. Not disting. from one or two others, presum. s. or grs. Timothy, in the Queen's service, m. 18 Dec. 1705 at Dover, Elizabeth Hall; in 1708 wit. Joshua Cromwell's will, same yr. Edward Evans and Timothy Carle for beating David Watson, in 1709 bot and in 1710 sold an ox common right on Dover Point. In 1720 Elizabeth Carrell sued by John Tibbetts. In 1718 one Carryle, a seafaring man, with two Sherburnes resisted the constable Henry Tibbetts. In 1734 Timothy of Dover, sailor, sold his town gr., presum. s. of Timothy and Elizabeth. Timothy first named presum. had sons **Timothy** and **Samuel**.

3 **SAMUEL** (2), Dover, carpenter, in court 1707 for fencing in commons. List 358d. Bot Samuel Beard's Scarb. lands and rem. there, self, wife and ch. m. and single bap. there in 1742. He m. Patience Evans(12). 8 ch. rec., besides 4 more bap., incl. **Timothy**, b. 6 June 1721, m. Deborah, d. of Phebe (Royal) Tanner-Tyler. Adm. 20 Feb. 1745-6 to her.

**CARLEY** (Kerly), **William**, mariner, m. Boston 7 May 1703 Mary Boaden(7), adm. 1739. Me. H. & G. Rec. iv. 279, Y. D. xii: 284.

**CARLISLE**, -lile, -line, Curloine.

**JOSEPH**, York, blacksm., antec. and sound of his name both unasc., first app. in 1688 having Charles Brisson in court for assault — poss. he was related bef. m. his stepd. Three yrs. later the ct. ordered Bris-

son to deliver her mother's things to Elizabeth Carline. J. C. m. 1st Elizabeth Bean (3); 2d 29 Mar. 1695 Rachel (Mains) Preble. Town gr. 1696. Pound keeper 1701. Highway surveyor 1701. Joseph -Curloine- (thus twice spelt in the inquisition, 14 May 1718) going over a pond near his house by accident fell in and was drowned. His s. John, who became coroner himself, and wrote very well, slurred the end of his name, as presum. he did the sound. Wid. was ±84 in 1749. Ch: **Lydia**, b. 8 Jan. 1696-7, m. Richard Gearing of Glouc.; 2d 12 Dec. 1723 Andrew Elwell. **Joseph**, b. 22 June 1699, fisherman, Glouc., m. 1 Jan. 1722-3 Deborah Elwell, who m. 2d (int. 21 Apr. 1739) James Russell of Yarm. 8 rec. ch. **John**, b. 18 Feb. 1700-1, joiner, 'gent,' List 279. Adm. 21 July 1741 to wid. Mary (Junkins, m. 29 Apr. 1724), who d. 22 Sep. 1784. 7 ch. **Mary**, b. 11 Mar. 1702-3, m. in Glouc. 26 Apr. 1723 Jonathan Smith. **William**, b. 2 Sep. 1705, mariner, Glouc., m. 17 Mar. 1727-8 Mary Springer. 3 ch. rec. **Elizabeth**, b. 1 Nov. 1708. **Esther**, b. 12 June 1712, m. (int. Glouc. 28 Feb. 1732-3) Solomon Hourd.

**CARMAN, Francis**, Kit. List 316. M. Abishag (Beale 1), wid. of Henry Barnes(3). **Carmell, Ann**, (monogram A. T.) wit. 18 June 1706 Dorothy Fryer's release of dower in Capt. Nathaniel Fryer's est.

**CARMICHAEL, John**, a Scotch prisoner, bot 40 a. and a house, later sold to James Grant, at York in 1660 from John Pearce and m. his dau. Anne, who m. 2d John Bracy. Of Cape Porpus in 1663, he was back at York in 1671 and had a grant at the bridge in 1674. Lists 356a, 254. K. by Ind. 7 Apr. 1677, his bro.-in-law Micum McIntire was app. adm. of his small est. 11 Sep. 1677. No kn. ch.

**CARPENTER**, common occupational surname, became 88th commonest in New England.

1 **AMBROSE**, prop. at Hampton, 1640. List 392a.

2 **CHRISTOPHER**, see Saml. Donnell's dep. Y. D. ii. 116.

3 **'JOHN** (Smith?) the Carpenter,' fined for drunkenness in Saco, 1636.

4 **LAWRENCE**, Isles of Shoals, sued by Nathaniel Fryer in 1671. See Babb(2). D. 4 July 1677, leaving will, 11 May—31 Nov. 1677, naming dau. **Grace**, ag. 3½ in Oct. 1677, for whom Richard Tope, whose wife her father had called a witch in 1674, and Tho. Jackson, to whom she was bound out, were app. gdns.

5 **PHILIP**, a Jerseyman, fisherman, of Cape Elizabeth in 1688, bot 20 a. there; of Isles of Shoals in 1702, bot the Peter Lewis plant on Smuttynose, and prob. kept his family in Kittery, where he was k. by Ind. at Spruce Creek with his w. and at least one ch. in 1707. Inv. taken 1 Aug. 1707 shows houses and land at Shoals and Kit. as well as 30 a. in C. E. Adm. 8 Oct. 1707 to Henry Barter, cr., whose acct. charges for 3 coffins. Lists 96, 296, 297. Only surv. ch: **Mary**, bp. 17 Apr. 1715, m. 1st bef. 1721 John Deering(9); 2d 17 Mar. 1729-30 Capt. Stephen Seavey (Wm.). 3 + 1 ch., of whom John Deering and Margery (Seavey) Googins surv.

**CARR**, common No. of Eng. surname. See also Carroe.

1 ——— (Kar), m. aft. 1696 Christian, wid. of Lewis Williams, who was Widow Kar in 1698 and later m. John Wyatt. List 330d. One Mary Car wit. 1698 Sherburne to James Randall.

3 **DANIEL**, commorant in Hampton Falls, late of Marblehead? Suff. Ct. files 25112 (no date).

3 **GEORGE**, nephew of (4), b. 15 Apr. 1644; Amesbury 1684; Portsm. 1697. Jury 1697. M. 8 Nov. 1677 Anne Cotton(4), who in 1685 was in jail for a spurious birth, and was bur. in Boston, Anne 'Johnson' 8 Dec. 1702. Wm. Johnson and Ann Carr were fined for forn. in York Co. Ct. June 1688. Ch. uncer. **James** and **Richard** of Salis. 6 Nov. 1706 deeded to Thomas Chase land of their father Geo. in Hampton. Hoyt conjec. John of Newbury, father of Dr. Moses of Somersworth, and Anna, m. 11 Nov. 1702 in Ames. Robert Beedle; and Mrs. Holman conjec. Dorothy, m. Freese, Clements and Adams.

4 **RICHARD**, came in the -Abigail- in 1635, ag. 29, Hampton gr. 30 June 1640, but remained at Salis., d. there 17 May 1689. One Richard Carr liv. at Ipswich 1678.

5 **RICHARD**, Capt., bro. of (3), b. 2 Apr. 1659, shipwright and mariner, Amesbury and Salisbury. D. 11 Sep. 1727. 4 ch. by 1st w. (see 6), 2 sons by 2d w. Sarah (Mayer) wid. of Thomas Haley, who d. 8 June 1726-7. **James**, b. 30 Nov. 1702. **John**, b. Aug. 1706. Both liv. 1731.

6 **SAMUEL**, mariner, app. s. of Richard(5) and Dorothy, b. in Amesbury 16 June 1686, was of Falm. in 1718, highway surveyor of Arundel chosen at the first town meeting 1719, still there 1731, perh. rem. to Sheepscot, d. bef. 1742. Revising Bradbury's higher than usual exub., Ruth Moody's hus. was not Benj., but James, m. in Newbury 25 Apr. 1712. He was not Samuel's grs., app. his first cousin. There wasn't any Benjamin, except by guessing great-grandpa's name. James came from Newbury to York ab. 1717, thence to Arundel ab. 1737. List 279. Samuel had no surv. sons. App. he had

an earlier w., perh. his stepsis., Sarah Haley, m. in Salisbury 24 Aug. 1709, who d. 14 June 1710, and their inf., **Sarah**, b. 12 June 1710, d. 25 Aug. 1711; certainly m. Mary Brown(3), who was liv. at Sheepscot, wid., in 1742, presum. with s.-in-law Job Averill, the Sheepscot litigant. His, or his wife's ch., paid £4 each by their uncle Allison Brown's will, may include three or more of the following: **Mary** (Carr, m. 17 Jan. 1743 Samuel) Fletcher, Sarah m. Job Averill, Anna m. John Leavitt, Elizabeth Hicket or Kincket.

**Carroe**, Jonathan, ±20 4 July 1673, bro. of Joanna 'Carr' who m. Robert Clemons 2 Apr. 1667.

**Carswell**, William, see Caswell.

**CARTEE**, Carty, Carter.

PHILIP, alias Teag, Exeter. In 1667 Philip Carty and Dennis Seahone (? Kelly?) were in poss. of land of John Sinkler in the Stratham - Hamp. section. In 1674 Philip Cartey was buying from Tege Drisco and Jeremiah Conaw, abuttors Cornelius Lare and Christian Dolhoff. Prior to the 'Jersey boy' period a small colony from Ireland appeared in Exeter, when shipmasters were bringing young men away and selling them for the Biblical period of 7 yrs. Philip Cartee m. Elizabeth York 23 Sep. 1668. Soldier in Philip's War. Ment. in tax lists or otherw. down to 1690. What end he made, or when, or what became of his wife, or his lands, is not found. Lt. Peter Folsom's estate showed some. Capt. Barefoot got afoul of him. See Cartee Gilman, Nehemiah Leavitt. Lists 376b, 381 - 383, 52, 57. One John Carty (aut.) was plaint. or deft. 1735-1766. In 1748 Anthony Pevey sued John Folsom 3d and John Cartee for false imprisonment.

**CARTER**, occup. surname, 49th commonest in Eng. and Wales. See also Cater.
1 **EDWARD**, fisherman, drowned, adm. 7 Mar. 1670-1 to conservators. The inv. of Gregory Churchwood, 'drowned in the boat with E. C.', was taken 7 Feb. 1670-1. App. an older man than (2)', (List 326c), his wid. and two daus. were in Eng., presum. never came over. The daus., Grace and another, by 1679 had sent separate powers of atty. to James Blagdon and Robert Townsend.
2 **EDWARD**, shipwright, a Great Isl. wit. in 1667, granted 1 a. in 1669, called -jr.- in 1671. Jury 1684, 1686, const. 1687, innholder 1686. Lists 330a, 326c, 14, 52, 55b, 312c, 313a, 319. His wife, wid. of Wm. Diamond(5) was Joan Carter, ±40 in the witchcraft trial in 1683. His est. was appr. 29 May 1691, and attested 25 Apr. 1693 by his wid., now w. of James Blagdon. He once gave a piece of land to John Martin, perh. his workman, whose w. Wilmot was ±75 in

Jan. 1726-7. App. his only ch. was **Ann**, m. Samuel Frost(8).
3 **HENRY**, fishing at Monhegan in 1651. List 111.
4 **JOHN**, mariner, in his pet. backed 11 June 1688, rep. that he had inhab. the west bank of the Saco over 26 yrs., had twice been driven off by the Ind. and his son wounded, had no land except by his wife's dower. He was one of the grantees just before Philip's War of a township back of Saco. Constable 1675. Fined for sailing out of Saco River on Sunday in 1686. Lists 245, 249. He m. 27 Dec. 1666 Ann (Bully 2), wid. of Wm. Scadlock. List 246. He had sold in 1680, then 'of Boston,' 140 a., but pet. gr. of lands on which to settle his ch., unkn. exc: **son**, b. 2 Dec. 1667. **Jonathan**, b. Boston 9 June 1678.
5 **JOHN**, poss. same as (7), in 1693 on Star Isl. rep. that he had had a letter out of Eng. saying his wife was dead, and furiously claiming that Ruth Welcome was his because she was with ch. by him. List 309. Adm. 19 Sep. 1726 to wid. Ruth, liv. 1734. One Ruth Carter m. John Wherrin 26 Aug. 1714.
6 **JOHN**, from Malden, soldier. List 267b.
7 **JOHN** ('Cater,' perh. Carter), antec. and subseq. hist. unk., acc. in Me. ct. Dec. 1691 by Mary Wittum; poss. (5, 6 or 8), or a scion of the Newington family who otherwise d. s.p. In 1712 John 'Cater' and Bartholomew Frost were up for fighting.
8 **JOHN**, York, had an uncond. gr. of 30 a. in 1714. Rebecca a wit. there 1725.
9 **JOHN**, tailor, by w. Frances (Perkins?) had ch. rec. in Dover 1726-29.
10 **RALPH**, sued in Me. ct. in 1682, likely of Boston, where Ralph, joiner, in 1691, 'at the request of the four daus. of Joseph Penwell,' sisters of Joseph jr., dec., was gr. adm. d.b.n. on est. of Joseph sr.
11 **RICHARD**, wit. (Charter) with Wm. Royal at No. Yarm. in 1646. In 1682 his wid. Agnes Madiver, ±82, dep. that they liv. divers yrs. in a house he sold to John Mains ab. 30 yrs. since. Michael Madiver's inv., 27 Aug. 1670, separates his cattle bef. he m. Wid. Carter from hers. Kn. ch: **Richard**, b. ab. 1645.
12 **RICHARD**(11), ±37 in 1682, dep. conc. No. Yarm. 30 yrs. since, again ±40 in 1684. A refugee in York, in Dec. 1676 he had dug the graves for two of James Jackson's ch. In 1679 he was appointed prison keeper. In 1695 he was fined for abs. from worship, and in 1698 was sued for 2½ yrs. rent by Capt. Raynes. Lists 267a, 294.
13 **SAMUEL** (Cater) and Hugh Allard had been committed by Roger Kelly to York jail, but at July 1690 ct., no prosec. appear-

ing, were disch. Not imposs., perh., the same that m. Elizabeth Rogers (Thomas).

14 **THOMAS**, Portsm., tailor, ±21 in 1673, was still there, fined for fighting, in 1675. Lists 327cd.

15 **WILLIAM** (Cater), acc. of drunkenness July 1662 in Me. ct.

16 **WILLIAM**, N. H. inhab. & train soldier. List 62.

**CARTWRIGHT**, common English occup. surname.

1 **EDWARD**, Isles of Shoals, fisherman. Three or less Edward Cartwrights, all with wives Elizabeth, all presum. mariners or fishermen, have not been untang. Edward of Boston, mariner, m. by 1663 to Elizabeth (Morris), in 1664 made a trust deed in her favor of a house and lot and a vacant lot (untraced). Adm. 24 Aug. 1671 to wid. Elizabeth, as he had miscarried in a boat at sea and not been heard from. She d. in Roxbury 4 Oct. 1673. Edward of Hog Isl., Shoals, by Maine Ct. in 1670 appointed grand juryman as Edw. -Carter-, dutifully reported, as Edw. Cartwright, a dozen Shoals men for fighting and drinking. June 11, 1673 (aut.E) he ack. indebt. to Mr. Vaughan, and with consent of his w. Elizabeth put himself apprent. to him until he should have paid him £13 in fish. In 1674 he was called Carter and Cartwright in the same handwr. Edward of Nantucket and w. Elizabeth (Trott by trad.) had ch. rec. 1678-1687 (bes. the eldest Nicholas), and d. 2 Sep. 1705, his will naming s. Nicholas, Sampson and Edward, and w. Elizabeth who d. 11 Aug. 1729.

2 **JANE**, fined in Hampton Ct. in 1672. Fled to Lampril River.

**CARVEATH**, Ezekiel. One E. C., gent., of Trenant in Menheniot, Cornwall, in 1669 left his s. E. C. £10. E. C. in Falmouth in 1671 was selling liquor to Ind. Boston, fishing master to the Eastward. Bur. 19 Mar. 1715.

**CARVER**, an infreq. occup. surname.

1 **EDWARD** (perh. Carter), signed probate bond est. of James Jones, 1686.

2 **RICHARD**, from Scratby, Norfolk, sailed from Yarmouth 1637, ag. 60, with w. Grace, ag. 40, 2 daus. and 3 booked as servants. Settled in Watertown. Will dated 18 Dec. 1638, with dates minuted 18 Dec. 1638 and 9 Sep. 1641. N. E. Reg. ii. 262. If either of these dates be the date of probate, then another R. C. came to Exeter with Wheelwright. Lists 374c, 375ab.

3 **ROBERT**, Boston, boatman. See Alger (7).

**CARWITHY**, Edward, mariner of Portsm., 1696, for whom and Samuel Cutt Elihu Gunnison contr. to build a ship; m. Rebecca Sloper, who was taxed as Mrs. Beck Carwithy in 1698. Lists 330de. Mortg. land bot

of Penhallow to John Knight -als- Chevalier of Dover in 1710, and was late of Portsm. 25 Nov. 1717. No kn. ch.

**CASAMENT**, John, sued in Boston by John Dollen, Dec. 1689, with Samuel Burnell and Wm. Phelps, for bringing away from Monhegan two anchors, etc., and two swine.

**Casawah**, James, Newcastle, 1690-93. Lists 57, 315a, 319.

**CASE**, pecul. to Norfolk.

1 **HUMPHREY**, Saco, ±50 in 1680, ±64 in 1693, first app., with extraord. welcome— jury, gr. of Edw. Colcord's forfeited grant (on Bidd. side), child b. in 1671; gr.j., clerk of the writs 1672; innholder, com. on county taxes 1673; town clerk. Fled with the rest to Salem, where adm. inhab. 11 Nov. 1675. Salem gr. 11 Apr. 1681, on which he built a house and shop. In 1712 and 1714 Salem was agreeing with the son to supp. his 'ancient father' during life. Lists 249, 27. His w. (Goody Case, List 246) was ppresum. a wid. Baldwin, as in 1675 he gave his 50 a. gr. to his 'dau. in law' Isabella Bawlden. How this land passed to John Abbott (1), who succeeded him as town clerk, is unasc. Kn. ch: **Margery**, b. 7 Aug. 1671. **Margaret**, b. 8 Jan. 1673-4, m. 9 Nov. 1699 Joseph Towne 3d, of Topsfield; d. 5 Nov. 1751. 12 ch. **Humphrey**, ag. 16 in 1693, m. 1st 11 Jan. 1698-9 Rachel Nichols of Topsfield; 2d 20 Nov. 1707 Mary Gloyd. 3 + 2 ch. bp.

2. **SAMUEL**, see Keais.

3 **WILLIAM** (Caice), owned land at New Harbor, Pemaquid, in 1686. Constable 1687. List 124.

**Cash**, Cosh, or Cost, George, see Coss.

**CASS**, Casse, rare surname found in Yorks.

1 **EBENEZER** (2), went with Roxbury settlers to Woodstock, Conn., of Lebanon in 1708, Norwich in 1720. He m. in Roxb. 13 Mar. 1689-90 Patience Draper. Ch: **Mary**, m. 1710 Samuel Wright. **Moses**, m. 23 Jan. 1717-8 Mary Haskins. **Jonathan**, m. 13 Nov. 1718 Bathsheba Williams. **Eliphalet**, m. 10 Dec. 1736 Martha Owen.

2 **JOHN**, age and antec. unk., held no share in Hampton commons in Feb. 1646, altho he sold land there in 1648, perh. having already m. Tho. Philbrick's young dau., b. 1633. Freeman 10 Oct. 1651. In 1664 he bot the Wheelwright farm. Selectm. 1653, 1657, 1668, 1672, 1674, and d. in office 7 Apr. 1675. Likewise gr.j. 1663, 1668 and at death. Jury 1654, 1662, 1667, 1670. Lists 393ab, 394, 392b. Will 4 May 1674—13 Apr. 1675. His wid. Martha (Philbrick), Lists 393a, 396, m. 30 Nov. 1676 Wm. Lyons sr., of Roxbury and took her younger ch. there. He d. 21 May 1692 (will), and she 4 Aug. 1694 (will). They must have kept the inn, as her will leaves 'half the drinks' to s. Ebenezer, half

to dau. Abigail. She rememb. also daus. Griggs, Radmon, Green, sons Joseph and Samuel, grs. John Cass, under age. Ch: **Martha,** b. 4 Oct. 1649, m. John Redman. **Mary,** m. 18 Feb. 1673-4 Isaac Green. **Joseph,** b. 5 Oct. 1656. **Samuel,** b. 13 July 1659. **Jonathan,** b. 13 Sep. 1663. Roxbury's half of Woodstock, in the lot drawing 26 Apr. 1695, incl. Jonathan Cass's heirs. Son John, of Roxbury, yeoman, in his will 4—16 Oct. 1711 rememb. his uncle John Griggs and his 'now captain' Henry Lyon, and made his chief heirs Jonathan, s. of Ebenezer Cass and Jonathan, s. of Joseph Cass. **Elizabeth,** b. 4 June 1666, m. in Roxb. 1682 John Griggs. **Mercy,** b. 1 Aug. 1668. **Ebenezer,** b. 17 July 1671. **Abigail,** b. 11 Jan. 1673-4, m. in Dedham 17 Nov. 1698 John Turbet. An Ind. captive Aug. 10, 1703, she d. in captiv. 15 Dec. 1705. Lists 39, 99. Also likely **Ann** (Case), m. in Boston 1 Nov. 1693 Thomas Lyons.

3 **CAPT. JOSEPH**(2), had half the homestead. Jury 1693. Selectm. 1707-1719. Liv. 1733. Lists 52, 57, 395, 396. He m. 1st 4 Jan. 1677 Mary Hobbs, who d. 3 July 1692; 2d, or poss. 3d, Elizabeth (Green) wid. of James Chase (3). Ch: **John,** b. 21 Aug. 1680, d.y. **Joseph,** b. 1685, d. 22 Jan. 1686-7. **Mary,** b. 26 Feb. 1686-7, m. Ichabod Robie. **John,** b. 19 Aug. 1689, m. Hannah Gove. In 1726 he sold out and rem. to Mendon (now Blackstone), Mass. 10 ch. Kn. ch. by 2d w: **Jonathan,** +14 in 1712, had the homestead, d. in Kensington. Adm. 27 Nov. 1745 to wid. **Tabitha.** 6 ch. **Joseph,** settled in Epping, m. 28 Nov. 1720 Phebe Nason, d. of Jonathan. Will Jan.—Feb. 1754 names 6 ch. **Amos,** liv. in Hampt. Falls. **Elizabeth,** m. by 1731 Wm. Macrease.

4 **SAMUEL**(2), had half of the homestead. In 1706 was disowned by the Friends as 'not of the true faith.' Lists 52, 396, 399a. In 1729 he deeded to s. Ebenezer, d. bef. 1736. M. 7 Dec. 1681 Mary Sanborn. Kn. ch: **Martha,** b. 25 Sep. 1682. **John,** b. 24 Oct. 1687. **Hannah,** b. 1 Mar. 1695. **Son,** killed by a falling tree 1 Mar. 1706, ag.±6. **Mary,** b. 10 Jan. 1702, m. in Salem 2C Mar. 1735-6 Josiah Southwick. **Ebenezer,** cordwainer. One Ebenezer m. at Glouc. 5 Jan. 1732-3 Lydia Sargent.

**CASSELL.** 1 **Gregory,** see Matthew Cannage. He was acquitted of murder as committed out of the jurisdiction. During 1657-1663, as Castle, Castell, Caswell, he was in the courts for fighting and not paying his bills at Marblehead.

2 **ROBERT.** List 391a. See Caswell.

**CASTINE.** 1 Jean **Vincent,** Baron de, husband of Madocawando's dau. List 5.

2 **SAMUEL** (Casteene), soldier in Philip's War, ran away; Berwick, 1684, fined for talking against Rev. John Emerson.

**CASWELL,** Carswell. A parish in Devon is Kerswell or Carswell.

1 **FRANCIS,** see Taprill.

2 **GREGORY,** see Cassell.

3 **HENRY,** bro. of 9. Boston, will 23 Oct.— 3 Nov. 1747. Sis. Susannah, cous. John of London.

4 **JOSEPH,** see Samuel Hill.

5 **RICHARD,** and s. Hopestill, see Cheswell.

6 **RICHARD,** of Dover (Madbury) 1744, Windham 1763.

7 **ROBERT** (Casell, Castell), Pequot soldier from Ipsw. 1637. List 391a.

8 **ROBERT** and Mary, Gosport, 6 ch. rec. 1711-1724.

9 **WILLIAM,** see Hon. Wm. Partridge.

10 **WILLIAM** (Carswell), see Robt. Mitchell.

**CATE.**

1 **EDWARD**(2), carpenter, b. ab. 1655, his mother's first child. Constab. 1693, 94, jury 1695, 96, gr.j. 1698. Lists 327d, 329, 52, 57, 335a (174), 330d, 331c, 339. Wife Elizabeth, only ch. of Philip Tucker. Lists 335a (176), 331c. She and s. James gr. adm. 24 Aug. 1732. Ch: **James,** oldest s. bp. with three foll. 5 Nov. 1693, m. Sep. 1715 Margaret Briard (1). Carpenter and farmer at Greenland and Stratham. 9 ch. **Elizabeth,** m. Jonathan Weeks. **Margaret,** m. John Wyatt. **Bridget,** bp. 5 Nov. 1693, m. 1st 20 Oct. 1709 Enoch Barker from Rowley, 2d 19 Mar. 1727 Daniel Donovan. **Edward,** m. 1st 9 Jan. 1717-8 Jane Jose (Richard); 2d Martha (Cotton, d. of Wm. (7 jr.), wid. of Obediah Marshall. List 339. **Tucker,** Greenland, m. 19 Jan. 1718, Mary Sanborn, d. of Mephibosheth. Will 1757 names wife and 9 of 10 ch. **William,** m. Dec. 1722 Elizabeth Cotton, dau. of Solomon (2); moved to Barrington ab. 1730. 7 or m. ch. 1723-1741. **Joshua,** b. 12 May 1702, m. 13 Aug. 1724 Anna Frost. **Mary,** m. 5 Jan. 1726-7 John Frost (see 8).

2 **JAMES,** b. ab. 1634, carpenter, Portsm., where first ment. in 1657. Lists 330ab, 326c, 327ad, 356l (Portsm.), 52. He d. 15 May 1677. Adm. gr. to wid. Alice, who m. 2d before 1679 John Westbrook, and thereaft. evid. used name Westbrook or Cate acc. to which family she was dealing with. Ch. named in settlem. in 1702, on her petn., after s. Edward had kept her out near 24 yrs.: **Edward. John. Rebecca,** m. John Urin. **Sarah,** m. Peter Babb (1). **Mary,** m. Samuel Whidden. **Elizabeth.** Also **William,** last ment. in 1690, d.s.p. Lists 329, 57. N. H. Hist. Soc. viii. 65. We must disregard Doctor Brewster's imag. list of Ind. victims, Rambles i. 73. Also presum. **Isabel,** m. Joseph Jewell 1681; in 1682 gave P. A. to Saml. Reed of Mendon to sell Portsm. land.

3 **JOHN**(2), housewright and owner of cornmill. First bot land in 1692. Portsm. se-

lectm. 1701, 1704-05. Lists 57, 62, 324, 330d, 335a, 338abcd. He m. 1st Joanna Johnson, dau. of John and Eleanor (Brackett) of Portsm., the mo. of at least one ch. William; m. 2d 29 Nov. 1710 Judith Emmons (4). He d. 4 Jan. 1748-9; will 24 Feb. 1740-1 — 25 Jan. 1748-9 names w. Judith, 5 sons, 4 daus. Ch: **William**, farmer and miller at Greenland; m. Elizabeth Sherburne (John). 7 ch. 1722-1735. **Eleazer**, m. bef. 1748 Deborah Philbrick, d. of Walter and Elizabeth (Tufton). Had the homestead. 4 or m. chn. **Samuel**, bp. 1714, m. bef. 1745 Mary White (Samuel). **Hannah** and **Judith**, both bp. 1716, neither in will. **Ebenezer**, bp. 1721, d. 3 Nov. 1742. **John**, capt. of ship -Lime-, d. of smallpox in Galway, Ire., Aug. 1738; his eldest son ment. in his father's will. **Jane**, m. Henry Beck (4). **Mary**, m. 13 Feb. 1727-28 Peter Matthews. **Martha**, bp. 5 Sep. 1718, m. 24 May 1739 James Brackett. **Rosamond**, m. 7 Dec. 1719 Moses Knight; d. bef. 1741.

**CATER**, see also Carter.
1 **EDWARD** (3), ship carpenter, bot in Portsm. in 1709. List 339. Adm. 25 May 1732 to Tho. Trickey, creditor. Order of dist. shows 1 s. and 3 d., incl. perh. the wives of Joseph Berry, who liv. in his house, and Joseph Cotton, boat builder, who bot it. He m. by 1708 Sarah Cotton (2), liv. 1740. Ch: **Mary**, bp. 16 July 1710. **John**, bp. 11 May 1712, shipwright, Kit., w. Mary. **Sarah**, bp. 18 Apr. 1714. **Edward**, bp. 15 July 1716, d.y.
2 **RICHARD**, early at Bloody Point, Newington. Memb. of Portsm. Ch. Gr. j. 1656, 1657, 1659, 1660, 1663, 1670. Lists 354bc, 355a, 356abceghkl, 311c (Dover), 359a, 331c, p. 50, 49. Wife nowhere ment. and may have d. early, as servants are named, James in 1651, James Muchemore 1655, Tho. Hayes ('my dame Mary') 1682. He made a mar. contract 16 Apr. 1672 with Mary Ricord of Portsm., who outliv. him, 1685. Lists 359b, 52. Ch: **Richard. Elizabeth**, m. John Bickford (13).
3 **RICHARD** (2), in 1694 was gr. a 20 a. addition to his father's plantation. At times liv. in Kit., and indist. from his son. One was const. of Dover 1700. One, app. the latter, joined Portsm. Ch. 20 Apr. 1693. He d. 23 Dec. 1702 of smallpox (List 96), and his son 15 June 1703? His ch. may have incl. John (Carter 7) if he d. s.p. His ch. Edw. Catter and Edw. Sheaf in 1726 released land sold in 1698 by R. C. of Kit. with wife Margaret. Surv. ch: **Richard. Edward. Mary**, m. Edward Sheafe.
4 **RICHARD** (3), liv. at Stony Hill, Newington, where his wid. Elizabeth still liv. 1722. Ch: **John**, bp. Portsm. 24 May 1696. Perh. of Kit. 12 Oct. 1719 pub. to Sarah Lary. Did m. in Newington 27 July 1721

Hannah Bickford. Ch: **Richard**, m. 12 Feb. 1718-9 Sarah Pevey. They joined the ch. 20 Sep. 1724 and had 3 ch. bap. **Mary**, unm. 1722, joined ch. with Richard. Also perh. **Elizabeth**, m. 12 Mar. 1716-7 Wm. Wittum.

**CAVERLY**
1 **MATTHIAS** (Cavele), garrison soldier (1704?). List 289.
2 **PHILIP**, cordwainer, in 1676 or 1677 dug a cellar and built a house at Oyster River. In Portsm. 1678 he and Mr. Stephen Munden were liv. in two ends of the same house. Tax abated 1683. In 1696, still of Portsm., he sold in Durham. Lists 94, 367a. Kn. ch: **Philip**, d. in Colchester, Conn., 16 Jan. 1778, ag. 91. First ment. in Colchester in 1712, he m. there 20 Dec. 1713 Hannah Adams, who d. 16 Aug. 1775. Will 19 Feb. 1772 names w. Hannah, their 3 ch. (recorded) and slaves.
3 **WILLIAM**, sued in Me. Ct. 1668; in 1691 and 1703 wit. Roger Rose documents; of Newcastle, sued in N. H. Ct. 1705. In 1709 was keeping one Andrews, a Portsm. town charge. List 316. He m. by 1696 Mary (Abbott 5) Guptill. She with 2 ch. in 1732 sold their father's common rights in Newcastle and Rye. Ch: **Moses**, Portsm., m. 30 Jan. 1714 Margaret Cotton. Will 1758—1765 names w. Margaret, sons Moses, Tho., Wm., Nathl., daus. Mary Nelson, Sarah C., Hannah C. **Elizabeth**, m. Aug. 1715 Tho. Wilkinson.

**CAWLEY**, see also Calley.
1 **RICHARD**, sued by John Frost 1667.
2 **ROBERT**, Sagadahoc 1674. List 15.
3 **TOBIAS**, Saco, d. 1685, when Henry Smith and Richard Peard inv. his clothing at £5.
4 **WILLIAM**, plaint. and def. on the Piscat. 1664-6 (Me. courts). List 78. In Dec. 1676 one Elizabeth, ±19, was hired at Digory Jeffery's house.

**Celkin**, Thomas, 1651. See Elkin.
**Center**, see Senter.
**Ceverne**, Janette, John Pickering's Jersey servant, in court 1673.
**Chabot**, Mathuus, ±18, ship's surgeon 1650. P. & C. i. 151-2.

**CHADBOURNE**, a typical English placename altho no such place is found.
1 *HUMHPREY (4) bot his first land from the Indian Rowles in 1643, later was an Ind. trader and in close relations with them. Although buying a house in Dover in 1645, he settled at Sturgeon Creek, Kittery, on land purch. from Nicholas Shapleigh, marrying his niece, Lucy Treworgy. There he was town clerk in 1650 and often thereaft., jury 1650, 51, selectm. 1651, comr. on Wells-York bounds 1657, Com.t.e.s.c. 1657-1661. Dep. to G. C. 1657, 59-60, associate judge under Mass. 1662-3. Lists 281, 283, 298, 24,

25. His will, of the 'Parish of Unity,' 25 May—13 Sep. 1667, names w. Lucy, 3 daus. under 21, 3 sons, unborn ch., cousin (niece) Mary 'Foss,' Sister Spencer. Wid. m. 2d Thomas Wills, 3d after 14 Mar. 1687-8 Elias Stileman; d. at Newcastle. Her will 8 Jan. 1699-1700—13 Apr. 1708, names with others her four surv. Chadbourne ch., all daus., and her sons' ch. Invent. of her large est. incl. five servant men and maids. Ch: **Humphrey. James. William,** capt. by Ind. and released at Pemaquid in 1676. List 298. D. s.p., perh. at a distance, or long since dead when adm. issued to his mo. 22 Sep. 1701. He is not named in her will. **Lucy,** m. 1st Michael Hicks, 2d Peter Lewis. **Alice,** m. 1st Hon. Samuel Donnell (4), 2d Jeremiah Moulton Esq. **Catherine,** m. 1st Edward Litten, 2d James Weymouth. **Elizabeth,** b. aft. 25 May 1667, m. Capt. Samuel Alcock (4). List 298.

2 **LT. HUMPHREY** (1), b. ±1653. Jury 1676, gr. j. 1687, selectm. 1692, 93. Lists 28, 33, 94, 298. His wid. Sarah (Bowles 3) settled his est. as insolv., adm. gr. to her 16 May 1695. Her cattle mark was recorded Kit. 1702-1712. Ch: **Humphrey,** Esq., b. 2 Sep. 1678. Lists 38, 296, 298. Marrying Hannah Abbot (4) 6 Nov. 1712, he surv. her and d.s.p. 26 Jan. 1763, leav. his large est. to sis. Mary Dyer, nephews and nieces. **William.** Jury 1714. List 296. Last noticed 1739, wid. Mary liv. 1766. 10 ch. **Elizabeth,** m. Amos Fernald (1). **Mary,** m. William Dyer (6). **Joseph,** Capt. List 298. He m. 14 Sep. 1738 Sarah Phipps; adm. 14 Nov. 1758, she liv. 1766. 9 ch.

3 **JAMES** (1), Sturgeon Creek, his prop. there adj. John Heard's farm. Gr. j. 1679, 85, jury 1680, List 298. His w. Elizabeth Heard (James), m. 2d Samuel Small. List 298. She was gr. adm. 30 May 1685, his inv. incl. 17 cattle, Abigail Heard's portion to be taken out of these. Ch: **Lucia,** b. 1681, m. 2 Dec. 1708 Jeremiah Calef. Both liv. 1729. **James,** b. 29 Sep. 1684, m. 24 Sep. 1713 Sarah (Hatch) Downing, wid. of Joshua (5 jr.). Selectm. 1732. Lists 291, 296, 297. He liv. in Sanford 1750, where he built a mill. Wid. liv. 1761. His 4 s. all fought in the F. and I. wars, Samuel dying in the service. 7 ch.

4 **WILLIAM,** with partners James Wall and John Goddard, under contract with Capt. John Mason, dated 13 Mar. 1633-4, to build mills in Berwick and run them on shares, arrived on the -Pied Cow- July 8. List 41. The Chadbournes both in Old and New England were housewrights, going wherever building was in progress. Their home app. in Winchcombe, Gloucestershire, Humphrey was bap. in Tamworth, Warwickshire. App. all came over together. One William was adm. inhab. of Portsmouth, R. I., in 1642,

both were at Boston in 1643. (In June, 1643, W. C. Senr. and others were up for drinking too much.) It was likelier the son in Kit. in 1652 (Lists 282, 283); both father and son may have gone back to Eng. Kn. ch: **William,** bp. in Winchcombe, 1610. Wife Mary. Kn. ch: Mary, b. at Boston Dec. 1644, mar. John Fost. **Patience,** bp. 1612, m. Thomas Spencer. **Humphrey,** bp. in Tamworth (1626?).

**CHADDER, William,** ±32 in 1674, fisherman for Elizabeth Seeley, Isles of Shoals. In 1700 the same or a son(?) was sailing under Nicholas Follett.

**CHADWELL.** 1 **Benjamin** (3), Dover 1659, retd. to Lynn. List 356e.

2 **MOSES** (3), b. Lynn 10 Apr. 1637, Dover 1659, retd. to Lynn. List 356e.

3 **THOMAS,** Lynn 1630, shipwright, rem. to Charlestown, d. Feb. 1683. By w. Margaret, who d. 29 Sep. 1658, had **Moses. Benjamin. Thomas.** He m. 2d wid. Barbara Brimblecom, who d. 1663, and 3d Abigail (Wyeth), wid. of Thomas Jones from Exeter. She joined Charlestown Ch. in June 1668, with her dau. Goose, and brought up her niece Sarah Bursley. Her will 8—19 June 1683 rem. sisters Ann Pearson of Piscataqua and sister Wheeler's dau.

**CHADWICK** (Chaddock). 1 **James,** poss. same b. Malden 15 Apr. 1653, wounded in the Swamp Fight, 19 Dec. 1675, m. Feb. 1677 Hannah Butler. Our James m. at Great Isl. Rachel Haskins (Wm.), adm. gr. to team on her fr.'s est. 15 June 1713. Lists 289, 316.

2 **JOHN** (Chadack), mentioned with Martha Sloper 1707.

3 **THOMAS** (Cadwick), Piscataqua 1670. P. & C. ii. 227.

4 **WILLIAM** (Chadwick), Somersworth, m. Abra Wentworth, both liv. 1753.

**Challis,** Hannah, Hampton. Warrant iss. June 1700; off. return 'Out of the Province.'

**CHAMBERLAIN,** occu. or offic. surname.

1 ——Capt. Chamberlain and Shop taxed, Portsm. 1707-8.

2 **RICHARD,** Great Island, ±50 in 1682, app. that Richard Chamberlayn of Gray's Inn, admitted 6 May 1651, s. and heir apparent of Wm. of London, gent. He was called to the bar 11 Nov. 1659, chosen ancient 17 Apr. 1676. He arrived in Dec. 1680, to be Secretary to the new provincial government, yet on refusing to keep the proceedings of the Council secret from the Home Office, was shut out; but served under Cranfield until Andros came, and when Dudley came in was reappointed. With almost no coöperation from his official associates, he maintained a high character for integrity, judgment and efficiency through this almost impossible pe-

riod. After returning home he wrote -Lithobolia, or the Stone-Throwing Devil-, which gives us a rare picture of Great Island at that time. (Ancestry of Lydia Harmon, Boston, 1924, pp. 91-108.) The dedication to Martyn Lumley, Esq. and reference to 'the relation I am now dignified with,' (the intermar. of their children three years before, Martyn Lumley jr. and Elizabeth Chamberlayn, made the parents 'brothers'), is what discloses his identity.

**CHAMBERS,** termed originally like Chamberlain.

1 **EDWARD,** ±29 in 1671, ±32 in 1672, Kittery from 1667. Wit. with Philip Swadden in 1669, appr. of John Tucker's est. in 1670. In 1672 he was before ct. for fighting with Rowland Flansell and for not going to his wife in Eng. Adm. gr. 4 Apr. 1676 of what they can find of his est. to Capt. John Davis and John Bray. Lists 82, 87, 287.

2 **THOMAS,** brought the Curtis family from Kent to Scituate, having m. 25 May 1632 in Ash-juxta-Sandwich, their mo., Richardene, her will at Plymouth 18 Nov. 1672—29 Oct. 1673. He is almost continually ment. in Scituate records Dec. 1638—July 1666, but in 1642 had come to York to buy the land on which Thomas Curtis and Richard Banks lived.

**CHAMBLET,** see also Champnois. Appar. the families of Henry Champnois of Winnegance (East Boothbay) and Morris Chamblet of Muscongus (Bristol) and Marbleh. all answered to the name of Chamb, and some were indifferent what end was put to it. A son of Henry m. as Champney and rec. his ch. Chamlet. Morris himself took O. A. in 1677 as Morris Chamlet (List 85), and witn. a Muscongus deed in 1717 as Maurice Champnye. The word -champenois- means a native of Champagne and poss. Chamlet stood for a little French highlander. Their genealogy is treacherous.

**MORRIS,** tailor, ag. 79 in Feb. 1720-21, dep. at Marbleh. conc. Muscongus 50 yrs. since. Ab. 1717 Wm. Hilton and James Stilson tore down his house at Muscongus, but said if their uncle **Samuel** Champney came he should have land. He m. Margaret (Brown 15), wid. of Alex. Gould. In the Eastern Claims hearings Morrice Chamles, now of Marbleh., formerly of Somersett Isl., tailor, claimed two miles square cornering on Broad Cove bot from Ind. 9 Jan. 1673-4, but John Pearce swore he never saw this deed. Maurice Champneys m. at Marbleh. 20 Oct. 1692 Elizabeth Taynour. Decs. of Hannah, who had 4 ch. bp. at Marbleh. 28 May 1710 (and presum. m. 20 Jan. 1712-3 Wm. Webber), call her w. of **Arthur** Chamblet,

and him s. of Morris, evid. not liv. when Morris's house was torn down.

**CHAMPERNOWNE,** a Norman placename.

1 **CAPT. FRANCIS,** bap. 16 Oct. 1614 at Dartington, Devon, s. of Arthur by Bridget, d. of Sir Tho. Fulford of Great Fulford. He was the 6th s. in this ancient landed family. Sir Humphrey Gilbert and Sir Walter Raleigh were cousins of his grf. The orig. counterpart deed of Champernowne's Isl. and 500 a. on the (N. E.?) side of Braveboat Harbor stream, made in England to Arthur Champernowne, Esq., 12 Dec. 1636 (Y. D. iii. 97) has on its back a memo: 'Cap. Champroun Boft his Iland of Mr. Bradbury in the year 1634 as apears under sidd Bradbury hand.' This is borne out by Edw. Johnson's dep. 21 Mar. 1682-3: 'About 48 yrs. ago Capt. Francis Champernowne desired him to go to Mr. Thomas Bradbury who was the agent to Sir Ferdinando Gorges,' and that he bought 'the Island Mr. Fryer now liveth on' and 500 a. on the other side of Braveboat Harbor stream. App. Mr. Champernowne sent over his youngest son, barely of age, with a cargo of cattle, to set up a branch of his fam. in the new world. In 1622 Sir F. Gorges had obtained for Mr. Champernowne (their wives at that time sisters), fishing and trading privileges in N. E. Adm. on the est. of Mr. A. C. was gr. to Capt. Francis C. 12 Apr. 1682, and lic. to sell r.e., altho he had already sold most of it and had repeat. mortg. the whole of it. App. he treated the prop. as his own from the start, only standing in his father's name. Mr. Francis Williams, an honorable man, who came over with an indenture signed by Sir Ferdinando himself dated 13 Nov. 1635, recites that he selected this land and Mr. Bradbury would not let him have it, but later 'for the lucre of a certain sum of money' sold it to Capt. Francis Champernowne. (Y. D. i. Pt. iii. 6). It had already been bargained for. Before this time, by 1640, F. C. was a captain, presum. bred to arms. He told the unk. author of List 88 that he was 'Commander at Sea in the same ship under the Lord of Malbrough many years ago.' This need not imply either a navigator or a sailing master, but a fighting man. James (Ley), 3d Earl of Marlborough, b. 28 Jan. 1617-8, was Admiral in command at Dartmouth in 1643, estab. a colony at Santa Cruz., W. I., obtaining a grant of the Carribee islands in 1645. Quite early F. C. himself lived in his 'lower house' above the Braveboat Harbor stream, later occ. by Capt. Richard Lockwood. This was bef. the mem. of Deborah (Lockwood) Phenix or Sarah (Andrews) Mitchell, who had been told so, and may

have been bef. he built at Greenland. In N. H. Ct. files is an acct. of an unnamed creditor dated 20 Nov. 1653 charging for a dozen debts paid for him and 'By the new house £15,' and crediting 'By 3 yrs. rent of ½ of the island.' Presumably this was John Heard, later of York and Dover. June 30, 1647, John. Heard was fined for speaking against Capt. C., and in Oct. 1650 he was sued by Withers, 'agent or attorney,' for burning a house. The judgment was for John Heard to rebuild the house he burned. Whether he had threatened to burn a house he had built on the island unless paid for it, and had occa. to fulfill his threat, is not fully discl. By 1640 Champernowne had certainly bot and built at Greenland. Elucidators have elab. two 400 a. 'farms' at Greenland (likelier two sets of buildings on one tract), and three or four dwelling houses for himself. He was given town grants by Kit. and Portsm. intended to cover his purchase from the patentees. His two houses, 'upper' and 'lower,' were at Greenland and near 'the stepping stones' at the head of Kittery Point. Neither Capt. C., nor perh. any other, liv. on the Island bef. John Heard. In the mortg. to Capt. White, 1648, Capt. C. agreed to 'put ashore upon the said island 15 head of swine,' at the halves. Presum. there were pig houses there then. Besides these he once had a dwellinghouse up Spruce Creek, on the right, ment. in Col. Archdale's grant 20 Oct. 1665, app. the same levied on and sold in 1645 by Edw. Saunders to Mrs. Sarah Lynn, soon m. to Hugh Gunnison, who had her land covered by a 300 a. town grant. Capt. C. in a deed of his land here started from 'Stage Point,' extending easterly from that place. This house may have been his earliest shelter. In 1641-2 he shipped fish in -The Hercules-, Hingston master, List 21. Y. D. i. pt. 2, 12, iii. 99, iv. 94. Perpet. in debt and careless of his obligations, he sought changes of scene, leaving unfit agents in charge. John Shapleigh in 1700 sued Capt. C.'s wid. on an acct. of Major Shapleigh, 1667-1675, debts paid for him, 10 s. paid him in money, 8 gal. Malaga, brandy, rum. (York Ct. files). See Y. D. i. 62, 63. He was accu. of selling his Greenland farm twice, and the pool who obtained the second deed had finally to pay costs. Yet he refused to take oath to an inventory, for lack of suff. inform., but readily gave his bond to answer for the estate. His treatment of what looks like a blunder, 'N. E.' for N. W., in the orig. grant from Gorges makes a comedy. Near the close of his life he had President Danforth confirm it to himself in the same course, after which he claimed Capt. Raynes's farm in York, resulting in a commission from Boston and a -compromise- by which the farm was en-

tailed on the heirs of Capt. Raynes's eldest son (Y. D. iv. 12). But Piscataqua was almost New Devon, and the Devonian idolizing of its ancient gentle families made him a kind of sentimental asset, to be elevated on a pedestal. Sir Ferdinando Gorges recognized his 'loving nephew' at every oppor. from Sep. 1639 on, but he took no part in that government. After Vines left he was on the bench in one court, at Wells, June 1647. Portsm. chose him a selectm. in 1654. After Charles II came in, Champernowne's fidelity to his cousin-in-law Gorges was unfailing. He accepted his first commission and acted at the courts at Wells 27 Dec. 1661 and 26-28 May 1662. He headed the warrant issued 11 Mar. 1661-2, and was ready to set his name to all papers brot to him by Jocelyn, Shapleigh or (when for the King) Rishworth,—except the petition which Jocelyn did and Rishworth would not, to throw over the Gorges charter and make Sir Robert Carr royal governor. Under the King's Commissioners he sat in three courts at York. He attended the invading court at York 7 July 1668 when Mass. again took possession, and signed the protest. In 1682 he personally delivered to Gov. Cranfield a petition to the King against Mass., and in 1684 Cranfield nominated him for the Council, altho liv. on the wrong side of the river. Randolph in 1676 knew of only three Eastern men to recom. for military officers: Champernowne, Shapleigh, Phillips. In President Dudley's commission, 8 Oct. 1685, Capt. C. was in his Council, but was no longer able to travel to Boston. In 1682 he was referee with Wincoll and Tyng, and in 1683 on an important probate com. with Hooke and Frost. That this man's conception of his place in the social firmament, as dispenser of good cheer to all humankind coming within the radius of his beams, included the red man, is shown by the Indians' demanding (Major Shapleigh and) Capt. C. as peace envoys. He must have gotten himself into the enemy's country somehow, (to 'the Smoaking Tree' in the Lygonia or Long Creek section of South Portland), to sign an execrable peace treaty on the enemy's terms, 12 Apr. 1678. List 32 would have had the Kittery trustees, Captains Champernowne, Hooke, Frost and Wincoll, and James Emery, named in an official copy of the orig. deed recently given to the Me. Hist. Soc. Lists 351b, 281, 288, 298, 311b, 323, 324, 26, 33, 47, 73, 88. After lifelong attention to the sex he finally m., by 1682, Mary (Hole) Cutt, wid. of Robert(7), sis. of John. The Me. Hist. Soc. has an earlier draft, as also his orig. last will, dated 16 Nov. 1686, both making his Cutt stepch. his heirs. He d. 15 Mar.—21 May 1687. His wid. app. made two or m. jour-

neys to her ch. in So. Car.; she was here in 1700, but by May 1703 had 'gone out of the country.' List 36.

2 **WILLIAM** (Champerown?), drunk at Isles of Shoals in 1671. In Dec., 1692, Wm. Brooking, 'being the person supposed to have entertained the criple Wm. Champernone in his first coming,' now for exemption from taxes agrees to maintain him for life. Wm. Walker's letter, 1711, called him 'one Champernoon a cripple who is since dead.'

**CHAMPION.**
1 **CLAUDE**, was late of Isles of Shoals 15 Sep. 1687 when Wm. Button of Jersey, merchant, Robt. Elliot, Esq. of Gt. Island, surety, was app. to adm. his est. List 307b.
2 **ROBERT**, carpenter, from Dartmouth, co. Devon, liv. 7 yrs. at Piscataqua, sending his wife and ch. nothing, until 1657 when on 7 May an Oyster Riv. jury brot in verdict that he had been drowned by accident. His wid. Elizabeth made Francis Champernowne her attorney to settle his est. 30 Sep. 1659, sending with her P. A. an int. testimony signed by the Mayor and other inhab. of the Borough of Clifton and Hardness. Y.D.i.102.
**CHAMPLIN**, William, Scarb. 1676. List 237e.

**CHAMPNOIS**, see also Chamblet.
1 **HENRY**, in 1639 was a wit. with Mr. Shurt at Pemaquid. In 1669 wit. -Champny-. He settled at Winnegance (East Boothbay) and bot a large tract from the Indians. List 12 (Chamnes). A fragment of his will 13 July 1679, 'formerly of Winnegance,' gave his lands to his sons **Henry, William, James**. The whole will may have named daus. Henry in the Eastern Claims hearing claimed for hims., his br. William and the dau. of his br. James. Robert Montgomery, sued for trespass in 1736, signed an agreem. to deliver poss. to the nine grch. not named.
2 **HENRY**(1), fisherman, Sagadahoc and Boston. List (Chamlett) 189. Died 1722. He m. in Boston 8 Dec. 1693 Elizabeth Worthylake. Ch: **Elizabeth**, b. 30 Sep. 1694, m. 8 Sep. 1735 Thomas Skinner of Milton, nailer. **Mary**, b. 5 Sep. 1696, m. 18 June 1734 Wm. Crompton, mariner. **Joanna**, m. 6 May 1718 Peter Wooden; 2d 18 Jan. 1727 John Tucker, mariner. **James**, b. 25 Dec. 1701, fisherman, Boston, m. 9 June 1732 Sarah Cleves. Adm. 1748. **Sarah**, b. 17 Dec. 1703, m. 9 Mar. 1726 Wm. Wadland; 2d 8 June 1732 Jonathan Smith, mariner. **Rebecca**, b. 8 Nov. 1705, executed 1 Oct. 1733 for concealing the birth of a child.
3 **JAMES**(1), d. early. Only child: **Mary** (Chambet), m. in Boston 24 July 1702 Benj. Averill(7) of Glouc., liv. 1746.
4 **WILLIAM**(1), master of fishing vessel at Sagadahoc in 1688. List 189 (Chamlett). Bur. (Chamblet) in Boston 7 Sep. 1709. Wife

Mary, presum. Curtis(1). Ch: **Curtis** (Camlet or Champnes), potter, m. 28 Apr. 1726, Mary Adams. Will Apr.–June 1738, w. Mary, 'eldest son' and 'ch.' unn. **Mary**, m. 14 Jan. 1722 John Biswarber, mariner. **Sarah** (Gamlet), m. 20 Apr. 1726 George Cross; s. Geo. b. 11 Mar. 1727; wid. in 1735.

**CHANDLER.** 1 **Henry**, Sergt., from Andover, soldier under Hill 1693-4. List 267b.
2 **JOHN**, sued Anthony Emery in Me. Ct. 1660. Poss. the same as 'Goodman C.' constable of Portsm. 1659, and 'old Chanler,' subs. for the minister's support 1659. Lists 323, 326a.
3 **JAMES**, from Newbury, under Hill 1693-4. List 267b.

**Chane**, Mr. Joseph (Chownes), master of coaster betw. Portsm. and Boston 1690-93.
**Channells** (Charnells), John, Isles of Shoals 1672-3, due bill to David Campbell.
**CHAPLIN**, William, Isles of Shoals, ±30 1672. In Me. Ct. 1675 won suit ag. Nathan Bedford. In Nov. 1679, he being in Mrs. Jane Jose's crew, with two ch. to support, she took the girl to bring up as her own.

**CHAPMAN**, an obsolete occup. surname, nearest to our market man (apple or cattle buyer). Common in E. of Eng. Became 70th commonest in N. E.
1 **ELIZABETH**, m. in Hampton 26 Oct. 1652 John Garland.
2 **FLORENCE**, sex unasc., late of York 23 Aug. 1647, gave P. A. to coll. £4 from Wm. Dixon.
3 **HENRY**, creditor of John Phillips' estate Dover 1642. Perh. had worked for a Boston merchant.
4 **NATHANIEL**, ±26 in 1679, s. of Edward of Ipswich. A housewright, he appar. moved about. In Ips. 1680 was appointed com. to inspect the jail. Was in Andover in 1686. In 1709 he was tenant of Edw. Ayers' farm in Eliot; later he bot land in 1725 deeded to s. Edw. with reserv. for life of self and w. Mary. Edw. sold in 1737. List 291. He m. at Ips. 30 Dec. 1674 Mary Wilborne, dau. of Michael, stepd. of Andrew Peters. Of the foll., John, Abigail and Edw. are cert. ch: **Mercy**, m. 8 June 1705 Adrian Frye(1 jr.). **Elizabeth**, b. 13 Feb. 1685-6 in Andover, m. 27 Aug. 1707 Joseph Wilson. **John**, carpenter or yeoman, living at Eliot, Spruce Creek, Falmouth, Spruce Creek. Lists 291, 296, 297. Adm. 15 Oct. 1734. He m. 10 Mar. 1710 Rachel Ingersoll, liv. 1743. 6 ch. incl. son Wellborn. **Abigail**, in 1713 accu. Samuel Hill jr., mar. 11 Feb. 1723-4 John Bridges; 2d Joseph Muzzett. **Mary**, m. 26 Dec. 1716 John Lord. **Nathaniel**, m. in York 27 Nov. 1735 Miriam Young. **Edward**, housewright, liv. at Eliot, Saco Falls, Falm. Will 3 Jan., d. 7 Jan. 1750, named wife, 2 ch.,

sis. Muzzett. He m. 1st 28 Oct. 1725 Abigail (Partridge), wid. of Noah Bradden(2); 2d (int. 2 Sep.1738 Biddeford) Elizabeth Libby of Eliot. 4 ch.

5 **ROBERT**, taxed Oyster River 1663, gone 1664. List 363c. M. Elizabeth Stevenson. Son **Robert**, b. 18 Dec., d. 6 Jan. 1664-5.

6 **SAMUEL**, bro. of (4), b. 1654, rem. from Ips. to North Hampton soon aft. 1700 with 1st wife's ch. and 2d wife. List 338b. D. 26 Jan. 1722[3, wid. Phebe cited, adm. to sons Joseph and Samuel. He mar. 20 May 1678 Ruth Ingalls of Ips. who d. there 22 June 1700; 2d by 1702 Phebe (Newmarch), b. ab. 1659, wid. of Peter Penwell of Ips., mariner. List 338b. Ch: **Samuel**, b. 12 Feb. 1679, liv. in No. Hampton and in Greenland, where d. 21 Apr. 1742. M. his stepmo's niece, Phebe Balch of Manchester, Mass., 11 Mar. 1702, who d. 11 Apr. 1738. 10 ch. **John**, m. 16 Mar. 1705 Dorothy Chase(3), d. 17 Oct., s. John, b. 20 Nov., all in the same yr. **Edward**, d. 17 Oct. 1688. **Joseph**, b. 6 Apr. 1685, d. unm. in Hampton Mar. 1750. **Ruth**, b. 10 Jan. 1687, m. 1 Mar. 1720-1 Timothy Eaton, liv. 1750. **Mary**, b. 2 Jan. 1691, d. unm. in Hampton 13 Mar. 1740. **Job**, b. ab. 1693, had the homestead, d. 1765. He m. 1st after 1716 Mary Chase(3), who d. 1 Apr. 1736; 2d 6 Jan. 1737 Rachel (Berry 5) wid. of Richard Goss, who d. 19 Feb. 1798, ag. 97. 4+4 ch. **Edmund**, b. about 1697; d. unm. in Hampton 20 Feb. 1739.

7 **WILLIAM**, Kennebec wit. 1651. Y. D. x. 252.

**CHAPPELL** (Chapple). 1 **Anthony**, Mr. Trelawny's servant, came to Richmond Isl. but would not stay. List 21. Doc. Hist. iii. 193, 124.

2 **WILLIAM**, master of The Hercules-, Plymouth and Richmond Island. Aut. Doc. Hist. iii. 107. List 21.

**Chappum**, see Clapham.

**CHASE**, an East of Eng. name, became 27th in N. E. An earlier Aquila and bro. Thomas were bap. in Chesham, co. Bucks, 1580-1585.

1 **AQUILA**, ±48 in 1666, mariner, altho forgotten by Edw. Colcord presum. came to Hampton with his br. Thomas 'the first summer.' See (6). He soon m. Anne Wheeler and in 1646 rem. with her fam. to Newbury, settling at Newburyport. Lists 391b, 392a, 393b. He coasted bet. Newburyport and Boston. Will 10, d. 27, Dec. 1670. His wid. m. 14 June 1672 Daniel Silloway and d. 21 Apr. 1687. For grch. who came back to N. H., see Chase Gen. Ch: **Sarah**, m. Charles Annis(1). **Anne**, b. 6 July 1647, mar. 27 Apr. 1671 Thomas Barber of Newbury. **Priscilla**, b. 14 Mar. 1648-9, m. 10 Feb. 1670-1 Abel Merrill. **Mary**, b. 3 Feb. 1650-1, m. 9 Mar.

1669-70 John Stevens. **Aquila**, b. 26 Sep. 1652, had the homestead; d. 29 July 1720. 9 ch. **Thomas**, b. 25 July 1654, carpenter, m. 22 Nov. 1677 Rebecca Follansbee(1); 2d 2 Aug. 1714 wid. Eliz. (Woodhead?) Moores. Will 3 Aug.—25 Feb. 1732-3. 10+1 ch. **John**, b. 2 Nov. 1655, cooper, d. in West Newbury 26 Feb. 1739-40. 2+9 ch. **Elizabeth**, b. 13 Sep. 1657, mar. Zachariah Ayer(9). **Ruth**, b. 18 Mar. 1659-60, d. 30 May 1676. **Daniel**, b. 15 Nov. 1661, wheelwright, d. 8 Feb. 1707; m. 25 Aug. 1683, Martha Kimball, who m. 2d (int. 9 May 1713) Josiah Heath. 10 ch. **Moses**, Ensign, b. 24 Dec. 1663, weaver, m. 10 Nov. 1684 Anne Follansbee(1), d. in West Newbury 6 Sep. 1743. 9 ch.

2 **LT. ISAAC**(6), put under gdnship. of br. Tho. in 1667, blacksm., Quaker, m. 1st 20 Feb. 1672-3 Mary Perkins, ae. 15, who d.s.p.; 2d 5 Oct. 1675 at Tisbury, Martha's Vineyard, where he settled, Mary Tilton, who d. 14 June 1746 ae. 88. Will 12 Feb. 1721-2, d. 19 May 1727. 12 ch. See Chase Gen. 482.

3 **JAMES**(6), millman. Lists 52, 396. Adm. 7 Mar. 1703-4 to s.-in-law John Chase(4). He m. 2 Nov. 1675 Elizabeth Green. One Elizabeth Chase of Hampton was in ct. in 1692 for two ch., no husband. The div. among 3 daus. 4 June 1705 ignores her, altho wit. by Joseph Cass(3), who m. her. Ch: **Hannah**, b. 22 Dec. 1677, d. bef. her grf. Green. **Abigail**, b. 27 Aug. 1681, m. John Chase(4). **Dorothy**, b. 17 Mar. 1686, mar. John Chapman(6). **Mary**, b. 17 Mar. 1686, m. aft. 1716 Job Chapman(6).

4 **JOHN** (s. of John 1), ±29 28 Feb. 1707-8; m. Abigail(3) and settled in Hampt., now Seabrook. List 399a. A war. issued 26 Aug. 1715 against his wid. for a ch., reput. s. of Henry Green, who carried thro life the name Daniel Chase alias Green. Five surv. ch. agreed to a div. 29 Nov. 1727. See Chase Gen. 49, 72-4, 138. **James**, b. 28 July 1698, d.s.p. **Jonathan**, b. 21 Oct. 1700. **Elizabeth**, b. 13 Apr. 1703, m. Wm. Russell. **Elihu**, b. 7 Sep. 1705. **John**, b. 18 Sep. 1708. **Hannah**, b. 10 May 1711, mar. 1 Oct. 1730 Thomas Fuller(2).

5 **JOSEPH**(6), ±26 in Apr. 1673, master of a coaster and followed the business of his uncle(1). ('Goodman Chase of Hampton boatman.') 1st selectm. in 1708 and in 1712. In 1709 Lt. Peter Weare and Mr. Joseph Chase were chosen a com. to stop lumbering on the commons. He became a Friend, not so his wife. Lists 396, 392b. He d. 12 Jan. 1717-8. Will 14 June 1704, codicil 19 May 1716, names w. Rachel (Partridge, m. 31 Dec. 1671), who d. 27 Oct. 1718, and ch: Anne Sinkler, Elizabeth Hilliard and Rachel Freeze, and more of interest. See N. H. Prov. Papers xxxi. 526. Ch: **Hannah**, b. 5 June 1672, d. 10 June 1674. **Elizabeth**, b. 11 May

1674, d. 8 Sep. 1675. **Jonathan,** b. 14 May 1676, drowned at Currituck 1 Feb. 1696. **Ann,** b. 9 Jan. 1677-8, m. Bradstreet Wiggin and John Sinclair. **Elizabeth,** b. 14 Feb. 1684-5, m. Benj. Hilliard and Capt. Joseph Tilton. **Rachel,** b. 27 Apr. 1687, mar. Lt. Jacob Freese(2) and Hon. Andrew Wiggin.

6 **THOMAS,** seaman, came to Hampton in 1639. Thomas and Aquila had grants there 30 June 1640. Thomas also bot of Thomas Jones and of Thomas Sleeper, and was allowed two rights in the commons. Thomas and Aquila sued Lt. Howard in 1648. Lists 391a, 392a, 393ab. Adm. 5 Oct. 1652 to wid. Elizabeth (Philbrick). List 393a. In 1653 she sued Wm. Furber, and in 1654 Christo. Palmer, and 26 Oct. 1654 m. John Garland. Surv. ch. 5 sons: **Thomas,** d.s.p. 23 Oct. 1714, ae. 72 (grst. in Seabrook). For a vivid character sketch of this Quaker preacher, see Thomas Story's Journal, p. 319. Selectm. 1695. Lists 52, 392b, 396. Inter. will 26 Apr. 1712. **Joseph,** b. ab. 1647. **James. Isaac,** b. 1 Apr. 1650. **Abraham,** b. 6 Aug. 1652, Quaker, d.s.p., killed in Philip's War on the Marlboro front. Adm. Apr. 1676 to Tho.

**Chaseling,** Anne (Ann Chaslyng, An Chesly), in Suff. County Ct. May 1680 accu. John Case. From Black Point in Suff. County Ct. Apr. 1681, confessed herself 4 mos. gone and accu. Wm. Burrage.

**CHATER,** Lt. **John,** probably the passenger listed at London 20 Nov. 1635, ae. 17. Settled in Newbury, freeman 1651. In 1659-60 he rem. to Wells (the part now Kennebunk), there lic. ferryman and innholder in 1662. Gr.j. 1661. Lists 244e, 264. In 1671 his admr. John Miller was sued by Nathl. Fryer, who lost. Wife Alice, dau. of John Emery of Newbury, liv. 1680. Ch. b. in Newbury: **Hannah,** b. 7 Aug. 1644, m. John Miller. **Lydia,** b. 12 Jan. 1647-8, liv. 1657.

**CHATTERTON,** Chatherton. Chadderton a chapelry in Lancashire.

1 **JANE,** Piscataqua, was warned to go to her hus. in 1642 and 1646, poss. the goodwife C. fined 5 July 1653.

2 **MICHAEL,** Piscataqua, 1640, sold house and lands to Wm. Palmer and Clement Campion bef. 1651. Wit. 1647. Lists 41, 321, 323, 330a. Goodman C.'s house and 10 a. ment. in 1652. 'One Michael Chatterton,' so called in the record, was cr. of Wm. Latham in New Haven in 1645.

3 **WILLIAM,** legatee and exec. of James Woodward of Saco in 1648, the will made in Portsm., was poss. of New Haven in 1646 et seq.

**CHAUNCY,** Rev. **Barnabas,** s. of Pres. of Harv. Col., H. C. 1657, A. M. 1660, minister at Saco 1665—. Lists 26, 249. In 1673 Elnation C. pet. the Gen. Ct. for arrear. due

their father needed for the relief of Barnabas. Starred in Harv. Cat. 1698.

**Cheater,** see Chater.

**CHEEVER.** 1 **Abraham,** Cape Neddick wit. 1662. Adm. gr. Suff. Prob. 12 Jan. 1669-70, bro. Bartholomew declining.

2 **REV. SAMUEL,** b. New Haven 22 Sep. 1639, s. of Rev. Ezekiel. H.C. 1659. Minister at Scarb. 1664—, at Marbl. from 1668. At Marbl. ±37 he wit. John Bonython's nunc. will. D. Marbl. 29 May 1724, his wid. Ruth (Angier) liv. to 95. 10 ch. incl. **Ruth,** bp. Salem Aug. 1672, m. Moses Wadlon and one Stacey. Folsom's Saco 133, 1 Me. Hist. Soc. iii. 154. Y. D. i. 153, 164; ii. 54.

**CHENEY** (Chaney). 1 **Daniel,** in 1662, having Edw. Colcord in custody, let him go in the night.

2 **DANIEL,** Wells, List 269c.

## CHESLEY

1 **GEORGE**(5). In 1699 he bot the land formerly Patrick Jameson's, and settled there. Lists 62, 94, 369. K. by Ind. 8 June 1710. Wid. Deliverance mar. Moses Davis (40 jr.). Ch: **George,** mar. Sarah Sampson. Will 1785-1790 names w. Sarah and 7 ch. **Elizabeth.**

2 **PHILIP,** b. 1606-08, ±77 in Nov. 1683. First ment. Dover Neck wit. 1642; he had a home lot there. At Oyster River by 1648. His and his 2d wife's share of existing records would fill a 'movie,' an alternating current of honor. and impuls. activ. His wife Elizabeth, liv. 1661, was presum. dead when he put everything in his sons' names. Soon his wife was Joanna, app. relation of James and Elizabeth Thomas. Both living 30 Apr. 1685. Lists 354abc, 355a, 356a, 359a, 361a, 362a, 363abc, 364, 366, 47. Ch: **Thomas,** b. ab. 1644. **Philip,** b. ab. 1646. By 2d w: **Hannah,** m. Thomas Ash(3). **Mary,** in ct. 1698, found at the house of Thomas Ash in Portsm.; m. 28 May 1701 Ralph Hall; 2d John Foye(3). **Esther,** m. 3 July 1699 John Hall.

3 **PHILIP**(2). Constable 1695. Will 13 Dec. 1695 omitted ch. names. He m. Sarah, app. d. of James Rollins, who was bap., an aged wid., 20 Mar. 1719. His sons were: **Samuel. James,** m. 29 Dec. 1704 Tamson Wentworth, s. James, b. 10 May 1706; k. in ambush 17 Sep. 1707; wid. by 1711 m. John Hayes. The conflict betw. Rev. J. Pike's diary and his mar. records, by which J. C. m. Tamson bef. his w. Sarah (Huckins) d., is expl. by subcon. pen action, substituting her father's for her husband's name James. As Philip Chesley's eldest son (Lemuel) was evid. by an earlier wife, we may take him for Sarah Huckins' hus. **Philip,** b. 1678, Lieut. Lists 368ab, 96. Liv. 1756. He m. 1st Sarah Huckins, who d. 14 Oct. 1705, (List 96), 1 son Lemuel; 2d 8 July 1706 Hannah Sawyer, 6

ch. bap. **Ebenezer,** named in will 1695, not aft. **Ichabod,** Lieut. Lists 368b, 369. Adm. 15 Dec. 1774 to wid. Temperance, his wife in 1729 and wid. down to 1786. 5 ch. \***Jonathan,** Capt., Rep. 1745. He m. 17 Nov. 1720 Mary Weeks, named in his will 4 Feb.—24 Sep. 1755. 5 ch. Daughters unkn., but presum. incl. **Lydia,** mar. 9 Jan. 1717-8 John Burnham(2).

4 **CAPT. SAMUEL**(3), selectm. in 1703 and capt. in the Port Royal exped. in 1707. Sep. 17, 1707, a lumbering crew were ambushed near his own house, and hims., br. James and perh. Ebenezer were shot down. He m. Elizabeth Smith, who m. 2d Amos Pinkham. His child. were: **Samuel,** eldest, d.s.p. 1717, by statem. of heirship in 1736. **Philip,** d.s.p. 1720. **Joseph,** m. Hannah (Peirce), wid. of Thomas Hanson. Liv. in Dover. Both dead, adm. 5 Aug. 1740 to Reuben Chesley and Timothy Hanson. **Benjamin,** d.s.p. 1718. **Reuben,** twice m. bef. 1735 to Ann and Margaret. Liv. in Madbury; d. bef. 1790. **Lilias,** m. Isaac Watson. **Keziah,** m. Timothy Hanson.

5 **THOMAS**(2), selectm. 1688, 1695. Killed 15 Nov. 1697. He m. 22 Aug. 1663 Elizabeth Thomas, liv. 1701. Ch: **Thomas,** b. 4 June 1664, d. by 1700, adm. 5 Sep. 1704 to wid. Ann (Huntress), who had m. Joseph Daniels(4) and had d. by Jan. 1704-5. 6 ch., incl. Samuel b. ab. 1691, who m. his stepsis. Anne Daniels. **George,** b. 1671. **Joseph.** Will 13 Apr.—7 Jan. 1730-1. He m. 1st Hannah Buss(1), who d. in 1717, 4 ch.; 2d 18 Dec. 1717 Sarah Cutt(3), who surv. **Elizabeth,** m. 1 Oct. 1688 Col. James Davis(14). **Sarah,** m. Abraham Bennett(1). **Susannah,** mar. bef. 1698 Capt. John Smith. **Mary,** m. William Jones of Dover.

**Chessemore,** see Chisholm.

**CHESWELL, Richard,** Newmarket, called 'Negro' in deeds to and from him in 1717, his **6** mark. Sons: **Wentworth,** in 1764 bot pew in meetingho. **Hopestill,** housewright, Esq., in Brewst. Ramb. called -Caswell- and half-bro. of Clement March, keeper of the almshouse.

## CHICK

**THOMAS,** in 1666 was bound to good behaviour towards Davie Hamilton's wife, —bondsman Tho. Doughty. Taxed Cochecho 1671, 1672. In 1680 he worked out 6 wks. to pay his fine for intox. A town gr. to Tho. Wills in 1671 for the benefit of T. C.'s ch. was laid out 1719-20 to Richard C., Tho. C. jr., John Holman or Holmes and Tho. Weed. Coroner's jury 1668. List 298. He poss. had an earlier wife, but m. by 1674 Elizabeth Spencer, who m. 2d by 1693 Nicholas Turbet. Ch: **Elizabeth,** in 1683 (last mem.) was assigned her mo.'s share in her grmo. Spencer's lands, subject to use of her parents.

**Richard,** eldest son, m. 11 July 1702 Martha Lord. Lists 290, 296-298. Will 1735—1737 names 8 ch., one of them -Winnefred-. (At Roxbury another Richard C. d. 13 Oct. 1686 aged 48, and in 1691 -Winnefred- Chick of Roxbury, living at the house of her mother, Alice C., widow, sued a man for slander.) Wid. liv. 1745. **Thomas,** ±21 in Aug. 1699; Mary, ±19, another wit. at the same time, may have been wife or sis. (She was then at Moses Goodwin's house.) Lists 289, 290, 298. Liv. 1713, not in 1719 tax list. 3 ch. incl. Mary who was unm. in 1736. **Margaret,** m. John Buxton, both liv. in Salem in 1729 and perh. **Mary,** m. 22 June 1717 John Randall of Berwick.

**CHILD,** one of the earliest of English surnames, indicating the heir.

1 **HENRY,** ±33 in 1681, wit. for Thomas Holmes in 1675, bot a house and 40 a. from him in 1679, and was hauling lumber for him in 1680. In 1686 he was given Tho. Parkes's land for life supp. Gr.j. 1688. Lists 96 (p. 81), 296, 298. K. by Ind. 28 Sep. 1691, adm. to wid. 9 Feb. 1691-2. He m. Sarah Nason who m. 2d 10 Nov. 1695 John Hoyt. Although the Court allowed her account as late as 4 Oct. 1726, 'to bringing up intestate's four children,' only two are cert. kn: **Sarah,** b. 26 Oct. 1680, mar. 20 May 1708 Philip Dore. **William,** mason, Stratham. Lists 68, 298, 388. His w. Elizabeth was a wid. by Jan. 1724-5. 4 or m. ch., incl. Richard, bp. 17 Jan. 1724-5, who was of Stratham in 1747. Ano. may have been **Richard,** who d. in Nottingham in 1758, formerly of Durham, est. insolv., leaving 'the woman Hannah' who had been liv. with him unm. This may have been the Richard who was formerly of Dover, working in the woods for Paul Wentworth. He could hardly have been the Richard m. to Sarah Dore of Dover 16 Sep. 1730 under her accu. The fourth may have been **Francis,** taxed in Newcastle ab. 1700. Lists 68, 315b.

2 **JOHN,** in July 1685 had gone away to the Eastward distracted. His w. Anne had been authorized to carry on. Samuel Wakefield his 'son-in-law,' Ebenezer Vaughan a servant. Suff. Co. Ct.

3 **JOSEPH** and **JOHN,** b. in Watertown 1680, 1689, claimed before the Eastern Claims Com. lands in Coxhall bot on spec. by their grf. Richard Norcross, consid. nephew of Rev. Nathaniel.

4 **DOCTOR ROBERT,** disting. savant, emigrated and went back. His brief presence, 1644-1647, was highly disconc. to the Bostoners; he headed an unsymp. petition. In 1645, 'Doctor of Phisicke,' he bot the Biddeford patent from Mr. Vines, (and more than 13 yrs. passed bef. it came again into

respons. hands.) Ag. 22 when he entered the Univ. of Leyden, 23 May 1635, he had had his degrees at Cambridge, 1631 and 1635. He d. in Ireland in 1654, 'living with Esquire Hill,' app. never m. His supposed parentage has been dispr. and not rediscov. He had a bro. Major John. See Col. Soc. Mass. xxi. 1-146.

**CHILSON,** name of a tything in Oxon.

1 **WALSINGHAM,** inhab. of Saco in 1659, had come from Marblehead where he and his w. Mary are recorded 1642-1652. In 1669 he gave his entire est. to his son William. List 247. Mary, who was in ct. for 'being in drink and drinking of an health' in 1659, was bur. 24 Aug. 1674 in Saco. List 246. Kn. ch: **William. Mary,** m. 23 Dec. 1658 John Cole(12).

2 **WILLIAM**(1), Saco, m. 167— Grace Briers(3); d. 1 July 1676, poss. an Indian victim, his wid. being gr. adm. that same month 'for the benefit of her child.' She soon m. 2d Samuel Oakman who deeded the Chilson farm to Humphrey Warren 12 Oct. 1677.

3 **JOHN**(1?), m. in Lynn 28 July 1667 Sarah Jenks, dau. of Joseph, the Lynn ironmaster, and took the O. F. in 1677-8. Rec. ch: **Joseph,** b. Aug. 1670. **Sarah,** b. 4 Aug. 1673, m. 2 Feb. 1693-4 Robert Burnell; also likely **William,** later of Mendon, m. in Lynn 23 May 1696 Jane Rhoads. As a connecting link of the whole fam., **Walsingham,** m. in Lynn 20 Oct. 1709 Susannah Edmunds and d. 15 Jan. 1760 in Bellingham in his 79th yr., is untraced.

**CHINICKE** (aut.), **William,** promoter of an 'illegal combination' at Shoals, 1677. List 306b.

**CHISHOLM,** Chessemore. Form. the name of a Scotch clan.

1 **DANIEL**(2), ag. 71 in June 1743, ± 75 at Newbury in 1746, liv. bef. 1690 at Chessemer's Hill. He dep. that he knew the Briers or Jacksons when they liv. at Spurwink, at Blue Point, Scarb., and at Marbleh. He m. Cyprian Sampson, b. in Beverly 13 Mar. 1672, whose f. later liv. in Scarb. across the river from Chessemer's Hill. She dep. at Newbury 24 Mar. 1745[6, ag. 73, that she had raked hay on the McKenney meadow near Dunkin's or Chezemore Hill. They were of Biddeford (Saco) in 1735, when they sold 20 a. at Chesmore Hill—wit. Joseph and Jacob Cheesemore. Their ch. incl: **Mary,** m. (int. Newbury 11 Aug. 1716) John Cornish of Boston and Newbury. Their sons Cyprian and John were at Newmeadows, Brunswick, with Jacob Chessemore. **Sarah,** b. Newbury 10 Sep. 1694. (**Elizabeth,**? b. 30 Nov.? 1696, d.y.?) **Elizabeth,** b. (30 Nov.? 1697). **Abigail,** b. 15 May 1699, m. 1 Dec. 1721 Daniel Rogers. **Joseph. Jacob,** of Biddeford (Saco)

in 1733, Newmeadows 1739; m. 26 Feb. 1732 in Biddeford Martha Smith. Ch. record. in Brunsw. 1733-1739.

2 **DUNCAN,** first app. 1659 (Jesson), fined for fighting with John Maccham, and wit. against Edward Colcord. Lawsuits in 1667 (Chesson), ind. a fisherman. Wit. at Spurwink (Jessum) in 1669. Lists 237ae (Chessom, Jeshmond). Presum. Chessemer's Hill, called by Capt. Daniel Fogg in 1741 Duncan's Hill, the rising ground east of and circled by Nonsuch River ⅛ mile north of Scarb. Beach station, took its name from him. Kn. ch: **Daniel.**

**Chownes,** See Chane.

**CHRISTOPHERS, Christopher,** Isl. of Shoals wit. 18 June 1660, ae. 26. List 302a. Presum. same m. at Churston-Ferrers, Devon, 16 Aug. 1654 Mary Berry, had ch. in Barbadoes, settled in New London. He d. 25 July 1687, ae. 55, she 13 July 1676 ae. 55 (grsts.) —the discrep. in ages humanly reconc. by a bast. son.

**CHUBB.** 1 **Ebenezer,** late soldier at New Casco fort 1711, sergeant 1722.

2 **JOHN,** soldier at Fort Wm. & Mary, Newc. 1695.

3 **CAPT. PASCO,** commandant at Pemaquid in 1696, outraged English pride by surrendering the fort without firing a gun. List 127. He had been Lt. under Andros, and as Captain, with Ant. Brackett his Lt., had commanded a marching company back of Wells and Saco. For the Pemaquid surrender he was imprisoned under suspicion of treason, but released. He settled in Andover, where the Indians in 1698 to avenge treacherous treatment killed him and his wife and wiped out his posterity. Thus Niles, pp. 238, 244, but this may not be true (List 96, p. 85), or some Chubb must have thought he was made a scapegoat, as —

4 **PASCO,** soldier under Captain Jeremiah Moulton, 1722.

5 **WILLIAM,** soldier in Philip's War.—Savage.

6 **WILLIAM,** soldier at New Casco fort, 1711.

**Chumley,** Nicholas, Pemaquid abut. 1686. Y. D. 17.314.

**CHURCH,** common in Mid. and So. Eng.

1 **JOHN,** Dover, admitted inhab. 1665-6, ±40 in 1681, m. 1st 29 Nov. 1664 in Salis. Abigail Severance, 2d one Sarah. Gr.j. 1667, 1668; j. 1672. Lists 49, 52, 54, 57, 62, 94, 96, 311c, 356ghkm, 357ad, 359ab. Cap. by Ind. 28 June 1689, he escaped only to fall victim 7 May 1696. Ch. by 1st w: **Jonathan, b.** (12 Apr.) 1666, d.s.p. **John,** b. (12 Apr.) 1668. **Ebenezer,** b. 25 Feb. 1669-70, d.s.p. **Abigail,** b. 12 Aug. 1672, m. 23 Apr. 1694 Samuel Piper. **Sarah,** m. 29 Dec. 1699 Nathan Folger of Nantucket, liv. in 1722 when she sold ⅓

of father's est. to Tho. Hanson, which he conv. to heirs of her bro. John in 1727. By 2d w: **Deborah**, b. 15 Aug. 1683, m. 26 Oct. 1704 John Roberts. **Benjamin**, b. 28 Oct. 1688, d.y.

2 **JOHN**(1), Dover, m. 1 Dec. 1699, Mercy Han'son who m. 2d bef. 1713 Nathaniel Young. Constable 1699, jury 1692, gr.j. 1698. Returning from church in the spring of 1711, he and Thomas Downes were k. by Ind. His wid. was app. adm. 5 Dec. 1711. Ch: **Abigail**, b. 15 May 1702, mar. Moses Wingate (John) before 1727. **John**, b. 1 Apr. 1704. **Elizabeth**, b. 2 Apr. 1706, unm. 1728, not in heirship deed 1744. **Jonathan**, b. 25 July 1708, m. Abigail Hanson (Nathaniel), 5 ch. b. in Barrington but rec. in Dover. **Mary**, b. 4 Aug. 1710, liv. unm. in 1730.

**CHURCHWELL**, Churchill, a So. of Eng. name.

1 **ARTHUR**, Saco, 1670, husb. of Eleanor Bonython(1). List 246. In Philip's War he escaped to Marblehead. List 85. D. at Glouc. 22 Jan. 1710. The 50 a. lot given his wife by her f. on the east bank of the Saco River next north of Haley's Gut came down by three or four conflicting titles. Richard Tarr of Glouc. in 1701 agreed with the town to maintain 'old father Churchill during his natural life,' and in 1730 deeded Churchill's Point to his s. Joseph. Sarah 'Churchill' m. 11 Aug. 1709 Edward Andrews(4) and by deed 2 Aug. 1720, reciting her mother's title but conspic. abst. from calling herself Arthur's dau., conveys 'a cert. neck of land.' Y. D. x. 99. Three months earlier Nicholas Roach gave a vague deed (Y. D. x. 51) under which John Bryant deeded land on 'Roach's Point.' In 1753, Blunt vs. Bryant, Hannah Blunt recov. the whole 50 a. She inher. as only ch. of Nicholas Roach (by a 2d wife), he from his infant son, (grst. in Charlestown), Bonython Roach, d. 28 Sep. 1719, ag. 7 weeks; he from his mother Elizabeth Gourding, m. 1st in Boston 22 Dec. 1707 Richard Sadler; 2d 26 Dec. 1714 Nicholas Roach; she from her mother Joanna, m. 1st one Gorden; 2d at Marblehead 21 Jan. 1702-3 Moses Phillips. But N. R. had also a deed, 15 July 1718, from Joanna Phillips of Marbleh., wid. woman, of the full 50 a. Y. D. ix. 69.

2 **ISRAEL** Church——? List 315a.

3 **JOHN**, Winter Harbor wit. in 1688, Y. D. v. 50, xx. 184, likely rel., not quite imposs. s. of (1), quite likely fled to Portsm. (List 237b, 267a).

4 **JOHN** (see 3), first cert. ment. in Hon. Richard Martyn's will, 27 Jan. 1692-3, carrying on his farm at Sagamore Creek. Jury 1695. Lists 318b, 315c. Presum. one Sarah Churchill (see Bickford 7), wit. with Elizabeth Hopley in 1693-4, and with Jacob Lavers in 1710-1, and as Sarah -Leach- in dep. 10 Feb. 1712-3, reciting 'I the said Sarah Churchwell,' was his wife or wid. Still presum., his ch. should incl: **John**, ack. covt. and bp. 26 Dec. 1714; m. 10 July 1718 Mary Jackson, d. of John, mariner; 2d 7 Nov. 1753 Elizabeth (Jackson), wid. of Thomas Cotton, who d. ab. 1775. List 339. Ch. **Martha** and **Elizabeth**, ack. covt. and bp. 1 May 1714-5; Martha, m. 13 Nov. 1718 John Kincade of Waterford, Ire., Elizabeth, m. 18 Sep. 1724 Patrick Lawley.

**CHURCHWOOD**, -ward, a South Devon surname.

1 **GREGORY**, b. in Kingswear, near Dartmouth, Devon, s. of Humphrey, drowned with Edw. Carter at Isles of Shoals 7 Feb. 1670-1. Adm. to conserv. 7 Feb. 1670-1, to his br. Humphrey 29 June 1675.

2 **HUMPHREY**, br. of (1), presum. came over after his br.'s est. In 1681 Francis Trickey and Capt. Barefoot were allowed for keeping and curing H. C., hurt in the country's service. His letter 3 Jan. 1682 to the Boston Baptists about ordaining Wm. Scriven is preserved. Lists 287, 30. He m. aft. 16 Nov. 1686 Mary Cutt(7), who m. 2d bef. 16 Dec. 1693 Lt. Richard Briar(5). His ch., if any, disap. with their stepf.

**Chwing** (Thwing?), Benjamin, 1660. Y. D. i. 120.

**CILLEY**. This spelling, standardized by Gen. Joseph of the Rev. Army, Nottingham, from Ceilly, Cilly, Cille, Scylla, Sellea, Silley, etc., who came from Joseph of Stratham 1729, likely either the son of Thomas and Ann (Stanyan) Silley, b. 6 Oct. 1701, or of Joseph Ceely, belonging to the ship, -Katharine- 1701. See Seeley.

**Circuit**, Katharine, Mr. John Cutt's maid, accu. Hugh Lattimer 29 June 1675.

**Claghorn**, James, N. H. 1697. List 68. Poss. same b. Barnstable 29 Jan. 1654.

**Clamperings** Island. List 323.

**Clampitt**, Edward, Kit. wit. 1717. Y. D. ix. 53.

**CLAPHAM, Arthur**, physician and writer of wills and deeds at Isles of Shoals, where he acted as agent for Wm. Sealey in 1664; ±50 in 1672; fined for drunkenness, 1666, and cursing, 1668; d. May 1676. Lists 82, 302b.

**Clarence**, Robert, Portsm. 1695. List 334b.

**CLARK**, the 9th commonest surname in Eng. and Wales (yet absent in Wales and scarce in the Welsh border counties); the 26th in Scotland; became the 3d in N. E. Altho Clark and Smith are of little use for the distinguishing purposes of surnames, they had perhaps the most honorable extraction of all. In every hamlet large enough to support a man of learning and a man of

applied science in the period when surnames were being taken on, they invar. took the names Clerk (spoken Clark) and Smith. So it is that when two Clarks meet, unless they know their ancestry, they have no more reason to look on each other as distant relation than if they were one Clark and one Smith. But they do show, among England's mixed races, distinctly Anglo-Saxon origin, except where emigrants from other countries bearing names of the same meaning have translated them into English.

1 **ABRAHAM**, Kennebec, 1674. List 15.

2 **ABRAHAM**, dep. at Oyster River, ±29 25 Mar. 1679, first taxed 1677. Often in company with Wm. Follett. Altho he appar. withdrew to Newcastle in the war, (taxed there 1691), he presum. was the Oyster River victim of 1694. Lists 359ab, 319, 358b. If his age be correct, Mary Clark, who mar. Bartholomew Stevenson could not be his dau. Deliverance Clark, creditor of Tho. Drew's est. in 1694, may have been his wid. or dau. Ch: **Deliverance**, m. Nathl. Lamos, 2d Joseph Hanson. Her will 1766—1773 names bros. James and Eli Clark and sist. Mary and Sarah Osborne, the latter dec. leaving ch. **Sarah**, m. at Salem 30 Aug. 1705 Samuel Osborn, d. 1738-1766. **James**, mar. 16 Jan. 1717-8 Sarah Leighton. Will 1754 — 1768 names 5 ch., also rec. in Quaker rec., incl. sons Jonathan and Remembrance. **Mary**, m. at Salem 10 June 1717 Samuel Osborn jr., her sister's stepson. **Eli**, ag. 69 in May 1763, 73 in Mar. 1767, knew Durham in 1703. Wife Elizabeth presum. d. of Robert Huckins.

3 **ABRAHAM**, 59 in 1738, carpenter, poss. br. of Mary (Clark) Stephenson, and they neph. and niece to (2), or ch. of (2) by a dif. mother, or omitted from the Friends' records by leaving them. Sergt. in Dummer's War. His Dover gr. of 1701 was sold in 1737 by Nathl. and Abigail Lamos and Wm. and Abigail Demeritt. Hannah Clark, Friend, m. John Reynolds 23 Dec. 1718. One Abraham with w. Anna had ch. rec. 1721-25, bp. in Dover 1740-42 with their mo.; sold to Remembrance, s. of James, who settled near him, in 1761; d. in Barrington 1762. Another Abraham was of Brentwood.

4 **ANTHONY**, fisherman at the Trelawny Plantation 1638-1640. List 21.

5 **ARTHUR**, a first-comer to Hampton 1639, appar. bro.-in-law of James Davis(12), made freeman at Salem 13 May 1640, settled in Boston by 1643, carpenter. Lists 391a, 392a, 75b. Adm. 31 Oct. 1665 to wid. Sarah. Kn. ch: **Sarah**, bp. 17 Mar. 1643-4, ag. 7 d. **Samuel**, b. 1 Nov. 1646, d. in Concord 30 Jan. 1729-30. Wife Rachel (Nichols) d. 1722. 7 ch.

6 **DAVID**. List 298, p. 38, 1744, likely bro. of (28), b. Haverhill 21 Aug. 1699, sons

of Joseph and Mary (Davis). See (49).

7 **EDWARD**, first ment. in Salem Qtly. Ct. for his wife Barbara in 1639, at Marblehead 1641. Next seen at Cape Porpus in first list of inhab. 1653. Jury 1656, gr.j. 1656, there in 1658, of Saco 1660. Lists 251, 263, 244c, 249, 24. Adm. 17 Sep. 1661 to widow Barbara. Rowland Thompson, citizen of London, in his will 31 May 1662 gave £5 to his wife Barbara's dau., Barbara Clarke of New Eng., wid. She next m. John Smith, the aged master carpenter. Div. of est. proves 2 ch: **Sarah**, m. 6 May 1658 or 1659 James Harmon. **Samuel**, a minor in 1666. Pope's Pioneers copies Bradbury's Kennebunkport in saying that they had also William and Edward. Edward was Edw. -Start- of York, many miles away and nothing to indicate con. if his name had been Clark. As Bradbury did not make Matthew(40), a son, he must have misr. him -William-, not otherwise visible. This horrible example of the inconseq. char. of early print. gen. must suffice for many passed unnoticed.

8 **EDWARD**, carpenter, of Doctor's Island, Portsm., by 1657. He and his w. were given 25 a. in the div. of 1660-1. Gr.j. 1663, 1665, 1666. Lists 330ab, 326ac, 331a, 311b, 323. Drowned shortly bef. 17 June 1675, date of inv. Adm. to wid. Mary. He m. 1st Elizabeth Fernald(2); 2d Mary Farrow(1), who m. 2d aft. 13 Sep. 1677 John Smith of York. Ch. enum. in dist. 27 June 1676, by 1st w: **John**, eldest s., to be bound out by Capt. Cutt and Mr. Stileman. **Sarah**, ±30 in 1693, to be bound to her aunt Sarah Waterhouse, m. Thomas Deverson(1), 2d one Ward. 'The three Children' by 2d w., unident. unless one or more of them were wives of Samuel Knight or John Bugg. In 1680 Joseph Lee sued John Smith, Sr. and John Bugg for a debt from E. C.'s est. Bugg liv. on Doctor's Isl., and Samuel and w. Amie Knight sold land settled on the wid. with warranty against all the heirs.

9 **EDWARD**, from London, m. in Portsm. 18 Oct. 1725 Christian (Egbear) Bushby, b. at Boston 30 June 1690, wid. of Robert, who m. 3d 18 Aug. 1728 Joseph Miller. She ack. covt. in So. Ch. 6 Nov. 1726, and had 3 ch. by two hus. bap. John and Elizabeth Bushby, Mary Clark.

10 **ELISHA**(15), carpenter, ±65 in Mar. 1729-30, dep. that he knew Salmon Falls in 1688. Benj. Clark, b. in Rochester 1797, told his grs. C. W. Tibbetts: 'my great-grandfather was Solomon, whose f. came from Scotland.' George Sawin Stewart called John Clarke of Wenham and Exeter a Scotchman. In 1696 and in 1705 Elisha liv. in Kittery. For many yrs. he liv. on Cochecho Point, ferryman, within hailing distance from the Maine shore and from Dover Neck. In 1727

he sold to s. John, reserv. 2 a. and ferry privilege for life. Liv. 1739. Lists 290, 298, 358cd. He m. Sarah Taylor, d. of John and Martha. Rec. ch: **Catherine,** b. 25 Nov. 1691, m. 20 Nov. 1712 Matthew James. One Mrs. James d. at Ichabod Clark's in Stratham 26 Jan. 1752. **John,** b. 20 Apr. 1694, of Kittery, shipwright, in 1727; 7 ch. by w. Judith, a wid. in 1737. John of Georgetown, Lincoln Co., in 1763 sold lands on Cochecho Point and in Rochester. **Sarah,** b. 9 Jan. 1696. **Abijah,** b. 7 Sep. 1699. **Elisha,** b. 16 May 1702. **Josiah,** b. 20 Feb. 1704. **Solomon,** b. 17 Apr. 1707, w. Judith, settled in Rochester, liv. 1760. **Stephen,** b. 10 Jan. 1709-11, d. 26 Aug. 1716.

11 **FREEMAN,** bro. of (49), b. about 1658, app. sailed with Joshua Fryer(3), aut. 1684 in N. H. Prob. 432. 'Sergt. Freeman Clarke of Ipsw.' was wounded at Maquoit 4 Aug. 1691. List 37. His neph., Nathaniel, s. of Sergt. Thomas jr., received a land gr. for his war service. Will 1692—1697, 'bound to the Barbadoes.' No ch. The list of his creditors, 30 Jan. 1698-9, incl: 'To the widow Clarke of Dover £1.' See (31).

12 **GEORGE**(30), joiner, chairmaker, mar. (int. 31 Dec. 1709) Elizabeth Jewett. He bot in Stratham in 1718, and in 1722, having rem. there, sold the Ipsw. homestead. Last ment. 1727. In a deed of Tho. and Rachel Moore, Edward and Anna Taylor and John and Hannah Pormort, 1747, he is called dec.

13 **CAPT. ISAAC**(52), taken on the surrender of Fort Loyal, was reckoned 102 at his death 26 May 1768. He was a capt. in Dummer's War. He mar. in Marlboro 1691 Sarah Stone, and liv. with her 70 yrs., chiefly at Framingham. Their prog. at his death was accounted 251. Ch: **Mercy,** m. 1 July 1712 Joseph Gibbs. 6 ch. **Martha,** m. 5 Jan. 1715-6 Maj. Joseph Willard, d. 3 June 1694. 12 ch. **Matthias,** mar. 17 Oct. 1729 Lydia Eaton, d. 1780 in Spencer. 7 ch. **Sarah,** b. 5 Aug. 1701, m. 10 June 1719 Tho. Drury, d. 10 Apr. 1743. 13 ch. **Mary,** b. 31 Dec. 1703, m. Wm. McCoy. **Jonathan,** b. 9 July 1706, d. 2 May 1709. **Isaac,** b. 25 Mar. 1709, m. 21 Apr. 1740 Mary Stone. 1 ch. **Jonathan,** d. in 1789. 5 ch. **Rebecca,** b. 30 Sep. 1716, m. 14 June 1737 Samuel Stone. 10 ch.

14 **JACOB**(49), sole heir and liv. on homestead; estate insolvent. Constable 1700. Lists 315bc, 316. Adm. 8 Oct. 1722 to wid. Alice (Davie 4), still his wid. 1748. 8 ch., not in order, liv. in 1738: **John,** eldest s., taxed 1720, fisherman 1725. In1736 of Newcastle, fisherman, with w. Elizabeth, presum. same called 'sister' in Nathl. Tuckerman's will. In 1751 he was liv. in a house on his father's land. In 1752 John of Portsm., chairmaker, sued his uncles as heir by primogen.

under will of his gt-grf. Presum. same of Newc. in 1763 with w. Abigail (Downes, d. of Gershom[6 jr.]). **Samuel. Isaac.** In 1760 his wid. Jemima, w. of Capt. John Pickering, and d. Mary q.c. to Stephen Batson. **Jacob,** bp. in So. Ch., Portsm. 13 July 1718. Adm. 1751. In 1774 his heirs were 3 daus. **Joseph,** in 1756 was of York, fisherman, with w. Sarah. Poss. the same in Portsm. poor house, blind, d. 25 Oct. 1781, ag. 70. **Love,** m. John Batson(2). **Mary,** m. one True; 2d by 1752 John Priddam, ropemaker, his wid. in 1757. **Elizabeth.**

15 **JOHN,** ±58 in 1678, ±60 in 1680, first app. in Wenham by birth of s. in 1665; he presum. had earlier ch., esp. Jonathan. Rem. to the Quamscot Patent near Hampton bounds by 1670. (Bot from John Gilman in 1696.) Lists 376b, (1670), 383, 52, 94. In 1674 Robert Smart's negro Bess acc. him. Kn. ch. (3 rec. in Wenham): **Jonathan,** b. ab. 1661. **Elisha,** b. 12 Apr. 1665. **Martha,** b. 28 Mar. 1667. **Sarah,** b. 14 Feb. 1668-9. **Solomon,** b. 19 Feb. 1672. **Ichabod,** b. 25 Dec. 1674. **Mary,** b. 18 June 1678.

16 **JOHN,** ag. 48 in June 1676, ±48 in Dec. 1677, mariner, yeoman, innholder, poss. the unident. s. of Lt. Wm. of Salem. See Furber(2). In 1674 his wife (from Gt. Isl.) and Wm. Furber jr. (from Dover) were both at Strawberry Bank protest. against Jane Furson and her grch. pulling up Richard Cummings' corn. He was of Isles of Shoals in 1664 when he bot at Newcastle, where he soon became active in town and probate bus. Jury 1682, 1683. Highway surv. 1692; selectman 1693; assessor 1698. Lists (323), 326bc, 330a, 331b, 49, 52, 54, 62, (82), 306b, 312cf, 313a, 315abc. Will 25 Apr.—20 July 1700 names only wife and 2 sons. His w. Elizabeth, ±34 in 1674, ±38 in 1678, ±42 in the witchcraft case, 1682, evid. boarded Walter Barefoote in his last yrs., liv. 1719, not taxed 1720. List 331c, 316. Ch: **Samuel,** wit. with his mo. in 1682, d. early. **Love** and **Isaac,** ment. in Barefoote's will, 1688. List 65. **Jacob. Joseph,** was drowned at Jamaica, a young man unm.

17 **JOHN,** seaman, lying in Hampton under Goodman Tucke's hands, d. 18 May 1658.

18 **JOHN,** Mr., small taxpayer at Cape Elizabeth, 1683-84. List 226. Poss. (16) or a transient from outside.

19 **JOHN,** Kittery, Oct. 1660, defamed his mistress, Mrs. Sarah Gunnison, innholder. Me. P. & C. i. 367.

20 **JOHN**(8), d. 13 Apr. 1694, ag. 29 (grst.), housewright liv. on Doctor's or Clark's Isl., Portsm. and his fam. after him. Lists 334a, 335a, p. 174, 330de. His will 13 Apr. 1695, unproven, is missing, adm. to wid. Mary, who refused to act as exec. Her bondsm. Edw. Ayers(1), apprs. Nathl. Ayers(6) and James

Leavitt. Lists 331c, 335a. Her will, 20 Jan. 1719-20—2 June 1725, devised the island as her prop., naming their 3 ch. and her s. Ichabod: **John**, shipwright, Kit., m. 27 May 1725 Lydia Fernald(5), both liv. 1737, she d. 17 Apr. 1743. **Sarah**, m. 1st 13 Sep. 1713 Capt. Wm. Nolar or Knowles; 2d 3 May 1723 Joseph Martin. Adm. 'wid.' in 1745 to her dau. Mary Nolar. 3+4 or 5 ch. **Elizabeth**, m. 13 Oct. 1716 Tho. Snow. 2 ch. bp. 1728. (Ichabod Clark, b. on Clark's Isl. May 1701, m. 15 Sep. 1723 Lydia Abbott, d. of John(1 jr.). 6 ch. bp. in Portsm. So. Ch., incl. Ichabod, bp. 20 Apr. 1735, who had ch.)

21 **REV. JOHN**(42), b. in Newbury 24 June 1670, H.C. 1690. With urgent calls from West Newbury and Exeter 1693-5, he chose the latter. His wife was adm. member of Hampton Ch. 9 May 1697 and with others of Exeter dism. to organ. a ch. there 11 Sep. 1698. Lists 376b (1697), 96. He d. int. 25 July 1705. Adm. to his wid. 2 Apr. 1706, her bond wit. by John Odlin. He m. 19 June 1694 Elizabeth Woodbridge, grn. of Rev. Samuel Dudley, b. 30 Apr. 1673, d. of Rev. Benj. and Mary (Ward), grd. of two preachers and m. two, the second, m. 21 Oct. 1709, Rev. John Odlin; and d. 6 Dec. 1729. 4 ch. by each hus: **Benjamin**, b. June 1695, master mariner, of Barbadoes in 1722, of Newcastle at death. Adm. 28 Dec. 1730. He mar. 30 Nov. 1720 Jane Pepperell, 'Aunt Clark' in 1737-8. She m. 2d Wm. Tyler and 3d 21 Aug. 1760 Ebenezer Tirrell of Medford, Mass. 2 sons. **Nathaniel**, b. 10 Dec. 1697, liv. in Cork, Ireland, later in Barbadoes; not in his br.'s will. **Deborah**, b. 3 Nov. 1699, m. 2 Oct. 1718 Dr. Tho. Dean, 11 ch., 1719-1742, incl. Deborah, d. 6 Sep. 1735. **Ward**, Rev., b. 12 Dec. 1703, H.C. 1723, first ordained min. of Kingston 29 Sep. 1725. Having lost his wife (Mary Frost, m. 20 Nov. 1727, d. of Major Charles jr.) and all their ch., his inter. will, 11 Mar.—7 June 1736-7, leaving benef. for four communities, the rest to his remaining rel., is printed. List 376b.

22 **JOHN**, impressed by a Portsm. captain in 1696, 5 mos. service in Dover( not Oyster River). List 336b.

23 **JOHN**, Stratham, b. 30 Mar. 1680 in Haverhill, s. of Matthew and Mary (Wilford). See (49). By trad. (Hist. Sanbornton), a sis. m. a Mudgett. List 388. Will 20 July 1750—12 June 1753 names w. Ann, sons John, Satchwell, Joseph, Daniel, daus. Mary, Ann, Martha. He m. 1st Mary, app. Rundlett, d. of Charles and Mary (Shatswell) Dale-Smith-Rundlett; 2d Ann Smith, d. of Nicholas and Mary (Gordon). Ch: **John**, b. 26 Feb. 1705, settled in Kingston. Adm. 1753 to wid. Elizabeth (Clifford). Div. 1758 to wid. and 10 ch. **Sachwell**, b. 30 Oct.

1706. By 2d w: **Mary**, b. 4 June 1712, m. Joshua Rollins. 5 or m. ch. **Anne**, b. 21 Mar. 1714[5, m. one Allen. **Nicholas**, b. 9 Nov. 1716. **Joseph**, b. 9 May 1719. **Daniel. Martha.**

24 **JOHN**, br. of (36 and 56), sons of Hanniel and Mary (Gutterson), b. in Haverhill 23 Apr. 1696, mason, Portsm. See (49). Sold in Barrington. List 339. Adm. 31 Jan. 1744-5 to widow Agnes, who became n.c.m.; adm. d.b.n. 23 Oct. 1749 to only s. **Josiah**, bp. July 1716, mason, who m. 14 Jan. 1747-8 Mary Moses. Ch. Daus. unk.

25 **JONATHAN**, br. of (49), taxed with him 1672. Wit. with Sergt. Tho. 1677. Wit. at Newbury 1679. ±21 in 1669, ±32 10 Mar. 1679. Ipsw. soldier in Philip's War, his Narragansett grant in Buxton was allowed in 1735 to Nathaniel, either of Newbury, grs. of (42), or of Ipsw., s. of his bro. Sergt. Thomas jr. One Jonathan had grants at Portland 1680. List 225a. Jonathan of Newbury, tanner, m. 15 May 1683 Lydia Titcomb. Rec. ch: **Oliver**, b. 6 Feb. 1683-4. **Samuel**, b. 18 Mar. 1686-7. **Jonathan**, b. 24 May 1689. **Lydia**, b. 17 May 1691. **Elizabeth**, b. 10 May 1694.

26 **JONATHAN**, this man seems to visualize, and to be s. of (15). Essex Qtly. vii. 288. 1679, wit. with Mr. Scammon and Armstrong Horne, conc. Rébecca Morgan—the neighb. where (15) settled. ±32 in Dec. 1694, Exeter soldier in 1696, ±75 in 1736, ab. 52 yrs. ago worked for Capt. Wadleigh. In 1713, of Exeter, he dep. that 27 or 28 yrs. since he helped build a mill on Lamprill River. Sep. 6, 1686, he was m. by Justice Wadleigh to Mary Magoon. In 1706 he sold his house at Lamprill River. Lists 57, (388), (67), 376b, 1698. In the 1725 Exeter div. he was gr. 40 a. Of Newmarket 1731, dec. in 1740. Ch. unkn. but likely incl. **Solomon**, gr. 30 a. in 1725, of Newmarket, laborer, ag. 44 in 1736. **Mary**, in the courts 1733-1743. Also perh. Jonathan(27), Josiah(35).

27 **JONATHAN**(26?), ag. 73 in 1760, apprent. to Wm. Moore sr. in 1700, 'jr.' of Swampscot in 1715, in 1744 mtg. land bot of Wm. Moore in 1715. (List 388). Rec. ch. by w. Zipporah: **Jonathan**, b. (24 Apr.) 1711, presum. m. 26 May 1741 Ann Cram. **Joanna**, b. (24 Apr.) 1713. **John**, b. 15 July 1715. **Mary**, b. 22 Mar. 1718. Also **Ichabod**, in 1754 was given part of the homestead. W. **Elizabeth** in 1760.

28 **JONATHAN**, List 298 p. 37, 1736, likely bro. of (6), b. Haverhill 25 Mar. 1690.

29 **'JOSEPH.'** List 331b. Error for (32) Josiah?

30 **JOSIAH** of Ipsw., b. ab. 1646, son of Thomas the cooper, and neph. of Edward of Haverhill, making him first cous. of Matthew, Hanniel and Joseph, whose sons came to the Pisc. See (49). In 1673 he bound out

to Henry Green of Hampton the 2-yr. old boy sworn on him by Sarah Warr. Tho. 'jr.', his bro., was his surety in 1671, and in 1667 Tho. 'sr.' was surety for Josiah(31) 'about stocks.' See (49). He was sheriff's deputy in Essex Co. He d. 27 Sep. 1691, adm. to wid. Mercy (Boynton, of Rowley, m. 14 Dec. 1670), who.m. 2d 4 July 1692 Dea. Joseph Goodhue, 3d, Nov. 1712, John Hovey, and d. 22 Dec. 1730. He liv. with his f. and did not come east, but his s. George, who bot out his sisters Mercy, Hannah and Sarah, wife of Nathl. Bailey, and his bro. Thomas, tailor of Boston 1715, rem. to Stratham.

31 JOSIAH, taxed at Portsm. with (49) in 1672, in 1675 was in the service of Mr. John Cutt(2). His excel. aut. is found on Mr. Cutt's papers in 1676. It is not easy to picture him as (32), who upon occasion m. a wid. with many ch. and little means, and of no known social position; and he merely vanishes. But his bro. Freeman(11) in his will left £10 to his son Josiah, liv. with Tristram Coffin in Newbury, poss. the Josiah who d. in Ipsw. 2 Feb. 1738, ag. 67. See Lists 326c, 331a.

32 JOSIAH, Portsm., could be the one taxed in 1674. In 1676-7 he worked on the road. In Oct. 1677 he and w. Sarah were in court, and in Nov. he was petit. to be let out of jail to provide for his large charge of ch. He had been a soldier. She was wid. of Richard Sampson. See Lists 326c, 331a, (1674), (331b).

33 JOSIAH(49), could not have been (31 or 32), but likely was the one gaining wit. fees by spotting unlicens. liquor sellers in Berw. 7 Jan. 1695-6. Surely it was he helping John Ford to break jail in 1702. Lists 330de. He m. in Boston 27 Sep. 1708 Elizabeth Summers. In 1717 Josiah of Portsmouth, husbandman, sold rights in common lands. See (35). Kn. ch: Summers, b. 19 Aug. 1709 in Boston, of Stonington, Conn., in 1731, when he q.c. land deeded to his grmo. Ann Clark by Richard Cutt. In 1733 he was of Portsm. buying land in Barr., later of Newbury, with w. Amme (Hills, m. 26 Nov. 1735), ch. 1737-1740.

34 JOSIAH(42), b. 7 May 1682, in Exeter in 1700, and in 1705, called tailor; in 1707 of Boston, tailor, where he d. 29 Apr. 1717. Adm. 1 Feb. 1719-20 to wid. Sarah (Chamberlain, m. 24 Jan. 1705), who m. 26 May 1720 Joseph Woodwell of Bridgewater. She had been liv. in Hingham. Ch: John, b. 21 Oct. 1710. Josiah, b. 1 Jan. 1713.

35 JOSIAH, petn. Stratham 1709, List 388; taxed in Greenland 1717-18, small, in 1719 'J. C. and farm' (leased). See (33). In 1722 Daniel Allen and J. C. of Greenl. parish were absent from meeting. One Josiah Clark m. Jane Berry in Greenl. 9 May 1728.

36 JOSIAH, b. 8 Mar. 1691-2 in Haverhill, bro. of (24 and 56) sons of Hanniel and Mary (Gutterson). See (49). Clothier, Portsmouth tax list calls him J. C. the Dyer. He m. 21 Apr. 1715 Mary Wingate of Dover, and in July both joined Portsm. No. Church. List 339. He d. in 1729, adm. 27 June 1734 to wid. Mary. They cert. were the parents of Anne, bp. 26 Aug. 1722, and of Sarah, ag. 3 y. 9 m. when her father d., and perh. also: Mary, George, Phebe, or Elizabeth, bp. 1720-1723. Pickering Gen., p. 102, gives them s. John, b. 16 Feb. 1718-9, shipmaster at Salem, who m. Sarah Pickering, d. of Timothy and Mary (Wingate), will 1801, parents of Rev. Dr. John Clarke of Boston. John Clark of Portsm., mariner, in 1746 deeded to his mo. Mary the house where she was liv., on Daniel and Middle Streets.

37 JOSIAH(10), of Somersworth 1731, Rochester 1733, Somersw. with w. Patience 1734, still there 1737, settled in Newcastle, Me. Later or earlier desc. call Patience's name -Blackstone-, and recite their 10 ch., incl. Ichabod of Falm. who did m. Sarah Blackstone, d. of Benj.

38 MARY, of Portsm., wid., poss. progenitrix of Presidents, but nothing kn. of whom, him or it, up for bastardy in N. H. ct. 26 Jan. 1685[6.

39 MATTHEW, ±30 in 1657. Boston mariner on the Kennebec. List 181.

40 MATTHEW, recur. fined for drunkenness 1671-1682 (return, Gone), at Saco and York courts.

41 NATHAN, N. H. Treas. acct. 1693. List 60.

42 NATHANIEL, bro. of (49), b. 1642, never liv. in N. H., but ch. did and wid. with all the younger ch. His post. well hunted by Geo. Kuhn Clarke. At 21 he m. into an important Newbury family and liv. his short but emin. useful life there. Will 21, d. 25, Aug. 1690. He m. 23 Nov. 1663 Elizabeth Somerby, who m. 2d Rev. John Hale of Beverly, who d. 15 May 1700, after which she liv. with s. (21) in Exeter and d. 15 Mar. 1716, ag. 71 (grst.). Ch: Nathaniel, b. 5 Dec. 1664, d. 6 June 1665. Nathaniel, b. 13 Mar. 1666, d. Oct. 1690 on the Canada exped., m. 15 Dec. 1685 Elizabeth Toppan, dau. of Dr. Peter. 2 ch. Thomas, b. 9 Feb. 1668, d. 25 Apr. 1722, mar. Sarah Noyes, dau. of Col. Thomas and Martha (Pierce), 2d 17 Oct. 1705 Lydia Moody, dau. of Samuel and Mary (Cutting). Ch. 6+3. John, b. 24 June 1670. Henry, b. 5 July 1673, d. 9 June 1749, m. 7 Nov. 1695 Elizabeth Greenleaf, dau. of Capt. Stephen; 2d 24 Jan. 1724 Mary Pierce. 12 ch., of whom Elizabeth m. 3 Mar. 1717 Daniel Thing of Exeter, and Mercy, b. 26 Dec. 1714, m. Jonathan Longfellow of Nottingham. Daniel, b. 16, bp. 19 Dec. 1675. Sarah,

b. 12 Jan., bp. 24 Feb. 1678, m. 9 June 1697 Judge Nicholas Gilman of Exeter. **Josiah**, b. 7 May 1682. **Elizabeth**, b. 15, bp. 18 May 1684, m. 1st Dr. Robt. Hale of Beverly, 2d John Gilman. **Judith**, b. Jan. 1687, unm., Exeter, 170—, m. in Boston 27 Jan. 1712. Israel How, who d. 27 Sep. 1735, 5 ch.; 2d 29 July 1737 Thomas Jenkins, mariner. **Mary**, b. 25 Mar. 1689, d.y.

43 **NATHANIEL**(49?), cordwainer, wrote, was bap. on becoming an orig. memb. in forming the Wells church. First app. 1692 in Wells, in the record of his oldest son's birth. Gr.j. 1701. Lists 268a, 269abc. Will 8 Feb.— 26 Mar. 1717-8 names w. Patience (Wells) and 9 ch. In 1725 the wid. deeded to s. Samuel for life sup. Ch: **Sarah**, m. (int. 2—Aug. 1715) Henry Burton of Salem. **Nathaniel**, b. 17 Sep. 1692, m. at Ipsw. 1 June 1715 Martha Treadwell. 12 ch. **Mary**, b. 8 Feb. 1694[5, Thompson in will. **Isaac**, b. 19 Mar. 169—. **Eleazer**, b. 30 Dec. 1699, m. 6 July 1727 Elizabeth Thompson of Durham, N. H. List 269c. **James**, bp. 12 Sep. 1702, m. 6 Nov. 1728 Sarah Littlefield. Both liv. Bidd. 1741. **Samuel**, b. 2 Apr. 1703, m. 26 Dec. 1728 Lydia Wells; both liv. 1768. List 269c, 1734. **Abigail**, bp. 7 Sep. 1707. **Abigail**, b. 13 Dec. 1709. **Esther**, joined ch. 26 Apr. 1730, m. 13 Aug. 1731 Isaac Southwick of Salem, living 1782.

43½ **NOAH**, N. H. Probate ii. 254, misr. of Barker.

44 **OLIVER**, came to the Trelawny Plant. in -The Speedwell- 1635, ran away with the others who went to the Piscataqua in June 1636. List 21.

45 **RICHARD**, ±19 in 1682, apprent. of Roger Rose at Lubberland, was there by several rec. until 1691. Evid. is lacking to connect him with the successful—

46 **RICHARD**, of Newmarket, or to connect either with (15, 26 or 30). Exeter gave him a large gr. 1725. From the Rix nar. we could surm. that he was b. around Greenland ab. 1693 and that his f. was of English stock. An easy way to leave a problem uns. is to surm. that Richard of Lubberland m. Elizabeth Footman, was an Ind. victim, and the wid. then m. John Phillips, a soldier from No. Kingston, R. I. In 1735 R. C. was calling her 'mother,' had her at his house, and Rev. John Moody, a newcomer, testif. that he was reput. her son. She soon d. at her neph. Footman's house, declaring that R. C. had tricked her into signing a deed to him of what she intended for her s. John Phillips. Likelier she was Clark's foster mother. He m. 23 Dec. 1725 Lydia Marston (Caleb). 4 sons.

47 **ROBERT**, Newcastle, about the fort as soldier and laborer 1694-98. In 1695 'of Kittery' was fined as a common drunkard and idler. The coroner's jury, 15 June 1697, found his death 'from overdrinking of rum.' Lists 65, 67, 68.

48 **ROBERT**, a boy, of 'Yorke,' a captive in Canada in 1695. List 99.

49 **SAMUEL**, ±27 in 1671-1672, ±40 in 1685, Portsm. tanner. Nathaniel(42) was cert. his br., and presum. also Jonathan and Josiah, taxed, with Samuel in Portsm. 1672. Their father was one of the Thomases of Ipswich, four in number. Three were made freemen, 1646, 1652, 1674. Three signed the protest in 1666 against the treatment of the King's Commissioners in Boston, there called Sr., Jr., and 3d. These were Sergt. Thomas the tanner, Thomas the cooper, who was br. of Edward of Haverhill, and Thomas the tailor, son of Sergt. Thomas, b. 1638, who m. Abigail Cogswell and d. 1682. Besides these three, there came to Ipsw. by 1670 the fourth Thomas, called 'Winnisimmet' when elected tythingman in 1679. Three of these four may have been totally unrel. The newcomer had been in 1658-60 the ferryman and innholder at Chelsea, and app. was 'Brewer Clark' and 'Corporal Clark' at Ipsw. Also the cooper was liv. in East Boston when his dau. m. Geo. Hiskett. His br. at Haverhill, b. ab. 1622, and w. Dorcas (Bosworth), by their sons Hanniel, Matthew and Joseph, had at least 6 grsons who settled on the Piscataqua. Sergt. Thomas Sen. and his sons carried on the tanyard at the foot of Summer St. some 60 yrs. Three of his sons liv. on his land there, John, Sergt. Thomas and Freeman(11); Nathaniel(42) and Jonathan (25) liv. at Newbury; and four, Samuel(49), Josiah(31), Jonathan and Freeman, were at Portsm. In 1682 by a sort of will he tried to arrange with Freeman for life supp. of hims. and wife Mary, and two years later changed to John. He d. 9 Jan. 1689-90, and his wife 27 weeks later. Thomas the cooper could have made only a brief try at Boston, in 1659 he was working up clapboards in Ipsw. His dau. m. Hiskett 11 June 1662. His will at Ipsw., 23 June 1688—inv. 14 May 1691, app. rememb. all his poster.: son Josiah, wid. and ch. of s. Thomas, dau. Sarah Hiskett and her ch., as recorded in Boston. Thomas the tailor also tried Boston, where his s. Thomas was born 7 July 1664, and Salem. His nunc. will, 19 Sep. 1682, left his house in Ipsw., on part of his father's land near the mill, to his wid. Abigail for life, who liv. in it until her death 2 Apr. 1728, ag. 87, after which releases reveal their poster., rep. 6 ch., incl. Thomas, tailor, of Ipsw., Thomas, tailor, of Marbleh., others of Boston, Cambridge, Isl. of Nassau. It seemed desir. to untang. these Ipsw. Thomases so as to know the relations betw. the Clarks here. Samuel's first app. was in Portsm. 10

Feb. 1667, already married to Sarah Leader, dau. of the dist. promoter, and niece of the wife of Capt. Richard Cutt. Whether he met her in Portsm. or in Barbadoes is undet.; her father dead after remar., she may have been liv. with her aunt or sis. here. By calling a tanner, he was otherw. active. Jury 1682, 1684, 1685; gr.j. 1683. In 1672 he and Mr, Mattoon were with John Clark at Ipswich, where Philip Mattoon was John Clark's apprent. Lists 326c, 329, 331b, 52, 55ab, 57, 92. His will 21 June 1686—8 Oct. 1691 left all to his w. for bringing up their 3 youngest ch. Her will 28 Sep.—4 Dec. 1723 left all to her (unfort.) dau. Sarah, thus shutting out our inform. She was given victualer's and innholder's licenses. In 1720 she was gr. adm. on est. of her f. and uncle Richard and George Leader. Lists 330d, 331c, 337, 335a, p. 175. Only 5 of their ch., perh. numerous, are disclosed: **Margaret, m.** by 1688 John Jackson, mariner; 2d Philip White, mariner; 3d Roger Swain. **Nathaniel,** bondsman for Josiah in 1702, and presum. bro., unident. but likely (43). The brothers Nathaniel (wife Priscilla) and Josiah in Boston 1707 were from Ipsw., app. (49 Sergt. Thomas jr.). Ab. 1711 Mark Ayers claimed his rights in Portsm. commons, and the selectmen ruled: no such man in the rate list. **Bridget,** mar. Joseph Miller, joined the No. Ch., and had 5 ch. bap. in 1714. **Sarah,** had a son (Richard Clark of Kit., of age, 1732, liv. in Boston, boat builder, 1736; of Dover, boatwright, in 1738; liv. 1740; d.s.p.). She m. 30 Jan. 1726-7 Sylvester Mantee, sailor, from 'Milford Haven in Wales'; 2d Capt. Robert Evans. In 1767 as heir of her son Richard she sold his rights bot in Canterbury. Among others poss. **Samuel**(50) is likely.

50 **SAMUEL,** likely s. of (49), in 1705, weaver, bot a 40-ft. houselot on Pickering's Neck. List 339. Agnes, his w., 4 July 1708 ack. covt. and was bap. with two ch. Samuel Clark's wid. was taxed in 1726. Her mar. contr. with John Meader of Durham 5 Apr. 1735, who soon d. In 1742 she was given lic. to sell her first husband's r.e.; liv. Portsm. 1746. The ch. sold their father's house in ninths: **Mary,** m. Dea. John Shorey of Berwick. **Elizabeth,** bp. 4 July 1708 with Mary, app. d.y. **Agnes,** bp. 2 Oct. 1709, m. app. Henry Terrell, cert. John Gorman, mariner, by 1751; his wid. 1762, of Portm. **Rebecca,** m. 24 Sep. 1730 Isaac Reed of Portsm. and Kit., shipwright. **Thomas,** bp. 16 Mar. 1711-2, weaver, m. 27 Jan. 1733-4 Sarah Seward. Sold two-ninths in 1762. **Samuel,** bp. 14 Feb. 1713-4, likelier an infant that d.y. **Sarah,** bp. 28 Oct. 1716, m. 22 June 1740 John Meserve. **Elizabeth,** bp. 29 Mar. 1719, m. Aaron Chick of Berwick. **Abigail,** bp. 12

July 1724, unm. 1760. **Priscilla,** joined So. Ch. 1742, m. Ichabod Cowell of Rochester.

51 **SAMUEL,** York, b. 13 Jan. 1690-1 in Topsfield, s. of Daniel and Damaris. Called by error 'of Wells' in 1743, he adm. est. of his bro. Jacob of Topsham. List 279 (1732). He m. 1 Dec. 1712 Dorothy Bradstreet, bp. in Topsfield 25 Oct. 1691, whose death record, 9 Feb. 1780, ag. 90, calls her 'grandchild of Governor Bradstreet.' Rec. ch. 1721-1734: **Dorothy, Daniel, Mary, Samuel, Mercy, Anna.** Of these Daniel m. Lucy, d. of Hon. Jeremiah Moulton, and desc. handed down a snuff box marked faintly with the initials of Anne Bradstreet, the poetess, and heavily with those of Lucy (Moulton) Clark.

52 *LT. THADDEUS, from Ireland, first ment. at Portland 1663. He liv. through Philip's War (see his letter 14 Aug. 1676) to die in the next. His house was on Clark's Point in the vicin. of Portland Bridge. Lt. 14 Nov. 1689. Rep. 1684 (misr. -Hadden and Clark- in List 226). Lists 25, 30, 32, 34, 35, 223b, 225a, 226, 228bc. In the siege of Fort Loyal he led a sally for observation and with 13 of his men was k. 16 May 1690. May 20 his wife and presum. all of his ch. exc. Elizabeth and Jonathan were taken captives. He m. Elizabeth Mitton, ag. 85 in Oct. 1728, ±90 in Dec. 1734, d. 1736, ag. 91, in Boston. Ch. (only 3 heirs): **Elizabeth,** m. by 1682 Col. Edward Tyng, bur. in Boston 4 July 1690. **Isaac,** b. about 1666. **Jonathan,** wit. with Elizabeth Tyng 1686, brot news 17 May 1690 of the battle at Portland. He d. early s.p., likely lost his life by returning to the scene. Doc. Hist. v. 99. **Rebecca.** Two daus. were exchanged, with traditions about others. See Barry's Framingham. **Martha,** app. m. 30 July 1700 in Boston John More (s. John b. 22 June 1701), 2d 23 Oct. 1712 John Harvey. She was of Boston, wid., in 1719.

53 **THOMAS,** List 41. Misr. of Black or Blake.

54 ‡*THOMAS, Major, Dorchester and Boston, ±48 in 1655, Commissioner to Maine, senior part. in Clarke & Lake, York town gr. 50 a. in New Mill Creek in 1658, Deputy (voted against hanging Quakers), Speaker, Assist., Capt. of Art. Co., Major of Boston Reg.; was a merchant in high credit here and in Eng. Most of his honors were by Savage given to an older man, earlier in Boston, Sergeant-Lieut.-Capt. Thomas, shopkeeper, whose s. Thomas, wife Hannah, was inconspic. Major Clark's wife was Mary in 1640, 1662, by will 15 Aug. 1679; and he d. 13 Mar. 1683. (The shopkeeper's w. was Elizabeth in 1646, Ann in 1678; he d. 28 July 1678.) Ch., b. in Dorchester: **Mehitable,** m. 1st Edmund Downe(1); 2d Humphrey Warren, Councilor. **Elizabeth,** b. 22

May 1642, m. 28 May 1661 John Freak; 2d Elisha Hutchinson.

55 **THOMAS**, impressed soldier, ag. 24, 20 Dec. 1689. Doc. Hist. vi. 23.

56 **WILLIAM**, b. 25 Mar. 1689 in Haverhill, bro. of (24 and 36), sons of Hanniel and Mary (Gutterson). See (49). He dep. 31 July 1754, ±65, that ab. 42 or 43 yrs. since he worked 2 yrs. for Capt. Paul Wentworth. In 1717 with w. Joyce he sold 40 a. in Somersworth and in 1720 bot Rev. C. Tappan's claim to the Batt farm on Berwick side. In 1747 he and his s. Wm. were lodged in the Pine Hill garrison. Lists 358d, 298. He m. Joyce Roberts, b. 21 Aug. 1693, stepd. of Ann (Tozer) Jenkins, the Indian captive. These were the people in Hon. James Sullivan's childh. memories (p. 200). Ch. (see Stack. Kit. p. 321): **Eleazer, William, Hanniel, Josiah, Mary**, five bp. 16 July 1724. **Mary**, bp. 2 Oct. 1726. **Jonathan** and **Joanna**, bp. 8 Nov. 1733. **Hanniel**, bp. 1737.

**Clarrian**, Anthony, wit. Jotham Lewis 1686. Misreading of Stanian?

**Clarridge**, Ambrose, Falm. 1725? Y.D.13.260.

**Clary**, William, Durham, 1715. List 368b.

**CLAY**, common in E. of Eng. One Jonas Clay m. Christian Sherman in St. Stephens, Ipswich, 15 Sep. 1636.

1 **JONAS**, something of a scamp in three provinces. First found at Wenham and in trouble in Essex ct. in 1643; before Dover ct. 1648-9. By 1652 he had gone from Wells to Sag. Creek with w. Mary Batson(3). List 330a. They returned to Wells and Cape Porpus where Mary had a continuous and discreditable court record. He d. abt. 1660, and she next found as wife of William Brockus of Barbadoes 1670; liv. 1673. Only kn. ch: **Jonas**.

2 **JONAS**(1), evid. brought up by Richard Tucker of Portsm. and with him a wit. there in 1669. Later he was a master mariner, of Boston, aft. marrying Mary Allen in Salem, 22 Oct. 1678. Lists 90, 333b. He was bur. in Boston 9 Nov. and she 16 Nov. 1704. Adm. on his est. to creditors. Ch. b. Boston: **Mary**, b. 27 Apr. 1680. **Rachel**, b. 3 Oct. 1683. **Rachel**, b. 28 Jan. 1688, m. 8 May 1707 Amos Murrel. **Jonas**, b. 29 Dec. 1690. **Stephen**, b. 16 May 1694, m. 27 Sep. 1717 Mary Allen. **Elizabeth**, b. 12 May 1696, m. 14 Nov. 1717 Samuel Haley, from Saco. **Hannah**, b. 28 May 1698, m. (int. 25 Feb. 1718) John Wharfe of Gloucester.

3 **JONAS**(2), gunsmith, m. Millicent Kingsbury in Boston, 18 May 1714. Ch. rec. at Ipsw. 1715-1729. Of Exeter in 1730, he bot land in Chester and rem. there. Will 1747, of Chester, named wife Millicent, and ch: **Jonas, Stephen. James. John. Mary.** Four younger ch. not in will.

4 **RICHARD**, cordwainer, Portsm. 1693. Lists 334a, 336b, 67. Dover granted him 30 a. in 1701. In 1710 his wife was Mary. Kn. ch: **William**, bot land at Oyster Riv. 1721, liv. 1742. Lists 368b, 369. **Richard**, of Biddeford 1735; m. Rachel Pennell.

5 **RULORD**, soldier at Pemaquid 1689. List 126.

6 **THOMAS**, fisherman, formerly of Cape Bonawagon, ackn. judgm. to Wm. Hoddy in Suffolk ct. in 1676. List 164. One Thomas was a young apprent. at Salem, 1668.

7 **WILLIAM**, Scarb., wit. Jocelyn to Oakman, 1668.

**Claypitt**, John, Pemaquid 1687. List 124.

**Clayton**, Thomas, Dover, 1650. Wit. Austin to Furber. List 354c.

**CLEAR.** 1 **Edward**, Isles of Shoals, 1677. See Wm. Bennett.

2 **THOMAS**, Kittery, m. Margaret Deering(9); both liv. 1723, wid. liv. 1743.

**CLEAVES**, Cleeve, latter the name of 4 parishes, Gloucester to Worcestershire.

1 †\***GEORGE** (Cleeve), b. ab. 1586, was apprent. in June 1600 to a fuller of Bristol for 7 yrs. to no purpose. His father John Cleeves, linen draper, was of Stogursey, co. Som. (7 m. from Stogumber) in 1582, and his mo. had become Anna Cary in 1591. In 1618 he repres. that his mo. held an estate worth £40 per an. The Shrewsbury tax roll for 1616-7 has Thomas Lewis and George Cleve taxed together as vintners. See Thomas Lewis. Disproof is lacking that he was the Geo. Cleoves of St. Peter's, Cornhill, marrying Alice Shortoll of St. Saviour Southwark, 22 Sep. 1614. He m. at Shrewsbury in 1617 the dau. of a burgess, Joan Price, ag. 16 in 1601 (77 in 1662 instead of 87, as stated by her hus.). List 221. There was nothing except his own statements to show his presence in N. E. back of the court of 1636 until after the Hist. of Portland was written, so that dates in the history and on the Cleeve & Tucker monument are false. The Trelawny Papers (Doc. Hist. III), discov. in Eng. in 1872, ment. 'the old Cleves' 18 June 1634, and show that he came to Spurwink in 1630 or 1631 and rem. to Portland in the autumn of 1633. Much has been written (one whole book) on this quest. char. with scant disclosure. See Asp. 272, Winth. Papers 175, 4 Mass. Hist. Coll. vii. 362. He went back to England several times, with misch. results as far west as Wells. In 1651 Ezekiel Knight and John Baker were making grants by authority of 'Mr. Cleaves gentleman Deputy President.' He joined readily in the subm. to Mass. in 1658, was placed on the local bench, and promptly resumed his litig. in the courts, with uniform adverse verdicts. In 1663, when other towns had

swung to the younger Gorges, he adhered to Mass., and was chosen Rep. by a disputed vote. The end this aged couple made is obscured by his blanket transfer in 1659 to Dea. John Phillips, with a lease back for the lives of hims. and wife. He continued in the courts down to 13 Nov. 1666, when he was refused judgment in a defaulted case for lack of assurance of the jury fees. Gr.j. 1640. Lists 21, 22, 23, 25, 221, 222abc, 231, 232, 34. As regards the allegation in a writ in (1735?) that Richard Tucker m. his dau., see Tucker. Kn. ch: **Cleombrotus**, bp. in St. Chad's, Shrewsbury, 13 Mar. 1620, bur. 30 Nov. 1621. **Anne**, bp. 24 June 1623, bur. 27 Apr. 1624. **Elizabeth**, m. Michael Mitton, 2d Peter Harvey.

2 **THOMAS** (Clives), fisherman at Cape Newagen. Bot from Ind. up Sheepscot River 28 Dec. 1662. Had his house on the oppo. side of the gully from Geo. Davis. Sold 5 June 1666 to Joshua Scottow.

**Cleg** (Cleag), John, taxed at Pemaquid 1687. List 124. App. m. Hope (Reynolds) Sanders, wid. of Thomas. Doc. Hist. vi. 366.

**CLEMENTS**, Clement once a not rare forename. Surname common on both sides of the Bristol Channel.

1 **ABRAHAM**(6), b. 14 July 1657, in 1675 was apprent. at the housewright's trade to Thomas (later Rev.) Wells. In 1693, of Salisbury, he sued that town. He became a contracting carpenter and millwright, and in 1695 built the addition and belfry of the Portsm. ch., and sued that town. He m. 10 Mar. 1683 Hannah Gove, dau. of Edw. and Hannah (Partridge). They liv. in what is now Seabrook most of the time, having ch. rec. in Newbury, Hampton and Salis., until ab. 1703, when having joined the Quakers they rem. to New Bristol, Pa. He had d. by 1706, altho adm. was not taken out until 31 Dec. 1716, to s. Jeremiah. 8 or m. ch. See Clement Gen.

2 **DANIEL**(1?), of Hampton, 1684. N. H. Prov. Pap. i. 551; Essex Qtly. Cts. viii. 266. See Clement Gen. 56.

3 ‡**JOB**, Esq., tanner, ±63 in 1678, s. of Robert of Anstey, co. Warwick, who fol. him to N. E. From Ipsw. he was one of the company to make the first clearing in Haverhill, and built the first house there. While there he was const., gr.j. and selectm.; freeman 1647. He was adm. inhab. of Dover 5 Apr. 1653. There he was repeatedly gr.j. and selectm. He was com.t.e.s.c., assoc. in the County Court, and from 1680 a Councillor. His reput. as a tanner attracted apprentices from a distance, and he was prosec. for practicing two trades—employing shoemakers to make up his leather. Lists 355a, 356-abcefghk, 357b, 359ab, 353, 341, 54, 49. Will

4 Sep., d. bef. 23 Oct. 1682. Thrice m., 25 Dec. 1645 Margaret Dummer; dau. of Thomas then of Salisbury—not an aunt to Judge Sewall, see Dummer(1); 'Lydia' his w. in 1658; 3d, m. 16 July 1673 Joanna, widow of Thomas Leighton, who d. 15 Jan. 1703-4. List 96. Ch: **John**, b. 17 Nov. 1646 mo. **Job**, b. 17 Apr. 1648. **Mary**, b. 12 Dec. 1651, called at m. dau. of Job and Lydia, m. Joseph Canney.

4 *JOB(3), Esq., tanner, inher. almost the whole est. of his f. Jury 1678, 1683; gr.j. 1681. Moderator 1694-1696. Rep, 1692. J.P. 1688-1708. Lists 357b, 353, 52, 55a, 62, 92. Will 8 Oct.—3 Dec. 1716. He mar. 28 Feb. 1688-9 Abigail Heard, d. of James and Shuah (Starbuck), liv. 1734. Ch: **Abigail**, possibly their dau., otherw. unk., d. 12 May 1706. List 96. **Job**, Capt., b. ab. 1691, capt. in 1st F. & I. War. Const. 1721. Will 14 Aug.— 26 Feb. 1752. He m. Hannah Emerson(7), who d. 3 Oct. 1725. 2 sons. **James**, b. 26 Mar. 1694, settled in Somersworth. Soldier in both F. & I. Wars, captive in 1749 and pensioned. Will 20 Sep. 1758—31 Oct. 1764. He m. Sarah Wallingford, d. of John and Mary (Tuttle), who surv. 7 ch. **John**, settled on Dover Point, liv. 1747, perh. same enlisted in 2d F. & I. War. He m. Sarah Bunker(4), who liv. to great age. 4 or m. ch. **Margaret**, m. Col. Tho. Wallingford, br. of Sarah. **Daniel**, mar. Frances Wallingford, d.s.p.

5 **RICHARD** (Clement), surveyor under Gov. Andros, presum. came and went with him. Doc. Hist. iv. 440-6, vi. passim. Lists 34, 221, 225a, 293.

6 **ROBERT**, br. of (2), ±30 in 1664, came with their father and remained at Haverhill, but most of his ch. either liv., d. or m. in Me. or N. H. See Clement Gen. 56.

7 **ROBERT**, mariner. See Clement Gen. 34. He m. 2 Apr. 1667 Joanna -Carr- and was drowned by upset. a canoe from Doctor's Isl., Portsm., in the night of 19-20 June 1673. Her br. Jonathan -Carroe- went up river and brought her down with their 3 ch. Inquest 4 July. Lists 326c, 327c, 328, 331a.

8 **WILLIAM**, List 225a, 1680.

9 **WILLIAM**, Isl. of Shoals 1684. Y. D. xi. 151.

10 **WILLIAM**, of Boston, m. bef. 1714 Eleanor, wid. of Edward Vittery. Me. H. & G. Rec. vii. 76. (Wm. Clements, m. in Boston 3d Mar. 1711 Eleanor Ela.)

**Clever**, Richard, early Exeter. Essex Qtly. Ct. vi. 139. Gutteral phonetic for Carver? The original was written and stricken out, looking like -Carner-, with -Clever- interlined.

**CLEVELAND. 1 Enoch**, from Woburn, soldier under Capt. John Hill, 1649. List 267b.

2 **ISAAC,** soldier at Saco fort 169--. List 248a.

**CLEVERLY, Thomas,** Scarb. debtor 1667, 1673. Lists 237ade, 238a. Adm. 28 June 1682 to John Palmer of Boston. Wife not ment. but 'her clothes' inv., house, not land —she poss. dau. of Palmer.

**Cliff,** William, wit. Ind. deed to Henry Curtis, 1666.

**CLIFFORD,** name of a parish (with ruins of a castle) in Hertfordshire, also places in Glouc. and Yorkshire.

1 **ISAAC**(3), b. 14 Feb. 1663-4 in Hampton, rec. a deed from his father in 1693 and d. 2 July 1694, leaving wid. Elizabeth who m. 2d Jonathan Prescott. Her will 24 Jan. —30 May 1755. Ch: **Elizabeth,** m. 12 Dec. 1720 Peter Garland. 5 ch. bap.

2 **ISRAEL**(3), Hampton, ±25 in Apr. 1675, took O. A. in 1678. Lists 395, 396. He m. 15 Mar. 1679-80 Ann Smith, app. dau. of Nicholas. Ch: **Ann,** b. 22 Feb. 1682, m. 21 Dec. 1702 John Gammage of Ipsw. **Israel,** m. Mary Garland, had at least 3 sons and liv. with son John jr. in 1733 at Hampton. **Mehitable,** b. 9 July 1686; in ct. 1705, 1716. **Samuel,** b. 28 Mar. 1689. Will 1760—1763, names wife Sarah (Dow 9), two sons, and daus: Abigail Carr, Sarah Prescott, Rachel Prescott, Hannah Palmer. **Sarah,** b. 10 May 1691, m. 1710 Joshua Prescott. **John. Isaac,** b. 24 May 1696, m. Sarah Taylor (William) and rem. to Kingston. Adm. to son Joseph 27 Sep. 1745. 9 ch., one of whom, Isaac, m. Sarah Healey and rem. to Chester and Rumney. **Richard,** b. 27 Mar. 1698, rem. to Kingston. He m. 1st 26 Dec. 1721 Hephzibah Basford; 2d Judith Woodman (Archelaus). Liv. 1762.

3 **JOHN,** both 60 and 66 in 1675, was orig. prop. of Salis. in 1640, but was of Hampt. 1 Mar. 1641-2, selling house lot in Salis. to Thomas and Mary Hawksworth in 1642 and buying in Hampt. in 1651. Gr.j. 1663, 1667, 1672, 1678, 1679. Selectm. 1660. Lists 392ab, 393ab, 394, 396, 398, 49, 52, 54, 80. He m. 1st Sarah, List 393a; 2d 28 Sep. 1658 Elizabeth Richardson who d. 1 Dec. 1667; 3d 6 Feb. 1672 Bridget, wid. of John Huggins, List 394, who as his wid. left will 1 Sep. 1679—26 Aug. 1680. Ch. by 1st w: **John. Israel. Hannah,** b. 15 Apr. 1649, legatee of Susannah Haborne-Leader in 1657, in court 1671, m. 20 Nov. 1677 Luke Maloon. **Elizabeth,** b. 4 Apr. 1650. By 2d w: **Mehitable. Elizabeth,** b. 31 Aug. 1659, m. Jacob Basford. **Esther,** b. 24 Feb. 1662, of Newbury 20 July 1686 when she m. James Stanley. **Isaac. Mary,** b. 8 Feb. 1665-6, d. 30 Oct. 1669.

4 **JOHN**(3), bap. 10 May 1646, m. 18 Aug. 1670 Sarah Godfrey, List 394. O. A. 1678. Lists 394, 396, 49, 52, 54. In 1676 he deeded

to his br. Israel 'my dwelling house standing in the woods.' Altho he gave his Hampt. prop. to s. Jacob for life support, he afterward liv. with s. Joseph, dying bef. 1722. Ch: **John,** b. 7 Feb. 1672, d. 7 Nov. 1683. **Sarah,** b. 30 Oct. 1673, mar. 24 Dec. 1702 Thomas Scribner. **Deborah,** b. 13 Oct. 1675, in court Mar. 1693-4 acc. Caleb Shaw, and Feb. 1697-8 acc. Benj. Batchelder, given life sup. in br. Joseph's will in 1724, but achieved mar. 29 Dec. 1726 with Joseph Welch. **Mehitable,** b. 20 Nov. 1677, d. 30 Jan. 1677-8. **Jacob,** b. 7 Apr. 1679, d. 9 May 1715, mar. Elizabeth Mayhew, who m. 2d 4 Nov. 1728 Ichabod Allen. 6 surv. ch. in 1729 at Martha's Vineyard. **Joseph,** Kingston, a carpenter, m. 1st 13 Apr. 1710 Sarah French (Simon); 2d 5 Jan. 1716 Lydia Perkins (James). List 400. Will 1724—1737. 2+2 ch. **Zachariah,** b. 15 Apr. 1685, Chester in 1721, mar. Mehitable Smith (Jacob) and had 5 ch. liv. in 1743. **John,** b. 6 Feb. 1686-7. In 1708 Israel sen. and jr., John, Jacob and Zachariah were taxed in Hampton Falls.

5 **RICHARD,** Pemaquid 1689. List 126.

**CLIFTON.** 1 Dr. **John,** of London, mar. at Hampstead, Middlesex, 14 Oct. 1709 Mary (Wentworth), wid. of Capt. Samuel Rymes. He d. bef. 1731, she 29 Jan. 1744. 2 ch.

2 **WILLIAM,** seaman, Piscataqua by 1637, had a w. in 1638. In 1640 he sold Mr. Francis Williams's land to Walter Abbott. See his dep. in 1642, P. & C. i. 105. 'Boatswain Clifton's marsh' on Gt. Is. ment. in 1656.

**Cling,** Thomas, Sheepscot abuttor. Y.D. 18.88.

**Cloade,** Andrew, Boston, Philip's War. List 237b. Dill 1682.

**Clother** (Cloder), Mr. Thomas, sued Joseph Pyler — writ served by Great Isl. const. 1668.

**CLOUDMAN** (Cloutman), **Edward,** Exeter 1696, had gr. in Dover 1702. He m. 22 April 1698 Sarah Tuttle, poss. born Tibbetts, who adm. his est., entering inv. 11 Nov. 1717. Capt. Samuel and Henry Tibbetts were cited for concealing assets and embezzling the estate in 1721. The widow also had difficulties with Wm. Blackstone, refusing to inventory 30 a. sold by him to E. C. on which £20 was due. Sued for fencing in common land in 1735, and bound to keep the peace in 1739, she was liv. in 1754 when she mtged. 20 a. in Dover. Prob. ch: **Sarah,** in ct. for having a bastard 1725-6. **Edward,** Falm., sold Dover land in 1739. **Thomas,** bot, but did not pay for, what seems a wedding outfit, Aug. 1720. **John,** with wife Mercy (Cook) in 1752. Ch.

**Clough,** Caleb, Cornelius, Jeremiah. List 400.

**CLOYES,** Cloyce, Clyes, Clayse. In Colchester Peter Cloyes, m. 1615, had Peter and John. Clyes frequent in Devon.

**1 JOHN**, seaman, of Watertown, where in 1652 he took O. F., was made freeman, and was member of Capt. Mason's train band. Sold Watert. homestead 'where my late mansion house was (by God's providence) burnt down' and bot house in Charlestown in 1656, but moved to Falmouth in 1658 where he settled on west bank of Presumpscot river, selling Charlestown prop. in 1660. Signed pet. to the King and twice refused to attend Wells ct. in 1665. Gr.j. 1664, 1671, 1672. Mutual suits with Francis Neale in 1671. Lists 25, 86, 222bc. K. on his land in Ind. attack of 1676. His 1st w. Abigail d. bef. 1656 as his 2d w. Jane released dower to the Watert. prop., and was adm. to Charlestown ch. that yr. She released dower in 1660 and wit. an Ind. deed to Geo. Munjoy in 1666. In 1667 Cloyes had a 3d w., Julian, quarrelling with 2 of her stepch., and 'a tale bearer from house to house,' ±53 in 1673, and in 1675 receiving stolen goods from her dau. Sarah Spurwell in Boston, where she retired after her husband's death, to sell beer and cider without lic. Feb. 1678-9. Ch: **John**, b. 26 Aug. 1638. **Peter**, b. 27 May 1640. **Nathaniel**, b. 6 Mar. 1643. **Abigail**, m. Jenkin Williams bef. 1667. **Hannah**, b. ±1650, m. Isaac Hallam of Boston, prob. as 2d hus., a soldier of Castle William at his death in 1722. In her old age she made many depos. as to Falm. lands, stating that she liv. there 7 yrs. bef. Philip's war, one yr. with Mr. James Andrews, and that bef. marrying and aft. she was a wid. she was at Scottow's garrison in Scarboro. Liv. 1735, ±84. 2 Hallam ch. b. in Boston, 1685, 1688. **Thomas**. **Sarah**, ±20, June 1673, m. Peter Housing. **Mary**, b. 1 July 1657, presum. the sis. of Hannah who m. Richard Burrough(2). **Martha**, b. 13 Oct. 1659, presum. m. Nathaniel Rogers 25 Nov. 1685 in Billerica. Julian(?); Julian Cloyes 'Jun' was p!f. with John sen. vs. Neale in 1671, a questionable record.

**2 JOHN**(1), Wells, 1663, Capt. of a coasting vessel plying from Boston to Maine settlements, m. Mary Mills (Thomas), who as his wid. conv. her Mills int. to her d. Abigail Wiggin in 1719. Lists 266, 268a, 269ab. Gr.j. 1687, 1689, 1693, 1698, 1699, 1702. Had town gr. of 150 a. next his br. Nathaniel in 1681. Ch: **Abigail**, m. 1st John Cousins(4); 2d James Wiggin, and wid. in 1719. **Mary**, m. 1st Thomas Baston jr.(8); 2d George Butland(1); ±67 in June 1750. **Dorothy**, mar. Samuel Hancock of Cambridge; q.c. to sis. Abigail Wiggin in 1721 in consid. of her care of their mother. **Elizabeth**, m. John Scribner of Exeter, their sons suing Abigail Wiggin in 1746 for ¼ of the Cloyes est. **Isaac**, had been supp. 7 yrs. by sis. Abigail in 1711 when he was presum. d., adm. being gr. her 7 Apr. 1746.

**3 JOSEPH**(2 or 4), 'of Wells' in 1711 in list of captives in Canada. List 99.

**4 NATHANIEL**(1), Wells, 1672, owning a lot the next yr., m. Sarah Mills (Thomas). Lists 33, 266, 268a, 269ab.. O. A. 22 Mar. 1680; jury 1680, 1688, 1689; gr.j. 1694, 1701. Received a parcel of marsh from his f.-in-law 6 July 1681. Petitioned to Mass. for Rishworth's retention 1686, and for aid to the town 1691. In 1692 he was presented for selling strong drink at retail, appar. keeping his family in Charlestown. At Wells 29 Oct. 1701 he joined the church. Liv. in 1722 when he dep. as to the use of the Ogunquit farm for 50 previous yrs. Ch: **Mercy**, bp. at Charlestown 25 Mar. 1699, with sis. Susannah and their mother, m. (Apr. Ct. 1706) Joseph Littlefield. **Sarah**, 'second daughter,' d. at Charlestown 1 Feb. 1694. **Susannah**, m. 15 June 1704 Caleb Kimball.

**5 PETER**, Wells, 1664, m. 1st Hannah Littlefield (Edmund) who d. ab. 1680. Lists 25, 28, 265, 266. Gr.j. 1666, 1668. During Philip's War retired to York and later to Salem, where he and w. Hannah sold their Wells land to Wm. Frost in 1679. About 1681 he m. 2d wid. Sarah (Towne) Bridges, who suffered imprisonment but escaped in the Salem delusion of 1692 and with whom he had been in Boston 'these many months' when he was dism. from Salem Village ch. to Marlboro 6 Oct. 1695. Again dism. to Framingham in 1701, he m. 3d wid. Susanna (Harrington) (Cutting) Beers 21 Jan. 1704-5, and d. 18 July 1708. Ch. by 1st w: **Sarah**, m. John Cunnable of Boston 13 Mar. 1688. **Hannah**, bp. with next three in Salem 5 Aug. 1677, mar. Daniel Elliot. **Peter**, mar. Mary Preston 13 Dec. 1693. **Mary**. **Abigail**. **James**, bp. 10 Mar. 1678-9. By 2d w: **Alice**, m. one Bridges. **Benoni**, bp. 2 Sep. 1683. **Hephzibah**, m. Ebenezer Harrington 3 Feb. 1708.

**6 THOMAS**(1), Falmouth, husbandman and cordwainer, m. Susanna Lewis (George), selling her int. in her father's est. to Richard Seacombe in 1685. Lists 34, 86, 223b, 225ab, 228b. Bot 70 acres at Capisic from George Munjoy in 1674, and also owned 6 a. and a house on the neck (Portland) which he rented and 2 a. near the fort, to which in prop. he returned from Salem 'among the first aft. Philip's War, as by his pet. to Gov. Andros, 1687. K. by Ind. in 1690, his w. retiring to Salem. Ch. as stated in depos. of Sarah White, Mary Wilkins, Samuel and John Felton, 1734-1738: **Thomas**, Boston, m. but d.s.p. ±1717. **Mary**, bp. 8 July 1677, m. Daniel Waters of Topsfield, Killingly, Conn., 1734, Sturbridge, 1758. **Hannah**, schooldame in Salem 1731, yet signed by mark when she gave deed to Phineas Jones of her ⅓ of her br. Thomas' land. **George**, Salem, husbandman, m. Lydia Deal 16 May 1717; deeded

his share of his father's realty to James Ross, 1718-9, and Thomas Haskell, 1730.

**COATES.** 1 **Elizabeth** Coots or Coote (Coates?) of Newcastle, up for bastardy, husb. abs. several yrs. 1705.

2 **ROBERT**, bot at Newcastle 1723, adm. to w. Jane 1 Sep. 1724. One Robert Coats (Robert), b. Lynn 17 Dec. 1683. Ch: **Robert**, shoemaker in 1738. **John**, minor ±14 in 1737. Presum. others, as Francis and James, adults 1742-52.

3 **THOMAS**, Portsm. 170-- selling without lic. Thomas C. and s. Tho. jr. taxed Portsm., milldam, 1707. Of Newbury, shipwright, died in N. H. 1709.

**COBB, Peter**, servant of Mr. Trelawny at Richmond Isl. List 21. Doc. Hist. iii. 170, 193.

**COBBETT**, *Thomas, Newcastle, ±21 in 1672-3, ±27 in 1681, ±30 in 1682. An apprent. of Mr. Nathaniel Fryer, he often accomp. his master's s. James on trading voyages. Jury 1686, master of the sloop -Fellowship- 1693, Assemblyman 1695, Com.t.e.-s.c. 1694. Lists 51, 52, 56, 57, 58, 66, 98, 315abc, 319. He m. Mary Lewis (John), and d. bef. 1707 when she had m. John Hinckes, Esq. See Hubbard for narrative of his Ind. captivity.

**Cobleigh** (Cobly), **John**. N. H. 1694. List 65. One J. C. in Philip's War.

**COBURN** (Colburn), **Ebenezer**, York. Lists 289, 279. D. 27 Dec. 1749, ag. 75 (grst.)

**Cock**, see Cox.

**CODDINGTON, Stockdale**, in 1648 bot from Henry Green land in Hampton, which was sold in 1650 by his eldest s. John, app. adm. 7 Apr. 1650 in Boston, to Edmund Johnson to pay for care of his late father. He had liv. in Roxbury when his w. Hannah was buried 20 July 1644.

**CODNER.** 1 **Christopher**, see Mary Bennett (John).

2 **JAMES**, Portsm., ±31 in Sep. 1679.

3 **MARY**, Portsm., ment. with Martin Hall 1667, wid. refused license to retail one hogshead in 1686. One Mary C. wit. with Charles Story 1706.

4 **THOMAS**, owing Mitchell est. 1666. List 78.

**COE**, a distinctive East Anglian name.

1 **JOHN** (2), m. Sarah Peabody in Duxbury 10 Nov. 1681; d. in Little Compton, R. I., 16 Dec. 1728. Claimed 100 a. at Back Cove, Falmouth, bounded on north by Great Falls Cove, the deeds being burnt in the first Ind. War when his grf. was slain and his house burned. Ch: **Lydia**, b. 26 Feb. 1683. **Sarah**, b. 25 Feb. 1686. **Samuel**, b. 12 Dec. 1692. **Elizabeth**, b. 28 Mar. 1694. **Hannah**, b. 28 Dec. 1696. **John**, b. 1 Feb. 1699. **Joseph**, b. 24 Mar. 1700.

2 **MATTHEW**, at Portsmouth in 1640. See Cole (21). Rem. to Gloucester. With other Gloucester men, as Phineas Rider, Jo: Jackson, Jo: Briers, Elias Parkman, Geo: Ingersoll, Thos: Skillins, Jo: Kettell, Thos: Wakely, Anthony Day, Jo: Wakely and Giles Barge, migrated to Falm. and Scarb. ab. 1658, Coe buying land on the Presumpscot in 1661. He m. Elizabeth Wakely (Thos.) K. on his farm in Indian attack of 9 Sep. 1675. Lists 41, 321, 75b, 25, 34. Ch: **John**, b. 30 June 1649. **Sarah**, b. 14 Mar. 1651, mar. Joseph Ingersoll who test. to her f.'s death in 1685. **Abigail**, b. 5 June 1658. **Matthew**, b. 3 June, d. 8 Feb. 1661-2. **Martha**, m. Jonathan Farnham of Boston, wid. in 1731, d. ch. rec. 1686-99. **Elizabeth**, w. of J. Tucker of Roxbury 1689 and his wid. 1731. **Isaac**, m. Martha Ramsey 11 Sep. 1706, in Roxbury; he with his nephew, John Coe of Little Compton deeded Coe lands in Falm. to Phineas Jones, 1731.

**COFFIN**, an ancient landed fam. in Devon. Coffinswell a Devon parish.

1 **CAPT. ELIPHALET** (5), by several deeds made his grfr.'s principal heir, m. 11 Feb. 1710 Judith (Coffin), b. 7 Oct. 1686, wid. of Parker Noyes, dau. of his cous. James and Florence (Hooke) of Newbury. Selectm. 1725, 1733. List 376b. See will 15 Jan. 1734-5—13 Sep. 1736. His wid. m. 11 Mar. 1742 Nathaniel Gilman; adm. 27 Sep. 1749 to Rev. Peter Coffin of Kingston and Dr. Josiah Gilman of Exeter. Ch: **Peter. Abigail**, m. Josiah Gilman. **Judith**, b. 22 Dec. 1717, m. 1 Jan. 1741 Rev. Nathl. Gookin, d. 24 July 1741, s.p.

2 **EZEKIEL** (Cossin) 1677. See Cousins.

3 **JAMES**, br. of (4), b. 12 Aug. 1640, brought over in 1642, liv. several yrs. in Dover bef. settling in Nantucket. In N. H. freeman 1671, jury 1669, 1673. In Nov. 1673 as merchant of the -Ketch Neptune-, David Kelly commander, Richard Cutt owner, he was captured by the Dutch. Lists 356ghkm, 357ad, 359a. He m. 3 Dec. 1663 Mary Severance. Among their 14 trad. ch., of whom 12 had fam: **Mary**, b. Dover 18 Apr. 1665, m. Richard Pinkham and James Gardner. **Dinah**, m. Nathl. Starbuck jr. **Benjamin**, drowned 20 Jan. 1703-4. List 96. In 1723 Mary, Dinah, **Deborah**, and Geo. Bunker, Esq., **Elizabeth** Bunker wid., and **Ruth** Gardner, all of Sherburn, Nant., sold the Dover lands willed to 'my five daus.' by their f.

4 **CAPT. ‡*PETER**, Esq., ag. 50 in 1680, ±54 in 1684-5, ±83 in 1713, s. of Tristram from Brixton, Devon, (whose aut. attests the Bishop's transcripts for that parish, 1639), was bred under Mr. Valentine Hill at Oyster River, taxed 1650, having app. been put in charge in place of Darby Field. Of 20 pur-

chasers of Nantucket, 1659, seven were his and wife's immed. rel., but he did not go, or if he went kept up his bus. in Dover; yet settled most of his ch. there and app. was an officeholder there. In 1653 Elder Starbuck deeded him a half int. in a mill priv. He was soon engaged in the Ind. trade. An import. fig. in N. H. hist. for half a century, for sketches see N. H. Hist Soc. viii. 377 and Allen Coffin 1881. Picking a course bet. two sides with sedul. attention to the law's letter, he was highly trusted and much employed. Auditing was commonly entrusted to him. In 1667 by contract he built the fort around the meet. ho. 100 ft. sq., with flankers. Com.t.e.s.c. in 1669; assoc. in the County Ct. 1670; J. P. from 1683-4; a judge of the highest court from 1697; and for one yr. chief justice. Councillor from 1692, except one yr. when he declined to serve, until his death. Under Mass. he was Rep. in 1672, under N. H. in 1680. In Dover he was selectm., treas., Lieut.; in Exeter moderator, Capt. Taken but spared by the Ind. in the Cochecho massacre, he rem. to Exeter, where he d. 21 Mar. 1715. Lists 354c, 355ab, 356-abceghk, 357a, 359ab, 364, 376b, 377, 311c (Dover), 353, 45, 48-53, 57, 59-61, 89, 81, 66, 64, 63. He m. Abigail Starbuck, their ch. not clearly kn. Having had his finger in numerous estates, no finger was in his,—no will, no adm. The Province vital records give 7 ch: **Abigail**, b. 20 Oct. 1657, m. Daniel Davison(1). **Peter**, b. 20 Aug. 1660, m. 15 Aug. 1682 Elizabeth Starbuck, d. 1699 on Nantucket. In 1724 and 1725 Ebenezer Gardner, Jedediah and Abigail Fitch, and Jemima Coffin, unm., all of Sherburn, deeded thirds of 100 a. given by 'our grandf. to our f.' Peter C. in 1696. **Jethro**, b. 16 Sep. 1663, blacksm., m. Mary Gardner, Nant. In 1713 his f.'s gr. of 240 a. in Mendon, 1672, was confirmed to him, where he settled. Will 29 July—10 Aug. 1726 names w. Mary, ch. John, Josiah, Robert, Margaret Terrey, Priscilla Gardner, Abigail Woodbury. **Tristram**, b. 18 Jan. 1665-6. **Edward**, b. 20 Feb. 1669-70. List 94. He m. Anna Gardner, Nant. **Judith**, b. 4 Feb. 1672-3. **Elizabeth**, b. 27 Jan. 1680-1, m. 5 June 1698 Col. John Gilman. List 385. Besides these the Nant. trad. gives three, **Parnel**, d. inf.; **Eliphalet**, d. unm.; **Robert**. The latter was deeded land by his f. in 1696. Capt. in 1708; selectm. Exeter 1705, 1708. Lists 376b, 385. Will 22 Oct. 1709—d. 19 May 1710, names br. Nicholas Gilman, sis. Abigail Davison, wife Joanna (Gilman, b. 30 Apr. 1679), who m. 2d Henry Dyer(4).

5 **TRISTRAM**, d. 2 Oct. 1681. In 1722 his living posterity numbered 908, in 1728 1218.

6 **TRISTRAM**(4), d. before 1695. Lists 94, 353. He m. ab. 1684 Deborah Colcord(1),

who was adm. to Hampton ch. in 1697 and dism. to Exeter Sep. 1698. List 385. His f. in 1695 deeded to her and their four ch: **Abigail**, m. Jonathan Thing. Was deeded lands by (4) in 1709. **Eliphalet**, b. 13 Jan. 1689. **Parnel**, m. Benjamin Thing. **Tristram**, Capt., m. 15 Nov. 1719 Jane Heard of Kit. Settled in Dover. Of 9 ch. bp. 1720-1745, five daus. are named in will 1761.

**Coggan** (Coggin), John, Boston, plf. in Me. Ct. 1640-1.

**Coham**, Thomas, Portsm. wit. 1646.

**Coker**, Samuel, Monhegan 1651. List 111.

**COLCORD**, See Foxwell.

1 *EDWARD, b. 1615. Here early, went back in 1656, and was at Teignmouth, Devon; farther up the Teign, at Bovey Tracy, one Edward, s. of Richard Colchard, was bap. 26 Aug. 1635. He must have learned the Ind. tongue, as Wheelwright empl. him to make his purchase in 1638. At Dover he was Com.t.e.s.c., and in 1642 was Rep. to the General Court in Boston. Later he claimed to be agent of the patentees for collecting their rents in Dover (Hubbard called him an 'apochryphal' governor), and in 1647 Richard Cutt, Pickering and Nutter were app. referees between Edward Colcord and the town of Dover. He had rem. to Hampton in 1645, and was then about rem. to Exeter. In 1651 he was bringing suits as attorney for Rev. Stephen Bachiler. In 1654 he was an owner in the Dover and Swampscot patents, and had bot James Wall's mill at Exeter, hiring it run by Anthony Day and Thos. Tyler the Indian. In 1661 he was arrested for barratry, and petition was freely signed to shut him out of the courts. In 1676 he was employed by Maj. Waldron to collect evid. against the Mason claim, and 11 Aug. 1681, in Boston prison, he was allowed £5 for 33 days service of self and horse under orders of Gov. Leverett. Feb. 10, 1681-2, he died. One of the best, and to many most unfavorably, known New Englanders of his day, he spent his life looking for trouble, reckless of all manner of abuse, except when accu. of picking a drunken man's pocket. Evid. sis. of Robert Page's wife, Anne Colcord was app. Anne 'Wadd' (Nudd?), who came with them ag. 15. She d. 24 Jan. 1688-9. Lists 392c, 393a, 394, 52, 96. Ch: **Jonathan**, d. 31 Aug. 1661 in 21st yr. **Elizabeth**, m. by 1664 Robert Evans(12). **Hannah**, mar. 28 Dec. 1665 Thomas Dearborn(5). **Sarah**, m. 30 Dec. 1668 John Hobbs. **Mary**, b. 4 Oct. 1649, m. Benj. Fifield. **Edward**, b. 2 Feb. 1652, k. by Ind. 13 June 1677. **Samuel**, b. 1656. **Mehitable**, m. 20 Dec. 1677 Nathaniel Stevens. **Shuah**, b. 12 June 1662, m. Richard Nason, John Douglass. **Deborah**, b. 21 May 1664, m. Tristram Coffin(5). **Abigail**, b. 23 June 1667, d.y.

2 *LT. SAMUEL(1), ±56 in 1713. Rep. 1682. A pioneer of Kingston, liv. there in 1702; d. 5 Oct. 1736 'in 81st yr.' He mar. Mary Ayer, 1st cous. of(9), d. 29 May 1739. Ch: Samuel, b. 11 Mar. 1682, Lt., Kingston; m. Sep. 1704 Elizabeth Folsom(7), who m. 2d in 1716 Samuel Sanborn. 5 ch. Jonathan, b. 4 Mar. 1683[4; Newmarket, d. 31 Dec. 1773. 6 ch. Elizabeth, b. 26 Dec. 1686, m. 5 Dec. 1710 Ebenezer Stevens of Kingston. Hannah, b. 17 Apr. 1689, m. Samuel Dudley(3). Edward, b. 1 Apr. 1692; Hawke, in Exeter, m. 1714 Mary Gordon. Will Aug.—Oct. 1756, names 1 s., 8 daus. Wid. d. bef. 1767. Ebenezer, b. 20 May 1695, miller at Crawley's Falls, Brentwood. Adm. 22 May 1766 to s. Ebenezer, wid. Hannah (Fellows 1) relinq. 7 ch. Mary, b. 24 Mar. 1698, m. Tho. Sleeper.

COLE, a very common So. of Eng. surname, became the 39th in N. E.

1 ABRAHAM, carpenter, br. of (8), b. 3 Oct. 1636 in Charlestown. First bot in Hampton in 1665. Jury 1675, 1676, 1694; Gr.j. 1678, 1679; selectm. 1680, 1696, 1702; const. 1693, 1694. Lists 393b, 396, 399b, 392b, 52, 54, 55b, 61. He was of Hampt. in 1719 and liv. until 1728, leaving only one ch. He m. 15 Mar. 1666-7 Mary Wedgwood, wit. in court 1667, 1671. List 394. Ch: Isaac, b. 15 Feb., d. 9 Apr. 1667-8. Abraham, b. 12 May 1671, d. early. Abigail, b. 5 Dec. 1673, m. Thomas Foss(6) and Samuel Folsom(9).

2 ANN, 1686. See N. Badcock.

3 CHRISTOPHER, one or more of him, in 1664 belonging to the pinke of which Mr. Clements was master, he was up in N. H. ct., drunk and disord. In 1673 Isaac Cole's bond was wit. by Richard Marten and Christopher Cole. Deed exec. in Hampton 13 July 1675, C. C. of Exeter to Saml. Whittemore 15 a. bot of John York. In Philip's War C. C. was in Major Appleton's Co., Ipsw. In 1679 Citt Cole shipped before the mast out of Newburyport.

4 EDWARD, Kennebec, in List 13, 1672, signed next bef. James; in List 15, 1674, named without James. Likely the same under Capt. Scottow at Scarb. in Philip's War, (enlisted in Boston). List 237b.

5 EDWARD and MARY, captives in Canada in 1711, listed 'Black Point.' List 99. See List 39 and Joseph(19). One Edward was rated to the New Meet. Ho., Portsm., 1717.

6 GEORGE, Isles of Shoals, abs. from meet. May 1685.

7 GILBERT, one or m. of him, likely a fisherman at Isles of Shoals (wit. there 1667, 1682) keeping his wife there, or at Ipswich (Frances fined 1672), or at Boston (ch. of Gilbert and Frances: Samuel, b. 30 Nov. 1678, Thomas, b. 14 June 1680.) G. C. free-

man 16 Oct. 1677. G. C. soldier in Philip's War.

8 ISAAC, ±30 in 1666-7, millwright, eldest s. of Isaac, ag. 58 in 1664, and Joan of Boston, Charlestown and Woburn. In 1661, 'of Exeter,' he bot in Hampton, and sold with house, barn and orchard in 1666. In Oct. 1662 Isaac and Abraham hired ⅛ of a sawmill of Francis Page. In 1671, still of Hampt., he was devel. the mill privilege in Greenland. Cape Porpus town meeting 4 Jan. 1681 gr. a mill priv. to John Batson, I. C. and Samuel York, and Cole settled there, last in Exeter (Quamscot). Hampt. appraiser 1666. Me. jury 1685. Lists 380, 396, 259, 57, 62, 388. His will 10 Feb., d. 13 Feb. 1706-7, rememb. br. Abraham and his dau., br. Jacob's ch., but chiefly the ch. of sister Fillebrown, poss. sis. of his w. if he had one.

9 JAMES, very early at Saco, at Falm. from 1636 to 1640 when Mr. Macworth petn. to have him banished. Last ment. Sep. 1640 as a wit. with George Cleeve. He had admitted giving false evid. against Thomas Cole, when accu. of John Packett's death. See Thomas(28).

10 JAMES, Woolwich, 1654-1672. One J. C. m. in Scituate 23 Dec. 1652 Mary Tilson and had Mary, b. 3 Dec. 1653. 'There was a James Cole in Scituate 1653. He removed to old York after that date'—Deane's Scit. Oct. 31, 1654, J. C. bot from Edw. Bateman the Bateman-Brown Ind. purchase, and 22 July 1658 sold to Clarke & Lake. Will 1664. Lists 11, 13. See Edward(4). See Suff. Ct. files 139100. It is undisc. whose was 'Wid. Cole' at Scituate with 'Strangers from Shipscot River' 26 Jan. 1676. She had aband. 2 oxen, --- cows, 2 heifers, and had sowed 6 bu. of wheat and planted 3 bu. of Ind. corn.

11 JOHN, Cape Porpus, submitted to Mass. 5 July 1653, fined for drunk. in Salem ct. Dec. 1654. Lists 251, 252, 255. Last ment. there 1668.

12 JOHN, Saco, m. there 23 Dec. 1658 Mary Chilson(1). He was bur. Mar. 1661, and his inv., attest. by Mary, shows 7 cattle, a musket, a saw, cooking utensils, no bed. Eliphal Cole was bur. 23 Oct. 1661.

13 JOHN, owner of the lighter cast away Nov. 1664 when Thomas Etherington and w. and 4 others were drowned. Nos. 11-15, instead of five J. Cs, may be but two. Almost any of them might be the one belonging to a shallop at Newburyport who lost his life trying to join his ship in a skiff and was found dead on the flats 1 Nov. 1681.

14 JOHN, 'of Pemaquid' 1672, lic. retailer; gr.j. 1674; grant from Andros 1679. Lists 13, 15, 187, (4, 80, 85?).

15 JOHN. List 4, likely same as (14), or same as either J. C. in List 85, Marble-

head or Lynn, or List 80, or J. C. of Marbleh., fisherman, adm. Mar. 1677 to John
Gardner sr., leav. one ch.; or J. C., mariner
or fisherman, who for 7 yrs. pd. taxes at
Marbleh., boarding his s. John there and
hims. when ashore.

16 **JOHN** (aut. Coll), Kittery, miller, m. 23
Sep. 1700 Elizabeth Allen(12). Apr. 5,
1701, 'of Kit.' he bot in Somersworth. In
1703 he was gr. 30 a. in Kit. which he sold
in 1711. List 290. In 1715 'of Kit.' miller, a
writ against him was served in Dover (Somersworth?) by leaving the notice at the
house of Tarbox, liv. on part of the same
est., deft. liv. out of the Province. In 1732
J. C. and Robert Coll (aut.) were sued. **Robert,** cordwainer, m. Judith Tuttle.

17 **SERG. JOHN**(18), York fisherman, was
in the Winter Harbor fight 21 Sep. 1707.
See Benj. Donnell. List 96 p. 150. His deed
6 Sep. 1712 was proved by witnesses 5 Jan.
1713-4. He m. Hannah Hilton, who m. 2d
Mark Shepard. Ch: **Mary,** b. 16 May 1708,
m. 8 Jan. 1724-5 John McLucas; 2d John
Bryant(9). **Joshua,** b. 23 Feb. 1709-10, liv.
1723. **Joseph,** b. 12 June 1712, m. in York
21 Mar. 1732-3 Hannah (the record says
-Cole-) Preble, b. 2 Sep. 1714, d. of Joseph,
both liv. 1741. List 279.

18 **JOSEPH,** liv. Cape Porpus? and York
1670-1680. First ment. wit. to John Sanders' will; 1673 abs. from meet. (York wit.);
1674 John Hunnewell, Wm. Barton and J. C.
for traveling from York on Sunday, Cole's
fine paid by John Smith of Cape Neddick;
30 a. gr. at York 25 Aug. 1679; sworn at
York Mar. 1679-80. Kn. ch: **John.**

19 **JOSEPH,** app. lost his life through m. a
Maine refugee in Mass. Nov. 20, 1702,
Sheriff Curtis trav. to Blue Point, Scarb., to
attach John Jackson's land, and left the
summons 'at the next house' (Bonighton
stricken out) Cole. In the massacre 10 Aug.
1703, 'Joseph Cole and his son killed, his
wife and one child taken'—listed last under
Saco. The French record of the bap. of three
daus. (one posth.) and the mother's turning
Cath., discl. her maiden name, Randall, and
the birthplace of the ch., Beverly. In 1727
Richard Randall's daus. Sarah and Priscilla
were the widows West and Presbury of Beverly, Y. D. xii. 177. Evid. the young couple
had been tempted east in the false peace.
The list of captives 1710-11 lists three Coles
taken at Saco. Lists 39, 99. Ch: **Son,** k. by
Ind. 10 Aug. 1703. **Deborah,** b. Beverly 9
Oct. 1698, bp. at Montreal 8 Dec.1703. **Mary,**
b. Beverly 28 Apr. 1701, bp. with Deborah;
m. 17 Jan. 1718 Pierre Rougeau. Ch. **Priscilla,** b. and bp. 29 Jan. 1704 at Boucherville.

20 **LEWIS** (Colle), seaman in 1674 on the
ketch -Dove-, Richard Martyn, charterer,
John Cutt(3), master.

21 **MATTHEW,** seaman on a Boston owned
ketch in Piscataqua River in 1642. Me.
P. & C. i. 105.

22 **MATTHEW,**(Cooe) List 34. See Coe(2).

23 **NICHOLAS**(35), ±52 in 1678. First ment.
1652 in Wells. In 1658 he occup. his father's farm. In 1664 he was gr. the ferry
priv. at Cape Porpus (Mousam) River for 7
yrs. By 1666 he was partn. with John Purington making oars and fishing, and built in
Cape Porpus. In 1672 they rem. to Harpswell where they obtained from the Ind., 26
Nov. 1672, a deed covering that town. When
the inhab. fled in Philip's War, N. C. brought
many of them away. Constable 1658; appraiser 1662; jury 1668, 1686, 1688, 1689;
gr.j. 1687, 1688. Lists 261-263, 24, 269b, 264,
255, 33. He d. 21 Dec. 1688, adm. to s. Nicholas. His wife's name 'Relief' in the Kit.
record (prtd.) of his dau. Jane's mar. is
misr. of -relict-. In 1668 his wife was Jane.
Ch: **Nicholas,** b. 1656. **Jane,** m. Joseph Littlefield, Capt. John Heard. **Thomas. Mary,**
m. 4 Dec. 1686 Samuel Littlefield.

24 **NICHOLAS**(23), ±23 in June 1679, ±24
in June 1681, carpenter, millwright, surveyor, had the advant. of apprenticeship to
Roger Plaisted up to the time he was killed.
In 1735 he had 94 a. laid out to him of 100 a.
gr. in 1682 to Wm. Frost and Jonathan Hammond, and in the same yr. deeded his homestead to his s. John for life supp. of hims.
and w. Mary. Jury 1696, 1700, 1714; gr.j.
1691, 1693, 1695. Lists 33, 269abc. As he
settled his large est. in his own lifetime,
his ch. are unk., except Mary and John, but
app. incl: **Nicholas,** k. by Ind. 9 May 1704.
**Mary,** m. Benj. Gooch, Robert Conoway, Jacob Rylance, Wm. Bracy(2). **Jane,** m. (Court
1706) Thomas Wormwood. **John,** m. 6 Oct.
1727 Bethia (Spencer), d. of John, wid. of
Andrew Rankin. His will 31 Oct. 1765. Hers
5 Mar.—4 July 1772. 5 ch. dau. **Keziah,** m. 27 Jan.
1725-6 George Goodwin.

25 **PHILIP** and his w. Mary were given letters by the Amesbury ch. to the Wells
ch. 4 June 1716. He was gr. 50 a. in Arundel
fronting on the ocean at Cleaves's Cove next
to Nicholas Barto, also from Amesbury. By
1720 he was dead and in 1722 she sold the
gr. to John Murphy. Ch. rec. in Amesb:
**Mary,** b. 18 Feb. 1698, in 1762 was Mary
Tucker of Pomfret, Conn. **Solomon,** eldest
s., b. 12 Feb. 1699-1700. **John,** b. 12 Apr.
1702. **Samuel,** b. 29 Aug. 1704. In 1769 Saml.
jr. was of Pomfret. **Sarah,** b. 24 June 1710.
**Elizabeth,** b. 27 Dec. 1712, in 1769 was w.
of Joseph Cheney of Newbury. Also likely
**Jane,** wid. Aubins of Newburyport, in 1769.
**Philip,** wife Dorothy, 5 ch. rec. in Amesb.
1740-1751.

26 **RICHARD,** Hampton grant 13 July 1642,
was in Boston in Dec. 1643 leaving the

country, and mortg. his grant to Henry Dow, then of Watertown, whose 2d w. was Margaret Cole of Dedham. List 392a.

**27 ROBERT**, at Barbadoes in 11th yr. with no parents, Mr. Saml. Stocker had ordered him aboard for Va. and in the cabin had him sign indentures for 9 or 11 yrs. Orig. indent. dated 1669 'by consent of Thomas Hare of Barbadoes.' The court, 1673, ordered him bound to 21 to be taught navigation.

**28 THOMAS**, Saco, an early tenant of Mr. Vines, on the same farm once occu. by Mr. Samuel Andrews(16) and in 1638 leased to John West for 1000 yrs. Allusions to him are all in the past tense, in reference to this farm or to the death of John Packett, not of record. See James(9). At Navestock in Essex, 15 Dec. 1639, John, aet. 3 yrs., 'which came out of New England,' perh. not Cole, was bap., grands. of Thomas Cole.

**29 THOMAS**, wit. with Philip Swadden at Muscongus in 1653; in 1669, deed of Elbridge to John Dollen, named as abuttor to land at Round Pond, near Musc. River. List 121.

**30 THOMAS**, shipmaster, from Nantasket at Sagadahoc 1675. Lists 3, 80. In 1685 one T. C. was late master of the sloop John & Mary- of Boston.

**31 THOMAS**(23), in court in 1682 for freeing Jonathan Ferguson(5) from the stocks. Gr. in Wells 29 Apr. 1684. Jury 1687; gr.j. 1694, 1695. Himself and his w. Abigail, m. by May 1685, were both k. by Ind. 24 June 1696. Adm. 7 July 1696 to Nicholas Cole and Josiah Littlefield. The latter in 1702 had two of their ch. bap. as his 'adopt. ch.' Lists 269b, 291, 96. Ch: **Samuel**, millman, squatted above Saco Falls bef. 1718, later bot and prospered. Jury 1712. He m. 1st 3 Nov. 1708 Rebecca Stimpson, d. of George and Alice (Phillips) of Ipswich; 2d (int. 14 Oct. 1731) Esther Brooks of Biddeford. 3+1 ch. **Elizabeth**, bp. with **Samuel** 12 July 1702, m. 25 Nov. 1708 Richard Stimpson, br. of Rebecca. **Abigail**, b. 1687, was liv. with Josiah Winn when Josiah Littlefield came out of captivity; in ct. 1709, 1711, m. 28 Dec. 1716 Thomas Haines of Hampton. **Ruth**, b. 15 Nov. 1694, m. Ichabod Cousins(4). **Twin** with Ruth, d. 21 Nov. 1694.

**32 THOMAS** (Daniel of Eastham), carpenter, m. (presum. in Eastham) Lydia Remick. 'Yeoman' of Eastham 13 June 1715 he bot 1-6 of est. of Nicholas Frost(10). 1716 of Eastham housewright. 1717 heavily rated to New Meet. House, Portsm., shopkeeper there 1718-1720. 1722 of Kit., storekeeper alias mariner. List 291. Adm. 5 Oct. 1725 to wid. Lydia, bondsm. John Thompson. The latter in 1723 took a mortgage on his lands, and in 1732 foreclosed and deeded back to Robert. Ch. rec. Eastham: **Remick**, b. 13

Feb. 1700-1, mariner, m. 2 Nov. 1732 Hannah Burrill. **Robert**, b. 27 Feb. 1702-3, fisherman, to whom five wives have been ascribed. The first was Phebe, b. 3 Aug. 1701, dau. of Margaret Shepard, later Spinney. Will, 1784, names 10 ch., incl. Remick. **Abner**, b. 23 June 1706, m. Patience Spinney. 9 ch. **Asahel**, b. 27 June 1708, by w. Lydia had 6 ch. rec. **Jerusha**, b. 23 April 1711, m. 1731 David Spinney. Will 29 Jan.—18 Feb. 1745-6 mentions cousins Margaret Cole and Susannah Knight. **Abial**, b. 27 April 1713, unm. Will 1759 gives 5 s. to 'my grands. the son of my dau. Susannah Tripe dec.', remainder to sister Charity Fernald. **Charity**, b. 18 May 1717, m. Moses Fernald of Kit., blacksmith.

**33 THOMAS** (Pots?). List 358c.

**34 WILLIAM**, b. ab. 1574, carpenter, Exeter and Hampton, and his wife, bonded servants of Mr. Matthew Craddock, were released from his service to come to N. E., with their passage furnished, for £10. The note dated Boston 16 Nov. 1637 was sued against Wm. Cole of Hampton in 1657. In Boston he was gr. 2 a. at Mt. Wollaston 20 Feb. 1737-8. He came to Exeter with Wheelwright and settled in Hampt. where he d. childless 26 May 1662, ag. 88. Lists 371, 373, 374a, 376a, 391a, 392a, 393ab. His w. Eunice, much in the courts, was at last impris. for life in Boston on the charge of witchcraft. She d. in Oct. 1680. Lists 392c, 393a.

**35 WILLIAM**, Wells. Lived on the farm which had been Wm. Wentworth's. The ownership of this farm between Wentworth and Harlark. Symonds, who sold it to Tho. Kimball shortly bef. 1660, is unasc., but he must either have owned or hired it. See Nicholas(23), who occup. it in 1658. List 262. Constable 1645. Jury 1647. 'Goodman Cole and Goodman Rawbone' appraisers 1648. Lists 261, 263, 72. In June 1648 Mr. Ezekiel Knight, John Wadloe, Wm. Cole and John White were sued for using Mr. Francis Raynes's canoe. This may refer to the s. Wm., but the f. is not afterwards ment. and must have d. bef. 1652. Kn. ch: **Nicholas**, b. ab. 1626. **William**, b. ab. 1627.

**36 MR. WILLIAM**, Saco, Wells, was from Sutton, Chew Magna, co. Som., and his br. **John**, b. ab. 1612, was still of Farrington, co. Som., in 1639. Wm. came in 1637 or soon aft., and in 1640 was given handsome recog. in Me. He and Mr. Boade rem. to upper Wells, where they had very large grants, app. under the Stratton patent. By May 1644 he was dead. He had sold 500 a. to Robert Nanny. Lists 262, 22. After her est. was spent Mass. Colony cared for his wife, terming her 'the gentlewoman Mistress Elizabeth Cole.' She bothered them much

and brought suits in our Me. Ct. She and her br. Rev. Francis, who came over, and their sis. Bridget, who didn't, were ch. of Francis Doughty, a Bristol merchant. In Oct. 1651 the Gen. Ct. voted her 50s., 'not likely to live long,' but she lived on.

37 **WILLIAM**(35), ag. 41 in 1668, appar. never m. In 1650, 'jr,' wit. Ind. deed; 1653 subm. to Mass.; from 1663 for 3 yrs. carried on John West's farm under his will for his grandch.; in 1668 and in 1670 was at Saco. Lists 261, 263, 264, 25. In old age he came back to Wells to the house of Jane (Cole 23) Littlefield, who bound herself to keep her uncle off the town, on which oblig. the town in 1700 sued her 2d hus. Capt. John Heard. Poss. it was this W. C. k. by Ind. in Wells 18 Sep. 1712.

38 **WILLIAM**, Sheepscot 1665-1672. Lists 12, 13. (Not in List 15, 1674). Poss. his was 'Wid. Cole' at Scituate. See (10).

**COLEMAN**, Colman, an Anglo-Saxon forename. General over England.

1 **ANNA** (Colman), 'vagabond' Quaker missionary, Dover and Kit. 1662.

2 **ELEAZER**, s. of Tobias(5). List 343. In 1713, at 23, fortified by a trust deed, he m. a maiden thrice his age, Mary Langstaff of Newington, who soon d.s.p.; 2d 1 Mar. 1716-7 Anne Nutter. 10 ch. bp., incl: Eleazer, m. Keziah Leighton; Joseph, mar. Abigail Downing. Rosamond, mar. Joshua Trickey; Lydia, m. Ephraim Pickering and d. 1832 at 94. His ch. in 1756 and 1759 and heirs in 1761 are discl. in N. H. Ct. files 4663.

3 **JABEZ**, son of Tobias(5), b. Rowley 17 Mar. 1668-9. At Hilton's sawmill in 1694, orig. settler at Kingston in 1700, taxed in Hampton Falls in 1709, settled in Kingston. Lists 384a, 400. May 24, 1724, he and his son, app. only ch., were k. by Ind. Adm. 2 Dec. 1724 to wid. Mary (Prescott, m. 2 Nov. 1699), who m. 9 Nov. 1730 Thomas Crosby(3). Son Joseph left 2 daus., the only heirs of his father: Phebe, ag. 1 yr. 11 mo. at death of father, m. 6 Feb. 1738-9 Abraham Colby of Amesbury and Concord; and Margaret, posth., ward of Tristram Sanborn in 1740.

4 **JOHN** (Collman), Oyster River, 1661. List 363a.

5 **THOMAS**, ag. 60 in Aug. 1662, arr. in Boston 3 June 1635 in -The James- from Southampton, accred. to Marlboro, Wilts. Freeman 17 May 1637. Lot layer Newbury 1638. He liv. in Hampton less than 20 yrs. After m. Wid. Johnson he app. liv. here, and signed against Colcord, yet was 'of Newbury' in deed 9 Oct. 1652. He was a memb. of Hampton ch. in 1671, yet had then rem. to Nantucket, where he was called 83 at death in 1682, adm. 1 Aug. to s. Tobias. He

was adm. one of the 20 Nant. prop. 2 Sep. 1659. Jury 1648, 1651; gr.j. 1653. Com.t.e.s.c. Hampton Nov. 1652; selectm. 1654. Lists 392b, 394. Susannah, the mo. of his ch. d. 17 Nov. 1650. His later wives were Mary, wid. of Edmund Johnson, m. 11 July 1651, d. 30 Jan. 1663; and Margery (Fowler) who had had two hus., Christo. Osgood and Tho. Rowell, and had a 4th, Tho. Osborne of Nant. Ch: Dorcas, m. 14 July 1648 John Tillotson; d. 2 Jan. 1654. Susannah, d. Jan. 1642. Thomas, fined for hitting and running in 1651. Tobias, b. 1638, m. 16 Apr. 1668 Lydia Jackson of Rowley. Of Rowley several years, Sherburne, Nant., 1673 until aft. his father's death, then back to Newbury or Rowley. 8 or m. ch., incl. Jabez and Eleazer. Benjamin, b. 1 May 1640, drowned in Newb. 21 Oct. 1650. Joseph, b. 2 Dec. 1642, m. by 1673 Ann Bunker of Nant.; d. 1690. See Edw. Allen(4 jr.). John, mar. by 1667 Joanna Folger, d. Nant. ab. 1715. 8 ch. Isaac, b. 20 Feb. 1646-7, at 12 went in the first boat to Nant., drowned out of a canoe bet. Nant. and Martha's Vin. 6 June 1669.

6 **WILLIAM**, Portsm., List 331a.

**COLESWORTHY**, Peter, Kit. 1675. List 287.

**COLFAX, William,** perh. a coastwise trader and later of Wethersfield, in 1640 was bound over in Me. Ct., his sureties Mr. Boade and Mr. Wm. Cole(36).

**COLLICOTT**, similar to several placenames.

*‡**RICHARD**, Boston merchant with trading and landed interests on Me. coast. Rep. for Falmouth 1669 and for Saco 1672. Owned half int. in Mr. Richard Dummer's 800 a. claim at Casco. Of Sagadahoc 1672, appointed alternate justice to keep Devonshire Co. court 12 May 1675, and petn. for garrison in that co. to be manned by deserting inhabitants 6 Sep. 1676. Lists 13, 15, 77a, 181. Died in Boston 7 July 1686. Grsons. Richard and Samuel C., Richard Miles, Samuel, Richard, Jonathan and Joseph Hall, and Richard Gookin claimed shares in his eastern lands ab. 1730. Kn. ch: Experience, b. 29 Sep. 1641, m. Richard Miles. Dependence, b. 5 July 1643, d. bef. 1686. List 191. Preserved, bp. 28 Jan. 1649. Elizabeth, m. Richard Hall. Bethia, m. Rev. Daniel Gookin, and poss. William, of Sheepscot 1672. List 13.

**COLLINS**, attributed to Cole, also distinctively South of England.

1 ——, List 90.

2 **ABRAHAM**, Oyster River (tax list) and Saco 1666, ±30 in 1669, led a busy life running away from old debts and contracting new ones, besides dodging fines for petty misdem. In 1669 as attorney for Dr. Morgan he sued Richard Smith. Exeter, 1670. Had fled the country, with Thomas Moun-

sell in 1671. Wells, 1677. Isl. of Shoals, 1678. In 1680 he had appar. gone to Northampton Co., Va., with Capt. Richard Lockwood and was leaving debts behind him there. He was back in Falmouth in 1683 as tenant of Sylvanus Davis & Co. and in 1687 claimed ab. 6 yrs. res. Only one kn. wife, Phebe Farrow(1), m. in Wells aft. 1676. They sold her est. 26 Mar. 1679. Last ment., Milton, 4 July 1690, when he had aband. his s. Benjamin, ag. 18 mos., promising to return and take the inf. to its grmother in Ipswich. His petn. in 1687 pleaded wife and ch. Doc. Hist. v. 130, vi. 305.

3 ANTHONY, N. H. gr.j. 1684 (Savage).

4 BENJAMIN, of Salis. mar. 5 Nov. 1668 Martha Eaton(3), servant to Henry Deering's wife. One son Benjamin, Portsmouth, helped on the meetinghouse in 1697, ±18 in 1699.

5 CHRISTOPHER, shoemaker, ±55 9 Feb. 1663-4, Boston 1640, Braintree 1645, Lynn 1648, Blue Point, Scarb. 1660. Aft. much diffic. in defending his rights thru life, his death occas. an inquest 29 July 1666 with the finding 'said Collins was slayn (by James Robinson) by misadventure & culpable of his own death.' Marshal's deputy, Lynn, 1650; const., Scarb., 1664. List 233. He m. in England Jane Greepe, to whom in 1645 money was due from Justinian Pearce of Plymouth, Devon. In 1651 she lay 10 wks. in jail under accus. of witchcraft, for which her hus. sued the accuser and appealed to the Ct. of Assist. In Me. she was fined for knitting on Sunday. Her dau. Williams was liv. with her in 1675. Ch: Deborah, m. Henry Williams. Moses, adult in 1670, was flogged as a Quaker. Adm. 6 Apr. 1675 to br. Timothy. Timothy, adult in 1675; of Newbury in 1680, he sold his father's Scarb. lands; wife Abigail; adm. gr. 25 Mar. 1690. Presum. Susannah, put under bonds to avoid Francis Shallet 6 Apr. 1675.

6 ELEAZER, cr. of John Young's est., Exeter.

7 GEORGE, Gosport 1733, Kittery 1742; m. Mary (Frost 8), wid. of Wm. Fox(6).

8 JOHN, N. H. jury 1694. One John and Sarah, Portsm., had sons John, William and Thomas, b. 1709-1713. List 339. Widow Collins's tax, Str. Bank, was abated in 1714.

9 NICHOLAS, with Capt. John Smith, 1614. List 7.

10 PETER, Sagadahoc, 1674. List 15.

11 ROBERT, York, had liv. with Mr. John Alcock over 2 yrs. prior to Oct. 1649. For crim. rec. see P. & C., Vol. I. He was cert. the same with same propensities in Essex Co., 1651-1654, and likely the same that m. wid. Hester (Fowler) Rolfe and had 5 ch. rec. at Ipsw. and d. in Haverh. 17 June 1688. If so, the career of 'fat Robert' in Maine

was off-line play of his adolescence. List 75b.

12 ROGER, Great Isl., ±30 1671. List 312c.

13 SAMUEL, Piscataqua 1675. List 286.

Collis, Benjamin, 1672. See Collins.

Colt, Richard, York, 1640. P. & C. i. 80.

Combe, see Coombs.

Comby, see Cumby.

COMER, see also Camer.

1 GEORGE, Pemaquid 1687. List 124.

2 RICHARD (Coman?), York, tailor, ±30 Dec. 1695.

COMFORT, Samuel, first app. with 'my cabin' aboard ship -America- 1690, ag. 24, ±32 in 1700, not noticeably here outside those years; 'oarmaker,' taxed Newcastle. Clerk of the Courts 1699. In that year he sued Col. John Pole of Boston for oars, who put in an account crediting '105 small pitifull oars judged thus by Capt. Job Alcock and Mr. Goudge, not worth a bone.' In 1697 he sued Mrs. Sarah Hopkins for withholding his chest containing his clothes, listed, enough for 10, also 'my articles of agreement with Samuel Allen Esq. Governor of the Province of New Hampshire.' The widow entered cross suit for 'one years diet' from which he claimed to discount 59 days for absences, 'when I went to meet the Lt. Gov.' etc. Lists 333a, 315bc, 318a.

Coming (Cummings?), Robert, master of the ketch -George-, Portsm., 1682.

COMPTON, John, Roxbury, Exeter, Boston. Grantee in Wheelwright's Ind. deed 1638. Rememb. in Rachel Bigg's will, Dorchester, 1647. Wit. in 1651 conc. Exeter's grant of mill priv. to Thomas Wilson. House formerly his was in 1650 conveyed by Stanyan to Edward Gilman. Lists 371, 376a, 378. See Savage.

Comston, Mary, widow, Boston, dau. of Amos Stevens. Y. D. 16.30.

Conett, Sarah, see Connell.

CONLEY, Abraham, was in poss. of a house and 6 a. in Kittery, bot of John Ugrave, on 5 Jan. 1638-9. His 1st w. was prob. that Elizabeth Conley who was with him a wit. against Thomas Crawley in 1664 and a troublesome female, for whose good behav. he was bound over in 1652. He m. 2d wid. Margery Everett-Nash. Constable 1646-7; selectm. 1651; jury 1647, 1649-50, 1651, 1665; gr.j. 1646-7, 1650, 1653, 1654, 1655, 1658, 1666; O. A. 1652, com. to adjust town grants 1652. Lists 24, 28, 281, 282, 283, 285, 298. Adm. was gr. 2 Apr. 1678 to Nathan Lord, who had m. his wife's dau. Martha Everett and who had brot the old man from his Sturgeon Creek farm to his own home over a yr. bef. his death. A will, later produced, 1 Mar. 1674[5—5 Mar. 1690-1], left prop. to Lord's 2 sons Nathan and Abraham, Adrian Frye 'with whom I now live,' John White and Robert Allen.

**CONNELL.** 1 **Thomas,** shipmaster, 1681. List 51.

2 **TIMOTHY,** Philip's War. List 237b.

3 **SARAH** (or Conett), 'the Irish woman,' Walter Abbott's servant, in 1655 had told 'her countrymen' about it and was transferred to Peter Coffin. In 1657, bastardy, accu. James Kidd.

**CONNER,** Conough. See Cartee.

1 **CHARLES** (Connaugh), in 1682 had been whipped with a Newbury man.

2 **CORNELIUS,** Salisbury, ±35 in 1672, app. brot over ab. 1656. Due to two blunders, (Mr. Dudley's man Cornelius, 1657, was not Conner, but Lary, and the births of C. C.'s ch. in the Norf. Co. rec. was a Salisbury, not an Exeter, record), this man, who began as Richard Goodale's servant and m. Robert Pike's milkmaid, all Salis., has been attrib. to Exeter falsely, to the geneal. obscur. of Jeremy, poss. his br. His will 21 Aug. 1684 —24 May 1687 names w. Sarah (Brown), liv. 1693, and 10 of their 11 ch. rec. 1659-1676, incl. 4 sons: **John,** b. 8 Dec. 1660, m. Elizabeth Purington, Quakeress, by whom ch. Joseph, Cornelius, Dorothy (mar. Jeremiah Green) George and Gideon (mar. Dorothy Bracy 2). He d. 1 May 1718. **Samuel,** b. 1662. **Jeremiah,** b. 6 Nov. 1671. **Cornelius,** b. 1675. One Cornelius m. 17 June 1720 Eleanor wid. of Wm. Brown.

3 **HENRY,** in N. E. Reg. vi. 249, is -Codner-.

4 **JAMES,** Little Harbor wit. 1691, poss. f. of Samuel of Newcastle, fisherman, 1711-1722, who was grs. of John Marden. He m. Sarah Jordan, his wid. in 1728, who mar. Thomas Brown(34).

5 **JEREMY,** Exeter. Oct. 14, 1664, Cornelius Lary's 15 a. gr. adj. Teague Drisco and Jeremy Conners, and Jeremy Conaugh's 20 a. gr., 31 Jan. 1680[1, adj. Teag Drisco and Philip Cartee]. In Apr. 1664 Robert Jones, James Kid, John Folsom jr., Dennis Skalion (Kelly) and Jerime Cano had gone Francis Pafat's bond. Jeremy was taxed in Exeter in 1680 and 1684. Lists 383, 52 (Conah), 376b. These records could not poss. relate to Jeremiah b. in Salis. 6 Nov. 1671, and unlik. the Exeter pet. of 1692, List 62, or the gr. jury of 1696. Yet the accepted Conner gen. ignores (5) and attrib. this large race in Exeter (6 grantees in 1725) all to the Salis. man, none to Jeremy. This unhappy cond. was unobserved until too late to invest.; even Jeremy's grants have not been traced, nor have the ident. of any of Cornelius's sons with those liv. in N. H. been confirmed, incl. (some of them likely recent emigrants): Cornelius, Ex. gr. 1699, m. Mary Gilman, ch. Moses, David, John, dau. Mary, m. Gale. **Samuel,** List 94. **Samuel,** in 1768 dep. that he and his bros. bet. 50-60 years

since brot logs to Exeter mill. **Timothy,** 1714, m. Mercy Drisco(5). **John,** Berwick, m. 5 Nov. 1722 Sarah Turbet. **Joseph,** cordwainer, Dover, m. by 1729 Sarah Forst(2), will 1768 —1771, ch. Benj., John, Sarah Hanson, grch. Whitehouse and Gage. **Joseph,** Rye, m. 25 Jan. 1738 Mary Seavey. **James,** Durham, List 369. **John,** Exeter, m. by 1749 Abigail Moulton. Some of these, or others, may have m. Abigail Leavitt by 1737, Mary Nock by 1737, Martha Dow by 1738, Bethia Wells or Wills by 1739, and Meribah Robie who d. bef. 1754.

6 **JEREMIAH,** presum. son of (2), soldier 1695, 1696; m. Ann Gove 3 July 1696; Exeter gr. same yr. He bot in Exeter in 1700. Lists 67, 376b. Will 20 Dec. 1737—24 Sep. 1740 names 6 rec. ch. His wife d. 12 Feb. 1722-3. Ch: **Jeremiah,** b. 18 Apr. 1697, d. Apr. 1722. **Jonathan,** b. 5 Dec. 1699. In 1744 the town of Exeter paid him for cloth furnished to Cornelius Lary. Ch. **Philip,** b. 3 Mar. 1701-2, m. Maria (Gilman) wid. of Joseph Dudley(3). Adm. 1761 to her. Ch. **Samuel,** b. 3 May 1704, liv. 1741, m. Sarah Gilman. Ch. **Hannah,** b. 20 Sep. 1706, mar. Jonathan Rawline. **Anne,** b. 30 Mar. 1709, mar. Thomas Lyford. **Benjamin,** b. 7 Sep. 1711, had the homestead. He m. 1st one Abigail; 2d Mary, wid. of Jeremiah Leavitt. Adm. 1771 to John.

**Conniers,** Walter, Boston, in 1685 sued Thomas Parker of Great Isl. for defamation.

**CONSTABLE.** 1 **Andrew,** Exeter, in 1661 knew Leonard Weeks. His land joining Hilton's in 1674 was sold by Samuel Hilton to his neph. Richard in 1699. Lists 383, 52.

2 **JOHN,** master of -The Charles- 1648. P. & C. i. 153.

**COOKE,** Cook, occup. surname, very common in East coast and S. E. counties. 40th in Eng. and Wales, became 20th in N. E.

1 —— Dr. or Mr. List 98.

2 **BENJAMIN,** N. H. petn. 1690. List 57.

3 **ED** (Cuck), Wells 1690. List 267a.

4 **JAMES,** mariner, Sheepscot 1684. List 163.

5 **JOHN,** York, had town gr. 1686; mar. by 1680 a dau. of Thomas Curtis(6). Ch: **Thomas,** joiner, mar. 8 Dec. 1725 Susannah Grover, dau. of Matthew. List 279. 12 ch. rec.

6 **JOHN,** Dover. Lists 359b, 92, 94, 62, 57, (315c?). Coroner's j. 1685. He mar. 25 Nov. 1686 Mary Downes(5). Kn. ch: **Rebecca,** m. event. John Drew(6) and 2d Samuel Starbird. **John,** b. 5 May 1692 (self recorded). List 353. Will 1752—1755 names w. Lydia (Young) and 7 ch.

7 **PEYTON,** gent., presum. same bp. 29 Sep. 1596 at Bury St. James, Suffolk, son of Richard Cooke and Eliz., d. of Sir Christopher Peyton. Relation of Mr. Jocelyn, he soon adhered to Cleeve, and was Secy. of

Lygonia Prov. By his wits or not at all, he found diff. in making a living. See P. & C. I, II, passim. Last ment. Aug. 1670, warned out of Saco. The name Peyton occurs in Cookes desc. from Mordecai of Glouc. Co., Va., 1648.

8 **PHILIP**, in 1686 one of Capt. Severet's crew. List 314.

9 **LT. RICHARD**, of Boston, tailor, Rep. Dover 1670. List 53.

10 **ROBERT**, one or more of this name: 1655-56 given 30 lashes for not keeping away from Mary Clay; 1659 Scarb. wit.; 1664 Saco; 1683-4 Sagadahoc. List 17.

11 **RUTH**, husband List 358c?, entered complaint 15 Feb. 1695-6 that Henry Hobbs entered 'my house at Bellemies Bank' (Dover), and forced her. Perh. mother of **Peter** who had w. Abigail and ch. Nathl., Joseph, Peter, Reuben and Abraham, rec. 1717-1725, besides app. Daniel of Rochester.

**Cooley**, Henry, see Cowley.

**COOMBS**, Coomes, Combe, in var. spellings a charact. English place-name and surname.

1 **ALEXANDER** (Coomes), Portsm. Adm. 15 Aug. 1707 to wid. Abigail, who had 'her child' bap. in No. Ch. and in 1709 was of Portsm. wid. She m. 2d Capt. Richard Thomas, mariner, will 1725—1728, Suff. Prob. Harvey Thomas, bp. No. Ch. 15 June 1712, m. Boston 14 Oct. 1736 Sarah Allen. Sarah Thomas wit. Elizabeth Combes's deed 1737. 2 ch. rec. It is undet. whether the mother, Abigail, was dau. of Edward Cowell(2) or of Thomas Harvey. When her 1st hus. d., her bondsman was Thomas Phipps, s.-in-law of T. H. E. C.'s s.-in-law, Nathaniel Ayers, and N. A. jr., wit. the will of her 2d hus. In 1730 she joined in a Harvey heirship deed. But in 1737 her dau. Elizabeth Coombs gave to the widow of Thomas Phipps jr. a warranty deed of the land deeded by Mr. Thomas Harvey to Mr. Edward Cowell (13 Nov. 1670), and the mother rel. dower. N. H. Deeds 23.151.

2 **ALLISTER**, Kennebec 1665, abuttor south of Thomas Stevens. List 182. Wit. 1673.

3 **ANTHONY**, blacksmith, apprent. of Lewis Allen(9). App. brot to Wells with him. By early trad. his parents, French, gave him to monks to be made a priest, but he got an English Bible and ran away. When Allen left Wells he left Anthony on his land. He m. in Wells 5 Sep. 1688 Dorcas Wooden. During the war he kept his fam. in different Essex Co. towns, while he spent much time in Wells, his section of the town in the hands of the Indians. Abandoning hope, he sett. in Rochester. His gr. there in 1704 was cond. on his practicing his trade of blacksmith. Lists 268a, (258?). Ch: **Mary**, bp.

Beverly 3 Nov. 1689, m. 20 May 1708 Rochester Thomas Raymond of Beverly. **Peter**, bp. Beverly 18 Oct. 1691, m. Joanna Hodgkins, d. Jan. 1768 at Newmeadows. 5 or m. ch. **Tabitha**, bp. Wenham 1693. **Anthony**, b. Wells 1 Mar. 1694-5, m. Glouc. 21 Oct. 1722 Mercy Hodgkins. Settled at Newmeadows. 7 or m. ch. **John**, d. inf. **John**, b. Rochester 18 Mar. 1699, m. 9 Jan. 1723-4 Lydia Wooden (Peter). 11 ch. rec. at Rochester. **Hannah**, b. 30 Nov. 1700, m. 24 June 1729 Nicholas Hicks of Rochester. **Rosanna**, b. 23 Nov. 1702, m. 21 Jan. 1722-3 Nathl. Whitcomb, d. Rochester 8 Mar. 1737. 7 ch. **Ithamar**, b. 20 Nov. 1704, m. 4 Nov. 1731 Hannah Andrews. 11 ch. record. at Rochester. **Joshua**, b. 28 July 1706, m. (int. Roch. 31 May) in Middleboro 10 Sep. 1729 Elizabeth Pratt. Settled at Newmeadows, near Foster's Point, ab. 1751. 9 ch., one rec. in Rochester, 7 of Joshua and Mary at Newbury. **Frances**, b. 20 July 1708, m. in Rochester 15 Apr. 1727 James Pratt of Middleboro. **Jane**, b. 29 Mar. 1710.

4 **HENRY**, likelier s. of Humphrey Coombs, ±60 in 1681, of Salem. He was in Boston in 1676, 'late of Kennebec, fisherman,' when he bot from David Oliver, adm. est. of Thomas Bowles(8), part of his lands on Georgetown Isl., which he claimed before the Eastern Claims Com. In 1688 he was constable of No. Yarm. His grant there in 1685 he sold (H. C. of York, tailor) in 1721. Me. jury 1702. Lists 80, 187, 214. He m. at York 25 Aug. 1713 Sarah (Preble) Parker, who d. 25 Oct. 1724. Will 29 Jan. 1723-4, d. 10 Feb. 1724-5, makes his chief benef. Samuel Ingersoll, of Marblehead in 1724, of Salem, cooper, in 1743, son of his sis. Mary, who m. John Ingersoll 17 May 1670.

5 **JOHN**, cooper, Boston, m. Elizabeth widow of Tho. Barlow, who m. 3d John Warren from Exeter. Her ch. by two husbands inherited land and a warehouse at Saco and called Joseph Royal uncle in 1685.

6 **JOHN**, pet. Andros for grant at Sheepscot ab. 1686, 'having been in these parts a considerable time.'

7 **PHILIP**, servant of Geo. Fabens(1), 1678, poss. hus. of wid. Abigail, who m. Thomas Avery(8).

8 **THOMAS**, from Newfoundland, 20 Oct. 1662, to pay his passage bound himself to 5 yrs. service for Tho. Beard, who assigned him to John Woodman.

9 **THOMAS**, perh. (8), at Kennebec 1665. List 182.

**COOPER**, occup. surname. 28th commonest in Eng. and Wales, yet uncom. in N. and S. W

1 **ALEXANDER**, Berwick, where he had town grants of 60 a. on the brook out

of Wilcox pond, bot 30 acres near White's marsh in 1662. Coroner's j. 1668. Lists 30, 288, 298. D. 11 Feb. 1683-4, leaving prop. to only s. John, ab. 16, by will dated 2 days before. Ch: John.

2 JOHN(1), b. ab. 1667, Berwick, mar. 13 Dec. 1692 Sarah Lord. Jury 1693; gr.j. 1693, 1694; const. 1694-5, 1696. Lists 290, 296, 298. Adm. est. of John Drisco in 1697. D. 18 Apr. 1758. Ch: Alexander, b. 28 Dec. 1697; d.s.p. John, b. 7 Oct. 1702, m. Mary (Goodwin), wid. of Richard Lord jr.; adm. 1792 to s. John. 5 or m. ch. Sarah, b. 29 Jan. 1704, m. Noah Emery s. of Daniel(2). Eleanor, b. 3 May 1708, m. one Horne and had a dau. Sarah who m. one Kimball by 1759.

3 PHILIP, 'the Walloon,' York, 1669, when he owed est. of Nicholas Davis, had a town gr. of 10 a. in 1673. He m. Anne Ingalls, who was slain with him in the massacre of 1690, adm. being gr. to Benj. Preble 31 Oct. 1692. Ch: Philip, 'eldest son,' Boston seaman, gave a P. A. in 1699 to Sarah Wright, whom he m. 29 Oct. 1700, to sell his father's York prop., which she did, to Lewis Bane and Andrew Brown. Son Philip, b. in Boston 21 May 1704. Mary, taken capt. when her parents were killed, bap. in Quebec, ag. 12, 25 Mar. 1693 with the additional name Frances, and redeemed in 1695. List 99.

4 THOMAS, N. H. 1694. List 65.

5 WILLIAM, Piscataqua, living 1633 with Mr. Wannerton, was drowned from his canoe with a boy in 1633-4 while going to fetch sack to be drunk at the Great House. List 41.

Coots, Elizabeth, see Coates.

COPELAND, Lawrence, wit. to Wheelwright Ind. deed 1638. List 371. D. in Braintree 30 Dec. 1699, ag. 100 (grst.)

COPPIN, Thomas, York patentee, neph. of Col. Walter Norton. List 272.

Coppleston, John, Shoals wit. 1684-5.

CORBER (Creber). 1 Richard, carpenter, came to Richmond Isl. in -The Hunter-1634. List 21 (pp. 38, 360-1).

2 THOMAS, Pepperell wit., (wrote), Kit. 1699.

CORBETT, Corbet, an anc. forename. Ancient landed family in Shropshire.

1 ABRAHAM, distiller, Kittery or Portsm. 1661. Wife Alice. Bot land near meet. ho. in Portsm. 1663, but app. generally liv. on his 11 a. homestead on Kit. Point, where he had warehouse, kept tavern and ran ferry to Great Isl. and Portsm. Led agitation against Mass. control in 1665 and warrant was issued 3 Aug. to produce him in Boston to answer charge of sedition. Indicted, under alias of Abraham Baker, for common fame of having two wives, 1670. Lists 26,

47, 87, 311b, 323, 326b, 327a, 330a. Sold Portsm. house by 1671 and moved to Sheepscot, whence he wrote to the N. Y. authorities 8 Sep. 1676 asking that ship be sent to collect the eastern refugees at Piscataqua, Salem and Boston. Before leaving Kit. he executed deed of trust 10 Sep. 1669 to Capt. Barefoot and Henry Greenland of his homestead and 440 other a. in Kit. for benefit of his w. Alice and their ch: Elizabeth, Alice, John, under age 1669.

2 FRANCIS, wit. deed Hilton to Barefoot 1669.

3 JOHN (also Corbyn). List 9.

CORBIN, Corben, an E. of Eng. surname, also Cheshire. One Robert C. had s. John bap. at Crediton 1607. One Richard of Maker had adult s. John in 1634.

1 JOHN, master of a fishing vessel, took letter from Wm. Hilton at Piscataqua to John Winthrop at Ipswich, 18 Apr. 1633. Lists 8, 9.

2 ROBERT, Falmouth 1657, poss. that R. C., master of the -Speedwell-, sued in Boston 1637, had gr. of land and took O. A. to Mass. 1658. Com.t.e.s.c. 1670, selectm. 1674, 1675. Jury 1667; gr.j. 1664, 1674. Lists 93, 111, 221, 222bcd, 232. He m. Lydia, d. of Dorothy, w. of Benj. Atwell and Richard Martin, appar. by her first hus., and she was captured when he was k. by Ind. 11 Aug. 1676. His heir was Clement Corbin of Muddy River and Woodstock, Conn., whom Robert 'often called cousin' when in Boston. James Corbin of Woodstock, 'now the only heir,' sold the Falm. land to John Rogers 1698.

CORBINSON, Samuel, Sagadahoc 1665—. House west bank of Sheepscot River below the falls. Lists 182, 78, 13. In Taunton, 11 Oct. 1693 Mary C. m. Wm. Ripley. Elizabeth C. housemaid in Boston 1699. Corbinson, -ison, -eson mar. there 1703-1719.

CORDING, Mr. Richard. Ipsw. wit. 1662, in court in 1663 Dr. Corden from jail provided he give security to depart that jurisdiction within one week. Sued by Thomas Canney 1666-7, Barefoote surety, he skipped his bail.

Cordy, Gilbert, Isles of Shoals. See Currier.

Cornall, James, wit. Wheelwright deed 1638. List 371.

CORNEY, John, of Gloucester, where he m. Abigail Skillins 18 Nov. 1670 and had gr. of house lot 1671. In Falmouth as tenant of John Ingersoll 1685, of Samuel Ingersoll 1686, and in 1687 bot 60 a. from Anthony Libby on south side of Casco river, east of Nonsuch Point, where he liv. 3 yrs. bef. retiring to Glouc. where his w. d. 15 Feb. 1722, ag. 70, and he d. 4 May 1725, ag. 80. Kn. ch: Elisha, b. 25 Sep. 1672, of Glouc. 1734-1753,

during which yrs. he testified thrice to location of lands in Falm. bef. the wars. Abigail, b. 8 Feb. 1676, m. at Glouc. 12 Jan. 1703 Capt. Tho. Sanders, and d. 12 Feb. 1767, ag. 90. **John,** b. 27 Sep., d. 12 Oct. 1678.

**CORNISH,** name for a Cornishman who settled in another county. Common in the nearer counties.

1 **JEFFREY,** at Damariscove from Virginia 162--, List 8.

2 **RICHARD,** York, 1640, coming from Weymouth where his w. Catherine had immoral record dating from 1634. Wit. to a Gorges gr. 1640. Found drowned in the river, his wife was accu. of his murder, tried by Mayor Roger Garde and executed, presum. bet. 30 Oct. 1644 and 17 Feb. 1644-5 (Winthrop).

3 **THOMAS,** Exeter, 1650, when he bot land from Tho. Jones, with w. Mary (Stone) whom he had m. in Gloucester 4 Sep. 1641 and for slandering whom he prosec. Exeter neighbors in 1652. List 376b. Ch: **John,** b. 1 Sep. 1642 in Glos. One John in N. H., 1688. **A child,** b. 1648 in Norfolk Co.

**Corrin** (Curran?), Richard. See Corwin.

**Corrine,** George, misr. of Burrine? List 314.

**Cors** (Corrs, Cusso?), James, alias Essex, taxed Great Isl. 1688, 1689.

**CORSON,** Courson, Cursonwhitt.

**CORNELIUS.** The only cert. fact ab. this person is that Samuel Courson was accounted his son. One Cornelius Cursonwhit was in a fight in New York in 1681. Cornelius Courson, s. of Jan Courson, mariner, bp. 10 May 1676 in New York, if an inf., could hardly be Samuel's father. In 1719 Hatevil Roberts, James Stagpole and Henry Hobbs dep. that Wm. Henderson and Cornelius Corsen were in quiet poss. at Cochecho Point by building and improving 34 years ago (1685). In Suff. Ct. July 1686 Cornelius Cossen late of Boston, and Joanna Armitage of Boston, both married people, had been found in naked bed together. One way to acc. for Samuel's getting £50 for his share of Richard Tozer's est. is that Elizabeth Tozer m. Cornelius bef. mar. Richard Randall, but this is impos. (forgetting infreq. divorces) if Cornelus Cosenwhit, inhabitant, in Lt. Frost's garrison ab. 1704 (List 289), was Samuel's father. See List 87. Poss. ch: **Samuel,** certain because, in 1729, he sold land gr. to Cornelius. First ment. 1707, wit. to Joanna Potts selling drink. Lists 358cd. He m. Mary Potts, d. of Thomas and Joanna (Roberts). Her stepmo., Ann (Tozer) Jenkins-Kincaid-Potts, may have deeded her father's lands to them. He was liv. in Berwick in 1739. 6 ch. b. or

bap. in Dover 1712-1722, incl. Hatevil. **Cornelius** (Cosenwhit) in Lt. Frost's garrison ab. 1704. **Abigail** (Cursonwhitt, Coursin), Dover or Kittery, Ind. capt. bef. 1695. List 99. **Hannah** (Courson), Portsm. wit. in 1702.

**CORWIN,** or Corrin, Richard, Portsmouth, servant of Mr. Richard Cutt. On 26 June 1660 he was ordered to maintain his child by Mary Poole (appar. 'Mary the Indian woman,' servant of George Walton). Dead in 1668. Ch: **Richard,** ag. 8 in 1668 was bound to Richard Cutt until 24. See N. E. H. and G. Reg. 10. 304, 26. 76.

**COSS.**

1 **CHRISTOPHER** (Cose), seaman on -The Dove-, Portsm., 1674.

2 **GEORGE** (Cost or Cosh), Portsm., wit. in 1669 (Cash), taxed 1688 and 1689, may poss. have been second hus. of Mary (Taylor) Hardison-Coss-Legrow, whose Hardison ch. had a half-br. **Thomas.**

3 **THOMAS**(2?), Portsm. mariner or fisherman, m. Abigail Banfield (Hugh 2), who m. 2d Samuel Brackett(5). He d. in 1740, adm. being gr. to the Bracketts 27 May 1752. Ch: **Abigail,** m. Thomas Sherborn. **Mary,** unm. in 1761. **Sarah,** b. 1734, m. Charles Butler of Berwick. **Hannah,** b. 1736, m. Jacob Shorey of Kittery. **John,** b. 1738.

**COTTLE** (Coettell), Edward, in Dover 1650 tax list, stricken out; accepted inhab. of Salisbury 1652; rem. to Nantucket ab. 1668. 13 ch., incl. **Mary,** m. Samuel Bickford.

**COTTON,** a common place-name in Mid. Eng., also Yorkshire and Suffolk.

1 **BENJAMIN**(1), Portsmouth, house carp., a minor in 1678, m. one Elizabeth, who m. 2d John Golden of Kittery. His est. was adm. by his 4 sons-in-law in 1724. Constable 1696, gr.j. 1695, 1697. Lists 59, 62, 94, 330d, 335a, 337, 339. Ch: **Sarah,** m. 1st 20 Dec. 1716 Capt. Thomas Waldron, 2d Samuel Pickering. **Mary,** m. June 1715 Matthew Nelson. **Elizabeth,** m. 1 Dec. 1715 Nathaniel Peverly. **Deborah,** m. 24 Sep. 1719 John Deverson(1).

2 **JOHN**(6), ±22 in 1674, Portsm., farmer, m. Sarah Hearle (William), who may have m. 2d 13 Dec. 1716 Henry Nicholson of Williamsburg, Va. Lists 41, 49, 52, 55b, 57, 329, 330ad, 331b, 335a, 336b, 337, 339. Jury 1683, 1692, 1697, 1699, gr.j. 1694, 1695, 1698. His will, 14 Sep.—9 Dec. 1714, names his wife and 12 ch: **William,** gunsmith, Portsm., mar. in Boston 6 Nov. 1699 Anne Carter (Ralph) and had a dau. Sarah b. in Boston 11 Aug. 1702. **Solomon,** shipwright of Kittery and Portsm., innkeeper of Greenland and Stratham, mar. 1st 14 May 1702 Margaret Fernald(5) who d. 12 Jan. 1719 or 1720; m. 2d Judith (Cutt 3) Pormort, who d. 5 Mar. 1744.

His will 25 Mar. 1754—27 Mar. 1755. 7 ch. **John**, butcher, Portsm., had lands in Me. bot of David Libby and Jacob Smith. He m. 6 May 1714 Elizabeth Davis(61) and d. in 1723. 5 ch. **Thomas**, joiner, Gloucester, when he m. 28 July 1718 Comfort Riggs (John). His will 2 Jan. 1768—7 Sep. 1770. 13 ch. **Elizabeth**, who with next 4 daus. had had her portion bef. 1714, m. bef. 1707 George Thompson. **Mary**, m. bef. 1707 Moses Paul. **Joanna**, b. 1685, m. John Jones (James), bricklayer, of Portsm., Kit. and Scarb. **Sarah**, m. by 1708 Edward Cater(1). **Hannah**, m. John Mead of Stratham. **Abigail**, d. 6 Oct. 1722 at Stratham at ho. of her bro.-in-law John Mead, leaving est. by nunc. will to niece Abigail Mead. **Margaret**, m. 30 Jan. 1714-5 Moses Caverly. **Susanna**, betrothed to Ebenezer Wallingford of Dover who d. in 1721 making her his exec. and prin. legatee, m. 27 May 1722 William Young.

3 **REV. JOHN**(4), H. C. 1678, and chosen a Fellow. Prior to his ordin., 19 Nov. 1696, he preached at Hampton and elsewhere (at Portsm. in 1692 and at Mystic). He d. 27 Mar. 1710, obit. in Boston News Letter 10 Apr. List 336c. The wid. Anne (Lake, dau. of Capt. Thomas, m. 17 Aug. 1686) moved to Brookline, and 30 May 1715 m. Rev. Increase Mather, D.D. She d. in Brookline 29 Mar. 1737, ae. 74 (grst.) Ch: **John**, b. 5 Sep. 1687, bp. by Dr. Inc. Mather, d. 8 Sep. 1689 at Boston. **Mary**, b. 5 Nov. 1689, bp. by Dr. Mather, m. Rev. John Whiting of Concord, d. 29 May 1731. 8 ch. **Dorothy**, b. 16 July 1693, bp. at Salis., m. 21 Dec. 1710, Rev. Nathaniel Gookin, from Cambridge, H. C. 1703, pastor at Hampt. 1710 till his death 25 Aug. 1734. She d. in East Kingston. 13 ch. **Thomas**, b. 28 Oct. 1695, bp. at Boston, d. in Brookline 4 Sep. 1770. He m. 14 Apr. 1725 Martha Williams, d. of Samuel of Roxbury, who d. 11 May 1744. 5 s. 4 daus. **Anna**, b. 13 Nov. 1697, d. at Boston 7 Aug. 1745. **Simon**, b. 21 Dec. 1701, d. 2 Jan. 1709-10. **Samuel**, b. 12, d. 16 Oct. 1703. **Lydia**, b. 14 Jan., d. 17 Feb. 1704-5. Dau. stillb., 19 Jan. 1706-7.

4 **REV. SEABORN**, son of Rev. John and Sarah (Hawkredd) Cotton, b. in transit from Boston, Old, to Boston, New, Eng., 12 Aug. 1633; H. C. 1651; candidated in Conn. (Wethersfield 1655), minister at Hampton from 1657 until his death 20 Apr. 1686. Elab. will 20 May 1684. Lists 49, 54, 392a, 394. Ch. by 2 wives, m. 14 June 1654 Dorothy Bradstreet, dau. of Gov. Simon and Anne (Dudley) the poetess, who d. 26 Feb. 1671[2]; 2d 9 July 1673 Prudence (Wade), d. of Jonathan, wid. of Dr. Anthony Crosby. Ch: One stillborn 21 Nov. 1655. **Dorothy**, b. 11 Nov. 1656, at Hartford, Conn., m. Col. Joseph Smith. **John**, b. 8 May 1658. **Sarah**, b.

22 Feb., d. 1 Apr. 1660. **Anne**, b. 22 Aug. 1661, m. 8 Nov. 1677 Geo. Carr(3), 2d Wm. Johnson of York, d. at Boston of smallpox 6 or 7 Dec. 1702. **Sarah**, b. 2 July 1663, m. 27 Aug. 1680 Richard Pearce, printer, of Boston; d. 2 Aug. 1690. **Elizabeth**, b. 13 Aug. 1665, m. Rev. William Williams of Hatfield; d. 1698. **Mercy**, b. 3 Nov. 1666, m. Dec. 1684 Capt. Peter Tufts of Medford; d. 18 June 1715. 12 ch. **Abiah**, b. 5 Apr., d. 11 May 1669. **Maria**, b. 22 Apr. 1670, m. 1st John Atwater of Salem; 2d Samuel Partridge of Hadley; d. June 1729. **Rowland**, Rev., b. 29 Aug. 1674, H. C. 1696, d. Warminster, co. Wilts, 1753. **Wade**, b. 6, d. 11 Oct. 1676.

5 **REV. THEOPHILUS**, nephew of (4), b. 5 May 1682 at Plymouth; H. C. 1701, first minister at Hampt. Falls, m. 1st Elizabeth (Elliot) Diamond, wid. of Andrew, who d. of a fall from a horse 13 Oct. 1710, ag. 45; m. 2d Mary (Gookin) Gedney of Salem, who m. 3d Rev. John Newmarch. He d.s.p. 16 Aug. 1726, leaving an interesting will, dated 1 Dec. 1719.

6 **WILLIAM**, Strawberry Bank, ±46 in 1660, ±60 in 1673, appears with Francis Rand et al. as def. in suit brot by William Whiting et al. 4 Mar. 1640[1. He m. Elizabeth Ham (William) and bot in 1650 at Str. Bk., where he was const. in 1651, selectm. in 1654 and 1671 and took the O. F. in 1659. Gr.j. 1651, 1655, 1657, 1659, 1671. Lists 41, 47, 49, 52, 57, 63, 239a, 311b, 323, 324, 325, 326ac, 329, 330abd, 331ab, 333a, 335a, 336c, 337, 339. He bot the Walter Abbot tavern in 1674 and kept it until his death in 1678 when his est. was distrib. to his wife and 6 ch. An admirable gen. in N. E. Reg. 58.294. **John**, double portion. **William**, homestead. **Solomon**, granted land by his grf. Ham in 1671; app. d.s.p. bef. his f. **Sarah**, m. Edward Beale(4) of New Castle. **Thomas**, a minor in 1678, Lt. Anthony Nutter his gdn., d. bef. 27 Sep. 1706. **Joseph**, Lt. Neal his gdn. in 1678. **Benjamin**.

7 **WILLIAM**(6), Portsm., ±79 in 1732-3, farmer, innholder, gent., m. Abigail, app. dau. of John Pickering (Lists 331c, 335a), who, tho named in his will, may have pre-dec. him. Jury 1684, 1685, 1692, 1694, 1695, 1699; gr.j. 1694, 1695; selectm. 1697-1701, 1717; Rep. 1702, 1705, 1707. Lists 324, 331c, 337, 339. In 1736 he deeded his Portsm. real est. to s. Thomas on cond. that he pay legacies in his will, 13 July 1733—6 June 1737. Ch., the first 7 bap. 19 Aug. 1696: Capt. **William**, Portsm., tanner, m. in Boston 31 Oct. 1706 Elizabeth Clark (George) who m. 2d James Clarkson. He d. in Portsm. 28 Feb. 1717-8 in 38th year. Will, made the day bef., ment. wife, 4 daus. and sons William and John. **John**, not in father's will. **Elizabeth**, m. 31 July 1707 William Fernald(5). **Jo-**

seph, not in father's will. **Abigail**, m. John Hardison between 1717 and 1720. **Thomas,** Portsm., shipwright, m. 14 Nov. 1721 Elizabeth Jackson who m. 2d 7 Nov. 1753, John Churchill of Portsm. His will, Nov. 2—Dec. 25, 1745. 12 ch. **Mary,** m. June 1715 Stephen Greenleaf (Stephen) of Newbury and d. 29 May 1733. 7 ch. **Sarah,** bp. 18 Apr. 1697, poss. m. Henry Nicholson from Williamsburg, Va., 13 Dec. 1716, altho not in father's will. Their s. Wm. d. 19 Mar. 1718-9 ag. 12 d. (grst.) Sarah Nicholson, perh. an inf., bp. No. Ch. 23 Sep. 1722.

**COUCH,** pecul. to Cornwall.

1 **JAMES.** One of this name was app. a scrivener's apprent. in Boston 1674-76. James of Isles of Shoals, fisherman, was drowned at Cape Cod 1720. His wid. Rebecca called John Downe bro. Adm. to creditors 4 June 1721.

2 **JOSEPH,** b. ab. 1646, son of Wm. 'of the County of Cornwall,' arrived at Kittery 26 May 1662 as apprent. for 7 yrs. at the shipwright's trade to John Bray, late of Plymouth, and wife Joan. Jury 1707, '10. Gr.j. 1708. Selectm. 1706, '07. Lists 313c, 292, 296-298. Inv. dated 22 Jan. 1713[4. He m. 1st Johanna Deering(7),ment. 1677,1699, mother of the older and likely all the ch. He liv. on Deering land. By 1712 his w. was Katherine, liv. 1720, dec. 1729. Ch: **Joseph. Roger.** Jury 1714. Adm. 5 Jan. 1719[20; m. in Greenl. bef. 1710 Bridget Bickford(15), who m. 17 Aug. 1720 Roger Mitchell. 2 s. **Sarah,** m. Richard Mitchell. **Joanna,** m. Joseph Mitchell. **William,** shipwright, Newburyport, mar. 1st 1 Jan. 1718-9 Elizabeth Richardson; 2d 21 Jan. 1725-6 Elizabeth Matthews. 3+8 ch. rec. **Mary,** m. 24 Aug. 1712 Tho. Allen(15?).

3 **JOSEPH**(2), sealer of leather 1696-7. He m. Anne Adams(1), who m. 2d 25 Oct. 1710 David Hill. Only ch: **Mary,** b. 3 Jan. 1696, m. James Spinney.

4 **ROBERT,** surgeon, of Stepney, Middlesex, bound for N. E., brot. P. A. dated 6 Apr. 1663. With w. Elizabeth he had ch. b. in Boston 1663-1671, **Robert, Elizabeth, Mary, Edward.** While still there he was making prof. trips to N. H. and may have rem. here bef. disap. Lists 82, 312b, 326c.

**Courser,** John, Philip's War. List 237b.

**Couse,** see Cowes.

**COUSINS,** var. spelled, South of Eng. and Yorkshire.

1 **EZEKIEL** (Cossin), soldier, fined at Hampton Ct., Aug. 1677, for stealing a new flint out of Abraham Drake's dooryard. Wrongly indexed as 'Coffin.'

2 **ISAAC,** an expert gunsmith and locksmith, and rolling stone, liv. in Rowley in 1647, Haverh. 1652, Ipsw. 1656, Portsm. where he was 'received as a tradesman' 1659, Boston and Dorchester, besides negotiating for settlement with New London, Conn., in 1651, and No. Yarmouth in 1678, always with a penchant for litigation. Warned out of Dorchester in 1691, he d. in the Boston poorhouse 23 July 1702. See -The Ancestry of Lydia Harmon-, 1924, pp. 47-53. Wife Elizabeth d. in Boston 14 Oct. 1656. He m. 2d Ann Hunt 'formerly wife of John Edwards,' and 3d Martha (Stanbury) Priest, by 1677. Ch. presum: **Elizabeth,** mar. in Charlestown 6 June 1664 John Barrett(3). **Thomas,** b. ab. 1649. **Isaac,** Wells, m. Susanna Mills (Thomas) who m. 2d 6 May 1678 at Exeter Lt. Peter Folsom(7). K. by Ind. in Wells 1675. List 269b. **Abraham,** settled in Sherborn, Mass. **Jacob,** b. 12 Sep. 1652 in Haverh. **Sarah,** b. 31 Aug. 1656 in Boston. **Rebecca,** b. 2 Apr. 1660 in Boston.

3 *JOHN, Casco Bay 1626, sailor, ±85 1682-3, ±87 1683, ±88 1684; dep. in 1640 that he had kn. Casco river for ab. 14 yrs. Assemblyman 1648, Dep. to Lygonia Assembly 1658, jury 1640, 1667. Lists 10, 21, 211. Had gr. from Richard Vines of two islands, totaling 500 a., (one of them still called Cousin's), and liv. thereon, deeding ½ of each to Richard Bray and Sabella, his w., in 1651-2. Retiring to York in the war, he liv. with Mrs. Mary Sayward, to whom he gave all of his est. by deed made 1679 and ack. 1682, for past and future care and maintenance.

4 **THOMAS**(2), Wells, wit. a deed for Morgan Howell, 1666, doubtless liv. in boyhood with his sis. Barrett, a neighbor of the Bowles fam., where Howell made his home. Served in Philip's War and was accused (and acquitted) of perjury for his evidence at Scottow's trial for not sending aid from Black Pt. garrison to hard pressed soldiers. Wells granted him 100 a. in 1684. Gr.j. 1708. Dep. Sher. 1711. Lists 236, 266, 269b, 33. Presum. he and his wife, name unkn., were k. in attack on Wells in 1690. Ch: **John,** m. 6 Apr. 1704 Abigail Cloyes(2), who m. 2d 11 May 1715 James Wiggin. She and her ch., **John,** bp. 17 Aug. 1707, Abigail, wife of Nathaniel Kimball, bp. 28 Aug.1709, and Mary, deeded their int. in Thomas's est. to Ichabod Cousins in 1726. **Elizabeth,** servant in the Wheelwright household 8 yrs., m. 22 May 1700 Zachariah Goodale. **Hannah,** m. 26 Dec. 1701 George Jacobs. **Ichabod,** ±60 in 1749, when he dep. as to Ogunquit and Wells lands. Bot int. of his sisters in their father's est. in 1726. Jury 1715. List 269c. Soldier in two wars and d. of smallpox in the service, adm. being gr. to his s. Nathaniel 3 Apr. 1764. He m. Ruth Cole(31) whose will, prov. 23 Nov. 1768, names 8 ch. of 10 rec. at Wells.

**5 WILLIAM,** Isles of Shoals, was a creditor of Stephen Sargent & Co. in 1649. June 24, 1649, he transferred an apprent., Philip Cox, to John Gill, 'to learn the misterie of mariner's art.' Gr.j. 1650. Sold house he had built to Mrs. Marie Mendum, 1659.

**Coventry,** Jonathan, lawsuit in N. H. Ct. 1649, Marshfield 1651.

**COWELL,** Cowle, Covell, an uncom. Eng. name.

**1 MR. BONEY,** Portsmouth tax list, 1672.

**2 EDWARD,** Portsm., shipmaster, commanded ketch -James- of Piscataqua River on voyage from Dartmouth, Eng., to Fayal in 1667. He had a house in Portsm. in 1667, purch. land from Thomas Harvey in 1670 and owned a warehouse in 1676. List 326c. As late master of the ship -Dolphin- of Portsmouth, he d. before 31 Oct. 1677 when adm. was gr. to his wid. Agnes, who m. George Snell and d. Dec. 1681, leaving will, 30 Apr. 1681-3 Jan. 1681-2. List 331b. Ch: **Mary,** mar. John Sherborn (Henry) aft. 29 Jan. 1677-8, presum. then receiving an adequate portion from her father, as she did not share in his est. **Abigail** (app. either Cowell or Harvey), mar. Alexander Coombs(1), Capt. Richard Thomas. **Amy,** m. 1st 19 Oct. 1678 Jethro Furber, who was named adm. of the Cowell est. 2 May 1682; and 2nd, bef. 1692, Nathaniel Ayers(6). **Edward,** adm. to Nathaniel Ayers in behalf of w. Amy, sis. of dec. 3 June 1692. **Samuel,** under 14 in 1682, Jethro Furber being his gdn.

**3 EDWARD** (poss. 2 jr.), Pemaquid, List 124.

**4 JOHN,** Portsmouth, 1715, when Zachariah Leach hired him to steal leather from Mr. Wm. Cotton's cellar. Lists 330de, 339.

**5 RICHARD** (-sic- in rec., Carle?), Kit. wit. 1671. Y. D. ii. 133.

**6 SAMUEL**(2). Either he or a Cowell with Christian name unkn. m. Hannah Miller (John), who as a wid. Cowell with at least 3 ch. m. 2nd 25 May 1715 Daniel Quick in Portsm. Ch: **Catherine,** m. 4 July 1718 Robert Lang. **Esther,** m. May 1724 Nathaniel Melcher, and named a son -Thomas Cowell. **Benjamin,** m. 27 Nov. 1729 Elizabeth Nelson. Prop. which he bot from his stepf. in 1737 was deeded by his daus. Mary Lear (m. Walker Lear 12 Jan. 1758) and Elizabeth, single, in 1764.

**7 THOMAS,** Kittery, m. Elizabeth, wid. of Wm. Sealey before Philip's War. 'Mr. Cowell' liv. in house on 10 a. of land adj. Gunnison's 11 June 1683. List 51. See (5).

**Cowen** (Cowine), Philip, won suit brought by Joseph Cross in Me. Court 1681.

**COWES. 1 Giles,** bp. at Stoke-in-Teignhead, Devon, 22 Oct. 1642, ±27 in 1672, dep. that he had fished at Isles of Shoals in 1666.

N. E. Reg. 85.387. 8 ch. incl. **Hannah,** b. 16 Oct. 1672, m. John Oliver of Kit.

**2 JOSEPH** (Cous), sergeant Falmouth 1689. List 228b.

**3 MARY** (Cous), of Portsm., single woman, 25 Mar. 1700-1 accu. Edward Dolbe, shoemaker.

**4 SARAH** (Couse), York, 1651, wit. Godfrey to Hethersey. One S. C. of Exeter, Devon, ±18, booked in 1634 Dartmouth for St. Christophers.

**COWLEY** (Cooly). **1 Abraham,** 1 Me. Hist. Coll. i. 298. Misreading of Conley.

**2 AMBROSE,** 1659, merchant or seaman between Boston and Nevis, by his inventory a travelling tailor. At Isles of Shoals 1665, adm. Dec. 1666 to bro. Henry, goods at John Hole's house.

**3 HENRY,** Marbleh. 1660, Boston 1668, plf. in Me. Ct. 1666-71.

**COX,** Cock, common surname in S. and W. of Eng., esp. Cornwall.

**1 ABRAHAM,** at Pemaquid under Captain John March in 1695, lost an arm; pensioned 1696.

**2 EDMOND** or Edward (aut. Edmond Cock), fisherman, Isles of Shoals 1664, boat master at Damariscove 1667, bot in York 1670, on which he built and liv. until the Ind. drove him off. Lists 303, 234a, 86. Adm. 2 Mar. 1682-3 to his widow's father, John Card(4), and again 3 Oct. 1699 to herself, now Agnes Kelly of New York. She gave P. A. to her s. **Edward** Cox of New York.

**3 GOWEN,** Portsm., prior to 23 Feb. 1696-7 owner of house and 2 a. north of Sagamore Creek, then in poss. John Lang, his wid. Mary, now wife of Peter Matthews of Ipsw., fisherman, sells it to the tenant.

**4 JAMES**(5), ±63 in June 1736, sworn in Boston, liv. at Cox's Head ab. 45 yrs. ago. One J. C. m. in Boston 11 Dec. 1695 Mary Roe, dau. of Richard of Kit. and rec. 10 ch.

**5 JOHN,** liv. at Tuessic, Woolwich, ab. 1658 or earlier, but moved down to Cox's Head, where he lived on land of his bro.-in-law Wm.(34), — unrel. exc. by m. sisters. See Lambert. He was twice a fugitive from the Ind., whither unasc. Lists 13, 15, 187, 191. Kn. ch: **John,** b. ab. (1658?) 1661. **Thomas,** b. ab. 1664. **James,** b. ab. 1673.

**6 JOHN,** creditor of Robert Weymouth in 1662, poss. at Canso. List 285. See Y. D. ii. 174. At a ct. held in Eliot, Sep. 1680, John Stover sr. was fined for striking Hannah Cocke, alias (Parnell?).

**7 JOHN,** sued by Robert Edge in 1666, poss. a fishingmaster from anywhere.

**8 JOHN,** poss. same as (6, 7, 9), m. about 1670? in Boston (but his affairs out of

the Province) Mary (Kirkland), b. 8 June 1640, wid. of Nathaniel Sherman, dau. of the widely kn. innholder Alice Thomas, who was his wid. in B. 1697. In 1672 in Suff. Co. Ct. he sued Richard Randall, one of his crew, for not going aboard ship when ordered. In 1680 Mary Cox was brewing and selling strong beer against her husband came home. The grmother's will names his ch: John, b. 12 May 1672, and Mary, not Philip, b. 9 Feb. 1674.

9 JOHN, Casco Bay 1672. List 86.

10 JOHN, Scarb., poss. same as (6, 7, 9). Lists 236, 237a. Adm. 2 July 1678 to Richard Hunnewell.

11 JOHN, poss. a trans. sailor, inquest 18 Aug. 1675 (the little canoe swamped), lower Kit. List 287.

12 JOHN(5), fisherman or shoreman, ±34 in 1695, ±78 in Sep. 1736, Woolwich, Phippsburg, and Dorchester, fished at Damariscove Isl. with John Parker ab. 168--. List 183. Deps. in Y. D. xiv. 193, vi. 141. He m. ab. 1680 Susannah Pope of Dorchester, living 1702; 2d in Salem 6 Nov. 1712 Christian Milliken, who d. in Dorchester 17 Dec. 1721. In 1736, with w. Rebecca, he sold his house and 3 a. on Squantum Neck, but reserv. the house built by his s. Joseph, with two rods on all sides and a way to the waterside. 'John Cox died Nov. 23d 1742 in the 85th year of his age.' Ch: Margaret. Mary. Sarah. John, Capt., m. 11 Dec. 1712 Tabitha Davenport(1). Rem. to Portland. K. by Ind. at Pemaquid 22 May 1747. 9 ch. Thankful, these five bp. Dorchester 5 Mar. 1692-3. William, Capt., b. 27 May, bp. 24 June 1694, m. 9 Feb. 1716 Thankful Moseley. 10 ch. James, bp. 18 June 1696. Thomas, b. 22 Aug. 1697, bp. 9 May 1698, m. 26 July 1722 Hephzibah Davenport, sis. of Tabitha(1). 3 ch. rec. Susannah, b. 29 Nov. 1698, bp. 9 Apr. 1699. Joseph, b. 8 Apr., bp. 4 Aug. 1700, m. 29 Nov. 1722 Elizabeth Blackman. Rem. to Portland. K. by Ind. with his bro. 5 ch. Submit, b. 20 Sep. 1702, bp. 28 Mar. 1703, m. Tho. Moseley jr. Benjamin, bp. 1 Apr. 1705. Besides the foregoing, three others, likelier ch. of their aunt Mary (Pope) Cock, father unk., were bap. in the same church: 'John s. of Mary Cocks' bp. 16 Nov. 1692; 'Ebenezer s. of Goodman Cock whose w. is dau. to sister Pope' bp. 10 May 1696; 'Elizabeth Cocks Sister Pope's grandchild' bp. 26 Sep. 1697. See Thomas(30). Ebenezer m. 26 Nov. 1719 Thankful Davenport, sister of Hepzibah(1), and was drowned from a canoe 7 Oct. 1753. 7 ch.

13 JOHN, Dover Neck poll tax ab. 1680-1684. Presum. same m. 22 May 1694 Hannah (Roberts) Hill of Oyster River, and was named as abuttor in a deed 1703. Lists 359b, 52. Wid. liv. 1720.

14 JOHN, Pemaquid 1687, taxed, personal. List 124.

15 JOHN, Kit. wit. 1703. Y. D. vi, 166. See (16) and Thomas(31).

16 CAPT. JOHN, Boston, see John Knight, Newington. In 1709 two John Coxes were taxed in Portsmouth, Str. Bk., shoemaker, (light), and mariner, (heavy); the latter abated 1713.

17 CAPT. MARCELLUS, see N. H. Prov. Pap. xix. 677. List 90?

18 MOSES, Hampton, relieved from training in 1662, called ab. 93 in the Province rec. at death 28 May 1687, had been in Ipswich, perh. in trans. from Watertown. Gr.j. 1668. Selectm. 1662. Lists 391ab, 392ab, 393ab, 396, 398, 49, 52. His w. Alice and s. John were lost in the catastr. of 20 Oct. 1657; also Wm. Swain, whose wid. Prudence (Marston), he m. 16 June 1658. List 393a. Will 1 Nov. 1682 names only w. and 4 daus. Ch: John, lost at sea 20 Oct. 1657. Mary, b. ab. 1644, m. John Godfrey. Sarah, m. 21 Jan. 1664 Nicholas Norris. Rachel, m. Tho. Rawlins. Moses, b. 2 Nov. 1649. By 2d w: Leah, b. 21 Apr. 1661, m. James Perkins and had the homestead.

19 NICHOLAS, wit. for Walter Mayer 1698. Y. D. ix. 65.

20 PHILIP, formerly apprent. for 7 yrs. to Wm. Cousins(5), assigned 24 June 1649 to John Gill of Boston, mariner.

21 PHILIP, taken by Ind. at Cape Sables in 1691 and sold to a French privateer. Doc. Hist. v. 376.

22 PHILIP, carpenter, m. Dorcas Hull, d. of Phineas and Jerusha (Hitchcock) of Berwick and Biddeford. In 1731 they were of the Blue Hills, Somerset Co., East Jersey, with an adult s. Philip. Y. D. xiv. 256, xvi. 83, xix. 116.

23 RICHARD, sworn with Shadrach in 1674, List 15. Unlik. the R. Cockes, and fam., for whom John Pierce became surety in Boston in 1685, nor the R. C. whose bed he usually slept on in Scituate was willed to him by John Williams in 1691.

24 SHADRACH, of Pemaquid in 1671, had bot goods from Capt. John Hull of Boston. Sworn in 1674, List 15. -Shadwath Fox- 1670, see Wm. Cox(33). One Shadrach, carpenter, was adm. citizen of Bristol, Eng., in 1651 by m. to Alice Hendris. Sydrack Cox, Bristol, will 1708.

25 THOMAS, first implied as 'Sen.' at Pemaquid in 1674, perh. the 'Sen.' to whom land was confirmed in 1686, and poss. the man often drunk in Essex Co. in 1677 or the fisherman in Beverly in 1678. Or he may have d. soon aft. the above date, so that one or all of these records belong to Thomas(26). Relation to Shadrach, Richard and John(14) unknown. Presum. he was father of Thom-

as(26) or Thomas(29). List 15, see Lists 13, 80, 85, 124. Thomas Coole, Pemaquid abuttor in 1669, (Cole 29) may poss. be Cock.

26 **THOMAS**, (see 25), as 'jr.' was sworn at Pemaquid in 1674. (A prom. note, not above susp., dated at Boston 29 Sep. 1675, of 'Thomas Cox Jr of Pemaquid, fisherman,' payable to Daniel Davison, was recorded with Lincoln Co. deeds 89 yrs. later.) Either he or (29) and w. Hannah were refugees at Beverly in 1690, and had the 1686 Pemaquid land script in possession.

27 **THOMAS**, Sagamore Creek wit. in 1679 (copy clear, but Beck?).

28 **THOMAS**, ab. 1685 pet. Gov. Cranfield, shipped from London, mate and boatswain, finds he has friends at Salem. Has his bro. with him as apprentice.

29 **THOMAS** (surely s. or grs. of 25, likely s. of 26), escaped in 1690 to Beverly. Presum. Capt. March's pilot at Pemaquid in 1693. Adm. 6 Feb. 1710 to widow Hannah. Ch: **Thomas. Elizabeth**, bp. with Tho. 8 June 1690. **Richard**, bp. 14 Aug. 1692, drowned in Beverly 1746, adm. to bro. Wm. **Hannah**, bp. 28 July 1695, 'Clark' in 1746. **John**, bp. 17 July 1698. **William**, bp. 18 Apr. 1703. 9 ch.

30 **THOMAS**(5), dep. at Salem with br. John in 1695, ±31, and in Boston in 1736, ±76. Unidentified, but did not m. Mary Pope, sis. of John's wife, as she was a wid. in 1700.

31 **THOMAS**, Kit. wit. 1703. See John(15). Presum. same with house and w. Margaret (Hillia---, m. 20 Dec. 1705) 1715-1718. Y. D. viii. 78, ix. 218.

32 **THOMAS**(29), bp. in Beverly on arr. from the East, m. in 1709 Judith Elliot, 2d Mary Woodbury. D. 5 Nov. 1738. 7 ch. incl: **Ebenezer**, b. in Beverly 27 June 1728, d. at Pemaquid in July 1795, whose s. Israel, b. 1755, told that his father's f. and grf. were both Thomas.

33 **WILLIAM** ('Cox'), Pemaquid? The contemp. doc. of that period and place suffered from an infection of forgery. When Mr. Shurt was back in Bristol, Eng., in 1635, his settlement with the Patentee was wit. by Wm. -Cock-, but it is unlikely that any W. C. was early at Pemaquid. Certainly the two John Brown deeds, antedated 1625 and 1660, with William -Cox- as a wit., were forged, and the dep. of John Pierce in 1735 was false. That aged man swore to other false evid. put into his mouth, assumably senile innocency, for a fee, and as against his oath, that no Cox but Mary, her father Thomas and his f. Wm. ever lived at Pemaquid, see Thomas(26, 29), John(14), Shadrach, Richard. Besides the forgery of the '1625' John Brown deed itself, ano. forgery, now in poss. of the Me. Hist Soc., was committed after the burning of the Sheepscot records in 1747. This pretends to be an at-

tested copy by Secy. Willard of a record of that deed made from those records before they were burned. Two other alleged documents received together 23 or 28 Sep. 1766 and recorded in the Lincoln Co. registry, Book 5, fols. 61-62, raise doubts. One is the due bill of 'Thomas -Cox- jr of Pemaquid, fisherman,' to Daniel Davison, dated at Boston 29 Sep. 1675. Why and by whom was the expense of such a record incurred 89 yrs. aft. the date? The other is the deed? not claimed under before the Eastern Claims Com. and not recorded for 96 yrs., dated 25 Oct. 1670, from John Brown 'mason' to Daniel Davison, and wit. William -Cox- and Shadwath Fox (Shadrach Cox?). This deed, if genuine, and the genuine assignment 31 Oct. 1654 from Bateman to Cole, wit. by Wm. -Cock- are the only evidence of a W. C. early. The land transf. by the latter deed is in Woolwich, on the Kennebec, where (34) liv. App. Thomas(25 or 26) was the first Cock or Cox at Pemaquid.

34 **WILLIAM**, wit. in Woolwich 31 Oct. 1654, bot from Thomas Atkins 1300 a. of his Ind. purchase, incl. Cox's Head, now in Phippsburg. Driven twice by the Ind., he was 'Senr. now resident in Salem,' when he sold out to John Higginson jr., 26 July 1693. Gr.j. 1666. Under Mass. in 1674 he was gr.j. and innholder. Liv. Salem 1699. Lists 181-183, 191, 15, 85. His wid. Mary (see John(5) and Lambert, Margaret) was of Boston, ±80 in Oct. 1719.

35 **WILLIAM**(34), Salem, m. Hannah Woodbury, b. 1 Apr. 1664, dau. of Andrew & Mary, who was wid. in 1708 and liv. Salem 1721. Ch: **Mary**, b. 13 July 1688, unm. 1721.

36 **WILLIAM**, Berwick abuttor 1708-9.

**CRADDOCK, Matthew**, London merchant, Governor under the Bay patent before Winthrop brought it with him. His very large investments here appear in the name of his widow, Rebecca, who m. Rev. Benj. Whitchcock (Wickott), D.D., liv. 1672. N. E. Reg. viii. 25, ix. 122.

**Craffort**, see Crawford.

**CRAFT.** Croft, name of 5 places Hereford to Yorkshire.

1 **EPHRAIM**. List 248b.

2 **RICHARD**. Richard White was fined 28 Oct. 1684 for accu. him of poisoning his son with pills which came from the doctor.

3 **WILLIAM**, Portsmouth taxpayer in 1681, but in 1684 victualer and innkeeper in Kit., where he m. Joane (Palmer), wid. of Roger Deering(7). In 1686 he was app. ferryman. Lists 329, 33, 298. After his death ab. 1694, when he had a gr. in Kit., his wid. kept the tavern as late as 1705, and in 1709 was presented for retailing.

**CRAM**, Crambe, the latter a Yorkshire par.

1 **BENJAMIN**(2), Hampton, jury 1694, gr.j. 1693, 1694. Lists 52, 55b, 396. M. 28 Nov. 1662 Argentine Cromwell, dau. of Giles of Salis., named in will 1 Mar. 1707-8—5 Dec. 1711, with 8 ch: **Sarah**, b. 19 Sep. 1663, m. 27 Mar. 1708 Jacob Basford(1). **John**, b. 6 Apr. 1665, m. 1st Mary Wadleigh, dau. of Hon. Robert, 2d 13 Jan. 1730 Susanna (Page) Batchelder. Will 1734—1742. 7 ch., of whom Benjamin m. Abigail Dearborn(4); John m. his cousin Mary Cram; Jonathan, had the homestead in Hampt. Falls and in will 1759 —1760 named 7 sons, 1 dau. **Benjamin**, b. 30 Dec. 1666, m. Sarah Shaw (Joseph); widow Elizabeth named in adm. to s. Jonathan of Exeter, housewright, 28 Dec. 1737. 10 ch., of whom Samuel m. his cousin Mary Cram; Sarah, m. Jonathan Norris jr. of Exeter, carpenter. **Mary**, b. 6 Aug. 1669, presum. same who in June 1696 accu. Jonathan Prescott. **Joseph**, b. 12 Apr. 1671. List 399a. M. 17 May 1700 Jane Philbrick. 2 ch. rec. **Hannah**, b. 22 Aug. 1673, m. William Fifield(4). **Esther**, b. 16 Oct. 1675. **Jonathan**, b. 26 Apr. 1678, d.s.p. 3 Dec. 1703, adm. to br. Benj. **Elizabeth**, b. 3 Jan. 1681, m. Samuel Melcher.

2 **JOHN**, bp. 29 Jan. 1596-7 in Bilsby, son of Thomas and Jane Crambe from Alford, Lincolnshire, came with Wheelwright. At Muddy River, Boston, 1637, he came with Wheelwright to Exeter but settled in Hampton. Selectm. Exeter 1648, 1649; gr.j. 1645, 1648, 1662. Lists 373, 374ac, 375b, 376ab, 377, 394, 57. In 1665 he deeded to sons Benj. and Tho. for life support, ±80 in 1674. The town clerk recorded his death 5 Mar. 1682 'good old John Cram, one just in his generation.' W. Hester (White, m. June 1624 in Bilsby), d. 16 May 1677. List 394. Richard Swayn gave J. C. land out of 'love and brotherly (perh. Christian) affection.' Ch: **Elizabeth**, bp. 11 Mar. 1625-6 in Bilsby. **John**, bp. 15 Feb. 1627-8, d. young. **John**, bp. 13 Apr. 1629 in Bilsby, bur. in Farlsthorpe 16 Apr. 1633. **Joseph**, bp. 5 Oct. 1632 in Farlsthorpe, drowned at Exeter 24 June 1648, ag. ±15. **Thomas**, b. ab. 1644. **Mary**, m. 25 Jan. 1666 Abraham Tilton. **Lydia**, b. 27 July 1648 at Exeter, liv. 1665.

3 **THOMAS**(2), ±65 in 1709, ±69 in 1713, Quaker. In 1687 'of Salisbury' bot there; later 'of Hampton.' Jury 1693. Lists 52, 396. In 1722 deeded to s. Thomas. M. 20 Dec. 1681 Elizabeth Weare. Ch: **Mary**, b. 14 Aug. 1682. **John**, b. 12 Jan. 1686. John and w. Sarah adm. to Hampton Falls ch. 13 Apr. 1711-2; dism. to Wilmington. **Thomas**, b. 9 Nov. 1696. Will 20 July—24 Aug. 1751 names wife Mary and 7 ch. **Elizabeth**, b. 15 Oct. 1702, app. same mar. 25 Sep. 1735 Ezekiel Dow(5). In 1708 there were taxed in Hampt. Falls: Benj. sr., Tho., John sr., Benj. jr.,

John jr., Joseph, Thomas and John (this perh. a lot owned in common).

**CRANCH**, a South Devon surname.

1 **ANDREW**, 70 in 1710, Piscataqua, brot 8 gal. of wine to Capt. Champernowne in 1667. At the Shoals in 1670, he was the Great Isl. constable in 1680, a Kittery gr. juryman in 1683 and Newcastle highway surv. in 1696. Lists 326c, 312c, 313abc, 52, 226, 228c, 315bc, 316, 318ab. By w. Elizabeth Lux (William), m. bef. 1678, he had surely 2 and poss. other ch: **John**, Newcastle, wit. with his f. to Nathaniel Fryer's will in 1704-5, m. one Frances bef. 1718 when he was listed among heirs of his gt-grf. Robert Mussell. List 316. **Elizabeth**, accu. William Allen(17) 27 May 1702, but m. Thomas Cosen bef. 1718.

2 **EDWARD**, Portsmouth, 1678. List 331b.

3 **JOSEPH**, a Newcastle sailor, whose wife, Elizabeth (Davis), gave birth to a child one mo. after mar., warrant being issued against them 18 Feb. 1700-1. In her petn. of 4 Mar. 1700-1 she states that her hus. is at sea. Gr.j. 1703.

**CRANFIELD**, **Edward**, after an active administrative career in Barbadoes and Jamaica, begun as early as 1639, was app. Lieut. Gov. of N. H., through infl. of Robert Mason, 9 May and arriv. at his post at Great Island 4 Oct. 1682. Lists 52, 59. Later called 'a most base Tory,' his admin. was unpopular and ended 15 May 1685. He was in Bristol Jan. 1685-6, but of Barbadoes 'formerly of St. Martin's-in-the-Fields, Middlesex' in 1688 when he sold his Gr. Isl. house to John Hinckes. Returned to Eng. and bur. in Bath Abbey 8 Nov. 1700, leaving a widow and issue.

**Crase**, Joseph, Richmond Isl. in -The Hunter- 1634. List 21.

**CRAWFORD**, Crafford, the former a parish in Dorsetshire. The 41st commonest Scotch name.

1 **JAMES**, 'of Hampton,' under Capt. John Hill 1693-94. List 267b.

2 **JOHN** (Crafford), app. came to Dover to take charge of the Quamphegon Mills. Taxed there 1670-71. Elizabeth Emery, b. 1658, former w. of James Goff and John Forst, dep. in 1734 that 63 yrs. since she liv. with .'my Master Craffot,' in the mill house. This resulted in cross suits in 1673 between him and Mr. Broughton in which the juries found £500 damages for both plaintiffs. In 1670-1673 he had grants in Berwick, and bot more, and soon was litigating with Tho. Holmes. Lists 356j, 298. In Philip's War he withdrew to Great Isl., and in Oct. 1676 was selling out in Berwick. He and w. Elizabeth were still on Great Isl. in

May 1677. Whence came, whither went, whether ch., unk.

3 **MORDECAI** (Craford, Crevit), mariner, ±50 in 1674, was a Salem freighter and trader to the Eastward who overtraded and lost by mortg. both his house and his barque, and was given an innholder's lic. He had bot at Damariscove, Sheepscot and Biddeford, and had been fined for overcharging for cloth. In 1649 he charged James Thomas with stealing his fish, and in 1651 bot an apprentice. Lists 244a, 80. His w. Edith, poss. a Maine woman, sometimes aboard with him, was unjust accu. of burning their house. Two daus. both went wrong: **Susanna,** exec. for infant. 1668. **Hester,** m. 23 Dec. 1669 John Homan. 3 ch. rec.

4 **MUNGO,** Scotchman, merchant, soldier in Philip's War, Boston 1680-1695, admit. inhab. 1686, later merchant at Great Isl. Plf. in York Ct. 1709. He m. 1st Mary (Roberts? of Dover), 2d in Boston 29 June 1694 Susannah, wid. of Richard Kennet, apothecary. Adm. in N. H., est. ins., 6 Dec. 1712 to Charles Story and Theodore Atkinson, and in Suff. Co. to his wid., who was bur. in Boston 1 Sep. 1713. Her will 27 Aug.—15 Sep. 1713 gives £20 to each grch., resid. to dau. Mary (Kennet) who m. 18 Jan. 1709 Stephen Paine. Rec. ch. by 1st w: **Elizabeth,** b. 19 May 1681. **Jennet,** b. 2 Nov. 1684. **John,** b. 18 Feb. 1686. **Hannah,** b. 7 Apr. 1688. **James,** b. 26 Apr. 1690.

5 **STEPHEN** (Crafford), fishing master at Isles of Shoals, partn. of Wm. Seavey, whose admir. accounting of fidelity to his partn.'s wid. and ch. is rec. at length, Me. P. & C. i. 120-123. Early had a house at Braveboat Harbor, either on York or Kit. side; later built at Oyster River, unpaid for at his death. He was cast away in a shallop bef. July 1642. Lists 281, 71. Wid. Margaret m. Tho. Willey. Ch: **Susan,** adopted by Wm. Seavey but aft. doctoring in Boston d. Adm. 6 Oct. 1649 to her sis. Sarah, whose m. and stepf. Margaret and Tho. Willey were app. gdn. **Sarah,** in 1692 was Sarah Rennels of Portsm.

6 **THOMAS,** see Graffort.

**CRAWLEY,** name of 4 places Sussex to Northumb.

1 **SAMUEL,** perh. alias Sayward or Seward, b. ab. 1668, s. of Aspira Sayward, stepd. of (2), to whom she laid her child. See P. & C. i. 288-9, ii. 431-2.

2 **THOMAS,** ±36 in Apr. 1654, of Stepney, Middlesex, ship carpenter, came over twice or more times. The first time, having lost his wife, leaving a child, he left a bond for £100 to a widow expecting to marry him, and came over in the same ship with a woman he did marry. Back there in 1646 he was sued on this bond, covering a board bill for himself, for 9 mos. nursing of his baby, brought by his mother to the widow, and £40 loaned him, the inheritance of her children. Over here, Exeter, Portsm., Eliot, he occup. much space in our records to no purpose. See Doc. Hist. iv. 109. He could run like a deer, otherw. beneath consid.; yet he did (1660) sue Tho. Canney for slandering his (or his wife's) dau. Phebe, and the Ind. when they plundered his house at Sagamore Creek in 1677, did not kill him, because he had shown kindness to Symon's grandmo. Lists 373, 376ab, 298. His last w. Joanna, who apprent. her grs. Samuel in 1671, was evid. wid. of Robert Sayers (Sayward or Seward), with whom T. C. appar. liv. in Exeter. In 1649 -Sowward- of Str. Bk. sold his house at Exeter, and while Richard Cummings was away bringing his family from Eng., Joanna Crawley and her hus. liv. in his house, and on his return were given leave to stay until they could provide for themselves. In 1667 he was punished for beating his wife, 'being a weake ould woman.'

**CREBER,** see also Corber. The parish register of Sheviock, Cornwall, 7 m. from Plymouth, reads as though that fishing village had been settled from our coast, instead of -vice versa-.—Devon-Cornwall, Notes and Queries, v. 57.

John Rundle m. Honour Creber 1620.
John Langdon m. Honor Hawkins 1628.
Toby Langdon m. Martha Welsh 1634.
Richard Comyns m. Jane Peter 1632.
Symon Toser m. Joane Bray 1629.
Henry Hancock m. Joane Sargent 1615.
Anthony Naunter m. Eliz. Harle 1610.
John and Philip, sons of Wm. Odiorne.
Jacob s. of Esay Odiorne 1655.
Eme d. of John and Eliz. Searle 1645.
Richard and Mary Shortridge 1628.
Richard and Joane Bray 1628.
Paul and Katharine Mitchell 1642.
William and Ann Reynolds 1625.
George and Elizabeth Harris 1651.
Henry Budge, Richard Hicks, Richard Randall, Wm. Letheby, Thomas Wills, Barret, Batten, Beard, Berry, Bligh, Gyles, Ham, Earle, Harle, Geffery, Genking, Lavers, Lockwood, Peprell, Pomery, Short, Symons, Tedey, Tinny, Trot, Wallis, Wakelye, Whiddon.

1 **RICHARD,** carpenter on -The Margery-1643, List 21, p. 361. See also Corber.

2 **THOMAS,** seaman, Portsm., m. by 1666 a dau. of Sergt. John Moses, settled on Moses land at Sagamore Creek. Lists 312c, 313a, 326c, 331b, 52. One Creber m. wid. Mary Pease of Martha's Vineyard. Ch: **Alice,** m. 16 May 1687 Richard Shortridge. **Moses,** only ment. 1668.

**CREDIFORD, Joseph,** Wells, where he had a 50 a. gr. on the Kennebunk river in 1693, m. by 1692 Rachel Bussy(3) who was his wid. in 1743 when she deeded inher. land to her s. Benjamin. Trad. connects this fam. with No. Carolina. Lists 269b, 290. He was dead by 20 June 1714 when his wid. had 6 ch. bap. in Wells ch., which she joined 18 Oct. 1719. Ch: **Elizabeth,** b. Aug. 1692. **Joseph,** b. 16 Feb. 1693-4, m. Esther Littlefield, settled in Arundel in 1729 and d. 1735, his wid. dying in 1793, ag. 90. 6 ch. bap. in Wells 1723-41. **Rachel,** b. 6 Mar. 1694-5, d.y. **Abigail,** b. 23 Feb. 1699-1700 (Kittery). **Benjamin,** b. 6 Mar. 1701-2, mar. (int. 4 Dec. 1736) Jane Gypson of Berw. List 269c. **Josiah,** b. 9 Feb. 1703-4 (Kittery), m. (int. 3 Apr. 1734) Mary Eaton. Ch. **Mary,** b. 13 July 1707, m. 31 Mar. 1726 Ichabod Dunham. **Rachel** (twin), b. 13 Apr. 1709, m. 15 Nov. 1733 James Bussy(2) of Dover. **John** (twin), b. 13 Apr. 1709, m. 1 July 1736 Judith Hamblen. Ch. **Nathaniel,** b. 20 Apr. 1713.

**CREEK** (Cricke). 1 **Cornelius,** m. Jan. 1704 Sarah Butland(1), liv. at Newport.

2 **CAPT. EDWARD,** ±25 in 1667, commanded the Wells garrison in Philip's War, as Ensign, Lt., Capt. In 1678 bot 200 a. at Maquoit. Later kept the Half Moon tavern in Boston, frequented by Eastern people. In 1679 'Edw. Creeke & his family' were exiled for trying to burn Boston, but the excitem. passed over. In 1689 he was again com. Capt. in active service. Francis Tebbott of Northampton, Eng., will 1670, called him 'cousin'; his own will, 18 Aug. 1701, favored the ch. of John Cunnable (who m. Sarah Cloyes 5) giving 'my land at Casco Bay' to Samuel Cun., £5 to Frances Patteshall, residue to bros. Abraham of London, John, 'now liv. with me,' and his wife Deborah, who bef. her m. at St. Christophers had been servant of Gov. Watts. He d. 6 May 1702. His wid. cont. the Half Moon and m. 28 Apr. 1709 Richard Christopher.

**Cressey** or **Creesy,** see Crucy.

**CRIMP, William,** boatswain, Richmond Isl. 1643. List 21, p. 361. In 1651 was sued in Me. Ct. by Mrs. Tamosine Matthews.

**Crimson, Mr. Hugh,** N. H. Prob. i. 24. Misr. of Gunnison.

**Crispe, Thomas,** gent., Damariscove 162--. List 8.

**CRITCHET, Elias,** ±25 in 1671, knew Greenland 8 or 10 yrs. since. Tax abated in Portsm. 1674, 1675. In 1674 he bot in Quamscot and was taxed in Hampton 1680; had settled in Durham by 1695. Gr.j. 1692. Lists 396, (358b), 368ab. D. by 1727. First w. unk., he m. 2d aft. 1715 Martha (Goddard) Thomas, will 21 Jan. 1729-30. Only kn. ch: **Elias,** shipwright, m. 12 Oct. 1714 Elizabeth Lane

of Hampton. Lists 368b, 369. In 1751 he deeded to John Davis 'part of a grant granted to my father' 19 Mar. 1693. List 358b. 4 ch. bap.

**CROAD, Mr. John,** Berwick, son of John (List 80) and Elizabeth (Price), was b. 14 June 1663 in Salem, m. 1st 1 Dec. 1692 in Marshfield Deborah Thomas, 2nd before 1707, when they joined Berwick church, Elizabeth. An innkeeper in Salem, he was called merchant in Maine where he speculated unfort. in land at Casco Bay, returning to Salem bef. 1717. Here he acted as attorney in court cases. Selectm. 1714. List 298. 10 ch., 5 of whom were bap. in Berwick.

**CROCKER,** occup., maker of crockery. An old Devonshire name.

1 **DAVID,** Kennebec, 1672. List 13.

2 **DANIEL,** Kennebec, 1680, next neighbor down river from Thomas Webber, acc. to dep. of his dau. One Daniel Crocker m. Sarah Balden 30 Nov. 1660 in Boston and, acc. to Savage, d. 5 Feb. 1692 in Marshfield, his whereabouts in the interim not stated. Ch: **Joanna,** b. ±1663, wit. in Kit. in 1684, possibly she who m. Michael Edgecomb(2) in 1687, surely wid. of John Gaskin and wife or wid. of Paul Williams in 1740. By her dep. 1728 and 1740 she lived in 1680 with her f., later with Mr. John Hole in Kittery.

3 **HENRY,** Piscataqua, got 6 qts. of rum for Capt. Champernowne in 1671 and was prob. 'his man Henry' in 1667. Abs. from meeting in 1674.

4 **JOHN,** Saco fort 169--. List 248b.

5 **JOHN,** Kittery, 1722. List 291. In 1715 he and Deborah Keene were up for aiding Paul Williams to escape from constable Joseph Crocket.

6 **MARY** (surname blindly written), Kittery, in court Apr. 1712.

7 **RICHARD,** wit. a Pickering-Plaisted deed in 1700. List 267b.

8 **SARAH,** in Maine ct. May 1685, William Presbury of Saco to maintain her child.

**CROCKETT,** a So. of England surname.

1 **ELIHU**(6), Kittery, fisherman, naming br. Ephraim in 1683, had 2 wives, the 1st Mary Winnock (Joseph), and was last ment. in 1690 unless he was called 'Elisha' by error in 1699; nor is his 2d wife, disclosed by dep. in 1721, noticed here at all. Ch: **Thomas,** b. ab. 1684.

2 **EPHRAIM**(6), Kittery, tailor, m. by 1667 one Ann who was still his wid. in 1695. Lists 287, 292, 298, 33. Jury 1680; gr.j. 1688. His will, 17 July–10 Sep. 1688, mentions his father, sisters Ann Roberts and Sarah Parrett, wife Ann and ch: **Ephraim,** eldest and under age, who had the homestead. **Richard,** 40 a. near the mastway. He m. bef. 1708 Deborah Haley and settled in Strat-

ham, d. 7 Jan. 1757. 4 or more sons in Cape Elizabeth, Gorham, Epping and Stratham. **Sarah,** m. Henry Barter(1). 4 ch. **Mary,** m. Francis Smart.

3 **HUGH**(6), fishing for Roger Kelly at Isl. of Shoals in 1672, and later a mariner, m. by 1697 one Margaret and d. aft. 1703. List 298. Rec. ch: **Margaret,** b. 12 May 1698, mar. 15 Nov. 1717 Noah Dodge of Portsm. **Samson,** b. 14 Mar. 1700. **Anne,** b. 3 Oct. 1702. **Elizabeth,** b. 24 Oct. 1703, d. 16 Jan. 1704.

4 **JOSEPH**(6), Kittery Point, m. Hannah Clements(6), who surv. him. List 291. Constable 1684. Lists 287, 290, 296, 298 (1694). His will, 12 Mar. 1713-4—29 Jan. 1716-7, ment. wife and 10 ch: **Joseph,** who had had his portion, m. 12 Oct. 1700 Mary Ball(5). Lists 296, 297 (1718), 298, 291. 4 ch. **Hannah,** m. John King bef. 1703. **Lydia,** 73 in 1756, m. Nov. 1712 John Edwards of Portsmouth and moved to Haverhill. **Dorothy,** m. John Ellingwood by 1715. **Mary,** liv. in 1716. **John,** b. 16 Mar., d. 23 Mar. 1692-3. **Eliza,** b. 15 Mar. 1693-4, m. Benjamin Hilton. **Abraham,** b. 14 May 1696, m. Eleanor Urine (John) of Greenland. He inher. his father's Kit. homestead, but was a mariner of the Isl. of Shoals. Liv. in 1735. **Anna,** b. 19 Aug. 1698, m. 19 Apr. 1721 James Titcomb. **Nathaniel,** b. 4 May 1700; apprent. 24 Feb. 1708-9 to John Jypson, tailor, who promised to settle at Kit. Point, but by 1715 had rem. to Newport, R. I., taking Nathaniel with him. **Sarah,** b. 8 Mar. 1702, liv. in 1716.

5 **JOSHUA**(6), Newington, working with John Trickey in 1683, m. Sarah Trickey, who was gr. adm. 2 Sept. 1719, and was liv. in 1730. Lists 298, 343. Ch: **Joshua,** m. 8 Dec. 1707 Mary Bickford (Benj.) who m. 2d 12 Apr. 1717 Samuel Thompson. 2 ch. **Thomas,** d.s.p. bef. 1717. **John,** shipwright, of Scarb. and Falm., m. 16 Mar. 1717-8 Mary Knight (Nathan). 6 ch. **Elizabeth,** m. John Frye bef. 1720. **Deborah,** bp. and adm. to communion 11 Mar. 1715-6, unm. in 1721.

6 **THOMAS,** ±43 in 1654, was brot over to the Piscataqua as a young man by Capt. Neale and app. in the 1633 accts. He worked as cattleman for Capt. Wiggin and for Robert Mendum and Capt. Pendleton as brewer, and for William Palmer. By 1640 he was liv. on Kit. Point, when Mr. Tho. Gorges gr. him the next point north, called Crockett's Neck, in 1643. His w. Anne, who with son Ephraim adm. his est. in 1679, m. 2d Digory Jeffrey and was liv., ag. 84, in 1701. In 1648 he was the Braveboat Harbor ferryman and from 1652-1654 liv. east of Capt. Raynes in York, where he took O. A. 1652 and had a 40 a. gr. 10 Jan. 1653. Returning to Kit. he was const. in 1657 and had the Pisc. ferry in 1659. Lists 41, 84, 275, 276,

298. Ch: **John,** dep. in York Ct. 1659 and in Essex Court 1663; d.s.p. **Ephraim. Hugh. Elihu. Joseph. Anne,** m. by 1673 William Roberts. **Sarah,** m. by 1675 John Parrott. **Joshua. Mary,** m. Elisha Barton(2).

7 **THOMAS**(1), in 1703, ag. ±19, was apprent. to Roger Rose at Lubberland. Sarah Hix and Hannah Crockett, present at his birth, test. to his parentage and grf. Winnock in 1721. He m. Dorothy Blake (John), in ct. Feb. 1711-2, and liv. in Portsm. Lists 338b, 339. Kn. ch: **Elizabeth,** b. 17 Jan. 1715-6. **Jonathan,** b. 2 Aug. 1717, m. 26 Apr. 1739 Elizabeth Rice of Kit. and in will, 1758, ment. her and dau. Elizabeth.

**CROCUM** (Crowckham), **John,** Boston, d. Dec. 1678. He m. Rebecca Jocelyn (Abraham), with whom, and her three husbands, Crocum, Thomas Harris, Edward Stevens, her mother prolonged her life.

## CROMMETT

1 **JOHN**(2), ±53 in 1713, was about Lubberland in 1673. In 1694 John and Jeremiah were among the Lubberland refugees pet. for soldiers to enable them to go back and rebuild their garrison. In 1710 John was a snowshoe scout. Jury 1697, 1699. Lists 62, 368ab. He m. 13 Jan. 1691-2 Elizabeth Thomas; 2d bef. 1715 one Mary, named in his will 22 May—1 Sep. 1724, and 8 ch., 2 or m. by 1st w: **Martha. Sarah. Mary,** bp., a maiden, 19 Sep. 1719. **Joshua,** m. 19 Sep. 1728 Elizabeth Kenniston. First Selectman 1765-1771. List 369. 5 ch. named in will 9 Feb. 1777. **Philip,** called 42 in army roll 1758. **Elizabeth,** twin with Philip, both bp. 6 Mar. 1719; m. John Durgin(3). **Margaret,** b. 6 Apr. 1715, m. Wm. Durgin(1). **John,** Sergt., List 369. K. by lightning 24 Jan. 1758. M. his cous. Sobriety Thomas, whose will made the sole benef. her dau. **Abigail,** w. of one Philip Crommett, presum. not uncle and niece; or Abigail may have been one of her ch. bef. she m. J. C.

2 **PHILIP,** Dover, taxed at Oyster River with Davey Daniel 1662-67. About 1666 he bot from Hugh Dunn. Lic. in 1671 ferryman at Lamprill River, in 1673 he had a gr. there. Lists 363bc, 365, 359a, 368a. In 1708 he and w. Margaret deeded their house and homestead, half to s. John, half to Cornelius Drisco. Kn. ch: **Jeremiah,** taxed 1681. Gr.j. 1696. List 368a. Shot and scalped by Ind. 1712, s.p. **John,** b. ab. 1660. **Sarah,** m. 18 Dec. 1691 John Footman(1). **Mary,** m. Cornelius Drisco.

**CROMWELL,** ancient family and name of parish in Nottingham. See also Crommett.

1 **DAVID,** or Davey, List 363b, 1662, app. sprang from Davey -Daniel- and Philip Crommett.

CROMWELL 173 CROSS

2 **GILES** (Cromwell and Cromlome), liv. in Salisbury, but all (two) of his ch. liv. in N. H. Tortured by geneal. writers -ad infin.-, he was not the father of Mr. Philip, the Salem merchant, cattle buyer and butcher, nor of Capt. Thomas, the Barbadoes and Boston mariner and merchant (will 1649). His rel. to Thomas(4) is unasc., plaus. a bro.; app. Giles came over to claim Thomas's estate. The deaths credited to Newbury vital records: 'Thomas Cromlome dyed 1635, ye wife of Thomas Cromlome dyed 1635,' is an interpolated entry of a later period and gives an incredible year, yet may indicate that (4) and his w. d. in one year. The entry in Mass. Rec. 14 June 1642: 'Crumwells girle of Newbury is referred to Ipsw. Court,' is unexpl. Charles S. Tibbetts's hypothesis that the same Giles m. in Erling, Hampshire, 20 Feb. 1629-30 Alice Weeks, is also plaus. and uninvgst.; but at Salem the will of Thomas Wickes, w. Alice, 1656, was wit. by Tho. and Anna Cromwell, he app. bro. of Mr. Philip the butcher, d. by dep. 1617-1625. In Newbury Alice, w. of Philip Cromlone, d. 6 June, and 10 Sep. 1648 he m. Alice Wiseman, who d. 6 June 1669. His will 7 Apr. 1672–25 Mar. 1673, app. exec. in Hampton, names ch: **Philip**, b. ab. 1634. **Argentine, m.** 25 Nov. 1662 Benj. Cram(1).

2½ **JOHN**, Chelmsford, Ind. trader up the Merrimac. Adm. 166-- to John Parker. Ch.

3 **CAPT. PHILIP**(2), ag. 32 in 1666, ship carpenter, taxed in Dover from 1657. The dep. making him b. about 1612 must have strayed from Mr. Philip, the Salem slaughterer; he dep. in 1666, Apr. 4, ag. 36, had kept 6 oxen logging around Quamscot in 1660. Jury 1662; gr.j. 1692. Selectm. 1670, '71, '77. Commissioned Captain 1683. Lists 352, 353, 356abcefhk, 357be, 359ab, 14, 49, 52, 55a, 62, 96. He m. by 1663 John Tuttle's eldest dau. and by 20 Sep. 1671 Elizabeth Leighton. Will 19, d. 26, May 1708, names w. Elizabeth and ch: **Alice, Elizabeth, Sarah**, said to have m. Timothy Wentworth, but poss.(?) mar. John Leighton. Sarah Wentworth by age in 1754 was b. ab. 1668. **Joshua**, town grant 1693. In 1709, of Dover, he sold the marsh willed by his grf. to Philip's oldest son. List 358d. D. bef. 1752. Wife Lydia liv. 1743. 7 or 8 ch., incl. Joshua of Arundel, Falm. and Harps. who m. 1st Elizabeth Larrabee, 2d Grace (Hodgkins) Tarr, grdau. of Haselelpony (Willix) Gee-Wood. **Mercy**, m. 14 Mar. 1706-7 Hatevil Hall. **Ann**, b. 19 Aug. 1674. **Samuel**, List 358d, m. 1st by 1710 one Elizabeth, 2d one Rachel. 2 ch. rec. **Joanna**, m. bef. 1700 Morris Hobbs.

4 **THOMAS**, some rel., likelier bro., of (2), partner of Samuel Scullard, orig. petitioners and grantees of Hampton. Dow's two lines of type incl. 3 Thomases. If T. C. and

Scullard settled in Hampton they quickly ret. to Newbury, and were incl. in the complete list of freeholders formally accepted by town vote 17 Mar. 1642. Will presented Sep. 1646 was objected to by (2). In 1647 his goods still remained in Scullard's estate —his lands untraced. Adding to the field of Thomases: In York Ct. files, on the back of a bill against James Barry found among the papers of the first Wm. Gowen are the words, in an obsolete hand: 'Brother Thoms Cromull my lov to you.'

**Crookdeack** (John), Damariscove. List 8.

**CROSBY**, name of 10 places Linc. to Cumb.

1 **JOHN**, Dover, 1715. List 358d.

2 **JONATHAN**, Dover, Oyster River, 1718, physician, by 1st w. Hannah (Wycom, m. in Rowley 5 Aug. 1718) had 3 ch. rec. 1719-1724. He m. 2nd 23 Oct. 1729 Mary Dill(3) and had 2 ch. bap. July 1731, selling his Dover prop. that same month. He d. soon aft., as his wid. was with her mo. and stepf. Charles Trafton in 1733 in York, where she was in ct. in 1734, acc. Dr. David Bennett. She m. 2nd 25 May 1738 John Crawley.

3 **THOMAS**, Kingston, schoolmaster, stepson of Rev. Seaborn Cotton, was b. 4 Mar. 1660 in Roxbury. He m. 1st 29 Oct. 1685 Deborah Fifield(3), 2d 9 Nov. 1730 Mary (Prescott) Coleman, wid. of Jabez(3), who was adm. to the ch. in Kingston 31 Mar. 1734 and m. 2 Nov. 1738 James Bean. 'The aged Mr. Thomas Crosby' d. 30 Mar. 1735. Ch. rec. in Hampton: **Hannah**, b. 27 Dec. 1687. **Abigail**, b. 2 June 1689. **Prudence**, b. 8 Mar. 1692, m. John Johnson of Greenland. **Jonathan**, b. 8 May 1694, d.y. **Mehitable**, b. 5 Jan. 1696, presum. mar. Samuel Haines, Greenl., 21 Jan. 1719-20. **Elizabeth**, b. 26 Apr. 1698. **Jonathan**, b. 24 Jan. 1701, of Nottingham 1742, of Exeter 1747. **Samuel**, b. 22 Jan. 1703. **Anthony**, presum. a son b. elsewhere, wit. Wm. Fifield's will in 1715; liv. at Hampt. Falls; adm. to Jonathan, 1753.

**CROSCUM**. 1 **Henry**, ±23 in Nov. 1701, dep. with Agnes Geage, Spruce Creek.

2 **WILLIAM**, Malaga, Isl., Shoals, fishing master? 1661. Ag. 56 in June 1676. In 1673 ordered home to his wife. Adm. 28 June 1682 to Roger Kelly.

**Crosley**, Henry. Falm. wit. 1687. Y. D. vi. 35. List 228c.

**CROSS**, common Mid. and East of Eng. name. One runs across Crosses at every crossroad, and yet some single emigrants to N. E. multiplied their surname more than all the Crosses. The very early Johns are here kept beyond hazard separate, but the grouped references to the later Johns around Portsm. (will 1739) may embrace several of the name.

1 **ABRAHAM**, m. in Portsm. 12 Feb. 1712-3 Abigail Rogers. Kit.-Portsm. 1703-1722. List 291.

2 **BENJAMIN**, mariner, List 339, mar. in Portsm. 16 Mar. 1720-1 Elizabeth (Treworgy) wid. of John Field(4). He continued the Field tavern, as did his w. after his death. Will 29 Jan. 1722-3—28 Dec. 1730 names only w. Elizabeth, who was living Portsm. 1740.

3 **CATHERINE** and Mrs. Elizabeth Clark wit. against Jeremiah Hodsdon selling liquor. Court Papers vi. 19.

4 \***JOHN**, Hampton, came from Ipsw., Eng., in 1635, ag. 50, with w. Ann ag. 38. Ipswich 1635, orig. grantee of Hampton, freeman 1639, Rep. 1640, highly useful several yrs., but ret. to Ipsw., gr.j. there 1645. Will 1650-1651, leaving w. Ann and dau. **Hannah**, b. at Ipsw. Apr. 1636, bp. at Newbury, m. Thomas Hammond. Lists 391a, 392ab, 393b. Across the Rowley line was another John and other Crosses, causing complic.

5 **JOHN**, of Watertown, d. 15 Sep. 1640. See Robert Sanderson.

6 **JOHN**. Poss. not, but likely the one who disapp. at Dover:

7 **JOHN**, at Wells. The Dover man signed the Combin. 1640 and had a 20 a. lot in 1642. Lists 351b, 352. John Cross first app. at Wells in 1647 as constab. and juryman, landowner (how?) in 1648. In 1649 he wandered from home distracted and was forbidden the use of the ferries. In 1650 he apprent. his s. John for 11 yrs. to Mr. Rishworth. Lists 261, 262, 269b. In 1657 his w. was Joan, supplying the magistrates; in 1662 Frances. He was k. by Ind. ab. 16 Oct. 1676, not long after his son. Adm. on est. of both was gr. Nov. 1676 to wid. Frances and s. Joseph. The inv. shows 8 oxen, 6 horsekind, 12 cowkind, and that the minister had been boarding with them. She was liv. 1681. Ch: **Mary**, m. 1658 Roger Hill. **John**, b. ab. 1640, called 'a kind of distracted fellow' when k. by the Ind. early in 1676. **Joseph**, gr. 1668. In 1680 m. Mary (Pendleton), mother of William Breeden(8), and her f., Major Pendleton, sold him three combined farms next N. E. of his father's farm. Jury 1670, gr.j. 1678. Lists 266, 269b. He d. 18 June 1684, codicil 11 June 1684, and the wid. soon m. Nicholas Morey. No ch. **Rebecca**, m. 1672 Francis Backus.

8 **JOHN** (one or more). Lists 52, 60, 67, 68, 307b, 315a, 316, 319, 330d, 337, 339. Fryer wit. 1679, 1681. Of Newcastle, Fort soldier, pet. for wages recd. by Hon. John Hinckes, capt. of the Fort, and not paid over, 1703 down to 1717. Petn. in 1704, 'himself and family.' Fisherman Portsm. 1707, in quarrel with Edward Cate. He m. Esther Manson, who m. 2d 2 Dec. 1728 Alex. Dennett(2),

3d 12 Dec. 1736 Anthony Roe. His will, Portsm. 2 Apr. 1724—5 Feb. 1724-5, wife, s. Joseph his house, sons George, Joshua and John 5s. each, daus. Mary and Lydia, grd. Mary Cross 5s. each. Ch: **George**, b. 24 July 1688; ?m. Greenland 28 May 1729 Charity Rhodes, who m. 2d 14 May 1739 John Groves. 2 sons bap. **Joseph**, carpenter, Kit. wit. 1723, mar. 22 Dec. 1723 Martha Lambeth. Will Portsm., laborer, 12 May—30 May 1739, w. Martha sole legatee. **Joshua**. **Mary**. One Mary, m. 19 Apr. 1715 Wm. Jones of Cochecho. **Lydia**. One Lydia m. 3 Dec. 1719 Alexander Lindsey of Forfaine, Scot. Also app. **Richard**, currier, rated to the New Meet. Ho. 1717, List 339, m. 10 Dec. 1719 Mary Rackley; d. bef. his father, but adm. not taken until 19 Apr. 1729 by br. Joseph; dau. Mary over 14 in 1739 chose for gdn. Wm. Parker of Portsm., gent., presum. the same who m. widow Mary Cross 31 May 1726.

9 **RICHARD** (Crose?), Cape Porpus witness 1687. Y. D. vi. 49.

10 **STEPHEN**, m. Boston 23 Jan. 1692 Mary (Phillips) wid. of George Munjoy and Robert Lawrence. One S. C. and Isaac Eveleth with Mr. John Penwill, were wit. in York Co. Ct. in 1684 agst. Timothy Yeals. Eastern Claims, Me. H. & G. Rec. v. 153. One S. C. m. in Boston 22 July 1708 Sarah Jackson. One S. C. adm. Suff. Prob. 1714.

11 **WILLIAM**, Monhegan, 1624. List 9.

12 **WILLIAM**, of Bideford, Devon, mar. 2 Jan. 1715-6 at Portsm. Abigail Briard(1). List 339.

**CROSSETT.** 1 **John**, Concord 1735.

2 **JOHN**, wit. Ind. deed to Geo. Davie 1669.

**CROWDER**, spoken Crowther, occup. surname, a player on the 6-string violin. Not rare in Eng. at the emigration, this name was as if pursued by fate in N. E.

1 **ELIZABETH**, in Suff. Co. Ct. Jan. 1676-7, acc. Thomas Horne.

2 **JOHN**, master of -The Jonas-, London for N. E. 1634 with goods for Gov. Winthrop, poss. same as (3), likelier Capt. J. C., overseer of Peter Andrews' will, London, 1650.

3 **JOHN**, early householder and selectm. at Portsm., was agent for Ambrose Lane and occup. Tho. Wannerton's house, owned farm and Crowther's Isl. at Little Harbor. App. while away his w. Anne entert. Henry Taylor, both of them executed. Adm. on his est. was gr. to creditors 8 Oct. 1652 without calling him deceased; he may have gone back and poss. was (2). His wife was ordered sent to Boston for (capital) trial as soon as her condition permitted. Lists 321, 323, 324.

4 **JOHN** (aut. Crowder). This quiet living man, taught to write his name in obsolete hand and never changed, was still liv.

about Spruce Creek in 1708. He may have derived his name from (3), been unack. by him, and cost both his parents their lives. Taxed Gt. Isl. 1688. Lists 313a, 315ab, 318b, 319, 66.

**CROWN**, a rare English surname.

1 **HENRY**(2), 1668 in Boston, wit. in the Lawson matter, in 1673 bookk. to Mr. John Cutt, in 1681 lic. innholder on Great Isl., having leased 'The Anchor' from Geo. Walton, with a brewhouse. Notary public 1693. Lists 52, 55ab, 62, 92, 313ef, 317, 331b, 335a. Adm. 24 June 1696 to wid. Alice— (printed Brown). Inv., late of Portsmouth, incl. land at Pemaquid, house lot at Str. Bk. His wid. a yr. later was in ct. for having a child in her widowhood. He m. here 1 May 1676 Alice Rogers, stepdaughter of Rebecca Wharf-Rogers, d. of Mr. Arthur Macworth, a distant rel. of his mother. List 335a. In 1713 she was of Portsm., in 1732 of Boston, where app. her daus. m. Ch: John, b. 10 Nov. 1679, presum. the same or father of John, carpenter alias fisherman of Newcastle, who was taxed in Newc. in 1726, in 1732 bot at Newc., in 1749 had w. Abigail (Kenniston), in 1766 of Portsm. adm. to wid. Mary. In '76 one widow Anne had gone from Newc. to Durham and in her will named sons James, William, John, Joseph. **Elizabeth**, b. 27 May 1684, bp. No. Ch., Portsm., 4 July 1708; (m. Boston 28 Mar. 1717 Elias Constance.) **Agnes**, b. 19 July 1686, m. Boston 5 Oct. 1710 James Addison; adm. Suff. Prob. 1751. 2 sons. **Rebecca**, b. 23 Jan. 1689-90, in 1722 wit. will of Edw. Lyde, Esq. (m. Boston 15 Dec. 1725 Robert Weston.) **William**, b. 1 Jan. 1691-2. In 1744 one Henry Crown was at Louisburg. Suff. Ct. files 59629.

2 **COL. WILLIAM**, in 1652 held a colonel's com. and was County Com. for Shropshire. John Crown came to Boston with the charter of Nova Scotia in the winter of 1657-8, either with or soon followed by his father, who still held the office of Rouge Dragon in the Heralds' College, which he sold when back in Eng. in 1661. At Mendon he became a regular pioneer, selectm. and the first town clerk. See N. E. Reg. 6.46, 8.287, 57.406, Doc. His. x. 74-84, Gay's Transc. He m. Agnes Macworth, a sister of Col. Macworth of Shrewsbury. In 1674 he was ordered back to Eng. to his wife. Dated 10 July 1682, shortly before his death, is a letter reciting his public services. Mass. Arch. 106.264-7. Of his ch. his will 24 Dec.—24 Feb. 1682-3 names only three: John, ±20 in 1660, 'member' of Harvard College, dramatic poet high in King Charles's favor. Liv. 1700. See N. E. Reg. vi. 47, Me. H. & G. Rec. iv. 188. **Henry**, b. ab. 1648. **Agnes**.

**Crowther**, see Crowder.

**CRUCY**, Cruce. A less hazardous treatment for ±18 named Crucy, Cressey, or other like names is merely to list them for minute search. Only three, John, Barnaby, and Mary, appear early enough to be the parents.

1 **BARNABY** (Cruce or Crucy), taxed Gt. Isl. 1708, 1721. List 316. Adm. 17 Feb. 1726-7 to wid. Margaret. He left 4 ch: **John**, **Barnabas**, **Abraham**, **Margaret**, and owned land. If Margaret (Jeffrey) was wid. or dau. of Barnaby Jeffrey, that perh. expl. his given name, also the parentage of Elizabeth(2), mother of Barnaby Roberts, bap. in 1718.

2 **ELIZABETH**, one or more, (Crusey) 1692 Y. D. 5.82, 1695 York Files; (Creesy) wit. with Mrs. Mary Hooke 1696, N. H. Records 1696; m. in 1702 (Crucy of Kit.) Wm. Roberts. In 1724, ±52, dep. that she liv. with Major Francis Hooke ab. 34 yrs. past.

3 **GEORGE** (Crucey), Spruce Creek 1698, List 295. (Cresy, Crusy) Kit. wit. 1700, 1703. Y. D. vi. 57, 158.

4 **HENRY** (Cressy or Crosley?), List 228c.

5 **JAMES** (Cressy), probate bondsman for Caleb Gilman of Exeter, 1735, app. came from Mass.

6 **JOHN** (Crassy), servant of Christ. Adams, father of Patience Jeffrey's child in 1673, was enjoined mar. with the woman. See Patience(10). One John Cresey in Suff. Co. Ct. Jan. 1676-7 adm. being absent from his wife several yrs., and was ordered back to Eng.

7 **JOHN** (Creasey), came from Conn., mar. Deborah Wadleigh in Boston and settled in Gorham by 1753. Many desc.

8 **MARY**, copied Broosy but more likely Creesy, wit. with Francis Hooke, 1683. Y. D. iv. 12.

9 **MICHAEL**, Isl. of Shoals, had s. **William** bp. at Newcastle 14 May 1710.

10 **PATIENCE** (Creasie), Kittery wit. 1694, app. with Francis Hooke, presum. dau. of or the same as Patience Jeffrey of 1673 and 1676. See John(6). Y. D. ii. 187, vi. 60.

11 **RICHARD** (Crucy), Pepperell wit. 1701. Y. D. vi. 163.

**Crumton**, Mary, Saco wit. 1721. Y. D. 10.268.

**Culling**, Ode, Shoals fishing master 1647.

**CUMBY**, Humphrey, mariner, Repeat. Piscat. wit. Ch. Boston 1651-57. Adm. 1675.

**CUMMINGS**, Commin. See Creber.

1 **JAMES**, late a soldier at Saco fort, adm. in Suff. Prob. 11 Jan. 1696-7 to br.-in-law Samuel Workman.

2 **RICHARD**, b. 1601-03, app. the same who came on -The Speedwell- in 1635 under a 3-yrs. fishing contract at the Trelawny plant., leaving his wife in Plymouth. See Creber. In 1642, fishing for himself, sold his fish to Mr. Winter to ship. Next app. in partn. with Turpin in 1645 buying a fishing

plant at Isl. of Shoals and a house and land in Portsm. Aft. this he went to Eng. for his family. In 1647 he was sued by Kittery fishermen. Fishing master and called mariner. In 1656 he entertained the magistrates. In 1649 he had Walter Muchemore for partn., in 1664 Gabriel Grubb. Gr.j. 1655, 57, 59, 63, 64. Selectm. 1656, 1664. Lists 21, 324, 325, 326ac, 356l (Portsm.), 330abc, 331ab, 54, 78. He gave the old schoolhouse lot to the town. His wife Jane d. 6 Aug. 1677, he 17 Jan. 1678[9. Will 19 June 1678 names only one ch. and her ch: **Jane**, m. Christopher Jose.

3 **RICHARD**, yeoman, first ment. 14 July 1647 when about to marry Elizabeth Bonython. Constable 1658, jury 1665. Lists 24, 243ab, 244f, 245, 246, 249. May 12, 1675, he was one of the petn. for 6 m. sq. at the head of Saco. It is not unlik. that he and his s. were both nameless vict. of Ind. Adm. July 1676 to s. Thomas and John Harmon. Ch: **Thomas**, b. ab. 1648, last ment. July 1676, d.s.p. Lists 237ab. **Elizabeth**, m. ab. 1672 John Harmon.

4 **RICHARD** (Coman) of Salem, tailor, in 1695 sold 10 a. of land in York, described Y. D. iv. 108.

5 **ROBERT** (Comins), master of the ketch -George- at Portsm. 1682.

**Cundy**, Simon. List 259. Misreading of Bussy?

**Cunlife** [? Curtise?], William, 1654, too lame to work, Dover to support him until able.

**CUNNABLE, John**, Boston, joiner, 1650-1724, will. By the 2d of 4 wives Sarah Cloyes(5), 4 ch: **Samuel, Abigail, Hannah, Elizabeth**, favored in Capt. Edward Creek's will. Samuel, m. 23 July 1713 Mary Diamond. See Me. H. & G. Rec. v. 211. By 3d? w. Martha Healey, bp. 9 Sep. 1660, m. 10 Dec. 1700, sis. of Wm. and Samuel of Hampton, 2 ch.

**Cure** (Lambert and) Jolly, French serv. at Passamaquoddy, 1688.

**CURHEET**, Mons. **Peter**, storekeeper and truckmaster at Penobscot Fort, sued the est. of Major Robert Sedgwick, writ 11 June 1657, with 3 yrs. int. and two voyages to Boston.

**Curling**, Richard, Sheepscot, 1689, read Lt. John Jourdan's letter to him.

**Curnow** (Curnew, Curnen?), Catherine, see LeCornah.

**CURRIER**, Curya, Kiah. See also Cordy.

1 **GILBERT** (Cardea, Cardye), ±36 in 1674, had 7 gals. of liquor from Roger Kelly, saw Giles Berry deliver to Tho. Trafton his share of fish.

2 **JEFFREY**, b. ab. 1635, fishing master, Isl. of Shoals, poss. br. of Richard of Salis. or Gilbert(1), first app. in Portsm. ct. 1664, last on Newc. tax list in 1698. His name occurs as Great Isl. abuttor in 1699. Lists 323, 326b, 330a, 315bc. Besides his s. Richard, he was presum. f. of John and Caleb and a swarm of grch. at Isl. of Sh.; his daus. not even surm. Ch: **Richard**, b. ab. 1671. **John** (aut. Curryer), b. about 1673, Newc. and Hog Isl. Adm. 5 Apr. 1709 to wid. Ann. **Caleb**, b. by 1680, Great Isl., cert. had ch.

3 **RICHARD**, in 1694, ±25 was a wit. for 'my father Jeffrey Curaya.' Fishing master Gosport. D. 12 Nov. 1707. Wife Elizabeth (Weymouth), stepd. of Thomas Diamond(3), m. 2d Nathaniel Lord of Gosport and Ipsw., will 3—31 Mar. 1725-6. Ch: **Diamond**, fisherman, adm. to creditors 13 May 1731. Perh. hus. of Eleanor (Urine) who by 1735 had m. Abraham Crockett(4). Ch. **Weymouth**, liv. 1726.

**CURTAIN, Mark**, mar. 9 Nov. 1717 Sarah Lewis, widow of George. Sued by Odiorne, the wit. were: John Card with wife Mary and dau. Mary, and Jacob Clark.

**CURTIS**, common in South and East of Eng. Became 26th commonest in N. E.

1 **HENRY**, Sheepscot, lived near the east bank of the river, near its mouth. First app. in Boston, record of son's birth. Jan. 20, 1666[7 he obtained from Robin Hood a deed covering from Winnegance westerly to the Sheepscot, reaching 7 m. up the river. This deed became the basis of the -Hawthorne right-, and was shown to the Ind. at the treaty in 1726. Of Beverly, seaman or fisherman, 15 Apr. 1690, deeded this 9000 a. to John Hathorne, Esq. List 15. In Feb. 1679-80 he was master of Thomas Heath's boat. At times kept his fam. at Marblehead. In 1697 Elizabeth Curtis took oath at Ipsw. that in 1695 her husband H. C. (perh. the son) contracted for a fishing voyage, and that she was with him on shipboard. The father's wife in 1657 was Jane. Kn. ch: **Henry. John**, b. in Boston, s. of Henry and Jane, 2 July 1657. **Mary**, presum. a dau., w. of Wm. Champnois(4).

2 **HENRY**(1), Sag. pet. with (1) in 1674. List 15. Perh. had w. Elizabeth in 1695. Presum. ch: **Sarah**, m. at Marbleh. 15 July 1687 Thomas Henly; 2d 1 June 1715 John Wescoat. Y. D. 23.174, 1735, is from Sarah Wescoat to Joseph Hendley of Marblehead quitclaiming her rights through her grf. Henry Cur--- (illeg.) of Winnegance, Nova Scotia.

3 **JOHN**, about the Dover sawmills 1657-8. Lists 356bc.

4 **JOHN**(1). Henry and John Curtis, coroner's jury, Marblehead 7 Oct. 1681. Perh. master of ketch -Mayflower- 1699, likely wit. to Muscongus div. 1717. Of Marbleh. fisherman, ±79 in 1736, dep. was an inhab. at

the mouth of the Sheepscot 60 yrs. since, made fishing trips with his father. Perh. f. of Sarah(2).

**5 JOHN**, York. List 279. M. Sarah Welch. Ch. rec. 1718-1731. See Y. D. 19.284.

**6 JOSEPH**(9), settled in Kittery at Spruce Creek. Gr.j. 1683, 1686. Innholder, and his son aft. him, 1697-1709. Several years County Sheriff. Lists 36, 92, 95, 291, 293, 296-298. D. 1705-1706. He m. Sep. 1678 Sarah Foxwell(5), liv. 1723. Ch: **Joseph**, b. 22 June 1678, liv. on the homestead, yeoman, gent., 1703 dep. sheriff. List 298. D. 20 Aug. 1751. He m. 7 May 1719 Sarah (Downing), wid. of Jonathan Mendum, who d. 4 Dec. 1757. 1 ch. Joseph. **Sarah**, b. 10 Aug. 1681, m. Jan. 1702 Tobias Lear. **Richard**, b. 2 Apr. 1684, d. 6 May 1686. **Elizabeth**, b. 16 July 1686, m. bef. Jan. 1706-7 Diamond Sargent from Ipswich. **Thomas**, b. 15 July 1688, d.s.p. aft. his f. Richard, twin, d. 15 July 1688. **Foxwell**, b. 16 July 1692, mariner, liv. in York and Boston. Will Suff. Prob. 1724-1727. He m. 30 July 1724 in Boston Elizabeth Goodridge, who d. Jan. 1742. No ch. **Lois**, b. 13 May 1695, mar. bet. 1723-1724 James Starrett of York. Ch. **Eunice**, b. 23 Dec. 1698, m. Hon. Richard Cutt(6 jr.).

**7 MARY**, ag. 36 in Dec. 1725. See George Norton.

**8 RALPH.** See Wm. Bickford.

**9 THOMAS**, bp. 2 Nov. 1619, s. of Thos. of Ash, Kent, bur. 11 Dec. 1631, and Richardene, who m. 2d Thos. Chambers(2). Brot to Scituate, Mass., he settled in 'Scituate Row,' York, ab. 1642. Gr.j. 1649, 50, 53-56, 61, 70, 75, 76, 83, 86-88. Selectm. 1667, 68, 74, 75, 83, 84. Lists 273, 275-277, 24, 25, 30. His will dated 19 Apr. 1680 was not proved until aft. his s. Joseph's death, but he was app. a vict. of the York massacre. Ch: **Elizabeth**, bp. Scit. 19 Aug. 1649, liv. 1671. **Joseph**, b. 1653. **Abigail**, m. by 1678 Benoni Hodsdon. **Benjamin**, carpenter, after buying in York and Newcastle, he m. ab. 1681 Martha Farrow, when he rem. to Wells and built on her land. When the inhabts. withdrew he went to Kit. or beyond (Kit. 1698, 1701), but returned in the false peace and was slaughtered 10 Aug. 1703. No ch. Lists 269b, 39. **Job**, called ±80 in 1736, had the homestead. List 279. Late in life he mar. Bethia Marston (Y. D. viii. 223) and had 3 ch. rec. 1718-1729. **Hannah**, mar. bet. 1678-1680 Jabez Jenkins. **Lydia. Dau.**, m. by 1680 John Cooke(5). **Sarah. Rebecca. Dodavah**, b. about 1669, presum. named for Dodavah Hull, settled in Kit., gr. 1699. Lists 291, 296-298, 96. He m. by 1700 Elizabeth (Withers), wid. of Benj. Berry(3), both liv. 1736. Her will 1743—1747. Only ch. k. by Ind. 4 May 1705. **Samuel**, bp. Scituate 4 Sep. 1670. Jury York Co. 1687. Settled in Scit., house

carp., liv. 1734. Ch. by w. Eliz. rec. 1694-1703. **Ann**, m. Alexander Thompson.

**10 THOMAS**, Kennebec milit. 1688. List 189.

**11 WILLIAM.** N. H. ct. 28 June 1650 ordered that Dover support W. C. and cure his lameness, he to repay when able.

**12 WILLIAM**, mariner, Shoals, 1686.

Curry, the Glazer, Portsm. tax abated 1713.

Custen, William, Kennebec, 168(8). Doc. Hist. vi. 371.

**CUTTS**, Cutt, called by Camden, before the emigration, a nickname for Cuthbert. The Cutt English ancestry has been so many times and falsely written up that correction seems worth while. Along with the Frosts, Parkers and others it suffered in an epidemic of fabricating boastful pedigrees— in this case from Sir Charles Cutts, baronet, and 'Lord Cutts, Baron of Gronsdale.' Yet all the while there existed two early and truthful traditional accounts, one (Brewster's Rambles ii. 143) written ab. 1790 by or for Samuel Cutts of Portsm., grs. of Richard(6), the other earlier by a Cutts-Hammond desc. b. in 1738. (N. E. Reg. v. 246). Both of these give the birthplace of the emigrants as Bath, where their baptisms are found recorded. Their ancestry has been traced no farther than their father's grf. Mr. John Cutte, a Bristol merchant, at times Mayor of the city, and indications point to a burgher, not a lordly, descent. This John Cutt is rememb. in the will of Richard Cutt, a London grocer, 7 Nov. 1569, a native of Wolverhampton, Staffordshire, whose f., Robert, was from Sheffield, Yorkshire. St. Michael's church in Burnett, between Bath and Bristol, has a memorial brass represent. the Mayor with his wife and ch. He d. 21 May 1575, his wid. Joane (Kelke) in 1590; both left wills. Joseph Whipple's paper does say that the father of the emigrants was a member of Parl. when he died. This has not been dispr., but cert. he was not Richard Cutts, member for Essex in 1654, but John Cutt, who by his own dep. in 1613, aged 50 yrs., then of Bath, before that of 'Eston-well,' co. Devon, was born where his f. and grf. had lived, in Burnett. He had sold the manor there in 1599. By the Cutts-Hammond trad. the mother of the emigrants, by two hus., Shelton and Cutt, had 23 ch. She was John Cutt's 2d w., Bridget, dau. of Arthur Baker of Aust, co. Glouc. (his will 8 Dec. 1613), wid. of Peter Sherston. She m. P. S. 11 Oct. 1598, (bur. 13 Aug. 1606), and 2d, J. C., his 2d wife. The baptisms show 3 Sherston ch., 1600-1606), and Cutt ch. down to 1625, 11 Sep., and the father was bur. 3 Nov. 1625. Of her Cutt ch. six appear in our N. E. records: **Baker**, he and John named in their Grf. Baker's will. **John**, bp. 1613.

**Richard,** bp. 23 June 1615. **Walter,** bp. 1617, was a London merchant in 1659. **Robert,** bp. 1619. **Ann,** bp. 11 Sep. 1625, m. John Shipway.

1 **BAKER,** eldest of the brothers, came and went back. He and Robert wit. a deed to Ambrose Lane, Strawberry Bank, 23 Sep. 1648, and bus. papers of his and Richard's were copied by Asp. 6 Feb. 1648-9.

2 ‡***JOHN,** br. of (1), (aut. N. H. Ct. Files 23299). First ment. with Richard at Str. Bk. in Sampson Lane's P. A. to collect from them 24 Mar. 1648-9. Selectm. 11 yrs. bet. 1657-1678. Dep. to Boston 1670, 1676. President of the Prov. Ct. 1680. Lists 251, 323, 324, 326ac, 328, 330abf, 331abc, 356l (Portsmouth), 359a, 311b, 285, 43, 48, 53, 54, 77b, 81, 88, 92, 335a, p. 172. Will 6 May, cod. 3 Jan. 1680-1, left the Great House to s. Samuel. John Cutt, First President, d. 27 Mar. 1681 (grst.) His wife Hannah, d. Nov. 1674 ag. 42 (grst.) Presum. he was not single until he m. 30 July 1662 Hannah Starr, bp. 22 July 1632 at Ashford, Kent, dau. of Dr. Comfort Starr of Boston. His wid. Ursula, m. by 1677, liv. on their farm, was k. by Ind. 21 July 1694. Lists 52, 329, 96. Ch: **John,** b. 30 June 1663, d. of smallpox on the return voyage of ship -Elizabeth- from London—Sewall's Diary 31 July 1685. List 51. Will names br. Samuel, cous. Reuben Hull. In 1680 ag. 17 he called Major Nicholas Shapleigh uncle, poss. thro a first wife of his father. List 329. **Elizabeth,** b. 30 Nov. 1664, d. 28 Sep. 1665. **Hannah,** b. 29 July 1666, mar. Col. Richard Waldron. **Mary,** twin, Lists 329, 330de, m. Hon. Samuel Penhallow. **Samuel,** b. 17 Nov. 1669.

3 **JOHN,** b. ab. 1650, presum. some relation to (2). In 1660 and '64 'John Cutt jr.' wit. a deed and a bond to (2), and in 1669 John Cutt jr. and Reuben Hull, both ag. ab. 20, had heard Mr. John Cutt give his orders to Tho. Dew. But in 1670 Mr. Fryer wrote to Eng. by hand of Mr. John Cutts of Dartmouth (Aut. 1667, N. H. Court Papers iii. 33b), and in 1672 Mr. John Bray had built that man a ship. John jr. of Portsm., mariner, m. 15 June 1672 Sarah Martyn. Jury 1682, 83. Lists 327d, 329, 54, 51, 52 p. 10, 55b, 57, 92, 331abc, 333b, 335a p. 173. He d. 30 July 1695. His wid. was lic. to sell drinks 1696-99, and was still a wid. 1724. Lists 330d, 331c, 335a, 337. Ch: **Sarah,** b. 26 Aug. 1673, m. Joseph Chesley(5). List 331c. **Mary,** b. 14 Nov. 1675, m. Humphrey Spencer, 2d Joseph Moulton. List 331c. **John,** b. 20 Sep. 1681, cooper. Selectman 1721-23. Clerk of Courts. List 324. Liv. 1747. He m. 20 Sep. 1715 Susannah Ayers(1). 6 ch. **Judith,** b. 10 July 1683, m. Joseph Pormort, 2d Solomon Cotton(2). **Margaret,** b. 16 June 1687, m. Nathl. Pike, 2d Capt. Thos. Landall.

She d. 15 July 1779, the last surv. member of Mr. Rogers' church. **Richard,** b. 16 Aug. 1691, mariner, d. 1729. List 339. He m. 18 Oct. 1713 Love Sherburne, who m. 2d John Almary. 3 ch. **Elizabeth,** b. 17 Mar. 1693, m. Wm. Fellows(4 jr.).

4 **JOSEPH,** m. bef. 1671 Sarah Raynes, who m.(?) 2d Joseph Hadley and had d. by 6 July 1675. P. & C. ii. 427, 308.

4½ **LAWRENCE,** Portsmouth, tax, Str. Bk. abated 1680, as he was not living there when the rate was made.

5 *CAPT. **RICHARD,** the 3d bro. Bap. in 1615, in 1626 his mother Bridget and br. Baker Cutt were bondsmen for £200 to apprent. him for 10 yrs. to Michael Wright, a Bristol merchant. By what Sarah (Mitchell) Sayward, b. in 1718, told her grdau. Sarah Sayward Wood, the Cutt brothers came over with letters of credit to Boston. In Boston 7 Aug. 1646 Sampson Lane, who had arrived with wine, gave his general P. A. to Richard Cutt, who may have come over with him. In Oct. 1647 the Maine ct. term him one of the chief of the fishermen and owners of the Isl. of Shoals. Capt. Lane had acquired a claim on Wannerton's Great House rights at Str. Bk., where all four Cutt bros. appear in 1648. Richard right away was buying and selling land and ships, and he and John began importing English goods at 'the Bank.' In his deed of Clement Campion's house, 1651, he is styled 'mariner,' which, if not an error, indic. a merchant navig. his own ships. His title of Capt. came from his position as commander of the fort, from 1669 until his death. Brewster's Ramb. have it that he liv. in the Great House, but the first Joshua Peirce dep. that he liv. in the house which had been Francis Raynes's, (earlier Roger Knight's?), recently Wm. Fellows' inn, and now (1742) occ. by Elizabeth Pike. He was selectman 8 yrs. btw. 1653-1666; Deputy to Boston 5 yrs. btw. 1665-1675; in 1664 was made a judge of the Court of Associates, at times with authority in Maine. Lists 76, 323, 324, 326ac, 327d, 328, 330ab, 331c, 356l (Portsm.), 303, 311b, 43, 44, 53, 79, 82, 83, 88, 3. His and his widow Eleanor's int. wills are printed, 10 May 1675 —27 June 1676, 12-29 July 1684. Lists 51, 329, 331b. The 1790 trad. said she was d. of an Eng. officer who left the country in the Civil War. Her will ment. ch. of her br. John Aldersey if they come or send; also her nieces Elizabeth Hole and Ann Clark, (Richard Leader's daus., whose mo. was her sister.) Also two daus. with three hus. left four wills. Ch: **Margaret,** ±20 in 1670, m. Maj. Wm. Vaughan. **Bridget,** m. Capt. Thomas Daniel(7), 2d Thomas Graffort.

6 *RICHARD(7), ±78 in 1738. In 1700 for £250 he sold his homestead to Tobias Fer-

nald and for £200 rec. from his mo. a deed of Champernowne's Island. May 24, 1742, he deeded to s. Richard 'the island where I now live.' Gr.j. 1690, 91, 93, 94. Foreman 1714. Selectm. 7 yrs. Dep. to Boston 1698. Lists 288, 290, 291, 296, 298. He m. Joanna Wills, liv. in 1738. Of 13 ch. only 6 surv.: **Robert**, b. 13 Nov. 1687, d.s.p., likelier young, but cf. Robert(8), 1712-1715. **Elizabeth**, b. 25 Nov. 1689, m. Nathl. Raynes. **Mary**, b. 28 Feb., d. 23 Mar. 1691. ‡**Richard**, Major, b. 5 Apr. 1693, d. 14 Nov. 1767. His will, 1 Mar 1765, is signed Richd. Cutt. He was major under Pepperell in the capture of Louisburg, and Councillor 1755-64. List 297. Wife Eunice (Curtis 6), m. 20 Oct. 1720, lived long a wid., some yrs. with Mrs. Sally Sayward Wood, her last yrs. with her sons in So. Berwick. She d. 29 Mar. 1795, aet. 97 (grst.) 10 ch. **Sarah**, b. 6 Sep. 1695, m. 3 Nov. 1717 Roger Mitchell. **Bridget**, b. 18 Feb. 1697, d. 13 Apr. 1700. **Thomas**, b. 16 Apr. 1700, Deacon, d. 10 Jan. 1795. List 297. He m. 23 Apr. 1724 Dorcas Hammond (8 ch.), 2d Sarah, d. of Dr. Nathl. Sargent. **Bridget**, b. 13 Dec. 1702, m. Samuel Hart. **Lucia**, b. 23 Apr. 1705. **Edward**, b. 9 July 1707, by trad. m. a Welch and had a son Edward— nothing seen of either. **Samuel**, b. 21 Sep. 1709. **Joseph**, b. 22 Apr. 1713. **Joanna**, b. 14 Apr. 1715, m. Capt. Timothy Gerrish.

7 ‡**ROBERT**, the 4th brother, was with the others in 1648-49; in Mar. 1652 was sued in Me. ct. by Capt. Champernowne for 'taking away' four oxen, arbitrated; but was not in Kit. in 1653, (List 282). App. he was a travelling merchant until his bros. decided him the Leader gr. in 1658, and at times afterw. In 1660 he was in Conn. dickering for a location; the records of Huntington, L. I., have app. his aut. His item. inv. shows a shop and brewhouse, but no shipyard, and indicates a plantation of the southern type. He may have had ships built of his own timber, but was not a shipwright. In 1665 Capt. Robert Cutt was acting with Col. John Archdale in the Gorges govt., and in 1666 he was serving as one of the Justices left by the King's Com. to govern Maine. Gr.j. 1661. Lists 88, 298. He made his will and d. the same day, 18 June 1674. By early trad. he had a first wife, m. in St. Christopher's, but his ch. were by Mary Hole, m. in Barbadoes, a sis. of John Hole who came later to Kit. She m. 2d by 1682 Capt. Francis Champernowne. Ch: **Bridget**, m. 23 July 1674 Wm. Scriven. **Richard**, b. ab. 1660. **Elizabeth**, m. bet. 1684-86 Humphrey Elliot, 2d Thomas Witherick. **Mary**, m. aft. 1686 Humphrey Churchwood, 2d Lt. Richard Briar. **Sarah**, m. by 1695 John Moore. **Robert**, b. 1673.

8 **ROBERT**(7), shipwright, presum. bred by his br.-in-law Scriven, but app. in 1712-

1715 was commanding one of Col. Pepperell's ships. Gr.j. 1697, 98. Lists 296-298, 291. Will 18 Sep. 1734; d. 24 Sep. 1735 in 69th year (grst.) He m. 18 Apr. 1698 Dorcas Hammond, will 26 May 1749, d. 17 Nov. 1757 ag. 82 (grst.) Ch: **Mary**, b. 26 Dec. 1698, m. 14 May 1722 Capt. Wm. Whipple, d. 24 Feb. 1783. 5 ch., incl. Wm., signer of Decl. of Ind., and Col. Joseph. **Catherine**, b. 30 Sep. 1700, m. 20 Aug. 1723 Hon. John Moffatt; d. Dec. 1769. **Mehitable**, b. 18 Aug. 1703, m. 29 Dec. 1725 Hon. Jotham Odiorne. **Elizabeth**, b. 20 Mar. 1709, m. 23 Oct. 1727 Rev. Joseph Whipple, 2d Rev. John Lowell, d.s.p. 22 Sep. 1805. 9 **SAMUEL**(2), gent., rented rooms in the Great House. Gr.j. 1694, 96. Lists 68, 96 p. 85, 330df, 337. Will 6 Aug.—25 Oct. 1698. He m. Eleanor Harvey who m. 2d 4 May 1699 Tho. Phipps. Ch: **John**, b. 22 Dec. 1694, was apprent. 12 Feb. 1707-8 for 7 yrs. to Capt. Robert Eason, mariner, of Ramsgate in Eng., commander of the ship -New Hampshire-. Adm. 23 Feb. 1717-8 to wid. Elizabeth and Saml. Penhallow, est. insolv. He m. one Elizabeth, called by trad. in 1790 a sis. of Col. (Samuel) Moore, but by the m. record, Boston, 22 Apr. 1712, Barnell; in 1719 had occasion to say she had m. Richard Gerrish; 1721 and 1725 gave her name Bryant; 19 Feb. 1733 as Elizabeth Manger m. John Savell jr. of Boston, feltmaker, and was his wife in 1747. Only ch: Samuel, mariner, adm. 30 Aug. 1738 to wid. Sarah (Savell) who m. Col. John Hart. Ch. **Samuel**, b. 23 Feb. 1697-8, brazier, Ipsw. and Boston. Adm. 17 May 1731 to widow Hannah (Perkins) who m. 12 Apr. 1740 Benj. Stokes, Boston, miller, both liv. 1748. Ch. 10 **WILLIAM**, 1640, wit. against Mr. John Winter for overcharging, in the service of Mr. John West, Saco. 11 **WILLIAM**, a boy, some relation, poss. a son, living with (5) in 1669. List 328.

**DAGGETT**, pecul. to Yorkshire. 1 **JOHN** (Doggett), Saco wit. Y.D. 14.154. 2 **THOMAS**, No. Yarmouth. List 214. 3 **WILLIAM**, by trad. Scotch, had gr. in Saco 1681, const. 1684, gr.j. 1687; of Winter Harb. gave P. A. 10 Sep. 1687 to John Watson to sue Abram Collins of Casco, Gilbert Endicott and Wm. Barton. He rem. to Marbleh. by 1689, d. bef. Jan. 1695. (?List 267b). Wife Rebecca (Wormstall), dau. of Arthur of Saco, liv. 1727. Ch: **Susannah**, b. Saco 1685, m. in Lynn 13 Mar. 1705 John Collins; d. Charlestown, R. I., 14 Jan. 1753. 10 ch. **William**, m. at Salem, 29 Nov. 1711 Mary Nurse, d. Jan. 1724-5. 3 ch. **Ebenezer**, b. ab. 1693, m. 10 Aug. 1722 Hannah Sibley, who d. 8 Feb. 1730-1, 2d 25 Nov. 1731 Hannah Burnap of Reading; d. Sutton 8 Apr.

1762. Ch. 4+3. **Samuel**, b. Salem 7 Jan. 1695, m. late, wid. Martha Sibley, d.s.p. 24 Aug. 1756. Of Sutton in 1731, he sold his father's Saco gr. of 1681.

**Dalby**, see Dolby.

**DALE**, John (also Deale), ±80 by several dep. bet. Feb. 1728-9 and Feb. 1736-7. An apprent. of Richard Hammond of Woolwich. He was at Arrowsic when the Ind. took the fort, but escaped to Sheepscot. Finally settling at Salem, he was first at Casco Bay several yrs. ab. 1678-79, was a Shoals wit. in 1681, and the same yr. ack. bef. Gedney in Salem his sig. as wit. to Neale's Ind. deed of 1672. Liv. Salem Feb. 1736-7. Wife Elizabeth. Ch. rec. Salem: **John**, b. 2 Nov. 1685. **Elizabeth**, b. 1 Mar. 1687. **Lydia**, b. 24 Feb. 1688. **Son**, b. ab. 1690. **Mary**, b. 7 June 1691. **Samuel**, b. 21 Nov. 1694. **Jane**, bp. 10 Nov. 1700. **Sarah**, bp. 10 Nov. 1700. **Ruth**, bp. 23 Apr. 1704.

**DALLING.** See also Darling and Dollen.

1 **JOHN** (Dealin), List 291. In 1737 John Bridges of Kittery from York compensated Alex. McIntire of York for life support of J. D. Daniel Deallin a York wit. the same yr.

2 **MARY** (Daling), wid., d. at Boston 4 Nov. 1717, ag. 85, perh. wid. of John Dollen.

3 **THOMAS** (Dalling), master of sloop -Dragon- from Fayal, entered Boston Apr. 1712. T. D. at Boston 29 Nov. 1709 m. Elizabeth Pitman of Manchester. Born in Portsm. 27 Sep. 1710 Stacy, s. of Thomas and Elizabeth Dalling; she m. at Portsm. 11 Dec. 1715 John Abbott, s. of (1). Bap. in Portsm. So. Ch. 8 July 1716 **Stacy** and **Samuel** Darling, ch. of Elizabeth Abbott. Stacy Dalling, m. 1 July 1736 Sarah Pevey. Capt. Samuel, d. 15 Oct. 1788, ag. 77 (Portsm. grst.) But: m. in Manchester 28 June 1723 Elizabeth Dalen and Joseph Woodbury.

**DALTON**, name of 14 places all in North of England.

1 **PHILEMON**, came in -The Increase- 1635, linen weaver, ag. 45, with w. Hannah 35, and Samuel 5½. Freeman 3 Mar. 1636 at Dedham, where he was well recog. but in 3 yrs. accom. his br. to Hampton. There he was app. marriage commis. 1645, and repeat. gr.j. Lists 391a, 392ab, 393a. Freed from training 1653. He d. 4 June 1662 at Ipsw. from an injury by the fall of a tree. Goody Dalton, List 393a. Wid. Dorothy, b. ± 1600, m. Godfrey Dearborn. Only ch. named in will: **Samuel**, ±42 Oct. 1671.

2 **DEA. PHILEMON**(3), const. 1686, gr.j. 1692, 1696, selectm. 1694, 1705. Mar. 25 Sep. 1690 Abigail Gove, aft. wife of Benj. Sanborn and James Prescott. Lists 52, 392b. D. 5 Apr. 1721; will 24 Mar. names 8 ch: **Hannah**, bp. 27 June 1697, m. 6 Mar. 1718

John Sargent, s. of Capt. Edw. **Timothy**, bp. same day, m. 2 Feb. 1721 Sarah Mason; will Feb.—Apr. 1756, names 8 ch. **Samuel**, b. 24 July 1694, m. 28 Apr. 1720 Mary Leavitt, dau. of Moses; d. 26 Dec. 1755. 10 ch. **Philemon**, b. 16 Aug. 1697, m. 15 July 1720 Bethia Bridges of Andover, who m. 2d 24 Sep. 1725 Samuel Morse. Three ch., Michael, Hannah and Philemon, were made wards to James Bridges and J. B. jr. in 1732, but app. all d.s.p. bef. 1739. **Abigail**, b. 2 Sep. 1699, m. 23 Feb. 1721 Benj. Carlton. **John**, b. 10 Feb. 1702, d. 10 Dec. 1717. **Sarah**, b. 19 Apr. 1704. m. Joseph Towle. **Jeremiah**, b. 25 May, d. 17 Dec. 1707. **Michael**, b. 22 Feb. 1709, m. 1st at Newbury 23 Nov. 1730 Mehitable Black of York, 2d 5 Feb. 1733-4 Mary Little. Michael, Esq., d. Newburyport, 1 Mar. 1770; wid. Mary d. 10 Dec. 1791, ag. 78. 3 ch. rec. **Mehitable**, b. 25 Sep. 1713, m. Benj. Prescott.

3 ‡***SAMUEL**(1), Esq. Jury 1654. Clerk of Court in 1662, from that time on he was foremost in public business. Deputy 1662-74, auditor 1663 and Com.t.e.s.c. from 1663, marriage commis., Associate in the County Cts. 1671-1680, Councillor 1680. Lists 48, 49, 53, 54, 392b, 393b, 394, 397a. He d. 22 Aug. 1681. M. Mehitable Palmer, dau. of Henry of Haverh., who m. 2d 26 Nov. 1683 Rev. Zachariah Symmes. List 394. She had 14 ch. all by her 1st hus.: **Hannah**, b. 11 Jan. 1655, d. unm. 12 Sep. 1674. **Samuel**, b. 19 Sep. 1656, m. 23 Nov. 1683 Dorothy Swan (Robert of Haverh.), 2d 6 Nov. 1701 Hannah (Davis 20) Kezar. By local Bradford trad. he was k. by Ind. He settled in Haverh. **Mehitable**, b. 3 Nov. 1658, m. Thomas Stickney of Bradford. **Elizabeth**, b. 11 Feb. 1661, m. one Scott by 1700. One Elizabeth Scott mar. in Hampton 8 Dec. 1709 John French(1), br. of Edward who m. Elizabeth's sister Mary. **Timothy**, b. 25 Jan. 1663, d. Boston 24 Oct. 1681. **Philemon**, b. 15 Dec. 1664. **John**, b. 23 Dec. 1666. **Caleb**, b. 29 Apr. 1668, d. 29 Aug. 1675. **Abiah**, b. 3 June 1670, twin, m. Bradford 23 June 1690 Gershom Haselton. Twin to Abiah, d. immed. **Joseph**, b. 2 May 1672, d. 2 Apr. 1673. **Abigail**, b. 21 Nov. 1673, m. 24 Apr. 1699 Richard Hall. **Mary**, b. 31 Oct. 1675, m. Hampt. 19 Sep. 1716 Edw. French of Salis. **Dorothy**, b. 6 Dec. 1677, m. 23 July 1701 Ebenezer Stiles.

4 **REV.\* TIMOTHY**, br. of (1). Their early home has not been ident., altho Jasper Blake or his w. was related to them, and Mr. Henry Boade called Mr. Timothy 'cousin.' He was grad. at St. John's Coll., Cambridge, 1613, and came here from the par. of Woolverstone, Suffolk, where he had been the incumb. from 1618 or longer, until suspended by the Bishop in Apr. 1636. At Woolverstone, in 1636, ag. 46, he dep. that he had many yrs. known Robert Wicks, clerk, and

his mo.-in-law Alice Ungle, wid. **These fig-ures** conflict with his age at death, but some misreading seems more likely than that there were two men. His w. **Ruth,** is shown by her will to have been near rel. to George and Phebe Parkhurst of Watertown, who came from Ipswich, 5 m. from Woolverstone. He joined his bro. at Dedham, where he was recd. on the underst. that he would not become the min., and on this basis was elected Dep. to the Genl. Court in 1638. He soon left for Hampt. with some of his friends, where he supplanted Mr. Bachiler. Freeman 1637. Lists 392a, 393b. He d. 28 Dec. 1661, 'aged about eighty-four;' his wid. Ruth, 12 May 1666, 'aged 88.' Her will made Nathaniel Bachiler, widower, her grand-nephew-in-law, her chief heir. List 393b. Ch. rec. at Woolverstone: **Samuel,** bp. 12 Mar. 1617-18, bur. same day. **Deborah,** bp. 3 June 1619, bur. 9 May 1624. **Timothy,** bp. 10 Nov. 1622, adm. gr. Apr. 1662 to Samuel Dalton. List 392a. **Ruth,** bur. 28 Aug. 1624-5.

**Daly,** Daniel, 1670, stole from his master, Richard Cutt, and ran away. List 328.

**DAM.** ———— See Creber.

**1 GEORGE** (Dam?) and Andrew Sampson appraisers ab. Sag. Creek in 1697. Misreadings excepted, there seems to have been an uncon. branch of this rare name. In 1692 **Elizabeth** Dam and Mary Moss complained of Jacob Lavers. In Portsm. 7 Mar. 1703-4 one Elizabeth Dam, former ch. member addicted to drink, was found drowned in the mill pond. List 96, p. 101. **Mary** (of Dover?) in court 1692. One Mary m. at Newbury 30 Nov. 1693 Thos. Titcomb. **Nicholas,** Portsm. shipwright in 1734.

**2 DEA. JOHN,** b. 1610. 2d dea. Dover, gr.j. 1646, Com.t.e.s.c. 1661. Lists 351ab, 352, 354abc, 355ab, 356abcefghk, 359ab, 311c (Dover), 49, 52, (54), 62, (92), 96. M. Elizabeth Pomfret who came in 1640, liv. 1682. He d. 27 Jan. 1689-90; will 19 May 1687—23 Mar. 1693-4 names 2 sons, 3 daus. Ch: **John,** by an earlier wife, ±68 in June 1702. **Elizabeth,** b. 1 May 1649, m. Thomas Whitehouse. **Mary,** b. 4 May 1651, m. Joseph Canney(1), 2d 22 Nov. 1701 Wm. Harford. **William,** b. 14 Oct. 1653. **Susannah,** b. 14 Dec. 1661. **Judith.** b. 15 Nov. 1666, m. Thomas Tibbetts.

**3 SERGT. JOHN**(2), gr.j. 1692, 94, 95, 99. Lists 356ceghk, 359b, 49, 52, 55b, (57), 62. He deeded half of homestead to s. John 28 June 1694; in 1705 deeded to s. and dau. Moses and Bethia. D. 8 Jan. 1705-6. Ch. by 1st w., Sarah Hall of Greenland: **Abigail,** b. 5 Apr. 1663, m. Thos. Starbird. By 2d w., Elizabeth Furber(2), m. 9 Nov. 1664: **John,** b. 11 Jan. 1665-6. **John,** b. 23 Feb. 1667-8, liv. 1734. **Alice,** b. 14 Dec. 1670. One Alice Stevens and Thos. Starbird in 1702 wit. a

deed of William and Martha Dam. **Moses,** b. 14 Oct. 1673. List 343. M. 22 July 1714 Abigail Huntress (9 ch. bp.), 2d, as her 4th husband, Elizabeth (Kennard), widow of Richard Waterhouse. Will 1751—1754 names 7 ch. **Bethia,** b. 5 May 1675, mar. George Townsend of Portsm. Will 1743—1761. **Jonathan,** appar. On the back of a town grant made in 1694 and put into court in 1702 is scribbling of Moses and Jonathan Dam. Lists 296, 297. M. in Kittery 25 Oct. 1711 Sarah Fernald(5), who d. 5 Nov. 1748. Will 1748—1749 names 3 sons, 2 of them shipwrights. One Jonathan Dam was bap. in Rochester in 1749.

**4 DEA. JOHN**(3). Constable 1696. List 343. In 1739 he deeded the homestead at Dam's Point, Newington, to son John. Wife Jane Rowe (Richard). 2 Nov. 1732 he m. as her 4th husb. Elizabeth (Haley), wid. of Nicholas Hilliard, who d. Feb. 1765, ag. 99, leaving the most of ab. 300 descendants living. Ch: **Zebulon,** Rochester, mar. 16 Aug. 1716 Abigail Bickford(4). 6 ch. bp. **John,** had homestead at Dam's Pt., Newington, d. 1768; m. 20 Feb. 1718 Elizabeth Bickford(4). 11 ch. **Richard,** d. 13 May 1776, m. 24 Jan. 1724 Elizabeth Leighton (Thos.) 8 ch. **Elnathan,** Dover, m. 1 Nov. 1736 Mary Rollins. 3 ch. bap. Also presum. **Alice,** or Eliza, m. 5 May 1720 Samuel Rawlins.

**4½ NICHOLAS,** Dover, 1690. Misreading of Dunn.

**5 WILLIAM**(2). Lists 352, 359b, 52, 62, 67. He d. 20 Mar. 1718 (grst. Nute farm), adm. 4 June to s. Pomfret. Wife Martha (Nute) d. 15 May 1718 (grst. Nute farm). Ch: **Pomfret,** b. 4 Mar. 1681-2, owned the Pomfret homestead, but liv. at Fresh Creek; m. 14 Jan. 1707-8 Esther Twombly (Ralph), 2d Elizabeth Tibbetts (Joseph), who was gr. adm. 6 May 1728, and m. 2d Gershom Downs(6), 3d Richard Goodwin. 6 ch. by both wives. **Martha,** b. 29 Mar. 1683, m. Jacob Allen(4). **William,** b. 14 Nov. 1686, m. 29 July 1708 Sarah Kimmin, d. 21 Apr. 1758 (grst. 200 yds. E. of Madbury R. R. station); will 1754—1758 names wife and 2 ch., 4 rec. **Samuel,** b. 21 Mar. 1689-90, d.s.p. bef. father. List 96. **Sarah,** b 21 Apr. 1692, m. John Twombly. **Leah,** b. 17 Feb. 1695-6, m. Samuel Hayes.

**DAMERILL. 1 Humphrey,** traveling merchant and mariner, at Boston by 1648, landowner. At death he was commander of the -Barque Sea Flower- of Boston. Adm. 27 Apr. 1654 to wid. Sarah, who m. 15 Sep. 1654 John Hawkins, mariner. Rev. H. S. Burrage, D.D., says, without references, he 'claimed to own a part or all of' Damariscove Island. Rev. H. O. Thayer thought Capt. John Smith may have found him there. With no records found to indicate age, it was likelier a fish-

ing master of the Newfoundland fleet of an earlier generation that gave his name to that harbor. The will of one James Damerell of Limehouse in Stepney parish 'deceased in parts beyond the seas,' was proved 24 Oct. 1631.—P. C. C. 106 St. John. The court ordering 100 marks to his son, the estate set off to **John** part of his father's land. Suff. Deeds iii. 69—untraced.

2 **JOHN**(1), presum. same ±22 in 1657, also ±25 same yr., came from Barbadoes with Jeremiah Cushing.

3 **JOHN**, not quite imposs. (2), was swearing drunk at Isles of Shoals in 1669, liv. there later. Presum. his w. Elizabeth, ± 23 in 1673, was liv. in a house of Edward Holland's. See List 191. J. D. in List 308b likely his s., and poss. Elizabeth -Wise- his wid., and desc. there later.

**Dane**, Wm., Cape Bonawagon 1672. List 13.

**DANFORTH**, Danford.

1 **THOMAS**, Mass. statesman, President of Maine 1680-1686. Lists 31, 32, 225a, 227.

2 **WILLIAM**, Newbury, never resided within our territory, but of his ch. the following had Me. or N. H. connections: **John**, b. 8 Dec. 1681, m. 2d Dorcas White (Nathaniel of Purpoodock), who d. 26 Mar. 1788, ag. 90 or 91. **Jonathan**, b. 18 May 1685, m. (int. 21 Jan. 1703-4) Mary White (Nathaniel of Purpoodock) who had been pub. 30 June 1702 to Richard Danforth who prob. d. in the interval. He was a carpenter of Pennacook, buying land in Canterbury in 1733. He and br. John sold White prop. at Maiden Cove to his s. Nathaniel who sold to Rev. John White in 1727. **Thomas**, b. 28 Dec. 1688, owned land at Casco Bay in 1723, when his br. Joseph adm. his est. **Francis**, b. 15 Mar. 1691, settled in Arundel where his wife, name unkn., d. in 1758. At least 5 ch.

**DANIELS**

1 **DAVY**, app. Scotch, Durham 1661. Lists 363ac, 364-366, 359a. M. Naomi Hull, who was a wid. in 1685. App. ch: **Joseph**, ag. 60, Jan. 1714-5. **John**, grants 1694, 1701. Lists 368b, 369. Wife Sarah was bp. 2 June 1723. 5 ch. bp.

2 **EDWARD**, List 57, petn. 1690.

3 **JAMES** (Teague), b. by 3 dep. between 1647-1654, about Lamprill Riv. 1660-1690. O. A. 30 Nov. 1677. Withdrew from Ind. to Stratham.

4 **JOSEPH**(1). Left his homestead in Durham to his two youngest sons, for which he was criticized by his sis. Sarah (Morrill) Darling and by Patience (Drew) Hill. Lists 368b, 369. M. 1st ab. 1700 Ann (Huntress), wid. of Thomas Chesley(5 jr), who d. late in 1704, 2d Jane, who outl. him. Ch., 2 or 3 by Ann?, 5 by Jane: **Joseph**, Dover. Lists 368b,

369. 7 ch. by w. Mehitable bp., 5 named in will 1773-1780. **Mary**, m. Morris Fowler of Dover. **Anne**, m. Samuel Chesley(5 Tho. jr.). **John**, b. 25 May 1709, settled in Barrington. **David**, b. 1713, m. Abigail Burnham. **Jonathan**, Barrington. Will 1779-1780 names w. **Elizabeth**, 7 ch. **Jacob**, Barr., m. Charity **Drew**. 5 ch. **Abigail**, b. 1722, mar. Henry Bussy or Buzzell(2), d. bef. her f., leaving 2 ch.

5 **SAMUEL**, ment. 1697 —Durham p. 90.

6 **SARAH** (Daniels, possibly? from York), m. at Hampt. 26 Mar. 1675 James Johnson.

7 ‡**CAPT. THOMAS** (Daniel), merchant, b. 1635, Portsmouth by 1664, from London. Captain of troop 1678-80, Councilor 1680, sesectm. 1673-75, 1677-80. Lists 48-51, 54, 83, 88, 89, 324, 326c, 329, 330a, 331b. Judge Sewall in 1714 was interested to transcribe his Latin epitaph, Thomas Daniel, Armig., d. 13 Nov. 1683 aet. 49. His br. Richard of the par. of St. Buttolph without Aldgate, London, had an only s. John, later citizen and mercer of London, who was rememb. in his uncle's will. M. Bridget Cutt(5), who m. 2d 11 Dec. 1684 her husband's kinsman Thomas Graffort. List 52.

**DARCY** (Dare). 1 **Edward**, Monhegan 1672-73. Lists 13, 15.

2 **JOHN** (Dare), Monhegan 1672-73. List 13, 15.

3 **ROGER** (Dari), Isles of Shoals 1677. List 306c.

**Darker**, Roger, Kit. wit. 1724. Y. D. xi. 126.

**Darley** (Durlen), Cornelius from Medfield, soldier under Hill 1693-4. See Cornelius **Darley**, b. Braintree 23 Mar. 1674-5.

**DARLING**, see also Dalling, Dollen.

1 **CORNELIUS**, son of Dennis Darling or Darley, b. in Braintree 1675, claimed ab. 1702, in right of Mary -Frebray- his wife, lands at Pemaquid granted by Palmer in 1686. See Friebury.

2 **JAMES** (George of Salem), ±43 in 1704, mar. at Marbleh. 16 May 1683 Hannah (Lewis) Mains, d. of Geo.; 2d in 1712 wid. Sarah Proctor. In 1695 he was bondsman for Mercy Lewis of Greenland. Liv. 1739 on the homestead in Lynn.

3 **JOHN**, Kingston, m. (int. 3 Nov. 1708) Mary Page (Onesiphorus), both liv. 1748. Ch. See Hoyt's Salis. 159.

4 **THOMAS**, Portsm., m. spring of 1720 Sarah (Morrell), wid. of Nicholas Frost(11). They rem. to Durham (now Lee). Both liv. 1739, she 1750.

5 **THOMAS**, and Joanna, Salem. See Liscomb.

**Darmer**, Thomas, see Dermer.

**Darmon** (misr. of -er?) Thomas, see Dermer.

**'Dauverne,** Mr. Philip—Mary Ricart,' memo. of marriage, with Stileman's court files ab. 1670, i. 469.

**Davadge,** William, Topsfield, wounded 1691. List 37.

**DAVENPORT,** a township in Cheshire.
1 **EBENEZER,** weaver, b. Dorchester 26 Apr. 1661, was at Falm. in 1680, a corp. at Ft. Loyal, liv. at Macworth's Point ab. 5 yrs. from 1684 or 85, then ret. to Dorch. His 1st w. Dorcas Andrews(6) d. in Boston 24 Nov. 1723, ag. 60. He d. 19 July 1738; will 26 Jan. 1729-30—21 Aug. 1738 cuts off his present w. Patience who had been abs. from his house 3 yrs., and names 3 sons and 6 daus., 3 of whom m. Coxes: **Tabitha,** b. 3 May 1688, m. Capt. John Cox(12 jr.). **Hepzibath,** b. 11 Apr. 1697, m. Thomas Cox(12). **Thankful,** b. 8 Mar. 1700, m. Ebenezer Cox. (See 12). See N. E. Reg. 33.27.
2 **JOHN.** Ladbrook est., Portsm. List 92.

**DAVIE,** see also Davis.
1 **GEORGE,** mariner, got Indian deeds at Sheepscot 1663-1669. In Philip's War escaped wounded, to Portsm., where Mass. Colony paid for his cure. See N. E. Reg. 18.71. Liv. there 1680. Only surviving ch: **William.**
2 ‡**MR. HUMPHREY,** son of Sir John, a newly made baronet, came from London 1662, Asst. 1679-86, died Hartford 18 Feb. 1689. Left ch. here by a young wife who mar. 2d Jonathan Tyng. Son by early wife, Sir John of Creedy, co. Devon, claimed his Kennebec lands.
3 **THOMAS.** In 1652 Joseph Atkinson ordered to keep away from the house of Thomas Davie (Sagamore Creek?) where appar. Mary (Batson) Clay was staying.
4 **WILLIAM**(1), prob. was killed in King Philip's War, as his two orphan daus. were brought to Portsm. where they were left some time. Y. D. x. 106. Wid. Rebecca (63 in June 1719), mar. Simon Hinkson (Peter), his wid. in Lynn 1719. Ch: **Alice,** m. Jacob Clark(14). **Mary,** m. John Witt of Marlboro, both liv. 1718.

**DAVIS,** Davies, 30th commonest name in Eng. and Wales, 3d (Davies) in Wales, became 5th in N. E. See also Davie.
1 **AMBROSE** (Dawes?) wit. with John Spinney, 1698.
2 **DANIEL,** from whom Daniel's Creek, Eliot, took name. Jury 1647, 1649-51, gr.j. 1650. List 282. In 1658 was fined for tardiness in reporting for jury service, fine remitted.
3 **DANIEL** (misr. for David?) N. E. Reg. vi. 35.
4 **DAVID,** servant of John Lang of Portsm. In 1678 was placed with Stephen Jones of Oyster River at the cooper's trade. David

3 **Davisson,** ±32 in Dec. 1692. Ab. 1688 he was tenant of Roger Rose's house at Lubberland, in 1694 had a gr. there, in 1696 his house was a garrison, 27 Aug. 1696 k. by Ind. Jury 1694, gr.j. 1695, coroner's 1694. Lists 367a, 368a, 94, 96. By 16 Jan. 1699-1700 his wid. had m. James Durgin, her name by Durgin fam. trad. Susannah S——h? from Island of Jersey. Kn. ch: **Abigail,** ±16 in 1703, given a calf in Tho. Morris's will, 1701. **David,** aged 49 in Feb. 1736-7. In 1756 he sold 14 a. of his father's 40 a. gr. Liv. at Packer's Falls. List 368b. He m. Elizabeth **Thomas.** 5 ch. bp. **Elizabeth,** bp. 20 Dec. 1719.
5 **EDWARD,** relation to (53). Having been in the service of the Duke of Albemarle, and served James II under command of the Earl of Plymouth, he came over 'to see his Relations', and stopped at Capt. Sylvanus Davis's, who sent his kinsman to wait on Gov. Andros. His gr. laid out at Scarb. has not been traced.
6 **EMANUEL** (19?), b. ab. 1655 (±21 in 1676, ag. 24 at York 28 July 1679). In 1680 he was held guilty of offering false evid. against Capt. Scottow and refusing to take oath. Of Wells during Philip's War and in 1682-4. In 1695, late of Cape Porpus, now of Newton, Mass., he sold land in C. P. Lists 236, 259, 266, 33. He m. Mary, wid. of John Turbet, d. of Margery (Batson) Kendall?—Young.
7 **HENRY,** Great Island, 1673, perh. an apprent. to a merchant. List 312g. In same yr. wit. with Tho. Seavey and Jeremy Tibbetts.
8 **HOPKIN,** Portsm., tanner, a Welshman; m. Ruth Roberts, d. of John of the village of Pamfret Aaikell in the town of Swansey, Glamorganshire, millwright. A mtg. by him to Edw. Bragg of Ipsw. was paid for only ch. **Timothy,** 31 Mar. 1693.
9 **ISAAC,** in 1655 was fined £3 for running away from his master. His father (who?) undertook to pay the fine. He mar. Lydia Black (John) in Beverly 28 Sep. 1659, she b. there 3 June 1638. In 1677 took O. A. in Beverly. In 1680 wit. a Falm. deed (Geo. Felt). Worked for Robert Lawrence. In 1687 rem. from Falm. to the Kennebec, with sons John and Ebenezer and son-in-law Richard Smith, and petitn. Andros for land grants. Both he and wife poss. Ind. victims. Ch. all d.s.p. but four: **John,** b. 1660. **James**(wrote), in 1733 was of Ipsw., husbandman. **Mary,** b. 1664, m. Richard Smith (2 sons), 2d Samuel Wood, (2 daus.), d. Ipswich 1731, ag. 67. **Ebenezer,** b. Beverly 7 Nov. 1671, with his father worked for Mr. Lawrence and rem. to the Kennebec. Jan. 29, 1700-1, late of Ken., adm. to br. John of Salem, fisherman. **Isaac,** bp. Beverly 5 July 1674. **Israel,** bp.

Beverly 3 June 1677. **Samuel**, of Glouc., mariner, in 1733, his deed of his father's land at Falmouth was wit. by Grace Tucker and Mary Davis. Presum. the same that m. Ann Robinson in 1704 and had 9 ch. (no Grace). 10 **JACOB**(39), presum. same with w. Susannah in Boston, adm. 1701. Ch: **Jacob**, b. 2 Nov. 1688, carpenter, Boston, grs. of (39). Presum. same m. 26 Mar. 1713 Elizabeth Howard. **Samuel**, b. 7 Feb. 1692, d.y. **Samuel**, b. 25 May 1695.

11 **JAMES**, 1607 Popham. List 6.

12 ***JAMES**, Newbury, Hampton, Haverhill, m. in Thornbury, co. Glouc., 11 June 1618 Cicely Tayer (Thayer), bp. there 1 May 1600, dau. of John and Joane (Lawrence). Himself, their three eldest children, and his younger bros., Samuel, Thomas, John and Ephraim, are named in the will of his father, John Davys of Acton-Turville April—Nov. 1626, this place a chapelry on the edge of Wiltshire, ab. 30 m. from Marlborough. Other wills of his relations in the same place are found, incl. his grmo. Agnes Davis, wid., 10 Mar. 1587-8—9 July 1589. Arthur Clark (5) was app. his br.-in-law. He was called ±60 in 1663, ±96 at death 29 Jan. 1678-9. Made freeman at Newbury 4 Mar. 1634-5. Hampton gr. 1639, rem. to Haverhill in May 1644. His gr. at Hampt. he sold 17 Aug. 1648, four years aft. his removal. Both at Hamp. and many yrs. at Haverhill he was Com.t.e.s.c. He was often selectm. and gr.j. and Rep. 1660. Lists 391ab, 392a, 393b. Will 17 Mar. 1675-6, cod. 22 July 1678. Wife -Sissilla- d. 28 May 1673. Ch: **James**, bp. at Thornbury 4 July 1619. **John**, bp. at Thornbury 28 Jan. 1620-1. **Sarah**, named in grfr.'s will, app. d.y. **Judith**, m. 1 Sep. 1647 Samuel Guild, d. May 1667, ch. **Ephraim**, m. 31 Dec. 1659 Mary Johnson. 9 ch. **Samuel. Sarah**, m. 18 June 1663 John Page, liv. 1714. 1 dau.

13 **JAMES**(12), gr. at Hampton 1640. In 1647 he and Mr. Stanyan were app. to lay out the road bet. Haverhill and Exeter. Lists 391b, 392a. Will 18, d. 18 July 1694. Wife Elizabeth (Eaton), d. 21 Jan. 1683. 12 ch. inc. **James**, who m. Sarah (Winnock?) Wiggin from Scarb., and **Daniel**, k. at Pemaquid in Apr. 1689. See Hoyt's Salis. p. 125.

14 **COL.** ***JAMES**(20), Esq. Oyster River, for many yrs. a leading citizen of Dover, leading man in Durham aft. it was set off, and influential in the Prov. Captain of scouting companies in the Ind. Wars and in a Canadian exped., he rose in military rank to Lt. Col. Early a J. P., from 1717 was a judge of the Court of Common Pleas. Repeatedly moderator of Dover town meetings, he was the usual moderator in Durham; was select. in both towns, and was Assemblyman from Dover nearly 20 yrs. Lists 52, 57-59, 62-64, 66, 67, 69, 94, 353, 368b, 369. Will 18 Oct.

1748, d. 8 Sep. 1749. He m. 1 Oct. 1688 Elizabeth Chesley(5) who d. first. See Jeremy Belknap's account of the longevity of his ch. N. E. Reg. 36.435. **James**, b. 10 July 1689, liv. in Madbury on his grf.'s gr. Lists 368b, 369 (358b). He m. 5 Nov. 1728 Ruth Ayer of Haverhill, who d. 28 Apr. 1730; 2d 14 Apr. 1743 Elizabeth Paine of York. Ch. 1+5. **Thomas**, b. 20 Oct. 1690, Major and J. P., Madbury, did not marry. Acc. by Sobriety Thomas in 1721 (and vig. contest.), and by Ann Nute in 1743, whose ch. was called Elizabeth Davis. In 1765 he deeded half his homestead to Joseph and Elizabeth Pinkham. **Samuel**, b. 26 Sep. 1692, Madbury, liv. on half of his grf.'s gr. Lists 368b. Will 26 July 1774, d. 26 Feb. 1789 'aged 97.' His w. Martha (Chesley 5 jr.) d. in 1791, called 102 yrs. old. 6 or m. ch. **Daniel**, b. 29 Jan. 1695, d. in Durham in Jan. 1759, est. div. in 1764 among wid. Elizabeth and 7 ch. Lists 368b, 369. **Sarah**, b. 3 Mar. 1697, m. Capt. Joseph Hicks, d. 20 Jan. 1788. **Hannah**, b. 28 Mar. 1699, m. 23 Mar. 1726-7 Clement Deering, s. of Clement(8). **Elizabeth**, b. 13 July 1701, m. John Hicks. **Ephraim**, b. 30 Apr. 1704, had the homestead. List 369. He m. (self record) 7 Dec. 1731 one Ruth. Selectm. 1743. 5 ch.

15 **JAMES**(9), Falm., Ipswich, unident. except by Y. D. xvi. 39.

16 **JAMES**, Kittery, yeoman, ±32 in July 1721, he dep. 'being an appr. to John Leighton of Kit. from ab. 8 yrs. of age to near 21.' List 291. He m. in 1715 Elizabeth Bradeen(1). In 1733 they sold part of his land in Eliot. Y. D. 18.30. Their s. **Samuel**, m. 8 Aug. 1744 Lydia Hoag, d. of Jonathan of Hampton.

17 **JOHN**, misr. of -Lavis- in Doc. Hist. iii. 329, 1642, and in Pope's Pioneers, p. 54, 1640, 1642, p. 24, 1651.

18 **MAJOR JOHN** (Davess), b. about 1613, first ident. at York in 1650, poss. some relation to (41). Sergt., Ensign, Lt., Capt., Major; Marshal, Councillor, Deputy (resident) President of the Province of Maine. He was gr.j. 1650 and often, and selectm. almost const. 1661-1681. Lists 275, 276, 77b, 92, 302b, 312f, 24, 26, 28-30, 32, 33. He m. the wid. Mary (Pooke) Purington, and cont. her tavern. See P. & C. i. 82, passim, and ii. note 59, passim. He d. just bef. the York massacre, adm. 6 Oct. 1691 to wid. Mary, who may have perished in the massacre, as adm. was regrant. to Joseph Weare 23 Jan. 1693-4. He adopted as his heir her d. Sarah 'Puddington', disclaimed in her first husband's will, which was not recorded until after Maj. Davis's death. Sarah b. ab. 1641 (aged ±46 10 Aug. 1687) m. John Penwell.

19 ***JOHN** (Davies), b. ab. 1619, blacksmith and doctor. He first app. with Henry

Sayward building a mill for the Lanes at Sag. Creek, and liv. in two of their houses there. In 1699 ag. ±80 at Portsm. he dep. that in the yr. '51 or '52 he liv. on the land where Mr. Mark Hunkin liv. then. In the latter yr. he was gr. a mill priv. in York, whither they both rem. In Jan. 1653-4, still 'of York,' he was gr. the mill priv. at Saco Falls, with an agreed price to the inhab. for his boards, and with the further stipul. that he set up his forge there. When Saco became uncomf. he went out to Cape Porpus and subject to Ind. dangers spent his remaining yrs. bet. that place and Portsm. (See Y. D. iii. 134, viii. 199). Beyond blacksm. and lumber milling, he also went into politics, doctoring and preaching, yet with leisure for sundry then unpop. relaxations. (See P. & C. i. and ii. Note 59 passim.) In 1672 he was First Selectm. of Cape Porpus. In 1682 he was elected Deputy from Saco and Cape P. to the Province Assembly, but the Court rejected him. Poss. he was J. D. Sen., N. H. grand j. in 1694. In Portsmouth 1680 the tax of 'Doctor Davis' was abated; in 1690 J. D. Sr. and Jr. were both taxed, equally light. Lists 275, 276, 245, 249, 259, 313af, (62). Unhap. wife Catherine ment. 1671-76. List 246. Ch. unk. except **John** and likely **Emanuel.**

**20 ENSIGN JOHN**(12), Hampton, Haverhill, Oyster River ±55 in 1679. Selectm. of Dover 7 yrs. Ensign from 1662, in 1680 he was com. Capt. of the Troop. Lists 391b, 375a, 46, 49, 50, 52, 54, 341, 311c (Dover), 330a, 353, 356a, 359a, 361a, 362ab, 363abc, 365, 366. He m. 10 Dec. 1646 Jane Peasley of Haverh., k. by Ind. 18 July 1694. Ten ch. outliv. their f. and were liv. or left ch. in 1736 (N. H. Ct. Files 17019). His son's sons are glossed over in Hist. of Durham, and but little untang. here. Ch: **Mary,** b. 6 Nov. 1647, m. 19 July 1671 Josiah Heath of Haverh. 9 ch., of whom John was reared by his grf. **Sarah,** b. 7 Mar. 1648-9, m. James Smith. **John,** b. 22 Aug. 1651. Three ch. rec. in Haverh., the following in Province V. R. **Hannah,** b. 24 Dec. 1653, m. 28 Sep. 1677 John Kezar of Haverh. (8 ch.), 2d 6 Nov. 1701 Samuel Dalton(3 jr.). **Jane,** b. 29 Dec. 1655, d. 23 Sep. 1656. **Moses,** b. 30 Dec. 1657. **Joseph,** b. 26 Jan. 1659-60. **James,** b. 23 May 1662. **Jane,** b. 15 May 1664. Three unm. ds. named in father's will. **Jemima. Judith,** m. 14 Dec. 1687 Capt. Samuel Emerson(7).

**21 JOHN,** Star Isl. constable 1655; fisherman 1661 (N. H. Ct. Files 1: 63).

**22 JOHN,** poss. same as last, in 1672, having served Geo. Walton 11 yrs. and growing towards decay, petitions to be set free.

**23 JOHN.** List 96, p. 102, of Jamaica (West Amesbury). His 1st wife was Elizabeth Boaden(9); 2d m. 19 Oct. 1702, Bethia Ash, d. of Mary Ash, referred to in List 96; 3d 28 June 1708 Elizabeth Beedle, who d. bef. 1746. Two, if not all, of his sons rem. to Maine. Ch: **Dau.,** unrec. **Martha,** m. 'Dan dau.' b. 26 Nov. 1686. **John,** Capt., b. 4 May 1689, m. in Hampton 2 Aug. 1711 Elizabeth Basford(1). By trade a cordwainer, in Biddeford he was a lumberman. Outfitted and com. a comp. of scouts. Will, 'gentleman,' 9 May, d. 12 May, 1752. 9 ch. **Mary,** b. 15 Nov. 1691. **Sarah,** b. 14 June 1694. **Ichabod Bowden,** b. 27 Apr. 1697, coaster, m. 28 Feb. 1717-18 Mehitable Chandler, d. of Capt. Joseph, of Andover. Living in Kittery 1721. Adm. 1 Oct. 1728 to wid. Mehitable, who m. 2d 6 Aug. 1730 John Rackleff of York and settled in Scarb. Ch. **Barbary,** b. 29 July 1699. By 2d wife: **Nathaniel,** b. 14 Apr. 1704. One Nathaniel by wife **Martha** had sons William and Robert b. in Scarb. 1726-1732.

**24 JOHN**(20), perh. succ. his father as Ensign—'Ensign Davis' juryman 1683. Lists 52, 94, 359a, 367ab, 368b, (358b). He lost a w., **Mary,** d. 12 Jan. 1684, and m. Elizabeth Burnham(5). Himself and all his fam., except two ds. taken captive, were k. by Ind. 18 July 1694. One dau. remained with the French, the other, **Sarah,** ±15 in 1716, mar. Peter Mason.

**25 JOHN**(64?), Kennebec, wit. with (67) Ind. deed to Tho. Stevens, 1675. Y. D. ix. 254.

**26 JOHN,** Portsm., mariner, had built his house bef. 1689, when his f.-in-law gave him the land. He mar. (Mary) Shortridge, app. in 1713 wid. Mary Davis of Boston, intrusted with the money of Edward Bickford(7 jr.). His house was sold by his son **John,** weaver and fisherman, Portsm. and Newc. List 339. He m. by 1712 Margaret (Bickford 7), wid. of Geo. Wright of Boston, to whom adm. was gr. 6 Nov. 1733, still his wid. in 1748—their only ch. Mary, bp. 15 May 1720, mar. Emanuel May. But see Richard(44).

**27 JOHN**(19), poss. same as (26), (28), (30) or others, joined in father's deed 1676. Presum. the same selectm. of Cape Porpus 1689, back there to be 'taken' 10 Aug. 1703, not ident. after. List 39. See 259, 313a.

**28 JOHN,** tailor of Portsm., sued Nathaniel Lammos in 1683.

**29 JOHN**(9), ag. ±83 in 1742, of Glouc., mariner, dep. that he knew Falm. before Philip's War and after the war went there to live on his father's gr., m. there, and liv. there until over 26. Of Salem, fisherman, 1701. Lived in Rowley ab. 1701-1705. Of Glouc. 1733, 1739, 1742. Babson deems him the same who moved from Ipsw. to Sandy Bay with w. and ch. in 1715, was 'old Mr.

John Davis' town charge in 1748, f. of **Samuel** who m. Deborah Harris in 1723 and perh. **Ebenezer** who m. Elizabeth Tarr in 1715. Deborah wit. his deed in 1733.

30 **JOHN**, Kittery 1700. Col. Pepperell to Mr. Somes: 'I had John Davis in custody and was going to put him in prison, but he promised so fair that I took his bond for £4 he owed me and his promise to work three months to pay it and to pay what he owes you. But he ran away, I understand to the westward. He is a great knave, which is pity having such knowledge as he hath.'

31 **JOHN**, b. in Salis., became 'Sen.' in York, where he m. Mercy Brooking(3) and had 6 ch. rec. 1718-1731. He was of Biddeford, laborer, 1732-1737, but of York, cooper, when his will was made, dated at Falm. 25 Nov. 1745—5 Nov. 1746, making Col. Cushing of Falm. sole benef., but the appraisers were all Biddeford men. Half of his ch. deaths are rec. with their births and all app. d.y. List 279.

32 **JOHN**, from Glouc., b. ab. 1698, became -Jr.- in York, where he m. 28 May 1724-5 Deborah Black(3). Liv. there 1768. 10 ch. rec. 1726-1750.

33 **JOHN**, of Bristol, Eng., m. in Portsm. 23 Oct. 1718 Mary Goodwin.

34 **JOHN**, Kittery, calker, adm. 7 Oct. 1732 to wid. Mary. 5 ch., 1 over and 3 under 7, 1 posth. She was presum. the Mary Davis and her ch. who in 1720 was sleeping in the house with Jacob Redington's wife when he was away and Wm. Moore's peddler was keeping his goods there. She perh. m. Jan. 1733-4 Joshua Chick.

35 **JOHN**, of Newington, acc. in 1723 by Susannah Rowe, Richard Downing his bondsman, and m. 29 Apr. 1725 Mary Place.

36 **JOSEPH**, cooper, s. of Thomas and Christian of Haverhill, presum. the same that wit. a deed of Henry Sayward of Portsm. in 1652 and dep. in 1669, ±32, that he was liv. at Piscataqua River when Christian Lawson first came, app. was cooper's apprent. here. By 1658 he had a cooper's shop in Kittery, const. in 1659, and Samuel D., here with him, app. was s. of (12). By 1665 he was of Haverh., adm. gr. to his father in 1673. Juryman, Norfolk Co., 1663, 1665, 1667.

37 **JOSEPH**(20), called Sergt. in Sep. 1736 and over 74, was Sergt. by 1694, Const. 1714, Lieut. in 1715. Lists 57, 368b. Wife Mary was bp. 10 Feb. 1716-7 and joined the ch., with her hus., 28 Sep. 1718. Liv. 1743. Ch. inc: **Mary**, m. James Basford. **Joseph**, ag. 56 by dep. 3 Feb. 1753. Had half the homestead. Corp. 1740. **Judith**, m. 3 Apr. 1718 Capt. John Tasker. **Jemima**, m. 27 Nov. 1718 Joseph Small. **Benjamin**, had half the homestead. List 369. He mar. 5 Jan. 1726-7 Miriam Roberts, liv. 1746. In 1748 he

deeded to s. Benj., both of Durham. **Jane**, m. 19 Jan. 1726-7 John Barber(4 jr.). Also consid. Moses Davis, bondsm. for Sobriety Thomas, 1721, and Sobriety, w. of Jonathan Bunker and d. of Joseph Davis, bp. 11 Apr. 1753.

38 **JOSEPH**, Portsm., joiner, m. after 1723 Christian, wid. of Benj. Green of Portsmouth and Rochester.

39 **LAWRENCE**, b. ab. 1625, wit. in York Ct. 1659, of Falm. 1662, came back from Ipsw., ab. 1681, fled to Beverly 1688, where he d. Apr. 1711 ag. ab. 86. Lists 25, 30, 34, 223b. His 100 a. farm in So. Portland was sold to Robert Means, from Ireland, by his wid. Elizabeth (Atkins 5), who m. (int. 15 July 1716) Geo. Nicholson of Marblehead. She was ±64 in 1709 (perh. not his 1st w.), liv. 1720. Kn. ch: **Jacob. Rachel**, b. ab. 1668, mar. Robert Haines of Falm., 2d Jonathan Wedgwood of Hampton. Also perh. **dau.** wife of John Holman of Falmouth whom Rachel called brother; **dau.**, mother of Mary, -cert. a gr.d., mar. as Mary Reed 4 June 1717 at Pembroke to Joseph Tubbs, both liv. 1736. **Zachariah.**

40 **MOSES**(20), 64 in 1721, m. in Haverhill 16 Jan. 1681 Ruhamah Dow (Stephen), and liv. there several yrs. Aft. 1693 was in Durham, until both himself and his s. Moses were k. by Ind. 10 June 1724. Jury 1696. Lists 57, 368b. Ch: **John**, b. in Haverh. 4 Jan. 1682, m. Abigail Meader. Lists 368b, 369. 7 ch. bap. together 28 Jan. 1720-1. **Moses**, b. in Haverh. 2 Nov. 1684, m. Deliverance, wid. of Geo. Chesley. Killed with his f. in 1724, adm. to wid. 8 Sep. 1725, whose est. was adm. by s. Moses in 1765. 5 ch., inc. Love and Aaron. **James**, ag. 41, when he m. in 1728, was dist. as 'widower.' He m. 1st 19 May 1719 Mary Stevenson; (1 dau.); 2d 4 Oct. 1728 Elizabeth Dunn(2), defined 'maiden ag. 39.' **Joseph**, 'grandson of Stephen Dow Sen.', bp. in Haverh. 8 Mar. 1695-6. **Joshua**, perh. same as last, m. bef. 1717 Esther Bunker(4), both liv. 1735. In 1737 he sued Ichabod Chesley for 9 mos. work 'done by my s. Joseph.' In 1744 he bot in Rochester and by 1746 had moved there and m. Jane (Hussey) who as Jane Lane 7 Mar. 1742 had her 3 ch. by former husband bap. at Dover. Adm. on his est. was gr. to her 29 Nov. 1752, ment. a s. 4 yrs. old. List 369. **Solomon**, ag. 70 in Mar. 1767 when he dep. that his br. Joshua built his house (and Joshua in a deed 1735 ment. his br. Samuel owning adj. land). List 369. He m. Elizabeth Davis, presum. not his niece, liv. in 1757 when they sold their homestead. In 1765 he (?) was of Nottingham; in 1770, with w. Hannah, of Lee. Ch. **Jabez**, in 1726 'brother' was deeded land by 'James Davis widower.' In 1727 one Jabez and w. Ruth of Dunstable q.c. estate of Thos. and Ruth

DAVIS 187 DAVIS

Blanchard. List 369. In 1734 grantee in Durham, in 1736 bot in Canterbury. His garrison is located on Doctor Stackpole's map. **Ebenezer**, b. 10 June 1702, adm. 7 May 1755 to wid. Susannah. List 369. Ch. **Abigail**, bp. at same time with last, 26 Nov. 1727. **Samuel**, 's. of James,' bp. 29 June 1729, rem. to Canterbury after. List 369, where he liv. on Ephraim Davis's lot, which he sold in 1745, having ret. to Durham in **Fr.** & Indian War. Liv. in Durham 1752. Perh. also (but consider Joseph) **Timothy**, Indian scout in 1712, pet. 1716-1719. Not in List 369. But in 1755 Rebecca Davis, hus. unkn. of Durham, deeded to her s. Timothy 11 a. in the Hook, who dep. in 1783 that in 1745 he liv. there, also William in 1783 that he liv. there in 1751. **Jeremiah,** in 1722 wit. deed from Moses(40) to s. Ebenezer; in 1732 Ebenezer deeded part of homestead to Jeremiah; in 1744 Jeremiah (w. Bridget) deeded it back to Ebenezer, adj. Jabez. In 1737 he sold to James jr. (s. of Moses) 10 a. adj. Deliverance Davis and Ebenezer. In 1735 Jeremiah of Durham bot from Benj. List 369. He m. bet. 1732-1734 Sarah Jenkins (2 sons). In 1761 his wid. Bridget q.c. his town gr. to Jonathan Hill.

41 **NICHOLAS**, Mr., tailor, of Wapping Hall, London, came in the -Planter- 1635, ag. 40, with w. Sarah, 40, s. Joseph 13, nephew Wm. Locke 6, and servants. From Charlestown he was an original settler of Woburn, where his w. d. 24 May 1643 and he m. 12 July Elizabeth, wid. of Joseph Isaacs. At York by 1650 (jury). In 1652 the warrant from the Mass. Comrs. was directed to him and John(18) Davis, and their court was held at his tavern. Gr.j. 1656, 1659, 1660. Selectm. 1653, 1656, 1658-59, 1662. Lists 275-277, 24, 25. Will 27 Apr. 1667—12 Mar. 1669-70, names his or wife's cousins besides his d. and her ch. and cous. Wm. Locke of Woburn. Ch: **Joseph**, bp. 18 Nov. 1621, called 15 in passeng. list, soon d. **Mary**, m. Geo. Dodd, Matthew Austin(5), Wm. Wright.

42 **NICHOLAS**, List 213. Illutherian 1686.

43 **RICHARD**, Kittery gr. 1685, gift from James Emery in 1687 (Y. D. iv. 88), sold both in 1702, late of Kit., deed executed in Portsm. (Y. D. vii. 66).

44 **RICHARD**, perh. same as last, m. 11 May 1708 Elizabeth Shortridge, and rented from Wm. Cotton sen. This man had been m. bef. Portsm. Selectmen's meeting 1 Dec. 1707, -Whereas Richard Davis's wife for sometime hath been taken care of and supplied by the town before her death, -her husband forced to spend his time to nurse her-, ordered that he be notified to refund 'or to choose his master with whome to live til such money be paid.' In 1743 Shortridge

Davis wit. a Berw. deed. Y. D. 23.222. But see (26).

45 **RICHARD**, br. of (52) who sold his 10+90 a. at Arrowsic in 1731. Y. D. 15: 65.

46 **ROBERT** (Davies), Capt. 1607. List 6.

47 **ROBERT**, carpenter, Sag. Creek, in 1648 was servant of and wit. against Henry Taylor. In 1651 ordered to produce cert. of his wife's death, next yr. he was ordered to go to her in England 1658, sold lot to Tho. Onion, 1660 land and bldg. to Edw. Bickford, 1667 house and 5 a. to Robert Purrington for life support.

48 **ROGER**, fisherman, Isles of Shoals. Lists 95, 307b. In 1711 his s. **John** of Dover, yeoman, q.c. to Richard Yeaton the house that was his father's on Star Isl.; Andrew Daniell also signs; wit. Geo. Blagden, Grace (Lewis?).

49 **SAMUEL**, perh. same as next, wit. in York Ct., July 1658, with Sarah Puddington against Mrs. Priscilla Johnson.

50 **SAMUEL**, Kittery 1661, with Joseph(36), ag. 28 in 1664, presum. s. of (12), m. in Haverhill in 1663 Deborah Barnes. His will 9, d. 10 Sep. 1696; she d. 14 Jan. 1718-9. 10 ch.

51 **SAMUEL**(9), of Glouc., mariner, 1733, his deed of his father's land in Falm. wit. by Grace Tucker and Mary Davis.

52 **SAMUEL**, of Falmouth, blacksmith, 19 Nov. 1729, sells grant. Of Boston, blacksm., 1 Oct. 1731, wife Katharine, sells 10+90 a. at Arrowsic, 'heretofore the right of Richard Davis my bro.' Y. D. xv. 65. Of Falm., blacksm. 25 Nov. 1734 or 1735, sells his town gr. in Falm.; ack. same day in Boston. Y. D. 18.77. M. in Boston 1 Oct. 1714 S. D. and Katharine Marion. 6 ch. rec.

53 **CAPT. ‡SYLVANUS** (Sil-), b. perh. ab. 1635, first ment. 14 June 1659 buying land from the Ind. up Damariscotta River. Highly ambitious and of ceaseless activity, this interest. char. inspired confid. and retained respect of import. persons, first on the Kennebec, then ab. Portland, finally ab. Boston, over a period of ab. 40 yrs. He was evid. a coastwise trader, with headq. at or below Bath. From ab. 1673 he was agent on the Kennebec for Clark & Lake, and by his offic. escaped the Arrowsic massacre, but with wounds. Presently he was in command of a ketch bringing relief from Boston, and next yr. commanded the fort at Arrowsic. As late as 1681 he secured a gr. of 60 ft. front to build a warehouse upon the westward side of the fishing island at Sagadahoc. Besides three Ind. deeds, 1659, 1665 and 1694, he acq. much land by grants and by purch. He organized 'the Town of Harwich' on the Maine side of the Kennebec. Upon Pres. Danforth's attempt to build a

city at Portland, his activ. shifted there. By articles dated 26 Nov. 1683 he took in as partners three Bay merchants, Capt. John Phillips of Charlestown, John Endicott and James English of Boston, turning in his warehouse at Sagadahoc, sawmill &c. at Falmouth, and livestock in the hands of Tho. Parker, Matthew Salter, Wm. Baker, Abraham Collins and John Parker. Able to accom. himself to shifting gov., he was J. P. under Andros, commanded the fort at Portland under Bradstreet and was made a Councillor of the Mass. Colony under the new charter. On the fall of Fort Loyal he was 4 mos. a prisoner in Canada. Lists 13, 14, 101, 182-184, 191, 225ab, 227, 228cd, 239a, 32, 34, 35, 97. His will 3 Apr. 1703—6 May 1704 recites that in recent yrs. he had been in the employ of Mr. John Nelson, whom he made his resid. legatee, and gives his Falm. real est. to the daus. of James English. His w. (unnamed, not imp. Jane Nichols, m. in Bristol 15 Oct. 1666), was to live in his recently built house at Nantasket.

54 **THEOPHILUS**, constable at Saco 1636, in several lawsuits 1636-37. List 242.

55 **THOMAS**, wit. in 1664 for Joseph(36).

56 **THOMAS**, Sagamore Ck. 1652. See Davie.

57 **THOMAS**, 1661 Y. D. 18.82. Improvised. See Larrabee, John.

58 **THOMAS**, Esq. Province Sec. 20 July 1692—14 Aug. 1696, 'went home for England' in 1693, by a contemp. letter, and in a hearing on the methods of government here, test. that a house levied on, which the people would not buy away from the owner, was knocked down for £4 to a man holding it at £200. The language of the letter implies that he was an Englishman, contrary to the implic. of jumbled and uncor. type in Savage. It does not appear that he came again, Wm. Redford acting as Deputy. List 65.

59 **THOMAS**, soldier from Haverhill. List 267b.

60 **THOMAS**, Portsm., cabinet maker, mar. bef. 1732. Timothy helped him in trouble; also Abr. Senter in 1734.

61 **TIMOTHY**(8), Portsmouth joiner, ±63 in 1714, liv. 1720, not in 1736. He was called by his contemp. a Welshman, and claimed, perh. secured, an inherit. in Wales. He was an orig. memb. of the Baptist Church in Kit. Jury 1684, 1685, 1699. Gr.j. 1692, 1693, 1698. Lists 52, 57, 62, 329, 330d, 333a, 339. He m. 1st Joanna Moses, 2d Constant, liv. 20 Mar. 1713. Ch. by 1st w: **Timothy**, b. ab. 1680; by 2d w: **Robert**, d.s.p. aft. 1715. **John**, joiner, Constable 1722. Adm. 10 Mar. 1723-4 to bros. Joseph Buss and Samuel Davis, s.p. **Samuel**, m. Elizabeth Small, d. of Joseph and Susannah (Packer), both living 1740. **Lydia**, mar. 25 Oct. 1711 Joseph Buss(1).

**Hannah**, m. John Paine, mariner, both liv. 1744. **Elizabeth**, m. John Cotton(2 jr.).

62 **TIMOTHY**(61), joiner, 62 in 1742, undersheriff 1713, m. 3 Nov. 1703 Elizabeth Badger of Portsm. Ch. rec.: **John**, b. 12 July 1704, app. same who m. Sarah Emerson (Rev. John), adm. to her 24 Feb. 1741-2; her will 1763-1765 shows 2 sons. **Mary**, b. 12 Oct. 1705. **Joanna**, b. 13 Apr. 1707. **Timothy**, bp. 25 Dec. 1715, joiner, m. Olive Goodwin, d. of Tho. and Mehitable (Plaisted); both joined Berwick ch. 11 Nov. 1733; they d. 12 May 1772, 10 June 1774. **Daniel**, bp. 25 Dec. 1715.

63 **TOBIAS**, adm. inhab. of Dover 22 May 1666. N. E. Reg. vi. 35.

64 **WILLIAM**, came as servant with Mr. Tho. Gorges, app. the same at the Kennebec in 1654 (List 11), as he had sold his York gr. to Richard Collicott bef. 1658, and the same whose wid. Margaret m. Richard Potts bef. 24 June 1661, when they sold land in Woolwich to Clark & Lake. Perh. f. of William(67) and John(25).

65 **WILLIAM**, Greenland, in 1671, ag. ±25, dep. 'ever since I came to my master Philip Lewis, which is 6 or 7 years ago.' Jury 1694. Coroner's j. 1694. Lists 52 pll, 57, 62, 326c, 330a (1667), 332b, 334a, 335a. Will proved 2 June 1707. He m. Elizabeth Hill, dau. of John of Durham, who mar. 2d John Avery(6). Ch: oldest s. **Samuel** and 'his brothers and sisters' unnamed in will, incl. likely **Wm.**(68) and **Daniel**. Of these names were m. in Greenland: 25 Jan. 1710-1 Samuel and Rebecca Fosket (Ficket?), 4 Dec. 1711 Daniel and Mary Bryant, 19 July 1717 Wm. and Rebecca Bryant.

66 **WILLIAM**, Damariscotta, see Davie(4).

67 **WILLIAM**, perh. s. of (64), Kennebec. List 161. Y. D. ix. 254.

68 **WILLIAM**, Piscataqua sailor, 1684-5. List 314. Likely s. of (65).

69 **ZACHARIAH, JOSHUA, GRACE, MARY**, in captivity in 1711 marked ·Casco-, have not yielded even an attract. hypoth. of their parentage. Presum. some Davis went back in the false peace not even reported in the casualties of 10 Aug. 1703. List 99, p. 92. See (51), (39). In Glouc. one Grace m. Wm. Burrage 11 Nov. 1723 and one Zachariah, s. of Wm., b. in 1719, presum. m. in 1741 Bathsheba Davis. A group of settlers in Friendship, Me., in 1760, are Wm. sen., Zachariah, Wm. jr., John. In Boston one Zachariah (unk. s. of Isaac or Lawrence?) had Samuel and Elizabeth 1691-1693. One Zachariah d. in Hampton 27 Dec. 1731, perh. f.-in-law of Samuel Batchelder(3). Et cet.

**DAVISON**, peculiar to Yorkshire.

1 ‡**DANIEL**(2), mercht. in Charlestown and Newbury, memb. B. Art. Co., major of Essex regt., m. 16 Dec. 1673 Abigail Cof-

fin(4). His will 18 Jan. 1717—11 Feb. 1717-18, names wife, s. Nicholas, grs. Daniel, 4 daus. Ch: **Abigail**, bp. 13 Feb. 1675-6, unm. 1717. **Joanna**, bp. 29 Apr. 1677, mar. John Lane. **Nicholas**, b. 16 May 1680. **Sarah**, b. 1 Feb. 1682, m. Stephen Dudley(3 jr.). **Daniel**, b. 23 May 1686. **Mary**, b. 21 May 1689, m. 22 Nov. 1710 Jacob Sheafe. **Peter**, b. 20 Oct. 1692.

2 ‡**NICHOLAS**, b. 1611. A typical Bay merchant, but bot the Pemaquid patent, came there and d. 1664. His grave was pointed out by the inhab. when his gt-grds. Abigail Fitch and Elizabeth Gorrod visited there. Home chiefly Charlestown, but 'of Pemaquid' 1658. His Pemaquid store books were evid. in court in 1810. Came over as agent of Gov. Craddock. His will 26 Mar. 1655—11 July 1664, named ch. of br. Jeremy, who had liv. in Lynn, Eng., and br. John, whereab. unkn., and other rel. M. Joanna Hodges alias Miller, ±65 in 1686, who d. 30 Oct. 1699. Whether she and her sis. or half-sis. Mary Anderson were Millers or Hodgeses has had consid. consid., espec. pp. 9-21 of Hodges Fam. of N. E., 1896, but more obviously they came of a double surnamed fam., using formally both or option. either. David Anderson, stepgrands. of the sis., acq. his Pemaquid interests by purch. The wid. m. 2d 6 Jan. 1674 Richard Kent jr. of Newb., but had only the two Davison ch: **Sarah**, b. 1647, m. 24 Mar. 1665 Hon. Joseph Lynde. 8 ch. **Daniel**, b. 9 Jan. 1650-1.

**DAY**, Dea, common in Mid. and So. Eng.
1 **ANTHONY**, b. ab. 1624-1627, worked about the mills in Exeter several yrs. ab. 1653. See Coe. At Glouc. he had 'contracted' to Susan Matchett in 1649, later at Ipsw. (marshal's deputy in 1660) and back to Glouc., where he d. 23 Apr. 1707 'aged 90,' and his wid. 10 Dec. 1717 'aged 93.' Besides the 7 ch. rec. 1657-1672, they had older: **Thomas**, b. ab. 1651, and presum. **Timothy**, soldier in Philip's War and father of
2 **ANTHONY**, grs. of (1), b. Glouc. 20 Feb. 1681-2, m. 20 Dec. 1701 Penelope Trafton, d. Glouc. 12 Jan. 1711-12; wid. m. 2d William Bracy(2). At least 2 ch: **Charity**, m. John Heard (Tristram) of Dover. +6 ch. **Elizabeth**, m. Ezekiel Wentworth (Gershom).
3 **JOSEPH**, br. of (2)? List 269c. M. Patience Hilton (William). 13 ch. 1735-6, all bap. at Wells, 1st one **Dorcas** rec. at Glouc. as b. at York 3 May 1713.
4 **SIMEON** (Dea), in 1666 with Edw. Rishworth wit. Wm. Dixon's will at York; in 1662 (Simon) swearing drunk; in 1659 (Symon Day), for disorder in the minister's house, ord. to pass through Wenham without stopping. List 47?

5 **THOMAS** (possibly Dew?), 1668 fighting with Hubertus Mattoon in Portsm.
6 **TIMOTHY**, br. of (2)?, member of crew capturing Ind. vessel in 1707. See Benj. Donnell. Wife Jane or Jean. Ch. rec. Glouc., incl. **Phebe**, b. at York 1706.

**Deacon**, John, at Penobscot 1630. List.

**Dealin**, see Dalling.

**DEANE**, name of 18 places all over Eng.
1 **JOHN**. (?Lists 267b, 96 p. 82). Liv. in house of Nathl. Hill, Oyster River, when k. by Indians (?1710). Dau. **Elizabeth**, m. Stephen Jenkins.
2 **THOMAS**, see Richard Scammon. N. E. Reg. 37.288.
3 **THOMAS** (Dane), a soldier looking for cattle a mile from Capt. Wheelwright's garrison, was taken by Ind. 13 May 1704. List 99. Prisoner 'Dean,' Wells, by Albany List 1710-11.

**DEARBORN**, formerly spoken Durbon.
1 **GODFREY**, weaver, came from Hannay, 3 m. from Bilsby, co. Lincoln, with Wheelwright, presum. the same bp. in Willoughby, 5 m. dist., 24 Sep. 1603, s. of William and Agnes (Hay). Gr.j. 1646, 1678, 1679. Lists 49, 54, 373, 374c, 375b, 376ab, 377, 378, 392b, 393a, 394, 396, 398. First wife, List 393a; m. 2d 25 Nov. 1662 wid. Dorothy Dalton(1), who outl. him. List 394. D. 4 Feb. 1685-6; will 14 Dec. 1680 names his sons but not 'my three daughters:' **Thomas**, bp. in Hannay 1 Nov. 1632. **Henry**, bp. in Hannay 22 Mar. 1633-4. **Esther**, m. Richard Shortridge. **Sarah**, b. ab. 1641, m. Thomas Nudd. **John**, b. ab. 1641.
2 **HENRY**(1), gr.j. 1678, 79, 83, 86. Lists 49, 52, 55b, 392b, 393b, 396, 397a. Wife Elizabeth Marrian. List 394. He d. 18 Jan. 1725. Ch: **John**, b. 10 Oct. 1666. **Samuel**, b. 27 Jan. 1670. Named in the charter of Kingston, he settled his sons there, but himself remained at No. Hampt., liv. 1746. Lists 399a, 400. 12 July 1694 Mercy Batchelder (3). 12 ch. **Elizabeth**, b. 13 Dec. 1672, d.y. **Sarah**, b. 9 Nov. 1675, m. Philemon Blake(1). **Abigail**, b. 1679, m. Samuel Palmer. **Elizabeth**, b. 19 Nov. 1681, m. Wm. Sanborn. **Henry**, b. 28 Oct. 1688, d. 26 Apr. 1756, fell dead in the road. Selectm. 1737, 1750. M. 1st 28 Oct. 1708 Hannah Dow(10), who d. 10 Feb. 1716 (5 ch.); 2d 12 Jan. 1721 Mary Robie, dau. of Samuel (1 ch.); 3d Esther (Fogg 6), wid. of -David- Fogg, who mar. 3d Joseph Wadleigh.
3 **JOHN**(1), had the homestead, gr.j. 1692, 95, 98. Lists 52, 392b, 396. Wife Mary (Ward), d. 14 Dec. 1725, he 14 Nov. 1731, 'good old John Dearborn.' Ch: **John**, b. 2 Sep. 1673, deacon, had the homestead. Wife Hannah (Dow 1), m. 10 Jan. 1695, d. 13 June 1733. He d. 19 Mar. 1746. 3 ch. **Thomas**, b.

22 June 1676, liv. in No. Hampton, d. 4 Apr. 1754. List 399a. Selectm. 1735. Wife Hulda (Smith) liv. 1754. 3 ch. **Mary**, b. 6 May 1678, m. Stephen Batchelder(3).

4 **DEA. JOHN**(2), ±26 in Aug. 1667, liv. on the S. G. Warner place, No. Hampt., m. 4 Nov. 1689 Abigail Batchelder(3), who d. 13 Nov. 1736. His will 22 May 1746, d. 22 Nov. 1750. Ch: **Deborah**, b. 8 Feb. 1690, m. Thomas Marston. **Jonathan**, b. 8 May 1691, sett. in Stratham, m. Hannah Tuck who d. 29 May 1738; he 29 Jan. 1779. 4 ch. **Elizabeth**, b. 31 Aug. 1692, mar. John Garland. **Esther**, b. 25 June 1694, mar. 1st Ebenezer Lovering, 2d William Norton. **Joseph**, b. 8 Feb. 1696, m. 27 Oct. 1719 Anna Dearborn (Samuel 5), d. 15 Jan. 1768; wid. d. 9 Oct. 1789. 7 ch. **Abigail**, b. 24 June 1700, mar. Benj. Cram. **Lydia**, b. 4 Apr. 1702, m. Jeremiah Sanborn. **Ruth**, b. 21 May 1705, mar. David Page. **Simon**, b. 31 July 1706, had the homestead, m. Sarah Marston. 12 ch., the youngest Maj. Gen. Henry. The Portland Argus for July 11, 1825, printed 1½ columns about 'The House of Dearborn,' listing the family connections in office; have recd. over $500,000 in salaries—more than any other family. **Benjamin**, b. 10 Nov. 1710, not in will.

5 **DEA. THOMAS**. Lists 49, 52, 62, 392b, 393b, 396. He m. 28 Dec. 1675 Hannah Colcord(1), who d. 17 July 1720. His will 10 Apr. 1710, d. 14 Apr. Ch: **Samuel**, b. 27 May 1676, d. 5 Feb. 1736-7. List 399a. He m. 16 Dec. 1698 Sarah Gove. Their 3 kn. ch. liv. in No. Hampt. and Greenland. **Ebenezer**, b. 3 Oct. 1679, Lieut., List 399a, d. 15 Mar. 1772; m. 7 Oct. 1703 Abigail Sanborn who d. 26 Feb. 1768. 9 ch. **Thomas**, b. 1681, m. Mary Garland, liv. at Hampt. Falls, later with s. Jacob at Old Orchard, Me. Wid. d. 1 Feb. 1749. 5 ch. **Jonathan**, Cornet, b. 18 Nov. 1686, m. 1st Mary Boulter(3), who d. 1 Apr. 1744, 2d Sarah Waite who d. 22 Oct. 1762; he d. 10 Sep. 1771. 7 ch.

Unident. Lists: Samuel 66, 68, Thos. jr. 66, 399a.

**Debeck**, James, east of Penobscot 1674. List 3.

**DECKER.** 1 John, Exeter 1672.—Coffin, Savage. Likely O. A. at Newbury 1678, ag. 32.

2 **JOHN**, Kit. Newington, Wiscasset, will prov. 1752 names 8 ch. bp. at Newington. Wife Sarah. Ch: **John**, b. Kit. 29 Mar. 1707, Wiscasset 1737, liv. 1787. **Sarah**, b. 10 May 1709, m. Clement Meserve. **Mary**, b. Kit. 1 Mar. 1710-1, m. John Hodsdon jr. **Hannah**, m. 1731 Hatevil Nutter 3d. **Elizabeth**, mar. Joseph Moody of Scarb. **Joseph**, these 6 bp. 30 Sep. 1716. Grst. at Wisc., perhaps misr. Capt. Joseph D. d. 17 Dec. 1742. **David**, bp. 4 Oct. 1719, liv. Portsm. Ch. **Abigail**, bp. 3 Feb. 1722-3, m. John Looe (Low?).

**DEERING**, Dearing. A magnif. search for the parentage of Roger(7), really making a textbook on English research, yields only a number of diverg. possib., altho his home and his wife's parentage were known beforehand. Altho widespread, it failed to ident. any one of the four others who came over.

1 **CLEMENT**(7), List 33, m. Joan Bray(2). From 1695 to 1708 she was a wid. lic. to keep tavern. Her will 20 June—22 Dec. 1707 names only three ch: **John**, b. 17 June 1680, sea captain. Lists 296-298. M. 12 Dec. 1705 Temperance Fernald(5). His widow 3 Apr. 1711 was gr. retailer's lic.; m. 2d Ebenezer Moore. Ch. **William**, b. 16 Sep. 1706, carver, m. Dorothy Mendum and Eunice Gunnison; **John**, b. 16 July 1710, m. Anna Dunn(3) and mov. to Falm. **Joanna**, b. 8 May 1687, m. Dominicus Jordan. **Miriam**, b. 22 Apr. 1692, liv. 1707.

2 **GEORGE** (Dearing), house carpenter at the Trelawny plant. 1634-37. Lists 21, 235. Settled at Blue Point, Scarb., liv. 1645. Wid. Elizabeth m. Jonas Bailey(6).

3 **GEORGE**, appar. a visitor at Kit. Point 1673-75. Me. Prov. & Ct. Rec. ii. 263,307.

4 **HENRY** (Dering), b. ab. 1638-9. He was at Salis. a lic. liquor dealer in Apr. 1664, innholder at Hampton 1665-67. In June 1671 he had hired Abraham Corbett's house and was just moving from Great Isl. to Str. Bk. Lists 312ce, 324, 326c, 330a, 331c, 87, 89, 90. Some time aft. his 2d mar. he rem. to Boston where he was prom. as a shopkeeper and in public affairs. There he was committed to prison in July 1689 for leading a riot— to overthrow Gov. Andros. Commissary General in Phips's Canada Exped. A man of high qualities, incl. resolute initiative, as stepfather-in-law he shared with Hon. Richard Martyn and Col. Mark Hunking the honor of founding the Wentworth political dynasty. He m. 1st at Salis. 8 June 1664 Mrs. Ann, wid. of Ralph Benning of Boston, 2d 15 Nov. 1676 Elizabeth (Mitchelson) Atkinson, wid. of Theodore(4), and was with her buried in one grave in 1717. Ch. by 1st w: **Ann**, b. Hampt. 31 May 1667, m. Nathl. Crynes, apothecary, of Boston; d. of smallpox 14 Dec. 1686. By 2d w. all rec. in Boston: **Elizabeth**, b. 18 July 1677, d.y. **Elizabeth**, b. 5 Jan. 1679, m. Boston 16 June 1709 William Welsteed, 1 son. **Mary**, twin, b. 18 May 1682, m. Boston 28 Apr. 1720 William Wilson, 1 dau. **Martha**, twin, d.y. **Henry**, b. 6 Oct. 1684, long a shopkeeper in Boston, descr. as a 'Gentleman famous for Liberty and Property,' d. 20 Oct. 1750; mar. 8 Feb. 1709 Elizabeth Packer (Thomas of Portsm.) 11 ch., of whom the oldest dau. Elizabeth m. Samuel Wentworth (Lieut. Gov. John.) See N. Y. G. & B. Rec. 52.40.

**5 HUMPHREY**, worsted comber and mill man, native of Old England, fort sold. at Saco 1696. List 248b. 'Of Winter Harbor,' husbandman, 31 Dec. 1717, selectm. Arundel 1719, 'now of Cape Porpus' June 1720. He mar. at Newb. 25 Dec. 1705 Sarah March (George), named in his will 13 Apr.—20 Oct. 1747, with ch: **Dorothy**, b. Newbury 2 Jan. 1706-7, mar. 1st Truman Powell, 2d Joseph Adams; liv. Arundel, 1771, ag. 64. **Mary**, b. Newb. 26 Jan. 1707-8, m. John Thomas. **Abigail**, m. David Hutchins. **Judith**, m. Andrew Lassell. **Elizabeth**, m. John Emmons. **Humphrey**, mar. Topsfield 23 Oct. 1738 Abigail Dwinell. Ch.

**5½ JOHN**, misreading of Veering.

**6 JOSEPH**(7), mariner, m. Mary Bray(2). Jury 1702. Lists 296-298. Adm. 7 Apr. 1719 to wid., who was liv. 1752. Ch: **Joseph**, b. 28 May 1698, d.y. **Bray**, b. 18 Oct. 1701. List 298. Fisherman, officer in Louisburg exped. M. Elizabeth Flye(1). 1 dau. **Clement**, b. 10 Nov. 1704, m. (int. 18 Dec. 1731) Miriam Hutchins (Benjamin). 6 ch. rec. **William**, b. 17 Sep. 1708, coaster, m. (int. 26 Oct. 1732) Mary Pine, dau. of Charles who came from Eng. to Marblehead by 1717, to Scarb. 1720. Murd. by her hus., he was sentenced to death. Orig. warrant returns that aft. being twice reprieved by Gov. Shirley, he broke jail where he was kept in irons on the night follow. 15 Sep. 1749, and though fresh pursued was not recovered. His escape was attributed to his disting. cous. Pepperell. 7 ch. **John**, d.s.p. at Damariscotta. Adm. 1743 to br. Clement.

**7 ROGER**, shipwright, from Townstall, Dartmouth, Eng. Suits in the Dartmouth courts up to 1663 show that he was a contracting shipbuilder there bef. coming to the Piscataqua, but he was also a mariner. Here he was called 'Mato Dearing' in 1665; and in the probate papers in Dartmouth, 20 May 1679, when his wid. was about to come over, he is termed mariner. He could build here, sail across, and sell in Dartmouth. Auto. documents show him here with John Jackson 4 Nov. 1663 and 19 Nov. 1665, and here in 1667. He was taxed in Townstall, Dartmouth, 1649-63 and 1671-72. Over here, 1 July 1673, he was in court for not going home to his wife. Lists 14, 286. Adm. gr. here to s. Roger 4 July 1676. He m. 30 Aug. 1647 Joane Palmer, whose parents, Clement and Sarah (Pettigrew), both left wills. Three yrs. aft. his death, her br.-in-law Jackson bro. her over, with Sarah and Joseph. Here she kept tav. on Kit. Point, both bef. and aft. m. William Crafts, and aft. his death. She liv. until ab. 1714, taken care of by her dau. Sarah for 14 yrs. Ch: **Roger**, bp. 2 Oct. 1648. **Joane**, named in her grfr's will 12 Dec. 1656, giving her the house aft. her mother's

death; d. unm., buried in Townstall 3 Apr. 1683. **Jonathan**, bp. 22 Sep. 1651, either d.y. or is misr. of Joane. **Clement**, bp. 16 Feb. 1653-4. **Johanna**, mar. in Kit. bef. 1677 Joseph Couch(2). **Sarah**, b. 9 Jan. 1656-7, m. Dennis Hicks. **Thomas**, bp. 4 Nov. 1659. **Jezreel**, bp. 29 Dec. 1662, bur. 24 Feb. 1662-3. **John**, b. ab. 1673, adm. gr. to his mo. Joane Crafts 23 Nov. 1691. **Joseph**, bp. ab. 1673.

**8 *ROGER**(7), shipwright, here by 1670. Jury 1674, gr.j. 1675, 78, 96, 97, 1702, Kit. auditing com. 1696-7. His w. Mary, b. 1649, outliv. him. Will 14 Feb.—1 Apr. 1718, names 4 ch., but not those who recd. 'part of my estate' before. Ch: **Sarah**, m. Robert Mitchell. **Roger**, Capt., Esq., b. ab. 1678, shipwright. Lists 296-298, 239b. Marrying Sarah Jordan (Dominicus), he bot in the other heirs to the famous Nonsuch farm, Scarb., and rem. there in 1716. At the outbreak of the Three Years War, 26 June 1723, the Ind. k. his wife and capt. her young cous., Tho. Jordan, her niece Mary Scammon, and a boy, John Hunnewell. Abandoning Scarb. in sorrow, he was 'of Portsmouth' in 1725, 'of Newcastle' in 1727, but later returned and became the leading citizen of the town, captain of the train band, J. P., and often Dep. to the Genl. Ct. He had been Lieut. at Kit. and was first selectm. after Scarb. was reorganized in 1720 and on his return in 1728. Having never had ch., his will, 3 Nov. 1741 —12 Jan. 1741-2, gave his large est. to his 2d w. Elizabeth (Litton) Skillings, mar. 16 Jan. 1723-4, except sums to the Scarb. church and 'the religious industrious poor of the town.' **Clement**, b. ab. 1680, m. 25 Sep. 1701 Elizabeth Fernald(5). They lived on the homestead. He d. in 1742, she 2 June 1745. 4 ch. [Joanna, mar. 25 Nov. 1700 Ebenezer Moore.] [Mary, mar. 12 June 1701 Tobias Fernald(5).] **Martha**, m. 5 Jan. 1708-9 Wm. Rackleff. **Margery**, b. 1689, m. Samuel Scammon (Humphrey).

**9 THOMAS**(7), shipwright. In 1678 was an apprent. with his uncle Jezreel Butcher, poss. m. in Dartmouth 29 June 1682 Hannah Vine. First seen over here on his marriage (March Court 1688). Wife Elizabeth, ±51 in 1720, dep. conc. John Moore of Spruce Creek 34 yrs. ago. Const. 1693-4, gr.j. 1694. Adm. 1 Oct. 1723 to wid. Elizabeth; her will 28 July—20 Sep. 1737. Ch: **Thomas**, b. 15 June 1692, d. bef. father s.p. **John**, b. 2 Apr. 1695. In 1719 he was at St. Johns, Newf., master of the sloop -Prosperous- of Piscataqua. Adm. to wid. Mary 12 May 1725. M. 22 Oct. 1719 Mary Carpenter(5), who m. 2d 17 Mar. 1729-30 Capt. Stephen Seavey (Wm.). 3 ch., of whom only one lived, John, m. Eunice Spinney, and lived in Saco and Paris, Me. **Roger**, b. 1 Jan. 1698, mariner, mar. by 1726 Martha Lydston (John). Only ch. **John,**

shipwright, mar. Miriam Boothby 28 Dec. 1754, both living 1764. **Margaret**, b. 2 Jan. 1701, m. Thomas Clear(1), wid. in 1739. **Sarah**, m. by 1727 Francis Deed of Kit., mariner. Ch. **Elizabeth**, m. 1st 18 Apr. 1727 Samuel Reeves of Kit., mariner, 2nd (int. 4 Sep. 1731) Samuel Moore, 3d by 1739 Benj. Welch of No. Yarmouth.

**DELACROY**, Peter, in 1659 sued Thomas Nichols in Me. Ct. In 1659 Pierre La Croix ack. judgment to Nicholas Shapleigh.

**Delaha**, John, Isles of Shoals 1706. See N. E. Reg. 35.249.

**Delano**, Philip, Piscataqua 1697. List 68.

**Delton**(?), William, wit. Hilton to Yeales, 1682. Y. D. iv.

**Delves**, John, 'now liv. in Portsm.', P. A. to Mr. Thos. Winter. Capt. Delves hired the old Cutt warehouse.

**DEMERITT** (Demrey), **Eli**, Jerseyman, had town gr. from Dover 11 Apr. 1694, soldier in 1712. Lists 368ab (358b?). Living 1745. Wife Hope, grdau. of Wm. Reynolds. Ch: **Eli**, b. 1 Mar. 1696, many yrs. selectm. of Dover and Madbury. List 368b. Will 10 Jan. 1758—5 May 1774. Wife Tabitha Pitman. 3 ch. **John**, b. 19 June 1698, m. 1 Jan. 1724-5 Margaret Bussy(2). Will 15 Feb.—13 Oct. 1773 names w. Margaret and 7 ch. **Job**, b. 29 Mar. 1705, m. Mary Bussy(2), d. 7 Aug. 1772. 6 ch. **Benjamin**, b. 29 Nov. 1708, liv. 1736.

**Demashaw**, see Shaw.

**Deming**, see Dennen.

**DENBO**, Denbow, Denmore, Dinsmore.

1 **SALATHIEL**, b. ab. 1642, d. bef. 1690. Our Denbo geneal. starts with a plausible hypothesis (Ancestry of Lydia Harmon, Davis, 1924, pp. 26-28), and ends with several too implaus. to print. It is cert. that Salathiel Denbo, 38 in 1680, m. a Roberts (who next m. Wm. Graves), and had at least 3 ch., Salathiel, Richard and Peter, of whom Richard, by a Quaker wid. b. by 1674, had ch., and the other two in old age were town charges. No less than five mar. records of Salathiels in that or poss. the next generation, are better left a snarl: 1. Salathiel (Denbow) and wid. Rachel Peavey of Newington 19 Dec. 1720, she b. by ab. 1670. 2. Salathiel (Dinbo), blacksm., and widow Mary (Drisco) Sawyer, by 1732. 3. Salathiel (Denmore) of Fairfield, Conn., and Ruth Rumsey, m. by 1734, she bp. 1709. 4. Salathiel (Denmore) and Mary Hill, both of Durham, m. in Newington 10 Sep. 1740. 5. Salathiel (Denmore) m. Jane Hambleton at Boston 26 July 1750, presum. the same that m. Wm. Fitzgerald 26 Dec. 1751. The first Salathiel was taxed 1666, 1669, 1677, last appear. in his aut. (a printed initial) 26 Dec. 1682. His successor last appears in his petn. 1696. The w. appears not at all with either of 3 husbands, Sias, Denbo, Graves. Lists 356j, 365, 366, 359a. Ch: **Salathiel**, was a pensioned soldier; thigh broken and skull fractured in a Canadian exped., the Province helped him in 1712, 1717, 1730; a town charge in 1751. In 1734 he sold his homestead and common rights, with reserv. for life, to Francis Drew, cordwainer, and Joseph Drew. He rec. no gr. that yr., but in 1737 was given a quarter share. He likely had earlier or later wives than the wid. Peavey, 1720-1724, and poss. ch. **Richard** (Denbo), m. in 1705 the Quakeress preacher, Mary, wid. of Joseph Bunker, who dep. 27 Jan. 1756, ag. 82 and upwards, that ab. 75 yrs. ago she liv. with John Meader. He was a helpful man: in 1719 accused of helping John Davis break jail, in 1726 endorsed for John Sias, jr., in 1740 was bail for Nathaniel, in 1742 bail for Salathiel the blacksm. Lists 368b, 369. Liv. 1754. He deeded his land to his sons Clement and Ichabod. Clement, who sold his homestead in 1764, was sued in N. H. ct. in 1742 for a beaver hat bot in Fairfield, Conn. One Salathiel was of Fairfield in 1734, and Mary Denbo m. there 24 Feb. 1754 Jabez Cable. Ichabod d. in Durham 20 July 1806, ag. 86 and 11 mos.; was prisoner in Canada in the last Fr. and Ind. war and escaped. Other grch. of the emigrant were: one or more Salathiels, one a scamp blacksm., wife Mary (Drisco) in 1732-1741, arrested for passing counterfeits in 1742, absconded. Cornelius, in 1771 a dep. sheriff indicted for stripping him of his clothes, 4th Sergeant (Denbo) in the Revolution, was presum. Cornelius Drisco's grson. Nathaniel, soldier in Dummer's War, pub. to Mary Smith of York 22 Nov. 1729, in prison for debt the same yr., in 1741 a mariner of Portsm., late of Durham. One Nathaniel of Durham in 1763 was accu. by Joanna Davis, his bail Clement (Denbo). Samuel, 1754, of Durham, blacksm., was sued by Salathiel on a note. Abigail, m. John Willey 3d 27 Feb. 1728-9 In 1740 John Willey jr., was bondsman for Nathaniel. John Wille, millwright, was bail for Salathiel Denbo jr., and John Sias jr., in 1742. **Peter**, taken captive 18 July 1694, when his stepf. was wounded, was in Canada several yrs. Laborer, sold his lands, a town charge in 1751. Lists 99, 368b, 369. No indic. of even illeg. ch.

2 **WILLIAM** (Denbo?, Denio?). List 15.

**DENHAM**, name of 3 places in Suff. and Bucks. See also Dunham.

**ALEXANDER**, ±26 in 1667, wit. in Hampt. 1660. Town herdsman in 1665. Bot land in partn. with Mark Roberts, and in partn. with Eleazer Elkins. In 1673 deputy for the

Marshal of Norfolk Co. List 396. M. 24 Dec. 1677 Elizabeth (Sleeper) Perkins, who mar. 3d Richard Smith of Salis. See Hoyt. Ch: **Sarah**, b. 9 Oct. 1678. **Abial**, b. 20 Nov. 1680. **DENIFORD, Walter**, shipwright, had cond. gr. in Kit. 16 May 1694, sold 1700. By 1703 he was located (through wife Joan?) on Broad Cove, Spruce Creek. Lists 290, 291, 296-8. Deeded homestead to grson William Hammet, cordwainer, who in 1743 had wife Margaret. Kn. ch: **Elizabeth**, mar. 1 Jan. 1716-7 Thomas Hammet from Shadwell, Middlesex, Eng.

**Denlo**, William, Pemaquid, see Denbo.

**DENMARK**, presum. sprung from a Danish emigrant to the British Isles.

1 **JAMES**(2), soldier under Capt. John Hill 1693-4. Lists 267b, 268a, 269b. M. 1 Apr. 1694 Elizabeth (Barrett) Littlefield(3). They sold the Barrett homestead in Wells in 1698 and moved to Bost. She liv. some yrs. with her dau. by 1st husb., Leah Gorham, in Bristol, R. I., where one Elizabeth Denmark was pub. to Christopher Greene 20 Aug. 1721. A dep. in 1728 test. that the mother kept the name Denmark till her death. James Denmark's town gr. in Wells 1694 was sold in 1748 by Peter and Elizabeth (Denmark) Rich. See Elizabeth(2). Ch: **Lydia**, b. 27 Feb. 1694-5, presum. serv. of Rev. Peter Thatcher of Milton, bp. in 1708, disciplined in 1717. **Mary**, b. Bost. 22 Jan. 1704. Also, by an earlier wife(?) **Elizabeth**(?).

2 **PATRICK**, ±40 in 1676, taxed in Dover 1662 (perh. in 1657 as Patrick the Scot), and at Oyster Riv. 1663-66. Rem. to Saco Falls, where in 1686 he petn. Andros for a land gr. to provide for his 'great charge of children.' But in 1676 he had sold land at Small Point, Kennebec, to James Middleton, who was selling it again. Lists 356a, 364, 365, 47, 236. Wife Hannah or Ann. Ch. presum. include: **Patrick**, b. 8 Apr. 1664 at Oyster Riv., in 1686 petn. for land at Saco which he had fenced and built upon for three yrs. Perhaps younger ch. in this list were his. **James**, b. 13 Mar. 1665-6 at Oyster Riv. **John**, b. 14 Oct. 1667 at Saco, bur. 12 Nov. 1669. **Bridget**, serv. maid of Duncan Campbell in Bost., convicted of accidental manslaughter by drowning Rice Griffin in the dock 10 Apr. 1691, and accu. in Dec. 1691 of stealing a stone gold ring from Mrs. Margaret Thacher of Bost. **Elizabeth**. The Elizabethan geneal. of this name is baffling. Perh. the foll. distribution is least impossible: Elizabeth of Boston (2) had bast. b. 11 Sep. 1697. Elizabeth (Barrett) pub. in Bristol in 1721 did not marry. Elizabeth(1) at Wells had a child by James Burnham, late soldier there, Oct. Ct. 1710; m. 1st 16 May 1712 Robert Sinclair (2 ch. bp.); 2d 25

Apr. 1718 Peter Rich, (one ch. bp. 17 Apr. 1725-6.) His will 1751—1760.

**DENNEN**, Deming.

**NICHOLAS**, b. ab. 1645, lived at New Harbor, where he bot Stage Point. Lists 15, 124. A refugee from the Ind., he was at Glouc. by 1697, d. there 9 June 1725, ag. ±80. He mar. Eme Brown(15), 2d 25 Nov. 1697 Sarah Paine. Ch., by Richard Pearce's dep. 1733: **Agnes**, m. 1st one Barrett, 2d at Glouc. 25 Nov. 1697 Richard Dolever. **Eme**, m. 21 Jan. 1696-7 Eleazer Elwell of Glouc. **Elizabeth**, m. 1st one Paine, 2d at Glouc. 29 Oct. 1733 William Hoard of Ipsw. **Nicholas**, m. 7 Dec. 1699 Elizabeth Davis, liv. Glouc. 1733. 5 ch. rec. 1703-1717. **Mary**, m. 1st 7 Mar. 1700 Thomas Day, who was lost at Isle of Sables with her br. George; 2d at Glouc. 5 Feb. 1722-3 Ebenezer Stevens. **William**, m. at Glouc. 5 Dec. 1706 Hannah Paine, both liv. Marb. Jan. 1733-4. 4 ch. rec. **George**, b. 1686, mar. at Glouc. 30 Mar. 1708 Hannah Dike, lost at Isle of Sables ab. mid. of Aug. 1716. 6 ch. rec. Unexp: Wm., pub. 26 Sep. 1724 to Mary Reading, m. 1 Dec. 1726 Susannah Galloway of Ipswich, drowned at Cape Sable 1729.

**DENNETT**, Demick. One Alexander Dennet was in Dorchester 1625, one John Dennett of Woodman Court, Sussex, in 1639.

1 **ALEXANDER**(3), came with br. (4), two house carpenters. May have moved across the river out of Cranfield's reach. By trad. d. on Great Island, presum. there for safety from Ind. Jury 1695, 1698. Lists 331ac, 52, 335a, 330d. Adm. to John(4), inv. 6 July 1698. W. unnamed church mem. List 331c, not in 335a. Ch. not John's presum. his: **Alexander**. **Sarah**, lived with Hon. Richard Martyn 1676, perh. m. Wm. Ham whose son Samuel in 1731 called John and Ephraim Dennett kinsmen. **William** (Denick). List 318b. **Grace**, joined ch. 16 Mar. 1693, mar. James Spinney.

2 **ALEXANDER**(1), b. years earlier than '1670,' perh. in Eng., yeoman and house carpenter, taxed Ports. 1681, lived on both sides of the Piscataqua. Constable Kit. 1684, 1686. Gr.j. Me. 1689, 1690, 1692, 1693; Gr.j. N. H. 1697. Lists 329, 296-298, 67, 337, 339. He mar. Mehitable Tetherly, b. 1663, List 331c; 2d 2 Dec. 1728 Esther (Mason) wid. of John Cross(8), who m. 12 Dec. 1736 Anthony Rowe. Will 26 Dec. 1729—26 June 1733 names 7 ch: **Mehitable** Stuart. **Elizabeth**, m. 1709-10 Enoch Sanborn of Hampt. Falls. **Ebenezer**, b. ab. 1692, mar. 10 June 1714 Abigail Hill (Samuel). List 291. 7 ch. rec. Kit. **Samuel**, called n. c. m. in fr's will, presum. d. bef. 1739 when Ebenezer, Moses, Sarah and Susannah deeded five-sevenths of

their mother's inheritance. **Oliver**, presum., otherw. unk., rated to New Meet. Ho., Portsmouth, 1717. **Moses**, had homestead, mar. 13 Feb. 1723-4 Lydia Fernald (Tho. 3). Will 25 Nov. 1745—d. 15 July 1749. 4 ch. The Buxton Dennett trad. unreconciled. **Sarah**, m. 13 Oct. 1720 Joshua Weymouth. **Susannah**, m. 17 Nov. 1724 Joshua Downing(2).

3 **JOHN**, 'Sen.' in List 331b. Hon. Mark Dennett, b. 1786, rec. the tradition that the emigrants were the two brothers, Alexander and John, but if their f. did not come with them he soon followed. Alexander is not named in this list, his f. must have been liv. with him. The only subscriber for the minister, 1658-1671, was John, 1671, List 326c. John Dennett, Portsm., freeman 1672. Gr.j. 1679. 'Denet Sen Wife' at the end of Rev. Joshua Moody's list of the early members is more lik. the aged mother, come up in the minister's memory, than a repetition of Alexander's w. List 331c. Ch: **Alexander. John**, b. 1646.

4 *****JOHN**(3), housewright, here by 1668, became highly trusted citizen of Portsm. Constable 1689, surveyor 1692, gr.j. 1692, foreman 1699, Deputy 1702. He was selectm. almost const. from 1697 until he d., 5 May 1709, aet. 63. (grst.) Lists 331abc, 335a (p. 173), 324, 329, 330d, 49, 52, 57, 316, 324. Will 17 Mar. 1708-9 names w. Amy, (see Sarah 1), (Lists 331c, 335a), and ch: **John**, b. 15 Dec. 1675, m. 5 Feb. 1701-2 Mary (Adams 5) wid. of Alexander Shapleigh. Lists 331c, 296, 297. Held town office in Kit. 1707-1729. In 1720 his house was a garrison. Will 28 Mar. 1738, d. 18 Nov. 1742. Large legacy to Sarah Hooper is unexp. In 1717 he called James Fernald kinsman. 5 ch. **Amy**, b. 9 Apr. 1679, m. John Adams(5). **Joseph**, b. 19 July 1681, cooper, Portsm., m. 24 June 1703 Elizabeth Meed; adm. 3 Dec. 1714 to wid. who m. 23 Dec. 1718 Samuel Hewey from Coleraine, co. Derry, Ireland. 5 ch. of whom one d. early: Elizabeth, Hannah, Amy, Joseph, bp. 29 July 1711, Nicholas, bp. 14 Dec. 1712. ‡*****Ephraim**, b. 2 Aug. 1689. Portsm. selectm. 1715-1718. Rep. 1718-1728, Councillor 1732. Lists 337, 339. Adm. 29 Apr. 1741 to wid. Catherine, who m. one Wise by 1768. 7 ch. rec.

**DENNIS**, common Cornw. to Yorks., an ancient landed fam. of Devon.

1 **DAVID**. List 52. 168--.

2 **(DENY?** List 98.)

3 **GEORGE**, wit. with Cleeve, 1640.

4 **JOHN**, 1675. Doc. Hist. vi. 84.

5 **JOSEPH**, Eliot wit. 1707. Y. D. 7:159.

6 **LAWRENCE**, J. P. 1680-1689, Arrowsic. Deed from Ind., 3 Aug. 1665, shown to Indians in 1726. In 1685, Aug. 3, he and John Bish secured an Ind. deed for Tuessic Neck. May have had two wives, as Law-

rence wrote his sister 'my father had Tuessic with -my- mother,' app. dau. of Robert and Mary Morgan. Lists 182, 13, 16-18, 186-189. Fled to Beverly 1689. In 1690 his wife was at the point of death from small pox, his three sons gone on the Canada exped., and he was asking pay for his cattle eaten by Maj. Church's army; was voted £30 in 1700: He lived in Bev. until death. Neighbors dep. he had 5 sons all supp. to have d.s.p. Kn. ch: **James**, ±26 1684. Lists 18, 189. **William**. Lists 18, 189. **John**, was pilot for Church. **Lawrence**, List 189, liv. 1717 in Charleston, S. C. **Mary**, m. Thomas Pitman of Manchester, mariner, both liv. 1729. Ch.

7 **PETER**, b. ±1670, List 238b. French boy.

8 **THOMAS**, 1650. Me. P. & C. i. 145.

9 **THOMAS**, b. ab. 1638, joiner, of Portsm. in 1663 bot house and land in Ipsw. from Wm. Searle; in 1664 bot land and in 1668 house at Str. Bk. Jury 1667. By 1669 had rem. to Ipsw., having m. 26 Oct. 1668 Wm. Searle's wid. Grace. In 1678 his tenant in Portsm. was Thomas Ladbrook. Lists 323, 326b, 356b. 1683 Portsm. tax abated. Wife Grace bur. Ipsw. 26 Oct. 1686 (±50, grst); he d. there 23 May 1706, ±68, (grst), leav. wid. Sarah who m. (int. 7 Dec. 1706) Capt. John How of Topsfield. Ch: **Thomas**, b. 30 Nov. 1669, d. 23 Jan. 1702-3. 1 son rec. Wid. Elizabeth presum. the one who m. (int. 6 Oct. 1705) Francis Sawyer of Wells. **John**, b. 22 Sep. 1672, m. 1st 31 Aug. 1699 Lydia White, who d. 10 June 1712; 2d (int. 21 June 1713) wid. Sarah Ward. Ch. **Elizabeth**, m. (ints. 23 July 1704) Ebenezer Hovey.

**Dennison**, Alexander and Elizabeth, had dau. **Abiah**, b. 20 Nov. 1680.—Hampt. Rec.

**DENTT**, **Abraham**, mar. in Portsm. 5 Sep. 1715 Sarah (Partridge) Langbridge, wid. of John. List 339. Ch: **John** and **Abraham**. Widow Dent taxed 1723, m. 3d 28 Oct. 1731 Edmund McBridge of Denfeniham, Ire.

**DERBY**. 1 **Joseph**, and Sarah Hodsdon, Me. Ct. Apr. 1706.

2 **ROBERT**, of Lancaster, 1724-1727. See Arthur Wormstall.

3 **THOMAS**, Falm. 1680. List 225a.

4 **WILLIAM**, Boston soldier at Scarb. 1676. Lists 236, 237b.

**DERMER**. 1 **Edward**, Kit. wit. 1661. Y. D. x. 15.

2 **CAPT. THOMAS**, explorer, 1615-1620. See Burrage -Beg. of Colonial Maine-. 138.

3 **THOMAS** (Dermon?), in a row, Piscataqua 1664; (Dermer), wit. to Wm. Lernon's nunc. will 1659.—N. H. Ct. Files i. 11. Dermit (?illeg.), William, with Wannerton at Piscataqua 1633. Gibbin's letter. List 41.

**DERRY**. 1 **James**, and John, were both taxed at Oyster Riv. 1681, both working about 1685 for Capt. John Gerrish, both had town grants 1693-94. James was jurym. 1695, d.

soon. The more plausible interp. of confus. deeds is that James was childless and no collat. heirs appeared; that Ezekiel Pitman with ch. by an unkn. wife m. the wid. Elizabeth and d. bef. 1701; that Francis Pitman sold his own place and liv. on Ezekiel's place with the widow; that she aft. 1709 m. John Pinder. Francis Pitman sold James Derry's land, and after changing hands that title was held in 1719 by Samuel Perkins and John Munsey, who liv. on it. F. P.'s title was undiscl. until 19 Feb. 1734-5, when a defective deed to him from Nathaniel Meader was recorded, dated 7 Apr. 1701, reciting a deed to Meader from Elizabeth Pitman, wid. A few mos. later a specul. obtained Elizabeth Pinder's q.c. and immed. negot. a release to Samuel Perkins and John Munsey jointly. Both these men had quieted the demands of Ezekiel Pitman's s. William, no wife ment., in 1721 and 1722.

2 **JOHN**, see James; see List 359a. Lists 359b, 52, 57, 62, 94. In the 1694 massacre his house was burned and most of ch. killed; self, wife Deliverance and one son carried capt. He d.; she retd, and 18 May 1697 was gr. adm., the ct. appar. thinking there were two heirs, no son. Six mos. later she had m. Nathaniel Pitman, and by Jan. 1698-9 she supp. her ch. all dead. Son John, List 99, app. was dead by 22 Sep. 1701.

3 **RICHARD**, in crew of -The Katharine- 1701.

**DEVERSON. 1 Thomas**, 1676, one of crew of -The Black Cock-, shipped 8 Sep. 1675, ordered back to get their wages in English court; 1684 in the ketch -Amity-. 1692 bot in Portsm., jury 1695. Lists 52, 62, 330d, 334b, 335a, 337. D. Nov. 1704, adm. to wid. Sarah (Clark 8), who was reared by her aunt Waterhouse. List 335a. By 1707 she m. one Ward, afterw. calling herself Deverson alias Ward; in 1717 'widow Deverson' was rated to the Old Meet. Ho. Adm. to s. John 22 May 1732. Ch: **Elizabeth**, b. 1684, m. Thomas Beck(4 jr.). **Sarah**, mar. 1st by 1706 Ebenezer Morse, 2d Walter Steward, both liv. Portsm. 1743. **Joanna**, unm., 'being a cripple.' **Mary**, m. 25 Feb. 1713-4 Joseph Mead. **John**, joiner, signed Davidson, m. 24 Sep. 1719 Deborah Cotton(1); adm. 1751 to creditors. 5 ch. bp.

2 **WILLIAM**. List 98. Likelier Thomas.

**Devine**, John. Y. D. iii. 23. See Veering.

**DEW**, Due.

1 **JOHN**, seaman of Pisc. Riv., in 1672 wit. with Samuel Keais. Will May—June 1674, sole benef. friend Robt. Rowsley.

2 **MARY**, Portsm. wit. 1661 conc. Goody Abbot and Goody Cate's baby's death.

3 **ROGER**, ±23 in 1677, Isl. Shoals, List 306c.

4 **THOMAS**, shipwright, sometimes went ship's carpenter. Owned house and wharf at Str. Bk. Lists 326c, 331b. M. 1663 Sarah Wall from Hampt., who mar. ab. 1679 John Baker(3). Among 'many ch:' **Elizabeth**, b. 1670, m. ab. 1696 Wm. Redford; 2d 10 July 1701 (thereby causing Dr. Richard Mills to bring breach of promise suit) Richard Wibird. After she became a grand dame, the usual detract. reaction was handed down even to Brewster's day, that herself, not her mother, once used to come in from Hampt. peddling vegetables.

**DIAMOND**, Dimond, Dyamont. Dev.-Som.

1 **ISRAEL**, Pemaquid 4 Aug. 1680, master of the ketch -Cumberland-, and John Rashly, held for the drowning of Samuel Collins(13). Of Bost. 1690 was about to m. Abiell Prowse of Amesb. See Hoyt's Salis. 131.

2 **JOHN**, of Stoke Gabriel, Devon, b. 1553. Popham Colony 1607. List 6.

3 **JOHN**, from Dartmouth, Eng., where he m. 2 June 1635 at St. Petrox, Grace Sammon, ment. here in 1652. In 1660 one Walter Winser from Hemick (Hennock), Devon, was apprent. to him. He was a ropemaker, but here built shallops and with his sons carried on fishing at Isl. of Shoals. In 1651 he bot by an imperfect deed a house and undescribed land at Crooked Lane, Kit.; the land he claimed was cut down by Thomas Withers and by town grts. to Dennis Downing, Richard Abbott, Wm. Leighton. Jury 1651, gr.j. 1653, selectm. 1659, clerk of the writs 1663. Lists 282, 24, 25, 79. Poss. a synthetic date, adm. on his est. is said to have been gr. to s. John 9 July 1667; but his wife surv. him. In that court 'John Dyamont' was a juryman. Ch: John, b. ab. 1639. *Thomas, Ens., Capt., bp. 30 Aug. 1641 at St. Petrox, Dartmouth. Settled on Star Isl., on the N. H. side of the Shoals, where he m. the innholder's wid. and cont. the bus., lic. 1685-1698. Rep. 1693. Lists 59, 95, 98, 307b, 308a, 309. Will 14 July 1707—27 Apr. 1708, shows no ch. M. 1st Mary, widow of James Weymouth, 2d (int. 19 Apr. 1707) Jane Gaines, who m. 2d (int. 11 Mar. 1709) Jonathan Wade. Andrew, J.P., b. ab. 1642, as a boy was in ct. for aggress., early at Smuttinose, where his w., her dau. and both hus. sold without license. Fishing master in partn. with Henry Mains. In 1673 he and his partn. had bot a house at Ipsw. and in 1681 he was providing a seat in the meetingho. for his wife. Constab. of Smuttinose 1670, selectman 1679, Com.t.e.s.c. 1685, J.P. 1690. Lists 95, 305a, 307b, 308a. The two bros., many yrs. leading fishing masters at the Shoals, were both childless by two wives. M. ab. 1668 Joan, b. ab. 1629, wid. of Roger

Grant; 2d at Marb. 24 July 1705 Elizabeth Elliot, who m. 2d (int. 5 Apr. 1707) Rev. Theophilus Cotton(5), later of Hampt. Falls, and d. 13 Oct. 1710 from a fall off horseback, ag. 45. Mr. Cotton bot his house from his sis. Grace and Peter Lewis. **Grace,** m. Peter Lewis.

**4 JOHN**(3), b. ab. 1639, eldest son. Pere et fils remain undist. A theory is that the 1667 juryman was the son and that he, deeming himself sole heir, undertook to dist. his father's est. among his brothers. Y. D. ii. 113, 80. He had laid out to him. in 1674, 40¾ a. next S. E. of Thos. Withers, 51 rods on the river. This became the Woodman-Moore ferry place, conveyed as 40 a., but with abuttors never named. William's wid. was obliged to repurchase their farm from the Downings. In 1685 John was shoreman of a fishing company on Pickering's island. Gr.j., foreman, 1688. Lists 298 p. 35, 313b, 30. Inv. 29 Aug. 1693, adm. 30 Aug. to Nathl. Raynes and John Woodman. His wife, a dau. of Capt. Francis Raynes, app. d. first. Ch: **Mary,** m. John Spinney, 2d Lieut. Jeremiah Burnham(2). **John,** Boston, m. 22 Aug. 1709 Mary Wilson. **Thomas,** Boston, mar. 2 Jan. 1706 Ann Webster. Ch. **William,** Boston, adm. to bro. John 11 May 1722.

**5 WILLIAM**(3), juryman 1672, gr.j. 1673. List 306c. Adm. 1 Apr. 1679 to wid. Joan, who mar. 2d Edward Carter(2), 3d, aft. 22 Dec. 1691, James Blagdon. His wid. by 1685 was Joan Carter of Gt. Isl., midwife. Jane Catter, ±40 in 1683 wit. ab. Goody Jones, witch. Liv. wid. 1702. Y. D. vi. 146. Ch: **John,** List 319, liv. 1691, d.s.p. before his mother; app. the one who came passenger from Bost. to Wells in time to be tortured to death June 1702. **Grace,** m. Richard Tomlin, 2d Richard Tucker. **Margaret,** m. Sylvanus Tripe.

**DICER, William,** from Salem, was in Saco in June 1680, then ord. to remove the old man and his fam. he had brot from Salem or secure the town; bot farm on west side of riv. in 1686. Constable 1688. Lists 33, 249. Rem. to Bost. where his 1st w. Elizabeth (Austin), m. Salem 20 Nov. 1664, was bur. 9 Feb. 1704; m. 2d Boston 28 June 1706 Mary Blewet, and d. there 11 Dec. 1707 nigh 80. Ch. rec. Salem: **Elizabeth,** b. 2 July 1667, m. Richard Tarr of Cape Ann. **Honor,** b. 2 Apr. 1673, petn. court to ord. John Bowden to supp. his ch.; m. 1st Joseph James, 2d Boston 17 Oct. 1705 David Ridley. Her dau. Rebecca, b. Boston, 1 July 1706, mar. there 1st (int. 13 Oct. 1729) John Langdon, 2d (int. 14 Jan. 1734) John Fling, and in 1743 sold ½ her grfr's 100 a. in Biddeford.

**DICKINSON. 1 John** (Diginson), Kittery Point 1701.

**2 THOMAS,** murdered in 1668 at Concord, N. H., by a drunken Indian, whom the Indians executed. List 357a.

**Dicurows(?),** Richard, Pemaquid garrison 1689. List 126.

**DILL, Dyll. See Creber.**

**1 DANIEL,** York, b. ab. 1628-1633 by sev. dep., was a York wit. in 1660 and serv. to Alexander Maxwell ab. 1662. He bot land from Roland Young in 1666 and had town grants 1680 and 1699. List 31. In 1678 he was drunk and threatening to kill his wife, who was Dorothy Moore, sister to Thomas; she d. bef. 17 Mar. 1693-4. He deeded all to s. John for life supp. in May 1701, John to pay the others' portions; d. bef. 1721. Ch: **John. Daniel. William. Joseph. Elizabeth.**

**2 DANIEL**(1), about 23 in Aug. 1702, had town grants 1699-1701, m. 8 Nov. 1698 Elizabeth Fost(1), who m. 2d Henry Beedle. He was k. by Ind. while fishing near the garrison 2 Apr. 1711. Ch: **Mary,** b. 25 Nov. 1699, had s. Thomas by Philip Carey in 1731. **Dorothy,** b. 9 Sep. 1700, m. Robert Lambert. **John,** b. 8 Nov. 1703. One John of York d. at Ipsw. 1 Nov. 1727. **Daniel,** b. 25 Feb. 1705-6, mar. 1 Apr. 1731 Hannah Bowden (Boody 1). 4 ch. **Dorcas,** b. 16 July 1708. **Joseph,** b. 14 Jan. 1710-11.

**3 JOHN**(1), mar. Sarah Hutchins (Enoch), who m. 2d Charles Trafton bef. 4 July 1716, when they gave bond to adm. his est. His York grants 1703-8 were laid out to his heirs in 1722. She was liv. 1739. Ch: **Mary,** b. 18 Oct. 1710, m. 1st Dr. Jonathan Crosby(2), 2d 25 May 1738 John Crawley. **Enoch,** b. 26 May 1712, chose Tobias Leighton gdn., acc. by Sarah Brookings 1732, m. by 1734 Ruth Parsons (Elihu). Ch.

**4 PETER,** List 96 p. 82. One Peter Dill d. Chelmsford 13 Aug. 1692.

**5 WILLIAM,** List 74, Scotch prisoner.

**DINALL. 1 Arthur,** wit. against Mr. Thomas Booth, Maine Ct., July 1663.

**2 JOHN,** O. F. Portsm. 11 July 1659.

**Disher,** Dermon, phonetic for Dermond Oshaw.

**Dison(?),** Thomas, N. H. train soldier 1692. List 62.

**Dispose,** Jennet, Jersey woman and her child, in Portsmouth 5 Oct. 1676, to be kept by Goodman Frye at the town's charge.

**DITTY, Francis,** Portsmouth, mariner, from Wimborne, co. Dorset, m. 26 May 1715 Elizabeth (Kennard), wid. of Joshua Furber(3), who mar. 3d Capt. Richard Waterhouse and 4th Moses Dam. List 339. Ch. bap. adult: **Mary,** bp. 24 Feb. 1734-5. **Sarah,** bp. 1 July 1739, m. her stepbr. John Dam.

**Divall** (Diuel), John, Oyster River 1657. Coroner's jury that yr. O. F. 1659. List 363a.

**DIXON**, Dixie, Dickson. Common on both sides of the Scottish border.

1 **ANNE**, Mrs. (Watts), wid. of Geo., d. of Ralph and Jane Watts, came from Ramshaw, Auckland St. Helen's, Durham, to Scarb. in 1665, to keep house for her br. whose w. had left him. See Allison(2). Liv. 1673. With her came app. one or two ds: **Anne**, w. of Ralph Allison and poss. one who m. Joseph Oliver.

2 **PETER**, Eliot, shipwright, first app. town gr. 26 Mar. 1679. In 1694 lic. to sell to churchgoers, in 1695 innholder and ferryman. Jury 1693-5, 1700, gr.j. 1688, 1693, 1694, 1711. Lists 30, 296-298. Will 1708, inv. 9 Apr. 1718. He m. Mary Remick, liv. 1704. Ch: **Mary**, b. 23 Sep. 1679, m. John Staples. **Hannah**, b. 3 Feb. 1684, m. John Morrell. **Anne**, b. 17 July 1689, mar. Tho. Jenkins. **Peter**, b. 29 Feb. 1692, had the homestead, m. 28 Sep. 1712 Abigail Flanders. Will 18 Feb. 1779 names 6 rec. ch. (3 liv.), also s. Benj., liv. 1783, and w. Elizabeth; and entails homestead on s. Peter.

3 **WILLIAM**, came in 1630, servant to Gov. Winthrop; in 1635 he had jumped his bail. Jan. 13, 1636-7, he bot a house at York, where he liv. 30 yrs., a cooper. Jury 1650. Lists 275-277, 24. His w. Joane, named in his will, was mother of Dorothy, w. of Wm. Moore, but app. his stepd. In 1686 the ct. ordered the Moores to take their mo. Joane Dixon to their home and maintain her out of the est. willed to her by her hus. Wm. Dixon. His will, 13 Feb.—16 June 1666, aided by deeds, shows four ch., poss. not all by one w: **James**, fishing partn. with Philip Hatch. Deed-will 9 Jan. 1666-7, going to sea, shows no fam. Liv. 1668. **Susannah**, m. one Frost, liv. at a distance. **Ann**, m. John Brawn. **Dau.** m. Henry Milbury.

**Doaks**, William, Kit. wit. 1720. Portsmouth almshouse ab. 1781, ag. 86.

**DOANE**. 1 **David**, N. H. 1697. List 68.

2 **THOMAS**, N. H. 1697. List 68.

**Doby**, James, Gt. Isl. merchant, 1684, sued Nicholas Baker, master of ketch -Diligence-.

**DOCKHAM**, John (usu. Dockum), of Greenland 29 Sep. 1691 m. to Jane, widow of John Bickford(14); 2d 13 Jan. 1713-4 Martha Fox(1), who joined Greenl. Ch. 1728. List 335a. See Arlot, Benedictus. In 1713 and 1721 he deeded land in Greenl. to son John, and in 1729 house and land there to sons Benj. and Jonathan; liv. ab. 1735. Lists 62, 335a, 338ac. Presum. ch: **John**, wife Jane joined Greenl. Ch. 1726. 4 ch. bap. 1728-1736. **Benjamin**, m. 18 Dec. 1719 Sarah Preston, both of Portsm., both liv. there 1767. A son Samuel m. Sarah, sis. of Susannah Martin, heirs of Clark's or Noler's Isl. **Jonathan**, mar. 3 Oct. 1717 Sarah Cotton, d. 11 Mar.

1753. 3 or more ch. **Mary**, m. 29 Sep. 1737 Richard Whitehorn. **Jeane**. **Margaret**, m. 27 Aug. 1724 Daniel Doe(1). **Dorothy**, mar. 22 Apr. 1725 Joshua Keniston. **Martha**.

**DODD**, George, perh. the one ag. 17 on -The Matthew- of London for St. Christopher's, 21 May 1636, was of Boston in 1648. In 1650 Tho. Trickey was building him a 50-ton ship. In Apr. 1651 he had been a partn. of Henry Parkes and Humphrey Chadbourne in a French voyage. Lists 71, 75b. D. in London bef. 31 July 1663 leav. wid. Mary (Davis 41) and 4 small ch. She m. 2d Matthew Austin(5), 3d Wm. Wright; liv. 1713. Ch: **Patience**, bp. 16 May 1647 ag. ab. 1 y. 35 d. **Isaac**, b. 3 Sep. 1651. **Mary**, b. 5 July 1653, was in Eng. in June 1680; d.s.p. **Elizabeth**, b. 5 Apr. 1657, m. 1st John Royal, 2d Thomas Southerin. **Mehitable**, b. 25 May 1660, m. Daniel Littlefield.

**DODDRIDGE** (spoken Dotheridge), **Philip**, Saco, 1665, up for working (and cursing) on Sunday. See Creber. See Richard Tucker.

**DOE**. The legal unkn. 'John Doe' is imag.

1 **JOHN**(2), ag. 68 in Mar. 1737-8, Durham. In 1706 he q.c. the homestead to Sampson. Gr.j. 1696, const. 1700. Lists 368ab, 369. He and w. Elizabeth joined the ch. in 1722. Their 7 ch. were bap. 29 Nov. 1719. Adm. to her 28 Apr. 1742. Ch., all living in 1742: (**Sampson?** One S. D. had a 20 a. gr. in Exeter in 1725. List 376b.) **Daniel**, m. 27 Aug. 1724 Margaret Dockum(1), 3 or m. ch. **John**, m. bef. 1736 Susan Wormwood. List 369. Ch. **Joseph**, m. Martha Wormwood. List 369. Ch. **Benjamin**, mar. Hannah Follett dau. of Benj.(6). **Mary**, m. John Mason. **Elizabeth**, m. Joshua Woodman. **Martha**, b. 13 June 1716, m. Edw. Woodman.

2 **NICHOLAS**, ±50 in 1681, landowner at Sag. Creek 1663, in Nov. 1666 wit. a Sag. Creek will, in 1667 gave his note to Charles Glidden of Piscataqua, in 1668 bot at Lubberland and was accepted a Dover inhab. Gr.j. 1679, const. 1682. Lists 356jm, 359a, 366, 57. Adm. 6 June 1691 to s. John. W. Martha must have d. Ch: **John**, b. 25 Aug. 1669. **Sampson**, b. 1 Apr. 1670. **Elizabeth**, b. 7 Feb. 1673-4, d. bef. f. **Mary**, liv. 1706, presum. Mary 'Dow' m. Wm. Richards 23 Aug. 1694.

3 **SAMPSON**(2) had homestead. Jury 1694. Ind. scout 1712. Orig. memb. of Durham Ch. He m. 1st one Temperance, 2d 4 Oct. 1716 Mary (Hopley), wid. of Wm. Ayers(8), bap. 19 Mar. 1717-8, who as Mary Stevens of Portsm. made her will in 1765. His will, of Newmarket, 4 Apr. 1748—29 May 1751, gives 8 ch. 3 sh. each, no r.e. ment., all else to w. Mary who sued for dower. Ch. by 2 wives, order of ages surmised: **Martha**, m. one Frost, perh. John, s. of Samuel(8). **Mary**,

mar. 1st one Wiggin, 2d Jonathan Smart. **Samuel,** m. 12 Nov. 1731, Abigail Wiggin. Liv. in Newmarket. List 376b. **Temperance,** bp. 8 Dec. 1718, ag. 9, not in will. **Nicholas,** m. one Elizabeth. 4 or m. ch. By 2d w: **Nathaniel,** bp. 19 Mar. 1717-8, liv. in Dover, m. Sarah Watson, d. of David and Mary (Dudley 2). **Elizabeth,** bp. 22 Jan. 1722-3, mar. James Stoodly of Portsm. **Zebulon,** bp. 15 July 1725, m. Deborah Wiggin. Ch. **Sarah,** bp. 6 Dec. 1727, m. Samuel Frost (see 8).

**DOLBEE,** -by, Dolberry.

1 **EDWARD** (Dolbe), shoemaker, Portsm., acc. 25 Mar. 1700-1 by Mary Cowes(Giles, of Ipswich), who was Mary Doliver when she receipted for share in her f.'s est. in 1702. Drowned by upsetting of a canoe, inquest 17 June 1701.

2 **NICHOLAS,** by Hist. Rye here bef. 1700, but not in Lists 315b, 316. He mar. in Hampton Falls 25 June 1713 Sarah Smith. Adm. 27 Mar. 1736. For desc. see Hist. of Rye, pp. 333-4.

3 **THOMAS** (Dolbe), Portsm. wit. in 1673 for Richard Waterhouse and John Partridge. Accid. drowned, inq. 10 May 1674. List 312h.

**DOLE** (Doole). 1 **Abner,** b. Newbury 8 Mar. 1671-2; mar. (1) in Newb. 1 Nov. 1694, Mary Jewett, d. 25 Nov. 1695; m. 2d in Boston 5 Jan. 1698[9 Sarah Belcher, who d. in Newb. 21 July 1730, ae. 59 (grst.) His will proved 12 Jan. 1740. Ch.

2 **BENJAMIN,** mar. Elizabeth, only ch. of Joachim Harvey, Portsm., bef. 1678. In settl. of her fr.'s est. she was given £100 and, aft. her mother's death, his house, untraced.

3 **BENJAMIN,** br. of (1), doctor, b. 16 Nov. 1679; m. Hampt. 11 Dec. 1700 Frances Sherburne; d. 8 May 1707, ae. 27 (grst.) List 96. Wid. mar. 2d 18 Jan. 1710-1 Wm. Stanford, from Ipsw., and d. 15 Aug. 1744. See N. H. Prob. i. 589.

4 **JAMES** (Dolle), soldier from Newbury, killed on exped. east, 1691. List 37.

**DOLIVER.** 1 **John,** b. Glouc. 2 Sep. 1671, dep. ±78 in May 1745 that 60 yrs. past he kept cattle on John Parrett's land, Cape Elizabeth.

2 **RICHARD,** of Glouc., m. Agnes Dennen.

**DOLLEN,** see also Dalling, Darling.

1 **EDWARD** (Dolen), Kit. soldier. List 289.

2 **JOHN,** ±49 in Mar. 1675-6, fishing master, was for 20 or more yrs. the princ. inhab. on Monhegan Isl., also in 1687 the 2d largest taxpayer in Pemaquid. **See Doc. Hist.** vi. 119. Besides Indian deeds, he bot from Tho. Elbridge 400 a. at Round Pond (for 3 gallons of liquor), and other lands on specu. Justice of the sessions ct. under the New York governor 1681-1686. Lists 3, 13, 15, 16, 18, 83, 124. In Suff. Co. Ct. Dec. 1689 he sued

Samuel Burnel, Wm. Phelps and John Casement for bringing away two anchors and two swine from Monhegan. He was liv. in Boston in 1700, 1706 and app. in 1715. His w. was dau. of Richard Gridley, ment. in his will 1674. He m. 2d by 1700 Mary (Waters), wid. of John Selman, d. of Wm. Waters of Boston, likely the wid. Mary Darling who d. in Boston 4 Nov. 1717, ag. 85. Kn. ch: **Joanna,** mar. Renald Kelly of Monhegan, 2d James Mander of Charlestown and Boston, who d. 8 May 1689. In 1717, of Boston, she made deed of gift to her nephew Richard Wildes of Lancaster. **Patience,** m. Walter Mander. His adm. in Suff. Prob. in 1700, she liv. at Martha's Vin. **Dau.,** mother of Richard Wildes.

**DOLLEY.** 1 **Jeremiah,** drowned 1663. Inquest by Portsm. jury. List 327a.

2 **JOHN,** Kit., m. Elizabeth Follett(4), Me. Ct. Jan. 1720-1.

3 **RICHARD,** Portsm., boatbuilder, m. Mary Haines (Joshua) of Greenland.

**DOLLOFF,** Dolhough. See Cartee.

**CHRISTIAN,** Exeter or Stratham, ±32 in 1671. Taxed at Cochecho in 1659-1664, settled in Exeter, where in 1666 he wit. Tho. King to Jonathan Thing. Soldier in Philip's War. Jury 1694, gr.j. 1698. Lists 356ch, 376b (1674), 381-383, 52, 57, 62, 96. Will 16 June, d. 18 Aug. 1708. He m. 1st Miriam Moulton who in 1661 wit. a deed of Ann, widow of John Moulton, and was called cousin in Tho. King's will. Presum. her f. was br. of John and of Miriam (Moulton), Tho. King's w. He m. 2d 10 Dec. 1674 Sarah Scammon, d. of Richard and Prudence (Waldron) who outl. him. Ch. by 1st w: **Mary,** b. 17 Sep. 1667, mar. James Gilman. **John,** b. 17 Feb. 1668-9, k. by Ind. in the woods 15 Sep. 1707. Lists 57, 99. **James,** b. 25 Dec. 1670, k. by the heathen at Casco 4 Aug. 1691 (grst.) App. by 2d w: **Samuel,** gr. 100 a. in 1698, was on Capt. Kinsley Hall's payroll in 1696. Lists 67, 376b. His homestead adj. his bro. Richard's in 1741, later occu. by their sons Samuel and Abner. Will 31 Mar.—29 Apr. 1741 names no w., 5 ch. (not Elizabeth, b. 1 Mar. 1706), and grs. Samuel. His s. Samuel, b. 1 Feb. 1703, m. Esther Beard(3 jr.) and their s. Samuel, named in the will, m. Rhoda Flanders by 1772 and by 1782 had moved from Freemont to Moultonboro with his wid. mother Esther. **Richard,** grants 100 a. in 1698, 20 in 1703. Lists 67, 376b. He m. by 1700 Catherine Bean(2) who outl. him. Will 1744—1750 names 6 of 9 or m. ch., the oldest b. premat. Dec. 1700. For his ch. taken capt. on their way to school by Ind., see Coleman's N. E. Captives, i. 373. **Thomas,** gr. 40 a. in 1703. List 376b. Will 11 Sep.—5 Dec. 1722, names 3 sons (b. ab. 1711-1721) and wife Lydia (Gordon), d. of Nicholas, who m. 2d

her cous. Jonathan Gordon. **Prudence,** liv. 1708. **Catherine,** liv. 1708.

**DONGAN,** †Col. **Thomas,** 1634-1715. Lt. Gov. of N. Y. and Pemaquid. Stuart adherent. Lists 163, 188. See Gen.

**DONHAM,** see Dunham, Denham.

**DONNELL,** (Dunwell?), often Daniels.
1 **HENRY,** b. ab. 1602-8, first ment. in 1641, but his dep. about Tho. Bradbury, 21 Mar. 1682-3, ±78, 'about 47 or 48 years ago,' shows him in York by 1635 or 1636, and dep. 25 Aug. 1676, ag. 68, shows he was over here, at least on a fishing voyage, ab. 1631. See Thos. Brooks. The names Henry Donnell and Geo. Jewell are in the church and borough records of Barnstable, co. Devon, 1631-4. Early fisherman, later innkeeper at the Stage Isl. ferry, his w. ran the inn while he lived at Jewell's Isl. in Casco Bay, where he made fish 16 or 18 yrs. until Philip's War (his s. Samuel said near 30 yrs. and that he bot the island of the Ind.; he mortg. it in 1644). In 1676 he was again innkeeper at York, but in 1678 was selling without lic.; again lic. 1686-1687. Jury 1650, 1653; gr.j. 1651, 1660. Selectm. 1661, 1667, 1673, 1677-79, 1683. Last ment. June 1687, inv. not till 25 Apr. 1693, after the massacre. Lists 84, 272, 275-277, 285, 24, 25, 86. W. Frances ment. 1656-1685. In 1671 she had furnished two barrels of beer for the County Courts. Ch: **Thomas,** b. ab. 1636. **John,** k. in 1664 by falling into an open pit at Kit. Point. Jane Topp ment. in 1660. **Mary,** Y. D. iii. 112, 1662, brot money from Boston to York for Capt. Tho. Clark. **Samuel,** b. 1645-46. **Joseph. Benjamin,** mariner, belong. to Mrs. Elizabeth Seeley's crew at the Isl. of Shoals in 1674. Inv. 26 Feb., adm. to br. Samuel 1 Apr. 1679. **Nathaniel.** List 30. Adm. 22 Dec. 1682 to his f. **Sarah,** poss. mar. Samuel Banks(4) who signed a joint note with Samuel Donnell in 1679, and later John Lancaster; or less likely James Johnson from Hampton. **Margaret.** Mrs. Godfrey 2 Apr. 1660 placed the Donnell property in the names of Sarah and Margaret for the benefit of their mother under trustees. Y. D. ii. 43. Adm. 5 May 1685 to br. Samuel.
2 **JOHN**(5), eldest son, had the homestead. List 279. He m. aft. 1712 Sarah, wid. of Henry Brooking(3) and John Linscott. Will 29 Mar. 1738—19 Feb. 1745-6: wife Sarah, homestead to only s. **Thomas,** ds. **Abigail, Elizabeth, Rebecca, Mary, Jemima,** all app. by an earlier w. Mary, late of York, now of Boston, m. 1st 28 Sep. 1727 Anthony Baker, and 21 May 1733 'Mrs. Mary Baker, d. of John Donnell' m. Wymond Bradbury, jr. of York. One Abigail Donnell m. (int. 15 Mar. 1734-5) John Curtis. John and Sarah Donnell, with Hannah Donnell also signing, per-

haps their minor d. who d. bef. her f., relinq. adm. estate of Henry Brooking. Why Francis Raynes signed with them is unexp.
3 **JOSEPH**(1), fisherman, first appears in deed from his f. of Jewell's Isl. and his fishing plant, 29 Feb. 1671-2. Aft. Philip's War he built on a Falm. gr. at So. Portland, which he sold in 1686. In the next war he fled to York, where the last ment. is a fine 1 July 1690 for abs. from meeting. Lists 30, 225a. He m. aft. Apr. 1675 Ruth Redding, who m. 2d Tho. Favor(2). Ch: **Henry,** m. ab. 1709 Elizabeth Wells (Peter). 4 ch. rec. **Patience,** m. 16 Feb. 1709 Miles Rhodes, 2d Ichabod Jellison. **Ruth,** m. 16 Nov. 1713 Wm. Sellers of York. Will 1756—1758: w. Ruth, 8 of 10 ch. rec. 1714-1733. **Sarah,** in 1745 was w. of Robert Ford of Boston, coaster, who may or may not have been her sixth hus. One Sarah Dunnel of Boston m. Robert Hewes of Ireland 30 Sep. 1714; Sarah Hurst m. Wm. Darracot (int. 1726); Sarah Dericott m. Jonas Strangman 1729; Sarah Strangman m. Robert Long 1731; Sarah Long m. Benj. Gold 1734; Sarah Goold mar. Robert Ford 29 Aug. 1742. **Mary** (Dunnell), m. in Boston 25 Oct. 1722 Abraham Smith, wid., of Boston, 1745.
4 ‡*SAMUEL(1), in his early yrs. went to sea (±27, 1672, Y. D. ii. 116). In 1717, ±70, he dep. 'for the most part of the time this 60 yrs. past he hath dwelt in the town of York.' Liquor lic. 1688, 1703, 1704, 1706-1709. Innkeeper 1690, 1699-1702. Gr.j. 1683, Rep. 1684, 1685. Councillor 1691, J.P. 1692, Judge of Com. Pleas 1699. Selectm. 1695, 1696, 1700. County Treas. 1711. Lists 86, 33, 38, 279. His will, 7 Mar., d. 9 Mar. 1717-8, names 7 of 8 rec. ch. Wife Alice Chadbourne(1), had tavern lic. in 1719 and m. 2d Jeremiah Moulton. Ch: **Samuel,** b. 11 Jan. 1681-2, shipwright, liv. 1735. **William,** b. 8, d. 18 Dec. 1684. **William,** b. 10 Jan. 1684-5; 50 a. gr. 1703; 'if he should ever return'— father's will; had not in 1734. **Alice,** b. 2 June 1687, m. 13 July 1709 Caleb Norwood of Glouc., of Boston, wid., in 1740. **Nathaniel,** b. 19 Nov. 1689, Col., Esq. While he did not, like his cousin Nathaniel, rem. to the Kennebec, he engaged in that specul. and in 1762 stood suit by the Prop. of the Kennebec Purchase. List 279. D. 9 Feb. 1780. W. Hannah (Preble), d. 22 Oct. 1767. 4 ch. **Elizabeth,** b 26 Mar. 1692, mar. 1st Joseph Harris, 4 ch. 1714-1717; 2d (int. 10 Sep. 1726) William Burnham; 3d 24 Oct. 1742 Geo. Jacobs of Wells. **Joanna,** b. 12 Apr. 1695, m. 1724 Wyatt Moore, liv. Biddeford 1736. **James,** b. 11 Apr. 1704, mariner. List 279. Adm. 14 Jan. 1745-6 to wid. Mary (Sayward), m. 29 Jan. 1729-30. 3 ch. rec.
5 **THOMAS**(1), eldest s. In 1662 of York with Andrew Haley of Isles of Shoals,

fishermen, bot Mr. Edward Johnson's former homestead. In 1672 he was hiring a fishing plant at the Shoals. Acting Ensign 1660. Gr.j. 1670, 1671, 1675, 1688, 1693, 1696, 1697. Selectm. 1693. In 1693 adm. the est. of James Adams(16). Lists 25, 87. Added name to Lists 275, 276. Inv. 28 Sep., adm. 3 Jan. 1699-1700 to wid. Elizabeth (Weare), living 1709. Ch: **John**, b. 1660. **Sarah**, b. 1663, she and Hannah, spinsters, of Boston, 1724. She d. there 3 Sep. 1734, ag. 71 (grst.). **Benjamin**, k. by Ind. at Winter Harbor 21 Sep. 1707. List 96 p. 150. Penhallow, N. H. Hist. Soc. Coll. i. Those engaged in this action were, besides Donnell: Capt. Matthew Austin, Mr. Harmon, Sergt. Cole, Timothy Day, three men and a boy. He m. Mary Harmon, who m. 28 Dec. 1709 Joseph Holt. 2 daus. **Hannah**, see Sarah. One Hannah left will Suff. Prob. 1762. **Nathaniel**, Capt., mariner. Of Boston 1710, Rowley 1716, Boston 1721, York 1725, Boston 1731, settled in Bath ab. 1734. List 279. He m. (int. 14 May 1711) Elizabeth Todd, d. of John of Rowley. By his will 1761–1761, naming 4 ch., he gave the Bath meetinghouse lot. One Benj. Donnell? was rated to the New Meet. Ho., Portsm., 1717.

**Donovan**, Crehor, sued in N. H. Ct. 1675. Surety Nicholas Lissen.

**DORE**, Door, the former the name of two places in Derby and Hertfordshire.
1 **PHILIP**(2), of Portsmouth, bot in Exeter 1715; of Newington 1717, sold in Stratham; 1735 Philip of Dover to Philip jr. land in Rochester; of Dover 1743 to Henry of Rochester. He mar. 20 May 1708 Sarah Child(1), his wid. of Lebanon in 1761. Ch., perh. not all theirs nor all of them, but of these all but Wm. and Sarah are sure: **William**, Rochester 1737. One W. D. of Cochecho m. 24 Apr. 1740 Mary Wallingford of Newington. W. D. d. Dover 23 Apr. 1785 ag. 78. Widow Dore d. Dover 29 Mar. 1799 of old age. **Sarah**, m. 1730 Richard Child (see 1). **Philip**, bp. 5 July 1730, signed Rochester petn. (1736), m. Lydia; 6 ch. bap. Rochester 1744, and more. **Henry**, Rochester, wife Mary in 1761. Ch. **Elizabeth. Frances**, bp. with Henry and Elizabeth 6 Aug. 1727 in Newington, m. Abijah Stevens, d. 1804. **John**, bp. 5 July 1730.
2 **RICHARD**, in 1669 bot what became his homestead at Sag. Creek. Started life as drinking, fighting tailor, taking his oath to kill Fryer; also subsc. for the minister. In 1673 his w. was a wit. that their neighbor was drunk. Lists 326c, 327b, 329, 52, 67, 330d, 331b, 335a, 336b, 337. For w. Tamsen, see John Jackson. List 335a. His will, 16 Feb.–17 Mar. 1715-6, gives all to her (liv. 1718) and aft. her to 'my children every one

alike,' presum. incl: **Mary**, m. 23 Dec. 1692 James Houston; possibly mother of Jennet Hueston bp. July 1718, and m. 2d (under mistak. name) 3 Nov. 1715 John Gardner of co. Glouc., Eng. **Joanna**, m. in 1692 David Cane(1), 2d John Bourne, 3d 25 Feb. 1716-7 Stephen Nole, or Knowles, from Lahant, Cornwall, fisherman. **Bryan**, m. by 1703 Martha (Jackson), wid. of John Boulter(1), who m. 3d 30 Sep. 1714 Philip Towle. For poss. ch. of Bryan see Philip. **Philip**, ±29 in 1713, m. (Aug. 1714) Mary Wiggin, both of Portsm. **Solomon**, wit. fam. deed in 1714, poss. a young grs.

**DORMAN**. 1 **Daniel**, (but see Daniel O'-Shaw), in 1671 with Bial Lamb was making trouble in Widow Moulton's house, Gt. Isl. N. H. juryman 1698.
2 **SETH**, soldier at Kit. 170--. List 289.

**Dorr**, Edward. List 15. See Darey? and Savage.

**Dotheridge**, Philip, see Doddridge.

**Doty** (Dotee), Edward, soldier N. H. 1697. List 68.

**DOUGHTY**, a Staffordshire name.
**THOMAS**, a Scotch prisoner, dep. in 1700, ±70, that ab. 40 yrs. ago he liv. with Mr. Valentine Hill. In 1663 he and John Wingate were partners in a logging contract. He gained high repute as a lumberman, and when Roger Plaisted changed his connection from the Great Works mills to the Broughton mills, he succeeded him, and later must have had a mill of his own at Doughty's Falls, Berwick. He was taxed at Oyster River 1661-1665. In 1667 he rem. to the Saco Falls mills, and bef. Philip's War had rem. to Wells where he stayed thro that war. In 1686 was tenant of Mrs. Bridget Phillip's mill at Saco. His petn. to Andros ment. grist mill built by himself. In the next war he withdrew to Malden. Gr.j., Kit. 1666, 1667. Town Treas. Saco, 1688. He was often bondsman for a Scot in trouble. Lists 356d, 361a, 363ac, 364, 28, 266, 249. His est. was not settled until 1710. He m. at Saco 24 Jan. 1669-70 Elizabeth Bully(2), liv. 14 Dec. 1711. Ch: **Elizabeth**, b. 14 Feb. 1669-70, m. Thomas Thomes of Stratham and Falm. **Margaret**, m. in Boston 3 June 1703 Edmund Chamberlain, 2d in Malden 6 Mar. 1711-2 Samuel Wilson. **Joseph**, mar. in Salem 4 Dec. 1707 Elizabeth Nurse. He adm. his f.'s est. Will proved 1751, 3 ch. **James**, b. ab. 1680, m. in Hampton 10 Apr. 1707 Mary Robinson. In 1712 he was of Stratham, aft. war ended moved to Falm. List 388. 6 ch. **Patience**, m. in Salem 13 Mar. 1706-7 Benj. Follet; rem. to Windham, Conn. **Benjamin**, settled in Windham, Conn. **Abigail**, m. in Lynn 28 Oct. 1717 Robert Edmunds, who d. 4 Feb. 1749-50, 3 ch.; 2d 28 Nov. 1752 David Potter.

DOUGLASS 201 DOW

**DOUGLASS.** 1 **Henry** (? of Boston will 1667), sued in N. H. Ct. 1651 by John Jackson.

2 **JOHN**, Dover, 1685, complained of Stephen Otis for beating him. Lists 52, 94. He m. 16 Sep. 1687 Shuah (Colcord 1), wid. of Richard Nason. Died bef. 1712, when she joined Hampton Falls Ch., and she and her dau. **Mary** Douglass are ment. in Thomas Chase's will.

**DOW,** Dowe.

1 **DANIEL**(2), Hampton. Lists 52, 54, 393b, 396. He m. 13 Nov. 1673 Elizabeth Lamprey, whose br. Daniel deeded land to all their ch. but Hannah. He d. 7 Mar. 1718. Ch: **Elizabeth**, b. 28 Jan. 1675, liv. unmar. 1731. **Hannah**, b. 13 Sep. 1676, m. John Dearborn(3 jr.). **Mary**, b. 7 Dec. 1678, d. unm. 30 July 1749. **David**, b. 20 Mar. 1681, d. 10 Jan. 1755. **Henry**, bp. 26 June 1698, mar. 8 Aug. 1723 Martha Sanborn. S. Daniel.

2 *HENRY, of Ormsby, Norfolk, was lic. 11 Apr. 1637 to emigrate to N. E., ag. 29, with w. Joan, 30, 4 ch., one of them hers, Tho. Nudd, by her former hus. Roger Nudd, and Anne Manning, ag. 17. One Henry Dow was on the Ormsby manor rent roll of 1610. At Watertown he was made freem. 2 May 1638, his w. was bur. 20 June 1640, and he m. 2d in 1640 Margaret Cole of Dedham. Having bot in Hampton he rem. in 1643-44. Jury 1648, selectm. 1651, Rep. 1655, 1656. Lists 392ab, 393ab, 53. Will 16 Mar., d. 21 Apr. 1659. His wid. m. 23 Oct. 1661 Richard Kimball of Ipsw., adm. on her est. gr. Mar. 1676. Ch: **Thomas**, bp. in Ormsby 27 Dec. 1631, bur. at Watertown 10 July 1642. **Henry**, b. 1634. **Child**, b. in Eng., d.y. **Joseph**, b. at Watertown 20 Mar. 1639. By 2d wife: **Daniel**, b. 22 Sep. 1641. **Mary**, b. 14 Sep. 1643. **Hannah**, m. Jonas Gregory of Ipsw., d.s.p. 22 Feb. 1671. **Thomas**, b. at Hampton 28 Apr. 1653. **Jeremiah**, b. 6 Sep. 1657.

3 **CAPT.** ‡*HENRY(2), Hampton, had the homestead, attorney at law, trader, shipowner, surveyor. Marshal of Norfolk Co. from 1673, Prov. Marshal 1680, Dep. Marshal under Cranfield. Selectm. freq. 1661-1699, town clerk 1681 till death. Judge of Com. Pleas. Member of the Constitutional Conv. 1690. Assemblyman 1693, 1697-1699, Clerk of the Assembly. Speaker pro tem. Prov. Treas. 1694. Councillor from 1702. Ensign 1689, Captain 1692. D. intestate 6 May 1707 full of public honors. Lists 392b, 393b, 394, 396, 49, 52, 54, 55ab, 56, 59, 61, 63, 64, 66, 67, 69, 96. He m. 17 June 1659 Hannah Page, who d. 6 Aug. 1704; 2d 10 Nov. 1704 Mary (Hussey) Green, who lived until 21 Jan. 1733. Ch: **Joseph**, b. 30 Mar. 1660, d. unm. 17 Aug. 1680. **Samuel**, b. 4 Nov. 1662. **Simon**, b. 4 Mar. 1667. **Jabez**, b. 8 Feb. 1672.

4 **HENRY**(7), Seabrook, but called of Salis. in his will 28 Dec.—12 Feb. 1738-9. List 399a. D. 22 Jan. 1738-9 (grst. in Seab.). He m. Mary Mussey, d. of the Quaker celebrity who left the garrison to go home with Ind. ab. and was killed. Mary d. 18 May 1739, in 62d yr. (grst.) Ch: **Joanna**, b. 4 Oct. 1696, m. (int. 16 Mar. 1716-7) Nehemiah Heath, 2d 21 Jan. 1719 Aaron Morrill; d. 18 Apr. 1736. **Lydia**, b. 31 Dec. 1699, m. 10 Dec. 1719 Samuel Gould of Amesbury. **Samuel,** b. 22 Jan. 1702-3, d. 9 May 1773. **Susannah,** b. 12 Mar. 1705, liv. 1738. **Ruth,** b. 4 June 1707, m. 13 Jan. 1735 John Morrill of Kit. **Judith,** b. 10 June 1710, m. 16 May 1728 John Mumford of Newport. **Henry,** b. 13 Dec. 1711, d. 11 Dec. 1729. **Daniel,** b. 4 Feb. 1714.

5 **CAPT.** *JABEZ(3), the usual moderator of Hampton town meetings 1720-1734, many years selectm., Rep. 1715. List 399a. Will 29 Dec. 1749, d. 14 Jan. 1752. He m. 24 Mar. 1693 Esther Shaw, who d. 25 Mar. 1739. Ch: **Benjamin**, b. 4 Dec. 1693; had the homestead; 5 yrs. selectm.; d. 19 Dec. 1762. **Lucy**, b. 26 Oct. 1695, mar. James Hobbs. **Ezekiel**, b. 5 Jan. 1698, settled in Kensington. He m. 1st 3 Mar. 1726 Abigail Roby; 2d 25 Sep. 1735 Elizabeth Cram(3). By both wives 9 ch. **Lydia**, b. 5 Nov. 1700, m. Philip Towle. **Esther**, b. 31 Oct. 1702, not in will. **Patience**, b. 15 Nov. 1705, m. 25 July 1749 Lt. Wm. Stanford from Ipsw., d. 10 Dec. 1762. **Comfort**, b. 28 Oct. 1708, m. Abraham Green.

6 **JEREMIAH**(2), Ipsw. His house, built by br. Tho. and hims. in 1676, was willed June, 1723, to his only ch. Wid. Susannah by will 1749 named the same. Ch: **Margaret**, under 18 in 1723, mar. 2 Nov. 1727 Henry Greenleaf; 2d (int. 8 Dec. 1733) John Lull.

7 **JOSEPH**(2), Seabrook. Selectman 1669, 1680, jury 1683. Lists 392b, 396. He was the first of the Dow Friends. Will 29 Mar., d. 4 Apr. 1703. He m. 17 Dec. 1662 Mary Sanborn, who outl. him. Ch: **Joseph**, b. 20 Oct. 1663. **John**, b. 12 Dec. 1665. Settled in Kensington. He m. 27 Nov. 1696 Hannah Page of Haverh., grd. of Judith (Davis 12) Guild. His will 6 Mar. 1737-8—28 Nov. 1744 names her and 8 ch., homestead to s. Benjamin. **Mary**, b. 15 Jan. 1668, unmar. 1703. **James**, b. 17 Sep. 1670, unment. **Hannah**, b. 25 Aug. 1672, m. Wm. Fowler of Amesbury. 7 ch. **Henry**, b. 7 Nov. 1674. **Jeremiah**, b. 24 Mar. 1677, liv. 1768. He m. 5 Apr. 1697 Elizabeth Perkins. 10 ch. **Josiah**, b. 2 July 1679, liv. in Seabrook, d. 18 Apr. 1718. He mar. 7 Nov. 1710 Mary Purington. 5 ch. Among dozens of Col. Winthrop Hilton's soldiers who named sons or grsons Winthrop or Hilton, he named his eldest s. Winthrop. His s. Abraham, b. 2 May 1715, was grf. of

Josiah, b. 1766, who in 1859 gave a typical family trad. Three Dow brothers came over, one settled in Haverhill, one in Salisbury, one, Abraham, in Seabrook, his birthplace. He had gathered apples from apple trees brot from Eng. by his grf. Abraham. The custodian of this trad. was a leading business man of Portland and f. of Gen. Neal Dow. **Thomas,** b. 26 Apr. 1682, liv. in Salis. 1721. **Charity,** b. 7 Dec. 1684, unm. 1721. **Samuel,** b. 4 June 1687, m. 2 Jan. 1711-2 Sarah Shepard. 7 ch. rec. at Salis. **Aaron,** b. 4 Apr. 1692, unment.

8 **JOSEPH**(7), ±57 in 1720, liv. in South Hampton, d. 5 Feb. 1734-5. He m. 1st at Amesbury 25 May 1687 Mary Challis who d. 14 May 1697; 2d one Hannah, an Indian reared by the Friends; d. in Hampton Falls ab. 1757. Ch. by 1st w., all liv. 1715: **Joseph,** b. 6 Feb. 1687-8. **John,** b. 16 Dec. 1689. **James,** b. 8 Oct. 1693, m. 24 May 1721 Mary Nichols. 7 ch. rec. in Amesbury. **Philip,** b. 26 Apr. 1695, reared by his grf. Dow, liv. in Kingston and Kensington. He m. 1st 2 Jan. 1723-4 Hannah Griffin, 2d ab. 1748 Sarah (Ayers) Freese(2), both living 1756. 10 ch. **Mary,** b. 11 May 1697, unm. 1715. By wife Hannah 4 or m.: **Eliphaz,** b. ab. 1705, hanged for murder 8 May 1755. **Noah. Bildad. Judah,** the last three of Hampt. Falls in 1747.

9 *****SAMUEL**(3), Deacon in 1747, had the homestead. Gr.j. 1692, selectm. 1693,1700, 1704, 1707, town clerk 1707 till death. Rep. 1696. Lists 52, 392b. Will 19, d. 20 June 1714. He m. 1st 12 Dec. 1683 Abigail Hobbs, who d., with twin ch. stillborn, 12 May 1700; 2d 13 Feb. 1708 Sarah (Taylor) Garland. Ch: **Hannah,** b. 12 Nov. 1684, d. 22 July 1687. **Joseph,** b. 13 Dec. 1686, d. 25 Aug. 1707. **Abigail,** b. 17 Apr. 1689, d. 23 Aug. 1707. **Sarah,** b. 22 May 1691, m. Samuel Clifford(2). **Samuel,** b. 25 May 1693, had the homestead. Town clerk 1730 till d., 29 Mar. 1755. He m. 12 Sep. 1717 Mary Page, who d. 10 Mar. 1760. 9 ch. incl. Samuel, b. 10 Oct. 1718, who had the homestead. **Rachel,** b. 20 Sep. 1695, m. Jonathan Garland. **Mehitable,** b. 10 Apr. 1698, d. 27 Feb. 1704. **Twins,** stillb. 12 May 1700. By 2d w: **Hannah,** b. 10 Jan. 1709, m. Shubael Page.

10 **SIMON**(3), Hampton. Jury 1695, selectman 1697, 1703, 1706. Lists 392b, 399a. Will, 18 Sep., d. 2 Oct., 1707, names all his ch. except Henry, posth. He m. 1st 5 Nov. 1685 Sarah Marston (d. 8 Mar. 1698); 2d 29 May 1700 Mehitable Green, who m. 2d 21 Nov. 1711 Onesiphorus Page. Ch: **Mary,** b. 19 Nov. 1686, m. Richard Jenness. **Hannah,** b. 7 Nov. 1688, m. Henry Dearborn(2 jr.). **Simon,** b. 5 Dec. 1690, rec. the homestead, d. 20 Feb. 1764. He m. 8 Jan. 1713 Mary Lancaster. 7 ch. **Sarah,** b. 23 May 1693, m. Benj. Lamprey. By 2d w: **Isaac,** b. Oct. 1701, liv.

in Rye, adm. 16 Aug. 1735 to wid. Charity (Philbrick). 3 ch. **Jonathan,** Deacon, b. 1 Oct. 1703, liv. at Kingston. He m. 20 Nov. 1729 Sarah Weare. 10 or m. ch. **Mehitable,** b. 13 Jan. 1706. **Henry,** b. 28 Mar. 1708, d. 30 Dec. 1727.

11 **THOMAS**(2), on his mother's remar. went with her younger ch. to Ipsw. With Daniel, then of Hampt., he was gr. adm. on their mother's estate Mar. 1676. Soldier in Philip's War, was wounded in the Great Swamp fight. His 1st w. Sarah (see Dew) d. Ipsw. 7 Feb. 1680-1; he mar. 2d bef. 1685 Susannah, who d. 29 Aug. 1724. Will 15 Nov. 1725, d. 12 July 1728. Ch: **Daniel,** m. Exercise, who d. 18 Dec. 1724. Will 1 Mar.—3 May 1725 names his bros. and sis. **Ephraim,** with Ebenezer and Thomas went to Voluntown, Conn. **John,** b. 24 Apr. 1685. **Ebenezer,** b. 26 May 1692. **Hannah,** b. 3 Oct. 1697. **Jeremiah,** b. 12 Dec. 1699, d. 20 Dec. 1731. **Benjamin,** b. 30 July 1706, not in br. or f. will.

In 1708 were taxed in Hampton Falls: Mehitable, John, Joseph, Thomas, Samuel jr. **Dowinge,** Joseph. In Edward West's book acct., 1667-1674, Barefoote is charged for money paid to him. **Dowling,** Samuel, Portsm. wit. 1688-89. **DOWNER.** 1 **Martha,** m. in Hampton 18 Oct. 1704 Richard Palmer of Bradford. 2 **MOSES,** d. Hampton 24 Oct. 1699. Widow Sarah was bap. and joined Hampt. Ch. 31 May 1703. In 1708, ±38, she was a nurse there. Ch: **Mary,** b. Newb. 18 Aug. 1694. **Moses,** b. Hampt. 17 July 1696. See List 291. **Ruth,** b. 28 Sep. 1698, all bp. 10 Oct. 1703. 3 **ROBERT,** sued in 1703 by Major John March, commander of New Casco fort.

**DOWNES,** common Middle Eng. surname. 1 **EDMUND,** Boston merchant with a warehouse at Saco. Had dealings with Wm. Phillips in Boston as early as 1656, and aft. his purch. of the Vines patent dealt with him here. Having m. Mehitable, d. of Maj. Tho. Clarke(54), he was his partn. in some of his shipping ventures. Lists 234a, 80. Adm. 29 June 1669 to wid., who continued to carry on, with Stephen Sargent as her agent. The papers show a large est., with a separate inv. for Winter Harbor. By 1674 she m. Hon. Humphrey Warren. 2 **JAMES**(Downe), with Capt. Wiggin, Wm. Hilton and Samuel Sharpe, wit. the livery of seisin of the Dover Neck patent, 7 July 1631. With Neale in Ashley trial. 3 **JOHN** (Downe). 1614. List 7. 4 **RICHARD** (Downe) alias Ford, ag. 40 in 1675, was in 1660 hiring the Dustin house in Crooked Lane, Kit.; he soon rem. with his w. to the Isl. of Shoals. Rebecca was militant, struck the const., Roger Kelly, scolded

the neighbors so that they complained. Arthur Beale fetched her and her hus. to York ct. in his boat, and he told the ct. the complainants were all drunk when they signed, and gave his bond to prove it. In 1684, 'Senior,' he mortg. his house and fishing plant on Hog Isl. in a fishing contract. In 1674 R. D., Gabriel Grubb, Wm. Pumery and Wm. Urine made a joint fishing contract with Francis Wainwright. Presum. the numer. fam. at the Shoals in the next century were his desc. William, gr.j. 1697. Wm. sued Elisha Kelly 1716. Wm. 1723. John called 'my brother' by Rebecca wid. of James Couch, (1720). John and Wm. bot together on Star Isl. in 1723. Richard, Eliot wit. 1707. Y. D. vii.159. Amey Downe and Richard Gumer, wit. (Elizabeth Currier), Shoals 1703. Elizabeth, dau. in Wm. Lakeman's will (1710). Rachel, dau. in John Muchemore's will 1718. John of Star Isl. and Ruth Coombs m. at Marblehead 12 June 1726, 2 daus. bap. there 1735. 3d selectm. of Gosport 1733. John jr. and Abigail, Wm. and Mary, Samuel and Joanna, had ch. bap. 1733. Capt. Robert, 1st selectm. 1731, widower, m. 1733 Martha Beckman (altered from Thompson). Ambrose, selectm. 1732, and Sarah (Bradbury 2 jr.), m. 3 Oct. 1728, 8 ch. 1729-1744. Wm. jr. m. 1748 Sarah, dau. of John jr. John, s. of John jr. m. 1750 Deborah Toombs. Elizabeth of Isl. of Shoals m. 23 Mar. 1737 Andrew Senter jr. of Wenham.

5 **THOMAS**, housewright, b. 1612, Boston and Dover. (T. D., shoemaker, was adm. inhab. of Hampton 25 Nov. 1654.) Gr. land at Cochecho in 1656, the next yr. he was up for water travel on Sunday, and for hims. and his man Christopher working on Sunday. Const. 1666. Lists 356abcefghk, 357d, 359b, 311c (Dover), 52, 54, 92, 94, 96. He d. 21 Jan. 1698-9, sick one month, lacking 12 days of 87. W. Catherine d. 23 Dec. 1702. List 96. An heirship deed in 1734 included 6 Downes and 2 Cooks. Kn. ch: **Rebecca,** b. 22 Apr. 1652 at Boston. **Thomas,** b. 17 Mar. 1653-4 at Boston. **Elizabeth,** b. 17 Nov. 1663 in Dover. **Mary,** mar. 25 Nov. 1686 John Cook(6).

6 **SERGT. THOMAS**(5), liv. with his father and had his lands, disting. from him as 'Sergt.' Constable. Lists 359b, 52, 57, 94, 353. In the spring of 1711 Sergt. Downes and 3 others working in a field were k. by Ind. Adm. Apr. 13 to s. Gershom. Thrice m., 1st one Martha, 2d Mary Lord, k. by Ind. 26 July 1696, List 96, 3d 24 Oct. 1698 Abigail (Roberts) Hall. Ch: **Gershom,** rec. his own birth, 's. of Tho. Jr. and Martha,' 10 Jan. 1680[1. Will 4 Apr.—27 June 1750. He m. 1st 24 Dec. 1707 Sarah Hall; 2d Elizabeth (Tibbetts), wid. of Pomfret Dam(5), who m. 3d Richard Goodwin. 7+2 ch., incl. Ger-

shom, k. by Ind. at Rochester 27 June 1746. By 2d w., Lord heirs: **Thomas,** lumberman. Highway surv. 1715. List 358d. Adm. 29 Nov. 1749 to 3 sons-in-law, all of Somersw. W. Sarah Ham had d. 9 daus. 1711-172--. **Ebenezer,** apprent. ab.1701 to Richard Pinkham; adult in 1715, housewright. List 298. His captivity in Dummer's War is much in print—Farmer's Belknap, p. 205, N. E. Capt. ii. 164. The letter of 25 Aug. 1725 printed in the -News Letter- says he had 5 ch. at Piscataqua. In 1746 he deeded half his homestead to his s. Ebenezer. Ab. 1760 Ephraim and Ebenezer Downes were liv. in Arundel, and went east. Wife Elizabeth 1737-1755. **Martha,** m. James Bunker(2), 2d by Dec. 1725 John Mackelroy, she bap. on a sick bed 17 Apr. 1744, both liv. 1750. **Samuel,** Somersw. Will 24 Mar.—30 May 1755 names w. Judith (his wid. in 1779) and sis. (app. wife's sis.) Martha Stackpole, who was widow of Tho. Stevens and d. 24 Sep. 1792, ag. 101. **William,** Somersw. Adm. 28 Aug. 1754 to s. Samuel. W. Mary Pitman, m. at Dover 3 May 1721. 6 ch.

7 **WILLIAM**, at Oyster River before 1640, rem. to West Indies. Lechford 282.

8 **WILLIAM**, (see 4), gr.j. 1697.

**DOWNING**, general name, esp. Norfolk, Suffolk, Cornwall.

1 **DENNIS**, blacksmith ('nailer') of Spitalfields, near Whitechapel, London, m. 17 Nov. 1634, at Stepney, widow Anne Daines. His first app. here was on a Me. jury 25 Nov. 1650, and a mo. later he bot the house in which he was then liv. which became the homestead. App. he came without his fam., and in 1656, when his wife quarreled with Francis Trickey's wife, they liv. in Crooked Lane, nearer his customers, on the 10 a. lot which his son 21 June 1679 sold to widow Joane Diamond. Jury 1656, const. 1656. Lists 282, 283, 285, 288, 298, 25. Jan. 16, 1676[7 he made over his est., with reserv. for life, to his son, lately m. to Patience Hatch, and confirmed it, with changed conditions, 20 Apr. 1690. W. Anne last ment. 1670. Ch: **John,** in court in 1653 for disobeying his father. He left homo and had a family, but has not been ident. Presum. he was the cr. of Robert Weymouth's est. in 1663, List 285, and not unlik. was the J. D. of Canso. Doc. Hist. iv. 372. The father's deed of 1677 was on cond. that Joshua pay to John's dau. Joanna a cow and a calf on her wedding day, which was not done, and the deed of confirm. in 1690 provided a payment of 12 pence each to his daus. Anne, Alice and Joanna if they demand it. **Joshua,** b. ab. 1644. **Dennis,** b. by ab. 1663, as his father signed 'Senior' ab. 1679. Lists 288, 94. Either this Dennis or

another, s. of (4), was k. by Ind. 4 July 1697. List 96.

2 *JOHN, CAPT., Esq., b. 1659, ag. 84 in Aug. 1742, dep. that ab. 62 yrs. past he came to Portsm. and soon aft. hired himself to Major Vaughan for one yr. and liv. with him. Ag. 78 in Sep. 1738, he dep. that in 1683 he leased Major Vaughan's farm at Cape Porpus for 7 yrs. and liv. on it 6 yrs., also owning five islands. Constable 1685; gr.j. 1687; selectm. 1688-9. In 1720 'Capt. John Downing and his son John Downing' each had a 50 a. gr. in Arundel. Driven off in 1689, he bot at Bloody Point, Newington, then in Dover. In 1701 he was a butcher, marketing in Portsm. In 1694 he and his w. held seats in the Portsm. ch., later he was a memb. of the Dover ch. In 1715 both f. and s. were orig. members of the Newington ch. He was Elder from 1724. Solectm. of Dover 1702, 1712, 1715; Rep. Dover 1714, 1715, Newington 1716. Lt. 1708; Capt. 1715. Lists 33 (J. D. sen. and J. D. jr. must stand for f.-in-law John Miller and son-in-law J. D.), 259, 335a, 336bc, 330def, 298, 343, 358d. He d. ab. 12 of the clock at noon 16 Sep. 1744, ag. 85 (his son's Bible). Will 23 Feb. 1743[4. He m. by May 1684 Susannah Miller, who d. 31 May 1733, List 335a; 2d Elizabeth (Stover) [Hunnewell] Walford, who outliv. him 'some yrs.' Ch. as named in will: John, b. 10 Apr. 1684. Richard, with John exec. of father's will. Will 2 Apr. 1747—30 Oct. 1754 names w. Alice (Downing 5) and makes his neph. and niece Richard and Alice Downing his heirs. List 343. Hannah, mar. by 1715 Jethro Bickford(15). Jonathan, m. 15 Mar. 1715-6 Elizabeth Nelson. Liv. Newing. 1765. 7 ch. bap. Joseph, m. 21 June 1716 Sarah Spinney, sole heir of James and Grace (Dennett 1). Portsm. 1 s. Joshua bap. Benjamin, m. 3 Dec. 1724 Elizabeth Fabyan(3). Settled in Ken'port ab. 1728. Deacon; town clerk 1750 till his death 1753. 10 or 11 ch. Joshua, Newington, m. 17 Nov. 1724 Susanna Dennett(2). Will 8 June—28 Oct. 1747, names 9 ch., of 10 bap. Josiah, father willed him land in Rochester.

3 JOHN, Pemaquid soldier 1696; List 127.

4 ‡COL. JOHN(2), had the homestead. In 1742-43 he liv. at Exeter, but ret. to Newington. Capt. 1740, Col. 1744. He was Councillor from 1740 till his death 14 Feb. 1766. List 343. Will 5 Sep. 1755—12 Mar. 1766. He m. 26 Nov. 1706 Elizabeth Harrison, who d. 27 July 1740; 2d 10 Apr. 1742 Sarah (Little), wid. of Maj. Barthol. Thing, who d. 11 Jan. 1754. 7 ch. of whom 3 outliv. father: Mary, b. 31 Aug. 1707, m. 7 Feb. 1726-7 Tho. Pickering. Susanna, mar. 5 Oct. 1727 Capt. Wm. Shackford. Harrison, b. 4 July 1710, mar., perh. 2d, 11 July 1750 Sarah Walker. Settled in Ken'port. John, b. 24 Sep. 1711,

joined the church, 'tertius,' 1736, mar. Patience Ham, d. 18 Aug. 1750. 5 ch. Wid. m. br.-in-law Shackford. 5 ch. Temperance, b. 12 Apr. 1713, m. Lemuel Bickford(15); 2d Jonathan Trickey, d. 28 Jan. 1770. Richard, Major, Esq., b. 24 June 1718, mar. 5 Jan. 1743-4 his cous. Alice, d. of Benj. 4 or m. ch. Alice, bp. 15 Apr. 1722, not in will.

5 *JOSHUA(1), came to Kit. ab. 1652, ag. ab. 8 by his petn. of 1680 (Doc. Hist. iv. 392, discl. a forerunner of the Revol. Yankee). He liv. with his father, had the homestoad and became a leading cit. Gr.j. 1687, 1693, 1694, foreman 1698, 1699, selectman 1692-97, commis. from Kittery to make the county rate, Rep. 1699. The Ind. 24 Aug. 1694 killed or took 5 persons at his garrison. Lists 30, 288, 96 p. 82, 296-298. For his 60 heirs at law see dep. ab. 1769 of Jonathan Fernald. N. E. Reg. 61.254. He m. by 1673 Patience Hatch, (poss. not his first wife), see Edge; 2d bet. 1709-1713 Rebecca (Rogers) Trickey, d. of Wm. and Sarah (Lynn) Rogers. In 1718 her grson Zebulon Trickey and Wm. Brooks were tenants of the est. In 1730 she was 'of Scarb.' liv. with Zebulon. In 1735 she was in Kit., deoding her all to Zebulon, now of Falm. (Stroudwater), and presum. ended her days there. Ch: Dennis, either s. or br., k. by Ind. 4 July 1697. Elizabeth, b. 22 Apr. 1669, m. Jonathan Woodman. Sarah, b. ab. 1675, m. Jonathan Mendum and Joseph Curtis(6 jr.). Joshua, jury 1710, k. by Ind. at Wells 18 Sep. 1712. Lists 296-298. He m. 28 Apr. 1709 Sarah Hatch of Portsm., who m. 2d James Chadbourne(3 jr.). 3 ch. rec., only 1 dau. grew up. Arabella, wit. with Joshua jr. in 1705. Alice, m. 24 Apr. 1709 Richard Downing.

6 RICHARD, made a fishing voyage to the Trelawny Plant. in 1634. List 21.

7 —— (Douning?), List 141.

Downton, William, 1667. Doc. Hist. vi. 8.

**DOWSE, Dowst.**

1 LODOWICK, soldier at Saco fort 1696. List 248b. At Sherborn, Mass., had ch. rec. 1683-1695.

2 SAMUEL, ±42 in 1707, m. 1 Mar. 1688-9 Sarah Berry (grdau. of 12). Gr.j. 1699. Lists 315bc, 318c, 316. 'Wid. Dowse & son Solomon' taxed 1717. Ch: Joanna, b. 2 Mar. 1688-9. Samuel, b. 4 Oct. 1690, m. Rachel. 2 ch. rec. John, b. 8 Feb. 1692-3, m. 27 Mar. 1718 Abigail Brown (Jacob), who m. 2d 16 Dec. 1724 Amos Knowles. Anna, b. 16 Feb. 1694-5. Solomon, b. 3 Jan. 1696-7, m. 31 Jan. 1723 Elizabeth Brown(33), 7 ch. of whom 5 d. 1735. Susannah, b. 6 Nov. 1699, mar. in Greenl. 11 Sep. 1720 Alexander Simes. Ozem, b. 12 Dec. 1701, m. Elizabeth Seavey. 9 ch. rec. Likely also unrec: Abigail, m. 29 Dec.

1726 Samuel Foss(5 jr.). **Priscilla,** m. 10 Oct.
1734 Samuel Wills.
**Dowt——,** William, Kit. List 298.
**Doyle,** Edward. In Me. Ct. May 1686 John
Brown accu. him of stealing silver from
his chest. Maj. John Davis paid his fine, to
be repaid in work. Of Falm. in 1687, ack.
judgment to Silvanus Davis & Co.
**Drafton,** Thomas, see Trafton.

**DRAKE,** common in Devon and Yorkshire.
Before Sir Francis Drake was knighted
(born near Tavistock, Devon, 1545), he had
his face slapped by Sir Barnard Drake for
using the arms of the Drakes of Devon. Sir
Francis d.s.p.
Drake's Island, Wells, from an early unk.
occup. or possibly ducks and drakes.
1 **ABRAHAM**(6), came to Exeter by 1643,
but later, when his f. came, he liv. with
him in Hampton, and had the homestead.
Gr.j. 1650, 1683, 1684. Jury 1651, 1674, 1693,
selectm. 1658, Marshal of Norfolk Co. 1660-
1673, volun. retired. Lists 374ac, 375ab, 376ab,
392ac, 396, 397a, 49, 54, 55b, 57. Wife Jane
d. 25 Jan. 1676. List 394. Ch. named in deed
14 Jan. 1708-9, exc. Elizabeth: **Susanna,** b.
ab. 1652, m. Capt. Anthony Brackett(2), 2d,
**John Taylor. Abraham,** b. 29 Dec. 1654. **Sarah,** b. 20 Aug. 1656, mar. Anthony Libby.
**Mary,** b. 15 Mar. 1658, m. Nathaniel Boul-
ter(3), 2d Richard Sanborn. **Elizabeth,** b. 11
July 1660, m. 18 Sep. 1679 Tho. Beadle of
Salem. **Hannah,** b. 14 Oct. 1662, d. unm. 18
Dec. 1716. **Robert,** b. 27 Sep. 1664.
2 **ABRAHAM**(1), liv. in Hampton at 'Drake
Side.' Soldier in Philip's War. Jury 1698,
selectm. 1696, 1703. Lists 57, 62, 392b, 395,
396. He mar. Sarah Hobbs, who outl. him.
Will 25 May, inv. 29 June 1714. Ch: **Sarah,**
b. 7 Nov. 1686, m. Jacob Garland. **Abraham,**
b. Dec. 1688, had the homestead. He mar. 2
Jan. 1711 Theodate Robie. Will 1752—1767
names all but one of 10 ch. rec. Wid. d. 12
Apr. 1783. **Jane,** b. 1691, m. 12 Nov. 1713
Lt. John Sherburne. **Mary,** b. 14 Feb. 1693,
m. Shubael Sanborn. **Nathaniel,** Capt., b. 7
May 1695, was given his father's new house.
Selectm. 1731, 1740, 1750. D. 11 Sep. 1763.
He m. 1 June 1716 Jane Lunt who d. 2 Dec.
1743, ag. 51, 6 ch.; 2d 22 Nov. 1744 Abigail,
wid. of John Foss(3).
3 **ENSIGN FRANCIS,** app. first in Portsm.
1657, Greenl. 1659, a hot royalist, favored
by Champernowne. Was in ct. in 1662 for
mowing a Hampton man's meadow. Jury
1661. Ensign 1666. Lists 47, 311b, 313a, 323,
326a, 327a, 330bc. Two sons cert. went with
him to Piscataway, N. J. (N.H. Files 17678)
where they have been much written up, his
w. called Mary Walker, his sons **George,** Assemblyman, (lists 47, 311b), and Rev. **John,**
Baptist preacher, and **Elizabeth,** w. of Hugh

Dunn, called his d. With w. Mary he sold
out here 5 Aug. 1668.
4 **JOHN,** Phippsburg bef. Philip's War. This
John or ano. must have been a fisherman
or coaster, drunk at Saco in 1672 (non appearance), in Marblehead before Nov. 1675
had his shoes tapped. At Kennebec he mar.
Rachel Atkins(5), where John Hanson left
them his lands and Gregory Mudge gave her
his house. List 191. She m. by 1687 James
Barry. Only ch: **Martha,** m. in Boston 21
Mar. 1703 Wm. Bewley; 2d 5 Mar. 1706 Peter
Soullard.
5 **ENSIGN NATHANIEL**(6), 78 in 1691,
app. came with his f. O. F. 1 Oct. 1650.
Gr. 30 a. by Exeter 1650, jury 1650, selectm.
1651. In 1653 of Hampt., he soon rem. to
Portsm. and again to Sandy Beach; liv. just
bef. the Ind. raid of 1691, he did not appear
as wit. to prove Anthony Brackett's will 11
July 1692. Portsm. selectm. 1656, 1661, 1663,
1671, 1676. Gr.j. 1660, 1680, 1684, 1687. Ensign 1666-1680. Lists 376b, 377, 47, 49, 50,
52, 55b, 57, 311b, 312cd, 313a, 323, 324, 326c,
330abc, 332b. He m. by 1657 (likelier 2d)
wid. Jane Berry(12) and fathered her younger Berry ch. List 323. See Locke. Ch: **Rachel. Jane,** mar. 15 Dec. 1673 Wm. Wallis.
**Son? 'Pd.** to Nathl. Drake & Son'—Town
Treas. accts. 1671. List 331a.
6 **ROBERT,** ab. 1580, serge maker, had
liv. in Colchester, Essex; followed younger s. to N. E. shortly bef. 15 Mar. 1649-50,
when he bot a house in Hampt. and 4 cow
common rights. He took O. F. 4 Oct. 1653,
freeman Apr. 1663. Jury 1653, gr.j. 1662.
List 393b. W. 18 May 1663, d. 14 Jan.
1667-8. Ch: **Nathaniel,** b. ab. 1613. **Abraham,** b. 1620. **Susannah,** in father's will.
7 **ROBERT**(1), liv. unm. with f. and sis. till
past mid. age. Had the homestead. List
399a. He m. 19 Oct. 1716 Sarah Knowles,
and d. 6 Feb. 1743; she had d. 8 June 1742,
ag. 65. Ch: **Robert,** bp. 2 Aug. 1719, m. 9
Jan. 1746 Dorothy Moulton, d. 4 July 1794;
she had d. 11 Nov. 1786. 4 ch. rec. **Hannah,**
bp. 28 Apr. 1723, m. Amos Towle; 2d Jonathan Marston.
8 **THOMAS,** sued in N. H. 1643, Isl. of Shoals
or Portsm.; early at Casco Bay, Yarm.,
bot from John Phillips, and sold by 1658 to
Richard Martin, and 24 Aug. 1664 sold his
farm at Prince's Point to Richard Bray.
9 (**William** Mr. —Folsom 110. Mr. Edm.
must have been misr. Mr. Wm.)

**DRAPER.** Occup., dry goods merchant.
Common in Bedfordshire and Lancashire.
1 **ANNE,** 20 July 1695, bond of Will Munsey of Dover and Nicholas Morrell of
Kit. to secure the town of Dover against lia-
bility by her residing there.
2 **ELISHA,** drowned 5 Apr. 1699 in trying

to recover his trout line at Mr. Wiggin's mill pond, Swampscot. List 387.

3 **NATHANIEL**, from Hitchin, co. Hertford, Sheepscot by 3 Feb. 1648-9. A wit. to earlier Ind. deeds, he bot from them himself 6 Mar. 1662. Perh. k. by Ind. in Philip's War. His heirs formed a land company which contested the Kennebec purch. Lists 12, 13. His wid., mo. of Lydia but perh. not all of his ch., was d. of Tho. Mercer; she m. 2d by 1680 Robert Scott. Ch: **Elizabeth**, m. one Stevens (Wm?) and had a son Samuel. **Nathaniel**, ±14 13 Mar. 1682-3, mariner, Boston, liv. 1736. Wife Elizabeth, liv. 1729; he m. 2d 26 Sep. 1733 Theodora Pomeroy. Ch: Lydia, b. 31 July 1699, Nathaniel, b. 30 Mar. 1702. **Esther**, ±64 in 1733, m. Joseph Roberts, Boston, shipwright, b. 24 Jan. 1673, liv. 1729, son of Simon and Christian (Baker). (See Savage, but the obit. which he scorns, printed in 1774, was written by a Harvard grad. Cong. clergy. b. 1718, whose father, b. 1694, lived to 80.) Wid. liv. 1736. 6 ch. incl: Joseph, b. 1694, d. 26 Feb. 1774, m. 29 Nov. 1716 Rachel Peck of Weston, 8 ch.; and Benjamin, b. 30 Apr. 1696 and recorded 'Samuel.' He and his mo. appeared in the Town Clerk's office and had the mistake corrected 27 Apr. 1736. 8 ch. Lydia, bp. at Charlest. 7 Jan. 1693[4, ag. ab. 20, then w. of Samuel Whittemore jr; mar. 2d 14 Mar. 1699-1700 Benj. Richardson of Woburn, and was Lydia Parker of Middleton, widow, in 1744. 1+3 ch.

**Drayton**, John, plf. in N. H. Ct. 1642-43.

**DREW**, a common name South of Bristol Channel.

1 **Bartholomew**, first app. as adm. of Gregory Jeffery's est. July 1663, later a rel., Charles Potum, joined with him. In 1666, at Shoals swear. drunk.

2 **FRANCIS**(17), ag. 31 in 1679, m. by 1673 Lydia Bickford(12). In the massacre, 1694, he was k. and his w. on the march was left behind to perish. Lists 366, 359a, 52. Adm. to br. John 16 Nov. 1694 but shifted to s. Thomas, back from captiv., 16 Nov. 1696. The deed from Francis to Thomas was a forgery. Ct. Files 25846. Ch: **Thomas**, b. ab. 1673. **Elizabeth**, mar. Tho. Footman(3). **John**. **Benjamin**, taken and k. 1694, ag. ab. 9. **Mary**, m. Samuel Green.

3 **FRANCIS**(6), m. 3 June 1713 Anne Wingate, d. 10 May 1717. She mar. 1 Jan. 1718-9 Daniel Titcomb of Dover, and d. in 1787. Only ch. by 1st hus: Joseph, b. 8 Apr. 1717, d. 1757. If wid. Tamsen Drew in 1758 was his wid., she app. was Tamsen (Meserve) wid. of Stephen Pinkham, who may have m. 3d Paul Hayes of Barrington, liv. 1789.

4 **FRANCIS**, of St. Sauveur, Isl. of Jersey, may have been the apprent. of John Drew

in 1724. He m. 21 Mar. 1726-7 Sarah Hunking of Portsm. Will 3 July, 29 Oct. 1746 names his Jersey parents. 9 ch. bap.

5 **JAMES**, br. of (11), ±30 in 1663-4, mariner, Portsm., bot at Sag. Creek 1656. Lists 330ab, 326c. He m. by 1663 Mary Jones (List 330b). Adm. 30 Dec. 1674 to widow Mary, who was given all to bring up the ch; 'Widow Drew' Lists 330def. Ch: **James**, ±24 in 1693, mariner. List 335a. **Nathaniel**, adult in 1695, feltmaker, deeded father's land with warranty against **Sisters**, incl. poss: Abigail, see (11). Also poss: John, see (7). Samuel, see Samuel White, Boston.

6 **SERGT. JOHN**(17), ±71 in 1721, cooper, settled at Back River, Dover. Jury 1696, 1697, 1699. Selectm. 1701. Lists 356j, 359a, 52, 57, 352, 358d. His will 31 Jan. 1721 provided for his whole fam. except the one born later. D. 27 Oct. 1723 ag. 73 (grst.). He m. ab. 1675 Sarah Field(1), but by 1709 was supporting two families, giving a good farm to Rebecca Cook(6). App. the community was dazed by the reckless enamourment of a responsible citizen. As soon as his w. d. he m. his concub., and as soon as he d. she m. a young man, Saml. Starbird. The Sergeant had explic. perpet. his 3 kinds of ch. on the town book. By 1st w: **Sarah**, m. 16 Jan. 1707 John Field(5). **Elizabeth**, m. Love Roberts. **John**, d. 1711. **Francis**. 'Children of John Drew': **Hannah**, b. 26 Feb. 1709-10, m. Henry Hill. **John**, b. 18 Oct. 1712, m. Patience Bunker(2). Liv. Middleton 1770. **Abigail**, b. 21 June 1714, m. James Bibber of Harpswell, d. 1783. **Rebecca**, b. 24 Apr. 1716, m. Clement Bunker(2). 'Children of John Drew by his wife Rebecca' (mar. 31 Mar. 1720): **Francis**, b. 9 Aug. 1720, d. 16 Feb. 1726-7. **Zebulon**, b. 9 Nov. 1721, blacksmith; an artisan in the Fr. wars, he was carried prisoner to France. **Lemuel**, b. 26 May 1723, d. 25 Sep. 1759. Soldier in 1st Fr. and Ind. war. Wid. Anna (Bunker) m. 17 Jan. 1753 Joseph Stevenson. Ch.

7 **JOHN**, of Portsm. 1717 or earlier, carpenter and painter, aut. N. H. Ct. files 20716, had done work in Boston, poss. an emigrant. Either he or his s. was a joiner in 1734. See (4). List 339. Hephzibah, joined Portsm. So. ch. in 1728, may have been d. or w. Kn. ch: **Ann**, m. 27 May 1719 Michael Whidden. **John**, taxed 1722, worked with his f. One John 'resident' of York, mar. 17 June 1736 Hannah Staples of Kit., who m. 2d 12 Nov. 1739 Edward Whitehouse.

8 **JOHN**(2), in the massacre was put out of a window and escaped. He liv. on his father's homestead and his daus. had it after him. K. by Ind. with likely his w. also, 27 Apr. 1706. Ch: **Mary**, m. 11 Feb. 1724-5 Joseph Wheeler. **Joanna**, mar. 11 May 1727 Zachariah Edgerly (John 1).

9 **JOHN**(6), liv. at Back River, Dover. He m. 24 May 1705 Elizabeth Hopley, who was his wid. by 10 July 1713, and soon m. James Pinkham. Ch: John, b. 17 Oct. 1707, Somersworth, k. by lightn. May 1745. He m. Abigail Wingate who was his widow in 1750. Ch. **Elizabeth**, b. 2 Nov. 1709. In 1731 she was 'now Twombly;' later presum. mo. of Hopley Yeaton, Philip Drew Y. and John Drew Y., m. in Portsm. 1766-1775—both hus. unident. **Francis**, b. 24 Jan. 1711-2, liv., w. Sarah, in 1751.

10 **MARTHA**, from 'Dedforard, Gt. Brit.', m. 11 Jan. 1727-8 James Abbott of Portsm.

11 **SAMUEL**, br. of (5), sailor. Liv. at Sag. Creek, but was building on Great Isl. when he d. List 330a. Adm. 3 July 1669 to Anthony Ellins(1) who had m. the wid. Abigail. His half-built house was conf. to his 'heirs,' incl. perh.: **Abigail**. One Abigail m. 4 Oct. 1689 Elisha Briard, who in 1715 was bondsman for Margaret (Ellins) Jackson. **Samuel**.

12 **SAMUEL**, in 1666-7 app. was in touch bet. Oyster River and Gt. Isl. Possibly bondsm. for widow of (17) in 1690. See (5 & 11).

13 **THOMAS**, br. of (17), b. 1632. Gr.j.1692. He took a mortg. from his bro's widow which she released to (6). List 366. K. in massacre 18 July, adm. to widow Mary 30 July 1694. In 1679 he wit. with Nathl. Fryer. Inv. shows trading goods. She mar. 2d Richard Elliot(4).

14 **THOMAS**(17), carpenter, cooper, ag. 69 in Sep. 1734. Settled at Back River, Dover. He mar. Mary Bunker(1), who d. ab. 1738, whereupon his son Tho. sold his own place and came back to live with his f., who d. soon aft. 1744. Jury 1697. One Thomas was selectm. of Dover 1732. List 367b. His ch. births, mostly made up for the Friends' records about 1786: **James**, b. 7 mo. 1687. **Thomas**, b. Apr. 1689, had the homestead in Madbury, w. Judith, both liv. 1762, he ag. 74 in 1763. List 369. 3 or m. ch. **William**, b. 9 mo. 1692, m. Mary Huckins. List 369. Ch. **Clement**, b. 28 Mar. 1694, 'aged 70' in May 1763. Madbury. He m. 20 May 1718 Mary Bunker(4). Their fam. record made by Abigail Dame 13 Oct. 1738 shows 8 ch. 1718-1736—**Samuel** b. later. **Lydia**, b. 10 mo. 1697 (spring of 1696 by the priest's record) was taken captive 22 May 1707. List 96. M. 28 Nov. 1720 Francis Matthews. **Hannah**, b. 2 mo. 1699, m. John Bunker(3 jr.), 2d Joseph Jackson, his wid. in 1760 when she sued her br. and neph. for calling her witch; liv. 1770. **Meshach**, b. 11 mo. 1702. List 369. Madbury. D. of a fall 7 Dec. 1785. 4 or m. ch. **Tamsen**, b. 5 mo. 1704. **Patience**, b. 11 mo. 1707, m. 21 Aug. 1729 Wm. Hill.

15 **THOMAS**(2), farmer, of Little Bay, Durham. He and w. Tamsen, recently mar., were taken capt. in 1694, dep. about very early Oyster River in May 1760, he ±87, she ±82; d. two days apart and were bur. in one grave, ag. 93 and 89. One Thomas was an Ind. scout in 1710. Lists 99, (358b), 368b, 369. Kn. ch: **Inf.** k. in the mother's captivity. **Joseph**, b. ab. 1704, joiner, m. Elizabeth Adams, d. of Rev. Hugh and Susanna (Winborn), both liv. in 1790. Ab. 1794 his narrative of the 1694 massacre was taken down. List 369. 5 ch. **Francis**, bp. 5 Apr. 1727, m. Phebe Adams, d. of Dr. Samuel and Phebe (Chesley). **Thomas**, bp. same d., was 'Thomas 3d' in the train band in 1732, rem. to Rochester bef. 1734, where he d. in 1806 ag. 95. 6 ch. bap. **Elijah**, bp. same d., was acc. of procuring by fraud a deed of his father's entire est., and app. absconded. **Tamsen**, bp. same d. **Martha, Abigail, Mary**, bp. same d., all had a deed of land in Rochester in 1744. **John**, bp. 6 Aug. 1727, app. living with Joseph in 1746. In 1773 Francis of Newington, shoemaker, q.c. est. of br. John of Durham. **Ruth**, bp. 6 Aug. 1727.

16 **WILLIAM**, fisherman, Isles of Shoals, adm. July 1657 to Capt. Brian Pendleton. Poss. f. of some or all of (1, 5, 11, 13, 17).

17 **WILLIAM**, br. of (13), b. ±1627, fisherman at Isles of Shoals keeping his fam. at Oyster River, had his house built there by Tho. Beard in 1648. He d. in Apr. 1669, adm. to wid. Elizabeth (Matthews, List 366), who m. 20 July 1671 Wm. Follett. Lists 354abc, 356a, 361a, 363abc, 365. Ch: **Francis**, b. ab. 1648. **John**, b. ab. 1651. **Hannah**, m. Godfrey Brooking, Nicholas Follett, Abraham Heseltine. **Thomas**, b. ab. 1665. (**Elizabeth**?, poss. a 1st w. of Abraham Clark, or w. of Thomas Phillips of Ipsw. 1717-1734.)

18 **WILLIAM**, soldier in Philip's War, if poss. s. of (17) he d.s.p. unless poss. he was father of Elizabeth, wife of Thomas Phillips of Ipsw., who in 1734 q.c. to Meshach Drew all rights in est. of our parent Wm. Drew late of Dover.

**DRISCO**, Thrisco. See Cartee.

1 **ANTHONY** (taxed in Exeter in 1683 only, -Frisco-, poss. error.)

2 **CORNELIUS**, Newmarket, first ment. in a deed, 1 Mar. 1708-9, from Philip Crommett, later confirmed by his s. John, of half the house and land on the no. side of Lamprill River, where grantor formerly lived. Scout service in 1712. Lists 368b, 376b. In 1718 his w. Mary and 2 daus. were bap. in Durham. 50 a. gr. in Exeter 1725. Will 10 Oct.—21 Jan. 1732-3 names w. (Mary, cited to adm. in 1740, sureties Stephen Pender-

DRISCO 208 DROWNE

gast and Geo. Grier) and 4 ch: **Mary,** called Denbo in will, Sawyer in 1740, alias Sawyer wife of Salathiel Denbo in 1741. **Keziah,** in 1732, under age, had been nursing Edw. Hilton's wife, mar. Theodore Willey. **James,** minor in will, adult in 1737, wife Mary in 1740. Had ±40 lawsuits. **Jeremiah,** bp. 2 Jan. 1722-3, had a dozen lawsuits. **Robert,** bp. 15 Feb. 1726-7, d.y.

3 **DANIEL,** Gosport, adult 1742.

4 **FLORENCE,** Portsm. 1670, List 328.

5 **JOHN,** Wells, 1683, d. 16 July 1697, adm. 10 Aug. 1697 to John Cooper of Berwick. Lists 266, 268a, 269b. His farm at Ogunquit was sold to Zachariah Goodale in 1716 by two daus: **Sarah,** m. 13 Dec. 1706 in Dover Zachariah Nock. **Mercy,** m. Timothy Conner. By trad. (Went. Gen.) they had a br. who went away unheard from, and their mo., an Emerson, was English.

6 **JOSEPH,** m. Mary Getchell, b. 12 Apr. 1687 in Salis., came with her br. John to Spurwink, in Scarb., and New Meadows in Brunswick, both liv. 1750. Presum. parents of Joseph, m. Elizabeth Mitchell (Wm.), who had d. in 1749 leaving sons Moses and John.

7 **THOMAS,** Rye, adult 1756.

8 **TIMOTHY,** alias Teague. Lists 383, 376b, 52. As -Tage Drescul- owed 2 s. to Geo. Carr's estate 1682. The hypoth. that Sarah Pitman, called Thrisco in her father's will, 1682, m. Timothy Drisco, Benj. Jones and Nathaniel Taylor is proven only so far as that Teage and wife Sarah in 1682 deeded their house and 8 acres in Exeter to John Sleeper, and that she had m. by 1696 Benj. Jones. No Jeremiah is found earlier than s. of (2). **Sarah,** -Trisco- had just m. in June 1700 Nathl. Taylor, b. 5 Feb. 1674. Witnesses Sarah Wadleigh, midwife, and Margaret Taylor. **John** Drisco in 1705 sold to Jeremiah Conner the 20 a. in Exeter gr. to -Timothy- in 1681. In 1724 Joseph Mason of Stratham and w. **Mary** q.c. the same. John was adult in 1705 and in 1715 with w. Mary sold land in Stratham bot of James Doughty. Teague, called Timothy only after his death, app. 1st in 1673 pledging his 8 a. as security for the child laid to him by Moses Gilman's servant, Mary Parker. In 1674 he sold to Philip Cartee. Taxed 1680-84. In 1771 Sarah Mason of Durham, wid., deeded house and 30 a. to dau. Mary -Disco- wid.

**DRIVER.** 1 **John,** from Lynn? soldier under Hill 1693-4. List 267b.

2 **ROBERT,** native of Orkney Islands, with Nicholas Favor executed in Boston for murdering their master, Robert Williams, on Gt. Isl., burying his body in the cellar, in Feb. 1674[5. The inventory says 'murdered in Spruce Creek.' Their master had flogged Driver. William Ferguson, Scotchman, was also arrested.

**DROWNE.** See Creber, also N. E. Reg. 53.224.

1 **LEONARD,** by trad. Welsh, (app. West Welsh, meaning Cornish or British), b. ab. 1647, shipwright. (Aut. in 1720 -Drowne-, Suff. Ct. files 14000). First app. 29 Mar. 1670, paying the fines of Mr. Henry Sherburne and w., in ct. for quarreling. In 1672 they deeded him land at Sag. Creek. In 1677, with w. Elizabeth (Abbott 5), he sold house and land there, having had a 60 a. gr. at Sturgeon Creek, Eliot, where he had a shipyard. Orig. memb. of the Baptist ch. formed in Kit. See Churchwood. Lists 329, 331b, 298. He withdrew from Indian dangers and was taxed in Boston 1689. His w. d. 5 May 1706; he m. 2d 4 Nov. 1707 Mary, wid. of Robert Colley of Malden, and was liv. there when he went bonds for her in court. Soon he was liv. with his d. in Charlestown. In 1715 he brot ejectment against Geo. Brawn for Sturgeon Creek land. He was blind for 7 yrs. bef. his d., 31 July 1729, ag. 83 (grst. in Copp's, Boston). His widow of Boston, ag. over 80 in 1736, told of her childhood at Pemaquid Gt. Falls, liv. in part of John Ridgeway's house. A geneal. letter written in 1776 by his grs. Tho., b. 14 Dec. 1715, gives but 4 sons and 2 daus. who m. Johnson and Kettle. Poss. ch: **Samuel,** b. 7 Mar. 1676-7. **Solomon,** b. 23 Jan. 1681, shipwright, d. in Bristol, then in Mass., 9 Oct. 1730 (yet Capt. Solomon, exposed to smallpox, was ordered to leave R. I. 25 Jan. 1730-1). He m. 8 Nov. 1705 in Bristol Esther (Jones?) Bosworth. 11 ch. **Shem,** Dea., coppersmith, b. 4 Dec. 1683, m. 18 Sep. 1712 in Boston Katherine Clarke, d. of Capt. Timothy and Sarah (Richardson) of Boston and Rehoboth, the mother an aunt of David Anderson of the Pemaquid patent named in his will. She d. 21 Apr. 1754, he 13 Jan. 1774. 8 ch., all but 3 d.y. Of these Thomas, the geneal., settled in Epping. **Simeon,** b. 8 Apr. 1686, shipwright, d. Boston 2 Aug. 1734. He m. 1st Mary Paine, d. of Col. Nathl. and Dorothy (Rainsford) of Rehoboth (5 ch., incl. Alithea, w. of Anthony Brackett(3); 2d 7 Oct. 1725 Mary Everenden, whose will 1752—1752, names her br. Geo. E. **Thomas,** m. 4 June 1710 Elizabeth Ham of Portsm. **Susannah,** m. 11 Jan. 1709 in Boston John Johnson. **Mary,** b. ab. 1693, m. 24 Apr. 1712 James Kettle of Charlestown, d. 24 Jan. 1732. **Elizabeth,** b. 2 Nov. 1699. **Hannah,** mar. in Boston 11 Apr. 1727 John Wardell.

2 **SAMUEL**(1), shipwright, d. in Eliot 25 Jan. 1720-1 (grst.). He m. in Boston 3 Feb. 1698 Elizabeth Morrill of Eliot. Wid. Elizabeth Drowne, ag. near 70, was bap. with her s. Samuel and grs. Solomon at Rochester 29 June 1740. Kn. ch., b. in Boston: **Elizabeth,** b. 20 Apr. 1700, m. 12 Mar. 1720-1 in

Kit. James Wittum. **Samuel,** b. 5 July 1704, in 1729 he and br. Solomon, of Dover, bot in Rochester, where they settled and he d. at 91. He m. in Durham 12 Jan. 1728-9 Martha Tibbetts. Ch. bap. in Dover and Rochester. **Solomon,** b. 26 Mar. 1706, ch. bap. in Roch. from 1743 on. **Thomas,** b. 23 Dec. 1708, d. 3 Aug. 1709. Poss: **Hannah,** mar. in Boston 1727. **Mary,** wit. in Durham, 1732.

**Druells** (Druelly?), George, in lawsuit with Richard Waldron, N. H. Ct. 1641.

**DRYLAND, Dennis,** wit. 1664 to Ind. deed to Maj. Wm. Phillips. Killed by a fall out of the chamber into the cellar. Coroner's jury of Berw. men Aug. 1668.

**Duckett,** Edmund, at Monhegan 1624. List 9.

**Duckworth,** Charles, Philip's War. List 237b.

**Duda,** see Durrell.

**DUDLEY,** a town with ruins of a castle in Staffordshire but rated in Worcestershire from which various noble families have taken their name.

1 REV. **\*SAMUEL,** bp. at All Saints, Northampton, 30 Nov. 1608, s. of Gov. Tho. by Dorothy, d. of Edmund Yorke, and halfbr. of Gov. Joseph (whose mother was a Dighton), and by marriage became son of another gov. and br. of two more. He was a merchant and budding magistrate when he turned to preaching, and app. never depended on that service to support his large fam. by 3 wives. Lieut. in 1631, he was at Ipsw. with f. and bros.-in-law in 1635, then at Camb., then with the first at Salis., where he was on the Co. Ct. bench and was Rep. 1641-1645. Evidence cont. through life of pub. conf. in his judgm. and impart. In 1650 Richard Martyn, Esq., Mr. Saml. Dudley, Mr. Seaborn Cotton and Elias Stileman were the committee to draw up the new laws. Exeter, aft. calling many, invited him to come and preach 13 May 1650, to bring his family when they had bot him a house. Portsmouth voted 27 Oct. 1656 to invite Mr. Samuel -Dudlow- to preach, and 10 Nov. agreed with him 'to come unto us this next spring' at £80 per yr. But he continued to preach at Exeter until his death, with no evid. of church records kept. Lists 376b, 379, 49, 52, 54. Inv. 10 Feb. 1682-3, adm. to widow's 'sonn in Lawe' Theophilus. He m. 1st Mary Winthrop who d. 12 Apr. 1643; 2d Mary Byley, who came in 1638, ag. 22, whose sis.-in-law mar. Dep-Gov. Sam. Symonds; 3d by 1651, one Elizabeth, ag. 43 in 1671, who in 1702 was liv. with their d. Dorothy Leavitt. The deeds of the 50 a. lots into which his 600 a. gr. was divided prove his 12 heirs, Theophilus not claiming a double share. In 1725, with only 2 s. liv. and all but 2 of his 10 s. childless, List 376b has 10 Dudleys. Ch: **Thomas,** bp. Boston 9 Mar. 1634, H. C.

1651, d. unm. 7 Nov. 1655, a tutor in the college. Will N. E. Reg. v. 444. **John,** bp. Boston 28 June 1635, d.y. **Margaret,** bp. at Camb., n.c.m. in 1683, if not always. Grd. of two governors, in 1664 she had a ch. by one Francis Pofat, who disapp., and a delegation of townsmen give bond to save the town from exp. Her f. on his death bed committed her care to her sis. Ann Hilton, the only one she would live with. **Samuel,** bp. Camb. 2 Aug. 1639, d. Salis. 17 Apr. 1643. **Ann,** b. Salis. 16 Aug. 1641, m. Edw. Hilton. By 2d w: **\*Theophilus,** Capt., Esq., b. 31 Oct. 1644, never mar. but fathered his father's young ch., even to fist fights. Jury 1679, 1694, forem. 1697, gr.j. 1679, forem. 1695, selectm., 15 yrs., Rep. 1699-1701, 1711-1713. Justice of Sessions Ct. 1707 till death. Lists 376b, 383, 387, 52, 54, 57, 62. Will 8 Apr.— 3 June 1713 names many kin. **Mary,** b. 21 Apr., d. 28 Dec. 1646. **Biley,** b. 27 Sep. 1647. Jury 1679, gr.j. forem. 1692, 1700, selectm. 1687, 1690, 1694-1698. Lists 376b, 377, 383, 52, 54, 55b, 57, 62, 67. Will 24 Jan. 1722-3— 4 Sep. 1728 leaves all to w. Elizabeth (Gilman), m. 25 Oct. 1682, who m. by 1729 Samuel Thing. No ch. **Mary,** b. 6 Jan. 1650, m. 24 Jan. 1675-6 Dr. Samuel Hardy of Beverly, living at Exeter in 1713, 4 or m. ch. **Thomas,** schoolmaster, liv. 8 Apr. 1713. In 1697 had w. Mary; m. 2d the returned Ind. capt. Rebecca, wid. of Edw. Taylor, liv. in Newmarket 1732. Lists 52, 57, 384b. By 3d w: **Elizabeth,** b. 1652, m. 25 Sep. 1674 Kinsley Hall. **Stephen. James,** Lt., b. 1664, merchant. Gr.j. 1703. Will 12 Feb. 1717-8, d. 14 Sep. 1720 (grst.). Sole benefic., w. Elizabeth (Leavitt), in 1697 sole surv. in a wreck (see Berry 2), liv. to m. 2d 8 Oct. 1724 Robert Brisco of Beverly; 3d 22 Sep. 1730 Rev. John Odlin; liv. 1746. No ch. **Timothy,** d. bef. 1702 s.p. **Dorothy,** m. 26 Oct. 1681 Moses Leavitt. **Rebecca,** m. 21 Nov. 1681 Francis Lyford. **Samuel,** b. by 1668.

2 **SAMUEL**(1), yeoman, m. Elizabeth Thing. In 1737 he deeded land to sons Samuel and Jonathan, providing a cow for d. Elizabeth. Lists 383, 67, 376b. Kn. ch: **Mary,** m. David Watson. **Samuel,** d. in the army. Will 1758 names 5 brs. and sis. **Jonathan,** m. 13 Oct. 1720 Dinah Bean (John 2 jr.). Liv. in Brentwood. Will 13 May—30 June 1762 names his w., 2 s., 7 ds. **Joanna,** bp. Hampton 24 Oct. 1697, not in br.'s will. **Elizabeth,** b. 9 Feb. 1714, unm. Adm. 1762 to Nathaniel Thing. **Sarah,** b. 9 Apr. 1716, m. one Leavitt. **Mercy,** m. by 1746 Nathaniel Thing, neph. of Joseph.

3 **STEPHEN**(1). Gr.j. 1695. Lists 52, 57, 62. He m. 24 Dec. 1684 Sarah Gilman, who d. 24 Jan. 1712-3 (grst.); 2d Mary Thing, 3d Mercy Gilman. Will 17 Feb.—13 May 1734-5 names w. Mercy, 3 sons, ch. of 3 dec. sons,

3 daus. Ch: **Samuel**, b. 19 Dec. 1686, d. 16 Feb. 1717-8 (grst.); m. Hannah Colcord(2), to whom adm. 8 May 1718. 4 ch. **Stephen**, Col. 1723, b. 10 Mar. 1688, apprent. to Tho. Webster, cordwainer, 1712 innholder, m. Sarah Davison(1). List 376b. 8 ch. **James**, Lt., b. 11 June 1690, cooper, m. Mercy Folsom(4), d. 4 Sep. 1746. 8 ch. **John**, b. 4 Oct. 1692, k. by Ind. 23 June 1710. **Nicholas**, Esq., b. 27 Aug. 1694, Brentwood, m. Elizabeth Gordon. Will 1763—1766. 8 ch. **Joanna**, b. 3 May 1697, m. Nicholas Perriman, d. 24 Nov. 1762. 5 ch. **Treworthy**, Capt., m. Hannah Gilman. Adm. 1751. 4 ch. **Joseph**, d. 8 Sep. 1727 ae. 25. He m. 26 Nov. 1724 Maria Gilman (Joshua), who mar. 2d in May 1729 Philip Conner(6). 2 ch. **Elizabeth**, m. Simon Gilman. **Sarah**, b. 15 Jan. 1706, mar. Ezekiel Gilman.

**Due**, see Dew.

**Duery**, Philip, see Durrell.

**DUGG.** 1 **Daniel**, see Duggin.

2 **JOHN**, k. by Ind., Dover, 1689. List 96, p. 80.

**DUGGIN.** 1 **Daniel**, Portsm. 1672. Lists 52, 57 (Dugg), 329, 331ab, 334a.

2 **SAMUEL**, servant in Rich. Martyn's will.

**Duk?**——, Philip, Portsm., drunk in 1673. Ct. Files ii. 351.

**DULEY**, Duly. In London a name Dule.

**PHILIP**, a sailor in Mr. John Cutt's service in 1679, m. ab. 1682 Grace Roberts and settled at Oyster River. In 1699 or 1700 he exchanged dwellings with Nathaniel Tibbetts. During the Ind. troubles he withdrew to Stratham. D. soon aft. 3 Aug. 1717 when he and his w. confirmed his 20 a. gr. of 1693 to the then owner. Lists 57, 368ab, 388. She was bap. 'an ancient widow' 11 Oct. 1719, soon m. Timothy Moses, and was liv. in 1736 'aged 68.' Ch: **Philip**, rem. from O. R. to Scarb. in 1719, where his wife Elizabeth (Eliza? bp. 10 Feb. 1716-7) d. 9 Mar. 1719, and he (aband. a logging contr.) moved back again, taxed in Portsm. 1722, lic. innholder in 1722, joined the ch. in Durham 3 Feb. 1722-3. At Scarb. he was a partn. of Hezekiah Phelps and clerk of the Proprietors. Lists 368b, 239b. Kn. ch: Sarah, apprent. 9 Apr. 1719, ag. 6, to Joshua Davis of Portsm., m. there 6 Sep. 1733 Peter Simpson, from parish of St. Clements Danes, London; a wid. and hanged for infanticide, with another on the same warrant, 27 Dec. 1739. Others, perh. Mary, bp. 28 July 1717, Samuel, mar. Susannah Perkins of Newmarket. **William**, of Oyster River 1715-6, town gr. in Scarb. 1721, soldier through Dummer's War 1722-1725, orig. memb. of Scarb. ch. 1728, was empl. by Crisp Bradbury at Biddeford 1738, d. in Durham ab. 1748. List 368b. Samuel and Mary, she a single woman, were of

Durham 1765. **Hannah**, ab. 1728 built hers. a house in Portsm., in 1736, of Durham, was in ct. for bastardy. **Sarah**, m. 25 July 1717 Tho. Harris. They moved to Scarb. where she d. and was bur. on Winnock's Neck. Of Scarb. 1724, Dover 1726-27. **Mary**, perh. the one bp. 28 July 1717, in 1721 was in Me. Ct. for bastardy, again in 1723 in N. H. Court. In 1724 she was accu. of liv. with her dec. sister's hus. as man and w. He could not m. her, as this was bigamy, as the law was then.

**DUMMER**, a double-surname family, Pyldren alias Dummer, from the time John Pyldren m. Maude Dummer, ab. 1515. Dummer a parish 5 m. from Basingstoke.

1 ‡*RICHARD**, Stephen and Thomas, sons of Thomas Pyldren alias Dummer of Bishopstoke, all have to do with N. H. or Me. altho they never liv. here. Two soon went back. Stephen, here at Newbury, was gr.f. of Judge Sewall and ancest. of the Maine Sewalls. Asp. pp. 50-66. He went back to Bishopstoke. Thomas, also here at Salis., was f. of Margaret who m. Hon. Job Clements(3). His will of North Stoneham, Hants, 1650. Richard came over at least twice, first in 1632 with w. Jane, d. of Rev. Tho. Mason of Odiham, Hants; next in 1638 with his bros. He largely financed the Company of the Plough, grantees of the Lygonia patent, and ack. relat. to their leader, Rev. Stephen Bachiler(5), whose 2d w. was widow Helen Mason. He then consid. leading a company to R. I., of whom Mr. Easton(1), Mr. Jeffrey and others went; but himself to Newbury. When first over he was made Assist., but was dishon. and disarm. with Mr. Wheelwright. Later he was Rep. 1640, 1645 and 1647 from Newb., where he d. 14 Dec. 1678. His 2d w. was Frances, wid. of Rev. Jonathan Burr of Dorchester, who d. 19 Nov. 1682, mother of all his ch. exc: Shubael, b. Ipsw. 17 Feb. 1635-6. His other ch. incl: Jeremiah, b. 14 Sep. 1645, Boston goldsmith, who in 1714 claimed 800 a. in Casco Bay gr. to his f. by Cleeve under the Lygonia patent. He was active in overthr. Andros. Ch. incl. Jeremiah the diplomat; William, Lt. Gov. during the three yrs. Ind. war, fought chiefly in Me. & N. H., called Dummer's War; Anna, mother of Jeremiah Powell, Esq. of No. Yarmouth; and presum. Shubael, d. a Boston deed 7 Nov. 1706. List 38.

2 **SHUBAEL**, ±15 in 1650, H.C. 1656, preaching at Salis. in 1660, 'Shubal Drummer priest' at Major Shapleigh's house in 1662, mildly ment. in Quaker hist., minister at York from 1668. Inst. to the Gen. Court—Mass. Arch. 69. 159a. Lists 34, 96. Wife Lydia (Alcock 1) and young son d. on the march to Quebec. In 1713 Jeremiah, Esq.,

claimed to be his 'only bro. & heir,' altho in 1680 their father's land was divided betw. Richard, Shubael and William, and later William's share (of Boston, dec.) was divided among bros. Shubael, Jeremiah and Richard; also note the other Shubaels.

**Dunbar,** Mr., operating at Shoals 1649.

**DUNCAN.** 1 **John,** Dover. Lists 94, 96. Killed by Indians 28 June 1689.

2 **JOSEPH,** servant of Capt. Thomas Wiggin, drowned 24 June 1648.

**DUNCOMB, Oliver.** List 14. Est. adm. in Suff. Co. by Wm. Waldron in 1672.

**DUNHAM,** see also Denham. [Jonathan m. at Barnstable 1655, ordained at Edgartown 1694], presum. the Mr. Dunham, minister at Saco 1659. List 249.

**DUNN,** a common name Devon to Northum.

1 **HUGH,** first taxed in Dover (Oyster River) in 1661 or 1662, adm. inhab. 1663, in 1664 was gr. land on Lamprill Riv. where he had already built. Was one of the four patentees of New Piscataway, East Jersey, 18 Dec. 1666. Lists 363abc. In N. J. he was a lay Baptist preacher. Will 7 Oct. 1691, d. 16 Nov. 1694. He m. Elizabeth Drake(3). 9 ch. b. 1672-1694. N. H. Gen. Rec. i. 149.

2 **NICHOLAS,** tailor, first ment. at Oyster River ab. 15 yrs. after (1) left. List 57. He m. Elizabeth (Roberts) who poss.(?) had lost a first hus. k. by the Ind. with her father, and was his wid. by 1699, when she was selling her land 'for my maintenance.' She m. 2d Tho. Allen(14). Ch: **Nicholas. Elizabeth,** b. 1687, mar. 4 Oct. 1728 James Davis(40).

3 **NICHOLAS**(2), shipwright, m. in Boston 6 June 1710 Deborah Grindall, their ch. bp. in Boston Second Ch. His wife joined Durham Ch. by letter 10 Jan. 1719-20. In 1722 they were liv. in Kit., in 1736 Edw. Hopkins of Portsm. was bound to the peace towards N. D. and fam., in 1737 they had been liv. 2½ yrs. in the house called Col. John Plaisted's house, in 1742 he was of Kittery. Rec. ch: **Nathaniel** b. 11 May 1711, Boston, with his w. joined Portsm. So. Ch. 2 Nov. 1735; marked -dead- on Portsmouth tax list 1738; s. Josiah bp. 23 May 1736. **Anna,** b. 26 Dec. 1713, m. John Deering jr.(1), 2d Dea. James Milk. **Samuel,** b. 24 Nov. 1715. **Deborah,** b. 13 Oct. 1716. **Dorcas,** b. 1 Nov. 1717. **Josiah,** bp. in Durham 3 Jan. 1719-20. In 1758 wid. Deborah (Skillings) Bailey, with her ch. Samuel, Josiah and Nathaniel Dunn and Lydia Atwood, sold at Long Creek, So. Portland. Besides these were: James, caulker, of Portsm., working for Richard King in Kit. 1731, and Alice, of Portsm., m. Caleb Beck 2 Dec. 1739.

4 **WILLIAM,** Boston, m. 15 Nov. 1723, Elizabeth (Parsons), wid. of John Hemenway, dau. of John of York, both liv. 1728. W. D. m. 20 Oct. 1730 Elizabeth Blancher. W. D. adm. 1749.

**Dunning,** William, York. List 279.

**Dunton,** John, master of -The Warwick- 1631. List 41.

**Dunwitt** (Dunnell?), Henry, soldier at Sagadahoc 1689. Doc. Hist. ix. 15.

**DURDAL,** Hugh, came 1638 with Edm. Littlefield's fam. Newport 1639. Hingham, millwright, 1641. Lech. 390.

**DUREN.** 1 **Edward** (Duren, During, Dowreing), see Eurin—Urine.

2 **JOHN,** train soldier 1690. List 57.

**DURGIN,** Durgen.

1 **JAMES**(2), eldest s., on his petn. in 1702 adm. was gr. to his stepmother Catherine on his father's est. By dep. of Tho. Drew, ±87 in 1760, James was consid. older. Ind. scout in 1710, d. bef. 1761. Lists 66, 368ab, 369. He m. 1697 Susanna, widow of David Davis. By elim. his nephews, his ch. incl: **Francis,** m. Susannah Durrell. List 369. Liv. in 1740. Ch. **William,** b. 1705, bur. 18 Apr. 1781. List 369. He mar. Margaret Crommett(1). 5 ch. **Jonathan,** b. 29 Sep. 1709. List 369: Adm. 1768 to wid. Judith (Edgerly, d. of Samuel(1). 9 ch. **James.** List 369. Liv. 1740. M. Dorothy Edgerly, sis. of Judith. Ch. **Treworthy,** ag. 69 in 1785, mar. Mary Durrell (Joseph 2). 7 ch. **Susannah,** m. James Goodwin of Newmarket.

2 **WILLIAM,** b. by sev. dep. 1643. First taxed 1663. His house at Lubberland was a garrison; was paid in 1695 for boarding soldiers; perh. some yrs. d. when adm. asked in 1702. Lists 363c, 359a, 52, 57, 94, 368a. Having lost his w., he m. 2d 25 June 1672 wid. Katherine (Matthews) Footman, liv. Sep. 1705 ag. 67. Kn. ch. by 1st w: **James.** By 2d w: **William,** b. ab. 1673. **Francis,** b. ab. 1675, d. 9 June 1735, Newmarket. List 376cb. Statement that his 1st w., mar. in Hampt. 24 Jan. 1703, was Sarah Marston, d. of Isaac and Elizabeth (Brown), has not been verif. He m. 2d Eleanor (Place) Satchell, whose will, of Stratham, 17 Feb. (d. 23 Dec.) 1747-8, shows no ch. By 1st w: 9 or m. ch., incl. Benj. d.s.p. bef. 1756, Francis and William, of Newmarket and Epping in 1766, and four ds. in q.c. deed 1738, Eliza-beth (m. 7 Nov. 1723 James) Kenniston, Mary Bracy (w. of Isaac Marston's grs. Joseph Bracy of York), Sarah Folsom and Susannah Kenniston.

3 **WILLIAM**(2), ±63 in Feb. 1734-5, dep. that ab. 45 yrs. ago he liv. with his uncle Wm. Follett. Lists 368b, 369. He m. Elizabeth Pinder, given 15 s. in Tho. Morris's will 1701, who d. in childbirth 24 Oct. 1721. Kn. ch: **John,** m. 6 Mar. 1728-9 Elizabeth Crommett(1). List 369. 4 or m. ch. **Joseph,**

w. Abigail d. 17 Sep. 1743, ag. 30. List 369. Benjamin, m. Elizabeth Edgerly, d. in Rev. army 7 Mar. 1778. Joshua, m. Hannah Perkins. 4 or m. ch. Josiah, bot the homestead in 1743, but liv. 1769 in Lee. His wid. Lydia (Coffin, m. 21 June 1749) was bur. 6 Sep. 1783. Elizabeth, liv. in Newington in 1754, m. 15 Dec. 1756 John Leonard. William, b. 24 Oct. 1721.

DURHAM. 1 Humphrey, b. ab. 1638, 1st ment. in deed from Cleeve, 25 Mar. 1658, 50 a. in Back Cove, Portland, adj. Phineas Rider, but later rem. to the east side of the Presumpscot Riv., now Fal., where he was k. by Ind. Aug. 1676. Lists 55, 222a, 223b. Wife unkn. Ch: John, liv. on his father's lands betw. the wars, d. bef. 1732 s.p. Samuel. Sarah, m. one Daniels, was late dec. of Mendon in 1734. Ch: John, Samuel, and Abraham, all of Mendon, and Sarah, w. of Simon Peck of Uxbridge. Anne, m. Samuel White, Boston boatbuilder, who d. bef. 1729. Ch. rec. 1697-1710, of whom Capt. Samuel, mariner, will Jan. 1736-7—25 Mar. 1740, ment. Ebenezer, Mary Webb, Lydia Chubb, with his mother Anne.

2 SAMUEL(1), taxed Bost. 1689, m. 6 July 1691 Elizabeth Reed, wid. 1736. Ch: Samuel, b. 1 Mar. 1692, d. bef. 1733. Elizabeth, b. 26 Nov. 1694, m. 12 Aug. 1715 Richard Lyne. John, bricklayer, Boston, 1734. 'Durum the mason' taxed Portsm. 1719. He m. 9 Dec. 1719 Abigail Wyman. Adm. Suff. Co. 1759. 6 ch. bp. Boston 1728-9. Anne, b. 22 Nov. 1698, d.y. Sarah, m. 9 Oct. 1723 Daniel Wyman. Anne, b. 14 Sep. 1702, m. 12 Aug. 1723 Caleb Pratt. Bethia, m. 27 Jan. 1726 John Inglesby. Mary, unm. 1733, (?m. Thos. More 11 Aug. 1745).

Durlen, Cornelius, see Darley.

DURRELL, Dueril, Durin, Duda.
1 MOSES (Durin, Dudey), was serv. of Robert Elwell in Glouc., and soldier in Philip's War. He rem. to Scarb. by 1683-4, his gr. there adj. John Sampson's whose dau. Sarah he m. 23 Dec. 1686. Lists 34, 85, 238a. (List 238a, Sc. gr. to Nic., error for Mo.). Sent back to Mass. by the Ind. troubles he was at Salem, leaving there aft. Oct. 1689. In Oct. 1699 he bot the land in Glouc. his house stood on, liv. there until he rem. to Biddeford ab. 1725. There he deeded land on the east side of the river to s. Nathl. 28 Jan. 1734-5, and half his right in Narragansett No. 1 to his dau. Sarah Rumery 25 Oct. 1736. Wife Sarah liv. 1734-5; adm. on his est. to grs. Benja. Durrell in 1753. Ch: Nathaniel, bp. Glouc. 15 Aug. 1703, m. 7 Feb. 1717 Hannah Elwell, dau. of Robert and Sarah (Gardner). Liv. in Bid., Scarb., Buxton and back to Saco 1762. 7 ch. Sarah, bp. with Nathl., m. 1st 30 Jan. 1717-8 Thomas Pennell, who d. Glouc. 31 Mar. 1723, 3 ch.; 2d Edward Rumery of Bid., 4 sons. Jonathan, b. Glouc. 30 Aug. 1702, d. there 10 Mar. 1725. Lydia, d. Glouc. 27 Nov. 1723, ag. ab. 14. Also poss. Moses, mariner, d. Boston 5 July 1730 aged 24, adm. 7 July to Caleb Beal, his acct. incl. item 'going to Salem.'

2 PHILIP (Dudey, Duda), by trad. from Guernsey, of Exeter in 1694. List 62. He rem. ab. 1700 to Arundel, where his fam. was taken capt. by Ind. 10 Aug. 1703, but wife and inf. s. sent back to Saco Fort. He ret. to Ex., was of Stratham 17 Aug. 1716 when sued for 5 years' store acct. by Samuel Penhallow, but soon returned to Arundel where hist. repeated, as he reed. his old gr. and his fam. was again capt. by Ind. in 1726 and wife k. In 1727 he bot 100 a. there. Abs. from meet., Jan. 1730-1, he was acquit. acct. age and distance; liv. there 1738. Ch: Joseph, blacksm., Durham, Lists 368b, 369, m. bef. 4 Mar. 1711-12 Rebecca Adams(4). 8 ch. Philip, Arundel, m. 27 May 1724 Keziah Wakefield. Ch. Benjamin, Arundel, List 99, m. Judith Perkins. Ch. John, m. widow Lydia Jellison. Ch. Rachel, captive, List 99, m. in Canada. Susan, capt., List 99, m. in Canada. Elizabeth, m. John Wakefield. Mary, m. James Wakefield. Lydia, m. Stephen Larrabee. Sarah, List 99, m. John Baxter(2). Dau., m. Joshua Purington.

DUSTIN, Thomas (aut. Duston), b. ab.1605. He was in Dover in 1640, was sued in Dover Ct. in 1643, and the same yr. bot from Edw. Colcord land formerly Wid. Messant's. Rem. to Maine by 1647. Trial j. 1647, gr.j. 1646-7, 1657, coroner's j. 1647, const. Kit. 1653-55. Lists 21, 351ab, 282, 298. Until his house burned he liv. on the 20 a. in Crooked Lane gr. him in June 1654; aft. in Portsm. where liv. Mar. 1659-60, brought there by Geo. Walton who gave bond to secure the town. He became indebted to Mr. John Cutt aft. the fire and the Kit. prop. was finally sold to him. Adm. 1 July 1662 to wid. Elizabeth (Wheeler, dau. of John of Newb.), who m. 2d 9 June 1663 Matthias Button of Haverh., d. there 16 July 1690. Ch: Thomas, Haverh. m. 3 Dec. 1677 Hannah Emerson, who later was the famous Indian captive and killer, Hannah Dustin. His will proved 27 Nov. 1732, hers 6 Mar. 1737-8. 13 ch., incl. Timothy, List 298 p. 35, m. 7 Nov. 1718 Sarah Johnson. Elizabeth, m. 1st bef. 1664 John Kingsbury, 2d 11 Dec. 1672 Peter Green.

DUTCH. 1 Osman, coastwise trader, sett. in Gloucester. See Roper. Lech. 109-114. Davis: -Ancestry of Charity Haley-.
2 ROBERT (Duch), mar. in Greenl. 7 Jan. 1719-20 Elizabeth King. Eliot wit. 1722.

DWIGHT, *Timothy, Hampton grant 1640. List 392a. Dedham 1636. Rep. for Medfield 1652. Fatally wounded in Ind. attack

on Dedham, d. 9 Mar. 1676. 3 ch. That T. D. disting. by his poster. was his neph. **Dwinthim**, Thomas. Sheepscot 1672. List 13.

**DYER**, a common name in S. W. of Eng. and Suffolk.

1 **CHRISTOPHER**(8), b. ab. 1640, of Sheepscot until 1676, Braintree 1680, with br. John was a petnr. in 1682 for re-settlem. of Sheepscot. He ret. there, was constab. 16 Sep. 1684, and k. in Ind. attack in Dec. 1689, after which fam. fled to Braintree again, never to return. Lists 12, 13, 17, 162. Wife Ruth m. 2d 25 Dec. 1692 John Hathaway of Taunton, d. 11 Sep. 1705 ag. 65. Ch. by 1st w: **William**, b. ab. 1663-4, m. 1st ab. 1692 Joanna Chard, 2d, of Bridgewater (int. 17 Apr. 1712) Mary Whitman. Of Weym. in 1738 he dep. ab. his grf.'s fam. and est. in Sheepscot. Will 10 Nov. 1749—15 Aug. 1750. Ch. **Grace**, b. ab. 1666, m. John Alliset. **John**. One John slain in the wars was f. of Abigail Ball's ch., Dorch., 1691. Ano. John, of Braintr., was drowned in June 1703. By 2d wife: **Rebecca**, m. Bost. 10 June 1695 William Briggs. Besides these, likelier ch. of 2d w. by former hus: Mary, m. 1698 Samuel Talbot of Taunton. Ruth, b. about 1683, m. Benjamin Paul of Taunton.

2 **EDWARD**, evid. from Ipsw. (Dear), ±17 in 1682. Lists 57, 67. M. by 1693 a dau. of Richard Morgan, presumably 'Old Goody Dyer,' d. in Stratham 13 Dec. 1744. Ch: **Katharine**, given 7 a. by her grf. bef. 1699.

3 **HENRY**, mariner, was at Portsm. 23 Mar. 1679-80, a wit. with Joshua Fryer 1681, master of the ketch -Prosperous- 1684. Wife Hannah Riddan, dau. of Thaddeus, was a wid. taxed in Portsm. 1690, vict. lic. 1692, m. 2d 12 Oct. 1693 Augustine Bullard(1). Ch: Henry.

4 **HENRY**(3), was a wit. with Geo. Jaffrey jr. in 1705. Of Portsm. in 1709 with five men he drove off Ind. attacking Sampson Doe's house—List 96. In 1715 he was a merchant of Boston, formerly of Exeter, but returned to Ex. where he d. Adm. 7 Nov. 1719 to James Jaffrey, the est. insolv. He m. Joanna (Gilman) Coffin, wid. of Robert(4). She d.s.p. 24 Dec. 1720, her will 23 Dec. 1720—7 June 1721.

5 **HENRY**, of Boston. List 37.

6 **JOHN**(8), b. ab. 1648. Lists 13, 162. Liv. in Braintree after leaving Sheepscot, he k. an Ind. who was trying to get into his house, and was found guilty of manslaughter 3 Feb. 1680-1. He joined in the endeav. to re-occupy Sheepscot, but escaped wounded to Braintree; bur. there 23 Apr. 1733, very aged. His will 9 Mar. 1731—30 Apr. 1733, reciting 'made incapable of labor by wounds from Indians in Eastern wars,' names wife Anna, 9 liv. ch., 1 decd. First w. Sarah, 2d

Anna Holbrook, dau. of Samuel; her will 2 Apr. 1745. Ch. by 1st w: **William**, b. Braintree 1 May 1683, left home early, says his fr.'s will in 1731. The only one of the fam. to live in Me., he was masting above Salmon Falls in Dec. 1707. He m. 1 July 1708 Mary Chadbourne(2) and lived in Berwick and Biddeford. Jury 1714. Dying in Bid. about 1741, adm. was gr. to his wid. Mary, who d. in Berwick ab. 1765. 7 ch. By 2d w: **Nathaniel**, bp. 8 Oct. 1693, d. 20 Mar. 1699. **Christopher**, bp. 19 Apr. 1696, m. in Boston 10 Nov. 1720 Anna Littlefield, dau. of Edmund and Elizabeth (Mott); lived in Randolph. Ch. **Samuel**, m. in Boston 12 Feb. 1717 Lucy Butcher; d. bef. 1731 leaving a s. Butcher, b. 11 Dec. 1720. **Anna**, bp. 5 June 1698, m. Ebenezer Pratt. **Jonathan**, bp. 3 Aug. 1701, m. 27 Apr. 1727 Mary Hayden, dau. of Nehemiah and Mary (Curtis). 2 ch. **Sarah**, bp. 5 Sep. 1703, m. 2 Dec. 1723 David Sloan. **Mary**, m. 1 May 1729 Gornil Price. **John**, m. Dorch. 15 Aug. 1727 Ruth Littlefield. **Deborah**, unm. 1731, prob. mar. (int. Bost. 31 Aug. 1738) Samuel Grice. **Peter**, d. at 11 mos. **Peter**, b. 4 Feb. 1711, m. 16 Oct. 1740 Dorothy Hayden. Ch.

7 **MATTHEW**, Cape Bonawagon 1672. List 13.

8 **WILLIAM**, Sheepscot, lived on 600 a. on Dyer's Neck conv. to him by Ind. deeds 11 Feb. 1662, 29 Mar. 1664, the latter shown to the Ind. in 1726. List 13. Associate, Court of Genl. Sess., and wealthy and prom. until Ind. attacks 1676 drove all away; that yr. he was in Scituate, all left behind, incl. 56 head of cattle, 30 swine. Altho only his sons signed the petn. in 1682, depos. show he did ret. to Sheepscot and was k. by Ind. in Aug. 1689. In 1712 Dyer's Neck passed to others by two deeds, his s. John and heirs of s. Christopher to Samuel Bolles and w., Samuel and Mary Bolles to Henry Flint. Ch: **Christopher**. **John**. **Mary**, m. S. Bolles(6).

**Dyver**, Jasper. Pemaquid 1687. List 124.

**Earle**, see Hearl, and Creber.

**EARTHY**, **John**, mariner, first appear. Pemaquid 1674, s.-in-law of Thomas Gardner, Esq. Lists 15, 4. Presum. Ind. interpret., he served as envoy and wit. treaty 13 Nov. 1676. Escaped to Salem, O. A. there in Jan. 1677-8. Allowed for house rent Dec. 1677. Wife Mary -Arthy- ment. in Salem fishing master's accts. that year. Taxed Boston 1688, where he was master of transport in the next war. Either his wid. or their dau. m. 10 Feb. 1713 Richard Taylor. Ch: **Thomas**, ±16 in 1696, chose Renè Gignon, goldsmith, his guardian, already his master. **Abigail**, b. Boston 28 Dec. 1687. (**Mary**? m. in 1713). **Ann**, m. 30 Dec. 1714 Isaac Gleason. Child of Mary Earthy, bur. Boston 31 Oct. 1704.

**Easly** or Eusty, Elisha, see Insley.

**EASON.** 1 ——, Capt. of the first mast ship, 1703. List 96.

2 **PETER**, ship carpenter, Portsm. List 319.

**Easter**, Daniel, wit. with Cleeve 1646.

**Eastknox**, Joseph, Jersey boy, 1691, replevined by John Alcock from Nathl. Keene.

**Eastman**, Samuel, at Gt. Isl. 1693. List 318b.

**EASTON**, ‡*Nicholas, 1593-1675, boarded ship at Southampton 14 May 1634, with sons Peter and John, b. about 1622-24. All three became governors of R. I. Peter left a valu. chron., summer of '34 Ipswich, spring of '35 Newbury, aft. 25 Mar. 1638 the father and two boys built the bound house at Hampt., same year was included among 'Mr. Richard Dummer and his friends' in a cond. grant in R. I., and rem. thither. Mr. Thomas Burwood in Eng. was his brother (1639).

**EASTWICK**, name of a parish in Hertfordshire.

**Phesant**, a physician otherwise employed, b. ab. 1630; in 1663 was given P.A. by John Paine, Bost. mercht.; in 1664 appr. a Portsm. est.; in 1673 in partn. with Thomas Thacher jr., merchts., bot Boston warehouse; dep. that for ab. 10 yrs. he hired a house of Mrs. Rachel Harwood, Bost., app. ab. 1670-80. In N. H. resisted Cranfield and was put out of office until Cranfield's removal; later was provost marshal, coroner, naval officer. Lists 47, 52, 55b, 66, 307a, 315abc, 319, 332a, 333b, 367a. Wife Sarah, b. ab. 1645, with hus. deeded land in Bost. 1700. List 315b. Ch. incl: Catherine, b. 12 Dec. 1671, Bost. **Sarah**, b. 24 Apr. 1674, in court 1702, app. m. John Evans(9) and had s. Richard, b. 1 Jan. 1706, whose poster. perpet. this surn. **Stephen**, b. 3 Oct. 1679, Camb., sea captain, Great Isl., Kittery. Jury 1715, foreman 1717. List 315c. M. by 1702 Elizabeth Fernald(4), who d. 26 Apr. 1714 ag. 31-2-20 (grst.); 2d 2 Dec. 1714 Sarah Shapleigh, both liv. 1754. **Nathaniel**, b. 7 Apr. 1682, Portsm. Also poss. John, Captain, Boston selectm., mar. 9 Sep. 1703 Grissel Lloyd, had stillborn twins 29 July 1704.

**EATON**, see also Yeaton.

1 **JOHN**, wit. Portsm. 1669 with 'Mr. Martyn's man Roger,' likely same as

2 **JOHN**, Salis, ±48 in 1694, working in York ab. 1670, wit. Y. D. ii. 146, 147, 159. Will 15, d. 17, Jan. 1717-8. 10 ch. incl. (5). See Hoyt's Sals. 148-9, 745-7.

3 **MARTHA**, sis. of (2), when young liv. in Hon. Richard Martyn's fam. in Portsm., was sick and her mother came to her. Suff. Ct. Files 1132. She m. Benjamin Collins. See Hoyt's Sals. 112, 148.

4 **TIMOTHY**, cousin of (2), m. in Greenl. 1 Mar. 1720-1 Ruth Chapman(6). Hoyt's Sals. 149.

5 **WILLIAM**(2), mar. Wells 19 Jan. 1709

Mary Littlefield. Jury 1714. List 269c. Suff. Court Files 137361 recites that she died 1745 leaving 4 ch: Joshua, of Wells. Ruth, w. of Josiah Crediford. Mary, wife of Joshua Adams. Joseph, in possession. Hoyt's Sals. 747.

**Ebbyns**, Gyles, see Hibbins.

**EBURNE**. 1 Husband of Elizabeth (Lewis) Phillips, b. ab. 1669, wid. of Israel, dau. of John Lewis, whom he m. aft. 1681, she a dry goods dealer in Portsm. 1698. List 330d. In a N. H. jury list, 6 June 1695, occurs the name Samuel Ebourn, crossed out. In 1702 she ack. judgm. to Mr. Samuel Eborne, presum. (2). Liv. 27 Sep. 1738, but dec. 1741. **Richard**, who may have been a son, m. 13 Aug. 1702 Mary (Morse) Sanders, widow of Richard, dau. of Obadiah Morse, he living 1712, she 1724.

2 **REV. SAMUEL**, minister at Isl. of Shoals in 1702, presum. the same who was min. at Brookhaven, L. I., from ab. 1685-88, and in 1690 in Virginia. List 309.

**Eccles**, see Egles.

**EDEN**. 1 Alice, ae. 18, came with John Moulton 1637.

2 **LUKE**, Damariscotta 162--. List 8.

**Edes**, Philip, Falm. 1689. House at Cape Porpus 1702. Lists 228c, 258.

**EDGE**, name of 3 places Glouc. to Cheshire. **Robert**, perh. the same who came in -The Hopewell- from London, 1635, ag. 25, was in York 1650, rec. 3 a. gr. there 1653. By 1661 he had rem. to Kittery side of the creek running into Braveboat Harbor, where he liv. ever aft. Last ment. 1680. Lists 275, 276, 30. Wife Florence in 1650. 'Gamar Edge' in 1690 had been liv. with Ann Crockett, partly or wholly at the charge of Joshua Downing. Ch: **Peter**, b. by 1644, last ment. 1665. **Florence**, appar. liv. with Robert Wadleigh in 1666. Appar. **Patience**, mar. Philip Hatch, perh. **Ann** mar. Ephraim Crockett, among 'children' of right age to be put out to service in 1655, accounting for poss. connections with Pulman or Dixon.

**EDGECOMB**, pecul. to Devon-Cornwall, where this fam. gave 16 sheriffs from 1487 to 1640.

1 **JOHN**(2), a Saco wit. 1680, selectm. 1686, 1688, on com. to build parsonage 1686; in 1687 bot 25 a. from John Bonython, the deed rec. 100 yrs. later; petnd. Andros 1688. He rem. to Marblehead and perhaps to Salem where one John taxed 1700. Wife Susanna Boaden, dau. of (3). Ch: **Nicholas**, m. 1st in Marbl., 25 Dec. 1712 Mary Gale, who d. 23 Oct. 1719, 2d 14 June 1720 Miriam Stacey. In 1752 as a Boaden heir he brought ejectment against John Rackliff and others. Liv. in Marbl. 1754, mercht. 3 ch. rec. Appar. children by an earlier wife: **Susanna**,

m. 5 Aug. 1696 to John Rhodes unless this a 2d mar. of Susanna (Boaden). **Mary**, m. 3 Dec. 1702 John Palmer. **John**, fisherman, mariner and innholder, of Marbl., m. 11 Dec. 1710 Grace Kelly, who was gr. adm. 8 Apr. 1723, and m. 2d 8 May 1726 James Perryman. 5 ch. rec. One Sarah E. d. in Lynn 7 Mar. 1743-4.

2 **NICHOLAS**, employed at the Trelawny Plant., Richmond Isl., 1638-9, and liv. on small est. at Blue Pt. in 1640, altho employed at Richm. Isl. at times during 1642-3 and marrying Wilmot Randall, a maid there. Selling his Scarb. land 3 Oct. 1660, he obtained a farm on the East bank of the Saco River, with 20 a. of meadow on Goosefare brook. In Philip's War he and his family resorted to Black Point garrison, until it was abandoned. His wife Wilmot was a wit. at Portsm. in 1678. Lists 21,222,235,244cef, 245. Nunc. will ordered recorded 6 Apr. 1681, s. Robert to have all to maintain his mother; 'rest of ch.' She dep. 1684 a. 64, liv. 8 June 1685. Ch: **Christopher**, b. ab. 1643. Lists 235, 237ab, 30. **Mary**, b. ab. 1647, m. 1st George Page, 2d John Ashton. **Joanna**, m. 1st Henry Elkins(6), 2d at Marbl. 1 May 1693 William Punchin of Boston. **Michael**, b. ab. 1651. Lists 237ab. M. (Ct. Sep. 1687) Joan Crocker(2?), both of Saco. **John**. **Robert**, b. ab. 1656.

3 **ROBERT**(2), ±73 27 Mar. 1729 dep. that he resided at Scarb. ab. 12 yrs. about 50 yrs. ago. He m. bef. 30 May 1682 Rachel Gibbins, dau. of James and Judith (Lewis), one of the heirs to half the Saco Patent. Gr.j. 1683, '88. Lists 237ab, 249. Liv. on homestead at Saco until finding refuge at Marbl. ab. 1690; returned to Saco perm. aft. 1718, but may have made an earlier attempt, as a son was taken capt. there 10 Aug. 1703. List 39. Wife d. Saco 13 Jan. 1724, ag. 63; he 1 June 1730, ag. 73. Ch., all bp. Marblehead: **James**, bp. 24 Apr. 1692, d. Marbl., 7 July 1704 in 17th yr. **Judith**, bp. 24 Apr. 1692, m. Abraham Townsend. **Nicholas**, bp. 24 Apr. 1692, d.s.p. bef. 1730. **Elizabeth**, bp. 22 Oct. 1693, d. bef. 1730. **Robert**, bp. 19 May 1695, liv. in Saco prob. on 600 a. laid out to him 1720; m. ab. 1721 Sarah Elwell, dau. of Robert and Sarah (Gardner), who d. 13 Dec. 1760; he d. 25 Sep. 1764, ag. 69. 7 ch. He and br. Thomas were original members of First Parish Ch., Saco, 1762. **Mary**, bp. 19 Aug. 1698, m. David Young. **Thomas**, bp. 25 May 1701, m. Bidd. 10 Dec. 1725 Sarah Fletcher (Pendleton 8 jr.); d. 17 Oct. 1778, she 16 Aug. 1790. 8 ch.

**EDGERLY**. Edgerley, a township in Cheshire.

1 **THOMAS**, Esq., an apprent. under Capt. Isaac Johnson of Roxbury, came to Oys-

ter River and m. a young wid. Received inhab. of Dover 19 Mar. 1665-6, freeman 15 May 1672. Under Cranfield he was a justice of the Ct. of Sessions, but soon was removed for insubserv. In the massacre, 1694, he was taken but escaped. Gr.j. 1667, 1668, 1672, 1675, 1679, 1680, 1699. Selectm. 1686. Lists 356m, 357c, 359a, 365, 366, 367b, 368ab, 336b, 353, 49, 52, 54, 56, 62, 92, 94. Liv. 1717. His wife Rebecca (Ault) Hallowell, m. 28 Sep. 1665, ±71 in Jan. 1711-2, was liv. 1715. He had much to do with other people's probates, but kept his own est. out of court, so that his sons given lands 1700-1715 are all his kn. ch. The early geneal. supplies dates at random, mostly wrong where records are found. Ch. presum. incl: **Thomas**, b. about 1670. **John**, m., by trad., Elizabeth Rawlings. Lists 62. 368ab, 369. D. in Durham 1739, leaving 2 sons, 4 daus. Their d. Elizabeth, w. of Benj. Durgin, sued Ebenezer Bickford and Zachariah E. for a seventh. In 1770 J. E. '3d' had w. Hannah. **Zachariah**, List 62. K. by Ind. 1694. **Rebecca**, b. about 1675, m in Durham 2 Aug. 1718 Aaron Hutcote (Hitchcock?), widower. **Samuel**, mar. Elizabeth Tuttle. List 368b. Adm. 7 Dec. 1725 to s. John, wid. Elizabeth Ambler (m. 20 July 1725 to Dea. John) relinq. 6 or m. ch., incl. John, called 'Jr.' in 1730, w. Elizabeth Wakeham. List 369. **Elizabeth** and **Susannah**, Ind. capt. brought home in Jan. 1698-9. List 99. **Joseph**, Ind. capt. 12 yrs., forgot his English, brot back to Boston 1706. Lists 99, 368b, 369. He m. by trad. Mary Green. 4 or m. ch.

2 **THOMAS**(1), ±31 in 1701, weaver, in 1700 had rem. to Greenland, in 1710 of Exeter sold in Quamscot. In 1719 was called millwright. Jury 1692, tythingman 1721, 1724, hayward 1722, 1727. Grant 20 a. 1725. Lists 62, 367b, 368b. D. 1738-1747. He m. 1st 3 Dec. 1691 Jane Whidden of Greenland; 2d Abigail Judkins. Abigail Perkins wit. his deed in 1726. Rebecca Judkins and Sarah Edgerly wit. a Bean heirship in 1721. In 1738, of Exeter, he deeded half his homestead to John Hutchins or Huckins of Exeter, cordwainer, and w. Abigail. In 1747 his wid. Abigail was keeping house for Dr. Odlin. Yet one record may indicate a wid. Jane liv. 1745, unexpl. Ch. by 1st w., by trad: **John**, k. by Ind. 1694. **Mary**, m. Tho. Kelly of Brentwood. **Samuel**, Brentw., will 1768—1769 names 11 ch. **Abigail**, m. Capt. John Huckins. **Joseph**, Stratham, cert. mar. Sarah Rawlings (Moses) and by trad. two more wives. Also poss: **Hannah**, m. in Greenland 28 Jan. 1724-5 James Urine. **Thomas**? By 2d w: **Thomas**, named in his grf. Judkin's will, 1738, presum. the same of Brentw. with w. Catherine in 1759, later of Gilmanton or Barnstead.

**Edling**, David Ludecas, see Ludecas.

**Edminster**, John and Hannah, ±26 and 22 in 1664. List 364.

**Edmondson**, Margaret, liv. at Mr. Geo. Jaffray's, in court Dec. 1700, ch. b. 12 weeks since, accu. Capt. Edward Willmot, commander of the -Charles and Sarah-.

**EDMUNDS**, Edmonds, a common Welsh and Eng. name, esp. on the Bristol Chan.
1 **HENRY**. List 21. Fisherman, runaway.
2 **JOHN**, Portsm. 1666. List 330d. Wife Mary. He, Mary (his wife?) and son Thomas k. by Ind. 26 June 1696.
3 **ROBERT**, b. ab. 1628, fisherman, at Kennebec 1664, gr.j. 1674, master of fishing vessel at Sagadahoc 1688. Lists 13, 15, 182, 189, 191. Bot land near Burnt Isl. of Thos. Atkins 1664, 1668, and sold to Wm. Hobby of Bost. 23 June 1713. As 2d wife, m. in Bost. 26 Mar. 1695 Rebecca Pasmore, wid. of Wm.; d. Bost. 19 Nov. 1717. Ch: **Thomas**, adm. gr. to father Mar. 1690-1.
4 **ROBERT**, Scarb., dec. bef. 10 Oct. 1687; had owned 160 a. at Blue Pt. taken upon execution by Edward Shippen of Bost. List 34.
5 **THOMAS**(2), Portsm., taxed Str. Bk. 1686, k. by Ind. 26 June 1696. Lists 335a, 330d (est.); wife 335a. One Thos. was in Lieut. Oakes' co. 24 June 1676. Ch: **Martha. Esther**, Jethro Goss's wife in 1734? **Hannah**, in 1714 q.c. to br. John the est. of her f. and grf. Edmunds. **Mary**, presum. mar. 26 Jan. 1717-8 Francis Mason. **John**, m. 1st 10 June 1713 Catherine Mason (John of Hampt.), 2d, Mar. 1720-1 Mary (Hodge?) Seavey; liv. 1762. List 339. 4 ch. **Thomas**, mar. 1st 22 Feb. 1721-2 Alice Locke, 2d, Feb. 1739-40 Mary Foss. Will 4 May—25 July 1744. 5 ch.

**EDWARDS**, 8th commonest Welsh name, 20th Welsh and Eng. Rare in No. of Eng.
1 **EWAN** (Evans?). 1663. List 285.
2 **JOHN**, List 7, 1614.
3 **JOHN**, adm. est. of br. Oads, 1651.
4 **JOHN**, bp. Salem 6 June 1639, mariner, mar. Elizabeth Price (Matthew). With Thomas Walters bot 100 a. at Falm. adj. Robert Stanford, 13 Sep. 1683; liv. Salem 1700. Only ch: **Elizabeth**, liv. 1712, d.s.p., her rel. on mother's side claiming her father's lands.
5 **JOHN**, Portsm., ±33 in Sep. 1667.
6 **JOSEPH**, Portsm. 1695. List 334b.
7 **MALACHI**, impressed twice at Newb. to come to Me. as a soldier. M. Elizabeth (Hilton) Littlefield. List 334b.
8 **OADS**, Isl. of Shoals, sued by Capt. Sampson Lane in Kit. Ct., 25 Nov. 1650, deft. in two suits 14 Oct. 1651. Adm. gr. 5 Dec. 1651 to br. John Edwards for the widow.
9 **ROGER**, Hampt. 1672, poss. same as (10). Wife Sarah d. 19 Mar. 1668.

10 **ROGER**, No. Yarmouth, List 214. Adm. to Thos. Blashfield 1686.
11 **STEPHEN**, Portsm., Robert Jackson's serv., drunk and fined 1662; m. Elizabeth Beedle(4), b. 1641. She mar. 2d bef. 1670 Peter Staples. List 298.
12 **THOMAS**, Spurwink, List 226, perhaps from Portsm.
13 **WILLIAM**, Sagadahoc 1674. List 15.

**EGGLESTON, Hezekiah**, of Boston, m. (int. 6 Dec. 1721) Sarah Martin of Marbleh., dau. of Samuel and Elizabeth (Fulford), yet John Brown called Sarah E. -sister- Y. D. 19.51. Son **Hezekiah** liv. in Bristol, Me., 1770.

**EGLES, Thomas**, commissioner in the County of Cornwall under New York, 1685. Y. D. x. 261.

**Ela**, see Ely.

**ELATSON, Jonathan**, Boston, merchant. Clerk of Ct. 1692-95, was obliged to go to the West Indies. Will 27 Feb.—18 Nov. 1697, wife sole legatee. He bur. one w. 6 Mar. 1694-5 and m. 27 June 1695 Elizabeth (Pemberton), wid. in 1682 of George Purkis, and in 1690 of Warner Wessendonk. She liv. in Portsm. with her dau. Sarah (Purkis), w. of Rev. Nathaniel Rogers, and in the burning of his house was fatally burned, with an infant grch., d. 31 Dec.—1 Jan. 1704-5, ag. 45 (both on one grst.). List 96.

**ELBRIDGE**, Albridge, so familiar here as a forename after Elbridge Gerry, is extr. rare in Eng. either as fore- or surname.
1 **GILES**, granted the Pemaquid Patent jointly with Robert Aldworth, 29 Feb. 1631-2, and became sole owner on death of Aldworth, childless, in 1634, although never here, but a mercht. of Bristol, Eng., engag. prin. in foreign trade. In 1639 he was to transport 80 to his fishing plantation. List 272. He m. ab. 1617 Elizabeth Aldworth, dau. of John, niece of Robert; d. sud. Feb. 1643-4. Ch: **Robert**, d. bef. father; 1 dau. **Martha**, was Wid. Martha Cugley 1646; m. 2d Rev. Richard Standfast of Bristol. **John**, father's heir and exec., d. unm. **Elizabeth**, mar. Tho. Moore of Bristol. **Thomas. Aldworth**, d. unm. aft. Sep. 1675. [**Mary**, d.y.]
2 **THOMAS**(1), merchant, Pemaquid, a minor and beyond seas in 1646 when he inher. from br. John much Eng. prop., incl. manor of Chelwood, co. Somerset, and 'one great continent of land in N. E.' The English posses. passed to his heirs intact, but he could not hold his Pemaquid lands which soon were in other hands through various mortgages and deeds, Richard Russell and Nicholas Davison of Charlestown owning one moiety in 1653, the other moiety deeded in 1657 to Davison, who soon owned alone. In 1650 he had been in jail five mos. for debt in a suit arising from sale of goods from the

wrecked -Angel Gabriel-, and was himself plaint. in various suits. In 1669, descr. hims. of Alderton in N. E., he sold 400 a. at Round Pond for three bottles of strong liquor. Lists 12, 13. By June 1677 he was of Marblehead, lic. out of doors; in 1679, having hired a large house, asked for lic. indoors. The next yr. a lic. was recom. for his dau. Elizabeth to provide for four small ch. left in her care, the father abs. in Jamaica, where he d. in 1682, will 9 June 1682; buried at Liguanee, parish of St. Andrew. Wife Rebecca d. in Jamaica Oct. 1684. Ch., the sons liv. in England, desc. here of two daus. only: **Aldworth**, evid. d. bef. 1733, leav. dau. Rebecca, who m. bef. 1739 Henry Woolnough, gent. **Thomas**, merchant, Bristol, will 9 June 1733—10 Oct. 1737, named surv. sis. and nieces in New Eng. Ch: Thomas, mar., but d.s.p., the last male member of the fam. **Frances. John**, Esq., Bristol, many yrs. Comptroller of Customs, wealthy benefactor of charities and schools, appar. never mar. Will 20 Feb.—27 Mar. 1738-9, gave £8,000 to daus. of late sis. Smith and their ch. liv. in N. E., £8,000 to sis. Saunders, her daus. and their ch. Sisters Smith and Saunders being one, (the late sister was Mrs. Russell), the Ct. of Chancery settled the claims of ten Smith-Saunders legatees; the Russell desc. were paid a sister's portion. **Elizabeth**, b. ab. 1652, d. in Marblehead 19 Sep. 1721 ag. 69 yrs., m. where d. 12 July 1711. Ch. rec. Marbl.: Samuel, bp. 27 Mar. 1687, not in will of either uncle. Elizabeth, bp. 13 Sep. 1691, d. Marbl., 'Madam Russell,' 4 Feb. 1771, m. 1st 23 July 1710 Benjamin Trevett, 2d 24 Dec. 1733 Capt. Giles Russell. Rebecca, bp. 13 Nov. 1692, d. Marbl. 3 Dec. 1737, m. 26 May 1715 Enoch Greenleaf. Of two ch. rec. Marbl., Elizabeth, b. 1 June 1716, m. 16 Dec. 1734 Capt. Thomas Gerry of Newton Bushel, Gt. Brit., and was the mother of Elbridge Gerry, Signer, b. Marbl. 17 July 1744. (One Rebecca E., likely a sick child from Pemaquid, d. in Newbury 15 Oct. 1657.) **Rebecca**, m. 1st Thomas Smith; 2 sons who d. bef. 1733, 1 dau.; m. 2d 7 Apr. 1697 Josiah Sanders of Boston; 3 daus. liv. 1733. She d. 4 Mar. 1745, ag. 86. **Giles** and **Robert**, both d.s.p. bef. 1733, perh. d.y.

**Elberson**, Elberd, Portsm. 1717, rated to New Meeting House.

**Elden**, Richard, Kit., Y. D. 18.276, misr. of **Endle.**

**ELDRIDGE**, a rare English name, confused with Eldred and Aldrich.
1 **JOHN** (Eldred), Hampton 1640. List 392a.
2 **JOHN**, Wells, b. ab. 1654, likely at Yarmouth, Mass., was at Wells abs. from meet. 1673 and 74, took O. F. there 6 Nov. 1677, appr. est. of Bryan Pendleton 1681,

gr.j. 1688, 1694-5, '98, 1701. List 266. He m. by 1681 Abigail Littlefield (Francis sr.). Bot from his f.-in-law 156 a. upland and housing on Ogunquit Riv. falls in 1683, selling to cous. Francis Littlefield in 1712 aft. ret. to Yarm., where he d. ab. 1728. Ch. b. in Wells: **Rebecca**, b. 23 Nov. 1681, m. Alexander McMillion, wid. in Salem 1728. **Abigail**, b. 2 June 1684, m. Zachary Rider of Barnstable. **Patience**, b. 3 Nov. 1686, mar. John Rider of Barnst. **Dorcas**, bp. 16 Nov. 1701, m. Gideon Gray of Barnst. **John**, b. 1 Aug. 1693, m. 15 Oct. 1716 Hannah Knight (Ezekiel jr.), liv. in Wells; on alarm list in 1757. List 269c. 5 ch.

**Elford**, Tristram, Eliot wit. 1651. Gloucester, ag. 40 in 1664.

**ELKINS**, uncom. Eng. surname, attributed to Saxon forename Ella.
1 **CHRISTOPHER** (11), first app. July 1663, with (11), called 'Sen.' 1 (5) 1664. Neither f. nor s. **Christopher**, ±25 in June 1667, fisherman, appears aft. Oct. 1667. Y. D. ii. 25 'planter' was app. the senior, and Y. D. ii. 23 'fisherman,' the son. Not imposs. also (6, 12, 9). Martha Elkins, who m. at Salem 4 Mar. 1680 Wm. Pincheon, may have been sis. or wid. of either. List 234a.
2 **'EDMOND,'** 1651. Y. D. vii. 187. This original deed is in Mass. Arch. 127. 244, and is clearly as printed in Doc. Hist. vi. 10, Thomas **1** Celkin. See (11).
3 **ELEAZER** (5), bot in Exeter in 1668. Soldier in Philip's War. Lists 376b, 381-383, 52, 57. D. ab. 1694 (Probate petn. 1734). He m. 31 Dec. 1673 Deborah Blake(1), who in 1708 (or their d.) was w. of Tho. Bigsby of Andover. Ch: **John**, b. 3 Dec. 1674. **Samuel**, b. 27 June 1677, had the homestead; m. Mercy Tilton. 3 or m. sons. **Abigail**, b. 22 June 1678, m. aft. 1708 one Martyn; liv. 1734. **Jasper**, liv. 1708. **Deborah?**
4 **GERSHOM** (5), ±68 in Feb. 1708-9, Hampton. Gr.j. 1693. Lists 49, 52, 392b, 396, 397a, 400. Will 9 June 1714, d. 12 Jan. 1718. Ch: **Jonathan**, b. 24 Jan. 1669. Lists 66, 399a. He d. 12 Feb. 1746 leaving wid. Joanna (Robie, m. 24 Dec. 1703) and 3 ch., incl. Henry of Rye. **Moses**, Deac., b. 4 Dec. 1676, Kingston. Lists 399a, 400. He m. 17 Nov. 1701 Ann Shaw, d. suddenly 10 May 1737, having lost several ch. by diphtheria. Adm. 3 June 1737 to s. Joseph who succeeded him as Deacon. 11 ch., of whom 3 s. divided his lands. **Joseph**, in 1684 was an apprent. to Rev. Seaborn Cotton. Not in will. **Mary**, b. 2 Sep. 1674, d. unm. 9 Feb. 1703-4. **Joanna**, b. 14 Mar. 1677, d. unm. 12 Jan. 1762. **Henry**, k. by Ind. 15 Sep. 1707. List 96. **Thomas**, b. ab. 1682, d. Hampt. 25 May 1760. He m. 8 Feb. 1711 Hannah Fogg(6) who d. 10 Sep. 1775. 7 or m. ch.

5 **HENRY**, tailor, adm. ch. in Boston 9 Nov. 1634, freeman 6 May 1635, disarmed in 1637, with w. Mary dism. to Exeter 3 Mar. 1639-40. Rem. to Hampton bef. 1650. Gr.j. 1647. Lists 373, 374c, 376a, 393a. W. Mary d. 17 Mar. 1659. List 393a. Will 27 Apr. 1667, d. 9 Apr. 1669. Ch: **Marie**, bp. Boston, 8 Apr. 1638. **Gershom**, b. ab. 1641. **Eleazer**. 6 **HENRY** (1?, 11?) wit. deeds and appr. estates at Scarb. 1663-1687. Escaped to Portsmouth in Philip's War, where tax was abated Feb. 1679-80. Lists 30, 237ade, 313a, 238a, 239a. See Ancestry of Charity Haley, Davis, 1916, p. 39. He m. by 1671 Joanna Edgecomb(2), who m. at Marbleh. 1 May 1693 Wm. Punchin (Pincheon) of Boston.

7 **JOSEPH**, will proved 1691—Banks.

8 **NATHANIEL** (Elkin), Boston merchant, s. of 'Old Mr. Elkin' of Boston, m. Esther Waldron. D. on a voyage, adm. to his f. in 1678, again to Major Waldron Apr. 1679. Wid. ret. to her f. in Dover, where she was in ct. 6 Nov. 1683 and m. 21 June 1686 Abraham Lee.

9 **OLIVER**, (11?, 1?), ±63 in Mar. 1713-4, first app. in Casco Bay 1674. With (12) and other refugees took O.A. at Lynn 1678. D. in Marbleh. 1722. He m. by 1684 Jane Purchase from Pejepscot, who d. in Lynn 28 Sep. 1716, ae. 53. Ch: **Mary**, bp. Lynn Apr. 1687, d. 8 Oct. 1694. **Thomas**, b. 30 Sep. 1689, m. 16 June 1718 Elizabeth Gale (Azor, Esq.), innholder at Marblehead 1731. 4 or m. ch. **Elizabeth**, pub. 25 Nov. 1710 to Tho. Owens of Marbleh., yet liv. unm. 1723. **Sarah**, pub. 25 Nov. 1710, m. 4 Jan. 1710-1 Wm. Peach. **Oliver**, d. 24 Sep. 1716, ae. 21 (grst.) **John**, liv. 1723. **Mary**, m. 11 Oct. 1722 John Lightfoot.

10 **ROBERT**, see Alkins.

11 **THOMAS**, presum. the same solic. by Catherine Gray in Boston 1634, might, in view of the surprising rarity of this surn., be grf. of Christopher ±25 in June 1667, and progen. of all in Maine and Essex Co., if the figures in Suff. Ct. files 1046, Tho. Elkins ±64, Geo. Taylor ±60, 4 Oct. 1659, are errorless; hardly if ±64 in 1668. He was around Mr. Gorges in 1640, dep. marshal around Mr. Cleeve in 1651, innholder in 1661 with w. Lists 281, 235. His last yrs. were in Black Point. 'Henry,' in poss. of oxen of Andrew Heffers is app. a misr. of Thomas. Y. D. i. 155. He and (1) signed Scarb. decl. 4 July 1663; sold marsh 8 Mar. 1664-5; d. bef. the deed bet. Scottow and Hinkson, 24 Aug. 1669, twice recorded Y. D. ii. 154, Y. D. iv. 40 to alter 'Thomas' to Christopher. The 'father' was Thomas, with **Christopher**, his only kn. ch., altho any or all of (6, 12, 9) are not imp.

12 **THOMAS** (11?, 1?), presum. in boyhood apprent. to Mr. Francis Neale, app. first at Salem, refugee from Kennebec, where he had m. Sarah Gutch, bp. 4 June 1654. With Oliver Elkins(9) and other Eastern men he took O.A. at Lynn 1678. Adm. 29 Nov. 1705, boatman, Salem, to wid. Sarah, still his wid. 1734, ±81. Ch. put on record in Salem: **Sarah**, b. 5 June 1674, m. 1st James Mayo; 2d 27 Feb. 1711-2 Deac. Edw. Knowles of Eastham; 3d (int. 24 Mar. 1743-4) Hezekiah Doane; d. Feb. 1753. **Thomas**, b. 11 Jan. 1676, coaster, Salem, m. 14 Jan. 1701, Sarah Miles. 6 ch. **Lydia**, b. 12 June 1679, m. 1st 10 Dec. 1700 Peter Cheevers; 2d John Stevens, fisherman. **John**, b. 17 May 1681, not among heirs 1718. **Margaret**, b. 26 Apr. 1683, m. Stephen Snow of Eastham. **Mary**, b. 1 Dec. 1686, m. 6 Jan. 1715 Nicholas Lydiard of Wells. **Magdalen**, b. 28 Apr. 1689, not among heirs 1718. **Henry**, b. 16 July 1691, mariner, d. bef. 30 Aug. 1718, leaving wid. Abigail. **Robert**, b. 2 Mar. 1695-6, not among heirs 1718.

13 'WILLIAM,' in jury list July 1664, with Samuel Oakman, presum. a mistake for one of the Scarb. Elkinses.

**Ellen**, Olive? List 72. See Ellingham.

**ELLICOTT**, **Vines**, s. of Thomas and Margaret (Vines) of St. Michaels, Barbadoes, came in -The Supply- 24 May 1679 for Boston, where in 1684 he was indicted for wilful murder, his riding horse having k. an aged man Henry Pease. A mercht. there in 1686, he was sued by Geo. Pearson in York Ct. that year, and himself sued Pendleton Fletcher in 1688. 6 Aug. 1687 he petnd. Andros about 'Hogg Island' in Casco Bay, posses. by Capt. Richard Vines his grf. near 50 yrs. since; and as Lt. Vines sgd. petn. in behalf of Eastern Parts 7 Jan. 1689-90, aft. wh. nothing known of him. Ch: **Vynes**, bp. Bost. 26 Sep. 1697, ag. ab. 12, had been brot up by a woman named Cable; mar. Mary Adams, dau. of Abraham(2); a wid. in 1718, she m. 2d 15 Jan. 1724 Ebenezer Allen.

**ELLINGHAM**, **William**, carpenter and husbandm., in partn. with Hugh Gale, millwright, built mills at Spruce Creek ab. 1648, in York 1652. Left in charge of mill by Capt. Shapleigh 1648, 49. 5 Aug. 1661 he was liv. (under 21 yr. lease) on part of the Small-Maverick gr. in Eliot, when Mr. Thos. Booth bot the whole, reserv. what was occ. by W. E. In 1668 his creditors were pressing him, was drunk at the Dover tav., collocted an old acct. from Champernowne, and disapp. just as Mass. resumed gov. Called dead in an abut. deed 1677. Lists 273, 275, 276, 285, 298. Two or m. wives, Christian in 1654, who was acc. of bigamy; a dau. or stepd. of Thos. Booth in 1663. No ch.

**Ellingwood**, John, Kit. 1715. See Crockett (Joseph).

**ELLINS**, very rare English surname.
1 **ANTHONY**(2), Portsm., bot a house from Wm. Seavey in June, another from Wm. Berry in July, 1648. Gr.j. 1650, 1654, 1664, const. 1655, selectm. 1660. Lists 323, 324, 326ac, 329, 330ab, 331abc, 356b (Portsm.), 49. In 1668 he deeded Ellens Point to his kinswoman Sarah Partridge, w. of Nehemiah; 3 July 1669 gr. adm. on est. of Samuel Drew(11), whose wid. Abigail he had m. as his 2d wife. She was adm. of his est. 8 Sep. 1681, and m. 2d (contract 13 Oct. 1691), John Jackson of Portsm. Ch., by 2d w: **Margaret**, m. 14 May 1694 Nathaniel Jackson.
2 **LAWRENCE**, List 41, early in Portsm., where he bot from Wm. Berry part of land later kn. as 'Anthony Ellin's Neck,' Anthony buying the rest of it from Berry ab. 1650. Ch: **Anthony**. Appar. **Judith**, who was acc. with Thomas Williams 3 Oct. 1648 and had a bast. ch. bef. 3 Nov. 1648, Sarah, who m. 1st Nehemiah Partridge, 2d James Levett.
3 **NATHANIEL**. 1690. List 267a.

**ELLIOT**, a general English and Lowland Scotch surname, except the East coast and Welsh border.
1 **GEORGE**, Portsm. In 1648 Elizabeth Roe was sued for calling another George Ellet's whore. He was plaint. and deft. in lawsuits 1654-56. Likelier another Geo. in List 51, 1681.
2 **HUMPHREY**, shipmaster, (master of the -Brigantine Joane- in 1685), m. Elizabeth Cutt(7). By early Cutt trad. she was taken to Eng. by her stepf. Champernowne, and went a voyage by stealth with one Elliot, whom she m. 1685. Witnesses in Y. D. v. 110 may indicate some rel. to (6). Tax abated Portsm. 1683, taxed Great Isl. 1688. What end he made is unasc., but one Elizabeth Elliot was a lic. liquor seller on Gt. Isl. in 1692. The wid. m. 2d by 1693 Robert Wetherick, and was liv. in So. Carolina in 1729. Ch: **Champernown**, d. in So. Car.; m. Elizabeth Elliot, who m. 2d Robert Booth. 1 d. **Robert**, d. in So. Car.; m. in 1721 his cous. Elizabeth Scriven. He had 4 s., perh. by an earlier wife.
3 **JOHN**. Popham, 1607. List 6.
4 **RICHARD**, b. ab. 1659, poss. drawn to Kit. by (2). Gr.j. 1688, 1689, 1691; constable 1690, 1691. Rem. to Portsm. in Indian war. Lists 331c, 330d, 337. App. bringing 1st w. with him, (List 331c), he m. 2d Mary, wid. of Thomas Drew(13); 3d Mary (Partridge) Moore, who m. by 1724 John Leach. Will 5 July—3 Sep. 1718. Ch: **Richard**, Portsm. List 339. Adm. 27 Oct. 1729 to wid. Abigail (Wilson, of Hampton, m. 2 Dec. 1716), who mar. by 1736 John Green, cordwainer, both liv. 1748 in Pelham. 6 ch. **Joanna**, mar. 11 Nov. 1714 Walter Warren. **Susanna**, m. 30

Nov. 1711 Nathaniel Ellithorp from Rowley, of Portsm., and s. John bp. 9 Mar. 1717-8. **John**, bp. 8 Nov. 1696, not in will.
5 *****ROBERT**, b. ab. 1631. carpenter, Portsm. 1659, const. 1662, 1664, sold his house at Sag. Creek 24 Mar. 1664-5 and rem. to Scarb. Lotlayer 1669. Selectman 5 yrs. 1669-1685. Rep. 1683, 1685. Lists 326a, 323, 330a, 341, 235, 237a, 238a. See Doc. Hist. vi. 254, 257; N. H. Prov. Pap. xvii. 527. Wife Ann in 1661, 1665: he was courting Peter Turbet's wid. in 1673; m. Margery (Batson), wid. of Richard Young, by 1683, the latter last ment. in deed 13 June 1687 to her d. Mary, w. of Emanuel Davis. He was liv. in Portsm. 22 Feb. 1695-6 with John Pickering jr., and deeded him his Scarb. lands for life supp. John Pickering in a dep. 14 Feb. 1715-6 called him dec.
6 ‡*****ROBERT**, b. ab. 1643, merchant. As a traveling merch. in the ship -Concord- of Bristol, he app. reached Great Isl. in 1669, when something induced him to aband. his voyage and consign certain of his goods to 'Uncle Wm. May.' Presently he had m. Sarah Fryer(4). In a London hearing in 1695 Richard Martyn jr. rated him 'the most eminent inhabitant of that province.' Jury 1680, 1682, gr.j. 1681, selectm. 1679, 1680; Rep. 1680, Province Assessor in 1680; Councillor in 1684 (under Mason, three of the five being Mr. Fryer and his sons-in-law), member of provisional government 1689 (List 56), Councillor 1692-1715, except one yr. when in support of Vaughan and Waldron he withdrew. Lists 312b, 313a, 331ab, 315b, 316, 319, 324, 326c, 329, 307b, 226, 34, 39, 51, 52, 54, 55a, 56, 57, 59, 60, 65, 66, 90-92, 95, 296, 297, 291. See P. & C. ii. 172, 213; Doc. Hist. vi. 328; N. H. Prov. Pap. xvii. 599, 703. After retirement he liv. on Gerrish Isl., Kit. and d. 24 Mar. 1723-4 in 82d yr. His w., not in will 10 Nov. 1718, proved in York Co., was liv. 1707. Ch: **Nathaniel**, shipmaster, m. 24 Aug. 1699 at Marbleh. Mary Cratey, and liv. there in 1705. He was taken by the French. **Robert**, in 1705 was given Gerrish's Island, with reversion if he d.s.p., as evid. he did. The strange deed Y. D. ix 259 is not unders., altho the title to Higgins Beach, Scarb., seems to come down through it. **Elizabeth**, b. 8 Apr. 1683, m. Geo. Vaughan. **Jane**, b. 1684, m. Andrew Pepperell and Charles Frost s. of Charles(2 jr.). **Sarah**, b. 1 Oct. 1687, mar. Timothy Gerrish. **Abigail**, mar. 16 Dec. 1708 Capt. Daniel Greenough.
7 **WILLIAM**, of Dover, in 1721 fell out of a gundalo and was drowned.

**ELLIS**. 1 **John**, fatally shot in the leg by Lodowick Fowler in Portsm. ab. 12 Sep. 1673. Called Fowler his own countryman. List 327d.
2 **JOHN**, Cochecho, ±24 about 1681, ±63 in

1717, first taxed in 1672. ·Lists 356j, 359ab, 52, 57, 62, 358d. The same J. E.(?) brought ejectment against Charles Kelly in 1716, and was rated to Old Meet. Ho., Portsm., 1717.
3 **LAWRENCE**, Gt. Isl., barber in 1724 sued Hon. John Hinckes for shaving him from 1716 to 1719. In 1725 bot the place John Fabes sold Wm. Broad 1673. D. July 1728. Adm. 16 Mar. 1730-1 to wid. Mary (Leach, dau. of John), who m. Stephen Barton. 1 ch. mentioned (besides?) (Robert?).
**Ellison**, see Helson.
Susannah, wit. with Charles Story 1709-14. See Allison(3).
**Ellithorp**, Nathaniel, see Elliot(4).
**Elson**, see Helson.
**Elston**, John, and two of Mr. Craddock's fishermen saved from drowning 1631.—Winthrop.

**ELWELL**, very rare, by form an English place-name, but not found.
1 **ELIAS**, of Exeter presum., cor. jury 1700.
2 **HEZEKIAH**(4), Newcastle 1693, had Kit. gr. 1699. Lists 315a, 318a, 290, 296-298. Wife Elizabeth Fennick, dau. of John, wid. in 1749. 7 ch.
3 **ISAAC**, Newcastle, around Sag. Creek ag. ±50 in 1702, was presum. Capt. Isaac of Glouc., bro. of (4).
4 **JOSEPH**, Great Isl., from Glouc. List 66.
5 **JOSEPH**(4), Newcastle 1693, fisherman. Lists 315a, 318a. Adm. 15 Sep. 1701 to wid. Margaret.
6 **ROBERT**, at the 'Eastward' 1635, wit. against Thos. Wannerton, presum. later of Glouc., father of (4). See -Ancestry of Charity Haley-.

**ELY**, Eli, Ela, the first a city in Cambridge.
1 **DANIEL** (Ela), Haverhill, N. H. lawsuit 1673, d. Boston 22 Dec. 1710 ±80.
2 **RICHARD** (Ely), a Plymouth, Eng., merchant and real est. holder, who became a large propr. at Lyme, Conn., was first at Great Isl., where he bot house and land from James Leach 24 Apr. 1663, sold in 1669 aft. rem. to Conn. The registers of St. Andrews and Charles par., Plym., show bur. of his 1st w. Joan and bap. of their four ch. He m. 2d in Bost. ab. 1664 Elizabeth (Fenwick) Cullick, wid. of Capt. John and sis. of Col. Geo. Fenwick, a large landowner at Lyme, where she d. 12 Nov. 1683, and he 24 Nov. 1684. Ch: **William**, bp. 15 Oct. 1647, m. May 1681 Elizabeth Smith, dau. of Simon, d. Lyme 2 Mar. 1717-8. 8 ch. **Judith**, bp. 6 Sep. 1652, buried 21 June 1655. **Richard**, bp. 19 June 1657, wit. will of John Sloper in Kit. 1692, taxed Bost. 1695, d. Lyme ab. 1698; widow Mary (Marvin), m. 2d 6 June 1699 Capt. Daniel Sterling of Lyme. 4 ch. **Daniel**, bp. 7 Jan., bur. 8 Mar. 1658-9.

3 **WALTER** (Eli), Portsm., 1681. List 329.
Emblen, Thomas, Elliot accts. 1689. List 90.
**EMERSON**, patronymic surname. Common in North of England.
1 **REV. JOHN**, s. of Nathaniel, b. Ipsw. in 1654, H.C. 1675, was minister at Berwick 1683-89 and chaplain under Major Swayne 7 Sep. to 23 Nov. 1689. List 298. Later of Charlestown and Salem, he d. in Salem 24 Feb. 1712, surv. by w. Sarah (Stowers) Carter, wid. of John, dau. of Richard and Joanna Stowers. Ch: **Sarah**, b. 1695, m. Richard Foster of Charlestown.
2 **JOHN**, Dover, 1674? List 357e.
3 **REV. JOHN**, s. of Rev. John of Glouc., b. 14 May 1670, H.C. 1689. Marrying Mary Batter at Salem 14 May 1696, he preached there 1697-1699, at Ipsw. 1703, was settled as min. at Newcastle 1703-1712, and at 2d Ch., Portsmouth, 1715 to his death, 21 Jan. 1731-2; his will 31 Dec. 1731—11 Feb. 1731-2. List 239b. Widow's will prov. 25 Oct. 1749. Ch: **Ruth**, b. 10 Nov. 1699, d. 3 Aug. 1721. **Mary**, mar. 12 Nov. 1724 Francis Winkley. **Elizabeth**, unm. 1738. **Anne**, m. Capt. Stephen Greenleaf. **Sarah**, mar. John Davis(62). **Margaret**, d. 5 Mar. 1718-9, ag. 6. **John**, b. 22 Nov. 1713, d. 17 June 1714. **Dorothy**, b. 17 June 1715, m. Elihu Gunnison. **Martha**, mar. Edward Flint. **Margery**, mar. Simeon Fernald.
4 **JOHN**, Sergt. at Wells, 1693. List 267b.
5 **REV. JOSEPH**, s. of Thomas of Ipswich, bap. in St. Michael's, Bishop's Stortford, Herts, 25 June 1620. Of York in 1648, he was at Rowley in 1649, when invited to Exeter, but had rem. to Wells by 1652, and there min. 1664-1667. Lists 261, 263, 277, 24, 269b. Returning to Mass., he was min. at Mendon 1669-1675; d. at Concord 3 Jan. 1680. He m. 1st Elizabeth Woodmansey (Robert of Boston), 2d 7 Dec. 1665 Elizabeth Bulkeley (Rev. Edward of Concord), who m. 2d Capt. John Brown of Reading. Ch: **Joseph**, Bost., w. Mary and 2 daus. **James**, Ipsw. and Mendon, m. Sarah Ingersoll. 7 ch. **Lucyan**, b. 2 Oct. 1667, m. Thomas Damon. **Edward**, b. 26 Apr. 1670, m. 27 Jan. 1697 Rebecca Waldo of Chelmsford. 5 ch. **Peter**, b. 1673, Reading, m. 11 Nov. 1696 Anna Brown. 10 ch. **Ebenezer**, Reading, m. 1st in 1707, Bethia Parker, 2d 2 May 1716 Mary Boutwell. 7 ch. **Daniel**, Boston, m. 19 May 1709 Jane Armitage. 3 ch.
6 **MARK**, soldier at Sagadahoc under Capt. Francis Nicholson, kil. July 1689.
7 **CAPT. SAMUEL**, s. of Michael of Haverhill, b. 2 Feb. 1633, m. 14 Dec. 1687 Judith Davis(20). List 99. He bot land in Durham 14 Dec. 1697, was of Dover 18 Dec. 1700, selectm. there 1705. Remov. ab. 1717 into Oyster River. par., he helped organize

the ch. there 3 Apr. 1718, made elder 16 Nov. 1721. Capt. of foot company 1718. Lists 358d, 269. Will 13 Mar. 1739—31 Aug. 1743. His wife was an Indian captive 1694-1699. Ch: **Samuel**, b. 21 Aug. 1688, appren. 15 Aug. 1701 for 8 yrs. to Noah and Eliz. Parker, ran away 28 Apr. 1707; in 1728, mariner, was sued for avoiding 2 yrs. as apprent. **Hannah**, b. 22 Dec. 1691. **Hannah**, b. 6 Jan. 1699-1700, m. Job Clements(4 jr.). **Micah**, b. 4 Jan. 1701-2, m. 5 Feb. 1725 Sarah Huckins. He d. ab. 1734; wid. m. 2d Joseph Tibbetts, d. 13 Feb. 1777. 3 ch. **Abigail**, b. 27 Sep. 1704, m. Robert Thompson. **Timothy**, b. ab. 1706, tanner, List 369, m. ab. 1732 Mary Smith, dau. of Samuel and Hannah (Burnham). He d. bef. 5 May 1754; wid. m. 2d Dr. Joseph Atkinson. 7 ch. **Solomon**, b. 1709, m. 1st Elizabeth Smith, sis. of Timothy's wife, 2d Mary, app. wid. of Saml. Meader. 9 ch. by 1st w.

**EMERY**, ancient forename. Common in S. E. of Eng.

1 ‡***ANTHONY***, carpenter from Romsey, Hants, came in -The James- from Southampton in Apr. 1635. First set. at Newb., he rem. by 1640 to Dover, where he had recd. 3½ a. from Capt. Wiggin in 1637. Lic. to keep ordin. and sell beer and wine bef. 1643, selectm. 1648, gr.j. 1649. Resid. at Cold Harbor in Kittery by 1651, he was active there the next ten yrs., tav. and ferry keeper, jury 1650-1, 1655, selectm. 1652, 1654, comr. to adj. differences about town grants 1654, comr. on York-Wells bounds 1658, and memb. of Godfrey's council dur. its last days; but in freq. trouble over Quakers, and fined and disfranch. 12 Nov. 1659 for telling a lie in the face of the court. Lists 351b, 352, 353, 354-abc, 282, 283, 298, 29. Prep. to rem. to the more liberal R. I., he sold his prop. in Kit. to s. James 12 May 1660, his (2d?) w. Frances suing him in Oct. for ⅓ of the purchase price. Recd. inhab. at Portsmouth, R. I., 29 Sep. 1660, he was prom. in town affairs and Deputy in 1672. Still of Portsmouth 9 Mar. 1680-1, he deeded his prop. after his own death to dau. Rebecca, then to her s. Anthony; was dec. in 1694. Three ch. ment. in petn. ab. 1643, but only two kn: James, b. ab. 1630. **Rebecca**, m. 1st Robert Weymouth, who d. bef. 24 Dec. 1661, 2d Thomas Sadler, 3d aft. 9 Mar. 1680-1 Daniel Eaton of Little Compton, his will 29 Apr.—21 Aug. 1704. She d. at Little Comp. 18 July 1719. The petn. made in her name for her late husband's prop. on Staten Isl., N. Y., 22 May 1676, represents that he had yrs. bef. aband. her and their three small children. Of her ch. we know only: William (Weymouth), called Weymouth alias Sadler in Maine rec. 1682. Joseph (Amory), presumably an unack. ch.

Anthony (Sadler), made his grf. Emery's heir by deed 9 Mar. 1680-1.

2 ***JAMES***(1), as a youth liv. some time in the house of and worked for Richard Waldron at Dover. In 1654 land was laid out to him in Kit., where often gr.j., selectm. 1666 and many times, lot layer 1665, 1698-99, assessor 1680, 1684-85, Rep. 1680, 1693, 1695. Lists 282-284, 25, 29, 33, 298. See Champernowne (List 32). Two wives Elizabeth, the 2d one Elizabeth (Newcomb) Pidge, wid. of John of Dedham, whom he mar. 28 Dec. 1695. He was living in Dedham 1700-1709, in Kit. 19 Sep. 1717, d. bef. 15 Oct. 1719. Ch. by 1st w: **Elizabeth**, m. 20 Apr. 1677 Sylvanus Nock. **James**, b. ab. 1660. **Sarah**, m. 1st John Thompson, 2d Gilbert Warren. **Zachariah**. **Noah**, liv. in Stone's garrison with Philip Hubbard 1690, d. before 1694. List 298. **Daniel**, Dea. and Elder, b. 13 Sep. 1667, mar. 17 Mar. 1695 Margaret Gowen alias Smith. Selectm. 1704-12, 1718, surveyor 1706-17. List 298. D. 15 Oct. 1722; will 5 Apr. 1722, gave both his old and new houses to s. Noah. 10 ch., all named in their mother's will 26 Mar. 1748. Job, Dea., b. ab. 1670, mar. 6 Apr. 1696 Charity Nason. Selectm. 1719-20, 1726. List 298. His will 26 Feb. 1736-7—26 Dec. 1738, named 13 ch.; her will 26 Mar. 1748—6 Jan. 1752.

3 JAMES(2), m. 1st Margaret Hitchcock (Richard and Lucretia [Williams]), 2d Elizabeth, wid. of John Fost(1). He was selectm. 1697-98, jury 1695, 1699, gr.j. 1693, 94. Lists 296, 298. Will 28 Dec. 1724—7 Apr. 1725, names w. Elizabeth, 2 sons, 6 daus. and s. James' ch.; inv. 24 Mar. 1725. Wid. liv. 5 Sep. 1730, but app. dead in Mar. 1737-8. Ch. by 1st w: **Margaret**, b. 18 Dec. 1686, m. Samuel Smith. **James**, b. 18 Feb. 1688, mar. Elizabeth, wid. of Isaac Spencer, d. bef. 19 May 1724; she m. 3d Thomas Abbott, s. of Joseph(4). 4 ch. **Lydia**, b. 28 Apr. 1691. **Frances**, b. 17 Dec. 1694, m. John Roberts. **Rebecca**, b. 7 Mar. 1697, m. 1st Capt. Daniel Smith of Bid., s. of Nicholas jr. of Exeter, 2d Capt. Nathaniel Ladd. **Samuel**, b. 2 Sep. 1700. **Elizabeth**, b. 7 Mar. 1703, mar. John Murch. **Thomas**, b. 2 Dec. 1706, m. 22 Mar. 1731 Susanna Hill (Dea. Ebenezer of Bid.). 3 ch. **Lucretia**, b. 6 Aug. 1709, m. William Dyer, s. of Wm.(6).

4 JOSEPH (Amory), grs. of (1), weaver, d. 31 Jan. 1711-12 at Little Compton, R. I. The town clerk evolved synthetic dates which have been printed as records. Adm. gr. to wid. Elizabeth (Washburn, d. of Philip and Elizabeth [Irish]), liv. 1714. Ch: **Patience**, b. ab. 1682, d. 10 Mar. 1749-50, in 68th yr. (grst.), m. 25 May 1704 Richard Grinnell 1669-1725. **Rebecca**, d. 8 Apr. 1712. **Daniel**, b. 24 Aug. 1695, mariner, Lit. Comp., Portsmouth, Newport. He m. 24 Dec. 1721 Lydia

Horswell. 8 ch. Besides the foreg. named in Daniel Eaton's will, perh. also: **John**, of Newport, freeman 1730, mar. (int. 18 June 1731) Judith Briggs. **Eliza**, m. 21 Sep. 1731 Aaron Sheffield. **Esther**.

5 **REV. SAMUEL**, grneph. of (1), b. Newb. 20 Dec. 1670, H.C. 1691, was chaplain at Wells garrison and min. there 1698, ordained 29 Oct. 1701. Lists 268b, 269a, 38. He d. in Bid. 28 Dec. 1724; wid. Tabitha (Littlefield) d. 27 Apr. 1736. List 269c. Ch: **Samuel**, b. 14 Aug. 1698, blacksm. in Falm., d. 1755. List 269c. M. in Bost. 22 Sep. 1726 Bathsheba Vose of Dorch., who surv. 7 ch. **Mary**, b. 7 Dec. 1699, mar. 1st Joseph Hill jr., 2d John Fairfield(2). **Hannah**, b. 10 Feb. 1701, mar. Francis Littlefield. **Sarah**, b. 29 Dec. 1702, m. 1st Nathaniel Gilman, 2d Hon. John Phillips. **Tabitha**, b. 23 Mar. 1704-5. **Stephen**, b. 3 Aug. 1707, H.C. 1730, pastor at Chatham, Cape Cod, 33 yrs., m. 8 Oct. 1742 Hannah Allen (Rev. Benj. of Falm.). He d. 24 May 1782, she 7 June 1799. 5 ch. **Irene**, b. 4 Mar. 1710-11, d. 1745, mar. Rev. Thomas Prentice of Ken'port and Charlestown, who d. in Camb. 17 June 1782. 5 ch. **John**, b. 2 Mar. 1715, d. in Exeter 1736, unm.

6 **ZACHARIAH**(2), b. ab. 1660. List 298. He m. 9 Dec. 1686 Elizabeth Goodwin, who mar. 2d 22 Dec. 1692 Philip Hubbard. Ch: **Elizabeth**, b. 27 Nov. 1687, m. Nathaniel Tarbox. **Zachariah**, b. 5 Oct. 1690, cordwainer, Chelmsford by 1711. First w. Sarah, d. 8 Oct. 1732, m. 2d 20 May 1733 Rebecca Reddington of Topsfield. 10 ch.

**EMMES.** 1 **Henry**, Boston, baker, owned land at mouth of Kennebec, bot from John Pritchet 10 Nov. 1686. Poss. never liv. on it but had a br. k. by Ind. there. List 183. Y. D. vi. 17, viii. 208, ix. 196, xiii. 175, xvii. 79. Petn. Boston 1694. Will 1725.

2 **SIMON**, soldier Kit. 170--. List 289.

**Emmett**, Richard, seaman for Pepperell 1717.

**EMMONS**, Emons, found about London.

1 **EBENEZER** (aut. Emons), app. same b. Boston 18 Apr. 1683, br. of Hannah who m. James Gooch, ch. of Samuel who d. 1685, br. of (2). In Kit. by 1712, tailor, he had m. Mary, sis. of Thomas or Grace (Ferris) Huff. Aft. Dummer's War he rem. to Arundel with his br.-in-law Huff, but soon settled in Kennebunk. Liv. 1737. List 291. Likely other ch. incl: **Samuel**, Kennebunk abuttor by 1729, m. Abigail Fletcher, d. of Pendleton(8 jr.), d. 1795 in Lyman. List 269c. Ch. bap. in Wells. **Hannah**, bp. Portsm. No. Ch. 15 July 1711, m. in Wells 1 Jan. 1730-1 Nathl. Wakefield. 9 ch. bap., also Abigail Emmons, infant, not their ch., bp. 29 Apr. 1750. **John**, m. Elizabeth Deering(5), settled in Arundel. Ch. **Jane**, in ct. Apr. 1747. **Joanna**, joined Wells ch. 29 June 1746. Removed.

2 **JOSEPH**, b. Boston 8 Mar. 1651, s. of Tho. and Martha who both left wills. In Marblehead 9 Oct. 1674, cordwainer, he took Christo. Codner apprent., whose stepf. later wanted him released, calling Emmons an idle fellow who would bring up the child for the gallows—an opinion agreeing with Joseph's mother's will. In 1694 he had a shoemaker's shop in Mr. John Stanyan's house, Hampton. The Emmons Gen. 1905 ascribes to Joseph a 1st wife and 3 ch. who cert. belonged to his br. Benj., and one app. bel. to his neph. Nathl. He did m. a mid. aged wid. with 6 ch., Mary (Webster) Swain, 12 June 1694 (mar. bond signed Emons, wit. Saml. Emons). She was liv. 1706, he in Hampton Falls 1728. Ch: **Martha**, b. 29 Mar. 1696. **Samuel**, b. 12 Nov. 1700, settled in Kingston. Reported dead 9 June 1757, adm. to Ebenezer Long. His wid. (Maria Norton, mar. Sals. 16 July 1723) m. 13 Oct. 1757 David Colby. Ch. incl. 3 who d. 1735.

3 **ROBERT** (Emens), belonged to -Pinke Lenham- 1670. List 82.

4 **RUTH**, Greenland ch. memb. 1721, m. 13 Dec. 1721 Benj. Estabrook. List 338b. Also in Greenl. 29 Nov. 1710 Judith, m. John Cate(3).

**ENDICOTT**, Indicott, Endacott, pecul. to Devon.

1 **GILBERT**, b. ab. 1658, weaver, soldier in K. Philip's War, was in Wells 1677, fined there for a lie in 1680; of Wells in Apr. 1683 he sold a sawmill on the little river at Cape Porpus to James Ross, and was a Cape Porp. wit. 2 Jan. 1687-8. List 269b. By 1696 he was in Reading, but was back in Wells, deposing, in 1698. He soon retd. to Mass., liv. prin. in Dorch., where he was selling without lic. in 1700 and selling liquor in 1713, and in Ponkapoag, though in 1708 he was of Bost., a house owner. D. 18 Oct. 1716, app. in Ponkapoag, his grst. the oldest in Canton. He mar. in Me., 28 Apr. 1686 Hannah Gooch (James), who mar. 2d 14 Nov. 1717 John Minot, d. 12 Oct. 1753, ag. 80. Ch: **John**, housewright in Boston 1716. **James**, housewr. in Dorch. 1717. **Sarah**, bp. Milton 27 July 1707, m. John Billings of Boston.

2 **JOHN** (Indicott), cooper, Boston, partn. of Silvanus Davis(53), m. Mary Talbot (Wm. of Boston). List 225a. He d. 7 Dec. 1711, ag. 70, wife Mary Sep. 1718 (grst.). His will, 1711–1712, gave ¼ of Falm. lands ch: **Sarah**, m. 21 Apr. 1708 William Halewell jr. Son **Bagworth**, b. 2 Apr. 1693, d.y. See Bagworth.

**ENDLE**

1 **JOHN**, in 1676 was adm. on est. of Wm. Ash of Kit.; if the same man, he was br.

of (3) who adm. his est. 7 July 1690. Inv. shows cattle, no land.

2 **MICHAEL**, ±60 in 1680. Invest. may confirm indent. with one Michael, s. of Michael, bap. at Stoke-in-Teignhead, Devon, 7 July 1621. At Isles of Shoals by 1648, later fishing master on Smuttinose, and m. Wilmot Bailey(5) by 1662. List 331c. Gr.j. 1659, const. 1666. Lists 302b, 305ae, 306c. In 1678 he sold his plant to the Olivers and retired to Spruce Creek, yet in 1683 he and Wm. O. still held a house together on Smuttinose. In 1691 he deeded his place to his next neighbors (John and Sarah Morgrage) for life supp. of self and Wilmot. In 1667 Richard's br.'s son had a jackknife from Mr. Jonathan Wade, poss. that **Ephraim**, who wit. turf and twig to Richard Cutt in 1685.

3 **RICHARD**, ±40 in 1674, in 1660 was fishing partn. with Stephen Ford; from 1665 on sold his fish to Mr. Jonathan Wade, acct. was not settled until 1682. In 1679-1681 he had been fishing for Roger Kelly. In 1667 he adm. on estates of Barthol. Priest and Christo. Monke. Lists 302ab, 305c, 298. In 1665 he bot at Spruce Creek and from that time kept his fam. ashore, self and w. bur. there. Adm. to s. Richard, inv. attested 5 Apr. 1694. He m. Agnes Turpin. Ch: **Hannah**, m. 1683 Joseph Wilson. Their s. Gowen occup. the homestead. **Richard**, b. ab. 1662, yeoman, had the homestead. Const. 1694-96. Gr.j. 1693, 1694, 1696, 1703. Lists 290, 295-298. W. Jane liv. 1707. D.s.p. 1716.

4 **WILLIAM**, swearing drunk on Sunday in 1662, poss. could do this young enough to be s. of one of the brs. Taxed Str. Bk. 1686.

**ENGLAND**. 1 **Stephen**. Ab. or bef. 1700 he built at Stratham, buying Wm. Morgan's land from a creditor. 1725-1732 bet. Biddeford and Stratham. In 1737, of Newbury, was sued on a note given in Scarb. List 388.

2 **WILLIAM**, owed Mitchell estate 1666. List 78.

**ENGLISH**, Inglish, Ingles, the latter the name for Englishmen settled in Scotland. 1 **JAMES** (Ingles), coastwise trader, partner of Silvanus Davis, ±63 in Jan. 1694-5, poss. the Scotch prisoner of war; in 1658 wit. turf and twig at Damariscove; in 1664 (Engless) was master of Anthony Checkley's barque; in 1667 Davis and he (Ingles —wrote) wit. a Kennebec deed. Lists 74, 91, 34, 225a, 227. His will, dated 2 Feb. 1702-3, indexed -Ingalls-, escaped atten. D. 6 Feb. ag. 70½ (grst. Copp's Hill, Ingles). M. 7 Jan. 1657-8 in Boston Joanna Farnum. His heirs who deeded away his Falm. lands were two daus., **Joanna**, mar. James Grant; **Jane**, m. 1st Smith, 2d John Stevens, both widows in 1716; ch. of dau. **Elizabeth**, who m. Benj. Brame; and ch. of son James.

2 **JOSEPH**, Salem soldier under Hill 1693-4. List 267b.

3 **JOSEPH**, Salem 1735, see Joseph Phippen.

4 **PHILIP**, Salem merchant. See Babb(2).

5 \***SERGT. WILLIAM** (Inglish), cordwainer, Ipsw. 1637, Hampton 1640, of Ipsw. 1652 sold in Hampton, of Boston 1653. Deputy from Hampton 1646-7. Jury 1647. Gr.j. Ipsw. 1650; jury 1651. Lists 391a, 392ab, 53. In Boston was at times a scrivener. Will 1682 names only w. Mary.

**Enow**, Thomas, Falm. 1689. List 228c.

**Ensly**, Elisha, see Insley.

**EPPS**. 1 Capt. **Daniel**, of Ipsw., called stepbr. of Wm. Symonds, owned large tract in Wells, now Kennebunk. 'Danniell Pearses upland,' Y. D. i. 86, is evid. phonet. for Eppes.

2 REV. **SAMUEL**(1), minister at Falm., b. Ipsw. 24 Feb. 1647, H.C. 1669, called 'our Reverend teacher Mr. Samuel Epps' by Mr. Munjoy and Walter Gendall in 1671, of Boston 1673, d. in London in Apr. 1685.

**Erington**, Abraham, at Kennebec 1688. Y.D. 8.25.

**ERRING** (Errin). 1 **Edward** (Erwin, Duren), see Urine.

2 **WILLIAM**, Saco, 1687. Special warrant issued for felony (stealing). Philip Foxwell had given bond for Richard Rogers and W. E. They fled this province, with hue and cry after them.

**Escot**, Richard, List 307b. See Westcott.

**ESMOND**, Robert, Kit. ab. 1673, adm. 6 Jan. 1712-3, perh. long since dead. Lists 293, 298. Ch. unk: except **Sarah**, m. (July Term, 1703) William Briar(7). Also presum: **Joseph**, in 1708 was master of -The Miriam-, Kit. to So. Carolina. His deed, dated 8 June 1710, of whole est. to w. Miriam was proved by wit. 31 Aug. 1711. List 296. The wid. m. 17 Mar. 1713-4 Joseph Simpson. **Henry**, Kit. wit. 1706. Y. D. viii. 44.

**Essex**, see James Cors.

**ESTES**. 1 **MATTHEW**, br. of (2), master mariner and Quaker, b. in Eng. 28 May 1645, s. of Robert and Dorothy, Portsm. tax abated 1675, m. 14 June 1676 Philadelphia (Jenkins) Hayes of Kit., wid. of Edward. He liv. on Great Isl., buying land there, in 1682, also buying in Salem that yr. Retailer Gt. Isl. 1686, taxed there 1688. He had mov. to Salem bef. 30 Mar. 1691, afterw. was of Lynn, of Salem again 1719. Wife d. 25 Dec. 1721; his will 4 June—8 July 1723 gave all to s. John and his fam., br. Richard exec. Ch: **Sarah**, b. 10 Apr. 1677, d. 28 Jan. 1682. **Philadelphia**, b. 9 July 1679, m. Salem 19 Mar. 1695-6 George Cornell of Portsm., R.I., d. before 1699. 1 dau. **Hannah**, b. 24 Oct. 1681, d. 30 Sep. 1683. **John**, b. and d. 6 Sep. 1683. **John**, b. 14 July 1684, d. Lynn 29 Sep. 1723, m. there 15 Feb. 1705-6 Hannah Bas-

set (Wm.), who d. 14 May 1762. 7 ch. **Richard**, b. 27 Sep. 1686, d. bef. 1723.

2 **RICHARD**, br. of (1), b. May 1647, sleymaker from Newington, East Kent, 'liv. in Eng. till the 11th day of the 7 mo. 1684,' arrived in the Piscataqua 11 Dec. that yr. Of Gt. Isl., he m. at Dover 23 June 1687 wid. Elizabeth Beck(3) of Gt. Isl. They were of Salem 1692-3, Lynn 1695-1726, Salem 1727. He d. at Lynn 'old' ab. 16 Jan. 1736-7. Of 11 ch., 3 came to Me. and N. H.: **Joseph**, b. 26 Aug. 1696, liv. at Dov., m. there 19 July 1719 Mary Robinson (Timothy and Mary [Roberts]). He d. 15 May 1770, she 26 Mar. 1771. 7 ch. **Benjamin**, b. 10 July 1698, of Salem until 1742, Berwick 1743, Wells 1759, of Berwick, Esq., at death, 1775. Wife Elizabeth, 6 ch. **Edward**, b. 20 Feb. 1703-4, m. 27 Aug. 1730 Patience (Carr) Peckham, wid. of Joseph, dau. of John and Waite (Easton) of Newport, R. I. Of Hanover 24 May 1748 he bot 100 a. at Merriconeag Neck, lived Harpswell 1750, Durham 1770, d. Durham 13 Feb. 1788. 12 ch.

**ESTOW, \*William**, s. of George of Ormesby St. Margaret, co. Norfolk, mar. there 15 July 1623 widow Mary Moulton. Newbury propr. 1638, orig. planter of Hampton. Freeman 13 Mar. 1638-9, selectman 1647, 1649, 1653. Jury 1648, 1651, gr.j. 1649, 1654. Com. t.e.s.c. 1649, 1650, 1652. Dep. to Genl. Court 1644, 1648, 1649. Lists 391a, 392ab, 393a(2), b. He was relieved from training in 1654, d. 23 Nov. 1655. Will 16 Oct. 1655—8 Apr. 1656, wife not ment. Ch: **Sarah**, b. 1625, m. Morris Hobbs. **Mary**, bp. at Ormesby 8 June 1628, m. Thomas Marston.

**ETHERINGTON, Thomas**, Ind. trader, had gr. in Kit. 1659. Lists 78, 298. He and his w. Mary Spencer (Thomas) were cast away in John Cole's lighter coming from Boston in Nov. 1664; adm. to br.-in-law Wm. Spencer 8 Sep. 1665. Ch: **Mary**, List 298, m. ab. 1675 Capt. John Wincoll. **Patience**, List 298, m. aft. 29 Feb. 1675-6 William Hearl.

**Eugsley**, Elisha, see Insley.

**Eureft.** Capt. John. List 122. Wit. 1695 to Maj. Francis Hooke's will; 'Capt. John Euret' recorded absent at proving.

**EVANS**, like all Welsh names, patronymic. 4th commonest in Wales, 8th in Wales and England.

1 **BENJAMIN**, misr. of Cram. N. H. Hist. Soc. viii. 47.

2 **EBENEZER**, Portsm. 1673, in 1685 received from Tho. and w. Mary Wacomb a deed of a house standing next their own. Adm. 26 Apr. 1686 to wid. Patience (Fernald 4), who m. 2d 9 Nov. 1686 Robert Alkins.

3 **EDWARD**(12), b. 28 June 1667, yeoman, was executor of his f's will and had the homestead by entail. Constable 1710. In

1729 'Edward' s. of Robert' ack. a deed given in 1712. Lists 94, 358d. By will dated 31 Oct. 1741, 'being advanced in years and laboring under the infirmities of age,' he gave his entire est. to his kinsman Moses Wingate. This will was never offered for probate, but he d. bef. 1751. Court files 16541, N. H. Deeds 47.330. The homestead passed to (10) under the entail.

3½ **EDWARD**(8?), cooper, recently extric. from (3), first ment. in the record of a child's birth in Kit., next in the exam. of his br. Joseph(10½), runaway apprent. in Boston. Called a centenarian at death, the newspapers said he perfectly remembered the revolution against Gov. Andros which occurred in the last yr. of his apprenticeship in Boston. List 358d, 1715, shows two: Edward liv. on his father's homestead, 'Edward Jun' liv. on the other side of Back River. In 1716 in suit on a bond payable to 'Edward Evins of Dover,' the writ has -Juninterlined. In 1724 E. E. of Dover, cooper, was sued on a store bill running from July 1709 to Jan. 1709-10. In 1726, with w. Dorcas, 'of Oyster River.' In 1729, of Dover, cooper, he bot 40 a. in Wells. In 1730, with w. Dorcas, q.c. estate of 'our father Simon Bussell'(3) in Wells. In 1734, cooper, wife Dorcas, sold his homestead (near Pudding Hill in Madbury). In 1737 E. E., cooper, and w. Dorcas, both sick, were presented for abs. from meet. in Wells. Four ch. of 'Edward and Dorcas' were recorded together about 1705. The warrant for Madbury parish meeting 1756 (appar. having come back from away) contains an article to see if the parish will vote a support for Edw. Evans or to send him out of the parish; 1756-1766 numerous items on Madbury records about supplying E. E. or letting him out; 1757 11s. for making his coffin and digging his grave. He d. in Barrington. It is quite poss. that the writer of the death notice, week of 20 Nov. 1767, found the other Edward's birth record in the Dover town book. Kn. ch: **Eleanor**, b. in Kit. 3 Mar. (1699-1700?). **Edward**, b. in Dover 23 Oct. (1701?); mar. in Wells 11 Oct. 1727 Sarah Larrabee, and settled with her fam. in the part now Kennebunk. 4 s. bap. of whom all but Jacob enlisted in 1758 and were k. near Fort Wm. Henry. **Rachel**, b. 6 Apr. 1703, mar. John Burks, 9 ch. bap. in Wells. **Joseph**, b. 29 Oct. 1704, Somersworth, was 'Jr.' till his death. He mar. Keziah Hall, d. of John and Esther (Chesley). Suits show a primer in 1733, a sick wife and 23 doctor's visits in 1734. Master Tate gives the wid. Keziah 4 ch. Also likely **Hannah**, m. (int. 1738) Tho. Wormwood of Wells, 5 ch. bap.

4 **EDWARD**, List 228d, killed in Casco battle 21 Sep. 1689. The name -Evans-, al-

tered from Greene, was read Gebens in Me. H. & G. Rec. i. 196, and poss. may have been Youine, for Ewen, or the same called Euin in Hub. Ind. Wars ii. 199.

5 **ELIZABETH**, from Bridgend, Glamorganshire, Wales, bound for 3 yrs. to Rev. John Wheelwright 25 June 1639.

6 **GILBERT** (Ifins), Kennebec militia 1688. List 189.

7 **GRIFFITH**, before Court at Saco in 1636.

8 **JOHN**, Mr., Capt., expert surveyor, of whom we know almost nothing except that he was a useful and highly respected inhab. and was k. by Indians 28 June 1689. Philip Benmore called him kinsman. He was adm. inhab. of Dover 10 Feb. 1659-60. Jury 1674, gr.j. 1676. Town clerk from 1686. Lists 353, 356j, 359ab, 49, 52, 54, 55b, 94, 96. Both will and heirship deeds are lacking, and his name is missing in some tax lists. In 1673 he had built on 2 a. which Mr. Waldron pract. gave him. In 1701 Richard Scammon deeded to Joseph Roberts sr. 26 a. described, 'which land or living was formerly the dwelling place of Mr. John Evans dec.', title not searched. We would know nothing of any ch. except for his note book and papers coming down among the descendants of **Thomas**, b. 1663 (in poss. of the late J. Q. Evans of Salisbury, not now access.), Capt. Gyles's account of his son **John's** death in captivity in 1692, and the traditions among the descendants of **Eleanor**, wife of George Ricker, older than the others. Nothing appears in the records but that the brothers, **Edward** and **Joseph** (3½ and 10½) were his ch. Abs. nothing appears of Mrs. Evans, unless poss. her mar. in Boston, Elinor Evans and John Sweeting, 7 Feb. 1694, poss. the same John -Sweeten- who m. Frances Child 8 Aug. 1700. The mother of Edw. and Joseph was dead in 1701.

9 **JOHN**, known only by the self-record of **Richard**, 'son of John & Sarah,' b. 1 Jan. 1706, Portsm., who in 1723 belonged to the watch on Gt. Isl., mar. 23 Sep. 1731 Mary Manson, and rec. 6 sons, some prom., incl. Eastwick, b. 12 Aug. 1740. Presumably the mother was Sarah Eastwick(1), Portsmouth wit. in 1708. Richard was bur. Portsm. Aug. 1788 'aged 84,' his w. Feb. 1784, ag. 77.

10 **JOSEPH**(12), b. 4 June 1682. Before his father's homestead came to him he had established his own farther inland, now called Wyanoke farm, on Littleworth road. List 358d. He m. 6 Apr. 1704 Mercy Horne (Wm. and Elizabeth [Clough]). Will 3 Dec. —21 Feb. 1750-1. Ch: **Robert**, b. 11 Jan. 1704-5, lived in Madbury near Barrington line. D. by 1758. W. Elizabeth. 6 ch. incl. William who liv. on the orig. Evans homestead. **John**, b. 3 Feb. 1705-6, scalped by Ind. 25 Sep. 1725, liv. to 80. He m. Eliza-

beth Kimming, wid. in 1776. **Joseph**, b. 28 Mar. 1708, d. in Madbury 16 Dec. 1786. W. Elizabeth (Hanson) d. 24 Sep. 1796, ae. 90. 5 or m. ch. **William**, b. 9 Feb. 1711-2, k. by Ind. 25 Sep. 1725. **Daniel**, b. 28 June 1715, had f.'s homestead. Will 14 Feb. 1781. Ch. **Mercy**, b. 6 Dec. 1717, not in will. **Mary**, b. 6 Mar. 1720-1, m. one Hayes.

10½ **JOSEPH**, br. of Edward(3½), both apprentices in Boston. Ident. only by Suff. Ct. files 5048, his exam., July 1701, for running away from his master, Wm. Tedman, brazier, this the fourth time. He was brot back by the constable of Sherburn—(Robert[13] was then liv. at Sherburn, Nantucket). He had stolen his indenture from his master's chest. His own copy, he said, his br. Edw. at Dover had kept since his mother died. He said he would be '19 next March.'

11 **PETER**, of Isles of Shoals, 1673. List 305b. Ordered home to Eng., Margaret Barter, Goodwife Boman, Goody Harris dep. about his wife liv. in Broad St., Plymouth, with another man, with 2 ch. by him.

12 **ROBERT**, Dover. In 1662 James Coffin, Robert Evans and John Church were taxed together at Cochecho in one assessment. By 1669 he had built at Bellamy's Bank, where the fam. contin. a century. His house stood in or close by the Catholic cemetery below the City Hall. Innholder 1689. Gr.j. 1694. Lists 356ghkm, 357c, 359ab, 311 (Dover), 49, 52, 57, (61), 62, 94, 96. Will 19, d. 27 Feb. 1696-7. He m. 1st Elizabeth Colcord(1); in 1675 she had d. and ch. been committed to their grmo. in Hampton; 2d Ann (Thompson), wid. of Israel Hodsdon, who long surv. him, kept tavern in his house, and left ch. by both hus. Adm. 30 May 1727 to Israel Hodsdon. Ch: **Robert**, b. 30 Sep. 1665. **Edward**, b. 28 June 1667. **Jonathan**, b. 10 Apr. 1669, perh. apprent. to Mr. Fryer 1688, in Dover 1694, d. in London s.p. by 1728. **Elizabeth**, b. 25 Jan. 1671-2, in will 1697. In 1728 sister Sarah Lewis deeded a ninth of Jonathan's gr. By 2d w: **Mary**, b. 1676, m. 2 May 1699 Samuel Hart, Esq. **Sarah**, b. 9 Nov. 1685, m. Wm. Lewis. **Benjamin**, b. 2 Feb. 1687-8, k. by Ind. 25 Sep. 1725. List 358d. W. Mary (Field) still his wid. 1740. 5 ch. rec. 1704-1720, incl. Benj., Ind. captive. **Hannah**, b. 21 June 1690, m. Zachariah Field(12 jr.), Richard Hussey. **Patience**, b. 5 Sep. 1693, m. Samuel Carle(3).

13 **CAPT. ROBERT**(12), ag. 84 in June 1750, a rolling stone. Ensign 1692, Lieut., Capt. Nantucket 1699-1701, Mendon 1711-1725, Dover, 1712, 1729, recom. by Dover selectmen for innholder 1750, warned out of Somersw. with wife 1752, liv. 1753. Lists 59, (61), 62, 94, 298. He m. 1st Ann (Heard), widow of Isaac Hanson; 2d by 1735 Sarah (Clarke),

wid. of Sylvester Mantee, liv. 1767. List
298. Kn. ch: **Anna,** b. at Nantucket 27 Feb.
1699-1700, m. by 1733 Job Hussey. **Edmund,**
b. Nant. 1 Oct. 1701, carpenter, m. in Mendon 9 Apr. 1722 Ruth Wood. Rem. to Enfield.
Wit. Y. D. 13.180 deed of Mary (Felt 2)
Wood. Ch.
14 **THOMAS**(8), Salisbury, m. 30 Sep. 1686
Hannah Brown, whose sis. m. Col. Paul
Wentworth. His will 21, d. 24, Jan. 1717-8.
Hers, 8 Mar. 1735-6—10 July 1738, names all
8 ch: **Anne,** b. 5 Nov. 1687, m. 8 Aug. 1718
Cornelius Clough of Kingston. **John,** b. 24
Aug. 1689, m. 26 Dec. 1714 Mary Tappan.
6 ch. rec. **Abigail,** b. 22 Aug. 1692, m. Icha-
bod Hayes, Wm. Twombly. **Tamsen,** b. 5
Apr. 1696, m. 9 Nov. 1721 Judah Hackett.
**Hannah,** b. 5 Apr. 1698, m. Benj. Twombly.
**Thomas,** b. 24 Mar. 1703, d. at Surinam 15
May 1743, adm. 5 Sep. 1743. He m. 14 Dec.
1721 Dorothy Stockman who m. 2d 7 Apr.
1757 Richard Fitts of So. Hamp. and d. 8
Nov. 1776. 8 ch. rec. **Elizabeth,** bp. 25 Jan.
1707, m. 1st 29 Jan. 1729 Theophilus Stevens; 2d 15 May 1735 Wm. Hackett. **Ezekiel,**
bp. 28 Jan. 1711, d. 6 July 1753. He m. 5
Oct. 1732 Judith French, who d. 28 Apr.
1777, ag. 65 (grst.) 8 ch. rec.
15 **THOMAS,** mariner. Inquest 1687. Lst 332a.
16 **WILLIAM,** Little Harbor, Portsmouth.
Grant 13 Jan. 1652. Sued in York Ct. by
Boston plaint. 1653. List 323. Oct. 12, 1658,
he 'delivered his wife to the town's hands,'
the case to be decided by the selectm. Four
years later she was sent down from Boston
jail, and her hus. bound himself for half her
support. Thomas Peverly was allowed 30 s.
for keeping her formerly, and to have £12
for the next year.

**EVEREST,** once common in Kent. In York
town records Averett.
1 **ANDREW,** York grantee in 1646. Sold
out in 1680-1682 and left York; in a deed
of 1715 is called 'old Master Everet.' O.A.
to Mass. 22 Nov. 1652, and again in March
1679-80. Constable 1672. Lists 25, 273, 275-
277. Wife Barbara 1670, 1681. Presum. ch:
**Isaac. Jacob,** Boston, glazier, in his will
1692—1693 ment. br. Isaac and sister Ruth.
**Job,** gr. 1674, rem. to Guilford, Conn. **Mary,**
in 1674 confessed to purloining goods from
Mr. Geo. Broughton. **Lydia,** in 1682 wit. for
Mr. Rishworth. **Ruth,** presum. blood sister
named in Jacob's will.
2 **ISAAC**(1), grant 1669; in Feb. 1675-6, with
w. Joanna, he sold his house and land at
York and rem. to Guilford. Ch: **John,** d.
1705. **Isaac,** b. 1675, d. 1751, w. Mary, no ch.
**Benjamin,** m. 1708 Hannah Jones, dau. of
Nathl. and Abigail (Atwater). **Lydia,** m.
1712 Daniel Mix.
3 **JOHN.** See Eurest.

**EVERETT,** called phonetic for ancient
forename Everard. Common in E. of Eng.
1 **JOHN,** ±60 in 1695, was at John Woodman's house, Kit. Wit. Francis Hooke's
will same year.
2 **THOMAS,** 'of Portsmouth,' drunk 1662.
3 **THOMAS,** m. Berwick 14 July 1724 Mary
Andrews(4).
4 **WILLIAM,** deft. in N. H. Ct. 1640. In
1646 with Dr. Renald Fernald appr. the
est. of John White. In 1650 his w. Margery
test. regarding Dr. John Reynold's affairs
three yrs. prior. Appar. they had come up
to Eliot with the others from the mouth of
the river. Innholder opp. Dover Neck from
1649, he entertained the Commissioners from
Mass. when Kit. submitted in Nov. 1652. He
d. bef. the next summer, and his wid. Margaret, m. 2d by 1656 Isaac Nash of Dover,
shipwright, 3d Abraham Conley. Lists 281,
282. Ch: **Martha,** b. ab. 1640, mar. Nathan
Lord. **William,** mariner, Lt. Charles Frost
his guardian in 1660, liv. 1671, d. at sea, s.p.
Adm. 12 May 1674 to Nathan Lord. List
298 (1671).
**Ewen,** Edward, called br. by Richard Pierce
of Marbleh. in 1717. Y. D. x. 265. Likely
same m. in Boston 6 Jan. 1736-7 Mary Purington.
**Exeter,** James, Pemaquid 1687. List 124.
**EYRE,** see also Ayers.
1 **BENJAMIN,** Portsm. wit. with E. Stileman 1671.
2 **JOHN,** Portsm. wit. with Richard Tucker
for N. Shapleigh 1659. List 326a?
3 **SIMON,** Portsm. 1674, nephew of John
Cutt(2). List 331a. Liv. in Boston, s. of
Simon and Lydia (Starr). See Savage.
4 **THOMAS, Elyanor** and **Eliezer,** London
shareholders in the Laconia Co. List 41.
**Fabens,** see Fabyan.
**FABES, John,** Esq., Star Island, b. ab. 1625-
28, a petnr. 18 May 1653, bot house and
fishing outfit from Wm. Weymouth 29 June
1654, was a fishing master and prom. man
at the Shoals many yrs. O.A. 11 July 1659.
Gr.j. 1664, jury 1682, J.P. 1683, retailer 1686.
Lists 301, 312c, 305b, 286, 306cd, 49, 95, 307ab,
308a, ?59. Nov. 29, 1667, Christopher Jose
and John -Fabins- bot marsh at Little Harbor from Tho. Seavey, which was later sold
by John Fabes's wid. Elizabeth. Mr. John
Fabes and Peter Twisden, both ag. ab. 53 or
54, 13 July 1681, were in the house of Mrs.
Jane Jose at the Shoals. Will, of Newcastle,
14 May 1696—1 Aug. 1698. Wid. Elizabeth,
Lists 315b, 316; adm. gr. 6 June 1711 to
only ch: **Deborah,** m. aft. 14 May 1696 John
Holden.

**FABYAN** (usu. Fabens), Feabens. See also
Fabes. See Creber.
1 **GEORGE,** weaver, Portsm., wit. deed to

Dr. Barefoot in 1667. In York Ct. 15 Sep. 1668 had not gone to his wife in several mos., and may have left her in Portsm. In 1678 he and John(2) were tenants of adj. lots on Pickering's Neck, where he owned a wharf in 1687 and unsucc. sued John Partridge sr. for wharfage. Jury 1688. Lists 52, 55a, 57, 329. Will 19 Feb. 1692-3—11 Dec. 1693 gave all to w. Elizabeth, who d. 23 Jan. 1698. Ch: **Richard,** liv.' 1687.

2 **JOHN,** Portsm., likely br. of (1), had gr. there in 1660. Constable 1678, gr.j. 1683, 1694-96, jury 1688, 1693. Lists 329, 55ab, 92, 57, 331c, 335a, 330d. D. bef. 1705. Wife Sarah Hall (John of Greenland). Lists 331c, 335a, 330ed. Ch: **John,** b. ab. 1681. **Joseph. Samuel. Sarah,** four bap. together 26 Mar. 1693. She liv. 1748.

3 **JOHN**(2), ae. 75 at death, 30 Mar. 1756. Lived in Newington, tailor and draper, Lieut., J.P., Deacon, Rep. 1745. Lists 337, 343. He m. 25 Dec. 1702 Mary Pickering (Tho.) His will 6 Aug. 1748 names w. Mary, sis. Sarah to be supp. by s. Samuel if she will live with him, and 7 ch: **John,** Capt., unm., d. in Scarb. 3 June 1782, ae. 76, 6 mo. (grst.) **Joseph,** settled in Scarb. **Elizabeth,** m. Benjamin Downing(2). **Mary,** four bap. together Oct. 1710, m. 11 Sep. 1732 John Woodman of Oyster River. **Samuel,** b. 3 Dec. 1710, m. 1st 29 Nov. 1733 Rosamond Nutter, 2d 12 Dec. 1745 Elizabeth Huntress. 4+2 ch. bap. **Phebe,** bp. 6 Sep. 1713, mar. 17 Sep. 1733 Jethro Furber(3 Jethro jr.). **Mehitable,** bp. 29 Apr. 1716, m. one Walker.

**FAIRFIELD,** poss. trans. of Beauchamp, Belcham name of 3 parishes in Essex.

1 **EDWARD,** Scarb. garrison 1676, misr. of -Hounsell-.

2 **JOHN,** from Ipswich, m. in Boston 18 Apr. 1693 Elizabeth Batson(1). Taxed Newcastle 1698. Lists 66, 315b. His wid. m. in Boston 5 Dec. 1718 Dependence Littlefield of Wells. See W. M. Emery: -Perkins, Fairfield and King-. Kn. ch: **John,** Wells 1722-1728, Arundel, mariner, coaster, millman, innholder. Lieut. in Louisburg exped. M. aft. 1725 Mary (Emery 5), wid. of Joseph Hill jr. 6 ch. Also presum: **Sarah,** of Wells, in court 3 July 1722.

3 REV. **JOHN,** b. at Boston 26 Dec. 1737, s. of Wm. and Elizabeth (Sweetser), H.C. 1757. Having preached at Arrowsic and Black Point, was ordained at Saco 27 Oct. 1762. D. 16 Dec. 1819 'aged 83.' He m. 20 July 1762 Mary (Goodwin), wid. of Foxwell Curtis Cutts. Grpar. of Gov. John Fairfield. See Me. H. & G. Rec. iv. 1.

**FAIRWEATHER.** 1 **John.** N. H. Prov. Pap. 23.65. See Savage.

2 **WILLIAM,** Portsmouth, m. 28 June 1716 Elizabeth Welch. Bap. No. Ch. (9 Dec.

1716). Corp. in Penhallow's Co. 1722. List 339. Ch. incl: **Nathaniel.**

**Faisey**(?), Ambrose, fined for swearing, N. H. 1646.

**FALL, Philip,** a Jersey mariner, b. ab. 1649, was in Portsm. 26 Jan. 1669-70. Of Jersey in July 1677 he gave P.A. to Joseph Hammond to recover a pair of shoe buckles from Samuel Clarke. Taxed Str. Bank 1688. Deposed in Essex Co. 15 Mar. 1691-2. Lists 328, 90, 314. Wife may have been Elizabeth Fall alias Elizabeth Basson, mo. of Joshua Basson of Beverly, and appar. recently decd. in Nov. 1702. Likely a son: **John,** yeoman, Berwick, mar. 26 Oct. 1710 Judith Heard (Saml.). Will 1 Aug. 1745—7 Apr. 1746. 10 ch., incl. Philip.

**Fandergoe,** John, 1655. See Vandergo.

**FANNING.** 1 **Joseph,** house carpenter. J.F. of Jamaica in 1686 sued Joseph Raynes of Piscat. on acct. stated in Boston 3 July 1683. 1696 sued Sanborn and Prescott. 1697 bot at Sag. Creek. 1698 taxed Portsm. D. bef. 1736. Lists 399a, 330de, 337, 339. M. 6 May 1697 Elizabeth Boulter(2). They deeded their homestead in 1726 to dau. Elizabeth and husb. Nicholas Norris, (of Exeter, m. 19 Dec. 1723).

2 **WILLIAM,** from Newbury soldier at Wells 1693-4. List 267b.

**Fargu** (Ferguson?) Gilbert, of Great Isl., bondsman for Mark Rounds 1685.

**FARLEY.** 1 **Anthony,** N. H. 1681. Of Isles of Shoals, bot there. Y. D. iii. 104.

2 **MESHACH** and **MICHAEL,** sons of Michael, of Ipsw., from 'Beverly Parks,' Essex. Grants at Portland 1680. List 225a. Meshach d. early, leaving sons Meshach and Michael. Y. D. 16.40.

**Farmer,** John, Penobscot 167--. List 3.

**FARNHAM,** Farnum, former the name of 8 parishes, Surrey to Northumb.

1 ———— Capt., killed at Pemaquid 1689. See Skinner.

2 **DANIEL,** York, br. of (5), m. Hannah Bragdon(3). List 279. 4 ch. rec. 1719--.

3 **EDWARD** (Farnum), vs. Robert Booth (by Richard Hitchcock), 1671. Me. P. & C. ii. 421.

4 **JOHN** (Farnum), miller, Boston, bot in 1675 101 acres above Braveboat Harbor which his s. **Jonathan,** miller, sold in 1718. Y. D. vi. 164, ix. 110. An early Baptist agitator, he may have come to Kit. and planted the seed of the early Baptist church there. See Scriven.

5 **RALPH, Daniel, Nathaniel, Barachiah,** sons of Ralph of Andover, b. 1689-1697, appeared in York 1711-14. Ralph m. 25 Dec. 1712 Elizabeth Austin(6). 10 ch.

**Farnsey,** Sarah, Portsm. 1694. List 335a.

**Farr** (Farre), James, 1614. List 7.

Farrand, Thomas, present at surrender of Pemaquid, Aug. 1696. See Coleman's Capt. ii. 349.

Farrell, see Farwell.

FARROW, George, poss. namesake of that G. F. of Fawleis in Wolsingham who in 1615, with wife Adelyn had a cottage there called Bridgend House, m. in Ipsw. 16 Feb. 1643-4 Ann Whitmore, ±40 in 1658, and liv. there until 1668 when he exchanged his farm there with Mr. Wm. Symonds for a house and land in Wells,—a decision that cost him his life, k. by Ind. 27 Sep. 1676. The farm here was the same Lt. John Barrett had liv. on and given up. His wid. app. became distracted at her hus. death and soon d. List 266. Ch: **Mary,** b. 6 Jan. 1644-5, m. Edward Clark(8) and John Smith of Cape Neddick. **Martha,** b. 25 Feb. 1646-7, mar. Benj. Curtis(9). **Phebe,** b. 7 May 1650, m. Abraham Collins(2).

Farthinge, John, Falm. casualties 7 Aug. 1691. List 37.

FARWELL. 1 **John,** Isles of Shoals wit. 1667.

2 **THOMAS** (Farrell), ag. 34 in June 1674, one of Mrs. Elizabeth Seeley's fishermen, Isl. of Shoals.

Faulkner, Paul, York wit. 1709. Y. D. 7.229.

FAVOR, Feavaugh.

1 **NICHOLAS.** See Robert Driver.

2 **THOMAS,** York, b. ab. 1668. List 294. Liv. 1721. He m. 9 July 1697 Ruth (Redding), widow of Joseph Donnell, who d. 27 Jan. 1729-30. Son **Joseph,** carpenter, soldier in Dummer's War; in 1724 sold the land his f. deeded him in 1721. 3 daus. rec.

Feaysts? William, Newington 1663. List 342.

FELLOWS, an uncom. So. of Eng. name.

1 **SAMUEL,** b. Salisbury 13 Jan. 1646, m. 2 June 1681 Abigail Barnard. See Hoyt's Sals. 156, N. H. Prob. iii. 60. Perh. only three ch. came to Kingston: **Samuel,** m. 14 Nov. 1710 Sarah Webster, b. 19 Sep. 1690. Adm. to her 8 Sep. 1715. 2 sons. **Ebenezer,** b. Sals. 10 Nov. 1692, m. 12 Nov. 1718 Elizabeth Brooks(4) of Kingston. Adm. 28 Apr. 1742. **Hannah,** b. 20 July 1697, m. Ebenezer Colcord(2).

2 **SAMUEL,** sadler, joined Hampton ch. 2 July 1699, d. summer of 1707, m. 15 Nov. 1698 Deborah Sanborn, who m. 2d 2 Oct. 1711 Benjamin Shaw, d. by 1728. Ch: **Isaac,** b. 12 Dec. 1699, of Kingston 1723, m. 9 Nov. 1721 Abigail Sleeper. **John,** b. 23 May 1701, d. 1723 in Kingston. **Joanna,** b. 29 Sep. 1702, mar. Hezekiah Blake s. of Moses(5). **Sarah,** b. 9 Apr. 1704. **Rachel,** b. 10 Mar. 1706, m. Samuel Shaw. **Samuel,** b. 3 Oct. 1707, ward of Jonathan Fellows, Ipsw., 1723. He and Sarah not in agreement of heirs 1728.

3 **THOMAS.** List 365.

4 *CAPT. **WILLIAM** (Ephraim of Ipsw.), innholder, Portsm., Rep. 1722-1727. List 339. He m. 7 Dec. 1693 Elizabeth Rust, dau. of Nathl. and Mary (Wardwell) of Ipsw., who d. 3 Oct. 1732, ag. 61; he d. 12 Apr. 1737, ag. 71. Ch. rec. Ipsw.: **Nathaniel,** b. 24 Apr. 1696, cooper, m. 16 July 1724 Hannah Ayers(1). **William,** b. 25 Feb. 1697, mariner, m. 15 Feb. 1721-2 Elizabeth Cutts(3), his wid. in 1743. **Elizabeth,** b. 29 Apr. 1700, m. Solomon Pike. **John,** b. 30 Mar. 1702, under sheriff, Portsm. 1737. **Mary,** b. 11 Oct. 1705, unm. 1743.

Felrik? John, Hampton 1695. List 393a.

FELT. One George Felce, (Felch or Felt), s. of Wm., bap. 28 Feb. 1609-10 in Leighton-Buzzard, Bedfordshire, was noted absent at the manorial muster 29 May 1634.

1 **GEORGE,** ag. 40 in 1654, ±87 in his petition to Andros 1688. The partic. statements in his pet. (Doc. Hist. vi. 336) discredit the recitals in a deed to the North Yarm. Com. in 1727 (Y. D. xii. 316), aside from which nothing is found to indic. his pres. in Maine till aft. 1662, when he was 'of Malden,' where he spent most of his life between 1633 and 1693, for 11 yrs. aided by Middlesex Co. or the town. The 1727 deed says G. F. liv. above 40 yrs. on 300 a. bot of John Phillips of Casco Bay, but his own pet. in 1688 says that he bot for £60 two thousand acres, from a dif. John Phillips, 18 yrs. since, having been tenant on it 3 yrs. bef. buying. His son evid. came East before he came, the earliest ment. of the name here 1658. No 'sr.' or 'jr.' is found until 1670. Lists 214, 34. He m. Elizabeth, dau. of wid. Prudence Wilkinson, d. 1694. Ch: **Elizabeth,** m. Nov. 1655 Wm. Larrabee. **George. Mary,** these bp. 26 Dec. 1639-40, m. Apr. 1660 James Nichols. **Moses,** bp. 20 Dec. 1640, app. d.y. **Aaron,** Falm. 1665. Was cutting hay near Stroudwater, Falm., in 1670. Had a deed from his f. at Broad Cove. For his ch. if any, see (5). List 93. **Moses,** b. by dep. 1650 or 1651.

2 **GEORGE**(1), 'mason or carpenter,' in Falmouth 25 Nov. 1662, m. Philippe Andrews(16); was as aggressive a pioneer as his father unag.; was fatally wounded in the old cellar on House Isl., Portland Harbor, 23 Sep. 1676, (Hubbard 166). Liv. in Falm., never in No. Yarm. His farm was divided in 1752 between Wm. Bartol and Wm. Bucknam. Jury 1666, 1668; gr.j. 1667; selectm. 1668. Lists 25, 222b. His wid. m. 2d in Rowley 19 Dec. 1682 Samuel Platts; 3d 9 Apr. 1690 Tho. Nelson; d. 29 Sep. 1709. Ch: **George. Mary,** m. in Rowley 17 Oct. 1689 Josiah Wood; wid. of Enfield, Conn., in 1729; d. there 4 Aug. 1753. 11 ch. **Sam-**

Dear Interlibrary Loan:

This book is from the Research Library Collection of the Boston Public Library. We are lending it to you for the use of your patron within your library. Our patrons can not borrow these books. We ask that you respect this restriction. Please note due date and any restrictions on copying on the pink band on the book.

Thank you,

Dorothy Keller
Interlibrary Loan Officer

uel. **Jonathan.** As the ch. sold sixths there was another ch.

3 **GEORGE**(2), blockmaker, came to Falm. bet. the wars but ret. to Salem. B. ab. 1663 but called ±52 in 1713 and 73 at death 24 Sep. 1729. Lists 34, 228c, 229. He m. 1st Hannah Holmes, bp. June 1667, d. of John and Hannah (Thatcher) of Watertown, who d. 29 Dec. 1693; 2d 27 Feb. 1695-6 Jemima (Bonfield), wid. of Oliver Luck—s of Marbleh. Ch: **Mary,** b. Falm. 13 Oct. 1687, m. 4 May 1714 Wm. Bartol. **George,** b. Salem 10 May 1690, mar. 26 Mar. 1713 Susannah Bacon. **John,** b. 8 May 1692, d.y. **Jonathan,** b. 21 Mar. 1693. By 2d w: **Jemima,** b. 19 Feb. 1696-7, m. 17 Nov. 1715 Jonathan Ashby; wid. in Salem 1756; d. 23 Nov. 1789. 4 ch. **John,** bp. 14 May 1699, liv. at Falm. and tended the Mussel Cove sawmill from 1718 'until the Indians broke out.' K. at Kennebunk in 1724. **Bonfield,** bp. 8 Feb. 1701-2, m. 1st 27 Oct. 1724 Margaret Armstrong, 9 ch; 2d 23 Sep. 1762 Mary Bacon. **Benjamin,** bp. 22 July 1705, m. 16 Feb. 1727-28 Abigail Knapp who d. 12 Nov. 1748, 5 ch.; 2d 15 Nov. 1750 Elizabeth Ropes.

4 **JONATHAN**(2), blacksmith, came back bet. the wars. List 34. Ret. to Salem, where he m. 3 Jan. 1694-5 Elizabeth Purchase; 2d Elizabeth Blaney. Adm. 13 Oct. 1702 to his wid., who m. (int. 15 July 1710) John Taylor. Ch: **Elizabeth,** b. 4 Nov. 1695, m. 1 Aug. 1715 Geo. Trask. 3 ch. **Jonathan,** b. 4 Mar. 1699, mar. 26 July 1721 Hannah Silsby. He d. bef. 1739. 6 ch. **Hannah,** b. 20 Apr. 1702, m. 11 Jan. 1727-8 Edw. Britton jr. (2 ch.); 2d 25 Nov. 1751 Joseph Ropes.

5 **MOSES**(1), made many dep. at ages from 63 to 93, all reck. to 1650 or 1651. By these he liv. at 'Casco Bay,' meaning either Falm. or No. Yarm., from ab. 1658 until Philip's War, and 7 yrs. bet. the wars. He was of Rumney Marsh as late as 1733, later in the adj. Lynn or Boston. His wife was a dau. of John Mains. The valuable family lore preserved by their gt-grs. Amos Atwell, b. 20 Oct. 1730, proves this, altho he called his name -Joshua-. Her name on the authority of Col. Banks and others, source unk., was -Hannah- Mains. The weird 'Origin of the Main family,' rewritten not printed in the Babcock & Main Gen., 1909, names 6 daus. of John Mains, -Lydia- m. -Felk-, Hannah m. Hayden. What the records show of Hannah is that at York, where her father stopped in Philip's War, in 1679 she had a ch. by a mar. man. Lydia Felt, ±61 in 1718, dep. in Boston, Moses then liv. at Rumney Marsh, practic. Boston. She dep. that in girlhood she liv. with Mr. Tho. Giles at Kennebec—quite nat. for one of 6 sisters liv. at No. Yarm. List 161. So Moses Felt

m. -Lydia- Mains. Their ch. may include: **Joseph,** weaver, m. (int. 12 Oct. 1700) Sarah Mills, d. of Joseph and Martha. They came to No. Yarm. where in 1722 he was k. by Ind. and his w. taken. She was ransomed by Capt. Peter Weare who mar. her only ch., Sarah. **Elizabeth,** called 'of Lynn alias Boston' in the Glouc. rec., m. there 21 Dec. 1708 (int. Boston) Wm. Tarr of Glouc. Their 7 ch. rec. 1710-1725 incl. Mary, Jonathan, Eunice, Abigail, Lydia. **Joshua,** cooper, of Rumney Marsh in 1712, m. (int. 15 Jan. 1712-3) Ann Walcott of Salem; 2d 18 June 1736 Dorcas (Gould), wid. of Anthony Buxton. 4 or m. ch. **Lydia,** m. (int. 11 Sep. 1703) her cousin-german Richard Atwell. **Sarah,** of Rumney Marsh, m. (int. 23 Dec. 1713) Joshua Preble. **Mary,** m. at Salem 6 Aug. 1712 Wm. Walcott. **Susannah,** m. in Boston 30 Apr. 1725 Samuel Sheldon.

6 **SAMUEL**(2), ret. to Falm. bet. the wars. List 34. He esc. to Salem and liv. later in Byfield and Rowley. His wid. Elizabeth m. 13 Sep. 1715 Benj. Plumer. Ch: **Mary,** m. in Rowley 6 Nov. 1707 Samuel Palmer, wid. in Mendon 1729, 6 ch.; m. 2d 5 July 1760 Samuel Walker of Hopkinton. **Elizabeth,** bp. Salem 7 June 1696, mar. in Rowley 9 July 1717 Benj. Poor of Byfield. 7 ch. **Samuel,** bp. 5 June 1698, m. 1st in Enfield Rachel Kebbe, who d. 24 July 1745; 2d 27 Feb. 1746 wid. Eliz. Bement. He d. 23 Mar. 1788. 10 ch. **Joseph,** bp. 26 May 1700, d.y. **Joseph,** bp. 20 July 1701, of Enfield 1729, m. 10 Aug. 1736 Hannah Bigbee. 13 ch. **Phineas,** bp. Rowley 9 Jan. 1703, of Enfield (ack. at Windsor) 1729. 1 ch. rec. **Mehitable,** bp. 1706, m. Elisha Kebbe of Enfield. 4 ch. **Abigail,** bp. 24 Dec. 1710, m. in Somers, Conn., 15 Nov. 1731, Ebenezer Buck.

**Felyn,** Thomas, of Pemaquid 1671. List 80.

**FENDERSON,** Finlayson, the latter a Perthshire surname from Finlay, an anc. Scotch forename, rendered Fender- in English.

**WALLIS.** As Willis Finderson, merchant, he arrived in Boston 6 June 1712 in Sloop -Tryall-, Jethro Furber, master, a passenger from Fayal. Settled at Portsmouth, where he m., started to build ships and soon died. 'Capt. Walter Fenlayson' rated to New Meet. Ho. 1717. 'Capt. Walles Fenleson' taxed 1722, perh. later. In 1720 he was given an 80 a. non-res. grant in Scarb., where the proprietors, 20 Sep. 1727, listed 'Widow Francies Fanderson' among those to settle in 3 mos. or forfeit. She m. at Scarb. 25 Aug. 1731 John Babb(1). A Portsm. creditor took adm. of his est. in 1738. He mar. Nov. 1715 Frances Bennett(5). Ch: **Wallis,** bp. 28 Oct. 1716, d.y. **Wallis,** bp. 17 Aug. 1718, d.y. **Nathaniel,** bp. 2 Aug. 1719, sett.

in Scarb., m. 1st 24 Nov. 1743 Hephzibah
Carter; 2d 11 July 1754 Mary Ayers. **Margaret Bennett**, bp. 9 Dec. 1722, d.y. **Sarah,**
m. Portsm. 21 Dec. 1740 Thomas Lang, and
named a son Wallis Finlayson L.
**Feneck** (Fenwick), see Phenix.
**Fenton,** Richard, Dover witness 1673, with
James Coffin.

**FERGUSON,** name of a Highland clan,
the 22d commonest Scotch surname.
1 **ALEXANDER**(3), Eliot, ±58 in 1730. Will
28 Apr., d. 11 Sep. 1731. His w. Elizabeth (Gowen m. 11 Feb. 1694-5), was liv.
1733. Lists 296-298, 291. Ch: **Daniel**, b. 18
Nov. 1695, d. 1752. Ch. **Elizabeth**, b. 3 Feb.
1699, m. 1 Feb. 1719-20 John Gowan jr., d.
bef. f. **Alexander**, b. 30 June 1701, unmar.
1734, d. bef. 1753. **Eleazer**, b. 29 Nov. 1703,
m. Anna Emery d. of Daniel(2). 10 ch. List
298. **Mary**, b. 18 Mar. 1705, mar. Nicholas
Hartford. **Sarah**, b. 17 May 1707, in 1731
acc. Joseph Furbush, m. 21 Nov. 1730 Tho.
Staples. **John**, b. 8 Aug. 1710, m. (pub. 2
Nov. 1745) Hannah Chase (Abraham and
Hannah [Barnard]) of Edgartown, where
he set. Ch.
2 **ARCHIBALD**, Muscongus 1717, presum.
from Marbleh.
3 **DANIEL**, bot land in partn. with Wm.
Furbush. List 25. His unproved will not
found, inv. 14 June 1676 has memo. of the
widow's 9 ch., ag. 21 to 1. Oct. 4, 1692 she
was captured with a dau. and a grandchild,
presum. the Sarah and Abigail redeemed in
1695. Still a wid. in 1708, she deeded the
homestead and outlands, with reserv. for
life, to her s. Alexander and grs. James. Ch:
**John**, b. 1655, gr. 1678, liv. 1686 near 'Little
Hill' (Suff. Ct. files 137480), had w. Mary
and child by July 1679, presum. the captive
Abigail. List 99. **Mary**, b. 1664. The spontan. Coiton Mather says one Mary F., Ind.
captive, was k. in 1690, ag. 15 or 16. If
younger she might be John's dau.; if older,
John's w., wid. or sis. List 99. What we
know is that one Mary mar. 16 July 1693
James Treworgy and d. 19 July 1696, and
that their two ch. liv. many yrs. with Alexander. **Hannah**, b. 1665. **Katharine**, b. 1666.
**Daniel**, b. 8 Jan. 1667-8. **Mehitable**, b. 1669.
**Alexander**, b. 1671. **Sarah**, b. 1673, presum.
the same who 16 May 1692 was gr. adm. of
Charles Penny's est. She was redeemed from
capt. in 1695 and m. 19 Dec. 1695 a fellow
capt. James Ross. List 99. **James**, 6 wks.
old at father's d., m. Elizabeth Hodsdon.
Both k. by Ind. 28 Sep. 1707, leaving son
James, minor in 1718, m. in 1727 Patience
Downing(5 jr.). 9 ch. Lists 96, 296, 297.
4 **GILBERT**, Great Isl., cooper, ±28 in 1673,
perh. the same who shipped at London,
cooper, on the Good Hope. 26 Feb. 1668-9.

He attended (3) in his last sickness, also
Philip Chesley in 1680. Lists 326c, 312cef.
5 **JONATHAN**, Wells. In 1682 Tho. Cole
was fined for freeing him out of the
stocks, Joseph Littlefield, bondsman.
6 **WILLIAM**, 'Scotchman,' ±22 in Mar. 1674-
75, arrested (executed?) for murdering
Robert Williams in Spruce Creek. See Robert Driver.

**FERNALD.** There is room for surmise that
Dr. F., a scholarly man, conformed his
surname to his forename. There was Farnold in co. Glouc., Farnell in London.
1 **JOHN**(2), cordwainer, of Portsm. in 1670,
granted land in Kit. 1671. Lists 326c,
331c, 298. D. 19 Apr. 1687, adm. to widow
Mary (Norman, who was stepdau. of Tho.
Spinney). Ch: **John**, deacon, cordwainer, d.
1754. Wife Sarah. Lists 296-298, 291. 9 ch.
**James**, Dea., farmer in Eliot, d. 1740, leaving w. Mary. In 1717 John Dennett called
him 'kinsman.' Lists 296-298. 8 ch. **Thomas**,
b. 1679, cordwainer. List 296. M. 28 Nov.
1700 Mary Thompson, both liv. 1739, he liv.
1747. 8 ch. **Lydia**, b. 1681, still Fernald 16
Nov. 1700. Wid. of (John) Harmon 19 Dec.
1702, as Lydia Harmon in ct. April 1705, m.
Benj. Miller. **Marjory**, b. 16 Apr. 1686, of
Portsm. 1711, m. John Marshall, cordwainer,
both of Portsmouth 1735. **Amos**, twin with
Marjory, cooper, Portsm. List 339. He m.
1st Elizabeth Chadbourne(2), sons Amos and
Humphrey bp. 27 May 1715; 2d 4 Nov. 1714
Mary Woodman, s. John bp. 24 July 1715.
Adm. 28 Nov. 1739 to s. Humphrey and John.
2 **RENALD**, Doctor, first in the records in
1640; so efficient a man, his name should
have app. earlier had he been here. His dep.
in 1656 shows him here in 1639. 'The old
doctor' was Mr. John Reynolds, liv. at Fort
Point on Newcastle. The oldest ch., Thomas, was a boy when his f. had the gr. of
Puddington's Islands made out in his name
in 1645. Nathaniel Fernald, tailor, in 1767
deposed: Grandfr. Renald Fernald claimed
several islands and gave them to his children, one now called Peirce's to one dau.,
another now called Mendum's to ano. dau.,
in whose rights they are still held. Renald
himself lived on Peirce's Isl. many years
and my father Wm. lived on Layclaim or
Fernald's Isl. about 50 yrs., moving off when
I was about 19 (1716). He then gave it to
my bro. Wm. who lived on it about 20 yrs.
and d. there. William's son Wm., whose son
now sues for it, lived on it till he went to
sea on the voyage on which he died. Dr.
Renald Fernald at his death in 1656 was
clerk of the county court, Com.t.e.s.c., town
clerk, selectman. His successor was elected
town clerk Oct. 7. Lists 41, 321, 323, 324.
His widow Joanna's will, 23 Apr.—28 June

1660, names the ch. Lists 323, 326a. Ch: **Thomas**, b. 1633. **Elizabeth**, mar. Edward Clark(8). **Mary**, b. 1643, mar. John Partridge. **Sarah**, Lists 330ab, m. 3 Dec. 1661 Allen Lyde; 2d 29 June 1672 Richard Waterhouse. **William**, b. 5 Mar. 1646. **Samuel. John.**

3 **SAMUEL**(2), shipwright, removed from Portsm. to Eliot in 1674. Jury 1696-7, gr.j. 1697, 1698. Lists 311b, 313b, 326c, 330ad, 331a, 94. D. 1 Dec. 1698. Will 24 Nov. 1698 names w. Hannah (Spinney) and four younger ch: **Samuel**, b. 9 Mar. 1676, d.s.p. **Sarah**, b. 17 June 1678. **Nathaniel**, b. 28 May 1681, shipwright, m. 10 Sep. 1702 Anne Allen(12). Will 15 Feb. 1742-3—4 Apr. 1748 names w. Anna and 5 ch. (7 recorded). Lists 291, 296-298. **Hannah**, b. 16 Oct. 1684. **Martha**, b. 18 Feb. 1692.

4 **THOMAS**(2), b. 1633, shipwright. Lists 330ab, 313b, 30, 52, 95, 296-298. Inv. taken 25 Aug. 1697. Wife Temperance (dau. of Mark Hunking) was liv. 1714. List 331c. Ch: **John**, shipwright, d. unm. 26 Feb.—21 Oct. 1701 (will in London). **Patience**, mar. Ebenezer Evans; 2d 9 Nov. 1686 Robert Alkins (Atkins). **Thomas**, mariner of Portsm. Adm. 20 Aug. 1711 to his widow Elizabeth (Hunking), dau. of John, who had been his wid. two yrs. or longer. No ch. **Mary**, mar. bef. Sep. 1697 Samuel Pray. **Samuel**, blacksmith, m. 12 Oct. 1699 Susannah Paul; 2d prob. (int. 27 Aug. 1743) Mrs. Elizabeth Seward. List 298. Will 9 Dec. 1745—20 Feb. 1745-6. 7(?) ch. **Joanna**, m. 25 May 1698 Charles Kelly. **Sarah**, m. 16 July 1700 William Henderson. **Hercules**, shipwright. Liv. 1719, his wid. Sarah (Hinckes, dau. of Hon. John) was liv. in 1746. 3 ch. **Elizabeth**, b. 6 Feb. 1682-3 (grst.), m. Capt. Stephen Eastwick(1). **Anne**, m. Capt. Stephen Seavey.

5 **CAPT. *WILLIAM**(2), b. 5 Mar. 1646-7, shipwright. Lieut. and Dep. 1684. Gr.j. 1682, 1693; jury, foreman, 1695, 1701. Selectm. 1674, 1692-1697. Lists 36, 52, 98, 239b, 291, 293, 296-298. D. 5 July 1728. Wife Elizabeth Langdon, m. 16 Nov. 1671, d. 11 May 1740. Ch: **Elizabeth**, b. 17 Aug. 1674, mar. Clement Deering(8). **William**, b. 31 Oct. 1676, d. 6 Dec. 1683. **Tobias**, b. 26 Dec. 1678, shipwright, m. 12 June 1701 Mary Deering(8), d. 18 Aug. 1701. 1 dau. b. 19 Mar. 1701-2. He bot 22 Aug. 1700 the Richard Cutt homestead, which his wid. 6 Apr. 1704 sold to his father, who made it his homestead. **Margaret**, b. 27 Mar. 1681, mar. Solomon Cotton(2). **Temperance**, b. 16 Sep. 1683, mar. John Deering(1). **William**, b. 11 May 1686, m. 31 July 1707 Elizabeth Cotton(7). He d. 12 Jan. 1728; her will 1756—1761. 7 ch. **Joseph**, b. 21 Dec. 1688, d. early. **Sarah**, b. 24 Apr. 1691, m. Jonathan Dam(3). **Lydia**, b. 19 Apr. 1693, m. John Clark(20 jr.). **Benja-**

min, b. 11 July 1695, shipwright, d. before 1743. List 291. Wife Catherine surv. 4 liv. ch. 1742. **Nathaniel**, b. 12 June 1697, tailor, d. 18 Sep. 1771, m. 7 Apr. 1720 Margaret Tripe. 7 ch. **Ebenezer**, b. 7 Oct. 1699, shipwright, m. 22 Dec. 1724 Patience Mendum, who d. 5 Jan. 1775. He d. 29 Jan. 1787. 12 ch. **Tobias**, Capt., b. 3 Dec. 1702, m. 22 Dec. 1724 Mary Mendum, who d. 16 Oct. 1767. He d. 11 May 1761. 7 ch.

**FERNISIDE, John**, accountant, Boston, b. ab. 1611, m. Elizabeth Starr, dau. of Dr. Comfort of Boston, and was drowned in millpond 13 Nov. 1693. Her will 8 Feb. 1703-4 names besides son and 3 daus., grdaus. Lydia Callender, Elizabeth Paine. She d. 4 June 1704, ag. 83. Ch: **Jacob**, joiner, will 1716—1716, (bur. 11 Oct.), sis. Elizabeth sole benef. **Mary. Hannah**, b. 8 May 1650, m. 1st Reuben Hull, 2d George Snell. **Lydia. Elizabeth**, b. 26 Oct. 1658, single 1704, helped in mother's shop. **Ruth**, b. 20 Aug. 1661. **Sarah**, m. Nathaniel Heard, 2d Wm. Fost(2).

**FERRIS, Aaron**, fisherman, first ment. 1668, of Isles of Shoals in 1669 bot land and a house frame on Great Isl. In 1683, of Great Isl., he bot 20 a. at Spruce Creek, but was still of Great Isl. when he sold his house there in 1695. In 1697, of Kit., he sold the rest of his land on Great Isl. to John Muchemore of Star Isl. Liv. 1712. Lists 313a, 319, 326c, 331b, 52, 290, 296-298. In 1709 with w. Grace he sold to dau. and son, Grace and Tho. Huff, their entire est. for life supp., and in 1712 Tho. Huff gave 1½ a. to br.-in-law Ebenezer and sis. Mary Emmons. Ch: **Grace**, m. Tho. Huff. **Mary**, likelier Ferris than Huff, wife of Ebenezer Emmons(1). (Edw. Vittery m. one Anna Farris in Boston 13 Nov. 1713.)

**Ferryman, William**, drowned at Oyster River. Inquest Sep. 1700. John Woodman bur. him. W. F., Beverly, in Philip's War.

**Ferson**, see Furson.

**Fesse** (fesee)? ———, N. H. jury 1696. For Seavey?

**FEVERILL, Thomas**, early at Piscataqua. Ralph Gee in 1643 test. that he was in charge of the cattle at the Great House (Odiorne's Point). List 41. Cf. Peverly.

**Feynell**, Rich., Y. D. x. 252. Misr. of Nich. Reynell.

**FICKETT**, see also Foggett.
1 **JOHN**, Scarboro, ±25 in Aug. 1670. Gr. 6 a. 1682. Lists 237e, 238a, 239a. Lists 57, 62, or 67 may ment. his son. He m. Abigail Libby. In the div. of her fr's lands, 1736, her share went to Tho. Fickett and Samuel Snell. Tho. Fickett had bot from his br. John and their aunt Rebecca Guy. Ch: **John. Rebecca**, m. at Marbleh. 8 Mar.

1707-8 Henry Guy, wid. in 1744. 4 or m. ch.
**Mary,** app. the w. of Samuel Snell or Snelling of Portsm. in 1724, when they were bap. with 7 ch., two of them adult.

2 **JOHN**(1), came to N. H. from Scarb. with his father or uncles in 1690. First clearly dist. as wit. of Tho. Westbrook's note in 1703. Bot land in 1708. He m. Susannah Ball(7), his wid. in 1730. Ch: **Thomas,** shipwright, of Kittery in 1731, later of Scarb. and So. Portland. Wife Mary, 6 or m. ch. **John,** of Portsm., tanner, 1731. Releases not found from **Margaret,** in 1732 wit. a Portsm. Moses will, mar. in Greenland 6 Dec. 1733 Tho. Quint of Newington. **Abigail,** of Portsm., mar. 1 Jan. 1733-4 Benj. Jackson. **Sarah,** of Portsm., m. Greenl. 23 June 1736 Geo. Taylor from Limerick, Ire. ?Rebecca (Fosket), mar. in Greenl. 25 Jan. 1710-1 Samuel Davis(65).

**FIELD,** a Mid. and East England surname.

1 **DARBY,** celebrated in his own day as the first white man (and an Irishman) to climb Mount Washington. In Boston in 1636, Marblehead 1637, he was an Indian interpr. by 1638; early hist. unkn. By 1639 he was a squatter in Oyster River, in 1649 was in poss. of 500 a. lately bot of Christo. Helme by Valentine Hill. His strenuous life was short, and its merriness marred by insanity. Lists 371, 373, 354ab, 73. Adm. 1 Oct. 1651 to Ambrose Gibbins. His wid. Agnes (List 354c), m. Wm. Williams. Ch: **Mary,** m. 15 July 1656 Capt. John Woodman. **Joseph,** b. ab. 1639. **Elizabeth,** m. 28 Jan. 1663-4 Stephen Jones. **Zachariah,** b. ab. 1645. **Sarah,** ±18 in 1719, ±70 in 1718, m. John Drew(6). If she was the wit. of 1672, called ±30, the age, clear in the orig., likely belonged to Joseph.

2 **ELEAZER**(1?), of Oyster River? in 1664. List 364.

3 **JOHN,** presum. an aged man, of Kit., merchant, 30 Aug. 1720, for life supp. deeded his entire est. to his well beloved landlord Michael Kennard. Poss. f. of (4 and 7), but see (4).

4 **JOHN,** Mr., dry goods merchant, Newcastle. Accts. of John Field & Co., (see Alcock 4) were sued 1715- --. Rated to New Meet. Ho., Portsm., 1717. Adm. est. of John Field gr. to wid. Elizabeth 23 July 1718, yet the next yr. Elizabeth -wife- of John gave a P.A. (York Files). Portsm. selectm. in 1717 approved him for innholder. His wife from 1715 was Elizabeth Treworgy (Samuel), who m. 2d Benj. Cross(2). By a poss. former w. he may have been f. of (7), or poss. br.

5 **JOHN**(12), had the homestead. He m. 16 Jan. 1706-7 Sarah Drew(6). List 358d. Adm. to s. John 1762. Ch: **John,** m. Mary Warren, d. of James and Mary (Goodwin).

He liv. on his grfr's. homestead until he lost it; d. 25 Feb. 1773. 7 ch. **Sarah,** mar. John Giles. **Abigail,** mar. John Jones; 2d Ebenezer Jones. **Elizabeth,** m. Samuel Jones. **Mary,** unm. 1763.

6 **JOSEPH**(1), ±30 in 1672, ±42 in 1681, was deeded land by his m. and stepf. in 1674. Lists 356a, 361a, 362b, 363abc, 365, 366, 359a, 358b, 52. Adm. 17 Nov. 1690 to (12). He m. Mary (Goddard), wid. of Arthur Bennett(3) who m. 3d Hans Wolford. Ch: **Mary,** m. Benj. Evans(12).

7 **JOSEPH,** of Newcastle, feltmaker, in 1715 sued Wm. Tucker, fisherman. In 1711 Abigail Tucker, ag. 5, had been apprent. to plaint. and w. and aft. 3½ yrs. her f. took her away. It is plaus. conjec. that a mercantile family (3, 4, 7), came to Newcastle, paid rent, but d. or rem. leaving few rec. (List 316).

8 **JOSEPH,** of Newcastle, fisherman, signed by mark, in 1720-21 had wife Hannah Thomas, dau. of Wm. and Mary (Barrett). Poss. the same, of Newc., mar. 5 Oct. 1735 Mary Roberts of Portsmouth.

9 **NATHANIEL,** N. H. Prov. Papers xxxi. 394, misreading of Zachariah.

10 **RICHARD,** Richmond Isl. 1638. List 21.

11 **ROBERT,** Boston merch., m. Mary Phillips, d. of Major Wm., Saco wit. 1661. List 244a. Parents of **Robert** of Dorchester, liv. 1733, Y. D. 17.98.

12 **LIEUT. ZACHARIAH**(1), ±34 in 1679, ag. 64 in Oct. 1709, liv. 1715?, dead 1720. He rem. to Dover aft. 1685, and in 1707 his house was a garrison, himself Lt. commanding. Jury 1695, selectm. 1695. Lists 363c, 365, 366, 359ab, 352, 353, 52, 57, 62, 96 (358d). Wife Sarah Roberts. Ch: **Dorcas,** m. John Bunker(3). **Stephen,** d. bef. his f., leaving an only ch., Stephen, who inher. two-sevenths of his grfr's. est. The grs., mariner, m. 10 June 1717 Mary King of Kit. and left 3 or m. ch., of whom Stephen, b. 16 Oct. 1722, shipwright, m. Jane Lary. **Abigail,** m. 24 Oct. 1697 Daniel Jacobs. **Zachariah,** Ens., m. 12 Jan. 1709-10 Hannah Evans(12), who m. 2d 16 May 1716 Richard Hussey. 2 s. sett. in Me. (List 358d). **John. Mary,** m. 13 Dec. 1706 Solomon Pinkham. **Daniel,** b. 9 Aug. 1690, accid. shot by John Waldron 23 Apr. 1708, d. that night.

**FIFIELD,** name of 3 places, Oxford-Wilts.

1 *BENJAMIN(3), ±52 in 1700, settled in Hampton Falls. Jury 1679, 1683, 1693. Const. 1698, 1699. Selectm. 1687, Rep. 1697, clerk of company 1699. Lists 396, 392b, 49, 52, 57, 62, 96. K. by Ind. 1 Aug. 1706 '& a lad, his kinsman, carried away.' Adm. 3 Sep. 1706 to the youngest son by agreement. He m. 28 Dec. 1670 Mary Colcord(1), who d. in Hampton Falls 23 Nov. 1741, ag. 93. Ch:

John, Ensign, b. 21 Nov. 1671, sett. in Kingston. Prop. clerk. Ch. incl. Elizabeth, b. 25 Nov. 1698, m. one Sleeper and one Webster; John, b. 1 Aug. 1701, with wife Dorothy joined church in 1733, called 'jr.' till 1748. Shuah, b. 27 Sep. 1673, d. 14 Nov. 1683. Dau., 3 May 1676. Joseph, b. 7 Mar. 1677, sett. early in Kingston. Lists 399a, 400. Will 25 July 1757, d. 7 June 1761, names 4 of 5 rec. ch. Wife Sarah (Sherburn), mar. 24 Apr. 1701, d. 3 Apr. 1765. Edward, Capt., b. 27 Mar. 1678, lot layer in Kingston in Apr. 1703, but withdrew to Stratham, where he m. Elizabeth Leavitt. Lists 399a, 400, 388. Will 25 July 1765—30 Apr. 1766 names all 9 rec. ch., 5 liv., ch. of 4. Benjamin, b. 10 Feb. 1682, d.s.p. bef. Sep. 1726. Jonathan, Dea., youngest son, lived at home and had homestead with his mother, until late m. July 1723 to Hannah Waite. Much trusted with probate business by his relations and by his br.-in-law Weare, Judge of Probate. Liv. 1749. Mehitable, b. 9 Nov. 1687, mar. John Sanborn. Abigail, unm. 1706.

2 GILES, Charlestown, mariner, tobacco winder, ±46 in 1675, m. 7 June 1652 Mary Perkins of Hampton, where later he may have liv. a short time. The connections betw. this man, Henry Green and Abraham Perkins are undisc. H. G. was repeatedly befriended by A. P., whose dau. m. G. F., who in 1660 called H. G. uncle. Presum. he was rel. to (3). He m. 2d 2 May 1672 Judith (Carter), wid. of Samuel Converse, d. of Rev. Tho. and Mary (Parkhurst), who d. of smallpox 3 Oct. 1678. He d. 5 Oct. 1676. Will ment., besides ch., cous. Elizabeth, Saml. Converse. Ch., all bap. together at Charlest. 19 June 1670: Abraham, Capt., mariner, liv. in Barbadoes, but ret. to Boston. Adm. 1711 to bros. Giles and Richard, all mariners. D. 11 Sep. 1711, ae. 57 (grst. in Woburn). Giles, Capt., ship carpenter, mariner, Boston, d. 29 Apr. 1718, ag. 60. 6 ch. rec., by w. Elizabeth, named in his will, who d. 16 June 1743, ag. 84. Mary, b. Hampt. 28 Nov., d. 9 Dec. 1659. Richard, b. Charlest. 20 Dec. 1663, and d. Richard, Capt., b. 6 Nov. 1665, Boston, mariner, will 1716—1718. He m. 1st 6 Aug. 1688 Mary Thurston; 2d 25 Aug. 1701 Mary Drew, who d. 12 Mar. 1712-13; 3d 6 Nov. 1713 Maria Green, who d. 24 Nov. 1746, will. 5 ch. by 1st w., incl. Mary, b. 7 May 1694, mother of Samuel Adams the patriot. John. Mary, b. 15 Sep. 1667. Joseph, twin with Mary, d. 4 Aug. 1668. By 2d w: Deborah, b. 6 July 1673, m. John Jackson. Thomas, b. 9 Jan. 1676.

3 WILLIAM, by several round-number ages from 40 to 85, was born 1614—1618. Came in -The Hercules- 1634, iñ 1639 rem. from Newbury to Hampt. Freeman 2 June 1641. Jury 1651, 1662, 1667, 1669, 1677, 1678. Con-

stable 1662. Selectm. 1652, 1659. Sometimes atty. for others in ct. The Quakers praised his humanity. Lists 391ab, 392b, 393ab, 396, 398, 49, 52, 54, 57, 62. He d. 18 Dec. 1700, after deeding his lands to his sons. Wife Mary, ±50 in 1673, among Mrs. Dalton's benef. in 1664. Dow has her death 9 Nov. 1683, yet in 1696 Wm. F. ±80 and Mary F. ±76 deposed together. Lists 393a, 394. Kn. ch: John, d. 8 Aug. 1665. (Both bros. named sons John.) Benjamin, b. ab. 1648. Mary, likelier Wm.'s, mar. 9 Jan. 1672-3 Samuel Haines. William, b. 1 Feb. 1651[2. Sarah, m. 31 July 1673 James Hobbs. Lydia, b. 12 Jan. 1654[5, presum. same m. Salis. 12 Sep. 1681 Benoni Macrease. Elizabeth, b. 7 Sep. 1657, m. 12 June 1678 John Tidd of Woburn. Hannah, b. 10 Dec., d. 1 Jan. 1659-60. Deborah, b. 6 Feb. 1660[1, m. Tho. Crosby(3).

4 WILLIAM(3), Hampton. Jury 1694, constable 1696. List 52. Will 18 Feb., d. 8 Mar., 1714-5. Wid. Hannah (Cram 1, m. 26 Oct. 1693) and 9 ch. were liv. 1723: Samuel, Mary, b. 3 Oct. 1695. Stephen, b. 29 Nov. 1696. Henry, b. 13 Aug. 1698, d. 4 Apr. 1789; mar. 26 Jan. 1726 Comfort Cram dau. of Joseph(1). 8 ch. Jeremiah, b. 8 Mar. 1700, d. 4 June 1773. Argentine, d. unm. 6 Feb. 1744. Hannah. Jonathan, cooper, adm. 15 Sep. 1738 to Henry. John.

Filman, John. List 189. See Sellman?

Filmore, Margaret, Kit. wit. 1671. Y. D. ii. 138.

Finlayson, see Fenderson.

Finson, see Vinson.

FISH, Gabriel, fisherman, came with Wheelwright. He left with James Carrington of Thoresthorpe, 1 m. from Bilsby, a bill due from John Hutchinson of Alford. Lech. 141. He accomp. Wheelwright to Exeter but was arrested there, Mar. 1639-40, for speaking against the King. He went (or was carried) back to Boston, where ch. of G. and Elizabeth are rec: Deborah, b. 2 Dec. 1642. Abel, b. 15 Dec. 1644.

FISHCOCK, Edward, Richmond Isl. 1633. Went off to New York and came back. Wife about Plymouth. List 21. Doc. Hist. iv. 36, 44, 45, 49, 56, 61, 114, 122, 468.

FISHER. 1 John, from Medfield? soldier under Hill at Wells 1693-4. List 267b.

2 ROBERT, Kit. wit. 1684. Y. D. iv. 12.

FITZGERALD. 1 ——, m. 22 Dec. 1720 Elizabeth Fletcher(7), who m. 2d after 1737 Charles Banfield, joiner and truckman, 1743-1768. Ch: John, d.y. Richard, mar. 13 Oct. 1748 Sarah Meed. Jane, m. Nathaniel Caverly(3).

2 MORRIS, soldr. under Westbrook in Dummer's War, m. 22 Nov. 1756 Sarah Weeks, both in Portsm. almshouse bef. 1781, ag. 75 and 70.

FLANDERS, Stephen, from Salisbury, tried

Maine, app. Kittery. The Court, July 1649, ordered a warrant served to bring his wife into the next court for abusing him and the neighbors; they went back. Son **Stephen,** b. Salis. 8 Mar. 1646-7, had 11 ch. rec. incl: Stephen, b. 31 Jan. 1671-2, who m. an aunt of Ebenezer Blaisdell of York; Daniel, b. 16 Mar. 1674-5, of Amesb., app. the same ±24 in 1699, who helped hang the Portsm. meetinghouse bell; and Abigail, b. 22 Oct. 1688, presum. m. Peter Dixon(2).

**FLANSALL** (Flansey), **Rowland,** carpenter, ±30 in 1671, formerly liv. with John Diamond. Oct. 3, 1660, he wit. a note payable to Barefoot. In 1668 he was in court for liv. in this country 6 or 7 yrs. having a wife in Eng. Was Henry Greenland's man in an appraisal. List 380. Christo. Banfield endorsed for him, 1672 in jail for debt.

**FLEET.** 1 Capt. **Henry,** came on -The Warwick- 1631, and remained several years about Virginia. List 21.

2 **JOSEPH,** m. Mary Pierce, Kit. 1670.

**FLETCHER,** occup. surname, arrow maker. General, but commonest in the Midlands.

1 **HENRY,** b. ab. 1662-3, appr. to John Lewis, Great Isl. 1682-4.

2 **JEREMY,** b. ab. 1664, serv. of Roger Rose 1682.

3 **JOHN,** Popham 1607. List 6.

4 **JOHN,** physician, Portsm., bot house and land there 13 Dec. 1667, evid. a new arrival from Eng., but soon prom. in local affairs. In 1669 adm. est. of John Tanner; selectm. 1681-85, town clerk 1681-83, 1686-92, jury 1684. Lists 324, 326c, 329, 330ad, 331abc, 49, 52, 54, 57, 62, 96, 335a. Will 3 Nov. 1694, cod. 7 Aug. 1695—21 Sep. 1695, named dau. and grdau. Mary Bennett, and gave s. Nicholas his part in his mother's prop. in Plymouth entailed upon Nicholas. Wife Joane, not named in will. Ch: **John,** b. 26 Mar. 1661. **Rebecca,** b. 6 June 1663, d. Sep. 1665. **Joanna,** b. 20 Aug. 1665. **Nicholas,** b. 22 July 1669. **Joseph** or Josiah, b. 23 July 1672. **Mary,** b. 30 Jan. 1674, mar. Nicholas Bennett(13). **Elizabeth,** b. 20 Oct. 1677, d. 4 Feb. 1678.

5 **JONATHAN,** Eliot, wit. to Eliot paper 21 May 1684; adm. June 1685 to wid. Catherine, James Emery bondsman. Inv. shows costly wardrobe, housek. effects, house and 46 acres, untraced.

6 **JOYCE,** Portsmouth. Lists 331a, 335a.

7 **NICHOLAS**(4), shipwright, Portsmouth. Lists 330f, 67, ?336b, 337. Sued by br.-in-law Nicholas Bennett 15 Feb. 1695-6. He m. 5 Dec. 1695 Agnes Banfield(2); she m. 2d 9 June 1713 Richard Parsley, who had Nicholas's town gr. in 1719. Ch. liv. 1734: **Mary,** b. 4 Sep. 1699, mar. William Nason.

**Elizabeth,** b. 29 Apr. 1701, m. 1st 22 Dec. 1720 —— Fitzgerald, (3 ch.); 2d Charles Banfield, (1 ch.). **Sarah,** b. ab. 1705, mar. William Cotton.

8 **LIEUT. PENDLETON**(10), b. ab. 1655, adopted son of his grf. Major Pendleton, lived prin. at Saco (Winter Harbor). Constable 1681, selectm. 1684-6, gr.j. 1687, 1691, com. Lieut. by Andros 1687. Of Wells in 1683, in June 1691 he was 'late of Winter Harbor now of Kittery.' Lists 96 (twice), 33, 36, 249. Taken by Ind., with his two sons, 7 Aug. 1697, he d. in Canada ab. 1699; adm. gr. to wid. Sarah (Hill, d. of Roger), 24 Feb. 1699-1700, who m. 2d William Priest, 3d Andrew Brown(3). Kn. ch: *Pendleton, b. ab. 1685, known to have been three times capt. by Ind., (Niles says four), but retd. home each time, where selectm. 1720, Rep. 1721, gr.j. 1723, Ensign 1731, d. 1747. Wife Hannah. 9 ch., incl. Pendleton who m. Hannah Powell and d. 17 Apr. 1807 aged 100 (grst.). (**James?**) captive 1697, d. unm. ab. 1699. **Mary,** m. 1st Joseph Sawyer, 2d in Boston 2 Sep. 1706 John Gibson. Her son John Gibson, Boston, sailor, in 1729 q.c. to uncle Pendleton Fletcher est. of grf. P.F. in Bid. **Sarah,** m. 1st in Boston 3 Dec. 1708 Walter Miller, 2d Matthew Robinson. **Abigail,** m. Samuel Hatch.

9 **RICHARD,** 336b? See Nicholas.

10 **REV. SETH**(11), was first instigated to preach by Rev. J. Brock of Reading, afterw. encour. by Wheelwright and by Dalton of Hampton, where he was teaching 1652-4 and liv. in May 1655. By Sep. of that yr. he was in Wells engaged to preach for one yr. without ordin., in 1660 had been their min. two yrs. The preacher at Saco in 1662, he last appeared there as a wit. 25 Nov. 1675. Lists 392b, 24, 236, 262, 247, 249, 254, 264, 269b. With Roger Hill he proved will of Andrew Alger sr. at Salem 30 June 1676, but was in Southampton, L. I., in Oct. 1677, writing ab. his visit to the mainland and 'my brother Stow.' Last move to Elizabethtown, N. J., where he d.; adm. 18 Sep. 1682 to wid. Mary. First w. Mary Pendleton, dau. of Major Bryan; she was a wit. with him 12 Feb. 1660, he wit. with her father in 1653; m. 2d (contract 30 May 1681) Mrs. Mary Pearson of Southampton, he then of Elizabethtown. Only kn. ch: **Pendleton,** who q.c. to his stepm., Henry Lyon of Elizabeth and Tho. Johnson of Newark.

11 **REV. WILLIAM,** minis. at Oyster River in 1656, but left because of difficulties with the town, intending to return to Eng. Appar. the one lately returned from N. E. who was ejected in Eng. in 1662; then back to N. E., altho Dover made a grant 6 Mar. 1661 to one Mr. Fletcher, poss. (10). In Saco -Mr.- William Fletcher, the only per-

son thus dignified on the town book, was buried 30 Jan. 1667-8. Kn. ch: **Seth. Hope,** m. by 1650 Rev. Samuel Stowe, her ch. rec. Middletown, Conn.

12 **WILLIAM,** soldier from Charlestown 1689, d. in N. H. on the way home.

**Flint,** John, corporal, Kit. garrisons(1704?). List 289.

**Flisson** (Stilson?), Magdelaine. List 99 (p. 123).

**FLOOD, Joseph,** Boston, ṁ. 10 Mar. 1698 Joanna Mitchell (Christo.). In 1707 owed est. of Joseph Curtis. 7 ch. incl: **Joseph,** b. 9 Aug. 1700. **Joseph,** b. 6 Aug. 1708. Will Joseph 1744 unexam.

**Fluen,** Thomas, Monhegan 1672. List 13.

**FLYE, Fly.**

1 **JAMES**(?2), housewright, Sagam. Creek 1705, Portsm. 1710, was liv. at Blue Pt. in 1717, there and at Portsm. in 1718 and recd. into Portsm. Ch. 2 May 1720, altho a Black Point juror in 1719. A sentinel at periods during 1722-25, men were posted at his house at the ferry, Black Point, 18 May 1723. Aft. the war he made Scarb. his home until death, adm. 1738 to wid. Elizabeth. Ch., the 1st 3 bap. Portsm. 2 May 1720: **John,** husbandman, Scarb. 1729, mar. 1st 2 Jan. 1736-7 Mary Bryant(8); 2d wife Hannah. 4 ch. **William,** liv. 1738. **Elizabeth,** m. Bray Deering(6). **Dorcas,** bp. Scarb. 28 July 1736.

2 **JOHN,** Isles of Shoals 1677, Falmouth by 1683, liv. there in 1689. He d. at 'Torbay,' Devon, 23 June 1696. The nunc. will of 'John Fly, mariner, late of Piscataway, N. E., belonging to his Majesties shipp the -Catherine- formerly the -Chester-, widower,' 22 June 1696—1 Mar. 1696-7, left half his wages to Wm. Taverner, executor, and half to 'my children.' Lists 306a, 226, 228c, 30. Presumably his ch: **James. Faithful** (also Faith), b. ab. 1685, serv. of Robt. Elliot in 1705, m. Jedediah Jordan jr.

**Foale** (Foley? Fowle? Howell?), John. Eliot wit. 1662. See his mark, Y. D. ii. 174.

**Fobes,** see Fabes.

**FOGG, Fogge,** a rare Eng. name, ancient in Kent.

1 **DANIEL**(4), b. 16 June 1660, blacksm., O.A. Hampt. 16 Dec. 1678, Scarb., Portsmouth, Eliot. See paper by his grs. Samuel, b. 1 June 1716—Me. H. & G. Rec. ix. 42. Aft. Philip's War he liv. in Scarb. till driven by the next war. Aft. hiring a farm in Portsm., of Richard Jackson, he bot in Eliot with two Libbys. Const. 1688. Lists 238a, 239b, 34, 334a, 330def, 290, 291, 296, 297. Will 14 July 1747, d. 9 June 1755. He mar. Hannah Libby, liv. 1730. By their grson's acct. they had 4 ch. b. in Scarb., 5 in Portsmouth, 2 in Kit. Ch: **Son,** d. inf. **Hannah,**

m. 21 May 1704 John Rogers. **Mary,** m. 11 Aug. 1709 Wm. Brooks(7). **Rebecca,** b. 1688, m. in 1726 Joseph Pilsbury, d. at br. James's house ab. 1780. Ch. **Samuel,** b. 1691, d.s.p. ag. ±21. **Daniel,** Capt., b. 12 Apr. 1694, cordwainer, in 1727 bot the Sheldon farm in Scarb. and sett. there. Orig. memb. of Scarb. church 1728. Commanded the Black Point company at Louisburg. List 291. He m. 30 July 1715 Anne Hanscom. In old age, 1774, the aged couple went to live with their s. Col. Reuben, where she d. 15 Apr. 1775 and he 1 Dec. 1782. 9 ch. of whom the eldest was the fam. hist. **John,** b. 12 Jan. 1696, m. 30 Sep. 1725 Mary Hanscom. Sett. on his f.'s homestead in Scarb. List 239b. Will 14 Aug. —7 Nov. 1749 names wife and 6 of 9 rec. ch. **Sarah,** b. Aug. 1698, m. 1 Jan. 1715 Tho. Hanscom. **Joseph,** b. Aug. 1700, settled in Scarb. on Libby land. He mar. 1st 13 Jan. 1725 Sarah Hill; 2d Eleanor Libby, who d. 3 Jan. 1799. No ch. **Seth,** b. Dec. 1701, sett. in Scarb. on his f.'s prop. grant. He m. 28 Nov. 1727 Mary Pickernell, who surv. Will 3 Sep. 1748—18 Oct. 1748. 7 ch. **James,** b. 17 Mar. 1703-4, had the homestead. List 297. He m. 23 Oct. 1728 Elizabeth Fernald, d. of James(1), who d. ab. 1766. He d. 24 Dec. 1787. 10 ch.

2 **JAMES**(4), Hampton. Jury 1696. List 399a. He m. 9 Jan. 1695 Mary Burren (See 1). On one day in Hampton church, 29 May 1698, three Mary Foggs, the wid. adm. a member, her d.-in-law and grd. bap. The wife, not bap. by her parents, may possibly have been dau. of Geo. She d. 14 Oct. 1750 ag. 80. His will 15 May 1754, d. 17 June 1760. Ch: **Mary,** b. 5 Jan. 1697, m. Joseph Wadleigh. **James,** b. 7 Feb. 1699, m. 1st 2 Jan. 1728 Elizabeth Robie, 2d 3 Mar. 1732 Hannah Page. Sett. in Kensington. Will 1762 —1767. 5 ch. **John,** bp. 11 Oct. 1702, d. 7 May 1754. He m. 6 Nov. 1729 Meribah Tilton who d. 23 Nov. 1795. 9 ch. **Sarah,** b. 7 Aug. 1705, mar. Tho. Robie. **Enoch,** bp. 27 June 1708, m. 21 Jan. 1749; sett. in Chester. **Hannah,** bp. 5 Apr. 1713, 'Rollins' in will.

3 **PETER?** List 336b. Error for Daniel?

4 **SAMUEL,** Hampton, brot over a boy, likelier somebody's stepson, first app. Sep. 1646 by his kinsman, Mr. John Legate, shifting his master from Wm. Fuller of Hampt. to Isaac Cozen of Rowley, at the locksmith's trade, with 4 yrs. longer to serve. Next yr. he was a wit. for his new master. Freeman 3 Oct. 1654. Stephen Sanborn and S. F. 6 Apr. 1650 bot from Christopher Hussey. Jury 1653, 1662, 1664; const. 1660; selectm. 1655, 1663. Lists 392b, 393b, 394. Will 9 Jan., d. 15 Apr. 1671-2. He m. 1st 12 Dec. 1652 Ann Shaw, who d. 9 Dec. 1663; 2d 28 Dec. 1665 Mary Page, who d. 8 Mar. 1699-1700, ag. 56. Ch: **Samuel,** b. 25 Dec. 1653. **Joseph,** b. 25

Mar. 1656, d. 17 Apr. 1660. **John,** b. 15 July 1658, d. 21 Apr. 1660. **Daniel,** b. 16 June 1660. **Mary,** b. 1 May 1662, unm. in Wm. Fuller's will 1691, 'married in Newbury and spent her days there,' she m. 1st Geo. Hardy who d. 6 Dec. 1694; 2d 13 Apr. 1696 Benj. Poor. 1+2 ch. By 2d wife, named in grfr's will 1679: **Seth,** b. 28 Nov. 1666. **James,** b. 18 Apr. 1668. **Hannah,** b. 6 Apr. 1671, d. 22 June 1680.

5 **SAMUEL**(4), is by family trad. diverg. treated; by Wm. of Eliot, b. 1790, he d. in Hampton in 1760 aged 107 'and has many desc'; by Samuel of New Glouc., b. 1716, appar. on inform. of his aunt Rebecca, b. 1688, 'when he came to be a man grown he sold in Hampton, moved to Pennsyl. and settled, had ch. and spent his days there.' New Jersey Foggs claim desc. Jury 1695. Lists 52, 57, 396, 397b, 399a. He mar. 19 Dec. 1676 Hannah Marston, rememb. in her father's will 1701. Ch. rec: **Samuel,** b. 18 Sep. 1677. List 399a. **Joseph** and a twin, b. and d. 9 Feb. 1679. **Rebecca,** b. 15 Sep. 1682. **Ann,** b. 29 Aug. 1688.

6 **SETH**(4), Hampton, jury 1700, selectm. 1704. List 52. Will 7 Mar. 1753, d. 6 Sep. 1755. Wife Sarah d. 10 Apr. 1756. Ch: **Benoni,** weaver, Hampt. Falls and No. Yarm. He m. 1st 22 Dec. 1714 Abigail ———; 2d 27 Oct. 1724 Mary Griffin. 4+6 ch. rec. **Hannah,** b. 1690, m. Tho. Elkins(4). **Seth,** m. 18 June 1714 Meribah Smith, named in his will 1738—1745 with 3 of 5 rec. sons and cous. Anne Moulton. **Sarah,** b. 27 Dec. 1694, d. 4 July 1701. **Esther,** b. 16 Mar. 1697, these five bap. together 27 May 1697; m. 1st (24 Oct. 1734 -David- Fogg—Dow); 2d Henry Dearborn(2 jr.); 3d Joseph Wadleigh. **Samuel,** b. 13 Feb. 1700, m. Mary Dearborn, d. of Thos.(3). 9 ch. **Simon,** b. 1 Nov. 1702, m. 28 Sep. 1724 Lydia Gove, d. Seabrook 18 Sep. 1749. 6 ch. rec. **Abner,** Capt., Esq., b. 18 Dec. 1704, d. No. Hamp. Aug. 1788. He m. 10 Dec. 1730 Bethia Robie, 7 ch. rec.; 2d 18 June 1775 Mary Moulton. **Abigail,** b. 31 July 1707. **Daniel,** b. 21 Dec. 1709, sett. in Rye, d. 7 Aug. 1757. He m. 5 Dec. 1734 Anna Elkins, d. of Jonathan(4), who m. 2d Dea. Tho. Marden of Rye. 2 of 4 ch. surv. Jeremiah, Rev., b. 24 May 1712, H.C. 1730, m. 17 July 1739 Elizabeth Parsons. Pastor in Kensington. 9 ch.

**Foggett** (Foget), Philip, adm. 28 June 1664 to Lt. Ralph Hall. See Marbleh. and cf. Fickett.

**FOLLANSBY,** a name found about London. Folensby in St. Dunstans, Stepney, 1591.

**THOMAS** (aut. N. H. Prob. files 432), b. 1637, joiner, finished Portsm. church and schoolhouse. In 1671 he had moved from

Great Isl. and hired the Abraham Corbett house near the meetinghouse, when Mr. Henry Dering, also removing to Strawb. Bank, hired the same house under a better title, whereupon the sheriffs turned T. F. out without notice in the depth of winter with no habitation provided for 'his wife and many smale children.' In 1673 his w. Mary ±34, ab. midnight hearing Rachel Webster cry murder, rose up and went to the window and asked said Webster why out of her house at that time of night. In 1674 his 'boy' had done work for the town. Rem. ab. 1677 to Newbury, O.A. there 1678. Lists 311b, 312a, 326c, 330a, 331a. First w. Mary, 2d Sarah (either she or a dau. d. 6 Nov. 1683), 3d (int. 4 Apr. 1713) Jane Moseman of Boston. Liv. 1717. Ch: **Rebecca,** mar. 22 Nov. 1677 Thomas Chase(1). **Anne,** b. 1668, m. 10 Nov. 1684 Moses Chase(1), d. 18 Apr. 1708 (grst.) **Mary,** b. ab. 1667, m. 1st 1 Dec. 1686 Robert Pike, 2d ab. 1691 Wm. Hooke. Ch. **Jane,** m. 1688 Lt. John Hubbard of Salis. and Kingston. **Thomas,** Capt., b. ab. 1674, m. 19 June 1694 Abigail Rolfe, supposed (Bond), wid. of Ezra; 2d 18 Feb. 1734-5 Mary Bancroft of Reading; will 1753, d. 1755. 4 ch., of whom William, b. Newb. 14 Mar. 1701, liv. 1753, m. (int. 18 May 1722) Mary Robinson (John of Exeter.) **Francis,** b. Newb. 22 Oct. 1677. **Hannah,** b. 10 Apr. 1680.

**Follen,** Abraham, 1658. See Jocelyn.

**Foll**——, young Goody. Hampton 1650. List 393a.

**FOLLETT,** a rare name found in Devon. Nicholases bap. in Dartmouth 1615, in Colyton 1617. Subsidy man Halwell 1624.

1 **ABRAHAM**(?), 1663. List 356h. Misr.? of (5).

2 **JOHN,** perh. br. of (8). Dover 1640. Lists 351ab. App. d. early leaving perh. Nicholas(5), but there was John, wit. for (8) in 1667; also John of Barbadoes called 'cousin' by Nicholas, s. of (6), in 1710, and Ichabod, taxed next to Ichabod Chesley in 1732, (full share in 1734 div., Lists 369, 368b); and John, who had deeds from Joseph and Elizabeth Meador in 1719-1732.

3 **JOHN,** wit. for (8) in 1667.

4 **JOHN,** m. in Boston 14 Mar. 1700 Sarah Gullison (Gunnison), perh. same ±22 in 1701. In 1707, of Kittery, butcher, w. Sarah, he sold 6 a. laid out to him 6 Oct. 1702. List 298. Sarah F. joined Kit. Ch. in 1718. He was bap., sick, 8 Nov. 1719. Ch. rec: **Elizabeth,** b. 23 Mar. (1701), mar. 14 Nov. 1720 John Dolley of Newcastle. **Frances,** b. 16 Feb. (1702), m. 13 Jan. 1725-6 Matthew Vincent. **Sarah,** b. 18 Dec. (1703). One Sarah m. in Boston 13 Mar. 1726 Charles Treleaven. **Martha,** bp. 5 July 1719. **Mary,** bp. same day, owned covt. 8 Sep. 1728. **John,** bp.

same day, m. (int. 16 Sep. 1731) Mary Tripe. Ch. **Charles**, bp. same day. One Charles m. in Boston 25 Oct. 1739 Lydia Doak.

5 **NICHOLAS**, perh. s. of (2), app. nephew of (8). His wid. dep. that his son Nicholas was 'second cousin' (grandnephew?) of (8). He d. early, last ment. perh. 1663 (see 1), and wid. Abigail m. Richard Nason and was ±80 in 1706. Kn. ch: **Philip**, wit. deed of (8) 1670, taxed 1671, assignee of John Cutt(2) 1672. **Sarah**, ±52 in 1706, m. John Meader. **Nicholas**, also perh. John(3).

6 *NICHOLAS(5), disting. shipmaster, Oyster River and Portsm., first app. 1675. In 1678 he was in poss. of Matthew Giles's field. Memb. of Constitu. Conv. 1690, leading inhab. of Portsm. Jury 1694, foreman 1699. Lists 359a, 56, 335a, 49, 52, 55b, 56, 62, 96, 330de, 333b, 335a. He d. in the Gulf of Campeche, will 29 Apr.—19 Aug. 1700. A man could have three wives all named Hannah. His s. Nicholas recorded his own birth and par., 5 Nov. 1677, mother Hannah. Dr. Stackpole, on grounds not stated or found says he m. Hannah (Drew), wid. of Godfrey Brooking who was drowned in 1681. His daus. Sarah and Elizabeth sold a full fifth of the lands of their uncle Joseph Meader in 1747, (perh. younger but there was Sarah Follett, ±22 in 1701). His wife named in his will was Hannah, who in 1705 had m. Abraham Haseltine, then of Portsm., but in 1694 his w. was honored merely as 'Mrs. Follett,' perh. then, cert. in 1697 and 1699, Hannah. Lists 52, 331c, 335a. We can state that one wife was (Hannah) Meader, d. of John and Abigail, who was mo. of Sarah and Elizabeth, and they may have taken the whole inherit. from their uncle as the only surv. The will named only 3 of his ch., Nicholas, Philip and Caleb, but Mary Bunker-Denbow in 1756 dep. that his ch. were Abigail, Nicholas, Benj., Sarah, Elizabeth, Caleb, Philip. Kn. ch: **Abigail**, m. 2 Sep. 1697 Hon. Andrew Wiggin. **Nicholas**, b. 5 Nov. 1677, Portsm., tailor, sanity doubted in 1714. He d. 29 Aug. 1722. Wife Mary (Hull, mar. 12 Sep. 1700) liv. 1738 widow. 3 ch. rec. d.y. **Philip**, in Me. court 1699, d.s.p. **Caleb**, d.s.p. **Sarah**, m. Theophilus Hardy, liv. 1754. **Elizabeth**, bp. 21 July 1695, m. 23 May 1718 Joseph Gilman. **Benjamin**, ag. 8 in 1705, cordwainer, lived in Stratham or Newmarket. Adm. 28 Sep. 1746 to wid. Deborah (Lyford, m. by 1722). 4 surv. ch.

7 **THOMAS**, from Isle of Jersey, mar. in Portsm. 1 Oct. 1730 Susannah Coolbroth, presum. the same who had her s. **Thomas**, bap. in Newington ch. in 1736, and m. 10 May 1739 Joseph Rollins jr.

8 **WILLIAM**, perh. br. of (2), cert. rel., app. great-uncle, of (6); cert. some conn. of Lawrence Avery(3). In Boston 19 Sep.

1654 administ. on estate of John Avery, a mariner, was granted to 'W. F. of Oyster River in behalf of his brother Lawrence Avery.' Earlier he had been at Dover Neck or Back River. In 1756 Elizabeth (Leighton?) Pinkham, ag. 77, dep. 'W. F. lived one summer at your deponent's father's house.' In 1651 he bot a quarter int. in the Bellamy's Bank sawmill which he sold to Richard Waldron in 1672. Oyster River gr. 1653. Lists 352, 354bc, 356acgh, 359a, 361a, 363abc, 365, 47, 49, 52, 92. He m. (presum. 2d) 20 July 1671 Elizabeth (Matthews), widow of Wm. Drew(17). Adm. 12 Nov. 1690 to her, still his wid. 7 Aug. 1705. No ch.

**Folloy** (Follett?), Samuel, Durham 1734. List 369.

**FOLSOM**, Foulsham, the latter a market-town and parish in Norfolk.

1 **EPHRAIM**(3), Newmarket. Selectm. of Exeter 1691. Lists 54, 382, 383, 384b, 376b, 377, 52, 57, 62, 96. K. by Ind. 11 June 1709. Inv. shows 30 a., said to be on the N. E. side of Hersey lane, now owned by Hon. Channing Folsom. Wife Phaltiel (Hall, d. of Lt. Ralph), liv. his wid. 25 yrs. As heirship deeds or releases were not recorded, their ch. are conject: **Ephraim**. **Lydia**, mar. Andrew Glidden. **Abigail**, m. Joseph Judkins. **Sarah**, b. ab. 1692, m. Thomas Young, Esq. **Phaltiel**, mar. John York. **William**, through whom the Hersey lane land came down. Will 1755—1755. He m. 1st Hannah Gilman; 2d Elizabeth (Gilman), widow of Benj. Sanborn. 6+1 ch.

2 **EPHRAIM**(1). Scout duty 1696, 1710. Lists 67, 376b. In 1741 and 1743 he adm. the est. of his sons Joseph and Edward, in 1742 he made deeds for the benefit of 6 other ch. Liv. 1755. He m. a dau. of Edw. Taylor. Ch: **Ephraim**, ag. 43 in May 1743, m. Eunice Smart. **Edward**, an invalid from 15, d. 1 Dec. 1740, ag. 36. **William**, ag. 39 in 1743, m. Mary Folsom (John 7). Will 1786 —1787. 10 ch. **Joseph**, trader, adm. 1741 to father. **John**, was given land in Durham by his father. **Andrew**, had the homestead, m. Eleanor Rust, d. in Ossipee 12 Apr. 1799. 7 ch. **Sarah**. **Rebecca**.

3 *JOHN, in deed to dau. Mary called himself 'Folsham alias Smith.' In 1673 he deeded to s. Peter land in Hingham, co. Norfolk (old Eng.) near Norrald Common, formerly called Fulsham. Ab. 1530 one Wm. Foulsham of Necton m. one Agnes Smith of Besthorp, both Norf., and had s. Adam. In Carleton-Rode, co. Norfolk, John Smith alias Foulsham m. Alice Newnham 29 Oct. 1616. One Peter Fowlesham alias Smith had son Adam bp. at Hingham 2 Dec. 1623. Our John Folsom, of two Hinghams and Exeter, mar. Mary Gilman (John Fowlesham alias Smith

and Maria G.) 4 Oct. 1636 at Hingham, and in 1638 came over with the Gilmans. Rep. from Hingham 1654. He sold out there and came to Exeter in 1659. He was fined at Hingham in 1645 for critic. the Dep. Gov., and on appeal the General Ct. stood only 15 to 14 against him. See Corbett. Jury 8 yrs. 1662-1678, gr.j. 1675, 1676, selectman 1660, 1668. Lists 75a, 376b, 377, 382, 47, 48, 52, 54, 55b, 57. He d. 27 Dec. 1681. His wife, ±54 in 1671, outl. him; adm. on both est. gr. to s. Samuel 7 Jan. 1692-3. Ch: **Samuel. John,** bp. with last 3 Oct. 1641. **Nathaniel,** bp. 2 June 1644. **Israel,** bp. Sep. 1644, d. infancy. **Israel,** bp. 26 Apr. 1646. List 376b. ±25 in June 1672. Joined the emig. to Piscataway, N. J. D. unm., inv. 6 Apr. 1677. Adm. to his kinsman John Gilman. His first-settlers' right was sold 12 Oct. 1687 by his br. Nathl. **Peter,** bp. 8 Apr. 1649. **Mary,** bp. 13 Apr. 1651, m. 12 June 1672 Capt. Geo. March of Newbury, who d. 1699, ag. 53, 13 ch.; 2d 29 Jan. 1706-7 Joseph Herrick of Salem. **Ephraim,** bp. 23 Feb. 1654-5.

4 **DEACON \*JOHN**(3), ±30 in 1671. Jury 1666, 1669, 1674, 1679; gr.j. 1683. Constable 1676 and under Cranfield. Selectman 1681, 1691, 1696. Rep. 1685, 1688, 1694, 1695. Lists 376b, 377, 381, 383, 49, 62, 69. He was a pillar, both of religion and common rights. See N. H. Hist. Soc. viii. 189, 211, 219. Will 24 Nov.—6 Dec. 1715, ment. w. Abigail (Perkins, m. 10 Nov. 1675). Ch: **Abigail,** b. 23 Dec. 1676, m. Edw. Gilman. **Abraham,** soldier 1696, scout duty 1710. Lists 67, 376b, 1698. He m. 27 Oct. 1703 Anna Chase(1 jr.). Adm. relinq. 24 Sep. 1740 by 'ancient' widow Elizabeth (Robinson), wid. of James Rundlett, m. by 1732. 4 surv. ch. **John. Sarah,** m. ab. 1703 Nathaniel Stevens. **Mary,** b. 27 Sep. 1684, m. 27 May 1707 Daniel Morrison of Newbury, d. 14 Feb. 1711. 2 ch. Deacon **Jonathan,** soldier 1710. Had the homestead. Adm. 25 Feb. 1740-1 to wid. Anna (Ladd). 12 surv. ch. incl. John (J. F. 3d in 1748) and Col. Nathaniel. **Jeremiah,** settled on 100 a. his f. gave him in Newmarket. Scout duty 1712. Minor town offices 1720-1730. He m. 26 Jan. 1709 Mary Basford(1), who d. 8 Oct. 1744, ag. 57 (grst.); 2d one Elizabeth. Will 19 Feb. 1746—26 Oct. 1757 names 8 ch., homestead to John. **Lydia,** m. Robert Stockman, b. 8 Aug. 1683, of Kingston, from Salis. His will, 19 Feb.—30 June 1741-2 names her and 5 ch. **Mercy,** m. Lt. James Dudley(3).

5 **JOHN**(4), scout duty 1710. List 376b. Drowned in crossing the river ab. a mile above King's Falls 31 Mar. 1725. Adm. to wid. Mary, who m. Stephen Sewall. Surv. ch: **Susannah,** b. 10 May 1718, m. Jonathan Bradley; in 1760 she was called wife of -John- Bradley. **Mary,** m. Samuel Bradley. **Josiah,** b. 24 July 1725; d. 27 July 1820.

6 **NATHANIEL**(3), ±27 in 1672, carpenter, Exeter gr. in 1664; Hingham 1674; at Rehoboth in 1676 he advanced money for Philip's War; 27 Aug. 1677 adm. inhab. of Exeter; in 1687 journeyed to New Jersey to sell his brother's lands. Later a mill man at Exeter. Death unknown, Nathaniel 'Jr.' was taxed in 1714. Jury 1678; gr.j. 1692, 1696. Lists 376b (1664), 52, 57, 62, 382, 383, 384b, 388. He m. 1st in Hingham 9 June 1674 Hannah Farrow; 2d by 1696 Mary (Jones), wid. of Geo. Roberts, who m. 3d Nicholas Norris. Only 3 kn. ch: **Samuel,** b. in Exeter 18 Apr. 1679. **Nathaniel,** soldier 1710, mar. by 1720 Susannah Jackson, dau. of John and Sarah from Scarb. and Bradford. Ab. 1730 rem. from Stratham to Brentwood where in 1743 he deeded his homestead to s. John, and in 1745 was k. by Ind. in Nottingham. 8 ch. attrib. to him, perh. incl. poster. of his uncle Samuel. **Israel,** of Stratham, w. Joanna, in 1724, presum. Joanna Rollins, d. of Jonathan and Lydia (Heard), s. Benjamin; also m. 2d in Greenl. 2 July 1734 Sarah Durgin (2 Francis). Liv. in Newmarket in 1738, he deeded to s. Israel in 1755. Likely also **Jeremiah,** mariner, Berwick wit. 1722 (Y. D. xii 11), of Stratham 1727 deeded his Bow rights to only son. Perh. his 'Widow Folsom' d. in Stratham 21 July 1743. Son Jeremiah, coaster, Kittery 1727, Dover 1729, Arundel 1733, Muscongus 1735. Wife Abigail, presumably same called dau. in Benj. Rollins' will 1736. Rachel Folsom d. at (Josiah) Rollins's 24 Sep. 1766.

7 **LT. PETER**(3), ±22 in 1671, served in Philip's War. Settled on the road to Hampt. Audit. com., com. on Hampt. bounds, com. to get minister. Jury 1677, 1694, 1698; gr.j. 1678, 1679, 1683, 1684, 1695, 1699. Ensign 1692, Lt. Lists 381, 383, 384b, 49, 52, 54, 55ab, 57, 59, 62, 67, 376b. Adm. 5 Mar. 1717-8 to s. John, wid. relinq. He m. 6 May 1678 Susannah (Mills) Cousins, widow of (2 jr.), liv. 1722. Ch: **Peter. John,** Lt. Will 1756—1757. List 376b. He m. 1st Sarah Lyford; 2d bet. 1730-1737 Mary (Eastman), wid. of John Burleigh. 7 ch. **Elizabeth,** m. 1704 Lt. Samuel Colcord(2 jr.); 2d Lt. Samuel Sanborn. **Susannah,** m. Caleb Gilman. **Mary,** m. Joseph Thing. **Benjamin,** b. 1696, d. Mar. 1752. Soldier Dummer's War. Perh. m. 1st Judith Lyford (T. L.'s will 1726); did m. Rachel Gilman who d. 16 Mar. 1785. 2 ch.

8 **PETER**(7), grant 1698. Lists 67, 376b. Adm. 4 June 1718 to wid. Catherine (Gilman), who m. aft. 1724 Richard Calley(2). Ch: **Samuel,** b. 27 Sep. 1704. **Elizabeth,** b. 20 Mar. 1706-7, m. 1 Feb. 1726 John Robinson jr. **John,** b. 14 Mar. 1708-9, 'jr.' in 1735, in 1750 sued Richard Calley for 1-12 of est. of (his half-br.) Nicholas Calley, glazier. He

m. Hannah Sanborn, Eleanor Brackett, and one Martha; d. in Raymond 8 Apr. 1790. 1+6 ch. **James,** b. 16 Oct. 1711, glazier. Adm. 27 July 1748 to wid. Elizabeth (Thing, m. 18 June 1735). **Peter,** b. 27 July 1714, joiner. **Catherine,** b. 24 Jan. 1716-7, mar. aft. 1739 Samuel Lamson.

9 **SAMUEL**(3), soldier in Philip's War. He sett. in the part of Greenland near Stratham. Lists 376b (1664), 381, 383, 52, 54, 337, 338ad. He d. bef. 6 May 1700, adm. 28 Feb. 1701-2 to s. Samuel, wid. Mary and eld. son renounc. W. Mary Robie mar. 22 Dec. 1664. Ch: **Mary,** b. 27 May 1664, m. 30 Nov. 1687 Ezekiel Ladd. **Ebenezer,** soldier 1694-96. Lists 67, 388. In 1712 bot land in Stratham on which he liv. and d.s.p. 22 Dec. 1749. He m. Hannah, d. of Nicholas Smith, whose son Thomas, by Thomas Odell, imprisoned for counterfeiting, retained the name Odell and was given the homestead. She d. 16 Dec. 1752. Poss. parents of Ruth and Sarah who d. 1786 and 1794 unm. **Ruth,** m. 4 Mar. 1692 Moses Norris. **Samuel,** m. by 1710 in Greenland Abigail (Cole 1), widow of Thomas Foss(6). They liv. on the Hampt. and Portsm. bounds, and he was memb. of the Greenl. Ch. D. bef. 1723, s.p. **Israel,** weaver, m. 30 Sep. 1713 at Hampt. Falls Rachel Berry of Greenl. He rem. to Conn., where he joined the ch. in Ashford in Oct. 1724, liv. later in Windham, and rem. to Piscataway, N. J. Will 1749—1749; his widow's will, Sarah (Hall) Drake, was proved the same yr. By 1st w. 7? ch., incl. a son who m. into the Choctaw Ind. **Deliverance,** joined Greenland ch. 1724, mother Mary and sister-in-law Abigail already members; liv. unm. 1745. **Ann,** m. 13 May 1697 Hezekiah Jenness.

**Fones** (Fownes), William, Kennebec militia 1688. List 189.

**Foote,** Robert, Pemaquid 1684.

**FOOTMAN,** name for two occup., a foot soldier, an unmounted escort. Rare.
1 **JOHN**(2), his mother's firstborn ch. by her dep. 7 Sep. 1705, he then ag. ab. 43. Lists 368b, 369 (heirs). He m. 18 Dec. 1691 Sarah Crommet(2), bap. 'elderly w.' 1720. In a deed in 1726 to dau. Margaret his wife is called Margaret. He was bap. 5 July 1727 and soon died. His est. was div. by cross deeds in 1756 bet. s. Joseph, d. Eleanor McCalvey, wid., and grs. Tho. Stevenson. Kn. ch: **John,** was given land by his grandf. Crommett in 1711. Lists 368b, 369. D.s.p. bef. 1756. **Margaret,** mar. 26 Sep. 1717 Joseph Stevenson. **Benjamin,** accu. in 1719 of selling a stolen horse, Lydia Tibbetts his bail. List 368b. **Joseph,** in 1735 accu. of bigamy, cleared by gr.j. In 1739 he deeded to John Welch and in 1765 Deliverance Footman of Lee deeded to grs. Jacob Welch. He sold out in Durham

in 1759. Lists 368b, 369. **Eleanor,** was the wid. McCalva 1756, 1760.

2 **THOMAS,** hailed from York from 1639 or earlier until 1648, and was back there acting as referee in 1653. From 1648 he was taxed at Oyster River. Gr.j. 1651. Lists 354abc, 355b, 356a, 361a, 363bc, 365, 47, (353). Maj. N. Shapleigh 20 May 1667 recommended him to Mason for a Councillor. Will 14 Aug. 1667 was disal. 30 June 1668 and wid. Catherine (Matthews) app. adm., who soon m. Wm. Durgin. Ch: **John,** b. ab. 1662. **Thomas,** b. ab. 1663. **Abigail,** mar. in 1676 Benj. York; 2d aft. 1715 Tho. Meakins. **Elizabeth,** m. John Phillips of North Kingston, R. I.

3 **THOMAS**(2), ±70 in 1733, liv. 1737. Aft. ab. 1710 he was liv. in a house of John Bickford(23), and fenced in Colley's marsh, which he and his s. Francis continued to hold. He was an impressed soldier in 1690 and met complete disabil. from wounds. Repeated approp. were made for him during a long life. Lists (353), 368b, 369. His wife was Elizabeth Drew(2). With their three ch. all five were bap. 22 Nov. 1719. **Francis,** will 1756 names 2 s. **Thomas, Elizabeth.**

**FORD,** a common English name. Name of 7 places in Mid., 2 parishes in N. of Eng.
1 **GEORGE,** about Portsm. 1673. List 327d.
2 **HUGH,** Rye Beach coroner's j. 1672. List 312d.
3 **JOHN,** Mr., 1661. List 311a.
4 **JOHN,** app. m. at Kit. Joanna (Andrews), wid. of John Searle. Rem. to Scarb. as tenant of the Jordans. Driven back, liv. at Newcastle, then at Braveboat Harbor, last ment. 1714 when he signed with Samuel the covenant in organizing the Kittery Point ch. Lists 239a, 289, 290, 294. His wid. dep. in 1735, ±78, conc. early days at Scarb. Kn. ch: **Susannah,** likelier a child liv. with Mrs. Jordan, poss. John's sis. or 1st wife, wit. Mrs. J.'s deed in 1685. **Samuel,** b. ab. 1679, test. ab. his boyhood at Scarb., liv. with his f. at Braveboat Harbor. Will 26 May 1752 —21 Oct. 1755 left entire estate to Richard Cutts jr., Esq. for life supp. of himself and w. Agnes (Geach), she liv. 1758. **Lettice,** m. by 1704 John Whitney. **Sarah,** m. ab. 1705 Nathaniel Whitney. As regards son John, see (5).
5 **JOHN,** escaped from Portsm. jail in 1702, assisted by Josiah Clark, whose bondsm. were Joseph Miller and Nathl. Clark; not ident., as also the following: John of Ipsw. in 1727 sold Scarb. 70 acre gr. 1721, deed wit. by John jr., presum. same bap. 7 Oct. 1705. Both wrote. — John, m. 4 Nov. 1704 at Sturgeon Creek (many miles from Braveboat Harbor) Hannah Tidy (from Scarb.), she a wid. having s. John bap. in 1713, b.

9 June 1708, and m. 2d Daniel Wittum. In this neighb. one Samuel wit. a deed by his mark in 1718 (Y. D. ix. 51), and a John in 1730, presum. the same mar. 15 July 1731 Mary Goodwin. — John, Portsm., fisherman, bot from Rebecca (Brookings) Rowse's dau. in 1721, presum. Barrington prop. (List 339), adm. to Joshua Peirce and in 1746 to Daniel Peirce. — John and w. Catherine had 2 ch. bap. at Portsm. So. Ch. in 1723, she, a wid., another ch. in 1726. — John jr., m. in Greenland 20 Sep. 1732 Sarah Sanborn, adm. 27 Nov. 1735 to wid. Sarah; inv. personal belongings only; presum. f. of Joanna bp. 1729, yet Joanna mar. 9 Jan. 1733-4 Aaron Hanscom.

6 **RICHARD**, Downes, alias Ford. See Downes.

7 **ROBERT**, adm. Apr. 1675 to John Boaden. Inv. 13 Nov. 1674 shows elab. wardrobe and two chests in Ralph Tristram's hands.

8 **STEPHEN**, Isles of Shoals, in Jan. 1651-2 had hands and feet frozen at sea, making 'the cripple' a public concern. But in 1655 the fishing masters assumed the burden and by 1660 he was a fishing master himself. In 1666 he was lic. innholder and retailer. Lists 302ab. Wife Joan. Ch. unkn.

9 **WILLIAM**, in 1669 was at Goodman Lux's house, Great Isl., ag. ±35, and sued Alexander Waldron.

**Forst** (sometimes Frost), see **Fost**.

**FORTADO, Antonio** (also Anthony), a Portug. from Fayal, at York was accu. with Mary Start in July 1673. She was his wife 27 Mar. 1674 when she shared in est. of her f. Edward of York. He was a wit. with the Plaisteds 1687. List 33. Kn. ch: **Elizabeth** (Hurtado), b. Aug. 1683, a captive in Canada, taken by Ind. at Salmon Falls 18 Mar. 1689-90.

**Fosque,** ———, Mr., Popham 1606. List 6.

**FOSS, Fosse.** See also Fost.

1 **JOHN**, Rye Beach, ±30 in 1666, ±46 in 1680, first app. in division of 1661 as of 1657, likely in his wife's right. In 1668 he bot John Warren's stake in the Shrewsbury Patent, and in 1675 defended it in a suit against Richard Morgan. Gr.j. 1675, 1678, 1681, 1692. Innholder 1694-1698. Selectman 1698. Lists 326a, 330c, 318c, 323, 312cd, 313a, 315be, 316, 49, 52, 57. He m. Mary Berry(12), grantor with him in 1673, liv. (or his son's w.) in 1700. His grs. Joshua, 1709-1809, as told by his grs. Jacob D., b. 1784, writing in 1854, gave his story. A calker, he deserted a British warship in Boston harbor, came to Rye, where he found a wife; Foss and Fost are two distinct names; he raised up 12 ch. who had families. Of this number, by taking every Foss in sight (not Fosts) we make but 10. His deed-will, 13 Sep. 1710, ment. by name only John, Joshua and Zachariah.

Ch: **John**, b. ab. 1660. **Elizabeth**, b. 1666, m. Nathl. Batchelder(4). **Samuel. Martha**, m. by Dec. 1693 Richard Goss. **Thomas. William. Joshua. Zachariah. Hannah**, mar. in June 1702 John Jenness. **Richard**, likely a grs., wit. in 1713 with Wm. Wallis, Newcastle. In 1745 one Richard, of Portsmouth, gave P.A. to wife Sarah.

2 **JOHN**(1), ±69 in 1729, Greenland. Jury 1694, 1697, 1702. Lists 57, 330d, 332b, 335a, 337, 338a. Died in Greenland 5 Apr. 1752, 'ag. 95.' He perh. m. twice, Mary bef. 1700; in 1719 his wife was Susannah, memb. of Greenland ch. bef. 1712. List 335a, p. 176. Kn. ch: **Josiah**, bp. 13 Nov. 1709, mar. 19 Apr. 1733 Elizabeth Weeks. 8 ch. bp. **Mercy**, bp. 1713, presum. m. in Greenland 2 Mar. 1731-2 James Locke. **Joseph**, mar. in Scarb. 23 Oct. 1750 and d.s.p. Wid. Abigail (Tibbetts) m. 2d 30 May 1754 John Harmon. **Thomas.** Poss. also Isaac of Chester. See (5). Also m. in Greenl.: Abigail, 25 Oct. 1711 to Samuel Seavey; Mary, 10 Jan. 1714-5 to John Rackley; Susannah, 20 Nov. 1723 to Joseph Grant.

3 **JOSHUA**(1), had the homestead. In 1726 he deeded the meetinghouse lot to the town. Lists 315b, 316. He m. Sarah Wallis. Ch: **John**, d. 15 Feb. 1731, ag. 24 (grst.) Wid. Abigail mar. 2d 22 Nov. 1744 Capt. Nathl. Drake(2). D. Sarah d. in Hampton 26 Feb. 1749, ag. ab. 17 yrs. **Joshua**, b. 26 Dec. 1709, d. 17 Apr. 1809. Of Rye 1 July 1737, bot in Barrington, subject to fulfil. cond. of grant. He m. by 1732 Lydia Rand. 8 ch. incl. Joshua, Esq. and Ephraim, b. 1744, father of Jacob D., who had the homestead. **Jane**, m. 27 June 1736 Wm. Palmer. **Wallis**, m. 25 Jan. 1739 Mary Dowst. Ch. **Nathaniel**, m. 16 Oct. 1740 Molly Tucker. 2 sons. **Hannah**, m. 21 Aug. 1741 Samuel Sanders of the Shoals. **Mark**, bp. 2 Aug. 1724, d. in Barr. 1811; mar. 18 Nov. 1745 Mary Thompson. 6 s., 1 d. **Job**, in 1756 received deed of the homestead, on which desc. cont. He mar. 1 Nov. 1750 Sarah Lang of Greenland.

4 **NATHAN**, in 1722, ag. 16, was liv. 2 yrs. since at Mr. John Pray's house. Joined Portsm. So. Ch. 7 Dec. 1735. Of Portsm., sadler, in 1731, he bot in Barr. from John Clark, mariner, but did not rem. bef. 1737. In 1739 his Portsmouth tax was abated for maintaining a sick brother. Taxed in Barr. 1753. He lived a few rods from Samuel, by trad. a brother, and had sons **Stephen**, bp. in Dover 1753, lived to great age, and **Nathan**.

5 **SAMUEL**(1), in 1682 was wit. to buying beer at Grace Spencer's house. He and w. Mary were members of the Portsm. ch. and original members of the Greenland ch. Taxed in Greenland 1708, 1712, 1715. S. F. was an added name on the Portsm. tax list

1726; 1731 list 'S. F. & farm' (leased). Taxed in Barr. 1753, small, with Samuel jr., large, and Samuel 3d, medium; in 1742 only 'Jr.' was taxed. Lists 315c, 338a. In 1731 Samuel of Portsm. and Isaac **1** of Greenl. gave a joint deed to James Berry, likely father and son; but John(2) wit. Isaac's deed when he sold out in Greenl. in 1729. This Isaac m. 5 Dec. 1717 Abigail Hinkson. In 1729, of Greenl., he bot in Chester, and in 1757 deeded to his s. Timothy. Isaac **1** of Chester in 1760 had w. Judith and sons Isaac, Timothy and Thomas. Aside from **Isaac**, there were kn. ch: **Samuel**, carpenter, of Portsm. 10 Mar. 1731-2 bot in Barrington, by 1735 he had settled there. M. 29 Dec. 1726 Abigail Dowst. 8 ch. **Hinkson**, bp. 1712; in 1742, of Rye, bot in Barr. from his 'bro. Saml. jr.' Taxed there 1753; mar. 7 June 1733 Rachel Berry. Had no ch. and made his sister's son, Hinkson Marden, his heir. **Mary**, bp. 1715. **Ichabod**, bp. 1716. Was taxed in Barr. 1753. His wid. Hannah d. in Gilmanton in 1819, ag. 103. Their s. Isaiah rem. to Me. 3 daus. **George**, b. 10 May 1724, bp. 25 Mar. 1724-5 in Portsm. Of Portsm. in 1748, bot in Barrington; taxed there 1753; m. 3 Apr. 1746 Mary Marden, b. 20 Sep. 1726; dau. Rachel, bp. Portsm. So. Ch. 8 Mar. 1746-7. 6 sons. **Priscilla**, m. 2 Jan. 1751 James Marden.

6 **THOMAS**(1). Liv. in Greenland on the road to Sandy Beach. He m. 5 Feb. 1696 Abigail Cole (Abraham) who m. 2d before Nov. 1710 Samuel Folsom(6 jr.). Ch: **Isaac**, Lt., Greenland. List 338d. Wife in 1749 was Sarah. Will 30 Aug. 1759—d. 2 Nov. 1761 names 7 ch. incl. s. Isaac Cole Foss. **Mary**, m. 17 Dec. 1724 Edw. Dearborn(5 Samuel).

7 **WILLIAM**(1). Lists 315c, 338a. He d. bef. 12 Dec. 1718. One Wm. (Foss) was accu. in the Sessions Court Mar. 1717-8 by Elizabeth Bird of Dover or Cochecho. He m. at Hampt. Falls 29 Nov. 1700 Sarah Buswell, b. 29 Nov. 1676, stepd. of Wm. Fuller(6). List 338b. Kn. ch: **Walter**, b. 10 Jan. 1708, in ct. in 1718 for bringing back from Scarb. by his mother's orders a colt which his f., now dead, had sold in 1717. He m. 13 Sep. 1726 Sarah Babb(1?), b. 18 Sep. 1711; was taxed in Newington 1727. 1 ch. bap. there, 6 in Scarb., incl. Joseph who m. 22 Dec. 1757 Elizabeth Parcher. **Benjamin**, bp. with Walter in Portsm. 30 July 1710, liv. Scarb. 1762, m. there 26 Oct. 1731 Silence Winch. 6 ch. bap. **William**, bp. Greenland 1712. **Sarah**, bp. 1714. **John**, bp. 1717.

8 **ZACHARIAH**(1), taxed Newcastle 1708, 1720. He had sold out at Sandy Beach to John Jenness. In 1722 he was occup. John Muchemore's house on Gt. Isl. In 1728 was culler of fish at Canso. In 1749 (wife Joanna) he deeded a house on Gt. Isl. to

Henry Foss, presum. a son. '**Zachariah** Foss of Newcastle and Sarah Waterhouse of Portsmouth,' m. 20 Aug. 1734, was presum. another son, mariner and later innholder, who m. 2d in Boston 2 Oct. 1765 wid. Hannah or Anna Adams, mo. of John Adams, shopkeeper. Ch.

**FOST**, Forst, phonetic or perhaps an older spelling of Frost.

1 **JOHN**, Dover 1663, tailor. Rev. Joseph ('Handkerchief') Moody, town clerk of York, a born genealogist, spelt his name -Foss-, yet guarded against the confusion of Foss-Fost-Forst-Frost by recording his dau. Elizabeth as 'd. of John Foss born in England.' The mar. rec. of one John Fost, 16----, at the home of the Chadbournes, has not been invest. First app. as atty. for Anthony Checkley in Dover ct. Aft. Mr. Goff's death he appar. had charge of Quamphegan mills and m. his wid. Gr. jury 1671, 1674. Lists 311c (Dover), 356km, 357c, 359ab, 49, 52, 96. Will 17 Dec. 1699, d. next day. He m. 1st Mary Chadbourne; 2d 25 Jan. 1686-7 Elizabeth (by error -Sarah- in the record), wid. of James Goffe, who m. 3d James Emery(3). Ch. by 1st w: **Mary**, m. ab. 1692 James Warren. **Humphrey**, app. d. or remov. **William**, b. 11 Mar. 1673-4. **Jemima**, wit. Berw. in 1702. **Elizabeth**, m. 8 Nov. 1698 Daniel Dill(2), 2d Henry Beedle(2). By 2d w: **Samuel**, mariner, Boston, mar. (Foss) 9 July 1714 Mehitable Lincoln (child bur. 25 July 1717); 2d (Fost) 15 Sep. 1726 Mary White. Will 1 Jan.—18 Oct. 1747-8 (Forst), son Samuel, ±19, under gdn. of uncle John Hill. **Lydia**, appar. m. 24 Feb. 1717 Capt. Peter Grant of Berw. 7 ch. bap., including Landers.

2 **WILLIAM**(1), recorded his own birth with his ch. by 3d wife. Bap. 22 Aug. 1725, joined ch. 9 Oct. 1748. Adm. (inv. 29 June 1764) to s. or grs. Wm. List 358d. He m. 1st about 1692 Margery Lord; 2d 26 Apr. 1703 Sarah (Ferniside), wid. of Nathaniel Heard, liv. 1714; 3d Mary (Horn), wid. of Benj. Hanson. Both liv. 1764. Ch. by 1st w: **William**, shipmaster, bap. 'Frost' in Portsm. in 1708, mar. there 1 June 1716 Elizabeth Snell, recd. into covenant 24 Mar. 1716-7. Both liv. in Dover 1741. 5 ch. (Forse) bp. in Portsm. 1717-27. **Humphrey**, likelier the same bap. Dover 31 July 1720, gr. 1734, not among Lord heirs 1737, widow Catherine (Wedgewood), d. Somersworth 19 Mar. 1776. **Mary**, m. John Waldron, he bap. 3 July 1726. **Sarah**, m. Joseph Conner(5), both bap. 31 Aug. 1729. **Benjamin**, bp. 31 July 1725, m. 2 Feb. 1735 Ann Hodsdon. Settled in Rochester. Will 1775—1787 names 11 ch. **Margery**, bp. with half-sis. Lydia 4 Apr. 1725, m. James Richards. By 2d w: **Lydia**, b. 7

Jan. 1705-6, bp. 4 Apr. 1725 (Foss). **John,** perh. a son, adm. 29 Oct. 1746 to Wm. Welland, s.-in-law of 2d wife. By 3d w: **Mary,** b. 24 June 1728. **Chadbourne,** b. 26 Mar. 1731. **Daniel,** bp. 26 Aug. 1733. **Lydia,** bp. 14 May 1738.

**FOSTER,** Forster, from an unknown occu. Numerous in Scotl. and No. of England.

1 **BENJAMIN,** Kit. grant 1699; Eliot wit. 1708. Y. D. 7.114; sold out 1719, Y.D. x. 14. List 298. Added name on Portsm. tax list 1713; listed to New Meet Ho. 1717. One Benjamin, perh. not a child, was bap. in No. Ch., Portsm., 12 June 1717-8, perh. s. of (1), or s. of (2), or (1) and (2) the same person.

2 **BENJAMIN,** (see 1), b. Ipsw., m. in Portsm. 1 Nov. 1716 Wilmot Griffith. Both were memb. of Greenland Ch. 1722. He rem. to Scarb. by 1737, presum. the B. F. of Portsm. who with Robert Hasty bot 100 a. in Scarb. in 1731. Known ch: **Hannah,** bp. 1724. One Hannah mar. in Scarb. 11 Nov. 1741 John Scammon. Col. **Benjamin,** bp. 1726, the Revolutionary hero of Machias, m. 1st in Scarb., 26 Nov. 1747 Abigail Milliken; 2d in Scarb. 29 Jan. 1750 Eliza Scott. Ch. **Sarah,** bp. 1728. **Wooden,** bp. 1730, settled in Machias, mar. in Scarb. 28 May 1753 Frances Scott. Ch. **Sarah,** bp. 1733, m. in Scarb. 17 May 1750 Joseph Milliken. **Isaiah,** bp. 1735, these six in Greenland; settled in Machias and Cherryfield; m. in Scarb. 18 July 1754 Lydia Fogg. Ch. **Ezekiel,** bp. Scarb. 2 Oct. 1737, settled in Machias; m. in Scarb. 17 Nov. 1757 Mary Fogg. Ch.

3 **ELEAZER,** Scarb. grant 1720, sold 1727, then of Ipsw., weaver. Y. D. 12.202.

4 **ISAAC,** Mr., perh. Rev., later of Hartford, or master of a coaster. Wit. at Capt. Francis Hooke's 1676. Y. D. ii. 187.

5 **WILLIAM,** Damariscove 162--. List 8.

6 **WILLIAM,** lost on fishing voyage out of Saco River. Adm. 29 June 1654 to br.-in-law Christo. Hobbs. List 244b.

**Founds?** Philip, Portsm. poll tax payer 1681. List 329. Cf. Fones.

**FOUNTAYNE, Edward.** Came in -The Abigail- 1635, ag. 28. Wit. Maverick to Bragdon, York, 1637. List 271. 4 Mass. Hist. Coll. vii. 18. Winthrop's Journal i. 75.

**Fovan,** John, of Wells selling in Glouc. 14 Oct. 1721 his 50 a. grant in Wells. Y. D. xi. 66.

**FOWELL** (Fovel), **John,** York. Y. D. xi. 270, xiv. 244. Br.-in-law of Samuel Johnson, mar. 19 Nov. 1727 Anna Burrill(2). 6 ch. rec.

**FOWLE.** 1 **Jacob,** Woburn, tailor, b. there 3 Apr. 1677, m. there 3 Nov. 1701 Mary Broughton(2), both liv. there 1738.

2 **JAMES,** br. of (1), sued Nathaniel Johnson in Maine Court 1697.

3 **THOMAS,** Boston, merchant and contestant for civil rights. Baffled, he went home Nov. 1646. See Savage. Prior to July in that yr. he sold a house in York. P. &. C. i. 110-11. In 1649 his 600 a. granted for a farm was re-granted to Valentine Hill and John Leverett.

**FOWLER,** Common English surname except S. E.

1 **LUDWIG** (Lodowick), usually at Portsm. Rarely in ct. Lists 52, 313e, 326c, 327cd, 329, 331a, 332b. See Ellis(1). Town charge Portsm. 1709-1714.

2 **RICHARD,** convicted of piracy 1674. List 3. See Peter Rodrigo.

3 **SAMUEL,** and ch. William and Mary. See Hoyt's Salis., p. 162, and Fowler Gen. Nothing is noticed to connect these with Portsm. The record of Mary's marriage calls her of Salis.

4 **THOMAS,** Boston, presum. same taxed there 1688, m. Sarah Barrett, will 1701 (unexam.), gave for love and affec. to Samuel Hill, who in 1708 was 'now of Portsm. gent., son of Wm. Hill of Boston, gent.', 50 a. of land in Kit. in the hands of John Frink.

5 **WILLIAM,** of Amesbury and Kingston, m. Hannah Dow(7) of Hampton, who had her 1st child there, **Hannah,** b. 4 Apr. 1692. See N. H. Prob. ii. 549, Dow's Hamp. 716, Hoyt's Salis. 164.

**FOX,** ancient general English surname.

1 **EDWARD,** in 1668 had bot a horse from Wm. Neff of Haverh., with Joseph Berry bound for payment. 'Of Hampton' in 1671, he bot from John Garland 140 a. at Hampton New Plantation, which he sold during Philip's War. 'Of Greenland' in an original acct. stated with Major Vaughan dated 18 Mar. 1684-5. In 1714 E. F. sr., wife Mary, Benj. Fox, w. Eleanor, John Fox, w. Sarah, all of Greenland, deeded to John Urine the land Benj. and Edw. were then liv. on. Lists 52, 62, 332b. He m. Mary Allen(2), who m. 18 Oct. 1716 Hance Whidden, and was liv. in Greenland in 1740. Lists 335a, 338b. Presum. besides sons they may have had daus. and grch., incl: **Benjamin,** taxed Greenland 1712. List 338a. Eleanor (Smart), his wid. in 1729, m. 18 Feb. 1730-1 Arnold Brick. One B. F. of Nottingham in his will 1766 named w. Mary and 8 ch. **John,** taxed Greenland 1712. Lists 338a, 376b. Newmarket, ag. 57 in May 1743. W. Sarah Kenniston, m. 24 Jan. 1711-2. One Sarah of Newmarket, m. 17 July 1755 John Willey of Durham. **Edward,** Newmarket, br. of last, ±45 in May 1743. One E. F. was Louisburg soldier under Capt. Samuel Hale. **Mary,** working for Mrs. Vaughan, Portsm., in court in 1706. **Martha,** m. 13 Jan. 1713-4 John Dockham. **Susannah,** m. 7 Mar. 1727-8 Samuel Triggs.

**2 REV. JABEZ** (Thomas), b. 1647, H.C. 1665. Dover Neck wit. 1670, 1677, Berwick wit. 1672-1675. In Dec. 1677 the Berw. selectmen were trying to get in arrears of taxes, and awaiting his answer whether he would continue his ministry there. List 298. His grst. in Woburn (he d. in Boston of smallpox) reads: 28 Feb. 1702-3, ag. 56, '23 years pastor of this church.' He went there as colleague of Rev. Thomas Carter. He m. Judith Reyner, who mar. 2d Col. Jonathan Tyng and d. 5 June 1736 in her 99th year. Ch: **John**, Rev., b. 10 May 1678 in Cambridge, H.C. 1698, min. at Woburn from 1703; he was blind 15 yrs. bef. his death, 12 Oct. 1756. His w. Mary (Tyng d. of Hon. Edw.), d. Feb. 1764. 7 ch. incl. Hon. Jabez of Portland, b. 25 May 1705, H.C. 1727, d. 7 Apr. 1755, who m. Ann Bradbury and Ann (Hodge) Jones. **Thomas**, b. 6, d. 10, July 1680 in Woburn. **Thomas**, b. 13 Nov. 1681. **Jabez**, b. 2 Dec. 1684, tailor, Boston, m. 8 Mar. 1705 Hannah Burroughs(1), his widow liv. near Bantam Point, Boston, in 1735. 4 ch. **Judith**, b. 19 June 1690, d.y.

**3 NATHANIEL**, 'mariner of New England' when married, later of Boston, sloopman. He was in litig. 1680, 1681, 1685. In 1684 he sued his wife's mo. and her second hus. for his wife's portion. He was mar. ab. June 1682 by Mr. Martyn at the house of Capt. Elias Stileman on Great Isl. to his stepd. Mary Stileman jr. (Richard), presum. a 2d m., as Nathl. and Mary had a dau. **Elizabeth**, b. 27 Dec. 1674. Adm. 1689, div. of est. 1702, wid., two eldest s. **Thomas** and **Nathaniel**, the latter's gdn. Timothy Rogers of Marshfield. One Nathl. m. in Boston 16 May 1706 Ann Lowder.

**4 OLIVER**, Isl. of Shoals 1664. List 303.

**5 THOMAS**, having absented himself from his w. several yrs., in July 1673 was ordered home. Wit. James Gibbins.

**6 WILLIAM**, Star Isl., Shoals, mar. Mary Frost(8), adm. to her 21 July 1720. Several ch. who all d. but one: **William**, bp. 10 May 1713 at Newcastle, of Southboro, Bolton and Lunenburg, Mass., who in 1733 released his stepfather Geo. Collins, and in 1744 sued Rev. Joseph Moody and James Grant for a third of 20 a. in Scotland, York, which A. Maxwell deeded to John Frost(6).

**FOXWELL.** The names Richard, George, Nathaniel, Philip, recur in S. E. Devon and adj. Somersetshire, incl: Bovey-Tracy on the Teign River, where Edw. Colchard and Geo. Jewell also occur—all uninvest.

**1 GEORGE**, nephew of (5), merchant, of Exeter, Devon, 1664, of Boston 1671, was plaint. for self and as atty. for Tho. Donnell in Me. ct. 1670. He d. in Va. and his br. Henry 'of Chesley,' England, wrote to Mr. Hull, the mintmaster, who sent a copy of his nunc. will from the Suff. Co. Ct. now missing. Adm. 29 Sep. 1674 to Robert Edmunds who cared for and buried him.

**2 JOHN**(5), ±30 in 1669, carpenter, signed as the eldest s. in 1664. Lists 233, 235, 279. Adm. 6 Nov. 1677 to his wid. He mar. Deborah Johnson of York, who m. 2d bef. 21 June 1680, John Harmon. Ch: **Philip**, ±19 in Boston 28 Apr. 1692, d.s.p. **Nathaniel**, b. 1676.

**3 NATHANIEL**(2), ag. 27 in Apr. 1703, grew up in York. His orig. deed in York Ct. files, 20 Jan. 1701-2, calls him 'now of York and belonging to Blue Point.' He was k. in the Hunnewell massacre at Black Pt. This was 6 Oct. 1703, and in the next court, Jan., appears an entry: 'Margaret Bowden the relict of Nathaniel Foxwell deceased, acquitted on account of several circumstances.' She was dau. of John(7), and liv. in Boston in 1726. Only ch: **Deborah**, m. in Boston 10 Aug. 1727 Wm. Corbin of B., mariner. 3 ch. rec.

**4 PHILIP**(5), ±17 in 1668, ±32 in 1684, likely first ment. as Geo. Norton's 'man Philip,' abs. from meeting in 1666. His bros. having d., he adm. his father's est. in 1677, and in 1690 was Captain with 6 soldiers in his garrison. Const. 1682, gr.j. 1685, selectm. 1685, and chairman 1686, 1687. Lists 90, 30, 36, 235, 238a, 249, 313a. He d. 20 Oct. 1690 'late of Kit.' Adm. to wid. Mrs. Eleanor (Brackett 2), m. by 1680, liv. in Boston in 1694, m. 2d Elisha Andrews(5). No surv. ch.

**5 *RICHARD**, ag. 72 in July 1676, ordered Ind. trading goods in London in 1629. In Boston 19 Oct. 1630 he desired adm. as freeman and 18 May foll. was sw. A letter of Wm. Hilton to J. Winthrop jr. 18 Apr. 1633 says: 'There arrived a fishing ship at Piscataqua the 15th of this present month where in is one Richard Foxwell who hath formerly lived in this country.' In London 6 Jan. 1632[3 he signed a note for goods bot in 1629. Whether he had m. Capt. Bonython's dau. by this time is unasc. In June 1640 he stated that 'these four years or thereabouts' he had lived at Black Point in the right of his f.-in-law. For Ind. trade he estab. a house on the western side of St. George's River, which was lost to the French, altho he cont. to trade with the French. (Essex Qtly. Ct. ii. 23-26; 4 Mass. Hist. Coll. vi. 570). Altho unsucc. in business he maintained an emin. char. during a long life. Courts were held at his house, which was a garrison in Philip's War. Suff. Ct. files 1526 contains a 2-page doc. in his hand stating Capt. Scottow's failure in defence, and adding 'Mr. Rishworth I pray faile me not to do your endeavour to put an issue to my busyness, for I have taken a hurt of late

which I Doubt will shorten my days.' Adm.
6 Nov. 1677 to s. Philip. He served as chairman of selectm., foreman of jury, clerk of
the writs, Lygonia assemblyman, member of
the Scarb.-Falm. court. Lists 101, 242, 231-
233, 235, 236, 337e, 28. His wife Susannah
(Bonython) is almost absent from the records. List 235. Ch: **Richard**, d. 4 June 1664,
carpenter's tools ment. in his inv. List 233.
**Esther**, m. in 1657 Tho. Rogers. **John**, b. ab.
1639. **Lucretia**, b. ab. 1644, m. James Robinson. **Susannah**, m. John Ashton. **Philip**,
b. ab. 1651. **Sarah**, in 1673 a wit. in Kittery
(Y. D. iv. 41), m. Sep. 1678 Joseph Curtis.
**Mary**, m. George Norton.

**FOYE**, Foy, the latter a parish in Hereford.
1 **GREGORY**, in 1661 test. that now that
her father is dead, Thomas Wedge's wife
is willing to come to her hus. via Barbadoes
or Newfoundland.
2 **JAMES**, fisherman, ±37 in 1695, ag. 53 in
Dec. 1710, was deeded 8 a. fronting 40
rods on Braveboat Harbor creek in 1686,
mortg. to Pepperell in 1707, discharged by
his grs. James, cordwainer, of Somersworth,
in 1748. Was wit. for the Pepperells down
to 1719. Lists 290, 296-298, 291. Wife Grace
in 1712, yet in 1715 -Martha- Foy joined
Kit. church. Ch: **Richard**, ship carpenter
and mariner, in 1711 bot land adj. his father's. In 1718 sold to Robert. List 298.
Wife Naomi Blake(5). Adm. 18 Feb. 1745-6
to s. James, cordwainer, of Somersworth,
who paid his grf.'s mtge. and bot in the
Hicksecs. **Martha**, m. (July Ct. 1711) Nathaniel Hicks, and was given 2 a. on the
creek surrounded by her father's land. **Robert**, b. 26 Aug. 1691, ship carpenter, in 1718
bot from Richard adj. their father. Adm. 7
Apr. 1724 to wid. Hannah (McKenney) who
m. 2d 27 Jan. 1724 Wm. Groves and rem. to
Wiscasset. In 1754 Elizabeth Foy test. 'my
father Groves,' and Robert Foy, 68 in 1786,
served his time with 'my master Wm. Groves.'
**Joseph**, twin with last, m. in 1729 Susannah
Jenkins. J. F. in 1737 wit. Richard Rogers'
will. **Charles**, b. 4 Mar. 1702, mar. (int. 27
Apr. 1728) Hephzibah Seavey, d. of Benj.
and Mary (Wallis), both living 1762. Ch.
**James**, b. 9 Jan. 1704-5. Unasc. whether he
or his f. or ano. was of Dover, Exeter and
Somersworth 1734-1741.
3 **JOHN**, poss. s. of (2), m. by 1717 Mary
(Chesley 2), wid. of Ralph Hall of Dover
(Somersworth). Lists 358cd. John of Dover
was a fisherman at Matinicus, in Vaughan's
schooner, Tho. Jordan master. J. F. was bap.
at Dover 25 Dec. 1738 upon a sick bed. J. F.
jr. of Dover pet. 1743 for separate parish
(Madbury); he m. ab. 1745 Ruth Huckins.
**Fraisey**, William, Dover. 164-- sued by Thomas Beard; 1643 absent from meeting;

1645 fined for fighting. Cf. Frayser, and
Freethy.
**FRANCIS**. 1 **David**, Pemaquid garrison 1696.
List 127.
2 **JOHN**, Kit. 1690, just out of captivity.
3 **ROBERT**, dft. Maine Ct. 1670, defaulted.
4 **ROGER**, wit. Indian deed to John Parker
1651. Y. D. x. 252.
**Frayser**? (Feaysts?), William 1663. List 342.
See Fraisey.
**FREDERICK, Christopher**, Great Isl. (aut.
in Ct. files 20064), in 1723 dep. he had
been going to sea for 40 yrs. List 316. W.
Mary (Palmer?) was a Mussell heir. Will
15 Mar. 1737-8—5 Oct. 1741, leaves all to w.
for life, entails lands on heirs of d. **Mary**.
**Freeby**, Nicholas, Falm. grant 168--. Me.
H. & G. Rec. v. 156.

**FREEMAN**, a common Eng. surname of
many origins, numerous in Mid. England.
1 **ANTHONY**, ment. in Black Will's will,
presum. the 'Tony' manumitted by Chas.
Frost in 1708 at Black Will's request.
2 **NATHANIEL**, b. ±1673, m. in Boston 18
Jan. 1699 Alice Peniwell (John of York.)
Both were wit. in York 16 Mar. 1701-2.
Bookkeeper for Mr. Daniel Weare of Boston in 1702, he was around Portsm. 1704-10,
engaged for schoolmaster south of the Mill
Dam 3 May 1708, and later schoolmaster at
York. Liv. 1719, but dead by Oct. 1727;
wife liv. 1717. Ch: **Nathaniel**, fisherman,
York, appren. to Benj. Stone in 1716, stole
and burnt his indent. 1719. List 279. M.
(int. 15 May 1736) Mary Perkins. **Sarah**, m.
bef. 4 Oct. 1727 Joseph Stover. **Mary**, m.
ab. 1734 Abraham Bowden jr., (Boody 1).

**FREESE**, if an Eng. surname, is extrem.
rare.
1 **JAMES**, ±16, 'Mr. Carr's man' in Salis.
1657, and later an Amesbury shipwright,
moved to Falm. ab. 1686, there to fall a victim of the Ind. List 228d. Unexplain. he
wit. a Falm. deed as James Fress Torgisen.
Y. D. 14.105. Wid. Elizabeth ret. to Essex
Co., m. 2d 30 Oct. 1695 Thomas Riggs sr. of
Glouc., d. 16 June 1722, ag. ab. 80. Kn ch:
**James**, b. Salis. 16 Mar. 1666-7, wounded at
Falm. 1689, m. in Newb. 2 June 1697 Mary
Merrill (Daniel). 3 ch. rec. in Newb.: Han-
nah, b. 24 Feb. 1697, m. there 14 Feb. 1716-7
Tho. Haskell of Glouc. and Falm., and d.
soon leav. only ch. Thomas. **Elizabeth**, b. 9
Oct. 1702, unm. 1743. **Isaac**, b. 6 Sep. 1716,
Newbury, mason, 1743. **John**, b. Amesb. 1
Oct. 1669, d. Newb. 29 June 1716, m. (int.
Salis. 25 July 1696) Dorothy Carr, who m.
2d 7 Mar. 1718 Fawne Clement; 3d 26 Aug.
1741 Archelaus Adams, and d. within 6 wks.
Rec. ch., Newb.: Jacob, b. 10 Nov. 1698,
'Jacob Jun.' m. at Hampton 30 Mar. 1725
Dorothy Moulton. 3 ch. rec. George, b. 27

Aug. 1709, mar. 19 Apr. 1737 Mary Atkinson. Ch. One John Freese of Wells, house carpenter, in 1728, m. 1732 Mary Wormwood. **Katherine**, b. 31 Jan. 1671, mar. in Topsfield 2 Mar. 1693 Daniel Foster, d. 3 Mar. 1694-5. 1 dau. **Frances**, b. 28 Sep. 1674. **Jacob.**

2 **LIEUT. JACOB**(1), Hampton, b. at Casco Bay 26 Sep. 1685 (self-rec. at Gloucester), d. 5 Nov. 1727 (grst.) He received a town grant in Falm. In 1707 was of Newcastle, shipwr. He mar. bef. 14 June 1704 Rachel Chase(5) and settled near her f. at the Landing. She m. 2d 4 Jan. 1737 Andrew Wiggin, Esq. Ch: **Joseph**, Ensign, b. 6 Oct. 1710, d. 8 July 1752, m. 20 Mar. 1735 Sarah Sherburn. 1 ch. **Benjamin**, b. 29 Aug. 1712, d. 26 June 1715. **Jonathan**, b. 27 Dec. 1714, joiner, d. 5 Apr. 1748, m. 1 July 1736 Sarah Ayers, of Portsm., who m. 2d Philip Dow(8). 5 ch. **Jacob**, b. 10 Oct. 1716, moved to Epping, d. 20 Apr. 1780. Wife Susanna grantee from Alex. Gordon's ch. 4 ch. bp. at Hampton. **Rachel**, b. 9 Oct. 1718, d. 16 Jan. 1736. **Elizabeth**, b. 18 Jan., d. 10 May, 1722. **Anna**, bap. 10 Mar. 1723. **Catherine**, b. 12 June 1726, five surv. in 1746. In 1760 Jacob, Sarah wife of Maj. Josiah Dearborn, and Catherine Moore of Stratham, seamstress, sold 6 a. near the Windmill Field, Hampton.

**FREETHY.** Freathy the name of a farm in St. John's parish, Cornwall. See Creber.

1 **ALEXANDER** and his br. Wm. were curing fish at Stratton's Isl., Scarb., in 1637. 'Sander' likelier came with Mr. Winter in the -Agnes- 1636, as he went home in 1638 bef. his 3 yrs. were up. See Doc. Hist. iii. 93, 97, 98, 120, 125, 137.

2 **AMBROSE**, in N. H. Ct. in 1646 fined for swearing.

3 **JAMES**(5), O.A. York 1680, in 1680 and 1685 had firewood grants with Wm. Rones and Wm. Wormwood, both k. by Ind., inv. taken 14 Oct. 1690. See Bragdon(2). Adm. 3 Dec. 1690 to wid. Mary (Milbury), who m. by 1695 Nathaniel Blackledge. Ch: **Mary**, m. by 1703 Andrew Grover. **Hannah**, mar. (Court Jan. 1703-4) Matthew Grover. **Elizabeth**, m. by 1706 Robert Gray. **Joseph**, List 279. Adm. 1758 to wid. Honor. He m. 28 Nov. 1710 Jemima Hatch, 5 ch. incl. James, b. 14 June 1712, List 279, and Hannah, b. 29 Apr. 1718, m. Nathl. Bray(7); 2d 24 Jan. 1733-4 Honor Stackpole, 4 ch. Also perhaps James, List 99, captive in Ind. hands in 1711, who may have been s. of (4).

4 **JOHN**(5), in 1674 a wit. at Yarmouth Falls (presum. there with Henry Sayward). Inv. 4 May 1692. Adm. 11 Dec. 1693 to wid. Hannah (Bray 4), who m. 2d at Bradford 10 June 1707 (-Mary- in record) Robert Hazelton of Rowley, and d. there 13

Mar. 1729[30 (grst.) Bef. adm. her husband's est. she was in ct. for retailing strong drink on a victualer's lic. Innholder's lic. 1696. In 1702 she pet. for the upper ferry, which her hus. had until forced to remove by the Ind. Ch: **Mehitable**, mar. by 1701 Aquilla Haines. **Joanna**, m. 1703 Capt. Joseph Bean(3). **Jemima**, mar. 13 May 1708 Jonathan Spofford of Rowley. 13 ch.

5 **WILLIAM**, fisherman, younger br. of (1), came over to Richmond Isl. in the -Speedwell- in 1635, ran away in 1636 but recanted and came back and served his 3 yrs. ending in 1640, when he left promising to pay to Mr. Winter 40 s. his mother had from Mr. Trelawny. Banks ident. him with W. F. who m. in Plymouth 13 Jan. 1639[40?] Elizabeth Barker. Sep. 15, 1640, just aft. leaving Mr. Winter, he and Henry Watts were fined for carrying boards on Sunday. In 1641 he was sued in N. H. court, and in 1643 he was called up for not leading an orderly life. He was liv. in Portsm. In Nov. 1652 he was liv. at York. His 'old field' is ment. in 1665. In 1683 he deeded his lands to sons Samuel and John, with reserva. for his own and their mother's lives. Next yr. appoint. ferryman. Lists 21, 323, 275, 276, (342?). His wife was Elizabeth in 1671, also in 1688 when he sold his town grant. Besides ch. Jane, Samuel and John, to whom he deeded lands, he presum. had others: **Jane** (or Joan), m. by 1671 Tho. Holmes. **Elizabeth**, m. 1st Isaac Botts; 2d, July 1679, Moses Spencer, whose s. Moses named his first ch. Freethy. **James**, town gr. 1680. **Samuel**, in 1683 with br. John recd. deed of homestead. Drowned 24 Nov. 1685. Adm. 23 Dec. 1685 to creditors. **John.**

**FRENCH**, name for emigrants from France to Eng. who lost their own names. Common in So. half of England.

1 **JOHN**, b. 12 Dec. 1660 at Salis., settled in Hampton Falls. First w. Lydia d. 15 Feb. 1708-9; he m. 2d in Hampton 8 Dec. 1709 Elizabeth (Dalton 3?) Scott, died 20 Feb. 1717-8. Ch: **Samuel**, b. 1 Mar. 1693-4, clothier, m. 20 Dec. 1722 Mary Perkins (Humphrey). 8 ch. **John**, b. 7 Jan. 1696-7, m. 11 Feb. 1725 Sarah Sanborn (Mephiboseth); liv. Hampt. Falls. 7 ch.

2 **JOHN**, Portsm. wit. 1698.

3 **JOSEPH**. List 399a.

4 **MICHAEL**, around Lubberland 1674-1680. Of Lamprill Riv. in 1679, had been abs. from his wife 4 or 5 yrs. List 92. Perh. a son: **James**, Boston, mar. Philippa (White) Greenwood, dau. of Samuel White, and had 4 ch. rec. Boston, 1st one Michael, b. 6 Jan. 1716, mastmaker in Boston 1738.

5 **NATHANIEL**, husbandman, Kingston, b. Salis. 8 Dec. 1678. Lists 399a, 400. Will 1747—1750 names w. Sarah, 4 sons, 3 mar.

daus., adopted son Thomas French, son of Mary Gilbert.

6 **PHILIP**, with wife, acc. in N. H. ct. 1695.

7 **SIMON**. List 400.

8 **THOMAS** 'French alias Yorke,' Portsm. 1672, staying in town without license.

9 **WILLIAM**, Stratham, b. ab. 1675, went to live at Exeter at Mr. Richard Hilton's ab. 1695. Lists 387, 388. He mar. ab. 1698 Abigail Wiggin (Andrew). 'Old Mr. Wm. French's wife' d. in Stratham 14 Nov. 1748. One **Abigail** m. in Greenl. 22 Feb. 1721-2 Joseph Kenniston.

**Frencham**, Henry, wit. for Clarke & Lake 1668-1673. Doc. Hist. iv. 336, Y. D. 8.160. (**Frenchman**), John the Smith, Portsm. 1681. List 329.

**FRIEBURY, Richard** and **Richard** jr., largest taxpayers at Pemaquid 1687. List 124. Lands claimed by Cornelius Darling(1) in right of his w. Mary Frebray ab. 1715.

**FRIEND**. 1 **John**, see Amee.

2 **JOSEPH**, seaman, Piscataqua 1684. List 314.

3 **PHILIP**, ±21 in 1694, this yr. saw Samuel Cutt take an axe and break in a door of the Great House, Str. Bank.

4 **RICHARD**, Damariscove 1672. List 13. R. F. in Philip's War under Major Waldron.

**FRINK**, if an Eng. surname, is extremely rare. See Briar(5).

1 **GEORGE**, Kittery, s. of John and Mary (Wood) of Ipsw., mar. Rebecca Skiljin (John); both living 1729, he in 1736. Lists 296-97. Ch: **Elizabeth**, b. 14 Jan. 1704, m. George Berry jr. **Mary**, b. 17 Jan. 1706, m. John Snow of Kit. **Rebecca**, b. 4 Aug. 1709, m. Ephraim Crockett of Stratham. **Sarah**, b. 2 Apr. 1711, m. Robert More.

2 **JERE**, soldier under Capt. John Hill 26 Aug. 1696. Me. H. & G. Rec. 3.109.

3 **JOHN**, br. of (1), yeoman, Kit., where he bot 50 a. 13 Oct. 1699. Lists 290, 296-7. D. by 1725. He m. 1st 10 Apr. 1700 Hannah Morgrage (John), 2d 25 May 1718 Jane Jackson, who mar. 2d (contract 13 Nov. 1730) Henry Barter. Ch: **George**, b. 19 May 1701. **John**, b. 12 Mar. 1702-3; he or a younger John liv. 1734. **Samuel**, of Newbury 1733, m. (int. 2 Sep. 1728) Ann Pugsley. **Hannah**, of Newbury unm. in 1733. By 2d w: **Andrew**, 5 yr. 11 m. when f. died, may have been the 1st wife's child. He was of Haverhill in 1740. **Jane**, 3 yr. 11 m. old when f. died. **Child**, d.y.

**FRIZZELL**. 1 **Alexander** (Frissell, Frossell), wit. three Ind. deeds 1660; charged with burglary (Frizell) 1669. List 13.

2 **JOHN**, Scotchman, fishing master at Spurwink between the wars. Later of Boston. Lists 226, 228c. Cf. Adams.

3 **WILLIAM** (Friswell), Kennebec 1665. List 12. Wm. Fresell a Scotch prisoner. List 74.

**FROST**, an ancient forename, common surname in So. half of England. See also Fost.

1 **ARTHUR**, N. E. Reg. 24.190, misreading of Hart.

2 **MAJ.** ‡\***CHARLES**(9), ±52 in 1683, first app. in acquit. for shooting Warwick Heard for a goose 24 Mar. 1646-7, next at the Submission to Mass., when he furnished the advance list of inhabitants and witnessed on that side. By 1657 he was Lieut. and gr.j., and always after was extrem. active in all lines of usefulness, except under the Royal Comrs. On the reëntry of Mass. he became Captain and a magistrate authorized to preside at the Associates' courts; in 1682 President Danforth app. him Councillor for 6 yrs.; he was a judge of Common Pleas Ct. 1692 till death; and in 1688 Sergeant-Major for all Maine. He was Rep. 1660, 1661, 1669, 1674, 1678; town clerk aft. 1669, often selectm. Lists 282, 283, 285, 298, 311a, 331c, 267a, 24, 25, 28, 29, 32 (see Champernowne), 33, 36, 83, 96. He was ambushed by the Ind. on his way home from meeting 4 July 1697. His will dated 7 Jan. 1690-1, while in active military service, names his w. Mary (Bowles, m. by 1664) who d. 11 Nov. 1704. 'Mrs. Mary Frost' was given innholder's lic. in 1698. Ch: **Mary**, d.y. **Sarah**, b. 1666, mar. John Shipway, Wm. Redford. **Abigail**, m. Joshua Fryer, Wm. Moody. Her will, May 1721—June 1723, names Frost rela. **Mehitable**, mar. 5 Jan. 1697-8 Tho. Peirce. Their sons Daniel and Thomas mar. their cousins, daus. of Charles. **Lydia**, m. 1692 Benj. Peirce of Newb'port; 2d 13 May 1716 John Greenleaf of Salis.; d. 13 May 1752, ag. 78. **Mary**, mar. 12 Dec. 1694 Capt. John Hill. ‡\***Charles**, Major, Esq., Deacon, b. 17 Apr. 1678. Gr.j. and Lt. in 1699, later was Captain, and Major until Hammond's appt. Register of Probate 1700 till death, and succeed. by his s. Charles. Rep. 1700, Judge of Common Pleas 1715 and Councillor 1719 till death. Lists 38, 289, 291, 296-298. Will 24 Sep.—d. 17 Dec. 1724. He mar. 1st 7 Feb. 1698-9 Sarah Wainwright, who accomp. 7 single childbirths in 8 yrs. and 2 more and d. 5 June 1714; 2d 25 Nov. 1714 Jane (Elliot) Pepperell, 3 ch.; her will 25 June 1747 —25 May 1749. ‡**John**, b. 1 Mar. 1681-2, Portsm., mariner, commanded the ship-of-war -Edward-. Province Councillor of N. H. Lists 296, 297, 316. Will 20 Jan. 1731-2, d. 25 Feb. 1732-3. He mar. 4 Sep. 1702 Mary Pepperell, who mar. 2d 12 Aug. 1745 Rev. Benj. Colman, D.D. 17 ch. (no Timothy) of whom 9 m. **Elizabeth**, d. 21 May 1696, ae.

14 (grst. Portsm.). **Nicholas**, d. bef. 25 Jan. 1699-1700.

3 **GEORGE**, Mr., respect. inhab. of Saco 1636-42. Gr.j. and referee 1640. In Sep. 1643 around Boston one G. F. was drunk, and the next March was distempered with wine. Lists 242, 22.

4 **JAMES**, read 'Tufts' by Joseph P. Thompson, ab. 1890, 'Huse' by another, mar. in Wells 1 July 1696 Hannah Woodin.

5 **JAMES** (see 15?), ag. 50 in Apr. 1733, first app. in dep. 1705 about men from upper Kit. getting hay from Wells. He m. 15 May 1707 Margaret Goodwin. Both joined Berwick ch. List 298. Will 17 Sep. 1744— 4 July 1748, names w. and 9 ch: **James**, b. 5 Nov. 1707, m. 25 Dec. 1729 Sarah Nason. List 298. 11 ch. bap. **William**, b. 15 Feb. 1710, m. Love Butler. 11 ch. **Nathaniel**, b. 14 Aug. 1713, d. in Gorham ab. 1763. 8 ch. **John**, bp. 22 Oct. 1716, of Berw., joiner with w. Lydia in 1751, went to Nova Scotia. See Y. D. 29.78. **Stephen**, bp. 12 Apr. 1719, d. ab. 1759. 8 ch. **Mary**, bp. 29 Sep. 1723, m. Maj. Charles Gerrish. **Jeremiah**, bp. 24 Dec. 1725, m. Miriam Harding. (List 298). Went to Nova Scotia. **Jane**, bp. 10 May 1728, m. 10 Mar. 1747 Caleb Emery, s. of Daniel(2). **Margaret**, bp. 13 July 1730, m. 18 June 1752 Wm. Haskell.

6 **JOHN**, York, fisherman. Town grant at the Harbor's Mouth in 1663, and in 1669 in a location aft. called 'Bricksome.' By right liv. he kept out of the records; in 1667 he sued Richard Calley and lost. K. by Ind. in Apr. 1677, adm. to sons John and Philip Nov. 6. Wife Rose outl. him 7 or m. yrs. Ch: **John**, b. ab. 1652. **Agnes**, m. by 1671 Alexander Maxwell. **Philip**, bp. at Brixham, Devon, 28 Mar. 1657.

7 **JOHN**(9), shipmaster and owner, Boston. Adm. 28 Mar. 1687 to wid. Mary. He m. 1st one Mehitable; 2d Mary Davis, dau. of Hon: Wm. and Huldah (Symmes), whose will 1727—1732 made d. Mary sole benef. Ch: **John**, b. 9 Jan. 1669-70. **Mehitable**, b. 15 July 1671, m. in Boston 3 Aug. 1689 Tho. Lincoln. 9 ch. incl. Mehitable, b. 25 Jan. 1690, who m. Samuel Fost(1). **Elizabeth**, b. 12 July 1677, m. 13 Dec. 1705 Tho. Short. By 2d m: **John**, b. 16 May 1681, d. bef. 1687. **Charles**, Boston, cooper. Will 6 Aug. 1705—3 Dec. 1722, names mother, sister Mary, 'other sisters,' aunt Margaret Davis. **Mary**, b. 22 Jan. 1684-5, of Boston, unmar., will 1748—1749 made her sister Short's ch. her heirs, but left her great Bible to Simon Frost of New Hampshire.

8 **JOHN**(6), ±22 in 1674, fisherman, Isles of Shoals. He m. ab. 1673 Sarah Kelly. Liv. on Hog Isl., later on Star Isl. List 309. Will 22 June 1713—7 Mar. 1718-9. Ch: **John**, in 1705 was helping Elizabeth Mainwaring

make a boarder pay, in ct. in 1707 for abusing his grf. Kelly. D. bef. 1713, leaving s. John, unident. (List 298, p. 34, col. 3, 1724). **Samuel**, Newcastle, in 1719, took out adm. on est. of his grf. John of York. Lists 315b, 316. He mar. Anne Carter(2), both liv. in 1726 when they sold land her father bot in 1670. She was his widow in 1739 and liv. Portsm. 1744. Ch: Mary, bp. at Newcastle 14 May 1710. It is undet. whether they had other ch., as Cater Frost, Gosport fisherman in 1729, m. Mary Urine in Greenland 9 May 1723, Samuel, mariner, of Portsm. So. Ch. 1744, 1755, or John, who m. 5 Jan. 1726-7 Mary Cate(1), who had d. by 1732 leav. 3 ch., of whom Elizabeth, bp. 1729, in her will 1755 named half-br. Cater and mother Martha (presum. the d. of Sampson Doe[3]), and her uncle Samuel Frost, mariner. **Ithamar**, s. Philip, bp. 14 May 1710. Only surv. ch. Sarah m. Arthur Randall of Gosport. **Mary**, m. William Fox(6).

9 **NICHOLAS**, mason, ±60 in June 1658, ±70 in Apr. 1662. His birth and birthplace as printed with grotesque partic. was the pen practice of a boy descendant, reckless where and improvising what he wrote. One Nicholas Frost of Goodleigh, near Bideford, Devon, in his will in 1638 named bros. Geo. (with 3 ch.) and Wm. Another Nicholas Frost of Bideford, merchant, was in 1613 lic. to marry Mary Bollen of Monckley, gent. Another Nicholas had w. Joan. Nicholas, the mason, wife's name totally unk., first app. 3 Oct. 1632 in the Boston court for compromising the English by misusing the natives at Damariscove, and was banished the province. In 1634 Mr. Wannerton had given him land in the neighborhood originally called 'Kittery.' On his second petition, 1643, Mass. removed the decree of banishment, and later he was an active support. of that govt. In 1648 he made a 7 yr. lease of his 'new house & ground at Kittery' to Jeremy Sheeres. Constable 1640. An efficient and aggress. man, he laid the foundation of this family's fortune. Jury 1647, 1650, 1655, 1662-64; gr.j. 1649-51, 1659, 1662; selectm. 1648, 1652, 1653, 1661. Comr. 1653 on Kit.-York bounds, 1654 on Kit.-Dover bounds. Lists 281-283, 24, 25, 298. Inv. 24 Sep. 1663. Ch: **Charles**, b. 1631-33. **Catherine**, b. 1633-34, poss. twin, m. Wm. Leighton and Joseph Hammond. **John. Elizabeth**, b. 1645-46, mar. Wm. Gowen alias Smith. **Nicholas**, b. fall of 1647, mariner or merchant, d. in Limerick, Ire., Aug. 1673, s.p. Lists 296, 297.

10 **NICHOLAS**, ±28 in July 1676, came from Bristol, Eng., in 1662. For his passage over he bound himself to serve 5 yrs., and was sold first to Wm. Scadlock, then to Francis Littlefield. By 1675 he had m. Mary

Small, and became an Ind. trader with her father. Gr.j. 1687. Lists 357d, 236, 99. His wife with 2 ch. was taken capt. 8 June 1693. The report 17 Jan. 1698-9 of a voyage redeeming Ind. capt. notes at the end 'Nick Frost drowned'—poss. went as interpreter. Adm. 30 May 1707 to wid. Mary who d., and regrant. to s. Bartholomew 26 Nov. 1712. Ch: Mary, a child in 1691. **Bartholomew,** liv. on homestead. Lists 291, 296, 297. Adm. 1 Mar. 1722-3 to wid. Hannah, who m. 12 Jan. 1723-4 David Clark. 3 daus. **Nicholas. Margaret,** m. 18 Oct. 1708 Wm. Merrifield of Cape Cod. Ch. **Katharine,** mar. Israel Young of Eastham. **Elizabeth,** m. 4 Mar. 1708-9 John Richardson of Kit. **Eleanor,** m. 28 Feb. 1711-12 David Sawyer from Newbury. Both orig. memb. of the Eliot ch., he orig. memb. of the Scarb. ch. 6 ch. rec.

11 **NICHOLAS**(10), mariner, Portsm., settled in Newington. Adm. to wid. Sarah 4 June 1718. He m. 1st Dorothy Mendum, who was found guilty of adult., fate unk.; he m. 30 Dec. 1714 Sarah (Morrell), wid. of Geo. Huntress, who m. 3d, spring of 1720, Tho. Darling. Ch: **Nicholas,** bp. 19 Sep. 1708, in 1730 was of Hampt., saddler, suing for his double portion. **Dorothy,** bp. same day. **Nathaniel,** bp. 11 Apr. 1711, liv. 1765 in Lee. Wife Elizabeth in 1735. **John,** with Nathl., both carpenters, were deeded by Tho. and Sarah Darling the house in Portsm. occu. by Richard Hilton, Esq.

12 **PHILIP**(6), had the homestead for caring for his mother. O.A. 1680. He mar. ab. 1677 Martha, wid. of Andrew Rankin, whose maiden name was Merry (or Merrow?). In 1678 he had a joint gr. with Arthur Beale. Jury 1687, gr.j. 1688-1690. Lists 33, 298. He d. ab. 1693 and in 1703 his lands were confirmed to his ch.; but one known **Agnes,** m. Wm. Shaw. †Philip, ment. 1710.

13 **SUSANNAH** (Dixon), dau. named in Wm. D.'s will, lived at a distance.

14 **THOMAS,** grantee at Newtown, Arrowsic, 13 Sep. 1686. List 189. His wid. in 1716 was Mary, w. of Joseph Soper, of Boston, blacksmith, presum. the same who m. Mary 'Monylex' 17 Apr. 1707. Ch. in 1716: **John** of Hebron, Hartford co., Conn. **Elizabeth. Mary,** wife of one Josselyn.

15 **WILLIAM,** cordwainer, not unlik. relat. to Rebecca (Frost) Booth, d. of Daniel of Fairfield. First app. at Saco, Oct. 1667, sued by John Budesert, but Goody Frost was assigned a seat in the meetingho. the yr. before. In Philip's War they fled to Salem, and aft. the war came back to Wells, where he was partn. in a sawmill grant and killed wolves. Const. Wells, 1682. Gr.j. 1684, 1687, 1689, 1690. Lists 27, 259, 269b. In May 1690 he was k. by Ind., adm. 25 Feb. 1690-1 to Israel Harding, now hus. of the widow

Mary (Wakefield). List 246. Kn. ch: **William. Nathaniel,** named with William in their grf.'s will. List 268a. Taken captive when his f. was killed, fate unk. **Mary,** b. at Salem 31 July 1677. **Abigail,** m. at Salem 14 Jan. 1702-3 Samuel Upton, both liv. Salem 1731. Poss. also: **James**(5).

16 **WILLIAM**(15), of age by Feb. 1691. Jury 1702. Lists 268a, 269b. Rem. ab. 1705 to Salem, where he was selling his lands at Wells and Cape Porpus in 1713 and 1718, and d. 23 Sep. 1721. He m. 1st at Wells 6 Dec. 1694 Rachel Littlefield, 2d 5 Apr. 1706 Elizabeth (Bush) Searle, wid. of Edw. Ch: **Rebecca,** b. in Wells 30 Sep. 1695, mar. Marbleh. 6 Nov. 1718 John Brown. **Rachel,** m. 2 Apr. 1724 Joseph Goodwin. By 2d w: **Elizabeth,** b. 22 Aug. 1708, m. Salem 1 Sep. 1726 John Brown. **Benjamin,** b. at Salem 24 June 1709, d.y. **Benjamin,** b. 24 Sep. 1710. **Hannah,** b. 4 July 1712, m. 23 Jan. 1734-5 John Prince. **Mary,** b. 2 Dec. 1713, m. Salem 13 Dec. 1733 Wm. Brown. **William,** b. 4 Oct. 1715. **Lydia,** b. 22 May 1717, m. 17 Nov. 1737 Wm. Cook.

**FRYE.** One Adrian Frye was of 'Hooke,' Wilts, in 1601, another of Lydiard-Millicent, Wilts 1603, another mar. Margaret Bryant in Henbury, co. Glouc., in 1627.

1 **ADRIAN,** first app. in 1663, in Eliot. In 1664 Abraham Conley, Adrian Frye and Elizabeth Conley were wit. agst. Tho. Crawley, and in 1675 A. C. was liv. with A. F. In Philip's War he moved to Portsm. Lists 30, 331b, 298. He m. **Hannah** White, d. of Robert. In 1692 they deeded their homestead to s. Wm. for life supp., deed proved by wit. 16 Sep. 1695. Adm. on her est. to grs. Wm. 23 Nov. 1709. Their poster. were largely Friends. Ch: **Eleanor,** b. ab. 1668, m. John Brooks(4), John Bishop. **William,** town gr. 1694. **Sarah,** m. (Court Apr. 1695) Nicholas Morrell, **Joseph,** taken capt. ab. 1695, ag. 15 or 16, still in capt. in 1711. See Coleman's Capt. i. 383-8. List 99. **Elizabeth,** m. 3 Mar. 1700-1 her'cous. James Thompson. **Joanna,** m. (Court Oct. 1700) Tho. Muzeet. **Adrian,** weaver, m. 8 June 1705 Mercy Chapman(4). In 1708 bot in Portsm., sentinel at the fort. List 298. They sold out in Eliot, 'glazier,' in 1717.

2 **JOHN,** in 1665 was servant to James Johnson. N. H. Deeds 2. 108a.

3 **WILLIAM**(1), had the homestead. Lists 290, 291, 296-298. He m. Hannah Hill, d. of John, liv. 1727. In 1713 he had the homestead, 'Frye's Point,' at the mouth of Sturgeon Creek, reserving the burying ground. Liv. 1745. Ch: **William,** b. 7 Jan. 1694, m. 1725 Abigail Varney. Will 1771. 8 ch. **John,** b. 26 Aug. 1698, m. Elizabeth Crockett(5). Ch. **Benjamin,** b. 10 Nov. 1701, m. 22 Dec.

1732 Sarah Dow(7 John). He died in Mar. 1754, she 12 May 1790. 8 ch. **Joseph**, b. 3 Feb. 1704, weaver, m. 24 Dec. 1735 Susannah Knowlton. 10 ch., named in will. **Sarah**, b. 9 May 1710, m. Tobias Hanson.

4 —— Goody (Frie?) 1674. List 246.

**FRYER**, common in Yorkshire and adjoining counties south.

1 **EMANUEL**, alias Nathaniel(4).

2 **JAMES**(4), master mariner, in Philip's War was fatally shot at Richmond Isl. Mugg himself came with him to Portsm., where he soon d. ab. Oct. 1676. List 326c. He m. Jane Scarlett, b. 21 Sep. 1653, dau. of John. Son: **James**, b. Boston 3 Mar. 1673, rememb. in his grf. Scarlett's will, chose Wm. Robie gdn. in 1691.

3 **JOSHUA**(4), master mariner, wit. papers from 1681. Lists 57, 315b. He m. by 1690 Abigail Frost(2). Will 19 Apr. 1703—1 Mar. 1703-4, made w. sole benef., who m. (int. 11 Dec. 1714) Wm. Moody. No ch.

4 ‡*CAPT. **NATHANIEL**, ±43 in 1669, ±54 in 1679, autograph -Emmanuel Friar- in 1653 (Middlesex Ct. files), changed to Nathaniel. John Hollicome's w. Joanna was d. of his own sis. Wilmot Tucker. In 1700 he dep. that he had been a dweller mostly on the Piscataqua river since the yr. 1648, but his ch. are recorded in Boston—a mariner and trading coaster until he brot his fam. to Great Isl. During many years he shifted his allegiance bet. the two provinces across the river, responsive to polit. or bus. consid. Selectm. of Portsm. 1664-66, 1669, 1670, 1673, 1675, 1677; selectm. of Kit. 1673, 1675, 1677. Com.t.e.s.c. Kit. 1676, 1677. He signed Maine petitions in 1662, 1686, was one of the Maine peace commrs. in 1678, sought probate appointments in either province. In 1686 he held lic. to sell liquors in Kit. and Cape Elizabeth and again in 1700. Aft. buying at the Shoals he was 'of Piscataqua in New Eng.' 1661, in Nov. 1664 of no place, in May 1686 'of Kittery,' 26 Oct. 1688, not knowing which way to jump, he was 'of piscataway river.' In the Maine courts from Oct. 1686 to Dec. 1687 he had been a judge on the bench. In Oct. 1694 he called himself 'Nathaniel Fryer, Sr., sometimes of Portsm. in New Eng. now of the Province of Maine.' In N. H. he was Rep. 1666, county treas. 1668-1680, Com.t.e.s.c. 1666-1670, Justice of the County Ct. under Dudley and Andros, usually Councillor under Gov. Allen until his death. His crowning glory was in 1695 as President of the Council. Lists 25, 303, 311ab, 356h, 356l (Portsm.), 225a, 226, 267a, 312bcfg, 313afg, 315b, 317, 319, 323, 324, 326bc, 330ac, 331b, 333a, 335a, 33, 48-51, 53, 54, 57-60, 64, 66, 79, 88, 91, 96. He d. 13 Aug. 1705, altho his will,

dated 10 Feb. 1704-5, was not proved until 1715. He m. 1st Christian, widow of James Allison of Boston, liv. 1674; 2d 29 Oct. 1679 Dorothy Woodbridge, a grdau. of Gov. Tho. Dudley. In 1718 she was liv. in Newbury, drawing on Mr. Elliot for her annuity; d. in Apr. 1723. Ch: **James**, b. 7 Oct. 1653. **Sarah**, b. 20 July 1656, m. Hon. Robert Elliot(6). **Elizabeth**, b. 1 Nov. 1657, unm. 8 Mar. 1671-2, m. by 1686 Hon. John Hinckes. **Nathaniel**, b. 9 Dec. 1660. **Joshua**. These do not expl. the record of 27 June 1673 when David Campbell was bef. Ct. for slurring 'Mr. Nathl. Fryer, Mr. & Mrs. Harve, with more of the said Fryer's family.'

5 **NATHANIEL**(4), extrem. unobtr. if he did not live away. Lists 57, 317, 315ab. Not taxed 1702. Must have been father of Nathaniel, given land in his grfr.'s will, and his br. **John**, fisherman, who sold it in 1725. Taxed 1720. Coroner's j. 28 Jan. 1720-1.

**FULFORD**, Richard, Round Pond, Muscongus, m. Elizabeth Pierce, who d. early. In Philip's War he fled to Salem, was there 1680, returned and driven away again in 1690. Lists 121, 124. Ch: **Francis**, fisherman, m. in Marbleh. 20 Feb. 1709-10 Elizabeth Welcome. Of Marbl. in 1739 he sold his int. in his father's land in Muscongus, but was of Boston 16 Nov. 1741 when adm. gr. to wid. Elizabeth. 9 ch. rec. **Elizabeth**, m. in Marb. 6 Jan. 1696-7 Samuel Martin. Liv. at Muscongus ab. 1715—1723-5. Dau. Sarah m. 31 Oct. 1721 Hezekiah Eggleston of Boston, altho called sis. by John Brown in 1735. Her son Hezekiah jr. claimed the Maine land later.

**FULLER**, occup. surname, finisher of cloth, in the E. and S. E. of England.

1 **GILES**, son of Roger of Topcroft in Norfolk (R. F. and Jane Gowen m. in Redenhall 24 Apr. 1600), his nearest kinsman in this county Dr. Matthew of Barnstable. He was first at Dedham and came to Hampton with the first from there. Dedham made a joint gr. to G. F. and Thomas Ward 23 Nov. 1638, and the latter was app. adm. on his death. In 1650 a seat in the meeting house was assigned to his 'wife appointed,' no further ment. Gr.j. 1648, 1660, 1667. Lists 391ab, 392ab, 393ab. He d. 'suddenly, in his own house' 6 Apr. 1676. Adm. was issued to T. W. and Richard Currier, but his nephew Thomas Thurton, s. of his only surv. sister Susannah, came over with suff. proofs to claim the estate.

2 **JOHN**, ±24 in 1668, ±38 in 1681, nephew of (5), s. of John of Ipsw., whose will discrim. against his sons John and Wm. because their uncle had promised to provide for them. Lists 54, 396. He m. 19 Mar. 1677 Rachel Brabrook, presently accu. of witch-

craft. 'Sister Cox' in Suff. Ct. files 1213 was evid. not his but Weare's 'sister,' Prudence (Marston) Swain-Cox, her husband Swain having been br. of Weare's wife. Will 9 July —2 Dec. 1719 names 5 ch: John, b. 12 Jan. 1678, d. 19 Jan. 1715. James, b. 27 Mar. 1679. W. Mary (Brown?). List 338b. 3 ch. rec. in Hampt., 4 in Rye, 6 liv. in 1761. Benoni, d.s.p. 25 Feb. 1761, 'ae. 83.' In 1760 he had deeded one-half of his homestead and livestock to David Batchelder whose purchases from the heirs include Love Wormwood of Epsom, Ithamar and w. Mary Seavey, Henry and w. Elizabeth Seavey, and Fullers, Tho. of Sandown, Joseph of Chester (m. Joanna), John of Epsom, Jeremiah of Portsm. Elizabeth, unm. in 1725. Rachel, m. (int. 29 July 1719) John Bond of Salisbury. Thomas, b. 27 Aug. 1695, m. Hannah Chase(4). Settled in Sandown, miller. Will 1765–1766 names all but 2 of 10 ch. rec.

3 JOSEPH, soldier Kit. (1704?). List 289.

4 SAMUEL, with wife Mary, of Salem in 1718, sold ½ of 600 a. on the Kennebunk Riv. Y. D. viii. 203. See Littlefield.

5 *WILLIAM, ±63 in 1671, gunsmith, came on -The Abigail- in 1635, ag. 25, with John, ag. 15, his br. who m. Elizabeth Emerson and sett. in Ipsw. Liv. at Ipsw. on his 4 a. lot at the west end of Heart Break hill. Soldier in Pequot war. In 1639 he kept the mill. Freeman 2 June 1641. Given Hampton gr. in 1640. Gr.j. 1641, 1663, 1664, 1669, 1672, 1675-1678. Selectm. 9 yrs. 1644-1677. Rep. 1661, 1667. Lists 391a, 392ab, 393ab, 394, 396, 398, 49, 52-54, 65. In 1663 the Court was held at his house. His w. Elizabeth d. 24 July 1642; 2d w. Frances d. 14 Dec. 1699, ag. 'above 80.' Lists 393a, 394. His d. Hannah, b. 8 Aug. 1641, must have d.y. He d. 26 May 1693. See int. will, 18 Mar. 1690-1, naming relations and others. He had already deeded lands to his nephews, William and w. Susannah in 1681, John in 1683.

6 WILLIAM, see his br. (2). App. liv. in Hampton with his uncle(5), 1671-1684 earlier or later, but ret. to Ipsw. or beyond. In 1679 Susannah (Perkins) Buswell, wid. of Isaac jr., had rem. his household goods, and 29 June 1680 m. W. F. jr. Kn. ch: Abigail, rec. in Ipsw. 10 Mar. 1690.

FURBER, Furbur, occurs in the southern counties, early in Cheshire.

1 JETHRO(2), mariner, Portsm. Lists 51, 52, 329. He m. 19 Oct. 1678 Amy Cowell(2). Inv. taken 29 June 1686, wid. lic. retail. 9 Oct. 1686, adm. to Nathl. and Amy Ayers(6) 26 Dec. 1692. Only ch: Jethro, 'master and mariner,' Portsm. List 339. D. 9 Apr. 1738, ae. 56 (grst.) He m. by 1708 Elizabeth Morrill, liv. 1740. Ch. 6 sons bap.,

incl. Jethro, 17 Oct. 1708, shipjoiner, Boston, m. 11 July 1728 Mary Manwaring.

2 *SERGT. WILLIAM, dep. in 1676 ±62, that he came in 1635 in the -Angel Gabriel- along with Mr. John Cogswell, whom he found liv. at Ipswich in Nov. aft. the wreck, and hired himself for one yr., sleeping on the same bed with Deacon Samuel Haines. At Dover Neck by 1639, he settled in Newington, where he and his posterity owned the ferry to Oyster River, the landing at 'Welch Cove' still pointed out. He was Rep. in 1648, often gr.j. and selectm., and was public adm. on several estates. In 1644 Edw. Starbuck, Richard Waldron and W. F. were app. weirsmen for life; in 1654 rent agent for the town, com. on Dover-Kittery bounds; in 1675 W. F., Anthony Nutter and John Woodman were the com. to act with other towns for relieving sufferers from the war. Lists 371, 351ab, 352, 354abc, 355ab, 356abcefghk, 359ab, 363b, 311c (Dover), 45, 46, 49, 52-54, 57, 62. He d. Apr. —Nov. 1694. In 1662 he acted for John, s. of Wm. Clark, late of Salem, in claiming a little neck of land on Ipswich river where a house formerly stood. (Ipsw. Deeds ii. 58 [117]). He m. bef. 1647 Elizabeth Clark, d. of Lt. Wm. Clark of London, Watertown, Ipswich and Salem by his 1st w. Elizabeth (Quick). She was ±47 in 1676, liv. 1683. How their dau. Bridget, w. of Tho. Bickford, in 1704 called Sarah, w. of John Pinder, and Eleanor, w. of Nathaniel Meader, 'cousins' has not been solved. Ch: William, b. ab. 1645. Elizabeth, m. 9 Nov. 1664 John Dam(3). Jethro. Hannah, m. (Court 1671) Roger Plaisted. Bethia, lived in President John Cutt's fam., given 50s. in his will. Abigail, liv. in Hon. Richard Martyn's fam. in 1677, m. Charlestown 28 Oct. 1687 Ebenezer Orton. She d. of smallpox 27 Mar. 1691 and he was drowned 7 Aug. 1694. Susannah, b. 5 May 1664, m. John Bickford(15). Bridget, m. Tho. Bickford(2). Moses, '3d son,' was deeded land by his father 1 Dec. 1686, taxed in Portsm. 1688, d. bef. his father, s.p.

3 *LIEUT. WILLIAM(2), ±30 in 1676, ±57 in 1702. Liv. with his. f. and had the homestead. Ensign 1695, Lt. 1697. Rep. 1692 till his death. Lists 353, 359ab, 52, 54, 57-59, 62, 68, 69, 96. He d. 14 Sep. 1707; adm. to wid. 4 Nov. 1707 and to s. Wm. 6 Mar. 1712. He m. 1st Esther, poss. d. of Edw. Starbuck, called 'dau.' by (2) in 1676; 2d 13 Aug. 1694 Elizabeth (Heard) Nute, who died 9 Nov. 1705 (List 96); 3d in 1706 Elizabeth (Martyn) Kennard, who m. 3d 27 Dec. 1708 Benj. Nason. Ch: William, d. 20 Mar. 1757, ae. 84. Lists 57, 343. Wife Sarah (Nute), d. 28 Apr. 1762, ae. 86. 6 ch. incl. Elizabeth who mar. James Webber. Jethro, had half of the homestead. Adm. 2 Mar. 1715-6 to widow

Leah (Nute), who m. 2d 16 May 1716 Hatevil Nutter. 6 ch. incl. Jethro who m. Phebe Fabyan(3). Joshua, mariner, Portsm. Lost in wreck 25 miles from home. Will 19 May 1708—6 Dec. 1712. Wife Elizabeth (Kennard), mar. 2d 26 May 1715 Francis Ditty from 'Winbird' (Wimborne?), co. Dorset. Ch. d.s.p.: Joshua, 5½ at father's death. Edward, 1 at father's death.

**FURBUSH**
1 DANIEL(2), ±35 in 1700, had the homestead. Lists 94, 291, 296-298. The Ind. 4 Oct. 1692 took his young wife and baby and her sis. captive. He m. Dorothy Pray. Adm. to her 11 Feb. 1745-6. Ch: Daniel, b. 9 Mar. 1690, m. 18 Dec. 1718 Anna Lord. List 298. Ch. Rebecca, b. 19 Apr. 1694, m. Benj. Goold. John, Lt., b. 1699, m. Hannah Littlefield (Dependence). Officer in Dummer's War. He bot in his uncle John's est. List 298. Adm. to wid. 5 Jan. 1756. Ch. Joanna, b. 14 July 1701, m. Saml. Fernald. William, b. 19 Mar. 1703-4. He and his s. Wm. enlisted in 1757. The father suffered impris. in France and d. soon aft. getting back. His wid. Sarah (Preble mar. 7 Oct. 1731), m. 2d 11 Dec. 1760 Samuel Holmes. Ch. Dorothy, m. Joseph Hartford. Sarah, m. 13 Apr. 1733 Hatevil Hall. Catherine, m. Robert Allen(12 Francis). Joseph, Berwick, d. 5 Apr. 1795. He m. 20 May 1734 Elizabeth Meads. 10 ch. Benjamin, Lebanon, m. Hannah Hussey. Ch. Mary, in 1736 accu. Zachariah Emery; m. 1743 Benj. Roberts.
2 WILLIAM, in 1659 taxed in Dover, by 1664 was settled on the fam. homestead in the N. W. corner of Eliot, 40 rods on the river. Here is a graveyard with ab. 30 unmarked stones. In 1674 in N. H. and in 1686 in Me. he was prosec. for getting Indians drunk. In the second war he withdrew to Newcastle. Lists 356e, 364, 30, 315a, 288, 298. In 1679 he was fined for abusing, and Rebecca for striking, the constable; in 1683 he and his wife for talking against the government. In 1695 the wid. Christian Furbush, ±43, was subp. as wit. with others of Newcastle, she had watched in Robt. White's sickness. His will was missing, dated 27 Aug. 1694, brought into ct. 2 Aug. 1722, was disal. bec. the estate had been dist. by an agreem. of the heirs dated 21 Mar. 1701. This provided that Daniel have the homestead and pay 'any thirds that may appear due,' but if any part of it should be recovered by Wm. Wittum, all should share the loss. Bethia Furbush to have her portion. Enoch Hutchins to have the land at Spruce Creek already in poss. The outlands to be divided by Andrew Neale, Tho. Thompson, John and William Furbush, John to be William's guard. Ch: Daniel, b. ab. 1665. John,

mariner, d.s.p. Adm. 24 Nov. 1701 to Daniel. Hope, m. 12 May 1693 Enoch Hutchins; 2d Wm. Wilson. Catherine, m. ab. 1694 Andrew Neale. Sarah, m. ab. 1698 Tho. Thompson. Bethia, m. in 1705 Joseph Goold. William, over 14 in 1701, d. in Craven, S. C. 20 Nov. 1724, leaving sons John, who d.s.p. 9 Oct. 1739, and William, 'late of Craven Co. but now (1755) resident in Kittery.'
FURNELL, John, sued by Richard Foxwell for debt, 1637. Arthur Browne denied that he and Mr. Mackworth owed J. F. ¾ lb. of beaver in 1640. See Fernald, of which the name is a variant.

**FURSON**
1 CHRISTOPHER, York wit. 1653. Allowed 1 yr. to have his wife come over.
2 THOMAS, at Bloody Point by 1642. The house and crop of corn, formerly the right of Thomas Furson, were sold in 1651 by John Lavis to Michael Brawn. He had rem. to Portsm., where he sold 'Furson's' (Noble's) Isl. in 1652. Lists 42, 78, 354a, 323, 325, 326a, 330b, 342. He mar. by 1656 Jane, wid. of Tho. Turpin, named in Mrs. Batchelder's will in 1660. In 1674 she and her (Turpin) grch. pulled up Richard Cummings' corn to make him start a title suit.
Fuz, Allen, see Virrs.
Gabsley, see Yabsley.
Gage, John, Wells soldier. List 267b. See also Hubbard (9).
Gager, John, had early Hampton gr. List 392a.

**GALE**, a South of Eng. name.
1 EDMUND, coaster, Beverly and Marbleh., bot John Lewis's land at Back Cove, Falm., from Nathl. Wallis in Feb. 1678-9, and liv. there bet. the wars. Ptn. Andros for 200 a. at No. Yarmouth. List 34. W. Sarah Dixey (Capt. Wm. of Bev.). 10 ch. bp. Salem and Bev., of whom Azor, Esq., of Marbleh., List 229, claimed the Me. lands, his heirs selling in 1731. Y. D. 17.83.
2 HENRY, Piscataqua witn. 1660. Y.D.1.98.
3 HUGH, millwright, prob. came with Wm. Ellingham from Norton Folgate in par. of St. Leonard, Shoreditch, London. They built mills at Sturgeon Creek by 1648, sold 15 Oct. 1651, and at York by 1652. Tr. j. 1653. York gr. 2 Jan. 1653-4; propr. 1655. Appeared last in June 1655 when sued by Capt. Clarke and Rishworth, who bot his int. in the York mills Oct. 1653. Lists 273, 275, 276. No fam. noted.
4 JOHN, tailor, Great Isl., liv. in half of Wm. he and Francis Tucker bot from Wm. Love. Roger Kelly acted for him in 1681, when sued by Lewis Tucker. Will 20 Dec. 1687—8 Mar. 1687-8 names only w. Sarah, who was taxed G. Isl. Dec. 1688.

5 **WILLIAM** (Geale or Heale), Saco 1688. List 249. One Wm. G. was rated in Wells 1726.

**Gallow**, Oliver, List 1. See Callow.

**GALLOWAY.** 1 **Benjamin**, m. at Kit. 31 Jan. 1699 Elizabeth Hodsdon (3), who m. 2d 19 Nov. 1702 Benj. Richards. See Garraway.

2 **HUGH**, Star Isl. 1694, with w. Anne. List 308b. One of the name, servant of Geo. Nowell, served in Philip's War. H. G., 'an aged man,' d. 14 Jan. 1729 in Ipsw., where younger Galloways found, incl. Hugh jr.

3 **THOMAS**, ag. 22, seaman at Portsm. 1690. List 333a.

**GALLUP.** 1 **Nathaniel**, at Monhegan 1654, List 112.

2 **SAMUEL**, List 112, prob. br. to (1) and son of John of Bost., who with others had P/A from Thos. Purchase in 1641 to sue Eastern men.

**Gamage**, see Clifford (2).

**Gambling**, see Penhallow.

**GAMMON,** found in Devonshire. Gamen or Gamon an ancient forename. One Robert Gammon m. Alice Norris at East Stower, co. Dorset, 17 June 1633.

1 **PHILIP**, b. ab. 1659-1660 (±71 in Mar. 1730-1), fisherman, Falmouth 1689, m. early Mary Parrott (John). Untraced foll. the War, he was liv. on Parrott's Point, Purpoodock, ab. 1702; York 1705 employed by Nathl. Raynes, who was his atty. that yr. in John Woodman's suit for trespass. One Gammon with his shallop taken at Winter Harbor 1705. Kit. 1707-1718, Portsm. by 1722 when Jethro Furber sued Capt. Nathl. Odiorne on acct., one item '2 gal. rum to father Gammon.' Again at Purpoodock on the Parrott farm 1738, when John and Sarah (Parrott) Green(17) q. c. to them, with ret. to Piscataqua, after deeding the dwg. and 30 a. to s. Francis. Kit. 1739; w. Mary at Portsm. 1743. Lists 228c, 339. Presum. ch., tho only the 1st by record: **Francis**, bound by his fa. in 1714 to pay a debt; Portsm. 1728-1732, Purpoodock by 1739. William, rated to 2d Par., Falm., 1743, poss. his son or bro. **Samuel**, drowned at Portsm. 26 Oct. 1728. **William**, Kittery, m. 31 Oct. 1717 Mary Hepworth of Portsm.; taxed Rye 1721-1728. 3 ch. bp. So. Church 1719-1723 One Mrs. Gammon, ag. 80, was in Portsm. poor-ho. 1781. **John**; his signa. on a paper in Richard Elliot's est. 1729. **David**, m. 26 Oct. 1732 Elizabeth Barnes of Portsm.; liv. there 1753. Ch. One Wm. Gammon 'so-called,' s. of Joanna Barnat, was b. at Braintree 26 Apr. 1715.

2 **ROBERT**, Cape Bonawagon 1672. Constable, Clerk of the Writs, Sergeant, Comr., all in 1674. O. F. at Pemaquid 22 July 1674. Alternate Associate 1675. Lists 13, 15, 83. Driven to Mass., he was sued in Essex Co. by Tho. Edwards in Nov. 1677, Henry Adams his bondsm.; at same Ct. John Ford ack. judgm. to him. Boston was his home aft. he bot near the Second Meeting-ho. in Dec. 1678; there boatman. Last found 1695. Wid. Grace d. in Boston 7 Aug. 1702, ag. 74. Ch: **Mary**, presum., m. bef. 1686 Wm. Shortridge, mariner, Boston. Her will, widow, 1703—1709, names son and dau. under age, br.-in-law John and sis. Grace Stevens. **Grace**, m. in Boston 6 June 1694 John Stevens. Rec. ch. incl. Gammon and Robert.

**Gansby**, see Gattensby.

**GARDE.**

**ROGER**, Mr., York, woolen draper from Bideford, co. Devon, where he m. Philippa Gist 4 July 1610 and she was bur. 1 Feb. 1634-5. He reached York bef. 11 June 1637, when he had gr. from the patentees in consid. of the great charge and travel he had bestowed for the advancement of the plantation. His ho. ment. Mar. 1639. Lists 272, 281. A promin. figure during his few yrs. here and highly trusted by Mr. Tho. Gorges, who left him agent to 'let and set his whole est.' when he went to Eng. (Y. D. 1.2.14). Recorder of York Ct. 1640; Alderman, Recorder and 1st Town Clerk of York 1641; Mayor 1644-5, and presiding officer at trial of Catherine Cornish, who named him in her accusations, thus prob. hastening his death and providing the reason he 'cried out much of the people they had broken his heart; and so grew some time mazed with it'; bur. with his arms, Mr. Hull preaching the funeral sermon, bef. 28 July 1645. Ch. bp. in Bideford: **Elizabeth**, bp. 16 Feb. 1613-4. **Rebecca**, bp. 9 May 1616, m. there 25 Nov. 1641 Wm. Champlain. *John, bp. 8 Nov. 1618, m. a dau. of Wm. and Christian Tetherly of Bideford, sis. of Gabriel of Me. A Boston merchant 1662, he took from John Davis(18) and w. Mary a q. c. to his fa.'s lands made over to her form. husb. for debt in 1645; at their ho. in York he confirmed their deed to John Lamb. (Y. D. 1.163). Rhode Island 1664, 1668, dealing with Wm. Tetherly in Boston; poss. the same Mr. J. G. adm. inhab. of Portsm., R. I., 19 Oct. 1666, Dep. 1667. **Thomas**, bp. 21 Jan. 1620-1. **Patience**, bp. 13 July 1623. **Mary**, bp. 1 Feb. 1626-7. Mr. John G., a Fayal merchant, 1647, undoubtedly closely relat. to Roger, and his w. Harte were at Newport, where both d., she 16 Sept. 1660, ag. 55; he 7 Aug. 1665, ag. 61. John Champlin, form. of Fayal, in 1675 was

heir to one of the R. I. Johns. See Hist. of York i. 104; P. & Ct. i. xiii; N. E. Reg. 82.69, 185.

**GARDNER**, a common English occupational name. Became 52nd in N. E.

1 **'SIR' CHRISTOPHER** (Gardiner), and his companion from Eng., Mary Grove, both much written of in Mass. as a Gorges agent. Both came to Me., she as the bride of Tho. Purchase of Pejepscot, he to stay in the Purchase ho. for months bef. reaching Bristol, Eng., shortly bef. 31 Aug. 1632. In Me. Ct. 1650 Richard Tucker sued Tho. Purchase for a warming pan borrowed by Sir C. G. in his name '9 y. since or thereab.' and a fowling piece bot of him 6 mo. later; knowl. of both transactions Purchase disowned. See 3 Mass. H.S.Col. 8.320, Proc. Mass. H. Socy. vol. 22.

2 **DAVID**, Portsm., tailor. List. 339. Will 21 May—7 Aug. 1723 names w. Margaret (Cate 1), 4 of 5 ch. bap. 1715-1723, br. James G., br.-in-law Joshua Cate. She m. 2d John Wyatt; again a wid. 1769. One Wid. G. was taxed in Portsm. Jan. 1731-2.

3 **HENRY**, owner in the Laconia Co. List 41.

4 **JAMES**. See (2).

5 **JOHN**, of co. Gloucester, Eng. Church rec. indicate that his w. Mary, m. in Portsm. 3 Nov. 1715, was dau. of John and Joanna (Dore) Bourne.

6 **NATHANIEL**, Bost. mercht., bot an int. in the Dover and Squamscot Patents in 1649 and sold in 1662, then of London. Suff. D. 4.51.

7 **RICHARD**, taxed Str. Bk. 1713.

8 **ROBERT**, mariner on a mastship and ab. the Piscat. several yrs., witn. deed from Barefoot to Robt. Wadleigh of Kit. 1666; twice sued by Thos. Withers 1666-7. Known to Henry Greenland, he dep. in 1670 ab. his plan to kidnap Mr. Rich. Cutt. App. the same Robt. who dep. an intimate knowl. of the Wadleigh-Lissen mill in 1669. List 380.

9 **THOMAS**, Esq., Lieut. and Capt., Pemaquid, evid. an untraced connec. of the Salem fam., bot a Beverly dwg. 13 May 1661, which housed him but a short time, if ever, and was sold by his atty. Thos. G. jr., of Salem, in 1675. Commander on the Penobscot 1662 and estab. a perm. home in Pemaquid. J. P. 1665 and later. On commit. to organize the Eastern govt., in May 1674, and lic. in July 1674 to keep ho. of entert. for his fishermen. County treas. 7 Oct. 1674 and same day put in command at Pema. as Lieut., altho next yr. he was susp. of trad. with the Fr. and Ind. Called Capt. 1675. In 1676 he was at Monhegan with the Pema.

force asking for help; 13 Sept. depos. at Bost. ab. affairs East, but was again in command at Pema. when Waldron arriv. there 22 Feb. 1677. Lists 2,13,15,4,83. Presum. going to Mass., he appar. was the T. G. of Salem who had P/A from John Earthy in June 1685 and the Capt. G. who was relieved at Berw. in Oct. 1689. Wife unkn. Only kn. ch: Mary, m. John Earthy.

**GAREY, Geary,** (See also Geare), **John,** York, was of Kittery when he m. (int. 21 Oct. 1720) Abigail Thompson (Alexr.). In 1723 he and Chas. White bot land and a mill site in York. 9 ch. 1721-1736.

**GARLAND.** One Peter G. had ch. bap. at Northam, co. Devon, 1601-1615. Ano. Peter, s. of Christopher, was bap. there 1613.

1 **FRANCIS**, at Mt. Desert with his ketch 1677. D. H. 6.183.

2 **GEORGE**, tenant at Nonesuch under Jordan, best kn. for his marital diffic. with Sarah Mills and Wid. Hitchcock. Found first in Ct. 2 July 1662, for freq. Sarah Mills's ho., when susp. of having a w. in Eng.; both indicted for liv. together in Nov. 1665, again in Sept. 1668, when ord. to mar. within a mo. Sarah G., 'a kn. vagabond Quaker coming from Black Point,' ord. whipped from town to town, Boston to Scarb., Aug. 1668. He was oft. abs. from meeting. Sued by John Parker for debt 1667. His intended mar. with Lucretia, wid. of Lt. Richard Hitchcock, was forbidden 10 Sept. 1672, he still owning hims. Sarah Mills's husb.; despite Ct. proceedings and his flogging, their relations contin. until her death, when he disapp., poss. k. at the same time. P. & Ct. ii. Ch. by Lucretia: **Jabez.**

3 **JABEZ**(2), Dover, witn. deed of br.-in-law James Emery(3) 2 Jan. 1694, and appar. liv. early at Berwick. An attempted ret. to his mo.'s old home ended in Aug. 1703 when his garri. at Winter Harbor was taken. In N. H. he sued Wm. Frost in Sept. 1705. K. by Ind. 1710, called by rumor -Jacob-. List 96. W. Dorcas Heard(5). Ch. rec. Dover: **Jabez,** b. 19 Feb. 1693-4, m. one Abigail who was liv. 1736. List 358d. Ch. rec.: **Reuben,** b. 20 Feb. 1723. **Dorcas,** b. 3 Apr. 1698, m. Ephraim Ricker. **Rebecca,** b. 25 Jan. 1699-1700. One Rebecca of Biddef. m. (int. 22 Aug. 1736) Walter Murch. **Ebenezer,** b. 14 Mar. 1703-4, m. 2 Mar. 1720-1 Abigail Powell, who d. 28 Feb. 1770. Will, of Somersw., 1777—1778. 5 ch. **Nathaniel,** b. 12 Apr. 1706, bp. on sick bed 8 Mar. 1740-1; adm. 27 Apr. 1742 to wid. Sarah. Ch. **Lydia,** b. 17 Feb. 1707-8. Presum. unrec. ch: ?**Elizabeth,** m. 16 Nov. 1720 Jos. Ricker. ?**Hannah,** m. bef. 1717 John

Ricker. ?John, m. Elizabeth Downes (Tho. 6 jr.). 3 or m. ch.

4 JACOB(6), farmer, m. in Newb. 17 Jan. 1681 Rebecca Sears, dau. of Tho. and Mary (Hilton 11), and liv. there a few yrs. bef. ret. to Hampt., where her mo. deeded them ho. and land, 1699. Lists 396, 400. Both liv. 1731. Ch., 1st two rec. Newb.: Jacob, b. 26 Oct., d. 19 Nov. 1682. Rebecca, b. 3 Dec. 1683, d.y. Jacob, b. 3 July 1686, m. 1st 26 Apr. 1708 Hannah Sanborn (Josiah), 2d 24 Oct. 1723 Sarah Drake(2). Adm. 25 Dec. 1735 to wid. and s. Jos. 5 + 1 ch. Mary, m. Tho. Dearborn (5 jr.). Sarah, b. 24 Feb. 1690. Tabitha, bp. with two fol. 11 Dec. 1698. Thomas, b. 9 Mar. 1692, d. bef. 1703. Joseph, b. 29 Dec. 1697. John and Elizabeth, twins, b. 28 Sept. 1700. Thomas, bp. 3 Jan. 1703, m. 23 May 1726 Elizabeth Moulton (John); mov. from Rye to Biddef. ab. 1731. 5 or m. ch.

5 JOHN, came in the -Fortune- 1638, returned. List 21.

6 JOHN, Hampton, b. ±1621. He was in Exeter 26 Aug. 1650, worked in Humphrey Wilson's mill, and in 1651 was acc. of taking the town timber without warr. and of making reproachful speeches ag. Mr. Dudley. Taxed Hampton 1653. Lists 376b (1652), 393b. M. 1st in Hampt. 26 Oct. 1652 Elizabeth Chapman(1), 2d 26 Oct. 1654 Elizabeth (Philbrick), wid. of Tho. Chase (6). List 394. His will 15 Nov. 1671, ag. ab. 50; d. 4 Jan. 1671-2. Wid. m. 3d 19 Jan. 1673-4 Henry Robie. Ch. by 2d w: John, b. 11 Mar. 1655. Jacob, b. 20 Dec. 1656. Peter, b. 25 Nov. 1659.

7 *JOHN(6), mill-owner, recd. the homestead. Constable 1693-94. Rep. 1693. Gr. j. 1695. Lists 396, 52, 399a. M. 1st 24 Dec. 1673 Elizabeth Robinson, who d. 15 Apr. 1715, ag. 62; 2d 29 Sept. 1715 at Greenl. Mary Philbrick. Ch: Elizabeth, b. 16 July 1674, unm. 1715. John, b. 12 Oct. 1675, d. 6 Oct. 1676. Esther, b. 6 Apr. 1679, m. 12 Jan. 1701-2 Wm. Powell. Peter, b. 10 Dec. 1681. Either he or Peter (9 jr.) m. Elizabeth Clifford. Mary, b. 14 Mar. 1683, m. Israel Clifford (2 jr.). Sarah, b. 18 Oct. 1685.

8 PETER, dep. in Saco Ct. 18 Sept. 1640 that he had freq. Casco Riv. ab. 14 yrs. A mariner with N. Y. connections, he was of Charlest. 1637, Boston 1638, Dover 1640. Walter Abbott(5) his atty. in N. H. 1645. Lists 21, 351b, 71. One Peter and w. Joan had dau. Mary rec. Bost. 1654. Peter a Mystic Side abuttor in 1662. Robt. Wyar and John Garland, called boys, and two girls were in Mass. Ct., 1643.

9 PETER(6), mariner, Hampt. First w. Elizabeth d. 16 Feb. 1688; 2d w. Sarah Taylor (John), outliv. him and m. 2d Saml.

Dow(9). Ch: Peter, b. 4 Oct. 1686. He (or his cous. 7), m. 12 Dec. 1720 Elizabeth Clifford, dau. of Isaac(1) and Elizabeth (Pulsifer), and had 6 ch. bp. Hampt. She was a wid. in 1757. Samuel, b. 2 Feb. 1688, shoemaker, liv. Kingston. Jonathan, b. 28 Oct. 1689, shoemaker, m. 21 Oct. 1714 Rachel Dow(9), who d. 22 June 1755. His will 25 Mar., d. 11 May 1760. 12 ch. *John, b. 13 Apr. 1692. Taxed Rye 1725, liv. there 1752. A large landowner in several towns. Rep. 1737. M. 12 Jan. 1716 Elizabeth Dearborn (4). 9 ch. rec. Hampt. James. In 1719, single, he sold share in Hogpen farm. James G., a sergt. in Col. Westbrook's co. 1724-5. One Garland had ch. bp. Falm. in 1727 and a s. Peter in 1731. James and w. Mary of Falm. 1733. Mary, b. 7 Sept. 1699, m. Henry Moulton. Abigail, b. 25 Feb. 1704, m. Worthington Moulton.

10 WILLIAM, Mr., called 'friend' by Winter, retd. to Eng. from Richmond Isl., July 1636, carrying letter from Winter to Trelawny.

Garman, see German.

Garnsey, see Guernsey.

Garraway, Benjamin, seaman on the Bristol ship —Charles & Sarah—; rioting, ct. Newc. Nov. 1699. See also Galloway.

GARRETT, James, a Charlestown mariner, gr. adm. in N. H. 1657 on est. of Henry Thorner of Wapping, Eng. The gunner of Mr. G.'s ship was in York ct. July 1C58, Mrs. Priscilla Johnson (8) acc. with him. 'Garretts Worke' in bill against town of Portsm., Feb. 1660-1.

GASKIN, John, Kittery, m. Joanna Crocker (2) and d. bef. 2 May 1690, when Mrs. Elizabeth Hole gave her a deed to 10 a. at N. E. end of the Hole plantation for which they had already pd. £10. She m. 2d (or 3d) Paul Williams. Ch., perh. not hers: Deliverance, m. in Berw. 6 Sept. 1710 Edward Walker. Elizabeth, ab. 17 in 1702, unm. in 1714. One E. G. m. in Kit. 28 Feb. 1722 Joseph Speering.

Gatch, see Geach.

Gatchell, see Getchell.

GATTENSBY. 1 Ensign John, Kittery. In Sept. 1661 he won suit against Francis Raynes of York for withholding a yr. of his time, and some stock. M. Susanna Spencer, whose da. Tho. deeded them land in Unity 20 June 1662. Of Wells 1664, bot half of Tatnick. Coroner's jury 1668; Ensign 1668. Keeping ordinary at Berwick bef. 1670. Adm. 4 Aug. 1671 to Richard Waldron; Capt. Rich. Cutt, a large creditor, added as adm. 1 July 1673; the est. insolvent. Wid. m. 2d Ephraim Joy (1). Ch: John, witn. with Wells men 1683; in Philip English's 1687 acct. for fishing supplies. Moses. Elizabeth,

acc. Jas. Warren jr. bef. Mar. 1689-90; m. William Wadlin.

2 **MOSES** (1), with bro. John had Berwick grants. Lists 62, 94. Wife unkn. Adm. 24 June 1718 to Peter Wittum jr., who had m. his dau. **Judith** 3 Aug. 1713. In 1723 they q. c. to Daniel Wadlin her gr.fa.'s right in Tatnick.

**Gaude**, Mark, 3-year man at Trelawny planta., who soon ran away. List 21.

**Gauge**, William, P. & Ct. ii. 398-9. See Gooch (7).

**Gavensey**, James, Kittery 1675. List 286. See Guernsey.

**Gay**, Elizabeth, a stranger at Mr. Toogood's, Portsm., 6 May 1695 (to give security).

**Gayer**, Edwin. List 41. See Guy.

**Gayneye**, William, 1614. List 7.

**GEACH, Geage, Gatch, Gage, Edmund**, ab. 40 Aug. 1687, Robt. Sanford's servant in Boston 1673; soldier in Philip's war; sued in Suff. Ct. Jan. 1683-4. By 1685 he was of Braveboat Harb. with P/A from John Farnum of Bost., his home thereaft. in Kit. where his life was not uncheckered. In 1686 he (Gach) witn. Capt. Champernowne's will; in 1712 he recorded a fraudul. deed as of Champernowne's, covering land at Braveb. Harb. Y. D. 7.232. Surv. highways 1692-3. Gr. j. 1695. Lists 290, 296, 297. See Andrews (9). In 1702 he sued Jos. Mitchell for tresp. and lost. W. Joanna (m. bef. 14 Apr. 1676), ab. 40 in 1687, was liv. 28 Feb. 1714-5. Will 18 Apr.—2 July 1717, w. (unnamed), dau. Agnes and husb. Ch: **Prudence** (presum.), ag. 16 in Mar. 1686-7, Robt. Mason's maid. Rec. in Boston: **Elizabeth**, b. 5 June 1677; may have m. Henry Croscum (1), who dep. in 1701 'my father Geage.' **Agnes**, b. 23 Jan. 1678, m. Samuel Ford (4). **Edmund**, b. 3 July 1681.

**GEARE** (**Geere**). See also Garey. **John**, cordwainer, Portsm. and Kit., ±46 in Jan. 1701-2. At Str. Bk. in 1685 he testif. with Walter Winsor who was appar. relat. to Edw. Melcher. O. A. 28 Aug. 1685, and taxed Oct. 1691, both at Str. Bk. Bondsman (Grure or Grare) with Edw. Melcher 1693. In 1694 fined for abs. from gr. j. (Me.); same yr. had Kit. gr., but was of Portsm. 1695, ±40. Taxed Kit. 1704 and 24 Jan. 1708-9. Lists 334a, 290, 296, 298. D. bef. 7 Dec. 1712. Wid. Sarah (Wills), dau. of Thos., liv. mostly in Portsm. In 1722 she was sued by Rich. Cutt (6), husb. of her half sis., for half of Crooked Lane land which had come from her own mo.'s fam. (Abbott 5), but lost to him. Liv. 24 Aug. 1738. Ch., order not kn: ?**Sarah**, o. c. and bp. No. Ch. 7 Dec. 1712, may have been the mo. instead. **Hannah**, ab. 14 in 1709, poss. ident. with **Joanna**, bp. 17

Apr. 1715; of Kit., m. 21 Nov. 1723 John Abbott jr., gr. s. of (1). **Samuel**, bp. 17 Apr. 1715, m. at Kit. 7 Jan. 1724-5 Abigail Hodsdon. He d. bef. 1735 and likely it was his wid. m. at Kit. 24 Dec. 1733 John Thomas. See Hodsdon (4). **Elizabeth**, m. 15 Nov. 1719 John Roberts of Portsm. **Mary**, m. 26 Mar. 1723 Benj. Langley (1).

**Gearing**, see Carlisle.

**GEDNEY**, a parish in Lincolnshire.

1 **BARTHOLOMEW**, Esq., (3), Salem, justice, military officer and land owner in Me., associated in No. Yarm. with Capt. Walter Gendall. Lists 34, 225ab, 227.

2 **EDWARD** (Gidney), a Piscat. witn. 1663 (Wall heirs).

3 **JOHN**, Mr. (Gydney) sued Nich. Bartlett in York Ct. 1654. P. & Ct. ii. Fa. of (1).

**GEE**, most freq. found in cos. Bucks and Cambridge.

1 **JOHN**, Boston, Martha's Vineyard, husb. of Hazelelponi (Willix), who m. 2d Obadiah Wood of Ipsw. Three daus., incl. **Mary**, w. of Tho. Pickering of Portsm. (m. by 1686). See Willix, Ugrove, Murrell.

2 **PETER**, from Newton Ferrers, co. Devon, where Peter, s. of John, was bp. 25 Jan. 1614-5. Shoals fishing master 1651, his fam. in Boston, where desc. prospered. List 301. W. Grace, both liv. Boston in Nov. 1681. Suff. D. vii, xi, xii. Ch: **Thomas**, eldest, whereab. unkn. Mar. 1670-1. **John**, Boston, app. of age 1671, d. 25 July 1693, leaving will. W. Joan d. 8 dys. bef. him. 7 ch. 1678-1692. **Joshua**, a captive in Algiers 1681. Mariner and shipwright, Boston. M. there 1st 25 Sept. 1688 Elizabeth Harris, 2d Elizabeth Thacher (Judah), who m. 2d Rev. Peter Thacher. His will 15 Jan.—11 Mar. 1722-3. 4 ch. by 1st w. 1689-1693; 5 by 2d w. 1697-1704, incl. Rev. Joshua, b. 29 June 1698, H. C. 1717, m. 1st 13 Dec. 1722 Sarah Rogers (Rev. Nathl. of Portsm.), 2d 17 Apr. 1734 Anna Gerrish (4), wid. of Saml. Appleton, 3d 29 Jan. 1739, Sarah Gardner. See N. Y. Gen. & Biog. Rec. vols. 42, 43. In 1750 Gee heirs were suing 11 Berw. residents for 2/9 of 1/2 of Quamphegan.

3 **RALPH**, Piscataqua, had been in charge of cattle on Capt. Mason's est. 1¼ yrs. bef. July 1643; recd. a small planta. near the est. Lists 41, 330a. D. 1645, adm. to Wm. Seavey, a creditor.

**GENDALL**, peculiar to Cornwall, or poss. a dialect. var. of Kendall.

*****WALTER**, Capt., J. P. See Banks' extend. biog. in -No. Yarm. Old Times, pp. 511-545. Writing in 1880, and printing docs. not now in the public archives, yet he

missed others still in place. Gendall did not come over in 1641, he was born that yr. It was not he at Richmond Isl.; it was she, Wilmot Randall, the maid. (List 21, Doc. Hist. iii. 350.) Instead of unnamed in any records from 1642 to 1665, he was the most prom. young man east of Scarb. from 1665 until his tragic death in 1688. Two of the vanished MS. are of great int., showing him at Spurwink 1663 and 1664, instead of his first record appearance at Purpooduck Nov. 1665. Two yrs. younger than Bedford(1) and both appearing first at Spurwink, did not these two young -go-getters- come over together to make their fortunes, take desperate chances, and both meet violent deaths? Both versed in court procedure, masters of the law of merchants at least, they may have been apprentices together to a Plymouth or London merchant, or even at the Inns of Court. At any rate the records show situations indic. their constant helping each other get ahead, which they did. The two docs. showing him living at Spurwink:—the Scarb. and Falm. petn. 4 July 1663 (N. E. Reg. 5. 264), and his dep. 11 June 1664, how he built the Tenney-Madiver fence 'ab. 3 yrs. since' (Banks, p. 512). Either the hero or the villain wherever present (or missing), the story of Gendall's dramatic life awaits the novelist, and he need not alter the facts to heighten his plot at all! His life was a picture of supreme confid. in himself to tackle every situation that presented and come out on top. Those who knew him knew this and made allowances. So when he was accused of looting, they knew he thought he was salvaging and preventing others from looting. When accused of betraying his own countrymen to the Indians, they knew he thought he was saving their lives. His belief that he could manage the Indians got him into his worst troubles, and finally cost him his life when life looked brightest. Only that he lived three centuries too soon, his name might have shone, or glittered, in high finance or in statescraft. Ag. ±35 31 July 1676, ag. 36 23 June 1677, he was killed 15 Sept. 1688, at 47. (Doc. Hist. 6. 445). Foreman of jury at 25, attorney for Scarb. at 26, he at 26 and Bedford at 28 accepted bondsmen in a murder case, at 34-35 in command at Spurwink, at 40 in charge of Indian trade, at 42-43 owner of large lumber mill, deputy to General Court, on both of Pres. Danforth's boards of Trustees for common lands, Falm. and No. Yarm. (List 32), provisional commander of Province Fort in Portland, largest taxpayer in Spurwink, at 45 Captain and Justice of the Eastern court under Andros, Judge Sewall notes his death 'of whom Justice Gendal

one.' Lists 236, 225a, 226, 214, 34, 97. Jury 1665, 1666, 1667, 1672, 1676; gr.j. 1671, 1673. He m. Joane Guy(2), whose fa. appar. gave his plantation, 2 Dec. 1668, to his new s.-in-law as her dowry. Whether the wid. sought refuge at Boston or poss. Marshfield is uncert. Thos. Scottow's letter 11 July 1689 reports Ind. killing swine at Mrs. Gendall's plantation. Theodosius Moore, upholsterer, was of Boston in Feb. 1689-90. She was at Marshfield, Moore's wife, 27 Nov. 1700, when he was granted adm. on Gendall's est. in Suff. court; he was again app. in York court May 1721, and by probate lic. sold all lands and proprietor's rights. Y. D. 11.89. Altho ch. are not mentioned and orphans and apprentices were contin. added to the Gendall household (Mills, Beale, Oakman, Boaden), a likely s. or gr.s. was John, m. in Boston 18 May 1722 Lydia Ingersoll(3), wid. of Elias Hart, and had two s. (Y. D. 16.19). Moore had 2 sons by 2d w. m. in Bridgewater 30 June 1725, Sarah Prior, who m. 2d 11 Oct. 1738 Josiah Hayward.

**GENT,** Jent. Ancient in Huntingdon and Essex, now found in Derbyshire.

1 **DANIEL**(2?), List 162.

2 **JOHN,** presum. the man in Essex County 1641, trading at the Eastward 1647, and indebted to Martin Stebbin's est. in Boston, 1657-9. Geo. Spear's ptn. to Andros called his predecessor an ancient inhab. of New Dartmouth, possess. of consid. tracts of land there, espec. on the Neck, which he enjoyed until the late Ind. War, and 'cast away' while his fam. was in Boston. D. H. 6.396. A deed given by his s. Thomas in 1715 recites that his mo. Elizabeth, while sole, bot large tracts there from the Ind. -1665-. (Y. D. 12.366.) She herself depos. that she liv. on the Neck, at times with her s. Thomas, at times with her daus. In 1688 she was there with 2d husb. Geo. Spear of Braintree; d. bef. Jan. 1715-6. N. E. Reg. 59.324. Kn. ch: **Thomas,** b. ±1642. **Mary,** m. 1st John Mason, 2d John Allen(5); see Burnett (1). **Elizabeth,** m. John Phips. **?Daniel,** List 162, if a son, d. s. p. bef. 1715-6. **?John.** One John was sued in Mass. on a note dated 16 Sept. 1676, payable in fish; if a son, he d. s. p.

3 **THOMAS**(2), brewer, ±37 in Jan. 1679-80, only son 1716, was perh. identical with T. G., servant of Mr. Martyn, Portsm. 1661. Bef. 1665 he was at Sheepscot and Damariscotta, where he built and liv., until the War, on land given by his fa.-in-law. Assoc. with an old neighbor Wm. Lovering (5), he was in Boston in May 1679, suing John Moors on a lighterage bill. Sheepscot 1683; in Jan. 1689-90, ±48, late Ensign, he

was in Boston testif. against Lt. Jordan, and there he stayed. Lists 12, 13 (Gympe), 17, 162, 163. In 1703 John Giles(3) sued him on a note dated 13 Apr. 1686. Thru his fam. and his w. Sarah Taylor (John), he was a large Eastern Claimant. Bur. in Boston 25 Dec. 1717; wid. Sarah liv. 11 Feb. 1734-5, ag. 86. Ch., all m. in Boston: **John,** eldest son, house carp., Boston, m. 5 June 1706 Abigail Scott (Peter of Braintree). 9 ch. rec. Boston, 2 in Braint., 1707-1729. **Mary,** m. 1st 17 Nov. 1699 Tobias Green (2 ch. rec.); 2d 27 Dec. 1709 Dr. Matthew Nazro (3 ch. rec.). Both liv. 1728. **Sarah,** m. 18 Mar. 1702 Peter Scott, was presum. a dau. who d. s. p. **Thomas,** m. 11 Feb. 1713 Mary Rogers; both liv. 1728. 1 ch. bur. 1714, 2 bur. 1720. **Elizabeth,** m. 2 Nov. 1704 Milam Alcock; d. bef. 1712. 1 dau. **Hannah,** m. 3 Feb. 1708 John Tuckerman jr., trader; both liv. 1728. **Abigail,** m. 17 May 1711 Saml. Mason; wid. in Boston 1728. **Rachel,** m. 29 Dec. 1715 Moses Walker; wid. in Boston 1728.

**GEORGE.** 1 ———Capt. of a mastship, aft. waiting at Piscataqua for soldiers to go to Casco Bay and being refused, sailed for Eng. in May 1690 with Benj. Bullivant aboard.

2 **JAMES,** taxed Portsm. 1698-1713. Lists 330de. One Thomas G. of Kingston 1725, bap. there with three ch. 1727.

**GERMAN** (Garman, Jerman). 1 John (Jarman), with Wm. Cock getting fishing supplies from Philip English 1684.

2 **JOHN,** surgeon, found nine badly wounded at Casco Fort, 12 Aug. 1703, and cured all.

3 **THOMAS** (Garman), Shoals 1664. List 303. Taxed Portsm. 1673 (Germaine). Place and time suggest Dorothy (Jarmin), witn. to Christo. Jose's will 1678, as his w.; as daus. **Priscilla,** m. one Bly (1) by 1692. **Elizabeth** (Garmine), m. 1st 20 Oct. 1692 Jos. Randall, 2d 19 Feb. 1704-5 Saml. Willey.

4 **WILLIAM,** Falmouth 1689, poss. the Marbleh. fisherman (Jerman) or from (3). List 228c. One Wm. soldier from York Co. 1722.

**GERRISH,** an uncommon English name, found early in Wiltshire, also in Monmouthshire.

1 **AGNES,** al. Pomery, Portsm., occupied one of Edw. Melcher's two small houses 1694, Walter Winsor the other. Seated at meeting-ho. as Goody Pumery al. Gerrish. List 335a. Presum. a wid. Gerrish, (see 2), remar. to one Pomery. In 1721 as Agnes Mathes, wid., form. Pomery, she q. c. common rights with dau. Hannah Langmaid(1).

2 **JAMES,** dep. Jan. 1685-6, ±37, Mr. John

Hunking, dec., his form. master; Walter Winsor also depos. Taxed Greenl. 1689-90; Str. Bk. 1691, and ho. List 332b. Connec. with (1) is indic., poss. her husb. Consid. as a son must be given to **James,** unplaced elsewhere, taxed Berw. 1713. He found one w. in Ipsw., so poss. was the James m. (int. Ipsw. 1 May 1708) Esther Standly; cert. m. at Berw. 17 Feb. 1714-5 Mary Wentworth (Timo.), next (int. Ipsw. 12 Dec. 1740) Mary, wid. of Matthew Perkins. Will 1770. 5 or m. ch.

3 *JOHN(8), Esq., b. Newb. 15 May 1646, m. 19 Aug. 1667 Elizabeth Waldron (Maj. Rich.) and settled in Dover. Quartermaster of the troops Oct. 1669, and rose steadily in importance, raising a prominent fam. Lieut.; Capt. 1680. Selectm. 1673-4, 1695-6; Moderator 1697, 1704-12, 1714; High Constable 1683-4; memb. of Special Assemb. 1684; Rep. 1684-94; J. P. 1686; named Counsellor 1692 and declined; Assoc. Justice 1696; Justice Superior Ct. 1699. Lists 353, 357c, 359ab, 48, 49, 50, 52, 54, 56, 57, 58, 60, 62, 64, 65, 66, 67, 94, 98. D. 1714. Will 12 July 1706—17 Mar. 1719-20. Widow's will 17 Oct. (d. 7 Dec. 1724 in 79th yr.) names surv. ch. and gr. dau. Elizabeth Henchman of Boston. Ch: **John,** b. 21 Aug. 1668. **Richard,** b. 17 Apr. 1670. **Anna,** b. 30 Jan. 1671, m. 1st Capt. Andrew Brock(1), 2d Jas. Jeffrey(7). **Elizabeth,** b. 28 May 1674, m. 1st 3 Sept. 1696 Rev. John Wade, 2d 5 Mar. 1718-9 Joshua Pierce. **William,** b. 8 Mar. 1675-6, not in fa.'s will. **Samuel,** b. 15 Mar., d. 6 Dec. 1678. Capt. **Nathaniel,** b. 19 Oct. 1679, mariner, Portsm., served at Ft. William & Mary 1708; mov. aft. 5 Apr. 1719 to So. Berw.; d. there 10 Apr. 1729 in 49th yr. (g. s.). List 298. W. Bridget Vaughan (Hon. Wm.) d. 15 Sept. 1743 in 65th yr. (g. s.). 7 ch., inc. Maj. Chas., 1st settler at Durham, Me. **Sarah,** b. 31 July 1681, capt. by Ind. 28 June 1689 and held 16 mo.; d. 29 July 1697. Lists 96, 99 p. 144. *Timothy, Esq., Kit., b. 21 Apr. 1684, m. 14 Nov. 1706 Sarah Elliot(6), who had western end of Champernowne's Isl. as dowry. Capt., Col., Rep. 1714, 1715. List 358d. He d. 19 Nov. 1755 (bill for 9 funeral rings); she 27 Oct. 1770. 13 ch. **Benjamin,** b. 6 Sept. 1686, gunsmith, Boston, taxed Portsm. 1708, m. 1st ab. 1711 Mehitable Plaisted (John), d. 3 Jan. 1715-6, ag. 21 (g. s. Pt. of Gr.); 2d 28 June 1716 Martha Foxcroft of Cambr., d. 14 Apr. 1736; 3d 22 June 1738 Abigail (Fowle), wid. of Benj. Bunker of Charlest., where he d. 28 June 1750. 4 ch. by 1st w. ‡*Paul, Esq., Dover, b. 13 Jan. 1688, m. 2 Oct. 1712 Mary Leighton(5). Town clerk 1728 to death; Rep. 1728, 1731, 1733-7, 1739. Capt., Major, Col., Counsellor, Justice. List 358d. D. 6 June 1743 in 55th yr., attended

to his grave by near 1,000 people. Adm. 21 June to s.-in-law John Wood and s. Saml., wid. Mary renounc. She d. 16 Apr. 1765. 8 ch.

4 **JOHN**(3), gunsmith, merch., ship-owner, Boston, d. 21 Feb. 1737-8 in 69th yr. Taxed Str. Bk., and shop, Oct. 1691. Moving to Boston, he m. 1st 19 Apr. 1692 Lydia Watts, sis. of Capt. John, d. 8 Jan. 1697-8; 2d (mar. portion 5 June 1700) Sarah Hobbs, niece of Nicho. Paige. Ch. 3+10. N. E. Reg. 64.185; 67.105.

5 **REV. JOSEPH**(8), b. Newb. 23 Mar. 1649, H. C. 1669. Minister at Wenham 46 yrs., he preached first at Dover. M. Anna Waldron (Hon. Richard). He d. at Wenham 6 Jan. 1719-20, leaving will; sons already had had £200 apiece; wid. d. 27 Jan. 1730-1, ag. 78. 6 ch., incl: **Joseph**, H. C. 1700. **Samuel**, Boston, town clerk, register of deeds. Capt. **Paul**, b. 1679-80, mariner, Portsm., shopkeeper 1719. M. by 1711 Mary Hoddy(2), she liv. 1719 when they sold the Hoddy ho. and shop to Saml. Winkley. In 1719 he wrote to Mr. Henry Sharpe, painter, Boston, describ. the Gerrish arms; in 1721 sued the Keais est. D. Wenham 20 Feb. 1729-30. No kn. ch.

6 **JOSEPH** (Garich), soldier, Casco Fort, cured by John German(2).

7 ‡*CAPT. RICHARD**(3), Esq., Portsm., taxed 30 Oct. 1691. Gr. j. 1694; Rep. 1709; J. P.; Counsellor 1716. Lists 62, 98, 335a, 330d, 337, 343. M. bef. 30 May 1695 Jane Jose(1). List 335a. His will 14 Oct.— 22 Nov. 1717. Saml. Hinckes, shopkeeper, sued his est. 1719 on bill 1708-1716. Her will 26 Nov. 1717—2 May 1719. Both cut off only ch. **Richard** if he m. Elizabeth, wid. of John Cutts(9), dau. of Richard and Mary (Partridge) Barnwell. In Mar. 1718-9 he was acquit. of illeg. liv. with her, she confessing they were m. ab. 8 d. bef. by Dr. Lucas, the witnesses gone to sea. One Richard of Piscat. and Abigail Paxton of Boston intended mar. in Boston 21 Feb. 1718.

8 **CAPT. *WILLIAM,** Newbury, selectm. Hampton 1663, their Rep. 1663-64. Lists 53, 392b. W. Joanna (Lowell), wid. of John Oliver. 10 ch. incl. (3), (5), and **Elizabeth,** w. of Capt. Stephen Greenleaf (4 jr.).

**GETCHELL,** Gatchell, a rare Eng. surname, found in Somersetshire in early 17th century.

1 **BENJAMIN,** shipwright, Portsm.; taxed 1708; m. that yr. bet. 4 Oct.—25 Nov. Bethulia Baker (3). W. Ann in 1718. In 1712 he was master of the bark —Richard—. Ch: **Benjamin,** bp. 5 Aug. 1711. **Sarah,** bp. 12 Apr. 1713.

2 **BEZALIEL,** fisherman, Marbleh., m. 14 Oct. 1705 Susannah Scadlock (Saml.),

and sold Scadlock rights at Arundel 22 July 1727, Y. D. 12.1.151.

3 **JOHN;** his w. Elinor memb. of Greenl. ch. 1713. List 338b.

4 **JOHN,** m. in Boston 26 Sept. 1729 Mary Benighton. See Bonython (2).

5 **SAMUEL,** Hampton propr. 23 Feb. 1645-6. Lists 392a, 393b. He soon made Sals. his perm. home, selling the Hampt. dwg. 17 May 1648. In 1678 he sued Saml. Fowler. Two yrs. later his w. Dorcas (m. by 1648) was assoc. with Mary Osgood, Philip Rowell and w. Sarah in action ag. John Ring and Martha Lampson. She d. 12 Jan. 1684-5. His will 2 Apr. 1684—6 Oct. 1697 names her and ch: **Susanna,** m. 10 Mar. 1662 Joseph Norton. **Priscilla,** b. Sals. 26 Feb. 1648-9, m. Solomon Rainsford of Boston. **Samuel,** b. 8 Feb. 1657-8.

6 **SAMUEL** (5), shipw., Sals., m. 27 Nov. 1679 Elizabeth Jones (Robert), who d. 24 May 1735. He d. 7 July 1710. Of 13 ch., 6 remov. to Me.: **Moses,** b. 15 May 1682. With w. Judith rem. to No. Yarmouth, Me., aft. 1719, liv. there 1734. Selectm. 1740 of Harpswell, where he d. Ch. **Mary,** b. 12 Apr. 1687, m. John (not Joseph) Drisco (6). 6 ch. rec. Salis. 1710-1722, inc. Joseph, b. 21 Dec. 1712. One Mary G. of Exeter up for bastardy 1710. **Samuel,** b. 12 Apr. 1687, taxed Berw. 1713, m. there 9 Nov. 1714 Elizabeth Nason. In June 1742, ±53, he dep. that 21 or 22 yrs. bef. he and Michael Thomas were sent with cattle from Newb., built a ho. on the Damariscotta Riv., and in 10 mos. he came away, leaving Thomas there. Liv. Berw. 1756. 4 or m. ch. **Joseph,** Wells by 18 Mar. 1713-4, m. 19 Dec. 1716 Eunice Hatch (5); m. 2d or 3d, in York, 28 Jan. 1753 Mary (Joy), wid. of Geo. Gray (10). 5 or m. ch. by 1st w. **Nathaniel,** m. Susanna Ladd; 5 ch. rec. Haverh. 1728-1736. Of Wells 1737, where he or a s. m. 10 Mar. 1746-7 Esther Low. **John,** rem. to Scarb. (gr. 22 June 1720), assoc. there with the Mitchells with whom he rem. to New Meadows ab. 1736. Corporal 1725, Capt. 1748, kn. Ind. fighter. W. Elizabeth d. 10 May 1771. He liv. 1760, gent. 7 ch. rec. Scarb. 1719-1734, and 4 m. Wheeler's Hist. of Brunswick says Mariners and Getchells came from Wales and relates the trad. that the gr. grfa. of the Marriners came with a patent to settle Monhegan. This trad., also attrib. to Getchells, does not apply to that name.

**GIBBINS,** Gibbons. Patronymic from Gilbert. See Harrod.

1 ‡**AMBROSE** (Gibbons), Mr., one of the founders of N. H., perh. had been over before at Glouc. Sent over by the Laconia Co. as a factor or steward with Walter Neale, he had reached the Piscataqua by 21

July 1630, and soon began the plantation at Newichawannock. He was still there in Aug. 1634, and has been termed an honest, capable, and faithful steward, who knew better than his employer what the planta. needed. His letters in Prov. Papers vol. 1 and Appendix to Belknap's Hist. of N. H.; aut. in Conc. Files 4.193. In 1634 land at Sanders Pt. bet. Little Harb. and Sag. Creek was gr. him for faithful services, and there he retired from Newich. Portsm. 1640; next yr. at Oyster River, his home thereafter. Land grants in 1652 and 200 a. near his ho. in 1654. Associate 1646, 1647; Selectm. 1647, 1648. Adm. Darby Field's est. 1651. Lists 41, 321, 352, 353, 354abc, 355ab. Will, on his sick bed, 11 July 1656—9 May 1657, beq. his prop. to his Sherburne gr. ch., tho their mo. was liv. W. Rebecca d. 14 May 1655. Wife and children had been sent over bef. May 1631, but his only surv. ch. was **Rebecca**, m. 13 Nov. 1637 Henry Sherburne.

2 **JAMES**, planter, Saco, came in —The Increase— from London in Apr. 1635, ag. 21, with Saml. Andrews (16), Robt. Nanny and Robt. Sankey, 'sent away' by Robt. Cordell, goldsmith in Limbert St. All went to Winter Harbor, where he and Tho. Mills bot the Boade est. in Aug. 1642. His mar. ab. 1646 with Judith Lewis (19), event. sole owner of her fa.'s half of the Patent, gave him a standing beyond his own, of which he did not take full advantage. List 246. Subm. to Mass. 5 July 1653, and among freemen ord. into Ct. 7 July 1663 for not subm. to their demands. Gr. j. 1654 and oft.; tr. j. 1656, 1669; jury life and death 1666; he or s. on Shoals coroner's j. 1677. Constable 1655, 1676; Com. t. e. s. c. 1663-4, 1668-70; Selectm. 14 yrs. to 1674 (?4 more to 1683). Master of magazine 1667. On commit. to view Casco prison for neces. repairs 1674. Lists 243ab, 252, 244cef, 245, 249, 26, 235, 306c. W. Judith dep. 18 Mar. 1681, ±55; liv. 15 July 1684, appar. dead 25 May 1687. F eeing the 2d War, he was at Kit. in July 1690, last found in Boston 7 July 1692. Y. D. iv. 22, 155-6; v. 1. 45. See 'Ancestry of Charity Haley', W. G. Davis, for div. of the whole Patent 1681, aft. they had sold the most val. part of their share, and adm. of her est. by Geo. Hibbort and Jos. Jewett 23 May 1729. Ch. (N. E. Reg. 71.125); James, b. 19 Mar. 1648. **E izabeth**, b. 23 Apr. 1652, m. 14 Nov. 1667 John Sharp. **Thomas**, b. 23 Nov. 1654. Son and heir, in Kit., 18 July 1690, he joined fa. in deed to sis. Elizabeth; no desc. liv. 1730. **Rebecca**, b. 30 Jan. 1656, d. 3 Jan. 1658. **Charity**, b. 5 Jan. 1658, no desc. liv. 1730. **Rachel**, b. 23 Oct. 1660, m. Robt. Edgecomb (3). **Hester**, b. 16 Aug. 1664, no dec. liv. 1730. **Anthony**, b. 14 Oct. 1666, d. s. p. bef. 1690. **Hannah**, not rec., m.

1st one Hibbert or Hibbard (1), 2d Robert Mace. May 21, 1729, as the 'antient liver' of the Gibbins est., she asked that her two sons be named administrators.

3 **LIEUT. JAMES** (2), Saco, m. Dec. 1668 Dorcas Seeley. List 246. Both had ch. seatings 18 Apr. 1669. Petty j. 1669; coroner's j. May 1670 (David May). In 1670 he helped raise security for John Bonython; in 1675 sued him for taking and detaining his goods. Sergt.; Lieut. 1674, when 'Lieut. G. his horse allowed on.' Lists 249, ?306c. D. bef. 1683; wid. m. 2d Francis Backus. Ch: **Patience**, m. 1st one Sands; 2d (int. Ipsw. 16 Jan. 1719-20) John Annable; both d. Jan. 1748. 4 ch. by 1st husb., incl. James of Biddeford and Hannah, m. John Bryant (9). **Rebecca**, m. James Wakefield. **James**, sailor, Boston, d. s. p. 8 May 1702 on ship —Margaret Galley— on voyage from Surinam. Nunc. will gave £5 to Aunt Sharp; rest to mo.; adm. to step-fa. 17 June 1702.

4 **WILLIAM**, mariner, in Casco Bay bef. the Patent. List 21. In Saco Ct. Mar. 1636 his case was referred to two men; sued by Henry Watts, June 1640, and in Sept. fol. he dep. ab. Casco River 17 yrs. ago or thereab. Ment. in Trelawny accts. 1638, 1643 (of Saco).

**GIBBS**, 1 **Henry**, York witn. 1715. Y. D. 8.106.

2 **JOHN**, shipmaster for the Laconia Co. List 41.

3 **RICHARD**, Mr., trading at Piscataqua 1673. List 312g.

4 **ROBERT**, ±33 in (1682?), Portsm. or York witn. 1663 (Y. D. i. 161), Fryer witn. 1672, fine penman.

5 **WILLIAM**, in Portsm. poor-ho. 1781, ag. 76. One Wm. (Gibes) of Biddef. m. Mary Hariel (int. Bid. 19 Feb. 1731-2).

**GIBSON**, patronymic from Gilbert, common in north of England.

1 **JOHN**, soldier at Scarb. 1676-7. List 237b. One John m. in Boston 2 Sept. 1706 Mary (Fletcher 8) Sawyer; s. John b. Boston 12 Oct. 1707, sailor there 1729. Y. D. 14.51.

2 **REV. RICHARD**, matric. Emmanuel Coll., Cambridge, 1627, and came to Richmond Isl. in the -Agnes- 1636, for 3 yrs., the 1st Episcopal minis. in Me. Soon beset by trouble with John Winter, so that in June 1638 he arranged to serve at Saco 6 mos. in the yr., by doubts of his w. Mary Lewis (19), m. soon aft. 10 May 1638, whose fa. he had sued for debt in June 1637, and by strife with John Bonython whom both he and his w. sued for slander in 1640; while J. B. also sued him. He was at Richmond Isl. in July 1639, planning to move to Piscataqua at Michaelmas, and became Ports-

mouth's 1st minister, but was soon embroiled with Mass. for marrying and baptizing at the Shoals, aggrav. by his corresp. with Rev. John Larkham of Dover. Imprisoned at Boston a few days in the summer of 1642, he made acknowledgm. and was discharged as ab. to leave the country. Tho. Mills dep. 20 July 1647 that he saw him sail from the Shoals and saw Capt. Champernowne deliv. him fish. Later life unkn., as his w. had no share in the Saco Patent. Lists 21, 249, 321, 322. Legatee in Robt. Trelawny's will of 1640, but not in his later one of 1643. 5 Mass. Hist. Socy. Coll. 1.267; D. H. 2.3.126, 156-61; Winthrop ii. 66.

3 **RICHARD**, Berwick 1669, addicted to drink; severely discip. in 1674 for mutinous carriages on training day and bound for one yr. to his bondsm. Tho. Doughty. One R. G. served in Philip's war at a distance.

**GIDDINGS.** 1 John, Ipsw., m. Sarah Alcock (1).

2 **NATHANIEL** (Giddens) ab. 18, working in the Hilton mills at Exeter 1694. List 384a. One Gidens was a Portsm. soldier 1708.

**Gidley**, Henry, witn. Major Phillips family deed 1668. Y. D. 2.132.

**Gifford**, John, Boston mercht., and w. Margaret sold lands and ho. to John Sargent 19 May 1685. Y. D. 4.42.

**GILBERT.** 1 **Capt. Raleigh**, Popham Colony 1607. List 6.

2 **ROGER** (Gilburd), Wells, 1677. List 266. One Roger sued Isaac Waldron in Suff. Co. 31 Oct. 1682. Liv. Boston 1688. W. Sarah; ch: **Sarah**, b. Bost. 22 Feb. 1683-4.

3 **WILLIAM**, No. Yarmouth, 1688. List 34.

**GILDEN**, Gilding, Gelding, John, Kittery, bot 30 a. near Sturgeon Creek 15 Apr. 1691; m. not bef. 1699, Sarah, wid. of Wm. Ham (9), and in 1701, of Portsm., bot Alex. Dennett's 20 a. gr. in Kit. Found only in Portsm. 1707-20, except Eliot witn. 1715. In 1720 he sold Kit. land and ho. to John Fernald, taking back a life lease. Kit. 1725. Lists 330d, 337, 297, 298. M. 2d 16 Aug. 1725 Elizabeth, wid. of Benj. Cotton (1) and 3 mos. later made over his rent. est. to her at his death. Both liv. 1727, he named in list of Kit. proprs. 18 Jan. 1730-1. No kn. ch.

**GILES**, forename, particularly in So. of England.

1 ———— (Jeiles), or a boy's given name, a yr.'s service due Gregory Jeffrey's est. 1666. See Giles Hibbins.

2 **JAMES**, ag. 42, arriv. Boston 9 Nov. 1668 in the —Peter— from London, with (8). His own story starts their trip from the Park, in par. of Challock, near Fever-

sham, co. Kent. Aft. a winter at Braintree, he went to Merry Meeting, and 3 yrs. later to his own ho. at Muddy Riv., Topsham, on land bot from the Ind. 31 Oct. 1671. List 191. Driven to Boston 18 Aug. 1676; soon at Southold, L. I., and at Piscataway, N. J., 1681. There Capt., Major, J. P. W. Elizabeth in 1668. Will, of Piscataway, 17 June 1688—Mar. 1690 ment. Kennebec land, w. Elizabeth, 4 ch: **Matthew. Elizabeth. Anna**, b. Braintr. 15 Apr. 1669. **Mary.** Not in will but app. ch: **Sarah, Jane.**

3 **JOHN**, b. ±1653, relat. to (2) and (8), likely bro., bearing out trad. that three came, James, Tho., John. Pemaquid, clerk, he witn. a Pattishall deed 3 Aug. 1685; liv. in ho. of (8). Personal tax 1687 (Jayles). List 124. His ptn. to Andros for land in 1688 gave as one reason, that he had been reading prayers in the garri. without compensa. Salem 1690, schoolmaster; Boston 1696; there, writing master, sued Tho. Gent 1703. D. 29 Aug. 1730, ag. 77 (g. s.) Wid. Mary, ±70 in July 1736, dep. ab. their life at Pemaquid over 50 yrs. bef. 7 ch. rec. Salem and Boston 1689-90—1705: **Sarah, John, Charles, William, Thomas, Mary, Mary.**

4 **CAPT. JOHN**, Esq. (8), ±12 when taken capt. in 1689, rejoined his fam. in Boston 19 June 1698. An interpreter and milit. officer, he gathered abund. material for his 'Memoirs' pub. 1736. Lieut. 1700, Capt. 1706, J. P. Of Casco, he m. in Sals. 26 Oct. 1703 Ruth True, who d. 1720. Innholder, Sals., during lulls. An old chief Terra Magnus in 1718 showed him and br. Tho. the bounds of their fa.'s lands; next mo. he bot from Tho. 60 a. at Merry Meeting where the ho. had stood. List 161. Stationed Brunswick by 1715, St. George's by 1725, retired to Roxbury, home of his 2d w. Hannah Heath, m. 6 Nov. (or Feb.) 1721. Will 9 Nov. 1751, d. Roxb. 29 May 1755, ag. 77. Ch. by 1st w.: **Dr. Samuel**, b. Sals. 30 June 1706, d. Brunsw. 11 Feb. 1738-9 (g. s.), m. at Sals. 2 June 1734 Elizabeth True, who m. 2d 1745 Capt. Wm. Allen. 2 ch. By 2d w.: **Hannah**, b. Roxb. 12 Aug. 1722, not in will. **Mary**, b. Boston 11 May 1724, m. 1747 Nathl. Loring of Boston.

5 **MARK**, Dover 1666, sued by Fryer 1668. In 1673 he bot 6 a. at Plum Pudding from Peter Coffin, and had 20 a. gr. near Broad Turn 1693-4. Lists 356jk, 359ab, 52, 94, 57, 62, 96. K. by Ind. 11 Aug. 1704. First w. unkn.; m. 2d 2 Sept. 1700 wid. Frances Perkins. Ch: **Mark**, eldest s. **Moses. Daniel**, b. ±1682, apprent. to Capt. Peter Coffin. Exeter 1708, Brentwood 1754, Raymond 1766, Brentw. 1769, ag. 87. List 376b (1725). In 1754 he sued neph. Mark, wid. Sarah G. and John Randall for 1/6 of 6 a., Pudding

Hill; same yr. q. c. to Mark land of fa. and br. Mark. W. Eunice 1721; she or a dau. a witn. 1730. Ch. incl: Daniel jr., Exeter 1724; Abigail, m. Kingston 16 June 1735 John Leavitt; presum. Mary, m. Kingston 10 Dec. 1740 Wm. Gilman; Joseph, m. Kingston 26 June 1742 Joanna Akers. **John**, k. by Ind. with his fa. List 96. Wid. Mary (Tibbetts m. 29 Dec. 1702) m. 2d Nathl. Goodwin (5). Ch: John, b. 30 Sept. 1703, m. by 1731 Sarah Field (5), both liv. Dover 1768. **Lydia.**

**6 MARK** (5), Dover, had 30 a. gr. near Broad Turn 1701, increased in 1702 by his fa.'s 20 a. Constable 1710. List 358d. With w. Sarah, m. by 1698, he deeded to Ichabod Hayes 1717. Adm. to her and s. Mark 4 Nov. 1735. She was liv. 1754. Ch: **Abigail**, b. 18 July 1698, m. Nathl. Lammos (2). **Ann**, b. 1 Oct. 1702, m. Jos. Bunker (2). **Mark**, Dover, b. 28 June 1706, m. Lydia Tibbetts (Jos.) See Danl. (5). 5 ch. rec. 1737-46. **Paul**, b. 1 Dec. 1708; of Dover 1737, q. c. to br. Mark land of fa. and gr. fa., prov. by witnesses 1756. **Sarah**, b. 9 Apr. 1711, m. Jas. Bunker (2 jr.). **Esther**, b. 21 Nov. 1713, m. John Randall.

**7 MATTHEW**, Dover 1642-1650, pd. largest tax 1648. At the Shoals, he owned a fish-ing plant, signed ptn. 18 May 1653, was sued for wages by Edw. Shaw 1657; at Oyster Riv., sold his Shoals dwg. 1659, sued Walter Matthews in 1660 for detaining his mooring place at the Shoals 4 yrs. and in 1661 with John Redman sued Wm. Seeley over a moor-ing place. Lists 354abc, 75b, 301, 355b, 356a, 362b, 363abc, 365. By 16— he m. one Eliza-beth, a jealous wid. with ch., who in 1663 acc. him and her dau. and was bound to good behav., he fined for provoking her. D. childless 21 Jan. 1666-7; adm. 25 June 1667 to Matthew Williams, 30 June 1668 to Ens. John Davis; div. to Matt. Williams and Rich. Knight (16), whose w. was a niece. John Redman and R. K. sold the ho. and fish. plant at Smuttin. 30 Nov. 1668.

**8 THOMAS**, Esq., came with (2), ag. 29, and mov. to a large tract bet. Merry Meeting Bay and Muddy Riv., in Topsham, bot from Tho. Watkins 1669. There he and (2) witn. for Tho. Stevens who m. Wat-kins's wid. Called to Eng., app. late in 1674, he went on his ret. to L. I.; later was with (3) on newly bot land at Pemaquid, an un-fort. move, as his death and capture of his w. and 4 ch. was a tragedy of 2 Aug. 1689. Magistrate there by appointm. from Don-gan and Andros. Custodian of Tho. Sharp's est. 1687. Lists 16, 17, 163, 124, 161, 191. W. Margaret, presum. sis. to husb. of Madam Ann Chalker of Canterbury, co. Kent, liv. in Boston aft. being redeemed; dead 'some yrs.' in 1698. Ch: **Thomas**, 19 in 1689. Lydia Felt dep. July 1718 that she liv. serv. with

Mr. Tho. G. at Kennebec and was there when his s. Tho. was b., 48 yrs. ago in June. **James**, b. ab. 1675, escap. from the Ind., re-taken and tortured to death at Penobscot Fort 1692. **John**, b. ab. 1678. **Mary**, m. 1st Andrew Ham (1), 2d John Brewer. **Mar-garet**, m. in Boston 31 Oct. 1717 Jonas Web-ber. **Samuel**, youngest s., not a captive, ac-comp. br. Tho. to Boston, where he met br. John on the boat when he ret. from Canada; liv. 1700, appar. still an apprent.; d. s. p. bef. 1727.

**9 THOMAS** (8), of age and improv. his fa.'s land, by Pemaquid tax list 1687, in dis-agreem. with other records. Left behind with br. Saml. when the others taken, he fled to Boston, later claiming the Me. land, but app. made no effort to return. In July 1700 he sent br. John to the Piscataqua to get a legacy in money sent from Eng. by Aunt Chalker in care of Capt. Long, who claimed it was stolen from his chest. Water-man, ferryman, Boston; m. there 18 Jan. 1699 Martha Bill. List 161. Retailer 1730-4. Dead 1739. Lists 124, 18, 161. Ch. 1701-1717: **Hannah, Martha, Thomas, Mary, James.**

**10 WILLIAM**, London, partner in Laconia Co. List 41.

**11 WILLIAM**, Scarboro, his 70 a. gr. adj. John Getchell and Wm. Mitchell laid out 1721. Poss. the same Falm. grantee dead in 1733, leav. wid. or dau. Margaret, or Re-becca, one w. of John Perry. Y. D. 16.89. One Wm. -Gibes- of Bid. m. (int. 19 Feb. 1731-2 Mary -Hariel- of Bid.

**GILL**, freq. found in Devon and Cornwall.
1 — Mr., shipmaster at Richmond Isl. 1633. List 21.

2 **ARTHUR**, bp. St. Stephen by Saltash, co. Cornwall, 14 Dec. 1608, s. of Thomas, came to Richmond Isl. in 1636, ship carpen-ter. List 21. A capable man, disagreem. over wages caused his removal, first to Dor-chester, then to Boston, in July 1639, altho the next summer he was working at Rich. Isl. See Hinkson (3). Appraiser of a wreck in May 1649. Bef. 1654 he had gone to Eng., his fam. here, his est. in the hands of John Sweet, who gave bond to adm. 16 Jan. 1654-5; Andrew Alger and Peter Hill among those named in accts. W. Agnes. List 21. Ch., the 1st two bp. at St. Stephen by Sal-tash: **Frances**, bp. 8 Mar. 1634-5, d. y. **Fran-ces**, bp. 2 Oct. 1636, evid. in her gr. fa. Gill's care in Eng. in July 1639; m. in Boston 17 Oct. 1656 Henry Boyen. Rec. Boston: **John**, b. 16 Nov. 1639, oldest s. in 1656. **Thomas**, b. Oct. 1644, his passage pd. to Eng. bef. 1655. **Nathaniel**, d. 2 Sept. 1652, likely the one b. 11 Apr. 1647.

3 **JOHN**, witn. a Jordan deed 13 Aug. 1658. Y. D. 1.76. Poss. s. of (2).

**4 PETER**, Richmond Isl., 1634, D. H. iii.40, misr. for Peter Hill.

**5 THOMAS**, mariner, Portsm., 1678, ±47 in Aug. 1682, knew the Whites and Harridons in Cornworthy, co. Devon. Master of the ketch -Amity- 1684. Taxed Str. Bk. 1688-1691. In Jan. 1702-3 he dep. that ab. 34 yrs. bef. he helped Maj. Nicho. Shapleigh run out his line. List 329.

**GILLAM, Zachary** (Benj.), b. Boston 30 Sept. 1636. In 1664 he delivered to the apprs. goods belonging to Thos. Etherington's est. M. 26 July 1659 Phebe Phillips, dau. of Lt. Wm. of Saco, who deeded 500 a. on West's Brook to Gillam and his br.-in-law Ephraim Turner. In 1732 his heirs were suing John Gordon (3). See also Gunnison (2).

**GILMAN.** While the New England family came from Norfolk, the name's chief home is Staffordshire.

**1 CHARLES**, br. of (9), was bp. 12 May 1642 in Hingham, co. Norfolk, Eng. First noticed in Exeter in town gr. 10 Oct. 1664, which was regranted 28 Sept. 1668 to br. John. List 376b. He removed to Piscataway, N. J., where he and br. were orig. grantees, and where one Charles was Constable 1687, Justice of town court 1688, and appraisr. est. of Maj. James Giles(2). Accepting New Jersey geneal., he had a fam. of ch. who might have been his gr. ch., mingling with sundry Charleses all dead bef. he would have been 80. Attributed to him are: w. Mary, m. 9 Jan. 1684, dau. of Thos. Alger, and wid. of David Bishop; ch: **Charles**, b. 2 Aug. 1686, **Joseph**, b. 10 Nov. 1689, **Mary**, b. and d. Dec. 1691; and a will 18 Jan.—l Mar. 1691-2, naming w., two sons under age, cous. Charles Gilman, stepdau. Mary Bishop, and w.'s mother. Hopewell Hull(6) was named an overseer, wit. the will, and apprais. the est., Benj. Hull (1) ano. appraiser. The wid. m. 2d 20 May 1692 Benj. Jones.

**2 DANIEL**(4), ±28 in Nov. 1680, called (8) 'my uncle John Gilman, Esq.' Exeter gr. 2 Apr. 1675. Lists 381, 54, 49, 55a. Wife Alice, m. bef. 2 July 1680. Adm. to her 7 Feb. 1683-4; adm. again 5 Mar. 1705-6 to Saml. Thing in behalf of Boston creditors. Alice was taxed, a widow, 25 Aug. 1684, List 52; m. 2d Nehemiah Leavitt(9). With Daniel's est. insolvent, proof of ch. is lacking, but fatherhood of several Gilmans, whose ancestry has been much sought with premature conclusions, lies bet. him and John(10); less likely with Daniel, whose early death throws doubt—a doubt which is deepened by the ch.'s lack of association with their mo. and step-fa., if they were Daniel's, and the improbability that their mo. would have removed to Hingham leaving young ch. behind in a town subject to Ind. raid in those yrs., tho taking with her s. Edward, a Hingham soldier in 1694. See also (10).

**3 EDWARD**, Exeter, b. near Hingham, co. Norfolk, ab. 1587. For ancestry see Gilman Gens. (1869) and (1895), both corrected in Am. Gen. (Jan. 1935). In court, shortly bef. leav. Eng., aged 50, he took oath that his fa. was Edward. He m. in Hingham 3 June 1614 Mary Clarke, and left Eng. with the large party led by Rev. Robert Peck, arriving Boston in the -Diligent- of Ipswich 10 Aug. 1638; thence to Hingham, with w., three sons, two daus. and three servants. Freeman 13 Mar. 1638-9. Partner with Hingham men in large gr. at Rehoboth 1641; by 1650 he had sold there to Joseph Peck the younger, whom his sons John and Moses called 'Cozen' in 1663. See Mayflower Desc. Mag. 25.65; 26.103. Liv. Hingham 20 Oct. 1647; Ipswich, Selectm. 1649; called of Ipsw. 1 Oct. 1652, when he sold out in Hingham (Suff. D. i.243), tho he had previously (8 May 1652) bot from Thos. Biggs at Lamprill River, and Mr. E. G.sr. and s. Moses were accepted inhab. at Ex. 10 May 1652. Signed Ex. ptn. 24 May fol. Lists 376b, 378. His entire est., except £30 each to sons John and Moses, he deeded to w. Mary 14 Jan. 1654-5, effective at his death. Adm. to her 10 Apr. 1655, the sons and sons-in-law agreeing to distrib. according to his deed. Wid. Mary signed a q. c. 7 Mar. 1663, appar. at Hingham, Mass.; d. there 22 June 1681. Ch: **Mary**, bp. Hingham 6 Aug. 1615, m. there John Folsom(3). **Edward**, bp. 26 Dec. 1617. **Sarah**, bp. 26 Dec. 1617. **Moses** and **Joshua**, bp. 15, bur. 19 Sept. 1619. **Lydia**, m. in Hingham, Mass., 19 Jan. 1644-5 Daniel Cushing, 6 ch. **John**, (b. 10 Jan. 1624†), bp. 23 May 1626. **Jeremy**, bp. 27 Nov. 1628, bur. 1635. **Moses**, bp. 11 Mar. 1630. **Sarah**, bp. 19 Jan. 1632-3. **Daniel**, bur. 21 Apr. 1634.

**4 *EDWARD**(3), came to Exeter bef. his fa. He left Hingham, Mass., aft. Mar. 1644-5, and was of Ipsw. when he m. shortly bef. 28 Sept. 1647 Elizabeth Smith, dau. of Richard of Ipsw., who went back to Shropham, near Hingham, Eng. At Exeter 4 Nov. 1647, E. G., the son, was accepted townsman and given mill and timber priv., he engaging to live there. He promptly began to buy up Ex. lands and build mills, mapping out works on a large scale. Lists 376b, 378, 75ab. In 1652 Mr. Saml. Dudley and E. G. were requested by the town to go as Deputies to the Genl. Ct. in Boston. In June 1653 he gave P/A, having urgent occasion to go to Old Eng.—to raise capital and buy machinery—and appar. had sailed

when writ was entered in Oct. term of Me. Ct. From this trip he never returned, being 'lost at sea.' Kn. ch: **Edward**, b. ±1649. **John**, b. ±1650. **Daniel**, b. ±1652.

5 **EDWARD**(4), ±18 or 20 in Feb. 1670-1, ±23 in Mar. 1671-2, ag. 32 in Dec. 1680. He was adm. inhab. of Exeter 1 Mar. 1672-3 and m. 20 Dec. 1674 Abigail Maverick (Antipas) whom he outlived. Selectm. Mar. 1676-7, 1680-3, 1690; Tr. j. Sals. 1679; Gr. j. 1683-4; aleho. or tav. lic. 1683-6. Lists 54, 49, 383, 55ab, 52, 57, 377. Will, yeoman, 2 June 1690—12 Apr. 1692, names 5 ch. and uncle Capt. John G. Ch: **Edward**, b. 20 Oct. 1675, m. (Ct. Sept. 1701) Abigail Folsom(4), who d. bef. him. Will, of Exeter, weaver, 24 Feb. 1748-9—28 June 1749 provides for 4 sons, 1 dau. incl.: (1752) Edward of Falm., Maverick of Brentwood, (1761) Antipas of Brentwood, Jonathan, innholder of Exeter. **Antipas**, b. 2, d. 27 Feb. 1677. **Maverick**, b. 11 Apr. 1681, m. at Newb. 16 June 1702 Sarah Mayo of Newb. He d. at Salis. 24 Oct. 1732. 11 or 12 ch., 2 rec. at Hampton 1703-5, the others at Newb. **Abigail**, m. Jonathan Thing. **Catherine**, m. Nathl. Ladd(5), gr. s. of John Gilman(8). **Elizabeth**, liv. 1690.

5½ **EZEKIEL**, wounded in Philip's War. Gilliam?

6 **JAMES**(14), Exeter, ±28 in Dec. 1694, m. Mary Dolloff (Christian). He was an Exeter soldier 31 Aug.—28 Sept. 1696. Selectm. 1696. Town gr. 1698. Jury 1706-7. Lists 57, 67, 376b, 377. Will 30 May 1738—28 Mar. 1739 names w. Mary, 6 ch. living, ch. of two dec. daus., and gr. s. Peter Hersey who recd. a sawmill at Piscassick and other land. Ch. (order in will): **James**, ag. 73 in 1768, was given the home place with br. Nehemiah. M. Elizabeth Lyford (Theophilus). 5 ch. **Nehemiah**, b. 1700, liv. in Gilmanton and Meredith, where he d. 1796. Wife unkn. 7 ch. **Elizabeth**, m. Peter Hersey(3). She was dead in 1738, leaving 5 ch. **Mary**, dead in 1738, leaving 4 ch. **Sarah**, Leavitt in fa.'s will. **Rachel**, m. Benjamin Folsom(7). **Ruth**, m. 18 Apr. 1725 Wadleigh Cram of Hampton. **Hannah**, m. William Folsom(1).

7 **CAPT. JEREMIAH**(14), Exeter, taxed Apr. 1682, m. 30 July 1685 Mary Wiggin (Andrew) who depos. in Sept. 1745, ±76, wife of Capt. J. Exeter soldier 31 Aug.—28 Sept. 1696. Town gr. 1698. Jury 1692; Constable 1698. Lists 94, 52, 57, 62, 67, 376b, 384a, 385. Ch: **Jeremiah**, taken by Ind. 6 May 1709, did not return. See Gilman Gen. (1869), p. 234; N. E. Captives 1.370-2. **Andrew**, b. 1690, taken capt. with br. Jeremiah; in Canada Mar. 1710-1. List 99, p. 92. He returned, and m. 1st 27 Jan. 1714-5 Joanna Thing (Saml.), who d. 16

Nov. 1727; 5 ch.; m. 2d 3 Apr. 1728 Bridget Hilton(24), who d. 10 Nov. 1736, 4 ch.; m. 3d by 1741 Jemima (Storer), wid. of Caleb Preble, who was liv. 1755. He d. in Brentwood ab. 1756. **Hannah**, m. Robt. Pike, gr. s. of Maj. Robt. Both liv. Salis. 1718. **A** dau. **Hannah**, b. 1714, m. Charles Hilton, and d. in 1794 (gr. st. at E. Andover, N. H.). **Simon**, m. Elizabeth Dudley(3). Adm. 23 Mar. 1749-50 to wid. Elizabeth and Wm. Moore, both of Stratham. 2 ch. under 7 in 1750; prob. others. **Israel**, m. Deborah Thing (Saml.), b. 14 Feb. 1708, dead in 1748; and had a 2d w. D. ±1768. 11 ch. Perryman's acct. 1724 charged Israel, 'your sis. Pike's maid, your br. Ezekiel.' **Thomas**, liv. 1723. **Benjamin**, m. Elizabeth Thing and had at least one s. Jonathan, called gr. s. of Capt. Jonathan Thing in 1746. **Ezekiel**, Major, d. at Louisburg. He m. Sarah Dudley(3). 3 or m. ch. **Joseph**, Newmarket, m. 23 May 1718 Elizabeth Follett(6). Adm. 22 Feb. 1748-9 to wid. Elizabeth and s. Constantine.

8 ‡*****JOHN**, Esq. (3), Exeter, first ment. in town books 12 Jan. 1648-9, and assoc. with fa., br. Moses and John Legat in 200 a. town gr. and mill priv. 1652. He m. 30 June 1657 Elizabeth Treworgy (James), who was ag. 33 in Oct. 1671. List 385. Selectman 1652 and repeatedly, also Com. t. e. s. c.; Rep. May 1669 (rec. Joshua); Lieut. for Exeter (60 soldiers) June 1669; Capt.; Deputy to Gen. Court, Boston, 1678; Associate for Norfolk Co. Ct. 1678, 1679; Clerk of the Writs 1679. Under the Royal Govt., he was Councillor 1680, Judge of Ct. of Common Pleas 1682, remov. from both by Cranfield in 1683. Rep. 1693 (Speaker), 1697. Victualer's lic. 1692, 1697; tav. lic. 1693-6, 1699, 1700. Lists 376b, 377, 379, 381, 383, 385, 48, 49, 50, 52, 53, 55b, 57, 62, 67, 80. Will 16 July 1700 (d. 24 July 1708) names w. Elizabeth, 9 liv. ch. Wid. d. 8 Sept. 1719 at 80; long obit. in News Letter of 21 Sept. 1719. The Gilman Gen. (1869) is devoted to his posterity. Ch: **Mary**, b. 10 Sept. 1658, m. 26 July 1677 Capt. Jonathan Thing; d. Aug. 1691. **James**, b. 6 Feb. 1659-60, d. y. **Elizabeth**, b. 16 Aug. 1661, m. 1st 12 July 1678 Nathl. Ladd(4), 2d 3 Dec. 1693 Henry Wadleigh. **John**, b. 6 Oct. 1663, d. y. **Catherine**, b. 17 Mar. 1664-5, d. 2 Sept. 1684. **Sarah**, b. 25 Feb. 1666-7, m. Stephen Dudley(3). **Lydia**, b. 12 Dec. 1668, m. 24 Oct. 1687 Capt. John White of Haverhill; 14 ch. rec. there. **Samuel**, b. 30 Mar. 1671, d. 9 Aug. 1691. List 57. *****Nicholas**, Esq., b. 26 Dec. 1672, d. 10 Mar. 1749, ag. 77. Often Selectm. and Moderator; Rep. 1709, 1711-15, 1732; Capt. 1708; J. P. 1715; Presiding Just. Ct. of Sess. Mar. 1732-3. Lists 376b, 377, 385, 63,

GILMAN

264

GILMAN

**67, 69.** M. 1st 9 or 10 June 1697 Sarah Clark(42), who d. 25 Aug. 1741; m. 2d Judith (Coffin) (Noyes), wid. of Capt. Eliphalet Coffin(1). She renounc. adm. on his est. 29 Mar. 1749 in fav. of Col. Saml. G. 10 ch. 1698-1720, incl. Col. Samuel; John (see Peter 12); Col. Daniel; Nathaniel, m. Sarah Emery(5); Rev. Nicholas; Dr. Josiah. **Abigail,** b. 3 Nov. 1674, m. 8 July 1696 Saml. Thing. **John,** b. 19 Jan. 1676-7. **Deborah,** twin, b. 30 Apr. 1679, d. 30 Sept. 1680. **Joanna,** twin, m. Robt. Coffin(4), Henry Dyer(4). **Joseph,** b. 28 Oct. 1680, d. y. **Alice,** b. 23 May 1683, m. Capt. James Leavitt(10), List 385. **Catherine,** b. 27 Nov. 1684, m. 1st Peter Folsom(8), 2d Richard Calley(2). List 385.

**9 *JOHN,** br. of (1), bp. 17 Feb. 1638-9 in Hingham, Eng., son of John, who did not come over, evid. related to (3). He was in Exeter 'Jr.' in 1659 (and in 1658 when (8) was called 'Sr.'). Ex. grants 1664, 1665 (List 376b); taxed Oyster River 1666; exchanged his Ex. land for a horse 1 Oct. 1668, and soon left for Piscataway, N. J., where he was an orig. grantee. In N. J., 1677, he was gr. adm. on est. of 'his kinsman' Israel Folsom(3). Rep. 1675, and chosen several times to treat with the Governor. Remov. late to Cesariae River, Salem Co., N. J. He m. 1st Elizabeth Goddard(3), 2d one Rachel who was named in his will 14 (inv. 25) Oct. 1695, with s. Edward and 5 daus. Wid. Rachel d. bef. 20 Mar. 1695-6. Ch., by 1st w., the first 3 b. in N. H., all rec. at Piscataway: **John,** b. 27 Jan. 1663; named in will of Uncle John Goddard(3); m. 9 Jan. 1684-5 Hannah Robinson, 4 ch. Nunc. will 1 June, inv. 23 July 1695. Wid. m. 2d John Lloyd. **Elizabeth,** b. 7 June 1666, m. 20 Jan. 1683 Wm. Richardson. **Sarah,** b. 9 Sept. 1668, m. Hugh Hutchings. **Charles,** b. 19 Dec. 1670, named in will of (1); m. one Joanna; d. 1710. **Edward,** b. 12 May 1673, m. 1st bef. 6 May 1697 Ann Bacon, 2d Hannah Sheppard. Will 13 Oct., inv. 7 Dec., 1715. **Mary,** b. 3 Mar. 1675-6, d. 27 Sept. 1682. **Anne,** b. 7 Apr. 1678, d. y. **Joseph,** b. 12 Apr. 1680, d. 9 Oct. 1682. **Mercy,** b. 23 Jan. 1682-3, unmar. 1701. By 2d w: **Rachel. Mary,** b. 18 May 1692(?).

**10 JOHN**(4), ag. 27 and called 'Jr.' in 1677, seems to have been brot up by (14) and his bro. (2) by (8). John in 1677 was doing business for 'his uncle' Moses. Adm. inhab. Exeter 1 Apr. 1678. Appar. liv. 1690. Lists 381, 54, 383, 52, 57. He m. 31 May 1675 Grace York (Richard). Her sister's mar. to Philip Cartee, and other considerations (see Daniel 2) make John and w. Grace the plausible parents of three, certainly bros., whose birth is not of

record or of absolute proof: **Stephen,** did military duty 1695-6; had Ex. gr. 1698, Kingston gr. 1708. K. by Ind. at Ki. 1712; adm. 7 July that yr. to br. Cartee. Lists 67, 376b, 96, 400. **Jacob,** cert. br. of Stephen and Cartee, m. 1 Sept. 1704 Mary Ladd (4), gr. dau. of John Gilman(8). Kingston gr. 1702. In 1725 his was the only Gilman fam. in Ki., where he was enterprising and prosperous. Lists 96, 99 p. 92, 400. Will, of Ki., 20 Sept. 1740—27 Apr. 1743, names w. Mary, 7 of 9 ch. **Cartee,** cordwainer, Exeter, wrote wills and deeds. Ex. gr. 1706, 1725. List 376b. Scout duty 1710. Adm. 1753 to Caleb G. jr. His wid. was Hannah. Ch. incl. sons Daniel and William who had land from their fa. in his lifetime. **?Daniel,** Portsm. wit. 1693-5 with Esq. Penhallow, seems ano. br. List 335b. Also **?William,** wit. with Cartee to Moses Gilman's will 1702. Also, poss. a sis. **?Elizabeth,** m. at Newcastle 7 Dec. 1702 Benj. Parker.

**11 *CAPT. JOHN**(14), 'Jr.' in 1697, ±82 in Feb. 1750-1. Lists 62 (jr.), 376b. Gr. j. 1695. Selectm. 1701-5 and at intervals thereaft. Lieut. by 1707, Capt. by 1735; Rep. 1716-1722. He m. Dorothy Wiggin (Andrew) in Hampton 19 Nov. 1695. She is not ment. in his will 2 May 1751—26 Jan. 1754 which names ch: **John,** m. Abigail Thing. **Jonathan,** m. 16 Jan. 1723-4 Elizabeth Leavitt; both liv. 1753. 11 ch. rec. **Hannah,** m. Capt. Treworthy Dudley(3). **Dau.,** m. bef. 6 July 1733 Nathaniel Webster; both dead in Mar. 1744-5, leav. 3 ch. under 21, one of whom, Deborah, w. of Theophilus Gilman, is named in gr. fa.'s will. **?Martha,** not in will, but called 'kinswo.' in Nathl. Webster's will 22 Jan. 1744-5, and poss. his wife's sis. or niece. Gilman Gen. adds two more not in will: **?David. ?Josiah.**

**12 COL. *JOHN,** Esq. (8), Exeter, ±34 in 1711. List 376b. Often Selectm.; Rep. 1716-1722; Magistrate Ct. of Appeals 1717; Presiding Justice Ct. of Sess. 1733. One of the grantees of Gilmanton, and a large landowner. He m. 1st 5 June 1698 Elizabeth Coffin(4), who d. 10 July 1720; 2d in Beverly, 29 Dec. 1720, Elizabeth (Clark 42), wid. of Dr. Robt. Hale. Will 19 June 1738—28 Apr. 1742 names 2d w., 6 sons, dau. Abigail Moore, gr. dau. Elizabeth Hale. Ch: **Joanna,** b. 20 Sept. 1700. **Elizabeth,** b. 5 Feb. 1701-2, m. at Ex. 12 Dec. 1723 Dr. Robt. Hale, jr., of Bev.; d. 19 Aug. 1736. ***‡Peter,** Col., b. 6 Feb. 1704-5, d. 1 Dec. 1788; Speaker of the Assembly; commanded a regt. at Crown Point 1755; memb. of Gov.'s Council. He m. 1st 8 Dec. 1724 Mary (Thing) Gilman, wid. of John (Nicholas 8). She d. 26 Apr. 1750. He m. 2d 8 May 1751

as her fourth husb. Dorothy (born Sherburne), wid. of Rev. John Tayler of Milton; she d. 25 Jan. 1761. He m. 3d Jane (Bethune), wid. of Dr. Moses Prince. 7 daus. **Abigail**, b. 19 Aug. 1707, m. Wm. Moore of Stratham. **Robert**, b. 2 June 1710, physician, m. Priscilla Bartlett. 3 ch. **John**, Major, b. 5 Oct. 1712, m. Jane Dean, dau. of Dr. Thos. and Deborah (Clark 21), who d. 1786. 12 ch. **Joanna**, b. 27 Oct. 1715. By 2d w: **Nicholas**, b. 20 Jan. 1721-2, d. 4 Apr. 1746, m. Mary Gilman (Col. Danl.). No ch. **Samuel**, b. 20 Apr. 1823, m. 1st Tabitha Gilman (Nicholas); 2d 4 May 1761 Lydia (Robinson), wid. of Col. Zebulon Giddings; she d. in Dec. 1791. 2 or m. ch. by 1st w. **Sarah**, b. 23 July 1724. **Nathaniel**, b. 18 June 1726; 1st w. a Russell; m. 2d (int. Boston 27 July 1749) Elizabeth Howe, grdau. of Clarke(42).

13 **JOSHUA**(14), Exeter. Back of him were two ghost Joshuas, one a blunder of the Colonial Secretary in Boston, 'Joshua' an extra Deputy from Hampton instead of John(8) from Exeter; the other, called son of (4), quite imaginary. The real Joshua did military duty at Exeter in 1695, had town gr. 1700, and m. 10 Nov. 1702 Mariah Hersey(2). Lists 67, 376b. He d. 26 Jan. 1717-8; wid. Mariah m. 2d Nicholas Gordon(6). Ch. rec. Exeter: **Mariah**, b. 2 Oct. 1704, m. 1st Joseph Dudley(3), 2d Philip Conner(6). **Sarah**, b. 20 Dec. 1708, m. Samuel Conner(6). **Hannah**, b. 14 Sept. 1712. **Joshua**, b. 2 Feb. 1716, m. 3 Feb. 1737 Esther Sanborn of Kensington; mov. to Gilmanton, where he d. 7 Jan. 1792. Ch.

14 **MOSES**(3), Exeter, ±46 in Mar. 1678, ±63 in Dec. 1694. He is first ment. in Exeter town books 10 Feb. 1647-8, but adm. inhab. with his fa. 10 May 1652. See John (8); also Hall(21). Selectm. 1653, 1660, 1673-4, 1677, 1693. Jury 1653; Gr. j. 1693. Sergeant 1680. Tav. lic. 1683. Lists 376b, 377, 379, 381, 383, 49, 52, 55a, 57, 62, 92, 94. He m. Elizabeth Hersey(1); his letter to her pub. in Essex Q. Ct. Records vi. 412. Will, 12 Jan. 1701—6 Aug. 1702 names w. Elizabeth, who was liv. 1714, and 10 ch: **Moses**, bp. at Hingham 3 July 1659. **Jeremiah**, b. 31 Aug. 1660; s. Israel named in Uncle David's will. **Elizabeth**, b. 19 Apr. 1663, m. 1st Biley Dudley(1), 2d Samuel Thing. **James**, b. 31 May 1665. **John**, b. 7 June 1668. **David**, had town gr. 1698. List 376b. Will 25 (Mar.?)—11 Apr. 1735 names br. Caleb chief heir, giving also to br. James's wife and several nephews. **Joshua**. **Caleb**, b. ±1682, ag. 86 in 1768, m. Susannah Folsom(7). Selectm. 1725, 1730-1, 1736-7. List 67. Son David, ±14 in 1735, inher. the homestead of his uncle David and was liv. 1768. Other ch. incl. Caleb (of age in 1733),

Israel, Susanna, Elizabeth. **Mary**, m. Cornelius Conner(5). **Judith**, m. Thos. Lyford (3).

15 **MOSES**(14), Exeter, taxed and had town gr. 1682. Jury 1694; Gr. j. 1698. Selectm. 1694; Constable 1700. Lists 376b, 377, 52, 57, 62. In 1682 Theophilus Dudley was beating him on account of an unborn child (presum. Theophilus Gilman, selectman of Exeter 1726). He m. 1st Ann Heard (3), 2d (int. Salem 6 June 1713) Elizabeth (Croade) (Bridges) Lambert. Will 4 Apr. 1741—28 Oct. 1747 names w. Elizabeth, 5 daus. 1 son: **Abigail**, b. 24 July 1693, m. 31 Oct. 1712 John Lord of Ipsw. Liv. Exeter. 16 ch. **Anne**, m. John Lougee. **Judith**, m. Nicholas Smith. **Shuah**, m. by 1721 Abner Thurston of Ex. **Elizabeth**, m. after 3 July 1729 Samuel Thurston of Ex. **Moses**, m. in Salem 3 Aug. 1742 Sarah Stacy; d. in Newmarket 9 Jan. 1769. 7 ch. See Y. D. 18.109.

**Gimison**, Patrick. List 362b. See Jameson.

**Gingden**, Ginden, John, Pemaquid 1671. O. F. 1674. Lists 80, 15.

**Giun**, Thomas, Oyster Riv. 1659. List 361a. See Gwinn.

**GLADMAN**, Elkanah, Mr., governor of Penobscot fort 1662, placed there by his kinsm. Capt. Thos. Breedon. List 2. Inven. filed in Suff. Co. 23 Nov. 1664 by Capts. Breedon and Lake, admrs. Lydia Goodyear (Stephen) was his intended wife. See N. E. Reg. 16.50, 48.127-8.

## GLANFIELD, a Devon-Cornwall name.

1 **DANIEL**, appar. Scarb., had m. Mary Moore by July 1676.

2 **HUGH**, in N. H. Ct. in 1669 for assaulting Martin Hall to the extent that his cure cost 50s. Jane Walford went his bonds. Scarb. 1681. Lists 238a, 226.

3 **JOHN**, Scarb., in 1674 sent to Boston with Amy, w. of Richard Willing, to be tried for adultery, at that time a capital offence; acquitted 3 Mar. 1673-4.

4 **PETER**, tailor, first appear. Dover tax list 1663, yet the same yr. 'of Isles of Shoals' and bot there. Constable 1666. Fined in Maine court for forcibly evicting Wm. Pitts, but sustained in jailing him. 1666 appraiser on Rev. Joseph Hull's estate. Next yr. bot 2 a. near Portsm. meeting ho. where he appar. liv. until going to Salem to live with his son. In 1670 he sold his ho. at the Shoals. Gr. J. 1670, 1672. In 1670 he took deed from Wm. Palmer of 12 a. in Kit. to bring up his dau. from 4 to 20, added to it by two other deeds in 1674 and 1682, and sold the whole in 1685. In 1684 was fined for expr. his opin. of Cranfield. O. A. at Str. Bk. 28 Aug. 1685. Last ment. 'of Salem' 30 May 1696. Lists 356h, 326c, 331b, 49. W. Margaret. Only kn. ch: **Robert**, b. 1643. **Abigail**, m. by 1664

Wm. Broad (4). **Ruth**, m. 1st Caleb Stevens, 2d Henry Kirke (2).

5 **ROBERT** (4), master mariner, first appears at Salem 1665. In 1696 his fa. called him 'only son,' yet others were poss. dead or disowned. In 1688 he commanded the ketch —Fellowship— in the European trade; in 1692 the pinke —Dove—. D. 1702. He m. 12 July 1665 Lydia Ward of Salem. Ch: **Lydia**, b. 3 Sept. 1666, m. Wm. Carkeet (4). **Abigail**, b. 20 Apr. 1668. **Peter**, b. 7 June 1670. In 1690 Peter (4) was 'Senr.' in the Portsm. tax list; his gr. s. may have been liv. with him or he may have had a s. Peter. **Robert**, b. 27 July 1672. **Sarah**, b. 16 Jan. 1674-5.

**GLASS, Richard,** Pemaquid, took O. F. there 1674, and at Marbleh. 18 Dec. 1677. Lists 4, 15, 85, 315c. Manchester 1684-87, Newcastle 1696. W. Elizabeth. Ch. 1st 5 bap. Salem 7 Oct. 1683: **Elizabeth; George; Nicholas; Richard, d. y.; William.** Rec. Manchester: **Mary,** b. 27 Oct. 1684, bp. Marbleh. 2 Aug. 1685; **Joan,** b. 13 Nov. 1686; **Richard,** b. 15 Mar. 1687, was jailed in 1708 for running away from his master John Carter of the Shoals and shipping on a voyage but escaped with aid of the O'Shaw fam. and was retaken at Wid. O'Shaw's. He or his fa. m. at Marbleh. 4 Mar. 1711-2 Elizabeth Curtis. One Mary G. of Newc. m. 29 Oct. 1732 John Noble of Portsm.

Glasson, Cornelius, ±28 in 1678, and Henry Burkes (1) depos. ab. Dennis Murphy and Henry Kirke.

Gleason, see Lissen.

Glicke, William, Scarboro wit. 1643. P. & Ct. ii. 398. See Lux.

**GLIDDEN,**

1 **CHARLES,** blacksmith, s. of Richard and Dorothy of Buckland-Brewer and Bideford, co. Devon, m. in Bideford 7 Apr. 1658 Eunice Shore, whose fa. Sampson Shore had already emig. to Boston. They soon foll. but quickly left Boston. Sept. 29, 1662 he was a Kit. witn. and soon a householder at Str. Bk. Constab. 1664. By 1668 he had sett. the perman. Glidden homestead in that part of Exeter now Newmarket. Lic. pub. ho. 1686, 1696-1700. He and w. Eunice ack. a deed 6 June 1707. Lists 323, 326b, 356L, 54, 383, 52, 92, 57, 67, 376b (1698). Ch: **Abigail,** bp. Bideford, Eng., 11 Feb. 1658-9. **Susanna,** b. Boston 16 Nov. 1661. **Richard. John.**

2 **JOHN** (1), Exeter, m. ab. 1695 Elizabeth Ladd (4). Lists 376b (1698, 1705). Inv. 17 May 1718, adm. 4 June to br. Richard. Kn. ch: **Elizabeth,** m. at Hampt. Falls 9 Aug. 1725 John Cilley. **Abigail,** m. 2 Mar. 1727 David Sanborn. **Nathaniel,** Exeter, m. 17 Feb. 1737-8 Anne Lord (Deac. John), who d. bet. 15 Oct. 1767 and 29 Aug. 1770;

he bur. 25 Oct. 1753. List 376b (1725). 7 ch.

3 **RICHARD** (1), Exeter, called Capt., but no official record found. Highway surv. 1699. Lists 62, 376b. Will 18 Oct. 1727 (d. 5 Oct. 1728) names w. Sarah, who was liv. 27 Feb. 1733-4 and ch: **Andrew,** b. ab. 1686, d. bef. 1 Jan. 1730-1. List 376b. W. Lydia Folsom (1), liv. 8 Nov. 1740. 1 dau. **Joseph,** cordw. Durham, b. ab. 1688, d. aft. 6 May 1761. Lists 369, 376b (1725). M. 1st Mary Smart (Robt.) who d. bef. 13 Apr. 1740; 2d Dorcas (Rawlins) wid. of Arthur Bennett (9). 9 ch: **Charles,** b. ab. 1690, d. bef. 18 Oct. 1727; m. Abigail Jones, who d. bef. 22 Feb. 1742-3. 2 ch. **Richard,** b. ab. 1692, recd. half the homestead. List 376b (1725). Liv. Brentwood 1749, d. bef. 17 Nov. 1755. W. Elizabeth Smart, sis. of br. Joseph's 1st w., was liv. 1741. 5 ch. **Benjamin,** cordw. Durham, b. ab. 1694, liv. 1739. List 376b (1725). W. Mary Wedgwood (John) liv. 26 Oct. 1736. 3 ch. bp. Durham 1724-1728. **Jonathan,** Epping, Brentwood and Deerfield, b. ab. 1696, m. at Greenl. 31 Dec. 1729 Margaret Bean (Jeremiah). She liv. 1756, he 19 Mar. 1771. 8 ch. **Josiah,** b. ab. 1698, incapac. and mainten. provid. by fa.'s will. **John,** b. ab. 1700, recd. half the homestead. Liv. Exeter 1749. **Susannah,** m. one Woodman bef. 18 Oct. 1727. **Sarah. Elizabeth,** both unm. 1727.

**GLINES (Gline), William,** s. of Wm. and Agnes (Grout) G. of So. Trent., co. Devon, cous. of Gabriel Grout, was working with Richard Manson at Portsm. ab. 1702. Settled at Oyster Riv. List 368b. Wife not found. Prob. his ch: **John,** bp. O. R. 26 June 1726. One John (Gline) m. at Dover 27 Nov. 1728 Mary Basford. **Abigail,** sister of and bp. with John.

GLOVER. 1 ———, 1676, List 4.

2 **RALPH,** Mr., Boston, York patentee, d. bef. 13 July 1633. Lists 271, 272.

3 **RICHARD,** Dover, m. Martha Moses (Timothy). See Moses.

Glydd. John, s. of John of Helson, co. Sussex, with consent of Robt. Lord, apprent. himself as husbandman in 1663. Y. D. 1.148.

Goage, Joan, 1682. List 185. See Gutch.

Goare, George, mariner, ship —Johanna— of Piscataqua, 1686. One Eliza Goar recd. into covt., So. Ch., Portsm., 1716.

**GODDARD,** a so. of England name.

1 *****GYLES,** Pemaquid, housewright, first found at Boston in July 1678 prosec. Benj. Ludden for striking him and drawing blood and striking his servant. Taxed Boston 1681; at Nevis 1683, and reached Pemaquid that yr. From Cornwall he was Rep. to the Genl. Assemb. in N. Y., 1684; the same yr. Lieut. and had a personal en-

counter with Capt. Nich. Manning; Com. t. e. s. c.; Capt. of a Foot Co.; Surveyor for the County and J. P. 1686. Of Pemaq., late of Boston, he was acquitted in Suffolk Ct. in Mar. 1685 on charge of selling at Nevis valuables entrusted to him at time of the Boston fire 1679, his former master in Eng. then ment. Lists 16, 162, 163. Taxed Boston 1691, bot there 1694, sued Gyles Dyer 1705. Adm. in Boston 9 June 1729 to s. John. W. Mary in 1678; he m. last in Boston 2 Aug. 1721 Lydia Chapin, who was liv. 1727. Kn. ch: **John**, cordwainer, Lieut., Capt., Roxbury, m. (int. Lynn 19 June 1697) Sarah Farrington; 2d 15 Nov. 1732 Mary, wid. of Jona. Sprague of Malden; 3d 16 Nov. 1738 Susanna (Gill), wid. of Obediah Lincoln of Hingham. He liv. 1741. 4 ch. rec. Lynn and Roxbury. **Elizabeth**. She or an unkn. sis. m. one Slaughter (poss. Geo. of Pemaquid 1687). A son John S., mariner, was liv. in 1718 in his gr. fa.'s home which his gr. fa. deeded to him, reserv. one end for life. **Mary**, youngest dau. 1685, m. John Vinal of Scituate; d. 18 July 1723 in 53d yr. Ch. rec. Scit., incl. Elijah, b. 19 Feb. 1694-5, who received Boston prop. from his gr. fa. in 1727. **William**, b. Boston 4 Aug. 1678, m. there 29 Oct. 1697 Elizabeth Fairfield (Daniel). 4 ch. rec. 1697-1707, incl. Gyles. One Wm. G. m. in Boston 21 Sept. 1709 Elizabeth Everton. See also Holman(5).

2 **HENRY**, weaver, came from Whaddon, co. Gloucester, to York, where his close assoc. with the Stover fam. suggests a relationship. First noticed in July 1687 witnessing a Weare fam. deed and Sylvester Stover's will, his name recorded -Webberby Capt. Wincoll when the will was proved. His 40 a. gr. beyond Cape Neddick for a fulling mill in 1688, he sold to Elizabeth Stover in Nov. 1690, and 3 mos. later was her atty. in Ct. Removing to Jamestown, R. I., he m. 12 Aug. 1693 Mary Howland (Henry of Marshfield). Adm. freeman there 21 June 1696, town sergeant many yrs. and often in minor office. A Quaker, his last appear. was as witn. to a Quaker mar. in 1736. 7 ch. 1694-1704: **Daniel. Josiah. Beriah. Ebenezer. Susanna** and **Mary**, twins. **John.**

3 **JOHN**, Oyster River, carpenter, b. ab. 1608, arriv. in the -Pied Cow- 8 July 1634 with his partners James Wall and Wm. Chadbourne(4) under contract with Capt. John Mason dated 14 Mar. 1633-4 to build mills at Newich. By 1642 he was sett. at Dover; that yr. got judg. against Francis Williams and Thos. Wannerton for false imprisonm., and as late as 1653 had counter suits with Jos. Mason, repres. Capt. John's wid., for breach of contract. In 1647 he bot from Jos. Miller on Goddard's Creek near Great Bay. Propr. 1648, freeman 1653, constab. 1655, gr. j. 1655, 57, 59, selectm. 1661. Depos. 25 June 1662, ab. 54. Lists 41, 352, 353, 354abc, 355ab, 356a, 361a, 362a, 363abc, 342, 47, 365. He met an 'untimely death' 12 Nov. 1666; adm. to wid. and s. John 25 June 1667. Wid. Welthen, ±60 in 1681, m. bef. 1670 John Symonds; liv. 1705 incapable. In 1721 her gr. s. Abraham Bennett was cited to disclose knowl. ab. her will. Ch: **John**, sickly, made his will 2 July 1672, giving all to br. Benj. aft. mo.'s dec. Lists 366, 359a. App. dead in 1678, altho will proved 4 June 1694. **Elizabeth**, m. John Gilman. **Mary**, m. 1st Arthur Bennett(3), 2d Joseph Field(6), 3d Hans Wolford. **Martha**, m. 1st James Thomas, 2d Elias Critchet. **Benjamin**, youngest son, liv. 1678, d. s. p. bef. 30 Apr. 1717.

4 **JOHN**, Mr., ±32, mercht. of the ship -Richard- on which Nicho. Frost (9 jr.) died, deposed in Portsm. 1674.

**GODFREY**, an ancient given name. The eastern counties, partic. Cambridge, are its principal home, but it is also rep. in Somerset and Gloucester.

1 §†‡**EDWARD**, York, Governor, Deputy Governor, Councilor, Assistant, and highly controversial subject, particularly as between the late Col. Charles E. Banks (his early 'Edward Godfrey, his Life, Letters and Public Services 1584-1664' and his treatment in his recent 'History of York,' Vol. I.), who perhaps overrates, and Mr. Charles Thornton Libby (Vols. I and II, Me. Prov. and Ct. Records), who perhaps underrates, the man's character and importance. Born in Wilmington, co. Kent, in 1584, of a Visitation family, son of Oliver Godfrey and his w. Elizabeth, dau. of Humphrey Toye of London, Edward Godfrey adm. his fa.'s est. in 1610, and was exec. of his mo.'s will 19, d. 21, Jan. 1621-2. Dr. Banks places him, a London and travelling merchant, in London by comtemp. record to 8 Oct. 1628. In the next 7½ yrs. there are four dated contemp. records of him (all ignored by Dr. Banks), three showing him in high position under the Laconia Co.—in London 17 Nov. 1629, over here 18 Oct. and 5 Dec. 1632. In London, he was just coming over as governor, bringing the patent and authorized to take livery of seisin in the Co.'s behalf (D. H. vii. 107); but before the -Warwick- sailed, they appointed Capt. Neale gov. instead (List 41). Winthrop's Hist. (p. 90) records Capt. Cammock and Mr. Godfrey in Boston in Capt. Neale's shallop with corn to be ground at their windmill. The Laconia Co.'s letter, seven weeks later, shows Capt. Neale recalled and E. G. left in chief con-

trol until further orders (Prov. Papers 1.68); this letter mention  him four times. The fourth record, 5 May 1634, shows Capt. Norton and Mr. Godfrey committed to Sir Ferdinando Gorges' activities in Agamenticus River; see the letter of Gorges and Mason to Wannerton and Gibbons, with a personal letter from Mason to Gibbons, giving instructions about dividing their patent (Prov. Papers 1. 88-90). Similar letters by the same ship to Capt. Walter Norton and Mr. Godfrey, in Sir Ferdinando's interest, were not preserved. Between these dates Councilor Godfrey's case in the first court in Saco (P. & Ct. i.3) shows him in Maine early in 1633, and Mr. Gibbons's letter 13 July 1633 (Prov. Papers 1. 81) shows he had abandoned the Laconia people some time before, and presum. had pitched on his chosen location up the 'sluggish tidal river' and built some kind of habitation. In his numerous recitals he never stated definitely the year in which he did this; the earliest take the date back to 1631 (his old-age figures Feb.—Mar. 1661, '30 years amongst them'), except his ptn. to the Mass. Genl. Ct., 30 Oct. 1654, written from Piscataqua, '24 years an inhabitant in this place (Piscataqua), the first that ever built or settled there' (meaning York). Godfrey's own 'Cattalogue of such Pattents as I know granted' (1 Me. Hist. Socy. Col. ix. 69-70) mentions no patent to himself, but only 'A Pattent to Sir Fir: Gorges Capt. Norton and others for the River of Accamenties wch was renewed to Edward Godfrey 1638 & populated with inhabitance most att his charge and regulated 25 years.' Every naming of councilors, commissioners, assistants, included him; even the Boston invaders named him 2d on their full county bench, altho the Genl. Ct. reduced them to Associates (P. & Ct. ii). In the period between Jocelyn quitting and Mass. coming in, he was Governor of the Province of Maine (then including York and Kittery), 1649-1652, with Wells appar. giving allegiance neither to his govt. nor to the Lygonia Prov. on the other side (P. & Ct. i. 133, 144, 166). While a long list of the leading inhab. of York and the most of Kit. could be made up who did not let Godfrey's court try a case in his whole three years, an exception (P. & Ct. i. 139) is four suits and executions issued against 'Thomas Turpine deceased,' hardly in a position to agree on referees or enter an appeal. Mass. came in, and in 1655 he went to England, spending four years in a fruitless endeavor to interest whatever govt. existed there in his claims. See also D.H. 3.240, 4.150, 152; 'New England's Vindication' (Gorges Socy. 1884); Prof. Andrews's 'The Colonial Pe-

riod of American History' (1934)—(Footnote, p. 429, was from a personal letter). Lists 41, 272, 273, 281, 71, 275, 276, 277. He m. 1st Elizabeth Oliver (Wm.) of Seale, co. Kent, who was liv. 1634; 2d, soon aft. 1640, Anne (Burdett?) Messant, who had come from Dover to York with Rev. George Burdett(2). D. in Ludgate poor debtors' prison 'of old age' 28 Feb. 1663-4. His widow, having remained here, soon gave her est. to Alice, w. of Major Shapleigh, and was liv. in Kittery in Jan. 1680-1; d. before June 1683. Ch: **Mary. Elizabeth. Oliver,** b. 1624; came twice to York and was about coming a third time, with his family, when delayed to assist his father (Doc. Hist. iv. 150), and soon d. He m. Mary, dau. of Richard Smith of Seale, co. Kent. Will, 10 Sept., bur. at Seale 23 Oct. 1661, names 7 ch., all under 18: Edward, ment. by (1). Mary. Elizabeth. Sarah, bp. 19 Oct. 1656 in Seale. Oliver, bp. 20 Dec. 1659, m. 14 July 1685 Hannah French. Charles, bp. 26 May 1661, bur. 16 Apr. 1664. Susannah.

2 **ISAAC**(7), farmer, inher. his fa.'s homestead. Gr. j. 1693, 94. Lists 394, 54, 49, 396, 52, 57, 62, 399a, 400. He m. 15 July 1670 Hannah Marion (John), and d. 27 Dec. 1717; will made 11 July 1710 names w., 2 sons (excrs.), 3 unm. daus. Ch: **Hannah,** b. 24 Apr. 1671, prob. d. y. **William,** b. 9 Nov. 1672, liv. No. Hampt. List 400. He m. 17 Jan. 1700-1 Priscilla Annis, who d. 31 Aug. 1768, ae. 88. His will 30 Apr. 1741—25 May 1743. 4 ch. **Sarah,** b. 29 Aug. 1674, not in fa.'s will. **Isaac,** b. Jan. 1677, d. 4 Nov. 1683. **Mary,** b. 7 Sept. 1678, d. 25 Mar. 1702 unm. **James,** b. 26 Feb. 1681, not in fa.'s will. **Abigail,** unm. in 1710. **Elizabeth,** unm. 1710. One Elizabeth m. 23 Jan. 1723-4 Thos. Briar(6) as his 3d w. **Hannah,** bp. with Jonathan 7 Mar. 1696-7, m. 12 Aug. 1736 Ephraim Hoyt (Thos.). **Jonathan,** b. 19 Apr. 1691. Will 2 Mar., d. 3 Mar. 1733-4. He m. 3 Dec. 1719 Mehitabel Blake(2), who m. 2d Enoch Sanborn. 6 ch.

3 **JAMES,** ±40 in 1680, ±65 in 1701, bot John Hilton's lot in Exeter and had 10 a. gr. adj. 4 Apr. 1666; in 1668 he sold ho. and land gr. by the town to Chas. Glidden. Henry Dering's acct. ag. him 1667-8 was largely for liquor and money deliv. to Wm. Graves. Nov. 1701 he dep. he had known Squamscot 42 yrs. Lists 376b, 380, 62, 384a, 67, 387, 388.

3½ **JOHN,** nephew of (1), bp. London 1619, s. of William, came to Piscataqua with his uncle; went with Capt. Norton on his fatal voyage to Conn.

4 **JOHN**(7), ab. 48 in July 1680. He went with his fa. to Hampt.; there m. 6 May 1659 Mary Cox(18), ±36 in 1680, liv. 14 Aug. 1707, ±65. He d. 19 Mar. 1696-7, adm.

4 June 1706 to s. John. Lists 392c, 54, 396, 397a, 57. Ch: **John**, b. 8 Apr., d. 16 Apr. 1660. **Mary**, b. 3 May 1661, m. in Haverh. 23 Nov. 1681 John Stockbridge. **William**, b. 28 May, d. 4 July 1663. **Sarah**, b. 26 July 1664, liv. 1680. **Rachel**, b. 28 Oct. 1666. **Mehitabel**, b. 15 Aug. 1668, liv. 1680. **Hannah**, b. 11 Dec. 1670, m. 25 Apr. 1695 Ephraim Hoyt (Thos.). **Deborah**, b. 14 Nov. 1672. In 1708 her ch. was charged to Maj. Joseph Smith in whose ho. she had been a serv. One Deborah soon m. Thos. Philbrook in Greenland. **John**, b. 5 May 1676, m. Abigail Greely (Andrew). 9 ch. 1706-1723. **Moses**, b. 11 Apr. 1679, d. July 1680 'murdered by witchcraft.' List 397a. 'And her (Deborah's) sist. Abiah,' ment. in Leah (Cox) Perkins's depo. 1707, unexpl.

5 **JOSEPH**, indebted to Jos. Mitchell's est. 1666. List 78.

6 **RICHARD**, soldier at Wells gar. 1677. D. H. 6.159.

7 **WILLIAM**, husbandman, came to Hampt. from Watertown where he was freem. 13 May 1640 and was liv. in May 1648 and May 1649 when he bot in Hampt., incl. Wm. Howard's house. He rem. to Hampt. before 4 Mar. 1649-50, selling in Watert. 1653. Selectm. 1654, deacon by 1660. Lists 392b, 393ab. June 22, 1648, in behalf of s. John he gave P/A to Mr. Antonie Lawrence of London to collect £10 legacy beq. to his decd. w. Sarah or ch. by Mrs. Betteris Key of Woburn, co. Bedford, a kinswoman. He m. 2d ab. 1638 Margery, mo. of Thos. Webster. List 393a. He d. 25 Mar. 1670-1; will made 2 Oct. 1667 names w. Margery and s. Isaac, excrs., the other 3 ch. and s.-in-law Webster. She m. 3d John Marion. Ch. by 1st w: **John**, b. ±1632. By 2d w: **Isaac**, b. Watert. 15 Apr. 1639. **Sarah**, b. Watert. 15 May 1642, m. John Clifford(4). **Deborah**, b. ±1645, m. 5 Dec. 1667 John Taylor. Also adopted ch: Nathl. Smith and sister.

8 **WILLIAM**, tax rebate Portsm. 15 Mar. 1679-80.

**Godin**, William, withdrew suit ag. Tho. Kemble for wages, Dover Ct., June 1661. See also Goodwin.

## GODSOE.

1 **WILLIAM**, mariner, ±50 Oct. 1698, b. 1644-5 by depositions made 1725-7. Capt. Geo. Corwin's servant in Salem bef. 1674, he made his home there until aft. the Corwin robbery 1683-4, in which he was implicated and which his w. Elizabeth, also a former servant, was cred. with conceiving. Removed to Great Island bef. 4 July 1685, and was made marshal under Cranfield in Jan. 1685-6, provost marshal in Apr. 1686. Taxed Gt. Isl. 1688, 1690. Foll. his last mar. he sett. at Spruce Creek, Kit. Of-

ten employed as surveyor and appr. of estates. Lists 330a, 319, 295, 296, 297, 298. Liv. May 1730 bet. 80 and 90. He m. at Salem 17 Apr. 1680 Elizabeth Lord (Wm.), 2d bet. 1 Apr. and 13 June 1691 Thos. Withers' wid. Jane, from whom he had bot land at Eagle Pt. Feb. 1687-8. Both were abs. from meeting in Nov. 1696. She liv. 1707; dead 13 or 14 yrs. in 1722. Ch: **William**, b. Salem 4 Mar. 1680-1. **James**, b. Salem 1 Dec. 1682, deposed 1725, witn. deed 1729. **John**, witn. deed with Elizabeth Surplice 1705; liv. 1711.

2 **WILLIAM** (1), Kittery, like his fa. was oft. a surveyor. List 298. He m. Elizabeth (Roberts), wid. of John Surplice, who was gr. adm. 25 Oct. 1731, and was liv. 6 Apr. 1745. Ch: **John**, b. 16 Oct. 1714, liv. 1769; m. 13 Sept. 1741 Mary Rogers (John). List 297. 1 ch. rec. **Elizabeth**, b. 2 Apr. 1716, d. y. **Alice**, twin to Elizabeth, m. (pub. 23 Oct. 1742) Nicholas Spinney. **James**, liv. 1745. **Joseph**, b. 23 Apr. 1719, shipwright. W. Hannah in 1743. **Dorothy**, bp. 10 June 1722, m. John Spokefield. **Elizabeth**, bp. 3 Oct. 1725, m. Joseph Spokefield. **Hannah**, m. (pub. 23 Aug. 1749) Saml. Wagling. **William**, n. c. m., supp. by br. John.

**Goe**, see Gove.

## GOFFE, Gough.

1 **ANTHONY**, Exeter 1677, acc. by Geo. Jones of stealing pipestaves; Hampt. witn. 1681. List 383. One Anthony of Billerica m. 29 Sept. 1686 Sally Polley of Woburn. 2 ch. b. Woburn, both d. y.

2 **DANIEL**. See Gott (2).

3 **JAMES**, Mr., agent for Sampson Sheafe, was running Quamphegan mills on halves as early as 1681; liv. in the Lovering ho. List 359b. D. Nov. 1685. In Oct. 1686 Henry Hobbs for hims. and Henry Child asked adm., the wid. Elizabeth (see Crawford 2) having refus. to deliver their partly sawn boards; adm. 7 May 1688 to John Fost (1), her 2d husb.; she m. 3d aft. 1709 James Emery (3).

4 **JOHN**, Portsm. 1672-3. Lists 327cd. One Patrick Goff taxed Newcastle 1720.

**Goit**, Peter, mariner, Boston, bound over in Portsm. 1683.

**Gold**, see Gould.

**GOLDING, Goulding. Peter**, Mr., attorney, ±50 in 1680, sued Capt. Champernowne in Saco Ct. Sept. 1664. Next Jan. with his fam. he hired a room in Boston, intending to ret. to Piscat. in six wks., but then or soon became resid. of Boston and was oft. in the cts. as atty. until disbarred 29 Oct. 1672. In June 1669 Walter Barefoot gave him P/A, 'my trusty friend,' and he repres. Barefoot in case ag. Edward Clements 1672. Boston 1686, Marlboro 1688, Hadley ab. 1690; d. Sudbury 11 Oct. 1703. First w. Jane,

2d w. Sarah, sist. of Joseph Smith of Boston, sadler. She surv. him. See Baxter (1). Ch. by 1st w. incl: **Mary**; in 1677 her fa. sued Richard Russell of Charlest. for not keeping and teaching her accord. to indent. Rec. Boston: **Martha, b.** 21 Jan. 1665-6; in 1683 her fa. in her behalf sued Andrew Smith for defama. **Peter,** app. twin to Martha. **Frances, b.** 22 Feb. 1667-8. By 2d w: 7 ch. rec. Boston and Marlboro 1673-1688, incl. **Windsor** and **Peter.** Sav. adds **Abigail, b.** Hadley 1691; and poss. there were others as **Palmer, b.** ab. 1695, was called the 15th ch. of Peter and Sarah.

**Golds,** ———, (Golde? Goold?), boatswain, his fine due Portsm. 1665.

**Goldwier,** George, Mr., taxed Dover 1658-59, came from and ret. to Salisb. Lists 356ce, Hoyt i. 176.

**Goliff,** Robert, rafted boards down Kennebunk Riv. on Sunday, in June 1688.

**Gomery,** Hugh, constable at Shoals (N. H.) 1696.

**GOOCH,** found in Norfolk, also a visitation family in Lincoln.

1 ———, Mr., List 191. See Gutch.

2 **JAMES** (4), inherited from fa. in addi. to the English prop., upl. in Wells adj. marsh already given him. Freeman 7 July 1670. Selectm. 1670; rep. Wells in protest to Mass. Sept. 1671; highway surveyor from Wells to Casco 1673. Tr. j. 1668-9; 1676; gr. j. 1670, 71, 72, 73 (foreman), 74. Lists 25, 265. K. by Ind. 24 Sept. 1676; his w. wounded then, d. in 3 dys. Her name not found; app. dau. of Wm. Hammond (5), who with w. and s. Jona, deeded to Jas. 3 Feb. 1667. Nov. 1676 Wm. and Jona. H. were ord. to take care of his ch., adm. to both 12 Dec.; his land still in Jona.'s custody 1681. Kn. ch: **James, b.** ab. 1666, oldest s. and h. 1698. **Hannah,** 80 at death 1753, must have been several yrs. older; m. 1st Gilbert Endicott (1), 2d John Minot. Br. James bondsm. for her 1716. One Rebecca G. bp. and adm. to 1st Ch., Boston, 29 Apr. 1694; Mary, adult, bp. there 28 Feb. 1696-7. See also (6).

3 **JAMES** (2), Boston mercht. and mariner, interested in Wells affairs until 1700. Tr. j. 1688. He asked aid for preaching there 1692; the next mo. with his sloop played an import. part repelling the attack on Wells; in Nov. 1696 with Saml. Hill and Tho. Walter took a Fr. vessel going E. from Piscat. York witn. 1697, and took a mtg. on Danl. Black's ho. 1700. Wells land laid out to him 1720. Lists 268b, 333b. In Boston he belonged to the First Ch. and held town offices. M. 1st 10 Feb. 1691-2 Hannah Emmons, sis. of (1), d. 15 Mar. 1694-5; 2d (int. 15 Aug. 1695) Elizabeth Peck, d. 1 Apr. 1702; 3d 12 Nov. 1702 Mrs. Sarah Tuttle.

He d. 30 May 1738 in 73d yr. leav. large est.; will 1732 names w. Sarah, 4 ch: James (by 1st w.), **John, Joseph** and **Elizabeth** Hubbart (by 2d w.), and gr. s. James Hubbart. See Hobby (1).

4 **JOHN,** Mr., propr. York 1640; and in June that yr. headed a commit. for settling their govt.; in 1644 Wm. Hooke deeded to him and Peter Wears 20 a. each near Cape Neddick. Alderman 1647-8. O. A. at York 22 Nov. 1652, at Wells 4 July 1653, member of 1st board of Wells selectm., yet of York 8 Mar. 1653-4 when he sold to Abra. Preble; settled perman. at Wells by 1655. Tr. j. 1640, 50, 55; gr. j. 1650, 57. Constab. 1656, 1662. Lists 273, 274, 275, 261, 276, 263, 269b, 24, 25, 266. W. Ruth among those acc. with Rev. Geo. Burdett (2). List 86. Will 7 May—12 July 1667 names her, sole exec., sons and gr. ch., gives to Jas. prop. in Slymbridge, O. E., bot from Wm. Hammond; br. Wm. Hammond, an overseer; this relationsh. thru the mar. of their ch. In 1663 he had given P/A to 'my lov. friend' Wm. H. Widow's inv. brot in with s. James' 6 Dec. 1676; a yr. later her est. given to the adm. Jona. Hammond for use of James' ch. Ch: **John. James. Ruth,** m. Peter Weare. **Elizabeth,** m. Saml. Austin (7). See also Hammond (2).

5 **JOHN** (4), had 10 a. gr. adj. his fa. from Wm. Hooke 18 Oct. 1644; inher. the home place at Wells. O. A. 4 July 1653. In 1665 Jona. Hammond was atty. for him in suit ag. Ens. Barrett. Lists 24, 269b, 265, 86. Adm. 2 July 1672 to wid. Lydia, poss. dau. of Wm. Hammond (5). His death caused gossip and inquiry. List 86. She soon m. Israel Harding (2), who was gr. adm. in her place 7 Oct. 1673 and ord. to make annual payments to Mrs. Ruth G. Adm. again 13 Mar. 1688-9 to Abra. Preble, invent. incl. old smith's tools, and listing what Lydia G. had dispos. of under pretense of next of kin, incl. a cow and heifer to Wm. Frost. She d. bef. Feb. 1690-1. Ch. ment. 1679, app. incl: **John,** named in gr. fa.'s will. One son was bound 19 Sept. 1679 to Abra. Preble who had then kept and educ. him many yrs. **Benjamin,** tailor, Wells, sold int. in his fa.'s est. 4 Dec. 1707. York Feb. 1695-6; soldier at Wells gar. May 1704. Jury 1705; fence viewer 1713. Bap. and adm. to Wells Ch. 13 Oct. 1713; d. bef. 20 Mar. 1716. List 269a. He m. bef. Dec. 1707 Mary Cole (24) who m. 2d Robt. Connoway; 3d 10 May 1720 Jacob Rylance, with him gr. adm. of 1st husb.'s est. 14 July 1720; 4th Wm. Bracy (2). 4 ch. **Elizabeth** who recd. from the mo. a horse belong. to the fa.'s est., can be acct. for only as a dau. One Elizabeth Gouge m. in Gloucester 15 Aug. 1695 Joseph Day of a fam. that sent members to Wells. See also (6).

6 **NATHANIEL**, pd. by York Mar. 1687-8 for k. a wolf. Presum. s. of (2) or (5).

7 **WILLIAM** (Guich, Gauch), Richmond Isl. July 1641-June 1643, creditor of Jonas Bailey (6), may have been hired here. List 21.

**GOODALE**, **Zachariah**, b. Salem 15 May 1675, s. of Isaac and Patience (Cook), bot in Wells 1699 a lot on the main highway near Ogunquit Riv.; in 1716 added to it the Drisco lot adj. Depos. July 1749, ±74, that he worked for the Cloyeses ab. 1701. Gr. j. 1703, jury 1708. Fence viewer 1721, 1723-4, constab. 1727. Lists 269ac. In 1747 he conv. his homestead and farm to s. John for mainten. M. 1st 22 May 1700 Elizabeth Cousins (4), 2d (int. 27 July 1747) Abigail, wid. of Jas. Tarrott of Peak's Isl., she liv. 1757. 8 ch. See 'Ancestry of Lydia Harmon,' by W. G. Davis.

**Goodenow**, Edw., Cape Porpus witn. 1658. Y. D. ii.123.

**GOODING**, **James**, shipwright, Falmouth, b. Boston 27 Dec. 1696, s. of James and Margaret (Davenport), m. 1st in Boston 7 Mar. 1718-9 Elizabeth Child, 2d in Falm. 1753 Mary (Oliver) (East), wid. of Henry Wheeler. He d. there in 1780. 7 ch., 6 rec. in Boston, the 7th bap. in Falm. 10 June 1733.

**GOODRIDGE**, Goodrich. Goodrich a parish in Hereford. Both found in Devon and So. Wales, and Goodrich in Suffolk.

1 **ISAAC** (Gutteridge), neph. of Christo. Adams (5). Lately from Eng., he bot ½ of Batson's Neck at Cape Porp. from Wm. Palmer in Aug. 1683; of Smuttinose bot in York 1685; of Kit. 1696 mtg. to aunt Margaret Adams part of land bot from Saml. King, giving her a deed in 1699. Adm. to her June 1701; inv. incl. ho. and 10 a. in Kit. besides the Cape Porp. and York land. Her acct. covered clothing 18 yrs., dieting, lodging, washing and attend. 6 yrs.

2 **JAMES** (Guttridge). Wells 1693. List 269b.

3 **JEREMIAH**, b. ±1636, s. of Wm. and Margaret, m. in Newb. 15 Nov. 1660 Mary Adams, and soon came to Kit. where Henry Greenland succes. sued him in 1667 for defama. and slander. In the foll. yrs. the Me. cts. saw him freq. for idling and not provid. for his fam. Fishing for Roger Kelly 1668-9. Witn. 1675 with Ephraim Crockett, who was bondsm. for him that yr. Lists 304, 286. In 1676 he was liv. in the Ladbrook ho., Portsm.; app. soon ret. to Newb. where he d. 20 Jan. 1707. In add. to the 5 ch. rec. in Newb. bef. and aft. his Me. resid., were two prob. b. in Kit. or Portsm.: **Philip**, b. 23 Nov. 1669, m. in Newb. 16 Apr. 1700

Mehitable Woodman; mov. to Lunenburg aft. 1723. 12 ch. rec. Newb. **Jeremiah**, Newb., ag. 76 in 1753, m. there 1703 Mary Rowe (Wm.) who q. c. Rowe interest to Thos. Cotton. 4 ch. rec. Newb.

4 **JOHN** (Gudridg), had fish on Pickering's Isl. 1685.

5 **JOSIAH**, from Newb., neph. of (3), a Berw. witn. 1700, m. Mary Abbott (4), Goodridge in fa.'s will. Both bp. and o. c. 20 Jan. 1716-7, he liv. 1750. Lists 289, 290. Ch: **Benjamin**, bp. and o. c. 17 Jan. 1719-20, m. in York 24 June 1725 Abigail Preble. 8 ch. **John**, bp. and o. c. 19 Mar. 1726-7, m. Dorcas Powell (Thos.), wid. 1750. 3 ch. bp. **Deborah**, bp. and o. c. with John. One Deborah a witn. 1720. **Mary**, **Sarah**, **Susanna**, all bp. 13 June 1717. **Abigail**, bp. 29 June 1718. **Anna**, bp. 2 Nov. 1721. **Margaret**, bp. 22 Apr. 1725.

**Goodwill**, Thomas and Rebecca. See Blackman (2).

**GOODWIN**, poss. from ancient forename Godwin. Scattered throughout the Midlands.

1 **ABIGAIL**, bp. at Oyster Riv. on death bed 26 Nov. 1718, with inf. dau. Abigail; poss. an early w. of (9).

2 **ABIEL**, York mason 1716, b. in Reading 11 Feb. 1693-4, s. of Nathl. and Susanna (Kendall?). List 279. 1st w. Hephzibah d. 30 May 1720, ag. 29; 2d w. Sarah Milbury (Richard). 10 ch.

3 **ADAM** (Goodens), ag. 20, came with John Moulton of Hampton, 1637. One Adam early at Providence, R. I.

4 **DANIEL**, Kittery 1652, long kept a pub. house with and without lic., at times with consid. disorder which brot him into ct., but he found time to give to town affairs. Town comr. and Sergt. 1659, constab. 1662-63. Coroner's j. 1668, gr. j. 1659, 1678. Orig. memb. of Berw. Ch. 1702. Lists 24, 25, 28, 296, 298. He m. 1st, mar. contract ab. 1654-55, Margaret Spencer (Thos.), 2d aft. July 1673 Sarah (Sanders), wid. of Peter Turbot. In Dec. 1711, both liv., he deeded homestead to s. Thos. for support; d. bef. 1713. Ch: **Patience**, m. 19 Sept. 1670 Danl. Stone. **Adam**, absent from meeting July 1675. **Daniel**, b. ±1656. **Thomas**. **James**. **William**. **Moses**, with br. Wm. was in Spencer's garrison (ab. 1693?); their fa. deeded to them jointly, Mar. 1696-7. Lists 296, 298. See Chick. M. 7 Sept. 1694 Abigail Taylor (John). Will 21 Apr.—9 June 1726 names her and 9 ch: Martha, Patience, Mary, Abigail, Phebe, Elizabeth, Margaret, Moses, Aaron. In 1738 Abigail, wid., of Berw., was accus. of receiving stolen goods. **Elizabeth**, m. 1st Zachariah Emery (6), 2d Philip Hubbard (9). **Sarah**, poss. by 2d w., m. in Berw. 6

Dec. 1694 Isaac Barron (Barnes by mar. rec.) of Chelmsford, who had been a soldier there. 4 daus. rec. Chelmsf. 1695-1703. She liv. Dec. 1711.

5 **DANIEL** (4), Berwick, ±30 Mar. 1686, ag. 70 Oct. 1725; ±37 Oct. 1700 obv. an error. May 24, 1679, his fa. deeded him land and a small ho. then occup. by Danl. Stone. Gr. j. 1687 and often. Surv. highways 1694-5; selectm. 1695-8. Lists 33, 298. He m. 17 Dec. 1682 Amy Thompson (Miles). She o. c. and was recd. into ch. 9 May 1714. Will 12 Apr.—12 May 1726 ment. w. (unnamed) and 10 ch. Ch: **Margaret**, b. 23 Aug. 1683, m. Jos. Hodgdon (1). **Daniel**, Dover, b. 13 June 1685, m. 30 Dec. 1708 Abigail Roberts (Hatevil). List 358d. He was drowned falling out of a canoe betw. Kit. and Portsm. 13 Aug. 1734. Adm. 1 Oct. 1739 to s. Daniel of Dover. Wid. Abigail had 26 a. gr. in Dover 1736. 8 ch. **Miles**, b. 31 July 1687, Berw. witn. 1711. Perh. mov. to Penobscot. W. Esther. 4 ch. bp. Berw. 28 Sept. 1736. **Nathaniel**, b. 29 Oct. 1689, m. (ct. Oct. 1713) Mary (Tibbetts), wid. of John Giles (5). 4 ch. bp. Berw. 16 Jan. 1723-4. **Amy**, b. 19 Apr. 1693, m. Moses Goodwin (12). **Samuel**, b. 24 May 1695, m. 1st 13 Sept. 1719 Sarah Davis, 2d at York 7 Nov. 1734 Judith (Preble) wid. of Benj. Smith. Ch. 6+2. **James**, b. 15 July 1697, liv. 1726. **Thomas**, b. 15 Aug. 1699, d. 3 Apr. 1769; m. in Portsm. 20 Dec. 1722 Abigail Seward. 6 or m. ch. bp. Berw. **Sarah**, b. 23 Sept. 1701, m. (int. 5 Dec. 1729) Josiah Paul. **Anne**, b. 19 Oct., d. 24 Nov. 1703. **Anne**, b. 16 Feb. 1704-5, m. 16 Jan. 1723-4 Wm. More.

6 **DAVID**, ag. 22 in 1670, had been servant of Rich. Cutt. List 328.

6½ **ELIZABETH?**, m. Robert Gray (10)?

7 **GEORGE**, Wells, presum. same b. Newb. 21 July 1695, s. of Rich. and Hannah, and same who m. Keziah Cole (24), m. at Newb. 9 June 1729 Mary Gooch, dau. of Benja. (5). She was a wid. in Wells in 1750. One Geo. (from Newb., w. Mary) was drowned with s. Wm., ag. 18, at No. Yarm., Apr. 1748. Geo. (Gooding) taxed Portsm. Aug. 1722. See (9).

7½ **ITHAMAR**, tr. j. 1689. Wooden?

8 **JAMES** (4), Kittery, with br. Thos. was given land by fa. 14 July 1683. Jury 1696-7. K. by Ind. 29 July 1697. Lists 298, 96. He m. 9 Dec. 1686 Sarah Thompson (Miles); adm. to her 24 Dec. 1697. Wid. Sarah adm. to Berw. Ch. Apr. 1703; soon m. 2d Wm. Hearl (5). Ch. rec.: **Adam**, b. 12 Apr. 1687. **Sarah**, b. 6 Jan. 1689, d. 16 May 1696. **Mary**, b. 23 May 1691; of Berw. m. John Davis (33).

9 **RICHARD**, cooper, Dover, app. br. to (7), m. 1st Sarah Hall (John jr., 10); 2d bef. 1753 Elizabeth (Tibbetts), wid. of Gershom

Downes (6). In 1721 with w. Sarah he gave deed to Wm. Twombly, ack. at Newb. 3 ch. bp. Dover 1721-26. See also (1).

10 **ROBERT**, Shoals fisherman, lost 30 Jan. 1677-8. List 306d. See Broad (4).

11 **THOMAS** (4), with br. James had land from fa. 14 July 1683. Living in Mr. Love's ho. when Salmon Falls sacked Mar. 1689-90, he was capt. with w. Mehitable, dau. of Lt. Roger Plaisted, and inf. son. Her br. James, ano. captive, wrote that Thos. had k. one French man and wounded ano. in the attack and was to be tried for his life by a council of war, yet he was free bef. his w. was redeemed in Oct. 1695. List 99. Gr. j. 1693, 94, 95, 1702. Lists 33, 296, 298. Ensign Thos. G.'s est. taxed 20 Nov. 1713; adm. to wid. 26 Mar. 1714, whose acct. incl. charge for bringing up two ch., one 5 yrs. old, one 3 yrs. old. She was liv. in 1740. Ch: **Son**, k. by Ind. 1690. **Thomas**, b. 29 July 1697, liv. Oct. 1755, m. 2 Dec. 1722 Elizabeth Butler (Thos.). 10 or m. ch. **Ichabod**, b. 1 June 1700, m. 25 Aug. 1729 Elizabeth Scammon (Capt. Humphrey of Saco). Will 1774-1777. 10 ch. **Olive**, bp. 14 Mar. 1707-8, w. of Timo. Davis, joiner, Berw., 1758. **Mary**, bp. 18 June 1710, m. 1st Richard Lord jr. (7), 2d John Cooper, jr. **James**, m. Margaret Wallingford; both liv. 1756. Ch. **Mehitable**, Portsm. Feb. 1721-2, w. of Thos. Butler 1758.

12 **WILLIAM** (4), m. Oct. 1687 Deliverance Taylor (John) and liv. on the Taylor homestead. With varying age she dep. late, ±75 June 1748, liv. at Salm. Falls ab. 60 yrs. ago; ±80 in 1750; ±87 in 1756; 90 in Apr. 1763. List 298. In 1706 he sold James Barrow's grants to Philip Hubbard. Gr. j. 1694. Lists 334b, 96, 296, 298. Will 26 Apr.—1 Aug. 1713, names w. and ch: **Margaret**, b. 19 Dec. 1687, m. James Frost (5). **Moses**, Berw., b. 18 Nov. 1689, m. 6 Nov. 1712 Amy Goodwin (5). W. Ann named in his will made 1769, he liv. 29 Dec. 1770. 10 ch. **William**, b. 11 May 1692, liv. 31 Dec. 1770, m. bef. 1720 his cous. Abigail Stone. 10 ch. **John**, b. 2 Sept. 1694, m. 12 June 1715 Patience Willoughby, both liv. 1758. 8 ch. **James**, b. 4 Mar. 1696-7, m. by 1718 Susanna Durgin (1). Liv. Oyster Riv. 1719-1725; later at Newmarket. Will 1757 names son, 2 daus. 2 gr. ch. (York). One Susanna Gordon or Gooden signed in 1721 as admx. est. of Robt. White, Exeter. **Elizabeth**, b. 17 Dec. 1699, m. Wm. Libby. **Hannah**, b. 29 Aug. 1701, m. Etherington Hearl (5). **Adam**, liv. 1763. M. 1st by 1729 one Sarah, 2d by 1734 Mehitabel Thompson. Ch. 1+9. **Taylor**. Est. adm. 1773. M. by 1733 Elizabeth Nason (Benj.), who m. 2d Peter Grant. 12 ch. **Mary**, m. Capt. John Libby (4).

**GOODYEAR, Moses,** Plymouth merchant, partn. with Robt. Trelawny in the Cape Elizabeth Patent which was vested solely in the latter aft. M. G. d. 26 Mar. 1637. List 21.

**GORDON,** one of the great Scottish clans.
**1 ALEXANDER,** Exeter. A Scotch pris. of war at Tuthill Fields, London, he was redeemed there by Danl. Stone of Cambridge, and came to N. E. with John Cloyes (1) under verbal agreem., working his passage with Capt. John Allen. Cloyes's sale of him to Saml. Stratton 15 Oct. 1652, aft. a yr.'s work without compensa., resulted in his appeal to the ct. in Feb. 1653-4. Mass. Hist. Soc. Proc. 61.25. His hist. unkn. for 10 yrs., he was mar. to Mary Lissen (2) bef. 10 Oct. 1664, when he had an Exeter gr. adj. land given him by his fa. Lissen. Deposed twice in 1678, ±40. Lists 383, 52, 57, 67, 376b (1664). Adm. 15 Aug. 1697 to s. John wid. Mary renounc. Ch: **Elizabeth,** b. 23 Feb. 1664, m. 26 May 1686 Thos. Emerson of Haverh.; both k. by Ind. with 2 of their 5 ch. 15 Mar. 1696-7. **Nicholas,** b. 23 Mar. 1665-6. **Mary,** b. 22 May 1668, m. Nicholas Smith. **John,** b. 26 Oct. 1670. **James,** b. 22 July 1673. Lists 67, 376b (1698). M. 7 Aug. 1700 Abiel Redman (John), who was gr. adm. 7 Dec. 1714, and m. 2d Moses Kimmin (2). 5 sons. **Alexander,** b. 1 Dec. 1675, m. (ct. 14 Sept. 1699) Sarah Sewall (Edward). Lists 67, 376b (1698, 1725). Wid. Sarah, exec. of his will (not found), deeded to Wm. Graves 25 Mar. 1729-30 half a lot owned in common with Graves; liv. a wid. 1732. 7 or m. ch. **Thomas,** b. 1678, m 1st in Haverh. 22 Nov. 1699 Elizabeth Harriman (Matthew), 7 ch., 6 rec. Haverh.; m. 2d aft. 10 Apr. 1709 Rebecca Heard (2), 5 ch. liv. 1756. Lists 376b (1699, 1725). Will 1757-1761, names 10 ch. **Daniel,** b. 1682, blacksmith, m. in Haverh. 15 Sept. 1708 Margaret Harriman. Liv. Kingston and app. sold out there 1717. Lists 358c, 376b (1725). Of 5 ch. rec. 1709-1716, 2 m. in Haverh. Wid. or dau. Margaret m. 17 Feb. 1736 Saml. Bradstreet, both of Suncook.
**2 GEORGE,** Newcastle, fisherman, with w. Hannah in 1715 sold town gr. from Dover 23 June 1701. Dau. Hannah G. named in will of John Yeaton, Newc., 1756-1757, also her dau. Hannah, w. of Thos. Blazo of Greenl.
**3 JOHN** (1), m. in Sals. 23 Dec. 1697 Sarah Allen (Lt. John); liv. Exeter, at times Sals., until 1722; thereafter divid. his time bet. Exeter and Biddeford. Lists 67, 376b (1698). Bot and sold much land in Exeter and Biddef., besides giving Biddef. land to two sons. Liv. Exeter July 1742. One Sarah G., wid. of Exeter, sued Saml. Dudley 18 Apr. 1746 on bond dated 4 Mar. 1742. Ch. incl: **Joseph,** Biddef., adm. 10 Nov. 1784 to s. Amos. His w. Mercy (m. by 1731) dep. 1766 she had kn. cert. Biddef. land ab. 50 yrs. 10 ch. **Allen,** Biddef., liv. 1760. **John,** m. in Newb. Dec. 1728 Hannah Willett; liv. Exeter, Newb., and Boxford bef. going to Biddef. in 1752. List 376b (1725). 4 ch. rec. Newb. Likely: **Hannah** (Goodin), d. Sals. 27 Sept. 1706. One John G. was pd. by Exeter for care of his dau. Mary 1741, 1744.
**4 JOHN,** York witn. 1717 (Y. D. 9.103), if not (3), may have been husb. of Elizabeth G., a York wid. in 1744, and fa. of **Nathl.,** of age 1744, and of **Robert.**
**5 LUDOVIC,** gent. mercht., a Greenl. witn. 1712. Of Portsm., Mar. 1713, he gave P/A to Rich. Wibird, and ord. to deliver his chest to Dr. Israel March; goods were sent over by his w. Next month he was in Boston.
**6 NICHOLAS** (1), constab. Exeter 1697, several times selectm. Adm. on est. of gr. fa. Nich. Lissen gr. to him 8 Dec. 1714. Lists 52, 57, 62, 67, 376b (1698, 1725). He m. aft. 20 June 1685, app. as 1st w., Sarah, wid. of Edward Sewall; sued on her acct. Jan. 1695-6; m. 2d Maria (Hersey), wid. of Joshua Gilman, who surv. Will 31 Mar. 1747, giving to w., numer. gr. ch. and dau. Mary, was contested by the wid., dau. Patience and ch. of Jona. Gordon. Ch: **Lydia,** m. 1st Thos. Dolloff (1), 2d Jona. Gordon (James). **Mary,** m. Edward Colcord (2). **Patience,** m. Saml. Stevens. **Elizabeth,** m. Nicholas Dudley (3).
**7 PETER,** Exeter 1684. List 52.
**8 ——,** see Churchwell (1).

Gore, George, taxed Dover Neck 1667. List 356j. See Gove(3).

**GORGES,** a Norman family, seated at Wraxall, co. Somerset, which ran out in the 14th cent. but whose name was assumed by a dau.'s son, Theobald Russell, 6 gen. back of the three bros. Edmund, Sir William, Sir Thomas. (Me. P. & Ct. i. xlix.).
**1 EDWARD,** Lord Gorges, knighted at Widerington 9 Apr. 1603, later Baron Gorges of Dundalk, bro. of Elizabeth, last w. of (3). Ch. of Sir Thomas, they were first cous. of (3)'s fa. and (10)'s gr. fa. Powerful and staunch friend of (3) bef. becoming bro.-in-law, and even bef. the patent to the Council for New Eng., his death soon followed Sir F.'s. As late as 1691 his s. and heir, **Richard,** Lord Gorges, the last Baron, was joining with (5) in the swansong duet of their hopes for rents from thousands of tenants whose ancestors had hewn homes in the new-world wilderness (N. H. Prov. Papers i.6.; Me. P. & Ct. i. xxvii, note; Baxter's Gorges, ii. 218). **Elev-**

en yrs. older, Richard d. 7 yrs. bef. (5); bur. at 'Stretchworth,' co. Camb., Sept. 1712.

**2 SIR EDWARD**, Knight, elder bro. of (3), bp. 5 Sept. 1564 at Wraxall; knighted at Bedington, at Sir Francis Carew's, in 1603. The mo. of the two boys, Cicely Lygon of Madresfield, co. Worc. (where the estate of Sir Richard Lygon, Kt., was adm. in 1556—not searched), m. 2d John Vivian, Esq., presum. an unident. younger s. of the anc. landed family of North Cornwall. Both evid. given the best schooling to be had, the heir to Wraxall was adm. to Hart's College, Oxford, at 18. High sheriff for Somerset 1609. Bur. at Wraxall 16 Dec. 1624. Of 12 ch. (6 boys) only one handed on the name. At the father's death (11) was called 4th s.

**3 SIR FERDINANDO**, Knight, b. ab. 1566, younger bro. of the senior Gorges line, s. of Edward, gr. s. of Edmund. This man, written up ad lib., was in truth Maine's worst enemy; had he had his way Maine would have been another Ireland. See his date line in one of his charters of his city of Gorgeana, not Anno Domini or Anno Christi, or in the year of his King's reign, but 'in the second yeare of my Principallity in Newe England'; and his assertion of 'absolute power over all the Inhabitants and People' living here then or in future; Rishworth's marginal notes to his patent; Povey's extracts from the records of the Council for New England (Me. P. & C. i. xxii, xxi note, xxxvii-viii, xxvii-viii note. Also viii, xxvi, xxviii, xxxiv-v, xxx, 30 note 20, 63, 89, 90, 116-117, 130, 278, 133). Even his enthus. biog. does not shield him. (Baxter's Gorges, i. 180-182, 170-172, 164-167, 174-175, 177-178, 159-161, 116-117, 126. See also iii. 266.) His career as an Englishman was highly important and creditable— admir. covered by Baxter. In York he appar. had not created his own manor in Gorgeana, except on paper, when he wrote his book, and his mirage of success (Baxter ii. 70) was gone while he wrote. Godfrey (1) must have written to him of the 'oppression' of his property here, or in 1637 embarked without orders. (P. & C. i. 109, 110, 116, 117.) Lists 41, 281, 29. He m. 1st 24 Feb. 1589-90 Ann, d. of Edward Bell, Esq., of Writtle, co. Essex, who d. 26 Aug. 1620, bur. in London. Licensed in Exeter 21 Dec. 1621, 'Sir Ferdinand Gorges, Knight, and Mary Fortescue of Pelynt,' m. rec. not found. Wid. of Thos. Achims (will proved 26 Mar. 1609), her parents were 'Mr. Thomas Fulford Esq. and Ursula Bampfield Gent,' licensed at Exeter 10 Oct. 1580. Adm. est. Dame Mary Achim, alias Gorges, was gr. to her bro. Sir Francis Fulford, Kt., 1 Aug.

1623, of Great Fulford, co. Devon. Her sister Bridget was mother of (3)'s nephew, Capt. Francis Champernowne. Licensed in Exeter 31 Dec. 1625, 'Sir Ferdinand Gorge of Plymouth, Knight, and Elizabeth Coffin, widow, of (blank),' m. record or other partic. not found. Uninvest. but likely she was mo. of 'Elizabeth Coffyn Jun. of Alwington' licensed to m. 'Hugh Fortesque of Weare Gifford, Gent.' As late as 1831 these two parishes, near Bideford, were in the patronage of Richard P. Coffin, Esq., and Earl Fortesque. He m. 6 Dec. 1627 at Ladock, co. Cornwall, Elizabeth (Gorges) his 2d cousin, d. of Tristram Gorges, Esq., (10's gt. uncle), who was 1st cous. of Gilbert and Raleigh thro the Champernownes; twice a wid., of Edw. Courtney of Landrake, co. Cornwall (d. 1623), and Wm. Bligh, who d. 21 July 1627. Adm. on wife's est. gr. to Sir F. 19 Mar. 1628-9. Her sis. Ferdinanda m. Edward Trelawny of Lanteglos by Fowey, Gent. (lic. 17 June 1615). Finally, at Wraxall 28 Sept. 1629, he m. his fa.'s 1st cous. Elizabeth (Gorges) Smyth, d. of Sir Thomas Gorges, wid. of Sir Hugh Smyth, whose lux. est. of Ashton Court, outside Bristol, was Sir F.'s home till death. Will 4 May, bur. in Long Ashton ch. 14 May, 1647. Her will proved 13 June 1659. Ch: **John**, b. 23 Apr. 1593. **Robert**, bp. 15 Nov. 1595, at Clerkenwell. **Ellen**, d. y. **Honoria**, d. y.

**4 CAPT. FERDINANDO**, bro. of (10). See (6) and (7). In 1673 bot the manor of Eye Court, co. Hereford, and built the manor house there. Bur. in Much Dewchurch, co. Hereford, 22 Apr. 1701. He m. Meliora Hilliard (Col. Wm.) of Barbadoes. Ch: **Henry**, entered St. John's Coll., Oxford, 1683. Many yrs. M. P. Bur. at Eye 18 Apr. 1718. **Barbara**, m. Thomas, Earl Coningsby, Lord Chief Justice of Ireland. **Meliora**, m. Sir John Hely, Chief Justice of Common Pleas in Ireland. **Ann**, m. Richard Hoper of Lucton, co. Hereford. Also (uninvest.) mar. lic. 25 Nov. 1682 Thos. Bache of Northfield, Gent., and Mary Gorges of Eye, co. Hereford, abt. 18, with parents' consent.

**5 FERDINANDO**(8), Esq., from childh. inde.. marked by his gr. fa. (3), he had put on his gr. st. 'sometime Governor of the Province of Maine.' Me. P. & C., Vol. I. xli-ii, li, 181-188, 195-210; Vol. II. xxiii, lll, 125, 129, 135, 140, 375 note, 283; Baxter's Gorges ii. 168-174. Lists 271, 272, 25, 26, 88, 29. Lived at Ashley, co. Wilts, a manor received from Lord Gorges(1), where he d. 25 Jan. 1718-9, ag. 89. See Richard(1). He m. at St. Bride's, London, 22 May 1660 Mary Archdale (Me. P. & C. i. xxxix, N. E. Reg. 54.191). Ch: **Mary**, b. 1661, d. 1689,

unm. **Thomas,** d. 1665 **Ferdinando,** b. 1665, bur. at Ashley 20 Feb. 1738. Leaving no ch. he devised the manor to his kinsman, John Beresford. M. in 1705 Catherine Foyle of Somerford, Wilts. 2 sons d. y. **Elizabeth,** b. 8 May, bur. 22 Sept. 1669. **Cecilia,** bp. 22 June 1670, m. 1st one Moody, 2d one Kingham. **Ann,** bp. 9 Jan. 1671-2.

6 **FERDINANDO**(10), Esq., came to Wells. Baxter would have him in Boston Aug. 1674. Y. D. ii. 158. His father's will left a large sum to apprentice him. Could he have been apprent. in Boston? Much likelier this wit. was his uncle(4), who was there from Barbadoes in 1663-4. Suff. Files 612. Ferdin. came to Wells with P/A from (7) dated 13 July 1685 and was here two yrs. at least. In Wells court 12 Oct. 1686 adm. was gr. to Mr. Ferdinando Gorges on the est. of Thomas Gorges. Dated 14 Dec. 1686 'Ferdinando Gorges of the Province of Mayne Gentleman Agent and Attorney unto Henry Gorges of the Island of Barbadoe Esq' leased to 'John Littlefield Sen (15) of Batcombe neere unto the Township of Wells in the Province aforesd yeoman' for 21 yrs. 200 acres 'being now in the tenure or occupation of him the said Ferdo. Gorges,' at £8 a year. (Orig. in York Files, 1722). Nathaniel Cloyes deposed that Capt. Littlefield had been in possession for 50 yrs. past. See in Me. P. & C. ii. 525, an agreement, owned in court 3 Apr. 1678, between Littlefield and the Town of Wells by which the town was to receive £5 yearly and protect him from the heir. He had occupied the land and the mill priv. since 1660 under a town gr. In 1688 favorable judgments were handed down in 3 of the 5 suits started in York court Oct. 1686 against persons settled on Batcombe lands. In Suff. court 7 Mar. 1687-8 adm. was gr. to John Davis, Esq., on the est. of Ferdinando Gorges, Esq., late of York, decd., whose ident. may be questioned. This was evid. the basis of Hutchinson's statement (Hutchinson, Hist. of Mass., i. 163) that (5) died in York, and it was surely (6) who 26 Mar. 1687 wit. a deed with Joseph Weare, whose wife was to be Major Davis's heir (Me. P. & C. ii. xvi), but was he poss. mistaking him for heir of (5), (10) or (3), and looking to collect old tavern scores?

7 **HENRY**(10), Esq., by death of eldest s. became the heir. In boyhood ran away to Barbadoes, where his uncle (5) had grown rich. There 1668. In 1679 he (or another Henry) had 125 acres and 58 negroes. See (6). (Me. P. & C. i. li-lii.). Adm. on his est. was gr. in York ct. 26 Mar. 1736 to Malachi Edwards(7), who occup. the dower of Capt. John Littlefield's son's wid., and had bot in heirs. Edwards had the lands appr., 25 a. of marsh and 170 a. of land on S. W. side of Ogunquit river, at £450, and took oath to his bill, no items, footing up £681: 0: 0. In 1740 a writ of ejectment to escheat 200 acres to the Crown was entered by the Province against Edwards, reciting that 'Henry George, late of Barbadoes, Esq. d. 'intestate and without heir to inherit the same,' and was dropped. (Suff. Files 51691).

8 **JOHN**(3), Esq., s. and heir, inherited the Province of Maine, only 2 townships at that time, and when he d., 9 yrs. later, the whole in poss. of Mass. But his will left his Patent of the Province of Maine to (5), with all other patents, maps and pictures. While his life looks vacant, he was under his father's wing while he lived, and as a loyalist helpless under Cromwell. List 271. He m. 1st at Clerkenwell 30 July 1620 Lady Frances Fynes, d. of the Earl of Lincoln, 2d Mary, d. of Sir John Meade of Wendon-Lofts, co. Essex. He d. 6 Apr., his wid. 15 Sept. 1657; both bur. at St. Margarets, Westminster. Ch. only by 2d w: **Ferdinando,** b. 19 Aug. 1630 at Wendon-Lofts, co. Essex. **Cecilia,** bp. in St. Margarets 14 Feb. 1631, m. 6 May 1652 Abraham Chapman of West Hampnett, co. Sussex. **Jane,** bp. in St. M. 24 July 1632. **Ann,** bp. 2 May 1635, unm. Will 8, bur. 19, Dec. 1655 at St. Margarets.

9 **CAPT. ROBERT**(3). In 1622 had 'newly come out of the Venetian War,' and was sent over by (3) in the name of the Council for New England as their 'Lieutenant Generall' with his illegal patent making him subject to knights' service. Between (1) and (3), they shipped him away with insuffic. supplies. The ship that brot him and his company brot other passengers booked for Virginia, and as his promised supply ship never came, he was left with none. Coming over with 'sundry passengers and families to begin a plantation,' and discharging at Weymouth after deciding to take over Weston's abandoned settlement, he quickly abandoned it again. He soon 'expedited some occasions' at the eastward and reshipped, with 'some that depended on him,' while some who came 'on their perticular,' (at their own charge), went south on the same ship, and some remained. See Bradford; Pratt's Relation; Baxter ii. 49-54. A sorry chapter of the irrespons. ineffic. in London. Pratt said he came with six gentlemen attending him and diverse men to do his labor and other men with their families. Of these Jeffreys and Bursley settled at Weymouth, Maverick and Thomas Walford went to Chelsea or East Boston. Capt. Walter Norton, one of the six armed gentlemen, evid. attended

his liege lord home, but later here again with Maverick or Jeffreys. (Doc. Hist. vii. 160; 2 Me. Hist. Coll. ii. 327; List 271. Godfrey 1).

10 †COL. THOMAS (3d cous. of 5), Esq., Speaker of Parliament at Cromwell's death. Here 1640-1643. See letters of Mr. Winter and Rev. Robert Jordan, July 27 and 29, 1641 (not '42), Doc. Hist. iii. 279-280, 314-319, notes pp. 316, 317-318, 253, also 309-310 and note; Winthrop ii. 9-10; Baxter i. 183. 'A young gentleman of the inns of court' when (3), his fa.'s 2d cous., sent him over to straighten things out, which he ably did, living 3 yrs. in York. The most important Englishman to come to Maine, except perhaps Rishworth (also in York and belittled), and in his mild way Jocelyn, Banks (p. 117) begrudg. mentions him. His high connect. were extraord. Besides all of (3)'s noble ancestry, his gt. gr. fa. Sir William, Vice Admiral, m. Winifred Burdockshead (Roger), 1st cousin of Sir Humphrey Gilbert and Sir Walter Raleigh, her mo. Frances and their mo. Catherine daus. of Sir Philip Champernowne. (Baxter ii. 163). Sir Arthur and presum. Edward Gorge who was a member of Sir Walter Raleigh's voyage south of Chesapeake Bay in 1585 were (10)'s gt. uncles. His gr. f. Robert, who m. Ann Webbe, heiress of Batcombe, founded that most talented and disting. Gorges line. His f., Henry, Esq., who was repeat. in Parliament for Taunton, m. Barbara, dau. of Thomas Baynard, Esq., of Wanstrow, co. Somerset, and Collerne, co. Wilts, by his w. Avice sis. of Sir Lawrence Hyde, Kt., of Dinton, co. Wilts. Besides (4), his bro. John was gov. of Londonderry, bro. Robert, Doctor of Laws, was Sec. to Henry Cromwell, Lord Lieut. of Ireland. Thomas, b. in 1618, was 22 when (3) sent him over, the best or only good thing he did for us. (Baxter ii. 186-192; Me. P. & C. i. xlix, li, lii, 74, 76, 77, 83). For his manor of Batcombe, now at Ogunquit, Wells, see Y. D. i. 2. 5; Me. P. & C. i. li-lii; ii, 525; Baxter ii. 191. Also (6) and (7). For letters and legal papers (Doc. Hist. iii. 255, 257; Winthrop ii. 9; Hutchinson Coll. 114; Bourne's Wells 9; Y. D. i. Pt. 3. 7, 8; Pt. 2. 3, 9, 10, 11, 12; Pt. 1. 13, 24, 28, 29, 140; Y. D. ii. 85, 6, 179, 109; iii. 74; iv. 46; viii. 244.) Also see his fine letter to Winthrop accred. to Godfrey (1 Me. Hist. Coll. ix. 40; Banks -Edward Godfrey-1887, p. 336.) He procured the earliest separate record book for deeds, later bound up as Part 3 of Vol. I, recording (except for Godfrey's invasions) only Gorges deeds; also 'The Great Book of Records,' which contained when he went back only Gorges deeds and the Vines patent. (Me. P. & C.

i. lix.) He was about taking ship (Mr. Abraham Shurt's?) when he wrote Winthrop, 28 June 1643, but did not finish his inventory of (3)'s possession until July 10, and was still here July 18. (Y. D. iii. 74). Lists 272, 235, 221, 71. Over there he was at once elected to Parliament from Taunton, and cont. until and after Charles II came in, Speaker during the debate on Richard Cromwell's election. D. 17 Oct. 1670, his wid. 14 Apr. 1671; a fit monumental stone in Heavitree ch. He m. 1st Mary, d. of Martyn Sanford of Ninehead Flory, co. Somerset, Esq.; 2d 23 Mar. 1656, at Heavitree, co. Devon, Rose (Alexander), wid. of Roger Mallock, Esq., of Cockingham, d. of Sir Jerome Alexander, Kt. Ch: Susannah, b. 1649, m. (lic. 25 May 1669) her stepbro. Rawlin Mallack, Esq.; d. 17 Apr. 1673. Thomas, b. ab. 1651, entered Wadham College, Oxford, 1668; d. soon aft. his f., s. p. Henry, b. ab. 1652. Ferdinando, b. ab. 1654. By 2d w: Alexander, b. 29 July 1660. Elizabeth, bp. 14 Apr. 1662. Edward, b. 15 May 1666, bur. 14 June 1667.

11 †CAPT. WILLIAM (2), sent over illeg. as Dep. Gov. in 1636, there is nothing to show that he attended more than the first ct. at Saco, nothing to show him at York except (3)'s jumbled Chap. XXV (Baxter ii. 58). He could not have gone back on the same ship with Cleeve in Sept., but soon foll. (Doc. Hist. iii. 98-105). His F. had not seen him 27 Jan. 1636-7 when he had fallen a victim to Cleeve (Y. D. i. 95), but his letter to Sir John Coke a month later, requesting that his nephew be ordered to sea to fight 'Turkish pirates,' is phrased as though he were back. (Baxter iii. 277). Bp. at Wraxall 2 Feb. 1605-6, he was bur. there 9 Feb. 1658-9, s. p. altho twice m.

Gorly, George, Exeter soldier Aug. 1696. List 67.

GORRELL. 1 Philip, Mr., several times sued for debt while engaged in fishing at the Shoals 1649-1652. P. & Ct. j. 1651. In 1652, late of the Sh., he drew bills on Eng. for £37 in fav. of Thos. Macy, Sals., proved by witnesses 1657.

2 ROBERT, Mr., sued by Saml. Maverick, Me. Ct. June 1647.

Gosling, Edward, receipted 11 Aug. 1676 for fish recd. from Mr. Francis Tucker and pd. to Nicholas Haskins.

GOSS, found in Devonshire.

1 RICHARD, Portsm., bot 11 a. on No. side of Sagamore Creek 22 May 1663. Taxed Oct. 1691; d. bef. his sons sold his land in 1694. Lists 356L, 313a, 331b, 52, 57. His 1st w. unkn., he m. 2d aft. 30 June 1670 Jane (Walford), wid. of Thos. Peverly, she liv. July 1686. Kn. ch: Robert, Richard, New-

castle, taxed Rye 30 Oct. 1691, jr.; bot in Newc. 1711. Constab. 1708. Lists 318c, 315c, 316. M. (Ct. Dec. 1693) Martha Foss (1), liv. Rye a wid. 1739. His will 23 Mar. 1718-9—3 Mar. 1719-20 gave all equally to her and s. Richard, they excrs. and to pay one ewe to each of the other ch. at 21, Mary, Jonathan, Thomas, John, Jethro, Martha, Margaret, Nathan.

2 **RICHARD**, from Ipsw., kinsman of and overseer est. of Mrs. Eleanor Welcome of the Shoals 1699, first noted in N. H. June 1693 as witn. ag. John Carter (5). Bot on Star Isl. 1694. Selectm. 1702. List 309. Selling at Star Isl. 1705, he ret. to Ipsw.; d. there 24 Jan. 1714-5, ag. 52. W. Mary. Ch. likely incl. three b. in N. H.: **John, Thomas, Eleanor**, in add. to **Richard** and **William**, bp. Ipsw. 1711-1714.

3 **ROBERT** (1), taxed Rye 30 Oct. 1691 (Jess), m. 5 Jan. 1692-3 Jane Berry (9). Lists 335a, 338b. Liv. Greenl.; constab. 1717. Lists 62, 335a, 330de, 338abc. Dec. 27, 1733 he gave a will-deed to s. Robt. Old Mr. G. d. Greenl. 1747; she d. 8 May 1752, ag. 84. Ch: **Robert**, Greenl., m. one Lydia. List 338b. 4 ch. bp. 1721-1732. **Margaret**, m. 3 Nov. 1720 David Smith. **Rachel**, m. Joshua Hill (9). **Joseph**, Exeter and Kingston, m. bef. 1736 Hannah Smith (Israel). **Ch. Jean**, m. 28 Jan 1722 Reuben Smith; not named with other ch. in fa.'s deed 1733. **Deliverance**, m. Simon Knowles (4).

4 **THOMAS**, Shoals, boatmaster for Thos. Diamond Oct. 1686. List 95.

**GOTT.** 1 **Charles**, Strawb. Bk., taxed 1717. Mary G. recd. into So. Ch. 11 Nov. 1716. Charles -Jos.- rated to No. Ch. 1717.

2 **DANIEL**, talked ag. the govt. at Ephraim Marston's ho., Hampton, and got into ct., 1694. Danl. -Goff- witn. will of Jas. Grant 1693, Danl. Gott prov. it. Weaver, York, Oct. 1699, when sued by Thos. Trafton; his atty. Arthur Bragdon sr.

**Gouge**, see Gooch.

**Gough**, see Goff.

**GOULD**, Goold, Gold, became 66th commonest name in N. E.

1 **ALEXANDER**, New Harbor, Pemaquid, m. Margaret, claimed to have been dau. of Brown (15) and to have recd. from him in 1660 an imposs. large tract of land, 8 m. sq. Y.D.15.233. Their dau. Margaret dep. in 1733 that her mo. recd. as part of her mar. portion Muscongus Isl., where her fa. liv., and her mo. long aft. his death. He was liv. 1672; likely k. in early part of the War bef. his fam. driven away. Lists 121, 13. They returned and were driven off a second time, permanently, to Marblehead. Wid. Margaret m. 2d Morris Chamblet. Ch: **Margaret**,

92 at death Feb. 1750-1, m. 1st James Stilson, 2d Thos. Pitman. **Elizabeth**, m. at Marbleh. 27 Oct. 1692 Edward Homan. 6 ch. rec. there 1694-1711. A wid. in Jan. 1735-6 she sold to Jos. Hendley her part of Somerset's or Gould's Isl. and cert. mainlands form. of her gr. fa. John Brown, since of her fa. **Mary**, m. Thos. Pinson; in 1729 was wid. Mary Shaw of Salem. Ch. rec. Salem (Pinson): Mary, b. 30 Sept. 1694, m. at Marbleh. 10 July 1715 John Coates; 6 ch. bp. Marbleh.; May 11, 1760, of Ashford, Conn., 'only surv. heir of Mary Gould', she gave P/A to the unscrup. James Noble of Boston to recover Muscongus est., incl. 1/3 of her fa.'s 1660 tract. Elizabeth, b. 9 Feb. 1697-8, d. s. p. bef. 1760. One Elizabeth Pinson m. Patrick Hickey at Marbleh. 2 Sept. 1726.

2 **BENJAMIN** (Goold), b. ±1693, br. of (6), s. of John and Mary (Crosman) Gold of Taunton, came to Kit. by 1714, bot there 1715 and m. 9 Feb. 1716 Rebecca Furbush (1). A Friend. His will 1769—1781; hers 1781—1782. Ch: **Benjamin, John, Sarah, Samuel, James, Nathaniel, Daniel, Mary.**

3 **CHRISTOPHER**, accused in Hampt. Ct. 2 Oct. 1660 of stealing breeches from James Philbrick; Portsm. 1670, drunk; in 1671 Hampt. would fine any person receiv. him into his fam. Last found in Aug. 1682 drunk all night at the ho. of Grace Spencer, Great Island.

4 **EDWARD**, Star Island, b. ±1641. First found in 1667 when Peter Lewis was his bondsm.; bot on Star Isl. from Peter Glanfield in 1670 and fined same yr. for stealing fish from John Fabes. Lists 306c, 307a, 308ab. See Broad (4). Constable 1693-94. Suppos. his s.: **Edward**, tailor, Star Isl., m. in Newbury (int. 1 Aug. 1704) Ruth Richardson. List 309. Will 20 Aug. 1724—7 Nov. 1727 names w. Ruth, daus. Anne, Dorothy, Ruth and chn. of decd. dau. Elizabeth. One Ruth orig. memb. of Gosport Ch. 1729. **Wm.**, s. of Elizabeth Gold of I. of Sh., bp. Newb. 28 Mar. 1725. See also (7, 8, 9).

5 **ISAAC** from Chelmsford, had 30 a. gr. at Oyster Riv. 19 Mar. 1693-4, which heirs in Mass. q. c. to Jona. Chesley in 1719.

6 **JOSEPH** (Goold), br. of (2), came to Kit. ab. 1702, ag. ±22, and m. in 1705 Bethia Furbush (2). In 1709 he bot Treworgy's or Thompson's Point in N. part of Eliot. D. 10 May 1762, ag. ±82. Ch: **Mary, Bethia, William, Samuel, Joseph, Hannah.** A sis. Elizabeth, said to have been in Kit. early, and unmar. 1717, is not identified.

7 **NICHOLAS**, Shoals 1687. List 307b. See (4).

8 **RICHARD**, Star Island 1692. Constable 1694. List 308a. See (4).

9 **SAMUEL**, Shoals, fought John Yelline in Apr. 1685; both attacked Rich. Sprittall; Wm. Lakeman their bondsm. (See 4).

10 **SAMUEL**, m. in Topsfield 20 Apr. 1697 Margaret Stone of Berw. (Danl.). With s. Samuel of Boxford she deeded 1/11 of her fa.'s est. 1715.

**Gouslde**, Henry, creditor of Wm. Button's est. 1687. List 307b.

**GOVE**, uncommon in England. Possibly a form of Gough?

1 **EBENEZER**(2), ag. 50 in Dec. 1720, m. 20 Dec. 1692 Judith Sanborn (John); liv. in the 'Bound House' in Seabrook on the State line. Soldier 1695-6. D. 16 Apr. 1758. List 399a. Ch: **Jeremiah**, b. 20 Mar. 1694-5, pub. 17 Nov. 1721 to, poss. did not marry, Dorothy Conner; m. 2 Feb. 1725 Sarah Cram (Benj.). Quaker. Will 15 Jan. 1766 (d. 19 June 1767) names w. Sarah, 7 of 8 ch. **Edward**, b. 29 May 1696, m. 1st 1718-9 Bethia Clark, who d. 19 Apr. 1727, ag. 30; 2d 16 Jan. 1728 Mary Moulton. Liv. Hampt. Falls; d. 10 July 1765, wid. d. in Oct. 1793. 4 + 4 ch. **Sarah**, b. 3 Apr. 1698, m. Benj. Brown (5 jr.). **Judith**, b. 18 Feb. 1700-1, m. 1st Capt. Jonathan Prescott, 2d Richard Sanborn. **Ebenezer**, b. 15 Feb. 1703; liv. Kensington; m. at Rowley 28 Mar. 1728 Elizabeth Stewart. 10 ch. **Lydia**, b. 3 Feb. 1705, m. 1st Simon Fogg(6), 2d 31 Oct. 1751 Nathl. Healy. Lieut. **Enoch**, b. 28 Oct. 1708, m. 1st 13 June 1731 Sarah Rowe, 2d 9 Feb. 1749 Hannah (Sherburne), wid. of Alex. Lucy. Liv. Hampt. F.; d. 24 July, adm. to widow 29 Aug. 1759. 10 + 1 ch. **Hannah**, b. 20 Jan. 1711-2, m. Enoch Clark. **Nathan**, b. 30 Dec. 1713, k. by Ind. 1730-1. **Mary**, b. 18 Apr. 1716, m. 20 Feb. 1733-4 John Green. **Rachel**, b. 26 Apr. 1718, m. 9 Oct. 1733 Winthrop Dow; d. 1738.

2 *****EDWARD**(4), Hampton, known lastingly for his leadership of a hopeless rebellion against Gov. Cranfield. Aged 35 in June 1676, ±38 in Jan. 1677-8, he was under age when he bot a common right in Salis. in Apr. 1657; perh. first apprent. to Mr. Saml. Hall, lawyer, who wit. his 1657 deed, wit. with him the next mo. and in 1669 from Eng. named E. G. his genl. atty. in N. E. Bef. 28 Nov. 1665, with w. Hannah Partridge (Wm.) he mov. to land in Hampt., now Seabrook, bot the previous April. List 394. There soon showed the traits which brot him much trouble. In Sept. 1674 he had been in Boston at the Ct. of Asst.; Freeman 4 Dec. 1678; Tr.j. 1679; Lieut. for Hampton bef. N. H. became a Royal Prov.; Rep. 1680; Selectm. 1682. The town 21 Mar. 1681 named Sergt. Jos. Dow and E. G. to prepare a statement and assert their rights against Mason, and chose him

as Rep. to the Assembly 14 Nov. 1682 aft. Cranfield's arrival. The Rebellion foll. 27 Jan. 1682-3, then his arrest, conviction, sentence to death for treason, removal to the Tower of London, and final pardon in Apr. 1686. See Proc. Mass. Hist. Socy. 45: 232-41, 628-40; The Gove Family (1922), pp. 16-49. Home again, he was Selectm. and on arbitration commit. 1688; Moderator 1689; Lieut. and Rep. Lists 392b, 396, 55a, 49, 56, 57, 58. D. 29 May 1691; adm. in Salem Ct. 25 June on motion of s. John to Mr. Edw. Thomas of Boston, the wid. relinq. She d. bef. 26 Mar. 1712. Ch., first 3 b. in Salis.: **John**, b. 19 Sept. 1661. **William**, b. 21 Oct. 1662, d. 1 Mar. 1663. **Hannah**, b. Mar. 1664, m. Abraham Clements (1). **Mary**, b. 14 Apr. 1666, m. 1st Jos. Sanborn, 2d one Morrill of Salis. **Abiel**, b. 23 July 1667, likely the ch. who d. 28 Aug. 1667 (Haverh. rec.). **Penuel**, b. 10 July 1668, d. 1 Aug. 1671. **Abigail**, b. 17 Apr. 1670, m. 1st Deac. Philemon Dalton(2), 2d Benj. Sanborn, 3d James Prescott. **Ebenezer**, b. 23 June 1671. **Edward**, b. 13 May 1673, d. 12 Nov. 1675. **Jeremiah**, b. Oct. 1674, d. 7 Sept. 1692. **Rachel**, b. 26 Jan. 1676, d.y. **Ann**, b. 9 Jan. 1677, m. Jeremiah Conner(6). **Sarah**, b. 5 Nov. 1678, m. Saml. Dearborn(5).

3 **GEORGE** (Goe), taxed Dover Neck 1667 (Gore); at Philip Chesley's ho., Oyster River, 1672, ±30; wit. (Gove) with Thos. Edgerly 1678; deft. with Thos. Drew sr. and jr. and Wm. Follett in suit for tresp. 1680; liv. 1684. Lists 356j, 359a, 52.

4 **JOHN**, brazier, Charlestown. Of St. Giles Cripplegate, London, he m. 6 Feb. 1630-1 Mary Shard (Humphrey, clothworker), in the par. where she was bap. 25 Feb. 1609-10, St. Nicholas Cole Abbey. Assisted by loan of £3 from Socy. for Propagation of the Gospel, repaid here, he brot his fam. over and bot in Charlest. in Sept. 1647, his first record here, tho ch. warden accts., St. Nich. Cole Abbey, 1642, show £3 loaned to help transport his two ch. to N. E.; same accts. 1644, 6d. paid for making John Gove's bond; 1647, 6s. 8d. paid for Mary Gove's lodging for two months. Will 22 Jan. 1647-8—13 Apr. 1648, gives dau. Mary to Ralph Mousall and w., 'their own ch. forever,' a silver porringer to Ralph M. and £5 out of the ho.; 50 s. each to two sons, out of brass in his ho. or to come out of Eng.; residue to w. Debts from 3s. to £5, some in Duxbury and Dedham. In 1653 James Astwood's est. (Suff.) was indebted to Mr. J. G. Wid. m. 2d John Mansfield, goldsmith, Charlest., by whom she had twins, ag. 8 in 1656, John Mansfield, put out to his aunt Mrs. Robt. Keayne, Elizabeth Mansfield, put out to Rev. Saml. Whiting. She was

±64 in Dec. 1671. Aft. J. M. d. in Charlest. 26 June 1674, she liv. with s. Edw. in Hampt. and d. there 4 Mar. 1681-2, Old Widow M. Gove ch.: **John**, Cambridge, bp. St. Botolph's, London, 25 Mar. 1631-2, m. 1st Mary Aspinwall, 2d Mary Woodhead, 3d 2 Dec. 1700 Elizabeth (Sanders) (Batson 1) Walden. He d. 24 Dec. 1704; she liv. 1725. 6 + 4 ch. **Humphrey**, bp. 30 Mar. 1634, bur. St. Paul's Ch. Yard 27 Nov. fol. **Edward**, b. ±1639-1640, bap. not found. **Mary**, bp. 19 Sept. 1641 at St. Nich. Cole Abbey.

5 **ENSIGN JOHN**(2), apprent. to Wm. Partridge. Carpenter and built a ho. north of his fa.'s, burned in 1913, the site now marked by a monument with names of owners 1713-1913, all Goves. He was implicat. in the Rebellion, convicted of treason, and pardoned, partly thru Wm. Partridge, who promised work on Gov. Cranfield's ho. in consid. of his pardon. Jury 1694; Constable 1696-97; six times Selectm. 1698-1712. Soldier 1708, called Ensign 1709. Lists 55a, 63, 64, 392b: In 1734 he ptn. for relief against a deed his son had obtained from him clandestinely. Adm. 15 Oct. 1737 to Jas. Norton. Wife Sarah. Ch.: **Mary**, b. 29 Oct. 1687, m. 14 Oct. 1705 Capt. Nehemiah Heath, master mariner; she d. 16 Apr. 1715, he m. 2d Mar. 1716-7 Joanna Dow; d. 14 Jan. 1717-8. 2 ch. **John**, Quaker, b. 29 May 1689, d. 23 Mar. 1759, m. 22 Mar. 1719-20 Ruth Johnson (Edmund 24), who surv. Liv. Hampt. F. Selectm., hog constable, highway surv. 7 ch. **Hannah**, b. 1 Apr. 1691, m. John Cass(3). **Jonathan**, b. 2 May 1695, d. 6 Aug. 1760. Liv. Hampt. F., Quaker. Selectm., highway surv., overseer, constable. He m. 1st 21 July 1720 Mary Lancaster (Thos.), 2d 23 Mar. 1729-30 Hannah Worthen, who m. 2d Abner Philbrick. 3 + 11 ch. **Sarah. Abigail**, m. 6 Jan. 1721 Joseph Norton.

**GOWDY, Goudy, George**, Newcastle, pd. by the town 1712 for keeping John Winsland 9 mos. List 316. Adm. 6 Sept. 1721 to Capt. Jotham Odiorne. One Amos G. m. in York 18 Feb. 1728-9 Miriam Card (6). List 279. Katharine G. acc. Jas. Evans, stranger, in Me. Ct. Jan. 1729-30, but m. Benj. Berry. Thos. G. m. Deborah Skinner in Gosport 1744. John G., Newc. 1749.

**GOWELL, Richard**, Kittery, by trad. from Wales, but loaned £40 in 1698 to a Devonshire man, Thos. Hoar jr. of St. Mary Church. Signed Kit. ptn. 1679. Often gr. j. Lists 30, 296, 297, 298. Bondsm. 1716 for Thos. Spinney, whose depo. with Jacob Remick, 26 Aug. 1729, has words 'Richard Gowell ag. ab. 83 y.' stricken out. Will 15 Dec. 1729—6 Apr.1730 names w. Hannah and

ch., giving Richard the homestead entailed on him in 1710 aft. fa.'s and mo.'s death. She was Hannah Remick (Christian), wid. of John Thompson, and declined to serve as exec. 7 Apr. 1730 in favor of 'my s. Richard G.' Ch. by unkn. w: **Tamsen**, m. 1st one Sheares by Mar. 1687-8, 2d Thos. Hanscom (3). **Martha**, in July 1694 had gone to live with Mrs. Crown (1) in Portsm. at £5 per yr. and sued for her pay 12 Nov. 1696. Last ment. witnessing fa.'s fam. settlement 14 Sept. 1714. One Martha Green assisting in Thos. Cole's (32) last sickness is unident. **Mary**, in 1705 was liv. with Mrs. Elizabeth Harvey of Portsm.; m. Job Hanscom (1). **Sarah**, m. 1st Thos. Worcester; Sarah Chase in fa.'s will. By w. Hannah: **Richard**, b. 28 Aug. 1685, d s. p. List 291. Land was laid out to him 1706, one abuttor 'his uncle Mr. Joshua Remick.' Will, gent., 26 Jan.—17 Apr. 1744 names w. Hannah, br. Wm., two nephews. **Hannah**, Hannah Taylor in fa.'s will. **Lydia**, b. 9 Oct. 1692, m. Saml. Adams (19). **William**, b. 28 Jan. 1694, liv. Kit., m. 25 Nov. 1714 Lydia Parker (John). 9 ch. **John**, b. 12 Sept. 1697, glazier, Portsm., m. 24 Nov. 1717 Elizabeth Polley (Edw.). Taxed Portsm. Jan. 1731-2. A suit was brot 1743 on bill of items ag. Mrs. Elizabeth G., wid., Sept. 1737—June 1739. Wid. in Kit. 1761. 1 son.

**GOWEN**, a Scotch given-name.

1 **ALEXANDER** (Gowing), Oyster River. List 363a.

2 **JOHN** (4), planter, mariner, Kit., d. 9 Jan. 1732-3, m. (ct. 3 Oct. 1693) his cous. Mercy Hammond (3). Gr. j. 1714; surveyor; selectm.; orig. memb. Berw. Ch. Lists 291, 296, 297, 298. Ch: **Dorcas**, b. 13 Aug. 1692; ab. 1724 acc. John Treworgy, who could not be found; unmar. 1732. **William**, b. 27 Apr. 1697, d. 7 July 1713. **George**, b. 10 Aug. 1696, d. 30 June 1712. **John**, b. 24 May 1698, mariner, m. 1 Feb. 1719-20 Elizabeth Ferguson (1), whose fa. sued him in 1728 for board of his dau. Jane 4½ yrs. Jane was liv. 1731, her mo. dead; he dead in 1732. **Mercy**, b. 27 Jan. 1700-1, m. in Glouc. 19 Mar. 1726-7 Moses Riggs. **Joseph**, b. 28 Nov. 1703, d. bet. 1717-1732. **Jane**, b. 13 May 1706, m. Wm. Gowen (3). **Lemuel**, b. 22 Sept. 1709, eldest s. 1732, d. at sea. Lists 290, 296, 297, 298. M. 25 Jan. 1731-2 Judith Lord, a wid. 28 Sept. 1738. His will 27 Dec. 1737, prov. 17 Oct. 1740. 4 sons bp. 1738. She m. 2d 22 Dec. 1748 Abel Moulton, York. **William**, b. 14 July 1715. One Wm. with w. Sarah and ch. Sarah Winkley (by ano. record, w.'s mo.) from Portsm. warned at Charlestown 1759; son Lemuel bp. there same yr.

3 *NICHOLAS (4), early an Ind. scout, was adm. to practice as an attorney in York Ct. Apr. 1703. Tr. j. 1695-6, 1702; gr. j. 1696-8, 1703. Auditing com. 1696-7; lot layer 1698-9; Rep. 1709. Lists 290, 291, 296, 297, 298. D. ±1742. Wid. Abigail (Hodsdon 1) liv. 1747. Ch: Abigail, b. 12 Apr. 1695, m. 14 Feb. 1712-3 Miles Thompson. Elizabeth, b. 5 July 1697, m. 8 Dec. 1718 Jos. Hart (4). Margaret, b. 19 Mar. 1699, m. 10 Apr. 1717 Abraham Lord (7). Hester, b. 20 Nov. 1701, m. 19 Feb. 1726-7 Hugh Ross. Nicholas, b. 12 Nov. 1703. William, b. 4 Apr. 1705, m. 26 June 1724 Jane Gowen (2). He d. 1748, she in Boston 20 Sept. 1750. 6 ch. Patrick, b. 30 Mar. 1707, m. Miriam Shackley. List 298. 10 ch. 1737-1756. Anna, b. 29 June 1709, m. 9 Dec. 1724 Richard Thurlo. *James, Esq., b. 14 Feb. 1715, Capt., Rep., Judge of Ct. of Common Pleas, m. 1st 29 Nov. 1738 Anna Smith, 2d Lois Woodbridge. D. ±1781. 7 daus.

4 WILLIAM, alias Smith, a. Scot, b. ±1634, ±51 in June 1685. Carpenter. Oyster River 1659, Kittery 1666, and m. there 14 May 1667 Elizabeth Frost (9). Tr. j. 1672; gr. j. 1673, 1681, 1683 (not sworn). Constable 1674. Lists 361b, 298. See also Cromwell (4), Barrow (1). In 1676 he bot from Jas. Middleton on the Kennebec Riv., incl. Small Point. Gr. adm. 11 Sept. 1677 on est. of Tristram Harris (26), q. v., whose relative Philip White sued him in 1684 and his wid. Elizabeth in 1695, for the part given the Gowen ch. In 1679 he was idling away time and drinking. D. 2 Apr. 1686, adm. 21 May to wid. Elizabeth, who was liv. 1733. List 290. Ch: Nicholas, b. 1667. John, b. 19 Nov. 1668. William, b. ab. 1672, k. by Ind. 12 Oct. 1691. List 298. Elizabeth, b. ab. 1673, m. Alex. Ferguson (1). James, b. 29 Mar. 1675, blacksmith, Wells, used the name 'Smith'; m. 3 Mar. 1701 Mary Wheelwright (Saml.) He d. by 1728; she n. c. m. 1741. Kn. ch: Mary, b. 25 Jan. 1702, m. Archelaus Hewett; Elizabeth and Margaret, both town charges 1746. Margaret, b. 15 Nov. 1678, m. Danl. Emery (2). Lemuel, b. 9 Feb. 1680, shopkeeper Kittery 1702; of Boston, m. 5 Jan. 1709 Sarah Mountfort. D. in Boston 21 Apr. 1727, she 20 Aug. 1736. 2 kn. ch. Sarah, b. 30 Mar. 1684, m. Wm. Smith.

Gracey, see Greason.

GRAFFAM (sometimes Grafton), Stephen, fished at the Shoals 1660-1; Ipswich bef. Mar. 1663 when sued by Jona. Wade; in May foll. bound over to Salem Ct. on charge of fornic. His ho. in Portsm. ment. Dec. 1663. He sold on Great Isl. to Roger Rose 1672; witn. a Nantucket deed 1678; boarded Peter Pisgrave, a Portsm. charge,

1682-3. Lists 323, 356L, 326bc, 330a, 312ac, 287, 313ab, 331b. Wid. Mary (his w. in 1673) m. 2d Rich. Abbott (3); a wid. again in Dec. 1712, she deeded 2 a. on Gt. Isl. in her poss. 50 yrs. to s. Caleb who would have to indemnify Portsm. for hers. and s. Stephen, and care for Stephen aft. her dec. One wid. Graffam taxed 1713. Ch: John, b. ±1664, jailed in 1682 for refusing to serve his master Roger Rose, his fa. claiming great abuse; depos. in 1682 (Grafton) that he was at Naomi Daniels' ho. in May; in 1685, ±21, depos. for Roger Rose. Mary, b. ±1667, m. 24 Dec. 1684 Jos. Grant of Watertown, br. of Roger Rose's w. He d. 1721; she was a wid. in Watert. 1751, ag. 84. 10 or m. ch., inc. Stephen. Stephen, incapable in 1712. Samuel, presum., bot in Portsm. 1707. Inv. 21 Oct. 1715; Capt. John Pickering and Jacob Lavers bondsm. for the wid. Agnes, who m. 2d 10 Nov. 1715 Thos. Russell. 3 ch. bp. 13 June 1708; 2 more bp. 1709-1711 may have been his. Caleb, b. ±1684, taxed Str. Bk. 1708, 1713 (and farm), went to Scarboro for a time, and app. liv. in Greenl. 1723-5. Lists 339, 234b. M. Rebecca Hinkson (6), who was adm. to Portsm. No. Ch. July 1715. Ab. 1731 he was liv. on Hinkson land at Scarb. and depos. there in Apr. 1735, ag. 51, that he was at Dunstan 20 yrs. bef., improv. land under Mr. Elliot and built and occup. a ho. until driven off by the Millikens. W. bur. at Scarb. 25 June 1759, he 16 Mar. 1767. 6 ch. bp., incl. Caleb of Windham.

GRAFFORT, Thomas, Mr., Esq., b. ±1648, merchant, kinsman of Capt. Thos. Daniel (7), and poss. here 1st by 1673 (List 327d?). Bef. Nov. 1683 he had been ransomed, presum. from Algiers, by money pd. by the Cutts fam. Depos. in Portsm. Nov. 1684, and m. 11 Dec. that yr. his kinsman's wid. Bridget (Cutts) Daniel. He belonged to Capt. Robt. Mason's troop 1685; J. P. 1686; named Councillor 1692, but never acted. Called merchant of Boston in Aug. 1691, and living there in Oct. 1693 when Mary (King) Vaughan sued him. In Suffolk Ct. 1692 his negro Tony was accus. of breaking open Mr. Thos. Wacum's trunk in his master's ho., and stealing money. Lists 52, 57, 337. D. in Boston 6 Aug. 1697; will names wife, kinswo. Mary Graffort and her br. Philip, who was in Boston in 1702, cooper. Wid. Bridget d. in Portsm. 29 May 1701; her will 1 Apr.—15 July 1701, giving largely to Saml. Keais (4), was contested by Vaughans. Lists 330de, 336c, 96.

Grafton, Stephen, large landowner at Sheepscot, his gr. s. Saml. of Boston selling in 1732. Y. D. 17.61. See also Graffam.

Granger, John, Kittery, carried a Court summons to the Point in 1671. ±30 in June 1677. Bef. the Ct. several times, drunk and idle, usually assoc. with Berw. men; and failed to appear in Apr. 1680. Next and last found in 1695, abs. from meeting. List 30.

**GRANT**, a great clan of Inverness-shire.
1 **CHRISTOPHER**, Berwick, wit. James Smith's will 10 Aug. 1687 and m. his wid. Martha (Mills). Gr.j. 1689. Pub. ho. lic. Mar. 1689-90, just bef. he was k. or captured in attack on Salmon Falls Mar. 24; adm. to Samuel Penhallow 24 Feb. 1690-1. His w., taken at the same time, was in Montreal in May 1698; Stackpole says 're-deemed.'
2 **FERDINANDO**, Winter Harbor, fired hay he was cutting for Tho. Williams; sued by Williams and Robt. Sankey in Sept. 1640. Tr.j. 1640.
3 **JAMES**, called 'Welsh James' by Dover record, was accepted inhab. there 1657. Lists 356abce. In Nov. 1659 he was rated for the minister from Dover Neck, Peter Grant(12) the next name; later he was with Peter on the Me. side, where in July 1661 either he or (5) was ord. home to his wife. D. or disappeared bef. 10 July 1664, when wid. Joan, liv. unmar. with Peter, was soon to have a child. Under ct. pressure they were m. 28 Nov. 1664. The unborn ch., Elizabeth, was repudiated by the new husb., called his dau. in Niven Agnew's will and called 'dau. of Joan the w. of Peter Grant' in the will of James(4); she m. 1st James Landers, 2d John Turner, 3d William Hearl(5). See also (4).
4 **JAMES**, carpenter, had a town gr. 11 Dec. 1662, which became his homestead, above Salmon Falls, Berwick. See also (7). Coroner's j. Oct. 1668. Lists 288, 298. Will 12 Nov. 1679 (d. 6 Nov. 1683) gave the home place to w. Elizabeth, dau. of James Everill of Boston; land to Elizabeth Grant, dau. of Joan w. of Peter(12); personal prop. to Peter and Peter's two sons. Complete untangling of the Jameses revolves around the young Elizabeth and the question whether her mo. Joan was actually mar. to (3). That James(4) was related either to (3) or (12), and, childless himself, took the unfortunate girl into his own home, is perhaps as reasonable as the theory advanced that (4) was identical with (3), vanished because of fam. complications, mar. himself after Peter and Joan were mar., and returned to Berwick, turning to Elizabeth who he thot might be his own dau. His wid. Elizabeth soon m. Edw. Toogood and d. s.p. by 1695. Toogood remained on her place until Salmon Falls was

destroyed and sold in 1705 to Timothy Wentworth.
5 **JAMES**, York, Scotchman, called also 'the drummer.' In 1658 he was gr. 20 a. below Quamphegan (Rollinsford). See David Hamilton. If there himself he had mov. to York by 1660; either he or (3) ord. home to his w. by Me. Ct. in July 1661; York gr. 1662; that yr. he was hauling for Henry Sayward on ord. of Mr. Thos. Clark who sent him money from Boston by Mary Donnell; in 1672 Sayward sued him for debt of £200 and lost. Tr.j. 1665, 1667, 1669; Gr.j. 1667, 1670, 1688 (fined). Constable 1675. Lists 25, 26, 33, 279. In 1681 Alex. Maxwell sold him the land his barn stood on and bot for him from Arthur Bragdon the land his ho. stood on. Will 14 Apr., inv. 4 Dec. 1693; sworn to 11 Jan. 1693-4 by wid. Hannah, then m. to Samuel Johnson(30). Ch., both under age 1693: John, m. (Ct. Oct. 1702) Dorothy Milbury (Henry). James, m. Patience Austin(6). 5 sons 1709-1723. In Apr. 1731 he sued John Sayward for 8 a. by the Mill Creek; in Oct. 1736 bot William Bracy's home place.
6 **JAMES**, York, 1662. Both James sr. and jr. signed ptn. then. List 25.
7 **CAPT. JAMES**(12), carpenter, Berwick, app. the James jr. wounded by Ind. 5 Oct. 1692. Tr.j. 1703, 1714. Lists 296, 298. Late collector of taxes in 1714 when sued by Berw. selectmen. Captain in Ind. war 1725; paid £200 in 1729 for bldg. the trading ho. up Saco River. In June 1734, ag. 63, he dep. ab. Quamph. and the Lovering ho. In 1735 the town laid out to him 70 a., 60 by virtue of gr. to James(4) of 13 Apr. 1671 (called in the rec. gr. to himself), the rest part of a gr. to hims. 10 May 1703. On 3 Nov. 1735 he o.c. and was bp. in bed, being at point of death. Adm. gr. 20 Oct. 1741, bondsm. Robert Patterson and John Brooks of Biddeford. He m. 1st 6 Oct. 1693 Mary Nason (Jonathan); 2d bef. 1709 Rachel Stone (Daniel). 5 + 6 ch., of whom **Peter**, Berw., b. 14 Dec. 1696, m. 1st 24 Feb. 1717-8 Lydia Fost, 8 ch. incl. Landers; m. 2d Mary (Lord) wid. of Jos. Stewart, 9 ch. Will 29 Apr.—12 July 1756. Lists 279, 298. **James**, b. 8 Dec. 1703, m. 9 Mar. 1724-5 Sarah Joy; Montsweag 1743. 4 ch. bp. Berw.
7½ **JOHN** Gr[-nt]?, Mr., Saco 1660. List 244c. Gray? N. E. Reg. 71.124.
8 **JOSEPH**, m. in Greenland, 20 Nov. 1723 Susanna Foss. 8 ch. bp. there 1724-1744.
9 **JOSHUA**, glazier, b. Watertown 11 June 1637, br. of Jos. who m. Mary Grafton (Graffam 1). Presum. he was the one acc. at New London 2 June 1674 by Elizabeth (Beckwith) Gerard, yet m. one Sarah there, Andrew Lester her bondsm., the bond forf.

He was k. at Arrowsic 14 Aug. 1676 when Rich. Hammond's ho. was attacked. Adm. est. Joshua of Kennebec Riv. to fa. Christo. of Watert. 19 June 1677. 1 son.

10 **MARY**, 'my old servant,' Saml. Winkley's will 1726.

11 **NICHOLAS**, witn. 1711 with Rich. Hilton and Thos. Pickering.

12 **PETER**, Berwick, a Scot, b. ab. 1631, taxed, Dover 1659, and ord. home to his w. in Me. Ct. 2 July 1661. In July 1664 he was liv. with Joan wid. of James Grant(3) altho not known that his own w. was dead. A certif. copy of Kittery town book, long lost, gives date of their mar. 28 Nov. 1664, she 'big with child.' He had previously bot in Kit. from Jas. Emery in Oct. 1659, and dep. in 1701, ag. ±70, that he had liv. in upper Kit. over 40 yrs. Named as trustee in Alex. Cooper's will 1683, and ret. the invent. Gr.j. 1687; surv. highways and fences 1693. Orig. memb. of Berwick Ch. Lists 356e, 30, 288, 290, 296, 298. Will 19 Oct. 1709 (inv. 2 Mar. 1712-3) names w. Joan and ch. 'them seven' (excluding Elizabeth): **William**, b. ab. 1670. **James**, b. 23 Mar. 1671. **Alexander**, b. ab. 1673; with Daniel recd. the homestead aft. their mo.'s death; single 1721. List 298. In 1734, ag. 61, he dep. ab. the Lovering ho.; liv. June 1737, ±63. **Grizzel**, m. John Key, jr. **Mary**, ±80 in Apr. 1756; m. Joseph Pray. **Daniel**, b. ab. 1680, taxed June 1701, 'Daniel and ye estate' taxed Nov. 1713. Single 1721, liv. 5 Apr. 1756, ag. 76. **Hannah**, unm. 1721.

13 **PETER** (Grout). List 3, p. 50. Read Grant.

14 **PETER**, Newcastle, fisherman, m. Mary Thomas (Wm.), gr. dau. of Lt. John Barrett(2). In 1720, with Jos. Field(8) and w. Hannah, they q.c. their fa.'s 1681 gr. in Cape Porpus; in 1722 all four relinq. adm. on the Barrett est. to Thos. Perkins. On 21 Mar. 1726-7 the Grants alone deeded to John Downing 5 a. near Miller's Creek. Widow G. taxed Newc. 1727-8; liv. 1743. Ch. presum. incl.: **Peter**, Newc., bot ho. from Jas. and Judith Marden 1739; m. bef. 1749 Ruth Seavey (Wm.). **John**, Wid. Grant taxed for him 1743.

15 **ROGER**, fisherman, Shoals 1662, fined in July 1667 for letting his w. sell without lic.; himself selling without in Sept. 1668 and July 1669, Peter Lewis wit. Wid. Joan m. 2d Andrew Diamond(3). She was ±44 in Mar. 1672-3. Ch. incl.: **Dau.** (Rebecca?), m. William Harris(27). **Roger**, appren. by his fa. 26 June 1662 to Ezekiel Northend of Rowley for 13 yrs. In 1674 he was sued by Francis Wainwright; in 1683 his ho. adjoined land of Peter Lewis on Smuttynose. Joan, struck by Joan Diamond 1676, may have been his w. or sis.

16 **THOMAS**, disorderly at Portsm. 1661. One of the name was sued by Nich. Weeks in Wells Ct. in 1673 for refusing to work as ordered.

17 **WILLIAM**(12), Berwick, ±42 in 1713. Lists 296, 298. In 1756 his br. Daniel dep. that Wm. improved Wm. Love's est. at Salmon Falls. Will 24 May 1721—27 Oct. 1722 names w. and s. Wm. exects., dau. Martha, and gives homestead to three sons. He m. 1st 4 Aug. 1690 Jane Warren (James), 2d 26 Dec. 1695 Martha Nelson (Charles), a wid. in 1730. Ch., by 1st w.: **Jane**, b. 26 Dec. 1692, m. 9 July 1708 Micum McIntire. By 2d w.: **William**, b. 27 July 1696, m. 26 Jan. 1717-8 Abigail Kennard (1). List 298. 11 ch. **Alexander**, b. 1 Aug. 1699, made over his int. in the homestead in Jan. 1729-30 to Micum McIntire who had pd. his debts; liv. 1732. List 298. **Mary**, b. 17 Oct. 1701, not in will. **Martha**, b. 18 Dec. 1704, m. 11 Feb. 1724-5 Ephraim Wentworth. **Charles**, bp. 19 July 1719, liv. Kit. tery 1732. List 298. W. **Kezia**. 6 ch. bp. 1735-1753.

18 ——, from Quebec, List 5.

**Grare** (Grure?), John, bondsm. with Edw. Melcher 1693. See Geare.

**GRAVES**, chiefly found in north-eastern counties of England.

1 **FRANCIS**, Portsm., br. of (2), Ipswich 1674-1682; m. in Portsm. 27 Aug. 1689 Amy (Onion), wid. of Robt. Purington. Of Salisb., form. of Piscat., 1690. Coroner's jury, Portsm., Mar. 1693-4; dissented to vote ab. schoolmaster's salary there 1696; liv. 3 July 1703. His w. was a memb. of No. Ch. 1699 and earlier; in 1715, wid. of Portsm., she deeded for life support to dau: **Hannah**, b. Sals. 29 Aug. 1690, m. 1st 23 Nov. 1712 Thos. Stephens, 2d Thos. Blashfield(2).

2 **JOHN**, Mr., b. ab. 1651, s. of Wm. and Beatrice of Bentley, co. York, sent over ab. 1673 by his uncle Mr. Saml. Hall, form. of Sals., to Mr. Saml. Symonds of Ipsw., and soon fol. by br. Francis(1). John did not refund his passage money to his uncle; Francis did, and was rememb. in uncle's will. Waters i. 780-1. John m. bef. 8 July 1677, perh. not in Me., Martha Mitton (Michael). He was of Ipsw. in 1678, and is noticed in Falm. only in June 1680, when he was gr. adm. on Michael and Nathl. Mitton's estates, sued Nathl. Masterson for defama., and witn. Geo. Felt's deed. Appar. gone the next month, poss. direct to Kittery, where he liv. on Champernowne's Isl. 1680-87. Recommended by Mr. Tyng in July 1686 as a marshal for the Prov.; Gr. j. 1687, 1688 (foreman). Lists 225a, 227. He depos. in July 1690, ±39, ab. Capt. Champernowne 14 yrs. bef. and money he had

engaged to pay Saml. Hall. His w. Martha was pd. £8 in 1682 from the money Mr. Hall left for relief of war sufferers. She d. in 1700 at Little Compton, R. I., where they remov. aft. 1690. List 225. He last found depos. in Kittery 15 May 1712, ag. ±60. Kn. ch: **Ebenezer**, living Kingston, R. I., 1722. W. Mary. **Martha**, m. at Little Compton 8 Jan. 1702 John Price, cordwainer; both liv. there 1734. **Dorothy**, b. 1684, m. 30 Jan. 1708 William Bailey, who d. at Little Comp. 17 Feb. 1730; she d. there 26 Nov. 1771. 10 ch. Poss. others as Martha and Dorothy were the 'two surv. daus' in 1722.

3 **JOHN**, 50 and upw., dep. in Salem Ct. Nov. 1704 that he was at Casco Fort Mar. 1703. Likely the Sergt. G. whose s. was k. there by Ind. 20 July 1704. List 96.

4 **SAMUEL**, Kingston, came from Andover, m. 1st by 1709 Sarah Perkins (James of Hampt.) who d. 16 July 1724; 2d 29 Jan. 1724-5 Martha Bond (Londonderry rec.), also called wid. of John Bowden. In 1742 he sold his homestead to s. James; liv. Haverh. at death; adm. in N. H. to wid. Martha 28 Oct. 1747. Ch. 6+2.

5 **THOMAS**, York patentee 1631. Lists 271, 272.

6 **WILLIAM**, ±60, Aug. 1685. If only one Wm., he moved around. Taxed Oyster Riv. 1659, a new name; in Kit. 1664 bondsm. for Geo. Palmer, and soon working in the Lamprill Riv. mills; of Oyster Riv. again in Dec. 1667, Abra. Collins gave him a due bill which he sold to Henry Kirke; appar. worked in Hampt. for Jas. Godfrey 1668-9; Portsm. 1670-2. Aft. his kn. marriages to two Oyster Riv. widows, 1st bef. Oct. 1680 to Elizabeth, wid. of Richard York, 2d to Salathiel Denbo's wid., he rem. there and in June, 1681, made an agreem. with s.-in law John York to leave the York land aft. his w.'s death. Last app. in ptn. 8 Jan. 1694-5 asking for money for the doctor and hims., his est. at Oyster Riv. demolished, himself wounded in last attack. His land ment. 1711. Lists 361a, 380, 326c, 312c, 52, 67. No kn. ch.

7 **WILLIAM**, Falm. List 227. Meant for John.

8 **WILLIAM**, husbandman, Exeter, ±22 in Aug. 1697, when he testif. ab. wid. Mary Gordon. He bot there from Benj. and Rachel Taylor in 1701; in 1730 bot from wid. of Alex. Gordon jr. half the land they had owned in common; his ch. were also intimately connec. with the Gordon fam. List 376b (1698, 1725). M. in Hampton 24 Sept. 1702 Margaret Redman, not in his will 10 Sept. 1744—25 Mar. 1747, naming ch: **Benjamin**, princ. heir and exec. **John**, b. -27 Mar. 1704-, bot in Exeter 1726; will, of Kensington, 1757—1757. List 376b (1725). He

m. 1st 26 Feb. 1740-1 Deborah Marston (Wm.), who d. bef. 24 Apr. 1751, 2 sons; 2d w. Elizabeth, 1 son. **William**, b. -19 June 1704-, d. Kensington 5 Aug. 1753. List 376b (1725). He bot in Exeter 1730, and his fa. deeded to him, of Kensing., 1743. M. 1st in Kingston 27 May 1731 Susannah Thing, 2d Margaret Lowe, who d. 11 May 1772 in 57th yr. 10 ch. **Joseph**, Exeter. Will 1 Apr.—28 Aug. 1745, names w. Mehitabel, 2 sons, 2 daus. **Mary**, unmar. 1744. **Deliverance**, m. in Kingst. 25 Jan. 1729-30 Edward Eastman; wid. 1744. **Margaret**, m. in Kingst. 16 Aug. 1733 Benj. Eastman.

9 **WILLIAM**, witn. Arundel and Biddef. deeds 1721. Y. D. x.

**GRAY**, a common English name, becoming 86th in N. E.

1 **ALEXANDER** (4), Berwick, ordered 3 Dec. 1705 to guard Capt. Hill in the woods. List 289. He soon m. Elizabeth Thompson (John) and cleared land in the wilderness for a home. D. suddenly 1725, adm. to her 7 Apr. The mo. of two illegit. ch. bef. her mar., see(2), Ball(5), Hilton, and left with 7 small ch. at his death, a colorful life with plenty of work and trouble was hers, her ptn. to the Govr. and Genl. Ct. in 1762 telling the story of her mar. life; her ch. all then dead but one, numerous gr. ch., but those liv. near in poor circum., the est. sold except her dower; yet her life was spun out to 14 Jan. 1777. In a fam. row in Jan. 1731-2 she sued Jos. Jellison and w. Sarah for assault and battery, the church susp. all three for their scand. quarrel. Deposed in Oct. 1755, ±74. 7 ch. liv. in 1734 of 9 rec. or bp. 1708-1726: **John, Nehemiah, Alexander, Timothy, Anne, Abigail, Lydia, Nehemiah, Daniel.** In 1743 her daus. and sons John and Danl. q. c. to her, while John Hooper jr., who was her bondsm. with Ebenezer Hilton 1731-2, q. c. the same yr.

2 **EBENEZER**, bp. as s. of Elizabeth Gray (1) 28 Feb. 1719-20. See Ebenezer Hilton.

3 **FRANCIS**, Great Island 1660, given to excessive drinking, tho appar. educated. Witn. 1668 with John Towle and John Tanner. Last found in Ct. 30 June 1669 giving bond for good behav., his form. bond violated. Lists 77b, 330a, 47.

4 **GEORGE**, Berwick, by trad. from Ireland, more likely Scotland, witn. deed to Peter Grant, Scotchman, 21 Oct. 1659. Signed Portsm. ptn. 1665. Kit. gr. 1671 and admon. there with Wm. Hearl in 1678 for not assisting the constable. Lists 311b, 288, 298, 296. M. (Ct. July 1672) one Sarah, who struck Patience Etherington in 1676, getting hers. into Ct. His will 31 Mar. 1692 (invent. 25 July 1693), names her exec., and

to have half his lands during widowhood; 4 sons, but not the dau. She m. 2d aft. 30 Aug. 1693 Francis Harlow (1); both liv. 1726. Ch: **Robert. George**, in captiv. when his fa.'s will made, was to receive his mo.'s half at her death or mar. if he ret. Remaining in Montreal 'for love of religion,' 1702; dead s. p. in 1723. List 99, p. 76. **Alexander. James**, husbandman, Berw., m. 30 Aug. 1711 Martha Goodwin, (dau. of Moses 4). Oct. 15, 1718 his step-fa. and mo. deeded to him for life supp., and a few dys. aft. his death deeded to his s. James. Will 18 June—4 July 1726 names w., 5 sons, dau. Mary. The wid. Martha was in Ct. Apr. 1729, acct. twin bastards; m., but did not accuse, Uriah Page. In 1756, wid., she sold common rights allowed her by the Genl. Ct. for mainten. of Francis Harlow; Elizabeth Gray, dau. of sist. Martha Page, was rememb. in will of Moses Goodwin, jr. 1759. **Sarah**, not in fa.'s will, m. 1st Joseph Jellison, 2d Nicholas Cane (2).

5 **GEORGE**, Sagadahoc. Lists 17. (228c?).

6 **JAMES**, mason or bricklayer; no kn. connec. with any Gray fam., poss. son of (8) or (14). Born 1691 by fam. rec., he was a soldier from Portsm. at Newcastle in July 1708, and with scouting party under Capt. Jas. Davis 1712. Bot ho.-lot in Portsm. 1712; taxed 1713-14, tax abated 1715. Newington 1717-1723, perh. longer; of Portsm. 22 Jan. 1731-2 when he bot in Barrington from John Shackford; but 'gone' by Portsm. tax list 15 Jan. 1731-2. W. Tamsen by 1717; both liv. Barr. 1758. Besides a dau., sons **George**, m. Martha James, liv. Barr. and Wiscasset, and **James**, these three bp. Newington 1717-1723, was s. **William** who 1st bot in Barr. 1752. One Mary G. m. in Newing. 4 Jan. 1724-5 Geo. Marriner and was in Eliot 1744 with sis. Elizabeth Gray.

7 **(JOHN?)**, Saco, O. A. 1653 (Sav.). Mr. John Gr.[nt] there 1660. See Reg. 71.124.

8 **JOHN**, Oyster River, soldier under Capt. John Woodman May—Oct. 1697; of Dover, surety for Saml. Perkins 1704. Lists 368b, 369. In Mar. 1726-7 he sold ¼ of 500 a. gr. in new township of Rochester, his w. then **Welthean** (Thomas), wid. of Robt. Huckins (2). As Wealthy, w. of John, she was bp. 1 Apr. 1728, d. bef. 21 Jan. 1729-30. He and last w. Elizabeth (m. bef. Oct. 1735) were liv. 1748. Presum. by an unkn. 1st w. he had ch. eq. unkn., but younger Grays in O. R. may tentatively be attrib. to him, incl: **Elizabeth**, m. 23 Nov. 1727 Joseph Whidden. **Mary**, bp. for herself 7 Jan. 1727-8. **George**, training soldier 1732. John in the same list poss. the fa. or a son. One Joseph had dau. bp. So. Ch., Portsm. 1740. One Reuben of

Madbury 1756, with w. Martha (Miller) q. c. land gr. to Jos. Miller in Barr. One Samuel liv. on no. side O. R. 1760. See also (6), (14).

9 **JOHN**, Esq., Biddeford, came from London with Saml. Shute, Esq. 1716. Commander at Ft. Mary 1720, Capt. in Fr. & Ind. War, d. 1755. W. Elizabeth (Emery) wid. of Nathl. Tarbox. 3 daus. 1727-1730. N. E. Reg. 71.211.

10 **ROBERT** (4), eldest son, under age 1693, m. by Rev. Saml. Moody of York 12 June 1701 to one Elizabeth (Goodwin and a 1st w., Stackpole says), but poss. the same Elizabeth Freethy (3), who was his w. by 1706 and his wid. in York, 1754. He sold out in Berw. to bro. James, 3 Mar. 1708-9; thereaft. liv. in York. Lists 289, 298, 290, 279. Ch. rec. Kittery: **Sarah**, b. 9 May 1702, m. Nathl. Lewis. **George**, b. 17 Apr. 1703, cordwainer, York, d. June 1737. List 279. M. in York 26 May 1725 Mary Joy, who m. 2d Jos. Getchell (6). 6 ch. **James**, b. 12 Apr. 1705, 'supp. to be drowned', Wiscasset, 29 Nov. 1739. Rec. York: **John**, b. 10 June 1707, m. Elizabeth Winslow (Nathl.), 1 s. rec. **Ruth**, b. 27 Mar. 1710. **Joseph**, b. 12 Apr. 1712, of Georgetown 1752, m. 1st at York 11 Apr. 1734 Sarah Stevens (Moses) of Kit., 1 dau.; 2d 8 Sept. 1737 Grace Lang (4). **Joshua**, b. 17 Nov. 1714. **Mercy**, b. 29 Nov. 1718, m. Jona. Sargent.

11 **ROBERT**, Berwick, Saco, from Ireland, says Folsom, and d. 1771, ag. 91. W. Jannet. 5 ch. bp. Berw. 1723-1732. In 1746-7 he deeded his 200 a. farm at Saco to s. James who gave back a life lease.

12 **SIMON**, Newcastle tax 1720 abated.

13 **WILLIAM**, in 1639 gave P/A to Philip White of Piscat. to collect from Jeremiah Willis.

14 **WILLIAM**, in 1681 leased from Wm. Shackford for 7 yrs. land so. of Turning Point, and asked Philip Lewis sr. to go with him to Luke Maloon's ho. to close the bargain. Sued by Shackford 1682. List 359b. No rec. of fam., but not impos. fa. of (6) and others.

**GREASON, Gracey, Robert**, Scotsman, Falmouth 1685-90, owning on Presumpscot River; with Dennis Morough witn. Sampson Penley's deed 1685; with Moses Felt did the stonework for Robt. Lawrence's ho. Lists 34, 228c. He was taken capt. 16 May 1690, not heard of aft. W. unkn. Ch: **John**, seaman, Boston, sold 90 a. of his fa.'s land 12 Sept. 1698 ; d. s. p. bef. 1734. **Esther**, m. John Stebbins. Both liv. Stoughton 17 Apr. 1734, when only heir, she deeded all int. to Phineas Jones.

**Grecians**, see Gresham.

**Gredon**, Chas. List 52. See Glidden.

**GREELY.** 1 **George,** soldier from Ipsw. 1693. List 267b.

2 **PHILIP,** Sals., owned land near Lamprell Riv., form. of Edw. Hilton sr., and sold to John Gilman 1680.

3 **THOMAS,** tanner, Portsm., bot and taxed 1698, likely there first as apprent. to Matthew Nelson to whom he assigned his pay as a soldier Dec. 1695—Jan. 1696. Bot in Kit. 1702 and had a gr. there 1703. Taxed Portsm. 1707 and sold his Kit. land 1708-1714. See Johnson(21). Lists 67, 330def, 336c, 337, 296, 339, 297. Wife Rebecca adm. to Berw. Ch. 1703. Will 27 Nov. 1723—9 Mar. 1723-4 names her and ch., giv. to Peter his est. in Jersey; Clement Hughes exec., Peter Mow, Frenchman, a witn. Ch: **Peter,** m. Mary Phipps (Thos. Esq.) He o. c. and had s. Thos. bp. No. Ch. 3 Mar. 1722-3. List 339. Adm. to her 24 Feb. 1741-2. 9 ch. surv. him, 7 dying s. p. bef. 1765. **John. Thomas,** bp. Oct. 1710, under age 1723, m. in Greenl. 19 Dec. 1731 Esther (Griffith 4) Wooden. 1 s. rec. **Samuel,** bp. 8 Apr. 1716. **Sarah. Hannah.**

**GREEN,** particularly common in eastern England, became 18th in N. E.

1 ———, Goodman, w. and chn. at Francis Trickey's in Portsm. 15 Apr. 1652; his house ordered cleared of them in a month's time. Poss. (11), while s. John got his house ready for him up river?

2 **ABRAHAM** (7), Hampton, m. 9 July 1668 Esther Swett (Capt. Benj.), who d. bef. him. Selectm. 1694, 1701. Lists 392b, 396. Will 3 Feb. (d. 27 Feb.) 1717-8, names ch: **Abigail,** b. 27 Feb. 1669, m. Edmund Johnson(24). **John,** b. 20 May 1673, m. 23 Dec. 1695 Abial Marston (Ephraim). 6 ch. 1697-1718. **Mercy,** b. 28 Mar. 1675, m. Thos. Lancaster (3). **Henry,** b. 19 Aug. 1678, liv. Hampt. F. 1727. List 399a. Wid. Abigail Chase acc. him 1718-9. See Chase(4). **Benjamin,** Hampt. F., m. 17 Dec. 1707 Elizabeth Brown (5). Will 11 Sept.—27 Dec. 1749 names her and 6 ch. b. 1709-1728. **Nathan,** b. 18 Dec. 1687. His fa. willed to other ch. prop. form. given him, in case he should never return more.

3 **ANN,** Newcastle 1672, ±19. List 312e. See also (11).

4 **BENJAMIN** (William), b. Charlestown 28 Apr. 1687, carpenter, Berwick 1712-1720, m. there 9 Sept. 1713 Christian Main (Thos.), who was liv. 1718. He bot from her br.-in-law Thos. Bond 1717, the two men bot together 1720. Rochester gr. 1722. His promissory note was endorsed by Daniel G. of Charlestown 1723. Of Dover, he m. Ruth Whittier of Salis. 4 Apr. 1723; dism. from Berw. Ch. to Salis., 1725. Haverhill 1727;

Salis. 1729. There Thos. Bond sued him Jan. 1730-1, and in Apr. fol. he gave T. B. a full disch. of all debts. D. Salis. 20 Oct. 1732, w. Ruth surv. See also (29). Kn. ch. by 1st w: **Abigail,** bp. Berw. 3 June 1716. **Christian,** bp. Portsm. 7 Apr. 1723; m. bet. 1738-1745 Joseph Davis (38). By 2d w: 3 rec. Salis. 1724-9.

5 **DANIEL** (23), ±18 in Jan. 1697-8, Christian Remick his master. Kit. gr. 1699. In 1704 his fa. deeded him the homestead with life reservation. M. 31 Oct. 1706 Sarah Knight (19), and in July fol. was acc. by Mary Morgrage, whose s. Danl. G. al. Morgrage was Edm. Geach's 'prentiss boy' in 1717. Lists 291, 298. Jury 1709. Will 11 Apr.—16 May 1749 names w. Sarah, 4 of 6 ch. b. 1708-1723 and gr. dau. Lydia G. when of age. Two months later Wid. Sarah waived dower, s. **Daniel** contracting to supp. her for life. He d. bef. 6 Apr. 1750 when his bro. **Andrew** repres. that his br. Danl's wid. Sarah (Cooper) had put their fa.'s will into Stephen Tobey's hands.

6 **EDMUND,** Newcastle, presum. belonged in Kit., the home of his master, Dennis Downing, who lost a suit against him in 1663 for deserting his service. M. Lydia Trickey (Thos.) Newc. gr. 1666; blacksmith there in partn. with Danl. Moore. Lists 323, 326b, 330a. See also (11, 22). His death occas. inquiry and the arrest of Stephen Jones and Philip Chesley; later the wid. recovered ag. Chesley for slander. Inv. 2 May 1668; adm. 30 June fol. to wid. and N. Fryer, declared illegal; to her and Isaac Trickey 3 July. She m. 2d Richard Webber; liv. in June 1718 ag. 68, b. at Bloody Point. Ch: **Sarah,** m. Nathl. Keene (2). In 1728 she sold her fa.'s Newc. gr.

7 **‡HENRY,** Esq., Hampton, ±30 in 1652, ±40 in 1659, ±54 in 1673. Ipsw. 1642; Hampt. in poss. of land bef. May 1644, and estab. his perma. home on S. side of Taylor's Riv. by 1653. Carpenter, millwright, mill-owner. Twice comr. to settle Salisb. line; Selectm. 1662, 1680; Moderator 1691, 1693-4, 1697; Asst. of Inf. Ct.; Justice Ct. of Sessions; Councilor 1685-9, 1692-8; Chief Just. Ct. Com. Pleas 1697-8. Lists 392ab, 393ab, 49, 396, 56, 59, 61, 64, 65, 68, 399a. Hampt. records his death 5 Aug. 1700, above 80 yrs., for several yrs. a memb. of the Council until by age he laid down that place, but a Justice till he d. Will 2—20 Aug. 1700, names 2d w., all ch., and dau. Elizabeth Cass's three Chase ch. First w. Mary d. 26 Apr. 1690. Lists 393a, 394. He or she was nearly relat. to the Perkins bros.; Abraham P. who was repeatedly his surety and whose s.-in-law Giles Fifield called him Uncle Green and young Mary G. his cousin,

and Isaac P., whose s. Ebenezer called Isaac G. cousin; while a connec. with Greens in Mass. may be indic. See also Moulton. He m. 2d 10 Mar. 1690-1 Mary (Hussey), wid. of Thos. Page, who m. 3d Capt. Henry Dow (3). Ch: **Abraham. Abigail,** b. 6 Oct. 1650, d. 13 May 1669. **Isaac,** b. 25 —— 1651. **Jacob,** b. ±1653. **Mary,** m. in Haverh. 4 Nov. 1678 Peter Green who had 3 daus. by his 1st w. Elizabeth (Dustin) Kingsbury. 4 ch. rec. Haverh. 1679-1687. In 1660 Wm. Edmonds of Lynn sued her fa. for the cure of her leg at expense of over £20 for 11 mos. time. **Elizabeth,** b. 11 June 1656, m. 1st James Chase (3), 2d Capt. Jos. Cass (3). **Hannah,** m. 1st 5 June 1676 John Acey of Rowley, 4 daus.; 2d bef. 1698 John Shepard of Rowley, 1 son. She d. 30 Mar. 1718.

8 **ISAAC** (7), Hampt. and Salis., where his fa. deeded him land in Mr. Hall's Farm 1668. M. 18 Feb. 1673-4 Mary Cass (2). Selectm. 1697. Gr. j. 1699, 1700. Lists 52, 392b, 399a. Will, Hampt., 20 Feb. 1712-3 (d. 12 May 1716, ag. 70, Seabrook Quaker gr. yard), names w. sole exec., 4 ch., br. Abraham. Ch: **Abigail,** b. 18 Feb. 1678-9 (Salis.), not in will. **Jonathan,** b. 4 June 1681, k. by Ind. bet. Hampt. and Salis. 17 Aug. 1703. List 96. **Mehitable,** m. Simon Dow (10), 2d Onesiphorus Page. **Jacob,** bp. Salis. 7 June 1691, m. 8 Oct. 1713 Mary Eaton of Salis.; liv. Hampt. F. 7 ch. **Isaac,** bp. with Jacob, d. y. **Isaac,** b. 28 Dec. 1695, m. 23 June 1724 Huldah Weare; d. 7 Jan., adm. to her 4 Mar. 1728-9. She was Huldah Davis in 1734. Of 3 ch., 1 was posth. and Mary was the only survivor 1737. **Mary,** bp. 24 July 1698, m. Jacob Brown (5).

9 **JACOB** (7), ±27 in 1680, d. 5 Nov. 1726. Wife Sarah d. 18 Apr. 1723. Selectm. 1695, 1702, 1705. Jury 1698. Called Capt. 1700. Lists 63, 64, 392b. Sarah Downer (2) was in his fam. as nurse for a sick child 1708. Ch: **Mary,** b. 17 Apr. 1693, m. 1st 28 May 1713 Nathan Longfellow of Hampt., who d. 15 Jan. 1731; 2d in Salis. 27 Aug. 1733 Jos. Macress. In 1736 she was the only surv. dau. and heir of her fa. Capt. J. G. In 1738 her s. Jonathan, eldest of her 9 Longfellow ch., was carrying on a lawsuit against her; liv. Salis. 1740. **Abigail,** b. 27 Sept. 1700, m. 29 Jan. 1719 Danl. Weare; d. 23 Apr. 1723. **Jacob,** b. 12 Sept. 1702, m. 17 Dec. 1728 Mary Gale. **Jonathan,** b. 23 Aug. 1704.

10 **JAMES,** Oyster Riv. 1675-6. List 359a.

11 **JOHN,** sr., Kittery, one of four arbitrators in Rice Thomas's suit against Mr. Francis Raynes 26 Mar. 1647-8, the same yr. that his gr. next to Geo. Rogers was confirmed to him, ±30 a. with the small island of Franks Fort, over and above. Subm. to Mass. Nov. 1652. List 282. See (1).

Last found abs. from meeting, and acquitted because of contin. weakness, 29 June 1654. Appar. soon d., poss. not bef. he, or else (12), sold to Robt. Weymouth the So. part of his land, which in 1679 became Jos. Hammond's homestead and the site of his garrison. Two ch. appear: John, whose constant association with Jas. Emery and Robt. Weymouth has suggested a Green-Emery relationship. **Richard.** Very poss. others. See (6).

12 **JOHN** (11), Kittery, junior 13 Oct. 1654, when gr. 50 a. in the place where Barnard Squire had a former gr., but had become senior by 1669. In 1668 he (w. Julian) deeded to the Abbotts the best and biggest part of his 1656 gr. of 20 a., on which he was then liv., next Peter Grant; he deeded to s.-in-law John Searle in Dec. 1675; with w. Julian deeded to s.-in-law Thos. Abbott, for their support, 1 Mar. 1679-80. Lists 30, 81, 284, 288, 298. Adm. 31 Jan. 1681 to Mr. Andrew Searle and John Green in behalf of the wid. Julian. In Oct. 1682 John Searle compl. against Thos. Abbott for not taking care of her properly; July 10, 1683 she deeded to John Searle sr. for John Searle jr. and John, s. of Nich. Jellison; and poss. was 'Gemmer' G., pd. for weeding Thos. Turner's garden (acct. of the admr. Christian Remick, 28 Oct. 1684); Richard G. had dug his grave. Kn. ch: **Elizabeth,** m. by 1664 Ens. Thos. Abbott (4). **Mary,** b. ±1651, ag. 44 in 1695; had a bastard in 1672; m. John Searle. **Barbara,** m. Nicholas Jellison.

13 **JOHN,** Kittery, s. of Richard Tozer's w. Judith, and gr. s. of Robt. Blott of Boston, m. 12 Nov. 1666 Mary Jenkins (9), and bot ho. and land on Eliot Neck. Inv. 27 Oct. 1686 by Christian Remick and Richard Gowell, incl. 58 a. and bldgs., was sworn to 30 Aug. 1693 by the wid. Mary, then w. of Humphrey Axall, who was gr. adm. same day. She was here in 1695, ag. ±43; soon remov. to So. Carolina. Appar. his ch., no dau. noted here later, but son John certain: **Mary,** b. 4 Oct. 1672. **Elizabeth,** b. 22 Jan. 1674. **Hannah,** b. 8 Jan. 1677. **John,** b. 10 July 1680; of So. C., only son and heir, he joined his step-fa. and mo., as admrs., in conveying his fa.'s land to Peter Dixon, 29 Jan. 1704-5. Y. D. 7.33. **Lydia,** b. 19 Dec. 1683. **Sarah,** b. 29 Sept. 1686.

14 **JOHN** (19), mariner, Boston, gr. adm. 4 June 1701 on est. of fa. Nicholas and step-fa. Sheares. Will 18 Jan. 1692-3—19 Mar. 1701-2 ment. land at the Eastward at present not valuable, and provid. that mo. Ann Sheares should live with his wid. or have £8 a yr. for life. First w. Priscilla by 1672; 2d Hannah (?Gallop) by 1680. The wid. and three surv. ch., all of Boston, **John,**

Samuel and Priscilla, (by 1st w.) w. of Saml. Grice, deeded the Cape Neddick land, 27 Mar. 1708, Y. D. 7.101.

15 **JOHN** (23), mariner, Kittery, m. Sarah Remick (Christian), prob. bef. 19 June 1687, when his fa., dwelling on his fatherly affec., tender care and love for this beloved son, gave him land at the Cove near Franks Fort, adj. his own land. D. bef. 1693. Wid. Sarah m. 2d Barnabas Wixon of Barnstable, who was gr. adm. on her first husband's est. 7 Jan. 1695-6, and put in a bill for two yrs. support of the deceased's wid. and dau. She had 5 ch. by her 2d husb. 1693-1700, and was liv. on Cape Cod 1715. Green ch: Sarah, Richard, n. c. m., app. left with gr. fa. Green who soon shifted him to gr. fa. Remick. The latter in Jan. 1711-2 ptn. for relief, had maint. for 22 yrs. a ch. which one Rich. Green, several yrs. past gone out of the country, left with him, now almost a crazy man. In Apr. 1712 he was 'a disobedient disorderly person in the fam. where he liveth;' in July 1714 R. G. 'a natural fool', committed to the common jail; his gr. fa. C. R. deemed able to supp. him and ordered that he be ret. to his gr. fa.

16 **JOHN**, taxed Str. Bank July 1690.

17 **JOHN**, m. Sarah Parrott (John); both liv. Newport, R. I., 1738. See also Gammon.

18 **JOHN**, cordwainer, Portsm., m. in Greenland 5 Apr. 1733 Abigail (Wilson) Elliott (4 jr.). Appar. he was not the same J. G. who had m. Elizabeth Haines in Greenl., 9 Jan. 1728-9.

18½ **MARTHA**, Kittery. See Gowell.

19 **NICHOLAS**, York, first noted as a witn. with Nicholas Davis, 16 Mar. 1650. Y. D. ii.177, 179. In June 1654, called Goodman G. who now lives at Cape Neddick, he, or his w., took away his boy who had been kept several yrs. by Thos. King of Exeter, and he was ord. to pay for his time or send him back. Town gr. 1654; gr. of 80 a. laid out to his heirs 1680. List 25. W. Susanna, perh. Goody G. who was feeding the Bay magistrates in 1662. Inv. 23 July 1663; adm. to wid. Susanna, who with her 2d husb. Jeremiah Sheares, was resisting the constable in Apr. 1664. Div. to her, eldest son (a double portion), and other ch. P. & Ct. ii. 140, 159-61, 392. See also N. E. Reg. 14.352. She was liv. 1693. Only kn. ch: John. Sarah, m. John Parker, jr. Ann, m. 1st (Ct. 24 Oct. 1673) William Barton(5), 2d Walter Penwell.

20 **PERCIVAL**, minister at Wells, b. Cambridge 29 Mar. 1660, s. of John and Ruth (Mitchelson); H. C. 1680. Poss. never ordained, he preached at Cambr. and Stowe bef. Wells engaged him aft. 20 June 1683 at salary of £50 in lumber and provisions and use of the parsonage. Loving friend Mr. P. G. named an overseer in Jos. Cross's will 2 Mar. 1683-4. His death 10 July fol. (gr. st. at Cambridge), makes Bourne's implication, pp. 168-9, an injustice, altho Bourne himself, p. 171, notes that his pastorate may have been short. Appar. unmar.

21 **PETER**, Haverhill. See (7); see also Dustin.

22 **RICHARD** (11), Kittery, found as 'Senior' once, in 1663. The complete abs. of any Richard from record until 1662 makes it poss. he was identical with, not fa. of Richard(23). One R. G. was cleared on Archibald Leamon's charge of felony 2 July 1662, and a creditor of Robt. Weymouth's est. (⸮List 285). See also (3, 6).

23 **RICHARD**, Kittery, (⸮same as or s. of 22), had a first w. Katherine, for whom Thos. Abbott was bondsm. in July 1669, when she and Mary Green (⸮12) were having trouble with Katherine Tobey. His last w. was Susanna in 1687, when he deeded to s. John at Franks Fort. Both were abs. from meet. 1696. In 1712 Christian Remick spoke of him as several yrs. gone out of the country. See (15) Lists (⸮285), 30, 31, 92, 296, 297, 298. She was liv. in 1724 when she ptn. for relief from Daniel, altho not named in her husband's deed of the homestead to Daniel 1 May 1704. Ch., appar. by 1st w: ⸮Richard, d. y. John. ⸮Thomas, witn. for Richard and Susanna, 19 June 1687. Y. D. 5.1.117. Samuel, Kittery, m. 6 Jan. 1708 Mary Knight (19). List 291. Both liv. 1739, when he was oldest surv. son; in 1743 he and br. Danl. q. c. to Danl. Emery 60 a. near York Pond laid out to John Green, sr., 2 Mar. 1673-4. Daniel, b. ±1679.

24 **ROWLAND**, taxed Portsm. 1707. Ruth, ag. 22 in 1708, a witn. with Nathl. Freeman 1709, perh. his w. Appar. ch: Robert, blockmaker, m. in Portsm. 28 Sept. 1727 Anna Martyn; will 1748-1749 names w. Ann, 3 ch. Rowland, tailor, m. in Portsm. 6 May 1733 Elizabeth Hall of Dover; 3 ch. bp. So. Ch., incl. Robert. One Priscilla G. recd. into So. Ch. 1719-1722.

25 **SAMUEL**, Stratham, taxed 1714. List 388. If he m. Mary Drew(2), who d. s. p. by 1744, she was not his w. Mary 1718-1726, nor his wid. Mary, who d. in Strath. 16 May 1753. His will 23 Apr. 1743 (d. in Strath. 31 Dec. 1743, old Mr. S. G.), names w., 5 sons, 5 daus., one of them Mary Drew. The Wid. Green's granddau., Mary Drew, d. Strath.. 11 Sept. 1744.

26 **SUSANNA** (Atkins 5), liv. distant from Boston in 1716 when her sis. Elizabeth Davis of Beverly receipted for her there. Y. D. 8.170.

27 **THOMAS**? List 361a. See Gwinn.

28 **WILLIAM**, Scarboro, sent down by Wm. Sheldon aft. Philip's War as tenant on his farm separated from John Libby's by Libby's river. His town gr. adj. that of Thos. Baker (9) 1686. List 238a. His land ment. 1729. Ment. also of 'John Libby's Nonsuch lot called Mary Green's.'

29 **WILLIAM**, witn. deed to (4) 1715; likely his br. from Charlestown. Y. D. 9.18.

30 **WILLIAM**, (and Jas. Jordan) paid reward for apprehending John Kenniston (1) 1717.

**GREENFIELD**, found in Nottingham and Sussex.

1 **SAMUEL**, ag. 27, weaver, of Norwich, Eng., arriv. Boston in the -Mary Ann- 20 June 1637 with w. Barbara 25, 2 ch. and serv. John Teed. Recd. inhab. of Salem 14 Aug. foll. and during the next few yrs. liv. in Ipsw., where he m. 2d Susanna, wid. of Mr. Humphrey Wyeth; Hampton, where he was an orig. settler; and Exeter. In Ex., he was the town's messenger to Boston 1643, lic. to draw wine 1644, Selectm. 1644-7, Com. t. e. s. c. 1645-6, and involv. in ct. cases with Ex. and Hampt. men. Lists 391a, 392a, 376ab, 377, 374c, 375ab, 378. Called late of Ex. in May 1649, the same yr. that Mr. Wheelwright sued him, Thos. King and Natl. Boulter, partners in a pipe-stave contract, and the same yr. Lt. Wm. Howard brot two suits ag. him, and depos. 29 Dec. 1649 ab. his altering a bill due his step-dau. Em Wyeth. S. G. was then in Boston jail and does not appear again. In 1651 his Ex. land was in poss. of Edw. Gilman who was bondsm. for him in 1649. Ch: **Mary**, ravished by Jona. Thing (Ct. 2 Mar. 1640-1), his fine of £20 to be pd. in 3 yrs. to her fa., who sued Henry Ambrose of Salis. 10 July 1644 for detaining him. She was unmar. 1649. **Barbara**.

2 **THOMAS** (Greenfild), 1658. Y. D. 2.46. See Greenslade.

**GREENHAM, Stephen,** Kittery 1650-52, liv. in wigwam near Sturgeon Creek, his land later owned by Thos. Broughton. There he sued Mary Batchelder, w. of (5), was sued by Ambrose Lane, and was cleared on charge of taking goods from the Shapleigh mill, the later charged with perjury. Winter Harbor 1653, keeping a disord. ho. there 1656, and with w. abs. from meeting. Falm. 1662-8. List 25.

**GREENHILL,** 1 **Robert,** ±32 or 34, cook and able seaman on navy vessels 1654-5, assigned his tickets to W. Barefoot 21 May 1657.

2 ———, Capt., named in Maj. Shapleigh's acct. ag. Capt. Champernowne, 1669.

**GREENLAND, Dr.** (and Mr.) **Henry,** physician, Kittery, ±42 in 1670, ±44 in 1672. Intimate of, and drawn to N. E. to be near, Capt. Barefoot, he practised first in Newbury (plaint. in a suit for slander Mar. 1662-3), uncert. where to settle until his wife came. In Nov. 1663 he wit. Capt. Lockwood's deed to Barefoot; Newb. wit. Apr.—May 1664. Bef. 17 July 1665 he and Thos. Wiggin had given evid. against Mr. Rich. Cutts for words spoken ab. the King's comrs. Liv. in Kit. ab. 1666, and continually in evid. or trouble, including a reported attempt in 1670 to seize Mr. Cutts and send him to Eng. for punishment for treason, and ransom. Convicted of many high misdemeanors in June 1672 and ordered by the Genl. Ct. to leave the jurisdic. within two mos. On ptn. of his w. Mary, this time was extended to Sept. 1673. The ho. he had built at Kit. Point was sold in 1689 by Maj. John Davis to Benj. Woodbridge, clerk, with special warranty against the heirs of H. G. and heirs of Mr. Wm. Bickham. Barefoot's will gives to H. G. the 1000 a. at Spruce Creek, bot from H. G.; the title to which was in dispute. Lists 82, 86, 92. See Me. P.& Ct., vols. i and ii; Y. D. ii; Proc. Mass. Hist. Socy. 39. 288-291. His w. Mary, who came aft. May 1663, was here aft. he had left for Piscataway, N. J., in July 1673, selling without lic.; the same in July 1675, but fine remitted as she had some assurance from the selectmen. At Piscataway he was a landowner, Capt., J. P. Wife liv. there 1684, not in his will 11 Dec. 1694—7 Feb. 1694-5, Benj. Hull(1) a wit. Kn. ch.: **Henry,** liv. 1694-5. **Frances,** m. 8 Oct. 1681 Daniel Brynson or Brymson of Millston River, who d. in 1696, leav. wid., dau. Frances, s. Barefoot. **Dau.** (presum. Mary), m. Cornelius Langevelt (Longfield), Esq. of Raritan. His will 1733 names w. Mary, s. Henry, 3 dec. daus. and gr. ch.

**GREENLEAF.**

1 **REV. DANIEL,** b. Newbury 10 Feb. 1679-80, s. of Capt. Stephen (4 jr.), H. C. 1699, was hired as school teacher at Portsm. in May 1701, and m. 18 Nov. foll. Elizabeth Gookin of Cambr. He left Portsm. ab. 1703, but was at Star Isl. in 1705 and again in 1707, bef. beginning his long pastorate at Yarmouth on the Cape.

2 **ENOCH,** saddler, Boston, bot the Howell prop. at Dunstan from John and Martha Morton of Boston in July 1695, for which his heirs Wm. G. and Wm. and Bethia Clear of Boston sued Chas. and Geo. Pine and Jos. Young in 1731.

3 **SAMUEL,** Newbury, m. in Kit. 10 Oct. 1723 Elizabeth Mitchell (Robt.). See Greenough.

**4 ENS. STEPHEN**, Newb., m. 1st 13 Nov. 1651 Elizabeth Coffin (5), 2d 31 Mar. 1679 Esther (Weare), wid. of Capt. Benj. Swett, who d. at Hampt. 16 Jan. 1717-8, ag. 89. 10 ch. by 1st w. incl: Capt. **Stephen**, b. 15 Aug. 1652, d. Newb. 13 Oct. 1743, m. 1st 23 Oct. 1676 Elizabeth Gerrish (8), 10 ch.; 2d 17 Sept. 1713 Hannah (Tristram), wid. of Dominicus Jordan (1). In Sept. 1746 she was in Boston ±92. **John**, b. 21 June 1662, m. 2d 13 May 1716 Lydia (Frost 2), wid. of Benj. Pierce.

**5 STEPHEN**, Portsmouth, s. of Stephen (4 jr.), b. Newb. 21 Oct. 1690. Lieut., Capt., Major. Selectm. 1724-5, 1727-8, 1732. Lists 239b, 339. He m. 1st June 1715 Mary Cotton (7) who d. 29 May 1733; 7 ch. bp. So. Ch. 1716-1729; 2d Anne Emerson (3), 4 ch. bp. 1734-45. Adm. 30 May 1749 to wid. Anne and s. Stephen, mathemat. instrument maker, Boston, called 'loving cousin' by John Banfield (Charles 2) in his will 1745. One Stephen of York, w. Mary, had ch. Lydia, Stephen, Joseph, Mary, rec. there 1722-1731.

**GREENOUGH,** Greenhaugh, **Robert,** Rowley, a Falmouth grantee 1680, but soon left Me. if he ever resid. there. List 225a. In 1684 of Salem he bot from Harlak. Symonds 100 a. in townsh. of Wells and Cape Porpus. Ch. by 3 wives, his 1st w. Martha Epps (Danl.) the mo. of two sons rec., but perh. not b. in Rowley: **Robert**, b. 28 Feb. 1682-3, m. 20 Jan. 1704-5 Hannah Dole of Newbury. 8 ch., incl. Saml., b. Rowley 25 Mar. 1707, m. in Kit. 23 Apr. 1729 Elizabeth, wid. of Saml. Greenleaf (3), who m. 3d 29 July 1754 Capt. Henry Kingsbury of Rowley; Epps, bp. Rowley 22 July 1711, joiner, Kit., m. (int. Newb. 11 Dec. 1730) Margery Moore (Ebenezer) of Kit. Capt. **Daniel**, b. 22 Feb. 1685-6, taxed Portsm. 1708, m. 1st 16 Dec. 1708 Abigail Elliot (6), who d. 5 June 1719; 2d 25 Jan. 1721-2 Elizabeth, wid. of Capt. Saml. Hatch (2), and liv. long at Newc., (Selectm. 1728), moving to Bradford, where he d. 25 (or 20) Apr. 1746; wid. d. 3 Dec. 1765 in 73d yr. Ch. 5+6, 9 named in his will 15 Mar. 1745, w. Elizabeth exec. His daus. Sarah Robins and Abigail Colfax recd. his form. dwg. ho. at Newc.; sons Simon and John ano. ho. there.

**GREENSLADE,** a Devon-Somerset name. **THOMAS**, mariner, fisherman, with crew of -The Margery- arriving 1642-3, perh. went and came again, as next found witn. Cleeve's deed in Falmouth 1 Sept. 1648; witn. again for Cleeve in May 1658 and for Elizabeth Mitton 7 Oct. 1661. Geo. Munjoy sued him for debt 1666; John Bateman for forf. of a mtg. 1667. Lists 21, 221? Liv.

Salem 1673, where either he or s. Thos. was admon. for breach of the Sabbath. D. July 1674; inv., incl. many and unkn. debts, sworn to 27 Mar. 1677 by wid. Ann, who m. 2d Jacob Pudeator of Salem and was hanged as a witch 22 Sept. 1692. Ch. named in step-fa.'s will: **John**, mariner, taxed Salem 23 Nov. 1683; in 1690 had been gone since Oct. 1689. Bef. this he was at the Scottow ho. in Scarb. with br. Thos. Adm. to wid. Abigail (Curtice) of Salem 30 Oct. 1693, inv. 24 Oct.; she m. 2d 1 Nov. 1693 Thos. Mason. Abigail and James Greenslade m. in Salem 1709, 1711, poss. his ch. One Anne m. in Topsfield 1710, Ruth in Salem 1724, Sarah in Wenham 1724. **Thomas**, mariner, b. ab. 1652, Cleeve's serv. in 1666. In 1678 he was in Salem from the Barbadoes; named in Philip English's acct. 1685. Sept. 15, 1692, ±40, he test. ab. Rev. Geo. Burroughs at Scottow's ho. in Scarb. ab. the beginning of the last war, when John Greensleit was among others there; the next wk. he was with his mo. when she was hanged. **Ruth**, m. in Ipsw. 19 Sept. 1677 Josiah Bridges. **Samuel**, at Falm. 1675-6. List 223b. **James**, in 1690 had left Salem since Oct. 1689. In 1692 he sued for his stepfa.'s legacy. **?Sara**, fined in Essex Ct. June 1673 on susp. of stealing and lying, not named in the Pudeator will.

**GREENWAY, Clement,** Saco, let his serv. Peter Hogg to Mr. Thos. Lewis in July 1635 and sued for his wages in Feb. 1636-7. List 242. Ment. in Trel. acct. July 1639 as master of the ship -Barnstable-, built in N. E. and reported lost.

**Greer,** Griers, **George,** Oyster River. 4 ch. bp. 1722-9 unless Mary bp. 1722 was his w., not dau. See Drisco(2).

**GREGORY, 1 David,** Portsm. witn. 1722. N. H. Prob. 1.678.

**2 GEORGE,** indebted to Capt. John Mitchell's est., Kit., in Feb. 1665-6, and likely —— Gregory whom John Moor of the Shoals success. sued for slander, abusing his w., in 1668. Of Scarb., abs. from his w. several yrs., he was ord. home to her 5 July 1670, yet was there without her 3 yrs. later, and a soldier under Scottow 1676-7. Lists 78, 237b.

**3 JONAS,** Ipswich. See Dow (2).

**Greinely,** Thos. List 221. See Greenslade.

**Gresham,** Noah, Shoals, lost in the great storm 30 Jan. 1677-8. See Broad(4).

**Gresling,** Peter, Popham colony 1607, master's mate of the -Gift of God-. Addition to List 6.

**GRIBBLE, 1 Elias,** Shoals, drunk and fined June 1666.

**2 ISAIAH,** Shoals, abs. from meeting July 1667.

**3 THOMAS,** Kittery 1728. See Grindle (1).

**GRIFFIN**, common except in No. of England.

1 ————, liv. 5 yrs. on the Champernowne farm at Greenland under Mr. Valentine Hill.

2 **EDWARD**, sued in 1686 by Wm. Sturt for ejecting him from Arrowsic Isl., and disclaimed title by letter. D. H. vi. 216.

3 **HANNAH**, wid., m. Wm. Partridge. See Griffith (4).

4 **JOSHUA** and **PRISCILLA**. She had 80 a. in Scarboro 1669-70. In Aug. 1729 Jos. Stevenson of Newport, R. I., calling them his predecessors, sold 80 a. in Scarb. form. in their poss. Y. D. 13.103.

5 **MARGARET**, Hampton; her dau. Elizabeth b. 25 July 1666, fa. unkn. (Ct. Salis., Apr. 1666).

6 **MARY**, witn. Saco deed Dec. 1671. Y. D. vi. 6.

7 **NATHANIEL**, Hampton soldier at Oyster River 1694, poss. serv. of Jos. Smith. List 66.

8 **PHILIP**, in Portsm. from Salis. 1659, soon went to Scarb. where assoc. with Wm. Snell in dealings with Henry Watts and Robt. Jordan. Lists 323, 326a. K. by lightning (Hoyt), tho a Griffin MSS attributes this fate to s. John. Adm. gr. Oct. 1667 to Rich. Foxwell and Christo. Pickett, again 6 July 1669 to John Budezert who had m. the wid. Agnes by 27 Oct. 1668; inv. incl. ho. and land. She d. 24 Nov. 1682 in Salis., where ch. rec: **Hannah**, b. 12 Mar. 1653-4. **Mary**, b. 24 Apr. 1655. **John**, b. 4 Nov. 1656, cooper. At Portsm. 17 Mar. 1692-3, describ. hims. as form. of Blue Point, he sold his fa.'s 100 a. there to Robt. Elliot. M. 1st (int. 17 Sept. 1695) Susannah Brown, 2d 28 Mar. 1706 Hannah Davis. Will 1730-1734. Ch: 5+5, incl. Philip, b. 16 Aug. 1696, m. 21 Dec. 1721 Sarah Brown (11), and liv. in Hampt. and Chester; Mary, b. 16 Oct. 1697, m. Benoni Fogg (6); Hannah, b. 25 Mar. 1702, m. Philip Dow (8); Phebe, b. 8 Oct. 1704, bp. Hampt. F. 2 Jan. 1714-5, being presented by Jacob Freese (2).

**GRIFFITH**, a common Welsh given-name.

1 **CALEB**, physician, Portsm., m. 30 Oct. 1701 Elizabeth Ayers(1), and bot there 1703. Adm. 24 May 1710 to the wid. and her 2d husb. Henry Lyon(2). Ch: Caleb, b. 8 Aug. 1702. Edward, b. 1 Feb. 1703-4, d. y. Joshua, b. 1 Feb. 1704-5, m. in Boston 21 Feb. 1725 Mary Lancaster; liv. there 1726. Gershom, b. 23 Sept. 1707, trader, Hampt. m. 1st 7 Jan. 1727-8 Mary Sheafe of Charlest., who d. 24 Sept. 1747; 2d Alice Neal (Joshua). 8+2 ch.

2 **DAVID**, Strawberry Bank 1681. List 329.

3 **GEORGE**, a London partner in the Laconia Co. List 41.

4 **HANNAH** (also recorded Griffin), wid., m. No. Ch., Portsm. Nov. 1710 Wm. Partridge. If Griffith, she may have been mo. of Wilmot, bp. and recd. into No. Ch. 22 Feb. 1714-5 with sis. Esther (Griffis); m. Benj. Foster (2). **Esther**, m. 1st 22 May 1723 John Wooden, 2d Thos. Greely (3 jr.). **John**, shopkeeper, Portsm. and Mary Wooden 1744, m. 28 Jan. 1724-5 Deborah Lang (5), who d. 20 Mar. 1771, ag. 65. His will 1775-1776. 11 ch., incl. Moses, David and Nathl. Sheafe. One Hannah of Portsm. was acc. 3 Dec. 1701.

**GRILL**, 1 **John**, worked at Ft. Wm. and Mary, Newcastle, 1694. List 66.

2 **WILLIAM** (Grills), drowned at Newc. Feb. 1695-6. List 318c.

**GRINDAL**, Grindle, 1 **Daniel**, Newcastle 1708, List 316, m. Elizabeth Blagdon; bot on Star Isl. 1713, liv. 1722. See Blagdon (1, 2). Others in the vicinity incl: James, Kit., on a Pepperell ship at Boston 1706, poss. belonged there; m. 3 May 1716 Sarah Barter (1) and bot 5 a. at Crockett's Neck 1725; List 291; she liv. 1743; his will 1 June 1754—5 July 1755 names two daus. gr. s. Jas. Raynes and sis. Tucker. (Alice G. of Kit. m. Wm. Tucker in Portsm. 27 Dec. 1711, int. in Boston). John, Portsm., List 339, m. 10 Aug. 1712 Sarah Savil; bot there 1715; adm. 31 Oct. 1739 to Timothy Batt; 3 ch. bp. 1714-1718. One Sarah m. at Portsm. 20 Dec. 1737 Christo. Skinner of Miley, co. Cornwall. At Gosport, Elizabeth m. Jas. Robinson 9 Feb. 1737-8, Saml. m. Mary Emmons 1 Feb. 1738-9. Thos. (Gribble?) m. at Kit. 14 Nov. 1728 Judith Weeks. See Dunn (3). One Jas. G. dec. in 1701, late of Boston, form. of Salem.

2 **RICHARD** (Gryndle), List 78.

**GROSS.** The Cornish Grosses 'came out of Norfolk.'

1 **ISAAC**, Mr., husbandman, adm. Boston Ch. 17 Apr. 1636, disarmed 1637, dism. with Mr. Wheelwright to Exeter 6 Jan. 1638-9. There one of the rulers 1 Apr. 1639, leaving office 1640, and ret. to Boston bef. 4 July 1647 when Mr. Jas. Smith was excommun. for fellowship with his w. Anne. Lists 372, 376a, 72. 5 Mass. Hist. Soc. Col. i.486. Will, brewer, 29 May 1649 (inv. 5 June) names w., 3 sons, gr. ch. and others, incl. Philemon Purmort and Wm. Wardwell, both of Wells. Her inv. 29 Dec. 1653; div. 29 Sept. 1654, to sons, all of Boston: Edmund, Clement and Matthew, who dep. 19 May 1655, ag. 25.

2 **THOMAS**, Capt., mariner, Charlestown, s. of Thos. and Elizabeth (Phillips) of Boston, gr. s., of Clement (1), poss. the unkn. husb. of John Hinckes' unnamed dau.

who d. early, leav. s. **Hinckes** Gross, mariner, of Billingsgate, Barnstable County, in 1729, when he sold half his inherit. from his mo. (Y. D. 13.161). Capt. Thos.'cert. m. in 1716 a Portsm. girl of the same social class, Phebe Penhallow (Saml.), who relinq. adm. on his est. 28 Mar. 1719-20 to his mo. Elizabeth Burroughs of Boston. As Phebe G. she witn. in Portsm. 1722 (Y. D. xi.157); m. next Leonard Vassall.

**GROTH** (aut., also Growth), **John**, Mr., physician, b. ab. 1637-8, ±35 or 36 in 1673, bef. Me. Ct. 12 June 1666 for riding bet. Kit. and York on Sunday, app. living in Kit., practis. in both. Maj. Robt. Pike called him a German. In July 1667 he withdrew suit ag. Rowland Young for treating his s. Saml.; forf. bond when sued by Dr. Francis Morgan in Apr. 1672. Taxed and practis. Portsm. 1672-3; Sals. 1674; adm. to pract. in Hampt. 1679; of Sals. 1680. Lists 87, 312e. D. bef. 30 Apr. 1685, when wid. Elizabeth (Eaton of Sals., m. 7 Jan. 1674) m. 2d Wm. Hutchins of Bradford. Ch: **Elizabeth**, b. Sals. 29 July 1674, m. in Bradford 31 Dec. 1690 Jas. Palmer. 5 ch. rec., incl. Groth Palmer, Newmarket 1749-1757. See also Rollins.

**GROUT**, **Gabriel** (also Groot), in 1679 took rum from Mr. John Cutts to his seaman Thos. Rice. If only one here, he long escaped record, and likely ret. to Eng. and came again. Gabriel, butcher, taxed Portsm. 1707, had lodged with Abigail Rowsley 5 yr. Nunc. will 13 Sept. 1707 gave his small est. to her and her s. Saml. Alcock, tho he had one or m. daus. in Eng. Adm. 15 Sept. to partn. Wm. Williams; one bondsm. Christo. Pottle, who dep. that G. G. was s. of Nicho. Grout of So. Trent, co. Devon, and 1st cous. of Wm. Gline, who in Ct. next mo. claimed the est.

**Grove**, Mary. See Gardner (1), Purchase.

**GROVER**, uncommon, found in Sussex.
1 **ANDREW**, York, br. of (3), their names poss. indicating desc. from fam. in Charlestown and vicin. In 1707 Elisha Hutchinson deeded to the bros. and three other York men 2/3 of 500 a. Y. D. 7.95. List 279. M. Mary Freethy(3), both liv. 1735. 9 ch. rec. 1703-24: **James**, m. 8 Feb. 1727-8 Mary Hutchins(3), and d. 29 Aug. 1730. 1 ch. As Mary Catherine G., the wid. acc. Moses Welch in Sept. 1732 and m. him, jr., 11 Oct. (or Nov.) 1733; **John**, **Samuel**, **Thomas**, **Benjamin**, **Mehitable**, **Matthew**, **Andrew**, **Samuel**.
2 **JOHN**, s. of Edmund of Salem, went East, app. with Isaac Davis(9); settl. on W. side of the great isl. (Georgetown) over ag. Newtown; with Davis ptn. Andros for gr. D. Beverly, Aug. 1716, ag. 88. W. Sarah

Barney (Jacob) m. 13 May 1656, was dead 1673, leav. ch: John, Beverly, m. in Ipsw. 23 June 1687 Sarah Low, 3 ch.; app. had 2d w. Margaret, his wid. in 1695; 1 ch. **Hannah**, b. 9 Nov. 1662, m. Hazadiah Smith from Tuessic. **Sarah** (an earlier Sarah d. y.). **Abigail.**
3 **MATTHEW**, York, br. of (1), m. (Ct. Jan. 1703-4) Hannah Freethy(3), who d. 9 Dec. 1726; 2d (int. 3 Feb. 1727-8) Mary Kirke(2), wid. of Saml. Brookings(3). Liv. York 1745. List 279. 11 ch. rec. 1703-26; **Hannah**, m. John Laiten(4). **Susannah. Lydia. Sarah. Elizabeth. Mary. Miriam. Samuel. Stephen. Ebenezer. Mary.**
4 **THOMAS**, Wells soldier from Malden, 1693. List 267b.

Groves, see Foye (2).

**GRUBB**, **Gabriel**, Shoals, fisherman, sued for debt in July 1664 with partn. Rich. Cummings; in 1666 with Isaiah Odiorne he gave bond to Thos. Bishop of Ipsw., who sued them in Essex Ct. 1670. When ashore he drank and quarreled. Lost in Great Storm 30 Jan. 1677-8. See Downes(4), Broad(4). List 306d. His w. was in Ct. in June 1666, P. & Ct. i. 264; his wid. was Frances. List 306c. Jos. Lee sold his ho. on Hog Isl. to Robt. Haines (9), who sued for posses. 1681. Portsm. pd. Wm. Cotton money for Goody Grubb 1695. Ch. unkn.

**Gruche**, Joshua, seaman 1684. List 314.

**Grure**, see Geare.

**GUERNSEY** (Garnsey). 1 **James** (Garnse), List 286. Not Gavensey.
2 **WILLIAM**, York, O. A. 22 Nov. 1652. Lists 275, 276. Gr. of 10 a. there 4 July 1659, tho then dead, if ident. with William, Shoals, lately dec., adm. 6 July 1657 to Wm. Rogers. Jan. 2, 1660-1 his wid. Elizabeth of Pinhoo, co. Devon, gave P/A to Bennett Oliver of Coffines Well, co. Devon, to try titles and collect claims at the Shoals and elsewhere; in 1671 at the Shoals he gave clearance to Rogers.

**Guich**, William, List 21. See Gooch (7).

**Gullett**, Peter, boatmaster, Richmond Isl., 24 May to 2 Oct. 1636, when he d. List 21.

**Gullington**, William, Pemaquid 1689. List 126.

**Gullison**, Gullishaw, see Gunnison.

**GUMMER**, **Richard**, Star Island, bot ho. and plant there from Rich. Goss of Ipsw., 1697; of Ipsw. bot ano. plant on the isl. from Wm. Lakeman 1700, a mtg. on this being assigned by Geo. Jaffrey to John Carter and Chas. Randall, 1713. Witn. bond of John Searle of Newc., 1702; Shoals witn. 1703; Star Isl. 1709. See Downes(4). List 309. W. unkn.; also ch., save presum. **Ezekiel** of Gosport, m. at Portsm. 25 July 1734 Hannah Williams; 5 ch. bp. So. Ch., incl.

Richard. ?**Richard**, taxed Newc., 1719, poss. a son or the fa.

**Gundry**, James, witn. (aut.) P/A Barefoot to Peter Golding, 1669.

## GUNNISON, Gullison.

1 *ELIHU (2), Esq., Kittery, Sheepscot, Pemaquid, Falmouth. A shipwright, he early worked for Mr. Henderson, and settled on his fa.'s 300 a. at Spruce Creek where he built a mill and had a yard; in 1695, only s. and h., he was trying to dispossess Rich. Endle as a tresp. on this gr. Taxed (and three men), Bloody Point, 1677; Portsm. minister's rate abated Mar. 1679-80. Constable, Kittery, 1680 (fined). Prepar. to move East, he mtg. his Kit. ho. in June 1683, discharged bef. Apr. 1697. Sheepscot Apr. 1684-1685; gr. Buckland's Neck at Jamestown 1686. J. P. for Cornwall Co. 1684-6. He signed a Pemaquid ptn. as a resid. in May 1689, but had just arriv. from Casco; at Falm. Aug. foll., and 13 Nov. memb. of a Council of War there when ord. that a garri. be erected ab. his ho. at Falm. to be the main court of guard. Rep. from Kit. 1693. Selectm. 1693-97, 1704. Audit. committ. 1696-7. Tr. j. 1702 (foreman), 1703. Lists 14, 359a, 30, 92, 16, 17, 163, 125, 35, 68, 290, 296, 298. Liv. 26 Aug. 1718; adm. to s. Elihu 7 Apr. 1719. He m. 1st 10 Nov. 1674 Martha Trickey; in 1680 his ptn. ab. Thos. Trickey's est. put on file; m. 2d by 1690 Elizabeth (Ingersoll), wid. of John Skillings. Ch. by 1st w: **Elihu**, b. ±1676, shipbuilder. Lists 291, 296, 297. M. 1st in Boston 6 Dec. 1705 Mary Rollins, d. 7 May 1726, ag. 42; 2d 3 Sept. 1730 Margery (Pepperell), wid. of Pelatiah Whittemore. He d. 13 Sept. 1752, she in 1769. Ab. 1750 he called Nathl. Keene cousin. Ch. 1706-1717; Elihu, Mary, Benjamin, Joseph (had s. Aquila), John, Eunice. **Child**, b. ±1677, k. by Ind. **Priscilla**, m. 7 May 1700, Nicholas Weeks. **Mary**, m. ±1702 Joseph Weeks. **Sarah**, m. John Follett (4). By 2d w: **Joseph**, b. 14 Oct. 1690. On sentinel duty 16 Sept. 1707, he fired in the darkness at a person who did not halt at command and killed, hurrying home, Grace Wentworth; acquitted; bondsm. Elihu sr. and jr. and Geo. Frink. List 96. Boston shipwright, 1716, where he m. 1st 11 Oct. 1715 Lydia Burnell, who d. 24 Feb. 1717; 2d in Boston 14 Apr. 1719 Susanna Shore, and ret. to Kit., she liv. 4 July 1728; appar. 3d 23 Oct. 1729 Elizabeth Lewis (9); last 26 Dec. 1734 Margaret (Swain), wid. of Wm. Nelson; in 1761 she was w. of Henry Sherburne. Will 18 Feb. 1745—18 Oct. 1748 names w. Margaret and all rec. ch. but 1st Saml. and Shore. Ch. rec. by 1st w. 1716-1717. Samuel, Joseph; by 2d w. 1721-1726: Samuel, John, David, Shore (in Boston); by

last w. 1735-1737: Margaret, William. Stackpole adds. William, Christopher, Benjamin, Elizabeth, bp. 1726-1742, none in will. **Elizabeth**, b. 15 June 1694, m. 24 Jan. 1714-5 John Walker; d. 4 Dec. 1715.

2 *HUGH, by tradition a Swede, as given by Dea. Joseph (Elihu jr.), 1713-1799, to his gr. son, he not unlik. may have been brought over from Holland by Capt. (Underhill?) and placed with Richard Bellingham, Esq. by 1634. Traditions given by Joseph of his other gt. gr. fa. Thos. Trickey were misapplied by the gr. son, and are attrib. to Gunnison in G. Gen. (1880), p. 13. Adm. to Boston ch. and freeman 1636. He was aggressive in business as a vintner and soon owned the King's Arms Tavern. Criticized by the courts for the way he ran it, he sold out (Apr. 1651) and two months later supplanted Mr. Hilton at Kittery. In Kit. he was much in evid., also his 2d w. with and aft. him, by whatever name. Comr. for Kit. 1656. Dep. 1654, but in 1657 judged unmeet as Dep. or for any judic. position. Lists 73, 75ab, 282, 283, 298, 24, 77a. P. & Ct. i. 251-3. Entert. without lic. 4 July 1659; d. bef. 20 July 1660. Adm. 1718 to gr. s. Richard Tucker. First w. Elizabeth d. in Boston 25 Jan. 1645-6; he m. there 2d 23 May 1647 Sarah (Tilley), wid. of Henry Lynn(2), ±51 in May 1670. Benj. Gillam of Boston wrote to Bro. and Sis. Gullison. She m. 3d bef. July 1661 Capt. John Mitchell, 4th Dr. Francis Morgan. Ch. rec. Boston, by 1st w.: **Sarah**, b. 14 Feb. 1637-8, m. Lewis Tucker. **Elizabeth**, b. 25 Apr. 1640, d. s. p. **Deborah**, b. 2d. d. s. p. See Lockwood. By 2d w.: **Hester**, bp. 20 Feb. 1647-8, d. s. p. **Joseph**, b. 31 Mar. 1649, app. outliv. fa. (Y. D. 3.107), altho writ calls Elihu the only s. who surv.; cert. d. s. p. bef. 1695. **Elihu**, b. 12 Feb. 1649-50. See also (4).

3 JAMES (Gallison), apprent. of Mr. John Hunking, delivered stolen goods to Wm. Richards and w. 1675, telling them his mo. sent the goods.

4 PHILIP (also Gullison, Galishens), Kittery, with Capt. Lockwood witn. Robt. Wadleigh's deed to N. Fryer 1665, and worked 9 mos. for Wadleigh at Lamprill Riv. bet. 1665-68. Lists 380, 298. W. Mary (Me. Ct. 1 July 1673), poss. a wid., as gr. mo. of Keziah Hooper (5). Invent. 3 Apr. 1676, incl. a ho. with pig ho., tools etc. at Ephraim Crockett's, Capt. Champernowne's and Jas. Wiggin's; adm. to John Bray. (Wiggin was having trouble with Mrs. Sarah Gunnison in 1660, and was bondsm. for Ephraim Lynn in 1670 when he and Elihu G. were fighting their step-fa. Morgan.) The wid. Mary, was willed a heifer and hog by John Hill (7), and owned at Braveboat Harb. passage adj. Jas. Foye in 1686, deeded

by her dau. in 1753 'which land was given by Mr. (or Mrs.) Franc. Champernowne to my hon. mo. -Sarah- Gullison.' Liv. ab. 1705. Ch: **Sarah,** m. John Amee (1). One Sarah Gullishaw, Kit., acc. of bast., Oct. 1695; in Ct. again next July. Presum. **?Aquila,** shipwright, Kit., bondsm. for Mary Martyn of Portsm. 1710; got search warrant from Pepperell 1712 (Gullison) for carp. tools stolen; deposed (Gunison). The name Philip G. is found later in Glouc., and Charlestown. See also Hooper(5), (10).

**Gunter,** Joseph, soldier at Kennebec 1688. List 189.

**Guott,** Robert, witn. 1664 (Y. D. ii. 8). Read Scott.

**GUPPY, Reuben,** York 1640, sent back to his w. in Salem, from whom he had run away. James Guppy, Dover 1715 and later, poss. from him or the Charlestown fam. List 358d.

**GUPTILL, Gubtail, Thomas,** Portsm. 1670, taxed 1672 (small). Lists 330a, 326c, 331a, 329, 52. With w. Mary Abbott(5) he deeded to Nathl. Fryer 1674, and had from her step-fa. and mo. in 1676 a little log ho. and half a. of land which they reserv. for him in deed 20 June 1680; liv. 1686. She m. 2d by 1696 Wm. Caverly (3). Ch. presum. incl: **Thomas,** Berwick, b. ab. 1675; fought on side of Ens. Thos. Abbott in 1701 to keep the fowling marsh; gr. 50 a. above Salmon F. 1703; taxed Berw. 1713. He and w. Mary o. c. and were bp. 8 May 1729. List 290. Liv. Apr. 1756 ±81. Only rec. ch: Mary, b. 16 Apr. 1705, m. 11 Feb. 1724-5 John Pearce. One Hannah G. of Berw. acc. Wm. Watson jr. 1736. **Hannah,** dep. June 1696 ±20; she and mo. concerned in the Thos. Pumery case at Portsm. In Ct. Dec. 1699; next Mar. when charged with having a bast., she was on Gt. Isl. and acc. Jas. Abbott. **Samuel,** witn. for Wadleighs 1698. **William,** witn. 1701 to Nicho. Meade, Jas. Booth. Sarah G., form. of Portsm., fined Mar. 1695-6, forn. bef. mar., poss. his or a brother's w. **Nathaniel,** mason, ±24 in 1709, m. in Portsm. 30 Sept. 1708 ——— Isselton (Heseltine? Islington?); neighbor of Mrs. Elizabeth Scott 1709. Tax abated 1713, then liv. Berw. List 298. There he and w. Mary o. c. and were bp., with 4 ch., 11 Nov. 1716; a 2d w. Mary bp. with s. Benj. 27 Apr. 1718, unless copies of Berw. Ch. rec. in error. 8 ch. in all kn., incl: Nathaniel, bp. 1716, m. Mary Brawn (Geo.); Thomas, bp. 1721, gave bond to supp. fa. and mo. in 1759; fa. liv. 1762. In 1750 Richard Hearl, Nathl. G. and w. Mary sold with full warr. 10 a. gr. 1669 to Jas. Grant, willed by him to Elizabeth Grant.

**GUSTIN.** See Legen.

1 **JOHN,** Falmouth, orig. Augustine le Rossignol Jean, bp. St. Owen's par., Jersey, 9 Jan. 1647, s. of Edmond Jean and w. Esther (le Rossignol). Jestin John, serv. of Jacob Barney of Bass Riv. 1670, poss. same as the Falm. man, who served in Philip's War as Gustin John. M. at Salem 10 Jan. 1676-7 Elizabeth Brown (16). Of Reading in June 1677, he sold his Jersey prop (Suff. D. x. 131). Falm. gr. with liberty for a brickyd. 1680; bot in 1686 from the Cloyes fam. and liv. on Presumpscot River until driven to Lynn, returning 1714-16. Lists 225a, 228c, 229. Will, husbandm., Falm., wit. by three York men, 3 July 1719 (inv. 4 Apr. 1720) names w. Elizabeth, 7 ch., favoring three youngest sons who had been helpful to them. She liv. 10 Apr. 1729, app. dead 21 May 1731. Kn. ch: **Sarah,** m. in Salem 20 July 1704 Jonathan Bly. **Samuel,** b. ab. 1681, mov. to Conn. **?Elizabeth,** poss. a dau., not in will, m. in Boston 12 Aug. 1708 James -Lowle-. In 1714 John Nicholson and Elizabeth -Lower- gave evid. ab. the Me. land. Rec. Lynn: **John,** b. 5 Nov. 1691, went to Conn. and N. J. **Abigail,** b. 9 Dec. 1693, m. (int. Lynn 1 Nov 1712) Thos. Fuller. **Ebenezer,** b. 4 Oct. 1696, shipwright. Falm. soldier 1722, 1725. With br. David indebted to Phineas Jones est. 1743; Gustin & Co. ment. same time. At Louisburg 1745; finally settl. at Phipsburg. W. Isabel. Ch. rec. Falm: Elizabeth, b. 31 Oct. 1723. **Thomas,** b. 5 Mar. 1698-9, went to Conn. **David,** b. 6 Feb. 1702-3, husbandman. Falm. soldier 1722, 1725. W. Jane or Jean; 9 ch. bp. Falm. 1728-50. Of Topsham, adm. to Saml. Winchell 11 June 1766.

2 **WILL,** Kennebec soldier 1688. List 189.

**GUTCH,** sometimes Gooch.

1 **JOHN,** Sergt. at Pemaquid 1696, unlikely s. of (2) aft. 24 yrs. abs.; if a gr. s. he d. s. p. List 127.

2 **ROBERT,** Mr., preacher to the Kennebec fishermen, came 1st with servant Hugh Jones to Salem, where he had gr. 1 Jan. 1637-8 by his fa. Holgrave's, whose dau. Lydia was his w. Freeman 27 Dec. 1642. Mr. Wilfred Gutch of London, desc. from his br. John, located the Eng. home at Glastonbury, co. Somerset, where Robert was bp. in par. of St. John the Baptist, 5 Apr. 1617, s. of John and Magdalen, gr. s. of Clement, who beq. to him 1632. His fa.'s will 1662 rememb. him, wife, s. John, and other ch; his mo.'s will 1668 beq. to his ch. if he were liv., if not, to his w. Lydia. At Pemaquid 14 Apr. 1657 he witn. an Elbridge deed, but estab. his home on a large tract on Kennebec Riv. oppo. Tuessic, now Bath, bot from

the Ind. 29 May 1660. O. A. to King 8 Sept. 1665 and empowered to adm. this oath. Lic. retailer 1665. Jury life and death, 1666; same yr. (in Me.) gr. adm. est. John Holgrave. Lists 12, 182, 191. Adm. to wid. Lydia Oct. 1667 (P. & Ct. i. 330-3); drowned by local trad., tho a gr. s.-in-law Nich. Lydiard claiming for the heirs 17.. stated he liv. on his land until driven off by Ind. Ch. bp. Salem: John, bp. 3 Oct. 1641, witn. two Ind. deeds with fa. 1660; bondsm. for fa. 1666 and had from him land which he sold to Thos. Watkins 1666. Lists 182, 13. Not found aft. 1672, unless same as (1). If mar., no desc. liv. to convey prop.; Joan, List 185, poss. his w., or unrec. sis. Patience, bp. 28 May 1643, d. s. p. Lydia, bp. 6 Apr. 1645, m. Wm. Rogers. Magdalen, bp. 7 Jan. 1646-7, m. John Tillman. Elizabeth, bp. 19 Nov. 1648, d. s. p. Deborah, bp. 16 May 1652, d. s. p. Sarah, bp. 4 June 1654, m. Tho. Elkins (12). Margaret, unrec., m. Wm. Lovering (5). ?Joan (Goage, List 185), if an unrec. dau., d. s. p.

GUY, 1 Edwin, (or Gayer), owner in Laconia Patent. List 41.

2 JOHN, fisherman, Purpoodock, called by Willis a faithful vassal of Jordan. Falm. 1660, and 1662, when Mr. Jordan deeded him 100 a. So. of Thos. Staniford incl. Purpoodock Point; this he deeded 2 Dec. 1668 to s.-in-law Gendall, who also had 3 a. he had bot from Nich. White. Ackn. judgm. to Mr. John Paine of Boston 1663, thru Francis Small, atty. Not found aft. 1668; w. not at all. Lists 221, 222b. Poss. same as John Guy of Lynn 1640 (Lechf. p. 418); and/or connec. with Nich. of Watertown. Kn. ch: Nicholas, consented to fa.'s deed 1668. Joan (Jane), m. 1st Walter Gendall, 2d Theodosius Moore. See also Fickett(1).

Guyer, ——, Mr., early at Casco Bay. List 21.

GWINN, Thomas, drunk in 1659, had the liquor from Ralph Hall's maid; Val. Hill bondsm. Appar. the man (Giun) taxed Oyster Riv. 1659, and poss. the same who had been with Saco men in Boston 1647 (Suff. D. 1.92). List 361a. One T. G. mar. in Boston by 1661 Elizabeth Gillam (Benj.). Hannah of Boston m. Abraham Boule in Portsmouth bet. Jan.—Apr. 1718. See also Mountfort.

Gymmison, see Jameson.

Gympe, Thos., List 13. See Gent.

GYPSON, 1 James, Lamprill Riv. 1719, d. bef. 25 Jan. 1726. Ch. bp. Oyster Riv. Wid. Ann m. 16 Jan. 1727-8 James Lindsey.

2 JOHN, tailor, m. at Kit. 20 Dec. 1705 Mercy Mason; liv. in Wm. Scriven's ho. 1708; jury 1707-8; lic. pub.-ho. 1707-8. 1 s. rec. See Crockett (4). One John of R. I. d. at Nantucket 23 Mar. 1717-8.

3 WILLIAM, Biddef. grantor 1721. Y. D. x. 268.

HABORNE, Raborne, Rawbone, etc. George, Exeter, 1639, went with the Wheelwright party to Wells, where grants he had held 5 or 6 yrs. were conf. to him 30 June 1648. Tr. 1647. As 'Rabone otherwise Haborne' of Wells, 6 Apr. 1650, he sold his ho. and lot there to Francis Littlefield; 2 mos. later was of Hampt. Freeman 7 Oct. 1652. Lists 373, 262. Nunc. will prov. 3 Oct. 1654 gave all to w. Susanna, who m. 2d Mr. Thos. Leader of Boston. Her will 24 May—6 Oct. 1657 names her husb., Mr. Rishworth, Thos. Wheelwright and several Hampt. residents. A fam. who spoke their name somehow bet. Haborne and Raborne, was early in Huttoft, co. Lincoln.

Hack?, William, had 100 a. at Nequasset from Dongan 1687. Hackett? One Wm. Hack of Taunton m. at Milton 13 Nov. 1694 Susannah Kingley of M.

Hackeley, William, Berwick witn. 1674, Y. D. ii. 191. Shackley? Hukeley?

HACKETT (sometimes Hoket, Horkett). William, Dover, Exeter, Sagadahoc, unless two confused, had a Dover gr. 1656, laid out 1659 and sold bef. 1666 to Thos. Hanson. Exeter gr. 10 Oct. 1664, 30 a. where he and Moses Gilman had logged; regranted 1671 to John Bean. At Sagadahoc he bot from Thos. Atkins(5) in 1666, m. early his dau. Mary, wit. her fa.'s deed (Hakith) 10 Jan. 1668-9 (Y. D. 27.301), and appar. liv. there until forced back to Exeter. O. F. at Ex. Nov. 1677, taxed there 1681, 1682, and was there or elsewhere in 1685-6. Lists 356abce, 376b, 54. Three wives appear, unless he m. Mary Atkins bef. going East; 1st, one who d. early; 2d by 1666 Mary Atkins(5); 3d one Margaret to whom he deeded his land E. of the Sagadahoc, claimed in 17— by Benj. Smith of Taunton in right of w. Sarah, nearest of kin to Mrs. Margaret H., form. wid. of Wm. H., since Margaret Smith —— deed Wm. H. to Margaret H. 5 Jan. 1686-7 (but Dr. Banks says 'willed to her. Pejepscot Papers vii. 372b') Kn. ch. by 1st w.: Mary, b. at Exeter 2 Dec. 1665. By 2d w. Mary three daus., called 'Haccat' in receipt signed for them by James and Rachel (Atkins 5) Barry in Boston 1718: Mary, prob. John Allen's maid in Salis. 1680, whose 'name by report was Hackit,' and the M. H. wit. there ab. John Allen's horse in 1682. Liv. 1718. Sarah, likely the Sarah of Piscataqua who m. 1st (int. at Boston 11 Oct. 1695) Joseph Rankin, 2d Samuel Canney(4). Rebecca, likely the R. H., whose s. Malachi was b. at Salis., 9 Mar. 1691, the same yr. Lt. John Allen was paid for keeping her twelve weeks, and the same R. H. who m. there 5

Aug. 1695 Jonathan Whidden of Portsm. She depos. in Portsm. in 1707, ±30; liv. 1719. But see Hoyt's Salis. i. 190, calling her prob. dau. of Capt. Wm. and Sarah (Barnard) H. of Salis.; not ment. in Capt. Wm.'s will 1713.

**HADLEY, 1 George,** of Rowley, m. Deborah, wid. of Thomas Skillins, sr.

2 **JOSEPH,** plaint. in York Ct. 13 Mar. 1673-4. In July 1675 he was a witn. ag. Mrs. Greenland, won two suits ag. Jeremiah Goodridge, and was himself acc. with (his wife?) Sarah (Raynes) Cutt (4), then dead; disowned the ch. and was acquitted.

3 **SAMUEL,** Amesbury, dep. Aug. 1734, ±82, form. liv. at No. Yarmouth, and knew John Moseley for 60 yrs. past to cultivate Mosier's Neck. See Hoyt's Salis. i. 191.

**Haggendy,** Haggeridg, see Hockridge.

**Haiffer,** Andrew, List 322. See Heffer.

**HAINES,** Haynes, common in the midlands.

1 **AQUILA,** York, where liv. his bros. (5), (16), and sis. Eleanor, w. of Matthew Young (Me. Ct. Jan. 1696-7); their fa. Thos. of Amesbury. Jury 1708. He m. Mehitabel Freethy(4); d. bef. Nov. 1718, she liv. 1736. Ch: **Aquila,** b. 17 July 1702, d. 2 Mar. 1750, m. 24 Feb. 1733-4 Mehitabel Young. List 279. **Mary,** b. 28 Nov. 1704, m. Aaron Banks (1). **Hannah,** b. 20 Dec. 1707, m. 5 Mar. 1732-3 Samuel Haines, 'now resid. in York'. **Dorcas,** b. 9 Mar. 1712-3, m. Wm. Babb(4).

2 **FRANCIS**(17), gunsmith, Falmouth 1689, went to Marbleh.; there m. 25 Dec. 1695 Elizabeth Hooper (John). List 228c. He claimed his fa.'s Me. lands and in Oct. 1713, form. of Casco Bay, sold 150 a. at Pine Point to John Ashley; 50 a. at Purpoodock to dau. Elizabeth in Sept. 1716. D. bef. 10 Mar. 1716-7. Ch. rec. Marbleh: **William,** b. 4 Dec. 1697, gunsmith; of Newc. bot at Spruce Creek from Ebenezer Emmons 1726; m. at Kit. 16 Mar. 1729-30 Joanna Marshall; liv. Kit. 1740. **Elizabeth,** b. 13 Aug. 1698, m. 29 July 1714 John Tarr of Glouc., mariner, who was liv. Boston 1734. **Isabella,** b. 19 May 1701, m. 5 June 1721 Ephraim Shelton. **Deborah,** b. 29 Apr. 1703. One Deborah m. in Glouc. 24 Dec. 1723 Saml. Davis(29). **Francis,** b. 18 May 1725. **Annis** (also Agnes and Anstace), b. 26 June 1707; m. 12 Sept. 1726 Nathl. Wallis of Beverly. **Sarah,** b. 14 May 1710. One Sarah m. at Marbleh. 24 Feb. 1724-5 Elias Cook. **Samuel,** bp. 26 Oct. 1712, cordwainer Falm. 1740, Brunswick 1742. **Hannah,** bp. 10 Mar. 1716-7. One Hannah m. at Glouc. 24 Dec. 1733 Richard Read of 'Putmouth'.

3 **IMMANUEL** (Haynes), constable Cape Porpus 1689. List 259. Dayves?

4 **JOHN,** Berwick, m. 7 July 1708 Hannah Key(1); taxed 1713, 1719. List 289.

5 **JOHN,** b. ±1680, br. of (1), (16), York 1706, weaver; in 1737 q. c. to John Sargent of Amesb. a gr. made to br. Thos., whose York land he was liv. on 1749. Liv. 1758. One Mary H. m. in York 4 Jan. 1737-8 Jos. Baker.

6 **MATTHIAS**(12), Greenland, ±21 June 1671, ±33 Sept. 1683, settl. near the homestead and carried on a logging business with br. Saml. Gr. j. 1679, 1682, 1683; Tr. j. 1683, 1685. Lists 331a, 54, 49, 55a, 52, 332b. Elias Philbrick dep. that he d. within a wk. aft. br. Saml. Wid. Jane (Brackett 1, m. 28 Dec. 1671) taxed July 1690; m. 2d 19 Apr. 1697 Isaac Marston. List 335a. In 1726 the selectm. summoned her gr. ch. to supp. her, altho she dep. 27 Dec. 1731, ±80, -wife- of Mr. I. M., ab. the Mitton fam. Ch: **Samuel,** b. 25 Dec. 1674, turner, Greenl., d. Jan. 1708-9. Gr. j. 1698. Lists 62, 330d. W. Alice Whidden (Saml.) in 1701, when Thos. Berry was apprent. to them. Lists 337, 338ab. She m. 2d 25 Nov. 1714 Wm. Jenkins(12). Ch: Saml., m. 14 Mar. 1720-1 Patience -Piner- (?Piper), mov. to Scarb., 11 ch.; Hannah, d. unmar. at Mr. Neal's in Strath. 1 Nov. 1747; Abigail, m. 23 Mar. 1720-1 Joshua Neal; Jane, m. 21 Mar. 1727-8 John Piper; John, bp. 6 Apr. 1707, blacksm., Exeter, w. Ann Thing (Jona.) in 1729 when his sisters q. c. to him, 2d w. Hannah Wiggin, ch. 2+7. **Joshua,** Greenl., b. 5 Apr. 1678, poss. m. 1st a dau. of Joseph Hall, and 10 May 1705 conv. to Mrs. Elizabeth Packer 2 a. in Portsmouth. Memb. of No. Ch. 1707. If Keziah, bp. in that ch. 14 Aug. 1709, was his ch., she d. s. p. He cert. m. ab. 1710 Sarah Whidden (Saml.); d. 10 Jan. 1736-7, adm. to her 1 Apr. 1737; she liv. 1757. List 338b. 9 or m. ch., 8 bp. Greenl. 1714-1729. **Matthias,** housewright, Greenl., m. Hannah Johnson (18); she d. 4 May 1755, he 1771. Selectm. 1706, 1715-20. Lists 324, 338a. 3 ch. bp. Greenl. 1718, 5 more 1719-1731. Haines Gen. adds Jane joined Greenl. Ch. 1724.

7 **REUBEN,** Falmouth 1689. List 228c. A soldier on ward at Newcastle Fort in 1692, he fired on Mr. Chowne's vessel which refus. to stop; in 1700 money was due him as a soldier (N. H.).

8 **RICHARD** (Haynes), tax abated Newcastle 1720.

9 **ROBERT,** fisherman, Hog Isl., bot Miles Pile's ho. in 1665. Constable 1667, tho drunk and abus. his neighbors 1666, 1671. In 1668, and again 1669 he sued Roger Kelly for forcibly taking away his goods; ag. ±70, in Mar. 1680-1, he sued Jos. Lee in Ipsw. Ct. for possession of the Gabriel Grubb ho.

at Hog Isl. which he had already pd. for. List 90. Fam. unkn.

10 **ROBERT**, Maquoit. List 191. Appar. should be Thos.

11 **ROBERT**(17?), poss. same who took O. F. at Lynn with Thos.(15) in 1678. Purpoodock 1680, and until the town was deserted, when he app. went to N. H., where his wid. Rachel (Davis 39) m. 2d 9 Feb. 1700 Jona. Wedgwood of Hampt. and d. 9 Nov. 1749. Lists 30, 85, 225a, 226, 60, 66, (191?). Only kn. ch: **Thomas**, b. ±1685, husbandman, weaver, Hampt. List 229. With his mo. in Mar. 1727-8 he sold part of his fa.'s Falm. land; s. and only heir of his fa. 2 Apr. 1733, he sold all rights to Phineas Jones. Y. D. 16.261, 15.206. M. 1st 9 Jan. 1712 Abigail Philbrick (Lt. Jas.), 2d 28 Dec. 1716 Abigail Cole(31); with her q. c. Wells land 1733-1752. D. 25 Mar. 1770, she 26 June 1772, ag. 85. 8 ch. 1717-1735.

12 **SAMUEL**, ±58 July 1663; ±65 Dec. 1676, dep. that he came on the -Angel Gabriel- in 1635 with John Cogswell whose serv. he had been in Eng. ab. 9 yrs., and went with him to Ipsw. The Haines Gen. is authority that he ret. to Eng. and m. at Dilton, co. Wilts, 1 Apr. 1638 Eleanor Neate, bef. sett. in Dover, where he signed the Comb. 1640; June 25 that yr. he did not appear at Saco Ct. In 1650 he rented the Champernowne farm in Portsm., now Greenl.; purchased and was gr. land adj. where he built his house; in 1670 bot a half int. in a sawmill. Selectm. 1653, 1663, often Gr. j., Deacon. Lists 281, 351ab, 352, 354ab, 323, 324, 326ac, 330b, 356L, 331ac, 54, 49, 52. On Dec. 28, 1682 he deeded his prop. to s. Saml., aft. him to his ch., for supp. of self and w.; ±78 in Dec. 1681; liv. 26 Sept. 1683, ±80; both sr. and jr. taxed 1684. Kn. ch: **Elizabeth**, m. Leonard Weeks as 2d w. **Samuel**, b. 1646. **Matthias**, b. ±1650.

13 **SAMUEL**(12), ±27 in 1673, ±37 in 1683, took O. A. at Portsm. 2 Oct. 1666. Farmer and miller. He m. 9 Jan. 1672-3 Mary Fifield(3) and liv. on the homestead in Greenl. Gr. j. 1683. Lists 331ac, 54, 49, 52, 55ab, 332b. Taxed 1688; appar. d. the next winter. Nathl. Huggins depos. that in 1689 he was hired by Wid. Mary Haines to build a sawmill on the lower falls of Winnicott Riv., and hired it of her 9 yrs. until the young men came of age. She was taxed July 1690, liv. 27 Apr. 1723, d. within two yrs. Lists 335a, 330d, 337. Ch: **Sarah**, b. 6 Oct. 1673, m. Nathl. Huggins(4). **Eleanor**, b. 23 Aug. 1675, m. Capt. Saml. Weeks. Lieut. *Matthias, b. 7 Mar. 1676-7, m. Mehitable Jenness(1), List 338b, and occup. the orig. homestead. Lists 62, 338abc. Selectm., Dep., Lieut., Deacon. Will 19 June 1741—24 Apr. 1745 names w. Mehitable (d. 1768),

and 6 of 9 ch. bp. 1715-1727 (5 together in 1715). Ensign **William**, b. 7 Jan. 1678-9, farmer, surveyor, mill owner, m. 4 Jan. 1704-5 Mary Lewis(8) of Casco Bay, liv. Apr. 1760. His will made 29 Oct. 1756; living, ag. 77 in June 1757, d. ab. 1761. Lists 338ac. 9 ch. rec. Portsm. 1705-1724. **Mary**, b. 27 Jan. 1685-6 m. Michael Hicks (4 jr.). **Samuel**, b. 5 July 1687, farmer, m. in Greenl. 21 Jan. 1719-20 Mehitable Crosby(3). List 338a. He d. 7 Sept. 1750. She soon deeded to dau.-in-law Ann (Jenness) H., reserv. one third of the homestead; d. May 1768. 7 ch. b. or bp. 1721-1738.

14 **SAMUEL**, York. See (1).

15 **THOMAS**, Maquoit, employed by Mr. Robt. Jordan to keep cattle on the land he had bot from Thos. Purchase; signed a certif. in Jan. 1645-6 with Purchase, Wm. Ryall and Rich. Tucker. Clerk of the band at Westcustogo Oct. 1667. Gr. j. 1667. Lists 221, 85. Driven off by Inds. he took O. F. at Lynn 1678; there the same yr. he and w. Joyce sold to Edw. Creeke of Boston 200 a. adj. Alex. Thwaite at Maquoit bot from Rich. Potts 20 Apr. 1675. Both, with Sampson Penley, 'ancient inhabts. in Casco Bay,' depos. bef. Edw. Tyng 21 July 1684 ab. Indian deed to Francis Small; neither found later. Relationsh. to others, and ch. unkn., but see (1), (11).

16 **THOMAS**, b. Salis. 27 May 1670, br. to (1) and (5), leased land in York from Mr. Wm. Hooke 4 Apr. 1695; grants 1697, 1703. Gr. j. 1703. He m. bef. 12 May 1698 Lydia Young (Rowland). Will 20 June 1721 (inven. 28 Sept. 1723), wife sole legatee; she m. 2d Saml. Bragdon(6). Aft. her death 1757, his bro. John, br.-in-law and sis. James and Mary Brickett, sued John Bean for his land

17 **WILLIAM**, Mr., schoolmaster, b. 1636-40, ag. 49 in Apr. 1685, ±50 in Aug. 1690; first found at Westcustogo. Tr. j. 1665; Gr. j. 1667; yet in 1666 John Lane's goods were found in and hid near his ho., and in 1667 Jos. Cousins acc. him as a common liar. He m. bef. 25 Nov. 1667—20 Aug. 1672 Margery, wid. of Nich. White, and liv. 8 yrs. or upward on Pine Point (Freeport) bot, with Bustin's Isl., from John Bustin. Here he sold in Jan. 1674-5, and was at Spurwink Apr. 1675. A refugee he drifted, with and without his fam., teaching and drawing papers; Lynn 1678; Kittery 1679; Boston 1680, his fam. then in Hampt., but in Boston Apr. 1681 when John Brookings was their surety; a Purchase witn. at Lynn 1683; Kit. 1684-5, going with Jona. Mendon to Spurwink to bring his fam. to Kit., but his wife refused to leave the land Mrs. Jordan had deeded them, her friends and neighbors, favoring Margery partic., in Jan. 1683-4.

He went on, Great Isl. 1686-7, Rowley 1688; last found in Oct. 1701, being sued by John Woodman of Kit. List 30. She bot at Purpoodock next Robt. Haines in Nov. 1686, moved there, and prob. to Marbleh. or Glouc. during the War; in 17-- claimed White prop. at Merriconeag for self and dau. John Redding depos. that several ch. were b. at Pine Point, naming only twins, who alone show in deeds: **Francis. Isabella**, m. in Glouc. 19 Jan. 1692-3 John Parsons; d. there 25 Nov. 1700; 5 Parsons ch., incl. **Mary**, b. 28 Apr. 1695, m. 26 Nov. 1719 Thos. Haskell, later of Falm. Poss. his son, not Margery's: **?Robert**(11).

**Hakens**, John, Wells soldier from Woburn 1693-4. List 267b.

**HALE.** (See also Hales, Haley, Healy. At times in error for Hall.) Common throughout England, became 94th commonest name in N. E.

1 **FRANCIS**, ag. 23 or 24, Great Isl. 1695; fine penman.

2 **REV. JOHN**, b. Charlestown, 3 June 1636, H. C. 1657, minister at Eastern parts bef. invited to Beverly 15 May 1665. Saco 1659, and perh. at Falm. as he witn. deeds for Cleves Dec. 1663—Apr. 1664; but cert. took his bride to Saco when he m. at Ipsw. 15 Dec. 1664 Rebecca Biley, dau. of Henry and Rebecca (Swayne) of Salisb. List 249. She d. at Beverly 30 Apr. 1683; 2d w. Sarah Noyes d. there 20 May 1697, and he m. 3d 8 Aug. 1698 Elizabeth, wid. of Nathl. Clarke (42). Ch. 2+4. incl. **Robert**, b. 3 Nov. 1668, H. C. 1686, minister and physician, Beverly, m. (int. 4 Feb. 1699) his step-sis. Elizabeth Clarke (42). He d. 12 Jan. 1718-9; she m. 2d Major John Gilman.

3 **JUDITH**, owned covt. and bapt. and s. John bp. Berwick 11 Nov. 1711.

4 **MARY**, witn. for Mrs. Prudence Scammon of Exeter 1691. See also Haley(4).

5 **NICHOLAS** (Heale), O. A. Kennebec 1674. List 15.

6 **SAMUEL**, witn. Thos. Hanson's will, 1666. Read Hall.

7 **WILLIAM** (Heale or Geale), Saco 1688. List 249. Wm. Haile taxed Newc. 1688.

**HALES**, a town in co. Norfolk.

1 **EDWARD**, shipwright, Newcastle 1696, selling without lic. 1699, Joanna Horne witn. Lists 315bc. Sued 1700 by Jos. Reyner, a Boston victualler, on note dated 1699; ack. judgm. to Wm. Morton of Boston 1699. Mariner, Portsm., taxed 1708 (and ho.), 1713; indebted to Dr. Robt. Pike 1718. In 1715 his w. was dau. of Danl. O'Shaw. N. H. Prob. i. 764. His **son's** shoes ment.

1708. One Jane (also Haly) of Portsm. m. 3 Dec. 1721 John Elliston, b. Boston. See also (3).

2 **PETER**, taxed Portsm. ab. 1708.

3 **RICHARD**, first app. with (1) at Newcastle 1696, where he and w. had a tavern 1700-2. Twice a witn. with Francis Tucker at the Shoals 1702; at Newc. 3 May 1703, the two witn. a note signed by Thos. Westbrook. Lists 315bc.

4 **THOMAS** (Haels also Harls), Sagadahoc 1674. List 15.

**HALEY**, a Devonshire and Yorkshire name, difficult to disting. from Hale and Healy.

1 **ANDREW**, Kittery, fisherman, early at the Shoals. With Thos. Donnell in 1662 he bot from John Pearce the Edw. Johnson homestead in York and sold his half in 1684, when he was liv. at Spruce Creek. Mr. Robt. Elliot pd. his fine in 1667 for swearing and blasphemy; in 1674 A. H. pd. a fine for Rich. Miller. Lists 293, 298. His w., poss. not 1st, was Deborah, dau. of Gowen Wilson, 2 June 1684, when her fa. deeded them her portion, incl. 11 a. at Spruce Creek east of Robt. Mendum's. Adm. to her and s. Andrew 24 Dec. 1697, Mr. Wm. Pepperell and Jos. Weeks bondsm. Wid. Haley taxed Kit. 1704. List 290. Ch: **Andrew. William**, shipwright, went early to Boston where he and w. Sarah Ingersoll, were liv. 1730. Y. D. 14.45, 16.19. List 298. Ch. rec. Boston 1707-1715: William, Mary, two Katherines, Samuel. **Elizabeth**, m. 1st (Ct. 1 Jan. 1694-5) John Nelson, 2d Wm. Hoyt (Thos.) 3d Nich. Hilliard(6), 4th Deac. John Dam (4). **Deliverance**, m. Geo. Berry (5). **Deborah**, m. Rich. Crockett (2). **Anna**, m. Richard Wescott. **Arodas** (also given Rhoda and Richord), m. 25 Dec. 1702 Saml. Skillings.

2 **ANDREW**(1), yeoman, Kit., had town grants 1694, 1699. Gr. j. 1699. Lists 296, 297, 298, 291. He m. 15 July 1697 Elizabeth Scammon (Humphrey), naming her exec. in will 8 Apr.—13 May 1725. She was pub. 14 Aug. 1742 to Nich. Weeks. Ch., all but Wm. in fa.'s will: **Elizabeth**, b. 25 June 1698, m. Peter Lewis (15). **Andrew**, b. 22 Jan. 1700, had from fa. his gr. fa.'s ho. and land; m. 7 Aug. 1727 Mary Briar (7). Will 2 Nov. 1775—25 Jan. 1776. 10 ch. **William**, b. 17 Feb. 1704, liv. 1722, not in will. List 291. **Samuel**, b. 17 Feb. 1706, with br. John had fa.'s home place; m. 21 Nov. 1733 Grace Lewis (2). Ch. **Sarah**, b. 7 Apr. 1700, m. (int. 23 Apr. 1726) Jos. Weeks. **John**, b. 14 June 1712; of Falm. in Apr. 1733 when acc. by Katherine Lewis (15). M. Margaret Briar (7) and liv. Kit. 11 ch. **Rebecca**, under 21 in 1725, m. (int. 19 July 1735) Chas. Smith.

3 JANE (Haly, also Hales), m. John Elliston in Portsm. bet. 5 Sept.—3 Dec. 1721.

4 MARY (Hayle) York or Kit., in York Ct. June 1654 acc. Christian Ellingham (1) of having two husbands; at same Ct. Joan Andrews (9) was acc. of stealing from her.

5 RICHARD (Haly). Adm. 15 Jan. 1677-8 to Maj. Nich. Shapleigh.

6 SARAH (Hailla), maid, loose, at Gt. Isl. 1672. Conc. Files 11.173.

7 THOMAS, Winter Harbor, had his farm near the mouth of Saco River, and was ferryman to the E. side as early as 1654; ord. in 1673 to provide better accommodations. He first appear. as juryman at Saco Ct. 8 Sept. 1640; O. A. to Mass. 5 July 1653; town grants the next wk., and in Dec. 1681 granted suffic. land more to make his home-lot 50 a. Apprais. Thos. Perkins' est. 1661. A mutilated Saco rec. 22 Aug. 1674 has the words 'till Thomas Healey comes home.' Either he or son appar. working in the mills at Wells 1679-1681; in 1681 he app. in Ct. for Abra. Collins and pd. his fine. Constable 1683, perh. earlier. Lists 243ab, 252, 245, 249, 33. M. as early as 1649 Mary West (John), who was bur. 24 Dec. 1658; List 244a. Obv. a 2d w. was Sarah who witn. Maj. Phillips' deed 22 July 1668. Y. D. ii. 124. Having outl. both wives and all but one ch., he deeded his est. 21 May 1683 to s. Thos. then liv. with and caring for him. Last found positively 6 July 1686, tho by implica. alive 1 Sept. 1687 when T. H. the younger ment.; supp. dead by June 1688 unless it was he and not the son then beating up the constable. The faint possibil. that he was the T. H. k. by Ind. 1724 is set forth in 'Thomas Haley of Winter Harbor and His Descendants' by W. G. Davis and Adelaide Haley, covering the first five gener. Ch., sole heirs of their gr. fa. John West who provid. that their fa. should have no voice in the management of his prop.: Ann, old enough 29 Sept. 1663 to mar. within 3 yrs.; d. s. p. by 1683. Lydia, d. s. p. by 1683. Samuel, d. s. p. by 1683. Thomas.

8 SERGT. THOMAS (7), ferryman, only heir in May 1683. In add. to his fa.'s est. he bot the John Henderson farm from Wm. Downes in 1684, and marsh on the E. side of Little Riv. (in Old Orchard) in 1687. Supposedly it was he and not the fa. who was fined in June 1688 for beating the constable. Wm. Dicer. Sergeant at the garri. near Saco Falls during the 2d War and until k. by Ind. in Aug. 1695. Lists 33, 96. See also (9). Wid. Sarah (dau. of Walter Mayer) and her ch. retired to Boston where she was liv. with her fa. 1698. She m. 2d 26 Feb. 1701-2 Capt. Richard Carr (5). Ch: Sarah, prob. m. in Sals. 24 Aug. 1709 her step-br. Saml. Carr; d. 14 June 1710. 1 dau. d. y. Samuel, Boston, painter by training, altho he accum.

a fortune thru real est. operations. Nov. 4, 1717 he transf. to br. Benj. his half int. in his fa.'s est., and 10 days later in Boston m. Elizabeth Clay(2). Adm. to her 17 Nov. 1743. She m. 2d 8 Nov. 1749 Deac. Henry Prentice of Cambr., where she d. 7 Apr. 1775. 15 ch. Benjamin, housewright, m. in Boston 25 Nov. 1709 Susanna Marsh (John) and kept his fam. there until aft. July 1717, altho hims. much in Me. Oct. 13, 1713 he was gr. the ferry bet. Black Point and Winter H. with liberty to erect a dwg. on his land adj., which app. he promptly did, as lic. for pub. ho. in Apr. 1714; in 1717 because of its dangerous location and his neglect, the ferry priv. was gr. to ano., higher up the river. Save for a few yrs. spent at Marbleh. during the next war, he cont. a prom. resid. of Biddef. until death, a fever ending his life at Cape Breton in 1745. 10 ch. Thomas, carpenter, Exeter, d. in 1790 at an age given from 98 to 107; cert. a son of Sergt. Thos. must have been at least 95 then. By trad. the Ex. man's fa. was k. going aft. the cows; his gr. fa. the first from Eng. In 1719 he bot 150 a. from Wm. Moore of Stratham; in June 1721 had 2 a. from Alex. Gordon (1 jr.) whose dau. was his 1st w. She d. 1727. 3 ch. He m. 2d in Glouc. 6 Aug. 1728 Mary Bartlett, and poss. had a 3d w. Mary, if the two ch. bp. Ex. 1744-7 were his and not his son's. W. Mary, liv. 1781. List 376b (1725).

9 THOMAS, soldier under Capt. Converse, resisted arrest at York Nov. 1692; poss. (8) or the T. H. k. by Ind. at Winter Harbor in the 3 Yrs. War (Folsom, p. 219), who cannot be reasonably placed in the Biddef. family.

HALL, scattered throughout England, but rarest in so. east and so. west.

1 EDWARD, Damariscotta or Kennebec 1659, in Sylvanus Davis's behalf took poss. of his Ind. purch. on Damariscotta River. Y. D. 16.113.

2 (EUNICE?). See Barber(5).

3 ISAAC, m. Hannah Hamilton. 2 ch. at York 1729-1731.

4 JAMES, 'a young fellow who calls himself by that name,' a runaway from his master (Fallshorn—Essex Q. Ct. 4.425) at Piscataqua, was bef. Wells Ct., Sept. 1671, for stealing at Cape Porpus and Scarb. Earlier that yr. he was in trouble with Brian Bradeen in Mass., where Danl. Whittemore depos. 'he said he came from Eng. and claimed kinship with us.'

5 JAMES, Spruce Creek 1708.

6 JAMES, Hampton 1717, from Sals.; with w. Mary sold land and bldg. in H. One Mary of H. m. Daniel McKenney of Kit. at Newb. 18 Dec. 1732. See Hoyt's Sals. 1.194.

7 **SERGT. JOHN**, of Greenland in the township of Dover. Signed Dover Comb. 1640; propr. 1642. Com. t. e. s. c. 1646, 1648. Sergeant by 1649, when he exch. his 20 a. lot on Back River for Hatevil Nutter's land and marsh in the bottom of the Great Bay near Capt. Champernowne's farm, where he made his home. In 1660 Leonard Weeks was calling him 'old dog.' Gr. j. 1664, 1666. Lists 281, 351ab, 352, 354abc, 356-abeghk, 359a, 356L, 323, 326ac, 331a. W. Elizabeth, named in his will 29 Aug.—31 Oct. 1677, with surv. s. and dau. and gr. dau. Abigail Dam. Kn. ch: **Dau.**, m. ab. 1662 Sergt. John Dam(3). **Joseph. Sarah**, named exec. with br. Jos. and gave bond with him 1677; m. aft. that time John Fabyan(2).

8 **DEACON JOHN**, b. ab. 1617, ±59 in June 1676, settled in Dover with br. Ralph (22), changing their first plan to go to York. One Thomas Hall, turner, of London, will 7 Oct. 1662—9 May 1663, had bros. John and Ralph, close to the age of our emigrants, bap. in Ecclesfield, John 7 July 1618, Ralph 4 Apr. 1621, and favored by John Hall in New Eng., but these records have not been verified or ident. attempted. John was taxed 1648, had the first of many gr. 18 Mar. 1648-9, and was liv. in 1652 on Dover Neck adj. the meet.-ho. lot and next to Back River. In 1651 a difference bet. the bros. and Robt. Knight over York prop. was adjusted by arbitrators, Knight to make good his covt. to them and confirm bargain of ho. and land, they to pay K. in shop goods at Boston. He was called Deacon 1655; lot layer 1657 and many times thereaft.; Selectm. 1660; Clerk of the Writs 1663, 1668-9, 1671; Gr. j. 1663, 1666, 1668. When as Deac. John he was chosen Town Clerk 6 June 1659, the Ct. refused to give him the oath, but he was holding that office 1670 (perh. earlier) to 1679 or later, perh. almost to 7 Jan. 1685-6, when, during the Mason controversy, a writ was issued against him for embezzling the records. Next month, in perfect health, but aged, he deeded half the homestead to s. Ralph, with other half at death. D. bef. 4 May 1692, likely aft. Jan. 1690. Lists 354abc, 353, 355a, 356abcefghk, 357e, 359ab, 49, 52, 54. Wife liv. 23 June 1662; she was named Elizabeth, if the mo. of Grace. Three sons proven: **John. Nathaniel. Ralph. ?Grace**, b. 16 Mar. 1663-4. One Grace was accus. of bastardy 9 Sept. 1701, when Bartholomew Stevenson, Peter Mason jr., Samuel Couson (Corson?) and Stephen Jenkins were charged with aiding her escape.

9 **JOHN**, taxed Bloody Point part of Dover 1650-7. Lists 354c, 356ab. In June 1668, of Bloody Point, he deeded ho., household goods, swine 'i. e. being my land, goods and chattels within doors and without,' with 12 a. gr. from Dover, to Henry Langstaff jr. and acknowl. deed 28 June 1669. See also (28).

10 **\*JOHN**(8), Dover Neck, witn. Tho. Beard's deed 8 Feb. 1664-5; next found in rec. 28 July foll. when he, his fa. and others were paid for k. a wolf in 1663. Constable Dover 1671-2, 'ag. 36,' nearer 26, Quint thot. Sylvanus Nock his apprent. 1676. In 1687 John Wingate named as execs. 'my very good friends and kinsmen,' J. H. jr., Mr. Job Clements, Zach. Field. Grants of 30 a. and 100 a. 1693-4. Ale and vict. lic. 1692, tav. lic. 1693-6. Rep. 1695, 1696, 1697. Rev. John Pike rec. his death 28 Apr. 1697, drowned coming up river in a little float near Green-point. Lists 359ab, 49, 52, 54, 55ab, 57, 62, 82, 96. He m. 8 Nov. 1671 Abigail Roberts, whose fa. John deeded to her 23 Mar. 1691-2; she m. 2d 24 Oct. 1698 Tho. Downes(6), and 26 Nov. 1700 relinq. adm. on her 1st husb.'s est., which was gr. 3 Dec. to sons Thos. and Jos. Ch: **John**, b. 27 June 1673, oldest s. 3 Aug. 1698 when he, w. Elizabeth and mo. Abigail deeded to John Tuttle land of his gr. fa. Deac. John, already in Tuttle's poss. Likely dead or incapac. in Dec. 1700, as not ment. then in connec. with fa.'s est. Wid. Elizabeth m. 2d 7 Sept. 1705 Benj. Pierce of Watertown, who m. next 30 May 1714 Hannah Ash. Only one ch. rec.: Sarah, b. 25 July 1696, m. Richard Goodwin(9); but appar. a dau. was Mary Sanders of Nantucket 1727. **Thomas**, b. 19 June 1675, liv. Oyster River. W. Mary in 1707. Adm. 2 Sept. 1732 to s. Thos., the wid. and eldest s. Jas. relinq. Besides s. James, O. R. 1735, whose wife was Tabitha; and Thomas, Dover 1741; was s. Joseph, b. 13 Apr. 1707, who conveyed an int. in his fa.'s land 1728 and was liv. 1741; and poss. John, b. 17 1726, who had w. Sarah, and s. John, b. 17 Dec. 1726; adm. to br. Thos., bond 13 Oct. 1732. One Ralph H., a young man, was bp. at O. R. 5 May 1728. **Joseph**, m. 3 Nov. 1707 Esther Beard(3). List 358d. Only rec. ch: Abigail, b. 3 July 1708. **Abigail**, b. 24 Feb. 1679-80. **Hatevil**, m. 14 Mar. 1706-7 Mercy Cromwell(3), and liv. on west side of Back Riv. By trad. drowned early, leav. one son; cert. dead 17 Nov. 1733 when only rec. ch. Hatevil, b. 15 Feb. 1708-9, q. c. his fa.'s int. in the 100 a. gr. of 1693-4. Hatevil (jr.) m. 11 Apr. 1733 Sarah Furbush(1); remov. to Falm. ab. 1753. 11 ch. rec. Dover 1733-1753. **Sarah**, m. Gershom Downes(6). **?Elizabeth**, m. 18 Dec. 1705 Timothy Carle(2).

11 **JOHN**, Newcastle, ±17 in Sept. 1713, went with Col. Walton and Mr. Usher to

take poss. of Berwick land. Y. D. 8.10.

12 **JOSEPH**(22), Exeter, taxed 1664; grants 1664, 1681; and in the latter yr. recd. from his fa. ¼ of a 400 a. gr. Taxed Apr. 1682, not in list Mar. 1682-3; d. 1684 by son's writ in 1764. List 376b. See also Huckins(1). W. Jane Hilton(2), m. 2d Richard Mattoon; adm. on her est., widow, to s. Edward Hall, 29 Mar. 1738. Ch: **Joseph,** Esq., b. ±1682, had ⅔ of his fa.'s land and liv. on it. Selectm. 1715-7, 1721, 1723-4. Lists 96, 376b. M. 1st Mary Lyford(1), who d. 1 Apr. 1755 in 73rd yr.; 2d Mrs. Eunice Parsons. He dep. in Nov. 1760, ag. 78, that he was in garri. with the ch. of Thos. Footman. D. in 1767. Wid. Eunice d. 27 Mar. 1790, ag. 94. Div. was to 5 daus. and heirs of ano. Capt. **\*Edward,** Esq., Newmarket, b. ±1684, ±78 in Dec. 1762, ±79 in Mar. 1763, inher. ½ the land, and liv. on it; in 1764 sued br. Joseph and several holding under him. Selectm. 1718, 1720, 1722, 1726; Rep. 1736. List 96, 376b. He m. 1st Mary Wilson, who d. 2 Dec. 1737, ag. 57 y. 22 d.; 2d Hannah (Lord) (Light), wid. of Josiah Hall(14). He was liv. 1769, over 85. Adm. 28 Mar. 1770 to dau. Elizabeth Weeks. 6 daus. by 1st w.

13 **JOSEPH**(7), Greenland, liv. in a new ho. on his fa.'s farm. His w. was 'Elizabeth Smith who came from Eng. upon the desire of her uncle, the orig. Maj. Richard Waldron of Dover,' (Brewster's Rambles ii. 66). He was taxed Portsm. 1673; memb. of No. Church. In 1676 he took Peter Babb an apprent., having already kept him two yrs. Lists 331c, 359b, 49, 52, 96. D. from smallpox 19 Dec. 1685; adm. to wid. Elizabeth, her bond 30 Dec. She m. 2d 7 Aug. 1687 Thos. Packer, Esq., of Portsm., and d. at Greenl. 14 Aug. 1717, ag. 62. In 1696 Peter Babb leased the farm and liv. there a yr.; final div. 1743 in three eq. parts to two daus. and heirs of ano. Ch: **Elizabeth,** b. ±1675-6, m. in Portsm. 24 Jan. 1694-5 Joshua Pierce; d. 13 Jan. 1717-8 ag. 42 (Pt. of Gr.). **Mary,** b. ±1679, m. Clement March, Esq., of Greenl.; d. 7 Apr. 1759 ag. 80 (Pt. of Gr.). **Sarah,** m. 1st Clement Jackson(2), 2d Joseph Hubbard. **?Dau.,** m. Joshua Haines(9)?

14 ‡\***KINSLEY**(22), Esq., Exeter, b. ±1652, ±44 in 1696. Town gr. 1672; adm. inhab. 10 Mar. 1672-3. He m. 25 Sept. 1674 Elizabeth Dudley(1), mar. contract dated 16 Feb. 1673-4, when his fa. made over to him ¼ a sawmill lately bot from Nich. Lissen; m. 2d in Beverly 29 May (bet. 1692-1702) Mary (Elliot), wid. of Nicholas Woodbury. He had ale and vict. or tav. lic. 1692-1700. Lieut. 1692, Capt. 1696. Selectm. 1681, 1690, 1693; Rep. 1694-5; Moderator 1700, 1704; Town Clerk 1720-5; Judge Sup.

Ct. 1696; Councillor 1698. Lists 376b, 377, 381, 382, 383, 385, 49, 54, 57, 59, 62, 67. Adm. gr. to Nathl. Ladd and Francis James 11 Sept. 1736, wid. Mary renounc. Div. 1738 shows ch: **Josiah,** merchant, eldest s., m. 1st in Beverly 22 May 1712 his step-sis. Mary Woodbury; 2d 10 May 1719 Hannah (Lord), wid. of John Light(4). Town clerk 1726-9. List 376b. D. 16 Oct. 1729, adm. 2 Feb. 1729-30 to wid. Hannah who m. 3d Capt. Edw. Hall(12). Ch., by 1st w: **Elizabeth,** m. 13 Dec. 1733 Tobias Lear (3 jr.); **Mary,** m. John Langdon(2), and d. 11 Apr. 1789, ag. 72; by 2d w., 1720-1728: Kinsley, Josiah, Dudley, Samuel, Abigail, Paul. **Elizabeth,** m. Francis James(2). **Mary,** m. John Harris(11). Repres. in div. by dau. Mary, w. of Jonathan Jones(4). **Paul,** turner. List 376b. Will 23 Dec. 1726—7 June 1727, names w. Mercy, one dau. Elizabeth, who m. (int. Newb. 12 Mar. 1742-3) Daniel Grant; liv. Ex. 1745. **Mercy,** m. 1st Dudley Hilton(2), 2d Nathl. Ladd(5).

15 **MARTIN,** miller, Portsm. 1667-1673, ±50 in Apr. 1670. In 1667 he sued Jas. Cate for talking ab. hims. and Mary Codner(3); next yr. was in Ct. for unduly freq. her company. See Glanfield(2). In Capt. Barefoot's suit against Edw. Clements (Suff. Ct. 1671) he depos. that he was on board the latter's ship when the two men had words over a debt. Taxed Portsm. 1673; abs. from w. there in 1673. Beverly miller 1677. There one Martin had m. 2 Nov. 1676 Susanna Chubb, who was bef. Ct. in June next; while he, from prison, asked abatement for himself, being in want. Great Island 1678, pawning his spectacles for drink. One M. H. d. Bev. 14 Sept. 1712. Only kn. ch: **Ralph,** wit. at Piscataqua 1671 (Jr.). He m. Elizabeth Dodge (John Jr.) of Bev.) in Boston, where her fa. took her to avoid scandal. A son b. there the beginning of winter 1676-7 was liv. in June 1677 as far as he knew.

16 **CAPT. NATHANIEL,** from Plymouth Colony, at Falmouth 1689. Lists 35, 228d.

17 **NATHANIEL**(8), Dover, taxed 1680-1, m. Hannah Swett, b. 16 May 1664, dau. of Capt. Benj. of Hampton, and receipted for her portion 9 Nov. 1682. Dover gr. 1694. Both liv. 16 Nov. 1696 when he sold out at Dover, prepar. to moving away. Lists 359b, 52, 57, 62, 352, 358a. Presum. it was their s. **Nathaniel,** who ret. to Hampt. and m. (his cous.) Elizabeth, eldest dau. of Moses Swett; she d. by 1729 when her fa. willed him 5s., but did not ment. Hall gr. ch.

18 **PAUL,** Newcastle, coroner's jury 1670. Lists 82, 312b. One Paul abs. from his w. in Eng. (Suff. Ct. Oct. 1671), had in-

forma. she was dead; ord. to ret. to her last abode, or bring certif. of her death.

**19 CAPT. PETER,** Portsm., m. in Newb. 10 May 1732 Elizabeth, wid. of Saml. Jackson(14). One Peter was a Portsm. soldier at Newc. 1708.

**20 PHILIP,** York, and Ruth Bush (Buck?), Boston, free negroes, m. in Boston 3 June 1727; likely the P. H. in Wells 1722. One Mary H., Portsm., m. (int. Beverly 15 May 1715) Anthony 'ye Freeman.' See Freeman(1).

**21 RALPH** (also Rodolphus; he wrote Ralfonsus), Exeter, signed Ex. Comb. 1639, and ptns. 1643, 1647. Hon. John Kelly found a trad. in Ex. that R. H., Thos. Wilson and Thos. Leavitt came bef. Wheelwright, and on their invitation Wheelwright came. Ralph was granted the ho. he had newly built in Nov. 1650. Lists 373, 375ab, 376b. In 1652 he sold all land to Moses Gilman; soon mov. to L. I., where he and his w. were acquitted on a witchcraft charge, 1665. One R. H. bot in No. Hempstead 1667 and was liv. 1679 on Madman's (Great) Neck in bounds of Hempstead. W. Mary in Exeter. Ch. rec. there: **Mary,** b. 15 Jan. 1647, d. middle of June 1648. Duplicate death rec., or poss. that of ano. dau., reads: Mercy, dau. of Ralph, ag. ab. — yr. and a half, d. July 1648. **Hildea,** b. 16 Apr. 1649.

**22 LIEUT. *RALPH,** b. ±1619-20, appar. the same Rafe Hall, 'pipe stave maker' at Mystic Side (Malden) in 1649 claiming lands granted in 1636 to John Hall and Richard Kettle. Losing his case he sold out and disappeared. See Hist. Charlestown and Malden. He came with or foll. br. John(8) to Dover, first taxed 1650. In 1651 he was shipping pipe staves from Dover, that yr. entert. the Court of Dover and Portsm., and was promin. in town thirteen yrs. bef. moving to Exeter. Ordinary lic. 1656. See also Gwinn. Lieut. by 1657. Selectm., Dover, 1657-1663; Com. t. e. s. c. 1658; Gr. j. 1659. Lists 354c, 355ab, 356-abefgh, 353, 46. Of Dover, 6 Oct. 1663 he bot half a sawmill at Exeter Falls; 16 dys. later, of Ex., bot Thos. Biggs's ho. and land. Ex. gr. 10 Oct. 1664; adm. inhab. same day. There he contin. in public service. Selectm. 1666, 1673-78, 1680; Com. t. e. s. c. 1668, 1679; lot layer 1675; Rep. 1680. Tav. lic. 1683. Aged ±51 in Feb. 1670-1; ±55 Oct. 1674. Lists 376b, (?379), 49, 50, 52, 54, 55ab. See also Foggett. W. Mary in 1663; both liv. 25 Mar. 1691 when he deeded to s. Kinsley. Ch: **Joseph. Mary,** m. 1668 Edward Smith. **Kinsley. Samuel,** a witn. 1674, surveyor 1678-9, in 1679 bot his fa.'s land Humphrey Davie had levied on; 50 a. gr. Jan. 1680-1. Lists 54, 383, 376b, 52.

D. s. p., adm. 11 Aug. 1690 to br. Kinsley. In Mar. 1691 his fa. recited that with no deed he gave s. Saml., dec., 100 a., part of his 400 a. gr. by Capt. Gilman's, 'and stood ready to give deed to whom it doth belong.' Kinsley sold it. **Phaltiel,** m. Ephraim Folsom(1). **Sarah,** d. in Dover 16 July 1663. **Ralph,** d. in Ex. 6 June 1671.

**23 DEACON RALPH(8),** Dover, first of record 1 Feb. 1685-6, when his fa. conveyed to him half the Dover Neck homestead, the other half at his death. Gr. of 20 a. on Fresh Creek, 1694. With John Pickering, jr., he was bondsm. for Thos. Tibbetts, tav.-keeper, 1694. In Jan. 1704-5 took q. c. deed from Richard Pinkham and w. Elizabeth of 3½ a. form. belonging to their gr. fa., Thos. Leighton, already in his occupation. Auditor 1702; Constable 1705. Lists 57, 62, 352, 96. D. 13 Nov. 1706, six days ill; adm. 4 Mar. 1706-7 to sons John and James. First w. poss. sister of Esther (Philbrook), w. of Joseph Beard(3), whose son called him uncle in 1713. He m. 2d 26 May 1701 Mary Chesley(2). In June 1710 a warr. was issued for her arrest for a bast. ch. She m. 2d aft. 23 Dec. 1713 John Foye (2); liv. 1737. Ch. by 1st w: Sergt. **John,** m. 9 Aug. 1705 Esther Chesley(2). Mov. to Somersworth by 1730; both liv. 1737. List 358d. See also Canney(3). 6 ch: John, Samuel, James, Keziah, m. Joseph Evans (3½), Esther, Betsey. **James,** d. bef. 11 Mar. 1716 when his wid. Mary, belonging to town of Portsm., m. there Jos. Holmes (3). Daus: Elizabeth, m. Rowland Green (24 jr.); Mary, spinster, Rye, 1734, likely M. H. of Portsm. (b. 24 Aug. 1709) m. 5 Dec. 1736 Thos. Goss of Rye. **Jonathan,** a sick and weak ch. 1708; n. c. m. 1736, when br. John had supported him 30 yrs. **Isaac,** by trad. went to Mass. By 2d w: **Benjamin,** b. 2 June 1702, apprent. to Wm. Dam, weaver, 1709. In 1718 he and br. Ralph were included with Wm. Davis's ch. in citation for concealing effects. Of Madbury 30 Dec. 1741, he, w. Frances (Willey, m. by 1730) and 5 of 7 or m. ch. were bp. m. by 1730) and 5 of 7 or m. ch. were bp. **Ralph,** Liv. Barr. ab. 1755; d. there 1779-80. Ralph, Madbury, Barr. ab. 1753, m. Elizabeth Willey of Lee. Liv. late in life with s. Jos. at Strafford, and d. there. 6 of 9 ch. bp. together 30 Jan. 1742. **Joseph,** b. 26 Mar. 1706, m. 19 Dec. 1731 Peniel Bean. He d. in Dover 14 Nov. 1782, ag. -80-; she 22 Dec. 1785. 9 ch.

**24 REBECCA** (Atkins 5), liv. Tarpolin Cove 1716. Y. D. 8.169.

**25 RICHARD, Samuel, Jonathan, Joseph.** See Collicott; also Dalton(3).

**26 SAMUEL,** Mr., in Me. Court records 1660-2. From Salisbury. See also Graves (1, 2).

**27 THOMAS,** in 1681 ptn. Council in Portsm. for his freedom, old age approaching; had served the Earl of Sandwich in Eng. and liv. in servitude in Va. and N. E. 28 yrs.

**28 THOMAS,** 74 in 1749-50, depos. ab. Zachariah Trickey and w. who liv. near Bloody Point in 1693 and in Newington ±22 yrs. See also (9).

**29 WILLIAM,** Strawberry Bank wit. 1653. **Hallam,** Isaac, m. Hannah (Cloyes 1), wid. of Edward Hounsell.

**HALLOWELL,** Hallwell, Holloway. 1 **Henry,** Oyster Riv., taxed 1661 (new name), m. Rebecca Ault (John). Adm. to her 30 June 1663. She m. 2d Thos. Edgerly(1). One child b. bef. June 1661. Lists 363ab.

**2 WILLIAM** (Halewell), Boston, m. Sarah Endicott (2). Y. D. xii.196.

**HALSEY,** Halce, Halsell. Halse a par. in co. Somerset.

**1 ———,** m. Margaret Phips, sis. of Sir Wm. She m. 2d 6 Aug. 1696 James Andrews (6) and was named in will of Sir Wm.'s widow, Dame Mary Sergeant late Phips, 19 Feb. 1704, also her two daus., perh. not all her Halsey ch: **Margaret** (Halce), m. in Boston 7 June 1694 Matthew Armstrong. 4 ch. rec., incl. Thos. **Dorcas** (Halce), m. in Boston 20 Nov. 1701 Aeneas Salter. Likely a son **Thomas,** s. of Margaret, b. Boston 18 Aug. 1682.

**2 GEORGE,** (Halsie), at Exeter 1651, had in his poss. 1/3 of the staves from mill on Humphrey Wilson's creek. Likely Geo. Halsell of Boston.

**3 JAMES,** Boston, mathemat. instrument maker, w. Anna, 1729, sold 1/32 of land bet. Sheepscot Narrows and Montsweag Bay bot of John Frost, Esq., of Newc.

**HAM,** most frequent in Somerset, Devon and Cornwall. See Creber.

**1 ANDREW,** Boston, m. 17 Nov. 1710 Mary Giles(8). List 161. She m. there 2d 6 Oct. 1719 John Brewer.

**2 EBENEZER,** taxed Portsm. 1713, next to Richard Nason. Poss. s. of (4) and d. s. p. bef. fa.

**3 ELEAZER,** bot in Rochester 1729 and liv. there. Will 1760—1760 names w. Elizabeth, 5 ch.

**4 JOHN,** Dover, witn. for Peter Coffin 1665-68. Aft. liv. many yrs. on a farm at Tolend, he bot on Garrison Hill from P. Coffin and mov. there. Jury 1671, 1688, 1694; Gr. j. 1703; Constable 1686; Surveyor; Town Clerk, leaving office Mar. 1693-4. Lists 356jk, 54, 359ab, 49, 52, 57, 62, 353, 358d. He m. 6 May 1668 Mary Heard(5), who d. 7 Dec. 1706. List 96. Will 29 Sept. 1727—19 Feb. 1727-8 names ch: **Mary,** b. 2

Oct. 1668, m. 1st John Horne(2); 2d John Waldron. **John,** gent., Dover, dep. 25 Mar. 1751 over 80. Town gr. 19 Mar. 1693-4 and inher. his fa.'s farm at Tolend. Lieut., Assessor and Lot-layer. List 358d. M. 14 Mar. 1697-8 Elizabeth Knight(6). Will 7 Dec. 1753, d. 11 Jan. 1754, having outl. his w. and 8 of 9 ch.; s. John alone surv. with numerous gr. ch. **Mercy,** m. Richard Nason. **Tryphena,** m. John Tucker. **Joseph,** b. 3 June 1678, gr. 20 a. 1701. Lists 358bd. He m. ab. Aug. 1704 Tamsen Meserve. He was k. by Ind. in 1723 (aft. 28 Sept.) and daus. Tamsen and Ann carried away. Adm. 1 Sept. 1724 to wid. Tamsen, who m. 2d John Tibbetts. 10 surv. ch. **Sarah,** m. Thos. Downes (6 jr.). **Samuel,** rec. £5 by fa.'s will, if in land of living, if hims. or heirs came and demanded it. **Elizabeth,** likely a 2d dau. of the name and not the one b. 29 Jan. 1674-5, m. Jeremiah Rollins. **Benjamin,** inher. the Garrison Hill farm and was exec.; d. 5 Mar. 1781, ag. 88. Constable, Surveyor of highways. M. 21 Apr. 1720 Patience Harford(2), who was liv. in 1758. 4 or m. ch. See also Ebenezer(2).

**5 JOHN**(6), fisherman, living mostly in Portsm., tho of Newington at least 1725-28, and located in Me. once, perh. twice. Of Portsm. in June 1730, ±71, he testif. ab. Scarb. bet. the Wars down to 1690; a few mos. later testif. ab. liv. at Cape Elizabeth several yrs. (ab. 1703?). Taxed Portsm. 1707. Lists 54 (?), 90, 226 (?), 228c, 334a, 330d, 339. M. 1st a sis. of John Lydston (List 335a); 2d 8 Jan. 1715 Judith Pitman of Oyster Riv. Ch. 6+5. Of Newington, 18-19 Oct. 1725, he deeded to w. Judith and her ch. the Dodovah Hull farm in Newington bot from John Snell; his old place in Portsm. to sons **William** and **Thomas,** already liv. on it, rights in new township to s. **John,** remaind. of form. w.'s portion in br. John Lidden's hands to daus. **Mercy** and **Dorcas.** Ano. dau. by 1st w. was **Elizabeth,** m. 16 Sept. 1713 John Remick, and not ment. in deeds of 1725, but named in fa.'s will, 6 Apr. 1731—1 Dec. 1735, giving princ. to w. Judith, exec., and her ch., incl. **Benjamin,** b. 10 Oct. 1716, settl. in Bath; **Tobias,** b. 23 Nov. 1717, of New Meadows.

**6 MATTHEW**(8), fisherman, Shoals, had Portsm. gr. 1654 next his fa.'s. Lists 323, 326a, 330ab. Constable, Isl. of Sh., 1657, 1658; Gr. j. 1658. Thos. Nicolls sued him in 1657 on acct. due for fishing voyage; his mare and colt figured in a case 1661. W. unkn. was taxed in Portsm. 1665 as Widow Ham; m. 2d Tobias Taylor and was liv. with him 11 Nov. 1667 in her 1st husb.'s ho. which he sold (or mortgaged?) 7 July 1670. Ch: **William,** of age 1677. **Matthew,** Portsm., ignored in gr. fa.'s will, but in 1678, cooper,

sold land adj. Rich. Jackson, form. of his
fa. Matthew. Mariner 1684, shipmate of
Joshua Jackson. Taxed Newc. 1688, liv.
there 1693. Lists 313e (?), 318ab. **Thomas**,
mariner of Rhode Island, on 2 Aug. 1680
deeded land belonging to his gr. fa. **John**,
b. ab. 1660.

7 **NATHANIEL**, Newcastle. List 313e.
?Matthew (6 jr.).

8 **WILLIAM**, fisherman, arriv. at Richmond
Isl. in the -Speedwell- 1635, and ran
away in June with five others. Sued by
Henry Taylor in N. H., 1646. He and John
Lander fished at Cape Neddick, app. bef. he
settl. in Portsm., where he was recd. inhabt.
and had gr. of land 13 Jan. 1652, his home
there on Ham's, now Freeman's Point.
Lists 21, 323, 326ac, 330b, 328. Gr. j. 1653,
1655; Selectm. 1656, and named in 1656 as
one of three 'men witches' there, 'Old Ham.'
Wm. Fifield appeared for him in Salis. Ct.
1662. His w. Honor found only 11 Nov.
1667, when he sold his dwgs. and fish. plant
on Malligoe Isl. now or lately in poss. of
Wm. Oliver, reserving land on which Tobias
Taylor liv. Poss. they were the W. H. and
Honor Stephens m. at St. Andrews, Plymouth, 20 Nov. 1622. Will 21 Dec. 1672—27
June 1673 names dau. Elizabeth and her ch.
and 3 of his Ham gr. sons, omitting Matthew. Kn. ch: **Matthew**, of age 1654. **Elizabeth**, m. ab. 1650 Wm. Cotton(6).

9 **WILLIAM**(6), cooper, Portsm., had his
gr. fa.'s ho. and was executor; deeded to
br. Matthew 1677. Taxed Str. Bk. 1690.
Lists 54, 331b, 49, 329, 52. His w. Sarah
was perh. dau. of Alex. Dennett(1); Lists
331c, 335a. His will 28 Dec. 1693, inv. 17
Mar. 1694-5, names her, exec., and ch., the
daus. all under age. She was a wid. in
Portsm. 1699, m. 2d John Gilden. Ch: **Samuel**, weaver, Portsm., eldest s. by will, but
app. only son; m. by 1710 Elizabeth Sloper
(John). List 339. Will 11 Sept.—9 Dec.
1731 gives prop. in Portsm. and Newington
to w. and ch., and names kinsmen John and
Ephraim Dennett. 10 ch., 8 surv. **Sarah.
Elizabeth**, m. Thos. Drown(1). **Mary. Hannah. Abigail.** One Abigail m. 20 Dec. 1711
Saml. Huntress(1).

**Hamer**, Samuel, witn. in Portsm. case, Apr.
1660.

**HAMILTON, David**, Dover, a Scotch
prisoner, ident. by the Hamilton Gen. as
prob. s. of Andrew of Westburn, not far
from Glasgow. He m. in Saco 14 July 166-
Annah Jackson(1), and built and liv. in
ho. on Jas. Grant's 20 a. gr. bet. St. Albans
Cove and Quamphegon bef. taking deed in
1669. Neither much in evidence. In 1666
Thos. Chick was bound to good behav. towards her. His Lists 74, 47, 57, 96. Rev.

John Pike rec. his death at hands of Ind.
28 Sept. 1692, not hers. Ch: **David**, oldest
son, town charge 1697, 'a poor person'
whose parents were destroyed by the enemy, the bros. refusing to supp. him; in
1698 the selectm. gr. the home place to Thos.
Potts to keep him for life. **Solomon**, b. 10
Aug. 1666. **Gabriel**, bot in Berw. Mar. 1702-
3, m. 1st Mary Hearle (5), dead in 1718, 2d
24 May 1721 Judith (Lord 7), wid. of Benj.
Meade. Lists 290, 296, 298. Will 22 Sept.
1729—6 Apr. 1730; hers 1775. By 1st w., 7
ch., 5 bp. 6 Sept. 1713, next one, Jonathan,
bp. 8 Aug. 1715, living Kit. 1742, remov. to
New London, later to Horton, N. S.; by 2d
w., 4 ch., 3 bp. 27 Aug. 1724. **Bial**, adm. to
Ch. with 1st w. Mary 24 May 1719; m. 2d
26 Dec. 1721 Abigail Hodsdon (Joseph 1).
Lists 289, 298. Will 1758-1763. Ch. 3+10.
**Jonathan**, b. 20 Dec. 1672; k. a deer on Sunday, Ct. 6 July 1691. **Abel** (Abiel), yeoman,
Berwick, had grants 1699, 1703. List 296.
W. Deborah 1709, if his only one, was liv.
17 Jan. 1740-1. 3 kn. ch: Joseph, had part
of the homestead 1737; Benjamin had part
in 1741, gave bond alone to take good care
of 'my aged mo.' and ano. with Joseph to
take care of fa., and aft. fa.'s death pay
sis. Mary, unmar., £20. Both bros. deeded
fa.'s marsh 1748. **Jonas**, bot and sold in
Dover 1703-7, rem. to New London.

**HAMLIN, 1 Thomas.** Hercules Hunking
sued him, Wm. Pitts and Rich. Boden
for assault and battery in York Ct. Oct.
1652.

2 **EZEKIEL**, Boston soldier at Scarb. 1676.
Lists 236, 237b.

## HAMMETT.

1 **NICHOLAS**, Scarboro, drunk and cursing
1 Oct. 1667.

2 **THOMAS**, Richmond Isl. 1638-43, settled
at Black Point, Scarb. In Sept. 1659
Robt. Jordan sued him and lost. He and
Jocelyn witn. for Joel Maddiver 25 May
1669. Lists 21, 232. M. by 1664 Avis
(Agnes), wid. of John Burrage (2). Adm.
to her s. Wm. Burrage 4 July 1676, the est.
to be improved for his mo.

3 **THOMAS**, (also Hammock), Cochecho,
taxed 1666-1677, liv. 1683-4 if s. Richard
gave his own age correctly. Lists 356k,
359a, 54. W. unkn. Kn. ch: **Richard**, ±21
May 1705, depos. ab. Wid. Heard's garrison; ±24, Feb. 1707-8, was at John Hayes'
garri. In 1719 the Coffins q. c. to him and
br. John land form. their fa.'s. Lists 358cd.
Rochester pd. Capt. Timo. Roberts for keeping him in 1749; John Weymouth, Somersw. was keeping him 1756, Wid. Weymouth was pd. for his winding sheet 1757.
**John**, Dover 1719. One Elizabeth recd. into
ch., Rochester, in 1739. One Thos. of Roches-

ter 1742-1757; the same or ano. of Berwick 1757, with w. Abigail running a lodging ho. there 1761. One Thos. had ch. bap. Newington 1753.

4 **THOMAS**, sailmaker, Portsm., from Shadwell, co. Middlesex, Eng., m. 1 Jan. 1716-7 Elizabeth Deniford (Walter). List 339. See Blashfield(2). Adm. to wid. and Henry Sherburne jr. 28 Oct. 1734. She m. 2d in Greenl. 22 Feb. 1735-6 Wm. Stevenson; liv. Portsm. 1737. Kn. ch: **William**, bp. 12 Jan. 1717-8, cordwainer, m. (int. 26 Sept. 1741) Margaret Fernald (James). **Elizabeth**, bp. 22 Nov. 1719. **Mary**, bp. 25 Feb. 1721-2.

**HAMMOND**, derived from Hamo, ancient given-name.

1 **ABEL** (Hamond), witn. Ind. deed to Lake and Spencer 1653. Y. D. 35.50. Cammond?

2 **LIEUT. JONATHAN** (5), b. ±1641, old enough to sign a ptn. in 1662 and sue Rich. Abbott for slander in 1663. In 1665 he was atty. for John Gooch jr. in suit ag. Ens. Barrett; witn. will of John Gooch sr. 1667; land of James Gooch was in his custody, 1681. In 1671 he exch. 100 a. at Stony Brook bot from John Barrett for Israel Harding's 200 a. gr. at Maryland, and had large town grants, incl. mill priv., besides receiv. his fa.'s est. Moderator, Selectm., Clerk of the Writs, Lieut., Deputy-Marshal for Prov. 1686, Deacon. Often Gr. j. and foreman. Lists 25, 265, 28, 266, 33, 267a, 268a, 269ab. Active to the end, he was chairman of the selectm. 25 Mar. 1717. His grave st. says died 17 Sept. 1717 aged 76, 'two wives and son Jonathan'. Likelier that one of them was d. of John Gooch (4); otherwise one or both of Gooch's sons mar. his sisters. W. Mary witn. with him 13 Mar. 1681-2; an Elizabeth witn. with Jona. sr. and jr. 1699 (Y. D. xi. 4) and one with Jona. and Mary 1701 (Y. D. viii. 40), poss. the 2d w., likelier his dau. He was excl. from jury for relationship when Nich. Shapleigh sued Mrs. Champernowne in 1701. Kn. ch: **Jonathan**, witn. deeds 1699, 1702; k. by Ind. with Isaac Cloyes 1704, prob. unm. **Elizabeth**, m. at Wells 26 Nov. 1701 Stephen Ford of Charlestown. 10 ch. 1703-1719, incl. Jona. Hammond, Y. D. 9.247, 13.139. **Mary**, m. (Ct. July 1709) James Welch; 2 daus. bp. Wells 10 Aug. 1712; m. 2d by 1718 Saml. Treadwell, a soldier at Wells 1711; s. Saml. bp. 28 May 1720. Y. D. 12.4, 16.

3 ‡*MAJOR JOSEPH** (5), Esq., 27 in June 1674, appar. was of York 1668 and settl. in Kit., the home of his w. Catherine (Frost 9) Leighton (m. Ct. 5 July 1670). First a carpenter, he was named Clerk of the Writs, Kit., 1 July 1673, and lic. 7 July 1674 and later to keep an ord., but soon engrossed in

pub. life, Town Clerk and Selectm. many yrs., Rep., County Treas., Councilor, Lieut., Capt., Major, Reg. of Deeds, Judge of Prob., Judge of Ct. of Common Pleas. Both he and s. Jos. orig. memb. of Berw. Ch. Lists 28, 256, 36, 96, 98, 99, 298. He d. 20 Feb. 1709-10 in 63d yr.; wid. Catherine 15 Aug. 1715 in 82d yr. Ch: **Mercy**, b. 1670, m. John Gowen(2). **George**, b. 11 Sept. 1672, d. 24 Apr. 1690. **Dorcas**, b. May 1674, m. Robt. Cutts (8). Col. ‡*Joseph**, Esq., Kit., b. 19 Jan. 1677, foll. his fa. in pub. life, Clerk of Courts, Reg. of Deeds, Col., Rep., Councilor. Lists 296, 297, 298, 221, 161, 291. His letter detailing the fam. hist. is in N. E. Reg. ix. 312. He m. 14 Sept. 1699 Hannah Storer (Jos.). Will 1 Aug. 1751, cod. 27 Dec. 1752 (d. 26 Jan. 1753) names w. Hannah (d. 21 May 1765) and 7 of 9 ch., incl. Joseph, b. 1 Feb. 1700-1, Clerk of Courts, m. 20 Sept. 1722 Mary Adams; George, b. 20 Feb. 1703-4, acc. in Apr. 1723 by Lydia Spinney (Spencer by Ct. rec.), whose dau. Dorcas Hammond was named in will of her gr. mo. Mary Burnham (2); m. 20 Nov. 1729 Hannah Coburn of York.

4 **RICHARD**, Woolwich, took O. A. to the King 5 Sept. 1665. Lists 12, 13. See Dale. He m. wid. Elizabeth Smith, whose 1st husb. James was alive 29 May 1660, and liv. on the Smith lands which became kn. as Hammond's Farm. As Mistress Hammond she was sending moose skins to John Winslow in May 1667. Indians attacked his ho. 13 Aug. 1676, k. him and k. or capt. the whole fam. (Hubbard says 16), except one girl, dau. or maid, who ran overland to give the alarm at Sheepscot. Mrs. H. was sent back with a letter from the Ind. dated 1 July 1677. List 185. She m. 2d (Capt.) John Rowden of Salem; liv., app. in Me., 1687, when she ptn. Andros. 3 Mass. H. C. 7.181.

5 *WILLIAM**, planter, Wells, bot or inherit. ho. in Slymbridge, co. Gloucester, which he sold here to John Gooch, who called him friend in 1663 and bro. in 1667, by an intermarriage of their children. One Wm. H., weaver, was liv. in Slymbr. in 1608, ag. 40. The Me. Wm. told his gr. s. he was b. in 1597, but depos. 5 July 1676, ±62, ab. Ambrose Boaden's resid. at Spurwink 30 yrs. bef. First app. in ptn. to Saco Ct. 21 Oct. 1645; of Cape Porpus in Dec. 1647 when he and R. Tristram held John Lee's cattle. By July 1649 he was perm. located in Wells and constantly in records there over 30 yrs. Often Selectm., Town Comr. and Gr. j. 1654-1679; Clerk of the Writs 1668; com. on York and Wells bounds 1655; lic. to keep ord. 1659; in 1661 he and Mr. Ezek. Knight were to conduct pub. meet. until the town could prov. a minister; overseer of prison 1673, and during this yr. was

in Ct. for marrying people contrary to law. Assemblyman 1682. Lists 269b, 261, 263, 252, 24, 262, 264, 25, 265, 28, 266, 33. W. Benedictus named in deed 11 May 1661; with her and s. Jona. 8 Feb. 1667-8 he deeded to James Gooch, incl. his 'now dwg. house and farm'; 23 Mar. 1680-1 deeded entire est. to s. Jona. to care for self and aged mo. then sick, her last appear. He witn. with Jona. 14 Apr. 1687, and by written word of gr. s. Joseph d. in 1702, ag. 105. Kn. ch: **Jonathan**, b. ab. 1641. **Joseph**, b. ab. 1647., Poss. a dau. or daus., the w. of James Gooch (2), or Lydia, w. of John Gooch (5), or both; none ment. in letter of Joseph (3 jr.), who named the two sons.

6 **WILLIAM**, soldier at Wells from Cape Ann 1694. List 267b.

**HAMMONS**, of same derivation as Hammond.

1 **BENJAMIN** (2), 50 in July 1731, witn. with Rachel Crediford 1707; adm. his fa.'s est., having a double share, and took care of his mo., with consid. friction, she exasperating, he unfeeling. In 1734 his surv. sis. q. c. to him their share in the mo.'s thirds and he mtg. the land he was liv. on, form. his fa.'s. Liv. Kit. 1758. Lists 291, 296, 297, 298. First w. unkn. was app. dead 1719; he m. 2d 19 Oct. 1722 Sarah (Esmond), wid. of Wm. Briar (7). Only kn. ch: **Benjamin**, old enough in 1719 to steal from his aunt Elizabeth Rose, who in 1732 sued both fa. and son for tresp.; m. 2 Sept. 1731 Elizabeth Grover (3), of York, who m. 2d (int. 26 June 1736) Thos. Rhodes. Poss. a ch. by 1st w: ?John, No. Yarm., m. there 26 Dec. 1732 Patience Webber, and had 13 ch., of whom Benj. m. Sarah Skriggins, her fam. and the Webbers from Kit. and York. Poss. by 2d w: ?Edmund, m. 7 May 1748 Elizabeth Pope. Edmund (sworn Benjamin) ag. 41, dep. in June 1766 that he liv. from a child next to the Curtis-Shapleigh-Keating house.

2 **EDMUND**, Kittery 1673, a newcomer, depos. 10 Mar. 1683-4, ±33. He liv. at Spruce Creek on land form. Thos. Withers', a. bot from T. W. 1679, the rest from John Hole 1681. Lists 30, 293, 298. Prob. a captive, he was called decd. 10 Jan. 1690-1 (Y. D. 7.85), but depos. 26 May 1694 ab. John Shepard's land 20 yrs. bef. If he and w. Jane (called Jeanne Montesse in bap. rec. of daughter Patience in Canada 1707) were the Edward and w. reported k. at Spruce Creek 20 Aug. 1694 (List 96), the report poss. was exagger. as to him, cert. as to Jane, taxed in Kit., widow, 1704. List 290. Adm. on his est. to s. Benj. 5 Mar. 1705-6, div. 1728. In 1719 the wid., liv. with Nathl. Keene, compl. that Benj. would not

care for her; in 1728, claiming he had supp. her ab. 25 yrs. since his fa.'s death, he tried to make other ch. contrib. She was dead in Nov. 1733; his bill 1734 for her maint. since 1702 disallowed. Ch: **Benjamin**, b. ±1681. **Abigail**, m. in Salem 9 Apr. 1713 Benj. Beadle; she liv. 1734, he 1752. 6 ch rec. Salem. **Patience**, a captive May 1705, in Canada 1711, was in Boston, spinster, 1719, running a boarding ho.; m. Daniel Jones and liv. in New York. List 99, pp 92, 127. Patience H.'s bounds ment. Jan. 1732-3; sis. Patience J. decd. ment. 19 Aug. 1734. Y. D. 16.213. **Elizabeth**, m. one Rose, likely Stephen, a witn. with her br. Benj. 1714. Y. D. 8.49. She was a wid. 1719, liv. 1745. One Elizabeth Rose in Ct. 1704 for cursing. **Margaret**, m. 25 Oct. 1716 Paul Williams; 2d aft. Aug. 1734 Wm. Dealing. **Jane**. She or her mo. abs. from meet. Jan. 1698-9, one or the other cursing and swearing and in Ct. 1704. In 1728 her br. Benj. was pd. for her 8 wks.' sickness and burial. Unlikely a son if he left desc., but poss. neph. was Edward m. Elizabeth Ball. See (3).

3 **EDWARD** (Hammonds) and w. reported k. by Ind. 1694. List 96. Unident. unless (2). If name correct, poss. fa. of **Edward** (Hammons) m. 20 Oct. 1700 Elizabeth Ball (5), who was at Nathl. Keene's ho. 1702; she m. 2d ab. 1707 Francis Pettigrew; 1 ch. rec. Joanna, b. 20 Apr. 1701. In 1760 Moses Wittum deeded to John H. of Kit., s. of Edward, late of Kit., decd.

4 **JOHN**, Newcastle 1696. List 315a.

**HANCE**, *John, carpenter, Dover witn. (neat signa.) with James Kidd and Timo. Waldron, 1657. Taxed 1657, next to Thos. Hanson; accepted inhab. 6 July 1659; bot from Geo. Walton 1665. Lists 356ab, 361a, 363ab (226 Ham?). With Tobias Hanson he subscr. for the purch. of land in Monmouth Co., N. J., and was at Portland Point in that Co. 1669-70; by 1672 at Shrewsbury, where he d. Dep., J. P. He m. Elizabeth Hanson (6) whose neph. Tobias Hanson gave P/A to uncle John Hance of Shrews. 4 Feb. 1698-9. Will 24 Mar. 1707-8—27 Jan. 1710-11 beq. to w. Elizabeth, 2 sons, 4 of 5 daus., and ment. Saml. Childe and Tobiah Hanson of Perscataway, N. E. Wid. d. 28 Oct. 1732. See N. Y. Gen. & Biog. Rec., vols. 35-36.

**HANCOCK**, commonly found in the south western counties of England.

1 **HENRY**, carpenter, Richmond Isl. 1638-1641. List 21. See Creber.

2 **JOHN** (Handcock, Han—, Hon—, Hunkett), Hampton, in company of John Fuller 1670. D. 16 Feb. 1670-1; inv. taken by Saml. Dalton, John Sanborn.

3 **REV. JOHN** (Nathl. of Cambridge), H. C. 1689, minister at York 1694...where

he was perf. marriages 26 July 1694—25 June 1695. He witn. Matthew Austin's deed in Dec. 1694, Henry Milbury's will 3 Sept. 1695; still there June 1696. Dec. 12, 1697 he began to preach tempor. at Lexington, Mass., and became their settled pastor until death 6 Dec. 1752. By w. Elizabeth Clark (Rev. Thos. of Chelmsford) 5 ch. 1702-1713, incl. **John**, H. C. 1719, fa. of John Hancock, Signer.

**4 ROBERT**, capt. of the ship -F(alk?)land- at Portsm. 1697.

**Handeside**, Robert, d. Portsm. 23 July 1705, ag. 28 (g. s. Pt. of Graves).

**HANDS, Mark**, nailer, from Boston, where he had ch. rec. by two wives 1645-1654, witn. against Thos. Furson (2) in 1652, and in York witn. Hugh Gale's deed 19 Oct. 1653. Y. D. i. 35. In a letter written at Barbadoes 1662 he ment. Cous. Everell of Boston and Sister (Abigail) Hanford. Will 1661-1664 (Suff.). In 1665 his dwg. in Boston was in poss. of Mr. John Winslow sr. N. E. Reg. 13.9.

**Hannah**, Robert, witn. at Little Harbor 1689. One of the name was soon in R. I.

**Hannet?**, Edward, and Elias White witn. Rich. Wharton to John Parker of Kennebec 15 July 1684. July 18 E. White, ±54, and Edw. -Skinner-, ±60, saw poss. given. Y. D. iv. 18, 19.

**HANNAFORD. 1 John**, Stratham, rated 1714 (Hannafer), likely the John (Honeyford) who m. Hannah (Anna) Robinson at Hampton 18 Jan. 1711. List 388. Bondsman with John Wiggin jr. for wid. Anna Wiggin 1749. Old Mr. John H. d. 9 Apr. 1764. 4 ch. rec. 1712-1726.

**2 WILLIAM** (Hannyford), master or owner of a ship here 1655. P. & Ct. ii. 141. In 1665 he and John Corbin owned two-thirds of the ketch -William and John- built here; Roger Deering and John Jackson owned the other third.

**HANSCOM**, very uncommon, not in Lower's or Guppy's handbooks. One Thomas H., of Sutton, co. Bedford, was bro.-in-law of Richard Clayton of Salem.

1 **JOB**(2), weaver, Kittery, sold his int. in fa.'s prop. to neph. Thos. 13 Feb. 1712-3. In 1724 he was sued in York Ct. by Saml. Penhallow, in 1735 had his br. John's 20 a. gr. of 1694, in 1738 deeded to s. Benaiah. List 298. Supp. to have mov. to Scarboro or Saco and d. late. His w. Mary Gowell (Richard) was liv., unmar., with Mrs. Elizabeth Harvey, innholder, 5 Dec. 1705, when John -Pickering- struck her; 13 Jan. 1707-8 as Mary Hanscom she sued John -Plaisted- for it. Ch. incl. **Aaron**, b. 10 June 1706, m. at Greenl. 9 Jan. 1733-4 Joanna Ford(5). Ch. **Benaiah**, m. 1739 Keziah Rogers (John);

mov. to Saco. **Elizabeth**, b. 16 Aug. 1716, m. (pub. 28 Dec. 1735) Saml. Odell. Prob.: **Uriah**, m. (int. 7 July 1744) Mary Hearl. One ch. liv. in 1745 when he was at Louisburg. **Zimri** (also Zimariah), blacksmith, had wife only in 1745 when he was at Louisburg, and likely d. there; adm. 20 May 1746 to wid. Mary; bondsm. Jos. Field, Mark Staples.

2 **THOMAS**, Kittery, b. ±1623. Wm. Hilton sued him for debt 15 Mar. 1649-50, and sued Robt. Mendum and him for tresp. 1651. In June 1654 the Ct. ord. him not to live with Mary Batchelder (w. of 5). App. he took little part in public affairs. He and his w. Ann (m. 16 May 1664) were abs. from meet. July 1669; he alone the next yr. Gr. j. (N. H.) 1661, 1662, 1663. Lists 288, 298, 30, 94. Depos. 23 July 1683, ±60, conc. Joshua Downing's fence; liv. 1688. Adm. to gr. s. Thos. 1713; div. 28 July 1719. In 1724 John Staples test. that Thos. was put in poss. of half the est. to care for his ancient gr. mo. She depos. Aug. 1695, ±49, as Goody Hanscom; 22 Nov. 1697 as Ann H., adm. of s. John, sold his 20 a. gr. to Rich. Gowell; m. 2d James Tobey who was k. 21 May 1705; living a widow 1719. Ch: **Thomas**, b. 17 Oct. 1666. **John**, b. 15 Sept. 1668, mariner, d. s. p. by 1697. List 298. **Alice**, b. 12 Mar. 1671, was liv. at Mr. Shapleigh's in 1691, the mo. of Black Will jr. As Alice Mathrell she was charged with bastardy in July 1693, and again in Apr. 1695, then accusing John Thompson. In 1695, called Alice Hanscom or Medril, under 24. Not repre. in div. 1719. **Samuel**, b. 10 Apr. 1675; he or his neph. a witn. 1717; d. s. p. by 1719. **Moses**, husbandman, ±50 in Apr. 1730. His cattle mark reg. at Kit. 1702-12. Jury 1712. Feb. 17, 1712-3 he sold his int. in his fa.'s est. to neph. Thos. Lists 296, 297, 298. Bot in Scarboro 1727; taxed there (Black Point) 1729; liv. 1738. M. Hannah Rackliff (Wm.). 6 small ch. in Jan. 1718-9, 2 or m. later. Job.

3 **THOMAS**(2), Kittery, d. intest. Feb. 1713. Lists 298, (?290 Thurcom). Gr. j. 1691, 1696; Tr. j. 1696-7. Constable 1698. He m. 1st Alice Rogers, ±30 in 1695, dau. of Richard, whose will 11 Jan. 1700 made no provision for Hanscom gr. ch., but named s.-in-law Thos. H. overseer; m. 2d by 1698 Tamsen (Gowell) Shears. Adm. to her 11 May 1713; a wid. 1729. Ch. by 1st w: **Thomas**, b. Dec. 1690, gr. adm. of his gr. fa. Hanscom's est. 1713, and had the homestead until it was divid. 1719. In probate case with his step-mo. were John Rogers, Abra. Cross. Lists 296, 291, 297. He m. 1 Jan. 1715-6 Sarah Fogg(1). 9 ch. **Hester**, b. 20 Nov. 1692, m. David Libby jr. **Anne**, b. 16 Aug. 1694, m. Danl. Fogg (1

jr.) **John** and **Priscilla**, twins, b. 26 Oct. 1695, d. y. By 2d w: **Samuel**, b. 25 July 1698, apprent. to Col. Jos. Hammond; m. 1st Jan. 1721-2 Hannah Libby(9), 2d 20 Nov. 1750 Mary (Fogg) Hanscom. Will 1 Dec. 1774. Ch. 7+2. **Mary**, b. 28 July 1700, m. 16 Dec. 1721 John Morrell jr. .**Martha**, b. 27 Sept. 1702, m. 4 Mar. 1724-5 Solomon Libby(3). **John**, b. 15 Apr. 1705, m. 16 June 1730 Mary Brooks(7). Will 4 Aug.— 1 Sept. 1790. 5 ch. **Joseph**, b. 13 July 1708, sold to br. John in 1730. He m. 18 Mar. 1732-3 Lydia Spinney (Saml.), 1 ch. rec. **Moses**, b. 2 Mar. 1711-2, m. 1st (int. 2 Aug. 1740) Mary Field (Stephen jr. 12), 6 ch; 2d Martha (Bartlett), wid. of John Shapleigh; d. 26 Feb. 1793.

**HANSON**, patronymic from Hans, peculiar to Yorkshire.

1 **ISAAC**(6), mariner, Dover, m. Mary Heard(3). Oct. 15, 1683 she attest. his invent. taken 17 Sept., and m. 2d Capt. Robt. Evans(13). List 359b. Kn. ch: **Isaac**, mariner, witn. Nich. Follett's will 29 Apr. 1700 at Treace in Bay of Campeach. Of Portsm. 14 July 1701 when his step-fa. deeded him Heard land at Thomp. Point; also in Jan. 1703-4 when he gave P/A to br.-in-law James Libby under which 30 a. at Thompson's Pt. were sold in 1707. Liv. 1717. **Mary**, b. 18 May 1679, m. 9 June 1698, 'sometime of Nantucket', James Libby(6).

2 **JOHN**, Dover, took O. F. 1655. List 355a. Poss. (3).

3 **JOHN**, liv. on the Kennebec at Small Point Harbor bef. the Ind. War, and left or sold his land to John and Rachel (Atkins) Drake(4). Y. D. 8. 167-8.

4 **JOHN**, Dover, deceased in 1716. Sons **Nathaniel** jr. (w. Mary) and **John**, both liv. 1746.

5 **LOVE**(10) Dover. W. Elizabeth. Ch. rec: **Hannah**, b. 10 May 1713. **Love**, b. 21 Apr. 1721.

6 **THOMAS**, Dover 1657, had 100 a. gr. near Salmon F. 11 Jan. 1658-9 and bot from Wm. Hackett and Capt. Barefoot. Freeman 5 June 1661. If not a Quaker hims., the founder of a fam. of Quakers. Constable; Highway Surveyor. Lists 356-abcegh, 47. Will (undated) proved 27 June 1666, names w. Mary, 6 ch. She was abs. from meet. 1663; k. by Ind. 'old wid. Handson' 28 June 1689. Lists 356jk, 359ab, 96. Ch: **Tobias**, oldest son, prob. of age 1662. **Thomas**. **Isaac**. **Timothy**. Two daus. under age by will, one **Elizabeth**, m. John Hance; the other poss. **Mary**.

7 **THOMAS**(6), planter, Dover, taxed 1663, m. at Salem 3 June 1669 Mary (Kitchen), wid. of Timo. Robinson, who brot her

s. Timothy to Dover. Lists 356hjk, 357c, 359ab, 94. She was named in his will 24 Apr., cod. 6 May 1710 (inv. 8 Nov. 1711), with ch. but Isaac: **Mary**, b. 3 Dec. 1670 (Salem); her fa.'s will gave her maint. and her mo.'s feather-bed, if she chose, or £20 and the bed. **Thomas**, Dover, m. 1st at Salem 9 Oct. 1701 Margaret Maule, 2d at Lynn 12 June 1719 Hannah Peirce, who m. next Joseph Chesley(4). His will 18 Sept. 1728 (d. ab. 13 Jan. 1728-9, Lynn rec.) names 6+3 ch., all liv. 1753 and all but two of Dover, Saml. of Epping, and Abigail, w. of Jos. Newhall of Salem. **John**, carpenter, Dover; m. 23 July 1703 Elizabeth Meader, whose tale of her experiences as a captive was pub. in 1780. List 358b. 10 kn. ch. (8 rec. 1705-1721), of whom Ebenezer and Caleb were k. by Ind. 27 Aug. 1724, the mo., 4 ch. and a maid carried to Canada, where the fa. redeemed all but one dau. the next yr. He d. ab. 16 June 1727 (Lynn rec.) while on his way to Canada a 2d time to redeem his dau. Sarah. Adm. to wid. Elizabeth 11 Nov. 1727; to s. John 27 Apr. 1737. Heirs (not incl. Nathl. jr.) signed an agreement 10 May foll., John, Isaac, Daniel, Hannah and Israel Hodgdon, Elizabeth and Ebenezer Varney, and Mercy and Abigail, minors, by their gdn. Jos. Meader of Nantucket. Sarah m. Jean Baptiste Sabourin and rem. in Canada. See Coleman's N. E. Captives, ii. 161-6. **Mercy**, m. 1st John Church(2), 2d Nathl. Young. **Abigail**, m. 12 May 1709 Jona. Young. **Nathaniel**, carpenter, m. Martha Bickford(17). Will 25 Dec. 1748—25 Jan. 1748-9 names her and 5 of 7 ch. rec. 1716-1729. List 358d. **Elizabeth**, recd. £10 by will. **James**, had the homestead and was joint excr. with mo. Prob. the James who had w. Ruth in 1737, and was dead in 1739, Ruth in poss. of homestead. Elizabeth, dau. of James, bp. Dover 18 July 1736. One James of Madbury 1768, adm. 28 June to wid. Abigail. **Isaac**, d. 22 Oct. 1706, 'a lusty young man.' List 96.

8 **TIMOTHY**(6), Dover, his 10 a. gr. in 1675 laid out near Wm. Sheffield and Jos. Sanders. Lists 359b, 52, 94. He m. Barbara, dau. of Benanuel Bowers of Charlest., (dau. Hanson in her fa.'s will 1693). He sold in Dover to Timo. Wentworth and took letter of removal for self and w. to Phila. 7 Mar. 1696; liv. there and at Abington. Will 17 Aug. 1710—4 Sept. 1711. Wid. d. 7 Nov. 1718. Ch. rec. Lynn, all in will but Joshua: **Timothy**, b. 9 Nov. 1679. **Mary**, b. 19 Feb. 1680-1, m. in Abington 16 July 1703 Benj. Barrett, the mar. rec. signed by her fa. and 3 bros. **Jonathan**, b. 29 June 1682. **Joshua**, b. 5 Feb. 1683-4, prob. d. bef. 1703. **Samuel**, b. 16 Aug. 1685. In 1717 of Frankford, Pa., yeoman, he sold to Thos. Downes ½ of 100

a. laid out to Thos. Hanson sr. 1658. **Elizabeth**, b. 9 Jan. 1686-7.

9 **TOBIAS**(6), Dover, eldest son; his bounds ment. 1660, taxed 1662. He early subscr. for lands in Monmouth Co., N. J., and poss. went there tempo. with John Hance, as he did not take the O. F. in 1669 with br. Thos. Lists 356ghk, 359ab, 52, 94, 96. He m. Elizabeth, dau. of Jos. Boyce, Quaker, of Salem (his will 4 Nov. 1684). She was bp. 6 Mar. 1641-2; carried capt. 28 June 1689 when his mo. was k. List 96. He met his mo.'s fate 10 May 1693. Kn. ch: **Tobias**, eldest s. 1718. **Joseph**, poss. husband of Deliverance Clark (2). One Deliverance Hanson witn. a Watson deed 1714. In 1747 he gave his homestead to neph. Wm. (Benj.). Dead 1749. **Benjamin**, blacksmith, ±80, 25 Mar. 1751. List 358d. In 1718 his br. Tobias deeded him 15 a. bet. his own land and Joseph's, part of 60 a. gr. to their gr. fa. M. at Salem 26 Nov. 1701 Elizabeth Trask. 8 ch. 1703-1719, incl. Jos. One Benj. m. at Salem (int. 21 Oct. 1732) Abigail King.

10 **TOBIAS**(9), Dover, m. 1st Lydia Canney(4); 2d 28 Aug. 1698 Ann Lord(6). Jury 1696; Constable 1697. Feb. 4, 1698-9 he gave P/A to uncle John Hance of Shrewsbury, N. J., as his gen. agt. in East Jersey. Will 1 June 1742—28 Aug. 1745, names w. Ann, 6 ch., 3 gr. ch. Ch. by 1st w: **Love**. **Benjamin**, m. by 1720 Mary Horne(2), who m. 2d by 1729 Wm. Fost(2). 3 ch. named in gr. fa.'s will: John, app. eldest, bp. 2 Aug. 1730; Lydia (Stiles by will) and Timothy, both bp. 26 July 1730. **Elizabeth**, m. (int. Salem 7 Jan. 1715-6) Saml. Buxton of Salem. By 2d w: **Mercy**, b. 4 Aug. 1699, m. Stephen Varney. **Tobias**, b. Mar. 1702, m. 1st 27 Dec. 1726 Judith Varney, 2d 25 Oct. 1750 Sarah Frye. Will 1762 (d. 27 Aug. 1765) names w. Sarah, 7 ch., all by 1st w. **Judith**, b. 7 Feb. 1703, m. 26 Nov. 1723 Saml. Twombley. **Joseph**, Esq., b. 10 Jan. 1703-4, innholder Dover 1738 (jr.); in Sept. that yr. was having a ho. built in Biddef.; trader Dover 1742; d. 5 Sept. 1758 (Dover). He m. 1st 23 Nov. 1727 Rebecca Shepard, d. 18 Apr. 1736, 1 son; 2d 25 Aug. 1737 Sarah Scammon (Humphrey of Biddef.), d. 2 Sept. 1738, 1 son; 3d 6 June 1739 Susannah Burnham (Robt.), d. 4 Mar. 1758, 2 ch. **Nathaniel**, not in will. **Isaac**, m. 31 Dec. 1741 Susannah Canney (Thos.). He d. 15 Jan. 1758; adm. 30 Aug. to wid, who d. 9 Aug. 1760. Est. div. 1771 to 2 sons, 4 daus. **Samuel**, not in will. **Aaron**, not in will.

**Hanworthy**, William, Piscataqua, mariner on the ketch -Endeavor- 1684.

**Harall**, John, Portsm. 1677; Mr. Haroll and w. 1684. Lists 54, 52. **Hearl**?

**Harben**?, James, 1665. List 47.

**Hard**, Harde, see Hardy, also Heard.

**HARDING**, mostly confined to south-west of England.

1 **ANNE** (Harden), in 17— claimed for self and ch. 140+20 a. in New Dartmouth on north side of highway leading to mill, and 15 a. on Eastern Riv., by Dongan patent 17 Aug. 1686. One Anne Harden d. at Boston 6 June 1722, ag. 80.

2 **ISRAEL**, blacksmith, Wells, had 200 a. town gr. at Maryland in 1670 provid. he settle there within three mos. and be the town smith. This he soon exch. for Jona. Hammond's 100 a. bot from John Barrett. The names of hims. and son, his occup., call to preach, and the acquaint. of Wm. Ashley (4) and w. Sarah with the R. I. fam., indicate that he was s. of Stephen of Providence. As a Baptist, he did not fit in well with the ch. in his new home; abs. from meet. in July 1679; in Aug. 1681 convicted the 2d or 3d time for reproachf. language towards ministers, in Mar. 1682-3 fined for preaching. Robt. Wakeham sued him in 1674 for a rapier bot and not pd. for. Gr. j. 1678. Appr. the Pendleton est. with John Eldridge in 1681. Lists 266, 33. Already m. to Lydia, wid. of John Gooch (5), he was gr. adm. of the Gooch est. in her place 7 Oct. 1673; she liv. 29 Jan. 1682-3; he m. 2d Mary (Wakefield), wid. of Wm. Frost (15); adm. on Frost est. to him 25 Feb. 1690-1; his end unkn. Only kn. ch: **Stephen**.

3 **JOHN**? See Herdin.

4 **MARTHA**, Portsm., 1713. See Almary.

5 **RICHARD**, Portsm. witn. 1663.

6 **STEPHEN** (2), blacksmith, Wells, Arundel, m. 28 July 1701 Abigail Littlefield (13) and in Mar. 1717-8 bot from Saml. (4) and Mary Fuller of Salem their half of her fa.'s est. Selectm. Wells 1713; lic. ho. of entert. Lists 269ac. In July 1720 he bot from John Reynolds of Oyster Riv. his right in the Reynolds 200 a. at Arundel, a resulting dispute with Thos. Perkins who had bot from other heirs being arbitrated 21 Feb. 1721-2. (Y. D. x, xi, xii.) By 1722 he liv. near the Galloping Place at Arundel and kept the ferry. During Dummer's War he was used as a skilled pilot, having hunted many yrs. from the Saco to the Winnipesaukee Ponds. W. Abigail d. 1 Oct. 1747; 13 Oct. he deeded to daus. Miriam and Elizabeth over and above their shares for their care of their mo.; d. 5 Dec. 1747. Ch: **Stephen**, m. Ruth Sampson. Ch. **Abigail**, m. 19 Oct. 1721 John Webber. **Sarah**, m. Robt. Cleaves. **Mary**, m. Abel Merrill. **Hannah**, m. Daniel Smith. **Lydia**, m. Lt. Thos. Perkins. **Miriam**, m. Jeremiah Frost(5). **Elizabeth**, m. Andrew Brown (Lt. Allison 3). **James** and **Israel**, d. y.

7 **THOMAS**, in one indictment Apr. 1681 with Nich. Bickford (21) and Augustine

Factor (or Parker), tried at Smuttinose 9 Nov., Jeffrey Currier informant.

**HARDISON.** Two probate papers 1697-8 spell the name Hareson, Harison, Hardiston, Harriss, Hardison. Harrison a patronymic common in north of England.
**STEPHEN**, Kittery. Of Hog Isl. in Apr. 1685, he sued Magnus White in Suff. Ct. for pine timber recd. of Mr. James Goffe; witn. will of John Taylor of Berw. 1687 and later m. his dau. Mary; ack. judgm. to Geo. Snell, and with Wm. Ardell was bondsm. for Edw. Hilton 1689; sued by Capt. John Pickering 1694, Philip Caverly his bondsm.; abs. from meeting 1696. D. 31 Jan. 1696-7; Thos. Starbird helped the wid. Mary ab. the est. In 1695, ag. 33, she witn. in case of Elisha Ingersoll and Dorothy Saterly; ment. as wid. 1698; m. 2d one Coss (Geo. 2?), 3d John Legrow. In 1730 her three sets of ch. sued for ½ of Niven Agnew's est. Ch: **John**, b. 22 Jan. 1691, mariner, Portsm.; bot there 1718. Lists 239b, 339. He m. 1st Abigail Cotton(7), whose fa. deeded them Scarb. land in 1720; she liv. 13 July 1733; m. 2d by 1745 Hannah, sis. of Nathl. and Saml. Odiorne, her will 1755—1755. His will 25 May—19 June 1753, names her; s. Stephen, boatbuilder, Portsm. (m. Mary Underwood); and dau. Abigail, w. of Saml. Tripe; but not dau. Mary bp. So. Ch. 4 Dec. 1720, and named in gr. fa.'s will 1733. **Stephen**, Berwick, b. 9 May 1693, apprent. to Col. Ichabod Plaisted 14 yrs. Owned c. and bp. Berw. Ch., 21 Dec. 1718. In 1735 he and Freethy Spencer bot Moses Spencer's homestead; bondsm. for Saml. Randall, Somersw., 1740; dep. July 1760, near 68; d. 25 Dec. 1769. List 298. W. Alice Abbott (Joseph 4), m. 23 Sept. 1724. 7 ch. bp. Berw. 1725-1736. (One Alexander H. taxed Portsm. 1731-2?).

**HARDY**, very ancient name in Midlands and East coast.
1 ———, Mr., Falmouth 1683. List 226.
2 ———, Lieut., Dover 1715. List 358d. Read Heard.
3 **CLEMENT**, fisherman, moved around. Appar. liv. in Saco Nov. 1665 when John Bonython sued him for debt; in Sept. 1666 he (Hard) and Nathl. Phillips defied Justice Hooke, who sued him for debt a yr. later. Of Winter Harbor, he sold the Page plantation at Saco to John Presbery in June 1670. Shoals 1677; in Apr. 1678 gave a note to David Campbell of Great Isl., witn. by Joanna Wescott and Wilmot Edgecomb, w. of Nicholas(2). Adm., fisherman, Richmond Isl., to Nathl. Fryer, July 1679. List 306a.
4 **DANIEL**, at Blue Point ab. 1696 with Saml. Savery, who pointed out John Jackson's farm.

5 **GEORGE**, Cape Porpus witn. Nov. 1651. Y. D. i. 37.
6 **GEORGE**, m. at Newb. 24 Nov. 1686 Mary Fogg (4).
7 **MARY** (Harde), dau. of (6), m. at Hampton 27 Jan. 1707 Jos. Lowell.
8 **RICHARD**, fisherman, York, bot 30 a. from Rishworth in 1667. Moses Worcester, adm., sold his marsh in 1705. Y. D. ii. 34, vii. 32.
9 **THEOPHILUS**, Exeter, bp. Beverly 1 Nov. 1691, s. of Dr. Saml. and Mary (Dudley 1), was beq. land in Ex. by his uncles Theophilus and Biley Dudley. List 376b. He m. 1st Rebecca Lyford (1), d. bef. Dec. 1723; 2d Sarah Follett (6). Ch.
10 **THOMAS**, fined as a common drunkard in Wells Ct. 5 July 1670, Chas. Potum witn.; on coroner's jury Saco 22 Dec. 1670. P. & Ct. ii. 202, 431. T. H. of Great Island acc. by Jos. Ring in his depositions in the Susanna Martin witchcraft case, 1692. The town pd. Rebecca Bell 18 Mar. 1700 for keeping him.

**HARFORD.** The county and town of Hertford are vulgarly so pronounced.
1 **JOHN**, Dover, kn. only by Quaker rec. of mar of s. **William** to Patience Long (John), 6 Nov. 1701.
2 ***NICHOLAS**, Dover, shopkeeper, presum. there because of the pres. of Wm. (4), altho no connec. found. He bot in Dover from Rich. Pinkham, 1706; in Feb. 1714-5 bot from Abra. Morrell in Kit., oppo. his own place in Dover, and kept the ferry, selling the Kit. land in 1718 to Nathl. Chapman. Kit. witn. 1727. Lists 358b5d. Selectm. 7 times 1724-33; Moderator 1728, 1731; Rep. 1732. W. Elizabeth (appar. Jenkins 12) was bound over to the March Sess. in Dec. 1701, bondsm. John Willey and Stephen Jenkins. Adm. on his est. to creditors 31 May 1737, wid. Elizabeth and s. Joseph cited; she liv. 1758. Ch: **Patience**, b. 16 Sept. 1701, m. Benj. Ham(4). **Joseph**, b. 9 Apr. 1703, m. by 1735 Dorothy Furbush(1). In 1747 his w. was Deborah. **Charity**, b. 5 May 1705. **Stephen**, b. 12 Apr. 1707. **Nicholas**, b. 1 Sept. 1709, m. 20 Feb. 1731 Mary Ferguson (1). **William**, b. 9 Oct. 1711, d. 10 Aug. 1716. **Elizabeth**, b. 18 Jan. 1713, selling liquor in 1736, bondsm. br. Benj. and Nathl. Roberts, jr. In 1737 her mo., bros. Benj. and Solomon, and Robt. Mace of Gosport, later her husb., rescued her from arrest by the dep. sheriff. **Benjamin**, b. 15 Apr. 1716, m. in Scarb. 9 Dec. 1737 Temperance Bryant (8). **Paul**, b. 24 Jan. 1717, m. by 1741 Lydia Heard (James 2); adm. to her 24 Apr. 1751. 4 or m. ch. **Solomon**, b. 31 Mar. 1720. **Ann**, b. 2 Aug. 1722, m. one Evans. **John**, b. 17 Dec. 1724.

**3 THOMAS**, with Kit. men witn. deed Joshua Crockett of Dover to Richard Cutts of Kit. 1697. Y. D. 4.157.

**4 WILLIAM**, tailor, Bellamy's Bk., Dover, drunk and idle in 1678, at Rich. Otis's ho. in 1680 coaxing for liquor, was first at Charlestown, where he was liv. in May 1673, his w. in Old Eng. List 359b. One Wm. (Hartford) served in Philip's War. He was hardly ident. with Wm. Haffut, 48 in 1668 (N. E. Reg. vi. 341), who would have been 81 when the Dover man m. 22 Nov. 1701 Mary (Dam) Canney(1). Will 16 June 1717—Mar. 1717-8, names aged w. Mary, s.-in-law Thos. Canney; no Harfords. May 27, 1719 she gave P/A to her s. Thos.

**HARKER, John**, York, fisherman on an island inside Stage Neck. In 1647 he bot the ho. of Allen Yoe & Co. from Thos. Fowle (3), but had to relinq. to E. Godfrey. P. & Ct. i. 110-6. Witn. Hooke's deed to Alcock and Heard 1650; grants 1653, 1659. Lists 75b, 275, 276, †328. He or s. John fined in N. H. 1670. Liv. 1 July 1673. He m. by 1647 a poor wid. with four small ch., Dorothy, wid. of Robt. Mills. Only kn. ch: **John**, fisherman, Winter Harbor, in July 1673, when his fa. sold him his island at York Harb., which John sold next yr. to Wm. Moore. Y. D. ii, 193, 160. List 328? One Harker (called both Ebenezer and John) m. early at Nantucket, Patience Folger (Peter), but was likely from the Boston fam.

**Harkine**, Harkins, Thomas, witn. Geo. Cleeves' deed to Michael Mitton 24 Feb. 1650-1. List 221. Note Harlow (2).

**HARLOW, 1 Francis**, husbandman, Berwick, 1698, swearing he would cut his wife's throat. His only kn. w. was Sarah, wid. of Geo. Gray (4). Town grants 1699, 1703. W. Sarah was recd. into Berw. Ch. 1716, he in 1720. Lists 290, 296, 298. Feb. 28, 1712 both deeded to his step-son Alex. Gray; in Oct. 1718 he deeded dwg. ho. and other prop. to step-son James Gray for supp. of hims. and w. Sarah; he alone deeded to gr. s. James Gray 16 July 1726 and to Uriah Page 16 Jan. 1730-1. In 1756 Martha (Gray) Page sold F. H.'s common rights allowed -us- by the Genl. Ct. for his maintenance. Appar. no ch.

**2 THOMAS** (Harlo), witn. Cleeves to Michael Mitton 1 Jan. 1650. Y. D. 3.76. Note Harkine.

**Harls**, see Hales (4).

**HARMON.** An ancient personal name. See 'Ancestry of Lydia Harmon', by W. G. Davis, for three Me. families.

**1 JAMES**, Saco 1655, for 20 yrs. perpet. bef. the Courts on charges oft. serious, from the day he first app. at Salem in Oct.

1653 on the -Happy Entrance-. In this ship or cargo he had some prop. right, and may have come first to Me. on one of its trading trips. M. in Saco 6 May 1658 or 1659 Sarah Clark (7), who naturally had a troubled life, and in 1664 was allowed to live with her mo. or with Jas. Gibbins where her husb. might go to her. List 246. A tempo. absence poss. foll. his 'suspitious words' in July 1660, which seemed to declare a speedy departure from the country; in Essex Co. late in 1661; soon in Saco, where last found 1 July 1673. Despite his behaviour, he was gdn. of br.-in-law Saml. Clark; atty in Ct. for Chas. Potum 1666; gdn. for ch. of Nich. Bully (3) bef. 1667; plaint. in several suits for debt, or fish taken away. Lists 245, 79. His wid. was in Boston in 1680 and July 1693, a few mo. aft. Jas. Gibbins gr. her land and marsh at Saco on Goose Fare Brook, form. occup. by her fa., which she claimed in 17—. Ch: **Child**, b. 1659 or 1660. **Jane**, b. ab. 1661, bound to Lt. Gibbins for 8 yrs. in Apr. 1671 aft. her fa. had been abusing her. One Jane m. 15 Nov. 1678 Saml. Doty at Piscataway, N. J., where the surname was unkn., and the Saco girl poss. accomp. some N. E. fam. there. His will, prov. 8 Nov. 1715, names her, exec., 13 ch., incl. James and Sarah. **James**, apprent. to Obadiah Emmons of Boston 1680, when ord. put to some other shoemaker; yet mariner, 17 July 1693 when adm. gr. to mo.; br. Saml. and Saml. Warkman, bondsm. He was in Ct., swearing and drunk, 1683-1685. **Samuel**, (good signature); cordwainer, Boston, where ch. bap.: Samuel 19 Sept. 1692; Sarah 2 Aug. 1696. **Barbara**, b. Saco 6 Dec. 1667. Not imposs. others, incl. Elizabeth and Naomi m. in Boston 1691-6.

**2 JOHN**, Wells, Scarboro. Servant of John Symonds of Kit., he was bef. the Ct. 9 July 1667 for swearing two oaths; next found at Narragansett Swamp fight 1675, place of enlistment unkn. He was gr. 50 a. in Wells 1677; O. F. there July 1676; worked in the Curwin mills 1679, boarding with Francis Littlefield. M. Sarah Roberts (Wm.) of Oyster River, the last home of his form. master Symonds, and liv. on a 100 a. farm at Wells bot from John Wentworth 20 Oct. 1680. This he deeded to s. Samuel in 1714, with life reserva. in 50 a. Lists 269ab. Soon aft. being adm. to Wells Ch. in June 1726, he and w. Sarah accomp. s. Samuel to Scarboro. Orig. member Scarb. Ch. 1728. She liv. 1727, he in 1734 when he sold his Narragansett grant. Ch: **John**, b. 27 Dec. 1681, m. aft. 16 Nov. 1700 Lydia Fernald (1), d. bef. 19 Dec. 1702. She m. 2d Benj. Miller, but prev. had been in Ct. in Apr. 1705 for having an illegit. ch., presum. John Harmon, Kit.,

witn. in a ram case 2 Jan. 1721-2, then 'of full age,' and servant of John Thompson. He was appar. at Newc. 1723; admonished in Apr. 1726 for voting in Kit., not being a voter; d. s. p., Thompson heirs conveying land John Thompson had deeded him 1725-6. **Sarah**, b. 15 May 1684. **Samuel**, b. 15 June 1686, m. 19 Mar. 1707-8 Mercy Stimson (George). Jury 1711, 1715. Surv. highways, Wells; lot-layer. A progressive millwright and mill owner, he acquired much land and mills in Wells, selling out in 1726 to move to the 500 a. farm near Dunstan, form. Andrew Brown's. Selectm. and on commit. to find their first minis. 1727. In Scarb. he contin. a princ. propr. and lumberman until reverses caused the sale of most of his prop. and homestead. Last ment. 18 July 1742; wid. liv. 1757, prob. Wid. H. bur. 19 June 1759. 7 ch. **Mary**, b. 2 May 1690; in Ct. Oct. 1708. **William**, b. 25 Feb. 1699. Indicted on charge of Mary Littlefield (5) in May 1722, he was acquit. thru lack of evid. In Capt. Wheelwright's co. 1722. Oarmaker of Boston, 1733, he sold his 1720 Wells gr.; m. there 12 Sept. 1734 Margaret Nichols, and aft. 1740 joined the others in Scarb., where he d. 30 Dec. 1766. 4 ch. bp. Boston 1735-40. Capt. **Nathaniel**, b. 1 Feb. 1702-3, d. 8 Oct. 1784, m. 30 Nov. 1727 Hannah Goodale (Zachariah), bur. 7 Oct. 1758; m. 2d 17 May 1759 wid. Betty Simpson of York. Settling in Scarb., he owned share in saw-mill at Mill Creek, sold 1732-3; propr. 1739; 2d largest taxpayer in 2d Par. 1751. Lieut. 1757, Capt. 1762, and grantee in Township No. 1 on Union River (Trenton) 1764. Ch. 9 + 4.

3 *JOHN, Mr., Saco, York, b. ±1639. A supposi. that he was bro. to (1) and brot to Saco by his tangled affairs, cannot be proved. First found in Ct. rec. 1 July 1673 aft. m. to Elizabeth Cummings (3). List 246. M. 2d Deborah (Johnson 8), wid. of John Foxwell (2), prob. bef. 21 June 1680 when gr. adm. on J. F.'s est., cert. bef. 18 Aug. 1680 when his fa.-in-law praised him in his deed of ho., 10 a. and other prop., for support. Records at Saco and York 1680-2 seem to overlap. At Saco, he was an admr. of R. Cummings's est. 1676; Tr. j. 1676; O. F. 2 July 1678; Rep. 1680, June 1681 (sick, appeared not); lot layer 1681; Gr. j. 1682. At York, O. A. 30 Mar. 1680; Gr. j. 1681, 1682, 1688; Rep. 1682; adm. Thos. Rogers's est. 1682; bondsm. for John Bonython 1682, John Ferguson 1682-3; Selectm. 1685, and ptn. for settlem. of Rich. Foxwell's est. same yr.; Tr. j. 1686-7; lic. pub.-ho. 1686-7; retail 1688. Dep. in 1694, ±55. Lists 237a, 249, 29, 33. Inv. 2 Apr. 1695 attested 8 May by Mrs. Deborah; she liv.

1697. Ano. inv. 2 Oct. 1706 of the Johnson land made over to him. In 1716 the ch. made agreem. for div. By 1st w: **Elizabeth**, heiress to one-eighth of the Saco Patent; m. Lt. Jos. Banks (2). By 2d w: **Johnson**. Capt. **John**, b. ±1687, m. 1707 Mehitable Parker (John), who had been a captive and was liv. 1743. See (5). List 279. Deacon and elder of Ch., York. Captain at Louisburg. Depos. July 1752, ±65. Ch: 1707/8-1722: **Deborah**, m. Johnson Harmon (5 jr.); **Benjamin**, List 279, m. Catherine Beale; **Elizabeth**, m. Ebenezer Moulton; Nathl., m. Mary Kingsbury; **Jerusha**, m. Edward Pell, who d. Harwich 1752; John, m. Sarah (Bragdon) Simpson; Napthali, m. at Cambridge 18 Oct. 1744 Anne Greenleaf. **Mary**, m. 1st Benj. Donnell (5), 2d Jos. Holt. See also (7).

4 **JOHN** (Heriman), and w. confessed fornic. in Hampton Q. Ct. Oct. 1674.

5 **LIEUT. COL. *JOHNSON** (3) m. Mary Moulton (Capt. Jere.), who was liv. 1731. Gr. j. 1702. He and br. John were on the fishing voyage at Winter Harbor 1707 when Benj. Donnell (5) was k. in Ind. attack; and there 8 Oct. 1710 he was taken capt., still in Canada 26 Mar. 1711. Lists 99, p. 92, 38, 279. Capt. in two exped. against the Norridgewocks 1722-24, earning his commis. as Lt.-Col. Rep. 1727. Peace Comr. at Falm. 1727. In May 1737 he was liv. with a dau. at Merriconeag Neck; d. 17 Apr. 1751. Ch: **Zebulon**, b. 2 Nov. 1702. **Mary**, b. 23 Mar. 1704-5, m. 10 May 1724 Ens. (later Lt.) Rich. Jaques. List 279; 4 ch. She m. 2d 8 Nov. 1750 John Littlefield. **Miriam**, b. 7 Jan. 1707-8, m. John Stover. **Johnson**, b. 2 July 1710, m. 11 Apr. 1729 his cous. Deborah (3), who m. 2d 8 Oct. 1738 Wm. Fullerton of Boston, and d. by 1743. List 279. **Joseph**, coaster, b. 1 Mar. 1712-3, m. 7 Nov. 1737 Mercy Sewall, who m. 2d 20 Feb. 1750 Simon Frost, Esq., of Kit. **Hannah**, b. 19 Feb. 1715-6, m. Josiah Webber. **Martha**, b. 13 Apr. 1720, m. John Raynes.

6 **PHILIP** (Horman), Falmouth witn. 1688. Y. D. 14.262.

7 **THOMAS** (Herman), York, blown off to sea and lost, in canoe, bet. Piscat. and York, 23 Dec. 1701. List 96.

**Haroe?** John, witn. with Jas. Kidd and Timo. Waldron 1657. John Hance?

**Harridon**, Tristram. List 298. See Harris (26).

**HARRINGTON**. 1 Ebenezer; m. 3 Feb. 1708 Hephsibah Cloyes (5). Likely the man b. Watertown 1687, cous. to (2).

2 **NATHANIEL**, Mr., Wells schoolmaster 1729, liv. there 1732, gent. Prob. from Watert., H. C., 1728, teaching at Watert. 1766.

**HARRIS**, sometimes Harrison, Harridon. Harris, a general English patronymic, became 56th in N. E.

1 **ABIGAIL**, m. Richard Morgan at Hampton 17 May 1699. See (11), (24).

2 **ABRAHAM**, m. 1st at Greenland 20 Dec. 1717 Elizabeth Vittom; 2d 10 June 1728 Abigail Avery.

3 **CHARLES**, sold a stage and swamp at Monhegan to Rich. Patteshall, 1683.

4 **GEORGE**, shipwright, b. 1623-4. See Creber. Aug. 17, 1669 a warrant was issued against him and Wid. Hart (2) for liv. together. Called sr. 1669 or 1670. He witn. a Fernald deed 1671; liv. in same ho. with John Bowman 1672; of Portsm. 1673, ±50. In 167- Goody Harris was recently from Plymouth, Eng. See Evans (11). He was appar. of Great Isl. 1678; in 1680, ±56, had a ho. there near Saml. Roby's shop. Lists 313ac, 331b (?315c). One G. H. in 1675 leased ho. and land on Fernald's Isl. for 13 yrs.; **George**, jr. and w. Joanna sold the lease to Thos. Fernald 28 Aug. 1682; G. H. receipted to Fernald 7 Aug. 1683. Y. D. 6.20-1. Poss. it was jr., not sr., who went in 1672 with John Hunkings' serv. Geo. Laskey to get apples for Mrs. Hunkings, put the Bowman boy out of the orchard and struck Gamer Bowman in the back. One Geo. d. in Boston 1686 leaving wid. Joanna; ano. Geo. was improving land at Little Harbor in 1705.

5 **HENRY**, d. 27 Oct. 1672; inv. 23 Feb. foll., clothing, a chest, 2 s. in money, left in hands of Grace Briars (3). Adm. Apr. 1673 to Giles Barge in beh. of gr. dau. Grace.

6 **HENRY**, seaman ±24, depos. at Great Isl. 26 Apr. 1673; prob. the same who depos. 7 Dec. 1680 that he saw Jas. Sharpe married.

7 **JOB**, Falm. 1717. List 229.

8 **JOHN**, poss. same as (9), came from Charlestown, where he m. Amy Hills, and had 5 ch. 1658-1665. He owned at No. Yarm. 1682; gr. land there 1685. Lists 32, 214. Taken capt. when Capt. Gendall k. in Sept. 1688; later fate unkn. He, or more likely s. John, weaver, Newport, R. I., was called decd. in 1730. His 10 a. ho. lot in No. Yarm. claimed in 17— by s. Jos. for self and br. **Thos.**, was sold in 1728 by Thos. (w. Eleanor), Jos. (w. Rebecca), Thos. jr. (w. Mary), all of Charlest., and Wigglesworth Sweetsir. Old John H's Assigns had Lot 45 in Proprs. drawing 1727.

9 **JOHN**, Falmouth, poss. same as (8). In Apr. 1688 he had ho. and lot near Peter Bowdoin's, ano. near the fort. Lists 34, 225b. In 17— John Comee of Cape Ann claimed at Falm. bet. John Aullwer (Oliver) and John Harris.

10 **JOHN** (27?), fisherman, Isles of Shoals, likely the witn. to a Smuttynose deed 6 Dec. 1685 (Y. D. 8.132), m. Mary Sparks (John of Ipsw. and Boston), mar. bond 24 June 1687, surety Jabesh Negus of Boston. Thereaft. he liv. in Ipsw. where his w. d. 6 May 1730, he 3 Dec. 1738. See 'Ancestry of Bethia Harris,' by W. G. Davis, pp. 37-8 for 5 ch. b. 1690-98, John, Joanna, Mary, **Thomas, Sarah.**

11 **JOHN**, Exeter, m. 1st Mary Hall, who d. 2 Mar. 1707-8; 2d bef. July 1711 Mary, app. dau. of John Robie of Haverh. Norf. Deeds 4.116. Liv. Ex. 1714. Ch. by 1st w: **Mary**, b. 25 July 1707, m. 1st in Boston 13 Dec. 1734 Herbert Walter, 2d by Oct. 1737 Jona. Jones. See (1), (24).

12 **JOHN**, merchant, Portsm., form. of Boston, bound for London with Capt. Martyn, d. at Portsm. Nov. 1710; adm. to Oliver Williams of Boston. List 90?

13 **JOSEPH** (8), weaver, No. Yarmouth, ptn. Andros in July 1688 for 100 a. at Broad Cove or elsewhere. He liv. then, and until driven back to Charlest. by Ind., on 10 a. given him by his fa. and in his poss. 6 yrs., with ano. 10 a. from the town. List 214. His first w. Naomi, b. ab. 1665, likely a No. Yarm. girl, had a illeg. s. bap. in Charlest. in 1695 as Benj. Stevens, ag. 7, poss. bearing his fa.'s name. Her husb. depos. in Charlest. in 1731 that ab. 44 yrs. past (in No. Yarm.) he built a dwg. ho. for Ann Stevens, wid. of Benj. and form. wid. of Thos. Shepherd. Naomi d. 16 Dec. 1710. He m. 2d 16 Apr. 1724 Rebecca Kettell. D. in Charlestown 24 Oct. 1732 in 67th yr. Ch: 8 + 2, incl. **Joseph**, eldest, b. No. Yarm. 4 Aug. 1689. **Amos**, b. 19 Aug. 1693, weaver, m. 8 Nov. 1722 Hannah Larrabee and settled in No. Yarm. Ch.

14 **JOSEPH**, joiner, bot in Portsm. in 1709. In Feb. 1711-2 he was almost murderously attacked by Ebenezer Morse; in June 1714, of Portsm., he and Jas. Johnson of Hampt. gave joint bond to pay Elisha Smith of Hampt. Portsm. tax abated 1714; and prob. then he rem. to York, the home of his w. Elizabeth Donnell (4), who was a wid. 10 Mar. 1725-6, and had two more husbs. Adm. on his est. 6 Apr. 1730. 1 son and 3 daus. rec. York 1714-17, of whom Saml., Phebe and Alice sold in 1739 their fa.'s 30 a. gr. of 1714-5. See also (23).

15 **NATHANIEL**, Kennebec 1672. List 13.

16 **NATHANIEL**, witn. deed from the Turbets to H. Symonds, in Berwick, 29 June 1687. Called of Rowley, he bot in York 1701-1703; served on jury at Kit. in May 1703, and was liv. in York the next mo., still there in 1706. Of Pembroke, Plym. Co., in Mar. 1714-5, he sold 50 a. at Coxhall to s.-in-law John Prichard of Boston; in May

calling hims. of York sold there to Prichard but ack. the deeds at Boston, and app. not then or later resident in Me.; d. Rowley 24 Apr. 1732. W. Elizabeth Hazen. 11 ch. 1670/1—1698.

17 NICHOLAS, ab. 22 in Aug. 1669, was at Goodman Lux's house (Great Isl.?); jury 1693. See Harrison.

18 ROBERT, on board Mr. Mead's ketch in the Piscataqua 1674. P. & Ct. ii. 493.

19 SAMUEL, cooper, Portsm., and Andrew Sampson bot at Sagamore Creek in 1670 from Geo. Jones sr. and sold to Jos. Berry in 1673; later he bot from Berry. Lists 312c, 331b. Liv. 1678; wid. Christian mar. her 2d husb. Lewis Williams bef. 24 Sept. 1681. See Carr(1). She was Wid. Christian Wyatt of Portsm. in 1734 when she deeded to gr. s. Thos. Mains for supp. of hers. and his mo. half the land and bldgs. bot of Jos. Berry, and land bot from Wm. Cotton; depos. 6 Dec. 1736, ±80. In 1698 she had two mar. daus: Patience, m. Thos. Mains, and in 1734 had the other half of the Harris land. Hannah, poss. Harris or Williams, m. Thos. Moore of York.

20 THOMAS, fisherman, bot John Brown's leasehold at Pemaquid from Wm. Bickford(24) 6 Nov. 1661. Y. D. 20.85. Poss. same as

21 THOMAS (Harries), adm. inhab. Saco 15 Mar. 1665.

22 THOMAS, late of Ditteson (Dittesham, see Tristram 26) near Dartmouth, co. Devon, boatswain on ketch -James- in Piscat. Riv., ab. to go to Fayal, made will 19 June 1667; w. Dewnes, 5 ch. under age, at Ditteson; d. that yr. Mar. 14, 1667-8 the wid. sent P/A to Thos. Jackson and Edw. Melcher, John Cutts a witn.

23 THOMAS, took O. A. at Kit. 6 Apr. 1680, witn. York deed 10 June 1681. Y. D. 6.16. He and w. abs. from meet. in May 1685; Francis and Nathl. Raynes sued him 1686. Jail-keeper, York, 1686; prison-keeper 1688-9; fined for swearing 1690. One Thos. was gr. j. 1702. Poss. fa. of William York, m. Tabitha (Moor), wid. of Thos. Vincent. 5 daus. 1721-1732. List 279. Others unattached in the vicin. may have belonged to him. See (14), (25).

24 THOMAS, Exeter 1714, where his connec. with Rich. Morgan, with whom he sold land in 1715, indic. relationship with (1). Of Stratham 1716, when sued by Westbrook. In suit of Morgan est. against Stephen England, he test. ab. the neighborhood 12 yrs. bef.; ano. witn. was Philip Duley whose sis. Sarah he m. at Oyster Riv. 25 July 1717. Of Dover 28 Sept. 1719 he sold Duley half the land in Scarb. recently bot from Wm. Burrage; witn. Duley's deed in Scarb. Feb. 1721-2; was sentinel at Black

Point 1723; liv. Scarb. Dec. 1723 with deceased w.'s sis. Mary (the law forbade their marriage), who had had several ch. by him. Of Dover, buying and selling in Scarb. 1726-9; not found later.

25 THOMAS, rated to No. Ch., Portsm., 1717; taxed Jan. 1731-2. One Thos. was drowned 1732, inq. at Portsm. Mary H., gone, Portsm. tax 1731-2. John and Abigail H. had two daus. bp. So. Ch. 1725-8. See (23).

26 TRISTRAM (also Harridon), Kittery 1659, s. of Tristram of Didsum (Dittesham), near Dartmouth, co. Devon. Thos. Gill depos. in 1682 that Tristram H. and Philip White's mo. were bros.' ch., both named Harradon, and both liv. with White's gr. fa. in par. of Cornworthy (2 m. from Dittesham), co. Devon. See also (22). In Kit. he took O. F. to Mass. 19 July 1669. Lists 25, 298. Impressed for Capt. Frost's co. against the Inds. in the Ossipee region in Sept. 1676; k. by Ind. prob. in that expedn. Inv. June 1677, inc. homestead 40 a., goods and clothing in John Brady's hands; adm. July-Nov. 1677 to Wm. Gowen al. Smith, a neighbor, to whose ch. he had told he would give his prop., and who divid. his lands; altho others made claims—the Bradys, John Turner who had m. his sis. Mary in Eng., and Philip White, who was gr. adm. in Prerog. Ct. of Canterbury, 22 Sept. 1681 and sued Wm. Gowen in 1684 and his wid. in 1695, while his s. Saml. White sued Gowens in 1729. Y. D. 3.16, 4.104. P. & Ct. ii.

27 WILLIAM, Smuttynose, witn. 1664, bot from Wm. Seeley in Apr. 1666 ho. and land already in his tenure. Fined in 1667 for letting his w., dau. of Roger Grant, sell beer by the pottle and by the gal.; the same yr. she was slandered by Stephen Ford. Poss. she was Rebecca H., atty. for one Wm. in action of debt ag. John Stover in York Ct. 1687. Adm. on his est. 27 Oct. 1668 to Andrew Diamond at req. of Capt. Francis Raynes; inv. 8 Oct. 1669, incl. one little ho. Poss. ch: John (10).

28 WILLIAM (Arise) of Boston fined at Saco 27 July 1676 for selling liquor to the fishermen. May have been the Boston man dealing with R. Elliot 1697. List 90.

HARRISON, general in north of England.
1 ———, Mr. & Co., taxed Portsm. 1713.
2 ABRAHAM, with Jas. Wiggin, witn. ag. Wm. Moore selling liquor, York Ct., May 1683. One Edmund H. int. mar. with Hannah Shaw at York 7 Apr. 1728.
3 NICHOLAS (often Harris), Dover, ±70 in 1703-4, yet appar. the same, ±36, who depos. with Benj. Matthews in 1681 ab. John York's land. See Nich. Harris (17).

He was first taxed in 1665 (Harris); once liv. in Walter Mathews's ho. built ab. 1669. When 70 yrs. old he depos. ab. this ho. and papers conc. it that were burned with his own ho. by the Inds. O. F. 1673, culler of staves 1674 (put out), witn. 1676-1704; sold strong drink to John Ault, ±70. In June 1679 Arthur Bennick mtg. to him land and part of a sawmill at Piscassick. Selectm. 1686, jury 1693; coroner's jury 1696. Lists 356j, 359ab, 365, 52, 92, 353, 57, 96, 358b. He m. Mary Bickford (12), whose fa. in 1677 deeded to them at Fox Point, where they liv. She d. bef. him. His will 5 Mar. 1707 (d. 11 Apr. 1708), gave prop. in N. H. and N. J. to daus. Ch: **Nicholas**, jr., d. 24 June 1704 (Downing Bible). **Elizabeth**, b. 4 Jan. 1679, m. Col. John Downing (4); recd. the homestead. **Temperance**, m. James Burnham (6).

4 **ROBERT**, had Kittery gr. 1671. He or ano., mariner, with his boat's crew tried to rescue a boat that upset, Oct. 1693. Lists 298, 318a.

5 **ROGER** (Harrissen), joiner, witn. ag. Henry Russell and w. at Great Isl. 1679.

6 **WILLIAM**, witn. Cleeves to Watts, 1648. Y. D. i. 84.

**Harrod**, see Harwood.

**HARRY**, 1 **Philip**. See Bryant (10).

2 **THOMAS**, witn. Parker fam. deed at Kennebec 1671. Y. D. 10.252. See Harwood (8).

**Harst**, John, Newcastle. List 315c. See Hurst.

**HART**. Poss. derived from the name of the male deer, and found throughout England.

1 **ARTHUR**, bondsm. for John Edwards (3) 10 Dec. 1651. P. & Ct. i. 173-4.

2 **JOHN**, shipwright, Portsm., adm. inhab. and gr. land 4 Jan. 1657-8. He had been in Boston; perh. earlier in N. H. as he gave receipt for Dover staves for Mr. Kemble, 1651. In Portsm. his w. Ann was on record more than he. In 1659 both witn. ag. Rich. Basson; she witn. ab. Mrs. Ann Batchelder's will 1661; he sold land in Hingham 1661; Geo. Jones fought with him and John Jackson and gave Ann a black eye, 1662. Lists 323, 326a, 330ab, 356L. Will 2 Mar. 1664-5—18 Sept. 1667 gave all to her, except to dau. the ho. and land in Boston she was then liv. in. The wid. liv. with Geo. Harris (4) in 1669; m. 2d Wm. Lucomb, and was in want in 1674-5 when Portsm. lent her supplies on acct. of the est. of her form. husb. Hart. He was called sr. in Boston 1656, but only one ch. seen: **Judith**, had three husbands in Boston, Robert Rachel by 1652, 3 daus; Thos. Reape, 1 son; Philip Bullis, 5 ch. If Ann's dau., she witn. in N. H. against her

own mo. for drinking in 1668. She and 3d husb. ptn. Gov. Cranfield ab. her fa.'s will, calling Ann 'our mother'; they had been twice to Piscat. to demand it, but Mr. Moody and Mr. Stileman refused them a copy.

3 **JOSEPH**, Ipswich, w. Jane Giddings. Son Thomas b. 20 Nov. 1705. N.H. Prov. Rec.

4 **JOSEPH**, blacksmith, b. Lynn 12 Sept. 1689, s. of Jos. and Ruth (Chadwell), bot in Berwick 10 Oct. and m. 8 Dec. 1718 Elizabeth Gowen(3). List 298. Adm. to James Gowen 10 Apr. 1769, she surv. 8 ch. bap.

5 **LYDIA**, sis. to (6), b. Ipsw. 10 Oct. 1671, m. in Portsm. 15 Sept. 1719 Wm. Parker.

6 **SAMUEL**, Esq., Portsm., b. Ipsw. 16 Aug. 1674, s. of Thos. and Mary (Norton), br. to (5), (8). He was taxed in Portsm. 1698 and bot there in 1702. Blacksmith. Selectm. 1714-15, 1728, Auditor, Surveyor of highways, Deacon of No. Ch. 1714, called Capt. 1714, Justice of Sessions Ct. 1733. Lists 330de, 337, 339. He m. 1st 2 May 1699 Mary Evans (12), who d. 23 June 1714, ag. 38; 2d 13 Jan. 1714-5 Mary Booth poss. wid. of James(2). She d. 1 Feb. 1755, soon aft. his own dec. 10 ch. 1700-1713, incl: **Mary**, m. Robt. Almary. **Samuel**, b. 20 Sept. 1701, carpenter, Portsm., m. 23 Dec. 1725 Bridget Cutts (6), who d. 5 Apr. 1773, ag. 70. Will 22 Nov. 1766—25 Feb. 1767, names w. and 6 ch. **Robert**, b. 16 Aug. 1704, Portsm., called tanner in 1747, m. 1st 19 Jan. 1728-9 Bethia Fitts of Ipsw., 2d 24 Oct. 1737 Elizabeth (Waterhouse), wid. of John Sargent, a wid. 1759. Col. **John**, b. 8 July 1706, blacksm. Portsm. and Newington, m. 1st 23 Mar. 1729 Abigail Landall(1), d. 21 —— 173-, in 31st yr.; 4 ch; 2d Sarah (Savell) Cutts, d. 24 Aug. 1757, ag. 42, 6 ch; 3d Mary (Dennett), wid. of Jona. Stoodley, 1 ch. He d. 30 Oct. 1777; she m. 3d 12 Nov. 1780 Nehemiah Furber. **Thomas**, b. 30 Aug. 1708, m. 1st 15 July 1731 Elizabeth Cotton (Wm.), d. 18 Sept. 1761, ag. 48; 2d 14 Nov. 1762 Anne Noyes of Newb. Will 19—28 Mar. 1781 names 6 ch.

7 **THOMAS** (Harte) signed testim. in fav. of Anthony Lamey in 1672. Prob. k. in the Ind. attack on York 24 Jan. 1691-2.

8 **ENSIGN THOMAS**, blacksmith, br. to (6), b. Ipsw. 15 Nov. 1667. Mar. 15, 1697-8 he and w. Mary released to Solomon Hughes, who in 1703 deeded ho. lot in Portsm. to them during Mary's life.

9 **WILLIAM**, in 163-, sent his regards by Rich. Foxwell coming from the French at Penobscot.

10 **WILLIAM**, ±23, liv. with Andrew Searle on Great Isl. 1702; taxed Portsm. 1719. One Wm. was drowned in York River in Oct. 1733.

**Hartopp**, Richard, witn. at Salmon Falls with John Wincoll 1679. Y. D. 3.47.

**HARTSHORN**, 1 **John**, clerk, from Haverhill, under Capt. Hill at Wells 1693-4. List 267b.

2 **JOHN**, son-in-law of John Brown (16).

**HARVEY**, an ancient Norman givenname.

1 ———, Goody, Saco 1674. List 246. One Widow H. was helped by Salem 1678-9. See also (16).

2 **AMY**, likely sis., poss. mo. of Thos.(14), witn. his deed to Edw. Cowell in 1666, witn. for him again in 1670. One -Ane- witn. by mark Lawrence Carpenter's will 1677, Roger Kelly ano. witn. Poss. a younger Amy, dau. of (14), was the legatee under Mrs. Eleanor Cutts' will, 1684.

3 **CLEMENT**, Greenland 1681; taxed 1714. List 52. The same as Clement Misharvie (Meserve) taxed there 1688, 1713?

4 **HENRY**, ±22, witn. ab. the Olivers at the Shoals in 1673; there in 1677, ±28. List 306a. Poss. the mariner ±43 at Salem, 1693 and later.

5 **JOACHIM**, Mr., Great Isl., ±40 in 1670-1, ±44 in 1675, often wrote his name Jo: sometimes appar. John. Evidently kinship of hims. or w. Clear to the Fryer fam. brot him to Gt. Isl., where first found in Aug. 1667, working for Mr. Fryer, and oft. a Fryer witn. during the next few yrs; 'Mr. and Mrs. Harve with more of the said Fryer's family' ment. 1673. Freeman 19 May 1669. Selectm. 1672, 74, 76. Ensign 1673. On Portsm. commit. 28 May 1676, and app. the -John- who appraised Edw. West's est. 1 Sept. 1677. Lists 330a (Jenkin), 326c, 312cf, 324, 83, 313a, 331b. Adm. 24 Sept. 1678 to wid. Clear and Benj. Dole in beh. of his w.; inv. incl. ho. and wareho. Only ch: **Elizabeth**, m. 1st Benj. Dole(2), 2d Robert Jordan(8). See also (13).

6 **JOHN**, witn. for Fryer 1668. Y. D. ii. 68. See Joachim(5).

7 **MIRTH** (Harvie?), Shoals fishing-master 1673

8 **ONESIPHORUS**, Isles of Shoals 1665, witn. H. Greenland's deed 1669; Mr. John Paine sued him for debt in Essex Q. Ct., 1671. Adm. 8 May 1672 to Thos. Daniel(7).

9 **PETER**, Falmouth 1662, witn. deed of Elizabeth (Cleeves 1) Mitton, 1 Mar. 1662-3, and prob. promptly m. her, tho she is first found as Harvey 26 July 1666, then adm. of Thos. Morris's est. He d. bef. 2 June 1671. List 25. No kn. ch., unless Peter(10) a son by an earlier mar. One John H. m. in Boston 23 Oct. 1712 Martha More, appar. P. H.'s step-gr.-dau. See Clarke (52). June 2, 1671, the wid. Elizabeth

deeded to Thos. and Mary Brackett, her dau., for life supp., he giving bond. She was fleeing from Casco Bay in Aug. 1676, List 224, yet Thaddeus Clarke addressed a letter to her in Boston 14 Aug. 1676, 3 days aft. the attack on Falm. (Reg. 31.288). In Falm. 8 July 1680 she assigned the Brackett bond to Thaddeus Clarke, made it void in Aug. 1681 and assigned it again to Clarke 5 Sept. 1683, in Falm.; not found later. Y. D. ii. iii. iv.

10 **PETER**, bearing name of (9), it may or may not be signif. that he appeared at the Piscat. the same time as did John Graves (2). On the other hand a poss. Kelly connec. may point to Thomas(14) as a kinsman. Taxed Str. Bk. 1681; in 1686 entert. his sis. and two ch. from Boston (John Kelly's w. and ch.?). Taxed Greenl. 1688-90. Lists 329, 330a, 332b. If same as (11) or (12), he is unobs. in N. H. nearly 30 yrs. One Peter and w. Sarah had s. Samuel rec. Weymouth, Mass., 27 Aug. 1696, who m. there, int. 25 July 1723, Ruth Howard, and d. 17 May 1733, leaving ch.

11 **PETER**, Capt. ship -Happy Return-, at the Piscataqua, drowned by upsetting of a boat 7 Mar. 1718-9; adm. to Capt. Joshua Pierce.

12 **PETER**, taxed Newcastle 1720, bot there 1726. In 1728 with w. Elizabeth he deeded to (her, poss. not his) dau. **Elizabeth** and husb. Abraham Sheriff. Liv. Newc. 1729-1732.

13 **RICHARD**, Great Isl. 1671, ±22 in 1673, gave same age in 1675. Lists 326c, 312f, 313a. On June 11, 1678 the selectm. of Portsm. made agreem. with Capt. Barefoot ab. the cure of his broken leg, but he d., Mr. R. H., 13 June; adm. next day to Robt. Elliott, inv. £18. His tax abated 5 Feb. 1679-80. No kn. w. or ch. See also (5).

14 **CAPT. THOMAS**, mariner, Portsm. 1663, bot in 1664 from Rich. Cutts and sold half to Edw. Cowell(2) in 1666. An indicated Cowell connection is unproven; poss. Cowell's w. Agnes was his sister. See also Amy Harvey(2). Mr. T. H. taxed Portsm. 1673; O. F. at Boston 27 May, 1678; witn. Mrs. Agnes Cowell's will; gave bond in 1682 not to take away men from Newfoundland; O. A. 28 Aug. 1685; lic. retailer 1686, 1692-4. Lists 326c, 331abc, 49, 51, 329, 62, 98. He m. 1st Elizabeth Wall (James) bef. 20 Aug. 1663 when they sold her land in Hampton; 2d bef. 7 Nov. 1681 Elizabeth Kelly, dau. of David and Elizabeth of Boston, b. ab. 1651. Suff. D. 12.145, 21.577, 30.270. Her depos. 10 Dec. 1721, ±70, conc. Maj. Vaughan's ho. 49 yrs. bef. may set the time of her mar. Thos. (jr.) depos. in Feb. 1733-4 that his fa. last sailed out of Piscat. Riv. 30 yrs. ago, was taken by the French

and d. in France. She was a lic. retailer 1695-97 (called widow 1697), lic. pub. ho. 1698 and later; in 1703 witn. will of Joshua Fryer, Wm. Kelly also a witn., prob. dead 30 Jan. 1726-7 when adm. on her husb.'s est. gr. to s. Thos. Lists 330d, 331c, 337. See Cowell. Ch., order and mo. not determ.: **Elizabeth**, m. 1st 11 Oct. 1689 Elisha Plaisted, appar. m. 2d aft. 6 July 1693 Elisha Ilsley, 3d in May 1709 Robt. Rutherford (Rutheson, Rediford), barber, Portsm.; adm. on his est. to Wm. Fellows, bond 19 July 1715. **Eleanor**, m. 1st Saml. Cutts(9), 2d Thos. Phipps. **Mary**, m. 1st Mark Hunkings(3), 2d 5 Dec. 1699 Rev. John Newmarch. In 1695 Saml. and Eleanor Cutts deeded to her, singlewoman. **Martha**; in 1695, single, witn. deed to her sis. Mary; m. 1st John Wilson, 2d bef. 13 Feb. 1699-1700 Geo. Veasey. **Hannah**; in 1699 her sis. Eleanor Cutts deeded to her, single woman; m. Joseph Jones; liv. Newport, R. I., 1716. **Agnes**, m. by 1708 Wm. Moore of Stratham. **Thomas** (cert. by 2d w.), b. ab. 1686. **?Amy**, willed two cows and six sheep by Mrs. Eleanor Cutts(5) in 1684, poss. a dau. or (2). **?Abigail**; appar. Harvey or Cowell (2). See Coombs(1).
15 **THOMAS**(14), innholder, Portsm., depos. in Feb. 1733-4, ±47, conc. his fa.'s death. He was taxed 1708; m. bet. 25 Feb.— 1 Apr. 1714 Anne Jose(2); adm. to her 13 Aug. 1736; invent. £807, 10s. 7d. List 339. She m. 2d 15 Feb. 1737-8 Capt. Wm. Slayton of Portsm., from Sandwich, co. Kent; adm. to her 25 Nov. 1740. Inventory of real est. of herself and 1st husb. taken 29 Aug. 1760, amt. £6625. **John**, boatbuilder, Portsm., eldest s. and admr., with other heirs petn. for div., had long been kept out of their shares. 8 ch. represented in div., incl. ano. son **Richard**.
16 **THOMAS**, soldier at Ft. Mary 1699, k. at Winter Harb. or Saco 1703. List 39. See also (1).
**Harwell**, Stephen, Shoals 1673, abs. from w. Portsm. tailor (Horwell), 1675. Lists 305b, 359a. See Horrell.

**HARWOOD**, Harrod. Harwood the name of six parishes and hamlets in England.
1 ————, Mr., breach of bond, Casco Ct. 26 July 1666. P. & Ct. i. 316. Likely (5).
2 **ANDREW** (Harrod), Oyster River 1643; witn. Darby Field to Wm. Roberts 1645; Newington 1663. He gave his name to a creek, cove and point, all ment. 1666-1686. Lists 42, 342, 330a. One Andrew in 1645 was fa.-in-law of Thos. Finson, mariner, late of Dartmouth, Eng. Reg. 3.79.
3 **LIEUT. HENRY**, shoemaker, was Ensign under Lt. Edw. Creeke at Wells in Oct. 1676 when Walter Gendall came urging

them to surrender. If the same Henry who was at Roger Rose's ho. at Oyster Riv. in 1681, a connec. with (2) may be indic. Falm. 1682; the next yr. at his own req. relieved from command of the Foot Co. He bot Rev. Geo. Burroughs' ho. at Falm. and mtg. it to Bozoan Allen in Boston 1 Aug. 1685. Tr. j. 1686. Witn. with and for Fryer and Jordans at Falm. 1685-8. Lists 225a, 226, 228c. Not found aft. 1689; if liv., prob. ret. to Boston, where he and w. Elizabeth (liv. 1685) had 5 ch. rec. 1665-1674, altho in 1671 he was app. in Milford.
4 **JAMES** (Herod). Smuttinose witn. 1706.
5 **JOHN** (Horwood), depos. July 1663 conc. action taken on Penobscot and Eastern forts when he was in London, 1661. Reg. 8.287. See also (1).
6 **JOHN**, soldier at Kennebec 1689. List 189. Poss. (7).
7 **JOHN** (Harrod), fisherman, Marblehead, m. Mary Parker (Thos. of Kennebec); both dead 27 Apr. 1730. Ch: Mary, m. in Boston 2 Feb. 1710 Jos. Clewly; dec. by Nov. 1732, leav. ch. **Elizabeth**, m. in Boston 17 Apr. 1724 Peter Gibbons; liv. 1732. Y. D. 13.212, 15.378-83.
8 **THOMAS**, Pemaquid 1672. List 13. See Harry (2). One Thos. was of Boston before and after 1672.
**Hasag**, John, with (Rev.) John Pike witn. (Rev.) Thos. Mighill's deed of Patrick Jameson's land to John Webster, 1670.
**Hasey**, Joseph, ship carpenter. List 14.
**Haskell**, John, coroner's jury, Portsm., 1663. List 327a.

**HASKINS** (Heskins, Hoskins). From Haw or Hal (Henry) with the diminutive 'kin'.
1 **ELIAS** (Hoskins). List 10.
2 **JOHN** (Hoskin), fisherman, Richmond Isl., in acct. 1634. List 21.
3 **JOHN** (Hoskins), Shoals 1664; drunk 1666; abs. from meeting 1667. List 303.
4 **JOHN** (Hoskins), Pemaquid 1687-8. Lists 124, 189. See (6).
5 **NICHOLAS** (aut. Heskins), ±36 Sept. 1673, ±40 Feb. 1678, ±45 Oct. 1681, appar. came to Boston bef. his br. (6) came over. Y. D. 4.100. Taxed Great Isl. 1671. Schoolmaster; bookkeeper for Robt. Elliot (6) and witn. Portsm.-Newc. deeds 1673-1703. Jury 1674. Lists 312cfh, 306b, 313ab, 317, 52, 319. Liv. a bachelor; as worthy as his br. unworthy, he evid. devoted his life to fathering his brother's neglected ch. Based on Savage's statement that Nicholas Haskins was of Dighton in 1708, a Taunton marriage rec. 2 Aug. 1686 of 'Richard Haskins of Providence' and 'Jane Feuster (or Fenster) of Taunton', and Miss Calkins's statements that Richard d. 1718 leaving 9

ch., John d. 1719 leaving 7 ch., the conclusion has been printed and reprinted that Nicholas with sons John and Richard went from Portsm., N. H. to Dighton and the sons thence to Norwich. But it was Nicholas -Stephens- at Dighton; with Providence only a day's walk distant the marriage rec. would have specified Piscataqua if so; and Miss Calkins's sources are undisc.

6 **WILLIAM**, Great Island, joiner, br. of (5); signed by mark. July 9-10, 1672 Wm. H., w. and ch. from Ireland 'admitted to sett downe in this Jurisdiction'; Wm. H., a joiner, lately arriv. in this place with his w. and ch., is adm., etc., in any such town as the selectm. shall approve. He bot his ho. and land 28 Oct. 1676, and at times had several apprentices. Tav. lic. 1683. Tax abated 18 Dec. 1683. Jury 1688. Lists 330a, 331ab, 313afg, 55a, 92. Last taxed Jan. 1688-9. His name appears freq. in records in ways to lose him the respect of the community. W. Christian (fine aut.), taxed Wid. H. 1690, 1691, may have been a namesake of Mrs. Christian Fryer. The Haskins ho. was deeded by Capt. and Mrs. F., and their s.-in-law Elliot for some reason relinq. adm. on his est. She m. 2d Henry Williams of Hampton (from Saco and Scarb.); liv. Williams 10 Apr. 1712. W. H.'s ptn. 1681, 'a charge of ch. to maintain'; named here not by ages, but by degrees of likelihood: **Lydia**, stepdau. in Henry Williams's will 1712, app. the oldest by Thomas Chase's will. **Elizabeth**, witn. a note to her stepfa. 1 May 1701, m. 3 Nov. 1701 Samuel Johnson(31). **Rachel**, m. James Philpott; 2d 6 or 7 June 1709 James Chaddock (Chadwick 1), who was granted 15 June 1713 adm. on her fa.'s est. These three are clearly proven; the following three presum. **Charles** and **Philip**, working ab. the bridge, Great Isl. 1683. N. H. Ct. Papers 7.43. **Zachariah**, taxed Str. Bk. list 5 Dec. 1688. **Jane**, under 18 in 1698, called 'my Kinswoman who lives with me' in Thomas Wacomb's will. So long as this relationship is undisc., she may have come from a distance. She m. bef. 1721 Nathaniel Odiorne, fisherman. **John**, taxed 1687 at Pemaquid, listed near others who escaped to Scituate, presum. the same of Scituate in 1695 and in 1716 who m. Ruth Atkins(5). Ch: Benjamin, Samuel, b. 1699, Martha, b. 1706. The roll of a Scarb. company in 1723 includes 'Benj. Horskins of Scituate,' who bot a farm near that of Benj. and Sarah (Johnson) Larrabee, she dau. of Elizabeth (Haskins) Johnson, and named his only ch. Sarah.

**Hastier?**, Nicholas, witn. in Portsm. or Kittery, 1712. Y. D. 8.144.

**Hastings**, Joseph, witn. Pendleton deeds 1660-1. Y. D. i. 102, 108.

**HATCH**, a place name, a 'hatch' being a gate across a highway.

1 **CHARLES**, s. of John, bp. at Newton Ferrers, co. Devon, 5 Sept. 1613; came to Richmond Isl. in 1633, a fisherman, then and in 1634 under his master Clement Penwill of Newton F.; came again 13 Feb. 1636-7 with br. (3), leaving a w. behind. The Trel. acct. 27 May 1639 shows money pd. to her; in 1640 he would not allow payment as she had not written an acct. of that already recd. Summoned as a witn. in 1641 and not found in Me. records again until adm. gr. to br. Philip 29 June 1654. Lists 21, 244b.

2 ***JOHN***, Mr., Capt., mariner, Portsmouth. Consid. by desc. an immigrant from England, the mar. of his dau. into the Downing-Hatch fam. may point to (3) as his fa. He was at Great Isl. 15 Jan. 1684-5, mate of the -Success-; in June sailed on the ketch -America-, John Jackson master. Taxed Str. Bk. Dec. 1688; from that time maint. his home in Portsm. and kept his goods in the old Cutts wareho. Taxed 1690, and house. His and his w.'s seating at the meetho. denoted a good social position. On Sept. 14, 1695, in London, he identif. the handwriting of Rich. Martyn, Speaker, and testif: 'being in N. H. ab. 2 yrs. since' heard great complaints among the inhabitants of apprehension of the Inds. Rep. 1696, jury 1699. In 1698 he bot near the Great House; in 1699 the Rymes wharf and wareho. Lists 314, 57, 335a, 330def. Adm. to wid. Sarah 2 May 1701. List 335a. She was taxed May 1707; in Portsm. acct. that yr., Mrs. Sarah Hatch credited 'by the use of your house.' Ch: Capt. **Samuel**, mariner, Portsm., taxed 1713, d. 22 Aug. 1716. Adm. 5 Feb. 1717-8 to wid. Elizabeth, who was rated to the No. Ch. 1717. List 339. She m. 2d Daniel Greenough (Robert), and d. in Bradford 3 Dec. 1765 in 73d yr. Ch: Thomas, hatter, Portsm., poss. the s. of Saml. and Elizabeth rec. in Boston 25 Sept. 1713. W. Mary in 1752, and m. by 1758 Alice Knight(10). (A son of this marriage transferred a Jersey tradition from his mother's to his father's ancestry.) In July 1757 he receipted for ⅛ of his mo.'s est., also for ⅛ for heirs of his sis. Sarah, b. 26 Mar. 1717, m. Wm. Odiorne, Esq. **Sarah**, m. 1st Joshua Downing (5 jr.), 2d James Chadbourne (3 jr.) **Anne**, recd. into covt., No. Ch., 29 Nov. 1713; m. in Kit. 17 Jan. 1716 Saml. Small. One Nathaniel (Hach), sailmaker, was of Portsm. 1719; of Newcastle alias Newport in 1722 when Danl. Greenough sued him on note for lodging and work done by his w.; presum. related; and poss. fa. of George (Hach), bp. No. Ch. 6 Jan. 1722-3. One Nathl. (Hatch) and w. Comfort had 3 ch.

rec. Newport, R. I., 1728-1732; he d. in Bristol, R. I., in 1739.

**3 PHILIP**, fisherman, York, bp. at Newton Ferrers 28 Dec. 1616, came to Richmond Island in -The Hercules- 13 Feb. 1636-7 with br. (1). Payments the first 4 yrs. were to his master Nich. Ball; last ment. in Trel. acct. 27 June 1643. In Nov. 1648 he bot Geo. Parker's ho. and land at York adj. Wm. Dixey's field; town grants 1653, 1659. Jury of life and death 21 July 1650; Tr. j. 1650, 51, 65; Constable 1663, the same yr. he was in Ct. with others for neglect of duty in not voting. He mtg. ho. and land to Maj. Pendleton in July 1663, Jasper Pulman buying from Pendleton and the widow in 1674; in 1668 mtg. 5 a. to Francis Johnson who had got judgm. against him and Jas. Dixey. Last found 4 July 1671 ackn. judgm. to Francis Wainwright; some few yrs. deceased in Aug. 1674. Lists 21, 275, 276, 244b, 24. His w. Patience, app. dau. of Robt. Edge, witn. as Hatch 27 Mar. 1675; m. 2d one Wolcott, prob. Edw., a witn. with Joshua Downing 13 Sept. 1680. She was in Eliot with the Nasons 24 Oct. 1709. Kn. ch: **Francis**, witn. for Robt. Knight 18 May 1667; in Ct. 15 Sept. 1668 with Jas. Dixey for attacking Isaac Everett on York Riv. **Philip**, ±22, 10 July 1673, at the Shoals, app. master of Peter Twisden's shallop; Mr. Philip in 1680; on coroner's jury there 1687. Lists 90, 307a. **Patience**, lately mar. to Joshua Downing(5), 16 Jan. 1676. Y. D. iii. 115. **Benjamin**. In 1684 John Brawn jr. was slandering him and Elizabeth Paine (Thos.); in Apr. 1685 he was in the woods making oxbows which Nathl. Adams brot out. D., or inv. taken, 21 Feb. 1689-90, clothing, gun, 1 cow; adm. next mo. to br. Saml. **Samuel**, b. ±1660-1. **Elizabeth**, m. by 1692 Baker Nason. One Patience Hatch m. in Gloucester, 1st 17 Jan. 1710-11 Richard York, 2d 15 Mar. 1719-20 Geo. Harvey; one Mary m. in Ipsw. 17 Nov. 1711 John Wood. These girls of a fam. name almost unkn. in early Essex Co. poss. were daus. of one of Philip's sons, separated from their kin by their fa.'s early death. See also John Hatch(2).

**4 ROBIN**, with crew of -The Margery- 1643. List 21.

**5 SAMUEL**(3), millman, b. 1659-62, was apprent. at the age of 7 in Wells, evid. to Saml. Wheelwright, and had his first home on 200 a. on Ogunquit Riv. bot from Mrs. Mary Bowles in May 1684; liv. later at Maryland Riv., where he bot from Caleb Kimball 10 July 1710. Lists 33, 269abc. Gr. j. 7 times 1692-1710. In Mar. 1749, ag. 90, and June 1750, ag. 94, he depos. that he had been an inhab. of Wells ab. 83 yrs. He m. 1st (Ct. May 1685) Mary Littlefield(12), 2d

one Lydia from the Ch. at York, adm. to Wells Ch. as Lydia Hatch in 1723. She was liv. 1737, not in his will 3 Feb. 1741-2—16 Oct. 1753, naming 8 ch. and ch. of decd. dau. Jemima; s. Jos. exec. and princ. heir, the others already provid. for. Ch: **Bethia**, b. 9 Apr. 1685, m. John Butland (1 jr.). **Benjamin**, b. 29 Sept. 1688, liv. 1750; w. Elizabeth, m. by 1714. In 1749 he and Saml. jr. were bondsm. for Ann Taylor. List 269c. 9 ch. **Jemima**, b. 29 Nov. 1690, m. Jos. Freethy(3). **Samuel**, b. 2 Feb. 1693, m. 22 Aug. 1715 Abigail Fletcher(8). List 269c. 8 ch. **Mary**, b. 25, d. 28 Mar. 1695. **Nathan**, bp. 12 July 1702; not in poll tax list or fa.'s will. **John**, bp. 13 Feb. 1703-4, m. (int. 29 Sept. 1723) Mary Low(4); his est. settled 1754. List 269c. 12 ch. **Philip**, bp. 2 Jan. 1703-4, m. 1 Jan. 1727 Elizabeth Low(4). List 269c. 11 ch. **Eunice**, bp. 13 Feb. 1703-4, m. Jos. Getchell(6). **Mary**, bp. 12 May 1706, m. (int. 8 Nov. 1735) Benj. Stevens. **Joseph**, b. 8 May 1709, m. 1st (int. 3 Oct. 1730) Hannah Sawyer, 2d 12 July 1739 Jerusha Young of York. Adm. to her 24 Apr. 1753. Ch. 3+6. App. it was ano. Joseph in Biddeford 1733, pub. to Abigail Fletcher there 18 Jan. 1734-5, and acc. by her in Apr. 1735.

**HATHERLY**, Henry, m. at Saco 4 July 167[1?] Elizabeth -Barlow-; prob. then of Cape Porpus, where he sold land on Batson's Riv. to Rich. Young in 1671, and was liv. in 1675. In Apr. 1672 he was sentenced for soliciting mar. women, and again in 1675. Lic.pub.ho. July 1673. He sued Simon Booth in 1673, was sued by Peter Weare, treas., in 1674, by Thos. Baston same yr. for tearing down his fence. Inv. 27 Mar. 1677 (N. H.); debts incl. funeral charges of hims. and w., poss. Ind. victims.

## HATHORNE.

**1 ELEAZER** (3), m. 28 Aug. 1663 Abigail Corwin (Capt. Geo. of Salem), and was in charge of the mills in Wells in the Corwin int. 1679 to death 31 Jan. 1679-80. List 269b.

**2 JOHN**, d. in service of Mr. Richard Cutts. Adm. in Essex Co. to his fa. Mr. John H. 24 June 1673.

**3 MAJOR WILLIAM**, Salem, comr. for Yorkshire 1662-63.

**4 CAPT. WILLIAM**(3), Salem. List 237a.

**Hatwell**, Benjamin. List 222b. Read Atwell. Bodge, p. 318.

**Haugham**, Francis, Newc. witn. 1698. N. E. Reg. 69.362.

**Haughton**, John, Boston, master of ketch -Endeavor- stole Inds. at Eastern parts and sold them at Fayal in 1676.

**Havercombe**, John, Popham colony 1607. List 6.

**Hawes**, Thomas. Scarboro soldier 1676-7. List 237b.

**HAWKINS**, a Devon-Cornwall name.

1 **CHRISTOPHER**, m. at Kittery 24 Jan. 1728-9 Margery Spinney (Thos.); liv. there 1733.

2 **EDMUND**, m. at Hampton 21 July 1715 Elizabeth Kelly.

3 **FRANCIS** (Haukins), witn. Moses fam. deed 1679.

4 **JAMES**, Dover, a minor (1680?). List 359b.

5 **JOB**, arrested in Dover 1652 on debt of Francis Smith, Boston. Prob. the one in the -Planter- from London, 1635, ag. 15. Kinsman of Maj. Wm. Holmes, Boston. W. Frances. Ch: **Martha**, rec. Boston 26 Mar. 1646-7.

6 **JOHN**, mariner, Boston. (See Damerill 1).

7 **NARIAS**, Mr., shipmaster, Richmond Isl. 1635-1640, came in the -Speedwell- 26 Apr. 1635 bringing Mr. Edward Trelawny and company of men on contract with hims. to fish and plant 3 yrs. Left in charge while Winter was in England, the Ct. 25 Mar. 1636 gave him author. to execute any Inds. proven to have k. swine of the English. List 21.

8 **STEPHEN**, mariner, Dover. Peter and Elizabeth Varney deeded to him 1719, 1725. M. 14 Apr. 1719 Rachel, wid. of Nich. Wallingford. Ch: **John**, b. 19 Mar. 1720. Likely s. by an earlier w: **Stephen**, w. Sarah, 12 ch. 1739-1756.

9 **THOMAS**, abuttor to Robt. Edgecomb, Saco, 1718. Jan. 5, 1731, s. **John**, weaver, Marbleh., and w. Abigail, sold land in Saco his fa. bot from Geo. Page. Y. D. 14.247.

**Hawkridge** (Hockridge, Haggeridge), Abel, Monhegan 1662; O. A. 1674. Lists 13, 15.

**Hawksworth**, Martha, Biddeford, witn. thrice with Wm. Graves, 1720-1. Y. D. 10. See also Willix.

**Haydon**, John, adm. gr. to br. Thos. 28 June 1670 at Portsm. court.

**HAYES**, parishes in cos. Middlesex and Kent.

1 **ANDREW**, taxed Newc. 1720.

2 **EDWARD**, Mr., Kittery, liv. near Cold Harbor. Lieut. 1661 to death; also militant by dispo. and found mostly in ct. records, in July 1659 for breach of the peace, 1671 threaten. to k. the marshal and constab., 1673 taking H. Chadbourne by the throat, also abs. from home over night. In Oct. 1660 he gave a bill to W. Barefoot, appar. in connec. with Henry Berkeley, whose est. was in his hands in 1661, and had trouble with Barefoot to 1673; in 1672 W. B. got judgm. for a debt ack. in Saco altho 'he never was in Saco in his life.' Tr. j. 1666; abs. from meet. 1668. Lists 285, 298.

In Nov. 1671 he gave P/A to his w. Philadelphia Jenkins (9), who was abs. from meet. July 1675. His will 2 July 1675, prov. 9 Mar. 1675-6, two days aft. her fa. ack. a deed to her of the ho. and land in her deed. husb.'s tenure. She m. 2d Matthew Estes (1). Ch. in will, all under age; **Joseph**, one Jos. Hays and Joshua Fryer witn. bond from Thos. Daniel, Wm. Vaughan and Rich. Waldron jr. to Mr. Joshua Moody 18 Apr. 1683. **William**, wounded in expedn. east 1691, liv. Kit. 1694. Lists 37, 298. **Elizabeth**. **Sarah**. **Ann**.

3 **JOHN**, Dover, by trad. from Scotland ab. 1680, while a br. Ichabod went So. and left desc. there. He witn. for John Ham 24 Jan. 1688-9 and had 20 a. gr. in Mar. 1693-4 near Tole-End adj. John Ham jr. Witn. John Gerrish's will 12 July 1706. In 1708 his s. Peter depos. ab. his fa.'s garrison. Lists 52, 57, 62, 96. D. 25 Oct. 1708. W. Mary Horne(?6), m. 28 June 1686, then 13 yrs. old by trad. Ch: **John**, b. ab. 1687, Deacon, liv. at Tole-End, d. 3 July 1759. List 358d. M. 1st by 1711 Tamson (Wentworth), wid. of James Chesley(3), who d. 30 Dec. 1753, ag. 66; 2d Mary (Roberts) wid. of Saml. Wingate. 11 ch: **Peter**, ±20 Feb. 1707-8, liv. at Tole-End. List 358d. In 1753 of Dover, husbandm., he deeded to sons Ichabod and Elijah land in Berw.; d. 1757. M. by 1718 Sarah Wingate (John). 11 ch. **Robert**. **Ichabod**, b. 18 Mar. 1691-2, liv. at Madbury; m. (int. 30 July 1715) Abigail Evans(14). He d. 1 June 1734, k. by a mill log; adm. to widow, her bond 7 Apr. 1735. 8 ch. She m. 2d 1737-1744 Wm. Twombley. **Samuel**, b. 16 Mar. 1694-5; owned and occup. part of the garrison many yrs., d. there ab. 1770. M. 7 July 1720 Leah Dam(5). 2 daus. rec. 1721-1728. **William**, b. 6 Sept. 1698, m. 23 Nov. 1720 Hannah Sanborn. Dover gr. 8 July 1734 to est. of Wm. H. 2 daus. rec. 1721-23, poss. other ch. **Benjamin**, b. 6 Sept. 1700, m. by 1726 Jane (Snell). wid. of Tristram Heard jr. (11 jr.); liv. Rochester, d. 16 May 1756. 9 ch. bp., 6 at Dover 1728-1735, 3 at Roch. 1739-1743. **Abigail**, m. 10 May 1720 Nathl. Fitts of Salis. 3 daus. rec. Salis. She d. 12 June 1738, he m. 2d Mehitable Dearborn. Her mar. suggests that two others mar. in Salis. were sisters, **Mary**, m. (int. 26 Sept. 1724) Henry Ambrose. 3 ch. rec. Salis. 1725-1730, incl. Robt. A wid. of Chester 24 June 1746, she renounc. adm. in fav. of the eldest s. Jona. (by a 1st w.), witn. Nathl. and Mehitable Fitts. **Elizabeth**, m. 6 Mar. 1729 John Ambrose. 1 ch. rec. Salis. The Hist. of Chester, where they liv., says 6 ch., incl. Robt. One Mary (Haise) m. in Salis. (int. 29 Feb. 1723-4) Jeremiah Flanders, 1 ch. b. 15 July 1725. He m. 2d 29 Dec. 1726 Mehitable Hoyt.

4 **ROBERT** (Haye?), Hampt. 1677. List 54.

5 **THOMAS,** ±28, depos. 4 Sept. 1682 ab. his dame Mary Cater's fence pulled down by Ephr. Trickey.

**HAYMAN,** a Devon name.

1 **ABRAHAM,** Bideford, Eng., step-son of Geo. Shurt of same (br. of Abraham Shurt) did not come, but through atty. Edmund Downes bot from Lt. Wm. Phillips, in his debt, ¼ the Vines patent 29 June 1663. July 26, 1681 his heirs, Henry Amory and Saml. Leache, gave P/A to Geo. Turfrey of Boston; in Mar. 1738-9 Wm. Pepperell jr. was atty. for Geo. Buck, Esq., and w. Sarah, executrix.

2 **JOHN,** witn. for Rich. Fulford at Muscongus 1653; at Monhegan Jan. 1655-6, ±40. Lists 121, 111. His age not in close agreem. with that of Maj. John, ropemaker, b. 1610-11, at Boston 1662, adm. inhab. Charlest. 1663, fa. of (5).

3 **JOHN,** ±18, 24 Oct. 1681; ab. 3 yrs. ago helped to raft logs to Mr. Goffe; his master Joshua Downing. Orig. by Capt. John Wincoll spelt Haymon, record by Rishworth spelt (Haymon altered to Heamon?, or vice versa).

4 **PENTICOST,** fisherman, Richmond Isl. 1638-40. List 21.

5 **SAMUEL** (2), one of the Mass. men named as Justices of York Co., by Sir Wm. Phips.

**HAYWARD.** See also Howard.

1 **JOHN,** plaint. in Dover Ct. 1661.

2 **JOHN,** Boston. List 238b.

3 **RICHARD,** coroner's jury, Newcastle, 1670. List 312b.

4 **ROBERT** (Heywood), planter, par. of St. Thomas, Barbadoes, W. I., mar. poss. not in Me., Elizabeth Lewis (19). Their int. in the Saco Patent was handled several yrs. by his br.-in-law Jas. Gibbins (2) under his P/A dated 10 Jan. 1660, and eventually was vested in Mrs. Gibbins. Widow Elizabeth made her will in 1680, prov. 10 June 1682, naming several gr. ch. in addi. to ch: **Richard. John. Robert. Nathaniel. Elizabeth. Martha. Hester,** m. John Orpen, and in 1689 recd. annuity of £50 under will of Thos. Lewis, Esq., a Royal Counsellor of Barbadoes, whose apparent relationship has not been established.

5 **SAMUEL** (Hayword), Falmouth 1703, depos. in Reading in July 1732, ±65, ab. the Phippens.

**HAZELTON,** Haseltine. Hazelton a par. in Gloucestershire.

1 **ABRAHAM.** Lists 98, 90. Likely the 3d husb. of Hannah (Drew 17) Brookings-Follett, and the Bradford man who d. 28 Apr. 1711; br. to (2), (4).

2 **GERSHOM,** Bradford, m. 23 June 1690 Abiah Dalton (3); d. 16 Oct. 1711. 1 ch. rec. She or a dau. m. in Bradford 12 Apr. 1715 Andrew Mitchell.

3 **MAXIMILIAN** (4), Bradford, b. 1687, m. 1st aft. 1717 Martha Jackson (13). 5 ch. 1724-1732.

4 **ROBERT,** Bradford, m. 1st 21 July 1680 Elizabeth Jewett; 2d 10 June 1707 Hannah (Bray 4), wid. of John Freethy (4). Y. D. 11.29, 12.273. He d. 8, she 13 Mar. 1728-9.

5 ——— Widow (Haslinton), Exeter rate 1714.

6 ——— (Issleton?). See Guptill.

**Heacock** (Hiskott), Stephen, 1681-5. List 122. See also Hiskett.

**HEAD.** The name is most frequent in Sussex.

1 **ANN** (and Henry Trefethen), wit. Edw. Carter's bond at Great Island, 1678. Poss. wife of (2) or (4).

2 **ARTHUR,** fisherman, Great Island, bot there in 1671, then of the Shoals. Deft. in suit 1677. Jury 1684. Sold on Gt. Isl. 1690. Lists 313a, 331b, 52, 318b, 66, 315ac. He was liv. in July 1696; dead by 1708. Poss. his first w. was Ann(1); certainly his last w. was Sarah, who swept the meeting-ho. in 1694 and 1697, and was a widow in Newcastle in May 1711, when James, Ann and Grace H. deeded to Capt. Philip Atwood of Bradford their fa.'s house, where 'our mo. Sarah Head now lives.' In 1718 (after her decease?) Atwood deeded it back. List 316. Ch: James, b. ±1683, m. 1st in Bradford 13 Feb. 1709-10 Sarah Atwood (Philip), who d. 25 May 1717, in 27th yr.; 2d, her sis. Elizabeth. He d. in Bradford 16 Sept. 1743 in 60th yr. Ch. by both wives. Ann, liv. Bradford 1711, Boston 1718. Grace, Bradford 1711, m. there 20 Mar. 1716-7 Andrew Cook. Arthur, fisherman, Newcastle; adm. in N. H. to br. James 7 May 1718. If he were that only s. of Sarah who d. in Bradford 25 May 1717, in 32d yr., and record correct, then James was his half-br. One Arthur H. and w. Esther had two Anns recorded in Boston 1707-9. ?Sarah (poss. the widow Sarah and not a dau.; or poss. widow of the younger Arthur), m. at Oyster River 3 Sept. 1719 Richard Blanchard. In 1722, they, John Buss(2) and w. Alice, in right of the wives, deeded with full warranty one-sixth of the Cape Porpus land of their uncle John Reynolds. Her illeg. s. James Head, bp. at O. R., 1 May 1720, m. 17 Jan. 1733-4 Sarah Danforth (sis. of Moses), and was liv. in Canterbury 1735 and 1761.

3 **NICHOLAS,** 1614. List 7.

4 **THOMAS,** carried goods belonging to John Lines's est. to Sarah Winsland on

Star Island in 1675. See also (1). One Henry H. was at Newbury in 1702 with w. Joanna, who m. there 2d 28 Dec. 1710 Joseph Pike.

**HOOKELY** (Hukeley, Huckley), **William,** former servant of Wm. Rawson of Boston, was working for Mr. Broughton in the Newichawannock Mills 1 July 1671—Mar. 1671-2; Kittery wit. 1672; Newich. 1676. In 1675, in Me. Ct., he sued James Barry for debt; in Sept. 1677 Geo. Broughton, assignee of W. H., sued Henry Hobbs for debt, two parcels of staves. Creditor of Abra. Conley's est.; Wm. Hilton's 1690. Wm. Ardell's account '1687, note to Wm. Hukeley.' Wife and ch. unkn. Presum. a younger man and his son was **William,** of Hampton when he m. at Salis. 30 Dec. 1700 Sarah Carr (b. 13 Aug. 1681), and had ch: Richard, b. at Salis. Nov. 1701, poss. the ch. of Wm. Hinckley (Hookely) k. by Ind. at Hampt. 17 Aug. 1703 (List 96); and two Williams, b. Sept. 27, 1705, and Sept. 5, 1706. One Wm. H. m. in Greenland 14 Apr. 1726 Keziah Sanborn (Joseph), who renounc. adm. in favor of Saml. Page 4 June 1734. One Wm. m. Hephsibah Rowell, int. Salis. 22 Dec. 1727. One Wm. of Amesbury, dangerously sick, was bap. 8 Apr. 1731; adm. granted 7 June 1731.

**HEALY,** a Yorkshire place-name.

1 **PAUL,** br. of (2), bp. Cambridge 3 Apr. 1664, served in K. P.'s War from Hampton; d. Rehoboth 12 Mar. 1717-8. W. Elizabeth. 14 ch.

2 **SAMUEL,** Hampton Falls, b. Cambridge 14 Sept. 1662, s. of Wm. and Phebe (Green). His fa. m. five times, he only four; 26 May 1685 Hannah Smith; 15 Sept. 1693 Judith Roby (Henry); 17 June 1725 one Elizabeth, d. 27 Nov. 1728, ag. 68; 28 May 1729 Joanna (Bickford 12), wid. of John Redman. 3 ch. rec. by 1st w: Samuel, b. 22 Oct. 1685 (Salis. rec.), drowned at Currituck with Jona. Chase(5) 1696. List 399a. Mary, b. 27 Feb. 1688-9. Capt. Nathaniel, b. 8 Feb. 1690-1; signed ptn. with Saml. 1713; bp., and joined Hampt. F. Ch. with w. 17 July 1715; m. 1st 12 Dec. 1712 Hannah Tilton (Danl.), 2d 4 Mar. 1722 Susanna Weare (Peter). Ch. 1+4. Unrec. possibly ?William, m. 12 Jan. 1715-6 Mary Sanborn (Benj.); witn. with Saml. 1719. 9 ch. See also Cunnable.

3 **WILLIAM,** blacksmith, half-bro. of (2), b. Roxbury 11 July 1652, served in Philip's War, and went from Cambridge to Hampton; there servant of Edw. Gove, joined in the Rebellion, arrested, and pardoned 8 Feb. 1683-4. Whether or not he m. a step-sis. Sarah Brown, dau. of his fa.'s last w. Sarah (Cutting) Brown, is unde-

term.; cert. he had w. Mary in Salis., Bradford and Boston, 1689-1696; neither ident. aft. July 1696. Kn. ch: **William, Mary,** twins, b. Salis. 29 Jan., d. 15-16 Feb. 1689. In Bradford: **Mary,** b. 2 Oct. 1691; **Sarah,** b. 18 Feb. 1693-4, both bp. 2d Ch., Boston, 7 June 1696, when their mo. admitted. In Boston: **William,** b. 19 July 1696; liv. Boston.

4 **WILLIAM** (Hely), Hampton, laborer, to serve Peter Coffin of Dover one yr., 1693.

**HEARD,** a Devonshire name, partic. in Bideford, 16th and 17th centuries; Hurd in Somersetshire.

1 **ARTHUR,** in Trel. acct. 1634. List 21.

2 **BENJAMIN**(5), cordwainer, Dover until 1696 or later. Gr. j. 1675, 89; Tr. j. 1694; Constable 1695-6. Lists 356jk, 357c, 359ab, 49, 52, 62. Will 20 Jan., d. Salis. 22 Jan. 1709-10. He m. 1st bef. 1673 Elizabeth Roberts (Thos.), 2d at Salis. 23 May 1690 Ruth Eastman who m. 2d 2 Dec. 1717 John Tappan. Ch., all but 1st and last in will: **Benjamin,** Dover gr. 1693-4, d. s. p. 10 Feb. 1696-7. List 96. **James,** inher. Dover land and liv. there. List 358d. W. Deborah d. bef. him. 7 ch. 1715-30, 4 in his will, no date, proved 31 Jan. 1749-50. **Lydia,** m. 1st (Ct. June 1696) Jona. Norris, 2d Jos. Rollins. **Rebecca,** m. Thos. Gordon(1). **Sarah,** m. 24 Nov. 1709 Simon French of Kingston. Ch. 1711-19. **Anne,** b. 1681. If the Anne of Cochecho recov. from Ind. up the Androscoggin Riv. by Capt. Church in Sept. 1690, she was taken again 25 Jan. 1691-2 and remained in Canada; m. 1705 Sebastian Cholet. 8 ch. List 99, pp. 72, 123, 6. Her fa. willed to her, Hannah, if she come for it out of her captiv. By 2d w. rec. Salis: **Elizabeth,** b. 25 May 1691; likely m. in Salis. 24 Sept. 1713 Wm. Baker of Ipsw. **Samuel,** b. 28 Feb. (1691-2?). **Benjamin,** b. 16 Dec. 1702, d. 8 Mar. 1705-6. **Benjamin** k. 29 Aug. 1723 (Hoyt i. 200) unplaced, poss. meant for Tristram (11 jr).

3 **ENSIGN JAMES**(4), Kittery, first ment. as lot layer 24 May 1652. Ensign by June 1656. Jury 1656; Gr. j. 1657, 61, 62 (foreman); Clerk of the Com. Ct. of Kit. and Clerk of the Writs 1659. Selectm. 1659, 1661, 1666-9; Town Clerk 1667-9, removed from both as a Quaker 1669. Lists 24, 298. D. bet. 6 July 1675—3 Mar. 1675-6. He m. by 1661 Shuah Starbuck (Edw.), who m. 2d bet. 28 Nov. 1676—5 Nov. 1677 Richard Otis. Ch: **John. Mary,** oldest dau., m. 1st Isaac Hanson(1), 2d Robt. Evans(13). **Elizabeth,** 2d dau., m. 1st Jas. Chadbourne (3), 2d Samuel Small. **John,** b. ±1667. **Katherine,** m. 1st Jas. Littlefield, 2d John Wooden. **Abigail,** m. Job Clements(4).

**Ann,** (these three under 18 in 1676), m. Moses Gilman. See Y. D. 9.266, 18.107-9.

4 **JOHN,** by his naming a son, and by selling 'Mosquito Hall,' a large tract on Great Isl., it is conject. that he came on -The Warwick-. From Great Isl. he removed to Sturgeon Creek on invitation of John Treworgye, representing Mr. Alex. Shapleigh. Goodwife Heard kept Mr. Treworgye's ho. while her husb. was building their ho. at the Creek. Altho on the Me. side of the river, he joined the Dover Combin. in 1640. He was always a devoted henchman of Maj. Shapleigh and was punished with him for opposing Mass. and for entert. Quakers. He was usually selectm. with Maj. Shapl. and in 1659 Com. t. e. s. c. Tr. j. 1640, 1645, 1647, 1650; Gr. j. 1645, 1649-51, 1653. Lists 41, 281, 282, 351b, 298. Recorder Rishworth disting. the two Johns, not uniformly, by spelling this one Hord, and he himself, altho usually signing by mark, in one deed appar. wrote his name Hord. Will 3 Mar. 1675-6—21 Feb. 1676-7 names w. Isabel, liv. 5 Nov. 1677. Ch: **Warwick,** accid. k. by Charles Frost 23 Mar. 1647 while shooting geese. **James.**

5 **JOHN** (Heard), master carpenter, never mariner nor captain. Age unkn., only as his w. was b. ab. 1628. In 1647 fined for calling Godfrey old knave and criticizing Capt. Champernowne; in 1650 he had lately been liv. on Champernowne's Isl. in Kit., and was buying lands in York. Appar. he had built a ho. on Champernowne Isl. and on not getting his pay had burnt it; judgm. of Ct. Oct. 1650 that he replace as good and as large a ho. His deed from Mr. Hooke, 18 July 1650, recites that he had already built and fenced there. He had left York in June 1648, (Y. D. 3.71) when he sold his York ho. to John Parker, carpenter, of Marblehead, which may imply a prior acquaint., but was back again in 1651 (Gr. j. 1651-2). In Dover, where he was perman. settled by 1654, he was much relied on by Major Waldron. Lists 352, 355ab, 356abceghk, 45, 311c, 54, 49, 359ab, 52, 96. Will 2 Apr. 1687, d. 17 Jan. 1688-9. His w. Elizabeth, dau. of Rev. Jos. Hull(6), is commen. by Revs. Cotton Mather and John Pike; d. 30 Nov. 1706. Lists 60, 65, 67, 96. Ch: **Benjamin,** b. 20 Feb. 1643-4. **Katherine,** b. ab. 1647, d. y. **Mary,** b. 26 Jan. 1649-50, m. John Ham(4). **Abigail,** b. 2 Aug. 1651, m. Jenkin Jones. **Elizabeth,** b. 15 Sept. 1653, m. 1st James Nute, 2d Lt. Wm. Furber(3). **Hannah,** b. 25 Nov. 1655, m. 6 Nov. 1674 John Nason; not in will. **John,** b. 24 Feb. 1658-9, liv. 1684, not in will. Lists 359b, 52. **Joseph,** b. 4 Jan. 1660-1, not in will. **Samuel,** b. 4 Aug. 1663. **Tristram,** b. 4 Mar. 1666-7.

**Nathaniel,** b. 22 Sept. 1668. **Dorcas,** m. Jabez Garland(3). Unident., poss. an unrec. dau. or a young widow: Elizabeth, b. ±1684, m. in Dover 29 Dec. 1708 John Horne (2 jr.). See also (7).

6 **CAPT. JOHN**(3), Kittery, ±53 Apr. 1720, depos. that he liv. with Jas. Chadbourne several yrs. bef. he d. Repeat. Gr. j.; Field driver 1694-6, 1698; Lieut. 1709; Capt. 1711; Selectm. 1713, 17, 21; Tavern lic. 1722. Lists 96, 38, 291, 296, 297, 298. He m. 1st 27 Apr. 1690 Phebe Littlefield(11) and was wounded when she was k. by Ind. 4 July 1697. List 96. He m. 2d 2 July 1698 Jane (Cole 23) Littlefield(17), 3d Dec. 1725 Ann Wingate (John), 4th 23 Dec. 1735 Maria (Cotton), wid. of Wymond Bradbury (3 jr.) Will 15 Jan. 1739, d. Nov. 1751; ch. and gr. ch. named, not wife. Ch. by 1st w: **Dorcas,** b. 26 Feb. 1690-1, m. 21 Nov. 1717 Hugh Tucker. **Phebe,** b. 15 Jan. 1692, m. 1st Abraham Morrill, 2d Thos. Stevens of Newc. **Shuah,** b. 25 Jan. 1694, m. 10 Mar. 1714 Nathan Bartlett from Newbury. 12 ch. rec. Kit. **James,** b. 21 Jan. 1696, m. 7 Apr. 1720 Mary Roberts (Hatevil). List 291. 4 ch. bapt. She was a wid. 3 Oct. 1725; m. 2d 1 May 1726 Saml. Wingate of Dover; adm. on 1st husb.'s est. to them 18 July 1732. By 2d w: **Jane,** b. 18 June 1699, m. Capt. Tristram Coffin (6 jr.) **Mary,** b. 24 Aug. 1700, m. Henry Barter (1 jr.) **Abigail,** b. 15 Apr. 1702, m. Moses Hubbard(9).

7 **NATHANIEL**(5), Dover, exec. of fa.'s will. Jury 1694; Gr. j. 1695; Constable 1696; Selectm. 1699. Lists 57, 62, 353, 96. He d. 3 Apr. 1700, ag. 31. Wid. Sarah (Ferniside) m. 2d 26 Apr. 1703 Wm. Fost (2) Kn. ch: **Tristram.** In 1701 his mo. applied for his portion; d. s. p. bef. 1720. **Hannah,** only surv. ch. 1720, m. 22 Mar. 1719-20 Wm. Willand. With her uncle Tristram (11) and his w. Abigail, they deeded in 1720 to 'our relative' Elizabeth, w. of John Horne (2 jr.), who is unplaced (See 5). 3 Willand ch. rec. Dover.

8 **SAMUEL**(5), Dover, d. 10 Feb. 1696-7. Constable 1692, Jury 1693, Selectm. 1694. Lists 57, 62, 96 (Jam:). He m. 20 Mar. 1685-6 Experience Otis (Richard), who was scalped by Ind. 26 July 1696, yet liv. to have adm. of his est. 31 Aug. 1697, and m. 2d Rowland Jenkins(11). List 96. Ch: **John,** ±14, 2 July 1706, when uncle Tristram app. gdn.; sold his fa.'s town gr. 1715. Adm. 9 Jan. 1716-7 to br.-in-law John Smith. One John m. Mary Beane in Kit. 17 Dec. 1711. **Samuel,** only surv. son 1718; of Berw., husbandm., 26 Feb. 1717-8, with w. Elizabeth, he sold ½ of John Holmes' gr. of 10 May 1703. 9 ch. bp. Dover 1720-37. **Judith,** m. John Fall. **Elizabeth,** m. by 1707 John Smith of Berw. **Martha,** Portsm. wit. 1704,

m. bef. 16 Dec. 1706 Richard Tobey.
9 THOMAS, drunk and disorderly, Saco Ct.
25 June 1640.
10 THOMAS and JAMES 1718. List 298.
Read Hearl.
11 LIEUT. TRISTRAM(5), husbandman,
Dover, only surv. son 1704. Town gr.
with Paul Wentworth 1694, and intim. assoc. with the Wentw. fam. Constable 1698,
Selectm. 1700-1. Lists 62, 94, 96, 358b,
(358d?). Will 18 Apr.—3 June 1734 names
w. Abigail, ch. and gr. ch. Ch: Joseph,
Dover and Rochester, b. 15 Feb. 1692-3, m.
9 Aug. 1722 Rebecca Richards of Newington; adm. to her 27 Aug. 1746. 4 or m. ch.
Tristram, b. 26 Mar. 1695, k. by Ind. 31 Aug.
1723; m. in Portsm. 4 May 1717 Jane Snell,
who m. 2d Benj. Hayes(3). 4 ch. 1718-23.
Nathaniel, b. 23 Jan. 1696-7, d. 10 Oct. 1723,
m. in Berw. 18 Dec. 1718 Margaret Warren.
His fa. in 1724 deeded to her, widow, and 2
ch. John, b. 1 Jan. 1700-1, m. Charity Day
(2), a wid. 1769. 8 or m. ch. Abigail, b. 15
Apr. 1702, not in will. Samuel, b. 28 Feb.
1703-4. Will 1756—1756 names w. Dorcas
and 8 ch. Elizabeth, b. 8 Feb. 1706-7, m.
Robt. Knight(17). Mary, b. 10 June 1709,
m. John Warren. Keziah, b. 1 Dec. 1712, m.
1st Spencer Wentworth, 2d Capt. Thos.
Pierce.
12 WILLIAM, (Hearl?), Dover 1649. List
354b.
13 WILLIAM, 1702. List 298. Read Hearl.

HEARL, Earl, also Harl. See Creber. Hearl
peculiar to Cornwall.
1 JOHN, Kittery, nearly relat. to William
(5) whose ch. held land in his right. Gr.
adm. (Earle) on Wm. Ash's est. 4 July
1676, Capt. Wincoll bondsman. (In 1677
John Harall signed a Portsm. ptn. List 54).
June 2, 1679, husbandman, he bot in Berw.
from Phineas Hull, sold to Abra. Lord 27
Aug. 1681, Thos. Hearl a witn. Y. D. 3.130.
Creditor of Abra. Conley's est. 1684, Lt.
Humph. Chadbourne's 1695. List 298.
2 RICHARD (Earl), sued for debt by Capt.
Nich. Shapleigh 5 July 1658. P. & Ct.
ii. 62. Mordecai Crawford's est. indebted
to one Richard (Hearle) 1660.
3 THOMAS, witn. for John (1) 1681.
4 WILLIAM, Portsmouth, b. ±1614, fisherman at Richmond Isl. 1638-40, reported
gone 29 July 1641, presum. with others to
the Piscataqua. Geo. Small withdrew a suit
against him 14 Oct. 1651. In 1652 he sued
Wm. Cousins (5) for debt. From 1657 on he
was of Portsm. Lists 21, 330b, 311b, 47, 323,
326d, 331ab, 49, 329, 52 (354b Heard?). He
depos. 3 Sept. 1674, ag. 60 or thereab.; in
1679 gave P/A to son John Cotton to collect from Mr. John Cutts; tax abated 1680.
Last w. Beaton, app. wid. of Hercules Hun-

king (2). List 331c. See Bickton. In 1677
they sold to Wm. Rackley land in Portsm.
where he had built; in Feb. 1680 both sold
20 a. in Kit. which Andrew Newcomb had
bot from Wm. Hilton. Will 17 May 1689—30
Mar. 1691 entailed his prop. on his dau. and
her ch. Only surv. ch: Sarah, m. John Cotton (2).
5 WILLIAM, Berwick, bot so. of Great
Works Riv. in 1690; 50 a. gr. in 1703.
Lists 296, 298 (p. 35 mispr. Heard). Undoubtedly relat. to (1) and (3). In 1678 he
and Geo. Gray were questioned, Phineas
Hull fined, for failure to assist the constable;
in 1712 (Earle) he test. for Mary, w. of
Rowland Jenkins of Newc.; in 1717 gr. adm.
on est. of Allen Furs (Fuz, Virrs) and called
him my cous. in 1729. M. 1st aft. 29 Feb.
1675-6 Patience Etherington (Thos.), d.
1697; 2d ab. Dec. 1703 Sarah wid. of Jas.
Goodwin (8); 3d bef. 5 Aug. 1714 Elizabeth
(Grant) Landers-Turner. Will 9 Aug. 1718—
16 June 1730 names w. and ch., all liv. but
Mary. In Apr. 1731 the wid. sued her step-
son Etherington for 1/3 the per. est. Ch:
Mary, m. Gabriel Hamilton. Her ch. q. c.
under grants to Patience Etherington 1671,
John Hearl 1679. Margaret, m. Nathan Lord
(7). John, Berwick. Lists 289, 291, 296, 297,
298. M. 17 Dec. 1711 Mary Beard(3), not
in his will 17 Jan. 1742—17 Jan. 1743, naming 5 of 6 ch. William, Berw., taxed 'junr.'
1713; his homestead app. Allen Fuz's 60 a.;
m. 15 Dec. 1717 Margaret Warren (Gilbert),
who was admx., bond 19 July 1725. 5 ch. bp.,
of whom Thos. and Mary, w. of Wm. Tibbetts, sold as heirs to Etherington gr. 1671,
John Hearl gr. 1679. Thomas, Berw., taxed
1713, o. c. and bp. 20 Dec. 1719; abs. from
meet. Jan. 1730-1. (James and Thomas, List
298, p. 35, mispr. Heard). Fa. willed 50 a.
near Jellison's place to him and br. James,
Berw., taxed 1713; m. 7 May 1717 Martha
Jackson. In 1732 they liv. next ho. to Jos.
and Sarah Jellison. Oct. 1755, ±55, she test.
that she liv. early neighbor to Rich. Lord.
His will 6 Jan. 1759—20 Oct. 1762 names w.
and 5 daus. of 9 ch bp. Etherington, Berw.,
taxed 9 Feb. 1718-9; d. 7 May 1770. Fa.'s
exec. and had the homestead. List 298. M.
18 Feb. 1723-4 Hannah Goodwin (12), liv.
1746. 8 ch. bp. By 3d w: Richard, under age
1718. Mar. 1729-30 the parents gave P/A to
'our trusty s. Ebenezer Boltwood and Richard Hearl' both of Berw. See also Guptill.
HEARN (Herne), 1 Joseph, took from Gov.
Allen lease of Esq. Dow's farm and 5
yr. lease of Wm. Vaughan's est., and in
1699 sued Vaughan for ejecting him.
2 NICHOLAS (Curren?), owned next to
the Magoon lot at Sligo 1708. One Richard in Dover Foot Co. 1740; George, Dover
1743 and later, w. Ruth Hanson; James

(Hern), bp. So. Ch., Portsm., 11 Oct. 1740.
Hearst, see Hurst.
HEATH, 1 John, Haverh., m. 14 Nov. 1666
Sarah Partridge (Wm.). Both d. Hampt.,
he 21 Sept. 1706, she July 1718. 1 ch. b.
Hampt., Martha, 30 Nov. 1677; 9 more in
Haverh. 1667-1688, incl. Capt. Nehemiah of
Hampt. F., and Ann, b. 30 June 1684, m.
Wm. Brown (5). See Hoyt 1.201.
2 JOSIAH, Haverh. See Davis (20).
HEDEN, 1 Robert 1665. List 47.
2 ROGER, Pemaquid soldier 1689. List 126.
Hederson (Parsons?), Mark, Kennebec 1664.
Y. D. x. 152.
Hedger, Henry, Pemaquid, taxed and se-
lectm. 1687. List 124. At Charlestown
-Hedge- with w. and 1 ch. 21 Oct. 1689.
HEFFER, Heifer, Andrew, Richmond Isl.
1637-1639, Piscataqua June 1640, on N.
H. side 1647, and built at Sag. Creek; Am-
brose Lane had his land 1651. Spurwink,
living on 50 a. leased from Jocelyn, 1659,
when he sued Robt. Jordan, and lost. W. in
Eng. 1637, not found here. Inv. 14 Apr. 1661
incl. cattle in hands of Henry Elkins, Rich.
Mayres; adm. 7 July 1663 to Jacob Rabskine and Arthur Alger; the form. sued
Andrew Thorne.
HEGEMAN, (Higiman), Dennis, Pemaquid
1687; taken capt. 5 Aug. 1689 with w.
Grace and appar. 1 ch. He was in Canada 5
Mar. 1693; she was telling her story in Boston 28 May 1695, just returned. N. E. Reg.
18.161. Lists 124, 125. Ch: Jane, prob. theirs
and b. here, a captive 1698-9. List 99, pp.
78, 172. Joseph, bp. in Quebec 5 Mar. 1693,
1 day old. See also Dollen.
Helborne, William, Richmond Isl., 1634.
List 21.
HELMAN (Hilman), Thomas, O. A. Sagadahoc 1674; Kennebec soldier 1688. Lists
15, 189. Prob. fa. of Mary of Boston, mo.
dead, fa. gone to the Eastward, m. in Marblehead 24 Nov. 1685 Wm. Clapp of Boston.
1 ch. b. Boston, d. y. One Mary Clapp m.
John Evans in Boston 7 Jan. 1694.
HELME, Christopher, s. of Mr. Wm. and
Priscilla (Wentworth) of Sutton St.
Mary, co. Lincoln, 1st cous. of Elder Wm.
Wentworth and of Christopher Lawson,
came to Exeter from Boston 1639. List 373.
Sued at Piscataqua in 1642, the Ct. in 1644
ord. the money sent to him, prob. then in
Warwick, R. I., where he witn. the subm. of
the Narragan. Ind. 19 Apr. that yr. In Nov.
1649 Val. Hill sold 500 a. near Oyster Riv.
purch. from him, then in poss. of Darby
Field. Suff. D. i. 106. D. at Warwick bef.
Dec. 1650. Wid. Margaret and four sons sur-
vived.
HELSON, Elson, Elsey. See also Hempson.
John, Saco 1653, fisherman. In 1666, in
consid. of 40 s. pd. 14 yrs. bef., he had deed

of Batson's Neck, Cape Porpus, from Thos.
Mercer of Sheepscot; in 1671 Roger Hill
confirmed to him 100 a. on Saco Riv. sold
him by Peter Hill. Signed a Cape Porpus
ptn. 1668; he or s. fined in July 1674 for
sailing out of the harbor there on Sunday.
In 1675 the Neck was owned by John Davis,
sr. and Ferdinando Huff. Witn. bef. coroner's jury, Saco, 1670; Constable 1671.
Lists 251, 263, 244ad, 247, 255, 249, 27. M.
3 Nov. 1658 Joan Waddock (Henry). List
246. During the War he went to Salem,
where was one John Elson or Elston, fisherman, in 1631. Adm. inhab. 1676. Will, of
Salem, 11 Mar. 1683-4—24 Nov. 1685, names
w. exec. The wid. and sons Samuel and Ephraim sold the Hill land to Wm. Dicer 28
July 1686. Ch. in will: John. Poss. the fa.
and not he at Black Pt. gar. 1676, taxed
Scarb. 1681. Lists 237a, 238a. Not named in
deed of 1686. One Mary (Ellson) was taken
by the Inds. at Black Pt. 1703. List 39 Will
of one Samuel of Black Pt., of H. M. S.
-Greyhound-, 25 Aug. 1706—11 Sept. 1707
(P. C. C.), gave all to friend Robt. Harding
of Peterhead, Aberdeenshire. Samuel, Salem.
W. Mary, perh. dau. of Nich. Potter. 4 ch.
1686-1692. Ephraim, b. Saco 4 Dec. 1667, liv.
1686. Dinah, m. Salem 2 Jan. 1690-1 Stephen
Ingalls. 7 ch. Margaret, m. Salem 22 May
1695 John Harris. Hannah, m. Salem 6 Nov.
1702 Robert Neal. 4 ch. Benjamin, b. Salem
20 May 1683.
Hempson (Imson), John, fisherman, Richmond Isl. 1636-7—Jan. 1640-1, his master John Fletcher. List 21. Same as John
Helson?

HENDERSON, a patronymic from Andrew, common in the north border counties.
1 JOHN, fisherman, Saco, obviously relat.
to (3), 1st found apprent. (Anderson)
to Wm. Seadlock; witn. with him 19 Feb.
1660-1. In 1664 he was pd. for work on the
meet.-ho.; 26 Sept. that yr. m. Ellen (Booth
3), wid. of Nich. Bully (3). List 246. Dep.
Constab. 1665; Road Surveyor 1671, 74; Gr.
j. 1673, 74. Lists 245, 249. He mov. to Salem
during the War; mtg. his 40 a. at Winter
Har. adj. Peter's land to Wm. Downe of
Boston in 1679, with w. Ellenor sold to
Downe in 1682; in 1690 mtg. the Salem
prop. he had bot in 1681. Old Widow Henderson taxed Salem Dec. 1701. Kn. ch: John,
b. Saco 15 Jan. 1665-6, mariner, late master
of ketch -Benjamin- in 1705; m. in Salem
6 May 1687 one Abigail. 3 ch. rec. Salem.
Peter, b. Saco 14 Jan. 1667, mariner, Salem,
m. there 2 Apr. 1687 Hannah Glover. Will
17 Apr. 1721—20 July 1722. Her will 13
Apr. 1751 not allowed. 9 ch. rec. Salem. See
Essex Inst. 48.328.

2 **JOHN** of Coleraine, co. Derry, m. in Portsm. 1 Jan. 1721-2 Sarah Keel. Ch: **Sarah**, bp. So. Ch. 7 Apr. 1723. **John**, bp. 17 Jan. 1724-5, s. of John decd. Poss. the wid. m. in Portsm 4 June 1727 John Savage. Susanna, ch. of one John, a town charge at Kit. 1727, Thos. Muzeet to take care of her.

3 **PETER**, Saco, had 12 a. gr. adj. John (1) 6 Oct. 1671, sold by his heirs 1729. Y. D. 13.51. Dec. 29, 167-, he m. John's step-dau. Abigail Bully (3). List 246. He too remov. to Salem. A master mariner, his ketch -Sara- was chased ashore by pirates at Funchal in 1683. Taxed Salem 27 Sept. 1700; d. ab. that time. Ch: **John**, app. single 1729. **Peter**, m. Salem 10 Nov. 1701 Elizabeth Beadle; adm. to her 2 Jan. 1718. **Ebenezer**, housewr., m. 1st 3 Nov. 1715 Elizabeth Marston, 2d 2 Dec. 1730 Wid. Mary Dolbear; adm. to her 11 May 1739. **Benjamin**, m. 22 July 1706 Abigail Beadle, who adm. 24 Jan. 1722-3. **Abigail**, b. Salem Oct. 1676, m. 31 Mar. 1699 Jona. Glover; many disting. desc.

4 **WILLIAM**, Mr., shipbuilder, Dover, likely from London; atty. in June 1676 to Wm. and Joanna Tapping of London, adm. of Capt. John Seeley; sued in Suff. Ct. 1677 by Robt. Oxe, atty. to Edw. Gosling of London, mariner, for money lent in Dec. 1672. He appr. Alex. Waldron's est. at Newc. 1676; in 1678 overhauled a ship for Isaac Waldron, who sued him and was sued in Suff. Ct. Constable, Dover, 1683; witn. deed of Kit. selectm. 1684. Fined in Portsm. 1694 for words against the govt.; taxed Newc. 1696-8. Dover gr. Mar. 1693 laid out to him in 1701. See also Corson. Portsm. witn. with Rich. Hilton 1708. Lists 14, 359ab, 52, 315bc, 98, 358c. Old Mr. H. d. at Greenland 1744. W. Sarah Howard. Kn. ch: **Howard**, mariner, shipbuilder, liv. Hilton's Point, the ferry there in his and his son's poss. many yrs. He depos. Jan. 1749-50, ag. 67, evid. understated, as he was on coroner's j. 1699; called 100 at death. Lists 387, 358cd. M. 8 June 1704 Sarah Roberts (Thos.), liv. 1740. 2 kn. ch., Capt. Howard and Richmond. One Mary of Dover m. Ebenezer Seward of Portsm. 15 Mar. 1732-3. **William**, shipwr., Fernald's Isl. His rate for the Newc. minister was abated 15 Aug. 1696 on his fa.'s compl. that he was not 16. M. 16 July 1700 Sarah Fernald(4); poss. she was the Wid. Sarah, creditor of Isaac Trickey's est. 1712. Both were dead 20 Mar. 1730-1 when only kn. ch. John, mariner, Boston, sold all rights in Fernald's Isl. and Berw. belonging to either or any of their ch. Adm. on fa.'s est. to him 18 July 1732.

**HENDRICK, Daniel**, Hampton propr. 1640, soon remov. to Haverh., where liv. 9 Nov. 1694, ±84. Lists 391a, 392a. John Wedgwood sold his 5 a. Hampt. gr. 1646; hims. sold Hampt. marsh 1649. Ch. 7+3 by two wives, Dorothy Pike (John) and Wid. Mary Stockbridge, m. in Boston 8 Apr. 1660.

**Hening, Shubael**, from Newbury, at Fort Mary, Saco, 1699; Kit. witn. 1700.

**Henly, ———**, Falm. 1683, poss. from Marblehead. List 226. One Jos. (Hendley), Marblehead, fisherman, bot half of Jewell's Isl., Casco Bay, 1735, and bot at Muscongus from Elizabeth (Gould 1) Homan, that yr. See Curtis (2).

**Henry, ———**, Mr., attorney for Adam Shurt, York Ct., 1648. P. & Ct. i. 118.

**HEPWORTH, William** (Hepworth), Portsmouth 1695. List 334b. One Wm. H. m. Mary Locke in Boston 3 Jan. 1697. Four Mary Hepworths of Portsm. or Newington m. in Portsm.: Joshua Remick of Kit. Sept. 1716; William Gammon (1); Capt. John Abbott (1); John Woodman 10 May 1723. One Hannah H. of Portsm. m. Wm. Bickum (5).

**Hept, John**, 1614. List 7.

**Her—y, Henry**, Shoals 1676, List 26.

**HERBERT**, an ancient given-name, found principally on the Welsh border.

1 **———**, Mr., Piscataqua early. List 41.

2 **JOHN** (Hurburt), Wells 1690. List 267a. One John, w. Elizabeth, in Boston, 1679-81.

3 **SYLVESTER**, tailor, Boston 1652-9, adm. inhab. Portsm. 22 Jan. 1660-1, mov. to Kit. and bot the Champern. ho. from Barefoot in Aug. 1661, sold to Fryer 1662. Sued in Me. Ct. 1663-70; in 1666 trav. with Rowland Young bet. York and Kit. on Sunday. Great Isl. 1671. Jury 1682; Gr. j. 1683; tav. lic. June that yr.; drowned 21 Aug. foll. going from York to Piscat. with his w., Robt. Young and Geo. Bentley, they escaping; adm. to Thaddeus McCarthy 1 Oct. 1683. Lists 330a, 312c, 326c, 331b, 91, 313f. A letter from London conc. the will of his w.'s mo. Mrs. Ramsey, Y. D. i. 116, is blind; app. he m. 1st a dau.-in-law of Mrs. Ramsey, who, and perh. he, had been at Barbadoes; m. in Boston 21 Sept. 1652 Lucy Adams (one Nathl. Ramsey, serv. to Alex. Adams, d. in Boston 22 Mar. 1662-3); w. Mary in 1662. Lists 313df. Only ch. rec: **Samuel**, b. Boston 12 June 1653, d. there 6 Nov. 1659. Poss. a son: **James**, depos. Newc. 1680, witn. with Elizabeth Cranch Jan. 1681-2; liv. 8 Oct. 1683; Y. D. iv. 6. ?List 313d. **Dau.**, legatee of Mrs. Ramsey, poss. Ramsey not Herbert.

4 **THOMAS**, Kittery-Newc. witn. 1677-8.

**Herdin, John**, Pemaquid soldier 1689. List 126.

**Hermitage**, see Armitage.

**Herne**, see Hearn.

**HERRICK,** 1 **Henry,** Beverly, m. Sarah (Alcock 1) Giddings.

2 **ISAAC,** Rye, m. Sarah Rand (Francis) by 1681, when she and Wm. Haskins were prosecuted. He was taxed in Aug. 1684, and was bondsman for his wife's fa. or br. in Nov. 1684; not found later. She was a wid. in Portsm. 1713; living 1732. Appar. no ch.

**HERSEY,** 1 **Judith** (Wm.), bp. Hingham 15 July 1638, m. at Exeter 21 Dec. 1665 Humphrey Wilson. Aunt of (2), (3), and sis. of Elizabeth, w. of Moses Gilman(14).

2 **MARIA,** sis. to (3), b. Hingham 12 Jan. 1677-8, m. 1st Joshua Gilman(13), 2d Nich. Gordon(6).

3 **PETER,** Exeter, **b.** Hingham 20 Aug. 1687 (John and Sarah), m. Elizabeth Gilman; adm. to her 5 Sept. 1722. 5 ch. liv. 1738.

4 **ROBERT,** Exeter, List 376b. Hethersay?

**HETHERSAY,** Hethersall, **Robert,** a rover of poor charac., early at Concord and Charlestown, was in Essex Ct. 1643, many yrs. abs. from w. Exeter knew him 1643-6, Dover 1648-9, during which time he conducted Balthazar Willix's w. on her fateful trip bet. Exeter and Dover, and was ord. back to his own w. in Eng. Bef. 25 Mar. 1650 he sold a ho. in Hampt.; York 1651-3; Wells 1654-8, and got as far as Falm., not found aft. 1658. Lists 376ab (Hersey?), 375ab, 354ab, 275, 262, 221. One Robt. Hethersaw lic. to m. Mary Smith at Gotham, co. Notts, 16 Jan. 1626-7.

**Hewes,** see Hughes.

**HEWETT,** a diminutive of Hugh.

1 **ARCHELAUS,** Wells 1720, b. Boston 27 Jan. 1695 (Archelaus and Jane), m. 29 June 1727 Mary Smith al. Gowen (gr. dau. of Wm. Gowen 4). List 269c. 6 ch. rec. Wells.

2 **EPHRAIM** (Huit), Mr., Windsor, Conn., owned in Dover and Squamscot Pat., sold by his wid. Isabel, Sept. 1647; Suff. D. i. 90.

3 **HENRY** (Hewet), Damariscove, 1622-1626. List 8.

4 **JAMES** (Huett), cred. of Stephen Crawford's est. List 71.

5 **JOSEPH** (Huit), Sergt., Falmouth 1690.

6 **NICHOLAS** (Hewit), shipwright, pd. for 10 days' work, Richmond Isl., 1641-2. List 21. Likely same in Boston 1644.

7 **NICHOLAS** (Huet), Wells 1690. List 267a.

8 **SAMUEL,** propr. Barr. List 339. Hewey?

**HEWEY,** Samuel, from Coleraine, co. Derry, Ireland, m. at Portsm. 23 Dec. 1718 Elizabeth (Meed), wid. of Jos. Dennett (4). List 339? Ch: **Margaret. Mary. Hannah** (Hughey) bap. Oyster Riv. 17 Sept. 1726.

**Hewland,** John, young Englishman, drowned Cochecho 1705. List 96.

**HIBBARD,** Hibbert, 1 ——— (Hibbert) of unkn. home and end, m. bef. 1689 Hannah Gibbins (2), who m. 2d Robert Mace and was liv. at Star Island 1733. Ch: **Mary,** b. 1689, m. 27 Mar. 1706 Jos. Jewett of Rowley. **George,** m. 24 Nov. 1709 Sarah Ellsworth of Rowley. Will 20 Feb. 1749-50 names w. Mary, 3 of 6 ch. See 'Ancestry of Charity Haley', by W. G. Davis, pp. 62-3.

2 **JOHN** (Hibard) k. Saco 1703. List 39.

**HIBBINS,** Giles, poss. servant of Gregory Jeffrey. See Giles(1). He m. at Saco 21 July 1670 Mary Pennell (Walter); convicted next Apr. of liv. together bef. mar. He liv. on land on Middle Neck gr. him 13 Oct. 1673, and had gr. of all the Neck adj. Little Riv. in 1674. Of Saco 8 Oct. 1675; refugee at Salem Jan. 1675-6. List 27. In Me. again, he liv. over -16- yrs. (his wid. deposed) on 100 a. up John Parker's Creek at Kennebec, until Oct. 1689 found him a refugee at Charlestown, with w. and 5 ch. There he d. from fever 11 Sept. 1693. The wid. claimed the Me. lands in 17-- and needed in Apr. 1718 with three daus., the only ch. ident: **Mary,** was Mary Abraham in 1718. **Sarah,** m. in Boston 9 Jan. 1704 Roger Wright. **Elizabeth;** one Elizabeth m. in Boston 19 Apr. 1719 Daniel Storer.

**HICKFORD,** John, his fa. Mr. H., a linen draper in Cheapside. In Feb. 1636-7 he was to receive debts here due Mr. Edw. Trelawny and turn them over to Capt. Thos. Babb; June 8 fol. witn. for Arthur Mackworth; sued Cleeve and Tucker in Saco Ct. in June 1640 on a 1637 acct. Last seen here 8 Sept. 1640 in counter suits with John Landers, tho John Jocelyn wrote he went back soon aft. 6 Sept. 1639.

**Hickman,** Nicholas, won suit in Piscataqua Ct. 1646. Dover 1649, 'Old Nickles'. Lists 354b, 386.

**HICKS,** a patronymic from Isaac, frequent in Cornwall.

1 **DENNIS,** Kittery, witn. in Ct. Mar. 1687-8. In 1689, with Jos. Crockett, he bot 36 a. at Kittery Pt., deeding his int. to Mary Ball, 1696. List 298. Called deed. 15 Nov. 1725. Y. D. 12.101. W. Sarah Deering (7). She was lic. July 1719; in 1721 test. that she was pres. at birth of Thos. Crockett (1); living Jan. 1727-8 with s. John in ho. form. her mo.'s; had taken care of her mo. 14 yrs. Y. D. 12.229-30. A q. c. deed to Nathl. in 1725 shows ch., poss. not all: **John,** shipwright, sold at Kit. Point to Wm. Walker 1739, then liv. at Braveboat Harbor where he bot 1721-3. M. (int. 13 Nov. 1723) Elizabeth Davis (14), wid. at Durham 1754, d. ag. 79. 2 or m. ch. Capt. **Joseph,** mason, Madbury, had a garrison ho. on 15 a. near Hicks Hill he bot from Lt. Thos. Davis in 1723.

In 1718 he purch. 100 a. at Oyster Riv.;
Sept. 1720 was lodging there at ho. of Mary
Thomas; in Feb. fol. was the princ. witn.
ag. Sobriety Thomas in her suit against
Thos. Davis. List 368b. M. by 1721 Sarah
Davis (14), who d. 20 Jan. 1788, ag. 91. His
will 6 Apr.—12 Oct. 1770. 6 ch., 1 surv. 1770.
**Nathaniel**, shipwright, Kit. List 291. At
Louisburg 1745. M. (Ct. July 1711) Martha
Foye (2); she liv. 11 Jan. 1748-9, not in his
will 7 June 1764—10 Apr. 1768. 6 ch. He
gave his real est. to gr. s. Nathl. jr. by deed
5 June 1764.
2 **JOSEPH** (Higgs?), mate of ketch -Pros-
perous- of Piscat. 1685.
3 **MICHAEL**, Kittery. Will 19 May—13
June 1688 left all, incl. prop. at Barbadoes, his birth-place, to w. Lucy (Chadbourne 1) who m. 2d Peter Lewis (15). See
also Landall.
4 **MICHAEL**, taxed Greenland 1688-1693.
List 335a. W. Sarah, dau. of Thos. Walford. List 335a. Of Portsm., widow, 1697,
she deeded to John Sherburne, John Peverly and Jos. Fanning; in 1699 q. c. to Matthew Nelson land of Tho. Walford given by
her mo. Jane Walford; liv. 1719, Sarah Savage. App. a son: **Michael**, Greenland, bot 25
a. in Stratham from Walter Philbrick 1713.
M. 10 Feb. 1714-5 Mary Haines (13), a wid.
1725-6. Both adm. Greenl. Ch. 1721. List
338b. Ch: Michael, bp. with two foll. 1721;
m. 15 Aug. 1734 Lydia Hill (see Hill 9). He
d. 3 Oct. 1735; 1 dau. bp. Samuel. Sarah,
unm. 1749. John, bp. 1723. In 1749 these
last three, of Greenl., sold the Stratham
land. Poss. ch. incl: ?**Mary** (Higgs) of Piscat., d. Boston 5 Nov. 1702, singlewo.
?**Sarah**, m. Portsm. June 1715 John Eals of
Isle of Wight; 2 ch. bp. So. Ch. 1716-1721.
?**Samuel**, taxed Newc. 1720. One Zachariah
witn. Christo. Rymes' will in 1740.
5 **PETER**, an Englishman living at Arrowsic, saw Edw. Tyng at Falm. 12 Dec.
1687. Poss. Peter, ±18 in 1680, on the ship
-Unity- from London, and (or) the man
called from Dorchester, who liv. on or
owned Harraseeket or Hicks Islands, No.
Yarmouth, sold in May 1699 by John and
Elizabeth Danforth 'who derived from P.
H.'
6 **RICHARD**, Cape Porpus 1660. Gr. j. 1661;
Constab. 1668-70. In Wells Ct. July 1675
he ack. judgm. to Nathl. Fryer, assignee of
Robt. Gutch. List 255. W. Susanna 12 Oct.
1669, when they made oath to Peter Turbet's nunc. will.
7 **RICHARD**, soldier on Kennebec River
1688; Sergt. in command of the garrison
at John Ingersoll's, Falm., May 1690. List
189.
**HICKSON** (Hixon), 1 **Richard**. See Watkins.

2 **ROBERT**, Greenland 1698. List 330d. See
also Hinksman. One Christian a Portsm.
witn. 1715. Y. D. 8.197. Margaret b. Newc.
8 May 1714. Samuel tenant on a Kit. farm
1730.
**Hidden**, Joseph, m. in Portsm. 4 July 1711
———— Crockett (No. Ch. record).
**Hidder**, Richard, Kittery. List 289.
**HIGGINS**, 1 **Beriah**, (fine aut.), b. 29 Sept.
1661, s. of Jona. of Eastham. Mariner on
a Newcastle ketch 1684; later master mariner; appar. of Dover 1689; Kit. witn. 1695;
bot in the heart of Portsm. 4 Jan. 1696-7.
Lists 314, 57, 333b, 358b. D: bef. 27 Apr.
1699. W. not found. Son **Joseph**, mariner,
Eastham, sole heir, sold his fa.'s Portsm.
land and 50 a. gr. in Dover 1718, 1727.
2 **JOHN**, coaster, York, m. 4 Mar. 1725-6
Mary Boody(1). 4 daus. As admx., she
and 2d husb. Jos. Stover sued Jacob Perkins 1737. List 279.
**Hight**, see Hoyt.

**HILL.** Became 14th commonest name in
N. E.
1 **AMBROSE**, took a knife away from Nich.
Frost in a fracas at the Gattensby tav.,
Berwick, in Apr. 1670; he and w. abs. from
meet. at Wells, July 1675. Witn. Wm. Hilton's note 1678 and ment. in his est. 1690;
sued by John Hinckes 1693. His statistics
1700 (London): ab. 700 families in N. H.,
50 sawmills in N. H. and Me.
2 **DAVID**, poss. first of Newcastle. See Jordan (8). M. Portsm. 25 Oct. 1710 Anne
(Adams) Couch, wid. of (3) and mov. to
Kit.; d. ab. 1717, adm. 6 Oct. 1724 to wid.
and 3d husb. Nich. Weeks, m. 6 Nov. 1718.
Two ch., 4 yrs. 8 mos. and 2 yrs. at his
death, were **Anne**, b. 31 July 1712, m. 24
Sept. 1728 Enoch Staples, and ?**William**,
Anne Weeks' s.-in-law by gr. mo. Adams's
will 1720, giving to him and her gr. dau.
Anne equally; her child (Y. D. xi. 127); yet
her deed of ho. and land 23 Oct. 1718 was
to two daus. only, Mary Couch, Anne Hill.
(Y. D. ix. 92).
3 **JAMES**, York, m. Mehitable Adams
(Philip). List 279. 6 ch. 1725-38.
4 **JOHN** (Hille), 1614. List 7.
5 **JOHN**, Dover (Oyster Riv.), 1649, ±35
in 1659, also in 1661; ±55 in 1680, depos.
ab. Drew and Giles land. Excused from
training in June 1661 on acct. of his small
stature. Gr. j. 1661-2, 1665, 1668, 1671, 1674,
1677. Taxed Greenland 1690-91. In 1698,
sr., of Greenl., form. of Portsm., he sold his
Portsm. gr. of that yr. Lists 352, 354bc,
355b, 356a, 361a, 341, 363a, 366, 359a, 49,
54, 57, 52, 62, 330d. W. Elizabeth. Poss. he
was the John in Boston 1647, and went back
to m. Elizabeth Strong 16 Jan. 1656. One
Elizabeth witn. a Crockett deed in 1683.

Y. D. 4.1. Kn. ch: **Samuel. Joseph**, b. ±1657.
**John, Benjamin**, b. 8 Apr. 1665, prob. d.
unm. **Hannah**, m. Wm. Frye (3). **Elizabeth**,
m. 1st Wm. Davis(65), 2d John Avery(2).
See also (22).

**6 JOHN**, witn. a Pendleton deed at Portsm.
1671. Y. D. 2.97.

**7 JOHN**, Kittery, from the Eastward, inv.
29 Nov. 1682; will prov. 3 Apr. 1683
gave all to Capt. and Mrs. Champernowne
except what given to Mary Gunnison. List
30.

**8 CAPT. JOHN** (17), partn. with Francis
Backus in bldg. sawmill at Saco 1686,
and began his milit. career there as Ensign
of Edw. Sargent's Co. 1689. Commis. Lieut.
aft. disting. hims. at Wells in June 1692;
com. Capt. by Phips 19 Apr. 1693 and stationed at the English outpost, Fort Mary
at Saco Falls. Reliev. at his own req., Apr.
1700. Of Saco Fort 4 Apr. 1698 he bot in
Portsm. from Saml. Cutts; of Portsm. Mar.
1699-1700, his dwg. ho. there ment. 1705,
but of Kit. 1700 and taxed 1701 at Berw.
where he estab. a perm. home. Lists 35,
267b, 248b, 289, 290, 38, 296, 298, 331c. Justice Ct. of Common Pleas 1711. M. 12 Dec.
1694 Mary Frost (2). He d. 2 June 1713; her
will 15 Jan.—23 Apr. 1753. List 298. See
Doc. Hist. 5.442. Ch: **Sarah**, b. 6 Dec. 1695,
m. Wm. Leighton (5). **Mary**, b. 15 Jan. 1701,
m. John Leighton (5). Hon. ‡***John**, b. 8 Jan.
1703. Capt., Major, Deputy, Senator, Councillor 1755-1771, Justice Ct. of Com. Pleas,
Judge of Prob. List 298. He m. Elizabeth
Gerrish, dau. of Capt. Nathl. (3), who d. 2
Jan. 1763; 2d Sarah, wid. of Rev. John
Blunt, dau. of Hon. John Frost (2). He d. 2
Mar.,she 13 May 1772. 7 ch. 1729-1748. **Abigail**, b. 5 Dec. 1706, d. bef. 1729. **Elisha**, b.
5 Feb. 1709-10, m. 16 Dec. 1736 Mary Plaisted (Elisha). List 298. D. 1 June 1764, she
d. 6 Aug. 1787. 14 ch. **Eunice**, b. 1 Nov.
1712, d. unm. 1737.

**9 JOHN** (5), Greenland, taxed jr. 1693.
Lists 332b, 62, 335a, 337, 338a, 339. W.
Sarah Brackett (6). List 335a. In 1709, of
Portsm., they q. c. to Joshua Brackett her
right at Casco Bay; in 1715, of Greenl., he
sold his int. in his fa.'s Dover gr. Adm. 11
Aug. 1718 to s. Joshua, wid. and three sons
renounc. She d. at Daniel Allen's in Stratham 26 May 1755 Ch: **Joseph**, turner,
chairmaker, Greenland. List 338d. M. there
24 Oct. 1717 Sarah Larrabee (6), both adm.
ch. 1727; 6 ch. bp. 1719-29. He owned in
Scarb. and bot and sold in Stratham, app.
liv. in Stratham 1740. W. Mary named in
will 9 Jan. 1755—28 July 1756, with 1 son, 2
daus. **Joshua**, ho. carp., Stratham, 1729; m.
Greenl. 24 Jan. 1723-4 Rachel Goss (3); d.
Stratham 13 Jan. 1774, she 7 Sept. 1784.
Ch., incl. Joshua jr., k. at Cape Breton.

**John**, ho. carp., Stratham 1729; m. bef. 21
Mar. 1725-6 Sarah Wiggin (Jona.); d. 12
Aug., adm. 2 Sept. 1752 to wid. and s. John.
4 ch. in div. John H. lost 4 ch. at Stratham
Oct.-Nov. 1742. **Benjamin**, liv. 1718, not in
q. c. deed with three bros. 15 Aug. 1729.
Daus. may have incl. ?**Lydia**, adm. Greenl.
Ch. 1728, m. Michael Hicks (gr. s. of 4),
and ?**Sarah**, poss. the mo. instead, o. c. 1735.
One Hannah of Portsm. m. 3 July 1718
Israel Smith of Stratham.

**10 JOSEPH** (5), ±25 in Sept. 1682; Constable 1682. In 1684 he compl. that the
sheriff had seized his cattle for his fa.'s
debt and put them in Capt. Mathews' pasture. In 1685 he sold his Oyster River farm
bot from his fa., and bot in Dover in 1689.
M. in Kit. (Ct. Dec. 1688) Catherine Knight
(19); 2d Susanna Beedle (1), prob. ab. 1696
when he bot at Long Reach. Jury 1693.
Selectm. Dover 1699 and sold there that yr.,
reserv. where his form. w. and chn. were
bur. Ch. bap. Portsm. 1709-1713. Will, yeoman, Kit., 30 Jan. 1712-3—5 Jan. 1713-4
names w. Susanna sole exec.; she m. 2d John
Lydston (1). Ch: **Samuel**, a Friend, m. 23
Dec. 1721 Hannah Allen (Francis 12). Will
24 Apr. 1764—1 Aug. 1775 names her, 4 liv.
ch., 3 decd. without issue. **Joseph**, m. 17
July 1725 Sarah Dennett (John); she liv.
1738, but d. bef. him. He d. s. p.; will 18
June—16 Oct. 1754 names 6 sisters (1
decd.), their ch; neph. Isaac (Saml.) exec.
**John**, under age 1713, not in bro.'s will
1754. **Elizabeth**, m. 9 Dec. 1714, John Emerson; 4 or m. ch. rec. Haverhill; wid. there
1755. **Hannah**, m. Thos. Hutchins(3). **Abigail**, m. Thos. Ham. **Sarah**, m. Nathl. Jackson (16). **Catherine**, m. 1 Aug. 1728 Edward
Ordway of Haverh. and d. 23 Nov. 1805, ag.
100 (Hav. Rec.) 8 ch. rec. **Mary**, m. Saml.
Jackson(16). **Dorcas**, m. (int. 29 Apr. 1729)
Joshua Remick.

**11 *JOSEPH** (17), Esq., Lieut. at Fort
Mary 1697-9; later Capt. Of Saco in Feb.
1699-1700, he bot the 300 a. Cross prop. in
Wells and mov. there; in 1707 bot the Bolles
homestead which became his home. Jury
1700; Gr. j. 1702, 1714 (foreman). Dep.
1705, 1718, 1724; Collector of the Excise
1734. Lists 39, 256, 267b, 269ac. M. 24 Jan.
1694 Hannah Littlefield(12) who d. 10 Oct.
1738, ag. 65; 2d 10 Apr. 1739 Sarah, wid. of
Daniel Sawyer. Will 23 Mar.—19 July 1743
names her; s. **Nathaniel** (List 269c) and
ch.; dec. s. **Joseph's** dau. Abigail Haley; s.-
in-law Wm. Sawyer, and nephews. 6 ch. rec.
Wells 1695-1708.

**12 CAPT. *NATHANIEL** (21), b. ±1660,
only surv. s. and heir 1697, had his fa.'s
500 a. farm, long the subject of litigation.
In 1745 it was occup. by ab. seven houses,
incl. Saml. and Val. Hill's and Thos. Ches-

ley's. A founder and Deacon of Oyster Riv. Ch. 1718. Gr. j. 1692; jury 1697; Selectm. Dover 1695, 1698; Rep. 1699, 1703, 1704, 1709. Lists 52, 94, 57, 62, 63, 64, 353, 368b, 369. W. Sarah Nutter (Anthony), adm. to ch. 1724; both ±78 in 1738. In old age he gradually lost his reason and spent his last six mos. with s.-in-law Capt. Mathews. Will 6 Jan. 1741—28 Apr. 1742. Ch: **Valentine**, liv. Nottingham 1765. Lists 368b, 369. **Samuel**, m. 12 June 1718 Sarah Thompson (John); d. bef. 2 Apr. 1767, 'benumbed in his senses' 12 or 14 yrs. 10 or 11 ch. **Sarah**, b. 18 July 1698, m. 15 Dec. 1720 Daniel Warner of Portsm. **Abigail**, m. 1st 17 Dec. 1716 Capt. Benj. Mathews, 2d bef. 1744 Eleazer Coleman of Newington. **Mary**, m. James Burnham (6); 4 sons bp. Oyster Riv. 2 Jan. 1723-4, gr. ch. of Capt. Nathl. H.

13 **\*PETER**, came over twice to Richmond Isl., sailor and fisherman, poss. same who had s. John bp. at St. Stephen by Saltash 26 June 1631. When time was up he settled in West Saco. Dep. to Ligonia Assembly 18 Dec. 1648. Saco gr. 12 July 1653. Lists 21, 243ab, 244a, 252. His 100 a. at Winter Har. bot from Mr. Jos. Bolles 12 Oct. 1659, and 100 a. from Mrs. Mackworth, form. Saml. Andrews, were confirmed to his s. by Maj. Phillips 8 Oct. 1667, also by the town. Bur. 29 Aug. 1667; adm. to only kn. ch. **Roger**; bondsm. 3 Sept. 1667 Mr. Thos. Williams, Rich. Hitchcock.

14 **RALPH.** List 355b. Read Hall.

15 **RICHARD**, Shoals, sued by John Pickering 1665; lost in the great storm 30 Jan. 1677-8. See Broad(4). See also (16).

16 **RICHARD**, O. A. Kennebec 1674. List 15. Poss. (15).

17 **ROGER** (13), ±33 Aug. 1668. Freeman 1653 and liv. in Saco until the War. In 1671 he confirmed to John Helson 100 a. sold by his fa., reserv. what his own ho. stood on. Salem June 1676—July 1680; at Wells early in 1681, and ret. to Saco bef. 3 Dec. that yr. when granted 20 a. Oft. Gr. and Tr. j.; Constable 1661; Fence Viewer 1674; Selectm. 1685-7. Lists 243ab, 24, 244af, 245, 249, 33. M. Nov. 1658 Mary Cross(7). List 246. From Wells 7 May 1690 he wrote to her at Saco to have s. John bring her and goods to Wells by water. D. 26 Aug. 1693, adm. 30 Aug. to s. Capt. John; wid. d. Wells 24 June 1696. Ch: **Sarah**, b. 7 Apr. 1661, m. Lt. Pendleton Fletcher (8), 2d bef. 7 Oct. 1702 Wm. Priest, 3d Lt. Andrew Brown (3). **Hannah**, b. 7 Sept. 1664, m. bef. 23 May 1681 Lt. Jos. Storer. **John**, b. 28 May 1666. **Samuel**, b. 14 Dec. 1668. **Joseph**, b. 1671-3 by depos., bp. Salem 19 May 1678 with John, Saml. and Mary. **Mary**, b. 25 June 1672, m. David Littlefield (5). **Benjamin**, b. 24 Feb. 1674, prob. d. bef. 19 May 1678. **Ebenezer**,

gent., b. 14 Feb. 1679-80, bp. Salem same mo., Corp. at Fort Mary 1699, taxed Kit. 1701. M. 30 Mar. 1702-3 Abiel Snell (Geo.) and mov. to his fa.'s land at Winter Harbor, where both taken 10 Aug. 1703 and carried to Canada. At Wells in Dec. 1706, Portsm. 1713, and ret. to Biddeford by 1724. There Selectm., Town Treas., Ensign, Lieut., Deacon. List 39. W. d. 10 Nov. 1750. His will 8 May 1757—2 Oct. 1758 names 6 (1 decd.) of 8 kn. ch. and gr. s. Ebenezer Jordan. See N. E. Reg. 12.139, 258.

18 **SAMUEL** (5), m. 28 Oct. 1680 Elizabeth Williams (Wm.); tavern lic. Oyster Riv. 1683. Bot in Kit. bef. 27 Apr. 1686; of Kit. in Mar. 1687-8 he and fa.-in-law sold at O. R. to Stephen Jenkins. Gr. j. (N. H.) 1696, 1697, 1700. Bricklayer, Portsm., 1703, turner 1705; there 1 Mar. 1707-8, he made a contract with Mr. Nich. Shapleigh ab. mills on Mill Creek. Of Kit. 1713, but in Portsm.; Kit. 1722, late of Portsm. Lists 52, 336b, 291, 296, 297, 298, 368b. Will 28 Aug. 1713— 28 Mar. 1723 names w. and s.-in-law Geo. Marshall exec., and all ch. but Elizabeth tho then liv. Wid. d. by 1737. Ch: **John**, b. 30 Nov. 1681, blockmaker, Portsm., m. by 1707 Hannah Almary (Robt.), who was liv. 1729. Adm. 24 Feb. 1762 to Jos. Low; div. to 6 daus., not incl. Elizabeth bp. with her mo. in 1708. One Elizabeth m. in Kit. 4 Oct. 1728 John Cole. **Elizabeth**, b. 7 Nov. 1683, m. 25 Feb. 1701-2 Geo. Marshall. **Mary**, b. 6 Apr. 1685, m. bef. Jan. 1707-8 Benj. Welch. **Hannah**, b. 29 Sept. 1687, m. Saml. More. **Abigail**, b. 29 Sept. 1689, m. Ebenezer Dennett(2). **Samuel**, b. 13 Dec. 1696; acc. by Abigail Chapman (4) in July 1713; m. in Newington 22 Nov. 1716 Mary Nelson (John). List 291. Chairmaker, Newingt., 1721, brickmaker 1724. 10 ch. **Sarah**, b. 28 July 1701; in Ct. Jan. 1724-5; m. Joseph Fogg (1). **Benjamin**, b. 2 July 1703, m. 12 Jan. 1726 Mary Neal (Andrew). 13 ch. **Joseph**, b. 28 July 1706, cordwainer Kit. 1735, m. 2 May 1728 Abigail Libby. 6 ch.

19 **SAMUEL** (17), Mr., Wells; Charlestown 1692, 1713; Portsm. 1698. Gr. j. 1688; tr. j. 1688-9. Capt. of a packet carrying supplies to East. Forts dur. the Wars, he helped take a French vessel in 1696. While liv. on the Austin farm at Wells 10 Aug. 1703, he, w. Elizabeth Austin (7), and chn. old enough to travel (younger ones k.) were taken by Ind. In letter written 1704 he sent respects to Cous. Pearce; paroled in 1705 with letters for Gov. Dudley, ret. perman. 21 Nov. 1706. Lists 39, 68, 268b, 269a, 330de, 333b, 336b, 337. Adm. 16 Nov. 1732 to s. Saml., wid. Elizabeth renounce. She, gentlewo., soon deeded to s. Saml. and to John Storer for life support. Two surv. ch: **Samuel**, Boston shopkeeper 1732, wrote to mo. in 1745, send-

ing regards from Grandma Simpson who would be 99 in Feb.; he liv. 1749. **Elizabeth**, m. 11 Oct. 1722 John Storer. Others incl.: **Rebecca**, m. at Charlestown 25 Nov. 1712 Jos. Caswell(4), d. Dec. 1713, leav. s. John, b. 15 Dec.; of Malden, cordwainer, 1744, he q. c. in Wells to John Storer. **Austin**, bp. Wells 26 Apr. 1702, must have been an Ind. victim.

20 **SAMUEL** (Mr. Wm. of Boston), legatee of his relative Thos. Fowler (4); ±19 in 1704. In 1708 he sued Nich. Tucker; of Portsm. Jan. 1708-9 success. sued John Frink for poss. of the 50 a. in Kit. and sold the land to Frink.

21 *\***VALENTINE**, Mr., merchant, Boston, Dover, Oyster Riv., interested in Eastern trade, land and mills at O. R., where he bot Christo. Helme's 500 a. bef. going there ab. 1650 from Boston. Town grants and the Champernowne farm in Greenl. purch. ab. 1657 increased his holdings, yet he left an involved est., many yrs. unsettled. A Lincolnshire man, he came to Boston with w. Frances (Freestone), bp. 13 Oct. 1610, d. 1644, dau. of Richard of Alford, a connec. of the Hutchinsons. N. E. Reg. 74.140. She was adm. to Boston Ch. 28 Dec. 1634; he 1636 and Deacon; freeman 13 May 1640; propr.; town officer. M. 2d Mary Eaton (Gov. Theophilus of Conn.). At Dover he was Selectm. 1651 (tho called of Boston Feb. 1651-2), 1657; Rep. 1652, 1653, 1654, 1655, 1657; Com. t. e. s. c.; memb. of Ct. 1653. Of Boston, late of Piscataqua, Gov. Eaton's will 1656. Lists 353, 354c, 355ab, 356a, 361a, 362a, 363ac, 323, 326a, 45, 46, 53, 73. Liv. 2 Nov. 1660; inv. filed 15 Apr. 1661, many yrs. bef. death of br. John, merch., London, will 1665—1687, mentioning Winthrope and Croft in co. Lincoln, and naming many, incl. br.-in-law Mr. Thos. Cobbett (of Lynn), who had taken mortgages on V. H.'s prop. and called him 'bro.' Waters i. 5. Wid. Mary brot several suits for dower; Capt. Thos. Savage held her int. in lands 1663 (Y. D. 3.101); in 1671 she liv. with Stephen Jones; m. as his 3d w. bef. 1679 Ezekiel Knight (2). She was of Dover 1703; d. 24 Apr. 1708, from age, infirmity and illness. List 96. Ch., all in Boston except the last: **Hannah**, b. 17 Mar. 1638-9; legatee 1651 of Robt. Turner, Boston, 'dau. of my w.'s sis'; m. Antipas Boyce(1). **John**, b. and d. 1 Sept. 1640. **Elizabeth**, b. 12 Dec. 1641, d. 9 Apr. 1643. **Joseph** and **Benjamin**, b. 29 June, d. Aug. 1644. By 2d w: **Joseph**, bp. 26 July 1646, ab. 8 days old, d. bef. fa. **John**, bp. 22 Aug. 1647, d. bef. fa. **Samuel**, bp. 10 Dec. 1648, liv. 1661, d. s. p. **Mary**, bp. 30 Dec. 1649, m. Rev. John Buss(1). **Elizabeth**, bp. 25 May 1651, d. bef. fa. **Nathaniel**, b. O. R. beginning Mar. 1659-60.

22 **WILLIAM**, Oyster River, ±34, 3 Sept. 1680, the same day that John (5) depos. ±55. Proof is wanting they were fa. and s., tho Wm.'s depos., ag. ±40, that he had kn. Bellamy's Bank Freshet since he could remem., places him here as a ch. Taxed 1675, 77, 82. Lists 359a, 358b. In 1696 Zachariah Pitman depos. that he had some corn of 'poor Wm. H.' W. Hannah Roberts (Wm.), m. 2d John Cox (13). Ch: **Henry**, John Knight's apprent. 1694, as was **William**, b. ±1678; Oyster Riv.; surveyor. Lists 368b, 369. W. Judith (Ct. Mar. 1698-9), adm. to ch. 1723. In 1720 he joined his mo. deeding her share in Wheelwright Pond gr. to Salathiel Denbo; in 1734 deeded 1/3 of his farm to son Henry; liv. May 1762, ag. 84. To his kn. ch: Wm. jr. m. Patience Drew (14), and Henry, m. Hannah Drew(6), poss. should be added: Eliphalet, Patience, Abigail, all bp. O. R. 29 Dec. 1720; Benj., an O. R. witn. 1720 in case ag. Amos Pinkham, when Wm. H. also witn. One Benj. had been murdered in 1744, Danl. Bryn accused. One Abigail m. in Portsm. 10 June 1714 Ebenezer Daniel; poss. oldest ch. of Wm. and Judith, or dau. of Wm. and Hannah. See also Daniels(4). One Mary m. in Newington 10 Sept. 1740 Salathiel Denbo, both of Durham.

**HILLIARD,** an ancient personal name.
1 —— Mrs., d. in Kingston 14 Sept. 1727, ag. 71, Abigail, w. of Richard, d. there 25 Sept. 1733.

2 **EDWARD** (Helier), Salem, at ho. of Mr. Gardiner at Pemaquid Nov. 1675; his vessel had been taken by Capt. Rodrigo. List 3.

3 **EMANUEL**, seaman, Hampton, bot ho. there 18 May 1649. Fisherman, of the Shoals, he sold Shoals ho. and stage to Wm. Seeley 24 June 1653. Lists 393ab. Adm. est. Saml. Parker 1656. W. Elizabeth Parkhurst (Geo. of Watert.) bp. at St. Margaret's Ch., Ipswick, co. Suffolk, 18 May 1628. List 393a. See N. E. Reg. 68.370. Her kinsm. Rev. Timo. Dalton deeded him 100 a., part of his farm, 10 Oct. 1657, 10 days bef. he left in a vessel lost bet. Hampt. and Boston. Adm. 13 Apr. 1658 to wid., who m. 2d, contract 13 Dec. 1659, Jos. Merry. Ch: **Timothy**, b. ±1645. **John**, b. 2 Mar., d. 7 Aug. 1651. **Benjamin**, b. 2 Nov. 1652, k. by Ind. 13 June 1677; adm. 9 Oct. to br. Timo. **Elizabeth**, b. 22 Jan. 1654-5. Francis Page recd. her and Benj.'s share of their fa.'s est. 23 June 1669. One Emanuel Helier m. Orange Adams, St. Andrew's, Plymouth, Eng., 2 Feb. 1626.

4 **JOSEPH**, m. bef. 9 July 1713 Mary Bickford (7). One Mary Helyer and Mary Ingraham witn. mar. of Saml. Cutts (9 jr.) and Hannah Perkins in Boston 11 Feb. 1718-9.

5 **MARGARET** (Hillia--?), m. Thos. Cox (31).

6 **NICHOLAS** (Hellier), m. at Portsm. 4 Aug. 1712 Mary Howard. See Howard 3. He or ano. Nicholas (Hilliard) of Portsm. m. in Newington 16 Dec. 1718 Elizabeth (Haley 1), wid. of Wm. Hoyt (Thos.). She was adm. to Newingt. Ch. 18 Aug. 1728, m. 4th 2 Nov. 1732 Deacon John Dam (4).

7 **TIMOTHY** (3), Hampton, ±64 Sept. 1709. Selectm. 1688, 1697; Constable 1693; Jury 1694. Lists 49, 396, 392b, 61, 399a. M. 1st 3 Dec. 1674 Apphia Philbrick (James); 2d (settlem. 20 Sept. 1712) Mehitable (Ayers), wid. of Thos. Philbrick; she was liv. 1721. Will 16 Apr. 1712, cod. 9 Jan. 1720-1; d. 17 Aug. 1723. Ch: **Elizabeth**, b. 29 Sept. 1679, m. 1st Caleb Shaw, 2d Joseph Tilton. Lieut. **Benjamin**, b. 19 July 1681, m. 1st 20 Apr. 1703 Mehitable Weare (Nathl.), 2d 3 Apr. 1706 Elizabeth Chase (Jos.). Will 16, d. 18 Nov. 1723. She m. by 1730 Capt. Jos. Tilton; wid. in Kensington 1753; will prov. 1765. Ch: 1+6. **Apphia**, b. 29 Aug. 1686, d. 14 Feb. 1699. **Mary**, b. 23 Aug. 1688, not in will. Dau., b. 24 June 1690, d. y.

**HILTON.** 'There are parishes and places so called in many counties and prob. several distinct families. The great baronial race which flourished in the XIV cent. derived their name from the castle of Hulton or Hilton, co. Durham, their ancient seat.' (Sharp's Hartlepool, p. 167.) The American Hiltons, like the Drakes and the Webbers, have been victims of a 'missing heir—estate in Chancery' fraud. The legend went that the last Baron Hilton (of co. Durham) had d. a bachelor and that, as his two brothers, William and Edward, had emigrated, the estate was in Chancery. About 1885 Nathan Hilton, a magistrate of Yarmouth, N. S., collected a fund and hired 'a woman in London to search the matter out' (letter of Capt. B. R. Hilton, 1924.) This woman, identity unkn., in order to connect the co. Durham family with the two brothers in London and America, must have invented probate records of two estates, 'Ralph Hilton, 1602,' and 'Roger Hilton, 1619.' Exhaustive searches by Mr. Hassam (1873-4), Col. Banks (1924) and the best professional Col. Banks knew, employed by him when he returned to America, failed to find any trace of 'Ralph' and 'Roger.' They did, however, find over thirty contemp. records supporting the origin of the American emigrant brothers in Northwich, co. Chester. The baronial pedigree was pub. in the Yarmouth Herald, Mar. 22-29, Apr. 5-12, 1898, and will doubtless charm the credulous for years to come.

1 §‡*EDWARD, first permanent settler of N. H., son of William, of Northwich, co. Chester, bro. of (13) and (17), prob. he who was bp. at Northw. (Witton chapelry) 9 June 1596. The record, now prob. illeg., was read 'son of Richard' by the vicar in 1920, and 'son of William' by a superannuated antiquary some yrs. later. The historian Hubbard's statement that Edward and William(17) were brothers, however, seems unquestionable. Apprent. to Marie, wid. of Charles Hilton of London, he was adm. to the Fishmongers Co. 9 Apr. 1621 ('nup. apprent. Marie Hilton'—late apprentice of Marie Hilton—a final reading from the original record), and in the subsidy list of the Lond. companies of 1641 'In New England' is marked ag. his name. He likely made a voyage to Piscataqua with trading goods and began a plantation, unrecorded, in 1628, the yr. set by his personal friends and purchasers of his patent for his arrival, and 9 June 1628 when the plantations agreed to send Thomas Morton back to Eng., he contrib. £1. The earliest contemp. rec. of him and Wm.(17) together, either in Eng. or here, are the livery of seisin of his Squamscot patent, dated 12 Mar. 1629-30, wit. by Wm. 7 July 1631 (N. E. Reg. 24.264; N. H. Court Files 21494), the Lewis-Bonython and Vines-Oldham patents at Saco river dated a month earlier, and the petn. of (18) (orig. in Suff. Ct. Files 362). E. H. was evidently back in London, waiting on Sir F. Gorges with Mr. Lewis, when the patents were gr. These doc. empower E. H., gent., to make livery of the two on the Saco, and Mr. Lewis to do the same for Hilton at Squamscot. Whether Hilton came over at once and went back to sell his patent to the Bristol men is quest. See Y. D. i. pt. 2. 9. Godfrey knew and told it best: 'A Pattent granted to Ed. Hilton, by him sould to merchants of Bristoll they sould it to my Lo: Say and Brokes, they to sume of Shrwsbury'; and confirm. by Winthrop: 'Pascataquack, which the Lord Say and the Lord Brook had purchased of the Bristol men.' The patent recited: Hilton's Point lying some two leagues from the mouth of the river, having already at his own cost & charge transplanted sundry servants . . . where they have already built some houses. Hilton was in control at Dover Neck 4 Dec. 1632 when Winthrop reed. letters from Capt. Neale and W. H. that they had sent 4 vessels and 40 men to protect Pemaquid from Dixie Bull. He contin. the Bristol men's gov. until 10 Oct. 1633, when Capt. Wiggin arr. in Boston to take over the patent for the two Lords. He then set up for himself betw. Dover and Exeter. When Mass. stepped in, the Gen.

Ct. in Oct. 1641 ordered that Francis Williams and E. H., with two magistrates from Boston, should constitute the County Ct., and he was named again in 1642. In 1652 Exeter voted that he go with Mr. Dudley to the Gen. Ct. to assist him. Cf. Prov. Papers i. 306. Selectman, Exeter, 1645, 1646, 1651. When Charles II came in, Hilton prov. to be a strong loyalist, and in 1665 was arrested for sedition. Lists 241, 375b, 376ab, 377-379, 47, 383, 384a. We know nothing of his wives until he m., soon aft. 1654, Catherine (Shapleigh) Trewargy. Last ment. alive 19 May 1669, his four sons adm. in their own wrong, and a yr. or more passed bef. the ct., on petn. of Chr. Palmer on behalf of their two sisters, summonsed them to bring an invent. to ct., which they did Mar. 1670-1. Inv. £2204. In June the wid.'s dower was set off and an order entered sequestering the real est. until debts were pd., and in Sept. the wid. was 'executrix.' She d. 2 May 1676; will ment. Edward, jr., and Jane Hilton. Ch: **Edward**, b. ab. 1630. **William**, b. ab. 1632. **Sobriety**, m. 20 Nov. 1651 Henry Moulton. (Savage mistook her name for Mary.) **Susannah**, m. 7 Nov. 1650 Christopher Palmer. **John**, gr. 29 + 1 a. 16 Mar. 1660-1, not laid out but sold to Godfrey(3) who had them laid out with 10 a. gr. to himself 4 Apr. 1666. List 276b. Not 'adm.' of his fa.'s est. See (3). **Samuel**, ±40 in 1680. In 1664 he and Charles dep. they had kn. Lamprill river, 'which is above our mills,' since earliest recoll. Road to S. H.'s mill ment 1687. 'Gent.' 1699-1702, sold to (14). Appar. never m., but numerous Samuels show how he spent his time. Jury 1685. Lists 94, 383, 384, 52(2), 57. **Charles**, ±25 in 1660, ±30 in 1672. He fell under the influence of Capt. Barefoot, to his harm. In 1668 B. was buying sack for him. Helped B. to resist constable Deering(4). In 1671 broke into ho. B. deeded to him without owning it in 1669. In 1679 'now of Hampton' he bound himself for 4 yrs. to Chr. Palmer who had got him out of Norfolk jail, wit. Henry Dow. Last taxed Apr. 1682. D. s. p. in winter 1683-4. Lists 312e, 52.

2 **EDWARD**(1), Exeter, 48 in 1678, had the homestead. Tav. lic. 1689, victualer 1692. Lists 49, 385, 52, 92, 94, 67, 385. He m. Ann Dudley(1), List 385. Will, prov. 10 July 1699, prov. for w. Ann, gave S.W. half of lands to s. Winthrop and a quarter each to s. Dudley and s. Joseph, £15 each to daus. Jane Mattoon, Ann, Mary and Sobriety Hilton. Ch: **Jane** (see 1), m. 1st Joseph Hall (12), 2d, aft. 1684, Richard Mattoon. **Winthrop**, b. 1671. **Anne**, m. Richard Hilton (14). **Mary**, b. 1678, m. (int. Salisbury 24 Oct. 1702) Thos. Bradbury(2). List 385. **Dudley**, b. 1679, m. (Ct. Dec. 1701) Mercy

Hall(14), who m. 2d Capt. Nath. **Ladd**(5). Last ment. 5 June 1710, by trad. never heard from after his bro. Winthrop was killed. Adm. given to cred. 1722. List 376b. 3 daus. See N. H. Deeds 20.348. **Joseph**, b. 1681, Ensign 1716. He m. 1st 16 Oct. 1709 Hannah Jose(3), 2d in Newbury 10 Oct. 1716 Rebecca (Atkinson), wid. of Israel Adams. D. 1765, ag. 84. List 376b. Ch. 1 + 4. **Sobriety**, m. Jonathan Hilton (19). List 385. **Judith**, **Bridget**, by trad. both d. y.

3 **JOHN**(17). See also (1). One of 4, 5 or 6 John Hiltons, none of whom had births recorded, only one had kn. ch., only two had kn. wives, only one had death recorded and one other death proved. At Newbury William(18) and John H. bot lands from several persons and in 1653 turned 2½ a. back to town commons to pay their 1652 taxes. Taxed only for his poll and a horse, John app. never married but shifted from place to place (marked 'gone' in 1664 tax list). Dover town records (i. 31) show a gr. on 4: 10: 1656 to John H. of 3 a. adj. Mr. Thos. Roberts, Sr., and refer to land 'formerly a lane to Mr. Hilton's house.' His father sold out bef. moving to Kittery, but John's right was neglected until 1721 when it was sold by the heirs of (20) to a Dover speculator. Lists 354a, 355a, 356abc, 361a, 363-abc(2), 47, 365.

4 **JOHN**(19), eldest s., adult by 1686; was not called dec'd. in 1703 when Capt. Pickering took oath that he saw him sign a bond in 1686. Y.D. 6.157-8. Tax abated ab. 1702. Lists 94, 57. See (5).

5 **JOHN** (see 23, 4, 3, 1, 18, 15), m. in Marblehead 10 Feb. 1694-5, 'both of Boston,' Abigail Snelling. Boston records: **Ruth**, b. 29 June 1697. Bur. a ch. of John H. 9 May 1704. John H. d. 16 Apr. 1705. Bur. Mr. John H. 21 Apr. 1705. Int. of mar., Mary H. and James Mirick 6 Apr. 1709-10, Mary H. and John Wilkey 30 Mar. 1711-2. Bur. 5 Aug. 1715 Mary H. If this were all, we would deem him an emigrant, altho poss. (very unlikely) identical with (4). And if his dau. Ruth was she who m. John Pierce in Gloucester 12 Aug. 1717 (especially if Pierce was not involv. in the Muscongus land frauds), we would deem William(23), who m. Mary Tucker, his near rel., poss. his son. But there is Y.D. 16.259, 7 Feb. 1733-4: Samuel Annis of Marbleh., fisherman, and w. Avis, quitcl. mtge. of ¼ of all eastern land claims in York or elsewhere of 'our fa. John Hilton late of Boston, dyer or clothier.' This vague deed is suggestive of fraud. Marbleh. and Glouc. were ablaze at that time with the money being made by forged deeds at Muscongus. If S. Annis of Marbleh. was s. of S. Annis of Glouc., and

if the Snellings, Tuckers and Martins of the two towns were related, we must ignore the deed as a swindle. Samuel Annis and wife were hired by Samuel Martin of Muscongus to live there with William Hilton(21) 7 or 8 yrs. See Hilton(21), Brown(15, 17), Chamblet, Fulford, Dennen. See Col. Soc. of Mass., vols. vi and viii, esp. viii, pp. 111, 114. Fact: Samuel Annis and w. Naomi, she ag. 60 or 70, were liv. at St. George's in 1769, and Samuel A., jr., coaster, of St. George's, m. at Boston 6 July 1743, Mary Humble of Wells. Ibid vi. 33, 34; viii. 105.

6 **JOHN**(18), Charlest., with bro. Richard and their mo., deeded to Elizabeth Cutler in 1701. With bro. Richard deeded to Thos. Graves in 1715, 1717; to Hannah Price 1716, 1717. He m. (int. 29 Aug. 1717) Sarah Parrock 'now res. in Boston,' b. 1681, adm. to Charlestown ch. 1723. He was keeping her mo., wid. Sarah Parruck, in 1721. Tax abated 1727.

7 **JONATHAN?**, Dover tax list 1659, List 356e. Presum. misread. for John(3), original now missing.

8 **JOSIAH**, wit. for (14) 1 Dec. 1703, likelier his bro. than son. An original bond given by him in Boston 1 Dec. 1708 to pay £5 to Sarah Tomlin of Boston, wid., is wit. by Susannah Knott and Dorcas Collings, and was sworn to by the latter in 1718.

9 **MAINWARING**(17). The surname of a great Cheshire fam., numerous about Northwich, where one John M. worked a salt privilege, as did M. H.'s gr.fa., in 1570, it is spoken 'Mannering' both here and in Eng. In June-July 1667, M. H. joined his step-fa. White, br.-in-law Beale and one Richard Sweat in securing a debt to a Boston merch. on the Hilton homestead, two dwellings, a 6-ton fishing-shallop and two cows, one of which was Mainwaring's. He m. Mary Moulton, dau. of Thomas, who took adm. of his est. 4 July 1671. Inv. shows stock, no house-hold goods. The wid. m. Samuel Bragdon(5) of York, who treated as his own ch. her dau. **Magdalene**, who had ch. by 3 husb., Nath. Adams(14), Elias Weare and John Webber, and d. 4 Feb.1725-6.

10 **MAINWARING** (Mannering, Mannerel) (20), ±20 in Apr. 1703, dep. that he had been hired by Benj. Donnell to help canoe away hay which Samuel Donnell, who sued 'Maurin Hilton' for it, had cut. Again in ct. July, 1705, sued by Kittery men for taking hay on Drake Isl., Wells. Lt. Jeremiah Storer dep. that Hilton had satisf. him for the grass he and Joshua Downing had cut. In that same term is ano. case which proves that Elizabeth Thompson, dau. of John and Sarah (Emery 2), is repons. for a large segment of those bearing the name Hilton. Having joined the church 23 May 1703 and

being about to marry Alexander Gray(1), she came into ct. and discl. the paternity, long shielded, of her two illegit. ch. The two young men involved, Thomas Ball(5) of Kit. and Mannerell Hilton of York, soon vanished for all time. (Mass. Acts & Resolves, 1762-3, ch. 253; Y. D. 39.52.) In the Wells case the writ was returned -non est inv.- but on 20 Dec. 1705 Joshua Downing of Kit. and 'Manuel Hilton of York, bachelor,' signed a joint note, which Downing paid when sued. Ch: **Ebenezer**, b. ab. 1703, first Gray, then 'alias Hilton,' finally Hilton. When ab. 17, Feb. 28, 1719-20, 'Ebenezer, son of Elizabeth Gray,' owned cov. and was bp. He m. Mary Lord (Wm. 7) and built on her fa.'s land. (Y.D. 19.80). As energ. as ambit., 'house-carpenter,' 'wheelwright,' 'millwright,' he soon made the contract, ab. 1735, with Rev. Christopher Toppan for vast virgin lands, beginning at Montsweag, near Murphy's Corner, Woolwich, which cost him and many of his blood their lives. (Lincoln Deeds 16.52; Suff. Ct. Files 140610). Ch: Abigail, m. Charles Libby; Mary, m. James Savage, jr.; Sarah, m. John Boynton; Joshua, k. by Ind.; William; Lt. Moses; Ebenezer, of Portland; Lt. John (these first eight bp. 3 Sept. 1736); Hannah, m. 1st John Bryant, 2d Bartholomew Fowler; Benjamin; Joseph; Daniel; Joshua, posthumous.

11 **'MARY** Hilton alias Downer,' likely dau. of (17), but, as she bore a ch. in 1675, was not the Mary bp. in Northwich. Her alias, so much discussed, based on the version in Coffin's Hist. of Newbury, 1846, indic. a 1st husb. named Downer, altho the county rec. reads 'Thomas Seeres m. Mary Hilton 11 Dec. 1656' and altho there were three other well-kn. uses of aliases. The Newbury rec.: 'Thomas Seeres & Mary Hilton alias Downer was m. Dec. 11, 1656.' Both records were by the same man, Bradbury(1), who knew Wm. Hilton(17) well and must have been familiar with the custom in many Eng. parishes of keeping a wid.'s maiden name with an alias. Sears d. 26 May 1661. 2 Sears ch. She m. last Abel Huse who d. 1690; will naming 7 ch.

12 **MATTHEW** (Matthias), Portsmouth, from Monkwaymouth, co. Durham, m. 13 Aug. 1738 Margaret King. Tax of 'Hilton at Wid. King's or Clark's' abated 1740. His w. was adm. to com. in So.Ch. 7 Feb. 1741-2; adm. on his est. to her 24th of same mo. One **child**, bp. So.Ch. 13 May 1739.

13 **RICHARD**, s. of Wm. of Northwich, co. Chester, and bro. of (1) and (17), bp. at Northw. (Witton) 11 June 1599. That he was with his brothers in New Eng. is prov. by the bapt. at Wooton-under-Edge, co. Gloucester, 16 Aug. 1636, of 'Richard, son

of Richard Hilton, aged 1 year ½, coming out of New England.' In the N. H. ct., June 1642, Wm. Hilton sued Geo. Walton for a debt against which Walton claimed to offset a draft on one Mr. Tomkins of Northhampton, Eng., for £10, given to 'Richard Hilton of Northwich.' The ct. allowed this offset, subject to proof that the draft was pd. (N. E. Reg. 31.182). His first w. Anna was bur. in Northw. 15 June 1638. On 8 May 1641 R. H., chapelry of Witton, was lic. to m. Alice Smith, wid., of Banbury. A petn. to Parliament in 1649 shows him a feoffee of the Latin school. 1669-70, Feb. 15, 'Richardus Hilton de Witton filius et heres etatis suae 71 sepult.' By the law of Borough English the youngest son, not the eldest, was the heir. Ch: Ellen, bp. at Northw. (Witton) 1 Apr. 1632; m. Thomas Huges and d. bef. 1676-7. Rev. Richard, b. prob. on Dover Neck ab. Feb. 1634-5, bp. as stated above, was vicar of Hanmer, co. Flint, in 1663 when lic. to m. Anne Whiteall at Banbury. He d. s. p. Will, 10 Feb. 1676-7—14 May 1680, directs he be bur. in the chapel of Witton, leaves est. to w. Anne, and names his three sisters. Sarah, m. Robert Steele. Alice, bp. at Northwich (Witton) 13 Aug. 1637, m. Thomas Revelt.

14 ‡CAPT. RICHARD(19), Exeter, 72 in 1736, 80 in 1742. Engaged in mast-making with (24). Gr.j. 1695; Selectm. 1693, 1701-3, 1707-8, 1715. Lists 52, 67, 98, 376b, 377, 385. Justice of Superior Ct. 1698-9, Councilor 1703-4, J. P. many yrs. His ferry betw. his ho. and Squampscot ment. in 1700. Made desperate struggle to save his fa.'s est. which was left deeply involved. In 1719 he and his w. were in ct. for resisting service of papers. They had attacked the Marshall's deputy on his first visit, and, going again in force, he found 20 men in the ho. in women's clothes with faces blackened. Of Newmarket 1734, Portsm. 1736, in 1739 was hiring a ho. of Thos. Darling(4). See (22). He m. 'ab. 58 yrs. ago last Dec.' (dep. 2 Sept. 1745 of Mary, w. of Jeremiah Gilman, who was present), his cousin Ann Hilton(2), who was in demand in Portsm. as a midwife in her later yrs. Litig. appar. promoted by Gov. Wentworth gives us a dep. (Ct. Files 24493, Mercy Lyford), taking oath to all R. H.'s heirs-at-law in May 1761: one or two ch., 13 or 14 gr.ch., 9 gt.gr.ch. If Ann Carter, wid., of Exeter, was not a dau., whether or not she was the Ann Hilton who m. in Portsm. 1 Nov. 1716 John Lobden, she is unident. Also one minor, Elizabeth Gilman, of Exeter, if not the young married sister of John and Amy Folsom, is unident. His other desc. were all thru four sons: Richard, m. by 1717 Elizabeth, only ch. of John Wilson. She d.

1723, he bef. Dec. 1735, perhaps long bef. No gr. in 1725 div. (List 376b). Ch: Martha, w. of Wm. Pearson 1760, w. of High-Sheriff Thos. Packer 1764; Ann, m. one Creighton, 6 ch.; Elizabeth, m. John Folsom (Jonathan 4), 3 ch. William. Samuel, 39 in 1736, coaster in 1732, liv. with Wm. List 376b. He m. 26 Jan. 1733 Prudence Page of Hampton, sole benef. in will 30 Apr. (d. 14 May, ag. 51) 1748. Edward, ±36 in 1736. Gt.-uncle and gdn. of 8 plfs. in 1760. He m. Elizabeth (Folsom?). List 376b. Will 1 June—30 Oct. 1776 names 5 of 8 ch. b. 1724-1752. Benjamin, appar. youngest, as given smallest gr. in 1725. His 5 ch. plfs. in 1760. List 376b. See also (19) for Rebecca (m. Smart?) and Josiah.

15 ROBERT, at Wells 1684, was gr. lot formerly gr. to Isaac Cousins. 'Apprehended to be deceased,' adm. on his est. was gr. to Wheelwright and Littlefield 29 Sept. 1685, but he was soon back. In 1695 up for drunkenness, and deeded marsh. Lists 269b, 127. In 1707 chosen constable in Boston, decl. to serve. A dep. was given in London 11 Mar. 1713-4 by Robert Hilton, late of New Eng., merchant, now lodging at ho. of Alexander Holmes in Duke's Place, near Aldgate.

16 SARAH, see (11, 18, 17), wit. deed to Thos. Sears in 1648. Likely sister to (11) and dau. of (17), yet Sarah (18), b. June 1641, would have been taught to write and might have signed as wit.

17 *WILLIAM, son of William of Northwich, co. Chester, and bro. of (1) and (13). He was 'of London' and indebted to his fa., by the accounts preserved with latter's will, in 1605, and was legatee of his bro. Arthur Hilton of Northw. in 1612. He arrived at Cape Cod in the -Fortune- 9 Nov. 1621, his letter, badly misrep. conditions, addressed to his 'cousin' and printed in Capt. John Smith's book, being dated two days later. The 'cousin' may have been a blind for Capt. Smith himself, or one of Hilton's own nephews or one of his w.'s, with directions to send her over. She arriv. at Plymouth, with two ch., ab. 10 July 1623. They were still there in 1624 when Rev. John Lyford bp. a ch. The historian Hubbard cared little about the eastern country, and his paragraph about the founding of N. H. (N. E. Reg. 31.179) is mostly false. Hilton did not come to the Piscataqua with David Thomson in 1623 and Chr. Levett's book proves that no settlement had been made up the river in the spring of 1624 (N. E. Reg. 76.315). It was later than this last season, therefore, when Hilton left Plym. and joined Thomson at Little Harbor with the purpose of starting salt works. Incidentally, salt making was the princi-

pal industry of Northwich, his fa.'s home. When his bro. Edward came over in 1628 he naturally removed up river and when Capt. Neale arrived he was liv. on Dover Neck, and planting his corn, safe from his hogs, on the other side of the river in Me. (N. E. Reg. 31.181; Me. P. & C. ii. 19). When (1) gave place to Capt. Wiggin, he appar. went with him to Newfields, but was soon back. Freeman, with Wm. Walderne, 19 May 1642, Com. t. e. s. c. 1642-4, Rep. 1644. He is first found at Kittery Point in June, 1648; bef. that, in Apr., Dover had allowed him and Thos. Turner to gather 70 loads of pine knots on Madbury Neck. In 1647 Mendum, the Kit. Pt. innholder, had bot and given up the ho. owned by Capt. Shapleigh, who got the lic. transferred to Hilton, who hired the ho. and liv. there until S. put him out, soon aft. 15 Oct. 1650, because of his w. Frances, who by her own dep. had been liv. there some yrs. bef. Removing to York, he was promptly given the ferry and tavern lic., made alderman of the expiring city, then selectman 1652-4, and referee in ct. Gr.j. 1651, 1653-5; j. 1650 (foreman). Evid. educated and suffic. familiar with the courts to almost invar. win his frequent suits, he was given his title of Mr. wherever he went. For letters, autographs, etc. see N. E. Reg. 31.179-82, 333; 36.40. Lists 376a, 352, 353, 53, 275, 276, 277. Besides the w. who foll. him to Plym., and Frances, poss. a wid. with ch. when he m. her ab. 1651, there may have been others. His fa.'s endorsing for him to Ellen Hewett bef. 1605 is unexpl., and if one of his wives should prove to have been a Winslow it would expl. his letter writing with Edw. Winslow, his assoc. with John Winslow, his removal to Piscataqua with Gilbert Winslow and the mar. of two of John Winslow's sons to his relations. Aside from this there is the railing of his w. Frances (for which the ct. sentenced her severely) that one John was his bastard. She was beneath his class. His other w., or wives, kept out of ct. and are therefore nameless. Between two cts., June 1655 and June 1656, he d. (ag. perhaps 75), and the wid. m. Richard White. Goody White called herself ±70 in 1688 (Me. P. & C. i. 267). Ch: John, perhaps his, bur. in Northw. 26 Nov. 1610. Elizabeth, bp. 27 June, bur. 1 Aug. 1616, in Northw. William, bp. 22 June 1617 in Northw. Mary, bp. 11 May 1619 in Northw.; see (11). John, see (3). Magdalene, m. 1st by 1646 James Wiggin; 2d, of Newbury, pub. 14 May 1698 to Henry Kenning of Salem. Mainwaring, b. bef. 1650. Agnes, (Anne), m. by 1667 Arthur Beale (2). By w. Frances: William, b. ab. 1653. See also (16, 5); also Richard Sweat, Y. D. 2.33; also George and Alice Walton,

who rem. from Exeter to Dover Neck, thence to mouth of the river.

18 **CAPT. WILLIAM**(17), bp. in Northwich 22 June 1617, disting. navigator and cartographer. We have his own story of his coming-over (N. E. Reg. 36.41,45), as full as would be expected of a six yr. old child, brot over by his mo. in 1623. Hubbard's careless statements must be attrib. to this boy, as we know only from Hubbard of the controversy over the bapt. of the Hilton infant in 1624. Hubbard must have known him and both his wives well. There is no rec. of him in N. H. except that his fa. was thrice called 'sen.' 1642-43. According to the statements in his petn., given credit by the Mass. Genl. Ct., he grew up with his fa., trading with the Inds. Freeman at Newbury 1653, his name recurring there 1641-1653; in Charlestown from 1654 on, his voyages must have kept him much from home. Joined Charlest. ch. by letter from Newbury 14 Aug. 1670. He pub. a book of surveys of the Carolina coast, where the present name of Hilton is attrib. to him. Loading at Boston for London 1672. He d. 7 Sept. 1675 (N. E. Reg. 31. 185-7). He m. 1st Sarah Greenleaf (Edmund, of Newbury); 2d 16 Sept. 1659 Mehitable Nowell (Increase) of Charlest. who m. 2d 29 Oct. 1684 Dea. John Cutler and d. 29 Sept. 1711 (gr.st.). Her will, 8 Dec. 1709 —22 Oct. 1711, left life int. in her est., except rememb. to sister Mary Long and wardrobe given to her step-dau. Elizabeth (Hilton)Cutler, to her two sons John and Richard to maintain their bro. Samuel. Ch., by 1st w., b. in Newbury: Sarah, b. June 1641, m. by 1661 Edward Winslow (John) and d. 4 Apr. 1667, ag. 26 (gr.st.); 3 ch. 1661-5. Charles, b. July 1643, d. y. Mary, m. at Charlest. 2 Oct. 1667 Wm. Marshall, and d. of small-pox 15 July 1678, ag. 33 (gr. st.); 5 ch. Anne, b. 12 Feb. 1648, presum. same as dau. Hannah who m. in Newb. 2 July 1668 Jonathan Woodman; 8 ch. Elizabeth, b. 6 Nov. 1650, m. in Charlest. 22 Dec. 1673 Timothy Cutler (Dea. John), who d. 21 Oct. 1694 in 42d yr. Her will 30 Nov. 1726—20 Apr. 1733; 11 ch. By 2d w., b. in Charlestown: Nowell, b. 4 May 1663, called 'our cousin' by the minister (Mr. Symmes? Mr. Shepherd?) who bp. him May 10. Shipped with crew of the -Success- 1683. His will 6 Oct. 1687, wit. in London, and prov. there 17 Sept. 1689, gives all to kinsman Nath. Cutler, sawyer, of Stepney. Edward, b. 3 Mar. 1666. John, bp. 24 May 1668. Richard, b. 13 Sept. 1670, m. 22 Jan. 1711-2 Elizabeth Lord, who d. 22 Sept. 1718. His will, 16 (d. 25) Jan. 1720-1, does not ment. w., ch., or bro. Samuel, but gives use of ho. and land to bro. John, and ho. and

land deeded to himself and w. Elizabeth by his aunt Mrs. Long in 1714 to two cousins Mrs. Mary Atwood and Mrs. Deborah Skinner of Boston, income to be pd. to Mrs. Long.

19 **CAPT. WILLIAM**(1), ±44 in May 1676, 47 and 49 in 1680. In 1663, as constable of Kittery, he tore up the special warrant for the election of a dep. to the Mass. Gen. Ct. Gr.j. (Me.) 1660, Constable (Kit.) 1661, 1663. Gr.j. (N. H.) 1671, 1673, 1681, 1684-5; tr.j. 1684; selectman (Exeter) 1690. Lists 298 (p. 36), 383, 52, 94, 92, 55b, 56, 57. Altho he signed by mark, he was Capt. and Provost Marshall under Gov. Cranfield (poss. a connection thru the marriage at Northwich, 4 Feb. 1589, of Humphrey Cranfield and Jane Hilton). His letter to Gov. Andros 7 July 1687 recites that his 'predecessors and himself' have been inhabitants of the Province 'neere upon 50 years,' that he was com. Capt. by Cranfield ab. 6 yrs. ago, and now declines a Lt.'s com. under Capt. Robt. Wadleigh. (Mass. Arch.) Adm. of his est., badly involved, showing unpaid notes dating from 1674, was gr. to s. Richard 9 Apr. 1694. The cellar of his ho. is located in N. H. Deeds 43.227. He m. Rebecca Simmons (John) of Kit., liv. 1715. List 385. Ch. incl.: **John**, eldest son. **Richard**, b. ab. 1664. **William**, apprent. to Roger Rose, mariner, and sent to jail in Boston for striking his master and quitting his service. Wit. 1681; fa. called 'sen.' 1687. Mariner, belonging to H. M. S. -Deptford-, adm. gr. to bro. Richard 25 Nov. 1700. **Samuel**, wit. 1687; had worked for Wm. Ardell bef. Mar. 1688-9. D. bef. his fa. **Jonathan**, called Richard's bro. in 1712; m. Sobriety Hilton (2). A 1750 deed shows his ch. or heirs: Jonathan, called 'jr.' 1724 (List 376b); Charles, m. Hannah Pike (Robert) and rem. to East Andover, N. H., where she d. 28 Mar. 1794 (gr.st.); John; Sobriety, m. in Beverly 25 July 1740 Ebenezer Sallows; Ann, m. Joseph Davis of Durham; Mary, m. Benj. Smart. **Rebecca**, called 'sister' in List 385, likely m. one Smart and wit. for (14) 1 Dec. 1703. Also **Josiah**, who wit. with her, could be a bro. or (14)'s son. Anne H., m. in Portsm. 1 Nov. 1716 John Lobden, could be a dau. of either (19) or (14) or neither.

20 **WILLIAM**(17), York, 24 in Dec. 1677, fully proven half-bro. of Wm.(18). (N. E. Reg. 36. 40). He grew up with his stepfa. White, without benefit of education. Sued by Capt. Francis Raynes 1675, judg. for def. York gr. 25 Aug. 1697; O. A. 22 Mar. 1679-80. In Philip's War, Nov. 1677, with his half-bro. Sampson White, Shadrach Walton (his cousin?), two Davises (19, 27), Robert Booth (3 jr.), John Leighton and

others, he went from Portsm. on a looting exped. to Cape Porpus. Lists 306a, 30. (See 3). Of the 105 a. in his poss. in 1682, he sold ½ to Timothy Yeales, and in 1688 mortg. the other ½ to Robert Elliot(6). In 1700 wid. Anne H. was liv. on the homestead 'between Thos. Trafton's and the Harbor's Mouth,' land formerly called Inglesby's Point, later Hilton's Point. In 1713 Elliot deeded part of it to her s. Benj., part to her dau. Hannah Cole. Liv. around Boston in 1737, ag. 80, she dep. about York 70 yrs. back. Appar. she was Anne Parsons, dau. of John P., for whose wid., Elizabeth, W. H. was bondsman in 1692. In 1699 the ct. ordered him to return a cow to her (then w. of Peter Hinkson). Ch: **William**, b. 1678. **Joshua**, wit. Benj. Trafton's will 4 June 1706. Taken by Ind. in Aug. 1707, still in Canada 1710-11. Lists 96, 99 (p. 92). Three bros., 2 sisters, their neph. Ebenezer all named 1st sons Joshua, as did Wm. his 2d son. **Elizabeth**, m. 1st Lt. Josiah Littlefield(18), 2d 10 Oct. 1716 Malachi Edwards(7). 4 ch. 1717-26. **Mainwaring**, b. 1683. **Hannah**, m. 1st John Cole(17) 2d Mark Shepard. **Benjamin**, m. Elizabeth Crockett(4). 6 ch. rec. **Patience**, m. Joseph Day(3). **Dorcas**, m. Samuel Moore.

21 **LT. WILLIAM**(20), b. 1678, fisherman, Ensign, scalp-hunter, land speculator, army officer. See N. E. Reg. 31. 188-94. In 1703 had gr. adj. the homestead and another at Braveboat Harbor. In 1706 Sergt. W. H., 58 men, 2 horses, crossed the Merrimac ferry. Bot in Manchester 1709, not selling in York until 1711. In Me. ct. 1710 for striking Robt. Oliver. Boston Newsletter, Nov. 19, 1711—'Boston Monday last Lt. Hilton brot in 3 Ind. scalps for bounty taken by him from 3 Ind. who with a Frenchman from Menis had sacked a part of York and carried away a sloop. They were followed and taken by Lt. Hilton and a dozen volunteers.' Presently it app. he had taken the Ind. prisoners into the woods, shot and scalped them. Indicted for false oath bef. Gov. and Council, the jury acq. him and his military career was not blocked. He had m. at Marblehead 2 June 1699 Margaret Stilson, a returned Ind. captive. In 1717 he and James Stilson tore down the ho. of his mo.-in-law's step-fa. at Muscongus (see Chamblet), but later took him into cahoots with them in their Muscongus land swindles. Every one of their deeds, which vanished as soon as recorded and are kn. only by certif. copies of the records made at the time, is under suspicion of crude forgery. This incl. not only the '1626' John Brown deed, now ack. a forgery of W. H.'s, but the equally imposs. deed (Y. D. 15.234), Hilton's two Ind. deeds and others. Befogged by fraud, the list of children of Brown(15), alleged

gt.-gr.fa. of Margaret (Stilson) Hilton, calls for scrutiny bef. acceptance. Meanwhile, calling himself coaster, mariner, fisherman, Hilton was reprimanded by Maj. Moody at Casco Bay for insolence. His gr.st. at Manchester, 'Lifnt. William Hilton, d. June the 21st 1723 aged 45 years,' marks the close of a strenuous and desperate struggle to rebuild the Hilton fortunes. The wid. m. 2d, 8 Dec. 1727, John Allen, and d. Nov. 1763, very aged. Ch: **Elizabeth**, m. 1st John Knowlton, 2d John Hassam, 3d John Day, sr. **Stilson**, m. Hannah Severy, who m. 2d Richard Day. His son Amos rem. to Yarmouth, N. S., aft. recording 3 ch. in Manchester, of whom Thomas, b. 8 Nov. 1765, was gr.fa. of Nathan (1819-1895) who investigated the 'lost heir' swindle. **Mary**, m. 1st Samuel Woodbury, 2d Benj. Presson. **Margaret**, m. Josiah Allen. **Joshua**, Sheepscot 1765; 2 ch. **William**, k. at Muscongus. See N. E. Reg. 46.120. **Samuel**, mason, m. 1st at Beverly 12 Apr. 1732, Eleanor Griggs of Salem; m. again. See N. E. Reg. 31.193 and Hists. of Newton and Lunenburg. **Thomas**, app. d. y. **Benjamin**, k. in 1st Fr. and Ind. War. **Amos**, k. by Ind.; 2 ch.

22 **WILLIAM** (14), would have been fa.-inlaw of Gov. Benning Wentworth (tho some yrs. his junior) but that he had lost his life in the capture of Louisburg. He m. 14 Apr. 1720, at Hampton Falls, Joanna Lane (6). His fa. quitcl. the Exeter homestead and 400 a. to him and his bro. Samuel in the spring of 1742, and he was liv. in the ancestral home, so stated in his deed of 20 Dec. 1742, when he sold to Capt. Jacob Tilton. List 376b. No doubt he moved to the Portsm. home of his widowed mo., whose dower in the Newmarket estate he was demanding, with Benj. Smart and John Pender for wit. She sued for it in 1743-4 and for dower in Kittery lands in 1745. Aft. Louisburg, the wid. left with 8 ch., most of them old enough to be helpful, collected her husb.'s military pay (1747). She d. in Portsm. Sept. 1784, ag. 90. Without dates, the list of ch. must be faulty: **John**, mariner, m. at Beverly 9 Mar. 1748-9 Judith Thorndike, whose will, 3 Apr. 1785, names only Hale and Love Ellingwood, out of 6 rec. ch. **Lane**, marked 'dead' in a Portsm. tax list 1760. **William**, mariner of Cape Ann in 1760, where likely he m. one of the 3 wives attrib. to (23)'s son; later sheriff's deputy at Portsm. **Love**, m. by 1743 Thos. Palmer jr. of Portsm., mariner. **Joanna**, liv. 1760, m. Capt. James Gilmore, who m. 2d Deborah (Meserve) Smith of Durham. **Mary**, m. 28 Nov. 1754 Capt. Thos. Stoodly of Portsm. Capt. **Henry**, Portsm., b. ab. 1735, d. ab. 1828, ag. 97; his w. Anne (Seaward) d. at 90; 9 ch. **Martha**, b. 1737, m. 1st 15 Mar.

1760 Gov. Benning Wentworth, in whose ho. she had been a maid. Descendant of Governors Winthrop and Dudley and of the patentees of Squamscot (Hilton) and Pemaquid (Davison), she was his equal in blood and never a simple ragamuffin, Mr. Longfellow's 'Lady Wentworth' to the contrary notwithstanding. Two sons d. y. She m. 2d 19 Dec. 1770 Col. Michael Wentworth; 2 daus.; d. in Portsm. 28 Dec. 1805, ag. 68. Her will, 12 May 1803—Feb. 1806, makes sole benef. her dau. Martha, who m. 7 Jan. 1802 Sir John Wentworth.

23 **WILLIAM**, see (5), m. at Gloucester 19 Nov. 1711 Mary Tucker. 'Wid. Hilton' d. there 10 May 1762, ag. 80. For posterity see Babson's Hist. of Glouc. (suppl.) and Riggs. Gen.

24 ‡**COL. WINTHROP** (2), Exeter, early a partner with (14) in mast cutting. When his kinsman, Gov. Dudley, came in, he was put forward in civil and military matters alike, a Judge of the Common Pleas from 1706 and in chief command of exped. forces ag. the French and Indians. The idol of his soldiers, scores of babies were named Winthrop or Hilton in his honor. Just appointed Councilor, he was shot from ambush while lumbering on his own land, aft. mastering the greatest perils in war, on 23 June 1710. Lists 65, 94, 98, 376b, 377, 385. His wid. (Ann Wilson) reared their 6 ch. until, by 1717, she m. Capt. Jonathan Wadleigh, and d. 8 Mar. 1744. Ch: **Judith**, m. 1st 29 July 1725 Wm. Pike (Joseph, of Barnstable, Eng.), who d. 25 Oct. 1726; m. 2d 1 Nov. 1731 Rev. Elisha Odlin. **Ann**, m. in Roxbury 19 Feb. 1722 Ebenezer Pierpont. **Deborah**, m. 26 Dec. 1722 Samuel Thing; 2d 21 Oct. 1725 Benjamin Thing. **Elizabeth**, m. aft. 1734 John Dudley. **Bridget**, m. Andrew Gilman (7). **Winthrop**, b. 21 Dec. 1710, liv. on the homestead; Lt.-Col. of militia, 1764; m. 9 Dec. 1736 Martha (Weeks), wid. of Chase Wiggin, who d. 31 Mar. 1769. 3 ch. He m. 2 other wives, is said to have marched to Lexington, and d. 26 Dec. 1781.

**HINCKES**, ‡**John**, Esq., bro. of Samuel of London (1700), appeared in Sagadahoc bef. Philip's War, ±21 in 1671; Pemaquid 1672. Escaping to Piscataqua, he soon m. Elizabeth, one of Fryer's daus. (Robert Elliot 'brothered' him in 1682), and all gave their support to the govt. hostile to local interests. His promotion was rapid. Councilor for N. H. and Asst. in Ct. of Chancery 1683 to May 1686, when Councilor under Pres. Dudley; Chief Just. Ct. of Pleas and Genl. Sess. N. H. 1686; Capt. of the Fort and Train Band, Great Isl. 1686, occupying these positions until Andros's overthrow 1689; Councilor (Pres.) again under Wm. III 1692, Capt. Fort Wm. and Mary

1696, Chief Just. Superior Ct. N. H. 1699. In (1702?) he had 'left the country', as far as Kittery, but soon came back. Bef. 4 Aug. 1707 he m. 2d Mary (Lewis 7), wid. of Thos. Cobbett. List 316. His 1st mar. saw his rise, his 2d his decline, as later yrs. find him princ. in various suits, usually deft.; in Apr. 1708, form. of Newc., his great new ho. was attached. Of Newc. in 1722 he sold there; taxed Grafford's Lane, Portsm., 1723; Kittery 1724 when sued by Lawrence Ellis for shaving him 1716-9, there in May 1725 he sued the town of Newc. for disbursem. in bldg. the meet.-ho. in 1704, and for his negro ringing the bell 3 yrs. Dr. Jackson was attending his w. in 1720; he is last found 15 June 1725, called decd. in Apr. 1734. Lists 13, 14, 49, 90, 317, 51, 55a, 91, 52, 34, 319, 59, 63, 64, 315bc, 336c, 296, 297. Ch: Capt. **Samuel**, gent., H. C. 1701, shopkeeper, Portsm. 1719, m. in Greenl. 29 Mar. 1712 Elizabeth (Winslow), wid. of Jos Scott of Boston, who had been liv. in Portsm. Capt. in Dummer's War. Roxbury 1728, there in 1734 he sold 2/7 of Champernowne's Isl.; Boston 1753; ret. to Portsm. where he d. List 339. Ch: Katherine Ann, bp. So. Ch., Portsm., 2 Jan. 1714-5, m. 25 Aug. 1736 Francis Skinner of Boston. Samuel, bp. 19 Apr. 1717, taught in Truro, mov. late to Bucksport, Me. **Christian**, m. Richard Jordan(5). **Dau.**, m. one Gross. See Gross(2). **Barbara**, m. John Pearce. **Sarah**, who claimed to be the w. of Capt. Temple reput. to have a w. in Eng., and was fined in Essex Ct. Dec. 1714; m. Hercules Fernald(4). **Mary**, m. by 1715 Wm. Seavey. At least one **son** d. s. p. as Saml. was called 'one of the sons' 1735. See N. E. Reg. 29.315.

**Hinckley**, William, Hampton. List 96. See Hookely.

**Hindrake**, Daniel. List 391a. See Hendrick.

**HINDS, 1** ——, his w. and 4 ch., 1688. List 5.

2 **ELEANOR** (Hy-es?) and John Frost witn. Wiggin to Lovering 1663.

3 **SAMUEL** (Hind), witn. Maverick deed 1663. Y. D. 3.109.

**Hinger**, Marker, adm. 26 June 1660 to Wm. Follett.

**Hinksman**, Robert. List 68. See Hickson (2).

# HINKSON, peculiar to Devonshire.

1 **PETER**, fisherman, Scarboro. App. the kinsman of Holbeton, co. Devon, to whom Philip's (3) wid. gave P/A 20 June 1662; he was here signing a Scarboro ptn. 4 July 1663, and bot 8 Mar. 1664-5. By Aug. 1669 he had acq. some kind of claim on the Elkins land; with John Mares leased from Jocelyn part of the flake yard on Prout's Neck. Grants 1668, 1671 and ano. 1686 adj.

Henry Libby. Lot-layer 1669; Selectm. 1669, 1688; Constab. 1673-4, 1685. Taxed 1681, land and consid. livestock. Lists 236, 237ade, 238a, 239a. See Boaden (2). He fled to Lynn, evid. at the outbreak of the second war. Of Lynn in Nov. 1699, he deeded his 23a. in Sc. to s. Peter of York, or to his w. Elizabeth for life if he d. s. p., then to revert to himself; went at once to York to make his home with them, and bef. the end of the yr. was having trouble with his son and striking him; soon returned to Lynn where he d. Will 27 Nov. 1701 (invent. 30 Sept. 1706) gives all to w. Elizabeth for life, then equally 'amongst my ch. and Joseph Felt if he the sd. J. F. dow live with my wife,' otherwise among the ch. His ptn. to Andros aft. Oct. 1687 for the land he had liv. and built on 16 yrs., ment. great fam. of ch. and gr. ch., but only 3 kn. surely: **Simon**, b. ±1653. **Honor**, m. Henry Libby (4). **Peter**, b. Jan. 1666-7. See also Naomi (6).

2 **PETER** (1), York. In Sept. 1691 he had been in govt. service a long time at Wells. Altho consid. her junior if he gave his age correctly, he m. in York 12 July 1698 Elizabeth, wid. of John Parsons. She liv. 5 Apr. 1720; he a town charge in 1730, the York selectm. selling his Sc. land to Thos. Bragdon who agreed to supp. him. 'Father Hinkson says he was 70 yrs. old Jan. 20, 1736-7.' No. kn. ch., unless one or m. of those m. in Lynn were his and not Simon's.

3 **PHILIP**, fisherman, Richmond Isl. 1639-43, one of Mr. Trelawny's own servants. In 1646 he gave P/A to Arthur Gill (2) to take poss. of inherit. ho. and land in 'Coskrum Halburto', co. Devon; likely the Philip bp. Holbeton 27 Mar. 1616, s. of Philip. West Saco 1653, the ground by his ho. to be div. bet. him and Thos. Haley. Lists 321, 243ab, 252, 78. W. Margaret. With 2d husb. Geo. Taylor she gave P/A 20 June 1662 to Peter Hinkson (1) to let out a tenem. in Holbeton form. in poss. of John Wedge and w., for use of her daus. both under age: **Sarah. Meribah.**

4 **ROBERT**, Greenland, ±25 in 1673, m. 26 Sept. 1679 Sarah Brewster (1). List 335a. Jury 1685. Sold to Jos. Berry sr. 12 Oct. 1700. Son John, but not he, in Greenl. Prov. rate 1711, 1722. In 1715 his 10 a. gr. was laid out, s. John having pd. the charges. Lists 326c, 52, 332b, 57, 62, 335a, 330c, 337. Kn. ch: **John**, soldier at Newc. 1708; taxed Greenl. 1711 and later; m. 13 Dec. 1716 Susanna Berry. In 1717 he owned adj. Jos. and Nathl. Berry. Lists 337, 338a. Ch. Sarah, Samuel, bp. Greenl. 1724-27, prob. others, incl. John, m. 26 Jan. 1736-7 Mary Lamprey, unless a 2d mar. of the fa.; **Robt.**, Epping, m. Ruth Chapman. **Abigail**, m. Isaac

Foss (see 5). Why Hinkson Foss (5), bp. 1712, recd. his name is unexpl.

**5 SAMUEL** (Hickson), tenant on a Kittery farm 1730.

**6 SIMON** (1), ±19 in Dec. 1672, his master John Lewis of Great Isl. Scarb. soldier 1676. Poss. he spent the next few yrs. in Newc., marrying there Rebecca, wid. of Wm. Davie (4), Scarb. 1681-88; grants 1682, 1686. Lists 312e, 237a, 238a, 226, 239a. If he surv. the 2d War, likely he was in Newc. or Lynn, unnoticed. From Lynn in 1719 his wid. wrote to her s. Jacob Clark (14), Great Isl., sending love to s. and dau. Graffam and sis. Clark. Ch: **Rebecca**, m. Caleb Graffam (Stephen). And likely the foll. m. in Lynn: **Naomi** or Amy (poss. sister), m. 26 Dec. 1700 Jas. Mills. **Peter**, m. 16 Sept. 1714 Elizabeth Jeffords (Jeffrey 5). 7 ch. rec. incl. Naomi and Rebecca. **Hannah**, m. 8 Aug. 1717 David Edmonds.

**7 THOMAS**, Portsm. 1657, propr. 1660. Lists 323, 326a, 330abc. M. Martha Walford (Thos.) by 1662 when, Hinkson, she test. for Geo. and Mary Jones. She was ±22 in 1667. His will 3, d. 4 June 1664; John Sherburne and Wm. Brookings overseers. She m. 2d John Westbrook. Only ch. in will: **Mary** (Hingson), named also in gr. fa. Walford's will 1666; in June 1678 she chose John Sherburne gdn., who sued her step-fa. that yr. and was still gdn. 26 May 1680.

**8 WILLIAM**, master of -The Hercules- 1638 and later; legatee of Trelawny. List 21. In May 1642 he was at the Piscat. taking fish at the Shoals; in 1648 cred. of Nich. Brown, Portsm. O. A. Saco 5 July 1653.

Hirst, see Hurst.

Hiskett, George, Boston, had two 150 a. lots laid out in Wells 1661-2, sold 1668-9 to Obadiah Reed. Y. D. 33.142. Master of the sloop -Exchange- at Sagadahoc 1689. See also Heacock.

**HITCHCOCK**, Lieut. **\*Richard**, planter, West Saco, depos. 18 Aug. 1668, ag. 60. Bound over in Mass. Ct. 5 Aug. 1634 bef. he came to Me. (here by Sept. 1636), he was set in the stocks 14 Feb. 1636-7 for abus. the Ct., likely thru his suit for slander against Robt. Morgan, but afterw. kept out of trouble. Town gr. Jan. 1653; in 1654 Rich. Vines confirmed to him the 100 a. where he was dwg. Often appr., admr. or bondsman. Sergt. 1653, Lieut. by 1662. Tr. j. 1640, 1645, 1646, 1656, 1660; Gr. j. 1645, 1658, 1660, 1668; Constable 1645; Com. t. e. s. c. 1653-9; Selectm. 9 yrs. to 1668; Rep. 1660; Road Surveyor 1666. Lists 242, 243ab, 252, 111, 24, 244bcdf, 235, 245, 247, 249. Old Shaw's boy was his servant in 1658. Will 6 June 1670 (bur. 22 June 1671), having an external malady. York people attending Ct.

were entert. at his ho. ab. 1643, so likely Lucretia Williams (Thos.), the mo. of his ch., was not his 1st w. As a wid., she liv. with, but could not marry, Geo. Garland (2). Presum. the Mrs. H., captive (Saco 1675?) who d. by eating poisonous root. Hubbard p. 210. List 246. Ch. in will: Jerusha, b. 28 Nov. 1653; in Berw. 1672 she knew ab. Zachariah Smith who worked for the Broughtons in 1670: witn. Christo. Hobbs's will; m. (aft. **28 Mar. 1673-4**) Phineas Hull (7). **Thomas**, b. 20 Jan. 1655-6, bur. 23 Dec. 1671. **Lydia**, b. 30 Nov. 1658, m. bef. 12 Oct. 1681 Lt. Jas. Plaisted. **Rebecca**, b. 20 Aug. 1661, d. s. p. **Ann**, d. s. p., and **Margaret**, m. James Emery (3), likely the two daus. b. 25 Sept. 1664. His twins sugg. a poss. connec. with Rich. Hickox whose twins Wm. and Ann were bp. at St. Chad's, Shrewsbury, 2 Mar. 1623. See Lewis (19). Y. D. 8.231, 14.147, 256, 17.133.

**HOAG** (see also Hodge, Hogg).

**1 BENJAMIN** (John), m. 1st at Newb. 23 June 1702 Sarah Norris (Nicholas) of Exeter, d. Stratham 30 Nov. 1717; m. 2d 21 Nov. 1718-9 Esther Swett (Moses). Liv. Exeter and Stratham 1707-17, Dover 1720-2, Strath. 1723-31, Amesb. 1732 until he went late to Dutchess Co., N. Y., where many of his ch. settled; d. there aft. 19 May 1760, wid. aft. 1780. Ch. (Friends Rec.) 6+10, incl. **Mary**, b. 5 Apr. 1704, m. Stephen Swett of Hampt. **John**, b. 30 Sept. 1706, m. 1st his cous. Mary(2), 2d Patience (Varney) Rogers; rem. to Oblong, N. Y. **Jonathan**, b. Dec. 1708-9, m. Comfort Stanyan; liv. Hampt. F. **Patience**, b. 26 Feb. 1710-20, m. 2d Moses Hoag(2) of Hampt. F. and Oblong.

**2 JONATHAN**, br. of (1), with w. Martha (Goodwin, m. Newb. 15 Sept. 1703), sold in Stratham 1715. Liv. Hampt. F. 1752, ±80. 12 ch. rec. Newb. 1705-1729.

**3 JOSEPH**, br. of (1), taxed Ex. 1714.

Hoalfe, Thomas, Cape Bonawagon 1672. List 13.

Hobart, see Hubbard.

**HOBBS**, a patronymic from Hobb, a nickname for Robert.

**1 CHRISTOPHER**, planter, West Saco, shared in the marsh 12 July 1653. Lists 243ab, 252, 244b, 245, 249. In Salem Ct. Nov. 1661 his atty. Wm. Beale sued **Mr.** Peter Oliver for money due on a fishing voyage. Constable 1672. His w. liv. 1666, d. bef. him. List 246. See Foster(6). His will 26 Nov. 1673 (inv. 11 Dec.); 4 ch. and dau. Jane's 4 ch. named. Ch: **Christopher**. **John**, if he came over to take poss., to have ½ the land Jane was liv. on, otherw. to Christo. One John witn. bill of sale to Job Clements and Henry Greenland 1670, Geo.

Norton ano. witn. **Jane**, m. 1st 2 Sept. 1664
Michael Nostras (Nossiter), 2d (Naziter) 8
July 1669 Richard Peard. **Robert**, by will
had his fa.'s upper plantation. Likely he
who took O. A. at Marbleh. 18 Dec. 1677,
Richard Peard in same list; and Geo. Norton's servant, time up in Mar. 1679, who
was impressed in the War, ran away and
was frozen. York Ct. 1 July 1679 ord. him
seized by constable of Marbleh. and deliv.
to Norton to serve out 2 yrs. which extra
time was allowed the surgeon for his pay
in Dover Ct. Mar. 1677. Sued for debt by
Geo. Jaffrey Mar. 1686. D. s. p.
2 **CHRISTOPHER**(1), had deed from Maj.
    Phillips 27 Dec. 1673 of his fa.'s 300 a.
where he was dwelling. Y. D. 2.182. O. A.
Salem Nov. 1678. In Me. 26 July 1687 he
witn. John Bowden's deed. List 33. Adm.
sometime of Saco, late of Boston, to Thos.
Barnard (1 jr.), Boston, 27 Jan. 1690-1. W.
unkn. Kn. ch: **John**, Boston, linemaker. In
17--, gr. s. and only heir of Christo. H., some
time of Saco decd., he claimed the 300 a.
homestead, selling to Abra. Townsend 25
Apr. 1718, John -Barnet- a witn. He m. in
Boston 22 June 1703 Susanna Sugers (Capt.
Gregory). 7 ch. rec. Boston, incl. Christopher Gregory. **Christopher**, minor, gdns.
10 Mar. 1690-1 Thos. Barnard, David Edwards of Boston; d. s. p.
3 **HENRY**, Dover 1657; grant 1658. By
    1661 he m. Hannah Canney(3), whose
fa. then deeded to them bet. Quamph. and
St. Albans Cove. Gr. j. 1675. In Ct.
1677 he sued Geo. Broughton and Benj. Barnard for taking away his ox; in same Ct.
Broughton as assignee of Wm. Hookely sued
him. For hims. and Henry Child he ptn. in
1686 for adm. on Jas. Goffe's est., the wid.
refusing to give up their partly sawn boards.
Lists 356abceghk, 359ab, 49, 62. Adm. 25
May 1698 to wid. Hannah; ±78 in 1719 she
depos. ab. Berw. 60 yrs. bef.; again in Apr.
1720, ag. 79, naming those who had been in
charge at Great Works. Ch. likely incl. 1
or m. sons, besides **Henry**, b. ±1670, only
surv. s. 1698, and a dau. m. Cornelius Corson (Cursenwhitt) who struck his mo.-in-
law Hannah Hobbs 3 Feb. 1685-6.
4 **HENRY**(3), depos. in Sept. 1717, ag. 47.
    He and John Wingate were in Ct. for
fighting 1695, he for forcing Ruth Cooke in
169-. **W. Mary** (Ct. Mar. 1698-9, Mary
Hobbs, Portsm.). Adm. to her 2 Dec. 1724;
she m. 2d 18 Dec. 1724 Deac. Jacob Remick
of Kit. As Mary Remick she signed by
mark her husb.'s deed of 13 Nov. 1714 selling 20 a. of his home place, which his mo.
had prev. signed. Kn. ch: **Thomas**, millwright, Dover and Berwick. In 1720 his
fa. deeded him half his land at Sligo, the
rest at his death. List 298. He m. at Kit.

2 Dec. 1721 Elizabeth Morrill (Nich.). Liv.
1755. Ch. **Hannah**, b. 2 Mar. 1704-5.
5 **JAMES**(8), m. 31 July 1673 Sarah Fifield
    (3); soldier in Philip's War; d. 22 Sept.
1679, adm. 7 Sept. 1680 to Wm. Fifield and
the wid. List 395. On Nov. 10, 1679 his
fa. deeded to the ch: **James**, b. 26 May 1674.
**Morris**, b. 1 Jan. 1677, m. Joanna Cromwell
(3). List 358d. Adm. 7 Oct. 1735 to s.
James, she relinq. 6 ch. rec. Dover 1700-
1720. **Sarah**, b. 27 Sept. 1679.
6 **JOHN**(8), Hampton, eldest son 1706, m.
    30 Dec. 1668 Sarah Colcord(1). Jury
1685, Gr. j. 1692. Lists 396, 52, 399a. In
1715 he deeded to his gr. s. Jos. Towle. D.
27 Jan., adm. 3 Sept. 1718 to Jos. Towle on
his est. and the widow's, she the form. admr.
Ch: **Sarah**, b. 30 Dec. 1669, m. John Leavitt
(3). **Mehitable**, b. 28 Feb. 1673, m. (Ct.
Sept. 1694) Jos. Towle, who m. 2d her cous.
Sarah(9).
7 **JONATHAN**, soldier, Kittery. List 289.
8 **MORRIS**, Hampton propr. 23 Feb. 1645-6,
    was at Newbury in 1642. At Hampt. he
liv. on the Estow land. Selectm. 1659, Constable 1667; Tr. j. 1650, 1669, 1673; Gr. j.
1663, 1677, 1683, 1684, 1693. Lists 392b,
393ab, 54, 49, 396, 55a, 398, 52, 56, 57, 62.
Adm. 3 Sept. 1706 to sons Nehemiah and
Morris, oldest s. John renounc. He m. Sarah
Estow (Wm.), ±44, 12 Oct. 1669. Lists
393a, 394. Ch: **John. Sarah**, m. Abraham
Drake(2). **Nehemiah**, b. ab. 1648. **Morris**,
b. 15 Jan. 1652. **James. Mary**, b. 11 Feb.
1657, m. Capt. Jos. Cass(3). **Bethia**, b. 28
Feb. 1659, m. 9 Jan. 1678 Deac. John Tuck.
**Hannah**, b. 9 Apr. 1662, m. 4 Jan. 1683 David
Wedgwood. **Abigail**, b. 29 July 1664, m.
Deac. Saml. Dow(9).
9 **MORRIS**(8), Hampton, liv. on the home-
    stead. Lists 392b, 395, 396, 52, 68. Con-
stable 1696, 1697. Selectm. 1700. He m. 13
June 1678 Sarah Swett (Capt. Benj.) who
d. 8 Dec. 1717; he 6 Apr. 1740. Ch: **Esther**,
b. 12 Apr. 1679, m. Peter Johnson(24). **Morris**, b. 13 Sept. 1680, m. 18 Nov. 1703 Theodate Batchelder(3), d. bef. him. Will 3, d.
7 May 1739. 9 ch. Capt. **Benjamin**, m. Mary
Marston (John); 4 ch. **Sarah**, m. Jos. Towle.
See Mehitable(6). **Mary**, b. 5 Mar. 1686-7,
sole legatee in sis. Sarah's will 1762. **John**,
b. 12 Dec. 1688, m. in Haverh. 24 Dec. 1719
Abigail Dow, who d. 5 May 1775; he 17 Mar.
1783. 8 ch. **James**, b. 16 May 1691, m. 1
Jan. 1720 Lucy Dow(5); d. 16 Jan. 1756.
9 ch., incl. Rev. James, H. C. 1748, 1st pastor at Pelham. **Joseph**, b. 15 May 1693, d.
21 Dec. 1717. **Jonathan**, b. 11 Feb. 1695, d.
20 Oct. 1715.
10 **NEHEMIAH**(8), Hampton, soldier in
    Philip's War. He m. Sept. 1693 Mary
Holmes, who d. 19 June 1706; he 7 Feb.
1730. Lists 396, 397b, 52, 399a. Ch: **Abi-**

**gail.** Her dau. Elizabeth b. ab. 1718 (charged to John Batchelder) m. Morris Lamprey. **Nehemiah,** b. 15 Jan. 1696, d. 24 Apr. 1753, unm. **Samuel,** b. 5 Feb. 1698, m. Rachel Knowles(4), liv. 3 Mar. 1759. He d. ab. 1753-4. **Stephen,** Kensington, b. 18 May 1700, m. 17 Feb. 1725 Patience Towle (Benj.); d. 1757. 5 ch. **Noah,** b. 22 Dec. 1702. **Bethia,** b. 8 Oct. 1705, m. Jos. Moulton.

11 **WILLIAM,** Wells petnr. 1668.

12 **WILL,** Wells soldier from Topsfield. List 267.

**HOBBY,** 1 **Sir Charles** (2), Boston. His insolvent est. 1715 listed deeds, set down at nothing, for half the Prov. of N. H., purch. from Thos. Allen, Esq., 1706. List 191. W. Elizabeth surv. and ch: John; **Elizabeth,** m. James Gooch (3 jr.); **Mary,** m. Zechariah Hubbard. N. E. Reg. 24.110, Col. Socy. Mass. 6.88.

2 **WILLIAM,** Boston merchant. Edw. Barton (3) ack. judgm. to him 1674, Thos. Clay(6) 1676. He witn. for John Dollen(2) in Ipsw. Ct. Mar. 1677; had been recently with Dollen in Boston. Dollen's deed for 1 m. sq. assigned in Feb. 1699 to John Foster and W. H. was exhibited to the Ind. at Falm. 18 July 1726. List 142. W. Ann. 3 sons, 4 daus., incl. **Charles; Judith,** m. John Coleman, Esq. In 1737 a gr. s. John Hobby of Richmond, co. York, tanner, q. c. to John Coleman, Boston, lands deeded his gr. fa. by Thos. Stevens, Robt. Edmunds (3), John Dollen, John Mitchell. Y. D. 20.105.

**Hobson,** Thomas, Scarboro soldier. List 237b.

**HOCKADAY,** 1 **Nathaniel,** Isles of Shoals, adm. 28 June 1664 to John Fabyan for use of widow and child: ?Samuel.

2 **SAMUEL** (1?), Portsm., tax abated Feb. 1679-80; taxed Str. Bk. 1690; Shoals witn. 1694. Lists 95, 332a. One Thos. (Hockedde), fisherman, had s. David bp. So. Ch. 7 Sept. 1735; Agnes (Hockedy), recd. into full com. Nov. 1743, poss. his w. In 1749 he was an owner in so. half of Ellins Point.

**HOCKING,** John, Mr., trading early at Piscataqua; Mr. Wm. Hilton deliv. his goods to Mr. Geo. Ludlow and took receipt 2 Aug. 1632. Y. D. i. 60. His quarrel with Plymouth Col. men at the Kennebec in Apr. 1634, when he was k., caused much trouble, his kinsman in Boston taking a hand. N. E. Reg. 9.80, Me. Hist. Coll. 3.2.322

**Hockridge,** Abel. See Hawkridge.

**Hocman,** Marie (Oakman?), b. Black Point, Scarb., bap. at Quebec 20 May 1709, then w. of Thos. Whore or Hoar; there 1713 a widow. List 99, p. 129.

**HODDY,** Hody. In 1630 John Hody, Esq., and Arthur, gent., bros., owned land in par. of Hawkchurch, co. Dorset.

1 **ARTHUR,** Mr., Portsm., mariner, presum. br. to (2), was master of the -Batchelour- 1686. See Lee(1). His ho. ment. 1683, land 1687. Gr. j. 1683, jury 1686. List 332a. Likely his wid. was Mrs. Hoodey taxed Dec. 1688, and as Mrs. Elizabeth 1689-91. Liv. Mar. 1693-4. List 335a.

2 **JOHN,** Mr., b. ±1648, Portsm. mariner 1672, taxed 1673. See (1). With John Tucker he appr. Robt. Braddock's est. 1677. Tr. j. 1682. Lists 54, 329, 331c. M. 21 June 1675 Mary Riddan (Thaddeus). Will 16 June, d. 17 July 1684, ag. 36 (gr. st.) As a wid. she was taxed Portsm. and lic. retailer 1686, 1692, 1694; tav. lic. 1693. Lists 331c, 335a. M. 2d Saml. Keais (4), and d. 17 Aug. 1711, ag. 58 (on 1st husb.'s gr. st.). Ch. in fa.'s will, the sons to be apprent: **Mary,** b. 1 Mar. 1677-8, m. Capt. Paul Gerrish (5); only surv. ch. 1 Aug. 1718. Capt. **John,** b. 27 Aug. 1679, mariner. His ho. near Mrs. Bridget Graffort's in 1700; taxed May 1707; his ho. 1708. One Mr. H. from Piscataqua was prisoner at Fort Royal, July 1704 (Penhallow). **Arthur,** b. 25 Aug. 1681. **Samuel,** b. 4 Oct. 1683, a Portsm. witn. 1703; mate on the -Wm. and Andrew- 1706. One Mary H., poss. a wid., m. Thos. Phipps in Portsm. 25 Feb. 1711-2.

**HODGE,** Hogg. See also Hoag. Hodge a nick-name for Roger, most commonly found in Cornwall and Devonshire.

1 **BENJAMIN,** Stratham 1709. List 388. Hoag?

2 **DANIEL** (Hogg), Scarboro 1687 (Col. Soc. Mass. 21.326). See Fogg (1).

3 **EDMUND** (Hogge), 1642. List 71.

4 **ELIZABETH,** m. Benj. Akerman (2).

5 **JOHN** (Hodg), Kittery witn. 1675. Y. D. ii. 184. See also Lewis (17).

6 **NICHOLAS** (Hodges), and Walter Knight sued by Mr. Val. Hill in Me. Ct., Oct. 1651.

7 **NICHOLAS,** fisherman, Little Harbor, m. Seaborn Reynolds (Nicholas, Esq. of Kennebec), adopted dau. of Richard and Margaret Tucker. In 1684 she had trouble with Francis Rand; in 1685 he tore down a fence set up by John Seavey and beat Nathl. Seavey in dispute over a ho. in poss. of Wm. Seavey sr. 28 yrs., by test. of Wm. jr., who added that in Oct. 1678 Wid. Margaret Tucker was at the ho. and begged that her gr. ch. might stay there a few yrs. aft. her death; others said the place was some time Wm. Berry's and that Rich. Tucker built the ho. Yrs. later he was kicking Thos. Seavey's dau. Rebecca Shute and pushed Thos. down. Lists 332b, 315bc, 316. In 17— Capt. John Wentworth claimed for him land of Nich. Reynolds who was -gr. fa.- of his w. Of Rye 4 Aug. 1735 both deeded their

int. in Tucker prop. at Falm. to s. Michael. He or s. Nicholas and John Edmunds q. c. Rye land in 1744. Kn. ch: **Nicholas.** apr. 4, 1682 Margaret Tucker deeded Portsm. land and bldg. to gr. s. N. H.; d. by 1688. Capt. **Michael,** b. ab. 1683, shipwright, mariner, Newb. and Salis., recd. the Falm. prop. and Rye homestead by deeds from his parents. Y. D. 14.76, 20.107, 21.117, 22.168. Will, Salis., 16 Sept. 1752 (d. Mar. 1756, ag. 73), names w. Joanna (Titcomb), who d. Mar. 1763, ag. 77, and 4 of 8 or m. ch. b. 1711-1732, incl. Ann, b. Newb. 16 Oct. 1713, m. 1st at Hampt. F. 31 Aug. 1735 Mr. Phineas Jones of Falm., and 2d Dec. 1746 Hon. Jabez Fox, gr. s. of (2); and Nicholas, b. 20 May 1719, H. C. 1739, taught in Falm., d. 1743. **Nicholas,** ±12 in 1700. **Mary,** poss. m. 1st Henry Seavey; cert. m. John Edmonds (5) by 1734 when her br. Michael deeded him the homestead; she depos. in May 1766 ab. her mo. Seaborn Reynolds and fam. **Sarah,** b. June 1701; w. of Thos. Watson of Rye 1766.

8 **PETER** (Hogg), servant of Clement Greenway, Saco. 1635.

9 **RICHARD** (Hodges), Boston soldier at New Dartmouth 1689. D. H. 5.38.

10 **WILLIAM,** Greenland 1714. List 338c. One Wm. (Hodges) and Anne Russell, both of Biddeford, int. mar. 27 Mar. 1737. One Samuel, shopkeeper Dover 1738, d. there 19 Mar. 1787, ag. 79. W. **Elizabeth;** 3 ch. bp. 1738-42.

**HODSDON,** Hodgdon, prob. a form of Hodgson, a patronymic from Roger, common in the northern counties of England.

1 *BENONI(6), Berwick, bot 50 a. from John Wincoll 1671. His ho. was burnt by Ind. 16 Oct. 1675; later he liv. on the homestead and cared for his parents. In 1690 he had a cow and goods belonging to Andrew Searle's est. Selectm. 1692-5; Gr. j. 1688, 1693, 1694, 1695, 1700-1; Rep. 1692, 1718. On commit. to build meet.-ho. 1701, and orig. memb. of the ch. Lists 288, 36, 38, 296, 298. W. Abigail Curtis(9). He d. ab. 1718; Mrs. Abigail taxed 9 Feb. 1718-9, not in agreem. of heirs 13 Oct. 1733. Ch: **Abigail,** m. Nicholas Gowen(3). **Joseph,** Berwick, ag. 63 July 1738, 65 June 1740; m. (Ct. Oct. 1700) Margaret Goodwin(5) who was liv. 1746. Lists 296, 298. Will 1756—1764. 9 ch. **Elizabeth,** m. James Ferguson(3). **John,** bp. Boston 24 July 1698, m. Elizabeth Wingate, dau. of John and Ann (Hodsdon 2); d. bef. 13 Oct. 1733. List 298. 2 ch. **Hannah,** m. 17 Nov. 1709 Richard Shackley. **Thomas,** m. 1 Dec. 1709 Mary Lord(7); d. bef. 28 Jan. 1716-7; adm. to her, bond 27 May 1717. She m. 2d 16 June 1720 Daniel Emery jr., gr. s. of (2). List 298. 4 ch.

**Esther,** acc. Jos. Abbott jr. 3 times 1716-1720; both in York Ct. Jan. 1719-20; m. Thos. Horne(4). **Samuel,** m. Prudence Scammon (Richard), both bp. 3 Sept. 1722. List 298. Est. adm. 1755. 11 ch. bp. 1724-41. See 7.

2 **ISRAEL**(6), m. (after Me. Ct. 4 July 1671) Ann Thompson (Miles); bot land with her fa., 1672. List 298. He and w. abs. from meet., Ct. 6 July 1675. He soon d.; she m. 2d Robt. Evans(12). Ch: **Israel,** Ensign, adm. fa.'s est. 1696, mo.'s 1727. Dover gr. 1696; of Portsm. bot in Dover 1697, and settled there; carpenter. Lists 352, 358d. Will 21 Jan. 1739-40—30 Jan. 1750-1 names w. Ann (Wingate), dau. of John, who surv., and 5 ch. b. 1697-1709. **Ann,** m. by 1691 John Wingate.

3 **JEREMIAH**(6), Dover 1666; Kennebec 1672-1677; Newc. 1680-4. He depos. in 1680, ±44; that yr. he and w. sold without lic. Gr. j. N. H. 1684; not noticed later. Lists 298, 356jk, 13, 184, 313a, 317, 52. W. Ann Thwaits (Alex.). In 17—, wid. of Boston, she claimed Thwaits land at Kennebec; depos. in Boston 10 July 1716, ag. 66; liv. there 10 Mar. 1723-4. Ch., by deed: **Alexander,** Newington, tailor, apprent. of Saml. Billings, Boston, in 1692; taxed Portsm. 1707; soldier at Newc. Sept. 1708; Greenl. 1708-14. List 343. He m. 1st Jane (called Shackford), 2d 5 Nov. 1728 Ruth (Foster) Grow of Greenl., wid. of Saml. of Ipsw. Liv. 24 May 1753 when s. John called him n. c. m. from a shock; wid. d. 25 Aug. 1756, ag. 84. 8 or m. ch. incl. Alex., cordwainer, Newingt., Rochester 1753; m. 9 July 1727 Mary (Shackford), wid. of Rich. Furber, and with her adm. the Furber est. **John,** blacksmith, Newington 1720, m. by 1723 Mary Hoyt (John), both liv. 1767. Y. D. x. 131. **Eliza-beth,** 'one of the sisters' 1720; m. 1st Benj. Galloway(1), 2d Benj. Richards. **Joseph,** (poss. gr. s.), m. 10 Nov. 1715 Patience Whittum; ch. incl. Alex., bp. Newington 30 Oct. 1723. Other sisters poss. incl. 1 or m. mar. in Boston: Rebecca, m. 9 July 1707 Edw. Bedford, 2d 3 May 1710 Saml. Kirby; Mary, m. 17 Apr. 1712 Milam Alcock; Sarah, m. 24 Sept. 1719 Morris Powers. See (5).

4 **JOHN**(6), taxed Boston 1689. See br. Joseph(5). In Suff. Ct. 1691, Grace Mallett, adm. of Hosea, sued him and David Edwards, owner of shallop -Grace and Sarah-. Boston 1695, then unobserv. till 1720-25, when shipwright, Kit., he deeded int. in fa.'s est., no w. ment., and bot from sis. Lucy et al. Kit. witn. Mar. 1727-8. List 298. Poss. fa. of some of those m. in Boston 1712 and later. In Apr. 1722 one John and w. Deborah had been liv. four yrs. on Mrs. Sarah Geare's land in Crooked Lane. One Abigail m. Saml. Geare. One John,

Berw., husbandman, had gr. s. Thos. Sanders liv. with him, 1744.

5 *JOSEPH(6), Great Isl. witn. 1674-6, Constable, Newich., 4 July 1676; sued by Jona. Nason in Apr. 1678. In 1680, Nonesuch Point, Falm., 100 a. each was gr. to Capt. Sylvanus Davis, Mr. Inglis and J. H. Deputy from Casco 1681. Gr. j. 1681. Lists 30, 225a. Returning to the home of his w. Tabitha Raynes (Francis), he liv. at head of Braveboat Harbor, York; with her sold out at Falm. in Apr. 1686 and June 1687. York gr. with John More 21 May 1688. Tr. j. 1689. In 1690 he had bot a shallop with br. John who was adm. 9 June 1691. Tabitha not in her fa.'s will 21 Aug. 1693, giving Joseph's ch. 10 s. each and naming two: Francis, willed his fa.'s plantation. Elizabeth, willed £10 at age beside her 10 s. One Elizabeth, m. in Boston 15 Sept. 1704 Robt. Scriven. Unprov., but strongly indic. by names, Nathaniel, cordwainer, Boston, m. 1st 5 May 1702 Susanna Clapp of Dorch. who d. 23 May 1730: ch. Tabitha, Joseph, Susanna, Patience, Elizabeth 1702-8; m. 2d 26 Nov. 1730 Ann Atwood who d. 9 June 1748; ch. Ann, Mary, Tabitha 1731-9; m. 3d 1 Dec. 1748 Sarah Porter. D. 5 Apr. 1757, ag. 76; adm. 30 Sept. to Thos. Stoddard and the wid. Poss: Patience, d. Boston 16 Nov. 1710, ag. 33, unless 1st w. of ?Joseph, taxed Portsm. 1719-1732, m. in Boston 29 Dec. 1715 Christian Mason; she recd. into No. Ch. 25 Feb. 1721-2; app. 2 ch. bp. there Sept. 1723. One Mary, b. in Boston (bp. 21 Jan. 1710-11), m. in Portsm. 4 June 1738 Giles Seward. See (3).

6 NICHOLAS, Kittery, first at Hingham 1635 and until aft. his 1st w. Esther Wines d. 29 Nov. 1647; Faintnot Wines's will 1663, giving to her 5 ch., called her cous. He m. 2d bef. 2 Oct. 1650 Elizabeth, wid. of John Needham who had d. in Va. Kittery 28 June 1655, abs. from meet.; liv. at Quampheg., later near Birch Pt. Brook. Lists 288, 298. In 1659 he was ord. to Boston for entert. Quakers; was hims. often abs. from meet.; he and w. abs. in 1675. In Oct. 1678 he deeded to s. Benoni for supp. of self and w.; 9 Dec. made agreem. with him ab. carrying on the farm both were liv. on; Y. D. 3.31, 41; alive 20 Feb. 1679. She was in Portsm. July 1686. List 330a. Ch. by 1st w., bp. Hingham: Esther, bp. 20 Sept. 1640; in Ct. July 1663, bastardy; m. 25 Dec. 1663 Edw. Weymouth. Mehitable, bp. Nov. 1641, m. at Salem 3 Nov. 1665 Peter Welcom, d. Oct. 1694. 3 ch. rec. 1666-1670 incl. Mary, b. 12 Aug. 1670, m. in Boston 15 Nov. 1694 Peter Townsend; deeded her right 24 July 1721. Jeremiah, bp. 6 Sept. 1643. Israel, bp. 19 July 1646. Elizabeth, bp. 19 July 1646, d. bef. Sept. 1663. Benoni, bp.

5 Dec. 1647. By 2d w: Joseph. Timothy. Sarah, m. by 1667 John Morrell. Hannah. She and her parents had been kind to David Wyatt, sailor, who gave her his all in N. E., Aug. 1674. John. Lucy, m. Geo. Vickers of Hull, who was liv. 5 Feb. 1716. Of Hull 24 July 1721 she deeded her fam. int.; d. at Hingham, widow, 25 Dec. 1725. 7 ch. 1683-99. See Y. D. 17.11-12.

7 NICHOLAS, soldier, k. at Wells 11 May 1704.

8 SARAH, m. Joseph Derby(1).

9 TIMOTHY(6), York, tailor. His fa. deeded him Berw. land 20 Feb. 1679 which he sold to Benoni in 1682. York gr. of 30 a. June 1685. Long dead in 1719 when adm. gr. to Edw. Beale at son's req. Wid. Hannah, poss. m. 2d 25 June 1695 Nicholas Smith of York, and admin. 10 Aug. 1697, Matthew Austin bondsm.; cert. m. (2d or 3d) Joseph Smith of York. His wid. 4 Dec. 1713, she deeded her 1st husband's 30 a. to Andrew Toothaker, who gave back a mtg. Ch: William, tailor, only s. and heir 1720 of Marshfield, m. Mary Eames at Dorch. 12 June 1713; Barnstable 1719. Under his P/A Edw. Beale sold at York 1720, 1721. One Wm., w. Margery, had s. Timothy b. Boston 25 Nov. 1725. Sarah, w. of Saml. Cox, Boston, 7 Apr. 1719, when they deeded to Wm.

Hogg, see Hodge, Hoag.

Hoket, William, List 356c. See Hackett.

HOLDEN, 1 Isaac (Holding), Saco fort soldier 1696. List 248b.

2 JOHN, joiner, Newcastle 1699. Lists 315b, 316. He sold in Newc. 1714, bot 1716 in Dover, where in 1718 his land adj. Wm. Weymouth and Jacob Allen. Dover witn. 1721-1728. A mtg. given in 1722 to Jos. Smith of Durham had been pd. bef. he d.; decd. in Mar. 1746-7, adm. 1749 to Richard Scammon. Wife Deborah Fabes (John, Esq.); with her mo. he deeded Fabes land on Great Isl. 1704. Two ch. kn. by deeds: Samuel, Dover 1734, q. c. fa.'s land 1739; of Dover train band 1740. Elizabeth, m. Nicholas Brock; in 1739 q. c. the homestead to Benj. Roberts jr. One Wm. of Dover 1730, likely the same who m. Elizabeth Walker in Newington 20 Dec. 1725, and had Elizabeth bp. Newington 1727, Jemima bp. Berwick 1732. One Holden (Isaac or John) m. Sarah (Tucker) Ingersoll.

HOLDRIDGE, Holdred, William, tanner, from par. of St. Alphage Cripplegate, London, came on -The Elizabeth- in 1635, ag. 25. Of Ipsw., Salis., Newb. and Haverh., bef. going to Exeter aft. 1667. Of Exeter 7 Nov. 1671, he and w. Isabel sold land in Haverh.; 12 days later, now resid. in York, he ack. debt to Thos. Holmes of York. He and Wm. jr. were at York in Jan. fol., he and w. Isabel at Str. Bk. 3 Apr. 1672, later

in the yr. at Exeter. In Hampt. Ct., May 1676, he won suit against Rich. Scammon for failure to give him a firm deed to 30 a. near Mr. Wheeler's creek where he had built. Liv. 1680, sr., poss. later. List 52 (?). W. Isabel, a princ. witn. in the witchcraft case ag. John Godfrey 1659, (Upham's Hist. of Witchcraft i. 429), met her end in tragedy, being k. in the Mast Swamp, where Strath., Hampt. and Ex. come together, by Negro Jack, who was hanged in Boston in 1690. Inv., wid. of Exeter, 16 June 1689; adm. 20 Feb. 1692-3 to Richard Morgan. Ch: **Sarah,** b. Salis. 1640, d. 1641. **Mary,** b. Salis. 22 Apr. 1641, d. 31 Jan. 1641-2. **Rebecca,** b. Salis. 20 June 1643; m. at Andover 21 May 1660 Richard Morgan of Dover. **John,** Roxbury, birth not rec., but his assoc. with N. H. people indic. he belonged here. In 1694 he witn. will of Martha Lyons, wid. of John Cass (2); in a case ag. his dau. Elizabeth the witnesses Ebenezer Cass, Isaac Morris, John Lyons and Martha Wintworth, were very well acq. with his fam. M. in Roxb. 16 Sept. 1663 Elizabeth Perry. 8 ch. **William,** b. Salis. 15 Mar. 1647-8, of Exeter m. 10 Apr. 1674 Lydia Quinby (Robt.). In 1677 Wm. Allen's maid Sarah Taylor was warned to keep away from Goodw. Holdridge and Susan Buswell. Lists 381, ?52. He rem. to Stonington, Conn., where he d. and wid. m. 2d bef. 23 Feb. 1696-7 Israel Dewey. Ch. ment. in Prob. Ct. order; two shown by Stonington land rec; William, b. ab. 1674-5, m. 4 Nov. 1696 Deborah Elliott; 12 ch. Gershom, b. ab. 1677-8, d. Stonington 1729; 5 or m. ch. **Sarah,** b. Haverh. 26 Dec. 1650, d. June 1651. **Mehitable,** b. Haverh. 14 Apr. 1652, m. there 25 Jan. 1669-70 Jona. Smith. In Apr. 1670 she was convicted of stealing from her form. master Lt. Geo. Brown and running away from his service. **Abigail,** b. Haverh. 12 Nov. 1654, d. 13 June 1657. **Mary,** b. Haverh. 24 Dec. 1656, m. Roger Kelly(12). She or sis. Mehitabel was John Ilsley's apprent. in 1666. **Samuel,** b. Salis. 6 Nov. 1659.

**HOLE,** Hoole, Hoel, a Somerset name.
1 **JOHN,** Richmond Isl. 3 yrs., had gone to the Westward to serve bef. 27 June 1640. List 21.
2 **JOHN,** Mr., ±36 Mar. 1671-2, ±47 Mar. 1683-4, mercht., Kittery, bef. and aft. of Barbadoes, where his sis. Mary m. Robt. Cutts (7) and his br. Robt. was liv. 1680. The Cutts story in Brewster's Rambles ii. 143 sends Mary to Ireland when 12 yrs. old, thence to the West Indies; dau of a clergyman. See 'Familiae Minorum Gentium', p. 1203. The merchant came bef. Dec. 1666, m. Elizabeth Leader (2), and was an adm. of her fa.'s est. 30 June 1668. He went

full lengths with Major Shapleigh in opposition to Mass. taking poss. of Maine under the Gorges charter. In May 1675, yeoman, he leased a ho. on Fernald's Isl. for 13 yrs. to Geo. Harris; in 1681 and 1684 sold his town gr. and land at Spruce Creek bot from Thos. Withers. O. F. 6 July 1669; Constable 1671, 1673; Gr. j. 1675, 1676, 1688; Highway committee 1676, 1679. Lists 298, 82, 31, 39, 92, 293, 296, 297. See Cowley (2), Beale (1), (8). In May 1690 his w. was his atty. in Kitt., he resid. at Barbadoes; in Jan. fol. she deeded Kit. land under his P/A. If he ret. he went again and d. away, his sis. Mrs. Champernowne putting hers. into mourning as soon as news of his death came. Wid. Elizabeth, 'a gentlewo. of good extraction', was k. by the Ind. at Spruce Creek ab. 4 May 1705, adm. 21 June to Wm. Vaughan. List 96. No ch., the Hole land going to the Cutts fam.

**Holgrave,** John, adm. in Casco Ct. 26 July 1666 to Mr. Robt. Gutch. P. & Ct. i. 312. Likely from Salem and fa. or br.-in-law of the admr.

**HOLLAND,** a district of Lincolnshire.
1 **EDWARD,** fisherman, Shoals, two of them, but not separated, except Edward sr., Hog Isl., abs. from w. 1673, List 305b; Edward jr. ±35 in 1674. Edward, no designation, gr. adm. 13 June 1664 on est. of kins. Oliver Wingate of Bridgtown, co. Devon, cast away at the Shoals, John Sanborn surety; in 1669 sold Hog Isl. dwg. to Jeffrey Currier; in 1672 on bond with Wm. Oliver and witn. conc. Elizabeth Oliver's ch. See Damerill(3). Adm. br. Roger's est. 1678. In 1683 Henry Mains sold him the land on which his ho. stood. Of Star Isl., inv. 24 Nov. 1684. Lists 305a, 329.
2 **FRANCIS,** depos. ab. John Parrott's refusal to deliver goods to John Frizzell at Richmond Isl. 1688.
3 **JOHN,** Mr., Dorchester, voyaged and traded at the Eastward. Complainant ag. Thos. Wannerton in Aug. 1635; named in Trel. acct. May 1639. List 10. Bef. May 1651 Wm. Cousins (5) had sold him the -Virginia Merchant- for use of Mr. Benj. Gillam. P. & Ct. i. 162, 167. Will, ab. to go to Va., 16 Dec. 1651—16 Sept. 1652. W. Judith. Ch., incl. **Thomas,** ±22, May 1656. List 131.
4 **JOHN.** His wife at the Shoals 1672. Essex Q. Ct. 5.228.
5 **PAUL** (Holand), Newcastle 1696. List 315c.
6 **ROGER,** drowned in Great Storm 30 Jan. 1677-8; adm. 5 Mar. to br. Edward. See Broad (4).
7 **CAPT. THOMAS,** Newcastle, mariner and purveyor for the English navy, m.

at Southwark, Eng., in 1692, Elizabeth (Very?) of Deptford. Here in 1693, surety with Capt. Geo. Long for Jas. Webb. By 1698 he had built ship -Mary-, 250 tons; in Mar. 1699 met with Hon. Wm. Partridge, John Bridger and Benj. Jackson in Boston, all agreeing at equal expense to fit out a trip Eastward in H. M.'s service. **Three ch.**, all liv. 1702, b. here in ab. 7 yrs., bef. his w. went to Eng. for a long visit. The birth of a dau. 3 wks. aft. her ret. in 1700 was fol. by his ptns. to the Genl. Ct. for a separation. In Oct. 1702, when ab. leaving for Eng., she was almost murderously assaulted by her boarding mistress Mrs. Elizabeth Eburne, one witn. Chas. Kirke in his 16th yr. His ship -The Bifron- was driven on Great Isl. rocks and sunk in Oct. 1703; in Feb. next he was gr. a final separation. Not identif. later. Lists 98, 315bc, 68. Prov. Papers 3: 272, 277.

8 **WILLIAM**, Damariscove. List 8.

**Hollard** (Hollett), George, Penobscot 1674. List 3. D. H. vi. 82.

**Holley**, Joanna, acc. with Richard Perrer, Me. Ct., June 1688.

**HOLLICOMBE**, Hollicum. 1 **John** (Hollicum), fisherman, West Saco, shared in marsh 1653. Adm. gr. 4 July 1654. Lists 243a, 244b.

2 **CAPT. JOHN**, mariner, Newcastle. Bef. the 2d War, he was at Cape Elizabeth, fisherman, and bot there in June 1688, N. Fryer a witn.; poss. placed there by Fryer if already m. to his niece Joanna, dau. of his sis. Wilmot Tucker. She was lic. in Newc. Mar. 1693-4; he had tav. lic. the fol. yrs. Jury (N. H.) 1694, 1695, 1697. Lists 90, 66, 315b, 316. Robt. Elliot's will 1718 named him overseer and gave Cous. H. a heifer; debts due from Mrs. H. Capt. H. and man taxed 1720. See Bradden (2). In 1721, fisherman, he and w. sold 85 a. at Cape Eliz.; his land there ment. 1741. Will 23 May 1718—16 May 1721 gives to Devonshire relatives and w. Joanna. She taxed 1723.

**HOLLIS**, 1 **Ben**, Portsmouth. List 54. Reuben Hull meant?

2 **WILLIAM**, Salem 1668, poor in 1678. He ptn. for relief in Nov. 1679, was going with his fam. to live at the Eastward; if he went, he ret. to Salem.

**HOLLOWAY**, 1 **Henry**. Lists 363ab. See Hallowell.

2 **JACOB**, at Kittery with Edw. Pattishall in July 1690, on way to Boston; both were escaped captives from Penobscot. D. H. 5.276.

**HOLMAN**, found in Cornwall and Sussex.

1 —— (Howlman), Mr., a surgeon, attended inquest on Nathan Bedford's body, 1681.

2 **DANIEL**, Exeter, w. Hannah. Ch: **Daniel** and **Hannah**, b. 3 Apr. 1715.

3 **HUGH**, York, weaver. List 279. A soldier under Col. Harmon 1725 and at Louisburg 1745; in 1757 one of the prisoners from Ft. William Henry taken to France, where he d., leaving wid. Keziah (Johnson 29), m. 21 Dec. 1727. 6 ch. rec. 1730-42.

4 **JAMES**, shipmaster 1638. List 21.

5 **JOHN**, Dorchester, from Swyre, co. Dorset, a trader on the Eastern coast with Rich. Collicott. Will 10 June 1652—18 Mar. 1652-3 names brethren R. C. and ano. overseers, and disinher. s. by 1st w. Ann: **John**, b. 23 Feb. 1637-8, poss. the witn. to Ind. deed to John Richards of Nequasset 22 Aug. 1654 (Y. D. 35.46); in 1685 his daus. Mary and Phebe and their cous. Abigail Mason test. in Boston ab. the wonderful things Giles Goddard's daus. had shown them at the Goddard ho. there. By 2d w. Anne (Bishop) two sons who had deed from Collicott 10 Apr. 1684 of half a large tract on west side of Kennebec River: **Thomas**, b. 6 Aug. 1641, cordwainer, Milton. Will 21 July—5 Sept. 1704 left his Eastern lands to his four sons. **Samuel**, bp. 6 Dec. 1646, barber surgeon, Boston. In 1716 his two surv. ch. conv. his Me. int. to the Pejepscot Proprs. N. E. Reg. 72.185; Y. D. 15.240, 8.167, 9.5.

6 **JOHN**, North Yarmouth, 1666, poss. the Nequasset witn. 1654 instead of (5 jr.), liv. on Holman's, now Prince's Pt., where he bot 60 a. in 1669, 50 a. adj. Wise's planta. in 1670, and expended much in bldg. and improv. One J. H. took O. A. Boston 11 Nov. 1678. Ag. ±35 he depos. in Boston in Mar. 1679-80 ab. Geo. Pearson's payment to Rich. Bray, but ±48 in depos. bef. Gendall 3 Apr. 1685 conc. Bray's former land. Land where he and John Main form. dwelt ment. 1681; poss. he was then at Purpoodock Side where he and John Edwards(4) liv. under Danforth. In 1688, of Falm., he owned at No. Yarm., at Stanford's Pt., and on so. side Casco Riv. adj. Lawrence Davis. Lists 211, 30, 225a, 34, 214. Last found at Piscataqua 19 May 1690, constable of Casco Forts, bringing word of the burning of Tyng's, Gendall's and Ingersoll's garrisons, and asking help to go back and save his chn. **W.** perh. sis. of Rachel (Davis 39) (Haines) Wedgwood, who deeded right in bro. Holman's land. Only kn. ch; **Elizabeth**, m. in Boston 3 July 1701 Wm. Cook, who m. Lydia Moor 22 June 1704. Her dau. Elizabeth, b. 5 Jan. 1702, spinster, Roxbury, gr. dau. and only heir of J. H. in 1728. Y. D. 13.110, 16.261, 23.146.

7 **JOHN**, Howell alias Holman. See Howell.

8 **JOHN**, Holman or Holmes, Kit. List 298. See Holmes(7).

9 **SAMUEL** (Howlman). His debts in hands of Humphrey Scammon, Doughty and others, seized in Oct. 1683, when he was acc. of trading with Inds., discharged in May 1684 as.he was forced to let them have liquor. In Nov. 1688, ±40, master of small bark sailing from Pemaquid to Monhegan. D. H. vi. 447.

10 **SOLOMON**, Englishman, West Newbury, d. 7 May 1753, ag. 82; m. 1st Mary, dau. of Wm.(5) and Ann (Green 19) Barton. Admr. of her br. Ebenezer's est. 1724; York witn. 1 Jan. 1724-5. 12 ch. Y. D. 11.179, 181; 14.24, 15.24.

11 **STEPHEN**, Portsmouth, witn. against Wm. Richards, 5 Dec. 1693.

12 **THOMAS**, Rehoboth, and w. Hannah Turner (Ralph), sold her fa.'s Falm. land 1729. Y. D. 13.234.

**HOLMES**, common throughout England, except in the south-west. A 'holme' is flat land near water. Holmes Island, E. of Kennebec, in Sylvanus Davis' census, Reg. 21.356.

1 **DAVID**, soldier under Capt. Hall, k. at Falm. 21 Sept. 1689. List 228d.

2 **HENRY**. His assoc. with Henry Sayward, who appar. pd. his fine in York Ct. 4 Dec. 1677, points to Thos.(7) as a relation. In Apr. 1679 Francis Shallot, Frenchman, was acc. of stealing two pieces of gold from him, Rich. Otis bondsm. for H. H.; that yr. in Dec. he was in Boston from Piscataqua.

3 **JOHN**, Portsm., ±26 in 1667, m. Mary Peverly (John), both named in her gr. fa. Walford's will 15 Nov. 1666; she was ±26 in 1672. Lists 331a, 335a. He took O. A. at Str. Bk. 28 Aug. 1685, taxed 1690-91. Lists 312c, 326e, 330a, 331b, 313a, 92, 57, 335a, 330cd, 337. June 4, 1700, he ±63, she ±55, depos. conc. Hannah Guptill; in Dec. 1703 they deeded to Thos. Westbrook their homestead ±15 a. at head of Sagamore Creek given her by her gr. fa. In 1707 he was liv. on road to Greenl. on land bot in 1705 from Sarah (Hall) Fabyan(2) and her s. John. Liv. 20 Oct. 1712, not in 1713 tax list. Three ch. found, prob. others: Jeremiah, sailor on ketch -Richard- of Newc. 16 May 1685; witn. Savage deeds 1686, 1694. List 314. He m. by Rev. J. Pike 22 Sept. 1689 Sarah Walker. **Joseph**, soldier at Oyster River 1696. In 1703 his parents deeded him land and bldgs. bot the same day from Nathan Knight's w. He bot in Barr. 1732. Lists 336b, 339. By 1st w. Anne, had Samuel and Mary bp. No. Ch., Portsm., 25 July 1708, Ephraim bp. 29 Oct. 1710. He m. 2d 14 Mar. 1716-7 Mary, wid. of James Hall; son John bp. So. Ch. 8 Oct. 1721. **Lazarus**, soldier at Newc. Aug. 1708; liv. 1748. List 339. W. Ruth bp. and recd.

into No. Ch. 25 July 1708; sons bp. with mo: John, and Jeremiah (m. Sarah Sherburne), Benj. bp. 29 Oct. 1710, James bp. So. Ch. 29 May 1720. Unplaced: Mary, Portsm., m. 28 Oct. 1728 Wm. Howard(3). Hannah recd. into So. Ch. 29 Mar. 1723-4; in 1733 one Hannah was liv. in a little ho. where form. stood a blacksm. shop near the gate that Henry Sherburne set up on Walter Abbott's land. See also Hobbs(10).

4 **JOHN**, Capt. of ship -America- 1690. List 333a.

5 **JOSEPH**, Casco, late of Cambridge, bot from Capt. Joshua Scottow 200 a. at Dunstan adj. Andrew Brown, 16 Apr. 1681, giving partly in exch. his Casco land bot from Francis Neale. Y. D. 3.96. Scottow sued him in Wells Ct. May 1682.

6 **ROBERT**, in Salis. Ct. 14 Apr. 1663 told ab. the dealings of Rich. White and w. with Capt. Barefoot.

7 **THOMAS**, sued Sylvester Herbert(3) 1667. In York 1668 he told that Peter Weare invited him to sue Henry Sayward; was sued by Sayward for breach of agreem. in 1672, when John Redman told falsely he was Sayward's servant; 7 yrs. later was one to set out Mrs. Sayward's 3ds. See also (2). Bef. June 1671 he built and liv. with w. Joan Freethy(5) on land her fa. gave them. Dover 1674-75, dealing with Maj. Thos. Clarke who sued him in Suff. Ct. 1679; succ. John Crawford(2) at Quamphegan mill and was a party to suits with Broughtons, Crawford and others. He bot on the Berw. side from Thos. Newbury 1676, Richard Abbott 1677. Taxed Dover 1677. Gr. j. (Me.) 1678, 1679, 1685-7; Tr. j. 1687; Constable, upper Kit. 1679-80. Lists 359a, 89, 33, 36. In Ind. attack 18 Mar. 1689-90, the only one liv. at Quamphegan, he retired to his own garri. near his mill, leav. his ho. to be burned; likely hims. an Ind. victim ano. day. Inv. 16 Jan. 1690-1, incl. ho.-hold goods at Portsm.; adm. 23 Feb. to wid. Joanna, who was at the Spencer garri. sick with the distemper, and next June was threaten. to destroy her husb.'s garri. then in use by the govt. Ch: **Mary**, m. Walter Allen(15), who receipted to the est. 25 Feb. 1695-6. **Thomas**, Berwick, depos. in Jan. 1733-4, ag. 63, ab. Lovering's place. In 1727 he sold a piece off his homestead, in 1733 gave the rest to neph. Thos. jr. Liv. 1736. Lists 290, 296. **John**, living on the Newbury land with s. Wm. in 1758 when s. Thos. made his will. List 298. W. Mary (York Ct. July 1701), liv. 1720. 8 ch. rec. or bp., not incl. **Sarah** bef. York Ct., Oct. 1720, who was poss. a dau.

**Holt**, Joseph, York, m. 28 Dec. 1709 Mary (Harmon 3), wid. of Benj. Donnell (5), and d. 1744, ag. 88. Lists 279, 298. 8 ch.

1710-1726, incl. **Lydia**, m. Edw. Ingraham.

**HOMAN**, 1 **Daniel**, Portsm., m. 21 Sept. 1714 Hannah Taylor. One Danl. of Exeter m. Love Nock at Kingston 28 Feb. 1738-9.

2 **DOWNING** (Homon), Cape Porpus 1702-3. List 258.

3 **EDWARD**, Marblehead, m. Elizabeth Gould (1).

4 **JOANNA**, Pemaquid, m. at Dover 3 June 1695 Edw. Sargent. A Homans fam. were among the 'poor' at Salem 1678-9.

**Home**, Fortunatus, Shoals witn. 1661-2. List 302b.

**Homer**, Joseph, Oyster River soldier. List 67.

**Homsly**, Thomas, Dover, drowned 1670. List 357d. Hornsby?

**Hones** (See Fones), William, had Arrowsic gr. 1679. List 187. Master of fishing boat tied up at Sagadahoc Oct. 1688. D. H. 6.442.

**HOOKE**, its princ. home early and now in co. Sussex, whence came the Bristol family.

1 **CORNELIUS**, master of the -St. Marea-. Inv. of the goods he left at Mr. Francis Morgan's ho. taken by Robt. Marshall and John Penwill in Dec. 1671.

2 ‡†***CAPT. FRANCIS**, Esq., Saco, Kittery, appar. near relation of (3) and had with him at times (7) and his s. Wm. He m. in Boston, 20 Sept. 1660, Mary (Maverick, dau. of Saml.), wid. of John Palsgrave; was in Boston in June, 1661, at Saco same yr., and bot 30 a. at Winter Harbor in Nov. 1662. A Gorges adherent, he was Com. t. e. s. c. 1663-4, (indicted by Mass. in 1663 for acting under Gorges' authority), Clerk of the Writs 1664, J. P. 1665, Treas. for eastern div. of the Prov. 1666; signed protest to the King 7 July 1668. He bot at Kit. Point in 1674, but was Selectm. there 1673, also 1676-7; Com. t. e. s. c. 1673 and later; Customs officer, Associate, County Treas., Rep., J. P., Councilor under Danforth 1681, Dep. Pres. 1691, Chief Judge 1692-4, Councilor under Wm. and Mary 1693. Capt. many yrs., Major 1694, and the mo. before he d. wrote three letters to Lt. Gov. Stoughton about Ind. affairs and his intended trip to York and Wells. Lists 26, 79, 87, 249, 29, 33, 88, 90, 225a, 267a, 278. See also Champernowne (List 32). No ch. Will 9 (died 10) Jan. 1694-5 names w. and 'my boy Samuel.' Wid. Mary, ±60 in 1695, was liv. 14 Nov., inv. 16 Dec. 1706. Lists 246, 296, 297. See also N. E. Reg. 8.334, 41.81.

3 **HUMPHREY**, Esq., called chief patentee of York by Edw. Godfrey in 1640, had paid E. G. bef. 27 June 1638 for obtaining the patent for himself, **William** and Thomas H. and Giles Elbridge(1), husb. of his dau. **Mary** (2d w.). A wealthy merchant, mayor,

alderman and M. P. for Bristol, where he remained. List 272. Y. D. 8.121-2; Suff. D. 1.115, 117; 2 Me. H. S. C. 2.319-327. N. E. Reg. 54.410, has his will 25 June 1658 (bur. 31 Mar. 1659), nearly 78 yrs. old, b. in Chichester, naming many daus. and gr. ch. (no son as living). Waters 1.640, has will of wid. Cicely, bur. 3 Oct. 1660, dau. of Thos. Young, merchant.

4 **PHILIP**, witn. a Parker deed at Kennebec, 1664. Y. D. 10.152.

5 **THOMAS**, bro. of (3), Bristol merchant and a York patentee. List 272.

6 ‡***WILLIAM**(3), Mr., York, Salisb., merchant, bp. at St. Stephen's, Bristol, 8 Apr. 1612, 2d son, presum. the W. H. who witn. the Pemaquid patent to Aldworth and Elbridge in Bristol, 29 Feb. 1631-2. He m. Eleanor, wid. of Lt. Col. Walter Norton, some time aft. 21 Jan. 1633-4, but first of record in Saco ct. 25 Mar. 1636. 'Citizen and merch. of Bristol, now of Agamenticus,' he was representing the fam. in June 1638, when Godfrey made over his one-third of the patent to him; 'governor' (business manager) in Mar. 1638-9; one of Sir F. Gorges's councilors in Sept. 1639; still 'governor' May-June, 1640, tho then on the verge of remov. to Salisb. against his fa.'s wishes, 'the state of religion and its superstitious ways' in York, the reason. Lists 271, 272. Freeman in Mass. Oct. 1640; visited his fa. in 1641 taking testimonials; Rep. 1643, 1647. In 1650 he was going to Eng. (see Jewell), and poss. d. there. Adm. 4 Oct. 1653 to wid. Eleanor, who went to Eng. when her s. Wm. was 'a pretty big lad,' was back 1660, and of Boston when Wm. returned; liv. 1669. Ch., the first two b. in York (dep. of Priscilla Johnson and Thos. and Mary Bradbury, Y. D. 8.261-2): **Humphrey**, **William**, b. ±1639. **Jacob**, b. Salisb., 15 Sept. 1640. His gr. fa. by will first gave him a larger legacy than his two bros. 'in hope he may prove better,' and by a later item made the bros. equal. **Josias**, unkn. except from gr. fa.'s will.

7 **WILLIAM**(6), Mr., merchant, Salisbury, was in Eng. in Dec. 1658, when he gave P/A to his mo., and in 1659 when his gr. fa. made his will, calling Wm. and his br. Josias 'a couple of most stubborn and unruly boys.' He m. Elizabeth Dyer in Eng., came over without her, was in Saco with (2) in 1666 (Y. D. 10.26), and of Salisb. in Apr. 1668, abs. from wife. In 1717 he deeded to his three sons his int. in York, includ. his fa.'s ho.-lot, the Scotland Farm and Cape Neddick Neck (Y. D. 15.189). His wife d. in Salisb. 26 Mar. 1717, he 3 Sept. 1721. Ch: **William**, b. in Eng., was with (2) in Kit. at times 1686-1690 and there admitted as atty. for inferior ct. of common pleas in

Sept. 1687, tho of Boston 14 Mar. 1687-8. He m. 1st ab. 1691 Mary (Follansby), wid. of Robert Pike, and liv. in Salisb. W. Sarah ment. in will made 23 June 1743. 8 ch. **Florence**, b. in Eng., m. in Newb. 16 Nov. 1685 James Coffin. Born in Salisb.: **Elizabeth**, b. 22 Feb. 1671, prob. m. (int. 28 May 1698) Ezekiel Craveath of Boston. **Eleanor**, b. 20 Feb. 1673-4, prob. m. (int. 19 Dec. 1702) Andrew Greeley. **Humphrey**, b. 28 Jan. 1675-6, m. 10 July 1700 Judith March who surv. him; Amesbury 1717; d. bef. 8 June 1741. 3 ch. **Jacob**, b. 7 Jan. 1677-8, m. Mary March; of Salisb. 1717. Ch. **Martha**, b. 18 June 1681, prob. m. 7 Apr. 1715 Wm. Buswell. **Josiah**, b. and d. 1683.

**HOOKER**, 1 **Benjamin**, taxed Str. Bk. July 1690, Hoocker; Oct. 1691, Hucker.

2 **DANIEL**, at Capt. Plaisted's garrison, Kittery. List 289.

3 **JOHN** (also Hucker), bot ho. in Portsm. from John White 1705; taxed Mill Dam 1707-1713. One John surety for Edw. Wells, 1724. List 339.

4 **WILLIAM**, Portsm., m. Sarah Pickering 24 June 1722. Taxed Mill Dam 1737. 7 ch. bp. 1723-1739.

**HOOPER**, principally found in the southwest of England.

1 **ELISHA**, Wells soldier. List 266.

2 **JOHN**, error for Thomas(10), whose name John Ham forgot in naming Elliot's tenants at Dunstan. Y. D. 16.37.

3 **JOHN**, cordwainer, Berwick, poss. the Portsm. soldier 1696; of Berw. bef. his 1st ch. born, and bot there in 1704. See also (5). Jury 1708, 1709; Deacon 1721. Lists 336b, 296, 339. In Mar. 1729-30 he was deft. with Deliverance Lord and John Goodwin in suit of Wm. Hearl and w. Elizabeth over Agnew land. W. Charity, liv. 1746, not in will 22 May 1756—7 Jan. 1762. 9 ch., incl. **John**, b. 14 Jan. 1701-2, shoemaker. List 298. Poss. he or w. Mary relat. to wid. Elizabeth (Thompson) Gray(1), for whom he and Ebenezer Hilton were bondsm. 1732; later both were bondsm. for Jos. Woodsum; **in 1743 he** alone q. c. to her. Of Arundel 1761, he and w. sold Berw. land adj. Gilbert Hearl; said to have liv. past 102. 7 ch., incl. Keziah. **Samuel**, cordwainer, b. 18 Apr. 1709. 1st w. Elizabeth, 8 ch. 1731-45; m. 2d at Kingston 11 Sept. 1746 Elizabeth, wid. of Josiah Plummer, 5 ch. Liv. Arundel 1763. **Joseph**, b. 29 Jan. 1712-3, not in fa.'s will. Mr. S. B. Shackford called him n. c. m. and provid. for in earlier, unprov. will of his fa.; the Hooper Gen. indentif. him as Jos. pub. in Bid. 16 Nov. 1737 to Elizabeth Locke.

4 **JOHN** of Apsum (Epsom?), Gt. Britain, m. in Portsm. 13 Dec. 1716 Mary Walden.

Of Portsm. 1733, they sold in Barr. Two ch. bp. So. Ch.

5 **KEZIAH**, gr. dau. of Mary Gunnison, w. of Philip(4). In 1701, having stolen from Nathl. Raynes, she was to serve him 9 mos.

6 **RICHARD**, physician, Hampton, built a ho. and gave note in part payment; sued on it in Essex Ct. in Sept. 1684. In July 1684 he sued Danl. Dow for curing him and 2 ch.; later that yr. had a knockdown fight with Capt. Sherburne. Rem. to Watertown, d. 8 Dec. 1690, adm. to wid. Elizabeth. Of Watert. wid., she sold the Hampt. land to Saml. Sherburne's wid. Love in 1697. Ch: **Hannah**, ±18 in Feb. 1701-2 when Mr. Foxcroft was her and bro.'s gdn. **Henry**, physician, b. 25 May 1685 at Watert. 5 ch. by w. Remember rec. there 1717-1722. Of Newport, R. I. 1735.

7 **ROBERT**, shipwright, Wiscasset, had Scarboro gr. in June 1720 and sold part 4 Jan. 1721-2, deed witn. at Kit., ack. at York. In Oct. 1736 he and w. Mary had liv. more than 6 yrs. on w/s of Sheepscot Riv. near Jeremesquam Isl.; Robt. Foye dep. 1789 that he was the first settler at Wiscasset; liv. 1754. Fam. of four persons in 1730. Kn. ch: **Mary**, test. in York Ct. May 1730 that her fa. came home from York in Jan., had tended Ct. 4 days, bef. the next Ct. had gone to Pemaquid. Likely: **Nathaniel**, under age in 1720, had Scarb. gr. in 1721. But see also Nathaniel(10).

8 **SARAH**, legatee of John Dennett(4); unkn. unless w. or dau. of Nathl.(10).

9 **THOMAS**, furnished boards to Peter Coffin at the Piscataqua 1659. Essex Q. Ct. 3.169.

10 **THOMAS**, ±34 June 1694, ±42 Apr. 1701, servant of Capt. Champernowne as early as 1665, and m. ano. serv. Elizabeth Small. Of York 5 Mar. 1697-8 they sold land beq. to her by Champernowne. Condi. gr. in Kit. 1699, taxed there 1704; depos. 1705 that he was at the Champernowne ho. 18 or 19 yrs. before. See also Gunnison(4). Lists 290, 298. Of Falm. 28 Aug. 1732 they deeded to s. Benj. for supp. He depos. Apr. 1735, ±76, ab. 32 or 33 yrs. since he hired the Elliot farm at Dunstan for 7 yrs., had been there a yr. when the war broke out, at that time no other person exc. his fam. at Dunstan, where he built ag. Nichols' chimney back; again in Aug. 1737, ±79, he went there at desire of Mr. Elliot who built the ho. for him, and is informed that Rev. Mr. Thompson's dwg. stands at or near the same old back. Wid. liv. 1738. Ch., 4 rec. Kit.: **Elizabeth**, b. 27 Mar. 1694. **Sarah**, b. 25 June 1697, m. 4 Jan. 1730-1 Solomon Rose. **Nathaniel**, b. 20 Mar. 1700, m. (int. 23 Apr. 1724) Sarah Bradeen(1); Falm. 1727; of

Scarb., decd., 1750, when two ch. in Kit. deeded to Nathl. Keene. See (8). **Joshua**, b. 7 Apr. 1703; w. Elizabeth; adm. 13 Oct. 1770 to Robt. Patten. 3 ch. rec. Bid. 1735-43, 2 or m. not rec. **Benjamin**, Falm. 1732; his mo. declined adm. 1738; bros. Joshua and Clement adm. **Clement**, Bid. 1731, int. mar. with Olive Welch 5 Sept. 1741, but d. unm., adm. 18 Oct. 1743 to br. John. Likely: **Abigail**, Kit. wit. 1714, acc. (Ct. Apr. 1715) Paul Williams, a neighbor of Jas. Bradeen (1).

**HOPKINS**, common in South Wales and the near-by counties. A nickname for Robert, with the diminutive 'kin'.

1 **BARTUE**, cutting wood for Geo. Walton at Little Harbor 1682.

2 **EDWARD**, taxed Greenland 1719, m. there 23 Jan. 1718-9 Charity Bryant(10), who m. 2d 23 June 1726 Moses Clough. Ch. b. Greenl., rec. Salis: **John**, b. 9 Dec. 1719. **Edward**, b. 29 Jan. 1721.

3 **EDWARD**, of Appledore, co. Devon, m. at Portsm. 3 May 1720 Joanna Ball(5). In Berw. Ch. 16 Oct. 1720, Joanna o. c. and was bp., -Frances- recd. into ch. Edw. taxed Portsm. 1728. See Dunn(3). 2 ch. bp. So. Ch. 1724-8.

4 **JOHN**, Pemaquid 1647, witn. Ind. deed to Lake 1653; with Wm. Cock witn. Edw. Bateman's assignm. to Jas. Cole 31 Oct. 1654, ack. by Cock alone Sept. 1666. List 10.

5 **JOHN**, taxed Newc. July 1690; Mr. H. taxed Oct. 1691. List 319. Presum. husb. of Mrs. Sarah, wid., Newc. 1697; tav.-keeper 1698-1700. List 315b. See Saml. Comfort.

6 **WILL**, taxed Dover Neck 1681.

**Hopkinson, William**, h. at Sagadahoc 20 July 1689. D. H. 9.15.

**HOPLEY, Robert**, mariner, Portsmouth, some time master of the brigantine -Endeavor- of Piscat. O. A. at Str. Bk. 28 Aug. 1685; taxed there July 1690; the widow's ptn. in June 1699 called him late of Boston, in reciting his 6 mos. service as a gunner on the -Amerith- in Canada exped. 1690. Will 16 Feb. 1691-2, proved at Barbadoes, gave all in N. E. or 'on this island' to wife for use of his two ch. She was Elizabeth Tucker (John and Ursula of Portsm.), m. by 6 Dec. 1687 when she witn. Michael Mann's will as Hopley; still witn. as Hopley 1703. Lists 331c, 335a, 330df. See Churchwell(4). She m. 2d Sergt. Thos. Roberts of Dover; liv. 1735. Several ch. ment. in 1699; two had deed from gr. fa. Tucker in 1705; **Elizabeth**, m. 1st John Drew (9), 2d James Pinkham; liv. Mar. 1733-4. **Mary**, m. 1st Wm. Ayers (8), 2d Sampson Doe (3), 3d one Stevens.

**Hord**, John. List 282. See Heard (4).

**HORNABROOK, John**, Kennebec bef. July 1677, when his atty. Lt. Rich. Way sued in Suff. Ct. Mary, admx. of Obadiah Walker, for his wages there. Guide and Ind. interpreter; his farm on Tuessic-Neck (now Woolwich) near John Bish's, tho named vaguely in 1718 as if Lawrence Dennis's tenant on his Ind. purch. W. of the Kennebec. Taken with w. and ch. in 1688 by Inds. incensed by Capt. Blackman; witn. Ind. treaty at Pemaquid 11 Aug. 1693. Of Boston in Aug. 1699, where his w. Mary then entert. comp. at 1 o'cl. at night; next mo. Eastern Ind. asked that he be settled as interpreter at Newtown; next June at Tuessic illeg. trading with Ind.; Kittery (1704?), and some time lived at Great Isl. in ho. built by Gov. Allen, not standing 1713. Lists 189, 190, 289. Ch. cert. incl. two daus: **Margaret**, indiscreet with Francis Shallot at Newc. Aug. 1708; m. bef. June 1710 Jos. Woodsum. Acquitted of adult. in Boston 1714, when her husb. was in Eng., she disappears, but prob. liv., as he waited until 12 Feb. 1723-4 to m. Abigail Abbott, dau. of John (4). He liv. 19 Jan. 1756; wid. Abigail d. 4 June 1776. By 2d w: 8 or m. ch. b. Berw., several bef. 1723. **Esther**, Newc., had a bast., Ct. Apr. 1717; the fa.'s name was Richard; 'they would not know his last name if she told it.' One Elizabeth H. drowned at Tiverton, R. I., inq. 16 May 1729; one Isaac m. Mary Larkin in Boston 16 Jan. 1732.

**HORNE**, found in Yorkshire, Norfolk and Kent. It is a personal name of great antiquity.

1 **ARMSTRONG**, Exeter, O. A. 30 Nov. 1677; depos. 23 Nov. 1680, ag. bet. -20 or 30-, calling Capt. John Gilman 'my master.' At Newc. 16 July 1694 he and Saml. Kenney were exam. ab. Capt. Geo. Long's trouble; Portsm. witn. 1700; liv. 25 Jan. 1713-4. Lists 52, 57, 67.

2 **JOHN**(6), Dover, m. 30 June 1686 Mary Ham(4); d. of malignant fever Mar. 1696-7. Lists 62, 96. In Apr. 1708, s. John sought adm. of est. of fa. (Wm. by published rec.), as the wid. had remar.; she had m. 29 Aug. 1698 John Waldron. Ch: **John**, eldest s. and rightful heir, exch. deeds with uncle Thos. 30 Oct. 1717, receiving 60 a. of gr. fa.'s land and releasing the rest; later his bros. and sis. q. c. to him. List 358d. His w. Elizabeth Heard, m. 29 Dec. 1708, d. 12 Feb. 1776, ag. 92; he d. 15 Nov. 1778. 6 ch. See Heard(5), (7). **William**, Quaker, Dover housewright, m. 1st 9 Sept. 1713 Mary Varney, who d. 18 Nov. 1735. Will 14 Dec. 1767—29 Aug. 1770 names w. Elizabeth, 11 ch. **Daniel**, b. 1689.

His great gr. s. Michael Read fathered the story that there were two distinct Horne families in Dover by telling the compiler of the Wentworth Gen. that Daniel came from Scotland, disprov. by his q. c. deed to br. John, 1748. W. Mary. 6 ch. 1716-1734. He d. in Dover 7 Apr. 1777, ag. 88; wid. d. 14 Oct. 1777, ag. 83. **Mary**, acc. Benj. Wentworth 20 July 1715, not proved; m. Benj. Hanson(10), 2d Wm. Fost(2).

3 **THOMAS**, Newcastle soldier at Ft. Wm. and Mary July 1694, liv. July 1696. Lists 66, 315c. Likely wid. or mo. was Joanna, Newc., who had pub. ho. lic. in June 1699, bondsm. James Leach, Rich. Tarlton; in Dec. fol. she witn. ag. Edw. Hales, selling without lic. List 315b. One Thos. was of Gosport 1732, w. Mary. One Joseph adm. So. Ch., Portsm., 3 Jan. 1741-2.

4 **THOMAS**(6), Dover, only surv. son 1717, m. 1st 14 Apr. 1699 Judith Ricker (Geo.), 2d in 1720 Esther Hodgdon(1). List 358d. In 1739, of Tole End, he and w. Esther sold near Puddling Hole, Kit.; in 1753 deeded ⅛ of her fa.'s land. His own est. was finally settled in 1777, she living. 4+9 ch. rec. or bp., incl. **William**, b. 7 Nov. 1702, d. bef. Aug. 1747; of Dover in 174-, when his w. Margaret had the small pox in Portsm.; she liv. to be old Wid. Margaret in 1777. Their dau. Eleanor b. 17 July 1726, oldest of 3 ch., q. c. in 1748 to mo. and bros. Wm. (his wid. another Margaret liv. 1777) and James (liv. 1777). **Thomas**, b. 23 Oct. 1705, bot in Rochester 1729. **Ichabod**, b. 25 June 1710. Likely an unrec. s. by 1st w. Judith was **George**, Dover, m. 1st 24 June 1735 wid. Mary Odiorne of Portsm., 2d 4 Oct. 1769 Katherine Woodin; d. Dover 19 Mar. 1783. Ch., incl. Judith.

5 **TOBIAS**, Newcastle. List 315c. Error for Thos.(3)?

6 **WILLIAM**, Dover 1659, bot 240 a. betw. Cochecho and Tole End from Edw. Starbuck 27 Sept. 1661. He had been of Salis., the home of his w. Elizabeth Clough (John), named in her fa.'s will 1691. Gr. j. 1679. Lists 356eghk, 359ab, 49, 52, 96. K. by Ind. 28 June 1689. Inv. 27 Feb. 1691-2, incl. 200 a. land, 16 cattle; attested 15 July 1699 by Wid. Elizabeth, who had the distinc. of being the only woman among many signers of petn. to Mass. 20 Feb. 1689-90 to set up a tempo. govt. She was taken by the Ind., old Wid. Horn, 30 Sept. 1707. Lists 57, 96. Ch: **Elizabeth**, b. Salis. 1 Feb. 1661-2, d. Newb. 6 May 1672. **John**, b. 25 Oct. 1663. ?**Mary**, m. John Hayes(5). ?**Joseph**. **William**, b. 11 May 1674, d. s. p. 12 Apr. 1697 of a malign. fever. Lists 62, 96. **Thomas**, b. 28 Nov. 1676. **Margaret**, b. 10 May 1679, d. soon aft. her br. Wm. List 96. **Elizabeth**, m. Moses Kimmin(2). **Mercy**, m.

Joseph Evans(10); in 1748 they sold to her neph. John (2 jr.) ½ her share, 10 a. in the land bot of Nathl. Starbuck.

**Horney**, David, from Galway, Ire., m. at Portsm. Nov. 1720 Elizabeth Bradden (2). 4 ch. bp. So. Ch. 1728-1734.

**Hornsby**, see Beale(2), Homsly.

**HORRELL**, 1 **Henry**, boy seaman under John Lewis, drowned at Salis. 17 Apr. 1657; Robt. Quimby indicted for thrusting him into the water.

2 **HUMPHREY**, sued by John Lavis in York Ct. Mar. 1650-1; Shoals witn. 1653. In 1658 he witn. livery of Damerils Cove Isl. to Nich. Davison, and acquired in 1667 Rich. Fulford's Ind. gr. at Muscongus, which Saml. Sturtevant claimed for the heirs bef. the East. Cl. Com. In 1719 John Pearce depos. that H. H. liv. next up Muscongus Riv. from his fa., on his land called Withbarne, until driven away by Inds. Lists 121, 301. Of Beverly in June 1678, when his w. was a witn., ±70. Son (poss. gr. s.): **Humphrey**, b. ±1650, mariner, Boston, Beverly. List 333b. At Bev. he or Humphrey sr. was freeman 16 May 1683; d. there 9 Feb. 1710, ±60. M. 1st Sarah, 2d at Bev. 10 Jan. 1687-8 Elizabeth Smith, who m. there 2d 12 Aug. 1715 Saml. Sturtevant, and went to Plympton with her ch. 4 ch. by 1st w. rec. Boston 1673-1684; 6 by 2d w. at Bev. 1691-1708.

3 **STEPHEN**, List 359a. See Harwell.

**Horsh?**, John. List 57.

**Horslee**, James, worked at Newcastle fort 1697. List 68.

**HORTON**, 1 **Barnabas**, baker, Hampton, propr. 1640, sold there Mar. 1641-2. In 1641 sold Ipsw. land. List 392a. York ptn. 1654. See N. Y. Gen. & Biog. Rec. 36.38.

2 **JOHN**, master of an Ind. slave ship, witn. in Boston 1676. List 4. He had w. and 2 ch.

3 **THOMAS**, with crew of Good Hope of London Feb. 1688-9. See Ferguson (4).

**Hough**, see Huff.

**HOUGHTON**, 1 ———, Mr. Houghton's marsh, Scarb., ment. 1685. Y. D. vi. 10.

2 **ROBERT**, London. List 41.

**HOUNSELL** (Hounslow, Hownsley), **Edward**, Scarboro, b. ±1653, one of three gay young men compl. of by Mr. Foxwell in Apr. 1675; likely sobered by the War in which he served at Scarb. Lists 237abe, 236. O. A. at Boston 21 Apr. 1679. His wid. Hannah (Cloyes 1) was there 30 Oct. 1683, admitting guilt, but asking mercy; had only her hand labor to supp. her. In Suff. Ct. Feb. next she acc. Thos. Saffin and ptn. that he be made to pay what the Ct. ord. to maint. her ch. She m. 2d Isaac Hallam. Elizabeth, (Hounsel), paternity shadowed,

m. Richard Lyn in Boston 15 June 1704.
One Richard Lyne d. in Bost. 16 July 1711
ag. 50; poss. his wid. m. Wm. Pierce there
20 Oct. 1712.

HOUSING, Peter, witn. in Falm. Mar. 1663-
4. Y. D. 1.144. Had m. Sarah Cloyes(1)
bef. Oct. 1667, when she test. against her
br. and sis. for ill-treatm. of their step-mo.,
whose bondsm. he was. Lists 86, 34. See
also Howsell. D. last of Apr. 1673; adm. to
wid., John Cloyes bondsm.; all given to her
while the ch. were minors. She depos. 2
June 1673 ±20, ab. John Stydson's words.
Only kn. ch: Peter, asked in 1687 for ±60
a. on W. side Presumpscot Riv. his fa. posses. many yrs. List 34. See also Howsell
and Hounsell.

HOUSTON, 1 James, m. Mary Dore(2) at
Dover 23 Dec. 1692. One Geo. (Hous-
town) taxed Berw. 1719. John Huson and
Mary Newman m. at Wells 21 Feb. 1733-4,
appar. the poor and ancient John and Mary
Huston there 1771. John Husten of Falm.
m. Mary Thompson of Scarb. 19 Nov. 1736.
2 ROBERT, Dover, met an untimely death;
inq. in Me. bef. 5 Mar. 1689-90. See
Littlefield(23).

Hovey, John, and Arthur Came apprais.
estates of Wm. Wormwood, Thos. Bragdon, Dec. 1690.

HOWARD, Haward, Hayward.
1 EDWARD, taxed Dover Neck 1681; m.
22 Aug. 1689 Martha Row.
2 EPHRAIM, fighting with John Page at
Maj. John Davis's ho. Oct. 1686. One
Ephraim, s. of Samuel and Isabel, was b. in
Boston 23 Feb. 1661.
3 JAMES, fisherman, Portsm. List 330d.
First w. poss. a Shortridge or Pitman.
List 335a. Adm. 7 Sept. 1708 to 2d w. Mary,
her bondsm. Tobias Lear, John Davis; aft.
her death to Geo. Banfield 3 Sept. 1718 at
req. of her stepson Pitman. Poss. she mar.
2d Nich. Hilliard (6), altho Wid. Howard
was on the Mill Dam tax list 1713. Ch: Pitman (cert. by 1st w.), the only one of age
in Aug. 1718, then liv. away; of Marbleh.
1720 he deeded to Reuben Abbott. M. at
Ipsw. 26 Mar. 1718 Lydia Davison. She was
gr. adm. in N. H. 1 Nov. 1728; m. 2d in
Ipsw. 10 Feb. 1729-30 John Bowles, 3d Benj.
Dyke. Two ch. bp. Ipsw: Mary, 21 Aug.
1720; Amos, 30 Aug. 1724; one Amos int.
mar. at Ipsw. with Anna Rollins of Exeter
20 Sept. 1746; d. there 20 June 1772, ag. 49.
James, q. c. to br. Pitman in 1721. Edward,
sailor, sold 1/5 of fa.'s est. to John Davis
in 1728, Edw. Kingman a witn. M. (int. 7
Dec. 1728) Susanna Mitchell (Christo.).
William, had sold to or was repres. by Reuben Abbott in fam. agreem. 1728; m. 28 Oct.
1725 Mary Holmes. 5 ch. bp. So. Ch., Portsm.

One Richard H. was bap. at Barrington 1
July 1741. One Amos in 1751 had w. Charity
Downs (Thos.), in 1761 w. Sarah Dam
(Saml.), and d. Dover 6 Mar. 1799, ag. 78.
See also Davis (10), (26).
4 JEREMIAH, late soldier at Casco Bay
garrison, testi. at Boston 29 July 1714
ab. the wreck of the ship -Three Friends-
from London Oct. 1711 'at a place called
Portland.'
5 MARY, Mrs., widow, mother of Sir Wm.
Phips, left an annuity by will of his
widow, Dame Mary Sargeant 19 Feb. 1704.
6 NATHANIEL (Haward), Exeter. List
392a. One Nathl. freeman at Boston 10
May 1643.
7 NICHOLAS, Pemaquid, 1687-8. Lists 124,
189. One Nich. and w. Elizabeth of Boston had ch. rec. there 1668, 1671.
8 RICHARD, Shoals, twice fined for abs.
from meeting 1666-67. Witn. ag. Roger
Kelly selling at retail, July 1667, and acc.
by R. K. at same Ct. in connec. with his
dau. Sarah.
9 ROBERT. List 94. Likely either the Notary Public 1660 (P. & Ct. i. 252) or his
son, both of Boston. Robert, N. P., witn. a
Boston deed with Wm. (10), 1661.
10 LIEUT. *WILLIAM, Hampton, ±52 in
Mar. 1661, ±56 in June 1665, assoc. with
Mr. Wm. Paine of Ipsw. and Boston 20 yrs.
and a legatee under his will, was with the
first comers at Hampt., already mar.; and
poss. had been first at Ipsw. Freeman 13
May 1640. Rep. 1641-45, Com. t. e. s. c. 1642-
43, Town Clerk 1643 for 4 yrs. In Mar. 1643-
4 a ptn. was presented to the Genl. Ct. for
his removal as Lieut.; he was estab. over
them without their knowl. or consent, and so
for ab. 3 yrs. Hampt. in Sept. 1648; in Oct.
1649 sued Saml. Greenfield for slandering
him in the meet.-ho. at Hampt. bef. a great
audience, but was of 'ye new meadows in
Ipsw.' 11 Oct. 1649, Topsfield 1650-1653,
Boston by June 1658, princ. his home thereaft., altho on gr. j. at Hampt. in Oct. 1663
and often in Essex Ct. In York Ct. 1 July
1662 he and Jas. Pendleton acted as agents
in seven suits for Capt. Bryan Pendleton
and Mr. John Payne, he alone was Capt.
Pendleton's bondsm. in his suit against Wm.
Phillips. Lists 391ab, 392ab, 393b, 53. W.
Alice witn. with him in Boston 15 Dec.
1664. Adm. to her in 1674, bondsm. Wm.
English (5) and Thos. Smith. In 1652 her
husb. had witn. English's deed of Hampt.
land. Of Boston, wid., she deeded land 19
July 1675, John Hayward, scr., a witn. See
(6), (9).
11 WILLIAM, Newcastle 1662. List 311a.
Poss. same as
12 WILLIAM, Scarboro soldier 1676. List
237b. Likely Ensign Howard at Wells

Nov. 1676 who had Nath. Masters' gun taken away from him. See (11).

HOWE, 1 **Anthony** (How) sued by Narias Hawkins, Me. Ct., June 1637.

2 **GEORGE**, Portsm. See Blackstone (2).

3 **JOHN**, Y. D. iv. 57; List 36. See Hoy.

**HOWELL**, a common Welsh baptismal name.

1 **ABRAHAM**, Portsmouth, late of London. Will, bound to sea, 29 Dec. 1699—17 Oct. 1700; all to Wid. Mary Clark.

2 **JOHN**, Mr. See Aldrich(3).

3 **JOHN**, blacksmith, Scarboro, b. ±1632-3, ±37 in 1669; 48 in 1681, when he depos. ab. Scarb. 30 yrs. past; his master Andrew Alger sr. Tenant farmer on Mr. Abra. Jocelyn's land 1660; bot Richard Shaw's ho. and land at Blue Point in Mar. 1661-2, and was his admr. next July; acquired some kind of a title to 100-a. farm at Dunstan, sold to John Morton in Feb. 1678-9, aft. fleeing to Boston. Scarb., Sept. 1680, Robt. Elliot's tenant at Blue Point and Dunstan several yrs. His ptn. to Andros asked for 50 a. bounding on Scottow's land, (Dunstan), in his poss. ab. 30 yrs. Again in Boston he liv. in ho., and worked with Isaac Hallam, whose wid. Hannah depos. in Oct. 1731, ±80, that she liv. in Scarb. ab. 60 yrs. ago with J. H., tenant to Mr. Scottow, and never heard that he owned any land. D. bef. July 1695. Lists 234b, 235, 237ae, 238a, 34. In a late depos., Nathl. Locke called him 'Howell al. Holman.' W. Prudence, m. by 1666, liv. 1679, taught school early. List 234b. Only ch. ident: **Prudence**, b. ±1666, m. at Concord 9 July 1691 Isaac Temple. 5 daus. Of Concord, she depos. in Aug. 1731, ±65, that her fa. liv. many yrs. on the land he sold to Morton, 'several of us ch. were b. there, I was nearly 9 when I came from there.'

4 **JOSEPH**, York 1711. Y. D. 7.192.

5 ‡**MORGAN**, Cape Porpus, first in rec. at Saco Ct. 6 Mar. 1636-7, suing and sued by Wm. Scadlock. His ho. was already standing on 100 a. at Cape Porpus granted him in 1643. Grant from Cleeve in 1648, 100 a., 30 'at home,' -60- up Eastern River, which was -70- when he sold, with a 40 a. town gr., to Ens. Barrett, 1666. Member of Rigby's Council. Gr. j. 1654-5, 1658, 1661, 1663-4; tr. j. 1662-6; Constable 1656, 1659-60. In 1661 he sent fish to Capt. Pendleton by John Snelling, who did not deliv. it. Freq. in Ct. as party to suit, witn., or in connec. with an est. Lists 23, 251, 252, 263, 24, 254. Leaving neither w. nor ch., his will 17 Nov. 1666 (inv. 22 Jan. fol.) gave all to Mrs. Mary Bolles (3) and her ch., except a bed, kettle and cow to Mary Frost sr., a heifer to Mary Frost jr.

6 **RICE**, Oyster River 1650; bot 12 a. on s/w side of York Riv. in York 1651; O. R. gr. 1653, and bot there from Thos. Footman 1654. Wm. Broomfield depos. in 1661 that Thos. Johnson bargained with R. H. to leave the place he was in, where he had good wages, and come with him, and he should have 4 a. as long as he liv. In 1661 he threw a glass bottle at Robt. Hussey. Lists 354c, (¶356a, 361a Rich), (¶356k), 363a. See also (7).

7 **RICHARD**, before Dover Ct. 1655. Same as (6)?

8 **STEPHEN**, List 359a. Horrell?

**Howett**, John, York witn. 1671. Y. D. ii. 104.

**Howsell**, Peter, around Saco 1661. Swearing and threaten. the constable. Witn. Richard Hitchcock. See Housing.

**HOY, John**, York, bot 50 a. from Capt. John Davis for two hogsh. molasses 17 Oct. 1679; built, fenced and planted an orchard; Jos. Abbott helped him raise his ho. at -Bixsom- ab. 32 yrs. ago (depos. 1721). Witn. 1681; 1686 (Howe, by mark). John Hoyes? selectm. 1685. Adm. (Howe) 1719 to Capt. David Robertson, mariner, Boston, chief cred., who sold one-fourth the land at Brixsom to Josiah Bridges. Lists 87, 36. Fam. not found at York. One John m. at Boston 4 July 1728 Sarah Clark.

**HOYT**, Hight, **Thomas**, b. Salis. 1 Jan. 1641 and liv. there, but sent five of ten ch. by 1st w. Mary Brown to Me. and N. H.: **Ephraim**, Hampt. Falls, b. Salis. 16 Oct. 1671, d. 1741-2, m. 25 Apr. 1695 Hannah Godfrey (4), and 1707 was surety for her sis. Deborah; m. 2d 12 Aug. 1736 her cous. Hannah Godfrey (2), 3d 4 Sept. 1738 Elizabeth Macrest. 9 ch. **John**, b. 5 Apr. 1674, m. 10 Nov. 1695 Sarah (Nason), wid. of Henry Child (1). List 298. In Nov. 1701 Mrs. Lucy Stileman's farm at Sturgeon Creek was in his occupation; in Feb. 1702-3 he exch. a Kit. farm for Geo. Brawn's in Newington, and bot more from John Downing. Dover constable 1705. D. bef. 1723 when only ch. Mary, b. Kit. 2 May 1697, and husb. John Hodgdon (3) began dispos. of his prop. **William**, b. 8 Apr. 1676, of Kit. 10 Mar. 1701-2 m. Elizabeth (Haley 1), wid. of John Nelson; mov. to Newingt. 1703, constable 1710, memb. of scouting party 1712. D. bef. 16 Dec. 1718 when she m. Nich. Hilliard (6). 6 ch. incl. Wm. b. ab. 1707, founder of Hight fam. in Berw. List 298. Sergt. **Israel**, b. 16 July 1678, soldier at Wells 1696. List 289. M. Grace Taprill (Robt.) and was in Newingt. by 1710; memb. of scouting party 1712; Sergt. in Capt. Hill's Co. Likely d. 1713. She o. c. and had 5 ch. bp. Newingt. 14 June 1719. See Babb (4). **Joseph**, m. 22 Dec. 1707 Hannah Chase, dau. of Aquila

(1 jr.). Of Stratham by 1713, where he d. 24 May 1753 in 69th yr., she 9 Mar. 1774 in 87th yr. List 388. 8 ch., 4 rec. Stratham 1713-9. See Bartoe (2); Ancestry of Lydia Harmon, by W. G. Davis, p. 57; Hoyt's Salisb. i. 206.

**HUBBARD**, Hobart, corruptions of Hubert, found in Norfolk, Suffolk and Leicestershire.
1 ———— (Hubord). List 90. Poss. (6) or (9).
2 **REV. GERSHOM** (Hobart), H. C. 1667, br. of (3), having been adm. freeman by the Genl. Ct., was given his oath by the York County Ct. July 1673. Why or how long in Me. unkn.; ordained minister at Groton 26 Nov. 1679.
3 **REV. JEREMIAH** (Hobart), H. C. 1650, br. of (2) and ?(7), s. of Rev. Peter of Hingham. His pres. in York in Apr. 1654 (Y. D. xii. 215) is unexpl. By 1656 he had begun at Beverly the first kn. of his troubled pastorates; in June 1660, ag. 28, had liv. in Lt. Lothrop's ho. more than 4 yrs. and contin. at Bev. until some time in 1664. In 1667 he served Wells as minis. less than 5 mos. of the 7 yrs. called for by their liberal agreem., incl. remov. of his hh. goods from Lynn. (Bourne, p. 104). Poss. he mov. only to Kit., where, if no other trouble devel., he could not collect his pay; in July 1669 the Genl. Ct. ord. the town to make a rate for his arrears, still partly held from him in July 1676. A Kit. witn. 2 Sept. 1670, altho at Amesbury 1669-1672, Topsfield 1672-1680. Lists 26, 82. Hempstead, L. I., called him 25 Apr. 1683, Haddam, Conn., 24 Aug. 1691; d. Haddam 6 Nov. 1715, ag. 84. Ch. incl. 4 b. Topsfield 1672-1679 by 1st w. Elizabeth Whiting (Rev. Saml.) of Lynn, m. 6 Apr. 1659; in 1664 they called Humphrey Woodbury's w. Elizabeth, kinswoman; Jan. 31, 1682-3 he had lic. at Jamaica, L. I., to m. Rebecca Brush; his wid. Elizabeth (m. by 1698) was liv. Hartford 1717.
4 **JOHN**, Boston merchant, took mtg. from Elihu Gunnison on 10 a. with Grantham's Isl. in Crooked Lane 23 Nov. 1685, released by s. Nathaniel 1719. Y. D. 6.60, 9.251-2. See (12).
5 **LT. JOHN**(10), blacksmith, Kingston, m. in Salis. Jane Follansby (Thos.). She adm. to Salis. Ch. 5 Feb. 1698-9, he 1 Aug. 1703. He bot in Kingston 14 Dec. 1702, liv. there 13 Sept. 1706. Will 25 Sept. 1723— 4 Mar. 1723-4 names w. Jane sole exec. and 10 ch. One Jane was dism. from Salis. Ch. to K. 26 Sept. 1725. Ch: Richard, b. 17 Mar. 1690, d. y. Jeremiah, Dea., b. 27 Aug. 1692; of Kingston m. at Haverh. 28 Feb. 1722-3 Mercy Johnson. 4 ch. rec. Mary, b. 29 Nov. 1694. Richard, b. 27 Dec. 1696, of

Kingston, m. at Haverh. 27 Dec. 1722 Abigail Davis, d. Ki. 25 Sept. 1733 of a consumption; 2d at Ki. 16 Oct. 1734 Abigail Taylor (Wm.), d. 9 Dec. 1758, ag. 56; 3d one Dorcas, d. 28 Jan. 1774, ag. 62. He d. 26 Dec. 1782 (gr. s.); appar. fa. of Martha, called niece, if not of Mary, m. in Cambridge 25 Dec. 1758 Thomas Durant, both found in his sis. Martha's will. Martha, b. 8 Oct. 1698, m. 26 Oct. 1725 Noah Champney of Cambridge. Her will 12 Jan. 1753— 11 Jan. 1776 rememb. bros. Jeremiah, Richard, John; Jeremiah's s. Richard; sisters Mary H., Anna Thompson, Keziah Libby, Jemima Meservey; neph. Noah Champney (?son of sis. Jane). Remaind. to niece Martha Hubbard of Cambridge and her s. Geo. Jane, b. 10 June 1700, m. Thomas Champney, bro. of above; wid. of Kingston, son Danforth of Boston. Anna, b. 22 July 1702, m. at Ki. 3 Oct. 1728 Rev. Wm. Tompson of Scarb. Keziah, b. 10 July 1704, m. John Libby(9). John, b. 21 July, d. 6 Sept. 1706. Dorothy, b. 8 Jan. 1708, liv. 1723. Jemima, b. 3 Mar. 1711, m. at Ki. 27 Dec. 1732 John Meserve of Scarb. John, b. 28 Jan. 1715, liv. 1753.
6 **JOSEPH** (Hubart), from par. of St. Saviour, Isle of Jersey, where a br. John had lately been in poss. of his field. Here he liv. with and was maint. by br. Philip(9) who recd. all by his will 24 Mar. (d. 1 Apr.) 1701. See (13).
7 **JOSIAH** (Hobart), ±33, 26 June 1667, was at Exeter in comp. with Andrew Wiggin and Capt. Barefoot; likely the Hingh. mercht., br. of (2) and (3).
8 **JOSHUA**, mate of the -America- at Portsm. 1690. List 333a.
9 **PHILIP**, Berwick, see (13) and (6). His 1st appear. is his m. rec. to Elizabeth (Goodwin 4), wid. of Zach. Emery(6) in Berw. 22 Dec. 1692. Lists 298, 296, 38. Fined (remitted) for non-appear. as Gr. j. 1698. Gr. j. 1699; pub. ho. lic. 1704-1709. Constable 1702; Selectm. 1703; Treas. of parish 1707; chosen Selectm., Town Treas. and Highw. Surv. 5 Aug. 1713, but soon d. Inv. 22 Feb. 1713-4 incl. carpenter and joiner's tools, much livestock, a negro woman. Wid. d. bef. 16 Dec. 1736 when her 3ds were divid., the homestead then val. at £1000. Ch: Philip, b. 9 Nov. 1693, k. by Ind. May 1722 (or 3); m. ab. 1717 Elizabeth Roberts (Jos.), who m. 2d Capt. John Gage of Dover. 3 ch. John, b. 25 Aug. 1696; had gristmill at Dover 1739-40; d. unm. Elizabeth, b. 13 Feb. 1697, m. 12 Nov. 1719 Jacob Redington of Topsfield. Moses, Berwick, Eliot, b. 8 July 1700, m. 26 Dec. 1723 Abigail Heard (6). 8 ch. In 1737 Elizabeth Trickey was schooling his ch. Aaron, b. 4 May 1702, tanner, Chelmsford 1728, Topsfield 1737,

where he d. 7 Sept. 1751. M. at Topsf. 1
June 1733 Mary (Curtis), wid. of Isaac How
of Falm. 4 ch. **Patience**, b. 30 Mar. 1704,
m. (Ct. Oct. 1724) Wm. Card(6), 2d at York
21 Aug. 1733 Danl. Farnham(2?), d. Georgetown 1751. **Mary**, b. 25 Jan. 1705, m. John
Bean(4); d. 1744.
10 **CORNET \*RICHARD**, [±40 1671-4 S. J.
C., prob. the Boston Richard b. ±1631],
presum. the same adm. inhab. of Dover Feb.
1658-9, List 356d, appears next receiv. a gr.
in Salis. 29 Jan. 1661-2, 'provided he stay
in the town 3 yrs. and improve hims. in his
trade for the good of the town'. He is
divided in the Hubbard Book into fa. and
son, b. 1620 and 1645. His gr. stone stands
in Salis. bur. ground, Cornet Richard Hubbard d. 16 June 1719 aged 88 yrs. See N. E.
Reg. 66.89. He was a blacksmith. Liv. in
Boston 1697-1700 and settl. his s. Joseph
there as a blacksm. Deputy; Cornet of the
horse troop many yrs.; in 1687 Quartermaster of the regiment. Mr. R. H. and Dorothy Stevens, his dau., were adm. to Salis.
ch. 16 July 1693. His w., a memb. in 1687,
was Martha Allen, dau. of Wm. and Ann
(Goodale), who d. 1 Oct. 1718, ag. 73 (gr.
st.). Ch: **Mary**, b. 19 Jan. 1667, m. Tobias
Langdon(2). **John**, b. 12 Apr. 1669. **Child**,
d. 1672. **Dorothy**, b. 19 Apr. (or 17 July)
1673; m. John Stevens of Salis. and Hampt.;
d. 5 July 1716. 11 ch. 1692-1716. **Joseph**,
b. 4 June 1676, m. in Boston 4 Aug. 1698
Thankful Brown of Sudbury. Their s.
Thomas 4 Aug. 1702—14 July 1773, was
Councillor and Treas. of Harvard Coll. 20
yrs. **Judith**, b. 9 July 1679, m. in Boston 7
Nov. 1699 Obadiah Emmons. **Comfort**, b.
17 Jan. 1682, m., in double mar. with last,
Joshua Weeks. **Jemima**, b. 11 Nov. 1684, m.
at Glouc. 26 Apr. 1712 Wm. Haskell. **Keziah**,
twin, m. 16 Dec. 1701 Joseph True, adm. on
his est. gr. 2 Oct. 1718. She and 6 ch. liv.
1728. **Richard**, b. 9 Mar. 1687; 'departed
this life An Dom 1687.' **Eleazer**, b. 27 Oct.
1689, m. 16 Dec. 1712 Dorcas Haskell of
Glouc. First at Kingston, ab. 1737 he had
remov. to Falm. and went by name of Eleaz.
Walton, app. to avoid debts.
11 **THOMAS** (Hobart). List 307b.
12 **WILLIAM**, Stack. Kit. p. 78. No trace
of such. See (4).
13 _____ Hubbard's Rock, Scarboro, lies
off the farm called 'Hubbard's house'
in Y. D. 6.132, east of Prout's Neck. Philip
(9), an educ. Jerseyman, appear. first in
Berwick shortly aft. Scarb. was evacuated
in 1690. This farm was then owned by
Mr. Robt. Elliot of Gt. Isl., who cert. had a
tenant on it, and was in position to pick his
men among the newly arriving Jerseymen.
This plaus. conjec. may include (6) also.
**Huch** or **Huck**, _____, Mr. List 92.

**Huches?**, Joseph, w. Mary; dau. **Mary**, b.
Hampton 25 Dec. 1659.

**HUCKINS**, prob. a diminutive of Hugh.
1 **FRANCIS**, a witn. with Thos. Beard and
Ezek. Pitman at Wm. Beard's ho. 1676;
twice a Sagamore Creek witn. in 1679. In
1680 Nehemiah Partridge sued him on a
bill for shoes, the writ attaching frame,
boards, land, being served at Jos. Hall's,
his last kn. place of abode; Jas. Robinson
bondsman had to pay the judgm. Mr. Wm.
Vaughan sued him the same yr.; last found
sending Vaughan (his best friend in this
strange country) a well written letter from
prison 3 June 1681, unable to get bond being a stranger; pipe staves were due him
from Ex. people, incl. Jos. Hall. Thos.
Rand then went his bond. Lists †359a
(Huckts), 329.
2 **LIEUT. JAMES**(4), Oyster River, husbandman, miller, first taxed 1664. In
1662 Wm. Furber sold on Dover Neck, partly his own gr., partly bot from Thos. Beard
and Thos. Austin, with warr. against claims
of J. H. Constable 1676; Gr. j. 1686; Selectm. 1688. Lists 363c, 365, 366, 359a, 49,
52, 55b, 94, 353, 382, 96. W. Sarah Burnham
(5), ±19 in Dec. 1673. Ind. k. him and 17
men from his garri. working in the field, 28
Aug. 1689, burned the garri. and k. or capt.
its inmates, incl. his w., who was returned
15 Sept. 1690, called -Robert- Hookins' wid.
in Capt. Church's report to Gov. Hinckley.
She m. 2d 17 Oct. 1700 Capt. John Woodman; not in his will 20 Dec. 1705. Obvious
errors in Prov. rec. of ch: **Sarah**, b. -12 Dec.
1672-, d. y., or else error for **Robert**, not rec.,
yeoman, miller, Oyster Riv.; Selectm., Assessor, Constable. Lists 62, 368b, 369. His
w. Welthean Thomas (James) was charged
9 Mar. 1692-3 with secretly burying a dead
ch. in Dec. 1692, not indicted. He was bap.
in his last sickness 17 Jan. 1719-20; will 9
Jan.—2 Mar., names w. Welthean, br.-in-
law Jas. Bunker(2) exec., 10 ch., incl. Mary,
w. of Wm. Drew, James under 21, Thos. under 14. She m. 2d John Gray(8). **Sarah**,
b. -12 Dec. 1674-, witn. for John Woodman
in 1701, m. Philip Chesley (3 jr.). List 96.
James, b. -15 July 1675-, d. s. p. ?List 99,
p. 92.
3 **JAMES**, Thomas, Mary, from Oyster Riv.,
in Canada 1710. List 99, p. 92. If gr.
ch. of (2), James was but a boy, Thomas a
small ch.
4 **ROBERT**, Dover, signed the Combination
and had a gr. in 1642 on W. side of Back
Riv., laid out in 1698 to his gr. s. Robert,
who was gr. adm. on his est. 7 Aug. 1705.
Geo. Parkinson's depos. in 1702, that his
master Kenne got perm. from Wid. Huckins
in 1656 or thereab. to cut all her late husb.'s

marsh, sets the time of his death too early, as R. H. was taxed at Oyster Riv. 1659. Lists 351ab, 361a. Wife's name not found as Huckins; likely she was Wm. Beard's w. Elizabeth in 1675, when they deeded to Jas. Huckins for love and affect., altho 5 June 1672 Sarah (Burnham) Huckins appar. said 'my mo. Jones.' Only kn. ch: James.

Huckts, Francis, Bloody Point. List 359c.

Huckins?

Huddy, John, List 329. See Hoddy.

## HUDSON

1 ———, dieted Stephen Crawford's wid. bef. Oct. 1647. List 71. Goodman H.'s lot, Dover, ment. 5 Dec. 1652; Hudson's lot in Edw. Patterson's hands 1669.

2 CAPT. DANIEL (Hutson). List 90.

3 ELEAZER, surety for Ruth, wid. of John Carter (5), Shoals, 1734. Mr. E. H. and Mrs. Mary Carter m. at Gosport 15 Dec. 1735.

4 HENRY, Mr., sued Mr. Nicho. Pape and Edw. Welch, York Ct., July—Sept. 1661.

5 JOHN, Newington, ±48 June 1701, taxed Dover ?1680, Bloody Pt. 1684, m. 25 July 1689 Mary Beard(4), who dep. in 1718 ab. the Langstaffs 60 yrs. bef. Gr. 10 a. adj. Wm. Furber sr., 1693-4. Dover constable Sept. 1697. Lists 359b, 52. Will, aged, 5 July 1717—6 Mar. 1723-4, names w. Mary, three Peavey gr. sons, cous. Jos. Beard overseer, and Joseph's s. Saml. Ch: Dau. m. by 1711 (?Abel) Peavey.

6 SAMUEL, m. in Boston 23 July 1713 Dorcas Miller, who m. 2d John Bradford (1). Ch: Izett, bp. Portsm. 15 July 1715, m. Isaac Bussy (2), presum. m. 2d Mark Hunking (9).

## HUFF, Hough. Hough a township in Cheshire, where the name is found as well as in Lancashire.

1 FERDINANDO, whose long and short names take strange forms, was of Portsm., mar. to Mary Moses (John) bef. 1 Mar. 1664-5, when she witn. fa.'s deed to s.-in-law Jos. Walker, partly 'in consid. of a little cornfield of J. W.'s which now doth belong to Ferdinando Huff'. He was ag. 41, she ±36, in Oct. 1681; he ±70 in Aug. 1702. Of Sandy Beach 17 Mar. 1671, he had been in Cape Porpus long enough to be Selectman (Off) 7 Dec. 1672, bot half of Batson's Neck 1674, was haying there (Nandy Hoof) in Sept. 1677, but had withdr. to Portsm. by 3 June 1678. In Oct. 1681 they liv. in John Sherburne's ho. and had charge of Henry Sherburne's mute dau. At Cape Porpus again, he had lic. for ordin. 29 May 1683, (Portsm. tax abated Dec. 1683), and was sued in York Ct. 1685-6, with no evid. that he came again aft. his 2d ret. to

Portsm., where liv. 1693. Taxed Little Harbor 16 May 1701; there Aug. 1702; last found in 17— claiming ½ of Barstow's (Batson's) Neck. Lists 312c, 313a, 331b, 52, 334a. Only prov. ch: Thomas, who deeded in 1712 to br.-in-law Ebenezer(1) and sis. Mary Emmons (more likely Ferris than Huff).

2 MARIAM (Hough), m. in Hampt. 8 Aug. 1709 Daniel (Dow says Saml.) Bailey.

3 THOMAS(1), b. ±1675, master of a sloop 1709-12, house carp. 1715, 1717, mariner 1732. He m. in Kit. 2 Jan. 1700-1 Grace Ferris (Aaron), made an attempt to settle at Cape Porpus and was liv. at Spruce Creek in Feb. 1708-9 when her parents deeded them the homestead and ¼ a sloop for life supp. Of Kit. in Mar. 1714-5 he mtg. to Pepperell 18 a. where he form. dwelt, and sold to Henry Barter in Mar. 1717, aft. perma. locating at Cape Porpus. W. Grace not named in his deed to Emmons 1712; w. Sarah named in, but did not sign, the 1717 deed, her only appear., and poss. error for Grace. Constable Cape P. 1719. In Apr. 1752, ag. 77, she testif. ab. the place in 1703. Ch. rec. Kit: Thomas, b. 18 Aug. 1703; of Arundel, m. 1st in Portsm. 8 Nov. 1729 Hephsibah Banfield (Geo.), 2d in York 14 Apr. 1746 Sarah Bowdy. Ch: Geo., Mary, Thos., and not unlik. several of those cred. to his fa. by Bradbury, whose report of the fa.'s service as pilot on the King's ship in 1745 applies more reasonably to the son. Joanna, b. 17 Sept. 1706, m. in Kit. 8 Oct. 1724 Jeremiah Springer, both of Arundel. Her fa. deeded him 50 a. in Arundel 25 Dec. 1732, she liv. 1 Mar. 1732-3. Sarah, b. 7 Sept. 1708; she or a niece m. John Hamer, Arundel. Unrec.: Mary, m. Miles Rhodes, fisherman, Arundel, deft. with her br. James, fisherman, in Pepperell's suit Apr. 1738. Of 4 m. named by Bradbury, George, Charles, m. Priscilla Burbank, John, d. y., Joseph drowned 30 Sept. 1749, the 1st two at least likely were ch. of Thos. Jr.

## HUGGINS, a Norfolk name, poss. a patronymic from Hugo.

1 JAMES, Lists 49, 363c, 365, 94; Robert, List 368b; Sarah, List 96. Should read Huckins.

2 JOHN, Hampton, came from Dedham where he sold in 1639; liv. near Hampt. Landing Place, and in Mar. 1643-4 pledged his ho. to deliver pipe-staves. Adm. John Legate's est. 11 Apr. 1665. Lists 391ab, 392a, 393a. W. Bridget, ±44 Oct. 1659, depos. in Essex Ct. ab. Henry Green's dau.; ±56 in June 1673. List 392c. His will, senr., ag. ±61, 31 May, d. 7 June 1670; w. Bridget and s. John exec., John to have the land in the woods called Mr. Legate's; younger ch. to

have Christian educ. Jacob Freese held some of his est. in 1724 when the Websters were acting for the heirs. She m. 2d John Clifford (3). Her will 1 Sept. 1679—26 Aug. 1680 names ch. and gr. dau. Mary Mattoon, how not appar., unless dau. of Martha. Ch: **Susanna**, bp. 6 Sept. 1640, m. Chas. Allen (2). List 392c. **Esther**, m. in Rowley 19 Oct. 1664 Anthony Austin; mov. to Suffield, Conn., ab. Dec. 1674, where she d. 7 Mar. 1697-8, he 22 Aug. 1708. 7 ch. **John**, b. ab. 1646-7. **Elizabeth**, m. in Rowley 3 June 1670 Timo. Palmer; of Suffield 1675, where he d. 28 Nov. 1696. She d. bef. 1724 when her ch. gave P/A to her br. Nathl. 7 ch. **Mary**, b. 29 May 1650. **Bridget**, b. 26 Dec. 1651, m. in Newb. 9 Mar. 1680-1 John Webster jr.; both liv. Salis. 1724, she not in his will 20 Sept. 1732—18 May 1737. 7 ch. **Martha**, b. 11 Nov. 1654. In Ipsw. Ct. 1 May 1672, ag. -16-, she depos. ab. trouble in ho. of her master, Quartermaster Perkins; Mr. Mattoon and Saml. Clark of Portsm. and Sergt. Thos. Waite were pres., she drew beer for them. In 1724 as Martha Mushal she gave P/A to br. Nathl., as did **Anna**, b. 15 Mar. 1658-9; m. in Newb. 24 Dec. 1678 Richard Woollery. 3 ch. rec. Newb. **Nathaniel**, b. 15 July 1660. 3 **JOHN** (2), ±25 in Oct. 1672, ±27 in June 1673, -30- in Sept. 1680, conveyed his int. in the homestead to br. Nathl. 7 Oct. 1680. Newbury in Feb. 1681; there in May fol. he gave P/A to Philip Fowler of Ipsw. to defend Nathl. Boulter's suit. First w. Hannah Buckley d. in Suffield, Conn. 1683; he m. 2d Experience Jones. Mov. bet. 1688-1691 to Springfield, where he d. in 1704; she liv. 1710. Ch. 1+5, incl. **Margaret**, b. 1686, a captive in Canada 1704-6, and **Bridget**, b. 1695.
4 **NATHANIEL** (2), Greenland, depos. in 1744, ag. ±84, that in 1689 Wid. Mary Haines hired him to build a sawmill on lower falls of Winnicot Riv., and he hired it of her 9 yrs. In 1696-8 he was working with Capt. Joshua Weeks. Jury 1694, 1699, 1700; Gr. j. 1698. Lists 62, 330d, 336b, 337, 338abc. M. 1st Sarah Haines (13), List 331c; 2d 10 Dec. 1716 Judith, wid. of Wm. Berry (13). List 338b. D. in Greenl. 28 Nov. 1744, old Mr. H. Wid. Judith in 1745 q. c. dower in the est. already in their hands to Thos. Marston, Wm. and John Huggins, and Nathl. Marston. She d. 19 Jan. 1753, old Mrs. H. Ch. by 1st w: **Samuel**, Greenl., decd. in 1733, m. 13 Feb. 1723-4 his step-sis. Frederica Berry (13), who m. 2d Philip Babb (1). 5 ch. bp. 1724-1732. In 1746 the oldest s. Wm. was in poss. of his gr. fa.'s premises and had q. c. deeds from his three aunts. **John**, o. c. and bp., Greenl., 1727. In 1733 his fa. deeded to his widowed dau.-in-law Frederica in case s. John did not return; app. he ret.

and m. Hannah Davis in Greenl. 30 Sept. 1736. **Nathaniel**, Greenl., m. 30 Dec. 1728 Sarah Weeks. 4 ch. bp. 1729-1737. **Bridget**, m. John Avery (2 jr.). **Eleanor**, o. c. and bp. 1727, with John and Sarah; m. by 1734 Jedediah Weeks. **Sarah**, adm. to Greenl. Ch. 3 Aug. 1735, unmar. 1746.

**HUGHES**, a patronymic from Hugh, common near the Welsh border.
1 **ARTHUR**, Saco. If he knew his age, ±68 twice in 1694, he was not the s. of Edw. Hughes of Ballunhatpin, Ire., gener., apprent. for 9 yrs. in 1627 to Thos. Walford, tailor, and w. Margaret at Bristol. Of Welchman's Cove (Dover), abs. from wife, he could not be found 24 June 1662. She may have been Dunie Stevens he m. in Saco 30 June 16— (1660-1663), who was fined in Saco (Denniss) 7 Nov. 1665 for having a bast., not then born. List 246. Both abs. from meet., Saco, 1669-70-71, she alone (Dwines) 1674. Refugee at Salem 11 Jan. 1675-6, his ordinary there ment. 1678. Poss. returning first to Saco, or Falm., he was of Portsm. 20 Jan. 1693-4, deeding the Angier homestead with his new w. Wid. Sarah Angier (2), both ancient; in March hired a room at the Great House; liv. Portsm. 6 Apr. 1696. Lists 245, 27, 93, 336b. Only kn. ch: **Arthur**, taxed Str. Bk. Oct. 1691, jr. June 15, 1694 his fa. 'late of Saco, at pres. in Portsm.' deeded to him 'of the same place' Saco land bot from John Bonython. Newcastle soldier 1693, at the garri. there 1697. Lists 60, 66, 68. Neither fa. nor son taxed Portsm. 1698. One A. H. m. in Boston 15 Aug. 1698 Ruth Bolton.
2 **CLEMENT**, Mr., from overseas, Portsm. shopkeeper. In Mar. 1705-6 thru Dr. Mills he was settling for a ch. with Mary Mansfield whose comp. he kept at John Hurst's ho. 18 mos. since and later; could not m. her without his mo.'s consent, for which he had written, and without angering his only friend here, Mr. Knight. Altho then she was the only one in this country he would mar., he soon m. Hannah Thompson (John) of Eliot, his wid. 1730, liv. 1751. His letters to John Jeffries 1716-17 show a crest. N. E. Reg. 31.61. Clerk of Courts 1718, Comr. of Excise, N. H., 1722. List 339. Ch: **Clement**, bp. No. Ch. 16 Oct. 1709, taxed Portsm. 1732, liv. 1734. **Charles**, bp. with Clement. With fa. or br. he witn. a Hubbard deed 1722; in June 1726 sailed for Cadiz with his uncle John Hughes, still gone in 1734. **John**, bp. 8 Apr. 1711. **Hannah**, bp. 26 Apr. 1713, d. y. **Hannah**, bp. 25 Apr. 1714, only surv. heir in 1761, liv. 1783 unmar. Likely: **Samuel**, bp. 5 May 1717. **William**, bp. 20 Aug. 1721. In Apr. 1743 John Brown of Boston recd. into his ho. Hannah Hughes, a Portsm. wom-

an, his sister and 2 ch. of Capt. Belden from Portsm.

**3 EMANUEL**, Kennebec 1654. List 11.

**4 JOHN** (Hues), Exeter witn. May 1671. Poss. (5).

**5 JOHN**, testif. at York Ct. 1672; took aboard boards at ord. of Henry Wright, claimed by Mr. Thos. Broughton. Likely the Hingham cooper (Hues) 1674.

**6 PHILIP** (Hews), witn. Ind. deed to Geo. Munjoy 1666. Y. D. 35.1.

**7 ROBERT**, Pemaquid, fisherman, mariner. List 123. One Robt. had w. Mary, s. Robt. b. Stow 23 Jan. 1688. One Robt. in Capt. Heath's co., under Westbrook, was decd. 17 Feb. 1723.

**8 SOLOMON** (Hewes), s. of Geo. of Salis., b. 2 Jan. 1674-5, bot in Portsm. from John and Dorothy Stevens 1697-8. Joiner, innholder. Lists 330de. M. in Boston 23 Sept. 1700 Martha Calef (Robt.). Sept. 1, 1719 he sold land in Portsm.; Wrentham 1720; Dorchester 1724, sold in Portsm.; Wrentham 1729, innholder, bot land on Damariscotta Riv. from Saml. Scott, sold to Wm. Vaughan in 1735. D. Wrentham 27 Aug. 1757, wid. Martha d. 4 Mar. 1759. 11 ch., 10 rec. or bp. at Portsm., the 11th b. at Wrentham 1720.

**9 THOMAS** (Hewes), ±22, in Oct. 1671, liv. at Moses Gilman's ho., Exeter, also Joel Judkins, John Young. In 1670 Thos. Meakins, Newmarket, had sold his ho. to one T. H.

**10 THOMAS** (Hues), Falm., a Munjoy witn. 1675, with Danl. Wakley receipted for Jas. Andrews's powder 21 Oct. 1675; ptn. against Geo. Ingersoll, Feb. 1675-6. One Thos. bur. in Boston 15 Sept. 1713.

**Hukely**, see Hookely.

**HULL,** old English for 'hill.' A city in Yorkshire.

**1 CAPT. BENJAMIN**(6), Oyster River, Dover, granted 100 a. on S.W. side Lamprill River Falls 1659; taxed O.R. 1659-1664. Jury 1657. Lists 361a, 363abc, 47; (List 331b Ben, must be Reuben; also Benjamin No. 20 in Hull Gen. p. 258). Of Dover, he sold his Lampr. Riv. land in Dec. 1678 and mov. to Piscataway, N. J., where he had signed the agreem. 11 May 1668 and had prev. bot land. There tav.-keeper, a busin. long carried on in the name. Overseer of br. Hopewell's est. 1693. He m. ab. 1668 Rachel York (Richard). 5 of 11 ch. app. b. in N. H., all m. in N. J., save 3 d. y.: **Elizabeth**, b. 5 May 1669. **Grace**, b. 5 May 1672. **Joseph**, b. 9 Jan. 1674. **Rachel**, b. 9 July 1676. **Sarah**, b. 27 Sept. 1678. **Benjamin**, b. 4 Apr. 1680. **Temperance**, b. 28 Dec. 1683. **Tristram**, d. y. **Tristram**, b. 18 May 1688. **Hopewell**, d. y. **Martha**, d. y.

**2 DODAVAH**(6), likely grew up in Ipsw. near sister Naomi; see Curtis(9). Gr. 15 a. in York 21 Sept. 1667, signed York ptn. in May 1668 (D. H. 4.215), but liv. in Portsm. List 327c. W. Mary Seward (Richard); adm. to her 6 June 1682, his will imperfect. She m. 2d Dr. Saml. Blagdon(3). Only ch: **Mary**, m. Nicholas Follett (6 jr.). The York gr. was laid out to him 25 Feb. 1702-3 and sold to Lewis Bane; in 1715 a ho. in Portsm., form. mtg. by him, was in poss. of his w., her mo. and half-sister.

**3 EDWARD** (?Hall), sued for debt in Dover Ct. 1651 (Pope).

**4 ISAAC**, a Baptist at Kittery 1665. Poss. the same at Beverly later, and/or the Bap. minis. at Boston 1675-1688. See (10).

**5 JOHN** (jr. to disting. from mintmaster), Boston, called by Mather a well bred merchant, m. Mary Spencer (Roger of Charlestown and Saco), and was trading in Saco in 1670. D. childless 1673; wid. m. 2d Sir Wm. Phips, 3d Peter Sargeant, merchant.

**6 REV. *JOSEPH**, York, Oyster River, Isles of Shoals, b. in Crewkerne, co. Somerset, s. of Thomas and Joanna (Peson) H., matric. at St. Mary Hall, Oxford, 22 May 1612; ag. 17, pleb.; B.A. 14 Nov. 1614. Teacher and curate at Colyton, co. Devon, then rector of Northleigh, dioc. of Exeter, 1621-1632 (resigned), he next app., ag. 40, leading the large comp., includ. his w. Agnes, ag. 25, 7 ch. and 3 servants, which arriv. Boston 5 May 1635 and went to Wessaguscus, soon Weymouth. Freeman 2 Sept. 1635. An Episcopalian, and also active in civil life, dissension soon came, even in his own ch. In 1636 he was liv. in Hingham (the part now Hull), Com. t. e. s. c., Dep. Sept. 1638 and Mar. 1639, tho still serving Weymouth, where he preached last in May 1639. Barnstable same yr., freeman 3 Dec. 1639, Dep. from Barnst. same mo. Yarmouth 1641, there excommun. for his act in leaving Barnst., a breach partly healed in Mar. 1643 when he and his w. were recd. back into Barnst. Ch. Gov. Winthrop, calling him 'an excommunicated person and very contentious,' shows him at York bef. May 1643; there both he and w. Agnes witn. Henry Simpson's deed in July 1645, he alone witn. H. S.'s will 18 Mar. 1646-7. List 274. See also Roger Garde. App. leaving all but his smallest ch. behind, he was at Launceston, co. Cornwall, in 1652, called Mr. Joseph Hull, minister; 10 yrs. later was ejected from the rectory of Buryan, co. Cornwall. He returned to his children at Oyster River; later at the Shoals, these islands owing him £20 when he d. 19 Nov. 1665; adm. to wid. Agnes, the chief item in the inven. 'His books £10.' Me. P. & C. i.

269-270. See also Stackpole's Hist. of Durham, N. H., 2.221-5. Ch: **Joanna**, 15 in 1635, m. 1st John Bursley(3), 2d Dolor Davis. **Joseph**, 13 in 1635; app. the son in disgrace at York in Feb. 1644-5; no later ment. **Tristram**, 11 in 1635, mariner, Capt., Yarmouth 1643, mov. with w. Blanche bef. 1648 to Barnstable, where a leading citizen, tho in trouble at times thru his sympathy with Quakers, whose belief many desc. adopted. Will 30 Dec. 1666—12 Mar. 1666-7 leaves large est. to w. and 5 of 6 ch. **Temperance**, 9 in 1635, m. John Bickford(12). **Elizabeth**, 7 in 1635, m. John Heard(5). **Griselda**, 5 in 1635. **Dorothy**, 3 in 1635, m. 1st Oliver Kent(4), 2d Benj. Mathews. Cert. by w. **Agnes: Hopewell**, Piscataway, N. J., one of its founders. His Quaker mar. to Mary Martin, dau. of John and Esther (Roberts), was not recog. by N. J. authorities, who ord. them re-mar. 29 Dec. 1669, they complying. He was active in public affairs until death; will 26 Mar. 1693 (inv. 27 Apr.) names w., sons Hopewell and Joseph, under age, daus., and br. Benj. She m. 2d 9 Apr. 1696 Justinian Hall. 12 ch., s. Benj. posthumous. **Benjamin**, bp. Hingham 22 Mar. 1639. **Naomi**, bp. Barnstable 23 Mar. 1639-40, placed in fam. of Saml. Symonds, Esq., at Ipsw., bef. her fa. went to Eng.; still there Apr.-June 1661. Bef. the Ct. as Amy H. in 1667, her fa.'s old neighbor Wm. Williams sheltered her and was fined for so doing; her ch. placed in care of John Church. M. Davy Daniel(1), and in 1682 was center of more trouble by speeches ag. her br. and sis. Mathews and others. See Stackpole's Hist. of Durham, ii. 222-4. **Ruth**, bp. 9 May 1641. **Dodavah. Samuel**, Piscataway, owned there adj. John Martin 1682; witn. Mrs. Martin's will 1687. M. 1st Oct. 1677 Mary Manning of N. J.; 2d w. Margaret bef 1702. Ch. 6 + 2. **Phineas**, b. ±1647. **Reuben**, b. ±1649. **Priscilla**, bur. at Launceston, Cornwall, 1652. Poss. **Sarah**, b. 1636 (Banks); d. 1647 (Stackpole).

7 **PHINEAS**(6), 27 in Aug. 1674. Carpenter, Berwick 1670, poss. working in the Broughton mills; there in June 1679 when he sold his Kit. gr. Saco 1680-1686 or later. Constable 1680; gr. 60 a. on E. side Little River near his mill, 1681; Townsman and on tr. j. (not sworn) 1683; Gr. j. 1684, fined same yr. for saucy and abusive language to Mr. Milburn, the minister; appraiser 1682-4; witn. Feb. 1685-6. Retired to York. M. bet. Nov. 1673—June 1679 Jerusha Hitchcock, liv. 17 Dec. 1681 when her gr. fa. Thos. Williams deeded to them for life supp.; not named in husb.'s deed 12 July 1683; m. 2d aft. 21 Dec. 1689 Mary (Rishworth) (White) Sayward, taken by Ind. 22 Aug. 1690, he escaping. List 96. Aft. the peace treaty at

Sagadahoc, her captors released her unwillingly, as she had written their letters. Named adm. of her fa.'s est. 25 Feb. 1690-1. Her husb. not found again; poss. perished in the York massacre; adm., of York, to Jas. Emery jr., 5 Apr. 1693. Lists 298, 249, 96. She m. a 4th husb. James Plaisted. Only surv. ch., by 1st w: **Dorcas**, m. Philip Cox(22).

8 **CAPT. REUBEN**(6), ±20 in June 1669, Portsm., mariner, merchant, 1st in view 1664 witn. for John Cutts(2) and was 'Reuben, Mr. John Cutt's man,' List 328. See Cutts(3). Taxed Portsm. 1672, soon m. Hannah Ferniside (John); in Boston Sept. 1673; of Portsm. bef. 24 Dec. 1674 when J. Cutts deeded to kinsm. R. H. and w. Hannah land on which he had already dug a well. On jury Mar. 1679-80, Mark Hunking v. Edw. Randolph; tr. j. 1682; Gr. j. 1684. Overseer of Pres. Cutts' will 1681, and gdn. of his s. John. Memb. of Portsm. Troop of Horse 1684. O. A. 28 Aug. 1685. Commit. on Trade and Navigation 1686. See also Hyatt. Lists 54, 306a, 331b (Ben), 331c, 49, 51, 329, 52, 55b, 89, 92, 330f. Unsigned will, sick and weak, -23 Dec.- 1689 (inv. -17 Dec.-), prov. 30 Oct. 1693, names w. Hannah, exec., s. Jos., other ch., sis.-in-law Sarah Ferniside. Mis H. taxed Oct. 1691; retailer 1692-3; Lists 331c, 335a. M. 2d by 1698 Geo. Snell; in 1705 they sued Roger Kelly for illeg. bldg. on R. H.'s est. at Maligo Isl. As exec., with daus. Elizabeth and Sarah, she deeded R. H.'s land 1719, half his ho. 13 May 1726. Ch., Prov. Rec.: **Elizabeth**, b. 9 Sept. 1673 (Boston), m. John Snell. **Joseph**, b. 31 Mar. 1676, named in step-fa.'s will May 1706; d. by 1711 when br. Dodavah was adm.; his common right laid out to Dodavah 1713. Lists 330de, 337. **Dodavah**, b. 31 Dec. 1681. List 337. Capt. Hull and ketch taxed 1707, D. H. and mo. 1708. In 1714 he swore to acct. from his fa.'s book 1686. Adm. 10 Dec. 1716 to mo. and br. John Snell; sis. Sarah ment. **Reuben**, b. 2 Aug. 1684, mate of ketch -Hopewell- 1706. One R. H. bp. No.Ch. 2 Aug. 1708. **Sarah**, b. 25 Sept. 1686, was Kinnecum (Cunningham) 1719-26. **Mary**, b. 1 Sept. 1688.

9 **RICHARD**, Portsm., mariner, no connec. found with (6) or (10), more likely relat. to (10), if either; signed by mark. In 1736 he sued Edw. Pendexter's w. Elizabeth, who had attacked his w. Patience (m. by 1729) with a pr. of tongs; Patience poss. sis. or niece of one witn. Thos. Mains. See Green(4). Ch. bp. So.Ch. 1730-33: **Elijah, Christian.**

10 **WALTER**, Portsm. mariner, wrote a good hand. Of Manchester, he had m. at Beverly 15 Dec. 1709 Ann Pitman of M.

Taxed Portsm., fisherman, 1713; mariner Newington 1716; Portsm. same yr. when she was recd. into covt. So.Ch.; witn. John Abbott's deed 1717, presum. one of his crew, and two deeds of Wid. Sarah Leavitt 1723; taxed 1727. 9 ch. bp. So.Ch. 1716-1729, incl. **James**, b. Manchester 27 Aug. 1710, m. ab. 1732 Hannah Matthews; **Elizabeth**, bp. 1718, m. 18 Apr. 1735 Thos. Harwood of Chatham, Kent, Eng.; two **Dionysias**. None bp. aft. 1729, tho she had lately had a ch. in 1734, when s. **William** bp. 1716, brot stolen sheep to the ho. to be dressed. See (4), (9).

**HUMBER**, 1 **Edward**, blacksmith, Salem 1665-72, had sent for his w. in 1669. In 1673 he bot on Smuttinose, where John Short agreed in Nov. to work for him six mo. Sold to John Shute 1675; same yr. as a Shoals fisherman was indebted to Robt. Paine, sr.

2 **HUMPHREY**, Mr., scrivener, Hampton 1645. In 1653 he witn. for Wm. Fifield; depos. Mar. 1653-4 ab. being in Rowley; fined Hampt. Ct. Oct. 1654 for telling a lie, bondsm. Wm. Fifield and John Sanborn. John Philbrook's depos. used in Salem Ct. June 1662, copy by H. H. List 323.

**HUMPHREY**, principally found in southeastern England.

1 **JEREMIAH** (also Umfress), Richmond Isl. 1648, pd. wages by R. Jordan. A link with (2) is Thos. Kennedy, a witn. with him to Jordan's deed 3 Mar. 1657-8; Y. D. i. 87. Saco 1658. Lists 21, 244a.

2 **THOMAS**, distiller, Oyster River, Kennebec. Taxed O. R. 1659, recd. inhab. 16 July 1660; O. F. 5 June 1661. He owned near Plum Brook Swamp with no rec. of gr. or purch., and abutted John Ault as late as Nov. 1678. See (1); see also Kennedy. At Kennebec he witn. a Parker deed 17 Dec. 1661, the same day his Head was named in ano. Parker deed. In 1664 swore to an acct. due him from est. of Mrs. Ludecas, whose adm. Jas. Middleton was later his partn. on Kennebec Riv. Jury N. H., 1661, 1663; Gr. j. Casco 1666. Clerk of the Writs for Kennebec, Sagadahoc and Pejepscot 1665; O. A. to King 8 Sept. 1665, Constable same date. Under Mass. he took O. F. in 1674, contin. as Constable and Clerk of Writs, and was made Sergt. for Sagadahoc and Kennebec; Marshal for co. of Devon. Lists 361a, 362b, 356g, 182, 15, 83, 183, 191. M. Hannah Lane (Geo.), 23 Dec. 1665, at Hingham, where one T. H., adult, had been bap. 19 July 1660. Both last found 9 June 1675, acknowl. a deed. Sarah (Hackett) Smith testif. he was k. by Ind. Her fa.'s will 16 Oct. 1688 named her sons, not her: **George**, d. Hingham 17 June 1732, ag. 68. Will names w. Elizabeth

(m. 16 Feb. 1686-7) and 6 of 8 ch., giving to Thos. and Wm. his land at Harwich on the Kennebec, yet in 1742 s. John deeded ¼ of his fa.'s land there 'willed to me.' **William. Ebenezer. Joseph**, Hingham.

**HUNKING**.

1 **BENTON**, N. H. Probate 1.41. Read Beaton, w. of (2).

2 **HERCULES**, fishing master, Star Isl., and cred. of Stephen Sargent's est. 1649; likely the same bap. at St. Stephens by Saltash, co. Cornwall, 13 June 1604, s. of Hercules, gr. s. of Roger, br. of (6). Fined for not serving on Gr. j. 1650; granted 50 a. in 1652. Com. t. e. s. c. See Boaden(9). Removing to Portsm. he occup. ho. and 50 a. bot in 1652 from Roger Knight, who confirmed to John Hunking 24 Oct. 1671. Selectm. 1658. Lists 301, 323, 324, 326a. If the man of Stonehouse, Plymouth, who m. Christian Leane 16 Sept. 1627, and had daus. Elizabeth and Joan, bp. 27 June 1634, his will 21 Aug. 1659 ment. neither but only w. (unnamed), dau. Ann and her ch. Inv. 6 Sept. 1659, incl. 3 boats, and ho. and stage on Star Isl. he had enjoyed 10 yrs.; sworn to in Essex Ct. by wid. Beaton Hunking 8 Nov. 1659. She m. 2d Wm. Hearl(4). Ch.: **Ann** (Agnes), b. ab. 1630, m. John Hunking (3).

3 **JOHN**, Mr., Star Isl., Portsm., poss. an outsider, or relat. to (2) bef. he m. his dau. Ann, who was liv. 1671-2, ±42. List 331c. Star Isl. 1652, selling without lic. Com. t. e. s. c., Shoals, 1660, 1670, 1677. Selectm. Portsm. 1663, 1667-8, 1671. Gr. j. 1669, 1677, 1680, 1681. See Broad(4). Guardian of Benj. Cotton(1) 1679. Master of the -Endeavor- and owner in other vessels 1681. Com. Ensign 1680, but called Sergt. 1681. Lists 326ac, 330ab, 323, 324, (347), 305c, 306cd, 331ab, 54, 49, 50, 51, 329. Will 25 Aug. 1681—7 June 1682 names 2d w. Richord (m. by 1679), 6 ch. She m. 2d Geo. Snell; will, resid. in Boston 24 Sept. 1691—23 Apr. 1695 names s. Geo. Littlejohn of Halwel, co. Devon, a sis. in Eng., and gives £10 to step-dau. Elizabeth H. Ch. by 1st w: **John**, b. 2 Mar. 1651-2, d. in Eng. July 1666. **Hercules**, b. 11 July 1656, not in will. **John**, b. 6 Apr. 1660. **Peter**, b. 20 Mar. 1662-3, inher. ho. and land where John Light liv. and 20 a. adj. Wm. Cotton. In 1688, at Barbadoes, bound sudd. to sea, he gave P/A to Rich. Hyat, mercht., Piscataqua, Nich. Hunking a witn. The way for 60 yrs. bet. land of Peter and Elizabeth given them by their fa., ment. in 1721. **Agnes**, b. 2 June 1665; inher. little ho. on Great Isl. adj. Fabes, and a seal ring marked A. H. Poss. she who o. c. No. Ch. 17 Oct. 1708, when Wm.'s w. and ch. bp. **William**,

b. 6 Jan. 1667-8. **Mark**, b. 17 May 1670, rec. by fa.'s will 120 a. near Salmon Falls bot of Ralph Hall. List 334a. M. 29 June 1697 Mary Harvey(14), who m. 2d 5 Dec. 1699 Rev. John Newmarch of Kit., and d. bef. Oct. 1727. No. kn. ch. but poss. a dau. was Agnes, m. 25 July 1716 Edw. Sherburne; or one of those named uncertainly under (9). **Elizabeth**, m. Thos. Fernald (4 jr.), 2d in Portsm. Nov. 1712 Capt. Saml. Winkley, whose will 1726 rememb. kinswo. Elizabeth Hunking liv. with him, and ment. silver cup bot of Capt. J. H.

4 **JOHN**, carpenter, in Portsm. with his fam. 8 Aug. 1672 when Edw. Clarke(8) engaged to save the town harmless. Poss. the Ipsw. man freq. in trouble in Essex Co. Lists (†47), 331a.

5 **CAPT. \*JOHN**(3), mariner, Portsm., was away, prob. at sea, when his fa. made his will, naming him princ. heir. June 27, 1682 (20 days aft. the will was filed), he sold to Jas. Blagdon the Star Isl. plant that had belonged to his gr. fa. Hercules and fa. O. A. 28 Aug. 1685. Rep. 1693. Jury 1699. Lists 52, 62, 335a, 298, 330d, 337. He was selling out in Portsm. 1712-1714; taxed there 1713 (Capt.), 1714. Deceased 1715, called late of Boston in 1720. He m. by 23 Sept. 1682 Mary Leighton(9), a wid. in Portsm. 9 Sept. 1723, d. bef. 10 May 1725. List 335a, 339. Only surv. ch. 1723: **Mary**, Portsm., m. 10 Jan. 1733-4 Geo. Pierce, blacksm. Her will 1764-1764 names dau. Mehitable Sherburne, kinsm. John Hunking. Poss. a son: **John**, jr., d. 6 July 1705. List 96.

6 **MARK**, shipwright, Little Harbor, presum. the -Marcus- bp. at St. Stephens by Saltash, co. Cornwall, 25 June 1615, bro. of (2). Appar. a later comer than his br., he and Rich. Shortridge were already liv. on the whole neck of land gr. them 22 Jan. 1660-1. In Ct. case 1660, John H. had borrowed, Mark (presum. the lad) driven to harm, Richard Abbott's oxen. Gr. j. 1663. Lists 330a, 47, 311b, 323, 326b. Both (10) and (3) witn. for him separately, 1666; John witn. his will, of Pascataway, 1 July (inv. 27 Sept.) 1667, naming w. Ann sole exec., 2 sons, dau. Mary, Thos. Fernald, all my ch. Wid. often styled Dame H.; taxed 1671, poss. liv. Mar. 1693-4; Lists 312c, 326c, 331c, (†335a). Kn. ch: **Mark**, eldest s. 1667; only surv. s. 1702. **Archelaus**. Fa.'s will gave him 20 a. land, marsh, 2 small guns, sword; not found later; d. bef. 1702. **Temperance**, m. Thos. Fernald(4). **Mary**, m. Thos. Wakeham; childless wid. 1711. **Margaret**, m Christo. Adams(5).

7 **\*‡MARK**(6), Esq., first a successful shipmaster, then merchant and public official, and shared honors in estab. the power-

ful Wentworth line. Taxed 1671, he m. ab. that time Sarah Sherburne (Henry), List 52. Master of a ship bef. 1679 and appar. ashore little until ab. 1692-3. Only surv. son 1702 and in poss. of his fa.'s Little Harbor lands, later the Wentworth estate. Jury 1693. Lic. 1693. Selectm. 1699, 1702, 1707, 1714; Rep. 1703, 1704, 1709 speaker, 1710; J. P.; Councillor 1710; oath as Just. of Superior Ct. of Judic. Jan. 1716-7; called Col. 1721; Prov. Recorder of Deeds 1722. Lists 326c, 312c, 331b, 313a, 49, 329, 92, 62, 334a, 335a, 330ad, 324, 69, 316, 337, 339. One Madam Sarah was recd. into So. Ch., Portsm. in Aug. 1720, ano. in Jan. 1728, one of them w. of (9). He was liv. May 1728, d. bef. 7 Jan. 1731-2. Only surv. ch: **Sarah**, m. 12 Oct. 1693 Lt. Gov. John Wentworth; d. 1 Apr. 1741 in 68th yr.

8 **ROBERT**, Kingston witn. 1714.

9 **WILLIAM**(3), Portsm., m. 12 May 1692 Sarah Partridge (John), named in her fa.'s will 1722. List 335a. See also (7). He bot ho. and land from Matthew Nelson 26 Dec. 1693. Gr. j. 1693, 1697; crossed out on jury list 1696. Subscrib. for Mr. Emerson 1713. Lists 62, 331c, 335a, 330d, 337, 339. With w. Sarah, 28 Dec. 1723, he deeded the form. Nelson prop., then having two dwg.-houses, to s. Mark, retaining half during life. Ch. incl. Capt. **Mark**, Esq., mariner, m. in Portsm. 30 July 1725 Mary Leavitt (3); both of Barr. 1760. 11 ch., 7 bp. So. Ch. 1733-42. Will 1776—1782 names w. Izett (presum. wid. of Isaac Bussy 2), 4 daus., 2 decd. sons, 2 gr. sons. **Archelaus**, bp. with twin at No. Ch. 17 Oct. 1708, when their mo. o. c. List 339. Mill Dam tax abated 1724. Of Portsm. (Hercules) he m. 3 Dec. 1724 Judith Sias of O. R. Ch. incl. Ann bp. Portsm. 1725, Agnes, Elizabeth, bp. O. R. 1727-9. **Agnes**, twin, poss. m. 25 July 1716 Henry Sherburne. See Mark(3). Others may incl., one or m: Mary, b. ±1704, m. John Ayers(1). Patience, bp. No. Ch. 16 Nov. 1712; one Patience m. Joshua Jackson(16). Elizabeth, legatee of Saml. Winkley. Sarah, m. Francis Drew(4). One John was of Portsm. 1764, kinsm. of Mary (Hunking) Pierce. Evidently of a Mass. fam. was John, Hampstead, d. 1754, leav. wid. Sarah, 5 ch.

10 **WILLIAM**, with Barnaby Jeffrey, witn. a paper for (6) 18 Aug. 1666; Mr. Wm. swore to it 28 Sept. Poss. he or (9) ment. 1693 as one who some time since improv. land adj. Saml. Penhallow's orchard for a shipyard.

**Hunkitt**, John, Hampton. See Hancock.

**Hunlock**, Henry, witn. Roger Knight to Cutts, 1662.

**Hunniborne**, Richard, 1666. List 78. Comp. Hunnewell.

**HUNNEWELL,** Honeywell, a local name in co. Devon, where at Buckfastleigh John H. had a son Richard bp. in 1632, and Jonas H. a son Roger bp. 1640.

1 **AMBROSE,** Sagadahoc 1661, less than 2 yrs. aft. one Ambrose m. Jane Homes at St. Andrews, Plymouth, Eng., 1 Nov. 1659, and disappeared. N. E. Reg. 54.140. In 1671, he bot a neck of land on S. part of the river, 250 a., claimed in 17— by s. Chas. for self and other heirs. O. A. to Mass. 22 July 1674; Gr. j. 1674. Lists 13, 15, 141, 183, 191. Driven to Boston, he took O. A. there 29 Oct. 1678; taxed 1681. In 1688 he was back home and selectman. If he surviv. the next war, he is not disting. from his son. Poss. his was Wid. Mary H. who defaulted suit of Saml. Walker, mariner, in Suff. Ct. Sept. 1699; she had witn. Walker's deed in Boston 19 Aug. 1697. One Sarah d. at the home of his s. Chas. in Charlestown 12 Aug. 1705. Ch. by deeds: **Ambrose,** b. ±1657, cooper, Boston 1719. Last found depos. in July 1731, ±74, that he liv. 60 yrs. ago with his parents on an islet called Hunnewell's Point adj. Small Point. W. Hannah. Ch. Abigail, Hannah, b. Boston 1686, 1693; others may incl. one of the Richards m. there 1723-5; Sarah, m. 1728; George, one of two mar. 1731, 1735. **Stephen,** fisherman, mariner, Boston, taxed 1688. He m. aft. 1687 Mary Shapley (Jos.) of Charlest., who d. 30 Oct. 1723, ag. 57. In 1718-9 he bot the Me. land from bros. Ambrose and Rich. and sis. Mary; and near there was beaten to death by Ind. in 1725, master of a vessel capt. at Damariscove and taken to Sagadahoc. Of 5 kn. ch., 1 son, 2 daus. deeded with uncle Chas. 1735. **Richard,** bricklayer, mason, Boston, the name 1st in tax lists 1689. Either older than appears, or younger than w., if he m. bef. 1690 Sarah Adams (Nathl.) who d. 30 July 1723, ag. 66. D. childless; will 24 June 1747 names w. Hannah, br. Chas.'s wid. and ch., neph. Stephen. Bur. near Sarah (Adams) and poss. a son, was Richard d. 27 Nov. 1742 in 61st yr.; mariner, adm. 10 Dec. 1742 to wid. Mary (Mudd appar., m. 20 Apr. 1732). The Richards m. in Boston 1723 are entangled. One Richard m. Hannah Belcher of Chelsea 29 July 1742, poss. Ambrose's s. Richard, or the Hunnewell working in Me. for Capt. Belcher; List 191. **Charles,** farmer, Charlestown, m. 17 Nov. 1698 Elizabeth Davis; d. 14 Dec. 1737. Old Mrs. H. d. 25 June 1763, ag. 91. 8 ch. 1700-1713. **Mary,** widow (Whiton) in Boston 1719. One Greenhill Henewell taxed Boston 1695.

2 **CHARLES,** k. by Ind. at Sagadahoc Point 20 July 1689. D. H. 9.15. Poss. br. of (1) or s. of (6).

3 **ISRAEL** (Honeywell); Ipswich, Westchester, N. Y.; unident. by record. A son of (9) or (6), if the latter had one, might be in Ipsw., where Israel in 1680 declared he was under the fam. govt. of Nathl. Emerson. If then under age, he could not have been s. of (9), but his 1st w. was b. 1656, and names used among desc. point to the two as fa. and son. A tablet in St. Peter's Ch., Westchester, commemor. one Honeywell line, beginning with Israel 1660-1720, by Royal Charter member of the First Common Council, and Mary, his w., of North Devon, Eng., who came to Westch. in 1693, was placed too late (1902) to accept the data without sustaining evid. Of Ipswich, Israel was wounded at the Eastward 1677; last found there in Sept. 1681, released from bond for good behaviour. He took to Westch. w. Mary Spofford (John) of Rowley, who d. s. p. Essex D. 53.137, 66.56. Ano. w. Mary (†Stevenson) in will 14 Dec. 1710— 17 May 1720. Ch., all but Sarah in 1698 census, all but Rich. in will: **Israel. Mary,** m. John Baxter of Westch., her ch. incl. Roger. **Samuel. Richard. Sarah.**

4 **ISRAEL,** Portsm., Berwick, Wiscasset. As Israel Hunnewell alias Nason, infant ab. 1 mo. old, Portsm. selectm. bound him to Geo. Vaughan, Esq., for 24 yrs., by advice and consent of Joanna Nason, the natural mo.; this was 7 Sept. 1703, the same day his twin Richard(8) was likewise bound to G. V. As the mo. alone was haled to Ct., the fa.'s first name is not of record, but susp. is strong he was the military hero (7) who set feminine hearts aflutter. The twins (Hunnewell) were reed. into covt., So. Ch., Portsm., 23 Feb. 1729; taxed 1730-2. Israel was of Berw. 1736-49; served at Louisburg from B. Wiscasset 1754, liv. there 1760. W. unkn.; poss. in her right he was deft. with several heirs of Wm. Lord in the Coopers' suit 1734-5. Ch. incl: **Richard, Lydia, Sarah,** bp. Berw. 1737-49. Found in Lincoln County were: Benj. of Pownalboro 1765; John and Israel in milit. list 1776; Wm. 1783. One Richard was high sheriff, Hancock Co., 1790.

5 **JOHN**(9), Middletown, Conn., moved around bef. the War; fought at Berwick 12 May 1674; two mo. later rode out of York on Sunday and abs. from meet. Mariner, Salem, 1677, and had a sloop there. In Mar. 1680 he was gr. land in Wethersfield to make and burn bricks, and there he dieted and lodged for a fortnight Rich. Haughton of Beverly who d. at Wethersf. that yr.; but was at Scarb. with br. Rich. in Apr. 1681, witn. against Weymouth Bickton. List 36. Of Middletown, brickmaker, 18 Dec. 1692, he closed his Me. connec., sell-

ing Hunnewell's Neck, Winter Harbor, with full warr., having bot out his br. 8 dys. bef. D. Middletown bef. 1710. By rec. he left his fam. in Salem 1678; is credited with a w. Lydia in Conn., m. 1 Jan. 1679-80, d. 10 Aug. 1683; m. last Elizabeth Harris (Capt. Danl.) of Middletown; adm. on her est. to s. John 4 Dec. 1710, again 7 July 1712 to Saml. Williams, John then at sea. Ch. by 1st or 2d w: Mary, b. 10 Jan. 1682. By last w: Abial, not in div. of mo.'s est. 1713; called dau. 1718 when she and husb. Abel Tryon of M. sold Harris land. Elizabeth, m. by 1707 Saml. Williams of Wethersf. John, b. 17 Apr. 1689, settl. in N. J. Bridget, b. 2 Oct. 1691, m. ab. 1716 Jona. Roberts, New Haven.

6 RICHARD, fisherman, Damariscove, b. ±1614. In Salem Ct. Nov. 1664, he ±50 and John Tapley ±25 depos. ab. fish Mordecai Crawford(3) recd. at Damariscove in 1652. Named as an early settler in depos. of John Cock(12), 1736, yet almost abs. from the records. In 1672 he headed a Damariscove ptn. List 13. W. and ch., if any, and connec. with others unkn.; presum. nearly related to (1); not imposs. that (2) or (3), or both, were his sons, while all in Boston are not placed.

7 CAPT. RICHARD(9), Black Point, Scarboro, the Ind. killer, pilot and military leader. Aged 31 in Aug. 1676. Poss. going to Scarb. when his mo. remar, he began in Philip's War the service which contin. until death 6 Oct. 1703, when he and his men from Black Point garri. were cut off by the Ind. Called Corp. in Aug. 1677, Ensign 1680, com. Lieut. by Andros 2 July 1687, signed as Capt. 24 June 1693. App. a fisherman early, he was at a Marblehead stage from Black Point in 1672, and m. a York girl (Ct. 31 Mar. 1674) Elizabeth Stover (Sylvester), of famous ancestry thru her mo. Elizabeth (Norton). All records of him are at Scarb. until 1690, except witn. Mar. 1680-1 at York, where his w. prob. was liv.; she depos. in June 1737, ±84, bet. 40 and 50 yrs. since liv. with her husb. Hunnewell in a stone ho. of Geo. Norton's; depos. again 8 Aug. 1738, ±85, ab. 64 yrs. past liv. in Scarb. He was contin. as Constable at Scarb. 1680; Gr. j. 1683, 1687-8, 1696; Selectm. 1685, 1686, 1688; Comr. Scarb. 1688. Lists 83, 236, 237ab, 238a, 32, 34, 35, 36, 37, 96. In 1690 at Saco Riv. he was shot thru the thigh. In 1692, late of Winter Harb. or Black Point, he deeded fa.'s est. to br. John, and ack. deed in Salis., his fam. there in 1693. Of York, a good pilot, ready for service, Aug. 1695; there in Mar. 1696-7 his ptn. for relief, wounded several times in arms and incap. of servile labor. Bet. 5 Sept.—14 Oct. 1700 he was at Scarb. witn.

possession to Mr. Vaughan; app. liv. there 20 Nov. 1702, and drove cattle eastward by Wells on Sunday in Jan. 1702-3. As wid. Elizabeth H., she was pd. in Mar. 1703-4 for a steer, and for disbursem. by her husb. in bldg. the fort; m. 2d Jeremiah Walford, 3d 1733-34 Capt. John Downing(2). Ch: Roger, b. ±1675, bp. at Salis. with two foll. 15 Oct. 1693. John, pd. July 1703 for 1150 lbs. beef furnished at Casco; served under Capt. Harraden in expdn. to Bay of Fundy Apr.— Aug. 1704. Elizabeth, m. by 1702 Capt. Benj. Hammond of Rochester, Mass. In 1730-1 she ptn. as Capt. Rich. H.'s dau. 8 ch., incl. Israel and Roger. Patience, m. 29 Sept. 1696 John Hathaway of Dartmouth. 10 ch. incl. Richard and Hunnewell. Their fa. and mo. Walford deeded to two sons-in-law 1 June 1722. See (4), (8).

8 RICHARD, alias Nason, twin to Israel (4), q. v. In May 1724, ag. 21 (Hunnewell), he depos. ab. going to Rich. King's with fellow-serv. Rich. Brooks, at ord. of his master Col. G. Vaughan. He m. in Portsm. 18 Sept. 1728 Jemima Alexander. Son John bp. Berw. 24 June 1739. Richard, s. of —— Hunnewell, bp. there 8 June 1735, poss. his or an earlier ch. of Israel(4). One Elizabeth (Honeywell) bp. So. Ch., Portsm. 29 July 1744. One Jemima, mo. or dau., was of Newington 1745.

9 ROGER, fisherman, mariner, West Saco, liv. on Parker's Neck near the entrance to the Pool, adj. point of land where later the fort stood. Likely there by 1650, but as obscure as his son was promin.; drowned bef. 4 July 1654. Lists 75b, 243a, 244b. Wid. Bridget m. 2d Richard Moore, and likely took her ch. to Scarb., where her s. Richard testif. 3 Apr. 1686, ±40, he had liv. ab. 28 yrs. In 1665 as B. M. she was accusing the neighbors; in Apr. 1671, ±50, depos. ab. the Sheldons. Ch: Richard, b. ab. 1645-6. Bef. Sept. 1681 he was caring for his step-fa., and gr. adm. 30 May 1682, chief creditor. John. See also (3) Israel.

10 ROGER(7), mariner, witn. 1702-1708 in York, where he m. 2 Oct. 1700 Mary Moore (John). In June 1714 his sloop -Yorkshire- entered Boston Harb. from Barbadoes. He ret. to Scarb., and d. there 13 June 1720 in 45th yr. Wid. liv. many yrs. List 239b. Ch. incl: Josiah, b. York 25 June 1702. Served under Sergt. Knight Sept. 1723—May 1724 and had gr. 20 Sept. 1727 as one who had abided in Scarb. during the War. Depos. in June 1755, had liv. there ab. 40 yrs., one of the 1st families then in town. M. 26 Nov. 1730 Rebecca Brown (Andrew 27). 10 ch. Richard, depos. in June 1755, had liv. there 39 yrs., in his 9th yr. when he first came, fa. liv. ab. 4 yrs. thereaft. Liv. 1774, ag. 68. He m. 1st (int. 7

Aug. 1731) Hannah Brown (Andrew 27), d. 15 Dec. 1760; 2d her sis. Sarah. 7 daus. rec. 1733-1752, of whom 3 with a br. Richard d. in 1754. **Zerubbabel**, b. 15 Apr. 1716 (1st birth rec. in new town). Liv. Windham. 1st w. Hannah (Haskell) d. 26 July 1753, ag. 33; 2d w. Hannah (Cobb) d. 24 Apr. 1791 in 80th yr.; he 23 Aug. 1803, ag. 89. Ch. 6+1 or m. **Roger**, b. 28 Dec. 1719, m. 7 Nov. 1750 Lydia Ervine, who d. Scarb. 14 Dec. 1811, ag. 83, he 13 days later, ag. 93. 8 ch. **Elizabeth**, m. 4 Jan. 1732 Robt. Gilmore. Likely s., poss. neph., **John**, Ind. captive 1723. See Deering(8).

**HUNT**, became 67th commonest name in N. E.
1 **BARTHOLOMEW**, Dover 1640. Lists 351ab, 386. One Barthol. of Newport, R. I., freeman 1655, d. 1687, leav. w. Ann and ch.
2 **CHARLES**, Kingston, m. Hannah, wid. of Thos. Scribner (d. 1718). One Mrs. H. brot ch. Margaret, Penelope, Sarah, to be bap. Kingston 1 Apr. 1730.
3 **GEORGE**. Lists 328, 329, 311b. See Huntress.
4 **RICHARD**, List 386, and
5 **THOMAS**, partners in Shrewsbury Patent. List 386.
6 **THOMAS**, Sagamore Creek witn. 1668; in 1671 had given false evid. ag. Geo. Jones, jr. and Wid. Webster; bondsm. Henry Sherburne, Jos. Walker. Cape Porpus 1675, where in Philip's War John Batson, John Sanders and Thos. Mussey compl. against John and Wm. Partridge and T. H. for salvaging their live stock.
7 **THOMAS**, Hampton, m. Elizabeth Stanvan (Jas.), who dep. 1741, ±48. Son James in gr. fa.'s will 1742.
**Huntaway**, Benjamin, named in will of Moses Gilman (14). An Indian.
**Hunter**, Leonard, York by 1636, owned land with John Barrett (1). Y. D. i. 118. One Leonard H. of Dalton-in-Furness, co. Lancaster, will 1614.
**Hunting**, Capt. Samuel, Charlestown, took off garrison men cut off on Arrowsic Isl., Apr. 1677.
**HUNTINGTON**, William, signed Hampton ptn. Mar. 1642-3; joint gr. at Exeter with Balthazar Willix June 1644-5. W. Joanna. Lists 392a, 391b, 376b. First taxed Salis. 1650, tho 2 of 3 ch. rec. there as b. 1643-8, prob. late entries. Hoyt's Salis. i. 213.

**HUNTOON**, Hunton.
1 **PHILIP**, Exeter, Kingston, from Jersey by one trad., Eng. by ano. The fam. gen. names a 1st w. Betsy Hall, dau. of his first employer, tho himself, ±16 in 1680, ment.

master (Capt.) Gilman. W. Hannah in 1702. Ex. gr. 1698; Kingston land laid out 1702; Exeter 1707; Kingston 1708, from where 22 July 1710 he and Jacob Gilman were taken to Canada, and earned freedom by bldg. a sawmill for the govt.; J. G. was in Canada in Oct. 1712, likely Philip, who had ret. and depos. in 1713 that 27 or 28 yrs. bef. he helped build a mill for Peter Coffin on Lamprill Riv. Lower Falls. In 1729 he deeded to s. Philip half his est., the bal. aft. dec. of self and w. She d. 22 Dec. 1741; he 10 May 1752. Lists 52, 57, 62, 376b, 400, 99. Kn. ch: **Samuel**, k. by Ind. 22 July 1710. **John**, by trad. their mo. saved him and br. Philip from the Ind. by calling them back that morning for their hymn and catechism. M. Mary Rundlett (Chas.) Corp. 1724; Selectm. 1740. Bur. 8 Dec. 1778, a very aged man. 12 ch. **Philip**, m. 22 Dec. 1720 Ann Eastman (Saml.), who d. 1750, and he m. again. Late in life went with s. Benj. to Salis., N. H., d. May 1780. 9 ch. **Sarah**, b. 21 Apr., d. 15 May 1703. **Elizabeth**, m. 2 Dec. 1725 Jos. Elkins. **Sarah**, m. 1 Jan. 1728-9 Darby Kelly.
2 **WILLIAM** (Hunton), List 392a. See Huntington.

**HUNTRESS**, often Hunt in early records.
1 **GEORGE**, Portsm., Newington, b. 1643-47, depos. (Hunt) 1 Sept. 1680, ag. 35, liv. servant of John Locke of Hampt. 13 yrs. bef.; ±38, 2 Nov. 1685; ag. 63 in Nov. 1706, he and Clem. Meserve depos. they liv. with Mr. Rich. Cutt to look aft. his cattle. Taxed Portsm. Oct. 1672; his man and 4 oxen in surveyor's acct. ab. 1677; O. A. Str. Bk. 28 Aug. 1685; taxed there, and farm, Oct. 1691. Soldier in King William's War 1696. Newington coroner's jury 1696 (Hunt), and surveyor (Huntress) for Bloody Point side. Jury 1688, 1692, 1694; Gr. j. 1697. Constable 1698. Lists 328 (Hunt), 329, 52, 57, 343. W., Mary Natt or Nott, depos. in 1675, ag. 27, as Mary Hunt(ress). Lists 328, 335a. In war time he having a bill ag. Saml. Clark, his wife collected by breaking open Clark's cupboard and taking powder. In 1681 he bot the Kenniston homestead in Greenl. and was bondsm. for Christo. K. same yr. Will, yeoman, 28 June—19 Aug. 1715, names w. Mary, sons Saml., John, ch. of decd. s. Geo., dau. Mary; others had recd. their portions. Kn. ch: **Ann**, m. 1st Thos. Chesley (5 jr.), 2d Jos. Daniel (4). **Mary**, m. 21 June 1694 Henry Seward. **George**. **Samuel**, b. ab. 1687, with br. John recd. the homestead, 150 a., part in Portsm., part in Newingt. Constable 1714. List 343. M. 20 Dec. 1711 Abigail Ham (9), adm. to Newingt. Ch. 17 Sept. 1727. Will 29 Mar. 1758 (d. 28 Apr. ag. 71, gr. st.) names 2d w. **Mary**,

with 5 liv., 2 decd., of 8 ch. by 1st w. bp. Newingt. 1717-1734. **John,** yeoman, Newingt., was drowned, coroner's jury 28 Apr. 1751. Will 11 July 1746—29 May 1751 names w. Mary (liv. 1761), 7 ch. bp. Newingt. 1716-1732, incl. Tamson, Hepworth (by bapt. rec., Hibbard by fa.'s will), Jonathan. **Abigail,** b. ab. 1694, m. Moses Dam (3). **Hannah,** m. by 1713 Maturin Ricker. Early desc. named both her parents, Geo. -Hunt- and Mary -Nutt-.

2 **GEORGE** (1), Portsm. soldier at Newc. 23 Aug.—6 Sept. 1708. He m. 4 Aug. 1701 Sarah Morrill (John) of Kit., who was taxed Greenl. in 1713 as Wid. Huntress and m. 2d Nich. Frost (11), 3d Thos. Darling (4). See Daniel (4). Ch. in gr. fa.'s will 1715: **Christopher,** eldest son; brickmason. Of Newingt., he m. (int. 26 Oct. 1724) Mary Chick (Rich.) of Kit., called Marcy in Ct. record a few mos. later, Mary in warrant. Ensign at Louisburg. Will 1 Oct. 1768—1 Oct. 1782 names w. Mary, 7 of 9 kn. ch., gr. dau. Martha Lord. **Elizabeth,** m. in Portsm. 7 Nov. 1725 Francis Merrill, b. in Wenham. **George,** under guardianship of step-fa. Darling 1724-5; m. in Portsm. 1 Jan. 1726-7 Elizabeth Seward; innholder, taxed Jan. 1731-2. Ch. **Deborah. Sarah.**

**Hupper,** see Hooper.

**Hurd,** see Heard.

**HURST,** Hirst, Hearst. 1 Mr. **John,** Newcastle 1693, blacksmith. Lt. John Hirst succ. Capt. Walton in command of the fort 1696. Witn. Fabes fam. deed 1704; both he and w. Rachel depos. Mar. 1705-6 ab. Clement Hughes and Mary Mansfield meeting at their ho. Mr. J. H. of Kit. pd. Saml. Penhallow a judgm. in iron, July 1706. Lists 318ab, 315bc.

2 **THOMAS** (Hirst), Newc., blacksmith, sued by Dr. Baxter 1695; he had brot drops from Eng., and called the patient, Robt. White, his countryman. Witn. at Portsm. 1693 against Wm. Richards. One Mary -Hurshe- bp. Portsm. 21 Oct. 1722.

**Huske,** Ellis, Esq. See Plaisted.

**HUSSEY,** a Wiltshire and Somersetshire name.

1 *‡**CAPT. CHRISTOPHER** (5), Hampton, orig. settler 6 Sept. 1638 with his mo. and fa.-in-law Rev. Stephen Batchelder (5), whose footsteps he foll. aft. mar. his dau. Theodate, meeting her by family tradition in Holland; coming on the same -Wm. & Francis- which arriv. 5 June 1632; settled first at Saugus (Lynn); freeman 14 May 1634; Newb., prop. 1637; Hampt. Com. t. e. s. c. 22 May 1639, the first of many times; lot layer 31 Oct.; called present Deacon 30 June 1640; Moderator 1641, 1663-4, 1672; Town Clerk 1650-3; Selectm. 1650, 1658,

1664, 1669. Often tr. and Gr. j., and foreman. Confirmed Lieut. 14 June 1653, Capt. 11 Oct. 1664. Rep. 1658, 1659, 1660, 1672; Councillor 1679 until Cranfield came in. Lists 391ab, 392abc, 393ab, 53, 394, 54, 48, 50, 397b, 398. Nantucket propr. July 1659, sold there to his sons in 1671 and 1681. In Apr. 1674 he and s. John were admon. for breach of the law called Quakers meeting. Colcord depos. that her fa. gave them all his cattle, goods and debts on going back to Eng., indicating his w. liv. beyond that time; ould Mistris Husse's dau. seated Mar. 1649-50, List 393a; and it was 9 Dec. 1658 bef. he m. 2d Ann, wid. of Jeffrey Mingay. She d. 24 June 1680. His will 26 Feb. 1684-5, codic. at Salis. 28 Oct., d. 6 Mar. 1685-6, ab. 90. Ch: **Stephen. John,** bp. at Lynn last day last mo. 1635. **Mary,** bp. at Newb. 2 Apr. 1638, m. 1st Thos. Page, 2d Hon. Henry Green (7), 3d Capt. Henry Dow (3). **Theodate,** bp. Hampt. 23 Aug. 1640, not in will, doubtless she who d. in 1649. **Hannah,** b. ab. 1643, m. John Smith.

2 **ELIZABETH** (8?), m. 12 July 1686 Rich. Blanchard, 2d Rich. Randall.

3 ***JOHN** (1), Hampton, now Seabrook, m. 1 Sept. 1659 Rebecca Perkins (Isaac). Friends, they were abs. from meeting; he in Apr. 1662, 26 times abs.; both in Apr. 1663, 20 days abs., in Mar. 1668 he worked on fast day. Named Rep. 1692, he declined to take oath, but aft. remov. to New Castle, Del., where he bot 1695, he served as Rep. 1696, the oath there unnecessary. In N. J. he adm. the est. of his mo.-in-law Susanna Perkins, as princ. creditor, 1699. Lists 396, 52, 392b. D. New Castle 1707, leaving a will. Ch: **Theodate,** b. 12 June 1660, m. 9 May 1682 Benj. Swett. **Rebecca,** b. 18 Nov. 1662, m. at Hampt. 4 May 1683 Jos. Howland of Duxbury, 2d at Duxb. 16 Aug. 1695 Saml. Collins. **Mary,** b. 8 Nov. 1665, m. 12 May 1687 Moses Swett. **Susanna,** b. 7 Sept. 1667, m. 1st Rich. Otis jr., 2d John Varney. **Ann,** b. May 1669, m. Jas. Stanyan. **Huldah,** b. 16 July 1670, m. 17 Nov. 1692 Nathl. Weare, Esq. **Bathshuah,** b. 21 Sept. 1671, m. Thos. Babb (2). **Christopher,** b. 17 Oct. 1672. **Hope,** b. 19, d. 28 Mar. 1674. **John,** b. 18 Jan. 1676. **Hope,** b. 22 Feb. 1677. **Jedediah,** b. 6 Mar. 1678. **Patience,** b. 4 Apr. 1679. **Charity,** b. 4 Aug. 1681. **Dau.,** b. 25 Sept. 1692, d. y. **John,** b. 30 May, d. 25 June 1684. **Content,** b. 29 Oct. 1685.

4 **JOSEPH,** List 392b. Read Capt. Christo. rep. 1672.

5 **MARY,** Mrs., widow, orig. grantee of Hampton, propr. 1638-1640. As Mary Wood she had m. John Hussey at Dorking, co. Surrey, 5 Dec. 1593, and, a widow, came with or foll. her son's fam. to N. E. Not unlikely her husb. was the early voyager Hus-

sey cast away upon Cape Florida and there devoured by the native cannibals, a fate attrib. to Christopher by his gr. gr. s. Jos. Marshall of Nantucket, in his signed 'Genealogy of the Husseys.' Christopher himself cert. d. in Hampt., if not in his bed. In Hampt. 25 Apr. 1648 she sold to John Woodin a joint possession until her death in 16 a., partly adj. Christo. She was liv. 4 Mar. 1649-50; Woodin sold alone 27 July 1657. Lists 392a, 393ab. In 1695 Thos. Leavitt and Jos. Marston drew in 3rd West Div. in her orig. right. Ch. bp. Dorking: **John**, 29 Apr. 1594, d. 8 Nov. 1597. **Christopher**, 18 Feb. 1599.

6 **MARY** (Husse), m. at Salis. 4 June 1678 Michael Towsley, who had been a Hampt. soldier. 1 dau. rec.

7 **RICHARD**, weaver, Dover 1690, had grants, incl. 50 a. in 1694 laid out in Somersworth and 30 a. at Sligo, sold to Benj. Weymouth, 1710. In 1696 he sold to Leonard Weeks int. in 30 a. at Great Bay bet. Wm. Furber and Thos. Willey except 3 a. disposed of or given Thos. Canney. Witn., sr., 1717; dead in Nov. 1729. Lists 358abd. Widow Jane; adm. to her s. Richard 21 Aug. 1733; dau. Jane Styles acc. of taking away est. Ch: **Richard**, b. 26 Oct. 1691, carpenter, Dover, m. in Newington 16 May 1716 Hannah Evans (12), wid. of Zach. Field (12 jr.). In 1717 when her br.-in-law Job Hussey and Job. Clements jr. were arrested for k. Thos. Ash's mare, she said 'our folks shot into the horses.' Jan. 8, 1753 he conv. the Dover homestead to s. Rich.; d. bef. Mar. 1757; she rem. to Lebanon with her sons. d. there 31 Jan. 1773. 4 ch. **Job**, b. 25 Dec. 1693, (5 Jan. by Tate), Somersw., but owned largely in Roch. M. 1st Margery Tibbetts (Jos.), 2d by 1733 Anna Evans (13). Will 10 Sept. 1761—9 July 1777 names w. Anna, 4 ch., 2 gr. ch. **Robert**, b. 28 Nov. 1695, liv. Charlestown where he m. 8 May 1729 Elizabeth Stone (Elias). In 1734 he bot in Canterbury from Job Clements. Adm. 17 May 1762 to s.-in-law Thos. Harris whose w. was the only heir, 1761. 5 ch. **Mary**, b. 1 June 1697, m. Benj. Varney. **Joseph**, b. 23 June 1699, Somersworth, m. 1st Sarah Canney (Saml.), 2d ab. 1736 Elizabeth (Robinson) wid. of Henry Tibbetts and became a Friend. Will 2 Jan. (d. 8 Feb.) 1762 names w. Elizabeth (d. 3 May 1773) and all but one of his ch: 5+7, incl. Saml., b. 12 Dec. 1742, m. 3 May 1769 Mercy Evans, and was fa. of the poet Whittier's mo. Abigail Hussey. **Elizabeth**, b. 28 Oct. 1701, m. 31 Aug. 1720 Jos. Farnham. **Eleanor**, b. 23 Apr. 1705. **Abigail**, b. 25 Apr. 1707. **Jane**, b. 27 June 1708, m. Saml. Styles, 1 ch.; 2d ab. 1736 Edmund Layn, 2 ch.; 3d Joshua Davis (40). **William**, b. 24

Mar. 1711, tailor, m. ab. 1730 'out of Friends orders' Hannah Robinson, sis. of his br. Joseph's w., but became a Friend. Will 27 July 1777 (d. 22 Jan. 1778) names w. Hannah (d. 20 Apr. 1793), 7 ch. **Margaret**, b. 28 Feb. 1712. **Benjamin**, b. 1 Apr. 1718; ag. ±16, he chose br. Wm. gdn.

8 **ROBERT**, Oyster River 1659. In 1661 Rice Howell threw a glass bottle at him. List 361a. Poss. fa. of (2), (6), (7), or none.

9 **STEPHEN** (1), Nantucket, m. there 8 Oct. 1676 Martha Bunker (Geo.). Bef. leaving Hampt. he was in Ct., Apr. 1668, for disturbing the congrega. on the Lord's Day and reviling Mr. Cotton, in Apr. 1669 and Apr. 1670 for not freq. pub. ordinance; in Apr. 1673 failed to appear in Ct. He d. at Nant. 2 Apr. 1718 (will made 1716); wid. d. 21 Nov. 1744. Ch: **Puella**, b. 10 Oct. 1677, m. May 1695 Shubael Gorham. 10 ch. **Abigail**, b. 22 Dec. 1679, m. 5 Apr. 1700 Thos. Howes who was soon drowned, 1 son; 2d Jos. Marshall, 1 son Joseph who wrote the fam. hist. as he had known it and heard it, naming Dorking as the Eng. home. She d. 26 Apr. 1763. **Sylvanus**, b. 13 May 1682, d. 10 Feb. 1767, m. 1st 7 Feb. 1711-2 Abial Brown, 2d 8 Nov. 1723 Hepzibah Starbuck (Nathl. jr.) Ch. 5+8. **Batchelder**, b. 18 Feb. 1685, m. 11 Oct. 1704 Abigail Hall; liv. Nantucket and Biddeford. 11 ch., a number mar. in Dover. **Daniel**, b. 20 Oct. 1687. **Mary**, b. 24 Mar. 1689-90, m. 1st 16 June 1707 Jona. Worth, 2d 24 May 1722 Ebenezer Barnard. Ch. 4+5. **George**, b. 21 June 1694, d. 7 June 1782, m. 12 Nov. 1717 Elizabeth Starbuck (Nathl. jr.). 14 ch. **Theodate**, b. 15 Sept. 1700, d. 25 Nov. 1744, m. 26 Sept. 1726 James Johnson. 4 ch.

**HUTCHINS,** found principally in Somersetshire.

1 **DAVID**, Spruce Creek, Kittery, owed est. of (2), in 1694 held part of gr. made to Rowland Williams who was closely connec. with (2), and m. bef. 13 Sept. 1706 a neighbor of (2) Mary Lewis (14), who depos. in Oct. 1709, ±50, liv. 34 yrs. ago at Turkey Pt. where Jos. Weeks now lives. He was k. by Ind. 19 Sept. 1708, adm. 7 July 1719 to s. John. Lists 298, 296, 297, 96. Ch. by deeds: **John**, yeoman, Kit., took q. c. deeds from sisters 14 May 1724. List 291. M. 11 Sept. 1718 Mary Downer; liv. 1734. Mary and John bp. 24 Oct. 1724 app. his ch. **Mary**, Kit. 1724 unmar. **Elizabeth**, Davis in 1724. Y. D. xi.

2 *****ENOCH**, Kit., liv. in garrison ho. near E. branch of Spruce Creek, where he bot from Thos. Withers 7 July 1675. Poss. brot to Portsm. by (4) in 1659, he signed a Kit. ptn. in fall of 1662, and was with Gowen Wilson at ho. of Goodm. Pickering, Portsm.,

an evening in Jan. 1663-4. Lists 25, 298, 30, 33, 293, 294, 296, 96. Gr. j. 1694. M. 5 Apr. 1667 Mary Stevenson (Thos.) of Oyster Riv., ±44 Aug. 1695, ±53 Oct. 1705, evid. much his junr. He made his will 7 June 1693, aged and weak in body, and was called by Niles an old man when k. by Ind. in his own door-way, and 3 sons taken 9 May 1698. Tradition carries the wid. to Canada at that time, dis-prov. by the fact that she showed his est. to apprs. 7 June 1698. In Feb. 1723-4 she had washed for Rowland Williams, dressed his diet, tended him near 30 yrs., her bill for 'house harbor' 36 yrs. Ch. in fa.'s will: **Enoch**, b. ±1671. **Joseph**, liv. 1693, not found later. **John**, liv. 1693. **Benjamin**, capt. 9 May 1698, ret. bef. 29 May 1701. He and br. Saml. recd. all their fa.'s cattle by will; together they first adm. br. Enoch's est., bondsm. Rowland Williams, Thos. Rice jr. M. 1st (Ct. Jan. 1702-3) Joanna Ball (5), 2d 12 Mar. 1718-19 Mary Dill (2), who was in Ct. Apr. 1721, -wife- of Benj. A wid. July 6 fol., she and his br. Saml. relinq. adm. to Chas. Trafton, the Ct. joining her as adm. with Trafton. Lists 99, 296, 297, 298. Ch. 5+1. She m. 2d 26 June 1723 Philip Carey. **Samuel**, taken with bros., but ret. the next Jan. Lists 99, 291, 296, 297, 298. Of Salis., he sold his Kit. dwg. 1724; of Arundel bef. 30 June 1729, where he d., will 20 Oct—28 Dec. 1742. Wid. Hannah, exec., d. 9 June 1747. 10 ch., incl. Caleb, m. 15 Feb. 1727 Sarah Bryars and repre. John Frink's ch. in 1734; Saml., Arundel, m. Sarah, wid. of John Baxter; Hannah, m. in Wells 7 June 1733 Geo. Perkins, 2d Lt. John Burbank. **Jonathan**, ±15 in May 1698, still in Canada May 1701. Lists 99, 291. Kit. 1714, 1734, York 1739. Adm. 20 May 1746 to s. Jos. of York. M. ——— Weeks in Portsm. bet. 20 Oct. 1709—20 May 1710. His only kn. w. was Judith Weeks (Jos.) of Kit., b. 3 June 1696, under 14 in May 1710; ch. of Judith H., decd., named in will of her step-mo. Mary Weeks 1763. 6 or m. ch. **Mary**, m. An-drew Lewis (2). **Sarah**, m. 1st John Dill (3), 2d Chas. Trafton.

3 **ENOCH** (2), ±28 in June 1699, m. 12 May 1693 Hopewell Furbush (2), and inher. from fa. ho. and 30 a. at head of Eastern Creek in Spruce Creek. Gr. j. 1693-4; Con-stable 1698. Lists 296, 297, 298, 96. His w. taken capt. with 3 sons 4 May 1705, was in Canada when he d. in Kit. 2 Apr. 1706, but was back and gr. adm. 13 Jan. 1706-7, dis-placing his bros. Benj. and Saml.; Saml. had waited on him 11 days and tended the cat-tle. Est. div. Sept. 1721 to wid. Hopewell (m. 2d 25 Apr. 1711 Wm. Wilson), sons Thos., Enoch, and dau. Mary; no provision made for s. Wm. if he should return. **Wil-liam**, b. 1 Aug. 1694, housewright, called

Nicholas in Canada, from where he returned unexpectedly in Jan. 1732 to be disowned by bros., accepted by mo. who depos. in 1732 that he was in his 12th yr. when cap-tured, in his 14th yr. when she left him in Canada. He won against his bros. in Ct., and Dec. 1736, of Kit., sold a double portion in fa.'s 1694 gr. M. 17 Oct. 1734 Mary Keene (2); 20 Apr. 1737 gave her genl. P/A. She m. bet. Mar.—Dec. 1739 Morris O'Brien of Kit., liv. Scarb. 1756. List 99. **Thomas**, b. 20 Sept. 1696. How and when he and br. Enoch ret. from Canada unkn. List 291. M. 5 May 1720 Hannah Hill (10), and in Jan. fol. was acc. by his kinswo. Meribah Hutchins (Benj. 2); m. 2d 13 Dec. 1764 Martha Jones, who m. again John Haley. Will 5 Aug. 1772—7 Jan. 1774. 7 ch. **Enoch**, b. 11 Sept. 1697, tailor, prob. m. Elizabeth Johnson (31). List 291. Adm. 1761 to s. David; div. 1770 to 2 sons, wid. living. **Child**, k. by Ind. 4 May 1705. List 96. **Mary Catherine**, b. Sorel, Can., 6 Sept. 1705, m. 1st James Grover (1), 2d Moses Welch, jr. See Coleman's 'N. E. Captives,' i. 391, ii. 404.

4 **JOHN**, carpenter, came to Boston on the -Bevis- in May 1638. Dec. 2, 1659 he contracted to build Portsm. meeting-ho.; in 1668 withdrew two suits ag. the town for satisfaction. Likely John of Newb. and Haverh., whose ch. incl. **William**, **Love**, b. 16 July 1647, m. in Haverh. 15 Dec. 1668 Capt. Saml. Sherburne of Hampt. One Mary m. 1 Apr. 1697 Isaac Webster of Hampt.

5 **MARY**, (Me. Ct. Jan. 1700-1) Joseph Young.

6 **NATHANIEL**, soldier at Oyster River Apr. 1696. List 67.

7 **NICHOLAS**, captive. List 99, p. 126. Ident. with Wm. (3).

8 **THOMAS**, redeemed Sarah Nason (Benj.) of Berw., Jan. 1699-1700. D. H. ix. 106.

9 **THOMAS**, husbandman, s. of Hugh of Old Eng. Nov. 6, 1718 his kinsm. Benj. (2) for love and affec. deeded him 5 a. at Spruce Creek; sold 20 Mar. 1718-9 to Jos. Wilson. App. the man pub. 26 July 1718 to Sarah Nason, likely dau. of Baker, who went the criminal bond of T. H., husbandm. of Berw., 14 Sept. 1721. In 1733 Kit. selectm. bound out Elizabeth, dau. of one Thos., to Rich. Chick.

10 **THOMAS**, depos. in June 1749, ag. ±47, hired near 20 yrs. ago by Mr. Wm. Vaughan to go to Damariscotta to build him a ho., the 1st ho. built there.

11 **WILLIAM**, Exeter, 1683-4. List 52. One Wm. (Houchins), afflicted with King's Evil, was at Portsm. in Sept. 1687, asking relief. See (4) and Groth. In 1733 one Wm. of Exeter had gone to Boston to get Jabez Allen al. Mead, of Exeter, out of jail.

**HUTCHINSON,** a name confined to the north half of Eng., most numerous in Durham.

1 \*‖**CAPT. EDWARD,** s. of Wm. and Anne (Marbury), bp. at Alford, co. Lincoln, 28 May 1613, came to Boston bef. his parents and went back to marry. In R. I. with the others, he was soon back· in Boston, where he led a highly useful life up to its close, shot down under flag of truce aft. success. closing an Ind. peace treaty. Deputy for Boston many yrs., in 1670-1 he was Dep. for Kittery. Betw. him and his br. Saml. and their sis. Bridget, the blood is brilliantly repres. in R. I. under numer. surn. Two of 4 ch. by 2d w. were: **Elisha,** and **Edward,** Boston, will 21 May—16 June 1692. Y. D. i. 57, 102.

2 **EDWARD**(7), with (10) at Piscat. on their fa.'s bus. in 1655. Y. D. i. 74. See Beex & Co. List 75a.

3 ‡**ELIAKIM**(7), over here in 1664 and went back; again in 1672. In 1673 he took Freeman's Oath. Assistant repeat. aft. 1692 and at death 22 Apr. 1717. Both on his fa.'s acct. and his own, he had large int. on the Piscat. and in Me. Will 3 Feb. 1716 names only one s: ‡**William,** H. C. 1702, Councilor.

4 ‡\*‖**COL. ELISHA**(1), retailer 1673, distiller 1674, O. A. 1676. On his fa.'s death he was quickly advanced. By 1678 he had m. 2d Elizabeth, wid. of Mr. John Freak, dau. of Thos. Clarke(54), partn. of Capt. Thos. Lake(3), and so concerned in Kennebec lands; also in Kit. and York. List 188. See Johnson(6). His s. **Thomas,** b. 30 Jan. 1675, Councilor 1717, was fa. of the Gov. Son **Edward,** b. 18 June 1678, active in Pejepscot matters.

5 **ENOCH** (Hutchison), Kittery. List 96. Read Hutchins.

6 **PETER,** boatswain on -Marigold- of Boston at Ports. 1695.

7 **RICHARD**(11), opulent ironmonger in London and partn. in Beex & Co.; repres. here by his sons (2), (3), (10), (12). His will in N. E. Reg. 51.125.

8 **RICHARD,** bro. of (1), bp. at Alford, co. Lincoln, 8 Dec. 1615; adm. First Ch., Boston, 9 Nov. 1634; Freeman 4 Mar. 1635; disarmed 1637 and went back to London, having been given letter 28 Dec. 1645 to Dr. Thos. Goodwin's ch. there.

9 **SAMUEL**(11). With Mr. Needham and others he was negotiating with Thos. Gorges for land in Wells, 1641. List 371. His will in N. E. Reg. 16.331.

10 **SAMUEL**(7). See (2).

11 **SUSANNAH,** wd. of Edward H., who was bur. in Alford, co. Lincoln, 14 Sept. 1631, may be the earliest born emigrant to d. in Me. (ab. 164-, in Wheelwright's home at Wells). Leaving most of her ch. behind, she came with Wheelwright to Boston, thence to Exeter, to Wells. Arriv. 26 May 1636, adm. First Ch. 12 June 1636, dism. to Ex. 3 Mar. 1638-9. Gr. mo. of Edw. Rishworth, Thomas and Samuel Wheelwright (b. 1631 and 1635), Bridget (Hutchinson) (Sanford) Phillips of Biddeford, for whose two husbands two Me. towns were named, also of Capt. Edward, Col. Elisha and Councilor Eliakim H. of Boston, she was back of much of Me. history. Of her Wheelwright gr. daus., Catherine's husb. acquired Sir Ferd. Gorges's ho. in York; Elizabeth's husb. owned at No. Yarmouth and elsewhere; Hannah's husb., Anthony Checkley, with her gr. s. Thos. Savage, acquired the Cammock patent at Scarb. Habijah Savage's poster. became large owners in the Pejepscot Proprs., and in the 'Drowne' Pemaquid Co. Of her 11 ch. 5 came over: **William,** bp. 14 Aug. 1586, husb. of the brilliant Anne (Marbury). **Samuel,** bp. 1 Nov. 1590. **Susannah,** bp. 9 Aug. 1601, m. Augustine Storre. **Mary,** bp. 22 Dec. 1605 (Mrs. Wheelwright). **Edward,** bp. 20 Dec. 1607. Of these, 3 came to Exeter, only Mary to Wells. From Ex., Samuel went to R. I., the Storres vanished, Edward went to R. I., and soon back to London. See also **Richard**(7), bp. 3 Jan. 1597-8.

12 **WILLIAM**(7), Kittery witn. 1670 (Y. D. ii. 123). List 298.

**Hutcote,** Aaron, widower. See Edgerly (1). This surname seen only in Rev. Hugh Adams's records, unaccess., presum. misread or phonetic spel.

**Hutton,** John, cook 1614. List 7.

**Hyatt,** Richard, merchant, Piscataqua 1688. See Hunking (3 jr.), Hull.

**Hyde,** Joseph (Hide), Scarb. soldier. List 237b.

**Hy--es,** Eleanor. See Hinds(2).

**IFINS,** see Evans.

**ILSLEY,** Insley, Ensley. **Elisha** (Ensley), Portsm., liv. in Morse's ho. in 1698, sued by Daniel Zackery in 1700, must be same as Elisha (Ilsley) of Portsm. 1702, and that s. of Elisha and Hannah (Poore) Ilsley of Newbury b. 21 Nov. 1668. Lists 330def. His wid. Elizabeth Ilsley (prob. born a Harvey, which see) of Portsm. 1708, m. (Robert) Rutherson (Rutherford) May 1709. Prob. ch: **Sarah,** bp. and recd. into cov. in No. Ch. 20 Feb. 1713-4.

**INGALLS, Henry** (Ingolls), Falmouth. List 225a. See also Cooper(3) and Parker.

**INGERSOLL,** a very uncommon English name. The emigrant, Richard of Salem, was married in Bedfordshire.

1 **ELISHA**(5), captured by Ind. in his youth, returned to Kittery 25 May 1695.

In 1715 his father deeded him his Stroudwater homestead to him and his bro.-in-law Chapman, both making their homes on it. The time of their removal is uncertain (both of Kit. in deed of 14 Mar. 1715). Elisha was dubbed 'Gov. Ingersoll' because he was already at Stroudwater when Moody and his soldiers resettled Falmouth Neck in (June?) 1716. Drowned in the Presumpscot Mar. 1722. Lists 229, 294, 295, 296, 297. His w. (Mary) surviv. him but in 1729 three daus. held his est. when they sold the Stroudw. mill-priv. Ch: **Elisha**, b. 2 Jan. 1697, d. Apr. 1698. **Mary**, b. 29 Nov. 1702 in Dover, was Mary Martin in 1729 but m. 2d bef. 1736 Patrick Tobin of Falm. and was liv. in 1753. **Elizabeth**, b. 12 July 1705, acc. John Clark of Berwick in 1724 and Arthur Mackleroy of Falm. in 1736 but m. the latter (int. 21 Mar. 1735-6) and as his wid. sold her Ingersoll prop. in Kit. to Tho. Cutt and her Falm. land to her bro.-in-law John Tenney. Again in 1740 she acc. Joseph Main of York who denied the impeach. successfully. **Deborah**, b. 3 June 1708, unm. in 1729, m. 23 Sept. 1732 John Tenney, whose first w. had been her cousin Deborah(6); liv., his w., 1739 (Y. D. 19. 243). **Elisha**, b. 3 June 1711, d.y. **Margaret**, b. 22 Feb. 1714, d.y.

2 *GEORGE, b. in England ±1618, s. of Richard and Anne (Langley) of Salem, spent early manhood in Salem and Gloucester, but was at Back Cove, Falmouth, with w. Elizabeth, as early as 1657. See Coe. Bot 55 a. in 1658 at Stroudwater, next Thos. Skillen, whose est. he app. in 1666. A townsman in 1668, he served as tr. juror in 1666 and 1668, selectman in 1668, dep. to the Gen. Courts at York 28 June 1682 and 24 June 1685, and measurer of land in 1684. Lists 27, 30, 35, 83, 86, 212, 222a, 223ab, 225, 226, 34, 93, 225b. His son killed and his house and prop. destroyed at the onset of Philip's war in 1675, he commanded the town's militia (commissioned lieut. 7 July 1668) and retired to Salem when Falm. was aband. One of a commission app. by Gen. Court to lay out a town-site on Falm. neck, he returned in 1680 but on out-break of next Indian war in 1689 again withdrew to Salem, too old for further military serv. He d. in 1694. Ch: a son, killed by Indians while shooting wild fowl in Oct. 1675. **George**, b. May 1643. **John**, b. 1645. **Joseph**, b. 4 Oct. 1646. **Elizabeth**, b. 1 Feb. and d. 9 Mar. 1648-9. **Elizabeth**, b. 19 Mar. 1651, m. 1st John Skillin, 2d Elihu Gunnison(1). **Samuel**, b. 1654, ±75 in 1730, of Charlestown and Glouc., had 200 a. at Falm., 100 of them at Capisic having been given him by his f. in 1689. Lists 34, 223a, 225ab, 228b. He m. Judith Maddiver (Joel of

Purpoodock). 11 ch. **Mary**, b. 12 Aug. 1657.

3 **GEORGE**(2), Falm., m. Catherine Nichols (Robert of Scarb.) c. 1674, d. in Boston 10 Aug. 1721, ag. 78 yrs. 3 mos. (Copp's Hill). They fled to Salem in 1675 and in 1689 to Boston, where he was a shipwright, he and his w. being bpt. when they joined the Charlestown ch. in 1696. The Eastern Claims describe his Falm. lands as 100 a. near the old fort adj. John Skillings; a house-lot in town near the old fort and a cornmill at Barberry creek 1½ miles from the fort. Lists 27, 30, 34, 223a, 225a, 226. Ch., the first three bpt. 10 Dec. 1693 and the last four 12 July 1696 at Charlest., their ages being given: **Elizabeth**, b. 1675. **Sarah**, b. 1677, m. William Haley(1). **Bethia**, b. 1679, m. by 1702 Richard Tucker of Charlest. and Boston. **Mary**, d. 14 Oct. 1693. **George**, b. 1683, m. 1st one Elizabeth and 2nd 2 Sept. 1707 Elizabeth Gourding. 1 + 3 ch. **Daniel**, b. 1690, settled in Falm. in 1717, built on his father's old house-lot on the neck and was selectman, but returned to Charlest. bef. 1730 and became wealthy shipbuilder. His 1st w. Sarah d. bef. 16 July 1741 when he was pub. with Hannah Tucker who m. 2nd 26 July 1764 William Nichols. 4 + 2 ch. **Catherine**, b. 1692, m. 4 Mar. 1713-4 Benjamin Eustis. **Lydia**, b. 1695, m. 1st 19 Dec. 1717 Elias Hart, 2d 18 May 1722 John Gendall.

4 **JOANNA**, Kittery, a wid. in 1720, when Andrew Poor, the schoolmaster, seduced her, promising marriage. Her petn. states that she was from Kinsale, Ireland, and that her husb. had d. soon after landing, leav. her with 4 small ch. Coming from Spruce creek, she and 2 ch. were warned from Boston in 1723.

5 **JOHN**(2), bot large tract from George Munjoy at Capisic in Falmouth in 1675 before the war caused his flight to Salem, whence he returned to Falm. in 1680 by way of Kittery (1676). Had a grant of 60 a. at Fort Loyal, but lived on his farm, operating the mill with his bro. until 1690, when his house, a garrison commanded by Sergt. Richard Hicks, was aband. and he, his w. Deborah (±83 in 1728) and his ch. retired to Kittery, where he became a carpenter. Lists 27, 212, 222, 225, 226, 291, 295, 296, 297, 298. His will, 27 Sep. 1714—4 Apr. 1716, names the ch: **Deborah**, b. ±1668 (64 in July 1732), m. 1 Dec. 1686 at Falm. Capt. Benjamin Larrabee(1). **Elisha**. **Nathaniel**. **John**. **Ephraim**, d. s.p. **Abigail**, m. 1st Morgan Lewis(14), 2d Joseph Junkins and 3d, bef. 1714, Ebenezer Blaisdell. **Rachel**, m. 10 Mar. 1710 John Chapman(4). A dau., m. John Brown(23). **Mary**, m. 1st Daniel Low(1) (ct. Oct. 1707), 2d, int. 25

Apr. 1724, Andrew Lewis(2).

6 **JOHN**(5), ±20 Sep. 1695, Kittery, m. 1st (ct. July 1703) Deborah Phoenix (John of Kit.), 2d Mary Roberts of Newcastle, int. 28 Sep. 1738. He was adm. to Kit. ch. 6 June and his w. bpt. 20 June, 1742. Lists 296, 297. Ch: **Deborah**, b. 20 Jan. 1702-3, m. 29 Dec. 1726 John Tenney, who m. 2d her cousin Deborah(1). **Mary**, b. 6 Jan. 1705, m. John Larrabee(6) 13 Jan. 1725-6. **John**, bp. 5 June 1715, m. Sarah Tucker, who m. 2d, after 1744, John or Isaac Holden. 3 ch. **Richard**, bp. 1 Sep. 1717; sailor; m. 17 Oct. 1747 Mary Henny who was his wid. in 1764 and prob. d. 2 Dec. 1809, ag. 86. 3 ch.

7 **JOSEPH**(2), Falmouth, and, aft. Philip's war, Charlestown and Glouc., carpenter, m. Sarah Coe(2), who d. 29 Jan. 1714. Lists 30, 223a, 225a, 228c, 34. His son Benj. entered Eastern Claims in his name for 100 a. at Capisic (part of the Munjoy purchase) and for a house and 2 a. ¼ m. from the fort, where he had lived. He d. 12 Mar. 1718 in Glouc. Ch: **Martha**, b. 5 Nov. 1670, at Falm., m. 10 Jan. 1695 Thomas Millet, who was drowned at Casco Bay Mar. 1722. **John**, bp. 13 Aug. 1676 at Salem. **Stephen**, Salem. 5 ch. **Benjamin**, b. ±1687, d. 11 Apr. 1755 at No. Yarmouth, m. 1st, int. 16 Nov. 1711 Mary Hunt of Ips., who d. 10 May 1733. He m. 2d Sarah (Ireson) Parker, who m. 3d Robert Johnson 18 Sep. 1755. Settled in Falm. on his father's lands and was innkeeper and prom. cit. being a member of Capt. Moody's Co. June 1—Nov. 22, 1725 and selectman 1727. 8 + 1 ch. **Joseph**, cordwainer of Glouc., m. 11 Dec. 1707 Mary Brewer. 8 ch. **Hannah**, poss. m. 19 May 1723 John Clements.

8 **NATHANIEL**(5) inherited his father's 36 a. homestead in Kittery, where he was adm. to the ch. in 1719. His wid. Joanna signed the deed from Newbolt to Gunnison in 1737 as Joanna Ingersoll, hence could not be the J. I. pub. with John Boaden 3 Oct. 1719, unless the mar. did not take place. Ch: **Nathaniel**, b. 22 June 1716. **Deborah**, m. Joshua Newbolt of Portsm., mariner, and was only surv. ch. in 1737 when she sold her gr. father's homestead to Elihu Gunnison.

**INGLESBY**, Ingoldsby 1 ———, presum. one of Sir Ferdinando Gorges's or Mr. Godfrey's disappearing tenants, gave his name to Ingleby's point and Inglesby's marsh at York, the former in poss. of Mr. William Hilton in 1651.

2 **EBENEZER**, s. of John and Ruth, b. in Boston 13 Dec. 1656, a Bos. soldier at Black Point 1675-8 and at Pemaquid 1696. Lists 236, 237b, 127.

**INGRAHAM**, an ancient personal name; also a par. in Northumberland.

1 **AARON**, poss. br. of (2), m. Elizabeth Dolbeer 17 Feb. 1708 in Boston, from where he, his wife and four small ch. were warned in 1714, coming from Newbury, but earlier from Portsm. where he was taxed in 1713.

2 **MOSES**, tailor, Portsm. and York, b. 9 July 1683 in Boston, s. of Henry and Lydia (Dowse), and m. there 25 July 1706 Mary Walton who d. in Portsm. 5 Dec. 1720, ag. 41. In No. Ch., Portsm., he m. 2d 23 Feb. 1720-1 Elizabeth Ayers (1), wid. of Caleb Griffith and Henry Lyon. Lists 279, 339. Ch. by 1st w: **Aaron**, b. 17 Mar. 1706-7 in Boston. **Samuel**, bp. 19 Dec. 1708 in Portsm., m. 16 Jan. 1728-9 Anne Pearce (Wm. of York). 10 ch. List 279. **Henry**, prob. he bp. 14 Oct. 1711, m. Bethia Young (Joseph) int. 17 Jan. 1735-6 in York. 2 ch. His 2d w., a Haskell, had 1 son. **Moses**, bp. 15 Feb. 1712-3. **Mary**, bp. 22 Dec. 1717. And prob. **Alice**, m. Rowland Young, jr. at York 11 Oct. 1738, and **George**, m. at York 8 Feb. 1738-9 Bethia Preble (Joseph). 2 ch. By 2d w: **Edward**, bp. 21 Jan. 1721-2, innholder at York, m. Lydia Holt (Joseph), int. 1 Apr. 1742. 8 ch.

**Inians**, see Onions.

**Instone**. An estate of this name listed in Scarb. in 1681 may have been that of John Ashton.

**IRELAND**, 1 **Jonathan**, in York court July 1718 with w. Sarah (More) on usual charges. She witn. will of John Wells in York in 1723.

2 **PHILIP**, formerly of Isles of Shoals, now (1695) of Ipswich, sued Edw. Dolbeare of Boston for money collected in suit from John Ireland of Charlestown, mariner, in 1684. His w. Grace d. in Ipsw. 13 May 1692. Ch: **Solomon**, b. 1691, and doubtless **Benjamin**, who m. Mary Hobbs int. 8 Aug. 1713, had among others a dau. Grace and d. 1778 'supposed 100.'

**IRISH**, 1 **John**, serv. of Timothy Hatherly and employee of Plym. Colony at Cushnoc in 1634 (Spencer). If that author. is good, Judge Savage was doubtless correct in his conject. that John 'Frish', on Kennebec with Howland in 1634, cutting the cable of the interloper Hocking, was John Irish.

2 **WILLIAM**, Portsm., apprent. of John Jackson deed., in 1667 chose to serve remainder of his time with Thos. Jackson, his master's son, and was still with him in 1671.

**Irons**, Thomas. List 237b. Prob. that son of Matthew and Anne bp. in Boston 5 Feb. 1643 and a tobacco-spinner there in 1666.

**Isles**, see Yeales.

**ISLINGTON**, Isleton. 1 **Benjamin**, ±19 in 1680 when he test. to the deliv. of shoes by his master Nehemiah Partridge to Francis Huckins, witn. a Remick deed in 1686 in Eliot and was taxed at Gt. Isl. in 1688. List 319. No w. or ch. rec., but 30 Sept. 1708 at No. Ch., Portsm. ——— Issalton m. Nath. Guptill, whose w. was Mary in 1716 and who named a son Benj.

2 **ROBERT**, Indian prisoner from Wells, still in Canada 1710-1, otherwise unkn. List 99, p. 92.

**Jack**, ———, Mr., his fine remitted by Portsm. 1665.

**Jacklin**, Rosamond, m. to Wm. Munsey by Rev. Mr. Pike 10 Jan. 1698-9.

**Jackman**, John, Casco witn. 1646. Y. D. i. 33.

**JACKSON**, common in the northern and rare in the south-coast counties of Eng.

1 **ANNAH** (Jaxson), likely rel. to (22), m. at Saco 14 July 166-, David Hamilton.

2 **CAPT. CLEMENT**, mariner, Portsmouth, witn. for Digory Jeffrey and with Andrew Haley 1694, m. 17 Oct. 1700 Sarah Hall; adm. to her 25 Mar. 1708. She was taxed a widow 1708-15; m. 2d aft. 1717 Jos. Hubbard; liv. Boston 1738. Lists 338c, 323. See also (11). Ch: **Mary**, b. 18 May 1703, d. 17 Aug. 1704. **John**, b. 20 Aug. 1704, d. 30 June 1713. Dr. **Clement**, b. 24 Mar. 1705-6, physician Hampt. and Portsm., m. at Hampt. 6 Aug. 1731 Sarah Leavitt; he d. in Portsm., Esq., 10 Oct. 1788, ag. 83 (gr. st.). 7 ch. **Joseph**, Col., Esq., b. 13 Dec. 1707, Boston hatter 1733, m. there 1 Mar. 1732 Susanna Gray; d. in Boston 10 Apr. 1790, ag. 84. 11 ch., incl. 3 Clements.

3 **DANIEL**, Casco Bay, m. at Gloucester 17 Nov. 1726 Abigail Day. Several unplaced in that vicin., incl: Francis, his 3 ch. bp. Falm. 1735-39, one of them Thomas. Henry, bot at Spurwink 1734. John, witn. a Purpoodock deed 1734. Thomas (Juxson), Casco Bay, m. at Newington 2 Apr. 1734 Mary Roberts; s. Benj. and dau. Bethiah bp. Newingt. 1735-7. See also James(22).

4 **ELEANOR**, Scarboro, wid. of John of Gloucester, who was liv. there 11 Oct. 1660. Essex Q. Ct. ii. 236, 249, 257. She came to Scarb. with s. John and the Briers; with John took lease of 50 a. at Spurwink from Jocelyn 20 May 1663, but m. bef. 11 Nov. that yr. Jonas Bailey(6), who soon d. Of Dorchester 3 Feb. 1682-3, she deeded to last husb. Gyles Barge(1) 500 a. at Blue Point for life, then to her gr. s. John J., but Gyles free to dispose of any part to gr. s. Jonathan and Peter J.; half the Spur. land, being her own, to Gyles outright. List 239a. She was ±76 in July 1676; d. Dorchester 15 Dec. 1691. Ch: **John**, ag. 34, 6

Feb. 1663-4. **Elizabeth**, ±30, Feb. 1663-4; 93 at death 2 Aug. 1722; called dau. of John in mar. rec. at Glouc. to John Briers(3). Evid. as to her age and standing in the fam. conflicts: Eleanor (Brackett 2) Pullen, Boston, depos. she had liv. in the same ho. with Eleanor Barge, a garrison; she had 3 gr. sons, no dau.; in 1732 John Boaden(8) and Susannah King, Marbleh., had liv. ab. 40 yrs. ago in same town with Eleanor Barge, and Elizabeth Briers was accounted her dau. Daniel Chisemore called them sisters, and never heard that widow Eleanor had a dau. Y. D. xii. 222.

5 **GEORGE**, physician, Pemaquid 1683-9, surgeon with the Canada exped. 1690, afterw. at Marblehead, poss. earlier home. He m. there 8 Dec. 1690 Mary (Aborne) Nick, who d. Feb. 1721-2. Lists 123, 124, 125. See also (11). Will 24 Aug. 1722—20 Apr. 1724 names three sons, the 1st surely, 2d prob. by earlier w: Dr. **Bartholomew**, oldest, poss. m. in Boston 5 Sept. 1706 Ann Hunt. D. 1757, leaving w. Jane and 6 ch., incl. George and Anne. In 1736 he (Mr.) had his fa.'s right in Lyndeboro, N. H. Dr. **George**, physician, Kit., m. 20 Mar. 1710-11 Joanna Pepperell, sis. of Sir Wm. Kit. 1724; prob. removed aft. his wife's death 17 Feb. 1725-6; Salem 1731, dead in 1760. One Dr. J. bur. Marbleh. 22 June 1744. Lists 296, 297. 8 daus., b. Kit. 1712-1721. **John**, m. in Marbleh. 5 June 1718 Mary Ryan. Ch., incl. George. See N. E. Fam. Hist. (Quinby), i. 28.

6 **JAMES**, Oyster River 1659-1662, freed from training 1661, having lost a finger. Lists 74(?), 361a, 363a. Poss. same as (7).

7 **JAMES**, Cape Neddick, see (6), m. a dau. of John Smith bef. 10 Oct. 1666, when land ord. laid out to J. S. and his son J. J. Other grants were, 28 a. by J. S. in June 1667, 50 a. beyond Cape Neddick 13 June 1674. D. bef. 16 Oct. 1676, inv. 25 Oct. by Rich. Bray and John Main; John Smith, sr., adm. Cattle had to be brot to York. Ch: **Two**, bur. bef. 12 Dec. 1676. See Carter (12). Goody Shears had nursed one sick child. **Elizabeth**; in Dec. 1676 Mr. Wollcott had recd. 32 lbs. pork for her schooling. Her discharge of her uncle John Smith jr., dated 16 July 1685, was rec. 10 July 1713; her gr. fa. and uncle put her cows out to John Barrett and John and Nathl. Cloyes of Wells.

8 **JANE**, m. 1st John Frink(3), 2d Henry Barter(1), unident.; also Martha, o. c. and bp. Berw. 23 Dec. 1716, m. James Hearle.

9 **JOHN**, Portsm., cooper, bot the Crowder farm from Ambrose Lane 2 June 1651; confirmed by the town 20 Mar. 1656, ho., land and island; in 1651 sued Henry Doug-

lass for 18 wks. of a son's time. Seven times Gr. j. 1652-1666. Constable and clerk of the market 1654. Selectm. 1656-7. O. F. 14 July 1657. Tr. j. 1666. Lists 324, 326ab, 330ab, 323, 43, 47. In 1662, having liv. peaceably in town so many yrs., he and John Hart were having trouble with a quarrelsome new neighb. Geo. Jones. Liv. 7 Nov., inv. 6 Dec. 1666; adm. 25 June 1667 to wid. Joan and s. Richard, div. aft. her death to be to three sons; Sept. 6, 1718 adm. gr. to s. John, the est. not fully adm. and Richard dead. She was liv. 1675; tax rebated 15 Mar. 1679-80, prob. then dead; line was fixed bet. John and Rich. 24 Dec. 1681. Lists 323, 326c, 331c. Ch: **Richard,** eldest. **Thomas,** b. ±1639. **John,** b. ±1641. **Daus.** escaped, gr. daus. almost escape rec.; deeds from the admrs. may reveal three daus.: w. of John Wyatt (deed 1669 of 2 a. out of the home farm); w. of Peter Ball(7) (deed 23 July 1672, the home part of the homestead, reserv. the E. end of the ho. and a garden spot for the wid., and ½ a. Rich. Dore had built on); Tamsen, w. of Rich. Dore(2), who made a ho. out of a bldg. 'called the shop' and added to it, bef. getting deed to the land, 1675.

10 **JOHN,** d. at the Shoals, adm. to John Cutts 12 July 1660.

11 **JOHN,** shipwright, mariner, paid £30 and his own work to bring from Dartmouth in the -Hannah & Elizabeth- arriv. Aug. 1679, hims., w. Sarah (Palmer), 3 ch., sis.-in-law Mrs. Joan Deering(7) and 2 ch. He was here earlier; with Roger Deering witn. N. Fryer's entry on Kit. land in Nov. 1663; in Nov. 1665 the two men owned 1/3 of the ketch -William & Mary- lately built here and likely sailed her to Eng. for sale. Appar. in Dartm. 1682. Lists under (14) may belong in part to this John, who, if here bet. 1665-1679, cannot be disting. Kn. ch., all but last in will of gr. mo. Sarah, wid. of Clement Palmer, of Hardnes, par. of Townstall, co. Devon, 12 Aug. 1665 (dau. Sarah Jackson exec.); all but 1st came with parents: **John.** Adm. on one John late of Dartm., mariner, to fa. John; bond, of Dartm., nautam, 1 Feb. 1681-2. **Sarah. Agnes. Clement;** whether ident. with (2) and George(5), a bro., uninvestigated.

12 **JOHN,** with Edward Woolcock and George Brooks(3) witn. orig. deed of Rascohegan Isl. 1672.

13 **JOHN**(4), Blue Point, Scarboro, witn. for fa. in Essex Ct., July 1660, ±30; m. 12 (or 22) July 1659 Susanna Jones (Thos.) in Glouc. where she d. 10 Apr. 1662. Sued in Essex Ct. June 1662, jr. Margaret, List 236, was likely a 2d w.; wid. Hannah of Blue Point in petn. to Andros told they improv. and liv. on their Scarb. land near 10

yrs. (One J. J. m. Hannah Hoppin in Dorchester 16 July 1679). Tr. j. 1666; Constable 1667; Gr. j. 1681, not sworn, being abs.; Selectm. 1682, 1685. Lists 235, (85, Gloucester?), 238a, 239a. Ch. by 1st w.: **John,** b. Glouc. 3 June 1660, liv. with the Barge fam. in 1683. In 1743 Daniel Chisemore called him John al. Henrys. In Bradford he told John Gage he was driven from Blue Pt. by the Inds., that his fa. was John, and he was the only s. liv. Gage told that he m. soon aft. coming there. Danl. Hardy describ. him a complete bodied man, ab. 6 ft., went to sea and never came back; but appar. he was in Scarb. 20 Nov. 1702. W. Sarah, mo. of 4 daus. rec. Bradford 1687-169(2?): Sarah, m. Ezra Rolfe. Susanna m. bef. 15 Aug. 1720 Nathl. Folsom (6 jr.); Y. D. xi. 235. Mary, m. Jas. Robinson of Stratham; deeded ¼ her fa.'s Scarb. int. Y. D. 12.1.142. Martha, m. Maximilian Haseltine(3). By 2d w: **Jonathan,** witn. Wymond Bickton's deed of Scarb. land 1683; k. by Ind. (Chisemore depos.), s. p. **Elizabeth,** m. in Marbleh. 25 July 1688 Crispus Squire; of Newark, N. J., in 17—, he claimed her Scarb. inheritance, thru atty. Saml. Barrett of Boston, to whom land was laid out much later by Edw. Milliken's fa. and Job Burnham. **Peter** (likely by 2d w.), named in gr. mo.'s deed 1682-3. Danl. Chisemore knew not what became of him. W. Hannah's ch. prob. d. s. p. and unkn., unless Peter one.

14 **JOHN**(9), cooper, mariner, ag. 84 in Dec. 1721. He bot ho. and garden lot in Old House Field, Portsm., living there most of the time; tho in Nov. 1666 his fa. deeded him part of the homestead adj. the Hunking-Wentworth est., where he liv. in Mar. 1700-1, ag. 59 or 60 (±60 in Sept. 1697), and where his s. and gr. s., both John, liv. aft. him. Tr. j. 1684, 1694 (foreman); Gr. j. 1682, 1692, 1696. Lists 330ab, 331ab, 326c, 54, 49, 51, 329, 55b, 314, 331c, 332a, 57, 334a, 335a, 330df, 316, 337, 323. See also (11). In 1719 for ¼ of his supp. and funeral exp., he deeded to s. Daniel half the ho. and use of the rest in common with br. Saml. John sr. recd. into So. Ch. 4 Mar. 1721-2, sued in 1722 for a sail borrowed in Boston 1707. His ch.'s mo. not found; he m. 2d (contract 7 Oct. 1685) Abigail, wid. of Anthony Ellins (1). Lists 331c, 335a. Kn. ch: **Mary,** b. ±1672, m. 25 Dec. 1689 Geo. Walker. **John,** fisherman. Lists 329, 314, (?334a), 330de, 337. W. Mary liv. 1723-4, when he and three sis. q. c. to br. Saml. List 335a. Son John, shipwright, b. ±1689, m. 10 Mar. 1716-7 Abigail Beek. Other ch. may incl. Martha, m. 10 Sept. 1713 James Moses. **Daniel,** mariner, liv. in Old Ho. Field; dead in 1744. Lists 330de, 323, 337, 339. W. Elizabeth in

1719. Ch. in ptn. 1744: Daniel, blockmaker, shopkeeper, Deacon, b. 16 Mar. 1699, d. 23 Dec. 1774, m. 30 Dec. 1722 Joanna Bennett of Ipsw.; Ebenezer, joiner, m. 23 Feb., 1728-9 Elizabeth Akerman; Elisha, blockmaker, m. 9 Nov. 1727 Abigail Hill; Mary, m. 10 July 1718 John Churchwell; Elizabeth, m. 8 Dec. 1737 David Mendum. Samuel, mariner, shopkeeper, will 17 Dec. 1729, d. 13 Apr. 1732, ag. 53 (gr. st.). List 67. In 1721 he and w. Elizabeth were selling strong drink at their ho. She m. 2d in Newb. 10 May 1732 Capt. Peter Hall. Ch. to be brot up incl. Elizabeth, who chose as gdn. her br. Saml., blacksmith, Boston, 22 Feb. 1733. A dau. Mary had d. 9 Aug. 1729, ag. 1 yr. 3 mo. Martha, m. 1st John Boulter(1), 2d Bryan Dore(2), 3d Philip Towle. Lydia, m. bef. 11 Dec. 1705 Christo. Noble.

15 JOSHUA, mariner, Piscataqua, depos. ab. the ketch -Swallow- 5 Dec. 1684. List 314.

16 RICHARD(9), Portsm., cooper, built a ho. on Christian Shore, occup. by six generations of his desc. He m. a dau. of Rich. Seward, poss. the Joan who was his w. in 1672 and 1675, altho R. S.'s will in 1662 names only s.-in-law Richard J. and ch. List 331c. In 1662 Stephen Edwards was his servant. Constable 1659. Gr. j. 1661, 1662, 1664, 1670, 1673; Tr. j. 1682, 1684. Lists 323, 326ac, 330ab, 356L (Portsm.), 327d, 54, 331b, 49, 329, 52, 55b, 92, 62. In 1694 he deeded to s. Nathl. land in Portsm. with Knight's or Jackson's Isl.; in May 1703 mtg. to Nathl. 1 a. on this Isl. near Mr. Phipps's dwg. D. bef. 6 Sept. 1718. Kn. ch: John, mariner, m. bef. 18 June 1688 Margaret Clark(49). Will 24 Jan. 1690-1 (d. 26 Jan., ag. 33), names w. and 'my child' John, who d. s. p. List 335a. She m. 2d ±1693 Philip White, 3d by 4 Jan. 1700-1 Roger Swain. Thomas, adm. to fa. 8 Apr. 1691; presum. d. s. p. Nathaniel, cordwainer 1703, master of the sloop -Hopewell-1706; taxed May 1707; at Ft. William & Mary 18—28 June 1708. Lists 330d, 337. He m. 14 May 1694 Margaret Ellins(1). She was taxed, a widow, 1713, and gr. adm. 21 July 1715. Div. 1727 to her and 4 surv. sons, all liv. 1752, she in 1742: Nathl., b. 26 Oct. 1702, cordwainer, m. 2 Mar. 1727 Sarah Hill(10); will 5 July 1769—26 June 1776 names w. Sarah, 4 ch. and prov. for br. John. Joshua, b. 6 Apr. 1705, blacksm., adm. to bros. 13 Jan. 1758; w. Patience Hunking, m. 25 Nov. 1728, liv. 1752. John, b. 11 Dec. 1707, d. y. Saml. 4¼ when fa. d., joiner; will 1758 names 6 ch. by 1st w. Mary Hill(10), m. 11 Jan. 1732-3; 4 by 2d w. —— Moore. John 2½ when fa. d., became distracted.

17 ROBERT, Pemaquid soldier 1689. List 126.

18 SAMUEL, mariner, Portsm., m. 12 Oct. 1693 Mary Melcher, whose fa. Edward in 1694 deeded her land at Str. Bk. on the street, and willed her the land her ho. stood on, her mo. to live with her. Samuel was Gr. j. 1696. List 335a. In 1704 Geo. Snell sued on his book acct. 1696-7, money to him when he sailed, supplies to her while he was gone. She was then m. to Peter Mann and was a wid. again in 1714. List 337. Her Melcher prop. descended in 7ths to Jacksons and Manns. Only kn. ch: Mary, m. 1st Abraham Ayers(7), 2d Jacob Lavers (2). In 1753 her Ayers ch. deeded her 1/7 to Hannah, ±14 in 1709, m. 22 Oct. 1718 John Symes of Exbourne, co. Devon; singlewoman 1753.

19 SARAH, member of No. Ch. May 1699, one of several connec. with that ch., not ident.; Sarah o. c. and obtained bap. for her ch. 1707-8; Sarah recd. into covt. at Boston, her s. Benj. bp. 18 July 1708; Sarah adm. bet. Nov. 1714—July 1715. Elizabeth and James bp. 16 Oct. 1709, Elizabeth bp. 22 June 1712, their mo. poss. Sarah.

20 THOMAS(9), cooper, ±50 June 1690, ±61 Mar. 1700-1, liv. on land on Jackson's Isl. given him by his fa. 25 June 1660, altho his w. Hannah Johnson(14) inherited half the Johnson homestead on Great Isl. In 1672 he adm. Peter Adams's est., and appar. John Larriford's. See Carpenter (4). Gr. j. 1665, 1666, 1675, 1683, 1687, 1700; Tr. j. 1683, 1696. Lists 330abd, 323, 326bc, 331b, 49, 329, 55a, 313f, 57, 335a, 316, 337. D. bet. 2 Apr. 1711—4 Dec. 1712; she liv. 1713. Lists 331c, 335a. Kn. ch: Hannah, b. ±1663, m. William Seavey. Thomas, took O. A. with fa. 28 Aug. 1685; cooper's mate on -Six Friends- in Canada Exped. 1690; saved from the wreck of a hospital ketch to which he was discharged, he was taken to Jamaica, impressed on a war vessel, and d. Mary, m. bef. 20 May 1700 John Sherburne. Ephraim, fisherman 1713, cooper. In Oct. 1709 his fa. deeded him half the Isl. where they liv., the rest at the parents's death. Selectm. 1719-21, 1728-9. Scarb. gr. 1720. Lists 67, 323, 337, 339. His w. Mary in 1712 (appar. Currier), m. ab. 1700 if 1st w.; 6 kn. ch. bef. he m. 5 July 1720 Elizabeth (Marshall), wid. of Jos. Smith, 1 ch. bp; m. last aft. Sept. 1725 Dorothy, wid. of John Moulton, 2 ch. bp., not incl. Eunice named last in his will 21 Sept.—30 Nov. 1748. In 1750 his wid. liv. in part of the old meet.-ho. on so. side of Pickering's Mill Creek; her will 1758—1761. Joseph, the only Newcastle Jackson, had half of the Johnson homestead from his parents 1700, and bot out the Odiornes in 1707. Joint owner of sloop -Adventure-with Christo. Amazeen, 1707. Selectm. 1728.

Lists 330de, 315b, 316. Mary Sargent (John) was his w. in Feb. 1716-7 and widow. Adm. to his s. Benj. 3 Apr. 1741; div. 1750 to 1 son, 3 daus. and heirs of 3 sons. Her will 10 Apr. 1755, d. 15 Jan. 1763 in 90th yr. (gr. st.). **Benjamin**, appar. husb. of Mary Ball(7), who m. 2d William White. In 1712 she deeded to his br. Ephraim the ho. her husb. built on Jackson's Isl. to enable her to bring up their ch.

20½ **THOMAS**, nephew of (11), at Kit. 1666.

21 **THOMAS**, signed ptn. with Exeter men 1689-90. List 57.

22 **WALTER**, Oyster River, his homestead on no. side bet. Wm. Beard and Philip Chesley. A Scotch prisoner and prob. first there in service at the mills. Recd. inhab. 10 Jan. 1658-9; gr. 20 a. at head of own lot 1666. Lists 74, 356d, 361a, 363abc, 364, 365, 366, 359a(2). His w. Jane and her form. master, Mr. Andrew Wiggin, were in Ct. 25 June 1667, he found not guilty. D. 1683; adm. 18 Mar. 1697-8 to s. William. Widow prob. m. 2d Henry Rice, but called 'Jackson' when k. by Ind. 169-. Ch: **William**, oldest, ±65 Feb. 1734, had 20 a. gr. at head of fa.'s land, 1694. Lists 62, 96, 368ab, 369. His w. Mary adm. to Oyster Riv. Ch. 24 May 1724, where he was bp. 24 Dec. 1727. Will 8 Feb. 1757—30 Jan. 1760, names her and 3 ch., all bp. 23 Aug. 1724: William, b. 1715 by depos., sued with his fa. in 1734; Meribah, m. Robt. Huckins; Benjamin. **Elizabeth**, m. by July 1701 Henry Marsh. **Mary**, m. by July 1701 Timothy Moses. **Jane**; July 15, 1712 Francis Drew gave bond to supp. her ch. 7 yrs. **James**, s.-in-law (stepson) of Henry Rice and adm. his est. Mary Tasker acc. him 12 Aug. 1698, her ch. b. 20 Apr. List 368b. He was bp. the day bef. he d. 3 Mar. 1717-8. Wid. Sarah bp. 21 Sept. fol. with her ch: Samuel (List 369), Joseph, Sarah, Abigail, Keziah. James, appar. eldest son and poss. not Sarah's, was gr. adm. of his fa.'s est. 8 Sept. 1725; m. Sarah Jordan(3). Ch. incl. James and Robt. bp. Dover 21 Mar. 1736, and poss. Solomon bp. 23 June 1728, m. (his cousin?) Sarah Jordan.

23 **WILLIAM**, Shoals, abs. from meet. 9 July 1667; sued by Thos. Wayle in Wells Ct. 1670, forfeiture of a bond. Of Portsm. adm. to Thos. Daniel 8 May 1672, inv. £8. **Hannah**, servant of Mr. Daniel in 1679, ±19, likely his dau.

**JACOBS**, most frequent in Somerset and Norfolk.

1 **DANIEL**, Dover, had gr. 19 Mar. 1693-4, laid out 19 Dec. 1701 to his wid. Abigail Field(12), m. 24 Oct. 1697. List 318b. She d. 14 Feb. 1704-5. List 96. Ch: **Daniel**, his

fa.'s gr. relaid to him in 1722; liv. Dover 1755. List 358c. See Bunker (3).

2 **GEORGE**, Wells, b. Salem 29 Sept. 1677, s. of Geo. and Rebecca (Frost), gr. s. of Geo., the witchcraft victim, and br. of Margaret the unhappy witness at that time. He m. in Wells 26 Dec. 1701 Hannah Cousins (4), 2d Elizabeth (Donnell 4) Burnham. Tr. j. 1703. List 269c. Will 21 Feb. 1750—24 Apr. 1751. See 'Ancestry of Lydia Harmon', W. G. Davis, p. 51, for 9 ch. 1702-1723.

3 **HENRY**, seaman, Portsm., 1689-90. List 333a.

4 **JOHN** (Jacob), Mr., from Ipsw., br. of (7), serv. of Mr. John Paine 1663, witn. a Hog Isl. deed to Thos. Daniel 22 Oct. 1670. Falm. grantee 1680. Lists 313a, 225a, 91.

5 **JOSEPH**, k. by Ind. at Winnegance Sept. 1697. List 96.

6 **JOSEPH** and **SUSANNA** (Jacob). Y. D. 8.227. See Symonds.

7 **Ens. NATHANIEL** (Jacob), br. of (4), Falm. grantee. List 225a.

8 **SKIPPER**, 1660. P. & Ct. ii. 367-8.

Jaffrey, see Jeffrey.

James, the Frenchman. List 356m.

**JAMES**, numerous on both sides of the Bristol channel.

1 **BENJAMIN** (Edmund), weaver, b. Newb. 15 Apr. 1673, came to Hampt. as John Stockbridge's apprent. Hampt. soldier at Oyster Riv. 1695-96, and at Ft. William & Mary 1708. List 399a. Constable 1728. M. at Hampt. 23 July 1702 Susanna Smith (John), who d. bef. him. Will 10 Aug. 1744, d. 5 May 1747. See Dow's Hampt. for 8 ch.

2 **FRANCIS**, Exeter, m. Elizabeth Hall. Ch: **Kinsley, Dudley, Francis**, rec. 1709-15, **Benjamin**. One Mrs. James d. at Ichabod Clark's at Stratham 26 Jan. 1752.

3 **MATTHEW**, m. at Portsm. 20 Nov. 1712 Catherine Clark (10). **Richard, Eleanor, John, Paddison**, bp. at No. Ch. 1713-1722, likely their ch. He was taxed, and ho., Grafford Lane, 1724. List 339. Both liv. Somersworth 1739.

4 **NATHANIEL**, sr., and Nathl. (James?). List 57.

5 **OWEL** (Howell?), Pemaquid soldier 1689. List 126.

6 **RICHARD**, of Charlestown, m. at Portsm. 16 May 1722 Abigail (Broughton 2) Walker, and left her. He was taxed Portsm. 1727, 'gone' in Jan. 1731-2.

7 **THOMAS**, adm. to James Blagdon 27 June 1671.

8 **WILLIAM**, fisherman, Shoals, sued Mr. John Seeley in 1647 for wages he had already recd. from Mr. Browne. If the man, and w. Elizabeth, held at Salem Ct. in Sept. 1636, and whose w. was disporting with

Philip Cromwell there in 1647, aft. which both disappeared (perh. to R. I.), he hims. was liv. suspiciously with Wm. Wormwood's w. in Me. in 1650 and Oct. 1651, altho he and Wormwood had been ord. to part households in June 1648. In June 1651, planter, he sold dwg. in Crooked Lane, Kit., recently bot from Alex. Jones. Going East, he took O. A. to Plymouth Govt. at Merry Meeting in 1654, to the King at Sheepscot in 1665; witn. Ind. deed to Geo. Davie 1668, and was liv. Sheepscot 1672. Lists 11, 12, 13. One Mary m. Randall Frierson at Beverly 16 Mar. 1687-8. Note (9), (10).

9 **WILLIAM**, sold liquor at Saco in July 1702, likely the same k. at Black Point 6 Oct. 1703, and the same who m. Honor Dicer (Wm.) at Wells, 26 Dec. 1700. List 96. She m. 2d in 1705 David Ridley, their dau. appar. her only heir.

10 **WILLIAM** (Guillaume), ag. 30, with Me. people at Montreal in Nov. 1702, remaining for love for the religion, app. not (9). List 99, p. 123. One Wm. had s. John bp. So. Ch., Portsm., 10 Feb. 1744-5, where one Ann was adm. to com. 3 Jan. 1741-2, and John, adult, bp. 29 Mar. fol. One Thos. was taxed Portsm. 1727, no William.

**JAMESON,** found in the counties of the Scottish border.

1 **JOHN**, (Jemson), ±24 in 1664, apprent. to Jos. Davis (36) 1659-1661, later of Amesbury. Essex Q. Ct. 3.58, 213.

2 **PATRICK** (Gymmison, Gimson, Jeanison), Oyster River, taxed 1657 as Patrick the Scot. Mr. Val. Hill conv. land to him in 1659 and told that he had been a useful servant ab. his mill; town gr. 1663. Lists 356d, 361a, 363abc, 365, 47, 357b, 366. In Sept. 1669 he was under indictm. in Boston for mistreatment of Grace Roberts, ag. 8, of Oyster Riv., which caused the enactment of the death penalty for such crime 13 Oct. 1669, tho his sentence, if any, permitted him to be in Saco, drunk 5 July 1670, when Maj. Pendleton paid part of his fine. At Yarm. Falls with Henry Sayward 1674; at Wells abs. from meet., 1675; adm. 2 Oct. 1678 to Saml. Austin (7). At Oyster Riv., yrs. later, one Wm. Jennison, 3 days old, was bp. 28 Jan. 1720-1.

3 **WILLIAM**, tailor, Charlestown, m. 18 Oct. 1677 Sarah Price of Salem, sis.-in-law of John Edwards (4); she d. 24 Mar. 1691. He bot 100 a. at Purpoodock Point from Joel Maddiver in Mar. 1697-8. Will 29 Jan.—9 May 1714, names w. Mary, and devises r. e., ½ to s. John, ⅛ each to two sons-in-law and two unm. daus. Ch. by 1st w: **William**, b. 26 May 1679, d. y. **Margaret**, b. 2 June 1680, m. Thos. Ferrand. **William**, b. 20 Jan. 1682-3, not in will, had Scarb. gr.

1720, and bot 50 a. in Spurwink from Jeremiah Jordan in Apr. 1723. Of Falm., he deeded to s. Martin 1733, his Scarb. gr. to gr. s. Wm. McKenney (Robert), 27 July 1734. 8 or m. ch. **Sarah**, bp. 29 June 1684, m. in Boston 5 Apr. 1722 Jos. Uran. **John**, b. 27 Oct. 1686. **Elizabeth**, b. 15 Nov. 1689, m. in Eng. 1714 John Haydon. **Mary**, b. 13 Mar. 1690-1, m. bef. 29 Jan. 1713-4 Benj. Purington.

**JANVRIN** (Jambrin).

1 **JOHN**, Capt., mariner, Portsm., from Isle of Jersey, his parents named by the Brackett Gen. as Jean Janvrin and Elizabeth LeCosteur, poss. intended for le Couteur, an armorial fam. there. He m. 12 Sept. 1706 Elizabeth Knight(9), whose fa. deeded to her in Feb. 1717-8 the Portsm. ho. she was liv. in and deeded to her husb. 23 Apr. 1719. Adm. to her, bond with Clement Hughes and Jos. Sherburne 13 Oct. 1720, when he prob. had been dead some time, as she m. 2d 23 Oct. 1720 Rev. Jos. Adams of Newington; d. 10 Feb. 1757. Ch., bp. No. Ch.: **John**, 2 Oct. 1709, H. C. 1728, schoolmaster Kit. 1732, Berw. 1743, Newington 1751, when heirs of Wm. Knight sold him ho. and 53 a. in Newington; d. 1780. Mrs. Mary adm. to Newington Ch. with him 5 Nov. 1738, poss. his sis., not w. **Elizabeth**, 30 Sept. 1711, adm. to Newingt. Ch. 19 June 1727. **George**, 19 July 1713, m. 10 Nov. 1738 Elizabeth Mendum of Portsm. Son Mendum bp. So. Ch. Jan. 1745-6. **Mary**, prob. the ch. bp. Dec. 1715, named in gr. fa. Knight's will; m. 19 May 1743 Thos. Pickering of Newingt.

2 **THOMAS** (Janverie) dealing with Clement Campion 6 May 1648.

**JAQUES**, 1 **Henry**, from Newbury, m. by Rev. Mr. Pike 28 June 1706 to Rebecca Pickering (Thos.). He subsc. for Rev. Mr. Emerson in 1713, she renewed bap. covt. in So. Ch. 16 Jan. 1716-7. Adm. on his est. to her br. Joshua 9 Mar. 1721-2, she renounce. M. 2d 24 Sept. 1724 Paul Wentworth of Kit. and in 1759 was a pauper at Ephraim Pickering's in Newington, trying to get supp. from her Brackett gr. sons. Ch: **Paul**, bp. So. Ch. 16 Jan. 1716-7. In 1731, ±19, (Jaquish), he was servant of John Woodman. **Sarah**, b. Newingt. 19 Sept. 1709 (mo.'s depos.), bp. with Paul; m. Samuel Brackett of Newmarket.

2 **LIEUT. RICHARD**, York. List 279. See Harmon (5).

**JARVIS**, 1 **Humphrey** (Jarvice) 1668. Y. D. x. 261.

2 **WILLIAM**, Portsmouth 1695. List 334b.

**Jassem**, Philip the Jassem (Jerseyman?), Newcastle 1693. List 313g.

**Jaye**, Thomas, 1650. See Joy (3).

**JEFFORD**, Jefferd, not in Lower's or Guppy's handbooks and must be extremely rare.

1 **FRANCIS**, Falmouth 1684, owned at the Neck and at Muscle Cove, where his ho. was. List 225a. His landing place ment. in Apr. 1689. Poss. soon an Ind. victim. In 17-- Dennis Murrough claimed a lot bot from Moses Durin bet. the grantee and Widow -Tefford-. He had served in Philip's War from Salem, where his ch. (mother not found) were later: **John**, had 6 ch. by 1st w. **Mary**, 4 bp. 1710-1714 at Salem, 1 bp. 1716 at Topsfield; liv. Topsf. 23 June 1719 when he agreed with his sis. and their husb. ab. the div. of the Me. land. He m. 2d in Salem 5 May 1721 Lydia Bailey; 6 ch. rec. Hopkinton 1722-1735. Will, of Hopkinton, 15 Jan., inv. 21 Sept. 1740, names w. and all ch. but 1st son. **Elizabeth**, w. of John Perkins of Andover, 1719. **Elinor**, m. bef. 1715-6 James Curtis of Boxford; liv. 23 June 1719, d. bef. Jan. 1723-4. 2 ch. Y. D. 11.68.

2 **JAMES** (Geffords). List 289.

3 **ROGER** (Jeffard), Portsm., liv. from w. Aug. 1668.

4 **REV. SAMUEL**, b. Salem 6 Apr. 1704, s. of Simon and Elizabeth (Cole), H. C. 1722, ordained 15 Dec. 1725 minister at Wells, where he cont. until death 2 Feb. 1752, and m. 27 Oct. 1727 Sarah Wheelwright (Rev. John). She d. 14 Feb. 1762. 10 ch.

5 **WILLIAM**, ±30, 12 June 1680, went with Wm. Harford to Rich. Otis's ho.

**JEFFREY**, Jefferies, have their principal home in the counties from Wiltshire to Cornwall. See Creber.

1 **BARNABY**, witn. for Mark Hunking 18 Aug. 1666. Patience, presum. w. or dau., may or may not have m. John Crucy, whose dame was Margaret (Hunking) Adams(5). As Jefferys she witn. deed to Francis Hooke 5 Feb. 1675-6. Y. D. ii. 187. See Crucy (1, 2, 6, 8, 10); Patience Bonython(2).

2 **DAVID** (Jeffries) Boston mercht. many yrs., with N. H. relations thru his fa.-in-law Lt. Gov. John Usher, and s. of ano. David, mercht., of Taunton, co. Somerset, Eng. N. E. Reg. 53.23. He was liv. in Portsm. 1727-1733; depos. there in May 1733, ±74, that he form. liv. with Mr. Sampson Sheafe late of Boston. O. A. in Boston 21 Apr. 1679. With John Usher he was bondsm. for Esther Jose(2) in Boston Feb. 1693-4; witn. in Newc. Nov. 1698; John Hunking was writing to him in 1712. List 98. Wife Elizabeth Usher, m. 15 Sept. 1686, d. 27 June 1698. See Legate(2). Ch: **Jane**, b. 4 July 1687, d. 1703. **John**, b. 5 Feb. 1688-9, Boston mercht. **David**, b. 15 June 1690, H. C. 1708, Boston mercht., m.

18 Mar. 1713 Katherine Eyre; d. in Gt. Brit. 13 Sept. 1715. Son David m. Sarah Jaffrey (4 jr.) whose gr. s. was her bro. George's heir. **Elizabeth**, b. 12 Feb. 1691-2, m. 1st Chas. Sheepreve, 2d Benj. Eliot. **Rebecca**, b. 9 Dec. 1693, m. Capt. Ebenezer Wentworth. **Sarah**, b. 4 May 1695, m. Geo. Jaffrey jr.(4). **Frances**, b. 12 July 1696, d. 1714. **Peter**, b. 18 Nov. 1697, d. 1698.

3 **DIGORY**, carpenter, Kittery, bot from Mr. Shapleigh 4 a. adj. the ho. he was liv. in and two small islands, Feb. 1662-3; sold and bot from Wm. Broad in June 1670 the Kit. Point ho. succes. owned by Geo. Palmer and Dr. Greenland, and with Broad won a suit brot against them by Palmer's adm. Jas. Neighbours. Constable 1664; Gr. j. 1674. Twice bondsman for Greenland 1671, 1672. Lists 380, 26, 286, 288, 30, 298, 33, 292. He m. Mary Rowe, wid., dau. of Robt. Mussell of Newcastle; she was liv. 5 June 1669, perh. not in 1676 when Mary (Pearce) Jones was suspected of being in his ho. and Ann Rowe, w. of his step-s. Richard, sent there in haste to find out ab. it. He was bondsm. for Elinor Pearce, admx., 1674; had a steer belonging to Jos. Pearce 1676. See Cawley(4). With last w. Anne, wid. of Thos. Crockett, he deeded the home place to Roger Deering 1 Sept. 1694, reserv. life est., and so concealing the identity of ch., if any. See Patience(1). 'His little boy' in his ho. 1676 may have been an apprentice. He was liv. 22 June 1695; she in 1701.

4 ‡*GEORGE (Jaffrey), Esq., Portsmouth, liv. on Great Isl., Councilor hims. and fa. and gr. fa. of councilors. A Scotch mercht., first at Boston, where his countryman Patrick Crawford gave him a P/A 25 Mar. 1676; he bot that yr. on Star Isl. from John Winsland; lic. retailer to fishermen 1677. In Portsm. tything list 1678; on committee asking for their own minister at Great Isl. 1679; in 1684, of Portsm., gave genl. P/A to John Macgowen resid. at Piscataqua. For his troubles in Cranfield's time see N. H. Prov. Papers 1.502 passim. Lists 331bc, 313a, 49, 317, 51, 90, 98, 324, 335a, 330df, 336c, 96. Portsm. Constable 1683; Selectm. 1695, 1700, 1702; Rep. (Speaker) 1694-95; Magistrate; Councilor 1702. D. at Ipsw. on way home from Boston 13 Feb. 1707, ag. 69 (altho ±27 in 1680). Adm. 20 Feb. to s. Geo., the wid. renounc. His 1st w. Ann (Agnes by deed 1682) d. 6 Dec. 1682, ag. 18 (Pt. of Graves); he m. at Mr. Peter Butler's ho. in Boston 28 Nov. 1694 Mrs. Hannah Porter. She was adm. to No. Ch. in Apr. 1709; m. bet. 20 Oct. 1709—20 May 1710 Col. Penn Townsend of Boston; buried 1 Nov. 1736. Ch. by 1st w: ‡*George, Esq., b. Great Isl. 22 Nov. 1682, H. C. 1702,

Portsm. Selectm. 1712-1717, Rep. 1710, Councilor 1716, Judge of Sup. Ct. Lists 324, 337, 339. He m. 1st 10 Jan. 1710-11 Sarah Jefferies(2), d. 12 Jan. 1734; 2d 9 Mar. 1738-9 Sarah (Wentworth, dau. of Lt. Gov. John), wid. of Archibald McPhedris, a Councilor. He d. 8 May 1749, ag. 66, adm. 30 May to s. Geo., the wid. declining. She liv. 1754; step-son ptn. for div. of her dower 16 Dec. 1783. 4 ch. by 1st w., incl. George, Esq., only s., b. 8 Feb. 1717-8, H. C. 1736, Councilor, Chief Justice, Treasurer of the Prov., who willed his prop. to a gr. s. of his sis. Sarah, bp. 1 Apr. 1722, m. David Jefferies, on cond. the young man take his name, make Portsm. his perma. home, and follow no occup. but that of being a gentleman.

5 GREGORY, Cape Porpus, gr. 200 a. there by Cleeve Nov. 1651, poss. newly arriv. as in Aug. 1661, ±60, he depos. conc. the place ab. 10 yrs. back. Constable 1658; town Comr. 1659. Suit in Portsm. Ct. 1660. Lists 251, 252, 24, 11, 244d, 254. On Jan. 7, 1661-2 he witn. will of Wm. Scadlock, whose s. John witn. his own will 14 Jan., 2 or 3 days bef. he d.; w. and kinsm. Chas. Potum (who called him uncle), execs.; Saco Church remembered. Inv. 17 Feb. 1661-2; adm. again 7 July 1663 to Bartholomew Drew. P. & Ct. 1.233 passim. Unlikely that his wid. Mary, who m. John Lux(3), was his 1st w., and he may have been the G. J. whose s. John was bp. 12 Sept. 1633, dau. Grace 23 Oct. 1636, both at Stoke-in-Teignhead, co. Devon, where one Chas. Potum, son of Robt., was bp. 3 Mar. 1632-3. Ch: John, b. ±1660, chose his step-fa. gdn. in Suff. Ct. 1674. He witn. John Leeds's will at York 1678; in Aug. 1690 he and Wm. Scadlock, both ±30, depos. at Boston that they saw plank delv. at Saco in summer of 1689. Liv. Lynn, and depos. May 1732, ±71, 45 or 46 yrs. bef. was at Scarb. in a brigantine for boards; d. bef. 10 Mar. 1734. W. Joanna. 8 ch. rec. Lynn (Jefferds) 1690-1714, incl: Elizabeth, b. 14 June 1690, m. Peter Hinkson(6); Joseph and Benjamin, coopers, who sold their share of their gr. fa.'s 200 a. in Cape Porpus to Jacob Wildes and Moses Foster 1734-5. Child, unborn by fa.'s will, not in mo.'s will 8 Sept. 1664; two ch. ment. in Ct. order July 1662.

6 GYLES (Jefferys) m. in Greenland 23 Sept. 1736 Joanna Benson(1). The same or ano. m. Mary Edwards in Boston 7 Dec. 1741. One Rachel (Jarfey or Jarfoy) d. Greenl. 6 Apr. 1738.

7 CAPT. JAMES, Portsmouth 1702, lawyer, N. P., Clerk of the Assembly, and memb. of import. committees, Capt. by 1712, m. by 1719, likely much earlier, Anna (Gerrish 3), wid. of Capt. Andrew Brock(1). Lists (?)289, 339. He witn. in 1733 with ?Cyprien,

shopkeeper, Portsm., who, if a son, was poss. by an earlier mar. Cyprien witn. Anna J.'s deed 1720; taxed so. side Grafforts Lane 1726. Like James (jr.) he kept a diary, and as dep. to David Dunbar, Surv. Genl. of H. M. Woods, compl. 5 Feb. 1738-9 ab. his treatment by millmen at Saco when John Bryant tore his wig off. He m. by 1743 Olive (Phipps), wid. of Saml. Winkley; both liv. 1766. Surely a son, James, Salem, d. 13 Feb. 1755, ag. 49, wrote his bro. from Salem 1745, sending duty to fa. and mo., and speaking of demand on Uncle Gerrish's est.

8 WILLIAM (Jeffries), Mr., gent., 'old planter,' at Weymouth 1623, and assoc. early with Salem, Manchester (Jeffreys Creek), Ipswich; s. of Wm. and Audrey J. of Chittingleigh, co. Sussex, grad. Caius Coll., Cambridge, 1606. He was named in Vines Patent Feb. 1629-30 to give poss., but did not; freeman 1631; York patentee 1637; with Nich. Easton built the first ho. at Hampton. Lists 271, 272. Of Weymouth 1640-1 he gave bond with his w.'s fa. or br. Jeremy Gould of R. I., removed to Newport by 1652 and d. there 2 Jan. 1675 in 85th yr., will 8 Dec. 1674 naming w. Mary, 5 ch. See Austin's R. I. Dict., also his Allied Families; Waters i. 5.

JELLISON (Gillison), Nicholas, liv. on 50 a. gr. him 13 Apr. 1671 near White's Marsh, now So. Berw., on road to Wells. Sept. 10, 1706 he deeded this place to three sons who in July 1715 were ord. to supp. their aged fa. and mo. Wid. Barbara (Green) ptn. for relief 4 Apr. 1721 as her ch. were not supp. her. In 1683 her mo. had deeded to her sons. Y. D. 7.77. Lists 290, 296, 298. Ch: John, given land by gr. fa. Green in 1680, not named in fa.'s deed 1706. Nicholas, Berwick, m. 23 Dec. 1707 Hannah Nason (John). Besides ch. John, Bridget, Hezekiah, all bp. 2 Nov. 1721, and Wm. bp. 14 Apr. 1727, was Mary, apprent. to John Tibbetts, Dover, who did not teach her to read, claimed she couldn't learn; she boarded 1730 to 1731 with Jos. Jellison who taught her to read and sued her fa. therefor in 1732. Charity, acc. Joshua Plaisted in 1744, poss. his or dau. of Joseph, Berwick, bot ¼ of fa.'s homestead from br. Ichabod 1719. M. Sarah Gray (4), who had a quarrel with Wid. Elizabeth Gray in 1732 so violent the Ch. took action; she m. 2d 11 Jan. 1753 Nich. Cane of Phillipstown. 9 ch., 8 bp. 20 June 1723. Ichabod, ±20 in 1710, servant of Sergt. Peter Nowell of York; m. in Portsm. 25 May 1714 Patience (Donnell 3), wid. of Miles Rhodes, and liv. in Kit. Will 18 Nov. 1752—1 Jan. 1753 names w. and 5 of 6 ch., incl. Benj., princ. heir who was to supp. his mo. (one Benj. m. Agnes

Patten, int. Wells 8 July 1749); Ichabod, m. Elinor Junkins at York 3 Nov. 1751; Nathaniel, m. Hannah Sedgley, int. York 20 Jan. 1746-7.

Jemson, see Jameson.

JENKINS, sometimes Jenks. Common in So. Wales and also found in Cornwall. See Creber.

1 ——, Cape Porpus, form. of Dorchester (Sav. says prob. Reginald), robbed and k. by Ind. while on a trading trip into the country, 1632.

2 HENRY, small inv. 30 June 1670 signed by Wm. Furber.

3 HENRY, Pemaquid 1687. List 124.

4 JABEZ (9), Kittery, ±27 in May 1682, m. bet. 9 Dec. 1678—19 Apr. 1680 Hannah Curtis (9). Constable 1683. Gr. j. 1690, 1691, 1693, 1694; tr. j. 1690. In 1695 he was bondsm. for Job Clements (4). Lists 30, 298. D. 2 Nov., adm. 24 Dec. 1697 to wid. Hannah, she liv. 1737. Ch: Reynold, d. 9 Jan. 1735, m. 19 May 1712 Elizabeth Canney (1), who was liv. 1765. In 1717 he and Wm. Fry, adms. of Moses Boody's est., were sued by John and Elizabeth Field and Elizabeth Alcock. Lists 296, 297, 298. 7 ch. Jabez, Quaker, Lynn 1703, was in the Liberties of Philadelphia Feb. 1710-11. Thomas, blacksmith, youngest son 1708, m. 14 Dec. 1708 Anne Dixon (2). In 1710 he had built a ho. and shop near Elihu Gunnison jr. Lists 296, 297. D. 25 Sept. 1740, wid. in May 1749. 11 ch. Sarah, m. 23 May 1711 Danl. Stone. Mary, m. 11 Mar. 1714-5 John Eldridge. Hannah, m. Francis Allen (12). Philadelphia, m. (int. Boston 27 Dec. 1710) Isaac Clark of Lynn, 2d (int. Boston 14 June 1715) Jacob Boardman of Gt. Brit.; liv. 1737.

5 JAMES (Jenkin or Jackin) witn. Jas. Cole's deed to Clark & Lake 22 July 1658.

6 JOSEPH, lawsuit in Piscataqua Ct. 1642.

7 JOSEPH. List 94.

8 JOSEPH, Oyster River, poss. came from Mass. with w. Hannah Merrow or Merry (Henry); she was b. in Reading 5 Mar. 1668-9, and depos. in 1704, ag. 36. He had Dover grants 1694, 1699, 1701. Lists 358bd, 368ab. Last w. Tabitha Weymouth (Wm.) m. 27 Apr. 1743, named in his will 20 Aug. 1754—12 Nov. 1755, was long a preacher among the Friends and d. of old age 18 Feb. 1777. Ch: Joseph, d. 26 Dec. 1730, unm. In 1727 Danl. and Deborah Meserve named Saml. Merry as uncle of Joseph jr., William and Sarah Jenkins, who were at the Meserve home; in 1732 his five bros. and sis. sold his Rochester gr. William, m. Phebe Hoag of Hampton. List 369. 8 ch. 1743-1756. John, left wid. Hannah and dau. Sarah Randall.

List 369. Sarah, m. Jeremiah Davis (40). Jemima, m. 23 Dec. 1736 Joseph Hoag. Keziah, m. 11 Dec. 1734 David Hoag.

9 REYNOLD, Kittery, b. ±1608. One Reynold m. Anne Gale in Broomfield, co. Somerset, 29 June 1635. If the Me. man, he left her behind while at Richmond Isl. 1636-1639; and his son Stephen's -grandmotherk. at Oyster Riv. in July 1694, as Stephen's wid. depos., could hardly have been mo. of either. He was in Kit. (Eliot) 1647, depos. 23 July 1683 ±75, that he bot 6 a. from John Newgrove bet. 40 and 50 yrs. ago, built and liv. upon it a time. Widow Everett invested her dau. Martha's 10 s. by buying this for her, but when she m., her husb. refused to accept it at the price, so her mother gave him a steer instead and sold the land to Wm. Leighton. A Quaker and prosec. 1668, 1675, abs. from meeting. Lists 21, 282, 283, 298. W. Ann, liv. 1661, likely d. bef. 10 Feb. 1678, when he deeded to s. Stephen for support. Ch: Philadelphia, b. ±1645, m. 1st Lt. Edw. Hayes (2), 2d Matthew Estes (1). Mary, m. 1st John Green (13), 2d Humphrey Axall. Sarah, m. 1st ab. 1670 Jona. Nason, 2d John Key(1). Stephen, b. ±1654, oldest s. in 1678. Jabez, b. ±1655.

10 ROBERT, P. & Ct. ii. 287. See Junkins.

11 ROWLAND, fisherman, Dover, Lower Kittery, Newcastle, of whom John Manson wrote 'Jenks, vulgarly called Jenkins.' Of Dover, he m. 1st (Ct. Mar. 1698-9) Experience (Otis) Heard, who d. 8 Feb. 1699-1700, List 96; m. 2d 10 Feb. 1700-1 Tabitha Joy (1) who depos. in May 1705, ±26, ab. Heards; 3d Mary Morgrage (John) bef. July 1710 when she (Jenkins) and John White were acc.; in 1707 (Morgrage) she had acc. Danl. Green. He was taxed in Newc. 1708, liv. there 1715. Lists 336c, 316. She was acc. of stealing ribbon in 1712; in 1714 her br. wrote to Mrs. Sarah Sheafe ab. a £5 note Mrs. S. had changed for her; next mo. Mrs. Katherine Weymouth depos. she never heard any good of her. In 1715 both charged with stealing. Uncert. marks his fam: one child by 1st w., who may have d. In 1710 he had two small ch., perh. not counting some who may have been in service; in 1712 he recovered dau. Ruth from her master Jona. Weeks of Portsm. Rowland, incl. bec. of his name, m. (int. 17 Aug. 1730) Mary Nason. 12 ch. ?Susanna (poss. named for Tabitha Joy's mo.), m. 1729 Joseph Foye (2).

12 STEPHEN (9), ±28 in May 1682, ±30 in Sept. 1683. Of Piscataqua, he was acc. by Mary Chelson in Suff. Ct. 25 Apr. 1676; of Kit. 23 Mar. 1686-7 bot from Wm. Williams sr. and Saml. Hill at Oyster River. Tav. lic. O. R. 1689. There his 1st w. Elizabeth Pitman (Wm.) drowned herself in

1687 (List 367a), and he and one ch. were k. by Ind. 18 July 1694. Lists 30, 57, 62, 298, 367ab. His 2d w. Ann (Tozier), taken with 3 ch., ret. in time to make a graphic depos. 11 June 1695, used at the trial in Boston of Chief Bomazeen, whom she had seen k. husb. and ch. List 367b. Adm. on his est. to br. Jabez 26 July 1694. She m. 2d David Kincaid (1), 3d Thos. Potts. Ch. incl. two or m. by 1st w.: **Stephen**, bondsman in 1702 for Elizabeth Harford (2), and in 1723 made over his int. in his fa.'s Kit. gr. to her husb. Nich. H. M. bef. 16 Dec. 1709 Elizabeth Dean(1). Lists 368b, 369. 8 or m. ch. **William**, depos. in 1737, ±54, that he liv. with Wid. (Stephen) Jones upw. of 20 yrs.; bot from br. Stephen in 1709. Presum. he who m. 25 Nov. 1714 Alice (Whidden), wid. of Saml. Haines (6), and was innholder, Greenland, where she d. 19 Jan. 1752; he m. 2d 9 Nov. 1752 Mrs. Mary Fernald of Portsm., named in his will 1757—1763 with 1 son, 2 mar. daus. Appar. a dau.: **Elizabeth**, m. Nich. Harford(2). By 2d w.: **Child**, k. by Bomazeen, and poss. all of the **three** carried away, incl. **Azariah**, still in Canada 1711. List 99, p. 92.

**Jenkinson,** ————, Dr., courting Lydia Spinney, k. by Ind. 172-.

**JENKS**, 1 **Ann**, witn. Hampton deed with Wm. Waldron 5 May 1645. Suff. D. i. 68.

2 **JOSEPH**, blacksmith, ironmaster, at York latter part of 1641; abutted John Alcock Mar. 1642-3. List 22. In N. H. 10 Nov. 1642 he sued John Phillips; Wm. Jones and Wm. Abington sued him. Lynn propr. 1645, where he depos. in 1681, ag. 81, ab. Richard Leader and d. Mar. 1682-3. Poss. an early w. was Ann (1), tho by trad. he came a widower, from Hounslow, co. Middlesex, or Colnbrook, co. Bucks. Elizabeth, his w. 1660, d. July 1679. Ch: **Joseph**, founder of the R. I. fam. **Sarah**, m. John Chilson(3). Rec. Lynn: **Deborah**, 11 June 1658. **John**, 27 July 1660. **Daniel**, 19 Apr. 1663.

3 **PETER** (Ginks), soldier at Wells. List 267b.

4 **STEVEN** (Ginks). List 367b. See Jenkins.

**JENNER**, poss. from the medieval 'Ginour', a craftsman.

1 **PATRICK**, Dover, bot. ho. from Val. Hill May 1659. See Jameson.

2 **REV. THOMAS**, non-conform. minis. at Saco, s. of ano. Thos., farmer, of Fordham, co. Essex, matric. at Christ's Coll., Cambridge, 1623-4. Possibil. that his fa. accomp. him to Roxbury 1634 (or 5), Charlestown and Weymouth 1636, is found in Weym. gr. 1636 to Mr. J. sr. and jr., and two men taking Freeman's Oath, 1636 (Mr. Thos. Jenner), 1639 (Mr. Thos. Gin-

ner). Dep. from Weym. 1640; from Saco wrote to Winthrop last mo., 1640, again 16 Apr. 1641 that he found the people superstitious and addicted to Papist practices; by Jan. 1641-2 minis. for both sides the river at salary of £47; on wings of removal 6 Apr. 1646, but knew not whither. 4 Mass. H. S. Col. 7.356-8. Settled at Cottishall, co. Norfolk, 1647-1658; d. in Ireland. W. was in Charlestown 1649-50, when as Mrs. J. she consented to s. Thos.'s sale of his fa.'s Weymouth land; if the Esther J. adm. to Charlest. Ch. 9 July 1648, without prefix of respect that was her due, she d. bef. husb., whose will 4 June 1672—26 May 1676 (Dublin Wills), names w. Ellen and ch., one s. and gr. ch. being in N. E.: Capt. **Thomas**, mariner, Charlest., of age 28 Jan. 1649-50, 28 in 1656, ±40 in 1670. M. 2 May 1655 Rebecca Trerice and was with Thos. Kemble (7) and John Phillips on a trading voyage at the Kennebec, when their ship -The John of Boston-, commanded by himself, was taken by John Pierce under authority of Capt. Allen of Penobscot Fort. News of his death in Eng. recd. 12 Dec. 1686. How he was s. of Wid. Wensley 1686 (Sewall's Diary) is unkn. 8 ch., incl. Thos., who went to Brookhaven, L. I., where was an earlier John Jenner. **David**. **Jonathan**. **Rachel**, Blackshaw in will, poss. the eldest dau. whose affec. Mr. Francis Robinson had secretly engaged, 1646. Daus. who d. bef. him may have incl. the **?Esther** at Charlest.

**Jennery** (Chenery?), ————, Hampton. List 392a.

## JENNESS, often Jennings early.

1 **FRANCIS**, seaman, baker, Hampton, first of Great Isl., where he took O. F. 2 Oct 1666. In Hampt. 15 Feb. 1670 he m. Hannah Swain (Wm.), List 394; bot the Wid. Mary Hussey place, sold in Oct. 1674 and settl. in N. E. part of town, now Rye, where his w.'s step-fa. had deeded 50 a. to him and s. Thos. in 1672; his he made over in 1674 to Thos. and his sis. Hannah, Mr. Cox to be feoffee in trust during his and his w.'s lives. Coroner's jury 1694. Had a garrison ho. 1704. Lists 330a, 395, 396. M. 2d 4 Feb. 1701 Salome, wid. of John White of Portsm., d. at Jos. Locke's in Rye 2 Aug. 1730. He d. 27 Aug. 1716; will 28 Oct. 1714 unproved, ano. 29 Dec. 1715—20 Aug. 1716, making good prov. for wid. and ch: **Thomas**, b 23 Feb. 1671, d. 24 Aug. 1696. **Hannah**, b. 26 Mar. 1673, m. Edward Locke (1). **Hezekiah**, b. 30 Mar. 1675. **John**, b. 14 June 1678, blacksmith, Rye, m. 1st 25 June 1702 Hannah Foss (1), 2d in Portsm. 25 Nov. 1718 Hannah Mason, named in his will 27 Sept. 1740—26 Aug. 1741. By 1st w.: 6 sons, 1 dau. incl. Joshua b. 14 May 1705, m. 16

Nov. 1732 Hannah (Jenness 2) Langdon; Job, b. 15 Oct. 1708, m. at Greenl. 12 Sept. 1735 Mary Jenness(2); Hannah, m. 13 Dec. 1733 Matthias Towle; by 2d w. 3 sons; all ch. in will but Hannah, whose two sons recd. 20 s. **Eleanor**, b. 30 Jan.1681, m. James Berry (5 jr.). **Mehitabel**, b. 1683, m. Matthias Haines(13). Capt. *****Richard**, b. 8 June 1686, first Rep. from new town of Rye. M. 9 Feb. 1710 Mary Dow (10) and was bp. 24 Apr. 1715 when both joined the ch. He d. 1769, she surv. 9 or m. ch.

2 **HEZEKIAH** (1), yeoman, Rye, m. 13 May 1697 Ann Folsom (9), who d. bef. him. Will 10—29 May 1745 names three daus., ch. of decd. s. Thos. and of ano. decd. son, sis.-in-law Deliverance Folsom; s.-in-law Job Jenness exec. Ch: **Thomas**, b. 10 Mar. 1698, m. 17 Oct. 1725 Elizabeth Norton (Bonus), who relinq. adm. on his est. to her br. Jos. 22 Oct. 1731 and m. 20 July 1732 Benjamin Swett. 3 ch. **Francis**, b. 30 Dec. 1699. **Hezekiah**, b. 8 Mar. 1702. **Hannah**, b. 30 Sept. 1704, m. 1st Saml. Langdon (2), 2d Joshua Jenness (John 1). **Anna**, b. 10 Dec. 1706, m. at Newc. 12 Dec. 1734 Thos. Parker. In 1768 her s. Wm. deeded to his fa. land she had bot from her fa. Hezekiah. **John**, b. 4 Apr. 1709, m. 30 Nov. 1732 Elizabeth Seavey (Wm.) who was n. c. m. 1749, liv. Oct. 1752. Will 15 Oct. 1744— 27 Feb. 1744-5 names her, 5 daus. **Mary**, b. 25 Jan. 1718, m. Job Jenness (John 1).

3 **JAMES** (Jeaneg?), m. Mary Pachren (Pickering?) at Rye June 1718. (N. H. Gen. Rec. i. 83). John m. Ann Webster. (N. E. Reg. 27.10); read John Jones.

**JENNINGS.** See also Jenness.

1 **ABRAHAM**, Mr., Plymouth mercht., operating with (2) and Wm. Cross (11) as Jennings & Co. at Monhegan, where they acq. title. In Nov. 1622 he had pd. £110 for his partnership in the mainland but not the ship. List 9.

2 **AMBROSE**, Mr., London mercht. List 9.

**Jent**, see Gent.

**Jerman**, Jermaine, see German.

**Jersie**, Mary, so-called, form. servant of Mr. Jose, wanted to stay with Elizabeth Bowman ab. 1675-6; (Hubertus) Mattoon had promised to take her to New York and mar. her. One Wm. J. taxed Portsm. 1731-2.

**Jesson**, Jessum, see Chisholm.

**JEWELL**, poss. a corruption of the French 'Jules'; found in Cornwall.

1 **GEORGE**, mariner. Bef. 23 July 1632 Capt. Cammock had visited his stage on Richmond or poss. Jewell's Isl., which Henry Donnell(1) held later. Both may have come from Barnstable, co. Devon, where one Geo. J. had ch. bap. as early as 1610; ch. of ano. or the same were bap. at Bovey-Tracy,

co. Devon, 1626-37. Saco 1637, sued by Mr. Gibson(2) and suing Theoph. Davis(54). Drowned in Boston Harb. Nov. 1637.

2 **JOSEPH**, miller, b. Braintree 24 Apr. 1642, s. of Thos. and 2d w. Grissell (Fletcher), Mendon, Watertown and Portsm., where in 1681, a widower with ch. **Martha** and **Joseph** by 1st w. Martha, he made mar. contract with Isabel Cate(2) and bot a ho. from John and Jane Preston. Of Portsm. Aug. 1682, Newb. 1684, Sudbury 1693, where two ch. **Sarah**, **Lydia**, b. 1699-1702; Stowe late; d. bef. 2 Sept. 1736, w. surviving. In 1719 they deeded to s. **John** for support. N. E. Reg. 22.43; Am. Gen. (Jacobus) 10.70.

3 **NATHANIEL**, mariner, Boston. See Weare.

4 **SAMUEL**, York 1650, Shoals 1653. On jury life and death 1650 in trial of Robt. Collins, whose alibi was he was at Mary Jewell's ho. that night. Lists 75b, 301. Inv. in Boston, 29 Oct. 1657, by Wm. Paine and John Sweet, bed and cooking utensils, all, his w. Mary said, but her clothing. She witn. Wm. Hooke's deed 16 July 1650, who 8 days later made her large gift of York land freely in case he did not ret. to N. E.

5 **WILLIAM**?, kn. only by deeds of John Legrow and w. Martha of Salem, John Chin and w. Mary of Marbleh., 1735, each for half of Jewell's Isl. form. the land of their fa. Wm. J. of Casco, decd. (Y. D. 34.123); only evid. a letter from the grantee Jos. Hendley that Wm. liv. and d. in poss. bef. the Ind. War, and depositions, incl. that of John Curtice, Marbleh., that 60 yrs. bef. he and his fa. stopped at Jewell's the only ho. on the island. David Mitchell in 1767 spoke of the grantors as Jewell's wife's two daus.; he was told the fa. was drowned going to the mainland. One John Legrow m. Martha Dutch in Salem 13 Apr. 1699.

**JOCELYN.** For ancestry and full account of this disting. co. Essex family, see N. E. Reg. 71.227.

1 **ABRAHAM** (Joslen), b. ±1619, s. of Thomas of Hingham and Lancaster, his fa. a remote cousin of (6). Liv. with his fa. at Hingh. until ab. 1652, when he mov. to Black Point and settled at 'Jocelyn's great hill' (Scottow's hill). Gr.j. 1658. (Subm. to Mass. 13 July 1658, ?Follen; P. & Ct. ii. 71). Lists 34, 232, 234b. Called of Scarb. 28 Oct. 1659, of Boston 8 June 1660, sold his Scarb. prop. and joined his fam. in Lanc. by 1663. He also owned and sold 'Joslin's Island' near Sheepscot. He d. at sea on ship -Good Fame- betw. 16 Mar. 1669-70 and 7 Apr. 1670, leaving wid. Beatrice (Hampson), dau. of Philip of London, m. in England about the time (1645) as 'one come from N. E.,' he visited a relative there. She

m. 2d, 6 Nov. 1671, Benj. Bosworth (see Austin 4), and was bur. in Boston 11 Jan. 1711-2, ag. 88. 9 ch., incl. **Henry**, b. ±1652, perh. left behind with (2) when his fa. left Scarb., as he is said to have mov. from Scarb. to Scituate in 1669. See also Crocum.

2 †*HENRY (6), Esq., b. 1606, called of Kent in his enrollment at Corpus Christi Coll., Cambridge, in 1623, ag. 17, evid. served time in one of the Inns of Court. Without him in Maine as conciliator our early hist. would have been sadly different. Later on Rishworth did partly the same work, but he was a freq. litigant, Jocelyn never; and without Jocelyn's co-oper., Rishworth could not have accompl. what he did. Jocelyn, the just Judge, whether on or off the bench, conducted so that everyone respected him, and as lord of the Cammock patent, his tenants loved him. His mellow kindness and helpfulness for all in trouble, so that the Indians, when he was in their power, would not harm him, must explain much; while his generosity beyond his means presently lost him his patent to Scottow. Also his consciousness of his background as an Eng. gentleman, to be upheld at any cost, must have figured in his ability to get on with such (eccentric) characters as Godfrey, Cleeve, Jordan. But behold: National Cycl. Am. Biog. vii. 215, 'who throughout his career both as a soldier and magistrate "displayed an unslumbering activity of courage and hate" towards both whites and Indians.' This scorching accus., quoted, with no citation, flies in the face of all kn. facts. Williamson (ii. 682) defended him; Willis (N. E. Reg. xi. 32) praised him. Here as Capt. Neale's lieutenant, 1630-1633, he came to the Piscataqua again the next yr. as governor. One writer contends that while there he liv. on the N. H. side of the river. No doubt the 'Thomson's Point house,' at the south entrance to Cochecho River, built by David Thomson for the salmon fishery, was in his care; 4 m. outside the Hilton patent and aband. by Thomson, it reverted to Gorges & Mason. But a single gentleman, unm., in control of the planta., liv. where he would be best cared for. He had his 500 a. grant laid out on the Me. side reaching as far north as 'Watt's Fort alias Point Joslain,' and also in behalf of the Plantation but from the Ind. on that side. Until the Cammocks left Piscat. he presum. boarded with them, but whether he left Piscat. bef. he knew he was made a judge at Saco is quest. Even aft. his removal he still exercised author. in N. H., and ackn. his liabil. to account to Capt. Francis Norton when he came as Mrs. Mason's agent in 1638. Member of first

court at Saco Mar. 1636. He settled at Black Point by 1637 and m. Margaret, wid. of Capt. Thos. Cammock, who had conv. to him at his death all but 500 a. of his patent there, on which he liv. No record of any Scarb. gr. to himself exists, tho in 1637 Mr. Winter wrote: 'Mr. Vines tells me that Mr. J. is to have 1500 a. above Mr. Cammock's patent in manner and form as Capt. C.'s' and his mortg. to Scottow, 16 July 1666, incl., in addi. to the Cammock land, 750 a. adj. (Y. D. 2.6). Councilor under Sir F. Gorges' first commission 1639; vice Dep. Gov. 1645; Dep. Gov. 1646-8. Adhering to the Lygonia govt., he was during part of the time judge for his own govt. and for the Prov. of Maine. With the coming of Mass., he was one of their strongest opponents, not submitting until 3 July 1658; accepted by them as Town Comr. 1658-9; Magistrate for County Ct.; Dep. from Falm. and Scarb. 1660. In happier times, when the coming in of Charles II brought back the Gorges rule, and later under Royal govt., he was Town Comr., J. P., Associate (with Shapleigh refused to take the oath of office 1662), Comr. for the Province, Chief Justice, until Mass. came again. King P.'s War and the desertion, during his abs., of his garrison ended his period of partial retirement at Black Point, and he was appar. at Kit. or Ports. (Great Island witn. with Robt. Jordan 19 June 1677) until he accepted New York's invitation to settle at Pemaquid. Justice there in August 1677 and contin. at the head of their civil govt. until his death (bef. 10 May 1683), tho at Kit. tempo. in Apr. 1678 (D. H. 6.202) and at Ports. in Nov. 1680. Lists 41, 281, 71, 23, 231, 111, 221, 232, 26, 235, 88, 237ade, 16, 162, 163, 239a. His w. liv. 12 May 1680. No. ch. See Me. P. & Ct. i, ii; Colls. Me. Hist. Soc.; N. E. Reg. 2.204, 11.31, 40.290.

3 **JOHN** (Josselyn) (6), b. ±1608, d. s.p. aft. 1675; traveller, writer and naturalist. He came to Black Point with his fa. in 1638 and ret. to Eng. in 1639, sailing from Boston in the -Fellowship- 10 Oct. 1639 (3 Mass. H. C. 3.211). Came again in 1663, visiting his bro. until Aug. 1671, when he went home. Abs. from meeting in Scarb. 1665, 1667, 1668. In 1672 he pub. 'New England's Rarities Discovered' and in 1674 'An Account of Two Voyages to New England.'

4 **MATTHEW** (Joslian), also Stephen Pearce and Thos. Snell, fined for excessive drinking at James Johnson's, 1649.

5 **RICHARD** (Joslin), Portsmouth, minister's rate rebated, Mar. 1679-80.

6 **SIR THOMAS**, Kt., b. ±1567, 2d s. of Henry, Esq., who was heir in the senior line back to the Norman invaders, but m.

Anne, dau. and heiress of Torrell or Torrell's Hall in Essex, and founded that line, while Sir Thos. himself by his 2d mar. founded the Kentish line. Called 'an ancyent old knight' by Winter, he arrived at Black Point 14 July 1638, brought over and taken back by (3), and sailed for home from Boston without knowing that Sir F. Gorges in his commission dated 2 Sept. 1639 (P. & Ct. i. 30-36) had named him head of his commission for the Province of Maine. He m. 1st Apr. 1589 Dorothy (Frank) Scott who d. 17 May 1602, by whom he had 11 ch., one of whom **Elizabeth**, b. 1597, m. one Francis Neile and had ch., Francis, John and Mary. His 2d wife Theodora (Cooke) Bere, m. ±1603, bur. 13 Aug. 1635, was the mo. of 4 ch., incl. **Henry** and **John**. See also Peyton Cooke(7), whose relationship is not confirmed, and who may have come to Scarb. bef. (2).

**Johns** (Jones?), Catherine, widow, adm. to John Fabyan 26 June 1660.

**JOHNSON**, became 4th commonest name in N. E.

1 —— Mrs. (Johnston), came from Newport, R. I., on visit in Mar. 1714-5, and brot Nathl. Crockett(4).

2 **ALEXANDER**, Scarboro soldier 1675-6. List 237b.

3 **SERGT. ANDREW**, may have come first to Scarb. as a soldier in 1677, poss. the same under Lt. Mosely at Dedham in 1675. Taxed Scarb. 1681, abs. from meet. 1682, witn. for or with Scottow 1685-6, still there 11 Apr. 1687. Lists 184, 237b, 238a, 239a.

4 **BENJAMIN**, apprent. of Wm. Pomfret, Dover, 1679; ran away.

5 **BENJAMIN** (wrote Johnston), weaver, m. in Portsm. 6 Sept. 1720 Sarah Bragdon(3); deed. in Apr. 1742. In 1725 Geo. King sued him for his passage Cork, Ire., to Piscat. 5 ch. rec. York 1720-1734. List 279.

6 **CORNHUTCH**, phonetic for Col. Hutchinson. Y. D. vii. 193.

7 **EDMUND**, Hampton, came in the -James- to Boston in July 1635, ag. 23; to Hampt. in 1639; had ho.-lot there in June 1640. See Coddington. Lists 391ab, 392a, 393ab. D. 1 Mar. 1650-1; adm. 8 Apr. to wid. Mary. List 393a. She m. 2d Thos. Coleman(5), who secured their portions 7 Oct. 1653 to the ch: **Peter**, bp. 1639. **John**, bp. 16 May 1641; had deed from step-fa. 29 Aug. 1662; d. s. p. leaving est. in R. I. **James**, b. ±1643. **Dorcas**, m. at Haverh. 16 Apr. 1672 Saml. Pearson. 9 ch.

8 *****EDWARD**, Mr., gent., York, an Old Planter who stated in 1676 he had liv. in this country 55 yrs.; 2d in list of those drawn to be freeman 30 Oct. 1630. Disaf-

fected, he left Mass. for Me. at an undeterm. date; lic. by Winthrop 1632 to trade (on the Merrimac River?). Tending to confirm that he came with Robt. Gorges to Weymouth, is the fact that in York ab. 1635 when Capt. Champernowne is the kinsm. Sir Ferd. G., and in May 1636 when Alex. Shapleigh wanted one, each had E. J. go to Mr. Bradbury for it. At York, he estab. his 1st home adj. Godfrey. Deputy at Saco 1640; Alderman 1641, 1651-2; Mayor 1647-8; Assoc. Just. 1650, and under Mass. 1652. Com. t. e. s. c. at York 1655, and many yrs.; Selectm. 1662, 1665, 1667, 1669-1673; J. P. 1665-8. Presented 1673 for marrying contrary to law. Lists 22, 274, 275, 276, 277, 24, 26, 33, 84, 88. Early life unkn.; he was been thot a London man, and poss. relat. to (11). Ag. ±82 in Aug. 1678, ±89 in June 1682, 90 in Mar. 1682-3; liv. 9 Jan. 1687-8. Only kn. w. Priscilla, ±65 1681-2. In 1681 both dep. ab. the news coming of Cammock's death; she was invit. to, but did not attend Mrs. C.'s wedding to Jocelyn; in 1682 ab. Burdett coming to their ho. ±1639. In 1699, ±80, she depos. ab. the birth of Mr. Hooke's two sons at York ab. 60 yrs. bef.; liv. 2 Oct. 1706, when inv. taken of the house and prop. he had turned over to John Harmon for life supp. in Aug. 1680. In earlier days, she was ord. to Boston in 1658 on susp. of adult.; abs. from meet. 1667 and acquit. as she had been visiting in Saco ab. 3 mos.; in trouble for abus. the Ch. and some members, and abs. 1674-5. Only kn. ch: **Benjamin**, witn. fa.'s deed 11 Nov. 1660; in Aug. 1669 his fa. deeded with consent of ' my w. Priscilla and my s. Benj.' List 87. In Feb. 1675-6 he mtg. ho., sawmill and 20 a. bot from fa. and Henry Simpson to Francis Hooke, who was gr. adm. 11 Sept. 1677; inv. incl. pers. effects, a mare, logs and marsh at Cape Neddick. **Deborah**, m. 1st John Foxwell(2), 2d John Harmon(3). See also (37).

9 **ELIZABETH** (Trafton) (Rackliff). See (20).

10 **ELIZABETH**, York, bastardy, York Ct. Apr. 1705.

11 **CAPT. FRANCIS**, merchant, Salem 1630, Marblehead, Boston, trading thru life at the eastward; his first yrs. in N. E. as manager of a Salem company. See Foxwell(5). York witn. 1658; freq. in Me. Courts in his own cases or atty. for others and often a York witn. 1678-1687; cert. there Dec. 1682, and July 1687, both times of Boston. In 1677 he sued Jos. Curtis for pulling down his ho. in York and the fences; in 1691 his garden abutted Sampson Angier. Lists 75b, 80. His Marblehead planta. was named Brooksby, poss. for that place in co. Leices-

ter; he had a sis. in Salem, Dorothy Norrice, and in 1660 called Christo. Coulson of London? uncle. 1st w. Joan, mo. of 7 ch. bp. Salem 1638-1654, incl: **Ruth**, bp. 9 Mar. 1640. **Elizabeth**, bp. 24 Apr. 1642, m. Thaddeus McCarthy. She willed in 1723 Medumcook Isl. and Hatchet Isl. near Georges River; inv. incl. lands in York Co. at the Eastward bot by -John- Johnson, her fa. **Francis**, bp. 16 June 1644. **Sarah**, bp. 19 Feb. 1654; her fa. bondsm. for her in Boston on susp. of infanticide Nov. 1682. (Poss. he brot her to York and she was the w. of John Morris there in Mar. foll.). He m. 2d in Boston 24 Oct. 1656 Hannah Madbury. Ab. 66 in 1672 'sr.,' 82 in 1686, d. 3 Feb. 1690-1, adm. at Boston 23 Mar. to the McCarthys.

12 **LT. FRANCIS**(11?), Pemaquid 1683-1690, had 100 a. gr. from Dongan 13 Sept. 1686; commis. Lt. of Capt. Nich. Manning's co. by Andros 1686; Selectm. 1687. Lists 17, 18, 124. No cert. connect. with (11) or earlier rec., and he disapp. as he came, but his Pemaquid resid., fam. names and perh. his connec. with Capt. Manning (from Salem) make this identif. probable. Poss. the same retailing at Marbleh. Neck 1673, and the F. J. (mark) bondsm. with Rune (Renald?) Kelly for John Roe in Ipsw. Ct. Nov. 1677. Poss. too he d. or was k. shortly bef. death of Francis sr., as not found in Scituate with his ch., kn. only by appearance bef. East. Cl. Com. of dau. **Ruth**, claiming for hers. and sis. Mary's ch. She m. 1st Thos. Sargent of Pemaquid, ch. incl. Thaddeus; m. 2d (int. Boston 13 May 1713) John Barry; wid. in Boston Oct. 1720. **Mary**, m. Thos. Warden of Pemaquid and Scit.; deed. in 1716, leav. ch.

13 **HENRY**, owned covt. No. Ch., Portsm., 7 Mar. 1713-4; taxed 1717. Ch: **Charles**, **Henry, Katherine**, bp. 1714-18.

14 **JAMES**, Great Isl., knew Kittery early; depos. 31 May 1652, ±50, ab. site of Capt. Mason's mill in Berwick. Signed Bloody Point ptn. 1642; in 1649 lic. to keep ord. at Dover and ferry to Str. Bk. and Hilton's; sold his ho. there in 1651. Sold at Sandy Beach 1660, and soon had 1 a. gr. on Gt. Isl. near ho. form. Alex. Batchelder's and bot from his widow. Selectm. 1652, 1655-7; Gr. j. 1657, 1659, 1661-2, 1664. Freed from training 1674. See John(16), Thomas (34). Lists 43, 323, 324, 326abc, 77b, 327a, 330abc, 342, 47, 311b, 312ch, 331a. Inv. 8 June, adm. 25 June 1678 to wid. Mary, who, remembering over 40 yrs. back, depos. 15 Feb. 1682-3, ±70, when she and husb. came over, old Thos. Walford liv. on Gt. Isl. on Little Harb. side. Lists 313a, 331b, 52. She was taxed July 1690; d. bef. 16 Nov. 1694, when eq. div. made to: **Mary**, m. John Odiorne. **Hannah**, m. Thos. Jackson(20).

15 **JAMES**(7), Hampt., Kit., carpenter, millwr., prob. learned trade with Henry Sayward and went with him to York and to Wells, where they and Thos. Paty had grants 1669. Of Hampt 23 Dec. 1670 he q. c. in Wells, and receipted for wages, to Sayward. At home he liv. on E. half of fa.'s homestead; of Hampt. bot 10 a. at Spruce Creek 28 May 1683, and one quarter of the Shapleigh mill 5 Apr. 1685. Lists 269b, 396, 62, 298. Gr. j. 1693; jury 1694, 1697. What actual time he liv. in Kit. is not appar.; but called of Kit. in Oct. 1699 and June 1700. His w. Sarah joined Hampt. Ch. 23 July 1704, he was in Hampt. in June 1714, and d. there sudd. 16 June 1715, ag. 72. First w. Sarah Daniels(6), m. 26 Mar. 1675, liv. 1704. See Sarah Donnell(1). Wid. d. Jan. 1718; she was Hannah in fam. agreem. made 1 mo. aft. he d. to give effect to his intended will. In June 1720, sons James and John were cited by Edw. Shaw to adm. Ch: **James**, b. 4 Feb. 1677, d. 6 Nov. 1752, m. 10 Nov. 1698 Elizabeth Mason (John); liv. on part of the home place. List 399a. 7 ch. **Samuel**, b. 18 Aug. 1678. **John**, b. 1679, d. 6 Jan. 1680. **Dorcas**, b. 16 June 1681, not in agreem. 1715. **Hannah**, m. 12 Dec. 1705 Jos. Shaw. **John**, b. 16 July 1687, d. y. **Mary**, b. 4 Nov. 1688, m. 27 June 1716 Edw. Shaw. **Benjamin**, b. 22 Nov. 1691, not in agreem. 1715. **John**, No. Hampton, b. 27 Oct. 1694, d. in Apr. 1750; m. 13 June 1718 Martha Redman (John). 10 ch.

16 **JOHN**, Greenland, 32 in June 1671, ±36 in 1673, depos. in June 1675, ±38, he took poss. of land for John Odiorne ab. 19 yrs. bef. Gr. 1 a. on Gt. Isl. 13 Jan. 1660-1; of Portsm. 21 Aug. 1668 sold to Fryer his dwg. on the Isl. bet. Jas. Johnson(14) and Jer. Walford's creek. Greenl. by 1673, many yrs. tav.-keeper. O. A. Portsm. 2 Oct. 1666; again 28 Aug. 1685. Surv. of Ways and Culler of Pipestaves 1692; jury 1693, 1697. See Barcley(2). Lists 323, 326ac, 330acd, 311b, 54, 49, 52, 332b, 57, 62, 335a, 337. He m. 26 Dec. 1661 Eleanor Brackett(1). Lists 331c, 335a, 338b. May 25, 1713, he deeded half his farm to s. James, the rest at their death; Jas. to pay his two bros. Son John taxed 'Jr.' in 1717, without 'Jr.' 1718. Ch: **John**, b. 2 Nov. 1662. **Rosamond**, b. 10 June 1665, unm. by gr. fa. Brackett's will 1691; m. John Nutter. **Hannah**, b. 7 Feb. 1670-1, presum. same as **Johannah**, m. 27 Apr. 1692 John Cate(3). Capt. **James**, Greenl., b. 13 Nov. 1673, called Lt. 1712, Capt. 1716; Selectm. 1707-8. Lists 62, 330d, 337, 338c. He m. 1st (int. Ipsw. 25 Sept. 1708) Elizabeth Thompson, 2d 19 Dec. 1734 Ann, wid. of Jona. Bill, sis. of Rev. Wm. Allen. Will, gent. or yeoman, 5 Mar. 1752 (d. 28 Mar., ag. 79) names w. Anna, 1 son and 3 daus. of

7 ch. bap. Deacon **Ebenezer**, Greenl., b. 27 Nov. 1676, memb. of Portsm. Ch. 1707. Lists 330d, 337, 338abcd. He m. 1st bef. 1703 Margaret Weeks (Leonard), List 338b; 2d 25 Oct. 1716 Susannah Martin, adm. to Greenl. Ch. 1717, appar. the same Susannah, dau. of Thos. Wiggin, who was his w. in 1725 and ag. 64 in May 1738. List 338b. D. 6 Sept. 1748; wid. Susannah 2 Apr. 1753, adm. to Thos. Wiggin. 6 ch. by 1st w., incl. Brackett, m. his cous. Mary (James).

17 **JOHN**, No. Yarmouth 1680. List 212.

18 **JOHN**(16), miller, Greenland, taxed 1688. Jury 1692, Constable 1698, Selectm. 1703. Lists 332b, 62, 335a, 67, 336b, 330d, 337, 338abc. His w. in 1696, prob. much earlier, was Hannah Lewis(16), who depos. Dec. 1731, ±76, that she was well acq. with the fam. of Mr. Mitton at Casco Bay, espec. Mary who m. Thos. Brackett. List 338b. She liv. 1738; he d. 7 Dec. 1747. Kn. ch: **Nathan**, or Nathaniel. Nathl. was on parish rate Feb. 1711-2, had deed from fa. in 1714, land and share in the sawmill. List 338a. Nathan m. 19 Feb. 1712-3 Mary Whidden (Saml.). List 338c. He d. 10 July 1745, adm. 25 Dec. to wid. Mary and s. Nathan. 9 or 10 ch. liv. 1748, incl. Philip. Ens. **John**, m. at Hampt. F. 24 Mar. 1714-5 Prudence Crosby(3). List 338a. 10 or 11 ch. bp. In 1729 Nathan and John J. and Henry Nutter agreed to div. marsh form. Henry Langstar's. One John had w. Jean in 1742. **Hannah** m. Matthias Haines(6); her fa. deeded to her adj. Nathan in 1736. **Eleanor**, m. 19 Jan. 1720-1 Wm. Burleigh, and had land in 1736 from her fa., who depos. in 1744 that some yrs. ago he gave his s.-in-law Wm. Burley of Stratham ¼ his mill. Perhaps: **?Joseph**, rated to Greenl. par. 1712; taxed 1713-4; poss. the same taxed Portsm. 1707-13. List 338a. **?Philip**, taxed Newcastle 1720. **?William**, Greenl., bondsm. for Nathan (jr.) in 1748; poss. the same who m. there 19 June 1734 Susanna Babb(4). See Jonathan(19).

19 **JONATHAN**, m. at York 29 Sept. 1731 Sarah Babb(4); settled at Sanford 1739.

20 **JOSEPH**, York, had k. Sampson Angier's horse in July 1690. He [or ano., poss. Nathl.(22), Stackpole says Samuel, but none eligible found] m. aft. 5 Nov. 1691 Elizabeth (Trafton), wid. of John Rackliff. She was Wid. Johnson, now of York, 26 Mar. 1720. Of Kit., 18 Oct. 1721, she deeded York land to s. Joseph; they then liv. with Wid. Sarah Curtis at Spruce Creek. In Apr. 1744, ag. 68, she testi. ab. Brave Boat Harb. 53 yrs. ago. Ch: **Joseph**, may have been the Jos. who m. 19 Nov. 1721 Hannah Dutteridge; later of Marbleh.

21 **JOSEPH**, Portsm. 1709, beat Mrs. Elizabeth Scott's son and threatened that he and Thos. Greely would burn her ho. bef. morning. John Bly called him 'the negro.'

22 **NATHANIEL**, sued by Jas. Fowle in York Ct. 1697; likely from Woburn. See also (20).

23 **PETER**, early adventurer at Sagadahoc. Winth. i. 58.

24 **PETER**(7), Hampton, of age 19 June 1660 when step-fa. deeded to him, eldest son; ±32 in Mar. 1670-1. If b. there, he was prob. the 1st white ch. b. in town, tho that distinct. claimed for Abra. Perkins. He m. 3 Apr. 1660 Ruth Moulton (John); drowned in Hampt. River with Jas. Philbrick 16 Nov. 1674, adm. to her 13 Apr. 1675. She joined Hampt. Ch. 27 Feb. 1697-8, liv. 12 Jan. 1702-3. List 52. 'His four ch': **Mary**, b. 7 Apr. 1663, m. at Haverh. 14 Dec. 1681 Saml. Ayer. **Ruth**, b. 13 July 1666, m. at Haverh. 24 (or 4) Nov. 1682 Timo. Ayer. **Edmund**, b. 3 July 1671, Quaker, millwright. Gr. j. 1695; Tr. j. 1698. Lists 57, 399a. He m. (25 Sept. 1693?) Abigail Green(2); both liv. 1718, and his wid. was Abigail. Will 9 Sept. 1737—16 Jan. 1737-8, names 7 of 8 ch: Abigail, b. (25 Sept. 1693?), m. John Brown(5); Ruth, m. John Gove (5 jr.); Esther Ruck; Dorcas, m. in Amesb. 18 Sept. 1724 Andrew Neal; Obadiah, had the homestead, m. 1st in Newb. 28 Jan. 1729-30 Judith Brown, 2d in Newb. 5 Nov. 1761 Ruth Rogers; Mary, m. Israel Hodgdon; Patience, m. in Amesb. 6 Aug. 1728 John Neal. **Peter**, b. 25 Nov. 1674, liv. on gr. fa.'s place; m. 1 Apr. 1708 Esther Hobbs(9). Lists 399a, 68, 400. Ch. Ruth, Peter, 1712-1714.

25 **PETER**, ±22, seaman 1690. List 333a.

26 **REBECCA**; verd. of jury on untimely death of Wm. Shipton, Robt. Tuck, Jos. Roberts and R. J., filed 27 June 1665.

27 **RETURN**, Hampton 1675, O. A. there 25 Apr. 1678. He m. Mary Johnson in Andover 7 Sept. 1673. He depos. in Ipsw. Ct. 5 Nov. 1678, ±25.

28 **SAMUEL**, soldier at Black Point garri. Jan. 1675-6, Wm. Griffith's hired substitute. List 237b.

29 **SAMUEL**, York, b. by 1656, prob. s. of Wm.(37), cert. step-son of Geo. Parker, had gr. 27 Feb. 1678-9; O. A. Mar. 1679-80. See Bass(2); Y. D. vi. 111. In June 1680 he and Peter Bass apprais. est. of John Foxwell(2); adm. to him 23 Jan. 1693-4 on est. of Geo. Parker, whose 1671 gr. Saml's wid. and ch. sold in 1719. His own town gr. 1696 sold by s. Saml. 1721. Selectm. 1698. The wid. was Elizabeth Adams(16); adm. to her 4 July 1711 (inv. 30 Dec. 1710). In 1725 she ptn. to sell the real est. Her will 12 July 1726—1 Apr. 1728 names sis. Sarah Black(2), in add. to her ch., all but 1st 2 rec. York, all liv. 1737: **Ruth**, m. ab. 1714

Benaiah Young. **Mary,** m. John Wilson; of Falm. 1739. **Sarah,** b. 5 Apr. 1695, m. (Ct. Jan. 1723-4) Henry Simpson. **Samuel,** b. 2 Feb. 1697-8. List 279. Apr. 15, 1726, with w. Sarah (Burrill 3) he sold 3 pieces of marsh form. his fa.'s. 5 ch. 1725-1735. **Keziah,** b. 11 Dec. 1700, m. Hugh Holman (3). **Hannah,** b. 6 Apr. 1705; in 1727 (Johnson) she deeded to br. Benj.; m. Zachariah Emery. **Benjamin,** b. 7 Mar. 1707-8; Merriconeag, 1737; Falm. 1738. List 279.

30 **SAMUEL,** Kit., husbandman, carpenter, s. of John, gr. s. of Capt. Edward, both of Woburn, b. there 29 Oct. 1670. Of York 11 Jan. 1693-4 already m. to Hannah, wid. of Jas. Grant(5). She was k. by Ind. 7 July 1694. In Cambridge 1695 he witn. the will of his br.-in-law Jona. Knight, but was in Kit. 30 Dec. 1696, then or soon aft. m. to Abigail Wittum (Peter) and liv. at Sturgeon Creek. He m. 3d (Ct. Apr. 1706) Amy Neal, a captive 1694-1700. As 'Sr.' he sold his 1699 gr. to Thos. Rhodes in 1706, and confirmed to Nich. Morrill in 1718, but was S. J., with no desig., in deeds 1700, 1714. In 1746, (w. Amy), deeded homestead to John Stanley. Lists 290, 291, 296, 297, 298. Two ch. by 2d w. rec.: **John,** b. 17 Oct. 1698. **William,** b. 25 July 1701. Prob. hers: **Abigail,** witn. Wittum deed 1723. By 3d w.: **Joseph,** laborer, 1745, when Rich. Chick got judgm. ag. his fa. and him; in 1754, liv. on the Sturgeon Creek lands and mtg. them to David Clark and Timo. Weymouth. **?Mary,** witn. a Neal fam. deed in 1724. **Amy,** m. (int. Bidd. 29 July 1739) Joseph Hill of Bidd. **Hannah,** w. of John Stanley 1745.

31 **SAMUEL**(15), had his fa.'s Kit. land and mov. there, millwright, miller, farmer. Lists 399a, 290, 291, 296, 297, 298. M. 1st 3 Nov. 1701 Elizabeth Haskins(6), 2d 23 Dec. 1734 Mary, wid. of Rich. King(12), who 6 mo. earlier had acc. James of beating his fa., also Saml. jr. Will 8 Feb. 1739—19 Nov. 1744 names w. Mary, 2 sons, 4 daus: **Sarah,** rec. Kit. 8 Nov. 1704, m. Benj. Larrabee(6). **Mary,** m. 26 Feb. 1729-30 Saml. Fernald. **Hannah,** m. 1740 John Peters. **Elizabeth,** m. Enoch Hutchins (3 jr.). **Samuel,** tertius Oct. 1735, m. 19 May 1748 Elizabeth Fernald, who m. 2d 2 June 1769 Edw. Ingraham; 6 ch. **James,** m. 1740 Lydia Fernald, 7 ch.

32 **SAMUEL,** with not even a guess as to his antec., m. at Kit. 28 Nov. 1715 Elizabeth (Mitchell), wid. of John Tinney. Lists 291, 296. In 1722, jr., he was in Jos. Curtis's garri. ho. at Spruce Creek; liv. 18 Nov. 1723 when her mo. deeded them 2 a. already in his poss. She was ag. 68 in Apr. 1744, liv. a wid. Jan. 1755. Presum. at least one child, who may have d. y.

33 **STEPHEN** (Jonsones). List 368b. See Jones.

34 **THOMAS,** planter, Dover, O. R., 1641-1661, at diff. times sued Abel Cammond, Oliver Trimmings, Robt. Tuck, and in 1660 had cross suits with John Hunking, adm. of Hercules; in 1649 sued by Jas. Johnson(14), who was bondsm. for Cammond in Thos.' suit. He sold ho. and all to Nich. Follett in 1652. Lists 42, 354abc, 355a, 356a, 361a, 326a, 363abc. Adm. 27 June 1661 to Wm. Furber, Wm. Follett. See Howell(6). **Dau.** under 10, 30 June 1663, to live with Goodm. Leighton; she soon d. and town took est. in 1665, no heir claiming.

35 **THOMAS,** Berwick witn. 1646. Y. D. i. 6.

36 **THOMAS,** k. by Ind. at Pemaquid 1695. List 96.

37 **WILLIAM**(8?), York, carpenter, b. bef. 1640, if Saml. his child. Cert. older than Benj., s. of Mr. Edward, descent by 'borough English' might explain Benj. as s. and heir (Y. D. ii. 88) and leave place for Wm. as eldest son; while young Samuel's connec. with est. of John Foxwell(2) possibly adds strength. Wm. had 10 a. gr. from the town 29 May 1659; 30 a. in 1661 to incl. this 1st 10; and 30 a. at the seaside in Mar. 1671-2. Constable 1665; Gr. j. 1674. Lists 25, 92. With w. Hannah he deeded to Isaac Everest in Jan. 1669-70, to Rich. Wood in Mar. 1674-5. In 1672 Geo. Parker, jr., sued him for shooting his mare, and there can be little doubt that it was his wid. Hannah who m. Geo. Parker bef. 10 Apr. 1685, when they deeded to Peter Bass for supp. and mainten. of Eleazer as his own ch. Two surely Hannah's ch: **Samuel. Eleazer,** under 21 in 1683; witn. for Jona. Bass, app. in Boston, 26 June 1701, but witn. in York bef. and aft., last found there 29 July 1703. **?Daughter** (poss. Parker), m. Peter Bass(2). **?William,** breaking the Sabbath on Boone Isl. in May 1685, when John Harmon was there; m. (Me. Ct. June 1688) Anne (Cotton) Carr (3), who d. in Boston of small pox 6 or 7 Dec. 1702. One Wm. m. in Boston 8 Dec. 1703 Abigail Weeden; ano. or the same m. Mary Grantam there 20 Sept. 1705. See Broughton(1).

38 **WILLIAM,** m. Margaret Lovering. Liv. Long Reach, Kennebec, 1738.

Joient, John. List 10. See Gent.

Joliffe (Jolly), John, Mr., Boston, agent for Matthew Craddock, acting in Rich. Williams's est. P. & Ct. i. 96, 102; Y. D. i. 136, iii. 5. A justice for York Co. by Gov. Phips' appointment 1692.

**JONES,** the patronymic from John which became the commonest Welsh name; 9th commonest in N. E.

1 **ALEXANDER,** early on Great Island, but confused with **Alexander**(2), his only known ch. Presum. the constable sued

in 1651 by Wm. Wormwood; not recognized later. No ment. of wife, unless she was 'Widow Jones' who had 1 a. laid out near the meeting-ho. in 1664-5. List 330a. See also (17).

2 **ALEXANDER**(1), seaman, Great Island, called 'the second' and 'son of Alexander' in 1660, m. Hannah Walford (Thos.) bef. or aft. 1 Jan. 1648-9, when her fa. spoke of her as Walford, cert. bef. 22 Oct. 1649, prior to which date he had given A. J. land on Gt. Isl. Earlier he was on Spruce Creek, Kittery, near Thos. Withers, wit. Vines's deed to T. W. 20 Mar. 1644, was sued by him in 1647, and was a party to suits in Me. and Dover cts. in 1651. On Gt. Isl. he and Hannah were involved in a long court dispute with Geo. Walton over certain marsh. He dep. in 1666 ab. the early deed to Withers; in Feb. 1667-8, ±52, ab. cutting and carrying away wood on Spruce Creek for Capt. Pendleton. Liv. 1671, dead in 1678. Lists 312ac, 323, 326ac, 330ab. Widow Hannah was acc. of witchcraft in 1681, and the next yr. was bonded to keep the peace on G. Walton's complaint. See Coll. N. H. Hist. Soc. viii. 99, 100. A midwife in 1685, liv. 1686. Widow J. taxed 1688. Lists 330a, 331b, 52. Poss. ch. by an earlier wife; see (3), (43). Ch. by Hannah, who ment. her boys in 1681, incl: **Jeremiah,** had a Great Island gr. in Feb. 1668-9, laid out in Mar. 1672-3 (List 330a); land Thos. Walford gave J. J. ment. in 1677. **Samuel** and **Sarah,** surely, both named in gr. fa. Walford's will 1666. Unless Sarah an infant then, she was app. too old to have been the first w. of Capt. Hugh Reed. Poss. Hannah's (or ?gr. ch. if she m. much bef. 1648): **?Cornelius**(7), and three m. who by all appearances were bros., **?William**(55), **?Thomas**(46), and **?Daniel** (8). If these last four, or three were ch. of Alexander(3) instead, Sarah Reed may have been their sister.

3 **ALEXANDER**, fisherman, liv. at the Shoals in 1661, when he sold a new ho. and flake room to Fryer and Pendleton, and poss. the man sued by John Ridgway in Middlesex Ct., an Eastern fishing case, in 1653; John Phillips his bondsman. Later up Spruce Creek, where Stackpole says A. J. was liv. in 1674 and d. bef. 1720. Land on Spruce Creek, form. A. J.'s, decd., ment. in 1722 (Y. D. xi. 35). His age unknown, relationship and records covering him and (2) may be hopelessly mixed; poss. too he was the fa. of the four or more younger Joneses named questionably as ch. of (2).

4 **BENJAMIN**(17), Stratham, b. 1660-3. If the Benj. app. at Pemaquid with (18), he was soon driven back. Signed N. H. ptn. 20 Feb. 1689-90. Jury 1693, Gr.j. 1699.

Lists 57, 62, 67, (?124), 376b, 384b, 388. In 1719 he deeded homestead and all, except one bed, to s. Joseph, who gave back a mortg. and was dead in 1720 when his br. Saml. deeded to their fa. Benj. for life. App. husb. of John Sinclair's dau. (Sarah?) whose two sons but not herself were named in J. S.'s will 1700, she was an early w., unless the Sarah he was m. to in 1696, formerly wid. of Timo. Drisco(8). In 1697 Benj. and Sarah dep. ab. the Folsoms; in 1710 the highway bet. his ho. and ho. of Jas. Sinclair sr., ment. Mrs. J. d. at Stratham 23 Jan. 1741-2, poss. his w. He dep. 11 Feb. 1736-7, ag. 74; in 1744, ag. 84. Old Mr. Benj. J. d. 29 May 1751; will made 1 Mar. 1749 names 5 liv. ch., 2 decd.: **John,** in gr. fa. Sinclair's will 1700, bot in Stratham 1710. List 388. Adm. 3 Mar. 1724-5 to wid. Mary, bondsmen John and Noah Clark; Noah Barker an appraiser. She d. bef. 31 Oct. 1759. 4 ch. **Benjamin,** in gr. fa.'s will, not fa.'s. One Benj., ag. 25, dep. in 1725 ab. Theoph. Smith's land. **Joseph,** d. 1720; legal repres. ment. in fa.'s will. One Joseph of Stratham int. mar. with Abigail ———— at Rowley 4 Mar. 172-. **Samuel.** One Saml. of Ex. m. in Glouc. 3 Nov. 1726 Mary Lane; he or ano. m. in Newb. 26 Dec. 1728 Mary Lunt. **Cornelius,** Stratham, m. in Lynn 22 Apr. 1729 Abigail Hawkes; mov. to Newcastle, Me. **Susannah,** unm. 1741, named in fa.'s will as 'my dau. Susanna.' **Abigail,** m. Chas. Glidden(3). **Jonathan,** fa.'s heir and exec., Jona. Barker bondsm.; he m. bef. 26 Oct. 1737 Mary Harris(11), wid. of Herbert Walter of Boston; d. 12 Feb., adm. to wid. 25 Feb. 1754. She d. 1 Sept. 1766. 4 ch. Benj. Ricker d. at his ho. 24 Jan. 1754.

5 **BENJAMIN**, Pemaquid 1687. List 124. Same as (4)? See also (18).

6 **CATHERINE**, 1660. See Johns.

7 **CORNELIUS**, Kittery, s. of ?(2 or 3, or even 17). His 20 a. gr. 24 June 1682 was limited in trust, to be improved for wife and her ch. In Feb. 1687-8 he was liv. on Joseph (John?) Waters's land at Spruce Creek, app. m. to Mary Waters. List 298. He was bound over in June 1687 on susp. of causing the death of Sarah Winslett of Gt. Isl.; in Dec. fol. he sued Abraham Spiller for abuse; last found in June 1688 fighting with Sydrach Leveridge. The 1682 gr. was laid out to his wife's 2d house. Henry Benson(1) in 1694; Tobias Leighton sold the 1683 gr. in 1736. Ch. untraced. Unplaced in Kit. are Hannah, m. 21 July 1709 Geo. Phoenix; William (58, 59); also Elizabeth (Barter 1) Jones.

8 **DANIEL**(?2 or 3), moved aft. 1696 from Newcastle to Spruce Creek, wit. Shapleigh's deed to W. Deniford 1700, taxed

1704. In May, 1732, ag. bet. 60 and 70, he dep. that he knew the blind boy Edmund Pendleton at Newc. ab. 50 yrs. past; liv. 1738. Wife Sarah in 1710, when they sold land at Jones' Cove, Newc., beginning at the head of Wm. J.'s land, to Capt. Hugh Reed, who, or his w., was app. related to one or the other. She wit. with or for Rices and Godsoes 1710-1715; John Morgrage was his bondsm. 1715. Lists 318a, 315c, 290, 296, 297. 7 ch. bp. 11 Sept. 1715: **Alexander**, fisherman, m. at Kit. 9 Nov. 1727 Elizabeth Beale, poss. relat. to Wm. Beale(8), if Alexander, Zaccheus, Sarah, Elizabeth, all bp. 18 July 1736, were her ch. But see his br. Daniel; see also Elizabeth (Barter 1) Jones. In 1738 his fa. deeded him 10 a. next Eagle Point. **Grace**. **Samuel**, m. (int. 8 Feb. 1728-9) Martha Barter (1), a wid. 1751. **Mary**, m. Wm. Barter(1). **Daniel**, fisherman, m. 1st 8 Dec. 1726 Elizabeth -Beale-, 2d 22 Nov. 1733 Martha Weeks (Jos.); with Martha sold ho. in 1738, land in 1754. She was a wid. in 1763. Ch. **Lazarus**, Kit. wit. 1734-8. **Hugh**. Prob: **John**, bp. 30 May 1719, d. 1755, m. (int. 3 May 1740) Abigail Hatch. 7 ch. **Sarah**, bp. with John.

9 **DANIEL**. See Hammons(2).

10 **DAVID**, soldier at Fort Mary, 1699.

11 **DAVIS**, wit. in 1670 against Geo. Jones jr. and Widow Webster.

12 **EDWARD**, Cape Porpus, drowned with Rich. Young just bef. 23 Oct. 1672; by drink and obstinacy access. to their own death. One Edw., s. of Edw. of Wellingborow, co. Northampton, Eng., came in May 1639 as serv. to Anthony Stanyan, and was a Boston carpenter 1641. Lechford p. 427.

13 **EDWARD**, Saco, swearing in July 1674. One Edw. redeemed at Quebec in Oct. 1695, is listed with Me. people. Coleman's N. E. Captives i. 74.

14 **ELIZABETH**, dep. in Portsm. in 1703 ab. Francis Trickey and Mr. Seeley in Crooked Lane 37 yrs. bef. One Elizabeth m. in Portsm. in Sept. 1710 Jos. Matthews; ano. was recd. into covt. No. Ch. 1716.

15 **EVAN**, hit by falling timbers while raising a barn, and asked help in 1682 from Portsm. govt.

16 **FRANCIS**(23), Portsm., b. ±1638, apprent. of Jeremy Sheres 1650, m. bef. 27 Apr. 1669 Susanna Willix (Balthasar). List 335a. He dep. 19 Nov. 1695, ±57. See N. E. Reg. 50.46; 68.81. Taxed Mill Dam, so. side. Lists 323, 330abd, 47, 311b, 326c, 329, 52, 57, 67, 68, 335a, 337. Will 22 Aug. 1713 names w. Susanna, exec., and ch. She d. bef. the will was prov. 7 May 1718, when adm. gr. to s. Abraham. The three sons-in-law wished to contest. Ch: **Abraham**, cord-

wainer, m. Hannah Sherburne (John). He was recd. into No. Ch. Jan. 1708-9, both into So. Ch. Jan. 1715-6. List 339. Adm. to wid. 25 Oct. 1728; div. 1734 to her, sons John, Nathl., Joshua, James, dau. Hannah Johnson (Ebenezer). **Abigail**, m. Hugh Banfield(2). **Sarah**, m. 1st ab. 1700 Saml. Whidden, jr., 2d bef. May 1718 John Savage. **Mary**, m. 12 July 1714 Edw. Phillips.

17 **GEORGE**, Sagamore Creek and Exeter, ±53 in 1683. At the first, in 1662, 'one lately come into this town' (tho here 1659), he fought with his neighbors John Jackson and John Hart. That five relatives of Alex. Jones's wife testi. ab. his and w. Mary's peaceable charac., is ground for belief he was relat. to Alex.(2); later events show the truth was stretched ab. both. In 1671 Geo. Purington swore the peace against him, s. Geo. and w. Mary, ±45. She dep. in 1662, ±34, ab. John Webster's clothes, and was in Hamp. 10 Apr. 1675, ag. 47. He mov. to Ex. by 1677 and soon quarreled with the Morgans, once wanting his w. to watch him all night so he would not shoot Rich. Morgan out of the window. In 1680 there was trouble with Mr. Rich. Scammon. Lists 323, 326ac, 330a, 312c, 327b, 383, 52, 57. Will, planter, 14 Mar. 1694, prov. 23 Sept. 1695 (date of death given 27 Sept.) names w. Mary, dau. Sarah Speed and her ch. Kn.ch: **Mary**, ±27 in 1678; m. 1st Geo. Roberts; 2d Nathl. Folsom(6); 3d Nich. Norris. **George**. In 1671, ag. 17, he and wid. Rachel Webster were prosec. for being unseemly together, so poss., despite his youth, he was husb. of Sarah Pearce (John), who m. Hubertus Mattoon in June 1673 while still mar. to Jones, yet sailed away to Barbadoes with Jones, and later was in R. I. with him. But Geo. J., ag. 59, dep. ±1681 that a letter addressed 'for my w. Sarah Pearce,' directed to Geo. Jones, was sent to Ex. 4 or 5 yrs. bef. Geo. jr. (and Benj. Tristram) poss. owned a fishing shallop in Jan. 1678-9; then disapp., unless the mariner of Boston 1683, and/or the man at Pemaquid 1687. (?List 124.) **Sarah**, ±19 in 1678, m. Thos. Speed. They were fighting with her sis. Mary and husb. in 1699, all in court. **Benjamin**, b. 1660-3. One William an Exeter soldier 1696. List 67. See (56), also (7).

18 **GEORGE**, Pemaquid 1687. List 124. ?(17) or his son? See also (5).

19 **GRIFFIN**, verd. of coroner's jury filed 6 June 1682.

20 **ISAAC**, with br. (24) bot from Thos. Cloyes at Falm. 1681. Y. D. 13.227. List 34. See Wyman's Charlestown i. 564.

21 **JAMES**(23), Portsm., signed Corbett ptn. 1665, taxed 1672. Jury 1684. Lists 47, 331ab, 54, 329, 52. Tax of 'Daniel Dug-

gin & James Jones' abated 1680. Duggin worked with him in 1682, was a neighbor in 1684 and was named in his est. He d. 1685. Inven. 6 May 1686 attest. by wid. Elizabeth, who m. 2d Abraham Bartlett(1). Citation was ord. sent to her and s. John to adm., 3 Sept. 1718, or adm. to issue to Capt. Pickering, who had letters 3 Dec., but s. John did adm., inven. 2 Mar. 1719-20. Ch: **John**, b. 1679, bricklayer, Portsm., Kit., had gr. (non-resid.) in Scarb. 1721 and bot more, moving there late. Lists (?68), 339. Of Kit. 1737, he deeded to s. John ab. 300 a. in Scarb. His w. Joanna (Cotton 2) d. at Scarb. 11 Oct. 1756, ag. 71; he d. there 20 July 1758, ag. 78. Adm. to s. Wm. whose bill for care of dec. and his farm 20y. 9m. 28d. was contested by three of the ch. Div. 1773 to 9 of 11 ch., the 1st one b. 10 June 1706. **Daughter**, m. Isaac Matthews, sailmaker, Portsm.; adm. of his est. to br. John Jones, mason, 3 July 1716. One Elizabeth J. m. -Joseph- Matthews, by record; see (14).

22 **JENKIN**, Dover 1666, both named 1673. Lists 356jk, 357a, 359ab, 54, 52, 57, 62. He m. Abigail Heard(5) bef. her fa.'s will made 2 Apr. 1687; in 1712 they deeded homestead to s. Joseph with life reservation. Ch: **Joseph**, m. 7 Feb. 1706-7 Mary Spencer (Moses), who m. 2d aft. July 1715 Jacob Allen(4). Dau. Elizabeth chose her step-fa. gdn. 1 Sept. 1724, and m. 3 Nov. 1725 Jona. Merrow al. Merry. **Elizabeth**, m. 24 Sept. 1702 Clement Meserve, who wit. her fa.'s deed to Jos. in 1712. **Samuel**, Somersworth, bot in 1718 from Ebenezer Downes ⅓ of 60 a. in Dover laid out to Saml. Heard; in 1726 he sold land gr. to Jenkin in 1701 and laid out to hims. in 1720. Wife Mary Cross, m. in Portsm. 19 Apr. 1715. 3 ch. bp. Dover 28 Sep. 1718, and 9 m., inc. Dorcas and Esther. Will 1758—1774 names w., 10 ch. (1 decd.) and gives homestead to s. Benjamin; also to Benj. the land adj. recently bot from Wm. J., whose fa. Wm. (?57 jr.) may have been a son of Jenkin instead; or even this Saml. a son of (57) instead of Jenkin. One Esther J. was bap. at Dover 28 Sep. 1718. See also (32).

23 **JOHN**, blacksmith, Portsm. His age, ±44 in 1660, ±50 in Oct. 1665, would permit him to be the J. J. ag. 20, who came in the -Susan and Ellen- to Boston 1635. At Portsm. early with w. Ann; both dep. in 1660 ab. Wm. Clifton's land and the talk at their ho. in 1637. In May 1647 he was in charge of Wannerton's ho. Gr. j. 1655. O.F. 11 July 1659. Lists 41, 321, 323, 326a, 330ab, 311b. Besides his trade, he cleaned the meet.-ho. and rang the bell, but liked to idle, and was censured in 1663. Will 2—

17 Sep. 1667 names as exec. w. Ann, who soon m. John Moses, and ch: **Francis**. **Mary**, m. James Drew(5). **Nathaniel**, not found later. **James**. **John**. In 1673 one John, ±20, was servant of John Lewis, Gt. Isl., who sued Dr. Francis Morgan for not curing him. Poss. the same taxed 1681. List 329.

24 **JOHN**, Falm. landowner from Charlestown, br. of (20). List 34. Inv. at Charlest., 1690, incl. land at Casco Bay now in the enemy's hand, val. 0000. Wid. Rebecca claimed in 17— for self and ch. and for heirs of (20).

25 **JOHN**, yeoman, Dover, granted 20 a. 19 Mar. 1693-4. Adm. 4 June 1706 to wid. Ann, bondsm. Rich. Pinkham and Hatevil Hall. She was lic. 5 Aug. 1707 to sell the real est. for supp. of his **two daughters**.

26 **JOHN**, Dover, d. 18 Mar. 1696-7. List 96.

27 **JOHN**, servant of Edw. Toogood, worked at Ft. Mary, 1697. List 68.

28 **JOHN**, k. at Casco 1703. List 39.

29 **LIEUT. JOSEPH**(39), Durham, dep. 30 Nov. 1734, ag. 60. Jury 1696. Selectm. 1702, 1703 (refused), 1706-10, 1714, 1717. Lists 353, 358bd, 368ab, 369. He m. Ann Nutter (Anthony). In 1733 they (he gent. of Dover) joined Nutter heirs in a land suit. She relinq. adm. on his est., of Durham, to eldest s. Joseph 22 Oct. 1744; div. 28 July 1746. Adm. on her est. 1762, div. 25 Oct. 1764. Ch., all bp. with their fa. 13 May 1722, the 1st 4 adult, the others in nonage: **Joseph**, had w. Mary, who m. 2d in Portsm. 27 Aug. 1755 Hercules Mooney. 1 dau. **Benjamin**, Lee, his est. divid. 1794. Wid. Elizabeth. 8 or m. ch. **John**, m. Abigail Field(5), a wid. in 1759; she m. 2d Ebenezer Jones(40). 'His heirs' shared in 1764 div. **Anthony**, Madbury, will 1781, no w. or ch. named. **Elizabeth**, not in either div. **Samuel**, m. Elizabeth Field(5), bp. a wid. with dau. Ann at Dover 23 July 1738. **Richard**, Madbury, m. Ursula Pinkham (James). 5 ch. bp. Dover 1739-54, two repres. in div. of his est. 1790.

30 **JOSEPH**, Newport, R. I., 1716, w. Hannah Harvey(14).

31 **LAWRENCE?**, J. P., Kennebec, 1688. Y. D. 8.24. List 18. See also Dennis(6).

32 **MARY**, k. by Ind. at Dover 26 July 1696. List 96. Other victims in the attack were associates of Jenkin(22).

33 **OWEN**, soldier at Scarb. in Philip's War. List 237b.

34 **RICE**, fisherman, Shoals 1651, sued Richard and Frances White in 1656 for slandering his w. List 301. Remov. to Boston; there he and w. Ann sold two houses, land and flake room at the Shoals to Christo. Jose in 1659. She attest. his

inven. 1 Feb. 1661-2; servants John Hues and Benj. Reden ment.; debts to the Eastward.

35 **ROBERT**, Dover 1657; granted 10 a. 1659. In Apr. 1664 he and Exeter men were bondsm. for Francis Pofat; see Dudley(1). In May 1679, of Ex., he ack. judgment, in boards, to Maj. Thos. Clarke of Boston. Lists 356abceg, 54.

36 **ROGER**, soldier under Scottow. List 237b.

37 **SAMUEL**, coroner's jury, Wells, 1697. List 268a.

38 **SARAH**, Goodwife, Hampton 1662. Essex Q. Ct. 2.420.

39 **STEPHEN**, b. ±1642, cooper, Oyster River 1660, recd. inhabt. 19 Mar. 1665-6, took F. O. 15 May 1672, and that yr. had gr. at Johnson's Creek. In 1668 he and Stephen Chesley were arrested in connec. with Edmund Green's death; in 1672, he, ±30, and w. Elizabeth (Field 1, m. 28 Jan. 1663-4) wit. in the Chesley cattle case. Adm. of Wm. Beard's est. 1676. See Hill (21), Davis(4). Lists 362b, 363abc, 356m, 311c, 365, 366, 359a, 54, 49, 92. In 1680 Jeremiah and Saml. Jordan were reaping for him. Widow taxed 1682, d. 10 Mar. 1705-6, long ill. Lists 52, 96. Three kn. ch: **Shephen**, b. ±1667. **Elizabeth**, b. ±1672-3, m. Lt. Jos. Roberts. In Aug. 1756, ag. 83, she dep., 'when liv. with my fa. 65 or 70 y. ago on Jones's Neck, Durham'; liv. 1757. **Joseph**, b. ±1674. ?**William**, m. Mary Chesley(5).

40 **CAPT. *STEPHEN**(39), Durham, ±87 in Aug. 1754; ±89 in Jan. 1756. Ensign 1690, and in 1694 defended his garrison, the refuge of many. Called Capt. 1729. Gr.j. 1696, 1698; Selectm. 1696, 1724, 1729-30; lot layer 1709, 1713; Rep. 1709-15; Moderator 1730. Lists 57, 58, 59, 62, 66, 63, 64, 353, 368ab, 369. He was an orig. memb. of O. R. Ch. 26 Mar. 1718; wife Abigail Nutter (Anthony) adm. 29 June foll. She d. bef. 16 Aug. 1733. His will 6 Aug. 1743 —29 Sept. 1756, names 4 ch., all of Durham 1745 when they q.c. the Nutter homestead: Major **Stephen**, b. 3 Mar. 1706, d. 8 June 1797. List 369. He m. 1st Sarah Dam (Wm. 5 jr.); her only surv. ch. Martha, under 21, was her gr. mo. Dam's heir in 1766. He m. 2d Susanna Millett (Thos.), b. 1740. Ch. 2 + 5. **Ebenezer**, fa.'s exec.; m. 1st Joanna Ham (John), who d. 4 May 1745, ag. 31; 2d 1 Jan. 1761 Abigail, wid. of his cous. John(29). List 369. Kn.ch. 4 + 1. **Mary**, m. 1 June 1727 John Smith jr.; wid. 1757. **Abigail**, m. Jos. Thomas.

41 **THOMAS**, Kittery, b. ab. 1609, named with York men in ct. record at Saco 25 Mar. 1636; creditor of Wm. Dixon(3) 1637. He was in service of Mr. Alex. Shapleigh

and worked for him at Sturgeon Creek in 1639 (his own dep. 2 May 1679, ag. 70), and for Mrs. Treworgy in 1644. In 1647 deft. with Thos. Duston for cutting grass at Eliot; in 1648 bot from Abra. Conley ho. and field adj. Wm. Everett. O. A. Kit. 16 Nov. 1652, residing 'farther northward.' Coroner's j. 1647; Tr.j. 1650-1; constable 1657. Lists 282, 283, 298, 24. Abs. from meet. and idling 1671. In 1686 he asked town help and arrangem. was made with John Leighton to keep him 4 y., for 6 a. of marsh, his only proper est., his deed to Leighton 20 Nov. 1686. No kn. fam. See also (43).

42 **THOMAS**, butcher, from Elsing, co. Norfolk, came in the -Mary & Ann- 1637, ag. 25. Propr. of Newb. bef. going with the first settlers to Hampton (List 391a), where gr. 100 a. 24 Dec. 1639. Herdsman 1640; signed Hampt. ptn. 7 Mar. 1642-3 (List 391b). In 1644 he had remov. to Exeter; gr. there 27 Jan. 1644-5. Lists 391ab, 392a, 393b, 374c, 375ab, 376ab, 378. 'My bro. Jones' turned a cow over to John Bursley(4) bef. 1649. In May that yr. he bot Saml. Greenfield's land, but remov. bef. 9 Oct. 1651 when his dwg. was in Edw. Gilman's poss. At Charlest. 3 Apr. 1654 he and Giles Fifield(2) were bondsm. for young Luke Perkins; there he dep. in 1654, ag. ±45, and bot in 1656-7. Will 24 Sept., d. 24 Oct. 1666. He m. Abigail Wyeth (Humphrey), who m. 2d Thos. Chadwell(3). Ch: **Susannah**, bp. Hamp. 29 Oct. 1639, m. ab. 1660 Wm. Goose, sea-captain, Charlest., and d. there 4 May 1674, ag. 34. 5 ch. He m. 2d 21 Sept. 1677 Mary King and soon d.

43 **THOMAS**, ag. 20 in 1660, then test. in Walton's suit that he saw the w. of Alex. J. tear down the fence about 2 yrs. bef.; Thos. Duston, ±55, test. at the same time. In 1665 he owned adj. Geo. Walton. Portsm. 1670 (when he sold on Great Isl.) and 1674. Lists 330a, 326c, 312c, 313a, 331b. See also (2) and (41).

44 **THOMAS**, abutter on Harriseeket River (Freeport) 1679. Y. D. 3.53.

45 **THOMAS**, abutter on Falmouth Neck (Portland) under Danforth. Y. D. 9.242.

46 **THOMAS**(†2 or 3), taxed Great Island 1690, abutted Richard Jackson in 1691. Jury 1688; highway surv. 1696-7. Abs. from meet. 1697. Lists 52, 315abc, 318ab, 319, 316. D. Jan. 1712-3 at ho. of Shadrach Bell (3). Nunc. will 23 Jan. gave all to the Bells, who had cared for him. Mrs. Sarah Reed, w. of Capt. Hugh, was at his ho. bef. he d., advising him to make his peace with God and settle his est.

47 **CAPT. THOMAS**, mariner, taxed Portsmouth 1718; had P/A from Timo. Davis (61) in 1720.

48 **TITUS** (wrote) wit. Gowen deed in 1702; Y. D. 7.19. Captive in Canada from Wells 1710, called negro. List 99, p. 92.

49 **WALTER**, Kittery wit. 1672. Y. D. ii. 118.

50 **WILLIAM**, Dover 1640. Money in his hands due Geo. Storey was attached by Edw. Colcord in 1642. He sued Wm. Pomfret and Wm. Hilton 1644; the same yr. was put under bonds to go to his w. in Old Eng. Lists 351ab. See also (51, 52).

51 **WILLIAM**, Portsm. Lists 41, 321.

52 **WILLIAM**, bound by Edw. Godfrey to appear at Saco Ct., 8 Sept. 1640. P. & Ct. 1. 81.

53 **WILLIAM**, owner in ship with Sampson Lane 1650. P. & Ct. 1.145.

54 **WILLIAM**, taxed Oyster Riv. 1659. In Dec. 1666 a joint warr. was issued ag. Benj. Hull (for abusing Stephen Paul) and Wm. J. (a common liar). In 1668 he was charged with adult. with Risby's w. (Sarah), both put in Dover jail. Lists 356e, 361a, 363ab, 342, 47.

55 **WILLIAM**(?2 or 3), fisherman, Newc., taxed Jan. 1688-9. First w. poss. Mary Marden (John and Rachel), called Jones in her mo.'s nunc. will 12 Feb. 1706-7; he m. 2d bef. 17 July 1714 Deborah (Bickford 22), wid. of Jeremiah Jordan(4). Constable 1698-9. Wit. with Hugh Reed 1709. Taxed 1743. Inven. dated 25 July 1750; the next Jan. his s. Jeremiah protested against adm. by wid. of a younger son. W. Deborah dep. in 1738, ±72, ab. the ch. of Robt. Tufton Mason — she had liv. with them. She was a wid. in Falm. in June 1752, aged bet. 80 and 90. Kn. ch., the sons cert. by a 1st w: **Jeremiah**, eldest, fisherman, likely the one taxed with fa. 1720, Wm. J. & Son. Liv. Newc. 1763. Wife poss. a Trefethen. At least two ch., Wm. and Saml.; poss. Robinson and Mary. **William**, mariner, Newc., taxed, jr., 1719-20, 1743, but app. liv. in Portsm. 1722, his ho. near the old meeting-ho. Adm., of Newc., 27 July 1748 to wid. Mary, who also adm. her fa.-in-law's est. and q.c. in 1752 to Jeremiah half the ho. and 2 a. of land. **Hannah**, m. one Perry; called of Newc., dec. 1753. Her sons Wm. Perry of Newc. and Richard Perry of Bradford q.c. 1753-4. Also taxed Newc. were: 1728, Daniel, Thomas; 1729 Samuel.

56 **WILLIAM**, Pemaquid soldier 1689. List 126. See also (17).

57 **WILLIAM**(39?), Dover, m. Mary Chesley(5), both liv. 1721. Poss. their sons: ?**William**, Dover, m. Hannah Ricker 28 July 1720; 3 ch. bp. 1723-28: Eleanor, William, Hannah. In 1748 the two sis. q.c. to br. Wm. their fa. and gr. fa. Ricker's est.; in 1756 he sold part of his homestead in Somersw. to Saml. Jones. ?**Thomas**. See also (22).

58 **WILLIAM**, Portsm., acc. by Mercy Brooking(3), 1712.

59 **WILLIAM**, Kit., wit. 1714-21 (wrote), sev. times with (8) and with Godsoes.

60 **WILLIAM**, caulker, from Rythyn in Wales, m. in Portsm. 11 Sept. 1720 Anna Mason of Newich; one W. J. taxed Berw. Feb. 1718-9; adm. to wid. Anna 1761. 5 ch. bp. Berwick and Portsm. 1721-1730, poss. others.

61 ——— (Jonas), Portsm. town charge 1722. Peter Abbott supplied her (Gimmer) with wood 1723, boarded her (Dame) 1726; her coffin bot 1727.

**JOPE** (Jupe), **Sampson**, able ship-carpenter, Richmond Isl., going home in July 1639, 'a good man to come back.' Ment. in acct. 1642. He was in England in July 1637, indebted to Winter's w., and poss. had been here earlier. List 21.

**JORDAN**, from Jourdain, an early Norman given-name.

1 **CAPT. DOMINICUS**(7), ret. by Sept. 1680 to the 1000 a. at Spurwink willed him by his fa. His ptn. to Andros 1687 recit. that he had built and improv. a consid. part for ab. 10 yrs. and settled four or six tenants along the river or creek of Spurwink. Selectm. Falm. 1685. A Kit. witn. in Aug. 1690, his w. Hannah in June 1692. Gr.j. 1690, 1691. Lists 221, 313a, 30, 32, 226, 34, 36, 29. An Ind. killer in war, their friend in peace, (his musket still on display at the Me. Historical Socy.) he met death unarmed in the treachery of 10 Aug. 1703. He m. Hannah Tristram (Ralph). Gr. adm. on her fa.'s and br. Nathl.'s est. 1 Apr. 1679. She was capt. with her ch. the same Aug. 10, (List 99), and ret. to Kit. M. (int. Newb. 17 Sept. 1713) Capt. Stephen Greenleaf of Newb.; depos. in Boston in Sept. 1746, ±92, ab. John McKenney being at her husb.'s mo.'s ho. at Spurwink to pay rent. See Miss Coleman's 'N. E. Captives,' ii. 25-30. His invent. 12 Aug. 1718 was attested by s. Dominicus, adm., 7 July 1719, and val. his 1000 a. at 5 s. per a. Ch: Major **Dominicus**, shipwright, b. ±1683, ret. from captiv. to Kit., buying there May 1710 the John Pearce ho. and 8 a. betw. the Stepping Stones and Mr. Roger Deering, whose niece Joanna Deering(1) he m. Lists 296, 297, 229. Kit. Apr. 1712. Selectm. Falm. 1719; there, Capt. D. J., gr. adm. on est. of uncle John in Jan. 1725-6; with w. Joanna sold the Kit. ho. 1727; in 1729 for self, bros. and sis. made agreem. with the town for the poss. of their lands. Y. D. 13.55. Will 10 June 1746, cod. 7 Mar. 1748, d. 20 May 1749 in 66th yr. (gr. st.). Wid. liv. June 1750.

7 ch. Capt. **Samuel**, b. ±1684, liv. Winter Harbor 1717. Ind. interpreter and agent, Capt. of militia, farmer, mercht. List 161. D. 20 May 1742, ag. 58; adm. 30 June 1743 to wid. Olive (Plaisted) and s. Richard. She m. 2d 1 Mar. 1743 Rev. Thos. Smith of Falm. 7 ch. **Sarah**, m. Roger Deering, Esq. (8 jr.). **Mary Ann**, or Arabella in ,Canada where she remained. In 1761 as Mary Ann, al. Arabella, single wo. of Three Rivers, she gave P/A to br.-in-law Jos. Calef. **Elizabeth**, m. Capt. Humphrey Scammon. **Hannah**, m. in Newb. 9 Nov. 1718 Jos. Calef(2). Lieut. **Nathaniel**, b. ±1696, ±66 in 1762, apprent. to Capt. Roger Deering. List 229. In 1751 he depos. that he had liv. in Falm. ab. 39 yrs.; in Nov. 1772 that he had been well acq. with inhab. of Spurwink since 1713; liv. Mar. 1782. He m. 1st ab. 1717 Dorothy Hill, 2d ab. 1741 Mary -Cutlevier-, who d. 10 May 1796, ag. 91. 5 + 2 ch.

2 **JAMES**. See Green(30).

3 **JEDEDIAH**(7), Kit., 4th s., recd. by will 1000 a. at Spurwink, where he ret.; taxed 1683-4. Driven away again, he was at Newc. 1697-1700, Kit. by 1704. Lists 226, 68, 315b, 290, 227. Will, of Kit., yeoman, 6 Mar. 1729 —16 Jan. 1735-6 gives his Spurwink land to ch. and gr. ch., wife not named; sons John, Robt. and Thos. execs. Ch: **Jedediah**, m. (Me. Ct. Jan. 1707-8) Faith Flye(2); d. bef. 6 Mar. 1729. 5 ch. **Hannah**, m. by 1714 John Moore of York. **Abigail**, m. by 1729 Danl. Robinson. **Keziah** (Saviah in will), d. unm. bef. 1740. **Sarah**, m. bef. 1729 James Jackson. **John**, Falm., m. there (int. 9 Apr. 1737) Deliverance Reading. She was gr. adm. 4 Oct. 1748; m. 2d (int. 11 Nov. 1749) Thos. Pollock. 3 surv. ch. **Thomas**, Falm., b. ±1701, capt. when his cous. Deering k. He depos. 1755 that ab. 1716, ag. ±16, he came from Piscataqua to Black Point as apprent. to Roger Deering; in 1773, ag. 72, ab. the early Boaden ho. List 229. M. (int. Falm. 23 Dec. 1736) Anne Simonton. 7 ch. **Mary**, m. aft. 1729 John Boulter(1 jr.). **Robert**, Kittery 3 Jan. 1726-7 when his fa. deeded to him at Spurwink; m. 14 Dec. 1727 Rachel Huckins. 12 ch.

4 **JEREMIAH**(7), youngest son. He and br. Saml. were reaping for Stephen Jones at Oyster Riv. in 1680; both must have ret. that yr. to Spurwink, where his portion was to be the old plantation willed to his mo. He m. 10 Mar. 1685-6 Deborah Bickford(22), who accomp. him to Newc. during the next war. Coroner's jury there 1693, taxed 1698. Lists 30, 226, 318a, 68, 315b, 39. Returning home during the false peace, his w. and 7 ch. were taken 10 Aug. 1703. The Jordan Mem. and Miss Coleman call him a captive, but it was his son, not he, who was kept long in Canada and France, and ret., unrecog. at first, to be kn. as French Jeremy. His w. was released by July 1706, was called his widow next mo., and cert. m. bef. 17 July 1714 Wm. Jones (55). Y. D. vi. 73. Of Falm. in June 1752, ag. bet. 80 and 90, she dep. ab. Scarb. 60 yrs. bef. Three of the seven ch. in 1703 appear: **Jeremiah**, b. ab. 1690, liv. Portsm. and Newcastle to 1726 or later; Falm. Apr. 1729, adm. of fa.'s est.; depos. there in 1752 ag. 62, liv. 1754. List 229. M. 1st by 1716 Catherine Randall (James), 2d at Greenl. 28 Jan. 1724-5 Sarah Rand (Nathl.), who prov. Jas. Randall's will in N. H., 12 Nov. 1753. Ch. 5 + 1, poss. 4 + 2. **Deborah**, m. James Randall of Newc., wid. 1731-3; 2d Saml. Wallis, wid. 1742; 3d by 1746 Henry Trefethen. **Child**, k. soon aft. capture.

5 **JOHN**(7), eldest son. Of Portsm., fisherman, 25 Jan. 1677, he deeded Richmond Isl., given him by his fa., to intended w. Elizabeth Stileman (Richard); witn. 1679 with Elias Stileman, but called of Richmond Isl. in July that yr. Accepting an old invitation of the N. Y. govt. to his fa. to settle in Pemaquid, he remov. there. J. P. for Cornwall Co. P. & Ct. ii. xxi. See also (6). Great Isl. in Dec. 1692, fined for refusing to obey the constable. Ret. when he could to Spurwink; k. there 10 Aug. 1703. In 1732 Henry Langmaid depos. that J. J. mowed cert. marsh at Cape Elizabeth 30 yrs. since; Thos. Marshall said 40 yrs. Y. D. 15.64-5. Lists 313a, 30, 226, 228c, 39. Three sons, being all the ch. he left, renounc. adm. of his est., late of Falm., 4 Dec. 1725; adm. next mo. to their cous. Capt. Dominicus. Ch., in will of Uncle Richard Stileman 1691: **John**, shipwright, m. Elizabeth Barnes in Portsm. 18 Sept. 1712. They were of Falm. in Nov. 1720; of Kit. 1728. Y. D. 10. 105, 12. 331. See Solomon (Nath. 1). **Richard**, mariner, Newc., had dwg., warcho. and land from his uncle Stileman; master of sloop -William and Mary- 1723; liv. 1740. He m. bef. 6 Mar. 1720-1 Christian Hincks. **Robert**, d. 1750, ag. 65; m. Mary Tobey (James). She was single 16 Dec. 1706; in 1707 acc. of robbing Newc. clothes-lines, and both were arrested. Both liv. Falm. 1736-42. List 229. 4 kn. ch. **Mary**, not in deed with bros. May 1716; likely one of the four members of her fa.'s fam. k. with him. Stileman J., m. 1742 Hepzibah Jordan (Jeremiah 3 jr.) must have been a gr. son.

6 **LT. JOHN**, Pemaquid, an (?English) officer ord. dism. with others to Boston 20 Apr. 1689, there charged with cruelty and treachery by Eastern residents; in London 1690. List 19. D. H. v. 35-46, vi. 476. See also (5).

7 ‡**REV. ROBERT**, Spurwink, prob. that s. of Edward of Worcester, co. Worc.,

'pleb.' enrolled at Balliol Col., Oxford, 15 June 1632. The will of Edward of Worc., bookseller, 1 June—2 Aug. 1637, left to s. Robert £35 to be added to his gr. fa.'s former legacy of £15, both to be pd. within one month of his decease. The fa.'s death may expl. his leaving Oxford instead of taking an A.M., getting a parish and remaining in Eng. The mother's fa. was Foulke Broughton, gent., of Worc. Feeble investig. to confirm this ancestry has failed, but the fact that on 24 Dec. 1661 the Maine Rev. R. J. was app. adm. on the est. of Richard Leader(2) ag. which Mr. Thos. Broughton(4) had a claim (Doc. His. iv. 12-3, 70-1) may lead to proof that he was the Oxford student, related to Mr. Thomas Purchase, not thru the latter's w., as Col. Banks suggests, but thru the Broughtons. Purchase was a native of Dorchester, co. Dorset, and appar. F. Broughton's sons liv. there and in London. Over here in 1639, in 1640 Jordan was in Brunswick with Mr. Purchase, the Pejepscot patentee, and a yr. later was still looking for a position. He attended the first ct. to be held and was a referee in an important case. Within 3 months of coming to Richmond Isl. as chaplain of the Trelawny plantation, he was acting as its lawyer in ct. Also Cleeve's repeated statements that leading men in Saco and Casco Bay were taking legal advice from him indic. that bef. leav. Oxford his ambitions had switched from the priesthood to the Inns of Ct. His pleadings and other legal papers drafted by him confirm this, yet he usually lost his cases. In 1663 Francis Small handled one for him, and won. (See references in indices of Doc. Hist. iii, iv; Y.D. viii; Me. P. & C. i, ii.) Sixteen months from his dau. Sarah's mar. to Jordan in Jan. 1643-4, John Winter, the Trelawny agent, gave a general P/A to his s.-in-law, embracing the entire plantation (20 May 1645). From that date 'Parson Jordan' was eminent, as Commissioner, Councilor, or Justice, under all governments. True he was dropped with the whole Lygonia gov. by Edw. Rigby in 1652, but he was quickly restored. The annexation of Scarboro and Casco Bay to Mass. took place at his ho. The King's Comrs. made him acting Chief Justice whenever Jocelyn was away. He was appar. content with any regime as long as he was in office. When New York took over Pemaquid and offered them magistracies there, Jocelyn accepted and Jordan sent a son. But there were limits to his compliancy. He wrote 'from the prison' in 1654, was taken to Boston jail by Joseph Phippen (his fee 19s.) in 1663, whence he wrote a letter on 4 Sep. (Jordan Memorial, pp. 72-3), and again

in 1669 the ct. ordered his arrest for defying Mass. authority. As a Ch. of Eng. minister he never weakened. Cleeve, as Rigby's deputy, prohib. his baptising, but he contin. He ignored the restrictions Mass. imposed on its own clergy. 'Mr. Jordan's meetings' were kept up until the Ind. drove him into the hands of the Bay brethren. His greed was a mastering passion, and no excuses can be made for his attempt to hound Cleeve from Machigonne and other settlers from lands beyond the Presumpscot. He set up a dubious claim to the Trelawny patent before the Lygonia ct., won it and was sustained by the Mass. ct. 16 July 1658, to the exclusion of both the Trelawny and Winter heirs. He intrigued notoriously for personal legacies among his own parishioners. His early estimate of Cleeve, 'wel nigh able to deceave the wisest braine,' was the judgm. of an expert. (See indices of Me. P. & C. i; Baxter's 'George Cleeve of Casco Bay'). Fleeing for safety in Philip's war, he went first to Eliot, poss. guest of Francis Small or hospitable Maj. Shapleigh, for whom he, 'sen.' and Mr. Jocelyn wit. a doc. now in an autograph coll. List 88, written by a stranger (likely Edw. Randolph) assumes he was dead. Actually he was mute, under protection of his lifelong foes. Lists 21, 221, 23, 111, 232, 222a, 223a, 222c, 182, 253, 88, 331b, 338a. Will 28 Jan. —1 July 1679, formerly of Spurwink, now of Gt. Isl., confirms Richmond Isl. to eldest s., Cape Eliz. to 2d s., gives the 'ould plantation' of ±1000 a. to w. Sarah with reversion to youngest s., and ±1000 a. to each of the others. The wid. was liv. 6 Oct. 1687. Lists 34, 226. 6 sons, perhaps the same in Jonas Bailey's will in 1663: **John. Robert. Dominicus. Jedediah. Samuel. Jeremiah.**

8 **ROBERT**(7), second son, mariner, late commander of the brigantine -Mary- in 1692. In Feb. 1675-6 his parents, then at Newc., gave tract called Cape Elizabeth to him; at Newc. 14 July 1679 he deeded half this to Nathl. Fryer. App. he did not ret. to Me. as early as his bros., but was there 20 Jan. 1684 deeding land with his mo.; of Cape Elizabeth 12 Nov. 1685 with w. Elizabeth (Harvey) Dole. July 3, 1687 he witn. Robt. Elliot's busin. at Newc. and Kit., poss., thru his wife's fam. connec., returning to Newc. bef. the Second War; cert. there 1690-1710. Lists 236, 90, 226, 319, 315abc, 316. Last found in 1710 when the Harvey land was in his poss.; dead 10 May 1716 and repres. by three daus: **Elizabeth,** m. John Larrabee(5). **Sarah.** She and Elizabeth Mansfield, both singlewo. of Newc., were bef. the Ct. 5 Jan. 1709-10, when her fa. and David Hill gave a joint bond. M. bef. 10 May 1716 Saml. Conner

(4), 2d bef. 16 Juy 1731 Thos. Brown(34). **Clear,** m. Wm. Lapish, 2d by 1740 John Martin.

9 **SAMUEL**(7), Kit., 5th son, b. ±1662, ±40 in Sept. 1702, served under Scottow at Scarboro, and was working with br. Jeremiah at Oyster River in 1680, but signed the Shapleigh ptn. that yr. in Me. Taxed there 1684. Selectm. Falm. 1685. Gr.j. 1687; tr.j. 1687. Leaving his 1100 a. at Purpoodock a second time he made a perman. home in Kit., tho taxed Newc. 1699-1700 and there 1702. Lists 237b, 30, 226, 227, 315b, 229. Of Kit;, adm. 4 Oct. 1720 to wid. Mary and s. Saml.; she relinq. 11 Oct. 1734. Wid. Mary depos. in Nov. 1741, near 77 (sworn by Pepperell), that she liv. in Falm. ab. 60 yrs. bef.; in 1751, ag. 84, form. of Falm., now of Spurwink, that she knew the ch. of Anthony Brackett(2) and Ann (Mitton). Prop. divided to 3 ch: **Samuel,** oldest, yeoman, Falm. His 1st w. Mary recd. into covt., So. Ch., Portsm., 25 May 1722, as w. of Saml. of Spurwink, tho of Kit. by deed Nov. foll.; m. 2d (int. Falm. 2 Mar. 1734) Frances Cranch. His house at Spring Cove, Cape Eliz., was a garrison, its site still kn. as Garrison Field. 2 kn. sons, the 1st and poss. both, by 1st w: Noah; Samuel. **John,** secundus, yeoman, Falm. 1736-7. Y. D. 18.112. In 1755 of Alewive Cove, he deeded to nephews Noah and Saml., tertius; of Alewive Cove depos. in 1749 that looking over his fa.'s papers aft. his death 30 yrs. ago, he found deed to John McKenney dated 12 Jan. 1673-4. **Sarah,** m. in Kit. 10 Dec. 1722 John Robinson.

**JOSE,** peculiar to Cornwall.

1 **CHRISTOPHER,** fisherman, mariner, merchant, Portsm., first at the Shoals 1651, selling wine there 1652; constable 1656-7. Portsm. propr. 1660, bot from Elias Stileman 1662, sold town gr. Oct. 1664. Taxed Portsm. 1672, Mr. C. J., tho called fisherman of Star Isl. 1670. Gr. j. (Me.) 1657; (N. H.) 1667-68, 1676. Lists 330b, 326c, 305c. Will 14 Sept. 1676 (d. Oct. 1676, or by s. Richard's fam. rec. 26 Dec. 1677), prov. 25 June 1678, disposes of much at Portsm., the Shoals and Great Isl., also ¾ of a ketch, to w. Jane (Cummings 2), exec., and 8 ch.; also remb. cous. Thos. (3), serv. Joan Knight, Portsm. Ch. and the college. Mr. John Fabes and Peter Twisden were at Mrs. Jane's ho. at the Shoals, 1681; she sued Ichabod Rollins in 1685 for cutting on her land on several islands; lic. out of doors 1686. Lists 329, 331bc, 51, 52. See also Chaplin. Will 31 Oct. 1689 names all ch. but Thos., little gr. s. Thos. and his two sis.; she had many rings and articles of silver, money, cows and a negro woman. Ch: **Rich-**ard, b. 10 Nov. 1660. **Thomas,** b. 27 June 1662, liv. on fa.'s place aft. his apprenticesh. with Mr. Robt. Eliot; d. s. p. bef. mo. (Ct. case), 27 Nov. 1684 (bro.'s rec.). Taxed Portsm. Dec. 1688. List 52. **Joanna,** b. 13 Mar. 1664-5, m. 10 Oct. 1680 Capt. Philip Severet. **Margaret,** b. 10 Oct. 1666, m. Capt. Wm. White; d. s. p. from small-pox 31 Jan. 1690-1, 3 wks. aft. her sis. Joanna. **John,** b. 27 May 1668. **Jane,** b. 18 July 1670, m. Richard Gerrish(7). **Samuel,** b. 6 May 1672; d. in France 1690 (br. Rich.'s rec.), s. p. **Mary,** b. 8 July 1674, m. 1st 5 Jan. 1692-3 Ichabod Plaisted; 2d aft. 1 Feb. 1715-6 John Brown Esq. of Salem, who d. 14 Apr. 1719, leaving large est.; she surv. and ret. to Berwick.

2 **CAPT. JOHN** (1), mariner, Portsm., Boston, on ketch -America- with John Jackson 1685. Under fa.'s will he shared in 300 a. at Long Reach with br. Saml. and sis. Jane; from sis. Joanna inherit. the Severet wareho. and wharf. M. aft. 19 Jan. 1690-1 Mrs. Esther (Waldron) Lee; d. Dec. 1693 (Jan. 1694-5 at Barbadoes, Richard's rec.); adm. in Suff. Ct., mariner of Boston, bond filed by Wid. Esther 27 Feb. 1693-4; adm. in N. H. to her 21 May 1694. She m. bef. Sept. 1695 Joshua Barnes. Only ch: **Anne,** b. Boston 18 Aug. 1692, gdnship to Capt. Rich. Gerrish 1 July 1707; m. 1st Thos. Harvey(15), 2d Wm. Slayton. Thos. Harvey was gr. adm. on her fa.'s est. 12 Oct. 1719. In 1731-2 he brot suit to evict Ephraim Jackson, Saml. Beck, Jos. Grant, who claimed under John Fabes, surv. joint tenant with Anne's fa.; but Wid. Sarah Leavitt and Col. Westbrook asked to be made defts., claiming that John Fabes took all by survivorship.

3 **\*RICHARD** (1), Esq., merchant, Portsm., liv. and d. on his fa.'s place. His inherit. incl. all the Shoals property. Selectm. Portsm. 1689, 1690-91; Rep. 1696; High Sheriff 1692-1707, exc. Jan.—July 1699 when displaced by Wm. Ardell on acct. of his sickness. Lists 313a, 329, 57, 324, 59, 62, 335a, 336b, 330df, 96, 337, 339. In 1679 he was adjudged the fa. of Joan Knight's (6) dau.; m. 16 Oct. 1683 Hannah Martyn (Hon. Richard). He d. 23 Sept. 1707 ag. 48 (gr. s. at Pt. of Graves); adm. to wid. 3 Feb. 1707-8. She m. 2d 2 Oct. 1718 Edward Ayres, d. 12 Jan. 1718-9, ag. 54 (one stone with 1st husb.). Lists 316, 337. Adm. again on his est. 19 Mar. 1721-2 to Edw. Cate; div. by agreement 18 Mar. 1722-3. Ch: **Richard,** b. 26 July 1684, d. 10 Jan. 1684-5. **Joanna,** b. 17 Nov. 1685. Her aunt Joanna Severet left her £20. M. 2 June 1709 John Pray. **Thomas,** b. 23 July 1687; inherit. ho. and land in Crooked Lane, Kit., from aunt Joanna; both he and sis. Joanna in will of their uncle Michael Martyn 23 Oct. 1700; d. s. p.

bef. 18 Mar. 1722-3. **Hannah,** b. 20 July 1689, recd. £10 from aunt Joanna. M. Joseph Hilton. **Jane,** b. 13 Oct. 1691, m. Edward Cate (1 jr.). **Mary,** b. 20 Jan. 1694-5, m. 28 Sept.—23 Oct. 1712 John Roberts. **Richard,** Portsm., b. 17 Oct. 1696, eldest s. 1723. M. in Boston 16 Mar. 1718-9 Damaris Dennis (Ebenezer), b. there 8 July 1701. Adm. to her 10 June 1734. She was a shopkeeper in Portsm. 1737, m. that yr. Jeremiah Wheelwright; both liv. 1758. 6 ch., 5 bp. So. Ch. 1721-1730. **Martyn,** Scarboro, b. 28 Dec. 1700, of Dover in May 1722 when acc. by Lucy Allen (Robt.) of Kit. as the fa. of her ch. Portsm. 1723-27. M. in Greenl. 1 Apr. 1725 Mercy Dearborn; she recd. 1 Oct. 1727 into So. Ch., Portsm., where he renew. his bap. covt. 9 Jan. 1725-6. 11 ch., 2 bp. Portsm., 1726-27, 9 bp. Scarb. 1729-30—1744, incl. Martin bp. 29 May 1737. Date of death unkn. One M. J. m. 4 Feb. 1744 Patience Haines and was bp. with a son James 26 Oct. 1746; other ch. bp. 1748-1776. **Sarah,** b. 20 Apr. 1704, m. Joshua Brewster(2). **Margaret,** liv. in 1720 at ho. of John Pray, her gdn; ±17, 20 Sept. 1722.

4 **THOMAS,** called cousin by (1) who left him 12 a. at Spinney's Cove. He or Thos. (1) depos. in Portsm. 23 Mar. 1679-80 ab. the ketch -Providence-, Mark Hunking master.

**Joully,** Henry, witn. Jas. Cole's deed of Nequasset land to Clark & Lake 22 July 1658. Y. D. 35.54.

**JOY,** poss. from Norman place-name Jouy; or a contraction of Joyce.

1 **EPHRAIM,** carpenter, Kittery, b. in Boston 7 Dec. 1646, s. of Thos. and Joan (Gallop) of Boston and Hingham. His fa. was dealing with Hugh Gunnison bef. the latter mov. to Kit. The son was in Kit. in Apr. 1670; worked in Portsm. 1671, ag. ±23; was fighting in Kit. with Danl. Goodwin and Nich. Frost in July 1672. M. Susanna (Spencer), wid. of John Gattensby bef. 1 July 1673, when she was abs. from meeting; and ret. to Hingham for a time, miller there 1675-6. She was liv. 13 June 1684; he 2 Nov. 1696. Kn. ch: **Ephraim,** b. ±1675, carpenter Kit. In 1693, ±18, he and his fa. ±42, went from Boston to Piscat. with Mr. Jos. Chownes. Lists 67, 298. M. 22 Feb. 1703 Sarah Nock; a wid. in Aug. 1715. 6 or m. ch., incl. Sarah, Mary, Ephraim, Susanna, Thomas, Samuel, and perh. Benjamin of Biddeford 1742. Sarah Joy, wid., was in Ct. Apr. 1717, bastardy; her s. Nathl., bp. 10 Oct. 1723, was named in John Key's will 1736 as my servant Nathl., called Nathl. Joy, under age. List 298. She appar. m. 2d aft. Oct. 1723 John Brown (17 jr.) of Bid-

deford. **Tabitha,** b. in Hingham 25 Sept. 1677, m. Rowland Jenkins (11).

2 **RICHARD,** carpenter, a good workman, but very spare (slow), Richmond Isl. 1638, with his boy who tended the carpenters. List 21.

3 **THOMAS,** associated with Jas. Johnson as bondsm. (Jaye) for Edw. Colcord in Portsm. Ct. 1650; several yrs. later jailed on Jona. Thing's excen. and pd. the money to Joanna Leighton's (2) 1st husb. (P. & Ct. ii. 97). List 75a. See (1).

4 **WALTER,** York grantee by 1650, removed to Milford. Wife Deborah 1652, related to Thos. Wathen and cous.-german to Wm. Sargent of Gloucester. In 1654 Mrs. Eleanor Hooke sued Robt. Collins on joint obligation with Sampson Angier, Edw. Start and W. J. Reg. 32.341.

5 **WILLIAM,** Portsm. 1685. List 334b.

**Joyce,** James, Great Isl. 1696; given life support by Hon. Robt. Elliot's will 1718. List 315c.

**JUDKINS,** a Northamptonshire name, poss. a diminutive from Jude.

1 **JOEL,** Exeter, appar. same b. Boston 30 Sept. 1643, s. of Job. and Sarah, or a younger s. of the name, age ±24 in Oct. 1671, liv. at Moses Gilman's ho.; 'over 30' in 1683. Ment. in the Judith Roby case 1671; fined in Hampt. Ct. 1672, swearing drunk. Lists 376b, 383, 52, 57, 67. Last found on minister's rate May 1714. He m. 25 June 1674 Mary (Bean 2), who was w. of David Robinson of Stratham in 1721. Ch: Job, b. 25 Jan. 1674-5, blacksmith, Exeter, had land from his fa. in 1700. Lists 67, 376b. His w. in 1715 and wid. was Elizabeth York (Benj.), who depos. in 1769, ag. 91, ab. early Exeter. Will 10 Mar.—26 Apr. 1738 names w., br. Benj., 5 sons as living, Job (ag. 66 in 1769), Joel, Josiah, John, under age, Jonathan, exec. and to have the home, dau. Abigail Edgerly (2) and her s. Thos., and Susanna, dau. of s. Benj. (not called decd.). **Sarah,** b. 13 Nov. 1676 (?). **Hannah,** her twin, m. 25 July 1709 Ebenezer Webster; ancestors of the great Daniel. **Mary,** b. 7 Nov. 1678 (?), m. in Haverh. bef. 1703 Saml. Welch; liv. Kingston in Jan. 1750, ±70. **Benjamin,** cooper, Kingston. His br. Job willed him 'my 10 a. right if he can get it.' W. Hannah Clifford (Jacob 4) in 1728. Will, bound for Cape Breton, 4 Mar.—27 Nov. 1745 gives all to her during widowhood, then to adopted son and apprent.; adm. to her, the execs. declining. **Samuel,** blacksmith, Kingston, freeholder 1706; had deed from br. Benj. in 1732. List 400. In 1731 he and Cartee Gilman were bondsm. for Saml. Scribner's wid. Anna. W. Abigail.

Will 26 Jan.—31 Mar. 1742 provides for w. (unnamed), 6 ch. and gr. s. Saml. J. Presum: **Joseph**, b. ±1695; Newmarket 1769, ag. 74, when he depos. that he liv. with Col. John Gilman from 9 yrs. old to 13. List 376b (1725). M. Abigail Folsom (1). 10 ch. One Rebecca (whether Judkins w. or dau. undeterm.), witn. receipt of David and Mary Robinson 1721; see Edgerly (2).
2 **JNO.**, 1695-6. List 67. Poss. Job or Joel. **Judson**, Randall (Randolph), convicted of piracy 1674. List 3. See Peter Rodrigo.
**Julius**, John, North Yarmouth 1686, a refugee from St. Christopher's. See List 213.

## JUNKINS.

**ROBERT**, York, was at Dover (Oyster River) with other Scots 1657-9, and bot there with Edw. Urine and Henry Brown, 1657. York by 1662 where he had a garri. ho. at Scotland. He and James Grant were bondsm. for Andrew Rankin 1667; his land adj. Grant's in 1686; O. A. 22 Mar. 1681. A town gr. of 32 a. by Curtis Cove was confirmed to his heirs in 1713. Lists 356a, 361a, 25, 87, 33. Will 2 Mar. 1696-7 (inv. 3 Dec. 1698) says 'my old age,' names w. Sarah and 'my ch.' She was dau. of John Smith, sr.; ag. 70 in Jan. 1715-6. In 1726 the two surv. sons divid. the homestead. Ch: **Alexander**. Town grants 1699, 1715. List 279. W. Catherine Stackpole (James) liv. 1747. Will 21 Feb. 1735-6—18 Jan. 1736-7 names w., 'me and my two bros.,' his 5 ch. rec. York 1701-1720, Joseph, Mary, Alexander, Martha, Mercy, and dau. Mary Carlile's s. John. **Joseph**. Town gr. 1701; leased John Frost's ho. and land at Scotland. List 279. M. Abigail (Ingersoll), wid. of Morgan Lewis (14). The Newsletter, Apr. 9, 1711, detailed his death: On Tuesday bef. Apr. 6 Danl. Dill and Joseph -Jenkins- k. by five Ind. near Scotland garrison. J. J. was stripped, scalped and left for dead, but arose and walked to garri., gave an acct. and liv. 2 hrs. The wid. and her 3d husb. Ebenezer Blaisdell gave bond to adm. 6 Jan. 1712-3; her acct. filed Jan. 1728-9. Ch: Joseph, 9 mos. old in Apr. 1711; d. bef. Jan. 1728-9, app. bef. he was 14. John, b. 21 Sept. 1711; adm. 1748 to half-br. Nathl. Lewis; left wid. Margaret, 3 ch. **Daniel**, Town gr. 1703. List 279. M. Eleanor Came(2). 8 ch. 1706-1730; Jonathan, Lydia, James, Daniel, Sarah, Eleanor, James, Mary, all but Jona. and 1st James in his will 9 Mar. 1746—17 Oct. 1749; widow's will 7 Sept.—21 Oct. 1755 names five ch. and dau. Eleanor's s. Joel Jellison; Peter Nowell also named.
**Justan**, John. List 228c. See Gustin.
**Jypson**, see Crockett (4), Gypson.
**Keais**, see Keyes.

**Keat**, William. List 332b. Presum. William Cate (2).
**Keates**, Richard, Kit., with Margery Pepperell witn. deed Crocket to Fernald, 1708. Poss. the Boston bricklayer and soldier of same name.
**Kecar**, see Kezar.
**KEEMER**. 1 **Edward**. List 161. See Camer.
2 **JOHN** (Kemar), of New England, friend of Francis Plaisted ment. in his will, executed in London 1707-8.

## KEENE. See also Cane and Canney.

1 **JOSEPH**(2), Scarboro and Kit., where he had his father's farm. The clerk who rec. the m. of Josiah K. and Mehitable Winch in Scarb. 25 May 1730 would seem to have made an error in his given name as it is the lone ref. to Josiah in the rec. Surely m. Abigail Andrews 19 Apr. 1733 in Scarb. where they liv. bef. ret. to Kit. after 1739. Will 1 Oct.—5 Nov. 1767. Ch., the 1st 4 bp. in Scarb.: **Jonathan**, bp. 5 Dec. 1734. **Deborah**, bp. 1736. **Miriam**, bp. 1738. **Aaron**, bp. 1739. **Simeon. Mary. Dorcas. Hepsibah. Lydia. Sarah.**
2 **NATHANIEL**, carpenter of Spruce Creek, Kit., b. 5 Aug. 1642, s. of Christopher of Cambridge, whose homestead he sold to John Hill in 1723. After working for Samuel Hall of Exeter 1680-1, he set. in Kit., where he was suing James Chadbourne in 1684 and Humphrey Chadbourne in 1686. He m. 2 Nov. 1688 Sarah Green(6), who surv. him. Charged with beating his negro slave in 1695. His title at Spruce Cr. brot him into court as deft. with sev. plfs., John Shapleigh, jr. in 1706, Samuel Spinney thrice 1713-6 and the estate of Christopher Adams in 1718. Will, 25 Oct. 1722—5 Jan. 1724-5, provides for his gr. dau. Mary Keene equally with his daus. Lists 291, 293, 296, 297, 298, 359b. See Hammons. A petn. dated 1706, describ. his life during the Ind. wars, states that he was 'obliged to lie in garrison and work hard to maintain his wife and 7 children,' of whom the foll. are ident.: **Nathaniel. Joseph. Deborah**, m. 1st 15 Dec. 1720 John Barter, 2d 9 Apr. 1752 Jacob Remick. See Crocker (5 John). **Lydia**, witn. deed Moore to Keene 1719-20, m. int. 8 Jan. 1724-5 Thomas Boothby, both of Scarb. 1756. **Abigail**, liv. unm. in 1767. **Sarah**, had illeg. dau. Mary who m. 17 Oct. 1734 Wm. Hutchins. A draft deed, dated 1713, from her father to John Proctor and Sarah, his now w., in York Files, may be evid. of her mar. **Esther**, single in 1725. She and Sarah were leg. of their aunt Deborah Kane, shopkeeper of Boston in 1711, their father not to finger a penny of it. **Jonathan**, witn. deed Williams to Weeks in 1714, depos. concern his fa.'s lands in 1716.

In 1715 his mo. made 2 trips to Newbury to collect his wages from Mr. Woodbridge. In No. Ch., Portsm., he m. 29 Nov. 1716 Martha Lydston(1), who m. 2d by 1726 Roger Deering(9).

3 **NATHANIEL**(2), yeoman of Kit., m. bef. 1725 one Grace, thru whom it must be that Elihu Gunnison called him cousin. Both liv. in 1742. Ch: **Richard** (prob.). **Isaac. Ephraim. Nathaniel. James** (prob.). **Grace. Sarah.**

**KELLY.** Our Kellys are both English and Irish. The Shoals family prob. came from Devonshire, where there is a par. of Kelly which gave its name to a family resident there since the 13th Century.

1 **AGNES** (Card 4), sis. of John Card who was a member of Roger Kelly's crew, wid. of Edmund Cox of Isles of Shoals, was Agnes Kelly of New York in 1699 when she adm. Cox's est., holding P/A from her son Edward Cox of N. Y., later of Salem.

2 **CHARLES** (11), Kit., where he liv. on 10 a. owned by his father, which he def. successfully ag. an ante-mortem gift to his br. Elisha and finally gave to his dau. Mary in 1722. Lic. to sell strong drink out of doors 1698-9 and 1709, but mariner 1718-23. Lists 296, 297. Juror 1709. His wife, Joanna Fernald (4) (m. 25 May 1698) d. bef. 1722. Only ch: **Mary**, b. 27 Dec. 1699, m. bef. 1725, when she sold her fa.'s Kit. property to Elihu Gunnison, James Scott of Boston, mariner.

3 **DANIEL**, Richard Foxwell's serv. at Blue Pt. in 1668. List 235.

4 **DAVID**, Portsm., s. of David and Elizabeth of Boston, b. 18 Dec. 1647, taxed in Portsm. 1672 and commander of the ketch Neptune, owned by Richard Cutts of Portsm., when it was captured by the Dutch in 1673. His mo. Elizabeth Smith, adm. of her 1st husb. deeded him, mariner now liv. in Piscataqua, a house and land in Boston, 1675-6. Still taxed in Portsm. 1679-80, but nothing further. See (9).

5 **DENNIS**, Exeter. In the first Exeter clerk's diff. hand, recording a gr. of 10 a. adj. the Hampt. line on the Salis. path. in 1664, the grantee's name has been read 'Davy' Kelley whereas it prob. is 'Denny' or Dennis. By a stretch of the imag. he is also Dennis Skalion, bondsman with others for Francis Pofat in 1664, and Dennis Seahone, partner of Philip Carty in 1667 in the Stratham-Hampton section. Names pronounced in brogue were hideously tortured in early spelling. Whether other Kellys of Exeter and vicin. were his descen. is unascer., as: Darby Kelly of Ex. m. Sarah Huntoon at Kingston 1 Jan. 1728-9; Stephen Kelly m. Anna Young at Kingston 1 Oct.

1729; Daniel Kelly and w. Catherine (Judkins?) of Hampton and Kingston 1721-40; John Kelly of Ex. 1724; Thomas Kelly of Brentwood, who m. Mary Edgerly (2).

6 **ELISHA** (11), Isles of Shoals, fisherman, ±31 in 1706, m. bef. 1702, when her sister gave him P/A, calling him bro. and gent., Susanna Sloper (Lt. Richard) who depos., ag. 32 and liv. in the ho. of her fa. Roger Kelly, in 1706. She was adm. to full com. in Gosport ch. 29 Aug. 1736 with her dau. Hannah. Lic. to retail in 1699 and to keep pub. ho. in 1700. Tried in vain to mtge. ho. at Crooked Lane, occup. by his bro. Charles, in 1715, but succeeded with his own ho. on Smuttynose in 1717. A writ was ret. 'non inventus' in 1719, but he was liv. in 1723 when he sold 6 a. on Star Isl., inher. from his fa. Ch. bp. at Newcastle 10 May 1719 as from Isl. of Shoals, were doubtless his: **Love. Margaret. Susannah. Hannah**, m. 28 Feb. 1736-7 Samuel Sewall jr. of York.

7 **GEORGE**, List 303. Isles of Shoals, 1664. Poss. misreading of (11).

8 **HOLDRIDGE** (12), Stratham, b. 10 July 1687 (Dow), m. bef. 1715 Hannah Whittacar (Abraham of Haverhill) who successfully sued Nicholas Gordon for share in Brentwood land of her gr. gr. fa. Nicholas Lissen (2), 1748-51. Judging by deeds, 4 of which he witn., he was liv. in 1705-1706 at Hampton with Henry Dow; Hampton Falls tax-payer, 1709; of Stratham 1749. By depos. of Nathaniel Johnson, Feb. 1750-1, he d. at Halifax. Ch. b. in Strat.: **Samuel**, b. 14 Aug. 1715, acc. by Abigail Morgan in 1736. **Jonathan**, b. 3 June 1719. **Joseph**, b. 31 July 1722. **Holdridge.** Dea. Samuel Lane's list of those who d. 1745-1746 at Cape Breton etc. incl. Holdridge Kelly. **Hannah**, b. 3 Mar. 1730. **Mary**, b. 17 Apr. 1733, m. Joseph Huckins. **Abigail**, b. 20 Apr. 1735.

9 **JOHN**, w. and 2 ch. ordered back to Boston from Portsm. 1686 (List 330a), may be bro. of (4) and of Elizabeth (Kelly) Harvey. He was a tailor, witn. his mo.'s deed to (4), m. Emm Jepson, who m. 2d Sylvanus Plummer 5 Nov. 1700, and had 6 ch. rec. in Boston. It is strange coincidence that Peter Harvey was also warned on same day for entertaining his sister and 2 ch. If the sister was Emm Kelly, sisterhood was at least once removed. One J. K. witn. a Portsm. note in 1687.

10 **RENOLD**, Monhegan, 1672. Lists 13, 15. His wid. Joanna (Dollen) m. 2d James Mander of Charlestown and Boston. See Dollen. No proven ch., but in view of fact that Robert Edmunds and R. K. were both at Monhegan, the record in Quebec of Jean Baptiste Edmunds, his w. Marie (Kelly) and dau. Marie Marguerite, b. in New England, captured betw. July 1694 and Nov.

1695 at a place unkn., is suggestive.

11 *ROGER, Isles of Shoals, ±76 in 1705, fisherman, first app. as mate of the ketch -Hope- on a voyage to the West Ind. 1662. On the death of the master at Nevis, he finished the voy. and made another voy. to Nevis, after turtles, in 1663 for owners, Francis Robinson and Edmund Brown. As a result of a civil suit growing out of this voy. he spent 15 weeks in Boston prison in 1664, and sued unsuccessf. for damages. On the turbulent Shoals he and his wife, Mary, led a turbulent life, constantly in the courts, he in civil actions with his crew and customers too freq. to detail, she as the result of an abusive tongue. First acc. of selling without a lic. in 1666, he afterward kept a pub. ho., lic. as late as 1693. Cons. 1667, Selectman 1679, local J. P. 1680 and 1699, County Justice 1692, 1693, 1695, 1696 and Dep. to the Gen. Court 1692. Lists 29, 52, 57, 304, 305a, 306ad, 308a, 309. Already a landowner in 1662, he bot land on Smuttynose from Nathaniel Fryer in 1668, and a ho. and 10 a. at Crooked Lane, Kit., in 1698. Part owner of the -Endeavor- in 1692-3, with William Partridge of Portsm., Henry and Samuel Dow of Hampt. and others. In 1707, in Boston, he deeded to his s. Elisha all his property, having made suff. adv. to his other ch., but his s. Charles, claiming that his fa. had been blind some yrs. and of impaired understanding, was able to upset the transfer of the Kit. land. Ch: **William**. **Sarah**, m. John Frost (8) ab. 1673. **Abraham**, presented for assaulting the constable of north I. of S. in 1690, Alex. Maxwell advancing his fine. His fa. was app. adm. of his est. 4 Apr. 1709. **Charles. Elisha.**

12 **ROGER** (see 11), first ment. in suit by Jane, wid. of Edward Eurine of Exeter, formerly of Shoals, for his wages on a 3½ mo. voyage to Nevis and Jamaica in 1677. M. 29 Sept. 1681 at Exeter Mary Holdridge, and was taxed then 1682-3. Deeded 10 a. at 'three pitch pines' to Benj. Taylor in 1696, and in 1701 q. c. 100 a. betw. his ho. and 'Jeremy's pocket' in the Stratham patent lands with warranty against 'any person that shall claim any legal right or title to my labor.' Ch: **Ruth** (prob.), m. 15 Nov. 1706 John Brown. **Holdridge**, b. 10 July 1687. **Mary**, b. 29 June 1689. **Sarah**, b. 10 Feb. 1692. **Abigail**, b. 3 Aug. 1694, d. 6 Oct. 1694 at Hampton. **Esther**, b. 12 Feb. 1698. **Roger**, b. 28 Apr. 1699.

13 **WILLIAM** (11), Newcastle, ±66 in 1738, mariner, m. Lydia Blagdon (2), both liv. in 1747 when they q. c. to dau. and s.-in-law Mary and Charles Treadwell all rights in est. of James and Martha Blagdon, deed., and Roger and Mary Kelly decd. Bot ho. at Gt. Isl. in 1698, mortgaged it 1710 and re-

deemed it 1727. Witn. will of Joshua Fryer in 1703, sued by Pepperell in 1706, app. est. of John Currier of Hog Isl. in 1709, and adm. est. of his fa.-in-law in 1722. Lydia Kelly relinq. adm. of est. of her bro. George Blagdon to Sampson Sheafe 16 May 1721. Ch: **Mary**, m. Charles Treadwell. **Lydia**, m. George Welch bef. 1727, when her fa. deeded them land.

**Kemp**, Nicholas, Pemaquid constable and tax-payer, 1687. List 124. See also Kim.

**KENDALL, William**, Cape Porpus, app. m. Margery Batson (3) bef. 1660, when as M. K. she witn. a Batson deed, who m. 2d Richard Young and 3d Robert Elliot (5). He was plf. or deft. in several small suits 1662-1665 over cattle, hay, etc., with Griffin Montague, Morgan Howell and Richard Hitchcock. Tr. j. 1665. In 1666 (last ment.) he was sued by John Lux for prop. left in his hands by Gregory Jeffrey. List 254. Dau. (either his or Young's): **Mary**, m. 1st John Turbet, 2d Emanuel Davis (6).

**Kendrick**, Joshua, burned to death, with Thomas Wilson, in their ho., inq. at Newcastle 12 Jan. 1661-2. Adm. to Nathaniel Fryer 24 June 1662.

# KENNARD. A line of Edward Kennards in Canterbury, co. Kent, is uninv.

1 **EDWARD**, Portsm., shipmaster, m. ab. 1680 Elizabeth Martyn (Hon. Richard), who m. 2d, contract 3 Apr. 1706, Lt. Wm. Furber, and 3d Benj. Nason, sr. Her fa. gave them a ho.-lot. Taxed in Str. Bank 1688, sued Joseph Couch Oct. 1694. Adm. to son John 6 Dec. 1712, Joshua Pierce bondsman. Lists 330d, 331c, 333b, 335a, 337, 66. Ch., the first 5 bp. in the No. Ch. 3 Sept. 1693; **John. Elizabeth**, had in 1706-7 an illegit. dau., prob. the Jane Kennard who m. 27 Mar. 1723, in the No. Ch., Daniel Cooper. She m. 1st Joshua Furber(3), 2d Francis Ditty 26 May 1715, 3d Capt. Richard Waterhouse whose wid. she was in 1738, 4th Moses Dam (3 John). **Sarah**, prob. d. bef. 1717-8. **Michael. Mary**, m. 10 Sept. 1710 in Berwick Benj. Nason, jr. **Abigail**, m. 26 Jan. 1717-8 in Berwick Wm. Grant, jr. **Richard**, bp. 5 July 1696.

2 **JOHN**(1), Portsm., mariner, m. 8 Aug. 1706 Elizabeth Alkins (Robert) whose fa.'s est. he adm. in 1711 and on whose lands, fronting on the great street, he liv. Taxed at Str. Bk. in 1713, rated in 1717 in the No. Ch., where his wife owned the cov. in 1708. In 1717-8 he, his br. and sisters q. c. their fa.'s ho. to their sister Elizabeth Ditty, a valuable geneal. doc. List 337. His will, 1753—1756, names the surv. ch: **Elizabeth**, b. 7 Nov. 1707, m. 1st 8 June 1726 Peter Mann, 2d 28 Dec. 1732 Mark Nelson. **John Wacomb**, b. 11 Feb. 1710, d. bef. 1753.

Alkins, b. 11 Sept. 1713, cordwainer, adm. to his fa. 1747. Thomas, bp. 30 Mar. 1718, mariner, of Rochester, co. Kent, in 1765, and had double share when the est. was div. Patience, bp. 13 Aug. 1721, m. Capt. Benj. Odiorne. Ann, bp. 25 Aug. 1723, m. Theophilus Dam.

3 MICHAEL(1), Kit., cooper, m. 1st Apr. 1711, in Portsm. Elizabeth Tetherly (Wm.), 2d 21 Dec. 1734 Sarah Varney (Peter of Dover), 3d 18 Oct. 1739 Rebecca Stanian (James of Hampton). Taxed in Portsm. 1713 and 1715, but settled at Sandy hill (now in Eliot) in 1717. Lists 291, 339. Will 30 June—July 1766 names w. Rebecca, 6 ch. Ch: Edward, bp. in No. Ch. 27 Apr. 1712, m. Elizabeth March 'from Black Point', liv. in Eliot and d. 22 Aug. 1788. 5 ch. George, bp. 8 July 1716. Michael, b. 22 July 1716, m. int. 11 June 1742 Dorcas Hammond (nat. dau. of George H. and Lydia Spinney), d. 26 Sept. 1797. 5 ch. Samuel, m. Elizabeth Allen (Francis jr.) 29 Nov. 1750; settled in Windham, Me. Mary, m. 3 or 5 Nov. 1743 Simon Lord. Susannah, m. int. 18 Feb. 1743-4 Joshua Small (Samuel). Ruth, m. 15 July 1749, in Newington, both of Kit., James Tucker.

Kennedy (Canade), Thomas, Falmouth witn. 1658, killed by falling tree, inq. 26 Dec. 1660. List 362b. See Bacon, Humphrey(2).

Kennells, Robert, taxed at Spurwink 1684. List 226.

Kennett, George, Str. Bk. witn. 1671.

KENNEY, see also Canney.

1 ELISHA, Scarboro, m. Lydia Grover (Matthew) in York 5 Jan. 1726-7. Sued Bray Deering, 1730, and his bounds in Scarb. ment., 1732.

2 SAMUEL, depos. in a Newcastle case, 1694. Poss. Samuel Canney(4 Thomas).

Kennicum, Sarah, formerly Cunningham, dau. of Reuben Hull(8), joined other heirs in selling his prop. 1719 and 1726, a widow.

KENNISTON, Kenerson. Kynaston an ancient Shropshire name. The third generation of this N. H. family should be the subject of further painstaking research.

1 CHRISTOPHER(5), Greenland, ±46 in 1701, served in Philip's war, m. 4 Dec. 1677 Mary Muchemore (List 335a) who witn. Coffin deeds 1707-11. In 1681 he laid the stealing of 2 pigs to his bro. John and Robt. Braines, but offered to pay Lt. Neale for 3 pigs rather than go to law. In 1682 Geo. Huntress asked to be relieved of a trust of £27 for the w. and ch. of C. K. Lists 52, 62, 33d, 332b, 337, 338a. Taxed as late as 1718. Ch: Alexander, ±21 in June 1701, m. Elizabeth Reed (Thomas). Lists 67, 336b, 338a. Had ch. Nathan, Judith,

Mary, Elizabeth, Elinor (b. in Hampton 3 June 1713) bp. in Greenl. in 1713, Deliverance bp. 1716, and doubtless others. William. With his bro. Christopher and Edward Bean he assisted his bro. John and John Fox to break Portsm. jail with an axe in 1716, all of them, after getting some good advice from his mother, fleeing to John Wiggin's in Stratham and later to Edw. Bean's in Exeter. Wm. may have been the groom of all or any of the foll. brides: Sarah Stanley, in Greenl. 6 July 1713; Bethia Trickey (both of Portsm.) 31 Aug. 1721; Elizabeth Ford in Portsm. 17 Dec. 1728. John, ±23 in 1718. After escap. from jail he was recapt. by James Jordan and Wm. Green, tried and acq. on the charge of murdering Hawnwick, a Penobscot Indian, near Furber's Point 1716-1717. And prob. Sarah, m. John Fox 24 Jan. 1711-2 in Greenl.

2 DANIEL, Wells, absent from meeting 1702, his master Thos. Barber(6).

3 GEORGE(5), Greenl., acc. of theft from Joseph Hall's wife, Thos. Pickering and others, he fled the juris. and was liv. with Joshua Brown, shoemaker, in Newbury in 1678. Taxed in Greenl. 1690, 1691. Tenant of the Hall-Packer farm in 1697, when he was ±40. Lists 62, 335a, 338a. D. 14 Mar. 1717-8, adm. being gr. 10 Nov. 1718 to wid. Bridget. She was taxed 1718-1719, and in 1720 she compl. that Jonathan Weeks, Tucker Cate, Jeremiah Lary and Abraham Sanborn stopped her 3 sons who were raising a house frame, assisted by Christopher Kenniston and Charles Allen. Ch: John, m. Sarah who was adm. to Greenl. ch. in 1728, and had a son John who m. Susanna Durgin (Francis) bef. 1738. List 338a. George, m. Elizabeth King, adm. to Greenl. ch. in 1726 and had ch. George, Elizabeth, William and John bp. 1727-1732. Samuel. Bridget, m. 11 Aug. 1719 Jonathan Smith. Mary (prob.), ±16 in 1696 when ment. with George.

4 JAMES(5), Stratham, m. bef. 1693-4, when his w. had a seat in Greenl. ch., and marked'gone' in Greenl. tax-list that yr. Grantee of Thos. sr., Thos. jr. and Elizabeth Reed in 1707. John Driseo sold him and John Satchell land in 1716 which he and wid. Eleanor Satchell divided in 1726. In 1732 his w. was named Dorcas. Old Mr. J. K. d. in Strat. 28 May 1747. In 1748 wid. Eleanor (Place) (Satchell) Durgin willed prop. to each of the ch. of J. K. of Strat. deed., naming: James, Greenl., weaver, m. 7 Nov. 1723 Elizabeth Durgin (Francis). Joshua, m. 22 Apr. 1725 Dorothy Dockum. His fa. deeded him prop. in 1736. Benjamin, m. 12 Dec. 1729 in Greenl. Abigail Bryant. Moses, m. Ann Lary (Samuel). His fa. deeded the homestead to him in 1746. D.

bef. 1768 leav. 2 sons, James of Greenl. and Bickford of Strat. **Abigail**, m. John Crown. Also **Joseph**, 18 in 1701. Adm. gr. to bro. Joshua in 1724 with consent of his fa. A Joseph m. Abigail French 22 Feb. 1721-2 in Greenl.

5 **JOHN**, Dover, 1663, but marked 'gone' in 1664 tax-list, was settled in Greenl. by 1665. Sued by Capt. Champernowne in 1666, Gr. j. in 1667 and 1668, subscr. toward Portsm. minister in 1671. Lists 326bc, 330a, 331a, 356b. On 16 Apr. 1677 his ho. was burned and he was k. by Ind. His wid., who had sat in the stocks for railing in 1676 and who was gr. adm. 1 Aug. 1677, was Agnes Magoon in 1681 when she and her son Christopher conv. land in Greenl. to Geo. Huntress. Ch: **William**, ordered that he should continue with his master Walter Abbott, accord. to his indentures, in 1663. **Christopher**. **John**, Dover, ±40 in 1697, ±48 in 1702, liv. with Lt. Anthony Nutter. Fined in 1681 for departing without a license, Joseph Hall bondsman. **Alexander**, drowned crossing above John Pickering's mill-dam on his horse, inq. 10 July 1671. List 327b. **George**. **James**.

**KENT**, an English county.

1 **JOHN**, Casco, 1703. List 39.

2 **JOHN**(3), Oyster River, m. Mary Wakeham (Edward) who was bp. 27 Sept. 1719, adm. to ch. 5 Apr. 1724 and liv. in 1757. Occupied the family homestead and d. betw. 1743 and 1748. Lists 368b, 369. Ch., the first 3 bp. 27 Sept. 1719: **Abigail**, prob. d. bef. 1748. **Ebenezer**, prob. d. bef. 1748. **Mary**, m. Moses Edgerly. **John**, bp. 30 Oct. 1726, bur. June 1781, adm. 17 Apr. 1782 to wid. Lydia who was liv. 1787. 4 sons. **Jemima**, bp. 30 Oct. 1726, prob. d. bef. 1748. **Benjamin**, bp. 30 Oct. 1726, sold rights in ests. of his fa. and gr. fa. to his bro. John in 1753. **Hannah**, bp. 5 Apr. 1728, m. James Durgin after 1753. **Elizabeth**, bp. 18 Apr. 1729, m. Reuben Bickford after 1753. **Joseph**, named in his uncle Robert's will. **Sarah**, q. c. to her bro. John in 1753.

3 **JOSEPH**(4), Oyster River, ±45 in 1705 when he depos. that he liv. with Benj. Mathes 35 yrs. past. Attested inv. of his bro.-in-law Robt. Watson's est. 9 Jan. 1695-6, and (erroneously Jacob in rec.) relinq. adm. 2 Mar. 1702-3. Gr. j. 1698. His plantation ment. in 1685 and 1703, he bot additional land from Henry and Sarah Nock (her fa. Charles Adams's grant of 1656) in 1712. In 1714 he q. c. 6 a. of marsh held by right of his fa. O. K. 'or any of his generation.' His w. Jane was adm. to the ch. 14 Sept. 1718 and he on 18 Oct. 1719, and our bro. J. K. was bur. 4 June 1727. Lists 57, 367b, 368b, 369. Ch: **John**. **Rob**-

ert, unm., q. c. to Oliver Kent part of an 80 a. Wheelwright pond grant in 1750; will 25 June 1748—27 Apr. 1759 names bro. Joseph, unm., sisters Dorothy, Sarah and Elizabeth, cousins (sister's ch.) Jonathan, Thomas and Hannah Langley, and John, Benj. and Joseph K., sons of his late bro. John. Lists 368b, 369. **Hannah**, m. Thos. Langley. **Dorothy**. **Sarah**. **Elizabeth**. **Joseph**, bp. 8 Nov. 1719, with 3 unm. sisters conv. all rights in their fa.'s est. to bro. Robt. 1 Apr. 1743.

4 **OLIVER**, Oyster River, m. Dorothy Hull (6) who m. 2d Benjamin Mathes. Taxed 1648, bot est. of Geo. Webb in 1651, had town grant (1656) laid out near Wm. Roberts in 1663, and ano. of 70 a. which still rem. in his family, laid out in 1658. Lists 354abc, 355, 356, 361a, 363a. The wid. and John Bickford app. adms. 28 June 1670. Ch: **Joseph**, b. 1660. **Hannah**, m. 1st Robert Watson, 2d bef. 1702-3 John Ambler.

5 **RICHARD**, a Newbury soldier under Lt. March, killed in skirmish with Ind. who had captured the Storer children at Cape Neddick the day before. (Pike's Journal, 20 Oct. 1705.)

Kerley, see Carley.

Kervorth, see Carveath.

**KETTLE**, John, Great Isl., cooper, ±33 in 1672, ±38 in 1678, paid town for his land in 1670-1 and sold it. Gr. j. 1665, 1666, 1673. Lists 312abcdh, 313ace, 323, 326bc, 330a, 331b, 312f. Twice witn. for James Pendleton in 1677, bondsman for Nicholas Paine and witn. to Nathan Bedford's bond in 1678. Corporal 1679. By w. Sarah he had: **Sarah**, b. 8 Mar. 1662-3. **John**, b. 6 Aug. 1666. See Coe.

**KEY**. See also Keyes. Found in Cornwall and the Midlands.

1 **JOHN**, Dover 1657 and bef., Berwick 1667, ±70 in 1703. O. F. 19 July 1669, jury of inq. 1668, Gr. j. 1673, 1674; tr. j. 1688. His wife (prob. 2d), Sarah Jenkins (9), wid. of Jonathan Nason, was still liv. 15 May 1731. Lists 30, 38, 81, 288, 289, 296, 298, 356, 99 p. 74, 290. His ho. was a garrison. He and his son John were prisoners in Quebec in 1695. Will 13 Apr. 1710—30 Oct. 1718, was witn. by 3 Warrens. Ch: **John**. **Elizabeth**, b. 1673, m. 3 Jan. 1694-5, Walter Abbott (Thomas 4). **Sarah**. **Abigail**, captive in Canada 5 Mar. 1710-11. List 99, pp. 75, 92. **Mary**, m. Sylvanus Wentworth. **Hannah**, m. John Haines(4), 7 July 1708. **James**, k. by Ind. ab. 1690, ag. 5.

2 **LT. JOHN**(1), Berwick, 65 in 1733, m. Grizzel Grant, and occupied the paternal homestead. Lists 99 p. 74, 298. Will 18 June 1736—20 Dec. 1737, names w., his servant man Nathaniel called N. Joy, and ch., the first 3 bp. in 1st ch. of Berwick 25 Apr.

1703: **James**, b. 18 Nov. 1697, not in fa.'s will. **John**, b. 22 Nov. 1699, m. Charity Hooper, int. 26 Oct. 1729, will 28 Feb. 1769 —4 Jan. 1779. With bros. Peter and Wm., sold part of their fa.'s lands in 1747. 7 ch. bp. in So. Berwick. **Mary**, b. 15 Dec. 1701, m. 18 Mar. 1724-5 Moses Tibbetts. **Peter**, d. 18 June 1769 (Tate's Journal). **William**, b. 4 Feb. 1703, m. Mary Hodsdon, 5 ch. bp. So. Berw. **Abigail**, given 20 a. by fa.'s will.

**KEYES**, Keese, Keais, Kaice, and even Case.

1 **HENRY**, early trans-Atlantic capt., at Piscataqua in 1629 and commander of the -Pied Cow-, which arrived with goods and passengers in 1631. Lists 1, 41.

2 **HENRY**, of Exeter, co. Devon, m. at Portsm. 19 May 1720, Sarah White of Topsham, co. Devon. See also (5).

3 **HENRY** (Keese), tax-payer in Str. Bk. in 1717 and later a wealthy merchant, m. Elizabeth Walton (Maj. Shadrach), with whom he adm. est. of Mr. Arthur Slade of Newmarket in 1747. List 339. Will 9 Aug. 1740—26 Oct. 1748, leaves estate to his wife, sister Mary, if liv., and his daus: **Mary**, unm. in 1740. **Elizabeth**, b. 1712, m. Hunking Wentworth (Lt. Gov. John).

4 ***SAMUEL** (Keais), Portsm., ±20 in 1663 and ±28 in 1671 when he was servant of Mr. Theodore Atkinson. Became landowner by 1673 and had long and active public career; Selectman 1681, 1682, 1683, 1686, 1687, 1698, 1699, 1700; Gr. j. 1676, 1683, 1694, 1698; tr. j. 1692, 1694, 1696; Town Clerk 1696-1713; Rep. 1692, 1697, 1698, 1699; member of the guard under Aaron Moses 1694. In 1701 he was a legatee of Mrs. Bridget (Cutt) Graffort for no stated or obvious reason. He m. 4 Feb. 1695-6 Mary (Riddan) Hoddy(2), (Lists 331c, 335a), who d. 17 Aug. 1711, ag. 58, and was bur. with her 1st husb. at Point of Graves. Lists 49, 52, 54, 57, 62, 83, 324, 327d, 330d, 331abc, 335a, 337, 330f (prob.). Will 1716—1720, ment. his dau. Gerrish (step-dau., born Hoddy) and his sons: **Samuel**, b. 11 Apr. 1697; **William**, b. 27 Aug. 1699.

5 **WILLIAM**? (or Henry?), of Exeter, co. Devon, m. at Portsm. 4 Sept. 1721 Elizabeth Perry. See also (2).

**KEZAR**, Kecar.

1 **GEORGE** (Kesare), witn. deed Payne to Coffin, 1670. The Salem man?

2 **RICHARD**, a Dover abuttor, 1657-8.

**KIDD, James**, very early at Dover, 1640+, where he had a ho.-lot adj. Lt. Hall, had grant on Dover Neck in 1658 and ano. in 1665. Adm. of est. of Edw. Urin of Oyster River, 1668. Sold much land to Job Clement in 1671, about the time of his removal to Exeter. Juror 1665, 1666, 1667, 1678, 1679.

Lists 52, 57, 62, 356abeg, 376b, 383, 384b. Ack. judg. to Capt. Thos. Clark in 1673, sued John Bray in 1669, John and Peter Folsom in 1672, John Clark in 1676, and was sued by Samuel Leavitt in the last yr. O. F. 1677. Liv. Oct. 1694. No record of a wife, but he had illegit. ch. by Sarah Connell or Connett, Walter Abbott's serv., in 1657.

**Kidder**, Stephen. List 41.

**Kiley** (Kelly?), Daniel, bp. 10 Aug. 1707, in Hampton.

**Kim**, William, Cochecho, 1664, and taxed there 1668-1671. Lists 67, 356j (Kemp), 356km, 359ab. His wid. Elizabeth m. Benj. Tubbs 12 Jan. 1698-9 by Rev. Mr. Pike. See also Kemp.

**KIMBALL**, Kemble, the latter a par. in Wiltshire where the name is localized. Kimball became 49th commonest name in N. E.

1 **BENJAMIN**, Portsm., ±20 in 1699, apprent. of Nathaniel Ayer.

2 **CALEB**, m. 15 June 1704 in Wells Susanna Cloyes(4); on Me. jury 1705, gone from Portsm. 1713, paid minister's rate in Exeter 1714, and back in Wells where he was a prop. as late as 1734. List 269c. See Hist. of K. Fam., pp. 1097-8. He was undoubtedly of the Ipswich stock, as were prob. John (5) and Thomas (8), and on the theory that he named his sons in an orderly manner, the 1st for his wife's fa., the 2d for his own fa. and the 3d for himself, it is suggested that he, at least, was a son of Richard and Rebecca (Abbe) K. of Wenham. 9 ch. rec. at Wells.

3 **DAVID**, Great Isl., 1670-1674, generally in trouble, was doubtless Campbell(2). In 1673 John Sherburne, jr. persuaded the constable not to whip him, 'as ye youth and myself were neighbors children ——— and in due respect to his good aged father,' the latter poss. the 'Long David' of 'Long David's house viz Kemble,' 1669. Taxed 1690-1691. Lists 87, 312c.

4 **HENRY** (Kemble), prob. bro. of (7), Boston anchorsmith, exec. of will of Giles Kemble in 1659, m. 1st 13 Nov. 1656 Sarah Founell who d. 10 Aug. 1657, 2d Mary Bridgen. In 1670 Rich. Selly of Winter Harbor owed him 10,000 ft. of pine board and gave him a mtg. on his prop. there, Thos. K. sr. and jr. being witn. List 82. To ch. **Zachariah, Henry, Giles, Abigail** and **Timothy**, b. in Boston 1663-1672, should certainly be added **Mary** Bucknell-Hough, who entered an Eastern Cl. for herself and other heirs of her fa. to 600 a. on the no. side of Cape Porpus, betw. lands of Maj. Phillips and Geo. Farrow, acq. in 1669. Wyman's Charlestown also lists **Sarah**, m. Philip Bass.

5 **JOHN**, a Wells witn. in 1707.

6 **THOMAS**, wheelwright, son of Richard of Ipswich, bot land in Hampton 1658 and 1659. He also owned a ho. and 200 a. in Wells, bot from Harlackenden Symonds, which he sold to John Wolcott in 1660, payment to be in corn and cattle deliverable in Rowley. Rem. to Bradford where he was k. by Ind. 2 May 1676, his w. (Mary Smith of Ipsw.) and 5 ch. taken and in captivity 41 days. Two ch. were b. in Hampt.: **Eliza-beth**, b. 5 Dec. and d. 27 Dec. 1658, and **Richard**, b. 20 Nov. 1659. 8 others named in K. Genealogy.

7 **THOMAS** (Kemble), prob. bro. of (4), ±57 on 28 June 1678, merchant and mill-man, of Charlestown 1653-1656 and 1658 (ment. his master, Mr. Rich, in England), was liv. in Dover in 1657 and had personal knowledge of Mr. Maverick's holdings there from 1647. He had bot a saw-mill on Oyster River from Valentine Hill of Bos-ton, ½ of which he sold to Randall Nichols in 1653-4, Gyles K. (ano. probable bro.) be-ing a witn., and ¼ to J. Pentecost in 16—, in return for maintenance of his family. In 1655 he and Thos. Jenner were suing John Pearce for detaining their vessel on the Kennebec. In 1658 he bot a ho. at Sandy Point, Dover, from Isaac Nash (sold to Peter Coffin in 1662), and also Hog Isl. in Casco Bay from George Cleeve (sold with Henry K., with consent of their wives, in 1663). He was 'of Kennebec' in 1660 and 1661, but in 1663 'of Boston', his head-quarters for the rest of his life, altho a 'resident of Damariscotta' in 1676 when he sold 400 a. to Walter Phillips. He d. 29 Jan. 1688-9, ag. 67 yrs. 14 d. (Copp's Hill). His w., Elizabeth Trerice, surv. until 19 Dec. 1712. His heirs entered East Cl. to 1000 a. in Coxhall, bot of John Sanders, land at Mere Point and an island adj., bot of John Sears in 1670, and an island at Cape Porpus bot of Henry Peas in 1673. Ch: **John**, b. 1 July 1656 in Charlestown. Prob. **Thomas**. Thos. K. jr. witn. with Thos. K. sr. in Win-ter Harbor in 1670. **Sarah**, b. 19 Apr. 1666 in Boston; m. Richard Knight. **Rebecca**, b. 12 July 1668 in Bost. **Henry**, b. 14 Mar. 1669 in Bost. **Elizabeth**, b. 8 Sept. 1671 in Bost. Poss. **Abigail**, m. 1st Philip Voden 22 Dec. 1692, 2d Isaac Jarvis 19 Jan. 1698.

8 **THOMAS**, York witn. in 1711, m. Bethia Bragdon (Ct. Apr. 1711), who m. 2d Charles White in 1717. Ch: **Thomas**, b. 28 Dec. 1710; with his mother's consent, sold land laid out to his fa. after his death, in 1731. One T. K. m. Mary Goodwin of Ber-wick in Wells, int. 23 Mar. 1737. **Abigail**, b. 29 Dec. 1713, d. 9 May 1728.

**KIMMING**, very rare and not in Lower's or Guppy's handbooks.

1 **JOHN**, bot ho. and 2 lots in Exeter in 1664 from Wm. Taylor, but was not ac-cep. as an inhab. until 1678-9. List 376b. Adm. 5 June 1708 to son **Moses**. **John**, b. 11 June 1670. **Sarah**, m. 29 July 1708 William Dam(5); her will 10 Dec. 1766—24 June 1767, div. the residue of her est. betw. Elizabeth Evans and Martha Flood, daus. of her bro. Moses, in event that her gr. dau. Martha Jones d. s. p.

2 **MOSES**(1), housewright and millwright, Exeter and Durham, m. 1st Elizabeth Horne(6), 2d, by 1720, Abial (Redman) wid. of James Gordon, who was liv. in 1760 when Benj. K. applied for aid for his mother A. K., now at the dwelling house of Stephen Flood, her sons Jonathan and Joseph (but notice served on -Nicholas-) Gordon having refused to help her. Lists 369, 67, 376b. D. bef. 1763. Ch: **John**, poss. son or the bro. of Moses, worked 8 mo. for John Scrib-ner, Exeter blacksmith, in 1733-1734. **Itha-mar**, blacksmith of Exeter, 1737. **Elizabeth**, m. 10 Aug. 1749 John Evans(10). **Martha**, had an illegit. son, Thomas Dolloff, by Thos. Dolloff, her sons Jonathan and Joseph (but a minor, 21 Mar. 1737; m. 26 June 1740, at Hampton, Stephen Flood of Exeter. Surely by 2d wife: **Benjamin**, Brentwood, m. 26 Feb. 1746-7, at Kingston, Sarah Moodey.

**KINCADE**, Kinket.

1 **DAVID**, came to Boston from Cambridge in 1680, employed by widow Neale to draw beer, Thos. Dewer being surety for him and his family to the town of Boston. Member of the Scotch Charitable Soc., 1684. Bef. 1690 he mov. to Oyster Riv. where his homestead, still kn. as Kinket's field, is now part of N. H. College. His 2d w. was Anne, wid. of Stephen Jenkins, who was adm. to the ch. 10 Feb. 1722-3, and who m. 3d Thomas Potts. In 1723 she deeded Kincade prop. in Lee called 'Camsoe', doubtless a corruption of Campsie, a par. in co. Sterling, Scotland, in which is a village of Kincaid-field. Lists 57, 67, 96, 368b, 399a (Daniel). Attacked by Ind. in 1708 he and his lad escaped (Pike). Will, 23 June 1719—6 Mar. 1722-3, ment. wid. and executrix and ch: **Naphtali**. **Hannah**, m. one Hay, adm. to ch. 1 Sept. 1723, and had ch. Mary, Samuel and Hannah bp. **Sarah**.

2 **JOHN**, taxed at Str. Bk. 1717, called of Waterford, Ireland, when he m. Martha Churchill(4) of Portsm. 13 Nov. 1718. Ch: **Susannah**, m. Job Jellison.

3 **NAPHTALI**(1), apprent. to Timothy Davis, jr. of Portsm. who sued Jeremiah Calef for flogging him for stealing corn. Bp. at Oyster River 31 Mar. 1716-7, m. 7 Dec. 1717 Christian Rand, who was bp. 18 July and adm. to ch. 7 Nov. 1725. Moved

to Sheepscot where in 1735 he bot land sold in 1740. Petitioned for garrison protection 17 Feb. 1743-4 and was k. by Ind. near Fort St. George 27 Sept. 1745. Lists 368b, 369. His wid., still of Sheepscot, sold dower rights in Durham 15 Sept. 1749. Ch: **David**, serv. in Louisburg exped. **James**, signed garrison petn. and was capt. when his fa. was killed. Returned in summer of 1747 only to be killed in attack of 24 Apr. 1748. **Elizabeth** (doubtless Carr(6) Kincket, niece of Allison Brown) was prob. his w.

**KING**, common throughout England, rarest in the north and so. west. Became 64th in N. E.

1 **DANIEL**(11), Kittery, carpenter, in 1674 sold to Gabriel Tetherly part of land granted his fa. Coroner's j. 1675. List 287.

2 **CAPT. DANIEL**, Salem, gr.-neph. of the wives of John Blaney and Thaddeus Riddan. List 37? He m. Mary Vaughan (William) of Portsm., where s. **William** was b. 17 Mar. 1698-9; m. Abigail Oborne, step-dau. of Saml. Penhallow, Esq. Will, mariner of Portsm., 24 Aug. 1745—26 Dec. 1753 names w. Abigail, 7 ch.

3 **EDWARD**, soldier at Saco Fort under Capt. Hill. One Edw. was of No. Yarmouth 1729. See also Larrabee (3).

4 **JOHANNA**, wit. (mark) with Benj. Bickford to Trickey deed, Newington, 1679; proved by B. B. alone 1682.

5 **JOHN**, from Weymouth, wit. Ind. deed to John Richards 1654. Y. D. 35.46. List 181.

6 **JOHN**, Portsm., tax remitted 1675.

7 **JOHN**, Kittery, m. bef. 1703 Hannah Crockett(4). Taxed 1704. List 290. She nursed Enoch Hutchins ab. 1705. Presum. had two more husbands, one Stanford m. in Portsm. bet. 3 May—4 July 1711, and Valentine Scates m. in Berw. 28 May 1722. One kn. ch: **Joseph**, b. in Kit. 11 Sept. 1704.

8 **JOHN**, 1720, gr. son of Richard Webber.

9 **PETER**, Pemaquid 1687; at Charlestown with w. and three ch. from Monhegan, Oct. 1689. List 124. One Peter m. in Marbleh. 12 Aug. 1723 Susanna (Oakman) Bennett, and d. in 1726, ag. 70; she a wid. there 1737, ag. 77.

10 **PETER**, Roi alias King. See Brackett(4).

11 **RICHARD**, Kittery, bot the Williams right to Champering Isl., Aug. 1649. 'Long Reach from Goodm. Green's to Goodm. King's' ment. 1651. Adm., of Piscataqua, 4 Oct. 1653 to Bryan Pendleton. Kit. gr. 1665 to R. K., his heirs or assigns. Lists 323, 298. Wid. Susanna m. 2d Gabriel Tetherly. She was ±67 in Jan. 1695-6. Ch: **Daniel**, of age 1674. **Richard**, b. ±1653.

12 **ENSIGN RICHARD**(11), seaman, shipwright, Kit., ±42 in 1695-6. Accus. of

abusing Richard Miller, Ct. Apr. 1673, he forf. his bond, and was sued by Mr. Weare therefor; in 1677 he sued Mr. John Cutt for wages on his last voyage on -The Return-. With Gabrigan Bonython(1) when he was drowned. Gr.j. 1688, 1693, 1695, 1699; Tr.j. 1704; Jury life and death 1693. Selectm. 1693-4, 1711-12; Surv. Highways 1694-6. Called Sergt. 1695-6, Ensign 1710. Lists 298, 30, 296, 291, 297. D. ab. 1723; bond of wid. Mary (Lidden 2) 7 Jan. 1723-4, with Jos. Curtis and Richard Gowell jr. She m. 2d Samuel Johnson(31). Ch: **Sarah**, b. 17 Mar. 1687, m. 1708 Joseph Young of York. **Susannah**, b. Mar. 1689, m. Thos. Knight (21). **Richard**, b. 26 Feb. 1692, shipwright, oldest s. 1725, liv. Jan. 1731-2, m. 19 July 1714 Hannah Preble (Abraham). 4 ch., incl. Richard, b. 20 Feb. 1719, who was not the founder of the Scarb. family. **Daniel**, b. 6 Feb. 1693, appar. the one who 'had but one hand' in 1710, when his fa. asked tax abatement for him. Adm. 6 Oct. 1729 to br. George. Town gr. of 30 a. 1699 divided bet. his br. and sisters. List 298. **Mary**, b. 9 Mar. 1695, m. Stephen Field, gr.s. of (12). **George**, b. 23 Mar. 1697, mariner, Portsm., taxed Jan. 1731-2, m. 28 May 1719 Margaret Adams (John 5). She m. 2d by 1740 one Clark; liv. Widow C. 1750, 1753. 4 kn. ch., 3 liv. 1753. **Joanna**, b. 12 Oct. 1699, m. 31 May 1721 Peter Staples.

13 **THOMAS**, Richmond Isl. List 21.

14 **THOMAS**, carpenter, Exeter. One of the young men to receive land in Hampton June 1640; in charge of bldg. the pound there Feb. 1640-1. Of Exeter 20 Sept. 1644, he sold Hampton land. Selectm. 1650, 1652, 1658, 1662. Lic. to sell beer and wine 1651; owned in mill being built 1659. Lists 21, 391a, 392a, 375ab, 376ab, 377. See also Green(19). He m. bef. Dec. 1641 Miriam Moulton, who had previously been accus. with Robt. Coker of Newb. Will 11 Mar.— 9 Apr. 1667 names her; neighbor and countryman Jona. Thing; cousins Henry Moulton, Christian Dolloff, and cous. Rachel, his w.; servant Wm. Willey; John Moulton; and the first ch. the Dolloffs should have.

15 **WILLIAM**, Isles of Shoals, poss. the W. H. ±40, wit. in suit John Ridgway v. Alex. Jones, in Middlesex Ct., 1653. D. at the Shoals, inv. 28 May 1664. Adm. to son **William**, under age, b. ±1646, who chose John Hunking gdn.; J. H. also apprais. with John Marden.

16 **WILLIAM**(15), late of Portsm., m. Sarah Palmer of Kit., their mar. portion from her fa. Wm., 24 Aug. 1669, 13 a. near his old ho. that was burned. Greenland 1666, when he bot 25 a. from Chas. Allen; sold to Philip Lewis, 1671; depos. Sept. 1671, ±25, that his dwg. in Greenl. was five yrs. last

winter. Abs. from meeting 1672. List 298. Adm. 6 Nov. 1677 to wid. Sarah; again 30 July 1681 to Wm. Palmer, Ephraim Crockett a bondsman. Ch: **Samuel**, Greenland, s. and h. 1706, confirmed to John Johnson the land his f. sold to Lewis, the deed lost. Portsm. soldier at Oyster Riv. 1696, Newc. 1708. Lists 67, 68, 330d, 336b, 338a. He bot from Christo. and Mary Keniston 1696; taxed 1698 next Leonard Weeks, whose s. Joshua gave life lease of 8 a. free of rent, to S. K. and w. Elizabeth 1724. She d. 3 Nov. 1735; he m. 2d 8 July 1736 Abigail Kelly, who d. 31 May 1742; 3d in 1743 ano. Elizabeth, named in his will 12 Dec. 1745—26 Feb. 1745-6, with daus., Elizabeth Keniston(3) and Sarah King; Dr. John Weeks and John Watson exec. One Elizabeth K. m. Robt. Dutch in Greenl. 7 Jan. 1719-20. **Sarah**, deeded to br. Samuel 1696; Wells witn. 1696; in Ct. Jan. 1697-8.

**KINGSBURY, 1 John**, York, b. in Newbury 16 Oct. 1690, m. there 29 Dec. 1715 Mary Stickney, who m. 2d 4 Dec. 1734 John Sayward at York. List 279. Ch: **Mary**, m. 24 Apr. 1737 Nathaniel Harmon. **Hannah**, m. int. 20 Sept. 1740 John Bane. **Sarah**, m. int. 17 Jan. 1740-1 Benj. Donnell. **Abigail**, m. int. 18 Oct. 1746 Daniel Grant.

2 **JOSEPH**. See Came(3). List 279.

**Kinneth**, Sarah, an adult, bp. 31 Mar. 1716-7 in Durham.

**KIRBY**, Kerby. 1 **Henry**, bot land from Philip Foxwell at Blue Point in 1676 and built a ho. and also had a town gr. in 1685. Sold 6 a. to John Sampson in 1689 and 72 a. to James Kent in 1727. A Boston tailor and 'an old man', he depos. about Edw. Bickford's will in 1713. List 238a.

2 **JOSEPH**. List 334b.

**KIRKE**, the northern pronunciation of 'church'. The name has spread from the border counties to the Midlands.

1 **EDWARD**, taxed Portsm. 1690. List 57.

2 **HENRY**, ±34 25 June 1672, first app. in Boston, called bef. Co. Court for keeping a disorderly family; next in Ipsw. (Keerke), allowed to settle in the town as a currier 14 Feb. 1664. In 1666 and 1667 he was lic. tavern keeper in Dover. He bot an Oyster River due bill dated 15 Dec. 1667. In 1671-1672 he app. as cr. or dr. in York Co. Court. At Maquoit in June 1672. In Oct. 1678 he was of Portsm., currier, selling his ho. and land at Cold Harbor, built on 2 a. given him by Abraham Conley. This deed was signed by wife Ruth (Glanfield) who in 1675 had adm. the est. of her husb. Caleb Stevens. In July 1675 he and his first w. had been ord. into York Co. Ct., for not attending church. The Stevens ho. became 'Kirke the currier's house', which the sole heir

sold in 1692, after coming of age. His death is indicated by a suit brot against his est. by dau. Ruth for silver money lent her fa. 1703-12. Lists 52, 57, 315a, 329, 330d, 331b, 335a, 337, 356jk, 318b. Ruth Kirke was adm. to the No. Ch. 20 Apr. 1693 and was still a member in 1699. In 1714 Goodwife K. was keeping Goody Bond. Lists 331c, 335a. His surv. heirs in 1728 are shown in deeds by which they sold their fa.'s pur- chase in Portland. See Allen(4). Which w. was the mo. is not clear. Ch: **Charles**, appar. working for Francis Huckins(1) in 1680, d. s. p. **James**, witn. 1689-1692 with John Libby(7) and Caleb Stevens. Likely the same who had been apprent. to Mr. Lad- brook 6 yrs. to poor advantage. He d. s. p. unless poss. fa. of Charles, in 16th yr. in 1702 (see Holland) and **Henry**, presum. s. or gr. s., d. s. p. Adm. on est. of H. K. of York, glazier, gr. in Suff. Probate Ct. 6 Nov. 1727 to Alexander Bulman, after which the remaining heirs sold their Portland inherit- ance. **Eleanor**, m. 29 Dec. 1692 Capt. John Libby(7). Likelier ch. of 2d w: **Elizabeth**, m. Daniel Libby; perhaps Jonathan Barlow; cert. John Meader. But if printed figures are correct, bp. 31 Dec. 1727, 60 yrs. old, sitting lame in her chair, then she was the 1st w.'s dau. **Ruth**, m. James Treworgye. **Mary**, m. 21 Sept. 1712 Samuel Brookings; 2d, int. 3 Feb. 1727-8 Matthew Grover. **Abi- gail**, m. 14 Mar. 1704-5 in Ipsw. George Smith of Kit.

3 **THOMAS** (Kirkes); taxed Portsm. and ho., 1691. List 62.

**Kirkeet**, see Carkeet.

**Kitto**, Edward, Falmouth, Oct. 1686, talk- ing too much.

**Kittredge**, James, ag. 28 in 1696, at Wells 1695-1696, prob. a soldier.

**KNAPP, 1 Henry**, informed against Francis Rogers in York Ct., 1704, and was him- self fined.

2 **JOSHUA**, gr. 20 a. in York in 1697, m. Sarah Beale(2) who m. 2d John Busher, int. 8 July 1727 in York. In 1714-5 an exec. ag. him was ret. -non est inventus- and in 1718 he, his w. and ch. were warned out of Roxbury. She was wid. Knapp in Dor- chester in 1725. James and Jonas Knapp of Falmouth, 1730, were his nephews. Kn. ch: **Samuel**, b. 26 July 1715 in Roxbury. **Ebenezer**, bp. 22 Aug. 1725 in Dorchester, of York in 1747 when his mo. deeded him land.

3 **PETER**, witn. a Berwick deed in 1687, called cousin by James Smith of Berw. who willed him 4 a., where he hath built his ho. adj. Richard Towzer, in 1687. List 94.

**Knapton**, Capt. Caesar, sent from N. Y. by Gov. Andros to command at Pemaquid in June, 1677. J. P. there 6 Oct. 1680. List 16.

Kneebene, James. See Neighbors.

**KNIGHT**, well distributed through central and southern England.

1 **DANIEL**, York, sued for slander by his former master, Rev. George Burdett, in 1640, lost the case, it would seem unjustly.

2 ‡\***EZEKIEL**, Wells. (An E. K. was appren. in 1619 and made free of the Fishmongers Co., London, in 1626). Of Salem in 1637 and in 1641 of Braintree, where his w. Elizabeth d. in 1642, he reached Wells in 1643, one of the first settlers, building a ho. near the mouth of the Mousam River. Selling in 1645 he was gr. land on the Webhannet and built there. Of Puritan inclination, he gained great prominence on the ascendancy of Mass., submitted willingly in 1653, was made freeman and immediately app. com. t. e. s. c., an office held for many years. From 1653 he was frequently gr. juror and selectman; Associate Justice 1662, 1663, 1664, 1668, 1669; Assistant 1647; Rep. 1680; agent for Rigby; signed all the petitions in favor of the Mass. govt.; and in the absence of a minister 'improved his best abilities in speaking out the word of God, praying, singing psalms and reading a good orthodox sermon.' Lists 24, 25, 28, 29, 33, 96, 261, 262, 265, 266. Three wives successively shared his Wells home, Ann (liv. in 1655), wid. Esther Lovering(2) who d. in or bef. 1675 and wid. Mary Hill, dau. of Gov. Theophilus Eaton and wid. of Valentine Hill(21) of Boston, who d. 24 Apr. 1708 in Dover. His old age was spent in Dover where he d. 1689. Will 18 Apr.—16 Sept. 1689, left 2/3 of his est. to his son Ezekiel and 1/3 to his dau. Elizabeth Wentworth, after a life est. in his w. Ch. by 1st w: Ezekiel, b. 1 Feb. 1641 in Braintree and d. 7 mo. later. By 1st or 2d w: Elizabeth, m. William Wentworth. Prob. by 2d w: Ezekiel, b. ab. 1650.

3 **EZEKIEL**(2), Wells, m. Sarah Littlefield, wid. of Thomas(23), who was his wid. in 1719-20 when she kept the meeting-ho. clean and decent for 40s. a yr. Wages were due him in 1677 for services in Philip's war. Signed petn. to Mass. in 1668 and took O. F. 7 July 1670. Constable 1679 and Gr. j. 1676, 1679, 1681, 1689, 1693, 1694. Lists 268a, 269a, 266. In 1717 he deeded all his marsh in W. to his d. Hannah, a dowry. Will 19 June 1717—25 Feb. 1718, ment. his w. Sarah and d. Hannah, who had m. 15 Oct. 1716 John Eldridge (2 John).

4 **FRANCIS**, bro. of (15), gent. and merchant, Pemaquid, 1647-8 to ab. 1658, ±47 in 1657. In 1648-9 he gave a bill for £23 to Hugh Gunnison of Boston who assigned it to Capt. Richard Davenport in 1650, Knight being arrested at his suit ab. 1658. See Asp. Lists 10, 72, 75b, 78.

5 **GEORGE**, Black Point, had w. Eleanor who was indicted for suspicion of adultery 7 Nov. 1665. He d. soon after making his will 5 Apr. 1671, the inventory being filed 27 May. By 10 Oct. his wid. had m. 2d Henry Brookings who was app. adm. 2 Apr. 1672. Ch: Nathan, b. ab. 1667. Elizabeth.

6 **JOAN**, sister of (8), was a servant in the home of Christopher Jose in 1676 and in 1679 brot to court her bastard ch. and in Richard Jose's presence acc. him as its fa. Witn. will of Richard Cummings in 1678 and a bond of Geo. Jaffrey in 1688, sworn to in Portsmouth in 1715. Ch: Elizabeth (Knight), m. 14 Mar. 1697-8 John Ham, named as grantor with her mother (but did not sign) in a deed to Benedictus Tarr in 1714.

7 **JOHN**, came over as servt. with Mrs. Annis Littlefield in 1638.

8 **JOHN**, Dover, ±26 in 1680, when he was reaping at Oyster River, m. Leah Nute (James), who m. 2d 17 July 1704 Benedictus Tarr, late of old England. His nuncup. will, 11 Nov. 1694, left £5 each to Zachariah Pitman, Wm. and Henry Hill (apprentices), cousin Leah Nute and to the Quaker Ch., and to his w. Leah and his sister Joan Knight a good est. incl. a 60 a. homestead farm and housing on Dover Neck, one called 'the great house' and the other 'the old house'. The wid. and sister agreed to divide the prop. 21 Apr. 1702. No ch.

9 **JOHN** (Chevalier), Jerseyman, b. 30 Aug. 1659 (gr. st.), m. 29 Mar. 1684 in Portsmouth Bridget Sloper (Richard). (It is worth noting that a John Chevalier from the Island of Jersey, mariner, of the Isles of Shoals and Boston, d. in Boston bef. 12 June 1686 when Abraham Gourdon, mariner, was named adm.) Taxed in Portsm. 1681; Gr. j. 1684. Lists 52, 57, 62, 329, 332a. Merchant and owner of much property in Portsm., he bought land in Newington, incl. ownership of the Hilton Point-Kittery ferry, from Bickford, Downing and Trickey from 1702 to 1707, and there d. 11 May 1721. Will 29 Nov. 1720—7 June 1721. Her son Capt. John K. was app. adm. of Bridget K.'s est. 30 July 1740. Ch: John, b. 29 Jan. 1684-5. Elizabeth, b. 8 July 1687, m. 1st 12 Sept. 1706 John Janvrin of the Isle of Jersey, whose est. she adm. in 1720; 2d 10 Oct. 1720 Rev. Joseph Adams of Newington; d. bef. Dec. 1760. Her ch. John and Mary Janvrin were ment. in their gr. fa.'s will. William, sole exec. of his fa.'s will, m. 29 Nov. 1722 in No. Ch. Deborah Penhallow, who adm. his est. on his death, 16 Nov. 1730, ag. 37. In 1737 his heirs were sons William and Temple and dau. Deborah (m. Henry Carter, merchant, of Gosport). Mary, given

a house formerly Edward Polley's by her fa., m. Capt. John Cox, Boston merchant and vestryman of King's Chapel, whose est. she-adm. in 1733. 2 daus. **Temple,** mariner, taxed in Portsm. 1722 and 1724, d. s. p., adm. being gr. 29 Apr. 1741 to his bro. Capt. John K.

10 ***CAPT. JOHN**(9), Portsm., merchant and Esq., m. Elizabeth Shapleigh (John), who was liv. in 1769. Member of Newington ch. but prom. cit. of Portsm., serving as moderator, selectman and Rep. List 343. Will 28 Dec. 1765—29 Jan. 1766. Ch: Ensign **John,** m. 1st 17 Apr. 1743 Patience Smith of Durham; 2d 15 Mar. 1759 Temperance Pickering; d. s. p. 23 Feb. 1770, leaving highly genealogical will. List 343. **Nicholas,** m. 28 Nov. 1744 Sarah Thompson. **Mary,** bp. 5 May 1717, d. y. **Daniel,** bp. 24 June 1720; not in fa.'s will. **Bridget,** bp. 1 Oct. 1721; m. 1st 6 July 1740 James Chadburne; 2d bef. 1769 one Allen. **Alice,** bp. 30 May 1723; m. Thomas Hatch(2). **Susannah,** bp. 18 Feb. 1727-8; not in fa.'s will. **Mary,** bp. 3 Aug. 1729; not in fa.'s will but poss. m. 24 Mar. 1757 Jonathan Hill of Durham. **George,** bp. 16 July 1732, m. 1st Mary, gr. dau. of Samuel Penhallow; 2d Susannah Chesley. Will 25 June 1785. **Deborah,** bp. 16 Mar. 1735; m. Nathaniel Adams, d. bef. her fa. **Elizabeth, m.** (Richard) Salter. Richard Knight Salter, s. of Richard, was bp. in Portsm. 15 July 1744. **Sarah,** m. 1st one Norwood; 2d 30 Jan. 1758 Samuel Brewster of Barrington.

11 **NATHAN**(5), Portsm. and Scarboro, was appren. 25 Nov. 1676 by his mo. and step-fa. for 12 yrs. 5 mo. to Samuel Whidden of Portsm., mason. Bef. Mar. 1693-4, when they were seated in the Portsm. meeting-ho., he m. Mary Westbrook. Gr. j. 1695, 1697; j. 1696, 1700. Taxed in Portsm. 1708 and in Greenland 1713, 1714. In 1707-8 he sold to Geo. Vaughan all his fa.'s land and rights in Scarb., but by 1720 he had moved to that town, where he kept the Black Point ferry and had a gr. in 1727 for abiding thru the war. He serv. as sergt. commanding Bl. Pt. garrison 1723-1725. Selectman 1723. Lists 239b, 330d, 335a, 337 and prob. 334a. Bur. 13 May 1746, ag. ab. 79. His wid. was liv. 1748, when his heirs deeded to Richard King (Y. D. 27.117). Ch: **Nathaniel,** m. 1st 26 Nov. 1724 in Greenl. Priscilla Babb; 2d 27 Aug. 1782 in Scarb. Hannah McKenney. D. bef. 18 Oct. 1787. **Mary,** m. 16 Mar. 1718-9, both of Newington, John Crockett (5 Joshua). **Margaret, m.** 1st 14 May 1713 in Greenl. Thomas Starbird; 2d 11 Dec. 1746 Axel Roberts. **Elizabeth, m.** Ebenezer Seavey of Scarb. **Martha, m.** John Elden of Biddeford, later of Buxton (Ct. Apr. 1727). **Hannah, m.** 1st Thomas Seavey; 2d

16 Nov. 1739 John Sellea of Bid. **Westbrook,** bp. 21 Nov. 1708 in No. Ch. Portsm., m. 23 Mar. 1735 Abigail Munson. Bur. 19 Nov. 1751. **Sarah,** bp. 21 Oct. 1711 in Portsm., m. 14 or 24 Feb. 1733-4 Anthony Brackett of Falm.

12 **RICHARD,** Hampton, carpenter and miller. Proprietor 1640. Contracted to keep a mill at the landing place, Aug. 1640. Lists 356c, 391b, 392a. Said to have built the meeting-ho. Suspected of theft in 1644 ('of Salisbury'), a warrant was issued to attach the body of R. K. 'of Hampton' in 1645, in which yr. he sold his ho. and mill in Hampt. to Christopher Lawson of Boston and departed for Rhode Island, where he was in 1647 when his Hampt. goods were attached. Doubtless the R. K., carpenter, of Newport, R. I., 1648, who m. there Sarah Rogers, a 2d w., as he had a son in England.

13 **RICHARD,** Dover, was taxed there with Thomas Kemble(7) in 1659, and was temporarily at Oyster River in 1668.

14 **RICHARD,** sworn at Great Isl. in 1696.

15 **ROBERT,** merchant and gent., bro. of (4), came over in 1633 with Abraham Shurt as agent for Giles Elbridge for purpose of accep. deliv. of the Pemaquid patent, and ret. to Bristol. From 1640 to 1649 he was mostly in Boston, but 'of Bristol' in all legal papers, for which see Asp. Whether he became 'of Boston' and was one of the two Robert Knights, merchants, of later yrs. in that town must be left to more particularized research.

16 **ROBERT,** York, mason, ±71 in 1658, ±86 in 1671, bot Robert Blaisdell's house and lands in 1642 and had town grants in 1648 and 1658. Took O. A. 1652; Tr. j. 1647, 1650, 1653, 1655, 1656, 1664; Gr. j. 1647, 1650-1, 1653, 1657, 1666, 1668; Selectm. 1653-6, 1658-9, 1661, 1663, 1667. Lists 24, 73, 275, 276, 277, 392a, 393b. He may have exch. lands with Mr. Edward Rishworth, for in 1653 John Pearce bot of E. R. a ho. and fenced field 'up the river of York which farm was ould Robert Knight's', while in the same yr. R. K. deeded to Thos. Marston of Hampton a ho. and lot 'formerly Robert Marston's now mine' and 35 a. of marsh and upland granted Mr. Rishworth by the town of Hampton, and in 1666-7 he deeded 7 a. in Hampt., bot of Rishworth, to his gr. son John Redman jr. His w., not named, testified in a ct. case in 1650. In 1668 Dr. Clapham sued him for care and medicine expended on his gr. son, Rowland Young's boy, 'which boy in time of his lameness R. K. took as his own', but withdrew the suit with costs to the deft. In 1673 he deeded land to his gr. son Rowland Young jr. Will 23 June—24 Aug. 1676, was exec. in Boston where he was liv. with his son. Ch: **Rich-**

ard, Boston, weaver. Sued by John Bursley in 1643, John Heard and William Pester in 1644, in York co. cts. His w. was an heir of Matthew Giles of Smuttynose, as was the w. of Matthew Williams. Having acq. the Williams share, R. K., then of Boston, weaver, and John Redman, Giles' partner, sold the Smuttynose fishing plant in 1667. Later history not untangled from several Richard Knights of Boston. **Joan**, m. ab. 1648 Rowland Young. Conv. her fa.'s homestead to her s. Rowland in 1685. **Margaret**, m. John Redman of Hampton; d. 30 May 1658. In 1671 her husb. conv. to Henry Sayward 50 a. gr. by Thos. Gorges Esq. to Margaret Knight, late w. of sd. Redman.

17 **ROBERT**, Berwick, cooper, son of Robert of Manchester, Mass., was ±70 in 1737. He m. 1st 3 Feb. 1686 Abigail Wilson (Shoreborn) in Ipswich where he liv. until 1704 when he sold his prop. and presum. moved to Berw. where he m. 2d 29 Aug. 1714 wid. Susanna Lord, thru whom he obtained the est. of her husb. Abraham Lord and of her son William who d. s. p. in 1712, being unsuccessfully sued by William's kin in 1719. The Abraham Lord est. was given by the Knights to K.'s sons Grindall and Robert by deed in 1718. His w. was recd. into Berw. ch. in 1716, and he, in his old age, was bp. and recd. at Rochester in 1739. Ch. by 1st w: **Grindall**, worsted-comber, of Cold Harbor, Berw., in 1719, m. int. 7 Aug. 1714 in Ipsw. Mary Harris ('Marshall John'), and was recd. into Berw. ch. with her 15 Oct. 1721. 2 ch. rec. in Berw. **Robert**, cooper, Dover and Berw., m. Elizabeth Heard(11), both liv. in Rochester in 1765. Ch. **Joseph**, b. 27 Feb. 1690 in Ipsw., of Kit. 7 Feb. 1712-3 when he m. Abial Herrick in Wenham; poss. d. bef. 1718. **Abigail**, liv. in 1718.

18 **ROGER**, Str. Bk., near 60 in 1656, very early on the Piscataqua, with w. Ann, who was sent over to join him bef. 31 May 1631, according to a letter from Thos. Eyres to Ambrose Gibbins. Recd. a grant from Thos. Wannerton 20 Jan. 1643-4 in consid. of faithful service to the patentees of the Great House. Lists 41, 323, 325, 326a, 330b, 331a. Successful in court vs. Mr. Francis Raynes in 1645 and 1647, he lost suits for wages vs. Capt. Mason and vs. Mr. Richard Cutt for a ho. and land in 1648. Bot ho. from Clement Campion in 1652 and sold it to Cutt the foll. yr. In 1671 he gave John Hunking a deed confirming a former gr. of 50 a. and a ho. to Hercules Hunking. His w. was liv. in 1656 when they made a joint depos. 'Old Knight' was a town charge from 1667, his last yr. being spent in the ho. of Thos. Onion, whose acct. for his coffin and funeral was closed Mar. 1672-3. No ch.

19 **SAMUEL**, Kit., 40 in 1699, recd. a gr. of 15 a. at Great Cove 27 July 1676 from his fa.-in-law Richard Carle, whose w. Amy was certainly mother of Knight's w. Amy. Altho Carle claimed that he deliv. this instrument while drunk, it was held good and K. sold to Samuel Spinney in 1686. An educated man, he drew local deeds, poss. too freely as he was once acc. of forgery. As tenant of wid. Jane Withers, he built and liv. on her Spruce Creek land. Lists 287, 330e. In 1682 he and his w. sold land which had been part of land of Edw. Clark, there being no explanation of their title. Ch: **Elizabeth**, m. 26 Sept. 1687 Thomas Spinney. **Catherine**, m. Joseph Hill(10), in ct. Dec. 1688. **Sarah**, m. 31 Oct. 1706 Daniel Green (5). **Mary**, in ct. July 1702 for having a bastard, poss. that Benoni Knight, laborer, who took Joseph Curtis's horse, rode him to Black Will's and turned him loose in 1721; m. 6 Jan. 1708 Samuel Green(23). **Thomas**.

20 **THOMAS**, witn. deed Obadiah Bruen to Rev. Thos. Larkham, 1640.

21 **THOMAS**(19), Kit., cordwainer, m. 1st Mary Rackliff (Wm.); 2d 14 Aug. 1710 Susanna King. Lists 296, 297. His will, 2 May—16 Oct. 1753, in add. to w. and ch., names 4 K. and 5 Barnes gr. ch. Ch. by 1st w: **Mary**, m. 29 Dec. 1726 in Portsm. Joseph Barnes of London. By 2d w: **Daniel**, m. 2 Aug. 1734 Mehitable Libby. His est. was adm. 12 July 1779 by John K. of Somersworth, 4 ch. ment. **George**, m. 1740 Elizabeth Cotton, who declined adm., which was gr. to his fa. 18 Feb. 1745-6. She m. 2d 4 Oct. 1746 Shadrach Weymouth. 3 daus. **Sarah**, bp. 5 May 1728; not in fa.'s will. **Gideon**, bp. 2 Nov. 1729; left wid. Mary who was adm. 1 Oct. 1776, and whose est. was adm. by Joseph Paul and Daniel K. 12 Apr. 1784. 5 ch. **Susannah** and **Phebe**, bp. 2 Nov. 1729; neither in fa.'s will. **Miriam**, m. 11 Oct. 1730 Nathaniel Libby.

22 **WALTER**, Braveboat Harbor, was adm. of est. of James Nichols in 1651, and appeared by his attorney, Clement Campion, in Norfolk co. court in that yr. Ordered to return to his wife by the first ship in 1652 and again in 1653, he nevertheless liv. and d. in the Braveboat Harbor ho. conv. in an unrecorded deed, Corbett to Champernowne, 10 July 1672. List 331a.

**Knill**, Charles. See Neal.

**KNOTT**, 1 **John**. List 304.

2 **MARY**. List 328. See Huntress.

**KNOWLES**, there are many knolls in many counties.

1 **REV. HANSERD** (Knollys), b. in Cawkwell, co. Lincoln, in 1598, grad. from Cambridge Univ. and held living of Hum-

berstone, co. Lincoln, bef. emigrating to N. E. in 1638. Of Baptist beliefs and an immediate adherent of Anne Hutchinson, he was denied residence in Boston ('a weak minister', said Winthrop) and proceeded to Dover and preached for 'some few loose men' (same authority). At first opposed by Rev. George Burdett, he organized a ch. when that worthy departed for Agamenticus, and wrote to England criticising the government in Boston. Signed the Piscataqua Combination in 1640, but left Dover that yr. and ret. to England, where he had an unhappy career as a Baptist pastor in London, suffering imprisonment many times bef. his death in 1691. List 351b.

2 **JOHN**, mariner, Hampton, m. 10 July 1660 Jemima Austin(1) who was legatee in wills of mo. and step-fa. Leavitt in 1692 and 1699. In 1664 he had land adj. Thos. Webster, acq. from Wm. Cole, and in 1666 he bot from Giles Fifield a house and 10 a. and 6 a. of marsh which had been for some yrs. in his poss. Gr. j. 1681. Lists 52, 54, 393b, 396, 49. Blind for his last 10 yrs., he d. 5 Dec. 1705. His will, 16 Mar. 1693-4—31 Dec. 1705, was witn. by 4 Dows. Ch: **John**, b. 6 Feb. 1661. **Ezekiel**, b. 19 Aug. 1663, d. 11 Dec. 1666. **James**, b. 20 Nov. 1665, d. 1 Feb. 1682. **Simon**, b. 22 Nov. 1667. **Joseph**, b. 11 June 1672, not ment. in fa.'s will. **Sarah**, b. 17 Apr. 1676, m. Robert Drake(7). **Hannah**, b. 18 Apr. 1678, m. William Locke(2).

3 **JOHN**(2), Hampton, had the homestead. List 399a. Will, 5 Dec. 1733—4 Jan. 1733-4, ment. w. Susanna, who d. 17 Oct. 1745, ag. 82. Ch: **John**, b. 14 May 1686, m. 31 Dec. 1713 Tryphena Locke(5). They liv. in Rye, but owned cov. and were bp. in Greenland in 1719. At least 5 ch. **Ezekiel**, b. 29 June 1687, m. 31 Jan. 1712 Mary Wedgwood (David). Betw. ch. and town rec. of Rye, 5 ch rec. **Amos**, m. 16 Dec. 1724 Abigail (Brown 11) Dowst, had the homestead and d. 24 Feb. 1746. 7 ch. of whom 6 surv. in 1746. **Reuben** (prob.), b. ab. 1691. **Abigail**, b. Dec. 3, 1695, m. Ephraim Marston.

4 **SIMON**(2), Hampton, m. 1st Rachel, who d. 11 Nov. 1696, and 2d 2 Aug. 1700 Rachel Joy. List 399a. Ch: **Simon**, b. 18 Mar. 1696; m. 26 May 1726 in Greenland Deliverance Goss; d. 22 Apr. 1753. **Rachel**, b. 10 June 1701; m. Samuel Hobbs. **Joseph**, b. 22 Jan. 1705, m. 1st Catherine Taylor (Richard) and prob. 2d 12 Jan. 1778 Lydia Randall. **Ruth**, b. 30 Sept. 1707. **Jonathan**, Little River, b. 22 Aug. 1710, m. 18 Sept. 1735 in Greenland Hannah Berry, but Dow names his w. Sarah. 7 ch. rec., the 1st in 1738. **Abigail**, b. 25 Aug. 1718, d. unm. 5 Aug. 1745. And in all prob. an eldest dau.

**Keziah**, who would have been named for her fa.'s aunt Keziah (Austin) Tucker, m. 17 Sept. 1714 in Greenland Ebenezer Berry.

5 **STEPHEN**, Portsm., fisherman, of Lahant (Lezant?), co. Cornwall, m. 25 Feb. 1716-7 Joanna (Dore 2) Cane-Bourne. Taxed in Portsm. 1722, had grant on Hog Isl. in 1725, and liv. at the Shoals 1727. Only ch. rec: **Samuel** (Noles), bp. 27 Mar. 1719-20.

6 **WILLIAM** (Knowler, Nolar and Knolen), Portsm., m. 13 Sept. 1713 in No. Ch. Sarah Clark (John 20), who m. 2d 3 May 1723 Joseph Martin. Ch: **Sarah**, bp. 22 May 1715. **Richard**, bp. 15 Aug. 1717. **Sarah**, bp. 18 Oct. 1719. **Mary**, adm. of the est. of her mo., Sarah Martin, widow, in 1745.

**KNOWLTON**, 1 Abraham, taxed in Portsm. in 1672. List 326c.

2 **BENJAMIN**, York witn. 1710. Y.D.7.195.

3 **JOHN**, of Ipswich, shoemaker, had a land grant in York in 1669 and had built a ho. bef. 1677-8. Y. D. 3.67, 7.210.

4 **THOMAS**, 1701, land now in poss. of Nathl. Batchelder.

**Knox**, see Nock.

**La**——, William, Kittery 1698. List 294, Landall?

**LABORNE**, Henry, a surgeon at Portsm. ab. 1700; sued Philip Payne that yr., when Margaret Bond ±69 and Sarah Follett ±22 test. that they liv. in same ho. with Dr. L. and his w.

**Lacroix**, Pierre. See Peter Delacroy.

**LACROW**, Abraham, Monhegan 1672. List 31. Poss. a clue to the origin or early history of Abraham Cross who m. Martha Beale 20 Sept. 1700 in Marblehead, they being called Abraham Lacroix, physician, and w. Martha in 1701.

**LACY**, Morgan. In Saco the birth rec. of his son (1642) is immediately foll. by those of the ch. of Ralph Tristram (1644-), suggesting that the wid. Lacy m. R. T. in 1643. Ch: **John**, b. 18 June 1642, ensign of the Saco company 18 July 1665.

**LADBROOK**, Thomas, Portsm. cordwainer, m. 1st bef. 13 July 1671, when she was ±54, Mary, wid. of John Barrett(1). His 2d w., contract 21 Feb. 1681-2, was Deborah, wid. of Robert Booth(3), her 3d marriage. He was fined for selling beer to soldiers, and Henry Kirke complained to the Pres. and Council that his ch., an appren. of Mr. Ladbrook's for 6 yrs., had recd. neither adequate food nor instruction. Bot of Rachel Webster 7 July 1676 a ho. and contents at the waterside near the meeting-ho. Freed from training 1676. Lists 92, 327b, 329, 331ab. Adm. bond dated 29 Sept. 1684, but d. bef. 27 Sept. 1683 when the wid., very ancient and with difficulty coming to court, petn. for her own prop., kept from her contrary to agreement. No kn. ch.

**LADD,** very uncommon. Ladds is peculiar to co. Huntingdon.

1 **DANIEL**(4), Exeter, m. 29 Apr. 1712 Mehitable Philbrick, who was adm. to Kingston ch. 10 Mar. 1728 and d. 23 Jan. 1779. Rated 18 May 1714. Called cousin by Stephen Dudley jr. in 1714 in deeding him ho. formerly gr. to Rev. Samuel Dudley. List 376b. Liv. in 1741. Ch: **Mehitable,** b. 30 June 1713, m. 28 Nov. 1732 Samuel Colcord. **Elizabeth,** b. 11 Feb. 1716, m. 21 Dec. 1731 John Nay. **Anna,** b. 25 June 1718, poss. the ch. who d. 18 June 1728 in Kingston. **Hannah,** b. 17 Apr. 1720, m. 6 (26?) May 1742 Samuel Huntoon. **Mary,** b. 3 Jan. 1722, m. 24 Apr. 1740 Samuel Dudley 3d. **Daniel,** b. 25 Jan. 1725, Kingston, blacksmith, carried prisoner to France after Louisburg, m. 1st Joanna Dudley, 2d Susanna Dow of Brentwood, 3d Ruth Bradley of Brentwood, d. Apr. 1809. 13 ch. **Stephen,** b. 30 Aug. 1728, Brentwood, m. 1st Abigail Webster, 2d Bethia Sweet. 6 + 7 ch. **John,** bp. 24 May 1730, d. 8 Jan. 1731. **Joanna,** b. 27 July 1735, m. 11 Dec. 1755 Josiah Huntoon. **John,** b. 24 Oct. 1737, Unity, m. Mary Moody of Brentwood who d. 25 Nov. 1715, ag. 73; he d. 15 Mar. 1784. 9 ch.

2 **EZEKIEL,** bro. of (4), Exeter, b. 16 Sept. 1654 in Haverhill, s. of Daniel, m. 30 Nov. 1687 Mary Folsom(9), who d. in Strat. 3 July (1742?). Sold Haverh. land in 1697, taxed and rated in Ex. 1714, of Stratham in 1718 when he bot pew in meeting-ho. He d. bef. 1723 when wid. Mary, as heir of bro. Samuel, deeded to Thos. Jenness. List 376b. Ch. rec. in Haverh.: **Lydia,** b. 18 Feb. 1688. **Mary,** b. 17 Jan. 1690. (**John?**), b. 6 May 1693. **Nathaniel,** b. 12 Nov. 1695.

3 **JOHN**(4), Kingston, m. Apr. 1714 Elizabeth Sanborn, who is said to have m. 2d Thomas Webster. Deeded to s. Nathaniel in 1745 and s. Trueworthy in 1750. Ch: **Love,** b. 25 Mar. 1716, d. 19 June 1720. **Benjamin,** b. 25 Apr. 1718, m. 11 Sept. 1741 Mary French (Timothy of Salisbury), both liv. 1760. **John,** b. 7 May 1720, m. bef. 1748 Alice Thing. **Nathaniel,** Alexandria, N. H., b. 17 June 1722, m. 12 Aug. 1741 Sarah Clifford (Isaac). 8 ch. **Jonathan,** physician, on Louisburg exped., unm. **Trueworthy,** bp. 29 May 1726, m. 1 Nov. 1750 Lydia Harriman who d. 8 Apr. 1819. A capt. in Canada exped., 1758; d. in Goffstown 26 Apr. 1778. 9 ch. **Love,** bp. 31 Mar. 1728, d. 18 June 1736. **Dorothy,** bp. 10 Jan. 1730-1, m. 4 Apr. 1746 Benjamin Sanborn. Was there also an eldest dau. Elizabeth who m. in Kingston 19 June 1729 Jeremiah Webster?

4 **ENSIGN .NATHANIEL,** bro. of (2), Exeter, b. in Haverhill 10 Mar. 1651-2, s. of Daniel, m. 12 July 1678 Elizabeth Gilman, who m. 2d 3 Dec. 1693 Henry Wad-

leigh. Rated in Ex. 1682. Lists 52, 57, 376b, 383, 37. Implicated in Gove's rebellion, he was never tried. Constable 1688. Mortally wounded in fight with Ind. at Maquoit and d. 11 Aug. 1691. Ch. who receipted to their fa. Wadleigh in 1712: **Nathaniel,** b. 6 Apr. 1679. **Elizabeth,** b. 6 Jan. 1680, m. John Glidden(2). **Mary,** b. 28 Dec. 1682, m. 1 Sept. 1704, at Kingston, Jacob Gilman. **Lydia,** b. 27 Dec. 1684, m. Charles Rundlett. **Daniel,** b. 18 Mar. 1686-7. **John,** b. 6 July 1689, m. 14 Apr. 1714 Elizabeth Sanborn. **Ann,** b. 25 Dec. 1691, m. Jonathan Folsom(4).

5 **NATHANIEL**(4), Exeter and Stratham, millwright, m. 1st Catherine Gilman, who d. 22 July 1717. No. doc. evid. is found for a 2d marriage to Rachel Rollins, but by 1719 (unless this is a 1st marriage of Nathaniel 2) he had m. Mercy (Hall) wid. of Dudley Hilton, adm. of whose est. she renounced. Lists 67, 376b, 388. Disposed of his land by deeds to sons, 1738-1747. Est. of Capt. N. L. declared insolvent 1763 and adm. gr. to s. Edward. Ch: By 1st w. **Nathaniel,** m. Ann Hilton (Dudley), d. 1730. 2 sons. **Daniel,** Epping, adm. 1758 to wid. Alice who deeded to 3 minor sons in 1762. **Edward,** b. 22 June 1707, m. 10 Feb. 1733 Catherine Thing (Samuel), d. 5 July 1787. 7 ch. **Elias,** m. 27 Nov. 1740 Ann Gilman (Capt. John jr.). Will 20 Apr. 1790—13 Mar. 1801. 7 ch. **Josiah,** b. 29 May 1713, m. 3 Jan. 1737-8 Sarah Morse (Philip of Newbury), who d. in 1780; millwright, carpenter, deacon, d. in 1785. 4 ch. By which w.? **Paul,** Stratham and Epping, m. in 1747 Martha Folsom (Nathaniel) who d. 17 July 1804. He d. Feb. 1783. 10 ch. By w. Mercy: **Love,** b. 6 Mar. 1719. **Dudley,** lost at sea. **Mercy.**

6 **ROBERT,** ship capt., entering Portsm. 1692. List 333b.

**Laflower,** —— and w., St. Robin's dau., liv. at Eggemoggin Reach 1688. List 5.

**Lafoleg?** James, witn. with Henry Lamprey, 1667. Concord Files 2.153.

**Laham,** Richard. Dover Comb. List 351b.

**Lahorn,** Henry. Dover Comb. List 351b.

## LAKE.

1 **SIR BIBYE**(4), Baronet, bp. 10 Apr. 1684 at Bishops Norton, co. Linc. By solicit. of Maj. Tho. Clarke's heirs he became the chief supporter of the Pejepscot Company. See Pejepscot MSS. in Me. Hist. Soc.; Suffolk Ct. Files 139154, pp. 100, 106, 108; N. E. Reg. 26.234. In 1741 he furnished Tho. Wotton's 'The English Baronetage' (Vol. IV or V, pp. 134-6) a full acct. of his parents and gr. parents, with his fa.'s epitaph, but made no allusion to New Eng. and called his gt.-gr.-fa. 'Stephen

Goodyear, goldsmith, of London.' He was bur. 6 Apr. 1744, his wid. (Mary Atwell) 23 Jan. 1752. 3 ch.; some descendants in America.

2 **RICHARD**, Eastern man gone. List 313d.

3 **CAPT. THOMAS**, partner in Clarke & Lake (see Clarke 54), in Boston by 1645, but m. in New Haven Mary Goodyear (Dep. Gov. Stephen). Capt. of the Artillery Co. The firm imported English goods, owned ships in the passenger trade and put £4000 into its Kennebec speculation. K. 14 Aug. 1676 in attempt to escape from his fort on Arrowsic Isl., just after appointment as Capt. of new co. to be raised out of Maj. Savage's co. App. com. to hold next co. ct. in Devonshire (Kennebec) in May 1675 and May 1676. Son of Richard and Anne (Morraly) of Irby, co. Linc., his older half-bro., Sir Edward, LL.D., already knighted, was created a baronet by Charles I. Their bro. John, merchant in Boston, m. here Lucy Bulkeley, and two ch. of another bro., Luke, named in the wills of John and Sir Edw., came to Boston, the girl, Mary, in nunc. will proved by Dr. Increase Mather, giving ½ to her Aunt Lake. A contemporary copy of Sir Edw.'s will and codicil was found among Dr. Mather's papers. For Eng. ancestry, see Lincolnshire Pedigrees, p. 577; Musgrave's Obit. (Harleian Soc., 1915), p. 149; N. E. Reg. 3.344, 61.189. Capt. Lake's will, made 12 yrs. bef. his death, named his sis. Lydia Goodyear, cous. Geo. Rokesby, w. and ch. Stephen, Thomas and Anne. His wid.'s will, 12 July—15 Sept., 1705, named cousins John and Richard Watts, abroad, cous. Mary Treworgy, gr. daus. Mary and Dorothy Cotton, s. Thos. and w., s.-in-l. Mr. John Cotton and made dau. Ann Cotton resid. leg. John Watts came over to rep. Sir Bibye Lake and m. Elizabeth Butler who m. 2d Capt. John Penhallow of Portsmouth. Also his sis. Lydia W. came over and m. 19 Apr. 1692 John Gerrish(4). Ch: **Stephen**, b. 13 Feb. 1649, enrolled in Gray's Inn, London, when named heir in Sir Edw.'s will, 1670, but d. first. **Thomas**, b. 9 Feb. 1656. **Ann**, b. 12 Oct. 1663; m. 1st Rev. John Cotton(3), 2d Dr. Increase Mather. **John**, b. 22 Feb. 1665; will, merchant, 24, d. 27, June 1690, mother sole benef.

4 **THOMAS**(3), after bro. Stephen's death was named heir in Sir Edw.'s will. Barrister, of Gray's Inn, London. List 188. He m. Elizabeth Story. D. 22 May 1711. 3 ch., incl. **Bibye**.

**LAKEMAN, William,** Star Island, boat-owner, was bondsman for two fighting sailors, Samuel Gould and John Yelline, in 1685. Gr. j. 1692-4; J. P. 1692. Lists 307a, 308a. Sold his houses, gardens, moorings, fish-ho., etc., to Richard Gummer and ret.

to Ipswich where he d. 24 Jan. 1707, ag. 56 (gr. st.). His wid. Margery d. 24 Mar. 1716, ag. 59 (gr. st.). Will 11 Dec. 1706—24 Aug. 1707 names 10 of 11 ch: **Agnes**, m. William Roberts. **Richard**. **Elizabeth**, m. one Downes and had ch. bef. 1706. **John**, m. int. 23: 8: 1706 Mary Newmarch. **William**, m. 17 Aug. 1705 Elizabeth Palmer. **Jonas**. **Archelaus**, m. int. 10 June 1710 Rebecca Ringe. **Sylvanus**, lieut., m. 23 Oct. 1714 Mary Lull. Attacked by Ind. in a captured schooner while fishing near Penobscot 10 June 1724, he escaped to Ipsw. and led a punitive exped. against them. **Solomon**. **Sarah**, m. int. 29 Oct. 1715 John Spiller. **Tobias**, not in will, helped carry away goods in his shallop from the -Three Friends- of London, cast away at a place called Portland (Portland Head, Cape Elizabeth) in Casco Bay Oct. 1711; m. int. 13 Sept. 1712 Margaret Pulsipher.

**Lakeslaw** (Lakesly, Lakestay), John, Richmond Isl. 1641-3, prob. hired here. List 21.

**LAMB.** Found throughout England.

1 **ABIELL** (Bial), went to Wid. Moulton's boarding ho. in Portsm. 1671, demanding to see Mr. Pormort. See Dorman. His rate for 1671 in Henry Dering's book acct. ag. Thos. Parker. Poss. the son of Thos., b. in Roxbury 15 Aug. 1646, and back in Mass. 1677 mar. to Jos. Buckminster's wid.; liv. Roxb. and Framingham.

2 **ANTHONY**. See Lamy.

3 **JOHN** (also Lame), Kittery, in Ct. Mar. 1651 as a thief and a liar, again in June 1653 for a lie. Grants 1655, 1656. List 298. Going to York, he burned charcoal at his landing place on Great Works Riv., and had mov. to New London bef. July 1666, when he sold ho. and land bot from John Garde to Edw. Start. Will made 14 Aug. 1673, not in Conn. records. W. Ann liv. May 1683. 3 kn. sons, likely other ch.

**LAMBERT.** 1 **Jonathan**, Kittery witn. 1684. Y. D. 4.44. List 33. One Jonathan and w. Elizabeth had rec. in Boston: Jonathan 1697, Benjamin 1699.

2 **MARGARET**, sis. to wives of John Cox (5) and William Cox(34), depos. in Boston in 1719, ag. 75, calling Wm. Cox bro.-in-law. Y. D. 18.262.

3 **ROBERT**, m. Dorothy Dill(2). 3 ch. rec. York 1724-8.

**LAMBETH, Philip,** Portsmouth, mariner, m. 14 Oct. 1697 Susanna Lear(1). Lists 330de, 337. D. ab. 1704; wid. m. 2d James Abbott(1), 3d Saml. Adams; see Adams(3). Ch: **Mary**, m. 25 Dec. 1721 Erick Erickson, b. in Phila., 2d 9 Dec. 1733 Edw. Gale of Waterford, Ire.; liv. 1740. **Martha**, m. 22 Dec. 1723 Jos. Cross(8); liv. 1740.

**LAMMOS**, Lomax, Loomis, Lummocks, and many others. See Loom.

1 **JABES** (Lumacks) taxed Portsmouth 1707.

2 **NATHANIEL** (aut. Lammos), Oyster River, s. of Edward of Ipswich, ±30 in Sept. 1679. Oyster Riv. June 1671 railing with Philip Chesley's w. Joan on Sunday; taxed 1672. See Davis(28). Juryman 1696. Dover gr. 1694; gr. with Richard Clay to be equally divided 1701. In 1702 he had made improvements by advice of Capts. Woodman and Tuttle on 7 a. gr. bordering his w.'s land and Storer's. Depos. Aug. 1713, ±60, that ab. 26 yrs. bef. he was around when the Exeter-Dover line was run. Dead in 1721. Lists 57, 356j, 358b, 359a, 367a, 368b. His fam. is taken up with misgiving. If only one man of the name, and, as appears, he m. Deliverance Clark(2), he could not have m. Mehitable Cowell in Boston in 1703 (Essex Inst. Coll. 53.137), while Deliverance must have been very aged when she made her will as Jos. Hanson's wid. in 1766, prov. 1773, no ch. or gr. ch. named. Ch. appear: **Nathaniel**. His fa.'s 1694 gr. was laid out to him in 1721. M. ab. that time Abigail Giles(6). See Clark(3). Will, of Madbury, 1 Aug. 1767—31 Aug. 1768. 7 ch. incl. Deliverance. **Elizabeth**, b. May 1698, dau. of Nathl. and Deliverance (Clark), by bap. rec. in Canada 11 Sept. 1707, foll. her capture at O. R. in May; m. 1st in Canada 25 Nov. 1721 Jos. Parent, 4 daus.; 2d 6 June 1735 Jean Baptiste Jetté. Bur. 5 Apr. 1737. Lists 96, 99 pp. 92, 127. Named by Essex Inst: **Sarah**, m. 2 Mar. 1721 Saml. Tibbetts (Sarah -Loo- by Dover rec. of mar.). **Deliverance**, b. 1705, taken by Ind. (unkn. unless same as Elizabeth).

**LAMONT**, **Archibald**, (also Leamon, Laymott), indebted to Robt. Weymouth's est. 1662; in July that yr. acc. Richard Green of felony in York Ct. A yr. later he sued Mr. Bolls for 250 lbs. sugar due on acct., Thos. Booth for forf. of a bond, and at the same time with Geo. Gray and Arthur Dinall witn. ag. Booth for swearing and slandering the country.

**LAMPREY**, Lamprill. See also Lempriere. If English, the fish fatal to Henry I.

1 **BENJAMIN**(3), Hampton, 76 in 1738, m. 1st 10 Nov. 1687 Jane Batchelder(3), 2d Mary, who d. 17 Sept. 1735, ag. 65. List 399a. Jury 1695, d. 3 Jan. 1752. Ch: **Benjamin**, North Hampt., b. 9 Oct. 1688, m. 7 Feb. 1711 Sarah Dow(10). 7 ch. **Deborah**, m. Samuel Palmer. **Daniel**, b. 23 Feb. 1692, d. 2 Apr. 1718. **Sarah**, b. July 1695, m. Robert Moulton. **Nathaniel**, bp. 26 June 1698, m. 1 Jan. 1734 Ruth Palmer (Samuel), d. 26 July 1769. 5 ch. **Jane**, bp. 30 Apr. 1699, m. Stephen Batchelder. **Henry**, Kensington, b. 25 Feb. 1701, m. 22 May 1728 Esther Palmer (Samuel), d. 10 Sept. 1772. 3 ch. **Elizabeth**, b. 18 Feb. 1703, m. Jonathan Moulton. **Abigail**, b. 3 May 1705, m. Josiah Batchelder (Benjamin). **John**, b. 17 Aug. 1707, m. 1st 14 May 1740 Mary Johnson (James), 2d 19 Sept. 1754 Hannah Johnson (John), d. 23 July 1788. 4+2 ch. **Hannah**, b. 13 Nov. 1709, m. John Moulton, acc. to Dow's Hampton, but note Hannah Lampere m. John Lane 28 Sept. 1732 in Rye. **Morris**, b. 20 Dec. 1711, m. 1st in Greenland 26 May 1736 Elizabeth Bachelder, 2d 6 Sept. 1738 Rebecca Moulton (John), d. 27 Oct. 1809. 1+6 ch.

2 **DANIEL**(3), Hampton, bot share in commons and right in no. div. from John Brown sr. in 1677. Freed from training in 1681. Lists 52, 54, 396. Gr. j. 1698. Traditionally unm., he recd. from the Prov. treas. in 1711 15s. to repay Roger Swain who had cared for D. L.'s son Benjamin when sick during military serv. He deeded land to Elizabeth Dow in 1732, and gave his homestead and stock to his bro. Benj.(1) in return for life support. Ch: **Benjamin**.

3 **HENRY**, ±50 in 1666, ±82 in 1697, cooper, of Boston in 1652, liv. in a ho. hired from the wid. of Mr. Bazial Payton bef. and aft. she m. Mr. Paddy. Creditor of estates of James Astwood and Joseph Shaw in 1653. Poss. he and his w. Julian were the Mr. Lampree and w. warned out of Portsm. in 1659, and the Lamprey who set up a ho. at Great Isl. in 1660. They moved soon afterward to Hampt., where he conv. all his movable goods to his 3 eldest ch. in 1668 and land to s. Daniel in 1673. Lists 77a, 52, 55b, 330a, ¶77b, ¶78. Gr. j. 1684. His w. d. 10 May 1670 and he surv. until 7 Aug. 1700. Ch: **Henry**. **Daniel**, m. 13 Nov. 1673 Daniel Dow(1), recd. 20s. by will of Wm. Fuller sr. in 1691. **Mary**, b. Mar. 1654 in Boston, d. y. **Mary**, b. 19 Mar. 1658 in Boston, d. 7 June 1663 in Hampton. **Benjamin**, b. 29: 9: 1660. Sarah Lamprey who m. Benjamin Hutchins 5 June 1694 in Haverhill is unplaced.

4 **HENRY**(3), Stratham, of Exeter 1666, m. at Hampton 24 July 1686 Elizabeth Mitchell, sold land in Ex. 1704 and petn. for incorp. of Strat. 1709. Poss. he, not his fa., was the H. L., cooper, of York, who bot land there from Thomas Curtis 18 Mar. 1683-4 (untraced), served on a coroner's jury 24 Nov. 1685, and was ment. as an abuttor in 1695 and 1707. Lists 388, ¶33. Only kn. ch: **Mary**, b. Aug. 1692 in Hamp.

5 **THOMAS**. In accts. of Maj. Shapleigh vs. Capt. Champernowne in 1667 is the

record of a payment to Capt. Thomas Lampre in fish.

**LAMY** (sometimes Lamb), **Dr. Anthony,** Portuguese, practising in York, Wells and Casco 1671-73, recovered £3 from Henry Sayward for two cures, 19 Sept. 1671. After John Gooch's death, he was bound over to Boston Ct. with a sample of his medicine. List 86. P. & Ct. ii, pp. xvii, 237. Last heard of 1673, in Apr. when his creditor Henry Dering sued John Parker, jail keeper, for letting him go out of custody, and in July acknowl. judgments to John Bray and Edw. Rishworth.

**LANCASTER,** an English county.
1 The husb. of Sarah Lancaster of Scituate, dau. of Elizabeth (Norton) Stover, so named in her mo.'s will 7 Dec. 1714. But she was called Sarah Longstaff when she m. John Roan 22 Oct. 1717 in Pembroke.
2 **JOHN,** Newport, R. I., shipwright, m. Sarah, wid. of Samuel Banks(4). His gr. stone in Newp. states that he d. 13 Dec. 1711, ag. 47 yrs. 6 mo. See Banks, Donnell (1), Butland(1). Ch: **Mary,** d. 29 Aug. 1703, ag. 5 mo. 14 d. **Sarah,** m. 23 Jan. 1717 Thos. Coggeshall.
3 **THOMAS,** Hampton, carpenter, b. 15 Mar. 1668-9, s. of Joseph of Amesbury, m. 3 Mar. 1695-6 Mercy Green(2), deceased by Ruth Shaw in same yr. Liv. near Nathaniel Weare's mill. K. by Ind. 17 Aug. 1703. Wid. Mercy deeded land to her Gove gr. ch. in 1732, and adm. was gr. to her s.-in-law 1 Mar. 1734. Ch: **Mary,** b. 1 June 1701, m. 21 Apr. 1720 Jonathan Gove. No doc. auth. is found for assigning to T. L. Jerediah, stated in fam. gen. to have been liv. in 1718.
4 **WILLIAM,** working in York in 1671, may have been any one, or none, of foll. Bostonians: W. L. sued by Thomas East, 1676. W. L. ack. judg. to Samuel Jacklin, 1676-7. Adm. on est. of W. L., single man, late of Boston, gr. to his former master, Robert Cox, bond 3 May 1677, Richard Knight and Wm. Kent sureties. W. L. Jane, dau. of Lionel Wheatley, and had ch. b. 1677-1680. W. L. and w. Sarah, dau. of John and Sarah Flood, ment. in heirship deed dated 1704, under will of Edward Barker (1674). W. L. m. Sarah Smith 3 Sept. 1705.
**Lancton,** Daniel, Corporal under Scottow at Scarb. List 237b.
**LANDALL,** 1 ——————, known only as the fa. of two sons, b. perh. afar, their mo. a dau. or step-dau. of Lucy (Treworgye) (Chadbourne 1) (Wills) Stileman, who willed £10 due from Rich. Stileman, if recd., to gr. s. Thos. Landall. As no Landall named in any other est., and Wm., not kn.

to have m., had land laid out at the head of his fa. Lewis, the possibil. exists that Lucy Chadbourne(1) m. a Landall as the 1st of three husbands. Ch: **William,** named as a Kit. abuttor 1703 and 18 June 1715. D. s. p., his Kit. gr. of 1699 descending to his br., whose wid. sold it in 1725. Y. D. xi. 253. Lists (?294 Wm. La.), 298. Capt. **Thomas,** mariner, Portsm., master of the sloop -Betty- arriv. Boston from Antigua, 1712. List 339. He m. in Portsm. 22 Oct. 1715 Margaret (Cutts 3), wid. of Nathl. Pike. Adm. to her 13 Mar. 1723-4. She was of Portsm., shop-keeper, 5 Aug. 1725, but acknowl. a deed in Boston the next wk.; taxed Portsm. 1732, Wid. L. She d. 15 July 1779, the last survivor of Mr. Rogers' ch., admitted Sept. 1714. Ch. bp. Portsm., liv. at fa.'s death: Elizabeth, bp. 1 June 1718, b. in the passage from Ireland. Lucy, bp. 10 July 1720. Thomas, bp. 25 Mar. 1721-2. Not identif. poss. dau. of Capt. Thos. by an earlier w., Abigail (Landale) m. in Portsm. 23 Mar. 1729 Col. John Hart(6). See Lundall.
2 **JAMES** (Lendall), ment. in Mungo Crawford's(4) est. 1712. N. H. Prob. i. 700.
**Landare,** Charles, witn. bill of sale of a ketch, Roger Deering jr. to William Follett, 1670. Prob. same as Lander(1).

**LANDER,** Landers, peculiar to Cornwall.
1 **CHARLES,** Dover, witn. at Oyster River 1670, drunk 1679. List 356j. See Landare.
2 **JAMES,** ±28 in 1681, leased the Barry-Agnew land at Salmon Falls from John Taylor 6 Apr. 1688. D. 23 June 1693; adm. 27 June to wid. Elizabeth (Grant, 3, 4) her bondsman Peter Grant. She m. 2d 28 Nov. 1694 at Berwick John Turner and 3d William Hearle.
3 **JOHN,** came to Richmond Isl. with Capt. Narias Hawkins in the -Speedwell- in 1635, but, after making trouble for Mr. Winter, departed in 1636 for Piscataqua where he was a builder of the chapel and parsonage of the Episcopal clergyman Rev. Richard Gibson. Lists 21, 281, 321. He and his partner John Billins div. their joint prop. and fishing outfit in 1639. Sued by Abraham Shurt and Robert Knight in 1640, and sued John Winter the same court for share of fish caught three yrs. since. Tr. j. 1640. He d. bef. 8 July 1646 when Thomas Withers sued his est. Y. D. 1.15 must have been dated 1649 in error.

**LANE.** Found principally in south western England. See also Hussey(7).
1 **AMBROSE,** Mr., merchant, Strawberry Bank, a Cutts wit. 23 Sept. 1648. Br. of (8) and (9). The latter gave him P/A 24

Mar. 1648-9, was his atty. the next Jan. and two months later for £1000 mortg. to Ambrose ho. and land, sawmill in bldg. at Sag. Creek (in 1653 'not yet perfected nor like to be'), ship in bldg., salt, and ho. in poss. of John Crowder. In Me. Ct. 1651, A. L. attached the prize -Sarah- and also Sampson's goods at the Shoals for £400. Assoc. for court at Str. Bk. Oct. 1651. Signed ptn. 1652. Lists 322, 323. Richard Tucker was his atty. 29 May 1655, and deeded 25 Sept. 1656 under P/A from A. L., sr. Yet his wid. Christian Lane of Teignmouth, co. Devon, (a 2d w., if he was the man of St. Marychurch, near Teignm. lic. to marry Mary Lackington 1631), appointed Thos. Jago of Dartmouth her atty. 4 June 1656 (Edw. Colcord(1) saw it done) and Jago at once named Capt. Champernowne, Nich. Shapleigh, Abraham Brown and Wm. Seavey agents here. Son (or nephew) **Ambrose**, jr. was here 1651 and wit. A. L.'s deed to John Jackson.

2 **JAMES**, Boston, late of Plymouth, Old Eng. (and appar. Str. Bank), made will 2 Oct. 1662, reciting debts due from Mr. Rich. Cutts, Mr. Bryan Pendleton for work done for Mr. Moody, John Pickering, John Hunking. Wife Dousabella was in Eng.: s. **Francis**, to have carp. tools left with Goodm. (Peter) Place; s. **James**, to come to N. E. See Hunking (1).

3 ***JAMES**, No. Yarmouth, came from London (memb. of Turners Guild 1654), and joined br. Job (see Reyner) at Malden; uncles liv. at Rickmansworth, co. Herts. Waters 1.472, 627; N. E. Reg. xi. 103, xlii. 141. A large landowner, and liv. on E. side of Cousins' Riv., a point and island still bearing the name; s. John depos. in 1733 that he mov. there with his fam. ±75 yrs. since and liv there 16 or 18 yrs. bef. driven away. Gr.j. 1665, tr.j. and j. life and death 1666. Sergeant and Clerk of the Writs (Mr.) 1665. Dep. to Genl. Ct. several yrs., ab. 7 yrs. bef. the Ind. war (son's depos. 1735). Lists 211, ?87. K. by Ind. at Casco Bay and fam. driven away. D. H. vi. 386. Nathl. Wharf, ±72, and Jas. Wallis, ±63, depos. in 1733 that he was slain in the first war. Wife unkn. Ch: **Ann**, liv. with but did not m. John Bray(3). Elinor Redding told in 1665 that she had two or three bastards and stole lace. **John. Henry.** He and br. **Samuel.** were attacked by an Ind. who had spent the night at their ho. at No. Yarm., 1688. List 34. **Samuel**, blacksmith, No. Yarm. 1688 (List 34); fled to Glouc.; land gr. there 1708. D. 30 Dec. 1724, ag. above 60. W. Rachel. 2 kn. ch: Samuel, m. in Glouc. 23 Oct. 1722 Mary Emmons; 8 ch. Rachel, b. 1708, d. y. Job, Billerica. List 34. Deeded Casco Bay est. 1719. W.

Mary Fassett (Patrick); 8 ch. 1707-1723. **James**, with Wm. Haines wit. Rich. Bray's deed 24 Dec. 1669, ack. by W. H. alone 25 Aug. 1679. Y. D. iii. 53.

4 **JOHN**, creditor of Richard Williams, the Saco clapboardman, 1640.

5 **JOHN**(3), No. Yarm., Falm., Gloucester, aged from ±73 in 1727 to ±84 in 1735. He ret. to Falm. ab. 1680-1; in 1687 liv. with w. Dorcas Wallis (John) on 7 a. on S. side Casco Riv. near Purpooduck. D. H. 6. 312. Lists 34, 228c. Aft. the next war he liv. in Glouc. (Lanesville), claiming his fa.'s and his own Me. lands. D. 24 Jan. 1738, ag. 86; wid. d. 9 Feb. 1751 in 93d yr. 11 ch., the first 5 likely b. in Me.: **James**, d. Glouc. 20 Apr. 1751, ag. 69, m. 1st in Glouc. 25 Oct. 1710 Ruth Riggs, 2d in 1715 wid. Judith Woodbury. Deacon. 7 ch., incl. Josiah, whose s. Francis settl. in No. Yarm. **John**, coaster, m. by 1714 Mary Riggs; k. by Ind. at Penobscot 22 June 1724, ag. 36. 8 ch. **Josiah**, m. in Glouc. 15 Jan. 1712-3 Rachel York (Saml.); d. s. p. 23 Nov. 1747, ag. 58; wid. liv. 1748. **Dorcas**, m. in Glouc. 8 Jan. 1713 Wm. Tucker. Ch. **Sarah**, m. in Glouc. 17 Dec. 1713 Thos. Riggs; d. 18 Nov. 1715. And rec. Glouc., 1694-1705: **Hepsibah. Mary. Joseph. Benjamin. Deborah. Job.**

6 **CAPT. JOHN**, Winter Harbor. By fam. trad., told to Geo. Folsom, Esq., he came a young man from his native Limerick, Ireland, and settled at Hampton; but is first found at Newb. marrying Joanna Davison(1) in Nov. 1692; there in 1699 he sold a Star Isl. plant bot from John Fabes. Hampt. innkeeper 1702; liv. in ho. of Mrs. Jane Sherburne who charged him with non-payment of rent. Mrs. Joanna lic. Mar. 1702-3. He wit. in York 1705-6. Capt. Lane and Co. were at Sebegoog Ponds 50 m. from Casco in Oct. 1705; a brave officer at Wells 1708; arriv. with men at wreck of -Three Friends- at Portland, Oct. 1711; Wells or York Jan. 1716-7; soon in command at Ft. Mary, where sued by a Boston man in Apr. 1718. His York land was levied on in Sept. 1719, he then dead. The wid. m. 16 Nov. 1718 Nicholas Mygood. Ch. rec. Newb: **Abigail**, b. 15 Aug. 1693; m. at Wells 31 Aug. 1715 Saml. Wheelwright. **Joanna**, m. at Hampt. Falls 14 Apr. 1720 Wm. Hilton (22). Capt. **John**, rec. as b. Hampt. 1 Mar. 1701-2, m. in Greenland 5 May 1724 Mary Nowell (Peter of York); of York in Jan. 1726-7, he filed bond as adm. of fa.'s est.; liv. there 1746. D. bef. 11 Oct. 1756, supp. to be bur. near Crown Point, N. Y. 5 ch., his 3 surv. sons all Capt. in the Revo., from Buxton. **Living**, b. 13 Nov. 1704. **Mary**, b. Feb. 1706. Lane Gen. adds: prob. **Jabez** and others whose names are lost. **?Sarah**, 'of Point or Harbour' (Winter Harbour),

m. in Marbleh. 9 Dec. 1717 Thos. Dennis, her ch. incl. Lane, Joanna, Abigail, John.

7 **JOSHUA,** cordwainer, Falm. 1687-9, m. by 1684, perh. in Boston, Sarah White (John), half sis. of Sir Wm. Phips, and had a later w. Elizabeth. List 228c. Of Boston in 1700, he sold 41 a. and a ho.-lot at Little Fall Cove, Falm., bet. John Coe and Robt. Murrell, and a ho.-lot adj. Thos. Cloyes. He and w. also sold early to Henry Bailey. Y. D. 16, pp. 127, 157. He d. in Boston 27 Nov. 1710, ag. ±57. Will 4 Nov.—25 Dec. 1710 gives his ho. there equally to w. Elizabeth and s. John and they execs.; Capt. Rich. Gridley overseer. Ch. by first w., rec. Boston: **John,** b. 26 Mar. 1684. Cordwainer, Boston, 1728, when he sold White land bet. Montsweag and Nequasset. Y. D. 12.375. **Sarah,** b. 6 Feb. 1685, d. bef. Nov. 1710.

8 **RICHARD,** br. of (1) and (9), wit. at Portsm. with Baker Cutt 1648; in England 1649, a wit. for (9). Likely the Richard indebted to John Mitchell's est. 1666. List 78. Me. P. & Ct. 1. 149, 151.

9 **SAMPSON,** Strawberry Bank, br. of (1) and (8), merchant, shipmaster, privateer under Belgium and Spain by letter of marque from Archduke Leopold made at Brussels 22 Apr. 1648. He had just arriv. at Boston 3 Aug. 1646, master of the -Neptune- of Dartmouth, with wines from Teneriffe; first found at Str. Bk. 5 July 1648, where he had an int. in Wannerton's Great Ho. There Mar. 24, 1648-9 he gave P/A to br. Ambrose to sue Richard and John Cutts, and is of record at intervals dealing princ. with the Cuttses and his br. List 72. The Mass. Gov. and Council, 1 Aug. 1650, ord. that S. L., 'an Englishman· a stranger in this jurisdic. and an inhab. of Spain by his own confession' take down bills he had posted inviting volunteers on a ship of war against French ships. In 1651 bef. the Genl. Ct., after taking the Frenchman La Tour's ship, he declared hims. a subject of the King of Spain. Last ment. in Me. Ct. 13 Oct. 1652. See also (1), Cutts(5), Me. P. & Ct. 1. 143-5, 149-156; Prov. Papers, 1. 45-8. Evid. of a Devonshire fam. (one S. L. was m. in Exeter as early as 1583), he may not have been the S. L., whose will made at St. Christopher's Isl. 3 Feb. 1665, prov. at Boston 15 Aug. 1666, disposes of large prop. at Sligo in Ireland and names friend Ens. John Lane of St. Christopher's exec. No w. or ch. ment. N. E. Reg. 15, 123.

10 **SAMUEL** (Leane?), Exeter, 1677. List 54.

11 **THOMAS.** List 315a. See Lang.

12 **THOMAS,** summoned into Great Isl. court Nov. 1699 with John Swallow and others, all prob. seamen.

13 **WILLIAM,** tailor, Hampton, b. in Boston 1 Oct. 1659, s. of Wm. and Mary (Brewer). Of Boston, he m. in Hampt. 21 June 1680 Sarah Webster, dau. of Thos. and Sarah (Brewer), and aft. the birth of their 1st ch. settl. in Hampt. near her fa. Gr.j. 1695. Lists 57, 66, 336c, 399a. She d. Jan. 1745, ag. 85; he 14 Feb. 1749. Ch: **John,** b. 17 Feb. 1685, m. 7 Mar 1708-9 Mary Libby (1). Son John b. 12 Oct. 1709, liv. Rye and Chester, m. 1st 28 Sept. 1732 Hannah Lamprey(1), 2d 9 Mar. 1738 Mary Knowles. 2 + 9 ch. **Sarah,** b. 6 Nov. 1688, m. Wm. Berry (13 jr.). **Elizabeth,** b. 12 July 1691, m. Elias Critchett. **Abigail,** b. 9 Dec. 1693, m. Wm. Vittum. **Joshua,** b. 6 June 1696, Deacon, m. 24 Dec. 1717 Bathsheba Robie (Saml.), who d. 13 Apr. 1765. He was k. by lightning in own doorway 14 June 1766. 16 ch. **Samuel,** Hampt. Falls, b. 4 Aug. 1698, d. 9 Jan. 1776, m. Elizabeth Blake (Philemon). 7 ch.; 3 d. in Aug. 1735. **Thomas,** b. 8 June 1701, d. 30 Aug. 1775, m. Elizabeth Bryant of Newington who d. 3 June 1798, ag. 91. 7 ch.

14 ———— (Lains), in acct. against John Hinckes 1680. List 90.

**LANG,** peculiar to Devonshire in England, but Laing and Lang are common in Scotland.

1 **JEREMIAH** (Lange), m. in Portsm. 16 May 1723 Hannah Towle, was poss. a stranger; likewise Immanuel (unless meant for Samuel), whose ch. Joanna and John (mo. Mary), were bp. 13 June 1731. Joseph, Aug. 1731, may have been the same who m. 25 Dec. 1734 Eleanor Jackson.

2 **JOHN.** See Davis(4). Should read 'one Lang'. See (9).

3 **JOHN,** from Kennebec, with w. and one ch. at Green's in Charlestown Oct. 1689. List 17 (Lange).

4 **JOHN**(7?), mariner, husbandman, liv. at Sagamore Creek, Portsm., close by (7), was bondsman in Nov. 1694 for Wm. Brookins's wid. Mary. Their dau. Grace became his wife (Ct. Mar. 1694-5). In 1697, already the tenant, he bot the Gowen Cox ho. and 2 a. at Sagamore Creek, and later acquired ±200 a. more. Witn. Nathl. Lang's deed 1698. Lists 68, 330d, 337, 339. W. Grace owned covt. and had all her ch. bap. at No. Ch. 30 May 1708; liv in Oct. 1715, and likely in Feb. 1719-20 when her step-fa. deeded to John for life supp. He m. 2d 10 May 1725 Ruth, wid. of John Sherburne, who surv. him and did not name Langs in her will 1759. His will 29 Oct. 1748 (d. 22 May 1752) gives to w. Ruth, ch. and gr. ch.; s.-in-law Jos. Gray exec. The est. invent. £3294. Elizabeth, w. of Stephen jr., and

Catherine, w. of John, were with him in his last hours. Ch: **Elizabeth**, m. 28 July 1716 John Wescom of Tiverton, co. Devon; liv. 1762. Ch. Thos. W. and Mary Bickford named in her fa.'s will. **Ann**, m. 9 Jan. 1717-8 her cous. John Savage; d. 7 Oct. 1722, leav. s. John named in his gr. fa.'s will. **Mary**, m. Wm. Adams(21). **William**, fisherman, farmer, m. 7 July 1721 Susanna Savage. Will 5 Apr.—29 Aug. 1759 names her, 7 of 9 ch., three Rand gr. ch. Son Mark adm. her est. 19 Oct. 1784. **John**, cordwainer, Greenland, m. by 1724 Sarah Bickford (Henry), who d. 1769. Will 5 Sept. 1767—27 June 1774. 10 ch. **Dorothy**, m. John Wells, and d. bef. her fa., who beq. to her ch. **Thomas**, bp. 17 July 1709, d. by 1714. **Grace**, bp. 16 Mar. 1711-2, m. (int. York 29 Oct. 1737) Jos. Gray. **Thomas**, bp. 4 Apr. 1714, mariner, m. 17 Nov. 1737 Mary Downs (Wm.). 4 ch. bp. **Hannah**, bp. 7 Aug. 1715, m. 5 Dec. 1734 Luke Mills, mariner, of Northampton, Va. Her fa. deeded to them in 1745, and beq. to her ch. in 1748, she then dead.

5 **NATHANIEL**(7), fisherman, was liv. at the Shoals in 1698 when he bot 9¾ a. on Sagamore Creek and moved there. This land with the bldgs. he deeded to gr. s. Daniel, mariner, in 1748. Lists 337, 339. Constable 1714. Added memb. of No. Ch. 1709; deacon 1720. His w. was Elizabeth (poss. Currier?) 1715-1748, as far as kn. the only one. In 1733 they deeded ho. and 58 a., the orig. right of John Jackson and Robt. Lang; he alone deeded entire est. to s.-in-law Stephen Marden in 1751, when last found. Ch., several bp. in No. Ch. 25 Sept. 1709: **Robert**, cordwainer, d. bet. 1737-1739, m. 4 July 1718 Catherine Cowell (6, John the fa., not Saml.); she was deced. in 1759. 7 ch. bap. **Nathaniel**, ferryman, d. in Portsm. poor-ho. in July 1785, ag. 84. Wife Hannah Beck(4), m. May 1724. 7 ch. bap. **Charity**, m. 21 May 1721 Stephen Marden. **Elizabeth**, m. 1st in 1722 Wm. White jr.; 2d in Newingt. 4 Oct. 1745 John Marshall. **Deborah**, m. 28 Jan. 1724-5 John Griffith (4). **Jeffrey**, b. 16 Jan. 1707, goldsmith, Salem, d. 14 May 1758, m. 1st in Salem 24 Aug. 1732 Hannah Symmes, d. 3 Oct. 1748, ag. 41; 2d in Rye 5 Dec. 1751 Wid. Esther (Ruck) Morrill of Salem. Ch. 9+2. **Samuel**, bp. 21 May 1710, m. 28 June 1733 Hannah Tout. **John**. **Agnes**, bp. 3 July 1715, m. 25 Nov. 1731 John Martin. **Benjamin**, bp. 30 Sept. 1716.

6 **RICHARD**, soldier at Kennebec 1688. List 189.

7 **ROBERT**, fisherman, Portsm., m. (Ct. 19 Aug. 1668) Ann Williams, who was seated in Portsm. Ch. in 1693. List 335a. Of the Shoals in 1670, he bot ho. and 13 a.

on Sagamore Creek bet. Rich. Goss and Henry Savage, afterw. his home. Francis Wainwright sued him in 1693. Lists 326c, 331b, 329, 92, 335a, 330d, 336c, 337. In 1712 he deeded 14 a. of commons to s. Nathl., and d. 16 Feb. 1715-6; adm., Senior, 5 Mar. to s. Stephen. A will was rejected and is not on file. Reckoned as ch., tho only Nathl. and Stephen surely proven: **John**. **Nathaniel**. **Mary**. In 1692 she had a ch., no husb.; in 1693 ptn. for pardon on paying fine. M. 8 Jan. 1695-6 Peter Staples jr. **Stephen**, fisherman, liv. on his fa.'s 13 a. at Sag. Creek. List 339. His w. belonged to No. Ch. in 1699. In 1716 she was Jane Wallis (Wm.) and was liv. 1723; he d. bef. 1739. Ch: Benjamin (poss.), taxed 1719-23. Stephen, d. May 1790, ag. 88; m. Elizabeth, wid. of Chas. Banfield(2). Samuel, Portsm., Lyman, w. Mary Sherburne by fam. trad. In 1736 he bot on Sag. Creek with br. Thos., who m. Sarah Fenderson in 1740. Wm., m. Lucy Bennett(5); d. by 1752 when Abra. Elliot was gdn. of his s. Jonathan. Deliverance, m. Matthew Nelson. Sarah, m. Nathl. Muchemore. Abigail, m. Abraham Elliot. ?Robert, (or gr. s.?) The fa. was senior 1708-1716. Robert and Stephen were added members No. Ch. bet. Apr. 1707—Aug. 1708. One Robt. witn. Edmund Geach's deed in Kit. 1714-5. **Anne**, new memb. of No. Ch. 9 Aug. 1708, may be the mo. **Deliverance**, m. 5 Feb. 1712-3 John Peverly.

8 **THOMAS**, Newcastle 1693. List 315a.

9 **CAPT. WILLIAM**, at the Shoals 1682. Y. D. iv. 13. Appar. the Wm. (Lange) of Plymouth, co. Devon, who sold his apprent. John Yeolland to John Odiorne in 1675, and another to Stephen Jones. (David Davis 4).

**Langberry**, Gregory. O. F. Pemaquid 22 July 1674. List 15.

**Langbridge**, John, m. in Portsm. 26 Nov. 1713 Sarah Partridge (Wm.), who m. 2d Abraham Dentt.

**LANGDON**. See Creber. Mr. Toby Langdon was buried at Sheviock, co. Cornwall, 10 Aug. 1654.

1 **TOBIAS**, Portsm., m. in 1656 Elizabeth Sherburne (Henry), the ancestress of two prominent families thru him and her 2d husb. Tobias Lear. She took a 3d husb. Hon. Richard Martyn and d. some time bef. Jan. 1692-3. Tobias in 1657 had gr. of 1 a. adj. that promised to Mr. Batchelder(1); in 1660 he had a lawsuit with John Odiorne over fishing accts. Lists 322, 323, 324, 326a, 330ab. D. 27 July, inv. 30 Nov., 1664. Adm. 27 June 1665 to wid. Elizabeth; eldest son under 21, other ch. under 18, ment. A certif. filed in 1734 by Joshua Pierce

names the wid. and ch: **Elizabeth,** m. Capt. Wm. Fernald(5). **Tobias,** b. ±1660-2. **Margaret,** m. 4 Aug. 1679 Nicholas Morrill. **Honor,** m. John Leighton(5).

2 **CAPT. TOBIAS**(1), wheelwright, Portsm. ±47 in Feb. 1709-10; ag. 64, 20 Feb. 1724-5 (gr. st.); m. in Salisb. 17 Nov. 1686 Mary Hubbard(10). List 331c. He was taxed Greenland 1688-1698. Ensign 1690; Lieut. 1692, yet styled Ensign in 1694 when his half-bro. Tobias Lear chose him gdn., also in 1695; Capt. 1696. Surveyor of ways at Sagamore Creek 1692 (Ens.); Selectm. 1693-6, 1706. J. P. 1699. Lists 52, 332b, 57, 58, 59, 323, 324, 335a, 336b, 330cd, 63, 64, 337, 316, 339. In 1694 his w. went to Boston to put out their niece Margaret Morrill, and he was gr. adm. on Nicho. Morrill's est. in 1697. Will 20 May 1724—3 Mar. 1724-5 provides comfortable mainten. upon the est. where he was liv. for w. Mary while a widow, and to have her thirds if need requires. She was liv. 1729. Ch., all in will: **Elizabeth,** b. 17 Nov. 1687, bp. at Salisb. 16 Sept. 1688, m. 28 Mar. 1706 Geo. Pierce of Newb. She d. 4 May 1732; he m. 2d Mary Hunking(5). Her ch: Tobias, Eizabeth, w. of Saml. Waterhouse. **Tobias,** b. 11 Oct. 1689, bp. Salisb. 18 Aug. (sic) 1689, cooper, m. at Portsm. 11 Feb. 1713-4 Sarah Winkley (Saml.). Both liv. Mar. 1749-50. Selectm. 1724, 1729-30. Ch: Saml., Mary, Tobias, Sarah, John (s. of Tobias and -Mary-), Richard, bp. or rec. 1716-1737; Elizabeth added by Wentworth Gen. **Martha,** b. 7 Mar. 1692-3, m. 7 July 1715 Nicho. Shapleigh of Kit. List 331c. Capt. **Richard,** b. 14 Apr. 1694, liv. in Boston where he m. 27 May 1718 Thankful Hubbard, who d. 5 Mar. 1732, ag. 32. He d. in Newtown, L. I. 3 ch. rec. Boston. Capt. **Joseph,** b. 28 Feb. 1695-6, m. 1st 1 Dec. 1720 Mary Banfield (Saml. 2), d. 10 Aug. 1753, ag. 49; 2d Ann, wid. of John Eyre. List 331c. Selectm. 1738. D. 10 Aug. 1767; will names w. Ann, s. Capt. Samuel (m. 29 Sept. 1748 Hannah Storer; one Saml. of Portsm. int. mar. with Mrs. Elizabeth Brown, Ipsw., 25 Oct. 1746), daus. Mary, w. of Amos Seavey, Elizabeth, w. of Jas. Seavey, Hannah, w. of Saml. Whidden; gr. ch. Jos. Seavey, Jos. Whidden. **Mark,** b. 15 Sept. 1698, d. 1776, m. 7 June 1722 Mehitable Jackson, who d. 7 Oct. 1762, ag. 63 (gr. st.), and had a 2d w. Mary. Selectm. 1736-8, 1743-53. Deacon. Ch: Joseph jr., merchant, d. 30 Oct. 17—, ag. 25 (Point of Graves), leaving insolv. est. and wid. Mary (Hunking), m. at Rochester 20 Dec. 1747; Tobias d. Aug. 1727, ag. 2 yrs. (gr. st.). **Samuel,** b. 6 Sept. 1700, m. 8 Oct. 1724 Hannah Jenness(2), who was gr. adm. 20 Dec. 1725, and m. 2d Joshua Jenness(1). Ann, dau. of Saml., d. in Rye 20 Jan. 1725; Anne,

dau. of Hannah, bp. Greenland 1726. **William,** b. 30 Oct. 1702, d. 1770; taxed Newc. 1720, Portsm. 1731-2. W. Sarah. 3 or m. ch. Mr. **John,** b. 28 May 1707, d. 27 Feb. 1780, ag. 73 (gr. st.). Wid. Mary d. 11 Apr. 1789, ag. 72. He had m. Mary Hall by 1745, poss. not his 1st w. Ch. incl. Hon. Woodbury and Gov. John Langdon.

**Langford,** John, ±20, 18 Nov. 1668, came from London to Piscataqua.

**LANGHAM,** 1 **John,** witn. a Walton deed 1659. Y. D. 2.38.

2 **THOMAS,** gent., pd. Arthur Hoddy £10, 13 May 1685, in part for passage London to N. E., £5 of it for Mr. Abraham Lee. See Lee(1).

**LANGLEY,** Longley. Parishes and places in eleven counties.

1 **BENJAMIN,** m. 26 Mar. 1723, No. Ch., Portsm., Mary Geer. List 339. Sold land in Barrington 1731.

2 **HENRY,** witn., Elizabeth Edwards of Portsm. to John Fernald, 1670. Y. D. 2.144.

3 **JAMES,** Portsm., m. Mary Reynolds (Job) c. 1705. He bot and settled in Oyster River in 1714 and sold share in Newcastle commons in 1721. Original member of ch. in 1718 and chosen dea. 17 June 1724. Lists 316, 368b, 369. Adm. to wid. Mary 16 Feb. 1730-1. Agreement of heirs, 1732, lists ch: **James,** of age in 1732, m. 31 Aug. 1727 Hannah Edgerly. **Thomas,** of age in 1732, m. in Newington 7 Sept. 1743 Sarah Trickey. List 369. **John,** with next bro. under guardianship of Capt. Francis Mathes in 1732. **Job. Elizabeth,** bp. 20 Apr. 1718, not in agreement. **Mary,** bp. 22 July 1722, with younger ch. under guardianship of Dea. Joseph Wheeler in 1732. **Samuel,** bp. 10 Apr. 1726. **Eldad,** bp. 12 May 1728.

4 **LYDIA.** Lidey Langley, still in captivity in Canada Oct. 1695, was not from Dover but from Groton. List 99.

5 **'OLD' LANGLEY,** Portsm., maltster, taxed 1722, 1724, 1725, may be same as (7) and fa. of (3).

6 **THOMAS,** Portsm., shipwright, had 1 a. gr. in 1657-8, sued for debt by Geo. Walton and by Capt. Pendleton and **Mr. John** Payne in 1662. Constable at Kit., 1680. List 330a. He contracted to build a bark for Francis Hooke and a series of counter-suits resulted 1662-1664. Elizabeth Langley, witn. to a bill, Thomas Nock to Walter Barefoot, 1662, may have been his w. Hannah Langley, witn. to Eleanor Pierce's will, 1675, and Anna Langley, w. of John Brawn of York (in ct. 1694-1695), are unplaced.

7 **THOMAS,** absent from meeting 1690, app. in Kit. or York, was not (6) but poss. was (5). List 33.

## LANGMAID.

1 **HENRY**, sued by Henry Dering in Wells Ct. Apr. 1672, Shoals witn. 1675, next found at Falm. 1683-4. Mr. Wm. Vaughan sued him in 1685, Anthony Brackett in 1686. Signed Falm. ptn. 1689. Lists 226 (Longman), 228c. Supposedly his wid. was Margaret who swept Newc. meeting-ho. 1697-9, and was awarded 40s. in 1698 in part for her son's wages at the fort. List 65. Ch. presum. incl.: **Henry**, Newcastle b. ±1669, soldier 1696; tax abated 1720. Lists 60, 66, 68, 316. He depos. in June 1732 that he liv. at Cape Elizabeth ab. 32 yrs. since and was then near 31 yrs. old. Adm. 24 June 1737 to Sampson Sheafe. **Samuel**, Newcastle, 1696, taxed Portsm., 1707, 1713. List 315c. One Saml. in 1721 had w. Hannah, dau. of Agnes (Pumery) Matthews; see Gerrish(1). Ano. or the same was of Newc. 1730-40 with w. Sobriety Nock (Jas. of Durham). One Saml. of Durham 1760, Lee 1770. **Kenny**. List 315b. Same as Henry? **Joseph**, o. covt. and bp. No. Ch., Portsm., 1707-8, Newc. soldier 1715, taxed 1720. One Sarah L. m. in Boston 27 July 1710 Jos. Penewell. Expenses of Wid. L. in Portsm. acct. 1730. Of next generation, parents unkn., or widows, were: Mary, witn. with John Penhallow 1731; Priscilla of Portsm. m. 25 Feb. 1732-3 Joshua Thomas; Hannah, Portsm., m. 4 Mar. 1735-6 Richard Stacy; Priscilla m. at Kingston 7 May 1736 Saml. Roberts; Hannah (Longmaid) o. covt. Greenl. Ch. 1742.

2 **JOHN**, fined in Me. Ct. Feb. 1690-1, abs. from meeting.

3 **WILLIAM** (Longmead), Timo. Yeals, Wm. Hilton, abs. from meeting Mar. 1689-90.

## LANGSTAFF.

Tho sometimes spelled Langstar, it should not be confused with Lancaster. Not ment. in Guppy's handbook, but Langstaff is pec. to York and Durham.

**HENRY**, Dover ±70 in 1682, ±90 in 1699, ±97 in 1702, by his own depos. arrived at the port of Piscataqua about the yr. 1635 in the service of Capt. Mason and liv. two yrs. with Mr. Walter Neale at Little Harbor, then called Rendezvous. Dover prop. 1642. Gr. j. 1643, 1650, 1652, 1655, 1661, 1662, 1671, 1673; tr. j. 1646; Selectm. 1651, 1655, 1659, 1663, 1664, 1665, 1669, 1672. Lists 41, 49, 52, 54, 57, 62, 96, 342, 352, 353, 354abc, 355ab, 356abceghk, 359a. Gr. of 200 a., and also his lot where Stephen Tedder's ho. was, laid out 5 Apr. 1658. Mr. Henry Langstar, ab. 100 yrs. old, hale, strong and hearty, d. from effects of a fall down the 4 steps of his leanto. (Pike, 18 July 1705). Ch: **John**, called eldest son, but, if so, his age, ±50 in 1718, was understated when he, of Piscataqua, Middlesex co., N. J., depos. that he had sold his fa.'s lands to Samuel and John Shackford and that it was his fa. and not his bro. who had bot land from John Hall. His s. Henry, b. 22 Aug. 1686, was in N. H. in 1716. **Sarah**, m. Lt. Anthony Nutter. **Henry**, capt., 66 in 1713, drunk in 1706. In 1716 he produced a deed, dated 1 June 1668, from John Hall to Henry Langstaff, jr., had it recorded, got his N. J. nephew to sign a release and sold the land to his kinsman Sampson Sheafe, all of which was aired in court. The degree of relationship to Sheafe is unkn. In 1718 he was dead, s. p. **Mary**, ±63 in 1713 when she m. Eleazer Coleman, aged 23.

**Lantrimony**, ———, Penobscot, prop. plundered and cattle k. by Peter Rodrigo. List 3.

**LAPISH, William**, taxed Newcastle 1720, prob. husb. of Clear Jordan(8), wid. of Newc. 1728-1731 (Lipsic, Lipsicha, Y. D. 14.206), who m. 2d by 1740 John Martin, Newc., mariner and fisherman; both liv. 1759. One Wm. L. taxed Newc. 1745; one Elizabeth (?Lapish) m. Elisha Bragdon in Scarb. 20 Sept. 1744.

**LAPP, Walter**, Mr., in Me. Ct. had acc. Wm. Warren of felony bef. July 1663. Late agent of John Frederick & Co. of London, their fishing plant on Star Isl. was in his occupa. in Dec. 1663 when they sold to John Pennywell of Plymouth, O. E.

**LAPTHORNE, Stephen**, one of Winter's fishermen at Richmond Isl., coming in the -Hercules- in 1636-7 and leaving a w. and ch. at home. 'Promising to be pliable, but being very stubborn', he left Winter and built on land rented from Cammock, from which Winter tried unjustly to oust him. His time being out 13 Feb. 1639-40, he sailed for home in the -Star-, June 1640.

**Lark?** (Cock?), Good. and two ch. at Portsm.; N. Fryer's bill 23 Feb. 1679-80 for their keep and provisions to carry them to Monhegan.

**LARKHAM, Rev. Thomas**, M. A., Dover, b. at Lyme, co. Dorset, 4 May 1601, matric. at Trinity Coll., Cambridge, 1619, and came as early as 1640 to Dover, then called Northam, the name of his former parish in Devonshire. First an associate of Rev. Hansard Knollys(1), who was soon driven away by dissension, he fought strenuously with George Burdett and had a controv. with Rev. Richard Gibson(2) during the few yrs. Dover knew him, and went back to Eng. under scandal (Winthrop), aft. 13 Nov. 1642. Lists 351ab, 386, 352. His diary as vicar of Tavistock, co. Devon, 1647-1660, has been published. Ejected, he appar. contin. to live there, and there he was bur. 23

Dec. 1669. Wid. d. Nov. 1677. Two kn. ch. were: Rev. **George**, educ. Trinity Coll., settled at Cockermouth in co. Cumberland, ejected 1662; d. 26 Dec. 1700 in 71st yr. His s. Thos. liv. 1658. **Jane**, m. 1652 Mr. Danl. Condy of Tavistock, d. 1671.

**LARKIN**, 1 **David**, Dover, had 10 a. gr. next Lt. Coffin 31 May 1673. Lists 357d, 359a, 384a. Part owner and member of comp. on sloop -Good Speed- of Piscataqua, attacked at Cape Cod in 1689 and robbed of Peter Coffin's boards. Witn. with Hiltons at Newmarket 1690-1710.

2 **THOMAS**. See Wm. Rowe.

**LARRABEE**, Leatherby, Norman French and English spellings of the same sound.

1 **CAPT. BENJAMIN**(4), ±66 28 Mar.—29 July 1732, d. bef. Apr. 1733. He m. in Falm. and liv. there most of his life, keeping his fam. in Lynn while Falm. was in Indian poss. Coaster and soldier, he was under Capt. Moody at Casco Fort, and at times, 1695-1704, his vessel was in the govt. service. He was com. to cruise the Acadian coast to keep the French from fishing. Lists 214, 225a. His w. Deborah (Ingersoll, m. 1 Dec. 1686), was liv. 29 July 1732, ag. ±64. See (3) and (4). Kn. ch: **Sarah**, m. (int. Lynn 15 Nov. 1712) Samuel Proctor. 2 ch. rec. in Lynn, later of Portland. **Deborah**, m. in Lynn 28 June 1714 James Mills, 2d Lt. Thos. Cummings, 3d James Donovan, 4th 9 Jan. 1755 John Libby(3). **Elizabeth**, m. Joshua Cromwell (3 jr.) **Benjamin**. In 1727 his fa. was called 'Capt. B. L., Sen.' List 225a. D. in Falm. 1784; m. Amy Pride; 8 ch.

2 **ISAAC**(4), liv. to great age and made many depos., ±67 in May 1730, 73 in Feb. 1736-7, 77 in Sept. 1740, 81, of Lynn, May 1745. B. in No. Yarm., when about 14 living with his fa., they fled to Jewell's Isl. to escape the Ind. List 214. Will 29 May 1753—July 1755, of the westerly parish of Lynn, w. Eleanor, 4 liv. ch., ch. of 3 dec. ch. He first m. in Salem in 1690. Bur. 10 May 1755; presum. his wid. bur. 25 Feb. 1756. Ch: **John**, m. 10 June 1735 Priscilla Townsend, who d. Lynn 21 Sept. 1759, ag. 53. 3 rec. ch. **Isaac**, m. Salem 30 June 1715 Martha Towne of Topsfield. He was 'drowned in our bay', Lynn, 19 Sept. 1746 leav. wid. Martha and 2 sons. **Benjamin**, mariner, settled in No. Yarm., when his fa. in 1729 deeded him half his rights. He m. at Lynn 16 Nov. 1725 Elizabeth Newman, appar. the 'wife of Benj.' who d. at I. L.'s 4 Nov. 1726. He was drowned 10 Sept. 1751; 1 ch. in gr. fa.'s will. **Sarah**, m. Lynn 2 Sept. 1731 James Parker of Reading. Her fa.'s will names gr. dau. Sarah Parker, dau. of his dau. Sarah, not called dec., presum. wid. of

James Parker of No. Yarm. who m. 2d one Ingersoll. **Samuel**, m. perh. 1st (int. 28 Nov. 1736) Elizabeth Hinchman, m. 5 Oct. 1741 Mary Brown. Adm. 1756 to wid. Mary, who d. 1773. 6 minor ch. **Eleanor**, unm. 1755. **Joanna**, m. (int. 30 Dec. 1753) Thomas Rhodes. Wid. in 1787 she deeded ho. and 24 a. to Lynn selectm. for £20 and life sup. Plausibly also a childless dau. **Mercy**, m. (int. Lynn 18 Feb. 1715-6) John Cummins of Topsfield. But see (3).

3 **SAMUEL**(4) m. Boston Nov. 1695 Lydia Biss, a wid. 'Formerly of Casco Bay, late of Boston', seaman, adm. was gr. to her 22 Sept. 1701. Her will, 13 Feb.—9 Mar. 1718-9, late of Boston, wid., left ½ to son John Biss (Bush?), ½ to Wm. Beardon. In 1727 adm. was gr. to his bro. Capt. Benj., as late of No. Yarm., evid. for the purpose of claiming the No. Yarm. grant made to him in 1685. List 214. Lot 33 was granted to his representatives, but who they were does not appear, poss. his brothers, nephews and nieces. He may have had ch. by an earlier wife. No deed is found, but Edward King, a surveyor and trader, owned Lot 33 in 1733. John Stearns in 1727 was licensed by the Proprietors to sell a lot to Edward King alias Rice.

4 **STEPHEN**, emig. ancestor of the Larrabees of Me., N. H., and Mass., whose name nowhere appears in the records during his lifetime. His son Isaac in 1733 took oath to his name and the names of his 9 ch. His brother William's will also named them. Capt. Benjamin in 1716 called his father 'Stephen Larraby which was one of the most anchant possessors in Casco Bay', and had Abomazeen execute a paper before Samuel Moody, J. P., confirming Warrumby's sale of land to S. L. In 1715 a deed was produced by which John Redding had conveyed 100 a. in No. Yarm. which his fa. had bot. from Stephen Larrabee and John Paine. See (2). He was one of the No. Yarm. men killed in the attack on Jewell's Isl. in Sept. 1676; the news reached Wells the 7th. Col. Banks conject. that he was a s.-in-law of John Mains. 5 or 6 of his sons had ch., almost all unrec. Ch: **Stephen**, b. 1652. **William**, b. 1657. **John**, mariner, will proved in London, 30 Apr.—19 June 1694. In Philip's War was a soldier from Malden, in gar. at Wading Riv. 1675. **Isaac**, b. 1663. **Thomas**. **Samuel**. **Benjamin**, b. 1666. **Ephraim**, k. by Ind. at No. Yarm. **Jane**, m. William Ashfield.

5 **STEPHEN**(4), in 1685 was a witn. at Winter Harbor with Geo. Pearson. Lists 30, 33, 214. Settled in Malden. In 1709-10 tenant of Gov. Usher's farm at the halves. Taxed there 1710. D. in Portland 1 Mar. 1718-9, ag. 66; his gr. st. is the 2d oldest

there. In 1694-1697 his wife was Isabella; his wid. was liv. in Portland 1722. Kn. ch: **Stephen,** b. 1682, called eldest s. in uncle's will, m. at Boston 10 Jan. 1704 Margaret Paine. Liv. in Charlestown, in Medford 1718-1719, in No. Yarm. Will 18, d. 20, Oct. 1737, names 4 of 7 or more ch. Wid. m. 27 Sept. 1738 Samuel Seabury and d. 18 May 1754. **William,** Dea., tailor, m. in Boston 12 Aug. 1708 Lydia Adams. Was dea. of Boston 2d ch. Will 5—24 Jan. 1757 names w. Mary (mo. of Mary Whitaker) and 3 of 10 ch. rec. 1712-1728. **John,** Capt. commanding the Boston harbor defences. See N. E. Reg. 16.15. He m. 29 Sept. 1710 Elizabeth Jordan(8). 3 rec. ch. Will 1760, bur. 12 Feb. 1762, names bros. Ephraim and Samuel and sist. Margaret Brock. **Ephraim,** m. in Charlestown 17 Apr. 1717 Anna Holden, liv. in Reading 1718-1722, tax abated in Charlest. 1723. Both liv. in 1749 when they sold their home in Stoneham and mov. to Reading, having then 3 adult ch.; and were both liv. in Woburn in 1763. **Samuel,** m. in Lynn 14 Jan. 1717-8 Sarah Breed. Both memb. of Lynnfield church, they were dism. to Lunenburg 1743. He rem. to Rindge, N. H., ab. 1762, where his son Samuel had settled. 7 or more ch. The fa. m. 2d, 19 Dec. 1758, wid. Mary Simonds of Shirley. **Margaret,** b. Sept. 1694 in Malden, m. one Brock. John and Margaret Brock had John b. 13 June 1734. **Abigail,** b. Sept. 1694 in Malden, presum. m. in Boston 13 Nov. 1718 James Trout. **Benjamin,** Capt., b. 11 Feb. 1696-7, rem. to No. Yarm., later Boston; was many yrs. in command of the fort in Brunswick, where he d. 9 May 1748. Wid. Mary (Elithorp, m. in Boston 18 May 1727) m. 2d John Oulton. 8 ch. rec. 1728-1742. In 1756 5 daus. q. c. to bro. Nathl.

6 **THOMAS**(4), soldier in Philip's War. (Arch. 100.300). He m. in Scarboro, where he had a 6 a. gr. in 1683 and liv. except during Ind. troubles. In 1690 he escaped to Portsm. where in 1696 he was working for Capt. John Pickering. On incorp. of Stratham 14 Mar. 1715-6, his was one of four families annexed to Greenland. Among the first to resettle Scarb., and Moderator of the first Proprietors' meeting. Lists 34, 214, 238a, 239b, 330d, 337, 338d. He and a son were shot by Ind. while working in his field 19 Apr. 1723. He m. Elizabeth Rowe (Anthony), and settled on the upper end of her fa.'s homestead. His wid. joined the church 26 Oct. 1735. Ch: **Jane,** (also Eleanor and Sarah) recd. into covenant and bap. Portsm. 1 May 1715. Liv. Scarb. unm. 1760. **Mary,** m. 1709 Henry Sherburne (Capt. Henry of the Plains). **Elizabeth,** b. 1690, m. Edward Pendexter of Portsm., d. 20 Aug. 1771, ag. 81. Ch. **Thom-**

as, ±61 in May 1752. In 1714 he was working for Col. Geo. Vaughan; rem. to Scarb., back to Portsm., again ab. 1730 to Scarb., in Portsm. 1733-1738. List 339. He m. in Portsm. in May 1715 Abigail Pitman. 10 or m. ch., incl. Isaac and Mary bp. in Greenland (printed Tetherlye) in 1729. **Eleanor,** m. in Portsm. 1 Dec. 1715 Christopher Mitchell, later of Cape Elizabeth. **Sarah,** m. 24 Oct. 1717 Joseph Hill(9). **John,** ag. 53 in June 1751. List 239b. He m. Mary Ingersoll(6). 10 ch., incl. Deborah who m. her cous. Isaac L. **Benjamin,** b. 1700, settled on Pleasant Hill. List 239b. See Me. Hist. Coll. iii. 152. He d. 17 Dec. 1763 and his wid. Sarah (Johnson 31), m. 4 Dec. 1724, d. 26 Dec. 1789, gr. sts. 7 ch. **Anthony,** k. by Ind. with his fa. 19 Apr. 1723. **Hannah,** m. in Scarb. 28 Feb. 1737 Benj. Richards.

7 **WILLIAM,** bro. of (4), ±45 18 Nov. 1668. First ment. in mar. in Malden, Nov. 1655, to Elizabeth Felt(1). These Larrabees are not known to be connected with the Larrabees of R. I. and Conn.; a New Haven record of Greenfield Larrabee was misapplied. William's home was chiefly Malden, but he must have been much at No. Yarm. with his bro. and his wife's relations. Constable of Malden 1678. Being childless, his will favored largely his bro.'s ch. N. E. Reg. 50.40. His w. outl. him. Inv. taken 4 Aug. 1693.

8 **WILLIAM**(4), ±27 16 May 1685, ±65 2 July 1722. His bro. Benj. depos. that he was 11 when No. Yarm. was abandoned, and on going back he liv. with his bro. William. Later he settled in Wells, where he married three wives, who with their ch. suffered much from the Indians. Jury 1709. Lists 214, 39. He m. 1st Joanna Milbury; 2d 14 Mar. 1699 Mary Came(2), List 39; 3d 14 Mar. 1706 Catherine (Ford) Adams(10). Will 25 Apr.—8 Aug. 1727 names w. Catherine, 3 daus., 1 son. Kn. ch: **William,** town gr. laid out to him 1713, d. s. p. bef. his fa. **Bethia,** m. bef. 6 June 1714, when she joined Wells church, John Look. 1 dau. bp. **Two ch.** massacred 10 Aug. 1703. List 39. **Stephen,** Sergt., b. ab. 1707, d. 177-. Bourne's Wells says: 'To him we are indebted in a great degree for the preservation of the [Kennebunk] settlement.' List 269c. He m. (int. 18 Apr. 1728) Lydia Durrell(2). A trad. acct. 1840 names his ch: Stephen, William, Jesse, Joel, Mary, Lydia, Catherine, Esther. **Sarah,** m. 11 Oct. 1727 Edward Evans (3½ jr.). **Esther,** bp. with Stephen and Sarah 14 June 1713; unm. 1727.

**LARRIFORD,** John, Portsm., sailmaker or tailor, called 'bro. Larefet' in John Martin's will 1664. Adm. 26 Mar. 1672 to Thos. Jackson, who gave bond to turn over to heirs who may appear. One Sarah Lariford

m. (int. Boston 11 Nov. 1696) Mark Round. **Larrison**, Thomas, wounded at the Eastward 1691. List 37.

**LARY**, Leary. See Cartee and Conner.
1 **CORNELIUS**, Exeter, was Mr. Dudley's man, appointed to keep the hogs out of the meadows 1 May 1657. Cornelius —ry sued Samuel Folsom and his w. for slander in acc. him of stealing, 3 Apr. 166–. He bot 10 a. from Ralph Hall which was in poss. of his s. Daniel in 1700, had a gr. of 15 a. adj. Teague Drisco and Jeremy Conner in 1664, a 20 a. ho. lot adj. Mr. Dudley's in 1680, and a 40 a. gr. in 1681. Lists 52, 54, 57, 376b, 383. His w., unkn., was prob. m. late in his life. Kn. ch: **Daniel**, witn. 1695, d. bef. 1755 leav. a son Daniel. **Thomas**, rated in 1714, adm. to bro. Daniel 25 June 1746. **Samuel**, rated in 1714, m. Agnes Bickford(14), who d. 31 Mar. 1759 at Stratham. Adm. to wid. Agnes 29 Feb. 1743-4, the papers naming ch. Samuel, Benjamin, John (of Portsm. 19 Dec. 1736, when he m. Rachel White of Stratham, where he d. Feb. 1745), Jane Field (Stephen), Anne Kennison (Moses), and Mary Fernald (John). **Sarah**, in ct. in 1712 and 1722 for bastardy, unm. in 1739 when she q. c. right in her fa.'s est. to Philip Cromet of Durham. Her ch. add to the difficulties of disentangling the 3d generation.
2 **JEREMY**, ±24 in 1725, Greenland 1720, Portsm. 1733.
3 **JOHN**, Kit. witn. 1696, m. Sarah Litten (2) who was his wid. in July 1698 and m. 2d Robert Allen (12). She was prob. the Sarah L. of Kit. who acc. Samuel Nelson in 1699, but the S. L. who m. John Cater or Cates 24 Dec. 1719 in Kit. likelier her dau., poss. illegit.
4 **JOHN**, of co. Cork, m. in Portsm. 16 June 1723 Hannah (Leighton 4) Tout.

**LASH**, 1 **Nicholas**, mariner, Saco or Scarboro 1664-1667, indebted to est. of Rich. Foxwell jr.; with John Rice appr. a little boat of Wm. Scadlock's est. Jan. 1665-6. Of Boston 1668, then sailing out of Cape Ann harbor on Sunday. Adm. in Boston 1679. W. Gertrude, in 1672, liv. 1676. Ch: **Robert** (presum.), b. ±1659, d. 9 Aug. 1712, ag. 53, in Boston, where he took O. A. Nov. 1678. First w. Mary, 2d by 1703 Elizabeth Stover (John jr. of York, Saco, Boston), poss. the E. L., wid., who depos. ab. the nunc. will of Edw. Bickford (7 jr.); wid., Boston 1719. Ch., by 1st w.: Mary, b. Boston 25 Nov. 1695; one Mary m. there 3 May 1715 Caleb Pratt. By 2d w.: Nicholas, b. 26 Apr. 1703, boatbuilder, Boston, m. 22 July 1725 Elizabeth Skillin; liv. 1747, as was his sis. Elizabeth, b. 9 Jan. 1705, m. 22 Oct. 1724 Wm. Stone. Y. D. 26.230. **Nich-**

olas, b. Boston 2 Sept. 1672. One Wm. Lash, mariner, Boston, will 26 Dec. 1687— 22 July 1693; w. Joanna, poss. the J. L. m. there 9 May 1695 John Manning. One Jone Tash (Lach?) dism. from No. Ch., Portsm., to Boston. List 331c.
2 **WILLIAM**, Mr., Weymouth shipmaster, early at Casco Bay. List 21.

**LASHLEY**, 1 **Frances**, Dover. See Allison (3).
2 **JOHN**, Mr. Robt. Jordan's man 1662. One J. L. d. at Boston almsho. Nov. 1738.

**LASKEY**, **George**, ±18 in 1673, servant to John Hunking(3). Poss. fa. of **John** of Kit., m. at Oyster River 31 Dec. 1718 Abigail Wakeham. 4 ch. bp. there 1722-1740. List 369.

**LASSELL**, **Joshua**, b. 15 Nov. 1686 in Hingham, m. ab. 1711 Katherine Gilman(3) and liv. at Hilton creek in York until 1722 when he moved to Arundel, where he was prop. in 1726. His w. was liv. in 1728 when her bro. Allison made his will but d. bef. 1731 when her two sisters were her fa.'s only surv. ch. He m. 2d 20 Aug. 1731 Sarah Bayley, and d. ab. 1750. Ch: **Joshua**, b. 5 Aug. 1711. **Mary**, b. 4 Mar. 1712-3, m. 1st 15 Apr. 1731 Noah Bailey and poss. 2d one Wood. **Jeremiah**, b. 7 Apr. 1715. **Andrew**, b. 20 Apr. 1717. **Elizabeth**, b. 1 June 1719; m. Jeremiah Miller. **Matthew**, b. 11 Aug. 1721. **John**. Allison. **Hannah**, m. Pierce Murphy. See genealogy in N. E. Reg. (1934).

**LATIMER**, 1 **Hugh** (Lattimore), Newcastle, ±17 in 1673, a Cutts witn. 1672-3. Thos. Ladbrook's servant in June 1675, when acc. by Catherine Circuit. In May 1685 he was sailing out of Saco River on Sunday.
2 **THOMAS**, John Chater's servant, found drowned in Saco River 1661. List 244e.

**Latin**, ——— (Englishman), servant of Martell, at Machias 1688 with w. and 3 ch. List 5. One John Lattine at Marblehead. List 85.

**Lattefar**, John, Portsm. 1671. List 326c.

**Lauener**, William, Great Isl. 1659. Conc. Ct. Files 13.15.

**LAURIE** (see Lowrey), 1 **George** (Lawry), adm. freeman 15 May 1672, with Portsm. names.
2 **MR. GILBERT**, signed agreem. with Portsm. 29 Oct. 1686 to come back from Boston as quickly as poss. and serve as minister 6 mo. or longer; with transporta. for w. and goods.
3 **SAMUEL** (Lawrey?), Exeter 1698. List 376b. See Lawrence.

**LAVERS**, Lavis. See Creber. Lavers an ancient name estab. in Somerset and Dorset.

1 **GEORGE,** Portsm., shoemaker, bot ho. at the Bank in 1671. Constable 1675; Gr. j. 1677, 1682, 1683. Lists 49, 54, 327d, 329, 331abc. Will, 30 Jan. 1683-4—24 May 1684, witn. by Samuel Keais and Obadiah Morse, leaves prop. to wife (not named), his shop to s. Jacob and names Mr. Richard Martyn and Mr. Richard Waldron overseers. Ch: Jacob.

2 **JACOB**(1), 58 in 1719-20, Portsm., cord-wainer, m. bef. 1698 Elizabeth Nutter (Anthony) who was liv. in 1733. In 1684 when the constable was taking a prisoner to the fort he hit him in the rear with the butt end of a musket, and was drunk in evil company (Elizabeth Dam and Mary Moss) in 1692. O. A. 1685; tr. j. 1693, 1694, 1695, 1699; Gr. j. 1697. Lists 52, 57, 62, 67, 33d, 332a, 333a, 335a, 337, 339. He d. intes. in 1733. His ch. are listed in a writ, 1755, for recov. of his 72 a. Barrington gr: **George,** eldest s., mariner, d. 1740, leaving an only dau. Elizabeth, w. of William Elliot of Pelham. **Jacob,** joiner, m. wid. Mary (Jackson) Ayers, sold the entire Barrington prop., without title, to Thomas Tuttle of Dover in 1747. **Eleanor,** m. 15 Aug. 1726 John Sibson of Durham, co. Cumberland (sic), d. in 1748 leaving 2 daus., Elizabeth Abbott (Henry jr. of Andover) and Mary Sibson of Portsm.

3 **JOHN,** see Davis(17), York from 1640, also had ho. at Bloody Point which he sold to Michael Brawn in 1651. Witn. in trial of Robert Collins in 1650, sued Humphrey Horrell in 1650, York gr. 1653. Lists 275, 276, 354bc. Old Goodman Lavesse in ct. in 1653 for liv. from his w. John Twisden app. to adm. his est. (John Laws) for town of York 2 Apr. 1678, John Stover and Abraham Preble, creditors.

4 **ROBERT** (Lavis). List 82.

**Law,** James, Sagadahoc 1689-90. List 18. See Loud.

**Lawde,** Robert. See Lord(9).

**Lawless,** Philip, taken prisoner with w. and 5 ch. at Casco 1703. List 39.

**LAWRENCE,** from the personal name, common in the south-western English counties.

1 *****DAVID,** Exeter, had 10 a. gr. 30 Mar. 1674 and bot from Israel Leavitt in 1677 land gr. to Jos. Taylor. Accepted inhab. 11 Mar. 1678-9. Gr. j. 1683, 1698, 1700; tr. j. 1698; Constable 1692; Rep. 1696, 1703. Lieut. Lists 376b, 54, 383, 52, 57, 62, 61, 384b, 67, 377. Will 16 Feb.—16 May 1710 names w. Mary, prob. dau. of Wm. Taylor, who was well provid. for, four surv. ch., gr. ch. David L., Mary Stevens, Jona. L., Nathl. Stevens, and son Rollins's eldest dau.; br. Benj. Taylor. He owned in Ex. and Hampt.

and a sawmill on Ex. Falls. Wid. L. taxed 1714. Ch: **William,** joint exec. of fa.'s will with mo. and br. Jos. No w. or ch. found, unless fa. of David, who was to receive the homestead aft. gr. mo.'s death. **Joseph,** Stratham, m. at Hampt. 14 May 1708 Mehitable Tilton (Daniel). List 388. In 1732 he took q. c. from Thos. Rollins's heirs, in fa. David's est., rights of Jona., s. of br. David, dec., rights of Nathl. Stevens and the Burleys. Will 1761 (d. 26 Mar. 1762) names w., sons: Tilton, exec., d. Stratham 22 Jan. 1767; w. Miriam. Joseph, poss. m. Sarah Young (Danl.). David Esq., Epping. b. 15 Dec. 1719, d. 4 Apr. 1791, ag. 76, m. Anna Gordon, who d. 24 Nov. 1797, ag. 82; 6 ch. rec. Daus.: Mary Smith, Catherine Bennett, Margaret Flanders, Mehitable Gooding. **David,** a witn. 1699. His fa. willed him £80 in case he ever ret. home. App. he did ret., as invent. filed 28 May 1724, adm. 3 June to br. Jos. Son Jonathan surv. Ano. son may have been David named in gr. fa.'s will. **Phebe,** m. 29 Nov. 1696 Thomas Rollins. **Dau.,** m. Nathl. Stevens, and d. leaving two ch: Mary, m. Jos. Burleigh (James), and Nathl. He m. 2d ab. 1703 Sarah Folsom(4).

2 **JOHN,** Lists 111, 181, and

3 **NICHOLAS,** List 111, prob. from Charlestown.

4 **ROBERT,** Falmouth, Mr., Lieut., Capt., m. bef. Apr. 1684 Mary (Phillips), wid. of Geo. Munjoy, and built a stone ho. on the Munjoy prop. east of the Grand Trunk Station, Portland, where they liv. until he was k. by Ind. and town destroyed in 1690. Noted as leader of the opposition to Capt. Sylvanus Davis and Edw. Tyng, Esq., adherents of Andros, and his long-drawn-out controv. with Capt. Davis, defending his wife's (formerly George Cleeve's) estate. In 1687 he was dealing with John Jollyffe of Boston (Y. D. ix. 175), and in Suff. Ct. 29 Oct. 1689 sued Edw. Hill, shoemaker, on bond dated 2 July 1687. Lists 32, 34, 35, 126, 225a, 228bc. Wid. Mary m. 3d Stephen Cross in Boston 23 Jan. 1692-3 and d. there 1705. No kn. ch.

5 **SAMUEL?** (Lawrey?), Exeter 1698. List 376b.

**Laws,** John, P. & Ct. ii. See Lavers.

**LAWSON, Christopher,** cooper, from Lincolnshire, b. ±1616 (±55 in 1671), s. of Rev. John and Ann (Wentworth) and relat. to Mrs. Ann Hutchinson; see also Helme. With his relatives he signed the Exeter Comb. 1639; betw. Ex. and Boston 1643-49; Ex. selectm. 1644 and gr. a fishing priv. there, tho prev. accus. of extortion by his townsmen. Haverh. propr. 1649, and bot twelve shares in the Squamscot and Dover patent from Robt. Saltonstall. Taking his

1st Ind. deed at Kennebec in Oct. 1649, he was there in July 1650 and many yrs. after, 'servant of' and assoc. with Clarke & Lake, with intervals at Portsm. and Boston. During this time, even aft. bringing her back from Eng. in 1656, he and his ch. were deserted by the w. and mo. Elizabeth (dau. of John James of Filton, co. Gloucester), m. ab. 1639, when she was Mrs. Scott's serv. in Boston. He was in Me. in 1667 and 1669, she in Boston in 1668, when her ho. had been burned. In 1670, she gone to Eng., he petn. the Mass. Ct. for divorce. (See Mass. Hist. Soc. Proc. 46.479). Of Boston, broker, he sold 1000 a. at 'Worsqueage or Wigby,' Kennebec; Boston Mar. 1680-1, ag. 65. Adm. 20 Nov. 1682 to Edw. Thwyng; inv. ment. 'old clothes he had on when he d.,' listing many better. Lists 373, 374a, 376ab, 377, 378, 77b, 182, 191, 330a (Sowton?). Ch. rec. Boston: **Thomas**, b. 4 May 1643; in 1661 he had run away from Thos. Lake of Boston who had his custody. **Mary**, b. 27 Oct. 1645, m. Edward Thwing, butcher, of Boston. 'Her children' liv. 1668; 'their dau.' in Jan. 1668-9.

**Lawton, Henry**, trafficking in Indians 1676. List 4.

**Layton**, see Leighton.

**Lazenby**, Margaret, Exeter, m. Robt. Goodale of Salem, mar. agreem. 30 Aug. 1669. She surv. him, liv. 10 Mar. 1682-3.

**LEACH**, most frequently found in Devonshire, less so in Cheshire, Yorkshire and Cornwall.

1 ——, Mr., fined in Saco Ct. Apr. 1671 for selling liquor to Inds. P. & Ct. ii. 422.

2 **JAMES**, weaver, Newcastle, m. Jane (Turpin), wid. of Walter Muchemore, and 26 July 1660 sued Rich. Cummings for W. M.'s share in a fishing voyage 11 yrs. bef. They, their four ch. and her mo., Jane Furson(2), were legatees of Mrs. Ann Batchelder(1) in 1660; they and s. James helped Goody -or widow- Furson tear up the Cummings corn and were bound over for it in 1674. His land incl. Leach's Isl. near Little Harbor, where he liv. See Ely(2). O. A. 27 June 1656. Gr. j. 1654-5, 1667-8, 1676, 1678, 1683; tr. j. 1682, 1683, 1685; Constable 1656; Deputy Provost Marshall 1688. Lists 323, 326ac, 330ab, 312c, 313a, 331ab, 49, 52, 319, 315ac. Will, of Portsm., 14 Jan.—30 June 1697, attested by w. Jane, names her and ch.: **Son**, either d. bef. fa., or incl. in will with 'my children.' **James**, b. ±1655. **John**, b. ±1658, named first in will but called 3d son. **Daus.** (unnamed), presumably include (or possibly step-daughter) the young widow of Henry Mansfield in

1678, and a daughter **Mary**, m. 1st Lieut. Aaron Moses, 2d John Sherburne, unless Mansfield was the first of three husbands. Another son, Thomas of New London, is claimed by desc.

3 **JAMES**(2), Newcastle, ±25 in 1680. By his fa.'s will he was to have half the 34 a. in the Great Bay if John had the home place from his mo. In 1694 the bros. and John Bickford went to Cape Porpus and Casco Bay, where they saw no Inds., but took away Ind. canoes. Lic. ho. of entertainm. 1686; innkeeper, Newc. 1706. Gr. j. 1692, 1695, 1698, 1699; tr. j. 1697. Selectm. 1697-8; Surveyor highways and fences 1699. Lists (?313a), 52, 319, 315abc, 318ab, 69, 316, 323, 339. He sold ho. in Newc. in 1712 with w. Mary, prob. a 2d w. if they were the couple later at Windham, Conn. Some Leach had m. Sarah Churchwell(4) bef. Feb. 1712-3, when she depos. in a Ct. case; one James L. depos. in the same case. His ch. are not disting. from John's; appar. ch. of one or both were kin or in-laws of Edward Bickford (7 jr.). **Mary**, dau. of James, bp. Newc. 5 June 1709. Not unlikely were: **Nathaniel**, Kit., surety for Rowland and Mary Jenkins 1715, took deed from Zachariah 1737. List 291. M. 1st 23 Dec. 1708 Magdalene Williams, 2d 9 Oct. 1746 Elizabeth Cowell. Ch. 11 + 1, eldest s. James. **James**, tailor, Portsm. Poss. the Str. Bk. taxpayer 1713 was he and not the fa.; cert. a young James m. 26 Sept. 1714 Sarah Pickering (Thos.); both liv. 1748, she a wid. 1761. In 1735 he and John Churchwell were surety for Mercy (Leach) Abbott. Ch. rec: Phebe, b. 16 Dec. 1717. George, b. 7 Dec. 1722. **Zachariah**, Portsm., next name to James in tax lists 1714, 1722. List 339. In 1715 he put up a boy to steal leather from Mr. Wm. Cotton (see Cowell 4); in 1733 he and Jas. Moses were surety for Margaret, wid. of John Davis (26 jr.). W. Elizabeth Mitchell (Christo. of Kit.), m. 23 Dec. 1721, was liv. 1740; his invent. 1761. 9 ch. bp. So. Ch., the 1st s. James. Daus. (or John's) may incl.: **Mercy**, m. John Abbott (see 1), yet in 1713 John Abbott and John Leach were bondsm. for Mary, wid. of Aaron Moses. **Sarah**, surely Mercy's sister, spinster in Boston 1713 (see Bickford 7). **Mehitable**, m. in Portsm. 18 Oct. 1716 James Berry of Dublin, Ire. One Mehitable Berry of Newc., m. John Talbot 3 July 1722; ano. m. Wm. Stiggins of co. Devon 7 Nov. 1727. Poss. other ch. in Conn., if there.

4 **JOHN**(2), weaver, Newcastle, ±62 in 1720; depos. in 1733 ab. Portsm. 60 yrs. bef. Of Newc. in 1733 he deeded to s. John, and of Portsm. in 1734 deeded Leach's Isl. to John. W. Sarah in 1699 was hardly Sarah Churchwell(4), whom he may have

m. later, but he surely m. by 1724 Mary (Partridge), wid. succ. of Rich. Barnwell, Saml. Moore, Richard Elliot(4). List 339. Constable, Newc. and Portsm., 1693-4. Gr. j. 1697; j. 1697, 1699, 1700. Lists 313e, 52, 315abc, 318b, 68, 316. If his est., and not son John's, that was divid. into five shares, then his ch. liv. 1764 were: John, fisherman, had two shares, m. jr., by 1729 Charity Salter (John); both liv. 1758-64 when he, s. of John, weaver, sold on Leach's Isl. Mary, m. 1st Lawrence Ellis(3), 2d Stephen Barton. Elizabeth, m. John Tucker. The 4th poss. Sarah, of Newc., m. 21 Jan. 1727-8 Oliver Tucker. Prob.: Elijah, taxed Newc. 1720, next aft. John & Son, and not found later; neither was ?Henry, member of the Newc. watch 1723; poss. a soldier from afar. See ch. named uncertainly under (3).

**LEADER.** This name is found at Salehurst, co. Sussex, in a district of iron foundries, a most likely place of origin for Richard and George Leader.

1 **GEORGE**, gent., bro. of (2), Berwick, shared in gr. at Crooked Lane in 1651. Tr. j. 1653; Gr. j. 1654, 1655. His servant Alex. Maxwell in ct. in 1654 for abuse of his master and mistress. Admon. for not attending meeting 28 June 1655. Lists 282, 298. He and his bro. gave bonds 5 Dec. 1655 that he would go to England within 18 mo. to render full acct. to John Beex & Co. concerning the Piscataqua saw-mills. He prob. took his wife and never returned. His niece, Anne Clark(49) was granted adm. of his est. in 1720.

2 **RICHARD**, gent., bro. of (1), was engaged in Ireland (or England) to manage the ironworks outside of Lynn in 1644, having had mining experience in Ireland and being 'a perfect accountant'. He came over with his w., 2 ch. and 3 servants (incl. Thaddeus Riddan, bookkeeper) and settled in a ho. built for him by his employers, John Beex & Co., his salary being £100 a yr., but proved unsuccessful in business and unpopular with the authorities. He left there in 1650 and liv. for a time in Boston, but by Mar. 1650-1 had come to Maine, obtained a large gr. on Little Newichawannock River and began the erection of the sawmills known as Great Works. Later in 1651 he went to England and on his return was charged with speaking against the govt., but, as the words were spoken 'in the midst of the sea', the court had no jurisdiction. As Gov. Godfrey asked the Colonial Office to grant audience to Leader as 'agent of the province' 6 Nov. 1652, he prob. spent that winter in England also. Magistrate 1651, 1652; Kit. grants

1651, 1653, 1654; O. A. at Kit. 16 Nov. 1652. Lists 75a, 282, 283, 298, 323. He mortgaged a ho. in Boston and a ho. at Str. Bk., lately bot from Mr. Ambrose Lane, to Mr. Thos. Savage in 1654, and sold both properties in 1655, the latter to John and Richard Cutt. R. Cutt's w. was sister of Leader's w., who prob. d. bef. he came to Maine. He had sold ¾ of Great Works to London capitalists (John Beex, Richard Hutchinson, Col. Wm. Beale and Capt. Thos. Alderne) in 1653, and, the venture proving a failure, he mortgaged his remaining ¼ on 14 Feb. 1655-6 to secure his appearance in London to render an acct. within 18 mo. Leaving Thos. Broughton as his attorney, he reached England 1 Sept. 1657 and remained there until May 1658 when he sailed for Barbadoes with a 2d w., 'a gentlewoman whom a long time had waited for me.' On 16 Jan. 1659-60 he was in the sugar-refining business, but intended to journey to New England in the spring. He did so, and d. soon after. Adm. was gr. on his est. to Rev. Robert Jordan 27 Dec. 1661, to John Hole and Samuel Clark, they having m. the daus. of sd. Leader, June 1663, and finally 6 Apr. 1720 to Mrs. Anne Clark and her dau. Sarah Clark. Ch: Elizabeth, m. John Hole(2). Anne, m. Samuel Clark(49).

3 **THOMAS**, Dedham 1638, Boston, had rights in Hampton. List 393b. He m. 1st Susanna, adm. to ch. in Boston 10 Apr. 1641 (Savage), 2d Rebecca who d. 16 Dec. 1653, 3d Susanna, wid. of George Haborne, 4th Alice who surv. him. The will of the 3d w., 24 May—6 Oct. 1657, seemingly made at Hampton, disposed of a ho. and land there, distrib. many local legacies and named Robert Smith exec. He d. 28 Oct. 1663, his will, 17 Oct.—3 Nov. 1663, naming s. Samuel, exec., and ch. of decd. s. John. Leane?, Samuel List 54.

**LEAR,** peculiar to Devonshire.

1 **HUGH**, Portsm., bro. of Tobias(2), who deeded to him 20 a. on Sagamore Creek over against Thos. Onion, in 1674. He witn. Tobias's will in Jan. 1677-8, and sued Thos. Barnes in 1679. O. A. 28 Aug. 1685. Not seen aft. witn. Henry Savage's deed in 1686. Lists 312c, 313a, 331b, 329, 52. W. Mary Savage (Henry), gr. dau. of Thos. Walford, was taxed in 1688 as Widow Lear; m. 2d by 1694 Peter Wells. Ch: John, cordwainer, Portsm., had gift of land from gr. mo. Elizabeth Savage in 1702; in 1708 he deeded to Hugh Banfield, reciting that his gr. mo. deeded marsh to his three sisters, one Lear, two Wells; the same yr. deeded to cous. Tobias. List 339. W. Hannah recd. into covt., So. Ch., in Jan., he in Aug.

1728. Both deeded to sons Benj. and Saml. in 1742, he to Saml. in 1746. If a Mrs. Lear d. in Portsm. in 1775, in 105th yr. (Sav.), or near that age, it would seem his wid. Kn. ch: Benjamin, bp. (?adult) 28 Jan. 1728, the hermit of Sagamore Creek. Granite Monthly vi. 66. Samuel, farmer, m. 22 Jan. 1730-1 Mary Lucy. Hannah, bp. (?adult) 28 Jan. 1728. Elizabeth, recd. into covt. So. Ch. 26 June 1726; of Durham, singlewo., she sued Abraham Bartlett(1) in 1733 for pay as housekeeper 1728-30. ?John. Susannah, m. 1st Philip Lambeth, 2d James Abbott, 3d Saml. Adams. In June 1713 Jas. and Susannah Abbott, Henry and Elizabeth (Wells) Donnell and Mary Wells deeded marsh given them by their gr. mo. Savage in 1702.

2 **TOBIAS**, bro. of (1), mariner, Portsm. (Sandy Beach), ±42 in 1674, then master of the -Richard- on which Nicho. Frost (9 jr.) was mate when he d. in Ireland. Here as early as 1659, he m. bef. 1 Jan. 1667-8 Elizabeth (Sherburne), wid. of Tobias Langdon(1), receiving as her mar. portion 28 Dec. 1668 one half an island or neck of land adj. her fa.'s. In 1669 he sued Wm. Croscom, who ack. judgment; in 1670 witn. ag. Richard Sloper, drunk. Lists 326c, 312c. 313a, 331b, 54, 49. Will 25 Jan. 1677-8—5 Dec. 1681, witn. by br. Hugh, ment. w. Elizabeth, fa.-in-law Henry Sherburne, and 3 ch. She was ±43 in Nov. 1681, was taxed a wid. in Aug. 1684, and m. 3d Hon. Richard Martyn. List 52. Ch: **Tobias**. **Elizabeth,** m. Nathl. Melcher. In 1730 Tobias q. c. to her, widow, ho. and 20 a. where she was liv., on so. side Sagamore Creek over ag. Nathl. Lang's, and she receipted for her full portion from her fa.'s est. **Joan.**

3 **TOBIAS**(2), late of Portsm., now of Hampton, certif. dated 26 May 1694, chose his br.-in-law (half-bro.) Tobias Langdon gdn. Under Hon. Rich. Martyn's will 27 Jan. 1692-3 he was given ho. and barn near Sagamore Creek which is....mother's. Jury 1695. Constable, Newc., 1699; Tr. j. 1695. Lists 315b, 316. He m. 1st in Jan. 1702 Sarah Curtis(6), 2d in Rowley (of Newc.) 10 July 1704 Hannah Smith (Saml.), 3d 14 Apr. 1714 Elizabeth Walker (Joseph). Invent., yeoman, 3 Mar. 1755; John Griffith admr.; settlement in 1756, the widow's dower, and two-thirds to gr. s. Tobias, he paying the other heirs, there being but two ch. She depos. in May 1760, ±80, that she and John Banfield's mo. Hannah Manson sat at his table five or six months; decd. by 17 June 1767 when the heirs receipted. Ch. rec. Newc., by 2d w: **Tobias**, b. 29 Mar. 1706, Capt., mariner, m. 13 Dec. 1733 Elizabeth Hall. Adm. to her on his est., jr., 27 Nov. 1751. She d. 21 July 1774, ag. 58 (Pt.

of Graves). Ch: Mary, bp. 30 July 1735. Capt. Tobias, d. 6 Nov. 1781, ag. 45, fa. of Washington's secretary Col. Tobias Lear. Elizabeth (poss. the ch. bp. 26 Aug. 1739), m. Nathl. Sherburne. See Granite Monthly 6.5. **Nathaniel,** Newc., b. 25 July 1712, m. 1739-40 Temperance Peverly. He sued his fa.'s est. for three yrs. service 1733-4-5, and cutting and hauling wood 15 yrs. to 1754. Liv. 1768. By 3d w: **Elizabeth,** b. 10 May 1716, m. 11 July 1734 Josiah Webster; d. 17 Aug. 1735 with inf. dau. **Mary,** b. 24 Nov. 1717, m. 12 Dec. 1734 John Banfield (Hugh 2); d. bef. June 1767 leav. ch. **Walker,** b. 25 Aug. 1719, princ. heir of uncle Capt. Geo. Walker, m. 1st by 1745 Mary Nelson (Joseph), 2d 12 Jan. 1758 Mary Cowell (Benj. 6, s. of John, not Saml.). Both liv. 1764, he 1767. Ch. by both wives.

**Leatherby,** see Larrabee.

**LEATHERS**, an ancient personal name. Leather is peculiar to Cheshire.

1 **EDWARD,** Oyster River, ±50 in 1696, ±70 in 1709, first app. in Ipswich in 1663 when Henry Russell withdrew a suit ag. him, but in 1666 E. L. ack. judg. Taxed in O. R. from 1666, he owned land next to Henry Brown(7) in 1667 and had a 40 a. gr. from Dover in 1693-4. Constable and tax-collector, 1681; Gr. j. 1679; Tr. j. 1685, 1694 (fined for absence). Lists 52, 57, 62, 94, 356j, 359a, 365, 366, 367ab, 368ab. Named overseer in will of Wm. Pitman in 1682, which, with other Pitman-Leathers asso., may indicate relationship. Liv. in 1716. His first w. and some ch. were victims of the massacre of 1694. Christian Leathers, witn. in 1701 and debtor to est. of Nathaniel Meader in 1705, may have been a 2d w. or a dau. Mary Leathers of Durham, ±90 in June 1741, when she test. to liv. at Black Point over 80 yrs. ago and until Philip's war, would seem to be his wid. Kn. ch: **William,** ±21 in 1696. **Mary,** liv. at home in 1696. And poss. **Robert,** ±75 when he depos. in 1766, a lone rec. which may be questionable. There was a Robert (Edward) in the 4th gen., who m. in 1756 and was liv. in 1775.

2 **WILLIAM**(1), Durham, ±78 in 1753, m. bef. 24 June 1701, when they gave a receipt to Margaret Squire, Abigail Willey (Stephen) who liv. to be 102. They were bp. 10 Dec. 1727 and adm. to ch. 4 Feb. 1727-8. He deeded his homestead to his s. Edward and other land to his s. Thomas in 1722, and ½ of his now ho. and 80 a. in Canterbury to s. Jonathan in 1753. Lists 66, 368b, 369. Liv. in 1754. Ch: **Edward,** 37 in 1736-7, bp. as adult 3 Dec. 1721, m. one Sarah and d. bef. 1773. He and 8 bros. (no Robert) deeded ½ of their gr. fa.'s est.

to a 10th, Jonathan, in 1753. Ch. **Thomas,** 65 in 1770, bp. 3 Dec. 1721, m. 1st Sarah Marsh, 2d 19 Nov. 1724-5 Elizabeth Marsh. List 369. **William,** bp. adult 15 Sept. 1728, cordwainer, Charlestown, m. 29 May 1729 Susanna Brett, who, lame and crazy, was of the town poor in 1783. **Ezekiel,** bp. 28 Mar. ˉ725, m. by 1729 Abigail (Thomas), wid. of ames Nock, legatee of her mo. Martha (Goddard) (Thomas) Critchet in 1729-30. List 369. He d. in 1801 aged 100, and she 4 Oct. 1807. **Abednego,** bp. 28 Mar. 1725, 85 in 1791, master mariner of Portsm., m. 1st Charity Boody, 2d one Hannah who d. 8 July 1800, ag. 71. List 369. **Abel,** bp. 26 June 1726, taxed Charlestown 1732-1734, of Nottingham 1753. **Abigail,** bp. 26 June 1726, m. 20 Nov. 1729 Ebenezer Spencer. **Ebenezer,** Barrington, m. 1st Ann who d. bef. 3 Apr. 1754 when he m. 2d Martha Brown. **Stephen,** Lee, had w. Margaret. **Benjamin,** Dover in 1752. **Jonathan,** m. at Newington 25 Dec. 1746 Keturah Trickey (Thomas). Ch. **Mary,** m. Robert Willey (Thomas) and liv. to be 102.

## LEAVITT.

1 **ARETAS**(11), Hampton, b. ±1646, m. 1 Aug. 1678 Ruth Sleeper (Thos.) and settled on homestead formerly Abraham Perkins's. Served in King Wm.'s War. Lists 396, 397ab, 52, 399a. In 1710 he deeded homestead to s. James for support of fa. and mo. and £5 paid to each of his two oldest sisters; other land to s. Thos., he to pay £5 each to two youngest sisters; both deeds confirmed 1733. D. 14 Jan. 1739. Ch: **Luther** (dau. by rec.), b. 1679, and **Elizabeth,** b. 9 Nov. 1680, both d. 6 Feb. 1684. **Mehitable,** b. 8 June 1682, m. Robert Rowe. **James,** b. ±1683, d. 13 Apr. 1760, m. 20 Feb. 1717 Ann Brackett(2), and had 2d w. Hannah. 5 ch. 1717-1728. **Thomas,** b. 15 Jan. 1696-7, d. in Hampt. Falls 16 Nov. 1761, m. 24 Nov. 1714 Elizabeth Locke(5). 9 ch. **Elizabeth,** b. 2 Aug. 1690, m. James Sanborn. **Ruth,** b. 19 May 1693, m. Stephen Sanborn. **Dau.,** liv. 1710. Dow questions also ?Reuben b. 1697, d. 18 May 1719, and poss. ?Benjamin, twin to Luther.

2 **CAPT. CHRISTOPHER** (Levett), of a Yorkshire fam. and notable here for his exploring trip along the coast of Maine in 1624 and his attempt to estab. a plantation in Portland Harbor, building the stone ho. on House Isl. There he left men in charge when he went back, not to return to the spot permanently, tho his name was remembered in the obsolete Fort Levett. He sold his patent, unrecorded, to two Plymouth merchants, who sold it to four fishermen in quarters, which Mr. Munjoy bought in. See Wm. Norman; see 'Christopher Levett of York, the Pioneer Colonist in Casco Bay' (Baxter); Me. Hist. Soc. Coll. I. 2.73; N. E. Reg. 67.66.

3 **HEZRON**(11), tanner, Hampton, ±30 in Oct. 1674, ±36 in 1683, m. 25 Sept. 1667 Martha Taylor (Anthony), ±53 in 1700, who was bap. with her ch. in Sept. 1675. Tr. j. 1684. Feb. 15, 1702-3, he made agreem. with s. Thos., provid. for care of self and w. and payments to four daus. D. 30 Nov. 1712. Lists 396, 52. Ch: **Lydia,** b. 5 Aug. 1668, m. Mephibosheth Sanborn. **John,** b. 26 Nov. 1670, shoemaker, d. 8 Aug. 1717, m. 30 Dec. 1691 Sarah Hobbs(6), who d. 13 Dec. 1701. Lists 399ab. Ch: Sarah, b. 29 Sept. 1694, m. Reuben Marston. Martha, b. 24 Apr. 1697, d. bef. Feb. 1720. Mary, b. 11 July 1699, unm. 1719, poss. m. Mark Hunking(9). Child (twin), b. 13 Dec. 1701, d. y. Hobbs, twin, chose Reuben Marston gdn. 1719. **James,** b. 31 Jan., d. 6 Apr. 1673. **Moses,** b. 30 Jan. 1673-4, m. 11 Dec. 1700 Mary Carr. As a widow, she kept his tavern, which was burned 1733 and rebuilt. 6 ch. 1702-1720, 5 liv. in 1724 when he deeded to w. and ch. Lists 67, 399a. **Thomas,** tanner, b. 8 May 1677, m. (pub. Newb. 4 Jan. 1703-4) Elizabeth Atkinson, who d. 27 Aug. 1749. List 399a. 6 ch. **Mary,** b. 20 Oct. 1679, m. Capt. Benj. Thomas. **Abigail,** unm. 1703. **Sarah,** unm. 1703

4 **ISRAEL,** own br. of (8). Of Hingham in 1677, he sold land in Exeter granted to Jos. Taylor. Family in Hingham.

5 **JAMES** (Levitt, Lovett) (11), Portsm. ±22 in June 1676, ±60 in Nov. 1714, made confess. of faith and was bp. in Hampt. 11 Oct. 1668, prob. then apprent. to Henry Dering, whom he called 'my master' in 1672, ±19. In 1679-80 he was tending store for Mr. John Cutt; later Cutt's bookkeeper. O. A., Str. Bk., 28 Aug. 1685. Dep. Sheriff 1694. Sergt. 1695. Selectm. 1696, 1698, 1703, 1708; Coroner 1697; Tr. j. 1699; J. P. 1699; Constable 1706. Lists 329, 52, 333a, 335a, 62, 67, 64, 324, 330d, 337. The richest memb. of his fam., he was childless, and by will 1 Apr. 1718 (d. 4 Apr. in 65th yr.), named as sole legatee his w. Sarah, form. wid. of Nehemiah Partridge, whom he m. bet. 18 Feb. 1690-1—4 Jan. 1691-2. See Ellins(2). List 335a. A midwife (Levett) she depos. in July 1707, ±59, was recd. into So. Ch. 29 Jan. 1715-6, and depos. in Apr. 1732, ag. 82, ab. Mary (Gee) Pickering. Will 10 Nov. 1733—27 Dec. 1738 gives to Partridge desc.

6 **JEREMIAH,** own br. of (10), bp. Hingham 1 Mar. 1645-6. List 376b (1670). Of Exeter 2 Dec. 1670 he gave P/A to Saml. (11), and ment. my part of the sawmill. Remov. to Rochester, Mass.

7 **JOHN**(11), Sergeant, Hampton, served in several campaigns ag. Inds. and m. late 28 May 1701 Deliverance Robie. In 1694 he was bondsman for Wm. Barton who defaulted. Tr. j. 1699. Lists 395, 52, 57, 67, 376b (1698). Will 23 Dec. 1726 (invent. 24 Feb. 1726-7) names w. exec. with Capt. Jabez Smith, his dau., and John Leavitt, (br. Aretas's gr. s., cous. Thomas's eldest son.) Wid. m. 2d John Nay. Ch: **Deliverance**, under 18 in 1726, m. at Hampt. Falls 7 Nov. 1734 Jeremiah Clough of Salisb., d. 31 Oct. 1736.

8 *****MOSES**, Esq., Exeter, one of five bros. and half-bros. who came from Hingham, (4), (6), (9), (10). He was bap. in Hingham 12 Aug. 1650, s. of John and 2d w. Sarah ———. Bot in Exeter 1676, and m. 26 Oct. 1681 Dorothy Dudley(1), who d. bef. him. In 1689 her br. Saml. deeded him one-half of 200 a. Selectm. 1682-3, 1691, 1696, 1717; Moderator 1707-8, 1713-15, 1723, 1726. Rep. 1693, 1695, 1698, 1702. J. P. 1699. Deacon. Lists 49, 52, 54, 57, 64, 67, 377, 381, 382, 383, 385, 387, 376b. Will 31 Dec. 1730—6 June 1731. Ch: **Moses**, Esq., Stratham, eldest son, recd. early 50 a. near the Great Hill and £45 as his portion. Gr. j. 1693, 1697. Justice, Sessions Court. List 388. W. Sarah Leavitt(10), d. bet. 1740-46; 2d w. Ann surv. him. He d. in Stratham 19 Feb. 1754. 8 ch. liv. 1740. **Timothy**, Brentwood. List 376b. Will 1756—1756 names w. Anne Lyford(1), 1 son, 2 daus. **Stephen**, Exeter, m. in Kingston 25 July 1726 Mary Gordon, both liv. 1752. List 376b. 2 or m. ch. **Joseph**, b. 22 Mar. 1699; some time of Kensington. List 376b. W. Mary. 6 ch. rec. Brentwood 1727-1740 incl. Wear. **John**, exec. with br. Dudley. List 376b. Will 1764—1768. 6 ch. **Dudley**, recd. the home lot, ±7a. adj. Capt. Jas. Leavitt on three sides. List 376b. Will 1765—1776. 3 ch. **Dorothy**, unm. 1730. **Elizabeth**, m. Capt. Edward Fifield(1). **Sarah**, m. Stephen Lyford(2). **Hannah**, unm. 1730. **Mary**, d. bef. fa., who gave her clothing, also the mother's to Dorothy. See Mary Lyford(3), m. one Leavitt.

9 **NEHEMIAH**, shipwright, own bro. to (8), b. in Hingham 22 Jan. 1655-6. His mar. record to Alice, wid. of Daniel Gilman (2) is not found, presum. at Exeter during the Andros period; witn. there 1689. They withdrew to Hingham where ch. were rec. 1693-1699. Betw. the two wars they started back to Exeter, were in Boston 23 July 1701 when they sold their ho. in Hingham, and in 1705 Exeter gave him an unconditional 50 a. gr. Lists 57, 376b (1705). Adm. 9 June 1715 to wid. Alice, her bondsm. Jos. Young and Benj. Jones. Kn. ch., first 3 shown by q. c. deed 1721, last 4 rec. Hing-

ham: **Nehemiah**, taxed 'jr.' 1714; later of Kingston (the part taken from Exeter). In 1721 he q. c. to bros. Daniel and Sealley; in 1740 Ex. gr. land to his heirs. **Abigail**, w. of Edw. Scribner in 1721. **Alice**, m. by 1712 Edw. West. **Mary**, b. 19 Aug., d. 6 Sept. 1693. **Selah** (Seally), b. 18 Oct. 1694. List 376b. Will 14—27 July 1748 names w. Sarah, 5 ch. **Daniel**, b. 30 May 1697, d. betw. 1721-1724. **Mary**, b. 7 Oct. 1699.

10 **LIEUT. *SAMUEL**, Exeter, now Stratham, half-br. of (8), bap. at Hingham in Apr. 1641, s. of John and his unkn. 1st w., joined relatives in N. H. bef. 10 Oct. 1664, when he was one of four to receive 15 a. a man, lying in old Salisb. way, beyond James Wall's ho. In Sept. 1668 he had 20 a. at head of Humphrey Wilson's land on Hampton highway, and settled on the Shrewsbury Patent 1667-8. Depos. in 1683, ±42. Selectm. 1675, 1691, 1696, 1704, 1707. Gr. j. 1684, 1694. Rep. 1685, 1692, 1696, 1703. Lieut. 1690. Lists 376b (1664, 1698), 377, 381, 383, 49, 52, 55b, 56, 57, 58, 388, 96. He d. 6 Aug., adm. 12 Aug. 1707 to s. James. Wife in June 1667 and wid. was Mary, liv. and called James's mo. when est. divided 3 June 1708, her share not indicating a recent wife, altho Lt. Saml.'s w. shows as -Ana- in 1701 when they acknowl. bef. Moses Leavitt. List 388. He may have m. a dau. of John Robinson, whose former land was in S. L.'s tenure in 1669, who his s. James called David Robinson uncle in 1714. Ch: **John**, b. 2 July 1665, not in div. **Mary**, b. 13 Jan. 1666-7, m. Thos. Veasey. **Elizabeth**, b. 9 Jan. 1668, m. 1st James Dudley(1), 2d Robt. Briscoe(1), 3d Rev. John Odlin. **Hannah**, b. 15 Aug. 1669, not in div. Elizabeth Dudley's sis. Hannah Leavitt and her ch. lost in the wreck 20 Oct. 1697, poss. this Hannah, or unkn. 1st w. of one of the bros. **Samuel**, b. 25 Dec. 1671, d. childless in Stratham, old Mr. S. L., 19 Dec. 1753. Lists 376b (1698), 388. Will 1739—1754 names br.-in-law Moses Leavitt, Esq., (admr.), and his ch. Dudley and Sarah; br. Ephraim; ch. of decd. bros. Benj. and Danl. **Jeremy**, b. 6 Apr. 1673, not in div. Unrec. but shown by div: **Ephraim**, Stratham. List 388. W. Martha in 1715; w. Sarah named in will 1757—1757, with 3 sons, 6 daus. **Daniel**, Stratham, innkeeper 1719. Lists 376b, 388. W. Abigail in 1710. Will 14 May—13 June 1737 names her, 4 sons, 4 daus. **Sarah**, m. Moses Leavitt, Esq. (8). **James**, Exeter, gent., Lieut. List 376b. In 1714 he deeded half of 200 a. bot of 'my uncle' David Robinson. Selectm. 1721-4, 1728-9, 1732. M. Nov. 1702 Alice Gilman(8), who d. 2 June 1721. Will 15 Dec. 1746—25 Mar. 1747, names w. Hannah, 6 of 9 ch. by 1st w., gr. sons (incl. two Obers, the ch. of dau. Joanna

by her 1st husb. Israel Ober, m. in Beverly 10 Mar. 1727-8), sis. Elizabeth Odlin, heirs of sis. Sarah Leavitt. **Benjamin**, Stratham, a Newmarket witn. 1701, innkeeper 1716. Lists 376b, 388. W. Elizabeth in 1709. Will 15 Aug.—7 Nov. 1733 names her and 11 ch. (10 rec. Stratham 1709-26). In 1739 she was w. of Nathl. Ambrose of Stratham. One Mercy m. at Hampt. Falls 30 Dec. 1706 Satchell Rundlett and liv. at Stratham.

11 **THOMAS**, Hampton, of no kn. relation to the prom. Exeter fam. from Hingham, was himself first at Ex. where he signed the Combin. in June 1639, but remov. bef. Mar. 1643 to Hampt. Mr. V. C. Sanborn's theory that he was s. of Thomas Leavitt, bp. at Melton, co. York, 8 July 1594, and neph. of Rev. Ralph L. of Grainsby, co. Lincoln, who m. Anne Hutchinson (Edward), is unconfirmed. By 1644 he had m. Isabel (Bland), wid. of Francis Austin(1), and liv. on the Austin homestead. List 393a. Selectm. 1657, 1667; Constable 1664; Gr. j. 1679; O. A. to Mass. 1678. Gr. j. 1679. Freed from training 1681. Lists 373, 376a, 391b, 392b, 393ab, 49, 396, 397a, 398, 52. D. 28 Nov. 1696, ±80. He was 60 odd in 1676. Will 9 July 1692, witn. by three Drakes, names w., 4 sons (John exec.), step-daus., and s. Hezron's s. Thos. Wid. Isabel's will 8 Feb. 1699-1700 (d. 19 Feb.) names only one s. John (exec.), her three Austin daus., and gr. dau. Sarah Knowles. Ch: **Hezron**, b. ±1644. **Aretas**, b. ±1646. **John**, b. ±1648. **James**, b. 10 Nov. 1652, rec. as s. of Thos. and -Elizabeth-.

**LeBRETTON**, 1 **Charles** (LeBritton), Dover, drowned 1695. List 358a.

2 **PHILIP** (later Britton), rigger, Falmouth 1686, a Fr. Huguenot, prob. arriv. with Peter Bowdoin; liv. there when the town was devastated and Philip Morrill taken (his depos.). He bot Dennis Morrough's gr. adj. Thaddeus Clarke and Jas. Freese, and had 30 a. gr. of his own. This land, he, al. -Brinton- of Boston, and w. Elizabeth deeded in Feb. 1715-6 to dau. **Elizabeth**, w. of John Young of Salem, joiner, m. in Boston 21 May 1713. In 1735 they sold the land -willed- to her by her fa. Y. D. 19.28. Other ch. were: **Philip**, d. in 1721, leav. wid. Lois. **Peter**. **David**, b. Boston 14 Mar. 1707. **Mary**, m. 14 July 1717 Edw. Dumaresq. **Rachel**, m. 30 July 1719 John Dumaresq. **Sarah**, m. 30 Nov. 1724 Henry Venner. **Jane**. **Ann**. He was liv. Boston 1734, ±74. Will 1737 (Brittaine). See Bretton(5).

**LECORNAH** (Curnow, Cornew), **Catherine**, acc. in Kit. Ct. in Apr. 1680 with Mark Roberts, who ran away, leaving effects with his bondsm. Wm. Fernald who settled. In 1684 (Cournew) she was acc. with Paul Wil-

liams and mar. him. Mr. Hooke's servant was Catherine -Curnen- in 1682. One John Lecornee, mariner, m. bef. 1743 Joanna, wid. of Capt. Pelatiah Whittemore of Kit.

**LEE**, common throughout England.

1 **ABRAHAM** (or Leigh), Mr., chemist, Dover, came in the -Batchelour-, Arthur Hoddy master, in 1685, with Thos. Langham of Boston, gent., and Benj. Arnold, chirurgeon. He was late of Cocheco in Nov. 1685, when Wm. Partridge was his bondsm.; Thos. Langham swore that in Deal, Eng., he saw him clip coin, and at the ho. of Wm. Partridge of Cocheco saw him make counterf. coin, and he told him he had committed highway robbery in Ireland. His career was cut short by Inds. at Dover 28 June 1689. List 96. See also Langham(2). He m. 21 June 1686 Esther (Waldron), wid. of Nathl. Elkins(8). The same Ind. capt. her and her child (poss. not Lee); soon ransomed, she was found by Capt. Church on a Dutch vessel near Peak's Isl., and ret. home to find a 3d husb. John Jose(2).

2 **JAMES**, m. by 1 June 1707 Sarah Tucker (Richard of Newcastle).

3 **JOHN**, senr., Mr., Saco 1640, with Capt. Bonython and Roger Garde witn. R. Vines' deed to Thos. Williams in Apr. 1642; sold wheat to Winter 1643. Geo. Cleeve early deeded to him and Ralph Tristram 100 a. and marsh at Cape Porpus, sold to Christo. Spurwell. Y. D. 1.58. Tr. j. 1640, 1645; Gr. j. 1645. Dec. 18, 1647, in Boston, late of Saco, he mortg. to Adam Winthrop cattle in hands of Ralph Tristram and John Hammond of Cape Porpus (Suff. D. 1.92); appar. Wells 1648 and in Me. Aug. 1650 when Winthrop gave P/A to Cleeve to collect from J. L., Thos. Mercer and Thos. Miles.

4 **JOHN**, Sheepscot witn. 1664. Y. D. ii. 8. Poss. same as (3) or (5).

5 **JOHN**, Sheepscot refugee at Scituate with fa.-in-law John White, 1676.

6 **JOHN**. List 92.

7 **JOHN**, mariner, Portsm., form. of -Chadwell- near London, 21 Nov. 1687, when his kinsm. Walter Barefoot deeded him 216 a. at Spruce Creek bot from Champernowne; called cousin in W. B.'s will 1688, leaving him £50. Of Boston, form. of -Shadwell- near London, 18 Sept. 1689, he sold the Kit. land to Thos. Fowler(4), whose deed 15 Oct. 1699 speaks of J. L. of Boston, not called deed.

8 **JOSEPH**, sued by John Smyth senr. of York, 1680.

9 **SYMON** (Lea). List 47. Simeon Day (4)?

10 **THOMAS**, took mortg. from John Stover of York, Jan. 1680-1. Y. D. iii. 86. In

Oct. 1681, ±33, he was at York helping about a wreck.

11 **THOMAS** (Ley). List 124. Read Vey (or Wey).

12 **TRYAL**, m. Susannah Knott at Portsm. 2 Jan. 1714.

13 **WILLIAM**, Damariscove 1672. List 13.

**Leecock**, ——, m. Abigail Moulton (Henry), who was b. 2 Oct. 1666, adm. to Hampton Ch. from Exeter July 1697, d. in Hampt., Widow Lecock, 7 Oct. 1705.

**LEEDS, John** (Leds, Leads), York husbandman. In ct. 1674 for absence from his w. for sev. yrs., and in 1677 ordered to get her or go back to her in Ipswich. Will, 15 Nov. 1678, left ho. and land at York to son John and made Mr. and Mrs. Henry Sayward exec., witns. being John Jeffreys and Timothy Yeales. Ch: **John. Abigail**, d. in Ipsw. 1 June 1676.

**Leekey**, Richard, Wells witn. 1694 (Y. D. 13.276). Richard and Anne L. had s. Richard b. Boston 17 Dec. 1688.

**LEGATE**, Lidget, peculiar to Lincolnshire.

1 **JOHN**, Hampton prop. 1640, sold his ho. lot to Anthony Taylor in Feb. 1642 and mov. to Exeter where he was clerk of the writs (1645), Town Clerk and com. t. e. s. c. (1649), and Selectm. (1647-1650). Called kinsman of Samuel Fogg(4). Lists 374ac, 375ab, 376a, 377, 392a. He taught school in Hampt. in 1649. Bot ho. from Robert Booth 29 July 1650, and sold 30 a. to Thos. Biggs bef. 1663. He m. bef. 1644 Ann, wid. of Thomas Wilson, but an Elizabeth Legatt witn. a deed, Biggs to Gilman, with him in 1653, poss. an error. Adm. to John Huggins 11 Apr. 1665. No kn. ch.

2 **PETER** (Lidget), prominent Boston merchant, 38 in 1667, was at meeting at ho. of James Whitcomb at Isles of Shoals that yr. As assignee of David Campbell, he sued Wm. Roberts in Me. ct. in 1674. Lists 14, 89. His wid. and exec. Elizabeth (Scammon), m. in the West Indies bef. they came to Boston, who m. 2d Hon. John Saffin, sued Francis Tucker for one-half of the pinke Prosperous of Piscataqua in 1677. Will. His dau. **Elizabeth** was 1st w. of John Usher, stationer of Boston and later Lt. Gov. of N. H. The son Col. **Charles** was an adherent of Andros and d. in London in 1698.

**Legen**, see Legindra.

**LEGINDRA, Gustain** (also Gustin Legen), Wells, sold ho. and land to Saml. Wheelwright bef. 1688. Invent. 20 Sept. 1688 by Jona. Hammond and John Cloyes sr., clothes, gun, sword, and small things.

**LEGROW**, 1 **John**, Portsm. tax for 1713 abated, being gone out of town; taxed Berwick Nov. 1713. List 298. M. Mary

(Taylor) (Hardison) Coss(2); both o. covt. and bap. Berwick 21 Dec. 1718. She d. ab. 1725; he m. 2d Rachel Tibbetts (Saml.): liv. Apr. 1756, ±73. Ch. by 1st w: **Mary**, bp. 21 Dec. 1718, m. by 1730 Thos. Abbott. 3 or m. ch. by 2d. w. The name found in Essex Co., where one J. L. took O. F. 1678. List 85.

2 **PETER**, taxed Portsm. 1717.

**Lehey** (Lewis?), Grace, Star Isl. witn. by mark, 1711. See Davis(48).

**LEIGHTON**, Layton. Of this name are two hamlets in Cheshire, parishes in Huntingdon, Shropshire and Bedfordshire (Leighton-Buzzard).

1 —— (Laiton), Old Goodman, taxed Kit. 1704. List 290. Poss. (3), (4), or none.

2 **JOHN**, West Saco, fined in Oct. 1645, drunk and swearing three oaths. Freeman 1653, senr.; town gr. 17 July that yr. Constable 1653-4. Signed ptn. 1657. Not appearing in Rich. Hitchcock's suit July 1659, the attachment on his ho. and land was cont. in force. Poss. it was he who m. in Boston (Laughton) 21 Sept. 1659 Wid. Joanna Mullins. Jona. Thing sued John and Joanna Leighton in York Ct. 1 July 1661 (see Joy), and as J. L.'s assignee and atty. brot suit a yr. later against Lt. Wm. Phillips for disposing of wine left in his hands; Lt. P. was also in poss. of some of his land in 1660; not found surely later. Lists 243ab, 249, 24, 244c, 247. Leighton's Point near Biddef. Pool, where tradition in Folsom's day said there was once a courtho., may take its name from him or John jr., called his son (Folsom) and only kn. ch.

3 **JOHN**, shipwright, Kennebec ab. 1648, liv. until the war on ±800 a. oppo. the mills at Arrowsic, and had enjoyed poss. near thirty yrs., when he sold 13 Apr. 1678, deed acknowl. in Boston, to Jos. Turrill and Nathl. Coney. Creek that runs towards Laiton's ment. 1685. In 1719 when this prop. passed to Pejepscot Proprs., Mary, wid. of Wm. Cox(34), depos. that her husb. sold the land to him more than 60 yrs. bef. Y. D. 18. 261-2. In 1739 by fraudulent deed, John Parker (w. Margaret) to J. L., 2 June 1666 (Y. D. xx. 257), James Noble tried to claim a large tract and defraud Isaac Parker. No kn. w. or ch. He had given land to Lawrence Dennis(6), still kn. as Leighton's. Lists 183, 191 (?290).

4 **JOHN**(2), West Saco (Winter Harbor), b. ±1638, ±39 in Nov. 1677, m. 2 Oct. 1663 Martha Booth(3), two mo. aft. he had 50 a. gr. above the bridge. She was seated in pew with Simeon Booth's w. 1669. List 246. Jury of life and death July 1666; coroner's jury 1670; one of six, headed by

Maj. Pendleton, gr. 6 m. sq. above Saco May 1675; abs. from meet. in July. Appar. at Portsm. 1677. Road surv. at home 1681 and appr. Jos. Pennell's est. 1682. Lists 245, 249. If he and w. liv. to flee the next war, it was prob. to Portsm., where John taxed 1698 (List 330d), John jr. (List 330e). Called late of Winter Harbor 5 June 1722; adm. 3 July 1722 to gr. s. Ebenezer Place. Ch., daus. by deed 1722 (Y. D. 13.119): **John** jr., presum., but not in deed, 1722. **James**, b. 19 Apr. 1675, liv. 1697, not in deed 1722. Lists 334a, 68. **Martha**, m. Richard Place. **Deborah**, unm. 1722. **Mary**, Wid. Woody 1722, husb. poss. Wm. Woody, Portsm. 1714. **Hannah** (Layton) of Portsm. m. 30 Sept. 1714 Henry Tout (Trout by deed) of Dartmouth in Gt. Brit.; wid. 1722; m. 2d 16 June 1723 John Larey of co. Cork, Ireland. **Ruth** (Layton), m. in Portsm. 26 July 1714 John Wherrin. Likely: **Robert**, Portsm., named for gr. fa. Booth; wounded at Eastward (Lighton) 1691. List 37. One John, jr., was stealing from John Libby in Portsm. Sept. 1700. (Lists 330de)? John Laiten, York witn. 1722, m. (Ct. Jan. 1723-4) Hannah Grover(3); her sis. Elizabeth Hammons gossiped ab. him and Sarah Brookings ab. 1730; 3 ch. rec. Sarah (Layton) m. 12 May 1731 Robt. Triggs, both of Portsm. Samuel (Layton) taxed Portsm. 1731-2.

5 **CAPT. JOHN**(9), Kit., m. 13 June 1686 Honor Langdon(1), memb. of Berwick Ch. 1708. Often selectman and moderator; by trad., sheriff of York Co. Town meetings were held at his ho. many yrs., also the 1st meeting of Ct. of Genl. Sessions. Gr. j. 1693, 1694, 1697, 1698. Called Ensign 1698; Capt. 1704. Lic. pub. ho. 1696-1702, retail 1703. Lists 291, 296, 297, 298. Will 7 Nov., d. 10 Nov. 1724 in 62d yr. Wid. d. 21 Mar. (or Nov.) 1737 in 75th yr. Ch. in will: **Elizabeth**, b. 30 May 1691, m. 22 Sept. 1717 Capt. Benj. Wentworth. **Mary**, b. 7 May 1693, m. Col. Paul Gerrish(3). **William**, b. 9 Sept. 1696, m. at Berw. 13 Nov. 1720 Sarah Hill. He inherited the homestead. Merchant. Selectm. 1728-35, 1741-2. List 291. D. 20 Aug. 1749, his wid. the next mo. 4 ch. **John**, b. 27 May 1699, d. 26 Apr. 1768, m. 29 Dec. 1726 Mary Hill(8), who d. 13 Apr. 1784, ag. 84. Planter, merchant. Deacon, Lieut. 1744. Of 8 ch., 5 d. 29 May— 21 June 1737. **\*Tobias**, b. 17 Nov. 1701, planter, merchant. Town Clerk. Rep. 1731, 1736, 1743. Served under Pepperell at Louisburg. Lists 296, 298. See Dill(3). M. 1st 15 Nov. 1727 Grace Staples (Peter), d. 7 Nov. 1736; 2d 20 June 1738 Sarah Chadbourne (James 3 jr.). His will 18 Nov. 1748; both d. that mo. Ch. 4(d.y.)+2. **Samuel**, b. 22 Nov. 1707, hatmaker, k. by fall

from tree 24 Dec. 1735, unm. His lands were divid. in 1739 into six parts, the mo. appar. taking an eq. share with her ch.

6 **THOMAS**, b. 1604-5, Dover 1640, where he signed the Combination; his land in 1642 list. Selectm. 1647-8, 1658. Gr. j. 1646, 1651, 1655, 1663-64, 1669. Constable. Bef. 1664 he deeded a 20 a. lot to apprent. John Wingate. Lists 351ab. 352, 353, 354abc, 355ab, 356abcefghk, 311c, 357b. See Johnson(34). Aged 60, Dec. 1665. Will 21 Sept. 1671, ag. 67, d. 22 Jan. 1671-2, names as exec. s. Thos. and present w. Joanna, who was appar. mo. of Thos., if not of all the ch. She m. 2d Job Clements, Esq. (3). Ch: **Thomas**. **Mary**, m. bef. Sept. 1671 Thos. Roberts, jr. **Elizabeth**, m. Capt. Philip Cromwell(3). **Sarah**, unm. 1671.

7 **THOMAS** (Lighton), propr. Saco 1653.

8 **THOMAS**(6), inherited the homestead bordering on Back River. Lists 352, 359a. First w. Elizabeth Nutter (Hatevil), liv. 13 Feb. 1670-1 when her fa. deeded to them, had d. bef. 28 Dec. 1674. Adm. 31 Oct. 1677 to 2d w. Elizabeth, Philip Cromwell and John Tuttle; on her ptn. Mr. Fryer and Lt. Peter Coffin were added admrs. 25 June 1678. Ch: **Thomas** (cert. by 1st w.), b. ±1670, was in Lt. Anthony Nutter's care 1677. Gr. j. 1697. Of Dover in June 1702, ±32, he depos. ab. Lt. A. N. 'whom I lived with.' Newington by 1714. Messenger to Earl of Bellomont in matter of Ind. depredations. Lists 62, 343. In 1735 he deeded to s. John and to s. Hatevil, in 1739 to gr. s. Wm., and later to s. Thos. for supp. of self and w. Deborah. Adm. 29 Aug. 1744 to wid. Deborah, ag. 61; she depos. that she had turned oxen into the Langstaff pasture by ord. of Eleazer Coleman ab. 2 yrs. bef. his 1st w. d. Ch: John, Elizabeth, Hatevil, Abigail, Olive, Keziah, Thomas (bp. 13 May 1720, his mo. Deborah), Deborah, and poss. Solomon. **John**, Dover. List 67. First w. Sarah, (poss. Cromwell 3); 2d Eleanor Meader, perh. wid. of Nathl. In 1692 James Nute ag. 13 chose him gdn., and 26 yrs. later was bondsm. for his s. Thos., named adm. 4 June (inv. 8 Apr.) 1718 aft. his fa.'s will of 24 Sept. 1712 had been disallowed. Ch., 1st three cert. by w. Sarah: Thomas, cordwainer, had the home place, m. by 1719 Susanna Chesley; both liv. 1762; 11 ch. Sarah, m. James Clark(2). Lydia, b. 19 Feb. 1703-4, m. in Salem 17 Feb. 1725 Isaac Meacham; wid. 1738; James Nute witn. her deed. John, Dover 1729-1735, Rochester 1737, remov. to Lincoln Co., w. Sarah. James, blacksm., Dover 1739, m. aft. 1723 Hannah Bussy(2). **Elizabeth**, m. Richard Pinkham by 1699, when Thos. q. c. to her, his only sis., lands on Dover Neck willed to his fa. by his gr. fa. In 1705 she and husb.

q. c. to Ralph Hall the orig. 3½ a. ho.-lot of fa. Thos. L., already in his poss. See Follett(8)

9 **WILLIAM**, Mr., Kit., called mariner in June 1656, but had a shop and stock of goods, incl. sugar, clothes, buttons, earthen jars. June 20, 1656, he bot land near Watts Fort from Isaac Nash and in 1660 had in his hands £13 due to Wm. Everett (4 jr.); granted 13 a. in Crooked Lane 1659. In 1661 Roger Plaisted sued him for detaining his servant; Lists 285, 298, 311c, 356hk. He m. in 1656 Katherine Frost(9). List 298. D. Sept. 1666. Adm. to wid. 13 Sept. 1667; in July 1669 Capt. Chas. Frost and Mr. Plaisted were joined with her in preserv. the est. and bringing up the ch. She m. 2d Maj. Joseph Hammond(3). Ch: **Elizabeth**, had gr. in 1671 (List 298) and likely was the witn. to John Heard's will 1676; d. s. p. bef. her br. who willed to sons John and Tobias 'my part of 50 a. form. belonging to my sis. E. L. decd.' **Mary**, had gr. 1679 (List 298), m. John Hunking(5). **Katherine**, m. 16 June 1681 Maj. John Whipple, maltster of Ipsw.; d. Ipsw. 15 Jan. 1720-1, ag. 62 yrs. 7 mo. 6 daus. **John**, b. May 1663.

**LEMON, William**, Piscataqua. Nunc. will 26 June 1660, ab. going up in the country, gave all to Mr. Antipas Maverick, who was adm., but 14 Oct. 1662 Wm. Furber and Rich. Otis, admrs., ord. to bring in invent.

**LEMPRIERE, Clement,** buried William Button, a Jerseyman, in Portsm. in 1693. Richard Anthony, of Jersey, now in Portsm. gave P/A to Clement (Lampier), now of Boston, 8 Jan. 1697-8. John (Lamprill) was in the boat when Mr. Button was drowned. List 318a.

**Leonard,** Hopestill (Lynard) of Rehoboth m. at Hampt. ab. Sept. 1695 Benj. Allen. Saml. (?Lenard), Exeter 1692. List 62.

**Leshaw,** Edward, Gr. j. (N. H.) 1699.

**Lesrier,** Edward. List 307b.

**LEVERDEUR** (Laverdore), **Peter,** Frenchman, at Penobscot. List 4. Wid. Priscilla, an English woman, liv. there 1676, was fined in Suff. Ct. July 1677, retailing wine without lic. List 4. Ch: **John**. Lists 3, 4. **Son,** liv. at Penobscot 1676.

**LEVERICH** (desc. are Leveridge), **Rev. William,** Dover, called by Winthrop a godly minister, was b. ±1603, s. of Saville L. of Drawlington, co. Warwick; matric. at Emmanuel Coll., Cambridge, 1622; B. A. 1626; ordained deac. at Peterborough 1626; priest 1627; poss. at Great Bowden, co. Leicester, 1628; M. A. 1631, then vicar of Great Livermere, co. Suff. There he may have met Thos. Wiggin, whom he accomp. back to N. E. in -The James- in Oct. 1633 and went with him to Dover. His stay in Dover

ended bef. 9 Aug. 1635 when adm. to Boston Ch. Duxbury briefly, foll. by long pastorate at Sandwich. App. he who was ment. in Oct. 1655 as chosen pres. of the new coll. at New Haven. Ab. 1658 he joined or led a migration to Oyster Bay, L. I., and d. at Newtown, L. I., 1677. A son was **Caleb** of Newtown, d. 1717, ag. 79, leaving wid. Martha, m. by 1663, form. wid. of Francis Swain of Hampton and L. I., and 3 ch. List 393b (1663). Ano. s. **Eleazer** d. s. p.

**LEWIS,** the Welsh personal name, became 22d commonest surname in N. E.

1 **ABRAHAM**(16), Portsm., ±19 in 1679, ±33 in 1693, ±42 in 1701, m. 1st Rachel Berry(9), 2d in Greenland 8 Dec. 1710 Sabina (Locke), wid. of Wm. Berry(14), who m. 3d 7 Mar. 1716-7 John Philbrick. Tr. j. 1693 (fined for absence); Gr. j. 1696. Taxed in Greenland 1708, Portsm. 1713, 1714. Lists 57, 62, 332b, 335a, 338a. In 1693 he and his partner John Johnson bot the sloop -Endeavor- from Wm. Ardell and in 1708 he was still coasting betw. Newbury and Portsm. Town charge, 1715. Prob. dau.: **Rachel**, m. in Greenl. 29 May 1718 Philip Babb(1).

2 **ANDREW**(14), Kit., ±40 in Jan. 1712-3, m. 29 Nov. 1701 Mary Hutchins(2), who surv. him. Tr. j. 1700. Lists 291, 296, 297, 298. Will 27 July 1758—31 Mar. 1760 names ch: **Andrew,** b. 2 Apr. 1703, m. int. 25 Apr. 1724 Mary (Ingersoll) wid. of Daniel Low(1), and poss. m. a 2d w., as he had a ch. b. as late as 1743. **Rachel,** b. 3 July 1704, not in will. **Mary,** b. 29 Jan. 1705, m. 1st int. 13 Apr. 1726 Joseph Webber, 2d 29 June 1753 Elias Weare. **Grace,** m. 21 Nov. 1733 Samuel Haley(2). **Dorothy,** bp. 1 June 1718, m. int. 12 Aug. 1738 John Main of York. **Thomas,** bp. 5 June 1720, m. int. 23 Nov. 1741 Susanna Hutchins. Ch.

3 **EDMUND,** Lynn, with Henry Dow bot land at Hampton from John Sanders and q. c. to Dow in 1649.

4 **GEORGE,** Casco Bay, 1640, liv. at Ferry Point in Back Cove, now East Deering, Portland, and worked for Mr. Mackworth, who paid him in beaver which Mr. Winter would take in trade only at a lower value. Bot land from Cleeve in 1657. Poss. he had been earlier at Pejepscot with Mr. Purchase. He depos. 1640 and 1645, and his w. (or poss. dau.) Anne witn. deed 1657. O. A. 1658; Constable 1659; Tr. j. 1667; Selectman 1668. In 1659 he was in ct. for drunkenness, and in 1667 for indecency with his daus. Lists 25, 221, 222acd. Lt. Clark (52) wrote that he and his w. were slain in the attack of 11 Aug. 1676. In 1683 Nathl. Wallis test. that bef. Philip's War Lewis had shown him his will, doubtless

destroyed, leaving his 30 a. of land to his 3 youngest daus., who sold to Richard Seacomb in 1685. Ch: **John. Philip,** b. ab. 1646. **Anne,** m. bef. 1667 James Ross. **Alice,** m. Benjamin Atwell(2). **Susanna,** m. Thomas Cloyes(6). **Mary,** b. ab. 1654, m. 1st Thomas Skillin, 2d bef. 1685 Jotham Lewis (10), 3d at Salem 22 Oct. 1718 Henry Wilkins(on). **Hannah,** m. 1st one Main, 2d at Marblehead 16 May 1683 James Darling.

5 **GEORGE,** Newcastle, fisherman for Jacob Clark, drowned bef. 9 Nov. 1717 when his wid. Sarah m. Mark Curtain.

6 **JENKIN,** rated in Portsm. 1717, 1718.

7 **JOHN,** Newcastle, cooper, ±50 in 1667, receipted to Edw. Colcord for 1600 staves in 1653. Gr. j. 1664, 1673, 1682-3, 1693, 1695 (foreman); Tr. j. 1682, 1684, 1685, 1694; sergt. 1678. Henry Fletcher and Arthur Wharf were his appren. Culler of pipestaves 1692-7. Lists 49, 52, 55a, 57, 65, 330a, 91, 312acefh. 313abdef, 315abc, 317, 319, 326c, 330a, 331ab, 356L. Will 22 Jan. 1700-1—27 May 1701 names w. Elizabeth exec. and directs that, if his 3 daus. d. s. p., his est. shall go to Theodore Atkinson. Ch: **Elizabeth,** m. 1st Israel Phillips, 2d after 1681, one Eburne. **Mary,** m. 1st Thomas Cobbett, 2d John Hinckes. **Hannah,** m. 11 May 1702 Joseph Simpson.

8 **JOHN**(4), Casco Bay, had land adj. his fa. in 1657, and a later gr. of 100 a. Lic. to keep pub. ho. 1674. Lists 25, 86, 222cd, 232, 237b. Prob. not the J. L. who sold 700 a. at Mere Point to John Lane in 1673. Last ment. as a soldier under Scottow at Black Pt. in 1677, he and w. Eleanor (List 86) may have been victims of the Ind. His land, sold to Nathl. Wallis, 27 Feb. 1674, was claimed by Azor Gale 13 Sept. 1679 and by Phineas Jones in 1732. Prob. ch: **Mary,** of Casco Bay when she m. in Portsm. 2 Jan. 1704-5 William Haines(13). 9 ch., the last 3, b. 1719-1724, being nam. Eleanor, John and George Lewis.

9 **JOHN**(14), Portsm., weaver, ±25 in 1699, m. Martha (Brookings 5), (Ct. June 1699), ±30 in 1699, wid. of John Wakeham, who m. 3d, contract 17 Oct. 1709, Joseph Rendle, a Frenchman. Bot a ho.-lot in 1701. D. 1708. Ch. ment. in their gr. fa's will: **Benjamin,** Portsm., shipwright, m. 14 Sept. 1727 Lydia Canney (Samuel 4) of Dover; liv. in 1747. **Grace,** m. 1st 28 Oct. 1718 John Bly, 2d 23 May 1723 Nathaniel Boulter(1), 3d Henry Dresser. **Elizabeth,** m. Joseph Gunnison(1). **Mehitable,** d. s. p. 1736.

10 **JOTHAM**(16), Greenland, m. bef. 1685 Mary (Lewis 4), wid. of Thomas Skillin, and appar. d. bef. 1698 when a wid. Mary L. was rated (Lists 330de, 335a). Constable 1686. Lists 52, 57, 330c, 332b. Ch., all un-

der 21 when ment. in will of their gr. fa. 1700; **John,** blacksmith, Portsmouth, 1711, Greenl. 1713, Mendon 1714. **James,** carpenter, had gr. 1714, sold out 1715. List 338a. **Philip,** Boston, mariner, m. 15 Apr. 1703 Martha Hender, poss. a wid. and dau. of Samuel Burrill. 5 ch. 1703-1721. **Hannah,** m. in Topsfield 1 Feb. 1710-1 Joseph Knight.

11 **MATTHEW,** Portsm. mill-dam tax 1707.

12 **MORGAN,** Piscataqua, mariner, 1639, sued Mr. Thomas Wannerton 1640. Gave power to John Pickering, witn. Christopher Hardy and Sampson Salter.

13 **OLD GOODMAN,** O. A. York 22 Nov. 1652. Lavis, List 275. See Lavers (Lavis) (3).

14 **PETER,** Isles of Shoals, ±29 in Sept. 1673, m. Grace Diamond(3), bot. ho., stage etc. on Smuttinose from Matthew Giles 30 Nov. 1668. Bot at Spruce Creek from John Phoenix in 1675, and sold at Shoals in 1683. Culler of fish, Shoals, 1680. Gr. j. (Me.) 1668-9, 1695, 1696, 1701, 1702; (N. H.) 1673. Lists 95, 293, 296, 306c, 298. Will 3 Feb. 1712-3—4 Apr. 1716. The wid. was a midwife in 1720. Ch: **Peter,** b. ab. 1670. **Andrew. William. John. Grace,** seduced by Philip Follett in 1698; had illegit. ch. in Oct. 1701; unm. in 1713. **Morgan,** m. (ct. Jan. 1705-6) Abigail Ingersoll, who m. 2d Joseph Judkins and 3d Ebenezer Blaisdell; d. bef. his fa. leaving a s. Nathaniel of York (Lists 279, 298) who m. Sarah Gray (Robert), int. 22 Feb. 1726-7, and had 8 ch. **Mary,** m. David Hutchins(1). **Ann,** m. bef. 1712 John Tapley. **Rebecca,** m. bef. 1713 Philip Pike. **Elizabeth,** unm. in 1715. **Sarah,** prob. m. in Portsm. 10 Sept. 1718 Peter Mow from Rochelle, France.

15 **PETER**(14), Kit., ±42 in 1712-3, ±59 in 1728-9, shipwright, m. 1st after 1688 Lucy (Chadbourne 1), wid. of Michael Hicks(4), 2d, after 1703, one Elizabeth, who was adm. to Kit. Ch. with him in 1731. His fa.'s deed to Wm. Mitchell, dated 1683, must have been witn. by Peter jr. and his w. Lucy in 1702, when it was ack. Culler of fish (Kit.,) 1692-3. Gr. j. 1714. Lists 291, 296, 297, 298. Of the ch. listed in his will, 17 May—21 June 1739, the first 4 can reasonably be assigned to his 1st w., but doubt increases with each of those following: **Lucy,** m. 1st in Portsm. 16 Apr. 1719 Samuel Briard, 2d 25 June 1724 Sylvanus Tripe, jr. 4 ch. ment. by her fa. **Peter,** Kit., husbandman, m. 29 Dec. 1726 Elizabeth Haley(2); will, 1772, ment. w., sons Peter and William, daus. Elizabeth Haley, Lucy Fernald, Sarah Fernald, Mary Young and Miriam Fernald. **Mary,** unm. 1739, but w. of Thomas Pillow, cordwainer, in 1753. **Catherine,** bp. with next two 1 July 1722,

acc. John Haley, late of Kit., now of Falmouth in 1733, m. John Phoenix bef. 1739. **Sarah**, unm. in 1739. **Abigail**, m. int. 5 Aug. 1738 Thaddeus Trafton. **Eunice**, bp. 16 July 1727. One E. L. m. Thomas Fernald 23 Feb. 1758.

16 **PHILIP**, ±40 in 1663-4, evid. closely rel. to (4), was app. at Str. Bk. bef. 1640. Taxed in Dover in 1649 and owned lot on Dover Neck in 1652. He m. Hannah Philbrick (Thos.) (Lists 331c, 394) and liv. in Greenland where he owned a sawmill and a cornmill. Bot in Hampton in 1663. Selectm., Portsm., 1660, 1661, 1662, 1668, 1676, 1681-1683. He and his w. were mem. of the No. Ch., seated 1693. Taxed in Greenl. after 1683. Lists 49, 52, 57, 62, 323, 324, 326, 330abc, 331a, 332b, 335c, 342, 354b, 355a, 356j. Will, 1 Nov. 1700—8 July 1701, names cousins John Tucke and James Philbrook overseers. Ch: **Philip**, jr., drunk in 1679, not in will. **Thomas**, had store bill in Portsm. in 1686, owed money to Wm. Ardell of Boston in 1687, drunk and disob. to fa. in 1692, taxed in Greenl. 1693; not in will. Lists 57, 334a, 335a. **Abraham. Jotham. Hannah**, ±76 in 1731, m. aft. Sept. 1673 John Johnson and had her fa.'s homestead for care of her mo. Depos. in 1731 that she knew the Mitton fam. of Casco Bay.

17 **PHILIP**(4), Casco Bay, ±37 in 1683, liv. for some time on Hog Isl. as ten. of Tyng, as test. by Elizabeth (Mitton) Clark (52). He and his w., name unkn., may have been victims of the 2d Ind. war. Their ch., ident. by a deed, 1701, conv. their fa.'s Casco Bay prop., were poss. brot up in Salem. Lists 30, 223b, 227. Ch: **Priscilla**, m. in Salem 14 May 1691 Henry Kinney, d. bef. 1714 when he m. Mary Curtis of Topsfield. **Elizabeth**, m. bef. 1701 John Hogg, mariner, of Boston. **Mercy**, b. ab. 1675, liv. as a child in the fam. of Rev. Geo. Burroughs and in 1692, when she was a dramatic leader of the 'afflicted' girls in the witchcraft trials, was a servant in the ho. of Thomas Putnam of Salem Village. After the delusion subsided she went to Greenland, where her aunt Mary (Lewis) Lewis, w. of Jotham(10) was liv., and in 1695, at the ho. of Abraham Lewis(1) she had a bastard ch., James Darling, husb. of her aunt Hannah, being her bondsman. Her aunt Mary, ±43, and Charles Allen jr., ±24, test. for her, and as she was Mercy Allen of Boston in 1701, it is prob. that Allen was the ch.'s fa. and m. her. **Mary**, unm. in Salem in 1701.

18 **RICHARD**, Portsm., ship-carpenter, liv. from his w. in 1673, said she kept other men's company and he could not live in peace with her. Walter Winsor was directed to supply wood to 'old father Lewis'

and the w. of Robt. Rowsley to 'dress his diet' in 1689. Wm. Mason kept him in 1691, Wm. Walker from 1692 to 1694, and Elisha Bryers was pd. for his coffin 2 Sept. 1695.

19 ‡**THOMAS**, partner of Capt. Bonython in the Saco patent, son of Andrew and Mary (Herring) of Shrewsbury, co. Salop, of an ancient Welsh fam., was b. ab. 1590, attended Shrewsbury School, of which he was listed as a benefactor in 1625, and was adm. to the Drapers Company in 1616. He was also a vintner, the business of his maternal gr. fa., and owned the 'Sextry', an inn still standing, where he empl. George Cleeve(1). On 29 Aug. 1618 at St. Chad's ch., he m. Elizabeth Marshall, dau. of Roger and Katherine (Mytton). Bef. closing with the Plymouth Company for a gr. of land in America, Mr. Lewis, at his own expense, made a voyage to the coast with companions, among whom may have been Arthur Mackworth, quite certainly his kinsman, and Michael Mitton, poss. a relation of his w., and must have picked the site of the patent which was gr. 12 Feb. 1629-30. Lewis arrived at Saco and took livery of seisin 28 June 1631. His w. and daus. did not come over until ab. 1637. Councillor 1636. Lists 241, 242. He d. aft. 1637 and his wid. bef. 1640. Both left wills, no longer extant, Francis Robinson being exec. of that of Mr. L. and Robinson and Capt. Bonython joint exec. of Mrs. L.'s. Ch., bp. at St Chad's, except Andrew (Correcting Ancestry of Charity Haley, W. G. Davis, pp. 53-5): **Mary**, bp. 28 June 1619, came to Saco with her mo., m. in 1638 Rev. Richard Gibson(2). **Susanna**, bp. 2 Nov. 1620, prob. d. y. **Margaret**, bp. 22 Apr. 1622, prob. d. y. **Elizabeth**, bp. 7 Apr. 1623, came to Saco and m. Robert Haywood(4) of Barbadoes. **Andrew**, bp. 22 Feb. 1624-5 and bur. 15 Nov. 1625 at St. Mary's. **Judith**, bp. 23 Oct. 1626, came to Saco, m. ab. 1646 James Gibbins(2). **Andrew**, bp. 25 Mar. 1628, d. y.

20 **THOMAS**, (see 8 and 16), late of Falmouth, since of St. George's Fort, had about 20 heirs liv. in Dedham, Walpole, Stoughton, etc., Mass., and Plainfield and Preston, Conn., 1738-1741. Y. D. 22.143, 24.10. List 223b.

21 **WILLIAM**(14), ship-carpenter, had Kit. gr. in 1703, of Spruce Creek when he bot in Portsm. in 1706. At Fort William and Mary in 1708. Bef. 1709, when they signed a deed, he m. one Mary, who d. aft. July 1716 when they were adm. to No. Ch., 2d, 17 Dec. 1719, Sarah (Evans 12) Low, wid. of (Jacob Low 3?). With her bro. Jonathan Evans they deeded in 1728 to Daniel Horn of Dover 1/9 of 60 a. to be laid out in Barbadoes Woods. Taxed 1732-

3. Lists 298, 339. Only kn. ch: **William**, bp. 22 Apr. 1722, Portsm., carver, d. in 1764, adm. to John Beck jr., leav. grown and young ch.

**LIBBY**, Lebbee, peculiar to southeast Cornwall.

1 **ANTHONY**(5), carpenter, soldier in Philip's War. In N. H. 14 Nov. 1678 he was app. adm. on his bro. See James(5). In 1681 was on committee to procure timber for building the Scarboro fort. Next yr. rem. to Falmouth (South Portland), where he m. Sarah (Drake 1), sis. of Capt. Anthony Brackett's wife, and in 1685 rem. to her native town, Hampton, where he settled in the region now Rye or Greenland. Lists 237ab, 238a, 332b. Will 20 Feb.—5 Mar. 1717-8 names w. Jane (Rackley, wid. of Wm., m. 6 Jan. 1717-8) and 7 ch. She was still his wid. 25 Mar. 1723-4. Ch: **Sarah**, m. 18 June 1701 Israel Smith. **Abraham**, b. ab. 1688, settled first in Hampton. In 1718, having bot a farm in Portsm., he sold his homestead to bro. Isaac. List 339. From 1757 until his death he was liv. in Portsm., North Hampt., Exeter and Epsom, where he died. Adm. gr. 1 June 1767 to Joseph L. of New Durham. 8 or m. ch., of whom Sarah and Mary m. bros. Penuel and Jonathan Chapman and Phebe m. Samuel Wallis. **Mary**, m. 7 Mar. 1709 John Lane. **Isaac**, m. in Greenland 9 Jan. 1718-9 Mary Bennick or Bennet(3). In 1725 he sold in Hampt. to his bro. Jacob and settled in Rye. From 1744 on he was active in settling Epsom, 1749 moderator, 1761 chairm. of com. for building the meeting ho., altho keeping his res. in Rye. Where or when he or his w. d. is unasc. 9 ch. rec. **Hannah**, presum. m. in Hampt. 9 Jan. 1719-20 Joseph Marston. **Jacob**, b. 25 May 1695, had the homestead. Either this was set off to Rye or he bot there, or both. Tried Epsom bef. the F. & I. wars, constable there 1746, but ret. to Rye. Last noticed in deed to s. Abraham 30 Oct. 1765. 11 ch. **Jane**, b. 5 Aug. 1700, m. 9 May 1720 Abraham Moulton of Hampt., later deacon in Kensington.

2 **DANIEL**(5), ±62 in 1728. Gr. j. 1687. List 34. In 1690 he fled with his wife's relations to Marblehead, where he was a carter. He depos. that about 1693 he moved into Col. Nordon's ho. and liv. there about 18 yrs. In 1731 he and his w. (Mary Ashton, m. 23 Feb. 1687) and gr. child were warned from Beverly, and she (or her dau.) at times visited her Norton cousins in Manchester; but 13 Sept. 1735 both were back in Marblehead, she still liv. there in 1737. Ch: **Daniel**, m. in Marblehead 22 Jan. 1713-4 Abigail Martin. 3 or m. ch. **Sarah**, m.

28 Dec. 1721 Charles Dennis. **Joseph**, ag. 21, 19 July 1723, with 25 others, was hanged as a pirate in Newport. A Marblehead fishing vessel had been taken by pirates and some of her crew were among those hanged. Joseph protested that he was forced but some of the witnesses testified they saw him 'fire'. The narrative of his more fortunate cousin, Philip Ashton, printed many yrs. later, tells how Joseph helped him from drowning. **Hephzibah**, bp. 23 Jan. 1703, m. 20 Sept. 1725 Henry Wittingham. **Beulah**, bp. same day, m. 22 May 1727 John Williams. **Mary**, bp. 10 Nov. 1706.

3 **DAVID**(5), ±71 in Dec. 1729, ±76 in Dec. 1735. In Scarb. he served on a commission to renew the Falmouth-Scarb. bounds. Gr. 6 a. in 1682 and 30 a. in 1685. On leaving the town he liv. ab. 10 yrs. in Portsm. until Dec. 1699 when he and his bro. Matthew and their bro.-in-law Fogg joined with Joseph Hammond, Esq., and Stephen Tobey in purchasing 'the Bay lands' on the river bank now in Eliot. The two bros. built close together on Libby Hill where in 1888 himself, his w. and five gen. of their desc. lay buried. Tr. j. 1710. Lists 238a, 34, 330def, 290, 296, 297. Will 6 May 1725—24 Dec. 1736 names w. Eleanor and 9 ch. Ch: **David**, b. presum. in Scarb., a big boy when his fa. moved from Portsm. to Eliot; liv. on part of his fa.'s land (lic. retailer) until ab. 1731 when he settled on Scottow's Hill, Scarb. List 291. He m. Hester Hanscom (3). In Scarb. also his ho. was garrison in 1745. By trad. he shot the Ind. that killed Nathl. Dresser. His w. d. in Mar. 1761. He was bur. 6 Feb. 1765. 8 ch. **Samuel**, b. ab. 1690, carpenter, m. his cousin Mary Libby (9), and built on her fa.'s land. Ab. 1731 he removed to Scarb. and settled on the homestead of Andrew Brown(2), his wife's gr. fa. Bur. 15 May 1754; she d. in Jan. 1774. 5 ch., or 6 if Elizabeth was one, and childless, 'of Biddeford', 17 Nov. 1743, m. Abraham Townsend (or poss. that Elizabeth was dau. of Daniel and Eleanor(6). **Mary**, m. 12 Apr. 1722 Joseph Small. **Solomon**, b. ab. 1695, carpenter, built on his fa.'s land, but later had David's place. He m. 4 Mar. 1725 Martha Hanscom(3). He d. in 1756, she in Feb. 1789. 8 ch. **John**, b. ab. 1697, was given his fa.'s homestead in Scarb. and mov. there. List 239b. He m. 14 Nov. 1724 his cousin Sarah Libby(9), and 9 Jan. 1755, as her 4th husb., Deborah (Larrabee 1) Donovan. Will 13 July 1761—d. 1 July 1764. Ch: 7 sons. **Elizabeth**, app. unm. by fa.'s will. **Ephraim**, b. 2 Feb. 1702 in Kit. Had the homestead and d. there in the winter of 1776-7. He m. in 1728 Mary Ambler, who outliv. him. List 358c. 5 ch. **Eleanor**, b. 21 June 1705, m. Zebulon Trick-

ey; 2d her cousin Lt. Andrew Libby(9). **Abigail,** b. 29 Sept. 1707, m. Nov. 1725 Richard Nason.

4 **HENRY**(5), ±78 12 Aug. 1736, near 83 in June 1731. Garrison soldier in Philip's War. Selectm. Scarb. 1686. Lists 237b, 238a, 239b, 30, 34, 226. In 1690 he escaped with his wife's family to Lynn where in 1701 he was a tenant on a farm of John Cogswell. In 1709 he was a creditor of Moses Hawkes's est. Among the first to resettle Scarb., his sons depos. that they came in July 1717 and that in 1718 they liv. in the Jordan garrison at Spurwink. They stood their ground in Dummer's War, and helped defend the garrison on Prout's Neck. In 1728, at 80, he joined the newly formed Scarb. church. His ho. stood near the east corner of the old Black Point burying ground, and the site was taken into it. Will 21 Feb. 1729-30, d. 21 Oct. 1732. He m. Honor Hinkson(1), who d. 24 Aug. 1724, ag. 60. Ch: **Mary,** m. in Marblehead 13 Jan. 1714-5 Richard Webber. **Samuel,** Lt., b. 1689, had the homestead. List 239b. Town clerk 6 yrs.; Proprietors' Clerk from 1727 until old age; Selectm. 1721-1742, except one yr.; often moderator. As lot-layer, he laid out most of the town. In 1726 divine service was held alternately in his ho. and in Col. Westbrook's ho. at Dunstan. In 1728 he was of the committee to build the meeting ho. D. 1 Jan. 1770. He m. 29 Feb. 1727 Abigail Meserve, who d. 10 Nov. 1734 (2 ch. d. y.); 2d 17 Jan. 1739 Mary Jones, who d. June 1754. 5 ch. **Sarah.** The Portsm. So. Ch. minister bap. in Scarboro 25 May 1722 Samuel, Sarah, James and John. She d. 1 Mar. 1723. **James,** turner, eldest of the three Jameses in Scarb. List 239b. He d. bef. 23 Dec. 1754. Of his daus. Abigail m. Elisha Douglass, Joanna and Priscilla m. bros. Isaac and Andrew Myrick, Hannah m. Jethro Starbird. **Hannah,** m. in Marblehead 15 Dec. 1720 John Pollow. **Elizabeth,** m. 16 Mar. 1727 Sampson Plummer. **John,** Capt., Lieut. in 1st F. & I. War, liv. on Oak Hill Scarb. Drowned by upsetting of a boat. M. 1st 15 June 1728 Mary Goodwin and 2d 24 Aug. 1738 Anne Fogg(1 jr.). Ch. 4 + 10 + 1.

5 **JOHN,** the only early emigr. of this name, was by early trad. (transmitted by Dr. Benj. Libby, b. 1777, written down ab. 1855) 'Welsh,' that is native British, not Anglo-Saxon. By this trad. he came over with 'the Plymouth company,' meaning the plantation at Richmond Isl. estab. by Trelawny. This trad. is borne out by the plantation accounts. He came on -The Hercules-, bringing ship's letters dated 30 Nov. 1636, arr. at Rich. Isl. 13 Feb. He had been in the service of Mr. John Sparke, merchant and Mayor of Plymouth, whose wife was from Fowey, co. Cornwall, the seaport of the Fowey river valley, where Col. Banks found several John Libbys who might have been the emigrant, presum. b. as early as 1615. The petition to the Boston authorities to release his sons from the Scarb. garrison was the work of a professional, worded regardless of truth to accomplish its object, and unnec. even to be read to the petitioner. He came under contract for three yrs. service, which expired 13 Feb. 1639-40, aft. which he settled near 'Libby's common landing place' at Anthony's hole near the eastern point of 'the Old Neck,' a spot shut out from view of the Prout's Neck summer settlement by Black Rock. Sometime bef. 1 Jan. 1663-4 he rem. inland and built on the bank of Libby's River, on the spot now marked as his homestead. In Philip's War 'Libby's buildings' were burnt. In 1661 J. L. and Wm. Sheldon were appraisers of Andrew Heffer's est. In 1664 he was constable and in 1669 J. L. sr. is named first of the selectmen in a town gr.; selectman 1676. Lists 21, 239a, 236, 237ade, 238a. His will 9 Feb. 1682-3 provides for 'my wife' and esp. for his 'two younger sonns' Matthew and Daniel. His sons David and Matthew were half-bros., acc. to early trad. in the fam. of their sister Hannah Fogg, all three liv. side by side in Eliot. Only once is either w. named in the records, 'Mary Libby's marshes.' Poss. she m. 2d Wm. Green (28). Heirship deeds and the div. of his est. in 1736 show that 12 of his ch. left ch., besides the two who lost their lives in Philip's War. Ch: **John,** b. 1637. **James,** garrison soldier in Philip's War, k. 1676-7. Adm. in N. H. court 9 Oct. 1688 to bro. Anthony. **Samuel,** soldier in Philip's War, sickened in Scarb. garrison, taken to Boston where he d. ab. July 1677. **Joanna,** m. Thomas Bickford(22). **Henry,** b. 1648. **Abigail,** m. John Fickett. **Anthony. Sarah,** b. ab. 1654; m. 1st Robert Tidy, 2d Richard Rogers, 3d Christopher Banfield. **Mary,** m. John Slaughter. **David,** b. 1658. **Hannah,** m. Daniel Fogg(1). **Rebecca,** m. Joshua Brown (27). **Matthew,** b. 1663. **Daniel,** b. ab. 1666.

6 **JOHN** (5), 'being 80 yrs. of age' 15 Mar. 1717-8, ±83 24 Mar. 1719-20. Soldier in Philip's War. In Scarb. he was selectm. 1669, 1673, 1674, 1676, 1684, 1688. Lists 235, 237ade, 238a, 34, 334a, 330dcf. In Portsm., miller, he and his sons ran (all and appar. built) the grist mill on the Vaughan privilege. Thinking that the Libby lands passed to him as eldest son under Eng. law, he deeded them to his eldest son, and deeded his own Scarb. lands to his son Daniel; so his other ch. are unnam. But the 1736 division of his father's lands among all the heirs shows that his bros. James and Sam-

uel left no desc., and all his other bros., except Daniel at Marblehead, left wills naming their ch.; so it seems cert. that all others about Portsm. of proper age were his ch., with poss. one or m. of the Libby girls who were likelier his gr. daus. He and w. Agnes depos. together in 1718, he that Winnock liv. in Scarb. over 60, she only 50, yrs. ago. Their ch. incl: **John**, b. 1669. **Joseph. Samuel**, taxed Portsm. 1698. Lists 330de, 337. Wid. Sarah (not Wells) had m. Samuel Waterhouse by 14 June 1712, when they sold her first husb.'s town rights to his bro. John. She was liv. in 1732. He was -not-father of Daniel sr. of Berwick, and may have been childless, but see his possible daus. or sisters. **James**, ±31 in Apr. 1707, ag. 60 in Apr. 1736, housewright, Portsm. He contracted with the Prov. for a line of fortifications near Portsm. From 1712 on he filled many town offices, up to selectm. Lists 67(2), 330de, 337, 339, 239b. In 1747 he sold his farm to Col. Nathl. Meserve and bot a ho. and lot in town. Will 27 May 1751—30 May 1754, ment. 9 ch., of 10 rec., by w. Mary (Hanson, m. 9 June 1698); by 1736 he had m. Elizabeth, liv. 1764. His s. James was post rider bet. Portsm. and Portland 6 yrs. His daus., called only by their forenames in his will, m.,—Mary in Newington 2 Dec. 1728 William Berry, Sarah in Newington 16 Dec. 1725 Col. Nathaniel Meserve, Shuah in Portsm. 11 Dec. 1729 John Marden, jr., Elizabeth in Newington 26 Nov. 1734 Capt. John Smith, jr. **Daniel**, miller, carpenter, taxed Portsm. 1707 for half the mill. D. bef. 1712 when his wid. sold his town rights to his bro. John. Lists 334a, 330de, 337, 239b. In 1697 he ack. and settled for a ch. by Elizabeth Nock: Daniel, b. ab. Feb. 1697-8, liv. with Elisha Plaisted, m. 6 Nov. 1722 Martha Trickey; d. in Berw. s.p. bet. 6 Sept. 1773—1775. By his w. Elizabeth Kirke he left 4 ch., incl. Daniel who m. 13 Jan. 1724-5 Eleanor Meader and d. ab. 1740 in Bid., where his wid. m. (int. Aug. 1740) John Brooks. Ch. untraced but see(3). Wid. Elizabeth (Kirke) L. may have m. 23 Oct. 1718 Jonathan Barlow; cert. was w. of John Meader in 1726, and d. bef. 1735. **Benjamin**, Dea., b. 4 June 1682, served 7 yrs. apprent. with Col. John Plaisted. Deacon of Cong. ch. 1725-1761, selectm. 1719-1736, often moderator. List 298(2). D. 9 Nov. 1768, his wid. Sarah (Stone, m. 25 Dec. 1707) d. Mar. 1774, ag. 88. Her obit. counted their post., 10 ch., 92 gr. ch., 152 gr. gr. ch. **Jeremiah**, ho. carpenter, ag. 77 24 Jan. 1766, shortly bef. his death. Active cit. of Portsm., repeat. moderator of town meetings. List 339. He m. 28 Apr. 1715 Lydia Badger, b. in Newbury 13 Apr. 1690. 8 ch., incl. Jeremiah, fa. of Jeremiah, Esq.,

1748-1824, postmaster of Portsm. under Washington, and friend of Jeremy Belknap. **Daughters**, unkn., may have incl. Elizabeth, m. 23 Oct. 1718 Jonathan Barlow; but see Daniel(6), Samuel (6).

7 **CAPT. JOHN**(6), ±68 in June 1737, ±74 in June 1743; depos. he was near 21 when Scarb. was abandoned. Dubbed usu. millwright, rarely ho. carp., wheelwright, gent. As Lt. Libby he was the hero of the Breakfast Hill attack in 1696, and in Dummer's War was Capt. of a Portsm. company. In 1738 he and w. Eleanor (Kirke, m. 29 Dec. 1692) depos. that from 1704 to 1729 they liv. on a farm hired of Major Wm. Vaughan on the road to Newington. But in 1697 he was lic. to keep tavern and retail liquors at the Creek, and about 1717, in part. with his uncle Matthew, Roger Hunnewell and Roger Deering, Esq., he went to Scarb. and built the first mill on Nonesuch River. Later he was half-owner and presum. the builder of the grist mill on Libby River, and in 1729 was part owner in the double sawmill farther up the river. Lists 337, 339, 239b. In 1746 he deeded to his three eldest sons the orig. Libby homestead, then occup. by Samuel Brown. He is not ment. alive aft. that yr., but d. bef. 3 Dec. 1748. The following were cert. his ch., except poss. Lydia: **Elizabeth**, Bethia and Agnes ack. covt. and were bapt. 20 Feb. 1713-4. Elizabeth m. Dea. Seth Ring. **Bethia**, m. 9 Sept. 1716 Samuel Brown(27). **Agnes**, m. 1 Dec. 1726 Capt. John Briard(4), a Jerseyman, ±69 in 1771. Son Samuel, Capt., b. 11 Sept. 1733, d. 1788. **James**, ±48 in 1747, ±76 in Nov. 1774, had the orig. homestead. List 239b. He d. 18 Feb. 1776. He m. Mary Furber (Jethro 3), who d. 29 Mar. 1777. 9 ch., incl. Capt. Anthony who had the homestead. **Mary**, m. 9 July 1721 John Peacock. Their s. Richard chose Capt. Briard gdn. **John**, carpenter, settled south of Oak Hill, Scarb. He m. 10 Nov. 1726 Mary Miller. He d. ab. 1767, she 23 Oct. 1780. Her unprov. will, dated 16 Mar. 1768 is with the Lancaster Ms., Me. Hist. Soc. 10 ch. **Eleanor**, m. Joseph Fogg(1), d. 3 Jan. 1799, ag. 95. **Jonathan**, Dea., b. 1706, settled next west of his bro. John. Ensign in 1st F. & I. War. He d. 28 Oct. 1759; his wid. Martha (Hasty, d. of Daniel, b. in Ireland 1711) d. 27 Nov. 1791. 10 ch. **?Lydia**, m. in Scarb. 28 Dec. 1729 Capt. Joseph Berry, s. of (9 jr.). In 1731 Joseph Berry, Samuel Brown and Capt. John Libby took a joint lease of 50 a. of marsh. **Josiah**, b. 1715, 'Trumpeter' in the F. & I. wars, settled on Oak Hill, later the Thornton place, d. 2 Feb. 1751. Wid. Anna (Small, m. 23 Mar. 1737) m. 2d 10 Jan. 1755 Nathaniel Milliken and d. 12 Jan. 1784. 6 ch.

8 **JOSEPH**(6). In 1696 he was servant to Capt. John Pickering, and signed as witn. for him in 1699. In 1710 fisherman. He app. d. soon aft. ack. the covt. at his home 5 Dec. 1718; had he liv. longer he would have had a Barrington right (List 339). App. his wid. Rebecca m. 21 Jan. 1723 Thomas Muzeet of Kit. The only kn. ch. are those named in the So. Ch. records: **Benjamin**, b. 1693, recd. into covt. 1 Mar. 1718-9, cordwainer. He m. Elizabeth Ham of Dover and settled there. She joined the church 16 Oct. 1763. He d. 3 Aug. 1781, ag. 88, she 17 Aug. 1788, ag. 84. 4 ch. **Joseph**. He and Joshua were bap. 18 Sept. 1720, the same day their mo. was recd. into covt., their fa. not named. He m. 29 Dec. 1726 Elizabeth Meserve (Daniel). Sailor and fisherman, except two or three yrs. 1731-1733 attempting a farm in Rochester. Both last ment. Nov. 1739. Two ch. bp. **Joshua**, bp. 18 Sept. 1720, shipmaster. W. Elizabeth. Adm. to creditors 1 Aug. 1736, his wid. decl. to act. App. it was she that joined the So. Ch. in 1742. They had 3 ch. bap. 1729-1734. **Sarah**, 'dau. of Joseph & Rebecca,' recd. into covt. and bap. 3 Oct. 1725. The three foll. are listed here because poss. their ch., and other parentage less likely: **Mehitable**, m. in Portsm. 5 Jan. 1732-3 Jeffrey Wells. **Hannah**, int. in Kit. 22 Oct. 173— 'both of Kittery,' m. in Portsm. 30 Jan. 1734-5, 'both of Portsm.,' Benjamin Welch. **Nathaniel**, m. in East Kingston 7 Aug. 1740 Deborah Ladd. In 1742 was a 'potter' of Portsm.; in 1743 bot in Exeter. Adm. Jan. 1752 to Josiah Thing; inv. shows a stock of pottery and general mdse. He wrote an elegant hand. If this Nathaniel was childless, he could have been s. of James(6), and his bro. John could have been fa. of Nathaniel, ancestor of the So. Car. Libbys, who might have learned the mastmaker's trade from his uncle John Marden. In 1761 Nathaniel of Portsm., mariner, was sued.

9 **MATTHEW**(5), 72 in Dec. 1735, 75 in Aug. 1738. In Portsm. aft. 1690 he hired Cutt's farm. See (3). Altho he joined with his nephew and others in erecting the first sawmill on Nonesuch River in Scarb., he sent his sons to and spent the rest of his life in Eliot. The graveyard near his ho. in 1880 held 6 generations (since been rem. to the cemetery). His ho. was a garrison. Tr. j. 1703, 1711. Lists 238a, 34, 334a, 330def, 290, 296, 297. He m. Elizabeth Brown(2), by his will given use of half of ho., by cod. altered to ⅓ of moveables indoors. In q.c. deed dated 5 Mar. 1742-3 she recited 'having for several months past been under great indisposition of body not capable of helping myself and my son Samuel Libby

having taken the whole care of attending on me in my helpless condition.' Ch: **William**, settled in Scarb. above Oak Hill; selectman, active in town and church affairs. Lists 298(2), 239b. He m. 11 Nov. 1722 his cous. Sarah Brown(27); both liv. to old age. 9 ch. **Matthew**, moved to Scarb. but in a few yrs. went back and settled on the back end of his father's farm. He d. in the winter of 1760-1, having outliv. his w., Mary (Nason, m. 3 Sept. 1730). 5 ch. **Mary**, m. her cous. Samuel Libby(3). **Hannah**, m. Jan. 1722 Samuel Hanscom(3). **Elizabeth**, estranged her fa., as his will shows. She did not m. John Smith, jr. (see James 6) but did prob. m. 'of Kittery' Edward Chapman(4) int. 2 Sept. 1738. **John**, b. 1698, settled on his father's homestead in Scarb. His ho. was on the site of the Abraham Plummer ho. at the railroad bridge near Scarb. Beach Station. He d. 7 Oct. 1756 (gr.st.). He m. in Scarb. 1 Jan. 1734 Keziah Hubbard, dau. of Lieut. John and Jane (Follansby) of Kingston, N. H. 6 ch. **Andrew**, Lt., b. in Kit. 1 Dec. 1700. Settled in Scarb. on the farm adj. Scarb. Beach R. R. Station. Lieut. from 1745, he app. served in the Black Point Company against Louisburg. He m. 7 Apr. 1731 Esther Furber (Jethro 3), who d. 1 Oct. 1756; 2d his cous. Eleanor (Libby 3) Trickey. He d. 5 Jan. 1773, his wid. 27 Sept. 1781 (gr.st.). 11 ch. **Sarah**, b. 7 Sept. 1702, m. her cous. John Libby(3). There was no dau. Rebecca; see Joseph(8). **Nathaniel**, b. 2 Nov. 1704, settled at Blackberry Hill, Berwick. List 298. W. Miriam Knight(21), m. 11 Oct. 1730; 13 ch., of whom 9 d. y. He d. in 1761, leaving wid. Hannah (Tobey) Staples, m. 16 Nov. 1757. **Dorcas**, b. 2 Feb. 1706, m. 24 June 1729 James Staples. **Samuel**, b. 5 June 1709, had the homestead. D. in 1788 or 89. W. Margaret Rogers, m. 12 Jan. 1736, is last ment. in 1782. 8 or m. ch. **Mehitable**, b. 14 Mar. 1711, m. 2 Aug. 1733 Daniel Knight. **Lydia**, b. 27 Apr. 1713, m. 17 Oct. 1730 Benj. Stacy.

**LIDDEN**, Litton, Liden. Lydden a par. in Kent, Litton pars. in Somerset, Dorset, Derby and York.

1 **EDWARD**, Kittery, bot back the land (2) sold to Edw. Clarke and liv. on it. Wid. Katherine (Chadbourne 1) was gr. adm. 18 Mar. 1691-2 and next mo. (wrote Letten) settled a controv. with her neighbor Wid. Sarah Trickey, over their divid. line; as K. L. made oath to inv. 27 Mar. 1693-4; m. 2d James Weymouth. Ch: **Elizabeth**, m. 17 May 1708 Josiah Skillings, 2d Roger Deering Esq. (8 jr.). **Mary**, unmar. Jan. 1706-7, m. one Long. See Long(4).

2 **GEORGE**, Kit.,mariner, bot John White's 20 a. and dwg. in Crooked Lane Dec. 1667 and 1670, and sold the E. half of the lot to Edw. Clarke in 1672. See (1). He dealt with John Tucker bef. 1670, sued Mr. Robt. Cutt for slander in 1672. List 287. Orig. memb. of Baptist Ch. 1682-3. Liv. Oct. 1691, when Sarah Trickey compl. of him for tearing down her fence several yrs. and preventing her planting; invent. at req. of the sons-in-law, King and Lary, 1 Sept. 1694, adm. to them 16 May 1695. W. Sarah in 1672, ag. 38 in 1678. See Boaden (10). A wid. 25 Aug. 1693 she made oath to John Alcock's nunc. will; d. bef. 20 July 1698 when heirs sold to Roger Kelly. Y. D. iv. 138. Ch: **Mary**, m. 1st Richard King, 2d Saml. Johnson(31). **Sarah**, m. 1st John Lary(3), 2d Robt. Allen (12 jr.).

**Lidget**, see Legate.

**LIGHT**, peculiar to Hampshire.

1 **HENRY**, Isles of Shoals, ±30 in 1673 when he took Edward Holland to the mainland aft. Elizabeth Oliver's baby was born. Lost in the great storm 30 Jan. 1677-8. See Broad(4).

2 **JAMES**, Portsm. 1695. List 334b.

3 **JOHN**, Newcastle 1669, called woolen-draper of Isles of Shoals in deed of ho. and 13 a. in Haverhill from Stephen Webster in 1673, was asso. in business with Maj. Wm. Vaughn. M. 11 Sept. 1674 Dorothy, d. of Maj. Robert Pike and wid. of Joshua Pierce of New Jersey, and made agreement with Capt. John Pike as to management of her prop. 18 Mar. 1678. Liv. in Portsm. from 1678; his wid. still there in 1695, when she conv. land, but of Newbury 1698-1714 (Hoyt). Lists 57, 305a, 312a, 329, 331b. Will, when bound on a voyage, 24 Feb. 1685-6—18 Mar. 1690-1, ment. w., unborn ch., step-ch. Joshua and Sarah Pierce, bro. John Pike of Dover and ch: **Joseph**, b. 21 Apr. 1676 in Salisbury; not in will. **Mary**, b. 20 Mar. 1677-8. **Robert**, b. 15 Sept. 1680; not in will. **John**, b. 8 Feb. 1682-3. **Dorothy**, b. 28 Apr. 1685, m. in Newbury 22 Jan. 1712-3 Richard Dummer.

4 **JOHN**(3), Exeter, m. in Ipswich 8 Nov. 1705 Hannah Lord, who m. 2d bef. 1718 Edward Hall. Had grants 3 Feb. 1697-8 and 1725, laid out to his heirs in 1740. List 376b. Adm. to wid. 7 May 1717. 6 surv. ch: **Robert**, eldest, m. 19 Sept. 1735 in Ipsw. Elizabeth Lord. **John**, capt., b. 3 Feb. 1712, m. in 1748 Deborah Smith (Daniel of Ipsw.), d. June 1757. **Ebenezer. Hannah**, m. 14 Oct. 1731 Jonathan Lord. **Mary**, m. Dudley James. **Dorothy**, Wells witn. 1732; m. Nathaniel Wells (Thomas).

**LIGHTFOOT**, 1 John, mariner, presum. J. Lightfoot in Kit. 1674 receipting 'from

Mistres Alice Shapleigh by ord. of Maj. Nich. S.' That yr. he bot 55 a. at Back Cove, Falm., from Rich. Pattishall, and sold half in 1682 to Zach. White of Salem, where he appar. liv. aft. m. Elizabeth Swasey there in May 1680; m. 2d 11 Nov. 1692 Elizabeth Fortune. Ch. 2+3 or 4 rec. Salem, incl. **John**, bp. 11 Oct. 1696, m. Mary Elkins (9).

2 **THOMAS**, Gr. j. (N. H.) 1697.

**Lilly**, George, wounded 1691. List 37.

**Liman**, John, 'from further Northward' took O. A. at Kit. 16 Nov. 1652.

**Lime**, Samuel, No. Yarmouth 1685. List 214.

**Lincoln**, John (Linkhorn), k. by Ind. at Pemaquid 1695. List 96.

**LINDSEY**, 1 **Alexander**, from Forfaine, Scot., m. in Portsm. 3 Dec. 1719 Lydia Cross; poss. same as Lydia Linsby, wid., m. James Kenney of Cadteen, co. Tyrone, Ire., 17 Nov. 1726. ?Dau. **Esther** (bap.?) So. Ch. 25 Feb. 1721-2.

2 **JAMES**, bach., and Ann Gypson, wid., m. at Oyster River 16 Jan. 1727-8, in clothes all borrowed. ?(List 368b, Lingley).

**LINES** (Lynes), 1 **John**, fined in Saco Ct. 7 Nov. 1665 for abs. from Ct. and contempt of author.; abs. from Gr. j. 1670; bot a fishing plant on Star Isl. 1672. Will 29 Sept. 1674—29 June 1675 names two sis. and a niece in Eng.; a minister and ano. of Dartmouth, Eng., execs.; overseers here Rev. Saml. Belcher and Dr. John Fletcher to collect his dues and have £10 apiece. Thos. Head carried some of his goods to Sarah Winsland, w. of John, whose ho. was searched by the constable. List 3.

2 **THEOPHILUS**, and John Parnell, their men and vessel taxed Oyster River 1666-7. He (Lyne) appr. Mark Hunkings's est. 1667.

## LINSCOTT.

1 **JOHN**, York, in pre-matrimonial difficulties Sept. 1690, m. 1st Lydia Milbury, 2d bef. 1712 wid. Sarah Brookings (3 Henry) who m. 3d John Donnell(2). He liv. on a part of the Donnell prop. and had various town gr. from 1691 until his death. Bondsman for wid. Sarah Masterson, 1691-2; Berwick witn., Emery to Searle, 1693-4; Portsm. witn., Elliot to Pickering, 1695-6. Adm. gr. to his s. John and Richard Milbury, bro.-in-law of decd., 6 Jan. 1712-3. Ch. **John**. **Joshua**, York witn., McIntire to Junkins, 17 Dec. 1716. Prob. d. in youth. Note that his bro. Joseph named a son Joshua in 1721-2. **Joseph. Ichabod**, 56 in 1763, husbandman, acc. by Sarah Bouden (Boody 1 Abraham) in 1732-3 and plead not guilty. He q. c. int. in est. of his fa. to bro. John in 1731, and later settled in Damariscotta.

**Josiah**, q. c. to bro. John in 1728; m. 1 Apr. 1731 Hepsibah Came(3). **Mary**, m. 1710-1. Nathaniel Ramsdell, having been in ct. with him Jan. 1709-10. **Lydia**, m. Jonathan Philbrick, int. 8 Feb. 1728-9, in ct. Oct. 1729 aft. their marriage, constituting a perfect example of the custom of pre-contract.

2 **JOHN**(1), York, husbandman, m. Tabitha Bragdon(3), received a deed from Samuel Donnell for a part of the land on which his fa. liv. 3 Apr. 1712. He sold 5 a. in 1729 and 40 a. where he then liv. to John McIntire in 1735. List 279. He lost his first 5 ch., all then born, betw. 7 Jan. and 31 Jan. 1728-9, doubtless of throat distemper (diphtheria). Ch: **Phebe**, b. 1 Oct. 1717. **Love**, b. 5 Oct. 1721. **Sarah**, b. 2 Jan. 1723-4. **Tabitha**, b. 29 Jan. 1725-6. **John**, b. 2 May, 1728. **Beriah**, b. 14 May 1730.

3 **JOSEPH**(1), York, m. Hannah Bragdon (4), ab. 1719. He q. c. share in his fa.'s est. to bro. John in 1726, and in 1729 he was listed as about to settle at Sheepscot. List 279. Ch. rec. at York: **Abigail**, b. 18 Nov. 1720, m. int. 18 Aug. 1739 Eleazer Wittum. **Joshua**, b. 22 Jan. 1721-2, m. 16 Nov. 1747 Hepsibah Kingsbury. **Joseph**, b. 2 Feb. 1723-4, m. 1st 31 Dec. 1742 Sarah Favour, jr., 2d 6 June 1748 Elizabeth Peake. **Mary**, b. 2 Nov. 1725, d. 5 Nov. 1726. **Molly**, b. 31 Aug. 1727 **John**, b. 10 Mar. 1729-30. **Samuel**, b. 7 Apr. 1732.

**LIPPINCOTT, Bartholomew.** One B. L. and Elizabeth Squyre were m. at St. Andrew's, Plymouth, co. Devon, 1 Nov. 1636. Suit in Piscataqua ct. 1644. Dover 1658-1662. List 356cg.

**LISCOMB** (Luscomb), **William**, Saco, cooper, had a grant of 100 acres from Maj. Phillips in 1662. Rated in Saco 1670; Tr. j. 1663, 1666. His w. Susanna was pres. for abs. from Saco meeting in 1669 and he was sued for debt by James Harmon in 1670. Soon moved to Rev. Robert Jordan's land at Nonsuch, seemingly as tenant, and his w. was in ct. for abs. from Scarboro worship in 1671, 1672 and 1673. Lists 26, 245, 249, 237a, 246. By 1680 he was in Salem and bot land, final payment being made by his w., during his abs. in England, in 1686. In 1729 his daus. Elizabeth Lewis and Joanna Darling, both widows, of Middleboro, sold 100 a. in Bidd. over against Cedar and Cow Islands, formerly their fa.'s prop., to John Gordon. Ch: **Sydrack**, drowned and bur. at Saco 1 Sept. 1660. List 244c. **Elizabeth**, m. 1st Thomas Parlour of Beverly, 2d 11 Sept. 1716 James Lewis of Middleboro, d. in 1744 in 90th yr. **Mary**, (on auth. of Sidney Perley), m. July 1681, in Salem, Daniel Caton. **John**, Lynn and Salem, m. ab. 1691 Abigail Brewer, d. bef. 1707. Ch. **William**, Salem, house-wright, m. Jane Garland, d. winter of 1733-4. 7 ch. **Joanna**, bp. adult in Salem 16 Jan. 1686-7, m. Thomas Darling of Middleboro.

**LISSEN, Listen.** Liston a par. in Essex.
1 **JOSEPH** (Lessen), Oyster River 1662. List 363a.

2 **NICHOLAS** (aut.), millman, Exeter, ±60 in 1678, ±80 in 1694. Salem and Marbleh. 1637; of Glouc. 10 Oct. 1648 bot Geo. Barlow's two houses and lands in Ex.; town gr. 12 Jan. 1648-9, the first of many, incl. mill privileges. One of three to collect town rent for sawmills 1653; Selectm. 1654-56, 1662, 1666; Commit. on Dover-Ex. bounds 1671-2. He bot ho. and land at the waterside 1654, int. in various new sawmills, and in May 1667 from Robt. Wadleigh half his 320 a. on Lamprill Riv., from which both had been disposs. and Mr. Saml. Symonds put in, bef. 30 Oct. 1668. For litigation in which Wadleigh held on, he didn't, see Dover Hist. Memo. pp. 402-4. Lists 376b, 379, 380, 377, 383, 52. Two wives in sight once each, Alice 1666, Jane m. in Ex. 14 Dec. 1682. He spent his last yrs. with Nich. and Mary (Gordon) Smith; and d. when their s. Richard was 8 or 9 yrs. old. Called deced. in deed 20 May 1697. Adm. 8 Dec. 1714 to gr. sons Alex. Magoon and Nich. Gordon; late div. to three daus. or repres.: **Hannah**, eldest, m. John Bean (2). **Elizabeth**, 2d dau., m. by 1661 Henry Magoon. **Mary**, 3d dau., m. Alexander Gordon(1).

3 **THOMAS**, 3-yr. man at Richmond Isl. 1638; ran away bef. 15 July 1639. List 21.

**LISTER, Francis**, Damariscove Isl. witn. with Abra. Shurt; witn. Thos. Elbridge's deed; both 1651. Suff. D. i. 24, ii. 73. Scrivener, he witn. Ind. deed to Lake 1654.

**Litchfield, Thomas**, Dep. Sheriff (N. H.) 1685; Kit. witn. 1690. Y. D. v. 1.56.

**Litford, Francis**, dealing with Wm. Ardell, 1680.

**LITTLE, Thomas**, had from Sir F. Gorges 500 a. bet. Saco and Black Point, recites deed of s. John of Newport, R. I., to Geo. Keniston, 10 Jan. 1728-9. Y. D. 13.133.

**LITTLEBURY, Capt. John**, invested £300 in the Laconia Co. in 1631, on persuasion of Capt. John Mason, and came over ±1649, when (as he wrote in 1669) he entered and laid claim to the Isles of Shoals and took poss. of the ho. and land at Little Harbor where Capt. Neale lived, and more lately of ho. and land at Gt. Isl., with Mr. Fryer's consent. During 20 yrs. he vainly strove to get poss. here, but strangely abs. from the records if in New Eng. much of the time. In 1651 he headed a commission for Newfoundland affairs; of Piscataqua in Oct.

1667, lately of Boston. Reaching 'great age' he had given up in 1668-9 and sought from the Mass. Gen. Ct. as relief only £200 to pay his debts and passage to London, thence to Holy Island, near Berwick, where formerly governor; the passage allowed in Oct. 1669. List 41. D. H. 4. 312, 318-9, 323.

**LITTLEFIELD**, a yeoman family of Hampshire.

1 ——— and ———, young Littlefields drowned on Wells Bar Oct. 1707. List 96. Bourne calls them Job and Moses, but cert. not Job(12) and Moses (19 jr.), the only ones known.

2 **ANTHONY**(8), planter, liv. at the Great Hill bet. Cape Porpus and Kennebunk Rivers (now Kennebunk) until death, by late depositions, altho 19 Oct. 1658 he sold (mortg.?) his land bet. these rivers, ±230 a., to Wm. Symonds. In June 1648 he won a land suit ag. Mr. Ezek. Knight. Lists 252, 261, 263. M. Mary Page (Thos.), ab. 1652 and in 1656 sued John Smith of Saco for goods recd. with her indenture. Invent. recorded July 1662. Wid. Mary liv. Saco 13 Mar. 1662-3. Ch. uncert., incl. surely: **Edmund. Caleb**, b. ab. 1659. **Samuel.** Also **?James**, and others.

3 **CALEB**(2), ±21 in June 1680, apprent. to Nehemiah Partridge of Portsm. Last found in N. H. in ct. case with Mary Allen (2) in Oct. 1681; next was warned out of Weymouth in Mar. 1685-6. Braintree 1692, Kingstown, R. I., 1714, New Shoreham (Block Isl.) 1715; liv. there 4 Sept. 1741, d. bef. 5 Mar. 1743-4, but poss. ret. once to Wells, where he, s. Caleb, Isaac Nash and three others had 100 a. apiece 18 Mar. 1713-4, provid. they settle. M. by 1692 Lydia, prob. dau. of Nath. Mott of Scituate and Braintr. Ch: **Caleb**, b. Braintr. July 1692; of Kingstown, m. 1 July 1714 Mercy Mott of New Shoreham, where he liv. In 1752 sold 200 a. on Mousam Riv. to Anthony L. of Wells. Will 1767—1769. 4 ch. **Lydia**, m. 14 June 1716 Robert Gardiner of Kingst., 2d Wm. Willis. **Samuel**, m. at New Shoreham 30 Sept. 1731 Sybil Wilcox; d. there bef. 25 Jan. 1750-1. 3 ch. **Nathaniel**, Esq., New Shoreham. Will 1780—1795. W. Margaret Mitchell. 8 ch. See N. E. Reg. 86.71.

4 **DANIEL**(11), Wells, under age 28 Mar. 1682-3 when fa. gave him 150 a. on N. side of Ogunquit River, form. Abraham Tilton's, with other land and marsh. Gr. j. 1689-90, 1693-7, 1699. Jury 1702, 1709. Orig. member Wells Ch. 1701. Selectm. 1713. Lists 90, 269ab. M. Mehitable Dodd (Geo.), liv. 1701. Invent. 5 June 1718, adm. to only kn. ch: **Francis**, bp. 3 May 1702, gent., his farm on Ogunquit Riv. List 269c. M. 1st 6 Nov. 1722 Hepzibah Littlefield, dau. of

Jonathan(12), 2d 26 Dec. -1734- (int. 10 Apr. -1731-) Hannah Emery(5). (One Francis was acc. by Sarah Bragdon 1720-1). Adm. to wid. Hannah 9 Feb. 1743; liv. 1746. Only ch. Mehitable b. 21 Oct. 1724, ptn. for adm. in place of her step-mo. 6 Feb. 1743-4, m. next day Joseph Sawyer, Esq., who adm.

5 **DAVID**(12), miller, Wells, ag. 76 in Nov. 1746, 79 in Mar. 1749, with br. Job inherited the Ogunquit land. He had deed of the Cross farm from Saml. Hill in 1713, one-fourth of Kennebunk Falls from Saml. L. in 1716. Constable 1697. Gr. j. 1698, 1699, 1710. Lists 268ab, 269bc. M. 15 Nov. 1694 Mary Hill(17), liv. 5 Aug. 1735; appar. he who m. (int. 6 Dec. 1746) Hannah Hutchins of Arundel. Adm. to s. Nathan 28 Sept. 1751. Ch., 1st four bp. 20 July 1707: **David**, m. 25 Jan. 1726 Sarah Sawyer (Danl.), 2d (int. 20 Oct. 1737) Sarah Butland, 3d one Abigail. List 269c. **Eleanor**, m. 15 Dec. 1715 Danl. Morrison. **Nathan**, m. 23 Sept. 1724 Lydia Winn. List 269c. 10 ch. **Mary**, m. Wm. Sawyer (Ct. Apr. 1728). **Jeremiah**, bp. 4 Apr. 1708, husb. of one or m. of foll: Lydia Sawyer 12 Nov. 1729; Abigail Wiggin 23 Nov. 1732; Sarah Hatch 26 Dec. 1739. List 269c. **Meribah**, bp. 20 Aug. 1710, m. 25 Dec. 1729 Joshua Wells. **Tabitha**, bp. 10 May 1713, m. Nehemiah Littlefield(7).

6 **DELIVERANCE**, List 38. Should read Dependence. See (7).

7 *DEPENDENCE(11), Wells, ag. 63 in 1734, 78 in 1749-50, but a boy in Mar. 1682-3 when his fa. deeded him the homestead, exc. what given to br. James. Lists 269ac. Rep. 1725; Selectm. 1726. His w. in Feb. 1706-7, poss. not 1st, was Hannah (Snell), wid. of John Ballard(2); m. lastly in Boston 5 Dec. 1718 Elizabeth (Batson) Fairfield(2), who liv. until aft. her Fairfield gr. sons were grown. Ch., all but last bp. 6 Aug. 1710: **James**, m. Lydia Littlefield (18). List 269c. A James and James jr. were at Louisburg. **Hannah**, m. Lt. John Furbush(1). **Samuel**, m. 1st Mar. 1725 Elizabeth Goodale, 2d 13 Mar. 1745-6 Sarah (Wiggin) Perkins. **Isaac**, m. 21 Feb. 1733-4 Jane Littlefield (?dau. of Joseph 17 jr.). List 269c. **Nehemiah**, m. 18 Dec. 1735 Tabitha Littlefield(5). List 269c. **Dorcas**, m. 29 Nov. 1733 Capt. John Shapleigh of Kit.

8 **EDMUND**, Wells, came 1st to Boston, likely with two oldest sons. W. Annis (Austin) ag. 38, six ch., and servants John Knight and Hugh Durdal foll. in the -Bevis- in May 1638 from Tichfield, co. Hants., where he was bap. 27 June 1592 and m. her 16 Oct. 1614. N. E. Reg. 67.343. At Exeter he signed the Combin. 5 June 1639, had two lots in the 1st div. of uplands, and remov.

to Wells bef. 14 July 1643, when Thos. Gorges gr. him 100 a. adj. the mill and the neck of marsh bet. that and Webhannet River. There he had a saw and gristmill, and headed a large and promin. fam. The 1st yr. he was agent for R. Vines to give poss.; in Nov. 1645 Vines gr. to John Wadleigh and E. L. 200 a. on S. W. side of Ogunquit River, not intrenching on town of Wells. Tr. j. 1645, 1647; Gr. j. 1645, 1647; O. A. to Mass. 5 July 1653. Com. t. e. s. c. 1654 to death, except 1657. Authorized 1654 to sell wine and strong liq. to Inds. Selectm. 1654, 1657. Lists 373, 376a, 378, 261, 252, 263, 262, 264. Will 11 Dec. 1661; fam. compromise signed 17 Dec. by s. Francis sr., his mo., and bros. Thos. and Francis jr.; inv. 24 Dec. Wid. Annis's will 12 Dec. 1677, inv. 7 Mar. 1677-8. Ch., all but Mary bap. at Tichfield: **Ann**, bp. 11 Feb. 1615-6, bur. 2 Jan. 1616-7. **Edward**, bp. 17 Feb. 1617-8; bur. 13 June 1635. **Francis**, bp. 17 June 1619. **Anthony**, bp. 7 Oct. 1621. **John**, bp. 1 Nov. 1624. **Elizabeth**, bp. 22 July 1627, m. John Wakefield. **Mary**, m. Lt. John Barrett(2). **Thomas**, bp. 10 Aug. 1633. **Anne** (Hannah), bp. 10 Aug. 1633, m. Peter Cloyes(5). **Francis**, bp. 24 Mar. 1635-6.

9 **EDMUND**(2), Braintree, as -Edward- of Cape Porpus was apprent. 7 Oct. 1662 for 12 yrs. to (11). Wells gr. 1674, 1680. In Mar. 1681-2 he and Joseph, both of Wells, took Nathan and Saml. as equal partners in their gr. from Cape Porpus, for sawmill and cornmill on Kennebunk Riv. Tr. j. 1687-1689. Lists 266, 269b, 256, 259. See (20). Remov. to Mass., prob. not long bef. he m. his 2d w. Elizabeth Mott (Nathl.), 30 Dec. 1690. Both were in Suff. Ct. May 1691 when Capt. Saml. White of Weymouth agreed to pay the fine. D. Braintr. 9 Apr. 1718; wid. Elizabeth and s. Nathl. admrs. Ch. by unkn. 1st w.: **Mary**, m. in Braintr. 6 Jan. 1703-4 John Harding, jr. **Samuel**, 'Fat Sam', Wells, m. one Frances by 1713; both liv. Apr. 1739. List 269c. In 1738 he sold land gr. to 'my honored uncle Caleb L. and Co.' 18 Mar. 1713-4, now descended to me. Ch. incl. sons Anthony, Samuel, Edmund, b. Wells 1713-8; Elijah added by Bradbury. **Edmund**, m. in Braintr. 6 Dec. 1711 Bethia Waldo; d. there 27 May 1717; adm. 17 Oct. to fa. and wid., who m. 2d Thos. Hayward of Bridgewater; 3 ch. By 2d w. at Braintr. 1691-1713: **Nathaniel, Elizabeth, Sarah, Anna** (b. 25 Mar. 1698, m. Christopher Dyer 6), **Abigail, Lydia, Levie** (son), **Deborah, Hepzibah, Ruth** (b. 6 Mar. 1709-10, m. John Dyer 6 jr.), **Dorcas.**

10 **ELIAB**(15), miller, Wells, Manchester, app. liv. also at Cape Porpus, where he bot the John Barrett farm in 1703, sold 1715. His form. ho. at Maryland ment.

1713. Fined 1698, non-appear. as Gr. j.; Gr. j. 1699; Tr. j. 1702, 1709. Lists 268a, 269b. M. in Manch. 29 Oct. 1696 Rachel Sibley; there their first ch., rec. Wells 23 Oct. 1697, was bp. 22 May 1698; there he ret. ab. 1711, and d., tho in 1713-4 in Me. he sued and was sued by br. Josiah's wid. Adm. 16 Apr. 1717 to s.-in-law Jos. Leach. Wid. d. bef. div. made Dec. 1718, when were liv. 8 of 9 ch. counted by Wells, Manch., and printed Beverly records, the last erron. naming -Josiah and Lydia- of Manch. as parents of the 7 ch. bp. Bev. 1712-3.

11 ***FRANCIS** sr. (8), Wells, innkeeper. The oft-told story of his separa. from his fam. was the imagining of some one trying to acct. for two bros. of the same name, and not unlikely he accomp. his fa. here, but moved around bef. settling in Wells, where gr. 50 a. by Gorges in 1643. Taxed Woburn 1646; Dover 1648; soon in Wells with 2d w., yet bot ho. at Charlestown 1653. Rep. from York 1660, Wells 1665, 1676, 1681. Gr. j. 1666, 1667, 1673, 1687. County treas. 1676, 1678, 1681. Selectm. 1677. Lists 354a, 261, 75b, 252, 263, 262, 264, 269b, 25, 254, 28, 88, 266, 36. Lic. innholder many times 1661-1691, afterw. presum. at Ipswich, where innholder 2 May 1700. Lic. at Wells Oct. 1700, 1701, 1702, tho in Essex Ct. Mar. 1701 when his step-son-in-law Cyprian Whipple was acquit. of selling liq., he did it only as one of his fa. L.'s fam. Inv. 15 Jan. 1712-3; adm. to s. Dependence, whose bill calling him lately decd., charged for two yrs. 'diet and attendance,' and transporting 'my dear fa.' twice from the westward to Wells. Three wives: Jane Hill, d. Woburn 20 Dec. 1646; Rebecca, b. 31 Jan. 1630, liv. 29 Mar. 1683 when he deeded homestead, with life reserva., to s. Dependence, exc. what given to sons James and Daniel; 3d by 1689 Mary (Wade), wid. of Wm. Symonds of Ipsw. Ch., by 1st w: **Mary**, b. Woburn 14 Dec. 1646, m. 1st at Billerica Nov. 1664 (or 2 Nov. 1665) John Kittredge, 2d at Biller. 16 Jan. 1677-8 John French. Ch. by both husb. By 2d w. (7 rec. together at Wells): **Sarah**, b. 15 Nov. 1649, m. John Wells, 2d by Nov. 1677 Wm. Sawyer. **Hanneth** (Hannah), b. 5 Jan. 1652. **Deliverance** (dau.), b. 5 July 1655. **James**, b. 2 Oct. 1657. **Isaac**, b. 23 Jan. 1660; k. by Ind.? **Abigail**, b. 26 Mar. 1661-2, m John Elbridge(2). **Dorcas**, b. 4 Oct. 1664. **Phebe**, m. 27 Apr. 1690 John Heard(6). **Daniel. Dependence**, b. ab. 1671. Also likely **Rachel**, m. 6 Dec. 1694 Wm. Frost(16).

12 **FRANCIS** jr. (8), ho. carp., Wells, had 200 a. gr. 1658. Ensign 1668. Tr. j. 1664, 1668. Gr. j. 1673, 1674. Lot-layer 1669-70. Lists 261, 252, 263, 262, 269b, 264, 25, 83. Will 5 Feb. (d. 6 Feb.) 1674-5,

names w. Meribah, dau. of Wm. Wardwell, and sons Jos. and Nathan execs. Inv. incl. saw and cornmill. In 1710 on ptn. of Jona. and David that their mo. Mrs. Meribah was liable to be chargeable to them beyond their propor., her ch. and gr. ch. were ordered to supp. her, altho only sons and sons-in-law named specif. in the order. Lists 266, 36. Ch: **Joseph. Nathan. Jonathan**, b. ±1662, inherited with br. Nathan all the Maryland lands. Lists 33, 268a, 269abc, 38. Often Gr. j. from 1693. M. Abigail Simpson (Henry); she liv. 1737. He was ±68 in July 1730; d. bet. 4 Oct. 1734—25 Feb. 1734-5. Ch., 1st five bp. 15 Nov. 1702: Abigail, w. of Robt. Monson of Scarb. 1739; Tabitha; Jonathan, d. y.; Hepzibah, m. Francis Littlefield(4); Mabel, m. in Newington 15 May 1730 Richard Boothby of Wells; Pelatiah, b. 26 Sept. 1704, List 269c, m. Mehitable Black(2); Priscilla, bp. 23 Feb. 1706-7, m. Nathl. Hill; Huldah, bp. 27 Nov. 1709, m. 7 Nov. 1732 John Winn; Jonathan, bp. 7 Mar. 1713-4. **Job**, d. bef. 13 Nov. 1694. **David** (once -Daniel- in fa.'s will). **Mary**, m. Saml. Hatch(5). **Joanna**, m. Thos. Penney. **Tabitha**, m. Rev. Saml. Emery(5). **Hannah**, m. Capt. Jos. Hill(11).

13 **JAMES** sr. (11), Wells, bot ho. and 150 a. form. Abra. Tilton's which with other prop. he deeded to fa. in Mar. 1682-3. Not sr., 14 Apr. 1687, he exchanged his home place in lower Wells for John Butland's 600 a. at mouth of Kennebunk Riv. K. by Ind. May 1690; adm. 24 Feb. 1690-1 to wid. Katherine (Heard 3) and her 2d husb. John Wooden. They were in Salem 1699-1701, perh. later. Ch: Abigail, m. Stephen Harding(6). **Mary**, m. in Salem, Apr. 1710 Saml. Fuller(4). In Mar. 1717 they sold half of the 600 a. to Harding. 6 ch., incl. James, Miriam, Abigail.

14 **JAMES**(2?), and Mary got judg. ag. Wm. Sawyer Feb. 1690-1. Y. D. v. ii. 8. Gr. j. 1693.

15 **CAPT. *JOHN**(8), had gr. from Gorges when his fa. did in 1643, which, and others, Henry Gorges later tried to recover. P. & Ct. i., li. lii. With this, his own purchases and town grants, he was a large land and mill owner, and active publicly almost to death. Oft. Tr. and Gr. j. and foreman; on commit. Kit.-Wells bounds 1658; constable 1661, 1663-4; Selectm. 1670, 1677; Rep. 1680; commis. Lieut. 29 May 1668 and placed in command at Wells 1675; Lt. L.'s mill taxed for Fort Loyal 1682; called Capt. 1690. Memb. of committee in Boston 1692 asking aid for a preacher at Wells and the garrison. Lists 261, 252, 262, 269b, 264, 25, 265, 83, 28, 266, 29, 36. Selling without lic. 1693, he was to answ. at the next Ct., being sick. D. 9 Feb. 1696-7; adm. 7 Apr. fol. to

wid. Patience, who was liv. 1701, when the heirs signed an agreement. Ch: **John**. **Josiah. Elijah. Lydia**, m. Saml. Storer. **Deborah**, m. Saml.Webber. **Mary**, m. Capt. Matthew Austin (6). **Charity**, m. Wm. Webb. **Elizabeth**, m. Edward Beale(5). **Mercy**, m. 1st Jacob Lufkin, 2d Richard Stimson. **Patience**, m. James Webber.

16 **JOHN**(15), eldest son, had 100 a. gr. 1683. List 269b. Long sick, his will 9 Sept. (inv. 16 Sept.) 1689, names w. Mehitable and ch: **Lydia**, to be brot up decently 'which I doubt not of'; she m. Josiah Winn and likely was the dau. of John jr. b. Wells 20 —— 1681.

17 **JOSEPH**(12), eldest son, under 22 in 1674-5, had the homestead. His mill taxed for Fort Loyal in 1682; in Jan. 1684 he made mill contract with Wm. Frost and Jona. Hammond. Y. D. xii. 4. Gr. j. 1685, 1687. Lists 28, 256, 259, 33, (?269b). M. Jane Cole(23), niece of (37); she was selling strong drink in 1693. ?List 268b. She m. 2d 2 July 1698 Capt. John Heard(6), and as admx., with him, made agreement with her ch.; Capt. Jas. Gooch of Boston had £38 belonging to the est. Ch: **Joseph**, millman, bot. in his sisters. Lists 38, 269a(?b)c. An early w., likely Mercy Cloyes(4) (Ct. Apr. 1706), must have been mo. of Sarah, who m. Danl. Cheney 12 Mar. 1723. He m. 2d 4 Aug. 1709 Abigail Storer (Joseph). Will 22 Mar. 1759—8 Oct. 1768 names her, s. Benj., daus. Sarah Cheney, Jane L. (?w. of Isaac 7), Hannah Hammond, Abigail Winn. **Meribah**, of Kit., m. (int. Newb. 22 Sept. 1705) Nathl. Bartlett, tanner; both of Exeter 1741. **Priscilla**, m. in Wells 24 Aug. 1710 Richard Ward; both of Portsm. 1742.

18 **LIEUT. JOSIAH**(15), Wells, m. Lydia Masters (Nathl.), and led a life beset by Ind. Gr. j. 1689, 1691, 1695, 1697-8, foreman jury 1701. Constable 1696. With the party when Thos. Cole(31) and w. were k., they escaped uninjured. Manchester, May 1698, perh. visiting; soon in Wells where he was Lieut., orig. member of the ch. 1701, and appar. it was their home until she and a son coming from Boston were k. by Ind. 10 Aug. 1707. List 96 (twice). He m. 2d Elizabeth Hilton, was hims. captured in Apr. 1708, spent two yrs. in Canada, writing letters and arranging his release, and ret. in Apr. 1710, only to be k. in Ind. attack, Apr. 1712. Adm. 2 July 1712 to wid. Elizabeth, who m. 2d 18 Oct. 1716 Malachi Edwards(7). See 'N. E. Captives' i. 435-7, Bourne's Wells pp. 267-274, 337-342, showing too his troubles with Josiah Winn aft. his own ret. and the controv. over the est. with the Edwardses. See Barber(6). Lists 268a, 96, 38. Ch. by 1st w. (Wells records, exc. bap. of Nathl.): **Josiah**, b. 15 Sept.

1688, bp. 28 June 1702, d. bef. fa., poss. the son k. with mo. **Anna**, bp. with Josiah, m. 17 Oct. 1717 Jacob Perkins. **John**, b. 7 Apr. 1695, eldest son 1732; m. 27 Oct. 1714 Sarah Stimson. Ch. List 269c. **Nathaniel**, b. 3 June 1697, bp. Beverly 29 May 1698; likely the reputed servant of Mr. Nathl. -Mastyn- of Salem 1717; sailor 1722. D. 1727 (ct. rec.), yet one N. L. int. mar. with Abigail Neal at Salem 20 July 1728. **Peter**, bp. with Josiah, joiner, Wells; w. Abigail in 1742. Lists 268b, 269c. **Esther**, b. 1 Feb. 1703-4, m. Jos. Crediford. **Lydia**, bp. 19 May 1706, m. James Littlefield(7). By 2d w: **Sarah**, bp. 30 Sept. 1711, brot up by mo. 4 y. 4 m.; m. James Clark(43). **Elizabeth** (posthumous), bp. 6 Dec. 1712, m. 26 Nov. 1730 Zachariah Goodale. Ch. of Josiah and Lydia of Manchester bp. 1712-3 (Beverly V. R. printed), belong to Eliab(10).

19 **MOSES**(23), m. (Ct. Dec. 1687) Martha Lord (6), his mar. portion from his fa. 100 a. lately purch. from Ezek. Knight jr. and one-third the homestead where he had already built. Gr. j. 1694-5, 1700, 1710; jury 1704-5, 1713. Constable 1696. Last ment. 18 Mar. 1713-4. Lists 33, 269b, 39. W. Martha and 3 ch. among captives of 10 Aug. 1703. She ret. in time to take adm. on his est. 24 Jan. 1714-5; m. 2d John Abbott(4), 3d Alexander Taylor. Still admx. in May 1726, but soon d., and s. Aaron filed adm. bond on fa.'s est. 2 Sept. 1727. ' N. E. Captives' names the captive ch: **Aaron** (Peter), b. 20 Oct. 1694, bp. as Pierre Augustin 27 Jan. 1704, then liv. with the par. priest of Boucherville. List 99, pp. 92, 125-6. Naturalized 1710 and m. (Lidfril) at Boucherville 3 Feb. 1717 Marie Brunel. 7 or 8 ch. He was here bef. and aft. his mo. d., and as Aaron L. of Montreal, only s. and h., in 1738 success. sued three Lords for her portion. Appar. in Canada aft. July 1751. **Tabitha**, supp. to have been k., but trad. (Bradbury p. 154) brings her back fleetingly as an Ind. squaw. **Ruth**, b. 23 June 1698, still captive 1710-11. List 99, p. 92. Her birthdate suggests she was Sister Angelique (Lidrefil) of the Hôtel Dieu, Montreal, d. 9 Jan. 1732, ag. 33. See Miss Coleman i. 403-10. **Moses**, bp. with fa. 13 June 1708, app. not a captive; d. s. p. bef. mo.

20 **NATHAN**(12), under 21 in 1674-5, shared fa.'s Maryland land with br., Jonathan; 100 a. town gr. 1680. List 269b. Adm. 13 Mar. 1688-9 to wid. Elizabeth (Barrett 3), who m. 2d James Denmark(1). Only ch. **Leah**, b. 16 Sept. 1687, m. by 1707 Jabez Gorham of Bristol, R. I., d. there 13 May 1739. 8 ch. N. E. Reg. 54.169.

21 **SAMUEL**(2), associated in 167- with Nicholas Cole sr. and Edmund L.(9) in

30 a. gr., while in 1680 the two L.'s and one N. C. had 100 a. apiece. List 269b. He m. 4 Dec. 1686 Mary Cole(23). D. 8 Dec. 1688; adm. to her 13 Mar. 1688-9, bondsm. -Edward- L. Only ch: **Samuel**, Wells, in 1720 sold Sebascodegan lands. Y. D. x. 29.

22 **SAMUEL**(15), partner 1695 in gr. with Jona. Hammond, Eliab L. and John Butland. D. bef. his fa., leaving w. Joanna called 'dau.-in-law' in div. by heirs 7 Oct. 1701. She was bp. on prof. of faith 3 Jan. 1702-3; her dau. **Abigail**, bp. 4 July 1703. Lists 36, 269b.

23 **THOMAS**(8), subm. to Mass. 5 July 1653. Constable 1661, 1663-4. **Gr.** of 100 a. 1665. Tr. j. 1680; Gr. j. 1688. Lists 261, 263, 252, 264, 25, 269b, 265, 28, 266, 30, 33. Inquest in Me. prior to 5 Mar. 1689-90 on untimely death of Saml. Lord(6), Robt. Houston, T. L. of Wells, drowned at Berwick; three coroners, three constables. His est. was left in widow's hands for mainten. of self and ch. W. Ruth in Jan. 1663-4; the wid. was Sarah, who m. 2d Ezekiel Knight (3). Ch: **Moses** (by 1st w.). By 1st or 2d w.: **Rebecca**, m. 1st at Salem 13 Mar. 1698-9 William Wakefield, 2d in Salem 19 Sept. 1717, Lt. Wm. King; both liv. Sutton 1718. **Dorothy**, m. Isaac Nash; both liv. Kingstown, R. I., 1718. Y. D. ix. 145-6. See (3). **Mary**, (by 2d w.), m. Wm. Eaton(5).

**Litton**, see Lidden.

**LIVINGSTON**, Daniel, m. in Braintree bef. 1680 Joanna, wid. of John Pray, who was convic. in Suffolk ct. for striking and abusing him in 1681, but acq. in 1683 of suspicion of selling liq. to Indians. Again in ct. in 1686 her bond was forfeited, she having joined her husb. in York, where he had been a witn. as early as 1666, they having signed an agreement 9 July 1685 that she and her 3 youngest (Pray) ch. should come to him and make a fam. Lists 33, 96. Tr. j. 1693, Gr. j. 1694. He was k. by Ind. 20 Aug. 1694, but she escaped and was liv. in 1699 when she filed in Boston a 2d acct. as adm. of her 1st husb.'s est.

**Lloyd**, see Lyde.

**Load**, Nathl. List 24. Read Nathan Lord.

**LOCKE**, found in many counties of so. England, but most frequently in Somerset.

1 **EDWARD**(2), Rye, farmer, m. Hannah Jenness, whose fa. Francis(1) in 1701 conv. land at Sandy Beach Point to them, then to their s. Francis. In 1738 he sold ho., barn and part of this land to s. Thos. D. ab. 1739. Ch: **Francis**, Rye, b. 18 July 1694, m. 1st in Greenl. 24 Jan. 1716-7 Deliverance Brookings(3), List 338b; 2d 11 Mar. 1733 Sarah Moulton. Capt. of Co. at Ft. Wm. & Mary 1746. He deeded homestead to s.

Francis 1750; d. ±1754. Wid. deeded to dau. Prudence Marden 4 Sept. 1760. Ch. 6 + 3. **Samuel**, Kingston, b. 4 Sept. 1698, m. 11 Feb. 1725 Margaret Ward (Thos.). 10 ch. **Edward**, Kensington, b. 28 May 1701, d. 29 Jan. 1788, m. 17 Dec. 1724 Hannah Blake (Moses 5), who d. 27 Nov. 1789. 8 ch. **Prudence**, b. 30 May 1707, m. 1st 3 Apr. 1735 Ebenezer Weare, 2d 29 Dec. 1742 Andrew Webster. **James**, b. 4 Oct. 1709, cordwainer, m. in Greenl. 2 Mar. 1731-2 Mercy Foss(2). Rochester 1737, mov. to Barnstead and d. there late. 8 ch. **Son**, d. Kensington 12 Jan. 1747, ag. 37. **Thomas**, b. 10 June 1713, m. (Abigail Berry?). Liv. prob. Roch. and Barr. 4 or m. ch.

2 **CAPT. JOHN**, Rye, carpenter, presum. nearly relat. to (4) and to Wm. Marston's w. Sabina. By trad. 1st at Dover, but seen 1st at Portsm. in Jan. 1656-7, getting 8 a. ho.-lot bet. John Jackson and Wm. Cotton. He had prev. m. Elizabeth Berry(12), with her sold his orig. gr. and the bldgs. in Mar. 1660-1. In 1661 she depos. ab. the fight bet. the Abbott-Cate wives. Capt. L.'s Portsm. fine remitted 1665. O. A. 2 Oct. 1666. Ab. 1666 he settled, without authority, on Jocelyn's, later Locke's Neck, now called Straw's Point, in Rye, then Hampt., and aft. much controv. was accepted inhabt. by Hampt. 8 Mar. 1667. No. Yarmouth witn. 1672. Tr. j. 1684, 1685; gr. j. 1698. Lists 323, 326ab, 330ab, 328, 312cd, 313ab, 331b, 52, 55b, 96. K. by Ind. 26 Aug. 1696, supp. ±70; Minister Pike then called him Lieut. Wid. liv. when div. made 4 May 1708, to be maint. by the adms. John and Jos. Ch., all daus. called Locke in div: **John**, b. ±1653-4. **?Elizabeth**, only one not in div. **Nathaniel**, b. ±1661-2. **Alice**. One Alice (Ellis) adm. Greenl. Ch. 1718 and had negro Peggy bp. 1721. **Edward. Tryphena**, m. at Haverh. 14 June 1693 John Webster. **Rebecca. Mary.** One Mary m. in Boston 31 Jan. 1697 Wm. Hepworth. **William**, b. 17 Apr. 1677, d. in Rye 22 Jan. 1768, m. 23 Nov. 1699 Hannah Knowles(2), who d. 12 Sept. 1769, ag. 91. Both adm. Greenl. Ch. 1716. List 338b. Lieut., Deacon. 11 ch. **James**, Rye, liv. 1742-3, m. 2d in Greenl. 3 Dec. 1713 Hannah Philbrook. Ch. incl. James m. in Greenl. 25 Oct. 1720 Sarah Remick. **Joseph**, gent., Rye, d. Mar. 1768, m. in Greenl. Salome White. Both adm. to Greenl. Ch. 1718. List 338b. Town officer. Called Ensign 1728, Capt. 1735. 7 ch. 1710-28.

3 **JOHN**(2), ±75 in Feb. 1728-9, liv. on homestead in Rye with w. Elizabeth. Gr. j. 1694, 1698; jury 1694, 1704. Ab. 1677 his fa. gave him half his right on Jocelyn's Neck; half of this he gave in 1707-8 to s. John, who was to pay Robt. Elliot's debt,

and the other half on cond. he maint. his mo. and pay bro. Jethro £5. Lists 316, 338b. Liv. Dec. 1733. Two kn. ch: **John**, Rye, b. ±1683, adm. Greenl. Ch. 1723. List 338b. W. Sarah and 4 of 8 or m. ch. d. in 1736 from throat distemper. **Jethro**, Rye, m. 7 Jan. 1720 Dorothy Locke(5), who d. bef. him. 2 of 4 ch., Jethro, Dorothy, in will 18 June —28 July 1737, br. John exec. Daus. may incl.: **Deborah**, m. Jude Allen(2) and named a s. Jethro. **Mary**, cert. sis. of Deborah, m. Geo. Banfield(2). **?**List 338b. Poss. one or m. of: Alice, m. Nehemiah Berry(8). Alice, m. Thos. Edmunds(5 jr.). Elizabeth, m. in Greenl. 28 Feb. 1710-11 Saml. Neal. Mehitable, adm. Greenl. Ch. 1725. List 338b.

3½ '**NATHANIEL**,' of whom no contemp. ev. is found, was traditionally the fa. of John(2), **Judith** Berry(13) and **Sabina** Berry (14). **Nathaniel**(4) would also be a poss. s. The theory is put forward that he came to Hampt. 1660 (preceded by his s. John) accomp. by a young w. Sabina (Hemins) and her ch., that he soon d., and that his wid. was that Sabina who m. Wm. Marston(10) and John Redman(1). In 1672 the will of Marston, naming his w. Sabina and making their dau. Tryphena (b. 1663) his chief heir, was wit. by John Locke(2) (who also had a dau. Tryphena), Locke's mo.-in-law and her 2d husb. Tryphena Marston m. Joseph Philbrook, and, after the death of her mo. (then Sabina Redman), Hampt. was disturbed by Philbrook's demands for 'rights sometime his w.'s mo.'s. A few yrs. aft. the death of that Sabina Locke who m. 1st Berry(14), 2d Lewis(1) and 3d Philbrook(4), a Berry gr.s. wrote in his Bible 'Sabina Philbrick b. on the ocean acc. to report d. 1761 ag. 95.' This indicates 1666 as the yr. of her birth, but as her supposed mo. Sabina (Hemins) Locke had m. Capt. Marston bef. 1663, either the yr. or age is doubtful. In 1810 Jonathan and David Locke depos.: Wm. Berry's w. Judith was the dau. of Nathaniel Locke and his w. who came from Eng., and Locke's w. bef. marriage was Hemins and she brot with her a coat-of-arms which referreth to John Hemins (N. H. Gen. Rec. i. 139). Poss. study of the lands of John Redman, Wm. Fifield, Richard Sloper etc. (especially of puzzling entries in Hampt. rec. 2: 125, 128) might confirm this trad.

4 **NATHANIEL**, Great Isl. 1671, worked on highways there Mar.—Sept. 1672; soon d. s. p. See (3½).

5 **NATHANIEL**(2), Hampton, ±45 in 1707, m. 22 Jan. 1688-9 Dorothy Blake(1), ±39 in 1707, who d. 28 Sept. 1737. He d. 12 Nov. 1734. His depos. 2 Feb. 1733-4, ±73, ab. Mr. Robt. Elliot's prop. in Scarb., that 50 yrs. bef. Mr. Elliott took him to Dunstan to build a barn, which Andrew and Arthur

Alger assisted in raising, and more, appears in part false evid., as Arthur Alger was k. in 1675. He or his s. Nathl. was in Scarb. yrs. later. List 399a. Ch. said to number 19, but that many have never been counted: **John**, b. ±1689, poss. went to R. I. **Dorothy**, b. 20 Mar. 1691, m. Jethro Locke(3). **Tryphena**, m. John Knowles(3). **Elizabeth**, b. ±1694, m. Thos. Leavitt(1). **Rachel**, b. 12 Dec. 1695, m. 6 Jan. 1715 Wm. Moulton and was named in codicil of Joseph Chase's(5) will 1716 as Rachel L. now Rachel M. If the Rachel L. who witn. the orig. will in 1704, she was but 9 yrs. old. **Nathaniel**, Falmouth, b. 18 Oct. 1698, m. 1st 6 Jan. 1726-7 Abigail Prescott (Jona.), lost in a vessel from Casco Bay to Cape Ann or Boston in 1735; 2d Mary Stubbs of Yarmouth. Ch. by both wives. **Joseph**, b. ±1700, m. at Block Isl. (New Shoreham, R. I.) 12 Dec. 1722 Mercy Nixon. 2 ch. rec. there. **Samuel**, Hampton, b. ±1702, d. 5 Dec. 1789, m. 11 Dec. 1729 Jerusha Shaw (Jos.). 9 ch. **Jonathan**, b. 22 Dec. 1705, went from R. I. to Chilmark, m. there 1 Jan. 1729-30 Mary Norton. Adm. to her Oct. 1731; m. 2d Matthias King. Son Jonathan remov. to Nova Scotia. **Deborah**, m. 19 Oct. 1732 Wm. Buckman; remov. to Falm.; lost with her inf. and br. Nathl.'s w. in 1735. **Abijah**, poss. mov. to R. I. **Timothy**, bp. 1720, poss. mov. to R. I. Poss. **?Alice**, m. either Nehemiah Berry 1705 or Thos. Edmunds 1722. See (3).

6 **PHILIP**, Dover, witn. for Richard Waldron 1672-1676, presum. apprent. to him as a merchant and later in his employ. Not found aft. 1676, he may have been one of the Ind. victims of that time. He appar. m. Elizabeth Bowles(3), who as E. L. had deed from her fa. in Oct. 1678, and as Mrs. E. L. had 100 a. gr. at Wells 4 Aug. 1679. List 269b. No ch. surv. if any. She m. 2d Wm. Pitman of Portsm. See also (8).

7 **WILLIAM**, ag. 6, came with his uncle Nicholas Davis(41) in 1635, and was named in his will 1667, then of Woburn, where he liv. with w. Mary Clarke (Wm.). She d. 18 July 1715, he 16 June 1720. Deacon. 10 ch. 1657-1684.

8 ——— Widow (of 4?), had permission from Great Isl., 5 Mar. 1674-5, to live in the schoolhouse and teach children to read and sew.

**LOCKHART, Capt. George**, commander of the fort at Falmouth in 1688 under Sir Edmund Andros, ordered to Boston 20 Apr. 1689 by the Council for the Safety of the People to answer charges. List 19, 228b.

**LOCKWOOD**, a township in Yorkshire.
1 **JOHN.** Name stricken out on N. H. jury list, 1685.

2 **CAPT. RICHARD**, mariner, Kit. App. his w. was in Kit. in 1655 (P. & Ct. ii. 40), but most improb. that either was there perman. and abs. from rec. until Nov. 1663, when he bot ho. and 30 a. form. Champernowne's; there he was liv. 1666, and with w. Deborah sold to Simon Lynde in 1671. She was bef. Saco Ct. for lying in Nov. 1665 and failed to app. on a like charge 6 yrs. later. Bet. these yrs. and in 1672 he kept in sight thru numer. suits and by selling without lic.; both were involved in long drawn out troubles with Joan Andrews(9), the Pearce fam. and Mr. Francis Morgan, the last affair causing all, incl. the Lynns, to be bound to the peace in July 1667. A major problem whether the Kit. Mrs. L. was poss. Deborah Gunnison, b. July 1642, and the older ch. by an earlier wife, is unsolved. Lists 82 (both), 298. Tr. j. 1666. See Creber. Some time aft. 12 Dec. 1671 (Hubbard says 24 Jan. 1671) she was carried away by the tide going in a canoe with a drunken fellow bet. Great Isl. and Kit., and never heard of. He was in Boston in May 1672 compl. ag. Barefoot; Kit. witn. 16 Dec. 1672, Boston 1673-4; in Jan. 1675 got judgm. ag. John Cavalier for passage Va. to Boston. Last found in Northampton Co., Va., where 10 Nov. 1680, mariner, ag. 48, he depos. ab. Abraham Collins(2) and John Bellamy, a Va. landowner and mercht.; test. in several of Bellamy's suits ab. conversa. heard in B.'s ho., and hims. got judgm. ag. John Michael 29 Aug. 1683, reversed 30 Oct. foll. His age in Va. tallies with his statement in Me. in 1672, ±40, but cannot be reconciled with ages of daus.: **Deborah**, May 1721, ±80 in 1728-9, ±86 in 1732, ±73 in May 1721, ±80 in 1728-9, ±86 in 1732, ±92 in 1740, m. John Fennick or Phenix. **Ann**, ±25 in 1673, m. Ephraim Lynn(1). **?Sarah**, connec. only by proping. In Oct. 1686 she acc. Christo. Beedle(1) who denied it; both in Ct. again Sept. 1687, perh. already mar. The question if Richard Logwood or Lockwood, gent., of Somerset Co., Md., will 1734, was a son, has been raised by desc., but not answered.

3 **SAMUEL**, 1694. List 98.

**Logan**, Alexander, witn. Hilton deed with Timo. Yeals Mar. 1681-2. Y. D. 7.194. One A. L. was of Charlestown.

**Loll**, Meribah (Sinclair). See Lull.

**Lombas**, Nathaniel. List 367a. See Lamos.

**LONG**, common in the so. of England, particularly in Wiltshire.
1 **CAPT. GEORGE**, in Portsm. in 1693, building a ship, doubtless the Falkland- on which passengers were embarked for England 5 Sept. 1694. Lists 60, 65, 98. Bef. he sailed Gov. Usher ordered his arrest, the

ship lying near Capt. Nathl. **Fryer's** wharf at Newc., and a free fight resulted. **George,** jr. was on board and, as G. L. of Romans Gate (Ramsgate?), Isle of Thanet, co. Kent, mariner, gave test. in regard to the events in 1703. The younger man was again at Portsm. in 1700 as 2d Lieut. on the Thanet mast-ship.

2 **CAPT. JOHN,** Portsm., depos. in 1695. List 334b.

3 **JOHN,** whose dau. **Patience,** m. Wm. Harford(1) 6 Nov. 1701 at Dover.

4 **MARY,** Newcastle, a wid., formerly Mary Lidden, prob. d. many yrs. bef. adm. on her est. was gr. to her sister Elizabeth and bro.-in-law Roger Deering of Scarboro 21 Oct. 1735. Her only heir was a dau. **Mary** who was an infant when her aunt took her and who was under guardianship of Danforth Phipps in 1735. She m. Thos. Larrabee, int. Falm. 1742. The prop. was in Kit.

5 **MICHAEL,** witn. at Great Isl. 28 Mar. 1670.

6 **RICHARD,** Salisbury, bot the Sheldon farm in Scarboro in 1693 from wid. Rebecca Sheldon, for which an Eastern claim was entered by Wm. Russell of Hampton in behalf of his w. **Sarah** and R. L.'s other ch., among whom were: **William,** b. 25 June 1682. **Richard,** b. 3 Jan. 1683-4. A Richard was of Kit. in 1717. **Eleanor,** b. 16 Jan. 1690-1, of Hampton in 1711-2.

7 **ROBERT** (Lang?), taxed in Portsm. in 1673.

8 **WILLIAM**(?6), signed bond to re-settle in Kingston, 30 Apr. 1705, which he did. Ch.

**Longfellow,** Nathan, Hampton. See Green.

**Longley,** Thomas. Lists 330a, 33. See Langley.

**Longman,** Henry. List 226. See Langmaid.

**LOOKE, John,** cordwainer, Wells, had town gr. 18 Mar. 1714 and m. bef. 6 June 1714 Bethia Larrabee(8). Born in Topsfield 25 Aug. 1690, s. of Jona. and Mary (Curtis), he was late of Wells 23 Jan. 1723-4, had 3 ch. bp. Byfield 4 Sept. 1726, but of Wells 5 Jan. 1729. List 269c. 4 ch. See 'Ancestry of Lt. Amos Towne', W. G. Davis, pp. 74-5.

**LOOM,** Looms, **John,** yeoman, Dover, was sued for a bbl. of mackerel in 1685 by John Bowman of Little Harbor. M. aft. June 1677 Mary (Canney 3), wid. of Jeremy Tibbetts. Old Wid. Looms d. 2 July 1706. List 96. See Lume.

**Lopes,** John, Richmond Isl., in acct. May 1639. List 21.

**LORD,** most frequent in Lancashire, Oxfordshire and Suffolk.

1 **ABRAHAM**(6), ±23 in Feb. 1681. W. Susanna, m. bef. 11 May 1695, when he settled a law controv. over land willed him by step-gr. fa. Conley and sold by his parents to Thos. Abbott and Jona. Nason; then deeding for a consid. to Abbott and Nason's wid. Jury and Gr. j. 1693, 1694, 1695, 1697. Constable 1695-6; highw. surv. 1698-9. Lists 30, 296, 298. Liv. 1 Feb. 1703-4; adm. to wid. Susanna, bound 5 Mar. 1705-6 with Wm. Godsoe and Nich. Gowen. She m. 2d Robt. Knight(17) and liv. on the land 1st of her husb., then of her son: **William,** d. unm., mo.'s bond as adm. 26 Nov. 1712, with Rich. Tozier and Saml. Smalley sureties. Aft. her death, his Lord uncles and aunts claimed his land. Saml. Tibbetts' depos. 1738 called him 'distracted.'

2 **DOROTHY,** wid., mar. at Dover 18 Oct. 1689 Wm. Rackliff.

3 **ELEANOR,** d. 11 Apr. 1716. (Pt. of Graves, Portsm.).

4 **FRANCIS.** List 18. See Loud.

5 **JONADAB,** York, granted 40 a. 17 Mar. 1711-2 provid. he settle and set up his trade as a clothier. List 279. M. (Ct. Apr. 1713) Martha Bragdon(3). 7 ch. 1713-1731.

6 **NATHAN** (a few times Nathaniel), Kit. 1652, when he had his 1st town grant, 60 a. at the heathy marsh, now in Eliot, and submitted to Mass. Called 87 at death, his age was exaggerated, or he was much older than his w. Martha Everett(4), m. bef. 20 June 1656, who was gr. adm. Feb. 1690-1, and was liv. 22 Feb. 1728-9; ±84 in Mar. 1723-4. Lists 24, 290, 298. In 1674 he adm. the est. of his br.-in-law Wm. Everett jr.; in 1678 the est. of his w.'s step-fa. Abraham Conley. Lists 298, 282, 283, 24, 25, 288. The wid. deeded at various times aft. his death, and 12 Mar. 1709 turned the home place and stock at Mount Misery, Berwick, over to s. Benj., with life reserva. Ch: **Nathan,** b. ±1656-7. **Abraham,** b. ±1658. **Samuel,** d. s. p. 20 Nov. 1689. See Littlefield(23). Adm. to br. Abraham, who attested invent. 1 Mar. 1689-90, Wm. Plaisted surety. **Margery,** m. (Ct. Nov. 1692) Wm. Fost(2). **Sarah,** m. John Cooper(2). **Martha,** m. 1st Moses Littlefield(19), 2d John Abbott(4), 3d Alex. Taylor. **Ann,** m. Tobias Hanson (10). **Mary,** m. Sergt. Thos. Downes(6). **Benjamin,** weaver or husbandman, Berwick. List 298. M. 10 Jan. 1709 Patience Nason (Benj.), named in his will 6 Aug. 1745—18 Feb. 1745-6 with sons, Benjamin (List 298), Samuel, Elisha and 'each and every one of my daus.' 11 or 12 ch.

7 **NATHAN**(6), Berwick, 'Elder Nathan,' ag. 25 in Feb. 1681, 29 in Mar. 1686, ±73 in Jan. 1729, m. 22 Nov. 1678 Martha Tozier (Richard and Judith). Tr. j. 1687; Gr. j. 1701; Constable 1692-3. Highway surv. 1694-5 (fences), 1696-7. Lists 288, 30, 296, 298, 38. Will 6 July—24 Sept. 1733 gives

£5 to gr. dau. Elizabeth (Chick), w. of Noah Emery, £20 to Berw. Ch. to buy plate for the communion table, a gold ring to the minister, and provides well for w. Martha and all the ch: **Martha**, b. 14 Oct. 1679, m. Richard Chick. **Nathan**, b. 13 May 1681, m. 1704 Margaret Hearl(5), who d. 22 Jan. 1772 in 89th yr.; he liv. June 1740. Lists 296, 298. Master Tate said she was the mo. of 18 liv. ch., Stackpole names 14. **William**, b. 20 Mar. 1682-3, m. (Ct. Apr. 1706) Patience Abbott(4), liv. 27 Aug. 1737. He liv., she dead, in Mar. 1756; poss. m. 2d w. Mary (List 298). 7 or m. ch., poss. incl. Elizabeth of Berwick in Ct. 1727. **\*Richard**, b. 1 Mar. 1684-5, Capt., four times Rep. to Genl. Ct., m. Mary Goodwin. Lists 296, 298. Est. adm. 1754; her will 1756-1763 names 6 of 13 ch. b. 1708-1732 and gr. dau. Olive, only ch. of decd. s. Richard. **Judith**, b. 20 Mar. 1687, m. (Ct. Jan. 1716-7) Benj. Mead, 2d Gabriel Hamilton. **Samuel**, b. 14 June 1689, m. in Berw. 19 Oct. 1710 Martha Wentworth (Paul). List 298. Will 1761, d. 11 May 1762. 6 ch., all in mo.'s will 1764—1776, with her gr. dau. Martha Marshall and br. Wm. Wentworth. **Mary**, b. 29 July 1691, m. Thos. Hodgdon(1), 2d 16 June 1720 Danl. Emery jr., s. of Danl.(6). **John**, b. 18 Jan. 1693, d. 1761, m. 26 Dec. 1716 Mary Chapman(4). List 298. 5 ch., incl. Tobias of Arundel. **Sarah**, b. 28 Mar. 1696, m. in Berw. 20 Sept. 1716 Saml. Roberts of Dover. **Anne**, b. 27 May 1697, m. Danl. Furbush (1 jr.). **Abraham**, b. 29 Oct. 1699, m. 10 Apr. 1718 Margaret Gowen(3), who d. 11 Feb. 1775. Will 11 Apr. 1772—20 Apr. 1779. List 298. 12 ch., incl. Benj. Meads L. of Arundel.

8 **NATHANIEL**, Gosport, from Ipswich, m. by 1708 Elizabeth (Weymouth), wid. of Richard Currier(3). Taxed Str. Bk. and Star Isl. witn. 1713. Will 3—31 Mar. 1725-6 names wife, her two sons and gr. son, his own four bros. and nephew.

9 **ROBERT** (Lawde), witn. ag. Redicum Wittum of Kit. 1661. P. & Ct. ii. 104.

10 **SARAH**, admitted to Berwick Ch. 1703 (Reg. 82.74).

**Loring**, John, Cape Porpus, contrib. towards erecting Davis's mill. List 259.

**Lotriell**, ————. Old L. and fam. taken 1704, Mt. Desert (Penhallow).

**Lott**, Thomas, witn. at Pemaquid or Kittery 1680. Y. D. 4.69. Servant of Jocelyn?

**LOUD**, 1 **Elias**, mariner, Great Isl., sued Nicholas Baker for his wages 1684. List 314.

2 **FRANCIS**, granted land at Arrowsic by Andros; liv. on Long Isl., Kennebec Riv., 1688; soldier there 1688-9. Lists 187, 189, 18. At Ipsw. with w. Sarah 1700. F. L., mariner, depos. in Boston in 1718 that he was at Casco Bay in Oct. 1711 when the

-Three Friends- was cast away, being then and several yrs. bef. and aft. master of the little sloop in which Thos. Stevens went down to the wreck, and contin. at Casco 12 mo. thereaft. Only kn. ch: **Francis**, b. Ipsw. 26 July 1700, liv. Weymouth.

3 **WILLIAM**, Portsm., m. 28 Feb. 1708-9 Abigail Abbott(1). List 339. 11 ch. rec. or bp. 1709-1730, incl. **Solomon**, b. 30 Sept. 1713. One early Solomon in K. P.'s War.

**LOUGEE**, 1 **Ellen** (Lougie). See Andrews (16).

2 **JOHN**, captive 1710 from Exeter, where he returned. Coleman i. 338, 374. List 376b. By trad. from Isle of Jersey. M. Mary Gilman. 8 ch.

**Louson** (Lonson, Larson), Roger, pd. (fish?) to Geo. Jaffrey on Rich. Tucker's acct., 1701.

**LOVE.** See also Lowe. Its principal English home is Kent.

1 **JAMES**, Saco witn. to Lewis—Bonython division 8 Oct. 1640.

2 **JEREMIAH**, Kit., 1675. List 287.

3 **JOHN**, Saco, sued Thos. Williams in 1640, and, by an account entered in ct. 11 Mar. 1668 Richard Williams was indebted to J. L. for £30.

4 **‡JOHN**, New Hamp. counsellor 1692. Belknap I. 124.

5 **\*WILLIAM**, Newichawannock, 1655, had Kit. grants in 1659 and 1671. Taxed in Dover 1658. York Gr. j. 1662, 1670, 1673, 1678, 1679, 1686; j. 1662-4, 1669, 1683; coroner's j. 1668; O. F. 1669; Kit. constable 1663, 1672; Selectm. 1674, 1675, 1683; deputy to General Assembly at York, 1685. Lists 356c, 25, 28, 33, 94, 298. In 1675 he was fined for travelling from Hampton to Newich. on Sunday. In ct. for trading with the Indians in 1676, but lic. to do so in 1683. In 1678 he bot a ho. on Great Isl. from Saml. Wentworth and opened a tavern, being lic. until 1679 when he sold to John Gale and Francis Tucker and returned to Kit. where he was lic. to keep a tavern until his death. Lic. to trade with Indians 1682. His w. was Mary Taylor (Anthony), who m. 2d 28 Nov. 1688 Saml. Wyllys, Esq., of Hartford, Conn., who, in 1695 aft. her death sold her Kit. prop. to her bro. John Taylor of Hampton. Will 25 Nov.—15 Dec. 1687 ment. his kinsmen Saml. Canney and Thos. Roberts, jr., his sister whose maiden name was Mary Love (b. at Tonbridge, co. Kent), his aunt Elizabeth Clubbs of Penshurst, co. Kent, and Joseph Love, gunner, of H. M. frigate -Rose-. No ch.

**LOVELL**, 1 (?John, Portsm. 1711. List 337). One J. L. a passenger on the -Three Friends- wrecked in Casco Bay, Oct. 1711.

2 **SPLANN**, Portsm., rang the bell and was grave-digger Feb. 1678-9; bot from Thos. Daniel 1686. Glazier. Gr. j. 1692, 1693; Jury of inquest 1694; Tr. j. 1695. Lists 52, 57, 60, 62, 67, 330df, 335a, 336bc. He was k. falling from Rich. Martyn's ho.; inq. 7 Nov. 1718. Adm. 20 May 1719 to Jos. Sherburne; wid. Mary L. renounc. 8 Aug. 1719, List 335a. Only kn. ch: **Mary**, b. ±1685, m. ±1706 Jos. Sherburne, Esq., to whom her fa. deeded in 1713; in Jan. 1745, widow, she made over her fa.'s ho. to s. Joseph. One Elisha -Lovell- taxed Newc. 1720; Mary, w. of Elisha -Loving- of Newc., bp. at Oyster Riv. 24 Nov. 1728.

**Loveridge**, Sydrath, fighting with Cornelius Jones at Kit. June 1688.

**LOVERING**, Loverell, peculiar to Devonshire.

1 **EBENEZER**, gr.s. of (2), Hampton, m. 26 or 27 Jan. 1712-3 Esther Dearborn (4) who m. 2d William Norton. Bot land from Benj. Shaw, jr. in 1712 and from Joseph Swett, sr., in 1713. His eldest ch. was b. at the ho. of Dea. Samuel Shaw and a local gossip, Mary Sanborn, said that the deacon was its father and found herself in court. Dea. Shaw called E. L. kinsman. Will 15 Nov. 1723—4 Mar. 1723-4 names 4 ch. (a 5th unborn): **John**, b. 31 Aug. 1715, m. 25 Oct. 1733 Anne Sanborn (Reuben). **Esther**, b. 2 Sept. 1718, m. Benjamin Marston. **Ebenezer**, b. 9 Dec. 1720, m. 19 Mar. 17-2 Mary Dearborn (Henry). **Abigail**, b. Apr. 1722, prob. m. Caleb Bennett.

2 **JOHN**, Berwick, witn. 1658, bot 50 a. at Quamphegan from Andrew Wiggin in 1663. Lists 285, 311c, 356abceghk. Gr. j. 1664. He was drowned 27 July 1668 and adm. was gr. to the wid. Hester and Capt. Waldron 29 Sept. 1668, the ch. being put under the guardianship of Mr. John Wincoll and Mr. Ezekiel Knight, whom she m. 2d. In 1675 she was dead, the ch. had been brot up by Mr. Knight and put out as apprentices. Only kn. ch: **Mary**, m. 4 Sept. 1682 William Thompson of Dover. **John**, appren. to Abraham Tilton 4 Apr. 1672 and accomp. his master to Ipswich where he m. 1st 1 Mar. 1686 Hannah Kilham, 2d 19 Mar. 1701-2 Love Parsons. He sold his fa.'s Quamphegan prop. to Thomas Abbott 21 June 1700. His ch. remained in Mass. except poss. Ebenezer.

3 **JOSEPH**, mason, taxed in Portsm. 1713, but had left town. One Joseph was rated in Exeter in 1714.

4 **SAMUEL**, Exeter, rated in 1714, surety for John Marsh 7 July 1715.

5 **WILLIAM**, Sheepscot 1672, m. Margaret Gutch(2) and had a gr. of 160 a., ±20 a. on the east side of Dyer's brook 20 Aug.

1686 under Col. Dongan. He had two sisters, Jane wife of John Pride, and prob. Sarah wife of John Place and mo. of Jane Underwood (of Boston in 1737). Y. D. 18.253. O. A., Boston 1678. Lists 13, 17, 162, 163. Samuel Williams, sr., of Roxbury was adm. of the est. of wid. Margaret Lovering (List 185) in 1690. Kn. ch: **William**, b. 26 Feb. 1676-7 in Boston, entered an East. Cl. for his fa.'s lands on behalf of himself, his brothers and sister. **Margaret**, m. William Johnson, liv. at Long Reach, Kennebec, in 1738. **Robert**, Boston, cordwainer, m. 3 Jan. 1704-5 Alice Crafts (Samuel), who m. 2d 4 July 1723 Ephraim Lyon, 3d 24 July 1729 John Greenwood of Newton, 4th 28 Sept. 1743 James Shedd of Newton, and 5th Capt. John Winchester, and d. in 1783 in her 102d yr. He conv. his fa.'s entire Sheepscot prop., no bro. or sister ment., 2 Mar. 1715-6 to Park Williams who in 1735 got a conveyance from R. L.'s ch. (Y. D. 18.62).

**LOVETT, Thomas**, w. and four ch. taken at Purpoodock 1703. List 39. Prob. from Beverly, and **Josiah** from Purpoodock in Canada 1710 his son. List 99, p. 91.

**LOW**, most common in the northern counties and the Midlands.

1 **DANIEL**, Merryland (Wells), bro., prob. younger, of Job(4). Their mo., Elizabeth (Howland), was widowed 26 Mar. 1676, when her husb., John Low of Marshfield, was killed in battle. In June 1678 she was bef. ct. for having an illegit. ch. As Job was at least 14 yrs. old on 3 Sept. 1691, carrying his birth back to or bef. Sept. 1677, it would seem that the ch. of 1678 was Daniel. He first app. in Me. as witn. to livery of seisin of the Andrews farm at Falmouth by Tobias Oakman to John Rouse of Marshfield, 29 June 1699. He m. bef. 1 Oct. 1707 (ct.) Mary Ingersoll, who m. 2d, int. 25 Apr. 1724, Andrew Lewis(2), many yrs. her junior. Wells gr. him 50 a. 22 Nov. 1699 and laid it out 23 May 1701, but, as it was not improved acc. to the conditions, it was re-granted to his bro. Job 18 Mar. 1714. He bot 60 a. on northern branch of Little River from Henry Maddox in 1721. Lists 269b, 289. K. by Ind. 11 May 1723. Only kn. ch: **Daniel**, Portsm. shipwright, sold his fa.'s Merryland farm in 1735, m. in Scarb. 26 Oct. 1735 Patience Mills.

2 **DOROTHY**, witn. deed, Bray to Pepperell, 17 Nov. 1682.

3 **JACOB**, Portsm., m. bet. 20 Oct. 1709 and 20 May 1710 an illegible bride who may have been that Sarah Low, recd. into co. 14 Aug. 1715, in which case, inasmuch as we find Wm. Lewis and Sarah Low, both of Portsm., were m. 17 Dec. 1719, it was

prob. a 1st mar. of Sarah Evans(12), who is known to have m. William Lewis(21). A widow Low was rated in 1717. Ch. of Sarah Lowe: **Jonathan,** bp. 14 Aug. 1715, m. 29 Dec. 1735 in Kit. Hannah More. **Sarah,** bp. 25 Mar. 1715-6, m. 6 Nov. 1734 Joseph Dennett.

4 **JOB,** bro. of (1), son, poss. illegit., of wid. Elizabeth (Howland) Low of Marshfield, chose Benj. Phillips his gdn. in 1691 when he was 14 or over. Settled in Wells and m. there 17 Apr. 1701 Mary Wormwood (Wm.), who was bp. on profess. of faith 23 June 1706 and adm. to ch. 22 Apr. 1722. Had a gr. of land in 1701, and in 1714 the 50 a. gr. to his bro. Daniel(1), which had lapsed, was given him by the town. List 269c. Jury 1714. Liv. in 1730 when he deeded half his homestead to his eldest s. William. Ch: **Mary,** bp. 27 July 1707, m. John Hatch(5) 29 Sept. 1723. **William,** bp. 27 July 1707, m. int. 12 Nov. 1726 Abigail Goodale. List 269c. **Elizabeth,** bp. 14 Sept. 1707, m. 1 Jan. 1727 Philip Hatch (5). **Job,** bp. 2 Apr. 1710, m. 1st 4 Sept. 1736 Elizabeth Hatch, 2d int. 5 Dec. 1741 Sarah Kimball. **John,** m. 6 Feb. 1740-1 Abigail Frost. **David,** bp. 18 Sept. 1715, m. 30 Aug. 1743 Sarah Matthews. **Tabitha,** bp. 9 Mar. 1717-8, had an illegit. ch. bef. July 1732, m. 25 Nov. 1736 Nathan Hatch. **Ephraim,** bp. 8 May 1720, m. 2 July 1741 Mary Frost. **Lydia,** bp. 13 Jan. 1722-3, m. 13 Dec. 1743 Samuel Cane.

5 **JOHN,** Portsm., ±39 in 1705, ho. carpenter, m. 16 Jan. 1701-2 Joanna Partridge, who m. 2d 8 Aug. 1716 Axwell Roberts. Selectm. 1710 to his death, 24 May 1713. Lists 324, 337. Adm. to wid. Joanna 14 June 1713, William Fellows and Samuel Hart, both from Ipsw., her bondsmen. The wid., who had owned cov. of No. Ch. in 1708, was taxed in 1713. Ch: **Sarah,** b. 1 Feb. 1701-2, m. 2 Mar. 1720-1 Samuel Tibbetts of Dover; d. bef. 1761, when he was liv. in Georgetown. **Mary,** b. 3 Apr. 1704. **John,** b. 10 Sept. 1706, Boston shipwright, d. by 1761, leaving wid. and exec. Sarah. **Joanna,** b. 6 Feb. 1708-9, m. James Springer of Falmouth, shipwright; liv. in Georgetown in 1761. **Nathaniel,** bp. 25 May 1712, Boston, mariner on H. M. ship -Norwich-; will 4 Jan. 1742-3—22 July 1746 (N. H. Prob. iii. 143). His wid. and exec. Mary Low of Boston joined his bro. John and his sisters Tibbetts and Springer in deeding the malthouse lot in Portsm. to Samuel Hart in 1754.

6 **JOSEPH,** Hampton, cooper, b. 18 May 1681 in Ipswich, son of John, m. 16 Nov. 1715 Elizabeth Pottle. He sold a ho. at Hampton Falls in 1721 and mov. to Stratham bef. 1731 when he sold other Hampton prop. His will, 16 Dec. 1738—25 July 1739 names

the ch: **Margaret,** b. 17 Sept. 1716 in Hampton. **Elizabeth. Ann. Susannah. Dorcas. Mary. Jacob,** to whom was left a com. right in Ipsw. which belonged to his gr. fa. **Joseph.**

7 **THOMAS,** Str. Bk., taxed 1713.

**LOWDEN,** 1 **Anthony,** Dover, cordwainer, wounded by Ind. July 1696, liv. to m. there 16 Sept. that yr. Elizabeth Osborne (Henry of Ipsw.). Rev. John Pike called her -Sarah-. Lists 67, 96, 336b. Portsm. 1697; sued by Pepperell 1702 on note of 19 Aug. 1701, when he was of Kit., and defaulted, poss. then at Ipsw., where liv. 1730. Ch. presum. incl.: **Jacob,** m. (int. Ipsw. 30 Dec. 1721) Mary Foster; York 1725; dau. Mary, b. there 2 May 1728, others in Ipsw. **William,** liv. Ipsw. 1725. **Elizabeth. John,** liv. Ipsw. 1729. **Sarah,** bp. Ipsw. 18 May 1718.

2 **ROBERT** (or ?Sowden) cond. gr. in York Mar. 1671-2, to build within a yr. R. L. a York abuttor 1719. Y. D. x. 17.

**Lowell,** John, soldier at Scarb. 1675. Lists 236, 237b.

**Lowrey,** ————, w. and ch. liv. near Mt. Desert. List 5. See Laurie.

**Lucar,** Robert, 1640, (Saco) dealing with Thos. Page. Lechford, p. 381.

**LUCAS,** distinguished with diff. from Lux.

1 **DR.** Elizabeth Cutt test. in 1718-9 that he had married her to Richard Gerrish.

2 **STEPHEN,** killed at Casco, 1703. List 39.

3 **WILLIAM,** confessed that he assisted Walter Gendall in alleged treasonable activities at Black Point in 1677. Lists 226, 228c. Prob. not William Lux(6).

4 **WILLIAM,** soldier under Lt. John Wyatt, taken prisoner at Saco in 1704, still in Canada in 1710-1. List 99.

**LUCKHAM,** John, planter, Kit., his field attached in suits of Hatevil Nutter and Danl. Davis(2) 19 June 1647. D. intest. ab. 8 July foll., adm. 27 June 1648 to Hatevil Nutter; est. indebted to Nich. Frost.

**Luckraft,** Walter, Portsm. 1673. Lists 327cd.

**LUCOMB** (Lucume), **William,** Portsm., his ptn. 1670 filed. Lists 326c, 331ab. W. Ann, wid. of John Hart, was in want Jan. 1674-5, and the town lent her supplies on acct. of her form. husb.'s est.; both in a sad and low condition Feb. 1678-9 when the town sent to her son and dau. in Boston to know if they would take the house and supp. them. He liv. Sept. 1679.

**LUCY,** anciently de Luci, from a parish in Normandy.

1 **BENJAMIN**(2), Portsm., m. Mary Savage (John), who owned cov. in So. Ch. in 1720 and was liv. in 1761. List 339. Will

1761. Ch: **Deborah**, bp. 20 Oct. 1723, m. 9 Apr. 1732 William Toby, but was Deborah Brown in 1761. **Alexander**, bp. with next five 22 Oct. 1727, m. 14 Oct. 1733 Hannah Sherburne (Henry) who m. 2d one Gove. He was a ship-owner and d. in Norfolk, Va., ab. 1745, leav. 3 sons, Col. Alexander of Nottingham, Benjamin and John, and a d. Hannah, w. of John Ayers of No. Hampton. **Benjamin. Esther. Mary**, m. 1st 22 Jan. 1730-1 Samuel Lear, 2d bef. 1761 one Atkins. Her son Alexander Lear was ment. in her fa.'s will. **Susanna. Lucy. John** and **Joseph**, bp. 13 Apr. 1729.

2 **THOMAS**, Portsm., called 'old goodman Luce' in 1679, m. Mary Brookings(5) who was his wid. in 1698. His ho. was in Greenland or Rye. Lists 52, 57, 335a. Sarah Lucy, member of No. Ch. aft. 1708 is prob. error for Mary. Her ch. settled her est. in 1717. Ch: **Benjamin. Mary**, m. 9 June 1709 John Shepherd of Kit. **Catherine**, m. 30 Sept. 1714 John Williams of Wandsworth, co. Surrey. **Elizabeth**, m. 2 Dec. 1714 William Chandler of Deptford, co. Kent.

**LUDECAS, David**, doctor in Boston and Hingham 1658, when he witn. Thomas Rowell's will as David Ludecus Edling; Dover 1658. Taxed as Mr. Ludeceus Edlin in 1659, when he was ạdm. inhab. Contracted to buy 150 lbs. of goose and duck feathers from Griffin Montague of Cape Porpus in 1659 and sued G. M. for debt in 1660. His land was next to Charles Buckner's. D. bef. 3 July 1660 when his wid. assigned Montague's bond to Richard Otis. List 356e. Elizabeth Ludecas, his wid., d. 16 Nov. 1663, and adm. on est. of Mrs. L. was gr. to James Middleton 28 June 1664.

**Ludgate,** ————, servant? to Squamscott patentees 1635-1661? 4 Mass. H. S. Col. 7.380.

**LUDLOW, George**, gent., recd. John Hocking's goods from Wm. Hilton 2 Aug. 1632. Y. D. i. 60. He remov. to York Co., Va.; there, merchant and Esq., dealing in 1647 with Mr. Alex. Shapleigh of Dartmouth and John Treworgye of Newfoundland. Aspinw. 205, 242.

**LUFKIN, Jacob**, m. Mercy Littlefield(15). She m. 2d in Wells 14 July 1702 Richard Stimson, and d. bef. 25 Nov. 1708 when he m. Elizabeth Cole(31). Ch. **Mary**, b. Wells 9 Oct. 1696.

**LUGG, Gilbert**, joint partn. with Weymouth Lydston in purch. of Jos. Alcock's ho. and land on Eliot Neck, Dec. 1662. D. s. p. bef. 8 July 1675 when W. L. sold his half to Chas. Nelson.

**Lukeford**, John, witn. 1637. See Hickford.

**Lull**, Meribah, dau. named in John Sinclair's will, 1700.

**Lumacks**, Nathl., List 359a. See Lammos.

**Lume?**, William, taxed Str. Bk. Jan. 1688-9. See Loom.

**Lundall**, Thomas, Dover. List 356d. See Landall.

**LUNT, 1 Daniel**, s. of Danl. of Newb., k. by Ind. at Dover 28 June 1689. List 96.

2 **SKIPPER**, bro. of Col. Joshua Wingate's w., ch. of Henry jr. of Newbury, taxed Portsm. 1707, witn. Thos. Phipps' deed 1708. Land of Phipps and Lunt in Great Ho. Field ment. 1709-12.

**Lurton** (?Hilton), Robert, witn. Littlefield deed 1682-3. Y. D. 6.142.

**Luscom**, see Liscomb.

**LUX.** A South Devon name, with Stokeinteignhead the logical parish to search in seeking to identify these emigrants.

1 **CHRISTOPHER**, ±40 in 1667, ±40 in 1669, Scarboro 1666, presented for being abs. from meeting and drunk on the Sabbath in 1667. List 317. Visiting a ship at Piscataqua in 1669 he test. that he heard David Campbell insult Mr. Robt. Elliot. Coroner's j. on his death 26 Aug. 1680.

2 **HUMPHREY**, appren. of Mr. Nicholas Brown(28) in 1648.

3 **JOHN**, fishing-master at Damariscove where he had a ho., flake-room, etc., sold to Nicholas Davison in 1664, first app. at Cape Porpus in 1662 when he m. Mary, wid. of Gregory Jeffrey, and carried her off to Damariscove to the consternation of Jeffrey's nephew, Charles Potum, who was left with her children and who acc. the couple of 'suspicion of adultery.' Lux had been named exec. of J.'s est., Jocelyn and Jordan of Scarb. being the bondsmen. Mary Lux d. in 1665-6, leav. a will naming her husb., her son John Jeffrey and her ch. Mary and Joseph Lux. In 1666 he entered suits vs. Robert Booth and Charles Potum. Lists 3, 234a. He failed to enter his writ vs. Sarah Turbat in 1672. Sent in 1676 from Boston, his headq. aft. the beginning of Philip's War, to recover the goods of the inhab. of Black Point, he begged Capt. Scottow to allow him to take soldiers to rescue the men fighting a losing battle on Saco sands. O. A. in Boston 1678. Sued successfully by Henry Ellis for detaining goods in 1679. Sued Henry Maire in 1680. Capt. John Lux bur. in Boston 13 Nov. 1714. Ch., the eldest by an early w: **John**, Boston. Had w. Agnes 1667-1671, but left at his death (John Lux, jr.) in 1677 a wid. Sarah to whom adm. was gr. 31 July 1677 and who m. William Dinsdale; bef. 1678-9 when she was ordered to pay one-half of Lux's est. to her fa.-in-law John Lux, sr. for the benefit of his ch. (doubtless her step-ch.) **Mary**, b. bef. 1665-6. A Mary Luex was cr. of Wm.

Button at the Shoals in 1687. List 307b.
**Joseph,** b. bef. 1665-6.
4 **NICHOLAS,** assisting the marshall, Robert Mendum, at Kit., 8 Mar. 1653-4. Depos. in Walton vs. Jones, 1660.
5 **THOMAS** (Luckes), witn. at Isles of Shoals, 1703. List 306c.
6 **WILLIAM** (Lukes) came over to Richmond Isl. with Stephen Sargent 10 May 1638 and fished for Winter for over 2 yrs., part of his wage going to his dame and his sister in Eng. Cr. of Jonas Baley Mar. 1642-3. Most prob. the W. L. who m. Audrey Mussell (Robert), who was 67 in 1686, and settled at Great Isl., where he took O. A. 2 July 1657 and was constable and juror the same yr. Her fa. deeded his ho. to Audrey Lux 10 Aug. 1667, and in 1668 Lux succeeded Mussell as water-bailiff. Gr. j. 1670, 1677, and again constable 1674. Lists 49, 311c, 312cfh, 313ac, 323, 326a, 330ab, 331b. Adm. to wid. Audrey·17 June 1684, James Robinson on her bond. The wid. aged 67, (List 52) was lic. to entertain on Great Isl. in 1686. Her will, 9 June 1688—1 Feb. 1691-2, ment. her land near the falls at Braveboat Harbor (Kit.). Ch: **Elizabeth,** 70 in 1710, m. Andrew Cranch (1) bef. 14 Mar. 1677-8. **Abishag,** had been engaged to Tobias Burnell(2) who d. 1674; m. 1st William Palmer aft. 14 Mar. 1677-8, 2d Thomas Marshall 4 Feb. 1686-7.
**LUXTON** (Luxon), **Capt. George,** fishing at the Shoals 1635, as he had done many yrs. (Winthrop). Shipmaster from Barnstable and Bideford, co. Devon, at Richmond Isl. 1639-40. List 41.
**Luyst,** William, Mr., taxed Portsm. 1672, there 1679.

**LYDE,** Lloyd. A long line of minor gentry named Lyde, an Allen among them, is bur. in the chancel of the church at Berry Pomeroy, co. Devon. An Allen Lyde, gentleman, had ch. bp. in the neighboring par. of Stoke Gabriel 1621-4, and Allen, s. of Edward and Rebecca Lyde, was bp. there 1 Nov. 1635.
1 **ALLEN,** Portsm., sailor, m. 3 Dec. 1661 Sarah Fernald(2) and had a ho. on her island (Doctor's, later Waterhouse's, now Pierce's). Adm. 25 June 1672 to wid. who m. 2d Richard Waterhouse. Only ch: **Allen,** b. 29 July 1666.
2 **ALLEN**(1), Portsm., mariner, m. Eleanor, d. of Gertrude Toogood, w. of Edward Toogood of Boston, by a former husb., poss. Francis Mercer. Taxed at Str. Bk. 1691. List 335a. Adm. 7 Feb. 1701-2 to Edward and Gertrude Toogood, who, as gr. fa.-in-law and their own gr. mo., were app. gdns. 16 Feb. 1701-2 of the ch: **Allen,** b. 15 Nov. 1691, d. bef. 13 Feb. 1719-20, s. p. **Frances,**

b. 28 Sept. 1695, m. Nathaniel Mendum. She sued the Waterhouses for a sh. in the Pulpit Point land of her gr. mo. Sarah (Fernald) (Lyde) Waterhouse in 1719-20.
3 **EDWARD,** prob. related to (1), Portsm., m. in Boston 4 Dec. 1660 Mary Wheelwright (Rev. John) who m. 2d Hon. Theodore Atkinson, ante-nup. agreement 21 Oct. 1667. Lists 330a, 311a. Sued by John Amazeen 8 Nov. 1662, and by Joshua Scottow in 1663, but the latter action could not proceed, the def. being dead. Adm. 30 June 1663 to Edward Rishworth, Samuel Maverick and Richard Stileman, confirmed 27 June 1665 to the last, the first being neglectful and the second dead.· Only ch: **Edward,** Boston, given lands in co. Lincoln by his gr. fa. Wheelwright's will, appren. to Col. Samuel Shrimpton in 1681. O. A. at Str. Bk. 28 Aug. 1685. M. 1st in Salem 29 Nov. 1694 Susanna Curwen, 2d, in Boston int. 24 Sept. 1696 Deborah Byfield who d. 31 Aug. 1708, 3d in Boston, 6 June 1709 Mrs. Katherine (Page) Brinley. Will 29 June 1722—12 Jan. 1722-3. 5 ch.
4 **CAPT. JOHN,** in command at Saco River, c. 1689. List 19.
**LYDIARD,** Nicholas, Newcastle witn. 1714, m. in Salem 6 Jan. 1715 Mary Elkins (12). Ch: **Mary,** bp. Salem 20 Oct. 1717. **Nicholas,** b. 11 Apr. 1720, and **Sarah,** b. 16 Apr. 1722, both at Wells, where he was invited as school-teacher 1717. Of Boston Jan. 1724-5, she a wid. there 1737.

**LYDSTON.** One John Lydstone of Dartmouth (St. Petherick), co. Devon, m. Elizabeth Worthley 30 Sept. 1610.
1 **JOHN**(2), b. ±1673, ±59 in 1732, Capt. John ag. 74 in 1747, -87- in 1750. Shipwright, worked for Gabriel Tetherly ab. 1687. Wounded by Ind. 1693, the Genl. Ct. in 1744 consid. gr. him 300 a., confirmed 1751 and laid out in Lebanon. Jury 1705, 1706, 1726. Lists 279, 291, 296, 297, 298. M. bef. 30 Aug. 1693 Mary (Roby), wid. of Wm. Tetherly; she retailed without lic. 1698-9, lic. Oct. 1699 and later. M. 2d in Newington 2 Jan. 1724 Susanna, wid. of Jos. Hill(10). Feb. 24, 1752 he deeded to gr. sons Roby L. and John Deering, his dau. 'Barshaby' to be supp. in old age, ment. gr. sons Danl. and Weyman L., to whom he had deeded 1748. D. bef. 1761. Ch: **Martha,** b. 1 Apr. 1695, poss. m. in Portsm. 29 Nov. 1716 Jonathan Keene(2), surely m. bef. 1726 Roger Deering(9). **John,** b. 25 Apr. 1697, m. 5 Apr. 1722 Abigail Paul (Danl.). Ch. prob. incl. Daniel and Weymouth, shipwrights 1748, both liv. 1766. **Bathsheba.** In Apr. 1724 she acc. Danl. Paul jr. as fa. of her bast. ch. b. 24 Dec. 1723. Liv. 1752, not named in suit brot by

fa.'s heirs in 1766 ag. Mary Littlefield.
**Gideon,** bp. 1721, he and his w. members of
Eliot Ch.; liv. 1728. He or an unkn. son was
fa. of Roby L., liv. 1752, decd. in 1761, leav.
wid. Sarah and 2 ch., Jos. Staples their gdn.
2 **WEYMOUTH,** Kittery, fisherman, joint
partn. with Gilbert Lugg 1 Dec. 1662 in
purch. of Jos. Alcock's ho. and land adj.
Goodm. Simmons and Goodm. Paul. In July
1675 he sold Lugg's half to Chas. Nelson.
In counter suits with Peter Staples, 1675,
for slander, each plaint. won. Fined at the
Shoals 1680, Kit. gr. 1681, taxed Falmouth
1683-4. Lists 90, 226, 298. D. 9 Mar. 1695-
6. His w. was a witn. ag. Geo. Jones jr. and
Widow Webster at Portsm. in 1670. She
was Martha in 1675; wid. Martha attested
inv. 7 Apr. 1696. Ch: Weymouth, ment.
1704. **John. Dau.** m. John Ham, likely older than or poss. same as **Sarah,** acc. with
Joshua Remick in July 1694; her ch. liv.
1695 when J. R. ord. to pay quarterly at her
fa.'s ho. 2s. 6d. a wk. for 7 yrs. from ch.'s
birth. She and John Tomson were named
together, same Ct. In Jan. 1698-9 Sarah L.
and Abigail Puddington at Elizabeth Redford's ho. saw John Woodman kick Thos.
Rice.

**LYFORD,** a chapelry in Berkshire, to
which co. the name is peculiar.
1 **FRANCIS,** mariner, Boston witn. 1667,
m. 1st ab. 1670 Elizabeth, dau. of Thomas
Smith, Boston shipwright, who deeded him
prop. in 1671. John Chandler mortgaged a
ho. and land in Roxbury to him in 1670.
Moved to Exeter, where he m. 2d 21 Nov.
1681 Rebecca Dudley(1), who surv. him.
Lists 52, 55b, 57, 67, 333b, 376b, 377. Had
deed for 60 a. kn. as Samuel Dudley's great
pasture in 1683, and a gr. of 200 a. in 1698.
Selectm. 1689, 1690; Gr. j. 1686, 1695, 1697;
Constable 1709, but excused because of infirmities. He served in Capt. Hall's co. 6
Feb.—5 Mar. 1696. Owner of sloop -Eliza-
beth- of Ex., 1692. Will 17 Dec. 1722-3—2
Sept. 1724. Ch., the first 3 by 1st w.: Thomas, b. 25 Mar. 1672 in Boston. Elizabeth,
b. 19 July 1673, spinster of Boston, lame
and infirm in 1714 when her bro. Thomas
q. c. to her the prop. of their gr. fa. Smith.
**Francis,** b. 31 May 1677 in Boston, not in
will. **Stephen,** b. ab. 1687. **Ann,** m. Timothy
Leavitt(8). **Deborah,** m. Benjamin Follett
(6). **Rebecca,** m. Theophilus Hardy(9).
**Sarah,** m. John Folsom(7). **Mary,** m. Joseph
Hall(12).
2 **STEPHEN**(1), Exeter, yeoman, 82 in
1769, m. Sarah Leavitt(8) who d. 13 Oct
1781. Selectm. 1734. D. 20 Dec. 1774. Will
23 Mar. 1773—13 Jan. 1775, the inventory
incl. negro woman and girl. Ch: **Biley,**
gent., exec. of his fa.'s est., m. 25 Aug. 1743

Judith Wilson, d. 10 Feb. 1792 in Brentwood. Will. 10 ch. **Stephen,** b. 12 Apr.
1723 in Newmarket, m. 20 Dec. 1753 Mercy
Pike, d. 14 Mar. 1805. 8 ch. **Moses,** Brentwood, tailor, m. 22 Sept. 1748 Mehitable
Smith (Oliver). Her will 15 July 1803—4
Dec. 1806. D. 13 Apr. 1799. 10 ch. **Samuel,** d. 8 Feb. 1778, unm. **Francis,** named in
will of his gr. fa. Leavitt. **Theophilus,**
Exeter, m. Lois James (Kinsley) who m. 2d
int. 19 July 1799, Gideon Colcord. D. 31
Jan. 1796. Will 19 June 1784—29 Feb. 1796.
7 ch. **Elizabeth,** m. Joshua Wiggin of
Stratham.
3 **THOMAS**(1), Exeter, mariner and husbandman, m. Judith Gilman bef. 1701
when she was 'daughter Lyford' in her
fa.'s will. List 376b. Will 29 Dec. 1726—
7 June 1727 gives ch: **Thomas,** Exeter, exec.
of his fa.'s est., m. 1st 5 Dec. 1728 Ann
Conner (Jeremiah), 2d bef. 12 Oct. 1778
wid. Mary James, innholder of Ex. Adm.
18 Mar. 1788. 4 ch. **John,** Epping, housewright, m. Lydia Folsom (Wm.), d. in Canterbury bet. 1788 and 1795. 9 ch. **David,**
Epping, perh. m. Abigail Dudley (Stephen).
liv. 17 May 1763 when he deeded to s.
Thomas (b. 1738). **Elizabeth,** m. Joseph
Sinclair ab. 1720. **Judith,** m. one Folsom,
perh. Benjamin(7). **Dorothy,** m. 26 Dec.
1720 Thomas Burleigh (James). **Mary,** m.
one Leavitt. **Abigail,** m. 14 Feb. 1722-3
John Kimball, d. 12 Feb. 1737-8. **Rebecca.
Susanna. Lydia. Hannah.**
**LYNCH,** 1 Eugene, Kit. witn. 1717 (Y. D.
8.204); sued by Pepperell Feb. 1717-8.
One Eugene m. in Beverly (int. 17 Oct.
1714) Martha Elliott; d. bef. May 1729. 4
ch. rec. She d. in Bev. 1740, poss. the M. L.
called by John Pearce gr. gr. dau. of Wm.
Cox of Pemaquid. Y. D. 17.131.
2 **JOHN,** Portsm. witn. 1698.
**LYNDE,** Simon, Mr., Boston merchant, with
many interests along the Me. coast, brot
suits ag. John Diamond and Dr. Francis
Morgan for debt in Sept. 1671. List 4. In
Feb. 1688-9 a voluntary div. of real est. was
made among his ch., mostly in Boston, giving **Samuel,** who witn. at Portsm. Sept.
1671 the Lockwoods' deed to his fa. (Y. D.
2.108), 1600 a. bot of Ashley on Kennebec
River; **Nathaniel,** 300 a. at Pennacook; dau.
**Elizabeth** Pordage, 3 parc. of land bet. Cape
Porpus and -Kenebeck-; dau. **Hannah** Bigg
of Hampton, ho. and land mtg. by Redman,
stage at Star Isl., 1/3 of Elizabeth Isl., ½
of Balston farm at Cape Porp., 30 a. at Kit.
bot of Lockwood. Hannah Bigg m. as her
3d husb. ab. 1697 Col. Edmund Goffe of
Cambridge.
**Lyndly,** Thomas, from Stoke Newington, co.
Middlesex, m. in Portsm. 17 Mar. 1722-3
Sarah Whidden.

**LYNN.** Lin is an early word for pool, Lynn a town in Norfolk and the name is peculiar to Lincolnshire.

1 **EPHRAIM**(2), Kit., m. bef. 1667 Anne Lockwood(2), a difficult woman who was in court for abusing her sis.-in-law and (step?) mother Lockwood in 1667. She fled the juris. in 1671 to avoid punish., her fa. going bond to produce her at York next training-day, and in 1673 she was again in ct. for lying and abusing Dr. Morgan. The entire fam. group, Capt. Lockwood, Dr. Morgan, E. L. and their wives were put under bonds to keep the peace in 1667. Richard Bickham was either his or his w.'s uncle. Lists 52, 82, 329, 331b. Sued by Nath. Reynolds for debt in 1660; sued Capt. Champernowne, John Diamond, sr., and Mr. Withers on a bill in 1665; fined for quarrelling with Dr. Morgan in 1665; sued Mr. Withers, Robt. Mendum and John Bray in 1667, and fined for not assisting the constable and opprobrious speeches in same yr.; under bond for good behavior toward Roger Kelly in 1672. Last ment. in Portsm. in 1680. No. kn. ch.

2 **HENRY**, very early in Boston, where he was whipped and set in the stocks for felony in 1630 and whipped and banished for writing letters 'full of slander against the government and churches' in 1631. Back in Boston in 1632 and fined for abs. from training. He settled in York by 1640 but prior to 1645 went as merchant, taking most of his property, to Virginia where he happened to die, leav. w. and 4 ch. in want. The Me. Ct. ordered his 5218 lbs. of tobacco and his ho. at Agamenticus sold for benefit of creditors. Lists 22, 272. The wid., who was b. Sarah Tilly (William) of Boston, was tenant of an old ho. at the mouth of the river (Kit.) belonging to Mr. Shapleigh in 1645, and m. 2d in Boston May 23, 1647, Hugh Gunnison, 3d ab. 1660 Capt. John Mitchell of Isles of Shoals, and 4th bef. 1665 Dr. Francis Morgan. Ch. b. in Boston: **Sarah**, b. 20: 6: 1636, m. bef. 14 Mar. 1658-9, William Rogers. **Elizabeth**, b. 27: 1: 1638, m. 1st William Sealey, 2d Thomas Cowell(7). Her step-fa. Gunnison was in ct. in 1653 for allowing her to stay away from meeting a whole month. **Ephraim**, b. 16: 11: 1639. **Rebecca**, b. 15: 12: 1645, but when all 4 ch. were bp. in Boston 23: 3: 1647 she was stated to be aged 5y. 3mo.

**LYON**, a Lancashire name.

1 **JAMES**, Pemaquid, soldier 1696. List 127.

2 **WILLIAM**, sr., of Roxbury, called of Rowley when he m. his 2d w. Martha (Philbrick), wid. of John Cass(2). His gr. s. Thomas (**Thomas**) m. 1 Nov. 1693 Ann -Case-, likely his step-gr.mo.'s dau. who d. in a yr. with her inf. Ano. gr. s. Ebenezer (**Samuel**) m. in Dedham 15 July 1700 Elizabeth Turbet of the Me. fam. and had 5 ch. rec. 1713-1723; prob. others earlier. Ebenezer's br. Samuel m. 24 Nov. 1742 as 2d w. her kinswo. Mary (Batson 1) (Prentice) Robbins. Ano. br. Henry, b. Roxb. 19 Nov. 1682, app. was Lt. Henry of York who m. at Portsm. ab. 3 Nov. 1709 Elizabeth (Ayers 1), wid. of Caleb Griffith(1). Called Capt. 1710 when selling without lic. Of York, 2 July 1711, he gave p/a to wife; of Roxb., 21 Nov. 1711, sold Thos. More's home-lot and other York lots; sued Benoni Boynton in Me. Ct. Apr. 1712. Mrs. L.'s tax abated Portsm. 1714. She m. 3d 23 Feb. 1720-1 Moses Ingraham(2). No ch. kn. and none repres. with Ayers heirs 1758.

**MACE**, chief homes Oxfordshire and Gloucestershire, but the name is found in Devon.

1 **ABRAM**, Kittery, List 289. A Mass. soldier or error for (2)?

2 **ANDREW**(5?), Isles of Shoals, bot Star Isl. ho. from (4) in 1713. Taxed at Newc. 1726, 1729. He was an orig. member of Gosport Ch. in 1729, and Johannah Mace, ano. orig. mem., was poss. his w. Lack of records makes difficult the identif. of his ch: Prob. **Andrew**, b. ±1709, m. 29 Nov. 1733 Deborah Moulton, both adm. to Gosport Ch. in 1734 and dism. to Hampton 3 July 1743; he d. 23 Jan. 1790. 7 ch. Prob. **Robert**, m. ab. 1737 Elizabeth Harford, inn-keeper in Dover in 1747, d. s. p.; wid. Betty's will, 1758, names Harford relations. Poss: **Agnes**, adm. to Ch. 1732-3, m. 27 Dec. 1733 John Volpy. **Mary**, bp. 1 July 1716. One Mary m. 24 Jan. 1731-2 William Robinson. Ano. Mary m. 10 May 1742 John Sanderson. **Joseph**, bp. 1 June 1718. **Joseph**, bp. 1 July 1722. **Richard**, bp. 10 May 1726.

3 **PETER** (Mase), lic. to retail (Me.) 1695. Macy or Massey?

4 **REUBEN**(5?), Newcastle, innholder, deeded ho. on Star Isl. to Andrew(2) in 1713 and bot in Newc. from Geo. Vaughan. He mtg. this land 6 Nov. 1713 to Jane Pepperell for ½ the sloop -Mary-, and 16 Jan. 1713-4 mtg. it and his int. in the sloop to Theodore Atkinson. R. M. and sons taxed 1730. By w. Margaret O'Shaw(1) he had: **Reuben**, Kittery, fisherman, m. 10 Nov. 1726 Mary Jenkins. Bot Kit. land from Pepperell in 1730. 7 ch. (Mary, Margaret, Anne, Reuben, Andrew, Eliphalet, Philadelphia) in Kit. 1728-1740. **Mary**, m. Bryant Davis. **Andrew**, Kittery, laborer, adm. of est. of gr.fa. O'-Shaw in 1763 and in 1764, with sis., surv. ch. of their fa. By w. unkn. had Levi, bp. in Kit. 1728.

**5 ROBERT,** Isles of Shoals, ±22 in 1674, ±24 in 1676 when he test. ag. Roger Kelly and Hugh Allard. In 1681 in Smuttynose ct. he compl. that Mr. and Mrs. Kelly had abused him. Prob. a widower when he m. ab. 1690 wid. Hannah (Gibbins 2) Hibbert. Owned pew in Ipswich meeting-ho. in 1700. He d. bef. 1720 when she conv. to her 6 ch. her share in the Saco patent. She was of Star Isl. in 1729 and was adm. to Gosport Ch. in 1733. Prob. ch. by a prob. 1st w: **Reuben. Andrew.** By w. Hannah: **Joseph,** m. Mary Salter (John) of Newcastle bef. 1726; adm. 1752 to Henry Carter. **Mrs.** Mary Mace, ag. 85, whose d. is rec. in So. Ch., Portsm., in 1789, was prob. his wid. **John,** m. Sarah Frost (Ithamar) who m. 2d 17 Mar. 1736-7 Arthur Randall. Taxed in Rye 1724. **Elizabeth,** m. at Ipsw. 8 Oct. 1720 Charles Miller. **Gibbins,** Gosport, had ch. by w. Judith bp. from 1732; m. 2d 1737 Elizabeth Emmons. Both he and his w. ended their days in Portsm. almsho.

**Maccham,** John, Scarboro, drunk and fighting with Duncan Chisholm(2) in 1657. See McKenney.

**Machin,** John, Exeter, depos. 17 May 1681 (Col. Papers 46: 141).

**MACKANEER** (McNair?). 1 **Alexander,** York, 1662, one of the prisoners of the battle of Dunbar, m. Dorothy Pearce(9) who m. 2d Micum McIntire(1) by 1671. List 25. He and w. absent from Ch. 5 weeks in 1666; the ct. excused him because of his lameness and weakness. Alexander Maxwell struck and abused him, 1666-7. Town gr. of 15 a. at Bass Cove, 1667, and 40 a. for firewood 1668-9. Inv. 1 Dec. 1670. No. ch.
2 **MATTHEW.** List 67.
**Mackerel,** John, Scarboro, 1680. List 30. See McKenney.

**MACKWORTH.** The Mackworths of Mackworth, co. Derby, sent a branch into Shropshire in the 15th century. There they were lords of the manor of Meole Brace, now a suburb of Shrewsbury. Arthur Mackworth, s. of Thomas, of Day House in the village of -Newton-, par. of Meole Brace, was appren. in the Drapers Co. of Shrewsbury in 1612. Born ±1598, he was a 2d cous. of Mr. Thos. Lewis(19) of Shrewsbury and Saco, and I (W. G. D.) believe him to be identical with **ARTHUR,** gentleman, who received a gr. from Sir F. Gorges for 500 a. 'for many years in his poss.' at the mouth of the Presumpscot river on Casco Bay, known as Menickoe 'but hereafter to be known as -Newton-,' together with a small island (still kn. as Mackworth's Isl.), on 30 Mar. 1635. He prob. came over in 1630 with Vines or in 1631 with Lewis and had an early unrec. gr. from Vines at Saco. He m. Jane

Andrews, wid. of (16). An outstanding member of the Gorges party, he acted for Sir Ferdinando in giving poss. to Cleeve, was magistrate in 1645 and often employed as arbitrator (Bonython v. Gibson, Cammock v. Winter, both 1640; Cleeve v. Winter, 1641). Gr.j. and j. 1640. Lists 21, 22, 23, 221. Alive 17 May 1657, he d. bef. 28 Mar. 1658, when his wid. gave a deed. His nunc. will was test. to by Rev. Robt. Jordan 17 Aug. 1660, all the prop. to go to his w. to distrib. equally among her ch., those whom she had had by her 1st husb. Andrews to have the advantage, if any. Mrs. Mackworth (Lists 221(2), 222b) obviously an intelligent and just woman, made various gr. to the ch. and in her will, 20 May, inv. 25 May 1676, gave all her lands and houses at Casco Bay to her sons-in-law Abraham Adams and Wm. Rogers, execs., her clothes to her four daus., small articles to daus. Rebecca Rogers, Sarah Adams, and (Elizabeth) Purchase. A codicil prov. that the ch. Rebecca Rogers had by Nathaniel Wharfe and that Sarah had by her now husband were to inherit as heirs. 'John' M., wit. with Francis Neale in 1660 (Y.D.12.191) is prob. error for Jane. Ch: **Rebecca,** m. 1st Nathaniel Wharfe bef. 1666, m. 2d William Rogers(16) after 1673. **Sarah,** m. bef. 1665 Abraham Adams(2). **Arthur,** wit. his mo.'s deed in 1658-9 and d. s. p. bef. her.
**Macnerener,** Matthew. List 67. See Mackaneer, Maranack.

**MACREASE,** Macress, Makrest.
1 **BENJAMIN,** b. Salisb. 16 Nov. 1685, s. of Benoni and Lydia (Fifield 3), m. Sarah Weeks (Leonard), who was adm. to Greenland Ch. in 1712 (List 338b), he in 1716 (Lists 338ab); both liv. 1748. Ch. bp. Greenl. 1712-1720: **Joshua. Mary.**
2 **JOSEPH,** br. of (1), b. 28 Aug. 1683, m. 1st in Hampton 12 Feb. 1708 Sarah Dole, m. 2d in Salisb. 27 Aug. 1733 Mary (Green 9) Longfellow; both liv. in Salisb. 1738. Ch. rec. Salisb. 1710-1712: **Mary** and **Lydia.** Prob. others. See also Cass(3).
**Macy,** Thomas, wit. Geo. Walton to John Heard in June 1656. See also Gorrell(1), Mace(3).
**Maddis,** Thomas, Scarboro, soldier 1676. List 237b.

**MADDIVER,** Maddaford, a name highly localized on the Devon-Cornwall border.
1 **JOEL**(2), Purpooduck, yeoman, signed a Scarboro pet. in 1663, pet. to Andros 1688, pet. to Bradstreet 1689. Walter Gendall took poss. of his ho. and lands for him from Walter Mare in 1671. Lists 34, 223b, 225a, 227, 228c, 39 (Joseph, in error). He took his fam. to Boston in Philip's War, and in the next Ind. crisis to Beverly, from where

in 1697-8 he sold the Purpooduck Pt. 100 a. to Wm. Jameson of Charlestown. Returning too soon he was k. in the Purpooduck massacre 10 Aug. 1703 and his w. Rebecca (m. bef. 1673) taken captive. Ch: Joel, signed pet. in 1689 which his fa. signed as Sr. Poss., with other ch. an Ind. victim. **Judith**, m. Samuel Ingersoll(2). **Mercy**, b. 12 Aug. 1677 in Boston. And poss. **Martha** (Matafor), m. at Chebacco 24 Mar. 1699 Samuel Parish.

2 **MICHAEL**, Spurwink, one of Winter's most trust-worthy fishermen, sent £4 to Eng. in 1642 and £5 in 1643, and poss. went home to bring back his 1st w., Judith, bef. 1657-8 when Jordan deeded him 150 a. on west side of Spurw. river to pay for his unrewarded services to Mr. Winter. Sub. to Mass. 1658, Scarboro constable 1660, abs. from church 1660, 1668 (twice). Lists 21, 232, 239c. Legal difficulties over bounds bet. his farm and Ambrose Boaden jr.'s, 1660-1664. He gave the farm to his s. Joel, but on 8 May 1669 he exchanged it for Capt. Gendall's 100 a. farm at Purpooduck Point and deeded this to Joel, 'my heir to the premises.' His 2d w. was Agnes Carter, wid. of Richard(11), on whose No. Yarmouth farm he ended his days. She was app. adm. 27 Aug. 1670, Tho. Stanford and Ralph Turner bondsmen, Stanford and John Wallis appraisers, the Carter cattle and his being kept separate in their return. The ct. ord. the est. of 'his father Maddiver' turned over to Walter Mare who settled it in 1671. Wid. Agnes dep. at York in 1682, ag. 82. Ch. by 1st w: **Joel**. A dau. m. Walter Mare.

**MADDOCKS**, Mattocks, Maddox.

1 **MR.** (Maddex), appar. a ship-master. List 71.

2 **CALEB**, Berwick 1724, where were Lydia and Thomas in 1727. Henry, Wells tailor 1719, sued by Edw. Emery of Newb. in Essex ct. 1721. List 269a. See also Low(1), John Wells.

3 **SAMUEL** (Mattocks), wit. with No. Yarmouth men 1679. Y. D. 3: 53, 54.

4 **THOMAS**, named in Eastern accounts 1681; Mass. Arch. 100: 300.

Madril. See Metherill.

**MAGOON.** See also the Scotch McGowen.

1 **ALEXANDER**(2), Exeter. Gr.j. 1693. One A. M. with Ex. scouting party in 1710 may have been he or a son. Lists 52, 62, 67, 376b (1698, 1725). See also Lisson(2). He m. 1st 7 Dec. 1682 Sarah Blake(1) who was liv. 12 Aug. 1701; m. 2d Ann (French), wid. of Tho. Mudgett. Adm. 21 Sept. 1731 to s. Samuel, wid. Anna renouncing. Kn. ch: **Samuel**, ag. 55 in 1746, Ex. scout 1712 and given land by fa. in 1716. List 376b (1725). Adm.

to s. Samuel 24 May 1753, wid. Abigail renounc. 8 surv. ch. The widow's dower was divided 26 May 1779. **Benjamin**, had land from fa. in 1721 and a gr. 1725 (List 376b). He m. Dinah Gordon (Tho.), she liv. 1757. **John**, Kingston, d. from a fever 14 July 1730, adm. to br. Benj. 15 June 1731; but poss. he was s. of (3) and it was his w. Sarah (b. Magoon and m. at Hampt. Falls 5 Dec. 1723), who was ch. of (1). Two sons bp. in Kingston 1727; also a bastard ch. of Magoon's (poss. not his), taken by Josiah Bachelder, was bp. Hannah 1733. Two Sarahs were adm. to Kingston Ch. in 1728; one m. John Kenniston there the night betw. Feb. 26-27, 1734-5. **Daughter**, m. John Roberts(1½).

2 **HENRY**, Exeter, a Scot, had a Dover gr. in 1656, taxed there 1657-8. In Oct. 1661 he bot from Thos. King the land in Ex. on which his ho. already stood, and the same day had land from his fa.-in-law with remainder to his s. John, then to his 2d son. He d. betw. 25 Aug. 1684-1701. Lists 356abc, 376b(1664), 380, 381, 383, 52, (¶94). His 1st w. Elizabeth (Lisson 2), d. 14 June 1675 and he appar. m. 2d betw. 1 Aug. 1677—19 Nov. 1681 Agnes, wid. of John Kenniston(5). Ch. rec. Exeter: **John**, b. 21 Oct. 1658. **Alexander**, b. 6 Sept. 1661. **Mary**, b. 9 Aug. 1666, m. Jonathan Clark(26). **Elizabeth**, b. 29 Sept. 1670.

3 **JOHN**(2), wit. in 1678 about a hog stolen in Greenland and sold in Portsm. Hampton 1695, that town being held responsible for him ag. Exeter in 1697 when he was liable to be a charge (his ptn., House Journals 1697-8). Exeter 1702, presum. the John to whom (1) sold land in 1707 and the same k. by Ind. at Ex. shortly bef. 2 Aug. 1708. Lists 68, 399b. Wife Martha Ash (John) in 1702. Ch. uncert., incl. appar: **Mary**, servant of John French(?), bp. at Hampt. Falls 6 Sept. 1713. **Dau.** of J. M. d. at Hampt. in June 1715 (poss. Mary). Appar. **Sarah** m. John Magoon, but see John(1). Cert. **Bethia**, Kingston 1729.

Magrady. See O'Grado.

Mahon, Denis (aut.), wit. bond of Joseph Trickey of Dover in June 1685; O. A. at Str. Bank (Mohon) 28 Aug. 1685.

**MAHONEY.** 1 **Daniel**, Dermond, Teague; see Me. P. & Ct. i: 159; Matthews(3). Teague, Boston, adm. of est. of Matthew Collane of the Shoals, 1651.

2 **ROBERT** (Meehony) and w. Rebecca had ch. rec. in Wells: **John**, b. 7 Dec. 1693. **Hannah**, b. 15 July 1695.

**MAINS**, Main, Mayne, found in several Devonshire parishes; Guppy names only co. Northampton.

1 **DANIEL**, named in Elliot-Hinckes account 1684. List 90.

**2 HENRY**, Shoals, fisherman, sued Stephen Ford 9 July 1667. Partn. with Andrew Diamond in purch. of a Smuttynose fishing plant from John Diamond in 1668, and the two took over Wm. Roe's Ipsw. ho. in 1673 (see Waters' Ipswich, p. 405-6); he alone bot the Lynes plant at Star Isl. 1675. 'Senior' 1683. Lists 95, 305c, 306c, 307ab. See also (8), Broad(4), and Tho. Symonds, whose friend, neighbor and legatee he was. Wife unkn. He was drowned 1687 (List 307a); adm. in Suff. Ct. 3 Aug. 1687 to only kn. ch: **Henry**, a Shoals fisherman; List 95. Poss. this son m. Joanna Rhodes 4 Nov. 1681 in Marblehead, where were many later Mains; or poss. he was the Boston man in poss. of personal effects of John Westbrook, late of Greenwich, co. Kent, 1692. One H. M. d. in Glouc. 3 Dec. 1724, ag. above 50. See also Lewis(4).

**3 JOHN** (Mayne), No. Yarmouth, b. ±1614-5. See Atwell(3). His home there was on 60 a. on Mayne's Point, w. side of Wescustogo River, bot from Richard Carter 'near ±30 yrs. agone' (depo. 1682). In Jan. 1684-5, ±70, he told that he had kn. the Point at least 36 yrs.; his w. Elizabeth said 35 yrs. J. of life and death, 1666. York 1676 (see Jackson 7); O. A. Mar. 1679-80; York gr. 1685, laid out in 1700 to s.-in-law Carlisle. Pres. Danforth confirmed the No. Yarm. land to J. M. of York in 1684, and from Casco Bay he ptn. Andros in 1687, stating that new-comers were laying out lots there. His w. Elizabeth was liv. Jan. 1684-5, ±61; she appar. at York 14 Apr. 1693. Lists 211, 214, 33, 93. Kn. ch: **Thomas. Sarah**, m. John Batten(4). **Daughter**, m. John Atwell(3); her s. John sold 1/10 of his gr.fa.'s land (Y. D. 13: 92). **Lydia**, b. ±1657, m. Moses Felt(5). **Hannah**, accus. Arthur Bragdon(2) in 1678, her sureties John Smyth, sr. and jr.; see Bragdon(4). She was of York 1679, unm. **Rachel**, ±57 in 1727, ±84 in 1748, m. 1st Stephen Preble(8), m. 2d Joseph Carlisle(1). **Priscilla**, m. 1st Nathaniel Preble(7), m. 2d in Salem July 1695 Joseph Carroll whom m. Rebecca Chapman there 9 June 1720; 3 Carroll ch. b. Salem 1696-1702 (Y. D. 14: 251). Another mar. dau., or an unkn. 1st husb. of one of the kn. daus., is called for by the fa.'s story of two sons-in-law killed in the First War, reckoning John Batten one of them. See also Lewis(4), or Larrabee(4).

**4 JOHN**, Piscataqua 1674, had effects belonging to David Wyatt.

**5 RICHARD**, Portsm., and Robt. Pike, chief creditors of James(2) George's est. 1716; Portsm. deft. 1719. One Richard Mean m. Sarah Marble 11 Dec. 1712 in Boston, where his s. **Richard** (Main) was b. 13 Sept. 1713. Sarah, from Portsm., warned at Boston 1725.

**6 THOMAS**(3), returned from York to No.

Yarm., was gr. land there, and had been an inhab. and propr. several yrs. in 1689. List 214. Slain by the Inds. (No. Y. Propr. Rec.). His w. Elizabeth was appar. a No. Yarm. heiress (Y. D. 16: 116). Only kn. ch: **Josiah**, only s. and h. 1732, had York grants in 1698 ('if he settle,' which he did) and in 1713. Lists 38, 279. His w. Dorothy Trafton (Thos.) was named in wills of her bros., Benjamin 1706, Charles 1721. 5 ch. b. in York 1700-1720: Dorothy; Joseph (List 279; see also Elizabeth Ingersoll 1); Amos (Rev.); Mercy; John (m. Dorothy Lewis 2).

**7 THOMAS**, started an acct. with Henry Deering(4) 4 Aug. 1669. The month bef. he had been in Me. ct. for slandering Andrew Diamond's w.; in July 1670 in same ct. unsucc. sued Richard Endle for slander and calling him thief. See also (2), (8).

**8 THOMAS**, fisherman, Portsm., presum. younger than (7), taxed 1698, m. Patience (see Harris 19), to whom her mo., wid. Christian Carr(1), deeded her ho. and part of the Harris land 3 Dec. 1698. She and 5 last-named ch. were rec. into cov. at So. Ch. 9 Oct. 1715. He was liv. 1726. Lists 330de, 337, 339. She was a wid. in Portsm. 1734. Ch. (N. H. deed 20: 115): **Christian**, m. Benjamin Green(4). **Williams** (dau.), m. in Berw. 11 Oct. 1714 Thos. Bond(3), who m. 2d in Portsm. 4 Dec. 1719 Patience Goodwin (Moses 4). He was of Arundel 1730; see Green(4). **Alice**, m. in Portsm. 10 Nov. 1726 John Mills, turner, of Bristol, Eng. She was a wit. in the Hull-Pendexter case. **Dorcas**, d. s. p. 1715-1734. **Hannah**, in ct. 1732, unm.; liv. May 1734. **Patience**, m. Richard Hull (9). **Thomas**, turner, m. 27 Apr. 1736 Mercy Cromwell of Dover.

**9 WILLIAM** (Mane), Greenland or Stratham wit. 1707.

**MAINWARING**, a disting. Cheshire fam. dating from Norman times. Dugdale found 131 variants of the name, which is pronounced Mannering, and was used as a baptismal name in the Hilton(17) fam.

**1 EDWARD** (Mannering), Falmouth 1663. List 222b.

**2 PHILIP**, had lawsuits in N. H. courts 1642-1649, and in Salisb. ct. ag. Exeter men 1649-50. Philip Swadden ack. judgment to him in 1643. Next yr. when in trouble in Salem he sent to Lt. Howard(10) for security. Last seen 1652.

**3 THOMAS** (Manery), Smuttynose (Y. D. 8: 224), m. Elizabeth Winchester, gr.dau. of John Andrews(9). See Y.D.16: 203; Card (4). Gr.j. 1690, 1693. 'Senior' in 1705, when John Shores was boarding with them (see John Frost jr. 8); also Saml. Frost left smuggled brandy in Elizabeth M.'s wareho. Adm. to s. **Thomas**, the only kn. ch., 9 May

1718, his mo. renouncing; Dr. Jackson and John Morgrage were bondsm. for him in 1719. The wid. was an orig. member of Gosport Ch. 1729; liv. in Kit. 1734.

4 **THOMAS**(3), fisherman, mariner, Great Isl. His 1st w. was perhaps a Kit. girl and they the couple Joanna Williams was scandalizing in 1715. Kit. wit. 1721 (Y. D. 10: 123). List 298. He m. 2d Sarah Briard (Briar 1). A 1732 store bill charged him for silk shoes for his dau., shoes for his w., mo. and Prudence, and several prs. each for Sarah Shaw and Sarah Wain, presum. relat. to Wm. Wain who m. Mary Briard(1), int. Boston 4 Jan. 1727. See also N. H. Prov. Papers 4: 7-8. He d. 1 Oct. 1733, adm. 29 Oct. to the wid., who was wid. Sarah Watson in 1756 (one Wm. W. of Portsm. left wid. Sarah, his adm. 1743). An old memo. names 3 surv. ch. By 1st w. a dau. (**Sarah**). By 1st w. a dau. (**Sarah**), m. by 1732 Ebenezer Jackson. (The **infant** of Thos., bp. Kit. Point 1714, was perh. Sarah or ano. ch. who d.) By 2d w: **John**; adm. to wid. Sarah 12 Jan. 1757. **Winchester**, ±14 in 1746, Joseph Pierce of Portsm. gdn.; d. Nov. 1747 in Jamaica. In 1756 his mo. sold his quarter of the ferry landing at the back of Gt. Isl., kn. as Mannering's place.

**MAJOR.** The fam. here came from the Channel Isl. Essex Q. Ct. 6: 346-8, 355-6, shows how many ways one man's name could be spelled. See also Masury.

1 **BENJAMIN**, blacksmith, Arundel, from Salem, m. (int. Wells 23 May 1702) Hannah Bailey(7). Newbury 1703-4; Newc.1708; bot at Cape Porpus 1720. He d. 11 July 1747 (Bradbury) leaving only his wid. Hannah. Ch. rec. in Newb: **Benjamin**, b. 1 Feb. 1703, had Cape Porpus gr. 1720, and is said to have been k. there by Ind. in 1725, appar. unm. **Priscilla**, b. 8 Nov. 1704, m. Lt. John Burbank of Arundel, d. 7 Nov. 1735 (gr.st.). 5 ch.

2 **GEORGE**, drowned at Newcastle Feb. 1695-6. Lists (?307b), 318c.

3 **H——**, 1694. List 98.

Makin, Joel, Dover wit. 1664 (Conc. Deeds 3. 107a).

Malardine (Mallandy), Peter, Scarboro soldier, 1676. List 237b.

**MALLETT.** Both Saxon and Norman; the Jersey fam. was represented in N. E.

1 **HOSEA**, fisherman, Sagadahoc, wit. deeds from Atkins(5) to Edmonds(3) in 1664 and 1673 (Oze); his own land adj. that conveyed in 1673. Called 'Frenchman' by Hubbard. Boston 1678. Lists 187, 189. In 1688 he was master of one of four fishing vessels tied up at Sagadahoc while the masters were in the garrison. David Edwards, interested in all four boats, was bondsm. for Grace, wid. and adm. of H. M., late of Kennebec, 2

Nov. 1690 (Suff. Prob.). See also Hodsdon (4). Only kn. ch: **Elizabeth**, b. Boston 19 Apr. 1678, m. Peter Wooding in Beverly 15 Oct. 1696. Wid. Grace m. 2d in Bev. 15 Mar. 1691-2 Benj. Balch as his 3d d.; 2 Balch ch. Note (2).

2 **JOHN**, Kennebec militia 1688, List 189, poss. son of (1). One Lewis M. wit. a Giles fam. deed in Boston 1718; List 161. See also Manning(8).

Maloon, Malone. See Meloon.

Malum. See Mansfield(7), Oliver(19).

**MANDER**, 1 **James**, Salem, Charlestown, Boston, m. Joanna (Dollen) Kelly(10). Appar. childless, she made deed of gift in 1717 to neph. Richard Wildes of Lancaster, s. of Richard and Margaret (Dollen) Wild (m. in Middlesex Co. 22 Aug. 1687).

2 **WALTER**, taxed at Salem 1683, **as was** (1). See Patience Dollen(2).

**MANN,** confined to so. half of England.

1 **——**, mar. a sis. of Richard Martyn, Esq. (15), perh. neither husb. nor w. ever here. 3 ch. appear: **Michael**. Son (see 2). **Sarah**; was Sarah White of Boston and the mo. of children in 1687.

2 **——**, son of (1), had w. Mary, presum. the M. M. of Boston, ±36 in Nov. 1672, when she ment. 'my husband.' She was called sister M. M. in will of (4) and appar. was mo. of three of the cousins named in this will: **Ann. Mary**, the younger. **Peter**.

3 **LAWRENCE** (or maybe a Manning), sued Samuel Treworgye in 1674.

4 **MICHAEL**(1), master of ketch -Prosperous- of Piscataqua in July 1685. Will, 'of Piscataway,' 16 Dec. 1687—14 Sept. 1691, names uncle Richard Martyn; sisters Mary Mann and Sarah White and each of their ch., Sarah's youngest dau. to have all owing to him in Eng.; three Mann cousins (see 2); and cousins Sarah Cutt, Elizabeth Kennard, Hannah Jose and Susannah Martyn; Elizabeth Hopley was a wit. (Suff. Prob.).

5 **PETER**(2), a minor in Dec. 1687, Richard Martyn, Esq., his overseer. A Portsmouth mariner in London 1697. In 1704 he sued Mrs. Mary Martyn, who had gone to Boston in 1693 and collected from Mrs. Grace Rankin £8 due him as a seaman. Taxed Portsm. 1707. He m. by 1704 Mary (Melcher 1) Jackson(18), who was taxed as Widow Mann 1713, 1732, and d. bef. 1754. Kn. ch: **Peter**, marked 'dead' in Portsm. tax list Jan. 1731-2. He m. 8 June 1726 Elizabeth Kennard(2), who m. 2d Mark Nelson(2). Son Peter, barber and periwig maker, Portsm., brot an ejectment suit (Melcher land), in 1754, against Francis Tucker, Edw. Mann and Henry Biggenden, whose w. was an Ayer. He was liv. 1765. **Michael**, Portsm., joiner, had deed from Geo. Jaffrey in 1728;

taxed Jan. 1731-2. In 1759 his wid. Salome and sons, Michael (dead in 1762) and John, blacksmiths, all of Boston, sold in Portsm. to Peter Mann. **Anne**, bp. No. Ch., 26 Sept. 1708, Hampt. wit. 1729, m. in Greenland 22 May 1731 Francis Tucker, hatter. **Edward**, bp. No. Ch., 29 June 1712, cordwainer, Portsmouth, m. 26 Sept. 1734 Alice Marden(3). Liv. 1754; see his neph. Peter.

**Mannering**, Mannery. See Mainwaring.

**MANNING**, an old given name, compounded in many place names. The fam. is most numer. in co. Essex and co. Devon.

1 **ANNE**, came as servant of Henry Dow(2) in 1637, ag. 17.

2 **DANIEL**, b. 1648, youngest s. of Thomas of Ipsw., inherited Wells land, but perh. never liv. there. His Wells marsh ment. 1683, 1712. Of Ipsw., he was gr. adm. on est. of Saml. Sayward of York in 1691, why not clear, but it is noted that his fa.'s est. was appraised by James Saward in 1668, and his bros. (6) and (9) liv. with James Sayer and w. Martha in Ipsw. in 1669. Liv. in Ipswich 9 Feb. 1724-5. No. kn. family.

3 **GEORGE**, mariner and trader along the Eastern coast, gave his age ±30 in 1675, 38 in 1683, and had a w. in or near Boston in 1674. Lists 3, 14.

4 **GEORGE**, Wells soldier 1676 (Doc. Hist. 6: 136, 143), was s. of George and Hannah (Everill) (Blanchard) Manning of Boston, b. 24 Nov. 1655.

5 **JOHN**, Mr., Boston merchant, and his fa.-in-law Richard Parker were creditors of Wm. Waldron in 1647. With Champernowne, he was interested in the Stephen Sargent est. at the Shoals, 1649. See Y. D. 1: 1: 62; Suff. D. 1: 252; 'The Manning Fam. of N. E.' (1902), pp. 780-2.

6 **JOHN**, br. of (2) and (9), wit. a Sayward deed in York in July 1671 (Y. D. 2: 162). Of Wells in Feb. 1673-4 when he bot there. List 269b. His inv. taken by Wm. Symonds and Jona. Hammond 5 Oct. 1674, incl. 200 a. and a ho., altho no w. or ch. appears to live therein; carpenter's tools were listed and John Wells was a debtor. Me. P. & Ct. ii: 496.

7 **LAWRENCE** (poss. Mann), see Mann(3).

8 **CAPT. NICHOLAS**, gunsmith, Sheepscot, b. in St. Petrox par., Dartmouth, co. Devon, 23 June 1644, s. of Richard and Anstice (Calley). Salem 1662, and m. 23 June (appar. 1663) a much older wid. Elizabeth Gray, who divorced him in 1683, aft. he had risen in civil life, served as capt. in Philip's war, and fled from Mass. to escape criminal punishment. Regardless, he was in favor with Sheepscot authorities, if not always with the inhabitants. Capt. of militia bef. Apr. 1684; marshal of Falm. and places adj., J. P.

for Cornwall, sub-collector and surveyor, all 1686; com. Capt. by Andros 1687; Judge Inf. Ct. of Cornwall 1688. A large landowner in right of self and 2d w., Mary Mason(5), m. 'bef. she and her br. went to Long Island' (Y. D. 20: 86-8). Lists 80, 16-19, 97, 163. See also Goddard(1). His ptn. for release from Boston prison after Andros's fall was gr. 12 July 1689. Bos. 1691-7, but wit. Ind. treaty at Pemaquid 1693, and was 'late of Scituate' in Mar. 1695-6. Staten Isl. and Long Isl. aft. 1702; appar. he and w. Mary liv. 24 Aug. 1725. Kn. ch: **Three**, b. Salem 1664-6, d. y. **John**, Boston, b. 28 May 1668, m. 9 May 1695 Joanna Lash(1), liv. 1 May 1721; w. -Susanna- d. 4 Dec. 1722. In 1724 he pub. int., but did not m., Ann Mallet, wid., named in his will, 16 Jan. (d. 3 Feb.) 1726-7; appar. s. p. No child of Capt. N. M.'s 2d mar. appears, but if Thos. of Moreland, co. of Phila., Pa., rightfully claimed ¼ of the Mason land in 1767 (SJC 131,790) one is indicated. This claim discussed in 'Manning Families of N. E.,' pp. 659-676, 690-4. See also Y. D. 12: 184; 14: 61; 20: 162, and D. H. 6.487.

9 **THOMAS**, carpenter, b. 1645, oldest br. of (2) and (6), bot in Wells from Francis Backus and John Barrett Oct.—Nov. 1674. He was one of Capt. Lothrop's men k. at Bloody Brook, Deerfield, 18 Sept. 1675. Adm. in Essex Ct. 28 Sept. to br. Daniel; the inv. incl. Wells land and marsh.

**Mannyard**. See Maynard.

**MANSFIELD**. A market town and parish in co. Notts.

1 **HENRY**, wit. in Shortridge-Jones case in 1671 with James Leach(2). Adm. 9 Oct. 1678 to fa.-in-law James Leach. Whether he m. a Leach dau. or was a step-son is uncert. See also (3).

2 **ISAAC**, Marblehead. See Ashley(3).

3 **JANE**, Portsmouth. In Maine ct. 5 Mar. 1651-2, a widow, she pet. concerning a debt due from Oades Edwards. Had Portsm. gr. 5 Dec. 1653, then vanishes. Not impossibly she was previously Jane (Turpin) Muchemore, and by an unkn. 2d mar. with a Mansfield was mo. of (1), if not of (7), marrying last James Leach(2).

4 **JOHN**, Charlestown, m. Mary (Shard) Gove(4). In 1672 John Gove sued him in Middlesex ct. for a legacy due under his fa.'s will. She d. in Hampton 4 Mar. 1681-2, 'old Mrs. Mansfield.' See Wyman's Charlestown 2: 653.

5 **PAUL**, from Salem, sold Falmouth land to John Smith bef. 1687. Me. Hist. Socy. Col. 2.6.298. See also Stileman.

6 **SAMUEL**, m. 9 Sept. 1707 Mary Bonython (2) in Lynn, where later liv. her half-sis. Patience, w. of John Collins and dau. of John(2) and Patience (Crucy 10) Bonython.

Wid. Mary Mansfield m. 2d Deacon John Bancroft, jr.

7 **WILLIAM**, Newcastle, ±22 at the Shoals in 1674, Falm. 1680-1689, yet taxed in Newc. in Dec. 1688, and in lists there, 1690-1, is named seco..d aft. James Leach and his sons. Wit. James Weymouth's deeds 1693 and his will 9 Jan. 1706-7, the last time seen. Lists 30, 90, 226, 228c, 315abc, 66. See also (3). Widow Mary depos. in Jan. 1710-1, ag. 59, about John Pearce's Stepping Stones bounds 40 yrs. ago; Andrew Cranch who carried the chain when bounds were laid out was also in Falm. and long a Newc. neighbor. She was ±80 in Jan. 1726-7 (see Martin 9); ag. 87 in Feb. 1734-5 she depos. ab. the Robinson(3) fam. in Blue Pt. and Newc.; ±89 in June 1738 ab. the Tufton Mason fam. Ch. presum. incl: **Mary**, complained in Jan. 1705-6 ag. Clement Hughes(2) who often saw her at John Hurst's ho., her mo. then liv. **Elizabeth** (surely), in ct. 1709-10 (see Sarah Jordan 8). In 1757 she was Elizabeth Carder, poss. w. of Samuel (q.v.) **Pasco**, in Newc. ct. 1713 on account of a bastard ch. Likely she, not -Roscoe-, saw Wm. Sanderson and Mary Cox married in Portsm. 23 Oct. 1711, John Niven ano. wit. See Oliver (19) for Pasco -Malum-.

**MANSON**, Monson. See also Munson.

1 **JAMES**, wit. deed to (5) in 1663. See also (6). In 1890 there was in Boston a copy of a traditional statement by a gr.s. of Samuel(3) that three bros., Richard, Robert and James came from Exeter, Eng., to Piscataqua.

2 **JAMES**(5), mariner, was bondsm. for br. John (in drink) 1700. Of Portsm. 1705, he q.c. father's est. to br. Samuel; in 1706 took deed from Samuel of part of the land 'where we all now live.' He m. in Boston 21 Apr. 1707 Joanna Thomas; both liv. there 1712. Son **James**, b. in Boston 8 Jan. 1707-8.

3 **JOHN**(5), mariner, Portsm. 1698, 1702, and later of Kit., where he had bot his fa.'s Ox Point land in 1701. Lists 330de, 291, 296, 297. His money which Mary (Morgrage) Jenkins(11) was accus. of stealing, caused a stir in 1714-5. Will 6 Dec.1734—5 Jan. 1747-8, names w. Lydia and 4 of 5 ch: **Samuel**, m. three wives betw. 1740-1750, Mary Parker, Eleanor Rogers, Jane Tucker. His s. Samuel, jr. settled in Georgetown. **Joseph**, see Samuel(7 jr.). **Anne**, b. in Kit. 21 June 1703, not in will. **John**, b. in Kit. 28 May 1705, m. Anne, wid. of Moses Rice(4); both liv. 1756. 1 son rec. **Lydia**, m. William Pettegrew (Francis).

4 **RALPH**. List 236. Read Allison.

5 **RICHARD**, b. ±1635, fisherman, Portsm., bot in 1663 and 1664 from the Drews the ho. and 8 a. formerly John Locke's; this place his fam. owned over 70 yrs. He and Jeffrey Currier, both ±36, depos. in 1671 ab. fish handled by Currier, and both apprais. Henry Hatherly's est. in 1677. He purch. at Ox Point, Kit., in 1680, selling to s. John in 1701. Retail lic. (N. H.) 1692, 1693; j. 1693; gr.j. 1694 (special), 1697. Lists 326c, 331bc, 329, 293, 335a, 330d, 52, 57, 98. Inv. 30 Nov. 1702, adm. 14 Dec. to wid. Esther (List 335a). Ch: **Richard**, jr., wit. delivery of the Kit. land 1681. Both sr. and jr. taxed Str. Bk. July 1690; R. M. only, in rate 30 Oct. 1691. **John**, eldest s. in 1702. **Samuel**. **James**. **Esther**, m. 1st John Cross(8), m. 2d Alexr. Dennett(2), m. 3d Anthony Roe(Rowe 2).

6 **ROBERT**, Shoals, named in H. Deering's account with Thos. Maine(7). He d. 10 May 1677; adm. 23 June fol. to Henry Putt; the widow as Elizabeth Putt attested the inv. three days later; Roger Kelly and R. Manson(5) appraisers. See also (1).

7 **SAMUEL**(5), mariner, Portsm. 1702. See his br. (2). Taxed for Mill Dam 1707; bondsm. with Wm. Cotton, jr. for Richard Dore's wid. Tamsen 1715; owned covt. So. Ch. 1721. Lists 337, 339. His w. Rebecca, m. by 1706, was liv. 1735. Betw. 1748-1758 he m. Mary (Jackson, dau. of Ephraim 20), wid. of Thos. Pierce. Will 1761—1761, names her, her dau. Ursula Pierce, his own dau. Mary, and gr.ch. Ch. bp. So. Ch. 16 Apr. 1721: **Samuel**. He and his cousin Joseph(3) seem all to choose from as husb. for Hannah (Bartlett 1) (Wells) Banfield(2) who evid. was older than either. His dau. Mary was named in his fa.'s will, but not he. **Mary**, m. Richard Evans(9). Her fa. deeded to him in 1735 and willed to her sons Daniel and Samuel. **Sarah**, m. 25 Nov. 1736 John Sherburne -tertius-; 4 ch. rememb. by their gr.fa. **Mantee**, Sylvester, Portsm. See Clark(49).

**Manuel**, Portsmouth 1670. List 328.

**Manus**, William, ±20 in 1664. List 364.

**Mapleton** (Mappulton), Thomas, Pemaquid soldier 1689. List 126.

**Maquerey**, Archibald, soldier under Capt. Hill 1693-4. List 267b.

**Maranach**, Matthew, Newcastle, worked at the fort in 1697. List 68. See also Mackaneer(2).

**MARCH**, a market-town in co. Cambridge, but our fam. evid. from co. Hants or co. Wilts. See Waters' Gleanings.

1 **GEORGE**, depos. in June 1694, ±19, his master Mr. Thos. Packer(2). Presum. son of George(2), b. in Newb. 6 Oct. 1674 and d. bef. 1698 when ano. George was born (see 6).

2 **HUGH**, reputed tenant of Shapleigh or Treworgye, plowed at Sturgeon Creek a little later than Thos. Jones plowed there 56 or 57 yrs. ago (Katherine Hammond's depos., 1703); John Shapleigh depos. that H. M. told

in his hearing that he plowed there, but whether for S. or T. he could not rememb. No Hugh is kn. except the Newb. carpenter who came with the Kents from Nether Wallop, co. Hants, in the ·Confidence· 1638, a servant, ag. 20; m. 1st one Judith, m. 2d 29 May 1676 Dorcas (Bowman) Blackleach or Blackledge, mo. of Nathl. B.(1), m. 3d 3 Dec. 1685 Sarah (Cutting) (Brown) Healey, and d. in Newb. 12 Mar. 1693. Ch. by 1st w: **George**, Newb., m. 12 June 1672 Mary Folsom(3). Will, 16 Mar. 1696-7—20 Nov. 1699. 13 ch. incl. (1) prob., (3), (4), (6), Sarah Deering(5) and Mary Hooke, w. of Jacob (7); see also (6) for what may be his 2d s. **George. Judith**, b. 3 Jan. 1652-3. **Hugh**, b. 3 Nov. 1656. **John**, b. 10 June 1658. **James**, b. 11 Jan. 1663-4. See Hoyt's Salisb. 1: 237; N. E. Reg. 53: 121.

**3 SERGT. HUGH**, unrec. s. of George(2), was k. by Ind. at Pemaquid 9 Sept. 1695 (List 96), leaving wid. Sarah (Coker) and s. **Joseph**, b. Newb. 24 June 1694. List 334a seems unlikely his; poss. in error for (1). The wid. m. in Newb. 18 Mar. 1697-8 Archelaus Adams.

**4 DR. ISRAEL**, Greenland, b. at Newb. 4 Apr. 1683, s. of George(2). Wealthy and influential. List 338c; see also Gordon(5). His w. Mary, adm. to Greenl. Ch. in 1716, must have been Mary Hall(13), regardless of what is appar. said in the distrib. of the Hall est. in 1743 (N. H. Prob. 3: 182), and the Portsm. inscription 'Mary, wid. of Dr. Clement March, 7 Apr. 1759, ag. 80.' She and s. Clement took adm. of the Doctor's est., of Portsm., 10 Sept. 1728. 6 ch. were bp. at Greenl. 1716: **Clement**, Col., physician, m. by 1730 Eleanor Veasey. **Joseph. Nathaniel. Paul. Mary. Elizabeth.** Ano. was **Thomas**, bp. 1718; and poss. others.

**5 LT. JAMES**(2), saddler, Newb., Salisb., York, m. Mary Walker of Bradford, and as Lt. James had a York gr. 29 Mar. 1701. Of York, they sold 22 a. at Bald Head in Aug. 1701. In Oct. 1705 he was engaged in an Ind. skirmish at Cape Neddick when two of his men were k. (List 96). He or (6), of Portsm., signed a bond with (7), of Newb., in 1712. Appar. a York wit. 1714 (Y. D. 8: 140); called 'late of said York, deceased' 12 Dec. 1721. The wid. m. John Emery in Newb. 2 Jan. 1723-4 when her late husb. was called Capt. James. Rec. ch., 1st 3 at Newb: **Benjamin**, joiner, Kittery, b. 23 Nov. 1690, m. in Kit. 10 Feb. 1713-4 Elizabeth Small. List 291. See also Y. D. 11: 234. One B. M. of Kit. was drowned, inquest 29 Apr. 1753. **Nathaniel**, b. 2 Sept. 1693. **Tabitha**, b. 20 June 1696. **Judith**, rec. Salisb. 13 May 1698. **Jane**, perh. b. at York, bp. at Salisb. 13 Jan. 1705. One John M. was sued by Jonathan Keene in Me. ct. 1715.

**6 LT. JAMES**, saddler, Greenland, Arundel, b. at Newb. 19 June 1681, s. of George(2). Appar. the Lt. M. taxed in Greenl. in 1708, 1712 (Lists 338ac), and as James in 1713-1716. See (5) for one James of Portsm. 1712. In Mar. 1717-8 Christopher Amazeen of Newc. and J. M. of Greenl. were prosec. 'for living with and entertaining those women by whom they have had bastard ch.' See Cheswell; also Brewster's Rambles i: 125-129, 318. He had an Arundel gr. 1719, but was 'form. of Greenl., now of Scarboro' in Nov. 1720. Arundel appraiser 1722, propr. 1728. Lt. under Westbrook 1724-5. Liv. 1730. His w. is unkn. On Bradbury's authority, she was shot by Ind., and all ch. d. of throat distemper, 1735. By same authority, George of Arundel (a soldier under Allison Brown 1725) was Lt. James's bro., m. Abigail Watson and had ch. Paul and Eunice b. aft. 1735, when all his older ch. d. from distemper. If identif. is correct, then George was b. at Newb. 24 Apr. 1698 aft. (1) died.

**7 COL. JOHN**(2), Newb., Salisb., had much of his military service in Me. As Capt., he was in the expedition ag. Canada in 1690, at Maquoit in 1691 (Lists 37, 96) and Commander at Pemaquid 1692-1694. As Major he succ. Maj. Frost in 1697 and was in the fight at Winnegance in Sept. that yr. (Reg. 12: 145; List 96). Commanded Casco Fort 1703-1707 (called Col. 1705), and Willis, pp. 313-4, says he took his fam. there, had a stock of cattle and cultivated the ground. His luckless expedition ag. Port Royal in 1707 ended his military life, and he liv. afterw. at Salisb. and Newb. See (5). His will 18 Apr.1707 (bound on an exped. to the Eastward)—25 Aug. 1712, names w. Jemima (True, m. 1 Oct. 1679, d. in Salisb. 24 May 1737). Two of seven ch. were **Judith**, b. 21 Mar. 1681-2, m. Humphrey Hooke(7), and Lt. **John**, b. 26 Sept. 1690:

**8 MATTHEW**, of the Charlestown fam., was warned there 14 Mar. 1708-9, 'late from Wells.' See Wyman's Charlestown.

## MARDEN. The name of seven parishes in Eng.

**1 JAMES**(2), in fa.'s will, not mo.'s. Taxed 1693, 1708; Newc. gr. 1698-9, 20 a. where he had built. Lists 318c, 315bc, 316. He m. 23 Oct. 1695 Abigail Webster (Stephen of Haverh. by 1st w.). See Broad(4). She m. 2d Samuel Berry(5), who 20 Oct. 1718, having liv. on Marden's place until some of the ch. were of full age, surrendered it to the s. James, with 3 cows, 2 oxen, 6 sheep, James to pay £4 to each boy, 20 s. apiece to the girls. 'The girls,' unless S. B. was including his own, indicate more than the 4 ch. rec. in Newc: **James**, b. 25 Sept. 1697, d. July 1777, m. Judith Bates(3) who d. 31 July 1796. 11

ch. at Portsm. and Rye. **Stephen,** b. 28 Aug. 1699, m. 21 May 1721 Charity Lang(5), both of Portsm. 6 ch. rec. **Rachel,** b. 20 July 1701. **John,** b. 30 Apr. 1703, not in 1725 tax list.

2 **JOHN,** Rye, an appraiser with John Hunking in 1664 (see King 15) and wit. for Mark Hunking in 1666. O. F. 1666. Taxed as J. M. 1690, as 'Sr.' 1693. Highway surv. 1696-7. Liv. 1702. Lists 323, 326bc, 330a, 312cd, 313a, 52, 332b, 57, 315abc. He m. Rachel Berry(12) who outliv. him. His will, 11 Aug. 1698—12 Feb. 1706-7, gives to s. James 'my right in the woods that I bought and paid for,' all else to w. Rachel for her disposal. Hers (nunc.) proved same day by John Foss, Sr., his w. Mary and Wm. Wallis, gives to 4 ch. (not James). Ch: **James. William. John,** b. 1671. **Elizabeth,** m. Nathaniel Rand(4). **Mary,** was Jones (see 55) in 1706-7. Presum. **Thomas.** In addi., a gr.s. Samuel Connor (see 3) mortg. Marden land in 1711; his mo. poss. one of the kn. daus. with an unknown husband.

3 **JOHN**(2), mastliner, carpenter, Newc. 1710, Portsm. 1712 and onward (first taxed 1714). Lists 316, 339. He m. at Hampt. 16 Nov. 1699 Alice Parker(26), both of Newc. She was liv. 23 Nov. 1732, he in Aug. 1749, ag. 78. Ch. appear; **James,** mastliner, taxed S. side of Grafford Lane 1727. He bot a Portsm. rigging wharf and plant where his fa. worked with him, his s. James aft. them. He m. 4 June 1729 Abigail White; a widow in 1762. 3 or m. ch. **John,** cordwainer, an added name (jr.) in 1728 tax list, Graf. Lane. He m. 11 Dec. 1729 Shuah Libby (James 6), called 'Sherburne' by printed rec., and liv. in Dover and Somersw.; liv. 1761. Master Tate names 6 ch. **Mary,** bp. Newc. 5 June 1709 (Salisb. rec.); see (4). **Alice,** bp. No. Ch. 16 Aug. 1713, m. Edward Mann(5). **Noah,** bp. 22 Sept. 1717, taxed Graf. Lane 1741. **Benjamin,** bp. 1 [7] Jan. 1719-20. **Benjamin,** bp. 2 July 1721. The Marden, bp. No. Ch. 7 Aug. 1715, was poss. ano. ch.

4 **THOMAS,** Newc., presum. (2), was taxed with the Fosses, Berrys and (1) in 1696. Lists 318c, 315c, 68. Also presum. he m. Sarah O'Shaw(1), who was Marden in 1716, as no other husb. appears for her. Ch. may have been: ?**Thomas,** m. 4 Mar. 1729 Mary Smith, both of Rye. Greenland 1733. 3 ch. rec. Portsm. 1732-5. See Fogg(6). ?**Mary,** Portsm., in ct. 1725, but see Mary(3). One Eleanor of Stratham, spinster, was in ct. 1739.

5 **WILLIAM**(2), Rye, liv. 1745. His mo. gave him a choice, the ho. and land where his fa. dwelt in his lifetime, or the place at Sandy Beach. Taxed Rye 1701, island side of Newc. 1720. Wife Dorcas. Ch. rec. in

Newc: **William,** Rye, b. 14 June 1705. In 1729 his fa. gave him all lands except marsh at Sandy Beach Pond and land at Breakfast Hill, he to pay £5 to each of his three sis. and give his fa. half the income. **Samuel,** b. 15 June 1707. **Jonathan,** b. 7 Sept. 1709. One Jonathan had w. Hepzibah and 7 ch. 1730-1750. **Mary,** b. 22 Apr. 1712. One Mary m. in Rye 27 Sept. 1733 Timothy Hardy of Bradford. **Dorcas,** b. 15 Feb. 1714. Unrec: **Sarah,** liv. 1729.

**Margoow,** ——, Frenchman at Mount Desert. List 4.

**Marinell.** See Marriner.

**MARION, John,** Hampton, likely related to but not same as John, cordwainer, Boston, whose fa. was Isaac of Stebbing, co. Essex, Eng., and whose w. was a Watertown girl, Sarah Eddy. Whether both men were once of Watertown is not clear, but John of N. H. was liv. there when he bot a ho. and 5 a. of upland in Hampt. from wid. Judith Parker, 23 May 1645. Gr.j. (N. H.). 1651, 1653, 1670; tr.j. 1665, 1667. Lists 392a, 393ab, 394, 396, 398, 49, 54. His w. Sarah d. 26 Jan. 1670-1; List 393a. Called widower, not -senior-, he m. 14 Sept. 1671 Margery, wid. of Deac. Wm. Godfrey(7), and 3 June 1681 deeded to his ch. for life supp. of self and her. He was liv. 2 Mar. 1683-4; she d. 2 May 1687, ±78; List 394. Two ch. of John and Sarah rec. in Watertown were perh. more likely his than the cordwainer's: **Mary,** bur. 24 Jan. 1641-2, two mo. old. **John,** b. 12, bur. 15 May 1643. Surely his: **Elizabeth,** m. 10 Jan. 1666 Henry Dearborn(2). **Hannah,** m. 15 July 1670 Isaac Godfrey(2). One Abigail M. d. 25 Sept. 1668 (Dow's Hampton).

**MARKHAM, 1 Jeremy** (Marcom), Dover. List 356e.

2 **JOHN,** seaman 1684. List 314.

**Markland,** Samuel, Mr., taxed in Newcastle 1699. List 315b.

**Marks** (Markes), William, Sheepscot 1665, wit. Ind. deed to Geo. Davie 1668-9. List 12. W. M. took O. A. at Lynn 1678; one John M. at Lynn 1677. List 85.

**Markvill** (or Marknill), widow, reported in Portsm. 1692, to be warned.

**Marlyn,** John (or Martyn), Newcastle 1699. List 315b.

**Marreday,** Jones, Corp., Pemaquid 1689. List 126.

**MARRINER,** Marrinell; see also Marvall. A French Huguenot fam. -le Marineur-, poss. from Jersey. See 'Descendants of Edward Small,' 3: 1197.

1 **ANDREW,** cordwainer, tanner (twice signed Andre Marine), evid. nearly related to (3) and to Joshua (Josue, and at times Joseph), saddler, Boston, whose deed he wit. 1689 and who took a Dover mortg.

1714. He bot a ho.-lot in Portsm. 1677; there at his trade 1678. Constable, May 1680. A ho. and shop stood on his Portsm. lot when he sold in 1681; the same yr., of Dover, he bot 50 a. at Casco River. Portsm. tax abated Dec. 1683. Boston 1684-1698, where 1st found at Geo. Cable's ho., as a shoemaker from New London. He and w. Ruth, dau. of Geo. Hollard, liv. in New York, 1703. See also Penny(4), Pastree, N. E. Reg. 63: 381. Ch. at Boston 1685-1690: Margaret. Ruth. Priscilla. George and Andrew, twins. One George m. Elizabeth Eelly at Narragansett, R. I., Sept. 1722; see also (2).

2 GEORGE, weaver, m. Mary Gray (see 6) in Newington 3 Jan. 1724-5. Only his name links him with (1). Taxed Portsm. 1725, a new name; bot there 1727 and sold 1730; 'gone' by tax list Jan. 1731-2. Dover 1733. Eliot 1739, lic. to keep ferry to Newington and Dover. There in 1744 he, w. Mary and s. George attacked Wm. Leighton and laid him up three wks.; Elizabeth Gray test. that her sis. Moll struck the first blow she saw. One George served at Louisburg.

3 JAMES, b. ±1651, mariner, rigger, wit. deed given by (1) in 1681. Of Casco (Marianell), he bot ho. and 5 a. there from Joseph Hodsdon in Apr. 1686 and sold a small lot to Henry Bailey in Apr. 1689. Deposed in Boston in Nov. 1705, former master of brigantine -Dover- (N. E. Reg. 69: 363). As an ancient Falm. propr., he signed three ptns. 1715-8 (his s. Adam also signing the last one), and depos. in Boston in Feb. 1731-2, ±80, that he had lived in Falm. bet. 40 and 50 yrs. ago, neighbor to Capt. Tyng. List 229. Will, 19 May—5 June 1732, gives his Falm. lands to his dau. Elizabeth and husb., the executors. She m. 1st in Boston 1707 John Lacooter (prob. -le Coutois-), 2d in 1713 Edward Masters. Joanna, m. there 1707 Philip Perreway. Adam, brewer, Boston, only s., m. 1st in Newbury 23 Sept. 1713 Hannah Nessbee or Nezby. He sold Falm. land in 1728. Hannah, appar. his dau., m. Richard Kent (jr.) in Newb. 1734 and in 1774 was called only surv. heir of James M., late of Falm.

MARSH. Henry, Oyster River 1692, a landowner bef. getting a 30 a. gr. in 1694 and ano. of 40 a. in 1702, above Coffin's mill. Ag. 44 in Mar. 1704-5. Lists 62, 368a. His wid. Elizabeth (Jackson 22) renounced adm. in favor of her s. John 7 July 1715; inv. £41 taken by Jeremiah Burnham and Stephen Jones. Mother and son sold to Jona. Thompson in 1715. Elizabeth (mo. or dau.) was adm. to O. R. Ch. in 1723. Widow Marsh living 1729. Ch: John, Exeter, suppos. the one, ag. 76 in 1779, who liv. as a boy with old Esq. Coffin, tho age or date must be changed to agree with facts. Scout in 1710; taxed

1714; List 376b (1725). He m. Elizabeth Pomery in Greenland 20 May 1714; she was an Ex. wit. in 1730. Zebulon, Newmarket 1769, and Henry, Exeter 1770, presum. spring from him. James, blacksmith, Glouc. 1738, where one James m. Sarah Griggs 29 Apr. 1728; 8 ch. One Isaiah was of Glouc. 1724-9, the only other Marsh there. Hezekiah, List 369, m. at O. R. 12 May 1729 Abigail York. Dinah, q. c. to Jona. Thompson 1738; single 1742. Sarah, 1st w. of Thos. Leathers(2); included on Stackpole's authority. Elizabeth, m. 19 Nov. 1724 Thos. Leathers(2); both q.c. in 1739. Lydia, single, q. c. to Thompson in 1737.

MARSHALL, well distrib. in Eng., most freq. in cos. Notts and Lincoln. See also Hilton(8), Hussey(9), Lewis(19).

1 CHRISTOPHER, singleman, adm. to Boston Ch. 28 Aug. 1634; freeman 6 May 1635; dism. 6 Jan. 1638-9 with the Wheelwright party to the Ch. at Piscataqua, where he disappears. Dau. Anna, bp. at Boston 13 May 1638. One C. M., minister at Woodkirk, co. York, d. Feb. 1673, ag. 59.

2 ELIZABETH, Mrs., poss. not a widow, m. Maj. Joseph Smith in Hampton 16 Feb. 1708-9 as his 3d w., and m. last Ephraim Jackson(20). Two Marshalls marrying in Hampt. were from Ipswich: Anna, m. Saml. Page(2); Abigail, m. Edward Shaw 3 July 1719. Ano. unident. Elizabeth m. in Portsm. (No. Ch.) 20 May 1710, her husband's name lost.

3 GEORGE, sailmaker, Portsm., m. 25 Feb. 1701-2 Elizabeth Hill(18), who owned covt. and had her ch. bap. at No. Ch. 24 Sept. 1710 and was adm. to full com. 1 Apr. 1714. He was bondsm. for John Cole in 1713; rated to So. Ch. 1717. Adm. 7 May 1718 to wid. Elizabeth, her bondsm. Saml. Shackford and John Hill. Chas. Kelly mortg. Crooked Lane prop. to her in Apr. 1719. Likely she m. 2d in Portsm. 2 July 1721 David Brown and d. bef. 1 Mar. 1739 when 6 surv. ch., all of Portsm., divided their fa.'s prop. Ch: Lydia, b. 19 Mar. 1702-3, m. Benj. Rackleff (1). George, sailmaker, b. 21 Aug. 1705. One George m. 17 Apr. 1740 Thankful Weeks of Greenland; 2 daus. bp. at So. Ch. Samuel, potter, m. 2 Dec. 1736 Eleanor (Mendum) Sherburne, who took adm. 22 Dec. 1749 and m. 3d Wm. Shackford. 4 or more ch. Obadiah, blockmaker, m. Martha Cotton, dau. of Wm. (7 jr.). Will, 6 (d. 12 Sept., ag. 37) 1746, names her and 3 of 4 ch. bp. She m. 2d Edw. Cate(1 jr.). Nathaniel, blockmaker, bp. 29 Apr. 1711. Adm. 13 Sept. 1748 to wid. Hannah, bondsm. John Dam and Geo. Libby. In Dec. 1758 the latter was gr. adm., d. b. n., on est. of both husb. and w. 3 or more ch. Elizabeth, (appar.) bp. No. Ch. 14 Dec. 1712,

not in 1739 div. Deacon **John**, boatbuilder, bp. Nov. 1714, d. in Mar. 1784, ag. 70, appar. had a 1st w. Martha, and poss. a 2d w. Elizabeth (Lang 5) White, m. in Newington 4 Oct. 1745. Ch. **Jane** (appar.), bp. No. Ch. 6 Apr. 1717, not in 1739 div.

4 **GRACE** (Record), w. of Philip M., form. w. of Joseph Bramhall(1), List 229.

5 **HUMPHREY**, Portsm. 1717-8, Berwick wit. 1719.

6 **JOHN**, Scarboro, wit. 13 June 1687 (Y. D. 6: 77); signed Falm. ptn. 1689. List 228c.

7 **ROBERT**, drowned 1663, adm. 30 June to Capt. Pendleton and Lt. Richard Cutts. List 327a.

8 **ROBERT**, shipmaster, about the Piscataqua (Me. side) 1671-2. Assistant to Marshal Richard Wayte in serving papers from Boston and Portsm. July 1672. Boston 1672-3, master of pinke -Lenham-. List 82. Y. D. 2: 96, 138, 167; Me. P. & Ct. vol. ii; Hooke (1).

9 **THOMAS**, fisherman, Newcastle, m. 4 Feb. 1686-7 Abishag (Lux 6) Palmer(24), who d. bef. Dec. 1695, when he denied an accusa. made ag. him by Margery Row, and soon m. 2d Joanna (Holley, or Hawley) Perry(4). Martha, a wit. in Esther Hornabrook's case 1717, seems a 3d w., yet ano. wit. was -Jsanah-, w. of Thos. He depos. in 1732 that he liv. in Cape Elizabeth ±40 yrs. since and was then near 30 yrs. of age. Taxed Newc. 1690, Oct. 1691. Newc. constable and juror 1695. Lists 66, 315abc, 316, 339. In 1731 old T. M. and sons Henry and Joseph were sued for supplies for a fishing boat owned jointly. Alive 20 June 1732. Ch: **Thomas** (by 1st w.). On Mar. 5, 1718-9 his wid. Sarah was cited to adm. by Jotham Odiorne, Esq., her bondsm. Daniel Greenough and Saml. Hinckes. She m. 2d Thos. Mitchell(14). (See also Mary, w. of Christopher Frederick, and Elizabeth, w. of Thos. Pierce (22), Mussell heirs, and either Marshalls or Palmers by birth.) Ch. rec. in Newc. with the Perry ch: **John**, b. 14 June 1697, cordwainer, Newc., had his fa.'s common rights in 1720. One John taxed in Portsm. 1732. See Margery Fernald(1). **Hawley**, b. 13 Apr. 1699. **Henry**, b. 14 Nov. 1701, hatter, Exeter, 1730-1750+, m. wid. Abigail Doran or Doring. **Joseph**, b. 3 Aug. 1703, Newc. fisherman 1731. **Mary**, b. 17 Nov. 1705. **Joanna**, b. 6 Sept. 1708; see Wm. Haines(2). **Martha**, b. 12 Sept. 1712.

**Marsill** (or Moursell), Richard, had supplies at Richmond's Island 1643. List 21.

**MARSTON**, parishes and places in 15 counties. The New Eng. Marstons came from co. Norfolk. See 'Marston English Ancestry,' by Mrs. Holman.

1 **EPHRAIM**, b. 30 Oct. 1643, s. of John of Salem, who was a cous. of the Hampton emigrants. On the Kennebec in 1661, at Damariscove in 1665. R. Pattishall sued him on account in 1673 and got a verdict of £107. Wit. deed Stevens of Kennebec to Sayward and Gedney of Wescustogo in 1674, and Ind. deed to Lawson of Swan Isl. in 1677. After Philip's war he was at Gt. Isl., carpenter, where he was sued by Isaac Bowde in 1683-4 and imprisoned. Moved to Black Pt. where Capt. Wincoll was ordered to send him home to his wife in 1685. Finally at Falmouth, where John M. of Salem sold ho.-lot of his bro., E. M. of F., late dec., in 1719, and one Nathaniel M. quitted his town gr. in Portland harbor in 1725. See also Benj. M. in List 229. His w. Elizabeth had 3 sons b. in Salem 1673-1683, and poss. other ch. One Elizabeth M. of Salem dep. in 1734 that she well knew David Phippen of Casco Bay when he liv. at Salem. Lists 225a, 228bc.

2 *****EPHRAIM**(9), brewer, had the homestead. He m. 19 Feb. 1677 Abial Sanborn (±41 in 1694). Gr.j. 1692, 1699; selectman 1698, 1705; constable 1693-1695; Rep. 1697, 1709, 1715-1717. Depos. in 1738 that he had always been an inhab. of Hamp., which separates him neatly from (1). Lists 52, 54, 55b, 68 (2), 69, 383, 392b (2), 395, 396, 399a. Ch., all but Phebe in deed 27 Jan. 1728-9: **Abial**, b. 18 Mar. 1677; m. John Green(2) 23 Dec. 1695, ag. will of her fa. who disowned her and named ano. dau. Abial; eventually reconciled. **Mary**, b. 9 Oct. 1678, m. Capt. Joseph Taylor 28 Nov. 1698. **John**, b. 17 Dec. 1680, m. Bethia Tuck (John) 4 Nov. 1703, d. 13 Nov. 1730. 5 ch. **Simon**, had land from John Redman, 1707; liv. at No. Hamp. Selectman 1721, 1725, 1730. He d. 4 May 1735. Will 1735, ment. w. Hannah and 5 ch., the eldest (twins) b. 1706. **Phebe**, d. 5 Sept. 1699. **Thomas**, b. 14 July 1687, m. Deborah Dearborn(4) 31 Dec. 1713. Liv. at No. Hamp. Will 1750—1755. 6 ch. **Jeremiah**, b. 5 Nov. 1691, m. Mary Smith (Lt. John) 23 Mar. 1720; had homestead; k. fighting the French at Louisburg. Will 1741—1745. His wid. d. 15 Jan. 1760. 8 ch. Capt. **Ephraim**, b. 3 Aug. 1695; m. 1st Abigail Knowles(3) 22 Jan. 1719; m. 2d Mary Nudd(1) 28 June 1727; d. 31 July 1763. 9 ch. **Abial**, b. 5 July 1697, m. Jabez Sanborn 29 Dec. 1716.

3 **ISAAC**(9), Hampton, m. 1st 23 Dec. 1669 Elizabeth Brown(14), m. 2d 19 Apr. 1697 Jane (Brackett 1) Haines, who depos. ±80, in 1731 ab. the Mitton family. Gr.j. 1686, 1698-9. Lists 49, 52, 54, 55b, 57, 396, 399a. Licensed to sell ale 1698, 1699, and ale and victuals 1700. Ch: prob. **Mehitable** (b. 1670?) m. Arthur Bragdon of York (2 jr.) 3 Nov. 1704, making three sist. mar. in York. **Caleb**, b. 19 July 1672, had homestead; se-

lectman 1725, 1738. List 399b. He m. 12 Nov. 1695 Anna Moulton(8); d. 18 Apr. 1747. Will, 1746, names 7 ch. **Abigail,** b. 25 Dec. 1673, d. 20 June 1674. **Elizabeth,** b. 30 Mar. 1675. **Mary,** b. 18 Apr. 1677, m. 30 Oct. 1699 William Bracy(2). **Thomas,** b. 21 Dec. 1678, m. 1 July 1702 Lydia Moulton(8) who was acc. of garden-thieving in 1713. Moved to Greenland in 1731, deeding Hamp. lands to neph. Caleb M. jr. and to dau. Abigail in 1732; Greenland prop. to son Nathan in 1739. Will 1745—1753, names, of 4 recorded ch., dau. Abigail Mordogh, sons Nathan, m. Eleanor Raines(4 jr.), and Nathaniel, m. Hannah Haines (Matthias). **Sarah,** b. 6 Nov. 1680. (See Durgin 2.) **Abigail,** b. 7 May 1682. **Bethia,** b. 6 July 1687, mar. cont. with Job Curtis of York 18 Mar. 1716-7, wit. by Samuel and Hannah Moody.

4 **JAMES**(9), Hampton, m. 23 July 1678 Dinah Sanborn who m. 2d John Brackett (4) of Newcastle 24 Nov. 1698. Lists 52, 396, 398b. He d. 3 Sept. 1693, adm. to s.-in-law Nathaniel Prescott 1 May 1705. Agreement of heirs 7 May 1706. Ch., the first three grantors to their uncle Ephraim M. in 1699, and all in heirship deed 1710: **Abigail,** b. 17 Mar. 1679, m. John Prescott(1). **Ann,** b. 16 Feb. 1681, m. Nathaniel Prescott(1). **Bethia,** b. 17 Mar. 1682, unm. in 1726. **Mary,** b. 22 Nov. 1687, m. Josiah Moulton(14 jr.). **Lydia,** b. ±1690, m. in Greenland Samuel Brackett(4).

5 **JOHN**(10), m. his w. Martha 15 Jan. 1653 and had four ch. b. in Hamp. before he sold his homestead to Francis Page and mov. to Andover, Mass., in 1664, dying there 2 Apr. 1708. His wid. who had a legacy of 20s. from William Fuller in 1690-1, no relationship stated, d. 11 Oct. 1723, ±87. Will, 19 May 1707—10 May 1708, ment. w. Martha, sons John, Jacob, Joseph (homestead) and daus. Sarah, Hannah, Martha and Bethia. List 393b. Ch: **Mary,** b. 28 Dec. 1655, m. 1 Dec. 1680 Stephen Parker. **Jacob,** b. 27 Dec. 1658, m. 7 Apr. 1686 Elizabeth Poor. **Sarah,** b. 15 Apr., d. 3 May 1661. **Joseph,** b. 24 June 1662. **John,** Andover, m. 28 May 1689 Mary Osgood; exec. of est. of his fa., 'sometime of Hampt.' **Sarah,** m. 24 May 1692 James Bridges. **Hannah,** m. 2 Jan. 1688 Benj. Barker. **Ephraim,** b. 14 Mar. 1673-4. **Benjamin,** b. 11 Jan. 1677. One B. M. entered an Eastern Cl. for Potts Neck (500 a.), 200 a. at Maquoit and an island betw. Jewell's and Small Pt. (1000 a.), but was prob. of the Salem fam. **Martha,** b. 23 Jan. 1679. **Bethia,** m. 22 Dec. 1703 Joseph West.

6 **SERGT. JOHN**(9), m. 5 Dec. 1677 Mary Wall (James) who joined the Hamp. Ch. 2 July 1699. Both his fa. and his gr.fa. Brown gave him land in 1678. Selectman 1681, 1693, 1697; gr.j. 1692. Lists 52, 54, 80, 392b, 396.

(Lists 212, 225a contain a Salem J. M.) He d. 24 Oct. 1699. Wid. Mary gave bond to adm. the est. 15 Feb. 1699-1700, John Tuck and Eph. Marston sureties. Her est. was div. in 1732 betw. s. Jonathan, s.-in-law Benjamin Hobbs(9) (w. **Mary**), dau. **Abigail** (m. Elisha Smith) and dau. **Mehitable** (m. 11 Dec. 1712 Joseph Batchelder 3). Lt. **Jonathan,** b. 27 Oct. 1678, m. 15 Mar. 1713 Abigail Smith; selectman 1706, 1709, 1720, 1721-32, 1740, 1744 (unless the latter terms were those of a later Jona.); d. 5 Mar. 1769. List 399a. Dow adds John and Bethia, of whom we find no record.

7 **ROBERT,** Hampton, bp. at Ormesby St. Margaret, co. Norfolk, 18 Sept. 1608, s. of Robert and Martha, was a neph. of (10). Hamp. proprietor 1640, had a 7 a. ho.-lot so. of meeting-ho. green, was gr. 3 a. of meadow 'near the Boars head' in 1641 and ano. 5 a. ho.-lot in 1643. He d. in 1643, unm., and his cous. John M. of Salem and Thomas(9) adm. the est. for the heir, his br. Simon M. of Ormesby. Wm. Moulton bot the lands from Simon and sold the first ho.-lot to Robert Knight who conv. it to Thomas Marston (10) in 1653. List 392a.

8 **ENS. SAMUEL**(11), No. Hampton, m. ab. 1684 Sarah Sanborn who d. 17 Apr. 1738. Gr.j. 1694-5; j. 1698, 1699; selectman 1704. Lists 52, 63, 64. He d. 8 Nov. 1723. Ch: **William,** bp. with 3 bros. 9 May 1697, m. Susanna Palmer(15) who was his wid. in 1747 and d. 21 Apr. 1749. Adm. 26 Apr. 1749 to s. Wm. and div. in 1751 to 2 sons and 5 daus. **Samuel,** b. 7 July 1687, ensign, m. by 1710 Catherine Carr who d. 10 Nov. 1763; d. 9 Mar. 1756. He wit. a York deed, Perkins to James Carr, in 1717. **Lucy,** b. 5, d. 10 Sept. 1689. **Stephen,** b. 2 Dec. 1690, d. y. **Joseph,** b. 27 Jan. 1693, m. 9 Jan. 1719-20 Hannah Libby (see 1). **Reuben,** b. 24 Sept. 1696, m. 14 Nov. 1717 Sarah Leavitt (John 3) who d. 7 Oct. 1767. **Sarah,** b. 29 May 1699, m. 29 Oct. 1719 Jacob Libby(1). **Hannah,** b. 17 Sept. 1701, m. 24 Oct. 1723 Wadleigh Cram. **Ruth,** b. 19 Apr. 1704, m. 24 July 1728 Israel James. **Mary,** b. 28 Oct. 1707, m. Moses Perkins(12). **Obadiah,** b. 18 Sept. 1710, Little Boars Head, had w. Elizabeth by 1736.

9 ***THOMAS**(10), ±52 in 1669, ±65 in 1681, liv. on original gr. of Robert(7) whose adm. he was. See Knight(16). He m. Mary Estow, Lists 393a, 394, who was liv. in 1700. Selectman 1649, 1656, 1659, 1664, 1667, 1670, 1673, 1680; gr.j. and j. 1684; Rep. 1677, 1680 (4 sessions); summonsed for the Gove panel 7 Nov. 1683. Lists 49, 52, 53, 54, 55ab, 376b, 391b, 392b (2), 393ab, 394, 396, 397a, 398. He d. 28 Sept. 1690. In 1730 his heirs settled his land titles with the grantee of the heirs of Walter Roper. (N. H. Deeds 23. 341.) Ch: **Isaac. John. Bethia,** d. June 2, 1655. **Eph-**

raim, b. 8 Oct. 1654 (or 1655). **James**, b. 19 Nov. 1656. **Caleb**, b. 23 Apr. 1659, d. 31 Oct. 1671. **Mary**, b. 9 Sept. 1661, m. 1 Jan. 1680 William Sanborn. **Sarah**, b. 20 Nov. 1665, m. Simon Dow(10).

10 **CAPT. WILLIAM**, Hampton, b. prob. at Ormesby St. Margaret, co. Norfolk, ab. 1590, s. of Henry, was in Salem in 1636. He had a land gr. in Hamp. 30 June 1640 and prob. had a ho.-lot earlier, near the present site of the town house. Selectman, 1652. He m. his 1st w., name unknown, in Eng. (she may have been the Goody Marston of List 393a) and late in life m. 2d a young woman, Sabina (see Locke 3½), who m. 2d John Redman; List 394. He d. 30 June 1672, his will, 25 June—8 Oct., left everything to his 8 yr. old dau. except 5s. to each son. His wid., executrix, claimed dower, and one son, prob. Wm. who is later found with the homestead, did not submit meekly, as in N. H. Ct. Papers is an attachm., undated and defendant blank, in behalf of Tryphena M., sole heiress, illegally pros. and arbitrarily dispossof. of her lands in 1674. Lists 392ab, 393ab, 391ab. Ch. by 1st w: **Thomas**, b. ab. 1617. **Prudence**, m. 1st William Swaine, m. 2d Moses Cox(18). **William**, bp. 11 Mar. 1626 at Hemesby, co. Norfolk. **Anne**, bp. 6 Dec., bur. 7 Dec. 1628 at Hemesby. **John**, bp. 20 June 1630 at Hemesby. By 2d w: **Tryphena**, b. 28 Dec. 1663, m. Joseph Philbrick(5).

11 **CAPT. WILLIAM**(10), near 80 in 1700, had the homestead. He m. 1st 15 Oct. 1652 Rebecca Page(6), m. 2d 5 July 1675 wid. Ann (Roberts 11) Philbrick(1) who surv. him. Selectman 1668, 1676-7, 1682, 1693; gr.j. 1693. He d. 22 Jan. 1703-4. His will 1701—1704, named his w., s. Samuel and daus. Rebecca, Hannah and Maria. Lists 49, 52, 392ab, 396, 397a, 391b, 393b, (List 80 prob. a Salem Marston). Ch: **Rebecca**, m. 23 Aug. 1676 John Smith. **Hannah**, b. 21 Aug. 1656, m. Samuel Fogg(5). **Mary**, b. 4 Apr. 1659, d. 2 Nov. 1660. **Samuel**, b. 8 Sept. 1661. **Lucy**, b. 21 Apr. 1665, m. Josiah Moulton (14). **William**, b. 7 Oct., d. 8 Nov. 1667. **Maria**, b. 16 May 1672, m. James Prescott(2).

**MARTELL**, 1 ———, and his servants, to Machias. List 5.

2 **FRANCIS** (Martel), and John Tapley were vilifying Mr. Saml. Eburne(2) at the Shoals, 1702.

**Martiel**, Thomas, List 315b. See Marshall.

**MARTIN**, Martyn, general in Eng., one princ. home in Cornwall. The prom. Portsm. fam., perh. from Exeter, co. Devon. Became 73d commonest name in N. E.

1 **BENJAMIN**, Casco, fined for abs. from court, 18 July 1665.

2 **CHARLES**, York, arrived ab. the time Thos. Trafton came over, the two suppos.

linked with Newlyn, co. Cornwall, tho the York Charles, ±50 in 1681, was not the one who m. Anne Traughton (Trafton) in Newlyn in 1644 nor their s. Charles, bp. 1649. York gr. next Dodovah Hull 18 May 1667; O. A. Mar. 1679-80. Sued by Arthur Beale in 1679 and ord. to pay for 7 weeks service performed by Hannah Wakeley. A sea capt. (Dr. Banks says), but in his last yrs. he was connected with the Saywards and their mills; in 1680 he and John Mitchell (see 6) were defts. in one of several suits brot by Abel Porter, atty. for Clarke & Curwin; the next yr. they and Samuel Sayward, ano. deft., sued, charging false imprisonment. Liv. 4 June 1683 (Y. D. 3: 125; 8: 234); inv. 24 Sept. 1684; adm. to Robt. Young. No kn. fam. His gr. was sold by Joseph Young, jr., in 1717.

3 **EDWARD**, fisherman, Smuttynose. See (9). Ag. 34 in July 1674, he testif. bef. Peter Twisden in Hugh Almary's favor, bot Rowland Young's Smuttynose prop. 1683, and wit. John Light's will 1685. Samuel Winsor liv. and d. in his ho. and by nunc. will gave all to him and his w. Gillian; his bond for adm. 6 Mar. 1687-8. Neither he nor w. seen later.

4 **FRANCIS** (Martyn), gent., from Plymouth, Eng., where his fa. had been mayor; perh. connected by mar. with Trelawney's sis., Mrs. Martin, and the one, ag. 35 in 1620, who m. at St. Andrew's, Plymouth, 10 Oct. 1619 -Priscilla- (appar. error for Prudence) Deacon. She and her ch. were rememb. in will of Thos. Fownes, Esq., of Plym., 1637 (Harl. Soc. Pub. 6: 180; N. E. Reg. 45: 154). Facing bad times, he came with two ch. to Richmond's Isl. bef. 27 June 1640 (List 21), soon settling at Casco, where his lack of means for subsist., thru poverty, age and unfamil. of self and ch. with work, worried Mr. Winter, who twice wrote to Trelawney and in June 1642 sent him a bill upon Mr. John Martin for his uncle. Tho without land, goat, pig, man, or wherewithal to pay a man, he managed to return to Eng., leaving his daus. in care of Mr. Michael Mitton, a choice which resulted in the execution of **Mary**, ag. 22, for the murder of her ch., b. in Boston 13 Dec. 1646. In her confession she named also (John) Sears (Winthrop, ed. 1853, 2: 368). Name and fate of 2d **dau.** unknown.

5 **JANE**, Portsmouth, recd. into cov. at No. Ch. and bp. with her children 10 Sept. 1710. These ch. poss. included one or all of: Elizabeth (see Neal 8); Mary (see Whidden); Anna (see Green 24); John (see Lang 5); while Jane, bp. 1713, and Keziah, bp. 1718, may have been hers. She depos. 1758, ag. 81, that she knew the Cutts wareho. on Deer Street from 1699, and had fruit from

it at her first lying-in. See (18).

**6 JOHN,** Capt., at Damariscove early. List 8.

**7 JOHN,** yeoman, Dover, on the Me. side by Oct. 1645 (P. & Ct. i: 94) and m. Hester (Esther) Roberts(11) bef. 7 Sept. 1647 when Thos. Tare sued them in N. H. for slander. Dover propr. 1648. Often petit and gr.j.; selectman 1666; called Sergt. that yr. Lists 353, 354abc, 355a, 356a, 361a, 362a, 363abc, 365. He sold his Lubberland home and a Dover gr. to Thos. Mounsell in Sept. 1667 and remov. to Piscataway, N. J. Will, made there 17 Mar. 1687, names w. Esther heiress and exec. with sons John and Benj.; Hopewell Hull and John Langstaff overseers. Her will, 9 Nov.—20 Dec. 1687, names ch: **John,** Piscataway, in will, 21 May (inv. 12 June) 1703, named w. Anne, 5 ch., 3 bros., 2 sis. **Joseph,** depos. in N. J. in 1718, ag. 63, that as a youth he liv. with Anthony Nutter at Welsh Cove. **Thomas,** liv. 1703. **Mary,** m. 1st Hopewell Hull(6), m. 2d Justinian Hall. **Martha,** m. John Langstaff(1); not in br.'s will. **Lydia,** was Smalley 1687, 1703. One John S. of Piscataway in will, 1731—1733, names w. Lydia, ch. and gr.ch. **Benjamin,** Piscataway, exec. of mo.'s will, mar. and left ch. Of N. J., in July 1718, ±58, he depos. that he once liv. with his uncle Thos. Roberts of Dover.

**8 JOHN,** made his will in Portsm. 5 Apr. (prov. 30 June) 1664, naming w. Sarah, ch. and servant Wm. Pierce who got his tools; wid. and bro. Larefet (Larriford) exec.; Capt. Pendleton and Mr. Richard Cutt overseers; wit. Joshua Moody, Richard Martyn. Ch: **Sarah. Mary. Mehitable. Hannah. Abraham.** One Abraham of Ipswich d. 2 Dec. (?1693); heirs in 1700 his wid. Hannah, and ch: Abraham (Smuttynose and York, Y. D. 12: 77; 13: 2), Hannah, John, Sarah, Samuel, Mehitable, Thomas. Cf. Wyman's Charlestown 2: 658.

**9 JOHN,** fisherman, mariner, Newcastle. Cor.j., Kittery Feb. 1674-5; in 1680 liv. in a ho. of widow Mary Matthews on Smuttynose. Of Great Isl., he sued Capt. Siveret for fish in 1685, and there, bef. 1690, Edw. Carter(2) gave him 1 a. of land next John Clark's. Last found deeding to son in 1705; Hannah Almary wit. the deed, proving it that yr. Lists 286, 315bc. See (3). His w. Wilmot, m. bef. Dec. 1685, ran into Capt. Barefoot's ho. with Edw. Carter's w. Joan when Thos. Wiggin was assaulting Robt. Mason in 1686. Ag. 75 in Jan. 1726-7, she and Mary Mansfield, ag. 80, depos. ab. their long-time neighbors, the Clarks(16). Kn. ch: **Edward,** shipwr., carpenter, old enough to buy from his fa. in 1705; List 316. His w. was Elizabeth in 1719; both liv. Apr. 1753. Ch. **Dau.,** m. James Randall(7). Poss. **John,**

who may have been the Kit. wit. 1707 (Y. D. 7: 67, 241), was taxed on island side of Newc. 1720, as was Edw.; presum. fisherman, mariner, and husb. of Clear (Jordan 8) Lapish; both liv. 1759. See also Brown(34). Note also Mary Stone (Daniel of Kit.) who was Martin in 1716.

**10 JOSEPH,** mariner, Portsm., m. 3 May 1723 Sarah (Clark 20) Nolar or Knowles (6); dead in 1737. Adm. on her est., widow, to dau. Mary Nolar 30 Jan. 1744-5. Ch. bp. So. Ch. 1724-1728: **Eliza. Susanna. Knowles.**

**11 MATTHEW,** sued Saml. Treworgye in June 1674. Adm. on his est. in N. H. 28 Mar. 1677 to Wm. Diamond, his bond for £50.

**12 MICHAEL** (Martyn) (15), mariner, London, perh. there in Jan. 1692-3 when his fa. willed him land if he come home. Portsmouth at intervals 1697-1699. That he d. s. p. in Boston 1699, where his sis. Cutts went to care for him (SJC 28272; 20920), his wills disprove. The first, made in Eng. 1 Feb. 1697 (bound to N. E.), prov. in Eng. 1 Nov. 1700, gives all to w. Sarah, then to s. Richard, or if s. p. to sis. (prob. wife's) Jane Rudkin; the 2d in Boston, 23 Oct.—14 Nov. 1700, gives Portsm. land to w. and s., with gifts to three sis., bro. Kennard, nephews, nieces, and cousins Edward (a wit.) and Susannah M. of Boston. His w. Sarah d. by 1721. Son **Richard,** (of Red Lion St.), bp. at Stepney, co. Middlesex, 9 June 1697, one day old. Late of H. M. S. -Salisbury-, he was coming to N. E. in 1721 (N. H. Prob. 2: 135), and later that yr., resident in Portsm., deeded to Geo. Jaffrey. One Michael was bp. at No. Ch. 8 Apr. 1722.

**13 NATHANIEL,** with Saml. Hart wit. a Hart deed in Portsm. in 1703, but was not Nathaniel(15) if SJC 28272 is correct.

**14 RICHARD,** Casco Bay, m. Dorothy, wid. of Benj. Atwell(1), liv. on her land, and tho he left no son, left his name to this day to Martin's Point. Employed at Richmond's Isl. 1637-1643, called of Black Point 1639, and bondsm. with and for Scarb. people 1666-7. Bef. Nov. 1658 he owned and sold Thos. Drake's planta. Cor.j. 1670. Lists 21, 221, 222bcd, 231, 232. His will, 11 (died 14) Jan. 1672-3, names w. Dorothy, s.-in-law Robert Corbin(2), Samuel White and Jos. Atwell (2), giving all aft. wife's death to Benj. Atwell(2) and Lydia Corbin (more likely Atwell than Martin). On 10 Dec. 1673 the wid. deeded to Corbin for supp. and d. bef. 1 Apr. 1679 when adm. was gr. on est. of Richard and -Deborah- in behalf of Jos. Atwell.

**15 ‡*RICHARD** (Martyn), Esq., Portsm. ±42 in Mar. 1672. First a Boston mariner, but not surely the factor of Robt. Hamon, merch., in July 1650, or the man going to the W. I. in 1651 (one Thos. M. was of this party), he emerges clearly when he m. there

1 Feb. 1653-4 Sarah Tuttle, dau. of John and Joan (Antrobus). In Boston liv. also his br. Michael, mariner, who m. Susannah Holyoke 12 Sept. 1656 and d. 26 Mar. 1682, ag. 60 (gr. st. with coat-of-arms, Copps Hill), his wid. and ch. Edw. and Susannah being named in Richard's will. See also (12) and Mann. Richard was in Portsm. 1658, bot in Great House field 1659, propr. 1660. His pub. service begins as gr.j. 1666; selectman 1669-70, 1673-75; com.t.e.s.c. 1671; Deputy 1672-73, 1679, 1692 (Speaker); Magistrate from 1676; Treas. of Prov. under Pres. Cutts; Councillor 1680 till remov. by Cranfield 1683; on Dudley's Committee of Trade and Navigation 1686; Judge Ct. of Com. Pleas 1692-3; Chief Justice Supreme Ct. of Judic. Oct. 1693 till death 2 Apr. 1694; also town clerk his last yr. Lists 323, 324, 326ac, 329, 330b, 331abc, 333a, 335a, 48, 49, 51-54, 57-59, 62, 88, 96. His w. Sarah, alive 18 Apr. 1670, had three successors: Martha (Symonds) Dennison of Ipsw., buried 15 Feb. 1683-4 (List 331c); Elizabeth (Sherburne) (Langdon) Lear(2); and, aft. Apr. 1691, Mary (Benning, sis. of Harry, q.v.) Wentworth (Lists 331c, 337, 339). His will, 27 Jan. 1692-3, names w. Mary, 5 ch., and others, incl. Tobias Lear(3) and step-dau. Dorothy Wentworth. Her will, 3 Feb. 1717-8—11 Jan. 1730-1, gives to Wentworths. Ch. by 1st w: **Mary**, b. 7 June 1655, not in will. **Sarah**, b. 3 July 1657, m. John Cutts(3). **Richard**, b. 10 Jan. 1659-60. **Elizabeth**, b. 31 July 1662, m. 1st Edw. Kennard(1), m. 2d Lt. Wm. Furber(3), m. 3d Benj. Nason(2). **Hannah**, b. 2 Jan. 1664-5, m. 1st Richard Jose(3), m. 2d Edw. Ayers (1). **Michael**, b. 3 Feb. 1666-7, only surv. son in 1700. **John**, b. 9 June 1668, and **Elias**, b. 18 Apr. 1670, neither in will. By 2d w: **Nathaniel**, a minor in Jan. 1692-3, wit. 17 Mar. fol. (Y. D. 5.1.113); d. s. p. bef. his fa. (SJC 28272).

16 **REV. RICHARD** (Martyn) (15), H. C. 1680, and like his classmate Green(20) minister at Wells, where engaged to preach 21 June 1689 (Sibley's Harv. Grad. 3: 179), tho then several yrs. resident. Historian Bourne could not determine the beginning or end of his pastorate. He made return of Anthony(3) Coombs's mar. in Sept. 1688, signed a letter ab. Ind. affairs in Apr. 1689, and on the following 30 June a pet. to Mass. asking aid for Wells. He d. from small pox 6 Dec. 1690 (List 96); adm. to fa. 2 Apr. 1691. No family.

17 **RICHARD**, Capt., master of -Thomas of London-, burned at the Piscataqua (Reg. 69: 360-1). In London 1695, he depos. that he lodged until July 1694 at the ho. of Mr. Elliot, 'the most eminent inhab. of the Province.'

18 **RICHARD**, Portsm., taxed 1713, paid for keeping John Bartlett to Mar. 1715, rated to So. Ch. 1717 (note also Richard, Wells schoolmaster 1716-7), taxed 1722 Grafford Lane. Tailor. In all probabil. husband of (5).

19 **ROBIN**, Richmond Island 1639 or 1640; Trel. Papers, p. 298.

20 **SAMUEL**, Great Island 1690. List 319.

21 **SAMUEL**, Marblehead and Muscongus. See Fulford.

22 **SUSANNAH** (also Martlin). See Johnson(16).

23 **WILLIAM**, wit. a Saco deed 1683 (Y. D. 4: 22).

**Marvall** (Marvill), James, abutted Bowdoin land at Falm. 1697-8 (East. Cl. 5: 152; Y. D. 17: 316), must be Marinall (Marriner).

**MASHON**, John, named twice in Robt. Temple's tax accounts, Saco, (1668?), 1672. See also N. E. Reg. 71: 124. His depo. (Meshan) and that of one Hobbs were wanted in case of Thos. Cousins, accus. of perjury by Scottow in June 1680; Maj. Pendleton was to locate them.

**MASON**, Tufton Mason. An occupational name general in Eng. except on S. coast and in extreme N.; also a Northumberland township. Became 79th commonest name in New England.

1 **ANNA** (see Jones 60) was instead Nason (2). Catherine (see Tibbetts), Elizabeth (see Roberts 12), Mary (see Gypson 2), are unattached.

2 **BENJAMIN** (Masson), taxed Dover 1677 next to (8). List 359a.

3 **EDWARD**, Berwick, d. 6 Nov. 1670; adm. in July 1671 to Capt. John Wincoll. Thos. Newbury made voyages for him in his sickness. See Me. P. & Ct. ii: 227.

4 **CAPT. JOHN** of London, Esq., patentee and founder of New Hampshire. Like his partner Sir F. Gorges in the patent from the Council of N. E., granted 10 Aug. 1622 and divided by new patents (to Mason, 7 Nov. 1629), he had a disting. career in and for Eng. and never came to his N. E. land, altho previously on this continent several yrs. as governor of Newfoundland. See 'Capt. John Mason, the Founder of New Hampshire,' pb. by the Prince Society (Boston 1887); N. H. State Papers, 29: 1-200; 2: 514-562. Lists 41, 52, 84, 283. Unlike Sir F. he was not of knightly descent, but not of the humble stock Col. Chester thought. Later invest. has carried his fam. back seven well-estab. generations to one Baldwin Mason, b. in Carnforth, co. Lancaster. Capt. John was bp. in St. Margaret's Ch., King's Lynn, co. Norfolk, 11 Dec. 1586, s. of John, merchant, and Isabel (Steed), and m. there 29 Oct. 1606 Ann Green, dau. of Mr. Edward, goldsmith, London. His will, London, 26 Nov.—

22 Dec. 1635, directs bur. in the Collegiate Ch. of St. Peter in Westminster, without funeral pomp or ceremony, gives to sis. Dorothy Moore and chn., various bros.-in-law and cousins and their wives, his wife (sole exec. with his br.-in-law Mr. [later Sir] John Wollaston as overseer), his dau. and her husband, and 4 gr.ch., and devises land incl.'my county of N. H. or Mannor of Mason Hall,' and ±10,000 a., being Masonia 'at Capeham of Wagen upon the south East side of Sagadahock in N. E.' John Winthrop wrote 10 June 1636: 'Capt. Mason is dead; therefore all their designs against us are (through God's great mercy) fallen asleep.' See also N. E. Reg. 56: 308; 59: 141; 'Old Kittery,' p. 211. His wid. Mrs. Ann made nunc. will 20 Feb. 1654-5; adm. 12 Nov. 1655 to gr.s. Robert. Her Lists 41, 283. See also (11). Only ch: Ann, m. (lic. 27 June 1626) Joseph Tufton who was of East Greenwich, co. Kent, Esq., when he made nunc. will, 14 Nov. 1653—29 Mar. 1654. She was Mrs. Ashurst in Feb. 1654-5, liv. 13 May 1659. The Tuftons had 5 ch: Mason, d. by 1633. Ann, ag. 6 in 1633, was given Masonia, ±10,000 a.; m. 6 Jan. 1647-8 Dr. Richard Gibbon of Kingston, co. Kent, and London. John, ag. 5 in 1633, his gr.fa.'s resid. legatee, but to alter his surname to Mason; dying under age his int. passed to his br. Mary, ag. 1 in 1633, liv. 1635. Robert (see Mason 16).

5 JOHN, Sheepscot, bought from the Inds. 20 Jan. 1652-3. Court was held at his ho. in Sept. 1665; liv. 17 Sept. 1666. List 12. Nathl. Draper who wit. his Ind. deed swore to it 15 Mar. 1666-7 and testif. in June 1669 that Mason intended his upper planta. for his son, his lower one for his w. Mary (Gent 2). She m. 2d John Allen(5) and in 17— claimed at Sheepscot for self and Mason ch: James, only s. and h., apprent. to Mr. Josiah Hobart of Hingham, going to East Hampton, L. I., with him ±1679. He m. there Mary Mulford (Wm.) and d. bef. 1736, leaving dau. Mary, b. ±1691, who m. Elias Mulford in East Hamp. 10 June 1713 (Y. D. 18: 70). See also Burnett(1). Mary, m. Capt. Nicholas Manning(8).

6 JOHN, named in early Saco records (N. E. Reg. 71: 124). See Mashon.

7 JOHN, Hampton, m. 11 July 1672 Elizabeth Ward (Thomas). In 1673 fined for disciplining Jacob Garland at the Robie ho.; ag. ±20 in Apr. that yr. Jury 1684, 1694; dep. Marshal 1684; lic. for beer and cider 1694; constable 1695. Lists 396, 399a. He d. 29 Feb. 1696. Widow Elizabeth (List 68) was k. by a horse she was trying to catch 21 May 1697 and her br.-in-law Jos. Swett took charge of the ch. Adm. to s. John 18 May 1698; div. 18 Oct. 1703 to all ch. but one: Elizabeth, b. 5 May 1674, m. James Johnson

(15 jr.). Margaret, b. 28 Apr. 1676, d. 29 Oct. 1694. John, Stratham, b. 30 Jan. 1678, liv. with Geo. Veasey ±1700. Lists 388, 400. Adm. 4 June 1718 to wid. Mercy, who prob. m. 2d Thos. Briar(6). Ch. at Strath. 1708-1717: Joseph, John, Benjamin, Hannah. Francis, Kingston, m. in Greenland 26 Jan. 1717-8 Mary Edmunds(5); d. 7 Apr. fol. She renounced adm. to his bros. Joseph and Benjamin 3 June 1718. Note Mary (not Hannah), 2d w. of John Jenness(1). Mary, m. Caleb Clough, int. Salisb. 29 Mar. 1707. Hannah. Catherine, b. 19 Sept. 1687, m. John Edmunds(5). Esther. Joseph, b. ±1693, weaver, Strath., wit. deed to Jona. Wiggin in 1714 and bought from him in 1721. List 388. Bef. 1724 he m. Mary Drisco(8); presumably m. 2d, 1738-1745, Catherine, wid. of Joshua Stevens, a widow again in 1763. Benjamin, b. ±1696, blacksm., Strath., m. Jean Masury, who d. by 1735 when Theophilus Smith deeded to her ch: Edward, Benjamin, Francis, Mary. Catherine, Elizabeth, Jane. Old Mr. B. M. d at Strath. 18 Mar. 1770. See also (18).

8 JOHN (Masson), taxed Dover 1677 next to (2). List 359a.

9 JOHN, soldier under Capt. Hall, slain at Falm. 1689. List 228d.

10 JONATHAN and RICHARD. List 36. Read Nason.

11 JOSEPH, Mr., kinsman of (4), came as his widow's agent with her p/a of 3 Mar. 1650-1, arriving bef. 4 July fol., when he entered a protest ag. R. Leader's occupa. of the Newichawannock land. See 'Capt. John Mason' (Prince Society), pp. 92-99. Lists 41, 283, 323, 330b, 326a. A letter from Salisbury (Eng.) to Rawson 6 Oct. 1652, signed Will Bridgewater, ment. 'my uncle Joseph Mason.' He contin. here aft. Mrs. M. died, but her gr.s. Robert, in letter 3 May 1664, wrote of him as formerly his agent, but 'by reason of his age not able any longer to act therein'; he was ±58 in 1652 when he produced Capt. M.'s will in Mass. Genl. Ct. He wrote to Robert from Piscataway 16 July 1665 (Doc. Hist. 4: 265); again 28 Sept. 1667 advising him to accept the offer of Mass. advanced thru Capt. Pike (London Transcr., N. H. Hist. Socy. 1: 114-147). In May 1667 he was about to ret. to Eng. in the -Great Duke of York-, but was here in Sept. fol., and 21 July 1668, form. of Portsm. (ack. in P.), sold his dwg. ho. in the Little Harbor. Mr. M. was liv. apart from his w. in N. H. 1661-1662.

12 JOSEPH, Pemaquid soldier 1689. List 126.

13 JOSEPH, Portsm. 1694, drafted in Apr. 1696. Lists 335b, 336b.

14 PETER, ag. 22, boarded at wid. Hannah Moulton's(2) in Dec. 1671. Of Cochecho,

he bot sole leather from Matthew Nelson 1678. Oyster River gr. 1694. In N. H., he refused oath as gr.j. 1693 and was lic. to sell outdoors 1695. Sealer of Leather (Kit.) 1698-9, and in 1700 bought hides stolen from Pepperell. Wit. as 'Senr.' 1707 (Y.D. 7: 152). Lists 359b, 55a, 52, 94, 318b, 368b. His wid. Mary, m. by 1692, was adm. to O. R. Ch. 7 July 1728, liv. 1739. Appar. ch: **Benjamin** (proved by deed 1730), cordwainer, Dover, Somersw.; List 358c. Will 1754—1754, names w. Elizabeth (m. by 1716, liv. 1765) and ch: Samuel, Abigail, Elizabeth, but not Benj. or Peter bp. 1718, 1725. **Peter**, ag. 15 in Oct. 1702, 'jr.' in 1709 (see Hall 8). His w. Sarah Davis(24) who was bp. at O. R. 21 Mar. 1717-8, admitted 3 Oct. 1725; he and daus. Hannah, Sarah, Mary, bp. 5 Mar. 1720-1. List 369. Living 1736 (see Randall 16). She was a wid. 1747, liv. 1772. **Joseph**, cordwainer, Durham, m. Mary Doe(1), a wid. in 1746. Sons John and Robert, bp. 1725, 1726, were of Durham 1748. **Patience**, dau. of Peter and Mary (Friends rec.), m. 8 Dec. 1724 Thos. Hanson, d. 3 Feb. 1772, he 17 June 1773. **John**, Somersworth 1738, br. of Benj. List 369. **Isaac**, little br. of Peter, bp. O. R. 5 Mar. 1720-1. List 369. See also (1).

15 **RALPH**, Boston, owned in York when he made his will in 1672; see Suff. D. 11: 278.

16 ‡**ROBERT TUFTON**, Esq., 9 mos. old when his gr.fa. (4) died, assumed the name Mason in accordance with will of gr.fa. who gave him 'my Manor of Masonhall in N.E.' His br. John's inheritance also passed to him. Adm. of gr.mo.'s est. 12 Nov. 1655. He m. Elizabeth, dau. of Wm. Taylor of Bradley, co. Hants, and had ch. b. in England: John, ag. 5 in 1664, came with his fa. (List 319) and d. unmar. in Va., drowned on a voyage, aft. 1690; not named in br. **Robert's** will (see 17). **Elizabeth**, named in Robert's will 1692 as E. T., but not ment. in fam. chart 1738 (Masonian Papers 1: 36). R. T. M. came to N. H. in 1680, Councillor for the Prov., signed the treaty of peace with the Ind. 8 Sept. 1685, and was of the Council of N. E. under Dudley and Andros. Lists 52, 84. He d. at Esopus on the Hudson 6 Sept. 1688, while visiting those settlements with Andros, and his claims to N. H., which he had steadily pressed, his sons sold to Samuel Allen, Esq.(13), by a conveyance eventually held illegal.

17 **ROBERT TUFTON**, Esq.(16), mariner, m. Katherine Wiggin (Thos.), perh. ab. 1686 when Wiggin was beating him. Lists 98, 319, 333b. Of Portsm., he depos. as Tufton in May 1695 ag. -27-; next mo. as R. T. M. took oath as Atty. Genl. of N. H., but signed as R. T., Atty. Genl., in 1696. Lost at sea 1696 (by 1738 chart), but in 1697

Katherine T. signed a deed by p/a from husband Robt. His will, 21 Oct. 1692, never proved, names w. Katherine T. M., sis. Elizabeth T., and son and dau., as Tuftons, charging them to carry it 'respectively' to their gr.fa. and gr.mo. and with all aunts and uncles. Wid. Katherine m. 2d (contr. 29 Oct. 1703) Simon Wiggin. Her will, 12 Sept. 1724—29 Mar. 1738 (when adm. gr. to John T. M. of Portsm., mariner), names dau. Elizabeth Philbrick, gr. sons John and Thos. Tufton and Tufton Philbrick, s. Walter Philbrick, Simon and Deborah Wiggin. Ch: **John. Elizabeth,** m. 1st Walter Philbrick (10), m. 2d Rev. Wm. Allen. **Katherine,** liv. 2 or 3 mos. (depos. of Deborah Jones(55) in 1738). The s. Capt. John, mariner, was bound to one Elliot, shipmaster, at age of 9 (widow's depos. 1738), went with his own shipments from Portsm. to Lisbon 1705, m. in Boston as Tufton (int. 31 Oct. 1710) Susanna Mossett, and d. at Havana 1718; widow m. 2d in 1720 Thos. Martin. 3 ch. b. Boston 1713-1718: Col. John, his gr.mo.'s adm., revived the Mason name and claim but sold out, later going to Eng.; will, of Bugden, co. Huntington, 1780-1787, gives to 2d w. Mary (Portsm. land), 4 Tufton nieces and neph. (Winnepesaukee land), dau. Catherine, w. of Saml. Moffatt of 'Damarera,' Esq., and 4 Livius gr.daus. Robert, d. by 1738. Thomas, Boston, m. twice and left ch., legatees of their uncle Col. John.

18 **ROBERT**, tailor, m. in Boston 30 or 31 Jan. 1693 Maria (also Mary and Mariot) Redman(2) and liv. in N. part of Hampton. Presumably related to (7). She d. in Hampt. Falls 8 Jan. 1735-6, a widow ag. -73-. 4 of 6 ch. joined in a q.c. that yr: **Nathaniel**, b. ±Jan. 1694-5, apprent. in Oct. 1710 for 5 yrs. 3 mos. to Edw. Sewall, cordwainer, Exeter, whose wid. sold him to Chas. Banfield (his gr.fa.'s report in 1713 when his fa. repres. he had no portion in land for him). He m. 12 Jan. 1716 Eleanor Long of Salisb., a wid. 1764. 6 ch. **Joseph**, bp. 14 Mar. 1714, not in deed 1736. **Sarah**, bp. 14 Mar. 1714, m. Timothy Dalton(2). **Benjamin**, b. 17 July 1704, d.y. **John**, b. 25 Feb. 1707, m. 28 Oct. 1736 Mary Sanborn; d. 12 Sept. 1771, she 25 Oct. 1778. 7 ch. **Benjamin**, b. 13 Dec. 1708, m. 17 Jan. 1734-5 Martha Rand(1); liv. on homestead. She d. 9 July 1782, he 22 Feb. 1799. 10 ch.

19 **THOMAS,** fisherman from Salem, a Falm. grantee under Danforth. List 225a. See Y. D. 14: 8; Essex D. 13: 217; Greenslade. One Thomas, weaver, Wells 1716-7 (Y. D. 9: 35, 104) was poss. the Scarb. propr. 1720 (List 239b), who was of Dover, trader, 1733-40, with Salem connection.

20 **WILLIAM,** tailor, Portsmouth. A memo on a ct. paper by Stileman in (?)1678

prob. shows his mar., 'William Mason, Elizabeth Perry 16 June.' His tax abated in Sept. 1680, -Manson-. He bot in 1693, tax abated 1695, sold without lic. 1696, and with Elizabeth mortg. Portsm. land to John White of Haverh. in 1699. Lists 329, 66. See also Lewis(18).

**MASTERS.** With Ruth (Pickworth) called both Masters and Masterson in Essex Co. probate records, the Wells and York families may well present difficulties.
**NATHANIEL,** Wells from Manchester, Mass., but earlier, Feb. 1649-50, a New London grantee, where his presence, also Cary Latham's, may reasonably connect him with John M. of Cambridge and Watertown, who willed to Nathl. and Abraham M. in 1639, without stating kinship. Nathl. had both Manch. and New London grants 1651; bef. June 1654 ret. to Manch. with w. Ruth, dau. of John Pickworth of Manch. and New London (Essex Q. Ct. 1: 360). York gr. 1666, but his w. still in Essex Co. in Nov. 1667. O. F. at Wells 1670. Lists 269b, 265, 266, 33. See also Howard(12) and Masterson. He signed a Wells letter ab. Ind., affairs 25 Apr. 1689 (Col. Soc. Mass. 8: 127). Manch. May 1702. Adm. to wid. Ruth 1 July 1708. Inv. (Senr. of Wells), including 150 a. upland (and ho. when sold in 1715), was sworn to 28 Apr. 1714 by gr.s. Nathl., whose acct. incl. '2 journeys from Manch. to Wells.' Wid. Ruth d. at Manch. 5 Apr. 1716. Ch., perh. not all: **Nathaniel,** unkn. except that the fa. was 'senr.' in 1676; poss. the wit. with Saml. Pickworth at Manch. 1675. One Nathl. served under Maj. Appleton ag. the Narragansetts. **John,** with fa.'s consent, apprent. for 4 yrs. in Sept. 1674 to Wm. Partridge of Wells, carpenter; swearing and fighting 1681. List 269b. **Abraham,** housewright, had Wells gr. 1681, m. Abigail Killam in Manch. 18 May 1691, d. bet. 24 Feb. 1712-3—16 Mar. 1713-4. Lists 368b, 269b. 9 ch. rec. in Manch. 1692-1711, the eldest Nathl. his gr.fa.'s admr. **Ruth,** m. Jeremiah Storer. **Lydia,** m. Lt. Josiah Littlefield(18). **Samuel** (List 267b), m. Ann Killam in Manch. 25 Dec. 1698. 5 ch. there. **Rebecca,** b. ±1675, m. Saml. Lee in Manch. 8 Feb. 1692. See also Barber(6).

**MASTERSON.** The N. E. fam. was from co. Kent and an offshoot of the ancient landed fam. in Cheshire.
**NATHANIEL,** York, marshal of the Prov., ±43 in Feb. 1671-2 (SJC 1073). Dr. Banks ident. him as s. of Richard and Mary (Goodall) M., b. in Leyden 1628, brot. to Plymouth as an infant, and later in Manchester and Ipsw. with fam. of his step-fa. Rev. Ralph Smith (Hist. of York, 1: 229; N. E. Reg. 10: 269). He m. in Ipsw. 31 July 1657 Elizabeth

Cogswell (John) and was there in 1658. York 1659, and there accepted marshal's office 3 July 1660. Remov. by the Gorges party, he submitted and was acquitted by the Carr court; restored as marshal by Mass. in 1668 and contin. until 1686+. His fence on Mr. Gorges' Neck ment. in 1661; in 1671 the town agreed to lay out his home place 'if it were not orderly granted' with 30 a. adj.; Rishworth and Thos. Moulton abutted. Constable 1666-7; gr.j. 1666, and either he or N. Masters in 1686-7. Freeman 1676; cor.j. 1685; selectm. 1687-8. List 25. Presum. he and w. Elizabeth perished in the Candlemas Day massacre, 1691-2. Adm. on est. of -Jonathangr. to Sarah M. 8 Mar. fol., her bondsm. Thos. Adams (replacing John Linscott first named) and Arthur Bragdon; inv. taken five days earlier by Linscott and Philip Babb incl. ho., barn, 160 a. of land, and other land adj. Only daus. appear, reckoning -Jonathan- as error for the fa. Nathl: **Elizabeth,** m. Samuel Young. **Sarah** (not Lydia), m. Capt. Arthur Bragdon(2 jr.) aft. 8 Mar. 1691-2. **Abiel,** an Ind. captive returned to N. E. but still in Ind. hands at Pennacook Jan. 1698-9 (List 99, p. 78). At York 1702-4; m. (int. Ipsw. 23 Dec. 1710) Isaac Foster Jr.
**MASURY** (see also Major), Edward, Exeter 1683, soldier Nov.—Dec. 1695. In 1698 when John Boulter was charged with passing counterf. money, he said it was paid him by E. M. Lists 57 (Meser), 67, 388. He m. bef. 9 Dec. 1712 Abiel, wid. of Wm. Morgan. One dau. kn. by an earlier w: **Jean,** m. Benjamin Mason(7).
**[Matershed],** Hannah, Great Island 1698. List 315b.
**Matson,** Ephraim, List 395, must be Marston.
**Matteford,** Joseph and w. (List 39), error for Joel Maddiver(1).

**MATTHEWS,** general over England except the North.
1 **AGNES** (Gerrish 1), depos. as Matthews in the Morse-Sloper case 1707; Obadiah Morse Jr. had been talking at her ho. In 1721 she was wid. A. M. of Portsm. (formerly Pomery), with a dau. Hannah, w. of Saml. Langmaid, who seems more likely to have been born Pomery than Gerrish or Matthews.
2 **CAPT. BENJAMIN**(5), Oyster River, ±47 in 1681. Cor.j. 1657, and sold marsh on Stony Brook to John Woodman in 1663. Then in Upper Kittery, where tr.j. 1664, constable 1666-7 and compl. of for neglect of duty. In N. H. again, freeman 21 June 1669; gr.j. 1670, 1673, 1675, 1695; j. 1665, 1680, 1682, 1685; tav. lic. 1683; called Capt. 1684. Lists 361a, 363a, 359a, 366, 357c, 49, 52, 57, 367b. See also Harrison(3). He m. aft. 28 June 1670 Dorothy (Hull 6) Kent, who was liv. in July 1685. He was ±80, 10 Mar. 1709-10, and

d. bef. 9 Mar. 1710-1, when his admr. and only kn. ch. **Francis,** was lic. to sell, his son and next heir Francis jr. consenting.

3 **DANIEL,** b. in Boston 4 Dec. 1646, s. of 'Dermin and Dinah Mahoone.' See Mahoney(1). The fa. was at times 'alias Matthews' and 'Matthews.' The s., always Matthews, was Sergt. in Philip's War and Dep. Sealer of Customs under Randolph, and aft. a more or less troubled career in Mass., entered upon ano. in N. H. as Provost Marshal and Sheriff under Cranfield 1683-4 until convicted of theft and dismissed. He was drunk in Boston in 1685, in prison for some reason in 1686, and there in 1688. One D. M. from Suff. Co. was a deserter from Wells garrison in 1690 (Doc. Hist. 5: 158). He m. Mary (Neighbors), wid. of John Windsor. Ch. rec. Boston: **Mary,** 3 Oct. 1669. **Elizabeth,** 30 June 1674. A dau. **Rebecca** Hannan claimed his Narragansett grant.

4 **DENNIS** (and Wm. Bickham), wit. deliv. of land, Withers to Godsoe, 25 Feb. 1687-8. One Dennis taxed in Boston 1687.

5 **FRANCIS,** Mr., Oyster River. On 1 Oct. 1637, Vines, Jocelyn and Wannerton as agents for Gorges and Mason (Narias Hawkins a wit.) leased to him for 1,000 yrs. 100 a. 'on the n.w. side of the great island commonly called Muskito Hall' (orig. in Fogg coll.). This passed from him to Wooton, to Tucker, and in 1664 to Geo. Walton, tho it is appar. Walton orig. claimed under John Heard(4). He signed Exeter comb. 1639, bot at O. R. from Wm. Beard in June 1640, from Wm. Hilton in 1645, and moved there. Bondsm. for Matthew Giles's w. Elizabeth and her s., 1644. Gr.j. 1646. Mr. F. M. to hear and decide local cases, 1647. Lists 41, 373. See also Brown(28). He d. betw. 10 May—19 Dec. 1648 with no rec. of adm. until it was gr. to s. Benj. 10 July 1704; inv. £119, claims £356. His wid. Mrs. Thomasine (Channon, m. at Ottery St. Mary, co. Devon, 22 Nov. 1622), sued John Heard of Sturgeon Creek in Me. Ct. Oct. 1652, and the writings were ord. deliv. to her; in 1653 she entered a caution ab. the land her husb. bot from Heard on Great Isl. See also Crimp, Shackford. List 354abc, 356a, 363b. She d. ±1690 (aft. 16 Oct. 1689); and s. Benj. entered claim for keeping her 25 yrs. Kn. ch., the 1st two bp. at Ottery St. Mary: **Elizabeth,** bp. 27 Dec. 1623. She or a 2d Elizabeth, ±50 in 1678, m. 1st Wm. Drew(17), m. 2d Wm. Follett(8). **Francis,** bp. 20 Feb. 1625. One F. wit. with (14) at the Shoals, 1665. **Walter. Martha,** m. 1st one Snell, m. 2d one Brown (see 18). **Benjamin,** b. ±1634. **Katherine,** b. ±1638, m. 1st Thos. Footman(2), m. 2d Wm. Durgin(2). See also Brookings.

6 **CAPT.** *FRANCIS(2),** Oyster River, m. 23 Feb. 1691-2 Ruth Bennett(3). Lists

368ab, 369. He refused office as selectman 1703, but served thirteen times 1704-1732; moderator 1728; Rep. 1728, 1731. Called Sergt. 1707, Ensign 1712, Capt. 1716. Rochester and Canterbury propr. He d. betw. 1749-1755. Ch. appear: **Francis,** oldest s. in 1711, m. in Newington 28 Nov. 1720 Lydia Drew(14), who took adm. 26 May 1742. List 368b. In 1749 his fa. deeded to 2 of the 4 ch., Gershom and Benj. jr., and to their mo., wid. Lydia, for life. **Benjamin,** O. R. scout 1712, m. 17 Dec. 1716 Abigail Hill(12), who was bp. with s. Benj. 20 Oct. 1717; List 368b. He was bp. and d. 11 Dec. 1724, ag. 31. She m. 2d Eleazer Coleman aft. 7 Apr. 1728 when she was admitted to ch., a wid. In 1748 their gr.fa. gave his homestead to 2 of the 4 ch., Valentine and Abraham, jr.; in 1755 their uncle Abraham q.c. to all 4 ch. all land his fa. had not himself deeded. **Abraham,** m. Phebe Davis(14) who was named in her fa.'s will and should be added to his ch. as given on p. 184. List 368b. Adm. to s. Francis in 1762. He and sis. Elizabeth were liv. 1764, but not Jonathan, bp. with Elizabeth in 1728.

7 **ISAAC,** sailmaker, Portsm., in 1713 tax list betw. Capt. Geo. Almery and Stephen Eastwick; this 1713 tax abated, he being dead. He m. a dau. of James Jones(21) and her br. John was his admr. 3 July 1716. See (9), (11).

8 **JOHN,** from Dartmouth, co. Devon, around Star Isl. and the mainland, 1650-2. P. & Ct. i: 154, 158, 174.

9 **JOSEPH,** by rec., m. Elizabeth Jones Sept. 1710, No. Ch. Portsm. **A daughter** of Elizabeth M. who was rec. into covt. and bp. at Boston, was bp. at No. Ch. 12 Aug. 1711. See also (7).

10 **NICHOLAS,** in Richmond's Island accounts 27 May 1639, and there aft. 18 July that yr. List 21.

11 **PETER,** fisherman, m. Mary, wid. of Gowen Cox(3); of Ipsw. in 1697 they sold to John Lang the Cox ho. and 2 a. on Sagamore Creek betw. Francis Jones and Abraham Bartlett. Poss. the same fisherman taxed in Newc. (List 316) and in 1720, and sold common rights with w. Mary in 1721. York had one or more Peters by 1714; soldier 1725; of York ord. out of Kit. 1726; incl. in a caution ag. town charges 1731. Peter, blockmaker, m. Mary Cate(3) in Greenl. 13 Feb. 1727-8; both liv. 1761. One Peter, ag. 80, was in Portsm. alms-ho. bef. Oct. 1781.

12 **SAMUEL(14),** fisherman, Smuttynose, had deed from gr.mo. Tamsen Matthews in 1678. Retired as Shoals constable in May 1685, and in 1690 was fined for abusing the then constable. In 1704 he sued (6) for ho. at mouth of O. R. built for his fa. Walter by Joseph Smith; Nicholas Harrison and the

wid. Tamsen had liv. there at times; in 1715 he q.c. to Nathl. Hill to confirm a deed given by his -mo.- Tamsen. Appar. childless when his fa. made his will in 1678, but had wife (dau. of Francis Raynes 1) and two or more ch. in 1693. Will, 18 Oct. 1719 (inv. 26 Sept. 1720), names sis. Joanna Raynes and 3 sons: **Walter**, given ⅓ his fa.'s Smuttynose and O. R. land. Shoals wit. 1717; of York 1727, he and w. Hannah sold Smuttynose dwg. and holdings; liv. York 1731. His dau. Hannah, from the Shoals, was bp. at Hamp. Falls 28 Aug. 1720; see Hull(10). Poss. a son: John, m. Abigail Averill at York 31 Mar. 1737. **Francis**, his inherit. in land the same as Walter's; liv. 20 May 1727 (Y. D. 12: 138). **Samuel**, given his fa.'s Smuttynose dwg. ho. and garden and ⅓ of the O. R. land. Newc. fisherman 1730 (Y. D. 16: 123). Samuel of Newc. m. Mary Bodge of O. R., 21 Nov. 1728, and of Newc. had s. Samuel bp. at O. R. 15 Feb. 1729-30. One Sarah adm. to Gosport Ch. 1 May 1737; Samuel, s. of Samuel, adm. 2 May 1742.

13 **THOMAS**, servant of Mrs. Bridget Graffort and beneficiary under her will, 1701. Gabriel Grout's est. was indebted to him in 1707. Taxed for Mill Dam, 1707-1713; tax abated 1714.

14 **WALTER**(5), Smuttynose, owned two houses there ab. 1652-3, occupied in 1680 by his wid. Mary and by John Martin as tenant (see depos. Y. D. 3: 71). Constable 1655 (in ct. for neglect of office in gathering rates) and 1658. Bondsman for Stephen Ford 1660. Gr.j. 1660, 1665 (absent). In 1671 he sued Wm. Croscum and was an appraiser of Wm. Seeley's large est. Lists 301, 366, 305c. See also Giles(7). His will, 15 Apr. (inv. 29 May —25 June) 1678, leaves housing, land and fishing plant on Smuttynose and at O. R. to w. Mary for life, then to s. Samuel (except what given to gr.s. Matthews Young and to sis. Martha Brown's son Thomas Snell), with cash to daus. and gr.ch. (3 Youngs and 2 Senters, but called -nephews- or -nieces-); wife Mary exec.; Saml. Belcher and Andrew Diamond overseers. Ch. in will: **Samuel**. **Susannah**, eldest dau., m. Rowland Young, jr. Her fa. gave her £10, and if her bro. d. s. p., ⅔ the est. One Susannah wit. an O. R. deed in 1669. **Mary**, b. ±1652, m. Wm. Senter. She also recd. £10 and was to have one third if her bro. d. s. p.

**MATTOON**. Evid. of continental origin; poss. a Walloon fam. in Canterbury or London. See N. E. Reg. 3: 389.

1 **HUBERTUS** (Rupert, Robert, or his own early signa. Hujbrecht), Portsm. tailor and fine gentleman of unkn. antecedents, first seen as wit. to Thos. Walford's deed 1 Jan. 1648-9. He took O. A. to Mass. in Me.,

16 Nov. 1652. Portsm. gr. Mar. 1654, and in 1657 served on cor.j., petit j., and as constable (also 1659). Dep. Marshal 1660-2. Lists 282, 323, 43, 325, 326ac, 328, 329, 330abde, 335. See Clark(49), Day(5). Devoted to women, he m. at least three, his w. Margaret noted only 5 Feb. 1663 when they sold dwg. and 8 a.; that she was Margaret Washington, an early Portsm. grantee, has been considered. In June 1673 he m. one equally devoted to men, Sarah (Pearce 8) Jones, whose husb. was liv. and undivorced. Mattoon divorced her in 1682, when she confessed misconduct, accusing him of the same and of desertion above 7 yrs. See Me. P. & Ct., vol. ii. He bot from James Gibbins in Saco in Apr. 1683, was there in Dec. next and poss. until the war. Taxed Str. Bk. July 1690 as Robert and appar. had with him ano. w. (List 331c); liv. Portsm. 1698. Ch. appear (4 indic. by the Pitcher deed): **John**, of age and a constable bef. Sept. 1676 in Ipsw., where prob. he had been apprenticed. Boston mariner 1678 (Jos. Stover's admr.) to 1693 (master of a brigantine). Had w. Dorothy. Only rec. ch: Joseph, b. Boston 2 Feb. 1687, but ano. must have been Richard, Boston blockmaker, who 25 Mar. 1728-9 q.c. the Saco land his uncle and aunt Pitcher had sold (Y. D. 12: 2: 295). One Eleanor M. m. Wm. Pollock in Boston in 1733. **Philip**, ±20 in 1675, his master John Clark of Ipsw. Going as a soldier to western Mass., he remained, m. 10 Sept. 1677 Sarah Hawks of Hadley, and d. in Deerfield 5 Dec. 1696; the wid. m. Daniel Belding. 10 ch., the 1st one Margaret. See Hist. of Deerfield, 2: 237. **Richard**. These sons, b. long bef. 1670, may well be ascribed to w. Margaret, but the mo. of **Grace**, b. not bef. 1670, nor aft. 1687, is uncertain. She m. Richard Pitcher in Boston 22 Dec. 1704; 4 ch. b. there 1707-1719. How she owned three fifths the Saco land sold by them 23 Mar. 1727-8 (Y. D. 12. 2. 294) and how relat. to John Pullen of Boston (will 1716, est. to w. Mary and sis.-in-law Grace Pitcher) not clear. That she evid. bot the portion of her oldest br. (his heirs later q.c.) conflicts with the 1753 writ (see 2). By w. Sarah (Pearce) cert. a **child**, b. ±3 wks. bef., and appar. liv. on 11 Nov. 1673. See also Mary Mattoon (poss. Maloon), gr.dau. of Mrs. Bridget Huggins(2) and Mary Jersie.

2 **RICHARD**(1), Exeter (Newmarket), had a Kit. gr. in June 1682 (Y. D. 31: 115) and worked at Madbury and Lampril River Bridge, 1686. Exeter highw. surv. 1690, 1693; j. 1695; tav. lic. 1695-6, 1698. Lists 218, 94, 57, 376b (1698), 96. He m., not bef. 1684, Jane (Hilton 2) Hall and with a son was k. by Ind. ab. 23 July 1706. Goods for 'Ma Mattoon' were charged to Richard Hilton in 1712. Wid. Matun taxed in Ex. 1716; dead

in Dec. 1735 (SJC 19971); adm. 29 Mar. 1738
to s. Edw. Hall. 4 of 6 kn. ch. were named in
a writ, entered and dropped in York Ct. in
Apr. 1753, Mattoon v. Scammon, reciting
that -Hubertus- d. ab. -1712- seized of ½ of
38 a. in Saco which descended to his ch: **Hubertus**, k. with his fa. (List 96). **Richard**,
Newmarket, carpenter, gentleman, Lt. at
Louisburg, m. bef. Aug. 1731 Ruth Bennett
(1), liv. 26 Sept. 1748. He d. betw. 3 May
1755—7 Jan. 1764. 4 or m. ch., the first two
bp. at O. R. 1723-4. **Mary**, m. Richard Smith;
not named in writ, but see N. H. deed 82: 258
(1758) given by the four sis. Appar. she liv.
with Richard Hilton, sr., in 1718 when R. H.,
jr., gave her an order on a Portsm. store.
**Ann**, m. Walter Neal(8). **Sarah**, m. Samuel
Sinclair. **Dorothy**, unm. in 1753, m. bef. 1758
Thos. Beck(4 jr.).

3 **WILLIAM**, bp. at Hampton 2 Aug. 1702,
presented by Martha Redman(2) as her
own.

**MAUDE, Rev. Daniel**, Dover, matric. at
Emanuel Coll., Cambridge, in 1603, and
arriv. here with Rev. Richard Mather in the
-James- from Bristol in Aug. 1635. Adm. to
Boston Ch. 20 Sept. 1635, freeman and chos-
en free-schoolmaster in 1636 and clerk of the
writs in Dec. 1641. He went to Dover bef. 1
Aug. 1642, when by town vote he and w.
Mary could enjoy for life their then dwg.-ho.
provided he remain as teacher or pastor. As
Marie Bonner, servant to Rev. John Cotton,
she was adm. to Boston Ch. 3 Aug. 1634 and
was dism. to Dover as his w. (prob. not 1st)
18 Aug. 1644. In July 1651 he was to remain
at Dover Neck and ano. minister to be chos-
en for O. R., each at £50 salary; there he remained till death. Belknap notes his serious
spirit and quiet and peaceful disposition; all
Dover ministers were not so endowed. His
will, 17 Jan. 1654-5—26 Jan. 1655-6, directs
burial by his last w. (a wid. with 4 minor
ch.), gives to her ch., Mr. Roberts and w., sis.
and bro. Cotton, four young Cottons, and
others; Susan Halstoe and -his- bro. and sis.
and sis.-in-law needed nothing and were all
in years. In Boston he had owned a small
lot adj. Mr. Cotton.

**Mauer.** List 375b. See Moore.

**MAUNDY, Richard**, Mr., merchant, Newcastle, 1698-9, had bill of sale of the -Mary-
from Thos. Holland(7) in 1698, declared
void in 1700. In Sept. 1700 Jacob Randall
(4) gave him (Capt.) a p/a to sue in Eng.
List 315b.

**MAVERICK.** For the Devon ancestry of
this prominent emigrant fam. see Reg.
69. 146. See also Parker(7).

1 **ANTIPAS**, Mr., ±50 in 1669, merchant,
son of Rev. John and Mary (Gye) of Bea-
worthy, co. Devon, was brot, a boy of ten, to

Dorchester by his parents. First at the Isles
of Shoals, he sold at Hog Island two houses
and a fishing-stage to Henry Sherborne in
1647 when he bot a dwelling-ho. and 100 a.
at Kittery from Edward Small. Francis S.,
son of the grantor, seems to have given Maverick constant trouble by claims against this
land, which A. M. mortgaged to Thomas
Booth for £520 in 1661. He put his equity in
the name of his br. Moses M. of Marblehead
in 1663 and in 1663-4 the mortgage was pd.
His w., name unkn., was ment. in a Kit. gr.
in 1654. O. A. 1652; inn-keeper's lic. 1659;
gr.j. 1646-7, 1654, 1655; j. 1647. See Lemon.
Lists 54, 73, 282, 298, 313b. In 1661 he sold
land and a mill formerly Wm. Ellingham's,
and by 1667 he had left Kittery for Exeter.
He was drowned 2 July 1678, having fallen
out of a boat while intoxicated. Adm. gr. 24
Apr. 1682 to his two sons-in-law to whom his
br. Moses gave a receipt in full. Ch: **Katherine**, m. Stephen Paul(2). **Abigail**, m. Edward Gilman(5). **Moses**, appren. to Robert
Couch of Boston for 8 yrs. 4 Sept. 1667 to
learn surgery, his fa. having given Capt.
Barefoot a p/a to apprentice him 29 Aug.
1667. Exeter wit. 1674. Presum. d. before
1682, s. p.

2 **SAMUEL** of Noodle's Island (Lists 73,
111, 271 [2], 272), Elias of Winnisimmet (List 272), and Moses of Marblehead,
brothers of (1). Elias and Moses did not
live within our territory, altho their names
occasionally appear in Me. records. Samuel,
the first of the family to come over, with
Robert Gorges, had much to do with Me. and
held land in York. In the period betw. leaving Boston and going to New York he never
had his home in Mass., and poss. it was here.
His w. Amias was in Saco with their dau.
Mrs. **Mary** Hooke(2) in 1666 (List 246), and
adm. on their son **Samuel's** Me. estate was
gr. to Francis Hooke at Casco Ct. 13 Nov.
1668, Tho. Williams and Roger Hill bondsmen. This s. Samuel m. Rebecca Wheelwright (2 daus.), and his older bro. **Nathaniel** (will 1670—1674) left a widow and ch. in
Barbados. Adm. on the senior Samuel's est.
was gr. in York Ct. 27 Sept. 1681. See Gorges
(9), Norton(6); Me. P. & C. Rec. i: xlvii,
184-194; N. E. Reg. 69: 157-159; 78: 448.

**MAXWELL**, sometimes Maxfield. A
Scotch border clan.

1 **ALEXANDER**, farmer, York, bot from
Thos. Moulton 23 Jan. 1657-8, and was
the first Scot to buy and settle in what became 'Scotland.' Previously, as Mr. Geo.
Leader's servant, he had been in ct. for
abusing his master and mistress. Kit. gr.
1656, York gr. 1659, 1668-9. Tr.j. 1668, 1676,
1688; gr.j. 1679, 1687, 1691; tav. lic. 1683-5,
1687. O. A. 22 Mar. 1679-80. On June 27,

1707 he sold to John McIntire 3 a. bounded S.E. 'by the orchard or garden of sd. Maxell where the Garison now stands.' This garrison the historian of York consid. to be the same, enlarged and improved, kn. later and now as 'the McIntire garrison.' See Y. D. 7: 87, and Hist. of York ii: 223-4. Lists 298, 25, 33, 87. See also his serv. Saml. Crawley (1), Dill(1), Fox(6), Grant(5), Kelly(11), Mackaneer. He m. bef. 4 Sept. 1671 Agnes Frost(6), who was liv. 23 Aug. 1704; both were abs. from meeting in 1696. He m. 2d (by Capt. Preble in 1707) Sarah Pennewell (see 3). His will, 15 May—8 Oct. 1707, gives her all for life, afterw. ½ the land and marsh to Mr. Moody, ½ for use of the church. No desc.

2 **JAMES**, an Eastern claimant (Me. Hist. & Gen. Rec. V: 151) must be Marinell. See Y. D. 14: 105.

## MAY

1 **ANDREW** (or Way), ±15 in Mar. 1668-9, apprentice of Joshua Scottow.

2 **DAVID**, Portsm. wit. 1670. His inquest held at Saco, 22 Dec. 1670, verdict suicide. Adm. in Saco Ct., 4 Apr. 1671, to Stephen Sargent as agent for Mrs. Mehitable(Clarke 54) Downes(1). Inv. incl. chiefly a large wardrobe, a hog and a sow.

3 **EMANUEL**, see Davis(26).

4 **GEORGE**, prob. the Boston man, by attorney Francis Johnson(11) unsuc. sued Maj. Shapleigh in 1672.

5 **GIDEON**, see Stone.

6 **JOHN** (Mays), Dover wit. 1661, Starbuck to Coffin.

7 **NICHOLAS**, and Wm. Ash, defts. in suit for trespass entered and dropped by Thos. Withers, in Me. Ct. July 1671. Portsm. wit. 1672; taxed there (10 s.) in Oct. that yr.

8 **WILLIAM**, and neph. Robert Elliot(6) came to Great Isl. in the Bristol ship -Concord-. He ret. with an order from Elliot, 4 Mar. 1668, to sell a schedule of hats and to collect bills.

**MAYER**, Mare, Marr, Mere and other variants, found in cos. Devon, Durham, Stafford, Lancaster. Some Eng. Mayers claim descent from Channel Isl. Maugers.

1 **JOHN**, (sometimes Meager), Black Point, ±25 in 1667, fisherman, with Peter Hinkson leased flake-yard on Prouts Neck from Mr. Jocelyn. In 1665 frequented Mary Oakman's company in a suspicious and unseemly manner. Sued John Tenney and sued by John Budesert (slander) in 1664, sued by Nathan Bedford for breach of contract and to account for a year's voyage in 1667, sued Tenney again in 1668 and 1669 and won cases against Bedford and James Harmon in latter yr. Sued commissioners of Scarb.

and Falm. in 1670. Attorney for Fr. Wainwright and James Harmon, 1669-1670. Deposed 12 July 1667 with Elias Oakman about a long fishing voyage. He must have been reported lost at sea in 1668 as on 29 Oct. Elias Oakman and Peter Shaw were gr. adm. on his est., but he turned up. List 234a. No ment. of w. or ch., but John Maire's wid. is in Philip English's accounts in Salem in 1683.

2 **RICHARD**, Black Point in 1661 when cattle belonging to Andrew Heffer's est. were at Richard Mayre's. Drunk in 1665.

3 **WALTER**, Saco. In Holberton, co. Devon, the home of several Maine immigrants, Walter Mares, son of Walter, was bp. 2 Mar. 1624, the only Mares entry in the register. Poss. he was brot over as a child by the Boadens. He m. a dau. of Michael Maddiver of Spurwink bef. 1654 and was a householder in Saco, on west bank of the river, in 1656. Constable 1663; selectman 1673, 1680-1683; appr. Henry Waddock's est. 1679. Gr. 50 a. at head of his lot, 1680: Lists 244a, 245, 246, 247, 249, 27. Fled to Salem in 1676 and in next war to Boston, where in 1698 he deeded his 100 a. homestead in Saco to his dau. Sarah Haley. Ch: **Judith**, b. 16 Mar. 1654, m. Giles Read(1) 10 Nov. 167-. **Mary**, b. 3 Sept. 1656, d. bef. 1704. **Walter**, b. 2 May 1659; d. bef. 1704. **Sara**, b. 5 Feb. 1661, m. 1st Sergt. Thomas Haley(8), m. 2d Capt. Richard Carr(5) 28 Feb. 1701-2. **Rebecca**, b. 12 July 1664, m. 1st Sergt. Nasiter 19 May 1688 at Marblehead, m. 2d Dr. John Baxter (1). **Ruth**, b. 20 Oct. 1666, in ct. 13 Mar. 1688-9 for bastardy, unm. in 1704. **Elizabeth**, b. 23 July 1669, d. bef. 1704. **Benjamin**, b. 16 Mar. 1671-2; soldier at Fort Mary Feb. 1699-1700; k. by Ind. bef. 13 Apr. 1704 when his four sis. asked adm. which was gr. to Capt. Carr, the inv. containing only one item, £7: 14: 0 in hands of Capt. James Gooch of Boston. In Oct. 1707, in suit brot by Carr as adm. ag. Wheelwright, Thos. Wormwood and Elizabeth Goodale testif. that Benj. Mairs did for seven yrs. make Mr. John Wheelwright's house his home as he passed to and fro on his business, and their mistress did his laundry and mending. List 268b. **Love**, b. 29 Sept. 1674, m. Henry Paine (see 4).

4 **WILLIAM** (Mares), bondsman for John West, N. H. tavern-keeper, in 1693.

**MAYHEW, Thomas**, Mr., agent for Mr. Matthew Craddock in the Richard Williams est. at Saco. See Me. P. & Ct. i: 96-99, 102; also Hist. of Martha's Vineyard, i: 80-3.

**MAYLEM** (also Milam), **Joseph**, at No. Yarmouth early (List 214), later bricklayer, innholder, Boston, where one Joseph, s. of John and Christian, was b. 26 Feb. 1651-2. He m. 1st at Charlest. in 1688 Hannah

King (Mark); 6 ch. rec. in Boston 1689-1703. He m. 2d at Boston, 11 Oct. 1711, Keziah (Brackett 2), who had m. her 1st husb. John Patteson in Roxbury 11 June 1706. List 229. See also Y. D. 9: 156 (J. M. and Hezekiah Phelps of Wells buy at Pemaquid, 1716); Y. D. 14: 198; 18: 139. Will, 13 Aug. 1730— 13 Feb. 1732-3, names w. Keziah, sons Joseph, Mark (whose wid. Elizabeth m. Anthony Brackett, 3 jr.) and John. Her will, wid. of Boston, 3—20 Mar. 1732-3, names two sis., nephew, nieces and aunt, giving residue to ano. neph. Anthony Brackett.

**MAYNARD, Ruth** (Mannyard), m. Elias Stileman 10 Apr. 1667 (N. H. Prov. rec.). Presum. one of the five Maynard gr.daus. named in will of Dr. Comfort Starr of Boston 1659, and niece of Pres. John Cutt's wife. (See also Pendleton).

**McBride.** See Dentt.

**McCalva.** See Footman(1).

**McCARTHY, Thaddeus,** Boston, m. Elizabeth Johnson(11) and gave bond as admr. of her fa.'s est. 19 Mar. 1690-1. List 14. See also Herbert(3). He d. 18 June 1705, ag. 65; her will 8 Apr., d. 7 June 1723, ag. 82 (Granary Bur. Gr.). Eight or more **ch.**

**McCARY, Matthew,** Portsm. rate abated Sept. 1695. In Mar. 1708-9 the town pd. for keeping Mati. Maccanarany.

**McCORMICK, Dennis,** Irishman, was sold to John Pickering for 5 yrs. in 1654, and the ct. ended his service in July 1659. Portsm. gr. 1660.

**McCUE, Timothy** (Markue), wit. Moore-Dill settlement at York 1694. List 37 (Machew).

**McDaniel.** See McDonald.

**McDONALD** (McDaniel).

1 **AENEAS** (McDaniel), had run away from his master Benj. Blackman(2) in June 1688.

2 **ALEXANDER** (Macdannel), a Scot of Oyster River, kinsman of John Roy of Charlestown, taxed 1661 or 1662; drowned in Jan. 1663-4. Lists 363ac, 364.

3 **RENALD,** m. Mary Bussey(3) and was of Falmouth in 1729. List 369. See Y. D. 13: 271; 15: 165. Poss. a son was Robert (List 369) whose ch. Margaret and William were bp. at Oyster River 1712-4.

**McElroy.** See Bunker(2), Downes(6), Ingersoll(1).

**McGOWEN, John** (also McGown), Portsm. 1683, a Scot in the employ of Geo. Jaffrey (4), who gave him a general p/a in 1684, calling him trusty friend. Member of No. Ch. (Magoon) and away in 1699 (Macgoon). List 331c. In Nov. 1701 he wit. James Treworgy's deed (Y. D. 6: 115).

**McGREGORY,** 1 **Daniel,** a Dedham soldier at Wells 1693-4. List 267b.

2 **LT.-COL.** List 19.

**McINTIRE.** A Highland clan.

1 **MALCOLM** (Micom), York, taxed Dover 1659, also in 1663 as Micom the Scotchman. Kittery gr. 1662, and bondsm. for Wm. Gowen(4) in 1667. On 22 June 1670 he bot two York tracts from John Pearce(9) whose dau. Dorothy, wid. of Alex. Mackaneer, was his w. bef. 4 Sept. 1671. Other holdings incl. James Carmichael's former gr. assigned to him by James Grant in 1670, and town gr. in 1673, 1696. Lists 356eh, 298, 81, 33. See also Carmichael, Reed(4), Roans. His wife was abs. from meeting in 1673. She d. bef. he made his will, 17 Apr. 1700 (inv. 22 Mar. 1704-5), giving his lands to three sons, with the homestead to **John,** who also had grants 1701, 1722, and bot more. List 279. For the McIntire garrison ho., still preserved, see Hist. of York, ii: 223-4, and Maxwell(1). John m. Susanna Young (Dea. Rowland) and was liv. in Apr. 1744, ±63. Ch. 1707-1721: Joseph, Susanna, John, Hannah, Ebenezer, Daniel, Samuel. **Daniel** had town gr. 1711, and was a soldier under John Penhallow in 1722. Appar. liv. in 1732, List 279, and in 1741 when his neph. was still 'jr.' **Micom** (Malcolm), innholder, had grants 1709, 1711. List 279. He m. 9 July 1708 Jane Grant (17), named as Jean in his will, 21 Oct. 1743 —21 Oct. 1755 (sic), with s. Alexander (b. 9 June 1709) and dau. Kezia (b. 13 May 1713), but not dau. Mary b. 1716.

2 **ROBERT** (MacKintire), ±24 in Jan. 1653-4, employed by Thos. Wiggin to cart coals.

**McKENNEY.** The Scotch prisoners may account for this family, which has also been consid. Irish. Henry McKenney, a Scot, ±21 in 1651, was Geo. Spear's servant in Braintree.

1 **HUGH,** k. at Casco in 1703. List 39.

2 **JOHN,** Scarboro, his name ranging from Maksharone, a Foxwell wit. 1664, to Mackemech otherwise Mackerell, a Sheldon abuttor 1693. See also (4) and Maccham. In 1675 (deed antedated to 1 Aug. 1668) Joshua Scottow confirmed to him 14 a. at Black Point, 1 a. of it adj. his ho.; but some suspic. of fraud attaches to deed 12 Jan. 1673-4, from Robt. Jordan to him, for good services in several ways, of ±15 a. meadow in his poss. several yrs. beginning at Chisemore's Hill (Y. D. 28: 79). John Jordan(9) depos. in 1749 that he found this among his fa.'s papers. See also Chisholm(1). As a refugee Salem aided him in 1677-8 and paid in 1679 for carrying the fam. to Black Point, where in 1681 he had a goodly amt. of livestock. Lists 237bde, 238a, 239a, 30. If same as (3) not kn. His w. not found, and only kn. ch. **Robert.** See also later Salem records.

3 **JOHN**, drowned in Ogunquit River 1697, by reason of his unacquaintance with the river. (List 268a). See (2).

4 **KENNEY**, Boston, by atty. Mr. Nathl. Phillips, sued (2) for debt in Saco ct. 1665.

5 **ROBERT**(2), m. at Dover 1 Dec. 1692 Rebecca Sparks, wid., who was abs. from meeting in Jan. 1696-7 and d. in Scarb. 19 Apr. 1724 (the day aft. an Ind. attack). He was in Boston 1698, Sagamore Creek 1705, Kit. 1707, York 1718, Scarb. propr. 1720, and d. in Scarb. a widower, 22 July 1725. List 239b. Ch., not in order: John, had a gr. in 1727 as one who had abided in Scarb. thru the war; eldest bro. 1737; depos. in June 1752, ±68, ab. Scarb. 37 yrs. bef. He m. (int. 23 Mar. 1728) Margaret Wright (Thos.) Ch. **Robert**, served under Sergt. Knight in 1723-4 and Capt. Gray in 1725, and had a gr. 1727. He m. (int. 1 Apr. 1727) Margaret Jameson (Wm. 3 jr.), who was gr. adm. 11 July 1758. Ch. See Y. D. 17: 231; 23: 141. **Henry**, had Scarb. gr. 1720, 1727; soldier under Westbrook 1724-5; taxed there 1729-30. He m. in Scarb. 15 Mar. 1729 Sarah Hanscom, settled in Cape Elizabeth and in 1732 owned adj. Sparks land; liv. 1757. Ch. **Eleazer**, in Capt. Gray's Co. 1725, had gr. 1727, of Scarb. 1731; of Falm., adm. to br. John 18 Jan. 1736-7. **Isaac**, taxed Black Point 1729, m. 1 Apr. 1731 Elizabeth, dau. of John and Mary (Getchell 6) Drisco (see 6); liv. 1783. Ch. **Hannah**, m. 1st Robt. Foye(2), m. 2d Wm. Groves. **Rebecca**, m. Daniel Burnham(3). Not imposs. one or m. ch. remained ab. the Piscat., where are found: James, taxed Portsm. 1728. Daniel, Kit., m. Mary Hall (see 6); of Berw. 1736-9. Thomas (Mackcheneium) at Chas. Trafton's in York 1730. Mary, a Kit. or Berw. wit. 1720 (Y. D. 10: 68). Ephraim Foster m. in Falm. 1735 Mary -Melony- by one rec., -Mackeney- by ano.

**McLucas**, John, List 279. See Cole(17).

**McMILLAN** (McMillion), Alexander, Wells, m. 15 Dec. 1698 Rebecca Eldridge(2), who was a wid. in Salem 1728 and liv. there 1734. His Wells gr. 1699 (List 269b) was laid out 1749-1754 to Lemuel Hatch, Benj. Crediford and Chas. Annis. **Six ch.** rec. in Salem 1702-1713.

**McPhedris**, Capt. Archibald. See Wentworth and Jaffrey (4 jr.).

**McPherson**, Angus, ±30 in 1664, poss. of Charlestown or vicinity. List 364.

## MEAD

1 **JOSEPH**, Hampton 1680. Lists 396, 397b.

2 **NICHOLAS**, tanner, Charlestown, Bristol, R. I., and Boston 1679-1696. By 1699 he leased the Vaughan farm at Greenland; Portsm. 1701, his tanyard taxed 1707; Dep. Coll. of Excise 1708; bot a Berwick tannery

1713, and, of Portsm. 1714, sold an Exeter ho. to s. John. In prison 1716, prob. for debt, when Samuel Chapman jr. of Greenl. was trying to get him out. Berw. 1717; in jail again 1720 (broke out) and ord. released on surety of two sons. His w. Elizabeth, adm. to Charlest. Ch. 1681, was liv. 1717. A Bristol census of 1688-9 counts 6 ch. Found are: **Susanna**, b. Charlest. 5 Sept. 1679. **Elizabeth**, b. Charlest. 14 Aug. 1681, m. 1st Joseph Dennett(4), m. 2d Samuel Hewey. **Ebenezer**, b. Bristol 22 Mar. 1685-6. **Katherine**, bp. Bristol 10 July 1687. **John**, bp. Bristol 13 May 1688, tanner, m. in Portsm. 2 Dec. 1708 Hannah Cotton(2). Exeter (Stratham) 1709, where Mr. J. M. d. 22 Dec. 1769. List 388. **5** ch. rec. Strat. 1709-1718, not incl. Nabby who was her aunt Abigail Cotton's heir. See also Hutchins(11). **Joseph**, currier, Portsm., on bond with Nicholas and John M. and John Odiorne 1715. Lists 339, 388. He m. 1st 25 Feb. 1713-4 Mary Deverson(1), and 2d, late, Mrs. Ruth Waterhouse. Adm. 21 June 1756 to Benj. Akerman and Richard Fitzgerald, the wid. renounc. in fav. of any of the next of kin. She m. (3) 16 June 1757 Thomas Skinner and d. in Portsm. 17 Apr. 1769, ag. 89 (see Moses 1). 3 daus. appear. **Benjamin**, bot his fa.'s Berw. tanyard in 1717. He m. (ct. Jan. 1716-7) Judith Lord(7), who gave bond as admx. 15 May 1718. She o.c. and was bp. in Berw. Ch., with ch. Elizabeth and Judith in Oct. 1720, and m. 2d 24 May 1721 Gabriel Hamilton. **Nicholas**, with br. John surety for fa. in 1720. Found in Portsm.: Elizabeth o. c. No. Ch. and had dau. Elizabeth bp. 25 Sept. 1709; Mary jr. recd. into covt. So. Ch. 1715. Thomas, m. in Newc. 20 May 1725 Hannah Stilson, renew. bap. covt. in So. Ch. 1726, admitted in 1727, she in 1728; 3 ch. bp. And Thomas, fisherman, appar. with w. Susanna, 1736; ch. bp. in So. Ch. See also Robert Moore(10).

3 **MR.**, his ketch at Piscataqua 1674. P. & Ct. ii: 492-3.

## MEADER

**MEADER**, not freq. in England. John Meader, a tailor, was of St. Andrew's Holborn, London, 1625.

1 **JOHN**, Oyster River, b. ±1630, knew Robert Huckins' land in 1647 or 1648 and depos. in Mar. 1709-10, ±80, that he liv. with Mr. Valentine Hill ±60 yrs. ago. Poss. related to a Boston blockmaker of same name who was dealing with Roger Rose in O. R. timber in 1676. The N. H. John had a 100 a. gr. with Wm. Sheffield in 1656, and alone in 1660 bot from Mr. Hill near the mouth of O. R., where he liv. Jury 1659-60: gr.j. 1661-2, 1665, 1670, 1678, 1693. Lists 356ab, 361a, 341, 362b, 363ac, 365, 366, 359a, 49, 52, 367a, 57, 62, 66, 368b. His garrison ho., burned in 1694, was appar. soon rebuilt. Bef. this, in

Nov. 1686, he deeded homestead to s. Joseph for supp. of self and w., with reversion to Nathaniel if Joseph should d. s. p., then to John, with payments to daus. Ag. ±70 in 1700, also 1702; ±82 in Jan. 1711-2; liv. 1715. His w. was Abigail from 1664 to 1671 at least. Ch. appear: **John**, b. ±1655-6. **Joseph**, b. ±1664. (**Hannah**), m. Nicholas Follett(6). And by Prov. rec: **Elizabeth**, b. 26 Mar. 1665, unm. in Mar. 1704-5. **Sarah**, b. 11 Jan. 1668, m. 16 Mar. 1691-2 Edw. Wakeham. **Nathaniel**, b. 14 June 1671.

2 **JOHN**(1), weaver, ±66 in 1721-2, m. 1st by 1680 Sarah Follett(5), who was ±52 in 1706 and liv. in 1714; m. 2d by 1726 Elizabeth(Kirke 2), wid. of Daniel Libby(6) and poss. of Jona. Barlow; m. 3d (contr. 5 Apr. 1735) Agnes, wid. of Samuel Clark(50). Jury 1681; gr.j. 1696, 1698; assessor 1699; selectm. 1702. Lists 359b, 52, 57, 62, 353, 368ab, 369. See also Richard Denbo(1). He was bp. at O. R. 3 May 1728, aged br. of Joseph. Will, 2 Nov.—17 Dec. 1736, names 4 surv. ch. and 2 Tibbetts gr.ch., but not w. Agnes, who q.c. to his s. Joseph in 1737 and was of Portsm. 22 Mar. 1745-6. Ch: **Joseph**, housewright, b. 10 Apr. 1681 (self rec. at Nantucket), m. there 29 Feb. 1703-4 Charity Nason (Joseph 5). 9 ch.rec. Nant.1705-1724 of whom Moses liv. in N. H. See also John Hanson(7). **Nicholas**, Dover Neck, b. ±1685 (77 in Nov. 1762). Nicholas Follett deeded to him in 1710, calling him 'cousin.' Lists 368b, 369. His 1st w. was Lydia. Will, 9 June 1759—29 June 1767, names w. Sarah and 4 of 6 ch., 5 of them rec. Dover 1709-1718, their mo. Lydia. **Elizabeth**, m. John Hanson(7). **Abigail**, m. John Davis(40). **Sarah**, m. by 1714 John Tibbetts; d. bef. fa.

3 **SERGT. JOSEPH**(1), ±36 in 1700. His w. Elizabeth, m. ±1690, was adm. 30 June 1723 to O. R. Ch., where he was bp. 4 Feb. 1727-8. Gr.j. 1692; Dover constable 1692; selectm. 1695, 1705, 1711-3, 1715-6. Called Sergeant 1711. Lists 52, 57, 94, 353, 367b, 368ab, 369. See also Follett(2), (6). With w. Elizabeth he deeded homestead to neph. Daniel for life supp. 20 Nov. 1729; d. s. p. and intest. by 1739 when his sis. Sarah Wakeham sold one-fifth of his land.

4 **NATHANIEL**(1), Dover constable 1697. List 368a. See also Derry(1), Leathers (1). Killed by Ind. at O. R., not far from Nicholas Follett's ho., 25 Apr. 1704 (List 96). Wid. Eleanor (app. Merrow 2) renounc. adm. to his bro. Joseph 3 Apr. 1705; div. 2 Apr. 1706 to wid., ch. (unnamed) and creditors. She may have been John(8) Leighton's 2d w. Eleanor. Ch. rec. in Dover (the last 4, not the mo., q.c. to Geo. Jaffrey 1723): **Lydia**, b. 25 Aug. 1696, m. at Portsm. 22 Dec. 1717 Elbert Elborton, b. at New York; see Elberson. **Daniel**, wheelwright, Durham, b.

3 Nov. 1698, m. 23 Aug. 1727 Elizabeth Allen (Francis 12). List 369. Will, 3 Aug.—25 Sept. 1751, names her (of Haverhill 1771) and 8 ch. **Nathaniel**, b. 8 Mar. 1700, m. at O. R. 17 Dec. 1724 Rachel Sias; liv. at Lee. List 369. Ch. **Elizabeth**, b. 3 Apr. 1702, m. 23 Jan. 1728-9 Henry Tibbetts. **Eleanor**, b. 3 June 1704, m. 1st Daniel Libby (s. of Daniel 6), m. 2d John Brooks.

**Meager**, John. See Mayer.

**MEAKINS, Thomas**, Exeter (Newmarket), had sold his ho. to Thos. Hewes in 1670; wrote his name Makins in 1679; creditor of Geo. Carr's est. 1682; named dep. marshal by Sherlock in Jan. 1683-4. Taxed 1714. Lists 383, 52, 94. Early wife or wives unkn. His wid., 1727-1738, was Abigail (Footman 2), form. wid. of Benj. York, whom he m. aft. 1715. One John Meekin had suits against Gershom Baston and Amos Jewett in York Inf. Ct., 1729.

**Meane**. See Mains.

**Medbury**, John, worked three days at Fort Wm. and Mary in 1697. List 68. One of the name was of Swansea in 1683.

**Meekell**, John, ackn. judgm. to Samuel Wentworth in 1681 (Conc. 5: 50).

**MEINZIES, James**, Mr., Boston, bot Easton's Neck, Great Boar's Head, 3000 a., from Nicholas Easton of Newport, gr.s. of the first Nicholas. In 1696 he was counsel in a Portsm. court.

**MELCHER.** The N. H. immigrant's connections here suggest a Devonshire origin. Co. Bucks also has the name.

1 **EDWARD**, baker, Portsm. 1657, ±46 in 1675. He wit. for John Cutts at times 1658-1664, took poss. for him in 1660, and in 1675 depos. ab. Katherine Circuit in the Cutts kitchen. Propr. 1660. Gr.j. 1679, 1683; constable 1679-80. Lists 323, 326ac, 329, 330b, 331ab, 332a, 335a, 52, 62. See also Geare, Gerrish(1), Harris(22), Williams. With w. Elizabeth, he deeded to dau. Mary Jackson in 1694, and by will, 5—24 Aug. 1695 (orig. in Ct. Files 27892), provid. that w. live with dau.; also that sis.-in-law Sarah Akerman (1) and Walter Windsor might live for life where they then dwelt. Lands were given to ch: **Nathaniel. Samuel**, Hampt. Falls, m. 16 May 1700 Elizabeth Cram(1). Lists 69, 399a. Will, 18 Apr. 1745—28 Apr. 1755, names w. and ch: Samuel (m. Esther Green), John, Hannah, Sarah, Esther, Mary (w. of Abel Ward), Elizabeth (w. of Ezekiel Sanborn). **Mary**, m. 1st Samuel Jackson(18), m. 2d Peter Mann(5).

2 **NATHANIEL**(1), Portsm., m. Elizabeth Lear(2). Taxed Str. Bk. 1690, rated to No. Ch. 1717. Lists 330d, 337, 339. Will, 20 Mar. 1722-3 (rec. as a deed 14 Mar. 1723-4), names w. and 4 ch. The wid. was taxed 1724,

rec. into So. Ch. as Elizabeth sr. 1729, and was liv. in 1730 when her br. q.c. to her the Sagamore Creek ho. and 20 a. where she dwelt. Both she and her s. Edward's w. seem unlikely the Mrs. M. taxed in Biddef. in 1737 next to Thos. Dyer. Ch., 3 bp. at No. Ch. 5 June 1709 when their mo. o.c.: **Edward**, cordwainer, m. in Portsm. 25 Dec. 1723 Elizabeth Bailey. Newc. 1724-5, 'gone' by Portsmouth tax list 1725. Arundel grant Jan. 1728-9, his ho. ment. in Mar. fol. (Y. D. 14: 133); liv. there Aug. 1733 and Dec. 1734, but ack. a deed in Boston in Oct. 1734; both of Arundel 1742. Ch. **Nathaniel**, m. May 1724 Esther Cowell (John; see 6), and d. bef. 25 Jan. 1740-1, she in Mar. 1790, ag. 84. 6 or more ch. In 1762 (or 4), Tobias M., glazier, and Mary, w. of John Lewis, sailor, sold half the Barr. gr., wid. Esther joining. **Elizabeth**, m. 25 Nov. 1729 Samuel Barnes, mariner, who in 1762 (or 4) sold half the Barr. gr. (willed to her bros. Edw. and Nathl.). **John**, bp. 26 Aug. 1711, renewed bp. cov. in So. Ch. 1732 and must have been -Jonathan- adm. to communion in 1732-3. He m. in Portsm. 1 July 1733 Mary -Mons- (or Morss?); d. in Mar. 1787, ag. 78, she in May 1790, ag. 76. 5 or more ch.

**MELLIN, William**, came to Richmond's Isl. in -The- Fortune- 1638. Landsman and seaman by accounts until last of May 1643, being furnished with much clothing. List 21.

**MELOON, Luke** (also Maloon, Malone), Greenland, taxed Bloody Point 1672, and of Dover when he m. Hannah Clifford(3) 20 Nov. 1677. Lists 356j, 359b, 62. See also Gray(14). He and John Partridge were bondsm. for tav.-keeper John Johnson(16) in 1689. Jury 1694. Portsm. rate abated Mar. 1695-6; of Hampton 1710; liv. in Greenl. 1723. Appar. his ch., only one dau. proved, all sons but George shown by fa.'s deed to **Joseph**, Greenl. 1723, he to pay his bros. (four named). List 338a. Elizabeth, who o.c. and was bp. at Greenl. 1716, poss. his w.; he o.c. and was bp. in 1726. 6 ch. bp. 1730 and perh. others older. Adm. on est. of one Joseph of Greenl. gr. to Gideon Walker in 1761. **Sarah**, b. ±1679, m. Samuel Nudd(1). **Hannah**, m. in Greenl. bef. Nov. 1710 Nathl. Watson. **Elizabeth**, dau. of Luke of Hampt., in ct. 1710, then mar. to Samuel Brown(11). **Jane** and **Abigail** (presum.), both recd. into covt. and bp. No. Ch., Portsm. 1 May 1715; Jane was there 1716. **Samuel**, m. in Greenl. 19 Nov. 1724 Mary Carter. He o.c. and was bp. in Newington 10 Nov. 1728. 4 ch. bp. there and in Greenl. 1728-1733. **Luke**. One Luke Mulloon m. Mercy Lufkin (int. Ipsw. 19 Feb. 1735). **Mark**, Greenl. 1722, m. there 21 May 1731 Abigail Robinson (Thos.). 4 sons rec. Exeter 1732-1737. **Nathaniel**. One

Nathl. was husb. of Rachel Robinson (Thos.) in 1745. **George**, taxed Greenl. 1719, not ment. in deed 1723, and name poss. an error. See also Huggins(2) for Mary Mattoon, poss. Maloon. One James Mulloon m. Anne Harris in Newb. 18 Sept. 1722.

**MENDUM**, also Mendall at Duxbury, where was an early Mark M. Neither Guppy nor Lower has either name. Mendham is a parish on border of the Eng. cos. Norfolk and Suffolk.

1 **JONATHAN**(2), only ch. named in fa.'s will, giving him (also exec.) the homestead for life, then to his younger sons David and Jonathan. He wit. with fa. 4 Apr. 1664; in 1673 he and John Shepard ack. a joint debt to Eliakim Hutchinson. Gr.j. 1688. List 312e. See also Phenix. He m. bef. 2 Mar. 1672 Mary Raynes(1), who was John Woodman's w. by Aug. 1693. Adm. to Woodman on his est. 3 Oct. 1699. Ch., the 1st three (minors) named in fa.'s will 1682: **Robert**, to have the homestead if his bros. d. He had been abs. ten yrs. and was supp. dead when adm. was gr. to br. Jonathan in 1701; his land was sold in 4ths in 1713 (Y. D. 8: 7, 8, 28.) **Jonathan**, shipwright, had Kit. gr. 1699 (Lists 298, 296); gr.j. 1714; liv. 19 June 1717. Wid. Sarah (Downing 5, m. bef. 20 May 1702) m. 2d 7 May 1719 Joseph Curtis (6 jr.). 7 ch. (no Robert) shared in distrib. 1725. As admx. the wid. had paid 'Bro. David' £31, but 'Bro. Nathl.' sued her in 1723 and got £19; still admx. in 1726. **David**, given £4 by gr.fa. Raynes in 1693. Blacksmith of Bristol, Eng., but here in June 1717 when he sold to br. Jonathan, reserv. small lot for use of self and s. Robert, who appar. m. —— Pray(3) 17 Nov. 1726. By ct. rec. May 1721, David was drowned at Winter Harbor ab. 2 yrs. bef., leaving a w. and ch. or chn. in Plymouth, Eng.; adm. to br. Nathaniel 6 Apr. 1720; no personal effects in inv. **Dorothy**, wit. as D. M. 1700, m. Nicholas Frost(11). **Nathaniel**, Esq., joiner, merchant, Portsm., b. 2 Apr. 1690 (Wentworth Gen.), agreeing with death rec., at Portsm., 30 Aug. 1771 in 82d yr., yet he depos. in Apr. -1702-, aged ±20, naming mo. Mary Woodman. List 339. He m. bef. 8 May 1712 Frances Lyde(2); see also Mercer(1). Daus: Eleanor, m. 1st John Sherburne, m. 2d Samuel Marshall(3), m. 3d Wm. Shackford; Elizabeth, m. Geo. Janvrin(1); Mary, m. Ebenezer Wentworth (Lt. Gov. John).

2 **ROBERT**, Kittery, ±50 in Apr. 1654, 76 in 1676. A Pequot volunteer from Duxbury 1637. By depos. he came ±1630, and by implication knew the Piscataqua long bef. disturbing events sent him there from Duxb. by or bef. 1644. Kit. ordinary lic. 21 Oct. 1645; in 1647 bot Thos. Crockett's ho. and 4

a.; earlier wid. Billing had sued him ab. a cellar, and lost. The tav. lic. went to Mr. Hilton in June 1648, with liberty to R. M. to sell what was in stock. Entertaining without lic. Oct. 1649; in Oct. 1650 had lic. where Mr. Hilton dwelt. He sold two houses and land on the Point, land at mouth of Spruce Creek, and town gr., to Gunnison in 1654. Sued for trespass or debt by Hilton, Shapleigh and others. Tr. and gr.j. often; constable 1651-2, 1654-5, 1663; called marshal in Mar. 1653-4. Selectman 1666, 1669-1673; lot-layer, surveyor. Lists 282, 298, 24, 25, 84. See also Hanscom(2), Lynn(1). His w. Mary could speak her mind and was familiar with Plym. and Me. courts 1639-1654. His will, 1 (inv. 16) May 1682, directed bur. in his field by his last w.; no living w. indicated, but Mary (poss. dau.-in-law) attested the inv. In 1658 Judith M. told how much H. Gunnison sold to Inds.; if w. and not dau., she was perh. mo. of Nicholas Weeks' w. Judith. In 1702 Mrs. Woodman depos. that her mo.-in-law Mendum wanted her fa.-in-law M. to give Weeks a deed to certain land, but he said he never would. Kn. ch: **Daughter**, d. bef. fa., leaving s. Robert Muchemore (see 1), who was willed a heifer. **Jonathan.**

**Menseene**, John. List 331b. See Amazeen.

**MERCER.** In Eng. a trade name. The Batchelder fam. connection was of French origin, -le Mercier-.

1 **FRANCIS**, carpenter, Portsmouth, had a given name liked by the Eng. relatives of the Batchelders(3), but not clearly of them; see also (2). If he is 'Mr. Mercer and rest yr,' 1678 (List 331b), it is his first kn. record here. Of Portsm. in Aug. 1681, he bot from Wm. Hilton(19) 3 a. in Kit. adj. Chas. Nelson; Jane, w. of Matthew N., slandered him in 1684. Taxed Portsm. 1681 (List 329) to 1691. Ale-ho. lic. 1683, 1685-6, 1692; jury 1685. In 1689 he bot land, wharf and warehouse from the Wills heirs. He d. 19 Dec. 1692, ag. 58 (gr.st., Messer, at Pt. of Graves), but was ±46 in 1683-4. His w. was called midwife in 1685 when Robert and Rebecca Smart of Newm. sold them a negro ch. of four whose life, also the mo.'s, she had saved. Wid. Gertrude had tav. lic. in Dec. 1693; soon m. Edw. Toogood. She was ±52 in 1695. Her dau. Eleanor (not surely Mercer) m. Allen Lyde(2). In 1718 Nathl. and Frances (Lyde) Mendum q.c. to Toogood lands of Allen Lyde, Francis Mercer, and Gertrude late w. of E. T., mentioning F. M.'s will, but no will is found.

2 **THOMAS** (also Messer), Sheepscot. One Thos. was of Lynn 1639-40. Thomas (s. of Peter, neph. of Francis, cous. of Nathl. Batchelder 3), was in N. E. 1685; whether

(2), Thomas of Boston, or ano., is uncert. See N. E. Reg. 27: 368; 47: 511-5; Waters 1: 520, 785. The Sheepscot man was somewhere East in 1650 (see Lee 3); his petty debt still due the Winthrop est. in 1652. Saco or Cape Porpus 1652 (see Helson); his Cape P. holdings also incl. 100 + 12 a. sold to Arthur Wormstall in 1666. Bef. 1660 he settled next Nathl. Draper west of Salt Water Falls, Sheepscot. With w. Edith was in Boston with Sheepscot refugees in Oct. 1676 and there with those planning to re-settle in 1682. Lists 12, 13, 162. The Thomas of unknown age who d. in Salisb. 5 Feb. 1688 was poss. he, son, or gr.s. Ch. incl. appar. a **daughter** who m. Wm. Wilcott, and as a wid. in 17-- claimed Sheepscot ho. and land given her husb. by T. M. See also Y. D. 23: 255. Surely, **Esther**, m. 1st Nathl. Draper (3), m. 2d Robert Scott. **Lydia**, b. at Sheepscot, (±75, also ±80, in 1737; ag. 79, also ±82, in 1742), m. there, at age of 17, bef. the first war, one Butler or Cutler. A wid. (called by both names), she m. Sergt. John Stanwood of Glouc. 9 Dec. 1680. 8 ch. He d. in Glouc. 25 Jan. 1705-6. She was wid. Stanwood of Boston, late of Glouc., in 1737; Glouc. 1742; and depos. late that she liv. with her fa. at Sheepscot until her mar., except one yr. with John Taylor at Damariscotta, when ten yrs. old. **Samuel**, apprent. by parents Thos. and Edith, 20 Oct. 1676, for 7 yrs. to Geo. Carr of Salisb.; of Amesbury train band, 1680.

**Merchant**, Walter, late of Bristol (Eng.), haberdasher, 1640-1, had been at Winnegance and Pemaquid.

**Meridaugh** (Meriday), John, Me. cor.j. 1647, tr.j. 1669, gr.j. 1670. List 92. See Ameri-deth.

**MERRY**, Merrow. Both Scotch and English.

1 **DANIEL** (Merrey), soldier at Saco fort, 1693 (Y. D. 5: 2: 24); see Daniel Meserve. One Daniel Merow of Reading, presum. unrec. s. of (2), was wounded in the Canada exped., 1691.

2 **HENRY** (Merrow), Reading, a Scot (incl. for convenience, as 6 or more ch. liv. in N. H.), m. in Woburn 19 Dec. 1661 Jane (Lindes), wid. of Nicholas Wallis; d. at Reading 5 Nov. 1685, Jane surviving. List 94. 1 ch. (unnamed) rec. Woburn 1662, 7 at Reading 1669-1680. Others were prob. b. 1662-1669, incl. **Sarah**, m. John Pinder, and **Eleanor**, m. Nathl. Meader(4). See also Furber(2). Among rec. ch: **Hannah**, b. 5 Mar. 1668-9, m. Joseph Jenkins(8). **Samuel**, b. 9 Oct. 1670; see (5). **Mary**, b. 22 Apr. 1673, prob. m. Edward Polley. **Deborah**, b. 11 Oct. 1677, m. Daniel Meserve. Deborah Merrow, Sarah Pinder, sr. and Elizabeth Pinder were rememb. in will of Thos. Mor-

ris(6); John and Sarah Pinder and Edw. Polley wit. the will. See also (1).

**3 JOSEPH**, carpenter, Hampton. Early a Haverh. propr., he sold there 1644, 1648. Hampt. by Apr. 1650. In Oct. fol. Edw. Gilman sued him for breach of contract in carting logs to mill; in 1654 he 'unadvisedly' signed the pet. favoring Robert Pike; sold a ho. near the Falls in 1655 and bot ho. and 10 a. from Thos. Coleman in 1657. Tr.j. 1664. His w. Mary dying 4 Apr. 1657, he m. 2d (contr. 13 Dec. 1659) Elizabeth (Parkhurst) Hilliard(3), and ±1670 mov. to Tisbury, Martha's Vineyard, where he d. 15 Apr. 1710, 103 yrs. old (gr.st.). See Hist. of Martha's V., vol. 2; Annals of W. Tisbury, p. 58. 5 ch. at Hampt. By 1st w: **Joseph**, b. 19 Dec. 1654. By 2d w. (all m. at the Vineyard): **Hannah**, b. 29 Nov. 1660, m. Benj. Skiff. **Abigail**, b. Oct. 1662, m. John Pease. **Bathsheba**, b. 16 June 1665, m. Thos. Pease. **Samuel**, b. 16 Nov. 1669, m. Remembrance Luce. His will 11 Sept. (d. 6 Oct.) 1727. Wid. d. 31 Jan. 1739. 8 ch. See also (4).

**4 MARTHA**, York, poss. connec. with a Scotch fam. there (but Dr. Banks consid. her a dau. of 3), m. 1st Andrew Rankin (1), m. 2d Philip Frost(12).

**5 SAMUEL**(2), yeoman, practitioner of physic, Dover, m. Mary Page at Haverh., 16 Dec. 1695. Of Reading, he leased Roger Rose's farm and stock at O. R. 16 Mar. 1702-3 and later that yr. was bound to the peace for beating Mrs. Abigail Rose, his bondsm. John Pinder. In 1722 Pinder sued him on a note dated 1717; Daniel Meserve was his bondsm. in 1725. See also Jenkins(8). He bot in Rochester, and in 1754 either he or his s. had been resid. there ±20 yrs. of his. rec. in Reading 1696-1710: **Mary. Joseph. Benjamin. Jonathan** (see Jones 22). **Ruth. Rachel. Samuel.**

**6 WALTER**, shipwright, Boston, had gr. of Chebeague Isl. in Casco Bay from Geo. Cleeve as Dep. Pres. 18 Sept. 1650. Drowned in Boston 28 Aug. 1657, leav. his 2d w. Mary (Doling), who soon m. Robert Thornton, and an inf. s. Walter. Called both Chebeague and Merry's Isl., it was sold by the Thorntons to Josiah Willes of Boston in 1675 (Y. D. 2: 186), confirmed to Edmond White of London by Pres. Danforth in 1685 (Y. D. 4: 46), and sold to John King of Taunton by the s. Walter, of Norton, in 1718 (Y. D. 11: 27).

**MERRYFIELD.**

**1 FRANCIS**, Shoals, fined thrice in Me. Ct. Nov. 1665, swearing, drunk, non-appearance. Of Star Isl., summoned to N. H. ct. in Mar. 1693-4 with Thos. and Elizabeth Wise, but none appeared. List 308b. See (2).

**2 JOHN**, Shoals, swearing in 1685. See (1).

**3 JOHN**, cordwainer, Boston. See Phillips (22).

**4 WILLIAM.** See Frost(10).

**Merritt.** See Ashton.

**Meser**, Edward. List 57. See Masury.

**MESERVE**, Meservey. An ancient Jersey armorial fam. In northern N. E. the first form is commonly pronounced in two syllables.

**CLEMENT**, ag. 54 in Dec. 1706, undoubtedly from Jersey and consid. s. of Jean and Marie (Machon), liv. early with Mr. Richard Cutts to keep his cattle. See also Huntress(1). Taxed Portsm. 1673; O. A. 28 Aug. 1685. Lists 331b, 332b, 57, 62, 335a, 336b, 330d, 337, 343. See Harvey(3). His w., Elizabeth, List 335a. Of Welch Cove in 1705, he deeded to her; aft. her death to s. John, with 1 shilling each to other sons and daus. Of Welch Cove in 1710, both deeded to s. Clement, to take effect aft. their deaths. The s. sold the Newington prop. in 1721. Kn. ch., not in order: **John**, liv. 1705, prob. dead 1710. **Elizabeth**, m. 6 June 1694 Michael Whidden. **Clement**, joiner, m. 24 Sept. 1702 Elizabeth Jones(22) of Portsm.; taxed there ±1707. Both o.c. and bp. at Newingt. 10 Mar. 1722-3, and she adm. to full com. With Daniel Moody(2), he bot 100 a. in Scarb., 1726; taxed Black Point 1729; Scarb. propr. 1737, as were sons John, Daniel and Clement jr. 1739. His w. Elizabeth was liv. 24 June 1730; Mr. C. M. and Mrs. Sarah Stone m. in Scarb. 14 Aug. 1738. Will, 18 Feb. 1739-40—5 Nov. 1746, names w. Sarah and ch: Clement, Nathaniel (Col., Esq., Portsm.), George, Joseph, Elizabeth Libby (w. of James, m. at Newingt. 23 Dec. 1725), Daniel and John, but not Peter, bp. at Newingt. with bros. George and Joseph 19 Jan. 1723-4, nor Abigail, m. Samuel Libby(4). **Daniel**. Daniel -Merrey-, Saco soldier 1693 (Y. D. 5: 2: 24) is in orig. document -Meservey-. He bot at Dover 1703; m. aft. 1 Dec. 1701 Deborah Merrow(2), ±24 in 1704, and sis. of Sarah Pinder. Both adm. to O. R. Ch. 29 Jan. 1720-1. Lists 67, 358d, 368b. Will, husbandm., Dover, 1 May 1747—30 June 1756, names w. Deborah and ch., all bp. at O. R., four with him 8 Jan. 1720-1, the others 9 Feb. fol: Daniel, Elizabeth Libby, wid., Mary Meader, John, Clement (officer at Louisburg), Anne Nute, Tamsen Pinkham. **Tamsen**, Mr. Waldron's maid taken by Ind. and left for dead 28 Apr. 1704 (List 96); m. 1st Joseph Ham(4), m. 2d John Tibbetts. (The Hist. of Durham adds ano. son, Aaron, Salem 1695; on what authority unkn.)

**Meshan**, John. See Mashon.

**MESSANT**, Mrs. Ann, wid. at Dover early, and owned there the ho.-lots form. of Thos. Barge(2) and Stephen Tedder (N. H.

D. 9: 747). Both in Dover and York she kept ho. for Rev. Geo. Burdett(2) and loaned him money, getting from him 18 Mar. 1639-40 a mortg. on his stock and farm in poss. of John Alcock (Y. D. 3: 116; 4: 20), which farm later became hers. Some time aft. Burdett left for Eng. she m. Mr. Edw. Godfrey (1), and aft. 1667 liv. with the Shapleighs. Consid. research has failed to prove her a Burdett or show how relat. to Mrs. Alice Shapleigh, to whom 14 Sept. 1667, for natural love and affec., also £100 and her husb.'s bond back to pay her £20 a yr. for life, she deeded the farm in York where she lived. Col. Banks found the names Measant and Egbeare (see Shapleigh) together in Lifton, co. Devon. Sussex also produced a Messant fam. She d. betw. Jan. 1680-1, when of Kit., and June 1683. See also Burdett(1), Margaret Donnell(1), Y. D. 2: 34, 42; Hist. of York 1: 242; N. E. Reg. 37: 246.

**MESSEN, Christopher,** List 66; John in H. Deering's surveyor acct. 1674, abs. from meeting in Newc. 1697 (Mescen); both must be Amazeen. See also Menseene.

**Messer.** See Mercer.

**Metcalf,** James (Meadcalfe), was at Piscataqua in Mar. 1638-9, when Mr. Samuel Maverick was to bring him in to the next Boston court, but did not.

**METHERELL, John,** Kittery, accus. by Alice Hanscom(2) ab. 1690 and denied it, but m. her, needlessly, as the ch. proved colored; see Black(5). Metherell disappears. A little mulatto, poss. her ch. called Jonathan in 1693, was at Mr. Hooke's in 1695. As Alice Madril and Mathrell, she was in ct. in 1693 and 1695 (accus. John Thompson), and she and her chn. were Kit. town charges in Oct. 1695. See also Remick(2). Peter Wittum read her fortune: if she liv. to be 24, she would be very good and live above her bros. Perh. it came true, as she quieted down, or died; more likely the latter. Not represented in Hanscom div. in 1719.

**Micom,** the Scotchman. List 356b. See McIntire.

## MIDDLETON.

1 **DAVID,** soldier under Scottow. List 237b.
2 **JAMES,** adm. inhab. of Dover 14 Feb. 1658-9, perh. there with the Ludecas fam., and all having some earlier tie with Thos. Humphrey(2). Adm. on Mrs. Ludecas's est. was gr. to him in June 1664, and soon he was at the Kennebec, assoc. with Humphrey. Corporal for Sagadahoc company 1674. Lists 356d, 361a, 326b, 363a, 182, 15, 83. See also Gowen(4). Of Great Isl. in Sept. 1676, he sold all Kennebec int.; on the Island in July 1677. Of Newichawannock in Sept. 1683 he sued Geo. Jaffrey in N. H. ct. and ab. then the two were bound to abide a judg-

ment obtained by Barefoot. No kn. fam.
3 **JAMES,** mariner, Portsm., depos. concerning the ketches -Swallow- and -Industry- in Dec. 1684. One James of H. M. S. -Winsor- d. in Boston 4 July 1711; will 10 June, of No. Britain, now residing in Boston, soldier, gave to two friends.
4 **MATTHEW,** wit. deed Blackman to Sheafe at Saco or Wells 9 Mar. 1685-6. **Charles,** s. of Matthew and Faith (Gillam), b. Boston 5 Oct. 1696. Est. adm. there 1701; wid. m. Wentworth Paxton.

**MIGHILL.** See 'Early Settlers of Rowley' (1933), pp. 234-237.
1 **JOHN** (also Migel, Mihill), older br. of (3), m. in Rowley 6 July 1659 Sarah Batt (Nicholas). Taxed Dover 1672; constable 1674; of Oyster River 1676 when 3 ch. were bp. at Newb. Lists 356j, 359a. Compare also Mitchell(6) (Michill). He and two oldest sons were at Suffield, Conn., 1681. Ch: **John, Thomas, Mary, Samuel, Nathaniel, Nicholas** (last 3 bp. Newb. 13 Aug. 1676), **Sarah.** The s. Samuel (also Migles, Myals), remained in, or ret. to N. H. An Ind. captive at Exeter 1706, but soon free; Ex. scout 1710; taxed 1714. Lists 96, 376b (1725). Will, of Newmarket, 20 July—25 Aug. 1736, names w. Sarah (Rollins 5), 6 ch. One wit. and appraiser was Edw. Hall, his fellow captive in 1706.
2 **THOMAS** (Mihell), wit., at Casco or Boston, Francis Small's deed to Isaac Walker, 1658 (Mass. Col. Rec. 5: 405), may be Mitchell(5).
3 **REV. THOMAS,** Oyster River, s. of Dea. Thos., b. Rowley, 29 Oct. 1639; see also (1). H. C. 1663. He m. in Roxbury 8 Nov. 1669 Bethula Weld, bot at O. R. from Patrick Jameson that yr. and sold to John Webster of Newb. in May 1671, then 'some time of O. R. in Dover.' Later at Milton and at Scituate, where he d. in 1689. Will, 26 July 1689, names w. Bethulia and 4 of 6 ch. bp. 1671-1688: **Elizabeth. Samuel. Mary. Grace.** The widow's will, of Boston, 11—27 Sept. 1711, names only Mary and Samuel.

**Milam,** John, Conc. 1: 88. See also Maylem.

**MILBURNE, Rev. William,** Saco, where the selectmen were empowered to treat with him 9 May 1685. In Aug. fol. he was bondsman there for Geo. Turfrey, accus. of trading liquor with the Ind.; the same yr. Wm. Daggett(3) was saucing him. Saco wit. 25 May—22 Sept. 1687 (twice with Turfrey); at Newc. 28 Dec. 1687 he proved Champernowne's will which he had wit. in Nov. 1686. List 249. Just when he left Saco is unkn. All his ch. were rec. at Boston and he was of Bos. in Oct. 1692 when he and Job Alcock (1) were bondsm. for Gabriel Tetherly of Kit. At Bos. he and Eliz. Pearson wit.

Mrs. Nanny's deed to Samuel Wheelwright 6 July 1694, and there he d. the month fol. Ch. by w. Hannah 1680-84: **Hannah. William. Jonathan. Mary.** By w. Susannah (see Turfrey) 1687-94: **Abigail. Susannah. Charles. William.** The widow evid. m. 2d one Watson, and as 'Susannah Milburne or Watson' she and her offspring recd. 1 shilling by Capt. Geo. Turfrey's will.

## MILBURY

1 **HENRY**, York, br. of (3) and presum. relat. to (2), was bp. at Stoke-in-Teignhead, co. Devon, 7 Aug. 1625, s. of Wm. He m. a dau. of Wm. Dixon(3) and had more than one ch. in Feb. 1665-6; poss. she was not his only w., as her gr.s. Wm. (5 jr.) in 1717 sold ⅓ of the land given by Wm. Dixon to the ch. He liv. on Alcock's Neck on what is now kn. as the Norwood est. O. A. 22 Mar. 1679-80. Grant of 20 a. in 1691. List 278. Will, 10 June—1 Oct. 1695, names 3 gr.ch. and his ch: **Mary,** m. 1st James Freethy(3), m. 2d. Nathl. Blackledge. **Joanna,** m. Wm. Larrabee(8). **Elizabeth,** m. Thos. Paine. Not in fa.'s will, but her two ch. were. **William,** decd.; 10 s. given to his s. Wm. **Lydia,** m. John Linscott(1). **Dorothy,** a captive (List 99, p. 78), returned, and m. John Grant(5). **Richard,** b. ±1674.
2 **JOHN**, wit. with Elias Stileman 1663. See (1).
3 **RICHARD**, York, br. of (1), was bp. at Stoke-in-Teignhead 23 Sept. 1628. O. A. at York 22 Mar. 1679-80. Killed during the Candlemas Day massacre 1691-2. His neph. Richard(4) had his land rights.
4 *****RICHARD**(1), York, his fa.'s resid. legatee and exec., ±28 in Aug. 1702, ±76 in July 1752. He m. (ct. July 1696) Mary Winchester (Robert), who was liv. in 1727. With Capt. Peter Nowell of York and Mr. Peter Weare of Hampt., he bot on the E. side of Saco River in 1713-4 and sold part in 1722. York selectman 1699; gr.j. 1702; Rep. 1729, 1731-40, 1745. Lists 38, 279. See also Linscott(1). Will, yeoman, 2 Apr. 1747—4 Feb. 1754, gives to ch. of decd. s. Joseph and to three surv. ch: **Samuel,** Lt., Deacon, b. 20 June 1696, m. Elizabeth Kingsbury (John of Newbury) and d. 26 Sept. 1777. His fa. left him the homestead. List 279. 7 ch. 1718-1738. **Sarah,** b. 31 Jan. 1699-1700, m. Abiel Goodwin(2). **Joseph,** b. 25 Dec. 1702, m. 16 Feb. 1737-8 Mercy Webber. List 279. 2 ch., also their widowed mo., liv. 1747. **John,** York, m. 16 Jan. 1728-9 Susannah Sayward (Joseph). List 279. Will, yeoman, 26 Nov. —31 Dec. 1759; names her, 3 sons, 6 daus.
5 **WILLIAM**(1), m. Hannah Preble(7), his admx. in 1691. Inv. 2 Oct. 1691, £39, incl. land and marsh at Bass Cove, which his s. sold in 1717 to his step-fa. John Burrill(3),

whom Hannah m. 28 Sept. 1694. Y. D. 9: 8, 150. Ch: **William,** b. 23 Oct. 1689, liv. in Glouc. and m. there 19 Aug. 1717 Susannah Rowe. 9 ch.

**MILES.** See also Mills; Mighill(1).
1 **HEZEKIAH**, alias Hector, Indian, taken prisoner at Maj. Frost's garr. in 1691; depos. in Boston 1695. See 'N. E. Captives,' 1: 282.
2 **JOSEPH**, Kittery. As -Milles- of Piscataqua, he bought 8 a. from Lander and Billings the last day of Feb. 1639-40; as -Mills- sold to Thos. Crockett 1647; by all other rec. noted he was Miles or Myles. He had cross suits with John Reynolds in N. H. ct. 1649-50. In Me., wit. Godfrey to Hethersay 1651; tr.j. 1651; abs. from meeting 1651, 1653 (H. Gunnison bondsm.); depos. in 1654, ±35, about Kit. Point. F. Raynes, Rice Thomas, Gunnison and John Diamond brought sep. suits ag. him 1651-3; name last noted 1655 when Rice Thomas sued Wm. Hilton for £10, non-payment of £5 debt due from J. M. List 282.
**MILFORD, Thomas** (also Milfort), Kittery Point, fighting at Richard White's ho. in Oct. 1686, and summ. into ct. in Mar. 1688-9 for breach of peace against Ann Billings. With crew of bark -Mary-, Robt. Mitchell (13) master, in 1693, and a deponent (Doc. Hist. 5: 383-392). Indebted to Richard Pope's est. His untimely death, inquest 3 July 1694. Adm. to Humphrey Scammon 29 Mar. 1694, and a wk. later to Wm. Pepperell at request of the constable; inv., a gun, Bible and clothes.
**Millard.** See Miller.

**MILLER.** England, Scotland and Ireland all furnish our Millers. Became 45th commonest name in N. E.
1 **ALEXANDER**, b. ±1663-4, butcher, taxed in Portsm. 1688 (next Wm. Cotton) to 1690. Boston 1691 to 1706, when, carter, he mortg. two ho. and land adj. the common. Portsm. Mar. 1706-7. See also (12). Fort Wm. and Mary soldier 10—20 Sept. 1708. In 1714 Richard Sloper accus. him and Wm. Williams of stealing a cow, but failed to prove it. In 1719 he owned a slaughter ho. with John Cotton. Bot in Scarb. 1721. List 339. Wife Dorcas, m. by 1691, was adm. to Portsm. So. Ch. 1715. He d. 3 Jan. 1724-5, ag. 61; she 5 Feb. fol., ag. 66 (Granary Bur. Gr., Boston). Heretofore of Bos., late of Portsm., husbandman, adm. on his est. was gr. in Suff. ct. in 1725 to John Bradford. Ch. rec. Boston: **Joseph,** twin, b. 15 Sept. 1691, liv. in Portsm. and Newmarket. He m. 1st in Rowley, 10 Dec. 1713, Martha Elithorp, m. 2d in Portsm., 18 Oct. 1728, Christian, wid. of Edw. Clark(9). Adm. to her 2 May 1755;

est. insolv. with many large claims, incl. John Bradford's £124. 2 + 2 ch. bp., all daus. In 1759 one Joseph of Boston, form. of Portsm., sued James Sterling for a dry goods bill 1758-9. **Benjamin**, twin, appar. d. s. p. bef. fa. **Dorcas**, b. 29 May 1695, m. 1st Samuel Hudson(6), m. 2d John Bradford(1). A wid. in 1761; gr. adm. on est. of Thos. Bradford of Portsm. in 1763. See also Y. D. 13: 155. **Samuel**, b. 25 Nov. 1696, appar. d. s. p. bef. fa. **Jacob**, b. 3 Mar. 1701, liv. Feb. 1724-5, appar. dead s. p. in 1729. See also Joseph Swett.

2 **BENJAMIN**(9), Portsm., m. aft. 1705 Lydia Fernald(1), wid. of John Harmon (2 jr.) and outlived her. B. M. and farm taxed 1707. In 1712 he bot from Samuel and Elizabeth Thompson. Selectman 1728. List 339. See also (8). Will, yeoman, 27 Jan. 1746-7—30 May 1750, names 7 ch., the first 5 bp. at No. Ch. 11 Aug. 1717, when he was recd. into covt: **Mary**, m. John Libby(7 jr.) **Lydia**, m. 10 Dec. 1728 John Hoyt of Newington. **Benjamin**, cordwainer, m. 23 Sept. 1731 Elizabeth Dennett. **Ch.** **Sarah**, was Skillin in 1747. See Mills(4). **Elizabeth**, m. 25 Jan. 1736-7 Nicholas Dennett. **Moses**, bp. 10 July 1720, m. and had ch. **Abigail**, m. 9 Mar. 1741-2 Jona. Trickey of Newington.

3 **EPHA.** (presum. Ephraim), soldier at Fort Wm. and Mary 1697. List 68.

4 **HENRY**, abuttor to John White, Sheepscot, 1686. must be Mills(3).

5 **HUMPHREY**, Charlestown and Reading, may have been with Capt. Wincoll at Arrowsic in Apr. 1677. Doc. Hist. 6: 167-8.

6 **JAMES**, cursing Esq. Pepperell in 1700, and a soldier at Casco in 1703 or earlier. James d. 23 Dec. 1764, ag. 100 (Saco Ch. rec.), perh. was the same, or one of the Scotch-Irish.

7 **JASPER**, wit. in the Hunking-Abbott oxen case at Portsm. in 1660, ag. ±29. Arrowsic 1679, Pemaquid 1687. Lists 187, 124.

8 **JEREMIAH**(9), Portsm. Little is kn. of him and nothing of his w. He was a soldier at Fort Wm. and Mary 19—29 July 1708; at Joseph Miller's nine-pin alley in 1711. Found taxed only in 1714, and that tax abated, he could not have been a ho. owner. Barnstead propr. 1727. Becoming incapacitated, he was carried in 1735 to his br. Benjamin's, where the town pd. for his care to 1742, or longer. Only kn. ch: **Jeremiah**, bp. No. Ch. 27 June 1714, m. Elizabeth Lassell and liv. in Kennebunkport. 12 ch. Unplaced in Portsm.: **Peter**, bp. No. Ch. 27 Apr. 1718, m. and had ch., not named in will of either (2) or (12). **William**, bp. 8 Oct. 1721, could belong to either (2) or (12), if he d. s. p. bef. fa., but neither Peter nor Wm. likely son of Joseph(1), whose ch. were bp. in the So. Ch. See also Hannah(12).

9 *****JOHN**, Cape Porpus, ±22 in Nov. 1661, ag. 45 in June 1685, came from Beverly (ano. J. M., tailor, was of Salem 1651-57). He wit. in Bev. cases in Dec. 1659—Nov. 1661, and was in Wells bef. 25 Apr. 1662, when represented in ct. by John Chater, whose dau. Hannah he m., and whose est. he adm. in 1671. Jeremisquam bef. Sept. 1665, his place adj. the Phipps home. This he and w. Hannah sold to Geo. Pearson in Nov. 1669, and mov. to Cape P.; see Y. D. 12: 223-4 for location of his home. Gr.j. 1670, 1680, 1683, 1687-8; constable 1671, 1675; with Gyles Barge bondsm. for Geo. Garland(2) in 1673; O. A. 17 Mar. 1679-80; Cape P. gr. 1681; tr.j. 1683; j. of inq. 1685; Rep. 1685; selectman 1688-9; surv. and lot-layer 1689. The first war sent him tempo. to Newbury, the second ended his pub. life save for military calls, and sent him perma., first to Portsm., then to Newingt. where cared for by the Downings until he d. bef. 18 Apr. 1720. The Miller adm. to Newingt. Ch. 28 June 1716 might be he or anyone. Lists 12, 259, 30, 256, 33, 334a, 67, 336b, 330def. Kn. ch. (3 q.c. at Cape P. to the Downings 1720; Y. D. 12: 224): **John**. List 259. In Mar. 1677-8 in Newb. the fa. compl. ag. his wife's relatives for keeping his ch. from him, resulting in John, jr. being apprent. till 21 to Joseph Bailey, and **Andrew**, to John Emery, jr. who was to teach him to read and write. Nothing kn. of Andrew. John jr. appar. alive 1693 when the fa. was 'Senr.' One John, a Portsm. soldier at Dover 1695-6. Adm. on est. of ano. or same gr. in Essex Ct. to Tristram Coffin of Newb., 2 Sept. 1700, the inv. incl. wages under Sir E. Andros. **Benjamin**. **Jeremiah**. **Susannah**, m. Capt. John Downing(2). **Hannah**, m. 1st John Cowell (Lists 330de), m. 2d Daniel Quick. See Cowell(6).

10 **JOSEPH**, a travelling merchant, wit. in York in July 1642 (Y. D. 3: 42), and that yr. was bondsm. in N. H. ct. for Mary Topp who defaulted. Lawsuits 1646. He left the country after conveying to John Goddard, 22 Sept. 1647, the ho. in Dover where he was then dwelling, and three pieces of land and marsh given by Dover to Rev. Thos. Larkham.

11 **JOSEPH**, who worked for John Goddard (3) 1647-1666, and depos. in Apr. 1660, ag. ±29 (Pope).

12 **JOSEPH**, Portsm. by 1702 (see Ford 5). Pub. ho. lic. at the Creek in Mar. 1706-7, bondsm. Wm. Cotton and Alexander(1), presumably a relative. Lic. 1708; served at Fort Wm. and Mary 17 June—28 July 1708, and had a nine-pin alley 1711 (see 8). J. M. and farm taxed 1708; later lists disting. him and Joseph(1) as Joseph of the Creek, and Joseph Alexander's son. List 339. He m. Bridget Clark(49), who was a Vaughan wit.

1707, adm. to full com. No. Ch. 1714, liv. May 1722, and d. bef. him. His will, 5 June 1756 —28 Sept. 1757, names two daus., s. Joseph if alive, 3 gr.ch., and gives residue to s.-in-law John Pendexter. Ch., the first 5 bp. No. Ch., 18 July 1714: John, not in will. Margaret, m. Thos. Noble(4); her s. Richard a benefic. Hannah, d. bef. 1756, leaving a dau. Susannah Wells. If Wells by birth, not mar., her mo. was not the Hannah who m. Pierce Bickford(15). Susannah, not in will. Anne, not in will. One Anne m. Joseph Berry, jr., of Portsm., 7 Dec. 1737. Alice, bp. 25 Sept. 1715, m. John Pendexter(1). Joseph, bp. 29 Sept. 1717, m. 1 May 1740 Abigail Moses. His s. John named in gr.fa.'s will; in 1751 Geo. Moses was named gdn. of John, s. of Joseph Miller, mariner, of Portsm., decd., yet his fa.'s will clings to possibil. that he was liv.

13 RICHARD, fisherman, Long Reach, Kittery, b. ±1649 (±30 in 1679), involv. somehow in a ct. case with Katherine and Mary Green and Katherine Tobey in July 1669, when the trio were ord. to pay him 3 s. apiece and costs. His w. Grace had him bound for good behav. and prop. mainten. in Sept. 1672, the ct. warning her to be more careful of appearances and to attend to her fam. He was abs. from meeting and fined for non-appear. in ct. 1674, Andrew Haley bondsm. In 1679 fishing for Mr. John Cutts under Wm. Pitt, master, and had fish on Pickering's Island in 1685. Lists 298, 30, 94. See also King(12). He d. 8 Oct. 1692; adm. to wid. Grace and s. Samuel 28 Nov. 1693. She m. 2d Christopher Banfield(1) and relinquished adm. to s. Samuel 6 Oct. 1696. Ch: Samuel, poss. the ch. unborn in Sept. 1672, m. (ct. Jan. 1693-4) Mary Neale(6), who was abs. from meeting in July 1696. Neither seen aft. 19—22 Oct. 1696, when he sold out to Joseph Hill and to his mo., his sisters' unpaid portions to be satisfied. See Y. D. 4: 90-92. Mary, m. Ephraim Wentworth, and Martha, m. 24 Dec. 1703 John Wentworth; both under 18 in 1696.

14 SIDRACH, cooper, made contract with Capt. John Mason et al., and came with two servants to Piscataqua, where they worked 18 mos. bef. he was called back to Eng. His ptn., of London[1631?], asked pay for self and his two men, who were suddenly discharged without pay aft. he left N. E. List 41.

15 THOMAS, Shoals wit. 1667; taxed Portsmouth 1672 (Mr. Th. Millard); depos. bef. Stileman in Nov. 1676, ±42, as commander of ship -Employment- belonging to Piscat., which was in Fayal the prev. April.

16 WALTER. See Fletcher(8).

17 MRS. (Miller?), sent a cheese to Rev. Daniel Maude the week bef. he made his will (N. H. Prob. 1: 89).

MILLETT, uncommon in Eng.

1 JOHN, Mr., Kittery in Aug. 1661, when Mr. Antipas Maverick sold a ho. there to Thos. Booth with proviso that houseroom should be allowed Mr. J. M. and fam. until May 1 fol.

2 JOHN, at Falm. from Glouc. 1732, with w. Bethia (Carter), step-dau. of John Benjamin(1) and form. wid. of Andrew Bennett of Glouc.

3 THOMAS, drowned at Casco Bay 1722, ag. ±47. See Ingersoll(7).

4 CAPT. *THOMAS, Esq., Dover, moderator 23 times, selectman 21 times, Rep. 11 times, to 1755. See Bunker(2).

Millions, James, a Kennebec soldier 1688. List 189.

MILLIKEN, John, Boston, Scarboro (propr. 1720, List 239b), became ancestor of a large and prom. Maine fam. by marrying Elizabeth Alger(6), who was called Elizabeth Mulligan in will of her maternal gr.mo., 1696. Deponents in 1734, including s. James, mariner, Martha's Vineyard, told that a ho. was built for him in 1717 at Dunstan, where he brot his fam. (within 14 mos., Edmund Ward said) and liv. until the war drove him off; s. James added that his fa. came down in 1716 to take poss., and that he himself went 'there in spring of 1718 to help him plow,' the first field that was there in my time.' Samuel, John, Nathaniel (77 in 1788) and Edward were Scarb. proprs. in 1737. Of these sons, John was a sadler in Bos. in 1720, and from Bos. he wrote to -Joseph- Burnham in Oct. 1723 regarding the care of their cattle. Edward was liv. with his fa. in Scarb. in 1720 or 1721, and m. Abigail Norman in Newbury 29 July 1726. Robt. Munson depos. that Edward came with his fam. in July 1727, Samuel came ±1729, Nathaniel ±1730. Others of 10 ch. b. Boston 1691-1711 were Thomas, Josiah, Benjamin, Joseph, Elizabeth. One John Milliken d. in Boston 20 Apr. 1734, ag. 79 (Granary).

MILLS, occas. Miles in early rec. A So. of Eng. name, usually Mill in Cornwall and Devon, where scarce.

1 EDWARD, came in the -Hercules- 1636-7; in Trelawny acct. 29 Nov. 1639. List 21. One Edw. was adm. inhab. in Boston 1645.

2 EDWARD, a wit. 1695 (Y. D. 6: 176).

3 HENRY, Sheepscot 1688. List 164. Late constable of New Dartmouth, he gave evid. ag. Lt. Jordan(6) in Boston 1689 (Doc. Hist. 5: 41-42). One Henry signed a Boston ptn. 1696 (N. E. Reg. 16: 86).

4 JAMES(11), was Mills. Of Lynn 4 May 1666, 'lawful heir,' he sold to James Grant land in York adj. Lt. Chas. Frost and Geo. Parker; and Robert Knight then depos. that he was lawful s. and h. of Robert, decd.

He m. at Lynn 1 Apr. 1671 Martha Alley and had there: **Martha,** b. 14 June 1672. **James,** b. 9 Sept. 1674, d. y. **Sarah,** b. 27 Feb. 1675, m. Joseph Felt(5). **James,** b. 11 Oct. 1678. **Dorothy,** b. 21 Apr. 1681. Poss. unrec.: **Mary,** m. in Lynn 31 Dec. 1707 Wm. Williams, and prob. **Patience,** m. (int. Lynn 27 Dec. 1712) Robert Burnel. The 2d s. James m. in Lynn, 1st 26 Dec. 1700 Naomi Hinkson, prob. dau. of (6), 2d 28 June 1714 Deborah Larrabee (1), who was bef. Essex ct. the next Feb. when he was at Casco Bay. List 229. He d. ±1719-20. She m. 2d Lt. Thos. Cummings, m. 3d bef. Oct. 1727 James Donovan, joiner, Falm. Adm. on the Mills est. was gr. to them 4 Jan. 1730-1. Ch. by 1st w. in Lynn 1701—1708-9: John, shipwright, Groton, Conn., 1734. Mary; one Mary -Miller- and Wm. Watson, both of Scarb., m. 16 July 1738. Sarah; Sarah -Miller- and Edw. Skillin m. in Scarb. 23 Mar. 1731-2, but see Miller(2). Rebecca. By 2d w., the 1st two in Lynn 1714-1716: Deborah, m. Christopher Mitchell(16); Scarb. rec. call her -Miller-, but surely Mills. Patience. Lucretia, b. Falm. 23 June 1719, m. there (int. 13 Apr. 1740) Benj. Ring of Georgetown.

5 **JAMES**(6), evid. the '-Mary- Mills her younger sunn' abs. from meet. in Oct. 1667. See also (8). John and James taxed together in Scarb., 1681. List 238a. Of Sandwich 12 Feb. 1693-4 he bought from his bro. 80 + 40 a. in Scarb., formerly his fa.'s; claimed at Black Point in 17--, and, of Sandwich, q.c. to John Dennison, Esq., in 1719 (Y. D. 9: 170).

6 **JOHN,** Black Point, wit. deed to Winter 12 July 1638 and depos. in 1640 that he had kn. Casco Bay 13 or 14 yrs. List 21. Long after, Francis Robinson depos. that ±1643 he bounded out the Cammock patent, one bound being on E. side of river called Mills river and near Mills' ho. on other side of river. See also Y. D. 4: 43; Doc. Hist. vol. 3 (by index). Scarb. wit. 1664 (Y. D. 2: 139). Geo. Knight's est. owed one J. M. in 1671. Adm. 7 Oct. 1673 to Walter Gendall on behalf of John (jr.). His w. Sarah was appar. called -Mary- in 1667 (Me. P. & Ct. i: 334). Poss. John d. long bef. 1673, as in 1665 one Sarah was sued for the minister's stipend. The wid. wit. in the Gendall case and Wm. Lucas depos. about Gendall meeting Sarah and her s.-in-law Winnock on the Neck. Turning Quakers, the fam. was often prosec. for abs. from meeting, and "Mary and Sarah became 'vagabond' 'travelling' Quaker missionaries.'' Ch: **Mary,** claimed Salem as her home in 1661 when exam. in Mass. as Mary Miles of Black Point, Quaker, but in Me. at later periods, and called of Bl. Pt. in Suff. ct. 1677; in 1719 she was wid. Mary Gifford of Sandwich (Y. D. 9: 170).

**Sarah.** See George Garland(2) whom she may have mar. By 1676 she m. Joseph Winnock whom her bro. John unsuc. sued in 1686. **James.**

7 **JOHN** (Mill), wit. Champernowne's deed to Capt. Paul White 14 Dec. 1648 (Y. D. 1: 8-9) and wrote him a dunning letter from Boston (several had been unanswered) 5 Nov. 1649 addressing him as 'Loving Friend.' He sued Champernowne in N. H. ct. 1650-1651. List 73.

8 **JOHN**(6), Walter Gendall's apprentice. J. M. was abs. from meeting 1665-1673, poss. always the fa., but certainly the son in July 1674 when he did not appear, being out of town. In July 1675 Sarah and her sons John and James were abs. In July 1679 John traded for Geo. Taylor's land, took poss., and of Scarb., made final payment in Boston 20 Mar. 1685-6. List 238a. Resident in Boston 12 Feb. 1693-4, he sold his fa.'s farm to br. James, and there, sometime of Bl. Point, in 17--, claimed the Taylor land. In 1704 he had served several yrs. as dep. sheriff (his aut. SJC 6066). Adm. 28 Nov. 1718 to s. John. The wid., formerly Joanna (Alger 1) Oakman(1), q.c. Alger prop. to the Millikens in 1727, depos. in Boston in Sept. 1728, ±77, and d. 26 Mar. 1733 in 83d yr. (Copp's Hill). Ch. rec. Boston: **Tamsen,** b. 30 Oct. 1686, m. there 15 Sept. 1712 Richard Hazely of Great Brit. **Jonathan,** b. 3 May 1689. **John** and **James,** b. 22 Feb. 1690-1. In 1718 the s. John and w. Sarah and the Hazelys q.c. in Scarb. (Y. D. 9: 173). Note also James, s. of John and Mary, b. Boston 10 Nov. 1679.

9 **PETER,** List 335a. Read Wells.

10 **DR. RICHARD,** Portsm. 1699, indebted to Dr. Wm. Davies of St. John in Wapping, co. Middlesex. As 'Jr.,' he was at College Green, Dublin, receiving letters dated Oct.—Nov. 1700 from Elizabeth (Dew 4) Redford whom he had courted. 'Poor sick and decrippled,' he asked leave in Aug. 1702 to sue her without fees (he had left £100 with her when going abroad) and next yr. sued her and her new husb. for breach of promise, event. losing. In 1710 Dr. Andrew Peterson of Aldgate, London, sued him on a bond dated 1708. See also Hughes(2). Taxed Portsm. 1708, bought 1712, tax abated 1714. Adm. 22 Dec. 1715 to wid. Anne, who soon d.; her mo. and admx., Mrs. Nicholson (Nichols 1), attested her inv. 30 Aug. 1716. Kn. ch: **Mary,** m. 3 Nov. 1730 James Turner of Kingsbury, co. Somerset, his admx. 12 Oct. 1737. Prop. her gr.mo. gave her was in poss. of a -True- in the 1760's, perh. -Trude- instead, suggesting ano. dau. **Anne,** m. 14 Dec. 1732 Thos. Trude of Tiverton, co. Devon. One Bethia M. was bp. at No. Ch. 5 June 1709.

11 **ROBERT** (Milles). Saco court 7 Feb. 1636-7 issued warr. for his appear. next ct. day. Apr. 4 fol. he sued John Heard for debt, and in R. Hitchcock's suit ag. himself for slander asked forgiveness and paid charges. He d., leaving **four** small **ch.** and a poor wid. Dorothy, who m. John Harker(1) by 1647 when she obtained an execution for debt of Vines (in behalf of Gorges) due her late husb. The only kn. ch. James deeded York land which was his father's, and thru this s. the Mills girls later in Scarb. trace to (11), not to (6). On the spot were: John, Mrs. Godfrey's disobedient apprent. 1659, whom she sued in Mar. 1661 for not serving out his time accord. to condition; but he perh. was son of (12). Mary, m. 1st Lewis Bane(3), m. 2d Chas. Brisson; her s. testif. that his mo. was Mary Mills bef. marriage.

12 **THOMAS**, fisherman, Saco, Wells, b. in Exeter, Eng., by Catholic rec. when his dau. Martha was bp. in Canada. In Aug. 1642 he and James Gibbins bought 100 a. at Winter Harbor lately Henry Boade's. Wells 1653, and granted land 1659 (Y. D. 12: 336). Lists 252, 261-263, 253, 244d, 28. See also Gibson(2), Lee(3). Wells constable 1664. Liv. 12 July 1681 (Y. D. 3: 105). He m. Mary Wadleigh (John), who in 1651 was with an eloping party arrested at Barnstable and sent home. In 1664 her fa. deeded to her and her chn. the ho. they were liv. in, and by will 7 July 1671 gave her a pr. of oxen, h.h. stuff and ⅔ his cattle. Ch: **John**, suppos. the wit. with Robert Wadleigh ab. John and Joan Andrews in 1657. Nothing surely kn. of him except that his relatives paid his debts (Y. D. 9: 250), but see Mrs. Godfrey's apprent. under (11). **Mary**, m. John Cloyes (2). **Sarah**, m. Nathl. Cloyes(4). **Susanna**, m. 1st Isaac Cousins(2 jr.), m. 2d Lt. Peter Folsom(7). **Martha**, b. at Saco in N. E. 18 June 1653 ('N. E. Captives' 1: 186); m. 1st James Smith, m. 2d Christopher Grant(1).

13 **WILLIAM**, soldier under Scottow. List 237b.

14 ——. 'Goody Mills and Mrs. Hammon's son came in with a Sagamore' (entry 9 Aug. in Scottow's narrative of a voyage to Pemaquid, 1677).

**MILTON**, 1 **Edward**, soldier under Scottow. List 237b.

2 **RICHARD** (Millton), at Saco, Apr. 1661. P. & Ct. ii: 375.

**MINGAY**. One Jeffrey M. m. Grace Hilliard at Fedingham, co. Norfolk, 3 Oct. 1623.

*JEFFREY, Hampton, with the early comers who were first at Dedham. Freeman 13 May 1640. Hampton gr. June 1640. Seléctman 1647, 1650, 1652, 1656; com. t. e. s. c. 1648-1650, 1652-1654; tr.j. 1649, 1651; Rep. 1650. Lists 391ab, 392abc, 393ab, 53. He d.

s.p. 4 June 1658. Nunc. will proved 5 Oct. fol., gives to w. Ann (Lists 392c, 393a), and much to Eliakim Wardwell. Wid. Ann m. 2d Capt. Christopher Hussey(1), and d. 24 June 1680.

**Minn**, John's wife and 4 ch. at Passamaquoddy, 1688. List 5.

**Minot**, Capt. George, at Pemaquid. List 19.

**MITCHELL**, a general Eng. name, more freq. in the So., partic. Cornwall, where often spelled Michell.

1 **BARTHOLOMEW** (Michell, altered from Drew) and Rebecca Downes, w. of (4), assaulted Constable Roger Kelly in 1668; Sampson Angier surety for both. See also Burrington.

2 **CHRISTOPHER**, Kittery, acknowl. judgment to Capt. Richard Cutts in May 1660, sued Robert Skinner in 1661, was bondsm. for Philip Atwell in 1672, and adm. est. of br.-in-law John Searle in 1675. Gr.j. 1678. His home was at the head of Braveboat Harbor. List 298. See also Me. P. & Ct. ii: 456-7. He d. in Apr. 1688; adm. to wid. Sarah (Andrews 9, who was ±40 in Jan. 1681-2), her bondsm. Capt. Hooke. She had pub. ho. lic. 1709; depos. in 1731, ag. 88, about Capt. Champernowne's lower ho., what she was told ab. it over 70 yrs. bef.; d. in Nov. 1732 (Jos. Billings's depos.). Lists 290, 292. Ch., as named in distrib. aft. her death, when s. Christopher was admr: **John**, eldest son. **Christopher**. **Joanna**, m. Joseph Flood. **Sarah**, m. one Pierce; her heirs in div. **Samuel**. **Robert**, ±24 in May 1693. **Richard**. **Joseph**. **Elizabeth**, 68 in Apr. 1744, m. 1st John Tinney, m. 2d Samuel Johnson(32). **William**.

3 **CHRISTOPHER**(2), Kittery. As Christopher, jr., he and his mo. prosec. John Billings, w. and dau. for felony in Dec. 1687. Gr.j. 1698, 1699; j. 1699. Lists 296-298. He m. 1st Mary Brackett(6), m. 2d one Sarah, named in his will, 28 June 1739—18 Oct. 1743, with all ch. but Benjamin. Ch. by 1st w: **Mary**, m. Charles Brown(27). One Mary of Kit. was in ct. on a bastardy charge in Jan. 1709-10; Mary M., dau. of Mary, was bp. at Greenland 1714. By 2d w: Capt. **Samuel**, b. 22 Jan. 1694, m. by 1730 one Elizabeth; his est. adm. 1756. List 298. 6 or more ch. **Joanna**, b. 14 Feb. 1696-7, m. Timothy Blake(5 jr.). Their s. Christopher was liv. with his gr.fa. in 1733. **Sarah**, b. 8 June 1699, m. Jonathan Partridge(2). **Elizabeth**, b. 27 Jan. 1701-2, m. Zachariah Leach(3). **Benjamin**, b. 23 Aug. 1704. **Miriam**, m. Andrew Phillips (see 24). **Susannah**, m. Edward Howard(3).

4 **ELIZABETH**, Hampton. See Lamprey (4).

5 **CAPT. JOHN**, Kittery. His mar., without publication, to Mrs. Sarah Gunnison(2)

brought Major Shapleigh, who mar. them, into ct. 1 July 1661. He first appeared in July, 1660, deposing with Tobias Langdon ab. Smuttynose land, and d. by 30 May 1663. As Mrs. Sarah Mitchell she was lic. in July 1664, was sued in Sept. fol., and m. Mr. Francis Morgan(2), bef. 21 Mar. 1664-5, when they were gr. adm. on the Mitchell est. The inv. 28 May 1664 shows much land. See Y. D. 10: 133; Me. P. & Ct. i: 227-8. List 78.

**6 JOHN**, Dover, servant of John Gerrish in 1675 with one yr. more to serve; withdrew a suit ag. Major Waldron; taxed 1680. Lists 359ab, 94. Poss. the same who had bot. half the woodlot of John Smyth, sr., in York, 1681, and the Newichawannock man fined for swearing in 1685. See also (8), Martin(2), and compare Mighill(1).

**7 JOHN**(2), eldest son, a Great Island wit. 1678, gave a bill to one of the Wentworths in 1681, the witnesses Sarah Tucker and Lucretia Robinson. Appar. he d. early, leaving one or m. ch., his **heirs** in 1733 receiving a double portion of the Braveboat Harbor land, while the old houses, the barn and gridiron went to his heirs and to those of his sis. Sarah Pierce. One ch. poss. was the unident. Christopher, cordwainer, Falm., whose deed of 1734 incl. phrase 'my right and my brethren which we have or ought to have in our gr.fa. Christopher M., late of Kit., dec.' (Y. D. 17: 49). This Christopher m. 1 Dec. 1715 Eleanor Larrabee(6); of Kit., he bot in Falm. in 1726, and was liv. there with her 1748 and later. See also (14) for others unkn.

**8 JOHN**, Pemaquid 1687; List 124. See also Hobby(2). Poss. from Charlestown (see 15); or (6).

**9 JOSEPH**(2), Kittery, had a 15 a. gr. laid out in July 1694, when he was called br. of (3). One Joseph, a captive named with Kit. youths, was in Canada in Oct. 1695 (List 99, p. 76). Lists 291, 296-298. Orig. memb. of Kit. Point Ch. Adm. to s. John 9 Oct. 1746. Ch., first 2 rec. in Kit. as ch. of Joseph and Joanna (Couch 2), all in heirship deed 1746 (Y. D. 26: 227): **Joseph**, b. 12 Feb. 1703; No. Yarmouth 1746. Capt. **Solomon**, b. 28 Apr. 1706, m. in Kit. 29 Jan. 1729-30 Mary Mitchell(12). A Kit. shipwright, he sold Cape Eliz. land to br. John in 1736; No. Yarm. 1746. 9 ch. rec. in Kit. **John**, mariner, York, Wells, b. 28 Apr. 1708, m. 2 Feb. 1735-6 Lydia Sewall of York, who d. in 1770, he in 1799. 13 ch. **Robert**, shipwright, Newbury 1746. **Benjamin**, ship carpenter, Newb. 1736, Kit. 1739, No. Yarm. 1746, m. 25 Feb. 1736 Mehitable Bragdon. 6 ch. **Joshua**, ship carpenter, Newb. 1736-1746. **Samuel**, m. 10 July 1745 Martha Rackliff (Wm.). His will 1790—1796; hers 1798—1801. Ch. **Joanna**, m. Joseph Goodhue of Newb. **Lydia**, m. Wm. Couch, jr.,

of Newb. **Mary**, m. James Titcomb of Portsmouth.

**10 MATTHEW**, a Kit. wit. 1667; soldier from Exeter 1676. List 381.

**11 PAUL**, sailor and fisherman, from Sheviock, co. Cornwall, where one Paul m. Richord Earle 29 Oct. 1634, came first to Richmond's Island in 1638 and was there in July 1641; his w. ment. in account, 1639. He came again in 1643-4 under a two yr. contract, and later was at Saco. Lost in a fishing disaster 1654. If any w. came over, she is unrecorded. Lists 21, 244b. See also Creber.

**12 RICHARD**(2), called br. of (3) in 1694, when his 15 a. Kit. grant was laid out. Highway surv. 1698-9. Lists 291, 296-298. Adm. to eldest s. Joseph 12 July 1756. Ch., first 3 rec. in Kit. as ch. of Richard and Sarah (Couch 2), all but John in div. 1759, by reckoning Joanna as Hannah; **John**, b. 14 May 1700. **Sarah**, b. 9 July 1702, m. Thos. Adams(19 jr.). **Joanna**, b. 19 Feb. 1704, accus. Robert Oram (ct. Jan. 1728-9), and was presum. same as Hannah, w. of Capt. R. O. in 1759. **Joseph**, m. in York 5 Jan. 1726-7 Isabella Bragdon(6). His will 1759—1764; hers proved 1784. 8 ch. **Richard**, m. 1st in 1736-7 Huldah Weare (Peter), m. 2d in 1740 Sarah (Deering) Jones. Will 1784—1786. 5 ch. **William**, m. 1st in 1741 Sarah Weare (Peter), m. 2d in 1756 Sarah Sellars of York. Will 1784—1788. 3 + 3 ch. **Mary**, m. Capt. Solomon Mitchell(9). **Temperance**, m. Wm. Rackliff(6 jr.); dead in 1759.

**13 ROBERT**(2), Kittery, early a mariner, later a tav. keeper. Of Kit. in 1693, ±24, he was master of Pepperell's bark -Mary- (see Doc. Hist. 5: 383-392); Portsm. 1702, master of sloop -Success-. Lists 296-298. Will, 23 Feb.1730—11 May 1731, names w. Sarah (Deering 8) and all ch. but the first Robert; her will, 6 Mar. 1734—14 Feb. 1735-6, names also 4 gr.ch. Ch. rec. Kit: **Roger**, b. 6 Dec. 1694, m. 1st in Kit. 3 Nov. 1717 Sarah Cutts(6), who d. 1718; m. 2d in Kit. 17 Aug. 1720 Bridget (Bickford 15) Couch (2); m. 3d (int. 18 Feb. 1726-7) Mary Gould (6), named in his will 1755—1762. Lists 291, 298. 1 + 2 + 7 ch. **Robert**, b. 14 Apr. 1697, d. 20 Aug. 1698. **Mary**, b. 20 Sept. 1699, m. Wm. Carswell or Kearswell. They were of Kit. 1722, Gosport 1736. Son James and dau. Sarah named in gr.mo.'s will. **Sarah**, b. 22 Mar. 1702, m. in Kit. 19 Jan. 1720-1 Mannering Beale(5). **Elizabeth**, b. 8 May 1705, m. 1st Samuel Greenleaf(3), m. 2d Samuel Greenough(1 jr.), m. 3d Capt. Henry Kingsbury of Rowley. Her s. Robert Greenough named in gr.mo.'s will. **Robert**, b. 27 Dec. 1710, cordwainer, m. Miriam Jordan (Dominicus 2 jr.); d. at Cape Elizabeth 7 May 1769. Ch.

14 **SAMUEL**(2), represented by heirs in 1733, perh. had liv. afar, but not unlikely was he of the same name dead in 1693, leaving wid. Rachel of Newcastle and **three small ch.**, with no estate, yet she possessed land on the Island in 1694. She had ale and vict. lic. in 1693, and the same yr. petitioned for and was given a pub.-ho. lic., as her mo., marrying out of the Province, had left her four beds; lic. 1694 and Dec. 1695; Dr. Bickham three times her bondsm. Her ch. are unident. by record, but found in Newc. are: Thomas, fisherman, taxed 1720, m. by 1721 Sarah, wid. of Thos. Marshall(9 jr.); David, fisherman, taxed 1726, gdn. of John Coates (2) in 1737. One George of Portsm. had w. Sarah in 1743. See also (7) for Christopher of Falm. and his unident. brethren.

15 **THOMAS**, at Spurwink in Feb. 1655-6, ag. ±25, and wit. Francis Small's deed to Isaac Walker in 1658. Lists 111, 112. Henry Putt was bef. Casco ct. in 1667 for embezzling Mr. T. M.'s pease. He may have been ano., but seems the same as Thomas, mariner, Malden, who m. in Nov. 1655 Mary Moulton, sis. of (9) and was of Pemaquid 1675 and later. For connec. with Peter Roderigo, see List 3. About Nov. 1, 1688, Richard Potts and T. M. went from Pemaquid to New Dartmouth for news. He d. in Malden 1 Sept. 1709, ag. 81 yrs. 10 mos.; wid. Mary d. there 7 Jan. 1711, ag. 76. Wyman names 5 ch., incl. Thomas, b. 1660, and John, b. 1664. In 17-- one T. M. and Robert Nichols wit. for Margery (White) Haines bef. the East. Cl. Com.

16 **WILLIAM**(2), has to be the 2d son if the fisherman who bot from Peter Lewis on Smuttynose in 1683, and with w. Honor sold in 1702, then appar. of Newcastle. See also (17). Liv. in Kittery 1715, Scarboro in July 1717 (SJC 73511) and there in Jan. 1723-4 when his mo. deeded him the Kit. place where she was dwelling. Scarb. selectman 1724. Killed by Ind. 18 Apr. 1724. Lists 95, 307a, 239b. Bef. 22 Aug. 1715 he m. Elizabeth Tinney (John), who was taxed a wid. in 1730, m. 2d Benj. Haskins (see John 6), and was liv. in Nov. 1750, ±64. A 1749 div. shows the ch., all of Scarb. in 1746, the mo. of the older ones uncert: Israel, oldest son in Apr. 1734 (Y. D. 17: 51, in which his bros. Christopher and John joined), m. in Scarb. 24 Dec. 1730 Mary Berry. He mov. to New Meadows and was drowned there in 1749. Christopher, m. (int. 5 Apr. 1734) Deborah Mills(4). He mov. to Brunswick. John, Scituate 1761. Elizabeth, m. (int. 21 July 1736) Joseph Drisco, s. of John (not Joseph) and Mary (Getchell) (see Drisco 6). Job, twin, b. 24 Apr. 1720, m. 5 Jan. 1743-4 Susanna Brown. William, twin, called gr.son of Wm. Tinney, m. 31 May 1744 Hannah

Berry. **Mary**, unmar. in 1745 (Y. D. 25: 167). One Mary was rec. (Scarb.) 1 May 1717, ano. 30 Sept. 1722; poss. one was Mary and one Mercy. **Relief**, b. 31 Dec. 1724, m. John Berry. **Mercy**, single in 1745, m. James Marr.

17 ——, and wife, Portsm., parents of **Prudence**, who m. 1st John Bradden(2), m. 2d Robert Tapley, and was Prudence Spoor in 1726. In 1708 the town agreed with Prudence T. to keep her fa. and mo. Mitchell and to finish a room in the back part of her ho. for them. The town also paid for subsisting Goodman M. at her ho. from 1713 to Apr. 1, 1714. Not imposs. his name was William and it was he, not (16), who bot on Smuttynose in 1683, selling with w. Honor in 1702.

**MITTON**. The disting. fam. of Shropshire and Staffordshire, to which the mo. of Mrs. Lewis of Saco(19) belonged, may have produced

**MICHAEL**, gentleman, sportsman and teller of tall stories to Mr. John Jocelyn. He prob. came over with George Cleeve when he returned from Eng. in 1637, and soon m. Cleeve's dau. Elizabeth, his fa.-in-law leasing to him Pond (Peaks) Isl., in Gorges' name, in Dec. 1637, the transaction being confirmed by Tho. Gorges in 1642 and by Cleeve for Rigby in 1650. Liv. at Clark's Pt. (foot of Brackett St., Portland). In 1640 constable of Casco, testif. ab. Winter's extortionate charges for powder and shot, and, 'a great fowler,' supplied the Trelawney Colony with geese, ducks, etc. For his seduction of Mary Martin, see Martin(4). Lists 22, 221(2), 232, 281. Subm. to Mass. and gr.j. 1658. Wit. ag. Joseph Phippen, Nicholas White et al. for fighting, and ag. his fa.-in-law for refusing to vote for magistrates, in 1659. He d. bef. 1662-3. Adm. 30 June 1680 to s.-in-law John Graves. Adm. Oct. 1728 to gr.s. Joshua Brackett of Greenland. Inv. lists 279 a. of land incl. Pond Isl. and a neck of land adj. to Lawrence's cove known as Clark's point. The wid. deeded 100 a. on so. side of Fore river to her s.-in-law Thaddeus Clark 1 Mar. 1662-3, and soon m. Peter Harvey(9). Ch: **Anne**, m. Anthony Brackett(2). **Dorcas** (not -Sarah-, a slip of James Ross's memory ab. 1735), m. James Andrews(6). **Nathaniel**, in ct. Oct. 1669; k. in Ind. attack of Aug. 1676 at Casco Bay with his Brackett bros.-in-law; adm. on his est. in hands of his mo., Mrs. Harvey, to Thaddeus Clark 28 June 1682. **Martha**, m. John Graves(2). **Elizabeth**, b. ab. 1645, m. Thaddeus Clark (52). **Mary**, m. Thomas Brackett(6).

**MOFFATT**. 1 **John**, Hon., from Dunster, co. Somerset, m. Catherine Cutts(8) and d. in Portsm., ag. 92 (newspaper of 3 Feb.

1786). One dau. was mo. of Gov. Langdon, ano. dau. was w. of Wm. Whipple, Signer of the Declaration of Independence.

2 **WILLIAM**, Newbury 1682, ±18, had w. Mehitable, poss. a Falmouth girl. **Six ch.** rec. Newb. 1692-1706. Of Killingsly, Conn., 1730, he and w. deeded right 'which we have' in Falm. (Y. D. 15: 207).

**MOLES**, Edward, and John Trick of Cape Newagon or Hope Harbor, claimed in 171- half of neck of land betw. Casco Bay and Kennebec Riv. adj. Thos. Stevens and Christopher Lawson, by deed from Richard Collicott 18 Feb. 1663-4, not signed or ack. One John Moles was taxed in Greenland 1719.

**Monday.** See Munden.

**MONK.** 1 **Christopher**, fisherman, Isles of Shoals, adm. on his est. gr. to Michael Endle 13 Feb. 1666-7. A later C. M., sailor, in Boston 1686.

2 **GEORGE**, fishing-master, Star Island, Shoals, asso. with the Sealeys and doubtless from a Teign parish, co. Devon, where the name is found. See Aspinwall, pp. 392-3. Robert the Frenchman threatened Mr. G. M., his commander, in 1647. Constable 1649. Sued Wm. and Frances Hilton for slander and was bondsman for Tho. Wedge in 1650.

3 **JOHN**, Isles of Shoals, with Antipas Maverick and Richard Cumming took inv. of est. of Stephen Sargent, 1649.

**Monson.** See Manson, Munson.

**MONTAGUE**, **Griffin**, carpenter, Cape Porpus, prev. of Muddy River, where accus. in 1635 of stealing clapboards and ord. to remove. Exeter in 1639, and evid. in 1643. Cape P. bef. 1647, his home on a point long kn. as Montague's Neck. Tr.j. 1647, 1655; gr.j. 1647, 1655, 1666; constable 1653, 1665; Cape P. comr. for building the prison 1654; Jonathan Thing's bondsm. 1655; and frequent plaint. or deft. in ct. Lists 376a, 378, 251, 252, 263, 24, 254, 79, 255. He apprais. the Bush and Sanders estates in 1670 and Edw. Barton's in 1671, not long bef. he made his will, weak and sick, 7 July 1671—1 Apr. 1672, giving all to w. Margaret and directing burial near grave of s. John, who wit. for his fa. in Aug. 1659 and was given 20 s. by gr.mo. Mrs. Ann Looman of Weymouth; likely maternal gr.mo. as no other Montague in her will, Oct. 1659. Wid. Margaret, m. bef. Oct. 1650, was dau. of Walter Kelway of Chelmsford, co. Essex (Waters 1: 759). She was evid. at Cape P. in 1677 (List 266); d. bef. 8 Sept. 1682 when her neph. Samuel Snow of Boston was her exec. and Griffin's admr.

**Montaway**, John, liv. in 1706 with Francis Allen(12) of Kit., who gave bond to save the town harmless (Y. D. 7: 65).

**MONTESSE**, 1 **Jeanne** (Jane), w. of Edmund Hammons(2) of Kit. (Ch. rec. in Canada). A French version of some Eng. name, but what one?

2 **PHILLIPPE** (Montase), in captivity 1710, named betw. Paul Otis and Adrian Frye. List 99, p. 125.

**MOODY**, Moodey. Old in cos. Norfolk, Oxford and Wilts; now also freq. in cos. Hants and Somerset.

1 **CLEMENT**, Exeter 1692, not of the Newbury family; perh. related to (5) or (4) and poss. a Jerseyman. In 1698 he was gr. land he had fenced by the river; in 1700 part of John(15) Clark's 1680 gr. was laid out to him and he may have m. 1st Clark's dau. Sarah; his w. was Sarah in 1706. Lists 62, 67. 376b (1698, 1725). Perryman's account ag. him in 1724 ment. 'your wife,' 'jacknife for David.' Adm. to eldest s. Clement 21 Apr. 1729, wid. Alice renouncing, Cartee Gilman and Jos. Smart bondsm. Ch. appear: **Clement**, Ex. scout 1712, taxed 'jr.' 1714, had deed from fa. 1715. List 376b. He or s. Clement (see Jonathan) m. Elizabeth Scribner (John). **Philip**, had deed from fa. 1717; head of a Kingston fam. 1725, liv. Kings. 1747. Perryman's account ag. him 1724 names several of his bros., mo. and w., and Benj. and Wm. Taylor. He and 3 ch. bp. 1727, 4 more in 1735. **John**, Ex., br. of Philip; Corp. 1724. List 376b. Adm. 10 Aug. 1731 to wid. Abigail, bondsm. Nicholas and Cartee Gilman. His heirs had a gr. in 1740. **Jonathan**, Ex. in 1725 his fa. deeded to him and to gr.s. Clement, 2d s. of Clement. List 376b. Will, 27 Feb. 1729-30—18 May 1731, names w. Joanna, s. Jonathan under age, dau. Sarah. Wid. Joanna m. 2d at Kingst. 21 Oct. 1731 Jonathan Wadleigh. **Josiah**, br. of Philip; presum. he who m. Sarah Scribner (John) by 1736; both of Brentwood 1747. **Elizabeth**, m. Jeremiah Brown(11). **David**, named in two accounts 1724, no kinship stated; in 1733 wid. Alice was his mo.-in-law (step-mo.). He m. in Kingst. 21 June 1733 Mary Gilman (Jacob 10); both o.c. and had 2 ch. bp. at Kingst. 10 Oct. 1735. Jane, adm. to Kingst. Ch. 3 Mar. 1727-8, must have belonged to this fam. by birth or mar.

2 **DANIEL**, maltster, Stratham, Scarboro, b. 16 Feb. 1683-4, s. of Daniel and gr.s. of Caleb, both of Newb., m. in Hampt. 19 May 1708 Mary Norton(1). Of Salisb. in 1713, he bot in Strath.; **six ch.** rec. there 1714-1724. List 388. In 1726 he and Clement Meserve bot 100 a. in Scarb., where he was taxed 1729, propr. 1737, and liv. 1741 when he sold a gr. in Bow.

3 **REV. JOSHUA**, Portsmouth, s. of Wm. of Newbury; H. C. 1653. Called to Portsm. 14 Feb. 1658, he was not ordained until 1671,

altho appar. there continuously until his conflict with Cranfield sent him to the First Ch. in Boston as asst. pastor in May 1684, aft. 13 wks. in jail. He soon declined election as Pres. of H. C., and contin. with Boston Ch. almost nine yrs. bef. his championship of Philip English and w:, accused of witchcraft, earned him both regard and criticism. In 1693 he ret. to Portsm., where as early as May 1691 he wrote both town and ch. he would return if desired. See Sibley's 'Harvard Graduates' 1: 367; N. H. Prov. Papers 1: 482 et seq.; Eliot's 'Biog. Dict.,' p. 327. Lists 311b, 323, 326bc, 329, 330abe, 331ac, 335a, 49, 54, 92, 96, 98. See also (7). His 1st w. Martha Collins (Dea. Edward of Cambridge) d. shortly bef. 24 Aug. 1674; List 331c. He m. 2d Ann, wid. of Samuel Jacobs of Ipsw.; Lists 331c, 335a. His will, 18 Sept. 1693 (d. Boston the Sabbath bef. 4 July 1697), requests bur. near decd. wife and their ch., names w. Ann, 4 ch., dau.-in-law Lydia Jacobs he had kept so many yrs., s. Winslow and money lent Eleazer Russell, decd., payable by heirs of br. Russell, decd.; only br. Caleb an overseer. Ch: Samuel, Martha, m. by 1681 Rev. Jonathan Russell, H. C. 1675, who was ordained at Barnstable 19 Sept. 1683, her fa. giving the sermon. Sarah, in 24th yr. in June 1688; m. Rev. John Pike(5). Hannah, m. bef. 1693 Edward Winslow of Boston, where 10 ch. rec. She d. ±1710. Abigail, d. from small-pox 2 Mar. 1686-7 (List 96). At least one more child, dead by 1693.

4 NICHOLAS (Mooedy), wit. a Hilton deed at Lamprill Riv. in 1679 with Robert Wadleigh and Michael French. See also (1), (5).

5 PHILIP, Exeter 1684, List 52. Note (1), (4).

6 MAJ. SAMUEL(3), better kn. as a military man than as Rev. Samuel, his change in profession poss. prompted by duty at times as chaplain, or a lasting memory of the refugees he had seen from childhood. H. C. 1689, and suppos. the S. M. preaching at Hadley 1693-4, Newcastle called him 19 Mar. 1694-5, where he was succ. by Mr. Emerson. At St. John's Fort, Newfoundland, bef. 1705, and succ. Col. March at Casco Fort bef. 4 Nov. 1707, being the agent between the Ind. and the government and receiving their flag of truce, resulting in the peace made 13 July 1713. Aft. the fort was dismantled, he settled on Falm. Neck (Portland) and has the fame of being the founder of the new town which he served as selectman, J. P. and Justice of Ct. of Com. Pleas. In the following war he was next in command with Col. Walton till both were dismissed by Lt.-Gov. Dummer. He m. 4 Apr. 1695 Esther, dau. of Nathaniel Green of Bos-

ton (her List 331c) and d. 5 Apr. 1729 in 59th yr. (gr.st. in Eastern Cemetery, Portland, long misread -in 52d yr.·). Adm. 30 June 1729 to s. Joshua, wid. Esther renounc. Lists 315c, 331c, 229, 161. Ch. b. in Newc. (Prov. rec.): Joshua, b. 11 Feb. 1695-6, d. 27 May fol. Joshua, gent., b.·31 Oct. 1697, H. C. 1716, m. (int. Falm. 3 Feb. 1736) Tabitha Cox; d. 20 Feb. 1748. Ch. bp: Houchin, William, Samuel. Major Samuel, Esq., b. 29 Oct. 1699, H. C. 1718, m. in Wells 12 Jan. 1724-5 Mary Wheelwright (John, Esq.). Will, of Fort George, Brunswick, 1756-1758, names w. Mary and ch. Nathaniel Green, Samuel and Joshua, but not William and Mary, bp. 1728, 1735. Mary, b. 16 Nov. 1701, m. Edmond Mountfort; d. 1751.

7 REV. SAMUEL, H. C. 1697, a frontier parson and fighting chaplain, and York's minister 50 yrs. despite eccentricities which at times must have caused consid. feeling. Nephew of (3), see also (8), he was b. in Newb. 4 Jan. 1675-6, s. of Caleb and Judith (Bradbury1) and went to York as a chaplain 16 May 1698, being ordained pastor in Dec. 1700. See Me. Hist. Soc. Col. 2: 4: 199; Doc. Hist. 5: 528-9, 9: 187; Sibley's 'Harv. Grad.' 4: 356; Hist. of York 2: 131. He m. 1st (int. Newb. 15 July 1698) Hannah Sewall (John), who d. 29 Jan. 1727-8, ag. 51; m. 2d (int. York 3 Nov. 1732) Mrs. Ruth Newman of Glouc.; d. in York 13 Nov. 1747. List 279. The town paid his funeral exp. £105-18-06, gave the wid. £40 to put herself in mourning, the son £15, the dau. £10. Wid. Ruth d. 20 Apr. 1764 in 76th yr. Ch. rec. York: Rev. Joseph, b. 16 May 1700, H. C. 1718, first minister of 'Scotland' par., town clerk, register of deeds, and the famous 'Handkerchief' Moody; see List 96 under date 25 Aug. 1708; Hist. of York 2: 80; Hawthorne's 'Veiled Parson.' The Me. Hist. Soc. has his orig. Diary 1720-1724, Suppos. to have been badly disappointed when Mary Hirst m. (Sir) Wm. Pepperell, he recovered enough to m. in York 11 Nov. 1724 Lucy White (Rev. John of Glouc.) who d. in 1736, he 20 Mar. 1753, ag. 55 (gr.st.). 4 ch. Mary, b. 28 Aug. 1702, m. Rev. Joseph Emerson of Malden. Lucy, b. and d. 6 July 1705.

8 WILLIAM, Exeter, gave p/a to Jarvis Ring in Nov. 1699 in connec. with a suit over Salisb. land (SJC 4028). Twice taken by Ind. in 1709, and suppos. to have been roasted to death. List 96; also 'N. E. Captives' 1: 370. Appar. he was the br. of (7), b. in Newb. 15 Dec. 1673, whose est. was divided to br. and sis. in 1710.

MOORE, general in Eng., but rare on S. coast except cos. Devon and Kent. Became 25th commonest name in N. E.

1 ANTHONY, fined for swearing in 1670, Capt. John Davis wit. Of the Shoals,

drunk and fighting, he did not appear July —Sept. 1671, when twice summoned.

2 **DANIEL**, blacksmith, Eliot wit. 1662, was partn. of Edmund Green(6) at Gt. Isl., and used the tools after Green died. Of Portsm. 1669, he sold to Andrew Newcomb ho. and 6 a. in Kit. near Thos. Spinney, form. occup. by James Emery, later by self. Mr. Fryer sued him for debt in Wells ct. 1672, and lost. Black Point resident in the garrison 1676. Lists 312a, 87, 237ac. Presumably m., but no fam. appears unless (3).

3 **DANIEL**, Portsm. 1694-1696. Lists 335b, 336b, 67. Note (2).

4 **EBENEZER**(8), shipwright, Kittery, with interest in sawmills, had gr. 1699; m. 1st 25 Nov. 1700 Joanna Deering (see 8), m. 2d Temperance (Fernald 5) Deering(1) by 1714, when as Temperance M. she was an orig. memb. of Kit. Point Ch. He liv. on the 50 a. on Spruce Creek deeded to wid. of (8) by John Fabes, defended his title ag. Richard Tucker 1718-1720, and mtg. it to Pepperell for £200 in 1725. Lists 291, 296-298. He d. bef. 28 Dec. 1733; adm. 15 Jan. fol. to Epes Greenough, the wid. renouc. In 1735 when Pepperell foreclosed, the land was in poss. of Greenough and John Jordan. Ch: **Margery** (surely), m. (int. Newb. 11 Dec. 1730) Epes Greenough, gr.s. of Robert (1). Appar: **Jonadab**, m. in Kit. 26 Sept. 1734 Mary Moore(11); he d. in the Fr. war, leaving wid. and ch. (See Bradbury's 'K'port'). Poss: **Joanna** (?Moore), m. 1st Peletiah Whittemore, m. 2d Capt. John Lecornee.

5 **ELIZABETH**, Portsm., rec. into cov. and bp. at No. Ch. with ch: **Samuel** and **Elizabeth**, 26 Mar. 1710, her husb. unident. An unnamed Moore (appar. a ch.) was bp. there 1711, Jonathan 1713, Sarah 1717, ano. Elizabeth 1720. See also Beale(4).

6 **GEORGE**, testif. at Portsm. 21 Dec. 1699 ab. lumber deliv. by (18) to Capt. John Ware at Antigua. N. E. Reg. 69: 362.

7 **JAMES**(?More), Saco 1674, when Humphrey Case had his boat and man.

8 **JOHN**, sr., fisherman, Star Isl., Kittery, b. ±1638-9, linked with (9) who must have been near his age. He was here and married in June 1665 when Peter Glanfield sued him and he sued Gregory Vittery. Star Isl. 1667. Gr.j. 1669, constable 1672-3. He depos. in 1674 ab. Giles Berry, Thos. Trafton and (25), and in Mar. 1676-7, ±38, ab. being at John Pickering's ho. the June bef. with Thos. Dyer and (9). Lists (?305c), 306d, 90. Of the Shoals, he and w. Margaret sold on Star Isl. 1681, and poss. then mov. to Kit., where he had bot in 1669 (Y. D. 3: 88, 104). His inv. 27 July 1686 incl. ho. and lands, 50 a. on Spruce Creek, and a ketch. In Sept. 1687, John Fabes, sr., having had livery of Star Isl. ho. and land from Moore, gave his wid. Margaret, admx., a deed to 50 a. on E. side of Spruce Creek betw. Richard Ambrose (see 9) and Richard Tucker, part of Hugh Gunnison's orig. gr. Margaret M. wit. a Deering deed 23 Mar. 1709-10. List 290. Ch. appear: **John**, b. ±1670-1. **Ebenezer.**

9 **JOHN**, jr., fisherman, Star Isl. See also (8). In 1668 he bot 20 a. at Great Cove, Kit., from John Symonds, and 50 a. betw. John Cutts and John Fabes at Spruce Creek, it being the Pendleton half of 100 a. Capt. P. and Fabes bot from Gunnison heirs. One Shoals John served on a cor.j. 1674 (List 305c). John (jr.) was summ. into ct. in 1675 for calling Mr. Belcher a knave. On Mar. 23, 1676-7 he was dangerously ill and not capable to give oath, being constable for the Shoals; adm. 5 dys. later to wid. Agnes and Capt. Thos. Daniel; inv. incl. much furniture, 50 a. at Spruce Creek with a frame on it, Star Isl. ho. and plant. The Symonds deed he had assigned to John Seward of Portsm. in 1674; wid. Agnes released dower 27 Apr. 1678. Ch., if any, unkn., but how Richard Ambrose(3) became a Spruce Creek abuttor (see Moore 8), unless he m. wid. or dau. of (9), is unexpl. See also John Seward.

10 **JOHN**(25), shipwright, York, O. A. 22 Mar. 1679-80; bot 30 a. at Braveboat Harbor adj. his own land, from Richard White, 1687; retailed without lic. 1695. Grants 1688-1700 were confirmed to his wid., Martha (Walford, dau. of Jeremiah, m. bef. 8 Mar. 1680) and two sons in 1718. Called 'cousin' by John Brawn (3 jr.) in 1703. A dispute over the land he liv. on was settled in 1703, when John Woodman, claiming under Capt. Raynes, gave him a deed to the place. Inv. 10 Mar. 1711; undated will, prov. 7 July 1713, names w. Martha, 2 sons, oldest dau. and 3 other daus. Ch. rec. in York, their mo. Martha: **Mary**, b. 23 May 1679 (oldest dau. -Marcy- in fa.'s will), m. Roger Hunnewell(10). **Martha**, b. 15 Oct. 1683. One Martha was summ. into Newc. ct. 1708 (or 1718) and was liv. with Christopher Amazeen 1720. **Sarah**, b. 7 Jan. 1685-6. See Ichabod Austin(6). Poss. m. 1st Jonathan Ireland(1), cert. m. Ephraim Ayers(2) and had 3 ch. rec. 1724-1728. **John**, b. 20 Dec. 1687, in 1703 was beq. ⅓ the est. of John Brawn(3 jr.) when of age. He m. 1st Hannah Jordan(3); s. John b. 5 Feb. 1713-4. He m. 2d bef. 1719 Mary Woodman (John); 4 daus. rec.; she liv. 1737, he 1757, List 279. In 1724 her fa. deeded to them for life supp. and voided her husb.'s bond in 1740. **Tabitha**, b. 20 Jan. 1689-90, m. 1st Thos. Vincent, who d. in Mar. 1719 (2 daus., both d.); m. 2d Wm. Harris (see 23). **Abigail**, b. 12 Feb. 1691-2; she or her sis. Martha d. bef. fa. **Samuel**, b. 14 Jan. 1694-5, impressed in 1717, m. (ct.

Apr. 1720) Dorcas Hilton(20). Liv. 1757.
List 279. 7 ch. rec.

11 **JOHN**(8), mariner, Kittery, mate on
Pepperell's bark -Mary- 1693, had gr.
1699, and m. Sarah Cutts(7), who was liv. in
1747, dead in 1748. In 1724 he deeded to s.
John the land betw. John Bray and Roger
Deering which (8) bot from Digory Jeffrey
in 1669. Depos. in 1721 ab. Braveboat Harbor near 40 yrs. bef.; in Jan. 1730-1, ±60;
and in 1732 ab. Christopher Mitchell 50 yrs.
bef. Lists 296-298. Will, 24 Feb. 1735-6—2
Apr. 1736, names w. Sarah, sole exec., and
ch: **John**, b. 9 July 1696, m. 10 Jan. 1721-2
Elizabeth Fernald (Tobias 5) who d. 7 May
1744; m. 2d Deborah Wilson (Joseph). 9 ch.
by 1st w. **Elizabeth**, b. 10 Feb. 1699-1700, in
ct. Jan. 1725-6, unm. 1735. **Edward**, b. 24
Aug. 1701, m. 5 Dec. 1722 Hannah Crockett;
both liv. 1740, he dead 1751. 3 surv. ch. **Abigail**, b. 31 July 1702, m. Roger Parker (see
26). **Robert**, b. 23 June 1704, shipwright, m.
1st 24 Dec. 1730 Sarah Frink(1), m. 2d 19
June 1736 Elizabeth Meads. In 1734 his
parents deeded him half the homestead on
Spruce Creek. Adm. to wid. 18 Feb. 1745-6.
A yr. later a lot was laid out to her as his
wid., and to Jonadab M. Ch. **Ebenezer**, m.
(int. 1 May 1736) Mary Ball; d. by 1748
when she was gdn. of 4 ch. **Mary**, m. Jonadab Moore (see 4), who was called son by
her fa., but given no part of the est.; Bradbury called them cousins.

12 **JOHN**, Boston, m. Martha Clark (see 52).

13 **MARY**. Mary Reed(9) was oft. called
Mary Moore, sometimes Kimball. John
Seeley saw M. M. in Nevis; Susanna Cross
testif. in 1671 ab. her under that name, and
Elizabeth Shute said 'this was when M. M.
was mar.'

14 **PETER**, List 339, was Peter Mow,
Frenchman. See Lewis(14).

15 **RICHARD**, Black Point, was of Cape
Porpus 20 May 1647 when gr. 400 a. by
Cleeve, who gave an ident. deed to John
Bush; Bush assigned to him in 1650, and he
to Gregory Jeffrey in 1652. He was at Winter Harbor with his boat 1654; Saco cor.j.
1661; betw. 1654-1664 m. Bridget, wid. of
Roger Hunnewell(9), bot at Black Point and
mov. there by 1664 (her s. Richard H. was
there ±1658). In 1665 she accus. the neighbors and did not prove it; abs. from meet.
1665, 1667-68; ±50 in Apr. 1671. He was constable 1674-5. Lists 251, 263, 244d, (255 is
Hix, not Moore), 237ae, 239. In 1678 Scottow succes. sued him and John Tinney for
taking away his shallop when the garrison
was deserted. In Sept. 1679, the town was
ord. to maint. him, lame and weak, and re-
imburse Richard Hunnewell for what he had
done; adm. to R. H. 30 May 1682. Ch. appear: **Joan**, but poss. Hunnewell; if Moore,

her mo. was an early w.; m. by 1667 Wm.
Batten(5). **Mary** (cert. Moore), called sis.
of Joan, her mo. likely Bridget. Henry Williams pd. her fine in 1673, and in same ct.
sued her fa. in her behalf. In 1675 she accus.
Robert Jordan(8), who was ord. to supp.
her ch.; m. (ct. 4 July 1676) Daniel Glanfield
(1).

16 **ROBERT**, Shoals wit. 1664 (Y. D. 2: 32),
poss. (17).

17 **ROBERT**(25), poss. same as (16) if age
permits. Not found aft. 1694, but must
have been he who m. Anna Penwill(5) and
had dau. **Anna**, who was a wid. Wakefield
of Newb. in 1749, when she sold to Wm. M.
of York the ho. her gr.fa. Penwill bot from
Lt. Job Alcock. One Ann M. m. Henry Wakefield in Boston 4 May 1704.

18 **SAMUEL**, Mr., mariner, Portsm., a newcomer, m. aft. Sept. 1694 Mary (Partridge 1), Barnwell. First seen here on a jury
Dec. 1696; in 1698 he bot from Sheriff Jose
land near the meet.-ho. adj. Aaron Moses,
and in 1704 from wid. Elizabeth Savage ho.
and land nearby, adj. Thos. Beck, which she
had bot from Moses. Lists 330def, 337. Sold
without lic. in June 1697, and lic. in Sept.
Master of brigantine -Endeavor- in 1699
(see 5); note too S. M. of Nevis (Reg. 64:
189). His w. was lic. 1698, selling without
1700, lic. 1704, 1706. One Samuel o.c. in No.
Ch. and had s. Samuel bp. 24 Feb. 1708-9. In
May 1711 he was voted 12 s. for cure of a
wound recd. in Prov. service on sloop -Speed-
well-, and d. bef. Oct. 1716, when wid. m. 3d
Richard Elliot(4). Ch: Ensign **John**, b. 16
Apr. 1696 (son's rec.), shipwright, farmer,
m. 15 Mar. 1719-20 Hannah Sias (John).
Oyster River aft. 1722; later, fol. reverses,
liv. in Canterbury. Lists 339, 369. He d. 10
Apr. 1786, 2 mos. aft. wife. 8 ch. Col. **Samuel**, Esq., Portsm., mariner, merchant, ship-
owner. Col. of N. H. regt. at Louisburg. His
br. q.c. the home place to him in 1722, their
mo. signing; he sold in 1725 to Henry Beck,
already in poss. Boston 1735, Portsm. 1742.
He d. in London; will, 7 Feb. 1744—31 May
1749, gives all to w. Mary (Pierce 13), m.
bef. 1734, d. 12 May 1753, ag. 45. No ch.

19 **SAMUEL**, cordwainer, and w. Hannah
(Hill 18), appar. of Portsm. 1721, Kit.
1729. One Samuel was rec. into cov. and bp.
at No. Ch. 30 Mar. 1718. Samuel of Kit. m.
Patience Knowlton of Newbury in 1730;
see also Hannah, w. of Jonathan Low(3).

20 **THEODOSIUS**, was at Casco Bay, perh.
tempo., in 1687, two yrs. bef. he could
have m. Joan (Guy 2) Gendall. Of Boston,
he bot 200 a. and ho. on Wescustogo River,
form. Thos. Redding's, and sold it in 1729
to John Smith of Boston. Liv. Bridgewater
1730. See Gendall.

21 **CAPT. THOMAS**, Boston, commander of ketch -Rose- went from Piscat. to the aid of the Eastern settlements in 1676; Maj. Pendleton called him an old acquaintance. Doc. Hist. 6: 142-8, 185.

22 **THOMAS**(25), York, admr. of fa.'s est. Grants 1695, 1699; ferry lic. 1695, 1696. Called cous. in 1703 by John Brawn(3 jr.) who left ⅔ of his est. to be improved for his s. Wm. till of age. He was with the York men attacked at Winter Harbor in 1707 (see Benj. Donnell 5), with party which recov. a stolen boat and took four prisoners in 1711, and served under Capt. Preble on Ind. exped. in 1712. He d. 22 Apr. 1718. He m. bef. 17 Feb. 1696-7 Hannah (either Harris 19, or Williams), dau. of wid. Christian Kar (see Carr 1). She was liv. 10 Jan. 1710-1, when he deeded his home place and the 1699 gr. to Capt. Lyons who had prev. bot Harker's Isl. from him. Ch., likely not all: **William**, eldest son (Y. D. 9: 46), minor in 1703, was apprent. in 1712 to Dr. March of Greenl. and ran away. He m. in Kit. 18 Jan. 1718-9 Mary Elwell (Hezekiah). List 279. Will 1781 names 10 (8 liv., 2 dead) of 11 ch. **Wyatt**, tailor, York, Biddeford (Y. D. 16: 255), must have been named for his mo.'s last step-fa. List 279. He m. 1st (ct. July 1725) Joanna Donnell(4), m. 2d (int. Bid. 16 Nov. 1740) Elizabeth Wormwood. Ch. **Patience**, apprent. to Benj. Stone; ill of small-pox in Dec. 1721; m. 7 Oct. 1727 Samuel Staples. **Jonathan**, d. at York 25 June 1731.

23 **THOMAS**, taxed for Mill Dam, Portsm., 1707, as Mr. More the carver; m. 8 Dec. 1715 Abigail Banfield(2), both of Portsm. where he was liv. 1717. List 339. Both of Boston 1725, where s. **Samuel**, carver, was liv. 1736. Portsm. taxes abated 1713, persons gone out of town, incl. one T. M.

24 **WILLIAM**, Exeter, shared in the divisions of Dec. 1639 and signed Ex. ptns. 1643, 1645. Selectman 1647, 1654, 1658; tr.j. 1654. Taking pipe-staves to Lamprill River for the Gilmans ±1651. Lists 374ac, 375ab, 376ab (1645), 377, 379. In 1654 relieved from ordin. training, paying 5 s., and from all training, without fine, in 1664, aft. he had mov. to Ipsw. where he made his will 14 Aug. 1660, sick and weak, yet liv. to 21 May 1671. Ipsw. inv., all personal, incl. £60 in the hands of Simon Thompson; the Ex. inv. was mostly land. Ch., but not w., named in will: **Ruth**, m. Henry Robie(1), who deeded an Ex. ho. to her fa. 20 Sept. 1653. **William**, b. 1631-4, oldest s., heir and exec. **Thomas**, received £10. **Mary**, b. ±1638, m. Robert Powell(5). In 1660 her fa., for love and affec., deeded her 100 + 10 a. in Ex. **Elizabeth**, of Ex. unm. 1673; m. bef. Apr. 1674 John Williams.

25 **WILLIAM**, York, fisherman, ferryman, had ct. actions with Mr. Godfrey in Oct. 1651 and 1653. With John Harker gr. 20 a. in 1653; in 1655 he and Philip Adams had 80 a. at Hull's Cove from Godfrey; town gr. alone 1674. Tr.j. 1655; j. 1678, 1691. O. A. Mar. 1679-80. Retail lic. 1687, retailing without 1690. In 1683 he compl. ag. others for ferrying, was given the monopoly and in 1684 sued Arthur Beale for taking away benefits. Lists 273, 275, 276, 28, 30. See also (8). His w. Dorothy was appar. step-dau. of Wm. Dixon(3), cert. his w.'s dau. His will, 31 Mar. (inv. 12 May) 1691. Wid. Dorothy liv. 5 Apr. 1693; adm. 28 Oct. fol. to s. John; div. 10 Jan. 1693-4, her 'five daus.' ment. Ch., all in will and div. but **Dorothy**, omitted for reason unkn., who must have been James Dixon's cous. D. M. given £5 in his deed-will 1666; m. by 1678 Daniel Dill (1). Her br. Thos., as admr., deeded him 20 a. near Scotland 'portion I am willing to allow to my own sis. D. M.' Other ch: **John. Robert. William**, a captive, uncertain if alive 1694; but in Canada 1711. List 99, p. 92. **Thomas. Elizabeth**, m. Thos. Trafton. **Sarah**, m. 1st Zaccheus Welcom, m. 2d bef. 1693 Henry Spiller of Ipsw. **Eleanor**, m. Richard Rogers(10); had but half portion in div. **Ann**, m. 12 Mar. 1697-8 Daniel Smith. **Mary**, a captive 1694, fate unkn.

26 **CAPT. *WILLIAM**(24), Exeter (±33 or 34 in 1666, ±60 in 1694), bot a q.c. of Mrs. Susanna Leader's Hampt. ho. with H. Robie in 1658, and poss. liv. there a time. Tr.j. 1664 and often, also gr.j.; Exeter selectman 1671-2, 1691, 1694, 1699; Ensign 1678-1689; rep. 1681, 1692; com. Capt. 1690; moderator 1698. Lists 381, 383, 49, 50, 52, 54, 55ab, 57, 58, 62, 388. He m. in Hampt. 7 Oct. 1673 Mary Wiggin (Thos.), wid. of Geo. Veasey, and soon aft. her br. Andrew deeded to him land in the Shrewsbury Patent promised to Veasey. She d. bef. him. His will, 25 Dec. 1700—2 May 1704, names br. Andrew Wiggin and ch: **Mary**, m. 17 Apr. 1707 Hon. Joseph Smith of Hampt. **William**, Esq. Stratham, was selectman 1709, 1711-2. Lists 376b, 388. He m. 1st bef. Jan. 1703-4 Sarah Wiggin (Andrew), m. 2d by 1708 Agnes Harvey(14) who d. bef. him (liv. 1730). His will, 14 Apr. (d. 11 Sept.) 1747, names 3 ch: Mary (by. 1st w.) m. bef. 1734 John Coker. By 2d w: Lt. William, Esq., m. Abigail Gilman(12); the Dudley Book makes him a son of the 1st w., but Hon. Joseph Smith's will, and names of 2 of his 10 ch., Agnes and Harvey, indicate the 2 w. **Thomas**, m. 19 Dec. 1734 Rachel Sinclair (John); 8 ch. See also Clark(12)

27 **WILLIAM**, merchant, Berwick, prosec. as a peddler in 1721, had goods come from Boston to York and mov. them to a room in

Philip Hubbard's ho.; understood to be Irish. See also Clark(34). He m. Anne Goodwin(5) in Berwick 16 Jan. 1723-4, and left ch: David; and Susannah, a legatee in will of Mrs. Jeremiah Wise, m. Wm. Rogers.
28 LT., taken prisoner at Saco in 1703. List 39.

Moregould, William, named in a Great Isl. acct. 1680. List 90.

Moreland, Thomas, seaman, ack. a debt. to Hugh Gunnison, 1655. List 78.

## MOREY.

1 NICHOLAS, carpenter, s. of Thos. and Mary of East Worldham, co. Hants, had a Wells gr. in Aug. 1684, was acting for the Curwin interests in Jan. fol. and m. betw. 28 Oct. 1684—31 Mar. 1685 Mary (Pendleton 2) Cross(7). He bot 150 a. at Cape Porpus in Feb. 1685-6; tav. lic. there Oct. 1686, 1687; gr.j. 1687; selectman 1688. His ho., which was being garrisoned, was burned by Ind. in Apr. 1689. Lists 259, 269b. Taunton 1692, Freetown 1716, Dighton 1722, where he d. 4 Mar. 1730-1; adm. to wid. Mary and aft. her death (her will 5 Oct. 1732—10 Jan. 1732-3) to John Smith of London now of Boston, his next of kin. Letters from N. M. to London relatives (N. E. Reg. 35: 235), name Eng. and Boston kinsmen, while a p/a given by a neph. John M. to Thos. Smith, both of London, to recover from the wid. Mary M., recites that Nicholas left a will, dated 15 Oct. 1722, naming these two men his heirs (SJC 33630, 40402). See also Pendleton Gen. pp. 40-41.

2 WILLIAM (Moree or Morce). See Morse (11).

## MORGAN, a Welsh name, and well spread over nearby English counties.

1 BENJAMIN, from Beverly and br. of (5), k. at the Eastward bef. July 1677.

2 FRANCIS, Mr., surgeon, Kittery, ±26 in June 1671, ±28 in Feb. 1671-2, not much more than of age when he m. betw. 5 July 1664—21 Mar. 1664-5 Sarah (Tilley) Mitchell(5), who was ±51 in June 1670, and thrice a wid.; Lists 78, 82. He kept much in evid., in numerous suits for one reason and ano., and troubles with his w., her ch. and the Lockwoods. Retail lic. at the Point 1665, tav. lic. 1670-2; she was lic. 1667-9. In 1673 on her ptn. the selectm. arranged for maintenance for her out of his prop.; she was then in a weak condition and may have d. soon. He was bound for Eng. in Aug. 1677 and is seen little thereafter. In July 1678 Russell heirs brot suit ag. him to foreclose the mortg. on the Gunnison prop.; last found on Kit. ptn. 1683. Lists 78, 82, 86, 288. See also Bartlett(7), Groth, Hooke(1), Lynde, and Me. P. & Ct. Rec. vols. i, ii.

3 JOHN, with crew of the -Margery- 1642-3. List 21.

4 JOSEPH, Purpooduck; his w. and 2 ch. k. List 39. Poss. from Beverly.

5 MOSES, br. of (1), slain at Black Point; adm. in Essex ct. June 1678 to br. Samuel.

6 RICHARD, Exeter, was of Dover, 1659, and when he m. Rebecca Holdridge(1) at Andover 21 May 1660. Exeter gr. 1664, 1681, 1698; O. A. 1677; gr.j. 1696. Lists 356e, 376b, 382, 384, 384b, 388, 52, 54, 62, 67. See also Foss(1) and his neighbor Geo. Jones (17) whose fence he tore down and w. had much strife. Called of Ipsw. 1693 when gr. adm. on the Holdridge est. Of Exeter 1699, he deeded to Peter Coffin his ho. and 100 a. on N. side of way to Quamscott, except what given to gr.ch. Katherine Dyer. Dead 22 Feb. 1711-2 (his son was 'Jr.' 1701, 1707); wid. Rebecca liv. 1714. Kn. ch: William, b. 23 May 1661 (Haverh.). Richard, b. ±1666. Dau., m. Edward Dear or Dyer(2) of Ipsw., an Irishman's son, who d. there 19 June 1703. One wid. Hannah D. m. John Waite (int. Ipsw. 16 Nov. 1712). John, d. at his br. Abraham's in Strath. 29 Sept. 1745, 'Old J. M.' He seems to be the blacksmith of Hampt. F., Chester (bot 1722), Greenland 1726, and Kingston, who m. Deborah Blake(5) at Hampt. (6 ch. incl. Luther, Kingston, who bot in Arundel 1731, but was there tempo. if at all); appar. m. 2d at Hampt. 31 Dec. 1724 Mary Dearborn (6 ch. at Kingston, the mo. called 2d w.). Abraham, had w. Damaris 1710-1730 at least. Ex. soldier 1710-1712; of Hampt., alias Portsm., 1715; Strath. 1719. He deeded his homestead, first in 1750 to s. Robert (d. 1752), then in 1756 to dau. Mary, singlewo., and d. 7 July 1758. 6 ch. in Strath. Two Bryant-Morgan marriages and a similarity with names in fam. of Bryant(10) are noted. Poss. a dau., old Rebecca M., d. at Strath. 4 May 1754, but see Rebecca(7).

7 RICHARD(6), ±48 in June 1714, m. in Hampt. 17 May 1699 Abigail Harris(1). In Capt. Gilman's co. 1710. In 1712 he and mo. sold grants made to fa. and self in 1698; he and T. Harris(24) sold in Ex. 1715. Lists 57, 67, 376b, 388. Turbet's Creek, Arundel, 1719 (Bradbury). His w. Abigail and two ch. were liv. there in 1721, when warrant was issued for her arrest and Mary Duley's; the Scarb. constable reported A. M. not found; Richard Smith of Bid. was her bondsm., either then or later. He d. appar. bef. Jan. 1726-7, cert. bef. Mar. 1732 when Joshua Lassell sold part of his grant (Y. D. 14: 239, 18: 270). Bradbury gives 5 ch., incl. Moses, shoemaker, and Luther, but Moses was from Beverly (Y. D. vols. 14, 15, 19) and Luther seems s. of John(6). Cert. a ch: Samuel, sold to Lassell Jan. 1726-7 what ap-

pears his fa.'s gr., had gr. of his own in 1730, and of Arundel (w. Hannah) sold half of it in Jan. 1731-2. Portsm. inquest 1732 on S. M. who d. in the jail, and Thos. Harris (drowned). Wid. Hannah (Bryant 10, m. in Greenl. 31 Aug. 1730) m. there 2d, 24 Apr. 1735 Philip Harris or Harry(1). **John,** liv. on Saco Road and d. bef. 1735 (Bradb.); see also John(9). **Rebecca,** unm. in July 1748 when she deeded br. Saml.'s gr. on Saco Road to Samuel Wilds; see Rebecca(6). This deed and Samuel's mar. suggest as other ch: Abigail, m. in Greenl. 16 Apr. 1725 Elisha Bryant(10); Elizabeth, o.c. in Greenl. 1729, m. there 24 July 1734 Samuel Wildes; and Robert, wit. Jacob Wildes's deed at Arundel 1732, but note that Moses of Beverly had br. Robert.

8 **ROBERT,** taxed Saco Sept. 1636; see Hitchcock. One of the Pemaquid men accused in 1641 of taking furs from T. Purchase's ho. (Gallop 2; Lechford p. 402). Early he had gr. of Tuessic Neck from Clarke and Lake and sold half to Lawrence Dennis(6) in 1664, tho he had no deed himself until Sylvanus Davis, agent for C. & L., gave him and w. Mary one 30 July 1673 (Doc. Hist. 4: 336). His and w.'s ends unkn., also their ch: Appar. a **Dau.** m. Lawrence Dennis. Poss. a gr.s. or gt.gr.s. was Robert M., Boston tailor, who in 1742 with John Bish(2) was bondsm. for Richard Hunnewell's wid. Mary of Boston, all Sagadahoc names. One R. M. m. Anne Swain in Boston 24 Oct. 1719.

9 **WILLIAM**(6), took O. A. at Exeter 30 Nov. 1677 and signed a N. H. ptn. Feb. 1689-90 (List 57), tho appar. at Wells 1689-1695 with w. Abigail (Abiel). He was fencing Strath. land ±1696-7, and d. ±1700. Adm. 9 Dec. 1712 to wid. Abiel and 2d husb. Edward Masury(1); Benj. Jones and Charles Rundlett sureties. In 1713 they sued Stephen England for Morgan land at Jeremy's Pocket which he had bot from Henry Williams, a creditor, a suit which brot the Morgan bros. to the wit. stand. Ch. rec. Wells: **Elizabeth,** b. 22 Aug. 1689. **William,** b. 3 Apr. 1692. **John,** b. 11 Mar. 1694-5. One John m. Mary Wescott in Berw. 20 Mar. 1725-6; one Mary m. Benj. Marshall in Wells 24 Dec. 1729; see also John(7).

**MORGRAGE,** Mogridge. Moggeridge 'a rare old Somerset name.' With varied spellings cos. Gloucester, Wilts, Surrey and Sussex have it.

**JOHN,** bricklayer, Kittery, a York wit. 1669 and fined 1671 for multiplying oaths. He m. Sarah Stevens (Thos.) and liv. on W. side of Spruce Creek. O. A. Apr. 1680. On Feb. 20, 1681-2 he was bp. and joined the Boston Bap. Ch.; his w. likewise in July 1682; in Sept. fol. both helped form the Kit. Ch. Lists

287, 30, 290, 298. Calling him friend, Richard Cutt deeded to him in 1695 the land he was liv. on, also the Endle land. Retail lic. 1694-9. Will, 6 Feb.—15 Mar. 1705-6, names w. and ch., John getting the Endle land, and aft. widow's death, the homestead. Widow Sarah sold drink 1706; pub. ho. lic. 1707, 1709; lic. 1718-9; of Newb. 12 Apr. 1733, ag. 72, depos. ab. her fa.'s land. Ch. rec., their mo. Sarah: **Hannah,** b. 8 Mar. 1679, m. John Frink(3). **John,** b. 12 Mar. 1682, blacksm., Kit., had w. Mary in 1710 (Stackpole says 'prob. Gammon'), and theirs is appar. the mar. in Portsm. betw. 28 June—16 Oct. 1709 (torn No. Ch. rec.). Provisional Scarb. gr. 1720, Falm. wit. 1721, Kit. 1725; Lists 296-7. Adm. 4 Apr. 1726 to wid. Mary, bondsm. Joseph Weeks, Samuel Ford. In 1733 Ruth M. was app. gdn. of his sons John (Portsm. 1736, sold 2/7), Samuel (Boston 1744), Benjamin (Bidd. 1744). Daus. incl. Sarah, **m.** Mark Pitman (see 4), and Elizabeth, Newb. 1738, unm. The gdn. Ruth, Kit. wit. 1725-6, Boston 1738, is unkn., unless oldest ch. **Mary** (John), bp. Newb. 1740, poss. ano. ch. if adult. **Sarah,** b. 9 Dec. 1684, app. m. Walter Denniford. **Mary,** b. 3 Aug. 1688, m. Rowland Jenkins(11); see Green(5). **Elizabeth,** b. 13 Sept. 1691, likely the Morgridge who m. Geo. Thompson 17—23 Dec. 1712 (No. Ch. rec.). **Thomas,** shipwr., b. 20 Feb. 1693, m. 1st 24 May 1716 Mary Weeks (Jos.), m. 2d bef. June 1725 Sarah Remick (Jacob), apparently dead in 1739; m. 3d by 1743 one Abigail, not in his will. List 291. Of Kit. 1739 he q.c. to Jedediah Preble ±£700 a. on Wigwam Point, Stevens Riv., Casco Bay (Y. D. 21: 72; SJC 139152). Somersw. 1743-53. Will, 10 Oct. 1753—29 May 1754, names 2 of 4 rec. ch: Benjamin, b. 1722 (in gr.fa. Weeks' will); William, b. 1737 (in gr.fa. Remick's will). Joseph, neph. of Samuel, bp. Newb. 1728, was poss. his Joseph, b. 1717, d. s. p. **William,** b. 1696, liv. 1705. If the one who m. Mary Whidden (Jona.) in Portsm. 22 June 1721, he gave his home as Chad, co. Somerset. They had 6 ch. in York 1721-1734, the youngest Burridge. List 279. **Samuel,** Newbury, b. 12 May 1699, m. Mary West in Newbury, 1 May 1724. 5 ch. rec. there, evid. others bp. Abigail, b. 3 Jan. 1703, m. Nicholas Hockrin of the Shoals; dau. bp. Kit. 3 Apr. 1721 (Newb. rec.).

**Morony,** Thomas, Portsm., rate abated 1695.

**MORRELL,** Morrill. In Eng. at present essentially a Yorkshire name. See also Murrell.

1 **JOHN,** plasterer, mason, Kittery, ag. 34 in 1674, 55 in 1695, m. by 1667 Sarah Hods don(6). Town gr. 1668. In 1674 her fa. deeded 7 a. out of his homestead to them and their ch.; they sold in 1676 and in 1678 bot

2 a. form. Anthony Emery's with a ho. at Cold Harbor and liv. there. Gr.j. 1672, 1679, 1694; constable 1674; Hugh Lattimer's bondsm. 1675; fined for accus. Sarah Wittum of stealing; lic. ferry and ho. of entert. 1686; j. of life and death 1693; highway surv. 1698. Lists 296-298, 30, 31, 36. One J. M. was taken into Berw. Ch. 1719. He depos. in 1721 ab. Thos. Jones' marsh 50 yrs. bef. and d. betw. 6 Sept. 1723—Jan. 1727-8, outliving his w. See their ch. and other Hodsdon heirs, 1734 (Y. D. 17: 11). Ch: **Nicholas**, b. 1667. **Sarah**, m. 1st Geo. Huntress(2), m. 2d Nicholas Frost(11), m. 3d Thos. Darling(4); see also Daniels(4). **John**, had deed from fa. 1699 and m. 18 Mar. 1700-1 Hannah Dixon(2). Lists 291, 296-298. He depos. in June 1759, aged 83. Will 1756—1763. 5 ch. rec. 1702-1713 and 2 more: John, Thomas, Peter, Jedediah, Richard, Keziah (m. a Roberts), Mary (m. Wm. Gerrish, Berwick). **Adah** (also Edah), m. Jonathan Nason(4). **Hannah**, m. John Tidy. **Abraham**, blacksm., Lists 296-297; see also Harford(2). ʻHe m. bef. 12 Feb. 1714-5 Phebe Heard(6), was here in Sept. 1718 and gone in 1720 when she had broken up housekeeping and turned apprentices adrift. His home, taken on exec. 1719 by Wm. Pepperell, John Frost and John Moore, was sold to highest bidder, 1724. She m. Thos. Stephens of Newc. 29 Aug. 1724, and was his wid. in Kit. 1737, when Jonathan Dam sued her as A. M.'s wid. No kn. ch. **Elizabeth**, m. Samuel Drown(2).

2 **NICHOLAS**, mariner, Portsm., m. 4 Aug. 1679 Margaret Langdon(1) and bot in Great Ho. Field same yr. In 1683 master of the ·Hopewell· belonging to Ambrose Fisher of Fayal. His wid. was taxed Dec. 1688—July 1690. In List 331c, Mary must be error for Margaret. She prob. d. by 1691, her br. Capt. Tobias Langdon having charge of the ho. and two ch. from that yr.; adm. on Nicholas's est. was gr. to him 23 Nov. 1697. Ch: **Margaret**. In 1694 Mrs. Langdon went to Boston to put her out. There she m. 23 Sept. 1697 John Kitt of Nevis, and in Nov. fol. with the admr. sold the Portsm. prop. to Col. Wm. Partridge. Presum. a dau. Elizabeth Kitt m. Nathl. Ayers(6 jr.) in Boston 5 Nov. 1724; their 4 ch. incl. a Margaret. **Elizabeth**, receipted for her share 19 Feb. 1704-5; m. Jethro Furber(1 jr.).

3 **NICHOLAS**(1), bricklayer, mason, Kittery, m. (ct. Apr. 1695) Sarah Frye(1) who was liv. 26 May 1727. Jury 1694, 1714; gr.j. 1699; constable 1698-9. Lists 290, 291, 296-298. See also Draper(1). He took a lease from Mrs. Lucy Stileman, and in 1703 was involved in a suit with Samuel Small who m. her son's wid. (SJC 5785). In 1728 bot 50 a. in Scarb. from Thos. Harris. Ag. ±57 in Jan. 1723-4; 73 in 1739; 76 in 1742; 81 in 1748.

Est. adm. 1757. Ch: **Sarah**, b. 1 Dec. 1695, m. Benj. Weymouth. **Elizabeth**, b. 18 Mar. 1698, m. Thos. Hobbs(4). **John**, b. 6 July 1701, m. 16 June (or Dec.) 1721 Mary Hanscom(3). Both bp. 6 Mar. 1736-7 at Scarb. where a dau. Martha was bp. 17 Dec. 1736, ag. 13; and Eleanor, 25 Aug. 1737. In 1737 he sold the 50 a. he liv. on, given him by his fa., and other Scarb. land; poss. ret. to Kit. **Robert**, b. 18 Feb. 1704, m. 1st 29 May 1729 Sarah Roberts, who d. 14 Aug. 1737, m. 2d in 1738 Patience Weymouth (Timothy), m. 3d 9 Nov. 1779 Anna Jones. In 1743 his fa. deeded him the Cold Harbor homestead, the whole farm on which the first John had liv. Will 1781—1784. 4 + 8 ch. **Anne**, b. 1 Dec. 1708, m. 2 Sept. 1728 John Hall of Dover.

4 **PETER** (also Murrell), Jerseyman, seaman, from Beverly, cert. related to (5), bot in Falmouth from Thos. Mason of Salem in Jan. 1680-1. Town gr. Dec. 1681, Mar. 1683 (on E. s. of Presumpscot River where he built betw. John Wakely and Humphrey Durham). Lists 85, 225a, 226. Philip Le-Bretton(2) depos. that he was taken by the Inds. when Falm. fell (Y. D. 20: 185); ʻN. E. Captives,' 1: 202, says he ret. to his w. and ch. at Bev. His wid. at Bev., Mary (Butler, from Jersey), in Salem 27 Sept. 1675) claimed the Casco land for self and ch. bef. the East. Cl. Com.; alive 8 Feb. 1713-4. Kn. ch: **Sarah**, m. 30 Mar. 1698 John Ellinwood in Bev. where ch. b. A wid. there, she q.c. Falm. land to Geo. Tuck jr., 13 Sept. 1725. **Mary**, m. by 1701 George Tuck; ch. at Bev. Living Falm. 1734, he, mariner, she only surv. ch. and h. of P. M.; both there in 1739 (Y. D. 21: 122).

5 **ROBERT** (also Murrell), Jerseyman, evidently went to Falm. with (4) and had Back Cove land next that improved by (4). He pet. Andros 1688, claiming lot with ho. near the Fort, 3 a. on the Neck adj. Sylvanus Davis, 80 a. with ho. near Stroudwater mills and several other houses. Lists 34, 225a, 228c. Aft. May 1689 he went to Salem where **three sons** (unnamed) were rec. 1690(?)—1696, the 1st one b. at Thos. Putnam's.

**MORRIS**, chiefly of Welsh origin. Morrish found in cos. Somerset and Devon.

1 **JOHN**, York, Apr. 1681; wit. Francis Johnson's deed in Dec. 1682. He was in ct. 6 Mar. 1682-3, then m. to Sarah Johnson (see 11), poss. the same John and Sarah who had ch: Sarah, d. in Boston 22 Sept. 1690; Elizabeth, b. there 20 July 1691. One John a Kit. wit. 1714 (Y. D. 8: 65). Newc. 1718 (Y. D. 9: 132, 11: 128).

2 **LENOARD**, Exeter wit. 1639 (List 372) must be Leonora. See (4).

3 **PETER** (Morrish), with Robert Tuck, wit. Colcord to Marion, 1653.

**4 CAPT. \*RICHARD,** a Wheelwright follower temp. at Exeter. As Direk Thomas (Richard, s. of Thomas), swordcutler, widower from Eng., he m. at The Hague 28 Nov. 1628 Leonora (Pawley) Underhill (see Underhill, Bulgar), thru her mo. connected with Capt. Boynthon(3). With w. and step-s. Capt. John Underhill he joined Boston Ch. 27 Aug. 1630; freeman 18 May 1631. Ensign and Lt. (called an experienced soldier); twice Rep. from Roxbury, until disarmed and allowed to withdraw, 6 Sept. 1638. In Ex. he signed the comb. and was a 'Ruler'; both he and w. (List 372) dism. to Ex. from Boston Ch. He was dealing in pipe-staves at Dover 1639-40. Called Lt. in July, Capt. in Nov. 1639. Lists 372, 373, 376a. He went to R. I. appar. bef. 1640 ended; in 1642 was at Portsm., R. I., where he had w. Mary in 1658, and was liv. 1667+. No ch. appear. See Lechford (index); Austin's Gen. Dict. of R. I.; Underhill Gen. (1932), 1: 14-27.

**5 THOMAS,** Falmouth 1652 (Y. D. 1: 64), signed ptn. 1658. Lists 23, 221. Deceased, adm. was gr. to Mrs. Elizabeth Harvey(9), 26 July 1666. His marsh ment. in deed from Mrs. Mackworth to her dau. Philippa in Feb. 1669-70.

**6 THOMAS,** Lubberland, taxed 1663, gone 1664, taxed again 1666, 1676-7. His land ment. 1669, 1681; last between John Daniels and T. M. 1694. Lists 363c, 365, 359a. Will, 1 Dec. 1701 (d. suddenly 30 July 1707, long sick, List 96), gives to friends James and Wm. Durgin ho. and land (they also resid. legatees and execs.); also to Deborah Merrow, John Footman, Elizabeth and Sarah (sr.) Pinder, Benj. York, David and Abigail Davis, and John Crommett, none called related; trusty friends Francis Matthews and John Doe, overseers; John and Sarah Pinder and Edw. Polley wit.

**7 WILLIAM,** Portsm., had 8 a. gr. 1 Jan. 1656-7; O. F. July 1657; Great Isl. 1659. Lists 323, 326a, 330a. Of Wethersfield, Conn., he deeded his 8 a. gr. to James Drew in 1667, but was named a Portsm. abuttor in 1672. See Hist. of Ancient Wethersfield (2: 512), where one Wm. d. 6 Apr. 1697 in 75th yr.

**Morrison,** Daniel, Wells, from Newbury. List 269c. Will, 24 July 1756—2 Jan. 1757, names w. Eleanor (Littlefield 5), **nine ch.** living and son of a deed. **dau.**

**MORROUGH.** Meroth, almost any spelling; years later appar. Munroe in Dorchester.

**DENNIS,** Falmouth 1675, apprais. Nathl. Mitton's est. in 1682 and wit. Sampson Penley's deed in Feb. 1684. By 7 Dec. 1686, likely much earlier, he m. Penley's dau. Jane and liv. at Purpoodock until forced out. Lists 223b, 225a, 227. See also Jefford(1),

LeBretton(2). Presum. it was he (Morrow) whose Milton land was taxed in 1705; cert. he and w. Jane were of Norwich, Conn., 13 July 1713, ab. the time he claimed at Falmouth 50 a. formerly Thos. Brackett's, a lot bot of Moses During 10 June 1689, a gr. betw. Thos. Cloyes and Thos. Jones, and 1½ a. between Durant (During) and Richard Broadrick. Deeds show one ch. **Dennis,** housewright, Lebanon, Conn., 1711 (Y. D. 12: 148); Coventry with w. Abigail 1719, d. there 1 Dec. 1767, in 79th yr. 4 daus. (Maraugh) rec. in Coventry 1719-1727, and likely older ch., incl. Phebe, who wit. his deed in 1734 (Y. D. 17: 35). Reasonably may be counted: **Hezekiah** (Meroth) at Dorchester with w. Sarah in 1705; d. there 16 Mar. 1749 in 74th yr. **Rachel** (Maroh alias Meroh), m. at Dorch. 26 Sept. 1700 John Everenden. **Mary** (Morah), m. at Dorch. 22 Sept. 1702 John Stiles. **Richard** (Maraugh), Coventry, Conn., 1725, with w. Deliverance.

**MORSE,** its princ. home in Wiltshire, whence came the Newbury fam. Became 41st commonest name in N. E.

**1 BENJAMIN,** Hampton wit. 1677, likely the br. of (6) who wit. Joseph Trickey's note to Thos. Rogers in 1687, and swore to it in Essex Co. as Dea. B. M. (of Newbury).

**2 DANIEL,** Hampton propr. 1640. List 392a.

**3 DEBORAH,** Mrs., taxed Portsm. 1698 betw. (9) and Richard Sanders, poss. all liv. in (9)'s ho. Most reasonably she was a widowed sis.-in-law, yet is not noted in the Newb. fam. Lists 330de. In Sept. 1707, ±56, she test. in Martha Sloper's suit ag. Obadiah, jr., as did **Deborah** Wincoll, ±28, w. of John, who seems surely her dau. If (9) outlived all his relatives, then **Mary** Eburne, ano. wit. 1707, ±30, was not his dau. and would seem to be the widow's. As Mary Morse, she was adm. to No. Ch. 20 May 1696 (List 331c), m. 1st 17 June 1697 Richard Sanders, m. 2d Richard Eburne(1); in 1712 Ebenezer (9 jr.) was bondsm. for her, shopkeeper. Not imposs. too, Obadiah jr. (see 9) was a son, or (10), if the two are not identical. A Wincoll acct. 1712 ment. 'brother Mosse,' indicating at least one son.

**4 JOHN,** constable Portsm. 1663, unless error for (6). Of Portsm., he ack. judg. to the Brattle est. in Suff. Ct. 1673. Godfrey Dearborn's will 1680 appar. gave his 2d w. Dorothy liberty to dispose of the pers. effects she brot with her to the w. of one John Morse (poss. of the Dedham fam.).

**5 JONATHAN,** Saco fort soldier 1696. List 248b.

**6 JOSEPH,** smith, Portsm., 30 in 1669 and s. of Anthony of Newb. Portsm. constable 1663-4, wit. there or Hog Isl. 1665; O. A. at Portsm. with his cous. (9) 2 Oct. 1666; **gr.j.**

1667, 1668. Wife Mary (Woodhouse), wid. of Geo. Pierce of Boston; see Moulton(2), Pierce(5). He bot on Great Isl. 1676, giving mtg. to John Davis of York, but ret. to Newbury, where he, ±40, took O, A. 1678. He d. there from small-pox 15 Jan. 1678-9, adm. to wid. 1 Apr. fol. Inv. at Newb., all personalty except a smith-shop; the Gt. Isl. inv. incl. a ho. and two small shops. Lists 312acfh, 323, 326bc, 330a, 356b. Wid. Mary m. 3d at Newb. 31 Dec. 1679 Francis Brown and was dism. from No. Ch. in 1682; not in F. B.'s will 19 Jan. 1690-1. Ch. (Hoyt's Salisb. 1: 258): **Benjamin**, b. ±1669. **Joseph** (poss.). **Joshua**. **Sarah**, d. at Newb. 7 July 1677. **Dau.**, b. 21 Jan. 1678-9. One child d. at Newb. from small-pox 5 Feb. 1678-9.

7 **JOSEPH**, owned at Muscongus. See Brown (17), Pierce(16).

8 **JOSHUA**, Newb., br. of (6), d. 28 Mar. 1691-2; inv. incl. Piscataqua land, also smith's tools.

9 **OBADIAH**, blacksmith, Portsm., s. of William of Newb., 49 in 1694, ±66 in 1713, 70 in Jan. 1719-20. O. A. 2 Oct. 1666. He bot land from Richard Cutt in 1670, and ho. and land on Great Isl. from his cous. (6) in 1678, but appar. never liv. there. Often on jury, a wit., appraiser and bondsm., usually with Samuel Keais. Freeman at Boston 1674; O. A. at Str. Bk. 1685; surveyor; selectman 1689-1692; clerk of the market 1692; lic. out of doors 1697-1700. In 1706 he sold primers and almanacs. Lists 324, 326c, 327b, 329, 330df, 331abc, 332a, 333a, 335a, 337, 339, 49, 52, 54, 55a, 57, 62, 98. He m. by 1670 a dau. of James Rollins(2), presum. Elizabeth, his only kn. w. (Lists 331c, 335a). Probate records indicate he outliv. all his relatives; adm. to Richard Wibird for creditors 4 Mar. 1723-4. Mary Eburne (see Morse 3) had bill for nursing -15 Aug. 1723 to 15 Aug. 1724-. Kn. s. **Ebenezer**, gunsmith, owned a Portsm. ho. 1705. He m. bef. 1707 Sarah Deverson(1), beat her with a dangerous weapon in 1712, and assaulted Jos. Harris (14); broke jail and supposedly took refuge in Mary Eburne's ho. He had been of Boston and poss. went back, as absent or dead in 1713; called late of Portsm. in 1715 (One E. M., blacksmith from Bos. was warned at Charlestown, 1715). She m. 2d 13 Sept. 1716 Walter Steward. Ebenezer who m. Mary Peavey in Portsm. 15 May 1729 was poss. a son. ?**Obadiah**, blacksmith, Portsm. (see 3, 10), m. Martha Sloper (Richard) aft. her ct. case ag. him in Sept. 1707 when many testif. incl. Agnes Matthews(1), at whose ho. he told that he had run away from Casco Fort to come home to marry Martha. Both liv. Oct. 1711. Ch. unident. In 1721 the town paid Mary Wallis £5 for Mr. Morse's gr.chn., whose chn. not clear.

10 **OBADIAH**, Portsm., had w. Hanna and ch. bp. No. Ch: **Lydia** 1694, **Benjamin** 1696. List 331c. He was hardly (9) and not clearly (9 jr.) who m. Martha Sloper. See also (3).

11 **THOMAS** (Mosse?), signed Shapleigh ptn. 1680. List 30.

12 **WILLIAM** (Morce or Moree) withdrew a suit ag. John Shepard, 1696 (P. & Ct. ii: 173).

## MORTON

1 **ABEL**; List 99, p. 79. See Moulton(6).

2 **JOHN**, carter, from Boston, bot John Howell's 100 a. farm at Dunstan in township of Black Pt. in 1679 and liv. on it some time. Scarb. wit. 1687. The war sent him back to Boston; there with w. Martha he sold at Dunstan to Enoch Greenleaf in 1695. Ch. rec. Boston, their mo. Martha: **John**, b. 13 Jan. 1678. **Samuel**, b. 3 Aug. 1693, and likely others were b. in Me. betw. these yrs.

3 **THOMAS**, of Merry Mount, famed in history, story and opera, spent his last yrs. in York, poss. through old friendship with Edward Johnson. He was liv. as late as 15 Aug. 1646, when he and Nicholas Frost wit. Clement Campion's deed (Concord 21,813), and Winthrop's Journal says d. within two yrs. aft. going there 'poor and despised.' His will, which he made 23 Aug. 1643 as T. M. of Clifford's Inn, London, gent., gives all, incl. a large tract in Conn. and 2000 a. in Prov. of Ligonia in Casco Bay, with the two Clapboard Islands, to his cousin-german, Tobias Milles, and niece Sarah Bruce, wid. See his 'New English Canaan,' pub. by The Prince Soc. 1883, with biog. and notes by Chas. Francis Adams jr.; and later articles by a writer not in sympathy with Puritan Mass., Col. Chas. E. Banks, Proc. of Mass. Hist. Soc. 58: 147-192; 59: 92-95; Hist. of York 1: 159. Also Y. D. 2: 86.

**MOSELEY**, Maudsley. Samuel Hadley(3) spoke of John Mosher as -Moseley-. See also Moses(3).

1 **CAPT. SAMUEL**, Dorchester, Boston. List 3. See also Roderigo.

2 **THOMAS** (Maudesley), Mary (Mosely) and Ebenezer Davenport supported Andrew Alger's claim for land next James Andrews at New Casco Fort, in 17—. The two men hired a Dorchester pasture in 1707. Rebecca, dau. of Thos. Stephens of the Carrying Place, was wid. of one Thos. Mosely of Dorchester, 1751 (Y. D. 29: 120).

## MOSES, Moyses.

1 **AARON**(2), Portsmouth, liv. in the homestead at Sagamore creek, which was a garrison in 1692. As marshal of N. H., he was sometimes called by the grandiloquent title 'Field Marshal.' Jury 1696. Lists 52,

57, 63, 330df, 335a, 339b. In the second and altered form of the Sloper fam. rec. (see Brewster 3) he is said to have m. 1 June 1676 Ruth Sherburne, whose birth is rec. in the original ms. All circumstantial ev., age, propinquity and the practical certainty that A. M. made an early first mar. are in favor of its truth, and there is no negative ev. By 1690 he had m. Mary (see Leach 2) who m. 2d 20 Oct. 1720 John Sherburne. Adm. 21 Nov. 1713 to wid. Mary, John Abbott and John Leach bondsmen, but the est. was not settled until after her death. Her will, 9 Oct. 1732, not proved, left small legacies to sons James, Josiah, Joseph and Mark, dau. Sarah Scott and three daus. (wives of three of her sons). Adm. d. b. n. on his fa.'s est. was gr. to James in 1733, Geo. Walker and John Jackson bondsmen, and div. into 8 shares contemplated, but in the account, 1734, div. into 7 shares is ordered. Giving James his double share leaves five other ch. to be identified, three being the kn. brothers, one the kn. sis. Sarah Scott. The fifth was undoubtedly **Ruth**, w. of Timothy Waterhouse, and, as she was liv. and not mentioned in Mary Sherburne's will, a dau. of A. M. by an earlier w. Mr. C. W. Brewster (Rambles about Portsm.), a gr.grs. of three of Ruth Waterhouse's daus., states that she was a 'Miss Moses.' She m. 2d Joseph Mead(2) and 3d Thomas Skinner. Other ch., poss. by 1st w., are **Elizabeth**, m. at Ipswich 25. 10. 1708 Joseph Smith and d. s.p. 7 May 1725, and **Aaron**, surv. his fa., but d. s.p. bef. the div. of the est. in 1734. By w. Mary: **James**, had the homestead, m. 10 Sept. 1713 Martha Jackson(14 jr.) who renewed bap. cov. 1715 and joined So. Ch. 1724-5; he joined 7 Jan. 1728; will 1772—1779. Ch. bp. in So. Ch: Mary 4 Aug. 1715, John 4 Nov. 1716, Aaron 14 June 1719, Sarah 10 Sept. 1721, George 31 May 1724, Martha 14 Aug. 1726, Ruth 3 May 1730, Dorothy 30 June 1734, Abigail 3 Jan. 1736. **Sarah**, bp. and rec. into cov. 4 July 1708, m. 21 Oct. 1714 Sylvanus Scott. **Josiah**, tanner, m. 12 Nov. 1719 Abigail Nelson(2). Ch. bp. in So. Ch: Abigail 4 Dec. 1720, George 5 July 1722, Mary 9 Apr. 1724, Nathaniel 15 May 1726, Daniel 31 Mar. 1728. **Joseph**, b. 1690, joiner, soldier at Fort Wm. and Mary in 1708, m. 1st 17 Aug. 1712, Rebecca Ayers, m. 2d bef. 1725 one Hannah, m. 3d 10 Aug. 1759 Eleanor (Jackson) Lang; d. Sept. 1773, ag. 83. Ch. by 1st w: Joseph, b. 9 Sept. 1713; prob. Robert, bp. 17 June 1716; prob. Mary, bp. 1 Sept. 1718. By 2d w: Peletiah, bp. 6 Mar. 1725-6; Theodore, bp. 4 Feb. 1728; Hannah, bp. 26 Oct. 1729; Hunking; Samuel, bp. 31 Aug. 1735; Katherine, Love and Elizabeth, bp. 19 Mar. 1737-8. **Mark**, Greenland, Arundel in 1732, Epsom; m. 1st 29 Oct. 1724 Martha Williams, m. 2d 12 Mar. 1735 Jane

Wallace; d. 2 Feb. 1789, ag. 86. Ch. by 1st w: Samuel, bp. 26 Mar. 1726-7; Elizabeth, bp. 1 June 1729. By 2d w: Samuel, Jane, Aaron, Sylvanus, William, James. A place must also be found in the 4th gen. for Ruth, an infant, bp. in Portsm. by the Kittery minister 6 Feb. 1731-2. **Samuel**, bp. 26 Sept. 1708; d. s.p. bef. 1732.

2 **JOHN**, Portsm., 70 in 1686 (not 1696), an apprent. of Geo. Cleeve and Richard Tucker who gr. him 100 a. at Casco Bay in 1646, and prob. came over with them in 1630. The first settler at Sagamore Creek, he had a deed from Ambrose Lane in 1651 and grants in 1652 and 1660. Sued John Lewis for unjust seizure of land and lost, in 1662. O. A. 2 Oct. 1666; sergt. by 1672; j. 1651; gr.j. 1651, 1655, 1657, 1659, 1664, 1674, 1681. Deeded prop. to s. Aaron, who was to pay his sis. Sarah, in 1679. Deposed about Richard Tucker's tenure of his house in 1686. Seated in the seat 'under the pulpit' in meeting-ho. in 1693-4, the last record. His w. Alice was slandered in 1648 by Elizabeth Roe whom he sued, winning the case. One Anne Crunther, poss. a relative, testif. with him. His 2d w. was Anne, wid. of John Jones (23). Lists 49, 312c, 313a, 323, 326ac, 330b, 356L, 52, 331b, 335a, 322, 330c, 337. Ch. by 1st w: **Aaron**. **Joanna**, m. Timothy Davis (61). A **Dau.**, m. Thomas Creber(2) by 1668 when her fa. deeded to them. **Mary**, m. Ferdinando Huff(1). **Elizabeth**, m. Joseph Walker by 1664 when her fa. deeded to them. **Sarah**, liv. in 1679.

3 **TIMOTHY**, Dover, traditionally and prob. from Conn., m. 1st by 1700 Mary Jackson(22), m. 2d after 11 Oct. 1719 Grace (Roberts 14) Duley with whom he deeded to s. Timothy in 1739. Liv. in 1741. List 368b. Ch. by 1st w: **Martha**, b. 5 May 1700, m. Richard Glover of Dover. They q.c. to her br. all rights in est. of their fa. (still alive) in 1739. **Timothy**, b. 2 Sept. 1707, liv. in Madbury. Desc. have changed their name to Moseley, and 'done over' their ancestors' gravestones.

**MOSHER**, Moshier, Mosier. Uncommon. Waters (2: 1185, 1066) shows Mosyer in an Exeter (Devon) will 1639; Moyser, Mosier, in a London will 1667.

1 **HUGH**, Casco Bay, came to Boston in the -James- of London 5 June 1632. Creditor of est. of the Saco clapboardman Williams, who d. in 1635. Tr.j. Saco Sept. 1640 and the same month he and Thos. Wise had deed from Cleeve and Tucker of 200 a. at the now E. Deering, N.E. of their ho. He left this land bef. Wise sold his int. in 1658 and evid. liv. on Harrisicket River near James Lane. List 23. See also Allen(1). Adm. at Casco to eldest s. **James** 26 Sept. 1666, when his br.

John, b. ±1640, and James Lane were sure-ties. Despite the unusual name, nothing is seen that actually connects Hugh Mosier, b. ±1633, of Newport (1660), Portsm. (R. I.) and Dartmouth with this fam. (see Austin's Gen. Dict. of R. I. p. 135). Note also Arthur Mosier, Boston, who first appears ab. the time Me. people were finding shelter there.

2 **JAMES**(1) eldest s. and fa.'s admr., but practically unkn. He evid. was in Brook-haven, L. I., in 1683 (see 3) and, on author-ity of Col. Banks, went later to New London and d. there 26 Feb. 1717-8. The compiler of the Hist. of Gorham, Me. (1903) called Daniel of Gorham (ag. 56 in June 1760), a son, but what link was found does not ap-pear, and James would have been 65+ when this Daniel was b.

3 **JOHN**(1), wit. a Felt deed in Nov. 1662, and in Oct. 1667 when fined for trav. on Sunday, said he did it because Mr. Lane was in danger of drowning. At same ct. bondsm. for Geo. Lewis; a No. Yarm. wit. Mar. 1673. List 93. In Nov. 1681, he was of Setauk, L. I., ±41, and of Brookhaven, appar. with w. Elizabeth, in May 1683, when he sold 300 a. on Harrisicket River with a ho. and frame of a barn; (2) also signed. Old neigh-bors depos. in 1733 that he occup. Mosier's Neck on W. side of river, also 2 islands (Great and Little Mosiers), 60-70 yrs. ago. At Brookhaven 1695, he sold land there to s. Hugh. Other ch. not found. One John M. depos. (SJC 69401) that Joseph Lamson, ±1734, had an unrec. deed from John M. of No. Yarm. to James Lane, of Mosiers Isl., and that J. M. once owned Wm. Thomas's farm.

4 ———, fisherman, Dec. 1684, went with others in Wm. Cotton's boat to the Great Isl. prison.

**MOULTON.** The N. H. fam. came from co. Norfolk. See Hotten's Lists, p. 291; N. E. Reg. 69: 342.

1 **BENJAMIN**(21), Hampton, m. Hannah Wall (James), whose sis., wid. Mary Marston (the mo. joining), deeded to him in 1700. Lists 395, 396, 52, 54, 57, 62. Will, 20 Feb. 1728-9—19 June 1733, names w. Han-nah, 6 ch., and Thos. Batchelder (given 5 s.). Wid. Hannah's will, 31 Aug. 1738—24 Nov. 1742, names ch: James, b. 13 Dec. 1686, m. 11 May 1714 Mary Redman(2). Second w. Lydia and 3 or 4 ch. named in his will, 11—24 Sept. 1755. Benjamin, Hampton F., m. 25 Aug. 1720 Elizabeth (Dearborn 2) Sanborn. Will, 23 Mar. 1749—24 Apr. 1752, names s. Benj., dau. Abigail Conner, and (his wife's?) gr.dau. Hannah Folsom (under 18 yrs. old), liv. with him. Mary, b. 5 June 1691, m. Thos. Batchelder(3). Joseph, b. 27 Sept. 1693, had w. Hannah; d. 4 May 1750. Elizabeth, b. 3

Mar. 1696, d. unm. 5 Jan. 1773. Ezekiel, m. in Newb. 4 July 1727 Sarah Moulton (Wm. 21 jr.); d. 12 Jan. 1783. 7 ch. Hannah, m. 1st in Portsm. 12 Nov. 1719 Richard Small of Jacobstown, co. Devon; m. 2d (contr. 17 Feb. 1730) Matthew Bradford; living Hamp-ton 1762.

2 **DANIEL**(20), Great Island 1667, land-owner 1668 when John Woodhouse (Woodis) bot adj. him. In 1669 he bot from Edward and Martha West. Constable 1668-1670. Lists 326c, 328, 330a. Inv. of £180 taken 22 June 1671 by Elias Stileman and Jos. Morse. Wid. Hannah (?dau. of Richard Woodis of Boston) was taking young men boarders in 1671, when Jos. Morse and Jos. Pormort were there; see also Dorman(1), Lamb(1). She was still Moulton in 1673; List 312f. H. M.'s land ment. 1674. Poss. she m. 2d bef. June 1681 Joseph Pormort(1); Suff. D. 12: 75. No ch. indicated, but see(3).

3 **DANIEL**, signed Great Isl. ptn. 1690, list 319.

4 **HANNAH**, m. Samuel Tilton. See (16).

5 **HENRY**(7), Hampton, had a gr. in June 1640 and shared in div. of commons 1645. He m. 20 Nov. 1651 Sobriety Hilton(1), List 392c, and liv. on third lot E. of his fa.'s. Selectman ten times 1653-1688; gr.j. 1683-4. Called Sr. 1683, but no Jr. appears in his fam. Lists 392ab, 393b, 394, 396, 49, 52, 54, 55ab. See also (16). He d. 8 Sept. 1701. Est. di-vided by agreem. 13 Sept., the homestead to s. John, he and Jonathan to maint. the mo. who d. 31 Jan. 1718-9, ag. 85. Ch: Miriam, b. 20 Mar. 1655, d. 11 May 1662. Joseph, b. 30 Dec. 1656, d. 17 May 1657. John, b. 22 Feb. 1659-60. Josiah, b. 26 Apr. 1662. Jonathan, mason, b. 25 Dec. 1663. Corporal, selectman. As Ens. J. M. he was on a committee of mili-tia given extraordinary powers for Hampt. in 1691. Lists 66, 68. He m. Sarah Paine of Gloucester; d. 3 July 1742. 3 ch. 1711-1716. Abigail, b. 2 Oct. 1666, m. one Lecock. Adm. to Hampt. Ch. from Exeter 1697; d. a wid. 7 Oct. 1705.

6 *****JEREMIAH**(20), Esq., York, m. betw. 12 Aug. 1673—24 June 1678 Mary Young (Rowland), who d. 3 June 1723; m. 2d in Sept. fol. Mrs. Alice (Chadbourne 1) Don-nell, who died 18 June 1744 in 81st year (gr.st.). He logged early for Henry Say-ward at Old Mill Creek and built a log ho. there; in 1684 got from Pres. Danforth a deed for Gorges Point which Rishworth claimed for Mrs. Nanny. Town gr. 1685; constable 1679; gr.j. often; Rep. 1692; joined with selectmen and James Plaisted to build the town-ho. 1698; selectm. 1700. Sum-monsed at times for retailing strong drink, threatening the constable, and abusing Mr. Hooke. Lists 87, 278, 38. Will, 9 May 1727 (d. 26 Dec. 1731), names w., only son, only dau.

and her husb., and 6 gr.ch. Presum. an unrec. s. **Abel** was arrested in Oct. 1696 for swearing, Arthur Bragdon and Jos. Pray bondsm., and had a gr. with Samuel Came in Mar. fol.; prob. the young Moulton taken at York in May 1697 (List 96) and the 'Able Morton' reported drowned in Jan. 1698 (List 99, p. 79). Rec. ch: Lt. **Joseph**, b. 18 Jan. 1679-80, m. 30 Dec. 1697 Mary Pulman(1) who d. 24 June 1722; m. 2d in Berw. 6 Dec. 1722 Mary (Cutts 3) Spencer. Berw. innholder 1727-8; York 1730; both liv. 1755. Lists 38, 279, and the only likely one for List 99, p. 92, tho cert. here in July 1711. Ch: Abel, appar. twin, b. 10 May 1701, m. 1st bef. July 1723 Eleanor Bane(4); m. 2d (int. 2 Dec. 1748) Judith (Lord) Gowen(2); List 279. Abigail, appar. twin, m. by 1722 Lewis Bane(4 jr.). Jeremiah 3d, m. (int. 19 Apr. 1729) Elizabeth Perkins of Wells; List 279. Mary, m. 24 Feb. 1731-2 James Grant jr. Miriam, m. in Newb. 11 July 1733 Abraham Lunt of York. Ebenezer (List 279), m. 7 Apr. 1734 Elizabeth Harmon (John 3 jr.). Mercy, m. in Newb. 10 June 1736 Joshua Grant of York. Elizabeth, m. (int. 28 Oct. 1738) Peter Grant. Samuel, m. (int. 22 Jan. 1736-7) Catherine Hamilton (Gabriel). Poss. Noah, List 279; see also Black(2). **Mary**, b. 14 Jan.1681-2, m. Johnson Harmon(5).

7 \***JOHN**, Hampton, older br. of (20), arrived at Boston 8 June 1637, ag. 38, with w. Anne, ag. 38, (Anne Green, m. at Ormesby St. Margaret, 24 Sept. 1623), 5 ch. and 2 servants (see Eden 1, Goodwin 3). He was one of those asking leave in 1638 to settle Hampt. where he was gr. 250 a. in Dec. 1639. Freeman 22 May 1639; lot layer; Rep. to Genl. Ct. in Boston 1639; with Goodman Cross made a valua. of Hampt. livestock for the Gen. Ct. 1640; com.t.e.s.c. 1641; selectman 1647. Lists 391a, 392ab, 393ab. Will, 23 Jan. 1649—1 Oct. 1650, names w. Anne (List 393a), the ch. brot from Eng., and John, but not Ruth. Ch: **Henry**. **Mary**, m. bef. Jan. 1649 Wm. Sanborn. **Anne**, prob. unm. 1649; see (16). **Jane** and **Bridget**, twins, liv. together in a small ho. many yrs., unm., and d. the same day 19 Mar. 1699, ag. ab. three score (see N. H. Hist. Soc. Col. 3: 122; Dow's Hampt. 2: 862). **John**, bp. at Newb. 1 mo. 1638 (Hampt. rec.). **Ruth**, bp. Hampt. 7: 1: 1640, appar. d. bef. 1649; see also (16).

8 **LT. JOHN**(7), Hampton, m. 23 Mar. 1666 Lydia Taylor (Anthony) and liv. on the homestead. Selectm. 1676-7, 1694; gr.j. 1683, 1694, 1696. Lists 49, 52, 54, 55a, 57-59, 62, 63, 396, 397b, 399a, 400. See also (16). He depos. in Oct. 1669, ±30; in 1694 as Ensign, ±55. Called Lt. in 1700. Adm. to s. John 4 Mar. 1706-7 and on that day the heirs signed an agreement. Wid. Lydia d. in 1729, ag. 83.

Ch: **Martha**, b. 16 Nov. 1668, m. Humphrey Perkins(8). **John**, carpenter, b. 30 May 1669, m. 11 Dec. 1713, Rebecca Smith (John). Tr.j. 1685, 1694; selectm. 1707; served in King Wm.'s war. He d. 1 Apr. 1740, his wid. 25 Feb. 1741. 5 ch. **Lydia**, b. 13 July 1671, d. 13 July 1678. **Daniel**, b. 16 Mar. 1672-3, d. 4 Jan. 1718; adm. 4 June fol. to wid. Mary and s. Daniel, bondsm. Hezekiah Jenness and Enoch Sanborn. Lists 62, 399a, 400. 10 ch. (6 bp. 13 June 1708). **James**, b. 29 July 1675, m. 15 Oct. 1702 Dorothy Clements(1), who d. 23 Mar. 1704, leaving dau. Dorothy, bp. 24 Sept. 1704, m. in Malden 31 Mar. 1725 Jacob Freese (John 1). List 399a. **Nathan**, allotted 20 s. if he demand it, having had his portion. He m. 26 Apr. 1705 Sarah Keaser of Haverh. 2 ch. rec. Hampt. were bp. in Haverhill 1706-1708. **David**, at his master Wingate's ho. 1704, blacksmith. He m. 2 Jan. 1710 Sarah Leavitt; d. 15 Feb. 1732-3, adm. 17 Mar. to Jabez Smith who was gdn. of 2 of 7 rec. ch., 5 in distrib. 1738. **Anna**, b. 2 Mar. 1679, m. Caleb Marston(3). **Lydia**, b. 19 July 1681, m. Thos. Marston(3). **Jacob**, b. 21 June 1688, m. 10 Dec. 1714 Sarah Smith, who d. 6 Apr. 1739, he 7 Mar. 1751. 6 ch. **Rachel**, b. 4 Oct. 1690, m. 21 May 1718 Capt. Jabez Smith.

9 **JOHN**, s. of Robert of Charlestown, and br.-in-law of Thos. Mitchell(15), was 'of Kennebec or elsewhere' in Oct. 1666, when his Malden land and ho. were sold by the mortgagee, John Payne of Boston, to Mitchell. Lists 186, 187. See also Sewall's 'Ancient Dominions,' pp. 181-2. He d. in Malden 8 Apr. 1707, ±76 (gr.st.).

10 **JOHN**, taxed Scarboro 1681, List 238a. Morton?

11 **JOHN**(5), Hampton, m. 26 Oct. 1692 Mary Perkins(2) and liv. on the homestead. Lists 57, 399a. She d. 14 Aug. 1707, he 21 Jan. 1741. Ch: Deacon **Abraham**, b. 8 Sept. 1694, m. 1st 9 May 1720 Jane Libby(1), m. 2d 13 Oct. 1736 Dorothy (Sanborn), wid. of Jethro Batchelder(4). Liv. at Kensington. 8 ch., incl. two Libbys. **Abigail**, b. 7 Jan. 1697. **Mary**, b. 1 Mar. 1699, d.y. **Henry**, b. 4 Sept. 1701; of York 1737, where one Henry m. 8 Feb. 1732-3 Martha Shaw. **Elizabeth**, b. 9 Apr. 1704, m. Thos. Garland(4). **John**, b. 6 Dec. 1706, d. 23 Aug. 1779, m. 7 Feb. 1734 Hannah Lamprey(1), who d. 14 Dec. 1772 in 64th yr. (gr.st.). 8 ch.

12 \***JOSEPH**(21), Hampton, m. 24 May 1677 Bethia Swain (Wm.), who d. 19 Dec. 1723 ag. 71 (gr.st.). He liv. on the homestead. Selectman 1682; j. 1692, 1696; Rep. 1693; gr.j. 1694, 1697, 1700. Lists 392b, 396, 399a, 49, 52, 54. In 1726 he deeded entire est. to four daus. and gr.s. Joseph (Samuel). Ch: **Mary**, b. 22 Feb. 1678, d. unm. 21 Feb. 1756. **Samuel**, b. 25 Dec. 1679, m. 8 Aug. 1706

Deborah Palmer(15), who d. 20 May 1716. List 399a. Will, 17 (d. 22) Jan. 1754, names 3 sons, 1 dau., gr.s. Nehemiah M. **Bethia,** b. 26 Nov. 1683, m. Ebenezer Philbrick(2). **Abiah,** b. 15 July 1689, unm. 1736 when she q.c. to Joshua Rand of Rye. **Sarah,** b. 10 Feb. 1692, called Moulton in deed 1726.

13 **JOSEPH**(20), York. O. A. 22 Mar. 1679-80; grant 1685; constable 1686, 1688; gr.j. 1686, 1691; j. 1691. In 1691 he entert. the gr.j. at his tav. and with James Sayward was bondsm. for Daniel Manning. List 33. In the Ind. attack 25 Jan. 1691-2, he and one or more sons were taken; his w. (probate records indicate she was dau. of Francis Littlefield 16) is not ment. as a captive or as alive later, and prob. was then k. He d. in captivity; his inv., 'who was taken by the Inds.,' 12 Oct. 1692. Francis Littlefield, sr., was admr. 12 Dec. 1692 to 1695+; Jan. 3, 1699-1700 adm. was gr. to the br. Jeremiah, who demanded (but did not get) the est. from John Heard (he had wintered cows for Joseph bef. his captiv.); in Oct. 1718 Mr. Jeremiah M. (poss. the son) asked for an addi. invent. 4 sons, all of York and 3 of age in 1706 (Y. D. 7: 51, 216). **John,** his keeping until he went out to service came to £12. Mariner, Portsm. (but of Kit. 1723), he m. Dorothy Cogswell (Wm. of Ipsw.), who as D. C. was at Moses Paul's in Portsm. in 1713. He d. at Antigua; appraisers Newc. men; adm. 20 Sept. 1725 to wid. Dorothy, who m. 2d Ephraim Jackson(20). Ch: Samuel, bp. So. Ch. 9 Dec. 1716, not in mo.'s will, 1758; Dorothy, bp. 9 Mar. 1717-8, m. in Ipsw. 18 Aug. 1737 John Whipple. **Joseph,** taken by Ind. 1691-2 ('N. E. Captives,' i: 227). Blacksmith, Portsm., he m. 25 Nov. 1709 Abigail Ayers(1) and bot the Ballard(2) prop. from the heirs. List 339. Both depos. 1 Mar. 1758, he 72, she 70. Adm. in 1762 to s. Joseph, b. 29 Sept. 171- (m. Sarah Sherburne). Other ch: John, 1713-1719; Alice, b. 4 June 1715 (m. James Holt of York); Abigail, bp. 1 Feb. 1718-9; John, bp. 8 Oct. 1721 (m. Eunice Sawyer of Wells and Ipsw., Lydia Smith of Hampt. and wid. Mary Pettengill). Capt. **Daniel,** mariner, Portsm. 1716, m. Lucy Cogswell (Wm.), who d. 27 Feb. 1733-4 in 37th yr. (Pt. of Graves); m. 2d by 1737 Elizabeth Vaughan (Wm.), both liv. 1743. Rec. ch: Daniel, b. Ipsw. 17 July 1719; Martha, b. Portsm. 17 July 1723. Col. ‡\***Jeremiah,** Esq., York, b. ±1688-9, taken prisoner 1691-2 ('N. E. Captives' i: 227), must have returned soon as the admr. kept him 4¼ yrs. Disting. in war and civil life, he first won fame as Capt. at Norridgewock. Col. of N. H. regt. at Louisburg; Councillor, Rep., County Treas., Judge Inf. Ct. Com. Pleas, Judge of Prob., Reg. of Deeds, and numer. lesser offices. His w. Hannah d. 26

Oct. 1760 (town rec.), 1761 (gr.st.), ag. 66; it is more than conjecture, but unproven, that she was Hannah Ballard(2). He m. 2d in Berw. 14 Oct. 1762 Mrs. Mary Lord; d. 20 July 1765, ag. 77 (gr.st.); ±70 in 1759. Ch: Jeremiah, Esq., b. 17 Jan. 1713-4 (m. 1st Hannah Sayward who d. 3 Dec. 1757, m. 2d Abigail Ruck); Daniel, 1715-6; Daniel, b. 17 Mar. 1716-7 (m. Hannah Preble); Hannah, b. 7 Feb. 1720-1 (m. Benj. Holt); Thomas, 1722-1736; Abigail, 1724-1736; Dorcas, b. 25 June 1726 (m. John Heard Bartlett); Lucy, b. 4 Sept. 1728 (m. Daniel Clark, see 51).

14 **JOSIAH**(5), Hampton, liv. south of the Green. Jury 1694; selectm. 1699, 1711, 1714, 1721. List 392b. He m. 1st 3 Dec. 1685 Lucy Marston(11), who d. 8 Mar. 1688; m. 2d 25 Apr. 1689 Elizabeth Worthington. Wm. Fuller(5) in will 1691 made his cousins Josiah M. and Elizabeth his w. his principal heirs, they to live with him and be as son and dau. to him and his w. Ch., by 1st w: **Josiah,** b. 21 Nov. 1686, d. s.p. 21 Nov. 1776 in 57th yr. of his office as Deacon; m. 28 Dec. 1709 Mary Marston(4) who d. 12 Sept. 1774 in 87th yr. (gr.st.). By 2d w: **William,** b. 18 Feb. 1690, d. 19 Nov. 1762, m. 6 Mar. 1715 Rachel Locke(5), who d. 20 Jan. 1774 in 80th yr. 6 of 11 ch. d. in 1736. **Simon,** b. 24 Feb. 1692, m. 2 Mar. 1722 Hannah Perkins(12). 3 kn. daus. **Sobriety,** b. 13 Aug. 1694, m. Ebenezer Brown(33). **Henry,** b. 1 Mar. 1698, m. 20 Nov. 1722 Mary Garland (9). Mov. to Sandown. 9 ch. **Elizabeth,** b. 10 Sept. 1699, m. 18 Mar. 1725 John Batchelder (Stephen 3). **Edward,** m. by 1727 one Mary. 9 ch. **Worthington,** m. 1st 9 Oct. 1735 Abigail Moulton (Corp. Jona.), m. 2d 8 Mar. 1739 Abigail Garland(9). Mov. to Me. 3 ch. bp. Hampt. **Sarah.**

15 **MARY,** widow. See (16).

16 **MIRIAM,** ag. 23, presum. sis. of (7) and (20), came in 1637 with them and other Moultons, Mrs. Mary, wid., ag. 30 (unident.), and Ruth, ag. 30 (unident.); also Wm.(21). Miriam m. Thos. King(14), whose will 1667 names her and others, incl. cous. Henry(5); cous. Rachel, w. of Christian Dolloff; John(18). Rachel Dolloff was presum. dau. of an unkn. br. of Miriam. Two others of uncert. place: Ruth, m. 3 Apr. 1660 Peter Johnson(24), cannot be reckoned dau. of (7) in view of his will; Hannah, m. 17 Dec. 1662 Samuel Tilton of Hampt. is not surely Anne(7) who must have been older than Hannah's husb.

17 **RACHEL,** m. Christian Dolloff. See (16).

18 **ROBERT**(21), Hampton, m. 29 May 1689 Lucy Smith. Gr.j. 1695; selectm. 1705, either he or son selectm. 1722, 1725. Will, Sr., 25 May 1727 (d. 11 Oct. 1732), names w. Lucy, s. Jeremiah principal heir and to main-

tain his mo., and 3 other sons: **William**, cooper, b. 8 Mar. 1690, m. 23 Dec. 1715 Abigail Page (Christopher 9), who d. 22 Jan. 1776. His will, 1762—1762, names her and 7 of 10 ch. **Robert**, b. 15 Feb. 1693, d. 3 Oct. 1778, m. 9 July 1719 Sarah Lamprey(1), who d. 21 Oct. 1767. Liv. at Bride Hill. 6 ch. **Jeremiah**, b. 1 Dec. 1696. See Dow's Hampton, 2: 864, 867. **Jonathan**, b. 5 June 1702, m. 21 Dec. 1727 Elizabeth Lamprey(1). Liv. at Little Boar's Head. Will, 20 (d. 22) May 1735, names w. and 5 ch. In 1749 she was the w. of Thos. Rand(6 jr.) of Rye.

19 **RUTH**, 30 in 1637, and a younger Ruth who m. Peter Johnson(24); see (16).

20 **THOMAS**, bp. at Great Ormesby, co. Norfolk, 16 July 1608, s. of Robert and Mary (Smith), came to Newb. 1637 and with the first settlers to Hampton, where he was gr. 80 a. in Dec. 1639 and liv. near the home of his older br. (7). See also (16). Freeman 31 Mar. 1638; selectm. 1644, 1652. Called of Hampt. in deeds to 12 May 1656 when he sold his ho. there, but owned in York in July 1654 and bot 70 a. with small bldg. adj. Arthur Bragdon in Mar. 1655; of York he sold this to Alex. Maxwell 23 Jan. 1657. Liv. on Gorges Neck until death. York gr. 1659, 1681; constable 1661; gr.j. 1666-7; tr.j. 1668; signed ptn. in favor of Peter Weare 1668; selectman 1679, 1680. Lists 391a, 392ab, 393ab, 25. His w. Martha, m. by 1638, signed with him 1650, 1653-4, and wit. with Rishworth 1661; List 393a. In 1684 they deeded whole est. to sons Jeremiah and Joseph for life supp.; he dead in 1703; she in 1711, s. Jeremiah having cared for her. Ch: **Thomas**, bp. Hampt. 24 Nov. 1639, no later rec. **Daniel**, bp. Hampt. 13 Feb. 1641-2. **Jeremiah**. **Abigail** (incl. without actual proof), m. bef. July 1669 Henry Simpson. **Mary**, b. Hampt. 25 Jan. 1651-2, m. 1st Mainwaring Hilton(9), m. 2d Samuel Bragdon(5). **Joseph**. **Hannah**, b. Hampt. 19 June 1655.

21 **WILLIAM**, Hampton, step-son of Wm. Estow. Listed as a servant, ag. 20, he came with fam. of Robert Page(6) in 1637, in same emigration as (7, 16, 20), accomp. the Pages to Hampt. and m. their dau. Margaret. List 393a. He had no Hampt. gr. until the div. of commons to proprs. of ho.-lots, 1645. Lists 392b, 393ab. Selectm. 1649, 1653, 1658; freeman 3 Oct. 1654. One of five Hampt. men who 'unadvisedly' signed the 1654 ptn. in fav. of Robert Pike. Will 8 Mar. 1663-4 (d. 18 Apr.) names w. Margaret, 7 ch. and unborn ch.; fa.-in-law Robert Page and br.-in-law Henry Dow exec.; inv. £478. Wid. Margaret m. 2d 2 Aug. 1671 Lt. John Sanborn; d. 13 July 1699. Ch., 4 liv. 1655 when Wm. Estow made his will, all under age 1664, all but Mary in gr.fa.'s will 1679: **Joseph**, oldest. **Benjamin**. **Hannah**, b. 15

Feb. 1651-2, m. Josiah Sanborn. **Mary**, d. 27 July 1664. **Sarah**, b. 17 Dec. 1656, m. 30 Dec. 1674 (-Mary- by Newb. rec.) Jonathan Haines; 9 ch. rec. Newb. and Haverh. He and 4 ch. were captured in 1696 (List 96) and he was k. by Ind. 22 Feb. 1697-8. See Hoyt's Salisb. 3: 979. **Ruth**, b. 7 May 1659, m. Richard Sanborn. **Robert**, b. 8 Nov. 1661. **William**, Newb., b. 25 May 1664, m. 27 May 1685 Abigail Webster (John jr.) who d. 24 July 1723, ag. 62. His will, trader, 12—30 Oct. 1732, names 2d w. Sarah. 9 ch., incl. Sarah, b. 4 July 1701, m. her cous. Ezekiel Moulton(1).

**MOUNSELL** (Moon-, Mun-), **Thomas**, ±30 in Oct. 1669, bot John Martin's Lubberland ho. and Dover gr. in Sept. 1667 and sold to Nicholas Doe in Feb. fol. At Exeter in Oct. 1668 he wit a Wadleigh-Gilman agreem.; in Oct. 1669 Nicholas Lissen withdrew a suit ag. him for failure to cart and haul logs as contracted, his bondsm. James Thomas and N. Doe. At same ct. Lissen sued him and Abraham Collins (2) for forf. of a bond. Both (he called Mounser) had fled the country in 1671. One Thos. Munsell, reckoned b. ±1650, was of New London 1680 to 1712, when he d. See also Munsey.

**Mountes** (see also Montesse). James and 'Sim:', both with crew of ship -Success- in 1685. List 314.

**MOUNTFORT**, **Jonathan**. About 1697 the est. of Capt. John Littlefield(5) paid Jonathan -Munford- for his mo.'s use. Jonathan, s. of the first Edmund, was b. in Boston 15 June 1678; see Bulkeley Gen. p. 879. See also Gowen(4), Moody(6).

**Moursell**, Richard (or Marsill). List 21.

**Movis**, William, Exeter. List 43. **Moore!**

## MUCHEMORE, an uncommon name.

1 **JAMES**. The fol. items are supposed to refer to one individual. In N. H. ct. 1651; also in 1655, when servant of Richard Cater (2). In 1658 Capt. Nicholas Shapleigh withdrew a suit ag. him for debt. Scarb. 1664; in ct. there on various charges, and in 1666 ordered to finish John Budizert's ho., as contracted, or forf. £10. He and w. Sarah, abs. from meet. in 1667, said they went to hear Mr. Jordan. She was perh. dau. of Robert Mendum(2) and mo. of **Robert** Muchemore, a minor in 1682. James frequented the comp. of Wm. Batten's w. Joan 1668-1670. One James sued Thos. Roberts in Suff. Ct., Feb. 1689-90.

2 **JOHN**, in 1668 wit. ag. George Jones at Portsm., where a John was taxed 1681, tax abated 1683. Poss. a younger John was the Star Isl. fisherman who bot a Great Isl. ho. from Geo. Ferris in 1697, but continued to live at the Shoals; this ho. was in occupa. of Zachariah Foss in 1722. Lists 329, 309.

The fisherman m. a dau. of Richard and Eleanor Welcom or Wilcomb, was willed a boat
by her mo. in 1699 and adm. her est. His
will, 11 Feb. 1717-8—3 June 1718, names w.
Anne and 7 ch: **Abigail**, m. one Priest by
1717. **Rachel**, m. one Downes by 1717. **John**,
(exec.), liv. at Gosport (Star Isl.), one of the
town's first selectm. in 1731. Had w. Abi-
gail. 6 ch. rec. 1716-1730, and poss. others,
incl. Samuel, who with Henry Carter, adm.
John's est. in 1752. **Richard**, Gosport, m.
Amie Tuckerman; adm. 3 June 1724 to br.
John. 3 ch. rec. 1718-1723 incl. Nathaniel
(see N. Tuckerman's will 1744). **Joseph**,
Smuttynose. Adm. 7 Apr. 1725 to wid.
Sarah, who m. 2d, one of her bondsm. Samuel
Preble(2); Abraham Martin was the other.
Deacon **William**, b. 27 Jan. 1703-4, one of
Gosport's first board of selectmen; liv. 1758.
His 1st w. Sarah, b. Mar. 1704, was adm. to
Hampt. F. Ch. 1726. 6 ch. rec. or bp. 1726-
1737. He m. 2d (int. Salisb. 26 Sept. 1737)
Joanna Bradbury, and had other ch. **Sarah**,
single in 1718.
3 **JOHN**, Oyster River, taxed 1677, the same
yr. a warr. was issued ag. him and Grace
Roberts(14), she a maid to Elizabeth Follett
(ag. ±50), he a hired man in same ho. Name
and fate of their child unkn. He (Michel-
more) was one of the O. R. men deposing ag.
Waldron in Apr. 1681. List 359a (twice).
4 **MARY**, of Portsm., but living at Greenl.,
m. 4 Dec. 1677 Christopher Keniston(1).
5 **WALTER**, Shoals, partn. of Richard Cum-
mings(2) in a fishing voyage by 1649. He
left a wid. Jane (Turpin, dau. of Thos.),
whose husb. James Leach(2) sued Cummings
in her behalf in 1660. Her 4 ch. were remembered by Mrs. Batchelder(1) in 1660; poss.
one or more a Muchemore. See also Mans-
field(3).
**MUDDLE, Philip**, taxed Portsm. Jan. 1688-
9; Newc. cor.j. 1693. List 318a. One P.
M. was of Salem bef. 1674; in 1680 he had
been long abs. from his w. and was planning
to marry ano. woman; taxed there 1683.
Thos. M. wit. a Berwick deed in 1713.
**MUDGE**, 1 **Gilbert**, fisherman, Hog Isl-
and 1661 (Essex Q. Ct. 3: 212); Shoals
wit. 1668. Several yrs. abs. from his w. in
1670 and ord. to go to her within twelve
mo. or forfeit £20, but here alone in 1671
and June 1673. Thos. Barnes was his
bondsm. in 1672 when Henry Deering sued
him for debt.
2 **GREGORY**, built at Small Point, and bef.
1676 gave the place to Rachel (Atkins 5)
Drake(4). Y. D. 8: 167; Doc. Hist. 24: 284.
3 **JAMES**, taxed Pemaquid 1687. Lists 124,
191.
**Mulford**. See Mason(5).
**Mullin**, James, with Wm. Pitman, wit. deed
of Abraham Josselyn to Scottow, 1663
(SJC 557).

**MUNDEN**, Munday.
1 **CAPT.** (Munday), took letter from Piscat.
to Barbadoes in 1669; likely Capt. Robert, commander of the -Richard and John-
of London at the W. I. in Feb. 1668-9, buying
Indians.
2 **STEPHEN** (Munday), Mr., Portsm. 1678,
when cleared on charge of entert. a Sunday drinking party, the host proving to be
Philip Caverly(2), who liv. in one end of
same ho. Tax of Munday's man rebated,
May 1679-80. List 331b. Presum. husb. of
Mrs. **Deborah** (Munden), b. ±1630-1, and fa.
of her ch: **Anne**, m. 1st Nathan Bedford(1),
m. 2d Richard Calley(1), and **Elizabeth**, m.
John Pickering(5). Mrs. Deborah, ±50, was
at Roger and Joan Brown's ho. in Boston in
Feb. 1680-1; bef. this, she and Edward Everett were in Suff. Ct. for scratching and
wounding Mary Hale with a great pin. Newcastle 1683 (List 313g); there in June 1684
she held as security for her charges the
goods of Sarah Winsland, who had been
badly burned. See also Bedford(2). One
Daniel M. of Boston d. by 1713, leaving wid.
Hannah and ch.

**MUNJOY**, Mountjoy.
‡**GEORGE**, Mr. ±47 in 1674, mariner, ship-
carpenter, s. of John of Abbotsham, co.
Devon, where he sold land in 1667, was adm.
to Boston Ch. and made freeman in 1647. He
m. by 1652 Mary Phillips(9) who m. 2d Robert Lawrence(4) and 3d Stephen Cross(10).
Coming in 1658 to Casco Bay, where his fa.-
in-law by the George Cleeve homestead in
1659, he acquired a tremendous prop. incl.
all of Munjoy hill, House Isl., Bustin's Isl.,
Pond (Peaks) Isl. and tracts at Saccarappa,
Capisic, Merreconeag, Tewissick, Ammon-
gungon, etc. He sold his Bos. ho. in 1663.
His ho. at Long Creek point was a licensed
inn for many yrs. Lists 3 p. 44, 25, 88, 93,
221, 222c, 225a, 236. In 1672 the surv. the
eastern boundary of Mass. for the Gen. Court
and advocated its extension to incl. the
Kennebec region. Associate 1662-1664, 1672-
1676; J. P. 1665, 1666; commissioner for
Scarboro and Falmouth 1661, 1662, 1664;
committee to build the prison at Casco 1669,
and to enlarge it 1674. For his many lawsuits, see P. & Ct. Rec. i, ii. One of Pres.
Danforth's trustees for the Province, 1680.
He d. bef. 1681 when wid. Munjoy was in
Bos. Adm. gr. 25 June 1684 to her and her
2d husb., inv. 24 Sept. 1685 listing the Me.
lands. See 2 Me. Hist. Col. 6, 200. Ch: **John**,
b. 17 Apr. 1653. Lists 27, 86, 223b. Adm.
Jos. Redding's est. and took inv. 1673. He
was k. in attack on Falm. in 1676. Temperance M., wit. 1675 (Y. D. 2: 174), may have
been his w. **George**, mariner, Bos. and Braintree, b. 21 Apr. 1656, m. Mary Noyes (Peter

of Sudbury) who m. 2d John Smith of Roxbury, innholder. Ch: Josiah, innholder, Bos., b. 14 Oct. 1687, m. 14 July 1709 Martha Cutler (m. 2d Stephen Pearkes), adm. to her 24 Nov. 1719, Pelatiah Munjoy bondsm.; Mary, b. 28 May 1690, m. 4 June 1714 Dr. Philip Thompson; Joanna, m. 25 Oct. 1738 John Gwynn. Josiah, b. 4 Apr. 1658. Philip, bp. 1 June 1662. Mary, bp. 9 July 1665, m. John Palmer(12). Hepsibah, bp. 9 Nov. 1673, m. 1st 1 Oct. 1691 Nathaniel Alden, m. 2d John Mortimer. Pelatiah, bp. 20 June 1675, mariner, m. int. 21 Dec. 1710 Rebecca Farr, d. s.p., adm. 23 Sept. 1729 to Wm. Lee, shipwright. Gershom, bp. 20 June 1675. Poss. Huldah Munjoy who m. in Bos., int. 25 Mar. 1696, William Norman, a barber from Carolina, who in his will, 1702, ment. his w. Huldah and dau. Huldah Mountjoy, was from Marblehead where there were Munjoys and Mountjoys 1669-1725.

**Munmer**, or Mummer, John, wore the clothes of John Webster of Portsm., decd. (deposition of Mary Jones 1662); Webster was liv. in Jan. 1657-8.

**MUNNINGS.** 1 George, Boston (Lists 77a, 181), and w. Joanna (List 181). See also N. E. Reg. 8: 354.

2 JOHN, at the Eastward with his vessel in 1675. List 3.

**Munns**, Mark, a Kittery wit. 1654, ag. ±30.

**MUNSEY**, Munsell. Note also Mounsell. **WILLIAM**, cooper, Kittery 1686, liv. on 30 a. S. of John Morrell sr. In 1687 with Nathl. Lamos wit. deed from Wm. Williams sr. of Oyster River and Samuel Hill of Kit. to Stephen Jenkins. In Dec. 1688 Jos. and Samuel Hill, Ephraim Tibbetts and John Hanson, in Ind. clothes, fired a gun to frighten him and fam. out of his ho., whereby they might take poss.; they were fined, while he sat in the stocks for threatening words to Justice Hooke. Abs. from meet. 1690 (Me.). Dover 29 July 1695. See also Draper(1). Of Dover, drowned in Piscat. River 10 June 1698; the cor.j. from Kit. (List 295). Wid. Margaret liv. in Dover 15 Apr. 1710. Kn. ch: William, Kit. gr. 1694 (List 298), m. in Dover 10 Jan. 1698-9 Rosamond Jacklin; d. s.p. perh. early. In 1761 his br. John, only heir, gave a warr. deed of the 1694 gr. Margaret, d. 29 Jan. 1708-9 aft. an illness of years (List 96). John, soldier under Col. Hilton 1710, liv. at O. R. where he and Samuel Perkins bot the James Derry 40 a. gr., he buying his half three times (see Derry 1). Rochester propr. Liv. 1758. Lists 368b, 369. His w. Margaret was bp. at O. R., 26 Nov. 1727; ch. Jonathan, David, Rachel, bp. 7 Jan. 1727-8. Near site of his old home not far from Durham-Lee line is now a bridge called Munsey's.

**MUNSON, Robert**, s.-in-law (step-s.) of Abraham How of Dorchester, asked release as a soldier at Fort Mary, Winter Harbor, in Sept. 1704, as in service over a yr. He m. Abigail Littlefield (Jonathan 12) and liv. in Wells and Scarboro, taking poss. at Dunstan under Mr. John Milliken in 1726 (SJC 55445). Aged ±55 in 1742, and d. bef. 13 Oct. 1758; she liv. 1762. Seven ch. bp.

**MURPHY, Dennis**, denied in 1678 that he had dealings with Henry Kirke(2). See also Glasson. One John M., an O. R. wit. 1726, poss. the same who had Arundel gr. 1733.

**MURRAY.** 1 Anthony, wit. a Cutts deed at Kit. 1658 (Y. D. 1: 163).

2 JAMES, admitted inhab. of Dover 10 Feb. 1658-9; k. by a falling limb in Nov. next. Lists 356d, 361b.

**MURRELL, Jeremiah**, Boston, with no kn. connec. except thru his w. Sarah, who was 'dau.-in-law' of John Ugrove or Newgrove, and somehow related to Pickerings and poss. to Rollinses. His will (Morrells), 15 Nov. 1676—4 Nov. 1679 (Jos. Farnum a wit.), names w. Sarah and 'my ch. all of them, being two sons and two daus.' Mrs. Sarah was gr. adm. on est. of her fa.-in-law Newgrove in 1694; John Pickering acted for her in 1695. She d. in Boston 7 Apr. 1709, ag. 77; adm. to Richard Stratton, her s. Amos declining; one bondsm. in 1710 was Jonathan Farnum. Ch: Sarah, oldest by will. Mary, b. and d. 1658. Lydia, b. 1659, d.y. Lydia, b. 14 Oct. 1661. Hosea, b. 25 July 1665. Amos, younger s., cooper, m. in Boston 8 May 1707 Rachel Clay(2); 3 ch. rec. there 1708-1712. In 1702 he was in Portsm. with Danl. Weare and Capt. Pickering; in 1721 as Newgrove's gr.s. he sold to Jos. Roberts jr. 60 a. marsh gr. to J. N., and also sold 'being the right owner,' 6 a. marsh gr. to James Rollins; each deed with full warr. Wid. Mary (Gee) Pickering(8), only surv. ch. and h. of John Gee of Martha's V., called him 'kinsman' in deed (copy of Duke's Co. deed 5: 68 in SJC 30516).

**MURREN, Richard**, Pemaquid, had gr. from Dongan 13 Sept. 1686 which had a ho. on it when claimed by John Starkey's heirs. His land abutted Francis Johnson's on E. side of Long Cove ('Brown Cove'). Mushal. See Huggins(2).

**MUSSEY**, Muzzey, Mussell.

1 BENJAMIN, a Sagadahoc wit. Nov. 1674 (Y. D. 4: 36), perh. belonged to a Salisb. fam. Elisha Bennett, attorney for John Bennett and Humphrey Davie, sued one B. M. in Suff. ct. 1679. In SJC 3614 (1691) is orig. agreem. of one Benj. Muzzy's heirs 'in case the ch. of his dec. daus. Mary Lunn and

Elizabeth Darlin' appear and claim. E. M. m. John Darling in Marblehead 4 Feb. 1680. See also Cambridge vital rec.

2 **JOHN** (Mussell), apprent. 28 June 1670 to Mr. Henry Deering for 7 yrs. to be a merchant. Still at Portsm. 1673-4 (Mussen).

3 **ROBERT** (Mussell), fisherman, Portsm., b. ±1589 (±80 in Mar. 1669), an early partner of John White, of whose est. he and John Reynolds were appar. admrs., 1646; see also Reynolds(2). The 4 a. adj. his Great Island ho. and in his poss. 15 or 16 yrs. were rec. in the town book at his request in July 1660. Water-bailiff 1652, resigned 1668; gr.j. 1656; O. F. 2 July 1657. In 1667 he deeded his ho. to dau. Audrey, or if she d. s.p. to heirs of dau. Mary. Bot in Kit. from Barefoot same yr. (Y. D. 2: 42). Lists 43, 311a, 323, 325, 326a, 330ab. See also Baker (5). Wife not noted. His will, 1 Mar. 1663—30 June 1674, names gr.ch. and Mr. Belcher, minister at Kit., in addition to ch: **Audrey**, b. ±1619, m. Wm. Lux(6). **Mary**, m. 1st one Rowe (see 12), m. 2d Digory Jeffrey(3).

4 **THOMAS**, Cape Porpus, s. of John and Lydia at Salisb. Wells gr. 1659 and signed ptn. there 1661. Cape P. constable 1663; selectm. 1672; O. A. Mar. 1679-80; gr.j. 1683, 1688; cor.j. 1685. Lists 269b, 264, 254-256, 259, 30. See also Hunt(6). If he liv. he prob. went to Salisb.; cert. dead in July 1703 (Y. D. 8: 125). His w. may have been (5). One son is kn. by deeds, and evid. a dau., **Lydia**, of Cape P., m. 1st John Randall (9), m. 2d James Purington(2). The s. **James**, b. at Cape P. 10. 8 mo. 1684 (Quaker rec.), m. 21 Nov. 1705 Judith Whitehouse (Thos.) of Dover, he then of Salisb. He bot on Dover Neck 1706, liv. there 1709; of Cape P. in Aug. 1715 was sued on a joint note with Zachary Newmarch dated 1706; Dover 1716-7; Arundel 1719 when his fa.'s 1681 gr. was laid out to him; town clerk 1719; sold out in A. 1728, then of Mendon, where his est. was adm. 1753, no w. ment. 8 ch. 1706-1723 (Quaker rec.). If (5) was wid. of (4), then Mary (Mussey) Dow was a dau., but Jeremiah (w. Elizabeth Perkins) named as s. of Thos. M. of Cape P. (Hoyt 1: 264) must have been instead Jeremiah Dow(7), br. of Mary's husb.

5 **WIDOW**, k. by Ind. at Hampton (Seabrook) 17 Aug. 1703. List 96. Penhallow called her 'a remarkable speaking Quaker.' See Henry Dow(4) who m. her dau. **Mary**, b. ±1677. See also (4), but John Mussey (jr.) of Salisb. also left a wid. in 1690.

**MUZEET**, Joseph (also Messeet, Moseet), Great Isl. 1677, m. bef. 8 Mar. 1680 Mary Walford (Jeremiah), who was ±25 in June 1681. He was liv. in 1699. Lists 313a, 331b, 315bc, 52, 66. Only kn. ch: **Thomas**, Kittery,

m. 1st Joanna Frye(1), who was fined in Oct. 1700; m. 2d 21 Jan. 1722-3 Rebecca Libby, appar. wid. of Joseph(8); m. 3d (int. 27 Sept. 1740) Mary Langley of Dover. Lists 290, 296, 297. See also Henderson(2). Of Newc. 1735, he q.c. to John Yeaton land of his gr.fa. Walford and two uncles. 6 ch. in Kit: Mary, b. 19 Jan. 1699-1700. Joseph, b. 1 Aug. 1702, m., poss. 2d, Abigail (Chapman 4) Bridges; both liv. 1751. Benjamin, b. 25 Nov. 1705. Sarah, b. 12 Mar. 1707, had an illeg. ch. in Feb. 1732-3, perh. m. 6 Aug. 1751 Miles Thomas (or Thompson). John, b. 14 Nov. 1710. Elizabeth, b. 25 Aug. 1713, m. Peter Brawn(2). Presum. a son: John (Meseet), wit. a York deed May 1703 (Y. D. 7: 3); in 1732 Kit. was to relieve him in his low and difficult circumstances, in future and for the past.

**Mygood**, Nicholas, Hampton Falls. See Lane(6).

**Myham**, Paul, Sergt. at Pemaquid 1689. List 126. He m. Eliza Tay at Boston 17 Dec. 1689.

**NANNY, Robert**, Mr., merchant, came in the -Increase- in 1635, aged 22. See Gibbins (2). Prob. first at Saco, he was of Dover in 1640 and, with Humphrey Chadbourne, bot a ho. there in 1645. In 1647 he took poss. of a ho. and 12 a. at York belonging to Sir Ferdinando Gorges to satisfy a debt of £11. Then at Wells, where he acquired much land and a w., Katherine Wheelwright (Rev. John). By 1652 he reached Boston, after a stop at Hampton. He had business dealings with the West Indies and made voyages thither. Lists 73, 262, 351ab, 354. Shortly bef. his death, 27 Aug. 1663, he estab. a trust for his w. and ch. His will, 22 Aug.—7 Nov., named his w., s. Samuel, dau. Mary and an expected ch. The inv., £1089, discloses prop. in Hamp., Wells, Bos., Jamaica and Barbadoes. The wid. m. 2d Edward Naylor, and, after her death, adm. on the Nanny est. was gr. to her s.-in-law, Benjamin Dyer, there being no surv. heirs, 10 Apr. 1716. The inv. incl. 500 a. bot of Wm. Cole, 150 a. bot of Wm. Hammond and 230 a. bot of Wm. Symonds. Ch: **John**, b. 16 Feb. 1653-4, d. 20 Sept. 1654. **John**, b. 12 Aug. 1655. **John**, b. 12 Aug. (sic) 1656, d. 10 Dec. 1658. **Joseph**, b. 1 June 1658. **Samuel**, b. 27 Aug. 1659, wit. at Wells 1688, sued Eph. Severance of Salisbury in 1689, d. in Bermuda 1690, s.p. **Mary**, b. 22 June 1661, m. 10 Mar. 1679-80 Benjamin Dyer, d. s.p. in Boston 15 Mar. 1690. Dyer m. 2d 10 Dec. 1691 Hannah Odlin, sister of Rev. John. **Elizabeth** (posth.), b. 2 Jan. 1663-4, d. 1 July 1664.

**NARRAMORE, Thomas**, a Dorchester fisherman 1664, had w. Hannah who joined Bos. Ch. in 1681 and had 5 ch. bp. 1671-86. In N.H. 1690 (List 57).

**NASH,** from the ancient preposition -atten- and ash, the tree. A place name in co. Bucks.

1 **ISAAC,** Dover, shipwright, had a gr. of 100 a. in 1650, later laid out to his step-s. William Everett. He m. by 1656 wid. Margery Everett(4) who m. 3d after 1664 Abraham Conley. Drunk at Wm. Pomfret's ho. and fell out of his canoe, 1657. Rated 1650, 1657, 1658. Lists 78, 354c, 356ab. He sold a ho. and 6 a. at Sandy Pt., Dover, to Thos. Kemble in 1658. Liv. 1660. Relationship, if any, to Isaac(2) is undetermined.

2 **ISAAC,** prob. of Wells, on whose est. adm. was gr. 4 Nov. 1662 to his wid. Phebe, who m. her bondsman, John Pearce(9) of York by 7 July 1663. Prob. ch: **Isaac,** m. Dorothy Littlefield(23) and moved to Kingston, R. I. Wells gr. him 100 a. on east side of Mousam river 18 Mar. 1713-4, sold in 1752 by Nathan Nash.

3 **JOSEPH,** Boston, bot 300 a. at Harrisicket from John Mosier in 1683 and, with w. Grace, sold to Enoch Wiswell in 1687. Appraised Jane Mackworth's est., 1676.

4 **ROBERT,** Boston, trader on Maine coast, got his own men and those of John Parker(12) drunk at Stratton Isl. in 1645 and fired guns disturb. the settlers from Blue Pt. to Casco. Sued Mr. Shapleigh and Mr. Henry Norton and was sued by Capt. Sampson Lane and John Alcock in Kittery court 1650-1. Lists 10, 78.

5 **WILLIAM,** wit. deed Charles Hilton to Capt. Barefoot, 1669.

**NASON,** a rare name, found in co. Warwick, where at Stratford-on-Avon a Richard, son of John, was bp. 3 Aug. 1606.

1 **BAKER**(5), Berwick, carpenter, ±30 in 1695, m. by 1692 Elizabeth Hatch(3) who was liv. in 1740. See (4). Gr.j. 1697-8, j. 1696-7. Sued for detaining Wm. Parsons' horse in 1695-6. Lists 94, 290, 296, 298. Will, 6 Jan. 1724-5—30 June 1729. Ch., first 5 rec. in Kittery: **Patience,** b. 3 Aug. 1692, m. 18 Dec. 1712 Joseph Wood (ct. Oct. 1713). **Elizabeth,** b. 23 Aug. 1694, m. 9 Nov. 1714 Samuel Getchell(6 jr.) (ct. Oct. 1715). **Sarah,** b. 4 Oct. 1696, pub. 26 July 1718 with Thomas Hutchins. **Hepsibah,** b. 5 May 1699, wit. with Joseph Wood in 1717. **Bridget,** b. 31 Mar. 1701, not in fa.'s will. **Samuel,** m. Sarah Abbott; will 1786—1787; 11 ch. bp. in So. Berwick from 1731, Bridget, Abigail, Samuel, Moses, Sarah, Daniel, Jacob, Prudence, Joshua, Stephen, Love. **John,** by w. Margaret had 3 ch. bp. at Eliot, John 1736, Abigail 1739, Rachel 1743; will, 2 Mar. 1744-5—4 Apr. 1748, bound on exped. to Cape Breton. **Joseph,** by w. Sarah had ch. bp. at So. Berwick from 1734, William, John, James, Molly, Betsey, Patience, Sarah,

Rachel. **Lydia,** bp. 11 Jan. 1727 at Berw. **Mary,** bp. 22 Sept. 1728 at Kit. **Prudence,** bp. and owned cov. 18 Jan. 1736 at Kit.

2 **BENJAMIN**(5), Berw., m. 1st 30 June 1687 Martha Canney(4); in 1705-6 his w. was named Sarah, and he m. 3d 27 Dec. (1708) Elizabeth (Martyn 15) (Kennard) Furber. Gr.j. 1696; j. 1689, 1694, 1699. Lists 30, 94, 296, 298, 359a. Ch. named in will, 28 June—11 Aug. 1714: **Lydia. Sarah,** captured by Ind. in 1694 and ransomed in 1699 by Thos. Hutchins, may have m. in Portsm. 8 Aug. 1725 William Divers of Devonshire. **Mary,** b. 25 Sept. 1689 (rec. in Kit. as were all later ch.), m. int. 13 Aug. 1730 Rowland Jenkins(11 jr.). **Benjamin,** b. 10 Oct. 1691, m. 10 Sept. 1710 his step-sis. Mary Kennard (1); had the homestead; will, 16 Jan.—12 July 1756; 14 ch. bp. in So. Berw. **Patience,** b. 10 Nov. 1693, m. 10 Jan. 1709 Benjamin Lord(6). **William,** b. 10 July 1695, of Portsmouth 1718-1726, m. 11 May 1718 Mary Fletcher(7); sold to br. Benjamin 6 a. so. of Pipe Stave Pt. given him by fa.'s will, 9 Oct. 1726. She was liv., a wid., 1737-1762. Their s. William was of Falmouth, his wid. Mary app. adm. 29 June 1748, and left a s. Samuel to whom his gr.mo. deeded in 1762. Wm. also had sons John Fletcher and Samuel, mariner, of Newbury, to whom his mo. deeded in 1756 and whose wid., Mary, of Newbury, adm. his estate in 1761 and deeded to his nephew Samuel (son of William jr.) in 1762. **Phebe,** b. 22 Jan. 1698. She seems a more available w. for Joseph Cass(2 jr.) of Hampton (m. 1720) than the gr.dau. of Richard(6). **Anna,** b. 2 May 1700, m. 11 Sept. 1720 William Jones(60).

3 **JOHN**(5), Berw., b. ±1640, m. 1st 6 Nov. 1674 Hannah Heard(5) and poss. had a 2d w. bef. he m. 7 Oct. 1687 Bridget Weymouth, who joined Berw. Ch. with him 7 Oct. 1716. In ct. for insulting the constable, 1687. Lists 30, 288, 290, 296 (2), 298, 388. Gr.j. 1692; j. 1687; town gr. 1676. His will, 10 Nov. 1715—6 Oct. 1719, names w. Bridget, ±63 in 1730, and 3 ch. Ch., by 1st w: **John,** d. s. p. By 1st or a poss. 2d w: **Joanna,** had no husb. but at least four ch., being bef. the N. H. ct. for bastardy 1699-1700, producing the Hunnewell twins (4, 8) in 1703 and another ch. in 1708 (ct. 21 June). By w. Bridget: **Richard,** So. Berw., m. Mercy Ham (4), 3 sons and 2 daus. bp. 31 May 1736. List 289. **Hannah,** m. 23 Dec. 1707 Nicholas Jellison jr.

4 **JONATHAN**(5), Berw., m. Sarah Jenkins (9), who m. 2d after 28 June 1703 John Key(1) and contin. to live on the Nason farm where she ran a tavern 1694-5. Kittery constable 1682; gr.j. 1674, 1688. Lists 30, 288, 298. He was k. by his br. Baker with an oar while in a canoe on the Piscataqua in

1691. Adm. to wid. 23 Mar. 1691-2; div. 17 May 1695; settlement Oct. 1702—June 1703. Ch: **Richard**, as eldest s. inherited 2/8 of his fa.'s est. but d. s. p., prob. an Indian victim, about 1696. See Emery v. Nason, Com. Pleas 8. 172, in 1730. A Kit. tradition, wrongly attached to a non-existent son of Richard(6), states that a R. N., captured and taken to Canada, m. his French master's dau. and lived to old age. **Alice**, m. Joseph Abbott(4). **Mary**, m. 6 Oct. 1693 James Grant(7). **Abigail**, m. 3 Jan. 1694-5 John Abbott(4). **Charity**, m. 6 Apr. 1696 Job Emery(2). **Sarah**, m. bef. 1707 Henry Snow. **Jonathan**, m. 27 Apr. 1702 Adah Morrill(1), both bp. and o.c. at So. Berw. 13 Apr. 1712. Will, 4 Nov.1745—7 Apr. 1746, of Kit., names w. and 11 ch., Richard, John, Jonathan, Jeremiah, Uriah, Azariah, Mary Libby, Sarah Frost, Philadelphia Rankin, Adah and Elizabeth. Lists 291, 296, 297.

5 **RICHARD**, Kittery, had 200 a. at Pipe Stave Landing. His 1st w., Sarah, may have been a dau. of John Baker(2) who was fined in 1645 for beating R. N. black and and blue (N. H. ct.). Coroner's j. 1647; j. 1649, 1653; ensign 1653; town commissioner 1654; O. A. 1652; a trustee for Gorges 1662; selectman 1659, 1666, 1667, 1668. A militant Quaker, he was constantly in difficulty after Mass. took over the gov. In 1653 he was disenfranchised for entertaining travelling Quakers, and in 1655, charged with blasphemy, he was in danger of losing his life, but the Gen. Ct. decided that he was not so guilty that he ought to die. Elected a Dep. to Gen. Ct. in 1656, he was not allowed to sit and the town was censured for choosing him. In ct. for abs. from meet. 1655, 1663, 1670, 1671, 1675, as were four of his sons, 1685. Rejected as selectman, 1669. Charged with being abusive toward officers, 1678. Lists 30, 282, 283, 298, 354b, 359b. After 1663 he m. Abigail Follett, wid. of Nicholas(5), who surv. him. In 1694 he deeded the homestead to sons Benjamin and Baker. Will, 14 July 1694—22 Dec. 1696, gave his w. a £12 annuity and div. the residue between his surv. ch. and her Follett ch. Ch. by 1st w: **John. Jonathan. Joseph**, Dover, m. Mary Swaine (John) and went to Nantucket where she d. 27 Sept. 1714, leav. a dau. Charity, b. 17 Sept. 1682, who m. Joseph Meader(2). List 356j. **Richard. Benjamin. Baker. Sarah**, m. 1st Henry Child(1), m. 2d John Hoyt. And prob. a Nason, not a Follett, **Mary**, m. 1st Ephraim Trickey, m. 2d William Wittum.

6 **RICHARD**(5), m. Shuah Colcord(1) who m. 2d 16 Sept. 1687 John Douglas(2). Trad. states that he was shot by Ind. in the entry of his ho. in 1675, but his fa. was called 'Sr.' in 1676 and the yr. of his w.'s birth (1662) necessitates advancing the date of his death some yrs. Conclusively R. N.

'Jr.' was absent from meet. in 1685. Stackpole must have guessed, and badly, at the birth yrs. of his ch: **Sarah**, m. Nathaniel Sanborn bef. 1709 and had a ch. as late as 1719. **Jonathan**, Hampton, m. 17 Oct. 1705 Huldah Sanborn who was bp. and adm. to full com. (Hamp. Falls) in 1727 and d. 7 Oct. 1758. His will, 1741—1750, directs that his mo. be maintained out of his est. and names his w. and ch: **Shuah**, b. 21 Nov. 1707 (m. 22 Feb. 1728 James Perkins); **Huldah**, b. 13 July 1709 (m. 13 Jan. 1731 Ebenezer Dearborn); **Richard**, b. 13 Nov. 1710 (m. 10 Feb. 1732 Elizabeth Tilton; 9 ch.); Mary. Two not in will, Phebe and Ann, bp. 28 Sept. 1727. If Phebe m. Joseph Cass in 1720 (see Cass 4 jr.), she must have been the eldest ch. and bp. by her maiden name. See Phebe(2). One Mary m. Elihu Shaw 28 Nov. 1739-40, and ano. m. Jonathan Moulton 14 Nov. 1744.

7 **WILLOUGHBY**, Ipswich, Lists 67 (2), 68, 336b, of no kn. connec. with the Me. and N. H. family, d. Nov. 17, 1724. Ch: **Robert, Willoughby, Thomas, Anthony** and **Elizabeth**.

**NAY, John**, Hampton, b. ±1660, m. Abigail Webster (Thomas) who d. 31 Aug. 1758. List 399a. He d. 8 Dec. 1750. Ch: **John**, b. 1703, m. 1st Deliverance (Robie) Leavitt(7), m. 2d Elizabeth Ladd(1). **Sarah**, b. June 1705, m. Joseph Philbrick(2). **Samuel**, b. 24 Aug. 1707, d. 29 June 1715. **Hannah**, bp. 3 Dec. 1710, m. Moses Perkins(12). **Ebenezer**, bp. 19 July 1713. **Abigail**, bp. 13 Jan. 1717. **Joseph**, bp. 22 July 1722. **Abigail**, bp. 6 Sept. 1724, m. Joseph Philbrick, her sister's stepson.

**NAYLOR, Edward**, ±32 in 1666, 38 in 1674, truck-master at the Penobscot fort under Lt. Gardner(9) in 1662 and in command at Negas for Col. Temple in 1666. Poss. he came from Barbadoes. He m. Catherine (Wheelwright) Nanny and liv. in Boston, a merchant, until 1672 when she divorced him and he was given two months to settle his affairs bef. being banished twenty miles from Bos., but this sentence was revoked that same yr. and his children restored to him. He had committed adultery with Mary Reade(9), whose dau., Deborah, was b. in Hampton 4 Sept. 1668, and who testif. in case. There was also evid. that his w. had been given poison. In 1674-5 he was in ct. for intruding into his late w.'s company. He settled accts. with Samuel Wheelwright in 1676. 'Mr. Naylor's brook' in Wells, 1678, was doubtless his, in Wheelwright territory. In 1679, in partnership with Obadiah Walker, he bot 1000 a. on E. side of the Kennebec over against Purchase's Isl. Lists 2, 14. She, 'a good woman' and blind, was cared for for 15 yrs. by Jonathan and Elizabeth Cary in Bos. Her will, 1 May 1700—1 Mar.

1715-6, dev. a ho. to her daus. and bequeathed to Mrs. Cary, the exec. Ch. b. in Bos: **Tabitha,** b. 2 July 1667, m. one Peak. **Lydia,** b. 26 July 1668, m. one Amee.

**NAZITER,** Nossiter, of Devon-Cornwall origin.

1 **MICHAEL,** Saco, m. 2 Sept. 1664 Jane Hobbs(1) who m. 2d 8 July 1669 Richard Peard(2). He was buried 13 June 1668. Lists 245, 246. He may have had an earlier w., mo. of **Agnes** (Noster), who m. John Curtis 12 Oct. 1680 in Marblehead. **Peter,** prob. his s., may have been a ch. of earlier w., or posthumous. Ch. rec. in Saco: **Michael,** b. 3 Apr. 1664(5?). **John,** b. 25 Feb. 1666-7.

2 **PETER**(1?), Boston, mariner, m. 19 May 1688, in Marblehead, Rebecca Mayer(3), both of Salem. He d. bef. 1696 and his wid. m. Dr. John Baxter(1) with whom she was gr. adm. 28 Mar. 1701. Ch: **John,** b. 16 July 1688. **Mary,** b. 23 June 1691, m. Stephen Badger in 1722, d. 1 Feb. 1743-4 in 53d yr.

3 **WILLIAM,** Saco. Ralph Tristram was ord. to give him warning 6 Aug. 1670.

**NEALE,** Neal, found throughout central and southern Eng.

1 **ANDREW**(6), Berwick, 68 in 1732-3, ±73 in 1738, ±74 in 1739, m. ab. 1694 Catherine Furbush(2) who was in ct. in 1696 for the heinous crime of sewing a shirt on Sunday. Tr.j. 1690-1; gr.j. 1691, 1696, 1714; public ho. lic. in 1705. Lists 14, 38, 290, 291, 296, 297, 298, 96. His ho., a garrison, was attacked in Jan. 1703-4 and successfully defended by Capt. Brown. Will, 28 Aug.—16 Oct. 1739, made his friend Samuel Shorey and his w. Catherine exec., left prop. incl. his negro 'Dillo' to her, and ment. his 4 surv. ch. and his gr.s. Andrew Austin. Ch: **Catherine,** b. 4 Dec. 1695, m. 22 Sept. 1714 Nathaniel Austin(8). **John,** Kittery, b. 18 Oct. 1698, m. Patience Johnson (Edmund 24); d. 17: 4: 1755; she d. 11: 1: 1800; his will 17 Apr. 1752, codicil 25 Jan. 1755, prov. 20 May 1755, made w. Patience exec., gave the homestead to sons John and Andrew and other prop. to sons James and Edmund and daus. Abigail, Mary and Patience. **Andrew,** Kit., husbandman, b. 4 May 1701, m. Dorcas Johnson (Edmund 24); will, 16 Mar. 1756—13 Feb. 1758, made very careful prov. for his w., named his s. James exec. and left him his negro Caesar, and named sons Johnson and Andrew and daus. Hannah Hubbard, Phebe Brown, Catherine and Dorcas. **Hannah,** b. 28 May 1704, d.y. **Rebecca,** b. 20 Jan. 1706-7, not in will. **Mary,** b. 17 Aug. 1708, m. 12 Jan. 1726 Benjamin Hill(18). **James,** b. 4 May 1711, d. 31 Aug. 1730.

2 **ARTHUR,** Pemaquid, taxed and obtained a 100 a. patent at Nequasset from Gov.

Dongan in 1687. At Charlestown in 1689, with w. and child. Lists 17, 124, 188, 189.

3 **CHARLES,** Piscataqua, made agreement with Capt. Walter Neale to serve Mason, the lord proprietor, from 1 July 1633 to 1 Mar. 1633-4 for £6 and then to have his passage home by first ship. He receipted -Nealebut Capt. Neale wrote him down as -Knill-. Wit. Thos. Blake's settlement 1 Mar. 1633-4. List 41.

4 ‡*****FRANCIS,** Casco, 68 in 1694, 'a gentleman born and bred,' in all prob. a nephew of Mr. Jocelyn of Black Pt., with whom he may have liv. ('near Casco Bay' in 1653) before going to Casco where he settled on Mr. Mackworth's prop. and m. Jane Andrews(16), his landlord's step-dau. In 1658 Mrs. Mackworth deeded 100 a. to him. He also had an Indian deed of questionable value to a large tract on the Presumpscot riv. with Geo. Felt and Jenkin Williams. His public services were continuous; O. A. 1658; Clerk of the Writs at Falm. 1658, 1665, 1668; gr.j. 1667; Commissioner Falm. 1658, (and Scarb.) 1659-1662, 1664, 1669, 1670; Secretary to Gorges gov. 1661; Gorges Commissioner 1664; Associate 1668-1671; Dep. to Gen. Ct. 1670. See indices of P. & C. Rec. of Me., vols. i and ii. Lists 27, 211, 222bcd, 224, 232, 235, 212. He took his fam. to Salem at the outbreak of Philip's war and was adm. an inhab. 11: 11: 1675, selling his Casco plantation in 1680. Conveyancer and schoolteacher. Will, 1 Aug. 1695, not prob., made his friend Capt. Bartholomew Gedney exec., and gave small legacies to his s. Samuel, his gr.dau. Sarah Neale, his sis.-in-law Mrs. Blaney and Mrs. Felt and their ch., Mr. John Blaney sr., Thos. Elkins 'formerly my serv.,' and Thos. Cloutman (a sermon book of Dr. Martin Luther). Mr. Gedney declined exec., and Samuel Neale was app. adm. of the insolvent est. 2 Jan. 1696-7. See 'Ancestry of Sarah Stone,' W. G. Davis, p. 58. Ch: **Francis,** cooper, signed petn. for township of No. Yarmouth, m. Sarah Pickworth, d. in Salem ab. 1691, leaving his wid. and an only dau. Sarah. List 212. **Samuel,** god-son of Jonas Baley in 1663, m. Abigail Collins of Salem, and was his fa.'s only surv. son in 1696-7. He had a s. John, of Marblehead, b. 1 Nov. 1689, m. Elizabeth Brown(20), and Abigail Neal who m. Henry Elkins(12) 6 Dec. 1714 must have been his dau. rather than his wid. **John,** d. s.p. in 1691, his br. Samuel adm. Two daus., named in Jonas Baley's will, not in fa.'s will.

5 **JAMES,** Isles of Shoals, ±19 in 1679, working for Roger Kelly who sued him for debt in 1685. List 306a.

6 **JOHN,** Berwick, first ment. 1660. All evid. indicates that his w. Joanna was a dau. of Andrew Searle. His s. Andrew adm.

Searle's est. in 1690 and Andrew's s. John named Searle as his (great) gr.fa. in a 1747 deed. That Andrew was the s. of a prev. w. would be a logical conclusion from the fact that the adm. papers describe him as -A. N. guard. of James Neale- (his minor br.), but, as James had no s. John, the 1747 statement must stand. Abs. from meet. 1668, 1685, prob. of Quaker sympathies. Lists 25, 30, 288, 298. He d. 18 Feb. 1704. Ch: **Andrew**. **Mary**, m. Samuel Miller(13). **James**, wit. deeds in 1694, 1701, but not found later. List 298. **Amy**, an Ind. captive in 1699, ret. and m. (ct. 1706) Samuel Johnson(30). List 99, p. 78.

7 **NATHAN** (Neill), Hampton, by w. Elizabeth had **Mary**, b. 23 Sept. 1663.

8 **SAMUEL**(10), Greenland, b. bef. 1703 when his fa. deeded to Samuel's ch. J. 1692, 1694; gr.j. 1693, 1694, 1696. He and his w. were seated in No. Ch. 1693 and he admitted 1695. Lists 52, 57, 62, 331c, 332b, 335a. He d. 1698. His wid. must have been that Jeane Neale adm. to Greenland Ch. in 1714, and the tradition that she was a dau. of John Foss(1), some of whose ch. are not identif., is most plausible. She would have been named for her gr.mo. Berry and herself would have named two of her sons, Thomas and Joshua, for her bros. Ch: **Samuel**, Greenland, m. 28 Feb. 1710-1 Elizabeth Locke (see 3) who was adm. to Ch. 1713, he adm. 1722; 9 ch. bp. 1713-1729, Mary, Jonathan, Jean, Elizabeth, Anna, Comfort, Margaret, Hannah, Ruhamah; will, 1755—1756, ment. his w. Elizabeth, br. John, gr.sons Samuel Neal Mason and Daniel Mason (ch. of dau. Elizabeth Mason, dec.) and gr.sons Jonathan Neal Berry and James Berry (ch. of dau. Jean Berry, dec.). Lists 338ac. **Thomas**, bp. No. Ch. 21 Apr. 1695 with next 3, no further ment. **Walter**, Exeter, m. 1715 Anne Mattoon(2); in 1712 Portsm. laid out to him a gr. made to his gr.fa., 'for a consideration for himself and mo.'; had Ex. gr. in 1725 (30 a.) and 1740; will, 1755, ment. w. Anne, who was liv. in Newmarket 1758, sons Walter, Hubertus, Samuel, John, Ebenezer and daus. Deborah and Anna. List 376b. **Jeremiah**, Portsm. carpenter, m. 13 Oct. 1720 Elizabeth Martyn (see 5). List 339. **John**, Greenland, deacon, m. 1 Mar. 1715-6 Margaret Whitten, both adm. to Ch. 1719; ch. bp. 1719-1738, Abigail, John, Walter, John, James, Sarah, Phebe, Joshua. Lists 338ac. **Joshua**, Stratham, bp. 11 Feb. 1697, m. 23 Mar. 1720-1 Abigail Haines (Samuel 6), d. 28 Apr. 1760; she d. 4 May 1785; will, 1760, names w., daus. Anna Veasey and Abigail Cate and gr.ch. Elizabeth and Olive Griffith, Joshua Veasey and Stephen Cate.

9 **§CAPT. WALTER**, comm. gov. of the Laconia Patent by Gorges and Mason and arr. at Piscataqua on the -Warwick- in 1630. By his own account he explored the coast and the interior of the country extensively, while making his head-quarters at Little Harbor. For the Council for N. E. he deliv. poss. of the Cammock and Trelawney patents in 1631 and of the Pemaquid pat. to Abraham Shurt in 1633. Recalled 5 Dec. 1632 he sailed for home from Boston 15 Aug. 1633. Lists 1, 41. For his later career as artillery officer, office-seeker and Lt.-Gov. of the Portsmouth (Eng.) garrison, see 'Dictionary of National Biography' (English), xl: 149, but note that his parentage, which has not been discovered, is there incorrectly stated.

10 **CAPT. WALTER**, Greenland, (Portsmouth), his age stated as 50 in an undated depos. incl. in N. H. court rec. of 1683, and 'signed in ct.' would seem to make the year of his birth 1633, coincident with the departure for England of the gallant artilleryman(9). That they were related has been, in view of their names and connect. with N.H., an obvious conclusion, and worldly experience teaches that where there are soldiers there are apt to be babies. He first appears in Dec. 1653 when Portsm. gr. him 8 a. on the neck of land by Winacont river. Other gr. foll. in 1655-6 and 1660. In 1657 he was working Capt. Champernowne's farm on the thirds while Capt. C. was in Barbadoes. By 1660 he m. his w. Mary who d. Apr. 1668. First Ensign of the Strawberry Bank trainband, he was elected Lt. in 1666 (but disallowed as he was not a freeman, which was soon remedied) and by 1689 was Capt. Gr.j. 1661, 1662, 1664, 1669, 1671, 1677, 1684, 1686; j. 1659; selectman (Portsm.) 1663-4, 1670-1, 1672-3, 1681, 1682, 1688, 1689-90, 1691; tythingman for Greenland 1678; O. A. 28 Aug. 1685; com. to seat the people in the (Portsm.) meeting-ho. 1693. Lists 49, 50, 52, 54, 55b, 57, 58, 83, 84, 323, 324 (2), 326ac, 330d, 331c, 332b, 335a, 337, 338a, 356L. In 1702-3 he deeded his homestead to his dau. Mary Philbrick and his other lands to the minor sons of his late son Samuel, their mo. to enjoy it as long as she rem. a wid. Ch: **Samuel**, b. 14 June 1661. **Mary**, b. 31 Mar. 1668, m. William Philbrick(10).

11 **WILLIAM**, Portsmouth ship-master, sued by Thos. Cole, 1719.

**NEEDHAM**, Mr. **Nicholas**, Exeter, had been a prop. of Braintree in 1636, came to Exeter with Rev. John Wheelright, signed the comb. in 1639 and was one of the 'rulers' of the settlement until his resignation 20 Oct. 1642. Moderator. With Wheelwright's group he negotiated with Capt. Thos. Gorges for land in Wells in 1641. John Legate's depo. made in 1652 (Norf. D. 1. 46) that he helped N. N. make bolts for Henry Roby(1)

in Piscataqua Great Bay 10 yrs. since and that Roby sued Ann Needham, app. over this bus., in Salem ct. 8 or 9 yrs. ago, would seem to give the date of his death and the name of his wid. Lists 371, 372, 373, 376a, 377.

**NEFF, William,** a Haverhill soldier who d. in service at Pemaquid in 1689, ag. 47. His wid. Mary (Corliss) was the companion of the intrepid Hannah Dustin in captivity and escape. List 37.

**NEGUS, Capt. Isaac,** a military officer at York in 1698. See Mass. Arch. 71. 380. While there he wit. Joanna Young's will and a deed, Hilton to Black.

**NEIGHBORS,** Nabors, James, a Boston cooper, who, as adm. of est. of George Palmer, sued Digory Jeffrey and William Broad of the Isles of Shoals in 1670. The wid. of Stephen Crawford owed James Kneebene (Neighbors?) 6d. in 1642. He had w. Lettice and more than five daus., of whom **Mary** m. 1st John Windsor and 2d Daniel Matthews (3), and **Rachel,** m. 1st Peter Codner and 2d one Pasco and was the mo. of Rachel (Codner) who had three husbands, 1st John Derby of Boston, 2d Andrew Sampson, 3d John Shores.

**NELSON,** a northern patronymic from Nigel.

1 **CHARLES,** Kittery, fisherman, prob. closely related to (2), bot land at Eliot Neck from Weymouth Lydston in 1675. Lists 296, 297, 298. He d. 14 Aug. 1688. His will, 7 Aug. 1688—30 Aug. 1693, ment. his w. Mary (List 290), his dau. Hannah, youngest s. Samuel, eldest s. John to whom he dev. the homestead, and two youngest daus. Martha and Lydia. Ch: **Mary,** m. William Rackliff(5), d. bef. 1688. **Hannah,** b. ±1667, m. 29 Nov. 1688 Stephen Tobey. **Samuel,** sailor, wrote a will 9 Sept. 1698 'bound to sea' and sent it to his sis. Hannah, ment. his mo., br. John, cous. (nephew) Wm. Rackliff and (br.-in-law) Wm. Grant. It was not prov. until 12 Feb. 1713-4. Acc. by Sarah Lary in 1699. Appar. d. s. p. **Martha,** m. 26 Dec. 1695 William Grant(17). **Lydia,** m. James Pickernell. **John,** m. 1694-5 Elizabeth Haley(1); common drunkard in 1696; 30 a. laid out to him in Berwick, 1699; d. bef. 1701-2 when she m. William Hoyt, the 2d of her 4 husb. List 298. Poss. Elizabeth who m. 1715-6 Jonathan Downing(2) was John's dau.

2 **MATTHEW,** Portsmouth, tanner, first ment. in 1678 as a serv. of Mr. Vaughan but employed by Job Clement, who acc. him of stealing hides and selling them, the pay to be left at Charles Nelson's in the Long Reach. The charge was not proven. Bot at Long Reach in Newington in 1679, opposite land bot by (1) in Eliot in 1675, but by 1685

had mov. to Portsm., Elizabeth Palmer keeping his ho. at Long Reach. O. A. 1685; constable 1697; gr.j. 1694; j. 1684, 1685, 1688, 1694, 1695, 1700. His serv. Dennis Crowley ran away. See Greeley(3). His 1st w. Jane had a sharp tongue and her husb. was in trouble with Francis Mercer on her account in 1684. Anne Clark, w. of Samuel(49), swore the peace ag. her that same yr. In 1690-1 his w. was Agnes Rackliff(4), and she adm. his est. 11 Apr. 1713, Thomas Westbrook and Nath. Tuckerman, bondsm. Div. was ord. to the six sons and their minor sisters. Lists 52, 57, 62, 67, 68, 329, 330cdf, 331b, 333a, 335a, 337. The wid. was taxed 1726; List 325a. Ch., perhaps by 1st w: **Martha,** m. 1708 or 1709 Nathaniel Tuckerman, d. bef. 1715. Surely by 2d w: **Matthew,** cordwainer, m. 1st June 1715 Mary Cotton (1) who was liv. June 1729; m. 2d 30 Mar. 1736 Deliverance Lang(7) who surv. him. Est. div. 1762 betw. wid. and rep. of 5 ch. **James** (prob.), taxed 1717 and 1726. A Priscilla Trickey had a s. called both James Nelson and James Trickey when he was apprenticed for 2 yrs. in 1751. **John,** taxed 1719, killed by a falling tree (inq. 28 Jan. 1720-1), unm. Adm. to br. Matthew 8 Feb. 1720-1. **Abigail** (prob.), m. 12 Nov. 1719 Josiah Moses(1). **Joseph,** tanner, had part of homestead, had w. Ann who was surely a desc. of Richard Leader(2) and prob. a sis. of Margaret Swain, w. of his br. William Nelson. Will, 1755, names dau. Mary, w. of Walker Lear, and sons Leader, Joseph, William, Samuel and Benjamin. **William,** had part of homestead, m. 29 Dec. 1726 Margaret Swain, who m. 2d 26 Dec. 1734 Joseph Gunnison of Kit., shipwright, and 3d, bef. 1762, Henry Sherburne, both of whom liv. on the Nelson prop. Adm. 14 July 1732 to wid., Samuel White and Joseph Nelson bondsmen. **Elizabeth** (prob.), m. 27 Nov. 1729 Benjamin Cowell(6). **Mark,** cordwainer, m. 1st 28 Dec. 1732 Elizabeth (Kennard 2) Mann, m. 2d after 1742 Mary (Jackson 20) Walton. Acc. by Elizabeth Abbot, his ho.-keeper, 11 June 1741, of seduction under prom. of mar. 2 ch. by 1st w.

**Nesfield,** Joseph, Gt. Island. List 312b.

**Neville,** Edward, Damariscove. List 8.

**NEWBERRY.** 1 **Thomas,** Dover, cordwainer, made a voyage for Edw. Mason during his sickness, in 1670. He suffered a £5 fine and ten lashes for light, uncivil carriages with the w. of James Smyth and Elizabeth Allen(15) and for profane swearing in their presence, in 1671. Moving to Berwick, he sold a ho. and land to Thos. Holmes(7) in 1675, 'being now bound for England.' Lists 298 (2), 356j.

**2 WILLIAM.** One William was rated in Exeter in 1714, poss. the same who had w. Mary who was received into cov. with him at So. Ch., Portsmouth, and had first 4 ch. bp. there 1 Apr. 1720. An original prop. of Scarboro in 1720, he had 100 a. gr., later laid out to Capt. Eliott Vaughan. In 1722 William Vaughan sued him for cattle deliv. in 1718. List 239b. Ch: **John,** of Shrewsbury, N. J., q.c. his Scarb. prop. in 17—. (Y. D. 32: 222). **Mary.** Rec. in Scarboro: **Susannah,** b. 22 Sept. 1716. **Sarah,** b. 16 July 1718. **William,** b. 17 Feb. 1720. **Thomas,** b. 27 Mar. 1723.

**NEWCOME,** Newcomen. In the Devonshire family the given-names Elias and Andrew occur.

**1 ANDREW** (Newcomen), mariner, s. of Andrew of Boston, ±32 in 1672, first at Isles of Shoals by 1666 (gr.j. -Anthony- in error), he bot a ho. and 6 a. at Emery's point, Kittery, in 1669, selling it to Samuel Fernald 1674-5. Constable at Shoals, 1671, when Mark Roe threatened to break his bones. List 82. Sued by Francis Small over a boat in 1673, by John Cutt in 1674. Sold his Hog Isl. ho. to Henry Putt in 1673 and mov. his large family to Edgartown, Martha's Vineyard, where he d. in 1706. Many ch. who liv. in Mass. incl. **Simon,** by 1st w. Sarah (liv. 1673), owned land at Sagadahoc, adj. William Cock, bef. 1690. Lists 13, 183, 303.

**2 ELIAS** (Newcomen), Isles of Shoals, bot half of Champernowne's (now Gerrish's) Isl. at Kittery from Thomas Withers in 1649. Constable (Shoals) 1650. Bondsman 1651 with John Edwards and Arthur Frost in estate of Oads Edwards. Gr.j. 1650-1.

**3 SAMUEL.** List 191.

**Newell,** Walter, Kittery, signed petn. to Cromwell 1657.

**Newgrove, see Ugrove.**

## NEWMAN.

**1 GEORGE,** wit. liv. of seisin of Pemaquid to Giles Elbridge, 1633. Sold a ho. at York to Samuel Maverick, Oct. 1634. Sued by Theophilus Davis, 1637. Wit., Vines to Winter, 1637. Still at Pemaquid as late as 1650. Lists 21, 73.

**2 JOHN.** List 237b.

**3 MATTHEW.** This name is written as a wit. on the forged '1625' Ind. deed to John Brown(15).

**4 ROBERT.** List 8.

**5 THOMAS,** Arrowsic Isl., trader, sued Geo. Brownell, schoolmaster, for £1000, the value of 15 men servants sent from England, in 1716-7. York wit. 1722.

**6 WILLIAM,** sued in Me. ct. in 1660 by Francis Raynes and in N.H.ct.in 1663 by John Frost, attorney for Anthony Checkley.

**NEWMARCH, Rev. John,** H. C. 1690, s. of John and Joanna (Burnham), b. at Ipswich 8 Oct. 1672, was the first ordained minister of Kittery, that ceremony not taking place until 4 Nov. 1714 altho he had been preaching at Capt. Wm. Fernald's and at Long Reach on alternate Sundays since 1695. Clerk of Ct., 1695. Liv. in Mr. Wm. Scriven's ho. in 1704 but in 1729 a parsonage was built for him. He also taught school. His 1st w., m. 5 Dec. 1699, was Mary (Harvey 14) Hunking, who d. 5 Mar. 1721-2; m. 2d 12 Oct. 1727 Mary (Gookin) (Gedney) Cotton(5). He d. 5 Jan. 1754. Lists 291, 296, 297, 298. Ch., b. in Kit: **John,** Portsm., boat-builder, b. 3 Oct. 1700, m. 1st 29 May 1726 Elizabeth (Wheelwright) Alcock (Samuel 4 jr.), 4 ch. b. 1727—1733-4. Selectman 1741. Will, 1771, names w. Sarah (poss. a 3d w., the name of the 2d not kn.). In 1742 'Sarah Fellows now Newmarch' was cr. of est. of John Pray of Portsm. He d. May, 1776. **Mark,** Portsm., b. 25 Mar. 1702, m. 14 Jan. 1724 Elizabeth Parker(26) who was liv. 1760 when she sold her ho. to Thomas Parker, shopkeeper. Will, 1744—1756, makes his w. sole legatee and exec., Thomas Parker her bondsman. Her will, 1763. **Thomas,** b. 15 Sept. 1703, m. 25 Dec. 1726 Sarah Spencer (Humphrey), d. bef. 1760. **Mary,** b. 18 Nov. 1705, m. 12 Nov. 1730 Caleb Cushing of Salisbury. ‡Hon. **Joseph,** H. C. 1728, Newcastle, b. 29 Oct. 1707, m. Dorothy (Pepperell) Watkins, who d. 8 Jan. 1763; Councillor; he d. 25 Sept. 1765. **Samuel,** b. 3 Sept. 1709, m. 1737 Sarah Eastwick. The above six in heirship deeds of 1742 and 1760. **Nathaniel,** b. 7 July 1711, d. 7 Oct. 1713. **Benjamin,** b. 18 July 1713, prob. d.y. **Joanna,** b. 12 July 1715, prob. d.y.

**NEWTON, 1 Thomas,** a lawyer in Me. ct. 14 Oct. 1695. Coming first to N. H., he moved to Boston and d. there. See Newton Gen., p. 799. List 60.

**2 WILLIAM,** taxed in Berwick 1713. A wid. Newton was head of a Kingston fam. in 1725.

**NICHOLS,** from Nicholas, found throughout central and southern Eng., with principal home in Cornwall. Became 38th commonest name in New Eng.

**1 ABIGAIL,** Portsmouth, left very poor with 4 ch., obtained tavern lic. 1694-1697, Mr. Wm. Partridge and Matthew Nelson bondsmen. She must have done well as she bot a ho. from Elizabeth (Partridge) Caswell in 1735, deeding it to her gr.dau. Mary (Mills) Turner, wid., of Portsm. in 1737. See (11). Lists 330def. Of the ch. only the foll. are ident: **Ann,** m. Dr. Richard Mills(10) and app. adm. of his est. 22 Dec. 1715. Her mo. was made adm. of her est. 30 Aug. 1716.

**John,** ag. 14 when bound appren. to Jacob Lavers and his w. Elizabeth in 1704.

**2 EDWARD,** in York ct. for drunkenness, 1660.

**3 ELI,** merchant and ship-capt. from Isl. of Jersey, at Piscataqua 1682. List 90 (2).

**4 ELIAS** and **NICHOLAS,** brothers, in N. H. ct. Sept. 1701 for drunkenness.

**5 FRANCIS,** Kittery, wit. Cutt deeds 1694-1695, and with w. Jane made deed of gift 19 Oct. 1695 to Mr. Richard Cutt of sev. lots at Falmouth 'granted me at my first settlement there.' Lists 225a, 228c. One F. N. was capt. of Sir Edmond Andros's guard.

**6 JAMES,** Piscataqua, sailor, sued in York ct. by Simon Overze in 1650. Adm. to Walter Knight 1 Oct. 1651.

**7 JAMES,** No. Yarmouth 1670, from Malden where he had m. Apr. 1660 Mary Felt(1). Ret. to Malden and d. 1694.

**8 PHILIP,** Pemaquid, taxed 1687. List 124.

**9 RANDALL,** Charlestown, bot ½ of a saw-mill at Oyster Riv. from Thomas Kemble in 1653-4.

**10 COL. RICHARD,** one of the King's Commissioners 1665. See Me. P. & Ct. Rec. i: xliv.

**11 SAMUEL,** taxed in Portsmouth 30 Oct. 1691, a poss. husb. for (1).

**12 THOMAS,** Isles of Shoals, drunk and calling the constable witch and devil and assaulting him with many bloody oaths in 1647. Swearing again in 1651. Cross suits in York ct. in 1657 with Matthew Ham over a fishing contract, and sued by Peter Delacroy in 1659.

**NICHOLSON,** the northern form of Nichols. The Dunstan Nicholsons were sometimes called Nichols.

**1 HENRY,** of Williamsburg, Va., m. 13 Dec. 1716 Sarah Cotton (2, 7) of Portsmouth, who prob. m. next, Nov. 1721, Jacob Treadwell. Rated in Portsm. 1717. Ch: **William,** bur. 19 Mar. 1718, ag. 12 days. **Sarah,** bp. 23 Sept. 1722.

**2 JOHN**(3), signed a Falmouth pet. in 1689 and active as deponent in Boston bef. Com. for Eastern Claims, ±1714, in regard to prop. at Casco Bay. Sold 60 a. on west side of Presumpscot riv. 1707-8. Of Boston, joiner, in 1719 when his sis. and br.-in-law Ingersoll q.c. to him their int. in his fa.'s Dunstan plantation. Lists 34, 225b, 228c. One J. N. took O. A. in Boston 1678. One John (Nichols) and w. Susanna had 5 ch. b. in Boston 1678-1695, and John (Nichols) and w. Dorothy had ch. b. 1695 (Wyman's Charlestown) and 1698 (Boston). That the last ch. of John and Susanna, -Alice-, was b. 8 Aug. 1695, while the first ch. of John and Dorothy -Mehitable-, was also b. 8 Aug. 1695

taxes credulity. There is prob. error here and we suspect that one John m. 1st Susanna and 2d Dorothy, and that Alice and Mehitable were the same ch., with a clerk or copyist at fault. Further Mass. research might clear this situation.

**3 ROBERT,** in Me. as early as 1650 (wit.), he owned a plantation on the end of Merryconeag Neck, alias Tuessic, in the town of Wescustogo, which he sold to George Munjoy 1 Oct. 1670. On May 20 of that yr. he had bot ±230 a. from Henry Watts, at Dunstan, Scarboro, where he is found as early as 1664, prob. a tenant. Sued John Palmer and had counter-suits with John Ashden (Ashton), 1674. Released from training, by reason of age, 1674. He and his w. were the first Scarboro victims of Philip's war, being slain in Sept. 1675. Adm. to his son **Robert,** July 1676, to improve the est. for the benefit of his br. **John** and the other relations concerned, of whom only **Catherine,** w. of George Ingersoll(3) is ident.

**4 ROBERT**(3), m. Winifred Bonython(1), ct. July 1673. She was abs. from ch. because lately brot to bed July 1674. Of Casco Bay, formerly of Scarboro, yeoman, he sold his fa.'s 230 a. at Dunstan to Robert Eliott 25 May 1685. His Casco land adj. that of his br. John on the Presumpscot. Driven west by war he settled his fam. at Marblehead, where the est. of R. N., fisherman, was turned over to his cred. 13 Dec. 1713. Lists 34, 212, 225b. The wid. Winifred was liv. 1729. Their ch. have not been separated from the Nicholsons who were Marblehead natives when our Me. refugees arrived there.

**5 WILLIAM,** Portsm., m. 1 Jan. 1721-2 Mary Benson(1). Poss. connected with (1).

**NICKS. 1 John,** husb. of Urith Waters, dau. of William of Boston, in whose will, 1684—1690, she is ment., prob. liv. at Damariscove and fled to Charlestown in 1689. She was adm. to Charlest. Ch. 21 (2), 1695. Wid. 'Eunice Neaks' was a poor person to be relieved, 1695-6, and a wid. 'Uriah Nick' d. in Boston 19 Nov. 1704.

**2 PHILIP** (Nick). Lists 323, 326b.

**NILES, Richard,** one of John Winter's boatmasters at Richmond Isl. 1637-1642. Lists 21 (2), 78. One R. N., prob. not the same, was indebted to Capt. John Mitchell of Kittery after 1661.

**Niven** the Scot, see Agnew. List 356e.

**NOBLE,** a Yorkshire name. The Boston fam. which gave its name to Nobleboro is of Irish origin and came to Maine too late for our purposes.

**1 CHRISTOPHER,** Portsmouth by 1677, gave testimony ag. Lt.-Gov. Cranfield in 1685. Lists 92, 313a, 331b. He escaped the records almost completely, but there are no

negative arguments ag. the assumption that he was the husb. of Martha Peverly(2) and that they were the parents of **Christopher, Lazarus** and **Stephen**, of proper age and neighborhood and for whom no other origin is found.

2 **CHRISTOPHER**(1), Portsm., m. bef. 11 Dec. 1705 Lydia Jackson(14) who renewed her bapt. cov. in the So. Ch. 19 Aug. 1716; both liv. in 1735. Her fa. deeded them in 1706 26 a. which they sold in 1724. List 329. She was arrested in 1730 for leaving a new-born baby, poss. a dau.'s ch., at John Churchill's door. Ch. bp. at So. Ch: **Lazarus**, bp. with next two 19 Aug. 1716, presum. that L. N. who m. Abigail Whidden, dau. of Capt. James of Portsm., and went with his fa.-in-law to Swan's Isl. in the Kennebec in 1750 and was captured by Ind. with his w. and 7 ch. and 2 servants on 8 Sept. 1750. See Miss Coleman's 'N. E. Captives,' ii: 248-259. **Lydia.** One Lydia m. Josiah Avlon of Stratham 11 Nov. 1733. **Mary.** One Mary m. 24 Feb. 1734 Nathaniel Rand of Rye. **Martha,** bp. 9 Oct. 1720. **Christopher,** bp. 7 Apr. 1723. **Thomas,** bp. 26 May 1728.

3 **LAZARUS**(1), Portsm., dissented from the school vote in 1696. A tenant of Mr. Vaughan in 1704, he bot a ho.-lot from him in 1706 and sold it back in 1724. Sold a Barrington rt. in 1726. The name of his w. is not found. Bondsman for John O'Shaw 1715. Lists 67, 336b, 339. He d. 9 May 1727. Adm. 13 Sept. 1727 to son Moses, whose bondsmen were Samuel Hart and Jotham Odiorne, and who pd. one Martha Noble (poss. his gr.mo.) for nursing his fa. 12 weeks. Only kn. ch: **Moses,** m. 1st 21 Dec. 1721 Mary Staples of Kittery. His will, 1750, names a 2d w. Elizabeth, sons Moses (exec.) and Mark, daus. Rachel, Rebecca, Keziah, and gr.s. John Churchill, s. of late dau. Mary (John Churchill m. Mary Noble 9 Apr. 1741). Poss. **Phebe,** m. ±1700, m. Joseph Brewster(2).

4 **STEPHEN**(1), Portsm., m. ab. 1705 a dau. of Thomas Barnes(13), prob. that Mary Noble who wit. a deed, Herrick (Rand) to Brackett, in 1713. In 1721-2 he, ship-carpenter, and w. Mary deeded land. He gave his ho. on Frame Pt. to his s. John in 1733, John to make certain payments to two bros. Lists 316, 339. Only kn. ch: **John,** m. Mary Glass of Newcastle 29 Oct. 1732. **Stephen,** m. 10 Dec. 1738 Sarah Partridge. **Thomas,** m. 1st 25 Dec. 1728 Margaret Miller(12), m. 2d 20 June 1739 Lydia Berry.

**NOCK,** early English 'atten oak' and related to the commoner name Noakes. Nock is localized in Shropshire. Later generations of the N. E. fam. have, in error, called themselves Knox.

1 **JAMES**(2), Oyster River, elder of the church and deacon (1721). He m. Abigail Thomas and was bp. with her and 5 eldest daus. 20 Oct. 1717. On 1 May 1724 'our worthy and desirable Elder James Nock was most surprisingly shot (off from his horse) and scalped by three Ind. enemies.' Adm. 2 Dec. 1724 to wid. who m. bef. 1729 Ezekiel Leathers(2). List 368b. **Ch: Elizabeth,** m. 8 Feb. 1727-8 Joseph Simons. **Patience,** m. 29 May 1729 Ichabod Tibbetts. **Mary,** m. one Conner. **Sobriety,** m. Samuel Langmaid(1). **Abigail. James,** bp. 7 Apr. 1717, d.y. **Anne,** bp. 17 Mar. 1719-20. **Love,** bp. 15 Apr. 1722, m. 28 Feb. 1738-9 Daniel Homan of Exeter. **James,** bp. 5 Apr. 1724.

2 **SYLVANUS**(4), Dover, chose Peter Coffin his guardian, 1676. Kittery gr. 1676. **Gr.** j. (Me.) 1690-1; j. 1688. See Hall(10). Lists 298, 358d, 359a. He m. 1st 20 Apr. 1677 Elizabeth Emery(2), List 96, who d. 6 June 1704 of a sore throat and other chronical distempers; m. 2d 12 Nov. 1705 wid. Esther (Philbrook) Beard (3) who surv. him. Will, 7 May, inv. 14 July 1716, lists ch: **Sylvanus. Thomas. James. Zachariah. Elizabeth,** b. 12 Feb. 1677-8, had a ch. by Daniel Libby(6) in 1697, m. 11 Feb. 1723 William Busby (Baisby, Bushby). **Sarah,** b. 4 May 1680, m. 1st 22 Feb. 1703 Ephraim Joy(1), m. 2d John Brown (17 jr.).

3 **SYLVANUS**(2), Dover, had the homestead, but was of Somersworth in 1730 when he, two bros. (not James) and two sisters gave a deed to John Hanson. Sold 5½ a. at Birch Pt., 1725. He m. 13 Dec. 1706 Sarah Drisco (correcting Drisco 5), who was b. in Wells 4 May 1683. List 358d. Adm. 12 Nov. 1750 to s. Drisco, there being 9 sh. for 8 ch: **Samuel,** b. 20 Sept. 1707, m. Abigail Ricker; his ch. Henry, Samuel, Sobriety Ricker (w. of Moses), Jedediah, Dorothy and Hannah gave a deed to their uncle Ebenezer N. in 1764. **Ebenezer,** b. 16 May 1710, eldest surv. s. in 1752, m. 1st Elizabeth Ricker, m. 2d Mary (Randall) Ricker. **Henry,** b. 23 Aug. 1714, d. bef. 1750, s.p. **Esther,** b. 21 Nov. 1717, m. Eliphalet Cromwell. **Drisco,** b. 11 Oct. 1723, d. s.p. in 1752, adm. to br. Ebenezer. **Sarah,** b. 11 July 1721, m. 1st Ezekiel Wentworth, m. 2d David Lyford. **Mercy,** b. 11 Oct. 1723, m. Nathaniel Ricker. **Sylvanus,** Berwick, m. and had ch. 1763-1768. **Rebecca,** m. Benjamin Varney.

4 **THOMAS,** Dover by 1652, rated 1657, town gr. 1657, 1659. See Langley(6). Lists 311c, 355ab, 356abcefgh, 359b(?). He m. Rebecca Tibbetts who m. 2d 28 Sept. 1669 Philip Benmore. He d. 29 Oct. 1666. Ch: **Thomas,** b. 26 Mar. 1654-5; will, 15 Feb., inv. 26 Feb. 1676-7, prob. 31 Oct. 1677, ment. his mo. Rebecca Binmore, sis. Rebecca, bros. Sylvanus and Henry and uncle Jeremy Tibbetts.

**Sylvanus. Rebecca,** m. 1st William Willey, m. 2d Samuel Tibbetts. **Elizabeth,** b. 21 Nov. 1663, d. 12 May 1669. **Henry,** b. 8 Feb. 1666-7, Berwick, weaver, m. 10 Jan. 1691-2 Sarah Adams(3) who m. 2d Eleazer Wyer. See Kent(3). Gr.j. 1695. List 368a. He d. s.p., his will, 23 May 1713—2 Mar. 1713-4, giving all his land to his wid. and other prop. to br. Sylvanus, nephews Sylvanus, Thomas, Zachariah.

5 **THOMAS**(2), Somersworth, carpenter, m. at Newbury 5 Nov. 1705 Abigail Brickett, both adm. to Dover Ch. 1726 and later dism. to Somersw. where he was deacon 1729 until death. Lists 298, 358d. Will, 1754. Ch: **Abigail,** b. in Newbury 11 Aug. 1707. **Elizabeth. Rebecca,** m. Richard Wentworth. **Hannah,** b. 9 Aug. 1714, m. James Stimpson and d. bef. 1754, 3 ch. ment. in her fa.'s will. **Nathaniel** (twin), b. 26 Jan. 1717-8. **Mary** (twin), not in fa.'s will. **James,** b. 1 Aug. 1720. **Mercy,** b. 4 Apr. 1723, m. Thomas Wentworth. **Love,** bp. 23 Oct. 1726, d. unm. with a Wentworth neph. in Lebanon. **Patience.**

6 **ZACHARIAH**(2), Somersw., carpenter, m. Sarah Pitman(7) who was bp. with her 1st 4 ch. 7 Apr. 1728. Lists 298 (2), 358d. Liv. in 1758. Ch: **Joshua,** b. 13 Oct. 1715, m. Elizabeth Stevens (Thos.). **Joseph,** b. 12 Nov. 1717. List 298. **Zachariah,** b. 1 Aug. 1720. **Benjamin,** b. 12 July 1722. **Mary,** b. 26 Mar. 1724. **Temperance,** b. 1 Apr. 1726. **Olive,** b. 28 Feb. 1728-9, m. John Hasson. **Thomas,** b. 23 Jan. 1730-1. **Jonathan,** b. 2 June 1733, d. on exped. ag. Canada, will, 1758—1759.

**Nolar, Noles,** see Knowles.

**Nolton,** see Knowlton.

**NORCROSS, Rev. Nathaniel,** A.B. (Cantab.), son of Jeremiah of Watertown, was candidate for ministry at Exeter in 1646, the town agreeing to purchase Mr. Wheelwright's ho. and land for him 25 May 1646, but it came to naught. In 1648 he was a candidate at Agamenticus, living with Mr. Godfrey, with like result. Ret. to Eng. and settled at Walsingham, co. Norfolk. Lists 375b, 376a.

**NORMAN,** a common name, its chief homes in Cambridge and Somerset.

1 **MATTHEW,** Pemaquid, 1640-1, when he gave bond with Robert Shute to a Bristol merchant.

2 **WILLIAM,** Cape Porpus, fisherman, pretending that he had been divorced from his w. in England, contracted a bigamous mar. with Marjorie Randall(13). In Wells ct. 11 Mar. 1650-1 they were legally sep., their common prop. div. and he was banished from the Prov. if he could not present legal ev. of his alleged divorce within 18 months.

As he failed to do this, she was gr. a 'divorce,' altho the ct. seemed doubtful if she had gone thru with a mar. ceremony, and for good measure Norman got 25 lashes at the whipping-post. At the same ct. poor Marjorie was fined for lying and for abusing the government, and was obliged to make due apologies to the w. of Thomas Withers for making 'threatening speeches' to her. Also she was warned to avoid the attentions of one Thomas 'Spleny,' but six months later Marjorie, the late w. of William Norman, and Thomas Spinney were 'keeping company together at unseasonable times' (N. H. ct.), which led to marriage. By Norman she had a dau. **Mary,** who m. John Fernald(1). Norman went eastward and bot House Isl. in Casco Bay with three other fishermen, John Wallis, Nicholas White and Geo. Bartell (Bartlett 3), selling his ¼ to Geo. Munjoy 10 Nov. 1663. Sued by Thos. Mills for 'disappointing his voyage' in 1662. Abs. from Scarboro meet. in 1672. Called of Black Pt. in 1674 when Ralph Tristram was app. adm. of his est.

**NORRIS,** a 'north-man,' widely spread in Normandy and Eng.

1 **JONATHAN**(3), Exeter and Stratham, m. (ct. June 1696) Lydia Heard(2), who m. 2d Joseph Rollins(6). Her ch. q.c. to Benj. Heard in 1751. List 388. His will, 20 Mar.—23 July 1718, names his w., his 3 sons and 'every one of my daus.' Ch., order unkn: **Benjamin,** Stratham, had homestead, m. Mehitable Stevens (Nathaniel). His unproved will, 20 Aug. 1762, names his w., sons Joseph, Benjamin, Jonathan, David and Nathaniel, and daus. Mehitable Smith, Sarah Wiggin, Lydia Smith, Mary and Abigail. He d. 11 Nov. 1764. **Jonathan,** Epping, joiner, m. Sarah Cram(1). Will, 19 Mar. 1768—27 Dec. 1769. 7 ch. b. 1744-1759. **James,** cordwainer, Stratham, Chester, Epping, by w. Joanna Chase (Norris gen.) had 8 ch. b. 1738-1755. **Sarah,** m. 4 Sept. 1718 Joseph Robinson(8) at Greenland. **Joanna** (not Rollins but Norris), m. Israel Folsom(6). **Lydia,** m. bef. 1732 Jeremiah Robinson. **Abigail,** m. bef. 1733 Joseph Prescott of Hampton. **Mary,** m. 1st 16 Nov. 1738 Timothy Hilliard, m. 2d 3 Nov. 1747 Walter Williams.

2 **MOSES**(3), Exeter, m. 4 Mar. 1691-2 Ruth Folsom(9), his fa.-in-law deeding 2 a. to him in 1698. Had the homestead. Taxed to and incl. Apr. 1732 after which wid. Ruth was taxed 1732-1740. Lists 67, 376b. Deeded land to children 2 Feb. 1720-1. Ch., order unknown: **Samuel,** had ½ of the homestead. His w. Ruth surv. him and gave a deed, with s. Samuel, as heirs-at-law, in 1754. **John,** Epping, b. 25 Dec. 1694. One John N. m. in Portsm. 10 May 1731 Sarah Roberts (Robin-

son 12). The Norris gen. names his w. Sarah
-Knight-. **Moses**, Exeter and Nottingham,
had w. Lydia Rundlett(3) by 1731; will, 23
Aug. 1750—16 Aug. 1751, s. James exec.
**Nicholas**, Portsm., m. 19 Dec. 1723 Elizabeth
Fanning; last ment. 1761. 4 sons. **Joseph**,
Epping, had ½ homestead, m. 1st Elizabeth
Bean, and 2d one Joanna. Ch. **Jonathan**, m.
Lydia Taylor. The Norris gen. exchanges
the marriages of Jonathan(1 jr.) and Jona-
than(2). **James**, Epping, m. 1st one Mary
who d. 19 Sept. 1766, m. 2d wid. Alice Mitch-
ell. Will, 12 Oct.—28 Dec. 1768. 15 ch.
**Ruth**, m. Richard Smart.

3 **NICHOLAS**, tailor, first at Hampton
where he m. 21 Jan. 1664 Sarah Cox(18),
who was bp. on confess. of faith 5 Apr. 1668.
Sold his ho. and 3 a. in Hamp. to his br.-in-
law John Godfrey in 1666, but must have bot
another as, after his removal to Exeter in
1671, he sold a Hamp. ho. bot from Thomas
Webster. He m. 2d, late in life, Mary (Jones
17) (Roberts) Folsom, who was liv., a town
charge, in 1741 when three of her sons, one
Roberts and two Folsoms, were questioned
as to their ability to care for her. Appar.
wid. Norris had formerly been with a s.-in-
law Samuel Akers, unless this was Ruth,
wid. of (2). In 1714 Norris deeded to his
son Moses, he to give 10 a. to his br. James,
if he ever returned, and to pay cash to his
br. Jonathan and sisters Abigail and Sarah.
Lists 52, 57, 67, 384b, 376b, 381, 383. Taxed
in 1718, but dead in 1722. Ch: **Sarah**, b. 20.
7. 1664, d. 10 Feb. 1667-8. **John**, b. 10. 5. 1667.
One J.N. wit. a Portsm. note, Joseph Trickey
to Reuben Hull, in 1686, and with Reuben
Hull wit. John Bickford's will (Dover),
1685-6. **Moses**, b. 14 Aug. 1670. **Jonathan**, b.
5 Mar. 1673. **Abigail**, b. 29 Nov. 1675, liv. in
1714. **Sarah**, b. 10 Apr. 1678, m. at Newbury
23 June 1702 Benjamin Hoag(1). **James**, b.
16 Nov. 1680; in 1730 land gr. of 1698 to J. N.
deceased was laid out to Theophilus Rundlett; appar. in 1714 his fate was unkn. List
376b.

4 **PHILIP**, cast away in the -Three Friends-
at Portland in 1711.

**NORROWAY**, James, Dover, wit. deed
Drew to Tuttle 1711. Lists 67, 330de,
336bc. By w. Elizabeth he had ch: **William**,
b. Portsmouth 2 Mar. 1697-8, sold gr. in
Rochester in 1729 and 1735. **Dorothy**, b.
Dover 9 July 1703. **John**, sold Rochester gr.
1729 and ack. the deed in Salem.

**NORTON**. The name of over 40 parishes
throughout Eng., meaning 'the northern
homestead.'

1 **BONUS**, Hampton, s. of William of Ipswich, where he m. Mary Goodhue bef.
moving to Hingham and later to Hamp.
where he bot land and buildings in 1695. He

kept a tavern and had lic. of various sorts
from 1695 to 1700. Jury 1696. His w. adm.
to Hamp. Falls Ch. in 1712 and he in 1714.
He d. 30 Apr. 1718, ag. 61 (Quaker cem., Seabrook). Ch: **Mary**, m. 19 May 1708 Daniel
Moody(2). **Sarah**, m. 26 Nov. 1713 Thomas
Waite. **John**, Kittery, m. 11 July 1717 Rebecca Wilson; at least one s., John, and one
dau. Joanna Billing. Lists 291. **William**, b.
9 May 1691 in Ips., m. 1st 19 Dec. 1716 Elizabeth Cotton, m. 2d 24 Dec. 1729 wid. Esther
(Dearborn 4) Lovering. **Joseph**, Portsm., b.
17 Nov. 1695, tanner, m. 6 Jan. 1721 Abigail
Gove(5), found dead (inq. 19 Feb. 1747-8).
**Samuel**, b. 12 Sept.1699; chose Nathan Longfellow gdn. in 1721. **Elizabeth**, b. 31 Mar.
1703; chose Thomas Leavitt gdn. in 1721; m.
1st Thomas Jenness(2); m. 2d Benjamin
Swett. **Lucy**, b. 10 Sept. 1706; with next sis.
chose Hezekiah Jenness gdn. in 1721; m.
John Jenness (s. of John 1). **Anna**, b. 20
Mar. 1708, m. Jonathan Towle.

2 **CAPT. FRANCIS**, in N. H. as agent of
Mrs. Mason, the patentee's wid., in 1638,
and went to London to give testimony as to
her affairs in 1640, but was settled at
Charlestown, where he had a disting. civil
and military career. In 1644 he bot land at
Great Bay, on the Piscataqua, from Capt.
Champernowne. He d. in Charlestown 27
July 1667 leav. a wid. Mary (Houghton),
who m. 2d Dea. William Stilson, and 4 daus.,
**Abigail** Long, **Mary** Noyes, **Deborah** Hill
and **Elizabeth** Symmes. Lists 41, 84.

3 **FREEGRACE**, Saco, miller, s. of George
of Salem, m. Lydia Spencer ±1660. Certainly in Saco by 1661, he mov. to Ipswich
by 1667 when he had permission to build a
ho. Lists 244e, 249. Gr.j. 1662, 1663; j. 1662,
1663, 1664. Serving as sergt. under Capt.
Appleton, he was mortally wounded in battle
at Hadley 19 Oct. 1675. No kn. ch.

4 **GEORGE**(5), York, shipwright, ±32 in
1672, m. Mary Foxwell(5). O. A. 17 Mar.
1679-80. Selectman 1686, outdoor lic. 1686,
gr.j. 1687, 1689. Lists 82, 272. A constant
litigant, details of his suits may be found in
P. & C. Rec. On the criminal side, he was in
ct. for vain swearing, abs. from meet. and
selling without a lic., and in 1689-90 was carried to prison by his fa.'s successor for some
unkn. offense. He owned the brigantine
-Beginning-, 50 tons burden, in 1691. By
1695 he was liv. in Boston, when some of his
w.'s Foxwell and Rogers relations visited
them, but in 1696 he was 'late of Boston now
of Manchester,' where he had had a gr. in
1695. Selectman there, 1698. One Mary Cur-
tis(7), who had liv. in the Norton fam. for
16 yrs., dep. in 1725, ag. 36, that she heard
her mo. say that she saw Mary Norton pay
money for Sue Black. If born a Curtis, she
may have been a niece of Mrs. Norton and

dau. of Joseph Curtis(6). If a mar. woman, she may have been a serv. of the Nortons who m. an Essex co. Curtis. The York authorities again got their hands on him in 1696 for leaving the harbor on Sunday. He d. 1 May 1717, ag. 77, his gr.stone giving the names of his parents. His will, prob. 27 May 1717, leaves his Manch. homestead to s. Shadrach after his mo.'s death, ½ of his York prop. to all or any of his sons Michael, Azarias and Joseph who shall return from the sea, and money to daus. Mary West, Elizabeth Woodbridge, who had lands at York already, and gr.dau. Mary (Joseph); w. Mary exec. Ch: **Michael,** of age in 1700 when he gave a depos. with Mary N. in his fa.'s suit ag. the Manch. tax-collector, d. s.p. **Azarias,** d. s.p. **Mary,** m. 1st in Bev. 13 Jan. 1701-2 Samuel West, m. 2d after 1725 Samuel Martin. Her death is rec. as the wid. of Samuel Martin, ag. 80, in 1762, but she was bur. beside her 1st husb. as Mary, w. of Samuel West, d. 28 Apr. 1762, ag. 79.' 8 West ch. b. in Bev. **Elizabeth,** m. 24 Feb. 1706, John Woodbridge of Newbury and York, liv. in 1749. **Shadrach,** with his fa. at York in 1696, m. Elizabeth Woodbury 25 Dec. 1709, sued his sis. Mary Martin in 1731, d. bef. 1749 leaving one dau. **Joseph,** by w. Miriam had a dau. Mary, b. 1710, d. bef. 1749, the dau. surviv.

5 **HENRY,** gentleman, bp. 26 Nov. 1618, s. of Henry and Sarah (Lawson) of Stepney, co. Middlesex, and neph. of (6), came to York after his uncle's death to look after the fam. int. First in Boston (bound to good behavior 4 Mar. 1634-5), he had a gr. in York in 1642. Provost Marshal of the Gorges colony in 1645, he held that office until Mass. took over the gov., when he submitted 22 Nov. 1652 and was app. Marshal in 1653. Recorder of the City of Gorgeana 1646-7, selectman 1650. He bot 30 a. of William Hooke in 1650 and 40 a. of Edward Godfrey in 1654. In 1650 he testif. for his cous. Jane (Norton) Bond when Robert Collins was charged with assaulting her. Lists 24, 273, 274, 275, 276, 277. In Oct. 1657 about to go to England, from which journey he never returned. Poss. he d. at sea, but note that H. N., a stranger, was bur. at Hodmersham, co. Kent, in 1659. On 14 Aug. 1659 the ct. conceived Mr. Henry Norton to be dead and adm. was gr. his wid. Margaret, who was liv. with her dau. **Elizabeth,** w. of Sylvester Stover, in 1660 and causing her s.-in-law such trouble that the ct. threatened to imprison her. No inv. was entered until 1679 when the s. **George** was app. adm.

6 **LT.-COL. WALTER,** of the fam. seated at Sharpenhoe, co. Bedford, a professional soldier of long experience in the Low Countries, was taken prisoner at the battle of Rhé in 1625, where his son was killed. His prop. lost, he, poss. on the advice of Capt. John Mason, decided to begin again in New Eng. where he is found at Charlestown in 1630, a candidate for citizenship. Bef. becoming a freeman, however, he seems to have visited the Piscataqua region, and, impressed by its possibilities he went back to England, enlisted the int. of his fam. and friends and secured, on 1 Dec. 1631, a patent for 12,000 a. on the E. side of the Agamenticus riv. Among the patentees were Robert Norton, Esq., Richard Norton, gent., and George Norton of Sharpenhoe. In 1632 he arr. at York to develop this prop., but in 1633 while journeying to Va. with Capt. Conn. riv., presumably to trade, he was murdered with all the ship's company by a band of Pequots, after putting up a stiff resistance. He was twice mar., his 1st w. being Jane (Reeve) Reynolds. His wid. Eleanor, authorized by the Gen. Ct. to sell his York lands in 1660, became the w. of William Hooke(6). Lists 271, 272. See Bradford's History, p. 203; Winthrop's Journal I. 122-3. By 2d w: **Jane,** m. 1st Henry Simpson, m. 2d Nicholas Bond(2).

**Nossiter,** see Naziter.

**Nott,** Mary, List 328. See Huntress(1).

**NOWELL,** Capt. *Peter, Esq., deacon, blacksmith, came from Salem to York ab. 1694. Had York gr. 1699; gr.j. 1700, 1714; j. 1703; sergt. 1696, capt. 1720-1; Rep. to Gen. Ct. 1723, 1724; special Justice of Ct. of Com. Pleas 1739. In 1696-7 he was in ct. for selling a horse on Sunday. He m. 1st ab. 1698 Sarah Weare who d. 9 (or 13) Sept. 1729, ag. 53 yrs. 9 m. His 2d w., m. 19 Feb. 1729-30, was wid. Mary (Preble 2) Preble, whose will was made 18 Jan. 1753, prob. 20 May 1755. He d. 10 May 1740, ag. 70 yrs. 10 m. His will, 28 Aug. 1738—30 May 1740, lists 9 ch., leaves the homestead to s. Ebenezer and makes gifts to gr.ch. John (eldest s. of John), Peter (eldest s. of Peter), Paul (eldest s. of Paul) and John Lane (s. of dau. Mary). Lists 38, 279. Ch: **Peter,** b. 24 Feb. 1698-9, d.y. **Sarah,** b. 29 Jan. 1700-1, m. Jonathan Bean(4). **Mary,** b. 15 July 1702. Her int. to m. Nicholas Winkley was pub. in York 27 Apr. 1724 but she appar. changed her mind and m. Capt. John Lane(6) in Greenland 8 days later. **John,** b. 18 Mar. 1705, m. 11 Jan. 1727-8 Tabitha Came(3) who m. 2d 26 Mar. 1747 John Frost. Dea. J. N. d. 9 Oct. 1743. List 279. 6 ch. **Peter,** b. ab. 1707, m. 19 June 1729 Lydia Junkins. List 279. Ch. **Ebenezer,** b. 12 Nov. 1709, m. int. 10 Jan. 1740-1 wid. Patience (Hamilton) Weymouth, dau. of Gabriel H., d. 1 July 1761. List 279. 4 ch. **Abraham,** b. 28 Feb. 1711-2, m. 24 Nov. 1736

his step-sis. Humility Preble, d. 24 Dec. 1790.
**Paul,** b. ab. 1714, m. Mary Nutting (Jonathan of Cambridge). Ch. **Silas,** b. ab. 1717, m. int. 20 June 1741 Hannah Came(3). 9 ch. **Esther,** b. 12 July 1721, m. 28 Nov. 1743 Jonathan Greeley of Kingston.

**NUDD,** a very uncommon Norfolk name.
1 **SAMUEL**(2), Hampton, farmer and capt. of a coasting-vessel betw. Hamp. and Boston, m. 27 Feb. 1701 Sarah Maloon who d. 14 Feb. 1756 aged 77. Selectman 1706, 1721. List 399a. He d. 26 Mar. 1748. Will, 8 Aug. 1746—29 Mar. 1749. Ch: **Mary,** b. ab. July 1705, m. 28 June 1727 Ephraim Marston(2 jr.). **James,** bp. 10 Aug. 1707, m. 10 Aug. 1726 Abigail Thomas and lived on her fa.'s place at No. Hamp. Both adm. to Greenland Ch. in 1727. She d. 13 Oct. 1749, he 27 May 1754, will dated 10 May 1754. 8 ch. bp. **Thomas,** b. 8 Oct. 1708, J. P., Esq., selectman, m. 23 May 1733 Deborah Marston who d. 28 May 1788. He d. 17 Mar. 1780. 5 ch.
2 **THOMAS,** Hampton, bp. 6 Jan. 1629 at Ormesby, co. Norfolk, s. of Roger and his w. Joan, who m. 2d Henry Dow(2) who agreed to treat her boy as his own and brot him to New Eng. in 1637. For many years he was a servant of Mr. Timothy Dalton, as he depos. 8 May. 1675. His step-fa. gr. him 10 a. of the home lot and other lands 3 Oct. 1649, he having grown to man's est. He bot land from Thos. Moulton in 1653. Clerk of the train band, 1676. Selectman 1644, 1663, 1668. Lists 49, 54, 392b, 393ab, 396. He d. 31 Jan. 1713 and his w. Sarah Dearborn(1) 21 Aug. 1714. Ch: **John,** b. 11 Jan., d. 22 Jan. 1661-2. **Sarah,** b. 23 Feb. 1662-3, d. 4 Oct. 1664. **James,** b. 24 Nov. 1665, d. 20 Oct. 1668. **Thomas,** b. 15 Feb. 1668-9, d. 1 May 1669. **Samuel,** b. 13 Sept. 1670. **Mary,** b. 1 Apr. 1673, d. 8 Nov. 1683. **Hannah,** b. 23 Oct. 1678, m. Francis Page(2 jr.).

**NUTE,** Newett, poss. from the given-name Knut, commonly but incorrectly spelled Canute.
1 **ABRAHAM**(2), Dover, ±80 in 1724, his fa.'s only surv. s. in 1699. Lists 52, 356jk, 359ab. It seems improb. that wid. Joanna Stanton, whom he m. 2 Sept. 1704, was his 1st w., but her predecessor escaped the records completely as did her ch., if any. Ch: Abraham, b. 9 Mar. 1705-6. His will, 1756, names his w. Rachel and 5 ch: Isaac, b. 29 Aug. 1731, exec. and had the homestead; Joanna, b. 5 Sept. 1733; Sarah, b. 12 Feb. 1738; Abraham, b. 10 July 1741; Mary, b. 3 Apr. 1744.
2 **JAMES,** Dover, signed the combination 1640; gr.j. 1643, 1651; cor.j. (Me.) 1647; selectman 1660. His w. Sarah was called 'a base jade' by William Storer in 1652. They

deeded the homestead to s. Abraham and other land to s. James in 1671, both deeds to take effect after their deaths. His gr.stone stands in the fam. gr.yard, 'Mr J Nute ae 78.' Lists 47, 49, 52, 351b, 352 (2), 353, 354abc, 355ab, 356abcefghk, 357b, 358b, 359ab. Ch: **Sarah,** m. James Bunker(1). **James. Abraham. Martha,** m. William Dam (5). **Leah,** m. 1st John Knight(8), m. 2d Benedictus Tarr.
3 **JAMES**(2), Dover, 26 in 1669, m. by 1675 Elizabeth Heard(5) who m. 2d 13 Aug. 1694 William Furber(3). Gr.j. 1678. Lists 49, 52, 356ghk, 359ab, 361a. His inv. was filed 24 Oct. 1691 by wid. (Mary—error), John Knight and Samuel Heard bondsmen. Ch: James, b. 27 July 1687 (his own record), 13 in 1699 when he chose John Leighton guard. Selectman 1725-1728, prop. of Rochester. His w. Prudence was liv. 1725. Will, 14 July 1752—31 Oct. 1759, ment. Robert Morrill 'brot up in my ho.,' and ch: Elizabeth, b. 28 Dec. 1706, m. John Tuttle who m. 2d her niece Anne Nute; James, b. 12 Mar. 1712-3, m. Anne Meserve, d. 4 Apr. 1776; Paul, b. 19 Aug. 1714, m. Judah Tibbetts, d. 7 Feb. 1796; Ann, b. 21 Mar. 1721, acc. Thomas Davis(14) in 1743 and had a ch. 'Elizabeth Davis commonly so called,' m. one Allen bef. 1752. Samuel, 18 in 1707-8 when he chose Jethro Furber guard., ±27 in 1716, m. 18 Mar. 1718-9 Elizabeth Pinkham(1). Prop. of Rochester. List 358d. Will, 29 Mar. 1764——26 June 1765. Ch: John, m. bef. 1750 one Hepsibah; Jotham, exec. of fa.'s will, b. 2 Mar. 1724, m. 1st Mary Hayes, m. 2d wid. Mary Canney, d. 6 Nov. 1801; Sarah, m. Josiah Clark; Martha, b. 17 Mar. 1734, m. 10 Oct. 1754 Benjamin Dam; Elizabeth, d. bef. 1764 unm. but leaving a s. Obed. Sarah, m. William Furber(3 jr.). **Leah,** m. 1st Jethro Furber(3), m. 2d Hatevil Nutter(3). **Nutt,** Jemima, acc. of bastardy in York ct. Apr. 1714.
**Nuttache.** There is seldom much humor in genealogy, but, when Mr. Pope personified 'Cap Nuttache' (Cape Neddick) as Capt. Nuttache and listed him as an inhabitant of York, he was unconsciously very funny.

**NUTTER,** peculiar to Lancashire. A dealer in nuts, or a corruption from Nuthalgh (a nut-grove).
1 ‡*LT. ANTHONY(2), Dover, ±50 in 1680, m. Sarah Langstaff ab. 1662. Bot a ho. at Sandy Pt. from Peter Coffin in 1664. Selectman 1666, 1667 (Corp.), 1672-1677; Rep. to Gen. Ct. 1674-1676, 1680-1684; Councillor 1679. Guardian of Thos. Leighton's eldest s. 1677, and of Thos. Cotton 1679. See Kenniston(5). Lists 48, 49, 50, 53, 54, 96, 353, 354bc, 355a, 356abceghk, 359ab. He d. 19 Feb.

1685-6 of small-pox. Adm. in 1720 to sons Hatevil and Henry. The wid. test. ag. Richard Otis jr. in 1688, and was liv. in 1698. Ch: **John**, b. 27 Dec. 1663. **Hatevil. Henry. Sarah**, m. Capt. Nathaniel Hill(12). **Mary**, m. Col. Shadrach Walton. **Elizabeth, m.** Jacob Lavers(2). **Ann**, m. Joseph Jones(29). **Abigail**, m. Stephen Jones(40).

2 **HATEVIL**, Dover, 50 in 1648, ±71 in 1674, first ment. in 1635. Prop. of Dover in 1642, gr. for a saw-mill 1647, 200 a. gr. in 1658. Exch. lands with Sergt. John Hall in 1649. Ruling elder of the Dover ch., he was a foe of the local Quakers. Selectman 1655, 1661; com.t.e.s.c. 1658, 1660; moderator 1659; gr.j. 1649 (Me.); j. 1649-50. See Luckham, Hall(7). Lists 44, 76, 311c, 352, 353, 354abc, 355ab, 356bcefghk, 357b, 375b. His w. Anne is called 'my present w.' (but no other is kn.) in his will, 29 Dec. 1674—30 June 1675, leaving his lands to his s. Anthony after his mo.'s death. Ch: **Anthony. John**, liv. 1669 but d. s. p. bef. 1674. **Mary**, m. John Wingate. **Elizabeth**, m. Thomas Leighton(8). **Abigail**, m. John Roberts(5).

3 **HATEVIL**(1), Newington, had a 1st w. whose name has not been found thus far, m. 2d 16 May 1716 Leah (Nute 3) Furber who surv. him and was liv. in 1748. She and his ch. named in will, 1745. List 343. Ch. by 1st w: **Hatevil**, cordwainer, m. 7 Feb. 1730-1 Hannah Decker(2). **Anthony**, m. 18 May 1740 Mary Downing. **Eleanor**, liv. unm. in Portsmouth in 1751. **Sarah**, m. 28 Dec. 1732 Edward Walker. By 2d w: **Abigail**, b. 15 Sept. 1717, m. 29 Dec. 1740 Jonathan Dam. **Elizabeth**, bp. 29 Nov. 1719, d.y. **John**, bp. 12 Mar. 1720-1, weaver, m. 17 Nov. 1747 Anne Symmes, d. 15 Sept. 1776. **Elizabeth**, b. 26 June 1723, m. 21 Nov. 1742 Edward Rollins. **Joshua**, carpenter, m. 22 Jan. 1748-9 Sarah Richards. **Olive**, m. 6 Jan. 1748-9 Ichabod Rollins.

3½ **HATEVIL**. In N. H. Prob. Minutes, under date 3 Mar. 1724-5, is the entry: 'Hate: Nutter's will brot & proved.' The will is not filed or recorded, nor are there any other papers. If the entry was not erroneous, there seems no place for this man except as an oldest s. (barely 21 yrs.) of (4).

4 **HENRY**(1), Newington, m. 1st 26 July 1703 Mary Shackford (ct. 1703-4); m. 2d Mary Hoyt. In 1732 he deeded to s. Samuel land bot from his kinsman Henry Langstaff. He sued for 1/9 of his fa.'s real est. in 1738-9. List 343. His will, 1739—1739-40, names his w. Mary, sons Samuel (homestead), Joseph and Valentine, daus. Elizabeth Crockett and Mary Pickering. Ch: **Samuel**, innholder, m. 18 May 1725 Sarah Hoyt. **Valentine**, Ports., carpenter. His will, 1756—1757, names w. Mary and 9 ch. **Joseph**, Durham, shipwright, m. bef. 1735 Bridget Barker

(Enoch). **Elizabeth, m.** 25 Dec. 1733 Joshua Crockett. **Mary**, m. 28 Aug. 1740 John Pickering. See also (3½).

5 **JOHN**(1), Newington, m. Rosamund Johnson(16), who as 'Rosaman Nitter' receipted to est. of Nicholas Frost in 1718 and was adm. to full com. in Newington Ch. 1724. Constable (Dover) 1692; gr.j. 1696; j. 1693-4. Lists 52, 57, 61, 343. He d. by 1719. Ch: **Anne, m.** Mar. 1716-7 Eleazer Coleman. **Mary**, m. 16 Jan. 1718 James Pickering(8). **John**, m. 8 Feb. 1718-9 Abigail Whidden. No ch. Will, 16 Aug. 1746—29 Apr. 1747, names bros. Matthias, James, Hatevil. **Matthias**, m. Hannah Furber (3 Jethro). **James**, m. 1 Jan. 1723-4 Abigail Furber. **Hatevil**, m. 28 June 1727 Rebecca Ayres. **Rosamond**, bp. 31 Jan. 1724-5, m. 29 Nov. 1733 Samuel Fabyan(3), and poss. an eldest dau. **Sarah**, m. Greenland 18 Jan. 1711-2 John Whidden.

**OAKMAN**, a Devon name, centered in par. of St. Nicholas.

1 **ELIAS**, Scarboro, 23 in 1667, fisherman, prob. a br. or neph. of (5), m. Joanna Alger(1) who m. 2d John Mills(8). Sued by Ambrose Boaden Sr. in 1667. Exec. of est. of John Mayer 1668. Refugee from Falmouth garrison 1675. His 'estate' was taxed in 1681, 20 a. of upland and 2 a. of marsh, but he may have been absent, not dead. Lists 223a, 234a, 238a. Only kn. ch: **Elias**, b. in Boston 21 Apr. 1680. Very prob. **Agnes**, who would have been named for her gr.mo. Alger, m. in Bos. 4 Nov. 1697 Joshua Kent. But no desc. of Elias appear as claimants or owners of Scarb. prop.

2 **JOHN**, Falmouth, his land ment. in 1730. Y. D. 15: 142.

3 **JOSIAH**(5), Spurwink, taxed 1681. List 238a. His fa.'s 'son and heir' in 1688-9 when he and his mo., his step-fa. Adams consenting, deeded 16 a. at Spurwink to his br.-in-law Edward Bennett. Poss. an Ind. victim or d. a refugee in Mass. His son cl. his Spurwink lands, for his 'heirs,' from Boston. His w.'s name does not appear. One Mary Oakman, wid., had a illeg. ch. by Anthony Sears in Falm. 8 Feb. 1703-4 in Bos., Martha Cox and Sarah Marshall on her bond, and buried ch. in 1701 and 1704. Only kn. ch: **Samuel**, Bos. and Marblehead, housewright, m. in Bos. 9 Aug. 1708 Sarah Shorey (John of Rehoboth), who m. 2d 1 June 1732 John Boaden(8) and 3d 19 Aug. 1746 Ambrose Grant. An absentee prop. of Scarboro in 1720 in which yr. he sold 50 a. at Spurwink to Richard Skinner of M'head. He had a 100 a. Scar. gr. in 1720 which Job Burnham bot 1748-1757 from Sarah Grant, Mary Andros, Sarah Oakman and Rebecca Oakman, wid. of his s. Samuel (m. at Salem 29 Nov. 1736 Rebecca Glover).

**4 ROBERT**, wit. deed Hunnewell to Hunnewell in 1692 in Salisbury, may have no Me. connection.

**5 SAMUEL**, Spurwink, fisherman, 25 in 1653, 34 in 1664, took O. A. and sub. to Mass. in 1658. He m. Mary Boaden(1), ±43 in 1679, who m. 2d Walter Adams(20). She was frequenting the company of John Mayer in a suspicious manner in 1665. He had a gr. from Mr. Jocelyn in 1668 and 50 a. at Spurwink from Mr. Scottow in 1675. Selectman 1671, 1673, 1674, 1676; gr.j. 1673, 1674; j. 1664, 1666, 1672, 1673. Lists 111, 232, 236, 237ac, 239ab. Adm. 30 June 1676 to wid. Mary. The inv. showed 120 a. of land, 10 a. of 'in-land' and 10 a. of marsh. Kn. ch: **Samuel**, in ct. in 1674 for sailing out of Cape Porpus harbor on the Lord's day, m. Grace (Briar 4) Chilson bef. 1677 when they deeded her 1st husb.'s farm to Hugh Warren of Boston. Selectman 1681. Lists 237ac. No kn. ch. **Josiah. Susanna**, b. ab. 1660, lived with (1) in her youth, m. 1st Edward Bennett(4), m. 2d Peter King. **Tobias**, b. ab. 1665. Mary 'Hocman,' b. in Black Point, w. of Thomas Hoar or Whove and a prisoner in Canada (see Hocman), may have been a dau. or a gr.dau. of (5).

**6 TOBIAS**(5), ±66 in 1731, ±69 in 1734, ±74 in 1739, 76 in 1741, was serv. of Walter Gendall at Yarmouth Falls in his youth and, in 1727, after his removal to Marshfield, W. G.'s adm. gr. him 50 a. on the Spurwink riv. Captured by Indians at Black Pt. in 1690. At first meeting of Scarb. prop., 1720. Lists 34, 214, 229, 239b. See Low(1). Made many depos. ab. Maine matters. He m. Elizabeth Doty who d. 16 (17 gr.st.) Dec. 1745. He d. 16 June 1750 in 86th yr. Will, 21 Mar. 1745—26 July 1750. Ch. b. in Marshfield: **Faith**, b. 15 May 1697, m. 1st Benj. White, m. 2d Thos. Foster. **Samuel**, b. 15 Mar. 1698-9, in trouble with Hannah Childs 1726, m. 6 Jan. 1725-6 Elizabeth Hatch. **Elizabeth**, b. 10 May 1701, m. Elisha Ford. **Sarah**, b. 1703, m. 17 May 1722 Samuel Randall. **Susanna**, b. Jan. 1705-6, m. 4 May 1732 Anthony Collamore. **Mary**, b. 3 May 17—, m. 1st Jedediah Ames, m. 2d Robert Sherman. **Mercy**, m. 1st Matthew Simonton, to whom her fa. deeded in 1741 150 a. gr. by Jordan to Maddiver at Spurwink; m. 2d John Hamilton. **Edward**, m. Sarah Doggett and had a s. Samuel, shipwright, of Bath and a s. Joseph who d. at Arrowsic.

**Oband**. List 13. See Osborne.

**O'Brien**, Dennis, in jail for stealing money entrusted to him by Newcastle people for purchase of goods in Boston, 1686.

**O'Cormack**, Denis, Great Isl. gr. of 1 a. 1660-1. List 330a.

**ODELL, Thomas** (alias Collins, alias Green or Grear, alias Fletcher), forger and counterfeiter, (?) m. Hannah Smith of Exeter who later m. Ebenezer Folsom(9). Discharged from ct. 1700; testif. to knowing Wedgewood ab. 6 yrs. ago in 1703; absconded from N. H. 1704; captured, a forger, in N. Y. 21 May, escaped in Newport 4 June and recaptured 8 June; in Boston jail 1707 and 1709. Only kn. ch: **Thomas**, s. of wid. Folsom, liv. 1757 (at Stratham?). One T. O. m. after June 23, 1737, at Greenland, Mary Rundlet.

**ODIORNE**. Our family is from Cornwall; another is found in Sussex. See Creber.

**1 ISAIAH**, Isles of Shoals, fisherman, ordered home 1670 for absenting himself from his w. for several yrs. See Grubb. List 305b. Inq. on his body 4 July 1681. At Sheviock, co. Cornwall, Jacob, s. of Esay and Judith Odyorne was bp. 12 Mar. 1655-6.

**2 JOHN**, fisherman, Boston to Great Isl. where he bot ho. and land from Oliver Trimmings in 1656 and had a gr. in 1660. One John, s. of Wm. and Agnes (Hickins), was bp. at Sheviock 1628-9. Sued by Philip Babb 1656, and by Stephen Ford 1661. Sold fishing outfit, stage etc. on Smuttinose Isl. 1660. Bot and settled at Odiorne's Pt. He m. Mary Johnson(14), Lists 331c, 316, who was wit. with Elias Stileman in 1661 and was adm. to No. Ch., Portsm., in 1694. Gr.j. 1684. Lists (poss. some refer to John jr.) 49, 52, 55b, 321c (correct James to John), 313a, 315c, 316, 323, 326ac, 327a, 330ab, 331b, 332b, 336a. Adm. 4 Feb. 1706-7 to wid. Mary, Mark Hunking and William Seavey bondsmen, the est. being insolvent. Ch., order unknown: **John. Hannah**, b. 30 June 1673, m. 1st Lt. John Batson(2), m. 2d James Stilson. **Jotham**, b. 1675. **Mary**, m. 1st John Swain, and 2d an unident. husb. and liv. in Haverhill.

**3 JOHN**(2), Odiorne's Pt. (now in Rye), farmer, had deed of homestead from parents in 1705. In 1711 his w. was Catherine, and in 1725 they and their s. John Jr. deeded to Nathaniel Rand. Deacon of Newcastle Ch., constable 1696-7, selectman 1699-1700. He d. 1741. Ch: **John**, eldest s., heir of his fa.'s lands (entailed), successfully defended his title ag. his bros. and sis. **Ebenezer**, mariner, m. Catherine Sherborne, who m. 2d Dr. Thomas Deane of Exeter. Adm. to her 25 Feb. 1746. Her will, 1766, names sons Thomas, Ebenezer and daus. Elizabeth, Mary Akerman. **Nathaniel**, his w. and daus. Sarah and Mary ment. in his sis. Hannah's will. **Benjamin. Samuel**, his w. and ch. ment. in sis. Hannah's will. **Hannah**, m. 1st one Stevens, m. 2d John Hardison, her will, 1755. **Elizabeth**, m. Richard Salter.

**4 ‡\*HON. JOTHAM**(2), Newcastle, wealthy merchant, 48 in 1723, m. after 1697 Sarah

(Barsham) Bickford(5) who d. 23 June 1752, ag. 76. He d. 16 Aug. 1748, ag. 73. Gr. 152 a. on Gt. Isl. in 1721. As J. P. from 1713, Dep. from 1715, Judge of the Inf. Ct. 1719-1730, Councillor 1724-1728, Judge of the Superior Ct. 1742-1747, he had a disting. public career. Lists 315c (2), 316. Will, 1737—1748, ment. w., sons Jotham, Wm., John, daus. Ann Rindge, Sarah Morrell, Mary Jackson. Her will 1751—1752 ment. s. Wm. (exec.), daus. Ann Packer, Sarah Fellows, Temperance (Bickford) Walton and Mary Meserve, and Mehitable Pevey dau. of wid. Sarah Pevey. Ch: *Jotham, Portsm., merchant, m. in Kit. 29 Dec. 1725 Mehitable Cutt(8) who was liv. 1762. He d. 19 May 1751, ag. 48. His will, 1751, ment. his w. and his mo., sis. Anne Packer, br.-in-law Nathaniel Morrill, sons Robert, Jotham, Samuel, Daniel, daus. Mehitable, Mary (m. Peter Pearse) and Sarah (m. Henry Appleton). William, shipbuilder, J. P.; Portsm., Durham, Epsom, Newmarket; m. 1st Sarah Hatch (Samuel 2), m. 2d Avis Adams (Rev. Hugh); d. 1798. 5 + 11 ch. John. Anne, m. 1st Hon. John Rindge, m. 2d bef. 1751 Thomas Packer(2 jr.). Sarah, m. 1st Rev. Nathaniel Morrill who d. 1735, m. 2d one Fellows. Mary, m. 1st (Ephraim?) Jackson, m. 2d bef. 1751 Col. Nathaniel Meserve.

5 NATHANIEL(7), mariner, m. Jane Haskins(6) who o.c. and was bp. at No. Ch., Portsm., 30 May 1708. He was at sea, an apprent. of Capt. Mark Hunking, in 1702-3. Taxed Portsm. 1707, 1708, 1712, 1713. He o.c. at So. Ch. 2 Jan. 1714-5. List 339. Ch. bp. in both churches 1709-1724, incl: Nathaniel, had w. Mary (poss. Yeaton 1), and s. Philip, bp. 1731. Elizabeth, bp. 7 Nov. 1714. Ann, bp. 13 Oct. 1723. John, bp. 26 July 1724. See also Elizabeth Yeaton(1).

6 PETER, fined 1673 for not appearing to serve on gr.j. Undoubtedly clerk's error (for Peter Lewis?).

7 PHILIP, Isles of Shoals, fisherman, prob. near relation of John (one Philip, s. of Wm., bp. at Sheviock 1664), sued Roger Kelly for kicking and dragging his w. in 1684. Lic. to retail 1686. Sued on a book debt in Boston 1690. Lists 305a, 306c, 307a, 308a, 326c. Prob. husb. of Elizabeth (List 307b), dau. of William Seavey, who was 'now Odiorne' in 1679. Adm. 11 Dec. 1703 to only kn. ch: Nathaniel.

ODLIN, Rev. John, Exeter, s. of Elisha (List 161) of Boston, b. 18 Nov. 1681, H. C. 1702, was ordained at Ex. 11 Nov. 1706. He m. 1st 21 Oct. 1709 Elizabeth (Woodbridge) Clark(21) who d. 6 Dec. 1729, m. 2d 22 Sept. 1730 Elizabeth (Leavitt 10) (Dudley) Briscoe. Had gr. 1725 (100 a.) and 1740. His sister Abigail O., 'once of Boston,' spinster, remem. his 4 sons in her will, 1735. List 376b.

He d. 20 Nov. 1754. Ch: Capt. John, b. 7 Nov. 1707, m. 27 Feb. 1734-5 Alice Leavitt (10 James), d. 15 July 1782. 8 ch. Rev. Elisha, b. 16 Nov. 1709, H. C. 1731, minister at Amesbury, m. 1 Nov. 1731 Judith (Hilton 24) Pike. 5 ch. Dudley, b. 22 Sept. 1711, d. 13 Feb. 1747-8, ag. 37. Samuel, b. 14, d. 31 Aug. 1714. Rev. Woodbridge, b. 28 Apr. 1718, H. C. 1738, ordained 1743 as fa.'s colleague, m. 23 Oct. 1755 Abigail (Gilman) Strong, wid. of Rev. Job of Portsm., d. 10 Mar. 1776. 9 ch.

Odrigue, see Roderigo.

Ogleby, James, a soldier at Scottow's garrison, Black Pt., 1676. Lists 237ab.

O'GRADO, Cormac or Charles, Portsmouth, yeoman, bot 10 a. at Spruce Creek from Ephraim Crockett in 1672 and sold it to Robert Elliot in 1689. Henry Kirke sued him in 1672. No w. or ch. ment. His names were a terror to the scribes, Cormac becoming 'Corromock' and 'Kerremuck' and O'Grado being found as Ogradas, Ograddos, Magradoe and Magrady—but never O'Grady.

Ohf, see Huff.

Okers, Rowland, fisherman at Richmond Isl., 1633, part of his wages being paid to someone in Eng. by Mr. Trelawney. List 21.

OLDHAM, John, gentleman, partner in 1629-30 with Mr. Richard Vines in the Biddeford patent, in which he may never have set foot. Arriving at Plymouth in 1623 he had an active and varied career in New England until his murder by Ind. on a shallop off the mouth of Narragansett Bay in 1636.

OLIVER, a common English name, most frequently found in co. Durham in the north, and in Devon and Cornwall in the south.

1 BENEDICT, Isles of Shoals, 31 in 1660, from Coffinswell, co. Devon, prob. br. of (16) and (21), had p/a from wid. Elizabeth Garnsey to settle her husb.'s est. See Guernsey(2). With (21) he bot from James Pendleton a ho. and half a stage at Smuttinose in 1669, the other half being Michael Endle's. Prob. returned to Devon. List 302a.

2 DANIEL (jr.), Boston, merchant, had deeded land at Sheepscot bef. 1726.

3 DAVID, Pemaquid, fisherman, O. A. 1674. As adm. of est. of Thomas Bowles, he sold part of Rascohegan Isl. at Sagadahoc to Henry Coombs, 1676, and ack. it in Boston 1676-7, being late of Kennebec. Lists 15, 187. He m. Grace Parker(25). Ch: Thomas, Boston ship-wright. David.

4 DAVID(3), Marblehead, fisherman, m. Sarah (Pedrick) Britnell, wid. of Henry, 3 Mar. 1691-2. List 189. Her son Henry 'Bricknell' fell from shrouds of a ship in 1707 and was injured. Joined his fa. in giving deed to Kennebec prop. Ch: Grace, bp.

12 Feb. 1692-3, m. Ebenezer Allen 25 Dec. 1712. **David,** ±72 in 1766 when he test. ab. Kennebec matters 46 yrs. bef., m. 29 Nov. 1716 Hannah Stacy. **Thomas,** bp. 10 Apr. 1698, m. 12 Mar. 1724 Ruth Oakes. **Miriam,** bp. 14 Apr. 1700, m. 29 Sept. 1720 John Rhodes. **Sarah,** bp. 15 Nov. 1702, m. 20 Sept. 1720 Joseph Bull. **John,** bp. 20 May 1705, m. 27 Dec. 1725 Jane Waters. **Jacob,** bp. 21 Sept. 1707, m. 1 Feb. 1727-8 Anstice Hawkings.

5 **GILBERT** (Oliver?), constable at Isles of Shoals, 1678.

6 **JAMES,** with Thomas Hawkins had p/a from Humphrey Damerill(1) to collect all debts in N. E., 1648.

7 **JOHN,** wit. a Penwill deed, Isles of Shoals, 1665. List 306c.

8 **JOHN,** Portsmouth, ship-carpenter, poss. that J. O. ±18 in 1686, apprentice to shipwright Seward. He m. Hannah Cowes(1) who q.c. to Robert Dutch of Ips., bricklayer, Ips. com. rights derived from her gr.fa. Robert Dutch, 1716. Had Portsm. com. rights 1711. Poss. the J. O. of Lists 57, 330def, 337. Taxed in 1717.

9 **JOHN,** Falmouth. See Harris(9).

10 **JOSEPH,** Black Point, Sergt., closely associated with Ralph Allison with whom he appr. est. of Richard Cummings and pet. for an increase of Bl. Pt. garrison in 1676. Slain at the garrison, adm. was gr. to Anne Allison, Nathaniel Fryer bondsman, 6 Apr. 1680, the tickets for his soldier's pay having been left in her hands. Lists 236, 237acd. That he had m. Allison's dau. Jane is very improb.

11 **MARY,** Newcastle, servant of Rev. Nathaniel Morrill, had a ch. by James Allard, a minor, in 1732.

12 **NICHOLAS,** Portsmouth, 1693. List 334b.

13 **PETER,** Boston, held mtge. on Stephen Batson's prop. in 1662.

14 **RICHARD,** Mr., Hampton, bot land and cattle from Edward Colcord in 1666 and Nathaniel Boulter's land, taken by levy, from James Pendleton in 1667, also 20 a. at Ass's brook on the Exeter line from Wm. Taylor in 1667. Fined for fighting with John Redman in 1667.

15 **RICHARD,** Mr., Pemaquid 1672, clerk of Cornwall Co. 1674, O. A. 1674, declared eligible for Associate 1675, refugee at Monhegan in Philip's war and wit. Mogg's treaty of peace 1676. Lists 4, 13, 15. Poss. same as (14).

16 **RICHARD,** br. of (21) and prob. of (1), Isles of Shoals and Newcastle, fisherman, wit. a Cutts deed 1658; with br. William(21) bot 50 a. at Thompson's Pt. 1664 which he sold to Thomas Rhodes in 1705. He was committed to York jail by Roger Kelly 1681,

Kelly's w. having acc. him of murder, but, as she was fined, he was appar. acq. Sued by Henry Russell 1682, ment. in Seaborn Cotton's will 1684, wit. deed Jordan to Elliot at Gt. Isl. 1695. He and William Tucker had fish stolen at Clark's Isl. in 1698. Prob. (22) was his w. and **Mary,** of the Shoals, who m. William Tucker 7 July 1684 his dau. Lists 90, 307a, 315c, 318a, 319.

17 **RICHARD,** poss. a s. of (16), by a special military ct. held 6 Oct. 1696, found guilty of mutiny at Fort Wm. and Mary, wit. Capt. Walton, Lt. Hirst, Ens. Rendle.

18 **ROBERT,** York, husbandman, in 1728 depos. ab. affairs at Quamphegan in 1700. Town gr. in 1703, 1704 and 1712. In ct. for cursing his dau.-in-law (step-dau.?) in 1712. Lists 228c, 267a, 279. Surety for James Wittum 1718. Liv. in 1740. By w. Mary, prob. a wid. when he m. her, he had ch: **James,** b. 17 June 1703, appr. 17 Jan. 1717-8 for 7 or 8 yrs. to John Sayward, whom he sued 1725. He and br. John were prop. of Sheepscot in 1728. He m. 1st 7 Aug. 1727 Mary Bradeen(1) who d. 13 Feb. 1728-9, m. 2d 27 Mar. 1728-9 Elizabeth Wittum. **Mary,** m. 11 Feb. 1727-8 James Bradeen(1 jr.). **John,** b. 14 Nov. 1709, m. 14 Oct. 1738 Lois Spencer. List 279.

19 **ROBERT,** of 'Yeatowe,' co. Northumberland, m. in Portsm. 7 Oct. 1715 Pasca Malum of Newc.

20 **SAMUEL.** In 1652 Edw. Gilman jr. sold to his bro. John ¼ of his right in the patent of Squamscott which he had bot of Mr. Samuel Olipher.

21 **WILLIAM,** br. of (16) and prob. of (1), Isles of Shoals fisherman, ±60 in 1680 when he depos. ab. affairs at Smuttinose in 1660. Gr.j. 1671, 1672. Lists 90, 305a, 306c. His w. Elizabeth was acc. of adultery with Edward Holland in 1672, but she and her husb. both declared the ch. to be his. Sued Wm. Snell for slander 1672. See Ham(8). With (16) he bot Michael Endle's share of the Smuttinose stage and flake-ho. in 1678. His part of the Thompson's Pt. prop. was mortg. to Wm. Goodhue of Ips. Liv. 1683. No kn. ch.

22 **WILMOT,** N. H., had dau. **Constance,** ±16, who lost a coat and both suspected Mary Richards of taking it, 1680. Poss. w. of (16).

**Oney,** Edward, fined in N. H. ct. 28 June 1664 with Jeffrey Currier(2).

**ONG,** Isaac, bound to good behavior in York Ct. 30 June 1653, John Bursley bondsman. An I. O., poss. a younger man, m. Mary Underwood of Watertown 18 May 1670.

**ONION,** Thomas, Kittery and Sagamore Creek, fisherman, bot Robert Davis's S. C. lot bef. 4 Jan. 1657-8, on which day he was received inhabitant. He and w. Margaret sold a ho. and 20 a. in Kit. to Gabriel

Tetherly in 1660. With Robert Puriﬂgton he bot land on east side of the Kennebec which they sold to Richard Collicot in 1664. Cared for Roger Knight 3 mo. in 1672 and supplied his coffin. Tr.j.(Kit.) 1651. Lists 312c, 323, 326ac, 330a (2)b, 331a. He d. bef. 1676 when his dau. sued Wm. Lucomb and his w. Ann for slander for saying -inter alia- 'she had seen our mother the wid. Onion often drunk.' Ch: Amy, m. 1st Robert Purington(4), m. 2d Francis Graves(1).

OPIE, Nicholas, owned fishing fleet at Isles of Shoals which he sold to Abraham Brown of Boston 16 Aug. 1664. Brown sold to Shapleigh, 1668, reciting his title.

ORCHARD. 1 John, List 314.

2 ROBERT, servant of Mr. Theodore Atkinson, poss. in Mass. and not N. H., 1662-1663. Bondsman in Boston 1674.

3 THOMAS (Archer), assigned indenture of Nicholas Frost(10) to William Scadlock bef. Justice Jocelyn, 10 July 1663.

ORDWAY, James, Dover, as servant of Maj. Richard Waldron helped begin the plantation called Cochecho, where lots were laid out to him in 164- and he was rated 1649. Later of Newbury. List 354b.

Org, Brugan. List 126. His identity is anybody's guess.

ORMSBY, Richard, referee in Cleeve v. Jordan, 1641, had a ho. at York often referred to in local deeds, but by 1644 he had moved to Salisbury. See Hoyt's Salisbury, pp. 267-8. List 392c.

ORR, 1 James. See Henry Brown(7). List 28, 33, 47, 266, 269b, 356d, 361a, 363ac.

2 JOHN (Ore) and w. Hannah, Portsmouth, had ch. bp. at So. Ch: Hannah, 2 Nov. 1718. Mary, 12 Nov. 1721.

ORRIS, Jonathan, blacksmith, maker of guaranteed saws. s. of George and Elizabeth of Boston, bp. 8 Feb. 1656-7, settled at Casco Bay under Danforth by 1680. O. A., Boston 1678. Lists 225a, 227, 228. Still at Casco in 1689, he retired to Gloucester and d. s. p. His heirs were the ch. of his 3 bros., Nathaniel of Barnstable (2 ch.), Experience of Braintree (1 dau.) and John of Boston (2 daus., Elizabeth Townsend and Sarah Puddington, w. of Elias 4).

OSBORN, 1 John, Scarboro, had gr. of 36 a. 1 June 1685 and pet. for more 28 July 1688. He m. 12 Nov. 1687 Lydia Rogers(13) and prob. d. s. p.

2 NICHOLAS, took O. A. 1674, having been at Damariscove (Oband) in 1672.

O'SHAW, Desher, Doseagh, Shehee, Usher, Osca, Leshaw, prob. all attempts at O'Shea in brogue.

1 DANIEL(2), Newcastle, ±28 in 1677, m. Damaris Seavey (Thomas). Gr.j. 1683, 1695, 1698-9; j. 1694, 1695; highway surv.

1690, 1691, 1695, 1698. Taxed as jr. 1690, without jr. 1691. He d. bef. 1708 when wid. O'Shaw was taxed (List 316). Adm. to s. John 20 June 1715, John Wilson of Newc. and Lazarus Noble of Portsm. bondsmen. The ch. are disclosed in a pet. for div. of their fa.'s est. in 1715. Andrew Mace, a gr.s., was adm. in 1763. John, cordwainer; with Joan and Mary O'S. he was in ct. in 1708 for aiding in escape of Richard Glass; will, 1763-4, ment. w. Sarah, sons James, John, Daniel, Joseph and daus. Margaret and Elizabeth. One Elizabeth, poss. a 1st w. or dau., was drowned at Gt. Isl. in 1727. James, adm. to br. John, hatter, of Gt. Isl., 15 July 1716. Margaret, m. Reuben Mace(4). Catherine, 'infirm' in 1715. Mary, m. Henry Treddick. Sarah, m. Thomas Marden(4). Dau., m. William Samors. Dau. (Joan?), m. Edward Hales(1).

2 DERMON, Newcastle, ±50 in 1660, ±60 in 1670 when he had been serv. to Geo. Walton for 15 yrs., but called +80 in 1677 when his s. Daniel testif. to an assault on him by Joseph Morse. 'Old Dermon' in constable's acct. in 1668. Lists 312c, 313a, 319, 323, 326b, 328, 330a, 331b.

Osten. List 341. See Austin(4).

Oswell, John. With Richard Bassey and John Bennett he was bef. Suffolk Ct. 7 Nov. 1682 for running away with a shallop belonging to John Dollen of Monhegan.

OTIS, Oates, thought to be a pluralization of the Teutonic given-name Otte or Otto, peculiar to Cornwall.

1 RICHARD, blacksmith, adm. inhab. of Boston May 1655, but settled at Dover where he had a gr. of land bef. that yr. was out. Not in sympathy with the estab. church and often in ct. for absence. Adm. est. of Wm. Lemon 1662 and of James Heard 1677. He admitted the Masonian claims and agreed to pay ground rent for his lands in 1683. Lists 46, 49, 52, 92, 96, 353, 355a, 356abeghk, 359ab. His 1st w. was Rose Stoughton, dau. of Anthony, a strong Puritan, who had come to Boston with her kinsman Israel Stoughton. She d. bef. 5 Nov. 1677 when he had m. Shuah (Starbuck) Heard(3) on whose 1st husb.'s est. he adm. His 3d w. was Grizzel Warren, m. ab. 1685. On the night of 28 June 1689 his garrison was attacked by Indians, admitted by treachery, and he was murdered. Some of his family shared his fate, but his w., daus. and at least three gr.ch. were taken captive. Three older daus. were retaken at Conway within a few days, but Grizzel Otis and the little ch. were carried to Canada where she embraced the Catholic faith, was bp. Marie Madeleine, and m. 15 Oct. 1693 Philippe Robitaille of Montreal by whom she had 5 ch. She d. 26 Oct.

1750. Adm. d.b.n. on the est. of R. O. was gr. 1 May 1705 to Susanna O., wid. of his s. Richard, and distrib. made to his creditors. Ch., by 1st w., order unkn: **Richard** (eldest s.). **Stephen**, b. ±1652. **Martha**, m. John Pinkham(1). **Anne**, m. Thomas Austin(8). **Solomon**, b. 15 Oct. 1663 and soon d. **Nicholas**, had gr. of 20 a. in 1694. He was k. and his w. captured by Ind. 26 July 1696 when ret. from church. Inv. 18 May 1697. She was set free near the Penobscot river and ret. to Dover, and was presum. the wid. Joyce Otis who m. 25 Feb. 1699-1700 Henry Tibbetts. List 96. A s. Nicholas shared his mo.'s experiences and d. s.p. about 1702, his aunts and cous. taking his share of his gr.fa.'s est. **Experience**, b. 7 Nov. 1666, m. 1st Samuel Heard(8), m. 2d Rowland Jenkins(11) and was scalped in the attack of 1696, but liv. to have a ch. **Judith**, m. John Tuttle. By 1st or 2d w: **Rose**, a captive in Canada, m. at Beauport 29 Oct. 1696 Jean Poitevin, d. 7 July 1729 having had 10 ch. The Otis Gen., followed by Miss Coleman, called the w. of John Pinkham -Rose-, without quoting any doc. authority for so doing, instead of -Martha- which was her name in fact, and therefore concluded that Rose Poitevin must have been a gr.dau. of (1) instead of a dau. By 3d w: **Hannah**, k. in the attack of 1689, ag. 2. **Margaret**, b. 15 Mar. 1689, taken with her mo. to Canada, bp. Christine in the Catholic faith 9 May 1693, m. 1st at Ville-Marie 14 June 1707 Louis le Beau, carpenter, who d. 26 Feb. 1713; ret. to New Eng. with Capt. Thomas Baker in 1714 and m. him; d. in Dover, where she kept a pub.-ho., Feb. 1773. List 99 (pp. 75, 125-6).

2 **RICHARD**(1), Dover, blacksmith, Quaker, in ct. for talking ag. Gov. Andros in 1688. Wounded in the attack of 1696. Lists 96, 359b. His only kn. w. was Susannah Hussey(3) who was at least 17 yrs. his junior, so there is a distinct poss. that he had an earlier w. whose name nowhere appears. His wid. adm. his insolvent est. 1 Jan. 1701-2, and in 1704 was app. gdn. of five ch., all under 14. She m. 2d John Varney. Ch: **John**, a captive in Canada, given the name Jean Baptiste, was recorded as the s. of Richard Otis, deceased, and Anna Otis, living, when he m. 1st in 1703 Cecile Poulin who d. 27 Apr. 1731; m. 2d 9 Feb. 1733 Marie Francoise Gagné; d. at Baie St. Paul 16 Sept. 1760. 1 + 6 ch. **Richard**, Charlestown in 1722, m. 1st Grace Hayman, m. 2d 2 Nov. 1714 Grace Smith at Watertown, m. 3d in Boston 3 June 1724 Sarah Dady. **Rebecca**, b. 11 July 1695, m. Richard Canney. **Stephen**, Madbury, weaver, b. 22 Aug. 1698, m. 1st 22 Feb. 1719-20 Mary Young, m. 2d 29 July 1736 Catherine Austin, m. 3d one Elizabeth who surv. Will, 1759, 4 ch. and ano. expected.

**Rose. Nicholas**, b. 8 Apr. 1701, tailor in Newport, R. I.

3 **STEPHEN**(1), Dover, ±33 in 1685, m. 16 Apr. 1674 Mary Pitman(11). In ct. for beating John Douglas 1685. Jury 1685. Lists 59, 96, 99 (p. 75), 359b. He was k. in the attack of 28 June 1689, and as his w.'s name does not appear again she may have shared his fate. Ch: **Stephen**, taken captive in 1689 and named Joseph Marie as a Cath. convert in Canada. He m. Louise 'Arel.' Liv. in Quebec in 1710 when he conv. to his br. Paul all rights in New Eng. Prob. later liv. in Lorette where his desc. became Huron tribesmen. List 99 (p. 158). **Nathaniel**, also a captive convert, took name of Paul. He m. 1st at Quebec 3 Nov. 1710 Marie Elizabeth Wabert (Michael Webber of Casco), who d. ab. 9 Sept. 1721; m. 2d 20 Oct. 1721 Madeleine Toupin who d. Oct. 1722; m. 3d 19 Sept. 1728 wid. Marie Anne (Perthius) Caron. He d., a master-cooper, in Montreal, ag. ab. 46, 24 Dec. 1730. He had released his int. to his fa.'s Dover prop. to his br.-in-law Ebenezer Varney in 1714. 7 + 1 + 2 ch. List 99 (pp. 159-164). **Mary**, m. Ebenezer Varney.

**Overzee**, see Voysey.

**OWEN, 1 John**, Portsmouth mariner, adm. 2 May 1704 to wid. Margaret, Geo. Jaffrey and Richard Wibird bondsm.

2 **RICHARD** (ap Owen). List 66.

3 **WILLIAM** (Owins). List 98.

**Pachecho**, Moses, engaged to pay James Randall 6½ bbls. molasses for a horse in Nov. 1668; wit. by Greenland and Geo. Norton.

**PACK. 1 John**, Great Island wit. 1669.

2 **NICHOLAS**, Kennebec soldier 1688. List 189.

**Packard**, Edmund, Mr., Shoals 1660. List 302a.

## PACKER

1 **CHARLES**, mariner, Portsmouth, in 1701 sued Elizabeth Eburne (her bondsm. Dr. Packer) for dry goods sold her in 1698, and Joshua Pierce for dry goods sold him at the ho. of (2) in 1698. Asst. Seizing Port Officer 1701.

2 ‡*THOMAS, Dr., Col., Esq., Portsm., b. ±1659 prob. in Eng., came to N. H. from Salem where his w. Hephsibah (Drake, m. in Marbleh. 23 Aug. 1681) d. -22 Jan. 1684- ag. 25 yrs. 5 mos. Of Salem, he m. 2d 7 Aug. 1687 wid. Elizabeth Hall(13). List 335a. He m. 3d in Marbleh. 1 Jan. 1719-20 Frances Noline who surv. him. Taxed Portsm. Oct. 1691; selectm. 1694, 1717; called Capt. 1694; Col. 1696; as -Capt.- lic. 1700; Justice Super. Ct. Judic. 1717; Rep. 1718, 1719 (Speaker); Councillor 1719. Lists 324, 330d, 332b, 335a, 337, 338c, 339, 57, 66, 68, 98. He d. 1 Oct. 1723. See N. H. Prob. 2: 197 (also 4: 214) for agreement betw. his son and dau. Eliza-

beth; the s. had prev. agreed with the older dau. and wid. Ch. by 1st w. at Salem (the daus. dead in Mar. 1752): **Susanna**, d. 21 Oct. 1683. **Susanna**, b. -1 Feb. 1684-5-, m. 1st Joseph Small, m. 2d bef. 18 May 1726 Benj. Rust. By 2d w: **Elizabeth**, m. Henry Deering(4 jr.). **Thomas**, Portsm., High Sheriff, b. ±1699, m. 1st 2 Jan. 1728-9 Rebecca Wentworth (Lt. Gov. John), who d. in Sept. 1738 (2 sons); m. 2d betw. 1740-1750 Ann (Odiorne 4) Rindge, who d. 12 Jan. 1762, ag. 61; m. 3d by 1764 Martha (Hilton 14 jr.) Pearson. He d. 22 June 1771 in 72d yr. (gr.st.), and s. Thomas contested his will giving his prop. to Gov. John Wentworth.

**Packett**, John, Casco, d. under suspicious circumstances bef. 25 June 1640. See Cole (9), (28).

**Padden** (Padon) Thomas. See Patten.

**PADDY, William**, Boston, owner and partner with Valentine Hill and Richard Leader in dam and mill on Lamprill River, 1657. See also Lamprey(3). And note Pafat.

**PAFAT, Francis.** Six Exeter bondsm. failed to bring him to Salisb. ct. in Apr. 1664 to meet charge of Margaret Dudley(1); ord. to pay for the child's keep. John Gilman had a constable's charge against him in 1679. Poss. he was the man-servant Francis Paddy (also Pavett) whom Geo. Felt bot from James Lane on his return from Eng., who stole from Felt's s. bef. 1659, ran away to R. I., and aft. imprisonment was sent eastward.

**PAGE**, confined to south half of Eng., particularly eastern counties.

1 **ANTHONY**, Dover, taxed 1663 and 1666, but gone in 1664. Lists 356hk.

2 **DEA. FRANCIS**(6), Hampton, m. 2 Dec. 1669 Meribah Smith (Robert). Selectm. 1677-8, 1695; tr.j. 1678; gr.j. 1682 and often, foreman 1694; moderator 1689, 1695, 1701, 1703, 1705. Ag. ±66 in Feb. 1699-1700. Lists 392b, 393b, 394, 396, 336c, 49, 52, 54, 55ab, 62. Will, 14 Nov.—2 Dec. 1706, names w. and ch: Lt. **Samuel**, b. 3 Mar. 1670-1, m. 1st 9 Jan. 1696 Hannah Williams, who d. 24 Dec. 1701, m. 2d 18 Nov. 1702 Anne Marshall (see 2); m. 3d 8 Mar. 1725-6 Mary (Smith) Thomas. 15 ch., at least 3 by 1st w. His will, 30 Apr. 1747 (d. 4 Dec. 1754), names w. Mary, 4 sons, 2 daus. and gr.ch. **Lucy**, b. 22 Sept. 1672, m. Ichabod Robie(2). **Susanna**, b. 20 Dec. 1674, m. 1st Benj. Batchelder(2), m. 2d John Cram (1). **Francis**, b. 14 Dec. 1676, m. 27 Jan. 1698 Hannah Nudd(2), who d. 12 Apr. 1751. Liv. at Little River. Lists 66, 399a. Will, 26 Apr. —8 Sept. 1755, names 1 son, 3 daus. liv., gr.s. Reuben Dearborn (mo. deed.), s.-in-law Wm. Locke. **Meribah**, b. 17 Mar. 1679, m. 1st Josiah Shaw, m. 2d Samuel Tilton, m. 3d Benj. Sanborn. **Rebecca**, b. 24 Nov. 1681, m.

Samuel Palmer(20 jr.). **Joseph**, b. 5 Nov. 1686, m. 14 Dec. 1721 Sarah Moulton, liv. at Little River, and d. 5 Feb. 1773, 9 ch.

3 **GEORGE**(7), too young to be bound out in 1645 but must have liv. with Mr. John Smith at Dunstan. He m. in Sept. or Oct. 1664 Mary Edgecomb(2) and dwelt near Saco River. Deputy constable 1666-7; helped lay out the upper way to Dunstan in 1674 and the Cape Porpus highway in 1681. Salem in Sept. 1677, deposing there in June 1678, ±36, ab. being on a lighter at Boston. At home, he appr. the Edgecomb est. 1681; selectman, 1683; j. 1685-6; he and John Sharp to see the new meet.-ho. shingled in 1686. Lists 235, 245c, 249. In the next war the fam. went to Marbleh., where his wid. m. 2d John Ashton(1). Ch. appear: **George**, ag. 6 in 1673 or 1674 when Mr. John Smith named him his heir; granted adm. on the Smith est. 1694. At Marbleh. in 1720 he sold his double right to his fa.'s land adj. Edgecomb's; dead in 1727. Poss. ch: Jane, m. in Marbleh. 31 Jan. 1711-2 Timo. Cummings. Sarah, m. there 20 Jan. 1717-8 Ambrose Grant. **Susannah**, m. at Marbleh. 3 Nov. 1698 John Prideaux. **Mary**, m. Joseph Ashton(1). **Christopher**, Marbleh., m. Mary Dutch, who m. 2d 25 Jan. 1713-4 Joseph Ashton(1). 2 ch. rec. Marbleh: Mary, b. 1710 and Abigail, both bp. 1716.

4 **JOHN**, 1686. See Howard(2).

5 **PAUL**, Kennebec soldier 1688. List 189.

6 **DEA. *ROBERT**, Hampton, s. of Robert and Margaret (Goodwin), reached Boston from Ormesby St. Margaret, co. Norfolk, 8 June 1637, ag. 33, with w. Lucy, ag. 30, 3 ch., and servants Wm. Moulton(21) and Anne Wadd aged 15, supposed to have been his wife's sis. (see Colcord 1), and went to Salem. N. E. Reg. 66: 180 has his Eng. ancestry; see also 69: 342. Hampt. by the 2d summer. Selectm. 8 times 1644-1671; allowed to build sawmill at Taylor's River 1656; Rep. 1657, 1668; marshal of co. of Norfolk; deacon 1660 to death; moderator 1667-8. Ag. 58, also ±59, in 1660; ±75 in Nov. 1676. Lists 391a, 392ab, 393ab, 394, 53. His w. Lucy d. 12 Nov. 1665, ag. 58. List 393a. His will, 9 Sept. (d. 22 Sept. ag. 75) 1679, names all ch. but Susanna, and many gr.ch. Ch: **Margaret**, m. 1st Wm. Moulton(21), m. 2d John Sanborn. **Francis**, b. ±1633. **Susanna**, came with parents. **Thomas**, bp. at Salem 1 Sept. 1639. **Rebecca**, bp. with Thos., m. Wm. Marston(11). **Hannah**, m. Capt. Henry Dow(3). **Mary**, b. ±1643-4, m. Samuel Fogg(4).

7 **THOMAS**, gentleman, tailor, Saco, from All Saints Stayning, London, arriv. at Boston in the -Increase- the last of July, 1635, ag. 29, bringing w. Elizabeth, ag. 28, 2 ch., and servants Edw. Sparkes, ag. 22, Katherine Taylor, ag. 24. Taxed in Saco Sept.

1636; sued John Richmond 1637; both tr. and gr.j. 1640. In Mar. 1640-1 he drew a bill of exchange for £40 on Mr. Christopher Phillin of Fanchurch St., London, payable to Mr. John Huxton of Wapping. Lists 242, 22. Dead 21 Oct. 1645. Ch. appear: **Thomas**, ag. 2, and **Katherine**, ag. 1, in Apr. 1635. **Mary**, bound to John Smith for 5 yrs. in 1645; m. Anthony Littlefield(2). **Christopher**, bound to Henry Waddock for 10 yrs. in 1645. His est. on Stratton Isl. apprais. 20 June 1667, incl. a boat and clothing. **Sylvester**, bound to Thos. Williams for 13 yrs. in 1645 and with him in 1654; liv. Aug. 1655. **George**, b. ±1641-2.

8 **THOMAS** (appar. 7), Cape Elizabeth, charged with Sabbath breaking in 1681; alive in Oct. 1683; List 226. He liv. and d. on the south side of Alewive Cove Brook, where his wid. and ch. liv. aft. him until driven away, evid. to Gloucester. Only 2 ch. proven, but perh. also **Tobias**, List 226. Cert: **George**, had w. Joanna and dau. Mary, b. at Antigua 16 Nov. 1705 and recorded at Glouc. where she m. Nathl. Travis, seaman, 28 Apr. 1727. Joanna, d. at Glouc. 7 Sept. 1707, likely his w. or ano. dau. In 1734 Nathl. and Mary Trafass, she dau. of George, decd., and only surv. heir of her gr.fa. Thos., deeded Falm. rights. **Joseph**, claimed the Cape Eliz. land where his fa. liv. 35 yrs. agone. He m. in Glouc. 6 Dec. 1705 Elizabeth Row; d. there 18 Mar. 1724-5, ag. ±48. Son rec., **Thomas**, b. and d. 1706. In Glouc. also were rec. ints., Mary with Wm. Bardens, seaman, 26 Dec. 1722; Mary with Philip Hammons 23 Aug. 1723. Note too ints. of Joseph P. and Margaret Rule in Boston 13 Nov. 1695.

9 **THOMAS**(6), Hampton, m. 2 Feb. 1664 Mary Hussey(1) and liv. on the homestead. Selectm. 1670. Lists 392b, 396, 52, 55a. Will, 31 Aug. (d. 8 Sept., gr.st.) 1686, names w. Mary, 5 surv. ch. She m. 2d Henry Green, Esq.(7), m. 3d Capt. Henry Dow(3), and d. 21 Jan. 1733, ag. 94, called in a Boston obit. 'a gracious gentlewoman.' Ch: **Mary**, b. 21 Mar. 1664-5, m. Samuel Robie(5). **Robert**, b. 17 July 1667, d. 25 July 1686 (gr. st.). **Christopher**, b. 20 Sept. 1670, m. 14 Nov. 1689 Abigail Tilton (Daniel); liv. on homestead. Gr.j. 1693-94; jury 1700; selectman 1700 and later. List 57. Will, 16 Aug. 1740—27 Feb. 1750-1, names w. Abigail (d. 5 Oct. 1759) and 8 of 9 ch: Robert (not in will), Abigail Moulton, Mary Dow(9 jr.), Lydia Towle, Jonathan, David, Shubael, Jeremiah, Tabitha. **John**, b. 15 Nov. 1672, named in a deed given by his mo. in 1714 'if he come to these parts to receive it.' Liv. Nantucket and Cape May. **Theodate**, b. 8 July 1675, d. 14 Aug. 1676. **Stephen**, b. 14 Aug. 1677, m. 3 Jan. 1701 Mary Rollins(6), she liv. 1722. His will, 26 Jan. 1713-4 (inv.

30 Mar. 1714), names her and ch: Thomas, Hannah, John, Rachel, Mary. **Bethia**, b. 23 May 1679, m. 3 Dec. 1696 John Swett.

10 **TOBIAS**, 1683, List 226, poss. son of (8).

11 **URIAH**, List 298. See James Gray(4).

**PAINE**, Payne. The S. E. quarter of Eng. its great home; co. Suffolk sent several to N. E. where it became the 95th commonest name.

1 **CORNELIUS**, at Merrymeeting Bay 1669 when Terra Magnus was a boy. List 161. See also (8).

2 **EDWARD**, from Essex Co. and cous. of (19), sued Wm. Bellew of Dover ±1643 and in 1644 got judg. for a ho. once Michael Chatterton's. Dead in Nov. 1645, when his assignee Wm. Paine sued Richard Waldron in Essex ct. See Essex Q. Ct. Rec. vol. i.

3 **GEORGE**, wit. will of Audrey Lux(6) 1688.

4 **HENRY**, fisherman, Newcastle, taxed 1708 (List 316) and bot there from John Searle in 1715. H. P. and **Son** taxed 1720, this s. poss. the Henry who m. Abigail Seavey in Greenland 4 Mar. 1721-2. See also Mayer(3).

5 **JAMES**, fisherman, Shoals 1664, Portsm. 1670. Gr.j. 1683. Taxed Great Isl. 1684-1691 and worked six days at Fort Wm. and Mary in 1694. Lists 303, 326c, 313a, 331b, 52, 319, 66. He d. bef. Oct. 1695 when Aaron Ferris deeded to his wid. Martha the Great Isl. ho. and garden spot already in her poss. In 1718 she deeded to only kn. ch: **Martha**, w. of Foster Trefethen.

6 **JOHN**, one or two. At Casco, a wit. in the James Cole case 1640 and fined that yr. for swearing. J. P. and Henry Webb wit. Cousins to Bray 1651 (Y. D. 3: 37). John, appar. of No. Yarm., was travelling on Sunday in Oct. 1667. Stephen Larrabee and J. P. deeded lands to Thos. Redding which his s. sold in 1715 (Y. D. 9: 32); in this connec. is noted the marriage of Stephen Larrabee(5 jr.) and Margaret P. in Boston 10 Jan. 1704; also that of Abigail P. and Miles Thompson 9 Nov. 1704.

7 **JOHN**, summonsed in the Dickinson case 1668, poss. a Mass. man. List 357a.

8 **JOHN**, at Merrymeeting Bay with (1), wit. deeds to Walter Phillips in 1674 and 1676 (John Brown ano. wit. each time), and was at Mr. Gardiner's ho. at Pemaquid ab. Nov. that yr. when Roderigo was there. It may have been ano. Mr. J. P. of Harwich who wit. Parker deeds 1684-5; was Mr. Randolph's deputy 1686 with whom all ships entering the Kennebec were to register; selectman 1688; Lt. 1689, and signed a Sagadahoc ptn. 25 Jan. 1689-90. Lists 161, 18, 190. See also Doc. Hist. 6: 424, 432, 480.

9 **JOHN**, mariner, Portsm., m. Hannah Davis (61), who was a shopkeeper. In 1747 he deeded land and bldgs. to s. **John**, the 'only ch. as yet,' and was liv. 1762. The s. chose Joseph Buss gdn. in 1752, and, a joiner, ch. s.p. and unm. at Jamaica in 1758. His aunt Buss ptn. that adm. be gr. to her two ch. Joseph B. and Hannah Horney, wid.

10 **NICHOLAS**, a York wit. 1667, Kit. or Portsm. 1670 (Y. D. 2: 33, 18). Roger Kelly sued him in 1670, Nathan Bedford in 1672 and again in 1678, action of review, when John Kettle and Thos. Rice were his bondsmen.

11 **PHILIP**, mariner, Portsm., form. of Jersey, was sued in 1700 by Dr. Labourne who had cured his leg. Taxed for Mill Dam 1707-1712; bot on Little Harbor side of Newcastle 1712-3 and moved there; taxed 1717; both Philip and John taxed 1724-5. His w. Christian (Ball 7) was rec. into cov. and bp. at No. Ch. 2 Oct. 1709. In 1738, of Rye, he deeded 15 a. to s. **John**, who was to pay his bros. **William** and **Amos**, these three bp. at No. Ch. 28 May 1710. He d. in Apr. 1746; adm. to s. John 25 June fol., when the s. Amos was in New York; left 3 sons, no. wid. Christian P. of Portsm., -wife- of John, bound to the peace towards Mary Bartlett in -1747-, may be error in date or meant for the younger John's dau.

12 **RICHARD**, Mr., Great Isl., test. 23 Jan. 1678 to what he heard Abisha Taprill say; also a wit. in the Gove case in 1683, ±37, and signed a Sheepscot pet. in 1684 as mastmaker and purser for His Majesty's use in Eng. (List 163). A Kit. wit. Nov. 1686, proved bef. Hinckes in June 1687. Of Newichawannock, shipwright, he was bondsm. for Sarah (Taylor) (Canney 4) Wingate in Nov. 1687-8 and m. her bef. July 1693, when, of Boston, he gave her p/a. Both of Boston 26 May 1705, where she d. 23 Dec. 1707 and he at Mr. Kenney's ho. 18 Apr. 1708, ag. 72. His will, very aged, 19 Mar.—24 Apr. 1708, gives his Boston ho. to cous. Thos. Pain of Rotherhithe, co. Surrey, or, if he die, to s.-in-law Samuel Kenney; ano. Boston ho. to S. K. and w. Abigail, and a third to Paine Wingate. See also Wyman's Charlestown, 2: 722.

13 **ROBERT**, Mr., feoffee in trust for Mrs. Ann Godfrey 1661-2; P. & Ct. Rec. ii: 100, 114. See also (14).

14 **REV. ROBERT**, Wells, s. of 'Elder' Robert of Ipswich, who was County Treas. 1665-1683; note (13). Altho of H. C. 1656, and a minister, the son is unseen over long periods. In Mar. 1665, Saco voted to send for him and pay necess. charges for his coming and going and while there; but he was evid. not a candidate, as in May Mr. Chauncey was chosen by 24 votes to Mr. Fletcher's

11. In Sept. 1667 he was engaged for 5 yrs. by Wells, where Bourne says, unlike his predecessor Mr. Hubbard, he did not claim rights or privilege, but only necess. compensation. He took to Wells a w., Elizabeth (Reynor), m. in Ipsw. 10 July 1666. Wit. John Wadleigh's will 7 July 1671. Later he was in Ipsw. at times, perh. perma., and Upham (2: 449) says was 'prob. foreman of the gr.j. that brought in all indictments in the witchcraft trials' at Salem in 1692. Liv. late in the 1690's and Judge Savage evid. noted him in 1704. Probably ch. b. in Me., but Ipsw. records all kn: **Elizabeth**, b. 16 June 1677, m. in Ipsw. 29 June 1702 Daniel Smith. **John**, b. 24 Oct. 1684. **Robert**, d. Dec. 1693.

15 **THOMAS**, Mr., trader, Dover (grant 1659), Newcastle. Kept Waldron's trucking ho. at Pennacook in 1668 when Thos. Dickinson(2) was k., and as late trader among Ind. there was fined in 1669 for selling them liquor; fined again for selling to Ind. in 1676. The first war sent him to Newe. tempo., the second permanently. Ho.-owner and taxed there 1690; retailer 1692-3; selectman 1696; cor.j. 1697, abs. from meeting that yr. Lists 356eghk, 357ad, 359ab, 331b, 52, 94, 319, 318ab, 315abc. His will, 27 Oct. 1694—22 Aug. 1700, gives all to w. Elizabeth for supp. of self and ch., all minors, and for their education. She m. 2d Richard Beazer (1). Ch: **Thomas**, York, b. by 1684, had the Cochecho, Berwick and Salmon F. lands, and of Newe. 1705, sold the Cochecho prop. his fa. bot from Richard Waldron in 1683. He m. at Sherborn 23 Jan. 1706-7 Mary Gookin (Rev. Daniel) and was at York by 1720. Lists 316, 279. Will, 12 June—19 Oct. 1742, names w. Mary and ch: Thomas, Daniel, Elizabeth, Mary Bradbury, Jane, Sarah. **Jane**, m. George Blagdon(1). **Elizabeth**, m. Nathan Raynes(4). **Catherine**, m. Francis Raynes(4). **Ann**, accus. her sister's husb. Geo. Blagdon, ct. Mar. 1717-8; m. 1st Joseph Preble(6 jr.), m. 2d Norton Woodbridge.

16 **THOMAS**, servant and legatee of Mrs. Ann Batchelder(1) in 1660; James Leach took over the bal. of his time to learn weaving in 1661.

17 **THOMAS**, York, likely the man abs. from meet. in July 1674 (Scarboro cases) and wit. Wm. Haines(17) to Geo. Felt in 1675, going to York in wartime with No. Yarm. men. York gr. 1679, 1683; O. A. 17 Mar. 1679-80; York wit. 1685, Bray to Atwell. Note also (16), (18). He m. bef. May 1685 Elizabeth Milbury(1); prob. it was she not his -dau.- slandered by John Brawn jr. in Feb. 1684 (see Hatch 3). Both were k. in the Candlemas Day massacre 1691-2 (Hist. of York 1: 271). Ch: **Bethia**, taken to Canada when her parents were k. and ret. to Casco Bay in Jan. 1698-9; List 99, p. 78. **Of**

York 5 Dec. 1711, unm., she deeded her fa.'s 1683 gr. to Richard Milbury, with full warr. Appar. m. Joseph Preble(6 jr.). **Samuel**, called a captive with his sis., but no rec. of him found in Canada. Their gr.fa. Milbury willed 10 s. apiece to them in 1695.

18 **THOMAS**, signed a Falm. ptn. in May 1689; List 228c.

19 **WILLIAM**, Mr. (Lists 323, 330a), and s. **John** (List 364), Ipswich and Boston merchants, with many interests northward and often found in the records. See also (2), Howard(10), Pendleton(1). Mr. John's inv., Boston, 21 Feb. 1693-4, incl. 600 a. at Tole End, Dover, purch. from Thos. Wiggin, and 500 a. near Edw. Hilton's sawmill that Mr. Wm. P. purchased.

20 **WILLIAM**, Gloucester, and Michael Webber, wit. for Joseph Page(8) bef. the East. Cl. Com.; see White. See also Dennen.

21 ——, of 'Canebeck,' d. at ho. of Capt. Thos. Lake(3) in Boston 15 Feb. 1663-4.

**Palfrey**, Peter, Salem, an early partn. in Eastern trading ho. with Anthony Pike and Francis Johnson(11). See also Foxwell (5).

**PALMER.** Essentially an East of Eng. name, tho many in cos. Devon and Somerset. Became 50th commonest name in N. E.

1 **SERGT. BENJAMIN**, Kittery. List 289. See also (25).

2 **BENJAMIN**, Stratham, with Thos. Rollins bondsm. in 1701 for Sarah, w. of Benj. Rollins(6); sued Jona. Norris 1708, sued by Geo. Chesley 1709; in 1712 gave a note to Mrs. Scott later Hinckes; bot adj. Nathl. Folsom and Wm. Norris in 1722. Old B. P. d. in Strath. 20 Apr. 1750. List 388. Note also (4).

3 **CHRISTOPHER**(22), Hampton, ±33 in 1660, ±43 in 1671, ±50 in 1674. In May 1699, ±73, he claimed he knew who liv. in the Great Ho. at Little Harbor under Mason. His fa. contracted with Hampt. in May 1640 for him to keep the calves. Acting for wid. Ann P. in 1647, and m. 7 Nov. 1650 Susanna Hilton(1); Lists 392c, 394. In 1652 he sued Hampt. for land gr. to his fa. and detained from him. Thereaft. freq. juror, wit. or party to suit (Essex Q. Ct. Rec. vols. 1-7). Selectm. 1655, 1677-8, 1681, 1692, 1697; called Corporal 1671. Lists 392bc, 393a, 396, 52, 54, 55b. See also (14). He d. 30 June 1699; s. Samuel cited in Mar. 1706-7 to adm. or renounce in favor of principal cr. Theodore Atkinson; return made 'non est inventus.' Wid. Susanna d. 9 Jan. 1716-7, ag. 82. In 1698 he deeded homestead to sons **Samuel**, b. 25 Nov. 1652, and **Joseph**. This, with the insolv. est., blocks knowl. of other ch., but likely seem **John**, sent to defense of Marl-

boro in 1676, and a wit. for Thos. Philbrick in 1678 (Dow, p. 224, and List 395), and **Benjamin**, twice a wit. for Christopher in 1679 (Essex Q. Ct. Rec. 7: 216-7); Christopher's son's est. 1680, List 396, may be one of these two; Palmer, List 395, may be anyone.

4 **ELIZABETH**, ±37 in Nov. 1685, testif. about Ichabod and John Rollins; she took care of Matthew Nelson's ho. and other concerns at Long Reach, Dover. Note also (2).

5 **GEORGE**, wine cooper, ±43 in 1663, Boston 1655, Kit. 1657, where in 1661 Barefoot entered a caution concerning land he, Edge and others had settled on. Freq. in ct. on varied charges, incl. an attack on John Billings with a knife. In 1663 he gave Capt. Shapleigh a bond, pledging ⅓ his est. in Boston or elsewhere; in Sept. 1666 his bondsman Captain Lockwood could not get him thither, tho in Oct. he sold Greenland a ho. and 100 a. bot from Barefoot; in Mar. fol. gave bond for his appearance, and of Kit. in July 1667 gave p/a to friend Roger Deering. His w. Elizabeth appears 1657-1666; in 1660 Boston ct. acquitted her of adult., leaving York ct. to deal with her for drunkenness. Richard Norton, Boston, called her husb. 'brother' and he was indebted to the Norton est. in 1657. He was dead and adm. gr. 25 Apr. 1670 to James Neighbors of Boston who had taken a mtge. on his Boston ho. in 1657; in July 1670 as adm. he unsuc. sued Digory Jeffrey and Wm. Broad for the Kit. ho. and land. No kn. ch.

6 **HENRY**, Haverhill, whose dau. **Mehitable** m. Samuel Dalton(3), wit. Dalton to Batchelder in 1657; Rishworth ano. witness.

7 **HENRY**(8?), took O. F. July 1674; liv. 1680. Lists 15, 4.

8 ‡**JOHN**, Monhegan, partn. in a fishing voyage 1661 (Essex Q. Ct. Rec. 5: 108). As 'Sr.' named one of five Associates for Devonshire in 1675. On the island 21 Aug. 1676 (Doc. Hist. 6: 119) and owned there with John Dollen(2) in 1686 (Y. D. 9: 230). A refugee at Charlestown in Oct. 1689. Lists 13, 15. Presum. his sons: **John**, jr. (11) and **Henry**(7). It has been suspected that the Marblehead Palmers derive from him.

9 **JOHN**, fisherman, Dunstan, Boston, b. ±1640, m. Elizabeth Alger(1) and had deed from the Algers of the 50 a. he was liv. on, 15 July 1662. He apprais. Giles Robert's est. 1661; Francis Hooke sued him for debt 1664; he and Robt. Nicholson quarreled over marsh 1670-4. Selectm. 1671. Boston 1679, adm. inhab. 1682. His ptn. to Andros stated that R. Elliot had fenced his 50 a. marriage portion that he had cleared by hard labor and liv. on -10- yrs. until driven away. Lists 235, 238a. See also Benmore(1). His will, 2

(bur. in Boston 7) July 1707, gives all to w. Elizabeth. Hers, of Boston, 11 Dec. 1717—21 Aug. 1732, gives all to daus. Abigail and Arminall, and names dau. Alice and 3 sons-in-law. Ch: **Elizabeth**, m. in Woburn 27 Dec. 1682, John Russell. **Mary**, m. by 1685 Eliah Tottingham (Totman) of Woburn. **Alice**, m. in Woburn 27 Feb. 1685 Joseph Covwell (Covill). **John**, seaman, b. Boston 28 Aug. 1679; adm. to fa. 28 Dec. 1705. **Abigail**, b. Boston 6 Feb. 1685, m. there 12 May 1709 Abraham Wacom. **Arminall**, b. Boston 4 Mar. 1687, m. there 15 Nov. 1709 Daniel Morse. In 1694 Ann, dau. of one John, Bost. fisherman, accus. Richard Collicott of Bost., who ackn. he had promised to mar. her. See also Cleverly.

10 **JOHN**, Exeter, worked in the mills. List 380. In Apr. 1669, ±26, he worked for Nicholas Lissen loading hay; in Oct. 1671, ±27, testif. in the Judith Robie case. Three yrs. later he or ano. John turned up in York, abs. from meet. Inv. (or d.) 27 Apr. 1677, livestock, food, pots and hooks. He owed Arthur Bragdon sr.; had given his horse to Nathl. Preble's s. and sold his colt to Jos. Sayward.

11 **JOHN**, jr., 1674, List 15; presum. s. of (8). Note too Ann, Boston, under (9).

12 **JOHN**, Mr., Falmouth, wit. Mrs. Harvey to Thaddeus Clark in July 1680, assisted in running the line betw. Mr. Robert Lawrence and the town of Falm. in Sept. 1684, and m. Mary Munjoy bef. 19 May 1686 when her br. Pelatiah chose him gdn. Tobias Oakman depos. that they liv. in her fa.'s stone ho. on Peaks or Pond Isl. Member of Sylvanus Davis's Co., 1689 (wounded). With others he signed a Falm. letter 28 Aug. 1689 and 11 Nov. fol. was one of the Council of War at Scarboro. Lists 225a, 35, 228bcd. His ho. and flake yard with accommo. for two vessels at Peaks Isl. were claimed by Mr. Joyliffe in 17—.

13 **JOHN**, Esq., a New York magistrate and official at Pemaquid under Andros. Lists 16, 124, 186. See also Y. D. 6: 58.

14 **JOSEPH**(22), appar. not brought up in Hampt., chose br. Christopher and Walter Roper of Ipsw. gdns. in 1661; in 1662 they sued several Newb. men for detaining prop. formerly his fa.'s, then his by gr. from John Sherman in 1661. He m. in Newb. 1 Mar. 1664 Sarah Jackman and d. in Bradford 8 Feb. 1715 in 72d yr. Will, 5 Feb. 1714, names w. Sarah, 3 sons als liv., s.-in-law Jona. Chase, dau. Rowling's ch., s. Joseph's ch. Ch. rec. Newb. 1665—1670: **Sarah**. If she was dau. Rollins and Benj. Rollins(6) was her husb., she was 13 yrs. his sr. Poss. she d. y. and there was another unrec. Sarah nearer Benjamin's age. **James**, blacksmith, m. 31 Dec. 1690 Elizabeth Groth(1) and bot in Strath-

am 1715; List 388. Will, of Stratham, 20 Aug. 1739—26 Mar. 1740, names w. Sarah and 4 of 6 ch. rec. in Bradford, but not Groth of Newmarket 1758, who must have been a gr.son. **Joseph**. Rec. Bradford 1672-1686: **Benjamin**, d.y. **Richard**, m. in Hampt. 18 Oct. 1704 Martha Downer(1); 9 ch. rec. Bradford. **William**, not in will. **Joanna**, m. (int. Newb. 11 July 1702) Ens. Jonathan Chase of Newb. and Stratham. **Mary**, 1683-1688. **Samuel**, fa.'s exec.

15 **JOSEPH**(3), Hampt., m. 25 Jan. 1677 Deborah Batchelder(3); liv. on the homestead. Lists 396, 52, 55b. In May 1694 Deborah, ±37, and Abial Marston, ±41, testified concerning Danl. Gott(2). Ch., all but Joseph and Ruth in a 1747 writ (20468): **Samuel**, b. 17 Dec. 1677, d. 25 Jan. 1761 in 84th yr. (gr.st.), m. 1st 28 May 1701 Abigail Dearborn(2) who d. 19 May 1747 ag. 68 (gr. st.); m. 2d 16 Nov. 1748 Martha Webber who d. 16 Jan. 1757, ag. 64. 6 ch. **Deborah**, b. 28 Apr. 1679, m. Samuel Moulton(12). **Susanna**, b. 16 Dec. 1681, m. Wm. Marston(8). **Joseph**, ±17 in 1701. Joseph Moulton deeded to him in 1713; liv. 1717. **Ruth**, b. 31 Aug. 1686. **Elizabeth**, b. 5 May 1692, m. Joseph Brown; both liv. Rye 1747. **Edward**, b. 12 Apr. 1694, m. in Greenl. 24 Mar. 1724-5 Bethiah Philbrick. She was dism. to Hampt. F. Ch., thence to new Ch. at Kensington, where he was liv. 1747. 2 ch. bp. Hampt. F. 1726-30. **William**, No. Hampt., bp. 26 June 1698, d. 19 Nov. 1776, m. 8 Feb. 1726 Hannah Sanborn (Stephen), who was dism. to Strath. Ch. 1760, and d. 8 Dec. 1776. 4 ch. rec. **Christopher**, b. 15 Feb. 1700, d. 11 Dec. 1775, m. at Hampt. F. 14 May 1729 Elizabeth Stanyan (Jacob) who d. 14 Dec. 1787. 4 ch. rec. **Mary**, w. of Joseph Moulton 1747.

16 **JOSEPH** (and James Webb), resisted the fort men boarding Capt. Long's ship at Newc. 1694. One Joseph in N. H. prison for debt, ptn. in 1703 for a new trial; he had been dispossessed of his freehold and his fam. impoverished.

17 **MARY**, wit. Withers to Rowland Williams, 1679 (Y. D. 4: 5).

18 **RICHARD**, Cape Porpus, wit. a Sanders deed in Oct. 1670, and was fined 4 July 1671 for marrying Grace (Sanders) Bush (1) when under fame of having a w. in Eng. They liv. on the land her first husb. deeded to Maj. Pendleton retaining a life int. for both. With George Pa(ge) bondsm. for James Harmon 1673; tav. lic. 1674. He was at Cape P. in 1677 when the Huff haycocks were taken, but of Great Isl. 1677-8. Lists 313a, 331b. Late of Cape P. 20 May 1680, he and Grace sold Elias Stileman half a ho., flakeroom and mooring, owned in partnersh. with Robert Williams and form. in poss. of James Pendleton; wit. and ackn. bef. Wm.

Vaughan. Presum. the York man who sued Thos. Doughty 1685; York cor.j. 1685. No ch. appear. See (23).

19 **ROBERT**, Newcastle 1695; prosec. in Dec. 1699 for fencing the highway. Lists 315b, 318c.

20 **SAMUEL**(3), mariner, Hampt., m. Ann Sanborn (Lt. John) who d. 4 Oct. 1745. He was liv. Mar. 1706-7; appar. dead 1724. Lists 52, 399a. Ch. (N. H. deed 33: 161): **Samuel**, Esq., b. ±1685, eldest in 1724, m. 1st 7 Feb. 1717 Deborah Lamprey(1), m. 2d 2 Mar. 1726 Rebecca Page(2) who d. 30 Apr. 1759. He was an 'eminent teacher of Surveying and Navigation and a practical surveyor and conveyancer.' He d. 8 June 1762. Will names 3 of 4 ch. **Christopher**, Rye, b. 12 Feb. 1686-7, liv. 1761, m. 24 July 1705 Elizabeth (Berry 13, by N. H. deed 33: 161); Locke by Rye rec., ibid. i: 95; see Locke 3½). In 1757 he deeded homestead to s. Jonathan (b. 1710), he to pay his br. William (b. 1712). **Stephen**, b. ±1689, m. 2 Dec. 1731 Sarah Cass. 3 ch. rec. **Mary**, b. 9 June 1691, m. Isaac Philbrick(2). **Jonathan**, b. 26 Mar. 1698, m. at Hampt. F. 26 Oct. 1725 Anna Brown (Wm. 5); liv. Kensington 1759. 3 ch. bp. Hampt. F. 1731-36. **Martha**, was Scofield in 1724. **Abigail**, unmar. 1724.

21 **SAMUEL**, wit. a Crockett fam. deed 1695 (Y. D. 4: 155); perh. Capt. P. of bark -Mary of Kittery- 1700, stormbound from Barbadoes.

21½ **THOMAS**, see Remick(3).

22 **WILLIAM**, with the first at Hampt., prev. of Watertown and Newb. Freeman 13 Mar. 1638-9; com.t.e.s.c. 1639; gr.j. 1640; hogreeve 1644. Lists 391a, 392a, 393b. In 1645 he deeded his Newb. and Hampt. prop. to John and Martha Sherman in consid. of dau. Martha's release of land in Great Ormesby, co. Norfolk, in which she had an int. of £105; hence likely he was the Wm. of Ormesby St. Margaret cited there in Sept. 1636 for abs. from Ch., who appeared not and was excommun. Wm. of Ormesby m. Mary Stamforth in nearby Ransworth 30 June 1608. See also Essex Q. Ct. Rec. 2: 347-9; N. E. Reg. 69: 342. Liv. 30 May 1647; 6 Oct. fol. his s. Christopher was acting for the wid. Ann, who was a very recent w. if not Joseph's mo. She m. in Newb. 21 Mar. 1649 Francis Plummer; d. there 18 Oct. 1665. Kn. ch: **Martha**, m. Capt. John Sherman of Watertown; he d. 25 Jan. 1690-1, ag. 76; she 7 Feb. 1700-1. 7 ch. 1638-1653. **Edward**, had Hampt. gr. adj. his fa. in 1640. **Christopher**, b. ±1626. **Joseph**, b. ±1643.

23 **WILLIAM**, planter, Kit., was at Str. Bank. 1640, sued by Walton 1649. There in 1651 he sold to Riddan ho. and land bot from Goodm. Chatterton, and went to Kit. where he had earlier connec. (Y. D. 2: 2).

Tr.j. (Me.) 1651; Lower Kit. constable 1661; lot layer 1667. Lists 41, 321, 323, 282, 298, 25. In 1675 he sold ho. and 40 a. at Palmer's Point to Christopher Adams and bot half of Batson's Neck at Cape Porpus and, of York 1683, sold this to Isaac Goodridge. Betw. times he wit. at Portsm. or Gt. Isl. in 1676, viewed a fence with Gowen Wilson in 1678, adm. Wm. King's est. in 1681, bondsm. Henry Brookings and Ephr. Crockett. He d. by 1696. Wife unseen. Kn. ch: **Sarah**, m. Wm. King(16) and in 1669 had marriage portion of 16 or 18 a. near her fa.'s old ho. that was burned. **Rachel**, ag. 3 yrs. 9 mos. 21 Apr. 1670, when her fa. bound her until 20 to Peter Glanfield to bring her up, deeding 12 a. to Glanfield at that time; in 1674 he sold him adjoining land. She testif. in Portsm. in Aug. 1684 conc. Glanfield.

24 **WILLIAM** (also Pamoth, Paymouth), mariner, Great Isl., m. (ct. May 1683) Abishag Lux(6) who was gr. adm. 6 Aug. 1685 and m. 2d Thos. Marshall(9). **?Mary**, w. of Christopher Frederick, and **?Elizabeth**, w. of Tho. Pierce(22), were her ch., either Palmers or Marshalls.

25 ——— Widow, and her **dau.**, Kit. sufferers 1703. List 290. Note (1).

**Pamoth** (Paymouth), William. See Palmer (24).

**Panco**, Sanco. List 312g. A Spanish or Portuguese sailor?

**PAPE**. 1 **George**, Saco cor.j. 1670 (on body of David May), presum. Page.

2 **NICHOLAS**, Mr., sued by Henry Hudson in York ct. July 1661.

**Pappoone**, Jean, a wit. 1674 (Thos. Guptill). A tortured French name?

**PARCHER**, Elias, soldier at Gerrish garrison, Dover, 6 Feb.—9 Mar. 1696; taxed Greenland 1698. Lists 67, 330de. He m. 12 Aug. 1708 Grace Allard(2), who o.c. and was bp. in Greenl. Ch. in 1717 with ch: **George** (Scarboro 1741) and **Deborah** (m. Edmund Webber). In 1725 **Elias**, **Elizabeth** and **Sarah** (Hampt. 1741) were bp. in Greenl. His was an added name on the Grafford Lane (no. side) tax list, 1725.

**Parell**. See Pearl.

**PARKER**, general in Eng. except in cos. Devon and Cornwall. Became 17th commonest name in N. E.

1 **ABRAHAM**(14), York, took O. A. 17 Mar. 1679-80. Indicted for theft in 1690; with w. Sarah abs. from meet. 1696. Grants 1699, 1703, the latter confirming land sold to Maj. Clarke and bot by A. P. from Capt. Job Alcock. See also (6). Adm. 1 Oct. 1706 to s. John and br. John, bondsm. Capt. Lewis Bane and Johnson Harmon. His 2d w. and wid., Sarah (Preble 1), m. 2d Henry Coombs (4). He was 'Sr.' in 1699, but only s. **John**

appears, who settled a differ. with his step-mo. in 1711. In Apr. 1732 he deeded to John Harmon(3 jr.) for life supp. No fam. seen.

2 **AUGUSTIN**, sent as a soldier to Scarboro, List 236. -Factor- in Shoals indictment in Apr. 1681, Parker at trial on Smuttynose in Nov. fol. See also Harding(7).

3 **BASIL**, York, also known as Thos. Brooks (5), which see. Lists 71, 298; also numer. references as Parker in Me. P. & Ct. Rec. vols. i, ii.

4 **DANIEL**(15), Kennebec, Charlestown. Wyman names -John-, w. (Ann who surv.) and dau. from Kennebec at Maj. Phillips' 21 Oct. 1689; they seem rather Daniel, w. Ann (Errington), and dau. He d. there 18 Oct. 1694, ag. 27 (gr.st.). Widow Ann m. 2d John May of Boston, mariner, m. 3d in Boston 22 May 1718 Thos. Coppin; liv. 1722. Ch: **Anne**, b. 4 Nov. 1687, m. Robert Ingalls (Wyman: but Rev. Mr. Thayer thot more likely he m. her aunt Hannah 15); s. Robert b. 1715 in Boston; she a wid. there 1719. **John**, bp. at Charlest. with Anne 22 Feb. 1690-1, is called by Wyman the one who m. 12 Jan. 1713-4 Mary Cutler. 2 ch. bp. 1728: Hannah (m. Wm. Sweetsir) and Stephen; neither noted in Parker deeds. **Isaac**, bp. 4 Dec. 1692, potter, Charlest., m. there 24 May 1715 Grace Hall; d. 7 Nov. 1742, ag. 50 (gr.st.). In 1744 his wid. and exec. called him only surv. gr.s. of John P., late of Kennebec; she liv. 1748. 11 ch., incl. Daniel, whose s. Isaac, H. C. 1786, was Chief Justice of Mass. See also Leighton(3).

5 **GEORGE**, carpenter, York, sold the ho. he was liv. in and enclosed field to Philip Hatch in Nov. 1648, and bef. 1650 bot from John Gooch ±8 a. adj. the Glebe and Henry Norton. York gr. 1653-1672. Tr.j. 1650, 1653; gr.j. 1650, 1651, 1653, 1658; constable 1659. Jeremiah Sheares was indebted to him in 1662, John West in 1663. Lists 273, 275-277, 24, 25. He m. late in life Hannah, appar. wid. of Wm. Johnson(37), and on acct. of their old age and decrepitude deeded all to s.-in-law Peter Bass for their supp. 10 Apr. 1683, the prop. being turned back in 1684 aft. Bass d. His inv. 6 Oct. 1693; adm. 23 Jan. fol. to Samuel Johnson, called his successor. No cert. child; the w. of Peter Bass(2) was a dau. or step-dau. (Johnson).

6 **ISAAC**, planter, York. In Aug. 1679 he bot from John Wentworth (giving back mtg.) two lots orig. Isaac Everest's with a small ho. on one. Francis Johnson sued him in 1680; in 1684 he ack. judg. to Johnson, payable in staves, (1) doing likewise. In 1687 one Isaac, an indent. servant, was beating his master Yeales.

7 **REV. *JAMES**, Portsm., poss. never ordained, first appears wit. delivery of the Saco pat. in June 1631. He left in Eng. two kn. bros. John, haberdasher, Joseph, skinner (b. at Leicester), both of St. Pancras, Soper Lane, London. At Dorchester (1633) and Weymouth (as late as 1641) he was devoted princ. to pub. life, and Str. Bk. named him Deputy 1642-3 aft. inviting him there as minister. From Portsm. he wrote to Winthrop 28 July 1645, telling ab. Roger Garde's death. Lists 241, 53. He was at Barbadoes bef. 24 June 1646 when asked to preach there tempo.; his w. Mary (dau. of Rev. John Maverick; see 1) and ch. joined him and there he d. Will, 1648—1652, names Mr. Richard Vines one exec. and directs his w. to go to N. E. with his ch: **John**. **Azricam**, of Barbadoes, form. of N. E., 1663. **James**, d. in Boston, adm. to Moses Maverick 13 Dec. 1666. **Thomas. Fearnot. Mary.** See Hist. of Weymouth 4: 456; N. E. Reg. 46: 308; 68: 202.

8 **JAMES**, (also Geo. Lewis and Francis Small), wit. R. Jordan's discharge to John Phillips in July 1658. List 221. See also (18).

9 **JAMES** and **JOHN**, Andover soldiers at Scarb., k. 29 June 1677 (Sav.).

10 **JAMES**, Sergt., sold goods from the wrecked -Three Friends- at Casco Bay to Joseph Bean's w. in 1711.

11 **JOHN**, Saco, taxed 1636; creditor of the Williams clapboard est. List 242. He must have given his name to Parker's Neck at the Pool, ment. 1650 (Y. D. 2: 11) and as late as 1733 (Y. D. 14: 56). See also (12), (13).

12 **JOHN**, fisherman, Damariscove, his men at Stratton Island 1645 (see Nash 4), might be consid. (and poss. was) same as (13), were it not for Robert(23). This Robert may or may not have been his son, but was cert. not s. of (13).

13 **JOHN**, fisherman, Sagadahoc, called of Bideford, co. Devon, in deeds given by his gr.chn. Many have placed him here at an entirely unsubstantiated date (1625 to 1628), while his kinsman John Phillips(10), calling him -Thomas- and uncle of his own fa., deposed in 1754 that he came as mate of the first ship from Eng. with the Plymouth people. Others have consid. him, perh. truly, as (11) or (12) or both. Whether or not, he was of Sagadahoc 27 Feb. 1650-1 when he bot Rascohegan, renamed Parker's Isl., from Robin Hood, while the same Ind. 7 May 1661 confirmed at the widow's ho. a deed to him of Sagosett alias Chegoney Isl. in 1648. Y. D. 15: 136 recites that he made a will the last day of Oct. 1651, giving cert. legacies to ch. and the Island and other prop. to w. Mary. She was liv. 28 June 1671. Surv. ch: **Thomas**, eldest s. **John**, b. ±1634. **Mary**, b. ±1639, m. Thomas Webber.

14 **JOHN**, carpenter, York, of Marblehead when he bot a York ho. and land from

John Heard 12 June 1648. See also (5). Prison keeper for the County, confirmed 4 July 1659 (but pub. whipper by 1656), and retired at own request, being ancient, 2 July 1678. Town gr. 1674, 1679. O. A. 22 Mar. 1679-80 (sr.). Lists 275-277, 24, 33. His wife, List 273; see also Adams(18). Robert Edge's w. was slandering her in 1654. He was liv. 21 May 1686, when Henry Dering levied on his prop. because of a judgm. obtained in 1673 for letting Anthony Lamy escape jail. Kn. ch: Mary, m. Wm. Roanes. John, b. ±1644-5. George, jr., sued Wm. Johnson in 1672 for shooting his mare; adm. 11 Sept. 1677 to fa. John sr.; no household goods or land in inv. The same day John sr. took adm. on the Roanes est. Abraham. Hannah, b. ±1658, m. Thos. Adams(19).

15 JOHN(13), seaman, fisherman, built by 1654 on 100 a. on Arrowsic bot from John Richards and sold to Clarke and Lake in 1659. Thereaft. liv., until the war drove him to Charlestown, on the west side of the Kennebec, a large tract betw. the river and Casco Bay bot from the Ind. Retailer 1665. Returning from Mass. he was with those on Stage Isl. for safety in Sept. 1679; from there went to his old home. In the second war he and s. James were k. at Falm. when the fort was taken. Lists 182, 13, 15, 183, 187, 190, 191. See also Davis(53). Ag. ±50 in 1684. (One John, a seaman, called ±25, was at Falm. with Col. Crown in 1662). Wife Margery or Margaret in 1661, -Mary- by error in 1664 (Y. D. 10: 152). She wit. in Charlest. in 1681 and a wid. was adm. to Ch. there 29 May 1692. Adm. on his est., of Falm., to dau. Elizabeth of Charlest. 14 Nov. 1700. John Phillips depos. in 1748 ab. the 6 ch. he had kn. in early visits East: Daniel, b. ±1667. James, k. with fa., s. p. and appar. single. Sarah, m. Wm. Baker(3). Hannah, not accounted for by Mr. Phillips; see her niece Anne(4). Elizabeth, m. twice in Boston, Wm. Bownd 13 Mar. 1700-1, John Eddy of Newport, R. I., 26 Nov. 1711. She d. in Newport bef. Dec. 1747, leaving s. Parker Eddy and at least one gr.ch., Ann Thompson, minor. Margaret, m. in Charlest. 19 Apr. 1699 Jonathan Carey(3), shipwright, Boston in 1718, of Augusta over ag. Georgetown, in 1720 (Y. D. 10: 146). She d. in Boston 1 Mar. 1723, ag. 43. Kn. ch., Jonathan, James.

16 JOHN(14), York, was hired out by his fa. to Wm. Roanes some time betw. 1657-1663; poss. also same as (17). In 1673-4 he was involved with Elizabeth Stover, but m. Sarah Green(19). O. A. Mar. 1679-80; constable 1679, 1680; tr.j. 1695, 1702; gr.j. 1695, 1696; selectm. 1700. He depos. in May 1721, ag. 76; in Mar. 1721-2 deeded all to s.-in-law John Harmon for supp. of self and w.; d. 1 Aug. 1723, ag. 79 (Father Parker aft. long

illness: Moody diary). Wid. Sarah d. 3 Jan. 1726-7. Ch. rec. York: Sarah, d. y. Mary, b. 1 Aug. 1676, taken 1691-2 and in captiv. Jan. 1698-9, List 99, p. 78. Susannah, b. 8 Oct. 1678, m. 30 Sept. 1698 Samuel Winch. Nathaniel, b. 16 Feb. 1680-1, only s. by fa.'s deed Mar. 1708-9. Adm. 10 May 1711 to wid. Hannah, who m. 2d one Barton, perh. John (5). Her acct. 1723 charged for bringing up the adopted child (appar. hers) one yr., the two youngest ch. two yrs. Two ch. liv. 1731: Hannah, m. 21 May 1730 John Foster of Billerica; Sarah, m. (int. 23 Feb. 1730) Jonathan Spinney. Mehitable and a twin, b. 28 July 1684. Mehitable, a captive, was back at Casco Bay Jan. 1698-9, List 99, p. 78; m. John Harmon(3 jr.). See also Mehitable (26). Abiah, dau., b. 18 July 1686. Elizabeth, b. 4 Nov. 1688. Mercy, d. ±2 yrs. old. Mercy, b. 14 May 1694. Lydia, b. 5 Aug. 1696, m. Wm. Gowell(1). John, b. 17 Feb. 1698-9, d. y. Abigail, b. 4 July 1700.

17 JOHN, servant of Mrs. Mitchell(5) 1661 (Essex Q. Ct. Rec. 3: 212). Poss. (16).

18 JOHN, sued John Phillips of Falm. for diet and attendance 1663; tr.j. 1667 (No. Yarm., Scarb. and Saco names). See also (8).

19 JOHN, Scarboro soldier; see (9).

20 JUDITH, widow, Hampton propr. 1640. List 391a. Of Charlest. 1645, she sold at Hampt. to John Marion, payment to be made at either of her houses in Charlest., Watert., Roxb., Dorch., Boston, Cambr., but doubtful if she owned in all, or merely thot of moving from Charlest. Dead 11 June 1651; appar. it was her will in Eng., 5—24 May 1649 (Waters 1: 265), which indicates no ch.

21 MARY, servant of Moses Gilman, laid her ch. to Teague Drisco(8) in 1673.

22 RICHARD, dealing with Exeter men 1639, was the Boston merchant. List 82; see also Manning(5).

23 ROBERT, Damariscove, took O. A. 1674. In 17— Clarke and Lake heirs claimed the ho., stage and other prop. he had deliv. them for debt, when the appraisers were Robert Gammon and Elias Tricke. Poss. the man on a Shoals cor.j. 1687. Lists 13, 307a. See also (12).

24 SAMUEL, adm. to Emanuel Hilliard of Hampt. 25 June 1656.

25 THOMAS(13), eldest s., always husbandman in legal documents, liv. on Parker's Isl., where his portion, about ⅓ of the island toward the sea and its northern boundary, was set off to him in 1664. In 1669 his mo. conveyed to him the fishing island, later Salter's, for his business. He took O. F. to the Plymouth govt. 1654, to the King 1665, to Mass. at Pemaquid 1674. Lists 11, 12, 13, 15, 187. See also Davis(53). In the war he appar. went first to Damariscove, then to

Charlest., and like (15) was on Stage Isl. in 1679. He d. at his Island home and was interred there, bef. the 2d war (Cox's and Hunnewell's depos. Y. D. 14: 193-4), aft. 13 Nov. 1684 (Y. D. 4: 34). Wife unkn. Ch. (div. of Parker's Isl. 1732, Y. D. 15: 136): **Grace**, m. David Oliver(3). **Sarah**, b. ±1656, m. 1st Matthew Salter, m. 2d in Boston 21 May 1703 Samuel Smith. **Remember**, m. Moses Pitman, a Marbleh. fisherman; he liv. 1732, she dead. 3 ch. in Marbleh. 1683-1688. **John**, eldest s., b. ±1665, shipwright, Boston, ret. to Parker's Isl. ab. 1720 and built, but soon driven back. He depos. in Boston in June 1736, ±71, that he liv. at Sagadahoc ab. 61 yrs. ago. Wife Sarah Vering (John) d. in Boston 9 Nov. 1711; he m. there 2d 13 Nov. 1712 Sarah Guille, wid. of Noah. He d. 27 Sept. 1744 in 80th yr., she 5 Sept. 1750 in 81st yr. (Copp's Hill). 7 ch. in Boston 1695-1707. **Jacob**, b. ±1666, mariner, Boston, deposed in Oct. 1730, ag. 64, that he was a soldier at Fort Loyal, Casco Bay, ab. 44 yrs. bef. He m. (int. Boston 13 Feb. 1695-6) Anna Randall. His s. Jacob deeded as his admr. 13 Jan. 1737. 6 ch. in Boston 1697-1709. **Margaret**, m. in Marbleh. 23 Oct. 1684 Samuel Dixey; he dead in Feb. 1721-2, she liv. 1732. 8 ch., in Marbleh. **Mary**, m. John Harrod (Harwood 7).

26 **THOMAS**, shoemaker, Great Isl., ±36 in 1672, matches a Boston ch. b. 3 Oct. 1636, s. of John and Jane, who had also ch. Noah and Alice. The mo. (then Thayer) was returning to Eng. in 1656 with Thos. and Noah, and supposedly went, yet Noah was here 1673 and Thos. too could have come back. Early in 1663 Hampt. gave our Thomas liberty to come there at his trade. Great Island Jan. 1663-4; gr. there 1667; m. before 28 Jan. 1668 Mary Shaw (Roger). Gr.j. 1681, 1686; tr.j. 1682, 1684, 1685; highw. surv. 1693-4. Jos. Alexander was bondsm. for him 1685 (see Pattee) and he for John Locke, sr. 1695. Lists 330a, 312ac, 326c, 313be, 331b, 315abc, 318b, 49, 52, 55b, 66, 91. See also Lamb(1). Last seen Sept. 1700 when he ack. a judg. to Pepperell. Ch., I proved, 3 more evid.: **Noah**, taxed Newc. Oct. 1691, sailed under Capt. Robert Mitchell 1693, d. at Lisbon 8 Feb. 1707-8, master of a brigantine. Lists 319, 96 (twice). See also Doc. Hist. 5: 383-392. Adm. 14 July 1708 to wid. Elizabeth (Treworgey, dau. of Samuel), who o.c. and had 2 ch. bp. in No. Ch. 17 Oct. 1708: Noah (b. 8 Mar. 1704-5) and a dau., prob. the dau. Elizabeth who m. Mark Newmarch. Wid. Elizabeth was the Parker of 'Mrs. Allcock & Parker' taxed at The Bank 1713. She m. 2d 26 Aug. 1714 John Field(4), m. 3d Benj. Cross(2). **Benjamin** (his fa. Thomas in 1694), cordwainer, Newc., Kit., m. 7 Dec. 1702 Elizabeth Gilman (see 10). She d. 5 May 1721,

bur. at Newc. where 'B. P. & Son & man' taxed 1720. Bot in Kit. 1719. Lists 315c, 316. Will, 1751—1752, names ch: Thomas, b. 25 Sept. 1703; Elizabeth, b. 24 Sept. 1709; Benj., b. 29 July 1713; but not Hannah, b. 13 Aug. 1718. **William**, currier, tanner, taxed Portsm. 1698, bot 1699. Lists 330d, 337, 339. He m. 1st 26 Feb. 1702-3 Zerviah Stanley, who d. 18 Aug. 1718; see Cutts for refer. to her fabricated pedigree (Brewster i: 118). He m. 2d 15 Sept. 1719 Lydia Hart(5), named in his will, 1731—1737, with ch: William, b. 9 Dec. 1703; John, b. 22 Dec. 1706; and 2 more, one likely his dau. Katherine, b. 5 Jan. 1704-5. Mary, bp. 10 Apr. 1709, was poss. ano. dau. **Alice**, m. John Marden(3); called aunt in will of Mrs. Elizabeth Newmarch 1763. Unattached: Mehitable, set fire to John Presson's ho. 1702, Rebecca Whidden persuading and assisting; see Mehitable(17). Nathaniel, o.c. and bp. in Portsm. 1707-8; Elizabeth, o.c. and bp. with ch. Elizabeth and Thos., 1707-8, was perh. his w. Wm., m. wid. Mary Cross (see Richard 8). Nicholas, Portsm. trader 1728-9. Grace, Newc., m. Francis Rand(3). Roger, mariner, m. Abigail Moore(11), both liv. 1744. John, m. at Greenl. 10 Dec. 1736 Bathshua Ward.

27 **THOMAS**, Berwick wit. 1680 (Y. D. 3: 92), must be Parkes.

28 **CAPT.** List 66.

**PARKES.** 1 **Henry**, partner with Geo. Dodd and Humphrey Chadbourne in a French voyage bef. Apr. 1651.

2 **THEOPHILUS**, servant to Walter Neal, Greenland, 1662.

3 **THOMAS**, Berwick, bot 40 a. near place called Post Wigwam near Newichawannock River from Richard Abbott in Jan. 1675; wit. Thos. Williams's deed to gr.dau. Plaisted 1680, and 25 Oct. 1686 deeded his 40 a. to Henry Child for supp.

**Parkinson**, Wm. See Perkins(24).

**Parkis**, Benjamin, wit. with Joseph Dow 1665, Philbrick to Sanborn.

**PARKMAN** (Partman), Elias, with the Gloucester men going to Falm. and Scarb. 1658; see Coe(2); sued Richard White in York ct. Oct. 1660. One E. P. sued Roger Rose of Piscataqua in Suff. ct., Oct. 1685.

**PARNELL.** Cornwall and Devon.

1 **FRANCIS**, Star Island, receipted to James Blagdon in May 1692 for three bags; Sarah Deverson saw them delivered. Likely the Salem fisherman.

2 **GILES**, fisherman, Beverly. List 85.

3 **HANNAH**, Cocke alias (Parnell?). See Cox(6).

4 **JOHN**, Oyster River, 1666; List 365. Petit j. (N. H.) June 1668.

5 **SAMUEL**, owed the Mitchell est. List 78.

**6 THOMAS**, took O. A. at Pemaquid 1674. List 15. One Goody P. had poor aid in Salem in 1679.

**7 WILLIAM**, sued Jeremiah Sheeres for defamation in York ct. Mar. 1649-50, case put to arbitration; plf. in N. H. ct. Oct. 1650. Partner with Thos. Way and Wm. England in deed from Ind. near Muscongus 1653 (Sewall's Ancient Dom., p. 104).

**PARR. 1 Giles**, Str. Bk., drunk and resisting the constable 1650-1652. Abs. from w., York ct. June 1653, also swearing and drunk. Drinking at Gunnison's, 1656.

**2 JAMES**, with Matthew Williams a wit. ag. Wm. Blake(6) and Christopher Cole (3), in June 1664.

**PARRETT. 1 John**, fisherman, Cape Elizabeth, ±33 in 1674, at Shoals and Kit. early, where he succ. sued Roger Kelly on an acct. in Oct. 1668, and m. bef. 1675 Sarah Crockett(6). In 1671 he struck John Dammeril on the Lord's day, being fined only for breach of the Sabbath; had suits ag. Arthur Beale (slander) and Rowland Flansell, and was sued for debt by John Pett 1679, by Geo. Davie's assignee 1683. Cape Eliz. in 1680, when N. Fryer was his bondsm. in Portsm. ct., and to Fryer he mtg. ho. and stage on Parrett's Point, S.E. side of Cape Cove, and 2 boats. Last found, being sued and jailed in Boston, in July 1691, for refusing to deliver goods from Boston to John Frissell (2). List 226. See also Dollin(1). His w. Sarah liv. 1688. Ch. (no male heirs, by deed 1725): **Mary**, m. Philip Gammon(1) and was liv. at Cape Eliz. 1738 when her sis. **Sarah**, w. of John Green(17), sold a half int. to them.

**2 RICHARD**, with Capt. Edw. Gosling's crew 1676.

**3 ROBERT**, Cape Elizabeth 1683. List 226.

**Parris**, George. His order figured in Capt. Pendleton's suit ag. Mr. John Paine in N. H. ct., June 1664.

**PARSLEY. 1 Richard**, tailor, Portsm., m. in Greenland 9 June 1713 Abigail (Banfield 2) Fletcher. Lists 337, 339. She was rec. into So. Ch. 4 Apr. 1725. Son **John**, bp. there 7 Mar. 1724-5, m. in Newington 1 Feb. 1740-1 Tamsen Huntress.

**2 WILLIAM** (Pursley) Ipswich, wounded at the Eastward 1691. List 37. One Wm. (Parsloe) was an abuttor to Frost land at Newtown, Sagadahoc, 1716 (Y. D. 9: 157; 10: 145.)

**PARSONS**, a purely south of England name. Became 100th commonest name in N. E.

**1 EDWARD**, St. Mary's co., Md., devised 500 a. at Kennebec by his will in 1715.

**2 JAMES**, bot land gr. by Berwick to James Frost and Thos. Guptill and d. s. p. His

wid. remar. and was wid. Elizabeth Pearcy of Berw. in 1734. Y. D. 16: 197, 200.

**3 JOHN**, cordwainer, York, at Portsm. 1674, poss. in Me. earlier if List 87 is his. Working for Nehemiah Partridge 1677 and a wit. ag. Geo. Bramhall. York gr. him 12 a. in Mar. 1677-8 if he buy the shoemaker's (Knowlton's) ho. and follow his trade, which he did. O. A. there 22 Mar. 1679-80; Portsm. tax rebated same yr. In 1681 he ack. judg. to Samuel Sayward payable in neat cattle. Lists 31, 33. He was k. in Ind. attack 25 Jan. 1691-2; adm., first, 4 days later, to Maj. Wm. Vaughan; 1 Nov. 1692 to wid. Elizabeth, bondsm. Wm. Hilton and Thos. Trafton; 13 July 1705 to s. John. Inv. (Y. D. 5. 1. 81). She m. 2d 12 July 1698 Peter Hinkson(2) and as E. P. compl. ag. Wm. Hilton in 1699 for taking a cow. Living 1720. Ch. rec. York: **John**, b. 31 July 1677, taken captive Jan. 1691-2, in Canada 1699, here 1705, and d. in Portsm. 3 Sept. 1722 appar. s.p. List 99, p. 75. **Elizabeth**, b. 9 Feb. 1679-80, m. 1st in Boston 1 Mar. 1705 John Hemenway; 3 ch.; m. 2d Wm. Dunn(4). **Mary**, b. 13 Oct. 1681, m. Nicholas Cane(2). **Elihu**, housewright, b. 31 Mar. ——, had gr. 1703-1721 and m. Ruth Wilson (Joseph). List 279. Will, 25 (d. 30) July 1730, names w. Ruth, br. Nicholas Cane, and 8 of 9 ch. Wid. Ruth's will, 11 Apr.—28 Sept. 1737, names 6 ch. Her exec. paid five doctors. **Rachel**, b. 30 Aug. ——, named in a Kit. acct. in 1710 and accus. Wm. Smith in July 1717, both of Kit. **Christian**, b. 16 Feb. ——, m. Caleb Boynton (2). **Mercy**, b. 6 Oct. ——, taken captive 1691-2, in Canada 1711; List 99, p. 92. 'Richard, boy, Dover,' List 99, p. 75 (1695), and Ruth, in captivity 1699; both unkn.; while Anne, w. of Wm. Hilton(20) may have been sis. of either John or Elizabeth, but not their dau. See also (7).

**4 JOHN**, Gloucester. See Haines(17).

**5 MARK**, a Parker's Island abuttor in Sept. 1664; by Eastern Cl. rec. bot there from Parker and Webber 26 Dec. 1664. Damariscotta River wit. 1665. A planter, living on N. W. part of Rascohegan, E. side of Little River, 26 Nov. 1672, he gave Wm. Parsons an (unrec.) deed to 100 + 20 a. below Hell Gate; his w. Elizabeth also signed. As a refugee, he took O. A. in Boston 11 Nov. 1678, was there in May 1682, and sold Eastern land to Edw. Woodman 7 Apr. 1687. His wid. as Elizabeth Parsons claimed on Rascohegan for self and **children**, yet Wm. Boardman(2), perh. later, claimed for his w. **Elizabeth**, as dau. of Mark, deed., and also as dau. of Elizabeth, w. of Mark, afterw. w. of John Spencer, late of Newton, decd. (?meaning Newtown), citing Palmer patent 1 Sept. 1686.

**6 PHILIP,** Mr., Pemaquid 1682. List 123. See Phipps(2).

**7 RICHARD,** wit. with Nicholas Haskins for R. Elliot 1697; wit. Fryer to Elliot 1698. See also (3).

**8 RUTH,** a captive. See (3).

**9 THOMAS,** fisherman, taxed Newcastle 1720, m. bef. 30 Dec. 1721 Mary Batson (2), who was gr. adm. 13 Sept. 1726 and m. 2d Richard Tarlton. Dau. **Mary** and husb. Richard Watton of Boston (m. there 1752) sold ½ his est. in 1754.

**10 WILLIAM,** Kennebec. See (5).

**11 WILLIAM,** Wells soldier, sued Baker Nason in Mar. 1695-6 for detaining his horse, and m. (ct. Jan. 1696-7) Hannah Wheelwright; her fa. Samuel deeded her a marriage portion in 1700. The husb. and 3 ch. were k., the w. taken, 10 Aug. 1703 (List 39). His heirs (Pearson), Lists 269ac. Hannah (List 99, p. 92) wit. a Montreal wedding in Feb. 1706, and was here in Jan. 1706-7 when John Wheelwright relinq. to her adm. on her husb.'s est. She m. 2d in Boston 19 Aug. 1708 Philip Rollins; d. by 1738. 3 kn. Rollins daus. See also 'N. E. Captives,' 1: 410-3. **Abigail,** evid. the oldest Parsons ch. and not a captive, was bp. at Wells 22 Sept. 1706, adopted dau. of John Wheelwright. She m. 1st in Boston 3 July 1713 John Johnson; m. 2d 25 Jan. 1727 Benj. Williams of Boston; in 1738 with her half-sis. Hannah Rollins they sold in Wells. Bourne names two of the Indian victims as **William,** ag. 5, and **Samuel,** ag. 18 mos. Perh. the 3d was captured, not k., and was the dau. **Hannah,** b. Wells, 6 May 1701 (Catholic rec. when bp. as Catherine 10 Jan. 1704), m. 17 Mar. 1729 Claude-Antoine de Berman, Esq., who d. in Quebec in 1761, ag. ±65. 10 ch. named.

**PARTRIDGE.** The N. H. fam. came from Olney, co. Bucks. See N. E. Reg. 63: 283; Essex Probate 1: 150.

**1 JOHN**(4), Portsm., ±28 in 1668, ±59 in 1695-6, a Boston seaman 1659, at Salisb. and also a Portsm. propr. in 1660. Cordwainer, innkeeper, vintner. Jury 1667, 1694-5; leather sealer 1668; selectm. 1696-7. In 1692 he liv. in the Great House; in 1696 the ferry right betw. the island his ho. stood on and Portsm. and Great Isl. was gr. to him and his heirs. Lists 311b, 323-4, 326bc, 329, 330abd, 331abc, 335a, 336c, 337, 49, 51-2, 54, 57, 62. See also (2). His w. Mary (Fernald 2, m. 11 Dec. 1660) d. 16 Aug. 1722. Lists 331c, 335a. His will, 28 Aug.—5 Sept. 1722, names 5 daus. and gr.s. Jonathan P. and his w. Sarah. Ch. (Prov. rec. except last 2): **Hannah,** b. 14 Oct. 1661, m. Robert Almary (1). **John,** b. 3 Jan. 1663-4. **Mary,** b. 26 Feb. 1665-6, m. 1st Richard Barnwell who was taxed in July 1690 next to her br. John, and

d. bef. Mar. 1693-4, leaving ch: John Barnwell(1) and Elizabeth, who m. 1st John Cutts (9). Wid. Mary m. 2d Capt. Samuel Moore (18); m. 3d Richard Elliot(4); m. 4th John Leach(4). Richard Gorish (Gerrish 7 jr.) in will made at Southhold, L. I., 21 Oct. 1719—4 Mar. 1719-20, made friend Elizabeth Cutts chief heir and exec., gave £20 to widow Mary Elliot of Portsm. to buy mourning, his new coat to Samuel Moore, s. of Samuel, and other clothing to Stephen and John King. **Sarah,** b. 3 Sept. 1668, m. William Hunking (9). **Rachel,** b. 4 Mar. 1670-1, **Elizabeth,** b. 4 July 1673, **Abigail,** b. 2 Feb. 1675-6, **Patience,** b. 4 July 1678, these four not in will. **Joanna,** m. 1st John Low(5); m. 2d Axwell Roberts. **Ruth,** m. 1st Rowland Rowlandson; m. 2d Wm. Tarrott or Terret; 4 Terrett ch. bp. So. Ch. 1729 when she renewed cov.

**2 JOHN**(1), Portsm. In Sept. 1669 his fa. deeded to him (minor) his gr.fa.'s Salisb. ho. and land, naming (3) and Abraham Corbett gdns. to care for the est. 'recovered if possible'; (the prop. had been deeded to (1) by mo. and step-fa. in 1659 in consid. of cert. legacies from his fa. and gr.fa., and deeded back to Stanyan, who appar. sold to Robert Downer). John, jr., taxed July 1690; jury 1697; vict. lic. 1697. Lists 52, 335a. He m. Abigail Plaisted(6), who was admx. 20 July 1698 and had pub. ho. lic. 1698-9, her fa.-in-law and James Leavitt sureties. List 335a. Kn. ch: **Jonathan,** perh. a Kit. apprentice, m. there 17 Jan. 1716-7 Sarah Mitchell(3). List 339. In 1728 Samuel Gammon was drowned wading from Jonathan's ho. to Mary Martin's island. 5 ch. bp. **Joshua,** 'youngest' s. in Nov. 1699, when his mo. deeded her Plaisted est. to (1) who was to keep the boy. In 1708 his gr.fa. compl. that Mary Clark (evid. wid. of 20) had abused his w. and gr.s., 'one of his fingers almost bit off.'

**3 NEHEMIAH**(4), cordwainer, Portsm., wit. deed betw. the John Pickerings, elder and younger, 7 Nov. 1665 (see also 6), and m. bef. 15 July 1668 Sarah, kinswo. of Anthony Ellins(1), who for love and affec. for Sarah deeded her husb. a ho.-lot; see also Ellins(2). Taxed 1672 next to A. E.; bondsman for John Baker 1681; cor.j. 1681; gr.j. 1683; j. 1684-5; O. A. 28 Aug. 1685; sealer and searcher of leather in 1688, 1692 (Sergt.). Lists 330a, 326c, 331b, 313c, 329, 333a, 52, 57. See also Bryant(10), Huckins(1), Parsons (3) and Rachel Webster who was perh. connected. Will, 9—18 Feb. 1690-1, names w. Sarah, bros. John and Wm., and s. **William,** who shares a gr.st. with one Nehemiah, who d. 12 Feb. 1709-10, in 47th yr., a rec. which fits no one. Our Nehemiah d. in Feb. 1690-1, in 47th yr., making a 19 yr. discrepancy, if he be the one. His wid. Sarah m. 2d bef. 4 Jan. 1691 James Leavitt(5). Her will, 10

Nov. 1733—27 Dec. 1738, gives to her Partridge desc.; see (6).

**4 WILLIAM**, Salisb., s. of John of Olney, co. Bucks, first at Lynn with relative Henry Gaines, Salisb. 1639, and d. there 5 July 1654. Adm. 3 Oct. fol. to wid. Ann who m. 2d 1 Jan. 1655-6 Anthony Stanyan and liv. at Hampt. In 1701 the dau. Hannah Gove and her s. John gave receipt of her three bros.' share in keeping the mo. from 1 Mar. 1684-5 to death (10 July 1689); the two surv. bros. with the Leavitts sued John Pickering (w. a Stanyan) for breach of contr. made 21 Feb. 1684, when he too agreed to pay. Ch: **John**, b. ±1638. **Rachel**, d. 1650. **Hannah**, under 21 in June 1659, m. Edw. Gove(2). **Elizabeth**, b. 14 Feb. 1642-3, m. Joseph Shaw of Hampt. **Nehemiah**, b. 5 May 1645. **Sarah**, b. 24 Aug. 1647, chose Maj. Pike gdn. in 1663, m. John Heath(1). **Rachel**, b. 10 June 1650, m. Joseph Chase(5). **William**, b. ±1654.

**5 COL. †‡WILLIAM**(4), Esq., Lt.-Gov. of N. H., ±39 in 1693, ±46 in 1700. A carpenter, and early at Wells (see Masters); Portsm., working on the meet.-ho. 1678; then Dover, where he fol. his trade, engaged in masting and became a succes. merchant. Ab. 1690 he ret. from Eng. with a contract to provide masts for His Majesty's service for 7 yrs. and offered Ichabod Plaisted, who refused, £200 a yr. to assume management (I. P.'s depos.). Portsm. 1693, Dover, 1695, Boston 1699. Capt., Col. When chosen constable of Portsm. 1692, he repres. it was in prejudice of his office as Treas., and Receiver Genl. of the Prov. Asst. Supreme Ct. Judic. 1693; Lt.-Gov. June 1696—June 1703. Councillor. Lists 359b, 330d, 335a, 336bc, 337, 52, 57, 62, 64, 65, 94, 98. See also Gove(5), Kelly (1), Lee(1). Salem 1709, Newb. 1713, where he had m. 8 Dec. 1680 Mary Brown (Lists 331c, 335a), and d. 3 Jan. 1728-9 in 75th yr. His will, 15 June 1723; hers, 8 Sept. 1737, d. 10 June 1739. Ch. (his Bible): **Richard**, b. 3 Dec. 1681, Clerk of Writs (N. H.) 1699. London merch. 1729, liv. there 1753. **Nehemiah**, b. 9 Mar. 1683-4, appar. of Boston 1713, a 'Japanner'; d. bef. 1737, leaving ch. **Mary**, b. 19 Oct. (1685: Sav.), m. 8 Jan. 1705-6 Gov. Jonathan Belcher, H. C. 1699; d. 6 Oct. 1736. 5 ch. **William**, b. 1 May 1687, m. in Boston 15 Nov. 1711 Rachel Goffe (Capt. Christopher), step-dau. of Samuel Wentworth; apparently d. 1717. 2 ch. rec. **Elizabeth**, b. 23 Sept. 1692, m. in Boston 10 May 1716 Wm. Caswell; a wid. 1729, liv. 1737.

**6 WILLIAM**(3), Portsm., ±25 in 1696, ±30 in 1701, planning to travel beyond sea when his fa. died. Taxed July 1690; j. 1693-1695; pub.-ho. lic. 1695, 1699, 1700. With James Leavitt he was surety for John Pickering jr. in 1693; he and Pickering sureties for Daniel Libby 1697 and for wid. Prudence

Tapley 1706. In 1702 J. P. deeded part of Pickering Point to him 'cousin,' for nat. love and affec. and in settlem. of all accts. betw. them. Lists 335a, 337. His w. Abigail (Riddan, m. 11 Jan. 1692-3) d. 29 Aug. 1704, and he m. 2d 28 Nov. 1710 wid. Hannah Griffith(4). He d. 13 May 1718 in 47th yr. (gr. st.); adm. to s. Nehemiah 3 Sept. fol., est. insolv. Wid. ment. in acct. 1721. His mo.'s will, 1733, names her two gr.sons and their wives, 3 gr.daus., 4 gt.gr.daus. Ch. (Prov. rec.): **Sarah**, b. 8 Dec. 1694, m. 1st John Langbridge(1), m. 2d Abraham Dentt(1), m. 3d Edmund McBridge. **Nehemiah**, cordwainer, m. Mary Philbrick (see 6) betw. Dec. 1718—June 1719 (3 dates found). 6 ch. bp. So. Ch.; 2 more bp. there in 1729 as ch. of Mary were his or his br.'s. **William**, b. 22 Jan. 1697-8, d.y. **Mary**, b. 9 Apr. 1699, m. Samuel Beck(4). **William**, b. 24 Dec. 1700, d.y. **William**, b. 25 Feb. 1702-3, m. 3 Oct. 1725 Mary Tapley. 5 ch. bp. So. Ch.; also see br. Nehemiah above. **Abigail**, b. 10 Feb. 1703-4, m. 1st Noah Bradden(3); m. 2d Edw. Chapman(4).

**Pasmore**, William, Portsm. cor.j. 1663. List 327a.

**PASTREE, Margaret**, Boston wid., depos. in 1738, ±64, that she knew Robert Tufton Mason(17) in 1686 and the circumstances of his death; other deponents were N. H. people. She was Geo. Hollard's dau., b. in Boston 23 June 1670, and wid. of John P. who d. 12 Dec. 1704, ag. 42 (Granary). In 1715 she sold Hollard land in Salem, Hampton, etc. Liv. 1748. The est. of Nathl. Kenney (see Canney 4) owned her a note of hand for £10 in 1749. See also Marriner(1).

**Patman**, Thomas, soldier at Gerrish garrison, Dover, Feb.-May 1696, in place of two Portsm. men. List 67. Pitman?

**PATRICK.** 1 **Christopher**, soldier, k. by Ind. 1703. List 96.

2 **PATRICK** (?Scot), Dover 1657. List 356a. Doubtless his given name.

**PATTEE** (Patee), **John**, mariner, depos. in Portsm. Oct. 1685 ab. Thos. Parker abusing his apprent. Thos. Spencer; wit. John Hole's p/a in Barbadoes 12 Aug. 1690 and swore to it in Portsm. 28 Oct. fol. (?List 90, Pette).

**PATTEN.** 1 **Andrew**, succ. defended suit brot by Bellgrave and Tremmels in York ct., 1666. Dealing in molasses with Maj. Shapleigh, 1667, 1668, poss. a sea-capt.

2 **DAVID**, Oyster Riv. wit., 1695.

3 **MATTHEW** (Y. D. 14: 105), in error for Matthew Paullen (Paulling); also in List 226.

**4 THOMAS** (Padden), in ct. (Me.) 1672, for fighting with Edw. Chambers, and was ordered to return to his w. in Eng. In 1673 he had forfeited his bond to the county

treas. Working at H. Deering's ho. 1674, ±50. Lists 286, 30.

**PATTERSON.** 1 **David**, and **James**, Scots, List 74.

2 **EDWARD**, taxed Dover 1657-8, O. R. 1659-1663, must have been ano. Scot. Gr.j. 1660. Lists 356abc, 361a, 362a, 363abc. Dover gr. 1660, an addition to his ho.-lot. In 1669 Goodm. Hudson's lot was in his hands.

**PATTESHALL.** See N. E. Reg. 72: 153.

1 **CAPT. EDMUND**, Esq., Kennebec, br. of (3), as citizen and salter of St. Mary-le-Strand, London, m., lic. 29 Dec. 1634, Martha Denham (Richard), bp. in that par. 26 May 1611, bur. there 16 Aug. 1667. A Kennebec wit. 26 Dec. 1664, and John Cox said that he liv. on Paddeshall's Isl. bef. his s. Richard did (Y. D. 18: 137 says the s. bot from Parker); Philip White described it as an island on eastermost side of Arrowsic. Retail lic., west side of Kennebec, Sept. 1665; Com. for town of Northampton Oct. 1667; O. A. to Mass. July 1674 and Com. for Co. of Devonshire; J. P. (acting) 1675, 1676. Reported k. at 'Quinebeck' 14 Aug. 1676. Lists 182, 15. Kn. here are 2 of 7 ch. bp. at St. Mary-le-Strand: **Richard**, 20 May 1636. **Mary**, 9 Aug. 1648, wit. three times in 1674 (Y. D. 2: 189-190), m. in Salem 6 June 1678 Eleazer Gedney who d. 1683, she 4 Sept. 1716. Ch: Eleazer; Edmund; Martha, m. 1712 James Ruck and was the only ch. in 1730. Others bp. London: **William**, 1639. **John**, 1640. **Martha**, 1641. **Samuel**, 1643-4. **Robert**, 1646-1649.

2 **CAPT. RICHARD**(1), Esq., mariner, merchant, Kennebec (his s. claimed land mtg. to him and [3] in May 1662), Boston, New York, owned largely at Kennebec and above Saco by inherit., purch. and Dongan patents (see also 3). Casco j. July 1666; liv. 'many yrs.' on Paddeshall's Isl., his fa. bef. him. When actually resident uncert.; he voyaged surely to Va. and N. Y. and at N. Y. had a gr. which was taken away by Andros; at Boston, was freeman 1673, took O. A. 1679 and had 7 ch. rec. J. P. for Cornwall 1684; called of Boston 1683, 1686. In 2d war his fam. went from Kennebec to Damariscove Isl., thence to Pemaquid, where he was k. on board of his sloop 2 Aug. 1689. Lists 89, 16, 17, 189, 141. Adm. in N. Y. 13 July 1692 to Matthew Marlow, cr. Wid. liv. in South Ward, N. Y., Aug. 1696 and Oct. 1697, appar. not there 1 Feb. fol., her ptn. 1700 in Mass. Arch. 70: 475. She was Martha Woody (Capt. Richard); d. Boston 21 Apr. 1713, ±61. See Alice Morse Earle's 'Two Centuries of Costume in America.' Ch. (all records in Boston) sold Damariscove in 8ths. By 1st w. Abigail: **Abigail**, b. 29 Sept. 1664, m. John Turner. **Richard**, b. 7 Feb. 1665-6; adm.,

late of Boston, sometime of Pemaquid, to sis. Frances 1 Apr. 1703. List 189. **Frances, m.** in 1703 Thos. Hitchborn; her dau. Deborah was mo. of Paul Revere. See also Creek(2). **Edward**, b. 27 Apr. 1670; at Kit. in July 1691, an escaped Ind. captive from Penobscot; liv. 1701, away from Boston. By 2d w: **Martha**, b. 31 Jan. 1673-4. **Ann**, b. 11 Dec. 1678, m. 1st in 1703 John Breck, m. 2d in 1717 Capt. Wm. Thomas. **Edmund**, b. 31 Mar. 1683. **Robert**, b. 26 Mar. 1685, leather dresser, Boston, m. 1st Jane Greenleaf in 1708, m. 2d Margaret Giddings in 1730. Will, 1753—1753, names wife, s. Richard (m. in Hampt. F. 6 Oct. 1748 Mrs. Ann Milford), s. Robert, and 5 daus. (willed his Eastern land). Unrecorded: **Elizabeth**, m. in 1701 Edw. White, m. 2d one Perkins; ch: Elizabeth (White) Townsend, John and Patteshall Perkins, and poss. ano. (Y. D. 32: 127). **Mary**, m. in 1704 Francis Peabody, m. 2d in 1716 Samuel Hodges, m. 3d in 1721 John Pitts. **Samuel** (or a gr.s.), mariner, Boston, joined Robert and sisters in lease of Damariscove Isl., 1728. A wid. Martha int. mar. with Richard Abbott at Ipsw. 1737.

3 **ROBERT**, Mr., merchant, Boston, Kennebec, br. of (1), 40 in 1654, ±40 in 1655, ±55 in 1665, wit. Richard Leader's mtg. to Thos. Savage 18 Dec. 1652; in 1656 wit. ano. Leader mtg. and dealt early with Mr. Gifford of Lynn Iron Works. Atty. in Dover et. 1655 for Richard Silley; in 1657, wit. with Waldron (perh. at Casco) and at Newc. Lists 221, 77b. Called of Boston in 1665 when he, (2) and Humphrey Davie bot at Kennebec, where he wit. in 1666 and was John Gutch's bondsm. Sued John Andrews(9) and w. Joan in 1668; also Richard Downe(4). No w. appears. Inv. 17 June 1671 incl. lands at Kennebec, Saco above the falls (Y. D. 2: 172) and Casco; adm. in Suff. 27 July fol. to (2).

**Paty**, Thomas, weaver, had Wells gr. 1669 and made a mill contract with Henry Sayward 1670 (Y. D. 2: 163). List 269b. See also Johnson(15).

**PAUL. Daniel**, bp. at St. Clement's, Ipswich, co. Suff., 24 Feb. 1590-1, m. there 9 Feb. 1617 Elizabeth Lever, bp. 30 Nov. 1590 in same par., where a dau. Thomasine was bp. 16 June 1624.

1 **DANIEL**, mariner, shipwright, Kittery. From Boston 26 Aug. 1640, late of Ipsw. Eng., he sent back p/a to sell his lands and deliv. the money to w. Elizabeth. He and Bartholomew Smith bot on Long Reach from John Andrews 21 Mar. 1647-8; in 1649 he bot from Rich. Cutts ho. and land adj. his own, form. Stephen Sanborn's. Gr.j. 1650, 1651. Grants 1653, 1665. Lists 282, 284, 298, 323, 326a. His w. Elizabeth was liv. in Oct. 1659 when he gave a mtg. to Cutts. On July 18,

1668, with no ment. of her he deeded all aft. he died to s. Stephen, except 15 a. given to Jos. Alcock; alive 22 Aug. 1672. Ch. here, poss. others in Eng: **Abigail**, m. 1st Joseph Alcock(3), m. 2d Robert Rowsley. **Stephen.**

2 **STEPHEN**(1), shipwright, Kit., compl. ag. Benj. Hull in 1666 for abusing him. He m. Katherine Maverick(1) aft. 18 July 1668 when in view of his coming marriage his fa. deeded him the homestead. She had a legacy from Mrs. Catherine Hilton(1) in 1676. He had tav. lic. at Long Reach 1680, 1682, lic. contin. in 1683 to wife. Lists 298, 92. Inv. 25 Sept. 1696. She had beer lic. 1695, tav. 1696, 1698, and was liv. in July 1706. Ch. (Y. D. 6: 162, 7: 52, 8: 63): **Elizabeth**, m. (ct. Apr. 1696) John Thompson. **Susannah**, m. Samuel Fernald(4). **John**, m. by 1706 Margaret Tobey (James). Lists 290-1, 296-7. In 1717 he deeded all to s. Amos (b. 19 Feb. 1712-3), he to pay £20 to sis. Katherine (b. 18 July 1707); wife not ment., but in 1737 John Thompson depos.: 'In 1717 at request of J. P. and w. Margaret.' He liv. up to 1735 (SJC 44026), appar. to 1737 (SJC 43978). **Daniel**, shipwright, m. 30 Mar. 1701 Sarah Bragdon(5), she liv. 28 Sept. 1732. In 1731 his home was half the Long Reach homestead; liv. 1736; marked 'moved' on Eliot Ch. list of 1727. Lists 291, 296-7. 8 ch. **Moses**, carver, Portsm., Boston, apprent. to Richard Knight, likely(14). Of Kit. 1701, still K.'s apprent., he bot in Portsm.; taxed there as late as 1727. He d. in Boston 5 Jan. 1730, ag. 53 yrs. 3 mos. Adm. in Suff. 1730, in N. H. 1731, to wid. Mary (Cotton 2, m. by 1703), who d. in Boston 7 May 1742, in 61st yr. Her will names dau. Mary (m. in Boston 1728 Jonathan Payson; d. there 1743 in 36th yr.) and gr.s. Moses Paul Payson. A s. Moses, ag. 27, and a dau. Sarah, ag. 18 yrs. 8 mos., both d. in Boston in Mar. 1730. **Abigail**, m. aft. 1701 John Skriggins. (With or near Moses' fam. was bur. Aquila, s. of Aquila and Sarah, d. 30 July 1714, acc. to Copps Hill rec. pub. 1878. This ch. was bp. in Charlest. 1712.)

**PAULLING, Matthew**, Falmouth 1682-1689; see Patten(3). Lists 34, 228c. In Nov. 1694 he was at Fort William Henry, N. Y., returning from a captivity of 4½ yrs. in Canada. In 1696 he sailed with Capt. Thos. Parker in pinke -John's Adventure-, England to Boston, and wit. Susanna Seacomb's deed in Boston 1698. His 1st w.'s fa., John Wallis, gave him 8 a. at Purpooduck on which he built two houses and made improvements. He m. 2d in Boston 15 June 1698 -Susanna- Walker, dau. of Saco with w. Sarah in July 1702 he sold a Boston ho. His will, made in Boston 26 Aug. (d. 13 Sept., aged 56) 1708, calls self a former soldier at Fort Mary, Saco, names friend Capt. Geo. Turfrey of Saco exec., and expresses the hope that his creditors be consid. of his only dau. Sarah: w. not ment. Ch. rec. Boston (mo. Sarah): **Sarah**, b. 25 Nov. 1699. **Hannah**, b. 16 Oct. 1701.

**Pavett.** See Pafat.

**Payton, Henry**, Mr., indebted to Mitchell est. List 78.

**PEABODY, Francis**, Hampton, Topsfield, came in the -Planter- in 1635, ag. 21, with certif. from minister at St. Albans, co. Herts. From Ipsw., he was with the first at Hampt., and sold there to Robert Drake in Mar. 1649-50. Freeman 18 May 1642. Tr.j. 1648; gr.j. 1649; com.t.e.s.c. 1649. Lists 391a, 392ab, 393ab. His w. in Hampt. was Lydia; List 393a. In 1645 Eunice Cole publicly ackn. her slanderous speeches ag. Susan Perkins (w. of 9) and Lydia Peabody; that these two were connec. seems poss. He m. 2d Mary (Foster) Wood, named in will of her fa. Renald Foster in 1680. Lt. F. P. d. in Topsf. 19 Feb. 1697-8. Ch. (Hampt. rec. show but one: several evid. b. there): **Lydia**, bp. Hampt. 30 Aug. 1640. **John. Joseph. William. Isaac. Sarah. Hepsibah. Mary.** And rec. in Topsf. 1658-1669, the mo. not named: **Ruth. Damaris. Samuel. Jacob. Hannah. Nathaniel.** See the Peabody Gen.

**Peach, John**, Marblehead, early on the Piscataqua, 'Old Father Peach.' List 41. See N. E. Reg. 54: 276; also Bennett(7).

**Peake, Symon**, a Portsm. wit. with Samuel Barrett(7) 1664, in suit of Richard Cutts v. Rachel Webster and Richard Allison(3).

**PEARD**, an ancient but rare name in Devonshire.

1 **JOHN**, Saco constable 1673 (P. & Ct. Rec. ii: 257); likely error for (2).

2 **RICHARD**, Saco, m. 8 July 1669 Jane (Hobbs 1), Naziter(1); List 246. Constable 1673. O. F. at Marblehead 18 Dec. 1677. Returning home, he was highw. surv. 1680; townsman 1682; constable 1688. Lists 85, 249. See also Cawley(3). Patrick Denmark jr. was in ct. for assaulting him in 1686; in 1687 his land adj. that form. Nicholas Bully's(2); named an abuttor in Apr. 1722 (Y. D. 11: 21). His ch. included presumably **Wilmot** who wit. deed of John Boaden(7) in July 1687. **Elizabeth** (surely), m. in Salem 28 Oct. 1703 Thos. Venney of Marbleh.; as Vinning of Salem they sold her rights as a Hobbs gr.ch. in 1749. One Wm. P. m. wid. Sarah Brown in Salem 25 Nov. 1723.

**PEARL, Nicholas**, Dover, s. of wid. Alice of Beverly Park, co. York, was of Salem and his br. John of Marblehead in Jan. 1683-4 when the est. of kinsman John P., intest. of Boston, sometime of Beverly Park, was settled on them, ⅔ to John, ⅓ to Nicholas.

He m. in Ipswich 25 Oct. 1686 Elizabeth Bosworth, who d. there 24 June 1702, tho he was resid. in N. H. earlier. Wm. Cotton had bill ag. him for leather 1689-1693; summ. as wit. in an O. R. case Sept. 1695; j. 1696; abs. from Dover meet. 1697. He was k. by Ind. 11 Aug. 1706, List 96 (both Penhallow and Niles say -William- Pearl). Wm. Dam jr. bur. him and with Jos. Meader was bondsm. for the admr. Wm. Rogers of Wenham. A wid. surv. and d. bef. 12 Feb. 1706-7. Ch: **John**, b. Ipsw. 17 July 1692, kinsman Wm. Rogers his gdn. 1706. Wife Mary, who gave bond to adm. 30 May 1753, 5 ch. 1714-1726. **Elizabeth**, d. Ipsw. 19 July 1702.

**PEARSON**, belongs to the English Midlands and the No., tho peculiarly strong in co. Kent. See also Hilton(14).

1 **GEORGE**, 38 in 1669, 43 in 1673, Boston merchant with Me. and N. H. connections and oft. there. Perh. first of Wells, he wit. for Littlefields in Oct. 1662, attested bef. Rishworth in July 1663, and m. Elizabeth Wheelwright (Rev. John). Owned at Winter Harbor in 1669. Sued Edw. Hilton's sons in Suff. ct. 1674. At Casco he had pub. ho. lic. Apr. 1680, 'by himself or some meet person'; on commit. to lay out No. Yarm. 1681; Falm. wit. 1683. Lists 266, 214. See also Holman(6), Miller(9), Sargent, Spurwell. Mr. G. P. deputy under Sheriff Tufton in N. H. 1685; in 1688 late farmer of His Majesty's Excise for this Prov. (N. H.). He d. ±1700; wid. Elizabeth depos. in Nov. 1707, ±74. **Three ch.** d.y. in Boston; others were: **Mary**, b. 19 Nov. 1664, m. by 1694 Robert Blabour (or Blaber), 1 ch. d.y.; m. 2d 21 Mar. 1700 John Butt; m. 3d 17 Nov. 1709 Samuel Hare; d. ±1720 leaving dau. Mary (Butt). **Thomas**, b. 30 Oct. 1669, liv. 1707, dead 1718, supposedly had w. Elizabeth and 5 ch. in Boston 1691-1705, tho none joined in suit ag. owners of Cousins and Littlejohn's Isl. (York Files 1762), the plf. being Mary, w. of James Moreton of Blanford, clerk, and dau. of Thos. and Mary (Butt) Rodgers. Two Georgetown deponents in 1760, Margaret Parker and Wm. Rodgers, knew the fam. hist. in Boston over many yrs.

2 **GEORGE**, Exeter, m. 2 Apr. 1677 Ann (Wyeth), wid. of Wm. Taylor, and ±1678 had 2 a. gr. adj. the Taylor ho. Lists 376b, 52, 57, 62, 67. In 1702 he deeded to s. Jethro aft. death of self and w. She depos. in 1714 ab. her 1st husb. 60 yrs. bef. See also Chadwell(3). Only kn. ch: **Jethro**, depos. in Mar. 1710-1, ±33, about Bride's Hill ever since he could remember. Lists 67, 376b, 388. Will, of Exeter, 30 Dec. 1738—26 Oct. 1743, names w. Jane, s. Jethro (63 in 1768; List 376b), daus. Anna Sanborn and Elizabeth Sanborn.

3 **SAMUEL**, Wells soldier 1693. List 267b, See also Johnson(7).

**PEASE.**

1 **HENRY**, collected from John Smith, Cape Neddick, 1662 (Y. D. 1: 141). A Boston mariner, he sold Redding's Isl., Cape Porp., to Thos. Kimball in Sept. 1673. See also Ellicott.

2 **SAMUEL**, Exeter, cor.j. Jan. 1693-4; j. 1695. He was k. by Ind. 23 July 1706; adm. 5 Nov. fol. to Richard Hilton. Lists 94, 384a, 376b (1698), 96. Elizabeth P. who m. Samuel Smith of Hampton 22 Jan. 1706-7 may have been his wid. Presum. a s. **Nathaniel.** Appar. it was his name in minister's rate 1714, betw. Richard Hilton jr. and Clement Moody, jr. List 376b (1725, 1740). He m. 4 Nov. 1725 Phebe Sanborn; 1 s. Samuel and 5 daus. rec. Ex. 1726-1735. Perryman's acct. ag. him 1724 has item 'your sister Rebecca Riding.' One Sarah P. m. Samuel Stevens in Greenl. 6 June 1728.

3 **THOMAS**, one of several Portsm. and Greenl. men dealing with Francis Huckins(1) in 1680.

4 **WILLIAM**, form. of York, laborer (but prob. Pierce 26), in Pepperell's warr. for stealing money from Capt. Raynes 1702.

**PEASLEY** (Peaslee), **Joseph**, Salisbury, Will, 1660—1661, names w. Mary, **five** ch. and gr.ch. Sarah Saier. Wid. Peasley was at the York home of Henry Sayward (m. **Mary** Peasley).

**PEAVEY.**

1 **EDWARD**, ±26 in 1696, taxed Greenland 1691, tenant on Hall farm with Richard Blanchard 1693, -Thomas Pavie- by one rec. At Oyster River in 1700 when sued by Pepperell and fined by Dover for fencing highway. Newington or Dover wit. 1711; subscribed for Newingt. minister 1713. Lists 62, 335a, 343. Wid. Rachel m. 2d in Newingt. 19 Dec. 1720 Salathiel Denbo(1 jr.). No specific proof of ch. but most, if not all, of the fol. likely: **Abel**, m. 1st in 1710 a dau. of John Hudson(5) and had, 1711-1716: Hudson, Thomas, Abel. He m. 2d in Newingt. 1717 Mary Clough of Strath. Durham 1736. Lists 343, 369. **Nathaniel**, adult 1713, List 343. His w. Annah o.c. at Greenl. 1727; 6 ch. bp. there, ano. at Strath. **Edward.** His w. Mary bp. at O. R. Feb. 1720-1; he adm. to Dover Ch. 1723, she 1727, both dism. to Berw. **Joseph**, signed a Newingt. ptn. 1713, bp. at Dover with dau. Esther 1728; Berw. 1732 with w. Elizabeth Powell (Thos. 6). **Peter**, incl. because one of his ch. was Rachel, recorded at Andover, where he m. 15 July 1720 Esther Barker (see 3) and d. 23 Nov. 1756 in 59th yr. As a young man he was a benefic. under Thos. Robie's(1) will. **Deborah**, m. James Rollins

(5). **Sarah,** m. Richard Cater(4 jr.). **Jane,**
m. Ebenezer Place(3). **Rachel,** m. in Newingt. 17 Jan. 1720 Thos. Row(18 jr.).
2 **JOHN,** drowned at head of Moses Paul's
Portsm. wharf in 1722. One Mary m.
Samuel Holmes there in 1727, ano. m. Ebenezer Morse in 1729.
3 **THOMAS**; see (1).
4 **WILLIAM,** mariner, Portsm. 1713. He
and w. Sarah recd. into covt. No. Ch. and
bp. in 1715 with ch. **William, Mary.** Ano.
child was bp. 1716, **John** 1719, **Mehitable**
1721-2. Wm. -Peverly-, List 339, prob. he.
He d. by 1734; Sarah surv. In 1765 John bot
from sisters Mary Stuart, **Sarah** Dalling,
Mehitable Dalling, **Abigail** Cario and **Elizabeth** Sayward; Samuel Dalling and Wm.
Cario also signed.
**PECK,** became 51st commonest name in
N. E.
1 **CAPT. JOHN,** master of ketch -Blessing-
about to sail from the Piscataqua in
June 1685. List 90.
2 **THOMAS,** shipwright, Boston, in 1718 sold
50 a. fronting on Back Cove, Falm., bot
from Philip Lewis in Feb. 1686-7.
**PECKER,** James, carpenter, Casco, certified
with Geo. Lewis and Francis Small in
Sept. 1659 that he saw John Phillips deliver
a cow to Mr. Jordan the prev. July. In 1662
he bot Phillips's oxen from Mr. Jordan. List
221.
**PEDELL,** Anthony, fisherman, Monhegan,
gave p/a in 1672 to Edw. Woolland, sr.
of Salem to sue Mr. Wm. Browne, sr. in Essex ct. List 13.
**Pedrick,** John, owned early at Falmouth,
East. Cl. v: 156; prob. from Marblehead.
See also Y. D. 14: 15.
**Pelham,** Edward, one of Lt. March's men k.
at Cape Neddick in 1705. List 96.
**Pelton,** James (and also Fairweather 1),
merchant and inhab. of N. H. 1684. See
Prov. Papers 23: 65.

**PENDEXTER,** Poindexter, a Channel Island family.
1 **EDWARD,** coaster, Portsmouth, depos. in
1766 that he had been there ±62 yrs.
Provis. gr. in Scarb. 1720. List 339. In 1748
trustee for widow Hannah Toogood. His
will, 7 Apr.—22 Aug. 1768. His w. Elizabeth
(Larrabee 6) was rec. into cov. and bp. No.
Ch. 27 May 1715; d. 20 Aug. 1771, ag. 81. See
also Hull(9). Ch: **Elizabeth,** bp. 27 May
1715, d. unm. **Margaret,** bp. with Elizabeth,
m. 13 Nov. 1729 Geo. Seward. **Mary,** bp. 25
Sept. 1715, m. 3 Nov. 1738 Richard Tibbetts.
**Philip,** bp. 7 Feb. 1719-20, bur. from St.
John's Ch. 18 Apr. 1799. 4 or more ch. **John,**
shipwright, bp. 7 Feb. 1719-20, m. 7 May
1738 Alice Miller(12); liv. 1765, d. bef. fa.
6 or more ch. **Edward,** Portsm., mar. and

had 3 or more ch.
2 **HENRY,** Biddeford, m. 20 Dec. 1727 Deborah Littlefield of Bid. 9 ch. rec. there.
3 **ISAAC,** Newcastle 1698, ±34; from St.
Hilary in Jersey and mariner on a Jersey
ship.

**PENDLETON,** the name of two Lancashire townships.
1 **MAJOR** †‡||\***BRIAN,** Portsmouth, Winter
Harbor (66 in 1668, ±70 in 1669), m. Eli-
nor Price at St. Martin's, Birmingham, 22
Apr. 1619 and in 1625 resided in St. Sepul-
chre's without Newgate, London. Here he
was adm. freeman 3 Sept. 1634 and was prom.
(Dep. and Lieut.) in Watertown and Sudbury bef. going northward, first to Ipsw. At
Portsm. acted for Mr. Paine 11 Aug. 1651,
Assoc. Justice in Oct. fol., Commander of
Portsm. train band 1652 and a Mass. comr.
to receive the Maine submissions. Called
Capt. 1654. Selectm. nine times 1652-1662,
Rep. seven times 1653-1663, town treas. 1654-
1663, com.t.e.s.c. In 1664 he was given
magistratical power for Me., where he had
long been buying largely and by 1665 was
liv. at Winter Harbor. The town's burgess
to the Genl. Ct., Surv. General of Highways
thruout the Prov. and com.t.e.s.c. 1667. Always devoted to Mass. int., under their rule
he was in 1668 named Associate and Major
(retired 1672) and occup. about every local
office. At Winter Harbor 13 Aug. 1676 (Reg.
1: 53), of Portsm. in Aug. 1677, but apprais.
Saco estates in July and Nov. 1677 and acted
for the town in July 1679. Councillor under
Danforth in Mar. 1679-80; presided as Dep.
Pres. 30 June 1680 (Y. D. 5: 1: 1). Lists 276,
263, 44, 76, 46, 253, 323, 324, 326a, 330a, 303,
311b, 364, 245,'249, 236, 313a, 3, 28, 29, 53, 54,
79, 83, 88. See Doc. Hist. 6: 20-31; Mass. Col.
Rec. 4: 2: 401; Howard(10), Leighton(4).
His will, 9 Aug. 1677—5 Apr. 1681, names w.
Eleanor (List 246); s. James and his s.
James; gr.s. Brian Fletcher; his son's daus.
Mary and Hannah; gr.s. Brian P. His wid.
signed a deed in June 1681 (Y. D. 3: 93) and
was called lately decd. 28 July 1688. Ch:
**James,** b. 1627-8. **Joseph,** presum. a s. and
the one who wit. Robert Turner's will in
Boston 1651. Portsm. gr. 1652. Lists 323,
330a. Dead in Aug. 1677. **Mary,** m. Rev.
Seth Fletcher(10). In 1671 her fa. deeded to
her s. Pendleton, 'my gr.son, now my adopted son.' **Caleb,** Portsm. 1661 (Lists 330ab),
dead in Aug. 1677; wife Judith. His son
Caleb d. in Boston 1 Oct. 1662. Gr.s. Brian
P. in will could have been either Joseph's or
Caleb's, but more likely was James' son.
2 **CAPT. JAMES**(1), freeman at Watertown
10 May 1648 (44 in July 1672), removing
from Sudbury to Portsm. a few yrs. aft. his
fa., first seen there as a wit. 20 Jan. 1656-7.

PENDLETON 538 PENLEY

Gr.j. 1659; constable 1661; town clerk 1663-4; selectm. 1663-4, 1667-8. Adm. freeman 11 Sept. 1666 and confirmed capt. of the military company a mo. later. Saco or Scarb. wit. Aug. 1671. Portsm. 1673 (Capt.). He remov. to Stonington (there in 1675; see also Y. D. 3: 93) and Westerly, R. I. Lists 323, 324, 326ac, 330ab, 312c, 331c, 356L (Portsm.), 81, 82. He m. twice at Sudbury, 22 Oct. 1647 Mary Palmer who d. 7 Nov. 1655, and 29 Apr. 1656 Hannah Goodenow. Will, of Westerly, 9 Feb. 1702-3 (d. 29 Nov. 1709), names w. Hannah (liv. 1725) and 8 ch. by 1st w: **James,** b. at Watert. 5 Nov. 1650, liv. Aug. 1677, d. s.p. by 1698. Lists 330a, 312b. **Mary,** wit. as Pendleton 16 Apr. 1680 (Y. D. 3: 82); m. (appar. 1st) Joseph Cross(7), m. (2d) Nicholas Morey(1). See Bretton (8). **Hannah,** m. in Sudb. 13 Jan. 1679 John Bush; liv. Sudb. and Maynard. (One Hannah Bush m. John Rutter in Sudb. 12 Mar. 1690.) By 2d w., first 5 in N. H. Prov. rec: **Brian,** rec. at Sudb. 23 July (27 Sept., Prov. rec.), 1659, presum. the Brian named in gr.fa.'s will; d. s.p. bef. 1703. **Joseph,** rec. Sudb. 29 Dec. 1661, m. at Westerly in 1696 Deborah Minor; m. 2d in 1700 Patience Potts; d. there 18 Sept. 1706. Called 'eldest son' in 1734, when 4 ch. were liv. **Edmund,** b. 24 June 1665, as a boy liv. with John Kettle(1), evid. a relative thru the Goodenows, when he was blinded by a stone thrown by Walter Wescott (Y. D. 15: 50). Of Westerly in 1734 he sued John Downing jr. and Thos. Trickey for 1/9 of ±70 a. in Newington (SJC 25043). He d. at West. 1750. Wife Mary, 6 ch. **Ann,** b. 12 Nov. 1667, m. 18 Oct. 1693 Eleazer Brown of Stonington. **Caleb,** b. 8 Aug. 1669, d. in Westerly 1746. Wife Elizabeth, 10 ch. **Sarah,** bp. Stonington 18 Apr. 1675, not in fa.'s will. **Eleanor,** bp. 20 July 1679, m. Wm. Walker of Westerly. **Dorothy,** bp. 3 Oct. 1686, m. Nicholas Cottrell; liv. 1734.
**Penfield,** Henry, at Gattensby's tav. with John Morrell one Sunday in 1670.

**PENHALLOW,** ancient in co. Cornwall.
1 JOSHUA, wit. Richard Endle's deed to (2), Sept. 1695 (Y. D. 6: 127).
2 ‡*SAMUEL, Esq., Portsm., historian of Ind. Wars, bp. at St. Mabyn ('Smabun' on his gr.st.), co. Cornwall, 20 Aug. 1665, s. of Chamond, gent. and Ann (Tamlyn). Rev. Charles Morton's pupil at Newington Green near London, he accomp. him to Charlest. in July 1686, with offer from Soc. for Propaga. of Gospel among Ind. of £20 a yr. for 3 yrs. to learn Ind. language, or £60 a yr. for life as a missionary. Instead he became a Portsm. merchant, marrying Mary Cutts(2) 1 July 1687, and began his history after a mission to the Ind. under commis. of Lt.-Gov. Partridge in 1703. Rep.; Selectman; J. P.; Coun-cillor; Prov. Treasurer; Judge Superior Ct.; Chief Justice 1717 to death. 'Now resid. in Boston' Nov. 1706 (SJC 7030). Lists 330d, 336c, 337, 339, 239b, 57, 58, 62, 64, 90, 98. See Mass. Hist. Coll. 2: 1: 161; N. E. Reg. vols. 32, 34, 76. His w. Mary d. 8 Feb. 1713; he m. 2d 8 Sept. 1714 Madam Abigail (Atkinson 4) (Winslow) Oborne of Boston named with ch., gr.ch. and her dau. King in his will, 15 Aug.—16 Nov. (d. 2 Dec.) 1726. Adm. on her est. to Capt. King(2) 30 Apr. 1740. He was called of 'ffilly,' co. Cornwall, when ch. rec. (Reg. 24: 115): **Hannah,** b. 3 May 1688, m. July, 1708, James Pemberton of Boston. **Mary,** b. 1 Dec. 1689, m. Nov. 1710 Hon. Benj. Gambling of Portsm., outliv. him and only ch. Her will, 1764—1764, names many of his and her relatives. **Samuel,** b. 4 Dec. 1691, Portsm. shipwright 1719, Boston mariner 1735, d. in Eng. by 1764, leav. ch. Capt. **John,** b. 13 Jan. 1693 (List 331c), partn. with John Watts as a Boston merch. and in settlement at Arrowsic where he commanded the garrison, m. Watt's wid. Elizabeth (Butler) aft. 1717. He d. in Portsm. 28 July 1735, she 25 July 1736; 3 ch. See Lake(3), Y. D. 12: 185. **Phebe,** b. 14 Jan. 1695 (List 331c), had 4 husbands, Capt. Thos. Gross(2), Maj. Leonard Vassall, Hon. Thos. Graves, Francis Borland. **Elizabeth,** b. 21 Dec. 1698, m. 1st as 3d w. June 1730, John Dummer, Esq. (see Pike 5), m. 2d 28 June 1739, Rev. Christopher Toppan; liv. 1764. **Lydia,** b. 11 Sept. 1700, m. Henry Sloper. **Deborah,** b. 2 Jan. 1702, m. Wm. Knight(9). **Benjamin,** b. 17 Dec. 1704, H. C. 1723, d. 1725. **Joshua,** physician, Portsmouth, b. 2 Sept. 1707; adm. 31 Oct. 1739 to Benj. Gambling. **Susanna,** b. 10 Jan. 1708, m. Wm. Winkley. **Joseph,** b. 5 May 1710, Portsm. mariner 1735, d. in Eng. **Olympe,** b. 12 Feb. 1711-2, d. 1743. By 2d w: **Richard,** b. 30 Oct. 1715. 'Very much out of order,' he made will at St. Christopher, 16 Jan. 1737-8, probated 30 July 1740, all to sis. Abigail King.
3 ——. Orig. laying out of lot at Pemaquid Harbor to Thos. Cox, sr., in 1686 was perh. misread, but, as printed in Cox pamphlet No. 3, p. 17, Cox and Penaller were adjoining lot owners.

**PENLEY.** One Sampson P. m. Margaret Standon at Plymstock, co. Devon, 29 Oct. 1639.
SAMPSON, Falmouth (Purpooduck) 1658, fisherman, prison keeper. In 1661 Nicholas White sold ¼ of House Isl. to John Breme, reserving liberty to S. P. to make fish there and to have refusal if sold. In 1663 he took by levy from neighbor Jos. Phippen(4) ¼ the Isl., half the old ho. and stages, and all the ho. Phippen had built; later sold his whole int. to Geo. Munjoy. Lists 221, 222b,

223b, 227, 25, 30, 34, 86. See also Greason, Haines(15). He testif. in 1684 as an ancient inhab. of Casco Bay; in Apr. 1687, 'senior,' sold ho. and land on Purpooduck Side betw. John Wallis and Nathl. White to Robert Lawrence, this proved by wit. 11 Jan. 1687-8. Lawrence sued the wid. and admx. Rachel in Dec. 1688. Ch., the daus. of Sampson and Rachel (his w. 1668) named in an ancient memo: **Sampson**, Boston mariner, sued for rent of a Boston ho. hired by his w. and occupied by her 1 yr. from 27 May 1691; liv. there Dec. 1694, ±30; d. s.p. **Jane** (Ann by memo), m. Dennis Murrough. **Dorcas**, m. Hugh Wilcott. **Mary**, m. Henry Bailey(2).

**Penmore**, Charles. Conc. D. 2: 219, quotes Robert Mussell's deed to him 10 May 1659. See Benmore.

**PENNELL**, Penwill. Devonshire sent those early in Me., where now are many descendants of the later comers to Gloucester from the Isle of Jersey.

1 **CLEMENT**, and s. **Walter** in the -Margery-, 1643. List 21. From Newton Ferrers, co. Devon. See Hatch(1).

2 **JOHN** (Penwill), Mr., mariner, at the Shoals in July 1661, ±47 in 1669. See also (5), Aldrich(3). Of Plymouth, co. Devon (Pennywell), he bot the Star Isl. fishing plant of John Frederick & Co. in Dec. 1663; mtg. all or part to Simon Lynde, 1665. Sued by Cutts 1669 for non-deliv. of 6 butts Madeira wine. He or his s. apprais. Cornelius Hooke's est., 1671. Sometime commander of ketch -George and Samuel- of Piscat. and dead some two yrs. in Aug. 1675 when his wid., thru atty. John Davis of York, his s. and h. **John**, jr. (b. ±1647), John Hunking and Christopher Jose gave discharge to John Cutt (also Robert Holmes), who had brot back Nevis goods, the last part of a cargo left there by J. P.

3 **JOHN**(2), Mr., York (Penwill) wit. in June 1670 with John Davis(18), whose adopted dau. Sarah 'Puddington' was his w. in 1673; see also Burdett(2). York gr. alone 18 Nov. 1674, tho deeds oft. ment. joint gr. made to him and John Puddington same day. Gr.j. 1683, 1687, 1690-1 (foreman). Joseph Weare his bondsm. 1685. He was ±40, wife ±46, in Aug. 1687; both wit. a York deed in Oct. 1689. List 312f. He remov. to Boston, there wit. will of Jacob Everest(1) in 1692, and depos. in Apr. 1695 that he wrote Geo. Norton's orders to his ship master. York, Jan.-Mar. 1693-4; late of York (not called dec.) in Feb. 1695-6. In Nov. 1697 one John occup. a small ho. of Capt. Thos. Berry's est. (Suff. Prob.); one wid. Berry in Boston list betw. Joseph P. sr. and jr. 1688. Adm. in Me. 29 May 1704 to Mary (Puddington) Weare, his w. being n.c.m. If she did not

recover and m. Alexander Maxwell(1) in 1707, that Sarah is unkn. Kn. ch: **Hannah**, m. Joseph Weare. **Alice**, m. Nathl. Freeman (2). One A. P. adm. to Boston 2d Ch. 1691.

4 **JOHN**(7), minor, had fished for Mr. John Bowditch of Salem bef. Feb. 1678-9 when his fa., thru atty., sued B. in Essex Ct. He went to Kennebec with or near Giles Hibbins, wit. a Parker deed with Abraham Errington(1) in Apr. 1688, and was at Josiah Smith's in Charlest. in Oct. 1689 with w. and **child**, Kennebec refugees. Note that one John (see 3) occup. a Boston ho., 1697.

5 **JOSEPH** (Penwill), b. ±1629-30, mariner, York 1670, would seem a br. of (2). In Jan. 1670 he sold 1/16 of the -True Love- of York to Mr. Abraham Browne of Boston and bot from Job Alcock ho. and land adj. land form. sold to Rishworth, and other land adj. R., with passage to fetch water; just bef. or aft. R. withdrew a suit ag. him for fetching it without his consent. Sued by Shapleigh 1674 on a bond payable in fish and pipestaves. Not noted in York again. Boston in Dec. 1679; there a mo. later, ±51, and ano. mo. later, ag. 50. Only one ch. located by deeds: **Anna**, m. Robert Moore(17), their dau. selling the Alcock prop. Yet note Joseph with w. Ann in Boston where a dau. **Mary** was b. 13 Feb. 1665; **Ann** d. 21 Dec. 1688, ±60 (Copp's Hill); and adm. on his est., mariner, was gr. to s. Joseph 1 May 1690, and in 1691 at request of four daus. to Ralph Carter(10), Joseph jr. being deceased.

6 **RACHEL** and **THOMAS** (see Clay 4, Durrell 1), came from the Gloucester family; as did ano. Thomas, later in Falm.

7 **WALTER**, Saco (Winter Harbor), may have been (1); List 21. He m. by 1649 Mary Booth(3); List 246. Her fa. and he had gr. of the neck called 'Stonie Stand' in July 1653, with ano. gr. to him alone. In 1659 he had deed from W. Phillips of 50 a. adj. Booth and Tristram; in 1663 he and Booth divid. their home lot. With John Davis apprais. the Booth est. Lists 243a, 24, 245, 27. A refugee in Salem, where his w. was adm. to Ch. 10 Mar. 1679. His son was 'jr.' in Apr. 1681. Inv. in Me., 4 Nov. 1682, incl. land and marsh at Little River, attested by wid. Mary 21 May 1683. Adm. to her and s. Walter 6 Mar. 1682-3, bondsm. John Abbott and Edw. Sargent; adm. two mos. later to s. Walter alone, bondsm. Scottow, John Sargent and Abbott. Kn. ch., 5 rec. Saco: **Walter**, b. 1 Dec. 1649. **Mary**, b. 12 Mar. 1652, m. Giles Hibbins(1). **Deborah**, b. 30 Dec. 1654. **Joseph**. Adm. 6 Mar. 1682-3 to br. Walter who returned inv. taken by John Leighton(4) and John Davis; clothes, two heifers, a horse, fish. **John**. **Sarah**, b. 2 Aug. 1661. **Susannah**, b. 29 Mar. 1669.

8 **WALTER**(7), weaver, Winter Harbor, prosec. with Giles Hibbins in 1673 for butchering Mr. Bolles' cow. Suppos. at Salem with the others, he ret. bef. Apr. 1681, when accus. of marking Mr. Watts' horse. Road surveyor 1682; in 1687 sold to Edw. Sargent the 50 a. his fa. bot from Mr. Phillips and gave poss. in July 1688. Lists 249, 33. Not noted during the 1690's, perh. at Newb. where he m. 15 Apr. 1700, Ann (Green 19) Barton(5). They had been cautioned in 1686 (Cape Porpus witnesses) and were liv. on the Barton land at Cape P. in 1701, he ±48, she 43. York 1719, he ag. 70; called of Cape P. the same yr., he sold his gr. there, but ack. deed in York. Of Arundel in Apr. 1722, they deeded Barton prop. to her. s.-in-law Solomon Holman for support. He depos. in 1724-5, ±74; dead in Aug. 1730 when S. H. of Newb. sold. If he m. early, Hannah Pennell, dau. of ——, bp. Salem 4 May 1679, could have been his ch.

**PENNEY**, Penny.

1 **CHARLES**, one of four soldiers in service 8 or 9 mos., writing a letter from Maj. Frost's ho. 27 May 1690. Late of Kit., decd., adm. 16 May 1692 to Sarah Ferguson(3).

2 **CAPT. HENRY** (Penny), merchant, Portsmouth, came out of Eng. because of his debts and liv. here ab. 26½ yrs. He had remov. a newly launched ship from Me. to N. H. in 1682, and sued Benj. Bagworth, a Boston mariner, in 1684. Active ag. Cranfield. O. A. 28 Aug. 1685. Sworn Clerk of Court Dec. 1692; Notary Public. Lists 59, 65, 68, 98, 336c, 96. Will (with armorial seal), 17 Feb. 1708-9—18 May 1709, gives English prop. to absent son Henry, and £10 to sis. Judith Clark if liv., else to her ch. The son, also Capt., at Dartmouth, co. Devon, made Capt. John Wentworth his atty. 2 Mar. 1709-10; Arthur Savage wit. the p/a and swore to it here.

3 **THOMAS**, Wells, wit. a Thompson deed in Berwick 1702, and had Kit. gr. 1703, sold 1710. Wells gr. Mar. 1713-4. Lists 298, 269c. He m. 1st Joanna Littlefield(12); m. 2d 17 Aug. 1732 Mary (Tidy) Brawn (2 jr.). Ch. bp. Wells: **Mary**, 23 Feb. 1706-7; **Thomas**, 27 Oct. 1710 (List 269c). One Thomas was early at Gloucester (List 80).

4 **WILLIAM**, in 1663 Matthew Giles's servant boy; in jail 1675 for not working for his living; perh. the Wm., removal of whose banishment was refused by Mass. Ct. in June 1680 when James Dennis's was removed. One Wm. and Sarah had Mehitable b. Boston 1678. Wm. and w. Ruth, appar. dau. of George Hollard, had a dau. Ruth, b. in Bos. 1681; he d. in 1683. See Andrew Marriner(1), the admr. in 1691.

**Pepper**, Mr. List 90.

**PEPPERELL.** In 1617 one Wm. and w. Johan were of Revelstoke, co. Devon, the par. named by Col. Wm. in his will, and from where Henry Roe wrote him 26 Nov. 1731, saying, 'Shall be glad to see your son in this country,' and 'Mr. Champernoon is dead,' also mentioning payments to Mary Nichols, Joan Grendal and others, and a visit to Pepperell's house. See also Creber and Aspinw. Not. Rec. p. 163.

**COL. *WILLIAM**, Esq., mariner, merchant, Kittery, of importance himself, but more as fa. of Sir William and ancestor of many (of other names) well placed here and in Eng. See N. E. Reg. 19: 141, 222; 20: 1. Born ±1647-8 (±80 in Jan. 1727-8) and first at the Shoals, he m. ±1680 Margery Bray(2) and made a home at Kit. Point. His persistence in going aft. Pearce(8) prop. in her behalf prob. shows how he advanced his fortunes. Gr.j. 1691, 1693, 1694 (foreman); selectm. 1693-4, 1698-9; moderator 1695-9; County Treas. 1696 and later; Rep. 1697; J. P. 1695 (Stoughton), 1699 (Bellomont); Judge 1699; clerk of both courts to Apr. 1725; and as an Esq. and Judge lic. many times to retail and keep pub. ho. Adm. to No. Ch., Portsm., 1696, and there young Wm. and Miriam were bp. in 1697; he and w. Margery orig. memb. Kit. Point Ch. in 1714. Lists 90, 36, 333b, 298, 331c, 289, 296, 291, 279, 297. His genealogical will, 19 July 1733 (d. 15 Feb. 1733-4 in 87th yr.), names w., ch., and gr.ch., 3 Phillips kinsmen (see 24), English relatives and poor of Revelstoke. Wid. Margery depos. 29 Sept. 1735, ag. 74. Her will, 1 Jan. 1739-40 (d. 24 Apr. 1741, ag. 81), names ch., Jackson gr.ch., sis. Mary Deering, dau.-in-law Jane Frost. Ch: Capt. **Andrew**, b. 1 July 1681, mariner, Newc.; inv. 14 May 1714. Lists 296-298, 316. He m. Jane Elliot(6), who m. 2d 25 Nov. 1714 Chas. Frost, Esq.(2 jr.). Ch: Sarah, b. 4 Dec. 1708, m. 12 Sept. 1723 her step-br. Chas. Frost; Margery, b. 25 Mar. 1712, m. Capt. Wm. Wentworth. **Mary**, b. 5 Sept. 1685, m. 1st Capt. John Frost(2); m. 2d Rev. Benj. Colman; m. 3d 6 Oct. 1748 Rev. Benj. Prescott; d. 18 Apr. 1766. **Margery**, b. 15 Sept. 1689, m. 1st Peletiah Whittemore; m. 2d Elihu Gunnison(1 jr.). **Joanna**, b. 22 June 1692, m. Dr. Geo. Jackson(5 jr.). **Miriam**, b. 3 Sept. 1694, m. 25 Apr. 1715 Andrew Tyler of Boston. 9 ch. Sir **William**, b. 27 June 1696, earned his baronetage at Louisburg. Lists 279, 291, 297, 298. He m. 16 Mar. 1723 Mary, dau. of Grove and Elizabeth (Sewall) Hirst of Boston; d. 'at his seat in Kittery' 6 July 1759. His will made two days bef., like his fa.'s, names all his kin. Lady Pepperell d. 25 Nov. 1789. Ch: Andrew, H. C. 1743, d. 1751; Wm. and Margery, both d.y.; and only surv., also oldest, ch., Elizabeth, b. 29 Dec. 1723, m. Nathl.

Sparhawk, Esq. Her 2d s. Wm. Pepperell S. dropped his fam. name, succ. his gr.fa. as 2d Baronet and as a Loyalist went to Eng., where desc. remain. **Dorothy**, b. 23 July 1698, m. 1st 26 Mar. 1719 John Watkins of Newc., adm. to her 16 Sept. 1723, 3 ch.; m. 2d Hon. Joseph Newmarch. **Jane**, b. 2 June 1701, m. 1st Benj. Clark(21), 2 ch.; m. 2d Wm. Tyler; m. 3d Ebenezer Tirrell of Medford.

**Percival**, Richard, owned in Shrewsbury patent; sold to Obadiah Bruen. List 386.

**PERKINS.** The Hampton and Ipswich families seem related; the latter came from Hillmorton, co. Warwick. Became 35th commonest name in N. E.

1 **ABRAHAM**, br. of (9), ag. 60 in Sept. 1663. Hampton 1639, freeman 13 May 1640. In 1648 he and Henry Green(7), apparently a relative, had a gr. near the Falls to build a water mill. Clerk of the market 1650; constable, com.t.e.s.c. 1651; ordinary lic. 1651 and later; lic. to still and sell by qt. 1665; marshal of Hampt. 1653-4; often on jury and gr.j. (foreman 1676-7, 1679). A good penman, he did business for others and the town. Lists 391a, 392abe, 393ab, 394, 396, 397a, 398, 49, 54. His w. was Mary, Lists 393a, 394. That she and Susanna, w. of (9), were daus. of Humphrey Wyeth, as often claimed, tho not true of Susanna, may have been true of Mary who had two sons Humphrey and knew ab. Em Wyeth's affairs, perh. only as Benj. Wyeth was her husb.'s apprent. His will, 22 Aug. (d. 31 Aug., ag. 70) 1683, names w., 7 ch., gr.s. John P. and gr.dau. Mary Fifield liv. with him. Wid. d. 29 May 1706, ag. 88. Ch: **Mary**, bp. 15 Dec. 1639, m. Giles Fifield(2). **Abraham**, b. 2 Sept. 1639, bp. with Mary (see Johnson 24). **Luke**, apprenticed self in Apr. 1654, ±14, to Samuel Carter, shoemaker, Charlest. (see Jones 42); m. 9 Mar. 1663 Hannah (Long) Cookery of Charlest., where he d. 20 Mar. 1709-10, she 16 Nov. 1715. 9 ch. **Humphrey**, b. 23 Jan. 1642, **James**, b. 11 Apr. 1644, **Timothy**, b. July 1646, all d.y. **James**, b. 5 Oct. 1647. **Jonathan**, b. 30 May 1650. **David**, b. 28 Feb. 1653-4, blacksm., Beverly, Bridgewater, m. Elizabeth Brown of Bev. who was dism. to Bridgew. Ch. in 1690 and d. 14 July 1735; he 1 Oct. 1736. Will, 5 ch. **Abigail**, b. 12 Apr. 1655, m. Deac. John Folsom(4). **Timothy**, b. 29 June 1657, d. 27 June 1660. **Sarah**, b. 26 July 1659, unm. 1683. **Humphrey**, b. 17 May 1661. See also N. E. Reg. 50: 34.

2 **ABRAHAM**(1), m. 27 Aug. 1668 Elizabeth Sleeper (Thos.). Constable 1674-6. K. by Ind. 13 June 1677 at North Hill where he liv.; adm. 9 Oct. fol. to wid. who m. 2d Alex.

Denham(1). Ch: **Mercy**, b. 3 July 1671, m. 12 July 1694 Samuel Chandler of Amesb.; in 1698 they q.c. to Jonathan Elkins. **Mary**, b. 20 Nov. 1673, m. John Moulton(11). **Elizabeth**, b. 9 Apr. 1676, m. Jeremiah Dow(7).

3 **CALEB**(9), Hampt., went to defense of Marlboro in 1676, m. 24 Apr. 1677 Bethia Philbrick(8) and in 1678 had his portion from fa. Gr.j. 1695. Lists 396, 52, 399a. In 1724 he deeded homestead aft. death of both to only surv. ch. Benj. Ch: **Rhoda**, b. 24 June 1677, m. Elias Philbrook(4). **Benjamin**, Hampt. F., b. 11 May 1680, m. 1 Mar. 1710 Lydia Macrease. List 339a. 6 ch. **Ann**, b. 19 Mar. 1682, d. s.p. bef. 1724.

4 **EBENEZER**(9), Hampt., in 1681 said 'my cousin Isaac Green.' Lists 395, 52. He and w. Mercy sold out in 1693, his mo. Susanna signing, and went to Delaware where he and br. Joseph bot in Brandywine hundred. Ch. rec. Hampt: **Daniel**, b. June 1685; **Abigail**, b. 11 Aug. 1687; **Jonathan**, b. 10 May 1691, all in fa.'s will, 20 July—16 Sept. 1703, with **four** more, but no wife. See N. E. Reg. 47: 483.

5 **EBENEZER**, in Capt. Hill's Kittery garrison, 1704. List 289.

6 **GEORGE**, fisherman, Shoals 1675, bot a Hog Isl. ho. in 1684, selling to Richard Tope in 1687. 'Friend Perkins' agent at the Shoals for Andrew Diamond of Ipsw. 1692. Constable 1693. List 316. Son **William**, Star Isl., bot back fa.'s place from kinsm. R. T. (jr.) of London, 1718. Smuttynose gr. 1725, the yr. he and w. Sarah sold a Great Isl. ho., bot from Broad. His ch. Mary and William, from the Shoals, bp. at Hampt. 1724, 1726; James, s. of Wid. P. of the Shoals bp. at Portsm. So. Ch. 1730. One Elizabeth was an orig. memb. of Gosport Ch. 1729. Thomas of Gosport, adm. to cr. Samuel Waldo 1735; left wid. Sarah.

7 **GEORGE**, paid by Wm. Ardell in 1689 for hauling boards for the Lamprill Riv. mill; poss. error for (24) or a son who d. early.

8 **HUMPHREY**(1), Hampton, m. Martha Moulton(8); had the homestead. Gr.j. 1693. Lists 52, 57, 399a. He d. 7 Jan. 1711-2; adm. 16 Sept. fol. to wid. Ch., all but John named in probate memo. 15 Sept. 1712: **John**, b. 12 Mar. 1688, his doctor's bill paid 1714. **Jonathan**, b. 24 Nov. 1691. **Mary**, b. 28 Nov. 1693, m. Samuel French(1). **James**, Hampt., Rye, b. 9 Sept. 1695, m. 24 Dec. 1717 Huldah Robie(5). 9 ch. **Martha**, m. 16 Sept. 1720 Ephraim Leonard of Bridgew. **Sarah**, m. 27 June 1726 Stephen Flanders of Exeter. **Abigail**, b. 4 Mar. 1708-9, m. ano. Bridgew. Leonard.

9 **ISAAC**, br. of (1), Hampton 1639, bot a farm next Salisb. line, now Seabrook,

from Rev. Mr. Dalton in June 1652 and prob. soon mov. there. Constable 1650; j. service often. Lists 391a, 393ab, 394, 396, 398, 49. In Jan. 1680 he deeded to s. Ebenezer for supp. of self and w. Susanna, and d. Nov. 1685. Susanna, List 393a, was not a Wyeth (see Bursley 4, Peabody). With her consent s. Ebenezer sold the homestead in 1693 and she went with him and other ch. to Delaware, where her est. was adm. in 1699 by s.-in-law Hussey, principal cr. Ch: **Lydia**, m. 17 Oct. 1659 Eliakim Wardwell. **Isaac**, bp. 8 Dec. 1639, drowned 10 Sept. 1661. **Jacob**, bp. 24 May 1640. **Rebecca**, m. John Hussey(3). **Daniel**, d. 1 Aug. 1662. **Caleb. Benjamin**, b. 12 Feb. 1649-50, d. 23 Nov. 1670. **Susanna**, b. Aug. 1652, m. 1st 12 May 1673 Isaac Buswell of Salisb.; m. 2d Wm. Fuller(6). **Hannah**, b. 24 Feb. 1655-6, m. James Philbrick(2). **Mary**, b. 23 July 1658, m. Lt. Isaac Chase(2). **Ebenezer**, b. 9 Dec. 1659. **Joseph**, b. 9 Apr. 1661.

10 **JACOB**(9), m. 30 Dec. 1669 Mary Philbrook(8) and had a mar. portion from fa. Temporarily at Holmeshole, Martha's V., in Feb. 1674-5. Jury (N. H.) 1685. Lists 396, 52. Ch. at Hampt: **Isaac**, b. 18 Dec. 1671. **Jacob**, b. 24 Dec. 1674. **Mary**, b. 18 Aug. 1678. **Benjamin**, b. 12 Aug. 1683. In 1693 he bot 330 a. on the Delaware River below Burlington, and went there, deeding this in 1711 to the three sons above, reserving life int.

11 **JACOB**, York, Wells, b. 15 Feb. 1685, s. of Jacob and Elizabeth (Sparks) of Ipsw., depos. in 1761 that he knew Cape Neddick lands near 60 yrs. ago. York gr. Mar. 1714-5; taxed Wells 1726. He m. 1st Lydia Stover (John); at least 1 s. **John**. He m. 2d in Hampt. F. 17 Oct. 1717 Anna Littlefield(18) and soon denied accusa. of Deborah Webber, whose s., b. 8 Feb. 1717-8, bore name Joseph Perkins. **Children**, by 2d w. Anna who was adm. to Wells Ch. in 1723. He was dead in 1772.

12 **JAMES**(1), Hampton, early at Exeter where his sis. liv. (O. A. there 30 Nov. 1677), returned, m. 13 Dec. 1681 Leah Cox (18) and liv. on her fa.'s land. Lists 381, 383, 399b. Will, 18 Mar. 1722-3—9 Dec. 1731, names w. Leah (d. 19 Feb. 1749) and ch: **Sarah**, b. 30 Oct. 1682, m. Samuel Graves(4). **Mary**, b. 2 Dec. 1686, m. Jonathan Taylor. **Lydia**, b. 30 Jan. 1689, m. Joseph Clifford(4). **Hannah**, b. 18 Aug. 1691, m. Simon Moulton (14). **Elizabeth**, bp. with 5 others 11 May 1701, m. Joseph Philbrook(2). **James**, b. 17 Mar. 1696, m. 22 Feb. 1727-8 Shuah Nason (Jonathan 6). Will, of Kensington, 12 Aug. 1754—30 Apr. 1755, names her, 9 ch. **Moses**, b. 30 July 1698, m. 1st 26 Feb. 1730 Mary Marston(8); m. 2d Hannah Nay; d. 14 Aug. 1765. **David**, b. 30 Nov. 1701, liv. 1728.

13 **JOHN**, indebted to Stydson est. 1673. List 87.

14 **JOHN**, of Old England, at Fort Mary, Saco, 1704. His w. and **two ch.** (small) were here.

15 **JOHN**, tailor, Newcastle, sued by Richard Rookes, Berw., for cloth, in 1716.

16 **JONATHAN**(1), Hampton, wit. Thurton to Robie, 1677. Liv. on homestead; d. 24 Jan. 1688-9. List 52. Wid. Sarah (m. in Exeter 20 Dec. 1682) m. 2d Josiah Sanborn. Ch: **Abraham**, b. ±1684, d. 14 Apr. 1715, and wid. Mary 6 Nov. 1738, ag. 53. Ch: Kezia, b. 25 Apr. 1709, m. James Towle; Anna 1714-1715. **Abigail**, b. 30 Apr. 1687, m. in Portsm. Geo. Ayers(5).

17 **JOSEPH**(9), Hampton, had w. Martha. List 52. See also Jacob Basford. Ch. at Hampt: **Joseph**, b. 28 July 1689. **John**, b. 4 June 1691. **Caleb**, b. 8 July 1693. These, and **four** more, but not w., named in his will, 4 Jan. 1706-7—19 Aug. 1707, in Delaware where he bot with br. Ebenezer(4), in Oct. 1693.

18 **MATTHEW**, Great Isl. wit. 1707, poss. the Ipsw. br. or neph. of (11).

19 **NATHANIEL**(21). Dover Neck, had fa.'s homestead 1693 and grants 1694, 1701. Gr.j. 1699. List 358d. In 1725 he deeded half his 1701 gr. to s. Joseph, the bal. in 1727 to Samuel (not called son), and his homestead in July 1727 to s. John, reserv. half the yield to self and w. Hannah (Tibbetts). She did not sign the deed to Samuel 13 Nov. 1727. Both Nathl. sr. and jr. ment. 1729. Ch: **Samuel**, had gr. 1701, 1702. Lists 358b, 368b, 369. See Derry(1), Munsey, **Gray** (8). In 1750 he deeded to gr.s. Dodovah Garland for supp. of self and w. Mary (Tasker); dead 1758. 6 ch. bp. O. R., 5 of them rec. Dover 1703-1723. **Mary** (prob.), m. Ichabod Rollins(1). **Nathaniel**, weaver, m. 15 Mar. 1715-6 Abigail Roberts (wid. of William) and liv. on the Roberts farm at Sligo. She liv. 1739; adm. on his est. 30 Mar. 1748. 4 ch. rec. 1716-1723. **Son**, d. 28 Oct. 1706, ag. ±14 yrs. 6 mo., appar. called Nathaniel in error (List 96). **Joseph**, List 99, p. 75. He and w. Eleanor were bp. at O. R. 1728; 2 ch. bp. 1728, 1729. Wid. Eleanor o.c. and 3 more ch. bp. at Wm. Buswell's ho. there in 1742. **Thomas**, a wit. 1715, Rochester 1744 with w. Martha, who was bp. there in 1791, ag. 93, 'a Quaker in her young days.' **Joshua**, Dover Neck, sued by Jeremiah Tibbetts in 1722 for supp. of dau. Lydia's ch. He m. in Greenl. 1 Sept. 1723 Dorothy Philbrick (see 4); 9 ch. rec. or bp. **Solomon**, weaver, Dover 1740, Rochester 1754. 4 ch. rec. in R. 1741-1753, and he bp. in 1785, ag. 83, a former Quaker. **John**, bp. 23 Oct. 1705, m. in Hampt. F. 21 Dec. 1727 Rebecca Draper of Hampt. He mtg. fa.'s homestead in 1744, and with w. sold part to s. John in 1760.

20 **NATHANIEL**, Kittery wit. 1694, Portsm. wit. (with Hugh Banfield) 1697. In 1701 he sold land below Salmon F. to John Cole of Kit.; Philip Hubbard his bondsm. 1713; Sergt. N. taxed Berw. 1713.

21 **THOMAS**, Dover, and John Adams, hayed for Capt. Waldron in 1665. In 1669 gr. a 3½ a. ho. lot on Dover Neck, N. of Isaac Stokes, form. laid out to Mrs. Ludecas; fighting with Stokes that yr. In 1674, ±46, he told about a man behind T. Beard's barn selling liquor to an Indian, but was ±56 or 55 in 1677 if the one deposing bef. Waldron ab. Tristram Harris. His w. Frances and Mary Beard depos. in 1678. Lists 357c, 359ab, 52. See also (24). 'Sr.' in 1693, he deeded dwg. and orchard on Fore River betw. widows Canney and Willey to s. **Nathaniel**, reserving half the produce. His w. had taken care of David Hamilton in 1697; a wid. in June 1699 selling without lic.; m. 2d Mark Giles (5). Ano. s. **Thomas**, is indicated by the fa.'s 'Sr.' See (23), (24).

22 **THOMAS**, Saco, inv. taken 13 Sept. 1660, lot, ho. and marsh, and ano. lot laid out at Blue Point by Capt. Bonython, for which he had served 7 yrs.

23 **THOMAS**, Greenland, Arundel, apprent. in Greenl. and liv. on Champernowne's farm on Great Bay 1706; presum. s. of (21), but it was (24) who depos. ab. Champernowne. He m. Mary Banfield(2). Greenl. 1718, Cape P. 1720, Portsm. 1721, Arundel 1722, appar. perma., tho w. Mary adm. to Greenl. Ch. 1726. Lists 330de, 335a, 337, 338c. (In Arundel was ano. Thomas, Capt., from Topsfield, his w. formerly Mary Wildes). Our Thos., ag. 62, depos. in Furber-Weeks suit 1733: 48 or 50 yrs. bef. Wm. Furber cut hay on his Greenl. marsh and at times lodged at 'my master's ho.' He and w. Mary of Arundel 1740, he alone in 1742. Deeds show: **John**, Arundel, Boston, had w. Jane. **Thomas**, Lt., Capt., m. Lydia Harding (6); d. 22 Feb. 1752, ag. 52. **George**, m. in Wells 7 June 1733 Hannah Hutchins, d. soon and she m. Lt. John Burbank. **Samuel**, m. in Greenl. 9 June 1734 Williams Bond (see Mains 8). Poss. daus.: **Sarah**, m. Joseph Urin in Greenl. 6 Sept. 1716; **Mary**, adm. to Greenl. Ch. 1726 (m. Murphy); **Chasey**, m. James Deshon of Arundel.

24 **WILLIAM** (also Parkinson), Oyster River, Exeter, b. ±1639-40, his master Thos. Canney. He bot at O. R. 1666, constable 1668, m. Elizabeth Ault(1) bef. 8 June 1669 (her fa.'s deed to them). In 1675 he bot from the Hiltons in Ex. (Newmarket). Gr.j. 1678. Dover gr. 1694. Lists 363bc, 365, 366, 357c, 359a, 49 (Dover), 52, 57, 92, 387, 376b. See also Rand(3), Huckins(4) (read Wm. P. for George). He depos., ±80 in 1715 (worked for

Matthew Giles 60 yrs. bef.); ±90 in Jan. 1722-3 (ab. Champernowne's old farm); poss. he was the Goodm. P. in an early Champernowne account. He perh. d. in 1732 (gr.s. not found as jr. aft. Sept. 1731), but not ag. 116, a record appar. set down in 1824. **Kn.** ch: **Elizabeth**, m. John Wheeler. **John**, poss. only s., as fa. in 1713 deeded all lands to him aft. his death. He m. Rebecca Smart (Robert), both liv. 1741, she dead 1749, he 1758. Lists 387, 376b. Joseph Burley named her ch: John (List 376b), Robert, Sarah Metcalf, Elizabeth Durgin, Rebecca Jenkins, Mary Neal, Eleanor Pike, Susannah Duley, 'and sundry others.' Two 'sundries' appear: Wm., jr. (List 376b), Newmarket 1724, his gr.fa. Wm. also there; called s. by John 1727. Benjamin called s. 1742, single. See also (7), (21), (23).

**Perrer.** See Perry.

**Perrum**, William, master of the -Samuel- at Richmond's Isl. 1638. List 21.

**PERRY.** Ap Harry, a Welsh patronymic, scantily repres. in early Me. and N. H. Became 59th commonest name in N. E.

1 **ELIZABETH.** See Holdridge, Keyes(5), Mason(20).

2 **JOHN**, Falmouth. So. Ch., Portsm., records that he and w. Elizabeth renewed bp. cov. at Falm. 2 May 1720 and had **Margaret** bp. John of Falm. bot Larrabee land in No. Yarm. 1727. See also Giles(11).

3 **MATTHEW**, Oyster River, had ch. bp. Feb. 1729-30: **James, William** (b. Dover 17 Apr. 1722; mo. Mary), **John, Paul, Elizabeth, Hannah.** List 369.

4 **RICHARD** (Perrer), in Me. ct. June 1688 with Joanna Holley (Hawley), not called wife. She m. 2d Thomas Marshall(9). Ch. by both husbands rec. together at Newc., the P. ch: **Christian**, b. 3 Aug. 1690. **Richard**, b. 18 Feb. 1695, blacksm., iron worker, much employed at Newc. fort. Presum. husb. of Hannah Jones(55) and fa. of William and Richard. Liv. 1743.

5 **ROGER**, bot in Scarboro from Elliot 1719 and propr. 1720, was from Marshfield. List 239b.

6 **SAMUEL**, his Newc. marsh taxed 1708, List 316, may be Berry.

7 **WILLIAM**, Portsm., and w. Sarah; s. **John** bp. So. Ch. 1723. Poss. Berwick 1731.

8 **WIDOW**, taxed at Graffort Lane, Portsm., 1720.

**PERRYMAN.** 1 **Edward**, lost in the great storm Jan. 1677-8. See Broad(4).

2 **NICHOLAS**, Exeter merchant, m. bef. Dec. 1720 Joanna Dudley(3); see will of wid. Joanna Dyer(4). List 376b. 5 ch. 'N. P. his book 1723' a valuable record to 1754, one item under 1726 'Capt. James Perry-

man, your wife.' See also Edgecomb(1 jr.).

**Pester,** William. See Knight(16).

**PETERS, Rev. Hugh,** Salem, bot at Cape Porpus with Richard Saltonstall, Esq., in 1639 (Lechford 209). On way thru woods from Dover to York, where Rev. John Ward was to be installed, he, Mr. Dudley and a York man were lost two days and a night. See his letters to Winthrop, Mass. Hist. Soc. Col. 4: 6: 103-108.

**PETERSON.** 1 **John,** in Pemaquid garrison 1689. List 126.

2 **NICHOLAS,** Kennebec, wit. a Parker-Webber deed in Sept. 1664; there in 1672. List 13.

3 ——, mariner, Great Isl., in crew of a Dutch ship. In 1682 servant of Mr. Geo. Jaffrey.

**Petfree,** ——, on the Piscataqua early. List 41.

**PETT.** 1 **Abraham,** in 1697 shot Abigail Pickering(8) with a pistol used for scaring away birds; her fa. brot action ag. him and his master John Fartridge, sr., in Dec. 1699. In So. Carolina in Jan. 1704-5, he, Richard Waterhouse and Benj. Windsor wit. for John Green(13 jr.) and the Axalls; the others ackn. for selves and for him in Kittery two mos. later.

2 **JOHN,** Kittery Point wit. 1672, 1677. In 1679 he sued John Parrett for debt; in 1681, ag. ±27, he and Ephraim Crockett depos. about being at the ho. form. Joseph Pearce's. (?List 90, Pette). One John, taxed Exeter 1714, owned at Quamscott 1715; List 388. See also Averill(5).

**PETTIGREW, Francis,** Kittery, b. ±1669 (±70 in June 1739), by trad. French (but note Deering 7), m. 1st, bef. 17 Apr. 1707 when her fa. deeded him ho. and 30 a., Elizabeth (Ball 5) Hammons (see 3), who d. 1 Mar. 1725-6; m. 2d 17 Nov. 1726 Elizabeth (Hutchins 1) Davis. Lists 291, 296-298. In 1747 wid. Elizabeth and the two surv. sons waived adm. in favor of Francis Allen. Ch: **Mary** (m. Francis Allen). **John. Francis. Thomas. William** (liv. 1747). **Joseph. Benjamin** (liv. 1747).

**PETTIT, Sergt. Thomas** (also Petty), Exeter, served Oliver Mellows in Boston 3½ yrs. from 1634; ord. whipped in Mar. 1636-7 for suspicion of slander, idleness and stubbornness. At the end of his service, he was gr. a Boston ho.-lot, but soon went to Exeter. Lists 373, 374ac, 375b, 376ab, 377. Drill officer at Exeter May 1645; also May 1647 (Sergt. -Samuel-). Tr.j. 1649-50, 1653-54. Se'ectman 1652. On 8 Oct. 1653 Edw. Gilman sold ho.-lots form. John Cram's and Thos. Pettit's. In Oct. 1654 he and Francis Swain were bondsm. for John Garland. His w. was Christian in 1647. Kn. ch: **Thomas,** jr.; his fa. had an Ex. gr. for him 20 May 1652. **Han-**

nah, b. Ex. beginning of Feb. 1647. **Mary,** wit. a Gilman deed with John Tedd 14 Jan. 1654-5, may have been a 2d w. or ano. dau.

**PEVERLY,** occasionally Peverell. The former sometimes a corruption of Beverly; Peverell dates from the Conqueror.

1 **JOHN**(2), Portsmouth, (±82 in Apr.1731), had a town gr. in 1674. Summonsed in 1679 for failure to pay rates for some yrs. past, and the only Peverly taxed in 1688. Jury 1684, 1692; O. A. Aug. 1685; selectm. 1696. Abs. from meet. 1698, when Thos. Beck was his bondsm. Lists 313a, 324, 330acd, 331b, 332b, 335a, 339, 52. See also Hicks(4). His wife, List 335a. His will, 5 Sept. 1730— 25 Nov. 1731, names 3 ch. (not w.): **John,** Portsm., b. ±1688, taxed for Mill Dam 1708 (jr.), m. 5 Feb. 1712-3 Deliverance Lang(7), List 339. Will, 26 Mar. 1753—26 Dec. 1759, names 6 ch. **Nathaniel,** housewright, Portsmouth, b. 14 Mar. 1690, m. 13 Nov.—1 Dec. 1715 Elizabeth Cotton(1), who d. **May 1765,** List 339. Will, 2 Jan. (d. 20 May) 1769, names 6 ch. **Grace,** rec. into cov. and bp. No. Ch. 10 Apr. 1709, m. Wm. Ross(4). William, List 339, is poss. a son who d. s. p. by 1730, or Peavey(4).

2 **THOMAS,** Portsm., m. Jane Walford (Thos.) as early as 1645 and had fenced land bef. 1651. Cf. Feverill. Town gr. 1652; O. A. 2 July 1657. By 1661 his land extended from Sagamore Creek to what is still kn. as Peverly's Hill; his ho. was on the Creek. Highway surv. 1664-5. Lists 330abc, 323, 325, 326a, 43, 313a. See also Evans(16). His widow, Lists 312c, 326c. His will, 19 Apr. (inv. 26 May) 1670, names w. Jane (m. 2d Richard Goss 1), and ch., only the first 3 of age: **Mary,** b. ±1646, m. John Holmes(3). **Martha,** m. betw. 1666-1670 Christopher Noble(1). **John,** b. ±1649, exec. **Thomas.** Thos. Dean of Salem sued one T. P. in Salem Ct. in 1701. **Lazarus,** b. ±1657. List 306c. **Samuel. Jeremiah. Sarah** (did she, not Sarah Walford, m. Michael Hicks[4]?).

**Phanin,** alias Pickering, List 330c.

**PHELPS.** Became 85th commonest name in N. E.

1 **HEZEKIAH,** Wells, Scarboro, found as both Phelps and Phillips. See Duley(1), Phillips(3).

2 **JAMES,** a wit. with the Davises at Kittery Point 1661 (Y. D. 3: 73). See also (4).

3 **JOHN,** s. of Edward of Newb. and Andover, k. by Ind. at Black Point 29 Jan. 1677.

4 **SAMUEL,** bondsm. for Joseph Davis(36) in 1661, with Samuel Davis(50) and John Bayden. See also (2).

5 **THOMAS,** paid the Stephen Crawford est. 4 s. in 1647; Damariscove 1649. Lists 71, 72.

6 **WILLIAM,** at Monhegan bef. 1689; see Dollen(2).

**PHENIX,** Fennick, prob. rightly the ancient name Fenwick. Col. Banks found Phenick at Paignton, co. Devon.

**JOHN,** mariner, Kittery, bot land on E. side of Spruce Creek in 1664, and had built on it bef. 1675 when he sold to Peter Lewis. Town gr. 1669. Lists 33, 297. In 1713 he and w. Deborah (Lockwood 2) were liv. for term of their nat. lives on part of the land Robert Mendum willed to his gr.s. Robert, and provis. for their continuance there was made when Samuel Skillings sold the prop. to their s. George in 1722. In 1728 he deeded all est. aft. they should die to s. Geo., he to pay his sis. Deborah. Depos. in 1720, ±70, 'when I came to live on the place I now live on ab. 50 yrs. ago.' His w. Deborah depos. many times; liv. 1740, ±92. Ch: **Elizabeth,** m. Hezekiah Elwell(2). **Deborah,** m. John Ingersoll(6). **George,** m. 21 July 1709 Hannah Jones (see 7), she liv. 1753. He depos. in Dec. 1767, ag. 83; liv. Apr. 1768. 8 ch.

**Philater,** Abraham, Jerseyman, met here by John Josselyn (see his 'Two Voyages to N. E.,' p. 73).

**PHILBRICK,** Philbrook. Uncommon. Nothing known supports tradition this fam. came from Lincolnshire or in the -Arbella-. Note Robert of Ispwich.

1 **JAMES**(7), mariner, Hampton, m. Ann Roberts(11); liv. on the homestead. See Gould(3). He was drowned with Peter Johnson, 16 Nov. 1674. Adm. 30 May 1676 to wid. Ann (List 394) and Timothy Hilliard who was replaced 14 Nov. fol. by the s. James, returned from sea. She m. 2d Wm. Marston(11). Ch: **James,** b. 13 July 1651. **Apphia,** b. 19 Mar. 1655, m. Timothy Hilliard (7). **Esther,** b. 1 Mar. 1657, m. 1st Joseph Beard(3); m. 2d Sylvanus Nock(2). **Thomas,** b. 14 Mar. 1659, Timothy Hilliard his gdn. 1676. **Sarah,** b. 14 Feb. 1660-1. **Joseph,** b. 1 Oct. 1663. **Elizabeth,** b. 24 July 1666. She, or Elizabeth(8), m. Nathl. Berry(9). **Mehitable,** b. 15 Nov. 1668. See also Hall (23).

2 **LT. JAMES**(1), mariner, Hamp., m. 1 Dec. 1674 Hannah Perkins(9). Had the homestead. Selectm. 1702, 1712, 1719, 1723; surv. and lot-layer. Lists 52, 396. See also Lewis (16). He d. 4 Nov. 1723, wid. 23 May 1739. A deed 1722 names ch. and gr.ch: **Hannah,** b. 30 Apr. 1676, m. Stephen Sanborn. **James,** weaver, Hampt. 1702, Newc. 1703. His w. Sarah joined Hampt. Ch. 1701; m. 2d Benj. Emerson 14 Jan. 1707-8 in Haverh., where

her 4 ch., b. 1701-1706, mar., tho the only s. Benj. m. his 1st w. in Salisb. **Daniel,** b. 19 Feb. 1678-9, and **Jonathan,** b. 9 Dec. 1680, neither ment. 1722, but one undoubtedly husb. of 'dau.-in-law' Penelope then liv. with (2) and fa. of her s. Jonathan, who m. Lydia Linscott(1) and had 6 ch. rec. York 1729-1742; List 279. Wid. Penelope m. 2d Elias Philbrick(4). **Sarah,** b. 11 June 1682, m. 1st John Sanborn, m. 2d Lt. Thos. Rollins (6 jr.). **Ebenezer,** Rye, b. 29 Oct. 1683, m. Bethia Moulton(12). Will, 1755—1760, names 4 ch. **Apphia,** b. 8 Apr. 1686, helpless 1722, d. 23 Sept. 1759. **Isaac,** b. 5 Aug. 1688, m. 27 Oct. 1717 Mary Palmer(20); d. 16 Oct. 1757. Dau. Hannah ment. 1722. **Abigail,** b. 1692, m. Thos. Haines(11); s. Malachi liv. 1722. Dea. **Joseph,** b. 3 Feb. 1694, m. 1st 5 Dec. 1717 Anne Dearborn (John 3 jr.), who d. 30 July 1718; m. 2d 26 Nov. 1719 Elizabeth Perkins(12), who d. 26 Mar. 1736; m. 3d 18 Nov. 1736 Sarah Nay. Will, 1760 (d. 2 Dec. 1761), names w. Sarah (d. 9 Dec. 1779), 4 ch. by 2d w., 1 by 3d, out of 14 rec. **Nathan,** blacksm., Hampt., Rye, b. 19 Aug. 1677, m. 31 Oct. 1721 Dorcas Johnson (James 15 jr.) who d. 22 Feb. 1764. His will, 12 (d. 23) Apr. 1749, names her and 7 ch. **Mary,** bp. 7 Dec. 1701, not ment. in 1722.

3 **JOHN**(7), Hampton, came bef. his fa. and had a gr. in June 1640. Lists 391a, 392a, 393b. He m. Ann Knapp (Wm. of Watertown) and was lost at sea with w. and dau. 20 Oct. 1657, going to Boston; see also Hilliard(3). Inv. recorded betw. 5 Oct.—24 Dec. 1658; ho. and land, 8 cow kind, 7 pig kind. His br. and admr. Thomas took charge of the ch: **John,** b. 22 Sept. 1650. **Hannah,** twin, b. 26 Sept. 1651, m. 1st Joseph Walker; m. 2d John Seavey. **Martha,** twin, m. John Brackett(4). **Sarah,** drowned with parents. **Abigail,** b. 8 Nov. 1654. **Ephraim,** b. 24 Apr. 1656, m. Elizabeth Barron; liv. Groton, Mass., where 3 ch. rec. 1689-1699.

4 **JOHN**(3), Greenland, m. 1st Prudence Swain (Wm.), her Lists 335a, 338b; m. 2d in Greeenl. 7 Mar. 1716-7 Sabina (Locke) Lewis(1); see Locke (3½). Taxed Greenl. 1690; gr.j. 1693, 1696; j. 1697; depos. in 1712, ±60, form. of Hampt.; in 1715 joined Greenl. Ch., which records death of old Mr. J. P. in 1737. Lists 330cd, 335a, 337, 338bc, 52, 57, 68. See also Elliot(5). Will, 15 Aug.—3 Oct. 1737, names w. Sabina, s. Elias and 3 ch. of decd. s. John; s. Joshua Berry exec. Ch: **John,** b. 22 Feb. 1679. Land was laid out to him and br. Elias on fa.'s acct. 1713 (Portsm. rec.); appar. last taxed Greenl. 1715; List 338a. **Martha** (List 338a) poss. his w. 3 ch. liv. 1737 (Susanna and John were bp. 1713, 1715). **Elias,** Greenl. ±68 in 1749, depos. in June 1756, ag. 75, ab. old Hampt. and the towns carved from it. Lists 338ab. See also

br. John. He m. 1st 24 May 1700 Rhoda Perkins(3), List 338b; 7 ch. bp. He m. 2d 2 Jan. 1722-3 wid. Penelope Philbrick; see (2). **Abigail**, b. 14 Apr. 1687. Perh. she as -Abiah-, or an unrec. sis., m. Joshua Berry (14), who was the fa.'s step-s., if not also s.-in-law. Unplaced in Greenl., poss. daus. of John(jr.) or of wid. Penelope: Ann, m. Ithamar Berry(8); Dorothy, m. Joshua Perkins(19).

5 **JOSEPH**(1), mariner, Hampton, Rye, m. Tryphena Marston(10); d. 17 Nov. 1755. Ch: **Joseph**, b. 14 Dec. 1686, d.y. **Joseph**, b. 19 Feb. 1688. **Zachariah**, b. 11 Mar. 1689; of Hampt., m. in Newb. 9 July 1715 Mary Lowell (Gideon). 7 ch. rec. **Sabina**, b. 1691, m. 14 Jan. 1713 Abraham Libby(1). **Ann**, b. 13 Jan. 1694, may have m. Stephen Berry(13) whose w. was not dau. of (9). **Ephraim**, b. 12 Aug. 1696, blacksm., Exeter (List 376b), m. Martha Wadleigh (Henry). Adm. 29 Apr. 1747 to s. Benj. 6 ch. **Hester**, b. 2 May 1699. **Phebe**, b. 9 June 1701, m. Danl. Moulton. **Joses**, b. 5 Nov. 1703, blacksm., Rye, m. 4 Jan. (or June) 1727 Abigail Locke; d. 24 Mar. 1757, she 12 Aug. 1783. 8 ch. rec. **Elizabeth**, b. 8 Dec. 1706.

6 **SAMUEL**(8), Hampton, d. 22 Apr. 1694, leaving w. Jane. Lists 396, 52, 62. One Samuel was accus. by Deborah Clifford in Mar. 1693-4. Rec. ch: **Thomas**, b. 3 Mar. 1688, m. one Abiah who surv. him. Will, 28 Mar.—29 Apr. 1747, gives to w. (unnamed) and 5 of 6 ch. **John**, b. 13 Oct. 1689. **Mary**, b. 1 Feb. 1694, poss. the one of Hampt. and Boston who m. Nehemiah Partridge(6).

7 **THOMAS**, Hampton. A Watertown propr. 1636, selling out in Jan. 1645-6 and joining his sons in N. H. Culler of staves 1655. Lists 393ab. See also(8). His w. Elizabeth (List 393a) d. 19 Feb. 1663-4. His will, aged, 12 Mar. 1663-4—8 Oct. 1667, names several gr.ch. and ch: **John**, d. bef. fa. **James. Thomas**, b. ±1625-6. **Elizabeth**, m. 1st Thos. Chase (6); m. 2d John Garland(6); m. 3d Henry Robie(1). **Hannah**, m. Philip Lewis(16). **Mary**, m. 1st Edward Tuck; m. 2d James Wall. **Martha**, m. 1st John Cass(2); m. 2d Wm. Lyon, sr.(2).

8 **SERGT. *THOMAS**(7), ±43 in 1668, ±46 in 1672, m. 1st one Ann who d. 17 May 1667; m. 2d 22 Sept. 1669 Hannah (French), wid. of John White of Haverhill; List 394. She was liv. 1694. In May 1647 he bot Wm. Sanborn's former ho. and in 1658 q.c. it to loving fa., who passed it on to a long line of desc. Gdn. of his Wall nieces 1659. Selectm. 1654, 1663, 1677-8, 1693; freeman 29 May 1668; Ensign (com. 1679); Sergeant; Rep. 1693; Deacon his last yr.; oft. moderator and on jury. Lists 392bc, 393b, 394, 396, 400, 49, 52, 57, 62. He d. 24 Nov. 1700, ag. 76. Ch: **Mary**, b. 11 Sept. 1651, m. Jacob

Perkins(10). **Bethia**, b. 15 Dec. 1654, m. Caleb Perkins(3). **Jonathan**, b. 4 July 1657, m. a dau. of Benj. Shaw, for whom, called his s.-in-law, he was buying Conn. land in 1713. Gr.j. 1698; selectm. 1701, 1704, 1711, 1718. Lists 331c, 396, 399a, 52, 57. He d. s.p. 1747, giving homestead to two gr.sons of (6); N. E. Reg. 38: 281. **Samuel**, b. 19 May 1660. **Elizabeth**, b. 1 Nov. 1663, d. 21 May 1667. **Elizabeth**, b. 3 May 1667; see Elizabeth(1). By 2d w: **William**, b. 27 June 1670. N. E. Reg. 38: 282, adds **Jane**, m. Joseph Cram(1). **Hannah**. One Thomas m. Deborah Godfrey(4) in Greenl. ±1710; in 1713 Wm. (10) deeded to s. Samuel land betw. Jonathan and Thomas. Also Walter(10) in will 1730 names uncle John P., perh. meaning gr.-uncle.

9 **LT. THOMAS**(1), cordwainer, Kingston, m. 14 Apr. 1681 Mehitable Ayers. Hampt. selectm. 1694. A Hampt. constable (new) in 1700 was Thomas. Lists 62, 392b, 400. He d. 1 Jan. 1711-2; adm. to widow 6 June fol., bondsmen Lt. James(2) and John Redman. She m. 2d Timothy Hilliard(7). Ch. rec. Kingston: **Daughter**, b. 13 Jan. 1681-2. **Son**, b. 30 May 1683. **Jeremiah**, b. 21 Sept. 1684. List 400. (One J. m. in Boston 25 Dec. 1712 Mary McCarthy). Dead 1715, leaving 4 heirs (br. and sisters); adm. 6 Dec. 1721 to Daniel Ladd. **Elizabeth**, b. 17 Oct. 1686, m. in Haverhill 18 Oct. 1705 Abraham Bradley (see Hoyt, p. 884). **Timothy**, b. 12 May 1689, d. 17 Nov. 1711; adm. 5 Feb. 1713-4 to br. John Sleeper. **Ann**, b. 14 Mar. 1691, m. 5 June 1712 John Sleeper. **Mehitabel**, b. 26 Mar. 1693, m. Daniel Ladd(1). **Hannah**, b. 19 Dec. 1695, d. 18 Jan. 1696-7. **Samuel**, b. 13 May 1698, d. 21 Nov. 1711. **Jedediah**, Kingston, b. 9 Aug. 1700, m. 25 Aug. 1721 Mary Taylor (Wm.). The Hon. J. P., Esq., departed this life 20 Mar. 1754, ag. 53 (Kingston). Will, made 4 days bef., names w. Mary, 2 sons, 1 dau., heirs of ano. son; 10 ch. were rec. **Thomas**, b. 9 June 1704, d.y. 10 **WILLIAM**(8), Greenland, m. 10 Oct. 1689 Mary Neal(10); both adm. to Portsm. No. Ch. 1693. Portsm. constable 1695-96; selectm. 1701; gr.j. 1698; j. 1699. Lists 330cd, 331c, 335a, 337, 338ab, 62. Her Lists 331c, 335a, 338b. In 1713 he deeded his Greenl. homestead, aft. he and w. should die, to s. Jonathan, he to pay four sisters. Last taxed 1714; wid. taxed 1715. She m. 2d John Garland(7). Ch: **Walter**, blacksm., b. 10 Nov. 1690 (he and sis. Mary bp. at Salisbury). In 1700 his fa. deeded him 'land that I have of my fa. Walter Neal.' Lists 337, 338abd. Will, 21 May 1730—8 Aug. 1732, names w. Elizabeth (Tufton; see Mason 17), 6 ch. (bp. 1715-1728), uncle John P., br. Jonathan. Wid. m. 2d aft. Jan. 1734-5 Rev. Wm. Allen. Her will, 22 Jan.—29 Apr. 1767.

**Mary**, b. 20 May 1692, m. (prob.) in Greenl. 18 Feb. 1713-4 James Whidden. **Jonathan**, bp. No. Ch. 25 Mar. 1694, m. in Greenl. 31 Jan. 1716-7 Elizabeth Whidden (Samuel); List 338b for both. Greenl. 1727, Arundel 1728, Bidd. 1733. 8 ch. bp. Greenl., the last in 1731. **Hannah**, bp. 31 Oct. 1697, not named by fa. 1713. One H. m. in Greenl. James Locke(2). **Samuel**, had land from fa. 1713. One S. m. (int Wells 20 Dec. 1726-7) Hannah Wells. **Honor, Abigail, Sarah**, all liv. 1713.

**Phillebrown.** See Cole(8).

**PHILLIPS**, from the given-name; freq. in Wales and S.W. quarter of Eng. Became 58th commonest name in N. E.

1 **EDWARD**, fisherman, Portsmouth, m. 12 July 1714 Mary Jones(16). List 339. Three ch. bp. Adm. on her est. to Abraham Jones 24 June 1728; on his est. d.b.n., 18 Feb. 1728-9 to br. Neal Phillips, who was called of Weymouth, co. Dorset, when he m. Elizabeth Snow, wid., in Portsm. 21 Oct. 1725.

2 **ELIZABETH**, to be whipped and ord. to leave town (Portsm.?) for entert. men at night in 1666.

3 **HEZEKIAH**, as Phelps, gent. of Wells, bot at Pemaquid with Jos. Maylem of Boston in 1716. As Phillips, a Scarboro propr. 1720, where **Parmeno**, s. of Hezekiah and Deborah, was b. 8 Jan. 1720-1, and d. (Promeno) 7 Dec. 1733, altho Hezekiah was of Western Hook, N. Y., in 1729 (Y. D. 13: 136). In Oct. 1738, ±58, he depos. ab. laying out Scarb. lots. See also Duley(1).

4 **ISAAC**, his Portsm. rate ment. 1674, List 331a. Poss. 'Old Phillips' 1677, List 313a.

5 **ISRAEL**, Portsm. 1672, constable 1676, 1677 and at death, the accounts made up with his wid. See Braddock(2). Adm. to wid. Elizabeth (Lewis 7) 24 Sept. 1678; apprais. Samuel Keais and Obadiah Morse. Lists 54, 327cd. She was Phillips in Dec. 1681; m. 2d one Eburne(1), and depos. in Dec. 1736, ag. 67, but must have been older.

6 **JAMES**, perh. two, Shoals wit. 1676, Eliot wit. 1686. Newc. shoemaker 1684, ±30, when he had beaten Frances Russell for calling people names (see Beale 4). Taxed Newc. 1690-1; in 1700 had been 4½ yrs. a soldier at the Fort. Lists 313f, 319, 318a, 65, 316.

7 **JOHN**, propr. Dover. List 351b. Drowned; inv. 20 Mar. 1641-2 by Geo. Smith and John Dam. Adm. 28 July fol. to (the Elders) Nutter and Starbuck to pay the debts. See also Jenks(2).

8 **JOHN**, millwright, Casco, called Welshman by Moses Felt, owned Martin's Point and upper Clapboard Isl. by 1643, selling to Thos. Wise, he to Rich. Martin (East. Cl. declaration); see also Drake(8). Cleeve deeded to him on Presumpscot River 1650-

1663, in 1657 for his intended mill or mills, in 1658 adj. his ho. His sawmill ment. 1658. Hannah Hallam depos. ab. his cornmill. For controv. with Jordan see Me. Hist. & Gen. Rec. 3: 114. He and Henry Williams were No. Yarm. wit. 1664; the two had cross suits in 1666 and he was sued in Casco Ct. in 1667. Not kn. to have m., but charge made in 1663 that he had kept a woman, not his w., 14 yrs. Lists 214, 232, 221, 222bc, 25, 227. Going to Kit., he bot from Withers on Spruce Creek 20 Sept. 1670, and sent for neph. Rowland Williams to live with him and be his heir, his only relative here. Inv. at Kit. 9 Mar. 1679-80. R. W. as admr. of J. P., blockmaker, sold at Presumpscot to Pepperell in 1701.

9 **DEA. JOHN**, biscuit baker, Boston, much with his s.-in-law Munjoy in Falmouth where he bot half of Capisic from Francis Small in 1658, and, of Boston, made it over to the Munjoys in 1664. See Me. P. & C. Rec. ii: xvi-xvii for him as recorder and atty. for and assistant to Munjoy. He depos. in Oct. 1681, ±77, conc. Robert Corbin. His w. Joanna d. in Boston 22 Oct. 1675, ag. 80, he 16 Dec. 1682, ag. 77 (Copp's Hill). Will, 15 Mar. 1680-1, gives to pres. w. Sarah and the Munjoys. Dorchester records their ch: **Mary**, 1633-1640. **John**, 1635. **Mary**, b. and d. 1636. **Israel**, 1642-1643. Unless an error in regard to the daus., a 3d **Mary**, m. 1st Geo. Munjoy; m. 2d Robert Lawrence(4); m. 3d Stephen Cross(10) who claimed Dea. Phillips' est. in Casco, viz. Casco Neck, Palmer's Isl., -Amacongin- Farm.

10 **COL. JOHN**, mariner, Charlestown, commis. J. P. for York Co. by Bellomont, 1699. Related to the Kennebec Parkers, and had fisheries at Sagadahoc Rock and Isl. One J. P. wit. Ind. deed to Lawson, Spencer and Lake in 1653. See also Thos. Jenner(2 jr.), Jones(3), Davis(53). Lists 225a (Capt.), 99, p. 77 (Col.). Wyman's 'Charlest.,' p. 740, states that he d. 20 Mar. 1725-6, ag. 90, and had two wives and ch., incl. Capt. **John**, who depos. in 1754, ±80 (d. 4 Nov. 1756 in 83d yr.), that when 12 yrs. old he went with fa. to Sagadahoc, alias Parker's Isl., named for Thos. Parker, mate of the first ship that came with the Plymouth people from Eng., uncle of his own fa., and fa. of Thos. Parker who then liv. on the Isl. (York Files Oct. 1754). List 123. He and younger br. **Henry**, Esq., sold in Falm.

11 **JOHN**, sued by John Parker for diet and attendance in Wells ct. 1663.

12 **JOHN**, wit. John Partridge's deed 1669 and evid. apprais. Richard Harvey's est. in 1678 with Wm. Partridge.

13 **JOHN**, soldier from the Southward, at Oyster River garrison, m. Elizabeth Footman(2), taking her away. She was at

Newmarket 1 Dec. 1735, wid. of John of No. Kingston, R. I. See Clark(46). Son **John** of West Greenwich, R. I., deeded Canterbury land to John Footman in 1747. One John, b. 27 Oct. 1696, had w. Sarah, 6 ch., in West Greenwich.

14 **MOSES**, Marblehead. See Churchwell(1).

15 **NEAL**, Portsm. See (1).

16 **RICHARD**, appar. an Eastern man 1647, List 10.

17 **RUTH**, Portsm. or Newc. wit. 1715.

18 **STEPHEN**, also Old Stiper. See (20).

19 **THOMAS**, fisherman, Pemaquid, gave bill to John Smith of Cape Neddick 13 Dec. 1652 (proved by the wit. Isaac Walker in Aug. 1671); wit. for Thos. Elbridge 6 Apr. 1657. If dead in 1671, it may have been his wid., of Hippocrass, in List 14, but see (23). Presumably sons: **Thomas**, took O. A. 1674, List 15. **William**(23).

20 **THOMAS**, shoreman, Ipswich, husb. of Elizabeth Drew (see 17, 18). In 1722 they sold a Star Isl. ho. to Joseph Mace. One Thomas d. in Ipsw. 23 July 1737. Poss. he was related to old Stiper (Stephen) P., a fisherman appar. from Ipsw., who carried away goods from a Portland wreck in 1711. See also Lakeman.

21 **WALTER**, liv. first at the Winnegance end of his land, later up the river at Damariscotta, having Ind. deeds in 1661, 1662, 1674. Recorder from 1665 till forced off in 1676. Lists 10, 12, 13, 85, 162. In June 1678 he depos. as if in Marbleh.; O. A. at Lynn, Nov. 1678; later, poss. aft. a stay East, he built at Salem Village, where he was an innkeeper and lic. as early as 1689. Christopher Toppan bot the Damariscotta land in 1702. Will, 21 Oct. 1704, then sick, gives all for life to w. Margaret, exec. Ch: **John**. Lynn, List 85, not in will. Adm. 22 July 1695 to wid. Hannah. 3 or more ch. **James**, Salem, given all housing and land aft. mo.'s death. He m. 12 Feb. 1693-4 Sarah Stevens; d. 1743. 8 ch. **Walter**, Lynn, List 85. His will, 15 Feb. 1730, names w. Ruth, sons Walter (eldest), Richard (decd.), Jonathan, dau. Ruth Graves (widow). **Tabitha. Margaret**, m. James Smith. **Sarah. Jane**, m. in Salem 14 Nov. 1689 Benj. Hutchinson. See also Pierce (12).

22 **MAJOR ‡\*WILLIAM**, innholder, vintner, Charlest. (with w. Mary adm. to Ch. 23 Sept. 1639), Boston, Saco. Both ment. by Danl. Field in letter dated Tring, co. Herts, 1642; in 1648 he gave p/a to ano. Wm. of Bedlam, shoemaker. Commissioner for Mass. in Me. 1653. As Lt. Wm. of Boston, he bot the Vines patent from Beex & Co. 11 Mar. 1658-9 and soon went there; 'of Boston now resid. at Saco' 15 May 1661; liv. on neck at the Pool, June 1662. Y. D. 9: 230 locates his Saco Falls ho. His name remained long

aft. him in Phillipstown or Phillipsburg, incorp. from his holdings; 19,000 a. were divid. to heirs in 1720 (Y. D. 11: 16-17). A Royalist and opponent of Mass. Lt., Capt., Major 27 May 1663; com. for town, selectm., Rep. (-Lt. John- 1664), Associate, J. P. Lists 244cd, 247, 249, 26, 83, 88, 224. See Downes (1). His w. Mary d. 1 May 1646; he m. 2d Susanna (ag.31 in 1641), wid. of Christopher Stanley. Her will 10 Sept. 1650 (d. 16 June 1655) ment. his of same date (see Wyman's Charlestown). He m. 3d bef. 10 Mar. 1657 Bridget (Hutchinson 1), wid. of John Sanford; List 246. Aft. his Saco ho. was burned in the War, he ret. to Boston bef. 12 June 1676 and d. there. Will, 28 Sept.—13 Nov. 1683, gives to w., daus. Mary Field and Elizabeth Alden; and to sons Wm. and Samuel ¾ his Saco prop. (see also Doc. Hist. 6: 16); he had portioned his four daus. Wid. Bridget was in Saco 1686. Her will, 20 Sept. —6 Oct. 1696—Aug. 1698, names ch: Samuel and Wm. P., Peleg Sanford and Eliphel (Sanford) Stratton. Ch: **Mary**, eldest dau., m. Robert Field(11). **William**, Boston, mariner, m. 24 Oct. 1650 Martha Franklin. Nicholas and Zachary P., the latter an abuttor, wit. his deed to fa. 1652. Liv. 23 May 1656. Ch. rec. Boston: William, Martha. **Martha**, 2d dau., m. Capt. Richard Thurston. **Rebecca**, 3d dau., m. Mr. Robert Lord. **Elizabeth**, 4th dau., m. 1st 6 July 1655 Abiel Everill; m. 2d 1 Apr. 1660 John Alden(1). **Phebe**, b. 7 Apr. 1640, m. Zachary Gillam(1). **Nathaniel**, b. 5 Feb. 1641-2. See Hardy(3); Me. Hist. Soc. Col. 2: 5: 189, has his 'Relation' of events in Me., dated Boston 1 Sept. 1668. Merchant there Aug. 1674, liv. 12 June 1676, d. s. p. bef. 23 May 1689. Adm. at Eastward to neph. William of Biddeford, 1719. **Mary**, b. 17 Feb. 1644, not liv. 1650, or poss. error for **Sarah**, youngest dau., who otherwise may have been 2d w.'s ch.; she m. Ephraim Turner. By last w: **John**, b. 18 Sept. 1656, d. Aug. 1657. **Samuel**, b. 16 Mar. 1657-8, d. bef. 1716. He and w. Sarah (liv. 1718) had in Boston 1682-1692: Sarah, Ann, William, Bridget (m. John Merrifield); his heirs in 1721 were Ann (single) and Bridget. **William**, Boston mariner, b. 28 Jan. 1659-60, d. 17 Apr. 1705. In 1683 had been four yrs. a captive with the Spaniards. He m. 13 Nov. 1689 Deborah Long, who m. 2d Wm. Skinner. Ch: William, Sarah (Y. D. 13: 83).

23 **WILLIAM**(19?), Pemaquid 1672, O. A. 1674. One Wm. wit. in 1674 the assignm. from Smith to Rishworth of the bill given by (19). One was taxed Pemaquid 1687. Lists 13, 15, 124. Geo. Jaffrey's claim for Hippocrass Isl. near Damerils Cove recites that it was gr. to Wm., decd., by Jocelyn and sold to claimant 20 Mar. 1693-4 by Geo. Snell and w., relict of said Wm. P. If this was Richord

Snell, form. w. of John Hunking(3), and also the wid., of Hippocrass, List 14, no William is found to fit; see also (19). Her son, perhaps not Phillips, List 14.

24 WILLIAM, ANDREW, JOHN, named as kinsmen by first Wm. Pepperell in 1733 (by trad. he had a sis. who m. a Phillips), while Sir Wm. in 1759 named kinsm. John and Andrew. William, m. 30 May 1719 Lydia Remick(2). Andrew, m. 1 Jan. 1727-8 Miriam Mitchell(3); both liv. 1760 in Kit., where 8 ch. rec. John, m. in York 23 Dec. 1725 Deborah Murch (Walter); daus. Tamasin, Deborah, at York 1726-1729, Sarah at Biddeford 1731, where he liv. on Pepperell land in 1759.

Phillipson, Robert, late Sergeant at Pemaquid; Marblehead inquest 12 Sept. 1682; Essex Q. Ct. Rec. 8: 443.

PHILPOTT, James, Great Isl. 1696, taxed 1699. Lists 315bc. He m. Rachel Haskins (6), who wit. an Elliot fam. deed in 1706 and m. 2d 6 or 7 June 1709 James Chaddock (Chadwick 1). Kn. son Capt. James, mariner, Newc., bot in Somersworth in 1737 and mov. there, where liv. also his half-br. Wm. Chadwick(4), mariner. He d. Sept. 1747 (inquest), leaving wid. Ruth, 8 ch.

PHIPPEN, Phippeny, Fitzpen. See N. E. Reg. 49: 244, or Waters "Gleanings' 2: 996; also Banks' 'Topographical Dict.' (1937) apparently connecting the Hingham fam. with Membury, co. Devon.

1 DAVID(4), shipwright, of Casco Bay in July 1667 when fa., then in Salem, deeded to him and (5). He too went to Salem and m. 26 June 1672 Ann (Cromwell) Ager. Both of Casco, late of Boston, in May 1702, when wid. Hannah Cromwell brot suit for dower ag. them and the Salem Pickerings. At Casco he liv. near the fort, and had a ho. and planted on Presumpscot River. He was k. 10 Aug. 1703. Lists 34, 39. The fam. ret to Salem and claimed the Falm. land. Besides s. John (unrec.), k. with fa., List 39, were rec. in Salem: David, b. 14 Apr. 1673. Thomas, bp. Aug. 1675; shipwright on Elk River, Cecil Co., Md., 1731; w. Sarah. Anna, bp. 19 May 1678, m. 1st in Salem Benj. Ropes; m. 2d John Green. Cromwell, bp. 5 Oct. 1679. Abigail, bp. 2 Aug. 1685, m. Wm. Furneux; 3 ch. Elizabeth, bp. May 1689, m. John Webb. In addi. 4 bp. at Salem 1681-1691 (parents not named) are credited to him: Joseph. Jane. Samuel. Sarah.

2 GEORGE, br. of (4), mariner, in Me. in Apr. 1660, signed a Falm. ptn. 1662 and was sued in Casco ct. by John Williams in Nov. 1666. Bef. 1672 he had mowed near Merriconcag Neck and liv. at Mare Point.

Lists 253, 25. See (3). Driven off, he took O. A. at Hull 21 Apr. 1679. He d. there 24 Dec. 1704. Wid. Elizabeth's will, 20 May (d. 20 Aug.) 1714, names s. James, exec., daus. Elizabeth Coms, Mary, Ruth, and gr.-dau. Elizabeth Coms. Ano. dau. Sarah d. at Hull 14 Jan. 1694. The s. James, boatman, Hull, had w. Joanna in 1693. In 1717 he depos. that he form. liv. at Mare Point and knew Nicholas White; in 1735 he sold 1000 a. there to Aaron Cleveland.

3 JOHN, Mare Point, List 191. Poss. should be George(2).

4 JOSEPH, seaman, blockmaker, s. of David of Hingham and Boston, br. of (2). Boston 1653, Blue Point 1658, Falmouth, where a friend of Cleeve and obnoxious to many who called him a man of contention and strife ever since coming. Me. P. & C. Rec. vols. i, ii, have many references. In Fogg collection is orig. of Y. D. 21: 22, Cleeve to Wallis, 27 Oct. 1650, wit. by Joseph and (1), the latter by mark. Falm. constable 1661; com. with Cleeve 1663; gr.j. 1664. Lists 212 (or his son), 221, 222ab, 25, 75b, 80, 34. See also Jordan(7), Penley. His s. David stated in 1687 that his fa. bot 100 a. from Cleeve ±37 yrs. ago (30 Sept. 1650; Doc. Hist. 6: 6, 242), which he and ch. poss. until disturbed by Ind.; but he was adm. inhab. at Salem 1 Nov. 1665 and d. there. His ch.'s mo. was Dorothy (Suff. D. 1: 280, 307). Will, 21 July—15 Sept. 1687, names w. Dorcas (Wood, by Salem rec.), 5 ch: Child, bur. Hing. May 1642. Joseph, bp. Hing. Aug. 1642. Mary, bp. Hing. 5 Mar. 1643-4. Sarah, b. Boston 11 mo. 1644, m. in Salem 24 Sept. 1665-1669 Geo. Hodges. David, bp. Boston 4 Apr. 1647, ±7 wks. old. Samuel (Joseph by Boston rec.), bp. 6 May 1649, ±7 dys. old, m. in Salem 1 Feb. 1676-7 Rachel Guppy, who d. there 1 Feb. 1710-1; he 1 Feb. 1717-8. 8 ch. rec. Elizabeth, b. Boston 10 June 1652, d. there 14 July 1653.

5 JOSEPH(4), Falmouth, Salem, was in Falm. aft. his fa. left there; see (1). Gr.j. 1667. Lists 25, 212 (poss. his fa.). Of Salem in Dec. 1700, mariner, he sold to John Higginson 100 a. on Purpooduck Side betw. Robert and Thos. Stanford, stating that he built and liv. there many yrs. bef. the first War; but Salem rec. show him there earlier. By 1st w., dau. of Thos. Stanford, is appar. Joseph 3d, of Salem 1687; cert. Mary, w. of Joseph English in 1735 (Y. D. 17: 150). He m. 2d in Salem 22 Dec. 1670 Seaborn Gooden and had 1671-1681: Daniel, Samuel, Sarah, Dorcas, Israel, while 3 ch. of Joseph bp. 1679-1684, their mo. not named, were prob. his: John. Rachel. Anne. He m. 3d 14 Apr. 1686 wid. Damaris Searle (see Bartlett 5) and had: Susanna. Benjamin. Elizabeth.

**PHIPPS,** Phips, most numerous in Gloucestershire, the home of the Maine fam. Cos. Worcester, Warwick and Northampton also have many.

**1 JAMES** (Phips), gunsmith, planter, Woolwich, may have been that s. of William Phippes who was b. at Margotsfield, a suburb of Bristol, Eng., and apprent. to John Brown of Bristol, blacksmith, for seven years from 1 Mar. 1625-6 (see Brown 15). Together, and early, he and John White bot from Edw. Bateman a large tract near the Kennebec River at Nequasset, with Montsweag River as the eastern bound, where both liv. many yrs., built houses and improved the land. This land had not been divided when Phips d. and his wid. Mary m. partner White, by 1661, if their s. Philip gave his age rightly in 1742. On 4 Oct. 1679, for love and affection, they deeded to her s. William, Jeremisquam Neck on which his fa. and White had liv.; in 1734 it was called that neck of land on which Gov. Phips and his ancestors formerly liv. She was Mrs. Mary Howard, wid., when her dau.-in-law Dame Mary Sargeant in 1704 willed her an annuity of £10. Altho singularly abs. from the rec., there is no reason to doubt that the father of the first native son to be knighted was an upstanding man, liv. with his fam. on his own land in as much comfort as the times and their remoteness from centers would permit. Only 6 Phips ch. can be counted of Mather's mythical 26, all by one mother: **Mary,** b. ±1637, by age at death; m. James Widger. **John. James,** appar. not known to be liv. in 1693 when Sir William by will left 5 s. to him or his heirs. **(Sir) William,** b. 2 Feb. 1650-1. **Margaret,** m. 1st one Halsey (see 1), m. 2d James Andrews(6). **Anne,** dead in 1693, leaving heirs, unknown, unless one was Elizabeth Hollard named in the Sargeant will. One George Hollard of Boston had wife Anne in 1687.

**2 JOHN**(1), m. Elizabeth Gent(2) and liv. at Sheepscot, near Mr. Wm. Dyer's ho. 'just over the river.' He was undoubtedly dead in 1682 when she was with Sheepscot people in Boston (List 162); his br.'s will 1693 called him deceased. Among 'Sheepscot Papers' at Augusta is an undated pet. of Elizabeth Phips, wid., reciting that her husb. was driven off by the Indians, that she has three sons and one daughter, and one of the boys, almost of age, is determined to go and live where he and his bros. were b. as soon as his apprenticeship is out; she asked for 150 a. upland with marsh to be next adj. the farm of John Tower, and a ho.-lot in the town that was form. Mr. Philip Parsons'. One s. was surely **John,** left £100 by his uncle William. Of Wrentham in Jan. 1738-9, 'being 70 years of age from last December,' he deposed that he liv. with his fa. at Sheepscot

above 60 yrs. ago; afterward liv. at Charlestown; went soldier under Sir Edmund. In 1742 he liv. in Dudley. Appar. he had w. Mary in Reading, where a dau. Mary was b. in 1699; a son William was b. in Medway in 1718, and there wid. Mary d. 14 Feb. 1754, aged 82. Ano. s., John of Sherborn, and 5 more daus. are apparent. The other ch. of John and Elizabeth (Gent) are not ident. As possibilities are noted: William, pilot of the -Marigold- of Boston 1695, and James, a Boston mariner in 1696. One James m. Sarah Tucker there 11 May 1711.

**3 RICHARD,** soldier, one of the garrison at Fort Loyal who deserted to Capt. Pound's company. He was wounded in the head at Tarpaulin Cove; later was in Boston prison and perh. died, as not brot to trial with the others in 1690. See 'Pirates of the N. E. Coast,' pp. 58, 66, 71.

**4 SOLOMON** (Phipps), List 364, of Charlestown, gr.fa. of (5) and fa.-in-law of John Roy (List 364).

**5 THOMAS** (Phipps), Esq., H. C. 1695, merchant, Portsmouth, b. in Charlestown 22 Nov. 1676, s. of Solomon(4) and Mary (Danforth), went to Portsm. in 1696 as schoolmaster and m. 4 May 1699 Eleanor (Harvey 14) Cutts. Selectman 1707, 1709, 1711; High Sheriff; Captain; J. P. Lists 324, 336c, 337, 339. See also Coombs(1). His w. Eleanor was liv. in 1709. On Feb. 25, 1711-2, he m. Mary (Plaisted 4) Hoddy, who with his s. Danforth and Peter Greely was gr. adm. on his est. 2 Oct. 1737. She was still Phipps 8 July 1740; m. 3d John Pray(2). Her will, 16 Apr.—28 May 1766, names four Phipps daus. Ch: **Eleanor,** b. 11 Aug. 1701, m. Joseph Sprague of Cambridge. **Mary,** b. 7 Nov. 1703, m. Peter Greely(3). **Elizabeth,** w. of Caleb Gardner of Newport, R. I., in 1739. **Danforth,** bp. 4 Feb. 1710-11, shipwright, and prom. resid. of Falm.; m. Elizabeth Skillings. Ch. By 2d w: **Thomas,** bp. 14 Dec. 1712, d.y. **Mehitable,** bp. 18 Oct. 1714; poss. m. Thomas Shepard and soon died. **Sarah,** bp. 1 Apr. 1716, m. Joseph Chadbourne(2). **Olive,** m. 1st Samuel Winkley, m. 2d Cyprien Jeffrey (7). **Thomas,** bp. 5 Mar. 1720-1, d.y. **John,** boatbuilder, bp. with **Bethia,** 8 Apr. 1722, both liv. in July 1740; he d. s.p. by 1761, she not in mo.'s will. **Hannah,** bp. 5 Jan. 1723-4, m. 16 Nov. 1738 Jonathan Sprague of Cambr. **Thomas, Jane,** both under 14 in Oct. 1737; he d. a minor, she m. aft. 1746 Wm. Doake.

**6 WILLIAM** (Phips), Penobscot 1631, List 1. John Deacon, ano. witness, said: 'Thomas Willett and William Fipps know more than I.'

**7 SIR WILLIAM** (Phips) (1), was b. 2 Feb. 1650-1 on his fa.'s plantation at Jeremisquam, and d. 18 Feb. 1694-5, at London, a Knight and Royal Governor of Mass.,

altho then in England facing an inquiry. Much has been written of his virtues and failings and of his life, as an apprentice, a shipwright working in Boston and at his home near the Kennebec (List 185), as master of merchant ships, as commander of a frigate with which he unsuc. sought sunken treasure, later finding wealth with an exped. under the patronage of the Duke of Albemarle, and receiving his title therefor, of his meeting with Increase Mather, of his two expeditions ag. Canada, and his much criticized administration as governor in a troubled time and amid many factions. Early in his career he m. Mary (Spencer) Hull(5), and having no ch., adopted her neph. Spencer, son of Dr. David and Rebecca (Spencer) Bennett of Rowley, who became Spencer Phips (H. C. 1703, Councillor 1721-1732, Lt.-Gov. 1733-1759; m. 1707 Elizabeth Hutchinson 3, whose fa.'s will ment. her ch.). See Roger Spencer of Charlest. and Saco. His will, made 18 Dec. 1693, gives est. to w. Mary, afterward, unless she made a will, to adopted s. Spencer; if he d. s. p., est. to be divid., half to his own sisters Mary, Margaret, Anne (her heirs) and half to wife's kin; neph. John, s. of his dec. br. John, was given £100. and br. James or his heirs 5 shillings. His widow m. 2d Peter Sargeant, Esq., of Boston, claimed the Phips lands at the East, and d. 20 Jan. 1705-6. Lt.-Gov. Spencer P. was buried 4 Apr. 1757, aged 73. Dame Mary Sargeant's will, 19 Feb. 1704—29 Jan. 1706, spoke of mar. contr. with present husb., 24 Sept. 1701, named s. Spencer as heir, and gave legacies to honored mo.-in-law Mrs. Mary Howard, widow (naming her s. Philip White); sis. Rebecca Bennett; husband's nieces Margaret Armstrong and Dorcas Salter; sisters-in-law Mary Widger and Margaret Andrews (see Halsey 1), and others, incl. Benjamin White and Elizabeth Hollard. See Waters' 'Gleanings,' i: 46; ii: 1142. Peter Sargeant, Esq., m. last Mehitable, wid. of Thomas Cooper of Boston (see 9) and claimed the Cooper lands. See also 'Dict. of Amer. Biog.' (1934), 14: 551-2, which gives many references.

**Pickard**, Edmund, fishing master, Smuttynose, party to suit ab. stage room, 1660. At Northam near Bideford, co. Devon, he sold out here in 1661. See Packard.

**PICKERING**, a North of Eng. name, and a township in No. Riding of Yorkshire.

1 **BENJAMIN**, Scarboro, List 238a, and a Scottow wit. 1681. See (3).

2 **JOHN**, Piscataqua, ±60 in 1660. Mason or carpenter, he enlarged a ho. for Ambrose Gibbons in 1633-4 and with Jocelyn was surety for Nicholas Frost(9) in Mass. ct. 1635. Not unlikely the John who had w.

Mary in Cambridge where dau. Lydia was b. 1638 and Abigail (rec. Picke) in 1642, being himself back and forth. At Portsm. in 1643 he was ord. to deliver up the old Combination; in 1647 an arbitrator in the Knight-Raynes suit. Selectm. 1652, 1654, 1656-7, 1660. Lists 41, 321, 323-325, 326a, 330b, 311b, 47. See also Lewis(12), Price(4). Conc. ct. 2: 65, has orig. unrec. deed to s. John, 7 Nov. 1665, of the house he was liv. in with 50 a., a neck of land and a water grist mill. Will, 11 (d. 18) Jan. 1668-9, giving principally to s. Thomas, also 4 daus., was disallowed 29 June 1669 and adm. gr. to s. John. Rev. Joshua Moody was gdn. of Thos., Rebecca and Abigail. Ch: **Mary**, List 330b, m. John Banfield(2). **John**, b. ±1644-5. **Sarah**. **Rebecca**, appar. m. Samuel Rollins(5). **Abigail** (not the Cambridge Abigail), wit. as Pickering 1670, appar. m. Wm. Cotton(7). **Thomas**, b. ±1656-7.

3 **JOHN**, List 212, a prominent Salem resident. Ch. incl. **Benjamin**, b. Jan. 1665-6, hardly(1).

4 **CAPT.** *JOHN(2), carpenter, miller, Portsm., York, depos. often from 1673, ±28, to Feb. 1715-6, ±70. He m. 10 Jan. 1665-6 Mary Stanyan (Anthony), she last noted in 1710; List 331c. In 1668 he gave a due bill for £6 to John Tanner, carpenter, to end all differences betw. T. and his fa. Selectman many times 1672-1708. Lieut., Capt., Rep. 1692-1695, 1697-1700 (Speaker 1693, 1697); Atty. Genl. 1695. Largest subscriber for Mr. Emerson 1713. Lists 323, 324, 326bc, 327b, 329, 331b, 267a, 330cd, 335a, 336c, 316, 337, 322, 38, 49, 52, 54, 56-65, 69, 82. Of Portsmouth, resident in York Sept. 1700, he deeded (entail) to s. John a York saw and cornmill with land adj., also a neck of land. Apparently betw. Portsm. and York until he d. 10 Apr. 1721. Will, 21 June 1720, names dau. Mary and ch., decd. s. John and ch. Ch., Prov. rec: **John**, b. 1 Dec. 1666. **Mary**, b. 18 July 1668, m. John Plaisted, Esq. (4). **Thomas**, b. 6 Apr. 1670, d. 3 July 1671. **Sarah**, b. 15 Feb. 1671-2, d. y. **Sarah**, b. 3 Jan. 1673-4, d. by 1691.

5 **JOHN**(4), miller, Portsm., York, m. 17 July 1688 Elizabeth Munden(2). Portsm. vict. lic. 1692, 1700; tav. 1693, 1695-98; j. 1695. Called of York 1700 (see 4); gr.j. (Me.) 1701. Lists 330d, 333a, 335b, 337, 57. Of Portsm., weak, he made his will 21 Mar. 1714-5, prov. 17 Sept. fol. when he was of York; w. Elizabeth and ch. named, w. and fa. executors; adm. to Thos. Phipps and Elisha Plaisted 2 Jan. 1721-2 at request of s. Thos. The wid. appar. d. by June 1720. Ch: **Mary**, m. by 1709 Ambrose Sloper. **Thomas**, accus. by Phebe Tanner (Me. Ct. Apr. 1722). Millwright, York 1727-9, Portsm. 1730. Will, of Portsm., bound to sea, 18 Mar. 1744-5 (k.

# PICKERING

## 552

# PIERCE

at Annapolis 1746), names w. Dorothy, 8 ch.; 3 ch. of Thos. and Elizabeth were bp. So. Ch. 1726-1731. **Deborah**, m. 1st aft. 3 May 1719 John Smithson (2 ch. bp. So. Ch.); m. 2d Joshua Pickering(8). **Sarah**, m. Wm. Hooker(4). **Samuel**, m. aft. Mar. 1724-5 Sarah (Cotton 1) Walden; he liv. 1742, she dead 1744. 3 ch. liv. 1754. **Daniel**, bp. No. Ch. 5 Aug. 1711, liv. 1721. Adm. on est. of one Daniel of Portsm. gr. 1765 to wid. Dorothy.
6 **MARY.** See Jenness(3).
7 **ROBERT**, cordwainer, from Barnstable, co. Devon, m. in Portsm. 13 June 1717 Sarah Abbott(1). List 339. In 1739 surety for Sarah, singlewo., suspected of shoplifting. One Christian, adult, was bp. So. Ch. 6 July 1740.
8 **THOMAS**(2), shipwright, Portsmouth, Greenland, Newington, ±23 in 1679, ±50 in 1706, m. by 1686 Mary Gee(1), a Newingt. wid. 1730; List 335a. See also Murrell. Portsm. constable 1700. Lists 329, 52, 332b, 57, 62, 335a, 330d, 334a, 337. Will, 14 Aug. 1719—20 Apr. 1720, names w. and all ch. but **John**, eldest, liv. 1713, dead s. p. 1717. **Mary**, m. John Fabyan(3). **Sarah**, m. James Leach (3 jr.). **Rebecca**, m. 1st Henry Jaques(1); m. 2d Paul Wentworth. Lt. **James**, Newingt. (List 343), m. 16 Jan. 1718 Mary Nutter(5). Will, 1766—1768. 5 ch. **Joshua**, Newingt., m. 18 June 1724 Deborah (Pickering 5) Smithson, and may have had 2d w. Mary. Will, 1767—1768. 9 ch. **Abigail**, a child in 1697 when shot by Abraham Pett(1); m. in Newingt. 12 June 1718 James Seavey of Newc. **Hazelelponi**, m. in Boston 4 Oct. 1716 John Chamberlain. **Hannah**, m. Wm. Blyth (see Bly 3). **Elizabeth**, m. 1st Capt. John Brackett of Greenl.; m. 2d 3 Jan. 1760 Rev. Joseph Adams; d. Feb. 1762. **Thomas**, b. 28 Nov. 1703, d. Newingt. 9 Dec. 1786, m. 1st 7 Feb. 1726-7 Mary Downing(4); 4 ch. in her fa.'s will. He m. 2d 19 May 1743 Mary Janvrin(1); 8 ch. **Martha**, m. in Greenl. 6 Dec. 1723 John Grow. **Mehitabel**, m. in Greenl. 19 May 1726 Samuel Weeks, jr.
**PICKERNELL**, James, Kittery 1704, bot there 1707 and m. Lydia Nelson(1). Lists 290, 296. Shot by Ind. 1 June 1712 (Niles); by trad. both husb. and w. were killed 'and their graves still pointed out on Pickernell Hill.' Stephen Tobey was gr. adm. on est. of br. J. P. 26 Nov. 1712. Ch. rec. Kit: **Samuel**, shipwright, b. 2 Sept. 1705, m. 19 Dec. 1728 Esther Rogers (Richard). Will, 1785— 1786. 10 ch. **Mary**, b. 20 Oct. 1708, m. Seth Fogg(1). Of Kit. 1729, only surv. dau., she q.c. to Samuel, only surv. s. Presum. an older deed. Son was fa. of James whose ch. Eleanor and Nelson were bp. 1745, 1748. List 297.
**PICKETT, Christopher**, Scarboro, from Muddy River (Brookline). He sold at M. R. to Joshua Scottow in 1662, bot in

Scarb. from Foxwell in Feb. 1663-4, with Foxwell adm. Philip Griffin's est. 1667 and sold in Nov. 1668 to Griffin's successor John Budizert. Ag. ±60, he was one of four Scarb. men proving Arthur Alger's will bef. Wincoll in Oct. 1675 and owed the est. £6. In 1676 he owned Jocelyn land. Lists 237e, 239a. O. A. at Muddy River, Apr. 1679; there in 1681 he mtg. Scarb. ho. and lands to Henry Williams for a debt. His w. Elizabeth was ±60 in 1685 (he m. Elizabeth Stowe in June 1647). He alive at M. R. in Aug. 1689. Only kn. ch. **John**, b. Boston 1657, d.y.
**Pickus**, John, Piscataqua, appeared at Saco ct. 25 June 1640. See Pike (4½).
**Piddock, Thomas**, at Monhegan 1624. List 9.

# PIERCE, or Pearce, the latter the favored form in Eng. and freq. in the S.W. Became 13th commonest name in N. E.
1 **BENJAMIN**, Esq., Newbury, gr.s. of (4), m. Lydia Frost(2). 11 ch. in Newb., incl. **Charles**, m. in Kit. 20 Nov. 1718 Sarah Frost (Chas. 2 jr.).
2 **BENJAMIN**, from Watertown, m. 1st in Dover 7 Sept. 1705 Elizabeth Hall, wid. of John(10 jr.); m. 2d 30 May 1714 Hannah Ash(5). 2+7 ch. rec.
3 **CHARLES**, joiner, in 1680 servant of Wm. Haskins who paid his passage money and sent him and Thos. Potts(2) to steal guns from a ship. Pierce was convicted in 1683, when his fa. (poss. 14) agreed to pay the fine, and Jos. Pormont was bondsm. Haskins won a suit ag. him as a runaway c. 1685.
4 **DANIEL**, Newbury, and Anthony Littlefield owned 300 a. betw. Cape Porpus and Kennebunk Rivers 1658 (Y. D. 1: 86); as John Spencer's admr., he sued Antipas Maverick in Me. Ct. 1660. 2 of 4 ch: **Daniel**, Newb., m. 1660 Elizabeth Milward; his ch. incl. (1), (6), (21). **Joshua**, Newb., m. 7 May 1668 Dorothy Pike(9), who m. 2d John Light (3). Ch: Sarah, prob. came to Portsm. with mo., m. 1st Dr. Humphrey Bradstreet of Newb., m. 2d in 1719 Capt. Edward Sargent of Saco and Newbury; Joshua(13) who sold the Cape P. land in 1711 (Y. D. 12: 74).
5 **GEORGE**, b. Boston 27 Jan. 1661, s. of George and Mary (Woodis), was in N. H. with his step-fa. Morse(6) in 1677, called a boy. Ch. he, ag. 17, and Morse took O. A. at Newb. 1678. Note also (16).
6 **GEORGE**, blacksmith, Portsm., b. Newb. 5 Mar. 1681-2, gr.s. of (4), m. 1st in Portsm. 28 Mar. 1706 Elizabeth Langdon(2), who d. 4 May 1732, ag. 45; m. 2d 10 Jan. 1733-4 Mary Hunking(5). List 339. Will, 1747—1753, names w. Mary, **four daus.**, three gr.ch. His wid. depos. in 1758, ±70, ab. the Cutts wareho. where she played when she went to school to Mrs. Jackson in the ho. Col. Vaughan later liv. in Her will, 1764—

1764, names (step) dau. Mehitable Sherburn, kinsm. John Hunking.

**7 JOHN,** Plymouth Company patentee, has no place in this book except as based on the depos. of Judge Samuel Welles, accepted by Willis, rejected by Folsom. See Me. Hist. Soc. Col. 1: 1: 38.

**8 JOHN,** planter, Kittery, ag. 55 in 1670. In 1639 he and w. Elinor (Ellen) were liv. 'disorderly' in Mass., perh. in part a liking for gayety, as in Kit. 1669 his ho. was disorderly on Sundays and he had music there. Bef. 1648 he bot from Champernowne 100 a. over ag. his island and remov. from Noodle's Isl. 'Senior' 1661. Constable 1667, fined for neglect of duty. List 26. Inv. 5 Dec. 1673; adm. to wid. Elinor 7 July 1674. Her will, 27 Aug. 1675 (inv. 5 Jan. 1675-6), shows a richly furn. ho. and gives to 3 ch., the daus. distant. Ch: **John.** In 1665 John jr. and Peter Edge assaulted Roger Townsend, but T. swore the peace ag. John, sr., w. and dau. Sarah. O. F. to Mass. 19 July 1669 (last found). **Joseph,** mo.'s exec. List 286. He was to m. Margery Bray(2), but d. bef. 29 Mar. 1676. No relation appearing, adm. was gr. 2 Oct. 1678 to John Bray, a creditor, and Capt. Hooke; again 29 Sept. 1680 to sis. Sarah P. alias Jones or alias Mattoon. The lands went to Maj. Shapleigh for debt. Col. Pepperell unsuc. brot suits 1681-5 for what he claimed as his w.'s inheritance. **Mary,** talked ab. H. Greenland's w. as a witch in 1669; m. Joseph Fleet(2) without being pub. in Kit.; Gowen Wilson pub. them in Portsm. where neither liv. Away, she gave T. Harvey(14) an order to receive her portion. **Sarah,** withdrew a suit ag. Robert Mendum in 1667; in 1670 ordered placed in good service as lack of home training was involving her relatives in scandalous defamation. She m. 1st one Jones (see 17 jr.); m. 2d Hubertus Mattoon (1); m. 3d Henry Seavey; s. Joseph S. sold his gr.fa.'s ho. and 8 a. See also Jeffrey(3), Mansfield(7).

**9 JOHN,** fisherman, York, bot old Robert Knight's ho. from Rishworth in 1653, paid the mtg. in 1656 and sold to John Carmichael in 1660, when he bot ho. and land from Edw. Johnson and added 40 a. in 1661. The Johnson prop. he sold to Donnell and Haley in 1662, the 40 a. to Micom McIntire in 1670. Town gr. 1653, 10 a. at Bass Cove, where in 1678 he bot ano. 10 a. from James Grant. Gr.j. 1666. O. A. 22 Mar. 1679-80. Gr. 1686. Lists 277, 25. Bondsm. for wid. Phebe Nash(2) 14 Nov. 1662, and m. her bef. 7 July 1663; she liv. 22 June 1670. The filing of his inv. 26 Sept. 1692 suggests he was a victim of the massacre the prev. Jan. Ch. by unkn. w: **Anne,** m. 1st John Carmichael(1); m. 2d John Bracy(1). **Dorothy,** m. 1st Alexander Mackaneer(1); m. 2d Micom McIntire(1).

**10 JOHN,** commis. by Capt. John Allen of Penobscot to range the coast for interloping traders; see Kimball(7). Poss. the Portsm. mariner who wrote to Mr. Rawson in 1665 (Mass. Arch. 106: 140).

**11 JOHN,** Dover, servant to Philip Chesley, sr. in 1672, was voted liberty by the town in May 1673 to buy 10 a. near Thos. Canney. Adm. 27 June 1676 to Robert Burnham and Stephen Jones.

**12 JOHN**(15), fisherman, Manchester, Mass., b. and raised till 18 on his fa.'s planta. at Muscongus, depos. thrice 1717-1721, making yr. of birth, ±1652, but ±1644-6 by deposi-tions in 1730's. See Cox(33). In 1721 he, also br. George, depos. that John Summer-sett, Ind., gave Hog Isl. to self and sis. Eliz-abeth, their fa. taking poss. for them, and that he took the S. half, leaving the N. for Elizabeth's ch. In 1736, ±90, he depos. ab. Muscongus and that he knew the Phillips (21) fam., having made love to one of the daus. Liv. Manch. 19 Feb. 1736-7. W. **Mary.** Ch. rec. Manch: **Thomas,** b. 23 May 1691. **Miriam,** b. 6 Aug. 1693. **Richard,** b. 25 June 1698. Unrec: **John,** shipwright, Kit., Newc., m. Barbara Hinckes(1); 5 ch. In 1719 his fa. deeded him half his Muscongus land and by descent he inherited all.

**13 CAPT. *JOSHUA,** Esq., joiner, b. Newb. 14 Jan. 1670-1, s. of Joshua(4), came to Portsm. when his mo. remarried. Jury 1696; constable 1698; town clerk 1700, and again 1714 to death; selectm. 9 times 1703-1732; Rep. 1718-21, 1728 (Speaker 1720-1); Regis-ter of Deeds; J. P. Lists 324, 330d, 337, 338c, 339. He m. 1st in Portsm. 24 Jan. 1694-5 Elizabeth Hall(13) who d. 13 Jan. 1717-8, ag. 42; m. 2d 25 Mar. 1718-9 Elizabeth (Ger-rish 3) Wade. Will, 13—15 Nov. 1742 (d. 7 Feb. fol.), names w. Elizabeth, 9 ch. and est. from his form. w. now improved by Thos. Ayers of Greenl. Ch: **Sarah,** b. 30 Apr. 1697, m. 1st 21 Sept. 1721 John Wins-low, step-s. of Samuel Penhallow(2); 2 sons named in their uncle Joshua's will. She m. 2d betw. 1743-1748 Dr. Nathl. Sargent. **Jo-seph,** Esq., physician, b. 21 Feb. 1698, d. 7 Feb. 1747-8. Wife Elizabeth in 1740; adm. to wid. Susanna. Ch. ment. Joshua, Esq., b. 31 Oct. 1700. Will, 18 July (d. 3 Aug.) 1754, names many kin, no w. or ch. **Anne,** b. 10 Sept. 1702, m. Joseph Green of Boston; d. there 28 Dec. 1770, a wid. **Elizabeth,** b. 31 May 1705, unm. 1742, called Osborne in 1754, d. 9 June 1764. **Mary,** b. 29 Oct. 1707, m. Col. Samuel Moore(18). Hon. **Daniel,** mer-chant, b. 2 May 1709, m. 29 Oct. 1742 Anne Rindge (John) who d. 19 Oct. 1748, ag. 25; he 4 Dec. 1773. 4 ch. Capt. **Nathaniel,** mari-ner, b. 7 Jan. 1711, d. 27 Aug. 1762; wid. Anne (Jaffrey, 4 jr.) Margaret, b. 25 June 1714, m. in Portsm. 24 Nov. 1737 Benj. Green

of Boston, but of Nova Scotia 1764.

**14 LANCELOT,** Pejepscot, m. Ann Stephens, dau. of Thos., who deeded land on Pejepscot River to them and to his s. Thos. S., 30 June 1676; Allister Coombs an abuttor. Wid. Nan d. at Milton 18 Feb. 1708, ag. 83. Ch. **William. Charles,** see (3). **Jane.**

**14½ LUCIUS,** soldier discharged at Falmouth 1686.

**15 RICHARD,** carpenter, Muscongus, m. Elizabeth Brown(15); unkn. where and when they d. List 121. In 1729 desc. had recorded an Ind. deed to him from John Summersett, 9 Jan. 1641, land betw. Round Pond and Pemaquid Point. Four of eight heirs signed an agreem. in 1717. Ch: **Richard,** eldest s., b. ±1647. **John,** b. ±1652. **William. Francis,** had w. Lydia and d. by 1729; called of Manchester, decd., in 1734, also late of Beverly. Only surv. ch. Elizabeth b. Manch. 22 Apr. 1700, m. 1718 Edw. Clark of Gloucester. **George,** ag. 55 in Feb. 1720-1, liv. Beverly 1734, where one George d. in 1746. W. Rebecca. Ch. rec. Bev. 1701-1716: Abigail, Rebecca, William, George, Elizabeth, Mary. **Elizabeth,** m. Richard Fulford(1). **Margaret,** d. in Suffield, Conn., 28 Dec. 1688, m. 1st one Long (dau. Elizabeth m. in Milton 1710 Simes Langley, later of Norwich, Conn.); m. 2d in Dorchester 18 Nov. 1681 Thos. Pope (ch: Elizabeth m. in Plymouth 1706 Nathan Ward; Mindwell m. Wm. Huxley of Suffield). **Mary,** m. in Marblehead 10 Apr. 1695 Nathl. Hamilton (Hamblin by deeds), both of Manchester; Suffield 1732. See York D. for numerous deeds and depos. by ch. and gr.ch.; Doc. Hist. 9: 451; Gen. Advertiser 1: 95; Col. Soc. Mass. 6: 21; 8: 104.

**16 RICHARD**(15), coaster, fisherman, Marblehead, Lists 15, ¶189. His w. was Mary; see also Ewen. (One R. P. and w. Mary of Manchester 1692 were gr.ch. of Richard Woodis; see (5) and Suff. D. 44: 165). In 1744 his s. Richard depos. that his parents liv. at Smelt Cove except during Ind. wars and he often visited them. The fa. was of Marbleh. 1717, ag. 70; Muscongus 1718-1721, and s. John depos. that he went there ab. 1722 and brot his fa. and fam. away. Marbleh. 1729; d. by 1734. Ch., order unkn., 1st 5 bp. at Marbleh. 27 Oct. 1700: **Richard,** 30 in 1720, m. 22 Sept. 1713 Hannah Bassett. Marbleh. 1734; Muscongus 1737, and mtg. the ho. he had built at Smelt Cove; in 1744, ±52, he depos. he knew the Ind. language and had been ab. 27 yrs. a trader with them at the East. Dea. **John,** baker, Marbleh., m. 30 Nov. 1715 Elizabeth Merritt, and had later wives. Ag. ±70 in 1764, ±76 in 1770, d. 1784. **Robert,** m. 10 Dec. 1717 Mary Merritt. **Joseph. Thomas. Benjamin. Mary,** m. Edward Surrigge. **Hannah,** w. of Joseph Morse, who

is a difficulty. In 1719 Wm. (25) deeded 100 a. at Muscongus to neph. J. M. of Marbleh., baker, adj. tract Morse had from his fa. and mo. Richard and Mary Pearce; see also Brown(17). Joseph Morse m. Hannah Man in Boston in 1735; in 1737 deeded Muscongus land to s.-in-law Alex. Young of Boston (m. Rebecca Man 1738), with ment. of 'my br. Richard Pearce.' See also Brackett(3).

**17 RICHARD,** Portsm., servant and legatee of Mrs. Ann Batchelder(1) 1660. List 330a. One R. P. and Sarah Cotton, both of Portsm., m. there 27 Aug. 1680; see Cotton (4).

**18 RICHARD,** a Kennebec soldier, List 189, may have been (16). Richard, a Falm. abuttor 1700, poss. (24). Richard in captivity 1713, List 99, p. 128.

**19 STEPHEN,** 1649; see Jocelyn(4).

**20 THOMAS,** Pemaquid 1687; List 124.

**21 CAPT. THOMAS,** cordwainer, Portsm., b. Newb. May 1674, gr.s. of (4), m. 5 Jan. 1698 Mehitable Frost(2). Portsm. selectm. 7 times; J. P. List 339. 3 ch. (Prov. rec.) and others.

**22 THOMAS,** Newcastle 1718, with w. Elizabeth. See Marshall(9), Palmer(24).

**23 WILLIAM,** Shoals wit. 1659, poss. servant of John Martin(8) in 1664, or Martin may have brot his Wm. from Charlestown.

**24 WILLIAM**(14), ship-carpenter, settler under Danforth at Falmouth. Lists 30, 227, 228c. He went to Milton (where one William and w. Miriam had ch. Miriam and Elizabeth, 1703, 1707, another or the same had w. Elizabeth and dau. Mary b. 1710). From Milton in 17— he claimed a 3 a. ho.-lot near Fort Loyal bot. from Samuel Webber in 1683, a ho. and 3 a. at Casco Bay bot from John Davis in 1687; and claimed also at Pejepscot for self as fa.'s heir and in behalf of cous. Thos. Stephens of Swansea. In 1730 (liv. 12 Jan. 1730-1) he deeded land at Falm. and at Stephens Carrying Place, Brunswick, to four ch: **William. Richard. Anne,** w. of John Spear of Braintree (m. in Milton 20 Nov. 1718). **Elizabeth.** One Jane P. of Milton m. James Bagley of Braintree 23 June 1713.

**25 WILLIAM**(15), Norwalk, Conn., 1719; d. by 1733. Deeds show ch: **Joseph,** Plymouth, late of Norwalk, 1719-1734; Rochester, Mass. 1735. **Thomas, Samuel,** both of Newton, Conn., 1733. Likely: **Sarah,** w. of Eleazer Stockwell of Housatonic 1732; **Francis,** Farmington, Conn., whose atty. in 1734 was Joseph of Plymouth.

**26 WILLIAM,** weaver, York. Pepperell issued a warrant ag. him as -Pease- in 1702. He m. Mary Beale(2), who was in ct. with him in Jan. 1702-3, not called his w. She d. 1 Apr. 1730. He kept the lower ferry in 1735. List 279. 6 ch. by York rec., the

first in 1707: **Ann. Mary. Andrew. Elizabeth. Hephzibah. Sarah.**

27 ——, master of the -Dover- owned by Waldron, ±1680. List 51.

28 ——, Samuel Hill's cousin Pearce; see Hill(19).

**PIKE**, a South of Eng. name; partic. frequent in Wiltshire.

½ **ANTHONY.** See Palfrey.

1 **CAPT. EDWARD**, sued by Nathl. Wallis in Casco ct. 1667, his bondsm. Capt. John Davis and Nathl. Phillips. List 234a.

2 **GEORGE**, Mendon; see Atkins(5). This name is found at Marblehead and Boston.

3 **HUGH**, Newbury, 21 in 1678, form. servant of John Knight, bot in Coxhall (Lyman) in 1694. His 2d w. Mary, gr.dau. of Richard Woodhouse or Woodis of Boston, and m. bef. 19 Dec. 1692, was a step-relative of his 1st w. Sarah Browne (Francis). See Hoyt's Salisb. i: 290; Suff. D. 44: 165; also Morse(6), Pierce(5).

4 **JOANNA**, Kittery, wit. in the Hammons case, 1719. Presum. she was the 2d w. of John Rackliff(3) and related to (7) or (12) or both.

4½ **JOHN**, Newbury, Salisbury, m. in Whiteparish, co. Wilts, 17 Jan. 1612-3 Dorothy Day of Landford. See Pickus; Hoyt's 'Salisbury,' i: 285; ii: 799; N. E. Reg. 66: 257.

5 **REV. JOHN**(9), H.C. 1675, Dover, preaching there 1 Nov. 1678, m. Sarah Moody (3) 5 May 1681, and was ordained 31 Aug. fol. His Journal (List 96) and marriage records of great geneal. value. 'Upon the desolation of Cochecho,' he mov. his fam. to Portsm. in June 1689; Hampt. part of 1690 and 1691, then Newbury; chaplain at Pemaquid Oct. 1694-July 1695, thence to Portsm.; Dover 1698; Salisb. 1702; Dover 1703, appar. until death. Lists 49, 358b. His w. Sarah d. 24 Jan. 1702-3. His will, 6—10 Mar. 1709-10, names 6 surv. ch., Joseph Stockman jr., nieces Dorothy Light(3) and Sarah Pike (Robert 9 jr.). Ch: **Son**, stillb. 30 Mar. 1682. **Nathaniel**, b. 3 June 1683, mariner, Portsm. (List 96), m. by 1708 Margaret Cutts(3). She took adm. in N. H. 5 June 1714, in Essex Co. 17 May 1715. 3 ch. bp., Sarah alone liv. 1717. Wid. Margaret m. 2d Capt. Thos. Landall(1), whose fa. or mo. may have been the —— Landall adm. to the Baptist Ch. in Bost. in 1682 when several Kit. people were admitted. Dr. **Robert**, Portsm., b. 6 Feb. 1685, m. 22 May 1711 Elizabeth Atkinson (5), who d. 5 Feb. 1719-20, ag. 27. Adm. on his est. 15 Dec. 1731 to Theodore Atkinson, his br. Solomon renounc. List 339. 3 sons bp.; will of eldest, Robert, 1737—1738, ment. uncles and cousins, no. br. **Abigail**, b. 3 Apr. 1688, d. 18 June 1694. **Hannah**, twin, b. at Hampt. 18 May 1691, m. at Bradford 28 Mar.

1714-5 Rev. Thos. Symmes, d. there 1 Feb. 1718-9, ag. 28. Dau. Sarah in uncle's will 1737. **Mercy**, twin, m. 1st 21 Nov. 1711 Rev. Joshua Gardner of Haverh., who d. 21 Mar. 1715-6; m. 2d in Bradford 12 Feb. 1721-2 John Dummer, Esq., of Newb.; see Penhallow(2). 2 sons (Gardner), Samuel alone in uncle's will 1737. **Joshua**, Portsm., b. 14 June 1693, List 331c; adm. 23 Jan. 1716-7 to Thos. Symmes. **Samuel**, b. 1 Apr. 1695, List 331c; d. 29 Nov. 1702. **Abigail**, b. 22 Dec. 1697, d. 21 Apr. 1699. **Margaret**, b. 31 Jan., d. 13 Mar. 1698-9. **Solomon**, cooper, innholder, Portsm., b. 23 May 1700, m. 18 Apr. 1726 Elizabeth Fellows(4). He and sons Nathl. and Joshua named in his br.'s will, 1737. Called 'deceased' 18 Aug. 1740; adm. to wid. 27 May 1741.

6 **MOSES**, Sheepscot 1665. List 12.

7 **PHILIP**, sued Roger Kelly for portlege and share of fish in 1700. Tailor of Kittery, he bot in Portsm. 1705; taxed there 1707-1713. His w. was Rebecca (Lewis 14), m. bef. 3 Feb. 1712-3, both of Kit. 1718. Note also (4), (12). Pike Fam. Rec. (1905) names s. **Philip**, m. Mary Maddocks of Wells, and also has: 'James P. of Hollis always told his ch. and gr.ch. that his fa. Philip of Kit. came to this country from Manchester, Eng.' Appar. it was the s. Philip, cordwainer, who bot in York in 1734. List 279. Other ch. may have incl: **Thomas** (m. Patience Stone) and **John**, both of whom o.c. at Berwick Ch. 1727-8.

8 **RICHARD**, liv. at Muscle Cove, Falmouth, and d. early, leaving wid. Elizabeth (Andrews 16) and appar. but one ch. **Samuel**, b. ±1654. Wid. Elizabeth m. 2d Thos. Purchase; m. 3d John Blaney, sr. See Doc. Hist. 6: 407.

9 **MAJOR ‡*ROBERT**(4½), Salisbury, ±52 in 1669. A Mass. magistrate and military man in Me. and N. H. and a liberal leader ahead of his time, his career is set forth in 'The New Puritan' by James Shepherd Pike. See also N. H. State Papers, 29: 163. His w. Sarah (Sanders), m. in Salisb. 3 Apr. 1641, d. 1 Nov. 1679; he m. 2d 30 Oct. 1684 Martha (Moyce), wid. of Geo. Goldwier. He d. 12 Dec. 1706 (List 96). Adm. 21 May 1707 to s. John; in Apr. 1714 to gr.son Dr. Robert of Portsm. Wid. Martha d. 26 Feb. 1712-3. Ch., all b. Salisb: **Sarah**, b. 24 Feb. 1641-2, m. 1st Wymond Bradbury(3); m. 2d John Stockman. **Mary**, 1644-1647. **Dorothy**, b. 11 Nov. 1645, m. 1st Joshua Pierce(4); m. 2d John Light(3). **Mary**, b. 5 Aug. 1647, m. 1st Jedediah Andrews(8); m. 2d Lt. John Allen. **Elizabeth**, b. 24 June 1650, m. 20 Aug. 1672 Wm. Carr, br. of (3), (5). Rev. **John**, b. 13 May 1653. **Robert**, b. 26 June 1655, m. at Newb. 1 Dec. 1686 Mary Follansby(1); d. Salisb. 22 Aug. 1690 (List 96). 2 ch. (see 10

and will of 5). Wid. Mary m. 2d Wm. Hooke (7 jr.). **Moses**, Salisb., b. 15 Mar. 1657-8, m. Susanna Worcester; 8 ch.

10 **ROBERT**, Exeter, b. Salisb. 3 Sept. 1687, s. of Robert(9 jr.), m. Hannah Gilman (7). List 376b. Ch.

11 **ENSIGN SAMUEL**(8), blacksmith, ±23 in 1677, ±27 in 1681. A refugee at Salem in Jan. 1675-6; in Apr. admitted to sojourn there during the war. O. A. at Lynn 26 Feb. 1677 and there in 1681. At Falm. he had 100 a S.W. of Muscle Cove River, a ho. and shop, and liv. there when he could. Falm. Ensign 1689. Lists 27, 85, 34, 228bc. He returned to Salem. Inv. taken 3 Apr. 1694; distrib. to creditors 15 Apr. 1695. Wid. Mary, dau. of Nathl. Wallis, was liv. in Salem 1718. Ch: **Richard**, blacksmith, ±53 in Nov. 1730, m. 1st bef. June 1710 Mary King (Daniel, sr., of Salem); m. 2d in Salem 26 Jan. 1715-6 Elizabeth (Pickman) Ormes; d. 25 July 1747. 1+7 ch. **Mary**, m. 1st in Salem 10 Sept. 1701 Richard Woodmancey (1 dau. rec.); m. 2d (int. 26 Mar. 1709) Richard Broadway, prob. related to the Sagadahoc Richard (1 dau. bp. 1722 as 'Broadway now Gray,' but m. as Broadway); in 1718 again a wid., Mary Gray of Salem, else her 2d husb. was alias Gray. **Samuel**, b. ±1681, m. in Boston 13 Feb. 1706 Mary Radmore (presum. a widow, formerly Bass); d. 3 Nov. 1711, ±30. Ch: Samuel, d.y., and Philip and Mary of Boston who sold a one-fifth int. at Casco Bay in 1730, the mo. signing. **Nathaniel**, shipwright, m. (int. Salem 22 Dec. 1711) Margaret King, presum. the unm. sis. of Richard's w. in 1710. 2 ch. bp. In 1718 Richard and Nathl. and sis. Mary Gray (their mo. signing) sold four-fifths of the Falmouth land.

12 **SAMUEL**, m. 6 Mar. 1712-3 Eleanor Rhodes(2). Liv. Berwick 1714; Georgetown, Me. 1716; Littleton, Mass., form. of Lexington, 1725. Ch. incl. 1 son bp. Berw., 2 sons bp. Georgetown, and 3 younger daus. See also (4), (7).

13 **WILLIAM**, Exeter. See Hilton(24).

**PILE**, Pyle, Piles. Exeter, co. Devon, the home of an ancient line.

1 **CAPT. MILES** (Pyle) from Dartmouth, co. Devon, one of several commis. in 1651 to take evid. ag. Sir David Kirke for extortion in Newfoundland (see Littlebury, Treworgye). Piscataqua 1662; merchant 1664, shipping tobacco there from Va. and being sued by John Bray for work on a ship. At Hog Isl. 7 July 1665 he sold ho. and fishing plant to Robert Harris already in poss.; his brew-ho. there ment. 1669, Mark Roe having occupied it.

2 **WILLIAM** (Pile, Piles), Dover 1657; wit. a Salisb. deed 1658, but Hoyt could not

find him resident; Kittery gr. 1659. **Gr.j.** (Me.) 1661, 1665; atty. for Kit. 1663; the same yr. he conv. to Richard Swain his Nantucket right, one-twelfth of the Patent. Richard Tozier sued him in 1667 for forcible entry on his land; bounds betw. W. P., now James Smith, and Tozier ment. 1668, and as late as 1707 he was named a Kit. abuttor. Lists 356ab, 25, 298.

**Pilgrim**, John, Mr., 1687. List 90.

**PILLIN** (Pillion), **John**, Dover, granted 40 a. on N.W. side of Stoney Brook in Oct. 1653. In 1659 John Goddard sold to Wm. Williams, sr., the lot that was John Pilline's (Dover T. Rec., 194), Hilons in deed dated 6: 4: 1659, Pillions in Conc. D. 2: 28b. List 355a.

**PILSBURY**. 1 **Abel**, soldier at Saco fort 1696. List 248b. Presum. the Newbury man who was dead in 1697, his ch. including **Joshua**, b. 1679.

2 **JOSHUA**, k. by Ind. at Winter Harbor or Saco 1703. List 39. See (1).

**PINDER**, **John**, bricklayer, Oyster River, depos. 15 Oct. 1675, ag. 26; ±50 in 1703, ±65 in 1715, ±73 in 1721. He bot from the Yorks at Lubberland next Thos. Morris in 1681, and had 10 a. gr. adj. in 1701. Gr.j. 1697. Lists 368ab, 57, 62, 66, 369. He and w. were among those called witches by Naomi Daniels in 1685; his w. was Sarah (Merrow) 1701-1705 at least (see Furber 2, Morris 6). Bef. 1724 he m. Elizabeth, wid. of Ezekiel Pitman(2). Will, 12 June 1724—31 Mar. 1742; wid. Elizabeth waived adm. 23 July fol. Ch: **Benjamin**, ag. 15 or 16 in Mar. 1704-5; w. Martha in 1736; liv. 1754. Lists 368b, 369. 5 ch. bp. 1729, not incl. John, named in gr.fa.'s will, who was of Newmarket in 1755. **Elizabeth**, given 15 s. by Thos. Morris 1701; m. Wm. Durgin(3). **Temperance**, m. Ichabod Follett (see 2). **Sarah**, m. Benjamin York. **Abigail**, ±8 in 1704, unm. 1724.

**PINKHAM**. Found in Alvington (Richard, s. of Richard bp. 7 Nov. 1613), Bideford and Roborough, co. Devon.

1 **JOHN**(2), Dover Neck, ±80 in 1724, m. bef. June 1674 Martha Otis(1), she liv. 1699. Lists 356jk, 357b, 358b, 359ab, 52. In 1715 he deeded to five sons (not Thos.), s. Amos to pay his sisters; in 1728 gave all except bed to s. Otis who gave bond to supp. fa. and pay £5 each to three sisters. Ch. (in 1740 all but Thos. and Sarah gave p/a to br. Otis to collect an Otis heirship; in 1741 the daus. q.c. to Otis their fa.'s est.): **Thomas**, as Richard's successor had lot 22 laid out in 1698; in 1703 had land at E. end of fa.'s and Thos. Williams', adj. Solomon; in 1715 land from his fa. He m. 2 Dec. 1700 Mary Allen (see 4). Kn. ch: Sarah, Richard, Benjamin, Ebenezer. **Richard**, carpenter, depos. ±30 in

1709, but must have been older. List 358d. He m. 1st by 1696 Elizabeth Leighton(8), appar. alive in Sept. 1756, ag. 77; m. 2d 27 Nov. 1757, when 85, Mary Welch of Kit., ag. 78. Ch. incl: John (b. 19 Aug. 1696), Tristram (in 1738 Richard and s. Tristram sued for land Philip Crommett sold to Richard in 1697), Richard. **Solomon**, upward of 74 in July 1757, m. 13 Dec. 1706 Mary Field(12), she liv. 1738. Lists 358d, 369. Ch. incl: Stephen and Abigail (m. 23 Jan. 1727-8 Samuel Austin 8). **Amos**, upward of 74 in July 1757, liv. May 1762, ag. 79. Lists 358b, 368b. First w. Katherine d. 22 May 1709, List 96; he m. 2d Elizabeth (Smith) Chesley (4). Thos. Millet accus. him of stealing rum, molasses, etc., in 1720, when Mary ·Janderstestif. 'he kept a noble house.' 2 daus. rec. 1714-1718. **James**, ±24 in 1709, ±52 in Feb. 1738-9. List 358d. **John** 10 July 1713 Elizabeth (Hopley 1) Drew (9). Will, 26 Oct. 1749—25 Apr. 1750, names her, 7 ch. **Rose**, m. 1st James Tuttle; m. 2d Thos. Canney(1). **Otis**, m. 22 Nov. 1721 Abigail Tibbetts (Ephraim). Adm. on his est. gr. 30 Nov. 1764, 5 ch. **Elizabeth**, m. Samuel Nute (3). **Sarah**, m. bef. 1728 Joseph Austin. One Ann m. Wm. Geddis, Betty m. Samuel Cromwell, both in 1727.

2 **RICHARD**, Dover 1640, beat the drum for service and swept the meet.-ho. in 1648. He liv. ab. a mile N. on Dover Neck. Freeman 1653. Lists 351ab, 352, 355a, 356fh, 357e, 359a. In 1660 he was in ct. for threatening to beat his w. if she came home by day or night. She was Gylian in 1663 when she sat an hour in the stocks as he refused to pay her fine for abs. from meeting; he was abs. himself in 1669. In June 1671, with no ment. of w., he deeded for supp. to s. John, who also agreed to supp. br. Matthew; John sold fa.'s land in 1688. Kn. ch. (one s. and John Barton, Wm. Ellingham's apprentices, ran away in 1659 and were not brot back): **John**, b. ±1644 (late depos.). **Thomas**, Lists 356jh. Presum. the pilot of ship ·Peter-. London to Piscat., in Nov. 1668, ag. ±24. **Matthew**, incapacitated 1671. **Richard**, Nantucket, m. Mary Coffin(3), d. 1718; she m. 2d James Gardner and d. 1 Apr. 1741. 9 rec. ch., 1 in 1684, 8 from 1691-1708.

**Pinmar**. See Benmore(1).

## PIPER.

1 **JONATHAN**, br. of (2), at Exeter tempo. about 1695-6.

2 **SAMUEL**, cordwainer, Stratham, b. Ipsw. 12 June 1670, s. of Nathl., br. of (1) and (3), m. in Dover 23 Apr. 1694 Abigail Church (1). Exeter 1698; sued by Pepperell 1703. Lists 67, 376b (1698), 388. Aged 75, he deposed in Strath. in June 1747 ab. Greenland 40 yrs. bef.; d. 31 Oct. 1747. Ch. incl. **John**

(see Samuel Haines 6), **Samuel**, and prob. **Sarah**, m. 17 Dec. 1719 Thos. Wiggin, who was gdn. of John's ch. in 1743.

3 **THOMAS**, b. Ipsw. 26 Nov. 1666, br. of (2), m. in Marblehead 21 Nov. 1692 Grace Hawley, both of Wenham. Taxed Greenl. 1717-1719; in 1719 bot in Strath., where both d., his will, 1767—1767. Ch. incl. **Thomas**, and **Nathaniel**, b. Wenham 1697, 1701, and **Patience**, b. Ipsw. 25 Feb. 1702 (see Samuel Haines 6).

**Pipon**, Joshua. Pemaquid commander 1686. See Doc. Hist. vol. 6.

**PISGRAVE**, Peter, Portsmouth 1670, List 326c. Thos. Wescott was paid in 1682 for keeping 'old Pitter' 13 months, then Stephen Graffam engaged to keep him from Aug. 1682.

**Pistor**, William, owned in the York patent. List 272.

**PITCHER**, 1 **Richard**. See Mattoon(1).

2 **SAMUEL**, Saco fort soldier. List 248a. Wit. Crocker to Pepperell 1699 (Y. D. 4: 151).

## PITMAN. A Dorset-Somerset family.

1 **ANNE**, wit. with Elizabeth Harvey, Portsmouth 1695. Mary, m. Wm. Woodman 1711; Abigail, m. Thos. Larrabee 1715, both of Portsm. Mary Coolbroth, Newington, had 7 ch. bp. 1725, incl. Pitman.

2 **EZEKIEL**(11), eldest s. 1664, depos. in 1677 ab. Teague Riall's nunc. will. His 1693 gr., 30 a., was ord. laid out to his s. Wm. in 1713 and order rescinded, as the fa. himself had alienated to Moses Davis. Dead in 1701. Lists 62, 367b. See also Huckins(1), Roberts(14). His 2d w. Elizabeth, appar. wid. of James Derry, and his br. Francis were cited to adm. in Feb. 1708-9, or adm. to issue to son Wm.'s gdn. Jeremiah Burnham who was named 4 Apr. 1709. She m. last John Pinder(1). See also Derry(1). Kn. ch. by unkn. 1st w: **William**, b. 16 Apr. 1691, chose Jeremiah Burnham gdn. 7 Jan. 1706-7, his master Thos. Edgerly consenting. Wife Joanna. 5 ch., first 3 bp. at O. R. with their parents 6 May 1719-20. **Ezekiel**, b. at O. R. and first a sailor, m. at Portsm. 23 May 1717 Elizabeth Shackford (Samuel). Of Portsmouth, blacksmith, 1751, he q.c. to Moses Davis (jr.) his fa.'s 1693 gr. Ezekiel, jr., m. there 13 July 1740 Elizabeth Peverly; Francis, bp. No. Ch. 1722, was presum. another son.

3 **FRANCIS**(11), taxed O. R. 1683, q.c. his int. in his fa.'s lands to Edw. Wakeham in 1695, and in Apr. 1701 bot from Nathl. Meader 40 a. on W. side of Beech Hill sold to Meader by wid. Elizabeth(2). Depos. twice in 1734, ag. 72; liv. 1735. Lists 358b, 368ab, 57, 62. See also Derry(1). He m. betw. 1711-1714, prob. not 1st, Elizabeth, wid. of Nathl.

Tibbetts; she was bp. at O. R. 21 July 1717. Only kn. ch: **Sarah,** m. at O. R. 28 Nov. 1728 Wm. Buzzell (see Bussy 2).

4 **JAMES,** Pemaquid landowner, husb. of Mary and fa. of ch. rec. Manchester 1676-1695: **Mark,** List 267b. **Sarah. James,** mariner, b. 25 Sept. 1681, m. in Manch. 27 Apr. 1704 Elizabeth Stocker; Portsm. 1709. His s. Benjamin b. Manch. 1707, was bp. at Portsm. in 1716, with ano. s. Mark. Of Portsm. 1717, for self and as atty. for br. Joseph, he sold his decd. fa.'s 104 a. near King's Bridge, Pemaquid. If the Barrington propr., List 339, he was a butcher in 1726; w. Elizabeth. James, bp. with 5 ch. at Newingt. in 1725, appar. ano. man. **Thomas,** b. 6 Apr. 1682, m. Sarah (not Mary) Dennis(6); d. in Manch. 21 Nov. 1753, ag. 70 or more; she 26 Oct. 1759, toward 80. 7 ch. 1701-1720. **Mary. Elizabeth,** b. 6 May 1688, m. Thos. Dalling (3). **Joseph,** liv. 1717. And presum. unrec., **Anna,** m. Walter Hull(10).

5 **JOHN,** wit. a Chesley fam. deed 1664.

6 **JOHN,** Marblehead. See Robinson(3); also (8), (10).

7 **JOSEPH**(11), ag. 30 in Dec. 1699. He had a gr. in Mar. 1693-4, and with Wm. Jackson was bondsm. for James Jackson(22) in 1699. Wife Elizabeth. Aft. his br. John was lost, he liv. on his place 'some years' until k. by Ind. not far from O. R. meeting-ho. 19 Aug. 1704 (SJC 28673). Lists 62, 94, 96. One 'Barnaba' (Sanders? Janders?), liv. there with the wid., reported mar. to her, but on some demur or affront he built himself a ho. some distance northward; see Amos Pinkham(1). Ch. in deed of the place to John Allen 1722: **John,** with sis. Ann a wit. in the Pinkham case 1720, when, in the argument, John was called 'infamous,' 'no one would believe him.' His w. was Elizabeth 1722; both liv. 1744, he 1752. **Zachariah,** b. ±1695 in the ho. his uncle John built; m. 13 Dec. 1723 Mercy Conner (Timothy). Will, 3 June 1783 (d. in Madbury 1 Feb. 1785, ag. 90), names 4 ch. **Nehemiah,** Scarb. 1728, had w. and 1 ch. in Durham 1751, when he ptn. for help. **Sarah,** m. Zachariah Nock(6). **Mary,** m. Wm. Downes(6). **Ann,** single 1722.

8 **MOSES,** Marblehead; see Parker(25); also (6), (10).

9 **NATHANIEL**(11), m. bef. 17 Nov. 1697 Deliverance, wid. of John Derry(2). Highway surv. for O. R. (south) 1699. Grant of 30 a. in Madbury 1701. List 358b. Dead 1728, she liv. Ch. by deed: **Tabitha,** m. by 1723 Eli Demeritt(1 jr.). **Abigail,** bp. 12 Apr. 1724, m. 13 Mar. 1729-30 Wm. Demeritt (1). **Derry,** bp. 24 May 1724; his w. Dorothy (Jackson, dau. of Dr. Geo. 5 jr.) was adm. to Dover First Ch. 14 Nov. 1736. One Nathl., ag. 19, was in Boston with Sampson Penley, jr., 1694.

10 **THOMAS,** of a Marblehead fam. (poss. early in Me.) that carried the name Mark as did fam. of (4). See also (6), (8). He m. in Marbleh. 30 Mar. 1696 Margaret (Gould 1) Stilson, who d. there 12 mo. 1750, ag. 92. Rec. ch: **Thomas** and **Elizabeth,** twins, b. 15 June 1697. **Sarah,** bp. 20 Nov. 1698.

11 **WILLIAM,** blacksmith, Oyster River (±41 in 1672), m. in Boston, 29 Nov. 1653 Barbara Evans. His w. was Ann 1661-1668 at least (when they had much to do with Philip Chesley), and Dorothy in 1673 (the sole rec. of her as wit. in a Chesley case). Poss. one w. was related to Zachariah Ayers (9). In 1657 he liv. on land of Wm. Roberts who deeded to him and s. Ezekiel in 1664, giving rise to suppos. that the w. Ann was a Roberts, but Wm. had no such dau. In 1677 at Thos. Wheeler's ho. he hit Roger Rose with a pint pot and was ord. to pay the surgeon. Lists 356a, 361a, 363abc, 365, 366, 359a. See also (5) and Leathers(1). Will, 30 Oct.—16 Nov. 1682, gives to w. (unnamed) two cows and her thirds, and to all ch. but Mary. The mothers of the ch. uncert. Surely by 1st w: **Abigail,** m. 1st by 1671 Stephen Willey, m. 2d 6 Oct. 1710 Edward de Flecheur in Canada, where she was sometimes Gabrielle, but bp. Marie Louise; List 99, p. 127. Presum: **Mary,** m. 16 Apr. 1674 Stephen Otis(3). **Ezekiel,** b. 1658. Poss: **Elizabeth,** m. Stephen Jenkins(12). **Sarah,** Thrisco in 1682; see Drisco(8). By w. Ann: **Francis,** b. ±1662, willed Giles's place bot by his fa. from Richard Knight. **John,** named sole exec., but had gdns. until 1684, Edw. Leathers and his br. Ezekiel. In 1685 he accus. Philip Chesley, sr., of threatening him so he would not testify for Burnham; built and liv. on N. side of Johnson's Creek until lost at sea; see (7). Lists 57, 94. **Joseph,** b. ±1669. **Ann** (presum.), of Wells, m. (Me. ct. Jan. 1698-9) John Sias. She depos. in 1734, ±62, that she liv. with Wm. Follett in 1689. (One Mary P., adult, was of Wells 1714-7). Appar. younger ch: **Nathaniel. Zacharias,** given £5 by John Knight(18) in 1694. Dover gr. 1694, sold 1697, then of Dover. See also Hill(22). **Hannah. Judith,** youngest, m. John Ham(5).

12 **WILLIAM,** Scarboro, twice a Scottow wit. 1667; wit. a Foxwell deed 1671 with Jocelyn and Ambrose Boaden sr., and sued Foxwell's admr., 1688. A Scarb. wit. with Thos. Scottow 2 Mar. 1689. See also (9).

13 **WILLIAM,** Mr., merchant, Portsm. (38 in May 1686) kept Mrs. Eleanor Cutts' books in 1680, and m. aft. 14 Aug. 1679 Elizabeth (Bolles 3) Locke(6). Gr.j. 1683, 1695, 1699; O. A. Str. Bk. 28 Aug. 1685; constable 1686; tr.j. 1697; town clerk. Lists 324, 329, 330d, 335a, 337, 52, 57, 62. Her Lists 331c, 335a, 337, 339. His will, 19 May 1693—Jan.

1699-1700, names w. Elizabeth, 4 sons under age, 'my children.' She had ale, beer and cider lic., 1700; in 1714 swore there were no credits in her husb.'s books ag. Joseph Trickey's note of 1684. Wid. P. and s. Jabez taxed 1722; she deeded to sons Joseph and Samuel 1730; taxed Jan. 1731-2. Only sons kn: **Jabez**, List 339, d. s.p. bef. 1751. **Samuel**, subscr. £2 for Mr. Emerson 1713; List 339; Portsm. 1730; d. s.p. bef. 1751. **William**, Boston mariner, m. there 22 Dec. 1715 Elizabeth Hincks. In 1730 Wells land was laid out to him by gr. to Mrs. E. Locke, 14 Aug. 1679. He d. 17 Dec. 1732, ag. 45 (Copps Hill). In 1751 his ch. Wm., Joseph and Elizabeth White, wid., all of Boston, deeded to uncle Joseph int. in est. of uncles Jabez and Samuel. **Joseph**, joiner, Portsm., List 339. Wife Mary 1736; w.Dorcas (Remick 3) 1746. Adm. to Dorcas 31 Oct. 1753 aft. his inquest. She m. by 1755 Nathl. Fernald jr.

**PITTS.** 1 **John**; see Pattishall(2).

2 **WILLIAM** (also Pitt), fisherman, b. ±1629-30, Shoals wit. 1663, 1668, sued Peter Glanfield in Me. ct. 1666 for turning his goods out of doors and putting him in prison. See also Pulman(2). Portsm. 1673. On the Shapleigh bark -Trial- in 1674 and bef. 1679 master of fishing voyages for John Cutts. List 3.

**PLACE.** See also John Plice.

1 **JOHN**, at York in Oct. 1676, but form. of Casco Bay where he owned at the Great Cove adj. John Holman(6), whose heir named him an abuttor in 17— and claimed 50 a. adj. Wise's old planta. bot from Place 12 Nov. 1670. Portsm. 1678; tenant on Vaughan farm 1703. Kn. ch: List 331b. **Richard**, b. ±1668. **Abraham**, apprent. to Matthew Austin at weaver's trade 19 Nov. 1684. **Eleanor**, m. 1st John Satchell; m. 2d Francis Durgin(3). Her will, 1747-8, names br. Richard P., 5 Kenniston step-gr.ch., and, no kinship stated, John Watson, w. Mary and dau. Eleanor.

2 **JOHN**, mariner, Boston, m. Sarah, sis. of Wm. Lovering(5), who was gr. adm. 27 Apr. 1686 and m. 2d John Bushnell(3). In 1703 as Sarah B., she was liv. on the Boston prop. her fa.-in-law Peter Place bot in 1650. Ch. rec. Boston 1674-1683: **Sarah** (m. Thos. Stevens), **Hannah**, **Joanna** (was mar. in 1703-4), **Jane** (m. Anthony Underwood). See Y. D. 18: 253-4.

3 **RICHARD**(1), aged ±8 and form. of Casco Bay, was apprent. in Oct. 1676 to Richard Wood of York, and m. Martha Leighton(4), who was liv. 1722. Taxed at the Bank 1713. Portsm. wit. 1719; he or a s. taxed at Graffort Lane 1720. Newingt. 1722; there in July 1747, ag. 84, he depos. ab. Greenland over 40 yrs. bef., and in 1748 deeded to gr.s. Joseph his homestead, being half his 1717 purchase. Presum. all those early in Newingt. were his ch: **John**, m. 5 Dec. 1716 Eunice Row of Newingt. J. P. and farm taxed Graffort Lane, Portsm., 1720. 3 ch. bp. Newingt. 1724. **Ebenezer** (surely), adm. of the Leighton est. 1722, when John Adams of Kit. was a bondsman. Of Newington, m. 31 Dec. 1729 Jane Peavey(1); liv. 1763. **Abigail**, m. 11 Dec. 1723 Joseph Walker. **Mary**, m. John Davis(35). **Samuel**, Newington, m. 5 Jan. 1725-6 Mary Row. **James** (surely: Y. D. 13: 119), m. 9 Nov. 1727 Mary Walker, both of Newingt. In 1734 his w. was Hannah. Presum. also **Susannah**, o.c. and bp. at Newingt. with five other Places in 1724; Richard who o.c. and was bp. at same time (named 1st) may have been the fa. or a s. not found later.

**PLAISTED**, Playstead. Gloucestershire has Playsteads; Roger of Me. m. in Wiltshire.

1 **ELISHA**(5), mariner, Portsmouth, ±24 in Oct. 1684 and mate of ketch -Diligence-. Taxed Portsm. 1690; wit. John Hole's p/a at Barbadoes in Aug. that yr. Lists 33, 57, 333a. Of Piscat., just ret. from Barbadoes, and very sick, he made will in Boston, 26 Oct.—6 Dec. 1690, giving all, incl. Newichawannock land and int. in the -Friends Endeavor- to w. Elizabeth (Harvey 14, m. 11 Oct. 1689). Of Portsm. in Oct. 1691, she gave his br. John p/a to collect £100 in Barbadoes. List 335a. Appar. she m. 2d Elisha Ilsley(1) and 3d Robert Rutherford.

2 **COL. ‡*ICHABOD**(5), Esq., m. 5 Jan. 1692 Mary Jose(1); List 331a. A Portsm. merchant and partner in masting with (4) until they dissolved in July 1704, but appar. ret. to Berw. earlier, or back and forth. Tr. and gr. j. (Me.) 1690; Capt.; Col.; in 1698 the Assembly's representative to meet the Earl of Bellomont at N. Y.; Rep.; Judge Inf. Ct. of Com. Pleas; Judge of Probate; Councillor at death (an office he declined in 1706, being engaged in His Majesty's Service, besides his own affairs). A founder of First Ch., Berw., and furnished the communion table. Portsm. 1713. Lists 33, 267a, 335a, 298, 330d, 336c, 289, 290, 38, 337, 296. See also Partridge(5). Will, of Berw., 2 Apr. (d. 17 Nov., ag. 52) 1715, names w. Mary, 4 ch., neph. Roger P., sis. Mehitable Goodwin. Wid. Mary m. 2d at Portsm. 1 Feb.-23 May 1717 Capt. John Brown of Salem. A wid. at Portsmouth 1724; of Berw. when adm. in N. H. was gr. 19 Oct. 1731 to sons-in-law, s. Samuel consenting. Ch. (N. H. Prov. rec.): **Samuel**, Esq., Berwick, b. 10 June 1696, m. 4 Aug. 1717 Hannah Wentworth (Lt.-Gov. John); d. 20 Mar. 1731-2 in 36th yr. (gr.st.); no ch. List 298. She m. 2d Theodore Atkinson, Esq.

(5 jr.). Col. **Ichabod**, Esq., Salem, Boston, b. 21 July 1700, m. in Salem 20 Oct. 1720 his step-sis. Sarah Brown; d. there 9 Dec. 1762. 3 ch. **Mary**, b. 6 Oct. 1702, m. in Salem 25 Oct. 1720 Ellis Huske, Esq., Portsm. merch., Councillor. She d. 8 Mar. 1745-6. His will, 1751—1755, 4 ch. **Olive**, b. 29 Aug. 1708, m. Dr. Nathaniel Rogers(7).

3 \*JAMES(5), Lt., Capt., Berwick, York, m. 1st bef. 12 Oct. 1680 Lydia Hitchcock(1), whose land he claimed. Kit. selectm. 1683; gr.j. 1687. Taken by Ind. at Salmon F. in Mar. 1689-90, and sent to demand surrender of the Holmes garrison, so escaping; see Goodwin(11). His w. -Mary- and 3 wks. old ch. were also captured (Niles), perh. her name an error for Lydia, as he had not then m. Mary (Rishworth) Hull(7) whom he m. bef. 25 Jan. 1691-2. Dates of her captivity as Mrs. Hull conflict with date she took adm. on fa.'s est. and attested inv. List 99, p. 74; ibid, pp. 71, 236-8, for her second captivity 1692-95. At York he was selectm. 1693, 1696, 1699; town clerk 1696-8; lic. 1696-8; Rep. 1701. Often gr. and tr. j. and foreman. Lists 298, 33, 278, 38. Adm. 18 Oct. 1710 to wid. Mary who liv. long. Ch. by 1st w: Capt. **Francis**, m. in Boston 28 Mar. 1706 Hannah Colman. Will, in London, 15 Jan. 1707-8, naming fa., br. Roger, w. Hannah, evid. reached Suff. Prob. long afterward and he is consid. the Francis who bot in Portsm. 1703 and had at Boston 1710-15: Francis (d. s.p. 1743), Hannah, James, both d.y.; and by 2d w. Hester at least William and Hester (m. Peck), who q.c. in Portsm. 1759. In 1732 s. Francis asked that uncle Francis Righton be gr. adm. on est. of fa., lost betw. St. Christopher and London ±4 yrs. bef., but it went to Capt. James Gooch(3 jr.) who had m. the wid. Hester at Newb. in 1729. Yet no repres. was heir of Capt. Francis' br. Roger unless Clark or Thayer. Lt. **Roger**, Berw., List 296. Adm. 12 Oct. 1767 to neph. Tristram Jordan of Saco, his heirs the Jordans, Jos. P.'s 2 ch., Mary Clark (w. of Wm. of Berw.), Sarah (Plaisted) (Tarr) Thayer of Boston. **Child**, k. by Ind. Mar. 1689-90. By 2d w. at York: **Lydia**, b. 4 Jan. 1696. **Olive**, b. 1 May 1698, m. 1st Samuel Jordan(2); m. 2d Rev. Thos. Smith; d. 3 Jan. 1763. **Joseph**, Esq., York, m. (int. 23 July 1724) Mary (Preble 3) (Bray 3) Craige; d. 25 Aug. 1752. List 279. Her will, Mary, jr., 10 Nov. 1752—15 May 1753, names ch. John and Sarah Swett. (Also Moody's Diary, 5 July 1723, Mrs. P.'s dau. Sarah d. at Salem).

4 COL. ‡\*JOHN(5), Esq. (74 in Jan. 1733-4), a def. in ct. 1680 and m. early Mary Pickering(4). Taxed Portsm. 1690; and there a wealthy merchant (see 2). In 1699 he bot the Great Works mill prop., selling one-third to Capt. John Hill. J. P., Lieut.,

Col., Rep.1693-97 (Speaker 1696), 1700, 1722-27; Judge Ct.Com.Pleas; Chief Justice 1716, one term; Councillor. Portsm. selectm. 1717-18. Lists 330d, 334a, 335a, 336b, 337, 296, 339, 52, 57, 62, 64. His w. Mary liv. 1727; Lists 335a, 331c, 337. He m. by 1731 Sarah (Purkis) Rogers(7) and mov. to Berw. by Aug. 1734, both there 29 Oct. 1746. Adm. on her est., wid., 27 Sept. 1749 to s. Daniel Rogers. Ch., 1st 4 bp. No. Ch. 27 May 1694: **John**, b. 2 Jan. 1682-3, m. in Boston 31 Oct. 1707 Jane Pemberton; d. 19 Oct. 1712. Will, 19 Feb. 1707-8, when going to W.I., gives all to w. unless a ch. be born. **Joshua**, b. 20 Sept. 1685, a wit. 1703 (Y. D. 7: 13), dead 1721. **Mary**, b. 29 Mar. 1687, m. 1st a s. of John Hoddy(2); m. 2d Capt. Thos. Phipps; m. 3d John Pray(2). **Elisha**, m. in Wells 16 Sept. 1712 Hannah Wheelwright (John), she liv. 1746, but not in his will, 26 Sept. 1750, ag. +60 (filed May 1771, not proved), naming 7 of 10 ch. He owned at Black Point. List 239b. **Mehitable**, bp. No. Ch. 16 Dec. 1694, m. Benjamin Gerrish(3); List 331c. **James**, in gr.fa. Pickering's will, 1721.

5 LT.‡\*ROGER, Esq., Berwick, m. Olive Colman in Preshute, co. Wilts, 25 Mar. 1648. First seen here as wit. to Nason's deed to Leader, 20 Feb. 1654. By one trad. he came as agent for Beex & Co., while his land in the Narragansett country, in his poss. many yrs. when confirmed in 1672, has led to the idea he was first in R. I. or Conn., negatived by the fact that it was part of a gr. made in 1658 to Harvard College and others (Y. D. 2: 195; Rec. of Mass. 4: 2: 229; Col. Rec., R. I., 2: 299; Col. Rec., Conn., 2: 227). He built 'The Garrison House' or 'Upper Garrison' on his 1659 gr. on N. side of Salmon Falls Brook, and until k. in ambush by Ind. 17 Oct. 1675 (Hubbard 121) led a useful pub. life. Gr.j. 1660; tr.j. 1666, 1667 (foreman); town comr. and selectm.; Associate 1663 to death; Dep. 1663, 1664, 1673; Lieut. 1668. Lists 24, 45, 298, 25, 83. See also Y. D. 6: 21, his purch. with John Hull, goldsmith, of the land and mills Capt. Wincoll had mtg. in 1662. An inscription on stone erected aft. his s. Samuel d., gives age as 70 in 1675. Adm. to wid. Olive and oldest s. Wm. 30 Nov. 1675; s. James added as admr. 5 July 1676. She m. 2d Capt. John Wincoll and made agreem. with her ch. 16 Sept. 1682 (Y. D. 8: 132) which was set aside (see 6). Ch: **Roger**. **William**, b. 1652. **James**. **Son**, wounded and d. a few weeks after fa. **John**, b. ±1659. **Elisha**, b. ±1660. **Ichabod**, b. ±1663. **Elizabeth**, not seen after 1682. **Mehitable**, m. Thos. Goodwin(11).

6 ROGER(5), eldest s., had a gr. in 1671 (List 298), m. (ct. 19 Sept. 1671) Hannah Furber(2) and was k. with fa. 17 Oct. 1675. Adm. to wid. 4 July 1676, her fa. bondsm.; at

same ct. his mo. agreed to maint. s. Roger's
w. and ch. until the wid. changed her condition; but her agreem. with other ch. in
1682 was disallowed as equitable provision
was not made for this fam: Frances, m.
Daniel Simpson. In 1702 they deeded to
Ichabod P. half the land gr. to her fa. Abigail, m. John Partridge(2), and in 1699 deeded half her fa.'s 250 a. to her fa.-in-law.
7 WILLIAM(5), eldest s. 1676, ag. 26 in
1678, was def. in a suit brot by Wm. Rawson in Suff. Ct. July 1678; John Broughton
was def. in ano. Rawson suit. In 1681 in Me.
he sued Geo. Broughton for knocking him
down; wit. for Mrs. Patience Spencer 1682.
Gr.j. 1678, 1686-7, 1689-90. Kit. constable
1683. Lists 28, 298, 33. In Mar. 1689-90 he
escaped from Capt. Wincoll's ho. and carried
news of the attack to Portsm. Bondsm. for
Abraham Lord same yr.; not found later;
appar. d. s. p. He had been m. to an unkn. w.
4 or 5 yrs. when a child (the first) was b. 5
Sept. 1683, called a monstrosity by Rev. J.
Moody (Mass. Hist. Soc. Col. 4: 8: 362). 'Mr.
William' (N. H. State Papers xiv: 1) very
likely an error for one of his brothers; note
N. E. Reg. 67: 188.
Plice (?Price), John, ±35 in 1674, depos. ab.
    drinking at Henry Russell's, Gt. Isl. See
    also Place(1), (2).
Plimpton, Henry, Dover. Adm. 8 Oct. 1652
    to Thos. Canney.
Pluckfoul, Joseph, Hingham, soldier at
    Wells. List 267b.
Plumley, Nicholas, taxed Portsm. about 1708.
Plummer, Jonathan, from Newbury, at Ex-
    eter Jan. 1693-4; Wells soldier; Lists 98,
    267b, 384a.
Pole, John, Boston, in Apr. 1700 sued Thos.
    Rice(3), who next mo. sued Pole for a
    bill dated 1678.
Polgreene, George, Mr., named by Nicholas
    Haskins as with the Gr. Isl. party cov-
    ered by List 312f.

## POLLEY.

1 EDWARD, tailor, innkeeper, Portsmouth,
    came from Reading by 1698. List 330d.
He wit. Thos. Morris' will 1701; but at Portsmouth from Vaughan 1705. In 1714 he was
out of the country and w. Mary (appar. Merrow 2) by his p/a first mtg. and then sold
his ho. for support, but did not give deed
until she knew he was dead. See Knight(9).
Innkeeper, she was gr. adm. 18 July 1715; m.
2d 1 Nov. 1716 Edmund Woollet, b. in Etham,
co. Kent. By 1719 she had d. and he had
gone off and not come back. Kn. ch., 1st 3
rec. Reading: Mary, b. 10 Mar. 1695-6 (m.
one Harris). Elizabeth, b. 3 Jan. 1697, m.
John Gowell(1) and q.c. a fifth her fa.'s est.
in 1761. Edward, b. 9 Sept. 1699. Sarah, m.
19 Dec. 1728 Francis Merrill from Wenham.

Joseph. David, mason, and Jonathan (bp.
No. Ch. 30 Dec. 1711), glazier, both of
Portsm. 1733.
2 THOMAS, Stratham. List 388.

POMEROY, Pomery, Pumery. Ancient in
    Devonshire. See Creber.
1 AGNES, Portsmouth, was Pomry alias
    Gerrish, 1693 (List 335a); Gerrish alias
Pomery 1694 (see 2); Matthews, wid., form.
Pumery, 1721. See also (10). Dau. Hannah
(presum. Pomery), m. Samuel Langmaid(1).
The Gerrish husb. must have been James
(2), named betw. Walter Winsor and Edw.
Melcher in 1691 tax list. See also Gerrish
(1).
2 JOHN (poss. 3), wit. bond to Geo. Jaffrey
    in 1688. In 1694 he and Richard Sloper
were prosec. for digging pits in the highway betw. John Holmes and John Sherburne. Indicted 1696 (orig. name appar.
Annis, altered to John) for selling without
lic.; see (1).
3 JOSEPH, Shoals 1669, when he and John
    Banfield bot ho. and land under lease to
Nehemiah Partridge. Taxed Portsm. 1672.
His w. Elizabeth wit. deed, John Hunking
to Weymouth, 1672; adm. to her 30 June
1674; adm. of both husb. and w. to John
Hunking 30 Dec. fol.; inv. incl. ho. and 15
a. Two ch. only: John, 5 in Jan. 1675-6,
bound to Mr. Hunking 27 June 1676 until
22. Abigail (to be nursed), bound to Goodman (John) Bowman until 19.
4 OWEN, master of the -Hunter- at Rich-
    mond Isl. 1633-4. List 21.
5 RICHARD, fisherman, Shoals, May 1660.
    In 1666 he failed to prosec. Richard
Symmons, who was given costs; in 1668 gave
due bill to Aaron Ferris who succs. sued him
in 1670, in which yr. he made over his Hog
Isl. plant to Thos. Daniel for debt. At Hog
Isl. 1672 with a new shallop built by John
Seward, and ackn. a paper as 'Mr. Pumry.'
Gr.j. 1674; Portsm. tax abated Mar. 1679-80.
Presum. he who wit. for (8) and (9) 1683-4,
but kinship can only be guessed at. Called
'Sr.' 1672, it might be assumed he had a s.
Richard.
6 RICHARD (poss. 5), Newington, where
    one of the name owned land in 1689. In
May 1694 he denied Elizabeth Twombley's
charge, his bondsm. Ens. Wm. Furber and
John Bickford; the latter and Nathan
Knight bondsm. when he was ord. to supp.
the child. Lists 60, 343. He m. 14 Feb. 1697-
8 Deliverance Berry (see 9); dead in May
1725 when 3 ch. sold in Newingt. to John
Knight: Richard, Falmouth, 'oldest son,'
but no other found, had w. Hannah. Elizabeth, m. in Newingt. 1 Mar. 1720-1 Nathan
Spinney. Jane, Newingt., of age and single
1725. Also Deliverance (appar. not the wid.),

m. at Oyster River 12 Sept. 1728 Joseph Wormwood. One Elizabeth m. John Marsh in Greenland 20 May 1714.

7 **THOMAS**, had joint p/a with Winter 18 Jan. 1631-2, but did not come over. List 21.

8 **THOMAS**, Shoals 1671, Portsm., m. Rebecca Brookings(5), whose parents deeded to them on Sagamore Creek 4 July 1679 with reversion to Thos., jr. See Wm. Robbins. Shoals constable 1681. He and (5) wit. for (9) 1683; (5) wit. for him 1684. In June 1685 his w. swore the peace on Wm. Walker and w. Alice. She m. 2d 6 Sept. 1687 Clement Rummeril; m. 3d Thos. Rouse; as wid. Rebecca Rouse took adm. on the Pumery est. 6 June 1713; Pumery and Rouse inventories taken together. Acct. incl. item 'to pd when wounded by the Inds.' and there were coroner's bills for both men. Ch: **Susanna**, 13 when fa. d., m. John Preston(1 jr.). **Thomas**, 11 when fa. d., 20 in Apr. 1695; stole wheat from his master Capt. Pickering in June 1696; in Dec. fol. signed a deed with mo. **Rebecca**, 9, **William**, 4, **Richard**, 2, **Elizabeth**, 5 mo., when fa. d.

9 **WILLIAM**, Shoals 1674 (see Downs 4). With w. Elizabeth he bot and sold a Hog Isl. ho. in Oct. 1683, wit. by (5) and (8). One Wm. was at the Gerrish garrison in 1696. Lists 67, 336b.

10 ———, 'Gimer' (Grandma), a Portsm. town charge 1722; poss. (1) gone back to the name.

11 **PUMPHREY'S** Point, List 323. See also Pomfret.

**POMFRET**, a corruption of Pontefract.

1 **LT. WILLIAM**, planter, Dover. A distiller in 1675, he was within reason the distiller who with Geo. Dugdale, tailor, offered himself to go to N. E. in 1622, and was at Monhegan 1624; List 9. At Dover Neck, he bot from Thos. Johnson in 1639; in Oct. 1640 sent security to Geo. Druell, mariner, London, for passage of w. -Hosanna- and dau.; w. Rose liv. 1675. Dover continually honored him, tho James Nute told ab. his deceitful heart. Com. t. e. s. c. 1643 and often; Lt. by 1646; gr.j. 1646, 1655-6; selectm. 1647-8, 1662; town clerk 1647 to 1665 or perhaps 1670; he, Thos. Leighton and John Dam had mill priv. at Bellamy's Bank 1649; Clerk of the Writs 1657; Comr. for the town. Lic. at times, and prosec. for selling without in 1670. Lists 351ab, 352-3, 354ac, 355ab, 356abcefghk, 311c, 359a, 49. In Mar. 1679 he deeded to (great) gr.s. Pomfret Whitehouse. He d. 7 Aug. 1680, leaving will proved 7 Sept. fol., not extant. Only kn. ch. **Elizabeth**, came with mo.; m. Dea. John Dam(2).

2 **PUMFRESS** Point (form.), now Batchelder's Point, Great Isl., ment. 1674, also in same deed Pomfres' Point. (Pumery?

Pomfret?). List 323. Pomry's Cove, adj. Sandy Cove, Dover, ment. 1662.

**Poole**, Mary, appar. dead in June 1660. See Richard Corwin.

**POORE.**

1 **AMBROSE**, a night-walker in 1670, disturbing the neighbors; wit. Thos. Spinney. In May 1671 Samuel Donnell agreed to pay his fine for swearing.

2 **ANDREW**, schoolmaster. See Ingersoll(4).

3 **EDWARD**, sued Leonard Weeks for wages, 1671.

4 **JOHN**, mariner, Hampton, m. 1st 13 Mar. 1661 Sarah Brown(14), who made confession of faith and was bp. with her ch. in Hampt. 6 Sept. 1668. He was adm. inhab. at Charlestown 15 Apr. 1662. Her br. John was with them there in 1669, and there she d. from small-pox in Dec. 1677. He m. 2d 12 Aug. 1680 Elizabeth (Burrage) Dean; d. in Charlest. 19 May 1686, ag. 50; wid. liv. 1693. 7 + 5 ch., incl. **Sarah**, b. Hampton 31 Dec. 1661, d.y., and **Richard**, b. there 28 Oct. 1666. See Wyman's 'Charlestown.'

**POPE.** See also Cox(12), (30).

1 **BARNARD**, Oyster River 1669. List 366.

2 **EXPERIENCE**, Saco fort soldier 1696. List 248b.

3 **RICHARD**, fisherman, Cape Elizabeth 1683, bot 25 a. from Robert Jordan in 1685 and sold in June 1688, then of Winter Harbor. List 226. Of Kittery in June 1691, he bot Middle Neck, Winter Harb., from Pendleton Fletcher, which his wid. Sarah (m. by 1688) sold aft. his 'untimely death'; adm. to her 17 Apr. 1694, bondsm. Wm. Pepperell and Humphrey Scammon; verd. of cor.j. accepted 3 July 1694. She was liv. in same ho. with Walter Denniford in 1710, and was a wit. that yr. when John White and Mary Jenkins(11) were accus.; the latter said Goody Pope slept with her. Liv. 1714. Presum. ch: **Mary**, m. 1st Wm. Rogers(17); m. 2d Richard Rice(3). **William**, m. in Portsm. 16 Aug. 1714 Joanna Tripe (Sylvanus). In 1719 he was 'going carpenter' under W. Fenderson; Portsm. shipwright 1726. 2 or more ch. **Hannah**, m. Wm. Stanley. **Richard**, shipwright (List 291), m. Sarah Spinney (Samuel). Will, 1760—1780. 6 ch. 1727-1740.

**POPHAM, Capt. George.** President of the short-lived colony at the mouth of the Kennebec, of which his uncle Sir John (fa. of Sir Francis) was patron. List 6. His will (N. E. Reg. 44. 383) names neph. Edward with him.

**PORMONT**, Purmont. One Philemon, s. of Thomas, was of Grimsby, Hull, in 1603.

1 **JOSEPH**(3), Great Island, ±21 in 1671, was at wid. Moulton's boarding ho. when Mr. Pormont, who was inquired for, was not there. See Lamb(1). When sued for taxes 1675, Jos. Morse(6) agreed to pay them; poss. he was Morse's 'servant Joseph' in 1673. He m. bef. June 1681 Hannah Woodis (Richard of Boston), suppos. the wid. Moulton(2); see Suff. D. 12: 75. Great Isl. constable 1675; gr.j. 1683; cor.j. 1683; tr.j. 1684. Lic. 1683, 1685, 1686 (appar. sick). Taxed 1688. Lists 312e, 313efg, 317, 331a, 52, 55b. Wid. Hannah taxed July 1690; lic. to June 1700. In 1691 Richard Stileman willed her £5 and a silver dram cup; in 1694 she and Mr. Web were prosec. for not securing their well. Lists 313g, 66, 336c, 315b. Kn. ch., the daus. summonsed as wit. with mo. in 1695; see Furbush(2): **Joseph**, feltmaker, of Newc. bot in Portsm. 1705; m. by 1710 Judith Cutts(3). She took adm. in Dec. 1721, and m. 2d Solomon Cotton(2). 3 ch. bp. No. Ch. 1713-1717: Hannah, John (joiner, Stratham), Abigail. **Elizabeth. Hannah.**

2 **LAZARUS**(3), Dover 1659-1670; broke jail there 1665. Lists 356eghk, 357d. Esq. Coffin paid his fine in Kit. 1673; servant of Mr. Ladbrook at Portsm. 1676, his w. ment. that yr.; with John Granger in York ct. 1679, drunk and idle, and he did not appear when summonsed in 1680. Bourne says he and Elias (not kn. otherwise) worked in Nicholas Cole's mill in Wells in 1680.

3 **PHILEMON**, schoolmaster, m. in Alford, co. Lincoln, 11 Oct. 1627 Susanna Bellingham, bp. there 1 Sept. 1601, dau. of Wm., and half-sis. of Balthazar Willix. Both adm. to Boston Ch. 18 Aug. 1634, he chosen schoolmaster in Apr. 1635 and made free in May. Dism. to Exeter Ch. 6 Jan. 1638-9, but his stay was appar. short. The Gilmans sold his ho. to John Robinson in 1652. Lists 373, 376a, 378, 72. Boston wit. 1644, 1648, and employed by Valentine Hill there in 1645. He rejoined Wheelwright, this time at Wells, and was there at least May 1649-Oct. 1650; see also Gross(1). Called late of Boston 1656; presum. the Mr. P. asked for at Newc. 1671 (see 1); cert. in Boston 29 Oct. 1679 (Y. D. 3: 65). His w. Susanna in Boston 29 Dec. 1642; one Elizabeth succeeded her. Ch: **Elizabeth**, bp. Alford 20 Feb. 1628-9, m. in Boston 1656 Samuel Norden. **Mary**, m. in Boston (Elizabeth by rec.) 24 Nov. 1652 Nathl. Adams. **Martha**, bp. Alford 24 Nov. 1633. Recorded at Boston: **Lazarus**, b. 28 Feb. 1635-6. **Anna**, b. 5 Apr. 1638. **Pedijah**, b. 3 June 1640. By 2d w: **Barshuah**, bp. 4 July 1647, her fa. a memb. of Exeter Ch. **Joseph**, not rec., b. ±1650. **Martha**, b. 16 June 1653.

**Portadoe.** See Fortado.

**Portegay,** Manwell (Manuel the Portuguese), a Kennebec soldier; List 189.

**PORTER, Abel**, pumpmaker, from Boston at Newcastle 1672, ±23; next neighbor of David Campbell 1673, and partner and adm. of John Stydson; Lists 312eh. With the Portsm. men adm. freemen at Boston May 1674. In June 1680 atty. for Clarke and Curwin (see Martin 2). He d. on a voyage from Scotland toward E. Jersey; adm. on his est., 'Jr.,' in Suff. to wid. Hannah 4 Mar. 1685-6, with Miles Foster of E. Jersey her substitute; Henry Dering wit. the bond. See also Jaffrey(4).

**Possell,** William, at Great Isl. with Joseph Curtis and Wm. Sanders, 1695.

**POTTER. 1 Anthony**, with men sent to Saco fort, Michael Edgecomb another.

2 **EDWARD**, chirurgeon, Great Isl. 1693. List 318a.

3 **VALENTINE**, Falm. wit. 1684 (Y. D. 4: 72).

**POTTLE.** One Christopher, merchant, of Totnes, co. Devon, d. 1636, leaving an only s. Christopher under 14.

1 **CHRISTOPHER**, tanner, ±30 in Sept. 1693, when he was adm. a share owner in Coxhall (Y. D. 5. 1. 85), m. at Ipsw. 12 Mar. 1693-4 Hannah Graves (Samuel) and in Nov. 1694 bot Benj. Swett's ho. on Falls side of Hampton, liv. there Dec. 1695. Gr.j. 1696, 1697; tr.j. 1697; with Henry Williams gave joint note to Pepperell 1699; selectm. 1706; depos. 1707 ab. Grouts in South -Trent-, co. Devon, and was bondsm. for Gabriel Grout's adm.; served at Newc. fort 1708. List 399a. Will, 19 Dec. 1709—8 Feb. 1709-10, names w. Hannah (dism. to form Hampt. F. Ch. Dec. 1711) and ch: **Hannah**, b. 21 Oct. 1694, m. at Hampt. F. 31 Aug. 1719 Thos. Richardson of Newb. **Elizabeth**, b. 29 Dec. 1696, m. Joseph Low(6). **Sarah**, b. 30 Apr. 1699, m. at Hampt. F. 5 Feb. 1722-3 Daniel Richardson. **Christopher**, b. 5 Apr. 1703, had the homestead. York grantee 1726, m. there Nov. 1727 Abigail Cane(2). List 279. 11 ch. at York. **William**, b. 30 Apr. 1705, blacksmith, Stratham 1729. His w. was Deborah in 1736; his w. (not named) d. in Stratham 23 Feb. 1767. 3 or more ch. **Ann**, b. 18 Nov. 1707 (but named bef. Sarah in will), m. 20 Apr. 1727 Henry Bodwell of Methuen. **Samuel**, b. 21 Apr. 1710, carpenter, cooper, Stratham 1733, m. in Methuen 27 Nov. 1734 Hannah Bodwell. Adm. to br. Wm. 8 June 1741. 4 ch. rec. Methuen, where wid. Hannah m. 2d John Hibbard.

2 **JOHN**, Portsmouth, propr. 1660. Drunk in 1662, he kicked out the head of his company's drum, Samuel Whidden bound for his fine. Committed to jail without bail 1667. In Mar. 1668-9 the gr.j. cleared Frank Negro,

accus. of aiding his escape from Boston prison, he having k. the cook of the ship -Golden Fox-. He gŏt to Me., where in 1670 there was a hue and cry for J. P., the murderer, and the Wells constable was paid charges. Lists 330b, 47.

**POTTS.** An old Northumbrian clan.

1 **RICHARD,** fisherman, Merriconeag, m. bef. 24 June 1661 Margaret, wid. of Wm. Davis(64). Tr.j. Casco 1666; bondsm. for Nathl. Cloyes 1667; see also Bartlett(7), Haines(15). Of Casco Bay he gave a bill to Edw. Creek(2) in 1671, and of New Damariscove ack.debt to Kimball(4) and Creek 1672. John Bacey depos. in 1703 that P. built and liv. on Potts Neck adj. Merriconeag over 30 yrs. ago until forced off by Ind. in Andros' time, and also improved and dried fish on New Damariscove. From a fishing boat, he saw w. and ch. taken by Ind. at Jewell's Isl., they not heard of again. In 1678 a partner with Thos. Stevens buying from John Hull. Last noted 1 Nov. 1688; see Mitchell(15). Of children, only **Thomas,** b. ±1667, is seen aft. Sept. 1676.

2 **THOMAS**(1), Great Island 1680, was Wm. Haskins' apprent. in 1683, when Timothy Carle(2) went his bond. In May 1686, ±19, he depos. conc. that apprenticeship; see also Pierce(3). He m. Joanna Roberts(12) 24 Mar. 1689-90, living thereaft. at Dover where gr. 20 a. on Fresh Creek Neck in 1694. In 1701 he sold to Benj. Marston of Salem his fa.'s prop., 500 a. at Potts Neck, an island of ±1000 a. betw. Small Point and Jewell's Isl. and 200 a. at Maquoit. Lists 313g, 358d. See also Blackstone(1), Corson, Hamilton. His w. Joanna sold disorderly in 1707 when Samuel Corson wit. ag. her; Sheriff Phipps was at her ho. in 1708 when he was searching for Portsm. goods and arrested Ebenezer Tuttle. She was liv. 14 Oct. 1729; List 358c. He was of Durham 1736 with w. Ann (Tozier) (Jenkins) Kincaid(1) who was still 'Kinket' in 1730. Ch. rec. Dover: **Mary,** b. 6 July 1690, m. aft. Apr. 1708 Samuel Corson(1). **Joyce,** b. 21 Aug. 1693, m. Wm. Clark(56).

**POTUM, Charles,** Cape Porpus, s. of Robert, bp. at Stoke-in-Teignhead, co. Devon, 3 Mar. 1632-3, nephew of Gregory Jeffrey(5), of whose will he was exec. and whose wid. and her new husb. caused him vexatious suits. J. 1669, 1670; constable and marshal's deputy 1671. List 255. Sued by James Wiggin, John Bateman and John Lux (crosssuits) in 1666, sued Richard Hitchcock in 1668 and by John Miller in 1673. Presented for leading an idle life, 1674. Adm. to John Barrett in 1678. No w. or ch. rec.

**Poulsen,** James, Shoals wit. 1674.

**Pound,** Capt. Thomas, a pirate who d. a gentleman. See Colonial Soc. Mass. 20: 24-

84; Pirates of N. E. Coast, pp. 54-72.

**Pow,** William, ±37 in 1684. List 123.

**POWELL.** The Welsh ap-Howell.

1 **ARTHUR,** Newcastle fort soldier 1697. List 68.

2 **JAMES,** soldier from York 1722, may have come from a Gloucester fam., as may also Truman Powell, corp. in Samuel Jordan's co. 1725, who m. in Wells 6 July 1725 Dorothy Deering(5) who m. 2d in Greenl. 20 Dec. 1729 Joseph Adams. See also Lebanon, Conn., records.

3 **JOHN,** granted Falm. land near the fort 1680; List 225a. John, taxed Pemaquid 1687, personal; List 124.

4 **MICHAEL,** had York gr. for fishing trade with Ball(4), Way and Stover, 3 July 1649; a yr. later John Alcock had built where Mighill P. had a lot. In Me. Ct. Oct. 1651 Mr. Wm. Hilton was plf. in suits: v. Thos. Way for £9, v. M. P. for £3. From Aspinw. Not. Rec. it appears he was Michael of Dedham and Boston. Mr. Powle of Boston was indebted to est. of Benj. Donnell(1). One M. P. of Ratcliffe and Agnes Hooke were m. at St. Dunstan's, Stepney, London, 27 June 1604.

5 **ROBERT,** Exeter, b. 1636, with fa.'s consent bound self in London 28 Apr. 1653, for 6 yrs. to John Cogswell the younger, and aft. he d., served Wm. Cogswell a time, redeeming bal. for £15. See Essex Q. Ct. Rec. i: 307-8. Wife Mary Moore(24). They had deed from her fa. 22 Jan. 1660, incl. ±10 a. on the neck on east side of Exeter River, where he built and liv. O. A. Nov. 1677. Lists 376b (1664, 1698), 54, 383, 52, 57. Essex Q. Ct. Rec. 1: 307; 6: 159. Culler of staves 1694. His minister's rate 1696-7 recorded as not paid. His w. Mary, liv. 1678, was freq. with Samuel Folsom's w. Mary and Judith Robie, and was at ho. of Geo. Jones(17) when he wanted to shoot Richard Morgan. She was ±23 in 1661, he 40 in 1676. Ch. appear: **Robert,** jr., taxed 1683. **Samuel,** hanged self to a tree 15 Jan. 1695-6; List 57. **William,** mason, worked at Newc. fort 1694, and m. at Hampt. 12 Jan. 1701-2 Esther Garland(7), he of Ex. Lists 67, 376b (1698), 388. Of Strath. 1719, he bot there from wid. Joanna Dyer, selling her 17 a. at Powell's Point; sold out in Strath. 1720; Chester 1726, and there in 1735 deeded to s. John for supp. of self and w. Esther; liv. 1740 (s. William was jr. 1743); other ch. were Samuel, Chester 1743, and Elizabeth (m. Jona. Goodhue and Nathl. Wood). **Thomas,** Strath., sold Ex. swamp to Robert Coffin in Feb. 1702-3; List 388. Adm. to wid. Abigail 6 June 1722, bondsm. Wm. Moore, John Clark; she liv. 4 Dec. 1723. Ch. from deeds, not in order: Mary (m. 1st in Portsm. 1 Sept. 1720 Isaac

Bosdit of Charlest., m. 2d Stephen Huggins); Abigail (m. Ebenezer Garland 3); Dorcas (w. of John Goodridge[5], 1732); Elizabeth (m. Joseph Peavey 1); Hannah (w. of Pendleton Fletcher of Bidd. 1733); Judith (w. of John Morgan, 1732).

6 **THOMAS**, Saco, with Robert Booth appraised Richard Hitchcock's est. Sept. 1671-Apr. 1672, and in 1671 had charge ag. the court for taking Mr. Bonython to Boston. Aged ±31 in 167- and may have been he who d. in Boston 29 Jan. 1717, ag. 78. One T. took O. A. there 11 Nov. 1678.

7 **TRUMAN**; see (2).

**POWNING**, Henry, shopkeeper, a Kittery cr. of John Phillips of Dover 1641 and gave p/a to Wm. Furber in 1647 to collect all debts on the Piscataqua. Adm. Boston Ch. from Dover 15 Oct. 1648, but had Kit. gr. 1651, 6 a. at his home lot. List 298. Inv. (Suff.), 20 Feb. 1664-5, incl. a large trading stock (Mr. Rouch his creditor in Eng.) and the Kit. land, sold by the wid. Elizabeth, adm., and 4 ch. to Jabez Jenkins in 1684. She d. in Boston 22 Oct. 1724, ag. 95. Ch. rec. Boston 1649-1663: Elizabeth (w. of Jona. Bridgham 1684). Mary, unm. 1684. Henry, not in deed, but see Wyman's Charlest. Two **Hannahs**, d.y. Sarah, unm. 1684. Daniel, shopkeeper, Boston, taxed with mo. 1688. One Daniel's will, 1732—1734, names w. Mary, sis. Sarah P. Anna (bp. Hannah), not in deed 1684.

**POWSLAND** (Pousland, Powsley), Richard, fisherman, Falmouth, bot 50 a. betw. Round Marsh and Capisic from Nathl. Mitton 5 Oct. 1674 and liv. there till 1689, his neighbors Thos. Cloyes and John Ingersoll, tho he is unnoted from Oct. 1675 to 1680. In 1687 he declared that he had poss. ±70 a. 13 or 14 yrs., had built, fenced and improved. In 1688, gr.j. and bondsm. (with John Holman and Richard Hunnewell) for Wm. Warren. Lists 223a, 225a, 226, 34. In Boston with w. Dorothy 1693. She, or a dau., m. Francis Crewe there 19 Dec. 1700. Son Samuel, shipwright, b. Boston 4 July 1693, m. 1st 25 Nov. 1714 Elizabeth Barnard; m. 2d 26 June 1722 Margaret Ruck, and sold his fa.'s Falm. land 1720-1732. List 229.

**Pratly**, Elinor, Exeter, m. Robert Smart, jr., 25 Sept. 1674.

**PRATT.** Became 36th commonest name in N. E.

1 **JOHN**, Saco, had a lot on east side of river adj. one claimed by John Sargent under deed of Jan. 1686-7 (East. Cl. 4: 279). Tr.j. 1688; gr.j. 1689. List 249. Appar. it was his s. Ebenezer who gave p/a to Edw. Sargent in Apr. 1720, wit. by Pendleton Fletcher and Matthew Brown. See Wyman's Charlest. 2: 770; Malden V. R.; also (3).

2 **PHINEAS**, arrived at Damariscove 1622. See Mass. Hist. Soc. Col. 4: 4: 474.

3 **THOMAS**, Saco, apprais. John Scolly's est. with John Edgecomb, Mar. 1688-9. Note (1).

4 **TIMOTHY**, wit. deed of John Penwill of Shoals to Symon Lynde, Nov. 1665, John Oliver ano. wit.

**PRAY.**

1 **JOHN** (Quinton), Braintree, m. 7 May 1657 Joanna Downam, who was gr. adm. 31 Oct. 1676, m. 2d Daniel Livingston(1) and brot to York her 3 youngest Pray ch: Samuel, b. 16 May 1669. Dorothy, m. Daniel Furbush(1); if she was his 1st w., by report a sis. was taken captive with her in 1692. Joseph, Berwick (60 in Apr. 1733), was wounded at York, 1698. In May 1703, already mar. to Mary Grant(12), he bot in Berw. Lists 96, 296, 298. Will, 11 July 1747—18 Oct. 1748, names w. Mary (±80 in Apr. 1756), and ch: John (w. Experience); Peter (m. Mary Roberts); Samuel (m. Dorothy Cromwell); Joanna Yeaton, Mary Wallingford, Martha Allen, Miriam Lord, but not Elizabeth, b. 12 Apr. 1704. One Elizabeth m. in Newington 26 May 1727 Samuel Walton.

2 **JOHN**, saddler, merchant, Portsm., of no kn. connec. with Me. Prays except that he bot from Roberts heirs, incl. Peter Pray (Joseph 1) and his w. Under-sheriff 1722; selectm. 1731-5, 1741. List 339. He m. 1st 2 June 1709 Joanna Jose(3), she liv. 1736; m. 2d bef. 24 Aug. 1741 Mary, wid. of Thos. Phipps, Esq., his old business associate. Adm. 30 Dec. 1742 for creditors (many); again 30 Mar. 1743 to s.-in-law Geo. Massey. Wid. Mary's will, 16 Apr.—28 May 1766, gives to Phipps ch. Two Prays rec: Richard, bp. No. Ch. 27 Aug. 1712. Elizabeth, b. 21 Nov. 1714.

3 **SAMUEL**(1), mariner, Kit. 1696, built on Elihu Gunnison's land bef. 23 Aug. 1699. List 296. His w. Mary Fernald(4) testif. in 1704, what her husb. told her. She was gr. adm. 19 Oct. 1708 and perhaps d. bef. 10 May 1722 when s. Samuel took adm. on fa.'s est. Ch: Samuel, of age 1722, m. 17 Nov. 1726 Alice Mendum (Jona.). She d. 20 Apr. 1757 and he may have m. 7 June 1759 Sarah Beaver; d. Jan.1762. List 297. 7 ch. Prob: Mary, m. 2 Nov. 1721 Samuel Stacy. Hannah, m. Thos. Rand(6 jr.). Daughter, m. Robert Mendum( see David 1).

4 **MR.**, slandered by Geo. Norton, 1666.

**PREBLE**, a yeoman family early established in co. Kent.

1 ‡**ABRAHAM**, Esq., founder of what York's historian calls the most disting. fam. of the town, was bp. at Wootton, co. Kent, 1 Jan. 1603-4, s. of Robert and Joan.

At Scituate bef. Oct. 1639, he m. there 3 Jan. 1641 Judith Tilden (Dea. Nathl.), bp. at Tenterden, co. Kent, 22 Oct. 1620, and came to Scituate Row, York, buying from Godfrey 20 Dec. 1642. See Banks(3), Chambers(2), Curtis(9), Twisden; N. E. Reg. 65: 322; 67: 44. Magistrate, Saco et. 1645; Prov. Councillor 1645-9; Associate 1646; Major; and last Mayor of Gorgeana. Under Mass., he was Magistrate; County Treas. 1654; Comr. for York 1655; Associate for Co. Court 1656 till death. Lists 273-277, 71, 34. Adm. 7 July 1663 to wid. Judith, named as wid. Preble in her step-fa.'s will, Dec. 1664. Ch., sons under 21 in 1663, daus. (prob. not incl. the first) under 18: **Daughter**, m. and had portion bef. fa. d. **Abraham**, b. 1642-6. **John**, had town gr. 1669. **Nathaniel**, bp. at Scituate 9 Apr. 1648. **Joseph. Stephen**, b. ±1656. **Benjamin**, b. ±1657. **Sarah**, b. ±1659, accus. with Joseph Weare in Dec. 1688 and acquitted; see Preble(9). She m. 1st Abraham Parker(1); m. 2d Henry Coombs(4). And at least one other married dau., not found, called **Mary** by Preble Gen. and Col. Banks, b. 1662, the latter says.

2 **CAPT. *ABRAHAM**(1), Esq., York, ±56 in 1702, d. 4 Oct. 1714, ag. 72 (gr.st.), m. Hannah Sayward (Henry), who was ±83 in Apr. 1748, and d. 9 May 1751. First noted 1667 when Richard Banks, Thos. Curtis, Samuel Twisden and he had a 200 a. gr. Constable 1672; selectm. 8 times, 1674-1697; town clerk 1674, 1681, 1685-95; O. A. Mar. 1679-80; Rep. 1680-2, 1698; Lt., Capt., and on committee to regulate the Eastern settlements; J. P.; Judge Inf. Ct. Com. Pleas; Deacon. Lists 28, 29, 32, 33, 38. See also Gooch(5). Ch: **Mary**, b. 8 June 1686, m. 1st Capt. Abraham Preble(3); m. 2d Capt. Peter Nowell. **Abraham**, b. 21 Aug. 1687, d. s.p. 30 Aug. 1720. Capt. **Caleb**, b. 7 July 1689, d. 7 Jan. 1734; m. by 1717 Jemima Storer (Samuel), who m. 2d (int. York 30 Jan. 1741-2) Andrew Gilman(7). List 279. 9 ch. **Hephzibah**, b. 28 Mar. 1691, m. Abiel Goodwin(2). **Miriam**, b. 14 June 1692 (List 331c), m. (int. Boston 28 May 1714) Benj. Stone; d. from small-pox by 1724. 2 ch. rec. **Jonathan**, mill-wright, b. 11 Apr. 1695 (List 331c), d. 1768 (gr.st.), m. 1st Rebecca (Harvey or Havey), who d. 1739, a native of Old Eng. (gr.st.). He m. 2d Mehitable (Storer), wid. of Nicholas Sewall; she d. 4 Mar. 1768 (gr.st.). Of Georgetown, he depos. in June 1765, ±69, that he first came there in 1716 and had liv. on Arrowsic since 1720. The three gr.stones are near his ho. there. 5 ch. **Ebenezer**, b. 26 Mar. 1698, accidentally shot by Jos. Moody, 1708 (List 96). **Samuel**, mason, b. 1 Apr. 1699, m. (int. 13 Nov. 1725) wid. Sarah Muchemore(2). Liv. at Newtown in York, d. there 22 Mar. 1746. List 279. 5 ch. incl.

Col. Esaias. Nathl. Donnell depos. that he went with Jona. P. and his br. Samuel to Damariscove Isl. in 1738.

3 **CAPT. *ABRAHAM**(7), Esq., York, d. 14 Mar. 1723-4 in 50th yr.,'Capt. of the town, Judge for the Co. of York, and at time of death sustained no less than nine offices of honor and pub. trust.' Grants 1697-1714. Town clerk 1699-1723; selectm. 1700; Rep. 12 times 1702-1719. Lic. out of doors 1704-6, 1709. List 38. His 1st w. Mary (Bragdon 5, m. 9 Aug. 1694) d. 1697; a 2d w. Hannah d. s.p. bef. Apr. 1699; the 3d was Susanna Sayward (John); the 4th, m. 1704-1711, was Mary Preble(2) who m. 2d Peter Nowell. His est. was div. in 7ths to s. Edward and 5 daus.; in 1728 the s. gave bond to pay £180 to John Kent of Newb. and to pay his sisters. Ch., by 1st w: **Mary** (orig. name Abigail), b. 17 Feb. 1695-6; m. 1st Samuel Bray (7); m. 2d William Craige; m. 3d Joseph Plaisted(3). **Hannah** (orig. name Humility), b. 13 May 1697, m. Richard King(12 jr.). Their names changed when bp. in 1699 'to bear up the names of a mo. and a mo.-in-law,' both dead. By 3d w: Capt. **Edward**, b. 23 Aug. 1702; accus. by Sarah Burrill(3) 1721; m. Hannah Simpson (Lt. Daniel). List 279. 6 ch. rec. 1724-1738. **Nathaniel**, b. 8 Apr. 1704, scalded to death. By 4th w., 3 named in mo.'s will, 18 Jan. 1753—20 May 1755: **Humility**, m. 24 Nov. 1736 Abraham Nowell; **Miriam**, m. 8 July 1739 Thos. Donnell; **Susanna**, liv. with mo. 1753; and **seven** d.y.

4 **BENJAMIN**(1), York (±70 in 1727), was in ct. in Aug. 1684. Adm. Philip Cooper's est. 1691, his surety Job Curtis. Grants 1696-1715. He m. Mary Baston(7) and was in Charlestown 1694-5 (his tax abated in Feb. 1705-6 and not seen there later), but served on gr.j. in Me. 1694, 1696, 1697. In 1721 he deeded Scituate land to s. John and his 30 a. homestead to s. Jedediah in 1729. Will, 16 Dec. 1723 (d. 25 Mar. 1732), names w. Mary (liv. 1734) and 5 ch., 2 rec. at York: **Hannah**, b. Charlest. 7 Feb. 1694, m. Rowland Young. **Judah** (Judith), b. 9 Feb. 1696-7, m. 1st Benj. Smith; m. 2d Samuel Goodwin(5). **John**, b. 26 Nov. 1699, m. 4 Dec. 1724 Hannah Young (Matthews), she liv. 1750. 7 ch. **Abigail**. One A. m. in York Benj. Goodridge(5). Brig.-Gen. **Jedediah**, b. 1707, settled in Falm., d. 11 Mar. 1784. List 279. He m. 1st 21 Mar. 1733 Martha Junkins (Alex.) of York who d. in Mar. 1753; 5 ch. He m. 2d 9 May 1754 Mehitable (Bangs) Roberts of Falm.; 7 ch. incl. Commodore Edward. Note too Benjamin(7).

5 **JOHN**(1), York, had grants 1669-1679. O. A. Mar. 1679-80. Cor.j. 1685; gr.j. 1685, 1688-90; selectm. 1688. List 33. Prob. killed in the Candlemas Day massacre; adm. to wid. Hannah 1 Mar. 1692, and aft. she d. 19 Aug. 1695, to his br. Abraham. Only ch:

**Hannah**, m. Nathl. Donnell(4). In 1719 they q.c. her gr.fa. Preble's estate.

6 **JOSEPH**(1),York,bot from Richard Wood on the Cape Neddick road in 1677 and had a town gr. (no date) that was confirmed to his s. Joseph. List 33. Lydia Smith accused him in 1684, her ch. appar. that ·Mary-P. who m. Job Averill(7) in Boston 26 Apr. 1700; Handkerchief Moody called her ·Sarah-, dau. of Joseph. Adm. gr. in Oct. 1691 (inv. 3 Oct.) to wid. Sarah (Austin 5) who m. 2d Job Young. In 1713 the ct. allowed Young £71 for bringing up the ch: **Nehemiah**, 'eldest,' from 3¼ yrs. to 7. **Joseph**, 'youngest,' from 5 mo. to 7. List 279. His 1st w. Bethia (appar. Paine 17) d. 19 May 1724; he m. 2d 11 Nov. 1725 Anne Paine (15), who m. 2d Norton Woodbridge. His will, 24 Apr. (d. 28 Apr. in 41st yr.) 1732, names her and ch., 5 by 1st w. 1714-1723: Hannah (m. Jos. Cole 17), Mary (m. Wm. Gerrish), Nehemiah (m. in Marbleh. Sarah Homan), Elizabeth (m. Samuel Donnell, jr.), Bethia (m. Geo. Ingraham 2), and by 2d w: Miriam (m. Joseph Parsons), Joseph, Anne, Timothy, these three dead in 1738.

7 **NATHANIEL**(1), York, had town gr. 1673. Selectm. 1677-1679; O.A. Mar. 1679-80; gr.j. 1681, 1686-7; tr.j. 1683. List 33. See also Palmer(10). Inv. taken 16 Oct. 1692; adm. to (3) and John Harmon. The wid. Priscilla (Main 3) m. 2d in July 1695 Joseph Carril and liv. in Salem. Ch: **Abraham**, eldest s., appar. of age 1692. **Hannah** (ag. 75 in 1748), m. 1st Wm. Milbury(5); m. 2d John Burrill(3). **Nathaniel**, weaver, m. (int. Salem 12 Mar. 1714-5) Rachel Preble(8). Stoughton 1732 (Y. D. 14: 251). S. of the. bp. Salem. He and br. **Joshua** receipted to eldest br. in 1713. Joshua m. (int. Boston 23 Mar. 1713) Sarah Felt(5); dau. Sarah b. there 7 Oct. 1714. Called sons: **Obadiah** and **Benjamin**, List 99, pp. 75, 92; Obadiah found in captivity 1695, 1711; Benjamin only in 1711; Niles named one Benjamin of York as the first who fell under Ind. cruelty in spring of 1708 (4 Mass. Hist. Soc. Col. 5: 325). In 1721 Wells Ch. examined Hannah Baston, feigning to be the w. of one Benjamin.

8 **STEPHEN**(1), York (±23 in Dec. 1679), had gr. 1678-1681 which were confirmed in 1701 to his heirs and successors. O. A. Mar. 1679-80; gr.j. 1687; tr.j. 1688, 1689. Adm. 6 Oct. -1691- to wid. Rachel (Main 3), her bondsm. (7) and Samuel Bragdon. She m. 2d Joseph Carlisle(1), and was liv. in Aug. 1748, ±84. Ch: **Rachel**, b. 7 Feb. 1687-8; her mo.'s account charged for bringing her up 3 yrs.; m. Nathl. Preble(7 jr.). **Jemima**, b. 6 Mar. 1690-1, brot up 4½ yrs.; m. in Lynn 21 Nov. 1710 Eleazer Rhodes, jr.; both of Dorchester 1724. **Stephen**, b. 15 Jan. -1692-3-, brot up 7 yrs., m. Hannah Weare

(Joseph). List 279. 6 ch. rec. 1724-1736. See Y. D. 9: 22.

9 **ZEBULON**, York, s. of Sarah(1), who accused Joseph Weare. In 1728 he settled with the admr. of his step-fa. Coombs, incl. the funeral charges of his natural mo. Sarah (Y. D. 12: 275). Gr. 1714-1719; in 1720 sold to Samuel Webber the land he was liv. on, bot from John Parker, jr. Wife Hannah Welch (Philip). **Ten ch.** rec. 1713-1732. In 1850 it was said that this line was reduced to a single head in York, Joseph, who had 7 or 8 ch.

**Prentiss**, Prentice. See Batson(1), Emery (5), Lyons(2).

**PRESBURY.** The Saco resident was also Presbyter, Praesbitery, and he and his sons sometimes Preston.

1 **JOHN**, shoemaker, Saco,in court Nov.1665 for common abs. from meet. That he was s. of early John of Sandwich and husb. of Dorcas Bessey is negatived only by the fact that the Saco man's dau.-in-law claimed for self and ch. the whole Page plantation at Saco which he bot from Clement Hardy in 1670, calling her husb. William 'only s. and heir' and that none of the Martha's Vineyard fam. appeared as claimants. Saco constable 1670, 1671 (negligent in gathering rates). Sued Doughty and Orr for taking away pine logs in 1671. Tr.j. 1674; gr.j. 1675 (abs. and fined), 1676. List 249. His w. was seated at Ch. 1674, List 246. His inv. 5 Mar. 1678-9 incl. 'things' at Pendleton Fletcher's; at his own ho. were a kettle and augurs of Walter Mayer's. Lately decd. and est. feared insolv., adm. was gr. 1 Apr. 1679 to Maj. Pendleton, who relinq. in July fol. to Francis Hooke, he in 1684 to s. **William**, bondsm. John Harmon(3). In 1679 s. **Nathan** was ord. to remain apprent. to Maj. Pendleton who bound him in 1680 to Jos. Cross(7). As Nathan Preston he contin. with Cross' wid., then with her new husb. Nicholas Morey, at the carpenter's trade. Cape Porpus wit. 1688. Boston records mar. of Nathan Presbury and Elizabeth Ganson 16 Feb. 1698, and their ch. 1699-1710: Nathan, Elizabeth, Dorcas. **Stephen** (Presby), who wit. deliv. of Kit. land from F. Hooke to Deering 8 Apr. 1686 (Y. D. 4: 134) can hardly be anyone but ano. son. See Hist. of Martha's Vineyard (Banks), vols. i, ii, for Stephen of Tisbury, m. ab. 1694 Deborah Skiffe, and d. 17 May 1730, ag. 58. Wid. Deborah d. 11 Mar. 1743, ag. 73. His will, 1730, names w., 7 daus. and ch. of decd. s. John. John, wounded at Saco 1691, lay 19 weeks under cover, seems ano. son.

2 **NATHANIEL**, of Blackfriars, London, m. in Portsm. 31 Mar. 1726 Parthenia Benson(1).

**3 WILLIAM**(1), Maj. Pendleton his gdn. in 1679; of age in 1684, called 'Presbury or Preston.' In May 1685 Saco ct. dealt with him and w. Priscilla (Randall 15), and also ord. him to maint. ch. of Sarah Crocker(8). The war sent the fam. to Beverly, where in 17— his wid. claimed the 50 a. Page planta. in his sole right. She d. there 23 Apr. 1752, ag. 86.' Presum. b. in Me. was s. **Edward**, who m. Catherine Pierce 27 Aug. 1713 in Newb., where 8 ch. were rec. (Presbury). In 1727 his mo. and aunt Sarah West (see Cole 19) deeded to him and br. Stephen. Rec. at Bev. (Presson, Preston): **Nehemiah**, b. 15 Jan. 1691-2. **Mary**, b. 5 Mar. 1694-5. **Stephen**, b. 3 May 1697, shipwright, m. Newb. 3 June 1723 Abigail Sargent (Capt. Edward). In 1730 he sold the Saco prop. to Nathan Whitney of York. **Benjamin**, b. 1 Jan. 1699-1700. **Randall**, b. 3 Apr. 1702. **William**, b. 1 Jan. 1704-5. **Nathan**, b. 18 May 1707. **Ruth**, b. 25 Mar. 1710. One David was of Bev. 1707, one Thomas 1720.

**PRESCOTT.** A Lancashire parish, a Lancashire and Cheshire family.

**1 JAMES**, Hampton ab. 1665 (±62 in Sept. 1709, ±64 in Sept. 1713), m. Mary Boulter(2); lived at the Falls. Kingston grantee 1694, and head of first board of selectmen 1695. Jury 1694 (sr.). James (no designation) on jury 1693, 1699, 1700; gr.j. 1694. He was adm. to Hampt. F. Ch. 20 Apr. 1712, dism. to Kingston 29 Sept. 1725, d. there 23 Nov. 1728, 'an aged father.' Lists 52, 400. Ch: **Joshua**, b. 1 Mar. 1669, m. (warrant 12 Oct. 1710) Sarah Clifford(2); liv. Hampt. F. 1722. 11 ch. **James**, b. 1 Sept. 1671. **Rebecca**, b. 15 Apr. 1673, m. Nathl. Sanborn. **Jonathan**, b. 6 May (or Aug.) 1675, liv. in Kensington. List 399b. Mary Cram (see 1) accus. him in June 1696 aft. he had m. Elizabeth (Pulsifer) Clifford(1). He d. 6 Jan. 1755. Her will made that month names her Clifford dau., 3 of 6 Prescotts b. 1696-1709, gr.ch., and Ruth Robie who had long liv. with her. **Mary**, b. 11 June 1677, m. 1st Jabez Coleman(3); m. 2d Thos. Crosby(3); m. 3d James Bean(2). **Abigail**, twin, b. 1 Sept. 1679, m. 2 Nov. 1699 Richard Bounds(1). **Temperance** (by Dow; or Patience, by Prescott Gen.), twin, d.y. **John**, Hampt. F., b. -19 Nov.- 1681, m. 8 Aug. 1701 Abigail Marston(4), who d. 30 Dec. 1760. Hampt. 1735, Kensingt. 1738; d. 1761. 10 ch. **Nathaniel**, Kingston, b. -19 Nov.- 1683. His w. Ann (Marston 4, m. 30 Dec. 1703) d. 10 Dec. 1761, he 26 Feb. 1771, s.p. Will.

**2 JAMES**(1), Sergt., Dea., liv. near fa. at Hampt. F. For poss. jury duty see (1). Selectm. 1726, 1729, 1733, 1737. Lists 60, 400. He m. 1st 1 Mar. 1695 Maria Marston (11); m. 2d 17 June 1746 Abigail (Gove 2)

(Dalton 2) Sanborn, who d. 8 May 1751 in 82d yr. and was buried with 1st husb. Ch: **Jeremiah**, b. 8 Dec. 1695, m. 14 Jan. 1720 Hannah (Philbrick 9, Dow says, but that Hannah d.y.); she adm. to Kingst. Ch. from Hampt. 9 July 1732. 5 ch. **Samuel**, Hampt. F., b. 14 Mar. 1697, m. 17 Dec. 1717 Mary Sanborn, who d. 28 May 1757, he 1758. 5 ch. **Elisha**, Hampt. F., b. 18 Mar. 1699, m. 13 Feb. 1723-4 Phebe Sanborn. He d. 9 Dec. 1781, she 28 Nov. 1788. 10 of 13 ch. d.y. **Sarah**, b. 20 Jan. 1701, m. 9 Mar. 1719-20 Joseph Lowell of Newb. **Lucy**, b. 6 Feb. 1703, m. Joseph Sanborn, jr. **Ebenezer**, b. 3 Dec. 1705, m. 15 Dec. 1726 Abigail Tilton; liv. on homestead; d. 1750. 7 ch. **James**, Hampt. F., b. 2 Dec. 1708, m. 14 Jan. 1730-1 Dorothy Tilton, who m. 2d 25 Oct. 1736 Benj. Sanborn. 2 ch. **Rebecca**, b. 27 Sept. 1711, m. Caleb Towle.

**PRESTON**, Presson. See also Presbury.

**1 JOHN**, cordwainer, Portsm. (±27 in 1673), bot from John Hunking in 1671 and with w. Jeane sold to Jos. Jewell in 1681. He rang the bell 1671-5, worked for Nehemiah Partridge 1677, and wit. with and ag. George Bramhall. Lists 80, 326c, 329, 331ab. Taxes abated Dec. 1683 for poverty or death, incl. his, and as no John seen for 12 yrs. thereafter, it was presum. the younger cordwainer and s. **John**, b. ±1675-6, on jury 1695 and 1698 and whose servant Mehitable Parker set fire to his ho. in 1702. Lists 330d, 336b, 337, 339, 67. His w. Susanna Pomery(8) was liv. 1721. He was bp. 9 Feb. 1745-6, ±70; alive 1749. Appar. daus.: **Susanna**, m. 14 Oct. 1716 John Parkes of Dublin, Ire.; **Sarah** (surely) m. Benj. Dockham(1), who had deeds from her fa. 1745, 1749, of half the ho. on Pickering's Neck he was liv. in, the 2d deed including the contents; **Elizabeth**, m. 24 Dec. 1724 John Boag of Kirkwell, co. St. Magnis, North Britain. One Wm. P., and several others, blackmailed Benj. Welch, Hannah Stephens and Martha Bly in 1715; see also (4). One John and Mary P. had s. Richard bp. So. Ch. 1722.

**2 RALPH**, Pemaquid soldier 1689. List 126.

**3 RICHARD**, Exeter 1712. List 376b (1725, 1740).

**4 WILLIAM**, posted at Capt. Gerrish's garrison with James Libby, Dec. 1695. List 67. Note also (1).

**PRICE**, the Welsh ap Rhys. See also Cleaves(1), Graves(2), Hilton(6), Pendleton(1).

**1 JOHN**, agreed in Aug. 1683 to pay 40 s. to Mrs. Mary Sayward, York; likely the Boston man from whose sloop Sylvester Herbert(3) fell. List 313f. See also Plice.

**2 LEWIS**, Scarboro soldier. List 237b.

**3 LOUIS** (or Samuel), a captive in Canada 1710, List 99, p. 126; poss. relat. to Elizabeth (also Pricer), List 99, p. 125, who was from Deerfield.

**4 RICHARD,** a tailor, b. at Shrewsbury, co. Salop, bound self to John Pickering(2) 25 Apr. 1639, for 4 yrs., and ran away.

**5 RICHARD,** a Kennebec soldier. List 189.

**6 SAMUEL;** see (3).

**7 WALTER,** merchant, Salem, called Capt. Wm. Gerrish(8) 'my br.' In 1659 Wincoll contracted to build a sawmill for him and Richard -Cooke- at Salmon F.; he and Richard -Coole-, assignees of Thos. Broughton, for selves and other creditors, sued Jona. Nason for tresp., 1671. In 1715 his gr.s. Capt. Walter of Salem q.c. the Wincoll homestead to John Smith of Berw.

**PRIDE, John,** fisherman, s. of John and Edith of Salem, stepson of Mordecai Crawford(3), under age in 1648, was fishing at Cape Bonawagon by 1661, resident there 1672, and m. Jane, dau. of Wm. Lovering(5). Gr.j. 1674. Lists 13, 15, 85. Late of Cape B., he ack. judg. to Clarke & Lake in Suff. ct. 1676 and took O. F. in Beverly 1677, but likely returned East a few yrs. bef. his fam. permanently settled at Bev. One John, fa. or s., wit. in Boston 8 Aug. 1699 the Turfrey-Foxcroft agreement to build Saco mills. Mrs. P., who d. at Bev. Dec. 1713, presum. his w. Ch., all bp. Bev. 12 Dec. 1686: **John.** **William,** m. (int. Bev. 22 July 1699) Hannah Thorndike. Norwich, Conn., 1737, eldest son (Y. D. 18: 253-4). **Peter,** m. (int. Bev. 22 Dec. 1700) ——— Thistle; d. there 17 July 1743, ag. 68. **Joseph,** m. 1st in Bev. 17 Dec. 1702-3 Elizabeth Bond, who d. in Glouc. 8 May 1716; his 2d w. was Sarah. Removed to Falm. by 1728. 5 + 7 ch. rec. or bp. Bev., Glouc., Falm., incl. Amy, m. Benj. Larrabee (1 jr.). **Mary,** m. in Bev. 5 Mar. 1694-5 John Lovett, jr. **Elizabeth,** m. in Bev. 14 June 1698 Lot Conant, sr.

**PRIEST.**

**1 ABIGAIL,** dau. of John Muchemore(2) 1718.

**2 BARTHOLOMEW,** Shoals, decd., adm. 13 Feb. 1666-7 to Richard Endle. See also Monke(1).

**3 RICHARD,** in Boston list 1687, following John Verin, sr. and jr., with John Lovering and Thos. Verin following him.

**4 RICHARD,** Portsm., from Clovelly, co. Devon. See Quick.

**5 THOMAS** (also Prust), shopkeeper, Portsmouth, from Northam, co. Devon, m. Sarah Collins 6 Mar. 1720-1. Adm. 30 Apr. 1740 to wid. Sarah, who wit. as Priest.

**6 WILLIAM,** m. bef. Oct. 1702 Sarah (Hill 17) Fletcher(8). Of Saco, he asked to be released from Fort Mary 13 Sept. 1704 as in service above a yr. Wid. Sarah m. 3d in Wells 23 Jan. 1709-10 Lt. Andrew Brown(3).

**Prine,** Isaac, a Braveboat Harbor wit. 1694 (Y. D. 7: 92); depos. in Me. ct. 1695 (Prenes, Prince).

**Prior** (Pryor), Edward, Kennebec, twice a Pattishall wit. 1665. List 182.

**PRITCHARD,** Pritchett.

**1 JOHN** (Pritchett), Sagadahoc, bot at Small Point from Thos. Atkins 16 Apr. 1660 and wit. for Atkins 1669, 1673. In Nov. 1674 he deeded land, half to w. Jane, half to son and daughter equally, and other land to br. Richard, provided that if neither w., ch., br., or sis. came to him while he lived, or, after he d., to look after est., all was to go to John Burrill(2), who was given outright land near Canoe Point. He ack. this in Boston 28 Mar. 1685, and, mariner, of Boston, with the Burrills, sold Small Point land to Henry Emons in Nov. fol.

**2 JOHN** (Pritchard), b. Ipsw. 28 Mar. 1680, s. of John, m. Sarah Harris(16). Falm., Sept. 1717, retailing without lic. 9 ch. b. in Topsfield, Boston, Falm., 1702-1721, the oldest **Elizabeth,** poss. the one who m. Edward Heal of Falm. at Topsfield 3 Dec. 1719.

**Procise,** William, sailed under Matthew Estes 1685. List 314.

**Proctor,** Edward and Samuel. See Sharp, Ashfield, Larrabee(1).

**Profeitt,** Walter, Pemaquid 1687. List 124.

**Prout,** Timothy, Kit. grant with Wincoll and Osborne 1659, forfeited. List 298.

**PROVENDER, John,** No. Yarmouth, List 214, presum. from Malden and the soldier under Capt. Mosely in Feb. 1675-6. Son **Isaac,** York, had grant 13 Mar. 1710-1 provid. he settle. Called laborer, cooper, husbandm., fisherman. In 1728 he sold his right to No. Yarm. lands laid out to heirs of his fa. Elizabeth P. depos. in July 1761 that she had liv. at Cape Neddick ±50 yrs. and knew Samuel Banks' ho. Ch.

**Provoe,** James, Frenchman, at Pemaquid fort 1682; ±45 in 1684. List 123.

**Prowse,** Michael, a Kennebec wit. 1664 (Y. D. 10: 153).

**Pucke,** William, Shoals wit. 1668 (Y. D. 2: 58); see Puggy.

**Puggy,** William (also Pugry, Puckry), ag. 44 in Sept. 1675; he heard John Moore, jr. call Mr. Belcher a knave. Shoals 1677, ±46. List 306c. See also Pucke.

**PUGSLEY,** an ancient fam. in Barnstable, co. Devon.

**1 JOHN,** Eliot, Scarboro (bot there 1727), m. at Dover 7 Mar. 1704-5 Elizabeth

Small. List 289. Membership list Eliot Ch. 1727: John, jr.; John, sr., removed. He and w. members of Scarb. Ch. 1728. Kn. ch: **John. Ann,** m. Samuel Frink(3). **Abraham, Kit.,** m. 1st 17 Nov. 1736 Abigail Cox; m. 2d Comfort Beale(8). (In Harwich, Mass., 1697, was one John, a Narragansett soldier, 'now grown old for hard work.' See also Bodge, p. 439).

2 **RICHARD,** a Kennebec wit. with Parkers 1664; wit. Clarke & Lake to Thoits 1668. He ack. a judgm. in Suff. ct. in July 1678 and took O. A. at Boston 11 Nov. fol. Desperate debts due Capt. Corwin incl.: Mr. P. Wid. Puglis taxed Boston 1687.

**PULLEN, Richard,** merchant, Boston, m. 6 Dec. 1705 Eleanor (Brackett) (Foxwell) Andrews(5). List 229. Will, 14 Jan. 1715-6 (d. 6 Feb. 1721, ag. 52); wife sole legatee. She depos. in Boston in June 1743, ±70. See also Jackson(4), Mattoon(1).

**PULMAN.** One Florence P., sex unkn., was bur. at Stoke-in-Teignhead, co. Devon, in 1635.

1 **JASPER,** fisherman, York, identif. by Col. Banks as the one bp. at Stoke-in-Teignhead, co. Devon, 18 Nov. 1633, s. of John, gr.s. of Robert. Not seen here as early as his br. (2), he bot Philip Hatch's ho. and land from the mortgagee in June 1674 and land at Great Isl. in York from the Angiers in 1675. A day in 1675 set apart for humiliation was to him a good day to go gunning; the court thought not. Constable 1678; O. A. Mar. 1679-80; gr.j. 1686, 1688, 1690-1; apprais. Wm. Moore's est. 1691; bondsm. for Thos. Adams 1692. Lists 30, 90. See also Edge. His w. Ann was slandered by Arthur Beale in 1685; some goods of Margaret Donnell(1), decd., were left in hands of Goody P. Adm. on his est. to her 7 Jan. 1700-1, John Pickering bondsm. Ch: **Thomas** (presum.), a youth fined for foul language in 1685. **Mary** (see 2), m. Lt. Joseph Moulton(6).

2 **JOHN,** br. of (1), fisherman, York, and perh. first at the Shoals, ag. 30 in 1669 when he caught Wm. Pitts stealing his money. In 1678 he bot ±10 a. S.W. of York River from Sampson Angier. Inv. of Aug. 1680 (adm. 29 Sept. to br.), incl. ho., meadow and island, heifer and calf. By oral evid., he gave all to niece Mary (Y. D. 5. 1. 4). In 1689 John Brawn deeded to her for love, but more especially in consid. of the love his mo. bore unto John P., Mary's uncle.

**PUNCHEON, William,** Scarboro in 1681, m. 1st in Salem 4 Mar. 1680 Martha Elkins (1); m. 2d in Marblehead 1 May 1693 Joanna (Edgecomb 2) Elkins(6). List 238a. Of Piscataqua in 1690 when he was resid. legatee in will of John Winnock of Black Pt. He was 'of Boston' in 1693 and his wid. was liv.

there, ±97, in 1738, ±98 in 1741. One Wm. Punchin (Punchard) m. Abigail Waters in Salem in 1669 and had ch. b. 1670-1682.

**PURCHASE.**

**THOMAS,** gent., Pejepscot patentee 18 June 1632 with br.-in-law George Way of Dorchester, co. Dorset, where he too had liv. (Aspinw. 147), supposedly s. of Oliver and Thomasine (Harris) of Holy Trinity par., that city. See Oliver Purchase of Dorchester, Mass.; Jordan(7); N. E. Reg. 20: 246; 61: 278; Waters 1: 310-2; Lechford, p. 219. Here bef. the patent (the exact time can be set no nearer than a recital in deed of July 1684 'near three score years since he came to this country'), he wit. livery of the Vines patent 25 June 1630, and in 1631 entertained Sir Christopher Gardiner(1) whose companion he mar. Comr. at first ct. at Saco 25 Mar. 1636. In 1639 he yielded to Winthrop and conveyed to Mass., with right of citizenship for self, a tract 4 miles sq. on both sides of Androscoggin River except what he might occupy within 7 yrs. (Col. Rec. Mass. 1: 272). Gr.j. Saco ct. Sept. 1640; this ct. two months before had issued a summons ag. him to answer what might appear, when statement was made that he had conveyed the greater part of his goods and chattels out of the country. He 'afterward acted with every government within reach.' Subm. to Plymouth Col. 1654. A Gorges comr. 1662, 1664, being one of those later dropped by the King's Commission. See Wheeler's Hist. of Brunswick, p. 788; Me. P. & C. i; Me. Hist. Soc. Col. 1: 3: 311-334. Lists 21, 11, 224. His w. Mary (Grove) d. in Boston 7 Jan. 1655-6; he m. 2d Elizabeth (Andrews 16) Pike(8), and d. at Lynn, his refuge during the war, 11 May 1678, ag. 101 by record. Will, 2 May 1677, gives one-third of all, except the silver plate, to w.; two-thirds to 5 ch.; Mr. Henry Jocelyn and cousins Mr. Oliver P. of Hammersmith (Lynn) and Mr. Edw. Allen of Boston, overseers. The inv. incl. 1000 a. at Pejepscot. Wid. Elizabeth m. 3d in Lynn Nov. 1678 John Blaney, sr. Ch. (Y. D. 4: 14-17): **Thomas,** mariner, eldest s. and exec. with mo. He m. at Salem 3 Dec. 1679 Elizabeth Williams. Lost at sea 1681, leaving s. Thomas, b. 29 Jan. 1679-80 (see Y. D. 16: 162). The wid. was still Purchase 30 June 1685. One Elizabeth of Salem m. Jonathan Felt(4) in Marbleh. 3 Jan. 1694-5. **Jane** (ag. 53 in Sept. 1716) m. Oliver Elkins(9). **Abraham** (±46 in Mar. 1713-4), anchorsmith, blacksmith, Salem, m. ab. 1695 Ruth Williams; d. by 1724; she liv. 1748. 5 ch. **Elizabeth,** m. in Marbleh. 20 Dec. 1683 John Blaney (jr.). The 5th one likely **Sarah, m. in** Marbleh. 27 Dec. 1688 Wm. Bartlett.

**PURINGTON,** Purinton, Puddington, the last old in Devonshire and the only form found in N. E. records during the first 30 years.

**1 GEORGE,** tavern keeper, York, s. of Robert and Joan of Tiverton, co. Devon, where he m. Mary Pooke in St. Peter's par., 5 Feb. 1630. Money difficulties which began bef. his fa. d. prob. sent him and his br. (3) to N. E. At York he bot his home lot from Henry Simpson 15 Apr. 1640. Tr.j. and one of four to appear for the town at Saco ct. 1640. Alderman 1641. Fined 1646 for exactions in selling liquor and victuals. He d. betw. 3 July 1647—5 June 1649. List 22. See Hist. of York 1: 100. His will, 25 June 1647, not proved until 18 Jan. 1695-6, named w. Mary, br. Robert, and specif. defined his 5 ch., excluding his w.'s dau. Sarah who wit. as Puddington 5 July 1658; see Burdett(2); Davis(18), (49); Pennell(2). Wid. Mary (List 72) sold at her tavern bef. Oct. 1649, was lic. that mo., m. 2d bef. 15 Mar. 1661-2 Major John Davis(18), and d. after 6 Oct. 1691, prob. bef. her 1st husb.'s will was filed. Ch., 1st 3 bp. at Tiverton: **George,** bp. 12 Feb. 1631, not in will. **Mary,** bp. 2 Feb. 1632-3, eldest dau. by will, m. Peter Weare; liv. Nov. 1717, ±83. **Joan,** bp. 22 Feb. 1634, not in will. **John,** b. ±1635-6, eldest s. by will, which gave the homestead to him and br. **Elias,** who helped appraise Wm. Endle's land in a levy 17 Nov. 1667; see also Y. D. 4: 47. **Frances,** 2d dau. **Rebecca,** youngest dau.

**2 LT. *JOHN(1),** ±44 in Jan. 1679-80. Cape Porpus 1666, a partner with Nicholas Cole(23) in fishing and oar making, and there in 1668 he had a ho. and w. Mary (see Barton 2, 5). The partners (he of Wells) bot at Merriconeag in Nov. 1672, built and liv. there till forced off by the war, as old friends depos. (see Doc. Hist. 23: 204), tho York gr. land to him and John Penwill in 1674 and he was 'now of York' in Nov. that yr. On Cape Porpus j. 1679; town clerk there 1679, 1681, 1689; gr.j. 1680-1; Assemblyman 1682; cor.j. 1685; j. 1686, 1688; selectm. 1688; Lt. 'now in H. M. immediate service' 1688; chosen first selectm., town clerk and lot layer Jan. 1688-9; ord. to Boston in Apr. foll. to account for discharging the garrison. Sometime of York 24 Feb. 1689-90, perh. at Salisb., where he d. in a few yrs. and s. James administered (Hoyt). Lists 255, 256, 259, 236, 19, 26, 30, 32, 33. In May 1720 when s. Joshua took adm., the inv. included: 600 a. on Chebeague Isl., 1000 a. on Merriconeag Neck, 100 + 12 a. at Arundel. Deeds indicate 7 ch: **John,** carpenter, evid. eldest s. as only one in Cape P. rec. Gr.j. there 1688 (jr.). Lists 33, 259. W. Sarah. Ch: Sarah, b. Salisb. 26 Jan. 1690-1. Poss. his: Daniel, Hampt. wit. 1710; Lydia, Salisb., m. 13 July 1713 Wm. Straw of

Amesb. **James,** b. ±1664, m. 1st one Elizabeth; m. 2d Lydia (Mussey 4) Randall. Lost at sea 12 July 1718 in 55th yr.; wid. Lydia d. at Salisb. 3 Dec. 1737. See Hoyt 1: 294, 2: 801, for 8 ch., incl. Mary, m. Josiah Dow(7); John, carpenter, eldest s. 1719, m. 1 Nov. 1720 Theodate Swett (Moses); Elias, bot in Hampt. 1723, m. 9 Jan. 1724-5 Phebe Swett (Moses), who adm. 1736. **Elizabeth,** m. in Salisb. 15 May 1691 John Conner(2). **Joshua,** Hampt. soldier 1695, List 399a. Cordwainer. Exeter wit. 1702; of Haverh., bot in Salisb. 1709; taxed Hampt. F. 1709 (added name); liv. there 1748 (Y. D. 10: 52) and appar. never of Arundel, where in 1720 a lot was laid out to him adj. 'brother Durrell,' how br. unkn. He m. (int. Amesb. 28 Oct. 1710) Damaris Jones. Will, of Epping, 1754—1754, names w. Judith, 4 sons, 5 daus. (1 decd.) **Mary,** m. (int. Salisb. 12 Feb. 1703-4) Sanders Carr. 9 ch. **George,** Salisb., form. of Cape P., d. Jan. 1692; adm. 30 Mar. 1693 to James. Dea. **Hezekiah,** Wells soldier from Salisb. 1696; at Fort Mary, Saco, July 1703, 'a Cape Porpus man, a shoemaker, lately mar.' Truro 1706, d. there 8 Jan. 1718. Wid. Mary (Scammon, dau. of Humphrey) m. 2d 29 June 1719 Jonathan Paine; d. Truro 17 May 1760, ag. 78. 9 ch., all b. Truro, except Dea. Humphrey, b. at Kit. 31 Jan. 1703, m. Thankful Harding, and d. at Gorham, Me., 27 June 1758 in 56th yr. See also Geo. Bixby; Y. D. 15: 217.

**3 ROBERT,** Portsm. 1640, br. of (1). Sued by Thos. Wannerton 1641; town committees 1648, 1655; constable for lower Str. Bk. 1649; gr.j. 1651; grant 1652. A deed to two sons 11 Feb. 1655, ho. and land on the plain south of the meet.-ho., was signed also by 'the mark of Agnes Puddington,' called 'my mo. Agnes' by s. Robert in Jan. 1656-7 when he sold to Pendleton. See also N. H. Hist. Soc. Col. 1: 255. He was last rec. here 4 June 1655 when, aft. he had remov., he gave a deed to Thos. Seavey. In 1676 Wm. Lucomb twitted his s. that his fa. was banished out of the place with main violence. The sons depos. in 1679 that he liv. several yrs. at Little Harbor, had land and marsh fenced, and when he remov., ±30 yrs., bef., sold all to Seavey. Lists 41, 321, 323, 324. Kn. ch: **Robert,** b. 1634-9. **John,** Shoals 1678, ±43. List 306b. Ab. 1677 Constable Diamond served a writ on him and Gabriel Grubb. One J. P. wit. with Richard Chamberlain and Jos. Rayn in 1681 (Y. D. 3: 91), while the John who once liv. in the Goff ho. (Elizabeth Emery's depos.) does not seem to be (2). In 1699 one Abigail P. and Sarah Lidston test. that at Elizabeth Redford's ho. they saw John Woodman kick Thos. Rice; one Abigail and Richard White m. 12 Aug. 1714 in Boston where other Puringtons mar.

4 **ROBERT**(3), ±30 in Oct. 1664, 35 in 1671, 42 in Aug. 1678, ±40 in Apr. 1679. Gr.j. 1667, 1668; freeman 15 May 1672. Liv. 1685, perh. later. Lists 312c, 313a, 326ac, 329, 330ab, 331bc, 49, 52, 54 (332b, poss. his son). He m. by 1665 Amy Onion (also Em and Emeline, Lists 331ac), with whose fa. he bot on Parker's Isl., Kennebec, in Sept. 1664, and soon sold. Wid. Amy m. 2d 27 Aug. 1689 Francis Graves(1), and in 1715 deeded to dau. Hannah (Graves) Stephens half a ho. betw. Edw. Toogood and Robert Walker, her s. Benj. owning the other half. Ch: **Thomas**, m. 20 Sept. 1689 Rachel Williams. Taxed Str. Bk. July 1690; long dead in 1710, s.p. Lists 332b, 57. **Robert**, taxed Sandy Beach Dec. 1688, July 1690; long dead in 1710, s.p. List 57. **Elias**, blacksmith, Boston, m. Sarah Orris (John) there 7 July 1694 and that yr. sold ho. and land of his fa. in Portsm. Boston cor.j. 1698, his aut. in SJC 3735. Arrested there in 1699 for stealing silver; Elizabeth Corbison test. that when the silver was taken he was courting her as Thos. Starbury and later called hims. Jarvis and Wm. Mann, but he, denying ever seeing her until arrested, was cleared. Liv. Boston with w. Sarah 1711, he there in Oct. 1720. Of 8 ch. rec. or bp. at Bos., 2 d.y. and 2 surely liv. to m: Hannah (m. Samuel Sprague 1720), Sarah (m. Ebenezer Ranger 1728). **Benjamin**, carpenter, m. Mary Jameson(3). Of Portsm. 1709, he gave p/a to his mo.; Boston 1716-7 assoc. with Thos. Pennell of Glouc.; lic. for 'town of Augusta' at New Meadows, and on j. from there in July 1719; Glouc. 1722; Boston with w. Mary 1735. Son Joseph b. Boston 20 Oct. 1716, was perh. the ch. bur. there 2 May 1717.

**Purston**, Thomas, from farther northward, took O. A. at Kittery 16 Nov. 1652. †Durston.

**PUTNAM. 1 John**, Oyster River soldier 1696. List 336b.

2 **JONATHAN**, Salem, partner in No. Yarm. grant. List 212.

**PUTT, Henry**, in much trouble at Scarboro 1667; a common swearer; uncivil carriages toward Joan Batten(5), his bondsm. Richard Martin and John Mare; embezzling Thos. Mitchell's peas; abs. from meet. He bot a Hog Isl. ho. from Andrew Newcomb in 1673, and that yr. was warned to go home to his w., having been absent 11 yrs. Adm. Robert Monson's est. 23 June 1677 and m. his wid. Elizabeth. Gr.j. (Me.) 1683. Liv. Oct. 1686. Lists 95, 307b.

**Pyle**. See Pile.

**Pyler**, Joseph, served on by Great Isl. constable, 1668. See Clother.

**PYNNE, Richard**, came to Richmond's Isl. in the -Welcome- 1633. List 21. In 1634 acct. is item 10 s. to w. of R. P., the gunner.

**Pyrie**, William, wit. Bragdon to Jeffries, 1637. List 271.

## QUICK.

1 **DANIEL**, tailor, taxed at Portsmouth ±1707, bot ho.-lot from Pickering in 1713. The name of his 1st w. is unkn. but he m. 2d 25 May 1715 Hannah (Miller 9) Cowell and 3d 22 June 1740 Elizabeth (Barnes 12) Shackford. Bondsman for John Abbott, 1722. Owned cov. of No. Ch. 26 Aug. 1711 and had sons **Daniel** and **Nathaniel** bp. Other ch., all by 1st w., were: **Charity**, bp. 22 May 1712-3, m. 24 May 1731 Richard Priest of Clovelly, co. Devon. A ch., bp. 6 Mar. 1714-5. The fa. was -non compos- in 1747 and the selectmen sold his ho. List 339.

2 **NATHAN**, ±35 in 1677, lost in the great storm of 1677-8. See Broad(4). Lists 30Cad.

**Quint**, Thomas, Greenland 1684 (List 52). One John taxed in Greenland, 1708+.

**Quire**, Matthew, verdict on his untimely death 4 Feb. 1679 (Prov. Papers 19: 657).

**Raborne**, see Haborne.

**RABSKINE, Jacob**, associated with the Algers at Dunstan. Adm. of est. of Andrew Heffer, 1663, and as such sued Andrew Thorne. Sued by Ambrose Boaden, 1665. Adm. on his est. gr. 5 July 1670 to Ambrose Boaden jr., A. B. sr. and William Sheldon, bondsmen. List 235.

**RACE, John**, s. of Judith Robie(1), b. 6 Dec. 1671 at Hampton, and nothing further. His fa. is even more obscure.

**RACKLIFF**, Rackley, poss. variants of Radcliffe, early in Lancashire.

1 **BENJAMIN**(4), Portsmouth, ho.-carpenter, rated 1720, m. 14 Dec. 1721 Lydia Marshall(3), and d. bef. 1729. The widow and three ch. were named in the will of George Richards, 1735. She was liv. in 1748 when she and two ch. deeded to Benj. Parker of Kittery. Ch: **Elizabeth**, bp. No. Ch. 21 Oct. 1722, d. bef. 1748. **William**, blockmaker. **Mary**, m. John Beck, felt-maker.

2 **JOHN** (see 4), York, tanner, m. ±1690 Elizabeth Trafton whose fa. deeded to them in 1691, William Rackliff (4 or 5) and Matthew Nelson, husb. of Agnes Rackliff(4) being wit. He was prob. slain in the York massacre and the wid. m. 2d one Johnson (see Johnson 20). Ch: **John**.

3 **JOHN**(2), York, tanner, m. 1st 10 Jan. 1714-5 Mary Foss(2) in Greenland where he was taxed 1715-1717. She d. 14 May 1718. He m. 2d Joanna Pike(4) who d. 7 Mar. 1729; m. 3d 6 Aug. 1730 Mehitable (Chandler) Davis(23) who m. 3d 1 Jan. 1746-7 Thomas Cummings in Scarboro. York laid out 20 a. to him and he bot 50 a., 1717. Corp. in the first Norridgewock exped., 1724. Sold out at

York and mov. to Scarboro, 1736. List 279.
Ch. by 1st w: **John**, b. 6 June 1715; **William**,
b. 22 Apr. 1717; both bp. in Greenland 1718.
By 3d w: **Benjamin**, b. 21 May 1731. **Joseph
Chandler**, b. 26 Feb. 1732-3. **Mary** and
**Joanna**, b. 15 Oct. 1734.

4 **WILLIAM**, Portsmouth, ±46 in 1676 when
he was boat-swain of ship ·Imployment·
of Piscataqua on a voyage to Fayal. In 1677
he bot land from William Hearle on which he
had already built a ho.; tax abated 1680.
Boston rec., under date 10 Nov. 1684, state
that W. R., carpenter, had come from Piscataqua and was liv. in the ho. of Magnus
White. Ret. to Portsmouth. Gr.j. 1693; j.
1694. Lists 329, 330d, 331b, 335a, 52, 355a
(Goody). It is apparent that he m. twice, his
1st w., name unkn., being the mo. of **Agnes**,
who m. Matthew Nelson(2). The 2d, **Jane**,
was a young w. of his old age, married bef.
1699, when he made a will leaving all to her
except two candlesticks to his dau. Nelson
and 1 s. apiece to his gr.ch. Jane's ch., b.
after this will was signed, were **Benjamin**,
and **Mary** (m. 10 Dec. 1719 Richard Cross).
Liv. in 1712 when he deeded to Col. Westbrook, he d. bef. 9 Jan. 1717-8 when wid.
Jane m. Anthony Libby(1). His will was
not proved, the wit. being dead, and his s.
Benjamin was app. adm. in 1723-4, wid. Jane
Libby declining. Yet, as Jane -Rackley-,
exec., she and Lydia, Benjamin's wid.,
deeded to Valentine Nutter in 1729. Altho
in this deed Lydia is described as 'wid. of
his (Wm.'s) only son,' there is room for
conjecture that (2) and (5) were sons by
W. R.'s 1st w. One and prob. both were dead
when he made his will, and Benjamin was his
only surv. s., his only s. with right of inheritance from his mo., Jane, and her only s. The
close assoc. of (2), (4) and (5) with the
Nelsons is more than chance.

5 **WILLIAM** (see 4), 21 in 1679, had a town
gr. in 1685. He m. 1st Mary Nelson(1)
and 2d 18 Oct. 1689 wid. Dorothy Lord(2).
List 67¶, 298, 336b¶ Ch: **William**, 'only son.'
**Mary**, m. Thos. Knight(21). **Hannah**, m.
Moses Hanscom(5).

6 **WILLIAM**(5), Kittery, ship-wright, m. 5
Jan. 1708-9 Martha Deering(8) who was
gr. adm. 6 Oct. 1724, Geo. Berry and Thos.
Allen bondsmen. List 291. Ch: **William**, b.
9 Aug. 1711, ship-wright, m. (int. 16 June
1739) Temperance Mitchell. **Nelson**, b. 12
Nov. 1713, m. in Newbury 27 Nov. 1739
Sarah Moodey. **Mary**, b. 4 Nov. 1715. **Martha**, b. 24 Nov. 1717, m. 10 July 1745 Samuel
Mitchell jr. **Hannah**, bp. 2 June 1728, m.
(int. 29 Dec. 1739) Enoch Plummer. **Samuel**,
bp. 2 June 1728, appren. to Clement Deering
when 2 yrs. 8 mo. old, m. (int. 26 Nov. 1743)
Mary Barter. **Roger**, posth.

**RADNER, Radver**, Abraham, fisherman, had
suit for wages ag. Thomas Turpin, dec.,
in York ct. 15 Mar. 1649-50. Taxed in Dover,
1650. Sued by Robert White, 1662. Deputy
constable of Saco, 1669. On 27 June 1670 the
Boston selectmen ordered Stephen Sargent
to transport him (Radford) back to the eastward whence he brot him. He d. in Saco 15
Sept. 1670. List 249. Poss. his name was
more properly Redford.

**RAGG, Jeffrey**, in Dover ct. 1642, and taxed
for a ho. in Newington in 1648, but listed
as non-resident. Lists 323, 354a.

**Rains**, see Raynes.

**Rainsford**, David, Pemaquid 1682, prob. a
transient Bostonian. List 162.

**RALPH**, Clement, Cochecho 1663 (Rafe),
was fined 1664. His will, 2 June—17 Sept.
1667, left all to William Follett but was not
proved as Wm. Roberts, a wit., refused to
swear. List 356h.

**RAMSDELL**, Nathaniel, York, took oath that
Mary Linscott(1) had had a ch. by him
and concealed it, in ct. Jan. 1709-10. She
denied it but m. him 1710-1. Had York gr.
and bot land 1711. Of Topsfield 1726, but of
York 1728 when he and w. deeded to her br.
John. List 279. Of their ch: **Lydia** m. 31
May 1733 John Wittum, jr., and **Nathaniel**
m. Sarah Wittum, int. 11 May 1734. A **ch.** d.
5 Sept. 1721.

**RAND.** Short form of Randall or Randolph.

1 **EDMUND**, Hampton, b. ±1686, of no kn.
relationship to other N. H. Rands, liv. on
Rand's hill. Bot from Thos. Leavitt, 1715.
He m. in Ipswich 27 Sept. 1708 Martha
Tuckerman who d. 21 July 1752, ag. 66. He
d. 12 Aug. 1769. Will, 1764—1769, names ch:
**Sarah**, b. 13 Dec. 1708, m. 25 Dec. 1728 Steph-
en Smith. **Martha**, b. 27 June 1711, m. 17
Jan. 1734-5 Benjamin Mason. **Mary**, b. 3 Oct.
1714, m. 13 Nov. 1735 Jonathan Leavitt, d. 5
May 1753, her ch. named in fa.'s will. **Thomas**, b. 7 Nov. 1717, m. 17 Dec. 1741 Elizabeth
Chapman (Job), had the homestead. 8 ch.
bp. in Hamp. **Abigail**, b. 31 July 1721. **Elizabeth**, b. 22 Apr. 1723.

2 **FRANCIS**, Sandy Beach, ±70 in 1686, here
by 1640-1 when sued by William Whiting.
Constable for upper Str. Bank 1649-1651;
O. F. 1657; gr.j. 1656, 1667, 1668. Lists 43,
47, 52, 54, 57, 311b, 312c, 313a, 323, 326ac,
330ab, 332b, 341, 356L. His w. Christian was
wit. ag. Anne Crowther bef. the gr.j. in 1648
and was sued for slander in 1655. On Sept.
29, 1691, while the younger men were out
fishing, the Brackett and Rand houses at
Sandy Beach were attacked by Ind. and 16
persons slain (including Francis and Christian Rand) or carried into captivity. One s.
or gr.s. was surely captured, and prob. other

Rand wives and ch. were among the victims. His will, 31 Dec. 1689—19 Feb. 1691-2, names his w., surv. ch. and the ch. of his s. Samuel by his now w. Mary; sons Samuel and Thomas exec. Ch: **Francis**, freed from training for 3 yrs. in 1668 'there being some distemper on him'; taxed 1675; wit. 1676; put under bonds to keep the peace on compl. of Seaborn Hodge in 1684; Lists 52, 313a; not in fa.'s will. **William**, appren. to John Partridge; his fa. gave bond for him in 1676; bot liquor of Richard Webber's w. in 1678; d. by 1680 (List 313d). **Nathaniel**, ±45 in 1683; of Portsm., laborer, jailed for debt, 1683; sued by Samuel Rollins and jailed for lack of security, 1685; List 94; in fa.'s will (5 s. only); poss. an Ind. victim. **John**. **Thomas**. **Samuel**. **Mary**, m. Thomas Barnes(12). **Sarah**, m. Isaac Herrick(2).

3 **JOHN**(2), Oyster River, ±24 in 1669, ±38 in 1683, m. Remembrance Ault, ±32 in 1682, bef. 1672 when Ault deeded to them and their ch. In 1682 he entered a pet. ag. his mo.-in-law stating that she, instigated by her s.-in-law William Parkeson (Perkins) who liv. with her, was demanding his lands on which he had liv. 15 yrs. Freeman 1672; constable 1673; j. 1685. Lists 49, 52, 54 (2), 57, 330a, 356b. Adm. on est. of both John and Remembrance (Ind. victims, List 99) gr. 5 Mar. 1694-5 to John Rand, Edward Leathers on his bond, raising question whether Christian Leathers, prob. w. of E. L., was not a childless dau. of (3). Proven ch: **John**, had w. Elizabeth to whom adm. was gr. 1 Aug. 1698 and who m. 2d William Glines. **J.** 1697. His dau. Christian m. Napthali Kincaid(3). His s. John (List 368b) chose his friend Francis Matthews gdn. 9 Mar. 1710-1, and m. 17 Dec. 1718 Joanna Willey. **Nathaniel**. **Samuel** (Jean-Baptiste Rain?) and **Remembrance**, captured when their parents were k. and never returned. **Hannah**, of Portsmouth, spinster in 1718. **Francis**, apprentice of John Searle, blacksm., at Champernowne's Isl. in 1710. Of Portsm., fisherman, he, Nath. and Hannah q.c. their int. in the land their gr.fa. Ault gave their fa. to Job Reynolds 18 Apr. 1718. He m. Grace Parker of Newc. 13 Oct. 1728. Wit. of will of br. Nath., 1740.

4 **NATHANIEL**(3), Sandy Beach, planter, in 1718. He m. Elizabeth Marden(2), in ct. Dec. 1701 for having a ch. 4 mo. after mar. Bot land of John Odiorne 1725. Of parish of Rye, 1728, he deeded his entire est. to s. Joshua, he to pay his bros. and sis. (named). He lived 30 yrs. longer, however. List 316. Will, 1740—1759, names w. Elizabeth, sons John, Joshua, Amos, Nathaniel, daus. Sarah Jordan and Elizabeth Philbrick. Ch: **John**. **Joshua**, b. 25 Dec. 1703, m. Ruth Philbrick who d. 13 Dec. 1752. **Amos**, m.

1726-7 Esther Philbrick. **Nathaniel**, either he or Nathaniel(5), m. 24 Feb. 1733-4 Mary Noble of Portsm. **Sarah**, m. 28 Jan. 1724-5 Jeremiah Jordan(4 jr.). **Elizabeth**, b. 2 Aug. 1716, m. James Philbrick.

5 **SAMUEL**(2), Sandy Beach, m. 14 Aug. 1679, wid. Mary Walton, poss. slain with her ch. in the 1691 massacre. He m. 2d, surely af. 1689, the date of his fa.'s will, one Susanna, who surv. him and m. William Webster. Constable 1694-1696; j. 1694; gr.j. 1699. Rated in Greenland 1698. Lists 52, 57, 313e, 315a(2)bc, 318c, 332b, 359a. His will, 25 Feb. 1706-7—1 July 1707, does not name ch. but states that sons are under age. Wid. Susanna gr. adm. c.t.a., Wm. Wallace and James Marden bondsmen. In 1719 she and Webster q.c. to 'my son Samuel,' he to pay his bros. and sis. (named). Ch., order and mo. uncert: **John**, q.c. to br. Samuel in 1719. **Richard**, q.c. to br. Samuel bef. 1726; 4 ch. rec.; adm. to s. Nathaniel 1769. **Nathaniel**. **Samuel**, adm. to w. Abigail 17 Mar. 1730-1; ch.'s deeds 1740-1752. **Esther**, q.c. to br. Samuel 1719. **Mary**. **Sarah**. One Sarah m. Nehemiah Berry(8).

6 **THOMAS**(2), Sandy Beach, ±68 in 1720. Rated in Greenland 1690; j. 1698; constable (Newcastle) 1699-1700. An early w. and fam. may have been wiped out in the massacre of 1691. In 1711 his w. was Hannah. Lists 52, 57, 313a, 315ab, 316, 332b. His will, 25 Feb. 1731-2—24 Oct. 1736, ment. land bot from his sis. Mary Barnes and Sarah Herrick and lists his ch: **Thomas**, m. 1st 14 May 1722 Hannah Pray, m. 2d bef. 1749 Elizabeth (Lamprey 1) Moulton(18) who surv. him altho not ment. in his will, 1756, naming sons Thomas, Ephraim (w. Mary), Reuben (w. Elizabeth), daus. Mary Chandler, Hannah Lock, Elizabeth Lang, Meribah Rand. **William**, liv. 1743. **Samuel**, d. s.p., adm. 17 Sept. 1740 to br. Joshua, his bros. Thomas and William asking permiss. of the ct. to sue him on his bond in 1743. **Joshua**, m. 23 Nov. 1738 Mary Moses, exec. of fa.'s will. **Hannah**. **Christian**, m. one Shute. **Mary**, m. 27 Nov. 1729 William Chamberlain. **Elizabeth**. **Lydia**, m. Joshua Foss(3 jr.).

**RANDALL**, diminutive of Randolph, of great antiquity in Cornwall.

1 **EDWARD**, Newcastle, fisherman, had a gr. of 1 a. in 1667-8 'if he build.' In 1669 he was acc. of getting Thomas Seavey's gun by fraud. Fined for swearing, 1681. On Isles of Shoals jury, 1681. In ct. 1687 for resisting the tax collector. Mary Randall, ±30 in 1679, when she test. in a Newc. case in which Edward R. was ment., was poss. his w. Lists 312c, 313a, 326c, 330a, 331b. Kn. ch: **James**, a subpoena was issued to James, s. of Edward Rendle, in 1681 and his fa. was ordered

not to go to sea. See (6). **Peter,** Falmouth in 1683, mariner, bot a plantation of 100 a. in Cape Porpus from John Reynolds in 1684; adm. 21 Feb. 1697-8 to his eldest br. James, who, of Newcastle, sold the Reynolds land in 1719 with a warranty ag. his own and Peter's heirs. **Anne,** m. John Card(5 jr.). Very prob: **Edward, John** and **Jacob.** Arthur, Charles, Daniel and John Randall, fishermen of the Isles of Shoals ±1720 (the wid. Elizabeth poss. the mo. of one, all or none of them) are guessed to be of the 3d gen. of this sea-going fam. Among many ch. Charles and Daniel each had a dau. Anne, and Arthur a s. Peter.

2 **EDWARD**(1?), Newcastle, tailor, his record separated from that of (1) with much hesitation, there being no rec. of the birth or death of either and no indication of their ages. Rated at Strawberry Bk. 1688, 1690, 1691. Constable (Newc.) 1695-1697; constable 'for the Province,' 1696; j. 1697. Abs. from meeting, 1697. Bot land in Newc. from Nathaniel Fryer in 1693. Of Newc. 1704-5. Lists 66, 315abc, 316, 319, 330de. Either he or a younger Edward, poss. a s., m. Hannah Wallis, bot a ho. in Rye in 1731 and sold it in 1738, and had ch. bp. as late as 1737.

3 **GEORGE,** Exeter, d. 15 Feb. 1666-7.

4 **JACOB**(1?), Newcastle, tailor, as was (2). Rated at Gt. Isl. 1690, 1691; j. 1695; gr.j. 1697, 1700; Ensign 1696; succeeded (2) as Newc. constable 1698; selectman 1700. Lists 315abc, 318ab, 319. Wit. will of John Fabes, 1696. See Maundy. Bondsman for Sarah Eastwick, 1701-2. Will, 23 Dec. 1702—30 June 1703, one of the wit. being John Card, husb. of Anne Randall(1), names w. Katherine (prob. dau. of Dr. Pheasant Eastwick) who m. 2d one Tucker, exec., and four ch. all under age: **Jacob,** Newcastle, devised ⅔ of the homestead by his fa., taxed by 1717, adm. est. of his mo. Katherine Tucker in 1718. Mr. J. R. was sued by Capt. Hugh Reed for his mo.'s funeral charges, the account being dated 24 Sept. 1716. He is the most prob. husb. for Mary, dau. of Col. Shadrach Walton, kn. to have m. a Randall of Newc. She, wid., pd. tax for her s. Benjamin in 1743. **Stephen,** got two gold rings and ⅓ of the homestead by fa.'s will, appren. to Capt. Roger Deering and went with him to Scarboro in 1717. Still there in 1733, but of Falmouth in 1741. **Susanna. Katherine.**

5 *****JAMES,** Newcastle, carpenter, ±46 in 1686, bot from Joseph Mason 20 July 1668 a ho. at Little Harbor and land reaching to Sandy Beach (1½ miles) for £207, which seems to place him in a higher stratum than that of his contemporary(1). Wit. a note of Capt. Barefoot to Geo. Norton, 1671. Took inv. of est. of Joseph Baker, 1672; of George Wallis, 1685. Bot land of Mr. N.

Fryer bef. 1674. Portsm. selectmen 1688, 1689, 1690; Newc. selectman 1693, 1694-1697 (Mr.); gr.j. 1696, 1697 (Mr.); j. 1698-9; assemblyman for Newc. 1699. Rated in Greenland (Rye) 1690, 1691, 1701. Lists 49, 52, 60, 69 (Mr.), 312c, 313ac, 315c, 316, 318c, 324, 326c, 330a, 331b, 332b. At this point genealogical judgm. quite dogmatically kills him off, first having gratuitously endowed him with two surv. ch: **James** and his proven sis. **Elizabeth,** w. of John Yeaton of Newcastle, living in 1757.

6 **JAMES**(1?), Falmouth or thereabouts bef. 1680 when he was a refugee in Kittery, signing a pet. with other Falm. and Scarboro men. Wit. by mark the deed of Wilmot (Randall) Edgecomb to Robert Elliot in 1685 in Newcastle. With John(9) and Peter(1) in Cape Elizabeth in 1686 (List 226), and signed pet. to Andros from there in 1689. Lists 30, 90, 226, 228c. Of Newc. in 1719 when he deeded land of Peter(1). He seems quite distinct from (5).

7 **JAMES**(5), Newcastle, carpenter, ensign in 1696, deeded to John Yeaton in 1713 'in consideration of the relation I bear to Elizabeth, w. of the grantee.' Bot a 1 a. gr. at Little Harbor from John Jackson in 1709. Took inv. of est. of John Locke, 1707, of Aaron Moses 1713-4. James Randall and son taxed 1719. He m. a sis. of Edward Martin (9) who d. bef. he made his will 10 June 1719. The entire est. in Newcastle left to only s. James, while to daus. Mary Tarleton and Katherine Jordan went a farm in Portsmouth that Samuel Seavey liv. on. Elias Tarleton to pay £14 and James £4 to the 'grand committee,' at a rate of 40 s. annually. His bros. Edward Martin and John Yeaton were named exec.; inv. of £985. The will was not prov. until 12 Nov. 1753, by Sarah Jordan formerly Sarah Rand, one of the wit. Ch: **Mary,** m. Elias Tarleton. **Katherine,** m. by 1716 Jeremiah Jordan(4 jr.). **James,** Newcastle, m. Deborah Jordan(4) who was gr. adm. 15 June 1731, John Sherburne and Elias Tarleton bondsmen; inv. of £1520. The wid. m. 2d Samuel Wallis, m. 3d Henry Trefethen. Four sons, Capt. James (m. Mary Sherburne), William (m. 24 Apr. 1745 Hannah Marston), Mark (m. 24 Nov. 1748 Abigail Philbrick) and Capt. Paul (w. Abigail in 1763) were dividing the land in 1753.

8 **JOHN,** Cape Porpus, wit. deed Messer to Wormestall, 1666.

9 **JOHN,** m. at Amesbury 23 July 1689 Lydia Muzzy(4) of Cape Porpus, and d. in Salisbury, 29 Sept. fol. He was indebted to Mr. Harmon of York and Caleb Littlefield of Braintree; James Littlefield and one of the Puringtons owed him. Wid. Lydia m. 2d James Purington(2).

10 **JOHN**(1?), at Cape Elizabeth with James (6) and Peter(1) in 1686 (List 226); still there in 1689 (List 228c).

11 **JOSEPH**, Portsmouth, not even a guess as to his origin, m. 20 Oct. 1692 Elizabeth German(3), both called bef. ct. 6 Dec. but did not appear. He d. bef. 19 Feb. 1704-5 when she m. 2d Samuel Willey of Dover. She prob. took with her at least one Randall s., **Nathaniel**, associated with the Willeys in Dover.

12 **JOSEPH** 'the Frenchman' (Rendle, Rendon), Portsmouth, ship-carpenter, m. 20 Oct. 1709 Martha (Brookings 5) (Wakeham) Lewis(9). A warrant was issued ag. her and four other women 7 Mar. 1709-10 'vehemently suspected of whoredom.' On 29 Nov. 1715 he pet. for a divorce but the case was dismissed for lack of ev. He abandoned her and went to Providence, R. I., where he m. Amy Estance 26 July 1716 (bigamously?). By Martha he had a dau., **Anne**, who m. Aaron Abbot of Berwick and in 1742 sued her half-br. Benjamin Lewis. The writ in this case stated that Martha Randall d. 1741. Lewis searched Randall out in Prov. and R. made a depo., sworn to in Rehoboth 9 Apr. 1743, giving the facts of his Portsm. marriage and ack. Anne as his dau. He d. in 1760; 4 ch. by w. Amy.

13 **MARGERY**, see Norman(2).

14 **NATHANIEL**(11?), Dover and Durham, b. ±1694, m. ab. 1720 Mary Hodgdon(2 jr.). Lands laid out 1721. Gr. of 1729, of 30 a. originally gr. by Dover to Richard Randall in 1694, is prob. fraudulent. List 368b. Prop. of Rochester. He d. Mar. 1748-9, ag. 54, the wid. waiving her right to adm. in favor of s. Miles. Ch: **Miles** and **Nathaniel**, bp. 11 Aug. 1723. **Simon**, bp. 9 May 1725. **Elizabeth**, bp. 21 Apr. 1728, m. Samuel Demeritt. **Jonas**, bp. 25 Oct. 1730, d. bef. 1749. **Jonathan, Ann,** and **Mary,** less than 14 in 1749, under Wm. Odiorne of Durham, gdn.

15 **RICHARD**, Cape Porpus and Saco, here by 1658. Appr. est. of Nicholas Bully, 1664. Bot land from Maj. Phillips bef. 1669. Coroner's j. 1670; gr.j. 1676, 1686, 1687; constable of Saco and Cape Porpus 1688; selectman of Cape Porpus 1688-9. Est. of John Ryce in his hands, 1676. Bondsm. for Elizabeth (Sanders) Batson, 1685. Lists 33, 244d, 259. Ch: **Richard,** b. 6 Mar. 1659; no heirs in 1727. **Sarah,** b. 24 Mar. 1661, m. 1st Joseph Cole(19), captured by Ind. in 1703 and entered Roman Catholic ch. in Montreal in 1704, returned to New Eng. and m. 25 May 1710 Capt. Thomas West of Beverly. **Priscilla,** ±66 in 1727, m. William Presbury(3). In 1727 Sarah West and Priscilla Presbury of Bev., widows, 'ch. and only heirs of Richard Randall late of Cape Porpus,' deeded a

Cape P. town gr. of 1681-2 to Edward and Stephen Presbury of Newbury, shipwrights.

16 **RICHARD**, Dover, m. 1st Elizabeth Tozier (see Corson) who d. 16 Apr. 1704 after long illness; m. 2d 10 Apr. 1705 wid. Elizabeth (Hussey 2) Blanchard. Lists 62, 298, 358b. In 1711 he released to br. Richard Tozier the share of his (late) w. in the est. of her fa. He and this br.-in-law deeded to their sons and nephews Richard and William Randall in 1712-3. Deeded to s. Samuel in 1720. Kn. ch: **Richard**, Berwick, m. 1st 10 July 1715 Sarah -Gase-, m. 2d 18 Dec. 1718 Leah Stone who was Leah Evans in 1736 (James Evans m. -Sarah- Randall 3 Jan. 1724-5). Adm. 25 Oct. 1723 to wid. Leah, Jonathan Stone and John Thompson bondsmen. Est. div. in 1737, when, of the three ch., Richard was dead, John had not been heard from for five years and Elizabeth survived (q.c. to uncle Samuel, who had been gdn. in 1743; m. Abner Clements of Berwick and was her fa.'s only heir in 1751). **John**, Berwick, m. 22 June 1720 Mary Chick. They o.c. in Berw. ch. 22 Apr. 1725 and had ch. -Jemoses-, John, Nehemiah and Ebenezer bp. His uncle William deeded Berw. land to John jr., cordwainer, of York, in 1751. **Samuel**, Dover, m. 1st 20 Nov. 1720 Elizabeth Macfield, m. 2d in Newbury 25 May 1733 Hannah Williams. He and w. Elizabeth and their ch. Mary, Samuel and Eliphalet were bp. in Dover in 1728 and a dau. Elizabeth bn. 23 Feb. 1728-9. Of Somersworth, 1740. **William**, Durham, bp.'batchelur' 24 Dec. 1721, m. 2 Feb. 1724-5 Hannah Mason who was adm. to Ch. in 1728. A dau. Elizabeth was bp. 1724-5 and there were sons William and Mason ment. in a deed from their gr.f. Peter Mason to their fa. in 1736.

17 **WALTER**, Isles of Shoals, 24 in 1670 when he test. that he had been a servant of Nicholas Leech and William Hobby on the Isle of St. Christopher in 1665, that his masters had traded in Indian and negro slaves and that he had come to New Eng. on their ship -Speaker-. George Wallis stood bond for him in 1677. Lists 288, 306b, 307a. Clerk of the writs, 1684. His 1st w., liv. in 1685, was a dau. of George Wallis. A 2d w., Joanna, renounced adm. on his est. 28 Oct. 1692, having m. Philip Ireland(2) of Ipswich, and asked that Mr. John Wainwright of Ips. be app. adm. Ch. by 1st w: **Elizabeth**, in Mr. Wainwright's service in 1692 when she also pet. that he adm. **Eleanor,** 'a girl called Nell.' for whom Mr. W. supplied keeping, clothing and schooling, m. in Ips. 7 June 1705 Samuel Ayres of Rowley.

18 **WILMOT**, Richmond Isl., b. ab. 1620, m. Nicholas Edgecomb(2). List 21. See (6). In Bigbury, co. Devon, a Nicholas and Wil-

mot R. had ch. bp. from 1621, and at St. Andrew's, Plymouth, a John R. and Wilmot Reed were m. 10 June 1621.

**RANDOLPH, Edward,** Esq., British agent, came to New Eng. in 1676 to report on the colony of Mass. and to demand that its agents be sent to London to answer the claims of the Gorges and Mason heirs. He was in N. H. shortly bef. he sailed for England in July, 1676. As a result of his report, control of Maine and N. H. was withdrawn from Mass. Again in N. H. in 1680, he installed the new gov. See Dic. of Am. Biog., XV. 356, for biography and bibliography.

**RANKIN,** diminutive of Randolph, found in Scotland.

1 **ANDREW,** York, admitted he was the fa. of Martha Merry's unborn ch. 12 Nov. 1667, James Grant and Robert Junkins his bondsmen. He m. her 4 Dec. 1667. Liv. in 'Scotland' among his fellow-countrymen. Gr. and deed from Arthur Bragdon, 1668. Adm. to wid. Martha 15 Jan. 1677-8, the inv. showing a 60 a. homestead. She m. 2d Philip Frost(12) and it was agreed that the Rankin prop. should be div. betw. any Frost ch. they might have and her 5 Rankin ch. of whom 4 are ident: Constant. Joseph, apprent. Mar. 1679-80 for 12 yrs. to Rev. Shubael Dummer; m. in Boston 11 Oct. 1695 to Sarah Hackett of Piscataqua who m. 2d 15 Mar. 1698-9 Samuel Canney(4). **Andrew,** Boston, mariner, apprent. to Mrs. Eleanor Cutt in 1684; m. 15 Apr. 1692 Grace (Newcomb) Butler who was bur. 25 Aug. 1713; one ch., Andrew, b. 13 July 1693, d.y.; will, 10 Aug. 1699—2 Nov. 1702, left ho. in Boston to wid. and £20 to sis. Mary Rankin of Martha's Vineyard on her wedding-day; wid. Grace's will, 5 June 1705 —2 Sept. 1714. **Mary,** m. at Chilmark, Martha's Vineyard, 8 Dec. 1699, Payne Mayhew; d. 17 Feb. 1753.

2 **CONSTANT**(1), York, near 61 in 1728, 71 in 1738, in 78th yr. in 1744, 82 in 1749; m. Hannah Wittum, in 75th yr. in Apr. 1744, 80 in 1749. They liv. in the ho. of John Frost, br. of C. R.'s step-fa., whom they called uncle. In ct. 1695 for not attending meeting. List 279. Ch: **Martha,** b. 21 Nov. 1688, d. 17 Sept. 1690. **Sarah,** b. 18 Mar. 1690-1, m. 1st Adam Mock. **Andrew,** b. 12 June 1693; m. Bethia Spencer who m. 2d 6 Oct. 1727 John Cole (24); York gr. 1713-4, 1716-7; d. 20 Apr. 1724; ch. James (b. 11 Sept. 1718), Martha (b. 25 Oct. 1720), Bethia (b. 18 May 1723). **Hannah,** b. 26 June 1697, m. one Shaw, m. 2d Edmund Harrison. **James,** b. 26 May 1701; reputed fa. of two ch. of Deborah Spencer 1722-1724; m. 21 Mar. 1728-9 Priscilla Shaw (Thomas of Norton, Bristol co.); ch. rec. in York and Norton. **Martha,** b. 6 Sept. 1703.

**Mary,** b. 19 Dec. 1704, m. Benjamin Wittum. **Joseph,** b. 23 Feb. 1708-9; d. 27 Aug. 1727. **Joshua,** b. 4 Sept. 1715.

**RASER, Richard,** ment. in early Saco record, was prob. not an inhab. but that R. R. of Boston who m. Exercise Blackleech in 1660 and d. bef. 1663. List 244d.

**RASHLEIGH.** 1 **Bartholomew** (Rusley), Pemaquid, 1647. List 10.

2 **JOHN** (Rashley), Pemaquid, charged with murder of Samuel Collins, 1680. See Diamond(1).

3 **REV. THOMAS,** minister at Exeter for less than a year in 1643, coming from Gloucester, Mass., and returning to England where he preached at Bishopstoke, co. Hants. His gr. of 14 or 16 a. reverted to the town. Lists 374a, 376ab.

**Rastell,** Humphrey, Damariscove. List 8.

**Rawlins,** see Rollins.

**RAY.** 1 **Caleb,** New Dartmouth, ±35 in 1689-90, was in Kennebec region by 1682. Ensign 1684. Test. ag. Lt. Jordan in 1689-90 in Boston where he settled and became prison-keeper, 1694. Of Edgartown 1704, but d. in Boston where wid. Anna Ray renounced adm. 3 July 1721 in favor of creditors.

2 **FRANCIS,** rated, No. Ch., Portsmouth, 1717.

3 **ISAAC,** of co. Kent, Eng., m. in Portsm. 1 Dec. 1720, Elizabeth Wells, prob. she who m. 11 Aug. 1724 John Hines of co. Kent.

**RAYNES,** Raines, Rayne. Col. Banks believed that the York emigrant was from co. Somerset where at Leigh-upon-Mendip a Francis, s. of William, gent., was bp. The theory that he was of French origin (Renaud) and the ancestor of New Jersey Rainos is highly improbable.

1 **CAPT. \*FRANCIS,** York by 1646, gentleman and surgeon, a leading citizen of the town and colony. Sued by Roger Knight, 1647. For some years he liv. at Strawberry Bank, selling his ho. and land to Clement Campion bef. 1652. Still there in 1653, poss. in the ho. Richard Cutt and his wid. d. in, where he is stated to have once lived. He m. his w. Eleanor bef. 1647. Gr.j. 1647, 1653, 1654, 1655, 1657, 1659, 1673, 1681, 1686; j. 1649-50, 1650, 1650-1, 1672, 1676; selectman 1652, 1663, 1673, 1675; Deputy and com. 1664; subm. to Mass., 1652; Lt. 1654; Capt. from 1659 until he resigned in 1663; magistrate 1668-1670; O. A. 1689; prop. of Dover. Lists 24, 38, 88, 275, 277, 279. See Gattensby (1), Knight(18), Harris(27). His will, 21 Aug. 1693—15 Oct. 1706, names his w., ch. and gr.ch., his w. and s. Nathaniel exec. Ch: **Sarah,** m. bef. 1671 Joseph Cutt(4). After his death she was involved with Joseph Had-

ley(2) and d. bef. July 1675, prob. in childbirth, her fa. being in ct. with Hadley and acc. of lying and acting as midwife. **Nathaniel**. A dau., m. John Diamond(4). A dau., m. Samuel Matthews(2). **Tabitha**, m. Joseph Hodsdon(5). **Mary**, m. 1st Jonathan Mendum(1), m. 2d John Woodman.

2 **JOHN** (Rayne), being kept by Goodwife Sampson, by agreement with Portsm. selectmen, 24 Aug. 1680.

3 **JOSEPH**, Newcastle, merchant and attorney-gen. of the Prov. under Gov. Cranfield. Wit. deed, Withers to Shapleigh, 1681. Sheriff. Lists 52, 319. In 1682 he said that Mr. Mason was coming over to N. H. and a gov. with him. In jail and assaulting the jailor, 1685. Substitute attorney for Philip English in 1685-6, in Tucker v. Nichols. Wit. will of John Gale, 1687. Legatee of Capt. Barefoot (£5), 1688. See Fanning(1). A lodger at Newc., no land, w. or ch. rec. His name is more frequently Rayne than Raynes.

4 ENS. **NATHANIEL**(1), York, surgeon, ±61 (over-estimate) in 1695, 70 in 1721, ±70 in 1727, 83 in 1730-1. His w. Joanna d. 5 Apr. 1732. Selectman, 1685, 1698; O. A. 1679-80; ensign, 1696; j. 1683, 1689, 1693; gr.j. 1679, 1690 (foreman), 1693, 1694, 1695. Lists 30, 279. See Gammon. He d. in 1734. Ch: Dea. **Francis**, heir of his grandfather's entailed estate, shipwright, married in Greenland 24 Nov. 1720 Catherine Payne (15) who was liv. in 1750. Origin of his right to adm. the est. of Henry Brookings in 1729-30 is a mystery. J. 1704. He d. bef. 1750. Of his 6 ch., b. 1722-1731, Elizabeth m. her cous. Robert Raynes, Mary was unm. in 1750, Daniel was only s. and heir in 17— and m. 17 Feb. 1749-50 Jane Frost, John and Joshua d.y., and Catherine d. unm. in 1750 leaving a will, 30 Aug.—31 Dec. 1750, in which she bequeathed a silver spoon to sis. Elizabeth and gold rings to each of her ch., gold buttons to br. Daniel, Daniel's note to sis. Mary, and the rest to her mo. and exec. **John**, kn. only from his gr.fa.'s will. As his br. Nathaniel was not ment., tho living, it has been suggested that John's name was changed to Nathaniel. **Nathaniel**, shipwright, m. Elizabeth Cutts(6). Will, 29 May 1745—6 July 1747, names w. and s. Robert (m. 1st his cous. Elizabeth Raynes, m. 2d Jane Gerrish; 5 + 1 ch.), s. Francis (about to go to Louisburg; m. 13 Sept. 1742 Joan Payne who d. 28 Apr. 1752; liv. on land given him by his gr.fa. Cutts), Eleanor (m. 25 Nov. 1735 Nathan Marston), Hannah (m. as ·Joanna· 29 July 1742 William Gerrish), Lucy Cutts, Sarah and Eunice. **Nathan**, m. Elizabeth Payne(15) who d. 30 Sept. 1746. Will, 21 Aug. 1747—16 Oct. 1750, names ch. (b. 1710-1727) Joseph, Nathan, John (m. Martha Harmon[5]; 10 ch. 1742-1763), Jane, Eliza-

beth Sergeant, Samuel (resid. legatee and exec.; m. 1st 27 June 1745 Miriam Jaques, m. 2d 7 Dec. 1750 Anne Grindall). Ch. who d.y. were Philip (b. 1720-1) and Anne (b. 1727.

5 **THOMAS**. In York there are two rec. which do not belong to the local Raynes fam: John Raynes, s. of Thomas and Mary, d. 12 Feb. 1727-8, ag. 1 yr. 21 dys. Ruth Raynes, dau. of Thomas and Mary, d. 15 Feb. 1728, ag. 3 yrs. 9 mo. 23 dys. It is our opinion that these items belong to the Rines fam., the clerk writing the familiar name for the slightly different sound. This also applies to Lists 368b (Thomas and William Raynes), 369 (Thomas Raynes).

**Read**, see Reed.

**Record**, Ricord, see Cater(2).

**REDDING**, Reading, a parish in co. Bucks.
1 **THOMAS**, in 1637 a soldier ag. the Pequots from Plymouth, where he m. 20 July 1639 Eleanor (Ellen) Pennoyer, ±55 in 1678, sis. of Mr. Wm. Pennoyer, cit. and cloth-worker of London, who remem. her and her ch. in his will in 1670. Of Scituate in 1644 but rem. only a yr. or less. First rec. in Saco 1653 (subm. to Mass. and took O. A.), but may have arr. earlier. Kittery gr. 1653. In 1654 he sold his homestead of 52 a. on E. side of Saco river to Wm. Carkeet and bot 3 islands at Cape Porpus, living on the 'great island' (±50 a.) and managing a fishing trade. One of his sons disappeared in 1655, but, after he had acc. Thos. Warrener of murder, the boy was found. Soon departed for Casco Bay where he owned 200 a. at No. Yarmouth (Redding's creek and Wescustogo river). He also liv. for a time at Mere Pt. under Mr. Purchase, and may poss. have owned lands there and on Jewell's Isl. His w. was admonished for slandering her neighbor Anne Lane in 1666. See Bustion. Lists 214, 243ab, 252. He d. about 1673, when the will. sold to James Andrews. When Philip's war broke out wid. Redding's house was attacked and burned and two of her sons murdered. She fled to Salem and in 1677 pet. the Gen. Ct. for aid, asking, quite naturally, that her br.'s legacy for 'instructing these Heathen' who had killed her sons be diverted to her. She and her dau. Rebecca were convicted of 'being abroad at night' in 1680 and Rebecca was advised to seek some good service. She raised money by mortgaging the No. Yarm. prop. to Mrs. Mary Higginson in 1680. By 1682 she was in Boston where she was receiving aid as late as 1686. Ch: a son, ag. 5 when he was left at Scituate in 1645 by his fa. who was charged with it in ct. Appren. to Gowen White. **Joseph**. Inv. 30 June 1673 taken at Falm. by John Munjoy, personal prop. in hands of John Inger-

soll. List 86. **Ruth,** m. Joseph Donnell(3). The Portsm. conveyancer who wrote deeds for her ch. in 1745, doubtless being familiar with Thaddeus Riddan and his Portsm. desc., called Mrs. Donnell's fa. -Thaddeus- Redding in error. **Rebecca,** m. John Taylor, Boston ship-carpenter, by 1681 (ct.). **John,** fisherman, ±30 in 1683, ±60 in 1713-4, prob. he who m. at Sandwich 22 Oct. 1676 Mary Basset and had dau. Eleanor b. there 22 Feb. 1677. Of Weymouth, 1678. Of Wells by 1689-90 when he appr. Philip Hatch's est. and was sued by Robert Stewart. Gave bonds to keep peace with Wm. Hilton, 1691. Mov. to Ipswich by 1698, when he had a 2d w. Jane, and finally to Gloucester, where he d. 17 Nov. 1716, ag. 62. The wid. m. 14 Oct. 1718 Richard Babson. He q.c. the Cape Porpus islands and the No. Yarm. prop. in 1715 and 1716. Ch. **Elias?,** debtor to est. of George Munjoy in 1685, prob. error for -Ellen-, the wid. of (1). **Robert,** Casco Bay wit. 1674-5, 1675, prob. one of the two sons k. by Ind. in 1677. The other **son.** And a plausible guess would be that Eleanor, w. of John Lewis(8), k. by Ind. in 1677, was a dau.

2 **RICHARD,** early settler on Damariscove Isl., m. Mary Brown(15). Wit. will of Mary Lux in 1664. Pemaquid commissioner in 1680. Lists 16, 41. Only surv. ch. in 1732 was **Margaret,** w. of Joseph Houghton, Milton.

## REDFORD.

1 **MR. ABRAHAM,** taxed in Dover 1650. List 354c. See Radver.

2 **HON. WILLIAM,** Portsmouth, ±28 in 1694, 30 in 1696, succeeded Thomas Davis as Sec. of the Prov. of N. H. in 1693. Coroner 1694, 1695, 1696; Clerk of Courts; Registrar of Probate 1693-1697; Registrar of Deeds 1695-1697; notary-public 1696; captain of militia; seated in the meeting-ho. in 1693 in seat where Capt. Fryer had sat. Lists 67, 318b, 336b, 68. He m. 1st Sarah (Frost 2) Shipway who d. 16 May 1695, ag. 29; m. 2d Elizabeth Dew, who, after his death in 1697, had an ale-ho. lic. until she m. 10 July 1701 Richard Wibird. Lists 330de, 335a. Ch. by 1st w., appar. brot up with affection by step-mo. and her second husb: **Hannah,** m. 1st 30 Apr. 1712 John Wainwright, m. 2d Matthew Bradford.

## REDMAN, found in Yorkshire and the northern counties.

1 ***JOHN,** Hampton, blacksmith, 43 in 1658, ±44 in 1661-2, mortg. his Hamp. ho. in Dec. 1641 having that summer built a ho. on Dover Neck on land which he did not own, with consequent trouble. The Dover land was gr. to him in 1642 and he was 'of Dover'

in 1647, but soon back at Hampt. He m. 1st Margaret Knight(16) who d. 30 May 1658, m. 2d wid. Sabina (see Locke 3½) Marston who d. 10 Nov. 1689. Freeman's oath at Salisbury, 1649. See Giles(7). Gr.j. 1684; j. 1679, 1694; selectman 1652, 1656, 1666, 1693; Rep. 1693, 1696. Again mtg. his ho. to Samuel Dudley in 1651. Sold to Henry Sayward 50 a. which Thomas Gorges had gr. to J. R.'s w. Margaret Knight, in 1671. Sold his Dover land to Richard Waldron in 1673. Deeded to s. John in 1680. He d. 16 Feb. 1700 ag. ±85. Lists 49, 52, 55ab, 302b, 392bc, 393ab(2), 396, 398, 399b; 'Goody,' 393a. Kn. ch. by 1st w: **John. Mary,** b. 15 Dec. 1649, m. Leonard Weeks. **Joseph,** b. 20 Apr. 1651, presum. d.y. **Samuel,** b. 12 Apr. 1658, presumably d.y.

2 ***JOHN**(1), Hamp., 66 in 1711, ±68 in 1713, ±70 in 1713, near 80 in 1722-3, m. 27 Mar. 1666 Martha Cass(2) who was ±47 in 1698. His fa. deeded to him in consid. of his marriage in 1666 and his gr.fa. Knight gave him 7 a. in Hampt. in 1667. J. 1684, 1692; selectman 1699, 1703, 1709; Rep. 1697, 1722-1726. Poss. it was his w. and not his dau. Martha who presented William Matoon for bapt. 2 Aug. 1702 'as her own,' which sounds more like adoption than illegitimacy. Lists 52, 392b, 396, 399ab. Ch: **Maria,** b. 12 Nov. 1669, m. Robert Mason(18). **John,** b. 7 Oct. 1672. **Martha,** b. 23 Dec. 1674. **Margaret,** m. 24 Sept. 1702 William Graves(8). **Joseph,** b. 28 Dec. 1678, d. 23 Apr. 1679. **Abial,** b. 17 May 1681, m. 1st James Gordon (1), m. 2d Moses Kimming(2). **Mary,** b. 3 June 1686, m. 11 Mar. 1714 James Moulton (1).

3 **JOHN**(2), Hamp., m. 12 Nov. 1696 Joanna Bickford(12) who m. 2d Samuel Healy(2). Joined Hamp. Falls Ch. 26 Feb. 1709-10. He d. Feb. 1718. Ch: **Joseph,** b. 6 Nov. 1697, m. 11 May 1727 Hannah Rollins, d. 4 June 1758. Ch. **John,** b. 20 Mar. 1701, m. 7 Feb. 1728 Sarah Godfrey. Ch. **Martha,** bp. with next 8 Mar. 1712, m. John Johnson(14). **Anna.**

**REDWOOD, Nicholas,** of Dartmouth, co. Devon, merchant, came to Isles of Shoals as agent for John Frederick & Co. of London to sell a fishing-plant to John Pennewell of Plymouth, co. Devon, 9 Dec. 1663, the deed ack. bef. Brian Pendleton.

**REED,** Read, Reid, from red, indicating the blonde complexion. Became 19th commonest name in N. E.

1 **GILES,** Saco, m. 10 Nov. 167- Judith Mayer(3) and both disappear.

2 ***CAPT. HUGH,** Newcastle, bot land from Daniel and Sarah Jones in 1710. Sold to Barnaby Crucy, 1716. Rep. from 1717 to 1720 when he and his family had gone to

Canso or Newfoundland without permission of the House and Newc. was ordered to choose ano. rep. His 1st w. Sarah (see Jones 2) depos. in 1734-5, ag. ±70, about the Fox-well-Robinson fam. He m. 2d Margaret Robinson(3), to whom he, gentleman, left all in his will, 15 Apr. 1747. Her will, tailoress, 27 Sept.—22 Oct. 1760, remembers her cous. Abigail Tarleton, Samuel Jones, Mary Jones, Elizabeth Branscomb, Lucretia Neale and Margaret Clark.

3 **JOHN**, Wells, wit. in 1661; had land in 1662; overseer of John West's will in 1663, Mary Reed, presum. his w., being a beneficiary. Wit. Morgan Howell's will, 1666. Gr.j. 1670; j. 1669. List 269b. The Prov. pd. him for sheltering a poor lame man in 1669. His 'former land' several times ment. in deeds. Disappears from Wells as (4), also with w. Mary, appears in Kittery, but poss. not the same.

4 **JOHN**, a Scot, had a Kittery gr. of 50 a. in 1673, sold by his s. John, of Lyme, to John Smith in 1713. Micum McIntire in 1705 stated that he had sold to J. R., 'his countryman,' 50 a. above Salmon Falls but it was not fully paid for so he gave Reed no deed. Reed cleared, fenced and liv. on this land until he was k. by Ind. there 18 Mar. 1689-90, whereupon his s. John leased it to one Stone and finally sold it to John Wentworth in 1714. A title from McIntire to Philip Hubbard was in conflict. Lists 60, 298. His w. Mary was captured when he was k., and redeemed, going to Braintree (there mistakenly said to have been captured at Casco) where she d. 16 May 1691. Ch. b. in Kittery: **Deliverance**, b. 26 Aug. 1670. **John**, b. 11 Apr. 1674. Captured with his mo., returned in 1695 and liv. at Lyme, Conn., his fa.'s only s. and h. Poss. he was the J. R. who depos. in 1721 ab. Kittery matters of 24-30 yrs. past. If so he may have been the fa. of Jacob, s. of John Reed, b. in Kit. 30 Sept. 1697 (supposedly the Jacob R. who m., int. 11 Mar. 1720-1, Agnes or Annis Tenney, was a Falmouth shipwright in 1735 and taken prisoner by Ind. in Gorham in 1745). **Elizabeth**, b. 4 Sept. 1677.

5 **JOHN**, Newcastle and Portsm., prob. several of them. J. R., servant of Thomas Walford, 1666. J. R., Strawberry Bk., took O. A. in 1685, taxed in 1688, rated in 1690, wit. in 1694. J. R., Portsm., hanged himself to a tree and was buried at the cross-roads in 1716.

6 **JOHN** and **SUSANNA** Reed wit. deed, Wm. Haines of Spurwink to Geo. Felt, and J. R. wit. Margery Haines to Felt, 1675.

7 **JOSEPH**, Newcastle, on bond of Mark Round, 1684. Taxed 1688. Lists 52, 315-abc. Wages were due him for work on Fort Wm. and Mary in 1693 and he served under Capt. Shadrach Walton in 1694. Wit., 1695.

8 **OBADIAH**, Boston, s. of Esdras, by purchase and inheritance from his w. Elizabeth (Broughton 4) became absentee owner of 450 a. in Wells and Kittery.

9 **ROBERT**, arrived in Boston by 1635 and came to Exeter by 1639 when he signed the combination. In Ex. between 1643 and 1645, taking O. A. there in 1644, but back in Boston in 1646. Thereafter he seems to have alternated between his houses in Bos. and Hampton. Lists 43, 373, 376a. He was lost on a voyage from Hamp. to Bos. 20 Oct. 1657. His 1st w. Hannah d. 24 June 1655. His wid. Susanna m. John Presson. Adm. on his est. gr. to Robert Smith of Bos. Ch: **Hannah**, m. 11 Jan. 1661 John Souther. **Mary**, had a dau. Deborah, b. 4 Sept. 1668 by Edward Naylor, coming to Hamp. to lie in at her sis. Hannah's. She was sometimes called Mary Moore(13). **Rebecca**, bp. 29 Sept. 1646. **Deborah**, bp. 28 Jan. 1648-9. **Sarah**, bp. 1 Sept. 1650. **Samuel**, bp. 3 Apr. 1653, d. 31 Mar. 1654. **Samuel**, b. 28 Feb. 1654.

10 **ROBERT**, schoolmaster at Kittery, was k. by Ind. at Spruce Creek in 1708. List 96.

11 **SARAH**, Portsm., wit. a Pickering mtge. in 1683, was assaulted by Richard Webber in 1684, and m. 2 Dec. 1686 Joshua Towle.

12 **STEPHEN**, Newcastle, working for Mr. John Bray in 1675-6, accidentally drowned (inq. 7 June 1679). List 313c.

13 **THOMAS**, Stratham, ±62 in 1701 when he depos. about matters 38 yrs. past. Wit. bill of Thomas Nock to Walter Barefoot in 1662. Before Philip's war he sold land in Greenland to get money for voyage to England. Back by 1680 when he wit. bond of Elias Critchet to Richard Waldron. Lists 52, 57(2), 62, 388. He had a ho. in Exeter in 1704, and he or his s. paid a minister's rate there in 1714. With w. Elizabeth he disposed of his prop., with life reservation, to s. Thomas and dau. **Elizabeth**, w. of Alexander Kenniston(1), in 1709. He d. bef. 1719 when his wid. signed a deed with his son. **Thomas**, Stratham, m. in Greenland 31 Nov. 1712 Rebecca Stacy. They were asso. with the So. Ch. in Portsm. in 1728 and had ch. bp: Thomas, b. 31 Aug. 1713; Samuel, b. 8 Sept. 1715; Rebecca, b. 17 Jan. 1717; Rachel, b. 22 May 1720; Love, b. 27 Oct. 1722; Solomon, b. 28 Feb. 1725; Love, b. 1 Sept. 1727; Mark, b. 3 Aug. 1730. One Rebecca m. in Portsm. 27 Nov. 1737 Joseph Seavey.

14 **THOMAS**, abandoned his w. and two ch. in Braintree and got into trouble with Elizabeth Brooks(2). Calling himself 'of London,' he m. her in Portsm. 4 Aug. 1716, and was given twenty-five lashes for his cumulative offenses in Jan. 1716-7. They continued to live together at Cape Neddick,

where a s. **John** was b. 23 Oct. 1716 and liv. to maturity and an inglorious end, dying in a drunken orgy at a ship-wreck on the York shore.

**Reekes,** Mr. Steven, mariner, wit. the deliv. of the Oldham and Vines patent at Saco (Biddeford) in 1630. Prob. he was a trans-Atlantic captain.

**REEVES.** 1 **Garrett,** sued by Capt. John Davis for debt and by Samuel Austin for breach of contract in York ct. in 1667, but was supposed to be out of the country.

2 **WILLIAM,** Kittery, ±38 in 1653 and 1654, was in John Treworgy's crew on the -Bachelor- 16 or 17 yrs. before. One Wm. Reeves, ag. 22, came on the -Elizabeth and Anne- in 1635. The same, or another, was bef. the Gen. Ct. in 1638 and Essex Co. ct. in 1640.

**REMICK,** not found in England and prob. of Teutonic origin.

1 **CHRISTIAN,** Kittery, ±67 in 1698-9, ±80 in 1718, settled on Eliot neck where he had a town gr. of 52 a. in 1651, six later gr. being recorded. Subm. to Mass. 1652. Gr.j. 1666, 1667, 1672, 1687, 1695; j. 1695, 1702. See Green(5). Selectman 1670-1673; treasurer. Lists 30, 31, 282, 283, 296, 297, 298. Adm. est. of Thomas Turner, 1684. Sued Samuel Spinney, 1697-1699. His w. Hannah was liv. in 1703 and he was still liv. in 1718. Ch: **Hannah,** b. 25 Apr. 1656, m. 1st John Thompson, m. 2d Richard Gowell. **Mary,** b. 7 Aug. 1658, m. Peter Dixon(2). **Jacob,** b. 23 Nov. 1660. **Sarah,** b. 16 July 1663, m. 1st John Green(15), m. 2d Barnabas Wixam. **Isaac,** b. 20 July 1665. Town gr. 1682, 1694. Constable 1693; gr.j. 1693-4, 1695-6. His fa. deeded him 30 a. and a ho. in 1686, and 10 a. in 1694. He also bot 20 a. from his fa. Sued by John Woodman for assault, 1695. List 298. Gr.j. 1694, 1696; constable 1692-3. Bef. 1698 he mov. to So. Carolina, selling his Kit. lands 2 May 1698. Adm. on his est. gr. at Charleston to his wid. Elizabeth (±23 in 1695), 26 Oct. 1700. Prob. ch: Isaac, planter, with w. Mary, liv. near Charleston in 1719. Poss. ch: Abraham, shoemaker, of Dover and Portsm. 1712-1713. **Abraham,** Eastham, b. 9 June 1667, m. Elizabeth Freeman who m. 2d in Eastham 7 July 1712 Joseph Myrick. Lists 298, 330de. 5 ch. **Martha,** b. 20 Feb. 1669, prob. m. Daniel Cole of Eastham and d. s.p. This marriage seems the only poss. explanation of the fact that Daniel Cole in his will (1735) called Martha (Remick) Knowles, dau. of Abraham Remick, cousin. **Joshua,** b. 24 July 1672. **Lydia,** b. 8 Feb. 1676, m. Thomas Cole(32).

2 **JACOB**(1), Kittery, shipbuilder, ±37 in 1698-9, 68 in 1729, had w. Lydia by 1684 and a 2d w. Mary by 1692. In 1695 gossip linking his name with that of the notorious Alice (Hanscom) Metherill, who was about to have a ch., his w. Mary, furiously jealous, attacked Alice in the Hanscom ho., in spite of Jacob's attempts to restrain her. The depos. in the resulting case give much local information. Gr.j. 1690-1, 1696, 1697, 1714; j. 1696; selectman 1706, 1708, 1709, 1713; treasurer 1722-1727. Will, 22 May 1739—26 July 1745. Ch. by 1st w: **Stephen,** b. 16 Jan. 1684, liv. in 1739. **Jacob,** b. 6 Mar. 1686-7, m. 1st 4 Jan. 1710 Rebecca Soper, m. 2d in Dover 18 Dec. 1724 wid. Mary Hobbs(4), m. 3d 9 Apr. 1752 Deborah (Keene 2) Barter. 7 ch. By 2d w: **John,** b. 7 Oct. 1692, m. 1st in Portsm. 27 July 1713 Elizabeth Ham(5), m. 2d 16 Sept. 1722 Mary Wilson. 2 + 3 ch. **Samuel,** b. 20 May 1694, denied acc. of Lydia Wixam of Eastham in 1716; m. 22 Oct. 1717 Elizabeth Mason. Will, 7 July 1755—26 Aug. 1765, leaves all to wid. and after her death to neph. Samuel. **Lydia,** b. 9 June 1696, m. William Phillips(24). **Tabitha,** b. 27 Dec. 1698, d.y. **James,** b. 23 Jan. 1701, m. in Charlestown int. 5 Sept. 1729 Abigail Benjamin. **Mary,** b. 25 Feb. 1703, m. 19 Feb. 1725 Capt. Isaac Johnson. **Sarah,** b. 21 Mar. 1705-6, m. Thomas Morgrage. **Timothy,** b. 9 Apr. 1708, m. in Newbury 18 Dec. 1729 Rachel Brown. 6 ch. **Elizabeth,** b. Aug. 1710, m. Amos Paul. Maj. **Nathaniel,** b. 16 Dec. 1712, m. 21 May 1741 Jane Libby. Will, 7 Dec. 1782—30 July 1783. 8 ch. **Joseph,** b. 7 Oct. 1715, d. bef. 1739. **Hannah,** shopkeeper in Portsm., b. c. 1717. Will, 4 Nov. 1767—9 Feb. 1768, of much genealogical interest.

3 **JOSHUA**(1), Kittery, ±23 in 1695, had the homestead, m. 1st at Amesbury 21 Dec. 1693 Ann Lancaster, m. 2d Sept. 1716 Mary Hepworth. Shortly after his 1st marriage, in July 1694, he was acc. of being the fa. of a ch. by Sarah Lydston and judged guilty, supporting this dau. thereafter. Gr.j. 1701, 1715; constable 1696-7. Lists 297, 298. Had town gr. 1694, 1701. Adm. to So. Ch., Portsmouth, 1720. His ch. ment. in will of their gr.fa. Lancaster. Adm. to wid. Mary, Apr. 1738. Ch. by 1st w: **Hannah,** b. 10 Mar. 1694-5, m. 1st Thomas Palmer, m. 2d Nathan Adams(19). **Sarah,** b. 27 Aug. 1696, m. in Greenland 25 Oct. 1720 James Locke(2). **Joshua,** b. 4 Sept. 1698, m. int. 29 Apr. 1729 Dorcas Hill(10). Will, 18 June—16 Oct. 1754. 6 ch. **Joseph,** b. 10 Nov. 1700, d.y. **Anne,** b. 19 Oct. 1702, m. John Coterel. **Ichabod,** b. 27 July 1704, m. 21 Nov. 1731 Abigail Scriggins who prob. m. 2d, int. 18 Dec. 1742, Robert Cole. **Isaac,** b. 14 Feb. 1705-6, m. 1st 26 Sept. 1726 Anne Allen, m. 2d 7 June 1753 Mary (Dixon) Pettegrew. 6 + 2 ch. **Dorcas,** m. 1st Joseph Pitman(13), m. 2d Nathaniel Fernald. **Lydia,** m. int. 15

July 1731 John Worster. Poss. by 2d w: **Mary**, bp. 28 Aug. 1720, d.y.

**Rencher**, Daniel, wit. Robin Hood's deed to Henry Curtis(1) in 1666. Printed -Benether- from John Pickering's copy, 1786.

**Rew**, Matthew, was late of Kennebec River, now of Staten Isl., in 1683 when he deeded 40 + 10 a. at Kennebec, bot of Thomas Webber, to Richard Pateshall of Boston.

**REYNOLDS**, Renalds, Rennals. Reynold an ancient given name, the patronymic being common, partic. in Cornwall.

1 **JOB**(6), appar. liv. in Portsmouth bef. 1679-80, when his tax was abated, and then moved to Cape Elizabeth where he was liv. in 1689, his chimney being a landmark after the Ind. wars. Lists 66, 313a, 228c. He m. Sarah Crawford(5), a Portsm. wid. in 1692, when as only heir of her fa. she deeded to her br. John Willey. In 1696 the Newcastle rec. state that the wid. of Job Renouls had several ch. and did not put them out as apprentices. They are ident. by q.c. deeds to their gr.fa.'s land: **Job**, Oyster River, where he bot 60 a. from Joseph Davis in 1713 and 30 a. from Naphtali Kincaid in 1719. Town gr. 1733-4. List 368b(2). Liv. in 1758 but d. bef. May 1763. He m. wid. **Hannah** (Huckins) Chesley who q.c. her right in her gt.gr.fa. Burnham's est. in 1747. Ch. **Mary**, m. James Langley(3). **John**, Oyster River, 38 in 1734, m. 23 Dec. 1718 Hannah Clark(3?). Lists 368b, 369. Will, 20 June 1756, names her, sons John, Abraham, William, Joseph (exec.), Stephen, Solomon, Winthrop, daus. Elizabeth Snell, Sarah Bunker, Deliverance, and (relationsh. not stated) Hannah and Elizabeth Willey. Adm. c.t.a. in 1767, to Joseph's wid. Lydia.

2 **DR. JOHN**, 'the old doctor,' an early arrival at Piscataqua. Wit. deed, Lander to Mills, 1639; bail in Str. Bk. ct., 1643; prob. Portsm. selectman, 1646; adm. est. of John White, 1646. With Rice Thomas, he sued Geo. Small and Richard Cummings in 1647. In 1647 he was liv. on Hog Isl., Isles of Shoals, and, contrary to law, had his wife, goats and hogs with him. He was allowed to keep the former, but the latter had to be sent to the mainland as they ate drying fish and defiled the springs. Constable there (or a s. of the same name?), 1647. With John Pickering, he arbitrated betw. Roger Knight and Francis Raynes, 1647. He and his family, of whom no knowledge, were abs. from meet., 1648. Cross actions with John Miles, 1649-50. Gr.j. 1646-7. Lists 41, 323, 324. Sued by Wm. Wormwood in 1650 for detaining goats and a sow, and lost, and his surety, Alexander Jones, had to pay judg., being repaid out of the Dr.'s goods left in Geo.

Walton's hands. Appar. he had gone away, prob. back to Eng.

3 **NATHANIEL**, sued Ephraim Lynn(1) for debt in 1660.

4 **CAPT. NICHOLAS**, Esq., Kennebec, 'the first Justice made in these parts,' had a deed from the Ind., Robin Hood, which covered land from the Kennebec river to Casco bay, in 1661. Took O. A. and oath as J. P. at Arrowsic, 1665. Lists 161, 191. Liv. in 1671 when he wit. deed of Mary Parker(13) to her s. Thomas. 'The late Capt. Reynolds, dec.' in 1696. By w. Dorothy he had: **Rebecca**, m. John Allen(6). **Seaborn**, adopted by Richard and Margaret Tucker, m. Nicholas Hodge(7).

5 **OWEN** (Runnals), Exeter by 1688 as he depos. in 1713-4 ab. matters 26 yrs. past. Gave note to Henry Williams, whose w. Christian sued on it, 24 Feb. 1700-1. Either he or his s. was member of an Exeter scouting-party in 1712. List 388. By unkn. w: **Owen**, Stratham, d. s.p. List 388. Adm. to br. Thomas 30 Sept. 1752. Div. to br. Thomas, sis. Mary and heirs of bros. Robert and John in 1755. **Judith**, in ct. for usual reason 16 Oct. 1713; d. 17 Nov. 1747, s.p. (legal). **Mary**, Stratham, spinner, had a male ch. which d. 6 June 1720, Mr. Jacob Trask its fa. Will, 15 Jan. 1755—29 Oct. 1760, made Judith, dau. of her br. Robert, sole legatee. **Robert**, of Chester 1728-1749, m. 21 Aug. 1730 Love Clifford, d. bef. 1755 leav. dau. Judith and prob. other ch. **John**, d. bef. 1755 leav. heirs. **Thomas**, ±57 in 1760, Stratham bef. and Deerfield after 1761; will, 27 Jan. 1766, names w. Elizabeth (exec.) and sons Owen, Thomas, Samuel, John.

6 **WILLIAM**, Cape Porpus, first at Plymouth where he had land on Duxbury side in 1637 and m. 30 Aug. 1638 Alice Kitson. At Kennebec with Howland in 1634 (see Hocking). In Cape Porpus he had a 200 a. gr. from Cleeve in 1654, bot Peter Turbat's ho. and 200 a. on the E. side of the Kennebunk riv. in 1657 and kept the ferry, being lic. as late as 1673. O. A. 1653. Lists 22, 24, 251, 252, 254, 255. In 1675 he settled his whole prop. on his s. John in return for life support for his aged parents, giving money to his sons William and Job bef. signing the deed. Ch: **William. Job. John**, ±30 in 1681, sold his fa.'s original 100 a. plantation(?) to Peter Randall in 1684. List 259. Appointed ferryman, 1687. He d. s.p. and prob. unm., and certainly intestate. By law his heirs were his nephews and nieces, and a series of deeds beginning in 1718 give us the names of 8 of them, but the same deeds leave us in hopeless confusion as to the number of William Reynolds' gr.ch. and the parentage of some of them. Job Reynolds (1 jr.) and his sis. Mary Langley q.c. their right

to Thos. Perkins in 1718. John Reynolds(1) q.c. to Stephen Harding in 1720. Samuel Reynolds(7) q.c. to Perkins in 1720. Perkins and Harding in 1721 proceeded to divide the whole 200 a. (specifically the Cleeve gr.), as if they had bot up all claims, thru arbitrators who awarded 1/15 to Harding and 14/15 to Perkins. From this it would seem that John Reynolds had conv. 1/15. But how could Job, Mary and Samuel conv. 14/15? In 1722 arbitrators are again at work, but this time 400 a. are mentioned (200 from Cleeve, 200 from Turbat). To add to the confusion Alice Buss and Sarah Blanchard appear in 1722, declare themselves nieces of John Reynolds and conv. 1/6 to Harding, and in 1725 Hope Demeritt and William Wormwood, niece and nephew, q.c. to Harding. Whereupon in 1726 Perkins and Harding divide all over again by exchanging deeds, but without disclosing what proportion of the land each claimed that he owned. Into the problem come the chance of unrec. deeds, the poss. that the arbitrators considered that they were dealing with Wm. Reynolds' heirs and not John's, involving a double share for his eldest son. A dau., mo. of Alice Buss and Sarah Blanchard. If Sarah Head was a maiden when she m. Richard Blanchard in 1719, this dau. was Sarah, 2d w. of Arthur Head(2). If Sarah was a wid. Head, her paternity is unkn. A dau., m. a Wormwood. And very prob. Hope, m. 1st in Saco in 1664 Thomas Sanders, app. m. 2d John Cleg.

7 WILLIAM(6), fisherman, prob. of age in 1663 when his fa. was sr. He had (by gr. from Cleeve?) 200 a. next his fa. which he mtg. to Francis Johnson in 1667 and never redeemed. He and Peter Turbat gave joint and several notes to John Cutt in 1668. Cutting wood at Spruce Creek with his br. John and John Turbat in 1676. After Philip's war he settled in Pemaquid (List 124). By an unkn. w. he had at least one ch: Samuel, Bradford, became adm. of the est. of his gr.fa. and his uncle John in 1721, giving a p/a to Thomas Perkins of Portsm. to manage his affairs. He had q.c. his rights in his gr.fa.'s est. to Perkins 15 July 1720. He m. Abigail Middleton; 9 ch. b. 1703-1726. Will, 5 Mar. 1744-5—25 Nov. 1745, ment. 'the lands that may fall to me in the Eastern parts, by my Grandfather or Father Runels,' his w. Abigail, sons Stephen, Samuel, Job, Ebenezer, dau. Sarah Lakeman and gr.s. William Atwood (s. of dec'd dau. Abigail).

## REYNOR.

REV. JOHN, from Gildersome, par. of Batley, co. York; A. B., Magdalen Coll., Cambridge, 1625; came to Plymouth ab. 1636 and was chosen teacher. Freeman 1637-8. Ab. 1655 he was called to be pastor at Dover and accepted. Lists 311c, 328, 356eg. His 1st w. was a Boyce, one of the co-heiresses of her br. He m. 2d Frances Clarke who had been a serv. in the ho. of Rev. John Wilson of Boston and was dism. to Plym. Ch. in 1642. He d. 21 Apr. 1669, and his will, made two days bef. his death, was prob. 30 June 1669. It made very careful provision for his w. and her ch. and stated that his ch. by his 1st w. had already been taken care of. They did not agree, however, and in 1678 Jachin Reynor and his br.-in-law Job Lane entered petitions stating that Boyce prop., entailed on Jachin as heir male, and prop. coming to them by will from the Boyces thru the death of their mo., had been enjoyed by their fa. until his death and was now withheld from them. Quite modestly they asked merely to share with their fa.'s second fam. Ch. by 1st w: Jachin (Joachim?), Rowley by 1651, m. 12 Nov. 1662 Elizabeth Dennison of Charlestown. Will 1708. 6 ch. Hannah, m. Sept. 1660 Job Lane of Malden. By 2d w: Rev. John, H. C. 1663, preached at Mendon ab. 1669 and later studied with and assisted his fa., being ordained 12 July 1671; m. Judith Quincy, dau. of Edmund Q. of Braintree (his mo., Mrs. Reynor, called Mr. Quincy -brother-, a relationship sometimes assumed by persons whose children had married); d. at Braintree 21 Dec. 1676, ag. 33. Adm. (c.t.a.?) gr. to his mo. 31 Oct. 1677, the exec. having declined to serve, Lt. Peter Coffin being assoc. with her as adm. 1 Apr. 1680. Elizabeth, d. unm. Dorothy, m. Capt. Job Alcock (1) and d. s.p. Abigail, m. 1st John Broughton(2), m. 2d Thomas Kendall of Woburn. Her ch. and those of her sis. Judith were the eventual heirs of her fa., br., and sis. Mrs. Alcock. Judith, wit. will of Henry Tibbetts, prob. 1676; m. 1st Rev. Jabez Fox(2), m. 2d Col. Jonathan Tyng. She, or ano. of the sisters, may have been the dau. b. 26 Dec. 1647. Joseph, b. 15 Aug. 1650, d. 3 Nov. 1652.

RHODES, found in Yorkshire and Lancashire, thought to be a contraction of Roadhouse.

1 JOHN. Two of them, Lists 3, 269b.

2 THOMAS, Kittery, ±33 in 1680, joiner, bot with £30 borrowed from James Chadburne on a note on the previous day, land in Eliot 2 Feb. 1680-1. He m. ab. 1679 Mary Thompson, who was bp., a wid., 1 June 1712. In 1680 he depos. ab. Kit. happenings of 1676. With Wm. Furbush he bot goods from Joseph Rayne in 1681, made joint note with Furbush in 1683, was sued by Rayne in 1684 and escaped from the sheriff's custody. See Johnson(30). Lists 290, 298(2). In 1704 he had suffered losses from Ind. attack. He mtg. 55 a. at Thompson's Pt. to Joseph Smith in 1707, it being redeemed by his s.-in-

law Shorey in 1712. He d. after 1710, when a writ was issued ag. T. R. sr., and bef. 1712. Adm. 1 Mar. 1719-20 to Shorey. The wid. d. 1 Apr. 1738. Six ch. surv. him out of: **Anne**, b. 19 Apr. 1680. **Mary**, b. 22 Sept. 1682, m. 28 Apr. 1702 Samuel Shorey. **Jacob**, b. 22 Feb. 1683, m. 7 Sept. 1704 Eleanor Brawn(2), d. within one mo. after his father. Ch: Mary, m. Samuel Place of Newington; Thomas, York, m. 1st int. 26 June 1736 Elizabeth (Grover 3) Hammons who d. 27 Nov. 1738, m. 2d int. 13 Nov. 1746 Mary (Pearce) Moody, 2 + 2 ch. **Thomas**, the fa. being sr. in 1710. **Charity**, b. 8 or 28 Nov. 1687. **Miles**, b. 28 Jan. 1689, m. 16 Feb. 1709 Patience Donnell (ct. Jan. 1710-1) who m. 2d 25 May 1714 Ichabod Jellison. He d. bef. his fa., leav. ch. Charity (m. 1st at Greenland 28 May 1729 George Cross, m. 2d 14 May 1739 John Grover) and Miles who m. Mary Huff (3) and was a fisherman in Arundel 1738 and of Sheepscot 1738-9. **Eleanor**, b. 8 May 1693, m. Samuel Pike(12). **John**, b. 28 Nov. 1697. One John was taxed in Portsm. in 1719.

3 **WALTER**, wit. Thos. Hinkson's will in Portsmouth, 1664. Poss. that Dr. Roads who was in ct. in 1665 for liv. in a suspicious manner in John White's ho. in Kittery. At the same session White's dau. Mary was acc. of having a bastard. He left Kit. and may have been the W. R. in Providence in 1668 and the Dr. R. killed by Mohawks in the wilds of central N. Y. in 1676.

**RICE**, from the Welsh given-name Rhys. Became 37th commonest name in N. E.

1 **HENRY**, Dover, had a town gr. 19 Mar. 1693-4. He m. wid. Jane Jackson(22). Wit. Huckins deed, 1698. Deeded in 1702 to Joseph Meader, who gave him a general receipt. Will, 'aged,' 31 Dec. 1711—13 June 1712, left entire est. (goods only) to Elizabeth Chesley(1) and named as exec. her mo. Deliverance Chesley, who relinq. in favor of James Jackson, step-s. of the decd. Lists 57, 94.

2 **JOHN**, Saco, fisherman. The town contracted with him 14 July 1662 for use of his ho. (bot from Wm. Tharell) for the minister. Sued by Pheasant Eastwick, 1663-4. Sued for debt by Isaac Walker in 1666, Rich. Hitchcock acting as his attny. Appr. a boat in Wm. Scadlock's est. in 1667. Wit. John Jackson's p/a to Giles Barge, 1671. Adm. on his prop., 'whether it be in the hands of Rich. Randall or others,' to Samuel Wheelwright, County Treas., 4 Apr. 1676. Lists 79, 244d.

3 **RICHARD**(4), Kittery, called gent. in 1711, m. 1st one Anne bef. 1721 when he was Joanna Pope's bondsman and Anne R. wit. the bond. He and br. Daniel bondsm. for Benoni Knight in 1721. He m. 2d 5 Sept. 1726 Mary (Pope) Rogers. His will, 4 Apr. 1752—12 Aug. 1754, left prop. to s. **Samuel** and dau. **Anne**, w. of Jonathan Hammond.

4 **THOMAS**, Kittery, seaman and shipwright, ±61 in 1702 when he depos. that he came to this country ab. 29 yrs. ago (±1673). He hired himself to Thomas Withers and m. his master's dau. Mary bef. 22 July 1675 when Withers deeded to them in consid. of their marriage, the deed not to take effect until his death. This took place in 1679, and in 1690 Wm. Haines test. that T. R. earned his land by work before he got it and was 'wont to signify spleen and rancor' ag. old Mr. Withers. He began going to sea on Mr. John Cutt's bark in 1679. Gr.j. 1690, 1691, 1692; j. 1690. See Grout, Lydston (2). He and s. Thomas were convict. and s. Richard acquit. of rec. stolen goods in 1698. Cross suits with John Pole of Boston, 1700. Sued Jona. Mendum, 1705. L.sts 30, 295, 296 (2), 297, 298. His will, 6 Feb.—17 Mar. 1711, leaves est. to w. and ch. except **Thomas** and **Richard**, who had had their sh. by deeds. Wid. **Mary**, ±44, in 1702, kept a tavern in 1719. Other ch: **Daniel**, Kittery, cordwainer, had a deed from his mo. in 1719; gave a mtg. on ho. and ¼ a. on Crooked Lane in 1731-2. **Mary**, m. 5 July 1715 John Dealin (Daland, Darling, Dolling?). **Jane**, m. Dec. 1712 Paul Wentworth, who was liv. at 'mo. Rice's' in 1717. **Elizabeth**, m. 23 Jan. 1715-6 Charles Banfield(2). **Margaret**, m. 22 Sept. 1720 William Taylor of Wells.

5 **THOMAS**(4), Kittery, shipwright, bondsman for Benj. and Samuel Hutchins, 1706. In 1709 Margaret Spinney, w. of Samuel, acc. T. R. jr. 'a married man' of being the fa. of her ch. List 297. He d. bef. 7 Jan. 1723-4 when wid. Mary took adm., her bondsmen John Woodbridge and Nicholas Morrell. The mar. of Samuel Spinney and Mary Rice in 1731 would seem to indicate a neat revenge by the wronged husb. and w. of 1709. She d. bef. 26 Oct. 1734 when the est. was distrib. Ch: **Sarah**, b. 11 Oct. 1702, m. 26 Oct. 1721 Nicholas Weeks. **Lydia**, b. 28 Feb. 1703-4, d. s.p. bef. 1734. **Moses**, m. in 1733 Anne Griffith who was gr. adm. in 1734, Nath. Keene and Nicholas Weeks, bondsmen, and m. John Manson in 1739. **John**, of Exeter in 1734. **Hannah**, m. 3 Dec. 1729 John Stevens of Wells. **Martha**, ±14 in 1725-6, m. in 1732 John Chapman. **Benjamin**, liv. in 1734. **Elizabeth**, b. 7 Nov. 1718, m. 26 Apr. 1739 Jonathan Crockett of Portsmouth. **Joseph**, had w. Ruth in 1755. **Eunice**, m. William Locke, joiner.

6 **WILLIAM**, ±24 in 1674 when he was mate of the -Richard-, Tobias Lear commander.

**RICH**. 1 **Deliverance**, a soldier k. at Saco fort Apr. 1695.

**2 RICHARD**, m. Sarah Roberts(11). Wit. sale of a sh. of a Portsmouth vessel, 1667. Wit. deed of his fa.-in-law to Zachariah Field, 1671. Bot ho. and orchard at Dover from Robert Mason, 1681. Sued by Edward Cranfield ab. 1685. Primarily a resident of Eastham, Mass., where he d. Lists 52, 87, 356j, 359ab. His ch. **John, Thomas, Samuel, Sarah,** w. of Isaac Baker, and **Lydia** (m. one Hopkins by 1708) gave a p/a to their br. **Richard** in 1706 to deal with their N. H. inheritance. He sold Trueworthy's Pt., 'descended to us from our fa. R. R.,' to Peter Dixon in 1708.

**RICHARDS**, patronymic from Richard, Cornwall and the Welsh border its chief homes.

**1 GEORGE**, of Topsham, co. Devon, mariner, bot a ho. in Portsmouth from James Jeffrey and had 96 a. at Barrington, all of which he left by will, 3 Dec. 1735—29 July 1739, to wid. Lydia Rackliff(1) for life, with careful remainders to a little girl called Mary Richards liv. with Samuel Moore in Kittery, and, if she d. s.p., to Lydia Rackliff's ch. Suspicion that Mary was his dau. by the wid. seems justified. Mary m. Joshua Downing of Newington, joiner.

**2 ‡*JOHN**, Pemaquid, s. of Thomas of Dorchester, sued Francis Knight in Saco ct. 1640, the case being subm. to arbitrators. In 1644 he bot from the sachem Robin Hood an island called Arrowsic or Richards' Isl. on which he was liv. and which he sold to Clarke & Lake in 1654. He rem. to Mass. and m. 1st Elizabeth (Hawkins) Winthrop, wid. of Adam, m. 2d 1 Sept. 1692 Anne Winthrop (Gov. John of Conn.). He d. s.p. 1 Sept. 1694, after a very active and successful political and military career, having been Rep. to Gen. Ct. for many yrs., Speaker, Assistant, Counsellor, Major etc., the details to be found in Mass. history. Lists 11, 181.

**3 JUSTINIAN**, Greenland, where he pd. the smallest tax in 1672. Bot land from Wm. Furber. Gr.j. 1693, 1694. His wid. Mary and s. Joseph q.c. his est. to his s. Benjamin in 1702, the latter to pay his fa.'s debts. Lists 52, 57, 331a, 332b. Ch: **Benjamin**, taxed in Greenl., 1707, the next name being Arnold Brick for whom (4) gave bond on his coming to town in 1694. He and w. Abigail (Hodsdon 3) (Galloway) sold his fa.'s ho. and 14 a. to Wm. Furber in 1719. List 343. **Joseph,** Rochester, 79 in 1749, m. 12 Aug. 1697 Abigail Rollins(5). On Newington coroner's j. 1696. Joseph and Benj., brothers, stealing fish from Col. Mark Hunking in 1722, were prob. gr.sons of (3).

**3½ THOMAS.** In Ashley case (List 1), A.'s servant Thomas Richards, lately dead, is ment.

**4 WILLIAM**, Portsmouth, currier, ±26 in Mar. 1671, m. by 1673 Mary Batchelder (5). In 1680 she was acc. of stealing Wilmot Oliver's coat. Received stolen goods from James Gallison in 1675, prob. deceived by him as to their origin. Test. ag. Geo. Bramhall, 1677. Sarah Sherburne test. that W. R. knocked Sarah Pearce down when she was going to his ho. (ab. 1681). Adm. of est. of Thomas Ladbrook, 1684. He rented a room for 6 yrs. to Dr. John Baxter in 1688. J. 1684. Lists 55b, 59, 60, 67, 313a, 327b, 329, 331b, 334a, 335a, 337. In 1693 he said at Mr. Fryer's ho. that Mr. Moody 'never did preach a sermon.' He d. 7 Nov. 1694 and wid. Mary was gr. adm. 10 Dec. Adm. on her est. was gr. 10 Feb. 1702-3 to s. Samuel and his br.-in-law Shackford. Ch: **Abigail, m.** (ct. June 1695) Samuel Shackford. **Samuel,** tax abated 1714. A Samuel with w. Sarah, a Wedgwood heir, liv. in Rochester where he had 4 ch. bp. in 1737 and others later. Perhaps **William,** m. in Portsm. 23 Aug. 1694 Mary Doe(2); j. Dec. 1695; nothing further.

**RICHARDSON**, a common patronymic, partic. in the northern counties. Became 30th commonest name in N. E. See also Benjamin Shaw.

**1 JOHN**, sued in Dover ct. for felling trees on Mr. Larkham's land in 1642. Wit. will of Thos. Wilson, 1642. His marriage with Elizabeth Fryer was declared void in Exeter ct. in 1644, he having a w. in Eng. Poss. she became the 2d w. of John Clifford (3) in 1658.

**2 JOHN** (Richisonne), wit. Cleeve to Phippen 30 Sept. 1650. See Doc. Hist. 6. 6.

**3 JOHN**, boat-builder, signed pet.ag. Gorges in 1666. Had gr. at Wells in 1673, which was sold in 1751 by Joseph R. of Medfield and Benj. R. of Medway, 'sons of John Richardson of Medfield.' Adm. to Walter Gendall July 1676. Lists 25, 269b, 291.

**4 MOSES.** List 237b.

**5 RICHARD**, with w. Elizabeth sold a ho. at Falmouth in 1721.

**6 THOMAS**, test. in 1676-7 ag. Capt. Walter Gendall, charged with treason. Prob. a Mass. soldier.

**7 LT.**, k. at Black Pt. June 1677, was Lt. James from Mass.

**RICHMOND**, a castle in co. York.

**1 EPHRAIM** (Ridgmond) sued Joshua Downing(5), 1683.

**2 GEORGE**, gentleman, merchant, from Bandonbridge, co. Cork, Ireland, was trading on the Me. coast in 1638, partic. with John Winter at Richmond Isl. When Winter was charged with extortion, Michael Mitton test. to hearing Mr. Richmond quote his prices for powder at Mr. Cleeve's ho. The

fam. of Richmond alias Shepherd, originally from co. Somerset, settled at Bandonbridge in the reign of Queen Elizabeth. Capt. Richard Richmond, a br. of George, and Lt. John Richmond, poss. ano. br. or Richard's s., were in command of the ship -Mary Providence- in Va. in Jan. 1623-4. That Richmond Isl. got its name from early voyagers of this fam. is an attractive but uninvestigated theory.

3 **JOHN**, Saco, sued by Mr. Theoph. Davis for slander and by Mr. Henry Boade for trespass, and sued Mr. Thomas Lewis for trespass and detaining his servt., Feb. 1636-7. Sued by Thos. Page for trespass, May 1637. Sued Theoph. Davis for debt, June 1637. Poss. the J. R. who was at Taunton by 1637 and later in R. I.

**Rickard**, see Ricker.

**RICKER**, Riccar, Rickard, Record. Rickard is peculiar to Cornwall.

1 **GEORGE**, Dover by 1672, br. of (2), bot land on the E. side of Garrison hill from John Wentworth in 1674 and from William Wentworth in 1677. Town gr. of 60 a. in 1693-4. He m. Eleanor Evans(8) about 1680. Lists 52, 57, 62, 96, 356j, 359ab. He was k. by Ind. in June 1706 'while running up the lane near the garrison.' Ch: **Judith**, b. 1 Feb. 1681, captured by Ind. in July 1696, but soon returned and m. Thomas Horne(4). List 96. **John**, b. 1 Apr. 1682, m. Hannah Garland(3) by 1714. Lists 331b, 358d. 14 ch. **Mary**, b. 22 Mar. 1685, m. William Twombly. She was with her fa. when he was k. but managed to escape. **Maturin**, b. 1 Feb. 1686-7, m. Hannah Huntress(1). 12 ch. b. 1713-1736. **Elizabeth**, b. 8 Aug. 1690, m. 1st Bartholomew Stevenson jr., m. 2d one Abbott. **Hannah**, b. 12 May 1693, m. William Jones(57 jr.). **Ephraim**, b. 15 Feb. 1696, m. 1st 1 Sept. 1720 Dorcas Garland(3), m. 2d Sarah Wentworth who d. Dec. 1788; d. Dec. 1773. 12 ch. **Eleanor**, b. 15 Feb. 1699, m. Benjamin Stanton. **George**, b. 10 Feb. 1702, m. Jemima Busby. Ch.

2 **MARY** (Record). See Cater(2). Name, age and propinquity suggest relationship to (1) and (3). See also Dauverne.

3 **MATURIN**, Dover, br. of (1), has slight history. Lists 52, 62, 96, 358d, 359ab. He was k. on the same day in 1706 as his br., 'in his field and his little son carried away.' Ch. by unkn. w: **Maturin**, m. Lucy Wallingford. The 'little son' is traditionally called Noah, but in the list of prisoners still in Canada 1710-1 appears 'John Ricor' of Cochick who can hardly be other than the Dover boy. He had been bp. as Jean Francois Ricard, aged 14, of a place near Dover called Quihecga, 11 June 1707. In 1710 he was at the seminary at Quebec, accounting for the Dover trad. that he became a priest. **Joseph**, Somers-

worth, m. 1st 16 Nov. 1720 Elizabeth Garland(3), m. 2d in Berwick 17 Dec. 1761 Mary May; will, 19 Jan. 1771—10 Dec. 1772, ment. his w., sons Tristram, Joseph, John, Noah, Joshua and Jabez and dau. Mehitable Brackett. **Sarah**, m. John Wingate.

**Rickword**, Stephen, wit. with Henry Crown a bond, Avery to Cutt, 1678-9.

**RIDDAN**, Thaddeus, ±56 in 1681, accountant and merchant, assoc. with Richard Leader(2) in his various enterprises, was first at the iron-works at Lynn, where he m. Elizabeth King (Daniel). In 1651, poss. after a visit to England, he came to the Piscataqua with Leader and bot a ho. in Portsmouth from Wm. Palmer. In 1652 he became clerk of the court. His stay in N. H. was short as he sold his ho. to Richard Cutts in 1653 and was in Lynn that yr. taking an inv. of the iron-works. Selectman of Lynn 1661-2. Ten years later he was at Marblehead where, among other activities, he kept an inn. Selectman of Marbleh. 1672, 1673, 1675, 1679, 1680. He d. 6 Jan. 1690-1 (gr.st.), his s. John app. adm. John bot in his sisters' shares and his mo. leased her int. to him for a £10 annuity. Lists 298, 323. **Ch: Elizabeth**, d. unm. 26 Apr. 1720 in 65th yr. **Mary**, m. 1st John Hoddy(2), m. 2d Samuel Keyes(4). **Hannah**, twin, b. 12 Aug., d. 13 Sept. 1660. **Sarah**, twin, liv. 1676 but d. s.p. bef. 1690. **Hannah**, b. 11 Nov. 1662, m. 1st Henry Dyer (3), m. 2d Augustine Bullard. **John**, b. 3 Feb. 1664-5, m. Joanna Hawkins (Thos.). **Abigail**, b. 4 June 1671, m. William Partridge(6). Desc. spell the name Raddin.

**RIDER**.

1 **BAKER**, acc. of theft and drunkenness in Wells ct. on compl. of Nathan Bedford in 1672. Of Damariscove in 1675 and later in the yr. a refugee in Boston where he was not wanted.

2 **FRANCIS**. List 87.

3 *****PHINEAS**, from Gloucester to Casco, where he had a deed for 55 a. from Cleeve in 1658. Deputy in 1670. Lists 25, 86, 87, 222acd, 317, 331b, 313a. Tr.j. 1662, 1663, 1664, 1666; gr.j. 1667; selectman 1668. Retired to Newcastle where wid. Alice was gr. adm. on est. of 'old Rider' in 1681. Only ch: **John** (Lists 222c, 223a, 227), left two sons, one who d. s.p., and John, and two daus. Elizabeth w. of William Dye of Stonington, Conn., and Mary who was w. of James Knapp of Falmouth in 1730 and the wid. of one Warren of Stoughton, Mass., in 1734. John the gr.s. was rep. by a s. John, weaver, of Swansea, in 1739. The 55 a. was in the hands of William Pote in 1735, ⅓ being deeded to him by Mary Knapp and ⅔ by Phineas Jones who had bot it from Elizabeth Dye and John Rider.

**RIDGWAY, John,** Pemaquid and Charlestown, ±32 in 1655, built a ho. on E. side of Pemaquid Great Falls, later owned by Thos. Giles. He had a fishing venture in 1651 with Rev. Robert Jordan whom he sued in 1654. Lists 111, 124. Sued Jordan, Rishworth, Richard Hitchcock and Wheelwright, 1655. He m. Mary Brackenbury who joined the Charlestown Ch. 27 Nov. 1652 and d. 24 Dec. 1670. Kn. ch: **John,** Boston, mariner, had a 100 a. gr. at Pemaquid in 1686. He d. 10 Nov. 1721, ag. 68, in Malden. Will. His sons John, brickmaker (w. Rebecca), James, housewright (w. Mehitable), Samuel, chairmaker (w. Naomi), deeded to James Woodside of Pemaquid, 1735. A dau. Elizabeth m. William Cox 23 Nov. 1719. **Alice,** bp. 27 Oct. 1667. **James** and **Hannah,** bp. 13 Oct. 1668. **Sarah,** bp. 12 Mar. 1671, ±56 in 1716, ±76 in 1736, m. Samuel Austin. Mary, w. of Robert Cawley(2) and Leonard Drowne, who test. to her girlhood in Ridgway's Pemaquid ho., ment. no relationship.

**Ridley, Mark,** sued for cattle in Wells ct. by Francis Morgan in 1672. List 312e.

**RIGBY, Alexander,** Esq., b. 1594, s. of Alexander and Anne (Asshaw) of Wigan, co. Lancs., and descended from an ancient county fam., lawyer, colonel in the Parliamentary army and Baron of the Exchequer (but neither -Sir Alexander- nor -Lord Rigby- as sometimes assumed by American writers). Adm. to Grays Inn in 1610; returned to Parliament as member for Wigan in 1639-40 and was very active; Deputy-Lt. for Lancs. 1641-1642; saw much action in the Civil War 1643-1644. In 1643-4 George Cleeve was successful in persuading him to buy the so-called Plough Patent covering the territory in Maine known as Lygonia, lying between the Sagadahoc and Kennebunk rivers, and in having Rigby appoint him Deputy-President thereof. He d. 18 Aug. 1650 and after the restoration of Charles II his int. was ignored, altho his son, Mr. Sergt. Rigby, entered a warning against so doing when Parliament was considering the Mason and Gorges claims. By w. Lucy, dau. of Sir Urian Leigh of Adlington, co. Chester, he had four ch. See Dictionary of Nat. Biog. 48: 299. The name Rigby has survived in Maine, alas, only as the designation of a defunct racetrack and of an active freight yard.

**Right,** see Wright.

**RILANCE, Jacob,** the 3d husb. of Mary Cole (24) whom he m. at Wells 10 May 1720. He d. bef. 4 Oct. 1729 when her int. to m. William Bracy(2) was pub. Jane Boothby and Elizabeth Rich test. in 1730 that it was a 'smock marriage.'

**RILEY, John** and w. Mary were refugees at Charlest. from the Kennebec in 1690 when he was impressed and taken to Wells, leaving her and 2 ch. without food. Lists 187, 188, 189.

**RINDGE, Daniel,** wit. deed Sarah Pope to Pepperell of land at Winter Harbor, 1694, Patience Creasie the other wit. John Rindge, a Portsm. merchant in 1729, wit. in 1720 with Barnabas Cruce.

**RINES, Rhines, Henry,** at Oyster River by 1695 when he signed a pet. Nothing app. as to his origin. Lists 368ab. He would seem to have been the fa. of **Thomas,** who signed a pet. in 1717, and of **William.** Both the latter were surely m. by 1720 when they and their wives (one named Elizabeth) were called as wit. in a case ag. Amos Pinkham for theft. One, at least, was m. sev. yrs. earlier and was the fa., not named in the record, of Joseph Rhines, ag. 14, and Thos. Rhines, ag. 11, bp. at O. R. 7 Jan. 1727-8. Christian Busby, single wo., compl. ag. Joseph in 1736-7 and he was not to be found, but subsequently ret. and m. her as they had two ch. bp. in 1741, when he o.c. at Dover Ch. Henry Rines, presum. a gr.s. of the signer of 1695, had ch. bp. in Berwick from 1739. See Raynes(5).

**RING,** very uncommon in Eng., poss. derived from residence near a baiting-ring.
1 **MERIBAH,** dau. of John, Salisbury, had liv. some time as servt. of Thomas Dean of Hampton in 1722, when she was acc. of murdering her bastard, George March its fa.
2 **ROBERT,** grantor with Abraham Shurt to John Brown(15). See Y. D. 20. 85.
3 **SETH,** Newington (Portsm. tax abated 1715), m. ab. 1716 Elizabeth Libby. He was neph. of Keziah (Brackett 2) Maylem who thus named him in her will, and therefore a s. of Mary Brackett who m. 1st Joseph Ring of Salisbury, 2d in 1710 Nathaniel Whittier of Salis. Among Seth's desc. a strong and early tradition persists that he was of Indian blood. If Mary was taken at Falmouth in 1690 or was with her Brackett grandparents at Sandy Beach in 1691 when they were k. and many unnamed members of their fam. taken prisoner, it is not imposs. that she had a ch. by an Ind. fa. during her captivity. Joseph Ring was at Fort Loyal in 1690, and was prob. that captive J. R. tortured and burned at the stake in 1704 by Ind. in revenge for their losses in the attack on Berwick. See 3 Mass. Hist. Soc. Coll. VI. S. R.'s will 5 Feb. 1756—30 May 1757 names his ch: **Joseph,** bp. 5 Jan. 1717-18, exec., Scarboro, mariner. **Benjamin. Eliphalet** and **Seth** and **Mary,** w. of one Huntress (all three in Halifax). **Jane** Alcock. **Elizabeth** Shackford. **Josiah. George.** Also **David,** bp. 24 Nov. 1734, not in will.

**RISBY, William,** Dover, taxed at Oyster River 1659, m. one Sarah late in the day in 1660 and left town to escape ct. action. See Jones(54). List 361a.

**RISHWORTH**, a Yorkshire name, Halifax its principal home.

‡*EDWARD, ±53 on 2 Mar. 1671-2, gentleman and distinguished civil servant, s. of Rev. Thomas and Esther (Hutchinson) of Laceby, co. Lincoln, gr.s. of Mrs. Hutchinson(11), came to N. E. as a young man with his Hutchinson and Wheelwright relations. Signed the Exeter combination in 1639 and in 1640 was chosen by Exeter to be 'secretary' (town clerk). Accomp. his uncle Wheelwright to Wells in 1640, had a gr. and built a ho., later sold to John Barrett sr. In 1643 Thos. Gorges named him as one of three agents to make gr. of land betw. Ogunquit and the Kennebunk riv. He owned land in Hampton in 1650 and prob. liv. there tempo. as he was Hampt. selectman, 1651. Owned a mill-site on Cape Neddick riv. in 1651. By 1656-7 he had settled in York, occupying Sir Ferdinando Gorges' house under Mr. Nanny, a more convenient residence for one who had become in 1651 Recorder of the Province, a place which he held with distinction thru many vicissitudes until 1686, when, although Scottow obtained the office, Rishworth as his deputy continued to do the work. Many York gr. from 1658 to 1687. Councillor, 1651; O. A. to Mass. 1652; Com.t.e.s.c. 1658; Justice 1664; magistrate almost all his life; Dep. to the Mc. and Mass. General Courts many terms and almost constantly selectman of York from 1657 to 1673. He m. his cousin Susannah Wheelwright, who was liv. in 1674 but not in 1679. An inv. of his est. was taken 18 Feb. 1689-90 and on 24 Feb. 1690-1 adm. was gr. to his dau. Mrs. Mary Hull. The est. was small and contained no real prop. altho much had passed thru his hands, poss. enriching his only child. His homestead had been mtg. to Mr. John Cutt in 1679. See Jocelyn(2), Nanny, Gorges(10), Godfrey(1). For more extended accounts of his life and estimates of his public service, see P. & C. Rec., I. xiv et seq., II. xi et seq.; York Deeds, I. 10-11; Banks' Hist. of York, I. 214-7. A more temperate estimate of Rishworth by Col. Banks appeared in the Portland Argus, May 22, 1915, in which he says: 'The reader will conclude that Rishworth was a capable official whose services were appreciated and desired by his fellow citizens . . . and posterity can clearly absolve him from the discredit of seeking and holding office by means of political charlatanry.' Lists 23, 24, 25, 26, 29, 32, 33, 78, 79, 82, 84, 88, 111, 221, 232, 235, 236, 254, 262, 275, 277, 276, 373, 376a, 392b, 393b. Only kn. ch: **Mary**, m. 1st by 1678-9 (William?) White, m. 2d by 1682 John Sayward, m. 3d Phineas Hull(7), m. 4th James Plaisted(3).

**Rix**, see Reekes.

**ROANES, William**, at York by 1659, **m. 1st** Mary Parker(14), m. 2d bef. 7 Oct. 1673 wid. Wilmot Start. In 1717 Thomas Adams test. that 58 or 60 yrs. ago he had helped his br. Roans. In 1718 John Parker test. that betw. 54 and 60 yrs. ago W. R. had hired him of his father. York gr. 1666 to his w. and ch. of 12 a. above Bass Cove. Tr.j. 1668. List 25. Adm. 11 Sept. 1677 to John Parker, sr., the est. being very small. Ch. by 1st w., both having been supported by John Parker sr. for 7 yrs. bef. 1678: **Elizabeth**. Dorothy Crew of Boston test. that she had had two bastards. In 1695, of Bos., only ch. of her parents, late of York, she deeded 10 a. to Samuel Came. She m. Philip Adams(19). **Esther**, wit. Hilton to Yeales 1682. In 1685 when she was liv. in Boston, Samuel Crawley was acc. of stealing her money from Joseph Weare's vessel bound for Bos. Presum. **d.** bef. 1695. See also Rounds.

**ROBBINS. 1 Edmund**. List 13.

2 **SAMUEL**. List 356h.

3 **WILLIAM**, Isles of Shoals by 1672, adm. 29 Sept. 1680 to Thomas Pumery who pd. for doctor and funeral.

**ROBERTS**, patronymic from Robert, most common in Wales and the border counties, but well kn. fam. in Kent and Cornwall. Became 81st commonest name in N. E.

1 **EDWARD**, Sheepscot wit., 1652-3.

1½ **GEORGE**, Exeter by 1678, **m.** Mary Jones(17) who m. 2d by 1698-9 Nathaniel Folsom(6) and 3d Nicholas Norris. In 1680 he and his Jones relations had an altercation with the Scammans, Roger Kelly and Robt. Steward over some timber. Ack. debt to Capt. Thos. Daniel, 1681. Lists 52, 57. Son **John** m. a dau. of Alexander Magoon(1); was called upon to help support his mo. Norris in 1741. Prob. **George**, cordwainer, Exeter, 1735+.

2 **GILES**, Scarboro by 1658, **m.** a dau. of Godfrey Sheldon. Gr. of 50 a. in 1662. Lists 221, 239a. Will, 25 Jan. 1666—20 June 1667, left his prop. for the bringing up of his five ch., three being with him and two with his br. Arthur Alger, who was named exec., Mr. Henry Jocelyn and br. William Sheldon overseers. Arthur and Andrew Alger agreed to care for all five, of whom three are ident. in est. papers of Arthur: **Abraham**, Reading, had w. Sarah. Sold 100 a. by Scottows Hill, had from his uncle Alger, to Aaron Jewett in 1730. **David**, Woburn, weaver; m. 2 Oct. 1678 Joanna Brooks. Entered an East. Cl. for a ho. and 54 a. at Scarboro. He d. 4 Sept. 1724. **Giles**, k. at Falmouth, 1689.

3 **HENRY**, Richmond Isl., baker, 1633. List 21.

4 **JOHN**, Richmond Isl. fisherman, 1637. List 21.

**5 JOHN**(11), Dover, ±43 in 1671, ±53 in 1683, m. Abigail Nutter(2). Sergt.; Lt. 1689-90; Marshal of the Prov. by 1670 (discharged because of age, 1681-2); delegate to the N. H. convention of 1689 to confer on methods of gov.; gr.j. 1683, 1692; selectman 1664, 1665, 1668, 1673, 1674, 1677. Lists 49, 52, 54, 55ab, 56, 57, 62, 82, 96, 311c, 353, 354bc, 355ab, 356abcefhjk, 357be, 359ab. In 1691 he deeded to the sons of his deceased s. John and to his s.-in-law Field, in 1691-2 to his s.-in-law John Hall and in 1694 to his sons Thomas, Hatevil and Joseph. He d. 21 Jan. 1694-5 of dropsy. Ch: **John**, by w. Mary had 3 ch. and d. bef. 1691. Lists 52, 57, 359b. **Thomas**, his 1st w. unkn., m. 2d c. 1711 wid. Elizabeth (Tucker) Hopley. In 1707 he conv. lands to s. Love and his homestead to s. Benjamin in 1734-5. 3 + 1 ch. ‡**Hatevil**, Berwick and Somersworth, 56 in 1717, m. his cous. Lydia Roberts. Dover constable, 1694; Councillor, 1699. Both adm. to Berwick ch. in 1721, and she dism. to Somersw. in 1731. Lists 63, 64, 96, 358cd. Constable 1694, 1695; gr.j. 1697, 1700. Will, 28 Oct. 1724— 3 Mar. 1724-5. 5 ch. Lt. **Joseph**, m. 1st Elizabeth Jones(39), m. 2d one Abigail. Selectman 1711-1714, Lt. 1713. Lists 57, 62, 94, 358ad. Adm. to s. Stephen and Wm. Ham, 25 Apr. 1744. 10 ch. **Abigail**, m. 1st John Hall (10), m. 2d Thomas Downes(6). **Mary**, m. Timothy Robinson(16). **Sarah**, m. Zachariah Field(12).

**6 JOSEPH**, Hampton?, inq. on his untimely death 27 June 1665. See Johnson(23).

**7 MARK**, Portsmouth in 1674, Hampton in 1676, Kittery in 1678, got Catherine Lecornah into trouble in 1680 and ran away, leav. his bondsm. Wm. Fernald to pay for her lying-in and 2 s. a wk. for the ch. See Denham.

**7½ MARY.** See Crawford(4). If a Roberts of Dover, her parentage uncertain.

**8 NATHANIEL.** See Robinson(12).

**9 SAMUEL**, Dover, accidentally drowned (inq. 29 Mar. 1669). Poss. that sailor s. of Robert Roberts of Ipswich, the inv. of whose est. was filed in Essex Co. 21 June 1670.

**10 THOMAS.** List 7.

**11 THOMAS**, Dover, said to have come with the Hiltons, which is very prob. as he was a fellow member of the Fishmongers Co. of London with Edw. Hilton, both marked 'in New England' in a list of 1641. Presum. that T. R., s. of John Roberts of Woolaston, appren. 29 Apr. 1622. In 1639-40 he was elected 'President of the Court,' an office of agency for the Bristol Co., the proprietors of Dover, from which fact he is sometimes called 'Gov.' altho the territory under his authority was only one town. Signed the Dover combination, 1640; gr.j. 1643, 1646,

1656. Various deeds, grants and suits. Sewell's 'History of the Quakers' states that he rebuked his sons for their official cruelty to that sect. Lists 47, 351ab, 352, 354abc, 355a, 356abcefghk, 357e, 358bd. In 1669 his w. was Rebecca, who d. bef. 1673. In 1670 he gave land to sons John and Thomas, and in 1671 half his remaining est. to his dau. Sarah Rich. Will, 27 Sept. 1673—30 June 1674, giving his homestead to Richard Rich and naming him exec., names ch: **John**, b. ab. 1628. **Thomas**, b. ab. 1635. **Hester**, m. John Martyn(7). **Anna**, m. 1st James Philbrick (1), m. 2d William Marston(11). **Elizabeth**, m. Benjamin Heard(2). **Sarah**, m. Richard Rich(2).

**12 SERGT. THOMAS**(11), Dover, ±25 in 1661, depos. 30 June 1659 that he had liv. with Geo. Walton nearly 5 yrs., beginning nearly 9 yrs. ago; m. Mary Leighton(6). Selectman 1670, 1671, 1694 (Corp.), ¶1703-10 (sr.). Prob. his s., not he, was constable, 1688. Chosen to select a minister 5 Dec. 1694. Lists 49, 52, 54, 57, 62. 90, 94, 353, 356abghk, 359ab. Gr.j. 1683, 1696, 1697, 1698, 1699; j. 1692, 1694. Liv. in 1705, ±70. Ch: **Thomas**, m. Sarah Canney(4) by 1687. See Love(5). He d. s.p. and by will, 3 Mar. 1745-6—31 Dec. 1755, left his prop. to his neph. Moses Roberts. **Nathaniel**, m. 11 Apr. 1706 Elizabeth Mason(1). Will, 3 Mar. 1745-6— 31 Jan. 1753, names w. and 7 of 9 ch. **John**, Somersworth, weaver, m. 1st Oct. 1704 Deborah Church(1), m. 2d 17 May 1720 Frances Emery(3). Will, 7 Apr. 1749—28 July 1756, names w. and ch. (b. 1705—1725-6) Joanna Wentworth, Sarah Wentworth, Mary (not in will), Phebe Tuttle, Deborah Roberts, Ebenezer, Alexander. **Joanna**, m. Thomas Potts (2). **Mary**, m. Thomas Young. **Lydia**, m. her cous. Hatevil Roberts. **Sarah**, m. Howard Henderson(4).

**13 THOMAS**, shipwright, late of New Dartmouth in 1689-90 when Edmund Perkins, his attorney, sued Geo. Hisket of Bos., mariner.

**14 WILLIAM**, Oyster River, in Str. Bk. ct. 1643, had from Darby Field in 1645 a deed of a farm in the occupation of Thomas Roberts(11), prob. a close relation. He sold the farm in 1646 and bot ano. which he lost in 1664 as endorser of Edward Colcord's bond. Town gr. of 100 a. each in 1662 and 1663. A strong Quaker, he was in constant trouble with the authorities. His last years were spent in a ho. first rented, then bot in 1673, from William Follett. Lists 46, 354abc, 355a, 356a, 357b, 361a, 362a, 363abc, 365. He was k. in the Ind. attack on O. R. in 1675. Adm. to Richard Otis 29 Mar. 1676. His wid., Dorothy, was liv., aided by the town, in 1687. See Ancestry of Lydia Harmon, by W. G. Davis, 1924. Ch: **William**, a 'simple youth'

in 1669, d. bef. his fa.'s est. was settled. A dau., m. 1st one Sias, m. 2d Salathiel Denbo (1), m. 3d William Graves(6). **Elizabeth**, m. 1st Nicholas Dunn(2), m. 2d Thomas Allen (14). **Sarah**, m. John Harmon(2). **Hannah**, m. 1st William Hill(22), m. 2d John Cox(13). **Grace**, had two illegit. ch., one by John Muchemore(3) in 1677, and one, laid to Ezekiel Pitman who denied it, in 1683, bef. she m. 1st Philip Duley and 2d Timothy Moses(3). See Jameson(2).

15 **WILLIAM**, Kittery, fisherman, 34 in 1674, prob. the W. R. in Arundel in 1660. Fishing for Roger Kelly in 1673, and shipped with Hugh Allard of Isles of Shoals in 1674. He m. Anne Crockett(6) and liv. on Crockett's Neck in Kit. Town gr. 50 a. in 1699. Mtg. his homestead to his s. George in 1706. It was assigned in 1708 to Pepperell to whom the wid., Anna alias Nan, relinq. her rights in 1714-5. Lists 297, 298, 317(?), 329(?). Kn. ch: **Mary**, m. William Ball(5) (ct. 14 Sept. 1687, their surnames being reversed in one rec.). **George**, Ipswich, m. Hannah Pettus of Haverhill. **Elizabeth**, m. 1st in 1702 or 1703 John Surplice (ct. Apr. 1703), m. 2d William Godsoe(2). **William**, fisherman, m. Elizabeth Crucy(2) (ct. July 1702). Ch. incl. William, b. 30 June 1701; George, b. 30 Mar. 1704; and Barnaby, bp. 27 July 1718. Lists 290, 291, 296, 298. Very prob. **Digory**, who would have been named for his mo.'s stepfa., Digory Jeffrey(3); fisherman at Newcastle, 1706-1710.

**ROBIE**, Roby, diminutive from Robert. Our fam. was from Castle Donnington, co. Leicester, where Thomas Robie, gent., was taxed in 1621.

1 **HENRY**, Hampton, ±50 in 1669, br. of (4), b. 12 Feb. 1618, s. of Thomas and Mary (Coxon) of Castle Donnington, came to Exeter from Dorchester in 1639, joined in building a saw-mill in 1649 and was selectman in 1650. Soon after 1650 he mov. to Hampton. He m. 1st Ruth Moore(24) who d. 5 May 1673, m. 2d 19 Jan. 1674 Elizabeth (Philbrick 7) (Chase) Garland who d. 11 Feb. 1677, m. 3d Sarah, a wid. with a s. John, otherwise unident., who surv. him and d. 23 Jan. 1703. Selectman 1656, 1660, 1665, 1681; constable 1661; j. 1679, 1684, 1685; J. P. many years; Justice of Ct. of Sessions. Lists 49, 52, 55ab, 373, 374ac, 375ab, 376ab, 377, 392b, 393b, 394, 396, 398. During his last yrs. he kept an inn, which his wid. continued. He d. 22 Apr. 1688. His will, 11 Jan. 1686—5 June 1688, made elaborate prov. for his w., named his ch. and a 'gr.s. Byall, in his mo.'s care,' who is not ident. Ch. by 1st w: **Mary**, m. 22 Dec. 1663 Samuel Folsom(9). ***Thomas**, b. 1 Mar. 1645-6, in Falmouth 1689. Constable 1697, 1698; gr.j. 1696; j. 1692, 1694,

1696, 1697; Rep. 1694, 1695, 1703. Lists 52, 54, 228c(?), 395, 399a. He m. 8 Dec. 1687 Martha Eaton who d. 26 Jan. 1719. Will, 30 Jan. 1719-20—6 June 1722, left £20 to br. Ichabod and the residue to Peter Peavey and Edward Wilmot. **John**, b. 2 Feb. 1648. **Judith**, acc. John Young and had s. John b. 6 Dec. 1671 (see Race); m. 15 Sept. 1693 Samuel Healey(2). **Ruth**, b. 3 Mar. 1654, liv. unm. in 1686. **Deliverance**, b. 22 Mar. 1657, m. 28 Dec. 1680 Nathaniel Haseltine at Haverhill; not in fa.'s will. **Samuel**, b. 4 Aug. 1659. **Ichabod**, b. 26 Nov. 1664. By 3d w: **Sarah**, b. 19 Apr. 1679, not in fa.'s will. See Sarah(3).

2 **ICHABOD**(1), Kingston, m. 1st 4 Jan. 1694 Lucy Page(2), m. 2d after 1717 wid. Lydia Spendlow who d. 21 May 1731. With s. Samuel and his w. (also a Spendlow), they sold the Spendlow homestead in 1739. Lists 68, 398a, 400. His will, 1753—1755, ment. all his ch. except Lucy: **Meribah**, b. 6 Oct. 1694, was wid. Conner in 1753; d. s.p. in 1757; will, of Kingston, ment. neph. Amasa Dow and his ch. **Lucy**, bp. 13 Mar. 1698, ment. in will of her gr.fa. Page in 1706. **Dorothy**, bp. 3 Mar. 1700, m. 1st 25 Nov. 1718 Edward Sanborn, m. 2d 17 Sept. 1729 Benjamin Prescott. **Lydia**, b. 23 May 1703, m. 1st 14 Aug. 1729 Amasa Dow of Salisb., m. 2d 8 Nov. 1738 Michael Brooks of Biddeford. **Samuel**, b. 12 May 1705, m. wid. Anna (Spendlow) Morrison. **Ruth**, b. 3 Sept. 1707. **William**, b. 6 Nov. 1709, d. betw. 1753 and 1755. **Susanna**, b. 2 Aug. 1713, m. Hezekiah Swaine.

3 **JOHN**(1), mov. to Haverhill in 1675 and liv. in part of town which fell to N. H. when the line was rectified. He m. 1 Nov. 1677 Anne Corliss (George) who d. 1 June 1691. Fifteen days later he was k. by Ind., leaving 7 ch., none over 12 yrs. of age. Ch. b. in Hav: **Ruth**, b. 14 Oct. 1678; see also Ruth(5). Col. **Ichabod**, b. 15 Jan. 1679-80, taken prisoner when his fa. was k., but escaped; Hamp. Falls; tanner; m. 10 or 13 Jan. 1706-7 Mary Cass(3); will, 1752—1753, names ch. John, Henry, Samuel, Sarah Tilton out of 7 b. 1708-1722. **Henry**, b. 12, d. 17 Mar. 1680-1. **Joanna**, b. 5 Mar. 1681-2, m. 24 Dec. 1703 Jonathan Elkins(4). **Sarah**, b. 6 Mar. 1683-4, more likely she than Sarah(1), m. 1st 21 Oct. 1702 Samuel Clough of Salisb., m. 2d in 1730 Ezekiel Morrill, m. 3d in 1734 Capt. Joseph Taylor of Hampton. **Deliverance**, b. 17 Feb. 1685, m. 1st John Leavitt(7), m. 2d John Nay. **John**, b. 25 Mar. 1688. **Mary**, m. John Harris of Exeter; in 1711 they deeded ⅛ of the lands of their fa. J. R., late of Hav., partly inherited from his fa. Corliss.

4 **SAMUEL**, Newcastle, cooper, ±40 in 1671, br. of (1), b. at Castle Donnington 12

Feb. 1628-9. In 1662 he bot from Christopher
Palmer 5 a. in Hampton adjoin. his br.'s
land, but in 1663 he was at Newcastle where
he set up his shop in the business section and
m. Mary Walton, ±32 in 1678, dau. of George,
who was closely assoc. with his br. Lists 52,
311b, 312acf, 313ae, 330a(2), 321b. Kn. ch:
Mary, m. 1st 13 Aug. 1683 William Tetherly,
m. 2d John Lydston(1). Thomas and Walton were both wit. in the 'Stone-throwing
Devil' case in 1682 and ment. in their gr.fa.
Walton's will, 1686. Thomas was taxed 1688,
1690. List 228c(?).

5 SAMUEL(1), Hampton, m. Mary Page(9),
   who d. 5 Sept. 1750. Jury 1695. Lists 56,
66. He d. 10 Aug. 1717. Will, 10 July—7
Sept. 1717. Ch. all in will: Ruth. One Ruth
m. 10 Dec. 1701 Hon. John Sanborn. Mary,
b. 25 Nov. 1686, m. Henry Dearborn(2 jr.).
Sarah, b. 27 Mar. 1689, m. Nathaniel Batch-
elder(4 jr.). Theodate, b. 5 Dec. 1691, m.
Abraham Drake(2 jr.). Huldah, b. 4 Mar.
1694, m. James Perkins(8). Bathsheba, b. 2
Aug. 1696, m. Jonathan Lane(13). Thomas,
b. 10 Oct. 1698, m. Sarah Fogg(2), d. 4 Mar.
1767. List 392b. Hannah, b. 26 Feb. 1701,
m. John Tilton. Abigail, b. 6 Apr. 1703, m.
Ezekiel Dow(5). Elizabeth, b. 19 July 1704,
m. James Fogg(2). Bethia, b. 28 Dec. 1707,
m. Abner Fogg(6).

6 WILLIAM, neph. of (1) and (4), was at
   Newcastle 1678-9 when he took inv. of
Martha (Walton) West's est. Subsequently
of Boston, where Mrs. Robe, his w., was bur.
27 Feb. 1712-3. His son, Dr. Ebenezer R.,
visited his Eng. relations in 1726 and copied
the entries in his gt.gr.mo.'s Bible.

ROBINSON, Robeson, patronymic from
   Robert, most common in the northern
counties. Became 48th commonest name in
N. E.

1 DANIEL, Kittery, wit. Johnson to Neal,
   1696. Perhaps Daniel(6) when a young
boy.

2 ‡FRANCIS, Saco, gentleman and merchant, ±52 (an under-estimate) in 1670-
1, was closely attached to Thomas Lewis(19)
and prob. came to Me. (here by 1631) with
him. Exec. of wills of Mr. and Mrs. Lewis,
and attorney to their s.-in-law Rev. Richard
Gibson in 1640. Attorney for John Bonython 1640. See Jenner(2). Gr.j. 1640, magistrate 1645, Councillor 1647. Merchant in
Barbadoes in 1650 when Adam Winthrop
gave him a p/a. In Nevis for some years
bef. 1666. See Kelly(11). Lists 22, 75a. Wit.
at Black Pt. 1669. By 1670 he was back in
Boston, freeman in 1671, 'a man of public
note that had his commerce and trading in
the chief places of trade, viz. in London,
Barbadoes, New England and elsewhere.'
Depos. ab. Paul Batt, 1674.

3 JAMES (also Robertson), Blue Point,
   cooper, acc. and acquit. of Christopher
Collins's murder in 1661, but Frances Russell was still calling him murderer in 1684.
Had a 40 a gr. in 1682-3. He m. Lucretia
Foxwell(5) who was ±24 in 1668, retiring to
Newcastle when Philip's war began. Portsmouth constable, 5 Feb. 1679-80. Lists 52,
55b, 238a, 313acfg, 315abc, 318ab, 319, 326c,
331b. Gr.j. 1683, 1687, 1692; j. 1682, 1683,
1684. The wid. relinq. adm. 6 Apr. and it
was gr. 1 May 1710 to dau. Elizabeth White.
Ch: Rebecca, m. John Pitman jr. of Marblehead. Elizabeth, m. Nathan White. Mary,
m. Henry Trefethen. Margaret, tailoress at
Gt. Isl., m. Capt. Hugh Reed(2).

4 JOHN, Exeter, blacksmith, ±45 in 1661, s.
   of John of Meppershall, co. Bedford, who
left him a legacy c. 1650, came first to Newbury, but soon moved to Haverhill where
he bot a ho. from Joseph Merry in 1644. Selling out in 1651 he went to Ex. where in 1651-
2 he bot from Edward Gilman a ho. formerly
Mr. Pormont's, which he sold to Moses Gilman in 1674. In 1667 he sold to Samuel
Leavitt 7 a. at Fort hill, by the falls. Selectman 1653, 1661, 1666, 1673; com.t.e.s.c. 1668;
gr.j. 1653, 1664, 1668, 1674; j. 1654, 1667.
Lists 376b, 377. Shot by skulking Ind.
while on his way to Hampton with one of his
sons, who escaped into a swamp, 10 Nov.
1675. Adm. gr. 30 May 1676 to wid. Elizabeth and s. David, the est. to remain undivided until her death. Ch: John, b. in 1641,
d.y. John, b. 1642, d.y. Jonathan, b. 16 May
1645. Sarah, b. 8 Jan. 1647, d. 18 May 1648.
David, b. 6 Mar. 1649, m. 1st 24 May 1680
Sarah Taylor, m. 2d Mary (Bean 2) Judkins
(1), who joined Hampton Ch. and was dismissed to Ex. in 1698. Sold 20 a. from his
fa.'s est. to John Sinclair, 1678. Depos. in
1714 ab. matters of 45 or 46 yrs. bef. Lists
52, 57, 67, 376b, 381, 382, 383, 384b, 388.
Deeded to his neph. Jonathan jr. in 1710. No
ident. ch. Elizabeth, b. 7 Mar. 1651, m. John
Garland(7). A dau., m. Samuel Leavitt(10).
And poss. Hannah, m. 1st 9 Jan. 1684-5 John
Gilman(9 jr.), m. 2d John Lloyd.

5 JOHN, Kittery, one of Mr. Pepperell's
   tanners, in ct. for working on Sunday in
1696.

6 CAPT. JOHN, now resident in Berwick in
   1709 when he bot from William Stiles.
Lists 296, 298. Killed while pursuing Ind.
who had attacked Wells in Sept. 1712. Adm.
to wid. Martha 12 Jan. 1712-3, Richard
Tozier and Philip Hubbard bondsmen. She
m. 24 June 1714 William Watson. Ch: John,
bp. Kittery 8 July 1709. Capt. Daniel, mariner and cooper, his fa.'s only surv. s. and
h., m. Abigail Jordan(3) who was liv. in
1749. Of Portsm., 1737; of Falmouth, 1738;
of London, 1747; again of Falm. 1749. Ano.

Daniel m. in Portsm. in 1747 Mary (Stephens) Church and was poss. the D. R. of Portsmouth whose will, 1761—1762, left all to s. John and dau. Mary.

7 **JOHN**, mariner, Boston, m. Rachel Almary ±1715. He sold a 1720 land gr. at Scarboro in 1729. He was taxed in Portsmouth in 1727 and sold a ho. and land there in 1733.

8 **JONATHAN**(4), Exeter, 66 in 1713, bot from Jonathan Thing in 1674. Tythingman, 1672; O. A. 1677; active in reorganizing the church in 1680; gr.j. 1693, 1697, 1699; selectman, 1695. Wounded in an exped. to the eastward in 1691. Lists 49, 67, 376b, 377, 380, 381, 382, 383, 388. His w. was Sarah in 1716. If, as seems prob., she was Sarah (Bradley) Bean(2 jr.), the mo. of his ch. was an unkn. 1st w. In 1710 he drew up a testamentary deed in favor of his w., five sons, two daus., and a gr.dau., Lydia, dau. of John. Ch: **John**, b. 7 Sept. 1671, m. Mehitable Stanyan; will, 7 July 1749—22 Aug. 1755, gent., Exeter, ment. his w., sons John (m. 1 Feb. 1726—7 Elizabeth Folsom 8), Jonathan, Jeremiah and Daniel (the homestead), daus. Lydia Morrison, Sarah Palmer, Mary Fo lansby (her ch.) and a gr.s. Jonathan Cauley. **Sarah**, b. 29 Oct. 1673, not in deed. **Hester**, b. 12 Aug. 1677. **Elizabeth**, b. 6 Sept. 1679, m. 1st James Runlett(3), m. 2d Abraham Folsom(4). **Jonathan**, b. 9 July 1681; will, 1754—1758, names sons Josiah (exec.), Jonathan, Ephraim, James (of Brentwood), and daus. Lydia Calef and Mary Chase. **David**, b. 28 July 1684, Stratham, m. at Hamp. 1 Jan. 1704-5 Sarah Sanborn who joined Hamp. Ch. in 1706; will, 1767—1769, ment. 2d w. Martha and several gr.gr.ch. Ch: Benjamin, bp. in Hamp. 21 Oct. 1705, and Hannah, Lydia, Sarah, David, Esther, Bathsheba, Abigail, rec. in Stratham 1708-1728. **James**, b. 7 Dec. 1686, Stratham, m. Mary Jackson(13 jr.). List 388. Ch. rec. in Stratham 1712-1721, Sarah, James, John, Joseph, Jonathan. **Joseph**, b. 1 May 1690, m. Sarah Norris(1); both liv. Ex., 1756.

9 **MARY**, who m. in 1707 James Doughty of Kittery, Stratham and Falmouth, is unident., as is Hannah m. 18 Jan. 1711 John Honeyford.

10 **MATTHEW**, m. at Wells 22 July 1716 wid. Sarah (Fletcher 8) Miller. Of Winter Harbor in 1719 when they deeded to her br. Pendleton Fletcher. Called himself soldier in 1722 when they sold a 30 a. town gr. to Nathaniel Tarbox. In 1750, Mary, w. of John Whitten of North Yarmouth, heir of M. R. of Biddeford, sold a ½ sh. in various pieces of Fletcher prop. Prob. also **William** and **Matthew** Robinson, bp. Wells 25 July 1731, brot by John and Elizabeth Storer.

11 **NATHANIEL**, Casco wit., Small to Phillips, 1658.

12 **NATHANIEL**, fisherman, b. in N. Y., now res. of Portsmouth, m. 29 May 1716 Sarah Broughton (Bradden 2). Taxed and rated 1716-1717. As Sarah 'Roberts' she m. 2d John Norris(2), but in deeding her 1st husb.'s Barrington rt. in 1763 she called him 'Robinson.' Ch. bp. as Roberts: **Elizabeth**, wid. Buck in 1762. **Sarah**, bp. with next in 1723, d. bef. 1762 s.p. **Mary**, wid. Sanderson in 1762.

13 **RICHARD**, a sea-capt. at Portsmouth, 1675. his mate, John West, in trouble.

14 **STEPHEN**, Oyster River, drunk in 1661; bot land in Eliot in 1663 and was of Kittery in 1669. Fined for swearing 1671 (Me. ct.). Of Oyster Riv. again in 1679. Lists 57, 356m, 363ac, 365.

14½ **THOMAS**, Falmouth, 1689, signed pet. to Andros.

15 **THOMAS**, Exeter, wit. in 1715, bot land in 1718 which he sold in 1742 to Ephraim Robinson, s. of (8 jr.). His will, 10 July 1745—25 July 1750, names s. John (homestead), daus. **Abigail** Maloon, **Mary** Judkins, **Rachel** Maloon, **Hannah** Bean and **Elizabeth**. Caleb Gilman jr. and Benj. Gordon, both of Exeter, were exec.'s sureties. Unless David (4) had totally undocumented ch. it seems imposs. to find a place for (15) in the 3d gen. of the large Ex. fam.

16 **TIMOTHY**, Dover, cordwainer, b. 15 Mar. 1667-8, s. of Timothy and Mary (Kitchen) of Salem, was brot to Dover as a baby by his mo. on her 2d marriage with Thomas Hanson(7) in 1669. Gr. 1694. Constable 1699. He m. Mary Roberts(5) and they were strong Quakers, the news of his death being rec. by Collins, the Quaker diarist of Salem. His will, 2 Feb. 1736-7—9 May 1737, names wid. Mary and surv. ch: **Abigail**, b. 23 May 1693, m. 5 Aug. 1712 Joseph Varney. **Mary**, b. 10 Apr. 1695, m. 19 Oct. 1719 Joseph Estes(2). **Elizabeth**, b. 14 Apr. 1700, d. 11 Apr. 1710. **Sarah**, b. 3 Oct. 1702, m. 26 Mar. 1723 John Varney. **Hannah**, b. 21 Nov. 1707, m. William Hussey(7). **Timothy**, b. 1 Aug. 1710, m. 24 Sept. 1730 Mary Allen who d. 8 Apr. 1792; found dead on the road 6 Nov. 1783. 13 ch. **Elizabeth**, b. 30 July 1712, m. 1st 13 May 1730 Henry Tibbetts, m. 2d Joseph Hussey(7).

17 **WIDOW** Robinson of Kittery and her ch. were drowned when Ambrose Berry's sloop went down on a voyage from Boston to Portsmouth in 1679.

18 **WILLIAM**, Kennebec?, wit. 1661 Parker to Davis.

19 **WILLIAM**, served writ in suit Thos. Newman v. Geo. Burnell, both of Arrowsic, 1716-7. Mr. W. R. d. at Georgetown in 1721, his wid. Sarah marrying one Denny that same yr.

Rocroft's men spent the winter of 1619-20 on the island (Monhegan). Am. Antiq. Soc. 31. 321 (1922).

**RODERIGO, Capt. Peter,** a 'Flanderkin,' was an officer under Capt. Jurriaen Aernouts, commander of a privateer commissioned by the Dutch gov. of Curacao, who plundered the French settlements from Castine northward in 1674. When Aernouts put in to Boston, after this expedition, Roderigo was left behind. With certain congenial spirits he bot the -Edward and Thomas-, estab. headquarters at Machias and began preying on New Eng. vessels trading with the French. Owners of captured vessels complained to the Boston magistrates, and Capt. Moseley was commissioned to hunt Roderigo out. Taking the Dutchman by surprise, Moseley captured him and brought his ships and men to Boston. A Court of Admiralty declared the ships lawful prizes, tried Roderigo for piracy, found him guilty and sentenced him to be hanged. He was pardoned, however, and is later found serving under Capt. Scottow at Black Pt. in Philip's war. Lists 3, 236, 237b. See 'Pirates of the New England Coast,' by Dow and Edmunds, 1923.

**Roe,** see Rowe.

**ROGERS,** patronymic from Roger. Common, partic. in so. western counties. Became 21st commonest name in N. E.

1 **CHRISTOPHER,** a servant of Sir Ferdinando Gorges, at York by 1643 when he wit. deed. Thos. Gorges gr. him marsh. Sold land to Mr. John Gooch in 1645. A cove and head-land at York retain his name.

2 **FRANCIS.** See Knapp(1).

3 **GEORGE,** one of Winter's fishermen at Richmond Isl. in 1638, settled at the Long Reach, Kittery, by 1641. Gr.j. 1650, 1651. Lists 21, 284. Convicted of adultery with Mrs. Stephen Batchelder in 1651, it was ordered that his prop. be held for the benefit of his ch. (their mo. appar. dead), and that they be put out as apprentices. One (a girl) went to Daniel Paul. Ano. girl was to be appren. by Mr. Rishworth at Hampton. One boy was to go to Anthony Emery and the youngest to Mrs. Shapleigh. Last ment. 1654. Of the four ch: **Benjamin,** was to have his fa.'s cow at Goodman Emery's. Thos. Crawley tried to have one B. R. indicted for suspicion of incontinency, ±1666. **Richard,** had the greater part of his fa.'s land. Prob. **Grace,** w. of Richard Miller(13) who liv. on so. part of G. R.'s land by 1667, m. 2d Christopher Banfield who sold 10 a. to Richard in 1697.

4 **JOHN,** York, alderman, aged 27, in 1640. His kinsman Robert Rogers of Boston was 23 in 1640. Cloth which he was sending to Boston to be made up by a tailor in 1640 was destroyed, as was the tailor, when the -Mary Rose- blew up.

5 **REV. JOHN,** Eliot, b. in Ipswich, s. of Rev. John and Martha (Whittingham), m. Susanna Whipple 16 Oct. 1718. H. C. 1711. Ordained minister at Eliot 25 Oct. 1721 after several yrs. service. His ho. a garrison. His diary may be read in 'Old Eliot,' vol. 7. He d. 16 Oct. 1773, his wid. surv. until 22 Oct. 1779. Ch: Rev. **John,** b. in Ips. 7 Aug. 1719, H. C. 1739, minister at Gloucester. Capt. **Timothy,** b. 8 Sept. 1721. **William,** b. 1 Oct. 1723, d. unm. 5 June 1747. **Katherine,** b. 2 Dec. 1725, d. 17 Mar. 1750. **Nathaniel,** b. Apr., d. 7 Aug. 1728. **Nathaniel,** Kittery, b. Aug. 1729. **Martha,** b. 14 Jan. 1731-2, m. John Hill. **Daniel,** Gloucester, b. 6 Oct. 1734. **Mary,** b. 4 Jan. 1737, m. Thomas Hammond.

6 **JOSHUA,** Newcastle, wit. for Edward Melcher 1667. Undoubtedly the Jos. of Lists 323, 326a, 330a(3). His w. may have been the goodwife Rogers who was a neighbor of Geo. Walton in 1667.

7 **REV. NATHANIEL,** Portsmouth, b. in Ipswich 22 Feb. 1669, s. of Rev. John, Pres. of Harvard, and Elizabeth (Denison); m. Sarah Purkis. H. C. 1687. After preaching a short time at Salem Village he was called to Portsm. and ordained 3 May 1699. In 1704 his ho. burned down and his mo.-in-law (see Elatson), infant dau. and negro servant lost their lives. After heated controversy the Ch. split in 1712, Mr. R. going to the new No. Ch. with his supporters, the new So. parish being estab. in the old meeting-ho. Lists 331c, 339, 96. He d. 3 Oct. 1723, ae. 54. Adm. 24 July 1724 to wid. Sarah, who m. 2d by 1731 John Plaisted, Esq. Adm. on her est. to her s. Daniel 27 Sept. 1749. Ch: *Hon. **Nathaniel,** H. C. 1717, doctor, speaker of the Assembly, m. 1st Olive Plaisted(2), m. 2d wid. Dorothy (Sherburne) Rymes, d. 24 Nov. 1745. **Sarah,** m. Rev. Joshua Gee(2). **Elizabeth,** d. in the fire, ag. 17 mos. **George,** Esq., Boston, m. Lydia Hutchinson. **Elizabeth,** m. 9 Apr. 1730 Rev. John Taylor. **Mary,** m. 2 Aug. 1733 Hon. Matthew Livermore. **John,** b. 5 Aug. 1714, d. aged 5. Hon. ‡**Daniel,** apothecary, member of the Royal Council, m. Mehitable Rindge. **Margaret,** d. unm., aged 22.

8 **RICHARD,** sued by Rev. Thomas Larkham of Dover in 1641. The town gr. him 20 a. on W. side of Back River in 1642. List 352.

9 **RICHARD**(3), Eliot, ship-carpenter, ±35 in 1678. O. F. 1669; town gr. 1671. His fa.'s land in the Long Reach laid out to him in 1698, on his pet. His 1st w. was prob. that Esther, w. of R. R. who was in ct. in 1675, included in a long list of Kittery offenders.

He m. 2d wid. Sarah (Libby 1) Tidy, who m.
3d Christopher Banfield. Either he or (10)
gr.j. 1688, 1693, 1694, 1697, 1698; j. 1696-7.
Lists 30, 298, 313ab, 331b; or (10) Lists 295,
297, 334a. His will, 11 Jan. 1700-1, inv. 28
Jan. 1701-2, names w. Sarah, only s. John,
s.-in-law (step-s.) John Tidy, and app. s.-in-
law Thos. Hanscom overseer. Ch. by 1st w:
Priscilla, w. of Jacob Smith of Kit. in 1716.
Alice, ±30 in 1695, m. Thomas Hanscom(3).
Rebecca, unm. 23 Sept. 1709. John, had the
homestead, m. 21 May 1704 Hannah Fogg
(1), wounded by Ind. 4 May 1705. Repeatedly on j. and gr.j. Lists 96, 268a, 290, 291(2),
296, 297. Will, 9 Mar. 1746-7—6 July 1747.
Ch. (b. 1705-1723), Richard, George, Hannah, Mary (m. John Godsoe 2), Margaret (m.
Samuel Libby 9), Keziah (m. Benaiah Hanscom 1), John.

10 RICHARD(13), Kittery, ±73 in 1735,
    was still of Saco in 1687, when, acc. of
stealing with William Erring, he had fled the
province, William Foxwell on his bond. Sold
10 a. of Saco marsh, 1687. Settling on the
w. side of Spruce creek, he m. Eleanor Moore
(25), who d. his wid. June 1747 in her 80th
yr. Lists 291, 298. He (Mr.) entered several
East. Cl. for the fam. prop. at Old Orchard.
He d. 8 June 1740 in his 78th yr. His will, 10
July 1737—30 May 1740, names w. and surv.
ch: Thomas, b. 29 Apr. 1694, m. 5 July 1723
Mary Fernald who d: 4 Feb. 1758. Had the
homestead. List 298. Ch. will, 1763—1776. Ch.
Eleanor, Elizabeth, Thomas, Mary, John,
Susanna, Margery, Richard. Hester, b. 25
Dec. 1696, d. 4 Jan. 1697. Elizabeth, b. 19
Nov. 1698, m. 16 May 1723 John Fernald, not
in fa.'s will. Sarah, b. 8 Jan. 1700, unm. in
1737. Mary, b. 10 Dec. 1704, m. 1st 5 Apr.
1722 Patrick Googins, m. 2d int. 10 Nov. 1739
Benjamin Parker jr. Richard, b. 4 Jan. 1705-
6, m. int. 10 May 1735-6 Sarah Fernald. Sold
Foxwell land to Paul Thompson, 1729; gave
Rogers land to Patrick Googins. Liv. in
1737. Esther, b. 4 Jan. 1708, m. 19 Dec. 1728
Samuel Pickernell. Dorothy, b. 8 July 1710,
m. bef. Dec. 1742 Samuel Willard of York.
Lydia, b. 7 Feb. 1713, m. int. 3 Apr. 1741
Daniel Junkins jr.

11 ROBERT, was too fat to tramp to Canada
    when captured by Ind. in attack on
Salmon Falls 18 Mar. 1689-90 and was
burned to death.

12 THOMAS, Saco, early near the mouth of
    Goosefair brook where Rogers' Garden
and Old Orchard, named for his surv. cherry-
trees, became place names. Wit. 1638. Dr.
Vines ment. him in a letter to Gov. Winthrop
in 1643. Subm. to Mass., 1653. Inv. of his
est. returned by Richard Foxwell and John
West, c. 1655. Lists 243ab. By unkn. w. he
had: William, Saco wit. in 1660, had quarrel
with John Bonython while walking up the

E. bank of the Saco with his br. Thomas in
1671. As Bonython, a close neighbor of
Thomas, did not recognize William and asked
who he was, it is apparent that he liv. at a
distance. He may have been (14) or (15-16)
or another. Thomas.

13 THOMAS(12), Saco, 36 in 1670, 38 in
    1671, wit. agreement betw. Henry Wad-
dock and James Gibbins, 1659. Constable
1659, 1665; gr.j. 1656; selectman, 1668, 1673;
com.t.e.s.c., 1673. He m. July 1657 Esther
Foxwell(5), List 246. In 1659 he had a town
gr. of 165 a. beyond Goosefair next to Richard Cummings, and in 1662 he had gr. from
James Gibbins of 200 a. from Goose Fare to
the next run of water, his ho. already standing on the land (which must have incl. the
former gr.). Lists 244cf, 245, 249(3), 252.
He was killed in Philip's war 13 Oct. 1675
going to the relief of Capt. Wincoll at Black
Pt., and his ho. was burned the next day.
Adm. gr. to his br.-in-law James Robinson in
1677. His fam. escaped to Kittery. Adm.
again to John Harmon 12 Apr. 1682, 'some of
the ch. now of age,' there being five of them:
Richard. William. Elizabeth, m. 1st Samuel
Carter, m. 2d John Benjamin. Lydia, m.
John Osborn. Mary, b. ±1674, in Boston with
Eleanor Foxwell in 1693, m. Evan Davis of
Southold, Long Isl. Her s. Sylvanus gave a
p/a to John Googins in 1755 to sell all rights
in the Old Orchard prop. The first ch.,
Thomas, b. 12 Jan. 1658, appar. d.y.

14 WILLIAM (see 12), Kennebec, m. Lydia
    Gutch(2) by 1670. List 191. Ch: Debo-
rah, 5 in 1675, was Deborah White in 1690-1
and m. 2d, int. in Boston 13 July 1695, John
Burnett (combine Burnett 1 and 4). Wid. in
Bos. in 1733. Lydia, m. John Orsment of
Manchester.

15 WILLIAM (see 12), York, subm. to
    Mass. 1652. Tr.j. 1651, gr.j. 1659. Had a
10 a. gr. on the far side of Mr. Gorges' creek
if he build within 1 yr. Adm. est. of William
Gurnsey of Isles of Shoals, 1657. Lists 275,
276, 313a, 331a. Very prob. same as (16).

16 WILLIAM (see 12, 15), Kittery, m. 1st
    bef. 1658-9 Sarah Lynn(2). Sued for debt
by Thomas Trafton in 1663 and in 1664 sued
Trafton for slandering his w., but bef. the
case was tried she had d. He sold the ho. and
½ the land he had received from his w.'s
step-fa. Gunnison to Elihu Gunnison in 1675.
Before 1676 he m. 2d wid. Rebecca (Mackworth) Wharfe and in 1681 was liv. in Falmouth, her old home, until driven away by
war. Lists 30, 93, 288, 299, 380(?). Ch. by
1st w: Alice, m. Henry Crown(1). Rebecca,
m. 1st Joseph Trickey, m. 2d Joshua Down-
ing(5), having an illegit. ch. in 1695, in the
interval betw. husbands.

17 WILLIAM(13), ±40 in 1723 when he
    test. ab. Kittery lands in 1702. Berwick

wit. 1703, Spruce creek wit. 1711. Kit. gr. 1699. He bot Alexander Thompson's gr. at Spruce Creek in 1714 and in 1715 bot from William Godsoe the 1 a. his house already stood on. He m. Mary Pope 17 Nov. 1706. List 291. Will, 29 Feb. 1719-20—10 Apr. 1725, named w. Mary sole legatee and overseers Capt. Wm. Pepperell jr. and Mr. Francis Pettigrove. She deeded the prop. to Richard Pope, in trust for her only s. William, 14 May 1726, and m. 2d Sept. 1726 Richard Rice. Ch: **Sarah**, b. 2 Apr. 1714, appar. d.y. **William**, sold all his right to lands in Old Orchard from his fa. and gr.fa. to William Googins in 1755. By w. Elizabeth he had 5 ch. b. 1748-1759, 4 ment. in his will of 1799.

**ROLFE.** 1 **Barbara**, an unruly dau. of George of London, was brot over by Thos. Babb(5) at request of her fa. ±1633. Edward Trelawney paid part of her expenses but her behavior here was so wild that Capt. Babb 'was forced to take her to another plantation.'

2 **BENJAMIN**, wit. with Capt. Scottow 1686 at Falmouth or Scarboro.

3 **SAMUEL** (Roff), ±21, at William Richard's ho. in Portsm. in 1693.

**ROLLINS**, Rawlins, Rawlings, derived from Ralph, found in Salop, Somerset and Wilts.

1 **ICHABOD**(2), Portsmouth, called cousin and kinsman by Capt. Barefoot who drew a draft on him in 1672. He m. Mary Tibbetts who m. 2d bef. 1700 Thomas Ash(3). Stephen Robinson of Kit. his bondsman, 1673. Dover gr., 1674-5. Lists 52, 57, 356j, 358b, 359b. Ch: **Ichabod**, Dover, m. 25 Dec. 1704 Mary Perkins(19), k. by Ind. 22 May 1707. List 96. One dau., **Hannah**, b. 16 July 1706, the mo.'s name rec. -Elizabeth- in error. **James**, Portsm., sailor, d. s.p. by 26 Oct. 1700 when his mo. renounced adm. in favor of Samuel Keais. Lists 67, 336b. **Jeremiah**, Somersworth, m. by 1714 Elizabeth Ham(4). Will, gentleman, 7 Dec. 1752—29 June 1768, disposed of large est., incl. two slaves Prince and Jupiter, to w., s. Ichabod (homestead), daus. Mary, Lydia, Deborah, Sarah, Elizabeth. Poss. **Elizabeth**, m. ±1697 John Edgerly(1).

2 **JAMES**, Dover (part later Newington), prob. he who was at Newbury 1634-1638. Signed Dover Comb., 1640; wit. a York deed, 1643. Town gr. in 1644 and 1656 (100 a. at Bloody Pt.). Bot a ho. at Long Reach from James Johnson, 1651. Presented for neglecting meeting in 1656 and for entertaining Quakers in 1659. In 1661 he was in London, where he received cloth to be deliv. to Mr. Cogswell of Ips. and Mr. Raynes of York. In 1663-4 he and sons Ichabod and

Joseph gave a bond to Mr. John Cutt, and in 1676-7 he mtg. his ho. and land to Cutt, excepting 8 a. already deeded to s. Morse and 18 a. to s. Samuel. Lists 52, 351b, 352, 354abc, 355ab, 356abceghk, 359ab. He d. bef. 13 Aug. 1687. Will, 16 Dec. 1685—25 July 1691, names w. Hannah, eldest s. Ichabod, sons Benjamin, Joseph, 'all my ch., sons and daus., every one of them,' Henry Langstaff, Obadiah Morse and Philip Chesley overseers. A lot gr. to him was laid out to Amos Murrell (q.v.) in 1722. Ch: **Ichabod. Rebecca**, m. Isaac Stokes and left him bef. 1663-4 when she promised to go back. **Joseph**, carpenter, charged with stealing a canoe in 1672, his bros. Ichabod and Samuel on his bond. No further rec. **Samuel. Benjamin**, ±23 in 1685, at Portsm. with Ichabod, who was responsible for his lodging, in 1678; gave a note in 1682; appren. to br. Samuel to learn trade of wheelwright 13 Aug. 1687, his fa. then dead. Sold 35 a. to John Pickering jr., 1689, with consent of bros. Ichabod and Samuel, and was prob. dead in 1690 when wit. prov. the deed. His sis.-in-law Rebecca Rollins(5) obtained his est. by paying his debts and deeded it to her sons in 1734. Lists 94, 359b. A **dau.**, m. Obadiah Morse(9). **Sarah**, m. Philip Chesley(3). Poss. **Thomas** (6), and **John**. Abigail (Rollins 5) Richards stated in a depos. in 1749 that she had liv. bef. her marriage with -John-, s. of James Rollins, poss. a scrivener's error. One John m. in Newbury 9 Oct. 1702 Mary Thomas of Oyster Riv., bot land there of Roger Rose and leased it back to him in 1705, wit. Obadiah Morse (strong ev. of some relationship to this fam., altho a cursory glance at the Newbury rec. would seem to place him as John, s. of Nicholas R., b. 1680). Lists 368b, 369.

3 **JOHN**, prob. a sea-capt., was permitted by Mr. Eliot to lodge in Mr. Isaac Bowde's wareho. as he was a friend of B.'s and had no fixed place of abode, 1683. List 52.

4 **RICHARD**, laborer, Oyster Riv., compl. of for beating Barth. Stevenson, 1685. List 95(2).

5 **SAMUEL**(2), Portsmouth, carpenter and wheelwright, appar. m. Rebecca Pickering(2), memb. of the No. Ch., who was gr. adm. 23 Nov. 1694 on his insolvent est., John Pickering and Wm. Cotton bondsmen. He d. 29 Oct. 1694. Lists 52, 57, 62, 94, 331bc, 333a, 334a, 356m, 359b. Some land rem. after payment of debts as it was held by 6 ch. in 7ths. The wid. was prob. that Rebecca who, ±60 in 1713, spoke of (2) as fa. in a depos. She deeded 60 a. bounded by lands of sons James and Samuel to her s. Joseph in 1744. Ch., order unkn: **Abigail**, ±73 in 1749, m. 12 Aug. 1697 Joseph Richards(3) who had a

deed from her mo. in 1729 and sold to her br. Samuel in 1734. **Joseph**, Newington, sold land inherited from his gr.fa., 1733. Will, 14 Feb. 1748-9—30 May 1749, names w. Sarah, sons Joseph, Samuel, Noah, daus. Sarah Allard, Mary Dam, Deborah, Elizabeth. **John**, drowned in the river, s.p. (inq. 22 Aug. 1718). His mo. deeded to Samuel her rights in John's est. in 1734. **James**, Newington, betw. 20 and 30 in (1). Will, 12 Dec. 1743—28 Mar. 1744, names w. and ch. Edward, Ichabod, John, Abigail, Mary. **Samuel**, Newington, m. 5 May 1720 Else (Alice) Dam, owned cov. 6 Aug. 1721 and had ch. Hannah, John, Alice, Lydia, Samuel, Jonathan, Hannah (again) and Paul bp. 1721-1735. **Sarah**, m. Samuel Migill (1). Poss. **Deborah**, bp. 14 Oct. 1694, m. 20 Mar. 1718-9 James Benson(1).

6 **THOMAS**(2?), Exeter, betw. 20 and 30 in 1671, his origin subject to some uncertainty. Taxed in Dover, 1662-1665, which is ev. on the side of relationship to (2), yet there is no doc. ev. to sustain flat statement of son-ship. An attempt to connect him with the Thos. Rawlins fam. of Weymouth, based on similarity of given names, has even more negative factors. Had a 30 a. Exeter gr. in 1670 and was adm. inhab. in 1673-4. Later gr., 1698. He m. Rachel Cox(18). Lists 52 (2), 54, 57, 356ghjk, 363c, 376b, 381, 384b. Adm. 19 Oct. 1706 to wid. Rachel, a memo. 'the children's names' among the papers. They made a div. agreement 28 Aug. 1707. Lt. **Thomas**, b. 14 July 1671, Stratham, m. 1st 29 Nov. 1696 Phebe Lawrence, m. 2d wid. Sarah (Philbrick) Sanborn who d. 30 May 1761. Lists 67, 388, 376b. Will, 8 Mar.—24 May 1753, names w. Sarah, s. Caleb, gr.s. Thomas, and daus. Dorcas (Bennett 9) Glidden, Tabitha Piper, Katherine Sanborn, Phebe Chase, Mary Coffin, Rachel Smith and names s.-in-law Daniel Sanborn exec. **Moses**, b. 14 Oct. 1672, Stratham, m. one Esther (ct. Dec. 1701) to whom adm. was gr. 4 June 1718 (d. 28 Feb. 1717-8), Moses Leavitt and Jonathan Wadleigh bondsmen. 9 ch. b. 1701-1717. Lists 67, 376b, 388. Sergt. **Joseph**, b. 6 May 1674, Stratham, m. 1st one Hannah, m. 2d wid. Lydia (Heard 2) Norris who sued for dower in 1749. He d. 20 Jan. 1749. Will, 11 Mar. 1746-7—25 Jan. 1748-9, ment. w. Lydia (d. 4 Oct. 1752), s. Joseph (exec.), s. Joshua (homestead), and daus. Hannah Redman, Elizabeth Marston, Charity Merrill, Mercy, Rachel, Mary Wright, all by 1st w. Lists 67, 376b, 388. **Mary**, b. 8 May 1676, m. Stephen Page(9). **Benjamin**, b. 6 July 1678, Ex., m. 1st one Sarah (ct. June 1701, Benj. Palmer and Thos. Rollins her bondsm.). She was poss. the 'dau. Rowlings' of Joseph Palmer(14)'s will. He m. 2d one Elizabeth. List 376b. Will, 7 Dec. 1736—16 Jan. 1740,

names w. and s. Josiah (joint exec.), sons John, Benjamin, daus. Abigail Folsom, Alice Selly, Dorothy Steel, Mercy, Anne, Elizabeth. **John**, ±60 in 1742, ±70 in 1752, poss. he who m. in Hampt. 27 Aug. 1706 Sarah Souther. 6 ch. b. in Stratham 1707-1719. List 376b. **Aaron**, Newmarket, m. a dau. of Edward Taylor, k. with a little dau. in Ind. attack 29 Aug. 1723, his w. and two ch. taken captive. Lists 376b, 388. See Coleman's 'N. E. Captives,' ii: 154-6. His br. Samuel app. adm. 31 Oct. 1723 with consent of other bros., no ment. of wid. **Samuel**, 16 in 1706, m. 21 May 1714 Elizabeth Palmer (James 5). **Alice**, m. at Hampton, 2 Mar. 1704-5 Roger Shaw. **Rachel**.

7 **WILLIAM** (Rawling), prob. a ship capt., wit. will of John Tucker in Kittery, 1670.

**ROMER**, Col. **Wolfgang William**, His Majesty's Engineer, recommended fortifications at South Portland for Casco Bay and at Stage gut, at Winter Harbor, Jan. 10, 1700-1. In 1703 he directed the construction of pallisades at the headquarters (where?) for a winter expedition against Norridgewock.

**ROPER**, **Walter**, carpenter, ±48 in 1661, ±50 in 1661-2, ±65 in 1676, and w. Susan, ±53 in 1669, settled in Hampton perhaps as early as 1640. Proprietor 1641. Freeman 13 May 1642. Selectman 1644. Had sh. in commons 1646. Bef. 1647 he sold out to Robert Sayward and moved to Ipswich. 'He often came to Hampton to see his brethren and neighbors.' See Palmer(15). Lists 392ab, 393b, 391a. Will, 1680, names w. and surv. ch. In 1710 Mary Sparks was the only surv. ch., and the only heirs, with her, were the ch. of Elizabeth Dutch and the wid. of John Roper. Ch: **John**, m. Anne Caldwell, d. s.p. 27 Nov. 1709 in 60th yr. (gr.st. in Ips.). Will. **Benjamin**, slain in Philip's war, 29 Sept. 1675, s.p. **Nathaniel**, d. s.p. at sea on voyage to Barbadoes in 1685. Nuncup. will left all to br. John and nephew Benj. Dutch who was W. R.'s only surv. gr.s. and male heir in 1711. **Mary**, bp. 22 Aug. 1641, m. John Sparks. **Elizabeth**, m. John Dutch. **Sarah**, in prison in 1665 for stealing from her former master Denison. Prob. d. unm.

**Ropes**, George, planted a little field 'away up the Presumpscot riv.' with David Phippen in 1703.

**ROSCOE**, **Robert**, m. Anna Willix of Exeter, who had been a servant of Rev. Timothy Dalton of Hampton, and rem. to Roanoke, Va. See Register 50. 46; 68. 81.

# ROSE.

1 **ROGER**, ±28 in 1667, ±37 in 1672-3, sailor, servt. of Lt. Wm. Hudson of Boston in 1660 when he was acc. as fa. of a ch. b. to Abigail Grant, ±26, dau. of Christopher G.

of Watertown. Rose was in Mr. Ford's vessel on a voyage to Jamaica when the baby
was born and m. Abigail on his return. Susannah Smith, ag. 15, called them uncle and
aunt in 1682-3. In York, but of Boston, 1675.
Sold Bos. prop. in 1678 and moved to Piscataqua. Had a ho. at Oyster Riv. in 1681.
N. H. j. 1684. Bound to keep peace toward
Wm. Graves, 1685. See Graffam. Lists 14,
57, 96, 312e, 358b, 367b. Late of O. R., now
of Watertown, mariner, 1695. Will, 30 July
—3 Sept. 1705, ment. w. Abigail, farm at
Lamprill riv., land in Portsmouth, and kinswoman Elizabeth Aysley of London (resid.
legatee). Only kn. ch: Dau., b. 6 July 1660, d.
in a week. Prob. Abigail, compl. in Sept.
1703 of her master Samuel Merry, who sued
Roger Rose in next ct. Yet Merry was
bound to the peace for beating Mrs. Abigail
Rose, w. of Roger, in 1703.

2 STEPHEN, Kittery wit. 1714, taxed Str.
Bank 1717, prob. husb. of Elizabeth Ham-
mons(2).

Roslings, Richard, Isles of Shoals. List 307b.

ROSS, primarily a Scottish name, meaning
red. Also a commune in Normandy and a
lordship in co. York.

½ ALEXANDER, Portsmouth, taxed 1688-
1690.

1 JAMES, Casco, shoemaker, here by 1658
and may have been a Scotch prisoner
who arr. in Boston in 1651 (List 74). He m.
Anne Lewis(4) and with her was k. in the
Ind. attack of 11 Aug. 1676. He had been
constable that yr. List 25. Of the 'children'
only one is ident: James, ±70 in 1731, ±81 in
1742, cordwainer, liv. on Andrews Isl. with
his uncle Skillin in his youth, was of Wells
as a young man, had a 100 a. gr. and bot a
saw-mill (at Cape Porpus) from Gilbert Endicott in 1683. In 1687 he petitioned Gov.
Andros for land his fa. had occupied 30 yrs.
ago. A soldier of Fort Loyal, he was made
prisoner when the fort fell in 1690 and taken
to Canada, being redeemed in Oct. 1695. Two
months later, in Berwick 19 Dec., he m. a
fellow captive, Sarah Ferguson. They mov.
to Salem, where he m. 2d 3 Nov. 1706 Martha
Darling. In 1711 he was ordered to serve
as pilot for the fleet going ag. Canada. Geo.
Cloyes deeded him Falmouth land in 1718-9,
and he sold ±160 a. at Back cove to Daniel
Epps in 1720-1. Made several depos. about
early days in Casco in his old age. Lists 34,
99 p. 74, 268a, 269b. No kn. ch. A James
Ross, poss. a Scotch-Irish emigrant, d. in
Kennebunk 16 Aug. 1749, ag. 35.

2 JOHN, Eliot, prob. a Scotch prisoner, had
a Kittery gr. 23 Nov. 1655 which he sold
to John Breathy (Brady) in 1672. John
Heard's will directs that he be permitted to
occupy the ho. which he had built on H.'s

land for life. Lists 34?, 74?, 298.

3 JOHN, late of Wells, dec., in 1734, leaving
ch: William, Wells, housewright. John,
Boston, mariner. Abigail, Boston, spinster.

4 WILLIAM, Portsmouth, m. Grace Peverly
(1). Taxed 1707 to 1726. Rated at So.
Ch. 1717. List 339. Ch: Jonathan, joiner.
William, carpenter.

ROUNDS, Mark, gunsmith and soldier, was
servant of Henry Kemble when he served
in Philip's war, being wounded in Rhode Isl.
Helped build the garrison at Kennebec in
1677. At Scarboro, 1681. Set up his forge at
Newcastle where he was in trouble in 1684
for kicking Joanne, w. of John the Frenchman, also for speaking contemptuously of
the Gov. and Capt. Barefoot. At the fort at
Pemaquid when it surrendered in 1696. Next
in Boston where he m., int. 11 Nov. 1696,
Sarah Larriford. In Feb. 1699-1700 at Fort
Mary on the Saco. Finally settled at Casco
near Capt. Samuel Moody at Casco Fort.
Lists 127, 184, 229, 238a, 268a. He d. bef.
1720. Kn. ch: Samuel, eldest s., of Boston in
1720 when he q.c. Falm. ho. and land to
Jonathan Sherman; of York 14 Dec. 1727
when he m. Mary Young; of Biddeford, carpenter, 1732; again of York 1737. Joseph, b.
4 Sept. 1699; blacksmith; of Biddeford in
1733 when he q.c. the Falm. ho. and land; m.
Susanna Homeyard; Boston. George, m.
Mary Webb.

ROUSE, from 'rous,' meaning red. Found
in Cornwall.

1 JOHN, Marshfield, bot from James Andrews in 1698 Portland (Cushing's) Isl.,
Ram Isl., 200 a. on the mainland and lands
at Androscoggin. He entered an East. Cl.
and sold to John Brown of Marshf. in 1711-2.

2 JOHN, York, fa. of Mary Averill (Job)'s
ch. called Lydia, b. 15 Oct. 1719 (ct. Jan.
1719-20).

3 NICHOLAS, of Wembury, co. Devon,
dwelt at the house at Casco in 1630.

4 THOMAS, Portsmouth, m. 2 Sept. 1689
wid. Rebecca (Brookings 5) (Pomery)
Rummerill as his 2d w. Taxed 1691. She and
her s. Thos. Pomery deeded to him in 1696.
Lists 330d, 337. He d. bef. 2 June 1713 when
the inv. of his est. and of that of his predecessor Pomery was taken. The wid. m. 25
Oct. 1714 George Alston. By a 1st w. he had
Joanna, m. Anthony Rowe(2 jr.).

ROWDEN, Capt. John, from Salem where he
had a 1st w. Mary, m. 2d wid. Elizabeth
Hammond(4) after 1677, and liv. on her
estate on the Kennebec, prob. on the west
side near Merrymeeting bay. Commissioner,
1687. Bef. 4 Sept. 1688 both were taken
prisoner by Ind. (her 2d captivity) and
Capt. Rowden, at least, never returned. Lists
124, 189, 97.

**ROWE,** most common in Cornwall.

1 **ANTHONY,** Scarboro, fisherman, 40 in 1676, bot 50 a. from Mr. Jocelyn in 1663 and had a gr. of 6 a. of marsh in 1671. Constable, 1670-1, 1673. Retired to Portsm. during Philip's war and again in 1690. Appr. Thos. Cleverly's est. at Black Pt., 1682. Selectman 1681, 1682, 1684. Sold his Scarb. prop. to John Waldron in 1700. Lists 30, 34, 236, 237ade, 238a, 239a, 330df, 331b. He d. bef. 1713. Only kn. ch. by unkn. w: **Anthony. Elizabeth,** m. Thomas Larrabee(6).

2 **ANTHONY**(1), Portsmouth, weaver, deposed in 1731 about Scarboro matters of 40 yrs. before. In 1697 he was the grantee of an extraordinary deed by which Nathan Knight and w. Mary (Westbrook) conv. 13 a. originally gr. to Anthony Ellins, Mary's br. Col. Thomas Westbrook signing it tho not named as grantor and the whole being ack. by the grantee, A. R., and his w. Martha. This may be only stupid conveyancing, but it provides a suggestion that Martha Row was b. a Westbrook. Propinquity and a deed from Rowe to John Brewster, on the other hand, have raised a conjecture that Martha was a Brewster(1). His 2d w. was definitely wid. Esther (Manson 5) (Cross) Dennett(2), m. 12 Dec. 1736. Lists 337, 339. In 1713 he deeded his homestead to his s. Anthony. In 1737 he and w. Esther sold the ho. in which they were liv. on Portsm. Plains, adjoining his son's land. Kn. ch: **Anthony,** m. 30 Jan. 1712-3 Joanna Rouse(4), both liv. in 1743. List 339. In 1717 they deeded to Samuel Brewster land adj. that sold to John Brewster by Anthony's fa. At least 4 sons, Lazarus, Noah, Anthony, Joseph. And quite poss. **Margaret** who m. 23 June 1709 their neighbor on Portsm. Plains, James Sherburne.

3 **EDWARD,** prob. a br. of (14), Exeter, fined 1664. Had land at Newmarket, 1676. Lists 52, 57, 367b. Hanged himself at Newington 24 Feb. 1695.

4 **EDWARD**(14), Newington, held ¼ of his fa.'s est. Had 200 a. gr. at Bloody Pt., 1693-4. His w. Mary. He settled his affairs by deed to s. Samuel in 1729, he to pay other named ch: **Samuel,** of Berwick in 1735, with w. Deborah (Canney), m. in Newington 13 Apr. 1730. **Richard. Susanna,** acc. John Davis(35) in 1723, m. in 1725 James Benson (1). **Eunice,** m. 6 Dec. 1716 John Place.

4½ **ELIAS,** owed est. of Hercules Hunking (2), 1659.

5 **GEORGE,** Portsmouth 1657. Gr. 1660. List 330b.

6 **GILES,** soldier under Capt. Davis at Falmouth fort, slain 21 Sept. 1689.

7 **JOHN.** Four unattached items: John, a wit. with Nicholas(13), 1658. John, ±35 in 1677 at Damariscove when they fled from the Ind. John, drowned in Piscataqua riv., Dec.1693. John, Newcastle wit.,1705. Lists, unassigned, 67, 90, 142, 318b, 330a, 336b.

8 **MARGERY,** Newcastle, acc. Thomas Marshall(9), Dec. 1695, but he denied it. Ordered in 1696 either to go into a family or back where she came from.

9 **MARK,** Isles of Shoals, 33 in 1672, generally Mr., neglected jury duty in 1665. Called Bartholomew Burrington a thief and lost the consequent suit, 1666. Gr.j. 1666. Fined for damaging a bridge, 1667. Threatened to break Roger Kelly's head, 1667-8. Fined for not going home to his w. in 1670 and again reminded of her in 1671, which poss. made him swear (ct. 1671). Portsm. minister's rate rebated 1679-80. List 305a.

10 **MARTHA,** m. 22 Aug. 1689 Edward Howard. Unplaced.

11 **MATTHEW.** See Rew.

12 **MICHAEL,** Newcastle, appr. Jeremiah Walford's est. in 1660. He is the most prob. husb. for Mary Mussell(3) who was a wid. Rowe when she m. Digory Jeffrey by 1664 and who had a s. **Richard** ment. in his gr.fa. Mussell's will.

13 **NICHOLAS,** Portsmouth, to whom, with Edward Barton, the town gr. Portsm. neck ±1640. In 1647 he drew a bill on Mr. George Smith in favor of John Billin. Sued Jonas Clay for killing a cow, 1649. Sued by Barton in 1657. In 1659 he sold his ho. and land at Sagamore creek to Richard Shortridge. Lists 8, 41, 321, 323, 326a, 330ac. His w. Elizabeth slandered Alice Moses in 1648, and in 1656 announced that there were three men witches at Strawberry Bank. His gr. of 1652 was laid out in 1674 to his s. **William,** his only heir.

14 **RICHARD,** Dover in 1669, at Welshman's cove. Bondsman for Richard Andrews, 1682. Gr.j. 1672, 1676, 1679. Lists 52, 54, 57(2), 311c; 356egh(2)k, 357c, 359ab. He d. bef. 1703 when his wid. Susanna, 'ancient,' relinq. adm. in favor of s. Thomas, Wm. Furber bondsman. In 1703-4 the prop. was div. betw. ch: **Thomas. Edward. Jane,** m. John Dam jr.(4). And 'others, if heard from.'

15 **RICHARD**(12), Kittery, successfully sued his step-fa. Jeffrey for 1½ a., £7 and 2 cows, in 1676. Age given as ±40 in 1678, but +30 in 1680. Boarding-master for Francis Hooke in 1680. List 298. He d. bef. 1684 when his wid., Anne, was selling without a lic. and permitting disorder in her ho. at Kit. Pt. Adm. to Francis Hooke, creditor, 1685. In 1710 the wid. was Anne Spiller of Boston, +16, stating that she had formerly liv. in Digory Jeffrey's ho. She d. in Bost. in 1722, aged -85-. Ch: **Mary,** m. 11 Dec. 1695 James Cox(4). 10 ch. rec. in Boston. **Elizabeth,** m. 12 July 1711 John Dorothy. Poss.

others, as Mrs. Cox and Mrs. Dorothy deeded their fa.'s whole prop. in 1713 with what seems to be a warranty ag. other heirs.

16 **ROBERT**, Isles of Shoals, fisherman, 1671. Lent (or sent) fish to Sylvester Herbert (3).

17 **ROBERT** and **ROBERT, JR.**, Hampton, both taxed in 1709. Robert sr. m. 1st 19 Dec. 1707 Mehitable Leavitt(1), m. 2d 3 Mar. 1726 Apphia (Shaw) Sanborn. For many ch., including a Robert, b. 11 Dec. 1726, see Dow's Hampton. Robert jr. m. 21 May 1708 Mehitable Swayne and had ch. b. 1709-1725.

18 **THOMAS**(14), Portsmouth, 75 in 1733, had double sh. (½) of his fa.'s Dover prop. and sold it in 1708-9 to Hatevil Nutter, including the ho. but reserving the family grave-yard. Taxed in Greenland 1708, 1713, 1714 (and a son). Lists 62, 343, 396. W. Elizabeth. Only ident. ch., poss. of many: **Thomas**, m. 17 Jan. 1720-1 Rachel Peavey, both of Newingt. Both adm. to full com. there 27 Feb. 1725-6. Ch. **Dau.**, m. a Quint. Thomas Quint bp. on his gr.fa. Row's account 1 Dec. 1723. Poss. **Mary**, m. 5 Jan. 1726-7 Samuel Place, both of Newingt.

19 **WILLIAM**(13), Newcastle, fisherman, 30 in 1675. He m. in Ipswich Nov. 1671 Sarah Woodward who, before and after marriage, had a serious flirtation with one John Leigh, aired in ct. in great detail. See Rec. and Files of the Quarterly Courts of Essex Co., Vol. V. In 1678 he sold a ho. he had bot in Ips. and in 1676 bot and built in Newcastle. Called merchant in later life. Lists 52, 54, 90, 313a, 319, 330ac, 331b. His est. was divided in 1728, in 5 shares. Ch: **William**, had ⅖ of his fa.'s and gr.fa.'s estates; d. in Jamaica; adm. 20 July 1724 to Thomas Cotton. **Ezekiel**. Benj. Morse of Newbury dep. in 1741-2 that he had known William Rowe who had sent two of his ch. to Newbury, and that Ezekiel was lost at sea, s.p. **Mary**, sent to Newbury; m. Jeremiah Goodridge(3); q.c. int. in his gr.fa.'s est. to Thomas Cotton. **Elizabeth**, spinster, of Boston in 1724 when she sold ⅕ of her gr.fa.'s est. **Sarah**, m. Thomas Larkin and was his wid., of Boston, in 1724.

**Rowelling**, Thomas, Exeter tax-list 1682-3. Rowell?

**ROWLAND**. 1 **John**, a Me. fisherman drowned in 1654. List 244b.

2 **MR.**, Cape Elizabeth, 1683. List 226.

**ROWLANDSON**, Rowland, shipped on the -Katherine-, Capt. Joseph Stephenson, 12 Mar. 1699-1700 at London and was one of the crew in Portsmouth 14 Nov. 1701. In Apr. 1703 Ruth Partridge(1) was his reputed w. She m. 2d bef. 1722 one Tarrott.

**Rowley**, William. List 386.

**ROWSLEY**, **Robert**, Portsmouth, sailor, m. wid. Abigail Alcock(3), about 1679. See Dew(1). In 1681 he was in the crew of the ketch -Prosperous-, Michael Mann master. She took lodgers. See Lewis(18). Both were seated in the meeting-ho. in 1693. Lists 329, 335a.

**Roy**, Peter, alias King. See Brackett(4).

**ROYAL**, a township in Northumberland. Royle and Ryle in Cheshire.

1 **CAPT. JOHN**(3), at York with his parents at out-break of Philip's war, but, instead of accomp. them to Boston, ret. to No. Yar. in 1680-1 and remained there until again driven off by war. Committee to get a minister, 1681. One of 4 trustees for No. Yar. in 1684. Arrested for selling liquor to Ind. in 1688 and taken to Boston for trial. Captured by Ind. in Sept. 1688 and redeemed thru influence of Baron Castine, acc. to trad. Lists 18, 32, 212, 214(2). A victualler in Boston in 1693. He m. Elizabeth Dodd (George), who was called kinswoman by Joseph Carlisle of York. She pet. Gov. Andros in 1688 on account of her husb.'s losses. She m. 2d at York 9 May 1699 Thomas Southerin. Two dau. surv: **Elizabeth**, m. James Baston(3). **Phebe**, m. 1st at Wells 30 June 1712 James Tanner who d. bef. 1721-2 when she had an illegitimate ch.; m. 2d James Tyler of Scarboro and was his wid. in 1756.

2 **TEAGUE**, Oyster Riv. Lists 359a, 363abc, 365, 366. Adm. gr. 23 June 1677 to John Woodman and Stephen Jones. Philip Russell and Wm. Pitman depos. 11 Dec. 1677 that he said that he had no kindred in this country and that Wm. Durgin was to have all his prop.

3 **WILLIAM**, North Yarmouth, cooper, engaged by Mass. Bay Co. 23 Mar. 1628 to go to N. E. and arrived in 1629 at Salem where he gave his name to Royal's Side. By 1636 he settled at Wescustogo, on a tract of 250 a. bordering on Royal Riv., gr. to him by Thos. Gorges in 1643. Had difficulties with George Cleeve 1636-1640. Lists 22, 211, 221. In 1665 the people of No. Yar., being without a minister, met at his ho. on Sundays. Clerk of the writs in 1667. In 1673 he deeded part of his lands to his sons William and John for support. At the beginning of Philip's war he abandoned No. Yar., of which he had been the leading citizen since his first settlement, and retired to Dorchester. His neighbors depos. that he was ab. 80 yrs. of age when he arrived there. He d. 15 June 1676. His w. Phebe (Green) d. 16 July 1678. His est. was not settled until 1722-3 when, on request of his sons William, Isaac and Joseph, his gr.s. Jacob was app. adm.

For clue to his English origin see will of Cicely Ambrose of Stepney, co. Middlesex, 1639 (Waters, p. 738). Ch: **William. John. Samuel,** Boston, cooper, was wounded at Black Pt. garrison in 1675 and d. a week later. By w. Sarah he had Sarah, b. 18 May 1664 and Samuel and Mary (twins), b. 17 Feb. 1666. **Isaac,** Dorchester, carpenter, soldier under Capt. Moseley in 1676; m. 1st Ruth Tolman who d. 1 May 1681; his 2d w., Waitstill Spurr, d. 29 Nov. 1732; bur. 17 Jan. 1729. 4 + 5 ch. **Joseph,** Boston, sailmaker, had w. Mary who was bur. 8 Mar. 1713-4; he d. 14 Jan. 1728, ag. 83; will, 1727—1728. 8 ch. Two ch. of Elizabeth (maiden name unknown), w. successively of Thos. Barlow, John Coombs and John Warren, called J. R. unc.e in 1685. A poss. dau. is **Margaret,** w. of Thomas Stevens who called William(4) br. in 1674.

**4 WILLIAM**(3), No. Yar. and Dorchester, carpenter. In 1721 he stated that in 1663 his fa. had given him a neck of land between two rivers in consid. of his keeping his parents and a maid for the term of their lives, and that he had complied with this condition until 1675 when harried away by the Ind., and that he had at his own cost given his fa. and mo. decent funerals. Deeded to s. Jacob in 1718. He d. 7 Nov. 1724 in his 85th yr. (gr.st. in Dorchester). Of his many ch. by w. Mary, col. **Isaac** acquired an enormous fortune in Antigua and returned to Mass. to live in great style on the Usher estate in Medford, **Jacob,** a Boston merchant, was adm. of his gr.fa. Royal's est., and **Samuel** removed with his w. Priscilla (Adams), and 5 ch. to No. Yar. in his middle age and perpet. the fam. name in Me.

**RUCK, Samuel** or **James,** wit. deed of Thos. Webber of Kennebec, planter, and Mary his w., to Richard Collicutt of land on Long Isl., Sagadahoc, 1663-1665. One Samuel was freeman in Boston, 1683.

**RUGG, John,** wit. for Christopher Lawson to his purchase of land for Clarke and Lake in 1658. O. A., Kennebec, 8 Sept. 1665. List 182.

**Ruiske** (Rusk?), **William.** List 271.

**RULE, John,** mariner, m. in Saco 13 June 1668 Emm Seeley. Wit. Richard Seeley's bill to Henry Kemble, 1670. Had a Saco gr. of 20 a. in 1684. Lists 235, 246, 238b. Moved to Boston where Rowland Story submitted a bill for 'graving Mr. Rule's barque' in 1684. An execution against him was returned -non est inventus- in 1708. He entered an Eastern Cl. to a ho. at Saco which he had bot from the est. of Humphrey Warren. Mrs. Rule was bur. in Bos. 29 Jan. 1717. Ch: **Margaret;** Rev. Cotton Mather told sensational ta'es of her as a victim of witchcraft in 1694; m. 1st 13 Nov. 1695 Joseph Page, m. 2d

23 Sept. 1700 Thomas Johnson, m. 3d 11 **Mar.** 1707 Benjamin Snelling. In 1698 she was exec. of the est. of William Brood, mariner, as 'my dearly well beloved friend.' **Sarah,** d. 1690, ag. 9 yrs. (Copp's Hill). **Dorcas,** unm. in 1729 when she and Margaret q.c. the Me. prop. to John Stackpole; m. 22 Mar. 1730 James Taylor. **Elizabeth,** m. 15 Nov. 1727 John Frothingham of Charlestown, shipwright. She q.c. the Me. prop. to Samuel Jordan in 1739. Poss. **Mary** (Role) who ran away to Rhode Isl. in 1702.

**RUMERY, Matthew,** a soldier who got his head broken in the fight aboard the -Falkland- at Newcastle in 1694. See Long (1). Lists 315bc. One Elizabeth Rumery was pd. for sweeping the Newc. meeting-ho. in 1704.

**RUMMERILL, Clement,** Portsmouth, m. Rebecca (Brookings) Pommery 6 Sept. 1687, the 2d of 4 husb., and d. bef. 1689 when she m. Thomas Rouse. Thomas Pickering had taken his personal effects.

**RUNLETT,** very uncommon, not in Lower or Guppy.

**1 CHARLES,** Exeter, ±20 in 1672, was servant of Philip Chesley in 1667. Captured by Ind. in 1675. He m. 10(11) 1675 Mary Satchwell, wid. successively of William Dale and Nicholas Smith. Lists 52, 67, 96. Drowned 1 Apr. 1709. Ch: **Charles** and **Jane,** twins, b. 9 May 1676. She m. at Hampton 24 Feb. 1699 John Anthony. **Mary,** m. John Clark(23). **James. Satchwell.**

**2 CHARLES**(1), Exeter, had a 30 a. gr. in 1697-8 and 50 a. in 1706. He m. Lydia Ladd(4) who was gr. adm. 6 Mar. 1722-3. Lists 376b, 388. Kn. ch: **Charles,** Newmarket, weaver, m. Lydia Ames. **Nathaniel,** Wiscasset, m. in Falmouth 13 May 1737 Mary Mitchell. **Mary,** m. John Huntoon(1).

**3 LT. JAMES**(1), Stratham, m. 21 Nov. 1699 Elizabeth Robinson(8) to whom, with s. Daniel, adm. was gr. 1723-4, and who m. 2d by 1732 Abraham Folsom(4). The heirs held his est. in ninths. Lists 67, 376b, 388(2). Ch: **Lydia,** b. 22 Oct. 1700, m. Moses Norris(2 jr.). **Daniel,** b. 11 Mar. 1702, m. at Hamp. Falls 9 July 1724 Lydia Cram. **Theophilus,** b. 11 Feb. 1704, m. 18 Aug. 1726 Leah Smith (Jacob). **Jonathan,** b. 19 Nov. 1705, m. Rachel Smith (Jacob). **James,** b. 15 Oct. 1709. **Mary,** b. 22 Apr. 1712. **Sarah,** b. 2 June 1714. **Charles,** b. 3 June 1716, Exeter, capt., blacksmith, had w. Dorothy. **Josiah,** b. 22 June 1719, d. 10 Jan. 1719-20. **Ruth,** who m. 14 Dec. 1727 Samuel Kenniston, may have been dau. of (2) or of (3), or a young wid.

**4 SATCHWELL**(1), Stratham, m. 30 **Dec.** 1706 Mercy Leavitt who d. 21 Jan. 1741-2. Bot 8 a. from Benj. Hoag in 1709 and ±77 a.

from Samuel Waldo in 1738. Lists 376b, 388. Will, 4 Mar. 1744—24 June 1746, made bef. his departure with his s. Satchwell on the Louisburg exped., directed his cous. Satchwell Clark to take charge of his ho. and land, and named ch: **Satchwell, James, Charles, John, Mary, Elizabeth.**

**Runnells,** see Reynolds.

**Rusley,** see Rashleigh.

**RUSSELL,** scattered throughout so. Eng. The 'de Rosel' claim of the Russells (Dukes of Bedford) has been disproved. Became 44th commonest name in N. E.

1 **HENRY,** at Casco Bay bef. 1631, presumably a ship capt.

2 **HENRY,** Newcastle, ±80 in 1681, was warned out of Portsmouth in 1671. He and his w. Frances, who scattered accusations of murder, bastardy, etc., among the neighbors with freedom and frequency, kept an inn of sorts where Thomas Skillings of Falmouth stayed in 1673 while his new broadcloth was being made up. He suspected Landlady Russell of stealing a yard thereof. Unlawful drinking there in 1674, the host drunk in 1678 and 'bad order' kept in the ho. in 1679. Jury 1684. Lists 55b, 313acf, 317, 330a, 331b. In 1681, his w. 'growing crazier,' he pet. for permiss. to keep a cook's shop and to sell penny beer. Frances was beaten by James Phillips, the shoemaker, in 1684, and assaulted by James Robinson in 1686. Three ch. emerge from the ev. in these cases: **John,** in ct. with an unnamed girl in 1686, taxed 1688, liv. in Newcastle with w. **Mary** in 1711. Lists 65(2), 94, 316, 318a, 319. **Frances,** 'one of the daus.,' unm. in 1684. **Andrew,** pulled Phillips away from his mo. in the 1684 battle.

3 **JOSEPH,** at Casco Bay bef. 1631, presumably a ship capt.

4 **NOEL** (Rusel), mariner, lately of Newcastle, in Boston 1699-1701.

5 **PHILIP,** Newcastle, wit. in 1666, had a 1 a. gr. in 1667 provided he build. Bot in 1672 land which he sold in 1687. Depos. ab. Teague Royal's will in 1677. Lists 312cd, 323, 326b, 330a. Dead in 1699.

6 **RICHARD,** Charlestown, distinguished merchant and officer, had large land interests at Monhegan, Pemaquid, etc., probably speculations. Thomas Elbridge mtg. Monhegan and Damariscove islands to him in 1650. In 1653 Elbridge mtg. ½ of his patent at Pemaquid to Capt. Paul White, who assigned it to R. R. and Nicholas Davison. Russell assigned his half to Davison in 1657. Capt. Gookin or Mr. R. R. were ordered to keep ct. at Portsmouth or Dover and at York in 1664. List 10. He d. 1674. See Wyman's Charlestown.

7 **ROBERT,** soldier at Gt. Isl., 1689.

8 **ROGER,** had built a ho. at Crockett's Cove in Kittery bef. 1674, later sold by Maj. Shapleigh to Mr. Fr. Hooke.

9 **THOMAS,** Wells, a prisoner in Canada in 1711.

10 **THOMAS,** Portsmouth, m. 10 Nov. 1715 wid. Agnes Graffam who was keeping an inn in 1722.

11 **WILLIAM,** Hampton, m. Sarah Long(9) and entered an East. Cl. for her to Scarboro prop. Ano. W. R. of Hamp. m. Elizabeth Chase(4) ±1725.

**RUST.** 1 **John,** m. at Hampton 12 May 1703 Hannah Swett.

2 **NATHANIEL,** to his heirs Wells laid out 206 a. at Tednick, 1720. See also Wardwell.

3 **SAMUEL,** wit. a Hampton receipt, Parker to Shaw, 1668.

**RUTHERFORD,** Rutherson, Rediford, **Robert,** barber, m. in Portsmouth May 1709 wid. Elizabeth Ilsley. Taxed Str. Bank, 1713, 1714. Mrs. Elizabeth was wit. in Scott v. Johnson, 1709. See Harvey(14).

**Ryford,** John, a N. Y. grantee at Arrowsic under Andros. Lists 186, 187.

**RYMES, Samuel,** Portsm., mariner, taxed 30 Oct. 1691, but at Isles of Shoals by 1692. He m. Mary Wentworth, who m. 2d Dr. John Clifton(1). J. 1696, 1697. He d. 6 Feb. 1709. Adm. 1 Oct. 1712 to John Wentworth of Portsm. and Samuel Wentworth of Boston, attorney for John Clifton, the est. being in the hands of S. R.'s mo.-in-law, Mrs. Mary Martyn. The real est. was div. betw. 3 sons, 1722. Ch: **Samuel,** b. 28 July 1693, m. May 1716 Mary Weymouth; mariner; d. 1755; will. 9 ch. **William,** b. 5 Apr. 1696; capt. of the -Juliana- of Bristol, England; will, Barbadoes, 13 May 1726, leaves £100 to his kinswoman Mrs. Mary Wentworth and other prop. to his mo., his bros. Samuel and Christopher and his nephew William. **Christopher,** b. 28 Feb. 1699-1700; mariner; m. Dorothy Sherburne (Henry), the 1st of her 4 husb.; his mo. liv. with him after Dr. Clifton's death; will 1741. 3 ch.

## SADLER.

1 **EDWARD.** See Sampson(2), Webber(8).

2 **JOSEPH,** soldier at Dover 16 Dec.—15 Feb. 1697. List 67.

3 **THOMAS,** Wethersfield 1649 (List 72) may be error for John, there early and d. there in 1673, appar. s.p.

4 **THOMAS,** Kittery. In York court 4 July 1659 Anthony Emery was bondsman for him, suspected of some misbehavior toward Dover ct. At same ct. he and Emery's dau., Rebecca Weymouth(8), were charged with riding about together on the Sabbath. He m. her after her husb. died, had left bef. July 1663 when Emery wanted relief from a for-

feited bond, and was in Flushing, L. I., in 1667. She was with her fa. at Portsmouth, R. I., from where in 1676, 'having been for several years in a widow like condition' and left with three small ch., she asked for restoration of her husb.'s est. on Staten Island in the hands of Jonas Halstead. In 1680, bef. she had m. 3d Daniel Eaton, her fa. deeded her his prop. with remainder to her s. **Anthony** (Sadler), who was of E. Greenwich, R. I., in 1714. Surely her son was William Weymouth alias Sadler, in York ct. for abusing ministers in 1681, when John Green paid the costs, but his position in the fam. seems as doubtful as that of her s. Joseph Amory (see Emery 1) who might have been either Weymouth or Sadler and brot up by gr.fa. Emery.

**SAFFIN, 1 Mrs. Elizabeth** (Scammon), List 89. See Legate(2); Scammon(3).

**2 THOMAS.** See Hounsell.

**Saffron**, John, worked in Cape Porpus mills 1679.

**St. Aubin**, Mr., List 123.

**St. Robin**, Charles, his wife and **son** at Passamaquoddy, his **son** and **dau.** (Laflower's wife) at Eggemoggin Reach; all in List 5.

**Sally.** See Solley.

**Salmon**, Peter, coroner's verdict filed Dec. 1700.

**SALTER**, common in the Exeter district of Devonshire; not uncommon in co. Suffolk.

**1 AENEAS.** See Halsey(1).

**2 HENRY**, servant of Roger Plaisted, Berwick, whipped for stealing in 1667; prob. the same who ran away, stole, and broke jail in Essex Co. in 1673. One Henry was named by several witnesses in connec. with Martha Sloper(3) in 1707. See Wyman's Charlestown ii: 842, for fam. of an early Henry.

**3 CAPT. JOHN**, wealthy mariner, Star Island, Newcastle, Rye, depos. in 1744, in 70th yr., that he liv. at the Shoals betw. 40-50 yrs. bef. List 316. His w. was Amy as early as 1722, when with her assistance and Joseph Mace's, he assaulted Constable John Barton and broke his staff. Will, 1752-1755, names w. Amy (liv. in Feb. 1757) and ch: **Richard**, m. 1st Elizabeth Odiorne(3), m. 2d by 1743 Elizabeth Knight(10). **Titus**, m. Elizabeth Bickford(10). **Mary** Mace, w. of Joseph(5). **Elizabeth** Roby, w. of Peter. **Charity** Leach, w. of John(4 jr.). **Margery** Hale. **Martha** Sanborn, w. of Ebenezer. **Sarah** Sloper, w. of Ambrose. Son **Alexander's** wid. Elizabeth (Sanborn) and 4 ch. Also gr.son John Randall (his mo. **Hannah**; see 'The Salters of Portsmouth, N. H.' by William M. Emery, 1936). Another **son** d. in 1728, his fa. admr. No s. John is named in will, but John, s. of John and Martha, was bp. at So. Ch. in 1730. This might be consid. the baptism of an adult son of (3) by an early w., except that Mary, dau. of ―― and Martha, was bp. in same par. in 1734, long after Capt. John's dau. Mary had mar. Martha S., of full age, testi. in the Hutchins case (see Wm. 3); she had been in Canada 7 yrs. bef.

**4 MATTHEW**, m. Sarah Parker(25) and liv. on Parker's Isl. List 189. See also Davis (53). In Oct. 1689, he, wife and **five ch.** were refugees at Josiah Smith's in Charlestown. Wid. Sarah m. 2d in Boston 21 May 1703 Samuel Smith. **Thomas** Salter, the Boston cordwainer and speculator (Y. D. vols. 13, 14, 18) was prob. a son. One Matthew was of Marblehead 1674-1678.

**5 SAMPSON.** See Lewis(12).

**6 THOMAS**, York grantee 1722, from Charlestown, where **six ch.** of Thomas and Mary were rec., the first two b. in Maine: **Mary** at Arrowsic 17 Dec. 1718, **Thomas** at York 2 Sept. 1721.

**7 WILLIAM**, wit. a Phillips(22) fam. deed in 1668 (Y. D. 2: 132).

**Saltridge.** See Shortridge.

**SAMPSON.** Devonshire and Cornwall have this name; frequent also in cos. Kent and Derby.

**1 ANDREW**, Portsmouth, with Samuel Harris bot from Geo. Jones at Sagamore Creek in 1670 and sold to Joseph Berry in 1673. (Sampson's Point on the S. side at the entrance of the Creek, was named for Sampson Lane.) Sued by Mr. Francis Wainwright in 1673 for a debt payable in cod. Lists 331b, 313a. Lame and unable to help himself and fam. in Mar. 1678-9. Goody S., who kept a poor man early in 1680 and made agreement with the town in Aug. that yr. to keep John Rayne, was presum. his wife. See also (2). By every sign there was a s. **Andrew**.

**2 ANDREW**(1?), mariner, Portsm. (a wit. in the Huff-Walton haycock case in 1677, ±27, unless (1) was incapacitated at the age of 30; wit. Jocelyn to Hinckes 1680). Taxed 1691, jury 1696. In 1697 Joseph Berry deeded to him for love and goodwill the land where his dwg. ho. then stood. He m., int. Boston 12 Dec. 1695, Rachel (Codner), wid. of John Darby; see Neighbors. Liv. 28 Dec. 1697 (see Dam 1). D. bef. 31 Mar. 1707-8 when wid. Rachel, then w. of John Shores, renounced adm. in favor of Wm. Cotton; the probate rec. calls him formerly of Boston. Ch. indicated: **John**, Portsm., m. Elizabeth Taylor 5 Mar. 1718-9. In 1720 John S. and 'her grandchild Samson' (a woman), were paid by the town for their trouble in regard to 'old mother E. Stone.' 7 ch. bp. incl Rachel and Andrew. **Mary**, m. in Portsm. 6

Nov. 1718 Edw. Sadler of Swansea, who m. 2d 20 Nov. 1723 Abigail Webber. Her ch. bp: Rachel, Edward.

3 **ELIZABETH**, with Richard Dore's w., wit. about Peter Abbott in 1673. See also Brown(29).

4 **HENRY**, a wit. against Edward Ashley in 1631. List 1.

5 **JAMES**, Wells, from Dartmouth, Mass. and descended from the Pilgrim fam., m. Ruth Sawyer (Wm. of Wells), who with **five** ch. was named in her fa.'s will 1718. They were of Arundel in 1754, he ag. 74, she 67. List 269c.

6 **JOHN**, Portsmouth 1670, List 326c. Ano. or the same was of Great Isl. 1695-96 (List 315c), but the John making oyster voyages to Billingsgate, from Boston to Piscataqua and other places in 1687, poss. came from Plymouth Co.

7 **JOHN**, Scarboro, from Beverly where he m. 20 Oct. 1667 Sarah Pease, step-dau. of Richard Haines, who was not his 1st w. as Salem adm. him inhab. 8 May 1660 provided he take effectual course to bring his w. to him. Taxed Scarb. 1681; on committee to treat with Mr. Blackman 1682; grants 1682, 1685; town clerk 1682; constable 1687. Lists 85, 238a(2). The war sent him back to Essex Co. from where he claimed 100 a. on N. side of Nonesuch River bot from Mrs. Jordan, and 6 a. betw. Thomas Larrabee and Henry Libby bot from Henry Kirby. In Jan. 1708-9, of Gloucester, late of Newbury, he deeded his Scarb. lands to w. Sarah, to be at her disposal if she surv., paying partic. regard to those ch. who had been most kind to them, only s. Jonathan's s. John to have the 16 a. parcel at Scarb. if he liv. upon it. He d. at the Durrell home in Glouc. 27 Jan. 1711-2 in 104th yr., but depos. twice in 1677, ag. 50 and ±50, and in 1679, ±53. Kn. ch., three rec. at Bev: **Sarah**, b. 18 June 1668, m. Moses Durrell(1). **Mary**, b. 15 Nov. 1670, m. Joseph Goodale. **Cyprien**, b. 13 Mar. 1672, m. Daniel Chesimore (Chisholm 1). **Jonathan**, not recorded, may have been the 1st wife's son. He m. 16 Nov. 1695 Mary Chandler in Newb., where s. John was b. 1696. Possibly by an earlier mar., Jonathan or an unknown older brother was fa. of several young Sampsons in Essex Co., notably William whose ch. incl. a Jonathan b. in Newb. in 1703.

8 **MARY**, see Akerman(1).

9 **RICHARD**, Portsm., taxed 1669, 1672, made freeman at Boston 27 May 1674. Lists 326c, 327b, 331ac. His wid. Sarah m. (ct. Oct. 1677) Josiah Clark(32) whose 'large charge of ch.' poss. incl. one or more Sampsons. One R., fisherman, Piscataqua, where he had liv. 16 yrs., depos. 9 Sept. 1698, ag. 23.

10 **SAMSON**, negro, List 94.

11 **THOMAS**, brewer, Richmond Isl., unwilling to work, unruly and a trouble maker, was sent home by Winter bef. 10 July 1637. He had a wife in Eng.

**SANBORN.** The late Col. Banks made a hard and unsucc. search in Eng. for the origin of this N. H. family.

1 **DEA. BENJAMIN**(2), Hampton Falls, was a Newbury wit. in 1687-8. List 400. He m. 1st Sarah Worcester, step-dau. of Henry Ambrose (2 jr.) who d. 29 Jan. 1720 ag. 54; m. 2d 7 Nov. 1721 Meribah (Page 2) Tilton; m. 3d 24 Nov. 1724 Abigail (Gove 2) Dalton. Will, 31 Oct. (d. 15 Dec.) 1740, names w. Abigail and all ch. but one: **Mary**, b. 27 Oct. 1690, m. William Healey (see 2). **Joanna**, b. 1 Dec. 1692, m. 13 Jan. 1713-4 Cornelius Clough of Kingston. **Sarah**, b. 30 Sept. 1694, m. Reuben Sanborn(5). **Theodate**, b. 1696, m. Jonathan Sanborn(4). **Dorothy**, b. 27 Oct. 1698, m. 1st Jethro Batchelder(4), m. 2d Abraham Moulton(11). **Abial** (Abigail), b. 22 July 1700, m. in Hampt. F. 16 Dec. 1725 Enoch Colby. **Jemima**, b. 17 May 1702, m. in Ipswich, 1st int. 15 Oct. 1720 John Stacy, jr., 2d int. 11 Nov. 1743 Samuel Lord, jr. **Susanna**, b. 20 Sept. 1704 (Sanborn in 1740), m. Joshua Blake. **Benjamin**, b. 1 June 1706, d.y. **Judith** (Judah), b. 26 Oct. 1708, m. in Hampt. F. 16 Dec. 1725 Robert Quimby. **Benjamin**, Hampt. F., b. 7 Nov. 1712, m. 1st 27 Dec. 1733 Hannah Tilton, m. 2d 25 Oct. 1736 Dorothy (Tilton) Prescott. Will, 17 Jan. 1747-8—27 Dec. 1752, names w. Dorothy, 2 of 4 rec. ch., and expected ch. By 2d w: **Ebenezer**, Hampt., b. 10 Oct. 1723. At Louisburg 1745. Will, 4 Mar. 1745—26 Mar. 1746 names step-mo., sisters and others, but not br. Benjamin.

2 **LT. JOHN**, Hampton, b. ±1620, s. of Ann (Batchelder 5) Sanborn, who was liv. in the Strand, London, in 1630-1, a wid. ag. 30 (see Waters' Gleanings i: 519-520, 783-788), and m. 2d at Strood, co. Kent, in Jan. 1631-2 Henry Atkinson of London. He and his bros. (9) and (10) shared in the Hampt. grants 1640, but their mo. appar. never came. John, the oldest, was active in town affairs, early and late, and in 1647 his gr.fa. Batchelder settled his Hampt. prop. on him and his posterity, he to pay his bros. and cous. Nathl. Batchelder £20 apiece. Often on jury, gr.j. and town committees. Selectman, 1650, 1661, 1665, 1668, 1672, 1674-5, 1678-9, either he or his son 1688, 1692. Com. t.e.s.c. 1667, 1669, 1672. When chosen Capt. for Hampton in 1664, it appeared he was not a freeman and the case was referred to the Genl. Ct. Called Ensign in Oct. 1665 and a yr. later legally chosen and confirmed Ensign. Commis. Lieut. 15 Oct. 1679. Ag. ±48

in 1668, ±60 in 1680. Lists 391b, 392ab, 393ab, 396, 397a, 48-50, 54, 57, 62, 83. He m. 1st Mary Tuck(3), who d. 30 Dec. 1668, List 393a; m. 2d 2 Aug. 1671 Margaret (Page 6) Moulton; d. 20 Oct. 1692. Ch: John, Mary, b. 12 Apr. 1651, d. Oct. 1654. Abigail (or Abial), b. 23 Feb. 1653-4, m. Ephraim Marston(2). Richard, b. 4 Jan. 1654-5. Mary, b. 19 Mar. 1656-7, d. 14 Mar. 1660. Joseph, b. 13 Mar. 1658-9. Stephen, b. 12 Nov. 1661, d. 24 Feb. 1661-2. Ann, b. 20 Nov. 1662, m. Samuel Palmer(20). Nathaniel, Hampt. F., b. 27 Jan. 1665-6, m. 1st 3 Dec. 1691 Rebecca Prescott(1) who d. 17 Aug. 1704; m. 2d bef. 1709 Sarah Nason(6). Lists 57, 400. Will, 25 Oct. 1721—4 June 1723, names w. Sarah (d. 1 Sept. 1748, ag. -85-), and ch. 5 + 6: Richard, James, Rachel, Jeremiah, Abigail, Nathan, Jacob, Eliphaz, Nathaniel, Jedediah, Daniel. Benjamin, b. 20 Dec. 1668. By 2d w: Jonathan, b. 25 May 1672.

3 ENSIGN JOHN(2), Hampton, d. 23 Sept. 1727. Selectman 1681 (he or his fa. 1688, 1692), 1702, 1708. Gr.j. 1695, 1697, 1699; j. 1698. Tav. lic. 1696. Lists 392b, 396, 52, 54, 55b, 57, 62, 68. He m. 19 Nov. 1674 Judith Coffin (Tristram) of Newb., who d. 17 May 1724. Ch: Judith, b. 8 Aug. 1675, m. Ebenezer Gove(1). Mary, b. 2 July 1677, m. Ebenezer Stevens. Sarah, b. 8 May 1679. Deborah, b. 1681, m. 1st Samuel Fellows(2), m. 2d Benjamin Shaw(2 jr.). John, Hampt. F., Kingston, b. 1683, m. 1 Jan. 1706-7 Mehitable Fifield(1). Adm. to her 4 Mar. 1723-4. 5 ch. Presum. she m. 2d Jacob Morrill of Kingston. Enoch, Hampt. F., ±18 in 1707, m. 1st in 1709-10 Elizabeth Dennett(2), m. 2d 1 Apr. 1736 Mehitabel (Blake 2) Godfrey. 9 ch. Lydia, b. .24 Feb. 1686. Peter, Hampt. F., m. 29 Nov. 1716 Apphia Shaw (Caleb 10). She took adm. 3 June 1724, and m. 2d Robert Rowe (see 17). 4 ch. Tristram, List 400, m. 25 Apr. 1711 Margaret Taylor(25); both d. in 1771. 9 ch. Abner, Hampt. F., b. 27 Apr. 1694, m. 5 Oct. 1715 Rachel Shaw (Caleb 10); d. 17 Jan. 1780. 13 ch.

4 CAPT. JONATHAN(2), Kingston. Jury 1694, gr.j. 1695; tav. lic. 1698. Lists 62, 400. He m. 4 Feb. 1691-2 Elizabeth Sherburne(8), who outliv. him. His will, 24 Jan. 1740-1 (d. 20 June 1741); estate insolvent. Ch: Elizabeth, b. 27 Dec. 1692, m. John Ladd (3). Lt. Samuel, Kingston, b. 7 Sept. 1694, m. 1st 19 Aug. 1718 Elizabeth (Folsom 7) Colcord (3 ch.); m. 2d 4 Aug. 1757 wid. Elizabeth Pettengill; d. 8 Apr. 1765. Achaicus, bp. with first two 9 May 1697, called dau. Acha in will, may have m. Thomas Dent in Kingston 10 Oct. 1714. Margaret, b. 20 Mar. 1698, m. Moses Sleeper(1). Jonathan, Kingston, b. 28 Apr. 1700, m. 31 Dec. 1719 Theodate Sanborn(1) who d. 10 Oct. 1756; m. 2d Hannah Griffin. Will, 1760—1760, names w.

Hannah, 6 ch. Love, b. 30 Aug. 1702, m. 8 Jan. 1719-20 Rev. John Graham of Kingston where 1 dau. rec. She d. in Stafford Springs, Conn., in 1725. Dorothy, b. 30 Aug. 1704, d. Nov. 1705. Dorothy, b. 22 Aug. 1706, not in will. Sarah, b. 18 Apr. 1708, m. Thomas Rollins (Moses) of Stratham. John, b. 19 Dec. 1710, d. Feb. 1711. Benjamin, b. 22 Jan. 1712, d. 7 Apr. 1718. Mary, b. 7 Dec. 1713, m. 14 Dec. 1732 Peter Sanborn. 8 ch. rec. in Kingston.

5 JOSEPH(2), Hampton F., m. 28 Dec. 1682 Mary Gove(2). In 1716 a warr. was issued ag. her for talking ab. Samuel Shaw and his w.'s niece Esther Dearborn whose 1st ch. was b. at the Shaw ho. Tav. or vict. lic. 1693, 1694, 1697-98, 1700; j. 1699. Lists 52, 57. Wid. Mary m. 2d, int. at Amesbury 25 Nov. 1727, Lt. Moses Morrill of Salisb., and had 'absconded' (returned to Hampt.) in 1731. Ch: Abigail, b. 1 Apr. 1686, m. Ebenezer Dearborn(5). Huldah, b. 3 May 1688, m. Jonathan Nason(6). Reuben, Hampt. F., b. 18 May 1692, m. 28 Dec. 1714 Sarah Sanborn(1), who d. bef. him. Will 17 (d. 22) Apr. 1756. 10 ch. Edward, Hampt., b. 7 Apr. 1695, m. 25 Nov. 1718 Dorothy Robie(2), who took adm. 26 Feb. 1727-8, and m. 2d 18 Sept. 1729 Benj. Prescott. 4 daus., one liv. in 1736. Abraham, Kensington, b. 10 Mar. 1696, m. 22 Jan.1718 Dorothy Smith (see 40); d. 2 Sept. 1757. 10 ch. Mary, b. 28 July 1697, m. Samuel Prescott(2). Lt. Joseph, b. 22 July 1700, d. 26 Jan. 1773, m. 1st 18 Jan. 1722 Lucy Prescott(2), m. 2d 23 Jan. 1724 Susanna James(1), who d. in 1761. He d. in 1773. 8 ch. by 2d w. David, Hampt. F., b. 16 Jan. 1702, m. 2 Mar. 1727 Abigail Glidden(2). 11 ch. See Bean(1).

6 *JOSIAH(10), Hampton, m. 1st 25 Aug. 1681 Hannah Moulton(21); m. 2d Sarah, wid. of Jonathan Perkins(16). Jury Oct. 1684 (jury accus. of violating its oath in acquitting Wm. Vaughan, tried for smuggling tobacco; 1694; Rep. 1695; selectman 1695; constable 1699. Lists 392b, 52. Will, 28 Mar. 1727—6 Apr. 1728, names w. Sarah (d. 1 Sept. 1748), 8 surv. ch. and ch. of s. William and of Jacob Garland. Ch. by 1st w: William, Hampt. F., b. 26 Mar. 1682, m. 20 Dec. 1704 Elizabeth Dearborn(2); d. 3 Apr. 1718, Rev. Mr. Cotton mentioning 'his awful death'; adm. to wid. 4 Mar. 1718-9. 6 ch. She m. 2d Benjamin Moulton(1 jr.). Hannah, b. 1684, m. Jacob Garland(4). Sarah, b. 1686, m. David Robinson(8). By 2d w: Jabez, Hampt. F., b. 24 Mar. 1691, m. 29 Dec. 1716 Abial Marston(2); 9 ch. Dow calls her a 2d wife, and questions a dau. Keziah, b. 1714, by a 1st wife. Keziah, b. 15 Mar. 1693, mo. of Winthrop Sanborn, b. ±June 1717. She m. Wm. Hookely in 1726 (see Hookely on page 321); d. 19 May 1785.

**Rachel,** b. 13 Mar. 1695, m. Joshua Brown (11); d. 17 Feb. 1742. **Jonathan,** b. 26 Apr. 1697, d. unm. 2 Mar. 1757. **Reuben,** Hampt., b. 10 Apr. 1699, m. one Margaret who was dism. to Epsom Ch. in 1760. 6 ch. 1728-1738. **Abner,** b. 3 Sept. 1702, d. at Louisburg, prob. unm. **Richard,** b. 9 Aug. 1705, d. 28 July 1764.

7 **MEPHIBOSHETH** (10), Hampton, m. Lydia Leavitt(3). Jury 1695. List 399a. He d. 5 Feb. 1749. Ch: **Mary,** b. 24 Feb. 1695, m. Tucker Cate(1). **Lydia,** b. 11 June 1697, m. 21 Apr. 1720 Robert Goss (see 3 jr.). **Sarah,** b. 1699, m. John French (1 jr.). **Nathan,** b. 8 Aug. 1702, m. Anna Moulton (John 8 jr.). He d. s.p. 25 Apr. 1784, making his wife's neph. John Moulton their heir. **Abigail,** b. 23 Oct. 1704, m. 11 Nov. 1736 Samuel Thorn of Salisb. **James,** b. Feb. 1707, prob. d.y. **Rachel,** b. 15 Feb. 1708, d. unm. 16 July 1736.

8 **RICHARD** (2), m. 1st 5 Dec. 1678 Ruth Moulton(21), m. 2d 20 Dec. 1693 Mary (Drake 1) Boulter. Jury 1694, gr.j. 1695; selectman 1695. Lists 392b, 396, 399a, 52, 54, 57. Ch: **Mary,** b. 30 Sept. 1679. Ensign **John,** Hampt., b. 6 Nov. 1681, m. 8 Aug. 1701 Sarah Philbrick(2). Will, 18 Aug. (d. 3 Sept.) 1727, names w. Sarah, 14 ch. She m. 2d Lt. Thomas Rollins(6 jr.) and at death in 1761 left, it is said, 182 liv. desc. out of 239. **Ruth.** **Shubael,** Hampt., bp. 19 Nov. 1699, m. 7 June 1716 Mary Drake(2); d. 3 May 1759. 7 ch.

9 **STEPHEN** (br. of 2), Hampton, Kittery, named second of the brothers in 1640 grants and in gr.fa.'s deed of 1647 (see 2). His Hampt. lot was in poss. of Aquila Chase and Wm. Fifield in 1644 and he did not share in the commons in Feb. 1645-6; perhaps then in Kit., where he wit., Andrews to Paul and Smith, 21 Mar. 1647-8, and was named constable for Piscataqua in June 1648. Of Hampt. 29 Aug. 1649, he sold his Kit. ho. and land adj. Daniel Paul to Richard Cutts, and 2 Oct. 1650 with Samuel Fogg bot a Hampt. ho. and land from Christopher Hussey; wit. with Fogg 10. 6m. 1654. Tr. j. 1651. By 28 July 1654 he retired as selectman (chosen 6 Feb. 1653-4) and by trad. returned to Eng. with gr.fa. Batchelder. 'Sometime of Hampton' 1 Aug. 1655. Lists 391b, 392a, 393ab. Wife. Sarah, List 393a. Two ch. rec. Hampt: **Sarah,** b. 12 June 1651. **Dorothy,** b. 2 Mar. 1653. Dau. **Lydia,** ±27 in 1680, made a trip from Newbury to Hampt. with James Brown of Newb. (Essex Q. Ct. Rec. 8: 359). If one dau. could be here late, another could, poss. **?Dinah,** who from her appar. age (m. 1st 23 July 1678 James Marston 4) does not fit easily into fam. of (2) and may have been dau. of (9) or (10).

10 **WILLIAM,** Hampton, br. of (2) and (9), appar. younger, but the one first seen in

Hampt., being named 27 Nov. 1639 to ring the bell. Lists 391b, 392ab, 393ab, 394, ?(395), 396, 49, 52, 54, 55a. Tr.j. 1649, 1652, 1664, 1668, 1674, 1678; gr.j. 1662, 1664, 1667, 1678. Freeman 8 Oct. 1651. Selectman 1651, 1660, 1667, 1671, 1677-8, 1683. See also Philbrick(8). He m. bef. 23 Jan. 1649 Mary Moulton(7), List 393a, and d. 18 Nov. 1692. The fragment of his will remaining names w. Mary and four sons, leaving other ch. uncertain. Ch., the first two on authority of the Sanborn Gen. (see also Dinah 9): **Mary,** m. Joseph Dow(7). **Mehitable,** m. Ens. Daniel Tilton(2). **William. Josiah,** ±18 in Feb. 1666-7. **Mercy,** b. 19 July 1660, m. Samuel Cass(4). **Mephibosheth,** b. 5 Nov. 1663. **Sarah,** b. 10 Feb. 1666-7, m. Samuel Marston (8). **Stephen,** b. 4 Sept. 1671, m. 26 July 1693 Hannah Philbrick(2) and d. 21 June 1750. Ch. 1694-1718: Stephen (m. Ruth Leavitt 1), James (m. Sarah Towle and Esther Shaw), Anne (m. Moses Chandler of Andover), Hannah (m. Wm. Palmer 15), Phebe (m. Elisha Prescott 2), Abiatha of Greenland and Parsonsfield, Me. (w. Mary), Zadoc of Brentwood (w. Sarah), Amy (m. Jacob Sanborn, s. of Nathl. 2), Abigail, Mary (m. John Mason), Jonathan (m. and had ch.).

11 **WILLIAM** (10), Hampt., may have been the constable of 1676. He m. 1 Jan. 1680 Mary Marston(9), who d. 11 Oct. 1686. No indication found of a later mar., altho he liv. until 9 Oct. 1744, then ag. 92 by rec. Jury 1685, 1695. William, sr. was selectman in 1717. Lists 395 (or his father's), 396, 399a, 66. Ch: Hon. *John, b. 6 Nov. 1680, a Rep. from Hampt. many times and Speaker, and gave his name to Sanbornton. He m. 10 Dec. 1701 Ruth Robie (see 5) who d. 19 Apr. 1753, ag. 74; he d. 30 Oct. 1767. Will. 5 ch. **Mary,** b. 1682-3, named in br. John's will 1760, d. unm. 22 Dec. 1770. **Dau.,** b. and d. 1686.

**Sanden,** Arthur, owed John Croad. List 80.
**Sander,** the Scotchman, List 14. See Alexander Waugh.

**SANDERS,** Saunders, frequent in S. half of Eng., partic. in co. Devon. The North has Sanderson. See Hall(10), Hodsdon(4).

1 **BARNABY** (Sanders? Jandes; N. H. State Papers xiv: 2), depos. in Aug. 1696, ±29, about selling goods to Joseph Pitman, whose wid. Elizabeth he reputedly married (see Pitman 7). Mary -Janders- a wit. in 1720 (see Pinkham 1).

2 **DANIEL,** an Illutherian at No. Yarmouth. List 213. See (12).

3 **EDWARD,** from Watertown, was sick at Piscataqua 5 Mar. 1638-9 when Mr. Nicholas Davison(2) was to bring him in to the next Boston ct., and did not. He was both

Sanders and Sanderson at Watertown (see Bond i: 416; ii: 930). Presum. the same Edward who wit. Thomas Wannerton's deed to Roger Knight in 1643, sold land as Capt. Champernowne's agent in 1644, and was successfully sued for slander in Oct. 1645 by Mrs. Sarah Lynn whom he claimed to have mar. and who said that for two yrs. she had liv. in fear of violence from him. In 1645 Mr. Robt. Saltonstall was assignee of E. S., agent for Capt. Champernowne. See also Me. P. & Ct. Rec. i: 85-90; Sanderson(1).

**4 EDWARD**, Saco 1663. List 244f.

**5 ELIZABETH**, a captive; see (16).

**6 GEORGE**, in Richmond Isl. acct. 1634.

**7 JOHN**, fisherman, came to Richmond Isl. in the ·Hunter· 1634 and liv. at Piscataqua in Nov. 1639; see Jonathan Weymouth's will, N. E. Reg. ii: 261. J. S., joiner, worked four wks. at Rich. Isl. betw. July 1641—June 1642. List 21(2).

**8 LT. JOHN**, Wells, Cape Porpus. Ipswich propr. 1635; freeman 25 May 1636. Admitted inhab. at Hampton 13 Dec. 1639. Called of Wells 14 July 1643 when he was gr. 150 + 50 a. by Thomas Gorges, but of Hampt. 27 July 1643 when he sold a ho.-lot to John Brown, to take poss. 1 May 1644. At Hampt. in 1643, he was fined for offensive speeches ag. the court, and pet. for relief, having a wife and six small ch. for whom he could hardly find bread or clothes, and was himself very sick. Hampt. friends, however, were willing to state he was fit to be made Sergeant. Of Wells 29 Sept. 1644, where a large land-owner; often gr. and tr.j.; selectman 1647, 1654-55; Sergeant 1653; Lieut. by 1657. Removed to Cape Porp. 1663. Lists 391a, 392a, 252, 254(3), 255, 259, 261-263, 269b. Will, 13 June (inv. 23 Aug.) 1670, gives to w. Ann for life, then entails homestead on s. **Thomas** and his heirs; to s. **John** immediately 1000 a. 8 or 9 miles above Cape Porp. River Falls; remaining prop. to 'all my ch.'; neighbors Simon Booth of Winter Harb. and John Barrett of Cape P. supervisors. Daus. appear: **Sarah**, m. 1st Peter Turbet(3), m. 2d Daniel Goodwin(4); **Grace**, m. 1st John Bush, m. 2d Richard Palmer (18); **Elizabeth**, m. 1st John Batson(1); m. 2d one Walden (see 7), m. 3d John Gove(4 jr.); leaving at least one **child** unkn. Wid. Ann had been dead ab. two yrs. when her gr.s. (16) sent in a pet. to Andros.

**9 JOHN**, had Exeter gr. 1645. List 376b. One John appar. an Exeter wit. in 1670, about Nicholas Lissen's note.

**10 JOHN**(8), fisherman, Cape Porpus. In York ct. July 1675 Sylvester Stover, J.S. and Matthew Barton ack. a judgm. to Richard Cutts payable in dry codfish. Cape Porp. selectman 1679; lot layer 1681, 1689; cor.j. 1685, tho he and w. Mary (m. bef. Oct. 1673)

were of Boston in June, 1684, when he deeded to Thomas Kimble the 1000 a. willed him by his fa. Scituate 1693+. He at least ret. to Cape Porp., was wounded by Ind. 10 Aug. 1703, escaped by getting among the bushes and d. of his wound ab. three days after reaching Wells. Lists 256, 33, 39. See also Hunt(6). Later the fam. throve in Gloucester, where wid. Mary d. 21 Dec. 1717, ±60. Kn. ch. (6 from deeds): Capt. **Thomas**, shipwright, Glouc., m. 12 Jan. 1703 Abigail Corney (John); see Brown(23). He d. 17 July 1742, ±67, she 11 Feb. 1767, in 91st yr. 7 ch. rec. Glouc., five of whom brot an ejectment suit for 4/7 of 50 a. ag. John Fairfield and Paul Shackford of Arundel in 1752; their fa. was 'disseized' by Samuel Averill's deed of 1728. **Nathaniel**, shipwr., Glouc. Wife Sarah. 9 ch. rec. 1704-1720. **Elizabeth**, m. at Scituate 7 Feb. 1701 Jonathan Springer. **Mary**, m. at Duxbury 18 Jan. 1703 Samuel Pierce; both of Glouc. 1713. **John**, shipwr., Pembroke, m. 23 Jan. 1709-10 Mary Pierce, both of Duxbury. 2 daus. b. at Pembroke, where he d. 10 Aug. 1724, and wid. m. Henry Perry. **Joseph**, d. at Glouc. 18 Nov. 1712; adm. to mo., later to br. Thomas. **Edward**, shipwr., Rowley, b. at Scituate 29 Dec. 1692-3, m. at Rowley 18 Dec. 1716 Elizabeth Gage. 13 ch. rec. **Lydia**, presum., d. in Glouc. 15 Dec. 1713.

**11 JOSEPH**, Dover, accepted inhab. 24 Apr. 1656. Town gr. 1660. He wit. with John Heard in 1660, and in 1669 sold Heard his right, up from Campion Rocks, adj. Tobias Hanson. Freed from training 1662, because hard of hearing. In 1672 he gave Christopher Snell a receipt for serge left aft. making his clothes. Killed by Ind. 28 June 1689. Lists 356eghk, 357d, 359ab, 96.

**12 NATHANIEL**, List 213. See also (2).

**13 RICHARD**, mariner, Portsm., m. 17 June 1697 Mary Morse (see 3), who m. 2d 13 Aug. 1702 Richard Eburne(1). Lists 330de. One Mary of Portsm. m. 16 Jan. 1717-8 James Wales of Dublin, Ire.

**14 ROBERT**, also Robin, from Plymouth, Eng., was at Richmond Isl. in 1638-9 and in June 1640 when he sued Henry Watts for debt. He came again aft. making a contract in Eng. 22 Nov. 1642 to serve three yrs. aft. arrival. List 21(2). See also Sanderson(2).

**15 SAMUEL**, one or more. Of Newington, robbed on the highway in 1718; at Star Isl. with John Ashley in 1719; had a Kit. gr. on Smuttynose in 1725; of Star Isl., deeded all to Abraham and Elinor Crockett 1744; Rye 1748. See also Foss(3).

**16 THOMAS**(8), Cape Porpus, m. in Saco 23 Oct. 1664 Hope Reynolds (see 6) and in 1665 was accus. of profane swearing by James Harmon(1) who neglected to press charge. Not seen aft. 21 Oct. 1670 when he,

as oldest son, and mo. sold 100 a. betw. Simon Bussy and Nicholas Cole's land. His wid., suppos. Hope, was w. of John Cleg (printed Cleay) of Pemaquid in 168-, when s. **John**, of Pemaquid, ±20, pet. Andros, reciting his gr.fa.'s entailing of the homestead on his fa., then himself, and so from heir to heir. List 124. He disappears, likely an Ind. victim. Elizabeth, a captive from Pemaquid, 1698-9, List 99, p. 178, is a prob. sis. or wife. No Reynolds claimant of later date can be traced to this line, and no Sanders claimant unless the J. S. who appeared bef. the East. Cl. Com. See also John(10).

17 **WILLIAM**, an early settler of Hampton (Dow), but name poss. an error. One William, carpenter, was bound in 1636 to serve Bellingham and Gibbins, of Boston, for 3 yrs.

18 **WILLIAM**, Monhegan 1673. List 13.

19 **WILLIAM**, Kittery, ±23 in May 1684, servant of Frost. Town gr. June 1682 (Y. D. 4: 24); in 1686 his land fronted on Sturgeon Creek. In Oct. 1686 he assigned to 'my late master Charles Frost' a note given him six months bef. by Wm. Stacy. He m. in Dec. 1687 Sarah Wittum(1), who was ±31 in Dec. 1695 when she knew a good deal ab. the Metherell—Thompson case. Both prosecuted in 1693 for trav. on Sunday. In 1695 she was abs. from meeting, and he had Esq. Hinckes arrested for breaking open his head with his cane. Wid. Sarah m. 1 Apr. 1700 George Brawn(2). No ch. appear.

**SANDERSON.**

1 **ROBERT**, Hampton, gold and silver smith (later a partner of John Hull, the mintmaster), had an 80 a. gr. in 1639. Lists 391a, 392b. Wife Lydia. He mov. to Watertown in 1642 where he m. 2d Mary, wid. of John Cross(5), whose dau. Mary, b. there 10 May 1641, m. in Boston 10 May 1659 James Penniman. In 1650, of Watertown, he sold his Hampton ho.-lot to Francis Swain. Dea. R. S. died in Boston 7 Oct. 1693. Dau. **Mary**, by 1st w., bp. in Hampt. 29 Oct. 1639. **Ch.** by 2d w. See Pope's 'Pioneers of Mass.,' p. 399; N. E. Reg. 52: 23, his will there naming br. Edward (see Sanders 3).

2 **WILLIAM**, Star Isl., Gosport, m. at Portsmouth 23 Oct. 1711 Mary Cox (see Mansfield 7). A Shoals wit. 1715 (Y. D. 8: 112; 9: 137); wit. Edward Gould's will 1724. One Robert (Sanders or Sanderson) and w. of Smuttynose helped raid the Frost brandy, see Thompson(8). Elizabeth S. of the Shoals was bp. at Newcastle 10 May 1719 with Kelleys. See also Robinson(12).

**Sandey**, John, taxed Portsmouth 1688. See Saudey.

**Sandord**, Thomas, a Berwick wit. 1669 (Y. D. 2: 81).

**Sands.** See Gibbins(3).

**SANFORD, John**, Boston, Portsmouth, R. I., m. Bridget Hutchinson (Wm. 11) who m. 2d Major Wm. Phillips(22), and named in her will only 2 of their 9 ch: **Peleg** and **Eliphel** Stratton. Ano. s. **Restrom** wit. a Phillips deed in 1662 (Y. D. 2: 36). See also Y. D. 1: 82; 11: 17; 12: 24.

**SANKEY, Robert**, Mr., came in the -Increase- from London in April 1635, ag. 30, and went to Saco where in 1636 his goods were attached for a debt due Trelawny. See Gibbins(2). One R. S. belonged to the Fishmongers' Guild in London (N. E. Reg. 61: 92). Saco constable Jan. 1636-7; in 1637 had cross suits with Ambrose Berry and was sued by Wm. Scadlock. Sold pork to Vines in 1639. Provost-Marshal 1640, in which year Thomas Smith accus. him and Mr. Arthur Browne of stealing a pig and was sued for slander. He was dead 2 Apr. 1642 (Y. D. 3: 124). Mr. Joseph Bolles afterw. held his est. (see Wright 12) and sold it, 200 a. adj. Peter Hill, to John Boaden in 1659. Lists 242, 281. See also Grant(2).

**SARDEN, Timothy**, a Kittery wit. 1675, ±50 in 1676, one of Mr. John Bray's workmen in 1677, and Bray and T. -Scardenapprais. Philip Gullison's est. Poss. a younger Timothy was Sylvester Stover's servant in 1685.

**SARGENT**, Sargeant. Scattered thru S. half of Eng., incl. Cornwall and Wilts, Sargent in both. Sergeant in Lincolnshire.

1 **BENJAMIN**(5), wit. David Tristram's deed to (3), all of Saco, in Jan. 1690-1. A refugee in Portsmouth, where he m. one Abigail (ct. Sept. 1694). He sold without lic. in June 1697, lic. in Sept. fol., Nathan Knight bondsman, and then pet. for remission of fine for not going bef. the ct.; giving reasons: had never been bef. a ct.; had an impediment in speech; was a poor man, driven from what he had by the enemy. He ret. to Winter Harbor where his w. was killed, **three ch.** captured, 10 Aug. 1703 (List 39). Oct. 6 that yr. he met death with a party from Black Point garri. looking for cows. Lists 334a, 330def, 39, 96. Two of his ch. were in Canada 1711 (List 99, p. 93). Son **John**, cordwainer, Portsm., not surely a captive. Of Newc. 1723, he q.c. his fa.'s Portsm. and Winter Harb. lands to Joseph Jackson, and must have been the cordwainer, sometime of Saco, who in 1715 claimed lots bot from Mr. Blackman in 1687, tho the wording suggests the claimant was (5). He m. 12 June 1726 Elizabeth Waterhouse(3). She was gr. adm. 3 Oct. 1737 (very small est.), m. 2d Robert Hart(6). Son Benjamin bp. 2 Apr. 1727.

2 **DIAMOND**, tailor, from Ipswich and gr.s. of Wm. of Gloucester (see Joy 4), a Kittery soldier in (?)1704, bot a ho. and land in Crooked Lane in Mar. 1707-8, having m. Elizabeth Curtis(6) bef. Jan. 1706-7. She was an organizer of Kit. Point Ch. 1714. He remov. to York bef. 1717. Lists 289, 296-298, 279. **Ch.**

3 **CAPT. *EDWARD**(5), Saco, Newbury, depos. in 1740 that he liv. in Saco until 27 yrs. old. In 1681 he and George Page made the Cape Porpus highway; in 1685 he and Goodm. Scammon collected the minister's salary. Gr.j. 1686, tr.j. 1687; com. Ensign 1687; tav. lic. 1686, 1687, Mar. 1689-90 (Capt.). Rep. 1688; town comr. 1688. In wartime he hired the town ho. in Portsm. where his fam. liv. 2⅔ yrs. from 22 Sept. 1689. Commanded Winter Harbor garri. 1690 (in May asked for vessels to carry off the women and ch.). Called of Saco in Jan. 1690-1 when D. Tristram deeded to him adj. his dwg. ho. Lists 249(3), 36. See also Y. D. 13: 226; Pratt (1), Pennell(7, 8). In 1693, ±31 he depos. about the last time Gov. Sir Wm. Phips went from Portsm. to Boston. Newb. vintner 1695; Capt. at Saco 1696; of Newb. bot the Love prop. at Salmon Falls in 1697, selling to Ichabod Plaisted in 1707. Wife Elizabeth (was she Elizabeth Plaisted 6?) d. in Newb. 12 Dec. 1718, ag. 56. He m. there 2d 9 June 1719 Sarah (Pierce, see 4) Bradstreet, and d. (Esq.) 31 May 1742, ag. 81; will. Wid. Sarah d. 12 Jan. 1743-4 in 74th yr. Ch. by w. Elizabeth, all rec. at Newb: **Edward**, twin, b. at Saco in Winter Harbor 2 Dec. 1684. **Ebenezer**, twin, m. Ann Sawyer at Newb.; d. 13 Jan. 1723. **Nathaniel**, b. at Saco 16 Jan. 1686, H. C. 1707, physician, Hampton, Portsm., m. 1st at Newb. 16 Oct. 1710 Dorothy Bradstreet (dau. of his step-mo.); m. 2d 1743-1748 Sarah (Pierce 13) Winslow, who d. 21 Aug. 1771, a wid. 9 ch. at Hampt. 1712-1729. **Elizabeth**, b. at Portsm. 3 Oct. 1689. **John**, not rec., m. 6 Mar. 1718 Hannah Dalton(2) who was dism. from Hampt. to Newb. in 1731. 4 ch. b. Hampt. and Newb. **Elisha**, b. 24 Oct. 1695. **Rachel**, b. 10 Oct. 1698. **Ichabod**, b. 5 Aug. 1701, d. in 1723. **Abigail**, b. 26 June 1704, m. Stephen Preston (Presbury 3).

4 **EDWARD**, m. at Dover 3 June 1695 Joanna Homan(4) of Pemaquid and three mos. later was k. at Pemaquid. List 96.

5 **LT. *JOHN**, fisherman, Saco (Winter Harbor). Of the Shoals, he mortg. to James Pendleton 28 Aug. 1658 a Great Isl. ho. and land formerly Alex. Bachelder's and land adj. form. Tobias Langdon's. Drunk and fighting in 1661, promised amendment and kept the promise. Winter Harbor bef. Aug. 1662, had gr. 1663, and bot from Wm. Phillips in 1669, George Pearson, Ralph Tristram

and Richard Randall abutting. Sued by Francis Hooke in 1664 (did not appear), by James Harmon in 1669. Tr.j. 1667; constable 1668. 'Near 36' in Aug. 1668. A Saco appraiser with Maj. Pendleton in Nov. 1677 and Mar. 1678-9; 'resident of Great Isl.' 14 Nov. 1677 he released his mortg. prop. there to the Pendletons. Lieut. for Saco and Cape Porpus 1680. Tav. lic. 1680, 1683; townsman 1681-82, 1684; road surv. 1683; Rep. 1684; -Capt.- John on committee 1686; gr.j. 1689. He found refuge in Portsm., ret. too soon, and was k. 10 Aug. 1703. Lists 323, 326a, 245, 249(5), 33, 334a, 67, 39. See also (1), Pratt(1), Pennell(7). His wife (List 246) was perh. not always the Ruth who wit. with him in 1684 (her mark A) and was adm. to Portsm. Ch. in. 1693; liv. 1699 (List 331c). Ch., 4 rec. at Saco, 3 more shown by div. 1721: **Edward**, b. 8 Mar. 1661. **Patience**, b. Dec. 1668, d.y. **Benjamin**, b. 15 Feb. 1671-2. **Mary**, b. ±1673 (gr.st.), her mo. appar. Ruth; m. Joseph Jackson(20). **Patience**, b. 1 May 1675, d. s.p. by 1721. **Joseph**, s. of Ruth, bp. at Portsm. 27 Aug. 1693, k. at Saco in 1703 (List 39).

6 **PETER** (Sargeant). See Hull(5), Phipps (7).

7 **STEPHEN**, Mr., fishing master, Richmond Isl., came in the -Fortune- bef. 11 June 1638. List 21(2). He wrote letters to Mr. Trelawney in 1639 and is ment. respectfully in Mr. Winter's letters to his chief, the last time 29 July 1641, 'Mr. Sargent and his two servants.' About 2 Aug. 1641 he took the ship -Richmond-, built here, to Eng. On Nov. 29, 1649 John Monke, Antipas Maverick and Richard Cummings appr. est. at Isles of Shoals lately in hands of S. S., dec., 'and was for account of Mr. John Maninge, Capt. Champernowne and himself,' houses, stage, boats, etc., with some items belonging to Sampson Lane, Mr. Thompson and Mr. Dunbar. John Thompson attested inv. at Boston 27 Aug. 1650.

8 **STEPHEN**, in Saco bef. June 1670 (see Radner), on cor.j. 22 Dec. 1670 (body of David May), and as agent of Mrs. Mehitabel Downes(1) took adm. on the May est. 4 Apr. 1671, Brian Pendleton bondsm. In 1675 he had a dwg.-ho., stage, etc., on Parker's Neck (Y. D. 2: 154) and was at Black Point in 1675 where Mrs. Downes' 2d husb. Humphrey Warren sent for him and gave him orders (List 236). In 1667 some of his goods had been stolen from the Downes wareho. in Boston and without doubt it was he who had w. Dorothy and **three daus.** rec. Boston 1670-1677. One Stephen was there in 1687. See also N. E. Reg. 48: 263-4.

9 **THOMAS**, Pemaquid, had gr. of 100 a. at Long Cove from Gov. Dongan 13 Sept. 1686. Taxed 1687, stock and land. Lists 17,

124. Wife Ruth Johnson(12). Ch. at Scituate 1690-1703: **Elizabeth. Thomas. William. Thaddeus;** in 1720, ±20 (sworn in Marbleh. as -Edward-) he depos. ab. being at Muscongus with Morris Champney and Pearces. **Mary.** Wid. Ruth m. 2d, int. Boston 13 May 1713, John Barry and claimed the Sargent prop. for self and ch. A wid. again in Boston 1720.

10 **WILLIAM,** grantee of Hampton 1638. Lists 391a, 392a. In 1652, of Salisb., he sold to John Brown of Hampt. land betw. Aquila Chase and wid. Bristow. See Hoyt's Salisbury, i: 310.

**SATCHELL,** Sachell, Shatswell.
1 **MARY.** See Runlett(1) and Haverhill records.
2 **ROGER,** expected to mar. Ann Atkinson, wid. of (3), but put in a bill instead. Appar. they did m. bef. 24 Sept. 1678, when Mary Beard and Frances Perkins had heard him say he would not kill his w. outright, but do his best to end her days quickly. His Portsm. tax abated in Feb. 1679-80. O. A. at Str. Bank 1685. Of Greenland 1686 when he and w. Ann had been fighting and he was bound to the peace. Wit. Samuel Cutts' deed 1694. Son **John** (or poss. step-son Atkinson using his name) was taxed at Greenl. ±1708 and was there 1713-4 with w. Eleanor Place(1). Stratham 1715, List 388. Undated will made when he was sick and weak (d. 11 Jan. 1725-6) gives all to w. who m. 2d Francis Durgin(2). See also Keniston(4).

**SATTERLY** (Saturly).
1 **ROBERT,** 1648 (Y. D. i: 69) is Roger (Trel. Papers, p. 375).
2 **ROBERT,** a Kittery wit. 1691 (Y. D. 6: 58), undoubtedly husb. of Dorothy, a mar. woman involved with Elisha Ingersoll at Kit. in 1695.
3 **ROGER,** fisherman, Richmond Isl., came in the -Hercules- in 1637, leaving his wife in Eng. List 21. In June 1640 he had left Winter's service for ano. man's. He (see 1) is in Mr. Robert Jordan's 1648 account.
**Saudey,** Henry, taxed Portsm. July 1690. See Sandey.

**SAVAGE,** ancient in cos. Gloucester, Cambridge and Norfolk, where yet well established.
1 **ARTHUR.** See Penney(2).
2 **CAPT. EPHRAIM,** s. of Maj. Thomas(5) and Faith, m. 2d 21 Feb. 1677-8 Sarah (Haugh), wid. of Obadiah Walker, and in 17— claimed in her right 1000 a. bounded E. by the Kennebec River. Lists 141, 191. See N. E. Reg. 67: 206.
3 **HENRY,** Portsmouth. (One Henry, Haverhill 1644, had land laid out there as late

as 1667). The N. H. Henry worked on Ambrose Lane's sawmill, and in consid., in May 1655 rec. from Lane's atty. a deed to two houses form. occupied by John Davis and Henry Sayward. In 1658 he sued Sayward for a debt. Declined to serve as gr.j. 1663. Lists 311b, 313a, 323, 326ac, 329, 330ab, 331b, 334a, 49, 52. See also Lang(7). He m. Elizabeth Walford(4), Lists 331c, 335a; see also Moore(18). In 1686 they deeded half their est. to s. John, except bedding, etc., intended for dau. Deborah, and in 1694 deeded to their s.-in-law Peter Wells. He was dead in 1702. Her will, 13 Nov. 1708, proved 1709, names s. John and his dau., and dau. Deborah and her fam., the deed to Peter Wells and her deed to gr.s. John Lear in 1702 having taken care of dau. Mary's fam. Kn. ch., two liv. 1666 when their gr.fa. made his will: **Mary,** m. 1st Hugh Lear(1), m. 2d Peter Wells(7). **Esther,** no later rec. **John. Deborah,** m. Edward Wells(3).
4 **JOHN**(3), Portsmouth, O. A. 28 Aug. 1685; taxed Jan. 1688-9. Lists 57, 330d, 335a, 337, 339. His first wife's name is not seen (List 335a). He m. 2d Sarah (Jones 16) Whidden (one Sarah rec. into So. Ch. in 1716) and was Jones's s.-in-law in 1718; w. Sarah liv. 1722. See also Hicks(4). He renounced adm. on fa.'s est. to Edward Wells 22 July 1724, and was rec. into cov. (So. Ch.) and bp. on his death-bed 12 Feb. 1724-5. Ch: **Esther,** named in gr.mo.'s will 1708, m. 2 Nov. 1710 William Amos (Joseph Ames by printed rec.); liv. 1717 when her fa. deeded to them. **John,** joiner, m. 1st 9 Jan. 1717-8 Anne Lang(4) who d. bef. 7 Oct. 1722 (ch. John and Mary bp.); 'J. S. widow' taxed 1725; m. 2d 4 June 1727 Sarah Henderson (see 2). Will, 1742—1742, names w. Sarah, sons Job, Josiah, John (had the homestead; was John Lang's gr.s. in 1748) and dau. Ann. **Deborah,** rec. into cov. So. Ch. 1716, m. Abraham Bartlett(1 jr.), had land from fa. in 1722. **Susanna** (presum.), rec. into cov. So. Ch. 1720, m. William Lang(4). **Mary,** m. Benjamin Lucy(1); called dau. in 1725.
5 **MAJ. THOMAS,** Boston, m. 1st Faith Hutchinson, dau. of William and Anne (see Hutchinson 11). In Apr. 1652 he and Thaddeus Riddan wit. Ambrose Lane's deed of a Str. Bank farm to Richard Leader; in Dec. 1652 Leader mortg. all in Str. Bank and Boston to him. His son and admr. (2) claimed a large tract on both sides of Saco River. List 19; Hill(21). See also N. E. Reg. 67: 198.
6 **TIMOTHY,** Popham colony 1607. List 6.
**Savane,** David, List 57, read Larance (Lawrence).
**Savell, Saville.** Wid. (Savel), List 52; see Sewall(1). See also Bryant(2), Cutts(9), Hart(6), Grindal.

**SAVERY, Samuel**, Berwick, worked with Humphrey Chadbourne in 1693. Ag. ±31 in Jan. 1695-6. About 1696 he was at Blue Pt. with Daniel Hardy, pointed out to him John Jackson's farm and said he was there when J. J. liv. there. Berwick wit. 1699; his ho. near Quamphegan ment. in Jan. 1702-3. In 1711 sold land with w. Hannah (prob. the Joanna who was adm. So. Berw. Ch. 1703). Liv. in Apr. 1727, ±68, when he depos. that ab. 30 yrs. bef. he worked with Capt. John Leighton.

**Sawers, Robert**; see Sayward(5).

**SAWYER**, usually Sayer in early records and easily confused with Sayward. Became 75th commonest name in N. E. See also Wallis(5).

1 **DAVID**, Kittery, nephew of (4). List 291. See Frost(10).

2 **FRANCIS**(4), Esq., shopkeeper, Wells, Ipswich, had his fa.'s right in Narragansett No. 1. Lists 38, 269ac. He m. four wives in Ipsw., 1st, of Wells, int. 6 Oct. 1705, Elizabeth Dennis (see Thomas 9 jr.); 2d, of Wells, int. 15 Jan. 1725, wid. Susanna Low; 3d in 1749 Mrs. Hannah Staniford; 4th in 1751 Mrs. Mary Knowlton. Will, of Ipswich, 17 Mar. 1754 (d. there 31 Aug. 1756) names w. Mary, 5 of 7 ch. by 1st w. Elizabeth, rec. at Wells 1706-1722: **Elizabeth** Appleton; **Joseph**, Esq., given the Wells land he was liv. on (m. 1st, int. at Wells 6 June 1730, Mary Calef of Ipsw., m. 2d in Wells 7 Feb. 1743-4 Mehitable Littlefield, dau. of Francis (4) and d. there 2 Mar. 1774); **Abigail** Gilman; **Mary** Harris; **Daniel**, Wells, given Wells land (m. in 1740 Frances Abbott of Ips.). And by 2d w. (2 rec.) **Samuel**, who was given Ipsw. and Rowley land. Ano. dau. **Eunice**, b. 1722 (Anis by Wells rec.) m. in Ipsw. John Moulton (see 13) and soon d.

3 **SAMUEL** (Sayer), at Stratham in 1699, ag. ±24. List 387.

4 **WILLIAM**, Wells, b. in Newbury 1 Feb. 1655-6, s. of Wm. and Ruth. Soldier in King Philip's War. He m. bef. 16 Nov. 1677 Sarah (Littlefield 11) Wells, and bot his first Wells land in 1679. Grant 1685. Gr.j. often 1686-1701; tr.j. 1687, 1696. Bondsman for Mrs. Sarah Fletcher, 1700. Lists 266, 33, 38, 269abc. Will, 4 (died 7) June 1718, names w. Sarah, s. Francis (given all lands), two daus. and gr.ch. Wid. Sarah was bp. at Wells 27 July 1718. Her will, 27 Apr. 1734—10 Feb. 1734-5, names four Wells ch. (incl. Sarah, w. of John Sawyer of Newbury), three Sawyer ch., gr. chn. and one gt. gr.ch. Ch. rec. at Wells: **Joseph**, b. 14 Aug. 1678, m. Mary Fletcher(8), k. by Ind. 10 Aug. 1703, List 39; adm. to br. Francis 29 May 1704. His w. Mary, reported killed, was in Canada in Mar. 1704-5 (List 99, pp. 123-4, 127), was bp. at Wells 28 Apr. 1706, m. 2d John Gibson(1). No. kn. Sawyer ch. **Francis**, b. 6 Mar. 1681. **Daniel**, Wells, b. 26 May 1683. List 269a. W. Sarah. Ch. rec. at Wells 1706-1714: William, m. 1st Mary Littlefield (5), m. 2d Love Bragdon(3); Sarah, m. David Littlefield, jr.(5); Lydia, m. Jeremiah Littlefield (see 5); Daniel, d.y.; Hannah, m. Joseph Hatch(5). He d. bef. 2 May 1714 when his wid. Sarah was bp. She m. 2d Joseph Hill, Esq.(11). **Hannah**, b. 9 Apr. 1685, m. Philip Chesley(3 jr.). **Ruth**, b. 26 May 1687, m. James Sampson(5).

**Saybrook.** See Seabrook.

**SAYWARD**, easily confused with Sawyer and Seward, by the early and varied spelling.

1 **HENRY**, millman, York, as -Harry Sawyer- had a Hampton gr. 23 Mar. 1640-1, with Abraham Morrill had an Amesbury gr. in Jan. 1641-2 to set up a corn mill which appar. was not done, and had a mill site gr. at Hampt. Sept. 1642. Col. Banks believed him a son of John and Anne Saward of Farnham, co. Essex, 6 m. from Hatfield Broad Oak, the home of Morrill. Of Sagamore Creek 1650, of Str. Bank adm. inhab. at Hampt. 6 Apr. 1654, of York 1656 when he sold Hampt. prop. He evid. had his first York gr. in 1658, owned timber lands by gr. and purchase and built mills which prospered until burned out in 1669 when he estimated his loss as £1000. Later ventures on the Mousam River and at No. Yarmouth with Gedney involved him in difficulties, his wid. aft. him, who strove with the aid of (6) to keep the mills ag. the mortgagees. In pet. for relief in 1669 he called it 32 yrs. since he left Eng.; his age, ±44 in Feb. 1670-1, an under-estimate. York lot layer 1661; constable 1664, 1665; selectman 1661, 1665-1667; gr.j. 1667-1669. Lists 392a, 393b(3), 25, 87, 88, 269b. See also Holmes(2, 7), Johnson(15), Leeds, Stevens(19); History of York, i: 226. Living in Nov. 1678 when his presentment was contin. by the ct. Adm. gr. to Clerk of the Writs 1 Apr. 1679, to wid. Mary 6 Apr. 1680; inv. incl. sawmills at York, Cape Porpus, Mousam and Casco. His w., Mary Peasley (Joseph) of Salisb., was ±48 in Aug. 1681, d. bef. 26 Dec. 1689. In 1679 John Cousins, by deed, gave all to her for past and future care and maintenance. Ch: **Joseph**, b. at Hampt. 16 Nov. 1655, liv. Dec. 1677 (see Palmer 10), d. s.p. by 1694. **Sarah**, named in gr.fa.'s will Nov. 1660; d. (inv. 14 July 1694) appar. at the Haverh. home of her cous. Dr. Joseph Peasley; adm. to br. James. **Mary**, m. 1st Robert Young(7), 2d Richard Bray(6). **John. Jonathan. Hannah**, b. ±1665, m. Capt. Abraham Preble(2).

James, 18 in Sept. 1685, chose Wm. Smith alias Gowen his gdn.

2 DEA. JAMES(1), Gloucester, had a York gr. 15 Mar. 1681-2 when only a boy. Tr.j. Feb. 1690-1; gr.j. 1691. See also (6). He m. Deborah Stover(5), and soon mov. to Glouc. where a dau. Deborah was rec. 14 June 1694 (Babson) and he had a gr. in 1696. Mrs. Deborah d. there 13 July 1734, ag. 67 (gr.st.). He m. 2d wid. Mary Davis; d. 13 Feb. 1736-7 in 68th yr. (gr.st.). His will, Capt. Thomas Sanders(10) an exec., names w., sons Samuel, Joseph, Henry (given No. Yarm. land), daus. Elizabeth (m. in York 27 Dec. 1722 Elias Weare), Deborah (m. James Stevens 9), Hannah (m. John Sanders), Mary, Abigail (poss. his s. Henry's w.), and gr. dau. Martha Somes. Ano. s. James (the 2d of the name), b. at Glouc. 18 Aug. 1699, d. at York 30 Nov. 1724.

3 JOHN(1), York, with Henry Simpson had a gr. near the Folly in 1679 which was laid out 26 Sept. 1689 to his wid. O. A. 22 Mar. 1679-80. Tr.j. 1683; gr.j. 1687; selectman 1685, 1686. List 33. He m. (ct. 6 Apr. 1681) Mary (Rishworth) White, who was gr. adm. 21 (inv. 17) Dec. 1689, and m. 3d Phineas Hull(7). See 'New England Captives' i: 236-243, or Hist. of York i: 304-306, for her captivity. Ch: Mary, b. 4 Apr. 1681, a captive (List pp. 75, 92), bp. Marie Genevieve in Canada. She remained there as Soeur Marie-des-Anges of the Congregation, and d. in Quebec 28 Mar. 1717. Susannah, b. 9 May 1683, m. Abraham Preble, Esq. (3). Esther, b. 7 May 1685, a captive (List 99, pp. 75, 92), naturalized in 1710 as Marie-Joseph, m. in Montreal 5 Jan. 1712 Pierre de Lestage, merchant, who d. s.p. in 1743. Several ch. d.y. She d. in 1770, long a member of the Sisters' household and a benefactress. Hannah, b. 21 June 1687, m. Joseph Swett (5 jr.). John, York, b. 2 Jan. 1690, m. 1st 31 Dec. 1713 Mary Bane(4), m. 2d 9 Dec. 1734 Mrs. Mary Kingsbury. Grants 1715, 1718; see also Y. D. 10: 3. List 279. Will, 8 Feb. 1742 (d. 11 Mar. 1743), names w. Mary, sons John, Ebenezer (m. Mary Bragdon), James (m. Bethula Bradbury), daus. Esther (m. Josiah Beale(5) and d. early), Hannah, Marah.

4 JONATHAN(1), York, m. (ct. May 1686) Mary Austin(5). Town gr. 1687. Tr.j. 1687. List 33. Adm. 25 Nov. 1689 to wid. Mary who m. 2d Capt. Lewis Bane(4). In Jan. 1706-7 they made a prop. agreement with her s. Joseph, the only surv. ch. in 1717. Ano. child was liv. in 1694. The s. Elder Joseph m. by 1709 Mary Webber(10). List 279. When 50 yrs. old he depos. that he built a mill and ho. for John Littlefield in Wells 1717-1719. Will, of York, 8 Dec. 1741 (d. 25 Dec., ag. 57), names w. Mary (d. 1 Aug.

1759), daus. Mary w. of James Donnell(4), Susanna w. of John Milbury(4), sons Jonathan, Esq. (m. Sarah Mitchell, dau. of Roger (13) and his 1st w.), Joseph, Henry (m. Hannah Sewall; d. 1748 leav. wid. and dau. Lydia), Jeremiah (m. Elizabeth Weare), and two youngest daus. Miriam, Hannah.

5 ROBERT (Sayers, Sawers, Sowward, &c.), perh. more properly handled under Seward. Bricklayer. He signed Exeter combin. in 1639, an Ex. pet. in 1643. Hampton gr. 1640; shared in the commons 1646. Lists 373, 374a, 392a, 393b. Of Str. Bank 8 July 1649, he sold ho. and 4 a. in Ex. where he form. liv. to Nicholas Davison(2), but was an Ex. hogreeve in 1652, dissented from an Ex. town vote in May 1652 and the same mo. had a sawmill priv. there with Thomas Crawley (2), whom he had sued in Salisb. ct. in 1650 over repairs to a ho. and fence they hired from Wm. Wentford. His wid. Joanna m. Crawley who had sued Ralph Hall for slander in 1650 for reporting he had called Sawer's wife a witch. She was liv. in 1671. Kn. ch: Aspira (Sayward), mo. of Samuel Crawley(1), who was ±3 in May 1671; see also Me. P. & Ct. Rec. ii: 239, 426. Note also Crawley(2), Phebe, dau. of Thomas C. or of his wife, 1660; also Elizabeth (Sowars) Wakely(3).

6 SAMUEL, York, s. of Edmund of Ipswich, nephew of (1), of whose est. he was an appraiser, and Mrs. Sayward's right hand man aft. her husb. d., was liv. in York in 1675 when John Knowlton(3) wrote to him sending 'my respects to your uncle and aunt,' and mentioning 'Dodavah.' He was Knowlton's atty. in 1679. O. A. at York Mar. 1679-80. Cor.j. 1685. Adm. 2 June 1691 to Daniel Manning, 24 Jan. 1691-2 to Wm. Spencer. Inv., personal effects only and est. in hands of Spencer. A debt was due to Arthur Bragdon. Apparently unm., and should not be connected with Aspira Sayward(5). See also John Leeds who willed him his broadaxe, Manning(2), Martin(2), Parsons(3).

SCADLOCK. Col. Banks found this name at Sutton-in-the-Forest, Yorkshire. See Me. P. & Ct. Rec. ii: 432, note.

1 SAMUEL(2), in Mar. 1653-4 wit. will of Godfrey Sheldon by which he rec. 5 s. Agent for mo. and sis. in Aug. 1667 when marsh form. his fa.'s was divid. betw. him and Capt. Pendleton. Signed Cape Porpus pet. 1668. Wm. Symonds sued him for debt in 1671; in 1673 he deeded 1/6 of his fa.'s place to Symonds who already had 1/6. O. A. at Marblehead 1677. Winter Harbor wit. 1688. Lists 255, 85. Ag. ±44 in Jan. 1693-4, he depos. ab. being at Richard Whiteridge's in Boston with Marbleh. and Beverly coasters, and presum. it was his w. Anne, ±27 in

1694, who was at Richard Way's in Boston when a fishing acct. was made up, being concerned on her husb.'s acct. Late of Cape Porp., he claimed land there bot from P. Fletcher in 1689, and his fa.'s 300 a. which his mo. and Rehoboth Gannett confirmed to him in 1671. Marbleh., form. of Cape P. in May 1714, ag. 67. There in Oct. 1717 he deeded ⅓ the Cape P. farm to dau. **Susannah,** w. of Bezaliel Getchell(2) and the fol. mo. mortg. the other ⅔ to Cyprian Southard. Liv. 18 Apr. 1719, ±76. In 1727 Getchell and Southard sold the whole 300 a. His w. (or wid.) Ann depos. at Marbleh. in May 1728 that she liv. at Cape P. ab. 40 yrs. bef. near John Jeffrey. Other ch. appear: **Anne,** m. 20 Nov. 1712 Joseph Masury of Salem. **Elinor,** m. in Marbleh. 7 Dec. 1715 Benjamin Gale. **Samuel,** b. 18 July 1698 and **Sarah,** b. 8 Feb. 1699, these two at Boston. Rebecca (Scarlett), a child, bp. at Marbleh. in 1715, and Norman (Scarlett), adult at Marbleh. in 1728, poss. gr.ch.

2 **WILLIAM,** planter, West Saco, Cape Porpus, had a ho. on W. side of Saco River adj. the Andrews(16) land in 1638, and not imposs. his w. Elinor was the Ellen Lougie (Hotten's Lists have it Longe) who came with the Andrews fam. in 1635, ag. 20. He was bef. Saco ct. in 1636 for drunkenness, and in 1640 was fined for misdemeanor (John Heard had bot liquor at his ho.); no other adverse rec. appears. In 1640 a wit. for Winter in his suit ag. Cleeve for slandering his w. some six yrs. bef. Tr.j. 1640; gr.j. 1653, 1654, 1657, 1660. Clerk of the writs 1653. In 1661 Wm. Phillips confirmed the 300 a. gr. to him by Cape Porpus in 1653. Lists 242, 243ab, 244bc, 249(2), 252, 24. Will, of Cape P., 7 Jan. (inv. 17 Mar.) 1661-2, names w. Elinor, 'our children,' and disposes of books and an assortment of personal effects (Me. P. & Ct. Rec. ii: 121; i: 247). She m. 2d in Haverh. 29 May 1663 Stephen Kent, later of Woodbridge, N. J., and was liv. in 1671. Ch: **William. Susanna,** m. Arthur Wormstall. **John,** wit. Flewellin's acknowledg. to Sanders, Bush and Turbet in Feb. 1660, attesting bef. Jordan in Apr. 1661; wit. Gregory Jeffrey's will in Jan. 1661-2; buried 29 Apr. 1664 (Saco rec.). **Rebecca,** 72 in 1714; m. William Sheldon(2). **Samuel,** b. ±1650. **Sarah,** m. by 1671 Rehoboth Gannett from Scituate, who was in N. J. in 1683 and d. there s.p. One Sarah G. proved Daniel Brymson's will in N. J. in 1696 (see Greenland).

3 **WILLIAM**(2), m. Anne (Bully 2) Berry. Tr.j. 1664. Lists 243ab, 79; see also Henderson, Orchard. Wife's List 246. He was bur. 17 July 1664 (Saco rec.); adm. 18 July 1665 to Capt. B. Pendleton, whose inv. incl. much later claimed by Stephen Kent as

admr. of (2)'s est. (Me. P. & Ct. Rec. i: 246-7). Wid. Anne m. 3d John Carter(4). Son **William** b. Saco 4 Mar. 1661. At Boston in 1690, ±30, he depos. in suit of Thomas Doughty of Malden vs. Henry Smith, over plank deliv. at Saco (see Jeffrey 5); on cor.j. (Boston waterfront) July 1693. From abs. of vital rec., deeds, and land claims, it would appear he d. s.p., but from his connec. with Doughty and the Jeffrey fam. who went to Lynn, it is perh. poss. he was the unkn. husb. of Hannah (Paul) S. of Malden and Lynn, and fa. of her 3 daus.

**SCALES, Matthew** and **William,** Piscataqua, Falmouth, No. Yarmouth. See Y. D. 12: 65, 354; 19: 83; 'Early Settlers of Rowley' (1933), p. 328-9.

**SCAMMON,** Scamman.

1 ***HUMPHREY** (see 2), Kittery, Cape Porpus, Saco, first seen in Oct. 1667 when wid. Sarah Abbott(5) withdrew a suit ag. him for refusing to satisfy her for lodging, etc., and for fish lent him in her husb.'s lifetime. In May 1674, no residence given, he bot in Wells from N. Fryer. Kittery 1677; chosen Cape P. constable Feb. 1678-9; of C. P., bot the Henry Waddock farm in Saco 4 Dec. 1679, and there given town priv. and a ferry lic. in June 1680. Tav. lic. 1680-1686; townsman and comr. to take the lists to York 1682; j. 1684; gr.j. 1685; Goodman S. and Edw. Sargent to collect the minister's salary in 1685; he to see the minister's cellar dug and stoned on 1686. Deputy 1686. Blackman's Falls on Dunstan River where Mr. H. S. formerly had a sawmill ment. in 1720. He ret. to Kit. in wartime, appr. Mrs. J. Bray's est. in 1694; culler of fish 1695-6; gr.j. 1699 (see also Milford and Pope 3) and ret. to Saco to be taken captive with w. and sons Humphrey and Samuel in 1703. One Humphrey was a resid. of Truro when that town incorporated. Lists 259, 249(3), 298, 39, 239b. He made his will in Kit. 12 Mar. 1713-4, prob. ret. to Saco as soon as poss., and there sold at Kit. Point in 1725. He d. 1 Jan. 1727, ag. 87. Ch. by will: Capt. **Humphrey,** in Kit. 10 May 1677, d. in Saco 31 May 1734, m. Elizabeth Jordan(1), who evid. outliv. sons Nathaniel and Benjamin. Ch., first two appar. by an earlier w., last six rec. at Saco 1717-1729: Hannah, Elizabeth, Mary (an Ind. captive; see Deering 8), Sarah, Humphrey, Dominicus, James, Nathaniel (d. 1745), Benjamin(d. 1745), Jeremiah (d. y.). **Samuel,** m. 1st Margery Deering(8), who d. 10 Oct. 1740, m. 2d (int. 5 Sept. 1741) Elizabeth Stimson of Bid. Will, of Bid., 23 Apr. 1751 (d. in May 1752 in 63rd yr.), names w. Elizabeth, ch: Samuel, John, Ebenezer. **Elizabeth,** m. Andrew Haley(2). **Mary,** three times a Penhallow wit. 1699-

1700, m. 1st Hezekiah Purington(2), m. 2d Jonathan Paine. **Rebecca,** m. one Billings, presum. John (2 jr.).

2 **JOHN,** a legatee with his dau. **Elizabeth** Atkins, under the will of his sis. Mrs. Elizabeth (Scammon) Saffin (see Legate 2, Scammon 3), may or may not have lived in Barbadoes, may or may not have lived in Kittery, but in all probabil. was the fa. of one son who did live here, **Humphrey.**

3 **RICHARD,** Dover, Exeter or Stratham, br. of Elizabeth Saffin (see Legate 2) whose will, 1682, gave £20 each to bros. John and Richard S. and sis. Anne Waldron, £40 to John's dau. Elizabeth Atkins, £60 to Richard's dau. Jean, and £5 to Hannah Gerrish. He mar. Prudence Waldron (13), evid. away from Dover (where first taxed in Dec. 1663). On his pet. to the Mass. Ct., as heir by mar. to the est. of Wm. Waldron, the ct. 23 May 1666 allowed him to take over the Shrewsbury patent provided he gave security to respond to the creditors and other partners. Lists 356h(2), 47, 54, 359ab, 383, 386, 49, 52, 57. On 24 Apr. 1691 he deeded to s. William 'my farm where I now dwelleth' near town of Exeter, and stock, reserving for dau. Mary the meadow called Jeremies Pocket and meadow by the river next land of Capt. Wm. Moore. Appar. dead 12 Oct. 1691 when Richard Talley and w. Sarah of Boston and Mary Hale wit. Prudence Scammon's consent to her dau. Jane's mar. in Boston. Unrec. ch: **Sarah,** m. 10 Dec. 1674 Christian Dolloff. **Richard. Thomas,** at Stratham in 1680 with fa. and br. Wm. (see later Marbleh. records). Ch. (Prov. rec.), their mo. Prudence: **William,** b. 29 Feb. 1664-5. **Jane,** b. 21 July 1667, m. 1st Thomas Stedman q.v.; m. 2d at Boston 12 Oct. 1691 Thomas Deane; see N. E. Reg. 13: 140; 37: 288. **Prudence,** b. 29 Aug. 1669. **Elizabeth,** b. 22 Apr. 1671. **Mary,** b. 31 May 1673, m. James Sinclair(2).

4 **RICHARD**(3), Dover, first taxed 1677. Constable 1694, 1695; highway surv. for Cochecho 1696; gr.j. 1697, 1698; assessor 1699. Appr. Robert Evans's est. 1697. Lists 52, 62. See also Evans(8). He m. Elizabeth Wakely(3); both called Quakers. Will, aged, 20 Dec. 1723—30 July 1724, names w. Elizabeth and ch. On Jan. 12, 1732-3 the wid. and only s. Richard deeded Wakely land to Phineas Jones. Ch: **Elizabeth,** m. James Wilmott(2); d. s.p. **Prudence,** m. Samuel Hodsdon(1). **Sarah,** m. aft. 1723 John Starbird. **Richard,** tanner, Dover, heir and exec., m. 1st 8 Dec. 1724 Susannah Varney(4), m. 2d 10 May 1753 Hope Tuttle; d. s.p. in Sept. 1764. In 1765 his sis. Sarah Starbird of Newcastle, wid., and the ch. of his decd. sis. Prudence brot an ejectment suit ag. wid. Hope

(d. 30 Sept. 1782) and Joseph Hanson for the whole of two 300 a. and 90 a. lots.

5 **WILLIAM**(3), Stratham. Exeter constable 1694-1696; selectman 1699, 1700. Rated for minister 1714. Lists 57, 67, 377, 388 (Jan. 1715-6). In 1720-1 he deeded marsh to br. Thomas Dean and w. Jane and must have been the same William who m. in Strath., prob. 2d, 4 Jan. 1721-2 Rachel Cleveland (Religious Hist. of So. Hampton: 'As early as 1720 one Scammon of Strath. had m. Rachel Thurber of Rehoboth, Mass., who agitated a Baptist church'). 4 ch. rec. Strath: **Richard, James, Elizabeth, Barnabas,** and their fa. deeded separately to sons James and **Samuel** in 1740. The same yr. he deeded the homestead, 226 a., to Daniel Lunt, who with w. Sarah deeded back to Wm. and Rachel for life with remainder to their 3 sons equally, Richard, Samuel, James. Wid. Rachel was gr. adm. 26 Oct. 1743.

**Scarden.** See Sarden.

**Scarlet,** John, List 82, prob. the Boston John. See also Adams(2), Scadlock.

## SCATES.

1 **HENRY,** Wells, had a town gr. in Mar. 1699 which he sold to Eliab Littlefield. Named a Wells abuttor, at Maryland, 1702. List 269b.

2 **VALENTINE,** a wit. in the Black Will, jr.—Elizabeth Turbet case 1715, and accus. by Sarah Turbet in Jan. 1716-7. With Thomas Westgate gave a bond to John Frost of Portsm. Taxed Berw. Feb. 1718-9 and m. there 28 May 1722 Hannah Stanford (see King 7). 3 ch. bp. 3 Nov. 1726: **Elizabeth, John, Abigail.** He was liv. in Berw. 1748; s. John was taking care of his mo. in 1764-5. One Mary, adult, bp. at Berw. 1736, wit. there in 1737.

**SCHOALES, Ralph,** a Portsmouth wit. 1699-1702, Plaisted, Partridge, Vaughan, Penhallow, etc. He was Mrs. Redford's bookkeeper in 1700 and wrote her letters to Dr. Mills.

**SCHOOLER, William,** a vintner from London, liv. at Merrimack, hanged for the murder of Mary Sholy with whom he was going as a guide to her master at Piscataqua, in 1637.

**Scobbel,** John, see Y. D. i: 137.

**SCOLLY.** 1 John, Saco, adm. gr. to (2) 13 Mar. 1688-9; appraisers John Edgecomb and Thomas Pratt. See Wyman's Charlestown, ii: 849.

2 **THOMAS,** Saco, Thomas Haley his bondsman 1689. See (1).

## SCOTT. See also Dalton(3), Gent(3).

1 **HENRY,** wit. a Young fam. deed at York 1712.

**2 JAMES,** Portsmouth (James Kidd?), was in court in June 1656 and had a Great Isl. gr. List 330a.

**3 JOSEPH,** merchant, Boston, m. there 18 Jan. 1693 Elizabeth Winslow, dau. of Edward and Elizabeth (Hutchinson). Portsmouth 1704. In June 1709, he wit. in Portsm. with Samuel Moody, but when sued there that yr. by Mark Newdigate for goods deliv. to his w. in 1697, return was made 'non est inventus.' Madam Scott taxed Portsm. 1707. In 1709, when she was at her own ho., Joseph Johnson (see 21; not a negro) beat her s. **Joseph,** ±16 (b. in Boston 23 Nov. 1694); she then beat Johnson while her son and her negro held him. When this got into ct., many neighbors test., and her **children** were ment. She m. 2d in Greenland Capt. Samuel Hinckes and was liv. in Roxbury in 1730. See also Palmer(2).

**4 ROBERT,** Sheepscot, wit. an Ind. deed to George Davie in 1663 or 1664, and bot half the Great Neck, up Sheepscot River, from Philip Bendall in 1665, which he claimed in 17—. Walter, Tabitha and Margaret Phillips and Thomas Gent supported his claim to other land on E. side of Damariscotta River above the middle falls, called Woodberry, while he supp. Brown, Gent, Taylor and Wilcott claims. He m. 2d Esther (Mercer) Draper(3). A refugee in Boston, he ret. to Sheepscot with the re-settlers in 1683. Lists 12, 17(?), 162-164. Ag. ±56, he depos. ag. Lt. Jordan in Boston in Jan. 1689-90. Thereaft. of Charlestown, where his w. was adm. to Ch. in 1699. In 1707 he was gdn. of her gr.s. Samuel Whittemore, ag. 15. Will, 15 Oct. 1705 (small personal inv. 12 Dec. 1711), gives all to w. except legacy to only s. **Samuel,** who was bp. (adult) at Charlest. in 1699, and whose s. Samuel was bp. there in 1707 on his gr.mo. Scott's acct. Poss. Thomas, Samuel, Sarah, Esther, b. Cambridge 1710-1717 (their mo. Sarah), were the elder Samuel's ch. also. Of Wrentham 1729, he deeded ⅓ his fa.'s land. In 1791 friends of Esther (Draper 3) Roberts, who d. ±1761, quoted her as saying that her mo. m. Robert Scott who had a s. Samuel when he m. her; that he wanted this son to share with her ch. in Draper land, but her mo. refused. Ch. by w. Esther: **Thomas,** b. in Boston 13 Oct. 1681, dead in 1705.

**5 SYLVANUS,** Portsmouth, m. 21 Oct. 1714 Sarah Moses(1). Will, 1754-1756, names w. Sarah, sons **Samuel, Sylvanus;** daus. **Ruth,** wid. of George Tompson; **Sarah,** w. of Joseph Seavey; **Elizabeth,** w. of Benj. Foster(2 jr.); **Frances,** w. of Wooden Foster(2). Members of his fam. went to Scarb. and to Machias.

**6 THEOPHILUS,** boatswain 1657 (Y. D. 1: 60-61).

**7 THOMAS,** at Damariscove early. List 8.

## SCOTTOW.

**CAPT. ‖‡JOSHUA,** merchant, Boston, Scarboro, owner of Scottow's farm and garrison in Scarb. where Scottow's Hill keeps alive his name. On 19 May 1639 he and br. Thomas were adm. to Boston Ch. which their widowed mo. Thomasine had joined 21 Sept. 1634. In 1649, as 'friend and agent,' acting for Mr. Thomas Lake(3), absent in Conn. His connec. with Scarb. began by 8 June 1660 when he bot the Abraham Josselyn prop. He later acquired the Henry Jocelyn prop. which was first mortg. to him in 1663, but appar. he was not resident until aft. 1670. Lic. to sell to his fishermen in 1671, on prison committee 1674, and that yr. indicted from Scarb. for an election irregularity. During the war in command at Scarb. where many held the opinion that he was more interested in the protecton of his own prop. than in the general welfare. Lists 234b, 236, 237bde, 238a, 239a, 266, 29, 32, 34, 77b, 80, 83. See N. E. Reg. 5: 78; 43: 64; 2 Mass. Hist. Soc. Col. iv: 100; Doc. Hist. 6: 47; Mass. Col. Rec. 4: 2: 208-9; Col. Soc. Mass. x: 369; York Deeds. His pet. in answer to complaint of Shapleigh, Rishworth and Wheelwright, the committee on military claims, who had severely censured him, was pub. in the Daily Eastern Argus (Portland) 16 Sept. 1911. See also Bedford(1), Cleaves (2), May(1), Moore(15), Pickett, Tucker (10), Wilmot(3). Aged ±40 in 1657, ±43 in 1659, ±66 in 1682 (Reg. 28: 68). Comr. for Scarb. 1676, magistrate 1676, 'of Boston' at times. Associate 1679 and impowered to give oath to Saco, Black Point and Casco jurymen and constables, on committee to manage new planta. at Casco Bay 1680, ord. to keep a better ferryman at Black Point 1682, Scarb. selectman 1683-1685, headed committee in charge of Fort Loyal 1684, J. P., Judge Inf. Ct. Common Pleas and Sess. 1687-1688. In addition, the author of two curious tracts. Of Boston 1690, d. there 20 Jan. 1697-8, ag. 83. Will, 23 June 1696, names w., 5 ch., 2 sons-in-law. Wife Lydia adm. to Boston Ch. 23 May 1641, d. 9 May 1707, ag. 86. Ch. at Boston (of Boston 6 May 1665, he made his Scarb. prop. over to trustees for his ch., Sarah, Mary, Rebecca, Thomas, Y. D. i: 163-4): **Joshua,** b. 30 Sept. 1641, d.y. **Joshua,** b. 12 Aug. 1643, appar. d. bef. May 1665. **Lydia,** bp. 29 June 1645, m. 1st Benjamin Gibbs, m. 2d Anthony Checkley. **Elizabeth,** bp. 1 Aug. 1647, m. Maj. Thomas Savage. **Rebecca,** bp. 10 Oct. 1652, m. at Malden 1 Apr. 1675 Rev. Benjamin Blackman(2). **Mary,** b. 11 May 1656, m. Capt. Samuel Checkley. Capt. **Thomas,** b. 30 June 1659, H. C. 1677, O. A. at Scarb. 17 Mar. 1679-80,

tr.j. 1681, Clerk of the Writs 1681; Scarb. gr., comr. for the town, Clerk of Courts (all in 1686); lic. 1686-1689, in command at Black Point 1689, Portsm. wit. Jan. 1690-1, Boston mariner 1694. Lists 225a, 238a, 18, 33, 97. Doc. Hist. 9: 10. Of Boston, chirurgeon, bound to sea in the -Gerrard- of London, when he made a will in England, 14 Nov. 1698—4 Sept. 1699, giving all in N. E. to sis. Elizabeth Savage, all else to loving friend Margaret Softley, wid., of St. Paul's, Chadwell, co. Middlesex. **Sarah**, m. Samuel Walker.

**SCRIBNER**, Scrivener.

1 **JOHN**, Dover, taxed 1662. Jury 1666, gr.j. 1670, 1673. Lists 356ghk, 357d. In 1685 his son sold the planta. on which he had liv., form. granted to John Lovering, 20 a. on E. side of Richard Otis. Will, 27 Nov. 1674 (d. 2 Oct. 1675), names w. Mary and ch: John, under 21. **Elizabeth**, under 18; m. 4 Nov. 1686 Samuel Eastman of Salisb. **Edward**. One Edward Screven was pressed for the country's service in 1679 (Essex Q. Ct. Rec. 7: 289). **Thomas**, yeoman, Kingston, List 400. In Jan. 1700-1 he went a stranger to Joshua Weeks' in Greenland, asking the way. He m. 1st in Hampton 24 Dec. 1702 Sarah Clifford(4) who d. 5 June 1706 (2 ch. rec. Kingston 1703-1705, bp. at Salisb: John and Deborah who liv. with their uncle Joseph Clifford in 1724); m. 2d 4 Feb. 1707-8 Hannah Welch (ch. rec. 1709-1716: Sarah, d.y., Elizabeth, Edward, two Samuels). Will, 28 (d. 30) Mar. 1717-8, names w. Hannah (m. 2d Charles Hunt 2), 5 ch., and prov. for ano. ch. b. about six mos. later.

2 **JOHN**(1), blacksmith, of age in 1685. Of Exeter, he was adm. to Hampton Ch. in July 1698 and soon dism. to Ex. Jury 1693, 1696. Lists 57, 62, 376b (1698). Paid for keeping Goody (Mary) Atkinson in 1729. He m. Elizabeth Cloyes(2) who was liv. 2 July 1730, but dead 1 Mar. 1733-4 when he deeded Cloyes land to his sons. Will, 2 Mar. 1735-6— 31 May 1738, names 3 sons, 5 daus. and ch. of decd. son Samuel. Ch: **John**, blacksmith, m. by 1713 Sarah Wadleigh(3). Will, 1756— 1756, names w. Sarah, son John, daus. Abigail Young, Martha Robinson, Sarah Robinson, Elizabeth Harper. **Edward**, blacksmith, m. bef. 1721 Abigail Leavitt(9). **Samuel**, m. Anna Taylor(25), who was gr. adm. 18 May 1731 (inv. 12 Jan. 1730-1), and was his wid. in 1742. Ch. in 1754: Benjamin, John, Elizabeth (w. of Abram Smith), Margaret, decd. (w. of David Sleeper). **Joseph**, took adm. on est. of s. Joseph, jr., of Exeter, 24 May 1756, the young wid. Elizabeth renouncing; sureties Joseph Lougee and Noah Emery. He and Elizabeth (wife, mo. or sis.) wit. Richard Glidden's will in 1727. **Eliza-**

beth Moody. **Mary** Gordon. **Abigail** Young. **Susannah**, m. 1st John Mudgett of Brentwood, m. 2d Nicholas Smith. **Sarah** Moody. In 1743 the surv. sons sued Abigail Wiggin and John Cousins for ¼ of 150 a. granted to John Cloyes.

**SCRIVEN**, Screven.

*****WILLIAM**, Mr., planter, shipwright, Kittery, founder of the Baptist Ch. in Me. and honored in the South as its founder there. Appar. from Somerton, co. Somerset. In 1668 he wit. a Salisb. or Amesb. deed and 10 May 1669, of Amesb., bound self for four yrs. 'after the manner of an apprentice' to George Carr, shipwright. He bot at Kit. in Nov. 1673, and m. 23 July 1674 Bridget Cutts(7). Abs. from Ch. (Me.) 1675 when it appeared he usually went to Mr. Moody's meeting. On 21 June 1681 he, w. Bridget and Humphrey Churchwood were bp. and rec. into the Boston Baptist Ch. Churchwood wrote from Kit. 3 Jan. 1682 (1681-2?) that W. S. had been called as pastor; lic. by the Ch. to preach 11 Jan. 1681-2; arrested in Apr. for preaching, and finally released on his promise soon to leave the Prov., but from Kit. later he wrote to Boston asking aid in organizing a Ch. there, which was done 26 Sept. 1682. If he went South early, he ret. and until at least 1695 did not perma. leave Kit. where active in more than the church. Constable for lower Kit. 1676; gr.j. 1678, 1679, 1682; foreman 1693, 1694; Deputy 1681, 1693, 1694; commis. Ensign for lower Kit. 2 July 1687; commissioner for Kit. 1692-3; moderator 1694-5; apprais. Thomas Crockett's est. 1679, John Moore's 1686; Kit. wit. June 1695. Lists 30(2), 288. See also Atwell(2); Y. D. vol. 5 (by index); 2 Me. Hist. Soc. Col. 1: 45; 5: 275; Doc. Hist. 5: 395, 398; 'History of the Baptists in Maine' (Burrage, 1904). About 1696 he went to So. Carolina, accomp. or fol. by others of his faith, incl. his wife's relatives, and there 7 Dec. 1696 had a warrant for 1000 a., where Georgetown stands, altho credited with first settling near Charleston in a place called Somerton (N. E. Reg. 43: 356). His Kit. homestead was sold in 1704 by his s. and atty. Robert (Y. D. 7: 14). He declined a call to Boston in 1707 and d. at Georgetown 10 Oct. 1713 in 84th yr. (gr.st.). Interested southern searchers credit him with 11 ch: **Elizabeth**. **Samuel** (a Kit. wit. in Oct. 1696, Y. D. 4: 132, 156). **Mercy**. **Sarah**. **Bridget**. **Robert** (shipwright, resid. in Kit. 20 Nov. 1704; mariner of So. Carolina, 16 Jan. 1704-5; see Hodsdon 5). **Patience** (by ano. rec. Parmenius). **Joshua**. **William**. **Joseph**. **Elisha**. But this does not include **Aaron**, a Cutts wit. Aug. 1700 (Y. D. 6: 82). One Saville S. found in S. C. has not been

connected with him. See also Elliot(5).

**Scullard,** Samuel, orig. petitioner and grantee of Hampton. See Cromwell(4).

**SEABROOK** (Saybrook), **Thomas,** Dover, and w. Mary, in 1667 q.c. to John Ault (for money paid by Thomas Edgerly) land that John Hill did purch. of Thomas Footman and did pass over to Richard Bray(5). Mary was poss. Bray's wid. or dau.

**SEACOMB, Richard,** and w. Joanna arriv. at Boston on the -Unity of London- bef. 20 Aug. 1680 when he and three others (incl. one James Ross) were unsucc. sued for slander by the commander George Penney. He was 35, Joanna 30, in Nov. 1680. Soon at Falmouth, where he had tav. lic. in Sept. 1681 (Wm. Rogers bondsm.) and 100 a. gr. by Lawrence Davis's, which he sold to John Edwards and Thomas Walter in 1683. In 1682 sued George Ingersoll, sr. and jr., for dragging and abusing his w., and lost. Gr.j. 1683, 1686; constable 1684; selectman 1685; called Capt. and late commander of Fort Loyal in Nov. 1686. In 1685 he bot the farm where George Lewis(4) liv. and d., and a Ross deed in 1721 ment. 'Lewis his Neck or Seacom's Point.' Lists 225a, 228c, 34. He retired to Lynn aft. May 1689. Will, 23 Aug. 1691—15 May 1693, ment. two daus., 4 sons, giving to **Susannah** all money whatsoever, and to **Noah** and **Richard,** under 15, land at Casco Bay. In 1698, as trustee, the dau. Susannah of Boston and single, sold to John Rogers. Richard had w. Ann and 3 ch. in Medford 1710-1715; weaver of Portsm., R. I., in 1715. Other ch: **John,** List 229, m. Mehitable Simons in Boston 26 Nov. 1706; ch. **Peter** (Seccomb), List 229, m. 25 Feb. 1702 Hannah Willis in Medford where he d. in 1756, ag. 78. Ch. incl. John, H. C. 1728, minister at Harvard, Mass., and Joseph, H. C. 1731, minister at Kingston, N. H. A chart of the fam. (c. 1856) has **Joanna** (instead of Susanna) who ret. to Eng., and **Mary.**

**Seahone,** Dennis. See Cartee and Sehand.

**SEALY,** Seeley, Cilley. See N. E. Register 85: 76.

1 **BENONI.** See (6).

2 **GEORGE,** one of four bros., sons of Andrew of Stoke-in-Teignhead and King's Teignton, co. Devon, all early fishing masters at the Shoals. See (3), (7), (10); also (8). Bp. at Stoke-in-Teignhead 19 Dec. 1622, he was a creditor of his br. John 1651, and signed a Shoals pet. in 1653. List 301. No later rec. found here, but living when his fa. made his will, 14 Apr. 1664—15 Apr. 1665.

3 **CAPT. JOHN,** Shoals, b. ±1618; see (2).

Chosen constable for the Shoals 26 Aug. 1646, and there a warr. from Boston was di-

rected to him and Antipas Maverick in Oct. 1647. James Rollins bot a ho. at Long Reach from James Johnson and J. S. in 1651. 'Of Kingstanton, Devon' he acknowl. debts to bros. (7) and (2) and to George Monk in 1651, in which yr. he sold Star Isl. prop. In 1652, of Star Isl., in consid. of £100 to be paid him in Eng., he assigned his debts, with a p/a, to (10). In Eng. in Sept. 1659, master of the -Dolphin-, about to sail for N. E. Bot on Doctor's Isl. 1660. List 354a. See also Brown(28), Wooton. Adm. gr. to (10) and to Elias Stileman 28 June 1670; informed he is dead; wife and **children** (in Eng.). In June 1676 adm. had been gr. in Eng. to William and Joanna Tapping of London, Wm. Henderson had come over with their p/a, and Mr. Stileman had been ord. to turn the Doctor's Isl. housing and land over to him. Heirs are not kn. to have come at all.

4 **JOHN** (see 7), mariner, Boston, ±31 in Feb. 1671-2, when a wit. in the Naylor divorce case; see Moore(13). List 3. Richard Starr (Tarr) pet. Andros for confirma. of 50 a. on W. side Saco River bot ab. three yrs. bef. from John Selly, fisherman; other land of Selly adj. (Doc. Hist. vi: 374); much later deeds say he bot from Richard S. Wife Margaret. Ch. rec. Boston: **Richard,** b. 17 Mar. 1667. **John,** b. 22 Sept. 1670. **Margaret,** b. 25 Mar. 1673. Prob. also **Dorcas,** m. in Boston 2 June 1698 George Courtney [mar. int. of James Sharp and D. S. rec. in Boston 16 Oct. 1696].

5 **JOSEPH** (Celly), with the (appar. local) crew of the -Katherine- in 1701.

6 **MARTHA** (Blaisdell) (Boaden 9), as Martha Selly of Amesbury deeded for love and affec. to dau. Elizabeth Davis(23) 1 Nov. 1684, and m. 3d at Hampt. 15 Jan. 1686-7 John Clough of Salisbury. She was liv. 1 Apr. 1707. Not imposs. mo. of **Thomas** (9) and of **Benoni,** joiner, who m. 1st (int. at Salisb. 28 Aug. 1703) Eleanor Getchell (6); m. 2d at Salisb. 9 Oct. 1739 wid. Rachel Tappan of Kensington. Will, of So. Hampt., 1745—1746, names w. Rachel and all rec. ch. but John: Mehitable, Elizabeth, Thomas, Martha, Samuel, Benjamin, Eleanor, Sarah, Dorcas, and by 2d w: Mary, Abigail; also son-in-law (stepson) Christopher Tappan.

7 **RICHARD,** bp. at Stoke-in-Teignhead 4 Feb. 1620-1 (see 2 and 3), was at the Shoals in June 1651 when Henry Shrimpton drew a bill of exch. for £300 on London, payable to Mr. R. S., for merchantable dry codfish. Com.t.e.s.c. 1653. Sued by Mr. Wm. Paine in Dover ct. in June 1655 when Mr. Pattishall appeared for him and his bond was forf.; acting at the Shoals for wid. Joan Bevill in Oct. 1657. List 301. Not named in fa.'s will 1664, but prob. then liv. in Saco where Gunner S. was indebted to the Scad-

lock est. in 1664 and the admr. sued Richard S. in 1666. Goody Sily 1666, 1674; List 246. In 1670, mariner, he dealt with the Kembles (see Kimball 4), and gave a bond for £30 15s., and mortg. to cover, to Robert Brimsdon who assigned it in 1697 to Capt. John Hill(8), he to his br. Joseph. Lived on W. side of river, N.W. of land Roger Hill sold to John Elson, he to Wm. Dicer. Gunner S.'s Creek ment. 1729. He was a refugee at Salem in Jan. 1675, List 27; O. A. at Boston 21 Apr. 1679. Certainly the logical fa. of: **John**, b. ±1642. **Emm**, m. 13 June 1668 John Rule. **Dorcas**, m. 1st James Gibbins(3), m. 2d Francis Backus.

8 **THOMAS**, Kennebec, wit. a Parker-Webber deed with Edmund Pattishall 26 Dec. 1664. O. A. to King 8 Sept. 1665. List 182. He may have been the youngest br. of the Shoals Sealys, who was bp. at Stoke-in-Teignhead 28 July 1638 and was liv. in 1664. The Kennebec man was a refugee at Braintree, where he sued Richard Thayer in 1678 and took O. A. 21 Apr. 1679.

9 **THOMAS** (see 6), Hampton, sea captain, m. 2 July 1697 Ann Stanian(3), whose fa. depos. 7 Mar. 1709-10 that he had 5 gr.ch. to take care of, ch. of his dau., w. of Thomas Cille, she dead, he gone out of the country 7 yrs. But J. S.'s will, 1718, spoke of his s.-in-law as if liv., and by fam. report, he died, aged, at home of his s. in Nottingham, while visiting there from ano. son's home in Andover. Ch. rec. Hampton: **Mary**, b. 2 July 1697, m. 14 Dec. 1724 Daniel Lovering. [Dover rec: James, s. of Mary Silley, b. 22 Aug. 1715]. **John**, b. 7 Jan. 1698-9, the only one named in gr.fa.'s will. He m. 1st 9 or 19 Aug. 1725 Elizabeth Glidden(2), was of Biddeford, form. of Hampt., in 1733, and as John Sellea of Bid. m. 2d 16 Nov. 1739 Hannah (Knight 11) Seavey of Scarb. **Abigail**, b. 19 Apr. 1700. Capt. **Joseph**, b. 6 Oct. 1701, m. Alice Rollins (Benj. 6). Of Stratham 1729, he bot in Nottingham. 6 ch., incl. Gen. Joseph; see Cilley. Hoyt's Salisbury ii: 567 adds: **Ann** (Sylle), m. Samuel Blake(5). **Thomas**, m. 7 Mar. 1729 Abigail Knowlton; liv. in Andover, N. H. Ch.

10 **WILLIAM**, bp. at Stoke-in-Teignhead 30 July 1632 (see 2 and 3). A wit. 1651 around Eliot; in June 1653 bot Emanuel Hilliard's ho. and plant at the Shoals, which he mortg. to Francis Wainwright in 1669. Ensign 1653; Shoals constable 1655, 1659; gr.j. 1656, 1660; O. A. 1658; Kit. selectman 1666-1668; highway surv. 1667. He and br.-in-law Rogers leased Spruce Creek land from H. Gunnison whose wid. gave them a deed in 1660. Bot on Smuttynose 1664, and legatee of fa. that yr. Kit. gr. 1667 (see Searle 5), which his wid. sold to Abel Porter in 1678. Selling without lic. 1669. Lists 301,

305a. He depos. 25 June 1670, ±39, and d. while carrying on vigorously at the Shoals. Inv. 13 Dec. 1671, adm. 2 Apr. 1672 to wid. Elizabeth (Lynn 2), m. by 1666. She was ±36 in June 1674, when she was at the Shoals, mistress of her own ho., and m. 2d bef. 16 June 1675 Thomas Cowell(7). No ch. appear.

**SEARLE**, has one home in Cornwall-Devon, ano. in Cambridgeshire. See also Creber.

1 **ANDREW**, Mr., Kittery, wit. in Portsm. with Sarah Abbott(5) in 1662, against her in Feb. 1663-4, when he was ±50. A wit. for Harvey(14) in 1663, 1670, the first time with Thomas Abbott. In Kit. he wit. a Spencer fam. deed in 1662 and had a gr. in 1665, either 50 a. beneath Quamphegan, if to be found, or 70 a. above Salmon Falls. Part of this he sold to Zachariah Nock jr., and Searle and Neale desc. sold more to Hamilton and Sullivan. An educated man, and often a wit. or appraiser to 1687. Surety for Francis Morgan 1667. Gr.j. 1667 (foreman); clerk of the writs 1668. In 1670 an accountant at the Shoals for Richard Endle (his testim. in 1671, ±50). Adm. of John Green's est. in 1681-2, with (4) as bondsm. Lists 298, 288, 30. He d. 25 Nov. 1690; adm. 10 Dec. to Andrew Neale as gdn. of James Neale. Inv., £38, incl. a loom, an ox in John Neale's hands, a cow, calf, chest, writing and books, all with Benoni Hodsdon; his shop built at the garrison; debts by book £9. Wife unseen. Ch. appear: **John**. **Joan**, m. John Neale(6). **Andrew** (the fa. was Senr. 1675, 1676, 1680). The younger man is more likely the A. S. (no prefix of respect) abs. from Ch. in 1676, 1679, cert. the one bound to good behav. in 1678 for turbulent and seditious practices toward authority. In 1701 A. S. liv. in Mr. Fryer's ho. in Prov. of Maine which in 1702 was in poss. of Mr. Robert Elliot; in 1702 Wm. Hart(10) liv. with A. S. at Gerrish Isl. Poss. Jemima of Kit., in ct. on bast. charges 1709, 1715, and Elizabeth, a Kit. wit. in 1720 (Y. D. 12: 20), connect with him.

2 **JOHN**, sued Mr. Nicholas Brown(28) for wages, in Me. ct. 1647. One Mr. J. S., master of a N. E. ketch, was buried at Barbadoes 7 Sept. 1691.

3 **JOHN**, fisherman, Kittery, perh. m. Joane Andrews(9) who m. 2d John Ford(4). (↑List 356m). See also (4). A coroner's j. made return 30 Nov. 1675 that he met death by drowning 4 Jan. 1675, partly by a blow in the face, partly by water. Adm. to br.-in-law Christopher Mitchell(2) 4 July 1676. One inv. at the Shoals, ano. of livestock in Mitchell's hands (Me. Prov. & Ct. Rec. ii: 326-7).

4 **JOHN**(1), Upper Kittery. (One John slandered all the women on the Piscataqua River in 1667). He m. Mary Green (12), who was ±44 in July 1695. Her fa. deeded to him 20 Dec. 1673; her mo. deeded to him and his s. John 10 July 1683. In 1682 he had his br.-in-law Thomas Abbott taken into ct. for not properly supp. his mo.-in-law, and T. A. was ord. to pay him for her board. Abs. from meet. 1685. Bot from James Emery 1693. Taxed Newcastle 1699-1700, but of Kit. in 1707 when John, jr., released int. in the Green prop. to his parents. Both abs. from meeting (Kit.) in 1712. In 1721 Wm. Rogers liv. on the land where J. S. lately liv. at Western Branch of Spruce Creek. Lists (†356m), ·288, 30, 52, 315b. Only kn. ch: **John**, blacksmith, Newcastle 1696, sued John Amazeen in 1702 for three yrs. rent from 1698. Lists 315bc, 68, 316(2), 388. See also Rand(3). With w. Elizabeth he sold at Newc. in 1715 and bot in Stratham; in 1720, of Strath., sold more in Newc.; sold in Strath. 1724; in 1736 of -Towns Kenel-, (Townsend), co. Middlesex, where the name is found later (see Y. D. 18: 29). One Elizabeth and one John S. d. in Strath. 17-19 July 1722.

5 **WILLIAM**. (The Kittery gr. 1667, List 298, in his name is more prob. Wm. Sealy's). One William signed, by mark, a N. H. pet. to the King 1665 (Prov. Papers 17: 512-3). See 'Ancestry of Bethia Harris' (W. G. Davis, 1934), for William Searle, joiner, form. of Boston, who assigned the deed of sale of his Ipsw. ho. and land to Thomas Dennis(9) in Portsm. 26 Sept. 1663, and whose wid. Grace m. Dennis in Ipsw. 26 Oct. 1668. Ch: **Grace**, m. Sergt. John Harris of Ipsw. **Samuel**, Rowley, m. Deborah Bragg. **William**, d. s.p. 1690.

**SEARS**, **John**, scalemaker, Casco Bay, sold Long Island to Isaac Walker in 1655 Munjoy wit. 1661. In 1667 unsuc. sued Wm. Haines for detaining his goods. Called planter, he sold Thomas Redding's island, land and marsh to James Lane in 1673. Kimball heirs claimed Mere Pt. land bot from him in 1670; he and Henry Webb owned there adj. Nicholas White. Robert Collicot and Nathl. Greenwood sued him in Boston in Sept. 1682. List 221. He was resident of Woburn. See Martin(4), Savage's Gen. Dict., Wyman's Charlestown.

**SEAVEY**, uncommon, prob. from West of Eng.

1 **BENJAMIN**(6), carpenter, Rye, wit. a Boulter deed with John Tuck in 1685. In 1693 money was due him for work at Fort Wm. and Mary. Gr.j. 1695. Lists 318c, 315bc, 316. In 1729 he and w. Mary deeded homestead to s. **William**, 3d (d. 1745, leaving wid. and ch.) except the part near Oliver's

Neck that s. **Benjamin**, jr. (m. Mary Wallis 23 Oct. 1712) used to mow, William to pay the daus: **Mary**; **Hannah**, w. of William Fernald (in 1762 she was Hannah Dixon); **Elizabeth**, w. of Ozem Dowse(2); **Sarah**, of Samuel Marden; **Hephsibah**, w. of Charles Foye(2); **Susannah** (Paine in 1762). The 1762 div. shows also s. **Moses** of Arundel.

2 **HENRY**(6), worked in the woods with Wm. Wallis in 1676, m. bef. 28 Feb. 1682-3 Sarah (Pierce 8) (Jones) Mattoon, and was liv. in 1685 when Col. Pepperell was suing for part of the Pierce est. See also Nath.(6). Both he and w. Sarah d. bef. 1697. **Joseph**, Portsm., was only surv. s. and h. 1710. In 1712 he and w. Hannah deeded the Pierce place to Dominicus Jordan. List 316.

3 **JOHN**(7), blacksmith, Rye. In 1673 he and Obadiah Morse wit. ag. John Bickford, jr.; in 1677 by atty. John Arnall he sued Morse in Suffolk ct. O. A. at Boston 21 Apr. 1679. He m. 29 July 1686 Hannah (Philbrook 3) Walker, List 331c. Jury 1684; gr.j. 1694; Newcastle constable 1696-1697. He sold the former Berry place to br. William in 1703, moving to Bradford, from where in 1704 he sold Newc. land to Tobias Langdon. Inv. in Essex Co. 4 Mar., adm. to wid. Mary, 4 Apr., 1709. Lists 329, 52, 332b, 57, 318c, 315bc. No kn.ch. Old Mrs. Seavey d. at Eldad Cheney's in Bradford, 27 Oct. 1738; see Walker(7).

4 **PHILIP**, with Anthony Nutter appr. Wm. Cotton's est. in 1678; N. H. Probate i: 229. Odiorne?

5 **SAMUEL**(6), Rye. Lists 57, 315ab, 318c, 316. In 1713 Samuel, sr. and Samuel, jr. subscribed for Mr. Emerson, the latter likely a son and he who m. Abigail Foss in Greenland 25 Oct. 1711; 9 ch. rec. in Rye. **Mary**, dau. of Samuel, accused Richard Swain in 1717, and perh. m. him. A poss. son was Henry who had w. Mary (List 338b) and d. bef. his s. Henry was bp. at home 27 Jan. 1718-9 (So. Ch. rec.); the wid. m. in Mar. 1720-1 John Edmonds(5); see Hodge (7). Note also Abigail (Paine 4), and Hannah, 2d wife of William(8 jr.) who may not have been a wid. Seavey when she m. him.

6 **THOMAS**, Rye, ±52 in 1679, was called 'cousin' by the ch. of (7). He had Portsm. grants in Jan. 1652 and later, and in June 1655 bot the Puddington home place next Wm. Berry at Little Harbor; (7) wit. this deed and he wit. deed of the adj. place to (7) in 1669. Gr.j. 1656; j. 1684. Constable 1663 for the Shoals, where he and (7) were at times plf. or deft. in suits over stages. In 1672, ±42, he depos. that he was at the Shoals when Thomas Turpin's w. and daus. came over. In 1687 he deeded 8 a. to s.-in-law Shute; in 1708 deeded to s. Benjamin,

effective aft. decease of self and w., Benj. to
pay his sis. Damaris, br. Samuel and neph.
Joseph. Lists 323, 43, 326ac, 330b, 312c, 54,
313a, 331b, 49, 52, 332b, 315abc, 318c. He d.
15 Mar. 1707-8, ±80. His w. was Tamsen bef.
1667; in Apr. 1711, ±70, she depos. about her
s. Henry and family. Ch. appear: **Samuel.
Henry. Benjamin. Nathaniel**, joined in one
tax with Thomas and Benjamin in 1681;
worked on highway 1683. Taxes abated 1683,
poverty or death, incl. his and Henry's. In
1685 Nicholas Hodge was bound over for
beating him. Lists 52, 57. **Rebecca**, m. John
Shute(1). **Damaris**, m. Daniel O'Shaw(1).

7 **WILLIAM**, Shoals, Portsm., Rye, depos.
in Sept. 1676, ±75, that he came to the
Shoals on a fishing account in 1632. Partner
of Stephen Crawford in 1640 and adm. his
est. He had a lot in Portsm. bef. Mar. 1646,
various grants later. Portsm. selectm. (1648
prob.), 1655, 1657; Shoals constable 1655;
gr.j. 1659. In 1660 he had a deed from
Joseph Mason of the Ralph Gee est. which
he had adm. in 1645, and in 1669 from the
Drakes(5) and John Berry(7) a deed of the
Little Harbor prop. where Wm. Berry had
liv. A ct. case with Nicholas Hodge over this
prop. in 1686 brot out deponents who told
that the ho. was orig. built by Richard
Tucker. Lists 312c, 313a, 323, 324(2), 326ac,
327a, 330ab, 331bc, 356b, 43, 47, 49, 52, 54,
71, 80, 84. See also (6), Crawford(5), Lane
(1). In 1679, with no ment. of w., he deeded
to s. William (b. ±1648), he to pay the others: **Elizabeth**, ±17 in 1669, Odiorne in 1679,
prob. w. of Philip(7). **John**, ±15 in 1669.
**Stephen**, taxed Bloody Point 1677, liv. 1679;
List 359a. William, sr., ±80, depos. in Feb.
1682-3 that he first knew Thomas Walford
over 45 yrs. ago. Not seen surely aft. 1684;
his son was 'jr.' 20 July 1686 and served on a
j. in 1687 (not jr.).

8 *WILLIAM(7), Rye, m. Hannah Jackson
(20); List 331c. One Wm. was adm. freeman at Boston in May 1674. Gr.j. 1682-83,
1695, 1698-99; j. 1684, 1687, 1692; highw.
surveyor 1683, selectman 1694; assemblyman (±1696). About 38 in 1686; of 60 odd
yrs. remembrance in 1719 (he and John
Hinckes were on Sheepscot River early);
±72 in 1720. Lists 312h, 315bc, 316, 318c,
330a, 332b, 52, 57. Will, crazy and infirm, 21
Mar. 1728-9—18 June 1732; provides well
for w. Hannah (exec. with Wm.), seven ch.,
and gives to Samuel Banfield and gr.dau.
Mary Langdon; his negro woman Ammi to
his wife. Her will, aged, 10 Sept. 1741—28
Feb. 1748-9 (s. Wm. exec.) gives to ch. and
gr.ch. and a cow to negro Amie. Ch: **William**, Rye, m. 1st Mary Hinckes (John), m.
2d 25 Sept. 1748 Hannah Seavey; d. betw.
28 Oct.—7 Dec. 1752, leaving ch. Wm., Amos,
Elizabeth Jenness(2). Wid. Hannah, liv.

1754, was perh. the H. S. who depos. in 1766,
±63, what she heard Seaborn Hodge tell ab.
the Reynolds fam. **James**, of Newc., m. at
Newington 12 June 1718 Abigail Pickering
(8); liv. 1741. Ch: Hannah, James, Paul.
**Hannah**, m. Samuel Wallis(8). **Hephsibah**,
m. in Portsm. 4 Nov. 1716 Thomas Wright of
London; her ch. in mo.'s will. **Mary**, m.
Capt. Samuel Banfield(2). Capt. **Stephen**,
taxed for Mill Dam 1712; at Portsm. in 1729
when he ment. 'my house at Canso.' He m.
1st Anne Fernald(4), her ch. 1712-1723:
Stephen, Michael, Nicholas, Hannah; m. 2d
at Kit. 17 Mar. 1729-30 Mary (Carpenter 5)
Deering; m. 3d aft. 18 Mar. 1735-6 Mary,
wid. of Obadiah True, who was gr. adm. 6
Sept. 1742 and named gdn. of ch. John and
Elizabeth, while Joshua, David and Mary
had their oldest br. Capt. Stephen, Portsm.,
as gdn. Triplets, **Ebenezer** and **Thomas**, bp.
21 Apr. 1695, and one who d. at birth. E.
and T. went to Scarboro (proprs. 1720)
where both depos. in Mar. 1734-5 ab. Scarb.
±17 yrs. bef. Lists 331c, 239b, for both.
Ebenezer m. Elizabeth Knight(11) and deposed in 1753, ±58, that he first trav. to
Scarb. in the company of Mr. John Libby, an
aged resident. Thomas m. Hannah Knight
(11) who took adm. 6 Jan. 1738-9. Unless a
Scarb. rec. of 1722 in error, he had an earlier
w. Elizabeth, while Thomas, s. of one Thomas and Mary, was bp. at Portsm. 31 Aug.
1718.

**Seay?**, William; see Me. P. & Ct. Rec. ii: 485.

**Seban**, Josiah, soldier at Great Isl. fort, 1695.

**SEDGLEY**, John, turner, York, m. 17 Jan.
1713-4 Elizabeth Adams(19). List 279.
Adm. 13 Jan. 1745-6 to oldest s. **John** who
had the homestead. The other surv. ch. were:
**Susannah** (w. of Jonathan Adams), **Hannah**,
**Elizabeth**, **Robert**, **Sarah** (John Booker her
gdn.), **Mary**, **Phebe** (d. young). Ano. s.
Thomas had died.

**Sedgwick**, Edward, a youth at Kittery
±1650.

**Seeley**, see Sealy.

**Seeth**, Richard, Cape Bonawagon 1672. List
13.

**Sefhens?**, Joseph, List 289.

**SEHAND, Anderos**, or Denis Seone, or
Dennis Sehone, ±25, Oct. 1671, worked
with Christian Dolloff. Andreas Sehand
named in the Judith Roby case. See also
Cartee.

**SELBY, Thomas**, Boston, owned at the
Kennebec. Ch. in 1731: **Thomas**, of Boston; **Jane**, w. of David Milvill of Newport.

**SELLERS. 1 Thomas** (Sallers), wit. livery
of seisin, Sears to Walker, Casco Bay,
1655.

2 **WILLIAM** (Sellers?), sued in Piscat. ct.
1642 (Pope). A very much later Wm.,

carpenter, was of York; see Ruth Donnell (3). List 279.

**SELLICK, David,** Boston, at Piscataqua; see Rec. of Mass. Bay Colony, ii: 129, 231-2; Suff. D. i: 252.

**SELLMAN, John,** Damariscove, Lists 15, 17, 141, 142. Widow Mary (Waters 6) m. 2d John Dollen(2). See 1 Me. Hist. Soc. Col. 8: 193; Waters(7).

**SENTER,** Center, Sentle, Sentall.

1 **ABRAHAM,** sailmaker, Portsm., wit. Snell to Milbury in 1715 (wrote Sentle), and Oliver to Dutch 1717 (-Setner-). Form. of Ips., he m. in Portsm. 29 Apr. 1718 Mehitabel Ayres(7) who was rec. into cov. and bp. No. Ch. Feb. 1718-9. Bondsm. for wid. Sarah Mainwaring 1733, Henry Sherburne, jr., 1734. List 339; sold in Barrington 1740. Both alive 1747. See Davis(60). Ch: **Abraham,** bp. 15 Mar. 1718-9, m. Sarah Jones. **Mehitabel,** bp. 27 Aug. 1721. Poss. **Ann,** bp. 25 Mar. 1732-3, **Hannah,** rec. into com. 7 Mar. 1741-2, both So. Ch. rec.

2 **ANDREW,** jr., see Downes(4).

3 **HUMPHREY,** depos. in Dec. 1677 that he bot liquor from Richard Welcom's wife.

4 **JAMES,** Hampton soldier, List 399a.

5 **JOHN,** boatman (Wyman: cordwainer), Charlestown Feb. 1726-7, when he q.c. land on Davis Brook, Biddeford, and a town gr., to Joshua Cheever, for advances and expenses in bldg. the meet.-ho. His mar. to Ruth Wright in Boston 2 Dec. 1708 indicates he was the John b. in Boston in 1682, whose step-mo. Ruth m. Ruth Wright's much older br. Joseph. Ch. at Boston: **Ruth, John, Samuel, Solomon.** Ruth and Patience, wives or daus., d. at Bidd. 7 Mar. 1721, 29 June 1723, respectively. See Wyman's Charlestown for last mar. and descendants.

6 **WILLIAM,** Shoals, his first name kn. only thru Catholic bp. rec. of his son, m. Mary Matthews(14), who was at Oyster River in Sept. 1683, ±29, and of the Shoals in May 1684 when she and sis. Susanna wit. ag. Roger Kelly and for Philip Odiorne's wife. Kn. ch: **Susanna,** 'eldest dau.' and **Nicholas,** both named in gr.fa.'s will 1678. **Samuel,** b. 1679 at the Shoals, an Ind. captive in spring of 1694 (Willis in Hist. of Portland says he was captured there), bp. in Canada as Jean Batiste Alexandre 21 Apr. 1696, having Martha (Mills 12) Grant as god.-mo. (List 99, p. 74). An English Marianne S. was bp. at Montreal 31 July 1708.

7 **WILLIAM** (Sentle, Sentall), shipwright, m. 1st at Kit. 2 Aug. 1706 Joanna Alcock (2). Soon aft. he and John Fennick divid. the land gr. in 1667 to John Ameredith and Fennick. List 298. He m. 2d in Boston 21 June 1708 Joanna Burnett, and, of Boston, 18 Oct. 1709, deeded 8¼ a. at Broad Cove,

Spruce Creek, to Walter Deniford. One Joanna m. Isaac Adams in Boston in 1731. Ch. by 1st w. at Kit: **William,** b. 1 Aug. 1706. **John,** b. 18 July 1707. By 2d w. at Boston 1710-1717: **Mary, William, John. Sentinall,** Sentle. See Senter.

**SERCUTT, William,** went out in a boat in May 1671 aft. drinking at Samuel Wentworth's ho. and Dr. Couch's shop; adm. in July to John Ameredith. See also Circuit.

**Ser..ente, Stephen,** sued by Wm. Parnell in 1650; action dropped as deft. was dead. Sargent?

**Sessor,** Daniel, List 74.

**Sever,** John, List 67.

**SEVERANCE, John,** Salisbury, dealt in staves with N. H. people 1653±. Sued by Robert Wicum in Wells ct. 1674. See Hoyt's Salisbury i: 314; also Ambrose(2), Bean (2), Broadbrook, Church(1), Coffin (3), Nanny.

**SEVERETT.** 1 **James,** in a Dover garrison, List 289.

2 **CAPT. PHILIP** (aut. Sivret), Portsmouth 1671, taxed 1672 next to Samuel Sheverick. Constable 1676. In 1679 witnessed p/a from Richard Calley of Richmond Isl. to Nathan Bedford; owner and commander of the -Joanna- 1680-1686; j. 1684; sued in 1685 by John Martin, and as a Portsm. merch. was deft. in ano. suit brot by a Fayal merch., in Suff. ct. Lists 326c, 329, 331a, 52. Will, 10 Sept. 1689 (d. 2 Mar. 1689-90, aged 40), gives all est. here to w. Joanna (Jose 1, m. 10 Oct. 1680) and all in Isle of Jersey to br. Thomas. His wid. was taxed July 1690; d. 10 Jan. 1690-1 from small pox, leaving a will made eight days earlier. No ch.

**SEVERN.** 1 **Ephraim,** Dover, List 359a.

2 **SAMUEL,** Newcastle cor.j. 1678, List 313b. See also Ceverne.

**SEWALL.** The Newbury fam. was from Coventry in co. Warwick.

1 **EDWARD,** cordwainer, Exeter, b. ±1640, must be that Edw. Seawell who m. Sarah Hale in Salem 3 July 1671. Exeter gr. 1675. Lists 376b, 54, 383, 52. Aged ±43 in May 1683. Vaughan's prison diary, 18 Feb. 1683-4: 'Sewall of Ex. is dead.' Adm. 7 Aug. 1684 to wid. Sarah, bondsm. Wm. Hilton. Wid. -Savel- taxed 1684 (List 52); pub. ho. lic. June 1685; m. 2d Nicholas Gordon(6). Ch., 1st two at Salem, others at Exeter: **Elizabeth,** b. 27 June 1672. **Edward,** b. 14 July 1674. **Sarah,** b. 17 Sept. 1676, m. Alexander Gordon(1 jr.). **Thomas,** b. 28 Mar. 1679. List 376b (1705). Died s.p.; adm. 19 Sept. 1712 to (2) and Alex. Gordon. **Joseph,** b. 28 Dec. 1681.

2 **EDWARD**(1), cordwainer, Exeter. List 62. See also Mason(18). Ex. gr. 1697, and bot 100 a. from Cartee Gilman who q.c.

to his heirs in 1723. Wife Sarah was adm. to Hampt. Ch. in Aug. 1697, dism. to Ex. in Sept. 1698. Adm. to her 6 Dec. 1712. She m. 2d by 1717 Samuel Lovering. The est. descended in 7ths (6 ch.); Nicho. Gordon was gdn. of four of the ch. and Alex. Gordon of Elizabeth. Ch: **Sarah**, ±16 in June 1715, m. in Beverly 10 Mar. 1724 Joseph Cole. **Edward**, cordwainer, Ex., ±14 in June 1715. List 376b (1725). In 1725 he and the Coles sold 3/7 of fa.'s est.; lĩv. 1743. **Elizabeth**, ±14 in Apr. 1717, m. in Bev. 4 June 1733 Wm. Tuck. **Thomas**, tanner, Salem 1726, when he sold 1/7 of his fa.'s and uncle's estates. One T. of Glouc. m. 29 July 1734 Mary Norton of Hampt. **Samuel**, Ex. 1729. **Stephen**, not shown by probate rec. List 376b (1725). He m. wid. Mary Folsom(5) who was his wid. in 1748. One Mary was in Ex. tax list 1743 betw. Edw. and John Scribner.

3 **NICHOLAS**, tanner, York, b. in Newb. 1 June 1690, s. of John and Hannah (Fessenden), br. of (4) and of Hannah (Sewall) Moody(7), 1st cous. of Elizabeth (Sewall) Hirst (see Pepperell). List 279. He m. Mehitabel Storer(3). 10 ch. in York 1714-1734. He d. ±1740 and wid. Mehitabel m. 2d Jonathan Preble(2).

4 **SAMUEL**, Esq., cordwainer, York, b. in Newb. 9 Apr. 1688 (see 3), m. 1st Lydia Storer(3), m. 2d in Newb. 29 Nov. 1723 Mrs. Sarah Titcomb, d. in York 25 Apr. 1769, ag. 81 (gr.st.). List 279. 6 + 8 ch. in York 1712-1740; 11 surv. him.

**SEWARD**, Seaward, a Devonshire name. See also Sayward, partic. Robert(5).

1 **HENRY**(2), shipwright, Portsmouth, m. 21 June 1694 Mary Huntress(1). Lists 330de, 337, 339. Will, 29 May 1734—13 Apr. 1737, names w. Mary and ch: **Mary**, m. 28 July 1715 Jonathan Studley or Stoodley. **John**, boatbuilder, m. 14 Nov. 1723 Catherine Drew of Deptford, Eng., bur. 22 Apr. 1785, ag. 88. **Abigail**, m. Thomas Goodwin(5). **Hannah**, m. by 1734 John Pulkinhorn, mariner, Portsmouth, and was gr. adm. 5 Aug. 1737. **George**, boatbuilder, m. 13 Nov. 1729 Margaret Pendexter(1); est. adm. Jan. 1759. 3 sons.

2 **JOHN** (aut. Sewer), shipwright, Portsm., an appr. of Mark Hunking's est. in Sept. 1667. Str. Bank constable 1671 (Sayword, by a Rishworth entry); taxed 1672; ale-ho. lic. 1683; j. 1682, 1684; gr.j. 1684, 1696. In 1687 his son and servants had made a complaint ag. Samuel Shackford. In 1697 he and w. Ann or Agnes (List 335a) sold to James Fernald land in Eliot assigned to him in 1674 by John Moore, jr.(9). In 1686 his w. called Timothy Davis a thief. Lists 49, 55ab, 329, 330d, 331b, 332a, 336b, 337. See also Oliver (8). Will, 21 Mar. 1704-5—3 Apr. 1705, wit.

by George Marshall and Reuben Hull, gives to w. Agnes for life, aft. her death to s. **Henry**, he to pay the other ch: **Samuel, Jane, Agnes, Charity, Love** (Seward 1729, Bush in 1746).

3 **JOSEPH**, Portsmouth. List 334a.

4 **RICHARD**, Portsmouth, on 7 Dec. 1652 gr. a lot on no. side of Str. Bank Creek against Mr. Campion's ho., prov. he build within a yr., and had other grants. Lists 323, 326a, 330ab. Will, 21 Feb. 1662-3—1 July 1663, gives Drake point to gr. ch. John Jackson, the next point to Richard Jackson and 'rocke' point to Mary Seward (these two not called gr.ch.). His other land and household goods to his son and son-in-law equally, his whole part of the vessel and cargo to his gr.ch., and names br. Roger. Ch: **Richard. Dau.** (perh. Joan), m. Richard Jackson(16).

5 **RICHARD**(4), Portsmouth, adm. an inhabitant of Boston in 1657 when Nathaniel Fryer was surety for him, rec. back at Portsm. and gr. 1 a. of land in Jan. 1660-1. Lists 323, 326a, 330ab. His will (disallowed), 1 Aug. 1667 (inv. 22 Apr. 1668), provid. that all land owned with Richard Jackson should be divid., his share going to w. Mary and ch., who were also to have the tobacco in the ship -Prosperous-, what was due him from Mr. Richard Cutts and Mr. Fryer, and tobacco in Maryland, aft. debts had been paid from it; loving friends, Maj. Shapleigh and Mr. N. Fryer overseers. Ch: **Mary**, b. at Boston 2 Oct. 1658, m. 1st Dodavah Hull(2), m. 2d Dr. Samuel Blagdon(3) by 1688, when she, her br. and sis. deeded to John Jackson. **Richard**, chose his master Wm. Vaughan gdn. 22 Nov. 1681. Mariner, Portsm. Wit. with John Barsham in 1686; with Nicholas Bennett in 1689, Margaret Adams to Wm. Fernald; evid. d. s.p. **Susanna**, m. Thomas Simpson(8). Her will, 20 Jan. 1737-8 (d. 12 Mar. 1739, ag. 72), gives principally and equally to cousins (nieces) Mary (Hull) Follett and Hannah Blagdon, the former sole exec.

6 **ROGER**, concerned in the Jordan-Ridgway fishing voyage in 1651 (Trel. Papers p. 489) and a wit. in the ct. case in 1655-6, 'he went to Monhegan.' Presum. the br. of (4) on whose land he was liv. in 1662 when given liberty to enjoy it for life, and owed £14 to (4) who willed the debt to his son. He or ano. was of Damariscove in 1672. Lists 13, 111, 141.

7 **SAMUEL**, Dover 1666. List 356k.

8 **SAMUEL**(2), List 335b, appar. the one around Spruce Creek in Jan. 1715-6, ag. ±39, calling Samuel Spinney 'my br.-in-law,' and occupying Diamond Sargent's place in Crooked Lane in 1717; John, Thomas and James Spinney wit. deed given by (2) in 1697. Both Henry and Samuel Seward

were taxed at the Bank in 1713. 'Sundry disbursements for Samuel Seward' in Portsmouth town account, 1729. In all probabil. Elizabeth (see also Samuel Fernald 4) and Elizabeth, jr. (see Huntress 2), who wit. will of Mrs. Mary Clark(20) in 1720 were his w. and dau.; John and Mary Shepard were the other witnesses. Poss. ch: Ebenezer, caulker, m. 15 Mar. 1732-3 Mary Henderson (see 4), and d. ±1761, George Huntress admr. (7 ch. incl. Love). Sarah, m. Thomas Clark(50).

9 WILLIAM, from Devonshire. See Shackford(1).

SEYMOUR. 1 Henry (Semor), Kennebec soldier 1689, List 189.

2 REV. RICHARD, chaplain with the Popham colony, List 6.

SHACKFORD, freq. on border of English cos. Norfolk and Suffolk, usually Shuckford.

1 JOHN(3), blockmaker, partner of (2) at Portsmouth where they owned a wharf. Ag. ±17 in Dec. 1694 and likely the son who was John Ballard's apprent. in 1693 and whose mo. was trying to have him set free in 1695; ±23 in 1702, ±27 in 1705. Lists 67, 330def, 337, 339. Will (Shuckford), 11 Sept. (d. 3 Oct., ag. 60) 1738, names w. Sarah (List 331c) and 6 ch., giving to w. £29 annually, household goods, and the use of the ho. during widowhood except the room reserved for dau. Toome; the two sons executors and princ. heirs. The est. incl. negroes and much prop. Ch: Mary, m. William Seward(9). Deborah, m. 1st bef. 1725 Isaac Summers (also Sumner), m. 2d Capt. Samuel Waterhouse(2). Paul, blockmaker, Newbury, m. there 29 Feb. 1727-8 Rebecca Hudson; 5 ch. rec., incl. Sumner. Both d. in Newburyport, she 24 Feb. 1776 in 66th yr., he 4 Dec. 1786 in 84th yr. John, blockmaker, Portsm., m. 20 Jan. 1731-2 Catherine Dennett. Major John d. in Portsm. 25 Oct. 1766, ag. 58. Catherine, wid. of one John, d. in Exeter 16 Dec. 1799. Sarah, m. John Flagg, mariner, Portsm. Elizabeth, m. 12 Nov. 1730 Andrew Toome (also Tomb), mariner, Portsm., from Minehead, co. Somerset. 2 SAMUEL(3), blockmaker, early in Portsmouth where he and (1) had a successful business. In 1687 Barefoot issued a warrant ag. him for breach of the peace. Ag. ±31 in 1705. Adm. to No. Ch. in 1716. Lists 334a, 62, 330def, 337, 339. He m. 1st (ct. June 1695) Abigail Richards(4), m. 2d 10 May 1716 wid. Frances (Hoyt) Peabody of Topsfield. His undated will, proved 11 Mar. 1730-1, gave her the E. end of his home and an annuity while a wid. She m. 3d at Amesbury Capt. James Pearson; m. 4th in 1746 Mr. John Johnson of Andover, where she soon d. Her will names Dorcas Shackford.

Ch. from fa.'s will: Elizabeth, with next sis. rec. into cov. and bp. (No. Ch.) Mar. 1716-7; m. Ezekiel Pitman(2 jr.). Abigail, m. Samuel Sherburne(6). William, bp. with two fol. in 1716. Father's exec., given Newington prop. and half the business int. at Portsm. Capt., Deacon, J. P. He m. 1st 5 Oct. 1727 Susanna Downing(4), m. 2d 7 May 1752 Patience (Ham) Downing (see 4 jr.), m. 3d Eleanor (Mendum) Marshall (see 3). Will proved 24 Feb. 1773; wid. d. 4 Feb. 1804, ag. 90. 8 ch. John, liv. in one end of fa.'s ho. and eventually had all. He m. 1st 26 Oct. 1727 Dorcas Lovejoy of Andover (3 ch. rec. there 1732-1742); m. 2d wid. Hannah Lancaster at Methuen 27 Nov. 1751; d. at Chester 2 Nov. 1786. Joshua, given Chester and Barr. rights. He m. 24 Dec. 1735 Lydia Lovejoy of Andover, where 2 ch. rec. Samuel, bp. 1716, dead 1731 leaving ch. at a distance. Mary, bp. Nov. 1716, m. 1st by 1723 Richard Furber, m. 2d Alexander Hodgdon (see 3). 3 WILLIAM, housewright, Newington (±37 in July 1679), depos. in Jan. 1709-10, ±70, that he liv. with Valentine Hill '58 yrs. agone'; in 1715, ±73, that Matthew Giles liv. on cert. land in Durham '60 yrs. agone'; in Apr. 1718, ±78, that he worked with Henry Langstaff at O. R. and built a ho. for him, and ±20 yrs. bef. went to N. J. himself and liv. with John Langstaff there. Trad. sets his early home in Ireland and in Bristol, Eng., with no evid. that either is correct. First taxed 1662. Constable 1671-2; gr.j. 1678; j. 1695. Nehemiah Partridge sued him in 1672; in 1675 he won a suit ag. Barefoot; sold without lic. 1678; sued by Francis Matthews next 1702. Nicholas Harrison's divid. line next W. S. at Fox Point ment. in 1707. Lists 356ghk, 357c, 359ab, 336b, 343, 49, 52, 54, 92. See also Gray(14), Taprill. He m. by 1671 Deborah Trickey(6). In 1680 they q.c. to her br. Zachary; in Nov. 1705, ±58, she depos. that she liv. at Benj. Matthews' ±40 yrs. bef. to take care of his mo. She was ±72 in June 1718. Both liv. 7 Aug. 1720 when they deeded to sons Samuel, b. ±1674, and John, b. ±1677, the deed proved by witnesses 8 Dec. 1720. Other ch. appear: Mary, m. Henry Nutter(4). Joshua, Newington, m. 4 Dec. 1707 Elizabeth Barnes(12). Of Dover, he q.c. Rand land to Thomas Rand, sr., in 1712; wit. with John Crockett in 1716. List 358c. Kn. ch: Sarah, o.c. and bp. at Newingt. 1727 (one S. m. at Portsm. 8 Apr. 1733 Joseph Welch from Ipsw.); Mary, o.c. and bp. 1732; Lazarus, a wit. for his Portsm. cousins in 1738; Samuel, Paul (Biddef., Arundel, Wells, int. m. with Sarah Day at Bid. in 1743), and John, these three bp. 8 June 1728 when their mo. Elizabeth owned the cov. She m. 2d Daniel Quick(1). In 25 yrs. research the late S. B. Shackford of

Dover found no evid. that Jane, w. of Alexander Hodsdon(3), was a Shackford; neither did he find his family name in Ireland.

**SHACKERLY.** 1 **John,** Portsmouth, sued Zachariah Taylor in 1661. In 1664 when Rachel Webster was in ct. for entertaining him, she said she had ordered him to depart. The same yr. he was ordered to return to his wife. One John S. and Peter Jackson were sued in Suff. ct. in 1674.

2 **WILLIAM,** from Plymouth, Eng., was fishing at Monhegan in 1661 (Essex Q. Ct. Rec. 2: 313).

**SHACKLEY, Richard,** Berwick, m. Hannah Hodsdon(1) 17 Nov. 1709. List 296. 10 ch. See 'Old Kittery and Her Families,' p. 713.

**SHAFFS** (Shafte), Thomas, at Pemaquid garrison 1689. Lists 126, 228d.

**SHALLOT, Francis,** Scarboro, Newcastle, a Frenchman, ±35 in 1685. Rishworth wrote his name Shullet. In 1674 he was ord. removed from Weymouth Bickton's ho. in a fortnight; in 1675 concealed iron work W. B. had stolen from the Alger mill. The same ct. ord. him to keep away from Susannah Collins, and he soon ret. to Mary Bickton's company. A soldier under Scottow. In York ct. 1679, with N. H. bondsmen, acq. on charge of stealing a gold piece from Henry Holmes and Mary Bickton. A poor Eastern person gone from Newc. in 1680; Scarb. wit. 1680; taxed 1681. In the next war he ret. to Newc., served several times as a soldier, and was at Newc. fort Nov. 1703—May 1705. Last seen in 1710 when arrested on compl. of Margaret Hornabrook alias Woodsum, and Mary Allard. Lists 237a(2)b, 238ab, 313d, 60, 66, 315b, 316.

**SHANNON.** 1 **Morris,** taxed Newc., 1720.

2 **NATHANIEL,** Mr. of Boston and Ipswich, m. 'Madam' Abigail Vaughan(4) at Portsm. 25 Nov. 1714, and d. ±1720-1723. Mrs. S. was taxed in Jan. 1731-2, adm. to So. Ch. in Aug. 1733, m. 2d Capt. George Walker (2). Ch. rec. at Portsm: **Nathaniel,** b. 17 Feb. 1715-6. **Cutts,** b. 17 Aug. 1717. See Shannon Genealogy (1905).

**SHAPLEIGH.**

1 **ALEXANDER,** gent., eminent merchant, Kingsweare, co. Devon, and Kittery, his large interests here looked aft. by the Treworgys and his s. Nicholas, whose transactions in his name, with the depositions of servants, would make it appear that he was here at times when actually he was in Eng. Here in person 26 May 1642 when he made over his entire est. to s.-in-law Treworgye, tho by rec. T. had deeded the same prop. to Nicholas Shapleigh 2 Apr. 1641. See Y. D. i: 1, 7; vii: 236, 237. In Oct. 1650 a statement

was made: 'The house where Mr. Wm. Hilton now dwelleth at the River's mouth was the first ho. built there, and was where Mr. Shapleigh's fa. first built, and Mr. Shapleigh now intends to rebuild and enlarge.' In May 1674 his dau. Katherine, pleading for her br., told that ±38 yrs. since in a time of great scarcity her fa. laid out a good est. for the supply of the country. In 1679 John White depos. that ±42 yrs. ago Mr. A. S. and Mr. James Treworgye agreed with the neighbors dwelling at and ab. Sturgeon Creek. He m. 2d at St. Saviour's, Dartmouth, 12 Dec. 1602 Jane Egbeare (see also Messant). His 1st w. is unkn., also the place and time of his death. Elizabeth Trickey's depos. made it appear he d. here, and appar. he was not long dead 6 July 1650 when the question to whom the est. belonged was brought bef. Godfrey. He ruled that Mrs. Treworgye was in no way poss. of the est. or responsible for any debts, as her fa. conveyed everything bef. he d. and no will was proved, no evid. considering the deeds, A. S. to J. T. and T. to Nicholas S., covered the same prop. and that the latter was the later deed. See N. E. Reg. 5: 345. Ch. appear: **Katherine,** b. ±1600, m. 1st James Treworgye(1), m. 2d Edward Hilton(1). **Alexander,** m. at Kingsweare 9 Apr. 1622 Elizabeth Tellman. **Elizabeth,** bp. at K. 16 June 1602, m. there 4 July 1626 John Bereford. By w. Jane: **James,** bp. at K. 16 Apr. 1608. **John,** bp. at K. 24 Nov. 1612. **Nicholas,** bp. at K. 1 Jan. 1617-8. One Avis S. was bur. at K. 1 Nov. 1615.

2 **HENRY,** Gosport, and w. Elizabeth, both b. 1726, m. by 1748, had 10 ch. there.

3 **LT. *JOHN,** Kittery, gr.s. of (1), neph. and heir of (4) who brot him over as a ch. aft. his fa. died. See depositions, Y. D. 4: 41. He depos. in June, 1678, ±36, ab. Antipas Maverick's poss. of ho. and land near 30 yrs. past; in Jan. 1700-1, ±56, that he liv. with (4) and in his ho. above 46 yrs. past. Sergeant for Kit. 4 July 1659; Ensign 18 July 1665; called Lieut. 1695. J. 1674, 1683, 1687, 1694; gr.j. 1674, 1675, 1693; j. life and death (Baker Nason) 1693; selectman 1676-77, 1683-84, 1692-1699; highw. surv. 1692-1699; town treas. 1694-1698. Deputy 1696. Overseer of Humphrey Chadbourne's will 1667, John Heard's 1676, John Ameredith's 1690. Lists 298, 290, 293, 82, 94. He was k. by Ind. and s. Nicholas taken prisoner in Apr. 1706 (Niles); Rev. Mr. Pike entered it under date 6 June 1706 (List 96). He m. Sarah Withers aft. 25 Apr. 1671, when her fa. gave her half his farm at Oak Point, Spruce Creek, as a mar. portion, and by T. W.'s will in 1679 he rec. a neck of land called Oak Point with the marsh next his ho. She was liv. in Nov. 1708, dead in Oct. 1723. In Dec. 1772 Edward Cutts, Esq., called a meeting of the proprs.

of Ossipee township on pet. of five heirs of Major N. S., Samuel, John, James, Dependence, Elisha (SJC 138062); a full list of the Shapleigh heirs is found in SJC 130076. See also 'Desc. of Edward Small and Allied Families' (1934), pp. 52-100. Ch., 1st two in gr.fa. Withers' will 1679: **Alexander**, m. Mary Adams(5); d. s.p. ±1701. She m. 2d John Dennett(4 jr.). **Alice**, d. s.p. by 1715. Major **Nicholas**, Esq., Kit., served his fa. 7 yrs. aft. becoming 21, m. 7 July 1715 Martha Langdon(2). Major in militia; J. P. Will, 17 Jan.—6 Apr. 1752, names w. Martha, 6 sons, 1 dau., Aunt Curtis. Inv. £4501. **Sarah**, m. Stephen Eastwick; eldest dau. in 1715. **Elizabeth**, m. Capt. John Knight(10). **Mary**, not named in list of fa.'s heirs 1733 (Harvard C. v. Harmon). Capt. **John**, gent., Kit., m. 29 Nov. 1733 Dorcas Littlefield(7). Will, 24 Feb.—9 Apr. 1759, names w. Dorcas, 4 sons, 4 daus. Inv. £2324.

4 **MAJOR \*NICHOLAS**(1), Kittery, merchant, a worthy representative of his family and noted for his ability in public life, his dislike of Massachusetts' government and his hospitable nature and tolerance for those not always in favor with others. Called merchant of Kingsweare in his br.-in-law's deed of 2 Apr. 1641 (Mr. Godfrey took poss. for him), he was here and a member of the court in Aug. 1644 but bound to England three months later when he gave his p/a to John Treworgye. By 1648 he had returned and was serving as selectman, an office he filled many years, until disallowed, with others, in 1669 because of Quaker sympathies. See York Deeds, Me. P. & Ct. Records, Documentary History, and Mass. Colonial Records for numerous references to him as Kittery's commissioner, County Treasurer, Magistrate, Assemblyman, Capt., Major and member of various civil and military commissions, also his dealings with Mass., including a stay in their prison in 1674, being released on his sis. Katherine's plea and his payment of £200. Also Lists 3, 30, 44, 76, 77b, 81, 92, 236, 282, 288, 298, 383; Alexander (3), Champernowne(1), Jordan(7), Lane(1), Mitchell(5), Nash(4), Small(3), Treworgye. How his w. Alice, married by 1651, was related to Mrs. Ann Messant, and why young John Cutts(2) called him 'uncle' are questions that arouse curiosity but are unanswered. He d. s.p. 29 Apr. 1682, being killed by a falling mast at a launching at John Diamond's, and leaving as heirs his wid. Alice and neph. John(2) whom he brot over from England as a small boy. The wid. was liv. 20 Dec. 1685.

**SHARP**, Sharpe, rare in the S.W. and So. coast counties of Eng., infreq. in the North.

1 **JAMES**, taxed Great Isl. or Sandy Beach in 1671 (List 312c). By depositions in 1721, he had a ho. in York in 1674 'near where Jonathan Bane now lives.' York constable 1676. The land on which he had built ment. in 1678. He m. Elizabeth Wentworth (11); see Harris(6). She had m. Richard Tozier bef. 18 Mar. 1690 when taken an Ind. captive to Canada, bp. there in 1693, and ret. bef. 3 Nov. 1698 when she and her husb. sold to Lewis Bane ±25 a. form. in poss. of James Sharpe (Y. D. 6: 42; also 3: 15).

2 **JAMES**, on Newcastle cor.j. 1693, List 318a. See also Sealy(4).

3 **JOHN**, Saco, presum. taxed at Dover in Dec. 1663, moving on to Saco in time to m. 14 Nov. 1667 Elizabeth Gibbins(2); List 246. Tr.j. 1668, 1674; gr.j. 1675. Absent from Ch. 1672. Wit. ag. Mr. John Bonython for swearing in 1675. Tempo. at Newc. and Kit., he returned to Saco by June 1683, when he appr. Gabrigan Bonython's est. Selectman 1685. Of Winter Harbor, sr., sold his Kit. gr. to Nicholas Morrill, sr., 1 Feb. 1685-6. Lists 356h(2), 249, 298, 313a. See Page (3). Wife Elizabeth a Saco wit. 1687. In 1690 her fa. deeded Saco land to her, reciting her descent from Mr. Thomas Lewis. She was in Boston in Nov. 1696, poss. a wid.; there in Oct. 1700, a wid. (aut. in SJC 4797); 'of the County of York' 26 July 1720; dead 2 June 1729. Ch: Capt. **John**, mariner, eldest son 1720, ag. 66 in Dec. 1736. One John of Boston sued John Cobbett of Salem in 1713 for a debt incurred at Martinique; his aut. in SJC 9245. In Saco his garrison was on Rendezvous Point. He m. 1st in Boston 6 Sept. 1697 Mary Brooks who d. in Saco 23 Feb. 1726, ag. 56 yr., 1 mo. (gr.st.); m. 2d in Saco 29 Sept. 1726 Elizabeth Gardner of Glouc.; both liv. 1748. Ch. rec. Boston 1698-1712: John, Elizabeth, William, Mary, Abigail, Elizabeth, Jonathan, all bp. in Boston, also Gibbins, James, Sarah and a 3d Elizabeth. **Gibbins**, mariner, Boston, m. 19 Jan. 1701 Sarah Goff, who d. 9 June 1756 in 78th yr. (Copp's Hill). Ch. rec. 1702-1709: Gibbins, James, Elizabeth, Sarah. Capt. **Jonathan**, mariner, Boston, but apprent. 10 Nov. 1696—20 Aug. 1703 to a Boston joiner, Thomas Hitchborne, sr., who d. bef. Oct. 1700 when his mo. wanted him freed. He m. 1st 22 July 1713 Deborah Thayer (4 ch. bp.); m. 2d 21 Aug. 1735 Margaret Putnam who d. 2 Dec. 1763, ag. 78. **Thomas**, of Great Britain, d. s.p. by 1748 when his 1/6 int. in his mo.'s est. was sold by br. John and Edward Proctor, the latter having bot out other heirs. **Elizabeth**, w. of John Mainwaring, Boston mariner, 1729.

4 **SAMUEL**, wit. livery of seisin of the Dover pat. to Edward Hilton by Thomas Lewis, 7 July 1631; see Downes(2).

5 **THOMAS**, commander at Pemaquid in May 1680, and wit. Matthew Rew's deed to Richard Pattishall in Nov. 1683. J. P. for Cornwall 1684. Lists 16, 124. See Bish(1), Giles(8), and his letters written from Albany to Gov. Andros and to Mr. John West in June 1688 (Doc. Hist. vi: 403-5).

**SHARPAM, Thomas**, drunk in 1659, Sagamore Creek witnesses. In 1670 (Sharpan), he wit. will of John Tucker(9) and swore to it bef. Stileman.

**SHAW.** No. of Eng. and north Midlands, also Scotland. Became 68th commonest name in N. E. See (5) and Rankin.

1 **ANDREW**, wit. a Scarboro deed in 1682, ack. it at Black Point in 1687, and signed a Falm. pet. next to (11) in May 1689; List 228c. A. S. was a York wit. in 1693, apprais. John Diamond's goods with Wm. Godsoe, and was indicted in 1695 as a common drunkard and liar.

2 **BENJAMIN**(13), trader, Hampton, m. 25 May 1663 Esther Richardson; liv. on homestead. Lists 49, 396, 52, 62. Goodwife Shaw, List 394, may be his w. or his brother's. In 1693 he refused oath as gr.j. Will, 27 Dec. 1717—12 Feb. 1717-8, names w. Esther who d. 16 May 1736, ag. 91, ten ch. and dau. Ruth's dau. Sarah; w. and s. Edward execs. Ch: **Mary**, b. 2 Dec. 1664, perh. m. Jonathan Philbrick(8). **Esther**, b. 17 Nov. 1666, m. Capt. Jabez Dow(5). **Sarah**, b. 22 June 1669, m. Seth Fogg(6). **Abigail**, b. 22 Aug. 1671, m. John Smith(27 jr.). **Ruth**, b. 24 Dec. 1673, d. unm. 13 Apr. 1715. See Lancaster(3), also her ch. Sarah Ward(10) and Reuben Smith(47). **Benjamin**, Hampt. F., b. 28 June 1676. List 399a. He m. 1st 2 Oct. 1711 Deborah (Sanborn) Fellows(2), she liv. 1722, dead 1728. Will, 26 Mar. (d. bef. 23 June) 1740, naming w. Mary (exec. with his cous. Benj. Dow) and 5 ch., was contested by daus. Ruth Sleeper and Esther Chase, and adm. gr. to wid. (Dow declining) 24 Sept. 1740, pending probate. In 1741, on the ground that the will was void and all ch. but themselves illegit., the daus. ent. suit ag. Mary Fifield, single woman, otherwise called Mary Shaw, wid., and Thomas Sillea; the wid. was admitted sole deft. **Roger**, b. 23 Sept. 1678, m. 2 Mar. 1704-5 Alice Rollins (6); d. 29 Oct. 1752. List 399a. 9 ch. **Joseph**, b. 1 Nov. 1681, m. 12 Dec. 1705 Hannah Johnson(15). Will, of Kensington, 24 Oct. 1743—31 July 1745, names her, 7 of 10 ch. **Edward**, b. and d. 1685. **Edward**, given homestead and to care for mo., m. 1st 27 June 1716 Mary Johnson(15), m. 2d in Newb. 2 July 1719 Abigail Marshall of Ipsw.; d. 24 Dec. 1764. 4 ch. 1720-1727. **Hannah**, b. 23 July 1690, m. John Wedgwood(1). **John**, Hampt., farmer, youngest son. Will, 21 May

1746—24 Sept. 1751, w. Sarah, 8 ch.; sons Edward and Stephen executors.

3 **EDWARD**, likely at Duxbury 1632-1639, was of Saco in 1645 when his w. Joan was to be whipped for slandering Capt. Bonython. In 1657 he sued Matthew Giles (7) for wages, sued Giles' wife, and was fined for being drunk at his ho. In July 1658, Richard Hitchcock compl. that 'ould Shaw' would take away his **Son**, a small boy he had kept five yrs., and the boy was ord. bound to H. A mo. later Alex. Bachelder, Henry Donnell and Richard Tucker arbitrated betw. Mr. Abraham Josselyn and E. S. of Piscataqua, form. of Blue Point, over his **Dau.**, Josselyn's apprent.; J. was awarded £8 and Shaw's Blue Point land was bound for payment. Josselyn assigned all papers to Christopher Collins, who took the land on an exec. in 1660. See also (6, 11).

4 **EDWARD**, a Kennebec soldier in May 1688, presum. the prisoner with the Ind. attacking No. Yarmouth in Sept. 1688, found useless because of a rupture and k. by his captors. List 189.

5 **HECTOR** (Demashaw), Frenchman, d. at the Shoals; adm. 23 June 1677 to Peter Shaw, surety N. Fryer.

6 **ISAAC**, Scarboro, servant of John Jackson(13) in 1671, when he rode from Saco to Black Point on the Sabbath. Absent from meet. 1674. See (3).

7 **JAMES**, in ct. May 1682, many times drunk; Capt. Hooke bondsman.

8 **JOHN**, deft. in Str. Bank ct. 1646-1650. In 1646 he ack. a judgment to Darby Field, in 1649 forf. his bond for appearance in Field's suit.

9 **JOHN**, York wit. 1705 (Y. D. 7: 228).

10 **JOSEPH**(13), Hampton Falls, m. 26 June 1661 Elizabeth Partridge(4); List 394, hers or w. of (2). His Lists 49, 55b, 396. Ch: **Abial**, b. Oct. 1662, m. Thomas Brown(33). **Elizabeth**, b. 23 Aug. 1664, m. Aaron Sleeper(1). Dea. **Samuel**, Hampt. F., b. 23 Aug. 1666. Gr.j. 1698; constable 1700. He m. 1st Esther Batchelder(3) who d. 24 Jan. 1715, ag. ±50; m. 2d 1 June 1716 Mary Tuck(2). Lists 94, 57, 399a. See Sanborn(5), Lovering(1). Will, 9 Nov.—4 Dec. 1723, names w. Mary and ch: Elizabeth and Samuel (to be brought up to learning and at college). Abigail, w. of Isaac Fellows, Mary Sleeper, sis. Sary Cram, and sis. Brown also named. **Child**, b. 11 Dec. 1669. **Caleb**, mariner, Hampt. F., b. 31 Jan. 1670-1. List 399a. See Deborah Clifford(4). He m. Elizabeth Hilliard(7), was lost at sea 19 Mar. 1715, and she m. 2d Capt. Joseph Tilton. Ch: Rachel, b. 1695, m. Abner Sanborn; John d.y.; Apphia, m. 1st Peter Sanborn, m. 2d Robert Rowe; Josiah, d. 1721; Samuel, m. Rachel Fellows(2); Elizabeth, m. Caleb Rollins;

Anne, d. 1724; Margaret, m. Jonathan Tilton; Joseph, m. Elizabeth Batchelder; Ebenezer, m. Anna Philbrick; Mary, posth., m. Joseph Worth. **Josiah**, b. 13 Jan. 1673-4, List 399a, m. Meribah Page(2) and was k. a few days later, 10 June 1700, running a race, his horse flinging him ag. a fence. She m. 2d Samuel Tilton(2), m. 3d Benj. Sanborn(1). **Sarah**, b. 5 Dec. 1676, m. Benj. Cram(1 jr.). **John. Ann**, b. 20 Oct. 1681, m. Moses Elkins (4). **Abiah**, m. 21 Sept. 1703 John Webster (6).

11 **PETER**, Scarboro, Spurwink; see (3, 5, 12). First seen 29 May 1668 as an admr. of John Mayre's est.; in 1680 appr. Joseph Oliver's est. Spurwink 1683. In 1685 Wilmot Edgecomb(2) sold Blue Point land, form. in poss. of -Peter- Shaw and J. Collins. Fined at Spurwink in 1687 for beating Wm. Lucas' wife, and there in May 1689. His fam. was in Beverly aft. Spurwink deserted, but he not seen there. Lists 237c, 30, 90(2), 226, 228c. Wid. Jane (Allison 2) m. 2d Wm. Bradford of Bev. (whose 1st w. d. bef. Feb. 1696-7), m. 3d in Manchester 13 Mar. 1717 Robert Leech. Kn.ch. in Beverly: **Sarah**, m. 8 Nov. 1694 John Tuck (Y. D. 16: 120, 121; 17: 107). **Walter**, m. 4 Dec. 1696 Anna Gale, who was gr. adm. 4 Oct. 1708 and m. 2d in 1710 Jonathan Williams. 3 ch. rec., incl. Anna, m. in 1723 John Thomas in Glouc. (Y. D. 17: 106). By his name: **Peter**, m., int. 14 Oct. 1705, Bethia Lovet who m. 2d Nehemiah Haward of Salem in 1711. Prob: **Mary**, m. 1st 29 Nov. 1711 Cornelius Balch, and d. 14 Apr. 1774, upward of 90, as wid. of Dr. Michael Dwinell of Topsfield (Balch Gen.). **Elizabeth**, ±18 in 1707, m., int. 10 Aug. 1712, Roger Haskins (Haskell?).

12 **RICHARD**, Scarboro, on 13 Mar. 1662 deeded his ho. and all land at Blue Point to John Howell(3), who was gr. adm. 1 July 1662. In June 1750 Daniel Burnham(3) depos. that ±26 yrs. ago he was at the ho. of Mr. John Tuck (see Shaw 11) and saw there an aged woman who told him she was the **daughter** of Richard Shaw, and b. on her fa.'s place at Dunstan.

13 *ROGER, Hampton, first at Cambridge, freeman 14 Mar. 1638-9, called R. S. sr. of Cambr. 15 Nov. 1647 when he bot John Cross' Hampt. houses and land (Essex Antiquarian i: 22). He had been selectman and town clerk in Cambr. Tr.j. (N. H.) 1648, 1649; gr.j. 1651; selectman 1649, 1654; Com. t.e.s.c. 1651; Rep. 1651, 1652, 1653; constable 1654; lic. to sell wine 1654. Lists 53, 66, 392b (2) 393a(2). His wife in Cambr. was Anne, his 2d w. Susanna, wid. of William Tilton (5), who d. 28 Jan. 1655, he 29 May 1661. Will, 25 Aug. 1660, cod. 20 Mar. 1660-1, names 2 sons, 4 daus. and 2 Tiltons. Called 'sr.' in 1647, but no 'jr.' seen. Kn.ch: **Joseph. Mar-**garet, m. Thomas Ward(9). **Ann**, m. Samuel Fogg(4). **Hester** (Esther), b. in Cambr. June 1638. **Mary**, d. in Cambr. 26 Jan. 1639. **Benjamin**, a minor in 1660. **Mary**, b. in Cambr. 29 Sept. 1645, m. Thomas Parker(26).

14 **WILLIAM**, York, had a gr. in Mar. 1699 and m. Agnes Frost(12). Jury 1714. List 279. Ch. 1701-1716: **Mary**, m., int. 7 July 1726, Joseph Smith. **Samuel**, m. Elizabeth Bowdy (Boody 2); List 279. 8 ch. 1727-1744. **John**, d. 6 Aug. 1726; he had been a student at H. C. about 3 yrs. **Martha**, m. 8 Feb. 1732-3 Henry Moulton (see 11). **Joseph**, d. 11 Dec. 1724.

**SHEAFE.** See English ancestry in N. E. Register, 55: 208; American Genealogist (Oct. 1938).

1 **EDWARD**, Charlestown, a Portsm. wit. 1702, m. 29 Aug. 1704 Mary Cater(3). His niece Mary (Wm.) m. Gershom Griffith(1). See Wyman's Charlestown, ii: 856.

2 **RICHARD**, Mr. Jacob's seaman, accus. of being fa. of Mary Agawam's ch. (George Walton's Indian), 1660.

3 ‡**SAMPSON**, Esq., merchant, Newcastle, bp. in St. Faith's par., London, 26 Dec. 1646, s. of Edmund and Elizabeth (Cotton), was in N. E. perh. tempo. in Nov. 1668, ag. ±21, and in Boston in 1672 but called of London. He 'visited' Newcastle in 1675, mov. there ab. 1693, but had Me. and N. H. interests earlier; see Goffe(3), Blackman(2). Dep. Collector of Customs for N. H. 1698-1707; Councillor and Secy. of the Prov. 1698; Clerk of Courts 1698; Commissary of exped. ag. Quebec 1711; in London in Apr. 1715, representing to the Lords of Trade 'if an enemy should possess themselves thereof (N. H.), as in the late war it was much feared, it would endanger the whole country.' Lists 48, 52, 315b, 316, 336, 382. He d. in Boston soon aft. 6 Dec. 1725. His w. Mehitabel Sheafe, b. in Boston 28 May 1658, dau. of Jacob and Margaret (Webb), was his 2d cousin. Ch. rec. Boston: two **Mehitabels**, b. 10 Dec. 1677, 27 Nov. 1680. **Jacob**, b. 18 Feb. 1681, m. in Newb. 22 Nov. 1710 Mary Davison(1), appointed as a Boston school-master 1712, d. there 26 Dec. 1760, ag. 79. 10 ch. rec. Hon. ‡**Sampson**, Newcastle, b. 14 Aug. 1683, H. C. 1702, m. 27 Nov. 1711 Sarah Walton(5) whc d. in Newc. 19 Aug. 1771, ag. 81. A merchant and West India trader; Councillor 1740-1761; d. 1772. List 316. 10 ch. See also Jeffrey(2), Langmaid, Langstaff, and 'Ancestry of Lydia Harmon,' (W. G. Davis), p. 90. **Matthew**, b. 1 Jan. 1684.

**Sheaner?**, Edward, an Eastern refugee at Salem, List 27.

**SHEARS**, Sheares, etc., found in co. Devon and distant Surrey.

1 **EDMUND** (Sheere), now resid. of Boston, gave a bill to Mrs. Sayward(1) in May 1683, wit. by Henry Williams and Samuel Wakefield (Y. D. 3: 130); but it was Edward Shoare in Y. D. 3: 134.

2 **JEREMY**, Kittery, York. In 1649 with Edw. Starbird he wit. deed, Bursley to Wall, which was ack. the same day bef. George Smyth; on 30 Mar. 1649 took a 7 years lease of a new ho. and land in Kit. from Nicholas Frost who sued in 1656 for breach of contract. Me. tav. lic. 1650; he and Wm. Everett had kept one without. With w. Elizabeth wit. ag. Michael Brawn 1652. In 1655 he depos. ab. a ho. Wm. Berry sold to Anthony Ellins in 1648. In Kit., Wm. Vittery sued him for debt, he sued Capt. Paul White for slander, and was fined at times for reviling Mr. Shapleigh and Mr. Hilton and being in drink. At Cape Neddick, where Geo. Parker sued him for debt in July 1662, idle in 1663, and m. wid. Susanna Green(19) bef. 29 Mar. 1663-4 when both got into trouble by resisting the marshal. Admr. of the Green est., his bondsm. Mr. R. Jordan and Mr. E. Johnson. He had grants 1666-1668, but liv. on the Green place. York people berated by him incl. Mr. Rishworth, who tried to collect from the Green est.; this time J. S. found a champion in Edw. Colcord. He and w. abs. from Ch. in 1666; in 1667 he had been abs. above 12 mos., and abs. at intervals to 1685. Surety for Humphrey Axall 1687; gr.j. 1688; Lists 282, 283, 298, 30, 92. See Jackson(7), Jones(16). Prob. dead in 1693, Susanna alive; see John Green(14) who took adm. in 1701. Kn.ch. by 1st w: **Son**, for whom his fa. sued John Heard for a cow and calf in 1651; note (4). **Elizabeth**, appar. only ch. not s.p., m. Humphrey Spencer(2). By 2d w: **Child**, b. betw. Mar.-July 1664.

3 **JOHN** (Jo.), sued Thomas Yowe for a debt of £4 in Me. ct., Dec. 1651 (Me. P. & Ct. Rec. i: 174).

4 **MATT.** (Sheires), wit. Thomas Roberts, sr., to Zachariah Field 1671. See (2).

5 **ROBERT**, on Portsmouth cor.j. in July 1663, subscr. 4 days' work to the minister in 1666. Lists 327a, 323, 326b. In Mar. 1669-70 wid. Sheares was in extreme poverty, having **two children** and nothing to relieve them. One may have been **Robert** (6). In 1671 'Gamer' Jones, calling her a prattling gossip, attacked 'Gamer' Sheeres in Samuel Robie's yard until he took her off. In Mar. 1672-3 Portsm. paid Mr. Francis Chirurgeon (Morgan?) for 'Desecting Goodw. Shears.' See also Snelling(1).

6 **ROBERT** (see 5), Falmouth 1689, List 228c. Poss. husb. of Tamsen Gowell

(Richard), who was Tamsen Shears (ct. Mar. 1687-8) and fa. of her dau. **Elizabeth** who m. 14 Feb. 1721-2 John Allen (see 15). Wid. Tamsen m. 2d 1695+ Thomas Hanscom (3).

**Shedroke**, Capt., Portsmouth, wounded at the Eastward, List 37. Sherburne?

**SHEFFIELD.** See N. E. Reg. 77: 193.

1 **ICHABOD**, br. of (2), taxed Dover 1658, List 356c, came from and ret. to Portsmouth, R. I.

2 **WILLIAM**, Dover, taxed 1657-1659. Grant 2 Apr. 1658. Lists 356abce; see also (1). He went to Braintree, thence to Holliston and Sherborn; d. at S. 6 Dec. 1700. 12 ch., incl. **Joseph**, b. 3 Mar. 1671, to whom in 1696 his fa. deeded all Dover lands, incl. ½ a 150 a. gr. made to himself and John Meader. Dover laid out land to Joseph in 1726, he was there in 1733, his land ment. 1742; d. 1750, leaving 1 br., 3 sis., as heirs.

**Shehee**, Dermond. See O'Shaw.

**SHELDON.** See N. E. Reg. 80: 378, for a Sheldon fam. in Bakewell, but no Godfrey.

1 **GODFREY**, planter, Scarboro, m. Alice Frost in Bakewell, co. Derby, 11 Mar. 1620-1. On 19 July 1660 Jocelyn leased 100 a. to G. S., sr., the deed mentioning G.'s dwg. and a great willow tree right ag. the dwg. of Giles Roberts. List 339a. Will (aged ±65), 13 Mar. 1663-4—3 Apr. 1670, gives equally to w. Alice and s. William (exec.), he to have all eventually, pay £4 to br., 10 s. to each sis. and to his w. Rebecca, and 5s. to Rebecca's br. Samuel -Scarlett- who wit. with Jocelyn. Aft. he d., neighbors depos. he wanted William to rememb. little Frank Small. Ch. (four at Bakewell): **William**, bp. 5 Feb. 1622-3. **Abraham**, bp. 28 Nov. 1624, bur. at B. 13 Dec. 1645. **Son** (stillb.), bur. 23 Oct. 1626. **John**, bp. 8 May 1628, with little or no doubt that he was that John of Billerica, Woburn and Billerica again, who m. 1 Feb. 1658-9 Mary (Converse) Thompson of Woburn, and d. 24 May 1690, ±63, leaving s. John, b. at Billerica 24 Apr. 1660. **Anne**, m. 1st Arthur Alger(4), m. 2d Samuel Walker(11). **Daughter**, m. Giles Roberts(2). No 'jr.' seen. Salem paid Goody True for keeping one Elizabeth in 1677; E. S. and child ment. 1678.

2 **WILLIAM**(1), carpenter, seen here before his fa., 28 June 1655, when Mr. Jordan sued him on a bond at Yorkshire ct. At Billerica he had a gr. in 1658-9 provid. he build a corn-mill in two yrs., and ano. of 44 a., void in 1663, as he and br. John had trouble with the town and he did not settle. At Scarboro, appraised the Heffer est. 14 Apr. 1661, and remained. Constable 1664; j.

1666; gr.j. 1675, 1676. Lists 26, 28, 236(3), 237a, 238a. Freed from training in July 1675, but his ho. a garrison 1675-1676, where Henry Brookings depos. he refused to receive hims. and fam., saying his ch. would eat the victuals right out of his pot. Marblehead 1679-1680. Daniel Fogg depos. that he ret. to Scarb., fitted up his ho. and put in one Green(28) as tenant; David Libby said he ret. and liv. there until the next war. Taxed 1681 for 100 + 12 a., 3 mares, 1 cow, 2 horses. He d. at Salem 2 Dec. 1691, ag. -80-, having fallen and cut his knee two weeks bef. Wid. Rebecca (Scadlock 2) and s. Ephraim sold the Scarb. land to Richard Long(6) 15 Nov. 1693. Her will, 1716—1720, names s. Ephraim, 4 daus. Ch: **Godfrey**, k. by Ind. 3 July 1690, ag. 24 (Salem rec.). At Salem, a s. of Godfrey was rec. —— 13 [1694-5?] **Ephraim**, List 267b, had w. Jane and 6 ch. at Salem, the first 3 bp. in 1700, incl. William (m. 5 Oct. 1714 Mary Roberts of Reading, dau. of Abraham 2) and Ephriam (m. Isabella Haines 2). **Mary** (Ray in 1716). **Lydia**, b. 1666 (death rec.), m. Ambrose Boaden(5). **Sarah** (Goodall in 1716). **Rebecca** (not in will). **Nathaniel**, d. at Salem 30 Nov. 1688, ag. 10; 'well Monday, sick Tuesday, distracted Thursday, died Friday.' **Hephsibah** (mo.'s principal heir), m. at Salem 29 May 1712 Skelton Felton. One Samuel and one Susan or Susanna, a girl, test. in the witchcraft trials.
**Shelling**, William, a Shoals wit. 1668 (Y. D. 2: 58).

**SHEPARD**, Shepherd, general in England except in Eastern counties S. of the Humber.

1 **ABRAHAM** and **JACOB** wit. at Hampton ct. in 1673 that Henry Robie was drunk.

2 **JOHN**, Kittery, b. ±1634, sold to William Seeley in 1667 a ho. and 10 a. sometime in Richard Carle's posses., had grants 1669, 1671, wit. Walter Boaden's will 1676. In April 1691, ±57, he depos. ab. building a fence for Mr. Francis Trickey ±16 yrs. bef. Highway surv. 1693-4. Vict. lic. 1695, cider and cakes 1696. He wit. with John, jr., in 1701 and 7 Oct. 1705 made over to him the home place, cattle and all land except 50 a. on York road. Called deceased in 1719. Lists 290, 293, 296, 298. See Hammons(2), Mendum(1), Morse(12). Ch: **Margaret**, in ct. Oct. 1701 (her dau. Margaret Shepherd, b. 3 Aug. 1701, m. 22 Nov. 1726 Robert Cole 32). She m. Samuel Spinney(3). See also Rice(5). **Elizabeth** (presum.), m. Samuel Seward(8). **John**, ±19 in Apr. 1702, ±29 in 1713, ±31 in 1715. Lists 291, 297, 298. He m. in Portsm. 9 June 1709 Mary Lucey(2), both liv. 1725. 1 son. **Anne**, m. 25 Dec. 1712 Gowen Wilson (7). Presum. **Mark**, m. Hannah (Hilton 20)

Cole and sold out in York 1727. 3 ch. rec. at Y. 1724-1727, 2 at Bid. 1730-1736. **Patience**, m. John Spinney(3). She and Margaret depos. that their earliest memory was of Spruce Creek.

3 **JOHN**, taxed Hampton Falls 1709, an added name.

4 **THOMAS**, No. Yarmouth. Two Wallis gr. daus. called their gr.fa. -John-, a gr.s. called him Thomas; cumulative evid. makes it clear the early No. Yarm. settler was Thomas, who came in the -Hercules- in 1636-7, had given three yrs. service at Richmond Isl. in 1640 and was there in 1642. Lists 21, 214. His wid. Ann m. Benjamin Stevens(3). See also Harris(13), who described her land as on E. side of Harrisicket River as far north as Little River and all first enjoyed by Thomas Shepard. In 171- her heirs claimed a 200 a. neck of land posses. ±50 yrs., a 10 a. town lot on Mains Point and 4 a. marsh. Kn. ch: **Bridget**, m. John Wallis (6). **John**, List 214(2). Granted 4 a. marsh 7 June 1686. Tobias Oakman depos. that when he liv. at No. Yarm. 50 yrs. bef. he knew J. S. and heard him say the marsh was his bef. it was granted to him. He had Lot 76 and d. s.p. 'without performing in the former settlement of the town' (No. Yarm. Rec.). This rec. calls **Margery** his only sis.; as wid. of Amos Stevens(2), she sold Lot 76 in 1728.

5 **THOMAS**, gent., with Theodosius Moore wit. Wm. Daggett's p/a to John Watson in Sept. 1687, when he had recently bot 100 a. betw. Little River and Goose Fare Brook. Saco selectman 1688. List 34.

**SHERBURNE**, the name of seven townships or parishes in Eng., incl. a par. in co. Hants. See also (4).

1 **GEORGE**, Portsmouth 1650 (Savage), but not seen, tho the Portsm. Sherburnes had a br. George at Odiham.

2 ***HENRY**, Portsm., bp. at Odiham, co. Hants, 28 Mar. 1611, s. of Joseph, reached Boston on the -James- 5 June 1632, wit. for Henry Jocelyn 20 July 1634, m. 13 Nov. 1637 Rebecca Gibbons(1), and in 1642 was lic. for a tav. and ferries incl. 'from the great house to the great island.' Large landowner by grants and purchase; see Maverick(1). Com. t.e.s.c. 1644; selectman 12 times 1652-1672; Associate for Str. Bank, 1651; in 1654 repres. for Piscat. region to search people and vessels for money coined here and being carried away; town clerk 1657-1660; Clerk of the County Ct. 1657; Comr. 1658-9; Deputy 1660. Ordered to Boston in 1665 on charge of sedition; see Corbett(1). Ag. ±48 in 1662, ±53 in 1665, ±58 in 1669 and 1671. Lists 321-323, 324(2), 326ac, 330abc, 331abc, 312c, 313a, 47, 49, 53. He and w. Rebecca

sold a Shoals ho. in 1660; in 1666 they signed an unrec. mortg. (SJC 15736). She d. 3 June 1667. Bef. the beginning of winter 1670 he m. wid. Sarah Abbott(5), kept a home not always serene, and d. bef. 26 Mar. 1680-1, 'by some strange accident being taken from her.' See Bickford(7). Ch. (Brewster's 'Rambles,' i: 51-52), all but last in gr.fa.'s will: **Samuel**, twin, b. 4 Aug. 1638; deponents much later set the yr. as ab. 1645. **Elizabeth**, twin, m. 1st 10 June 1656 Tobias Langdon(1), m. 2d 11 Apr. 1667 Tobias Lear(2), m. 3d Hon. Richard Martyn (15). **Mary**, b. 20 Nov. 1640, m. Lt. Richard Sloper(3). **Henry**, b. 21 Jan. 1642, d. at sea 10 July 1659. **John**, b. 3 Apr. 1647. **Ambrose**, b. 3 Aug. 1649, a Shoals wit. 7 July 1670; adm. to fa. 27 June 1676. **Sarah**, b. 10 Jan. 1651, m. Mark Hunking(7). **Rebecca**, b. 26 Apr. 1654, deaf and dumb, had a ct. case ag. Peter Abbott in 1681, d. 29 June 1696, ag. 43. Her fa. gave land for her mainten. to his s. Samuel who deeded it in 1685. See also Huff(1). **Rachel**, b. 4 Apr., d. 28 Dec. 1656. **Martha**, b. 4 Dec. 1657, d. 11 Nov. 1658. **Ruth**, b. 3 June 1660, appar. m. Lt. Aaron Moses(1).

3 **HENRY**(5), wealthy farmer, innholder, owned the Glebe Tavern on the Plains and much land in Portsm. and nearby. Selectman 1704; assessor. Lists 330df, 331c, 332b, 335a, 339, 52, 57. He m. Sarah Wiggin (6) who was adm. to No. Ch. 17 Dec. 1693, Lists 331c, 335a. In May 1700 her fa. deeded to him 100 a. in Exeter which he sold to Richard Wibird. In May 1738, he ag. 72, she 69, depos. ab. Robert Tufton Mason. His will, 1738 (cod. 20 July), names wife, 8 ch., gr.s. Thomas, niece Mary Matthews; sons Thomas and Joseph execs., to act jointly when here, separately when one away. Adm. 30 Aug. 1738 to wid. Sarah, both execs. beyond seas. Ch: Capt. **Henry**, a scout in 1712, rose to be the 'valiant Capt. H. S.' at Louisburg. In 1715 his fa. conveyed a double portion of land in the Plains to him as oldest son and as a bar to further claim. Lists 337, 339. He m. 1st 3 Nov. 1709 Mary Larrabee(6), m. 2d wid. Margaret Nelson (see Wm. 2). Liv. 1771. Ch. bp. 1714-1718: John, Portsm., Epping, d. aged at Readville, Me.; Hannah, m. Alexander Lucey(1). **Sarah**, bp. 24 Dec. 1693, unm. 1738. **Thomas**, bp. 22 Mar. 1696-7, mariner, Portsm., m. an Ayers 13 Feb. 1721-2, was here 1739, d. bef. 20 May 1742 when Henry S. was named gdn. of his s. Thomas. Capt. **Joseph**, mariner, merch., Portsm., prob. the Capt. J. S. at Louisburg, m. 15 Feb. 1721-2 Phebe Ayers(1); dau. Phebe m. Bradstreet Wiggin. **Elizabeth**, was Wilson (see 6) in 1738. **Susanna**, b. 13 Mar. 1703, m. 6 May 1728 Lt. Simon Wiggin(4 jr.). **Catherine**, b. Mar. 1705, m. 25 Aug. 1734,

Samuel Sherburne(6). **Mary**, unm. 1738.

4 HON. ‡\***HENRY**(8), Portsm. mariner, shipmaster, merch., selectman, Rep., auditor, Col. of militia, Councillor, Treas. of the Province, Chief Justice of Supreme Court. Lists 337, 339. He used the arms of the Sherburnes of Stonyhurst, and in 1710 drew up a pedigree tracing thru Joseph of Odiham and Henry of Oxford to Sir Richard of Stonyhurst who d. in 1513; this pedigree, enlarged and continued, was filed at the Heralds' College in London in 1770 by his gr.s. With w. Dorothy (Wentworth 8), List 337, and **seven ch.**, he liv. 'in almost Royal style.' She d. 3 Jan. 1754, ag. 74; he 29 Dec. 1757, ag. 83.

5 **JOHN**, mariner, 'of Little Harbor, Newcastle,' br. of (2), was bp. at Odiham 13 Aug. 1615. Portsm. gr. 1646, a ho.-lot next to his br. Assessor 1653; selectman 1653, 1658, 1669, 1670; freeman 14 July 1657; Portsm.-Hampt. boundary committee 1660. Sergt. 1675. Lists 323, 324(3), 326abc, 330b, 311b, 331ab, 332b, 43, 47, 49, 52, 54, 55a, 57, 90. Wife Elizabeth Tuck(3). He deeded his orig. homestead to s. John in 1687, his pres. homestead to s. Henry in 1689. Will, of Portsm., 12 Nov. 1691—27 Nov. 1693, names w., 4 ch., s. John's w., decd. cousin(8), and directs s. Henry to pay his mo. half what he was bound to pay his fa. during life. Ch: **John**, b. ±1650. **Elizabeth**, poss. mar. in 1691. **Mary**, called Sherburne in 1691. Unless she m. 1st Gowen Cox(3), 2d Peter Matthews(11) and had a dau. Mary, it is unkn. how Mary Matthews was her brother's niece. See also Brewster(1). **Henry**, b. 1666, ag. 72 in 1738. Prob. a decd. son: **Joseph**, seaman 1673-4 (Essex Q. Ct. Rec. V: 340), m. 19 Oct. 1678 Amy Cowell(2), who soon m. 2d Jethro Furber(1).

6 CAPT. **JOHN**(2), mariner, shipmaster. On 29 Jan. 1677, his fa. for love and affec. deeded to him the Little Harbor homestead 'upon his mar. with Mary Cowell to which I have freely consented'; see Cowell(2). Of Sandy Beach 1688. Lists 52, 55b, 57, (†62), 312c, 332b. Will, of Portsm., 25 Nov. 1690—10 Oct. 1718 (he d. in 1698), gives est. to w. Mary (exec.) while a wid., to revert to s. Joseph and his heirs, £5 each to other ch. In 1709 she leased the Little Harb. farm to s. John, he to pay £10 each to Samuel, Edward and Ambrose; in 1729 she gave him a deed, he to pay £15 to Samuel and £15 to Edward's dau. Sarah. Her Lists 330d, 337 (& son), 339. She was liv. 31 Mar. 1736. Ch: Hon. ‡**Joseph**, Portsm., mariner, merch., Col. of militia, Councillor, Justice of Supreme Court, d. 3 Dec. 1744, ag. 64. Wid. Mary (Lovell 2) d. 6 Mar. 1745-6, ag. 61; will; 5 ch. Capt. **John**, mariner, Newc., Rye, m. Hannah (Jackson by Reg. 58: 231, but none seen).

Adm. 30 Mar. 1748 to wid. Hannah, liv. 1759.
5 ch. **Mary,** m. Col. Thomas Westbrook(2).
**Edward,** m. 25 July 1716 Agnes Hunking
who d. 10 Oct. 1726, ag. 33, poss. dau. of (9).
He was dead in 1729. Surv. ch: Sarah, m.
Joseph Moulton (see 13). **Ambrose,** liv.
1709, appar. d. s.p. by 1729. **Samuel,** blacksmith, innholder, Portsm., m. 1st 11 June
1719 Abigail Shackford(2), m. 2d 25 Aug.
1734 Catherine Sherburne(3). 4 ch. bp. 1736-
7, incl. Henry who settled in Conway, where
wid. Catherine d. in Jan. 1808, ag. 102 yrs.
10 mos., by record. **Elizabeth. Catherine.**
7 **CAPT. JOHN**(5), of 'the Plains,' ±26 in
Nov. 1676, ±70 in 1721. Selectman 1694-
1696, 1702, 1703. Deacon. Lieut. 1704, Capt.
1715. Lists 52, 57, (†62)(6), 63, 64, 68, 331c,
335a, 337, 339. He m. 1st Mary Jackson(20),
adm. to No. Ch. 24 May 1694 (Lists 331c,
335a), whose parents, in 1700, deeded to
them 73 a. form. her gr.fa. Johnson's. He
must have m. 2d 20 Oct. 1720 wid. Mary
Moses(1) who outliv. him, tho his will, 17
Dec. 1723—16 Feb. 1730-1, names only ch.
and gr.s. Nathaniel. Ch: **Priscilla,** bp. 20
Aug. 1693, not in will. **John,** housewright,
24 in 1710, m. ±1706 one Ruth, d. bef. Dec.
1723. She m. 2d John Lang(4). Her will,
proved 10 Feb. 1761, names Sherburne ch:
Nathaniel, John, Mary Philbrick, Priscilla
Sanborn, Ruth Rowe, and s.-in-law Matthias
Haines (m. Abigail). Deacon **James,** of the
Plains, 22 in 1710, m. 23 June 1709 Margaret
Roe(2); d. 7 Nov. 1760; will names w. Margaret, 10 of 11 ch. Lists 338b (and wife),
339. **Ephraim,** Portsm., Kit., owned ship-
yards in each; m. 8 Sept. 1726 Hannah Skillings (see 1), d. 1781, ag. 79 (gr.st. at Lee);
2 daus. bp. **Ruth,** m. Thomas Ayers(7 jr.).
Capt. **Thomas,** mariner, Portsm., 21 in 1710,
drowned, falling from his ship into the water; inq. 22 Dec. 1724. Wid. Margaret (Swett
5, m. 15 Nov. 1710) m. 2d 13 Aug. 1729 Benjamin Rust of Portsm., d. at Newport, 27
Mar. 1761, ag. 70. 7 ch. **Elizabeth,** bp. 8
Mar. 1696-7, m. William Cate(3). **Hannah,**
m. Abraham Jones(16). Dea. **Samuel** of the
Plains, b. 10 Aug. 1698, m. 27 Feb. 1726
Mercy Wiggin(1 jr.); d. intest. 14 Nov. 1760.
4 of 11 ch. d.y. **Mary,** under 21 in 1723.
8 **CAPT. SAMUEL**(2), Little Harbor, Portsmouth, Hampt., chief heir of gr.fa. Gibbons. He had a 60 a. gr. and ferry priv. in
1670, a ho. and land at Little Harb. from fa.
in 1674, and in 1678 bot the old Tuck inn at
Hampt., where he was selectman 1683, 1688.
List 312c, 313a, 326c, 330ac, 392b(2), 396,
49, 50, 52, 56-58, 37, 96. Capt. of militia and
k. 'by the Heathen' at Maquoit 4 Aug. 1691.
Adm. 28 Oct. 1691 to wid. Love, dau. of
John Hutchins, b. at Newb. 16 July 1647, m.
15 Dec. 1668, d. at Kingston in Feb. 1739.
She was lic. as a wid. List 66. Ch: **Frances,**

1670-1675. **Elizabeth,** b. 5 Feb. 1672, m. Capt.
Jonathan Sanborn(4). **Henry,** b. 16 Feb.
1674, bp. at Newb. **Frances,** b. 29 Sept.
1676, bp. at Newb., m. 1st Dr. Benj. Dole(3),
m. 2d Lt. Wm. Staniford(1). **John,** b. 2 Feb.
1678, d.y. **Margaret,** b. 15 Feb. 1679, m. Capt.
Joseph Tilton(2). **Mary,** b. and d. 1680.
**Sarah,** b. 14 Jan. 1682, m. Joseph Fifield(1).
**Samuel,** b. 21 July 1684, poss. the scout in
Capt. Phipps' co. 1712. **Love,** b. 5 July 1686,
m. 1st Richard Cutts(3), m. 2d John Almary.
Lt. **John,** Hampt., b. 2 Feb. 1688, bp. at
Salisb., m. 12 Nov. 1713 Jane Drake(2);
mov. to Epping (Dow), d. at Northwood
(fam. rec.); 9 ch. **Achaicus** (dau.), b. 23
Feb. 1692, did not share in est.
**Sheriff.** See Harvey(12).

**SHERLOCK.** 1 **Francis**? [**Frances**?]. Adm.
gr. to Col. Shadrack Walton 9 Mar.
1721-2.
2 **‡JAMES,** Provost Marshal and Sheriff of
N. H. 1683, Councillor 1684, one of Robert Mason's justices 1685. List 313f. Sheriff
for Suff. Co. under Andros (taxed Boston
1687) and imprisoned aft. his overthrow, his
pet. 13 June 1689 asking release from Boston prison. He used an armorial seal.
**Sherman,** see Palmer(22). Became 69th
commonest name in N. E.
**Sherwood,** of Pentucket, List 72.
**SHEVERICK** (Sheverett), **Samuel,** blacksmith, taxed Portsm. 1672 next to Philip
Severett, and wit. with N. Fryer that yr.,
Cater to Record. Absent from his w. in
1673, when he spoke of 'my master John
Coots.'
**Shewder,** William, owed the Mitchell est.,
List 78.
**Shierly?,** John, at the East in 1689-90, List
18.
**SHILAND.** 1 **James** (or Shirland), sued in
Me. ct. by John Webster 1653.
2 **JOHN,** Dover Neck, drunk in 1652.
**Shinn,** John (Shinne), in York ct. 1653 for
swearing, Goody Davis the wit. John
(Shind), a Pemaquid soldier 1696. List 127.
**Shipley,** John, Oyster River, a boy captive
1695, List 99, p. 75, ident. by Miss Cole-
man as John Shepley from Groton.
**SHIPPEE.** 1 **Thomas,** ag. 25, a wit. in the
Nelson-Rollins suit 1685.
2 **MR.** (Shippy), List 14. Shipway?
**SHIPPEN, Edward,** Mr., merchant, Boston,
Philadelphia, bondsm. for Robert Ed-
munds(4) as admr. for George Foxwell(1)
in 1674; later acquired by exec. Edmunds'
lands at Blue Point; taxed Scarb. 1681
(Sheppia) and sued Matthew Alger(7) in
Suff. ct. that yr. In 1683 Nathaniel Draper
chose him gdn. to recover his fa.'s est. at
Hitchin, co. Herts.
**Shipton,** William. See Johnson(26).

## SHIPWAY.

1 **JOHN**, Mr., Portsmouth, early at Barbadoes from where Samuel Winthrop wrote to his fa. 18 Mar. 1658-9: 'This is by Mr. Shipway, who m. the sister of Mr. Cutt of Pascataway,' i.e., Anne Cutts bp. 11 Sept. 1625 (List 331c). Portsm. wit. 1659, Great Isl. grants 1671, 1673, Portsm. selectman 1672, appr. Nicholas Frost's est. 1674. J. 1682. Lists 324(2), 326c, 327cd, 329, 330a(2), 331b, 14, 49, 54. He was ±46 in 1672, ±50 in May 1675, when he, w. and son were named in her br. Richard's will. Pres. John Cutts' will 1680 named only the son. His nunc. will was proved 9 Nov. 1683. Inv., £440, attested by s. **John**, b. 26 July 1662.

2 **JOHN**(1), merchant, Portsm., took O. A. 28 Aug. 1685, bot a Portsm. ho. and land from Thomas Dennis(9) in 1685, taxed July 1690. Lists 52, 57, 330f (his ho.), 337. Wife Sarah Frost(2) named in her fa.'s will 7 Jan. 1690-1, when her husb. was lately deceased. His will, 15 Dec. 1690, names w. Sarah and dau. **Mary**, ag. 13 in Dec. 1701, Joshua Fryer then her guardian; she m. Rev. Jeremiah Wise(1). 'Mis Shipway' was taxed in Oct. 1691, m. 2d Hon. Wm. Redford(2), d. 16 May 1695. By depos. in 1720 the first Shipway liv. on his land on Spring Hill until he d., his s. John then did same, his wid. the same, and the only ch. Mary Wise owned it in 1720.

**Sholey**, Mary, a maid at Piscataqua 1637. See Schooler.

**Shoredee**, Joseph, a Portsm. wit. 1702 ab. the disaster to ship -Catherine-.

## SHORE, Shores. See also Gunnison(1), Shorey.

1 **EDMUND** (Shore or Sheare), 1683; see Y. D. 3: 130, 134.

2 **JOHN**, Portsmouth, suspected in connec. with Christopher Jose's Jersey maid in 1674, when Charles Glidden was his bondsman, should it seems be related to Glidden's w. Eunice (Shore), but no John is found in the fam. of her fa. Sampson S. See also Shute(1). John was drunk at Lamprill River in 1679, wit. the Graves-York agreement with Thomas Broughton in 1681. Presum. the J. S. in a Dover garrison and on a Newington cor.j. in 1696. Also presum. in Portsmouth in 1708, then husb. of wid. Rachel Sampson(2) to whom he, fisherman, gave a p/a in 1711. Taxed for the Mill Dam 1708+, rated to No. Ch. 1717. Rachel Showers was to keep 'Gamer' Brown for the town in 1727; John Showers' tax abated same yr. In 1730, fisherman, he sold his Barr. right. Lists 67, 339. See also Mainwaring(3). Poss. a son: **Peter** (named for Rachel's fa. Peter Codner?), m. in Portsm. 31 Mar. 1737 Su-sannah Ball (Peter 7 jr.). One James S. m. Mary Snow in Portsm. 12 Nov. 1738.

3 **SAMPSON** (Shoar), gave p/a in N. H. to w. Mary in 1694, proved by witnesses 1705. See Glidden(1).

**SHOREY, Samuel**, Kittery. Undoubtedly the soldier at Piscataqua, Samuel Shore of Braintree, ord. home in 1690, and the soldier at Saco in 1696 (Shorey) were the same. He m. 28 Apr. 1702 Mary Rhodes(2), had a gr. in 1703, and liv. in what is now Eliot. Lists 248b, 290, 291, 297, 298. In 1724 gr. adm. in Bristol co. on est. of br. John, shopkeeper of Rehoboth. Mary Davis of Westerly, R. I. (m. Peter D. in Boston 1706) and Sarah Oakman of Marbleh. (m. Samuel O. in Boston 1708) were their sisters. Samuel and w. Mary had **ten ch.**, incl. **John**, b. 10 Aug. 1704 (List 298; see also Clark 50) and **Miles**, b. 23 Feb. 1710-11, m. Elizabeth Walker in Rehoboth 28 Oct. 1731.

## SHORT, found in a few scattered Eng. counties, incl. Devon. See Creber.

1 **CLEMENT**, Kittery, m. in Boston 21 Nov. 1660 Faith Munt (Thomas) and 11 Dec. 1662 had a 50 a. gr. in Kit. on which he lived, adj. George Veasey's, later Mr. Wincoll's. Cor.j. 1668. Lists 25, 30, 94, 288, 298. He, w. and 3 ch. were k. by Ind. and 6 or 7 ch. carried away 18 Mar. 1689. Historian Niles reported this, calling him an 'esteemed and honest man.' Adm. in Nov. 1705 to s. Thomas, bondsm. Christopher Banfield and John Key. Inv., land only, 50 a. where he dwelt, 60 a. not laid out. The adm. sold the 1662 gr. to John Key and Wm. Grant. Kn. ch: **Three** reported k. in 1689, perh. incl. **Clement**, jr., who had a gr. in 1685, List 298. **Mary**, m. by 1692 Bartholomew Green, printer, Cambr., Boston. **Mercy** (see 'N. E. Captives,' i: 192), m. in Bos. 29 July 1694 Joseph Marshall, d. by 1708, and he m. 2d Abigail (Hussey 9) Howes. **Patience**, m. in Bos. 27 Dec. 1694 David Copp, barber. **Rachel**, m. in Bos. 7 July 1699 Micah Coars or Michael Coares. **Thomas**, printer, m. in Bos. 13 Dec. 1705 Elizabeth Frost(7). List 298. New London 1709, and issued in 1711 'The Saybrook Platform of Church Discipline,' the first book pub. in the Colony (Thomas' Hist. of Printing i: 405). He d. there 27 Sept. 1712, ag. 30 (gr.st.) Wid. Elizabeth m. 2d Solomon Coit, d. in New L. 25 Mar. 1715. Ch: Elizabeth and Mary, b. Bos. 1706-1708; Catherine and (Capt.) Charles (List 298), b. New L. 1709-1711. In 1766 Charles of New L., s. of Capt. Charles, was 'now residing in Berwick.' **Jane**, unm. 1708, when the sisters and Joseph Marshall of Nantucket (by atty. Bartholomew Green) released to Thomas. Poss: **Richard**, a boy, Dover, in Canada 1695-6; List 99, p. 75.

2 **JOHN**, Shoals 1673. See Humber(1).

3 **REV. MATTHEW**, b. at Newbury, H. C. 1707, m. Margaret Freeman at Taunton 27 Dec. 1711. Attleboro 1712-1715; soon chaplain at Fort Mary, Winter Harbor, also preaching to and marrying the settlers. List 368b. He left the fort 21 Nov. 1722; d. at Easton 15 Apr. 1731. Ch: **Anna** and **Judith** at Attleboro 1712-1714. **Matthew** and **Margaret**, twins, at Newb., 1716. **Matthew**, b. 20 Apr. 1719, and **Ebenezer**, b. 21 Mar. 1721, both at Biddeford.

4 **RICHARD**, No. Yarmouth, wit. livery, Sears to James Lane, in May 1673. Lane succes. sued him in 1674 when Jenkin Williams and Oliver Elkins were his bondsm. In July 1688 he pet. Andros for 100 a., stating that he served his apprenticeship in No. Y., had since been an inhab. several yrs. and had not a foot of land. Two mos. later he and John Royal were taken captive from a canoe and carried Eastward (Doc. Hist. vi: 446). Lists 223a, 226.

5 **TOBIAS**, fisherman, came to Richmond Isl. in the -Agnes- in 1636, List 21. Winter sent him, 'my servant,' home bef. 18 July 1639, but wanted him back and asked that he be fitted out with clothes, if desired. He returned. Accounts 1641-1643 show much clothing deliv. to him.

**SHORTRIDGE**, Saltridge, Sawtridge. See Creber.

1 **RICHARD**, fisherman, basketmaker, Portsmouth, bot ho. and land at Sag. Creek from Nicholas Roe in Oct. 1659; of Portsm. or the Shoals, mortg. it to Roe 1661, redeemed it 1673. See also Hunking(6). A wit. in ct. with John Locke and John Moses 1659. He and w. Esther (Dearborn 1) liv. at Sag. Creek in 1670. He was ±40 in 1671 when he swore the peace on the Jones(17) family; he had been threatened with a knife, his w. slandered. Freeman 15 May 1672. Gr.j. 1675. Lists 312c, 313a, 326c, 329, 330a, 331b, 49, 52, 54. In 1689 he deeded to s.-in-law Davis the land his ho. stood on; witnesses proved the deed in 1694. The Davises sold to Mark Hunking who in 1726 sold it to Richard Shortridge(2 jr.). Kn. ch: **Mary**, b. in Hampton 4 Oct. 1661, m. John Davis(26). **Richard**. **Ann**, liv. with gr.fa. Dearborn in 1680, m. 18 Nov. 1686 George Wallis(2). See also Howard(3).

2 **RICHARD**(1), mariner, Portsmouth. Lists 330d, 331c, 334a, 335a, 337, 316. He m. 16 May 1687 Alice Creber(2), Lists 335a, 337, and appar. d. long bef. 19 Dec. 1712 when she was gr. adm. Widow S. was taxed for the Mill Dam 1707, 1713; Alice was 're-ceived into cov.' So. Ch. 22 May 1715, Alice 'received' 7 Aug. 1720; if two persons prob. mo. and dau. Wid. Alice liv. 13 Dec. 1721

(Y. D. 10: 227). Kn. ch: **Elizabeth**, m. Richard Davis(44). **Miriam**, m. George Banfield(2). **Richard**, cooper, deacon of So. Ch., m. 12 Nov. 1719 Abigail French of Salisb., who joined So. Ch. in 1724. List 339. Will, 1756—1756, names her and ch: **Samuel** (exec.), **Richard**, **John**, **Miriam** (w. of John Sherburne), **Elizabeth** (w. of Wm. Brown), **Abigail** (w. of John Phillips), **Mary**, **Sarah**. **Esther**, in 14th yr. in 1702 when Mrs. Mary Martyn's servant; m. in 1712 Ephraim Collins of Salisb. **Susannah**, m. 1st 9 Oct. 1715 Reuben Abbott(1), m. 2d one Pitman.

3 **WILLIAM**, Boston, ±28 in Jan. 1689-90, master of ketch -Elinor-, Nevis to Boston; d. by 1703. See w. Mary Gammon(2). Ch., under age in 1703: **William**. **Mary**, m. in Boston 17 Nov. 1709 Thomas Hunt.

**SHOVE**. 1 **Edward**, Y. D. 15: 103, and 2 **JOHN**, both N. Yarmouth, List 214.

**Shu——**, Will, List 363a. Shackford?

**Shuller**, William, Portsmouth, bookkeeper for Mr. John Cutts 1679. Taxed 1680 (Sheller). List 329.

**SHURT.**

1 **ABRAHAM**, Mr., merchant, Pemaquid, called the 'Father of American conveyancing.' See 1 Me. Hist. Soc. Col. 5: 195; 4 Mass. Hist. Soc. Col. 6: 110, 570; Doc. Hist. 3: 59; Aspinwall; Y. D. 1: 41; Suff. D. i: 252. He was bp. at Bideford, co. Devon, 11 Oct. 1584, s. of John, sometime mayor there, and in Dec. 1662, ±80, depos. that he was sent over by Alderman Aldworth and Mr. Giles Elbridge in 1626 to buy Monhegan from Mr. Abraham Jennings, that in 1629 they sent over a patent of which Capt. Walter Neale (9) gave him possession (in 1633). Winthrop spoke of him as of Pemaquid in Sept. 1631 and June 1632, and he wit. deliv. of the Commock pat. 23 May 1633. Aldworth's will 1635, gave £200 to A. S., 'my servant if he live till my decease and return to Bristol.' Here 13 June 1635; in Bristol and of Bristol 11 Nov. 1635, he released Elbridge (Aldworth's exec.) of all claims, and bound self as a covenant servant to serve 5 yrs. in N. E. and not to trade on his own acct. He sued Thomas Wannerton in Me. ct. in May 1637, was agent for Elbridge and Hugh Yeo in 1640, gave a receipt to Elbridge in 1646, a p/a to Robert Knight who was residing in Boston, in 1647, took a mortg. on Monhegan from Thomas Elbridge in Sept. 1650 (Suff. D. i: 131) and in Dec. that yr. gave T. E. a bond to abide an arbitration on accts. Called of Charlestown Oct. 1653. List 77a. See Cox(33), Lander(3). No evid. of w. or ch. is seen. Brother A. S., 'now in N. E., God sending him home from thence to live in Bideford,' had a bequest by will of br.

George in Bideford 9 Feb. 1655; others ment. incl. sis.-in-law Mary, her dau. Mary, and Abraham Hayman(1).

2 ADAM, Mr., as attorney for mo. Mrs. Mary Shurt, brot suit ag. Edward Small for debt in Wells ct. 30 June 1647 when the case was contin. and finally dropped in June 1648 when charges allowed ag. 'Mr. Henry,' atty. for Shurt. No evid. appears that he was ever at Pemaquid. His parents were John (d. 1628) and Mary (Lugge) S. of Bideford, his gr.fa. Adam Lugge of Barnstable. See (1) for will of George Shurt.

SHUTE.

1 JOHN, Shoals, Newcastle (Rye), blacksmith, fisherman, boarded at Michael Endle's Nov. 1673—July 1674. About this time Chas. Glidden was his bondsm. (but see Shore 2, poss. a confusion). He bot a Smuttynose ho. from Edw. Humber in 1675 and was there with w. Rebecca (Seavey 6) in 1687 when her fa. gave them 8 a. at Little Harbor, part of Oliver's Neck, where he prob. soon removed. In 1700 she sued Nicholas Hodge(7) for assault. In 1708, form. of the Shoals, he deeded to Benjamin Seavey, mentioning fa.-in-law Thomas S. In 1714, of Portsm., (or poss. a son), with w. -Sameon- (Tamsen?) sold ho. and gr. at Sandy Beach. Lists 95(2), 315b, 318c. James, taxed 1721, who m. a neighbor's dau., Christian Rand (6), was prob. a son; both liv. 1750 when they deeded to their s. James. ?Johanna of Newc., with her ch. deported from Kit. in 1722, could have been dau. or dau.-in-law. One Hannah of Portsm. m. James Fadden from Ireland 8 Apr. 1726.

2 RICHARD, mariner, Pemaquid, Boston, liv. near Pemaquid in 1650-1, see (3), and in 1672, ag. ±39, was East associated with Edw. Naylor and Thaddeus McCarthy, List 14. His w. Elizabeth, a wit. in the Naylor divorce case (see Moore 13), d. in Boston 8 Sept. 1691, ag. 63½ yrs. He d. there 2 Oct. 1703, ag. 72. Will, 1703, names w. Katherine (in 1695 as K. S. late Guttridge, she and Daniel Smith presented will of Richord Snell(3) for prob.), and ch: Michael, Richard (b. Boston 1666), Joanna Buckley formerly Nichols, 14 gr.ch. and kinsman Wm. S., but not dau. Elizabeth or s. William, b. Boston 1667, 1670. Wid. -Shoot- was bur. 18 Sept. 1709. The s. Richard, mariner, Malden, Boston, bot in Falmouth and No. Yarm. (List 229) and depos. in Jan. 1737-8, ag. ±72, that ab. 50 yrs. bef. he 'happened to be at Pemaquid.'

3 ROBERT (also Shutt), Winnegance 1641, accused with others of taking Thomas Purchase's furs; see Morgan(8), Norman(1). Will, Suffolk, 24 Mar. 1650-1—29 Apr. 1654, gives to br. Richard, liv. near Pemaquid, all

debts due from the Ind. about those parts; to br. Thomas (allowed exec.), to sis. Marie and to sis. Sarah Holly's ch.; also to Sarah Phippen, Richard Russell and Boston and Charlest. ministers.

SIAS, very uncommon.

1 ——, mar. a dau. of William Roberts(14), who mar. 2d Salathiel Denbo(1) and 3d William Graves(6). Son John appears. See also (2). One John Size, residence unkn., was a soldier under Capt. Moseley in 1675.

2 HENRY (Sise), Oyster River 1690. List 57. See (1).

3 JOHN(1), Oyster River. As John Cyas, credited to Ipswich, he was a soldier at Wells in 1693-4, m. there (Ct. 3 Jan. 1698-9) Ann Pitman(11), remov. to O. R. and in 1701 had a 20 a. gr. adj. his ho. She was bp. 7 June 1724, and depos. in Sept. 1755, ±89. In 1747 he deeded homestead to s. Joseph who sold in 1756 to Samuel Demeritt. Lists 267b, 386b, 369. Ch: John, bp. adult 8 Oct. 1721, adm. to O. R. Ch. 1723, m. 16 July 1728 Hannah Sampson(5), who d. in Danville, Vt., in 1794. In 1742 he and Salathiel Denbo, jr., were charged with counterfeiting in Newport, R. I. 4 or more ch. Hannah, b. 21 Aug. 1700, m. John Moore(18). Samuel, Lee 1765, ±64 in 1768. Will, 1774—1775, names w. Phebe, 6 liv. ch., gr.s. John Hill. List 369. Judith, bp. adult 7 June 1724, m. Hercules Hunking(9). Rachel, m. Nathaniel Meader (4). Solomon, bp. adult 25 July 1725, of Lee 1765, w. Hannah. List 369. Clement, List 369; of Canterbury 1737. Capt. *Joseph, m. Ruth Matthews (Francis 6 jr.). 2 kn. daus. Often moderator and selectman at Durham; Rep. from Lee 1776-7; Justice of Inf. Ct. of Com. Pleas.

Sibley, Richard, wit. Hampton deed, Howard to Sayward, 1647.

Silloway, Henry, List 68.

Simes, Mr., d. at Hampton 6 Feb. 1711-2, ag. 76.

SIMMONS, Simonds. See also Symonds and Creber.

1 ANDREW (Symmons), a Portsm. wit. 1670, fine penman, servant at ho. of John Clark in 1677.

2 JOHN (at times Simonds), Kittery. At Richmond Island 1635, leaving with other disaffected men in 1636, but returned. His Kit. land adj. that laid out to Robert Beedle in May,1641. Bondsm. for Mr. John Reynolds 1648. Constable for river of Piscat. 1650-1; selectman 1659; lot layer 1661; j. 1652-3, 1664(abs.), 1667; gr.j. 1653, 1655, 1658, 1665 (abs.), 1667. Lists 21, 282, 284, 298, 52. See Harmon(2), Moore(9). Ag. ±47 in June 1662; ±52 in Dec. 1669 (depos. ab. Rev. Joseph Hull and ch.); ±58 in 1672. First w.

unkn.; he m. 2d by 4 June 1668 wid. Welthen Goddard(3). Of Kit. in July 1669 and June 1670, but mov. to Oyster River. He ack. judgm. to John Cutts in N. H. ct. 1669, wit. a Goddard will in 1672, gr.j. 1674, taxed O. R. 1684. See also (3). Only dau. **Rebecca**, m. Wm. Hilton(19), who with her fa. and Thomas Turner appr. a Weymouth est. in 1663. The homestead in Kit. was settled on her in Apr. 1667.

3 **JOHN** (Symons), signed a pet. in 1690, with Exeter men. List 57.

4 **MICHAEL**, Oyster River 1666. List 356j, 365. See also Nock(1).

5 **RICHARD**, given charges ag. Richard Pomery in York ct., Sept. 1666. One Richard Simons wit. John Whinnick's will.

6 **THOMAS** (Simonds), Shoals. Will, 7 May—16 June 1674, wit. by Michael Endle and Arthur Clapham, gave all due him in N. E. to friend and neighbor Henry Maine(2).

**Simpkins,** Pilgrim, List 3.

**SIMPSON,** Simson, belongs to North half of Eng. and to Scotland. See also Duley, Hill(19).

1 **LT. DANIEL**(3), cordwainer, York, had town gr. 16 Oct. 1696, and m. about that time Frances Plaisted(6). County treasurer 1725. Lists 279, 298. She d. 11 Feb. 1746, he 5 Oct. 1747. Ch., all sons liv. 1747 (Y. D. 26: 212): **Samuel**, b. 17 July 1697, m. 28 Oct. 1725 Joanna Webster (Stephen) of Newb. List 279. Ch. rec. 1726-1740. **Henry**, b. 13 Apr. 1698. One H. m. ±1720 Mercy Young (10), 11 ch.; ano. H. m. (ct. Jan. 1723-4) Sarah Johnson(29), 4 or more ch. **Abigail**, b. 25 Feb. 1699-1700, d. 20 Oct. 1716. **Hannah**, b. 25 Dec. 1702, m. Edward Preble(3). **Joseph**, b. 27 Apr. 1705, m. Abigail Webster (Stephen), altho Hannah Bane forbade the bans. Ch. 1729-1747. **Daniel**, b. 30 Sept. 1707, m. Mary Coburn (Ebenezer). List 279. Ch. 1735-1739. **Jonathan**, b. 7 Apr. 1709. In 1747 his brothers were to support him. **Mary**, b. 13 July 1712, m. Joseph Simpson(7 jr.). **Jeremiah**, b. 15 Jan. 1717-8, m. Sarah Whitney (Nathl.). Ch. rec. 1737-1739.

2 **HENRY**, York, m. Jane Norton(6) and rec. land from Mr. Wm. Hooke as a mar. portion 13 Mar. 1638. He sold land to George Puddington in Apr. 1640 and Mar. 1641, when Ralph Blaisdell's land abutted. In the Shuttleworth fam. accounts in co. Lancaster, Col. Banks found Ralph Blaisdell (1582) and Henry Simpson (1591), and found Henry B. and Henry S. in par. of Goosenargh, but could not trace any sure connec. with the York men. He was one of the eight aldermen of Agamenticus under the Gorges charter, 1641. Attorney for Mr. Hooke 1645. Being sick, he made a will 18 Mar. 1646-7,

giving half to w. Jane (List 274), half to s. **Henry** (±6 in 1650), and the unborn child; friends John Alcock, Edw. Johnson, Abraham Preble, Richard Banks, overseers; w. Jane exec. Adm. gr. to her 3 July 1648. Lists 22, 274. She m. Nicholas Bond(2) bef. May 1650 when she made a crim. charge ag. Robert Collins(11). Her chn. were then ment. and Henry was called the 'eldest boy.' He was evid. the only ch. in 1655, and was her only son in Dec. 1688 when he had cared for her ab. 15 yrs. and expected to do so longer.

3 **ENSIGN HENRY**(2), York. In 1655 for the better improvement of his small est., the ct. ordered Mr. Preble, Mr. Johnson and Mr. Hilton to dispose of half the upland and meadow and such cattle as were in young John Parker's hands, acc. to their discretion. He m. Abigail Moulton (20) bef. 6 July 1669, without publication, causing trouble for Capt. Raynes who mar. them. Constable 1670; j. 1672, 1687, 1688, gr.j. 1673, 1687, 1689; selectman 1675, 1676, 1687, 1688; grants 1679, 1686; O. A. 22 Mar. 1679-80; Ensign 1680. In 1679 his ch. appar. had been kidnapped; see James Adams(16); Me. P. & Ct. Rec. ii: 351. He served on the gr.j. in Dec. 1691 and undoubtedly he (and prob. his w.) was k. and two sons captured, one mo. later in the Ind. attack on York. Inv. 7 May 1692 (Y. D. 5: 1: 79); adm. to Lt. Abraham Preble. Div. 26 Dec. 1695 to four ch: **Henry**, ret. from Canada in Oct. 1695; killed by Ind. while coming post from Wells, about 4 July 1697; adm. 10 Aug. 1697 to br. Daniel and Jonathan Littlefield. Lists 99, p. 74, 96. See also Susanna Young(10). **Daniel**, ±63 in Apr. 1737. **Joseph**, ag. 75 in 1754. **Abigail**, m. by 1695 Jonathan Littlefield(12). In Oct. 1700 the heirs here agreed that br. **Jabez** should share equally upon his ret. from Canada; he was still there in 1711. List 99, p. 72.

4 **JAMES**, Falmouth, m. by 1726 Elizabeth Stanford(2). Will, 27 Oct. 1748, not proved, gave all to her with remainder to Josiah Stanford's heirs. She was a wid. in Falm. in 1750. See (5).

5 **JOHN**, Scarboro, signed the pet. favoring Scottow in 1676 and liv. near Black Point garri. in Oct. that yr. Scarboro 1680, taxed 1681, selectman 1680-1682, constable 1683, gr.j. 1686, selectman 1688, not seen again until he and two of his fam. were captured by the Ind. at Black Point in Aug. 1703. Lists 237ae, 238a, 30, 39. Note also (4) and Boaden(8).

6 **JONATHAN**, Oyster River 1715 (List 368b), and Joseph, there in 1734 (List 369). See also Bickford(4).

7 **JOSEPH**(2), haberdasher, feltmaker, J.P., Newcastle, m. there 1st, 11 May 1702,

Hannah Lewis(7), who d. 26 June 1712, m. 2d 17 Mar. 1713-4 Miriam, wid. of Joseph Esmond of Kit. She was liv. in 1754. J. S., Esq., ag. 75, deposed in June 1754 about Scituate Row. Lists 279, 316, 339. No ch. by 1st w. are rec., but Mr. Marshall called Henry (m. Mercy Young) a son; see (1). By 2d w., b. at Newcastle: Joseph, b. 16 Jan. 1714-5, m. 1st 14 Jan. 1740-1 Mary Simpson (1), m. 2d by 1750 Alice Donnell (Nathl. Esq.). Ch. by both wives. Abigail, b. 14 Oct. 1716, m. Benj. Underwood. John, b. 14 Feb. 1722-3, m. Sarah Sheafe. Mary, b. and d. 1724. Theodore, b. 14 Feb. 1726-7. Miriam, b. 29 Mar. 1728. Mary, b. 7 Sept. 1732, m. Mark Fernald.

8 THOMAS, shopkeeper, Portsm., prob.— Simpson, an added name in the 1716 tax list. 'Of Borough senes in Scotland,' he m. Susanna Seuer (Seward 5) in Portsm. 17 Sept. 1718. List 339. Will, 1734—1735, names her (exec.) and s. William of Boston (her step-son). Her will, 1738—1739, names cous. Thomas Butler of Boston who had given a note to her late husb., and her Seward relatives.

SINCLAIR, ancient in Scotland. The English cos. Herts and Surrey also have many.
1 GEORGE, in N. Perryman's acct. book 1725 'for your s. Joshua.' One George m. Hannah Brown in Newb. 1722; will in N. H. 1767.
2 JAMES(3), liv. near Wheelwright's Creek, Exeter. He served in Philip's war, at a Newbury blockho. in 1704, and as sergeant in a scouting party in 1710. O. A. 30 Nov. 1677. Grants 1681, 1689, and was willed by fa. 20 a. (formerly Robinson's), £10 and a feather-bed. J. 1692, 1700, 1703, 1712; gr.j. 1720; constable 1693-4; selectman 1695, 1700, 1706, 1721. Lists 52, 57, 62, 376b(1725), 377, 384b, 388. He m. Mary (Scammon 3), 13 yrs. his junior, poss. not a first wife. Will, 23 July 1731—15 Feb. 1732-3, names her, 11 ch. (Ebenezer exec.) and gives to s. Joseph his right from Mass. as a Narragansett soldier. Ch., order in will: Capt. John, had grants 1705 and 1725 (List 376b), m. aft. 22 Sept. 1709 Anne (Chase 5) Wiggin, d. 11 Sept. (adm. to Thomas Moore 30 Oct.) 1745; wid. liv. 1746. Ch. at Strath. 1711-1719: Anne (m. Edw. Taylor 3); Rachel (m. Thomas Moore, see 26); Mercy; Hannah (m. John Purmont, Abner Dolloff). Joseph, So. Newmarket, Pembroke, taxed Ex. 1714, bot land with Thomas Young 1715. List 376b(1725). He m. Elizabeth Lyford(3); liv. Sept. 1767; 4 sons. Samuel, List 376b(1725). Wid. Anne (poss. Hobbs m. in Amesbury 1740) waived adm. in favor of John Sleeper 27 Feb. 1748-9. Jonathan, a Wells wit. 1717. Of Exeter, but

liv. in W., he authorized his fa. to sell his Wells gr. in 1729. His fa. willed him 20 s. Richard, List 376b(1725). In 1727 his parents deeded him land in Strath., where he m. 27 June 1728 Catherine Stevens(Nathl. 16 jr.). Will, 25 June—27 Aug. 1751, names her, 9 ch.; w. and br.-in-law Benj. Norris execs. Ebenezer, Ex., under age in 1731 when willed the homestead and named exec., m. Abigail Folsom, d. 1754. 3 ch. Benjamin, younger than Ebenezer. Wife Elizabeth; d. s.p. shortly bef. 26 Mar. 1759. Mercy, m. (?Paul) Hall(14). Martha, m. John Bean (1). David, given 20 s. Keziah, had £5. Mary, had £5 and a feather-bed.
3 JOHN, Exeter, whose name suggests a Scotch prisoner, bot 10 a. adj. Thomas Biggs from John Warren in Jan. 1659 and in 1672 had a suit over bounds ag. Lt. Ralph Hall who had bot from Biggs. Grants 1664, 1681. Tr.j. 1670, 1693. O. A. 30 Nov. 1677. In 1678 bot 20 a. from David Robinson. Gr.j. (or his son) 1699. Lists 376b, 383, 52, 57, 62. With 1st w. Mary he sold 15 a. betw. Samuel Folsom and Samuel Leavitt, 27 Apr. 1667. His 2d w. Deborah was adm. to Hampton Ch. from Ex. 14 Nov. 1697 and dism. when the Ex. Ch. was incorp. in Sept. 1698. Will, 27 Jan.—14 Sept. 1700, names her and their mar. contract, 4 ch., gr.sons John and Benjamin Jones (given £2 at 21); s. John exec. Ch: James, b. 27 July 1660. Mary, b. 27 June 1663; Mary Wheeler in 1700. Sarah, b. 15 Sept. 1664, not in fa.'s will; prob. m. Benjamin Jones(4). John. Meribah, was Meribah Lull in 1700.
4 JOHN(3), Exeter, m. Elizabeth Bean(2), who was liv. in 1733. Lists 57, 67, 384b, 376b (1705, 1725), 388. Will, 28 Dec. 1730— 16 Nov. 1731, names w. Elizabeth (exec.) and ch: John, husbandman, coaster, Exeter. In 1729 his fa. deeded him half his est. Adm. 28 Sept. 1747 to Nicholas Perryman, principal creditor. Samuel, So. Newmarket, willed the remaining half of his fa.'s est. at mo.'s death. He m. by 1733 Sarah Mattoon (2); both alive 1758. 3 sons. Abigail, Margaret, Elizabeth, all unm. in 1730.
5 ROBERT, Wells, m. 16 May 1712 Elizabeth Denmark(2), who was bp. on prof. of faith 17 Oct. 1714. Conditional gr. 18 Mar. 1713-14. He d. by 1718 and wid. m. 2d 25 Apr. 1718 Peter Rich. Ch. bp. 14 Apr. 1717: John, m. 19 Apr. 1739 Mary Wakefield. Elizabeth. One Robert was of Boston in 1688; Archives 129: 126.
Singleman, Henry, Cape Porpus. Morgan Howell had his land in 1648. One H. S. was fined for swearing in Salem ct. 1641.
Skalion, Dennis, Exeter. See Conner(5), Kelly(5).
Skellito, Thomas, List 237b.

**SKILLINGS.** Uncommon.

**1 JOHN**(2), carpenter, Falmouth, signed a pet. in Aug. 1665. In 1673 at Newcastle having his broadcloth made up (see Russell), appar. a w. Mary with him. From Falm., he was adm. inhab. of Salem 11 Jan. 1675-6, made agreem. in Sept. 1677 to finish Salem meet.-ho., and was paid for work in July 1678. Working for the Pickerings in Portsmouth in Mar. 1677-8. Falm. 1680; taxed Scarb. 1681; gr.j. 1681, 1687; constable 1686; liv. 1688; prob. an Ind. victim in Falm. in 1689. Lists 222c, 223a, 27, 30, 235a, 238a, 34. His s. John claimed marsh up Capisic River, land leased to Collins(2) in 1685, 5 a. and ½ of a mill on Long Creek, and ho. and 7 a. exchanged with Rev. George Burroughs. Wid. Elizabeth (Ingersoll 2), m. 2d Elihu Gunnison(1). Ch: **John**, Portsm. (taxed 1722), Boston 1726, when he sold his double share, ⅔, to Thomas Westbrook. List 339. Wife Elizabeth, adm. to No. Ch. 1713, liv. 1726. Kn. ch., bp. in Portsm., mar. in Boston: Elizabeth, m. Nicholas Lash (Robert 1), d. 14 Aug. 1750 in 44th yr. Simon, bp. 1711. Simeon, bp. 1716, m. Ruth Phillips. Mary, bp. 1718, m. Thomas Adams. Sarah, bp. 1721, m. Jonathan Crosby. Prob: John, m. in 1739 Elizabeth Farmer; Peter, m. in 1744 Mary Sargent. Poss: Joseph of Richmond, m. Eleanor Youngman in Roxbury 1731. Note also Hannah, w. of Ephraim Sherburne(7). Lt. **Samuel**, shipwright, Exeter, Kit., Falm., b. 25 July 1679, d. at Long Creek 2 Jan. 1757. In 1744, ag. 66, he depos. that he liv. in Falm. until the spring bef. Fort Loyal was taken. Lists 388, 291. His w. Richord (Haley 1, m. 25 Dec. 1702, liv. 1730), was not named in his deed to s.-in-law Roberts in 1736. See 'Old Kittery,' p. 731, for ch: Mary, Rebecca, Samuel, Katherine, Dorcas, Elizabeth, Deborah, Joanna, Susanna. **Rebecca**, m. George Frink(1). **Josiah**, shipwright, Kit., m. 17 May 1708 Elizabeth Lidden(1). She was gr. adm. 7 July 1719; m. 2d Roger Deering, Esq. (8 jr.). Lists 296, 297. Ch: John, b. 15 Aug. 1709, poss. one of three bur. about 7 mos. aft. the fa. died. Edward, Scarb., b. 25 Mar. 1711; see Miller (2), Mills(4). Elizabeth, b. 24 Dec. 1713, m. Danforth Phipps(5). One Elizabeth was w. of Isaac Winter in 1736 when Roger Deering was her bondsman.

**2 THOMAS**, Salem, Gloucester, Falm., wit. ag. James Smith sr. in Salem ct. 31: 1: 1640; had Salem gr. 1642, to be laid out in Wenham; sued Wm. Brown and w. of Glouc. for slander in 1652; of Glouc. 1657 when w. Deborah, ±34, wit. ag. Brown in behalf of Goodw. Prince. See Essex Q. Ct. Rec. i: 286, 320. On 25 Mar. 1658 he bot from George Cleeve 55 a. at Back Cove betw. George Ingersoll and Richard Tucker, and liv. there.

Wit. Cleeve to Munjoy 1665. Tr.j. 1662-1664, 1665 (did not appear); gr.j. 1663. Lists 222ac, 25, 225a. Will, very weak, 14 Nov. 1666—2 Oct. 1667, gives livestock and tools to sons Thomas and John, all else to w., but only ⅓ if she mar., the rest then to be eq. divided to all the ch. Inv. £186 (see Me. P. & Ct. Rec. i: 329). Wid. Deborah m. 2d at Ipsw. 29 June 1668 George Hadley. Ch: **Deborah**, b. 22 Aug. 1640 (pub. Glouc. rec.), but Babson who found the rec. illegible said '1640 or 1648.' She is the logical w. for John Ingersoll(5) but if the D. S. who wit. for Joseph's East. Claim, she was then unm. **Thomas**, b. Nov. 1643 (Salem rec.; see Essex Q. Ct. Rec. i: 93). **John**. **Abigail**, b. 1652 (age at death), m. John Corney(1). **Joseph**, Marblehead, claimed for self and br. Benj. 100 a. at Back Cove given them by their fa. and posses. by their mo. and br. John until they were of age; Deborah Skillings, Elizabeth Clark and George Ingersoll his witnesses. He and w. Elizabeth sold half to Edmund Clark in Sept. 1719. No ch. appear, unless it was a son and not he who m. Elizabeth Gott in Salem 22 May 1713, and unless Elizabeth Clark was his dau., not Benjamin's. **Benjamin**, youngest son, had a Rowley freehold, m. 1st one Susanna, m. 2d (int. at Ipsw. 24 Apr. 1708) Mary Jewett. Of Marbleh. in Sept. 1719, he and w. Mary sold his 50 a. at Back Cove to John Wass. Kn. ch. by 1st w: Elizabeth, b. at Ipsw. 25 Dec. 1693; one E. m. at Marbleh. 21 Dec. 1714 Edmund Clark who was of Falm. in 1719 when he bot and sold Joseph Skillings's 50 a. John, b. Ipsw. 29 Mar. 1704; of Marblehead m. Eunice Kimball (int. at Ipsw. 1727); ch. By 2d w: Nehemiah, named in gr. fa. Jewett's will; of Marbleh., m. Mercy Kimball, int. Ipsw. 1730; ch. Mary, bp. at Ipsw. 13 May 1711; one M. mar. John Brooks at Marbleh. in 1727.

**3 THOMAS**(2), Falmouth. Lists 3 (p. 45), 222bc, 224, 93. John Allicet sued him in Suff. ct. in Oct. 1676 for wages for making his fish at Cape Sable. He m. Mary Lewis (4), d. at Salem, a refugee, 30 Dec. 1676; adm. to her in Essex ct. 14 Mar. 1676-7. Inv., by Francis Neale and Henry Williams, incl. personal prop. at Salem; goods left at Boston, incl. 2 guns, 2 Ind. swords, 2 or 3 lbs. of feathers, 60 lbs. of shot; at Piscataqua, molasses, salt and a bear-skin. She m. 2d Jotham Lewis(10), m. 3d Henry Wilkins, and depos. at Salem in Sept. 1731, ±77 (Y. D. 14: 210) and in Mar. 1732, ±78; of Middleton, depos. in June 1735, ±80. **Three ch.** were b. at Falm. bef. she had to take refuge in the Andrews garrison. Appar. only **Benjamin**, b. ±1671, survived. Of Portsm. when land was laid out there to him and his mo. 17 Mar. 1713, and when he, w. Deliverance and mo.

sold land to Samuel Folsom in Sept. 1717. Lists 330de, 337, 338ac, 229. Soon remov. to Falm., where he was ±81, Deliverance ±70, in May 1752. · He was bur. 11 Dec. 1764; 'he reckoned he was in his 100th year' (Smith's Journal, p. 202). Ch., all bp. at Greenl. 1717: Isaac, Benjamin, Lydia, Mary, Jean.

**SKINNER.** See also Champnois(2), Phillips(22), Waterhouse(4).

1 **EDWARD**, ±60, wit. delivery of Sebascodegan Isl., Wharton to Parker, 1684. See also Hannet.

2 **CAPT. FRANCIS**, commander of Pemaquid Fort, 1682+. Taxed 1687, land and cattle. Lists 123, 124. Killed by Ind. with Capt. Farnham ab. 2 Aug. 1689, as they landed on a rock at Pemaquid, having come from an 'island ab. half a mile distant (Niles). One Francis and w. Mary had a dau. Sarah rec. at Boston 1670.

3 **GABRIEL**, Cape Bonawagon 1672, List 13. One G. was a mar. man at Marblehead in 1660.

4 **JAMES**, at Damariscove in 1676 where he had friends or relations. Lists 142, 85. He was then or later of Marblehead, as also his s. **Richard**, ag. 16 in 1677, List 142. See N. E. Reg. 54: 413; SJC 138271.

5 **ROBERT**, servant of Capt. Paul White, for whose services on the ship ·Jane· for one yr. Capt. Champernowne paid £10, had run away from the ship bef. Feb. 1648-9. Likely the R. sued by Christopher Mitchell in 1661 for money paid for him.

**Skipper**, John, List 78.

**Skorck**, John, Newcastle cor.j. 1670, List 312b.

**SKRIGGIN, John**, shipwright, Kittery. Oyster River wit. 1704, Welthen Simonds to her gr.s. He m. Abigail Paul(2), and in 1716 bot ½ a. houselot, part of the Tetherly land, from Richard King. See also Y. D. 8: 63. His w. d. ±1733, he bef. 1747, when ch. **John, Paul** (m. Dorothy Cloudman), and **Abigail** (w. of Robert Cole; former w. of Ichabod Remick), were liv., and **Mary** (m. Thomas Fernald, jr.) was dead, leaving a s. **Benjamin**.

**SLACK, William**, of Attleboro, once of Boston, entered an East. Cl. for 105 + 20 á. at Newton . . . Nequasset, deed from Wm. Stevens 1686, and 109 + 20 a. in same place, deed from John Palmer, Esq., 1686. List 188. He and w. Mary had **four sons** rec. in Boston and Braintree 1683-1690.

**SLADE. 1 Arthur**, Mr., Portsmouth, Newmarket, from Deptford, co. Kent, d. 12 Jan. 1746, ag. 64 (Atkinson platter). See Keyes(3), N. E. Reg. 43: 160, 428. He left a wid. Elizabeth in Eng. One Benjamin S. m. in Newc. 8 Jan. 1736 Mary Perry, wit. Henry

Keese's will in 1740, the codicil in 1741, and d. by 1744.

2 **JOHN** (Slades, Slead), Scarboro soldier, fisherman; Lists 236, 237b. A Shoals fisherman in Oct. 1678 when sued by Roger Kelly.

**SLAUGHTER**, Slafter, Slater.

1 **GEORGE**, Pemaquid, where his land adj. Thomas Warden's. List 124. Supposed the husb. of Giles Goddard's dau. and fa. of **John**, mariner, Boston, who had a deed from gr.fa. Goddard in 1714. John m. in Boston 22 Oct. 1711 Elizabeth Bradstreet (John of Rowley). As E. S., wid., 20 Dec. 1736, she deeded land adj. Elijah Vinal, to Samuel Butler (m. Mary Slaughter in Boston in 1732), mar. one wk. later John Wass and was Wass' wid. and still admx. of the Slaughter est. in 1750.

2 **JOHN**, swearing many oaths in July 1662 (York ct.). He or a younger J. was at Scarboro, m. Mary Libby(5) and had a 6 a. gr. near the meeting-ho. in Aug. 1682. Lists 34, 238a. They retired to Lynn, where J. S. in 1713-4 hired from the town 2½ a. of land for 7 yrs.; later went to Mansfield, Conn., thence to Wellington (Y. D. 15: 167). By trad. he d. at great age. Ch., from 'Memorial of John Slafter' (1869): **Mary** (m. int. Lynn 23 Aug. 1717 Isaac Wellman). **Anthony**, ·(m. at Lynn 30 Dec. 1712 Mary Eaton). **Elizabeth** (m. at Lynn 2 May 1711 Thomas Hutchinson). **Samuel. Joseph. Sarah. Moses. Abigail. Benjamin**, yet this last willed his est. to his nine bros. and sis. and their heirs.

**SLEEPER.**

1 **AARON**(3), m. 1st 23 May 1682 Elizabeth Shaw(10) who d. 27 Oct. 1708. He liv. on Shaw's Hill in Hampton until 11 ch. had been born, afterw. in Kingston. O. A. 1678. Jury 1695. Lists 52, 57, 400. Of Kingst. in 1709 he deeded homestead to s. Thomas, who in 1723 gave a deed to his fa., 'in case he outlives me.' 'Aaron ye aged' was head of a Kingst. fam. in 1725, a member of K. Ch., and d. there 9 May 1732 'an aged father.' The aged Mrs. Sleeper d. of a fever 3 Jan. 1736. Ch. rec. Hampt: **Moses**, b. 2 (or 22) Jan. 1684-5, m. in Kingst. 9 Jan. 1714 Margaret Sanborn(4). Sergt. 1725. List 400. Will, 12 Jan.—27 Feb. 1754, names w. Margaret, 14 ch. **Thomas**, b. 3 Nov. 1686 (List 400), m. at Kingst. 6 Dec. 1714 Mary Colcord(2). She was gr. adm. 30 Dec. 1723, m. 2d 5 May 1726 Ebenezer Eastman. 4 ch. **Aaron**, b. 23 July 1688, cordwainer, Kingston. Wife Sarah and ch. Daniel and Edward, 1715-1719. Adm. to Edward 25 Apr. 1753. Mary Kenniston and Hannah Sleeper, her dau., released claims for a consid. **Jo-**

seph, twin, b. 14 June 1690, m. in Kingst. last day of Dec. 1713 Sarah Hutchins. Both adm. to K. Ch. 1726. Will, 1752—1753, names wife and 4 of 5 or more ch. **John**, twin, of Kingst., m. 1st 5 June 1712 Ann Philbrick (9) who d. 30 Aug. 1716 (3 sons); m. 2d 18 July 1717 Mary Towle(1), at least 1 dau. She relinq. adm. to his br. Thomas 23 June 1720, was adm. to Hampt. F. Ch. 27 Aug. 1721, m. 2d 29 Mar. 1727 Thomas Page. **Samuel**, b. 1 Dec. 1692. **Elisha**, b. 9 May 1694. **Hezekiah**, b. 11 May 1696, m. Elizabeth Fifield (John 1), d. 30 Sept. 1722. 2 ch. rec. 1717-1720. Widow m. 2d by 1729 Jonathan Webster of Kingston. **Ebenezer**, b. 1697, d. 1698. **Jonathan**, b. 17 Mar. 1699 (one J. of Bridgeton, N. J., d. by 1736, leaving a family). **Abigail**, b. 17 Apr. 1700, m. Isaac Fellows(2). Rec. in Kingston: **Mehitabel**, b. 25 Apr. 1701. **Ebenezer**, b. 24 Apr. 1702, bot in Kingst. 1723, head of a fam. and Ch. memb. 1725. Mrs. Sleeper, his w., adm. to Ch. in Dec. 1727. Will, 1761—1768, names w. Sarah, 1 son, 2 daus. **Daughter**, b. and d. 1704. **Mary**, b. 21 Feb. 1705-6; one M. m. Elisha Winsley at Kingst. 4 Jan. 1725. **Ithamar**, b. and d. 1708. See also (2) for Elizabeth, w. of Joseph Young.

2 **JOHN**(3), Hampton soldier 1676, took O. A. 1678, taxed at Hampt. 1680, at Exeter 1682, when he bot Teague Drisco's Ex. ho. and ±8 ɑ. of land. A participant in the Gove Rebellion and one of those indicted; his fa.'s pet. in this connec. called him 'my eldest son.' Of Ex. in Aug. 1689, he bot ±80 a. adj. Moses Gilman from John Bray(5) and his mo., sold in 1693 and disappears. Lists 395, 396, 62. No fam. appears, unless Elizabeth who m. Joseph Young in Kingston 24 Dec. 1705, was a dau., but names of 3 of her 8 ch., Aaron, Hezekiah and Jonathan, suggest she was an unrec. dau. of (1).

3 **THOMAS**, weaver, Hampton, bot from Christopher Lawson 15 July 1645 a 5 a. ho.-lot in Hampt. betw. Thomas Leavitt and Goodm. Marion, but in Oct. 1649 liv. on 1 a. of Henry Dow's land that had been deeded to Thomas Nudd. In June 1657 he bot Joseph Peaslee's ho. in Haverh. and mov. there, selling out in Hampt.; sold at Haverh. in 1659 and bot at Hampt. again in 1660. In his later life, Dow says, his was the frontier ho. on what is now Shaw's Hill, that part of the town being called Sleeper-town, since corrupted to Sleepy-town. Jury 1651, 1662; gr.j. 1670, 1673, 1676, 1677. Freed from training in Oct. 1665. Ag. ±75 in Feb. 1682-3. Lists 392a, 393ab(3), 394, 396, 398, 49, 52. He d. 30 July 1696. His w. Joanna (±33 in Sept. 1656) d. 4 Feb. 1702-3 (Kingston rec.) Lists 393a, 392c, 394. Ch: **Elizabeth**, m. 1st Abraham Perkins(2), m. 2d Alex. Denham, m. 3d Richard Smith. **Mary**, m. 15 May

1667 Gershom Elkins(4). **Ruth**, b. 1 June 1650. Ag. ±21 or 22, she depos. in Dec. 1671 that she had liv. at Moses Gilman's, but went back to her fa.'s ho. in Hampt. She m. Aretas Leavitt(1). **John**, b. 10 Sept. 1652. **Naomi**, b. 15 Apr. 1655, m. Timothy Blake (5). **Moses**, b. at Haverh. 13 Mar. 1657-8; adm. to fa. 7 Sept. 1680. **Aaron**, b. at Hampt. 20 Feb. 1660-1. **Luther**, b. 14 Nov. 1668, d.. 19 May 1670.

**SLEW, Leonard**, in 1678 had not long since mar. Tabitha Hoar (Wm.) of Beverly. A Purpooduck settler under Danforth, where in 1683 Richard Seacomb sold to Edwards and Walter 100 a. by Lawrence Davis', except 12 a. of L. S.'s. In the 2d war he ret. to Salem and there in July 1700 took oath that he sold Purpooduck meadow and marsh to Margery Haines for a heifer. Reported k. at Purpooduck, with w. and **three ch.**, 10 Aug. 1703, but Miss Coleman identifies '——— Slew from Casco' in Canada 1710 as Leonard. Lists 227, 39, 99, p. 92. A s. **Leonard** who may not have ret. to Purpooduck with his fa.'s fam., m. Abigail Johnson 23 Nov. 1703 in Beverly where in 1744 he q.c. half his fa.'s 12 a., having sold the other half to James Noble. One Mary S. m. Joshua Beans in Salem in 1701.

**Sligins, James**, Falmouth 1683. Lists 226, 228c.

**SLOPER**, sometimes Soper. A Wiltshire family.

1 **JOHN** (also Soper), Kittery, consid. the J. early in Portsmouth, presum. related to (3) whose s. John was 'Jr.' in 1688. A Portsm. constable's acct. 1668 has item: 'Richard Sloop alias John Soapr 0: 5: 0.' John subscr. a bu. of corn for the Portsm. minister in 1671; 'himself and oxen' in acct. 1672. On 14 Feb. 1679-80, 'now in New England,' he bot in Kit. from Stephen Paul, betw. James Fernald and Richard Gowell, describ. in 1720 as 'at a place called Gowell's Bridge.' Portsm. abatements 1683 incl. John Soper (see 2). Lists 326c, 296, 297. Will, of Kit., 9 Feb. (d. 24 Feb. or Mar.) 1692-3, gives all lands to w. Sarah (exec.) for life; witnesses, Jacob and Isaac Remick, Richard Carle; apprais. Richard King, Jacob Remick. Wid. Sarah m. 2d Moses Worcester(1). Ch: **Elizabeth**, given all lands eventually, to pay her sis. half the value. She m. Samuel Ham (9). One Elizabeth Soper was serv. of Elizabeth Eburne(1) in 1702. **Rebecca**, m. Jacob Remick(2 jr.). See Y. D. 8: 18; 9: 263; 11: 24-26.

2 **JOHN**(3), Portsmouth. John Sloper in Wm. Seavey's highway acct. in 1683; John Soper's tax abated that yr. (see 1). Richard's John took O. A. 28 Aug. 1685; taxed 1688 (jr.), 1690, 1691; wit. deed to

br.-in-law John Knight in Nov. 1692; taxed 1693 (poll); seated at ch. in Mar. 1693-4. Lists 312c, 313e, 52, 332b, 335a. His tax abated in Mar. 1694-5. No later rec., no evid. of wife or ch. One John sued Joseph Pitman in 1730, on a bill for 20 days' work in 1729; one Mary m. John Thompson in Portsm. 31 Oct. 1737.

3 **LT. RICHARD**, Portsm. In Nov. 1649, Ipswich ct. ordered him whipped for challenging and threatening to shoot Wm. Cogswell; John Cogswell, jr. went his bond. In June 1650 admon. in Salem for threatening speeches. Dover 1657-1658, of Portsm. aft. he m. 21 Oct. 1658 Mary Sherburne(2) who kept the fam. record first printed in Brewster's Rambles ii: 51-2. Her fa. gave land as a mar. portion 29 Sept. 1659. O. A. 2 Oct.1666. Selectman 1667-68,1672,1674; constable 1680; O. A. 28 Aug. 1685; gr.j. 1693, j. 1694. Sergt. 1674, 1680; Ensign 1685; Lieut. 1693. Ag. 70 in Nov. 1701 when he denied that he knew of John Cogswell deeding land to Wm. C. Ag. ±84 in Mar. 1713-4 and Sept. 1714 (SJC 15076), but he was then dead. Lists 356abc, 322-324, 326abc, 330abcd, 331b, 311b, 312c, 313a, 332b, 335a, 336b, 337, 47, 49, 52, 55a, 67. See also (1). Wife, List 335a. See Brewster(3, 1), Miller(1). Will, 26 Oct. 1711—28 Dec. 1713 (adm.'s bond 1 Feb. 1712-3), names w. Mary, 6 of 11 liv. ch.; w. and dau. Elizabeth execs.; br. Mark Hunking and cous. Tobias Langdon overseers. Wid. Mary d. 22 Sept. 1718. Ch. (mo.'s rec.): **Bridget**, b. 30 Aug. 1659, m. John Knight(9). **John**, b. 13 Jan. 1661. **Mary**, b. 11 Feb. 1663, m. John Brewster(2), depos. in 1720, ag. 53. **Sarah**, b. 26 July 1667. **Susannah**, b. 21 Mar. 1669, m. Elisha Kelly (6), depos. in 1706, ag. 32. **Elizabeth**, b. 26 June 1671, willed £10 and to have what mo. left. Of a weak capacity in Apr. 1720 when she asked that br. Henry be cited to account for part of the est. In June 1721 she deeded her int. to Ambrose. **Rebecca**, b. 23 Oct. 1673, m. Edward Carwithy. **Martha**, b. 26 Dec. 1676, in 1702 gave p/a to br. Elisha Kelly to sue Nathl. Solley who accus. her of stealing. In 1707 her suit ag. Obadiah Morse, jr. (see 3, 9), who m. her, brot out much scandal. **Tabitha**, b. 17 Dec. 1679, m. Wm. Bridgham. **Richard**, twin, b. 16 June 1682, willed £20, but to revert to br. Henry, 'in case he be dead,' or d. first. Payment was made to Henry bef. 14 June 1721. Capt. **Henry**, twin, mariner, had land from fa. in 1707, m. 1st by 6 Oct. 1716 Lydia Penhallow (2) who d. 17 Aug. 1718 ag. 16 y. 11 m., m. 2d bef. 1725 Miriam Thompson (see 7). Liv. 29 Aug. 1760. List 339. His son by 1st w., **Samuel**, b. 6 July 1717, a sailor on the -Fanny and Sally-, in will, 23 Aug. 1738—24 Jan. 1739-40, named fa. and mo., br. Henry, and

sis. **Lydia** (w. of John Bean of Brentwood in 1760). **Ambrose**, Portsm., b. 20 Jan. 1684. Lt. S. and Ambrose S. taxed for the Mill Dam 1708. List 339. He m. 1st bef. May 1709 Mary Pickering(5) who was liv. in 1721. Wife Sarah in will, 1759-1772. See Reg. 64: 13 for ch: Ambrose (accus. by Rachel Burrill(3) in 1732), William, John, Richard, Samuel, Joshua, Daniel, Benning, Mary, Sarah, Susannah, Olive, Elizabeth.

**Slowman**, Simon, a Kennebec soldier 1688. List 189.

**Sluce**, Lawrence, master of the -Hopewell-. List 122.

**SMALL**, from Devonshire, often Smalley on Cape Cod. See 'Descendants of Edward Small and Allied Families' (Underhill).

1 **EDWARD**, Mr., Piscataqua, from St. Mary's parish, Bideford, co. Devon, appeared at Saco ct. 25 June 1640, when he served on both gr. and tr. jury, and had a ho. at Sturgeon Creek bef. 25 July 1643 when he had a deed from Thomas Gorges for 100 a. lying betw. two creeks on each side of his ho. His son's depos. in 1685 sets the time he had lived in N. E. as upward of 50 yrs., but as he had overstated his age by 5 yrs., calling himself 65, his estimate of '50 upward' may be ano. overstatement. Mr. Edward was a magistrate in 1645. Cor.j. 1647. In 1647 he sold his Sturgeon Creek place to Mr. Antipas Maverick, suing him in 1649 for a debt of £20, likely the bal. of the purchase price; a judg. was ack. and execution granted. His actual later resid. does not appear, but it was near by. Foreman on j. 1651, signed Shoals pt. 1653, 'Mr. Small' had tav. lic. 28 June 1655. Following this he disappears and was plausibly the Edward later in Virginia. Lists 281, 301. See also Shurt(2). Elizabeth, w. of Edward, was bur. at St. Mary's, Bideford, 10 Feb. 1665. She was prob. related to the Shurts. Ch. bp. at Bideford except the first: **George**. In Mar. 1645-6 the ho. of John Whitfield in York was attached for two debts, Mrs. Lynn's and George Small's, in 1647 he had an exec. ag. ho. and land of John Lander. See also Reynolds(2), Heard(4). **Francis**, bp. 6 Oct. 1625. **Elizabeth**, bp. 6 July 1627, d.y. **Mary**, bp. 5 May 1629. **Edmond**, bp. 2 Mar. 1630. **Elizabeth**, bp. 10 Oct. 1632, bur. 27 Dec. 1635. **William**, bp. 4 Feb. 1634.

2 **EDWARD**(4), depos. at Scarb. in 1676, ±22, and was also at Kit. in 1676, not long aft. employed at Dover masting and m. Mary Woodman(2) prob. bef. 1685 when he signed a pet. with Woodmans. Oyster Riv. gr. 19 Mar. 1693-4, 40 a. adj. his plantation. In 1695 at Manomoisett on Cape Cod, afterwards Chatham. In Dover Public Library is

an orig. letter, dated Oyster River, July 26, 1700, from John Woodman to 'Son Edward and Daughter Mary Smalle,' at Monamoy, 'Smalle's horse not yet sold.' Lists 236, 52, 94. He d. the last day of Apr. 1702. See also Broadbrook. Wid. Mary was of M. in June 1707, and of Oyster River 24 Oct. 1721 when 20 a. were laid out to her in compensation for care of Archibald Smith. In 1742 she conv. this land, with the buildings, to gr. sons Edward and Joseph of Durham. Kn. ch: **Edward**, m. 3 Apr. 1704 Sarah Nickerson of Manomoisett, who was gr. adm. 8 Jan. 1706; 1 dau. **Jonathan**, m. at Harwich 30 July 1713 Damaris Winslow, d. ±1778; 5 ch. **Elizabeth**, m. at Eastham 1 Sept. 1705 Caleb Lombard. **Joseph**, m. at Oyster River 27 Nov. 1718 Jemima Davis(37); 8 ch. incl. Edward and Joseph named above. **Zachariah**, m. 1st at Oyster River 31 Mar. 1720 Jane Davis, liv. at Harwich, where he m. 2d in 1742 Hannah (Hopkins) Paine and d. 1778; 7 + 1 ch. **Benjamin**, m. 29 June 1726 Patience Baker of Harwich, where he d. bef. 1788; 9 ch.

3 **ELIZABETH**, servant to Capt. Francis Champernowne, m. Thomas Hooper(10).

4 **FRANCIS**(1), planter, fisherman, noted Ind. trader, first seen in a Dover tax list of Dec. 1648, but by his depos. 1685 (Prov. Papers 29: 136) he knew Capt. Mason's planta. and servants upward of 50 yrs. and ±40 yrs. bef. was employed by Capt. Norton to drive cattle toward Boston. Aged ±43 in Mar. 1670-1; ±56 and w. Elizabeth ±49 in May 1683; ±57 in Nov. 1685. Of Casco Bay in July 1657 he had an Ind. deed of Capisic, sold half to John Phillips(9) in 1658 and re-affirmed his deed aft. Cleeve had unsucc. sued him for building and settling on his land. On Sebascodegan, or Small's Isl., early, which he bot for Major Shapleigh, long an intimate friend, to whom in 1669 he made over half his Ossipee interest. He dealt early in furs and with the Ind. and had land and housing at Ossipee bef. Feb. 1662 when he made over all to Munjoy and agreed to make an accounting every time he came back. For the litigation years later and the Ossipee proprs., see 'Descendants of Edward Small' (1934 ed.), pp. 51-100. Lists 354a, 221(2), 222b, 232, 298, 25, 87, 94. See also Jordan(7), Newcomb(1), Sheldon(1), Y. D. 9: 221. Gr.j. 1660. Of Casco 1662, atty. for Mr. Robert Jordan and others in ct. 1663, but poss. never gave up his Kit. home where he ret. A Portsm. wit. in Mar. 1670-1, Kit. gr. 1671, liv. at Sturgeon Creek 1674, impressed to go to Ossipee in 1676. He laid claim to the land his fa. had sold to Antipas Maverick whose heirs succ. sued him in 1683. His last yrs. were spent on Cape Cod where he and w. Elizabeth were liv. with s.

Daniel in 1712 and where he soon d. Kn. ch: **Edward**, b. ±1654. **Mary**, ±21 in June 1677, m. Nicholas Frost(10). **Francis**, 'little Frank Small' in 1671. **Samuel**, b. ±1664. **Benjamin**, m. ±1694 Rebecca Snow of Eastham, liv. in E., Truro (1701), Lebanon, Conn. (±1712), where he d., adm. to Rebecca 4 June 1721. 10 ch. **Daniel**, carpenter, Truro, had supported parents 6 or 7 yrs. in 1712 and would have to do it as long as they lived. A purported deed from his fa. 31 Oct. 1712, conveying all he owned or thought he owned, has generally been consid. fraudulent, but Daniel mortg. and sold prop. under it; liv. Provincetown 1729. Wife unkn. 5 of his ch. came to Cape Elizabeth: Anna Dyer (w. of Henry), ±86 in Aug. 1781; see N. E. Reg. 35: 366; Isaac, John, Edward and Abigail Strout (w. of Anthony). Two sons Daniel and Elisha liv. in Mass. and Conn., and Benjamin is untraced aft. 1730. **Alice**, m. 1st one Wormwood (see her br. 5), m. 2d 19 Apr. 1711 Beriah Smith. **Elizabeth**, m. John Pugsley(1).

5 **FRANCIS**(4), carpenter, Kittery, Truro. In 1681 Major Shapleigh sued Stephen Jenkins and F. S., jr., for cutting and carrying away his timber. Before York ct. in Feb. 1691-2 for not paying his rate for the poor, and he promised to pay. List 94. At Truro by 1702. His will there, 22 Aug. 1709—5 Apr. 1710, names w. Elizabeth (considered prob. dau. of Samuel Hicks), ch. (2 by name), and sis. Alice Wormwood. His ch., Francis, Samuel, Daniel, Joseph, and poss. Alice, liv. on Cape Cod.

6 **JAMES**, signed an Exeter pet. 7 Sept. 1643 (Mass. Arch. 112: 8).

7 **JOSEPH**, Portsm., m. Susannah Packer(2), d. 4 Oct. 1720, ag. 40 (Point of Graves); wid. m. 2d Benjamin Rust. Ch: **Elizabeth**, m. by 1730 Samuel Davis(61). **Joseph**, d. s.p. by 1736. **Hephzibah**, Boston 1738, unm. **Thomas**, bp. at Portsm. 28 May 1721, of Boston and of age in 1740.

8 **RICHARD**, from Jacobstown, Devonshire, see Moulton(I).

9 **SAMUEL**(4), Kittery, m. bef. 28 Aug. 1688 Elizabeth (Heard 3) Chadbourne. As S. S. and E. C. they were bound over in York ct. for an assault on Nicholas Frost; he fined, she not guilty, 12 Oct. 1686. At the same ct. Frost and his w. were fined for assaulting them. He depos. in Apr. 1721, ag. 55, that he worked for Thomas Jones 37 or 38 yrs. bef.; in May 1737, upward of 70, that 60 yrs. bef. he and others liv. at Major Shapleigh's; in Nov. 1737, ag. 73, that he was Mr. Henry Jocelyn's servant at Pemaquid several yrs. Appr. Joseph Moulton's est. 1692. Jury 1700. Kit. grants 1694, 1699, 1703, but liv. on prop. near Ferry Landing, Sturgeon Creek, 16 a., ho. and orchard, he

bot from Peter Wittum in 1696 and conv. to
s. Joseph in 1728. Orig. member of Berwick
Ch. Lists 94, 290, 296-298. See also Lord(1),
Morrell(3). His ch. and gr.ch. claimed and,
aft. long litigation, settled on Ossipee land
his fa. deeded to him in 1711, but which he
made no effort to claim. Ch: Prob. one of
more had d. bef. **Elizabeth** was b. 9 Nov.
1695; she m. Benjamin March(5). **Samuel,**
Kit., Scarb., b. 17 Apr. 1700, m. 17 Jan.
1716-7 Ann Hatch(2). List 291. At age of
68 he (w. Ann) conv. all Scarb. prop. to gr.s.
Benjamin (s. of Samuel) for life supp.; liv.
1775; 9 ch. **Joseph,** b. 3 Dec. 1702, m. 12 Apr.
1722 Mary Libby(3); liv. at Kit. (List 298)
and Falm. (by 1746); 8 ch. **Mary,** bp. with
her brothers 27 May 1708, m. 24 Nov. 1720
Solomon Davis of Gloucester.

**SMALLEDGE, William,** sued by Mr. Jordan
in 1659. List 253. See William -Small-
all-, Scarb. or Falm. 1663 (N. E. Reg. 5:
264); also Boston and Marbleh. records;
Storer(1).

**SMART,** located in Oxfordshire in 13th
century. 'Smart' in Doe(3) should read
'Swett.'

1 **FRANCIS,** husbandman, Kittery, m. Mary
Crockett(2). In 1718 Jonathan Partridge
was charged with stealing eels from his boat.
List 291. In 1723 bondsm. for Elizabeth
Deering(9). Will, 10 May 1743—31 Dec.
1750, gave all for life to w. Mary, afterw. to
belov. kindred, Wm. Barter, Sarah Grindle,
Elizabeth and Martha Jones (see Barter 1).

2 **JOHN,** Exeter (Newmarket), came from
co. Norfolk to Hingham in 1635 with w.
and two sons (Cushing mss., Reg. 15: 27).
He did not sign the Exeter comb., but shared
in divisions in Dec. 1639. Lists 375ab, 376ab.
In 1647 Thomas and Esther Biggs succes.
sued him and w. Margaret for slander; in
Mar. 1648 in ct. for abusing John Stanyan
while serving an execution and at same ct.
Stanyan sued him (sr.) for assault. Abraham Perkins was allowed costs in suit of
John sr. in Apr. 1649. In Oct. 1649 John (not
called 'sr.') and Robert were sued for the
meet.-ho. debt. Edward and Wm. Hilton
dep. in 1678 that 'old goodman Smart deceased several yrs. bef. 1652.' His wid. was
liv. 24 Nov. 1654. Ch: John. Robert. Daughter (or poss. step-dau.), m. John Wedgwood
(2). The s. John was poss. the deft. with
Robert in 1649, and in Christopher Lawson's
suit same yr. In 1653 he deeded to neph.
John Wedgwood land form. his fa.'s. In a
suit over marsh on s.w. side of John Goddard's Creek, in 1678, John Ault, ±73, depos.
that John S. mowed it 12 yrs. bef. Dover was
a township, 16 yrs. together; the Hiltons
depos. ab. the two brothers there aft. their
fa. died.

3 **PRISCILLA,** a lame girl at Boston in Mar.
1703-4, driven by the enemy from Black
Point. Supplies were furnished her at Boston Nov. 1706—Dec. 1707.

4 **ROBERT**(2), Exeter, was bound for appearance of w. Rebecca in Salisbury ct.
in Oct. 1654; owned a mill with Thomas
Kimball and Wm. Hilton in 1657. Lists 376b
(1664), 377, 379, 383, 49, 52, 54, 57, 92. Gr.j.
1673; j. 1694. In Nov. 1677 Sergt. Robert
(List 381?) and Robert jr. took O. A. Inv. 1
July 1703; wid. Rebecca renounc. adm. to
step-son Robert 11 Dec. 1703, his bondsm.
Winthrop and Jonathan Hilton. See Rebecca Hilton(19), Mercer(1). Kn. ch: **Robert,**
b. ±1646 by depos. Capt. **John,** mariner, perhaps the quartermaster on the -John and
Mary- of London in 1675, bot at Oyster River
in 1685; O. R. wit. 1686; in 1689 master of
the -Good Speed- of Piscat. taken by pirates
on way to Nantucket; poss. of Barbadoes
1698. Elizabeth of O. R., a redeemed captive 1695 (List 99, p. 74), presum. his w. In
1701 they gave p/a to Joseph Smith of O. R.,
who sold the O. R. land in 1703, when husb.
and w. were called of New York. Will, of
New York, 15 Oct.—20 Dec. 1703, did not
name her, but gave all est. in N. H. or N. Y.
to loving br. Robert of O. R. and to his
youngest son or youngest dau.

5 **ROBERT**(4), Exeter, m. 1st 'Elnell Pratly' of Ex., 25 Sept. 1674 by one rec., 1673
by ano., that it was 30 May 1676 when he and
w. 'Hellena' (also Eleanor) were ord. into
ct. (Essex Q. Ct. Rec. vi: 142, 213.) See also
Rebecca Hilton(19), likely one w. of (5) or
(4). His 1674 gr., 300 a., was laid out in
1698 bounding N.W. on Piscasset River.
O. A. in Nov. 1677. Gr.j. 1697. Of Oyster
River in 1703. Lists (381, or his fa.), 383, 387,
52, 57. Ag. ±67, he depos. in June 1713 that
50 yrs. ago he went back and forth over
Lamprill River bridge. Of Exeter, adm. gr.
to s. William 23 July 1718; appraisers Edward Hall and James Burley; inv. £413. 8. 6.
Wid. Mary twice named in 1740, and mention of 'widow Elizabeth Burley's dower
in est. of Robert Smart' is not understood
(suit of the s. Robert ag. John Perkins, sr.
and jr. in 1741). Ch., order in probate rec.
1740: **William,** Ex., oldest son, m. Martha
Veasey(2) who d. bef. Aug. 1751. Adm. on
his est. gr. to br. Robert 17 Jan. 1723-4.
Only ch. Elizabeth, m. 1st by 1740 Thomas
Tufts, m. 2d by 1747 Anthony Pickering.
**Robert,** Newmarket 1747; wife Ann. **John,**
Durham 1747. **Joseph,** b. 8 Dec. 1700, sold
uncle John's est. to br. Robert in 1730; Durham 1747. Wife Mary in 1735; wid. Abigail
and dau. renounc. adm. to his br. Robert in
Feb. 1754. One of the Smarts m. Mary Marston (Caleb). **Richard,** Exeter, Epping, m. by
1727 Ruth Norris. **Benjamin,** Durham 1747;

m. Mary Hilton (see Jonathan 19). **Charles,** Durham 1747; m. Mary. **Ann,** b. ±1676, m. John Barber(4). **Rebecca,** m. John Perkins (24). **Eleanor,** m. 1st Benjamin Fox(1), m. 2d Arnold Brick. **Eunice,** m. Ephraim Folsom(2 jr.). **Elizabeth,** m. Richard Glidden (2 jr.). **Mary,** m. Joseph Glidden(2).

**SMITH,** Smyth, the No. 1 name in N. E. See also Gowen, sometimes Gowen alias Smith or just Smith; Bland; Clark.

1 **ALEXANDER,** had Saco gr. 1657; Scarboro 1660-1661. List 233.

2 **ARCHIBALD,** Durham, List 369. See Small(2).

3 **ARRIS,** named as an early Jamestown abuttor in Ruth (Johnson 12) Barry's Eastern Claim.

4 **BARTHOLOMEW,** Dover 1640, had a lot on West side of Back River 1642. Lists 351ab, 352. In Mar. 1647-8 he and Daniel Paul bought in Eliot.

5 **CHRISTOPHER,** coaster, at the Eastward in 1671. List 14. Sued by William Waldron, admr. of Oliver Duncombe, in Suff. ct. 1672. See also George Bucknell(1) who deposed in 1673 that C. lodged at his house.

6 **DANIEL,** probably several. One had a Falm. gr. next Fort Loyal in 1680, List 225a. In 1682 D. S. was sued for debt by Thomas Holmes in Wells ct. and wit. a Plaisted family agreement. D. S. had York gr. 1698, m. Anne Moore(25) 12 Mar. 1697-8, wit. Joan Young's will in 1698 and was a York abuttor in 1722 (Y. D. 11: 1). Daniel, wife and ch. taken captive at Winter Harbor or Saco 1703, List 39.

7 **EDWARD,** Mr., Exeter, first seen 9 Mar. 1666-7 as a wit. King to Thing, m. 13 Jan. 1668-9 Mary Hall(22) and had a town gr. in 1670. Presum. he or (40), or both, related to Gilmans. Bondsman for Ralph Hall 1670; ag. ±27 in Mar. 1671-2 when he and Edw. Gilman, ±23, test. ab. John and Sarah (Wadleigh) Young's wedding, to which they were invited; constable 1672, fined in 1673 for not clearing his accts.; on committee ab. the town debts in 1679; selectman 1679, 1680; complained of as an associate of Gove, but not indicted; (?Sagamore Creek j. 1684, 1685); to record births 1686. Engaged in logging and sued for debt at various times (see Essex Q. Ct. Records). Wife Mary joined him in a deed 1680; he last seen 27 June 1689 (Y. D. 6: 148). Lists 376b, 377, 383, 49, 52. Land formerly Mr. Edward Smith's, decd., ment. in 1706.

8 **ELIZABETH,** ±17, testified in 1655 with Robert Pattishall ±40. Appar. too old to be Major Waldron's reputed niece and w. of Joseph Hall(13).

9 **GEORGE,** Mr., Exeter, Dover, Lists 372, 353, 354ab, 355a, not seen aft. 17 Nov.

1653 when Recorder of Courts, and no rec. of a family. See History of Durham ii: 329-330, answering 'No' to question asked there, if identical with George of Ipswich. Com. t.e.s.c., Associate for Dover Court, Clerk of the Writs. In 1650 he sold Kit. land, acting for John Newgrove. See also Phillips(7), Webb(1).

10 **GEORGE,** weaver, m. Abigail Kirke(2) at Ipsw. 14 Mar. 1704-5. His br. Joseph m. Elizabeth Moses(1). George was taxed at Portsm. (and ho.) 1708; he and w. liv. 1734 in Kittery where at least one ch. Charles liv. (Y. D. 16: 189; 17: 71).

11 **HENRY,** List 74.

12 **HENRY,** Hampton, living with Mr. Cotton, was to clean the meet.-ho. and ring the bell, 1658.

13 **HENRY** (also Smeath), shipwright, Little Harbor 1683 when sued by Thomas Pickering; surety Wm. Williams. He had boarded at John Jackson's at the Bank. Saco 1685, see Cawley(3). Of Saco 1689, when he bot oak plank from Thomas Doughty, and was sued in Suff. ct. for breach of contract dated 18 Mar. 1688-9. Called sometime of Saco in suit of Doughty (then of Malden) ag. him in 1690, when ¼ the brigantine -Industry- was attached and summons left at ho. of wid. Henley, Boston; see John Jeffrey(5) and Wm. Scadlock(3 jr.), witnesses. List 319 presum. his. In Aug. 1694 a writ was served on him in Portsm. bef. John Ballard(2). One H. traveled from Wells to Saco on the Lord's Day 6 July 1701; one was k. at Saco in 1703, List 39.

14 **HENRY,** chirurgeon, late of New Dartmouth, test. 31 Oct. 1688, ag. ±44, that 5 Sept. last he was in his own ho. at New Dartmouth when Ind. took himself, wife and son.

15 **JAMES,** Maquoit 1641, among those accused of taking T. Purchase's furs (Lechford, p. 402). Nequasset 1648 and bot his land that yr. (2 Me. Hist. Soc. Col. 1: 268); in May 1660 owned near the land then gr. by Robin Hood to Robert Gutch, in Kennebec River over ag. Tuessic (Y. D. 2: 32); d. by 1667. Recorder of Deeds 1654 (Y. D. 35: 52). Christopher Lawson dep. in 1664 that when he bot from James Cole for Clarke & Lake in 1658, J. S. and his w. were much displeased that he had bot over their heads by which they might be turned out of doors. Lists 11, 181 (and w.). Y. D. 20: 22 recites that his wid. (Elizabeth) m. 2d Richard Hammond(4), who had his lands, and there were two sons liv. with them as boys: James, later of Salem, -Harediah-, later of Beverly. In Smith v. Hutchinson 1738, Deborah Burnett and Joanna Williams depos. that they knew the ch. of James and Elizabeth, naming five: **Elizabeth. James. Samuel,** k. by

Ind. 14 Aug. 1676 when the Hammond ho. was attacked and his step-fa. killed (Doc. Hist. 6: 149), but List 185 shows him as liv. **Mary**, taken captive with mo. in 1676. **Hazadiah**, m. 27 May 1684 Hannah Grover(2), d. in Bev. 21 June 1735; ch. See also Mills(14). Widow Elizabeth Hammond m. 3d Capt. John Rowden and ret. to her Me. home.

16 **JAMES**, and James Gooch apprais. the Wadleigh est. 1671 (Me. P. & Ct. Rec. ii: 246). List 248b.

17 **JAMES**, tailor, Oyster River 1662, ±30 in 1673. See also (26). In 1663 he was set by the heels for keeping his hat on in ct. aft. admonition; fined next day for abs. from meeting several months and going once to a Quaker meeting. In 1669 bot from Brown and Ryall on south side of Oyster River above the falls. Tav. lic. 1686. Lists 363bc, 365, 366, 357c, 359a, 367a, 47, 49, 52, 57, 94. He d. of a 'surfeit,' running to assist Capt. Floyd in an Ind. fight at Wheelwright Pond, 6 July 1690. Widow Sarah (Davis 20) and two sons were k. by Ind. 18 July 1694. Son John adm. his est., filing bond 26 Mar. 1714. Ch: **John**, Oyster River, m. Elizabeth Buss (1). Adm. 27 Mar. 1729 to s. John, and again 25 July 1739 to s. James. Widow Elizabeth liv. to be old. Ch: John (his wid. Hannah m. Charles Facey 1739), James, Joseph, Elizabeth, Mary, Hannah. **James** and **Samuel**, k. by Ind. **Sarah**, b. 31 Oct. 1679, m. 26 June 1702 Joshua Harding; of Eastham 1729. **Mary**, b. 24 May 1685, m. 1st 13 Nov. 1707 Thomas Freeman of Cape Cod who d. 22 Mar. 1717-8; m. 2d Hezekiah Doane. In 1729 Hardings and Doanes q.c. to their br. John Smith.

18 **JAMES**, Berwick 1668 when bounds between Miles Piles, now J. S., and Richard Tozier, mentioned. Wife Martha Mills (12). Lists 298, 28, 33. See Newberry. Will, 10 Aug.—14 Sept. 1687, names w. Martha (m. 2d Christopher Grant 1), two sons under 21, two daus. under 18, cous. Peter Knapp. Ch: **James**, blacksmith, m. (ct. July 1693) Martha Bragdon(7). Called both 'of Salmon Falls in Kit.' and 'late of Kit., now of York' 24 May 1703 when he rech. farms with Joseph Pray of York and sold him his fa.'s homestead. Appar. of Scarb. 1727-8 when w. Martha was liv. In July 1738, ag. 63, he deposed ab. going from Berwick to York. Ch. rec. at Y. 1694-1714: Joseph (m. Thankful Smith; see 42); James, 'Jr.' of York 1722, Y. D. 11: 51; John, unrec. and poss. oldest ch., see Y. D. 9: 100 (m. 1 July 1724 Judith Thompson); Daniel; Mary (m. Shubael Hinckley; 1 ch. rec. at York); Martha (m. Tobias Ham 5); Ebenezer. **Mary. Elizabeth. John**, b. 26 July 1685, taken captive with mo. and bp. in Montreal 3 May 1693, depos. in July 1760, ±76, that he was ap-

prenticed to Col. Ichabod Plaisted, m. Elizabeth Heard(8) and liv. in Berwick. Lists 296, 298. See 'Old Kittery,' p. 735, for 11 ch. 1708-1732. 'Family Records of Berwick' (typed) adds a dau. Mary bp. 7 Aug. 1737.

19 **JAMES**(15), blacksmith, m. Margaret, dau. of Recorder Walter Phillips(21) and had a ho. near his at Damariscotta bef. the first war (Y. D. 18: 2). Salem 1676. Dead in 1704 (one J. died in Salem 1702-3), leaving wid. Margaret and ch: **Samuel. Elizabeth. James. Sarah. John. Walter. Benjamin. Hazadiah. Jacob**. See Perley's Hist. of Salem, 3: 104. In 1735 Solomon Martin of Andover q.c. ¼ Smith's or Hammond's farm on East side of Kennebec, ¼ of Dennis's, ¼ of Lightning's farm, ¼ of Sagatock Island, all bot from heirs: Samuel Smith of Andover, Walter and James S. of Salem, Benj. Pope of Salem and w. (Sarah Smith), Stephen Ford of Charlestown and w., Thomas Pitman of Manchester and w. (Sarah Dennis), John S. of Providence, -Hezekiah-S. of Killingly, Jacob S. of Preston.

20 **JAMES**, Wells. See Gowen(4).

21 **CAPT. JOHN**. List 7.

22 **JOHN**, Damariscove, List 8.

23 **JOHN**, Mr., carpenter, Saco, connected with the Williams(26) est. and taxed in Sept. 1636, Gr.j. and tr.j. 1640. In 1642 R. Vines deeded him 100 a. on south side of Saco River, gave him two more deeds 1642, 1643, and Mr. T. Gorges deeded him an island and 100 a. of mainland at Cape Porpus in 1643. 'Mr. Smith our magistrate for Saco' (Letter of Vines 29 Jan. 1643-4). In 1650 he sold his plantation where he liv. to Nicholas Bully, reserving one room for two yrs. Saco 1656. The ho. of Mr. Smyth ment. in Abraham Josselyn's deed 11 June 1660; of Dunstan 2 Sept. 1661 he sold houses, lands, etc. (place not stated) to James Gibbins. Of Saco on Mar. 1662, his ho. near Mr. Gibbins's; a freeman there 1663. Lists 235(2), 242, 243ab, 244cf, 245, 263. No rec. of an early w. (see Clark 7). Ab. 1673-4 he named as heir a boy, George Page(3 jr.), whose fa. and aunt Mary(7) had liv. with him (depos. of Arthur Hughes, John Bonython and John Harmon 1694; York ct. 6: 111); Page took adm. 5 Apr. 1694.

24 **JOHN** (Sr.), Cape Neddick, b. ±1612, may be assumed that runaway serv. of John Alcock's, ord. whipped and ret. from Saco to Agamenticus 9 Sept. 1640, and surely was that John liv. at Casco Mill in June 1646 with w. Joan who had as a dowry a York ho. and land. This prop. they then sold to Richard Bulgar for Mr. Henry Walton of Portsmouth, R. I., whom Smith owed (himself or for a former husb. of Joan's?). Casco Mill was evid. Yarmouth, as Wm. Royal and Richard Carter wit. deed. In 1685, J. S.,

±73, depos. that he was a marshal under Cleeve ±40 yrs. bef. York grants 1654, 1668(2), attended ct. as 'the drummer' in 1655, in 1657 had deed from br.-in-law Edward Wanton (how so related unkn.) of Cape Neddick land already in his poss. several yrs., and by Wanton's depos. 1716 took W.'s cattle to keep for halves. O. A. 22 Mar. 1679-80. He led an active life up to Mar. 1685-6 (Y. D. 8: 4) and was the 'executioner,' whipping York people 1684-5; see Me. P. & Ct. Rec. i, ii; Hist. of York, ii: 23, 27. Lists 22, 24, 25, 33 (or his son's). See also Clark(8), Hannah Mains(3), Phillips(19), Bugg, Lee(8). His w. Joan or Joanna was liv. 23 Oct. 1674 when they deeded the home place to s. John with a life reservation. He m. 2d betw. 13 Sept. 1677—26 Mar. 1679 Mary (Farrow) Clark(8) and d. bef. 3 Feb. 1687-8 when wid. Mary and his only kn. s. John signed an agreement. Kn. also are a dau. who m. James Jackson(7) and Sarah (ag. 70 in Jan. 1715-6, when she depos. ab. her fa.'s home place 48 yrs. ago) who m. Robert Junkins. See also (39).

25 JOHN, Hampton briefly ±1640, came from Watertown and went to Martha's Vineyard. Lists 391a, 393a may belong to him and w., or to (60). Will, 14 Feb. 1670 (d. bef. 9 June 1674), names w. Deborah (Parkhurst) and ch: John and Samuel, given land on Nantucket and to pay their sisters. Deborah, m. Nathaniel Batchelder(3). Abigail. Philip, given land at 'Martin's Vineyard,' a Hampton wit. 1668, but liv. on M. V., as did Samuel and Abigail. See Dalton(4); N. E. Reg. 68: 370.

26 JOHN, Oyster River 1662. His connec. with Matthew Williams and various circumstances indicate that he, (17), (36), and Rebecca (Smith) Adams(3) were bros. and sister. In 1667, he, (17) and M. Williams were fined for nonappearance at the Bussy inquest. In 1668 fined for stealing from pocket of Mr. Deering's servant, James Leavitt, and the same yr. was at the Deering ho. with Wm. Pitman and w. Ann; Mr. John Woodman then paid his fine. In 1672 the ho. of Williams and J. S. was attached, and summons left 'at the house.' In 1673 the two were sued by Philip Follett, assignee of John Cutts; both were out of the jurisdiction when this came up again in 1674; Richard Nason was bondsman and the 'usual place of abode of M. W. and J. S.' was mentioned. Not ident. later; no rec. of family. Lists 363bc, 365, 366, 357d.

27 LT. *JOHN(25), cooper, Hampton (±57 in Aug. 1700), m. 26 Feb. 1666-7 Huldah (not Hannah) Hussey(1) and in 1674 deeded to her br. Stephen the Nant. land willed him by his fa. Selectman 1674-5, 1678-9, 1687, 1696 (Lt.). Rep. 1684, 1692 (Lt.), 1694,

1695, 1697-1699. On military committee 1691 (see Jonathan Moulton 5). Lists 376a, 392b, 396, 49, 55b, 59, 64. Wife, List 394. Lists 52, 54, 57, 62, may belong to (29). Will, 8 Apr. 1709—8 Mar. 1709-10. Widow Huldah d. ±1740. Ch: Theodate, b. 16 Dec. 1667, d. 2 Oct. 1675. Capt. John, b. 21 Aug. 1669, m. 11 Apr. 1695 Abigail Shaw(2); d. 24 July 1752; 9 ch. His fa. willed him the 40 a. where his ho. stood at Brambly Hill. Deborah, b. 7 Apr., d. 11 Aug. 1671. Samuel, b. 31 Oct. 1672, List 399a, m. 1st 8 Dec. 1696 Ruth Haskell who d. 20 Jan. 1700, m. 2d 22 Jan. 1706-7 Elizabeth, wid. of Saml. Pease (2); liv. at North Hill Plain. Will, 22 (d. 23) Nov. 1738 names w. Elizabeth, sons Samuel, Stephen, gr.s. William, br. Elisha. Stephen, b. 23 Apr. 1674, d. 22 July 1692. Huldah, b. 6 July 1676, m. Thomas Dearborn (3). Christopher, b. 12 Dec. 1677, List 399a, d. 18 Aug. 1701. Deborah, b. 12 Apr. 1679, d. 21 Feb. 1682. Philip, had the homestead and to care for mo.; d. s.p. 14 Jan. 1745. Lt. Elisha, farmer, m. Abigail Marston(6); d. s.p. Feb. 1759, naming in will w. Abigail and Elisha Marston (Jonathan). Abigail, b. 19 May 1687, m. Lt. Jonathan Marston(6). Mary, m. Jeremiah Marston(2). After br. Philip died, she sued Elisha Smith and Elisha Marston for ⅛ and 1/6 of ⅛ of the homestead that Capt. Christopher Hussey got with wid. Mingay (SJC 27874).

28 JOHN (Jr.), (24), York, Gloucester, had grants 1667 (next his fa.), 1674, and deeds from his fa. in 1674 and 1684. Abs. from meeting 1673 when his fa. promised his amendment. Lists 33 (or fa.), 279. See also Weare(1), York Deeds, Me. P. & Ct. Records, i, ii. Of York 3 Feb. 1687-8 (Y. D. 4: 78); of Gloucester 4 Mar. 1709-10 when he sold the York homestead, 100½ a., to the Webbers (10), and of. G. in 1713 when James Jackson's 1674 gr. in Y. was laid out to him. His w. is not identified. Four ch. are kn. by their q.c. deed of 19 Feb. 1727-8 (Y. D. 12: 244) when they called their fa. 'late of York, decd.' (one J. wit. Samuel Webber's will there 1716): Elisha of Boxford. Elizabeth, Lull of Ipsw. (m. Thomas Lull, sr., 29 Oct. 1705). Hannah of Ipsw. Patience Curtin of Ipsw. (int. with Robert Curtin 14 Apr. 1716). As the fa. called himself 'Sr.' in 1710, there may also have been a s. John.

29 JOHN(52), tailor, Hampton, depos. in May 1695 that he liv. a servant many yrs. with Mr. Timothy Dalton. Dow gives him a 1st w. Rebecca Adams, m. 14 May, d. 15 Sept. 1675. He m. 23 Aug. 1676 Rebecca Marston(1). Selectman 1692. Jury 1694. On 24 May 1694 adm. to Portsmouth No. Ch., where 7 ch. bp. 1694-1696. Lists 376a, 392b, 396, 331c, 49, and see uncertain Lists under (27). Ch: David, b. 8 Mar. 1678, not

bp. with others. One D. m. 3 Nov. 1720 Margaret Goss(3); Kingston 1722; will, of Brentwood, ancient, 1747-1758; w. Margaret, s. Joseph, 6 daus. **Israel**, tailor, Hampton, b. 12 Apr. 1680 (List 399a), d. 20 Mar. 1706. Adm. to wid. Sarah (Libby 1, m. 18 June 1701). Ch: Mary, David of Rye, Sarah. **Susanna**, b. 14 Oct. 1682, m. Benjamin James (1). Capt. **Jabez**, Esq., m. 21 May 1718 Rachel Moulton(8); d. 28 May 1761. Ch: Lydia (m. Moulton), Hannah (m. Clough), John. **Rebecca**, b. 25 June 1687, m. John Moulton(8). **Meribah**, m. Seth Fogg(6 jr.) and **Hannah**, both bp. with Sarah 24 May 1696. **Sarah**, b. 28 Aug. 1695, prob. m. Jacob Moulton(8).

30 **JOHN**, Falmouth (see Mansfield 5), sent pet. to Andros 18 Jan. 1687; he was and had been for many yrs. past in poss. of 50 a. at Back Cove. In 1734 John Davis(29) deposed that J. S., decd., was a settler under Danforth several yrs. Lists 34, 227. See also (51).

31 **JOHN**, a red coat belonging to Pemaquid fort 1689 (Doc. Hist. 5: 37).

32 **CAPT. JOHN**(36), Oyster River, m. 17 June 1694 Susannah Chesley(5) who was adm. to O. R. Ch. 17 Mar. 1722-3 as Lt. J. S.'s wife. Selectman, Capt. of military company, large landowner. Lists 368ab, 369. Will, 10 Mar. 1739-40 (d. 14 May 1744), names wife (d. 24 Mar. 1746, aged 68), ch. and br. Samuel. Ch: Capt. **John**, b. 18 May 1695, m. 1 June 1727 Mary Jones(40); d. s.p. 17 Dec. 1747. Lists 386b, 369. **Elizabeth**, b. 1 Aug. 1697, m. Robert Burnham(2). Col. **Joseph**, Esq., Newmarket, b. 7 Sept. 1701, d. 29 Mar. 1781, m. 20 Nov. 1729 Sarah Glidden (Andrew 3), who d. 25 Nov. 1785. Ch. **Hannah**, b. 30 Sept. 1703, m. 24 Nov. 1726 as 2d w. Tristram Coffin(6 jr.). **Samuel**, b. 6 Feb. 1706-7, List 369, m. 17 Mar. 1733 Margaret Lindall; ch. Capt. **Benjamin**, Lubberland, b. 22 Mar. 1709-10, d. 1791, had ch. by three wives, Jemima Hall, Anna Veazie, Sarah Clark. List 369. Deac. **Ebenezer**, Lubberland, b. 6 June 1712, d. 25 June 1764, m. Margaret Weeks (see 2) who is said to have m. 2d Hon. George Frost of Newcastle. Ch. **Winthrop**, b. 30 May 1714, d. 1728.

33 **CAPT. JOHN**, surveyor of the town (Kittery) 1703, Y. D. 7: 227.

34 **JONATHAN**(52), brickmaker, Exeter. Of Hampton, he bot 15 a. and a ho. at Ex. from Samuel Leavitt in June 1667, and m. at Haverhill 25 Jan. 1669 Mehitabel Holdridge (Wm.). He prob. had his trade from John Wooden from whom he bot land at North Plain, Hampt., in 1671. Constable 1699. Lists 383, 376b (1698, 1702), 52, 67. In 1706 he deeded to s. Israel flats in Hampt. which he had of his fa., the flats never to be sold, but to go to I.'s heirs. Aged ±68 in Aug. 1708, ±72 in 1712. Ch: **Israel**, Exeter, Stratham, b. 16 Jan. 1670-1, ±40 in Mar. 1710-1. Lists 67, 388. Adm. 7 Sept. 1723 to s. Reuben, wid. Hannah renounc. in favor of 'my eldest son,' Mehitable Lawrence a wit. Ch. by deed 1736: Israel, Reuben, John, Mehitabel, all of Ex., Jacob of Kingston, Hannah (w. of Joseph Goss of Ex.), Mary (w. of Abraham Stockbridge of Strath.), Deborah (w. of Robert Wadleigh). **Jacob**, b. 10 Aug. 1673, Kittery 1698-1716, ag. ±38 in Mar. 1710-1. Lists 67, 298, 376b (1702). Will, of Exeter, 1741—1744, names w. Priscilla (Rogers 9, m. bef. 12 Jan. 1701-2), 6 ch., gr.ch., and Mehitable Clifford. **Ithiel**, depos. in June 1714, ±38, ab. Quamscot in 1703. Lists 376b (1702), 388. 'Of Hampt.' when adm. gr. to wid. Mary 5 Mar. 1717-8; 'of Exeter' by inventory. She was liv. in 1732 when sons Josiah (as admr.) and Solomon (w. Abigail 1725) sold; other ch. inc. Ithiel of Brentwood, Joseph of Stratham, William and Abigail (w. of Benoni Gordon) of Exeter. **Abigail**, b. 22 June 1678, m. Moses Blake(5). **Joseph**, b. 7 Feb. 1680, List 376b (1702); see will of (37). **Leah**, b. 7 Apr. 1683. **Mehitabel**, b. 14 Aug. 1685, m. Zachariah Clifford (4). **Oliver**, had deed from fa. 1715, m. 6 June 1717 Ruth Blake(5), d. 1757-1760, leaving wid. Jane and ch. (one O. m. Jean Yeuren at Kingston in 1750). See also Bell's Exeter for one Jonathan who m. Mary Ames in 1714 (2 ch.), Bridget Keniston(3) in 1719 (12 ch.) and N. H. Probate 3: 62, for his will 1741—1742; yet in 1741 Bridget, form. wid. of Isaac Clifford, was now w. of Jonathan S.

35 **JOSEPH**, List 268b.

36 **JOSEPH**, Oyster River, at Wm. Pitman's in June 1661, ±22; ±61 in Mar. 1703-4; depos. 1719 ab. Valentine Hill 63 yrs. ago. See also (26). He wit. a deed in 1657, bot 40 a. from Matthew Williams in 1660, and was gr. a small piece of waste land for a ho.-lot betw. Matthew and Wm. Williams, jr. Jury 1669; constable 1670; selectman 1699, (†1700 or 1701). His ho. was a garrison. Lists 353, 358b, 359a, 363abc, 365, †380, 49, 52, 66. He owed Nicholas Pearl for shoes 1690-1695 for his own fam. and for Hance's ch., and also for Godfrey, Francis Drew, Stephen Jenkins, Wm. Hill, Henry Marsh, Henry Rines, Thomas Ash. Mary Tasket owed him in 1697. Wife Elizabeth Bickford(12) d. 25 May 1727. See Matthews (12). His will, 7 July 1727—26 Dec. 1728, names gr.ch. Sobriety Crommett and Patience Tash, and ch: **John**, b. 9 Jan. 1669-70. **Mary**, m. 1st James Thomas(6), m. 2d Lt. Samuel Page(2). **Elizabeth**, m. 1st Capt. Samuel Chesley(4), m. 2d Amos Pinkham (1). Col. ‡*Samuel, b. 16 June 1687, selectman, Rep., Councillor, bot in Scarboro 1720

(see Y. D. 15: 79); m. 16 Feb. 1709-10 Hannah Burnham(2) who d. 14 July 1750. Will, 16 May 1755 (d. 2 May 1760). Lists 368b, 369. 12 ch. **Joseph**, liv. 1694 (gr. of 40 a.), not in will. One Joseph, Jr., List 358b.

37 **COL. ‡*JOSEPH**(52), Hampton, liv. on fa.'s homestead. Selectman, moderator, Rep., Justice Superior Ct., Chief Justice, Councillor, Judge of Probate, Province Treasurer, Capt., Major many yrs., Col. 1716-7. Lists 392b, 395, 396, 399a, 49, 52, 55a, 66, 68. See also Deborah Godfrey(4). He m. bef. 1694 Dorothy Cotton(4) who d. 20 Dec. 1706, m. 2d 17 Apr. 1707 Mary Moore(26) who d. 15 Oct. 1708, m. 3d 16 Feb. 1708-9 Mrs. Elizabeth Marshall (see 2). Will, 28 Oct. 1712 (d. s.p. 15 Nov. 1717), names w. Elizabeth (m. next Ephraim Jackson 20); cousins Jabez, Jacob and Joseph Smith (the last at Dedham); three Page cousins, giving homestead to Saml. Page's eldest son; Mary Moore (Wm. 26 jr.); Nathaniel Locke (his oldest feather bed or 40 shillings).

38 **JOSEPH**, York, m. Hannah, wid. of Timothy Hodsdon(9) and also appar. wid. of Nicholas Smith(42). Town gr. 1701; j. 1703. He d. bef. 4 Dec. 1713 (Y. D. 8: 247). List 279. In 1747 heirs sold land gr. to him in 1700-1. Ch: **Joseph**, mariner, b. 11 Feb. 1699-1700, liv. 1748. **Benjamin**, b. 24 Apr. 1702, lost at sea with Elisha Allen 1 June 1724. Widow Judith (Preble 4) m. 2d Samuel Goodwin and was again a wid. in 1748 when an unmar. dau. Mary Smith was liv. **Hannah**, b. 17 Feb. 1705-6, m. Benj. Thompson (2).

39 **LYDIA**, York 1684, see Joseph Preble(6).

40 **NICHOLAS**, Exeter, b. ±1629, bot a ho. from James Wall in Sept. 1658, John and Elizabeth Gilman wit. Selectman 1658; Comr. 1659; gr.j. 1659, 1670; j. 1665; tav. lic. 1659; constable 1668, 1669. In 1668 sued Nicholas Lisson for mowing his flats; in Apr. 1669, ±40, depos. that he offered Abraham Collins what corn he wanted on Lisson's acct.; Richard Smith depos. in same case. Lists 377, 379. See also (7). His 1st wife unkn.; he m. 2d aft. Oct. 1665 Mary (Satchell) Dale, and d. 22 June 1673, adm. to wid. 14 Oct. foll. Her 3d husb., Charles Runlett(1) ack. a judgment for her to Mr. John Cutts who in 1677 sold part of the homestead to Nathl. Folsom. Ch: **Nathaniel**, b. 9 June 1660, taken as a child by Dea. Wm. Godfrey, in 1677 ord. to remain with John Marion till 21. He depos. at Goody Fuller's trial 14 July 1680. Drowned, inquest, List 397b. **Nicholas**, b. 3 Sept. 1661. **Ann**, b. 8 Feb. 1663. In 1672 Goody Cole, by report, appeared in various forms and enticed a girl (A. S.) to live with her. Of Hampt., she m. Israel Clifford(2). Appar. by 2d w: **Theo-**

**philus**, Esq., b. 14 Feb. 1667, m. Mary Stanyan(3) who was liv. 13 Feb. 1717-8. Exeter constable 1694, 1695. Lists 57, 67, 376b (1698, 1706), 377. Ex. selectman 1699, 1706, 1711-2, 1717-8 (he or son 1727 and later). Will, 14—23 Mar. 1736-7; ch: Theophilus (m. Sarah Gilman), Mary Tilton, Dorothy Sanborn, Elizabeth Gilman, Lydia Wadleigh, dec. (her husb. and 2 ch.). **Hannah**, b. 10 May 1673, m. 1st Thomas Odell, m. 2d Ebenezer Folsom(9).

41 **NICHOLAS**(40), Exeter, m. Mary Gordon(1), see Lissen(2). Jury 1699. Lists 52, 62, 67. Will, 13 Feb.—6 June 1716, names w. Mary, 13 ch.; w. and son Richard execs. She d. 1737 (SJC 10940). Ch: **Richard**, tanner, Ex., first taxed 1714, m. Mary Mattoon (2) who d. 21 Jan. 1772; he was bur. 22 Apr. 1765. 7 ch. **Nathaniel**, b. 15 Sept. 1695. Will, of Kingston, 12 June 1753 (d. 6 Aug. 1757), names w. Elizabeth (see Stone 3), 5 of 7 rec. ch., gr.s. Nathl. Weare. Capt. **Daniel** (List 388 and Y. D. 9: 230); m. in Biddef. 1 Jan. 1719 Rebecca Emery(3) who m. 2d 28 May 1755 Nathl. Ladd of Falm. 8 ch. rec. **Nicholas**, taxed 1718, m. 1st Judith Gilman(15). Exeter 1749. Will, of Brentwood 1753—1758, names 2d w. Susannah (Scribner 2) Mudgett, 9 ch. **Benjamin**, Exeter, b. 1 Feb. 1702, adm. 28 Dec. 1756 to wid. Mehitable; 9 ch. **Edward**, Biddef. 1749; see Stackpole Gen. (2d edit., 1920), p. 88. Capt. **John**, Biddef. 1749, Dayton, liv. 1789. Wife Sarah Stackpole; 4 or more ch. **Ann**, was Clarke in 1716 and the only mar. dau. **Mary**, m. Daniel Lovering; Ex. 1749. **Elizabeth**, m. Thomas Mudgett of Brentwood; wid. in Ex. 1749. **Patience**, m. 9 Feb. 1729 Joseph Eastman of Kingston. **Comfort**, m. Wm. Lovering; Kingston 1749. **Abigail**, w. of Richard Berry of Biddef. 1749.

42 **NICHOLAS**, an Indian captive 1691, was at Fort Wm. Henry in N. Y. with Matthew Paulling 10 Nov. 1694; both said they had been taken in 'Province of Wells.' Poss. the same N., husbandman, York, who m. there 25 June 1695 Hannah Hodsdon and was k. (Trooper Smith) with young Simpson coming post from Wells (List 96, July 4, 1697). Adm. to wid. Hannah 10 Aug. 1697, Matthew Austin bondsman. If as appears, she was 1st the wid. of Timothy Hodsdon(9), then she m. 3d Joseph Smith(38). Poss. fa. of (43) by an earlier w.; by w. Hannah, cert. one **child**. Thankful, dau. of one Nicholas, m. Joseph Smith (James 18 jr.) by 1719.

43 **NICHOLAS**, wounded by Ind. when James Ferguson and w. (members of Berwick Ch.) were killed; he escaped and was cured (List 96, Sept. 28, 1707). See also (42) but Dr. Banks suggested he might have been a Gowen.

44 **OBA.**, a navy boy 1657 (Y. D. 1: 60-1).

45 **QUINCH** (or Quince), Portsmouth 1658-9, sued Edward Hayes(2) in Me. ct., July 1659, for striking him and calling him a rogue and Hannah Battle (Beedle?) a whore. Lists 323, 326a, 78.

46 **RALPH**, tailor, Boston, and w. Huldah, sold 2000 a. at Muscongus 1733 (Y. D. 16: 178).

47 **REUBEN** (Smith alias Shaw), son of Ruth Shaw(2), whose br. Edward deeded to him in 1726.

48 **RICHARD**, wit. delivery of the Cammock patent 23 May 1633 (Y. D. 2: 85).

49 **RICHARD**, Ipswich, fa.-in-law of Edw. Gilman, jr., 1651, List 378. See also Richard ment. under (40).

50 **RICHARD**, Kittery, servant of Mrs. Mitchell 1661 (Essex Q. Ct. Rec. 3: 212); ag. 27 in 1661, ±30 in 1664; sued by Roger Kelly 1667 and by Abraham Collins as atty. for Mr. Francis Morgan in 1669. Richard, York, drunk in 1678 when Mr. Dummer would pay his fine.

51 **RICHARD**, Falmouth (see 30), m. Mary Davis(9), remov. with her fam. to the Kennebec, on the western side of the Great Island over ag. Newtown, ±1687, and joined them in a pet. to Andros asking for 100 a. each. List 189. Marblehead 1689. Widow m. 2d Samuel Wood. Ch. rec. at Gloucester: **Thomas**, b. at Falmouth 26 Feb. 1684. **Richard**, b. at Marblehead 15 July 1689, evid. the R. at Biddeford 1723-1754+ (w. Mary liv. Oct. 1752), who was gr.s. of one Davis of Falm. In 1733 he and w. Mary were arrested for complicity in counterfeiting, when Richard Stimson and Saml. Smith(56) were their bondsmen. See also Morgan(7); Y. D. 14: 49; 20: 222; 26: 224; 30: 382; N. E. Reg. 71: 128.

52 **ROBERT**, tailor, Exeter 1639, Hampton by 1654, ±61 in Oct. 1673, ±83 in May 1695 when he depos. ab. the Willix daus. (Reg. 69: 361). Com.t.e.s.c. 1643. O. A. 17 Apr. 1644. Gr.j. 1650, 1666, 1669, 1670, 1674; j. 1651, 1653, 1664-5. One of three magistrates for Ex. named by Mass. in 1652. Hampt. selectman 1654, 1660; constable 1671. Freed from ordinary training 1673. Gr.j. 1683. Lists 373, 374ac(2), 375b, 376ab (1645), 378, 392b, 393b, 394, 396, 398, 43, 49, 52. See also Leader(3), Reed(9). Wife Susanna k. by lightning 12 June 1680. His will, 22 Mar. 1699-1700 (d. 30 Aug. 1706), names 5 ch: **John**, willed ½ the land given his fa. by Robert Mason, Esq. **Jonathan**, b. ±1640. **Asahel**, given 40 a. at the new plantation, £4 and ⅕ the cattle. **Joseph**, given ½ of the Mason land. **Meribah** m. Francis Page(2). A decd. son was **Israel** of Boston; adm. 20 May 1676 to fa., who wrote 24 July

1676, agreeing that the est. be divided among his five sons, including s.-in-law Page as one.

53 **SAMUEL**, shipwright, North Yarmouth 1665, ret. to Eng. and m. wid. Eleanor Beale of Badock, co. Cornwall, 26 Jan. 1666 (Banks).

54 **SAMUEL**, 1693, List 98 and prob. List 334a.

55 **SAMUEL**, Saco soldier, Lists 248ab, and poss. List 39, may have been same as (56).

56 **SAMUEL**, Berwick, Dover, Biddeford, depos. with James Frost ab. Upper Kit. men in 1705, m. (ct. Apr. 1708, his 'wife') Margaret Emery(12), and was of Dover 5 Mar. 1714-5 when he bot from his br.-in-law James Emery ½ his Hitchcock lands in Biddeford. List 358d; see also (55). Biddef. 1733 (see 51 jr.). In 1736 Benj. Haley depos. that Richard Stimson addressed him as 'Brother Smith' and they talked about Abel Smith of Boston. Ch. included four bp. at So. Berw. 4 July 1715: **Joel**, mariner, had deed from parents, 1 a., part of Hitchcock lot, 'being the very spot on which the old fort stood.' **Samuel. John. Daniel.** Ano. s. **James** had land from his fa., of Biddef., 1743.

57 **SARAH** (?Berwick), had an illeg. **child** 1671 (Me. P. & Ct. Rec. ii: 221).

58 **SOLOMON**, Kittery (List 289), Kit. wit. 1708 (Y. D. 7: 98), m. at Wells 16 Sept. 1718 Susannah Barton(5) who m. 2d 14 Jan. 1730-1 John Whitney. See Y. D. 15: 24. At least one ch. **Rebecca**, b. at Biddeford 28 Mar. 1723.

58½ **SUSANNA**, ±15 in Feb. 1682-3 (N. H. Files 6: 349), dau. of Daniel and Mary (Grant) S. of Watertown. See Rose(1).

59 **THOMAS**, with Henry Jocelyn wit. for Narias Hawkins 6 July 1639, and in Saco ct. 1640 sued Capt. Cammock and Mr. Jocelyn for a debt which he came over to collect and had been forced to stay to the hindrance of his affairs in Eng. Gr. and tr.j. 1640. The same yr. a bondsman for James Cole and an arbitrator betw. John Richards and Francis Knight. See also Sankey.

60 **THOMAS**, Hampton 1640, prob. the tailor sued in Str. Bank ct. 1642. In 1653 his land abutted that of Edmund Johnson, decd. List 392a; Lists 391a, 393a (Goody), prob. his, but see (25). In 1652 John and Joan Andrews sued one T. S. in Me. ct. for slander and assault.

61 **WILLIAM**, Mr., Black Point, was constable from Cape Elizabeth Eastward in 1636, wit. Capt. Bonython's deed 1642, and was a Cammock appraiser 1643. In Sept. 1651 George Cleeve as agent for Alex. Rigby, Esq., granted to W. S. and Andrew Brown

500 a., see Brown(2); he sold his half to Scottow in 1662 (the orig. deed 'in York Files, 1730, Pickering v. Harmon). Selectman, confirming Foxwell land (SJC 26124). Before 1663 he had sold John Burrage's land to Thomas Elkins. Aged ±69 in July 1664 when he depos. ab. the Burrage est., but was ±72 when he made his will 25 Oct. 1661 (prov. 3 July 1676), giving to br. Richard of Westchester, Eng., 'and two sisters in Eng.; Henry Jocelyn, exec., who stated when he filed the inv. that W. S. d. in Mar. 1675-6, ag. 88. Mr. William was abs. from meet. in 1672. Lists 22, 231, 235.

62 WILLIAM, Dover 1659-1660, frequented taverns with Philip Chesley and Thomas Footman and fought with James Middleton. Lists 356e, 362b.

63 WILLIAM (Me.), given costs ag. Roger Kelly for not prosec. his suit in July 1667, and at same ct. wit. ag. Kelly for selling beer. Note also (50). One Wm. and John Puddington fined in York ct. Sept. 1670 for refusing to testify. Wm. and (24) were pres. when Joseph Tibbetts was apprent. to Matthew Austin.

64 WILLIAM, Scarb. soldier, List 237b.

65 WILLIAM, Oyster River garrison, List 399a.

66 WILLIAM, Kittery, had grants 1699, 1703, m. (fined Oct. 1699) Sarah Gowen (4). Lists 290, 296-298. In 1760 they deeded to s. Elisha of Berwick 20 of 30 a. bot from Peter Wittum. 'Old Kittery,' p. 735, names ch: William (see Parsons). Elizabeth. Lemuel. Anne. James. Elisha. Stephen. Sarah. Margaret.

67 ZACHARIAH, s. of Thomas of (?Watertown), worked at Piscataqua for the Broughtons in 1670. George Broughton ±28 and Jerusha Hitchcock (Richard) ±18, test. in suit of Richard Satle, gdn. and gr.fa. of Z. S.'s bast. ch., ag. the Smith family. Z. had been k. by an Ind. (Middlesex Files 1672).

68 SERGT., slain by Ind. betw. York and Cape Neddick, List 96, 10 Aug. 1707.

69 WIDOW, carried off by Ind. from a Sturgeon Creek garrison 8 June 1693.

70 ——, s. of Lt. Smith of Winnisimmet, k. near York ab. 7 Apr. 1677 (Hubbard).

SNAWSELL (also Snowsell), Thomas, Boston merchant 1669-1671, with w. Judith sold 1 a. on Great Isl. to Christopher Jose. (Was she Caleb Pendleton's wid.?) See also Essex Q. Ct. Rec. 3: 348-9.

SNELL, Devon-Cornwall, a few in co. Suffolk.

1 CHRISTOPHER (±26 in 1672), wit. Edw. West's bond to Philip Chesley, sr., 9 July 1666, and as West's runaway servant was ord. in 1667 to serve him an extra yr.

Great Isl. 1669. In July 1670 he liv. at Thomas Chesley's and in 1672 was at Thomas Beard's with Philip Chesley. This last compl. that Snell went to his ho. whenever he was not there, and the ct. warned him to keep away from Chesley's wife. Stephen Jones was his bondsm. in 1672, Thomas Edgerly in 1673. See also (2) and Sanders(11).

2 ELIZABETH, in Dover ct. 1679, poss. connected with (1) or (8).

3 CAPT. GEORGE, mariner, York, Portsm., sold ⅓ of a Shoals stage in 1663. York gr. 24 July 1663. Portsm. by 1678, taxed 1690, adm. to No. Ch. from Ch. at York 16 Mar. 1693-4. Adm. on Mr. Shubael Dummer's est. was gr. to him 19 Mar. 1691-2 and removed to Mr. Jeremiah Dummer 28 Nov. 1693 (Me. ct.). Portsm. selectman 1692-1694; tr.j. 1694, 1696, foreman; gr.j. 1695, foreman 1698, 1699. Lists 51, 52, 57, 60, 62, 65, 324 (2), 329, 330d, 331c, 332a, 334a, 335a, 336b, 337. The mo. of his ch., Hannah (Alcock 1), was succeeded by three or more widows, Agnes Cowell(2); Richord Hunking(3) aft. Oct. 1681 (List 52) who evid. left and liv. in Boston; and Hannah Hull(8) by June 1698 (List 331c twice). See also Phillips(23). Will, 9 May 1706—Mar. 1707-8 names w. Hannah (liv. 1726), his and her ch., several gr.ch., br. Job Alcock; wife and s. John execs. Ch: Samuel, mariner, Piscataqua, List 314, m. Hannah Hubbard (Hobart) of Hingham, mar. bond in Boston 12 Jan. 1687. Dau. Hannah, b. and d. in Hingham 1689-1690. Of Boston, he d. bef. 28 Oct. 1690; adm. 4 Nov. to wid. Hannah who appar. m. 2d John Doane of Billingsgate. John, b. 1667-8. Mary, m. Hon. John Wheelwright (3). Hannah, m. 1st John Ballard(2), m. 2d Dependence Littlefield(7). Abiel, m. Ebenezer Hill(17).

4 LT. JOHN(3), cooper, Portsm., taxed Jan. 1688-9, in 1692 bot from S. Penhallow land near the great ho. Culler of pipestaves 1692. Jury 1695. Ag. 27 in 1694, ±30 in 1698, 38 in 1705. Aft. his fa. d. he evid. liv. in his ho. Lists 57, 61-64, 330d, 331c, 335a, 336c, 337. He m. Elizabeth Hull (8) who was adm. to No. Ch. 2 Apr. 1696, List 331c. Adm. to her and s.-in-law Wm. Forss 3 Sept. 1718; inv. incl. 'dwelling ho. Alexander lives in.' She was liv. a wid. in 1726. Ch. appear: George, bp. 5 Apr. 1696, named in gr.fa.'s will 1706. Elizabeth, m. William Forss (see Fost, 2 jr.). Jane, named in gr.fa.'s will, m. 1st Tristram Heard(11 jr.), m. 2d Benjamin Hayes(3). Reuben, b. 6 Apr. 1732 Sarah Barnes. One John of Portsm., m. 7 Oct. 1731 Sarah -Catu-, but see John(6), and Cater(1).

5 MARTHA (Matthews). See (7), (8), and Snelling(3).

6 **SAMUEL**, Portsm., Greenland. Lists 67, 330de, 336bc, 339. Samuel and farm taxed for the Mill Dam 1713, he or son taxed as late as 1731. In 1717 (Snellen) he sold Portsm. common rights. He and w. Mary (appar. Fickett 1) were rec. into cov. So. Ch., 29 Jan. 1723-4. In 1741 he or his son, of Durham, sold a 1721 Scarb. gr. and in 1742 sold Barr. right to Thomas. Ch: **Samuel**, jr. and **Thomas**, both rec. into cov. with their parents. Thomas, cordwainer, Barr. 1736, Durham, m. Joanna Pinkham who was gr. adm. 26 Sept. 1750; large est. (?List 229). Bp. together 29 Jan. 1723-4: **Abigail**. **John** (see 4). **Martha**. **Mary**. **Solomon**, Barr. 1736, m. Elizabeth Reynolds(1).

7 **THOMAS**, fined for overdrinking in 1649 (see Jocelyn 4), prob. the Shoals fisherman and poss. fa. of (8), yet in July 1657 Brian Pendleton was gr. adm. on his and Wm. Drew's estates, they lately decd. and no one appearing to administer.

8 **THOMAS**, Smuttynose, son of Martha (Matthews 5) (Snell) Brown, was willed by his uncle Francis Matthews in 1678 the ho. his mo. Martha was then liv. in. His ho. on Smuttyn. ment. in Oct. 1683. See also (7), (2).

9 **WILLIAM**, prob. of Scarboro. In June 1661 Henry Watts gave a receipt, in part, to him and Philip Griffin, and a release in full in Feb. 1664-5. Both were sued for debt by Mr. Jordan in Nov. 1665. In 1672 Wm. Oliver sued him for slander in York ct., getting £10 and costs. One Wm. was taxed in Boston in 1687; Wm. d. there 10 Nov. 1726, ag. 91.

**SNELLING**. See Fickett(1), Hilton(5). Samuel Snell of Portsm. is found also as Snelling.

1 **ANN**, ±19 in 1669 when assaulted by David Campbell. Goodw. Sheares(5) had sent her to him to buy wine.

2 **JOHN**, Saco 1655 when he slandered James Harmon, who in 1656 as Snelling's endorser was sued by R. Hitchcock and in turn sued Snelling. In 1661 sued by Thomas Mills for detaining fish, and by Morgan Howell for not deliv. fish to Capt. Pendleton; in 1662 sued by Wm. Batten for £12. Prob. the Boston resident who is ident. as son of John and Frances (Hele) S. of Plympton St. Mary, co. Devon (N. E. Reg. 52: 342). Sarah, w. of this John, was gr. adm. 13 Nov. 1672. Ch. b. Boston: **Sarah**, b. 4 Oct. 1657. **John**, blockmaker, b. 17 Mar. 1664, m. Jane Adams(2), who m. 2d John Chamberlain and d. in 1738, ag. 68. 6 ch. in Boston 1689-1699. **Joseph** (not rec.), mariner, m. 19 July 1694 Rebecca Adams(13). He d. 15 Aug. 1726, ag. ±59, she 7 Nov. 1730,

ag. 56 yrs. 7 mos. 20 d. (Copp's Hill). 7 or more ch. He may have m. 1st in 1693 Sarah Sedgwick who liv. but a few mos. **William**, b. 9 Apr. 1671. **Benjamin**, blockmaker, b. 18 Aug. 1672, m. 1st 29 Jan. 1694 Jemima Andrews(7); m. 2d 11 Mar. 1707-8 Margaret (Rule) Johnson, both liv. 1729. 7 + 2 ch. in Boston.

3 **MARTHA** (Sneling), a Shoals wit. (by mark) 1672. See Snell(5).

4 **THOMAS**, Shoals 1660, List 302a. One Thomas, a ship-carp., liv. at Dartmouth, Old Eng., d. intest. in Boston 16 Oct. 1661.

**SNOW**, became the 80th commonest name in N. E. See Frink(1), Montague.

1 **HENRY**, b. at Torbay, co. Devon, in 1674, m. Sarah Nason(4), d. in upper par. of Kittery during week ending 4 May 1771, ag. 97. Lists 290, 291. 7 ch., the first b. 22 Nov. 1703.

2 **THOMAS**, 1670. List 82.

3 **THOMAS**, from Ilfracombe, co. Devon, m. Elizabeth Clark(20) 13 Oct. 1716. See also Phillips(1).

**Soddans**, Elias, a commissioner for Cornwall under N. Y. rule 1685; see Y. D. 10: 261.

**SOLLEY, Nathaniel**, Portsmouth merchant, form. of London, bot adj. Hart's wharf in 1702, and the same yr. gave p/a to George Jaffrey(4) whose gr.dau. Elizabeth Jaffrey m. in 1741 Samuel Solley (Councillor). She d. in Portsm. in 1753, he in Eng. in 1785. See also Sloper(3).

**Soper**. See Sloper, Frost(14), Tilman; Y. D. 16: 149; 17: 35, 36.

**Souden**, Robert, York, had a 20 a. gr. next John Frost's in 1671, if he build within a yr., and ano. gr. in Mar. 1672-3. Wit. Wm. Moore's will, 1691.

**Soul**, Edward, a Shoals appraiser in 1672.

**Soullard**, Martha, w. of Peter, d. in Boston 14 Oct. 1717, ag. ±38. See Drake(4), Y. D. 8: 168.

**Southard**, Thomas, and wife, Casco, taken by Ind. 10 Aug. 1703; List 39. See Southerin.

**SOUTHER**, Souter, John, m. in Boston 11 Jan. 1660-1 Hannah Reed(8), lived in Hampton by 1666. Ag. ±39 in 1671-2, when he depos. that his wife's sis. Mary (see Naylor) liv. with them 15 mos. Pub. ho. lic. 1674; prison keeper 1685. Lists 54, 57. Wife Hannah d. 15 Jan. 1675. A 2d w. Mary and ch., Mary, James, Sarah, Rebecca, were named in his deed of real and pers. prop. 3 July 1705. Ch: **Hannah**, rec. at Boston 31 Aug. 1663; liv. in June 1667 when Nathaniel Boulter deeded to her and br. John 1 a. of his home-lot. Rec. at Hampt: **John**, b. 13 Apr. 1666, dead or abs. in 1703 when his fa.

had his land. **Mary,** b. 25 Aug. 1668, m. John Berry(8). **Rebecca,** b. 5 Dec. 1670, d. 26 Sept. 1675. **Sarah,** b. 27 Feb. 1672-3, d. 6 Oct. 1675. By 2d w: **James,** b. 4 Mar. 1678, had w. Sarah. List 399a. 1 ch. rec., Benjamin, b. 6 Aug. 1715. **Isaac,** b. 9 Mar. 1680, d. bef. 1703. **Sarah,** b. 8 Aug. 1682, m. 27 Aug. 1706 John Rollins (see 6). **Robert,** d. 30 Oct. 1703, ag. 17. **Rebecca,** b. 11 Sept. 1689.

**SOUTHERIN, Thomas,** soldier at Saco fort 1696 (List 248b), m. at York 9 May 1699 Elizabeth (Dodd) Royal(1). Both of York in Sept. 1700 (Y. D. 6: 75). See Southard.

**Sowtherick,** John, List 80.

**SOWTON.** 1 **Christopher.** Souton, Conc. D. 13: 340 (1660). [?Sowton], List 330a.

2 **CAPT. WILLAM** (Sowtone), liv. at Mr. John Cutts' in 1667; see Squire(1).

**Sparhawk.** See Pepperell.

**SPARKS, Sparke.** See Harris(10), Moses (1), Perkins(11), Roper.

1 **EDWARD,** ag. 22, came as a servant with Thomas Page(7).

2 **HENRY,** fought with Cromwell the Indian in 1667, both fined at Cochecho. Taxed 1671. Fined in 1673 for taking Samuel Leavitt's bridle from Goodm. Robie's. Lists 356j, 381. Of Exeter, he m. Martha Barrett at Chelmsford 10 July 1676. In Feb. 1677-8 'late of Ex. now sojourning at Chelmsf.' ack. judg. to Simon Bradstreet. See Chelmsford Records.

3 **HESTER,** wit. John Pickering's bond to Abraham Corbett in 1665. One Esther -Sparhawk- m. Samuel Adams in Chelmsford in 1668.

4 **JOHN,** Saco 1653, his lot ment. 1656. Lists 243a, 244be. Town rate made 28 Aug. 1669 towards maintaining old Goodman S., who was bur. 24 Oct. 1669.

5 **JOHN,** a Barrington propr. List 339. Susanna rec. into Portsm. So. Ch. 4 Oct. 1719 and s. John baptized.

6 **ROGER,** gunner at Pemaquid 1689. List 126.

7 **THOMAS,** started and dropped an action ag. Nicholas Tuckerman in York ct. 1666. One T. S., resident in Cape Elizabeth in 1685, bot from Clement Swett a ho. and 20 a. next north of John Parrott. One Rebecca, wid., m. Robert McKenney(5) at Dover in 1692. In 1732 land was laid out to their s. Henry McK. out of the land deeded by Mr. Fryer to Mr. Hollicomb; (Thomas) Sparks' old ho. was nearby.

**Spear,** George. See Gent(2).

**SPEED, Thomas,** Exeter, b. ±1650, m. bef. Mar. 1694 Sarah Jones(17). They were fighting with the Folsoms(6) in Mar. 1698-9; in 1699 he got judg. ag. Nathl. Folsom, and Henry Williams credited the amount on his

acct. Williams also wit. a mortg. on the homestead they gave to her br. Benjamin in 1703. Ag. ±59 in Dec. 1709. Lists 376b (1698), 384b, 388. She was liv. in 1718. Poss. it was the s. **Thomas** (List 388) and not the fa. who sold marsh with s. **John** (List 388) in 1714. John's will, 1766—1766, names w. Elizabeth, 4 sons, 4 daus. One J. m. Ruth Allen in Greenl. 1 Dec. 1720.

**SPENCER,** rare in No. and So. of Eng., numerous in the midlands. An ancient baronial fam. derived from a steward -le Despencer- to the King. Became 92d commonest name in N. E.

1 **GEORGE,** with Rishworth wit. a Smith fam. deed 1 Aug. 1684. 'John alias George' was sued by F. Gorges in York ct. 1686, consid. by Col. Banks the same as (6); see 'Hist. of York' ii: 9. George S. and Brawn, his now w., were bef. York ct. 6 Apr. 1697 and fined as G. S. and wife, 4 Jan. 1697-8; see Brawn(1).

2 **HUMPHREY**(11), carpenter, tav. keeper, Kittery, Great Island, b. ±1646 (ag. 43 in Apr. 1689), m. 1st Elizabeth Sheares (2), m. 2d one Grace by 25 July 1676 when his parents gave him a ho. and 30 a. in Kit. (Berwick). Of Gt. Isl. they bot land from the Mussell est. in Mar. 1677-8. Sold liq. there in 1678. Me. lic. 1680, also in 1681 with ferry lic. to Gt. Isl. and Str. Bank. Pub. ho. lic. and taxed Gt. Isl. 1682-1690. Jury 1684, 1688; gr.j. (Me.) 1694. Lists 298, 313a, 331b, 52, 92. He d. 19 Dec. 1700. Wife Grace wit. in contest over est. of T. Harris (26) in 1684; wife 2 Apr. 1686. In Sept. 1687 Wm. Haines told that H. S. and his mo. poisoned his w. who died. As Grace outliv. his mo., Haines must have referred to the 1st w. Elizabeth Emery depos. in 1738, ag. ±82, that his 1st w. left two sons: **Humph-**, **rey,** Berwick innkeeper, constable 1696-7, m. bef. 17 June 1701 Mary Cutts(3) who m. 2d Joseph Moulton(6). His will, 22 Jan.—11 July 1712. List 296. Ch: William, brot up by mo. 2 yrs. 6 mos.; m. Mary Gerrish (Benj. 3). Sarah, brot up 4 yrs. 6 mos.; m. Thomas Newmarch. Samuel, brot up 6 yrs. 3 mos.; liv. 1737. **Thomas,** a small boy in Oct. 1685 and apprent. to Thomas Parker(26) who was accus. of abusing him. He d. a young man (Emery depos.). Stackpole adds **Mary,** unmarried. One Mary of Berw. d. 19 or 20 Apr. 1704, 'aft. some months' sickness with a disease called Strangury' (List 96).

3 **JOHN,** Mr., Newbury. On 3 Mar. 1636 the Genl. Ct. gave permis. for a planta. at Winnacunnet and for Mr. Dummer and Mr. J. S. to impress men to build a ho., they to be reimbursed from the treasury or by those coming to inhabit. See references in Essex

Q. Ct. Rec., vol. i; also Essex Prob. i: 107-8, for his will (left with Mr. Dummer when he went to Eng.), 1 Aug. 1637—29 Mar. 1649, naming (4) his chief heir.

4 **JOHN**, Mr., Newbury, neph. and heir of (3). Presum. the foreman of a Kit. cor. j. (death of Warwick Heard) in 1647, as his sis. Penelope m. in Newb. 15 Jan. 164- John Treworgye(4). They were bp. in Chertsey, co. Surrey, ch. of Thomas and Penelope (Jernegan) (Fillioll) Spencer. In Dec. 1650, a half-sis. in Eng., Anne Fillioll, was gr. adm. on his est., late of Jamaica, bachelor (Waters' Gleanings, i: 553; see also p. 467 for will of fa. Thomas in Eng.). The admr. here, who was called his uncle, Daniel Pierce (4), sued Antipas Maverick in Me. in 1660.

5 **JOHN**(9), wit. deeds to Wm. Phillips in Saco, 1660, 1664, and was at the Eastward at times, but his career is not closely followed. Lists 186, 18, 34. In 1687, living at Falmouth, tired of rambling about and wishing to settle down, he asked Andros for confirmation of 100 a. at Stroudwater near the Davis mills where he wished to live (Doc. Hist. vi: 308). On 25 Jan. 1689-90 he signed a pet. to the King from 'Prov. of Me. and co. of Cornwall.' Edw. Woodman claimed 20 a. at Newtown bot from him 26 July 1690. One John's est. adm. in Suff. Co. 1701. Not named in his sis. Mary's will. He appar. m. Elizabeth, wid. of Mark Parsons(5). One wid. Elizabeth d. in Boston 1 Jan. 1712-3, ag. 72. Ch., if any, unkn.

6 **JOHN**, husbandman, York, wit. Weare to John Smyth, jr., 18 July 1683, had a 40 a. gr. beyond Cape Neddick in May 1687, ano. gr. in Mar. 1701-2. See (1). His home was near Bald Head. He m. wid. Mary Wormwood(3) whose s. Thomas depos. in 1749 that over 40 yrs. ago 'Nicholas Cane and myself helped my fa.-in-law' Mr. J. S., fence land. Killed by Ind. 1 Sept. 1712; adm. to s. John 30 June 1729, wid. Mary renouncing. She was liv. in Wells in July, 1736, ±69. Ch. appear: **John**, coaster, York, List 279, liv. 20 May 1732. Supposed lost at sea, unmarried; adm. gr. 25 Oct. 1734 to the Coles. **Bethia**, m. 1st Andrew Rankin, m. 2d John Cole(24). **Deborah**, had ch. John and Hannah, b. 1722-1724, their reputed fa. James Rankin; she m. 8 May 1734 Ichabod Wittum. **Ebenezer**, shipwright, Durham, m. 20 Nov. 1729 Abigail Leathers(2). List 369. See also Lois, m. John Oliver(18).

7 **MOSES**(10), Berwick, one of several young men fined for fighting in May 1674. He m. Elizabeth (Freethy) Botts bef. 1 July 1679 when adm. on the Botts est. was removed from N. Masterson to him. Abs. from meeting 1685. Lists 298, 289, 296. The writ in SJC 53374, Jacob and Mary Allen v.

Moses S., for ⅓ of ½ of 50 a. at Pipe Stave Hills laid out to Moses sr. in Mar. 1673-4, recites that he d. about 1693 leaving 4 ch: **Isaac**, List 298. One Isaac m. Bethia Gerrish in Boston 10 Dec. 1701. His wid. Elizabeth m. 2d James Emery(3 jr.), m. 3d Thomas Abbott. Only surv. ch. in 1736, both of age, Moses and Hannah, both bp. 24 July 1720 as ch. of Elizabeth Emery. **Moses**, gr. adm. on fa.'s est. 19 Apr. 1720. List 298. He m. Elizabeth Abbott (Joseph 4), deeded homestead to s. Freethy and to Stephen Hardison in 1735, d. in 1746. 9 ch., the first 5 bp. 20-24 Dec. 1719. **Patience**. **Mary**, m. 1st Joseph Jones(22), m. 2d Jacob Allen(4).

8 **PENELOPE**. See (4).

9 **CAPT. ROGER**, Charlestown, Saco, was dealing with Francis Knight(4) in 1649; in May 1653 had an Ind. deed as partner with Christopher Lawson and Capt. Lake, and two Ind. deeds the next mo., one of them with Lake. Saco made him a sawmill gr. in Sept. 1653 but appar. his fam. was in Charlestown until he and Capt. Pendleton bot a neck of land at Winter Harbor in 1658. Called seaman 1654. In 1660 Wm. Tilley depos. that he saw him show two bills to Francis Knight at Pemaquid in 1655. Saco 1658-1662. Y. D. 1: 113 (28 Jan. 1659-60) and 2: 63 (26 May 1669, when he was of Boston) show his Saco interests. He also owned and sold at Falm. (Y. D. 10: 264). Lists 75b, 244a, 3. Wyman's Charlestown ii: 886. His w. Gertrude was adm. to Charlestown Ch. in June 1652. As 'Mis' S. she wit. ag. Mary Clay in 1660; lic. at Saco in July 1662; in 1672 sold strong drink in Boston, her husb. being indicted therefor. His est., diminished by mortg. and sales, was adm. in Suff. ct., wid. Gertrude's bond 14 May 1675. In Me. ct. the next July Maj. Pendleton was allowed charges on acc. of an attachment not prosec. by her. On Charlest. tything list 1677-8, off 1680-1. Ch. appear: **John**. **Sarah**, d. 30 Oct. 1662, appar. at Charlest. **Lydia**, m. at Saco 3 Aug. (±1660) Freegrace Norton (3). **Mary**, m. 1st John Hull(5), m. 2d Sir William Phips(7), m. 3d Peter Sargeant, Esq. **Rebecca**. As Rebekah Buller [did she m. 1st John Bully(1) ?], she m. at Rowley 14 Feb. 1682 Dr. David Bennett. 3 sons b. at R. 1683-1687; David, rememb. in aunt Mary's will. Spencer, Sir Wm.'s adopted son and heir (see Phips 7). Dr. William, also rememb. by aunt; fa. of Dr. David of York.

10 **THOMAS**, Kittery (par. of Unity 1662), depos. in Aug. 1676, ±80, that he had liv. in this country 46 yrs.; 'old father Spencer . . . was sent over as a serv. by Capt. John Mason' (Samuel Allen v. Humphrey S., 1704). He prob. came from Winchcombe, co. Gloucester, the home of the Chadbournes,

where one T. S. bot a messuage in 1624. Sued for debt by Wm. Scadlock in Saco ct. 7 Feb. 1636-7, Mr. John Treworgye bondsman. In 1647 he and Thomas Withers were called on to acct. for rates and fines collected. Disenfranchised 1659 for entertaining Quakers. In 1661 he and Daniel Goodwin were accus. of trading with Ind., but no ground appeared. In 1662 Barefoot got a judgm. ag. him for debt, which was discharged in 1663 by Humphrey Chadbourne in behalf of the s. Wm. Cor.j. 1647; gr.j. 1651, 1653, 1656; j. 1653. Tav. lic. 1659, 1680. Lists 24, 41, 281-283, 298. Wife Patience Chadbourne(4). Both abs. from meet. 1663, 1675, he in 1665. He d. 15 Dec. 1681; will, 5 June 1679—1 May 1682. Wid. Patience was lic. in 1682 (s. Moses bondsman); d. 7 Nov. 1683; div. to 3 sons, 2 sons-in-law (Joy, Chick); Daniel Goodwin was given 10 s. as a token of remembrance. Ch: **William. Margaret,** m. Daniel Goodwin(4). **Mary,** m. Thomas Etherington. **Susanna,** m. 1st John Gattensby (1), m. 2d Ephraim Joy(1). **Humphrey,** 2d son. **Elizabeth,** m. 1st Thomas Chick, m. 2d Nicholas Turbet(2). **Moses.**
11 **WILLIAM**(10), Berwick, eldest son, presum. mar., but left no w. or ch. Kit. gr. 1651. Tr.j. often from 1662, gr.j. from 1664; cor.j. (foreman) 1668; surv. highway 1673 (charged with neglect; did not appear and fined for contempt); selectman 1674-75, 1677; comr. for Kit. 1677. Deliverance Taylor was a maid in his ho. ±1685. With fa. adm. of the Etherington est. in 1665; adm. of Saml. Sayward's est. 1690. Mrs. Hannah Hobbs named 'Wm. Spencer and Walter Allen' among those having charge of Great Works mills. Lists 24, 25, 28, 36, 298 (2). He d. 15 May 1696. Will, 18 June 1687, named neph. Humphrey sole heir; a cod., 11 Mar. 1695-6, provid. that his serv. Moses Spencer serve his time out with Humphrey and then receive a meadow and 50 a.
**SPENDLOW, Philip** (Spindler, Spinderlow), Exeter, ag. ±29 in Dec. 1694, served on jury 1696, had a 20 a. gr. 1698. He gave a deed (mortg.?) to James Dudley in 1713. Liv. 14 Jan. 1715-6. Lists 67, 376b, 388. Wid. Lydia m. 2d by 1739 Ichabod Robie(2). Only ch. **Anna,** wit. as Spenlow 20 Mar. 1717-8, m. 1st bef. 26 Nov. 1723 Ebenezer Morrison, m. 2d 1736-1739 Samuel Robie(2).
**SPILLER.** 1 **Abraham,** a wit. in the Turpin-Cummings case 1674. Of Kit., given a pub. ho. lic. by N. H. in 1686. Wit. a Fernald fam. deed 1689. Kit. gr. 1694, List 298. Great Isl. 1695 and paid by that town for carpenter's work in 1697.
2 **ANN.** See Rowe(15).
3 **HENRY,** m. Sarah (Moore 25) Welcom, and was a wit. in the Carter-Welcom case in 1693. Of Ipsw. in 1700 when gdn. of the

Welcom ch. Ch: **John,** b. 3 May 1693 in Ipsw., where Martha, dau. of one Henry, was bp. in 1711.
**Spindler.** See Spendlow.

**SPINNEY,** uncommon. A spinney is usually a thicket, but in co. Bucks is a brook.
1 **JAMES**(4), cordwainer, had a Kit. gr. in 1682, constable 1695-6, gr.j. (Me.) 1696. Ag. ±35 in Nov. 1697. Portsmouth 1700, taxed at the Bank 1713, rated to So. Ch. 1717. Lists 298, 339. W. Grace Dennett(1), List 331c. Will, of Portsm., 13 June 1720—18 Feb. 1724-5, names her and only ch. **Sarah,** m. Joseph Downing(2) who in 1740 was seized of the whole est. in her right.
2 **JOHN**(4), Kittery, had a gr. in 1694 and inherited the homestead. Ag. ±29 in Dec. 1697, ±30 in Mar. 1698-9. Jury 1694; gr.j. 1694 (fined for non-appearance). With br. Samuel bondsm. for Mrs. Lucy Stileman, admx., in 1701. Lists 296-298. He d. ±1705 (Stackpole). His wid. Mary (Diamond 4) m. 2d Lt. Jeremiah Burnham(2) and as his wid. ret. to Kit. Her will, 4 Dec. 1733—12 Mar. 1734-5 (cous. John Fernald exec.), names s. Jeremiah Burnham, gr.dau. Dorcas Hammond, and Spinney ch: **Andrew,** oldest son, m. 25 June 1726 Abigail Wingate(2). Adm. to her and Wm. S. in 1753. 8 ch. **Mercy,** m. Wm. Tetherly(4 jr.). **John,** m. 10 July 1729 Mary Waterhouse(4), both liv. 1757. 6 ch. **Margery,** m. Samuel Tetherly (4). **Mary,** m. Samuel Tobey(4). **Lydia,** liv. 1731 when land was laid out to the six heirs, not in mo.'s will. Dr. Jenkinson courted her, but it was George Hammond (see 3) she accus. in 1723. Samuel Tetherly was gdn. of her dau. Dorcas Hammond 15 Apr. 1735.
3 **SAMUEL**(4), Kittery, had gr. in 1694, constable 1693-4; gr.j. 1694. Lists 296-298. Ag. ±36 in 1696, he depos., telling what Richard King told John Woodman at Katherine Paul's ho.; ±38 in Jan. 1697-8; ±77 in Apr. 1736. He m. 1st 26 Sept. 1687 Elizabeth Knight(19), m. 2d 27 Sept. 1708 Margaret Shepard(2), m. 3d wid. Mary Rice (see 5), m. last 26 Sept. 1734 Jane McClure. Will, 10—22 Mar. 1737-8, names Jane and gives homestead to sons David and Samuel. Ch. by 1st w: **Samuel,** b. 13 Oct. 1688, d. bef. 1716. **James,** b. 8 Mar., d. 24 Sept. 1690. **John,** b. 17 July 1691, weaver, oldest s. in 1716, was drowned; adm. 4 July 1726 to wid. Patience (Young, Rowe 5, cov. Nicholas Rowe, liv. Newington int. in 1725. Ch. **Jeremiah,** b. 19 Oct. 1699, List 291, m. Hannah

Pettigrew; his w. was called Anne in 1739. Ch. **Elizabeth**, named last in fa.'s will, 'if she be living'; poss. came betw. Jeremiah and David. One E. o.c. and was bp. in No. Ch. 16 July 1721; one was in Me. ct. Jan. 1721-2. **David**, b. 12 Sept. 1706, m. Jerusha Cole(32), d. s.p. in 1745, she soon aft.; both left wills. **Jonathan**, b. 28 June 1708, m. (int. 23 Feb. 1730-1) Sarah Parker (Nathl. 16). Ch. By 2d w: **Sarah**, m. Richard Pope (3 jr.). **Lydia**, b. 17 Dec. 1710, m. Joseph Hanscom(3). **Patience**, b. 3 Dec. 1713, m. 13 Oct. 1731 Abner Cole(32). **Samuel**, b. 3 July -1717-, liv. 1739. **Margaret**, these last four bp. with their mo. 29 Sept. 1717.

4 **THOMAS**, weaver, Kittery, ag. ±67 in Nov. 1697, first seen when John Webster wit. ag. him and Margerie, late w. of Wm. Norman, in N. H. ct. 30 Sept. 1651. She was orig. Margery Randall and soon became his wife; see Norman(2). A tradition was pub. in 1863 to the effect that the first Spinney here was b. near Manchester, Eng., went to Wapping Stairs near London, shipped as a fisherman for the No. Am. coast and was carried thence to the Piscat. by a Capt. Fernald, ±1630. Kittery constable 1656. A wit. in 1658 (Edw. Melcher and the Websters). Gr. of 200 a. on both sides of Great Cove, afterw. Spinney's Cove, in 1659. Gr.j. 1660, 1666 (did not appear), 1670, 1688, 1692-3, 1695, 1698-9; tr.j. 1669; ferry lic. 1668, 1671; selectman 1674. Lists 282, 283, 298, 25, 96. Margery was liv. 23 Mar. 1694, but not in will, 9 July—23 Sept. (d. 31 Aug.) 1701, naming ch. and 2 gr.ch.; wit. by Thomas and Mary Fernald. Ch: **Hannah**, m. Samuel Fernald(3). **Samuel**, b. ±1658. **James**, b. ±1662. **Thomas**, b. ±1665. **John**, fa.'s exec., b. ±1668.

5 **THOMAS**(4), cordwainer, Kit., had a gr. in 1699. Lists 296, 298. Wife Christiana or Christina was ±49 in 1724; he was ±61 in 1726, ±64 in Aug. 1729, liv. 1732. Ch: **Hannah**, b. 16 Jan. 1700-1, m. by 1723 John Cane, and as H. C. accus. Wm. Brooks in 1733 when Thomas S. went her bond. **Joseph**, b. 18 June 1703, m. in Newb. 12 Oct. 1725 Jane McClure. Bridget Rashford or Rishford with her baby liv. with them 8 or 9 mos. and in 1740 sued him for a yr.'s work. **Thomas**, m. (int. 28 Aug. 1731) Tamsen Ham (Joseph 4), who d. 21 May 1799, ag. 90 (newspaper rec.). **Margery**, m. Christopher Hawkins(1).

**Spofford**, David, taxed Portsm. (Mill Dam) 1707.

**SPRIGGS.** 1 **Daniel** (Spregg), a Kit. wit. 1672 (Y. D. 2: 128).

2 **WILLIAM**, fisherman, mariner, Portsmouth, m. in Sept. 1714 Ruth Abbott(1). Liv. 1723. Adm. on est. of one W. S. to w. Abigail 26 Oct. 1748.

**Springer.** See Huff(3), Low(5), Sanders(10).

**SPRITTALL.** 1 **Richard**, Shoals, attacked by Samuel Gould and John Yelline in 1685.

2 **THOMAS** (Spridel), bondsman for John Bugg of the Shoals, 1673.

**Spur**, John, Saco wit. 1662, Williams to Wormstall. List 247. See also Bradden (2), Mitchell(17).

**SPURWELL, Christopher** (also Spurrell), Cape Porpus, took O. A. to Mass. 5 July 1653. Bef. 11 Dec. 1655 he bot land from John Lee and Ralph Tristram and sold to Richard Ball. Lists 251, 252. Widow Julian m. 2d John Cloyes(1). She was ±53 in June 1673. Ch. appear: **Abigail**, m. in Saco 8 Sept. 1664 Arthur Batten(1). **Timothy**, had land from John Cloyes bef. 30 June 1675 (Y. D. 2: 174). List 223b. **Sarah**, in 1675 had stolen goods from George Pearson of Bost. and brot them to the Falm. home of her mo., who sent part of them to ano. Dau. in Boston. **Christopher**, around Scarboro in 1680, List 30.

**SQUIRE.** See also Jackson(13).

1 **BARNARD**, Portsmouth, Oyster River, but first at Kit., his former gr. ment. in 1654. He had a bill ag. Portsm. in Feb. 1660-1; abs. from meeting 1664; in 1667 abused Capt. 'Sowtone' at Mr. John Cutts' ho. and frightened Mrs. Cutts. Ag. ±40 in June 1672, when he cut wood at Spruce Creek. He appar. m. aft. 1681 wid. Margaret Willey(4) and sold land to Stephen Willey bef. 1696. She was liv. in 1701 (see Leathers 2). Lists 298, 311a, 312c, 323, 326a, 327c, 330a, 331a, 57, 62. Presum. a son by an unkn. w: **Philip**, was drunk and fought with John Willey at O. R. in 1678; left the Province. One P., Newbury 1681, ag. ±25, had ch. rec. there by w. Mary: Mary, 1686, Thomas, 1694. More likely of the 3d than the 2d gener. were: Sarah, accus. of bastardy in 1710, return made to Dover ct. 'non est invent.' Elizabeth, b. at O. R., away some yrs. (List 99, p. 75), back at O. R. in 1706 and had a ch. b. there, no husb. appearing; also named in warr. 7 Mar. 1709-10 with Martha Randall(12) and others. Joseph Stevenson of Great Brit. and Elizabeth S. of Portsm. int. mar. in Boston 11 Oct. 1716; also Richard Williams and E. S. (no resid. given) 22 June 1717, John Pike and E. S. m. in Boston 16 Aug. 1717.

2 **JOHN**, and Nicholas, fishermen, York, also Sampson Anger, made a joint contract with Thomas Foule of Boston in July 1640 for the next yr.'s fishing. John sold fish to Winter in 1642, and bought pork.

3 **NICHOLAS.** See(2).

**STACKPOLE.** See 'History and Genealogy of the Stackpole Family' (2d edit. 1920).

**JAMES,** Dover, a squatter in 1680 in the part now Rollinsford, built on land gr. to Joseph Austin in 1656 and cleared part of the adj. lot that was gr. to Henry Tibbetts. In 1710 he got a deed for 100 a. from Austin's s. Thomas. By one trad. he was brot here (abducted) from Ireland as a boy of 14. He signed a Kit. pet. in 1680 and m. Margaret Warren(4), indicating that he had prev. liv. there; later he liv. in Berwick a few yrs., having tav. lic. 1693-1698. Dover 1699. Dover gr. 1694, Kit. gr. 1702. Lists 30, 298, 358d, 359b. Wife Margaret liv. in Dec. 1712. In 1732-1734 he divid. his homestead betw. sons Philip and Samuel, keeping 3 a. and the ho. he was liv. in. Ag. 80 in Aug. 1732 when he depos. ab. Edw. Toogood at Salmon Falls; ±80 in 1734. Inv. 12 Aug. 1736; adm. 14 July 1737 to s. John. Ch: **James,** d. unm. Interesting will, of Berwick, 11—30 Nov. 1706. He had been a soldier. Lt. **John,** soldier at Saco and Ind. captive ab. 1710; see Miss Coleman's 'N. E. Captives,' ii: 21. In York, 1711—May 1717, later that yr. in Biddeford (constable). He m. by Dec. 1715 Elizabeth Brown(3) who was liv. in Bidd. in 1759, he in 1767. 3 or more ch. **Catherine,** m. Alexander Junkins. **William,** named in br. James' will. **Margaret,** m. 7 Jan. 1707-8 Jonathan Young(10). **Philip,** m. 1st Mercy Thompson(12) with whom he was accus. and acq. in Apr. 1713; m. 2d betw. 1750-1755 wid. Martha Stevens (see Downes 6). He built on the Tibbetts land and was sued in 1717 by Samuel Tibbetts, jr., who was awarded the ho. and land, but to pay S. £200 and costs. List 358d. Will, of Somersworth, 25 Aug.—30 Sept. 1761, names w. Martha, 6 of 8 ch. **Honor,** had a s. Joshua Roberts, b. in 1721. She m. 24 Jan. 1734 Joseph Freethy(3). **Samuel,** not named in br. James' will, but of lawful age in 1723; d. s.p., adm. to br. Philip 22 Feb. 1758.

## STACY.

1 **MARK,** tailor, Oyster River, Stratham, ag. 25 in Aug. 1682, poss. that s. of John and Eleanor of Marbleh. who served in King Philip's War. In 1683 he worked for Philip Chesley, sr. O. R. cor.j. 1687; Exeter (Stratham) by 1689. Lists 57, 67, 367a, 388. Ano. tailor, Philemon of Newc., had w. Elizabeth who was gr. adm. 11 June 1730. Richard, b. in Exeter, N. E., m. Elizabeth Sutton in Portsm. 9 Aug. 1733; see Langmaid(1). One Eleanor of Hampt. m. Philip Lewis in 1722. See also Reed(13).

2 **THOMAS,** Portsmouth 1656.

3 **WILLIAM,** ho. carpenter, Kittery 1679, likely that s. of Thomas and Susanna (Worcester) b. at Ipsw. 21 Apr. 1656, m. Mehitable Weymouth(2). He wit. in a Sturgeon Creek case at Wells ct. in 1684, gave a

note to Wm. Sanders in 1686, ack. judg. to Wm. Pepperell in 1703. Lists 290, 296-298. Rev. Mr. Pike recorded his death 17 Oct. 1705 (List 96), a man of more understanding than common among mechanics, but irreligious. Adm. to wid. Mehitabel 5 Mar. 1705-6, div. 29 Mar. 1726. Her will, of Kit., now residing in Berwick, 13 Jan.—20 Apr. 1753, gives 1 s. each to sons Samuel and Benjamin and Thompson gr.ch., residue to dau. Mehitabel. Ch: **Mary,** b. 6 Apr. 1690, m. John Thompson(12 jr.). **Hester,** b. 22 Nov. 1693, and **William,** b. 12 Jan. 1696, neither in div. **Samuel,** b. 19 Apr. 1698, carpenter, m. 2 Nov. 1721 Mary Pray(3). List 296. 6 ch. **Elizabeth,** b. 10 Aug. 1701, not in div. **Benjamin,** b. 17 Nov. 1704, m. 1st 7 Oct. 1730 Lydia Libby(9), m. 2d in June 1738 wid. Sarah Tidy. Lists 291, 297, 298. Will, of Kit., 10 Oct. 1757—9 Nov. 1758, w. Sarah, 8 ch. **Mehitabel,** b. 4 Apr. 1706, m. 10 Oct. 1726 Joseph Emery (Job).
**Standege,** Joseph, at John Key's garrison ±1704. List 289.
**Standers,** Lidivine, a captive, named next to Rose Otis. List 99, p. 123.

**STANFORD,** Staniford. The Falmouth fam. often found as -Sanford-.

1 **JOHN** (Staniford), wealthy resid. of Ipsw. (w. Margaret Harris), bot Hunnewell's Neck at Winter Harbor in 1692. John and Margaret were Star Isl. wit. 1697, **Thomas** and J. in 1705. Hannah (prob. w. of Thomas) and J. wit. in Hampt. 1715. Ano. s. Lt. **William** settled perma. in Hampt.; see Sherburne(8), Dow(5); 3 ch. by 1st w. See also 'The Ancestry of Bethia Harris' (W. G. Davis), p. 30.

2 **ROBERT**(3), Falmouth (Purpooduck). In 1660 Mr. Jordan deeded to him 50 a. over a small creek and near 80 a. adj. his fa.'s ho., this 80 a. being deeded to his fa. at the same time. J. of life and death 1666. At Falm. in Feb. 1675-6; O. A. at Beverly in Dec. 1677; ret. to Falm. by 1680 when he and fa. had a gr. Gr.j. 1686. Lists 222b, 223b, 225a, 85, 30, 214, 34. He and fa. joined in pet. to Andros. In the 2d war he went to Glouc. where he d. 15 May 1709 and his wid. 6 July 1721, ±72. Ch. by deeds: **Mary,** m. Josiah Wallis(5). **Martha,** m. James Wallis (3). **Rebecca,** m. in Glouc. 20 Feb. 1701 John Sawyer. **Elizabeth,** m. James Simpson (4). **Bethia,** d. in Glouc. 20 Feb. 1719-20, ±28. **Josiah,** m. 19 Nov. 1719 Hannah Day of Manch., liv. in Glouc., aft. 1724 in Falm. Living in Apr. 1772. 7 or more ch., lst 3 b. in Glouc. 1720-1724; see also Simpson(4). **John,** Glouc., claimed the Me. lands and in 1730 sold to Samuel Stevens ⅛ of 204 a. on Purpooduck side, naming his fa. and gr.fa. In 1743 he and his br. exch. interests, he tak-

ing Glouc. and Josiah taking Falm. lands. Wife Abigail Butman, m. 8 Nov. 1722 in Glouc.; 8 ch. bp.

3 **THOMAS,** Purpooduck, with (2) made claim to Andros in Nov. 1687 that they had been in posses. on so. side of Casco river over against the fort ±35 yrs. In ct. for swearing in 1659; had Jordan land in 1660 (see 2). Dep. constable 1661, when Col. Crown, who had a suit ag. Mr. Jordan, charged him with not executing his office. The same yr., Joseph Phippen, John Wallis and he gave joint bond to Mr. Munjoy, payable in merchantable codfish. Called a common swearer and drunkard in 1663, and accused of breach of oath of freedom and fidelity, the ct. discharging this case. Apprais. M. Maddiver's and J. Richardson's estates, and surety for Maddiver's wid. His w. and Nicholas White's railed at each other in 1659, on the Sabbath. She or Robert's w. was in Salem early in the war, List 27. O. A. at Beverly in Dec. 1677. Back in Falm. in 1680 (see 2). In Jan. 1683-4 wid. Sarah Jordan deeded to Wm. Haines and w. 30 a. at the 'place commonly called Stanford's old House.' Not seen aft. 1687. Lists 221, 222b, 225a, 232, 85, 30, 34. See Guy(2). Kn. ch: **Robert. Daughter,** m. Joseph Phippen(5 jr.). (Note also Thomas, List 85, and Marbleh. V. R.)

4 ——, m. in Portsm. 1711 Hannah King (see 7) who was in ct. as Hannah S. in 1720 and m. last Valentine Scates(2).

**STANLEY.** See also Clifford(3), Kenniston(1).

1 **JAMES,** d. at the home of Mrs. Abigail James in Portsm. and the town paid for his burial in 1729.

2 **JOHN,** Portsm., wit. Wm. Ham's will, 1672.

3 **WILLIAM,** blacksmith, Kittery, m. 20 Oct. 1714 Hannah Pope(3). Lists 291, 298. He bot in Eliot in 1723; Wells gr. by 1726. 7 ch. rec. at Kit.

4 **ZERVIAH.** See William Parker(26); Topsfield records.

**STANTON, Benjamin,** Pemaquid soldier 1689, List 126. He may or may not have been the husb. of wid. Joanna who m. Abraham Nute(1) in 1704, but in all probabil. it was her s. **Benjamin** who m. Eleanor Ricker (1), had ch. Benjamin and Eleanor in Dover 1725-1727, was of Somersworth 1740, and bef. Dec. 1751 m. Sarah (Walker) Farrow. See also Broughton(2). One Benjamin from N. H. served at Louisburg under Capt. Samuel Hale.

**Stanwood.** See Mercer(2).

**STANYAN,** Stanian, etc. See Waters' Gleanings, i: 224; ii: 999.

1 *****ANTHONY,** Mr., glover, Exeter, Hampton, ag. 24, 6 Apr. 1635, when about to embark on ·The Planter· from London for N. E. He shared in the Ex. div. in Dec. 1639; 'sometime of Boston, now of Ex.' in July 1641 (see Jones 12). Assistant ruler 1639; Ex. constable 1645, 1648; selectman 1645, 1646; Com.t.e.s.c. 1646; Clerk of the Writs 1647. Of Hampt., he sold Ex. prop. in 1650. Hampt. selectman 1649, 1662, 1669, 1676-7; Com.t.e.s.c. 1650, 1654; Rep. 1654, 1680, 1684; constable 1665; ord. lic. 1667, 1668; j. and gr.j. often. Ag. ±59 in Feb. 1666-7, ±65 in 1672, ±68 in Apr. 1675. His man Cornelius was ±50 in 1660. Lists 374c(2), 375ab, 376ab (1645), 377, 378, 392b(3), 393ab, 394, 396, 398, 43, 49, 52-54. First w. Mary, List 393a. He m. 2d wid. Ann Partridge(4), List 394, who d. 10 July 1689. His inv. 21 Feb. 1688-9; £45. 18. 2. Ch: **John,** b. at Boston 16 July 1642, bp. there ±6 days old as s. of A. S. of Exeter Ch. **Mary,** m. Capt. John Pickering (4).

2 **JAMES(3),** Hampton, m. Ann Hussey(3). List 399a. Will, 7 June 1742—26 Oct. 1743, gives half his est. to her for life; John Gove sole exec. She was liv. in 1749. Ch: John, Hampt. Falls, named w. Mary, 7 ch., in will, 23 Dec. 1748—25 Jan. 1748-9. **Elizabeth,** m. 19 July 1727 Thomas Hunt(7). **Joseph. Mary,** m. 17 Mar. 1726-7 George Newbegin of Nantucket. **Lydia,** m. John Davis. **Susanna,** m. Ichabod Canney(2) of Dover. **Huldah,** ±34 in 1741-2, m. 1st 19 Oct. 1729 John Canney of Dover, m. 2d 17 Oct. 1745 Samuel Eaton. **Comfort,** m. 22 May 1733 Jonathan Hoag(1). **Anne,** m. 22 Nov. 1738 Stephen Otis. **Rebecca,** m. Michael Kennard (3). **Bathsheba,** m. 14 Sept. 1742 Jonathan Hardy.

3 **JOHN(1),** Hampton, m. 17 Dec. 1663 Mary Bradbury(1); liv. on homestead. In 1678 Henry Bennett of Ips. wrote letters to 'Cozen' J. S., signing 'your loving uncle '; see Essex Q. Ct. Rec. vi: 390. In 1694 Joseph Emmons had a shoemaker's shop at his place. Selectman 1692, 1699, 1701, 1709, j. 1695 (foreman). Lists 392b, 396, 52. He d. 26 Sept. 1718 (gr.st.). Will, 13 Feb. 1717-8, names w. Mary, 5 ch., gr.s. John Silley. Wid. Mary was adm. to Hampt. F. Ch. 20 Nov. 1718; wid. Staniell of Hampt. d. 29 May 1724 (Salisb. rec.). Ch: **Mary,** b. 22 Oct. 1664, m. Theophilus Smith(40). **James,** b. 26 June 1667. **Jacob,** b. 11 Jan. 1669-70; verdict on his untimely death filed 6 Dec. 1681. **Joseph,** b. 5 Dec. 1672, not in will. **Mehitable,** b. 1 Jan. 1676, m. John Robinson(8). **Ann,** b. 17 Feb. 1678, m. Thomas Silley (Sealy 9); not in will. **Jacob,** Hampt. F., b. 31 Mar. 1683, depos. in June 1761, ag. 78. First w. Dorothy, m. 29 Oct. 1704, d. 16 Nov. 1723, ag. 39 yrs. 10 mos.; 2d w. Lydia. Ch: Elizabeth,

Mehitable, John, Mary, Joseph, Jacob, Dorothy, Rachel and Ann (twins), Sarah (by 2d w.). **Elizabeth,** m. in Salisb. 6 Jan. 1697-8 Jeremy Stevens.

**STAPLES,** often Staple in early records. 1 **PETER,** Kittery, had a gr. in 1671 and bot from Thomas Turner on Long Reach in 1674. He m. Elizabeth (Beedle 4) Edwards and in Sept. 1675 was gr. 10 a. adj. the 5 a. gr. to her in her widowhood 13 Dec. 1669. In cross suits with Weymouth Lydston for slander in 1675, each pl. won, but L. got the larger award. Highway surv. 1673 (in ct. for neglect of office); constable for lower Kit. 1676; gr.j. 1686, 1689-90, 1699; tav. lic. 1704, 1706-9. Lists 291, 296-298. Will, 6 June 1718—7 Apr. 1719, names w. Elizabeth and sons: **Peter. John,** carpenter, Kit. (±60 in 1737), m. (ct. Oct. 1696) Mary Dixon(2). Lists 290, 291, 296, 297. See Hanscom(2). Will, 21 Nov. 1744—16 July 1746, names w. and ch: Hezekiah (m. Ann Thompson), Solomon (m. Martha Tobey), Samuel (m. 1st Patience Moore 22, and 2d Mercy Cane 2), 3 ch. of s. Thomas (m. Sarah Ferguson 1), Hannah Whitehouse (w. of Edw.; her 1st husb. was John Drew 7 jr.), Annah Brooks (Joshua), Elizabeth Thompson (John), Mary Hanscom, Mark. **James,** tailor, Kit. See Bennett(13). He m. 15 Apr. 1701 Mary Tetherly(4). Lists 290, 291, 296, 297. Adm. 4 July 1726 to s. James. Ch: Elizabeth (m. John Tobey), James (m. Dorcas Libby 9, and a 2d w. aft. 1742), William (m. Elizabeth Jones), Samuel (m. Elizabeth Sawyer), Mary (m. Timothy Richardson), Joseph (m. Sarah Shores), Katherine (m. John Fernald), Abigail (m. Azariah Nason). 2 **PETER**(1), carpenter, Kit., had deed of the former Turner land from his parents in 1694, m. 8 Jan. 1695-6 Mary Lang(7). List 298. See also Beedle(1). Bondsm. for Thomas and John Abbott 1702. Will, 6 Dec. 1720—4 Jan. 1720-1, names w. Mary, honored mo. and all ch.; inv. £1108. Ch: **Mary,** b. 20 Sept. 1696, m. 21 Dec. 1721 Moses Noble(3). **Peter,** b. 20 Aug. 1699, m. 1st 31 May 1721 Joanna King(12), m. 2d in Portsmouth 20 Aug. 1741 Abigail Winn. Capt. at Cape Breton 1745; d. 1768; 6 ch. **Elizabeth,** b. 10 Oct. 1701, m. 18 Oct. 1719 Wm. Ham. **Robert,** b. 1 May 1704, m. 7 Jan. 1724-5 Hannah Tobey(4). Will, 8 Sept. 1743—17 Apr. 1744, names w., 7 daus. She m. 2d Nathl. Libby(9). **Anne,** b. 16 Mar. 1705-6, m. 25 Oct. 1726 Stephen Tobey(4 jr.). **Enoch,** b. 12 Mar. 1707-8, m. 24 Sept. 1728 Anne Hill(2). She d. 23 Apr. 1742 in 31st yr.; adm. on his est. to br. Peter 19 Mar. 1743-4. 6 ch. **Grace,** b. 17 Apr. 1710-1, m. 15 Nov. 1727 Tobias Leighton(5). **Joshua,** b. 16 Sept. 1712, m. 1st 17 Jan. 1734-5 Abigail Fernald (John),

m. 2d aft. Aug. 1761 Margaret Ross. 6 + 4 ch. 3 **SAMUEL** (Staple), Kit. Mrs. Mendum and S. S. wit. ag. Wm. Norman in Oct. 1651.

**STARBIRD,** -board, -bolt. **THOMAS,** weaver, Dover, in Dec. 1680 won a verdict ag. George Huntress for a year's service. O. A. at Str. Bank 28 Aug. 1685, taxed there 1691. In 1695 fishing with John Tenney, and ±48 in 1695 wit. in the Saturly case. He helped S. Hardison's wid. as admx. Abs. from meeting Jan. 1697-8. Prob. soon a settler in Dover, and ±1701 concerned in a farm of James Nute. In 1714 he sued Nicho. Wallingford for stealing his purse. Ag. ±68 in June 1714, ±70 in May 1716. Lists 332a, 358d. He m. 4 Jan. 1687-8 Abigail Dam(3) and in will, 3 July 1722— 18 Apr. 1723, provid. for 'my widow.' Abigail, wid., was bp. 22 Aug. 1740. Ch. rec. in Dover: **Jethro,** b. 28 Aug. 1689, not in will. **Thomas,** tailor, b. 19 Oct. 1691, m. in Greenl. 14 May 1713 Margaret Knight(11), taxed for Mill Dam 1713, Dover 1726, Scarb. 1727 where he made a deed in Apr. 1738, sick in body. Wid. Margaret m. 11 Dec. 1746 Axwell Roberts. 7 ch. at Dover 1714-1725, a q.c. in 1761 shows 4 more. **Agnes,** b. 4 Oct. 1693, not in will. **Abigail,** b. 29 Sept. 1695, w. of John Pinkham in 1747. **Elizabeth,** b. 15 Feb. 1699-1700, not in will. **John,** carpenter, b. 16 Mar. 1701-2, m. Sarah Scammon(4). Dover 1749; d. at Brunswick 20 June 1753 in 52d yr. (gr.st.). Will, made same day, names w. Sarah (a wid. at Newcastle in 1765), 3 sons, 4 daus., homestead on Merriconeag River. **Samuel,** Dover, b. 22 Apr. 1704, m. Rebecca (Cook 6) Drew(6), who was liv. in 1734, he in 1761 at Dover. Ch. at Dover 1725-1727: Elizabeth, Samuel.

**STARBUCK.** 'Banks Topographical Dictionary' names Draycot, co. Derby, and Attenboro, co. Notts, in connec. with **ELDER *EDWARD,** Dover 1640, agent for Mr. Valentine Hill in 1646 and partner with Richard Waldron in lumbering on the Me. side in 1648. His grants incl. one jointly with Mr. Thomas Wiggin in 1650 and 200 a. with Elder Nutter in 1659. In 1653 he sold ½ his sawmill gr. to Peter Coffin, in 1657 sold to Thomas Broughton ¼ the mill above Capt. Waldron's mill at Cochecho, other owners being Capt. Wiggin (½), Peter Coffin (¼). Dep. to Gen. Ct. 1643 (fined for 3 weeks absence), 1646. In 1646 Mr. George Smith and Mr. E. S. to take charge of the writings that were in custody of Mr. Waldron. Gr.j. (Me.) 1647. Com. on Dover-Kit. bounds 1654. Dover Commissioner, 1658. Lists 281, 351ab, 352, 353, 354ab, 355a(2)b, 356abce, 53. See Furber(2), Phillips(7). In

1648 bound to the peace towards the minister and to appear at Boston for violating the law conc. Anabaptists. Appar. no later action was taken, but holding to his opinions, he deeded his Cochecho ho., goods, cattle, etc. to s.-in-law Coffin 9 Mar. 1659-60, and mov. to Nantucket where he d. 4 Mar. 1690, ag. 86. His w. Katherine (signed with him in July 1653) is repeatedly called Katherine Reynolds, but no doc. evid. of the 'Reynolds' has been seen. In a deed 1659 Mr. Broughton excepted the ho. and land on Newichawannock river of Goodwife S., 'being formerly given her,' . . . 'in' wife's right.' She was liv. 19 June 1678. Nothing lists his ch., who are picked up one by one: **Sarah**, m. 1st Joseph Austin(4), m. 2d Humphrey Varney. In 1664 her fa. confirmed to the Varneys the 20 a. he had form. given her 1st husb. **Nathaniel**, ag. ±26 in June 1661, last taxed at Dover in 1659 (Lists 356abce), but 'of Dover' in Sept.-Oct. 1661 when he sold out there to Wm. Horne and Peter Coffin. His w. Mary (Coffin 5) d. at Nantucket 13 Nov. 1717, ag. 73, he 6 Aug. 1719, ag. 84. Ch. at Nant., the 1st one rec. 30 Mar. 1663. **Abigail**, wit. her fa.'s deed with Nathl. 20 July 1653; m. Capt. Peter Coffin (4). **Jethro**, d. at Nant. 27 May 1663. **Shuah**, m. 1st Ens. James Heard(3), m. 2d Richard Otis(1). **Dorcas**, wit. an Ind. deed to proprs. of Nant. 29 June 1671, m. Wm. Gayer of Nant. as his 1st w. 3 ch. 1673-1677 (see N. E. Reg. 31: 297). And poss. **?Esther**, w. of Lt. Wm. Furber(3).

**Stariot**, List 291. See Starrett.

**Starke**, Peter, wit. Wilmot Edgecomb to Robert Elliot 1685 (Y. D. 7: 55); see also Start.

**STARKEY, John**, Pemaquid, from Boston and Malden, where he had had dealings with John Ridgway and Robert Cawley(2) whose wid. Mary m. Leonard Drown(1). Clothier; ag. ±39 in 1677. First seen at Pemaquid in his undated pet. to Andros asking that land be confirmed to him and mentioning his cattle. Signed a Pemaquid pet. 11 May 1689 and 2 Aug. foll. was taken by Ind., his fate unkn. List 125. Tryall Newberry of Malden ent. an East. Cl. in behalf of the heirs for 104 + 20 a. at Jamestown, Pemaquid Neck, by Dongan patent to Richard Murren in 1686, also for 104 + 20 a. next to R. M.'s, Dongan patent to Nicholas Denning 1686. See N. E. Reg. 46: 144, for **six ch.**, incl. **Mary**, m. at Charlest. 28 Jan. 1685-6 William Case(3) whose Pemaquid land adj. her fa.'s, and **Andrew**, of Attleboro in 1716 when he sold the Eastern land.

**STARR**. See also Ferneside, Eyre(3).

1 **BENJAMIN**, Portsmouth, wit. for Mr. John Cutts in 1670 (presum. related to Mrs. Cutts), taxed 1672, jury, etc., 1673-

1676. Rate rebated 1675. Lists 326c (Mr.), 327c, 331a.
2 **EDWARD**, List 351b.
3 **RUTH**, wit. a Trickey fam. deed at Newington 1682.

**STARRETT, James, James, jr. and Peter**, all in List 291. See Y. D. 10: 182; 11: 160, 242; Curtis(6). In 1734 James of Falmouth was app. gdn. of William, minor son of James, jr., late of Kittery, mariner. See also 'Maine Wills,' p. 532.

**START**. See also Starke, Sturt.
1 **EDWARD**, fisherman, York, s. of Peter of Brixham, co. Devon, where he was bp. 23 Nov. 1614 and m. 23 June 1645 Wilmot Lamsytt. Jury of life and death in July, 1650; O. A. 22 Nov. 1652. In 1653 he bot ho. and land on Ferry Neck and liv. there. Grants 1653, 1659. In 1666 he bot from John Lamb and sold this the same yr. to John Card. Selectman 1667. Lists 275-277. See also Clark(7), Joy(4). He d. 19 May 1671; adm. 4 July to wid. Wilmot, bondsm. Wm. Roanes and Matthew Austin. Inv., ho. and lands, 5 cow kind, 1 mare, 6 swine, and debt due from John Card, sr. and jr., for a boat (Me. P. & Ct. Rec. ii: 228, 478, 483). Wid. Wilmot m. 2d Wm. Roanes. Ch: **Thomas**, only son, bp. at Churston-Ferrers, co. Devon, 31 July 1646. In Feb. 1673 he bot 18 a. adj. Robert Knight from Richard Burgess. List 86. Adm. 30 Dec. 1674 to Capt. Richard Cutts. **Sarah**, m. Henry Wright(2). **Elizabeth**, abs. from meeting, Wells, 1674; m. Moses Worcester(1). **Mary**, m. Antonio Fortado.
2 **JOHN**, b. ±1633, at the Shoals in July 1661, sued for debt by Richard White in 1663, drunk and telling a lie in 1666. Of Scarboro (Blue Point), drunk in 1673 (Mr. Neale bondsman) and 1674. His vessel was at Black Point in 1676. Scottow wit. 1681. Black Pt. ferry lic. 1682. He may have m. a Taylor heir, as in Feb. 1685-6, called ferryman, he sold 30 a., form. land and marsh of George Taylor, decd., to Thomas Scottow, one wit. being Henry Elkins. 17 Mar. 1686, Thomas Scottow admr. Lists 236, 237b, 238ab. See also Peter Starke who wit. with Henry Elkins in 1685 (Y. D. 6: 11; 7: 55).
3 **WILLIAM**, Y. D. 4: 69, List 124. See Sturt.

**Stathon**, John, Dover 1659. List 356e.

**STEADMAN, Thomas**. Records seem to disclose more than one. Thomas, Exeter, taxed 1680, bot from Robert Wadleigh 1685, if husb. of Jane Scammon(3), could not be the man killed in Hilton's sawmill, or the T. of Ex. who sold the Wadleigh land 12 Jan. 1695-6. List 383, 384a. One Thomas and Jane had s. Thomas rec. at Boston 8 Jan.

1687. Jane (Scammon) m. 2d 12 Oct. 1691 Dr. Thomas Deane.

**STEARNS.** 1 **Isaac,** sued John Wittum and George Brawn in York ct., 1710.

2 **SHUBAEL,** m. 29 Dec. 1704 Rebecca Larrabee (Kittery rec.). See Bond's Watertown.

3 **THOMAS,** List 57. Read Stevens.

**STEEL, Francis,** of Exeter 1694 and working at Newcastle fort. Land was laid out to him 7 Mar. 1697-8 and he bot from Thomas Rollins, jr. in 1698. Rated for the minister 1714. Lists 67, 376b (1698; his heirs 1740). Will, 20 Aug. 1717—3 Dec. 1718, names w. Elizabeth and sons: **Clement,** given the homestead on No. side of Great River, m. 7 Mar. 1721-2 Joanna Avery. In 1757 bondsm. for John Dow, gdn. of James Gordon(jr.). **John,** husb. of Dorothy Rollins (Benj. 6) in 1736. **Henry,** accused by Mercy Taylor(25) in 1734. See also Stevens(16), Allen(13).

**Stent,** George, Dover, List 94.

**STEVENS,** Stephens, generally in south half of Eng., adding -son in the north. See Dam(3) and Samuel Pease(2) whose dau. Rebecca was w. of Nath. Stevens of Durham in 1742.

1 **AGNES,** wit. Brackett to Munjoy 1668 (Y. D. 4: 34). Note Ann, w. of (3).

2 **AMOS** (see 3, 19), No. Yarmouth, a Boston sailor in Nov. 1682 when he bot from John Royal 15 a., being a small neck adj. Royal's own land. In June 1686, 4 a. of marsh each were gr. to A. S. and John Shepard, to be laid out on east side of Harrisickett. No. Yarm. trustee 1686. List 214, self and w. Margery (Shepard 4). His heirs entered an East. Cl. In 1727 a home lot of ±7 a., being a town gr. and the first lot from Mains Point, was sold by the wid. and admx. Margery of Boston and the only surv. ch: **Mary** Compston, wid., Boston (m. Edward C. there 11 Oct. 1721) and **Rachel,** w. of Henry Woolfe of Boston, mariner (m. in Boston 1st 24 July 1709 James King, m. 2d 28 Oct. 1719 H. W.). Woolfe remov. to No. Yarm., will, 1759—1759. A son John d. 27 Aug. 1713, ag. 23 yrs. 9 mos. (Granary Bur. Gr.). In Dec. 1728 wid. Margery sold No. Yarm. lot 76, orig. her brother's; liv. in Boston 24 Mar. 1732.

3 **BENJAMIN,** Richmond's Isl., No. Yarm., from Landrake, co. Cornwall, came for 3 yrs. in 1636-7, here in June 1640 (his wife in Eng. 1639-1640), and came again aft. signing a 3 yr. contract in Eng. 22 Nov. 1642. A wit. 11 Mar. 1642-3 for Jonas Bailey. Likely he went and came a 3d time, as unseen until Apr. 1666, in No. Y., prob. then m. to wid. Ann Shepard(4). Lists 21, 211; wife 214. In 1731 Joseph Harris(13) depos. that

±44 yrs. bef. he built a dwg. ho. for Ann, wid. of Benj., her land on east side of Harrisickett River, and taking in 4 a. marsh of hers and 4 of her s. Benjamin's, all enjoyed first by Shepard, then by Stevens, then by Ann until Ind. drove her off. An East. Cl. was ent. by the heirs of Ann Shepard. Not imposs. ?**Amos** and perh. ?**Edward** were ch. by his 1st w. By w. Ann: **Benjamin,** adult in 1687. See also Naomi, w. of Joseph Harris (13), and her son Benjamin Stevens.

4 **CALEB,** fisherman, Portsm., bot a ho. from John Banfield in June 1671; fined 1672, taxed 1672; with w. Ruth (Glanfield 4) sold the Banfield prop. to (20) in June 1673. One half of wid. Stevens' 1674 rate abated. Appar. he d. on a fishing voyage; adm. 29 June 1675 to Ruth and her fa. Lists 326c, 331a. She m. 2d Henry Kirke(2) who occup. the Stevens ho. until the only ch. Caleb, cordwainer, sold, deed ack. 20 June 1692. Caleb wit. a Pickering deed with James Kirke in 1692. In Dec. that yr., one C. wit. John Hunnewell's deed, appar. in Ipsw. (Y. D. 4: 115).

5 **DUNIE,** Saco. See Hughes(1).

6 **EDWARD** (see 3, 19), tailor, No. Yarm., now resid. of Boston 12 Mar. 1678-9 when he sold to Edw. Budd a planta. on Harrisickett River betw. John Holman and Thomas Jones, Isaac Cousins a wit. In Boston in Sept. 1684, ±56, he depos. that many yrs. bef. he was at John Cousins' ho. in Casco Bay and saw and heard read a deed from Vines to Cousins. One Edward and w. Mary had Thomas, rec. in Boston 1669; Edward and Esther had 3 daus. there 1680-1687; Edward d. in Boston 5 Oct. 1689. One Thomas, shipwr., m. in Bost. 13 July 1695 Sarah Place (2), liv. in Joseph Royal's Charlest. ho.; see also (19) and Crocum.

7 **EPHRAIM,** wit. for (13) in Aug. 1702. At Piscataqua in Oct. foll., ag. ±20.

8 **JAMES,** taxed Pemaquid 1687, two cows. List 124. See (17).

9 **JAMES,** coaster, Durham 1723, innholder 1731 when he receipted in full to Jeremiah Walford on a note. In Sept. that yr., J. W. repres. to the legislature that being very aged he had intended to make a deed in the nature of a will to J. S., who defrauded him in the wording of the deed; the legis. found it fraudulent. List 369. He m. 1st in Glouc. 15 July 1717 Deborah Sayward(2); in 1737 in N. H. app. gdn. of their ch: **Mary** Stevens al. Sanders, **Deborah, Abigail, Elizabeth, Samuel** (Samuel James, b. in Durham 1723); **James** (b. in D. 1724-5), **Susannah** (b. in D. 1726). He appar. liv. in Mass. with a 2d w.; m. 3d in Glouc. 20 Jan. 1754 Mrs. Mary -Dow- of Portsm. who must have been Mary (Hopley) (Ayers 8) Doe(3). Will, of Portsm., 1759—1759, names her, s. Samuel

James, dau. Elizabeth Elwell; br. William exec.

10 **JOHN**, wit. a Hampton mill contract 18 Jan. 1669-1670.

11 **LT. JOHN**, d. at Casco Bay 4 Mar. 1688-9. See Hoyt's Salisbury i: 323.

12 **JOHN**, b. Salisb. 28 Dec. 1670, s. of John and Joanna, br. of Jeremiah (w. Elizabeth Stanyan 3), neph. of (16). He m. Dorothy Hubbard(10), liv. in Hampt. 1694-5, bot in Portsm. 1695, sold there to Matthew Nelson in 1697 and Solomon Hewes in 1698. See Hoyt's Salisbury i: 327, for 11 ch., incl: John, b. in Hampt. 5 Jan. 1693-4. **Martha**, bp. in Portsm. 30 Aug. 1696, her mo. of the Salisb. Ch., List 331c. And rec. at Salisb: **Hubbard**, tanner, Oyster River, b. 20 Oct. 1698, m. bef. 24 May 1724 Mary Thompson (11); will, 1770—1771; 5 or more ch. List 369. **Joshua**, Stratham, b. 22 Aug. 1701; adm. 31 May 1738 to wid. Catherine who m. 2d Joseph Mason(7). 4 ch. **Moses**, tanner, Dover, Somersw., b. 17 Aug. 1708, m. Hannah Thompson(11); liv. 1764. **Benjamin**, b. 6 Nov. 1710, perh. of Durham 1734 (List 369).

13 **CAPT. JOSEPH**, of the -Katherine- at Portsm. 1700-2. See (7); N. E. Reg. 69: 363.

14 **MOSES**, Wells, in ct. in July 1701 for travelling on Sunday, m. 16 Nov. 1703 Elizabeth Butland(1). Grants 1713, 1734. Lists 269ac. Will, 10 Jan. 1758—8 Jan. 1767, names w. Elizabeth, ch: **Jeremy, Elizabeth** Trow, **Hannah, Hepsibah, Joseph, John** (List 269c), **Moses** (List 269c), **Benjamin**.

15 **MOSES**, Berwick, wit. a paper for Charles Frost in 1708, taxed 1713, wit. a Keene fam. deed in 1722, depos. at Kit. in 1726. List 291. A ch. Moses, s. of Joanna, was bp. at Berw. 25 Oct. 1713. Sarah, Ann, John, Enoch and William, m. in Kit. 1733-1748, were perh. his ch. See also (22).

16 **NATHANIEL**, Dover, Exeter, b. at Salisbury 11 Nov. 1645, s. of John and Katherine; see also (12). Taxed Dover 1666-1684; in 1672 bot from R. Waldron the land his house stood on; appraised John Scribner's estate 1675, Isaac Hanson's 1683; deposed there in 1681, ±35, altho all his children but the 1st were recorded in Salisbury. First w. Mary. Of Dover, he m. 2d 20 Dec. 1677 Mehitabel Colcord(1). Late in life he liv. in Ex. Adm. 6 Dec. 1708 to sons Nathl. and Samuel. Lists 356k, 357d, 359ab, 52, 54, 94; or son 376b(1698). Ch. (in 1716 the 3 bros. deeded Dover Neck land with full warr.): **Mary**, rec. at Dover 4 Oct. 1672. **Nathaniel**, Stratham, b. 12 June 1674, was going post to Haverh. with John Gilman in 1696. Lists 67, 388; or fa., 376b(1698). He m. 1st a dau. of David Lawrence(1) who willed to his gr.ch: Mary (m. Joseph Burley)

and Nathaniel (Newmarket 1740). He m. 2d Sarah Folsom(4); ch. rec. Dec. 1704—Dec. 1717: Samuel (Newmarket 1740), Catherine (m. Richard Sinclair), Mehitabel (m. Benjamin Norris), John (Falm. 1743), Jonathan (not in div. 1742), Benjamin (Falm., Gorham), David (Stratham, adm. to wid. Mary 1757), and unrec: Sarah (m. Ebenezer Barker), Ann (unmar. 1742), Abigail (m. Benjamin Whitcher). Adm. gr. to wid. Sarah and s. David 28 Jan. 1740-1. **Katherine**, b. 23 Apr. 1676. By 2d w: **Samuel**, Exeter, b. 18 Jan. 1680 (twin). Ind. captive, Lists 96, 99 (p. 92). Will, 1 Oct. 1735—30 Aug. 1738, names w. Patience (Gordon 6, liv. Brentwood 1762) and ch. under age: Samuel (d. early, leaving 2 sons), Healy (d. by 1758), Edward, Nathaniel, Sarah (m. John Gilman), Mehitabel (m. Samuel Colcord), Patience (m. Ebenezer Colcord). **Mehitabel**, (twin), m. John Thing(2). **Edward**, Exeter, b. 4 June 1684, Ex. wit. 1701-2. Adm. 3 Dec. 1718 to wid. Elizabeth (Thing 2), who m. 2d by 1725 Daniel Young. The land was div. in 1737 by the sons Samuel and Edward (Epping, will, 1756—1757), who had sisters: Mary (w. of Philip Wadleigh 1736), Elizabeth (w. of Israel Young 1738), Mehitabel (wid. of James Gordon 1741-1746+, later w. of one Steele).

17 **ROBERT**, Pemaquid, taxed 1687, land and stock; List 124. How related to (8), and which, if either, was fa. of the three captives taken there 5 Aug. 1689, is unkn: Samuel, in Canada 1711; John, a boy, and Katherine, a girl, there 1695. List 99, pp. 91, 75 (2). Katherine was appar. the Marie Francoise (p. 127) who m. 1 Aug. 1697 Jacques Pacquet and liv. near Quebec; ch. She was ±19 when mar., and did not rememb. the bap. names of her late fa. and mo. or the surname of her mo. who d. in her infancy.

18 **SARAH**, Portsm., had money from the town for her necessity in 1713.

19 **THOMAS**, Pejepscot. O. A. to King 8 Sept. 1665; gr.j. 1665, 1666; retail lic. 1665; wit. an Indian deed in 1670, another 26 Nov. 1672 with 2d w. Margaret, wid. of Thomas Watkins(2). In Jan. 1670 he had from the Indians a large tract at Wescustogo, which he and Margaret deeded to Gedney and Sayward in 1674, when he empowered 'loving friend' Wm. Royal to give poss., and also called him 'brother.' By ano. Ind. deed 1675 he got land on Pejepscot River, adj. his own and Allister Coombs', running to the Carrying path or place. O. A. at Dorchester 21 Apr. 1679. In Feb. 1680, he ±60 and Margaret ±38, depos. that the Ind. John Dyer(6) had killed had attacked their home the same night; she ment. 'my children.' He ack. a deed to Kelland and Hobby in Boston in Sept. 1681, she in July 1682; the

fam. was in distress at Milton in Nov. 1683. He ret. East and depos. 4 Sept. 1688, ±70, ab. going by canoe from his ho. to John Bish's with two of the Bish ch. and all made prisoners in the Bish ho. by Ind. Their end unkn. Lists 161, 182, 13, 189, 191, 214. See Giles (10), Potts(1). Ch. owned in 6ths and 5 are kn. By unkn. w: **Thomas**, with sis. Ann had Pejepscot land from fa. in June 1676. Of Scituate in 1701, he gave a bond to Robert Cock; Newport 1718; coaster of Boston 1719, when sued on the Cock note. A son, Joseph, shipwright, m. Ann Hallowell in Bost. 1711, was there 1718, of Newb. 1750 when he deeded 1/6 of his gr.fa.'s farm, with warr. ag. 'heirs of my fa. or any of my bros. and sisters.' Thomas, Swansea, was called cousin by Wm. Pierce(24); see also Thomas(6). Abigail, w. of Samuel Fowle or Fowler of Newb., 1739 (Y. D. 21: 73), may belong here, and 'Stevens son at New Haven mar. to Parker's dau.,' List 191, is not figured out; Jacob Parker(25) was bondsman in the Cock suit 1719. See also Gammon(2); Y. D. 13: 28-29. Daus. of the 1st Thomas: **Ann**, m. Lancelot Pierce(14), her age at death, 83 in 1708, evid. overstated. **Sarah**, m. John Morgrage of Kit. **Abigail** (not Rachel), m. Samuel Lane(3), lived first at Salem where a ch. d. 10 Feb. 1690-1, ag. 18 days, 4 ch. incl. Samuel were bp. in 1700 and ano. in 1701; at Glouc. a dau. Rachel was rec. in 1708. By w. Margaret, if age at death correct: **Rebecca**, wid. of Thomas Moseley(2) of Dorchester 1751, d. there 29 Oct. 1755, ag. 79. T. M. of Dorch. m. Rebecca -Mason- of Milton 4 July 1700.

20 **THOMAS**, Portsm., at the Shoals in 1672, ±28, prob. related to (4) from whom he bot a Portsm. ho. and land in June 1673. Taxed Portsm. July 1690, Oct. 1691; his land ment. 1695. Lists 331b, 329, 57. His wid. Joan m. Thomas Barnes(12) by 1696 when they sold the Stevens ho. and 1¼ a. adj. Edw. Cate and Philip Tucker, decd. Son **John**, cooper, Newc., signed off his int. 16 Sept. 1697; appar. m. Abigail Alcock(2); taxed 1728, 3 polls; liv. 1758. Lists 315c, 316. 2 ch. appear: Alcock, cooper, had deed from fa. 1753. Thomas, b. at Kit. 11 Sept. 1700, may have m. Phebe (Heard 6) Morrell(1) in 1724. Poss. an unkn. br. m. Hannah Odiorne (3), who m. 2d John Hardison, and named Alcock Stevens of Newc., her resid. legatee in 1755. Henry, s. of one John, was bp. in So. Ch., Portsm., 1722. See also Alcock(2). ?**Mary**, Newc., in ct. on a bastardy charge in 1710.

21 **THOMAS**, Hampton, at Oyster River garrison Oct. 1696; List 399a.

22 **THOMAS**, Portsm., m. 23 Nov. 1712 Hannah Graves(1), a wid. in 1715 (see Preston 1), m. 2d bef. 10 Oct. 1716 Thomas

Blashfield(2). One Moses S. (see 15) wit. a paper for her in 1733. A dau. **Mary**, m. 1st 26 Dec. 1732 George Church of Rumford, co. Essex, Eng., m. 2d Daniel Robinson (see 6). In 1719, Thomas, ag. ±16, s. of one Thomas, of Piscataqua, mariner (living?), was put under guardianship of Samuel Adams, maltster (Suff. Prob.).

23 **THOMAS**, Dover, m. by 1717 one Martha (see Samuel Downes 6). Both living at Somersworth 1746, he dead 1762, she Philip Stackpole's widow 1765. 8 or more ch. One T. of Boston gave a note for £19 in 1717 (interest since 1709) and was of Dover in 1718 when sued on it.

24 **WILLIAM**, built and liv. on 100 a. on west side of Sheepscot River at head of Wiscasset Bay. The depos. of John Phips (2 jr.) 1738 ident. this William as the one who m. Elizabeth Draper(3) and had at least one ch. **Samuel**. As Widow Stevens she entered an Eastern Cl. for this land (wit. Robert Scott and Thos. Gent), but ano. Eastern Cl. was entered by Wm. Slack of Attleboro for 105 + 20 a. at Newtown ... Nequasset, by deed from Wm. Stevens of Boston, shipwright, 16 Dec. 1686 (ack. bef. Nicholas Manning), Stevens' deed being from Dongan 1 Sept 1686.

25 **WILLIAM** (Stephens), and Joshua Crockett helped John Trickey repair a Crooked Lane fence ±1683. At Hog Island, agent for Francis Wainwright in Mar. 1691-2 (Doc. Hist. 5: 357).

**STEVENSON**, Stephenson, at times Stimson. See also Worcester(1).

1 **BARTHOLOMEW**(5), Oyster River, m. 10 Oct. 1680 Mary Clark (see 2, 3). Jury 1695; constable 1695. Lists 52, 94, 376a, 368b(2). See also Rollins(4). Will, 22 Apr.— 4 June 1718, names w., ch., 2 gr.ch. Mary, an aged wid., was adm. to O. R. Ch. 5 Apr. 1724. Ch. rec. Dover: **Mary**, b. 21 Sept. 1681, as an 'elderly maiden' m. 19 May 1719 James Davis(40). **Bartholomew**, b. 30 June 1683, k. by Ind. about 30 June 1709 (List 96). See Hall(8). His wid. Elizabeth (Ricker 1) m. 2d one Abbott. Dau. Deborah, b. 11 Apr. 1709, named in gr.fa.'s will was D. Wentworth, 1753. **Joseph**, b. 13 Sept. 1686, m. 26 Sept. 1717 Margaret Footman(1). He was adm. to O. R. Ch. 10 May 1719, she 5 Apr. 1724. He d. ag. 80 (gr.st.). Lists 368b(3), 369. 7 ch. **Elizabeth**, b. 8 Dec. 1688, m. Samuel Williams(36). **Thomas**, b. 28 Dec. 1691. List 369. Will, 1753—1755, names w. Sarah, bros. and sis. Joseph, Abraham, Sarah, nephews, nieces. 4 ch. d. in 1735. **Sarah**, b. 21 May 1695, m. Samuel Willey(2). **Abraham**, b. 8 Nov. 1700, depos. in Sept. 1768, ag. 68. Lists 386b, 369. Wife Mary. 2 daus. bp. 1724, 1729.

2 **JOHN** (Stevenson?), List 248a.

3 **JOSEPH**. See Griffin(4).

4 **MARMADUKE**, a Quaker, executed with his companion, Wm. Robinson, in 1659. They had spent the preceding weeks on both sides of the Piscataqua.

5 **THOMAS**, Oyster River, owned on the so. side by July 1643, was gr. 30 a. at Oyster Point in 1649, and had ano. gr. in 1654. Lawsuit 1655. Lists 354abc, 355b, 356a, 361ab, 362ab, 363ac. Wife Margaret d. 26 Nov., he 7 Dec. 1663. Adm. 28 June 1664 to s. Joseph, a minor. He chose as gdn. Wm. Follett, who gave bond to pay the other ch. In Dec. 1667, Joseph was ord. to allow his 3 sis. and 2 bros. £6 apiece but to have the bros.' portions for bringing them up and all the rest of the est.; Mr. F. to be reimbursed £6 for physick for sis. Chapman. Ch: **Margaret**, m. William Williams(36). **Joseph**, ±26 in June 1673, in 1678 and later had difficulties with Nicholas Follett and the Thomas Drews over bounds; served on j. in June 1694. Adm. on his and br. Thomas' est. gr. to br. Bartholomew 4 Aug. 1694. A p/a given by the Williamses 7 wks. later recites that they were k. by Ind., s.p. Lists 356j, 359a, 365, 366, 52. **Elizabeth**, m. Robert Chapman(5). **Mary**, ±44 in Aug. 1695, ±53 in Oct. 1705, m. Enoch Hutchins(2). **Thomas**, ±29 in Aug. 1680, prob. nearer correct than ±26 in Sept. 1683, as he was drunk in 1670. Lists 359a, 52. Killed by Ind., s.p.; see br. Joseph. **Bartholomew**.

6 **WILLIAM**, master of the -Pied Cow- out, 1632, List 41.

7 **WILLIAM**, sued by John Lux in N. H. 1676. See Hammett(4) for a later William.

**STEWART**, Stuart, Steward, a Scottish clan. See 'Early Settlers of Rowley' (revised by A. E. Jewett, 1933), p. 356.

1 **DUNCAN**, m. Ann Winchurst in 1654, both being in service of George Hadley(1), and liv. 30 yrs. on the Dummer est. in Byfield, moving to Rowley ±1689. Perh. he first consid. removing to Scarboro, where he bot 100 a. at Blue Point from T. Collins(5) in Dec. 1680. Taxed 1681 (List 238a), but the fam. historian, Mr. George S. Stewart, said he never liv. there, and he sold to Francis Wainwright in 1708. Ag. ±75 in 1698 (SJC 3784). He d. in Rowley 30 Aug. 1717, wid. Ann 9 July 1729. 12 ch. incl: **Katherine**, b. in Ipsw. 8 June 1658. Mr. Stewart thot she prob. m. Paul Wentworth(7) and her sis. **Martha**, b. in Newb. 4 Apr. 1659, perh. m. John Wentworth(5). **Elizabeth**, b. 2 Nov. 1662, m. Sylvanus Wentworth(9). **James**, b. 8 Oct. 1664; his ch. incl: Charles, Hampt. Falls (m. Mehitable Dennett 2); Edward liv. in Wells with a 2d w. Bethia Batten of York;

Elizabeth Gove (see 1). See also (2). **Anna**, m. Colin Fraser (see Wentworth 7). **Ebenezer**, sent several ch. to Kingston. **Samuel**, carpenter, innholder, Wells, had town gr. 1699, m. 30 Jan. 1700-1 Dorcas Baston(7); j. 1701. Lists 269abc. Dorcas was a wid. and school-mistress in Mar. 1752. Ch. at Wells: Samuel, b. 4 June 1704, m. Dorothy Allen and Elizabeth (Littlefield) Goodale; List 269c. Joseph, b. 28 Nov. 1706, List 269c, m. Mary Lord who was gr. adm. 15 Apr. 1735 (ch. Wentworth and Dorcas); see Peter Grant(7). John, b. 5 Aug. 1709, List 269c, m. 1st Mary Preble, mov. to Scarb., where he m. Mary Bragg(1) in 1735, Mary Holmes in 1751, wid. Jane Anderson in 1777. Zebulon, b. 20 May 1713, m. Penninah Getchell. Jeremiah, b. 27 May 1716, m. Sarah Paul and Abigail Jones. Dorcas, b. 26 Aug. 1718. Amos, bp. 28 Oct. 1722. Ano. Amos, bp. 4 Oct. 1724, served at Louisburg.

2 **JAMES**, Portsmouth, see Wells(7). James, br. of Charles (James 1), b. 1688, is not placed.

3 **ROBERT**, Exeter, Wells, ±30 in 1680, was not the R. of List 74. Admitted Exeter inhab. 1678, taxed 1680. In 1682 atty. for Daniel Davison in Me. court, and fined (lightly) in Me. that yr. for illegally pursuing a thief and getting back stolen goods. Wit., Champernowne to Joan Andrews, 1685; wrote letters to Mr. Curwin ab. the mills in 1686; of Wells, sued John Redding in 1690. Gr.j. 1687, tr.j. 1687, 1689. Lists 383, 33. See also Brown(7). Will, of Wells, husbandman, 9 Aug. 1690, gave prop. at Wells or elsewhere to friend David Johnson of Boston; prov. in Suff. ct. by Johnson's son Robert 1 Dec. 1715.

4 **WALTER**, mariner, Portsmouth. See Deverson(1), Morse (9).

5 **WILLIAM**, List 74. One W. took O. A. at Str. Bank 28 Aug. 1685.

**STILEMAN**. Robert Stileman of London had p/a from John Stratton's wid. and ch. in 1641 to collect money in co. Suffolk. Note also (3). Yet only one Stileman is listed in Col. Banks' 'Able Men of Suffolk, 1638.' One Robert was in Ipswich, N. E.

1 ‡**ELIAS**, Esq., Portsmouth, Newcastle, b. ±1616, s. of Elias who came to N. E. from par. of St. Andrews Undershaft, London. Freeman's oath here 3 July 1632 and soon at Salem. See also (2). Elias, jr., was clerk of the county ct. and prom. in Salem until he remov. to Portsm. Com.t.e.s.c. at Portsm. 1658; of P. when gr. adm. on fa.'s est. in Essex Co. 30 Sept. 1662. Selectman almost contin. 1659-1695; town clerk 1664-5—1681; Recorder County ct., Comr., Associate and Magistrate for Me. and N. H.; Deputy 1667-8, 1671, 1673, 1677, 1690, 1692,

1693 (not sworn), 1695. Lieut. for Great Isl. 1673; succ. Capt. Richard Cutts as Capt. of Great Isl. fort 21 Feb. 1675-6; taxed as Capt. Oct. 1691; called Major 1692. Councillor 1680 (secy.). Judge ct. of Common Pleas. Lists 311b, 312c, 313ae, 317, 323, 324(2), 326c, 329, 330ab, 331abc, 356L (Portsm.), 46, 48-50, 52-54, 55b, 57, 59, 80-84, 94, 96. He depos. in Aug. 1686, ±70; in Feb. 1694-5, ag. 79, ab. Portsm. cts. in 1655. His w. was Mary 1662, 1672, (Perley names his 1st w. as Deborah Wolfe); he m. by 1684 Mary, wid. of (3) who was a midwife in Aug. 1685; m. last Mrs. Lucy (Treworgye 1) (Chadbourne) Wills (List 215b). Will, 18 (died 19) Dec. 1695, names w. Lucy (exec.), her ch., his gr. dau. Ruth Tarlington and her sons Elias and William T.; Mr. Samuel Donnell and Mr. John Shapleigh overseers. Her will, 1700—1708, gives to her own ch. and to her gr.s. Thomas Landall £10 due from Richard Stileman(3 jr.) if received, or the bill for £10 if she d. bef. recovering it. Only kn. ch: **Elias,** bp. at Salem 15 Mar. 1640-1. ?A dau. who d. s.p., dau.-in-law, or gr.dau., List 335a, 'the seat where Major Stileman's daughter satt,' Mar. 1693-4?

2 **ELIAS**(1), little known. In 1650 Thomas Lambert of Salem was fined for striking him. In 1662-1663 either he or his fa. appraised Essex co. estates. He m. in N. H. 10 Apr. 1677 Ruth Mannyard (see Maynard), had a Great Isl. gr. in Mar. 1668-9, d. bef. fa. Lists 330a, 331c. Only kn. ch: **Ruth,** m. 1st in N. H. 5 Sept. 1687 William Bussell, m. 2d aft. 1 June 1691 Richard Tarlington (Tarlton); see (3 jr.). Her will, 1708, names cous. Mary Atkinson of Newc. (whose maiden name is unkn.) and cous. Ruth Langford of Salem. The latter was form. Ruth Mansfield, dau. of Paul and Damaris (Stileman) (Laskins) M. of Salem. It is poss. Damaris was a much younger sis. or half-sis. of (1), and it is noted that Mr. Elias S. was bondsm. in Salem ct. 1654 for James Harmon(1) who had quarreled with and made advances to Damaris Laskins and Bathshua Raymond.

3 **RICHARD,** Portsmouth, Newcastle, b. ±1611, Cambridge 1644, Salem. No kn. rec. calls him son of the 1st Elias or br. of (1), the natural assumption; N. E. Reg. 51: 346, calls him cous. of (1). In 1646 he ack. judg. to John Horne, atty. for Nicholas Pacey of Lowestoft, co. Suff., merchant; had a Great Isl. gr. in Feb. 1660-1, but evid. considered returning to Salem, where an ordin. lic. was asked in his behalf in 1662, when it was ruled 'if he come,' etc. In 1663 an adm. of Edw. Lyde's est. with Rishworth and Samuel Maverick, why not appar.; as admrs. he and R. sued Capt. Champernowne in 1672. Clerk of Associate Ct. Feb. 1663-4; O. A. Oct. 1666; he and w. Mary were Kit. wit. in 1669;

with (1) apprais. Richard Cutts' est. 1674. Ag. 51 in 1662, ±55 in 1666, ±61 in 1672, ±64 in 1675. Lists 304, 312c, 313a, 323, 326bc, 330a, 331b, 54. His 1st w. was Hannah, the last one Mary, ±34 in 1668. He d. 11 Oct. 1678, leaving 4 ch.; adm. 24 June 1679 to wid. Mary who m. Elias(1) by 1684 when Nathaniel Fox sued for his wife's portion. Ch., by w. Hannah: **Samuel**, b. at Cambridge 23 May 1644; he or a 2d Samuel bp. at Salem 20 July 1651; d. bef. fa. By w. Mary (N. H. Prov. rec.): **Mary,** b. 6 Jan. 1657, m. Nathaniel Fox(3). **Elizabeth,** b. 8 May 1663, m. John Jordan(5). **Sarah,** b. 30 June 1665, liv. 1679, not in br.'s will 1691. **Richard,** b. 20 Mar. 1667-8, as only s. had the ho. and land, but mo. to have use of half the ho. Will, going to Barbadoes, 1 June 1691—19 Apr. 1703, names sis. Mary, sis. Elizabeth and her ch., cous. Ruth Bussell, and wid. Hannah Pormont(1). See also wid. Lucy (1); Tucker(3).

**STILES, William,** Dover, and w. Deborah had ch. there 1702-1710: **Elizabeth, Abigail, Deborah, Mary, William, Samuel** (m. Jane Hussey 7). He was an Eliot wit. in 1709 and the same yr. sold several Berwick lots. Adm. to s. William 30 July 1740. Lists 358cd.

**Stillet,** Thomas, a captive in 1713, List 99, p. 128.

**STILSON.** See N. Y. Hist. and Biog. Rec. 51: 30; Miss Coleman's 'N. E. Captives,' i: 175-179.

1 **JAMES,** Muscongus, from Marblehead, m. Margaret Gould(1), but how early and how long East does not appear. At Marblehead, at intervals at least, 1677-1686, and in pet. to Andros from Boston, 14 Apr. 1687, told that his w. inherited Somerset's or Muscongus Isl. where he made improvements and laid out money; he also ment. a certif. from Jocelyn in 1681. List 85. See also Doc. Hist. vi: 262. He was k. at or near Pemaquid and members of his fam. taken or k., the time uncer., but perh. 2 Aug. 1689. Wid. Margaret was redeemed in 1695 (List 99, p. 74), m. 2d Thomas Pitman(10). 4 ch. bp. at Marbleh. 16 May 1686: **James,** called a boy from Pemaquid in 1695, m. in Canada 4 Oct. 1705, ag. 25 or 26, Anne Marguerite Odiorne, ag. 30, otherwise Hannah (Odiorne 2) Batson, was in Portsm. 1710-1, a fisherman, liv. principally in Newcastle; d. ±1772 at home of s. James in New Durham. Lists 99, p. 75, 316. Ch: Hannah, b. in Canada 2 Aug. 1706, bp. the next day as Marie-Anne, m. Thomas Mead. Anna, m. Abraham Trefethen. Alice, m. Samuel Clark. Capt. James, m. Mary True. **John,** may have been Jean of List 99, p. 123. **Margaret,** m. 1st Lt. Wm. Hilton(21), m. 2d John Allen. **Mary,**

bp. in Canada as Marie Magdelaine 28 Oct. 1695, m. 31 Oct. 1702 Jean Baptiste Cardinet, her br. James being a wit. 16 ch. at Quebec. List 99, pp. 75, 127. And by trad. a nursing baby was torn from its mo. and burned at the time of capture.

2 **JOHN** (Stilsone), Mr., adm. inhab. 21 Dec. 1671, List 330a.

**STIMPSON,** Stimson. See also Stevenson, Stinson.

1 **GEORGE,** Ipswich, came from Eng. as Mr. Wm. Cogswell's servant and in ¼ yr. went to Mr. Theodore Atkinson in Boston; John Atkinson(1) test. he was there in 1653. Daniel Eppes' servant 1664. Soldier under Major Appleton 1675 and wounded in the Narragansett fight; a soldier credited to Exeter in Oct. 1676. List 381. He m. in Ips. 22 July 1676 Alice Phillips. Ag. ±31 in June 1676, 32 the next Oct. when she was ±20. Neither's death is rec. in Ips. and neither is seen in Wells where lived several of the ch. rec. at Ips: **George,** b. 17 Aug. 1677, d.y. **Richard,** b. 10 Mar. 1678, of Wells and Saco (by 1714). He depos. in 1722 ab. Ogunquit river channel from 1696 to 1713; in 1735 had fa.'s right in Narragansett No. 1. He m. twice at Wells, Mercy (Littlefield 15) Lufkin 14 July 1702, Elizabeth Cole(31) 25 Nov. 1708. Ch. **Elizabeth,** b. 11 Jan. 16[80?], m. in Ips. **Mercy,** b. 11 Mar. 1682, m. Samuel Harmon(2). **Alice,** b. 18 Feb. 1684. **Prudence,** b. 16 Feb. 1686, m. Daniel Baston(1). **Rebecca** (unrec.), m. Samuel Cole(31). **Sarah,** b. 14 June 1691, m. John Littlefield(18). **George,** b. 27 Aug. 1693, and **Mary,** b. 4 Mar. 1695-6, both m. in Ips. See also (3).

2 **JAMES,** taxed Portsm. 1724. See also Nock(5).

3 **JONATHAN,** Saco fort soldier 1696, List 248b. Jonathan -Sympson- d. at Wells 30 Mar. 1703. Jonathan Stimpson and w. Abigail Allen(15) bef. York ct. in Oct. 1709; liv. in Berw. where ch. bp. and they joined the church.

**STINSON, John,** and Aaron Felt wit. Mrs. Mackworth's deed to her dau. Philippa Felt in Feb. 1669-70. Mr. John S., ±24 in 1671, bot liquor of David Campbell(2) or Kimball(3).

**STOCKBRIDGE.**

**JOHN,** Hampton, b. in Boston 19 July 1657, s. of John and Mary, stepson of Daniel Hendrick, m. Mary Godfrey(4) 23 Nov. 1681 (Haverhill rec.). Taxed Hampt. 1684, bot land there 1693. List 52. See also James(1). The writ in his dau. Mary's suit in 1746 recites that he d. in 1716 leaving 5 ch., but Capt. Jona. Marston depos. that the s. Abraham was b. aft. his fa. d. Samuel of Dorchester (Gloucester?), oldest s., renounced

adm. 23 Nov. 1715 in favor of the next br. John who took adm. 15 Aug. 1716; inv. incl. land only. Ch: **Ruth,** b. in Haverhill 9 Jan., d. 26 Feb. 1681-2. **Samuel,** clothier, m. Mary Villars 31 Oct. 1708 in Glouc., where 5 ch. rec. 1709-1715; ano. ch. Charles was bp. at Arrowsic 15 Dec. 1717. **John,** b. 18 Feb. 1685, an Exeter wit. 1702, Berwick 1715, m. 11 Dec. 1718 Jane Warren(1); 5 ch. bp. at Berwick. **Moses,** b. 9 Jan. 1688, of Hebron, Conn., 1719. **Charles,** b. 5 Mar. 1690, not named in writ 1746. **Mary,** b. 19 Mar. 1692, m. in Scituate 9 July 1717 James Northy. In 1746 she sued Richard Clifford (he had bot from Joshua Prescott) for 1/6 of her fa.'s land. **Abraham,** b. 17 June 1694, liv. in Stratham (List 388), appar. d. at Cape Breton. Will, 15 July 1745—25 Mar. 1746, names w. Mary (dau. of Israel Smith), s. John (b. in Stratham 24 Feb. 1717-8), two unmar. daus. Moriah (w. of Timothy Gordon in 1746) and Comfort; also gr.sons John and Abraham.

**Stocker,** Samuel, Mr. at Barbadoes 1669 (see Cole 27), at Portsmouth 1673 when he sold sugar to John Stydson. 'Mis' Stocker at Portsm. 1686, List 330a.

**Stocklenes,** John, a Berwick wit. 1716 (Y. D. 8: 158). Stockbridge?

**STOCKMAN,** Mr. **John** d. 1686, Dorothy d. 1696 (List 96), son-in-law and gr.dau. of Major Robert Pike(9). See Hoyt's 'Salisbury,' ii: 328; Jacob Bradbury(2), Folsom (4).

**Stockwell,** William, List 289.

**STOKES.**

1 **HENRY,** Monhegan. Lists 13, 15.

2 **ISAAC** (also Stocks), Dover, adm. inhab. 13 June 1660, in 1661 had gr. of 3½ a. with the river east, the common on all other sides. In 1669 Thomas Perkins was gr. the next lot north; the two neighbors were fighting that yr. and arrested. Eliot wit. 1674. A 4 a. addition to his ho.-lot was laid out in Mar. 1674-5. Lists 57(2), 356eghk, 359a(2)b. He m. Rebecca Rollins(2) who left him but promised in ct. 2 Feb. 1663-4 to go back. Two appear who were prob. his ch: **Hannah,** a ch. drowned in 1674, List 357e. **Deborah,** m. 15 Aug. 1687 Richard Kenney (see Canney 2).

**STONE,** became 28th commonest name in N. E.

1 **BENJAMIN,** York, m. 1st (int. at Boston 28 May 1712, he of Boston) Miriam Preble(2); 2 ch. rec. Y. 1715-1721; m. 2d 13 May 1723 Abigail Swett(5), 8 ch. List 279; see also Freeman(2), Moore(22).

2 **DR. DANIEL,** Cambridge, Boston, land-owner in Wells, his gr.s. Daniel Edwards of Boston selling in 1723.

3 **DANIEL,** Kittery (par. of Unity), b. ±1643, called 'Wadelstensteen alias

stoone' in George Broughton's suit in 1672, m. 19 Sept. 1670 Patience Goodwin(4) whose fa. gave bond for his good behav. in July 1673; he then owed £6 to John Crawford(2). Jury 1691; gr.j. 1691; sealer of leather 1692-3; constable 1698-9. Creditor of Humphrey Chadbourne. Lists 356j, 290, 296, 298, 33, 36. See also Wadlin. Will, 28 Mar.—23 Apr. 1713, names w. Patience, sons Jonathan, Daniel, 8 daus. Widow's will, 18 Feb.—4 Apr. 1716, omits Jonathan. Ch: **Mary**, m. one Martin, see (9 jr.). **Jonathan**, b. 21 Oct. 1673, was at fa.'s garrison about 1693; a bondsm. for wid. Judith Mead in 1718. List 298. Will, 3 Apr.—26 May 1742, names w. Sarah (exec. with Paul and Joseph who had the homestead and other prop., Joseph to maint. the mo.) and ch: Jonathan (b. 8 Feb. 1699, Exeter 1725, List 298), Paul, Skinner, Joseph, Elizabeth Neal, Mary May, Patience Pike (see Pike 7), Sarah Libby. **Margaret**, b. 6 Oct. 1674, m. Samuel Gould (12). **Rachel**, b. 13 July 1680, m. James Grant(6). **Patience**, b. 23 Mar. 1683, twice a Penhallow wit. 1699, m. Timothy Weymouth(2). **Sarah**, b. 23 Aug. 1686, m. Benjamin Libby(6). **Daniel**, cordwainer, b. 13 Mar. 1689, m. 28 May 1711 Sarah Jenkins(3). Scarb. 1730. Adm. 1 Sept. 1735 to wid. Sarah who m. 2d Clement Meserve. Ch. bp. 1712-1727: Solomon, Hannah, Daniel, Archelaus, Mary, Sarah, John. **Abigail**, b. 29 Nov. 1691, m. Wm. Goodwin(12 jr.). **Elizabeth**, b. 13 May 1694, m. 16 Nov. 1720 Nathl. Smith(41). **Leah**, b. 31 Dec. 1698, m. 1st Richard Randall(16 jr.), appar. m. 2d James Evans.

4 **E——**, 'old mother E. Stone,' Ports., see John Sampson(2).

5 **CAPT. JOHN**, at Damariscove early, List 8. Poss. the Capt. J. ment. by Winthrop in 1633, and the same belonging to Virginia, who went from Boston to Agamenticus, taking aboard Lt. Col. Norton(6) and all k. by Ind. in Conn. on way to Virginia.

6 **JOHN**, perh. several. At the eastward, took O. A. to Plymouth gov. in 1654. In 1656 compl. ag. John Bonython for beating his servant. In 1669 had long since dwelt on, improved, and sold to Thomas Walford, ±1 a. on Great Isl. Dover cor.j. 1670. Lists 11, 357d.

7 **JOHN**, Wells soldier from Malden 1693-4, List 267b.

8 **RICHARD**, at Mr. Gunnison's ho. in Kit. with Wm. Reeves(2) in 1653; ±19 in Apr. 1654.

9 **SIMON**, s. of Hugh of Andover, b. 1671, had a remarkable experience at Exeter 1690; see Mather's 'Magnalia,' ii: 606; 3 Mass. Hist. Soc. Col. 6: 218.

10 **WILLIAM**, Kittery 1683, named with John Broughton and Nathl. Keene. Gr.

1699. List 298. See also Lash(1).

**STONEMAN, Elizabeth**, Portsmouth, depos. in 1711, ag. ±65, about the parents of Timothy Davis(61); see also Branscomb. One John S. of Portsm. was br.-in-law of Samuel Banfield in 1734; adm. 31 Jan. 1738-9 to wid. Mary.

**STOODLEY, James** (also Studley), Portsmouth, wit. (Stoodleygh) a Spinney deed in 1700. Rated to So. Ch. 1717; taxed 15 Jan. 1731-2. List 339. Son **Jonathan**, b. in Lyme, co. Devon, m. 28 July 1715 Mary Seward(1), his name printed -Shedely- in error. Her fa. deeded to them in 1721. List 339. See also est. of Mary Cameron (N. H. Prob., iii: 152).

**STORER, a Derbyshire family.**

1 **LT. JEREMIAH**(4), carpenter, mastmaker, Wells, Boston, receipted for his share 28 Oct. 1671, and m. Ruth Masters (Nathl.) who was wounded by Ind. in June 1696, List 96. She d. 17 Aug. 1701. Jury 1687-1689, 1695, 1696; gr.j. 1691, 1692, 1694, 1695, 1697, 1699, 1702; an organizer of Wells Ch. 29 Oct. 1701. Called Lieut. 1695. Of Wells 1705; see Hilton(10). Lists 266, 269ab, 96, 39. Of Boston 1713, he deeded to s. Jeremiah his right in mill priv. gr. by Wells in Mar. 1701-2; in 1719 sold land on Mousam river granted to self and Jos. Littlefield. Ag. 71 in Feb. 1721-2. At the Smalledge ho. in Boston early in 1730. Will, 23 Jan.—6 July 1730, names 6 ch., Benjamin and Nathl. execs. Ch. at Wells: **Jeremiah**, b. July 1681, eldest s., to have an equal sh. if he adjust accts. with execs. He m. 1st in Boston 13 May 1708 Margaret Wardwell; 3 daus., b. in Charlest. 1709-1713, all d.y.; of Boston 1714, Wells 1723, m. there 2d 12 Sept. 1728 Abigail Wilson. Heirs in 1757: Jeremiah, eldest s.; Abraham, 2d s.; William 3d s. (bp. in Wells 1723); Amos youngest s. (bp. in W. 1729); Sarah Baston (w. of James, 3 jr.) oldest dau.; Priscilla Hatch (w. of Jona.), youngest dau. **Elizabeth**, b. 1 May 1683, m. 1st in Wells 22 Jan. 1711-2 (1701-2?) Thomas Barber(6), m. 2d in Boston 26 Oct. 1727 Peter Ray. **Benjamin**, b. 17 Nov. 1684, shipwright, Boston, m. 2 Dec. 1712 Susanna Wardwell; ch: John and Susanna, bp. 1714, Benjamin, Samuel, Jonathan, b. 1716-1725. He wanted a lic. in 1735, having a w. and 4 ch., and not able to dress himself since falling into a saw pit. Liv. Mar. 1750-1, ag. ±66. **Rachel**, b. 16 Oct. 1686, bp. at Wells 3 May 1702. An Ind. captive (Lists 39; 99, pp. 92, 126), bp. in Canada as Marie Francoise 16 May 1706, ±19, m. next day Jean Berger; 2 ch. d.y. Unseen in Canada later, and poss. ret. here, as her fa. willed to her as Rachel Bargee, but not to her sis. Priscilla. **Nathaniel**, b. 17 Nov. 1689, shipwr., Boston, m. there 11 Jan.

1711 Margaret Smith; ch: Nathaniel, John, Margaret, b. 1712-1717. One Nathl. Storer pub. int. with Sarah Howard (Hayward) of Braintree 25 June 1724; 5 ch. rec. as Story. **Ruth**, b. 25 Feb. 1692, m. in Boston 22 Nov. 1709 Wm. Smalledge. Not in fa.'s will: **Priscilla**, b. 4 Sept. 1694, bp. at Wells 24 May 1702, and in Canada 21 Nov. 1705 as Marie Priscille, m. 26 May 1711 Jean Baptiste Dagueil; 4 ch. liv. 1749. She was bur. in Montreal 13 May 1768, ±76. Lists 39; 99, pp. 92, 127. **Abraham**, b. 28 Feb. 1697, bp. in Wells 28 June 1702; either he or Rebecca was k. 10 Aug. 1703. List 39. **Ann** (twin), b. 22 Aug. 1699, d. 12 Nov. 1700. **Rebecca** (twin), bp. at Wells 24 May 1702; see her br. Abraham.

2 LT. *JOSEPH(4), Wells, one of the heroes of Ind. times. He was an eq. partner with br. Benjamin, whose est. he adm., and by agreem. with the heirs had the ho. he had built, all cattle and moveables that were B.'s except a horse, and half the meadow. Apprais. John Wells' est. 1677, adm. George Farrow's 1678. Exch. farms with step-fa. in 1682. O. A. Mar. 1679-80. Gr.j. 1678, 1679, 1694, 1695; j. life and death 1693. Deputy 1681, 1684, 1685. Called Ensign 1680, Lieut. Feb. 1690-1. Deacon. Selectman 1713. Retail and tav. lic. many times. Ag. ±29 in Sept. 1678, ±79 in May 1727. Lists 262, 266, 267ab, 268b, 269ab(3), 28, 36, 38. See also Y. D. 2: 91; 3: 108; 12: 259; 'Old Eliot,' i: 12, 43. His w. Hannah (Hill 17) surv. him. Aged and infirm, he made will 20 Feb. 1721-2, naming w. and all ch. but Joseph; liv. to 12 Jan. 1729-30; inv. £1481. Ch: **Hannah**, b. 6 May 1680, m. Col. Joseph Hammond(3 jr.). **Sarah**, b. 9 Dec. 1682, m. Ebenezer Coburn; he d. in York 28 Dec. 1749, she 21 Jan. 1770. Ch. rec. York 1707-1726. **Mary**, b. 11 May 1685, wit. with sis. Hannah in Nov. 1700. A captive (List 99, pp. 92, 127), bp. at Boucherville as Marie 25 Feb. 1704, m. 26 Nov. 1708 Jean Gaultier, dit St. Germaine; d. 1747. 10 ch. Calling her Mary St. Germaine, her fa. willed her £50 if she ret. to N. E., otherwise 10 sh. See Proc. of Mass. Hist. Socy. 2: 55: 228. **Abigail**, b. 29 Oct. 1687, m. Joseph Littlefield(17 jr.). **Joseph**, b. 29 Aug. 1690, bp. at Charlest. 8 Nov. 1696, drowned going over Wells bar in a small sloop about Oct. 1707 (List 96). Col. **John**, b. 5 Sept. 1694, m. at Wells 11 Oct. 1722 Elizabeth Hill(19). Fa.'s exec. and had the homestead (entailed). List 269c. See 'Hist. of Wells,' chapter XXV; 'Maine at Louisburg' (Burrage). 9 ch. rec. or bp. at W. 1723-1743, incl. Bellamy. He d. 28 Sept. 1768, ag. 74; by newspaper report left a w. to whom he had been mar. 46 yrs., 1 s., 3 daus. **Keziah**, b. 2 May 1697, m. at Wells 3 Nov. 1715 Benjamin Plummer. See Essex

Inst. Col. 50: 270. **Ebenezer**, Esq., Boston, b. at Saco fort 4 June 1699; of York, m. at Boston 12 June 1723 Mary Edwards; d. 22 May 1761, ag. 63 (obit. in Boston Gazette). 8 ch. rec. Rev. **Seth**, b. 26 May 1702, H. C. 1720, adm. to So. Ch., Portsm., Mar. 1721-2, ordained at Watertown 1724, m. 9 May 1734 Mary Coney (John), d. s.p. 27 Nov. 1774, aft. a pastorate of 50 yrs.; will, 1774, names w., Storer kin.

3 **SAMUEL**(4), mariner, Wells, Charlestown, receipted for his portion in upland and meadow 9 Oct. 1674. From Wells he wrote to Mr. Curwin in Nov. 1680 to introduce Jonathan Orris, and there, in 1685, master of brigantine -Endeavor-, sold half the vessel to Lewis Allen. At Boston 1692, asking aid for a preacher at W., having 40 soldiers, no chaplain; with his sloop helped defend W. in the Ind. attack that yr. (3 Mass. Hist. Soc. Col. 6: 228-230; Gooch 3). Lists 266, 269b, 333b. He d. in Charlest. 10 June 1700; wid. Lydia (Littlefield 15) filed bond 23 Dec. 1700; inv. incl. ho. and garden at Charlest., land at Wells. On pet. to sell (he left 6 ch., 5 of them small) she was authorized to sell the W. land and keep the C. prop. for supp. of her 5 ch.; £20 were voted her by the Genl. Ct. Of York 15 Feb. 1721-2, she and 4 last named ch. q.c. Wells land to John Storer. Ch: Oldest **child** in 1700, poss. not Lydia's, is unkn.; perh. Daniel, see Hibbins. **Patience**, d. 8 July 1690, ag. 7 mo. (Charlest. gr.st.). Rec. and bp. at Charlest: **William**, b. 22 June 1691, not seen aft. 1700. **Lydia**, b. 4 Mar. 1693-4, m. Samuel Sewall (4). **Mehitabel**, b. 5 May 1696, m. 1st Nicholas Sewall(3), m. 2d Jonathan Preble(2). **Jemima**, b. 30 Aug. 1698, m. 1st Caleb Preble (2), m. 2d Andrew Gilman(7). **David**, b. 23 Oct. 1700, cordwainer, York, Feb.-Aug. 1722. Miss Coleman did not see him as a captive, but credits to Parson Moody the statement that he ret. from captiv. in Aug. 1724, having 'been long mourned as dead.'

4 **WILLIAM** (or Story), Dover 1640, kept a commonplace book into which he copied a eulogy of Rev. Arthur Hildersam, an eminent Puritan preacher at Ashby-de-la-Zouch, co. Leicester. If an indica. that he came from that section of Eng., knew Dr. H. by reputation, or had sat under his preaching, the bp. of William, s. of William Storer, at Wirksworth, co. Derby, in 1611, may be promising. A page of this valuable book, giving the births of his ch., is reproduced in 'Annals of the Storer Family' by Dr. Malcolm Storer, 1927. At Dover, he signed the combin., had grants, and wit. Heard's deed to Walton in Mar. 1649-50. Clerk of the train band 1650. As marshal, held John Crowther's goods and was allowed 5 s. by the admrs. in 1652 'for his pains and service

and venturing his life thereby.' Chosen commissioner 30 Mar. 1657. Last taxed 12 Oct. 1658. Lists 351ab, 352, 354abc, 355a, 356abc. See also Nute(2). Widow Storey (Sarah) in rate made 22 Nov. 1659, List 356e. Inv. 8 Oct. 1660; adm. 27 June 1661 to Samuel Austin(7) who m. the wid. and took care of the estate. Ch. (Storer), from commonplace book: **Samuel**, b. 29 Dec. 1640, d. bef. ano. Samuel was born. **Sara(h)**, b. 16 June 1642, d.y. **Hannah** (Hana), b. 15 July 1644, and **Sara(h)**, b. 13 Dec. 1645, both d. by 1661. **Joseph**, twin, b. 23 Aug. 1648, called oldest son. **Benjamin**, twin. On 31 Jan. 1670, the twins receipted to step-fa. for their portion in lands and agreed to maint. and winter 5 neat cattle for fa. and mo. as long as either liv. B. was killed by Ind. at Wells 13 Apr. 1677, adm. to Joseph 4 Dec. 1677. Lists 266, 269b. **Jeremiah**, b. 4 Oct. 165[1 is doubtful]. **Samuel**, not rec., youngest s., of age in Oct. 1674.

**STORRE, Augustine**, Mr., Exeter, s. of Rev. Thomas, vicar of Bilsby, co. Lincoln, and br.-in-law of Rev. John Wheelwright(2) who m. his sis. Mary. He m. at Alford 21 Nov. 1623, Susanna Hutchinson(11), was at Boston in 1638, Assistant Ruler at Exeter 1639, and soon vanishes. Lists 371, 373, 376a, 377. John Legate sold land that was formerly his in 1650.

## STORY.

1 **CHARLES**, Esq., Portsmouth, Secretary of the Province, being appointed at request of Samuel Allen made 14 Aug. 1696. Admitted attorney-at-law in York Co., 1701. Ag. ±36 in June 1700; ±37 in Mar. 1700-1, also in Aug. 1702. Lists 98, 337. Will, 4 Mar. 1714-5—17 Mar. 1715-6, names w. Susannah, his beloved kin Robert, Barbara, Elizabeth and Margaret Foster, and gives 5 s. to Barbara Booth. Wid. Susannah succ. him as admr. of the Mungo Crawford est.; Madam Story rated to So. Ch. 1717; liv. in Portsm. 1720 (sold property).
2 **GEORGE.** Monies due him in Wm. Jones' hands attached in E. Colcord's suit 1642. See also Essex Q. Ct. Rec. i: 28.

**STOVER**, found in several co. Suffolk parishes. See Hist. of York, ii: 20.
1 **DEPENDENCE**(5), shipwright, York, had a gr. in 1680 which was conf. to him in 1719; in 1699 bot ¼ a sawmill and land at Cape Neddick from Samuel Webber. Wounded by Ind. in 1712 when John Spencer was killed. In 1732 John Spencer(jr.) q.c. to the gdn. of D.'s dau. Deborah land gr. to Henry Goddard and laid out to D. S. He m. Mary Young(10), d. 25 Sept. 1723, and she m. 2d 20 May 1725 John Wells. Division was made 4 Apr. 1726. Kn. ch: **Mary**, b. 8 June

1702, eldest dau. 1726, m. Isaac Stover(2). **Susannah**, b. 5 Nov. 1705, 2d dau. Adm. gr. to Isaac Stover 1 Jan. 1727-8; an extraord. wardrobe, 2 a. salt marsh, 21½ a. land inventoried. **Joseph**, b. 29 Jan. 1712-3, only s., rec. ⅔ the homestead, Samuel Came his gdn. in 1725. One J. m. Sarah Freeman(2), ano. or the same m. Mary (Boody) Higgins(2). See (2). **Deborah**, b. 14 Apr. 1717, youngest dau., Richard Milbury her gdn.; m. in Wells 11 Oct. 1733 John Wells. Ano. dau. **Abigail** d. 30 June 1723. Dependence 2d, List 279, is unkn.
2 **GEORGE**(5), of York 15 Nov. 1714 when he exch. deeds with br. John, but form. of Glouc., where he m. Abigail Elwell 25 Jan. 1692-3. He m. 2d (int. at Y. 29 Aug. 1741) wid. Elizabeth (Young 10) Webber. In June 1739, over 70, he depos. that he was bred at Cape Neddick and that Jeremiah Sheares owned adj. his fa. as long as he could remember; in Apr. 1748, over 80, depos. about (3). List 279. Will, 23 Mar. 1747—2 Apr. 1753, names w. Elizabeth (m. 3d Samuel Came 3), 5 ch. Rec. in Glouc: **Jonathan**, b. 12 Apr. 1696, d.y. **Isaac**, b. 3 June 1697, m. July 1724 Mary Stover(1); List 279. **Joseph**, not rec., named with Isaac as 'two elder sons'; see Joseph (1). **Hannah**, b. 19 Feb. 1701-2, d.y. **Abigail**, b. 20 Apr. 1703, m. 16 Sept. 1725 George Rodick. **Mehitabel**, b. 15 Feb. 1705-6, d.y. **Abraham**, b. 23 Feb. 1706-7, d.y. **George**, unrec., d. 10 Dec. 1729, ag. 19 yrs. 3 mos. 14 d. **John**, b. 26 Aug. 1709, **David**, b. 13 Nov. 1712, neither in will. Unrec: **Josiah** and **Abraham**, 'two youngest sons' by will. One J. m. Sarah Webber, int. 2 Jan. 1741; one A. m. Deborah Webber 2 Jan. 1749.
3 **JOHN**, butcher, York, Saco, Boston, presumably illeg. son of (5) whose w. in 1655 accus. him of having a bastard at Tom Crockett's. In 1748, (2) depos. that there was ano. John in York older than his br., who as long as he could rememb. called deponent's fa. 'uncle.' Rachel Carlisle depos. he liv. on S.W. side of York river. Presum. east in 1674, List 15 (2). In settlem. of John Lawes' (Lavers 3) est., the ho. and land were set off to him, appar. as cred.; called L.'s assignee in 1679. York gr. 1680, which heirs q.c. in 1747 (orig. deed in SJC 63476). Of York, he bot at Saco Falls in 1681; ack. judgm. to George Norton in 1683; of Saco in 1684 ack. debt to Wm. Vaughan and sold York land to Thomas Wise; of Boston in 1691 sued Wise. List 33. He m. 2d (int. Boston 13 Aug. 1696) Mary Blanchard of Charlestown; (2) often saw him in Boston and said he had 3 daus., forgetting the 2d wife's ch. The oldest dau. claimed the Saco land which was sold in 1719 by ch: **Elizabeth** Lash, wid. (m. Robert L., surely s. of (1) and d. 12 Oct. 1727, ag. 58). **Mary Pitts**,

wid. (Mary -Stafford- m. Thomas P. in Boston 18 Dec. 1702). **Grace Rowles**, wid., but ack. as -Lawless-; she was Grace -Jepson-, wid., in 1747 (in Boston, Grace -Stanford- m. Robert Rowles 1706, Grace R. m. Wm. Mingham 1712, Grace M. m. John -Gibson- 1720). **Dorothy** (by 2d w.), b. 23 Mar. 1699, m. 1st in 1725 John Lawrence of Charlest. and Boston, m. 2d Thomas Wharton; wid. 1739-1747+. Ano. **Dorothy**, b. 16 Oct. 1697, d.y.

4 **JOHN**(5), Cape Neddick, had a 30 a. gr. 22 Apr. 1680 which he deeded to little gr.s. John Perkins(11). Bot from Henry Donnell in 1686. Wife Abigail had tav. lic. in Jan. 1704-5, he was lic. 1705 and later. Lists 33, 279. See Harris(27), Lee(10). In 1714 he had built a new ho. on his fa.'s land; see (2). He depos. in May 1730, ag. 77, ab. the Cape Porpus land Dr. Davis liv. on 59 yrs. bef. Wife d. 9 July 1730, he bef. 12 Apr. 1748. Ch: **Four** taken or k. by Ind. in Oct. 1705; Pike (List 96), Penhallow and Niles disagree as to the number k., but Gov. Dudley in 1706 demanded release of three little boys, John Stover's ch., supp. held at Penobscot. One of them **Joseph**, was bp. in Canada 24 Feb. 1707, naturalized 1710, ret. home and depos. in 1733 that he saw Wm. Hutchins(3) in Canada. List 99, pp. 126, 279. See also Joseph(1). **Lydia**, m. Jacob Perkins(11). **Dorothy**, b. 10 Dec. 1704 (?m. Thomas Pickering 5). **John**, b. 4 Aug. 1709, m. 11 Jan. 1728-9 Miriam Harmon(5). List 279. York 1734, No. Yarm. 1736 and 1740 when her fa. deeded him 100 a. on Merriconeag Neck (Y. D. 19: 317), but the two deeds, 19: 37, must have been conscious or unconscious errors. See Wheeler's Hist. of Brunswick, p. 855, for ch., incl. Wanton and Alcott, and a garbled account of his youth.

5 **SYLVESTER**, fisherman, ferryman, York (Cape Neddick), with partners Ball, Way and Powell had gr. of a neck on so. side of Cape Nedd. river for a fishing stage 3 July 1649. The neck where he dwelt ment. in 1650. Grants 1653, 1665. Exempted from training as a ferryman in 1661. Abs. from meet. in 1664, he and w. in 1666. Censured in 1673 for over-indulging his dau. O. A. Mar. 1679-80. Lists 273, 275-277, 24, 25, 33, 75b. See also (3). He m. bef. 1655 Elizabeth Norton(5), whose mo.'s presence in their ho. evid. caused many of the troubles of their early ‚mar. life. Will, bound to old Eng., 21 July 1687—14 Feb. 1689-90, names w., 4 sons, 'the rest of my ch.' Her pet. (Doc. Hist. V: 432), stating that she lost her husb. the beginning of the war, indicates he ret. from overseas. She remained in York until forced off, poss. to Scituate. See Goddard(2). Will, at Scit. 7 Dec. 1714, gives to all ch., liberally to her negroes; the three

execs., incl. Michael Wanton, decl. to serve 4-17 Sept. 1722. Ch., order in will: **John**, 77 in May 1730. **Dependence**. **Josiah**, of Tiverton, R. I. in 1709 when he q.c. to Dependence; Joseph Coggeshall a wit. Named by mo. as an exec.; liv. 1722. **George**, ±80 in Apr. 1748. **Elizabeth**, 85 in 1738, m. 1st Capt. Richard Hunnewell(7), m. 2d Jeremiah Walford(3), m. 3d Capt. John Downing(2). **Sarah**, called Lanchester in mo.'s will, not identif. More likely she m. 1st Butland(1) than Banks(4), if either. **Deborah**, m. Dea. James Sayward(2). **Mary**, m. John Wanton, later gov. of R. I., tho their mar. int. in Boston were forbid 15 Nov. 1695. **Hannah**, appar. m. twice in Scituate, 1st Richard Church 2 Feb. 1696-7, 2d David Bryant 31 July 1706.

**Stowe**, William, Hampton, com.t.e.s.c. 1643, must be William Estow.

**Stower**, Joseph, List 57.

**Stranguidge**, Arthur, worked in the Lamprill River mills. List 380.

## STRATTON.

1 **BARTHOLOMEW**, Mr., Boston, and son, List 82. His w. was Eliphel (Sanford), step-dau. of Major William Phillips(22).

2 **JOHN**, gent., of Shotley, co. Suffolk, and associates were gr. 2000 a. on Cape Porpus River by the Council of N. E. 1 Dec. 1631; he had been in N. E. three yrs. past and had expended £1000 transporting and maintaining cattle and servants. He was then with his mo. in Dedham, co. Essex, leaving that month to take posses., poss. then being cast away at Cape Porpus (±10 yrs. bef. Nov. 1640). In Mar. 1636 he had owed a debt to Mr. Edw. Godfrey for three yrs. and his brass kettle was in Mr. G.'s hands. Fined in Boston in Sept. 1636 for lending a gun to an Ind., fine remitted in Dec. fol. 'if he go to the Merrimack.' Salem 1637-1641, where were his mo. and two sis. In 1639 he mortg. 100 a. in Salem Vill. to Valentine Hill and sold to Richard Saltonstall and Hugh Peters all Cape P. lands not already sold to Matthew Craddock. Ag. ±34 in 1640. Abs. in 1643, not seen in Salem again. Two islands called Stratton's Islands were incl. in Jocelyn's mortg. to Scottow in 1666, the name remaining in Stratton's Isl. off Old Orchard Beach. A dau. **Anne** was w. of Wm. Lake of Salem in 1660. See references in Lechford; 'A Book of Strattons,' i: 77; Essex Inst. Col. 54: 177; Andrews(17), Stileman.

**Streeke**, Samuel, ag. ±28, depos. in Apr. 1675 that the Churchwood bros. were born and brot up at Kingsweare, co. Devon.

**Strobbs**, William, Casco. His w. was killed 10 Aug. 1703. List 39.

**Stroton**, Henry, a captive, List 99, p. 126.

**Stuckley,** Capt. Charles of H. M. S. -Depford- in 1706 carried away by force Jethro Furber, master of pinke -Wm. and Richard-. N. E. Reg. 69: 363.

**Studley.** See Stoodley.

**STURT, William,** Pemaquid, wit. (Start) Nathan Bedford's bond to Mrs. Jocelyn in 1679. Recorded Andros' Arrowsic grants (List 187). In Boston with Sheepscot people in 1682. In 1686 sued Edward Griffin for ejecting him from Arrowsic Isl. which was gr. to him by John West. Town clerk, Pemaquid (1 Me. Hist. Soc. Col. 5: 137), taxed there 1687, personal only. Lists 162, 124.

**STYDSON** (also Stidson, Stetson), **John,** Mr., merchant, had bot a broadcloth coat from Mr. John Munjoy in 1673 and Goodwife Trafton of York had washed for him. Adm. in Wells ct. 25 May 1673 to partner Abel Porter; inv. 1 July 1673 by N. Fryer and H. Deering. List 87. See Me. P. & Ct. Rec. ii: 258-261, 271-2, 473.

**Suite,** John, Isles of Shoals (Me.) in Sept. 1680, a former constable.

**SUMMERS.** 1 **Charles,** a Kittery wit. 1671 (Y. D. 2: 133).

2 **CHRISTOPHER,** Henry Hobbs' servant in 1673.

3 **ISAAC,** shopkeeper, Portsm., m. Deborah Shackford(1) who was rec. into cov., So. Ch., 7 Mar. 1724-5, and was gr. adm. 30 Dec. 1737. She m. 2d Capt. Samuel Waterhouse (2). Dau. **Mary,** ±14, chose Wm. Shackford gdn. in Oct. 1740.

**Sumner,** William, Portsm. or Shoals wit. 1667 (Y. D. 2: 101).

**SUNDERLAND.** 1 **John,** a traveller, in N. H. ct. 1659 for driving a hired horse to death.

2 **NATHANIEL.** See Doc. Hist. 5: 406.

**SURPLICE** (Surplus), **John,** Kittery, m. Elizabeth Roberts(15), who m. 2d Wm. Godsoe(2). Ch: **Katherine,** b. 9 Mar. 1703, m. 16 July 1719 John Marr; see Stackpole's 'Old Kittery,' p. 604. **John,** b. 30 Nov. 1719.

**SWADDEN, Philip,** Piscataqua, St. Georges river. Mass. ct. ord. him whipped in June 1631 for running away from his master Robert Seeley of Watertown, intending to go to Virginia, and freed him from Seeley's service two mos. later. His wigwam at Braveboat Harbor ment. in 1636. In 1639 Thomas Hett of Hingham gave p/a to Lt. Morris(4) to levy 56 s. on his dwg. near Piscataqua River. Dover 1640. Wit. Sylvanus Davis' Ind. deed at Damariscotta 1659. Sued in Middlesex ct. by Nicholas Davison's wid. wit. 1666. Great Isl. wit. 1669. Ag. 54 in 1654; 73 in Aug. 1673 when he depos. that 38 or 39 yrs. ago Mr. Wannerton gave Nicholas Frost land to come to be his

neighbor. No evid. of w. and fam. Lists 35lab, 281, 101, 121, 41, 75ab. See also Mainwaring(2). One Philip S., clothier, was of Hilmerton, co. Wilts, in 1619.

**SWAFFER, Thomas,** willed £10 by Capt. Barefoot in 1688; he and John Lee certif. that the will was read to B. Edward Randolph, Esq., had a neph. of this name. See Register, 48: 487; Waters' 'Gleanings,' ii: 923.

**SWAIN.** Perh. partly descriptive, partly an old Scandinavian personal name Sweyn.

1 **FRANCIS**(4), Hampton, Exeter, seems connec. with both towns at the same time. Sued by Ralph Blaisdell for debt in 1649, by Wm. Bartholomew in 1653 for 4000 hogshead staves, Abraham Perkins being co-deft. In 1650 he rec. staves from N. Boulter for the Gilmans; in 1653 sued Thomas King for false reports about himself and Mary Cornish, when they settled by agreeing to pay their own charges and never renew the suit; in 1654 he was bound to keep away from her. Evid. in Charlestown in Jan. 1654-5. He sold Hampt. land to Henry Green in 1655, poss. moving away then, tho ment. in connec. with Sarah Jones in 1662. J. 1650. Lists 391b, 375ab, 376ab(1646), 393ab, this last showing he d. bef. 23 Mar. 1663. See also Pettit. Adm. in N. H. 11 Apr. 1665 to Nathl. Weare, who 25 May 1669 had p/a from the wid. Martha (sole exec.) and her 2d husb. Caleb Leverich (Rev. Wm., Dover) of Newtown, L. I.

2 **JOHN**(4), Hampton, Nantucket, ±70 in Apr. 1703, wit. ag. Nicholas Lissen in 1653; drawn for tr.j. 1660. List 393a. He m. 15 Nov. 1660 Mary Weare(5), mov. to Nant. aft. Apr. 1662, when in ct. for abs. from pub. worship, and d. there in 1715; will. Ch. incl: **Mary,** b. at Hampt. 11 Sept. 1661, m. Joseph Nason(5). Rec. at Nant. 1664-1679: **John, Stephen, Sarah, Joseph, Elizabeth, Benjamin.**

3 **JOHN,** mariner, Piscataqua, bot land at Maquoit from Robert Jordan in 1688 and depos. that yr. about John Parrett and John Frissell. Bot (at Newcastle?) from Fryer in 1696. Newc. cor.j. 1697. Lists 68, 315b. Wife Mary (Odiorne 2), List 315b. As Mrs. M. S., she was gr. adm. 21 Apr. 1699, m. a 2d husb. in Haverh., and soon died, inv. filed in N. H. 3 Sept. 1704. Adm. had been regranted on the Swain est. to John Odiorne 25 June 1703, when he was app. gdn. of the ch. **John** and **Richard,** the former not seen again. The Maquoit land was claimed for Richard, who had a provis. Scarb. gr. in 1720 which he, of Portsm., turner, q.c. to Nathl. Keene in 1728. List 339. Mary Seavey(5) who accus.

him in 1717 was poss. the w. Mary who d. bef. 10 Nov. 1728 when ch. John, Mary and Richard were bp. (So. Ch.). Appar. he had a 2d w. Margaret and liv. in Barr., but was of Durham 1747. Roger, a ch., was bp. in Roch. 28 June 1737. See also (5).

4 **RICHARD**, Hampton, was gr. 100 a. in Dec. 1639 and in 1641 had a 30 a. gr. in Exeter which he evid. sold to Nathl. and Abraham Drake. Presum. the R., ag. 34, who came in the -Truelove- from London in Nov. 1635, tho the age seems understated. Hampt. com.t.e.s.c. 1639; lot layer. Plf. or deft. several times (see vol. i, Essex Q. Ct. Rec.). Selectman 1650; j. 1650; gr.j. 1653. Freed from training in June 1653. In July 1659 he was a purchaser of Nant. In Nov. foll. fined and disenfranchised for entert. Quakers. In Sept. 1660 he deeded prop. to Nathl. Boulter, also giving him a p/a, and in Oct. 1661, late of Hampt., sold a Hampt. ho. and land to Benj. Swett and other prop. to Nathl. Weare, tho he depos. bef. Thomas Wiggin in Sept. 1662, ±67. Of Nant., by deed to the Boulters in July 1663. Hampt. Ch. excommun. him as a Quaker in May 1668: Lists 391ab, 392ab, 393ab(2), 376b (1647). See also Cram(2). His 1st w. Basille (List 393a) d. 15 July 1657; he m. 2d 15 Sept. 1658 Jane, wid. of George Bunker of Topsfield, with whom he sold Tops. land in 1660. She d. at Nant. 31 Oct. 1662, he 14 Apr. 1682. Kn. ch: **William**, ag. 16, and **Francis**, ag. 14, came in the -Rebecca- from London, arriving at Boston 8 June 1635. **Nicholas**, had Ex. grants with br. Francis in 1641, 1650, and in the latter yr. had a 2d gr. of 5 a. at the end of his ho.-lot. Lists 391b, 374c, 375ab, 376ab(1647). He d. 18 Aug. 1650. **Grace**, oldest sis., m. Nathaniel Boulter(2). **John**, b. ±1633. **Elizabeth**, bp. at Newb. 9 Oct. 1638, m. Nathaniel Weare(6). By 2d w: **Richard**, b. Hampt. 13 Jan. 1659-60, admr. of fa.'s est. in Nant. 1 Aug. 1682. He remov. to Cape May where adm. was gr. to his oldest s. Jonathan 22 May 1707; other sons were Ebenezer 19, and Lemuel 16, in 1708.

5 **ROGER**, joiner, Portsm., taxed 1698, m. bef. 4 Jan. 1700-1, prob. by 1698 (List 330f), Margaret (Clark 49) (Jackson 16) White, who was adm. to full commun., So. Ch., 28 Aug. 1715. Lists 330de, 337 (and w.), 339. See also Lamprey(2). He was liv. in 1726, marked 'dead' on tax list of Jan. 1731-2. Adm. gr. 31 July 1734 to John Morse; inv. incl. ho., barn and 23 a. in Portsm., 80 a. in Barr. Wid. Margaret was liv. in Kit. in 1741 when she depos. that she formerly liv. in the ho. in which the late Elizabeth Eburne, wid., dwelt, and it was ±48 yrs. since she went out of that ho. into her own near by. Ch. bp. at Portsm. 15 May 1709: **Dorcas**, m. 30 June 1726 John Morse of Kit., from Newbury. **Margaret**, m. 1st William Nelson(2), m. 2d Joseph Gunnison(1), m. 3d Henry Sherburne (3 jr.). **John**; one J. m. Miriam Banfield in Portsm. 17 Mar. 1740-1.

6 **WILLIAM**(4), Hampton, m. Prudence Marston(10), List 393a, and liv. on part of his fa.'s home lot. Jury 1650, 1653; selectman 1651, 1654. Lists 392b, 393b. Sergt. Wm. was lost on a vessel that left Hampt. for Boston 20 Oct. 1657. Est. of William -jr.,- apprais. 10 Nov. 1657, was attested 12 Apr. 1658 by wid. Prudence who m. 2d Moses Cox(18). Ch: **Hezekiah**, oldest s. 22 Apr. 1658 when gr.fa. Swain deeded land to him, ⅓ the income to be for the use of his mo. while a wid. Inv. 2, adm. 6 May 1670 to br. **William**, who had a double portion of his est. **Hannah** m. Francis Jenness(1). **Elizabeth**, b. 14 July 1650, d.y. **Bethia**, b. 22 Nov. 1652, m. Joseph Moulton(12). **Noah**, twin, b. 29 Dec. 1654, d. 23 July 1658. **Prudence**, twin, m. John Philbrick(4). **Elizabeth** (posth.), b. 24 Jan. 1657-8, d. by 1670.

7 **WILLIAM**(6), Hampt., m. 20 Oct. 1676 Mary Webster(6). Lists 396, 52. Inv. 9 Apr. 1692. Wid. Mary m. 2d (contr. 12 June 1694) Joseph Emmons(2). 6 ch. in div. 1702: **Mary**, b. 10 Nov. 1677, m. Edward Williams (6). **William**, b. 28 Dec. 1679, d. 4 Jan. 1718. List 399a. Wife Mary, who may have m. 2d 11 Nov. 1725 John Rollins of Ex. 3 ch. 1709-1714. **Mehitable**, m. Robert Rowe (see 17). **John**, m. 1st 25 Nov. 1714 Mary Sargent, m. 2d 24 July 1716 Martha Tongue. Will, 1757—1758. 1 + 8 ch. **Caleb**, Hampt. Falls, m. in Salisb. 24 Jan. 1711-2 Hannah Brown. Will, 1753—1757, w. Hannah, 8 ch., b. 1710-1725. **Sarah**, ±15 in 1706-7, ran away from mo. and step-fa. and was entertained by Samuel Fellows; her sis. Mehitable took her part. One Sarah of H. m. 25 Jan. 1719-20 Isaac Clough of Salisb.

**Swallows**, John, at Newcastle in Nov. 1699; see Garraway, Lane(12).

# SWAN

1 **JOSHUA**, soldier at Saco fort under Capt. Hill when Michael Edgecomb was there. Poss. from Rowley.

2 **SAMUEL**, taxed Portsm. 1713, depos. there in Dec. 1722 that he was at Lt. Joseph Roberts' ho. in Dover when Mrs. Susanna Cotton was there and employed him to do some business for her.

**SWARTON**, John, No. Yarmouth, where 50 a. were ord. laid out to him 29 June 1687 in answer to his pet. to Andros, dated Beverly 16 June 1687, stating that he had visited No. Y. and found favor with Capt. Gendall. In July 1688 he depos. ab. John Royal. He

had served in Flanders under Charles II and Capt. Church in his exped. East 1689 saw 'one Swarton a Jerseyman.' He was k., w. and ch. taken captives at No. Y. 1689. Lists 34; 99, pp. 74, 75, 126. See also Doc. Hist. 6: 264, 415. The mo. of his rec. ch. was Hannah, his captive w. was Johanna (called Anne Ebal by Catholic rec. when her dau. was mar.) and it seems certain that he m. in Bev. 8 Jan. 1671 Joanna Hibbert or Hibbard, b. 1651 (not Abigail, as by mar. rec.), and that her sis. Abigail, b. 1655, m. Thomas Blashfield(1). She was redeemed in 1695, her famous 'Narrative' being first pub. in 1697. See 'N. E. Captives,' i: 204-206. **Mary**, dau. of John, d. at Bev. 14 Sept. 1674. Ch. of John and Hannah bp. there: **Samuel**, bp. 8 Nov. 1674, was k. bef. the captives reached Norridgewock on their way to Canada. **Mary**, bp. 17 Oct. 1675, m. in Canada 9 Sept. 1697 John Lahay or Jean Laha, an Irishman. 11 ch. there. **John**, bp. 22 July 1677. His mo. parted with him the day after their capture, his later hist. unkn. One John m Abigail ――kins in Bev. 4 July 1702, and appar. soon d. **Jasper**, bp. at Bev. 14 June 1685, redeemed with his mo. in 1695, when she was called 'of York,' he 'of Casco.'
**Sweeting**, John, Pemaquid soldier 1696. List 127.

**SWETT.** Dorcas, Stephen, Joseph, Benjamin, ch. of John, were bp. at Wymondham, co. Norfolk, 1618-1624.
1 **CAPT. BENJAMIN**, Hampton, s. of John of Newb., prob. the B. bp. at Wymondham 12 May 1624, m. in Newb. 1 Nov. 1647 Esther or Hester Weare(5), living there until aft. he bot a Hampt. ho. and land from Richard Swain 16 Oct. 1661. At Newb: com. Ensign in Oct. 1651; j. at Hampt. ct. 1653; signed the Pike pet. 1654, giving as his reason bef. the inquiry board that 'every free subject has liberty to pet. for any that had been in esteem without offense to any.' At Hampt: j. 1664, 1666; foreman gr.j. 1664, 1668, 1673; selectman 1666, 1670, 1675-6. Lists 45, 392b(2), 393b, 394; wife's 394. Called Lieut. 1666. A resolute executive, he was commis. Capt. 22 June 1677 and ord. to repair to Black Point where he was soon slain (see Bodge, 342-346). Adm. 9 Oct. 1677 to wid. Hester; eldest s. to have the land, the other 8 ch. £30 apiece as they came of age. She m. 2d 31 Mar. 1679 Ens. Stephen Greenleaf(4). Ch., 1st 7 b. at Newb., last 4 at Hampt: **Esther**, b. 7 (or 17) June 1648, m. Abraham Green(2). **Sarah**, b. 7 Nov. 1650, m. Morris Hobbs(9). **Mary**, b. 7 Jan. 1651, d.y. **Mary**, b. 2 May 1654, m. Richard Waterhouse(1). **Benjamin**, tanner, b. 25 (or 5) Aug. 1656, apprent. to Mr. Samuel Clark of Portsm., m. 9 May 1682 Theodate Hussey

(3). Lists 395, 396, 52. He sold Hampt. prop. in 1695, bot at Newcastle, Del., in 1704 and. d. there; will, 1719—1719. Ch. here 1684-1689: Sarah, John, Stephen. **Joseph**, b. 21 Jan. 1658. **Moses**, b. 16 Sept. 1661. **Hannah**, b. 16 May 1664, m. Nathaniel Hall(17). **Elizabeth**, b. 2 July 1667; one E. m. James French 8 Dec. 1709. Lt. **John**, Kingston, b. 17 May 1670, m. 1st 3 Dec. 1696 Bethia Page (9), who d. 16 Apr. 1736, m. 2d 10 Nov. 1736 Mrs. Sarah Brown, who surv. him. List 66. Will, 16 June 1748 (d. 3 Sept. 1753). 7 ch. at Hampt. and Kingston 1699-1714. **Stephen**, tailor, b. 13 Sept. 1673, m. Mary Kent (int. at Newb. 27 Dec. 1695). Will, 1739-1746. 13 ch. at Newb.
2 **CLEMENT**, fisherman, Cape Elizabeth, sold a ho. and ±20 a. next north of John Parrett and near his own ho. to Thomas Sparks in May 1685; named an abuttor in July 1685. List 226. Not found in person again, and prob. Sarah whose land adj. that bot by Philip Carpenter in June 1688 was his wid. He was named an abuttor in Jan. 1713-4 (see Vittery): land form. owned by Sarah Sweat ment. in 1751. See also (6, 9).
3 **GEORGE** (also Swett, aut. Swett), was Charles Hilton's man at Great Isl. List 312e. In 1672 he wit. a note given by Arthur Bennick and Francis Thorne; the same yr. sued Thorne for wages. Bondsm. for Robert Smart, jr., 1676. In 1679, of Exeter, he did not answer a ct. summons; was sued by George March of Newb. for victuals, drink and horse meat, at which time he gave a p/a to Christopher Palmer; and, of Lamprill River, was in ct. for abs. from w. 7 or 8 yrs. Sued by Vaughan in 1680. In 1683, ag. ±30, he depos. ab. the York-Doe fence. Here in 1684. Lists 396, 52. Rebecca Sweat who wit. Mrs. Catherine Hilton's will (proved 1676, N. H. Prob. i: 173) may have been Rebecca Smart.
4 **JOHN**, Shoals, sued by Samuel Rowland in 1672 for withholding two hides. See also Gill(2), Jewell(4).
5 **LT. *JOSEPH**(1), Hampton Falls, m. 1st Hannah Ward(9), who d. 14 Aug. 1701, m. 2d 20 Nov. 1701 Sarah Andrews (Thomas) of Boxford. Constable 1686; j. 1685, 1694, 1695; on committee of militia 1691 (see Jona. Moulton 5); selectman 1693, 1698, 1712, 1717; Rep. 1693, 1698, 1699-1701. Called Sergt. 1693, Lieut. 1698; led a comp. of militia to Saco (N. H. Prov. Papers 3: 424). Lists 392b(5), 396, 399a, 52, 57, 63, 64. Will, 29 Sept. 1720—4 Jan. 1721-2, named w. Sarah, their ch., and four by 1st w. She m. 2d 15 Jan. 1722-3 Charles Treadwell of Wells. Her will, of Hampt. F., 12 Dec. 1743—30 Oct. 1745, names 5 ch. By 1st w: **Hannah**, b. 13 Sept. 1682, not in fa.'s will. One H. m. John Rust in Hampt. 12

May 1703. Lt. **Joseph**, tanner, Hampt., York, where he bot in Jan. 1717-8. Lists 279. He m. 1st Hannah Sayward(3), who d. 15 Nov. 1761 in 74th yr.; m. 2d 11 July 1762 wid. Patience Nowell; d. 2 Aug. 1776. 7 ch., 3 in H. 1715-1718, 4 in Y. 1719-1729. **Esther**, m. 18 Nov. 1708 John Eaton. **Margaret**, b. 2 July 1690, m. 1st Thomas Sherburne(7), m. 2d Benjamin Rust. **Abigail**, b. 29 Mar. 1692, m. Benjamin Stone(1). By 2d w: **Lydia**, b. 22 Mar. 1704, m. 1st 3 Apr. 1729 David Lee of Boston, m. 2d 25 Sept. 1746 Samuel Smith. **Hannah**, b. 23 May 1708, m. 2 Feb. 1728 Moses Swett of Newb. Capt. **Benjamin**, b. 2 May 1710, m. 20 July 1732 Elizabeth (Norton 1) Jenness, who d. 25 Mar. 1759 in 57th yr. Will, 1762—1762, w. Mary, 3 of 4 ch. Capt. **Jonathan**, b. 17 Nov. 1712, m. 1st 19 July 1733 Deborah Tilton, m. 2d 26 Oct. 1738 Jane Rowe, who d. 5 Jan. 1751 in 33d yr., m. 3d Mary (Doe 3) Wiggin; both liv. 1768; 10 ch. **Moses**, b. 13 Dec. 1716, not in mo.'s will. **David**, m. 25 Sept. 1746 Dorothy Currier who m. 2d 12 Sept. 1751 Andrew Wiggin; 2 daus. rec.

6 **JOSEPH**, and w. Jane, Portsm. Rated to No. Ch. 1717. One Joseph (Sweet) was a Deering wit. in Kit. 1717 (Y. D. 9: 20); Joseph (? of York) and Abner Perkins were bondsm. for wid. Mary (Carpenter 5) Deering in 1725. See also (2). Ch: **Alexander**, d. 20 Mar. 1716-7, ag. 5 days (Point of Graves). **Joseph**, bp. 30 June 1717, **Icet** (dau.), bp. 19 June 1720 (So. Ch. rec.).

7 **MOSES**(1), Hampton, a Quaker, m. 12 May 1687 Mary Hussey(3). He depos. in 1720, ag. ±60. Lists 52, 399a. Joseph Chase willed him £10, his dau. Elizabeth £5• Will, 15 Apr. 1729—19 Jan. 1730-1, names w. Mary and ch: **Elizabeth**, eldest dau., m. Nathl. Hall (see 17 jr.); d. bef. fa. **Mary**, b. 2 Feb. 1689, m. 6. 1 mo. 1711-2 John Swain of Nant. **Esther**, b. 10 June 1690, m. Benjamin Hoag(1). **Daniel**, m. 4 Feb. 1730-1 Hannah Cass. 4 ch. rec. **Deliverance**, m. 20. 8 m. 1718 Solomon Coleman of Nant. **Theodate**, m. John Purington (James 2). **Stephen**, m. 23 Dec. 1723 Mary Hoag(1), mov. to Mass. and R. I. Ch. **Phebe**, m. Elisha Purington (James 2). **Huldah**, m. 28 Sept. 1726 Benj. Coleman of Nant. **Patience**, m. 20 Apr. 1731 John Dow. **Benjamin**, blacksmith, given the homestead, went to R. I. and Mass., but returned. Wife Mary Davol. Will, of Hampt. F., 26 Oct. 1757—23 Feb. 1758, gives to sis. Deliverance and Huldah Coleman of Nant., all the rest to s. Jonathan.

8 **RICHARD**, 1667; see Hilton (9, 17); Y. D. 2: 33. List 3, Sweat?

9 **SAMUEL**, Falmouth or vicinity 1684. List 226. See also (2).

**Swind**, John, Falmouth or vicinity 1683. List 226.

**Swinnerton**, John, Falmouth wit. 1657 (Y. D. i: 98).

**Sygus**, John, Scarboro 1670, ag. 28. List 235.

**SYMONDS**.   See also Simmons, Simonds.

1 **HARLAKENDEN**(2), gent., Wells 1655-1660. He bot the Boade est. with br. Wm. in 1655, and from Bush and Turbet in 1660. In 1656 Robert Clemons sued him for selling a mare and foal he had already sold to plf. Late of Wells 17 Apr. 1661 when he deeded large tracts to fa. and other relatives. Interested with fa. and br. at Lamprill River. Lists 24, 269b. See Lissen(2); Y. D. 5: 1: 84, and references in Y. D.; Essex Q. Ct. Rec. 4: 303. Ipsw. 1662; Glouc. 1664 with w. Elizabeth Day (Wentworth); Ipsw. 1670, 1694. She d. in Glouc. 31 Jan. 1727-8 in 90th yr. His fa. willed to him the Lamprill Riv. farm and other N. H. land and to his dau. **Sarah**, b. at Glouc. 2 July 1668, the Coxhall land form. her fa.'s. She m. Thomas Low, jr., in Ipsw. 2 Dec. 1687. Wells land was laid out to her s. John in 1731.

2 **DEP. GOV. SAMUEL**, Ipswich. He was one of the Mass. comrs. receiving Kittery submissions in 1652, and as a Mass. magistrate held ct. in Me. and N. H. Owned largely at Wells, Lamprill Riv. and outside Ex. and Dover. List 379. See also Lissen(2), and Essex Prob. iii: 263, for his will, 1673-1678. Ch. incl: Harlakenden. **William**. **Samuel**, d. s.p. bef. him. **Elizabeth**, m. Capt. Daniel Epps(1). **Martha**, m. 1st Maj. John Dennison, m. 2d Hon. Richard Martyn(15). **Ruth**, m. Rev. John Emerson. **Priscilla**, m. Thomas Baker.

3 ‡*WILLIAM(2), gent., Wells 1655 (see 1), a large landowner and long resident there. Gr.j. 1659, 1662, 1663, 1675 (abs.), 1676 (sworn in, fined for abs. later); j. 1662-1666, 1668; Deputy 1676; Associate 1677-8; selectman 1678. Named an overseer in wills of John Gooch 1667, Francis Littlefield, jr., 1674, Joseph Bolles 1678. Of Wells 19 Nov. 1678. He inher. in N. H. from his fa. Lists 24, 25, 262, 266(2), 269b. See also Lissen(2), Manning(6). He m. Mary Wade (Jonathan) of Ipsw., where he d. 26 May 1679, adm. 17 June to wid. Mary and Jona. Wade; a div. made 7 Feb. 1688-9. Called late of Wells in 1706, when his farm was ment. ' at the Easterly end of the town.' During the war he had remov. to a garrison ho. in the center of the town. Ch. rec. and mar. at Ipsw: **Susanna**, b. 3 Jan. 1668, m. 18 Dec. 1690 Joseph Jacob(6). **Dorothy**, b. 21 Oct. 1670, m. 19 Dec. 1695 Cyprian Whipple; of Stonington 1710. **Mary**, b.'6 Jan. 1673, m. 10 Dec. 1697 Joseph Whipple; dead in 1706. **Elizabeth**, b. 20 July 1678, Boston 1710, m. there 7 July 1715 Ichabod Allen of Chilmark.

**Tain**, Thomas, York abuttor 1709 (Y. D. 7: 135).

**TAINTOR**, *Michael, Mr., Kittery, laid bounds between Maj. Shapleigh and Nicholas Frost ±1640. Wit. Shapleigh deed 1642. Removed to Branford, Conn., where he was prominent citizen.

**Taire**, see Tare.

**TALLEY**, Richard and w. Sarah wit. consent of the bride's mo. to Jane (Scammon) Stedman's marriage to Thos. Deane at Exeter 1691. One R. T., ±30 in 1683, was a Boston baker 1675-1699.

**Tamling**, John, wit. deliv. by turf and twig of Sheepscot land, Thos. Cleaves(2) to Scottow, 1666.

**Tankin**, David, drunk 1662. Isles of Shoals. See Y. D. 2: 99.

**TANNER**. 1 James, Wells, m. (York ct. Oct. 1712) Phebe Royal(1). See Y. D. 8: 140. Wit. 1714. She, of York, 'accounted a single woman,' was in trouble 1721-2. Still Tanner, she kept a shop 1723; m. 2d James Tyler. Dau. **Deborah**, poss. illegit., m. Timothy Carle(3).

2 **JOHN**, Portsmouth, carpenter, fined 1664, in ct. for absence from w. 1666, 1668. Adm. to Mr. John Fletcher 30 Mar. 1669. Lists 47, 311b, 330a. See Gray(3), Pickering (4).

## TAPLEY.

1 **JOHN**, ±25 in 1664, Damariscove. See Hunnewell(6).

2 **JOHN**, s. of John and Elizabeth, b. Salem 7 Apr. 1669, taxed there 1691, considered to be the J. T. at the Shoals 1702 (see Martell 2) and the husband of Anne Lewis(14). Poss. ch: **William**, Kittery, mate in Pepperell's service 1717. One W. T. was ordered pinioned at Canso in Sept. 1718 by Capt. Andrew Robinson on charge of stealing goods from the French. One W. T. m. 19 Mar. 1726-7 Rebecca Briar(7), was a Kit. tailor in 1745 when he and Rebecca deeded Briar prop. to John Haley. **Mary**, m. 1725 William Partridge(6 jr.).

3 **ROBERT**, br. of (2), b. Salem 17 Dec. 1673, taxed there 1692. He m. wid. Prudence (Mitchell 17) Braddin(2) by 1706 when they adm. the Braddin est. and she sold a ho. on Star Isl. She was taxed 1707 (mill-dam), 1709 (Str. Bank), 1722 (house on s. side Graffort Lane). In 1709-10, a Portsmouth inn-keeper, she was suspected of keeping a disorderly-ho. She renewed her bap. cov. at No. Ch. 18 Nov. 1716 and had two Braddin and two Tapley ch. bp. Her Lists 337, 339. She m. one Spoor by 1726. Ch: **Robert**, not in mo.'s will. **Samuel**, of Boston 17 June 1729 when his mo. deeded to him; legatee in her will 1729; in York ct.

for selling spirits 1737; signed Portsm. petition 1737.

**TAPRILL**, Robert, Mr., mariner, prop. of Portsmouth, m. Abishag Walton(1) after 1659. Wit. Champernowne to Walton, 1661. In 1672 they liv. in Boston in Alexander Waldron's ho. She seems to have left her husband and returned to her fa.'s ho. at Newcastle soon afterward, opening a shop to maintain her family. Taprill was capt. of the pinke -Hopewell- in 1676 when he was sued for wages by Francis Pallot, and of the ketch -Providence- when he d. at sea in Nov. 1678. Lists 302b, 311a, 313a, 330ab, 331b. The wid. d. Jan. 1678-9. See 'Ancestry of Lydia Harmon' (W. G. Davis, 1924). Ch., named in gr.fa. Walton's will: **Alice**, suspected of having had an illegit. ch. 1685. **Priscilla**, m. Boston 18 Aug. 1699 Francis Caswell; d. bef. 1714 when his w. was Jane. **Grace**, had illegit. ch. 1700 which she laid to John Tomson of Kittery; m. 1st Israel Hoyt and prob. m. 2d Sampson Babb(4).

**Tarbell** (Turbell), Benjamin, Cape Elizabeth 1683. List 226.

**TARBOX**, Nathaniel, Berwick 1713 (tax), Biddeford ab. 1720, b. Lynn 25 Jan. 1684, s. of John and Mary (Haven). Killed by Ind. 1723. By w. Elizabeth Emery(9) who m. 2d John Gray(9), he had: **Joseph**, m. 22 Feb. 1732 Mary Belcher. 10 ch. **Benjamin**, m. 1st one Abigail, m. 2d Hannah Smith. 9 ch. **John**, m. one Abigail. 9 ch. **Haven**, m. 20 Nov. 1746 Miriam Dempsey. 9 ch. **Sarah**, m. 25 July 1745 Job Roberts.

**TARE**, Taire, Tayer.

1 **JOHN**, very poss. br. of Cecily (Tayer) Davis(12) and s. of John Tayer of Thornbury, co. Glos. Bloody Pt. by 1642; gr.j. 1646, 1649; j. 1650; wit. at Gt. Isl. 1668. Lists 342, 354a.

2 **THOMAS**, Dover, blacksmith, ±21 in 1678, ±26 in 1680, by propinquity and name would seem related to (1). Supplied iron work on Isaac Waldron's -Primrose- and sued for payment 1678. Working for Richard Paine at Gt. Isl. 1680. Taxed Dover 1681, 1682. Sued in Suffolk Co. 1681-2 by Wm. Henderson. List 359a.

**TARLETON**, Richard, Newcastle, m. 2d ±1692 Ruth Stileman(2). Constable 1694, 1695; j. 1695; cor.j. 1697; gr.j. 1699. Lists 66 (Tarrington), 96, 315abc. See Horne (3). Drowned 18 Mar. 1705-6 at launching of a ship at Capt. Fernald's yard in Kittery. Her will, 4 Jan.—4 Mar. 1707-8, left ho. and Stileman heirlooms to minor ch., made prov. for her husb.'s dau. by his 1st marriage, if she came from Eng., contingent legacies to cous. Ruth Langsford of Salem and Mary Atkinson of Newc., and app. Mr. John Emerson and Theodore Atkinson Esq. trustees,

the latter and his w. to bring up the two youngest ch. Ch: **Elias**, b. 13 Aug. 1693, m. Mary Randall(7); taxed Portsm. 1727; signed pet. for setting-off Rye 1724. He d., ag. 95, in 1785 (newspaper of June 3). **William. Richard**, Newc. wit. 1720, m. wid. Mary (Batson 2) Parsons. **Ruth**.

**TARR**, Torr.

1 **BENEDICTUS**, Dover, 'late of Old Eng.' m. 17 July 1704 wid. Leah (Nute 2) Knight, whose 1st husb.'s garrison-ho. he rebuilt. List 298. Liv. 1732, when they sold 50 a. near Love's brook to Samuel Row. Having no ch., he made his neph., Vincent Torr, ±18 in 1726, from Blackawton, co. Devon, his heir. Vincent m. ±1739 Lois Pinkham; 7 ch. b. 1740-1758.

2 **RICHARD**, ±84 in 1730, liv. 5 yrs. on Elliot's farm at Blue Pt. bef. Philip's war, later at Saco where he 'improved' a sawmill under Blackman and Scammon. Of Gloucester (Sandy Bay) 1693 when he sold 50 a. in Saco that had belonged to Richard Sealy. He m. 2d Elizabeth Dicer (Wm.). Will, 7 Jan. 1729—13 June 1732, names w. and ch. By an unkn. 1st w: **William**, m. 21 Dec. 1708 Elizabeth Felt(5). **John**, Biddeford 1730, Boston 1734, m., int. 8 Apr. 1714, Elizabeth Haines(2) whose fa. deeded them 50 a. at Purpoodock in 1716; master of sloop -Mary- 1711. By w. Elizabeth, rec. in Gloucester: **Elizabeth**, b. 10 Jan. 1691, m. Ebenezer Davis; d. bef. her fa., her ch. in his will. **Honor**, b. 10 May 1693, m. 1st John Wise (see 4), 2d John Wonson, 3d Isaac Prince. **Richard**, b. 26 Aug. 1695. One Richard m. 29 Sept. 1719 Sarah Beale of Marblehead and had ch. 1722-1734. Ano. Richard m., int. 20 Feb. 1721-2, Grace Hodgkins who m. 2d 10 Nov. 1726 Joshua Cromwell (Joshua 3) after R. T.'s murder by Ind. at Fox Harbor 22 June 1724, and had ch. 1722-1724. Study would prob. identify them. **Joseph**, b. 16 Jan. 1697-8; his fa. deeded him 1729-30 100 a. at Saco, granted by Bonython to Arthur Churchwell(1). **Benjamin**, b. 9 Apr. 1700. **Caleb**, b. 4 July 1703. **Samuel**, b. 25 June 1706. **Abigail**, b. 11 June 1709, not in fa.'s will. **Sarah**, b. 11 Sept. 1716, m. Thomas Dresser.

Tart, John, taxed at Dover 1648. Prob. Tare(1).

**TASH**. 1 Jacob. List 339. See Thomas(6). 2 **JOAN**. See Lash(1).

**TASKER**, Taskett.

1 **ISAAC**. List 75b.

2 **MR**. List 328.

3 **WILLIAM**, Oyster River, ±40 in 1696, m. Mary Adams(3) whose fa. deeded 50 a. (in Madbury) to her and her ch. 1 Mar. 1693-4. Taxed Dover 1675. J. 1693. Joint

gr. with John Derry 1693-4. He d. ±1697. Lists 52, 57, 94, 359ab, 368a, 382. The wid. had an illegit. ch., b. 20 Apr. 1699, by James Jackson, her bondsmen James Bunker and Robt. Huckins. Adm. on her est. to Henry Nock 2 Feb. 1699-1700. Ch: **Samuel**, k. by Ind. 1 June 1704. List 96. **Mary**, m. Samuel Perkins(19). **Capt. John**, served in Crown Pt. exped., m. 3 Apr. 1718 Judith Davis(37). Will 12 June 1755—25 Nov. 1761. Ch., the first two bp. 6 Aug. 1721, others 21 Mar. 1736, Dover: William; Elizabeth, m. Samuel Davis; Samuel, d. bef. 1755 leaving w. Rebecca and ch.; John; Ebenezer; Rebecca, m. Samuel Huggins.

**TAYLOR**, an occupational name which became the 15th commonest in N. E.

1 **ALEXANDER**, taxed Berwick 1718-9. See Lord(6).

2 **ANTHONY**, feltmaker, Hampton, a young man with the first-comers. The new 'Banks Topographical Dict.' names Cobham, co. Surrey, in connec. with him, but imposs. to tell whether a positive identification or a good clue. He sold Hampt. land to John Legate in 1642, the first of many transactions. O. A. 1648. Signed the pet. in fav. of Robert Pike. Tav. lic. 1654. O. F. 1655. Selectman 1658, 1666, 1670, 1682; fence viewer 1660; j. 1665, 1675, 1676, 1678; gr.j. 1679, 1680. Dismissed from milit. training and watches 1666. Prison keeper 1668, 1672-1674, constable 1673, on special enforcement committee 1677. O. A. to Mass. 1678. Lists 391ab, 392ab(2)c, 393ab, 396, 397ab, 398, 49, 52, 54. Wife Philippa (Phillip in 1658) d. 20 Sept. 1683, he 4 Nov. 1687, ag. 80. No probate rec., but Joseph Dow once wrote to Judge Savage that he expected to find a will. Ch: **John**. **Lydia**, m. John Moulton(8). **Sarah**, m. 1st Thomas Canney(4), m. 2d John Wingate(1), m. 3d Richard Paine(12). **Martha**, m. ±1647, m. Hezron Leavitt(3). **Mary**, m. 1st William Love(5), m. 2d Hon. Samuel Wyllys of Hartford.

3 **BENJAMIN**(24), liv. on land he bot from Roger Kelly 1 Oct. 1696, a short distance from Asse Brook, in what became Stratham. Gr.j. 1699; selectman. In 1701 he and w. Rachel deeded to Wm. Graves. Called 'my br. Taylor' in David Lawrence's will 1710 and had deed from Joseph Lawrence in 1716. Lists 67, 376b(1698), 388. He d. 30 Jan. 1747, his w. 19 Oct. 1749. Ch: **Nathan**, had deed from fa. in 1723; m. Anne Chase (Jonathan) who d. in Mar. 1740, ag. 37; he d. in Sanbornton 11 Mar. 1784, ag. 88. 4 ch. **Benjamin**, had deed from fa. 1723, m. bef. 11 Apr. 1726 Elizabeth Wiggin (Bradstreet) who d. in 1749. His will, 1767 (d. in Strath. 14 Apr. 1768), names w. Patience, 5 ch. **Ed-**

ward, deacon and elder, had deeds from fa. 1729, 1740; m. Anne Sinclair (John 2) who d. 6 Apr. 1768, and had a 2d w. Mary.

**4 EDWARD**(24), ship-carpenter, liv. long at Salmon Falls where his w. Rebecca was born. In 1673 fined in Me. for taking Wm. Furbush's horse; ack. judgm. to Mr. George Broughton in 1676. His S. F. land ment. in 1683. In Mar. 1693-4 Dover gr. him a strip of land betw. his own and Mr. G. Broughton's fence. Of Exeter 20 July 1699, he sold 50 a. at S. F. to Thomas Roberts and soon took a q.c. from George and Jethro Pearson of 50 a. adj. his own land that was Edw. Rowe's. He liv. at Lamprill River, where he was k. by Ind. ab. 26 Apr. 1704, w. Rebecca and child captured. Lists 359b, 94, 96. See 'N. E. Captives,' i: 367-9. She ret. and m. 2d Thomas Dudley(1) bef. 7 June 1711. In 1720 she and s. Nathan renounc. adm. on the Taylor est. to Aaron Rollins, and again in 1726 to Nathan Pilsbury. The land was in 7ths in 1762. Ch. incl: **William**, b. at Newichawannock in 1691, bp. in Canada 25 May 1706, bur. there 11 Jan. 1712, a shoemaker. List 99, pp. 92, 125. **Nathan**, Exeter, m. 18 May 1727 Mary Barber(5), liv. 1762. **Daughter**, m. Ephraim Folsom(2). **Daughter**, m. Aaron Rollins(6). **Hannah**, m. Nathan Pilsbury. **Sarah**, called Souter in 1762. Rev. Mr. Pike reported one John Taylor severely wounded by Ind. betw. Ex. and Lamprill River ab. July 1706, who recovered.

**5 EDWARD**, New Dartmouth, where his ho. (empty?) was plundered by Ind. 6 Sept. 1688. Richard Adams and Edw. Ewster pet. Andros for land adj. his in Sheepscot River. See Doc. Hist. 6: 240, 443. Ag. ±38, he gave evid. ag. Lt. Jordan(6) in Boston in Jan. 1689-90. John Slaughter was liv. in a Boston ho., formerly one E. T.'s, in 1718, when his gr.fa. (see Goddard 1) deeded it to him. See also (10), (12).

**6 ELIZABETH**, taxed Pemaquid 1687. List 124. See also (12).

**7 GEORGE**, Black Point, ±60 in 1659 (see Elkins 11), ±70 in 1681, liv. at Casco with Cleeve in 1636. He sued Rev. Richard Gibson for trespass in 1640. Sued for debt by Richard Hitchcock in 1661, and sued Joseph Winnock for marsh in 1675. Lists 232, 235, 237ac, 238a. See also Boaden(2). His only kn. w. was wid. Margaret Hinkson(3), m. aft. 1653. She abs. from meeting 1665. They sold their land, for future payments, to John Mills 29 July 1679. He d. bef. 1685-6, but adm. was not gr. until 3 Oct. 1699 to John Tenney. Only kn. ch: **Andrew**, mariner of Boston, +21 on 20 Mar. 1685-6 when he receipted to Mills for final payment. See also John Start who sold Taylor land (Y. D. 6: 10).

**8 HENRY**, Portsmouth by 1640, sued Wm. Ham in 1646. In ct. for adultery with Ann Crowder(3) in 1648, taken to Boston jail and executed. Adm. 5 July 1649 to John Webster for creditors. Lists 41, 321, 330a. See also Davis(47), Storer(4).

**9 HERCULES**, Newcastle, sailor. List 312a.

**10 ISAAC**(12), poss. at Salem tempo. after the war, at Sheepscot 1683-1689 (List 164), signed a pet. ag. Lt. Jordan in Boston 28 Jan. 1689-90 (Doc. Hist. 5: 40). Later at Scituate (see 27) and ret. to Boston where he d. ±1720, leaving a will. He ent. an East. Claim for his fa.'s Damariscotta land held over 50 yrs. and enjoyed peaceably until the 1st war; his wid. and exec. Sarah deeded Sheepscot and Damariscotta lands to s. David of Scituate in 1731. She depos. in Boston in July 1737, ag. ±77, that she liv. at Sheepscot when ±20 and knew Elizabeth Gent, wid.; in May 1738, ±74, that they were neighbors together with Wm. and Margaret Lovering. Kn. ch: **John**, b. in Boston 16 Jan. 1691-2. At Scituate: **Isaac**, b. 20 Feb. 1693. **Mary**, b. 10 June 1696. **Jonathan**, b. 15 Jan. 1698-9. **David**, b. 15 Mar. 1700-1. **Rachel**, bp. 1 June 1707.

**11 JOHN**, boatmaster for John Winter when he fished at Casco, was liv. at Jalme (Yealm?) near Plymouth, Eng., in 1640. List 21.

**12 JOHN**, planter, Damariscotta River, was with Nathl. Draper 2 June 1651, wit. with Edw. Hall and Walter Phillips in 1659. Gr.j. 1666. John Pearce depos. that Phillips liv. near the Salt Water Falls and T.'s fence was ab. ¼ m. below the Falls. See Y. D. 16: 112, for bounds of land where he liv. until the war, and Y. D. 18: 281, for depos. of Lydia (Mercer 2) Stanwood, ±80, who liv. with him when she was 10 yrs. old. Lists 12, 13. His w. is not seen, unless (6), and he not aft. wartime, but one of them was related to Rev. John Oxenbridge's wid. Susanna of Boston (her form. husb. Mr. Abbott), whose will, 6 June 1695, gave to (John Taylor's ch.) kinsman **Isaac**, kinswoman **Mary**, kinswoman **Elizabeth** Gent (w. of Thomas 3); see N. E. Reg. 44: 83-88; 59: 324. Lydia Stanwood spoke of the sons, one of them presum. **William**(27), altho not named in the Oxenbridge will, and no ch. of his kn. to have held or claimed east of Arundel. As a possibility **?Joseph**, whose 1683 rate was abated in Salem, where the rate of one Wm. was abated in 1679, of one Isaac in 1684. See also (5).

**13 JOHN**, Berwick, had Kittery gr. 1655, 1669. By depos. of dau. Deliverance, both he and w. Martha had been servants of Mr. Leader. Constable 1665. One of those who used 'profane language' in ordinary speech (see Warren 4). Gr.j. 1671, 1672. Allowed

20 s. for service to the ct. in 1679. Lists 30, 81, 288, 298. Will, 7 May 1687—28 Jan. 1690-1 (inv.), named w. exec. (Stephen Hardison and John Turner bondsmen), ment. land given by Niven Agnew to him and his ch., and left 30 a. apiece to five daus. The wid. was abs. from meeting 1696, 1697. Her will, 7 Sept. 1702—10 Feb. 1703-4 (inv.). Ch: **Catherine**, m. Charles Cahan bef. 1687; not in mo.'s will. **Mary**, b. ±1662, m. 1st Stephen Hardison, m. 2d one Coss (see 2), m. 3d John Legrow(1). **Sarah**, m. Elisha Clark (10). **Deliverance**, b. ±1670, m. William Goodwin(12). **Abigail**, m. Moses Goodwin (4).

14 **JOHN**(2), Hampton, m. 1st 5 Dec. 1667 Deborah Godfrey(7) who d. 10 July 1699, m. 2d 30 Oct. 1700 Susanna (Drake 1) Brackett who d. 14 Nov. 1719. O. A. 25 Apr. 1678. Gr.j. 1683, 1694, 1697, 1699; j. 1695. In Mar. 1695-6 he bot the former Love ho. and 200 a. at Salmon Falls from his br.-in-law Wyllys and sold to Edw. Sargent(3). He d. 15 Dec. 1712. Lists 396, 397b, 399a, 52, 57. Ch. (w. Deborah had her ch. bp. 14 Mar. 1696-7): **Sarah**, m. 1st Peter Garland(9); m. 2d Samuel Dow(9). **John**, b. 26 Oct. 1673, d. 8 Oct. 1683. Capt. **Joseph**, North Hampt., b. 20 June 1677, m. 1st 28 Nov. 1698 Mary Marston(2) who d. 19 July 1732, m. 2d at Salisb. 10 Jan. 1733-4 wid. Sarah Morrell. Lists 66, 68, 399a. Will, 25 Sept. 1750 (d. 17 July 1752). Ch: Deborah (m. John Weare 7), Mary (m. 1st Daniel Weare 7, m. 2d Thomas Wiggin). **Richard**, No. Hampt., carpenter, m., int. at Newb., 23 Dec. 1704, Sarah Carr (James). Will, 13 Jan. 1753—26 Jan. 1757, gentleman, names w., sons John (exec.), Joseph (decd.), daus. Sarah Dearborn, Catherine Knowles(4), Anna Marston (decd.). 3 sons, James, Benjamin, Jonathan, d. bef. their fa., s.p. **Jonathan**, m. Mary Perkins (12), liv. on his gr.fa.'s 1669-70 gr. Adm. 1 Sept. 1724 to wid. Mary. 9 ch. 1708-1723. **Mary**, b. 3 May 1687, d. unm. 5 Feb. 1735.

15 **JOHN**, boarded with wid. Moulton(2), Portsmouth, in Dec. 1671, ag. ±23; at Great Isl. in 1672, ±25.

16 **JOHN**, Mr., masting for the Royal navy and for Mr. Peter Coffin 1694. List 66.

17 **JOSEPH**(24), millwright, Exeter, Wells. As son of Wm., he was gr. 40 a. at Asse Brook in Mar. 1658-9, when only a boy. Employed in an Ex. sawmill 1671. O. A. 30 Nov. 1677. Taxed Ex. 1683, appar. not later. In May 1692 partner with John Wheelwright and Thomas Cole in a mill gr. at Mousam Great Falls where a mill was built bef. 1701. Partner in ano. gr. with Thomas Cole 1693; grants alone 1699, 1700. Wells constable 1693; j. 1694; gr.j. 1694, 1695; highw. surveyor 1696. Lists 376b, 383, 268b, 269b. See also Y. D. vols. 12-13; Lawrence(1), Leavitt

(4). His wid. Rachel had a Wells gr. 23 Mar. 1714-5, was adm. to Ch. 31 Aug. 1718, cert. alive 13 Sept. 1727 and appar. 25 May 1728, altho the three grantors (Rachel named first) were called 'children' of Joseph. Ch. b. at Wells: **William**, b. 8 June 1694 (mo. Rachel), m. 22 Sept. 1720 Margaret Rice(4), deeded homestead to s. Nathl. 26 Feb. 1755 and ack. 12 Jan. 1759. List 269c. 6 ch. **Nathan**, clothmaker, Salem, m. Abigail Foster there in 1720, Mary Ray in 1748. Ch. **Joseph**, b. 18 Feb. 1699-1700, cordwainer, Wells, m. 5 Dec. 1734 Elizabeth Jacobs. 7 ch. **Benjamin**, b. 23 Mar. 1704, weaver, Wells, sold his int. to br. Joseph 15 Nov. 1725. **John**, b. 17 Sept. 1706, sold and ack. at Wells 22-25 May 1728.

18 **KATHERINE**, 1635, see Page(7).

19 **MATTHEW**, Pemaquid soldier 1689. List 126.

20 **RICHARD**, List 99, p. 128, may not have belonged here.

21 **THOMAS**, had Exeter gr. 1652. List 376b.

22 **THOMAS**, hindered Wm. Seeley in the building of a Kittery highway in 1667, when Sarah Trickey paid his fine for her husband. In 1670 he went to church drunk, also abused Capt. Raynes, 'theeing and thouing' him; non-appearance in each case. Ch.

23 **TOBIAS**, Isles of Shoals, indebted to Mr. John Payne of Ipsw. in 1663. He m. the wid. of Matthew Ham(6) by 1667, evid. the w. Sarah from Malaga Isl. who was washed out of a boat going over Ipsw. bar, inquest 27 Feb. 1667-8. He sold the Ham ho. to Mr. Fryer in 1670. **Tobiah**, in 1682 servant of Samuel Bishop of Ipsw. who had lately brot him from Salem, was poss. their son.

24 **WILLIAM**, knew Exeter ±1646, owned land bef. 26 June 1650 when part was bot for the minister's ho., and m. Ann Wyeth (Humphrey) after 25 Mar. 1648. Foreman of a Gilman mill 1653; excused from training and watches in 1666. He sold a ho. and two lots partly gr. by the town, to John Kimmin in 1664, 20 a. at Asse Brook to Richard Oliver in 1667, and by son's depos. had land at Asse Brook in 1673. Lists 376b (1659), 379. Widow Ann m. 2d 2 Apr. 1677 George Pearson(2). In 1683 her sis. Chadwell (see 3) willed her a serge gown and petticoat; in 1714 she depos. that her 1st husb. planted at Asse Brook 60 yrs. ago, and ment. her s. Joseph. Ch., order unkn: Joseph. **William**. **Edward**. **Benjamin**. **Sarah**, in July 1677 had run away from her master Wm. Allen,sr., ord. placed in a good fam. and to keep away from her evil advisers Goodwife Holdridge and Susan Buswell; because of her family's poverty, each side to pay its cost; she m. David Robinson(4). Two ch. of Wm. rec. in Ex. are credited by

Mr. Edgar Yates, in his fine work on this fam., to (25) and a 1st w., but more reasonably ch. of this Wm. and w. Ann, who was young enough to have a ch. ±1677. These rec. ch: **Mary**, b. 26 Oct. 1667, poss. m. David Lawrence(1). **Nathan**, b. 5 Feb. 1674, carpenter, m. (ct. Mar. 1699-1700) Sarah Drisco (8), and appar. was he who was k. in Me. in 1703; Lists 67, 376b (1698), 400, 39.

25 **WILLIAM**(24), ho. carp., taxed 1680, liv. near the Kingston line. Lists 52, 57, 67. Jury 1694; Exeter gr. 1698; gr.j. 1698; constable 1702. In 1703 school was to be kept at Richard Hilton's and at his ho. His wid. was Margaret (Bean 2), presum. his only wife (see 24). She renounc. adm. to her oldest son Joseph 22 Mar. 1735-6; div. was made to them and to five daus. The wid. was liv. 29 Dec. 1761. Ch., order unkn: **Joseph**, Exeter, m. in Salisb. 6 Sept. 1718 Penelope Favor, d. bef. 9 June 1763. 10 or more ch. incl. Willoughby. **Benjamin**, drowned by falling into the river, inq. 19 June 1728. See also Moody(1). **William**, in prison 1730 when his fa. evid. had paid out money for him; Biddeford 1734-1736, and there sold all right in fa.'s est. to Robert Patterson; of Exeter 1737, q.c. all int. to his br. and sisters; Ex. tax abated 1737 'being run away.' **Margaret**, m. 25 Apr. 1711 Tristram Sanborn (3). **Anna**, m. Samuel Scribner(2). **Mary**, m. Jedediah Philbrick(9). **Sarah**, m. Isaac Clifford(2). **Abigail**, m. 16 Oct. 1734 Richard Hubbard(5). **Mercy**, accus. Henry Steele in 1734, not in division.

26 **WILLIAM**, murdered at the Shoals in 1677. List 306c. Adm. to John Hunking 25 June 1678. Inv. of £7.

27 **WILLIAM**(†12), Wells, Scituate, perh. of Salem 1679, cert. bot from Nathan Littlefield near Kennebunk Falls 9 June 1684, when he was of Wells, had a W. gr. in 1685 (List 269b), and in July 1685 bot marsh on W. side of Kennebunk River from John Butland. Of Scituate 1689-1696+. Deane's Scituate calls him br. of (10), but locates the fam. home as prob. in Concord, Mass. Ch. rec. and m. at Scit., their mo. not named: **Lydia**, b. 20 Mar. 1688-9, m. John Wright in 1709. **Elizabeth**, b. 5 July 1692. **Mary**, b. 13 July 1696, m. Nathl. Brooks, jr., in 1717. Y. D. 27: 112 (1748) recites that Wm. willed his Me. farm to his three daus.; by Y. D. 29: 209 (1748), Mary Brooks (w. of Nathl.), Wm. Brooks and Mercy Wright, spinster, all of Scit., deeded as heirs of -our fa.- Wm. T., who formerly liv. in Arundel.

28 **WILLIAM**, appar. the name of one Taylor, an old man, in want at Portsm. in 1692, whose sickness and funeral were to be paid for 29 Mar. 1693, when Wid. T. was in want and not able to work. In Feb. 1694-5 she was to be 'shipped' to Ipswich, but the town to accept her back if she came again. Also in Portsm: Henry m. Deborah Ferdinando 1710, Hannah m. Daniel Homan(1), Elizabeth (evid. gr.dau. of old mother E. Stone) m. John Sampson(2), and Deborah at the almsho. in 1718.

29 **ZACHARIAH**, 1661. See Shackerly(1).

**Tebbs**, George. List 57. Tubbs?

**TEDD**. 1 **John**, Exeter, had a ho.-lot bef. 1649 (Tide), poss. the John Teed, servant, ag. 19, who arrived in Boston with Samuel Greenfield on the -Mary Ann- of Yarmouth June 20, 1637. Wit. Gilman fam. deed 1653 (Ted). Commissioner 1658-9. Sold to John Folsom 1662 (Tid), and to John Bean (ack. in Boston) 1664 (Ted). Lists 364, 375a, 377, 378. One John (Ted) of Woburn m. Elizabeth Fifield(3) 12 June 1678.

2 **THOMAS** (Teat), ±21 in 1678, a smith at Dover.

**TEDDER, Stephen**, assoc. with Ambrose Gibbons, here by 1633, gave his name to Stephen's Point ('Stephen Tether's point'), a little above Bloody Pt. Signed Piscat. Comb. 1640. Sold land to Mrs. Messant (N.H. Deeds 9: 748). See Langstaff. List 351b.

**Tedman**, Thomas, Exeter 1684. List 52.

**Tefford**. Wid. Tefford of Falmouth in East. Cl. rec. should be Jefford(1).

## TEMPLE.

1 **ROBERT**, Saco by 1664, poss. from Salem where one R. T. wit. 1659 and sold land 1660. Cor.j. 1670; constable 1671; selectman 1672. Goodwife T. seated in meeting-ho. 1674. He was k. by Ind. in Philip's war and the widow Temple, going to Mr. Scottow at Black Pt. for aid in saving her crops, was refused and shortly afterwards all was destroyed (SJC 1526). Lists 245, 249(2), 236 (wid.), 246 (goodwife). Supp. ch. (poss. others): **Richard**, Reading, servant of Thos. Bancroft, m. Deborah Parker, d. 28 Nov. 1737, ag. 69. 10 ch. 1695-1716.

2 **COL. SIR THOMAS**, Gov. of Nova Scotia (including that part of Me. as far south and west as St. George's and Muscongus), bp. 10 Jan. 1614, s. of Sir John of Stanton Bury, co. Bucks. On 20 Sept. 1656 Sir Charles St. Etienne made over to Temple and Wm. Crowne his interests in Nova Scotia, which gr. was confirmed by Cromwell and Temple app. gov. He came over in 1657. At the restoration of Charles II his claims were disputed, but, on his personal appearance in Eng., upheld. Created baronet 7 July and a new commission as gov. issued 10 July 1662. When by the Treaty of Breda Charles II ceded Nova Scotia to the French, Temple was commanded to transfer the territory, which order was not entirely fulfilled until 1670. He retired to Boston and became a benefactor of Harvard College. He

d. in London 27 Mar. 1674, s.p. For his two
wills see Temple Gen., by Temple Prime,
1894, pp. 61-65. Lists 2, 3.

**Tennehill,** Andrew, Portsmouth. A fine due
from him, 1665.

## TENNEY. See Creber.

1 **JOHN,** Black Point, husbandman, ±40 in
1676, settled ab. 1657 on 50 a. on west
side of Spurwink riv. bot from Ambrose
Boaden. O. A. 1658; constable 1668; com.
t.e.s.c. 1682, 1683, 1686; selectman 1671,
1673, 1679, 1683-1686, 1688; j. 1675; trustee
under Danforth 1684. Gr. of 80 a. 1671.
Sued by John Williams 1666, by Capt. Scottow 1678, by Capt. Hooke 1682. 'Sr.,' ack.
judg. to Mr. Francis Tucker in York et.
1694. His 1st w. was Agnes Boaden(2).
When Scarb. was aband., he fled to Gloucester where on 17 Jan. 1692-3 Jane Waddock,
the mo. of his 2d w., Margaret Waddock,
gave him a p/a. See Carkeet(3). Settled at
Kittery by 1694, selling the Waddock prop.
to Scammon in 1700. On 22 Aug. 1715 he
deeded the Spurwink land to his dau. Elizabeth Mitchell, appar. for life-support, tho
not so stated, and some yrs. later he and his
w. left Kit., went to their dau.'s home and
both d. there (SJC 73511). Lists 30, 32, 34,
232, 236(3), 237abc, 238a. See Mayer(1),
Moore(15). 'The Dath of John Tenney
Husbant to Margaret Tinney march 22th
day 1722.' Ch. by 1st w: **John,** b. ab. 1665.
**Agnes,** m. Glouc. 2 Jan. 1691 John Hammans
who d. at Casco Bay 1717-8, ag. ±54. By 2d
w: **Sarah,** ±23 in 1702 when John Amee was
acc. of trying to rape her, the ct. judging her
to be at fault. **Mary,** ±18 in 1702, wit. in
Sarah's case. **Elizabeth,** ±64 in 1750, m. 1st
William Mitchell(16), m. 2d Benjamin Haskins. In 1752 the Boadens disputed the Haskins title at Spurwink.

2 **JOHN**(1), ±30 in 1695. Sued by Capt.
Scottow 1683 and appealed (jr.) but did
not prosecute it, bondsmen Ambrose Boaden
and Weymouth Bicton. Taxed for a sloop at
Glouc. 1693. 'Late sojourner at Gloucester
now dwelling at Berwick alias Kittery' he
was acc. by Agnes Barrett, wid. (see Dennen) in Aug. 1694; her ch. would be that
Agnes Tinney who m. Glouc. 9 Dec. 1713
Constantine Joslin and had 8 ch. rec. 1714-
1735 incl. a s. Barrett. He m. ab. 1698 Elizabeth Mitchell(2) who m. 2d 28 Nov. 1715
Samuel Johnson(32). List 290. Ch: **Agnes**
(Annis), b. 15 Mar. 1699, m., int. 11 Mar.
1720-1, Jacob Reed(4); both of Falmouth
1735; liv., a wid., at Gorham 1752. **John,** b.
30 Oct. 1702, Falmouth, ship-carpenter, m.
1st Kittery 29 Dec. 1726 Deborah Ingersoll
(6), m. 2d 23 Sept. 1732 her cous. Deborah
Ingersoll(1). Stating the names of his Tenney gr.parents, he and his sis. q.c. Scarboro

prop. to Paul Thompson, 1735 (Y. D. 17:
246).

**Terrett,** William. List 339. See Ruth Part-
ridge(1).

**Terrill,** William, Saco, in ct. for selling
liquor 1661.

**TERRY.** 1 **James.** Error for Derry(1) in
List 57.

2 **JOHN,** Portsmouth, carpenter, living
away from his wife, 1668; bondsman for
Joseph Rollins, 1672; wit. deed Spencer to
Spencer (Y. D. 5). Lists 312c, 326c, 330a.

## TETHERLY. William Tetherly, mariner,
of Northam, co. Devon, m. 1st 1618-9
Christian Thorne, 2d 1636 Mary Harges.
His will, 30 Apr.—9 Dec. 1651, ment. among
his ch. sons Gabriel (bp. 4 Jan. 1622-3), William and John, and named w. Mary exec.

1 **GABRIEL,** shipwright, Boston by 1656,
Kittery by 1659. Bot land near Boiling
Rock at Eliot Neck 1660. Gr.j. 1674. Lists
25, 30, 31, 92, 298. He m. wid. Susanna King
(11), ±67 in 1695-6; d. 10 Dec. 1695, adm. 20
May 1696 to step-s. Richard King who sold
the land and ship-yard to Richard King jr.
1714-5. Ch: **William. Mehitable,** ±32 in
1695, m. Alexander Dennett(2). **Elizabeth,**
m. 1st John West(3), m. 2d Col. Peter Weare
(10).

2 **JOHN,** Isles of Shoals, br. of (1), ±30 in
1668, ±40 in 1672, ±50 in 1680, mariner,
familiar with the Shoals from 1630. Drunk
1661. Poss. sailed back and forth to Devon.
No fam. found here.

3 **WILLIAM,** Boston, transatlantic sea-
capt., br. of (1), bot land at Abbotsham,
co. Devon, from George Munjoy 1667. Salem
1668-1671. Adm. to br. Gabriel 21 Oct. 1692.
No fam. found here. See John Garde.

4 **WILLIAM**(1), Kittery, had town gr.
1678; m. 13 Aug. 1683 Mary Robie(4),
who m. 2d John Lydston(1). He d. 18 Dec.
1691. Lists 30, 36, 297, 298(2). Adm. to her,
1693. Ch: **Mary,** b. 8 May 1684, m. James
Staples(1). **William,** b. 3 Nov. 1685, shipwright, deacon, m. 13 June 1710 Mercy Spin-
ney(2). Will, 9 Nov. 1745—4 July 1748,
names ch. Mary (m. John Dennett), Mercy,
Ruth, Elizabeth, Susanna, Eleanor, William,
Anne, John, Catherine. **Samuel,** b. 26 Feb.
1686, shipwright, m. 12 May 1715 Margery
Spinney(2). Ch. listed in div. agreement
with ch. of his br. William (Y. Prob. 18656)
and in will of his s. Daniel: John, Samuel (m.
Elizabeth Kennard), William, Diamond
(d.y.), Daniel (will, going on expedition,
Feb. 1757-8—24 Apr. 1758), Mary (d.y.),
Elizabeth (bp. with last four 13 Sept. 1736).
**Elizabeth,** b. 20 July 1689, m. Michael Ken-
nard. **Daniel,** b. 20 Mar. 1691, schoolmaster,
d. s.p.

Tew, Henry, Kittery wit. 1710 (Y. D.7: 245).
**Tharall,** See Turrell.
**Thayer,** See Tare.

## THING.

1 **JONATHAN,** ±46 in 1667, ±50 in 1671, ±56 in 1673, apprent. of Henry Ambrose of Hampton 1641 when sentenced to be whipped at Boston and Exeter for ravishing Mary Greenfield(1), but in 1644 her fa. was admonished for 'entertaining the boy Jonathan Thing' contrary to ct. order, so all would seem to be forgiven. Settled in Wells; O. A., sergt. and constable 1653; fined for political libel 1655. Had Wells gr. of 100 a. in 1660 but by 1658-9 had rem. to Exeter where he became prom. cit. Ex. gr. 1667; com.t.e.s.c. 1668 and later. He m. Joanna Wadleigh(2) who m. 2d Bartholomew Tipping. See Leighton (2), King(14). He d. 29 Apr. 1674. Adm. to wid. Lists 261, 263, 269b, 376b, 377, 379, 381, 382, 383, 392a. Note the extraordinary affinity of Gilmans and Things. Ch. (dates from Bell's Exeter): **Jonathan,** b. ±1654 (by an earlier w.?). **Elizabeth,** b. 5 June 1664, m. Samuel Dudley(2). **John,** b. 20 Sept., d. 4 Nov. 1665. **Samuel,** b. 3 June 1667. **Mary,** b. 6 Mar. 1673, m. Stephen Dudley(3).

2 **CAPT. \*JONATHAN(1),** Exeter, m. 1st 26 July 1677 Mary Gilman(8) who d. Aug. 1691, ag. 33; m. 2d July 1693 wid. Martha (Dennison) Wiggin(7) who m. 3d Matthew Whipple of Ipswich. Gr.j. 1684, constable 1686, town clerk 1689, deputy 1693. Lists 49, 52, 54, 55b, 56, 57, 58, 59, 62, 98, 376b, 384. See Wentworth Gen. i: 201-2. He d. 31 Oct. 1694, ag. 40, shot by his own gun when falling from his horse (inq.). Adm. 22 Feb. 1695-6 to Nicholas Gilman, the wid. Martha renounc. Ch. by 1st w: **Jonathan,** b. 21 Sept. 1678, m. Abigail Gilman(5); adm. 8 June 1720 to wid. and br. Bartholomew; div. 1736-7 to ch. Jonathan, Edward, Anna, heirs of Mary (late w. of Benjamin Gilman), Abigail, Elizabeth, Sarah. Lists 67, 376b. **John,** b. June 1680, m. 1st Mehitable Stevens(16) who wit. will of David Lawrence 1709-10; m. 2d bef. June 1719 wid. Love Wentworth (see Thomas 3, and Reg. 41: 312). List 376b(2). 4 + 2 ch. Maj. **Bartholomew,** b. 25 Feb. 1681-2, m. 1st 7 Dec. 1705 Abigail Coffin(6) who d. May 1711, m. 2d 3 Apr. 1712 wid. Sarah (Little) Kent who m. 3d 1742 Col. John Downing, d. 28 Apr. 1738. List 376b. Adm. 31 May 1738 to wid. Sarah and s.-in-law (Rev.) Nicholas Gilman jr. 2 + 1 ch. **Joseph,** b. Mar. 1684, m. Mary Folsom(7). 6 ch. **Elizabeth,** m. 1st Edward Stevens(16), m. 2d Daniel Young(3). **Benjamin,** b. 12 Nov. 1688, m. 1st Jan. 1711-2 Pernal Coffin(6) who d. 2 June 1725, m. 2d 21 Oct. 1725 wid. Deborah (Hilton 24) Thing

(3). Liv. 1768. 2 + 6 ch. By 2d w: **Daniel,** b. 2 May 1694, his step-fa. Whipple his gdn. in 1700, m. 3 Mar. 1717-8 Elizabeth Clark (42 Henry); will 1765—1766.

3 **SAMUEL,** Esq.(1), Exeter, blacksmith, ±27 in 1694, ±30 in 1697, 78 in 1746; m. 8 July 1696 Abigail Gilman(8) who d. 7 Nov. 1728, ag. 54; m. 2d Elizabeth (Gilman 14) Dudley, 78 in 1746. J. 1686, 1693; gr.j. 1695; constable 1696. Various deeds to ch. Will, 21 Sept. 1748—25 Jan. 1748-9, leaves his brick ho. to his ch.; div. 21 Feb. 1755. Lists 57, 62, 98(2), 376b, 384b. Ch: **Joanna,** b. 22 June 1697, m. Andrew Gilman(7). **Samuel,** b. 28 Mar. 1699, m. 26 Dec. 1722 Deborah Hilton(24) who m. 2d Benjamin Thing(2), d. Sept. 1723. 1 s., Samuel, d. 14 Mar. 1723-4. **Abigail,** b. 1 Dec. 1700, m. John Gilman(11). **Elizabeth,** b. 19 Dec. 1702, m. Benjamin Gilman(7). **Sarah,** b. 8 Jan. 1704-5, m. Daniel Wormall. **Lydia,** twin, b. 14 Feb. 1707-8, m. Antipas Gilman (s. of Edward jr. 5). **Deborah,** twin, m. Israel Gilman(7). **Catherine,** b. 19 May 1711, m. Edward Ladd(5). **Josiah,** b. 15 Sept. 1713, Keensboro (Brentwood), blacksmith; m. Hannah Dudley. 10 ch. **John,** b. 17 May 1716, d.y. **Mary,** b. 18 May 1718, unm. in 1748. **Alice,** b. 14 Feb. 1722-3, m. John Ladd(3).

**THOITS,** Thwait, Alexander, came in the -Hopewell-, 1635, ag. 20, and settled in Watertown where two yrs. later he was convicted of selling fire-arms to the Ind. Gone by 1640, when Rev. Peter Bulkley was ord. to take charge of his corn against his return, he next appears on the Kennebec where Lake deeded him part of Lawson's purchase in 1650. O. F. 1654, lic. to sell liquor 1665. His dau. depos. that he liv. at Winnegance against Arrowsic Isl. 8 or 9 yrs., but, Richard Pattishall attaching his cattle, he gave P. a deed (7 Dec. 1665) and mov. farther up river, poss. to land for which he had an Ind. deed 28 May 1660. On 10 Aug. 1668 Lake and Clarke made a gift of land to his ch. (Y. D. 8: 159), prob. that entered as East. Cl. by Mrs. Hodsden 17—. Lists 11, 181, 182. Ch. by w. Anne (5 of 9 had d. s.p. by 1724): **Elizabeth.** One Elizabeth ment. her sis.'s husb. Joseph Smith, 1720. **Ann,** 66 in 1716, m. Jeremiah Hodsdon(3). **John. Rebecca,** m. 2 Dec. 1686 John Phelps. Y. D. 3: 58. **Alexander. Lydia. Jonathan,** ±24 in 1689-90; Lynn 1688-1691; by w. Hannah had dau. Sarah b. 1691. **Mary,** in York ct. for usual cause 3 July 1694, m. Boston 25 Dec. 1696 Edward Gilling, tailor; both liv. 1724. **Margaret.**

**THOMAS,** became 53d commonest name in New England.

1 **CAPT. BENJAMIN(5),** North Hampton, feltmaker, had garrison on so. side of

Winnicut road. He m. 12 Sept. 1700 Mary Leavitt(3) who d. 24 Sept. 1747; he d. 13 Nov. 1766. Lists 66, 399a. He q.c. his fa.'s Topsham land to s. Benj. 1755. Will, 1758—1766, ment. all ch. except John, b. 13 June 1702. Abigail, b. 22 Oct. 1708, m. 1726 James Nudd(1). Jonathan, bp. 5 Oct. 1712. 5 ch. bp. 1733-1742. James, Nottingham, bp. 3 Feb. 1717, m. 4 Jan. 1737 Alice Jenkins of Greenland; adm. gr. to his fa. 31 Dec. 1746. Ch: James, Molly, William, Anne, Olive, Elisha. Benjamin, b. 22 June 1720, hatter, of Stonington, Conn., 1756, of Falmouth 1758, of Topsham 1758. Acc. of cheating the Pejepscot Prop. out of 900 a. of land, a compromise was reached in 1758 (Doc. Hist. 24: 373). Elisha, bp. 24 May 1724, had w. Anne who d. 4 May 1771.

2 DAVID, at Star Isl. and too sick to work in 1694, but was maintained by a group of boat-owners until he recovered and liv. with James Blagdon. Of Kittery, he m. 28 Jan. 1705-6 Elizabeth Brawn(2), who depos. 1759, ±80, that 40 or 50 yrs. ago her husb. took poss. under Michael Hodge, built a ho. and liv. there until his death. York wit. 1716.

3 HONOR, a poor wid. driven from the eastward, wandering from town to town, 1717 (Essex ct.).

4 JAMES, 1649. See Crawford(3).

5 JAMES, Dover, prob. a br. of Elizabeth who m. 1663 Thomas Chesley(5) and related in some way to Joanna, 2d w. of Philip Chesley(2). He m. by 1670 Martha Goddard(3), who m. 2d by Dec. 1718 Elias Critchet. On 20 July 1670, with Samuel York, he bot from Ind. a great tract with a frontage of 2 miles on the Androscoggin river (Topsham) and mov. there, but was driven back by Philip's war. Lists 52, 57, 80?, 94, 191. Liv. 1715. The wid. div. her est. by deed 1729-30. Ch: James. Elizabeth, m. 1691-2 John Crommett(1). Welthean, m. 1st Robert Huckins(2), m. 2d John Gray(8). Anne, m. James Bunker(2). Abigail, m. 1st James Nock(1), m. 2d Ezekiel Leathers(2). Benjamin. Mary, m. John Rollins(2).

6 JAMES(5), Durham, m. Mary Smith (Joseph) to whom adm. was gr. 3 June 1719 and who m. 2d 3 Mar. 1725-6 Samuel Page (2). Named in will of his gr.fa. Goddard. Lists 366, 368ab(2). Ch. in gr.mo. Thomas's deed: Capt. Joseph, m. Abigail Jones(40). As a little boy had been a captive in Canada, ransomed after 1710. List 369. Selectman ten terms. He d. 1795. Ch. Elizabeth, m. 28 June 1717 David Davis(4). Sobriety, whose name belies her career, laid her first ch. to Thomas Millett; as fa. of her second (1720) she acc. Lt. Thomas Davis(14) whose friends test. in no uncertain terms to her intimacies with Richard Clark and John Perkins and

to the fact that 'she had been in Boston,' appar. considered pertinent in view of her propensities. She m. her cous. John Crommett(1). See Davis(37). Patience, m. 21 June 1727 Jacob Tash. Mary, m. 1st Samuel Perkins, m. 2d Samuel Veasey; liv. 1763 when they sold 1/6 of Thomas est. Claude and Jean Thomas, prisoners in Canada 1702, are not ident.

7 JOHN. List 3.

8 JOHN, Portsmouth wit. 1662, 1674. List 336b.

9 JOHN, Exeter 1680. List 383.

10 JOHN, Cape Porpus?, m. Mary Deering (5).

11 MICHAEL, sent from Newbury with Samuel Getchell(6 jr.) ab. 1720 with cattle to Damariscotta river where they built a ho. Had w. and family there several months later.

12 MILES. List 336b, Portsmouth 1696 (Thompson?). One Miles depos. at Spruce Creek 1725.

13 NICHOLAS, Pemaquid 1686, taxed 1687. List 124.

14 RICE, Kittery, ±38 in 1654, worked for John Treworgy brewing for the fishermen. Fishing partner of John Reynolds 1647. Sued Francis Raynes 1647-8. Beer lic. 1650; O. A. 1652; gr. 1652 confirmed 1655; tr.j. 1647, 1650, 1651. He m. by 1647 wid. Elizabeth Billings(1). Sued her s. John 1664 and 1669 and lost, giving bond 1671. Sold ho. and land 1672 to Maj. Shapleigh and by 1684 was desperately poor and 'under deep suffering,' the selectmen ordered to take speedy means for his relief. No kn. ch. Lists 30, 282, 288, 298.

15 RICHARD, Boston ship-capt. See Coombs(1), Cowell(2).

16 ROBERT. List 95. Poss. a Mass. man.

17 ROGER, Kittery, came over ab. 1682 by his depos., but one R. T. appr. est. of John Andrews of Kit. 1671; ±40 in 1695, ±50 in 1697, ±48 in 1701-2; was boarding with Mrs. Sarah Trickey 1685. List 290. Acc. of stealing from Mary Dixon 1697, but no ev. ag. him. Lost suit vs. Richard King for dispossessing him of land, 1699. Ch. by w. Mary: John, b. 12 July 1686. Roger, b. 6 Mar. 1688, m. Portsm. 6 July 1717 Mary Allard(2). Mary, b. 9 Nov. 1692. One Mary m. Portsm. 30 Aug. 1716 Michael Brooks. Hannah, b. 8 Oct. 1697. One Hannah m. Portsm. 3 June 1718 John Tomas of Jersey. Joseph, b. 7 July 1704.

18 ROSE (a man), Casco 1703. List 39. Error or misreading?

19 SARAH, wit. Elliott to Penhallow 1713 (Y. D. 8: 1).

20 THOMAS, Gt. Island, acc. of taking William Waldron's canoe, 1686.

21 **WILLIAM,** Cape Porpus, m. (ct. June 1680) Mary Barrett(2). Had 100 a. gr. 1681. Cor.j. 1685. Lists 256, 259. Ch: **Hannah,** m. Joseph Field(8). **Mary,** m. Peter Grant(14).

22 **WILLIAM,** Boston, mariner and merchant, claimed 300 a. on Harrisicket riv., bot 9 Nov. 1714 from Job Otis, 1 Feb. 1714-5. His w. Ann Patteshall(2) inherited large interests in the Kennebec region. Bot in Falmouth (Mussel Cove) 1718. List 229.

**THOMES.** 1 John. List 3.

2 **JOHN** (Tome), petn. for cancellation of sentence for misbehavior on ship -Peter-, (1668?). N. H. Files 1: 275. O. A. Exeter 30 Nov. 1677.

3 **RICHARD,** Isles of Shoals, abs. from his wife 1673. List 305b.

4 **ROBERT** (Tomms), Isles of Shoals. Lists 306c, 307a.

5 **THOMAS,** Stratham, m. Elizabeth Doughty (Thomas of Salem) bef. Mar. 1712. Stratham wit. 1708, 1714-5. Liv. in a Brackett ho. at Falmouth 1716. Stratham, 1717. List 229.

**Thomling,** see Tomlin.

**Thomly,** John. List 62.

**THOMPSON,** Thomson, Tompson, the 23d commonest English name and became the 16th commonest in N. E.

1 **ALEXANDER.** List 74.

2 **ALEXANDER**(19), at the Stone garri. in Kittery when Noah Emery was there, had a Kit. gr. in 1694 (List 298) and a York gr. in 1701 which his br. James bot. His homestead was at 'Bricksum' (Y. D. 17: 158). He depos. 31 May 1720, ag. ±50, d. 13 July fol., adm. 4 Oct. to wid. Anne (Curtis 9). Unrec. ch: **Elizabeth,** m. John Allen (see 15). **Abigail,** m. (int. 21 Oct. 1720) John Garey or Geary (see Y. D. 12: 306). **James** (presum.), wit. as jr. 1719 (Y. D. 10: 17), d. at York 22 Oct. 1724. Rec. York 1702-1715 (mo. Anna Curtis): **Benjamin,** m. Hannah Smith, had q.c. from the Gareys. List 279. **John,** m. Priscilla Davis of Haverh. List 279. **Samuel,** m. Hannah Brackett, will 1759. List 279. **Joseph,** m. Mary Welch. **Jonathan,** m. his cousin Dinah (James 19). **Curtis,** m. Sarah Junkins (Daniel).

3 **BARTHOLOMEW**(13), Berwick, had town gr. 1694 and land from fa. the same yr., presum. d. betw. 28 May 1722—28 Mar. 1726 (Y. D. 12: 12). Lists 290, 296-298. Wife unkn. Rec. ch: **Miles,** b. 15 Feb. 1689, m. 14 Feb. 1712-3 Abigail Gowen(3), liv. 1753. He depos. in June 1768, ag. ±80. 11 ch. bp. **Bartholomew,** b. 7 Dec. 1690.

4 **CORNELIUS,** Dover 1678, apprent. to Wm. Henderson; one of several who took their masters' horses and ran away to Newbury in 1679.

5 **DAVID** (Thomson), Mr., has been called a fishmonger of London, and of Scotch birth, but was of Plymouth, co. Devon, apothecary, in a mar. settlem. made by his fa.-in-law Wm. Cole of Plymouth 1 Apr. 1615 (he m. Amias Cole 13 July 1613), and of Plymouth, gent., in the N. E. patent to self and others 14 Dec. 1622. See Aspinwall N. Rec. 128; N. H. Gen. Record, 2: 1; Mass. Hist. Soc. Proc. 14 (1876): 358. He began a planta. at Piscataqua in 1623 (Hubbard); of Piscat. in 1626 when Bradford wrote ab. his going to Damariscove with Plym. men. List 41. Ab. 1626 he bot Trevour's, later Thomson's Isl., in Boston Harbor and removed there, dying soon. Lack of dates and details of his time make imposs. a true knowledge of his work in founding N. H., of whom he brought and how many. Dr. Stackpole, in his History of N. H., locates a ho. at Thompson's Point, on w. side of the Newichawannock which empties into the Piscataqua at Hilton's Point, and ano. settlement at Odiorne's Point, both abandoned in a few yrs. His wid. Amias m. Samuel Maverick(2); see Reg. 69: 158. In her letter to Mr. Robert Trelawny, dated Noodles Isl. 20 Nov. 1635 (Doc. Hist. 3: 76), she ment. her fatherless children. One is kn., **John,** an 'infant' when his fa. died, to whom Mass. conf. Thomson's Isl. 10 May 1648 (Records of Mass. 2: 245). A master mariner, making trips across the Atlantic, and often at the Piscataqua. His fam. as far as known never here; he once liv. at Limehouse, co. Middlesex, also in London. See Me. P. & Ct. Rec. 1: 144; Aspinwall's Not. Records; Sargent(7).

6 **REV. EDWARD** (Tompson), minister of Berwick, b. at Braintree 20 Apr. 1665, s. of Samuel(18) and Sarah(Shepard), H. C. 1684, at Simsbury, Conn., 1687. As a student, he had taught at Newbury where the 'new town' was about to call him 14 July 1691, perh. then resident with his Newb. w. Sarah Webster (John). As minister of Berwick, he performed marriages betw. 20 Nov. 1694—17 Mar. 1695-6, wit. Miles Thompson's deed 4 Dec. 1694, James Emery's 2 Mar. 1694-5. Ordained at Marshfield 14 Oct. 1696, d. there 16 Mar. 1705 (List 96). His wid. ret. to Newb. Ch: **Sarah,** 1st dau., b. at Simsbury 11 May 1688, m. Percival Clark at Newb. **Ann,** b. at Simsbury 31 Dec. 1689, m. Isaac Thomas of Marshfield at Newb. Rev. **Samuel,** b. at Newb. 1 Sept. 1691, H. C. 1710, d. at Glouc. 8 Dec. 1724, pastor of the 2d Ch. **Abigail,** m. at Newb. 25 Mar. 1714 Stephen Longfellow, ancestor of the poet. Dr. **Edward,** b. at Newb. 14 May 1695, d. at Haverh. 20 Apr. 1751. Rev. **William,** Scarboro, b. at Marshfield 26 Apr. 1697, H. C. 1718, wit. John Hubbard's deed at Kingston in 1723

and m. his dau. Anna(5) aft. he had settled in Scarb. Invited to preach at Wells 26 Jan. 1724-5 (see Bourne's Hist. of W., p. 357). He d. at Scarb. 13 Feb. 1759. **John**, b. at Marshfield 17 Sept. 1699, liv. in Conn. **Joseph**, m. in Newb. 7 Nov. 1727 Priscilla Noyes, liv. in Falmouth.

7 **GEORGE**, Portsmouth, and w. Elizabeth (appar. not Cotton 2); see Morgrage and Samuel Thompson(10). In 1719 one Sarah was rec. into cov. So. Ch. and m. Barnard Bosdet of London. See Brewster(2) for Margaret and Sloper(3) for Miriam; one Martha wit. in 1725 when Sloper's boy Scipio had stolen Mr. Rymes' beaver hat. John, Portsm., adm. to wid. Sarah 17 Oct. 1732, appar. Scotch-Irish.

8 **ISRAEL** Beckman (Tompson), Star Isl., one of the fishermen raiding Samuel Frost's smuggled brandy stored in the Mainwaring(3) warehouse. See Downes(4).

9 **JOHN**, carpenter, Portsmouth, undertook to pay doctor's bills of Susanna Avorta, Mr. Martyn's maid, 1672. Admitted freeman 15 May 1672. Lists 327b, 328, 331ac.

10 **JOHN**, 'the Scotchman,' ag. ±22 in Sept. 1677, was with Tristram Harris on a scouting party commanded by Capt. Frost in 1676. Lists 28, 298. He m. Hannah Remick(1), whose fa. was gr. adm. on his est. 17 June 1684. She m. 2d Richard Gowell. Ch: **John**, 'of the Reach,' weaver. Lists 289, 296-298. See also John Harmon(2 jr.), Lydston (2), Metherell. In 1695 his fa. was dead, mo. liv., no wife. He m. (ct. Apr. 1696) Elizabeth Paul(2), depos. in June 1737, ag. 62, ab. Pauls, and in June 1743, ±73, ab. his mar. 52 yrs. ago. No surv. ch. Will, 13 Aug.—15 Oct. 1751, names w., br. Samuel, two sisters, Parker Foster (under 21, his mo. Hannah), neph. Amos Paul and his s. Joseph. **Samuel**, carpenter, apprent. when eleven to Mr. John Dennett of Portsm., m. Elizabeth (Cotton 2) who o.c. No. Ch. as E. T. 8 Aug. 1708. Of Newington 1713, m. there 2d 16 Apr. 1717 Mary (Bickford 4) Crockett (liv. 1742), ret. to Portsm. ab. 1717, liv. there 1758, ag. ±81. Ch. appar. incl: Charles, bp. at Portsm. 9 Oct. 1709; Elizabeth (surely), bp. Newington 6 May 1716, and poss. some of those who m. in Newingt. later. **Mary**, m. Thomas Fernald(1). **Hannah**, m. Clement Hughes(1).

11 **JOHN**(19), Oyster River, m. 1678-1680 Sarah Woodman(2). In 1684 he gave bond to clear admr. of fa.'s est. and to provide for br. James; in 1708 he and James sold the Cold Harbor homestead to Francis Allen, with warr. ag. other heirs; in Nov. 1715, of Dover, he q.c. his fa.'s 50 a. gr. there to John Tuttle, and must have been he of Berw. 1716 (Y. D. 8: 158). He depos. in 1719, ag. ±60. John, sr., and w. Sarah adm. to O. R.

Ch. 7 Apr. 1728. Lists 94, 368b, 369. Will, 12 Apr. 1733—24 July 1734. names w. Sarah. Ch: **John**, m. Mary Davis; 2 sons bp. 21 Mar. 1717-8 at O. R. Ch. where she was adm. from Dover 25 Sept. 1718. He was ±57 in Dec. 1745, liv. 3 Feb. 1753. 8 ch. Capt. *****Jonathan** (±60 in 1753), selectman Dover and Durham, Rep., Deacon, Lt., Capt., m. 23 Jan. 1717-8 Sarah Burnham(2), both adm. to O. R. Ch. 4 Feb. 1727-8. List 369. Will, 10 Sept. 1756—23 Feb. 1757, w. Sarah. 8 ch. **Robert**, had the homestead by deed of gift, m. Abigail Emerson(7). He dropped dead in 1752, she d. 1757. 5 ch. bp. Lists 96, 368b (2). **Sarah**, m. Samuel Hill(12). **Mary**, m. Hubbard Stevens(12). **Hannah**, m. Moses Stevens(12). **Elizabeth**, m. at O. R. Eleazer Clark(43).

12 **JOHN**(13), m. Sarah Emery(2), d. bef. 6 Mar. 1702-3 and she m. 2d Gilbert Warren(1). List 298. In Oct. 1718 they renounced adm. on the Thompson est. to **John**, the only son, poss. the J. T. of Kit. who was accus. by Grace Taprill in Mar.1700-1. In Mar. 1702-3 his gr.fa. deeded him his 1671 gr., 100 a. at York Pond. List 298. He m. 22 June 1709 Mary Stacy(3); both joined So. Berw. Ch. 1712. No w. named in his deed of 22 Mar. 1738-9. In 1744 his w. was Elizabeth. 10 ch. bp. 1710-1725. **Elizabeth**, m. Alexander Gray(1); in 1748 she sold her inheritance to Samuel Wentworth, 1/6 of 50 a. gr. to fa. John in 1678-9. **Mercy**, m. Philip Stackpole.

13 **MILES**, carpenter, Kittery, liv. on 1st lot no. of Thompson's Point Brook in 1655, had a gr. there in 1656. (One M. was in Boston in 1643; one was fined in Middlesex ct. in Apr. 1651 for playing cards aft. 9 o'clock at night). Gr.j. 1656; Sergt. 1659; selectman 1659, 1661; on commit. to lay out lands 1661. Bot land from John Morrell in 1663; see also Hodsdon(2). Sued for minister's rate 1663. Lists 24, 87, 288, 298. His w. Ann was b. 1632 by depos. and rememb. Great Works when Mr. Leader was there. They were abs. from Ch. 1663 (ab. half a yr.), 1671, 1675. In Dec. 1694 he made over homestead, ±80 a., stock, etc., to s. Thomas for life supp. of both, tho the deed reads as if Ann were not Thomas' mo. He d. betw. 6 Mar. 1702-3 (see 12 jr.) and 30 June 1708. She was liv. 19 Sept. 1717, ±85. Ch: **Ann**, m. 1st Israel Hodsdon(2), m. 2d Robert Evans(12). **Miles. John. Bartholomew. Mary**, m. Thomas Rhodes(2). **Amy**, m. Daniel Goodwin(5). **Sarah**, m. 1st James Goodwin(8), m. 2d Wm. Hearl(5). **Thomas**, wheelwright, ±23 in Jan. 1695-6, Lists 296, 298, m. Sarah Furbush (2) who was his admx. 27 Sept. 1715, Andrew Neale and Joseph Goold bondsm., John Neal gdn. of two of the daus. Ch. 1699-1712: Miles, d. bef. Sept. 1727; Sarah, m. 4 July

1723 Moses Hodsdon (Israel, 5 jr.); Anne, m. 22 Feb. 1727 Hezekiah Staples (John 1); Mehitable, m. Adam Goodwin(12); Thomas, only surv. son in Sept. 1727 (Saml. Lord gdn.), m. Abigail Smith who sold by p/a in 1756 when he was on the Crown Point expedition; later of Bristol, Me.; ch.

14 **MILES**(13), had no gr., as far as noted, but is identif. by 'Old Kittery and Her Families' as that 'One Thompson (Niles, p. 349, said Miles) k. in Apr. 1724 and his son captured. They liv. at Love's Brook on road from Quamphegan to Wells.' Canadian records show the captive as **Miles**, a boy, who ret. to N. E. with Hansons bef. 25 Aug. 1725. One Miles was a Penhallow wit. 1693-1695 and served in O. R. and Dover garrisons 1695-1696. List 67. One M. mar. Abigail Paine in Boston 9 Nov. 1704 and d. there 2 Nov. 1713, ag. ±31, leaving ch. See also Thomas(12).

15 **PAUL**, evid. a newcomer, wit. a Gunnison fam. deed in 1721, with w. Margaret was adm. to Kit. Point Ch. in 1726 and had ch: **Margaret, Sarah, Paul**, bp. there 1723-1726. He had older ch., as a dau. **Jane** (Y. D. 17: 245) m. Joseph Poak 19 July 1732 in Scarb., where Paul bot from Bonython heirs in 1726 and soon remov., had grants and bot more. In 1774, Job Burnham, ±73, depos. that a few yrs. bef. P. T. died he divid. his 100 a. at Blue Point betw. his sons **John** and **Paul**.

16 **PETER**, worked ab. Lamprill River bridge 1686-7. List 94.

17 **ROBERT**, York patentee. List 272. See also Me. P. & Ct. Rec. i: 161.

18 **REV. WILLIAM** (Tompson), York, Braintree, matric. at Brasenose Coll., Oxford, 28 Jan. 1619-20, ag. 22, from co. Lancaster, pleb., B.A. 28 Feb. 1621-2, settled as curate of Newton, a chapelry of Winwick, Lancashire, in 1623, and was in Winwick in Oct. 1635. Over here, he joined Dorchester Ch. under his former superior in Eng., Rev. Richard Mather, and went to York, prob. not long aft. Mr. Hooke and Mr. Bradbury appealed to Gov. Winthrop 13 Sept. 1637 'to solicit in our behalf some godly minister.' He wit. Mr. Hooke's deed at York 13 Mar. 1638 (Y. D. 6: 74). See also Hist. of York, ii. 111-2; 2 Me. Hist. Soc. Col. 3: 52. Ordained at Braintree 19 Nov. 1639, d. there 10 Dec. 1666, ag. 68, melancholia having forced retirement for seven years. He had here early a w. Abigail (not dau. of John Collins, N. E. Reg. 89: 78), who d. 10 July 1643, while he was on a mission to Va. for Mass. Bay. His last w. Anne (Brigham), wid. of Simon Crosby, d. 11 Oct. 1675, ag. 68. Reg. 15: 115-116 has agreement betw. her as admx. and 5 ch: **Elinor**, m. 1st Wm. Veasey of Braintree, m. 2d John French (see Reg. 12: 353). *Sam-

uel, eldest son, m. 25 Apr. 1656 Sarah Shepard (Edward), Rep. many yrs., Deacon, d. 18 June 1695, his ch. incl. (6). **Joseph, b.** 1 May 1640. **Benjamin, b.** 14 July 1642, H. C. 1662. By w. Anne: **Hannah, b.** 1 m. 3. 1648. See also 'Rev. William Thomson of New London, Conn.' in 'The American Genealogist,' Oct. 1937, which does not take into acct. the fact that Rev. William of Braintree had a s. **Eleazer**, bp. at Winwick 21 Oct. 1635.

19 **WILLIAM**, Kittery, had a 50 a. Dover gr. in 1656, laid out in 1659 beyond Cochecho log swamp. Lists 356abce. In Kit., John White's 1651 gr. was assigned to him in 1656, a short way below the mouth of Sturgeon Creek. List 298. He m. White's dau., was in York ct. 1659 for rebellion ag. fa. and mo.-in-law, and bound to good behavior, espec. towards fa. and mo. Also in ct. several times for drinking, abs. from Ch., idleness and not provid. for fam. He d. 22 June 1676. Inv. incl. 23 a., ho. and orchard in Kit., and 50 a. ab. Cochecho which he 'gave to his two sons living at Dover William and Robert as John White.' See Me. P. & Ct. Rec. ii. 338. Adm. to Capt. Wincoll and James Emery, all to be improv. for ch.'s use and the selectmen to place them out; no w. ment. Ch., age and where placed in 1677: **John**, oldest, ag. 18, not placed out. **William**, ag. 16, with Richard Otis. **Robert**, ag. 13, with Tobey Hanson. List 94. **James**, ag. 11, a lame boy, not placed out. A 'lame, impotent brother' in 1684, he became a tailor, m. 3 Mar. 1700-1 Elizabeth Frye(1), of York 1710 sold Kit. gr. of 1694-1699, in there 1717 on land he bot from (2) 4 Jan. 1713-4. Lists 290, 298. Of Biddeford in Sept. 1733 he deeded Bid. and Scarb. land to s. Cornelius for supp. and ack. at York 18 Apr. 1734. John, lame man, List 279 (?James). 13 ch., desc. incl. Brig.-Gen. Samuel T. and many at New Meadows and beyond. **Alexander**, ag. 6, **Judith**, ag. 2, not disposed of.

20 **WILLIAM**(19), m. 4 Sept. 1682 Mary Lovering(2), List 90(?). In Aug. 1685, ag. ±24, he and Stephen Otis depos. ab. clearing land 5 yrs. bef. (See Doc. Hist. 5: 401, for pet. in 1694 of one W. T. impressed in Me. and wounded in service). Lived in Somersworth. List 359b. In 1732 Thomas Downs and Elizabeth Alley wit. a bond for William, or for his s. **William** who sold his fa.'s land to Samuel Alley 30 Aug. 1735 and whose wid. Elizabeth and ch. had a deed of 20 a. in Rochester from Alley in 1749.

21 **WILLIAM** (Tomson), taxed Great Isl. 1688. Note pet. mentioned under(20).

22 ———, 'the maid Tomson,' drowned at Richmond Isl. bef. 10 July 1639. List 21.

23 **THOMSON'S** Point house, List 354a. Thompson's Point, Piscataqua River,

ment. 14 Oct. 1651 (Me. P. & Ct. Rec. 1: 170).
**THORNE.** 1 **Andrew,** 1667 (Y. D. 2: 14).
See Heffer.
2 **FRANCIS,** Exeter, wit. deliv. of Ind.
lands to Edward Hilton, 1669; gave joint
note with Arthur Bennett(3) 1671-2; sued
by Deering 1672.
**THORNER.** 1 **James,** sued by Roger Rose
1681.
2 **HENRY,** of Wapping, Eng., ship-carpenter, killed by a rolling mast (verdict cor.
j., N. H., 19 Aug. 1657). Adm. to Capt.
James Garrett and Edward Thorner who carried est., incl. goods in Mr. Pendleton's
wareho., to Eng.
**Thornton.** See Merry(6).
**THORPE,** Rev. **John,** Black Point, wit. a
Jordan deed 1658 and in ct. (Mass.) 4
July 1659 for abusing Rev. Robert Jordan
and preaching unsound doctrine. Acc. of excessive drinking and referred by Mass. magistrates to York ct. 1660 (SJC 369). Sued
Andrew Brown and Christopher Collins, and
forbidden to preach, 1661. List 233. See
Reg. 13: 195.
**THRASHER,** Henry, formerly of Salem,
killed by Indians at Purpoodock 1703,
soon after he had bot 100 a. from Joel
Maddiver. See Putnam's Quarterly Mag.,
1902, pp. 143-6. Ch: **Joseph,** only s., tanner,
of Salem when he entered East. Cl. for self
and three sisters; m. Dover 31 July 1711
Mary Watson(5); of Hampton 1736. **Mercy,**
int. Salem 21 Oct. 1710 with Jonathan Buffum. Others unident.
**Thrisco,** see Drisco.
**Thurlay** (Thurlow), Thomas, Newbury, sold
farm in Wells to Thomas Wells jr. 1667-8.
Y. D. 2: 140.

## THURSTON.

1 **JOHN,** Kittery, blacksmith, m. 15 Aug.
1688 Hannah Carey(2). Mr. Benj. Woodbridge gave them land at Kit. Pt. which they
mtg. to Pepperell 1689.
2 **STEPHEN,** Stratham, s. of Daniel of
Newbury, where he m. 1st 14 Oct. 1706
Mary Knight. Adm. in N. H. 26 July 1728 to
s. **Moses,** Moses Leavitt and Joseph Mason
bondsmen, wid. Sarah renounc. Ch. **Daniel,
Robert, Rebecca, Mary, Nathaniel, Stephen**
and **Abigail** were minors. **John,** b. 1709, and
**Sarah,** b. 1722, were appar. dead. See also
White(18).
3 **THOMAS,** in Boston from Piscataqua
1682, and of bad report. Same as Thos.
Thurton?
**THURTON, Thomas,** Hampton, ±35 in 1683-
4, s. of Thomas and Susanna (Fuller) of
Croydon, co. Surrey, came in ·Mary and
Sarah· from London 1677. Fined for fighting with David Wedgwood 1679, sued Christopher Palmer 1681. App. 'Deputy Search-

er' by Randolph 1681-2, Provost Marshal 25
June 1684. Lists 55b, 396. Innholder, late
of Boston, adm. to Wm. Bolderson, creditor,
14 Feb. 1688-9. See Fuller(1), Thurston(3).
**Thwaits,** see Thoits.

## TIBBETTS, Tippetts, Tybbotts, etc. Gup-
py gives Tibbett (Cambridgeshire), Tibbetts (Warwickshire), Tippett (Cornwall).
See N. Y. Gen. and Biog. Rec. 50: 354.
1 **ELIZABETH,** had escaped from Great Isl.
prison 29 Dec. 1684 when Wm. Cotton or
his men, Wm. Cotton's man Meshac, Sara
Beal of Gt. Isl. and one Broadhead that lived
at Cochecho, were accus. of helping her. See
also (4), (13).
2 **EPHRAIM**(6), blacksmith, Dover, m. Rose
Austin(8). Cor.j. 1695, j. 1697. List
358a. See also Munsey. Called of Dover in
1726 when dau. Mary m. at Nantucket where
he and w. Rose were pres. at the Worth-Hoag
wedding 2 July 1729. Ch: **Ephraim,** blacksmith, b. 31 Dec. 1694, m. 6 Nov. 1722 Anne
Allen (Francis); of Rochester, adm. to wid.
Ann 28 Aug. 1754. She was dead 1760, when
div. made to 2 sons. **Ann,** b. 8 July 1697, m.
at Nant. 26 Nov. 1718 Paul Starbuck. **Henry,**
b. 29 July 1699, m. 13 May 1730 Elizabeth
Robinson(16) who was gr. adm. 7 June 1736;
m. 2d Joseph Hussey(7). In 1748 her br.
Timothy was gdn. of Peter Tibbetts, +14 and
of Hepsibah, –14. **Abigail,** b. 12 Aug. 1700,
m. Otis Pinkham(1). **Joseph,** b. 4 Nov. 1702,
m. Sarah (Huckins), wid. of Michael Emerson; d. at Rochester 20 Jan. 1776. **Elisha,** b.
16 Feb. 1704. **Aaron,** cooper, b. 26 Feb. 1705,
m. aft. Apr. 1727 Penelope Richardson.
**Mary,** b. 16 Nov. 1707, m. at Nant. 29 Dec.
1726 Matthew Barnard. **Elijah,** b. 23 Mar.
1711, m. 23 Dec. 1738 Love Drew (Wm.).
**Rose,** b. 4 Feb. 1713, m. Joseph Tibbetts(9).
**Elizabeth,** b. 30 Oct. 1716, m. 4 Sept. 1735
Thomas Canney.
3 **HENRY,** shoemaker, Dover, arrived in the
·James· from London the last week in
Sept. 1635, ag. 39, with w. Elizabeth, ag. 39,
two ch., and Remembrance, ag. 28, who came
in Mr. Thomas Wiggin's service, m. John
Ault, and with him sued Mr. Wiggin in
1645 for wages to 14 Dec. 1638, the date
when she came to Piscataqua. Henry had
one of the 20 a. Dover lots in 1642. Gr.j.
1651, 1657, 1659; j. 1653; sealer of leather
1661. In 1653 he succ. sued Philip Lewis for
taking away cocks of hay from his marsh
near Capt. Champernowne's farm; 'planter,'
sold land to John Tuttle in 1657; sued
Charles Allen in 1659; signed a pet. in 1665;
taxed 1675-6. Lists 352, 354abc, 355a(2)b
(2), 356abcefgh, 311c (Dover), 359a. See
also Stackpole. A record often quoted from
N. H. Province records, but not in printed
N. H. Probate: '27 June 1676, Last will of

Henry Tibbetts brought into court proved by Mrs. Judith Reyner allowed John Roberts an inventory of the estate amounting to £207. 5. 0.' Kn. ch: **Jeremy,** ag. 4 in 1635. **Samuel,** ag. 2 in 1635. **Rebecca,** m. 1st Thomas Nock(4), m. 2d Philip Benmore. In 1659 her fa. deeded 100 a. to his sons Jeremiah T. and Thomas Nock. See also (4).

4 **HENRY** (or Tippett), fisherman, Portsmouth. No record links him or a contemporary Henry of Kingston, R. I., with (3) who is not kn., by evid., ever to have had a son of his own name. The Portsm. Henry, who appar. connects with Tucker(11), wit. Thomas Harvey's deed in 1670 (see also 13), was in ct. 1679 for not going home to his w., his rate for the minister rebated 15 Mar. 1679-80. Able to take oath bef. Cranfield 9 Nov. 1683 (N. H. Prob. I: 266). Inv. 10 Dec. 1683, old clothes and shoes, 13 s. 6 d. in cash, 2 quintals of refuse fish, total £2.6.6., claims against est. £3.4.9. Mrs. Ursula Tucker had washed for him formerly, and cared for him when sick. Wine and sugar were bot for his burial.

5 **HENRY**(6), Dover, m. 1st 25 Feb. 1699-1700 wid. Joyce Otis (see Nicholas 1); m. 2d 1713-1717 Mary (Akerman 1) Sampson; see Williams(38). Scarb. gr. of 60 a. in 1720 sold by his sons in 1736. Will, 14 Aug.—6 Sept. 1727, gave Portsm. houses, land, goods to w. Mary for life, except to Richard the ho. Mr. Croswhite was liv. in and R. to have all aft. his mo. died; to other sons Dover and Rochester prop., to dau. Susannah £10 and a bed; Benjamin exec., bros. Capt. Samuel and Joseph trustees. In 1724 Mary T. named as an abuttor to wid. Elizabeth Eburne; in 1741 the abuttor was 'formerly M. T. now Richard T.' Ch., three sons liv. 1751: **Benjamin,** b. last of Oct. 1700, w. Abigail. Dover 1728; of Rochester 1736, deeded to br. Edward the homestead E. was liv. on, part of fa.'s homestead, ±10 acres. **Edward,** b. 2 Feb. 1702-3, had wives Charity and Mary. Dover, 1728-1736; of Rochester 1742, sold to Capt. John Gage 22 a. and ho. on Dover Neck. **Paul,** b. 26 June 1705; Dover 1728, Rochester 1736; adm. 25 May 1743 to wid. Sarah. Ch. Nathaniel, Henry and Joyce of Rochester 1754. And more? **Susannah,** b. last of Oct. 1707, m. Samuel Canney. **Richard** (by 2d w.), joiner, Portsm., m. 3 Nov. 1738 Mary Pendexter(1). In 1751 he sued John James and John Gage for 1/6 of certain Dover land (SJC 19793).

6 **JEREMIAH**(3) or Jeremy, Dover, ±38 in 1670, m. by 1655 Mary Canney(3). Granted 100 a. in 1658 which James Clements owned in 1719. Witnessed ag. Richard Pinkham in 1660. Prison keeper of Dover 1670, when he wit. in suit H. Symonds v. Barefoot. Lists 356abcefghk, 311c (Dover), 312e, 357e,

359a. Will, 5 May—20 June 1677 (inv.), gives to s. Jeremiah 10 a. and two yearling steers in his poss. on acc. of £13 given him by his gr.fa. Canney which the testator used in his own behoof; to w. Mary half the ho. and barn for life, and all else to bring up 'our small children'; w. and s. Jeremiah execs., Job Clements and John Roberts overseers. Widow's Lists 359ab, 52. She m. 2d John Loome. In 1709 the s. Jeremiah and his s. John were cited to adm. his fa.'s est. Ch. (1st 5 by Prov. rec.): **Jeremiah,** b. 5 June 1656. **Mary,** b. 15 Apr. 1658, m. 1st bef. 5 May 1677 Ichabod Rollins(1), m. 2d Thomas Ash(3). **Thomas,** b. 24 Feb. 1659. **Hannah,** b. 25 Feb. 1661, m. Nathaniel Perkins(19). **Joseph,** b. 7 Aug. 1663. **Samuel. Benjamin,** joined 4 bros. and sis. (Perkins) in deed to br. Ephraim for mo.'s supp. 1703 and was liv. 14 Dec. 1706. See also (8). **Ephraim. Martha,** in fa.'s will. **Elizabeth,** m. John Bickford(17). **Nathaniel. Henry.**

7 **JEREMIAH**(6), Dover, m. bef. 28 Feb. 1684 Mary Twombley(2), who was liv. 10 May 1720. Gr.j. 1693. Constable 1698, 1699. In 1735 he deeded to s. Timothy. His s. Jeremiah was 'jr.' in 1736. Lists 357e, 359ab, 358a, 52, 94. Ch. incl: **Mary** (presum.), m. 1st John Giles(5), m. 2d Nathaniel Goodwin(5). **Jeremy,** accid. shot by br. John and d. 31 Aug. 1709 (List 96). **John,** cited with fa. 1709, List 358d, m. 1st Sarah Meader(2) whose ch. were rec. 1711-1721: John (m. Tamsen Ricker), Jeremiah (with br. John deeded est. of gr.fa. Meader 1736), Nathaniel. He m. 2d Tamsen (Meserve) Ham (see Joseph 4), her dau. Sarah b. 1725. **Timothy,** had deeds from fa. 1717, 1735. See also (8). **Lydia,** in 1722 her fa. compl. ag. Joshua Perkins(19) for refusing to supp. her ch.

8 **JOHN,** wit. a Perkins deed with John Tuttle in 1693. Theod., 1697 (N. H. Prov. P. 2: 256), Margaret, whose earmark was registered at Dover 1720, are unkn., names poss. misread.

9 **JOSEPH**(6), Dover, was apprent. by mo. and (7) to the weaver's trade with uncle Matthew Austin for 7 yrs. 12 Nov. 1677, when he was called -youngest- son, but depos. in Jan. 1729-30, ag. ±66, that he liv. with Austin from 9 to 21. In 1688 he bot from John Pinkham the 20 a. lot P.'s fa. had in exch. with George Webb; in 1724 Pinkham called it Lot 13 which J. T. now lives on. Lists 352, 358a. His 1st w. Elizabeth d. 24 Feb. 1706-7, ag. 35 y. 2 m., wanting one day (List 96). He m. 2d Catherine (Mason) by Quaker rec. 1786). Will, 13 Feb.—28 May 1746, which his w. got him to make after his mind was weak, and Abraham Nute steadied his hand in making his mark (SJC 27422); James Nute and Samuel Young the widow's

bondsm. as exec. Ch., all but Margery liv. 1746; by 1st w: **Elizabeth,** b. 10 Mar. 1697, m. 1st Pomfret Dam(5), m. 2d Gershom Downs(6), m. 3d Richard Goodwin(9), liv. 1762. **Margery,** b. 18 Jan. 1700, m. Job Hussey(7), left sons Robert and John. **Judith,** b. 3 Feb. 1702, m. John Bickford(17 jr.). **Lydia,** b. 4 Aug. 1704, m. Mark Giles (6 jr.). **Joseph,** b. 2 Feb. 1706-7, m. Rose Tibbetts (2). By 2d w: **Catherine,** b. 24 Aug. 1713, unm. 1761, appar. m. in 1764 Benjamin Larrabee(1 jr.). **Mary,** b. 11 Oct. 1716, m. 1st 27 Sept. 1739 John Pearl, m. 2d Benjamin Allen. **Hannah,** b. 23 June 1721, m. Jacob Allen.

10 **MARY** (Tappett), List 89.

11 **NATHANIEL**(6), Oyster River, had 30 a. gr. 16 Apr. 1694 to be laid out on the west side of Johnson's Creek. Bot from Thomas and Mary Ash in 1700. Carried away by Ind. ab. 4 Nov. 1705. Lists 358b, 96, 99 (p. 92). Widow Elizabeth m. 2d Francis Pitman(3). In 1717 Philip Duley, sr., reciting that in 1699-1700 he and N. T. exch. dwellings, confirmed to her his own 20 a. gr. of 19 Mar. 1693. Kn. ch: **Henry,** Dover 1722, sold the Johnson's Creek gr. to Thomas Davis with warr. 'by and under me and from any of the heirs of N. T.'; m. 23 Jan. 1728-9 Elizabeth Meader(4); Durham 1734, Dover 1738, depos. in 1754, ±54, that for many yrs. he liv. near Johnson's Creek. Will, 1753—1766, names w. Elizabeth, 6 ch. incl. Weymouth. **Bridget,** b. 28 Sept. 1700, m. 7 Feb. 1727-8 John Williams, jr. **Martha,** m. Samuel Drowne(2 jr.).

12 **CAPT. SAMUEL**(6), tanner, Dover, was apprent. to Mr. Job Clement and ran away to Newbury in 1679; see Thompson (4). He m. 1st 1 Sept. 1686 Dorothy Tuttle (2), m. 2d by 1708 Rebecca (Nock 4) Willey, and left a wid. Rachel. Constable 1696, 1697. Lists 358abd, 62, 67. See also Cloudman. He depos. 9 Feb. 1733-4, ag. 67. Will, 8 Nov. 1738—31 Jan. 1738-9, names w. Rachel, ch. and gr.ch. and gives homestead and tanyard to s. Ichabod. Ch: **Samuel,** o.c. and bp. on death bed 23 Dec. 1724 (Berw. Ch. rec.), d. next day, adm. to wid. Judith (m. by 1718). 4 ch. bp. His fa. deeded to her in 1728. See also Stackpole. Capt. **Ichabod,** tanner, m. 1st by 1722 Abigail Tibbetts(14), m. 2d at Portsm. 29 May 1729 Patience Nock(1). Will, 30 Dec. 1746—25 Feb. 1746-7, names w. and exec. Patience (w. of Humphrey Pooler in 1748), 6 ch. **Sarah,** m. Thomas Tibbetts (14); dead in 1746, her s. Thomas in will. **Dorothy,** m. John Wingate(2 jr.); her 4 sons in fa.'s will, she dead. **Rachel,** m. by 1728 John Legrow. **Martha,** m. 1st Benjamin Varney (her s. Ichabod in will); m. 2d one Whitehouse. **Mary,** m. by 1721 William Chamberlain. **Esther,** m. Ephraim Tibbetts (14).

13 **THOMAS,** Portsmouth 1671. List 326c. Error for (4)?

14 **CAPT. THOMAS**(6), Dover, m. 6 July 1684 Judith Dam(2), who d. 22 Oct. 1728. Jury 1694, 1696, 1697. Bondsman for John Varney 1694. Tav. lic. 1694 and later, Ralph Hall a bondsm. in 1694, Joseph Hall in 1700. In 1701 the town gr. him a gore at the head of his 20 a. lot on west side of Back River, to square it. He depos. in Jan. 1738-9, -ag. ±70-, ab. Roberts land and fam.; in Sept. 1748, ag. 88. Lists 353 (1696, Corp.), 358b (Capt.)d(2), 52, 57. Will, 13 July—26 Oct. 1748, gives to w. Sarah (sole exec.) half his moveables unless she 'shall elope or unlawfully depart from me,' then only what the law allows. His lands and buildings had already been deeded to 5 sons, of whom 3 surv. with 1 dau. Ch: Ens. **John,** b. 29 Aug. 1685. Will, of Somersworth, 21 Jan. 1742-3—30 Mar. 1743, names w. Mary (exec. with friend Benjamin Mason), 13 ch. In 1741 he and s. John, tertius (b. 29 Mar. 1711), gave a mortgage to Walton who forecl. on the widows Mary and Joanna in 1746, both Johns being dead. **Thomas,** b. 4 Nov. 1687, m. 12 Aug. 1708 Sarah Tibbetts(12), s. Thomas, b. 7 Jan. 1716, all three bp. together 1725. In 1745 with w. Elizabeth he deeded land bot from John Frost to s. Thomas of Somersworth who was of Berwick when he sold in 1749, his fa. having d. bef. July 1748. **Ephraim,** b. 4 Mar. 1690, m. 16 Nov. 1721 Esther Tibbetts(12). In 1717 one E. and one Samuel, jr., of Dover, were prosec. by Foxwell heirs for cutting grass on their Scarb. land; in 1735 Richard Plummer, innholder, prosec. E. and w. Esther for setting fire to his ho., their bondsm. Thomas and Samuel T., gent. Living 1748. 5 or m. ch. **Elizabeth,** b. 8 Sept., d. 12 Oct. 1692. **Samuel,** b. 8 Oct. 1693. As son of Capt. Thomas he deeded to br. Ephraim 1718, had deed from fa. 1729, m. 2 Mar. 1720-1 Sarah Low(5); 4 ch. rec. at Dover. Scarb. 1741, Georgetown 1761. **Elizabeth,** b. 25 July 1696, m. Benjamin Mason (4). **Moses,** b. 27 Jan. 1701, m. 18 Mar. 1724-5 Mary Key(2), liv. in Somersworth. Ch. **Abigail,** b. 12 Sept. 1705, m. Ichabod Tibbetts(12); her ch. in fa.'s will.

**Tibs,** Mary, York, prisoner released from Quebec 1695. List 99.

**Tickener,** Stephen, slandered Mrs. Wheelwright 1660, and made public confess. at Wells, Scarboro and York.

**Tickson,** in List 267a, should be Pickron.

**TIDY.** See Creber.

1 **JOHN**(3), Kittery, ±67 in 1750, m. ab. 1712 Hannah Morrell(1), d. Jan. 1766. Scarboro prop. and gr. of 100 a. on east side of Nonesuch river, 1720. Lists 239b, 296,

297. Ch., b. 1713-1724: **Sarah, Edah, Hannah** (d. unm. ab. 1799), **Robert** (m. 1743 Hannah Goold, d. s.p.), **Meribah, John** (d. unm. 1749).

2 **RACHEL**, a Jersey woman, at Edward Peavey's in Portsm. (prob. a servant) when she had a bastard 1698, and another in Dover 1710 when she acc. John Dam jr.

3 **ROBERT**, Scarboro, m. Sarah Libby(5) who m. 2d Richard Rogers(9) and 3d Christopher Banfield(1). Lists 34, 237ab(2), 238a(2). Had 6 a. gr. 1682. Selectman 1686. Ch: **John. Hannah**, m. 1st 4 Nov. 1706 John Ford (see 5), m. 2d Daniel Witham(2). **Elizabeth**, m. 8 Jan. 1708-9 John Witham(2). **Mary**, m. 1st George Brawn(2 jr.) m. 2d Thomas Penney(3). One Sarah dep. 1705 at Daniel Weare's ho. in Boston, where she m. 9 July 1706 Benjamin Varney (see 4).

**TILLEY, William**, Boston, had w. Alice, ±62 in 1665, a popular mid-wife and a trial to the magistrates, who having put her in jail for some offense, ±1649, were showered by petitions from Boston and Dorchester women in her favor. She, under his p/a, sold their Boston ho. 1649, he prob. at Cape Porpus where he was in 1650 and 1652. Both liv. 1665. Only kn. ch: **Sarah**, m. 1st Henry Lynn(2), 2d Hugh Gunnison(2), 3d Capt. John Mitchell(5), 4th Dr. Francis Morgan (2).

**Tillman**, John, liv. on west side of Kennebec from 1665; wit. 1675. He m. Magdalen Gutch(2). Lists 78, 182, 186, 189. Only ch: **Mary**, was wid. Soper in 1734.

# TILTON. A parish in co. Leicester.

1 **ABRAHAM**(5), Wells, carpenter, 72 in 1714, appren. 5 Dec. 1653 to John Hood of Lynn, who, going to Eng., had the boy's time transferred to his br. Peter Tilton, who in accordance with a ct. order sent him to Hampton to his step-fa. Shaw. He m. 25 Jan. 1665-6 Mary Cram(2). Bot in Kittery from Nathan Lord in 1668 (sold 1672-3), but in 1671 settled in Wells on 150 a. bot from Francis Backhouse, also leasing a farm from Samuel Wheelwright ab. 1674. J. 1674, gr.j. 1675. Town gr. 1678. Lists 229, 265, 266, 269b. Ab. 1676 he m. 2d Deliverance Littlefield(11) and moved to Ipswich where he d. 28 Mar. 1728, ag. 90. Wid. Deliverance's will, 9 Nov. 1730—2 July 1733. Ch. by 1st w: **Abraham. Isaac**, drowned at Pemaquid 28 Mar. 1695. List 96. **Jacob**. By 2d w: **Sarah. Abigail**, b. 1 Apr. 1679. **Samuel**, b. 14 Apr. 1680-1. **Ebenezer** and **Mary**, twins, b. 8 Aug. 1683. **Joseph** and **Benjamin**, twins, bp. Wenham Sept. 1685. **Daniel**, bp. 8 Nov. 1687-8. **Rebecca**, b. 8 Mar. 1692-3. **Isaac**, b. 2 May 1695.

2 **ENSIGN *DANIEL**(5), Hampton, his br. Samuel his gdn. 1662, asked 'liberty to sit down as a smith' in Hampt. 1667. He m.

23 Dec. 1669 Mehitable Sanborn(10), adm. to Hampt. Ch. 10 Dec. 1703. Gr. 4 a. on Hampton hill 1669, bot 50 a. from Christopher Palmer 1671. J. 1683, 1684, 1694; gr.j. 1683. Deputy 1693-1695, 1702 (Speaker), 1709, 1711-1714. App. Justice of Ct. of Sessions Dec. 1698, but did not qualify. He d. 10 Feb. 1714-5. Lists 49, 52, 57, 62, 392b(2), 396, 399a. Ch: **Abigail**, b. 28 Oct. 1670, m. Christopher Page(9). **Mary**, b. 9 Mar. 1672-3. **Samuel**, b. 14 Feb. 1674-5, m. 7 Jan. 1703 Meribah (Page 2) Shaw who m. 3d 7 Nov. 1721 Benjamin Sanborn(1). At Fort Wm. and Mary, Newcastle, 1708. Est. div. 21 Jan. 1725-6 to ch. Samuel (b. 1 Nov. 1703, m. 31 Jan. 1731 Abigail Batchelder), Abigail (b. 20 May 1706, m. 15 Dec. 1726 Ebenezer Prescott), Meribah (b. 23 Dec. 1707, m. 5 Nov. 1729 John Fogg 2), Josiah (b. 1 Apr. 1709, m. 8 Feb. 1732 Sarah Flanders). Capt. **Joseph**, b. 19 Mar. 1697, m. 1st 26 Dec. 1698 Margaret Sherburne(8) who d. 1 July 1717, m. 2d 5 Dec. 1717 Elizabeth (Hilliard 7) Shaw who d. 19 Apr. 1724, m. 3d 17 June 1725 Elizabeth (Chase 5) Hilliard who d. 14 Aug. 1765. Her will 1753—1765. He d. Kensington 24 Oct. 1744. Will, 14 Oct. 1742—31 Oct. 1744, names ch. Sherburne, John, Mary Batchelder, Sarah Swett (dec'd.) Jonathan, Joseph (all by 1st w.), Timothy, Margaret Batchelder, Joanna (by 2d w.). **Mercy**, b. 25 May 1679, m. Samuel Elkins(3). **Daniel**, b. 23 Oct. 1680, d. Stratham 16 Sept. 1722, adm. 5 Dec. to w. Elizabeth who d. 19 Apr. 1724, adm. d. b. n. to bros. Joseph and Jethro 4 Dec. 1724. 5 ch. **David**, b. 30 Oct. 1682, m. 8 Jan. 1708 Deborah Batchelder(4) who m. 2d 14 June 1733 Jonathan Fellows. He d. 26 May 1729. 10 ch. **Mehitable**, b. 2 Oct. 1687, m. Joseph Lawrence(1). **Hannah**, b. 27 Apr. 1689, m. Nathaniel Healey(2). Capt. **Jethro**, m. 4 Nov. 1712 one Mary; sons John and Benjamin, daus. Dorothy Sanborn, Mary Leavitt, out of 8 ch. rec.

3 **MARY**(?5), m. at Martha's Vineyard 5 Oct. 1675 Isaac Chase(2) and had ch. b. 1677-1703, d. 14 June 1746 in her 88th yr. (gr.stone). Her parentage is a mystery, but there can be no doubt of her kinship to the family of William(5) as she m. a Hampton man closely assoc. with Samuel(4) who also settled at the Vineyard. Her age at death, if correctly stated, makes her birth yr. 1659 and her age at marriage 16. Each of the five sons of William(5) had daus. named Mary, dau. of Daniel(2), b. 1672-3, only three yrs. bef. the Chase marriage. That she was a cousin sent over from Eng. is poss., but seems hardly prob. in view of the early death of the emigrant William and his w., to whom a young girl might have been entrusted. Could she have been a dau. of William himself?

Gravestone records are notoriously faulty. William d. early in 1653. If Mary were his posthumous ch., b. in 1653, she would have been 22 at marriage, 50 at the birth of her last ch., and 93 at death. The best that can be said for this theory is that it is within the realm of possibility.

4 **SAMUEL**(5), Hampton, carpenter, m. 17 Dec. 1662 Hannah Moulton(see 16) who d. 11 Apr. 1720. Deeds from step-fa. Shaw 1660, from Robert Tuck 1661, from Nathaniel Batchelder 1662, from John Sanborn 1670. Receipted for Shaw legacy 1661. With Hampton neighbors in 1673, he settled in Martha's Vineyard where he d. 29 Nov. 1731 in his 94th yr. Lists 386, 399b. Will, 15 June 1718—7 Mar. 1732. Ch: **Hannah**, b. 15 Sept. 1663. **William**, b. 11 Nov. 1668. **John**, b. 23 Oct. 1670. **Josiah. Mary. Rachel.**

5 **WILLIAM**, Lynn, placed here for convenience, first in Mass. records 1643, freed from training 1649 on acc. of age. Inv. 16 Apr., will (missing) prov. July, 1653. Wid. Susanna, exec., soon m. Roger Shaw(13), their contract ment. (missing), and d. Hampton 28 Jan. 1654-5. On 8 Feb. 1653-4 the Shaws sold the Lynn land, 2 a. and a ho., bot from John Wing, 3 a. on Sagamore Hill, 4 a. marsh and 12 a. planting lot. Ch. by a 1st w: Hon. *‡**Peter**, Windsor, Conn., and Hadley, Mass. **John**, (prob.), Lynn and Gravesend, L. I. By w. Susanna: **Samuel**, b. ±1638. **Abraham**, b. ±1642. **Daniel**, b. ±1646. ?**Mary.**

**Tinney**, see Tenney.

**TIPPIN**, Lt. *Bartholomew, employed by Scottow to proceed to Black Pt., discover the state of the fort, transport recoverable goods and impress inhabitants and others to hold the place, authority being given by Mass. Gen. Ct. 25 Oct. 1676. Agent of Maj. Thos. Clarke in N. H. 1679-1680. Rep. 1680. Of Exeter, planter, 1683; m. wid. Joanna Thing(1) who was liv. 1703. Lists 49, 237b, 377, 383.

**TITCOMB**. 1 **Daniel**, York wit. 1709.

2 **JAMES**, Portsmouth. See Mitchell(9).

**Titterson**, John, Portsmouth 1695, prob. an English sailor. List 334b.

## TOBEY.

1 **HENRY**, Exeter 1639+, is in every case an error for Henry Robey(1).

2 **JAMES**, Kittery by 1669 when his w. Katherine was sentenced to pay 3s. to Richard Millard and, at same ct., said she would be revenged on Richard Green and his w. if it cost her life. See Miller(13). Town gr. 1687, 1694, 1699. Lists 96, 288, 290, 298 (2). Deeded to s. Stephen and to sons John and William for support, 1695. Killed by Ind. 21 May 1705, his w. and s. Stephen adm.

Ch: **Stephen. James**, 17 in 1685, appren. to Ichabod Rollins, slain with fa., s.p. **John**, had town gr. 1694; d. s.p. List 298. **William**, no further rec. after 1695 deed. **Richard. Isaac**, named in deed of his bros. and sis. to br. Stephen 1706, but did not sign or ack. it; prob. d. s.p. **Margaret**, m. John Paul(2). **Mary**, m. Robert Jordan(5).

3 **RICHARD**(2), Portsmouth, cordwainer, m. bef. Dec. 1706 Martha Heard(6), who was bp. 14 July 1708. At Fort Wm. and Mary 1708. Constable 1720 (pd. fine); tythingman. List 339. Deeded ½ ho. 1735 to s. Isaac who conv. it to Edward Brooks 1741, five of his bros. and sis. conveying their int. to Brooks in 1746. Adm. to wid. Martha 26 Sept. 1739. Ch., from deeds and bp. rec: **Samuel**, turner, m. Mary Pickering; rem. to Portland, from where his wid. and ch. sold Portsmouth rights to Jacob Waldron 1788. **Martha**, m. Solomon Staples. **William**, bp. 30 Sept. 1711, m. 9 Apr. 1732 Deborah Lucy (1). **Isaac**, bp. 31 Jan. 1713-4, m. 13 Jan. 1736-7 Elizabeth Page. **Catherine**, bp. 15 Jan. 1715-6, m. 17 Apr. 1735 Edward Brooks (1). **Experience**, bp. Dec. 1717, prob. d.y. **Lydia**, bp. 29 Nov. 1719, m. John Waldron. **Mary**, unm. in 1746.

4 **STEPHEN**(2), Kittery, shipwright, 66 in 1732, m. 29 Nov. 1688 Hannah Nelson(1). Liv. at Maj. Shapleigh's ±1677. Gr.j. 1690, 1691. Lists 291, 296, 297, 298. See Green(5). Bot in Long Reach (Eliot) with partners, 1699. Deeds to sons 1735, 1743, and all personal est. to Stephen jr. 19 Oct. 1748. A will, dated 3 May 1729, was turned over to the ct. 2 Jan. 1748-9, but not proved. It names s. John, s.-in-law Robt. Staples and a gr.dau. Catherine Tobey (under 18). Ch: **Katherine**, b. 25 Oct. 1689. **Samuel**, b. 31 Jan. 1692, m. 29 Dec. 1720 Mary Spinney(2) who was liv. 1773; he liv. 1762. 5 ch. **James**, b. 21 Oct. 1694; app. d.y. **John**, b. 2 Jan. 1699, m., int. 9 Nov. 1723, Elizabeth Staples who d. Sept. 1769; he d. 6 Dec. 1778. Will. 3 ch. **Stephen**, b. 3 Jan. 1702, m. 1st 25 Oct. 1726 Anne Staples(2), m. 2d 30 Nov. 1749 Margaret Emery. Her will, 1788—1795. 6 ch. by 1st w. **Hannah**, b. 10 Jan. 1705-6, m. 1st Robert Staples(2), m. 2d Nathaniel Libby(9).

5 **THOMAS** (Tobbe). List 7.

**Tocker**, Brian, 1612. List 7. Tucker?

**TOMLIN**. 1 **John**, creditor of est. of George Knight(5) of Black Pt., 1672. List 228c.

2 **JOHN**, on N. H. j. 1694, gr.j. 1703.

3 **RICHARD**, Newcastle or the Shoals, m. Grace Diamond(5) who m. 2d Richard Tucker (see 16). She ( Tomlin) had victualler, retailer or tavern lic. 1693-1697. Her list 315b. Ch: **Richard**, of Boston, over 14 in 1709 when John Harris(10) was his gdn.

**TOOGOOD,** later form of Towgood, confined to co. Somerset.

1 **EDWARD,** m. after 1683 Elizabeth (Everill) Grant (4), she b. 1641. E. T. and family adm. inhab. of Boston 1684 (authority of Col. Banks). They came to Salmon Falls and liv. on the Grant place until driven off by Ind. An amusing story is told of his disarming a threatening Ind. who followed him for miles begging for his gun back. By 1695 she had d. s.p. and he had m. Gertrude (Urin) Mercer(1), she b. 1643, and was liv. in Portsmouth, where he had land from Samuel Cutts, 1694. Tavern lic. 1694-1698, constable 1696, gr.j. 1689, j. 1694, 1695 (foreman), 1700. They adm. the est. of Allen Lyde, 1701-2, and were gdns. of Lyde's ch., gr.ch. of Gertrude Toogood. E. T. Lists 60, 67, 68, 330d, 335a, 337, 339. See Gay, Jones(27). He sold the Grant prop. to Timothy Wentworth, 1705, and took a mtg. back, discharged 1732. Hannah Toogood who wit. a Hall heirship deed 10 Dec. 1711 (rechecked), may have been a dau. or a new wife, but, if the latter, she soon d. if (1) was that E. T. who m. 16 Oct. 1711 Hannah Ayres (7), she b. 1680, almost 40 yrs. younger than the Grant and Mercer wives. The will of E. T., brick-layer, 14 May—6 June 1737, left prop. to w. Hannah for life, then to dau. Mary (m. 4 Aug. 1731 John Cotton and d. 1 May 1758). Hannah, wid. of E. T., non compos, was ward of Edward Pendexter 29 Apr. 1748 when he pet. for permiss. to sell her lands, and 13 July 1748 he reported that he had sold them, buried the wid. and paid Mr. Benjamin Pitman's claim of £59. This leaves the death of one Hannah Toogood, 1 Aug. 1745, a very detached record (if not an error). She was hardly a dau. of the testator of 1737 as he made no mention of her. In no kn. rec. are 'Sr.' or 'Jr.' attached to E. T.'s name, and James Stackpole, deposing in 1732, said that the E. T. then living in Portsmouth was he who lived in Salmon Falls before the wars. Nevertheless, on the evidence now at hand, probability is stretched to the limit in regarding all the records of E. T. as referring to one man and not to a father and son.

2 **RICHARD,** Pemaquid 1647. List 10.

**Tookey,** Job, wit. Me. deeds 1679, 1680 (Y. D.: 53, 82). Later of Beverly where acc. of witchcraft, 1692.

**TOOTHAKER, Andrew,** York, in ct. with w. Abigail July 1707. Bot land 1713, leased Frost land 1719, sold various town grants 1722. 6 ch. rec. 1707-1722. List 279.

**TOPE, Richard,** Isles of Shoals, fisherman, here by 1663, sued by David Campbell 1673. In 1689 bot from George Perkins a ho. on Hog Isl. which his s. **Richard,** sailor of London, sold to Wm. Perkins 1718. See

Carpenter(4), Perkins(6). Lists 307b, 327a. See also Topp.

**TOPP, Mary,** wid., first at Strawberry Bank where, bound over to answer charges, she forf. bond (Joseph Miller bondsm.). Took O. A. 22 Nov. 1652 (a unique instance?) at York where she liv. between Alcock and Preble. Lists 275, 276. Her dau. **Jane** was slandered July 1660 by John Smith who said she was with child by John Donnell. In Shepton Mallett, co. Somerset, Jane, dau. of Richard and Mary Tope, was bp. 26 Mar. 1636. See also Tope.

**Torgisen,** see Freese(1).

**Torr,** see Tarr.

**TOUT** (or Trout). 1 **Henry,** of Dartmouth, co. Devon, m. 1714 Hannah Leighton(4) who m. 2d 1723 John Lary(4). Dau. **Hannah,** m. 1733 Samuel Lang(5).

2 **JOHN.** See Towle(3).

**TOWER, John,** s. of John and Margaret of Hingham, had a 2 a. ho.-lot next to Dartmouth or Sheepscot fort and 104 + 20 a. east of Dyer river from Col. Dongan 1686, all claimed by his s. **Benjamin** in 17—. List 164. See Tower Gen. (1891), p. 46, for ch.

**TOWLE,** not in Lower or Guppy. Descendants say the name is Irish, poss. a variation of O'Toole.

1 **BENJAMIN**(6), Hampton, ±27 in 1700, ±85 in 1754, m. 7 Nov. 1693 Sarah Boaden (9) who d. 22 June 1759, ag. 88; he d. 29 May 1759. Will, 1758—1759. Ch: **Mary,** b. 20 May 1695, m. 1st 18 July 1717 John Sleeper(1), m. 2d 29 Mar. 1727 Thomas Page. **Tabitha,** b. 1 May 1697, m. 22 Feb. 1721 Jonathan Tuck(2). **Abigail,** b. 16 Sept. 1699, d. 13 May 1716. **Martha,** d. unm. 1 Mar. 1730. **Patience,** b. 8 June 1704, m. 17 Feb. 1725 Stephen Hobbs(10). **Hepsibath,** b. 2 Oct. 1706, m. 27 Feb. 1729 John Page. **Sarah,** b. 2 May 1709, m. 22 Jan. 1734 William Clifford. **Benjamin,** b. 24 May 1711, d.y. **Benjamin,** b. 3 May 1713, m. 30 Jan. 1735 Rebecca Garland, d. 24 June 1768. 7 ch. **Elisha,** b. 23 July 1715, m. 1 Mar. 1739 Ann Vittum. 11 ch.

2 **CALEB**(6), Hampton and Chester, of which he was an original settler, m. 19 Apr. 1698 Zipporah Brackett(2) who d. 14 Aug. 1756. List 399a. He d. 20 Sept. 1763. Will, 1763, named 8 liv. ch. and heirs of s. Matthias and of dau. Elizabeth Brown. Ch: **Philip,** b. 18 Aug. 1698, m. 4 Mar. 1724 Lydia Dow(5). **Elizabeth,** b. 2 Dec. 1699, m. 1st John Fellows(2), m. 2d 1 Jan. 1724 Josiah Brown(33). **Caleb,** b. 9 May 1701, m. 18 Jan. 1727 Rebecca Prescott(2). **Anthony,** b. 30 Apr. 1703, m. 7 Nov. 1734 Sarah Hobbs. **Zachariah,** b. 13 Aug. 1705, m. 15 May 1728 Anna Godfrey. **Matthias,** b. 13 Aug. 1707, m. 13 Dec. 1733 Hannah Jenness (3 Hezekiah)

and had ch. Sued Henry Trefethen 1744.
**Jeremiah,** b. 12 Dec. 1709, m. 1st Hannah
Dearborn, m. 2d Sarah (Sanborn) Tuck.
**Francis,** b. 13 Jan. 1711, m. 1st one Prudence,
m. 2d 4 June 1738 Judith Sargent. **Hannah,**
b. 28 Mar. 1714. **Nathaniel,** b. 25 May 1716,
m. 17 Sept. 1740 Lydia Tilton. **Abraham,** b.
29 Nov. 1719, d.y. **Samuel,** b. Sept. 1722, d.
14 May 1736.

3 **JOHN,** Piscataqua, fisherman, ack. that
he had sworn falsely ab. Geo. Walton,
1652. See Gray(3). Rishworth wrote his
name -Toutte-, Bacon copied a missing record -Towte-. He or ano. wit. Tanner for
Fletcher, Portsm. 1668, and wit. for Withers
1675.

4 **SERGT. JOSEPH**(6), Hampton, ±85 in
1754, m. 1st 14 Dec. 1693 Mehitable
Hobbs(6), m. 2d 27 Jan. 1707-8 Mary (Ward
or Wardell?), m. 3d 4 Mar. 1731 Sarah Hobbs
(9). Lists 66, 399a. He d. Sept. 1757. Will,
20 Sept. 1754—26 Oct. 1757, names w., 6 of
7 ch. and gr.ch. (ch. of Amos, decd.). Ch:
**John,** b. 26 June 1694, m. 15 Nov. 1721 Lydia
Page (9 Christopher). **Joseph,** b. 31 Mar.
1696, m. 11 Nov. 1724 Sarah Dalton(2).
**James,** b. 10 Dec. 1698, m. 22 July 1725 Kezia
Perkins(16). Will, 8 Apr. 1750—9 July 1756.
**Mary,** b. 11 Mar. 1701, m. 4 Jan. 1720 Jona-
than Page. **Jonathan,** b. 5 Apr. 1703, m. 10
Feb. 1728 Anna Norton(1). **Mehitable,** b. 14
Aug. 1706, m. 2 May 1729 Thomas Brown
(5). **Amos,** b. 13 Nov. 1711, m. Hannah
Drake(7). Adm. to wid. 13 Sept. 1754.

5 **JOSHUA**(6), Hampton, ±30 in 1700, m. 2
Dec. 1686 Sarah Reed(11). List 52. He
d. 25 Sept. 1715. Will, 2 Nov.—8 Dec. 1715,
names wid., ch. and app. br. Caleb and s.
Joshua, exec. Ch: **Hannah,** b. 23 Sept. 1690,
m. bef. 1715 one Gilman (a s. of John 10?).
**Joshua,** m. 6 Feb. 1713 Sarah Brown(33) who
d. 8 Aug. 1767. He d. 24 Nov. 1752; adm. to
s. Joshua 27 Dec. 1752. **Sarah,** given 2 a. of
land in fa.'s will.

6 **PHILIP,** Hampton prop. in 1657, when he
m. 19 Nov. Isabella Austin(1) who d. 7
Dec. 1719. Bot a ho. and land 1664. Lists 52,
396. He d. 19 Dec. 1696, ag. 80. Will, 18
Dec. 1696—25 May 1697, app. sons Joseph
and Caleb exec. Ch: **Philip,** b. 3 May 1659,
m. 30 Sept. 1714 wid. Martha (Jackson 14)
(Boulter) Dore who was liv. 1724. He d. 17
June 1717. Will, 31 May 1709—6 Sept. 1717,
going to war, gives all to br. Caleb, but inv.
ment. the wid. **Caleb,** b. 17 May 1661; slain
13 June 1677 by 'the barbarous heathen.'
**Joshua,** b. 29 June 1663. **Mary,** b. 12 Nov.
1665, not in fa.'s will. **Joseph** and **Benjamin,**
twins, b. 4 May 1669. **Francis,** mariner, b.
1 Aug. 1671, original grantee of Kingston
1694 (List 400). For some unexpl. reason he
seems to have been disinherited, moved to
Charlestown (where he m. 26 July 1698

Prudence Russell) and changed his name to
Dowell or Dowle. On 25 Feb. 1705-6 she was
adm. of his est. (Towle alias Dowle), and his
br. Caleb gave up 'any right he may have.'
Ch. Francis, bp. 6 Apr. 1701, liv. 1724; and
poss. Philip Dowell who had a case in Com.
Pleas 1719 (Wyman's Charlestown). **John,**
b. 23 July 1674, not in fa.'s will. **Caleb,** b.
14 May 1678.

**TOWLTWOOD.** 1 **Henry,** in York ct. 1677,
suspected of setting fire to ho. of his master Mr. John Broughton, 'may be sold for
four yrs. in any Eng. plantation.' Wit.
1680 with Henry Simpson. Not guilty of
ravishing Elizabeth Horsley at Newbury,
1690. Also Towlthead and Toltwood.

2 **WILLIAM** (Tulted), York wit. 1671.

**TOWNSEND.**  See Jeffrey(4).
1 **CALEB,** soldier from Lynn at Wells 1693.
List 267b.

2 **GEORGE,** Portsmouth, mariner, m. Bethia
Dam(3). List 339. Will, 12 Mar. 1742—
25 Mar. 1761, bound to sea, ment. w. Bethia
(exec. with Wm. Parker), George Dam
(Moses, of Newington), Bethia Loud (Solomon). Appar. no ch.

3 **HENRY,** Richmond Isl. 1633. List 21.

4 **ROBERT,** Isles of Shoals, ±32 in 1668, bot
land in 1664 in Portsm. which he sold
1670. Wit. 1669. See Carter(1). List 356L.

5 **ROGER,** assaulted at Kittery 1664. See
Pierce(8).

**TOWSLEY, Michael,** in Boston from Hampton 26 Apr. 1675, a Hampt. soldier 1676.
He m. 4 June 1678 Mary Hussey(6), and liv.
in Salisbury. List 395.

**TOZIER,** a cleaner of wool. Peculiar to co.
Devon.

**RICHARD,** Berwick, first at Boston where
he m. 3 July 1656 Judith Smith, dau. of
Thomas and gr.dau. of Simon of Stepney, co.
Surrey, who named her and her husb. in his
will 3 Oct. 1665. Barring divorce, it is impossible that he was the husb. of 'dau.
Tozier' (with eldest s. John Green) who
was alive and legatee of her fa. Robert
Blott of Boston in 1662. Taxed Cochecho
1659 but that yr. mov. to Salmon Falls where
he had Kittery gr. Bounds dispute with
Wm. Piles 1667. Killed by Ind. 16 Oct. 1675,
adm. to wid. 16 July 1676. Lists 25, 33, 298.
Adm. on est. of his mo. Judith to s. Richard
18 June 1683. The real est. was conveyed in
sixths. Ch: **Thomas,** b. Boston 5 May 1657,
poss. killed with fa. **Richard,** ±70 in 1732,
±73 in 1733-4; m. wid. Elizabeth (Wentworth 11) Sharp; d. s.p. Gr.j. 1694, j. 1701,
constable 1702, moderator 1713 and 1716,
sergt. 1715. Lists 267b, 296. See Lord(1).
Original memb. Berwick Ch. 1703. Deeded
to Randall neph. 1712-3. Traditionally he

was twice an Ind. captive, she thrice, but only rec. is her capture 18 Mar. 1690. Bp. in the Catholic faith and servant to M. Pierre Boucher, she returned in 1695; liv. 1734 when they sold to Samuel Lord. **Simon,** Watertown, d. 30 Dec. 1718; by w. Mary had 6 ch. who (of Southboro) deeded to Samuel Lord 22 Sept. 1735. **Judith,** no rec. of her except that the mo. was Judith 'sr.' in 1683. **Elizabeth,** m. Richard Randall(16). **Ann,** m. 1st Stephen Jenkins(12), m. 2d David Kincade(1), m. 3d Thomas Potts(2). See Corson. **Martha,** liv. as a girl with the Loverings(2), m. 1678 Nathan Lord(7). **John,** apprenticed to Capt. Francis Littlefield and ±18 in 1683 when Capt. John Wincoll was app. his gdn. No heirship deed from him; presum. d. s.p.

**TRAFTON,**Traughton, Draughton. A family at St. Newlyn, co. Cornwall, named sons Thomas and Charles. See Martin(2).
1 **THOMAS,** York, fisherman, sued Sarah Mitchell for slander and Wm. Rogers for debt, 1663. He m. Elizabeth Moore(25). Town gr. 1673, 1697; bot 40 a. 1678. Selectman 1673, 1678, 1679, 1683, 1685, 1686; gr.j. 1692-1695; ferryman from 1688 and poss. earlier; inholder 1695-1700. See Gott(2), Martin(2). He d. by 1707 when his est. was div. in tenths for nine named ch. His house was burned in 1708. Another div. took place 1723-4, in sevenths for six named ch., three sons having d. s.p. in the interim. Lists 30, 278. Ch: **Jane,** 65 in 1737, m. William Beale (8). **Elizabeth,** m. 1st John Rackliff(2), m. 2d one Johnson (see 20). **Dorothy,** m. Josiah Mains(6). **Charles,** captured by Ind. 1695, ag. ±15, taken to Montreal, bp. as 'Charles Louis Marie' and entered service of his godfa., M. de Frontenac. Altho naturalized Frenchman in 1706, he returned to York on his fa.'s death and m. wid. Sarah (Hutchins 2) Dill; gunsmith. List 99. Will, 12 Oct. 1721—17 May 1748, names w., br. Hezekiah (no br. of this name in above divisions or any other rec.—scribe's error for Zacheus), sis. Johnson, Beale, Maine and Bracy. **Joseph,** had town gr. 1701-2, d. s.p. Their br. Charles was app. adm. of the estates of Joseph, Benjamin and Thomas 7 July 1713. **Penelope,** b. ab. 1683, m. 1st Anthony Day (2), m. 2d William Bracy(2). **Benjamin,** b. ab. 1685. Will, 4 June 1706—6 Oct. 1713, going to sea, names br. Wm. Beale, sis. Beale, Mane and Day, bros. Zacheus and Thomas (both under age), exec. Capt. Lewis Beane. **Thomas,** d. s.p. by 1713. **Zacheus.**
2 **ZACHEUS**(1), York, blacksmith, succeeded his fa. at the ferry. He m. 1st Annabel Allen, m. 2d int. 17 Sept. 1748 wid. Mary (Bickford 15) Walker. List 279(2). Ch: **Thaddeus,** b. 3 Dec. 1716, m. int. 5 Aug. 1738

Abigail Lewis(15). **Thomas,** b. 11 Aug. 1718. **Joseph,** b. 8 Dec. 1720. **Ch.** d. 19 Apr. 1723. **Annabel,** b. 6 Mar. 1724, m. Ephraim Blaisdell of Amesbury. **Olive,** b. 4 Dec. 1725, m. Stephen Lovejoy. **Charles,** b. 27 Apr. 1728, m. wid. Lydia (Bragdon) Gordon. **Zacheus,** b. 16 Apr. 1736, m. Eleanor Hutchins. **Jotham,** b. 6 Apr. 1741, m. Abigail Lewis.
**TREBLE, John,** at Piscataqua 1631 or 1632 on way to Eng., fleeing arrest in Mass. for attempting to assault Thomas Moulton's wife.
**TREBY.** 1 **Edward,** Richmond Isl. List 21.
2 **PETER** (also Trevy), adm. (Me.) 11 Nov. 1673 to Geo. Bartlett(3), debts due to est. from Black Point men.
**Tredby,** Nicholas, Falmouth wit. 1682. Y. D. 4: 65.
**TREDICK.** 1 **Henry,** m. bef. 1715 Mary O'Shaw(1).
2 **THOMAS,** List 356e.
**TREE, Richard,** Lynn, on garrison duty at Dover 1667. Ano. Richard, taxed Portsmouth 1698; Lists 330de, 336b, (67?).
**Treedel,** William. List 7.
**Treeweek,** John, N. H. 1689. List 57.

**TREFETHEN,** a typical Cornish name.
1 **FOSTER**(2), Newcastle, ship-carpenter, m. Martha Paine(5). Bot in Portsmouth 1705; sold to s. Henry 1736. Lists 315abc, 316, 318b. He and son taxed 1715; appr. est. of Diamond Currier 1731. Will, 30 Mar. 1751—28 Aug. 1754, names heirs of dec'd sons **Henry** and **James,** sons **John** and **Foster,** gr.dau. (dau. of s. **George** dec'd), gr. ch. John, Elizabeth and Sarah Trundy, gr.ch. Thomas, Love, Richard and Mary Toull, daus. **Elizabeth** and **Martha** Card, and appoints John Card (husb. of Elizabeth) exec. Foster jr. had w. Margaret in 1738. The two daus., mothers of the Trundy and Towle ch., are unident.
2 **HENRY,** Newcastle by 1678, had w. Joanna who was liv. 1708. J. 1695. Lists 313abc, 315a(2)bc, 319, ?90. Wit. will of Capt. Barefoot 1688. See Head(1). Only kn. ch: Foster. Henry.
3 **HENRY**(2), Newcastle, gr. land (in poss. of his mo. Joanna) by Penhallow, 1708. Constable 1697. He m. Mary Robinson(3) and is a more likely husb. than his neph. Henry(1) for Deborah (Jordan 4) (Randall) Wallis, who was w. of a H. T. by 1746. List 316. **Robinson,** inn-keeper at Rye, with w. Abigail (Locke) 1753-6, of Dover 1761, of Somersworth 1764, is a prob. s., and a prob. dau. is the w. of Jeremiah Jones(55) who had a s. Robinson. **Abraham,** a Newcastle mariner and capt. of marines at Louisburg, more likely a s. of (3) than a gr.s. of (1) or (3).

Trefry, see Turfrey.

Trego, Thomas, debtor to est. of Stephen Crawford, Isles of Shoals, 1642.

**TRELAWNEY**, a name borne by a long line of Cornish gentry.

1 **EDWARD**, br. of (2), came to Richmond Isl., inspected the patent, made an inventory of its goods and wrote a report to his br. from Boston 10 Oct. 1635, the language of which indicates a distinct Puritan tendency. His last letter from New Eng. was dated at Piscataqua 12 Aug. 1636. In 1637 he was in London and in 1643, with w. and ch., he was liv. in poverty. See index to Trelawney Papers, 2 Me. Hist. Soc. 3. List 21.

2 **ROBERT**, Esq., b. in Plymouth, co. Devon, 1598, s. of Robert and Eleanor (Mayne) Trelawney, his father an eminent merchant and thrice mayor of Plymouth. He m. at Megavissey, co. Cornwall, 1623, Ann Voga. Plymouth being the seat of the Council for New England, it was most natural that he, succeeding to his fa.'s mercantile interests, should seek gain in colonization, and on 1 Dec. 1631 he and another merchant, Moses Goodyear, obtained a patent for Richmond Isl. and a large portion of the adjacent mainland. On 21 July 1632 his agent, Mr. John Winter, was put in poss. of this territory by Dr. Richard Vines of Saco, acting as the agent of the Council. Trelawney never came over to his patent, but he took an active int. in its affairs through correspondence with Mr. Winter, whose letters and accounts, published by the Me. Hist. Soc., give a fascinating and unique picture of pioneer life on the Maine coast. An M. P., a staunch Royalist and supporter of the established church, the advent of the Commonwealth caused his political and financial ruin, and, twice imprisoned, he probably d. while confined in Winchester House in London, where he had made his will 24 Aug. 1643 (prov. 19 Nov. 1644). His s. **Robert**, a small boy, was given the Maine lands, but neglect on the part of Mr. Trelawney's exec., the uncertainties of the times and finally Mr. Winter's departure and death brought the small colony on evil days, and in 1648, Rev. Robert Jordan, who had m. Winter's dau., laid claim to it as payment for his fa.-in-law's salary and advances and obtained a favorable decision from the Ligonia court, the justice of which, however, has been subject to strong doubts. **John**, heir of Robert jr., tried to recover the patent from the Jordans in 1676, 1696, and 1700, but time and neglect were held to have made their title good. Lists 21, 221.

Treleage, Thomas, ship's carpenter on -The Hunter-, Richmond Isl. 1634. List 21.

Tremills, William, see Belgrove, Patten(1). Tremouille?

Trennick, Thomas, Dover wit. 1660.

**TRESCOTT**. 1 **John**, wit. Ellacott to Stevens, 1688. One J. T. was of Dorchester 1651-1741.

2 **ZACHARIAS**, captured at Merrymeeting bay 13 June 1722. See Y. D. 15: 3.

**TREWORGYE**, Cornish, but Brixham, co. Devon, had the fam. by 1593, Kingsweare (a hamlet in Brixham) by 1605. In Maine this name has become Trueworthy.

1 **JAMES**, Mr., Kittery, m. Catherine Shapleigh(1) at Kingsweare 16 Mar. 1617. At Kit. bef. June 1640, List 281. Summonsed for the gr.j. at Saco in 1640, accus. of divulging its secrets to John Winter and found unacceptable. His exact relations with his fa.-in-law cannot be known, but 2 Apr. 1641, resid. in N. E., he sold all fishing trade belongings and all est., real and personal, for £1500, to Nicholas Shapleigh, livery being given to Mr. Godfrey in behalf of N. S. 22 Apr. 1641, yet the similar deed from his fa.-in-law to himself is dated 26 May 1642 (Y. D. i: 1, 7; Shapleigh 1). His dau. Lucy's depos. in 1704 sets the yr. of her arrival here as 1646. By court rec. it seems he was here ±1647, but like other males of the fam. he vanished early and without rec.; cert. dead 2 July 1650 when Mrs. T. agreed to turn the est. in her hands over to her br. See N. E. Reg. 5: 345; 27: 266; references in Lechford, Aspinwall, Me. P. & Ct. Rec. and early Y. D. Widow Catherine (List 298), had an Ind. deed of Thompson's Point 3 Oct. 1651. She m. 2d Edward Hilton(1). Her nunc. will, proved 30 May 1676, named daus. and gr.ch. but only two Treworgyes, James, s. of Samuel and James, s. of John. Ch. found here: **John**, bp. at Kingsweare 30 Sept. 1618. **Nicholas. Samuel. Joanna**, m. John Amerideth. **Lucy** (±46 in June 1678, ±72 in July 1704), m. 1st Humphrey Chadbourne(1), m. 2d Thomas Wills(5), m. 3d Elias Stileman(1). **Elizabeth** (ag. 33 in 1671), m. John Gilman(8).

2 **JAMES**(4), tanner, Kittery, Portsmouth, more likely the James (in N. H.) who chose Maj. Shapleigh gdn. 24 June 1673 than (3) whose fa. then appar. had a home in Portsm. or Great Isl. In 1676 his paternal gr.mo. willed him a silver cup with no provis. that it be kept until he be of age. List 329 may be his or (3)'s. Gr.j. (Me.) 1687. He came into poss. of the John Brady(2) prop. by mar. the wid. Sarah, as 1st or 2d w. (Y. D. 8: 26; 9: 221). On 16 July 1693 he m. Mary Ferguson (see 3; also Y. D. 12: 218), the Kit. mar. rec. calling him 'son of John of Dartmouth.' She d. 19 July 1696. He was Pep-

perell's tanner in 1696, wit. an Emery fam. deed 1 Mar. 1696-7. Of Portsm. 18 Nov. 1701, he sold in Kit. to Thomas Greely (Y. D. 6: 115), and was ab. to m. Ruth Kirke(2) 8 Nov. 1702 when he released all int. in her prop. Taxed for the Mill Dam ±1708; called late of Kit. (but not deceased) in Mar. 1713-4. The selectman paid for shoes for one James in 1718. Widow Ruth at Portsm. 1734+. Ch., by w. Mary at Kit: **Penelope**, b. 1 June 1694, m. 17 Jan. 1720 Joseph Kilgore, 6 or more ch. in Berw. and York. **John**, b. 1 June 1696, adm. to Berw. Ch. 27 Mar. 1720, accus. by Dorcas Gowen(1) in 1721, Berw. soldier 1724, dism. to Arundel 19 Oct. 1730. As far as known, no one has proved Bradbury's statement that he was Allison Brown's hired man and m. his wid. Hannah (Scammon), see Brown(3), but he cert. m. Mary Bracey(2) 9 Apr. 1731, was of Bid. in Mar. 1732-3, and in 1744 sold a ho. and 1 a. there adj. Dyer. Bradbury, p. 145, names him as one of the Arundel men (he s.p.) cast away and drowned at Mt. Desert in 1746, on way to join regt. at Nova Scotia (his wid. m. 2d in 1753 John Davis of Bid.), but a s. Spencer. bp. at Bid. in 1743, m. there in 1769. One Jacob m. Catherine Libby in Bid. in 1756; one James was serv. of Thomas Dyer 1756 (Folsom, p. 271). By w. Ruth: **James**, bp. at Portsm. 11 Apr. 1714 when his mo. owned the covt.

3 **JAMES**(6), willed a silver beaker by his gr.mo. (Hilton) in 1676, to be given him when of age. See (2). A mariner, m. Mary Watts(2), and liv. in Boston, his aut. there in Nov. 1695 and Feb. 1695-6 in SJC 3218 and 3261. In 1698 master of the -Mayflower-, Jamaica to Providence or Boston. In 1716 one Thomas Smith depos. that ±1696 Florence McCarthy and J. T. borrowed £200, John Gerrish(4) endorsing for J. T. who d. by 1699; the creditor claimed that Gerrish ought to pay, being T.'s br. and atty. (SJC 11114). Kn. ch. in Boston: **Samuel**, b. 24 Jan., d. 19 Apr. 1697 (Copp's Hill). **Samuel**, bp. in 2d Ch. 21 Aug. 1698. Cousin Mary T. named in will of Mrs. Lake(3) in July 1705 was prob. Mary (Watts) T. and not a young dau. In Boston one Mary Treworgye and George Jones, belonging to the Reserve, pub. int. in 1709, the same or ano. Mary m. Samuel Kill in 1712.

4 **JOHN**(1), Mr., merchant, Kittery, ag. 33 in Mar. 1650-1, appar. here 5 May 1636 when Thomas Bradbury, agent for Sir F. Gorges, deeded to Edw. Johnson for use of J. T. of Dartmouth 500 a. described in Y. D. 1: 11. In 1678 Mr. Johnson depos. that the land was purch. by J. T. as Mr. Alexander Shapleigh's agent and for A. S.'s sole use. Bondsman for Mr. Thomas Spencer at Saco ct. in Feb. 1636-7, and appar. here steadily until ±1651. In 1644 he held Nicholas Shapleigh's p/a while S. went to Eng. Cor.j. 1647; tr.j. 1647. Having failed in a contract to deliver fish, he pledged Kit. prop. to Major Sedgwick (Y. D. 1: 3: 9); in 1649 ack. a transaction done for his uncle in Newb.; depos. in Boston 25 Oct. 1650, and of Dartmouth, depos. 19 Mar. 1650-1 ab. the -Prosperous- coming to N. E. ±1640 when he had been here ±5 yrs. In Apr. 1651 named on a Newfoundland commission, not seen here again except in Lists 72, 73, 78, 80, and was of Dartmouth in Apr. 1654. See also all references under (1). He m. Penelope Spencer (see 3, 4) 15 Jan. 164-, in Newb., where a s. **John** was rec. 12 Aug. 1649. Only other known ch: **James**.

5 **NICHOLAS**(1), Mr., sailor, Piscataqua, depos. 3 Feb. 1650-1, ag. 22. If age correct, he could not have been the Mr. N. T. who came ±1640 as master of the -Prosperous- (see N. Y. Gen. & Biog. Rec. 47: 113) who could have been the Nicholas bp. at Kingsweare 29 Sept. 1609, son of Nicholas. One N. wit., Shapleigh to Treworgye 26 May 1642, Gorges to Withers 1 Mar. 1643. In 1648 Richard Hogg of Boston had a p/a from England to collect from John Pease and N. T. In a Mass. ct. that yr. Robert Knight got a verd. of £183 ag. John T., Nicholas Shapleigh and N. T., the case ag. Shapleigh being reheard in 1653 when the judg. ag. him was reversed. Mr. N. T. plf. in a suit ag. Thomas Turpin, decd., York ct. 15 Mar. 1649-50. List 73. See also references under (1).

6 **SAMUEL**(1), Mr., mariner, depos. in 1661, ag. 33, that he was lately at Samuel Wentworth's ho. on Great Isl. (Reg. 27: 272). Both men were taxed there in 1671 and it is poss. the yr. -1661- is an error. A Berw. wit. in Feb. 1664-5 (Y. D. 3: 27), in 1669 took a letter from Barbadoes to Piscataqua. On 2 Nov. 1674 his mo. deeded him the former Thompson's, now Treworgye's Point, which he, a Portsm. mariner, and w. Dorcas (Walton 1) sold to Richard Rich four days later. Deft. in suits brot by Andrew Cranch and Lawrence Mann in 1674; his aut. 1674 in Concord files 3: 89. Lists 298, 312c, 326c, 330a. Last seen as a Boston wit. with Thomas Kemble 16 Mar. 1674-5 (Suff. D. 12: 99); not in mo.'s will. Wife Dorcas also drops from sight, not in her fa.'s will. Kn. ch: **James**, a minor in 1676. **Elizabeth**, named in gr.fa. Walton's will in Feb. 1685-6, List 315b, m. 1st Noah Parker(26), m. 2d John Field(4), m. 3d Benjamin Cross (2). As E. C., wid., of Portsm., only surv. ch. of Samuel Treworgy of Kit., she sold an 18 a. addition to his ho.-lot 7 Mar. 1739-40.

**TRICK**, Tricke. 1 **Elias**, Damariscove 1672, had a Devonshire name. Gr.j. 1674. O. A.

at Pemaquid 1674, at Marblehead 1677. In Essex ct., Nov. 1681, thru atty. John Putnam, he sued Wm. -Cook- for entert. and detaining his servant over a yr. In York files, 1737, Savage v. Patteshall, is indenture, 16 Aug. 1686, betw. Patteshall and E. T. of Damariscove, who was to live in his own ho. there for life, keep stock limited to 40 sheep and lambs, 4 cows and calves, and what swine he could raise; at death all to go to P. for his debt. By depositions in 1736 he appar. d. on the isl. bef. long. Lists 13, 15, 85. See also Parker(23).

2 **JOHN**, Cape Newagen. See Moles.

**TRICKER, Israel**, wit. in Wells 1729 (Y. D. 13: 80), and of Boxford depos. in 1730 ab. Wells marsh in 1725, prob. the inhabitant of 1726 named by Bourne as Israel -Tucker- (see 27). He and Hannah Smith, both of Wenham, were m. at Ipsw. 22 Mar. 1725. One Marks Tricker took O. A. at Beverly in 1677.

**TRICKEY**, Devon-Somerset. Much work is needed on the 3d generation, a scant count being found and not surely placed. See also Gunnison(2).

1 **BETHIA**, see Keniston(1). Martha rec. into cov., So. Ch., 1718. Priscilla, appar. adult; the town paid a good sum for her nursing, 1731-2; see also James Nelson(2). Elizabeth m. in 1741 Peter Miller. All these of Portsm. One Mary and Michael Row pub. int. in Boston 1736.

2 **EPHRAIM**(6), Bloody Point, pulled down the fence of a neighbor Mary Cater(2) in 1682. See also Bickford(22). Last seen in tax list 25 Aug. 1684. Lists 359b, 52. Widow Mary (prob. Nason 5, not Follett) m. 2d William Wittum(4) who was liv. on E.'s land in June 1701. Adm. 24 Sept. 1701 to John Pickering to whom the s. Thomas was apprent., and to (4), the wid. renouncing. Kn. ch: **Thomas**. In 1701 Dover conf. to him all the land his fa. had improved; had deed from (7) in 1706. Appar. he was Capt. T., shipwright, Newington, who m. Mary Gambol in Portsm. 28 Aug. 1712. Both o.c. and bp. at Newingt. 18 Apr. 1725 with 6 ch: Isaac m. 24 Oct. 1734 Elizabeth Wells and was presum. the oldest son who was beyond seas in 1747, s.p.; Jonathan, shipwr., Newingt., near 25 in Jan. 1745-6 (one J. m. Abigail Miller 2; see also Temperance Downing 4); Sarah, m. 7 Dec. 1732 Hatevil Leighton; Abigail; Elizabeth, m. 23 Oct. 1737 Thomas Tripe of Kit.; Mary, m. 16 May 1742 Abraham Fernald of Kit.; and at least 4 more: Thomas; Joseph (one J. m. Elizabeth Dam 1748); Keturah, m. Jonathan Leathers(2); Lemuel (5 yrs. 7 mos. when fa. died; of Durham 1756). The widow Mary was gr. adm. 27 Sept. 1738, div. 1747. She m. 2d 4

Apr. 1751 John Bickford of Durham; liv. 1758. **Isaac**, a minor in 170-.

3 **FRANCIS**, Mr., fisherman, Kittery. Taxed Dover 1649, Exeter wit. 1650, Portsm. 1651 (see Green 1), Kit. by 1656 where he bot from H. Gunnison bef. 14 Mar. 1658-9. The Dennis Downings sued him and w. Sarah for slander in 1656 foll. a quarrel betw. the wives. Cor.j., lower Portsm., 1657. In 1667 George Lidden bot Crooked Lane land betw. his and John Ameredith's. Lists 354b, 323, 325, 330a, 286, 287, 298, 25, 30, 92. Inv. 11 Apr. 1682, ho. and land, debt due from Richard Downes of the Shoals; adm. to s. **John**, whose own inv. was taken 17 May 1686 with adm. to mo. **Sarah**; Lists 30, 298. A dau. **Sarah** m. Samuel Winkley(2). In 1685 Roger Thomas boarded with Mrs. Sarah T. See also Lidden(1, 2), Taylor(22). In 1702 the 20 a. gr. reaching from Crooked Lane to Spruce Creek was laid out to Samuel Winkley who adm. the widow's est., his bond 15 Apr. 1703.

4 **ISAAC**(6), of age 1668 (see Green 6), taxed 1670, Bloody Point constable 1686. Jury 1692; cor.j. 1696; gr.j. 1698. In 1695 he and Wm. Redford wit. at Portsm. for Andrew Wilson, shipmaster. Lists 356j, 359ab, 52, 54. See also Rebecca(5). Of Dover 1701, and called of D. 13 Aug. 1712 when adm. gr. to s. John, appraisers John Dam and John Downing; est. insolvent. His w. is unseen, 2 ch. seen: **Thomas**, ment. in list of claims in fa.'s est., wit. with Joseph Gunnison 1707 (Y. D. 7: 111), had deed from br. in 1717; poss. it was he who had a fam. in Newingt. and not Thomas(2). **John**, Newingt. 1712, List 343, presum. the one with w. Mary adm. to full commun. at Newingt. 4 Apr. 1725, and who left will, 1753—1756, naming her and ch: Joshua, exec. (bp. at Durham 21 Apr. 1728, young serv. of Joseph Edgerly, m. Rosamond Coleman(2) who was R. Bracebridge in 1772); John; Ephraim (given Rochester land by fa. 1746, not in will); Mary (m. James Smith of Durham 1737); Alice (m. Joseph Smith of Durham 1734; her ch. in will); Sarah (m. Thomas Langley 3); Elihu (bp. 1726; in will, if alive and returns); Deborah (not in will). One Joanna was bp. and o.c. there in 1728.

5 **JOSEPH**(6), carpenter, gave a q.c. to (7) in 1679; a Dover shipwright 1685 (see Mahon). Nehemiah Partridge had a bill ag. him in 1682, wid. Mary Hoddy had a reckoning with him in 1689. He gave various notes, to Wm. Pitman 1684 (see 13), Reuben Hull 1686, Thomas Rogers 1687. Jury 1684. Lived near Bloody Point ferry. Lists 359b, 52. In June 1695 his wid. Rebecca (Rogers 16) was accus. of having an illeg. ch.; she was then very sick at ho. of (4). She was called Trickey 1704, took adm. and gave bond as

widow T. 1 Sept. 1713, swore to inv. 21 Oct. 1714 as Rebecca Downing (w. of Joshua 5). Of Kit., 17 June 1735, she deeded cow, chest, etc., and wearing apparel aft. her death to (gr.son) Zebulon. Ch. appear: **William,** York, m. Mary Andrews (Robert), in 1735 owned at Braveboat Harbor, in 1743 depos. that he lumbered and built fences for Richard Mitchell; wid. Mary liv. 2 Oct. 1761. Only ch. rec: Zebulon (see Downing 5), went to Scarb. ±1727 and Falm.; adm. 17 July 1744 to wid. Eleanor (Libby 3) who m. 2d Lt. Andrew Libby(9). Note also Martha(7). **Elizabeth,** unm. 1704; one E. m. John Ambler 6 Nov. 1706.

6 **THOMAS,** shipwright, Bloody Point, here by 1640, bef. ct. with w. Elizabeth in 1646, taxed 1648. In 1650 George Dodd of Boston sued him over a 40-ton vessel he was building. He sued Michael Brawn in 1652, George Elliot in 1656. O. F. ±1655. His 1656 gr. on Bloody Point side was rebounded in 1674 when Trickey's Cove ment. and the neighbors were John Bickford, Richard Cater and Henry Langstar. Gr.j. 1659. Aged ±54 in 1668, w. Elizabeth ±52, tho she was ±64 in May 1688 when she depos. that she liv. with Mr. Alexander Shapleigh in Eng. ±52 yrs. bef. (see N. E. Reg. 5: 349). Both wit. about Edw. West selling liquor, 1671. Inv. 3 Dec. 1675; adm. to wid. 27 June 1676, the whole est. left in her hands for her comfort and care. In Dec. 1680 Elihu Gunnison's pet. ab. the est. was filed. Lists 351a, 354abc, 355a, 356abceghk, 342. Widow's Lists 359b, 52. Ch., not in order: **Isaac. Joseph. Ephraim. Zachariah. Deborah** (±58 in 1705, 72 in 1718) m. William Shackford(3). **Lydia** (68 in June 1718), m. 1st Edmund Green(6), m. 2d Richard Webber(8). **Martha,** m. Elihu Gunnison(1). **Sarah,** m. Joshua Crockett(5).

7 **ZACHARIAH**(6), b. ±1651 (±50 in 1701), first seen drunk and fighting at training in 1671, when Thomas Beard was his bondsman. He had a q.c. from (5) in 1679, from the Shackfords in 1680. Portsm. 1700, Bloody Point 1706. In Oct. 1715 the body of Z. T. had been taken up at Kit. List 359a. See also Williams(38). He left a wid. Elizabeth (Wittum 1). No son of his name is seen, tho he was 'Senior' in 1709. The wid. Elizabeth liv. much in Berw. 1730-1738, so poss. **Martha** who m. Daniel Libby (see 6) was their dau.; see also Zebulon (Wm. 5) who m. a Libby. Elizabeth T. was schooling Moses Hubbard's ch. in Berw. 1737; 'old Mother Trickey' adm. to So. Berw. Ch. 1742. In 1749 Kit. and Newingt. disputed over her care, a sick and indigent aged widow; see Hall(28) and Howard Henderson(4) who said Z. T. and w. liv. at Bloody Point in 1696 and for 8 yrs.; Kit. lost and had to keep her.

**TRIGGS, Robert, Samuel, Jane, Elizabeth,** bros. and sis. at Portsmouth. Robert wit. 1711, adm. to br. Samuel 1743. Samuel m. 1727-8 Susannah Fox(1); sold ⅓ Robert's land. Jane, wit. for Penhallows 1705, 1709; was wid. Jane Cox 1758 when she sold ⅓ Robert's land. Elizabeth m. 28 Apr. 1723 Joseph Allen; sold ⅓ Robert's land 1758.

**TRIMMINGS, Oliver,** in Piscataqua ct. 1643 for trespass, 1652 for perjury. Portsmouth gr. 1652; sold to John Odiorne 1655, to Thos. Seavey 1656. Walter Abbott sued his w. Susannah for slander 1655. She charged Jane Walford(4) with witchcraft in 1656, when Oliver test. that his wife came home all-a-tremble and laid her **child** upon the bed. Lists 323, 330a(2), 342. See Johnson (34).

**TRIPE, Sylvanus,** Kittery, weaver, m. ±1695 Margaret Diamond(5). Lists 290, 296, 297; her list 291. Will, 29 Dec. 1714—10 May 1716, left all to w. for maintenance of herself and eight ch. (named) until they could be apprent., Mr. Robert Cutt and Mr. John Newmarch overseers. Her will, 4—19 Jan. 1741-2, bequeaths to surv. ch. and gr.ch. Ch: **Joanna** (Hannah), m. Portsm. 16 Aug. 1714 William Pope(2). **Margaret,** m. 1720 Nathaniel Fernald(5). **William,** wit. Gunnison deed 1713, d. bef. mo., s.p. **Sylvanus,** m. 25 June 1724 Lucy (Lewis 15) Briard, d. bef. mo., leaving ch. Samuel, Abigail, Anne and William named in her will. Adm. on est. of wid. Lucy gr. to Peter Lewis jr. 26 July 1738. She left an illegit. baby, Lucy Tripe, who was a poor ch. in the family of Richard Evans, bp. 20 June 1742. **Samuel,** b. 13 Apr. 1704, d. bef. mo., leaving by unkn. w. ch. Sarah, Samuel and Anne. Either Elizabeth Tripe who m. 1733 Joseph Dill, or Eleanor Tripp who m. 18 Mar. 1735-6 Nathaniel Seavey may have been his wid. **Thomas,** b. 12 May 1706, had homestead from his mo. 1739, and her exec. **Mary,** b. 2 Apr. 1708, m. John Follett(4). **Robert,** b. 4 Sept. 1710, had w. Mary who m. by 1764 Jonathan Johnson. Given ho.-lot by mo. (Y. D. 23: 20). 12 ch. b. from 1733.

**Trippier,** Isaac. List 3, p. 47.

**TRISTRAM, Ralph,** Mr., Saco, had early gr. from Cleeve and poss. m. 1643 the wid. of Morgan Lacy. O. A., Clerk of the Writs and constable, 1653; selectman 1659. Acquired Richard Randall's land, adjoining his own. Lists 24, 243ab, 244adef, 245, 246, 249, 252. See Boaden(7), Ford(7), Lee(3), Naziter, Norman(3). Adm. 4 Mar. 1678-9 to Dominicus Jordan, husb. of dau. Hannah who saved the blood but not the name from extinction. Ch: **Samuel,** b. 2 Feb. 1644. **Nathaniel,** b. 10 July 1650; inv., entered same day as his fa.'s, incl. a ho. and land. **Benjamin,** b. 8 May 1653, depos. 14 Nov. 1676,

inv. 25 Jan. 1678-9 incl. fishing boat and outfit tendered by Sylvanus Davis, agent for
Maj. Thos. Clark who was to adm., but adm.
was gr. to Capt. Francis Hooke 1 Apr. 1679,
Dominicus Jordan and John Harmon bondsmen. List 236. **Ruhamah**, b. 18 Dec. 1655,
poss. same as **Hannah**, ±92 in 1746, m. 1st
Dominicus Jordan(1), m. 2d Capt. Stephen
Greenleaf(4 jr.). **Rachel**, b. 23 Aug. 1658.
**Freegrace**, b. 7 Oct. 1661. **Ruth**, b. 10 Aug.
1664. **David**, with sis. Hannah sold fa.'s land
to Edward Sargent (who sold to Pepperell)
1684 and 1690-1. Adm. to Dominicus Jordan
30 Aug. 1693.
**TROTT, Simon**, Cape Porpus, took O. A. 5
July 1653. Lists 251, 252, 255. He prob.
m. twice, 1st a dau. of Stephen Batson(3),
2d one Elizabeth. The latter attended a wild
party at Winter Harbor in 1656, other par-
ticipants being Mary Clay(1), James Har-
mon(1), Robert Cook(10) and John Davis
(19), all of whom were constant sources of
scandal to the community. In 1658, vehemently suspected of adultery, she was taken
to Boston for trial, result unkn. 'An old wigwam that Goody Trott did make and live in'
is ment. in Morgan Howell's deed to John
Barrett in 1666. See Creber. Ch. by 1st w:
**John**, took O. A. 1670, legatee of gr.fa. Batson 1673, of Wells 1674, moved to Nantucket
by 1679-80. List 269b. Deeded to Jonathan
Littlefield 100 a. and ho. at Wells, bounded
by Charity Webb and Wm. Ashley 1685.
Will, 5 Jan. 1722-3—17 July 1728, weaver,
names w. Anne, sons John and James (where-
abouts unkn.), Benjamin, daus. Tabitha,
Elizabeth, Rachel, Mary, Abigail, Priscilla.
**Mary**, in Batson will, given same legacy as
John tho not specifically called gr.ch.
**?Sarah**, Ashley in Batson will. See Ashley
(4). **?Elizabeth**. Nantucket genealogists
say that Edw. Cartwright (see 1) m. a sis. of
John Trott.
**Trout**, William, Kennebec, 1674. List 15.
**Trowills**, see Twowills.
**Trowtte**, Timothy, York ct. 6 July 1657
(original lost), must be misreading of
Timothy Prowtte (Prout).
**TRUE, Henry**, Salisbury, m. 16 Mar. 1667-8
Jane Bradbury(1) and dau. **Mary** was
b. Hampton 30 May 1668.
**Trumbull**, Joseph, York wit. 1712 (Y. D. 8:
184).
**TRUNDY, George**, Newcastle by 1696,
caulker. Lists 315bc, 387. **Sarah**, dau.
of George, in ct. for stealing food from Jere-
miah Walford 1702. One Elizabeth, w. or
dau., a Berwick wit. 1711. In Boston 8 May
1720 the w. of George Trundy was bur. and
22 Feb. 1721 he m. Sarah Watts. Prob. s.
**John**, Newc. 1722, 1726 (w. Jane). **John**,
Falmouth, formerly of Newc., with w. Catherine 1743. Falmouth marriages: John T.

and Elizabeth Maher 4 Sept. 1748, George T.
and Olive Jordan 30 Nov. 1757. See also
Trefethen(1).
**Tubbs**, Benjamin, Kittery, m. 12 Jan. 1698-9
wid. Elizabeth Kim. List 290.

**TUCK**, see Lower's 'Patronymica Brittanica' for various theories of origin.
1 **EDWARD**(3), Hampton, m. Mary Phil-
brick(7) who m. 2d James Wall(1); d.
6 Apr. 1652. Lists 391b, 392a, 393a. Ch:
**Edward**, b. 8 Sept. 1649, d. between 12 Apr.
1653 and 11 Apr. 1665. **John**, b. 12 Apr. 1652.
2 ***JOHN***(1), Hampt., carpenter and miller,
m. 9 Jan. 1678 Bethia Hobbs(8) who d.
29 May 1738. Gr.j. 1694, 1696, 1698; Rep.
1717, selectman 10 yrs., town clerk 15 yrs.,
deacon 27 yrs. Lists 52, 54, 55a, 57, 62, 85,
392b, 396, 399a. Called cousin in will of
Philip Lewis(16). He d. 4 Jan. 1742. Ch:
**Bethia**, b. 28 July 1682, m. John Marston
(2). **Mary**, b. 27 Jan. 1684, m. Samuel Shaw
(10). **John**, b. 19 Apr. 1687, d. 25 June 1688.
**Samuel**, twin, b. 30 Apr. 1689, not bp. 1697
with twin **Sarah**, who m. Thomas Batchelder
(3). **Hannah**, b. 10 Apr. 1692, m. Jonathan
Dearborn(4). **Edward**, Kensington, carpenter, b. 7 Feb. 1695, m. 24 Nov. 1720 Sarah
Dearborn, d. 15 Jan. 1756. 11 ch. ***Jonathan***, b. 11 Sept. 1697, had homestead, miller,
deputy, deacon, selectman, m. 22 Feb. 1721
Tabitha Towle(1), d. 3 Feb. 1781; she d. 12
Aug. 1766. 10 ch. Rev. **John**, b. 23 Aug. 1702,
H. C. 1723, m. 26 Nov. 1724 Mary Dole. For
41 yrs. pastor at Gosport, Isles of Shoals,
where he d. 12 Aug. 1773. 6 ch.
3 **ROBERT**, Hampton, vintner, came from
Gorleston, co. Suffolk, to Watertown
where he was a prop. 1636. Original settler
of Hampt. 1638, freeman 7 Sept. 1639, Clerk
of the Writs 1648, selectman. His inn on
Rand's hill was the first in the town. Made
a trip to England 1652. Lists 391ab, 392ab
(3), 393ab. See Clark(17), Johnson(34). He
d. 4 Oct. 1664, adm. 11 Oct. to s.-in-law John
Sanborn and wid. Joanna who d. 14 Feb.
1673-4. Ch: **Robert**, remained at Gorleston.
He had a s. William, 24 in 1670, with whom
Sanborn made an agreement in 1674. **Elizabeth**, m. John Sherburne(5). **Mary**, m. John
Sanborn(2). **Edward**.

**TUCKER**, occupational, belongs to the
West of Eng., espec. Devonshire. Became
96th commonest name in N. E.
1 **ADRIAN**, got judgm. ag. Sir Ferdinando
Gorges in 1639 for wages due 17 June
1633, services to Gorges and Mason at Piscataqua. List 41.
1½ **BRIAN?** See Tocker.
2 **ELIZABETH** (Coe 2), wid. of John; see
Y. D. 15: 170.

3 **FRANCIS**, Mr., merchant, Great Isl., here in July 1672, 'cousin' of Wm. Bickham (2), given p/a by Vickers, Bickham & Co. of Bristol, in Mar. 1674-5, was presum. gr.s. of Hugh Bickham whose will (in Eng.) names sons William and Richard B. and dau. Margaret Tucker. As a Bickham agent he was plf. in suits ag. Me. and N. H. fishermen, and often a Newc., York and Shoals wit. to 1703. Ag. ±28 in 1679, ±30 in Oct. 1681 (Y. D. 3: 103). See Legate(2) and John Gale(4) whose will he wit. Poss. at York by chance, he was captured in the Ind. attack of Jan. 1691-2, but soon ret. ('N. E. Captives,' i: 226). Wit. will of (21) in 1694. Cor.j. 1683; gr.j. 1685; selectman 1693, 1695-1697. Coroner for the Prov. 1697. Lists 312f, 313af, 315a(2)bc, 317, 319, 326c, 331b, 336c, 52, 60, 65, 91. Admr. of Richard Stileman's est. 19 Apr. 1703 (the will, 1693, named T. trustee); last seen 7 Mar. 1704-5 complaining that Newc. still taxed him and the Stileman est., altho 4 Aug. last he left there and hired a chamber at Mr. Samuel Fernald's in Kittery. The logical husb. for Mr. Fryer's sis. Wilmot T., if she were in N. E., but if so, might not have been fa. of her dau. Joanna who m. John Hollicomb (he wit. Fryer's deed to J. H. in 1694). And he dealt with and in 1690-1 was taxed next to Jacob Randall(4) whose wid. Katherine was Tucker at death, adm. in 1718. See Mann(5) for Francis 1731; note (14), (26) and Ann Carmell.

4 **GEORGE**, sailor at Newc. 1684. List 314 (2).

5 **HENRY**, York wit. 1639 (Y. D. 1: 119); see also Me. P. & Ct. Rec. ii: 58. One H. signed a Kit. petition ±1673 (Doc. Hist. 4: 340); abs. from meeting 1674; sued by Capt. Hooke and by John Bray in 1678, and again absent from meeting.

6 **HUGH**, Mr. (Tucker?). List 312f.

7 **HUGH**(16), fisherman, Kittery, eldest son. He and his now w. were accus. in July 1698 and did not appear. A captive 1706; still away in 1709 when w. Bridget sold liquor (Me.). She was liv. 13 May 1712. A son John was bp. at Glouc. 10 Mar. 1705-6. Other ch. of this mar. poss. incl: **Stephen**, signed a bond with Hugh and John in 1730, all Kit. fishermen. **Elizabeth**, m. Thomas Allen (see 14). **Mary** (Mercy?), int. mar. with John Collins of Portsm. 1733. He m. 2d 21 Nov. 1717 Dorcas Heard(6) who had ch: **Phebe**. **Samuel**. **Hugh**. **Joseph**. **James**. Ano. **Joseph**. In 1734 he and half-sis. Elizabeth Bragdon (half-br. Lewis named a grantor, but did not sign) sold half of all their Falm. common right as heirs of fa. Lewis, a settler under Danforth. In 1736 he deeded his full share, ⅛, of his fa.'s town right. Widow Dorcas liv. 1762.

8 **JAMES**, List 57, with Portsmouth names, poss. from Salisb. One J. of Tiverton got an exec. ag. Peter Wittum, sr., in 1713. See also (13).

9 **JOHN**, fisherman, Kittery, Star Isl., assisted the Marshal in 1653. In York ct., Oct. 1660, he had a suit ag. Richard White; at the same ct. the two men ack. a judgm. to Samuel Hall(26), £180 on a bond, the orig. debt £95:15:0. Will, 31 Oct. 1670—3 Jan. 1670-1, of Star Isl., but by God's providence at John Ameredith's in Kit., gave £1:10:0 to Thomas Wells, the minister, all else to the Amerediths. See Me. P. & Ct. Rec. ii: 206-8.

10 **JOHN**, fisherman, Cape Annawaggon near Sheepscot, bot on north side of Montsweag River from Robinhood in 1662, wit. Ind. deed to Dyer(8) in 1664, depos. in Mar. 1668-9, ag. ±36, that he accomp. Scottow up Sheepscot River when he took poss. of Thomas Clive's est. Of Tisbury, late of Cape A., 2 July 1675, he sold Eastern land, and 'Hist. of Martha's Vineyard,' vol. ii ('Annals of W. Tisbury'), reports him a town officer 1675-1680, dead in 1681 when wid. (Susanna) was living (Plym. Col. Rec. 6: 65). Son John sold half the Ind. land to Hussey(9) (ack. bef. Thomas Mayhew 1695, Hussey's East. Cl.), and as fa.'s heir claimed a large tract for self. Dr. Banks found him at Harwich 1716; of Newb., shipwright, 1729, he sold at the East to Christopher Toppan and ack. with w. Susanna. Will, 1730—1732, names her, dau. Mary Butler (m. Philip B. 1726). In 1786 Susannah (Butler) Pearson, ag. 57, depos. that her gr.fa. John who sold to Mr. Toppan was s. of John, who, her gr.mo. said, foll. fishing at Sheepscot and had two more ch: **Noah** (deponent never heard that he left ch.) and **Susannah**, who d. unm. (SJC 140612). One Noah test. in Boston ab. Edw. Bickford(7 jr.) in 1713; one (or two) mar. there 1707, 1721, and had ch.

11 **JOHN**, Mr., cooper, Portsmouth 1671, liv. in Great House Field with w. Ursula in 1673. In 1677 he had a confirmatory deed from the Cutts(5) est., in 1681 a deed from Thomas and Bridget (Cutts) Daniel; not imposs. his w. was related to Pres. Cutts' wid. Ursula, also to John Shipway and Henry Tibbetts(4), with whom she test. ab. the Shipway est. in 1683. Gr.j. 1673, 1692, 1694, 1696; O. A. 28 Aug. 1685; culler of pipestaves 1692; Mr. John impressed 1695. In 1696 he mortg. prop. to Rev. Mr. Moody's step-dau., Lydia Jacob of Boston, selling it to Wm. Lakeman in 1699. He d. aft. a languishing illness (List 96, 2 May 1706); wid. Ursula liv. 1713. Lists 326c, 328bcd, 329 (3 heads), 330d, 331b, 335a, 337, 49, 52, 54, 57, 62, 92. Mrs. Tucker, Lists 335a, 316. Surely

a ch: **Elizabeth,** m. 1st Robert Hopley, m. 2d Thomas Roberts(5). Likely: **John,** jr., List 57. (John, sr., was taxed in 1690; one John, no designation, in 1691). Richard, at John's (List 329) may not have been a Tucker.

12 **JOHN**(23),fisherman,Falmouth,Gloucester, at the Shoals in 1677, went later to Falm., where he had 100 a. at Muscle Cove for which he ent. an East. Cl., giving as bounds, br. Lewis west, Elisha Andrews east, 40 pole front. On 9 May 1681 he m. Sarah Riggs at Glouc. where his ch. were rec., but spent his early mar. life in Falm., as fined there in 1684 for abusing Mr. Davis and Mr. Tyng, and in 1730 deeded to s. John of Glouc., 60 a. at Falm. 'on which I did dwell and my s. John, jr., was born' (27 Dec. 1686, Glouc. rec.). Except for rec. of his mar. and his ch.'s births, Babson did not find him in Glouc. until 1707; liv. there 12 Apr. 1736, ag. ±80. Lists 225a, 34. See also (18). Ch. rec. at Glouc. 1682-1706: **Mary,** see Hilton(23). **Sarah. John,** m. 14 Dec. 1714 Mary Lane (5). **William,** see Dorcas Lane(5). **Thomas,** drowned at Carolina 1717. **Richard. Abigail. Joseph. Grace.**

13 **JOHN,** captured by Ind. at Dover 26 July 1696 (List 96), soon found his way home from Penobscot ('N. E. Captives,' i: 164). Poss. J. of Providence who deeded a 30 a. Dover gr. to Morris Tucker of Tiverton in 1716; also poss. the husb. of Tryphena Ham (4). See (8). Hoyt's Old Salisbury, i: 337.

14 **JOSEPH,** and Nathaniel Fryer, jr., wit. a Cape Elizabeth deed, Jordan and Fryer to Vittery, 1685. See also (3).

15 **KEZIAH.** See Austin(1).

16 **LEWIS**(23), fisherman, Shoals, Kittery, Falmouth, b. ±1648-9 (±25 in Sept. 1673, ±33 in Feb. 1682-3), first found swearing at the Shoals in 1670. Constable 1674. By one acc. he took up a Falm. lot and built a ho. bef. Philip's War, Moses Felt building his chimney, but no rec. seen actually places him there then. Of Piscataqua 1680, late of the Shoals, he sold a Smuttynose ho. to Roger Kelly, partly for a debt due to K.; sued John Gale in 1681. One Sarah was a Gt. Isl. wit. in 1681, he was there with Elihu Gunnison in Feb. 1682-3. Falm. until the 2d war where he had 200 a. on the main, midway from Broad and Muscle Coves; there again 1703 when w. and dau. killed (List 39). Of Piscataqua 1709; at Salem in 1713, ±70, depos. ab. Merriconeag and Richard Potts 40 or 50 yrs. ago; Glouc. 1716; Falm. 1719 when sued on a bond to Pepperell, dated 1709, his ho. and land attached and a copy left with his dau.; late of Falm., decd., 1734. Lists 305ac, 30, 290, 228c, 39, 229, 227. Sarah Gunnison (2), the mo. of his older ch., was more reasonably an unrec. dau. of Hugh G. and his 2d w., b. ±1653 (Sarah, ±20 in 1673, wit. with

mo.-in-law Allard), than the Sarah b. in Feb. 1636-7. The w. killed at Casco may have been another. Wife Joanna living 1716. Ch. by w. Sarah: **Hugh,** eldest son, gave p/a to br. Richard to act in the Gunnison est. suit; see (7). **John,** outliv. mo., dead in 1719-20. **Richard,** shipwr., Boston, gr. adm. on gr.fa. Gunnison's est. 4 Nov. 1718 and in Feb. 1719-20 sued Gowen Wilson et al. for 30 a. at Goose Creek. If he m. **Grace** (Diamond 5) Tomlin, she soon d. or was a later w., as his w. Bethia (Ingersoll 3) had at least 4 ch: Bethia, bp. at Charlest. 1702; Richard, b. in Aug. (Glouc. rec.), bp. at Charlest. in Oct., 1704; Daniel and John, rec. at Boston 1707, 1709. **Joseph,** liv. 1719-20. **Grace,** m. at Boston 5 May 1708 Isaac Pierce; in 1739 they sold ⅛ her fa.'s Falm. town right. **Daughter,** killed at Falm. 1703, poss. not Sarah's, as the 1719-20 writ stated she 'had' (perhaps meaning 'left') 4 sons, 1 dau. By w. Joan or Joanna, b. at Kit. but rec. at Glouc: **Elizabeth,** b. 12 May 170-, m. Jethro Bragdon(4); see Tucker(7). **Lewis,** b. 29 July 1706, of Newc. 1734. **Joshua,** b. 14 Dec. 1708; one J. depos. in 1732 that he knew Wm. Hutchins(3) in Canada. **Isaac,** b. 30 Nov. 1709; one I. was drowned, Kit. inq. 1729, no est. **John,** b. 31 Dec. 1711, d.y. at Kit. See also Y. D. 3: 77; 9: 199-202; 10: 89; 14: 249; 17: 37.

17 **NATHANIEL,** a Shoals wit. 1677, Allard to Wainwright. See (23).

18 **NICHOLAS**(23), cooper, Kittery, apprentice to Wm. Diamond(5), was at the Shoals in Sept. 1673, ±22, but ag. 21 in 1674. In 1682 the est. of John Turner of Salem brot suit in Me. ct. ag. him, (25) and (12). In 1686 he bot 40 a. on north-east side of Spruce Creek from Capt. Champernowne (Y. D. 7: 17) and 20 yrs. later defended his title ag. Samuel Hill who claimed under Champernowne's deed to Barefoot (Y. D. 1: 77). Gr.j. 1694, 1701; j. 1701, 1708; bondsman for Thomas and John Abbott 1702; culler of fish 1707, 1710; of fish and pipestaves 1714. One N. T. and Wm. Wentworth were among the wounded men at Casco Fort 1703 (Doc. Hist. 9: 150). Lists 305a, 30, 294, 296, 297, 298 (2). See also Y. D. 4: 94; 6: 163; 7: 214; 8: 43, 204, 213-4; 10: 112. Will, 21 Jan.—2 Apr. 1717, names w. Jane (an Endle wit. 14 Sept. 1695, liv. 4 Dec. 1719), 3 ch., gr.s. Wm. Wentworth. Ch: **William,** shipwr., Kit., List 291, m. 27 Dec. 1711 Alice Grindal (see 1), a wid. 1755. Ch. incl. Josiah, b. 14 Oct. 1727 (see Willis' Hist. of Portland, p. 844). **Joseph,** Kit., 1720. **Grace,** m. Wm. Wentworth (7). **Margaret,** unm. in 1717.

19 **PHILIP,** fisherman, Shoals, Portsmouth, adm. of the John Bickford(11) est. in June 1662, owned a stage in 1664, was with the party when Robert Clements(7) was

lost, bot a ho. formerly Abraham Corbett's in 1677, and in 1687 of Portsm., late of the Shoals, bot in Portsm. List 329; he and w., List 52. He was bur. at Salisbury; adm. 6 Sept. 1699 to Edward Cate(1) and w. **Elizabeth**, mar. by 1687. The wid. was in Boston when an acct. was rendered 9 Aug. 1701. His premises were in poss. of Hugh Banfield's wid. Hannah in 1749 when Cate started an ejection suit, the writ calling his w. the only ch. Note (26).

20 ‡**RICHARD**, gent., shares with Cleeve the honor of founding Portland. He alone bot R. Bradshaw's Spurwink claim from which Trelawny's agent ejected him and Cleeve in 1632. The two were in Eng. in 1636 (Matthew Craddock's letter to Winthrop), and there 27 Jan. 1636-7 Sir F. Gorges gr. them 1500 a., also Hog Isl., to begin at Machigonne Point where they had planted divers yrs., henceforth to be called Stogummor (Stogumber, co. Somerset, considered T.'s home). They took poss. 8 June 1637, 'their house' ment. 1640, and also in Alex. Rigby's deed to them of Hog Isl. 3 May 1643. Gr.j. 1640; that yr. sued Thomas Purchase for a warming pan borrowed by Sir Christopher Gardiner ±1631. York wit. 1642. Assistant under Rigby 1645; in later yrs. adhered to Mass. About 1646 T. and C. parted, without dividing, and the (by comparison) inconspicuous T., even called by Mr. Jenner 'as it were, a servant hitherto for Mr. C.,' went to the Piscataqua (4 Mass. Hist. Soc. Col., vol. 7, by index). Portsm. selectman 1654, agent for Ambrose Lane 1655, connected with the Leader mills 1655-7, liv. at Great Works aft. Mr. L. left (Y. D. 8: 236), of Newich. in 1657 sold to George Walton his Great Isl. ho. and land, and in 1664 sold to W. 'Muskeeto Hall' (see Wotton). He had a deed from Cleeve 1658, now of Casco Bay 1661, Saco wit. 1662 (Y. D. 1: 75, 108; 2: 68). Ag. ±60 in Mar. 1668-9, working up Seavey accts. Lists 22, 221, 323, 324(2), 326b, 330a, 331ab, 356L (Portsm.), 312c, 313a, 54. See Clay(2), Seavey(7); York Deeds; Doc. Hist. vol. 3; Me. P. & Ct. Rec., vol. i, ii; N. H. Hist. Soc. Col. 8: 120-2. Inv., Portsmouth, 19 Sept. 1679, five cattle, an old ho., 20 a.; adm. 30 Sept. 1679 to Mrs. Margaret, as far as kn. the only w., mar. bef. 1646, called Margaret 1661; see Allen(1). No evid. appears that any w. was Cleeve's dau., this claim resting on 'minutes' filed in a late Vaughan suit. She was in want 26 Feb. 1679, and Wm. Seavey, sr., ordered to supply her; his son spoke of her 5 Oct. 1686 as 'now deceased.' List 331c. Having no ch., they adopted Seaborn Reynolds(4) who m. Nicholas Hodge(7). See Reg. 53: 84, article by Col. Banks who had not seen the later deeds and depositions giving the facts ab. Seaborn.

21 **RICHARD**(23), fisherman, Newcastle. Y. D. 8: 43 (1706), Adams to Carpenter, conveys land that (18) sold to br. Richard in Jan. 1698-9. Lists 307a, 315b. Will, bound to sea, 15 June 1694—2 Apr. 1707, gives a dwg. ho. near the meet.-ho. at Str. Bk., a dwg. and 12 a. in Spruce Creek, formerly br. Wm. Broad's (if Broad did not return to N. E.), and a dwg. ho. on Great Isl., all to dau. **Sarah**; if she d., then to Richard(16) and Richard(25). How Wm. Broad(4 jr.) was 'brother,' unless Tucker had mar. his sis. Abigail Broad, b. ±1667, is not clear. The dau. Sarah m. James Lee bef. June 1707.

22 **WILLIAM**, Richmond Isl. 1634. List 21.

23 **WILLIAM**, fisherman, Shoals, sued by Thomas Wescott for slander and defamation; fined as a common swearer and drunkard, a first conviction; fined for striking the constable's deputy, on Mr. Rishworth's compl.; and w. Grace fined for railing speeches ag. the neighbors, all in 1665. Lately decd., adm. gr. to Nathaniel Fryer 12 June 1666; inv., with widow's consent, by Capt. John Davis and Edw. Vittery, £73: 19: 06 (Me. P. & Ct. Rec. i: 277). Widow Grace m. 2d aft. Oct. 1666 Hugh Allard(1). A midwife, ag. 46 in 1673, ag. 47 in 1674. Of 'many ch.' only sons appear: **Lewis**, b. ±1648-9. **Nicholas**, b. ±1651. In 1670 his master Wm. Diamond sued Allard for detaining him. **William**. **John**, b. ±1656. **Richard**. See also (17).

24 **WILLIAM**, Kittery. His inv. 7 Mar. 1671-2 indicates a single man (Me. P. & Ct. Rec. ii: 452). Adm. in Apr. 1672 to Wm. Rogers (surety Ephraim Lynn), who succeeds. sued Digory Jeffrey in 1673 for detaining the est.

25 **WILLIAM**(23), fisherman, Shoals, Newcastle, poss. too young to be the W. who gave a bond to David Campbell in Apr. 1673, but cert. a deft. in the Turner suit in 1682 (see 18). At Marbleh., 7 July 1684, he m. Mary Oliver (see 18). Of Newcastle 1715. List 315c. No count of his ch. is seen. He, wife and s. **William**, all of Smuttynose, were with those raiding the Frost brandy (see Thompson 8); one W. mar. Mary Archer in Rye 5 Apr. 1721; 7 or more ch. **Oliver**, with the same raiding party and prob. a son, bearing his mo.'s fam. name; of Portsm., he m. Sarah Leach(4) 21 Jan. 1727-8. **Richard**, named in will of (21). **Abigail**, ag. 5 when bound in 1711 to Joseph Field; taken away by fa. 3 yrs. later (Field's suit ag. him in 1715). One Thomas of Portsm. was Henry Sloper's 2d mate in 1722; John and w. Elizabeth had ch. bp. in So. Ch. 1729 on, incl. William; -Han-taxed Portsm. 1732; Mary, adult, bp. there 1733.

26 **WIDOW**, taxed Portsm. July 1690 bet. Francis Jones and John Snell and near Edw. Cate. See (21).

27 **SERGT.**, an Ind. captive at Wells at the time of the Plaisted-Wheelwright mar. 1712, and soon back, indexed in Hist. of York, as 'Francis.' See Doc. Hist. 9: 325-331, Bourne's Hist. of Wells, pp. 278-281; also pp. 331, 350 for Israel 1725 (elsewhere given Tricker), and an incapacitated, but appar. young, Daniel, 1728 and long aft.

**TUCKERMAN**, peculiar to co. Devon.

1 **NATHANIEL**(2), mariner, Ipswich and Portsmouth. By w. Martha had ch: **Nathaniel**, b. Ips. 9 Sept. 1684, m. 1st Martha Nelson(2) whose fa. deeded to them 1712, m. 2d by 1734 one Mary. Sold land of gr.fa.(2). Portsm. selectman 1722. List 339. Will, 1744—1755, ment. br. John (real-est. at Gt. Isl.), sis. Elizabeth Clark (silk gown), neph. Nathaniel Muchemore (real est. at Portsm.). **Martha**, b. Ips. 27 June 1686, m. Edmund Rand(1). **John**, gr. adm. on Nathaniel's est. 1758. **Elizabeth**, m. Jacob Clark(14). **Amy**, m. Richard Muchemore(2).

2 **OTHO**, mariner, first at Boston, was a Portsmouth prop. 1660. Lists 330ab. Constable 1662. 'Lately cast away,' adm. was gr. to his wid. Eme 24 May 1664. Ordered that, in case the wid. marry, the children's portions be secured. Ch. (poss. others): **Nathaniel** (surely). **Nicholas** (prob.), wit. 1669 at Kittery and Hog Isl.

**Tucking**, Joel, an abuttor in Exeter deed 1695, prob. error for Joel Judkins.

**Tufton**, see Mason.

**Tufts**, James, soldier at Saco fort, 1696. List 248b.

**Tuley**, Christopher, sued Samuel Treworgy 1674.

**TURBAT**, Turbert a given-name in Domesday Book.

1 **JOHN**(3), Arundel, ±30 in 1681, m. Mary, dau. of Margery (Batson) (Kendall) Young (by which husb. uncert.), who m. 2d Emanuel Davis(6) and took her ch. to Newton. Lists 256, 331b. Had 200 a. gr. 1681. Adm. on his est. gr. to Capt. Francis Hooke, chief creditor, 24 Oct. 1683. Ch: **Sarah**, m. 31 Aug. 1693 Thomas Hastings of Newton; with her sis. and husb. they q.c. to their cous. Moses Banks their fa.'s rights under their gr.fa.'s will, 1719. **John**, m. Dedham 17 Nov. 1698 Abigail Cass(2) who was taken by Ind. at Arundel 10 Aug. 1703 and d. in Montreal 1705, embracing the Cath. faith on her death-bed. He d. s.p. 1704. **Elizabeth**, m. Dedham 15 July 1700 Ebenezer Lyon(2) of Roxbury.

2 **NICHOLAS**(3?), Berwick, of whose paternity there may be reasonable doubt.

Not ment. in Peter's will, yet in 1687 Peter's wid., Sarah Goodwin, calls him 'my eldest son living of the said Peter Turbett Sr.' Peter's dau. Elizabeth and his s. John's daus. go out of their way to state that John was 'eldest and only surviving son of Peter Turbit' and that he was 'only son of Peter Turbot that left issue,' yet Nicholas had two daus. when these statements were made. A Narragansett soldier, his dau. Sarah sold his rights to bonus lands to James Pike, 1730. He m. by 1693 wid. Elizabeth (Spencer) Chick, selling Spencer land 1693-4. Both abs. from meet. 1696, 1698, 1699, 1703; he in ct. for profane swearing 1707-8. Lists 289, 290. He d. bef. 1715. Ch: **Sarah**, in ct. for usual cause 1711-2, acc. Valentine Scates 1717, m. 5 Nov. 1722 John Conner(5). **Elizabeth** 'lawfully pub. with William Black' (5 jr.) otherwise 'black Will' 22 Nov. 1714, liv. with but did not marry him. Haled into ct. 1718, Elizabeth (sr.) and Sarah Turbot wit. ag. her, and she was sentenced to be whipped.

3 **PETER**, Cape Porpus, poss. earlier at Plymouth (Talbot), took O. A. 5 July 1653. He m. Sarah Sanders(8). Sold ho. and 200 a. to William Reynolds 1657, bot of his fa.-in-law and sold 1660. Lists 71, 251, 252, 254, 255. Will, 19 Oct. 1669—15 Mar. 1669-70, names w., sons John and Peter, dau. Elizabeth who was to be brot up by her gr.fa. Sanders, but wit. stated that he revoked this direction, in his w.'s favor, on his death-bed. Robert Elliot, about to m. the wid., was app. adm. July 1672, but on changing their minds, the appoint. was annulled and s. John substituted July 1673. She m. 2d Daniel Goodwin(4). Ch: **John**. **Peter**, appren. by his mo., his fa. consenting, to Maj. Champernowne for 11 yrs. 8 Nov. 1661. One Peter (unless error for Nicholas) fined for swearing, 1713. **Elizabeth**, m. John Banks (1), only surv. dau. in 1727. See also (2).

**TURFREY**, Capt. *George, Boston merchant, with business int. at Saco. Sued Benj. Blackman in York ct. 1686, wit. Winter Harbor deed 1687. Deputy 1685, J. P. 1687-1688. Lists 34, 249. In 1687-8 Mr. Wm. Blaithwait at Whitehall sent his 'services to cous. Treffrey,' and Mr. John Povey (friend of Samuel Pepys) sent his 'humble services to Capt. Trefry.' In prison for talking against authority 1689. Residing in Saco 1699, building a mill with Francis Foxcroft. App. to command at Fort Mary in Saco in 1700, to succeed Capt. Hill, and was still there 1704. See also Paulling. Will, 15 Oct. 1712—17 Nov. 1714, left 1 s. to Susanna Milburne or Watson and her off-spring, and residue to w. Mary, adm. on whose est. was gr. to John Briggs 26 Sept. 1717. The simplest explanation for **Susanna**, cut off with

a shilling, is that she was a dau. by a 1st w. (she did not share in the wid. Mary's est.), m. 1st Rev. William Milburne by 1687 and m. 2d after 1694 one Watson, to her fa.'s displeasure. By w. Mary: **Edward**, Boston, gent., will 2—19 Jan. 1702-3 names mo. sole legatee. **Katherine**, m. 1st 29 Oct. 1700 George Ball, m. 2d 1705 John Briggs of Boston, trader.

**TURNER**, common occupational name.
1 **JOHN**, Berwick, m. 28 Nov. 1694 Elizabeth (Grant) Lander(2) who m. 2d Wm. Hearl(5). Ch: **Mary**, m. Ebenezer Boltwood.
2 **PHILIP**, Portsmouth, attacked his master 1673; lately in prison in Boston in 1675 and was to be returned to county ct., the town of Portsm. to satisfy the Boston jailor.
3 **RALPH**, Falmouth; wit. 1659, 1668, 1674; in ct. for swearing 1667; constable 1670. Lists 34, 85, 223b, 225a. See also Maddiver (2). His dau. **Hannah**, w. of Thomas Holman of Rehoboth, sold his land (200 a. at Barberry creek, etc.) to Thomas Magoon et als. 1729.
4 **ROBERT**, at Hampton ct. 1662. See also Hill(21) for ano. of the name.
5 **THOMAS**, Kittery, here by 1648 (see Hilton 17), his age wildly guessed at (±48 in 1672, ±56 in 1673, ±73 in 1683). Sued by John Cutt, 1666. He m. Mary, wid. of Robert Beedle(4) and Rev. Stephen Batchelder(3), and sold her Gorges gr. to Peter Staples(1) in 1674. Lists 25, 285. Christian Remick accounted as adm. 28 Oct. 1684. Goody Rogers was pd. for curing his leg and Staples was reimbursed for the funeral expenses.
6 **WILLIAM**, of full age 1716 and servant of John Rollins of Lubberland.
**TURPIN, Thomas**, Isles of Shoals, with Richard Cummings bot a plantation at Salt Creek from Francis Williams in 1645, Cummings buying him out in 1648 acc. to a depos. by Roger and Ann Knight. Drowned 29 Oct. 1649, adm. to William Payne who seems to have laid claim to ½ of the Williams land, poss. never pd. for by Cummings who settled for £14 in 1652. The est. was heavily indebted to Mr. Nicholas Treworgy, Mr. Wm. Hilton, etc. The wid. Jane m. 2d Thomas Furson. In 1665 Cummings pd. her 20 s. for her dower thru her s.-in-law Adams, but in 1674 she, her daughters and gr.ch. raided his corn-field, demonstrating her further claims, and had opportunity to explain in ct. She finally sued in an orderly manner. Ch. (Leonard Weeks had kn. them in Eng.): **Elizabeth**, m. James Leach(2). **Jane**, m. Philip Adams(16). **Agnes**, List 330b, m. Richard Endle(3).
**TURRILL.** 1 **Daniel**, with John Conney bot ±800 a. on the Kennebec from John Leighton(3) in 1678. The heirs, thru Joseph

T., entered an East. Cl. and sold to the Pejepscot Prop. 1719.
2 **MR. WILLIAM**. List 244d.
**Tutherington**, Elizabeth, Newcastle, summonsed 1711 to answer 'what may be alleged.'

**TUTTLE.**
1 **JOHN**, Dover, planter, liv. on 20 a. lot laid out to him 1642 on east side of Dover Neck. Helped drive Capt. Wiggin's cattle from York to Dover, 1641. Lists 351a, 352, 353, 354abc, 356abcefg. Adm. 30 June 1663 to wid. Dorothy (her List 356h). Ch: **Thomas**, killed by falling tree (verdict 31 Mar. 1654). Eldest **dau.**, m. bef. 1663 Capt. Philip Cromwell(3) and her portion paid. **John**, under 21 in 1663. Youngest **dau.**, under 18 in 1663.
2 **CAPT. *JOHN**(1), Dover. Constable 1686; selectman 1686-1688; town clerk 1694-1717; Deputy 1698, 1699, 1705-1707; Judge of Ct. of Com. Pleas 1695; capt. of the Dover militia from 1695. With Ezekiel Wentworth he bot a mill privilege on the west side of Salmon Falls, 1701. Lists 49, 52, 55a, 56, 58, 59, 62, 63, 64, 67(3), 69, 336c, 353(2), 357be, 358bcd, 359ab. He d. June 1720. Will, 28 Dec. 1717—12 July 1720, names w. Mary exec., s. Ebenezer (60 a. at Indigo Hill), gr.sons Thomas (to pay his two sis.), John, Nicholas and Elijah T. and Samuel Edgerly. See Hall(10). Ch. (N. H. ct. files 27: 467): **John**, m. Samuel Tibbetts(12). **Mary**, m. 6 Dec. 1687 John Wallingford. **Elizabeth**, m. 1st Samuel Edgerly(1), m. 2d John Ambler. **James**, b. 7 Apr. 1683, m. Rose Pinkham(1) who m. 2d Thomas Canney(1), d. 15 May 1709. Ch: Phebe, b. 26 Sept. 1706, m. 26 Mar. 1708 Moses Varney; Elijah, b. 14 May 1708, m. Esther Varney, 4 ch., d. 23 Oct. 1787. **Sarah**, m. Edward Cloudman. **Ebenezer**, arrested for theft 1708, m. Hannah Abbott.
3 **ENSIGN JOHN**(2), Dover, m. Judith Otis (1). Killed by Ind. 7 May 1712, adm. 1725-6 to s. Thomas, the wid. renounc. Ch: **Mary**, b. 7 Jan. 1697-8, m. James Canney(2) who was bondsm. for his mo.-in-law 1725. **Thomas**, b. 15 Mar. 1699-1700, m. Mary Brackett(5) who d. 28 Feb. 1773, d. Feb. 1777. 11 ch. **Judith**, b. 10 May 1702, m. Robert Cole(16). **John**, b. 8 May 1704, m. Elizabeth Nute, d. Feb. 1774. 10 ch. **Dorothy**, b. 21 May 1706, d. bef. 1717. **Nicholas**, b. 29 (or 27) July 1708, m. 1st Deborah Hunt, m. 2d Bethia Davis, d. 1793, 10 ch. **James**, b. 9 Feb. 1710-1, m. Mary Allen, had homestead, d. 9 Nov. 1790. 12 ch.
Twisdell, James, Arrowsic 1679. List 187.

**TWISDEN**, an estate in co. Kent.
1 **JOHN**, York, first at Scituate 1638-1641,

settled in York by 1642 selling out at Scituate 1645. Deed of 20 a. from Wm. Hooke 1645 and town gr. of 120 a. 1653. He or s. John called cousin in will of James Cushman of Scit. 1647. Subm. to Mass. 1652; selectman 1650; gr.j. 1649, 1650; j. 1649-1651. Lists 273-277. He d. bef. 12 Nov. 1660. His wid. Susanna and sons John and Samuel deeded land to Joseph Moulton 10 Apr. 1685 for an annuity to the survivor of them, and she and Samuel were subsisted by Arthur Bragdon(2) in their old age. Ch: **John**, ±54 in 1678; sergt. 1659 (or his fa.); j. 1653, 1656, 1662-1664, 1666; gr.j. 1653, 1666, 1671, 1683; selectman 11 times 1663-1684; Clerk of the Writs 1677-1681 (poss. before and later). Lists 24 (or his fa.), 25, 26, 30, 275, 276. Presum. killed in York massacre 1692, unm. Adm. to nephew Arthur Bragdon jr. (2 jr.) 8 May 1695. **Peter. Ellice,** m. Scituate 20 Nov. 1649 Joseph Tilden. **Samuel,** constable 1660, had town gr. 1667. Lists 24, 25, 33. Appar. d. unm., his est. adm. 1695 with John's by Arthur Bragdon(2 jr.). **Lydia,** m. Arthur Bragdon(2).

2 **PETER**(1), Isles of Shoals, fisherman, ±45 in 1673, 53 or 54 in 1681; m. Mary Alcock(1), ±41 in 1673. Wit. with (2) at York 1642, bot in York 1662. Lists 89, 301, 305a, 306ac, 307b. Com.t.e.s.c. 1671. Liv. 1683. The wid. ack. in Boston 1696 deed for marsh, bot by her husb. from Robert Edge in 1662, sold by her to Samuel Small. No ch. appear, but the Twisden fishermen at Marblehead 1690± should be investigated.

**TWOMBLEY,** Twambley, not in Lower or Guppy.

1 **JOHN**(2), Dover, m. 1st 18 Apr. 1687 Mary Canney(4), m. 2d 3 Oct. 1692 Rachel Allen(4). Gr.j. 1695, 1698. Lists 94, 358ad. Bp. two days bef. signing his will 18 July (prov. 3 Sept.) 1724, which names w. and 10 ch: **John** (surely by 1st w., the others uncert.), m. ab. 1711 Sarah Dam(5), sued for share of self and three bros. and sis. in gr.fa. Canney's est. 1747. Joint will with w., 20 Dec. 1747—27 Apr. 1748, names 4 ch. **Joseph,** cooper, had w. Martha 1732, liv. 1748. **Benjamin,** m. 10 July 1721 Hannah Evans, named with 7 ch. in his will 1761—1762. **William,** had w. Elizabeth in 1734, prob. Elizabeth Drew(9) who was Twombley in 1731 and m. 2d a Yeaton. **Samuel,** b. 10 Mar. 1699-1700, m. 26 Nov. 1723 Judith Hanson(10). **Sarah,** prob. m. Gershom Wentworth(3). **Mary. Rachel. Esther. Hannah.**

2 **RALPH,** Dover, cor.j. 1657, sued by Ralph Hall 1660. Lists 47, 52, 356abceghk, 359ab. Abs. from meet. 1669. Excused from training 1670. Will, 28 Feb. 1684-5—7 Oct. 1686. His wid. Elizabeth deeded to s. John 17 July 1724 all her est. except legacies in

her will (not proved). One Elizabeth was bp. 6 May and adm. to Dover Ch. 3 June 1722. Ch. in will: **John. Joseph,** ±73 in 1734, had w. Jane 1726, liv. 1741, d. s.p. **Mary,** m. Jeremiah Tibbetts(7). **Ralph,** d. s.p. 4 Oct. 1700. His sis. Sarah Giles listed his heirs 1765 (ct. files 17, 117). **Elizabeth,** acc. Richard Pomeroy 1694, again in ct. 1703, spinster 1730, d. s.p. **Hope,** d. s.p. **Sarah,** under 18 in 1684, wid. Giles in 1765. Mark Giles(6) had w. Sarah by 1698. **Esther,** under 18 in 1684, m. 14 Jan. 1707-8 Pomfret Dam. **William.**

3 **WILLIAM**(2), Madbury, m. 1st Mary Ricker(1), m. 2d by 1744 wid. Abigail (Evans 14) Hayes. List 358d. His will, 14 Sept.—29 Oct. 1763, names sons Ralph (executor), Isaac, William, daus. Elizabeth Pearl and Eleanor Ricker, gr.dau. Tamsen (dau. of John decd.). Ch: **Ralph,** b. 13 Sept. 1713. **Isaac,** b. 18 Dec. 1715, had homestead; w. Lydia surv.; will, 25 Nov. 1784—12 Jan. 1785. Ch. **William,** b. 25 July 1717. **Mary,** b. 25 Feb. 1721. **Elizabeth,** b. 1 Nov. 1723, m. Benjamin Pearl. **John,** b. 19 Sept. 1725, m. Tamsen Chesley who m. 2d Col. Otis Baker. Only ch: Tamsen. **Eleanor,** m. Nicholas Ricker.

**Twowills,** Thomas, sued by Mr. Andrew Searle Dec. 1665, but bill was withdrawn. Wills?

**TYLER.** 1 **Abraham,** Hampton wit. 1674.

2 **ELIZABETH,** ±23, at Goodman Tenney's ho., Kittery, 1702.

3 **JONATHAN,** York wit. 1696-7.

4 **THOMAS,** an Indian, prob. servant of Edw. Colcord for whom he wit. 1655.

**TYNG, Lt. Col. ‡Edward,** b. 26 Mar. 1649, s. of Edward, wealthy Boston merchant, m. by 1682 Elizabeth Clark(52) and thru her acquired great interests in Falmouth. His fa. had bot Hog Isl. in Casco Bay in 1663. After distinguished service in the Narragansett exped., he was made commander at Fort Loyal on Falmouth Neck 1680. Councillor 1681-1683, 1685, 1686; J. P. 1689. Lists 13, 19, 32, 97, 225ab(2), 228cd, 229, 239a. Her dist 225a. Appointed Lt. Col. by Sir Edmund Andros and placed in charge at Sagadahoc, but soon afterward being named governor of Annapolis, Nova Scotia, he was captured by the French while proceeding to his post, carried to France and d. in prison. Adm. to br. Jonathan April 1701. Tyng's garrison at Falm. was burned 1690. Ch: **Edward,** Boston, mariner and merchant, commander of the colonial squadron at the siege of Louisburg. **Mary,** m. Rev. John Fox (2). **Elizabeth,** m. 16 May 1705 Samuel Franklin. **Jonathan,** d.y.

**Tyson,** Claus, Pemaquid tax-list 1687. List 124.

**UGROVE,** Ugroufe, Newgrove, **John,** Kittery, mariner, sold 6 a. and a ho. to Abra-

ham Conley, in grantee's poss., 5 Jan. 1638(9), Mary Ugroufe a wit. Lists 281, 351b, 352. Absent 19 Apr. 1641 when he wrote to George Smyth, sending respects to 'my master and mistress,' Smyth appar. renting his ho. for him to Dennis Downing who bot it in 1650. Gr. of 20 a. in Dover, 1642. No further rec. until 27 June 1694 when adm. was gr. to his dau.-in-law Sarah Murrell of Boston. Inv. incl. ±400 a. lying between Watsfort and Franksfort. John Pickering acted as her atty. in claiming lands in 1695. Sarah (parents unkn.) was wid. of Jeremiah 'Morrills' of Boston, whose will, 15 Nov. 1676—4 Nov. 1679, left est. to her and ch. Sarah, Lydia, Hosea and Amos; she d. (Morrell) 7 Apr. 1709, ag. 77, adm. to Richard Stratton, s. Amos refusing. Amos M., Boston, sold Cochecho marsh, gr. to 'my gr.fa. Mr. John Newgrove,' to Joseph Roberts, 1721. See Rollins(2).

Umfrees, see Humphreys.

## UNDERHILL.

1 CAPT. *JOHN, s. of John and Honor (Pawley), of a good co. Warwick fam., spent his early life in Holland where he m. 1st at The Hague 12 Dec. 1628 Helena de Hooch. They emigrated to Boston where he took the Freeman's oath 18 May 1631, began his disting. military career and served in the first Gen. Ct. The religious controversy of the day caused his banishment on 6 Sept. 1638, and he foll. Mr. Wheelwright to Exeter, where he served as 'Governor of Exeter and Dover' for almost a yr. Lists 351ab, 371. In Sept. 1639 he was considering joining the Dutch in N. Y., but after his submission to the Bay authorities in 1641 and the remission of his banishment, he left Ex. for Stamford, Conn., where he was settled in Oct. 1642. The Boston Ch. had dism. him and his w. (after his admission of error) to Ex. 22 Aug. 1641. He m. 2d Elizabeth Feke and d. 21 July 1672. For his ancestry, life and desc., see the monumental genealogy by Mrs. Frost (1932), prepared for Mr. Myron Taylor.

2 SAMPSON, York wit. 1712 (Y. D. 10: 46), (No. Yarmouth?) wit. 1721 (Y. D. 27: 322). A clothier, Chester, N. H., adm. to w. Elizabeth 1732, Jacob Stanyan and Joseph Norton bondsm. Ch.

UNDERWOOD, John, Newcastle, bot from Benj. and Elizabeth Parker 1714, and m. by 1718 Temperance Bickford(5) who m. 2d George Walton(2 jr.). Adm. to her 27 May 1727, John Rindge and Samuel Hart bondsmen. Ch: John, Portsm., Kittery, had w. Mary in 1762. Benjamin, Newc. Mary, m. Stephen Hardison (John) bef. 1743 when she sold Newc. land to br. Benj. Poss. Sarah, m.

25 Dec. 1740 Nathaniel Furber, both of Portsm.

Undery, Edward, List 95. See Vickery.

URIN, Urine, Uran, Urann, Euren, Youring, etc., etc.

1 EDWARD (Eurin, Errin, Duren, During, Dowreing—all poss. attempts at Irwin), Oyster River, 1657, a Scot. See Brown(7), Junkins. Lists 356d, 361a, 363abc, 364. John Roy receipted for boards on his account (Duren) 28 June 1664. Sued by Philip Lewis, 1665, and by John Bray, 1667. In Salisb. ct. Apr. 1668 the cor.j. on untimely death of Ed: Evrin was ordered paid. Adm. to Geo. Veazie and James Kidd, Apr. 1668. The est. (Dowreing) was sued by John Roy 6 Apr. and by Roger Collins Oct. 1668, sued John Bray 1669, and was sued by Henry Sherburn as husb. of the wid. and exec. of Walter Abbott in 1672. Appar. no w. or ch.

2 EDWARD(4), Star Isl., Sagadahoc, Boston, fisherman and coaster, bot from adm. of (4)'s est. ½ the ho., fish-ho. and boats at Star Isl. 4 Mar. 1667-8 and, with w. Jane, sold to James Blagdon(2) 6 Nov. 1668. Bot in Boston 1674 and sold 1675. His shallop -Philip-, chartered to Dutch privateers and charged with piracy, 1674, was released on his ev. of innocence, but in Mass. ct. 1675 he and Thos. Mitchell, acc. of stealing Mr. Geo. Munjoy's sheep, were sentenced to 20 lashes and to pay treble damages. Lists 3, 12, 79 (or Edw. 1), 80, 83. Adm. at Boston 31 Oct. 1676 to wid. Jane, who mov. to Exeter. See Kelly(12). Ch. rec. Boston: Edward, b. 2 June 1669. Matthew, b. 16 Nov. 1672. Benjamin, b. 25 May 1676.

3 JOHN(4), Greenland, ±34 in 1697, cordwainer, pet. that his half-br.-in-law John Muchemore adm. his mo.'s est. 25 Dec. 1699. Gr. of 8 a. by Portsm. in 1695-6 in confirm. of his fa.'s 1653 gr. J. 1697. Lists 57, 330d, 332b, 335a (and w.), 337. Rec. into cov. So. Ch. 9 Jan. 1715. He m. 12 Nov. 1686 Rebecca Cate(2) who d. his wid. in Greenl. Nov. or Dec. 1745. He d. bef. 13 Apr. 1734 when the wid. and 5 ch. div. the land. Ch., all bp. So. Ch. 25 Sept. 1715: James, cordwainer, m. 28 Jan. 1724-5 Hannah Edgerly (2). 8 ch., 5 in deed of their fa.'s and gr.fa.'s Epsom rights 1 Jan. 1771. William, with sisters sold int. in fa.'s est. 2 May 1734 to James Brackett. Joseph, Greenl., m. 6 Sept. 1716 Sarah Perkins(23) (adm. Greenl. Ch. 1723) who was his wid. 1 Jan. 1771 when she q.c. to her s. George, who also bot the Epsom rights of bros., sis., and cousins that day. (N. H. Deeds 102: 372, 373, 379). 9 ch. Eleanor, List 338b, m. Diamond Currier(3), was his wid. 1734, m. 2d Abraham Crockett (4). Mary, m. Carter Frost (see 8), poss. m.

2d Samuel Wilson. **John**, not in 1724-5 div. Richard, ag. 90 in 1776, Boston, Concord (N. H.), Haverhill, Newbury, called eldest s. in Urann gen. (N. E. Reg., 1910), not ment. in div. or deeds, is unplaced; of Haverhill, he was sued in 1717 for a Boston board bill incurred in 1716; more likely an unrec. s. of Francis(4) or s. of an unkn. s. of (4).

4 **WILLIAM**, fisherman, Star Isl. by 1653 when also rec. in Portsm. where he had a ho.-lot 1657 (Gt. Isl.). Lists 301, 303, 323, 330a. He d. Apr., adm. to cr., later declared illegal, 13 May, inv. 11 July 1664. His wid. Eleanor m. Richard Welcom who bot part of the est. 17 July 1672. Her will, 1699, ment. her 5 ch., 2 kn. to be Welcoms (q.v.), and Joseph Youring who was to be brot up in faith of God and to such learning as was convenient for one of his degree. Joseph, too young to be her s., must have been a gr.s., poss. orphaned, who liv. with her. Ch: **John** (surely). Very prob: **Edward**. **William**, ±20 in June 1673. List 305a. Fisherman, of R. Downes & Co., in contract with Fr. Wainwright of Ips. 19 Nov. 1674. See Erring 2. **Francis**, fisherman, Ips. by 1681; w. Alice; adm. to eldest s. William 9 Apr. 1713. 5 sons rec. Ips. 1681-1694, of whom William, fisherman, sold a Star Isl. ho. and garden next Dea. Muchemore to Benj. Damerill of the Shoals 25 Feb. 1745-6. Poss: **Gertrude**, w. of Francis Mercer and Edward Toogood. On back of probate doc. of Eleanor Welcom, Gertrude's name and those of her ch. appear, with no comment. She was too old to have been a Welcom. She named a dau. Eleanor.

**Urington**, see Yarington.

**USHER**, †*Lt. Gov. **John**, b. 17 Apr. 1648, s. of Hezekiah, the Boston magnate, aft. a long judicial, military and political career in the Bay, during which he negotiated the purchase of the Prov. of Me. from the Gorges heirs, became Lt. Gov. and Commander-in-Chief of N. H. in 1692. He was succeeded by Wm. Partridge in 1697, but reapp. by Gov. Dudley in 1702, serving until 1715 when he retired to his estate at Medford where he d. 25 Sept. 1726. His regime was unpopular because of his personal pomposity and arbitrary methods. He m. 1st 24 Apr. 1668 Elizabeth Lidgett(2) who d. 17 Aug. 1698. Of their ch., **Elizabeth** m. 15 Sept. 1686 David Jeffries(2). Gov. Usher m. 2d 11 Mar. 1699 Elizabeth Allen(13) who was liv. 5 May 1732 in Charlestown when Capt. Ebenezer and Rebecca (Jeffries) Wentworth's three sons were called her gr.ch. (actually step-gr.gr ch.). Her ch: **Frances**, m. Rev. Joseph Parsons; **Hezekiah**; **Elizabeth**, b. aft. her sis. Mrs. Jeffries d., m. 25 Apr. 1728 Stephen Harris.

**Utter**, Nicholas. Lists 356gh.

**Vallack**, Nicholas. List 15.

**Vandegar**, John. Indictment against him quashed, York Ct. 1653.

**Vanderhill**, James. Gr.j., Isles of Shoals, 1686.

**VARNEY**, poss. from Vernai, a parish in Normandy; peculiar to co. Bucks.

1 **EBENEZER**(2), Dover, ±55 in 1727, m. Mary Otis(4). Constable 1690, Gr.j. 1696. Will, 22 Oct.—28 Nov. 1753, names 13 ch., 11 liv., 2 decd. Ch., births from Quaker rec: **Mary**, b. 6 June 1693, m. William Horne(2). **Sarah**, b. 10 Nov. 1695, m. Samuel Gaskill of Salem. **Stephen**, b. 7 Nov. 1697, m. 7 Oct. or Nov. 1721 Mercy Hanson(10) who d. 1790; d. 21 May 1771; will 1771 names 10 ch. **Abigail**, b. 11 Apr. 1699, m. 15 Sept. 1724 William Fry(3). **John**, b. 15 Jan. 1701, m. 26 Mar. 1723 Sarah Robinson(16). **Ebenezer**, b. 31 Mar. 1704, m. 24 Feb. 1729-30 Elizabeth Hanson (John 7). **Nathaniel**, b. 17 Mar. 1706, m. 1727 Content Gaskill, d. 9 June 1776. 11 ch. **Thomas**, b. 7 Apr. 1708, m. Dorothy Martin; will 1763 names 6 ch. **Judith**, b. 11 Apr. 1710, m. Tobias Hanson(10). **Samuel**, b. 2 Apr. 1712, m. 30 June 1736 Mary Varney; will, 1759-1760, names 9 ch. **Martha**, b. 18 Mar. 1713-4, m. 30 Oct. 1734 John Twombly, jr. **Paul**, b. 18 Mar. (sic) 1715-6, m. Elizabeth Mussey. **Anne**, b. 6 July 1718, m. Solomon Hanson.

2 **HUMPHREY**, Dover 1659, s. of Wm. and Bridget of Gloucester, ment. in her will 1671. Prob. a Quaker, as many of his desc., he pleaded non-conviction to charge of abs. from meeting 1663. He m. 2 Mar. -1664- Sarah (Starbuck) Austin(4). The recorder called her Sarah -Storer-, doubtless having in mind the wid. Sarah Storer of Dover who had m. Samuel Austin(6) in 1661. Note birth of s. John in Nantucket 1664. His fa.-in-law Edward Starbuck confirmed to him 11 May 1664 20 a. formerly given to s.-in-law Joseph Austin. Lists 49, 52, 356efghk, 359a(2)b. His will, 17 Sept. 1713—2 June 1714, aged, ment. w. Sarah, dau. Abigail Brackston, sons Ebenezer, Peter (all sons). Ch: **John**, b. Nantucket 5 Sept. 1664, d. 14 Aug. 1666. **Peter**, b. 29 Mar. 1666. **Joseph**, b. 8 Oct. 1667, no further rec. **Abigail**, b. 10 July 1669, m. Wm. Blackstone(2). **John**, in ct. 1694 for passing counterfeit money, his fa. and Thos. Tibbetts bondsm.; Dover gr. 1702 laid out 1721 to neph. John; m. Susanna (Hussey 3) Otis (2). His will, 21 Feb. 1713—22 Mar. 1715-6, ment. bros. Peter and **Ebenezer**, neph. John (Ebenezer), sis. Abigail Blackstone and his w.'s ch. Nicholas, Rebecca, Stephen and Rose Otis; br. Ebenezer exec., Tobias and John Hanson his bondsm.

3 **JOHN**, Dover inhab. 6 (4) 1659. Error for (2)?

**4 PETER**(2), Dover, cordwainer, had w. Elizabeth, the mo. of his ch., in 1721 when they deeded 15 a. to s. Joseph Varney. List 358a. See Hawkins(8). Will, 2 Mar. 1731-2—18 May 1732, names w. and ch: **Joseph**, m. 5 Aug. 1712 Abigail Robinson(16). 4 ch. **Benjamin**, d. bef. 1731-2 leaving wid. Martha (Tibbetts 12) who m. one Whitehouse bef. 1747. Ch. in 1745 incl. Moses, Ichabod, Phebe w. of Richard Hussey, jr., Esther w. of Elijah Tuttle. One Benj. Varney, m. Boston 9 July 1706 Sarah Tidey (see 3), poss. an early mar. of our man. **Moses**, exec., m. 26 Mar. 1728 Phebe Tuttle who d. 23 June 1774; his est. div. 1765 among 11 ch. **Sarah**, m. 21 Dec. 1734 Michael Kennard(3). **Rachel. Susanna**, m. 8 Dec. 1724 Richard Scammon(4). **Lydia**, m. 23 Nov. 1728 Robert Hanson.

**VAUGHAN**, a Welsh personal name, common in Wales and border counties.

**1 GEORGE**, factor of the -John- 1631-2, trading for the Laconia Co. Lists 41(2), 241. See N. H. Prov. Papers, ii: 514-562.

**2 LT. GOV. †\*GEORGE**(4), Portsm., H. C. 1696, wealthy merchant and disting. public servant, m. 1st 8 Dec. 1698 Mary Belcher, dau. of Andrew, the Boston magnate; she d. 3 Feb. 1699, her **ch.** dying a few days later; m. 2d 9 Jan. 1700-1 Elizabeth Elliot(6), adm. to So. Ch. 4 Apr. 1725, d. 7 Dec. 1750, ag. 68. Constable 1699; selectman 1701, 1720, 1721; Deputy 1703; Col. of the N. H. forces; agent of N. H. in England 1707 until 1709 when he retired but was reappointed; Lt. Gov. of N. H. 1715 until 1717 when removed from office by Gov. Shute aft. a conflict over authority in N. H. His fa. had bot from Andrew Brown 600 a., formerly Henry Watts', in Scarboro in 1699, and he added to it at Blue Pt. 100 a. formerly Watts', 100 a. Edgecomb's and 100 a. Griffin's by purchase from his fa.-in-law Elliot in 1702. In 1681 he had acq. from James Pendleton 300 a. and five islands at Cape Porpus. His home farm at Portsm. cont. 562 a. Lists 90, 239b, 330df, 337. He d. Dec. 1724, leav. a vast est. by will, 1 Nov. 1724—25 Jan. 1724-5, the inv. very interesting. Ch. by 2d w: **Sarah**, b. 8 Feb. 1701-2, m. 5 Sept. 1721 Dr. John Ross. **William**, b. 12 Sept. 1703, H. C. 1722; d. unm. London Dec. 1746; will, 23 Mar. 1744-5—20 Oct. 1747. Settled at Damariscotta ab. 1729 (Thos. Hutchins' depos. 1749) and is said to have conceived the idea of the Louisburg expedition in which he served as Lt.-Col. His last yrs. were spent in Eng., seeking recognition of his services. See Hughes(2), Hutchins(10). **Margaret**, b. 21 Aug. 1705, m. 1743 Hon. Hunking Wentworth. **George**, b. 22 July 1706, d.y. **Elizabeth**, b. 8 Oct. 1707, m. William Bennett. **Abigail**, b. 11 Mar. 1709-10, d. 9 Sept. 1719. **Eliot**, b. 12 Apr. 1711, merchant, m. 14 Mar. 1738-9 Anna Gerrish who d. May 1786, he 1 July 1758. 10 ch. **Mary**, b. 7 May 1713, m. 1 Dec. 1741 Cutts Shannon. **Jane**, b. 27 Dec. 1714, m. May 1747 Maj. James Noble of Boston. **George**, b. 18 Feb. 1720, d. ag. 22 months.

**3 WILLIAM** (also Vengam), Monhegan planter, 1624. List 9. Col. Banks found ment. of this man in the Admiralty Rec., Pub. Rec. Office, London.

**4 MAJ. ‡WILLIAM**, Portsm., ±31 in 1672, appren. to Sir Josiah Child of London, merchant, first rec. in N. E. Sept. 1664 when he sued Richard White in York ct., sued Champernowne and was app. to audit. ship accts. with Fryer, 1665. (One Wm. Vaughan marked 'gorn' in Council Minutes, Va., 1666). Lic. to sell strong waters 1666. He m. 8 Dec. 1668 Margaret Cutts(5), ±20 in 1670, who d. 22 Jan. 1690. Lt. of troop of horse 1672, Capt. by 1680, Maj. 1681. Selectman eleven yrs. 1677-1706. Councillor 1675 to 1683 when removed and imprisoned by Gov. Cranfield as a vigorous opponent of the Masonian claims (see his very informative prison diary, N. H. Prov. Papers, vol. i), 1692 to 1698, 1701 to 1715 (Pres. from 1706). Justice Ct. of Com. Pleas 1680-1686, Chief-Justice Superior Ct. 1706-1715, Treas. of the Prov. 1696-1698, Register of Deeds 1696-1702. He d. 12 Nov. 1719, ag. 78. For a fuller acct. of him, see Vaughan Gen. (1918). Lists 48, 49, 51, 52, 54, 56, 57, 58, 62, 63, 64, 67, 68, 69, 83, 88, 89, 267a, 323, 324(2), 326bc. 329, 330adf, 333a, 335a, 336a, 337. See Graffort, Huckins(1). Ch. b. in Portsm: **Eleanor**, b. 5 Mar. 1669-70, m. 6 Feb. 1692-3 Col. Richard Waldron(11). **Mary**, b. 6 Mar. 1671-2, m. Capt. Daniel King(2). **Cutt**, b. 9 Mar. 1673-4, d. Barbadoes, unm. **George**, b. 13 Apr. 1676. **Bridget**, b. 2 July 1678, m. Nathaniel Gerrish(3). **Margaret**, b. 30 Dec. 1680, m. 1st 23 Feb. 1721 Capt. John Foye of Charlestown, m. 2d 10 Feb. 1735-6 Charles Chambers of Charlest. **Abigail**, b. 5 May 1683, m. 1st 25 Nov. 1714 Nathaniel Shannon, m. 2d Capt. George Walker(2). **Elizabeth**, b. 26 Apr. 1686, m. Capt. Daniel Moulton(13).

**VEASEY**, Veazie, very rare and not in Guppy or Lower.

**1 GEORGE**, Dover prop. 1659, bef. ct. same yr. for being more than ½ hr. at the tavern. Of Kittery 11 Dec. 1662, sold gr. there to John Wincoll in 1664 and gave deed for it 1672-3 (Y. D. 2: 128). Late of Berwick, 1676. See Urin(1). Lists 298, 356a. His wid. Mary (Wiggin 5) m. 2d Oct. 1673 William Moore(26). Only ch. seen: **George. Thomas**.

**2 GEORGE**(1), Stratham, innkeeper, m. by 1699-1700 Martha (Harvey 14), wid. of John Wilson(4). Deeded to br. Thos. Har-

vey 1713. See Mason(7). Lists 57, 62, 388, 376b (1705). Ensign G. V. d. 29 Nov. 1752. His w. d. 28 Jan. 1752. His will, gent., 1751— 1752, ment. 6 daus: **Eleanor** March (w. of Clement(4), who was buying out the other heirs 1757) and her s. George, **Miriam** Fifield (yet Edward Fifield m. -Elizabeth- Veasey 9 Nov. 1727), **Amy** Leavitt, **Hannah** Colcord, **Martha** Smart and her dau. Elizabeth Pickering, **Mary** Wiggin and her dau. Martha Brackett, and gr.ch. Jonathan and Elizabeth Fifield.

3 **HENRY**, Shoals 1687. List 307a.

4 **THOMAS**(1), Stratham, ±75 in 1744, m. Mary Leavitt(10). Had deeds from Benj. Leavitt 1709 and Simon Wiggin (100 a.) 1713. 'Old Mr. Thomas V.' d. 7 Aug. 1750. Lists 57, 62, 388, 376b (1705). Ch., order not kn: **George**, had deeds from fa. 1718 and 1732 (homestead). With w. Hannah (Wiggin 4) deeded to br. Samuel 1719; both liv. 1752 when they deeded to s. George. Ens. **Jeremiah**, Exeter, had w. Elizabeth and s. Samuel (bp. Ex. 5 Apr. 1747). **Benjamin**, had deed from fa. 1727; will, Brentwood, 1763—1764, ment. w. Deborah (Blake, m. Hampt. F. 30 Dec. 1725) and 4 ch. **Thomas**. One Thomas had daus. Abigail, Agnes and Sarah, gr.daus. of Nathaniel Ambrose of Chester, 1745. One Thomas jr. had w. Anna Neal (Joshua 8), 1760, 1761. **Samuel**, 55 in 1757, 59 in 1760, m. 1st 13 Jan. 1725-6 Hannah Robinson; his wid. was Mary (appar. formerly a. wid. Perkins) in his will, 1763— 1764, which ment. dau. Hannah (a minor), gr.ch. David Folsom, Samuel Smith, Hannah Thurston, sis. Hannah V., neph. Samuel (Jeremiah), s.-in-law John Folsom and w.'s s. Joseph Perkins. **Hannah** and **Sarah**, to whom their fa. deeded 1748, both single 1758 when they sold; Hannah in br. Samuel's will.

**VEERING**, Vering, **John**, associated with the Parkers at Sagadahoc (Harwich in Devonshire Co.), 55 in 1684, wit. Ind. deed to Thwoits 1660; had deed to Colley's swamp 1661 and to Vering's high head 1664, both from John Parker; deed from Thomas Kemble 1668 to land on which V. was building a corn-mill. He and w. Eleanor deeded 200 a. near Sheldrake cove to Ichabod Wiswell 1675. Harwich gr. 1688, and that yr. pet. Andros for 200 a. possessed 20 yrs. In 1684 he (misread 'Voanny') and Wm. Baker went to Casco Bay to get news about rumored Ind. rising. Lists 182, 183, 187(2), 191. He d. bef. Jan. 1689-90 when wid. Eleanor, ±57, depos. that 'ab. June 1688 Sir Edmund Andros came to my ho.' Adm. in Boston 10 Jan. 1700-1 to s.-in-law John Parker, the wid., then w. of Anthony Gulliver of Milton, relinq. Ch: **John**, god-s. of John Parker who deeded him land, 1661. Prob. he, not his fa.,

k. by Ind. with five others while searching for cattle on W. side of river 1689 (Doc. Hist. 9: 15). **Nathaniel**, millwright, his est. adm. by John Parker with his fa.'s. **Sarah**, m. John Parker(25). **Eleanor**, m. John Daniel of Milton by 1730 when they q.c. 'Verin's farm' on expiration of Christian Snowman's lease. Ano. John Vering, sailmaker of Boston, had w. Mary (Wiseman) and d. 5 Nov. 1713, ag. 83.

**Veeton**, John. List 239a.

**VENNER, Thomas**, cooper, at Salem by 1638, Boston by 1645, was at York a few yrs. bef. returning to Eng. by 1656. List 75b. Sold his ho. and lot to Edward Start 25 July 1653. His w. Alice had at least three ch. in N. E. He was the 'Preacher at the Conventicles of the Fifth Monarchy Men and Seducer of Libertines, Captain of the seditious Anabaptists and Quakers in the City of London,' and was beheaded and quartered 19 Jan. 1661.

**Vennion**, Thomas, Richmond Isl., 1642-3. List 21.

**Vernall**, Mary. List 66. See Fernald(1).

**VICARS, Roger**, Black Point, sued Andrew Alger for slander and won, 1659. Had built ho. and fences on Wm. Smith's half of the Smith-Brown gr. bef. 22 Oct. 1662 when he sold to Scottow, who sold to Andrew Brown. Lists 85, 231 (both Vickery), 238ab. Wife Mary, ag. 50 in 1685; List 238b. Ch: **Joseph**, ag. 21 in 1685 (List 238b), and presumably **John** (Lists 236, 237ae) and **Samuel** (List 238a). In Marblehead a Roger (Vicary) and w. Grace had ch. b. 1685-1710, and a Roger (Vicary) m. 4 Dec. 1694 Amy Willen (wid. or dau. of Willing 2).

**Vickery**, Andrew, signed petition with Mr. Thos. Jocelyn 1653. See also Vittery and Vicars.

**Vie**, John. List 37.

**VIGARS, Thomas**, York, ±45 in 1695-6 when he went with Nathaniel Raynes to run his lines. (York Files). Vicars?

**VINCENT, Thomas**, York, m. Tabitha Moore (10); town gr. 1714; adm. to her 7 July 1719. She m. 2d William Harris (see 23).

**VINES**, a Devon name.

†‡**DR. RICHARD**, gentleman, servant of Sir F. Gorges. Considered to have been of a west-country fam., the only Eng. rec. of him yet found is the baptism of his s. in a London church 1625-6. In or about 1616 he headed an expedition for Sir Ferdinando to explore the New Eng. coast and country and partic. to remain throughout a winter. Vines made his headquarters at the mouth of the Saco, in the vicinity of Biddeford Pool, penetrated the interior and found the winter climate bearable. Poss. he made other voyages to Me., but, having been gr. with John

Oldham a patent for a tract 32 sq. miles (now Biddeford) 12 Feb. 1629-30, he came over to found a permanent settlement soon aft. and was delivered poss. 25 June 1630. Agent to give poss. of Trelawney patent, 1631-1632. Estab. a trading post at Machias with Isaac Allerton 1633. Commissioned councillor 1635, but appar. absent at the ct. of 25 Mar. 1636 when Mrs. Joan Vines pet. for the island which she had formerly planted. On 2 Sept. 1639 Vines was made 'steward general' (deputy gov.) of Maine, and after the departure of Thomas Gorges the Gen. Ct., sitting in Saco 1645, elected him to the same position. He was already planning to leave Maine, however, and on 20 Oct. 1645 he sold the patent to Dr. Robert Child and soon sailed for Barbadoes where he bot two plantations and prac. medicine. Two of his letters to Gov. Winthrop, 1647-1648, are printed in Folsom's Hist. of Saco and Biddeford. He was bur. in St. Michael's par. 19 Apr. 1651. His will, 21 May—13 June 1651, directs burial in the Church, names w. Joan (⅓ of est. to be at her disposal at her death) and s. Richard exec., gr.ch. Belinda Parrasite, under 15 yrs. old (legacy for her education; to be put in charge of Mr. Lindsay), s.-in-law Thomas Ellacott (overseer), dau. Joan Ducy, dau. Elizabeth, and Will Maxwell (an apprent. who was to make up accounts, get in debts, practice the remainder of his time from which 2 yrs. were to be deducted); wit. Mr. John Lee, Mr. Joseph Onslowe, John Moody. Ch: Richard, s. of Richard and Joan, bp. 22 Feb. 1625-6 at St. James Clerkenwell, London; nunc. will, 26 Aug. 1657—26 Mar. 1658, bound to sea and being at Mr. Joseph Onslowe's ho., gave ½ his prop. to ch. of br. John Deuce 'who taught me navigation,' ¼ to John Paris his child, ¼ to Mr. Ellicott's child ('the names of the children I have forgotten'). Dau., m. John Parrasite or Paris. Joan, m. John Ducy or Deuce. Margaret, m. 18 Oct. 1649 Thomas Ellicott; see her s. Vines Ellicott. Elizabeth, unm. in 1651, not ment. in br.'s will.

VINNEY. 1 Roger (Venney), Cape Porpus wit. 1669 (Y. D. 2: 131).

2 WILLIAM, his York gr. of 28 Mar. 1699 had been improved acc. to condition in 1715-6. Of Wells, he sold land and buildings at Merryland to Richard Stimpson 29 May 1702, ack. by s. and adm. William of Sutton, 1728. Wid. Abigail m. one Rider of York bef. 1728 when she relinq. adm. Lists 39 (hardly his), 269b.

VIRRS (Fuz), Allen, planter, Newichawannock, wit. will of Martha Taylor, Mar. 1688-9. Bot 11 June 1695 30 a. from Robt. Elliot who had it from Humphrey and Grace Spencer. Adm. 2 Oct. 1717 to William Hearl

(5) who called him cousin. List 290.

VITTERY. 1 Edward, Shoals by 1666 when he acted as appr., fisherman, ±50 in 1673. Appr. John Searle's est. 1675. Gr.j. 1679. List 95 (Vickery), 226, 305c, 306c. On 7 July 1685 he bot 'Clem's Pt.,' Cape Elizabeth, from Jordan and Fryer. His wid. m. 2d aft. 1698 David Ela of Haverhill who left his est. to her in 1710. She m. 3d Boston 30 Mar. 1711 William Clements(10). She cl. the Cape Eliz. prop. in 17—, Clement Sweet, John Parrott and Richard Pope abuttors (East. Cl. vii: 76).

2 GREGORY, see Moore(8).

3 PETER, of London, d. at sea; adm. 6 June 1682 to Reuben Hull of Portsm.

Vivion, John, Richmond Isl. 1635. List 21.

Voanny, John, 1684. See Veering.

Vodard, William, Cochecho wit. 1666.

Voden, Vooden, Moses. List 267b. See Boody.

Vorce, John. List 68.

VOTER, Capt. John, commander of H. M. S. -Samuel and Henry- in 1692 when he sent his lieutenants and men to the Shoals, brot Capt. John Pickering's ship -Dove- by force of arms to Portsm. and remov. 14 bbls. of gun-powder.

VOUCKLIN, John, had suits in N. H. courts 1642-1644. In 1644 ct. ordered that money be sent to Christopher Holmes for him.

VOYSEY (Overzee), Simon, a Dutch merchant liv. in Va. who sued James Nichols (6) in York ct. 1650. For biog. see Edward Small and Allied Fam. 2: 842.

Wadd, Anne. See Colcord(1), Page(6).

WADDOCK (Warwick, Warrick), Henry, Saco. The Williams(26) est. owed him £7. 17. 6 and for a like debt he sued Williams(32) in May 1636. Sold seed corn to Winter 1643; his lot ment. 1654. Jury 1640, 1665; gr.j. 1645, 1656, 1659. Comr. for Saco 1653-1664, 1667; selectman 14 yrs. to 1672. Tav. and ferry lic. 1654; tav. lic. 1672, 7 July 1674. Lists 242, 243ab, 244bcef, 245, 249, 252, 24, 75b; wife, List 246. See also Page (7). Inv., incl. 250 a. upland and 30 a. meadow, taken by John Sargent and Walter Mayer 16 June 1679. The wid. Jane attested at Kit. 9 Oct. 1679, sold 200 + 20 a. on no. s. Saco River to Humphrey Scammon, and was lic. 30 Mar. 1680 to sell any or all of the lands as 'her sons by whom she was to be provided have very little or nothing left.' Of Glouc. and admx. of H. W. sometime resid. in Scarb., she gave p/a to s. John Tenney 17 Jan. 1692-3 to recover from Scammon ±200 a. and £30 or £40. The Tenneys deeded 400 a. to him 4 July 1700, mentioning H. W.'s deed from Richards, Lake and Scottow, 1 Nov. 1657. Ch. appear: James, a Saco wit. 1664 (Y. D. 15: 74). John, a Saco townsman

in 1674 when 'his horse allowed on.' Black
Point 1676; Newcastle 1677, his tax there
abated 5 Feb. 1679-80; Scarboro 1681-1682.
Lists 237a, 313a, 238a, 239a. **Joan,** m. in
Saco John Helson. **Margaret,** w. of John
Tenney(1) in 1692, and may have had one or
more earlier husbands; see Carkeet(3), Y.D.
10: 246.

**Waddy,** Nicholas, fisherman, adm. gr. in
York ct. July 1658 to John Diamond(3),
not of right.

## WADE.

1 **REV. JOHN,** Berwick, b. in Ipsw. 15 Feb.
1674-5, s. of Col. Thomas, H. C. 1693, m. 3
Sept. 1696 Elizabeth Gerrish(3), List 298.
Minister of Berwick (par. of Unity) 12 May
1697 (see 2), also in Nov. 1699 and Sept. 1700
when he bot there near the meeting-ho., tho
bef. May 1698 he had been chaplain at
Brunswick. He wit. John Fost's will in 1699
and wrote and wit. Mrs. Bridget Graffort's
contested will. Ordained at Berw. 18 Nov.
1702; his w. adm. a member in May 1703.
He d. 13 Nov. 1703, ill two days, and Rev.
Cotton Mather paid tribute to him. Lists
298, 96. Wid. Elizabeth of Dover m. 2d Capt.
Joshua Pierce(13). Ch: **John,** b. 16 July
1699, d. ab. 1720, unm. **Sarah,** b. 20 Sept.
1701, wit. for her mo. 12 Dec. 1722, m. Capt.
Nicholas Winkley(2) by 1730 when she was
the only surviving child.

2 **COL. JONATHAN,** Ipswich, List 303, fa.
of Col. **Thomas,** his admr., whose sons
Jonathan (m. wid. Jane Diamond 3) and
Thomas, as their fa.'s execs., gave p/a to
their br. (1) to collect from John Diamond
of the Shoals. See also Graffam.

**Wadelstensteen,** see Stone and Wadlin.

**WADLEIGH,** Wadley, the latter now
found in Gloucestershire.

1 **EDWARD** (Wodley), Richmond Isl. 1641-
2, hired here. List 21.

2 **JOHN,** planter, Saco, Wells, of unkn. origin, but by Catholic rec. his dau. Mary
was b. at 'Bristol near London.' Taxed
Saco 1636, and appr. the Williams(26) est.
Vines gr. him a lot 'in Yeapskesset River' in
1639. An arbitrator betw. John Richards
and Francis Knight, 1640. Tr.j. 1640, 1645;
gr.j. 1645. Evid. of Wells 20 Nov. 1645 when
Vines gr. 200 a. on s.w. side of Obumkegg
River to him and Edmund Littlefield. Wells
selectman 1647, 1648. Took Ind. deed in
1649, and in 1650 took poss. and made deliv.
to s. Robert as joint purchaser. In 1654
Thomas Wheelwright and Ezekiel Knight
wit. ag. him for swearing; the next yr. he
was fined for defaming a gr.j. man, a sequel
to this case. Comr. for Wells 1659. Lists
242, 252, 261-264, 22, 23. Wife Mary abs.
from meeting 1654, liv. 18 Apr. 1664. His

will, 7 July 1671 (Me. P. & Ct. Rec. ii: 244),
directed bur. beside decd. wife, names 3 ch.,
the son exec., Edw. Rishworth and Samuel
Wheelwright overseers; inv. 20 Sept. 1671
by James Gooch and James Smyth, £453. Ch:
**Robert. Mary,** m. Thomas Mills(12). **Joanna,**
m. 1st Jonathan Thing(1), m. 2d Bartholomew Tipping. Her fa. willed her 1/6 of his
cattle.

3 **ENSIGN HENRY**(4), millwright, Exeter,
m. 3 Dec. 1693 Elizabeth (Gilman 8)
Ladd. Gr.j. 1694, 1695; selectman 1695. Lists
376b (1698, 1725), 377, 400. Adm. 20 Feb.
1732-3 to s. Joseph of Hampt., the wid. renouncing. Ch: **Sarah,** b. 3 Sept. 1694, m.
John Scribner jr. (2). **Abigail,** b. 2 Sept.
1696, appar. m. Samuel Magoon(1). **Joseph,**
b. Sept. 1698. One Joseph m. Lydia Smith
(Theophilus) who d. bef. 1737 leaving ch.
Theophilus and Lydia. See also Dearborn
(2). He was liv. in 1768, ag. 70. **Martha,** b.
Jan. 1700-1, m. Ephraim Philbrick(5). **Benjamin,** 1703-1716.

4 **‡*ROBERT**(2), Esq., millwright, Exeter,
went with fa. to Wells and had left for
Kittery, or was ab. to depart, 17 June 1654,
when he was 'at present in the town of
Wells.' Kit. wit. 15 July 1654; constable
1656; ferryman and tav. keeper; gr.j. 1665;
Clerk of the Writs 1665. In May 1666 he bot
320 a. at Lamprill River, sold out at Kit. two
mos. later, and of L. River sold half his 320
a. to Nicholas Lisson in 1667 (see Lisson and
Dover Hist. Memo., pp. 400-5). Dover gr.
him a mill priv. on L. River and rec. him
inhab. 3 May 1669. Adm. inhab. of Exeter
26 Sept. 1676. Rep. 1681, 1684. The partici-
pation of his sons John, Joseph and Robert
in the Gove Rebellion, resulted in his trip to
Eng. in their behalf and also on account of
his own troubles with Mason. On his return
Cranfield feared his influence and a report
was made 23 May 1684 'he hath put the
people of the Prov. into such ferment and
disorder that it is not poss. to put His Majesty's commands in execution, or any way
govern them.' Councillor 1684; Capt. by
1687 (see Hilton 19); Justice Ct. Com. Pleas;
Judge Superior Ct. Lists 252, 261, 263, 269b,
356m, 376b (1668), 377, 380, 381, 383, 385, 24,
49, 52, 54, 56-58, 92. Wife Sarah, m. bef. 17
June 1654, was liv. in 1698. He was liv. in
1701, his son was 'Jr.' 1702-1710. Kn. ch:
**Sarah,** m. John Young(3). Capt. **John,** oldest
s., ±20 in 1683, millwright, Ex., Salisb., was
pardoned for his part in the Rebellion bef.
May 1684; Ex. selectman 1687; Salisb. 1701.
Lists 376b (1681), 377, 52, 57, 296. Wife
Abigail Marston (John of Salem). Will, 13
Jan. 1725—1 Mar. 1727-8. See Hoyt's Salisb.
ii: 605, for ch. rec. there 1684-1700: Abigail,
Joseph, John, Alice, Ephraim, Ruth. **Joseph,**
had Ex. gr. 1681 (List 376b), taxed 1682, d.

in prison bef. 23 May 1684. In 1722 his sis. Mary sold 1/6 of his 100 a. near Deer Hill. **Robert**, in prison 23 May 1684, m. in Rowley 8 Sept. 1696 Sarah Nelson (Capt. Philip). Farmer, Ex. constable 1699, liv. 1734. Lists 62, 376b (1725). Ch. appear: Robert, Stratham, m. 18 Dec. 1718 Deborah Smith; will, 1733—1733, 7 ch. Benjamin, Kingston, w. Judith; liv. 1745. Philip, Ex., List 376b (1725), w. Mary Stevens (Edw.); will, 1765—1767, w. Mary, 2 ch., 2 gr.sons. Jonathan, Brentwood, List 376b (1725), appar. m. 1st wid. Joanna Moody(1); will 1755—1756, w. Sarah, br. Joseph, 5 ch. Joseph, Ex., b. 17 Sept. 1711, m. 5 Jan. 1737 Ann Swain, 5 ch. **Mary**, m. John Cram(1). **Henry. Jonathan**, Ex., bondsm. for Nicho. Gordon 1696, constable 1697, selectman often 1705—1732, called Lieut. 1709, Capt. 1725. Hannah, a wit. with him 1698, was likely his 1st w.; he m. 2d ab. 1717 Anna (Wilson) Hilton(24). Will, 1748—1756, names dau. Mary Leavitt (w. of Joseph), and ch. of decd. dau. Hannah Noyes (m. Joseph N. of Newb. by 1716).

**WADLIN, William**, Berwick, his name poss. from Wadelstensteen (see Stone 1), first appears as Nicholas Hodsdon's apprentice (Wadleigh) in Dec. 1678 (Y. D. 3: 42) and m., not before 1690, Elizabeth Gattensby(1). Kit. gr. 1694. Member of Berw. Ch. in 1703, his w. in 1716. In 1709 (Wadley), he sold mill rights on Wilcox Pond Brook. Taxed 9 Feb. 1718-9. Lists 290, 296, 298. Dame Elizabeth Wadlin living 1723. The s. Daniel, with Nicho. Gowen and Elisha Plaisted, gave bond as fa.'s adm. 5 Oct. 1725. Ch: **Daniel**, adm. of gr.fa. Gattensby's est. 15 May 1717, taxed Feb. 1718-9, ag. 44 in Sept. 1741, depos. in 1750 that he heard a dispute betw. Moses Spencer and Mrs. Mary Spencer in 1710. List 298. See also Gattensby(2). Wife Hannah. 4 ch. bp. 1736 and 4 betw. 1742—1753. Parents of 4 Wadleys bp. in 1741 were not named. **Sarah**, bp. with 4 fol. 25 Oct. 1716. **Mary**, m. 14 July 1726 John Rowell. **Ebenezer. Moses**, bot in Bid. 1734; m. (int. Bid. 15 Oct. 1737) Jane Perry(5) of Bid. List 298. **Patience**. And poss. **John**, List 298. See also Cheever(2), Marbleh. records.

**Wain**, William. See Briard(1), Mainwaring (4).

**WAINWRIGHT, Francis**, Ipswich merchant, an early Hampton grantee, and later largely concerned in Shoals fisheries. Lists 392a, 308a. See also Grant(15), Lang(7), Mayer(1). His ch. incl. **John** of Ips. who test. in a Seavey case at the Shoals in Nov. 1681, ag. ±32, and d. in 1708, Lists 95, 96. See also Randall(17); Redford(2) for a later John; Col. Soc. Mass. 20: 152.

**WAITE** (Wayte), **Richard**, from Boston, List 312c. As Marshall R. W., he and his assistant, Robert Marshall, were sued by Barefoot, Greenland & Norton in 1672; in the same ct. the three sued him alone for carrying away plank, etc., in the pinke -Lenham-, and he had a suit ag. George Norton. See also List 82.

**WAKEFIELD**, a market-town in Yorkshire. Estab. as a fam. name in cos. Gloucester, Lincoln and Warwick. See also Moore(17).

1 **JAMES**(2), Wells, ag. 16 in June 1680 (Essex Q. Ct. Rec. 7: 401), and evid. younger than his br. Henry, signed a Wells pet. in 1686, had a gr. in Mar. 1693-4, ano. 100 a. on Kennebunk River, at the landing, in 1699, and with w. Rebecca (Gibbins 3) wit. Wheelwright to Gooch in Nov. 1700. Drowned going over Wells bar with br. Wm. and others 25 Oct. 1707. Lists 33, 269b, 96. Wid. Rebecca deeded her int. in the Saco pat. to three surv. sons 8 Nov. 1728. Ch: **James**, had a Wells gr. in 1716, m. 18 Dec. 1719 Mary Durrell(2). List 269c. **John**, List 269c, m. Elizabeth Durrell(2), and **Keziah**, m. Philip Durrell(2 jr.), both on 27 May 1724. **Nathaniel**, m. 1 Jan. 1730-1 Hannah Emmons(1). List 269c. **Gibbins**, served in Norridgewock exped.; not named in mo.'s deed 1728.

2 **JOHN**, Wells, Scarboro, Saco, at Marblehead by Jan. 1637, at Wells bef. June 1647 when he helped appraise Mrs. Cole's swine. Selectman 1654, 1657. Form. of W., he sold ho. and land there to Samuel Austin in May 1658, and of Scarb. 3 Apr. 1661 confirmed to John Gooch land sold him 5 or 6 yrs. bef., form. Stephen Batson's. A Saco wit. with dau. Mary 31 May 1664. Tr.j. 1656, 1666; gr.j. 1656, 1661; j. life and death 1666. Abs. from meeting 1669; he and w. abs. in 1670, when he promised to be more careful. Lists 252, 261, 263. Saco wit. 10 Dec. 1673; d. there 15 Feb. 1674. His will, recorded on a folio now missing, but which Historian Folsom must have seen over 100 yrs. ago, named 4 sons, 3 daus., 2 Frost gr.ch. His w. Elizabeth (Littlefield 8, m. by 1661), by his p/a of 9 Aug. 1670, sold Marbleh. land a mo. later. She was a refugee at Salem in 1676, Lists 246, 27. Ch., Folsom's order: **John**. The Wakefield Gen. says he m. Hester Harbor of Mendon and d. by 1693, leaving a dau. Elizabeth who m. Jonathan Hayward of Mendon by 1706-7. **James**, b. ±1664. **Henry**, a Wells wit., Hill to Cross, 30 Mar. 1677. **William**, m. in Salem 13 Mar. 1698 Rebecca Littlefield(23). York gr. 1702, 2 or 3 a. swamp betw. his own land and John Stover's. Of York 29 Sept. 1705, he sold 100 a. at Cape Neddick. Drowned with (1), 25 Oct. 1707, List 96. Wid. Rebecca was bp. at Wells on prof. of faith 9 May 1708, m. 2d at Salem 19 Sept. 1717 Lt. Wm. King and

remov. to Sutton. Her ch. were bp. at Wells 23 July 1710, William, Joseph, Benjamin, Jonathan, all but William locating at Sutton or Dudley. **Mary**, m. 1st William Frost (15), m. 2d Israel Harding(2). **Katherine**, named in gr.mo. Littlefield's will 1677. A mistaken idea that she m. Mr. Robert Nanny is attrib. to deed of July 1694 by which N.'s wid. Katherine conv. in part 'all that land lately in poss. of John Wakefield,' betw. John Sanders and Mr. Cole (Y. D. 4: 111). **Daughter**, unidentified.

3 **JONAS**, Portsmouth, his tax (Wigfield) abated in Feb. 1679-80, taxed 1698, List 330d.

4 **SAMUEL**, a (?Boston) wit. with Henry Williams, Sheares(1) to Mrs. Sayward, 1683. See also Child(2).

5 **WILLIAM**, came in the -Bevis- in 1638, ag. 22, with Anne W., ag. 20, and was with those first at Hampt., a young man. Freeman 13 Mar. 1638-9. Dow calls him the first town clerk, chosen 31 Oct. 1639 and serving ±3 yrs.; lot layer 1 yr.; succ. by Wm. Howard as Clerk of the Writs in June 1642. Lists 391a, 392ab. Newbury 1646 (Coffin). In Mar. 1649, Stephen Kent, his atty., won a suit for tresp. ag. Walter Roper, in Essex Ct., but the fol. Oct. W. W., evid. in person, sued Wm. Fuller for tresp. and won. In 1652 Stephen Kent sold land for him. Wm. Fifield depos. in 1660 ab. the time 'when Mr. W. was going for England.'

**WAKEHAM**, Wacom.

1 **EDWARD**, weaver, Oyster River, b. ±1663, m. 16 Mar. 1691-2 Sarah Meader (1), had Dover gr. Mar. 1693-4, bot 'Giles old field' on so. side of O. R. in 1695, and adj. land in 1699. Ag. ±40 in Sept. 1703. Lists 62, 368ab(3). See also Pitman(3). He and w. Sarah adm. to O. R. Ch. 18 Oct. 1719. She was a wid. in 1739 (see Meader 3). Ch: **Mary**, m. John Kent(2). **Sarah**, bp. at O. R. with Abigail 14 Dec. 1718, sisters and maidens; m. John Buss(2). **Abigail**, bp. with Sarah, m. John Laskey (see George). **Elizabeth**, bp. with mo. 11 Oct. 1719, m. at O. R. 11 Jan. 1725-6 John Edgerly, Jr. **Mehitabel**, bp. 21 May 1721, m. betw. 16 Nov. 1734— 17 Feb. 1735-6 John Jones, jr., of Kit. **Caleb**, bp. 21 May 1721, in 1732 wit. a Langley (Reynolds) div. with Stephen Buss. Wife Mary. **Prudence**, m. Ichabod Follett. The est. of William Wakham, decd., List 369 (?Edward's).

2 **JOHN**, Portsmouth, taxed 1681, 1684, 1688. In 1683 Reuben Hull called him 'my servant John Wackum.' Lists 329, 52, 57. Adm. 15 Mar. 1691-2 to wid. Martha (Brookings 5), who m. 2d John Lewis(9) (called Martha Lewis or Wacomb 1695-6), m. 3d Joseph Randall(12). Apparent are

daus. **Mary** and **Martha**, liv. in 1710.

3 **JONAS**, Wells soldier 1693-4, from Dedham. List 267b.

4 **MARY** (Wacom), appar. one of Richard Cutts' servants. List 328.

5 **ROBERT** (Wakam by his will; Rishworth wrote it Wacom), a Portsm. wit. with w. Hannah 1668 (Joseph Mason's deed) and had a fight there with David Campbell the same yr. Plf. in Me. ct. 1673-1674, against Christopher Gould (withdrawn), against Israel Harding, against John Severance. List 266. Will, 1677—1677 (Suff. Prob.), gives house, land, goods, horses, mares, all at Wells, to w. Hannah, and 5 s. to each ch. at 21, **Robert, William, James, Hannah** (all bp. at First Ch., Boston, 6 Feb. 1675-6, ch. of sister Wakum); 'my gr.fa. Everet to assist my wife.' Two ch. had d.y: **Hannah**, b. Boston 1665, **Elizabeth**, bp. 1675-6.

6 **THOMAS**, Mr. (Wacomb, Wacom, seldom with 'k'), merchant, Portsm., bot ¼ a. of land from Richard Cutts in 1667 and m. by 1677 Mary Hunking(6), List 335a. Constable 1687; j. 1693; retail lic. 1692, 1694, 1695, outdoors 1697. Lists 326c, 327b, 329, 330d, 331ab, 335a, 336b, 52, 57(2), 62, 98. See also Evans(2), Grafort. Will, 27 Sept. 1698— 15 Dec. 1709, names w. Mary, kinswomen Jane Haskings (see 6), Elizabeth Alkins (the homestead, but if she d. s.p., then to Jane Haskins), Mary Adams and Patience Alkins. Wid. W. and ho. taxed 1713, her tax abated in 1714.

7 **WALTER**, Shoals, his inquest 2 Aug. 1674. List 305c.

**WAKELY.** See also Coe(2), Creber.

1 **HANNAH**, York 1678 (see Martin 2), is unkn. unless one of the Falm. fam. who escaped the massacre. See (3).

2 **HENRY**, sued by Francis Williams in N. H. 1641.

3 **JOHN**(4), Falmouth, m. at Glouc. or Salem (rec. at both) 10 June 1657 Elizabeth Sowars (Joanna), bot at Back Cove in 1661 (see 4) and mov. there, afterw. living on the east side of Presumpscot River below the Falls. In 1665 he and other Casco men were fined for non-appear. at ct. and contempt of authority. Lists 25, 222c. His w. was abs. from meet. in July 1674. He, w., parents and three ch. were reported k. in Sept. 1675. 3 ch. rec. both at Glouc. and Salem: **Hannah**, b. 12 Mar. 1657-8. Did she escape in 1675? Note (1). **Thomas**, b. 3, d. 7, Sept. 1659. **Elizabeth**, b. 31 Jan. 1660-1. She or a younger Elizabeth, called aged 11, was taken captive in Sept. 1675, returned to Major Waldron and m. Richard Scammon (4). And at least **two more ch.**, if three were k. by Ind.

4 **THOMAS,** Hingham, Cape Ann, Falmouth. Freed from training at Cape Ann because of lameness in 1651, 10 yrs. later he, two sons and s.-in-law Coe bot 200 a. at Back Cove, Falm., from Richard Tucker and mov. there. Fined for non-appear. at ct. in July 1665; wit. Thomas Skillings' will in 1666. He and his w. were k. at Falm. in 1675 when (3)'s fam. was almost wiped out. In 1688 his gr.s.-in-law Joseph Ingersoll(7) pet. Andros for confirmation of the Falm. land. Lists 25, 222c, 34. See also Y. D. 14: 210, 255. Kn. ch: **Elizabeth,** m. in Glouc. 15 June 1647 Matthew Coe(2). **John,** oldest son. **Isaac,** bot in Falm. in 1661, but appar. was the Isaac cast away at sea with Glouc. men ab. Mar. 1662, adm. in July fol. to Thomas Very (Essex Q. Ct. Rec. 2: 368, 413). **Thomas,** bp. at Hingham 14 June 1640, evid. liv. 1647-9 when his fa. was 'Senr.' at Glouc. **Sarah,** bp. at Hingham 13 Mar. 1641, bur. there 13 May fol. Also, if time and place indicate anything, **Daniel,** k. by Ind. at Martin's Point 11 Aug. 1676, with Benj. Atwell, jr., Robert Corbin, Humphrey Durham and Goodman Lewis. List 223b. See also Hughes(10).

**Walden,** see Waldron.

**WALDO,** Thomas, Hampton ±1645, List 392a, wit. Sanborn to Philbrick in May 1647. One T. W., ag. 24, depos. bef. Jocelyn and Godfrey in 1647 that Wm. James(8) and John Batten(3) asked him to be their atty. ag. Wm. Seeley.

**WALDRON,** Walden. Warwickshire the home of the Walderne fam., who often lost their 'r' in early records and finally became Waldron. See N. E. Reg. 8: 78; 43: 258. Walden is found in co. Dorset.

1 **ALEXANDER,** gunsmith, Dover, Great Isl., s. of Foulke of Coventry, Warwickshire (his will in Reg. 43: 60), br. of (5, 14), neph. of (3, 10, 13). He and (14) were taxed together at Dover 1664, he alone 1666. In 1666 he sued Thomas Nock, in 1669 was sued by Wm. Ford, in 1670 wit. Payne to Coffin, in 1671 sued David Campbell, in 1672 of Piscat. bot Boston ho. from (14), was at Great Isl. 1674, elected constable 14 Mar. 1675-6. Lists 356hk, 312h. See also Henderson(4). As a 'sojourner' at Great Isl., he made his will 7 June 1676 (d. same day), naming br. Isaac and w. of Boston; bros. William and George to have Boston ho. and land aft. death of Robert Taprill's w. Abisha (she also received two gold rings and her oldest dau. Alice £10); br. Edward in Eng.; sis. Mary, br. Samuel, and Joan Barker of Coventry, if unmar.; Isaac exec. and overseer. The bros. George and Samuel liv. in N. E., but are not noted in N. H. or Me.

2 **ANTHONY** (Walden), ±22, and Ann Burdis depos. in Mar. 1671-2 about Thomas Parker slandering Mary Wentworth. Falmouth 1676, List 223b.

3 **GEORGE,** Mr., Dover, br. of (10, 13), was bp. at Alcester, co. Warwick, 26 Apr. 1603, m. at A. 31 May 1635 Bridget Rice, and had ch. **Elizabeth, Mary** and **William,** bp. there 1636-1639. An Eng. pedigree shows him at Alcester, a chandler, 1650. Taxed Dover 1659-1677. Of Cochecho, he was bef. the ct. in June 1661 for abs. from his w., and again in June 1662 when she 'was dead before twelve months this fall.' Lists 356eghk, 359a. Little appears of him except his trials with his only ch. seen here, **John.** Poor and aged and almost quite blind, he pet. 1 June 1680 that he might be rid of this son who 'instead of holding me hath rather destroyed me and what I had in drinking,' and that a guardian might be appointed for himself. A week later Mrs. Waldron(10) had taken him in until her husb. should return.

4 **HENRY** (Walderne), Cape Bonawagon 1672. List 13.

5 **ISAAC,** physician, br. of (1, 14). Judge Savage noted him in York in 1670; Col. Banks thought he was there only professionally from Dover and not resident. He ret. to Eng., m. in London 25 Feb. 1674 Priscilla Byfield (sis. of Nathl. of Boston and Bristol) and was back bef. 27 June 1676 when he attested his br. Alexander's inv. in N. H., but liv. in Boston where ch., **Isaac** and **three Priscillas,** were rec. 1677—1682. In Suff. ct. Feb. 1677-8, he sued Wm. Henderson(4) for delay in overhauling a ship and was sued by Thomas Tare for iron work done on the ship. See also Gilbert(2). Wid. Priscilla and John Usher were admrs. in Oct. 1685, Chas. Lidget admr. 22 Apr. 1686 when Walter Barefoot signed his bond; the next day L. receipted for £130 due the est. from Thomas Paine(15). List 89. See also Reg. 42: 107.

6 **JOHN**(3), hornbreaker, Dover 1672, List 356j. In June 1678 Jonathan Watson and Joseph Beard saw him overtaken in drink, a habit which brought distress to his fam. In 1680 the ct. took drastic steps, ordering him confined with one leg chained to a post, and supplied with materials for his trade, the proceeds to go for his and his children's maintenance. His letter to his w. 29 Jan. 1682, still in confinement, ment. only his child; see N. H. Hist. Soc. Col., 8: 42, 43, 115. In Boston drunk and abusing the constable 1684; not seen again unless he is (7). Kn. ch: Capt. **John,** Dover (±30 in 1705), willed a cow by John Heard(5) in 1687 if he served his time faithfully, m. 29 Aug. 1698 Mary (Ham 4) Horne(2) who joined the ch. 1 Aug. 1742. Gr.j. 1699. Owned at Black Point (50 a. bot from Anthony Row in 1700), Roch. and Barr. Lists 289, 358d. See also Daniel Field

(12). Will, gent., 12 May—30 July 1740, names w. Mary, gr.ch. and ch: John (d. 4 July 1778, ag. 80), Elizabeth (w. of Ezra Kimball), Anna (w. of Timothy Roberts), Mehitable (w. of James Chesley; d. 21 Aug. 1776, ag. 68), Sarah (w. of Isaac Libby), Richard (resid. legatee). By trad. the two oldest ch. Sarah and Bridget were k. by Ind., ag. 9 and 7. **Elizabeth**, m. 1st Joseph Beard (3 jr.), m. 2d Ephraim Wentworth(2).

7 **JOHN** (Walden), from Wells, played cards at a Boston tav. in Feb. 1689-90 and paid a fine in ct., saying 'There is something for you to make merry with,' and they sent him to jail. Jonathan Dawes sued J. W. in Suff. ct. in Aug. 1690 on a bill dated 22 Mar. 1689-90. Perh. the 2d husb. of Elizabeth (Sanders) Batson(1), or same as (6). ?Lists 91, 92.

8 **JOHN**, Marblehead, Lists 90, (?91, 92). His mar. to Dorothy Dolliver in 1653 and Marbleh. records show he was not (6).

9 **NICHOLAS** (Walden), tailor, Portsmouth ±1680. Gr.j. 1683, j. 1688; O.A. 28 Aug. 1685. In 1685 he had a Portsm. ho. lately built, in 1690 John Knight(9) bot a ho. from him. In June 1693 N. W. and Elizabeth Sherburne were summonsed, he for keeping a wench in his ho. not proper to be entertained. He soon had a w. Mary (ct. Dec. 1693). Fine aut. in 1695, with John Barsham. Lists 52, 57, 67, 329, 336b. Given no share in commons 1711 and wrote a protest 13 June 1712, had been here 32 yrs. Taxed for Mill Dam 1713, soon d., wid. Mary being rec. into So. Ch. 19 Dec. 1714. Adm. on his est. gr. to s. **Thomas**, mariner, 19 May 1720, Thomas Sherburne surety. This son was master of the -Douglass- from Nevis in May 1714, tho under age; m. 20 Dec. 1716 Sarah Cotton(1); List 339. Will, 18 Jan.—6 Mar. 1724-5, names w. Sarah (m. 2d Samuel Pickering 5), and ch: Thomas, mariner, adm. to wid. Anne 31 Mar. 1756, large est., ch.; John, shipwright, m. Lydia Tobey; William, shipwright, d. s.p., adm. 28 Aug. 1754 to wid. Priscilla and her 2d husb. John Partridge. Daus., ch. of Mary: **Elizabeth** and **Hannah**, rec. into cov., So. Ch., with mother; Hannah m. Henry Beck(4). **Mary**, bp. 19 Dec. 1714, rec. into cov. 3 June 1716, m. John Hooper(4).

10 §†‡*MAJOR RICHARD, Dover, eminent beyond his home and Province, was bp. at Alcester, co. Warwick, 6 Jan. 1615, (±33 in 1648), s. of William and Catherine (Raven) who were m. there 26 Nov. 1600. See his bros. (3, 13) and nephews (1, 5, 14). A Mass. adherent, his activities in peace and war and his land and mill holdings were too numerous to list. His own testi. locates him in the Ind. trade at Pennacook ±1635 (Doc. Hist. 4: 228), and Lechford (p. 289) shows he had his ho. at Dover in Aug. 1640 when

he and (13) held p/a of John Jordan, grocer, London, dated 21 May 16 Charles. In 1644 Mr. Edw. Starbuck, R. W. and Wm. Furber were named wiersmen for life for Cochecho Falls and River. Selectman often 1647—1675; Dep. 1649, but unable to serve, being very sick; Associate, Dover ct., by 1650; Dep. almost contin. 1654—1679 (Speaker 1666—1668, 1673—1675, 1679); Com. t.e.s.c., Treasurer, Magistrate for Me. and N. H. Capt. early; Major in 1674, and in command in King Philip's war; called Col. in 1682. Councillor under Pres. Cutts, Dep. Gov., and succ. Pres. Cutts, serving until Cranfield arrived, under whom he was suspended and restored as Councillor, and finally suspended permanently and a warr. issued for his arrest as a perturber of the peace 24 Aug. 1685. Not again in office. With it all, Quakers detested him, and the Ind. on at least one memorable occasion found him treacherous. Lists 351ab, 352, 353, 354abc, 355ab, 356abceghk, 357a, 359ab, 184, 221, 223a, 236, 311c, 28, 44-46, 48-50, 52-54, 76, 81, 83, 89, 94, 96. See also Gattensby(1), Lovering(2), Paine (2, 15), and Starbuck. His early wife or wives unkn. The last w. Ann (Scammon, see 3) d. 7 Feb. 1685-6, List 96; he was k. in an Ind. attack on Cochecho 28 June 1689. No probate. Kn. ch: **Timotheus**, wit. Philip Lewis' deed with John Hance and James Kidd 4 June 1659; said to have d. as an under-grad. of H. C. **Paul**, employed at the Pennacook truck ho. in 1668, List 357a, and depos. ab. liquor taken from his fa.'s cellar; see also Mass. Col. Rec. 4: 2: 414. Said to have gone abroad and been taken by the Algerenes ±1669. **Elizabeth**, m. John Gerrish(3); presum. not Ann's dau. as by rec. ano. dau. was given this name. Her ch. incl. Timothy and Paul. **Richard**, unrec., his mo. poss. Ann; only son and heir in sis. Esther Barnes' deed (N. H. Deeds 10: 68). **Anna**, b. ±1653, m. Rev. Joseph Gerrish(5); appar. dau. of Ann as named in the Lidgett will. Ann's ch. rec. in Boston: **Elnathan**, b. 6 July, d. 10 Dec. 1659. **Esther**, b. 1 Dec. 1660, had husbands Nathl. Elkins(8), Abraham Lee (1), John Jose(2), Joshua Barnes (see 8). **Mary** (bp. as Marcy), b. 14 Sept. 1663; d. at 14 (Savage). By N. H. Prov. rec. **Eliazer**, b. 1 May 1665. **Elizabeth**, b. 18 Oct. 1666. **Marah**, b. 17 July 1668.

11 ‡*COL. **RICHARD**(10), Portsmouth, bred a merchant under Lt. Gov. Willoughby of Charlestown (N. H. Hist. Soc. Coll. 8: 348), who by will 1670 gave to 'man Richard Walden.' Rep., J. P., Councillor, Justice Ct. of Com. Pleas, Judge of Probate, Colonel in Provincial militia. Lists 49, 51, 52, 55b, 56, 57, 59, 62, 64, 89, 329, 330df, 335a, 336c, 337, 339, 353, 358d. His 1st w. Hannah Cutts(2) was bur. 16 Feb. 1682-3 on the

1st anniversary of her mar. (List 96); he m. 2d 6 Feb. 1692-3 Eleanor Vaughan(4) who d. in Sept. 1727, he 3 Nov. 1730. Ch. by 1st w: **Samuel,** d.y. By 2d w: ‡\***Richard,** b. 21 Feb. 1693-4, H. C. 1712, Councillor, Sec. of the Prov., Judge of Prob., Rep. (Speaker), m. 31 Dec. 1718 Elizabeth Westbrook(2); he d. 23 Aug. 1753, she 16 Oct. 1758; ch. **Margaret,** b. 16 Nov. 1695, m. 18 May 1721 Eleazer Russell of Portsm., from Barnstable. Rev. **William,** b. 4 Aug. 1697, H. C. 1717, pastor of New Brick Ch., Boston, m. there Elizabeth Allen, d. 11 Sept. 1727; 1 dau. **Anna,** b. 29 Aug. 1698, m. Rev. Henry Rust of Stratham. **Abigail,** b. 28 July 1704, m. 6 Jan. 1725-6 Richard Saltonstall, Esq., of Haverhill. **Eleanor,** b. 7 Apr. 1706, d. 26 Aug. 1726.

12 **RICHARD,** Portsmouth, soldier at Newcastle 1708 (Prov. Papers 13: 239).

13 \***WILLIAM,** Mr., Dover, bp. at Alcester 18 Oct. 1601, oldest of 11 ch., incl. (3, 10), was with (10) in 1640 at Dover where his few yrs. were well filled. Freeman 19 May 1642; Assistant to the Magistrates and Com. t.e.s.c. 1642; sworn Recorder of the Prov. of Me. 21 Oct. 1645 and serving 6 July 1646; Clerk of the Writs and Recorder at Dover 1646; Deputy 1646. As a partner with the Shrewsbury men, he gave a bond to Mr. Whiting et al. in 1645 and a mortg. on his Dover ho. and land to (10) who had signed with him. Sued by Lt. Edmund Greenleaf for debt in 1643 and 1646; with Mr. Robert Saltonstall an agent for Mr. Shurt in 1645. He wit. Francis Matthews' deed 5 Sept. 1646 and that mo. was drowned at Kennebunk on his way back from Saco, leaving many creditors. Winthrop called him a good clerk and subtle man, while noting his inclination for drink and contention. Lists 351ab, 352, 353, 386, 53. See also Jenks(1). Only kn. and only surv. ch: **Prudence,** m. Richard Scammon(3); see Mass. Col. Rec. 4: 2: 303.

14 **WILLIAM,** gunsmith, Dover, Boston, br. of (1, 5), ±37 in 1679, first seen in Dover in 1664 taxed with (1). In 1672 he deeded to (1) a ho. in Boston and appar. made Bost. his principal home, tho dealing much at the Eastward. Lists 356b, 3, 4, 14, 142. See also Duncomb, and Peter Lidget (Legate2) whom he called 'cousin.' A non-suit was gr. in his case ag. John Woolcott, sr., in Suff. ct. Jan. 1678-9, the deft. being of Newbury and the plf. in a former attachment having called hims. of Dover, where he appar. was not on partic. good terms with (10) as in 1682 he made answer 'I did not use to come to his (10's) house,' 'I informed the next magistrate Mr. Coffin.' In May 1686 Thomas Thomas had taken the canoe of W. W. of Dover, smith, his last kn. rec. No rec. of fam., no probate. In 1723 'heirs of Wm. W. of Cochecho' mentioned.

**Waldrop,** see Woodrop.

**Wales,** Lists 212, 223a, 307b, see Wallis. One James Wales of Dublin m. Mary Sanders in Portsm. 16 Jan. 1717-8. See Wincoll(2).

**WALFORD.** One Thomas W. lived at Waltham Parva, co. Essex, 7 Charles I. See also Hughes(1).

1 **HANS** (also Hance Wolford) depos. 10 Aug. 1720 that he liv. with Edward Hilton(2) above 40 yrs. ago. He m. Mary (Goddard 3) (Bennett) Field(6) and liv. at the Bennett ho. at Lamprill River about 1698. Lists 376b (1698), 387. In 1700 they sold his 30 a. Exeter gr. Taxed Ex. 1714. He m. last 18 Oct. 1716 Mary (Allen 2) Fox who was liv. at Greenland in 1740 and d. there Oct. or Nov. 1743 'Granny Woolford.' One Elizabeth W. of Ex. was in ct. on a bast. charge in 1731; one John, husbandman, was of Durham in 1733.

2 **JEREMIAH**(4), Great Isl., had land from his fa. bef. 22 Oct. 1649, and a gr. of 20 a. near his ho. on Great Isl. in July 1651. Lists 323, 326a. Will, 16 Apr. (d. 21 Apr.) 1660, names w. Mary, 4 ch., his fa. and Mr. Henry Sherburne trustees. Inv. by Michael Rowe and Wm. Powell, £95. 6. 11. Wid. Mary and ch. were benef. under will of Mrs. Ann Batchelder(1), 1660. She m. 2d bef. 26 June 1666 John Amazeen. Lists 330a(2)b. Ch: **Mary,** ±25 in June 1681, m. Joseph Muzeet. **Thomas,** willed his gr.fa.'s dwg. ho. and to have learning at school. Taken suddenly by death, adm. 25 June 1678 to John Amazeen as gdn. of the br. **Jeremiah** who was of age 1 Mar. 1680. **Martha,** m. John Moore(10).

3 **JEREMIAH**(2), Newcastle, taxed in July 1690, constable 1691, j. 1695, gr.j. 1696. Lists 315a(3)bc(2), 316, 319, 336c, 52, 60, 66. He m., prob. not 1st, betw. 1704-1714 Elizabeth (Stover 5) Hunnewell. His pet. in Sept. 1731 stated that being very aged, he intended to make a deed in the nature of a will to James Stevens(9) who defrauded him in the wording of the deed; the legislature found it fraudulent. No ch. Will, 13 Jan.— 2 May 1733, names only w. Elizabeth who m. 3d Capt. John Downing(2).

4 **THOMAS,** blacksmith, see Gorges(9), the earliest and sole inhab. of Charlestown, being there when the Spragues and others arrived in 1629. He did not find favor with new comers, or they with him, and was fined 40 s., 3 May 1631, for contempt of authority, and ord. to leave the jurisd. with his w. bef. 20 Oct. In Sept. 1633 his goods were sequestered to pay the debts he owed in the Bay. He remov. to Portsm. (Great Isl.) as old friends test., incl. Henry Langstaff who depos. in 1683 that T. W. liv. and planted on Great Isl. over 50 yrs. ago, and also built at

Sandy Beach in Capt. Neal's time, without disturbance from Neal. Mrs. Mary Johnson depos. that he liv. on Little Harbor side when she and her husb. came over, afterw. at Sagamore Creek, his s. Jeremiah living on his Great Isl. land. Gr.j. 1650, 1652, 1655, 1659, 1660; selectman 1655, 1658, but for yrs. trouble fol. them in N. H. thru contests over land and charges of witchcraft ag. his w. Jane. Lists 321-324, 326a, 330abc, 43, 47, 312c. By Oct. 1649 he had given land to his dau. Jones and to his son. Will, senior, 15—21 Nov. 1666, names w. Jane, ch., many gr.ch. Wid. Jane depos. 27 June 1667, ag. ±69; liv. 1671, d. bef. 7 Sept. 1681. See also Glanfield (2), Reed(5), Trimmings; N. H. State Papers, i: 217-9; Reg. 43: 181-3. Ch: **Jeremiah, Jane,** m. 1st Thomas Peverly(2), m. 2d Richard Goss(1). **Hannah,** m. Alexander Jones (2). **Elizabeth,** m. Henry Savage(3). **Mary,** ag. 32 in 1667, ±46 in 1680, ±72 in 1702, m. 1st William Brookings(5), m. 2d William Walker(17). **Martha,** ag. 22 in 1667, m. 1st Thomas Hinkson(7), m. 2d John Westbrook (1).

**WALKER,** became 46th commonest name in N. E. An Elizabethan statute ment. a 'Clothe-Fuller otherwise called Tucker or Walker.'

1 **BENJAMIN,** Mr., Boston, entered claim for the Falm. prop. Rev. George Burroughs exch. with Henry Harwood, who sold to Bozoan Allen, he to claimant in 1687.

2 **CAPT. \*GEORGE**(7), Portsmouth, son and heir, m. 1st 25 Dec. 1689 Mary Jackson(14), List 335a, who d. 1 June 1734, ag. 62; m. 2d by 1736 Abigail (Vaughan 4) Shannon. O. A. 28 Aug. 1685; constable 1692; j. 1694, 1697; gr.j. 1699; selectman often 1698-1733; Rep. 1727, 1728. Called farmer in 1705 when gr. adm. on bro.'s est., baker 1713 and later; Capt. 1720. Prov. gr. at Scarb. 1720. Lists 324(2), 330cd, 332b, 335a, 316, 339(2), 52, 57, 61. See also Moses (1). He d. 7 Dec. 1748, ag. 86 (Atkinson platter). Will, gent., 18 Aug. 1740, gives to w. Abigail (ag. ±70 in 1758); to Joseph Banfield and cous. Ichabod Cheney and Hannah (Cheney) Spofford, £50 each; neph. Walker Lear, chief heir, he to pay his mo. Mrs. Elizabeth Lear £100. He owned a good many negroes; see Reg. 81: 436, 452. Walker Lear was not in the good graces of the wid. who was quoted as saying that he could thank his uncle for what he received, she would not have given him one groat. Her will, 1756—1762, names Shannons only.

3 **ISAAC,** Mr., Boston merchant, much in Me. from Kit. to Sheepscot, first noted as a York wit. in 1650 and 1652. He bot Long Isl. in Casco Bay from John Sears in 1655, bot from Francis Small in 1658, and took a mortg. on Foxwell land at Blue Point in 1668. Agent for Mr. Thomas Elbridge in 1667 when sued by Mr. Foxwell in Casco ct. List 221. See also Mighill(2), Mitchell(15), Phillips(19), Rice(2), and Me. P. & Ct. Rec., vols. i, ii. Will, of Boston, 1672—1674; ch: **Isaac, Nicholas, Stephen, Susanna** Stanbury; -nevew- Thomas Stanbury, jr.; York and Sheepscot lands to w. Susanna for life; br. Nicholas Cowlings. Inv. incl. 'debts due to the Eastward.'

4 **JOHN,** s. of Richard of Ipsw., m. Lydia Colburn (Edward) and liv. many yrs. at Chelmsford and Ipsw. Appar. it was he, and not his s. John, at Newington 1723 and liv. there in the ho. with Benj. Patch in 1727, when he had 7 cows and oxen. Ch. rec. Chelmsford 1686-1706: **John,** said to have liv. at Dracut. **Edward,** Berwick, Newington, m. in Berw. 6 Sept. 1710 Deliverance Gaskin (John). **Andrew,** Berwick, m. 18 Dec. 1718 Mary Grant(7). **Lydia,** m. in Ipswich 27 Mar. 1718 Benjamin Patch. **Hannah. Joseph.** One J. m. Abigail Place(3) in Newingt. 11 Dec. 1723; one m. Martha Greenough in Ipsw. in 1724. **Sarah,** m. William Waterhouse(3). **Richard,** Berwick, m. (ct. Apr. 1728) Martha Smith, and, of Wells, m. 2d Sarah Gypson of Berw., int. 1739. **Elizabeth,** m. William Holden (see 2). Note also mar. of James Place and Mary W., both of Newingt., 9 Nov. 1727.

5 **JOHN,** glover, Portsmouth, Newington, b. 13 May 1667, s. of John of Charlestown, was 'now out of the country' in 1690 when Mary Phipps of C., sis. of (5), had a ct. case ag. him there. Taxed Portsm. Oct. 1691, deposed in May 1693, ±25, bot from Richard Jose 1695. Dep. sheriff 1695 and long after, altho once of Casco Bay, his pet. 23 Feb. 1704-5 reciting that a few yrs. bef. he built a ho. near the first fort, which was taken as a hospital when Col. Romer enlarged the fort. In 1711 he protested ag. having no share in Portsm. commons altho 'here near 22 years.' Tax abated 1713, gone out of town; but called of P. in 1715. Of Newingt. in Jan. 1715-6 he adm. fa.'s Charlest. est. Conditional Scarb. gr. 1720, which he sold in May 1727, then 'late of N., now of P.' Last seen in 1734, of Portsm., when he sued Joshua Downing(2). Lists 315b, 335a, 336c. W. Elizabeth 1700-1727 at least. No cert. count of ch., but credited to him: **John,** shipwright, Kit., prob. apprent. to Elihu Gunnison(1), whose dau. Elizabeth he m. 24 Jan. 1714-5 (1 ch. d.y.). He m. 2d in Newingt. 24 Oct. 1717 Mary Bickford(5). Will, 13 May—19 July 1743 (d. 3 June -1745- in 51st yr., gr.st.), names w. Mary, 4 of their 8 ch. She m. 2d Zacheus Trafton. **William,** shipwright, Kit., m. 1st 16 Jan. 1723-4 Deborah Berry (George 5), m. 2d by 1742 Mehitabel Fabyan

(3); ch. **Gideon, m.** in Portsm. 21 Oct. 1721 Lucy Weymouth (see 6), taxed there 1732. Her will, 1766—1766, names ch: Joseph, Elizabeth, Katherine Stavers. **Joshua,** Arundel 1722, had wives Hannah and Mary. Will, 1767—1768, names wife, 8 ch. **Samuel,** m. 4 Oct. 1724 Anna Bickford(15) who o.c. at Newingt. and had dau. Bridget bp. 1 Aug. 1725; a wid. in 1731. **Anna,** bp. at Portsm. 1709, m. there 31 July 1727 Moses Furber of Newingt. Note also the two Place marriages under (4).

6 **JOHN** (Jun.?) 1689, List 125.

7 **JOSEPH,** Portsmouth, granted 1 a. and rec. inhab. as a newcomer 22 Jan. 1660-1, tho he subscr. for the minister in Feb. 1658-9. He m. 1st Elizabeth Moses(2) bef. 1 Mar. 1664-5 when her fa. deeded to him; in 1669 he and br.-in-law Thomas Creber(2) had a suit in York ct. ag. Philip Lewis who was given costs. His 2d w. was Hannah Philbrick(3). Gr. of 13 a. in 1671. Gr.j. 1671. Lists 323, 326ac, 330ab, 356L (Portsm.), 312c, 313a, 331bc, 49, 52. See also Huff(1), Hunt(6). Inv. 7 Nov. 1683; adm. 10 Dec. to wid. Hannah and s. George. She m. 2d, 29 July 1686, John Seavey(3). Kn. ch: **George,** b. 1662 (age at death). **Joseph,** a lad apprenticed to John Endicott, Boston cooper, in Apr. 1679, when Rev. Joshua Moody wrote to Rev. Increase Mather asking him to bp. the boy, saying 'His fa. Joseph W. has lately joined our Ch. and the rest of his ch. bp. with us.' **Samuel.** Adm. gr. to br. George 8 Jan. 1704-5 on est. 'lying and being in said Prov. or elsewhere,' he being 'form. of said Prov., dec.' Cert. by 2d w: **Mary,** m. at Newb. 31 Dec. 1707 Eldad Cheney. Her mo. d. at their home in Bradford 27 Oct. 1738. See also will of (2). **Elizabeth,** b. ±1680, m. Tobias Lear (3).

8 **OBADIAH,** Boston, partn. of Edw. Naylor in the purch. of 1000 a. at the Eastward and later bot from Naylor. His wid. Sarah (Haugh) m. in Boston 26 Feb. 1677-8 Capt. Ephraim Savage (gr.s. of Wm. Hutchinson 11), who claimed the 1000 a. bounded east by the Kennebec, west by Thomas Stevens' land. See also Hornabrook; Reg. 67: 206. Only surv. ch. **Samuel,** bp. in Boston 19 Dec. 1675, made a will when 18 yrs. old (copy, no date, no probate, in SJC 139152), naming three Savage sis. and other relatives, tho a probate rec. names his heirs-at-law as Richard and Nathaniel W., sons of Shubael, late of Bradford.

9 **ROBERT,** mariner, Portsmouth. See Broughton(2), James(6). His wid. Abigail, List 339.

10 **SAMUEL,** Exeter, signed the comb. and shared in the 1640 division. On committee to distrib. corn to the needy in 1643. O. F. at Piscataqua ct. 1644. Lists 373, 374a, 376a, 43.

11 **SAMUEL,** Woburn. See Alger(4). (?List 238a).

12 **CAPT. SAMUEL,** merchant, mariner, Boston, Scarb., m. Sarah Scottow bef. 24 Sept. 1672 when her fa. deeded him Boston property. One S. was a Scarb. soldier in Jan. 1675-6, List 237b. As Mr. S. W. of Boston he was bef. Wells ct. in May 1684 for Sunday travel, Wells to Saco; as Capt. S. W. of Scarb. lic. out of doors in 1686 and bondsm. for Benj. Blackman, with whom he and Sampson Sheafe had built a mill on Saco Falls; he bot Sheafe's third in Mar. 1687. In Sept. 1687 he wanted to cure fish on Stratton Isl. where he had built a ho. and made a stage. Referee betw. Blackman and Capt. Turfrey in 1688; he and B. petitioned Andros from Boston 1688. After 1690 he mov. to E. Jersey, and was late of Boston in 1699, when he sued Mrs. Mary Hunnewell(1). Lists 236, 238(?a)b. Ch. rec. Boston 1679-1690: **Sarah, Mercy, Samuel, William, Mary, Elizabeth, Susannah.** The s. Samuel of E. Jersey filed admr.'s bond in Boston 16 July 1708; inv. incl. land on Scottow's oblong and Scottow's Creek. See Y. D. 8: 185-6, 220, 258.

13 **SAMUEL,** Sagadahoc soldier Jan. 1689-90, List 18. Note also the Scarb. soldier 1675-6, List 237b.

14 **SARAH.** See (17).

15 **THOMAS,** Newcastle, d. 15 Mar. 1707-8. List 334a.

16 **WILLIAM** (Walker?), sued by (3) in York ct. 1653 for debt of £46. One Wm. wit. Richard Bulgar's assignment to Henry Wanton in 1646 (Y. D. 1: 33), perh. not Maine.

17 **WILLIAM,** Portsmouth, m. 1st by 1670 one Alice, evid. both working for Mr. Richard Cutts (see White 1); m. 2d ±1698 Mary (Walford 2) Brookings(5). Taxed 1673. Lists 326c, 328, 329, 331ab, 335a, 337, 52. Wife Alice, Lists 328, 335a. See also Champernowne(2), Lewis(18), Pomery(8). His w. Mary depos. in June 1702, ±72, abt. the Cate fam. 47 yrs. bef. He had been here more than 45 yrs. in 1711. Both liv. 16 Feb. 1719-20 when, in consid. of life supp. for both and also £100, he deeded to John Lang(4) 'land I formerly (in 1678) bot of Wm. Brookins dec.' No ch. appear unless poss. **Sarah** who m. 22 Sept. 1689 Jeremiah Holmes(2).

**WALL.** One James Wall m. a certain Johanne at Dartmouth St. Saviour's, co. Devon, 1 Nov. 1627.

1 **JAMES,** carpenter, millwright, Exeter, Hampton, came with Wm. Chadbourne (4) and John Goddard(3) under a 3-yr. contract with Capt. Mason dated 14 Mar. 1633-4. In 1652 he depos. that Mr. Jocelyn, Mr.

M.'s agent, brot them to cert. lands at Ashenbedick Falls, where they ran a sawmill and a stamping mill for corn 3 or 4 yrs., that he built a ho. there, and Chadbourne did also. Signed Exeter comb. 1639; Com.t.e.s.c. 1645, 1646; selectman 1647, 1649, tho taxed in 1649 at Dover where he had bot a mill and rights at Cochecho Falls in 1647. Tr.j. 1649, gr.j. 1651. He mov. to Hampt., but was called of Ex. in 1653. In 1654 he was closing up his affairs, sold mill prop. and cattle, and deeded his farm at Hampt. to two daus., their mo. dead. Of Ex. in Sept. 1658, he sold 'my now dwg.ho. in Ex.' to Nicho. Smith and agreed to groundsill it by 29 Sept. 1659. Lists 41, 373, 375a(2)b, 376ab, 377, 354b. See also Colcord(1); Essex Q. Ct. Rec., vol. i, for various suits. His 1st w., named with Rev. George Burdett, was prob. the w. Margaret liv. in 1647, dead bef. 18 July 1654. He m. 2d Mary (Philbrick 7) Tuck, named in his will, of Hampt., 20 Sept. (d. 3 Oct.) 1659, with his 4 daus.; Henry Robie trustee for the 1st w.'s ch. His wid. was a midwife in 1671, Lists 394, 52, and d. in Oct. 1702, adm. to s. John Tuck. Her ch. (1 Tuck, 2 Walls) made an agreement 12 Feb. 1702-3. Ch. by 1st w: **Elizabeth**, m. Thomas Harvey(14). **Sarah**, m. 1st Thomas Dew(4), m. 2d John Baker (3). By 2d w: **Mary**, b. Hampt. 8 Jan. 1655-6, m. Sergt. John Marston(6), d. 12 Dec. 1708. **Hannah**, b. 17 Mar. 1658-9, m. Benjamin Moulton(1).

2 **JOHN**, Portsmouth. Lists 41, 321.

3 **MARY**. See Amos, Bartlett(1), Morse(9), Watts(4), Wincoll(2).

**WALLEN**. 1 Capt. **John** (or Walwin), Pemaquid wit. 1686. List 97.

2 **THOMAS**, with the eloping party from Winter Harbor 1651; see Warner. Kittery wit. 1666. Anne wit. at Kit. ±1665.

**WALLEY**. 1 **John, Mr.**, List 225a.

2 **THOMAS**, Dover, List 365.

**WALLINGFORD, John**, b. in Newbury 7 Apr. 1659, s. of Nicholas and Sarah (Travers), m. 6 Dec. 1687 Mary Tuttle(2). His fa. was neph. of Wm. Gore or Goore, gent., of Nether Wallop, co. Hants; see Waters' 'Gleanings' i: 146-7, and assignment of £40 each, as legacies from gt.-uncle, given by John and his br. and sis. to Wm. Longfellow in 1686 (N. H. Probate, i: 308). He was liv. in 1705, she in 1717, neither named in s. Ebenezer's will. Ch. b. at Bradford: **John**, b. 14 Dec. 1688, had w. Charity. He depos. in June 1750 that he was b. at Bradford, mov. to Newingt. ±40 yrs. ago, to Somersworth ±7 yrs. ago, and to Rochester ±4 yrs. ago. Will 1761—1762. 10 ch. **Nicholas**, b. 28 Oct. (or Nov.) 1691, liv. in Dover where John Hill's 50 a. gr. was laid out to him in 1715. See also Starbird. Wid. Rachel m. 2d in 1719 Stephen Hawkins(8). Dau. Margaret, b. 4 Apr. 1714. **Sarah**, b. 29 Dec. 1693, m. James Clements(4). **Ebenezer**, b. 30 Sept. 1695. Will, of Dover, 19 Aug.—6 Sept. 1721, gives wearing apparel to bros. John and Thomas W. and James Clements, all else to beloved spouse (betrothed) and friend Susannah Cotton(2). Col. and Hon. *****Thomas**, Somersworth, b. 28 July 1698, m. 1st Margaret Clements(4), m. 2d bef. 21 July 1730 Mary Pray (Joseph 1), m. 3d aft. 1751 Elizabeth (Swett) Prime of York, d. at Capt. Stoodley's in Portsm. 4 Aug. 1771. Selectman, moderator, Rep., Judge Sup. Ct. Judicature. List 298. 6 + 5 + 2 ch. See Clement Gen. i: 98. **Judith**, b. Mar. 1699-1700. **Abigail**, b. 27 Sept. 1702.

**WALLIS.** Wallace in Scotland and north of Eng., Wallis elsewhere. See also Carkeet(3), Creber, Tenney(1), Waddock.

1 **GEORGE, Mr.**, Portsmouth, 'gent.' in 1656 when he bot from Samuel Bennett of Rumney Marsh his dwg.-ho. called Rumly Hall which he conv. back to B. aft. litigation. Sometime of Newfoundland, he bot at Little Harbor from James Johnson in 1660, in div. of 1661 he and Johnson together had 112 a. Gr.j. 1669, 1672, 1684. Bail for Walter Randall 1677. Ag. ±60 in 1679. Lists 311b, 312ch, 313a, 323, 326bc, 330ab, 331ab, 49, 52, 55b. He d. 14 Dec. 1685; adm. 2 Jan. fol. to wid. Eleanor, her bondsm. Robert Elliot. Settlement was made on s. **George**, evid. the second s., with consent of wid. and other ch: **William**. **Honor**, may have m. James Allard (2). **Caleb**. **Daughter**, w. of Walter Randall (17); one Margaret Woollis wit. with Elias Stileman in 1678. Daughter (**Eleanor**), w. of James Berry(5). In Greenland tax list, Dec. 1688, one line 'James Allerd Widow Wallis.' She was also taxed in July 1690. List 307b.

2 **GEORGE**(1), Little Harbor, m. 18 Nov. 1686 Ann Shortridge(1) who was liv. in Apr. 1726. Jury 1695; gr.j. 1693, 1696. Constable 1698. Lists 315a(2)c, 316, 57. Adm. 8 Jan. 1724-5 to s.-in-law Nathl. Berry. Ch., all the daus. mar. by 1726: **Caleb**, only s., an 'idiot.' **Ann**, m. Abraham Barnes(12). **Mary**, m. Benjamin Seavey, Jr.(1). **Esther**, m. Nathaniel Berry(13). **Deborah**, m. Christopher Scadgel. **Hannah**, m. Edward Randall (see 2).

3 **JOHN**, Falmouth, Purpooduck, fisherman. He wit. Cleeve to Phippen, 30 Oct. 1650; Y. D. 21: 22, has deed from C. to him 27 Oct. 1650, 100 a. next Michael Mitton's, but neither he nor (6), who is consid. a br., is seen again for sevrl. yrs. In 1667 he bot the Nicho. White planta. at Purpooduck. Robert Jordan succ. sued him for tresp. in 1659; he was given costs in ano. suit brot by Jordan in 1664. On joint bond with Joseph Phippen and Thomas Stanford 1661; he and

T. S. were Phippen's bondsm. 1663. Selectman 1674, 1680. A refugee in Salem and Glouc. in the 1st war; in the next he retired to Glouc. and d. 13 Sept. 1690. Wid. Mary and s. Josiah, with David Phippen (?her br.) as surety, gave bond 29 Mar. 1691. Lists 212, 221, 222a, 223a, 225a, 228c, 232, 25, 27, 30. 34, 85. See also Maddiver(2), Norman (2). In 1724 the heirs made a div., but leaving House Isl. and 3 or 4 a. called Purpooduck Point in common (Y. D. 11: 209-211). Ch: **Josiah**, ag. 67 in Oct. 1730. **Dorcas**, m. John Lane(5). **James**, weaver, Glouc., m. Martha Stanford(2). This fam. evid. escaped in the 1703 attack, altho he then had a ho. on Spring Point, as did his bros. Benjamin and Joseph. He depos. often ab. early Falm. Aged 62 in Oct. 1730, ±63 in May 1733, near 70 in Apr. 1736, liv. in June 1737. List 228c. See also Y. D. 14: 41. 7 ch. rec. at Beverly and Glouc. 1693-1711. **Daughter**, m. Matthew Paulling. **Benjamin**, m. 1st 23 Mar. 1695-6 Elizabeth Morgan of Bev. who was k. at Purpooduck with three ch. in Aug. 1703 (List 39); m. 2d 26 Dec. 1704 Sarah Sallows in Bev. where ch. Samuel and Elizabeth b. 1708-1711. In 1755 Andrew and Elizabeth Ellingham q.c. estates of her fa. Benjamin, uncle Joseph and aunt **Susannah** who was liv. unm. in 1724. **Elizabeth**, b. Glouc. 12 Sept. 1678, m. (int. Bev. 11 Aug. 1700) Joseph Morgan(4). **Rebecca**, m. 1st at Bev. 23 Feb. 1703-4 John Graves and as R. Groves m. there 2d (int. 4 Sept. 1708) Joseph Foster. **Joseph** (List 228c), m. in Bev. 13 Jan. 1701-2 Elizabeth Black who was reported k. in 1703 (List 39), but was in Canada 1711 (List 99, p. 91) and redeemed by July 1716 when her fa. deeded them land in Bev., partly in consid. of the great charge her husb. had lately been at to redeem her.

4 **JOHN**, Shoals 1671, drank excessively. John -Wallis- (?Wells) took O. F. at Wells in July 1670 (Me. P. & Ct. Rec. ii: 194).

5 **JOSIAH**(3), eldest son, shoreman, went to Beverly during 2d war, then to Glouc., and ret. to Purpooduck where his w. Mary (Stanford 2) and **three ch.** were reported k. in 1703 (List 39). On 19 Dec. 1706 he m. a 2d w. Sarah in Glouc., where he contin. to live. Lists 85, 228c. He deposed often (see Y. D. 14: 41); ag. ±66 in 1727, 67 in Oct. 1730, ±72 in 1734 when he depos. that his earliest memory was of Falm.; near 80 in Aug. 1739. Will, 31 Dec. 1739 (d. Glouc. 7 Feb. 1740-1, ag. 70 or 'uperward'), names w. Sarah, 3 ch., and ch. of deced. dau. Mary. Kn. ch: **Mary**, dau. of Josiah and -Elizabeth-, bp. at Bev. 25 Feb. 1693-4, m. Paul Dolliver. **Sarah**, bp. with Mary, m. in Glouc. 2 Feb. 1715-6 Jacob Sawyer who settl. in Falm. —**hm**, son, b. at Glouc. 23 Aug. 1696,

poss. was **John** who m. in Glouc. 8 Jan. 1719 Patience Hodgkins and settled in Falm. (of Glouc. 1733; Y. D. 18: 84). Of Falm., in May 1751, and again in Feb. 1770, ±68, he depos. ab. the fam. history, the fate of his mo. and others, and his own escape from the Ind. **Susannah**, b. at Glouc. 25 Aug. 1699, prob. k. with mo. By 2d w: **Josiah**. **Samuel** (fa.'s exec.)

6 **NATHANIEL**, shoreman, Falmouth, No. Yarm. (see 3), here by July 1657 (Y. D. 1: 83), bot the Thomas Wise planta. at Martin's Point in 1660 and at No. Yarm. from the Brays and John Cousins in 1672. Ag. ±52 in July 1683, and b. in co. Cornwall, Gt. Brit., by his death rec. Constable 1658; gr.j. 1658, 1670, 1671; tr.j. 1666, 1667; fined for non-appear. 1665. He had suits ag. Lawrence Davis (trespass) and Edw. Pike (for pork) in 1666-7; appr. the Skilling est. 1667; on commit. to lay out a Scarb. highway 1669. Lists 212, 214, 221, 222acd, 225a, 232, 25, 30, 34. See also Brown(23), Gale(1), Lewis(4), Rand(5), Doc. Hist. vi: 454-5. In both wars he retreated to Beverly and d. there 18 Oct. 1709, ±77. His will gave Me. lands to sons Caleb and Joshua and gr.sons John and Nathaniel. Wid. Margaret d. in Bev. 14 May 1711, ±84. One Margaret wit. Jane Waddock to Scammon in 1679 (Y. D. 3: 103). Ch: **John**, mar. Bridget Shepard(4), List 214. Both were fined in Mar.1674, the rec. indicating he was blind; ano. rec. of him, ag.22 in 1678 (Essex Q. Ct. Rec. 7: 74) indicates he was not blind. Dead in 1720. 8 ch. rec. Salem 1675-1693. See also Y. D. 10: 193; 14: 166. **Bartholomew**, d. in Bev. 17 Jan. 1676, ag. 19; List 223b. **Caleb**, m. 12 Dec. 1687 Sarah Stone in Bev. where 9 ch. rec. or bp. **Joshua**, m. 1 June 1691 Abial Conant in Bev. where a dau. Mary was b. in 1694. A cordwainer of New Sherborn in 1734 when his s. Caleb, mariner of Salem, deeded land as his atty. See Y. D. 17: 89; 18: 41. **Nathaniel**, m. Anna Rich, int. 21 Mar. 1698 at Bev. where 5 ch. rec. **Mary**, m. Ensign Samuel Pike(11).

7 **PETER**, Shoals, fined in 1653 for swearing, in 1661 drunk and fighting. In 1660 Henry Sherburne sued him for keeping his boat at his landing. Of Smuttynose, he bot on Hog Isl. in 1670. Lists 307b, 327a.

8 **WILLIAM**(1), Little Harbor, m. 15 Dec. 1673 Jane Drake(5). In 1676, ag. ±28, he worked in the woods with Henry Seavey; Mr. Stileman had told them to fell his bound tree. Constable 1694, 1695, 1697; assessor 1695, 1696; examiner 1698. Lists 313a, 315a (2)b, 316(& son), 318c, 332b, 52, 57. In 1723 he deeded his est. to his s. Samuel who was to pay **Jane**, w. of Stephen Lang(7), and **Sarah**, w. of Joshua Foss(3). The s. **Samuel**, m. Hannah Seavey(8) who was liv. in 1732.

His will, 1 June—26 Aug. 1741, names 4 sons, 2 daus., no wife, yet in 1746 his wid. Deborah (Jordan 4), then w. of Henry Trefethen, brot suit for dower ag. the s. and exec. Samuel. Appar. a s. **William**, Greenland, jr. in 1715, w. Martha by 1717, liv. 1762. Ch. bp: Jean, 1716 (m. Mark Moses 1), two Nathaniels, Martha and William, 1723-1729.

**WALTER**, Walters. See also Waters.

1 **HENRY** (Walters), Mr., wit. seisin to Mr. Richard Wharton at Pejepscot Fort, 1684.

2 **JOHN** (Walter, -s), Portsmouth, wit. with Richard Stileman 1669-1670, sued John Bickford for nursing his ch. in 1670. Portsmouth town item 4 Dec. 1671: Expense on the body of John -Waters-. Adm. on the est. of one John Walter, sometime of Monhegan, sometime of Damerell's Cove, dead ±4 yrs., was gr. at the Eastward to George Burnett in 1674, List 15. But see Waters(2, 7).

3 **JOHN**, Falmouth, List 225a. Wallis?

4 **LAWRENCE**, List 75b. Waters?

5 **THOMAS**, mariner, Falmouth, at Salem in 1679, husb. of Hannah Gray, step-dau. of Capt. Nicholas Manning(8). Settler under Danforth at Falm., where in 1683 he and John Edwards(4) bot 100 a. from Richard Seacomb and 12 a. from Leonard Slew. Lists 225a, 229. In the war he went to Salem, then to Charlest. where w. Hannah joined the Ch. 1692. In 1696 bef. York ct. for loading his sloop on Sunday; see also Gooch(3). Of Charlest. 1700 when he and Edwards div. the Falm. land (Y. D. 12: 320, 363); both later ent. an East. Claim. Sold in Charlest. 1704. Of Boston in 1723, he depos. ab. Mr. John Bean, a Boston merch., hiring his sloop in 1716 to go to Arrowsic. Will, of Boston, 25 June—6 July 1724, names w. Hannah, s. William (land at Casco Bay), gr.sons Herbert, Wm. and John Walter. In Mar. 1732-3 wid. Hannah of Boston, ±75, depos. ab. Falm. (Y. D. 15: 250). Adm. on her est. to s. Wm. 31 Oct. 1734. Ch. bp. at Salem 10 Nov. 1689: **Elizabeth. Thomas. Welthean**, m. in 1701 Jeremiah Snow of Charlest., d. 11 Apr. 1704, ag. 20 yrs. 8 mos. **William**, mariner, Boston, apprent. of Thomas Rand of Charlestown 1693, York wit. 1714, m. 1st at Reading 8 Jan. 1701-2 Sarah Herbert (s. Herbert, b. 21 Sept. 1702, m. 2d Mary Harris 11; see also Jones 4). One or more wives succ. Sarah; his ch. by 2d w. (Loise Adams, m. in 1705) incl. Welthean, Abigail, Wm., John. See also (2), Y. D. 15: 207.

6 **WILLIAM**, List 15, see Waters.

**WALTON**, usually from north of England.

1 **GEORGE**, Great Island, tailor, vintner and inn-keeper, ±70 in 1685, first fqund in Boston ct. for swearing 4 Dec. 1638, but in Exeter in time to sign the combination 5 June 1639. Had inn-lic. in Dover 1647 and moved down to Gt. Isl. by 1649 where he bot Mosquito Neck from John Heard. His title was supplemented by a deed from Richard Tucker 1664, but he had to defend it 1669. Mtg. all his real-est., incl. two houses, inn, warehouse and wharves, to Henry Robie in 1662. Gr.j. 1659. Town gr. 1652. See Jones (2). Lists 52, 77b, 311ab, 312c, 313a, 323, 325, 326a, 330ab, 331b, 352, 354a, 373. He and w. Alice, 'one of the most godly women thereabouts' and poss. related to the Hiltons or the Waldrons, were convicted as Quakers 1663-4. In 1680 he deeded the bulk of his prop. to s. Shadrach. The 'stone-throwing devil' case, a local sensation, had its setting in his inn in 1682. See 'Ancestry of Lydia Harmon,' by W. G. Davis. Will, 14 Feb.— 9 Mar. 1685-6, names w. Alice exec. and gives legacies to gr.ch. Ch: **Abishag**, m. Robert Taprill. **Martha**, m. Edward West(1). List 330b. **Dorcas**, m. Samuel Treworgy(6). **Mary**, ±32 in 1678, m. Samuel Robie(4). **George**, 22 in 1671, ship-master, d. bef. 14 Aug. 1679 when his wid. Mary m. Samuel Rand(5). Only kn. ch: Samuel, in gr.fa.'s will. Lists 313ad, 331b. A ch., drowned 5 May 1657. **Shadrach**, b. ab. 1658.

2 *****GEORGE**(5), Esq., kept the inn in Newcastle in 1706, moved to Newington by 1715-6. Took bankrupt's oath 1717. Newcastle town clerk 1704, Newington town clerk 1717 and later, Rep. 1730—1741-2, J. P. 1745-6. Deeded the Newcastle est. to s. George in 1756. He d. 13 Dec. 1769 in 89th yr. List 316. Will, 24 Sept. 1764—28 Mar. 1770, names w. Frances Allen(13) and all the ch: **John**, had the Newington lands. **Samuel**, Somersworth, shopkeeper, m. 25 May 1727 Elizabeth Pray(1). Will, 25 Oct. 1753—30 Jan. 1754. 9 ch. **George**, Portsmouth, shopkeeper, sold the Newcastle est. to Thomas Bell 21 Mar. 1766. His slaves, Sabina and Sylvia, bp. 1741-2. He m. wid. Temperance (Bickford) Underwood. Would seem to have been the G. W., ag. 78, confined to bed in Portsm. alms-ho. bef. 1781, and his w. the Mrs. W. who d. in Kittery in her 93d yr. (newspaper of 16 Dec. 1786). **Shadrach**, Durham, joiner. **Frances**, bp. Newington 22 Jan. 1715-6; d. bef. her fa. **Elizabeth**, m. 27 Oct. 1734 William Hoit of Berwick.

3 **HENRY**, soldier at Pemaquid 1689. List 126.

4 **JOHN**, Damariscove. List 8.

5 **COL.** ‡**SHADRACH**(1), Newcastle, 20 in 1677, 83 in 1741, carried on his fa.'s tavern and business interests, but is notable for his military career. Ensign 1691, Capt. at Fort Wm. and Mary bef. 1694, Maj. at Port Royal in 1707 and Col. of the N. H. Forces there at its fall in 1710. Commander of New Eng. forces

in eastern Me. from 1720 until his resignation in Jan. 1722-3 after heated controversy in the Mass. House in which he was supported by the Gov. and Council. Selectman (Portsm.) 1688-1692; Judge of Ct. of Com. Pleas 1695-1698, 1716-1737; Judge of Supreme Ct. 1698-1699; Councillor 1716-1733 and Pres. of Council in the latter yr. Lists 52, 55b, 57, 58, 65, 66, 315abc, 316, 319, 324 (2). He m. Mary Nutter(1) who was taxed as Madam W. in 1752. He d. 3 Oct. 1741. Will, 5 Dec. 1737—28 July 1742. Ch., order unkn: **Shadrach**, d. bef. 1737, s.p. **George. Elizabeth**, m. Henry Keyes(3), d. Portsm. 9 Sept. 1769 in 83d yr. **Abigail**, m. Pierse Long, Esq., wealthy merchant of Irish birth, delegate to Continental Congress and Constitutional Convention; parents of Mary, w. of Col. Tobias Lear. **Sarah**, m. Sampson Sheafe(3 jr.). **Mary**, m. (Jacob?) Randall (4 jr.). **Benjamin**, H. C. 1729, Portsm. Latin School master, m. Mary Jackson (Joseph 20) who m. 2d after 1742 Mark Nelson(2). 4 ch.

**Walwin**, see Wallen.

**WANNERTON**, Capt. **Thomas**, gent., Str. Bank, here in 1633 in charge of Gorges' and Mason's ho. at Piscataqua, and later traded along the coast, wherever drink was easily got, Judge Savage said. In 1635 when trying to collect Henry Way's debt from John Holland(3), he expressed an opinion of the Bay rogues. Sued by Mr. Abraham Shurt in 1637 and sued Robert Purington in 1641. Named comr. at Piscataqua by Mass. in 1641; assistant to the magistrates 1642, and commis. to seize powder from those trading with the Ind. Lists 41(2), 84, 323. See also Goddard(3), Knight(18), Lewis(12), Matthews(5). He was k. in the summer of 1644 leading an attack of La Tour's forces against D'Aubnay's Penobscot farm, and the several mortgagees instituted litigation over his property (See Suff. D. i: 52; Mass. Col. Rec. i: 150, 168, 231). In 1643 he had been fined at Str. Bk. for striking his w. (Ann) with a stool. She m. 2d Thomas Williams(33) and was liv. 1671 when they brot a suit for dower ag. Richard Cutts.

**WANTON**, **Edward**, York, in Nov. 1651 bot land on Cape Neddick River he was then clearing and sold it in Nov. 1657 to br.-in-law John Smith who had been in poss. several yrs. By trad. he came from London with his mo. at age of 19. Lists 273, 275, 276. A Boston shipwright 1658; resident in Scituate 1661 (Deane), altho ch. were rec. at Boston 1658-1664. A Quaker at Scituate. There he depos. in Apr. 1716, ag. 84, that ±64 yrs. ago he dwelt at Wells and that John Smith took divers of his cattle to keep at halves. He d. 17 Oct. 1716 in 85th yr.; will. Through ch. by wives Elizabeth and Mary rec. at Boston and Scit. 1658-1686, he was ancestor of

many leading R. I. merchants and governors, his ch. incl., by w. Elizabeth: Gov. **William** of R. I., b. 1670, and Gov. **John** of R. I., b. 1672, who m. Mary Stover(5), altho he forbade the ints. pub. at Boston 15 Nov. 1695. Ano. s. **Michael** (by w. Mary), b. 1679, one of Scit., was one of the execs. named in will of Mrs. Elizabeth Stover(5). See also Hist. of York ii: 27 (which says he had a kinsman in Saco), Deane's Scituate, and Arnold's Gen. Dict. of R. I.

**WARD**, from a ward or keeper. General in Eng. except in extreme north and a few southern counties.

1 **EDMUND**, Scarb. propr. and proprs.' clerk 1720. List 239b. Ipswich 1722 (Y. D. 11: 264). In 1734, of Scarb., he depos. that in 1717 he and the Seaveys built a ho. at Dunstan for John Milliken.

2 **ELEAZER**, a Wells soldier 1693-4 credited to Cambridge. List 267b. One E. was a Berw. wit. 1710, taxed there 1713, but not in 1719. In York ct. for swearing 1714.

3 **REV. JOHN**, minister at Agamenticus and s. of Rev. Nathaniel of Ipswich. Called to the Maine settlement by Dec. 1640, he and two companions, Rev. Mr. Peters and Rev. Mr. Dalton, on way there from Piscataqua in Apr. 1641, were lost two days and a night in the woods. Col. Banks says he had left by Mar. 1642 (see Hist. of York ii: 119). Long minister at Haverh., where he and w. Alice (Edmunds) had daus: **Elizabeth**, b. 1647, m. Nathaniel Saltonstall. **Mary**, b. 1649, m. Rev. Benjamin Woodbridge(1).

4 **JOHN**, taxed Island side of Newcastle 1720.

5 **RICHARD**, Portsmouth, m. in Wells 24 Aug. 1710 Priscilla Littlefield(17) who was at Moses Paul's ho. in Portsm. in 1713. York wit. 1717, rated to Portsm. So. Ch. 1717, taxed Greenland 1719, Portsm. prison keeper 1724, sold Dover prop. in 1733, and figured in law-suits to 1743. She was a wid. in 1748. Ch. incl: **Nahum**, Portsm. mariner 1747. **Miriam**, m. Paul Sherburne, Portsm. mariner, his admx. 7 July 1748, and d. bef. 30 Nov. 1748 when adm. on his est. was gr. to mo.-in-law Priscilla Ward. And appar. a dau. **Priscilla** (see N. H. Prob. 3: 578).

6 **ROBERT**, fisherman, mariner, Portsmouth, m. 11 Nov. 1713 Sarah Ball(7). He bot in Portsm. from John Davis in 1714, bot Fernald Isl. with bldgs. from Richard Webber 1717, beat Edw. Phillips in 1719, was sued in 1722 by Thomas Cole of Kit., whom he had accus. of stealing corn from his sloop, and in 1723 mortg., and then sold, Webber Island. Wife Sarah rec. into So. Ch. 1718. Both of Boston 1730 when they q.c. as Ball heirs. The Barr. right of R. W., late of Portsmouth, ment. 1745. List 339. Ch. appear:

**Robert**, bp. 15 Aug. 1714 (No. Ch.), wit. parents' deed 1730. **Sarah**, bp. 5 Mar. 1720-1 (So. Ch.).

7 **SAMUEL?** (—well), Portsmouth, taxed for Mill Dam 7 May 1707. See (8).

8 **SARAH**, Portsmouth, see Deverson(1). Mrs. Ward taxed for Mill Dam Jan. 1711-2, 1713. See (7).

9 **THOMAS**, weaver, Hampton, a young man receiving a lot the first yr. He prob. liv. first on the north side of the Exeter road, moving to a lot on the road from the Meeting-ho. Green to the Falls, bot from Lt. Howard. Selectman eight times 1650-1672. Lists 391a, 392ab, 393ab(2), 394, 396, 49. His wife, List 393a, wid., List 52. See also Fuller(1). Called 'loving br.' in will of Samuel Fogg(4). Will, 18 June 1678 (inv. 27 July 1680), names w. Margaret (Shaw 13) and ch: **Elizabeth**, b. 10 Dec. 1651, m. John Mason(7). **Mary**, m. John Dearborn(3). **Hannah**, b. 29 Dec. 1655, m. Lt. Joseph Swett (5). **Thomas**, b. 3 Jan. 1666-7.

10 **CAPT. THOMAS**(9), Hampton, liv. on the homestead. Jury 1693. Lists 52, 399a. Will, 27 Dec. 1738 (d. 15 Mar. 1743), names w. Sarah (d. 23 Dec. 1763), 5 ch., 2 gr.ch. Ch: **Thomas**, Hampton Falls, b. 9 Jan. 1692, m. Rachel Sanborn (Nathl. 2) and d. bef. fa., whose will names his ch. Daniel and Rachel, but not Jeremiah, the oldest. **Abel**, b. 1 Jan. 1694, m. 23 Oct. 1724 Mary Melcher of Hampt. F., where he liv. 9 ch. **Noah**, b. 16 May 1696, had the homestead. He d. 5 June 1774; wid. Sarah, appar. dau. of Ruth Shaw (2), d. 3 Nov. 1788. 2 ch. rec. 1728-1734: Noah (d.y.), Cotton. **Shadrach**, b. 22 Oct. 1699. Will, of Kensington, 27 Sept. 1746—25 May 1748, names w. Margaret, 4 sons, 2 daus. **Sarah**, b. 20 May 1702, m. a Sleeper. **Margaret**, b. 2 July 1705, m. Samuel Locke (1). **Mary**, b. 14 Sept. 1707, d. unm. 4 Mar. 1736.

11 **CAPT. ——**, at Monhegan in the -Samson- 1619, fishing (Register 31: 397).

12 (——)**MS**, Saco 1661. List 244d.

13 **——**, butcher, taxed Portsmouth (the Bank) 1713.

## WARDEN.

1 (**ANTHO.?**), List 226.

2 **THOMAS**, Pemaquid, taxed 1687 for a colt and lands, m. Mary Johnson(12), and fled from the Ind. to Scituate where he liv. 1690-1698+. Late of New Harbor, he ent. an East. Cl. for 100 a. betw. Arthur Neale and Wm. Case, on w. side of Long Creek, 50 a. adj. George Slater and 20 a. meadow, under Dongan patent 13 Sept. 1686. His wife d. by 1716 when her sis. claimed Johnson lands for self and the Warden her. T. W. d. in Boston 30 Sept. 1730, ag. 78 (Granary B. Gr.). (One Mary W., wid. d. there 1 Jan.

1717-8, ag. 72). Ch., of Boston, the 1st and last unrec., but probable: **John**, bur. from Christ Ch., Boston, 8 June 1732, ag. 45. One J. m. Katherine Hutchins in Boston 17 Feb. 1723. **Thomas**, b. Scituate 11 Jan. 1690-1, d. 1747-8. First w. Anna. Will names w. Mary, dau. Anna; 10 or 11 ch. d.y. **Elizabeth**, b. Scit. 5 Mar. 1692-3. **Francis**, b. Scit. 22 Sept. 1695, ho. carpenter, Boston, m. 1st 23 Dec. 1718 Elizabeth Crowell, and had 2d w. Sarah. Will, 1765—1766. 6 ch. **Samuel**, b. Scit. 28 May 1698, m. 7 July 1720 Sarah Davis; ch. **Ruth**, adm. to First Ch., Boston, 26 June 1720.

**Wardhackines**, Edward, boatswain 1657 (Y. D. 1: 61).

## WARDWELL,
found in various Lincolnshire parishes, incl. Alford. One Thomas, an excommun. person, was bur. at Louthe in that co. in 1631.

1 **ELIAKIM**(2), Hampton, wit. with John Wheelwright in 1654 and was willed much by Jeffrey Mingay in 1658. He m. 17 Oct. 1659 Lydia Perkins(9), and the same yr., with Nathl. Weare(6), bot Hampt. prop. from Thomas Kimball. As Quakers he and w. encountered trouble and made a new home in New Jersey aft. he was fined in 1662 for abs. from meeting 26 days, both fined in 1663 for abs. 20 days and she ord. whipped in May 1663 for going into Newb. meet.-ho. naked. Evid. he was at Hampt. in Oct. 1663, called sometime of Hampt. 1669, at Shrewsbury, N. J., 1670. Monette's 'First Settlers of Piscataway and Woodbridge', 5: 873; 6: 1232, names ch: **Joseph** (b. at Hampt. 29 Dec. 1660), **William**, **Margaret** (b. at Hampt. 23 May 1664), **Elizabeth**, **Esther**, **Lydia**, **Mary**, **Meribah**, **Patience**, **Eliakim**.

2 **THOMAS**, shoemaker, Boston, Exeter, consid. br. of (3), was adm. to Boston Ch. 9 Nov. 1634, made freeman 4 Mar. 1634-5. Disarmed in 1637, he went to Ex. with Wheelwright adherents, was dism. to Ex. Ch. 6 Jan. 1638-9 and signed their combination. Sergeant; com.t.e.s.c. 1643. Lists 373, 374a, 376a. He ret. to Boston and d. there 10 Dec. 1646. Wife Elizabeth. Ch., rec. at Boston: **Eliakim** (poss. only one), b. Nov. -1635- (bp. 23 Nov. -1634-). **Martha**, b. Aug. 1637. **Benjamin**, b. Feb. 1639-40, soldier under Scottow (List 237b), O. A. at Boston 11 Nov. 1678. **Samuel**, b. 16 May 1643, m. at Andover 9 Jan. 1672 Sarah (Hooper) Hawkes. He was hanged for witchcraft 22 Sept. 1692 and prop. confiscated. She was condemned, but not executed, and sentence revoked in 1703. 6 ch., perh. not all, rec. at Andover 1673-1691: Marcy (by town rec., Mary by ct. rec.), Elizabeth, Samuel, William, Eliakim, Rebecca. The s. Eliakim, b. 17 Aug. 1687, m. (ct. Oct. 1710) Ruth Brag-

don(5) and was gr. 20 a. at York in 1714-5.
Will, 7 Mar. 1749—16 Oct. 1753, names w.
Ruth (liv. 1754) and 8 of 11 ch., all rec. at
York except the 2d ch. Abigail, rec. at An-
dover in 1715. List 269. Judge Savage evid.
noted a Joseph Wardwell at Lynn in 1669
and Mr. Monette reported a Joseph at
Shrewsbury, N. J., in 1670.

3 **WILLIAM**, Boston, Exeter, Wells, adm.
to Boston Ch. 9 Feb. 1633-4 as Mr. Edmund Quincy's servant, m. a wife Alice,
was disarmed in 1637 and dism. to Ex. Ch.
with (2). Wells Oct. 1649 (lic. retailer)—
Mar. 1656-7. O. A. to Mass. at W. 5 July
1653, altho the day bef. when called to come
in and answer his name, he refused and contemptuously turned his back on the ct. In
1654 he refused to subscr. for the college as
not an ordinance of God. Lists 373, 376a,
72, 252, 261-263. See also Gross(1); Doc.
Hist. iv: 74, 75, 78. Despite his dislike of
Mass., he ret. to Boston, m. 2d 5 Dec. 1657
wid. Elizabeth Gillett (form. wid. Perry)
and by mar. contract agreed to bring up her
dau. Hannah, ag. 2, for half the Gillett ho.
(Reg. 12: 275). Lic. at Boston. 'Descendants of Henry Rust,' p. 22, has his will, 18—
30 Apr. 1670, naming w. Elizabeth, her daus.
Hannah.and Deborah and his 6 ch.,friends
James Everell and Wm. Bartholomew overseers, s. Uzal exec. The wid. was lic. alone
to 1691 when her dau. Deborah (Perry)
Mann was also included. 'Mis Wardel an
antient widow' d. 12 Feb. 1697. Ch. rec. Boston: **Meribah**, b. 14 May (bp. 25 June) 1637,
m. Francis Littlefield(12). **Usal**, carpenter,
b. 7 Apr. 1639, m. 1st Mary (Kinsman) Ringe
3 May 1664 in Ipsw. where ch. rec. 1665-
1677: Abigail, Hannah, Alice, Mary. Salem
constable 1681, taxed there 1683, ch. rec. at
Bristol, R. I., 1684-1693. Will, of Bristol, 10
Jan. 1728—7 Sept. 1732, names w. Grace, 6
mar. daus., 5 sons; see R. I. Hist. Soc.
Col., 5: 89. **Elihu**, bp. 5 Dec. 1641, **Elihu**, b.
Nov. 1642, poss. the same and error in dates.
Wells wit. 1662 (Y. D. 1: 128), m. in Ipsw.
26 May 1665 Elizabeth Wade (Col. Jonathan), depos. there in June 1681, ±38. Ch.
at Ipsw: Elizabeth (1666), Elihu (1668),
Prudence (1670), Jonathan (1672), Susanna
(1684), John (unrec., d. in 1688), and prob.
several others; see Adams(6), Storer(1);
Wyman's Charlestown, ii: 995. **Mary**, bp. 14
Apr. 1644, ±9 days old, m. Nathl. Rust of
Ipsw. **Leah**, b. -7- (bp. -6-) Dec. 1646, m.
Wm. Tower of Boston. **Rachel** (presum. by
1st w.), named in fa.'s will, unmar. By 2d
w: **Abigail**, b. 24 Apr. 1660, d. 23 Aug.
1661.

**Wareham**, ——, Capt., List 90.

**WARNER, Thomas** (also Warriner), fisherman, Cape Porpus, the only Warner

found in early Me. or N. H., altho it became the 60th commonest name in N. E. One
T. was fined for fighting in Mass. ct. 1639.
The Me. Thomas was here by 1647 when
James Woodward had worked for him. Sued
by Ambrose Lane in Dover ct. 1651 and defaulted. The same yr. his w. Katherine went
with an eloping party from Winter Harbor
to Barnstable. In 1655 he was imprisoned on
a false charge of murder (see Redding 1),
the Mass. Genl. Ct. later allowing him £5 for
his suffering (suggesting that he look to
Redding for further redress) and exonerating Richard Hitchcock who issued the hue
and cry ag. him. Lists 111, 252, 253. See also
List 255. Drowned on a fishing voyage; adm.
gr. to Morgan Howell in July 1660 and revoked, as Mr. Richard Russell and Mr.
George Corwin had taken adm. for the creditors in Suff. ct. Inv. 23 Apr. 1660, called 'of
Boston,' where the only kn. ch. **Thomas**, was
b. 24 Dec. 1658. Wid. Katherine m. John
Searle there 26 Nov. 1661. A deed 1661 recites the John Littlefield homestead had
been bot by him from Thomas Warriner,
deceased.

**WARREN**, became 83d commonest name
in N. E.

1 **GILBERT**(4), Berwick, m. Sarah (Emery
2) Thompson. Prob. the Wells soldier
credited to Haverhill in 1693-4. Lists 267b,
290, 296, 298. Adm. to So. Berw. Ch. 1725.
He gave his age as ±69 in Oct. 1725, ±73 in
1730, and also 76 in June 1730, when he depos. that he had kn. Plaisted meadow over
60 yrs. Will, senior, husbandman, 2 Apr.
1728—17 Apr. 1733, names w. Sarah, s.-in-
law (step-son) John Thompson, 2 ch. In
Feb. 1744-5 wid. Sarah deeded ½ of 10 a.
adj. Benjamin Nason to dau. Jane. Ch:
**Jane**, m. 11 Dec. 1718 John Stockbridge.
**Margaret**, m. Wm. Hearl (5 jr.).

2 **HUGH**. See Oakman(5).

3 **HON. HUMPHREY**, Boston merchant, m.
by 1674 **Mrs**. Mehitabel (Clarke 54)
Downes. In June 1674 he contracted with
Major Phillips to collect the rents from all
fishermen on stages on Parker's Neck, except Ralph Tristram's. In 1675 among those
who succes. pet. for a large gr. above Saco.
Sued Henry Williams for debt in Wells ct.
1676, Richard More jr. in Suff. ct. 1677. List
236. Adm. in Suff. ct. 20 Dec. 1680 to the
wid. and Capt. Elisha Hutchinson; inv. incl.
land and a wareho. at Winter Harbor; debts
'which we hope some time to receive' £321;
debts of fishermen and others, little worth,
many of them left by Mr. Downes, £1623.
See also (6). In Kittery ct., 1695, Mehitabel
W. et al. sued Joshua Downing for 5 a. betw.
Watts Fort and Franks Fort. She d. in Bos-

ton 20 July 1701, and E. Hutchinson claimed Scarb. land adj. John McKenney for self and her heirs. List 188.

**4 JAMES**, Kittery (par. of Unity), prob. a Scotch prisoner, had land laid out on so. side of John Taylor's lot 'by the water side,' in July 1656. Constable 1664; j. 1665, gr.j. 1666, cor.j. 1668. In 1670 his w. Margaret (called a native of Ireland) and other Scots were admon. for using profane speeches, Divil-a-bit, &c.; in 1674 he was bound to good behav. and disciplined for abetting Richard Gibson(3). Lists 288, 298. See also James Barrow, who was sick at his ho. bef. going to Gowen's. In Mar. 1700-1 he deeded 40 a. near York Bridge, laid out 17 Mar. 1698-9, to s. Gilbert, he to pay 30 sh. yearly to fa. or mo. as long as either liv. Upward of 80, he depos. in Sept. 1702 that he had liv. in upper Kit. near 50 yrs. Will, 9 Dec. 1700—15 Dec. 1702, names w. Margaret, 4 ch., gr.s. James Stackpole, gr.dau. Jane Grant. Her will, very aged, 13 Dec. 1712—15 Oct. 1713. Ch: **Gilbert**, b. ±1656-7. **Margaret**, m. James Stackpole. **Grizel** (or Magdeline, List 99, pp. 123, 126), b. 24 Feb. 1661-2 (Catholic rec.) m. 1st Richard Otis(1), m. 2d Philip Robitaile; not named in mo.'s will. **Jane**, m. Wm. Grant(17), not named in either will. **James**.

**5 JAMES**(4), Berwick, accus. by Elizabeth Gattensby(1) in Mar. 1689-90, but m. (ct. 1 Nov. 1692) Mary Fost(1). Surv. highways and fences 1692-3, 1698-9; constable 1693-4; gr.j. 1695, 1702 (foreman); selectman 1696-1698; auditing commit. 1696-1699; on commit. to divide Kit. from Berw. lands Feb. 1713-4. Lists 289, 296, 298, 38. Adm. to wid. Mary 6 July 1725. She depos. in 1734, ag. 67, that it was 44 yrs. since she first knew the Lovering ho. at Quamphegan; in June 1750, ag. 84, she depos. ab. early Chadbournes. Ch: **Mary**, b. 23 Feb. 1692, wit. John Key's will 13 Apr. 1710. **Margaret**, b. 5 Nov. 1694, m. Nathl. Heard(11). **James**, b. 8 June 1698, m. Mary Goodwin (Moses 4). 'Old Kittery' names 9 prob. ch., not incl. the dau. Mary who m. John Field(5 jr.). **Rachel**, b. 26 Aug. 1700, d. 13 Sept. 1703. **Gilbert**, b. 30 Apr. 1703, liv. in Berw. with w. Abigail who surv. him. Quaker. Will, 1755—1755. 8 ch., incl. Alden. **John**, b. 16 Dec. 1705, m. Mary Heard(11). List 298. Will proved Jan. 1769. 8 ch.

**6 JOHN**, planter, cordmaker, Exeter by 22 Apr. 1649 and gr. 5 a. in 1650. Sued John Cass, John Garland, and Humphrey Wilson (for a debt due from Mr. John Legate), 1653-1664, and was summonsed in 1661 for felling trees on the Shrewsbury men's divisions. On committee to lay out county way betw. Ex. and Hampt. 1661,

Squamscott bounds 1668. Selectman 1655, 1657; j. 1663. In Oct. 1668 the town sued him and John Folsom as bondsm. for Mary Folsom, sr. Of Boston in 1673 when he sold his int. in an Ex. mill. Lists 376b, 377, 379. See also Foss(1). He m. 1st 21 Oct. 1650 Deborah Wilson(10) who d. 26 June 1668; m. 2d wid. Elizabeth Coombs(5) and took adm. on her est. in Jan. 1671-2. Will, 10—31 July 1677, gives to 3d w. Elizabeth to bring up her ch. Nathaniel and Abigail, acc. to pre-nupt. contract (or, by ano. abstract, 'my s. Nathaniel and Abigail'), to sons Joshua and Thomas, and 'the rest of my ch.' She m. successively, Samuel Sendall, John Hayward, Phineas Wilson of Hartford. Her will, 5 Jan. 1724-5—Aug. 1727, gives to dau. Abigail and ch., dau. Warren of Boston and her s. Thomas, dau. Mary -Bird- of Hingham, and many others, several called 'daughter' and poss. one or more a Warren. See Early Conn. Prob. Records, Hartford District, ii: 619-624. Kn. ch. by 1st w: **Joshua**; his fa. willed him 'the engine I cut tobacco with.' **Thomas**, as 'jr.' had an Ex. gr. in 1664, List 376b. T. W. an Ex. abuttor 1680-1697. **Mary**, m. 24 Dec. 1685 John Burr of Hingham, where she d. 26 July 1742, ag. 77. By 2d w: **Nathaniel**, b. in Boston 27 May 1670. His mo. willed to her ch: Sarah Barlow, Elizabeth and Mary Coombs, Nathl. W. In 1685 their uncle Joseph Royal(3), gave bond as gdn. of Mary and Nathl.; the inv. incl. Winter Harbor land and wareho. and debts of fishermen and others, many of them left by Mr. Downes (see Warren 3). By 3d w: **Abigail**, b. in Boston 10 May 1676, m. 1st ±1693 Richard Lord, m. 2d by 1716, Rev. Timothy Woodbridge, both men of Hartford. **John**, b. in Boston 10 Feb. 1677, not in will of any step-fa., tho two of them named his sis. Abigail.

**7 RICHARD**, Monhegan 1672, O. A. 1674. In 1676 Wm. Waldron hired R. W. and his boat to go from Monhegan to Damariscove. R. W., who wit. Thomas Burrage of Falm. to Sylvanus Davis 10 Feb. 1685-6, was perh. a younger man and s. of (10). Lists 15, 225a.

**8 THOMAS?**, senior at Exeter, when Thomas(6) was junior, in 1664?

**9 WALTER**, blacksmith, Portsmouth, m. in Nov. 1714 Joanna Elliott(4), owned Portsm. land in 1718. He endorsed a note for John Roberts of Portsm. in 1718; bondsman for Elizabeth (Barnwell) (Cutts) Bryan of Portsm. in 1725. List 339. Will, 27 Oct. 1736—26 Jan. 1742-3 (inv. £668); w. Joanna and ch: **George**, blacksmith, m. 24 June 1736 Martha Noble. **John**. **Walter**, blacksmith, liv. 1748. **Amos**.

10 **WILLIAM,** bound over in York ct. 1663, forfeiture of bond to Mr. Walter Lapp. In Oct. 1671 Saco gr. him a lot S.E. of Peter Henderson, 12 a. His wife seated in Ch. there 1674. List 246. In June 1688 he ack. judgm., £27, to Sylvanus Davis, his bondsmen, John Holman, Richard Powsland, Richard Hunnewell. Presum. fa. of **Mary,** in Boston in Sept. 1684 going to Piscataqua. She had come in a boat with Francis Backaway without the knowl. of her fa. and mo. who liv. in Casco. See also (7).

11 **SIR WILLIAM,** List 48.

12 **WILLIAM,** Portsmouth, from Devonshire; List 339. See Bretton.

**Warwick,** Warrick, see Waddock.

**Washford,** James, sailor 1684, List 314.

**Washington,** Margaret, Portsmouth 1661, List 330b. See Mattoon.

**Wastill,** see Westall.

**Watels?,** Will, Wells soldier. List 267b.

**WATERHOUSE,** primarily a Yorkshire name, but found in eastern counties to London.

1 **RICHARD,** Portsmouth, tanner, first at Boston 1669-1671, m. 1st Portsm. 29 June 1672 wid. Sarah (Fernald 2) Lyde and liv. on her prop. on Doctor's Isl. Gr.j. 1682-3, 1688, 1695, 1696; j. 1682-3, 1684; signed pet. ag. Cranfield 1685. Lists 52, 54, 55b, 57, 68, 98, 329, 330de, 331b, 335a (and w.), 337. A fine penman. Deeded to sons Sam'uel and Timothy, 1700. See Clark(8). He m. 2d Hampton 3 Dec. 1701 Mary Swett(1), who was rec. into So. Ch. 3 June 1716. Will, 14 Mar. 1717-8—23 July 1718, left small est. to wid. Mary, exec., and sons: **Richard,** b. 19 Apr. 1674. **Samuel,** b. 9 May 1676. **Timothy.**

2 **RICHARD(1),** Portsm., sea-capt., liv. on Doctor's Isl. in 1703 but in 1709 bot ho. and land on Pickering's Neck. Owned brigantine -Dove- in 1707. Served at Fort Wm. and Mary, 1708. Subscribed to Mr. Emerson's salary, 1713. See Bryant(7). His 1st w. Sarah, who owned cov. 1710, was liv. 1728. He m. 2d Elizabeth (Kennard 1) (Furber) Ditty who m. 4th Moses Dam(3). Lists 330d, 334a, 339. Adm. on his est. gr. to his s. Capt. Samuel 25 June 1731. Ch. by 1st w: **Richard,** bp. with next two 23 July 1710, d. bef. 1744 s.p. Capt. **Samuel,** mariner and shop-keeper, m. 1st Elizabeth Pierce (see Langdon 2) who d. 1736, ag. 29; m. 2d bef. 28 Nov. 1739 Deborah (Shackford) Sumner who m. 3d John Ayers. One Capt. W. brot Irish emigrants to Portsm. in Oct. 1732. He d. 1 Jan. 1744-5, ag. 38 (Point of Graves). Will, 26 Dec. 1744—30 Jan. 1744-5 (inv. £3901), names w. and daus. Elizabeth and Sarah (m. John Titcomb of Dover). **Hannah,** was wid. Scott of Hampton when she q.c. to br. Samuel in 1744. Capt. **Arthur,** bp. 16 Aug. 1711, mari-

ner, m. 1st 15 Jan. 1737-8 Hannah Bickford (10), m. 2d Deborah (Leighton) Collins, wid. of Capt. Wm. She adm. his est. 30 July 1746. 1 + 2 ch.

3 **SAMUEL(1),** Portsm., cordwainer, bot ho. and lot from Richard Webber, 1700. Served at Fort Wm. and Mary, 1708. Subscribed to Mr. Emerson's salary, 1713. Had w. Sarah in 1700 and m. 2d after 1702 wid. Sarah Libby(6) who was poss. S.W., ±29, who test. in Martha Sloper's case in Nov. 1707 and who o.c. and was bp. in No. Ch. 1707-8. He d. bef. 14 Aug. 1732 when the wid. sold his Barrington right. Four ch. conveyed his Portsm. real-estate to Jotham Odiorne 27 Feb. 1746-7. Lists 331c, 339. Ch., prob. three by each w: Capt. **Samuel,** Boston, mariner, m. 1st 7 Oct. 1724 Rachel Young who d. 23 Jan. 1726-7, ag. 22 (Copp's Hill); m. 2d 7 May 1728 Mary Berry; m. 3d 20 Oct. 1741 Elizabeth Stoddard who was app. adm. 6 June 1751. 1 + 4 + 2 ch. **William,** cordwainer and school-teacher, Portsm. until 1730, Berwick 1731, moved to Arundel 1742, finally Georgetown where he d. bef. 23 Dec. 1767 when his 2d w. Mary was app. adm. He had m. 1st Newington 4 July 1726 Sarah Walker(4). List 298. 5 ch. **Elizabeth,** m. 1st John Sargent(1), m. 2d Robert Hart(6). **John,** Boston, peruke-maker, m. 16 Oct. 1733 Anne Gee who m. 2d 1 Sept. 1747 Uriel Rea; d. 1 Jan. 1746-7. 2 sons. **Jacob,** bp. 14 Sept. 1712, and **Nathaniel,** bp. 24 Apr. 1715, d.y.

4 **TIMOTHY(1),** Portsm., tanner and cordwainer, received in 1700 from his parents his mo.'s land at Pulpit Reach which she had as her Lyde dower. Sold Doctor's Isl. to Joshua Pierce in 1735. He m. Jan. 1700 Ruth Moses(1) who o.c. and was bp. in the No. Ch. in 1707-8, and who m. 2d Joseph Mead(2) and 3d Thomas Skinner. Lists 67, 339. Will, 3 June—28 Dec. 1748, named 9 liv. ch., 4 having d. in infancy: **Timothy,** bp. with next two 25 July 1708, d.y. **Margaret,** m. Samuel Brewster(2). **Mary,** m. 10 July 1728 or 1729 John Spinney(1 jr.). **Ruth,** bp. 18 June 1710, m. 1st 18 Jan. 1727-8 John Gaines, m. 2d James Nudd. **Joseph,** b. 11 Apr. 1711, Scarboro, m. 1st 12 June 1735 Mary Libby, m. 2d 10 Feb. 1757 wid. Rachel (Norman) Smith. 12 + 3 ch. *****Timothy, Esq.,** Newport, Rhode Island, cabinet-maker, Deputy 1781, Justice of Ct. of Com. Pleas 1781-1791; m. 11 May 1738 Hannah Proud; d. 20 Mar. 1792; 8 ch., incl. Dr. Benjamin, M.D. (Leyden) 1780, M.D. (Harvard) 1786. **Sarah,** bp. 9 June 1717, m. Capt. Zachariah Foss(8 jr.). **Elizabeth,** bp. 19 Apr. 1719, m. William Ham (John). **John,** b. 15 May 1721, Barrington; m. Alice Babb who d. 26 Nov. 1795; he d. 19 Aug. 1797. 11 ch. **Lydia,** m. 1st 23 Aug. 1747 Capt. Spencer Colby; m. 2d 24 Feb. 1751 Capt. Ephraim Dennett, m. 3d Hon. John

Plummer. **George Walker**, bp. 2 May 1725, d.y.

**WATERS.** See also Walters, two names which can cause confusion and error.

1 **DANIEL**, Killingly, Conn., sold Falm. land which his wid. Mary of Sturbridge, Mass., q.c. to six in K., S. and Brimfield, 1755.

2 **JOHN**, fisherman, Kittery, dead in 1674–1676 when Thomas Withers gave the deed for 8 a. on so. side of Spruce Creek adj. Alexander Jones' land which had been sold to Waters in 1651. Dau. **Mary**, appar. m. 1st Cornelius Jones(7), m. 2d Henry Benson(1). In 1688 Jones was liv. on land 'commonly called Joseph Waters' land,' Joseph poss. a son, but more likely error for John. See also Walter(2).

3 **NATHANIEL**, Capt., wit. delivery of the Vines patent 25 June 1630. List 10?

4 **RICHARD**, Falmouth wit. 1657 (Y. D. 1: 98), in all probability from Salem. Corp. Richard, a gr.s. from Salem, was at Wells 1693-4 List 267b.

5 **THOMAS** (Warteres), sent in custody of Thomas Hall to the constable of Hampton 1683.

6 **WILLIAM**, fa. of at least two who liv. at Damariscove, but poss. never liv. Eastward himself. List 80. Will, aged, now of Boston, 20 Aug. 1684—25 Feb. 1689-90, wit. by Henry Harwood and Thomas Gross, gives to gr.s. William (s. of **William**) of Damariscove and mentions the real est. 'which I have already made over to my three daus. for my life': **Mary**, w. of John Sellman of Damariscove (see also Dollen 2), **Urith**, w. of John Nicks (her 1st husb. was John Whitway), **Ann**, w. of Richard Narramore; gr.daus. Eleanor Waters and Elizabeth Whittaway. His w. had impoverished him 'by carrying away for Eng. all that I had or she could procure and running me in debt.' In Suff. ct. in July 1680 Elizabeth W. comp. ag. her husb. Wm. for non-support; in Jan. 1683-4, blind and aged, she charged neglect.

7 **WILLIAM**(6), fisherman, Damariscove, as Waters took O. A. 1674, as Walters was named constable and Clerk of the Writs the same yr. Liv. in Apr. 1677, when his w. Abigail was ±23. Lists 15(3); 142 for both. His son depos. that the fam. was driven off to Boston where his fa. died; the 'estate brought to Waymouth' was apprais. by Samuel White and Jacob Nash 20 Aug. 1679; attested by wid. Abigail, admx. 28 Aug. In May 1680 the two ch. had been taken off the mo.'s charge by the fa.'s relations, a son and dau., both named in will of (6): **William**, had Stephen French, sr., of Weymouth as gdn. in 1684. Of Boston in July 1736, ±63, he depos. that he was b. on Damariscove Isl.,

from where the fam. was driven off, and after the war his aunt Mary Sellman sent for him to come and live with them; he was then ag. 5 and liv. on the isl. until ±15. One Wm. of Boston, weaver, in will, 1749—1757, named w. Rebecca and ch: William (undutiful to parents), Rebecca Wimble, decd., Abigail Walcott, Seward Waters. **Eleanor**. One E. m. Robert Grandee in Boston in 1707.

**WATKINS.**

1 **JOHN**, mariner, Kittery. Adm. 1 Feb. 1707-8 to Capt. John Frost of Newcastle. Presum. fa. of Capt. **John**, Newc., m. 26 Mar. 1719 Dorothy Pepperell (Col. Wm.) who was gr. adm. 16 Sept. 1723. D. W. and two of her three sons were named in her fa.'s will 1733; she m. 2d bef. 1 Jan. 1739-40 Hon. Joseph Newmarch.

2 **THOMAS**, Kennebec, was of Boston when he had Ind. deed of High Head west of Merry Meeting, in 1661. In 1664 he depos. ab. Christopher Lawson and in 1667 wit. Ind. deed to him. Gr.j. 1667. Fined same yr. for trading liquor with Ind. on the Sabbath, John Mosher and John Payne informers. Lists 12, 161, 191. See also Gutch. From East. Claims it appears he had d. and wid. Margaret had m. Thomas Stevens(19) by Aug. 1672. Ch: **Thomas**, cordwainer, Boston; adm. 5 July 1690 to Richard Hixon of Milton, in right of two sis: **Margaret**, m. Richard Hixon in Milton 14 Sept. 1686. **Mary**, a female servant (but not a negress) in trouble in Boston 1692-3 for slandering her dame Mrs. Swift and may have been sold in Va. (see details in N. E. Reg. 44: 168).

3 **THOMAS**, Kittery 1669-1673, wit. for Barefoot, Champernowne, Corbett and Greenland; a Dover wit. 1671. Ag. ±25 in 1671, ±27 in 1672, List 82. He and Richard Alexander, called 'Maj. Shapleigh's men,' were drunk in Nov. 1673; they kept the Shapleigh books.

**WATSON.**

1 **CHRISTOPHER**, Portsmouth 1695. List 334b.

2 **GEORGE**, Penobscot 1630-1. List 1. One George wit. Ind. deed to Christopher Lawson in 1649 (Y. D. 35: 46-7), and swore to it in 1666 (East. Cl. of Clarke and Lake heirs).

3 **JOHN**, had p/a to bring suit for Wm. Daggett(3) in Sept. 1687, and was allowed an atty. in any ct. in Maine in Mar. 1688-9. A creditor of the Gendall est. In 1698 Robert Bronsdon gave p/a to J. W. of Boston to sue Nathl. Fryer, sometime of the co. of York. See also Milburne, Turfrey.

4 **JOHN**, Arundel, b. in Rowley 15 Nov. 1671, s. of John and Eunice (Barker) Watson (see also 7), m. in Bradford 25 Feb.

1691-2 Ruth Hartshorn, bot in Cape Porpus 1718, living there 1719. Ch. rec. Bradf. 1693-1717: **John, Thomas** (?List 269c, Thad), **Ruth, Abigail, Hannah, John, Samuel, Shadrach, Ebenezer.** In 1720 John Hartshorn of Rowley deeded rights in Coxhall to gr.sons John and Samuel W. of Arundel, having already given half to their br. Thomas.

5 **JONATHAN,** tanner, Dover 1676, depos. with Joseph Beard in Sept. 1678, m. bef. Dec. 1678 his sis. Elizabeth Beard(4), and owned land on the Upper Neck and near Tole-End. Jury 1694, Lists 358c, 359ab, 52, 94. In Oct. 1714 he deeded all prop. to w. Elizabeth. She was a wid. in May 1720, conv. prop. to sons David, William and Isaac, 13 Sept. 1721, and d. by 1736, when Joseph Thrasher of Hampt. sued Isaac for 1/9 of 15 a., the writ (SJC 12380) reciting that Jonathan d. in 1714 and left ch: **David,** eldest son, compl. in 1707-8 ag. Edw. Evans and Timothy Carle for beating him up at John Hayes' garrison, Evans being convicted. He m. Mary Dudley(2) who was liv. in 1737 when her sons Jonathan and Winthrop deeded to her for life ⅓ of cert. Exeter land. He d. bef. 13 June 1747. The writ in SJC 11674 (1749) names his heirs: Dudley, Dover; Jonathan, Exeter; Winthrop, Ex. (b. at Dover 11 Jan. 1723-4); Sarah, w. of Nathl. Doe(3); Mary, w. of Wm. Cushing of Ex.; Mercy, Dover, unm. **William,** at some time a mariner of New York; see (12). **Jonathan. Isaac,** rec. the homestead by the 1721 deed, had ch. by two wives, Lilias Chesley(4) and Joanna. Adm. 26 Apr. 1753 to wid. Joanna and s. Joseph, both of Dover, their sureties John Hart and Wm. Earl Treadwell of Portsm. **Elizabeth. Hannah. Alice,** m. Eleazer Young (12). **Mary,** m. (int. Salem 26 May 1711, she of Dover) Joseph Thrasher, q.v.

6 **JONATHAN,** Medford, Middlesex co., a No. Yarm. propr. 1727 (Y. D. 12: 352), belonged to the Cambridge family.

7 **NATHANIEL,** Greenland, poss. the br. of (4), b. in Bradford 2 Dec. 1676, m. in Greenl. bef. 29 Nov. 1710 Hannah Meloon (see Luke). Taxed 1713+. Both adm. to Ch. 1715. Lists 338abc, 388; wife 338b. Kn. ch., the first 4 bp. together in 1715: **John,** Greenland, Newmarket, had deed for half his fa.'s land in 1736; of Newm., he and w. Mary sold out in Greenl. in 1767; see also Durgin(2 jr.), King(16), Place(1). **Nathaniel; see** Deborah Bryant(10). At Lamprill River in Feb. 1763, ±48. **Hannah. Ann. Mary,** bp. in 1722. Also **Samuel** to whom his fa. deeded land and h.h. goods in 1736.

8 **PHILIP,** boatswain on the -Good Hope- of London in Feb. 1668-9. See also Ferguson(4).

9 **RICHARD** (also Wadsone), wit. ab. a Berwick fight in 1670 (Hull, Frost, &c.)

and was paid for physic by admr. of Edw. Mason(3). In 1671 Thomas Crawley escaped from R. W. and Christopher Batt who had been charged by the constable to secure him.

10 **ROBERT,** Oyster River, 1665, b. ±1641, poss. related to (5), as in 1667 he, Wm. Beard, John and James Smith and Matthew Williams were fined for not coming into ct. and taking oath on untimely death of Simon Buzal. In 1668 he wit. a Jackson deed. In York ct. 1671 one R. W. ackn. judgm. to Capt. John Davis. Bound to the peace in 1685 on compl. of Joanna, w. of Philip Chesley, who swore she feared injury from him. Jury 1685, constable 1686, gr.j. 1692. Lists 47, 365, 366, 356j, 359a, 52, 57. He was prob. k., poss. with ch., in 1694 when his w. Hannah (Kent 4) and son were captured. Inv. 9 Jan. 1695-6. Wid. Hannah was ransomed and m. John Ambler bef. 2 Mar. 1702-3 when they took adm. Only kn. ch. **Joseph,** a captive with his mo., List 99, p. 92, was bp. in Canada 8 Apr. 1697, ag. 17, keeping his own name; m. 1st in Montreal 15 Nov. 1711 (ag. +28) Marie Madelene Demers, 2 ch.; m. 2d 11 Apr. 1717 (±33) Angelique Benard Carignan, 3 ch. He was bur. 14 July 1749.

11 **ROBERT,** whose acct. of the taking of Falmouth 1690 is in Mass. Arch. 242: 400, is likely the same who m. Susanna Prior in Boston 13 Feb. 1690. In 1691 he adm. that he was in drink when he beat Col. Shrimpton's negro, and 'now engaged to go under Capt. Samuel Adams against the French.'

12 **WILLIAM,** Portsmouth, m. there 24 June 1714 wid. Martha Robinson(6). Taxed Portsm. 1717, Berwick Feb. 1718-9; Martha taxed Portsm. Jan. 1731-2. Adm. on est. of Wm., Portsm. shopkeeper, gr. 28 Sept. 1743 to wid. Sarah (see Mainwaring 4); Samuel Hart and two others signed the list of claims. See also William(5). Presum. a s. **William,** jr., whose Portsm. tax was abated in 1740; see Hannah Guptill. Elizabeth, dau. of Capt. Watson, was bp. in Portsm. So. Ch. 7 Mar. 1741-2. See also Mills(4).

**WATTS.** The prominent Maine settler was from co. Durham, where Guppy found Watsons numerous, replacing in the No. the more southern Watts.

1 **MR. *HENRY,** fishmonger, Blue Point, ±67 in 1669, ±71 in 1675, 82 in 1684, was bp. at Cockfield, co. Durham, s. of Ralph and Jane and br. of Mrs. Anne Dixon(1). Adm. to freedom of Fishmongers Co., London, by service, 12 Dec. 1625. Here by 1631 and wit. deliv. of the Saco Patent; a creditor of the Williams est. 1635; gr. 40 a. by Bonython and Lewis in 1636; a Saco rec. 1660 ment. the lot betw. John West and Mr. Watts. Jury 1640. In 1648 he had deed from Cleeve of 100 a. at Blue Point adj. his ho. where he had

liv. 15 yrs., and ano. deed from Cleeve (for Col. Rigby) for 500 a. at Black Point. Deputy to Lygonia Assembly 1648. O. A. to Mass. 1658. Commissioner for Scarb. 1658-1659, altho admonished in 1659 for criticiz' ing the governor and scandalizing other Comrs. Constable 1659; town clerk 1660; Comr. 1660-1662, 1664 (not allowed). One of Mr. Gorges' Deputies or Comrs., 1664. Abs. from meeting 1664 (did not appear), 1665, 1667-68, 1671. Growing old, in 1673 he deeded half his farm, called Cockell, and half his mill to Ralph Allison(2), he to have all eventually; at Portsm. in June 1680 he sold to Nathan Bedford 100 a. at Blue Point where he form. liv.; having outliv. Allison, conv. his 500 a. at Black Point to Andrew Brown for support 12 Nov. 1687. Lists 22, 34, 91, 111, 231, 232, 235, 237c, 238a, 241, 242. See also Pennell(8); Y. D. 2: 149; 5: 1: 109; 7: 117; 12: 164; 15: 257. No wife appears until 1665 when she had left him and he accus. Mr. Jordan of influencing her ag. him. Y. D. 15: 269, cites his deed of Scarb. land 20 May 1670 as successor and owner by marrying George Barlow's wid. He d. s.p. and Mr. Thomas Bowes(1), son of his sis. Barbara, came over and took adm. 27 June 1697.

2 JOHN, a Great Isl. wit. with Francis Tucker in 1678, perh. the Mr. J. W. who was in trouble in Boston in 1677 for trading powder and shot to Ind. and ab. that time shipped a master and crew in Boston and went on a fishing trip in his barke to Cape Sable where taken by Ind. The Boston John m. ±1668 Lydia Goodyear (see Gladman) and had ch: John, b. 22 Jan. 1668-9. Rebecca, b. 22 Feb. 1670-1, both in Boston. Unrec: Lydia, m. John Gerrish(4), d. 8 Jan. 1697-8, ag. ±27. Richard. Mary, m. James Treworgye (3). See Lake(3). Mrs. Lydia d. in Boston 29 Sept. 1700, ag. 55, and was bur. on Copp's Hill beside or near her dau. Lydia. The son, Mr. John, merchant, Boston, Arrowsic, representative of Sir Bibye Lake, m. in Boston 13 July 1711 Elizabeth Butler, joined Boston Second Ch. 6 Jan. 1711-2, had ch., Elizabeth, John (Portsm. mariner 1735, will 1750) and ano. Elizabeth (w. of Caleb Richardson of Boston 1735) bp. there 1712-1715. Will, 20 Nov. 1713 (d. at Arrowsic 26 Nov. 1717), beq. est. in par. of Westharrock, co. Essex, in Charlestown, Mass., and in par. of Stone, co. Kent. Madam Watts had their dau. Lydia bp. at Arrowsic 15 Dec. 1717, and soon m. 2d her husb.'s partner Capt. John Penhallow (2), who was Lydia's gdn. in 1735.

3 JOHN, owned at No. Yarmouth 1706; see Salem vital records.

4 MARY, Portsmouth, -Walls- in 1721 (see Morse 9), -Watts- in 1722 (see Wincoll 2). See also Wm. Amos and Wales.

5 RICHARD, smith, Strawberry Bk. 1681, sued by Wm. Haskins for assault and battery 1682. Lists 329, 52.

6 SARAH, Charlestown, her dau. Sarah bp. at Hampt. Falls 1712. See Benjamin in Wyman's Charlest. ii: 1002.

7 THOMAS, a Lamprill River wit. 1673.

8 WATTS FORT, Y. D. 11: 231.

Waugh, Alexander, the Scot, List 14.

## WAY.

1 ANDREW (or May), Joshua Scottow's servant in Mar. 1668-9, ag. ±15.

2 GEORGE, Mr., merchant, Dorchester, co. Dorset, subscr. £50 for the Mass. Bay Colony in 1628, and with br.-in-law Thomas Purchase obtained the Pejepscot patent 16 June 1632. Waters i: 310, and Reg. 43: 151, have his will, of Dorchester, Eng., 1641, naming w. Sarah, ch. Sarah, Mary, Elizabeth, Martha (m. Edw. Allen in Boston 1652), and Eleazer, under 26, who was given, in part, all at Pejepscot and Dorchester, N. E. Eleazer's suit ag. Purchase in a county ct. at Boston in 1657 was dismissed for lack of jurisdiction; in 1669 he gave his uncle T. P. authority to sell (Reg. 43: 49), and in 1683 himself sold to Richard Wharton (Y. D. 4: 18). His inv. at Hartford Aug. 1687; div. to wid. Mary and 4 ch., one wit. Edw. Allen (jr.). Note also E. A. in T. Purchase's will.

3 GEORGE, with the eloping party from Winter Harbor in 1650, evidently a boy. See Wallen, Warner.

4 PETER, fisherman, Monhegan, List 111.

5 RICHARD. See (6).

6 THOMAS, fisherman at the Shoals by 1649, List 72, partner with Ball, Stover and Powell in a Cape Neddick gr. July 1649, and had 12 a. from Godfrey in Feb. 1650-1. Jury of life and death (Collins) 1650. Sued by Wm. Hilton on account, £9, in 1651; owed John Webster(3) in 1652. One T. was at Marbleh. liv. abs. from his w. in 1652; one wit. in Boston 1666 for Richard Way (List 77a; see also Hornabrook).

7 THOMAS (Ley, Vey, Way?), Pemaquid 1687, List 124.

8 WILLIAM, with Abraham Spiller wit. Thomas to Wm. Fernald 1689.

Wayle, Thomas (also Weale), drunk at the Shoals 1666, here 1670 (see Jackson 23).

## WEARE, from the South of England.

1 DANIEL(8), mariner, Boston, a minor 28 Oct. 1684 when John Smyth, jr., assaulted him in a dispute over logs and his fa. collected the fine. In 1687 his parents deeded to 'our son' 60 a. bot from Mr. John Gooch, called Gooch's Neck. York gr. 1701. He m. 1st Hannah Boaden(7) who d. in Boston 4

May 1697, m. there 2d, 31 Oct. 1698, Lydia Hillier who d. 2 Jan. 1704-5, ag. 43 (Copp's Hill) and 3d 19 Nov. 1705 Mary Vial. In Apr. 1714 he deeded his homestead in York on the shore betw. Thomas Avery decd. and Mr. Peter W., decd., to Joseph Bragdon who later sued for it (SJC 33650). In 1727 relinq. adm. on fa.'s est. to kinsman Elias W. See also Freeman(2), Murrell. Ch. b. in Boston, by 1st w: **Daniel,** b. 26 Nov. 1692, d.y. **Hannah,** b. 5 May 1694, m. in 1712 Wm. Marshall. **Elias,** b. 20 Oct. 1695, a Rhode Isl. merchant when he and his sis. joined in a Boaden heirship deed. By 2d w: **Daniel,** b. 12 Oct. 1700. By 3d w: **Lydia,** d.y., **Mary, Lydia, Joseph,** 1707-1717.

2 **ELIAS**(8), York, had town gr. 1699. Ferry lic. at Cape Neddick 1701. Killed by Ind. betw. York and Cape Neddick, List 96 under date 10 Aug. 1707. He m. (York ct. Apr. 1697) Magdalene (Hilton 9) Adams, who m. 3d John Webber(10). Ch: **Ruth,** b. 6 Jan. 1696-7, m. (ct. Oct. 1713) Moses Banks(1). In 1728 they q.c. to her br. Elias as heirs of her fa. or gr.fa. and of her bros. Jeremiah and John. **Elias,** b. 10 Jan. 1698-9, gr.fa.'s admr. 1727, m. Elizabeth Sayward (2); 5 ch.; m. 2d Mary (Lewis 2) Webber. List 279. **Jeremiah,** b. 13 Feb. 1700-1, Boston, mariner in Apr. 1726, and **John,** b. 16 Jan. 1702-3, both d. s.p. bef. 30 Aug. 1728. **Joseph,** b. 17 Mar. 1704-5, with br. Elias bot in other heirs of fa. Wife Mary (Webber) d. from small pox in Sept. 1778 in 69th yr., aft. a mar. life of 50 yrs. 7 days; he d. 18 Oct. 1791, ag. 86; will. 10 ch. **Mary,** b. 27 Mar. 1706-7, m. 6 Feb. 1728-9 Alexander McIntire. **Elizabeth,** unrec., m. by 1735 Dr. David Bennett of York (see Spencer 9). See also N. E. Reg. 55: 55.

3 **HOPEWELL**(8), had York gr. in 1703, m. (ct. Jan. 1718-9) Lydia Young(2), d. 7 June 1721, adm. to her 6 July. See Y. D. 11: 40. In 1724 her br.-in-law Joseph Favor made compl. in her behalf ag. Nathl. Abbott of Andover, but she m. 2d John Wells(6). Ch: **Joseph,** b. 25 Oct. 1718, m. Miriam Grover. In 1745 he sold ⅔ of 10 a., his br. **John,** b. 9 Sept. 1720, owning ⅓. List 279 for both sons.

4 **JOSEPH**(8), York mariner in 1685 when Samuel Crawley stole money from his vessel bound for Boston, and Arthur Beale accus. Jasper Pulman's w. of kissing him. Town gr. 1685-1699, wit. with John Penwill (3) in 1687 and m. his dau. Hannah. See also Preble(1). Gr.j. 1691, 1695; selectman 1696. Admr. of Maj. John Davis' est. 1694, John Harmon bondsman. Adm. on own est. gr. 7 Jan. 1700-1 to wid. Hannah, her bonds. Abraham Preble, Esq. and Johnson Harmon. As wid. and admx. in 1705, she sold Cape Neddick land that was gr. to Capt. Davis;

liv. 6 Dec. 1723 and appar. a yr. later. The writ in suit Weare v. Milbury, 1743, names the ch: **Joseph,** eldest s. and plf., of age 20 June 1710 when he deeded ¼ a. where Major Davis' wareho. stood. Town gr. 1721 (partly gr. to John Davis, his gr.fa.), 1722. See also Y. D. 7: 47. In 1731 he said 'my honored gr.fa. John Davis, Esq.' Ag. ±66 in July 1752. Wife Sarah Black(2). 4 ch. 1718-1731. **Peter,** York 1724 when he and sisters q.c. to Joseph their fa.'s, but not their mo.'s, est. Liv. 1748. **Mary,** m. Hezekiah Adams(19). **Hannah,** m. Stephen Preble(8 jr.).

5 **NATHANIEL**(5), Newbury, Nantucket, where he d. 1 Mar. 1680-1. Wid. Sarah liv. 23 Aug. 1682. Ch. incl: **Hester,** m. 1st Capt. Benjamin Swett(1), m. 2d 31 Mar. 1678-9 Ens. Stephen Greenleaf of Newb., d. at Hampt. 16 Jan. 1718-9, ag. 89. **Nathaniel, John,** d. at Newb. 12 Oct. 1653. **Mary,** m. John Swain(2). Aft. long research in Eng. Col. Banks could not place Nathaniel surely but consid. him nearly related to (8). At Bristol he found the apprenticeship in 1618, for 8 yrs., of one Nathaniel, s. of Peter of Barkenborough, Wiltshire, clothier.

6 †**NATHANIEL**(5), Esq., Hampton (±66 in 1699, ±70 in 1703), m. in Newb. 3 Dec. 1656 Elizabeth Swain(4). Of Newb. in Oct. 1659 when he and Eliakim Wardwell bot in Hampt. from Thomas Kimball, and in Sept. 1660 when his fa.-in-law deeded to him. At Hampt. he became one of the influential men of the town and province. Selectman (1st in 1667) and moderator; chosen to run the so. line of the town in 1669 and to lay out the land lying more than 4 m. no. of the meeting-ho. As strong an opponent of the Cranfield-Mason party as his townsman Edward Gove(2), he chose instead an orderly and effective course of opposition, going to Eng. twice as representative of the petitioners (see Dow's Hist. of Hampton, i: 96-117; N. H. Hist. Soc. Col. 8: 380). Councillor 1692, resigning in 1715 because of age; Chief Justice of Supreme Ct.; J. P. Called Capt. 1694. Lists 392b, 393b, 394, 396, 45, 48, 49, 52, 54, 56, 64, 65, 68, 69, 94. Wife Elizabeth d. 10 Feb. 1712-3, ag. 75; he 13 May 1718, ag. nearly 87. Ch: **Elizabeth,** b. in Newb. 5 Jan. 1657, m. Thomas Cram(3). **Peter,** b. in Newb. 15 Nov. 1660. **Mary,** b. in Hampt. 23 Sept. 1663, d. 6 Sept. 1682. **Sarah,** b. 17 Aug. 1666. **Nathaniel,** b. 29 Aug. 1669. **Hannah,** b. 7 Jan. 1672-3. **Abigail,** b. 13 Sept. 1676. **Mehitabel,** m. Benjamin Hilliard(7).

7 *****NATHANIEL**(6), Esq., Hampton Falls, m. 1st 17 Nov. 1692 Huldah Hussey(3), m. 2d 24 Aug. 1703 Mary Waite. As Nathl., jr., he was constable 1695; selectman 1701, he or fa. in 1714. J. P., Justice of Superior Court, Speaker 1727, re-elected 1728 but withdrew. Deacon. Land and mill owner in

No. Yarmouth. List 392b. He depos. in Sept.
1754, ag. 85. Will, 26 Feb. 1754 (d. 26 Mar.
1755), and an early will, dated 24 Feb. 1737-
8, in N. H. Prob. 5: 47-53 (State Papers, vol.
35). His w. Mary d. betw. these dates. Ch:
Daniel, b. 12 Sept 1693, m. 1st 29 Jan. 1719-
20 Abigail Green(9) who d. 23 Apr. 1723; m.
2d Mary Taylor (see 15). She was gr. adm.
8 May 1733, m. 2d by Nov. 1738 Thomas
Wiggin. Ch., Nathaniel, Daniel, Joseph Taylor, named by gr.fa. in 1738. Capt. Peter,
No. Yarm., where he had his fa.'s mill. In
1738 he made oath that he mar. Sarah Felt
(Joseph 5) at No. Yarm. 30 May 1720 and
as town clerk made entry of the mar. at that
time. Drowned there 13 Apr. 1743. Ch. John,
b. 12 Nov. 1696, m. 6 Dec. 1720 Deborah
Taylor (see 15), 8 ch. Hannah, b. 12 Jan.
1698-9, m. (int. Salisb. 1 Feb. 1717-8) John
Allen. Huldah, b. 16 Jan. 1701, m. 1st Isaac
Green(8 jr.), 2d one Davis. By 2d w: Nathan, b. 22 Sept. 1705, d. 17 June 1725. Mary,
b. 19 Nov. 1706, m. Jeremiah Brown(5).
Mercy, b. 22 Mar. 1708, d. bef. 1738. Sarah,
b. 5 July 1709, m. Jonathan Dow(10). Elizabeth, b. 11 Oct. 1711, m. 13 Dec. 1733 Joseph
Tilton, jr. Hon. Meshech, b. 16 Jan. 1713,
H. C. 1735, d. 14 Jan. 1786, m. 1st Elizabeth
Shaw, m. 2d Mehitabel Wainwright; see
Dow's Hampton ii: 1030-1. Abigail, b. 17
May 1716, m. Col. Abraham Drake. Mehit-
abel, b. 18 Dec. 1720, m. Caleb Sanborn. Susanna, b. 28 July 1723, m. Nathl. Healey.

8 *PETER, Mr., York (±40 in 1658), from
  Charfield, co. Gloucester (his fa. prob.
ano. Peter of C.), was here ±1638 when he
and Thomas Brooks, alias Basil Parker, bot
John Wilcox's land at Great Works. In
early yrs. he trav. to Winnipesaukee and the
Merrimack for furs, settled at York by 1643,
and on the homestead on Cape Neddick River by 1650. Favoring Mass., he was often a
storm center and is now consid. unqualified
for some of his pub. positions, but York evid.
found him useful, as he was chosen selectman 18 times 1653-1683. Tr.j. first time 1640,
gr.j. 1645; York comr. (in place of selectman) 1657, 1660, 1664; town clerk; Rep.
1660, 1665, 1669; Recorder; County Treas.
Imprisoned by the Royalists in 1668, and had
been in prison for some reason in 1675 when
George Norton sued the prison keeper for
letting him out. In 1685 as the exec. he went
to Eng. to prove the will of his br. Thomas
of Charfield. In 1688 had Cape Ned. ferry
lic. Lists 281, 273, 275-277, 235, 22, 24, 25,
88, 92. See also (5) and Hist. of York ii: 16,
by a desc., Col. Banks. Wife Ruth Gooch(4)
d. bef. 7 May 1667; his 2d w. Mary Puring-
ton(1) was not liv. with him in July 1675,
but would if he would provide for her. In
Dec. 1715, ±80, she depos. that ±66 yrs. bef.
she liv. with her husband's 1st w., being

then ±14 yrs. old. He was k. in the York
massacre, inv. 18 Apr. 1692 ret. by wid. Mary
(Y. D. 5: 1: 79-80). Her will, 21 (d. 29 Jan.)
1719, names 4 ch., s.-in-law Nowell. In 1730
adm. on P. W.'s est. was given to heirs of s.
Elias, heirs of the older sons having declined,
Elias' heirs to pay the others' shares, each
£41.6.7. Ch. by 1st w: Elizabeth, m. Thomas
Donnell(5). Mary, m. John Drury; dead in
Dec. 1716 (Y. D. 9: 36). Hannah, m. 1st Nathaniel Jewell of Boston, mariner; m. 2d
(int. 28 Jan. 1696-7) Michael Shuller of Boston. Phebe, m. Isaac Marion of Boston; adm.
to neph. Nathl. Cunningham 2 Nov. 1724.
Peter, b. ±1650-1. Nathaniel, cooper, Bos-
ton, d. on the pinke -Society-, Thomas Ed-
wards, master; adm. in Suff. ct. to br. Peter
9 July 1677. Ruth, m. bef. 1690 Timothy
Cunningham of Boston who was k. by Ind.
at Exeter 16 Apr. 1712. By 2d w: Daniel.
Elias. Joseph. Mary, m. 1st by 1695 Charles
Roberts, m. 2d Peter Brown of Boston.
Sarah, m. Capt. Peter Nowell. Hopewell.
A Child liv. in 1702; heirship deed in 14ths
(Y. D. 7: 105).

9 PETER(8), carpenter, Boston, ±29 in Jan.
  1679-80. By Boston rec. he had a 1st w.
Elizabeth, and a 2d w. Abigail who on 21
Jan. 1722-3 relinq. adm. to John Cobbett.
Ch., by Elizabeth: Peter, b. 28 Nov. 1682.
By Abigail: Hannah, b. 3 Jan. 1684, m. 2 Oct.
1712 John Cobbett, tailor.

10 COL. †*PETER(6), Hampton F., m. 1st
   6 Jan. 1691-2 Elizabeth Wilson(4) who
d. 29 June foll., m. 2d 30 Dec. 1698 Elizabeth
(Tetherly 1) West, List 315b. 'Taverner.'
Hampt. selectman 1694. Temporarily at
Great Isl. where lic. in Mar. 1697-8. Councillor, Justice of Superior Court, Rep. and
Speaker. Called Major in 1716. Lists 62,
392b. Adm. 25 Feb. 1746-7 to Andrew Webster. 'History of Hampton' (1893): 'now no
desc. of Col. P. W. who bears his name.' Ch:
Peter, b. 22 Dec. 1698. Nathaniel, b. 1700 or
1701, d. 15 May 1715. Susanna, b. 1 Aug.
1702, m. Nathl. Healey(2). Lt. Ebenezer, b.
4 Mar. 1708, m. 3 Apr. 1735 Prudence Locke
(1). She was gr. adm. 24 Feb. 1741-2, m. 2d
Andrew Webster. A son Nathaniel, b. 1736,
d. by 1763, leaving 3 daus. Stephen, b. and
d. 1710.

11 RICHARD, a wit. (Wiere) with Robert
   Pattishall in 1668; Dover 1673, wit. for
Thomas Seavey. In 1700 Richard Ware,
Shoals, was sued by Roger Kelly for goods
deliv. 1699-1700, Wm. Lakeman bondsman.

## WEBB. See also Rounds.

1 GEORGE, Dover 1640, in ct. 1643 for liv.
  idle like a swine. In 1649 he called
Frances Emery a witch and was sued for
slander by her husb. Anthony. Exchanged
Back River lots with Richard Pinkham.

Lists 351b, 352b, 354abc (ho. and land), 71. Adm. 8 Apr. 1651 to George Smith, who sold to Oliver Kent land already in his possession. 'All the marsh above 12 a. in the two creeks that was form. given by Dover to G. W. and Mr. Rogers,' was awarded to Henry Langstaff in Philip Lewis' suit in 1651.

2 **HENRY** (and Hilkiah Bailey 3) sued by Capt. Cammock in Saco ct. Sept. 1640. No. Yarmouth wit. 1651 (see Paine 6). Sued for slander in 1666 by Thomas Wise who lost. List 211. James Russell, Esq., ent. an East. Cl. for a Casco Bay planta. bot from Isaac Walker, bounded E. with cove going to Henry Webb's. Y. D. 27: 172 describes his land next S.W. of Nicholas White who liv. on upper end of Mere Point. See also (7, 8).

3 **HENRY**, Mr., wealthy Boston merchant, interested in mills at York where a mill gr. was made to Mr. H. W. and Capt. Thomas Clarke, both of Boston, Edw. Rishworth and Wm. Ellingham 20 Jan. 1653-4. He bot from Ellingham in 1654, from Henry Sayward in 1658 and 1659. N. E. Reg. 10: 177 has his will, 5 Apr. (d. bef. 13 Sept.) 1660. Only surv. ch. **Margaret**, m. Jacob Sheafe (see 3). See also Savage's Gen. Dict.

4 **JAMES**, Great Isl. Ale and vict. lic. June 1693, sureties Capt. George Long and Thomas Holland. Selling drink without lic. in 1694; constable's return 5 Sept: 'he and fam. on board the Forkland, Capt. George Longe, mr., to go to England.' See also Pormont(1).

5 **JOHN** (Webb or Wells), and John Dalle, appraised Joseph Bailey's ho. when taken into Casco fort in Sept. 1704. See also (8).

6 **RICHARD**, List 226, must be Webber(9).

7 **THOMAS** (Web), wit. Wells deed, Ashley to Jonathan Littlefield, 6 Oct. 1684. See (8)

8 **WILLIAM**, Wells. One W. W., likely from the East (see 2), was on 20 Sept. 1675 adm. inhab. of Salem, where Daniel, John (Perley says fa. of John, coaster, who m. Elizabeth Phippen 1), and Benjamin, were married 1675-1683. William m., appar. bef. 1680, cert. by May 1685, Charity Littlefield(15). List 269b. Wells abuttor Mar. 1681-2. Boston 1694-1696. Of Wells, in Nov. 1699, with approval of w. Charity, sold to Zachariah Goodale, 60 a. betw. Nathl. Cloyes and John Drisco. Me.j. Oct. 1701. She was bp. and rec. into com., Wells Ch. 28 Dec. 1701; her ch. **Josiah**, **William**, **Joseph** (b. Boston 7 Mar. 1694), **James** (b. Boston 13 Nov. 1696), bp. there 22 Nov. 1702. Appar. an older s. was **John**, carpenter, Salem 1705, when he sold to Jonathan Littlefield 150 a. in Wells, the same described as Charity Webb's in 1685. Francis Littlefield sued

John Webb in York ct. in 1727, when Jonathan Littlefield, George Jacobs and Charles Annis were excluded from the jury. See also (7) and Salem Records.

**WEBBER**, a weaver in Southwestern Eng. Early N. E. Webbers were English, and desc. cannot claim kinship with the Dutch Webers of New Amsterdam. See Aspinwall's 'Notarial Records,' pp. 259, 363, for Thomas Webber, master mariner at Boston, 1649-50.

1 **EDWARD**, Portsmouth, depos. in 1678, ±22, what he heard Thomas Ladbrook say. Poss. the Edward at Kennebec 1679-1688, List (†92), 187, 189. This name is found in Beverly later.

2 **HENRY**; see Goddard(2).

3 **JAMES**(12), mariner, boatman at Falmouth 1689, List 228c, prob. tempor. at Wells or York, as he m. Patience Littlefield (15) who was bp. at Charlest. as his w. 23 Apr. 1699. A York grant 1699, provid. he settle, was never laid out. Of Boston 19 Mar. 1715-6; of Charlest., but sworn at Portsm. in Mar. 1718-9, he test. that he liv. at Casco at or bef. the time Casco fort was taken and knew for a certainty that (10) sold half of Long Creek sawmill to John Skillings. He d. 19 Mar. 1729 in 64th yr. (gr.st. at Medford). Adm. to wid. Patience, liv. at Medford 1748. Wyman's 'Charlestown' names ch. b. 1696-7—1712-3: **James**, **Joseph**, **Benjamin**, **Jonathan**, **Nathan** (s. of James and Patience, rec. at Glouc. 20 Aug. 1704), two **Elizabeths**, **Josiah**.

4 **JOHN**(12), mariner, eldest son, ±28 about 1684 when he went from Wells to Boston with John Cloyes. Cape Neddick wit. in Feb. 1687-8 (see 10). Taxed Boston 1688 next to Verins. He d. bef. 21 Feb. 1715-6, leaving only s. and heir, **Nathan**, Boston, mariner 1716 (N. m. Ruth Cobbett there 7 Apr. 1709, m. Rebecca Burbank 20 Oct. 1713), and only dau. **Abigail**, m. John Newman in Boston 15 Sept. 1710, a wid. 1716.

5 **JONAS**, sawyer, Boston, List 161. See Giles(8), Doc. Hist. 24: 369.

6 **JOSEPH**(12), Falmouth 1680 and until war time. Wit. (10)'s deed there in 1685. Lists 34, 225ab. He appraised a Yarmouth (Barnstable Co.) est. in 1693 and was there in July 1700 when his mo. deeded him 1/7 of the Kennebec land given her by her br. This he soon sold to Thomas Sturgis, with 60 a. at Falm. at head of Long Creek River, two other Falm. lots and Parker's Neck in Saco, yet later ent. an East. Cl. for the Kennebec land. Appar. his son was **James**, cordwainer, Kittery, but once of Yarm., who bot a Crooked Lane ho. in 1717, m. 1st 18 Dec. 1719 Elizabeth Furber (Wm. 3 jr.), m. 2d 13 Feb. 1728-9 Keturah Jenkins

(Thomas 4). One Samuel W. was of Yarmouth, Mass., in 1743.

7 **MICHAEL**, Purpooduck 1683, m. 14 Aug. 1686 Deborah Bedford(1). Driven off by the war, he was a Kittery fisherman 1695, at Glouc. 1701, and mistakenly ret. East where his fam. was k. or captured 10 Aug. 1703. A Wallis depos. placed his home as at Spring Point. Lists 226, 39. He ret. to Glouc., in Feb. 1717-8 testif. for Joseph Page (see Paine 20) and d. 12 Jan. 1728-9, ±90 by rec. His w. and six ch. were k. in 1703, by report, but at least four ch. were captured: **Michael**, ret. to Piscataqua in 1704, m. in Boston 11 May 1710 Sarah Green, liv. in Glouc., where 11 ch. rec. Adm. to wid. Sarah 11 Feb. 1760. Descendants came to Me.; see George Walter Chamberlain's Gen., 1935. **Nathan**, in Canada 1710-11. **Elizabeth**, as Marie Elizabeth Wabert, ag. 19, m. Nathaniel (or Paul) Otis (3); see 'N. E. Captives' i: 159. **Child**, in Canada 1710-11. The only rec. ch. was **Mary**, b. in Glouc. 16 May 1701, whose age makes it improb. she was the unnamed ch. carried away. List 99, pp. 92, 127.

8 **RICHARD**, Portsmouth, b. ±1641 (±37 in 1678). Shoals 1669, bot in Portsmouth that yr. from the Samuel Drew est. and from James and Mary Drew in 1672. A tailor in 1684 when he attacked Sarah Reed(11); a butcher later, unless two Richards. He m. by 1674 Lydia (Trickey 6) Green who sold liquor in 1678. Tav. lic. 1678, 1681; Pheasant Eastwick informed ag. him in 1690. Summonsed for Gove panel 1683; j. 1684; gr.j. 1684, 1693. Constable 1693-1695. In 1693 cautioned for selling sheep skins without their ears. In 1700 he and Lydia sold 1 a. and a ho. near the meet.-ho. to Samuel Waterhouse; in 1717 sold Fernald's Isl. to Robert Ward, called Webber's Isl. in 1723. Lists 326c, 329, 330d, 331ab, 333a, 335a, 336b, 337, 52, 54, 55ab, 57. Goody W., List 335a, was ag. 68 in June 1718. His will, butcher, 24 Feb. (d. 25 May, ag. 82) 1720, gives all to w. (Lydia) except 5 s. each to 2 daus., 3 gr.ch. Her will, 6 Aug. 1720 (d. 30 Apr. 1721, ag. 69), gives all to dau. Abigail, but if she sold the ho. or had ch., to give sis. Hannah £10. Ch. appear: **Mary**, m. Wm. Bickham(3); her dau. Mary, but not self, in fa.'s will. **Hannah**, appar. m. in 1721. The mo. of John King, named in gr.fa.'s will, presum. was **Elizabeth**, m. in Boston 14 Sept. 1704 John King, d. there 20 Nov. 1715, ag. ±38; rec.ch: John, Elizabeth, William, Richard, Lydia. **Daughter**, mo. of John Abbott named in gr.fa.'s will. **Abigail**, m. in Portsmouth 20 Nov. 1723 Edward Sadler(1).

9 **RICHARD**, Casco Bay by 1683 (List 226, Webb), m. Damaris Boaden(3) and liv. long at Marblehead where in 1726 they q.c. to s. John land at Black Point adj. Spur-

wink River. At Salem 27 Nov. 1733 he deposed that ±38 yrs. bef. he liv. at Casco Bay and knew Ralph Turner. Damaris was liv. in 1752, called 100. Their s. **John**, coaster, Wells, m. there 19 Oct. 1721 Abigail Harding (6) and in 1731 sold to Joseph Poak his gr.fa. Boaden's land. List 269a. Other ch. may have incl. four who m. at Marbleh: **Mary**, m. Samuel Bowden. **William**, m. Sarah Mercer in 1707, Hannah Chamneys in 1713. **Richard**, m. Mary Libby(4). **Sarah**, m. Richard Oakes, jr., in 1717.

10 **SAMUEL**(12), millwright, York. Wells 1679 and apprais. Mousam mill with John Littlefield in June 1680. His Casco mill taxed 1682; he sold ho. and mill at Long Creek to Skillings and to Davis 1685. Wit. mill deeds at Bid. in June 1686, with br. John a Cape Neddick wit. in Feb.1687-8, his mill ment. 1688, York gr. 1690, commanded Cape Neddick garrison that yr. In Aug. 1692, ag. ±36, he depos. in the Burroughs trial at Salem. Gloucester 1695, and of G. 21 Mar. 1698-9, bot from Joseph Weare 20 a. at York near Weare's ho. Me. j. 1700-1702; gr.j. 1703. Partner with Capt. Pickering and Matthew Austin in York mill 1702. In 1709 he and s. Samuel bot the Smith homestead. Either fa. or son was shot by Ind., but not killed, in 1712. Lists 36, 225a, 279. Will, 5 May—13 Nov. 1716, names w. Deborah (Littlefield 15) and 9 ch., Waitstill and Joseph event. to have homestead; wife exec. Her will, 23 Apr. 1737—19 May 1747, gr.s. Jonathan Sayward exec. Ch., order in fa.'s will: **Samuel**, had York gr. 1702-1722, and willed, over and above the others, 6 a. Black Point marsh bot of Mr. Andrew Brown. List 279. Owned at Kennebec 1716. Will, 25 Mar.—29 May 1735, names w. and exec. Elizabeth Young(10), 12 ch. (the 1st ch. Elizabeth b. 12 Oct. 1705, had d. in 1721). The wid. m. 2d George Stover(3), 3d Hon. Samuel Came(3). **John**, had gr. 1702-1714, List 279, m. 1st in 1709 Magdalene (Hilton 9) Weare (ch: Hannah 1711, m. George Colesworthy in Boston 1732; Josiah 1713); m. 2d, int. 21 May 1726, Elizabeth Gypson of Wells (ch: Deborah, 1727-1740; Lydia 1729). In 1716 his fa. deeded him 100 + 10 a. at Kennebec. **Thomas** and **Benjamin**, had Cape Neddick land from parents in 1716. Thomas sold to B. bef. 24 July 1720, d. 26 Feb. 1723 (Mr. Marshall); see (13). Benjamin, millwright, had York gr. 1713-4, List 279, and when ±54 depos. that ab. 18 yrs. bef. he went to Damariscotta and built the first mill there for Mr. Wm. Vaughan. He m. 1st (ct. Oct. 1715) Mehitabel Allen, m. 2d Martha Day (int. at York 3 Feb. 1738-9 'published to satisfie such persons as are dissatisfied and think he is not married'); 1 ch. **Waitstill**, b. 18 Jan. 1697-8 at Glouc. where his twin **Pa-**

tience, d. the next mo. He had York gr. 1721-2, List 279, m. Meribah Hutchins (Benj. 2); 3 ch. 1723-1726. **Joseph,** youngest son, had (mortg.) land and livestock from mo. in 1726, m. (int. 13 Apr. 1726) Mary Lewis (2) who m. 2d 29 June 1753 Elias Weare (2 jr.). List 279. **Mary,** m. Joseph Sayward (4). **Deborah,** m. Andrew Wescott(3). See also Perkins(11). (Ano. **Deborah,** b. at Glouc. 2 June 1695, d. there 6 July 1698). **Dorcas,** m. (int. 5 Feb. 1724-5) John Baker. **Barsheba,** in Canada 1735, in mo.'s will, not fa.'s. Likely the Eng. girl Wabert, dau. of Samuel, bp. in Canada as Marie 17 Feb. 1714, m. 11 Mar. 1720 Joseph Saleur; see 'N. E. Captives,' i: 250.

11 **THOMAS,** one of Capt. John Smith's quartermasters 1614, List 7.

12 **THOMAS,** fisherman, Kennebec, took O. F. to Plymouth govt. 1654. His s. Samuel in deeding 100 + 10 a. to his s. John located his fa.'s home place as on S.W. side of the Kennebec over ag. Arrowsic Isl.; of this he had a deed from Robin Hood in 1660 and his w. Mary Parker(13) had land from her fam. In Feb. 1663-4 they sold Long Isl., butting on Sagadahoc Point of Entrance, to Richard Collicott (orig. in SJC 68), and in Mar. 1666-7 he deeded to Wm. Brown of Salem ⅔ of Rascohegan Isl., ⅓ for self, ⅓ for John Brown. Lists 11, 182, 183, 4. See also Benmore(2), Crocker(2), Purington(4). Reported at Charlestown early in the first war, then Falm. His wife's pet. to Andros in Feb. 1687, List 34, stated that for several yrs. she had been in poss. at Falm. and made no ment. of him; his dau.'s deed 1741 called him 'of Lynn, dec.' Widow Mary, ±53, test. in the Burroughs trial at Salem 2 Aug. 1692, joined Charlest. Ch. 28 Apr. 1695, of C. deeded to s. Joseph in July 1700, and later, as wid. of Thomas of Casco Bay, claimed 130 a. at Falm. (a town gr.), also the land deeded by Robin Hood, and land adj. Sylvanus Davis and Winnegance Creek deeded by her br. John in 1661, while Wm. Brown, Richard Hall and Clarke & Lake heirs claimed land deeded by Webbers died. b. def. 14 Feb. 1715-6. Ch., 5 sons and 1 dau. left at their decease (Y. D. 8: 149): **John,** eldest son, ag. ±28 about 1684. **Samuel,** ag. ±36 in 1692. **Nathaniel,** Falm. 1689, List 228c, in 1697 owned cov. at Charlest. Ch., his w. Elizabeth joining in 1714. A Boston sawyer 1716, living 1717. His w. d. 11 Mar. 1731-2 in 60th yr. (Copp's Hill). See Wyman's 'Charlestown,' ii: 1004, for 8 ch. 1697-1711. **James. Joseph,** b. ±1665. **Mary,** York, tailoress, single 21 Jan. 1741-2 when he q.c. fa.'s and mo.'s estates to James Donnell.

13 **THOMAS,** of 'Augusta,' mortg. and sold land on Bigbuary Isl., a dwg. and three schooners to Capt. Penhallow 1718-1720;

four of the five witnesses were York men. In Suff. Co. jail 1721, on suit of Wm. Young, and a bankrupt, having been at much charge in building and improving lands to the Eastward. Mary of Boston, wid. of one Thomas, depos. in Nov. 1749, ag. 60, that she liv. with her husb. on a 300 a. farm at Kennebec ten yrs. past, and when he d. deliv. the farm to James McCobb in behalf of the heirs of Isaac Parker, gr.s. of John Parker; and John Snowman of Boston, ag. 21, form. of Kennebec, depos. that he liv. on this farm with his fa.-in-law T. W. and mo. Mary Webber. See also Thomas(10).

**Webley,** George, verdict filed 29 June 1669, 'drowned going over the bar.' N. H.?

**WEBSTER,** ano. form of Weaver.

1 **SERGT. EBENEZER,** Kingston, m. there 25 July 1709 Hannah Judkins(1) and d. 1 Feb. 1736, ag. 67. Jury 1693, grantee of Kingston 1694, constable Mar. 1696-7. Lists 399A, 400. Will, 12 Jan.—16 Mar. 1735-6, makes ample provis. for w. Hannah and 7 of 9 ch: **Rachel,** b. 17 Mar. 1710. **Susannah,** b. 9 July 1712. **Ebenezer,** b. 10 Oct. 1714, fa.'s exec., m. 20 July 1738 Susanna Batchelder (2); they in time became the gr.parents of Daniel Webster. **William,** b. 26 Aug. 1716, and **John,** b. 4 Aug. 1719, these two not in will. **Hannah,** unrec. **Joseph** and **Mary,** twins, b. 15 Sept. 1724. **Iddo** (son), b. 9 Feb. 1727-8. See N. E. Reg. 9: 159.

2 **ISRAEL,** List 66, credited to Hampton, is unkn. in the Hampt. or Ex. families. The name occurs in the Ipsw.-Newb. fam.

3 **JOHN,** brewer, Strawberry Bk., in Aug. 1646 bot from Roger Knight 8 a. that had been Michael Chatterton's. See also (9). Constable 1648, apprais. Henry Taylor's est. 1649, lic. to sell wine 1649. Before Me. ct. 1651 for selling beer at the Shoals. Pub. ho. lic. Str. Bk. 1656, 1657, 1659-1661; j. 1650; selectman 1655; gr.j. 1659. He exch. land with John Jones in 1655; sold on Gt. Isl., to John Cutts 1658, to Isaac Cousins 1661. In 1658 gave a bill to Barefoot who sued his wid. in 1662, Samuel Hall her atty. Lists 323-325, 326a, 330ab. See also Munmer. Wife Rachel first seen 16 Dec. 1658. In 1659 he was accus. of abusing her, also of keeping Mr. Batchelder in his ho. three days; his defense: he could not get him out. Adm. on his est. 24 June 1662, to Capt. Waldron and Elias Stileman; Capt. Waldron took adm. alone in 1663. As a wid. she had a pub. ho. lic., was much in evid. and rather unruly; last seen 7 July 1676. A persistent Batchelder-Richards relationship is noted. See also Allison(3), Hunt(7), Jones(17 jr.), Ladbrook, Peake, and Mary Follansby who heard her having an altercation with Martin Hall (15). One ch. seen: John, by an unkn. wife.

In Jan. 1650-1 his fa. deeded him all, house, brew-ho., furnace, livestock, boat, land; sued his fa.'s admr. 1665; pub. ho. lic. 1667; ord. to take down his sign in 1668. List 47.

4 **JOHN,** blacksmith. See Mighill(3).

5 **STEPHEN,** tailor, Haverhill, of the Ipsw.-Newb. fam., m. 2d 26 May 1678 wid. Judith Broad(4). List 331b. Judith wit. John Marden's will in 1698. Ch. by 1st w., Hannah Ayer, incl: **John,** m. Tryphena Locke (2). **Abigail,** b. at Haverh. 27 May 1676, m. 1st James Marden(1), m. 2d Samuel Berry (5).

6 **THOMAS,** planter, Hampton, bp. at Ormesby St. Michaels, co. Norfolk, 20 Nov. 1631, s. of Thomas W., who was bur. there 30 Apr. 1634, and his w. Margery who m. 2d Wm. Godfrey(7) and 3d John Marion. In 1656 he bot from Wm. Cole whose sole legatee he was in 1662. Gr.j. 1683, 1693, 1696. Lists 393b, 394, 396, 397b, 49, 52, 54, 57, 62. See also Knowles(2), Norris(3). He m. 2 Nov. 1657 Sarah Brewer, aunt of Wm. Lane. She joined the ch. 15 Oct. 1699. He d. 5 Jan. 1715, ag. 83; no rec. of adm. Ch: **Mary,** b. 19 Dec. 1658, m. 1st Wm. Swaine (7), m. 2d Joseph Emmons(2). **Sarah,** b. 22 Jan. 1660-1, m. Wm. Lane(13). **Hannah,** b. 27 Dec. 1663, d. 1 Feb. 1663-4. **Thomas,** b. 20 Jan. 1664-5. **Ebenezer,** b. 1 Aug. 1667. **Isaac,** b. 12 Apr. 1670, m. 1 Apr. 1697 Mary Hutchins. Newbury 1706. Ch. bp. at Hampt. 1697-1704: John, Jonathan, Hannah, Elizabeth, and by 2d w. Sarah, rec. at Kingston 1715-6, Samuel and Gideon, besides two older ch. who d.y. He d. at Kingston 21 Feb. 1717-8; adm. to s. John. List 399a. **John,** b. 16 Feb. 1673-4, m. 1st 21 Sept. 1703 Abiah Shaw(10) and had a 2d w. Sarah, m. perh. betw. 1706-1712. Ch: Jeremiah 1703, Charity and Josiah, twins, 1706, and from 1712-1724: John, Thomas, Caleb, Abiah, Elizabeth. Adm. on his est., mariner of Rye, to sons Jeremy and Josiah, bond 8 July 1734. Calling him late of Amesbury and herself advanced in yrs., the wid. 11 Nov. 1754 asked that adm. be gr. to her oldest s. John. **Joshua,** b. 8˙Nov. 1676. **Abigail,** b. 1 Jan. 1678-9, m. John Nay.

7 **THOMAS(6),** Kingston, d. 7 Mar. 1733, an aged man who fell dead in the street. Lists 66, 399a, 400. Wife Sarah d. 15 Feb. 1717-8. Ch: **Sarah,** b. in Hampt. 19 Sept. 1690, m. Samuel Fellows(1 jr.). **Thomas** (unrec.), had land from fa. in 1713, m. 19 June 1717 Mary Greely of Haverh.; d. 13 May 1772 in Kingston where 6 daus. rec. **Mary,** b. in Hampt. 19 May 1696, m. 16 Aug. 1716 John Fifield of Kingston. **Alice,** b. in Hampt. 5 Aug. 1698, d. in Kingston 30 Oct. 1722. Rec. at Kingston: **Benjamin,** b. 24 Aug. 1701, m. 1st in Feb. 1725 Elizabeth Stuart, m. 2d 1 Dec. 1737 Mary Stanyan. **Joshua,** b. 2 Sept. 1703. **Abigail,** b. 15 Apr.

1706, m. 26 Dec. 1724 David Quimby. **Samuel,** b. 3 Apr. 1708, had land from fa. in 1729, m. 1st at Ipsw. 6 Feb. 1732-3 Elizabeth Burnham of Chebacco, m. 2d 10 May 1740 Dorothy Stanyan. **Elizabeth,** b. 11 Jan. 1710, m. 20 Apr. 1730 Josiah Fowler.

8 **THOMAS,** Exeter (bot 5 a. in 1700), b. in Boston 11 Jan. 1661, s. of James, a Scotch brewer, and his Irish w. Mary Hay, who were m. in Boston 14 Feb. 1658. Merchant, cordwainer, innholder. List 376b (1700, 1701, 1725). In 1717 he q.c. fa.'s est. to br. Wm. of Boston. Wife Deborah liv. 1728. Betw. 1728-1738 he deeded to each ch.; s. Thomas called jr. 1743. Ch: **Deborah,** b. 11 Nov. 1701, m. 12 Oct. 1724 Zebulon Giddings of Ex. **Nathaniel,** had ho. and land from fa. 1728, m. a dau. of Col. John Gilman(11). List 376b (1725). Will, 22 Jan. 1744—27 Feb. 1744-5, names 3 ch., kinswo. Martha Two Giddings, fa.-in-law Gilman gdn. of the ch. **Thomas,** had land from fa. 1733, d. 1749, leaving wid. Susanna, 6 ch. **Elizabeth,** appar. unm. in 1733, w. of Francis Bowden by Jan. 1734-5. See Putnam's Gen. Quarterly Mag., vol. 5 (1904), pp. 139, 183.

9 **WILLIAM,** brewer, Strawberry Bk., List 72, may be error for (3).

10 **WILLIAM,** taxed Newc. 1708, m. wid. Susanna Rand(5). List 316. Of Newc., farmer, he sold common lands to George Walker 1722.

**WEDGE, Thomas,** Strawberry Bk., sued by Henry Sherburne 1650; George Monk bondsm. for him 1650. In 1661 ordered to bring his wife or go to her; Wm. Seavey depos. that he had sent for her several times; Gregory Foye depos. that now her fa. is dead, she is willing to come either via Newfoundland or Barbadoes. Lists 323, 326a. See also Wegges, Hinkson(3).

**WEDGWOOD,** a Staffordshire hamlet which gave its name to the fam. and the ware.

1 **DAVID(2),** Hampton, m. 4 Jan. 1683 Hannah Hobbs(8) who was liv. in 1707, ag. ±44, he then ±54. He and Thomas Thurton fined for fighting 1679; j. 1694; sold Hampt. prop. 1716; d. 25 Jan. 1742. Lists 52, 396, (?399a, error for David), 399b. Ch: **John,** b. 8 Aug. 1688, m. 31 Jan. 1712 Hannah Shaw(2), d. 31 July 1755, 2 ch. rec. **Mary,** b. 5 Apr. 1694, m. Ezekiel Knowles(3).

2 **JOHN,** Hampton by the 2d summer, but first an Ipsw. landowner 1637-1639, during which time he went ag. the Pequots. By 1644 he bot a ho.-lot orig. gr. to Wm. Sargent, sold in 1650, and bot from Rev. John Wheelwright, and liv. on, 15 a., called 'the Elder's lot.' Jury 1652. Lists 391a, 392a, 393ab. He m. a dau. of John Smart(2), cert. the mo. of his s. John and presum. that

Mary who was his w. in Ipsw. in 1639 when they were in the company of Ann Cross(4), and his wid. (List 393a). Will, 24 Nov. (d. 9 Dec.) 1654, names w. Mary (exec.) and ch., giving to eldest s. John his Ex. ho. and land, part to be his on the death of his gr.mo., but if he died, all to w. Mary. She had a legacy from Susanna (Haborne) Leader(3) in 1658, wit. in a Goody Cole case (with 1673 depositions), d. 24 Aug. 1688, ag. 70. Ch: **John**, b. ±1640. **Jonathan**, blacksmith, Hampt., soldier at O. R. in Sept. 1694. Lists 52, 54, 396, 397b. His w. Sarah d. 16 June 1680; he m. last 9 Feb. 1700 Rachel (Davis) Haines (11) and by deed ackn. 5 Apr. 1723 conv. all to her, and aft. her death to her gr.s. Malachi Haines, or if he d., to her s. Thomas H., and if he d. to his own br. John's sons, if any liv., else to his dau. Yet Daniel, List 399a (unless error for David), and Jacob, List 399b, poss. were sons who d. s.p. bef. 1723. Wid. Rachel d. 9 Nov. 1749, ag. 88. **Mary**, called the prettiest girl in town 1663, m. Abraham Cole(1). **Abigail**, b. 12 Sept. 1650, d. 16 July 1669. **David**, b. 12 Dec. 1652.

3 **JOHN**(2), Exeter by 1674; ±40 in 1680. He had land from uncle John Smart in 1653, and in 1678, of Exeter, sold it. Intimately assoc. with Hiltons. Gr.j. 1692, 1699. In 1698 sued by Reuben Hull's est. on an acct. that started with an old bal. 1681. Edw. Hilton and one John W. were abs. from meet. 1698. Two deeds, 1700-1701 may have been his or his son's. His wife is unseen and fam. uncertain. Jonathan(2) ment. br. John's **sons** and **daughter**, and poss. Daniel, List 399a, and Jacob, List 399b, were his ch. More reasonably, by age and from the fact that (3's) dau. (not daus.) was ment., it was a s. **John** (presum. the captive 1712, List 99, p. 92) who in 1717 deeded to Richard Clarke 150 a. 'granted me by Edw. Hilton,' and in 1717-8 deeded to s. John, a minor, who was to pay £4 to each sis., and d. by 1736, leaving ch: John (Newmarket 1747, when he q.c. est. of Uncle Jonathan of Hampt.); Catherine, unm. (w. of Humphrey Fost(2) in 1747); Abigail, b. 22 Mar. 1701, m. at O. R. 11 Apr. 1728 Abraham Bennick(1 jr.); Mary, m. bef. 15 Feb. 1730-1 Benj. Glidden(3); Salome and Ann, both unm. 1736; also Sarah (w. of Samuel Richards of Rochester 1739; see Richards 4).

**WEED, Thomas,** weaver, and w. Joanna, Kittery, Berwick; see Hoyt's Salisb. i: 346, ii: 808; Y. D. 10: 6; 12: 12. In May 1729 he depos. that he knew Capt. Thomas Abbott to be in poss. of land at Quamphegan ±30 yrs. ago. Lists 291, 298. See also Chick.

**WEEDEN,** Weden, -don. See also Barnard(1).

1 **GEORGE,** Dover 1659, List 356e.

2 **JOHN,** his letter to John Butler ab. collecting from 'old White,' dated York. Jan. 1680-1, is quoted in Hist. of York ii: 55, with reference SJC 2057.

3 **JOSEPH,** York, wit. mortg. given by John Stover, sr., to Thomas Lee in Jan. 1680-1, fined for selling without lic. in Apr. 1681 (see Annay), sued by Wm. Wright, jr., in Oct. 1681. A man of this name, ±39, test. in Boston in 1685, in the case ag. Gyles Goddard(1), accused of wrongfully selling goods at Nevis.

**WEEKS,** from South of England. See also Winkley(2).

1 **JOSEPH**(3), Kittery, m. 1st Adah Briar (see 5), m. 2d ±1702 Mary Gunnison(1). Grant 1694. Jury 1693-4; gr.j. 1693-4, 1695; constable 1696. Lists 291, 297, 298. In 1704 Richard Briar called him 'my beloved bro.' and the same yr. gave p/a to 'br.-in-law' J. W. Ag. ±50 in 1720 (Y. D. 10: 84). Will, 19 Nov.—14 Dec. 1741, names wife, 5 ch., br. Nicholas, gr.s. Benj. Morgrage. Widow Mary's will, 25 Oct. 1763—13 Apr. 1767, names dau. Martha Jones, wid., and gr.s. Joseph Jones, exec. Ch., by 1st w: **Judith,** b. 3 June 1696, m. Jonathan Hutchins(2). **Mary,** b. 8 Sept. 1697, m. Thomas Morgrage (John). **Nicholas,** b. 27 Aug. 1699, m. 26 Oct. 1721 Sarah Rice(5). **Benjamin,** b. 8 July 1701, m. 1 Feb. 1727-8 Elizabeth Wilson(7). By 2d w: **Joseph,** b. 25 Feb. 1704, not in fa.'s will. **Abraham,** m. Sarah Elwell, both liv. 1746. **Martha,** m. Daniel Jones(8 jr.).

2 **LEONARD,** Greenland, ±1646, serv. of Capt. Champernowne, said to have been bp. at Compton-Martin, co. Somerset, 7 Aug. 1639 (Reg. 75: 321), but he deposed, ±40 in 1672, 48 in 1681, ±65 in 1699, ±70 in 1703, 73 in 1705. See also Turpin. Berwick wit. 1655 (Y. D. 1: 57); Portsm. gr. 1656; O. A. 1666, 1685; on Greenl.-Bloody Point highway com. 1669; j. 1679, 1694, 1695, 1697; constable 1682; surv. of fences 1692; gr.j. 1693. Lists 323, 326ac, 330abcd, 331a, 332b, 335a, 337, 356L, 49, 52, 54, 55a, 57, 62, 67, 90. See also Hall(7), Hussey(7). He m. 1st Mary Redman(1), List 331c, and depos. in 1682 that 20 yrs. bef. he put his horse in his fa. Redman's pasture; m. 2d Elizabeth Haines (12) whose fa. and bros. depos. in 1683 that he had poss. for 23 yrs. without molestation the place where he had set up his ho. In 1706 he gave deeds to sons Samuel and Joshua, but making provis. for w. Elizabeth and certain ch.; see 'Leonard Weeks of Greenland, N. H.' (Chapman 1889) p. 118. He d. betw. 15 May 1706—24 May 1708 (Joshua had his deed rec. 4 Sept. 1707); adm. to s. Samuel 4 June 1718. Ch., by w. Mary: **John,** 'eldest son,' b. 14 June 1668, outliv. fa., d. s.p. by 1718. Given £10 in 1706, no land, he

prob. liv. away. **Samuel,** b. 14 Dec. 1670. Capt. **Joseph,** cordwainer, Greenl., b. 11 May 1671; see (5). Lists 338ac. Taxed as Capt. 1719. Wife Hannah. Adm. 27 Nov. 1735 to s. Jedediah. Ch. in 1748: Jedediah, Jonathan, Joshua, Joseph, Leonard, Abigail, Elizabeth (m. Josiah Foss 2), Sarah (m. Nathl. Huggins 4 jr.). Capt. **Joshua,** Greenl., b. 30 June 1674, m. in Boston 7 Nov. 1699 Comfort Hubbard(10), List 338b. Taxed as Capt. 1717. Lists 337, 338abc. See also Huggins(4), Samuel King(16). He d. 13 June 1758; will, 2 Nov. 1752 (cod. 11 Jan. 1757) names w. Comfort (d. 20 Mar. 1756) and ch: John; Joshua (decd.), his s. Joshua; Mary Chesley (Jonathan 3); Martha Hilton (w. of Winthrop 2 jr.) and her s. Joshua Wiggin; Comfort Weeks (w. of Walter 5); Thankful Marshall (w. of George), lately decd., her 2 sons and 2 daus.; Margaret Smith (w. of Ebenezer); William and his s. Joshua. Sons Ichabod and Richard had d. s.p. **Mary,** b. 19 July 1676, m. Joshua Brackett(6); the plf. in SJC 15120 (1734); both liv. 1748. **Margaret,** b. 4 June 1679, m. Ebenezer Johnson(16). Appar. by 2d w: **Jonathan,** Greenl., m. Elizabeth Cate(1) by 1718 (List 338b). His Lists 338abcd. See also Jenkins(11). Will, 29 Sept. 1746, proved 22 Sept. 1748, altho John Brackett and Samuel Weeks ent. protest, gives to w. Elizabeth, two Allens, two Cates, and David Haines' w. Lydia. SJC 25962 (1748) names the next-of-kin. Will. Elizabeth's will, 11 June 1754—20 July 1755, gives to Cates; see also SJC 25951. **Sarah,** m. Benjamin Macrease(1).

3 **NICHOLAS,** shipwright, Kittery, sued by Mr. Robert Cutts in 1666 as 'Wix.' Gr. 1671, bot E. of Spruce Creek 1672. In Jona. Mendum's suit ag. (1) in 1702, John Ball depos. that N. W. liv. on the land in controv., always called Weeks Point, and aft. his ho. was burned by Ind., rebuilt on same spot bef. old Robert Mendum d., who never claimed the land. Others called the spot Turkey Point. His son claimed poss. of over 40 yrs., and Joseph Couch depos. that N. W. liv. in Spruce Creek when he came to Kit. 40 yrs. ago. Constable 1673; sued Robert Cutts 1674; j. 1686, 1690, 1693; gr.j. 1687, 1688, 1690; j. life and death 1693. List 298. See also Grant(16). Adm. to s. Joseph 11 Jan. 1693-4, sureties Mr. Wm. Scriven, Mr. Richard Cutts. His w. was Judith in 1666 (see Woodman 5). In 1705 she depos. ab. old R. Mendum's bounds (see Judith Mendum 2). Surv. ch. 1720: **Joseph,** b. ±1670. **Nicholas,** shipwright, b. ±1672 (±59 in July 1731), named in br.'s will 19 Nov. 1741. Lists 291, 296, 297. He m. 1st 8 May 1700 Priscilla Gunnison(1), m. 2d 6 Nov. 1718 Ann (Adams 5) Hill, and was pub. 14 Aug. 1742 to Elizabeth (Scammon) Haley(2). Ch. 1702-1714:

Joseph, had the homestead, m. Sarah Haley (2); Judith, m. Thomas Gribble (see Grindal 1), Joseph Richardson and Joseph Wilson; Priscilla, in court as P. W. 1721, m. one Toolee; Elizabeth, m. Wm. Briar (7 jr.); Mary, m. Nathl. Fernald.

4 **OLIVER,** sailor, Richmond Isl., George Cleeve's serv. 1633, afterw. employed by Winter for whom he test. in 1640. Swearing in 1640, Thomas Elkins and George Deering bondsmen. In Trel. acct. 27 June 1643. List 21.

5 **CAPT. SAMUEL**(2), Greenland, m. Eleanor Haines(13) who d. bef. he made his will. In Aug. 1701 he and br. Joseph depos. that they liv. with their gr.fa. Redman of Hampt. 5 or 6 yrs. and drove the cows with their cousin John Redman. Gr.j. 1696, 1700; constable 1699; selectman 1701, 1705, 1709-1712, 1714. In 1744 he depos. ab. Ens. Wm. Haines and his int. in a sawmill near Greenland bridge over 40 yrs. Lists 324, 336b, 337, 338ac, 62, 67. Will, 15 Sept. 1745—30 Apr. 1746, names 6 surv. ch. also named in SJC 25962. Ch., first 6 bp. at Greenland 1712, their fa. called Capt. W: Lt. **Samuel,** tanner, Greenl., m. 19 May 1726 Mehitabel Pickering(8). He depos. in 1748, ag. 47. Will, 1762—1763, 7 ch. **Walter,** m. in Greenl. 14 Dec. 1725 Comfort Weeks (Joshua 2). **John,** m. in Greenl. 21 Dec. 1727 Abigail Forse. **Matthias,** m. in Greenl. 17 Dec. 1735 Sarah (Sanborn) Ford. **Joseph,** not seen aft. 1712. **Mary,** m. Paul Chapman. **Eleanor,** bp. 1714, d. unm. **William,** bp. 1717, not seen again.

6 **WILLIAM,** employed at the Shoals by Francis Wainwright in 1674, ag. ±45. William, ag. ±35, depos. in Apr. 1675 that the Churchwood bros. were b. and brot up at Kingsweare. See also Streeke.

**WEEMS, Lt. James,** commissioned commander at Pemaquid Fort by Gov. Andros 30 Nov. 1687 (Doc. Hist. 6: 304), from where he wrote to Gov. Bradstreet 11 May 1689 telling that Mr. Gullison had arrived from Casco (Mass. Arch. 107: 33). In Nov. 1689 he and Lt. John Jordan(6) created a disturbance at the Boston tavern of Richard Phillips, but only Lt. Weems was ord. arrested. Lists 19, 125, 126. See also Doc. Hist. 5: 179-183, 486-490, 521, and references in vols. 6 and 9.

**Wegges,** Thomas, ordered home to his wife in England by Dover ct. 1653. See also Wedge.

**Wel--,** Ralph, Dover 1674, List 357e.

**Welby,** Thomas, signed Dover petn. 1654.

**WELCH.** For origin of Ipswich fam. see Essex Q. Ct. Rec. 2: 294-297, 310; 6: 192, 360; Essex Probate 3: 230. See also N. E. Reg. 19: 55; 23: 417.

WELCH 734 WELCOM

1 **BENJAMIN**, tailor, Portsmouth, Kittery, a York or Kit. wit. 1707 (Y. D. 7: 81), m. bef. 20 Jan. 1707-8 Mary Hill(18). Poss. he was ano. unrec. br. of (7), as Philip, sr., moved around. Taxed Portsm. 1713; see also Preston(1). In Apr. 1719, of Kit., he bot 70 a. in Berw. from Nicholas Morrell and the same day bound half of it to his fa.-in-law in sum of £50 for his w. and ch. He, w. Mary and dau. **Elizabeth**, one of the **daus.** and **children**, were liv. 6 Dec. 1735, but the wording of Y. D. 17: 283, implies this Mary was ano. wife. Other ch. unidentified. Widow Mary of Kit., ag. 78, m. Richard Pinkham (1).

2 **EDWARD**, a London shipmaster, sued by Mr. Henry Hudson in York ct. Sept. 1661. John Pickering's bond for his appearance in 1662 was forfeited.

3 **GEORGE**, Pemaquid 1687, List 124. See Kelly(13) for George, taxed Newcastle 1720, whose s. William was bp. at Portsm. (So. Ch.) 19 Mar. 1726-7.

4 **JAMES**, m. (ct. July 1709) Mary Hammond(2) who joined Wells Ch. 13 July 1712 and m. 2d by 1718 Samuel Treadwell. Her ch. bp. at Wells 10 Aug. 1712: **Katherine**, m. at W. 6 Dec. 1726 Enoch Davis of Haverhill. **Beriah**, m. at W. 24 Oct. 1738 Caleb Kimball.

5 **JOHN**, a captive at St. John's River 1695 (Doc. Hist. 5: 403). One J. wit. Terra Magnus' depos. 1719. List 161.

6 **MOSES**, Portsmouth, Kittery, b. at Ipswich 25 Nov. 1685, br. of (7), m. there (int. 13 Apr. 1706) Rebecca Dod. Of Portsm. when his s. John was a little boy and started a fam. row with Benj. Miller, jr. Moses and Joseph taxed Portsm. Jan. 1731-2. Will, of Kit., 7 Jan.—19 Oct. 1756, names w. Rebecca and ch. (the 1st 7 bp. at Ipsw. 31 May 1719): **Joseph, Moses, Benjamin, Thomas, Daniel, John, David, Samuel**, bp. at Ipsw. 14 Aug. 172-, **Sarah** Page, **Hannah** Vinnen.

6½ **NATHANIEL**, Pemaquid wit., 1687.

7 **PHILIP**, York, b. at Ipswich 27 Dec. 1668, s. of Philip (List 85) and w. Hannah (Hagget, m. 20 Feb. 1666), br. of (6) and (10). Of York by Oct. 1693, m. Elizabeth Came(2) and in 1698 had town gr. of 30 a. for self, w. and ch., which he and Elizabeth sold in 1716. In 1733 Samuel Came deeded the place where Philip was liv. to him and Elizabeth for life, with remainder to their s. Benjamin; all three sold to Josiah Linscott in 1736. List 279. See also Hist. of York, ii: 93-94. Ch. at York: **Hannah**, b. 15 Aug. 1694, m. Zebulon Preble(9). **Elizabeth**, b. 14 Nov. 1696; see Fairweather(2). **Sarah** (b. at Beverly 15 Aug. 1698), m. John Curtis(5). **Abigail**, b. 15 Aug. 1700. **Deborah**, b. 16 Oct. 1702. **Samuel**, b. 28 Oct. 1703. **David**, b. 8 Oct. 1705, pub. int. with Catherine Soomes

(Ichabod), d. 3 Dec. 1727; s. David b.-12 May 1728. **Joseph**, b. 12 Oct. 1707. **Benjamin**, b. 17 Sept. 1710, m. Martha Conoway (Robert); 10 ch. **Mary**, b. 17 Mar. 1714-5, m. Joseph Thompson.

8 **RALPH**, at Richmond Isl. 1643, List 21.

9 **RALPH**, Dover, Hampton, Greenland or Rye, 1677-1684. Lists 359a, 396, 52.

10 **SAMUEL**, Kingston, unrec. br. of (6) and (7), and br. or br.-in-law of Hannah W. who m. there Thomas Scribner(1) as a 2d wife. Of Portsmouth, he m. (ct. Dec. 1701) Mary Judkins(1) who depos. in Kingston 28 Jan. 1750-1, ±70, about her mo.'s fam. Ch. rec. Feb. 1702-3—Mar. 1724-5, the 1st 2 at Haverh., others at Kingst: **Joseph, Hannah, Benjamin, Tabitha, Samuel, Martha, Philip, Martha, David, Abigail**. One Martha poss. should read Mary, as a Mary m. in Kingst. 2 Oct. 1740 Elisha Clough of No. Yarmouth. In York Inf. Ct. 1737 Benjamin W., lately of York, now of Kit., sued Samuel W., lately of Kingst., now of Berwick.

**WELCOM**, Wilcomb, Woolcomb. See also Fulford, Hodsdon(6).

1 **RICHARD**, Shoals, bot the Wm. Urin est. from the creditors and m. the wid. Eleanor by 1667. She sold liquor in 1677. He was constable for Star Isl. when John Winsland's ho. was searched for goods of the Lynes est.; gr.j. 1678; Shoals tav. lic. 1681, 1685, 1686; bondsm. for Wm. Chaplin 1681. Lists 308a, 312c. See also Broad(4). He signed a Shoals pet. 26 Jan. 1692 (Doc. Hist. 5: 331); prob. d. bef. Mar. 1692-3 when Eleanor had a Shoals lic. with John Westbrook and John Urin as bondsmen. She was lic. also 1694, 1695; taxed at Great Isl. 1698. Lists 307b, 315b. Her will, Wilcomb, 19 Sept. (inv. 12 Oct.) 1699, gives to s. John Muchemore her new boat of which John Currier is master, the rest to be divid. to 'my five ch.,' but provis. made for care of young Joseph Urin; Mr. Roger Kelly and kinsm. Richard Goss(2) overseers. Adm. was gr. to Muchemore 1 Feb. 1699-1700. Ch. appear: **Zaccheus**, first born. **Daughter** (poss. Amie), m. John Muchemore(2). **Ruth**, m. John Carter(5).

2 **ROBERT** (Waylkumm), a Wells wit. 1672 (Y. D. 2: 122).

3 **WILLIAM**, Pemaquid 1674, List 15. One W. ag. ±27 was at Wm. Brown's ho. in Boston 1670. See also 'Wilcome' in Savage.

4 **ZACCHEUS**(1), Shoals, m. Sarah Moore (25) who m. 2d Henry Spiller by 1693. In 1700 H. S. was gdn. of the three ch. who m. and liv. in Ipsw: **William**, m. 1st Charity Dodd who d. 18 Dec. 1724; m. 2d Rebecca Harris who d. 10 Feb. 1725-6. He d. 3 Dec. 1726. Will. Ch. **Deborah**, m. (int. Ipsw. 24 Mar. 1721-2) Daniel Smith. **Richard**, m.

(int. Ipsw. 22 Apr. 1710) Elizabeth Hodgkins; liv. Beverly 1760. 7 ch. bp. at Ipsw.
**Weld,** John, several times in error for Wells (5). See Hubbard, p. 230; Me. P. & Ct. Rec. ii: 337.
**WELDEN** (or Welding), **John,** a Falmouth settler under Danforth; helped run the line betw. Mr. Robert Lawrence's land and the town. Lists 30, 225ab. Gr.j. (N. H.) 1699.
**Welland** (or Willand), William, Dover. See Heard(7), Fost(2).
**WELLMAN.** 1 **Abraham,** List 142.
2 **THOMAS,** Lynn, soldier at Wells, List 267b.

**WELLS,** general in Eng., anciently usually Welles in cos. Oxford and Cambridge. Became 54th commonest name in N. E.
1 **ANTHONY,** d. intest. and without heir; adm. to Walter Gendall 1 Apr. 1673 (Wells ct.).
2 **EDWARD,** List 75b.
3 **EDWARD** (often Wills), mariner, Portsmouth, m. bef. 1694 Deborah Savage(3), and presum. br. of (7) who m. her sister. Lists 330d, 335a, 337, 339. Deborah (also Deborah, jr.) wit. John Lear's deed 1708 and was liv. 1711; Lists 335a, 337. In 1715 Edward, jr. deeded to fa. the land and old ho. willed him by his gr.fa. Savage; in 1717 James Stewart and w. Mary (Wells 7) deeded to uncle E. W., and he was Stewart's bondsm. in 1718. Admr. of Henry Savage's est. 1724, his bondsm. John Hooker and Richard Parsley. Adm. on his est. gr. to s. John 16 Feb. 1737-8. Ch. (1739 division): **Edward,** m. 9 Nov. 1713 Hannah Bartlett(1), d. bef. 1 Sept. 1717. Widow Hannah m. 2d Hugh Banfield(2), and 3d one Manson. Ch. bp: Elizabeth; Edward (had 2/9 in div.). **John,** fisherman, mariner, Portsm., m. by 1725 Dorothy Lang(4); adm. on his est. (Wills) gr. to John Lang 28 Jan. 1740-1; 6 ch. liv. 1754. **Samuel,** Portsm., m. 10 Oct. 1734 Priscilla Dowse(2); 7 ch. rec. at Rye. **Jeffrey,** Portsm., m. 5 Jan. 1732-3 Mehitabel Libby; ch. bp. at So. Ch. **Anne,** named in gr.mo.'s will 1708, not in div. One Ann was rec. into So. Ch. 3 July 1720. **Deborah,** wit. brother's deed as D. W. in 1715 and attested it as Brown in 1724. She had m. Henry Brown(9) by 1722 when her fa. borrowed a bed for her from Hugh Banfield. **Elizabeth,** m. 1st Isaac Ray(3), m. 2d John Hines, m. 3d 8 Oct. 1733 Robert Drought from Ireland. **Bethia,** renewed bp. cov. as B. W. 11 Feb. 1728; m. one Connors by 1739. **Zebulon,** at Halifax, N. S., 1751, when he q.c. fa.'s est.
4 **ISAAC,** Mr., preached at Kittery a short time in 1673, then disallowed. See Doc. Hist. 4: 338.

5 **JOHN**(10), had gift of fa.'s Wells land, ±350 a., and m. Sarah Littlefield(11) bef. 31 July 1666. Gr.j. 1670, 1671; j. 1676; ferry lic. 1671; indebted to John Manning's est. 1674; bondsman for Hammonds, and assoc. with Phebe Farrow in care of her mo. 1676. Lists 28, 266, 269b. Killed by Ind. 11 Apr. 1677. Adm. gr. first to bros. Nathaniel of Ipsw. and Thomas of Amesb. and the wid. Sarah; to the wid. alone 4 Dec. 1677. See Me. P. & Ct. Rec. ii: 337. She had m. William Sawyer(4). Her will, 1734, named 4 Wells ch., 2 Sibley gr.sons and a gt.gr. dau. Mary Clark; the ch. divid. the land in 1702 (Y. D. 6: 146): **John,** b. ±1670 (64 in Nov. 1734), mariner, m. 1st in Bost. 18 Feb. 1696-7 Mary Peck. Of Bost. until 1707+, and likely the Capt. W. at Black Point with his sloop when Capt. Hunnewell was k. in 1703. Wells by 1719, innholder, and m. 2d 20 May 1725 wid. Mary Stover(1). Lists 333b, 269ac. Will, 10 May—22 July 1748, names w. Mary, gr.ch., 3 ch: Mary, b. Bost. 22 Nov. 1697, m. by 1722 Henry Maddox (see 2). John, List 269c, m. 11 Oct. 1733 Deborah Stover(1); his s. John rec. the homestead. Hannah, wid. of Thomas Goodwin 1748 (see also Samuel Philbrick 10). Deacon **Thomas,** b. ±1672 (62 in Nov. 1734), tanner, m. 1st at Newb. 14 May 1696 Sarah Brown. Joined Wells Ch. from Newb. 21 Dec. 1701; jury 1701. At Newb. tempor. aft. w. and ch. were killed in 1703 and m. 2d at Salem 12 Oct. 1704 Lydia (Ropes) Gale. Wells mill-owner 1713; chosen Deacon 3 Mar. 1717-8. Lists 39, 269ac. Will, 19 July (d. at Wells 26 Aug.) 1737: w. Lydia (d. at Wells 6 Mar. 1746), 3 ch. Two of the four ch. reported k. were Sarah, b. at Newb. 9 Mar. 1698-9, and Joshua, b. at Wells 9 Oct. 1701. Ch. by 2d w., rec. at Newb., all in will: Nathaniel, b. 21 Aug. 1705, m. 26 May 1736 Dorothy Light(4); Joshua, b. 6 Mar. 1707, List 269c, m. 25 Dec. 1729 Meribah Littlefield(5); Lydia, b. 29 May 1709, m. Samuel Clark(43). **Sarah,** m. 1st at Salem 13 Sept. 1695 Samuel Sibley, m. 2d (int. at Newb. 25 Nov. 1710) John Sawyer, her step-fa.'s nephew. **Patience,** m. Nathaniel Clark(43).
6 **JOHN,** soldier, m. at York 3 Aug. 1725 Lydia (Young 2) Weare. List 279. Ch. 1728-1737: **Lydia. Job. Sarah. Nehemiah.** One John, soldier, from Suffolk, in Old Eng., made his will at Elisha Allen's ho. in York 13 Apr., prov. 3 Oct. 1723.
7 **PETER** (often Wills), mariner, Portsmouth, taxed Oct. 1691, m. Mary (Savage 3) Lear by 1694 when her parents deeded to them 10 a. adj. land form. Hugh Lear's and Robert Lang's with a way to the waterside. Lists 57, 335a (also his wife). Prob. both dead in 1698 as neither in tax list. Ch: **Elizabeth,** m. Henry Donnell(3). In 1736

they sold half her fa.'s 10 a. **Mary,** single in 1713, w. of James Stewart in 1717 when they deeded her half of 10 a. to uncle Edward Wells. See also (3) and Lear(1).

8 **PHILIP,** land surveyor in Maine for Sir E. Andros in 1687, and had been his steward. Lists 34, 221.

9 **GOV. THOMAS** (Welles) of Wethersfield, and Mary Willis of Hartford, owned in Squamscot patent, selling to Christopher Lawson in 1648 (Suff. D. i: 126).

10 **DEACON THOMAS,** Ipswich, bot 200 a. at Wells from Mr. Wm. Symonds in 1657, but was not resident there. See Y. D. 10: 91-92. By will, 1666—1666, he gave 50 s. to 'our Cussen Marye Baker (alias Loue) of Colchester.' See Essex Probate, i: 63-73 and i: 241-243 for wid. Abigail's will, 1671. See also Hoyt's Salisb. i: 348, for 8 ch. by w. Abigail (Warner), incl: **Nathaniel. John,** 2d son. **Thomas,** b. 11 Jan. 1646-7. **Lydia,** m. John Ropes of Salem.

11 **REV. THOMAS**(10), bot in Wells 1667-1669; of Wells in Dec. 1669. 'Minister of the town of Kittery' when John Tucker made his will 31 Oct. 1670. He served Kittery ab. a yr., and Mr. Francis Hooke was called chiefly responsible for his removing; see Doc. Hist. 4: 338; Y. D. 6: 36. Long minister at Amesbury, where he d. 10 July 1734. He was one of the first to receive an honorary degree from H. C., and poss. once of the class of 1669, but not a graduate. See Hoyt's Salisbury i: 351 for ten **ch.** by w. Mary (Perkins, m. 10 Jan. 1669), incl. **Luke,** b. 19 Mar. 1673-4, Lists 67, 336b, 96 (carried away by Ind. in 1697).

**WENTWORTH.** It is noteworthy that 'The Homes of English Families,' Guppy, 1890, does not ment. this family name which once flourished in England.

1 **BENJAMIN**(11), ±47 in Mar. 1716-7, ±57 in June 1727, had deed from fa. in 1693, covering corn he had sown on his fa.'s lot, the black cow he had chosen, and the land his br. Sylvanus had liv. on. Dover surv. of highways 1703, 1717; constable 1711, 1713. List 358d. Wife Sarah Allen(4). She drowned 25 July 1728; at 11 o'clock at night, going home from Dover Neck, he missed the boom and drove into the river. Adm. 10 Sept. 1728 to wid. Sarah, who depos. in Jan. 1756, ag. 76; d. 12 July 1770, ag. 91. Ch. rec: Capt. **William,** Somersworth, b. 14 Aug. 1698, m. 1st Mary Wentworth(4), m. 2d in Salisb. 25 Nov. 1737 Abra Evans; will 1778. **Sarah,** b. 16 Apr. 1700, m. Dea. Daniel Plummer. **Tamsen,** b. 4 Jan. 1701, m. Aaron Riggs of Glouc. Lt. **Benjamin,** b. 1 Dec. 1703, had the homestead, m. Deborah Stevenson(1), both d. 1790. **Ebenezer,** b. 9 Sept. 1705, m. 1st Sarah Roberts (John 12) who d. 1770,

m. 2d Elizabeth (Monroe) Young. **Susannah,** b. 9 Dec. 1707, m. Stephen Harford(2). **Joseph,** b. 22 Dec. 1709, d. 1765 leaving wid. Rachel and ch. See Y. D. 18: 1. **Elizabeth,** b. 8 June 1712, m. John Yeaton, jr. **Dorothy,** b. 26 July 1714, m. Ezekiel Wentworth (2). **Martha,** b. 25 July 1716, m. Elihu Hayes (John, 3 jr.). **Abra,** b. 14 Feb. 1718, m. Wm. Chadwick (see Haskins 6, Philpott). **Mark** (Markes), b. 30 May 1720, m. Elizabeth Wentworth (Capt. Benjamin 3); inv. 1757.

2 **EPHRAIM**(11), Dover, Lists 96, 358d, held minor town offices. He m. 1st Mary Miller(13), m. 2d Elizabeth (Waldron 6) Beard bef. 10 May 1726 when he q.c. to her br. his right in 40 a. of upland gr. to his fa. in 1652, with warr. ag. all persons that doth or may bear the name of Wentworth. She was liv. 5 Oct. 1737, but not in his will, 16 Mar. 1738-9—29 June 1748, from which his unrec. ch. are learned: **Ephraim,** m. Martha Grant(17). **Spencer,** m. Keziah Heard(11); d. s.p. **Ezekiel,** had the Dover homestead, m. 1st Dorothy Wentworth(1), m. 2d Sarah Nock(3). **Samuel,** m. Patience Downs, the 1st of 3 wives and mo. of his ch. **Jonathan,** m. Abigail Heard. **Mary,** m. Nehemiah Kimball. **Anna,** m. Ephraim Ham. **Martha,** m. Joseph Twombly. **Elizabeth,** unmar. 1738.

3 ***EZEKIEL***(11), first taxed 1672, had grants 1694, 1696, 1701, and lived in part of Dover incorp. as Somersworth. Jury 1687 (fined), 1699; constable 1693, 1694; highway surv. 1695; selectman 1702; assessor 1705; died while in office as Rep. betw. Oct. 1711—May 1712. In 1720 three sons were cited to take adm., on compl. of the Things. Lists 353, 356j, 358b, 359ab, 52, 54, 57, 62, 94. He m. one Elizabeth bef. 27 June 1676 when she depos. that she wit. the indenture of Sylvanus Nock to John Hall, jr., who deliv. the paper to Sylvanus in the presence of his mo., his fa.-in-law (Benmore) and herself. In Nov. 1715 sons Benjamin and Gershom were to care for her; prob. d. bef. 9 Mar. 1726. Deeds and s. Paul's will show fol. ch: **Thomas,** mariner, had portion from fa. 3 Feb. 1708-9. His wid. Love, then w. of John Thing(2), was gr. adm. 3 June 1719; one dau. Elizabeth, her gdn. Capt. Paul W. **John,** liv. at Sligo, m. 24 Dec. 1703 Martha Miller(13), had part of his portion 2 Apr. 1711, d. betw. 24 Dec. 1717—20 July 1718; adm. on prop. in Me. and N. H. gr. to Wm. Cotton, wid. Martha decl. She was liv. 3 Jan. 1755. 5 ch. Col. **Paul,** wealthy merchant, lumber dealer, J. P., and public official, m. in Salisb. 24 May 1704 Abra Brown, had deeds from fa. 1705—1709, and in 1705 bot from cous. Timothy a ho. and 14 a. near Salmon Falls in Dover. List 358d. Will, 3 Feb. 1747-8 (d. 24 June 1748 in 70th yr.), names many but no w. or ch. Capt. ***Benjamin,*** Dover selectman,

Rep., d. in office betw. 18 Sept. 1724—14 Apr. 1725. Adm. 10 May 1726 to wid. Elizabeth (Leighton 5), m. 23 Sept. 1717. He had bot the John Lovering(2) prop. which his wid. improved, herself or by tenants. She d. in 1779. 4 ch. See also Mary Horne(2). Deac. **Gershom**, Rollinsford. Will, 1758—1759, named w. Sarah (by trad. Twombly), 2 sons, dau. of a decd. dau. **Tamsen**, m. 1st James Chesley(3), 2d John Hayes(3 jr.). **Elizabeth**, m. 3 Nov. 1713 Nathl. Brown of Salisbury.

4 **DEACON GERSHOM**(11), first taxed 1670; gr.j. 1676, 1677, 1694 (special); j. 1694, 1695. Gr. 30 a. near Reyner's Brook and 10 a. nearest the head of his lot at Cochecho 1696. Lists 356j, 358d, 359ab, 52, 54, 57, 62. See also Wm. Thompson. His w. (perh. not 1st) was Hannah French, m. at Salisb. 18 Mar. 1695-6. On 26 May 1730 they deeded homestead and stock to s. Samuel for support. He d. 2 Mar. 1731. Ch: **Mary**, b. 14 May 1697, m. Capt. Wm. Wentworth(1). **Samuel**, Somersworth, b. 5 Dec. 1699 (Salisbury), m. 1st 9 Dec. 1731 Elizabeth French of Salisb. who d. with all 3 of her ch. bef. 3 Nov. 1737 when, of Hampt., he m. 2d Sarah Williams (Newb. rec.). Widow Sarah filed bond as admx. 28 June 1758. **Ezekiel**, Somersworth, b. 4 Feb. 1702, d. bef. 29 June 1757, leaving wid. Elizabeth (Day 2) and s. Moses who d. s.p. bef. 20 July 1768. Her unproved will, 1768, names 3 sis. and kinsm. Moses Wentworth Downs, Daniel Heard. **Gershom**, b. 4 Apr. 1705. **John**, Rochester, k. by Ind. 1746. Widow Jane (Richards) m. 2d Daniel Palmer. **Sarah**, m. Ephraim Ricker(1). **Thomas. Moses.**

5 **JOHN**(11), first taxed 1668. Of York, form. of Cochecho, 5 Feb. 1675-6 and until 10 Feb. 1690-1 at least, acc. to deeds. In 1680, he and w. Martha (m. by 28 Aug. 1679; see Steward 1), sold 100 a. in Wells which he had of Ezekiel Knight; in 1685 he sued Charles Brissum for damage done by turkeys. A fam. rec. says his s. Edward was b. in 1693 in Newb., but by 1704 he was located at Ponkapoag, now Canton; last seen, of Boston, 6 Oct. 1716, giving p/a to s. John. His w. Martha was in Boston in Jan. 1709; see John Holdridge. Lists 356m, 357c, 269b, 33. See also Parker(6). Ch. appear: **John**, Stoughton, b. ±1676, m. Elizabeth Bailey (2) whose fa. in 1717 willed her half his land at the Eastward; d. at Stoughton 6 Jan. 1772, ag. 95. **Charles**, d. at Canton 8 July 1780, ag. 96. **Edward**, d. at Stoughton 12 Feb. 1767, ag. 74. His 1st w. was Keziah Blackman (Dea. Benjamin of Stoughton). **Shubael**, Stoughton, d. in 1759. **Mary**, m. James Wright in Boston 1712. **Abigail**, m. Benj. Jordan in Dorchester 1715. **Elizabeth**, m. John Kenney in Stoughton 1728.

6 **LT. GOV. †‡JOHN**(8), Portsmouth, was fortunate in his step-relatives and in-laws, Deering(4), Martyn(15), and Hunking (7) whose dau. Sarah he m. 12 Oct. 1693, and that he and his, alone of all the Wentworths, rose to great power to form what has been called the 'Wentworth political dynasty' may be ascribed to their guidance and influence. First a mariner, then merchant. In 1699 loading masts for Spain (Lt. Gov. Partridge owner) when Bellomont threatened to send both to Eng. for trial for treason. Councillor 14 Feb. 1711-2, Justice of the Ct. of Common Pleas 1713-1718, appointed Lt. Gov. 7 Dec. 1717, holding this office until death, and having full control in N. H. 1723-1728 when there was no Royal Governor here. Lists 330df, 337, 339. See also Penney(2). Will, 7 Aug. (d. 12 Dec.) 1730, left large est. to w. Sarah and ch. Her will, 20 Mar. 1740-1 (d. 1 Apr. 1741 in 68th yr.). Ch: Gov. §†‡*Benning, Portsm., b. 24 July 1696, H. C. 1715, Rep., Councillor, Governor, m. 1st Abigail Ruck of Boston where he was a merchant in 1720; m. 2d Martha Hilton(22), d. 14 Oct. 1770. **Hunking**, Portsm., b. 19 Dec. 1697, m. 1st Elizabeth Wibird(2), m. 2d Elizabeth Keese(3), m. 3d Margaret Vaughan, d. 21 Sept. 1784. **Hannah**, b. 4 July 1700, m. 1st Samuel Plaisted(2), m. 2d Theodore Atkinson(5 jr.). **Sarah**, b. 24 June 1702, m. 1st Archibald McPhedris, m. 2d George Jaffrey (4 jr.). Major **John**, b. 19 Oct. 1703, H. C. 1723, Judge Ct. Com. Pleas, Judge of Probate, m. Sarah Hall of Barbadoes, d. 24 Nov. 1773. Capt. **William**, Kittery, b. 10 Dec. 1705, m. 1st Margery Pepperell (Andrew), m. 2d Mary (Hall) Winthrop, d. in Kit. 15 Dec. 1767. **Mary**, b. 7 May 1707, m. 1st Temple Nelson, m. 2d John Steele. **Samuel**, b. 15 Jan. 1708-9, H. C. 1728, Boston merchant, m. Elizabeth Deering (Henry 4 jr.). He d. 16 Sept. 1766, she in 1785 in London where she was liv. with her s. Benning. **‡Mark**, Portsmouth, b. 1 Mar. 1709-10, m. Elizabeth Rindge. A wealthy merchant, Councillor, and fa. of Gov. John, a Loyalist who found rewards in Eng. **Elizabeth**, b. 16 Feb. 1710-1, m. 1st John Lowd, m. 2d Capt. Benj. Underwood. **Rebecca**, b. 16 Apr. 1712, m. Thomas Packer(2 jr.). **Ebenezer**, b. 1 Aug. 1714, physician, shopkeeper, m. Mary Mendum (Nathl. 1), d. 3 Feb. 1757. **Daniel**, b. 5 Jan. 1715-6, Portsm., merchant, m. Elizabeth Frost, d. 19 June 1747. **George**, b. 12 June 1719, d. at sea unm. 1741.

7 **PAUL**(11), taxed at Dover ±1680, there 1684. Lists 359b, 52, 94. See also Heard (11). Newb. in Apr. 1696 when he sold to br. Benjamin land 'formerly my seat in Dover'; adm. to Rowley Ch. 30 Aug. 1696, with w. Catherine (m. bef. 21 Apr. 1681, see Stewart 1) dism. to New London Ch. 29

July 1707. Norwich 1715, where in 1726 he deeded for supp. of self and w. to s. Edward who soon d., and in 1746 to s. Benjamin for supp. of self alone. He depos. ab. Rowley in Apr. 1739, ag. 79 (SJC 49033). 13 ch. bp. at Rowley, 11 together 16 May 1697. As rec. at Dover at one time they were: **William,** b. 25 Dec. 1680, living Berwick 1764, m. Grace Tucker(18); see Joseph Gunnison(1), List 96. Her fa. willed her portion to her s. William. **Sylvanus,** b. 28 Feb. 1681, List 289, of Berw. until 1723, Norwich by 1727, liv. 4 May 1762. He m. 1st Mary Key(1), 2d in Rowley 3 Apr. 1723 Eleanor Davis. **Paul,** Kittery, b. 10 May 1682, m. 1st Jane Rice(4), 4 ch.; m. 2d 24 Sept. 1724 Rebecca (Pickering 8) Jaques(1). In 1730 his fa. deeded him all his Dover lands; liv. 7 July 1736. **Ebenezer,** b. 18 June 1683, List 289, liv. in Conn. **Martha,** b. 9 Feb. 1684, m. Samuel Lord(7). **Mercy,** b. 18 July 1686, m. in Rowley 23 Apr. 1707 Joseph Chapman. **Aaron,** b. 1 Jan. 1687, liv. in Conn. **Moses,** b. 17 Apr. 1689, liv. May 1697. **Mary,** b. 25 Dec. 1692, liv. May 1697. **Katherine,** b. 28 July 1694, m. 1713 Daniel Chapman of Colchester, Conn. **Sarah,** b. 8 Apr. 1697, m. at Norwich 1718 -Colen Ffresior-; see Steward(1). **Benjamin,** b. 28 Dec. 1698, bp. at Rowley 1 Jan. 1698-9, liv. in Conn. **Edward,** b. 20 June 1700, bp. at Rowley 31 Aug. 1700, liv. in Conn.

8 **SAMUEL**(11), Portsmouth, ±32 in June 1674, ±39 in Sept. 1680, first taxed 1659, m. by 1666 Mary Benning, sis. of Harry, and step-dau. of Henry Deering(4). From them spring the Wentworths eminent in N. E. and abroad. By 1669 (or 1661, by Samuel Treworgy's depos., Reg. 27: 272) he remov. to Great Isl., had tav. lic. to 1678 when he sold, and was there 1678-1679 when he acted for George Munjoy in Me. Ct. Lic. also at Portsm. and selectman there 1683. Jury 1682, 1685; gr.j. 1683. O. A. 28 Aug. 1685. Capt. S. W. one of Walter Barefoot's overseers 1688. Lists 356eghk, 357c, 312eh, 313abf, 324(3), 326c, 331b, 49, 51, 52, 54, 55ab, 57(2), 82, 90, 92, 98. See also Meekell; Y. D. 3: 82. Will, 13 Mar. 1690-1 (d. of small pox 25 Mar., ag. 50); w. Mary, 3 surv. ch., gr.ch. Widow Mary m. 2d Hon. Richard Martyn(15). In 1671 Thomas Parker called her vile names and said she and her mo. never left their country for their goodness. List 312e. Ch., Prov. rec: **Samuel,** merchant, Portsm., Boston, b. 9 Apr. 1666, m. 1st Hannah Wiggin(1) who d. at Portsm. 21 Feb. —, ag. 24 (Pt. of Graves); m. 2d at Boston 12 Nov. 1691 Elizabeth Hopson; m. 3d at Boston 28 Oct. 1699 Abigail (Phillips), wid. of Capt. Christopher Goffe; d. in 1736. A son Samuel, by 1st w., d. bef. 6 Mar. 1712-3 when adm. was gr. to his fa. **Daniel,** b. 21 Oct.

1669, List 57, d. 5 Jan. 1690, ag. 22 (Pt. of Graves). Col. Banks reported from Records of Privy Council: Ebenezer and **William** depos. that their br. Daniel liv. at Sheepscot with Elihu Gunnison. No William was rec. or in fa.'s will and ano. br. may have been meant. **John,** b. 16 Jan. 1671 (Lt. Gov.). **Mary,** b. 5 Feb. 1673, m. 1st Capt. Samuel Rymes, m. 2d Dr. John Clifton. Capt. **Ebenezer,** b. 9 Apr. 1677, mariner, Portsm., Boston, commanded a storeship at Port Royal in 1707, m. 9 Aug. 1711 Rebecca Jeffries (see Jeffrey 2), d. 14 Sept. 1717, she 2 July 1721. 3 ch. **Dorothy,** b. 27 June 1680, m. Henry Sherburne(4). **Benning,** b. 28 June 1682, d. bef. fa.

9 **SYLVANUS**(11), Dover 1684, m. in Rowley 7 Nov. —— Elizabeth Stewart(1), signed a pet. at Dover in Feb. 1689-90 and likely was soon an Ind. victim. Lists 52, 57, 94. In May 1693 his fa. deeded to (1) 'the land my s. Sylvanus lived upon.' Ch: **Elizabeth,** rec. at Rowley 27 Aug. 1689, m. there 13 Nov. 1707 Nathaniel Dresser.

10 **TIMOTHY**(11), Dover, Berwick, signed a N. H. pet. in Aug. 1692, bot in Dover in Apr. and had land from fa. in May 1696; gr.j. 1696; called of Dover 1702; of Berwick 1705, where he bot the former Grant homestead from Edw. Toogood, giving back a mortg. which was released to his sons in 1732. In 1718 he recited that he had a share in his gr.fa. Ezekiel Knight's lands by virtue of his fa.'s will. Lists 62, 296. Will, 3 May—8 July 1719, names w. (Sarah, ±86 in Jan. 1754; see Cromwell 3), 4 ch: **Timothy,** m. Elizabeth Hodsdon, who was gr. adm. 15 July 1735 and m. 2d by June 1739 John Pierce. Dea. **Samuel,** liv. on the Berwick homestead, m. 29 Aug. 1725 Joanna Roberts (John 12), both d. 4 July 1780. **Mary,** m. James Gerrish(1). **Sarah,** m. 1st Benj. Hossum, m. 2d John White.

11 **ELDER WILLIAM,** Dover, ag. ±54 in Sept. 1670, is consid. the same bp. at Alford, co. Lincoln, 15 Mar. 1615-6, s. of William and Susanna (Carter), gr.s. of Christopher and Katherine (Marbury). In Apr. 1636 Richard Filkin transferred to the trustees of Hansard's Free School the right to the rents of a long list of houses, one of them tenanted by 'Wm. W. or his assigns' in Bilsby (the Wheelwright par.). See English material in the Wentworth Gen.; Harleian Soc. Pub. (Lincolnshire Pedigrees) 52: 1062; Col. Soc. Mass. 11: 61; N. E. Reg. 22: 135. Altho the revised edition of the W. Gen. was pub. 60 yrs. ago, so well was it done that few addi. facts are known. One of a large fam. connection to come over, young William foll. his kinsman Rev. John Wheelwright to Exeter and Wells bef. settling perma. at Dover. He signed the Ex.

Comb. and from a ct. rec. and List 376a was appar. there in Sept. 1643, but soon at Wells. Tr.j. (Me.) 1647, 1649; gr.j. 1647; Wells constable 1648, and had three grants adj. Edw. Rishworth (See Y. D. 1: 62, 147). Taxed Dover 1650. Selectman 1651, 1657, 1660, 1664, 1665, 1670; moderator; constable, Com. t.e.s.c., lot layer, on important committees, Ruling Elder, and as 'Elder Winford' was made freeman 5. 2m. 1653. His land holdings are listed in the Wentworth Gen., much of it in the present Rollinsford. Preaching at Ex. 1683-1693, but liv. in Dover, where in 1689, altho over 70, he is credited with saving the Heard garrison from the Ind. 'Of Cochecho, now liv. in Ex.' in May 1693; of Dover 27 May 1696. Lists 373, 376a, 72, 262, 353, 354c, 355ab, 356bceghk, 359ab, 311c, 46, 49, 52, 54, 57, 62, 94, 96. His 1st unkn. w. had at least one ch.; his last w. Elizabeth Knight(2) was liv. when her fa. made his will 18 Apr. 1687. He d. 15 Mar. 1696-7; inv. by Nathl. and Tristram Heard and Thomas Downes, attested by wid. Elizabeth 4 Apr. 1697. Ch: **Samuel** (by 1st w.), b. 1641-1642. **John**, first taxed 1668. His connec. with Wells and the Knight fam. (Y. D. 3: 84) indicates he was son of E. K., who was cert. mo. of Ezekiel, Elizabeth and all the younger ch. **Gershom**, first taxed 1670. **Ezekiel**, first taxed 1672. **Elizabeth**, b. ±1653, m. 1st James Sharpe(1), m. 2d Richard Tozier, jr. See Y. D. 9: 92. 'New England Captives,' i: 193. **Paul**, taxed ±1680. **Sylvanus**, adult 1684. **Timothy**, see Y. D. 12: 17. **Sarah** (appar.), m. 1st Benjamin Barnard(2), m. 2d Samuel Winch. **Ephraim. Benjamin**, b. ±1670.
**Wescom**, John, see Lang(4).

**WESCOTT**, Westcott, Westgate. Old in cos. Devon and Somerset, and in various forms a common place name in S. of Eng.

1 **DANIEL**, Shoals, Portsmouth, held Thomas Dew's note of 20 Mar. 1675-6 and sued John Baker on it in 1682. At the Shoals liv. from his wife in June 1678 and had been abs. 6 or 7 yrs. in 1679 when he put in as evid. a letter dated 20 June 1679 from w. Esther to loving husb. Daniel, saying 'our dau. **Elizabeth** is dead, rest of our **children** well' and 'must consider whether I leave my native country.' In 1680 in Me. ct. he ackn. judgm. to Henry Williams in Edw. Hounsell's behalf, and for himself sued John Parrot in Portsm. ct. Taxed Portsm. 1681, O. A. 28 Aug. 1685, hired the Glebe in Portsm. for one yr. in Apr. 1691, D. W. and shop taxed 1691, last seen 1694. Whether w. or ch. came unkn. Lists 52, 57, 95(2), 329, 335a.

2 **RALPH**, his name endorsed on back of bond 1668 (case Richard Endle v. Jona. Wade, Mar. 1682; Essex Q. Ct. 5: 11).

3 **RICHARD** (Escot), 1687, List 307b, m. Anna or Hannah Haley(1). (Note 'Yescutt' in Ipswich vital records). A mariner of Piscataqua in 1704 when plf. in a suit; disorderly and bound over to York ct. by Pepperell in 1707, Henry Barter bondsman. Newc. wit. 1714. Widow Hannah receipted for her Haley inheritance 4 June 1724, liv. June 1725. Ch. appear: **Josiah**, Kittery, accused by Margaret Tucker in Apr. 1727. **Richard**, shipwright, York, m. 10 July 1729 Mary Wardwell. Ch. rec: Anna, Prudence, Josiah. See 'Maine Wills,' p. 788. **Andrew**, housewright, York, accus. by Margaret Tucker 1730-1732, altho he had m. (int. 19 Apr. 1729) Deborah Webber(10) and had a s. Josiah, b. and d. 1730. **William**, wit. deed to Andrew 1730.

4 **THOMAS**, sued Wm. Tucker in Saco ct. in Nov. 1665 and was sued in 1668 by Dr. Arthur Clapham for curing his w. Joan. Scarb. bef. 1676 where Hannah Hallam deposed he kept the ferry when she worked for Scottow. Portsm. or Great Isl. with w. Joan in 1678 (see Hardy 3) and in Oct. 1682 had kept Peter Pisgrave 13 mos. Lists 236, 237e, 331b. No ch. surely kn., but presum. fa. of **Walter**, servant of James Robinson (3) in 1683, ag. ±19 in June 1684 (see Edmund Pendleton 2), and of **Sarah** who was with Sarah Read(11) when she was attacked by Richard Webber in 1684. See also (3), (5).

5 **THOMAS** (Westget), a Portsmouth wit. 1716. In 1749 his wid., then Mary Levallee, and son **Thomas** (Westgate) of Berwick (m. Margaret Davis in 1745) sold his Rochester land. One Mary W. m. John Morgan in Berw. 20 Mar. 1725-6.

**Wesley**, John, Newcastle cor.j. 1670, List 312b.

**WEST**, scattered thru East and West of Eng., most numerous in Northamptonshire.

1 **EDWARD**, b. ±1639, vintner, Great Isl., wit. George Walton's p/a 22 Oct. 1662, m. his dau. Martha and had a s. John by 1665 when he conv. his ho. in trust for them and any other issue to Nathl. Fryer and Henry Robie, they to choose a third. Pub. ho. lic. 1663-1675. In 1666 he gave a bond to Philip Chesley, sr., wit. by his servant Christopher Snell; the next yr. Joanna Chesley test. ab. 'Mr. West coming up to our ho.' and borrowing a canoe. Sued Rowland Flansell and Christopher Banfield for forf. of a bond in Me. ct. 1667; ag. ±29 in Dec. 1668; sued by Richard Wharton 1671; wit. ag. David Campbell 1673. Called Sergt. 1673. Lists 47, 311b, 312abcf, 313a, 323, 326bc, 330a. See Moulton(2), Wise(3); note (4, 7, 8). Inv. (£540) 1 Sept. 1677, adm. 31

Oct. to wid. Martha (List 331b) and aft. her death to George Walton 24 June 1679. Her inv. (£762) 29 Jan. 1678-9, adm. to her fa. who leased to Henry Crown a ho. called 'The Anchor,' a brew-ho. and a log storeho., terminable on the oldest s. John coming of age. Other ch: **Elizabeth**, liv. 1679; she or (3)'s w. wit. with him 1689. **Mary**, presum. m. Richard Archer(2). **Edward**, 'infant son,' Capt. Thomas Daniel named gdn. 24 June 1679; see Edward(3).

2 **JOHN**, West Saco, Wells, prob. came in the -Speedwell- in 1635. Saco before 4 Apr. 1637 when his corn on the isl. in the river had been harvested contrary to law. In Nov. 1638 he leased from Vines for 1000 yrs. a ho. and 100 a. on so. side of the river reaching from Cole's Brook to 'what shall now be called West's ditch' (see Cole 28). Sued Thomas Roberts in Piscataqua ct. 1641. Jury 1640, 1645; gr.j. 1640, 1645, 1655 (for Saco). In 1643 as 'Deputy for the country' he and Francis Robinson, Magistrate, laid out the bounds of Black Point patent for Capt. Cammock. Submitted to Mass. and named selectman, com. t.e.s.c. and had gr. of Cow Isl., all in 1653; selectman also 1654. Apprais. Thomas Rogers' est. 1655. By Mar. 1651-2 he owned in Wells adj. John Wadleigh, inhab. there 15 June 1658, and sold in Saco to Capt. Pendleton in Mar. 1658-9, w. Edith signing; in 1653 he was suspected of having two wives. Wells constable 1660, 1661; freed from training 1 July 1661, being 73; apprais. John Barrett's est. 1662. Lists 22, 24, 25, 243ab, 249, 252, 262, 264, 235. Will, 29 Sept.—5 Oct. 1663, places his est. for 3 yrs. in hands of Wm. Cole for use of his gr.ch., their fa. to have nothing to do with it; Francis Woolfe got his best clothes and Mary Read certain articles; Wm. Cole, exec., Thomas Littlefield and John Read overseers. Only ch. **Mary**, m. Thomas Haley(7).

3 **JOHN**(1), Great Island, b. by 1665, bp. 19 Mar. 1676 in par. of St. Martin Outwich, London, chose Wm. Partridge gdn. 24 June 1679 and depos. in Sept. 1687, ag. ±23, that 5 or 6 yrs. ago he was Mr. P.'s apprentice. He m. Elizabeth Tetherly(1), prob. bef. 1689 when he and Elizabeth (w. or sis.) wit. together. Taxed 1690; ale ho. lic. 1692, tav. 1693, 1695; cor.j. 1693. (In 1695 one John was master of the -Bedford Galley- of London; see 4). Lists 315a, 318b, 319. Inv. 27 Dec. 1695, adm. to wid. Elizabeth who had tav. lic. 1696 (Capt. Cobbett and Wm. Ardell sureties) and 1697 (List 97), and m. 2d Col. Peter Weare(10). **Edward**, cooper, Newcastle (List 316), Hampt. Falls, Rumford, seems more likely a son than identical with (1 jr.). Of Newc., he sold land and shop near West's Cove in 1708, other prop.

to Benj. Parker 1712, w. Alice (Leavitt 9) joining in latter deed. As -Ellen-, she joined Hampt. F. Ch. 2 Nov. 1712. He sold out in Hampt. 1738, bot ho. and land in 'Rumford, Essex Co., Mass.' 1739; w. -Ellis- dism. to Rumford Ch. 16 Apr. 1739. He was dead in 1762 when s. Nathl. took deed from bros. Edw. and Daniel and the Dolloffs. Ch., bp. 1712-1724: Elizabeth (m. Nicholas Dolloff), William, Nathaniel (d.y.), Edward (Exeter 1743, Brentwood mason 1762), Nathaniel (blacksmith, of Rumford form. Pennycook, 1762), Noah, Daniel (Brentwood 1762).

4 **JOHN**, Capt. Richard Robinson's mate at Newc. in Sept. 1675 when a warr. was issued ag. him and Elizabeth Woodard, sis. of Wm. Rowe's wife. John (of Portsm., altered to Dover), borrowed money for 15 days on his note to Philadelphia Estes(1) who in 1679 sold stockings for the daus. of (1). Perh. the master of the -Bedford Galley- of London 1695.

5 **JOHN**, Mr., named by Andros as J. P. for Pemaquid and parts Eastward 1680-1682. Secretary of the Andros govt., at New York and Boston, and sent home with Andros. Lists 16, 225a.

6 **SARAH**. See Cole(19), Presbury(3), Randall(15), also Norton(4).

7 **STEPHEN** (Weste) ±40 in 1685, built a fence for Philip Chesley, sr.

8 **WILLIAM**, cooper, in 1671 patient of Dr. Morgan(2) who was frequenting the ho. of (1) about that time; see Y. D. ii: 138. Ag. ±23 in Mar. 1672-3, he depos. ab. John Jones (see 23 jr.) and Dr. Morgan.

**WESTBROOK.** One John, yeoman, was of Harting, co. Sussex, in 1620, ag. 46. Suff. Probate has the will of one John, form. of Greenwich, co. Kent, 1692; see Main(2).

1 **JOHN**, Portsmouth, m. Martha (Walford 4) Hinkson (List 331c) and had one ch. by 15 Nov. 1666; m. 2d bef. 18 June 1679 widow Alice Cate(2), her Lists 330c, 331c, 335a. In 1671 he bot 13 a. from Anthony and Abigail Ellins which were sold by his heirs in 1697 (see Rowe 2). Sued in 1678 by John Sherburne, poss. of his step-dau. Mary Hinkson(7); in 1681 he sued Sherburne for withholding Walford land. O. A. 28 Aug. 1685. Jury 1685, 1692, 1694; surv. of fences 1692; selectman 1697. Lists 324(2), 326c, 330ac, 331b, 332b, 335a, 356L (Portsm.), 49, 52, 54, 57, 92. With John Sherburne, he apprais. estates of John and Thomas Edmunds 27 June 1696. Westbrooks, Sherburnes, Brewsters and the Edmunds were neighbors, and indications are that young Mary Hinkson was the w. of Thomas Edmunds(5), the mo. of his ch., and the Ind. victim. Adm. on his own est. 11 Aug. 1697

to s. Thomas, wid. Alice renouncing. She was liv. 1702, at times called Cate aft. his death. Ch. appear: John, b. bef. 15 Nov. 1666, last seen in July 1690, when both John, sr. and jr., were taxed, but John, sr. was ment. in Mar. 1693-4; cert. d. bef. fa. Lists 57, 332b. Job, List 57, unless an error, must have been ano. son who d. bef. 1697. Mary, m. Nathan Knight(11). Thomas, b. ±1676. And perhaps ?Martha (see Rowe 2).

2 COL. ‡THOMAS(1), Portsmouth, Scarboro (lumbering there by 1720), Falmouth, oldest son in 1697, ag. ±33 in Feb. 1709-10. Portsm. selectman 1711-1716, taxed as Capt. W. 1713, 1715, Councillor 1716, and kn. for his military career in Dummer's War (see 'Letters of Col. T. W. and Others, Relating to Ind. Affairs in Me. 1722-1726,' N. E. Reg. vols. 44-49). Lists 229, 324, 330d, 337, 339. See also Fickett(2), Nelson(2). He m. Mary Sherburne(6) and d. ab. 11 Feb. 1743-4 in a one-story ho. next to 'Harrow House' (at Stroudwater in Falmouth), his prop. lost thru speculations and his assoc. with Waldo; 60 acres inventoried. In 1744 the wid. and only ch. Elizabeth, with her husb. Richard Waldron(11 jr.), gave a p/a to Jabez Fox to prosec. an appeal from probate decree. Widow Mary d. 23 Oct. 1748, ag. 75 (Atkinson platter).

Westell, John (also Wastell), Dover 1640-1642, Lists 351b, 352. See Hist. of Wethersfield, Conn. ii: 752.

Weston, Thomas. See Proceedings Mass. Hist. Soc. 54: 165-178.

WETHERICK, Robert, m. by 1691 Elizabeth (Cutts 7) Elliot(2), who wit. a Fryer deed in 1694 (Y. D. 7: 261). Newcastle soldier 1694. List 318a. Of Summer town in Carolina in Aug. 1700, when his w. was at Kit. with his p/a and sold land to Richard Cutts.

WEYMOUTH, a town in co. Dorset. In 1665 Miles Pile gave a bond to pay one Robert Weymouth of Dartmouth in Devonshire.

1 BENJAMIN, Dover. His connec. with Kittery and his son's mar. suggest relationship with (2), but no evid. found. With Wm. Munsey he wit. a Coffin deed in 1696, was sued by Kit. selectmen for mowing the Fowling marsh in 1700, and sued the selectmen in 1701. Dover gr. 1701 adj. Edw. Cloudman; in 1708 bot from Richard Hussey 20 a. and bldgs. near Sligo garrison, and from Jethro Furber 30 a. next west. Lists 358d, (?298, B. Weymouth). Wife Mary, m. by 1693. In 1717 they deeded to s. Benjamin, b. at Dover 1 Feb. 1693-4, who was gr. adm. on fa.'s est. 3 Mar. 1724-5, and was of Somersw. by 1743. Will, 1754—1756, names

w. Sarah (Morrell 3, m. 14 June 1716), 3 sons, 5 daus.

2 EDWARD, tailor, b. ±1639 (40 in 1679), was taxed Dover 1662, 1663, m. 25 Dec. 1663 Esther Hodsdon(6), and lived at Kit. Abs. from meeting 1668, swearing 1669, offences that brot him into ct. several times, Wm. Furbish bondsm. in 1671. Kit. gr. 1671, 1694; liv. next neighbor to Jona. Nason who succ. sued him for slander and defama. in 1675. His ho. was burned by Ind. in 1677. Gr.j. 1688. He and w. abs. from meet. in 1696, but said they sometimes went to Dover Ch. Lists 356gh, 298, 290. In Mar. 1704-5 he deeded homestead to s. Timothy, effective aft. he and Esther should die. She wit. a Hodsdon deed 11 Mar. 1723-4. Deeds prove 2 ch: Timothy, had Kit. gr. 1703. From Y. D. 12: 331 (1726-7), it appears he lost his farm and John Hooper and Joseph Hodsdon recov. it for him. Lists 290, 291, 296-298. The printed rec. naming -Rachel- as mo. of his 1st ch. Rachel, b. 10 Aug. 1705, must be an error, as his w. Patience Stone (3) was adm. to Ch. as P. W. 25 Apr. 1703, took adm. 4 Oct. 1731, and was liv. in Feb. 1745-6. He.was thrown from his horse and killed (inquest). See 'Old Kittery' for 9 ch. and add a 10th ch. John, cordwainer, Kit., 1749. All ch. but Mary in div. 1738. Mehitabel, ±60 in Jan. 1729, m. Wm. Stacy (3). Edw. and Esther are also the logical parents of Bridget who m. John Nason(3), and gave her age as ±63 in 1730, but poss. she was the ch. b. to Esther Hodsdon bef. July 1663, or a young widow. One Edw. is named several times as if liv. in suit, Emery v. Nason, 1730. See also (1).

3 GEORGE, gunner of the -Margery-. List 21.

4 ICHABOD, a wit. in 1699, either at Newbury, or for George Chesley at Oyster River.

5 JAMES, Shoals, fined at Saco 21 Oct. 1645 for breach of the Sab. and the peace, was perh. older than James of Star Isl. who had pub. ho. lic. 1667, 1668, 1670-1677, and bot on Great Isl. 1672. Wife Mary and Edw. Beale wit. a Stevens deed in June 1673. In 1703 James (jr.) and his sis. called her 'my fa. Weymouth's widow,' indicating she was not their mo. His will, 'now on the Isles of Shoals,' 10 Apr.—25 June 1678, names her, four ch., the sons under 21, the dau. unm. Y. D. 3: 104 (1681) locates his former Shoals ho. Widow Mary had pub. ho. lic. 1678, 1679, m. 2d Capt. Thomas Diamond(3). Ch., order in will: William, bot on Star Isl. 1693, bondsm. that yr. for John West. Lists 95, 309. Adm. gr. to fa.-in-law and mo. Thomas and Mary Diamond after relinquishment 22-27 Apr. 1703 by the Curriers and James, who 23

June fol. q.c. to Capt. Diamond. **George**, dead or gone 23 June 1703. **James. Elizabeth**, m. 1st Richard Currier(3), m. 2d Nathl. Lord(8).

6 **JAMES**(5), Mr., Newcastle, m. aft. 27 Mar. 1693-4 Catherine (Chadbourne 1) Lidden(1) and poss. liv. a while on Lidden prop. in Crooked Lane which he, his w. and her daus. sold to Samuel Skillings in 1705. Newc. selectman 1699, innkeeper 1702, bot there 1703. List 315b. Will, 9 Jan.—4 Feb. 1706-7, names w. Catherine, 3 daus. under 21, two step-daus., bros.-in-law Capt. Samuel Alcock and Mr. Richard Cutt, and ment. 'plate lately given me by my mo. Diamond, dec.' Widow Catherine, a midwife, ±62, depos. in a Kit. case in Apr. 1727. List 316. See also Jenkins(11). Ch: **Mary**, m. Samuel Rymes. **Katherine**, unm. 1721. **Lucy**, near 13 in Jan. 1714-5, liv. 1718; one Lucy m. Gideon Walker (see 5).

7 **ROBERT**, Richmond Isl. 1634, List 21.

8 **ROBERT**, mariner, fisherman, Kittery 1652, had grants in 1653 (by James Emery's) and 1656. Adm. br. William's est. 1654. He m. Rebecca (Emery 1) who was riding abroad with Thomas Sadler on the Sabbath in 1659. 'R. W. and some others of his company dying intest.,' by ct. order 24 Dec. 1661 Maj. Shapleigh was to administer. Inventory 1662, £60. 5s., with 5s. in hands of Laymotte. James Emery took adm. 7 July 1663. Lists 282-285, 298, 24. Widow Rebecca m. 2d Thomas Sadler(4), 3d in R. I. Daniel Eaton. No certain ch. appears, altho (13) and Joseph Amory of R. I. (see Emery 1) were cert. Rebecca's ch. That the latter was b. a Weymouth (Robert's son) and used the fam. name of a gr.fa. who brot him up, is not imposs.

9 **SAMUEL**, Portsmouth, and Mary Burnham pub. int. in Ipsw. 10 Dec. 1709.

10 **WALTER**, servant of George Walton 1666.

11 **WILLIAM**, Shoals, owned a ho., stage and mooring place which he sold to John Fabes (Y. D. 1: 41). Adm. 27 June 1654 to br. Robert(8).

12 **WILLIAM**, owed the Mitchell est. List 78.

13 **WILLIAM**, Dover, appar. the 'William Weymouth alias Sadler' who was bef. Wells ct. in Jan. 1681-2 for abusing magistrates and ministers, and escaped, John Green paying costs. If an ackn. s. of (8), it is cert. strange that the name of a worthless step-fa. clung to him as an alias. His w. Sarah d. ab. 17 Feb. 1704-5, having fallen into the fire. He m. 2d in Salisbury 1708 wid. Elizabeth Maxfield. Lists 57, 96. In 1741 he deeded ho., barn and 17 a. to dau. Tabitha. Ch. (Dover Friends Records): **Rebecca**, b. 15 June 1686, m. Elisha Andrews(4). **William**,

weaver, b. 10 Sept. 1689. Of Dover, he bot in Rochester 1731, living there 1736. **Robert**, b. 15 Feb. 1691-2. **Joshua**, weaver, b. 11 June 1695, taxed Berw. 1719, m. Oct. or Nov. 1720 Sarah Dennett(3). Shoals 1726, Kit. 1736, both of Richmond, York Co., 1739. Ch: Mary m. Nathan Hoag; Mehitable, b. 25 Apr. 1731 ('Old Kittery'), at Richmond on the Kennebec (Quaker rec.), liv. with her aunt Tabitha, m. Elijah Jenkins; Abigail, bp. at Kit. 23 May 1749. **Tabitha**, b. 14 Oct. 1698, m. Joseph Jenkins(8). **Samuel**, b. 13 Oct. 1701. Dover 1729; of Somersw., sold com. rights to John Mason 1733, his deed saying 'I being a town born child;' adm. to Mason 1759.

14. ——, Dover, List 37.

**WHARFE, Nathaniel**, Falmouth, wit. a Felt deed 27 Nov. 1662 and m. Rebecca, eldest dau. of Mr. Arthur Mackworth. He signed a Falm. pet. 1663, was fined 1665 for abs. from ct., with wife q.c. int. in cert. marsh to Francis Neale 1666, and apprais. Richard Martin's est. 21 Feb. 1672-3. List 222b. His own est. was apprais. by Robert Corbin and Jenkin Williams 23 June 1673; adm. in July to wid. Rebecca who m. 2d Wm. Rogers(16). See Me. P. & Ct. Rec. ii: 269, 476-7. Two ch. proved by deeds; **Nathaniel**, Falm., Gloucester, b. ±1661 (near 70 in Oct. 1730, 71 in Apr. 1732, ±72 in July 1733), depos. that he liv. at Falm. from earliest recollec. until the first Ind. war and for 7 yrs. betw. the wars, and built a ho. on his fa.'s farm, Wharfe's Point, up Presumpscot River, next above Mackworth's. He m. Anna Riggs 30 Jan. 1683 in Glouc. where 11 ch., incl. Arthur, were rec. to 1701 when his w. died. In 1735 he deeded all int. in Falm. to Nathl. Noyes; liv. 12 Apr. 1736, upward of 75. **Rebecca**, adm. to Second Ch., Boston, in Jan. 1690, m. there 15 Feb. 1693 Francis Holmes. 11 ch. rec. at Boston, incl. Isaac, Nathaniel and Ebenezer. In 1742 the last named, under his mo. R. H., late of Boston, q.c. Mackworth farm and isl. Incl. because of his name, **Arthur**, ±20 in 1684 when an apprentice of John Lewis, cooper, of Great Isl., where he beat up Mark Rounds, 36 Charles II, 10 Sept. His presence there suggests also Isaac, Great Isl. 1692, List 319, while in Second Ch., Boston, two ch. of (John and) Martha Wharf were bp: Margaret, b. 15, bp. 19, May 1695; Susannah, bp. 14 Mar. 1697.

# WHARTON.

1 **EDWARD**, glazier, who became a noted Quaker in Salem, was sued by Anthony Emery in Piscataqua ct. 1642, 1644, and sued Capt. Champernowne in same ct. 1643. Mass. tried on him all its cures for Quakerism and banished him 11 Mar. 1660-1, tho

he did not stay banished. He made freq. trips to the Piscat. and in 1663 went from Salem to Casco Bay and back; see Batson (3). He d. in Salem 3. 1st mo. 1678, his nunc. will (James Mills one wit.) giving £10 to Sarah Mills(6) and her ch. (Essex Prob. 3: 201). See also Me. P. & Ct. Rec. ii: xxxviii; Perley's Hist. of Salem, 3: 261-267.

2 RICHARD, Esq., Boston, sued Edward West(1) in 1671, bot the Pejepscot Patent 1683-4 and had a large gr. from Mass. Genl. Ct. See vol. iv of York Deeds; Lists 80, 191. He d. in London in May 1689, leaving, by 1st w. Bethia Tyng, a son William (Y. D. 4: 19) whose wid. Eunice was at Pejepscot 1730. By 2d w. Sarah Higginson: Sarah and Bethia. By 3d w. Martha Winthrop: Ann, Martha and Dorothy, all rec. at Boston with others. See Doc. Hist. 24: 231; Waters' Gleanings, i: 170.

WHEELER, found chiefly in Gloucestershire and bordering counties. Became 23d commonest name in N. E.

1 DAVID(3), of Hampton in Sept. 1646 when he and the Chases(1) were charged with gathering pease on Sunday. By Mar. 1647 all had gone to Newb. where he m. 11 May 1650 Sarah Wise or Wieth (Humphrey). He wit. Dustin to Cutts 1660 (Y. D. 3: 20). See Hoyt's Salisbury, i: 354, for eleven ch., incl. Jonathan, b. 6 Jan. 1657-8, m. one Mary (see 5) in Rowley 15 Mar. 1683; see 'Hist. of the Wheeler Fam. in America' (1914), p. 1008, for his will, of Byfield, 12 Aug. 1720.

2 JACOB, Exeter soldier 1676, List 381.

3 JOHN, from Salisbury, co. Wilts, where he m. Ann Yeoman 1 Dec. 1611, was early at Hampton, soon at Salisb. and ±1650 at Newbury where Ann d. 15 Aug. 1662. His will, of Newb., 28 Mar. 1668—11 Oct. 1670. See Hoyt's Salisbury, i: 353, for eleven ch., incl: David. Anne, m. 1st Aquila Chase(1), m. 2d Daniel Silloway. Elizabeth, m. 1st Thomas Dustin of Dover and Kit.; m. 2d Matthias Button. Roger. See also 'Desc. of Aquila and Thomas Chase' (1928), p. 521, for English data, incl. his fa.'s will.

4 JOHN, Oyster River, b. at Concord, Mass., 10 May 1668, s. of William and Hannah (Buss), m. Elizabeth Perkins(24) bef. 10 June 1694 when her parents deeded them a ho. and 60 a. over ag. Little Bay, reserving half the mowing land and half the apples; this was his home. Jury 1695, 1696; gr.j. 1699. In 1705 he bot land from the Follett est. He and wife k. by Ind. 27 Apr. 1706. Adm. on his est. to Wm. Parkins(on), bond 6 May 1706. The acct. shows funeral exp. for one child, prob. k. with the parents. Sons William and Richard went to Concord and chose their uncle Wm. of Concord as

their gdn. in 1711. Joseph, liv. on the home place, added to it and passed it on to his son. Tailor, farmer; adm. to O. R. Ch. in Aug. 1722 (many yrs. Deacon); m. 11 Feb. 1724-5 Mary Drew(8) who was adm. to Ch. in July 1728. Est. adm. 1769; wid. Mary m. 2d Francis Edgerly. 5 ch.

5 MARY, dau. of John Sinclair(3), m. one Wheeler unkn., unless Jonathan(1). One Mary of Ipsw., wid., bot in Nottingham 1723, sold 1727.

6 RACHEL, Boston, wid. of Henry (gr.s. of 3), m. Benjamin Allen 1686 (Hampt. rec.).

7 ROGER(3), m. in Newb. 7 Dec. 1653 Mary Wilson, and was sued in Piscataqua ct. 1657 by Thomas Beard for slander and detaining his servant, one Wilson. He sued George Walton in 1657. Wife Mary d. in Newb. 27 Dec. 1658; he m. 2d in Boston 23 Nov. 1659 Mary Stone, wid. of John; d. there 7 Dec. 1661 (Reg. 18: 331), leaving wid. and ch. Mary and Joseph, both by 1st wife, both named in will of (3).

8 ROGER, wit. an Ind. deed at the Kennebec with Robert Gutch 7 May 1662 (Y. D. 11: 139).

9 S——, at Scottow's garrison 1675, List 236.

10 THOMAS, see Pitman(11), his ho. prob. in Boston.

WHEELWRIGHT, from Lincolnshire. See N. E. Reg. 68: 73; 74: 51, for English pedigree.

1 JAMES, Mr., List 88. Samuel?

2 REV. JOHN, celebrated Antinomian and founder of Exeter soon aft. his banishment from Boston 2 Nov. 1637 and the disarming of those seduced and led away by the 'opinions and revelations of Mr. Wheelwright and Mrs. Hutchinson' (Mass. Col. Rec. 1: 207, 211). See Col. Soc. Mass. 1: 271-303; 'Life of John Wheelwright' (Heard, 1930); Dict. of Am. Biog., vol. 20 (1936) with references, for annals of his life, beginning in Lincolnshire ab. 1592-4 (his fa. Robert of Cumberworth and Saleby) and ending in Salisb. 15 Nov. 1679 'in an advanced age and the 17th yr. of his ministry.' Educ. at Sidney Coll., Cambridge, B.A. 1614-5, M.A. 1618, and vicar at Bilsby, Lincolnshire, 1623 to 1633, when replaced, altho appar. not resigning. At Boston he, his w. and her mo. were adm. to Ch. 12. 4m. 1636. Of Boston, Braintree, Exeter (until Mass. came in), and Wells where a large land owner (Y. D. 1: 28, gr. from Thomas Gorges 17 Apr. 1643; Y. D. 1: 137; 8: 14), and where he was liv. in May 1644 when Mass. remov. its ban (Mass. Col. Rec. 2: 67). From 12 Apr. 1647 to latter part of 1656 he was Mr. Dalton's colleague at

Hampton (see Dow's Hampton, i: 352), and aft. a stay in Eng. went to Salisb., where yrs. later in conflict with Major Robert Pike whom he excommunicated (see 'The New Puritan,' pp. 67-81). Lists 371-373, 375b, 376a(2)b(1644), 269b, 262, 24. Y. D. 8: 16, has the much quoted, but forged Ind. deed of 1629. He m. 1st at Bilsby 8 Nov. 1621 Marie Storre, sis. of Augustine of Ex., who was bur. at B. 18 May 1629; m. 2d Mary Hutchinson(11), List 393a, outliving her. Will, 25 May 1675; much Wells and English prop.; his plate to be divid. among 'my latter wife's ch.' Ch. by 1st w: **John**, bp. at Bilsby 6 Oct. 1622, remained in Eng., and in 1645 pub. a work in vindication of his fa. **Thomas**, bp. 5 Oct. 1624 (Banks). **William**, bp. at B. 10 Feb., bur. 19 May 1627. **Susannah**, bp. at B. 22 May 1628, m. Edward Rishworth. By 2d w. Mary (see will of their uncle Samuel Hutchinson 1667): **Katherine**, bp. at B. 4 Nov. 1630, m. 1st Robert Nanny, m. 2d Edward Naylor. **Mary**, bp. at B. 19 May, bur. 28 July 1632. **Elizabeth**, bp. at B. 19 May, bur. 28 July 1632. **Elizabeth**, bp. at Laceby, co. Lincoln, 9 June 1633, ±39 in Sept. 1673, m. George Pearson(1). **Mary**, bp. at Boston 25 June 1637 (see 5), m. 1st Edward Lyde(3), m. 2d Theodore Atkinson of Boston, fa. of (4). **Samuel**, 'sister's oldest son' 1667, ±40 in 1678. Rebecca, m. 1st in Boston 1660 Samuel Maverick(2 jr.), m. 2d William Bradbury(2). **Hannah**, m. by 1664 Anthony Checkley of Boston, who m. 2d Lydia (Scottow) Gibbs. **Sarah**, m. bef. 1671 Richard Crispe of Boston. In 1677 her fa. deeded to her land in Nawthorp, Boundthorp and Cumberworth, co. Lincoln.

3 **COL. ‡*JOHN**(4), Esq., Wells, ±53 in Jan. 1716-7, ±68 in Jan. 1732-3. His fa. willed him, aft. his mo.'s death, lands in Croft, Eng., if Mr. Lyde had not sold them. Ensign in July 1687, gr.j. 1687 and often. Lieut. 1693, Rep., J. P., Judge of Probate, Judge Ct. Common Pleas, Councillor for the Province, Capt. and Col. in Ind. service at home, Eastward, and in Dummer's War. See Westbrook Papers in N. E. Reg. vols. 44-49; Y. D. 12: 233. Lists 267a, 268ab, 269ac, 36, 38, 39. He m. in Wells 28 Jan. 1688-9 Mary Snell (3). Will, 11 Apr. 1739 (d. 13 Aug. 1745); his large farm where he lately dwelt was already given to sons Samuel and Nathl. Wid. Mary's will, 16 Nov. 1750—16 July 1755. Ch. at Wells: **John**, Esq., b. 10 Dec. 1689, Boston merchant, m. 1st 20 Oct. 1715 Mary Allen (s. Jeremiah named in will of gr.fa. Jeremiah Allen, Esq., Boston, 1736); m. 2d 20 Nov. 1718 Elizabeth Green (5 ch. rec.); m. 3d 13 Oct. 1741 Elizabeth (Winkley 2) Weeks, who d. 23 Feb. 1748, ag. 45 (1 son). Will, 1751—1760. **Samuel**, Esq., b. 2 May 1692, m. 31 Aug. 1715 Abigail Lane(6) at Wells, where ch. rec: John, b. and d. 1716;

Abigail, b. 1717. List 269c. Capt. in Dummer's War. Liv. Wells 1757. **Hannah**, b. 1 May 1694, m. Elisha Plaisted(4) at Wells 16 Sept. 1712, the wedding festivities being broken up by an Ind. attack and the groom's capture (Doc. Hist. 9: 327). **Esther**, b. 31 Mar. 1696, Lists 39, 99 (p. 92), became Sister Esther Marie Joseph of the Infant Jesus and later Mother Superior of the Ursulines of Quebec. Both parents willed to her if she came home; in 1739 'not heard of these many years.' See 'N. E. Captives,' i: 425. **Jeremiah**, b. 5 Mar. 1697-8, cooper, Boston, Portsm., m. 1st (int. Bos. 6 Sept. 1727) Mary Bosworth (dau. of Bellamy) of Bristol, R. I., who was liv. in Apr. 1735 (ch. Jeremiah), m. 2d ±1737 Damaris (Dennis) Jose (see 3). Will, 1768—1768; dau. Mary Oram (bp. 1742), sons John (bp. 1740), Jeremiah, gr.s. Jeremiah. **Elizabeth**, b. 10 Apr. 1700, m. 1st Samuel Alcock(4 jr.), m. 2d John Newmarch (Rev. John). **Mary**, b. 11 June 1702, m. Samuel Moody, Esq.(6 jr.). **Nathaniel**, b. 15 June 1704, m. 28 Jan. 1729 Abigail Hammond (Joseph 3 jr.). List 269c. Of Wells, gent., 1757. **Sarah**, b. 27 July 1706, m. Rev. Samuel Jeffords(4). **Job**, b. 6 Sept. 1708, d. 1 June 1709. **Lydia**, b. 7 Sept., d. 6 Oct. 1710.

4 **‡*SAMUEL**(2), Esq., ±40 in Sept. 1678, 'now resid. at Wells' 15 July 1663, when his fa. deeded him half his farm there, comprising his gr. from Mr. Gorges in 1643 and from the town 25 Nov. 1651. He also inherited most of his fa.'s remaining Wells prop. and land in Croft, co. Lincoln. Tr.j. 1662, 1663, 1664; gr.j. 1664, 1671; Clerk of the Writs 1663; Lieut. for Wells 1665, Lieut. of Horse 1680; O. F. 5 July 1670; Deputy 1671, 1677, 1684; selectman 1677, 1678; Comr. for Wells 1679; County Treasurer, altho he decl. appointment in 1674; J. P. 1665 (named by King's Comrs.); Associate; Judge of Probate; Judge Inf. Ct. of Com. Pleas; Councillor. He had a garrison and was active in Ind. affairs locally and in seeking outside aid. Lists 236, 265, 266, 267a, 29, 33, 36, (788), 96. He m. Hester Houchin (Jeremy). Will, 30 Jan. 1699—1700 (d. 13 May 1700), provided well for her and ment. her portion in hands of Bozen Allen of Boston. Ch: John, willed ¼ the farm his fa. liv. on except 20 a. where the ho. stands, already deeded to **Joseph** who was also willed ¼ the farm. Joseph had w. Alice who was liv. in 1741, he in 1744. Gr.j. 1703. Lists 268a, 269ac, 38. Ch. 1708-1723: Thomas, Lucy, Mary, Esther, Alice, Joseph, Benjamin. See Y. D. 20: 6; 22: 259. **Hannah**, m. 1st William Parsons(11), m. 2d Philip Rollins. **Mary**, m. James Smith (see Gowen 4). **Samuel**, jr., wit. 1685 (Y. D. 6: 6), not in will.

5 **THOMAS**(2), Mr., closely assoc. with Mr. Rishworth and in favor with Mass., was of Wells and adult in June 1650 (Y. D. 1: 146). Jury 1651; with Peter Weare surveyed cert. marshes for the Genl. Ct. in 1651 (Me. P. & Ct. Rec. i: 171); gr.j., foreman, 1653-1655; Wells selectman and Com. t.e.s.c. 1653; York wit. 1654; agreed to pay Robert Hethersay's fine 1655; with Rishworth wit. Sayward to Colcord 1656; late of Wells, gave p/a to Rishworth 20 Jan. 1656-7; last seen 1657. Lists 263, 275, 276, 24. See also George Haborne with whom he dealt early. No fam. appears, unless Mary who wit. with Rishworth in 1657 (Y. D. 1: 60) and was slandered by Stephen Ticknor in Mar. 1659-60 (Me. P. & Ct. Rec. ii: 365) was wife and not sis. Bourne, p. 50, knew of or imagined a blighted romance.

**Whelden,** John, Falmouth settler under Danforth, Lists 225a, 227.

**WHELPDELL, William,** kinsman of Capt. Cammock, consid. coming over with his w. in 1632 and may have come. Trel. Papers, p. 20.

**Where,** Henry, wit. Peter Coffin to Gov. Samuel Allen, 1698.

**WHERRIN, John,** Portsmouth, m. 26 July 1714 Ruth Leighton(4), prob. the John drowned in the Piscat. River, the town paying his funeral bill in 1732 and having his sick w. on its hands. One John was a Portsmouth mariner 1738, when John Rindge, Esq., went his bail; William, laborer, was there 1745; James, blacksmith and ferryman, in 1750.

**WHIDDEN,** Whitten, the former old in Devonshire. See also Creber.

1 **JOHN,** bricklayer, Portsmouth, of unkn. age, might have been fa. of (2) by an early mar., but presum. was older br. and here as early, altho first noted in 1665. In 1667 he and (2) wit. with Richard Tucker for Moses and Drews; in 1668 he wit. ag. wid. Hart(2); in 1669 bot land adj. his ho. from James Cate; taxed 1673; in May 1681 with w. Elizabeth gave deed to s. Jonathan to be effec. after they d. Lists 47, 49, 326c, 329, 331b. Adm. 7 Sept. 1681 to wid. Elizabeth, List 335a. On 20 Mar. 1695-6 Jonathan made over the prop. to br. Michael, partly in consid. of her care and maintenance. In 1683, a poor wid., she took up a contribution for the ransom of her **son** in Algiers, who may have been one of the foll: **Jonathan,** bricklayer 1681, appar. eldest son at home, wit. two Champernowne deeds with John Penwill in May 1686, poss. then of York, where he had a ho. bef. 1691 when 'Whidden's Beck' mentioned. Taxed Portsmouth 1691; of P., m. in Salisb. (prob. not first) 5 Aug. 1695 Rebecca Hackett (see

Wm.). Of P. 1696-1703; form. of Newb. now of P. 1708. Lists 60, 67(2). His w. Rebecca (see Parker 26), ±30 in 1707, was a Portsm. charge 1718-1719. Ch. appear: Elias (presumably), m. in Newb. 27 Dec. 1711 Rachel Jackman, ch. incl. Jonathan; see also Rowley records. Mary (Jonathan's dau. by York rec.), m. William Morgrage (see John). And prob. one of three Sarahs: one m. James Roe, ano. Thomas Lyndly, both 1722; one m. Jonathan Look 1727. **John,** perh., (1) being sr. in 1681. Lists 337. Of Portsm., he had a deed of land there from Daniel Allen 5 June 1712. **Michael,** joiner, Portsm., m. 1st 6 June 1694 Elizabeth Meserve (Clement), m. 2d 20 Dec. 1715 Rebecca Howlett of Topsfield. Lists 330df, 337, 339. He or son selectman 1729, 1730. Will, gunsmith, 26 Sept. 1738—28 Mar. 1739. Wid. Rebecca d. bef. Oct. 1745. Ch. (5 bp. 5 June 1709): Michael, joiner, taxed 1716, List 339, m. 27 May 1719 Anna Drew(7) and had 2d w. Sarah; liv. 1764. John, m. 24 Oct. 1723 Mary Martin (see 5), taxed Jan. 1731-2, d. by 1738, wid. Mary and ch. liv. 1745; one Mary, ±80, was in Portsm. almsho. ±1781. Samuel, adm. to fa., bond 5 July 1732. Abigail, m. John Nutter(5 jr.). Elizabeth, not in will. Mary, m. 15 Apr. 1725 Abraham Perkins of Ipsw.; son Nathl. liv. with his gr.fa. See also Gray(8) for one Joseph.

2 **SAMUEL,** bricklayer, mason, Portsmouth, Greenland (see 1), here 24 June 1662 (see Pottle 2), ag. ±20 in Jan. 1663-4. He bot from Anthony Ellins 27 Jan. 1669, adj. land E. had sold to Nehemiah Partridge, sold this in 1672, bot more from Ellins 1673 (selling 1680), and in 1682 bot from George Huntress land and bldgs at or near Greenland. Kittery wit. 1675 (Y. D. 3: 107). Mary Cate(2) was his w. in Aug. 1680 (Lists 331c, 335a, 338b) and his wid. Lists 47, 49, 52, 62, 326c, 329, 330cd, 331bc, 332b, 335a, 337, 338a. See also Knight(11). Appar. last taxed 1713; Samuel's wid. taxed 1715-6, was perh. the dau.-in-law. Will, ancient, 3 Mar. 1713-4— 7 May 1718; ment. w. Mary and all ch. but first two: **Thomas.** No rec. calls him son, but 7 Feb. 1687-8 Samuel and Thomas of Greenland were bound to the peace by Ludovick Fowler; taxed 1690 betw. Samuel and Fowler; Portsm. wit. 1694, Dr. Fletcher to Bennett. Lists 67, 68, 330de, 336b. **Samuel,** m. Sarah Jones(16), List 338b. As 'Jr.' taxed for Mill Dam 1707, 1708 (and farm), Lists 337, 338a, alive 22 Aug. 1713, dead 3 Mar. 1713-4 when his fa. willed 20 s. apiece to his three sons and the 2 a. where his ho. stood. Widow Sarah m. 2d John Savage(4). Ch., 4 bp. 1713: John (Arundel), Samuel (Greenland), James (Truro, N. S.), Sarah (see Bucknell 3), Ichabod (Newmarket), bp. 1714. John and desc. were Whittens,

others remained Whiddens. **Jane,** m. Thom-▪
as Edgerly(2). **Alice,** m. 1st Samuel Haines
(6), m. 2d Wm. Jenkins(12). **Abigail,** m.
William White(32). **John,** Greenland (see
John 1), taxed 1708, m. 18 Jan. 1711-2 Sarah
Nutter (see 5), willed part of his fa.'s homestead. Called 'Ensign' 1729. Will, 1767—
1767, names ch: Samuel, John, Anna Jones
(w. of John), Hannah Jenkins (w. of Wm.),
Sarah Haines (w. of Samuel), Elizabeth
(Neal in 1771), Mary, dec. (her ch.). In
1734 Samuel Nutter and w. Sarah deeded
to the sons Samuel and John, jr. Capt.
**James,** willed the homestead, m. 18 Feb.
1713-4 Mary Philbrick(10), List 338b for
both. Captain at Louisburg. Of Portsm.,
gent., in 1750, he bot Swan's Isl. in the Kennebec, which was soon attacked by Ind. (Me.
Hist. Soc. Col. 2: 10: 187-210; 'N. E. Captives,' vol. 2). Said to have ret. to Greenl.
and d. bef. 1770. Ch. bp. there: Abigail (m.
Lazarus Noble), Eleanor, Timothy, Mary,
Martha, James, ano. Timothy, Solomon.
**Sarah,** m. Joshua Haines(6). **Mary,** List
338b, m. Nathan Johnson(18). **Elizabeth,**
m. Jonathan Philbrick(10). **Margaret,** bp.
at Portsm. 22 Sept. 1695, m. John Neal(8).
**WHITCHALLS, Emanuel** (also Witchall,
Witshall), Damariscove 1672 (White-
chance as printed); O. A. 1674. Lists 13, 15.
His w. Joanna must have been the Kennebec wit. (Witrhall) in June 1675 (Y. D.
9: 74). They had rec. at Marblehead: **Mary,**
b. 17 Aug. (bef. 1674); one Mary m. there
27 Nov. 1712 James Widger, likely from
Maine. **Daughter,** b. 10 Oct. 1674, may have
been **Elizabeth** who m. John Collier of Salem
at Marbleh. 28 May 1705, or **Sarah** who m.
Josiah Sikes there 6 Dec. 1711.
**Whitcomb,** James, Boston merchant interested at the Shoals; see Legate(2), Essex
Q. Ct. Rec. 5: 10.

**WHITE.** Became 7th commonest name in
N. E. See also Wight.
1 **ALICE,** a Cutts servant. List 328. See
Walker(17).
2 **ANDRAH,** Wells soldier 1693-4. List 267b.
3 **CHARLES,** York, List 279, m. Bethia
(Bragdon 7) Kimball. Arundel 1745.
Ch. in York 1717—1723: **Mary. Charles** and
**Bethia,** twins. **John.** See Y. D. 11: 101; 12:
306; 14: 248; 25: 31, 271.
4 **EDMOND.** See Merry(6).
5 **ELIAS** (Whitte), wit. deed John Parker
to Richard Wharton 15 July 1684, and
that month, ag. ±56, wit. deliv. of Sebascodegan Isl., Wharton to Parker. One E. was
of Marblehead, List 85. See also Codner(7).
6 **FRANCIS,** Scarboro, absent from meet.
in Oct. 1667 (he went to hear Mr. Jordan); a Great Isl. wit. with Christopher Lux
and Henry Williams 1669; drunk at Scarb.

1670, Williams and Tenney witnesses. Scottow got a judgm. ag. him in 1680; in 1684
John Davis made a contract with Scarb. to
cure him for £11. Lists 237ade, 238a, 239a.
7 **HENRY,** at Kittery in Oct. 1690, recently
back from captivity. John Chevalier
alias Knight(9) bot a shallop from him and
his fellow captive John Francis.
8 **HENRY,** ±21 in June 1699, his master
Nathl. Ayers of Portsmouth.
9 **JOHN,** Kittery bef. 1640, one of the
Shapleigh servants, depos. in Dec. 1662,
±58, ab. Mr. S.'s marsh ±22 yrs. bef.;
±66 in June 1672; ag. 70, 5 May 1679, when
he depos. ab. Shapleigh matters ±1637. He
sold a Sturgeon Creek ho. to Anthony Emery
in 1648; in 1650 a ho. to be built for him by
Mr. Shapleigh out of Province funds. Called
'neighbor' J. W. in Abraham Conley's will
1674. Lists 281-283, 298, 25, 30. With w.
Lucy 2 Dec. 1667 and 9 May 1670 he deeded
to Geo. Lidden his Crooked Lane gr. of
1654; in Nov. 1678, with no ment. of w. or
support, deeded all aft. his death to John
Allens, with reversion to their oldest surv.
son. Kn. ch: **Daughter,** m. William Thomp-
son(19). **Hannah,** m. Robert Allen(12).
**Sarah,** m. Adrian Frye(1). **Mary,** had an
illeg. ch. in 1665; see Rhodes(3).
10 **JOHN,** sailor at Richmond Isl. 1642-3.
List 21.
11 **JOHN,** Strawberry Bank 1643, sued by
John Redman in 1644. Adm. 26 Aug.
1646 to John Reynolds and Robert Mussell,
his partner; Wm. Everard and Reynold
Fernald appraisers.
12 **JOHN,** partner with James Phips in
early purch. of a large tract near the
Kennebec River at Nequasset where both
liv. and d. (Y. D. 12: 375). Lists 11, 12. In
June 1676 he wit. Thomas Stevens's deed to
Lancelot Pierce; on 4 Oct. 1679 he and 2d
w., wid. Mary Phips(1), at Boston, deeded
Jeremisquam Neck to her s. (Sir) William;
one John and Wm. Haynes wit. Purchase
heirs to Wharton in 1683. See also Reg. 73:
237; Y. D. 35: 55. His wid. was Mrs. Mary
Howard in Feb. 1704-5. How many of his
surv. 8 ch. (Y. D. 11: 15) were hers does not
appear, but surely Philip and prob. Benjamin, both named in Lady Phips' will.
**Four** of the surv. ch. d. s.p. bef. 1722, evid.
incl. **John,** jr. and **David** who with John, sr.,
wit. Miller(9) to Pearson in Nov. 1669. One
would expect any John White found with
Wm. Phips to be his half- or step- br., yet
John of List 185 was appar. too young (see
also 14). In 1722 the oldest surv. s. was
**Peter** of Milton, innholder there 1686, ag.
67 in 1727, bp. with w. Rachel in June 1730,
both above 70. She d. 20 Oct. 1732, he 23
Jan. 1736-7 in 77th yr. (gr.st.); 10 ch. at
Milton 1683-1705. **Sarah,** m. Joshua Lane

(7); Y. D. 12: 375. **Philip,** carpenter, house-wright, Beverly 1688, Newton 1711, Dedham 1743, depos. in Boston in July 1737, ±76, that he was b. at Kennebec, liv. there until 14, knew Richard Pattishall well, and Thomas Elbridge often came to his fa.'s ho. In Dec. 1739, ±77, he depos. ab. the Dyer fam. and his own birthplace, Jeremisquam Neck. Betw. 80 and 81 in June 1742. 7 ch. by w. Deborah (liv. 1713) dau. at Beverly 1686-1705. Will, 1743, names w. Anna whose admr. in 1749 was Isaac Whitney. See also Y. D. 18: 254; 20: 87, 278; SJC 50542. **Benjamin,** named in Lady Phips' will; husband-man of York 1729 (Y. D. 13: 61). That Peter of Milton named two sons Paul, suggests a connection with Paul taxed at Milton 1681-1683.

13 **JOHN,** Wells, wit. Ezekiel Knight's deed to John Sanders in Aug. 1645 and depos. in July 1647 ab. land granted to Knight. In June 1648 Mr. Francis Raynes sued E. K., John Wadleigh, Wm. Cole and J. W. for taking a canoe. Lists 252, 261, 263. Poss. same as (14) and foll. the course of John Lee (see 3, 4, 5) East.

14 **JOHN,** Sheepscot 1665, easily confused with (12) who liv. so near him, but not identical and evid. not a son. This John was at Scituate in 1676 with s.-in-law John Lee; he had left behind 17 head of cattle, 16 swine, 1 horse. Appar. at Boston in 1682. Land at Sheepscot for one John was surveyed by Giles Goddard in Aug. 1686. Lists 12, 13, 162, 164. Note also (13). Ch. incl. a **Dau.** m. John Lee (unless L. was instead a stepson) and at least one **Son** (see 12 jr. and List 185). Deborah Rogers(14) mar. 1st either a son of (14) or of (12). In 1733 (Y. D. 24: 96) Thomas Laworthy or Loworthy and w. Lydia (White, m. in Boston 16 Aug. 1722), gr.dau. and only surv. heir of John W., late of Sheepscot and Damariscotta, deeded one-half of a neck of land on East side of Sheepscot River where J. W. dwelt.

15 **JOHN,** tinker, Kittery, accus. with Rowland Jenkins' w. Mary in 1710, when believed aboard a ship in the harbor.

16 **JOSIAH,** Purpooduck, where he and br. (19) had 100 a. under Danforth, each living on his own part. In 1688 two houses stood on the land. In 1738 Josiah Wallis gave the bounds: Little Brook north, Maiden Cove Brook south, Penley's west. Altho the bros. were neighbors of John Wallis who bot the land of (20), nothing indicates relationship with (20) except the Paine deed ment. later, but it is noted the bros. bore Wallis names. Hannah (Tristram) (Jordan) Greenleaf depos. in 1738 that she well rememb. the bros. and Josiah d. within the township of Scarb., of small-pox, at least 52 yrs. ago. List 30. A dau. **Miriam** m. in Boston 30 June 1713 Richard Sundery who (as Suntay) claimed her Purpooduck land. Presum. ano. **Dau.** was mo. of William Paine of Glouc. (w. Elizabeth) who in Mar. 1724-5 deeded to John White of Glouc., clerk, ±30 a. near Maiden Cove form. Josiah White's, the warranty incl. 'from, by and under me and my mo. who gave it me.' Yet by deeds others must explain, Wm. Paine in 1720 deeded Mere Point land as gr.son of (20), and in 1724-5 Hannah, wid. of Samuel (20), deeded half of Josiah's land at Maiden Cove to the Gloucester John White (Y. D. 10: 125; 11: 212, 225).

17 **MAGNUS,** sloopmaster at Piscataqua 1674-5, later of Boston. In 1681 he and Nathl. Fox had a suit ag. Roger Rose(1). See also Hardison.

18 **NATHAN,** mariner, Portsmouth 1667, m. aft. June 1670 wid. Salome Wyatt(2). Lists 326c, 331b, 329, 52, 319, 318b, 335a, 68, 315bc. Wife, 331c, 335a; see also Jackson (9). As his wid., she owned at Little Harbor in 1699, and in 1700, bef. her 3d mar. to Francis Jenness(1) deeded ho. and land to s. William, he to pay 40 s. to each of her other ch. In 1728, of Rye, she deeded to 'my two sons in Portsm.,' Nathan and William, the prop. which her husb. Wiatt bot of John Jackson and already in Wm.'s possession. She d. at her dau. Locke's home 2 Aug. 1730. Kn. ch: **William,** ±39 in 1715-6. **Nathan,** Portsm., Newc., cooper, culler of staves, Deacon, List 316, m. by 1710 Elizabeth Robinson(3). Will, 12 May—24 June 1747, names w. Elizabeth (living 1754) and ch: Solomon, exec., Nathan, Joshua, Robert, Elizabeth Branscomb (see Reed 2). **Richard,** Greenland, taxed 1708, kinsman and legatee of Nathl. Wright(6), d. 19 Mar. 1717-8, adm. to wid. Sarah, bondsm. Jonathan Wiggin and Nathan Johnson. Lists 338ab (and w.) d. She was Sarah Thurston in 1737. Kn. ch: Rachel, m. John Lary (Samuel 1). Elizabeth, n.c.m., a town charge 15 yrs. in 1759; her br. N. W. W. had sold his fa.'s lands without right. Salome, bp. 1712, appar. m. Thomas Gaines of Ipsw. Nathaniel Wright, bp. 1716, d. bet. 1749-1759. Richard, bp. 1718. **Salome,** m. bef. 29 Nov. 1710 Joseph Locke(2).

19 **NATHANIEL,** Purpooduck, br. of (16), liv. on his half of the 100 a. until driven away by Ind. and afterwards was k. by Ind. (Y. D. 12: 170-1). Sergeant in command of Half Moon Garrison at Falm. in May 1690 (Doc. Hist. 5: 95); a tortured captive (his ear cut off) in Nov. 1691, when aft. a treaty at Sagadahoc, 10 captives were to be delivered, but not Mrs. Hull(7) their secretary, or N. W. Lists 34, 228c. By Wallis depositions 1737, he had 2 ch. that liv: **Mary,**

presum. the one 1st pub. to Richard Danforth, but m. his br. Jonathan Danforth(2). The Wallises named her husb. as Nathaniel D. **Dorcas**, m. in Newb. 24 Nov. 1714 John Danforth(2).

20 **NICHOLAS**, at Richmond Isl. 1637-1640, had a master, Mr. John Sparks, and a sis. in Eng. Assuming there was only one N., he perh. went and came once or twice, as unseen for long periods. Lists 21, 75b, 221, 222a, 232. Also Norman(2), Phippen(2). Drunk in 1659. In 1661 he sold ¼ of House Isl. to John Breme with reserva. to Sampson Penley; and 25 Nov. 1667, of Wescustogo (last seen), sold his Purpooduck plantation to John Wallis. By Eastern Cl., he owned at Mere Point (the upper part towards Maquoit), meadow at Sears Creek, etc., Pulpit Isl., alias New Damaris Cove, and a tract at Merriconeag Point. His w. was Margery bef. 4 July 1659 when Mr. John Thorp had lost a case ag. her in Comrs. ct. and appealed to the County ct. She m. 2d Wm. Haines (17). See also Stanford(3). Ch: **Daniel**, eldest son 25 Nov. 1667 (Y. D. 2: 181). **Samuel**, later of Boston (see 16), willed £4 by Richard Martin(14). Perh. **Nicholas**, who wit. a deed of Kennebec refugees in Boston in Dec. 1676 (Y. D. 11: 29), and prob. a **Dau.**, as Margery Haines claimed White land at Merriconeag for self and daughter. See also (16)·for Wm. Paine's deed as gr.s of Nicholas.

21 **CAPT. PAUL**, merchant, mariner, Pemaquid, Newbury. On 14 Dec. 1648, no resid. given, he bot from Capt. Champernowne half his Island and bldgs., and half the ho. and land called Capt. C.'s lower ho., ±500 a., all in Prov. of Maine, and in poss. of Capt. R. Waldron (assignee Thomas Kelland) in 1664. In York ct. 1650-1, he had suits ag. Jeremy Sheares, Simon Overze, Capt. C. or any agent of his, Clement Campion, and others; Sheares and Campion had suits ag. him. In Feb. 1651 he bot half the Pemaquid patent, goods and cattle from Thomas Elbridge, took poss. at once, and sold to Russell(6) and Davison(2) in Apr. 1653. List 73. Newbury 1654, from where in 1657 his w. Mrs. Bridget wrote to Davison (who was suing for possession), speaking of her husb. and his partner Mr. Elbridge. She d. in Newb. 31 Dec. 1664. He m. 2d, 14 Mar. 1664-5, Mrs. Anne Jones and d. at Newb. 20 July 1679, above 89; will, 14 Aug. 1674, gave all to her and step-ch. He owned at Barbadoes, likely Jones property.

22 **PHILIP**, mariner, Portsmouth, bound to Eng. in 1639, had p/a from Boston parties to collect in Plymouth; in Nov. 1640 had p/a from a London man to collect from Wm. Quicke.

23 **PHILIP**, mariner, Portsmouth. As cousin-german and next of kin of Tristram Harris(26), he was gr. adm. by the P. C. C. 22 Sept. 1681. Over here, he sued Wm. Gowen for the est. in 1684, sued Gowen's wid. in 1695, and his s. Samuel sued Gowen heirs in 1729. Thomas Gill depos. that Harris and P. W.'s mo. were brothers' ch., both named Harridon, and both liv. with P. W.'s gr.fa. in Cornworthy, co. Devon. Master of the ketch -Endeavor- of Piscataqua 1684; bot a Portsm. ho.-lot from Harry Benning in 1688; liv. 23 Dec. 1696. Lists 335ɑ, 98. He m. Margaret (Clark 49) Jackson (see John 16). Lists 335a, 330d. She m. 3d Roger Swain(5), in 1718 renounced adm. on the White est. to s. Samuel, and in 1732 deeded Clark prop. to him. Ch: **Joseph**, joiner, d. s.p. at and of Antigua, will, 18 Apr.—24 June 1718, giving all to br. **Samuel**, joiner, Portsm., who m. 26 Apr. 1720 Abigail Brewster(2). Will, 2 Mar.—27 Nov. 1745; names w. Abigail, dau. Mary (w. of Samuel Cate 3), son Joseph under 14. In 1757 the wid. and Samuel Cate were liv. on the homestead.

24 **RICHARD**, Kittery, m. wid. Frances Hilton(17) bef. 30 June 1656 when he was gr. adm. on the Hilton est. Both kept in evidence, Me. P. & Ct. Rec. vols. i-ii having many references. Lic. in 1659 to entertain and 'sell beer but no further'; lic. again in 1660 when he had been selling under Gunnison's lic. Aged ±44 in May 1669, ±50 in 1676. In 1679 he bot from Ephraim Crockett 50 a. in Kit. adj. York line near Braveboat Harbor and gave a mortg. to Capt. Hooke. Frances was last seen in Oct. 1687 when named in, but did not sign, a deed of his 30 a. York gr. He mortg. Braveboat Harbor land to Henry Deering in 1688; tr.j. 1689; apprais. Joseph Hodsdon's est. 1691. At Boston, but 'of Kittery' 28 Sept. 1692 when he q.c. to Henry Deering, but also called 'late of Kittery' the same day. Lists 285, 288, 298, 30. See Hilton(20), Milford, Tucker(9). Kn. ch: **Sampson**, ag. 21 in Dec. 1677 when a wit. in the Huff-Walton case; ag. 23 in Nov. 1678. Lists 298, 306a, 30. Abel Porter sued him in 1679; in 1682 he and fa. ackn. a judgm. to Mr. Henry Deering and he was bondsm. for Timothy Yeals. See also Y. D. 3: 39, 79; 4: 29; Craft(2). In 1736 Tobias Leighton sold land that had been deeded to him by S. W.'s heirs. **Frances**, punished for a slanderous lie ag. her half-br. Wm. Hilton in Sept. 1671. She and fa. abs. from meet. in July 1673 when he promised amendment for both,—she was abs. again in July 1674, her parents in 1675.

25 **ROBERT**, Saco, named with Eleanor Redding(1) in Oct. 1653 when both were fined and bound to good behavior, wit.

Thomas Redding's deed 1654 and a Redding depos. 1655. In 1658 he had been abs. from his w. six or seven yrs., she in Eng. Last seen in 1662 suing Abraham Radver for taking away fish.

26 **ROBERT**, Newcastle, called 'my countryman' by Thomas Hurst in 1695 when he had been Dr. Baxter's patient; in 1696 Hannah Pormont, sr., deposed: 'Mr. R. W. being at my house very sick.' He may or may not have liv. One R. wit. for Hiltons at Newmarket 1712-1714; in 1721 his admx. was Susannah Gorden or Gooden.

27 **SARAH**, in Canada 1695, a girl from Oyster River. List 99, p. 75. Miss Coleman could not place her.

28 **SARAH**, of Salem in June 1735, ag. ±79, form. of Falm., knew Thomas Cloyes who was k. by Ind.

29 **WILLIAM**, ag. 14, came with Rev. Philemon Dalton in 1635.

30 **WILLIAM**, and Edward Rishworth, wit. poss. given Beex & Co. to William Phillips 13 June 1659 (Y. D. i: 82). One W. was foreman of a Hampton j. 1662. Mr. Rishworth's dau. Mary m. one White (William?) bef. her gr.fa. Wheelwright(2) made his will in May 1675, and m. 2d John Sayward (3).

31 **CAPT. WILLIAM**, prob. a mariner, m. bef. Oct. 1689 Margaret Jose(1) who d. from small-pox 31 Jan. 1690-1. Her sis. Joanna willed him a silver basin and a jointed ring in 1690.

32 **WILLIAM**(18), fisherman, cooper, Portsmouth, m. 1st Abigail Whidden(2), m. 2d 15 Nov. 1716 Mary (Ball 7) Jackson (see Benjamin 20). Lists 315c, 330d, 337, 339. See (18) for prop. his mo. deeded to him. In 1732 he deeded ho. and land to s. Richard, in 1738 sold in Barrington, in 1740 deeded again to Richard for supp. of self and w. Mary. Ch., all bp. at Portsm. 30 Sept. 1711: **William** (m. in 1722 Elizabeth Lang 3). **John. Richard. Samuel**, went with his fa. when he moved Daniel Hasty to Scarb. in 1732. **Abigail. Salome**.

33 **WILLIAM** (Guillaume), naturalized in Canada in 1713, his former home not named. List 99, p. 128.

34 **ZACHARIAH** (also LeBlanc), mariner from Salem, bot at Back Cove, Falmouth, from John Lightfoot in 1682 (see also Whitefoot); of Casco Bay, bot 20 a. from Henry Bailey. List 227. A neph., Philip White of Salem, sold both lots in 1729. Y. D. 14: 261, 262.

**WHITEFOOT.** 1 **John**, Falmouth, Lists 223b, 93. Same as John Lightfoot, which see, and compare Salem records. Prob. a Jerseyman. In 1734 his s. **Joseph** (Whitefoot, b. 14 Apr. 1683), Salem shipwright, and w. Elizabeth sold half of 50 a. at Back

cove sold to his fa. by Richard Pattishall 13 Oct. 1674. See also Y. D. 14: 261 (two deeds).

2 **ROBERT**, Newcastle, taxed 1720, k. by pulling a gun out by the muzzle (N. H. Ct. files 15376).

# WHITEHOUSE.

1 **JOSEPH**, Dover, List 356j. Error for Thomas?

2 **THOMAS**, blacksmith, Dover, taxed 1663, adm. inhab. 10 Oct. 1665, m. Elizabeth Dam(2). Gr.j. 1677; highw. surv. for Dover Neck 1695. Thomas Story, the Quaker, went to his ho. from Hampt. in 1704. He d. aft. a three weeks' illness, ab. 3 Dec. 1707. Lists 356hkm, 359ab, 352, 49, 52, 57, 62, 96. See also (1). No probate for husb. or wife. Philip Cromwell's will, 1708, locates his own dwg.-ho. as betw. Thomas Whitehouse and Abraham Nute on west side of Dover Neck. Kn. ch: **Pomfret**. Lt. Pomfret's 20 a. Back River lot was laid out to him in 1694. 10 ch. by w. Rebecca rec. 1703-1720. List 358h. **Thomas**, weaver, first seen 1699, prosec. for fencing highway in 1707, gave deed to br. Edward in 1717. He m., likely not first, Rachel, appar. wid. successively of Nicholas Wallingford and Stephen Hawkins. Will, 1744—1750, names her and dau. Elizabeth, b. 1 Nov. 1725. **Edward**, bot from Philip Cromwell's est. 1710, wit. Humphrey Varney's will 1713, bot from br. Thomas 1717 and in 1722 he and Nathl. Austin bot and divided land. **Judith**, m. James Mussey (4). See also Connor(5), Drew(7), Tibbetts (12).

**WHITFIELD, John.** In 1645 his ho., appar. at York, had been attached for debts due to Mrs. Sarah Lynn and George Small, and Mr. Godfrey ordered that Mrs. L. should occupy it (see Me. P. & Ct. Rec. i: 255).

**WHITING.** 1 **Capt.**, wounded at Winnegance 1697, List 96.

2 **JOSEPH**, Mr., ±18 in 1663 when Mr. Richard Cutts put him aboard one of his ships 'to be merchant of the said cargo' (SJC 746).

3 **WILLIAM**, Mr., Hartford, br.-in-law of Capt. Thomas Wiggin(5) and owner in the Squamscott Patent. In 1640 W. W., Edw. Holyoke, et al. sued Wm. Cotton, Francis Rand, et al.; ab. 1642, W. W., E. H., and Henry Clarke sued the inhabs. of Northam on acct. of John Redman's building a ho. on the point of land. See 'Early Conn. Probate Records, Hartford District,' i: 40, for will 1643, cod. 1646, in which he gave to sis. Wiggin and her ch. In 1649 Mistress Susanna W. sued James Rawlins on a bill for freight of staves, etc.

**Whitlock, Mary.** See Bray(5).

**WHITLY, Samuel,** Portsmouth, wit. in' the Webster-Jones case 1670. In 1675, formerly John Pickering's man (Whittly), he was accus. with Honor Bennet, Richard Cummings' maid. In June 1676 (Whitwell, q.v.), he was to be sold for four yrs. unless he paid for the two ch. which R. C.'s servant Honor laid to him.

**WHITMARSH, Onisephorous,** ag. 5 when his fa. John of Weymouth and fam. came with Rev. Joseph Hull's company. A Berwick wit. 1651 (as read for Y. D. 1: 18, Wouessefferos Whitmasse). One Simon W. was taxed Berwick, Feb. 1718-9. See Hist. of Weymouth (Chamberlain), 4: 758.

**WHITNEY,** became 61st commonest name in N. E.

1 **BENJAMIN,** tailor, Dover, York, b. at Watertown 6 June 1643, s. of John and Elinor. Taxed Cochecho 1666. In Mar. 1670-1 he sold to a br. the int. in the Watert. homestead given him by his fa. in the hope he would return to it. York 1672, gr.j. 1679, O. A. Mar. 1679-80. A 10 a. gr. was laid out to him by Philip Cooper's, on which he had liv. 'these several yrs.' when he and w. Jane sold, with ano. 10 a., to Jonathan Sayward 24 Mar. 1684-5. York wit. 1686? (Y. D. 4: 159). Of Sherborn 1687 where w. Jane d. 14 Mar. 1690. Of Framingham, he m. 2d at Marlboro 11 Apr. 1695 Mary Poore; d. at Sherborn 1723. Ch. appear: **Jane,** b. at Watert. 29 Sept. 1669, m. Jonathan Morse in Mass. **Benjamin,** Framingham, m. in Boston 7 Aug. 1705 Esther Maverick, wid. of James. **Jonathan,** Sherborn. **John,** York, had 20 a. gr. 1714, liv. near Braveboat Harbor 1724, at Kit. 1732. List 291. He m. 1st Lettice Ford(4); ch. at York Mar. 1704-5—May 1719: Mary, Samuel, Elizabeth, Mercy, Mehitabel, John, and 'Old Kittery' adds Benjamin b. 22 May 1725 (see Hist. of Brunswick, p. 760). He m. 2d at Kit. 14 Jan. 1730 Susannah (Barton 5) Smith. **Nathaniel,** weaver, b. at York 14 Apr. 1680, of Kit. bot in York 1708, York gr. 1713, 'late of York' bot there 1717, depos. in May 1731 ab. the land John Ford liv. on. List 279. He m. Sarah Ford(4). Ch. rec. Jan. 1706-7—Mar. 1729-30: Nathan (see Presbury 3), Nathaniel, Abel, Sarah, Isaac, Amos, Lydia, Joanna. **Joshua,** b. at Sherborn 21 Sept. 1687.

2 **JONATHAN,** Saco fort soldier, Lists 248ab.

**Whittaker,** Abraham, Wells soldier from Haverhill 1693-4. List 267b. See Bean (2), Kelly(8), Larrabee(5).

**Whittell,** Robert, Monhegan 1672, List 13. One Thomas Whittle was taxed at Newcastle 1720. See also Whitwell.

**WHITTEMORE.** The Charlestown fam. was from Hitchin, co. Herts. See also Draper(3), N. E. Reg. 21: 169.

1 **JOEL,** mariner, Portsmouth, b. in Charlestown 15 June 1677, s. of John and 1st w. Mary; adm. 9 Jan. 1711-2 to (2).

2 **PELATIAH,** Kittery, Portsmouth, Boston, b. in Charlest. 7 May 1680, half-br. of (1). Commissary at Kit. 1703, and m. 4 (or 14) Nov. 1706 Margery Pepperell (Col. Wm.). Mr. W. and ho. taxed Portsm. 1708, merchant there 1711-2; he, w. and 3 ch. warned at Boston 23 June 1715, having come there from Kit. six mos. bef.; Boston 1717. Lost in a shipwreck near the Shoals bef. 3 Sept. 1730 when wid. Margery m. 2d Elihu Gunnison (1 jr.). Adm. on her est. to Wm. W. 14 Aug. 1769. Ch., all but Margery rec. at Kit. and in Col. Pepperell's will: Capt. **Pelatiah,** Kit. Pt., b. 26 Jan. 1707-8, m. Joanna (?Moore 4). Adm. to her 21 July 1741 (bondsm. Wm. and John Deering), 3 ch. bp. She m. 2d bef. 21 Oct. 1742 Capt. John Lecornee, mariner, from Isle of Jersey. **William,** goldsmith, b. 10 Mar. 1710-1, of Portsm. 1748. **Mary,** b. 2 Nov. 1712, m. Edmond March of Amesbury. **Margery,** d. at Boston 8 July 1715. **Joel,** b. 15 Dec. 1716, m. at Newington 15 June 1739 Abishag Hoyt, both of Portsm.; of Kit. 1748.

3 **SAMUEL,** wit. bill from Arthur Bennick to N. Fryer in Mar. 1671-2; in 1675 bot from Christopher Cole 15 a. he had bot from John York, having Charles Glidden's old field on the north. List 356j. He was from Charlest., son of Thomas and uncle of (1) and (2). See Wyman's Charlestown, ii: 1027, for nine ch. by w. Hannah, all rec. at Charlest. except the oldest s. **Samuel,** b. at Dover 24 Dec. 1672, m. Lydia Draper(3), and d. early, leaving an only ch: Samuel, b. 23 Jan. 1692-3, whose gdn. in 1707 was Robert Scott(4).

**Whittredge,** William, Ipswich, had a 20 a. Exeter gr. with Thomas King in 1649, which was regranted in 1651, he not having come to dwell acc. to condition.

**WHITWELL, William,** abutted Mitton lands in Falmouth 1671 (Y. D. 2: 132). He was from Boston where he had w. Joanna (s. **Samuel,** b. 1653), and 2d w. Mary (ch. **Mary, William,** ano. **Mary,** 1669-1671). His wid. adm. in 1686. List 225b, Mrs. Whitwell's. See also Wittell, Whitly, Waters(6).

**WIBIRD.**

1 **JOHN,** named as John Vybird in Charles Story's bill ag. Mungo Crawford in 1710. Adm. on est. of John of Portsm., who seems a br. of (2), was gr. to (2) or his son 22 Jan. 1730-1. One Thomas who may never have

seen N. H. was master of the pinke -Mary-in 1707 (Reg. 31: 67). One Sarah m. John Bussy(2) 4 Jan. 1724-5.

2 ‡*RICHARD, Esq., Portsmouth, wealthy and prominent, came first (quoting Wentworth Gen.) 'as poulterer under the steward to one of the King's ships.' He m. 10 July 1701 wid. Elizabeth (Dew) Redford (2) and in Dec. that yr. was prohib. from selling liquor. Capt. W. taxed 1707. Select-man 1712, 1713 (1714 election annulled); Rep. 1716; Councillor 1716. Lists 324, 337, 339, 239b. See also (1), Gordon(5), Mills (10), Owen(1); Wentworth Gen. i: 292. Will, 19 Oct. 1732—25 Apr. 1733, names br. Anthony and his dau., and Mehitabel Wain-wright, under 18, in addition to wife, 2 sons, son-in-law and gr.ch. Widow Elizabeth's will, 1 May 1739 (d. 12 Feb. 1742-3, ag. 73), names also Mehitabel Wainwright and Mrs. Hannah Bradford. Ch: ‡Richard, Esq., b. 4 July 1702, H. C. 1722, Councillor, Judge of Probate, etc., m. in Boston 30 Nov. 1738 Elizabeth Wendell (Hon. Jacob). He d. in Portsm. 25 Sept. 1765, she shortly bef. 7 Jan. 1785, ag. 66. John, merchant, b. 20 Oct. 1705, m. Elizabeth Fitch (Rev. Jabez), who was gr. adm. 7 Apr. 1732 and d. 14 Jan. 1774, ag. 68, leaving a son Rev. Anthony, H. C. 1747, long minister at Quincy. Thom-as, b. Oct. 1707, H.C. 1728, d. (Thomas, Esq.) 12 Nov. 1765 in Portsm., unm.; see N. E. Reg. 32: 35. Elizabeth, b. 27 Aug. 1709, m. Hunking Wentworth(6).

Wiborne, John, List 82.

Wickam, John, Hampton wit. 1671, John Wooden to Jonathan Smith. See also Wakeham.

WIDGER, uncommon.

1 JAMES, fisherman, Sagadahoc, m. Mary Phips(1); see also Phips(7). O. A. there 1674 and again at Beverly in Dec. 1677. At Kennebec in 1688. Lists 15, 85, 186, 189. He d. in Boston 18 June 1715, ag. 89; wid. Mary d. there 8 Dec. 1721, ag. 84. Little appears of them and nothing of their fam. Hannah Widger and sis. Mercy Due, ag. ±32, in Boston 1698, may have been ch. of (1), (2), (3), or none. This is true also of Robert (Wiger) who had been five weeks in Boston jail in 1689 and asked for 'enlargement' and of John Widger who m. Bethia Sweet in Marblehead 12 Nov. 1685 (see Marbleh. V. R. for later Widgers). See Witshall; also Y. D. 17: 171 for John (Wiger) and w. Eliz-abeth Hunnewell (Stephen 1), of Boston 1735.

2 PETER, fisherman, Monhegan 1672, List 13. O. A. at Boston 11 Nov. 1678, deft. in a suit there 1691. See also (1).

3 WILLIAM, fined in Me. ct. 1647, with other Shoals men, for trying to collect

pay a second time from Mr. Nicholas Brown (28).

Wier. See Weare.

Wigfues, Jonas, List 330e, must be Wake-field.

WIGGIN. Col. Banks found a Wiggin fam. at Creeting, co. Suffolk, ab. 11 miles from Great Livermere where Rev. Wm. Leveridge was rector in 1631. See also Pope's Pio-neers of Me. & N. H.

1 ANDREW(5), Mr., J. P., Stratham, ±65 in Aug. 1700, m. at Andover 3 (or 8) June 1659 Hannah Bradstreet (Gov. Simon). Freeman's oath Oct. 1669. Pub. ho. lic. 1678, 1679, 1683; jury 1684. Lists 356e, 377, 396, 331c, 384a, 388, 49, 52, 54, 57, 62, 67, 96. See also Prov. Papers 17: 673. Hannah, liv. when he made his will 13 Jan. 1703-4, was appar. dead 18 Apr. 1707 when he added to it; he d. 9 Jan. 1708-9. Ch: Thomas, b. 5 Mar. 1660-1. Simon, b. 17 Apr. 1664. Han-nah, b. 10 Aug. 1666, m. Samuel Wentworth (8 jr.). Mary, b. 22 Mar. 1668, m. Capt. Jere-miah Gilman(7). Andrew, Col., J. P., Strath-am, b. 6 Jan. 1671-2, Ex. constable 1698, Lists 57, 62, 331c, 377, 388. He m. 1st 2 Sept. 1697 Abigail Follett(6), m. 2d 4 Jan. 1737 Rachel (Chase 5) Freese, named in his will, 20 July 1753—6 Feb. 1756. Ch. by 1st w: Hannah (m. in Ipsw. Wm. Cogswell, James Burnham and Andrew Burley); An-drew, not in will; Martha (m. as 2d w. Rev. Henry Rust, see Waldron 11); Abigail (m. Samuel Doe 3); Nicholas, d.y.; Mary (m. Theophilus Smith, see 40); Mercy (m. Sam-uel Sherburne 7); Caleb, not in will; Brad-street (m. Phebe Sherburne, d. by 1754, 7 ch.); Nicholas (m. Mary Doe 3, d. by 1754, 6 ch.; wid. m. 2d Capt. Jonathan Swett); Elizabeth, not in will. John, b. 4 Sept. 1674, not in will. Bradstreet, b. 25 Mar. 1675-6, d. 18 Jan. 1708-9. Adm. to Hampt. Ch. 4 Apr. 1697, j. 1699, 1700, selectman 1706. Lists 62, 387. He m. 21 Aug. 1697 Ann Chase(5), List 388, who m. 2d John Sinclair(2). Ch: Chase, bp. at Hampt. 26 Nov. 1699 (m. Martha Weeks who m. 2d Winthrop Hilton 24 jr.); Thomas, bp. at Hampt. 19 Apr. 1702; Elizabeth, bp. at Hampt. 1 Oct. 1703 (m. Benj. Taylor, jr.); Joseph, a minor in 1726. Dorothy, b. 13 Sept. 1678, m. Capt. John Gilman(11). Jonathan, Stratham, 22 in 1701, Lists 376b (1705), 388, m. in Newb. 9 Nov. 1703 Mary Emery. Will, 23 Mar.—31 May 1738, names wife, 1 son, 5 daus. Abi-gail, m. (ct. Sept. 1698) Wm. French(9). Sarah, m. Wm. Moore(26 jr.).

2 JAMES, Kittery, Blue Point, ±34 in 1669, ±37 in 1674, ±39 in 1675-6, m. Magda-lene Hilton(17) by June 1656. York gr. 1659 east of Edw. Godfrey's dwg. ho.; Marshal's deputy 1659; late marshal under the Comrs.

Noyes, Libby & Davis
Geneal. Dictionary of Maine & N. H.

7 July 1663, and took unkindly to his removal by Mass. (see Me. P. & Ct. Rec. ii: 140-1); marshal again 1666-1667 when accused by Rishworth of abusing him and authority. He and the Whites were bound to the peace towards Mrs. Gunnison in 1660; with Mr. Jordan bondsm. for Edw. Colcord 1662; bondsm. for Capt. Lockwood 1666; sued by Mr. Francis Johnson 1670, 1677, by Mr. Henry Deering 1675. In Feb. 1678-9 he mortg. livestock to Robert Elliot; at Scarb. 1681, prob. on Mr. Elliot's Blue Point farm which Richard Tarr said he occupied five yrs. bef. his own lease began. Scarb. gr. Mar. 1682-3; he and Tarr sued on a note by Scottow 1685; defaulted a suit in June 1688; Lists 288, 298, 238a, 30, 92, 93. See Gunnison(4), Potum. Widow Magdalene of Newbury m. 2d in 1698 Henry Kenning of Salem. Only kn. ch: **James**, ±21 in Sept. 1679.

3 **JAMES**(2), Kittery, Blue Point, had taken Major Hooke's canoe and not returned it in 1677. Accused by Deliverance Adams(3), 1679. Kit. gr. 1681. As 'Jr.' sued in 1681 by Robert Elliot whose will 1718 ment. 'debt due from Wiggins.' Lists 288, 298, 30. Accused by Sarah Winnock in June 1687, made denial, but ord. to pay her 2 s. a week. Called late of Blue Point 16 Aug. 1693 when wid. Sarah (?Winnock) of Newb. m. 2d James Davis(13 jr.). She was liv. 1726. Ch: **James** (surely, Y. D. 17: 130), Wells 1714, m. there 11 May (1715) Abigail (Cloyes 2) Cousins(4). Jury 1714-1715; W. constable 1716. She was a wid. 1719-1746, dead 1748. Ch: Abigail, bp. 23 May 1715 when her fa. recog. bp. cov.; m. Jeremiah Littlefield(5). Sarah, b. 14 Feb. 1717, bp. 18 May 1718 as dau. of Sarah; m. 1st 4 Sept. 1736 Jacob Perkins, jr.; m. 2d Samuel Littlefield(7). Poss: **Ann**, of Haverhill, m. 16 Feb. 1707 Joseph Merrill of Newb. and Stratham. **Sarah**, m. by 1707 George Hadley of Haverh. and Amesb. See also Mary, w. of John Dore(2).

4 **LT. SIMON**(1), Stratham. Jury 1695; constable 1696; adm. to Hampt. Ch. 23 May 1697; selectman 1701-1705. Lists 52, 57, 62-64, 384a, 385, 388. He appar. m. 1st Judith Wilson(4), m. 2d (contr. 29 Oct. 1703) Catherine (Wiggin 6) Tufton-Mason, who was adm. to Hampt. Ch. 14 Apr. 1706. Will, 9 Feb.—9 June 1720, provides that what he had from her should return to her immed. after his interment. See Mason(17) for her will. Ch. by 1st w: **Hannah**, bp. at Hampt. with her sis. 24 July 1698, m. 17 Dec. 1719 George Veasey, jr.(4). **Deborah**, bp. with Hannah, unm. in Sept. 1724 when her step-mo. called her 'my well beloved dau.-in-law.' Lt. **Simon**, b. 12 Aug. 1701, d. at Stratham 11 Aug. 1757, m. at Portsm. 16

May 1728 Susannah Sherburne(3) who d. 9 July 1763; 7 ch.

5 **CAPT. ‡\*THOMAS**, gent., wit. deliv. of the Vines patent 25 June 1630, the Hilton patent 7 July 1631, and of Piscataqua 22 Oct. 1631 when he wrote to Winthrop ab. Bagnall. In Eng. 31 Aug. 1632, and there 19 Nov. fol. when he wrote to Sec. Cooke, estimating the English in N. E. as ±2000. A week later granted a patent by the Council of N. E. In Mar. 1632-3 he was called the chief agent (in Eng.) of the honest men about to buy out the Bristol men's plantation at Piscataqua and plant 500 people bef. Michaelmas, and Winthrop, 10 Nov. 1633, records his arrival at Salem in the -James- with ±30 men, incl. Rev. Wm. Leveridge. He went directly to Piscataqua from where he wrote a letter in Nov. 1633. As agent for Lords Say and Brooke and in his own interest, he was opposed to the Mason claims, and in time became a strong adherent of Mass. and a help in extending their power. His land was long outside the limits of any town, but in 1657 he was ord. taxed in Hampt. and was moderator there that year. Comr. for Piscataqua ct., Assistant, J. P. See Records of Mass. Bay, vols. 1-4; Me. P. & Ct. Rec., vols. i-ii; N. E. Reg. 26: 234; Winthrop's Letters; Savage. Lists 241, 263, 276, 356abcegh, 372, 375a, 392b, 53. See also Starbuck. His w. Katherine was willed £5 and each ch. £5 by her br. Mr. Wm. Whiting(3). Will, of Squamscott and aged, 16 June 1664 (proved 1666), names w. Katherine and ch.; friends Samuel Haines and Elias Stileman overseers; his son depos. as 'jr.' 29 Mar. 1666. Ch., all bp. at Hampt. 20 Sept. 1641: **Andrew. Mary**, with Samuel Hall wit. Pike to Bradbury 1657; m. 1st George Veasey(1), m. 2d Capt. William Moore(26). **Thomas**.

6 **\*THOMAS**(5), Sandy Point, depos. in Mar. 1666, ag. 26; in Nov. 1684, ±42; in Aug. 1700, ±60. In 1662 Thomas, sr. and Thomas, jr. for £400 gave deed to Capt. Barefoot, ½ of ho., mill, land gr., utensils, cows, etc. Rep. 1684; gr.j. (foreman) 1694. Lists 377, 384a, 387, 49, 52, 57. He m. by 1665 Sarah, sis. of Capt. Walter Barefoot (see his will). She was gr. adm. 19 Dec. 1700, bondsm. Thomas Wiggin and John Pickering and was liv. 1711. Ch: **Thomas**, b. ±1664, recited his parentage: his mo. was sis. and only heir to said Barefoot, himself son and heir to his fa. Ag. ±60 in 1724. Will, of Stratham, 4 Jan. (d. 6 Mar.) 1726-7, gives much to wife (she was Sarah in 1719, Y. D. 9: 184) and ch: John, Walter, Thomas, Henry, Andrew, Tufton, Samuel and three daus., naming only Mary who was under age. **Catherine**, m. 1st Robert Tufton Mason(17), m. 2d Capt. Simon Wiggin(4).

**Sarah**, ag. 69 in May 1738, m. Henry Sherburne(3). **Susannah**, ag. 64 in May 1738, single 10 Oct. 1692, w. of Ebenezer Johnson (16) in 1725, presum. the Susannah -Martlin- he m. in 1716.

7 **THOMAS**(1), Stratham, m. Martha Dennison (John) of Ipsw., and d. early; inv. 18 Feb. 1695-6, the same day adm. was gr. to the wid. Martha, then w. of Jonathan Thing(2). She m. 3d 11 June 1697 Matthew Whipple and d. in Ipswich 12 Sept. 1728 in 60th yr. Only one ch. seen, and only one named in gr.fa.'s will: **Hannah**, m. in Ipsw. 23 Oct. 1717 Jonathan Cogswell, d. 13 June 1723 in 32d yr.

**WIGHT**, Thomas, Exeter 1639, prob. of Lincolnshire origin; see N. E. Reg. 68: 77. He was fined for speaking contemptuously of magistrates in 1642, signed a pet. in Sept. 1643. Lists 373, 375ab, 376ab(1645). Prob. d. bef. 25 Mar. 1648 when w. Lucy gave p/a to George Barlow. As a wid. she sold a ho. and lot to John Tedd which he sold to John Bean in 1664. She m. 2d in Boston 24 Dec. 1652 John Samuel (see Records of Mass. Bay, 3: 420; 4: 1: 283), whose est. was apprais. 8 Dec. 1662, and was liv. 1665 when there was a suit over a Boston ho. which Samuel had left to her for life with remainder to her ch: **Israel**, a Boston wit. 1656. In 1664 sued his former gdn. Capt. R. Waldron for withholding his est., got judgment, levied on Squamscott land, and sold to Christopher Palmer, 20 a. marsh and meadow; the deed also incl. a q.c. to a Boston ho., and ho. and land of Charles Buckner in Dover. See Records of Mass. Bay 4: 2: 283, 322; Rec. of Ct. of Assistants 3: 142-4, 170. On 11 Apr. 1665 he was gr. adm. on his fa.'s est. (N. H.); in Sept. 1666 had gone out of the country. **Elizabeth**, had John Joyliffe as gdn. in 1665.

**WILCOCK**, -cox. Wilcox became the 72d commonest name in N. E.

1 **JOHN**, here early, List 41. Sued by Thomas Johnson in Saco et., June 1640; £10 in the hands of Thomas Brooks and Peter Weare of Piscataqua to be attached. He sold land (?house) to Brooks (or Basil Parker) and Weare (Y. D. i: 30). 'Will Coxes Pond,' Berwick, ment. long aft. One John later in Essex Co., List 85.

2 **THOMAS**, Portsmouth 1693, List 334b.

3 **WILLIAM**, and Theodore Atkinson, wit. for Mr. Leader(2) in Mass. Genl. Ct. 1651.

**WILCOTT.**

1 **HUGH**, named in an old memo. as husb. of Dorcas Penley (Sampson), was prob. the seaman who sued Joshua Ward, master of the pinke -John and Elizabeth- of Salem,

for six months' wage in Essex Q. Ct. 1679. Taxed Salem 1692. An aged wid. of Boston, she made a will (uninvest.) naming dau. Pringle, Ballard gr.sons and others. Kn. ch: **Dorcas**, m. in Boston 28 Sept. 1704 Daniel Ballard. **Elizabeth**, called Pringle in 1722, m. 1st in Boston 17 July 1711 Wm. Hall, m. 2d 4 Apr. 1715 James Prignall. Esther m. in 1704, John in 1708, Lydia in 1710, Hannah in 1715, all in Boston, may have been other ch., but note that two of them bore Mercer-Draper names. See (4).

2 **JOHN**, wit. a Wells gr. 1660 (Y. D. 11: 203).

3 **THOMAS**, ±30 in 1672, List 14.

4 **WILLIAM**, Sheepscot bef. the first war. Ag. ±45, and late inhab. at New Dartmouth, he test. ag. Lt. Jordan(6) at Boston 27 Jan. 1689-90. Lists 162, 164. His wid., appar. dau. of Thomas Mercer(2), ent. an East. Cl. for 100 a. on west side of Sheepscot River below the falls given by Mercer to her decd. husb., who improved several yrs. until the wars. In 1737, a son or gr.s., William W. of Billingsgate, mariner, sold half this 100 a.; see also Reg. 44: 24. Not imposs. Philip W. of Scituate (m. Deborah Gannett 1711) and Hingham was connected. See also (1).

**Wild**, Wildes, Richard. See Mander(1).

**Wildgoose**, John, O. A. 1674, List 15.

**Wiles**, John and Philip, sailors, both List 7.

**Wilkey**, Mr., an early shipmaster; Me. P. & Ct. Rec. i: 122.

**WILKINS.** 1 **Henry** (or Wilkinson), see Lewis(4).

2 **JOHN**, a Portsm.-Berwick wit. 1676 (Y. D. 3: 22).

**WILKINSON.** See Wilkins(1); Waters' English Gleanings, ii: 1257.

1 **BRAY**, a wit. ab. the Wannerton-Holland trouble at the Eastward in 1635.

2 **JOHN**, came to Richmond Isl. in the -Welcome- 1633. He and others depos. at Saco in June 1641 that they were servants of Mr. John Winter when Mr. Cleeve left Spurwink and did not know that Mr. Winter ever forced him to depart. Sued by John Baple at Saco 1640; Black Point constable 1640. One J. was at Monhegan 1653 (Essex Q. Ct. Rec. i: 325). Lists 21, 22, 281. He seems the J. W., decd., on whose est. Richard Collicott took adm. in Casco ct. 26 July 1666, altho George Felt was a bondsman.

3 **JOHN**, No. Yarmouth. Before Philip's War the farm betw. Redding's Creek and Mosier's land was 'called by the name of Lane's and Wilkinson's farm and by no other' (Y. D. 26: 161). Moses Felt heard old Mr. Royal say he had sold all his land

E. of Redding's Creek to James Lane and J. W. Prob. the son of wid. Prudence W. and br. of Elizabeth (Wilkinson) Felt(1), who d. in Malden in Dec. 1675. In 1730 Isaac W. of Rumney Marsh sold No. Yarm. land bounded by Redding's Creek. See Wyman's Charlestown, ii: 1031.

4 **THOMAS**, Portsmouth, from London, List 339, taxed 1732. See Caverly(3).

**Will** (Black Will), Lists 94, 297 (est.), 298. See Black(5).

**WILLARD**. 1 Josiah, Secretary, List 256.
2 **CAPT. SIMON**, Lists 35, 36.

## WILLETT.

1 **ANDREW**(6), servant of Mr. Humphrey Davie at Swan Isl., Kennebec, ±1668, and served out his time there. See Rec. of Ct. of Assts., Mass. Bay. In 1685 he had gone to R. I., from there to sea. Depos. in Boston 21 Apr. 1696, ag. ±42, ab. the Kennebec and Thomas Giles 20 yrs. bef.; again 22 July 1718, ±67, ab. Mr. Giles and his own service under Mr. Davie ±50 yrs. bef. Andrew of Boston m. Susannah Holbrook of Braintree 6 Mar. 1693-4; **children**. In Boston A. m. Rebecca Bushell 25 Oct. 1705; A. m. Martha Hamon 18 Nov. 1719. See also Reg. 11: 376.

2 **FRANCIS**, Exeter 1694, List 384a, prob. from Newbury.

3 **JACOB**, Mr., London merchant, creditor of the Broughton est. 1670, took over most of Mr. Thomas B.'s prop. in Boston ±1674-5, and as Mr. Peter Cole's assignee sued Jonathan Nason for tresp. in Wells ct. 1676. Will, of Barbadoes, 4 Sept. 1677 (proved in Me. 1 May 1733), gave all in trust for w. and children in Eng. He d. much earlier, his exec. in 1721-2 suing many in Berwick (Abbotts, etc.) for 2/9 of ½ of Quamphegan.

4 **JAMES**, Wells, see Butland(1). Son James.

5 **NATHANIEL**, Black Point, 1675-1678. Lists 236, 237ab(2). One N. wit. John Hoddy's deed at Portsm. 1678.

6 **CAPT. THOMAS**, left in charge of the Penobscot trading house when Edw. Astley went to New Plymouth, List 1, had a ho. at Penobscot a yr. aft. Capt. Neale left the country, from which he was ejected by the French, and was master of the Plymouth trading ho. at Kennebec in 1639. Ch. incl. Andrew, b. 5 Oct. 1655. See also Savage; Rec. of Mass. Bay 4: 2: 447, 455; Rec. of Ct. of Assts. (Mass.), 3: 185, 257.

**WILLEY**, peculiar to Lincolnshire (Guppy).

1 **GEORGE**, Dover, List 356m.

2 **JOHN**(4), weaver, Oyster River, ±24 in Sept. 1683, ±60 in 1715 and 1718, ±65 in 1721, 80 in Feb. 1734-5. Gr.j. 1700. His w. was Alice by two deeds 1717, Dorcas when bp. 7 Apr. 1717, Alice Dorcas when adm. to Ch. 6 Mar. 1719-20 and in deed 1735. He receipted to his mo. (see Leathers 2). In 1718, sons Samuel and John, jr., having had deeds from him, q.c. fa.'s est. (he liv.) to his heirs. He deeded to s. Wm. in 1735, and to s. Stephen, incl. the homestead, in 1737. Dead 10 Sept. 1739. Lists 52, 57, 94, 367b, 368ab, 369. See Harford(2), Reynolds(1). Ch: **John**, bp. with minor s. John 6 Apr. 1718; with w. Christian adm. to Ch. 5 Apr. 1724. Lists 368b, 369. 8 ch. **Samuel**, m. Sarah Stevenson(1) who was adm. to Ch. 12 Nov. 1727. List 368b. He depos. 23 Jan. 1753, ag. 60, and soon d., a release to Samuel (jr.) that yr. showing 4 of the heirs: Samuel, Mary (w. of Benj. Heard), Sarah (w. of Wm. Smart), Hannah (w. of Josiah Doe); ano. s. Joseph deeded to Samuel in 1756. **William**, shipwright, m. at Hampt. F. 9 Dec. 1718 Margaret Basford (Jacob); both adm. to O. R. Ch. 4 Feb. 1727-8, he living 1730. Lists 368b, 369. 4 or more ch. **Stephen**, bp. with mo. 7 Apr. 1717, ag. 12, m. 12 Dec. 1728 Lucy Allen. List 369. 2 or more ch.

3 **STEPHEN**(4), mariner, ±30 in Sept. 1679, m. by 1671 Abigail Pitman(11) and liv. on homestead. In 1683 he was murderously jealous of her and John Bickford, jr., at which time (2) protected her. She and two daus. went to Canada as captives in 1689 and remained. When bound to sea (Barbadoes), 4 July 1696, he made a deed to the two ch. at home, in case death seized him or he never ret., giving the homestead, other land and stock to his son, the land he bot from B. Squire to dau. Abigail. This was rec. 27 Jan. 1700-1. Lists 359a, 57. The wid. m. in Canada 6 Oct. 1710 Edw. de Flecheur. List 99, pp. 75, 255. Ch: **Thomas**, weaver, had w. Frances by 1702, both bp. 25 Mar. 1721-2. Lists 368ab. See also Hussey (7). He depos. 1 May 1738, ag. 67; d. bet. 1746—July 1753. 'Hist. of Durham' names ch: Joanna, Benjamin, Ezekiel, Stephen, Thomas, Robert. One Thomas and appar. two Abigails wit. in the Amos Pinkham case 1720, one Abigail poss. belonging to this fam.; note also Hall(23). **Judith**, b. 11 June 1676, (List 99, p. 75), bp. in Canada as Marie Magdeleine, m. there 29 Sept. 1698 Jean le Conte, bur. 1 Feb. 1703. Ch. **Abigail**, likely 'one Willis' dau. of Oyster River' recovered from the Ind. up Androscoggin River (Capt. Church's report 15 Sept. 1690); m. William Leathers(2). **Elizabeth**, List 99, p. 75, as Marie m. 3 husb. in Canada, Charles Arnault 1702, Pierre Perot 1704, Barthelemy Cotton 1741; bur. at Quebec as Marie Wellis 17 Sept. 1776, ag. 96.

4 **THOMAS**, Oyster River, b. ±1617, had a
'breadth of land' at Oyster River Point
in 1645, prob. from Darby Field, and m. bef.
6 Oct. 1649 widow Margaret Crawford(5).
Gr.j. 1651, 1652, 1655, 1666. Dover gr. 1654.
Lists 354abc, 355ab, 356a, 357c, 359a, 361a,
362b, 363abc, 366, 92. In Sept. 1680, he ±63
and Margaret ±65 depos. ab. Stephenson's
Neck or Point ±40 yrs. bef. Adm. 7 Sept.
1681 to wid. Margaret and s. John. She m.
2d Barnard Squire(1), (see also Leathers 2).
Ch. seen: **Stephen**, b. ±1649. **Samuel**, with
Nicholas Doe bondsm. for Elizabeth and
John York, execs., 1674. List 359a. Reported dead 21 May 1679; adm. to fa. 24 June
1679 when he and s. Wm. gave bond to pay
the debts. **William**, b. ±1656. **John**, b.
±1659. At one time the s. Stephen had a
**sister** in Kittery, poss. his half-sis. (Crawford) or a sis.-in-law, tho it seems that there
must have been unkn. daus. in the early generations.

5 **WILLIAM**(4), servant of Thomas King
of Exeter, who willed him land in Mar.
1666-7. In 1678, ag. ±22, he depos. bef. Waldron. Portsm. tax rebated 15 Mar. 1679-80;
he prob. had mov. to Dover Neck with w.
Rebecca Nock(4), on whose mo.'s est. he
was gr. adm. 1 June 1680. Gr.j. 1679, 1680.
Living Feb. 1689-90. Lists 359b, 52, 57. His
s. Samuel as fa.'s admr. sold Nock prop. in
Aug. 1706 and the former King prop. in
Feb. 1707-8. Widow Rebecca m. 2d Capt.
Samuel Tibbetts(12). Ch: **Samuel**, Dover,
(List 358d), m. 1st 8 June 1702 Mary Can-
ney(1) who d. 2 June 1703 (List 96), m. 2d
19 Feb. 1704-5 Elizabeth (German 3) Ran-
dall(11), who was living 27 Oct. 1715. But
Randall desc. call her dau. of Richard Ran-
dall(16) and sister, not mo., of Nathaniel
(11), relying for proof of Nathaniel's par-
entage on a deed considered fraudulent, N.H.
Deeds 17: 223 (1729), Richard Randall to s.
Nathaniel, 30 a. gr. from Dover 1694 (see
N. H. State Papers, 9: 161-167). Samuel's
will, 21 Dec. 1753—30 Jan. 1754, names s.
Samuel, b. at Dover 25 Feb. 1702-3, and dau.
Mary, unm. Presum. **William**, d. 15 Oct.
1706, ag. 22 (List 96).

**WILLIAMS**, princ. from Wales and border counties, but co. Cornwall an inde-
pendent home. Became 8th commonest
name in N. E.
1 **ANN**, m. Robert Lang(7) in 1668, the
first of several unplaced. In 1670 Martha (wrote) and Elias Stileman wit. Anthony Ellins' deed. Rachel, see Purington
(4). Sarah 'lately called Williams now
Sarah Bodge' named in a Portsm. warr. with
others 7 Mar. 1709-10; see Randall(12) and
Benj. Bodge, her husb., appar. a neighbor of
Samuel Williams(36) at O.R. Rebecca,

Portsm. 1719, see (39). Hannah (see Page
2), poss. from Essex Co., but see (6). Margaret (see Ayer 1), prob. from Essex Co.
2 **CHARLES**, see Y. D. 1: 136.
3 **DANIEL**, taxed Newcastle 1719-1723, innkeeper 1723. One D., w. and ch., warned
from Beverly 1731.
4 **EBENEZER**, fought with Josiah Winn
1710, York wit. 1716 (Y. D. 8: 183).
5 **EDWARD**, br.-in-law, and Wilmot, sis., in
John Lines' will 1674, perh. not in N. E.
6 **EDWARD**, Hampton, a wit. 1691 (see also
Hannah 1), sold without lic. 1707-8. Perhaps tempo. at Portsm. where one E. went
bond for Wm. Jones(58) in 1712 and was
taxed 1713. Hampt. innkeeper 1720. In
1738 his aged w. Mary (Swain 7) in pet.
stated that he lost his eyesight more than
29 yrs. ago. She was liv. 1740. Adm. on his
est. 20 Aug. 1746 to s. **Walter**, mariner, b. 12
Aug. 1711, m. 1st 11 Apr. 1734 Rachel Hilliard (Benj. 7), m. 2d Mary (Norris 1) Hilliard. Other ch: **Anne**, b. 23 Mar. 1714, m.
24 Jan. 1733-4 John Robie. **Edward**, b. 15
July 1718.
7 **FRANCIS**, gent., and w. Helen had gr.
from Sir F. Gorges 13 Nov. 1635, 6000 a.
where he should choose. He chose, took
poss. bef. witnesses and brot over 11 in his
fam. within a specif. time, yet Mr. Bradbury sold the land to Capt. Champernowne,
whereupon Mr. Thomas Gorges (deed recorded 13 Aug. 1644) gr. him 1000 a. on
N. H. side of the Piscataqua over ag.
Thompson's Point (bounded, Y. D. 1: 3: 5).
He was here 13 Mar. 1638-9 (Mass. Col. Rec.
1: 254) and as 'Governor' was the first
signer of the Glebe gr. at Str. Bank. Lists
321, 323, (171). See also Goddard(3). Winthrop called him 'governor of those in the
lower part of the river' at time of the
Knollys-Larkham trouble, but no author.
seen for Belknap's statement that he was
contin. as governor 'by annual suffrage.'
Associate for Piscataqua ct. 1641, 1642,
1643, 1645. Com. t.e.s.c. 1644. See Mass.
Col. Rec. 2: 136, 3: 49, for his negro from
Guinea. Last seen 8-10 Sept. 1645 when he
sold his plantation near Salt Creek to Turpin and Cummings, and ack. deed in Boston.
His Str. Bk. marsh ment. in July 1648. Said
to have gone to Barbadoes, dying soon. Who
comprised his 'family' unkn. In 1674 Joseph Atkinson depos. ab. land fenced by
his order.
8 **GREGORY**, Shoals constable 1672-1674,
±37 in 1674, with Elias Stileman wit.
Moore(9) to Seward, 1674. One G. had a
w. and **child** at Marblehead later (Essex
Q. Ct. Rec. 8: 345-6).
9 **HENRY**(32), Saco, Scarb., Boston, Hampton, had trouble with Mr. Jordan in
July 1664, was a No. Yarm. wit. the same yr.

and thereaft. seldom out of sight. See Me. P. & Ct. Rec., vols. i, ii. A Great Isl. or Portsm. wit. in Dec. 1667, there in Dec. 1669. Scarb. selectman 1669, 1671, 1673, 1674; town clerk 1669; lot layer 1669; gr.j. 1670; Clerk of the Writs 1671. Hubbard, 10 Oct. 1675, reported him wounded at Saco Sands or Downs. Sued in Wells ct. 1676 on a debt payable in fish and oil. At Boston 1678-1686, marshal's dep. 1678, 1679 (wit. his fa.'s deed at Saco 1680), sued in 1684 on a note given to Samuel Sayward(6) 2 Jan. 1678-9. In N. H. 1688. Gr.j. (N. H.) foreman 1696, 1699; j. 1699. 'Yeoman alias merchant trader' in 1701. Thomas Chase (6) willed to him and w. the land his ho. stood on. Lists 222c, 235, 236, 57. See Moore(15), Morgan(9), Pottle(1), Reynolds(5). He m. 1st Deborah Collins(5), was bondsm. for her mo. in 1666 and in controv. with her over the est. in 1675. Deborah was in Boston 13 May 1680. He m. 2d wid. Christian Haskins(6), liv. 1716. Will, of Hampt., 1 Feb.—10 Apr. 1712, gives her ⅓, her dau. Lydia H. ⅓, his son Henry £15 if he liv. and came for it, and ⅓ to s. Thomas; widow and Thomas execs. The son renounced. Prob. the T. of Newb., List 267b, who m. 1st 15 Jan. 1695-6 Mary Lowell, m. 2d 30 Dec. 1713 Ruth Woodman; will 1756—1757; 8 ch., the oldest s. Henry (Hoyt's Salisb. i: 361).

10 **JENKIN**, Falmouth, m. bef. 1 Oct. 1667 Abigail Cloyes(1) whose sis. Hannah depos. in 1735 that he hired his place on Mackworth Point from Mrs. Mackworth and later built and cleared on Presumpscot River above John Wakely's. See also Neale (4). In Jan. 1672-3 he and Nathl. Wharfe apprais. Richard Martin's est., in June 1673 he and Robert Corbin apprais. Wharfe's est. Bondsman for Richard Short 1674. Falm. wit. 10 Dec. 1673—12 July 1675. Adm. inhabitant at Salem 11 Feb. 1675-6 and appar. did not ret. East. Lists 223a, 85. Lic. to sell real est. was gr. to Abigail and s. **Daniel**, admrs. est. of J. W., late of Manchester, decd., in Nov. 1697. Poss. other ch.

11 **JOANNA**, a wit. with Deborah (Rogers 14) Burnett 1738; see (24), Lovering(5).

12 **JOHN**, around Falmouth, Scarb. and Saco, seen only as a plaint. or deft. In 1660 he started a suit ag. Nicholas White and did not enter the writ; sued by Francis Hooke 1664; sued Joseph Winnock, George Phippen and John Tinney separately, in 1666; sued by Capt. James Pendleton in 1672, by Major Brian Pendleton 1672, 1673, and had a suit ag. the Major in 1674. In Sept. 1674 one John W. and Edw. Shippen were bondsm. for Robert Edmunds, admr. of George Foxwell(1), Suff. ct.

13 **JOHN**, Exeter, m. by Apr. 1674 Elizabeth Moore(24). His bondsm. in 1674 were Wm.(jr.) and Benjamin Fifield, Jacob Brown.

14 **JOHN**, a Cornishman with Rodrigo, List 3.

15 **DEACON JOHN**(36), Oyster River, granted 60 a. near Wednesday swamp 19 Mar. 1693-4. His parents gave him a p/a in 1694 and deeded all to him for supp. in 1701. Gr.j. 1697; constable 1700. Lists 62, 368ab, 369. In 1721 he brot an ejectment suit ag. Joseph Smith for land gr. to his fa. in 1658 and deeded to self in 1701. Wife Ruth adm. to O. R. Ch. 10 May 1719, he 7 Feb. 1719-20. Will, 23 May 1735—27 Mar. 1745. Ch., all bp. 7 June 1719: **Hannah**, m. bef. 30 June 1723 James Huckins (Robert 2). **Elizabeth**, not in will, but appar. mo. of Elizabeth Badger who was given her mo.'s unpaid portion. Ens. **John**, m. 7 Feb. 1727-8 Bridget Tibbetts(11). In 1748 Wm. and Elizabeth (Badger) Brown q.c. to him. In 1753 he was distracted, with no personal est. to supp. w. Bridget and 4 or 5 ch. Lists 368b, 369.

16 **JOHN**, with crew of ketch -Prosperous- of Piscataqua, 1685, Michael Mann master.

17 **JOHN**, signed a Pemaquid pet. 11 May 1689 (Doc. Hist. 6: 479). Poss. the Wells soldier, List 267b.

18 **JOHN**, of Wandsworth, co. Surrey, m. Catherine Lucy(2) at Portsm. 30 Sept. 1714. 'Katherine Lucy alias Williams' was above Sagamore Creek 1715. Presum. he soon went off, leaving a dau. **Hannah** who m. Ezekiel Gummer (Richard).

19 **LEWIS**, Portsmouth, taxed 1681, m. bef. 24 Sept. that yr. wid. Christian Harris (19). In Apr. 1692 they put in a bill for attending Thomas Footman, a wounded soldier, nine months. Jury 1693; gr.j. 1693. Wit. a Moore deed in Mar. 1693-4 (Y. D. 6: 45). Lists 329, 52, 57, 335a (self and w.). She was a wid. 22 Aug. 1696 when Wm. Cotton deeded to her ±6 a. on North side of Sagamore Creek formerly Robert Puddington's, and was Christian Kar (see Carr 1) in 1698. Williams was cert. not fa. of her dau. Patience Mains(8), and appar. not., but poss. was, fa. of her dau. Hannah Moore(22). Note also Rachel(1).

20 **MARTIN**, Pemaquid 1689, N. H. 1693. Lists 125, 60. Oue M., a stranger, was counterf. money at Salem in 1691.

21 **MATTHEW**(35), old enough to trouble girls in 1646, taxed 1657, had a gr. by 1658. Lists 341, 356a, 361ab, 363abc(2), 365, 366. See also Parr(2). Not surely kn. to have married. Either Mary or Elizabeth W. (see 35) may have been w. or sis. or neither, their ages not appearing; in 1667

he adm. est. of Matthew Giles(7) which was divid. betw. him and Richard Knight (m. Giles' niece). See Joseph Smith(36), to whom he deeded 40 a. in 1660, and John Smith(26), co-deft. in suits 1672-1674. He and John evid. liv. in one ho., where in July 1674 the marshal found no moveable prop. In 1672, ±47, he depos. that he met Joan Chesley at Maquoit, and poss. was the Williams who once liv. with his w., no ch., on north side of Merrymeeting Bay, List 191.

22 **MATTHEW**, wit. Kittery deed, Voden to Johnson, in Oct. 1702, taxed Str. Bk. ±1707, 1708 (next William W.). Rang the bell at Newc. in 1709; in 1722 his wid. Elizabeth sold his com. right there. List 316.

23 **OWEN**, deft. in one of two actions brot by Mr. Isaac Walker in Saco ct. 1669. H. Greenland took both on himself and executions issued ag. him. One Owen was around Salem.

24 **PAUL**, Kittery 1680, had town gr. 1699, m. 1st (bef. ct. 25 Mar. 1684) Catherine LeCornah, m. 2d aft. 2 May 1690 Joanna (Crocker 2) Gaskin. Living in Apr. 1715, prob. dead in Jan. 1732-3. Lists 30, 290, 291 (or his son), 293, 296, 298. An indicated Keene connec. is unsolved. W. Joanna, an orig. memb. of Kit. Point Ch. 1714, depos. in 1728, ±65, that she liv. with Mr. John Hole, and in May 1740, ag. 77, that 60 yrs. bef. she liv. at Kennebec with her fa. In Smith v. Hutchinson 1738 (Suff. ct.), Joanna W., ±74, depos. ab. the Hammond-Smith fam. at Arrowsic. This agrees with age of Joanna of Kit., but Deborah (Rogers 14) Burnett was ano. wit., and Joan Goage (List 185) and a strong Williams (Roxbury)-Lovering connec. are noted. See also Mainwaring(4). Ch., by 1st w: **Child** who may have d.y., or poss. was that Magdalene who m. Nathl. Leach (see 3). By 2d w: **Joanna**, b. 20 Feb. 1692. Joanna W. (sr.) and one Joanna Pike (see 4) wit. in the Hammons case 1719. **Paul**, mariner, b. 23 Oct. 1695, accus. by Abigail Hooper(10) in Apr. 1715 (his fa., Nathl. Keene and Benj. Hutchins bondsmen), m. 25 Oct. 1716 Margaret Hammons(2). List 297. Both of Kit. in Jan. 1732 (Y. D. 15: 186, but ack. in Newc.); of Boston, he gave her p/a in Feb. 1732; both of Kit. in Aug. 1734 and there July—Sept. 1735 she sold by p/a. She m. 2d Wm. Dealing of York (1736: Stackpole). **Mary**, b. 31 July 1697, wit. parents' deed 18 May 1714, Jona. Keene ano. wit. **Daniel**, cooper. Kit., b. 4 Oct. 1699, Scarb. grantee 1720, m. 24 Dec. 1724 Deborah Elwell(2). He built his ho. on Walter Deniford's land and rec. a deed of the 20 ft. sq. it stood on 4 Nov. 1725. Both liv. 1746 when Elwell heirs deeded to Richard Clarenbole land on

Spruce Creek; Deniford abutted. **Martha,** b. 18 Nov. 1702, poss. the M. bp. at Kit. 15 Nov. 1715 when one Lazarus W. was also bp.; m. Mark Moses(1).

25 **PHILIP**, wit. Robin Hood to Bateman and Brown at Nequasset 1 Nov. 1639 (Y. D. 35: 55).

26 **RICHARD**, Saco, known as the 'clapboardman,' presum. br. of (32) to whom he entrusted his goods bef. he d. 15 June 1635. Inv. taken in behalf of Mr. Matthew Craddock, the sponsor. Adm. gr. 25 June 1640 to Peyton Cooke for self and other creditors. As late as 1666 Cooke sued (32) for withholding est. See Me. P. & Ct. Rec. i: 96-102; Love (3).

27 **RICHARD**, mariner, Great Isl. 1679, cor. j. 1683, deposed ab. the ketch -Industry-in 1684. Lists 313cef. One R. was taxed for the Mill Dam 1707; R. taxed Newc. 1717, added name.

28 **ROBERT**, called of Great Isl. but murdered at Spruce Creek by his servants (see Driver 2, Ferguson 6), supposedly for his money judged ab. £40, List 286. The servants had told that their master had gone to Cape Porpus. Adm. 27 June 1676 to Elias Stileman; inv. by N. Fryer and Richard Stileman £36. 2. 9. See also (29), Palmer(18).

29 **ROBERT**, joiner, Portsmouth, drinking with Philip Caverly 1678; his rate for minister abated 1680. Lists 331b, 329. Robert, Kit., was bp. and united with the Boston Baptist Ch. in July 1682, and was an organizer of the Kit. Ch. in Sept. fol. See (28).

30 **ROGER**, Me. P. & Ct. Rec. i: 251. Roger Spencer?

31 **ROWLAND**, blockmaker, Kit., nephew of John Phillips(8) who sent for him to live with him and be his heir. In Nov. 1679 he bot land from Thomas Withers abutting his uncle. Tr.j. 1694; gr.j. 1694, 1695. He and one John W. among debtors of Enoch Hutchins' est. 1698; in 1706 he and Thomas Rice were bondsm. for Benjamin and Samuel Hutchins. Lists 294-298. Also Y. D. 13: 1-2. Adm. 26 Apr. 1713 to Mary Hutchins, a creditor; later to Samuel Hutchins whose acct. showed £48 due Mary H. for 36 yrs'. house harbor, washing, and dressing his food.

32 ‡**THOMAS**, Mr., Saco (Winter Harbor) early, see (26), and prominent until age and poverty came to him. At ct. held at his ho. 9 Feb. 1636-7 Mr. Thomas Lewis(19) was to appear in connec. with the combination,prob.leading up to his words of defama. ag. Mr. Lewis for which he was bound a mo. later. Jury and gr.j. 1640. In 1642 Vines gr. him 120 a. at Winter Harbor adj. Robert

Sankey, evid. already in his poss. as he and Sankey had a suit ag. Ferdinando Grant in 1640. Freed from debts of (26) in 1645 and given a full discharge by the Craddock est. in 1653. Assistant or Councillor under the Ligonia govt. Selectman by 1653 and often; Comr. for Saco 1655, 1656, 1664, 1665; town treas. 1656; constable 1657; often apprais., admr. or bondsman. See Me. P. & Ct. Rec. i, ii, by index. He was freed from rates during his or w.'s life 29 June 1674. At Newichawannock with gr.dau. Lydia Plaisted (see 3) in Oct. 1680 when he deeded Winter Harbor prop. to her. Of Saco River he deeded all est. to Phineas Hull(7) for supp. 17 Dec. 1681; last seen when he ack. this at York 4 May 1682. Lists 242, 243ab, 244aef, 245, 247, 249, 252, 23, 24, 26. See also Love (3), Page(7). Mrs. Williams was liv. 29 June 1674, but not in ch. seatings in Dec. fol., List 246. Ch: **Lucretia,** m. Lt. Richard Hitchcock; see also Garland(2). **Lydia** (presum.), see Woodward(2). **Henry,** ±43 in Jan. 1679-80.

33 **THOMAS,** Portsmouth, was gr. Clampering Isl. 25 Aug. 1645 and assigned all right to Richard King(11) 11 June 1649. Father of Judith Ellins' **child** in Nov. 1648 (see Ellins 2), and bef. or aft. this date m. Thomas Wannerton's dau. Ann who was liv. 27 June 1671. Around Sagamore Creek 1663. Lists 72, 323, 331a. T. W. and John, his partner, taxed 1673. In July 1674 he compl. ab. the leather sold by Richard Waterhouse and Mr. Job Clements. 'A shroud for T. W. 1674' must have been for his w. as he was in want and sick at Wm. Richards' ho. in Jan. 1674-5, liv. sick and poor in Oct. 1675. He may or may not have had legit. ch. See (1) and others.

34 **THOMAS,** Exeter, his wife's dau. **Mary** bp. at Boston 11 Aug. 1650.

35 **WILLIAM,** sr., Oyster River bef. 1646 when his son (21) was in trouble, m. (not first) wid. Agnes Field(1), who was liv. 18 June 1674, m. last betw. 25 Mar. 1679—23 Mar. 1686, wid. Mary Beard(4). He had grants of 20 a. in 1651, 5 a. in 1660, 100 a. in 1662. Freeman 1655. In 1659 John Goddard sold him the lot that was John Pillines' at O. R., being the neck of land betw. Stony Brook and the meeting-ho. lot. Highway surveyor 1659. Lists 355a, 356a, 361a, 362ab, 363abc, 365, 359a, 46, 52, 57. On 23 Mar. 1686-7 Wm., sr., of Durham, and w. Mary, Samuel Hill(18) of Kit. and w. Elizabeth (appar. a gr.dau.), gave a joint deed of the 40 a. Wm. was liv. on to Stephen Jenkins. He prob. went to live with the Hills who in 1713 as execs. to the will of Wm. of Kit. gave a deed to Samuel Penhallow to replace a lost deed to John Cutts. 'Old Sister Williams,' ill and crazy three yrs., d. in June

1704 (List 96). Two ch. kn: **Matthew,** ±47 in 1672. **William,** ±50 in Aug. 1680. Poss: **Mary** and **Elizabeth,** ct. witnesses 1665 ab. the Ann Denmark—Ann Pitman quarrel (see 21).

36 **WILLIAM**(35), Oyster River, gr. 10 a. in 1653, a small lot betw. Matthew and William Williams in 1658, 5 a. in 1660. Freeman 1655. He or his fa. constable in 1657. Jury 1696. Lists 355a, 361a, 363abc, 365, 359a, 52, 367a, 368a. He m. Margaret Stevenson(5), with her gave p/a to s. John 29 Sept. 1694 in connec. with Stevenson prop., and 12 Dec. 1701 made over all est. to s. John for their support. Ch: **William,** b. 22 Dec. 1662, depos. 25 Mar. 1679, ag. ±16, in the suit over Nicholas Follett's field, d. s.p. bef. 1707. **John,** b. 30 Mar. 1664. **Elizabeth,** b. 25 Oct. 1665, appar. the one who m. Samuel Hill(18). **Thomas,** had 30 a. gr. 11 Apr. 1694, wit. parents' p/a that yr., his land ment. 15 Jan. 1702-3. List 368a. In 1707 his bros. John and Samuel sold his gr. to Thomas Davis, calling him 'our dec. brother.' **Samuel,** m. Elizabeth Stevenson(1) by 1712 when they had Valentine Hill arrested for putting her out of the (Stevenson) ho. violently; both liv. 1738. Lists 368b, 369. Dau. Mary named in gr.fa.'s will 1718, and 8 more ch. bp. 1720-1729 are credited to them (Hist. of Durham, 2: 390). An older dau. Elizabeth was adm. to Ch. in 1728. See also the husb. of Sarah Bussy(2).

37 **WILLIAM,** plasterer, drunk in 1668, a Portsm. presentment.

38 **WILLIAM,** blockmaker, butcher, Portsmouth 1681, O. A. 28 Aug. 1685. Summonsed with Elizabeth Akerman in June 1693 when he admitted he had liv. in the ho. with her 9 yrs. or more. In 1696 he bot Zachariah Trickey's ho., ferry right, etc., at Bloody Point, and in 1699 exchanged his claim on this for T.'s 30 a. gr. Gr.j. 1699. Partner of Gabriel Grout and gr. adm. on his est. 15 Sept. 1707, when called 'blockmaker and butcher.' Bondsman for wid. Mary Polley in July 1715. Lists 329, 52, 62, 335a, 330def, 337. See also Miller(1). Adm. 9 Mar. 1721-2 to Henry Tibbetts(5). A small Newc. lot adj. Benj. Parker was inv. and most of the est. went to Mary Tibbetts for attendance on him.

39 **WIDOW, ——,** Portsmouth, her tax abated 1713. Town order, 9 Apr. 1716, Goody Allston to prov. for and take care of Goody W. during her sickness. One Rebecca was rec. into cov., So. Ch., at home, 8 Mar. 1718-9.

40 **'WILLIAMS** ye joiner' taxed Portsmouth (the Bank) 1713. **William,** s. of 'Mr. Williams, joiner at ye Bank,' bp. at Newb. Oct. 1717.

**WILLIAMSON.** 1 Lt. **Caleb,** List 68.

2 **DAVID,** Wells soldier 1693-4, List 267b.

3 **CAPT. STEPHEN,** at Great Isl. 1673 when John Skillings lost his broadcloth, and Frances Russell(2) accus. him of breaking open her chest, but her dau. spoke up: 'No, mother, it was broke before.' Portsm. rate rebated in Mar. 1679-80.

**WILLING,** a Devonshire name.

1 **JAMES** (Wellin), wit. for Jocelyn at Black Point 4 July 1663.

2 **RICHARD,** mariner, Scarboro, indebted to George Knight 1671, m. bef. spring of 1672-3 one Amy (see Glanfield 3). Granted 20 a. adj. Peter Hinkson 1674; sued by Nathl. Fryer 1674; owed £1 to Arthur Alger's est. 1675. Constable 1676. On an expedition Eastward with his shallop 7 Nov.— 14 Dec. 1676. Taxed 1681. In 1742 his daus. deeded to Joseph Moody 20 a. in Scarb. laid out to fa. 24 Oct. 1685. Lists 237ade, 238a, 239a. Presum. wid. Amy, and not a dau., m. Roger Vicary in Marblehead 4 Dec. 1694. Kn. ch: **Elizabeth** (Woolen), m. in Marblehead 29 Dec. 1709 Peter Pollow: both liv. 17 Mar. 1741-2. **Naomi,** m. 1st 5 July 1703 Edw. Homan, m. 2d 28 Jan. 1706-7 George Girdler, both of Marbleh., a wid. there 1742. **Hannah** White, a Salem wid. 1742 (Hannah Wellin m. John Baxton in Marbleh. 1708, Hannah Blaxton m. Benj. White in Feb. 1710-1). Also one Susannah (Woollen) m. Samuel Salter in Marbleh. 11 May 1710.

3 **ROGER,** Richmond Isl. 1635, and was there 1638-1639, his mo. in England. Called one of the first inhabitants of Cape Porpus by John Bush in 1670 when he sold 10 a. marsh bot from him. Abutted Morgan Howell's land 1648. In Dec. 1658 he depos. bef. Francis Neale that 21 or 22 yrs. bef. he helped row up the river which runs by Mrs. Mackworth's, Mr. Vines, Mr. Mackworth, Mr. Winter and others, and saw Mr. Vines give poss. to Winter. No rec. of a fam. but (1) and (2) may have been his. Lists 21, 221.

**WILLIS,** Wyllys. 1 **Jeremiah,** in 1639 owed Wm. Gray who gave a p/a to Philip White of Piscataway.

2 **SAMUEL,** Esq. (Wyllys), Hartford, see Love(4), Y. D. 4: 117, Reg. 37: 33.

**WILLIX,** supposed of continental origin. See N. E. Reg. 50: 46; 68: 79-82; 69: 361.

1 **BALTHASAR,** Exeter 1640, bp. at Alford, Lincolnshire, 27 July 1595, s. of Balthasar and Anne, and half-br. of Susanna (Bellingham) Pormort(3). Bell called him a man of more than ordinary education. Townsman 1647. Lists 375ab, 376ab (1645), (?378, Wits). He and w. (Annah) wit. ag. Edw. Hilton in 1645. In 1647 he won a suit ag. John Legate and Humphrey Wilson, and Legate won ag. him and the Walls in a suit over cruelty to his cattle. About June 1648 his w. was robbed and murdered betw. Dover and Ex. and her body thrown into the river. In Hampt. ct. the next Sept. he and Robert Hethersay had cross suits for defama., he charging that H. had raised an evil report of his decd. wife; he also sued for breach of contract in carrying her to O. R. in a canoe and not bringing her back, as agreed. He soon m. wid. Mary Hauxworth of Salisb. and mov. there; taxed 1650; d. 23 Jan. 1650-1. She was gr. adm. in Apr. 1651 and was sued by Robert Tuck in 1652 for diet of 2 ch., one ab. a yr., one ab. 8 wks. Crazy and distempered, she was under a gdn. in 1664; wid. Willix a Salisb. abuttor 1667. Ch: **Hazelelponi,** servant of Henry Waltham of Weymouth, see N. E. Reg. 5: 303. She m. 1st John Gee of Boston and Martha's Vineyard, m. 2d aft. 19 Nov. 1671 Obadiah Wood of Ipsw., d. 27 Nov. 1718, ag. 78 (gr.st.). Gee ch: Mary, m. Thomas Pickering(8); John, b. in Boston 1662; Anna, m. Samuel Hodgkins of Gloucester; Martha, m. Thomas Cotes. See vol. 2, Hist. of Martha's Vineyard (Annals of Edgartown, p. 70, of Tisbury, p. 13); Essex Antiq. 8: 164. **Anna,** serv. of Rev. Timothy Dalton whose wid. Ruth in 1663 willed her £5. She m. 1st Robert Roscoe, had 3 more husbands in the south, James Blunt, Seth Southwell, Esq., Col. John Lear, and d. s.p. **Susannah,** a serv. near her sis. Anna, m. Francis Jones(16).

2 **SAMUEL** (Wellex), master of the -Good Hope- of London at Piscataqua, Feb. 1668-9.

**WILLOUGHBY.** See also Nason(7).

1 **FRANCIS,** Salem, in right of gr.fa. Henry Bartholomew ent. an East. Cl. for Damariscove prop. and fishing stage and 'Little Neck' at Sheepscot, by deed 21 Mar. 1663-4.

2 **RICHARD,** Kennebec soldier 1688, List 189.

3 **WILLIAM** (Liloby), at Monhegan 1653, Essex Q. Ct. i: 325. Willoughby?

4 **WILLIAM,** small tax at Greenland 1693, he and w. seated at Ch., List 335a. In Sept. 1697 Abigail W. (w. or dau.) and George and Bridget Keniston made one depos. ab. a fracas on the Joseph Hall farm. One Mary Willibe, serv. to Thomas Bradbury, d. at Salisb. 16 Nov. 1709; one Patience of Berwick m. John Goodwin(12). Someone named Wilely was at Josiah Moses' in 1726.

**WILLS,** from S.W. corner of England. See Creber; Wells(3), (8).

1 **BENNETT,** liv. at or near Plymouth, Eng., in Oct. 1640, a former boatswain

and boatmaster for John Winter at Casco.
List 21.

2 **HUMPHREY**, from Alphington, co. Devon; see Burnell(2).

3 **ROBERT**, at the Eastward in 1675. List 3.

4 **ROGER**, Monhegan 1672. List 13.

5 **THOMAS**, Mr., shipmaster, Kittery, m. 1st by 1662 Sarah Abbott(5) who was liv. 16 May 1667, m. 2d Lucy (Treworgye 1) Chadbourne, who depos. in June 1678, ±46. His Kit. land was ment. in Thomas Leighton's inv. 1666; in 1667 his land was N.W., and Robert Cutts' E., of Wm. Diamond's Crooked Lane home. Lot layer and surv. 1669-1673; O. F. 6 July 1669; j. 1669, 1672; gr.j. 1670, 1673; selectman 1670, 1671; owned in the Great House Field 1679. List 298. See also Chick. One T. W., master of the -Robert-, was sued by 7 of the crew for 13½ months' wages in Salem ct. 1662. Inv., £46, attested 14 Mar. 1687-8 by wid. Lucy who m. 3d Elias Stileman(1). Ch. by 1st w: **Thomas**, liv. 30 Jan. 1688-9, d. s.p. **Sarah**, b. bef. 16 May 1667, m. John Geare. By 2d w: **Joanna**, ±69 in June 1738, m. Richard Cutts (6). In 1689 the Stilemans, Geares and Cutts sold to Francis Mercer prop. Mr. Wills had bot from John Cutts, one piece adj. Mr. Snell's land, one adj. Cutts wharf, with wharf and storehouse. See also Y. D. 8: 143.

6 **WILLIAM**, Shoals, abs. from wife several yrs. (wit. Jeffrey Currier) and ord. home in 1670. Here in Sept. 1671; with John Bugg wit. (as Wells) a Spruce Creek deed in Dec. 1672, George Lydden to Edw. Clark; taxed Portsm. 1673, and fined that yr.

**WILMOT**, Wilmett, ancient and titled in cos. Derby and Herts.

1 **CAPT. EDWARD**, commander of the -Charles and Sarah-, was accus. in Dec. 1700 by Margaret Edmondson who liv. at Mr. Jaffrey's. Appar. her ch. then 12 wks. old was Edward, Hampton (see Thomas Robie 1), m. 1st 18 Mar. 1731 Elizabeth Marston (Wm. 8), m. 2d 30 Sept. 1746 wid. Mary Whittaker, d. 22 Dec. 1761, ag. 62. 5 ch. by 1st w. were bp.

2 **JAMES** (also Welmett), liv. on Dover Neck near Campion's Rocks, m. 1st Elizabeth Scammon(4), who d. s.p., m. 2d Rebecca Downes (Gershom). In 1729 he and 4 others signed a pet. to the Gov. and Council, stating that they 'had been settled on a cert. tract or neck of land, some over 40 yrs., some over 30 yrs.' List 358c. Inv. 26 June 1746, adm. to Gershom Downes. Widow Rebecca d. a few months aft. him. Dau. **Sarah**, of Somersworth, m. Jonathan Bickford.

3 **NICHOLAS**, Boston, where Judge Savage found rec. of four daus. 1650-1660, and Scarb., where his stay was appar. short, but he of more than passing interest as an ancestor of the Millikens. In May 1665 he apparently liv. on Scottow's Hill farm and had Scottow's cattle in his care; Wilmot's Brook also ment. Hannah Hallam depos. in 1728 that she was told ab. N. W. as a tenant on the farm. Back in Boston, he sold without lic. 1673 and forf. bond; licensed later. Wit. Robert Knight's will in June 1676 and swore to it in Boston in Aug. Taxed Scarb. 1681. Lists 234b, 238a. Will, Boston innholder, 27 Sept. (inv. 16 Oct.) 1684, names w. Mary, 6 ch., 2 Alger gr.ch.; Philip Squire an overseer. Widow Mary m. 2d aft. July 1685 Abraham Smith and brot in ano. Wilmot inv. in 1690, incl. articles 'In the Green Draggon.' Her will, wid., 13 May— 27 Aug. 1696, names 5 ch., gr.dau. Elizabeth Mulligan. Ch: **John**, in mo.'s will; a deed 30 June 1697 says 'John W. if living.' **Samuel**, charged with stealing money from his master David Adams in July 1685; not in mo.'s will. **Mary**, b. 5 Mar. 1650, m. John Alger(6), d. bef. fa. **Elizabeth**, b. 26 Sept. -1657-, m. 1st by 1684 Caleb Rawlings, m. 2d by 1695 Richard Newland. **Abigail**, b. 2 Oct. -1657-, m. by 1684 Abraham Adams (see 2), both of Boston 1697.ʼ **Hannah**, b. 10 Feb. 1660, m. by 1681 Nathaniel Adams, both of Charlest. 1697 where she d. 24 Jan. 1699, ag. 39. **Ann**, youngest and at home 1684, m. by 1696 Joseph Allen.

4 **RICHARD**, had Falmouth gr. 1719; of F. Feb.—May 1722. List 229. Called late of Falm. in 1726 when John Wass of Boston, form. of F., sold there, incl. the homestead on the Neck which he held as heir of R. W. Wass had m. **Ann** Wilmot bef. 9 Feb. 1711 when a s. Wilmot was b. in Boston. See also Slaughter(1).

**WILSON**, became 34th commonest name in N. E.

1 **ANDREW**, commander of the -Marigold- of Boston 1695 (Portsm. Notarial Rec.).

2 **EDWARD**, Newcastle. Lists 318b, 315c.

3 **GOWEN**, Exeter, Kittery, by trad. from Paisley, Scotland; Col. Banks found the name in Stoke Bruerner, cò. Northampton, in 1604. The Gowen of Boston 1641-3 likely moved on to Ex. by 1647, cowherd 1649, with Thomas Cornish bot prop. from Thomas Jones in 1650 and sued for it in Oct. 1651. Going on to Me., he took O. A. at Kit. in Nov. 1652, 'residing further northward'; depos. in Apr. 1654, ag. 36. Goose Cove gr. 1658. Constable 1658, 1669; gr.j. 1672, 1685; selectman 1674, 1675. Excused from training by age in July 1674. Deeded dau. Deborah's portion 2 June 1684; d. bef. 6 Aug. 1686. Lists 376b (1650), 282, 286, 298, 28. See also Hutchins(2). In 1657 he was attentive to John Andrews' w. Joan to the

neglect of his own w. and fam. Kn. ch: **Son**, b. and d. at Ex. 1647. **John**, a Spruce Creek wit. 1672, List 298. In Aug. 1686 he took as his portion from br. Joseph, 3 a. with a ho. on it, a cow and a sow, agreeing if Joseph had to care for him, the prop. should go back to him. This was rec. 7 Feb. 1710-1, but adm. gr. to Nathaniel Keene 24 Feb. 1690-1. **Rebecca** (appar.), m. 1st Henry Barnes(2), m. 2d Henry Bodge. **Joseph**, b. ±1655. **Deborah**, m. Andrew Haley(1).

4 **HUMPHREY**(10), Exeter, of age at fa.'s death or soon aft., and ran the mill bef. 1647. Partner with Edw. Gilman, sr. and jr., and Edw. Colcord in a mill gr. 1652. Tr.j. 1651; gr.j. 1662, 1677, 1678, 1683, 1693 (foreman); selectman 1653, 1658; constable 1673, 1694 (fined). Lists 374c, 375ab, 376ab (1645, 1674), 377, 383, 385, 49, 52, 54, 55a, 57, 62. See also Garland(6), Leavitt(10). Inv. 26 Aug. 1698, £641. Will, now missing, was prov. 13 Oct. 1698 when adm. gr. to wid. Judith (Hersey 1, m. 21 Dec. 1665); a copy shows it was dated 4 June (10 Wm. & Mary) and named w. Judith, 4 ch. Widow Wilson rated in May 1714, d. in 1716 (SJC 20329). Ch: **Judith**, b. 8 Nov. 1664, d. 3 May 1667. **Elizabeth**, b. 11 Jan. 1665, m. Col. Peter Weare(10). **John**, Exeter, selectman 1693, gr.j. 1693, 1696, retail lic. 1695; Lists 57, 62, 377. He m. Martha Harvey(14), List 385, a wid. 23 May 1698 when his fa. deeded to her and her dau. Adm. 13 Feb. 1699-1700 to her and 2d husb. George Veasey(2). Only ch. Elizabeth m. Richard Hilton(14 jr.). **Hannah**, b. 12 Nov. 1670, d. bef. fa. Deac. **Thomas**, Exeter, b. 20 May 1672, Lists 67, 385, 376b (1725), single when fa. made will, soon m. Mary Light(3), List 385. Will, 1753—1754, names ch: Humphrey (List 376b, 1725), Joshua (exec.), Anna Rice (w. of John), Sarah Kimball (w. of John), Mary Blunt (w. of Jonathan), Judith Lyford (w. of Biley 2), out of 14 rec. 1699—1718. Heirs of Elizabeth (Wilson) Hilton sued Joshua for 2/6 of the homestead which had been willed to Deac. Thomas for life (SJC 20329). **James**, b. 27 Aug. 1673, d. bef. fa. Unrec., named in will: Judith, m. a Wiggin (see Simon 4). **Ann**, m. 1st Col. Winthrop Hilton (24), m. 2d Capt. Jonathan Wadleigh(4). **Mary**, b. Nov. 1680 (age at death), m. Capt. Edward Hall(12).

5 **JOHN**, Dover 1666, List 356k. One Wilson was Thomas Beard's serv. in 1657 (see Wheeler 7).

6 **JOHN**, cordwainer, Newcastle, bot ho. and shop at the Bank in 1716 and sold with w. Elizabeth (see Sherburne 3) in 1726 when he was a Newc. innholder. See also O'Shaw. Will, 24 Feb.—28 Mar. 1738-9, names w. Elizabeth (a Newc. wid. 1752)

and ch: **Joseph. William. Sarah. Elizabeth. Abigail.**

7 SERGT. **JOSEPH**(3), Kittery, (±48 in 1703), m. Hannah Endle(3). Highw. surv. 1693-1698; sealer of leather 1695-6; j. 1699; gr.j. 1694, 1698 (fined for abs.), 1699, 1701; selectman 1703-1705. Lists 290, 293, 295, 298, 36. Died Mar. 1708-9. In Feb. 1714-5 wid. Hannah (List 291) sold to Ebenezer Moore ¼ a Spruce Creek sawmill form. her husband's. She d. in 1748. In 1754 a div. was made betw. Thomas Hobbs, Thomas Hammett and John Godsoe, who had bot out several heirs, and Wm. and Gowen W., Joseph Billings and Benj. Weeks who had not sold. Ch. (Y. D. 18: 91): **Hannah**, b. 19 Nov. 1683, m. Joseph Billings(2). **Joseph**, b. 28 Oct. 1684, m. 1st 27 Aug. 1707 Elizabeth Chapman(4), 4 ch. In 1733, a widower, he had liv. a yr. with Mary Cloff, singlewoman, and m. 2d 3 July 1733 Mary Clear (3 ch.); m. 3d 2 Apr. 1751 Judith (Weeks) Richardson. Lists 296, 291, 297. See also Hutchins(9). Will, 2 Jan.—3 Apr. 1758. **William**, b. 28 Aug. 1686, carpenter, m. 25 Apr. 1711 Hopewell (Furbish 2) Hutchins(3). Lists 291, 298. A widower in June 1766, d. intest. 1770. 5 ch. **Ruth**, b. 19 Apr. 1688, m. Elihu Parsons(3). **Gowen**, b. 29 Jan. 1690, List 291, m. at Portsm. 25 Dec. 1712 Anne Shepherd(2), mov. to Falm. where she joined the Ch. in 1739. 7 ch. rec. or bp. in Kit. **Agnes**, b. 1 Mar. 1692, d. s.p. bef. Feb. 1723-4. **John**, b. 13 Jan. 1694, List 291, m. Mary Johnson (29). Falm. 1739—1746+, ret. to Kit., d. 1757. 1 ch. bp. at Falm. **Rebecca**, b. 16 Feb. 1696, m. John Norton(1). **Deborah**, b. 19 Apr. 1698, m. Capt. John Moore(11 jr.). **Mary**, b. 25 Feb. 1700, m. 16 Sept. 1722 John Bennett, both liv. 1739. **Anne**, b. 29 Mar. 1702, unm. 1748. **Elizabeth**, b. 23 Sept. 1705, ag. 3½ when fa. d., m. Benjamin Weeks(1).

8 **MARY** (Deering 4), wid. of William of Boston, was of Greenland 1749, distracted (see N. H. Prob. 3: 729; 4: 116); d. 15 Apr. 1753, ag. 71 (Atkinson platter). Dau. **Mary**, b. at Boston 1722.

9 **NOAH**, Wells, m. 27 June 1715 Abigail Brown; wit. Samuel Littlefield's deed 1720; dead in 1733 when S. L. deeded to his sons Michael (b. 1721) and Noah (b. 1723) 25 a. near Kennebunk River by the ho. where their fa. liv. Ano. ch. was **Mehitable**, b. 1717. One Wm. W. m. Margaret Brown at Wells in 1734, and d. by 1746. See also (12).

10 **THOMAS**, miller, Exeter, seems br. of Edward, miller, the testator of 1638 (N. E. Reg. 7: 30; Lechford's Note Book, 10-13). Roxbury 1633, freeman 14 May 1634, and as a Wheelwright follower left Roxb. Ch. for Exeter, later making peace with Roxbury. He built the first gristmill at Ex., his

gr. described as the 'creek or water course at the higher falls, also the little island by the falls on which his ho. and mill stand.' Chosen 'Ruler' 20 Oct. 1642. Lists 373, 376ab, 377. Will, 9 Jan.—18 Feb. 1642-3, names w. (Ann), 5 ch., and commends them to churches of Roxb., Hampt. or Ex., or wherever their lot fell. A dispute betw. the oldest son and the wid. was referred by Boston ct. to Ipsw. ct. 7 Mar. 1643-4. She m. 2d John Legate(1). Ch: **Humphrey**, his mo. poss. an earlier wife. **Samuel** and **Joshua**, both under 21 in 1643. **Deborah**, b. at Roxb. Aug. 1634; her mo. deeded cattle to Anthony Stanyan for her benefit; m. John Warren(6). **Lydia**, b. Nov. 1636.

11 **THOMAS**, Newcastle, burned to death, List 311a. Adm. 24 June 1662 to N. Fryer.

12 **THOMAS**, Wells, d. bef. 25 Dec. 1714. In Nov. 1746 his wid. Sarah (then Allen) depos. in York that he liv. at Merriland until driven off by the Ind. and soon aft. was k. by them; he liv. there ±1702-3 and two of their ch. were b. there. She named her ch. in 1746 as: **Samuel** of Phillipstown (m. at Greenl. Dec. 1735 Mary (Urin) Frost, and had a son-in-law John Frost with him at P. in 1741). **Sarah**, w. of Joseph Clark and **Joanna**, w. of Charles Davenport, both of Worcester. See also (9); Y. D. 12: 116; 13: 134.

13 **WILLIAM**, Hampton. Adm. 26 Apr. 1710 to wid. Elizabeth, bondsm. Lt. Joseph Swett and John Gove. She m. 2d 16 Aug. 1716 Nathaniel Lovejoy of Andover. Distrib. of fa.'s est. ordered in 1716 to 4 daus., all rec. at Hampt: **Abigail**, b. 17 May 1694, chose Lt. Joseph Swett gdn., m. 1st Richard Elliot(4 jr.), m. 2d John Green(18). **Martha**, b. 31 Aug. 1702. **Hannah**, b. 22 Aug. 1705. **Elizabeth**, b. 1 July 1708.

**WINBORNE, William** (also Wenborne), Exeter 1639. Earlier at Boston where the **John**, b. 22 Nov. 1635, s. of Wm. and Elizabeth Wen, is considered his, and the **John**, b. 21 Sept. 1638 (mo. Elizabeth) was surely his. Clerk of the Writs, Exeter and Com. t.e.s.c. 1643. Freeman May 1645. His fine for drawing beer without lic. was abated in May 1646; called very poor in Nov. 1646. Lists 373, 374a, 376a, 378. Boston constable 1653, of Malden 1687 (Midd. D. 8: 219). The s. John m. Elizabeth Hart at Malden 11 Apr. 1667, was minister at Manchester, Mass. 1667—1686, leaving there 1690—1693, poss. for So. Carolina. Susanna, w. of Rev. Hugh Adams of Durham, and her br. Ebenezer W. of Boston, are consid. Rev. John's ch. (See Stackpole's Hist. of Durham, ii: 4).

**WINCH, Samuel**, York, wit. an Emery fam. deed in Mar. 1696-7 and m. in York 30 Sept. 1698 Susannah Parker(16). His ho.

ment. 1714 (Y. D. 10: 38). Sold his York gr. to Pepperell in 1728. **Hannah**, who accus. Daniel Carr of Salisb. in York ct. Apr. 1726, was prob. a dau. and the H. W. who m. Rowland Le Page, mariner, in Salisb. 7 Feb. 1733-4. Samuel may have come to Me. from Framingham, where a Winch fam. carried the name Silence, and may have remov. to Scarb. where Mehitable Winch m. appar. Joseph Keene(1), Silence m. Benjamin Foss (7), Samuel m. Alice McCarthy 1736. One Samuel m. Zerviah Parker in Newb. 28 Aug. 1732.

**WINCHESTER, Robert**, fisherman, York, Shoals, was sued in 1665 by Capt. John Davis on a bond endorsed by John Andrews (9), whose dau. he married. Sued by Capt. Lockwood 1667, 1668, by Francis Wainwright's atty. 1669, by Capt. Raynes 1671, 1673. Resident of the Shoals 1673; dead in Apr. 1681. List 79; see also Ball(2). Widow Elizabeth m. 2d John Card(4) who agreed not to meddle with her former husband's est. or anything that belonged to her (Y. D. 3: 138). Ch: **Elizabeth**, m. Thomas Mainwaring(3). That she alone of the ch. deeded Andrews prop. is ground for questioning if the wid. Elizabeth were not a 2d w. and mo. only of the other kn. ch: **Martha**, m. Thomas Card(6). **Mary**, m. Richard Milbury(4). **Robert**, a lad of ±14 when taken an Ind. captive ab. July 1696; in Canada 1704 (Doc. Hist. 9: 186).

**WINCOLL**, found in co. Suffolk, England. 1 **CAPT. *JOHN**, Kittery, where outstanding citizen and a military leader, came from Watertown where he was a propr. in 1636-7 and made freeman in 1646. Kit. selectman 1652, 1654, and engaged to build a mill on Great Newichawannock River for Walter Price and Richard Cooke in 1659, but not here perma. until ±1662, as Watert. selectman 1656, 1661, 1662; Rep. 1658, and there in 1657 he settled the estates of his fa. Thomas and of Ann Fleming. Here interested in mills and timber lands, and assoc. with Thomas Broughton(4) whom he called 'brother' (and George Broughton 'cousin'), Roger Plaisted(5) and John Hull (the mintmaster). See Me. P. & Ct. Rec. vols. i, ii; Y. D., incl. 3: 1; 4: 8-9. Kit. selectman and comr. many yrs.; lot layer and surveyor; Deputy 1653-1655, 1675, 1677, 1678; Assoc. Judge; J. P.; Crier of the Prov. Ct. 1692; Clerk and Register at time of death. Called Sergt. at Watert.; elected Lieut. at Kit. 4 July 1653; com. Capt. of Militia 16 Aug. 1665. Lists 282, 283, 298, 236, 237d, 25, 28, 29, 33, 80, 81, 83, 88. See also Champernowne, Lovering(2), Mason(3). His 1st w. Elizabeth, liv. 24 Sept. 1673, d. s. p. He m. 2d, contract 29 Feb. 1675-6 (Y. D. 4: 86)

Mary Etherington (Thomas) who d. bef. 5 June 1679; m. 3d bef. 16 Sept. 1682 wid. Olive Plaisted(5). Mounting his horse to ride with Maj. Hooke and others from Newich. to Kit. Pt., he fell from his horse and d. immed., 22 Oct. 1694. Ch., by 2d w: **John.**

2 **CAPT. JOHN**(1), mariner, Portsm., sailed betw. Boston and London in 1698 and m. bef. 5 Apr. 1699 Deborah Morse, dau. of (3) or (9). In 1708 he had a Portsm. dry-goods store; called mariner 1709, 1712, when he sold 90 a. gr. to Wincoll and Veasey in 1662 to John Smith (see also Price 7), and 65 a. gr. his mo. on Wilcox Pond to the Lords. Widow W. taxed at the Bank 1713, her tax abated 1714 when Mrs. W. was an innkeeper. Adm. gr. to her 12 Nov. 1715, the est. insolvent; in Oct. 1717 John Wentworth and George Jaffrey took adm.; the ho. was sold to Benning Wentworth in 1738 to pay the debts. From a torn No. Ch. rec. it appears the wid. Deborah m. 2d in Feb. 1716 one Dennett. Kn. ch: **Olive.** In 1722 the town arranged for Mary -Watts- to care for Olive -Winckley- and her sis. **Deborah** (bp. 22 May 1709) and in 1723 for James Holegate to carry them back to Haverh. for treatment with Dr. Peasley; he had cured them in 1724. One Deborah Winkle m. Ebenezer Wright in Boston 17 Oct. 1728. **Isaac,** bp. 27 Oct. 1711, worked for John Drew, joiner, in 1724; of Kit. in 1744 sold his part of 100 a. gr. his gr.fa. in 1671; m. and had at least 1 ch. See also Capt. John, mariner, Boston, m. 22 Apr. 1725 Lucy Lee who was gr. adm. 20 Mar. 1738-9 (Reg. 15: 273). One Mary m. Jonathan Road (or Read) in Boston 1724.

**Winforth,** John, York gr. 1686, addi. to Isaac Everett's lot. See John Wentworth.

**WING.** 1 **Deborah,** wid. of Rev. John, came to N. E. with **four sons.** See Batchelder (5).

2 **JOHN,** wit. Ind. treaty at Pemaquid 11 Aug. 1693 (Doc. Hist. x: 11).

**WINGATE,** townships in cos. Durham and Northumberland. One ancient family is first found in co. Bedford.

1 **JOHN** (also Winget, Windet, Windiet), Dover, ±44 in Aug. 1683. A 20 a. lot was laid out to him twice, 11 Jan. 1658-9 and 1664 when described as the lot given him by his master Thomas Layton(6). Ano. 10 a. gr. was laid out in 1669. A new partner with Thomas Doughty in a logging contract 1663. Freeman 15 May 1672. Selectman 1674, 1686, 1687. Lists 353, 356hk, 359ab, 49, 52, 54, 94, 96. Called one of the principal landowners in Dover in Cranfield's time, and one of the 'loyal subjects and freeholders' who signed the Weare pet. to the King. He m. 1st Mary Nutter(2) who was liv. 28 Dec.

1674 (her fa. deeded him land on Dover Neck in 1670); m. 2d Sarah (Taylor 2) Canney(4). Will, 12 Mar. 1683-4, cod. 1 Dec. (d. 9 Dec.) 1687, names w. Sarah, 7 ch., 5 Canney ch. (unnamed); see also Hall(10). The widow's bondsm. were Richard Otis and Richard Paine(12), who later was her 3d husb. Ch: **Ann,** b. 18 Feb. 1667-8, m. Israel Hodsdon(2 jr.). **John. Caleb,** willed land, lived in Piscataway, N. J., where he and w. Hope had 7 ch. rec. 1706-1719 and two more. See Monette's 'First Settlers of Piscataway and Woodbridge,' part 5, p. 874. **Moses,** mariner, Lists 335b, 352. Will, made at London, 20 Jan. 1695-6—10 Mar. 1697-8, gives his clothes to Nicholas Follett, then in London, all else to sis. Ann. **Mary,** presumably by 2d w., as willed the feather bed and furniture given to her mo. aft. her mo.'s death. Surely by 2d w: Col. *Joshua, a disting. citizen of Hampt. where he was b. 2 Feb. 1679, and returned to as an adult aft. a boyhood in Dover. Selectman, Rep., Capt., Major, Col., and in command of a regt. at Louisburg. He m. at Newb. 9 Nov. 1702 Mary Lunt (see 2); d. at Hampt. 9 Feb. 1769 (will 3 Mar. 1764); wid. Mary d. 27 Mar. 1772. Ch: Rev. Paine (H. C. 1723, minister at Amesbury, m. Mary Balch); Sarah (m. Dr. Edmund Toppan); Mary (m. Timothy Pickering of Salem); Joshua (m. Dorothy Freese); Jane (m. Rev. Stephen Chase); Abigail, twin, (m. John Stickney of Newb.); Anna, twin, (m. Daniel Marston); Martha (m. Dr. John Weeks); Love (m. Rev. Nathl. Gookin); Elizabeth (m. Dr. John Newman); John, H. C. 1744, unm. **Abigail,** b. betw. 12 Mar. 1683-4—1 Dec. 1687, m. Samuel Kenney (see Canney 4, Paine 12).

2 **CAPT. JOHN**(1), Dover, inherited the homestead and liv. there with w. Ann Hodsdon(2). Evid. belligerent and had fights at times with Edward and Jonathan Evans, Henry Hobbs and Ephraim Wentworth. As Capt. commanded a company in a Port Royal expedition. Lists 62, 94, 358d. Will, 28 Dec. 1714—16 Feb. 1714-5, names w. Ann, 11 ch., giving homestead and other prop., incl. his part of a new mill, to wife and s. John to bring up the small ch.; if John refuse, to have nothing until the ch. had been brot up. She m. 2d Capt. John Heard(6). Ch: **Mary,** b. 3 Oct. 1691, m. Josiah Clark (36). *John, b. 10 Apr. 1693, Lt., Capt., Rep., m. 1st in 1717 Dorothy Tibbetts(12), m. 2d Sarah Ricker(3). 13 ch. (at least 5 by 1st w.), 10 named in will, 1764—1764, with w. Sarah. **Ann,** b. 2 Feb. 1694-5, m. 1st Francis Drew(3), m. 2d Daniel Titcomb. **Sarah,** b. 17 Feb. 1696-7, m. Peter Hayes(3). Lt. **Moses,** b. 27 Dec. 1698, cooper, m. 1st Abigail Church(2), who was liv. in Apr. 1745; m. 2d Deborah (Cushing), wid. of

Daniel Watson. See also Evans(3). Will, 1780—1782. 8 ch. **Samuel**, b. 17 Nov. 1700, blacksmith, Kit., List 298, m. Mary (Roberts) Heard (see 6) who m. 3d John Hayes (3 jr.). **Edmund**, b. 27 Feb. 1702-3, liv. 1714, d. s.p. bef. Dec. 1726. **Abigail**, b. 2 Mar. 1704-5, m. Andrew Spinney(2). **Elizabeth**, b. 3 Feb. 1706-7, m. John Hodsdon(1). **Mehitabel**, b. 14 Nov. 1709. **Joanna**, b. 6 Jan. 1711-2, m. Ebenezer Hill (Ebenezer 17). **Simon**, b. 2 Sept. 1713, m. Lydia Hill (Ebenezer 17); liv. in Biddeford.

3 **OLIVER**, of Bridgtown, co. Devon, cast away at Isles of Shoals in Apr. 1664, adm. in behalf of wid. to kinsman Edw. Holland 13 June 1664.

**Wingfield**, Thomas, a 'Shrewsbury man,' List 386.

**WINKLEY**, ancient in Lancashire. Devonshire has a township Winckleigh.

1 **NICHOLAS**, wit. will of Richard Seward (4) 21 Feb. 1662-3 and proved it bef. Comr. Pendleton 1 July 1663.

2 **CAPT. SAMUEL**, mariner, merchant, Kittery, Portsm., Boston, said to have come from Lancashire. About Jan. 1683-4 master of the ketch -Mary- of Kit. which brot tobacco into N. H., m. Sarah Trickey(3) and evid. first liv. in Kit. Master of ketch -Adventure- 1686; bound for Jamaica 1691. Portsm. (Great Isl.) 1692—1698+, retail lic. 1693—1695. Boston 1703, where w. Sarah d. 14 May 1705 and he m. 2d 12 Dec. 1705 Hannah Adams (wid. of John), who d. bef. Feb. 1707-8. Boston mariner 1706, trader 1707; late of Boston, now of Kit. in May 1709, and m. 3d in Portsm. Nov. 1712 Elizabeth (Hunking 3) Fernald who d. 6 Aug. 1723 (Point of Graves). Rated to So. Ch. 1717, taxed Grafford Lane 1722. Lists 60, 66, 297, 315abc, 296, 297, 339. Ag. ±70 at death. Will, of Portsm., Esq., sick and weak, 13 Nov. 1726—6 May 1736; much real est. and interesting pers. prop. to 6 ch., incl. to s. Francis the ho. and land in Crooked Lane, Kit., 'where he lived & I formerly lived.' Kinswoman Elizabeth Hunking living with him and old serv. Mary Grant were remembered. Ch: **Samuel**, b. 28 Oct. 1687, in 1707 master of sloop -Sarah and Hannah- which his fa. owned, Va. to N. H.; d. s.p. ±18 May 1708. **Francis**, boatbuilder, m. 12 Nov. 1724 Mary Emerson(3), who d. 17 Mar. 1745, ag. 41, he 23 Apr. 1776. In 1724 he liv. on the Crooked Lane prop., but not in 1726 (Y. D. 12: 168-9). Kittery 1739. List 291. 7 ch., first 4 bp. in Portsm. 1726—1733. Capt. **Nicholas**, mariner, Portsm. (but of Boston 1726), m. by 1730 Sarah Wade(1), who was gr. adm. 13 July (he d. 1 June) 1739. See also Nowell. In 1746 she and his br. Wm., as admrs., pet. for div. of ho. left to Sam-

uel(jr.), for payment of N.'s creditors, and supp. of his minor ch: Sarah (d. s.p. 1758), Elizabeth (m. Wm. Hill of Portsm.). **Sarah**, m. Tobias Langdon(2 jr.). **John**, d. in Boston 18 Oct. 1703. **Michael**, b. 13, d. 18, May 1699. **William**, boatbuilder, Portsm., m. Susanna Penhallow(2); she liv. 1762, he in 1770. **Elizabeth**, b. ±1703, m. 1st bef. Mar. 1724-5 Samuel Weeks of Boston m. 2d John Wheelwright(3 jr.). **Samuel** (by 3d w.). His fa. willed him much pers. prop. and 'my now dwg.-ho. in Portsm.' but to be divid. among the other ch. if he d. s.p. He m. Olive Phipps(5), a minor when he died, who was gr. adm. 9 May 1737 and m. 2d aft. 16 Apr. 1740 Cyprien Jeffrey(7).

**WINN**, Josiah, Wells, had 10 a. of meadow laid out 9 May 1698 and m. bef. Oct. 1701 Lydia Littlefield(16). List 269c. See also Cole(31), Littlefield(18). He was b. in Woburn 15 Mar. 1674, s. of Joseph and Rebecca (Reed), and went back for his 2d w., Mary Wyman, m. 17 Aug. 1733. Will, 9 Oct. 1734—10 Feb. 1734-5, names her and 4 of eight ch. rec. at Wells: **Lydia** Littlefield (w. of Nathan 5; she b. 10 Mar. 1701-2); **John** (List 269c, m. 1st in 1732 Huldah Littlefield, dau. of Jonathan 12; m. 2d in 1736 Abigail Littlefield); **Abigail** (b. 14 June 1714); **Joseph** (b. 15 June 1722, pub. int. with Sarah Littlefield in 1743).

**WINNOCK** (Whinnock), **Joseph**, fisherman, Black Point, built there bef. 1666, his land described by Y. D. 12: 67. Sued for debt by Thomas Kimball in July 1662, by Richard Cutts in 1663 when Francis Small was his atty., and plf. or deft. in later suits for debt, trespass, etc. Fined 1665 for saying he was no more drunk than Mr. Hooke and calling him 'moon-calf'; abs. from meeting 1674. In July 1676 he appraised the Chilson est., but bef. or aft. was an Ind. captive, one of those recovered before Feb. 1676-7. List 238a. In 1684 sued by Mr. Wm. Vaughan, in 1686 by John Mills who lost. Killed in the second war; adm. gr. 18 June 1690 to wid. Sarah (Mills 6, a 2d w., m. by 1676), who attested the inv., no land, at Kit. 15 July 1690. At Boston in Nov. 1694 she q.c. to Richard Hunnewell ±40 a. at Black Point her husb. had sold him by verbal agreem. ab. 15 yrs. bef. In Nov. 1702 Sheriff Curtis had a writ to serve at Scarb. ag. the wid. of Joseph W. and left it at Mr. Hunnewell's. In 1715 Scarb. land was inv., ±40 a., and adm. gr. 1717 to Elisha Plaisted by p/a from Thomas Crockett; see also Y. D. 9: 50-51. Ch. appear: **Daughter**, killed with fa. and bur. with him on his own land. **Rachel**, accus. Hugh Alley at Lynn in 1681. **Mary**, m. Elihu Crockett(1). **John**. Will, at Boston, late of Black Point, 26 Nov. 1690—10 Jan. 1690-1, gives wages in Canada

and gun to Wm. Puncheon who was resid. legatee. **Sarah**, accus. James Wiggin(3) in York ct. June 1687, presum. m. him and m. 2d at Haverh. James Davis(13 jr.); liv. 1726. One Joshua W., a Boston jeweler, m. Mary Houghton of Boston at No. Hampt. 17 Feb. 1724-5 (Newb. rec.).

**WINSLAND** (Winslett, at times Winslow), John, Star Isl., Newcastle. John Winslade wit. a Casco Bay deed in 1658 and depos. in Nov. 1668, ±48, ab. Thomas Mitchell's fishing trip, but John Winsland, the Shoals fisherman who sold without lic. in 1667, was ±41 in July 1673, ±40 in 1674. He and Edw. Bennett bot 50 a. at Spruce Creek from Capt. J. Pendleton in 1668, and sold to John Moore, jr. Wife Sarah in 1675; see Head(4), Lines(1). John, sr., of Star Isl. 1675. In 1681 Thomas Andrews, Anthony Farley and John, jr., bot John Moore's fishing stand at the Shoals, but plain John et al. gave a bond to Moore. In 1684 when he was gone, she knew not where (perh. around Falm.), his w. Sarah fell into the fire and was disabled (see Munden 2); in May that yr. he sued his employer Fryer for not providing for her. Sued by Mr. Wm. Vaughan in Wells ct. 1685. In June 1687 Sarah had been murdered at Great Isl. (see Jones 7). He liv., abs. from rec., until 1712 when Newc. paid Goody Gowdy for his care 9 mos. and paid for his funeral, Lists 306c, 226, 313e. Son **John** indicated by 'sr.' and 'jr.'

**Winsley.** See Boade; Hoyt's 'Old Salisbury.'

**WINSLOW.** See also Gray(10), Hilton (18), Scott(3). Winsland and Winsley cause confusion.

1 **EDWARD**, and Thomas Humphrey, wit. John Parker to Clark and Lake 1657 (Y. D. 35: 54).

2 **GILBERT**, at the Piscataqua early, engaged in salt works (see Hilton 17).

3 **JOHN**, sr., Boston, one of the purchasers of the Plymouth Colony interests on the Kennebec and partner with Edw. Tyng in a trading ho. more than 20 miles up the river, from where he wanted Mr. Checkley's barque to bring off his people and goods (Josiah W. and peltry), in 1664.

4 **JOHN** and sis. Elizabeth, b. in Boston, came to Portsm. when their mo. Abigail (Atkinson) m. Samuel Penhallow(2). Elizabeth, m. in Portsm. in July 1715 Alexander Todd, mariner (Suff. D. 34: 268). John was of Boston when he m. in Portsm. Sarah Pierce(13). He d. at sea 31 Oct. 1731, ag. 38. 3 ch. rec.

5 **JOSIAS**, and Christopher Lawson, wit. Spencer to Clarke & Lake 1654 (Y. D. 35: 52). See also (3).

6 **NATHANIEL** and Gilbert, Swansey; see Wiswell(1).

7 **LT. SAMUEL**, ag. ±23, depos. bef. Fryer 1 Aug. 1691 that he was on the Great Isl. the last of July. Poss. about then and there he m. a wife Amy (Moses Furber's wid.?) and they were the S. & A. who had a s. **Samuel** rec. in Boston 28 June 1692. A warr. was issued in Boston 5 Nov. 1697 ag. Amee W., her ch. b. June 1697, her husb. long absent. In Nov. 1698, calling herself of Boston, wid., she gave Samuel Weeks a lease of what was evid. Moses Furber's prop. This lease was used as evid. in suit Wm. Furber v. Joshua Weeks, 1733, for 2/4 of 1/6 the land the orig. Wm. Furber(2) had deeded to his s. Moses. But also the statement was made that Weeks held the Moses F. title thru Vaughans.

**WINSOR.** See also Matthews(3), Neighbors.

1 **SAMUEL**, Smuttynose, a single man liv. at Edw. Martin's, gave all to him and w. Gillin; his friends in Eng. had enough in their hands. Inv. 28 Dec. 1687, £39.

2 **WALTER**, Portsm., depos. in Jan. 1685, ag. ±64, that he was in the employ of Mr. John Cutts a great many yrs. since and erected a fence for him. O. A. 28 Aug. 1685. In 1689 gr. the use of the garden belonging to the minister's ho., he to keep up the fences and deliv. two cords wood to old Lewis. Taxed 1690-1691. In 1694 liv. in a small ho. belonging to Edw. Melcher whose will, Aug. 1695, allowed him the use of it. See also Geare, Gerrish(2).

3 **WALTER**, s. of John of Hemiock (or Hennock), co. Devon, apprent. to John Diamond(3) for 5 yrs. 3 May 1660. If a lad, he was not (2).

**WINTER.** The S.W. corner of Eng. sent Mr. John Winter, but the name is not found there now to any extent. See also Skillings(1).

1 **EBENEZER**, a Scarboro soldier, List 237b.

2 **JOHN**, Mr., early a shipmaster, here at Richmond Island in charge of the Trelawney patent and called the 'Governor of Mr. Trelawnie's people' in Sir F. Gorges' letter 11 Aug. 1636 to his neph. Capt. Wm. Gorges in N. E., in which he requested that Mr. J. W. have such authority as the rest of the Justices. 'The Trelawney Papers,' Col. Me. Hist. Soc., Doc. Hist., 2d Series, vol. 3, devoted to the plantation, Mr. Winter and the correspondence, must be seen by all interested. Lists 21, 221. He m. in Holberton, co. Devon, 29 Jan. 1609-10 Joane Bowdon (see Boaden 2) who joined him here in

1636-7, List 21, and was his capable assistant. See also Me. P. & Ct. Rec. vols. i, ii, by index. His last letter to Mr. Trelawney was from Boston, 19 July 1642, his last letter to anyone was to his dau. Mary 13 June 1644, his w. being then alive. On 20 May 1645 he gave p/a to s.-in-law Robert Jordan and d. prob. not long aft., leaving a will, not on rec., by which he left £10 to his gr.s. John Jordan (Y. D. 3: 34). Inv. 10 Oct. 1648, after Mr. Jordan's pet. to the Ligonia Govt. in Sept., in which he said 'for the satisfying of whose (Winter's) legacies, he hath emptied himself of his proper est.' and that most of the est. lyeth in the execs. of Mr. Trelawney (Y. D. i: 67-72). By divers persuasive letters and mediation of friends, Mr. Jordan finally obtained poss. of the patent to the exclusion of Trelawney and other Winter heirs. Two ch. came with their mo: **Sarah**, m. Rev. Robert Jordan(7), and **John**, jr., who left the country and had recently ret. (appar. to Eng.) from East India in June 1644. An older dau. **Mary** Hooper remained in England.

3 **JOHN**, about Falmouth, wit. John Sears to Isaac Walker of Long Isl. 1655; wit. Cleeve to John Phillips 1659; signed a pet. in 1663. List 222b.

4 **THOMAS**, Mr., Portsm., had p/a from friend John Delves of Portsm. 1700. Peter (and Richard Gull) wit. a Hugh Banfield paper there in 1712. Richard, had an apprent. 1744, sold Portsm. land 1748.

**WINTHROP.** 1 **Adam,** List 78.

2 *****STEPHEN**, Mr., Rep. for Strawberry Bk. 1644, List 53.

**WISE.** See also Wyeth.

1 **REV. JEREMIAH,** Berwick, s. of Rev. John of Ipsw., H. C., A.B. 1700, A.M. 1703. He was called to Berw. in 1706, ordained 26 Nov. 1707, m. bef. 1709 Mary Shipway(2). Lists 296, 298, 337. Her will, 1 Mar. 1747-8—1 Jan. 1749; his will, 17 Jan.— 9 Apr. 1756. Five of **eight ch.** d.y. or unm. bef. their mo. The 1st ch. **Abigail**, b. 22 June 1709, m. Wm. Moore(27) who had by his 1st w. Ann at least 1 ch. Thomas, and by Abigail, 2 ch., David and Susanna, both named in wills of their Wise gr. parents, their mo. being dead. **John**, m. Elizabeth Malcolm; ch. **Sarah**, m. James Plaisted.

2 **THOMAS**, Saco 1636, had made Mr. Lewis' boat tight in 1637. Of Casco, 1640, he wit. ab. Mr. Winter's charges for aquavitae, was sued by John Hickford, and with Hugh Mosher had deed from Cleeve and Tucker of 200 a. N.E. of their then dwg.-ho., adj. wid. Atwell and George Lewis. He assigned his int. in this to Nathl. Wallis 21 Feb. 1658. Sued Henry Webb for slander in Casco ct. July 1666; wit., Brackett to Munjoy, 13 Oct.

1668. See also Brown(23), Phillips(8). No kn. family. Note (4).

3 **THOMAS,** taken to Boston by Charles Glidden, Portsm. constable, in 1664 and committed to prison, charged with embezzling rich goods belonging to the ship -Blue Dove-. A warr. had been issued to search the houses of John Greek, Mr. Corbett, and one West, the ordinary keeper. Before the Governor 14 Sept. 1664 he ackn. himself to be of Deale (Deal, co. Kent) and ag. 24.

4 **THOMAS**, fisherman, York, bot there from John Stover(3) in July 1684 and sold to Isaac Goodridge in Dec. 1685. Of York in Apr. 1691, in Dec. that yr. compl. ag. Wm. Hilton and wit. a Spruce Creek deed with Newcastle men. Gr.j. 1691. In 1694 he and w. Elizabeth were named in a Star Isl. warr., but did not appear. Lists 90, 308b. Of Ipswich in 1698, they sold 11 a. of the Burnt Plain in York (York witnesses); both ack. in Ipsw. in Sept. 1700. Bot in Glouc. 1705 and as **Mr. T. W.** ack. his 1685 deed to Goodridge there 8 Nov. 1715. Living Glouc. 1723. If his w. Elizabeth was wid. of John Damerill(3), they were not the T. and E. whose dau. Dorcas was b. at Glouc. in 1705, but appar. were parents of **John**, fisherman, who m. Honor Tarr in Glouc. in 1712 and bot land there with his fa. in 1713. See also (2); Glouc. and Attleboro vital records.

**WISWELL.** See N. E. Reg. 40: 58.

1 **ENOCH**, tanner, s. of Thomas of Dorchester, br. of (2), bot the Mosher prop. at No. Yarm. from Joseph Nash 25 June 1687, improv. Mosher's Neck (±50 yrs. ago, Tobias Oakman's depos. 1731), and sold 8 July 1698 to Nathl. and Gilbert Winslow who soon sold to Job Otis. List 34. By w. Elizabeth Oliver a large fam. was rec. at Dorch. where he d. 28 Nov. 1706, ag. 73. Ch. incl: **John**, b. 10 Dec. 1658, a No. Yarm. wit. 11 Sept. 1683 (delivery Royall to Nash) and ackn. in Boston a mo. later. **Oliver**, b. 25 Jan. 1665, depos. in Boston in Dec. 1733, ±69, that he liv. and worked with Capt. Gendall at No. Yarm.

2 **REV. ICHABOD**, br. of (1), once a student at H. C., leaving in 1657. Early dates are uncertain. He wit. a Sagadahoc deed, Parker to Veren, dated 17 Dec. 1661, poss. not until it was ack. in Aug. 1676 (Y. D. 15, p. 178); preached for a time at Sandwich, removing 'from hence to Sagadahoc and then next to sea.' Of Kennebec (Sagadahoc), he bot from Thomas Humphrey in June 1674, from John Veren in June 1675, was 'the minister of the place' and from there 6 Sept. 1676, he, James Giles and Richard Collicott pet. for a garrison. Lists 15, 183, 191. Later Duxbury's minis-

ter, active in pub. life and d. there 23 July 1700 in 63d yr. A w. Remember, seen but once, in Sandwich, left a dau. **Elizabeth** who m. Elisha Wadsworth. **Six ch.** by 2d w., Priscilla Peabody, were rec. in Duxb., incl. **Mercy** whose husb. John Wadsworth claimed the Eastern land for her and three sis., and **Peleg**, fa. of Rev. John of Falm. See also Me. Hist. Soc. Col. 2: 9: 113. In Oct. 1691, one Thomas W., ±21, depos. that Ind. were brot to the pond near his fa.'s ho. and remained there the rest of the summer till his going to the service at the Eastward when they went and ret. with him. Reg., vol. 40, does not give a Thomas of this age.
3 **CAPT. NOAH**, br. of (1), slain in N. H. near Wheelwright's Pond 6 July 1690, on march for relief of Falm.

**Witham**, see Wittum.
**WITHERELL.** 1 **Sackford**, Damariscove, List 8.
2 **CAPT.**, List 41.
**Witheridge**, John. See Burgess(4).
**WITHERS**, *Thomas, gent., Kittery, depos. 25 Aug. 1676, ag. 70 odd, setting the time he had liv. here as ±45 yrs. In Mar. 1643, for faithful service and long abode, Mr. Thos. Gorges, as rep. of Sir F. G., granted him 400 a. on N.E. side of Piscataqua River with two islands next adj. to his ho., containing ±200 a.; Mr. Vines, Steward General, confirmed this 20 Mar. 1644. Tr.j. 1640, gr.j. 1645, constable 1648, and influential from then to death. Lists 41, 281, 282, 298, 25, 44, 52, 76, 84, 92. See also Adams(21), Gardner(8), Hutchins(2), Jones(2), Lander(2), Lynn (1), Phillips(8); Y. D. 5: 43; 8: 37; 10: 34; Me. P. & Ct. Rec. vols. i, ii. He was acting under Capt. Champernowne's p/a in 1650. In 1651 Wm. Norman and Margery Randall were abusing his wife. Selectman 11 times from 1651, Deputy 1656, Comr. for Kit., Magistrate, one of Gorges Deputies or Comrs. 1664, being dropped by the King's Comrs. Lot layer and surveyor, and member of important committees. Y. D. 1: 115, locates his ho. at Braveboat Harbor. In Apr. 1671, he deeded to dau. Sarah, intending mar., half the ho. and land where he liv. and other land (Y. D. 2: 156). The same year he deeded an island to daus. Mary and Elizabeth, and in 1675 Kit. land to Elizabeth alone and to Thos. Rice. (Y. D. 2: 133, 184; 3: 90). Will, 26 Sept. 1679—30 Mar. 1685. Widow Jane m. 2d Wm. Godsoe(1); in 1707 they deeded Withers land. See also Knight(19). Ch: **Sarah**, m. John Shapleigh(3). **Mary**, ±25 in 1685, ±44 in 1702, m. Thomas Rice(4). **Elizabeth**, ±65 in Feb. 1728-9, List 293, m. 1st Benjamin Berry(3), m. 2d Dodavah Curtis (9).
**Withington**, Capt., List 19.

**Withrington**, Thomas, Berwick wit. 1705 (Y. D. 7: 71).
**Witter**, Thomas, a Kittery wit. 1666 (Y. D. 2: 92), sued by Richard Lockwood 1667 (Me. P. & Ct. Rec. 1: 306). See also Wittum (3).
**Wittey**, George, Saco fort soldier 1696, List 248b.

**WITTUM**, Witham.
1 **PETER**, Kittery, m. Redigon Clark at Boston 17 June 1652. At Kit., abs. from meeting in July 1659, 1660, 1671, 1685, he and w. in 1673, 1682. In 1660 he had taken in the highway betw. Kittery House and Sturgeon Creek, in 1661 slandered James Heard's w., in 1664 was sued by Richard Cutts, in 1684 drunk and put w. and ch. out of doors, in 1696 sold to Samuel Small the ho. and 16 a. on S.W. side of Sturgeon Creek where he form. liv. Living 15 Jan. 1696-7, his son called 'Sr.' in Jan. 1705-6; Redigon liv. 18 Mar. 1699-1700, ag. ±73. Lists 290, 298. Ch., 1st 3 at Boston: **Mary**, b. 15 Apr. 1653. One Mary was in ct. in Mar. 1687-8, Dec. 1688 and 1691 (see Carter 7). **Elizabeth**, b. and d. May 1654. **Peter**, b. 15 May 1656. **Ichabod**, ment. 1675. **William. Sarah**, ±31 in 1695, m. 1st Wm. Sanders(19), m. 2d George Brawn(2). See Morrell(1), 1685. **Hannah**, b. ±1669, m. Constant Rankin(2). **Elizabeth**, as a ch. played with Abigail (Heard 3) Clements who was ag. 80 in June 1750; m. Zachariah Trickey(7). **Ruth**, m. Moses Bowdy (Boody 2). **Abigail**, ±21 in 1695, m. Samuel Johnson(30).
2 **PETER**(1), yeoman, turner, Kittery, deposed in Apr. 1729, ±72, that he was a soldier at Blue Point under Capt. Wincoll 52 or 53 yrs. before; ±77 in Mar. 1730-1. Wife Agnes or Annis (ct. May 1684). Abs. from meeting 1685. Lists 298, 38. See also Y. D. 3: 65. In 1686 he exch. land with br. William, getting 50 a. on Sturgeon Creek between Leonard Drown and Wm. Sanders, and a 20 a. gr. In Mar. 1723-4, he deeded to s. John, effective aft. death of self and w. Eunice. She was also called Eunice in deed of Feb. 1726-7, but in July 1730 he and w. Anniss were ord. removed from York where they had liv. six months; the constable remov. him, Anniss could not be found. Ch. appear: **Peter**, turner, Kit., in Jan. 1705-6 agreed to live one yr. with Mr. Frost to pay his fa.'s bill for sheep; m. 3 Aug. 1713 Judith Gattensby(2). He was 75 in June 1759, both liv. 1761. Y. D. 20: 205 (1738) shows ch: Moses, Peter, Gansby, Bartholomew, Daniel, Jeremiah, Judith, Naomi. **John**, York, m. 8 Jan. 1707-8 Elizabeth Tidy(3). Lists 296-298. Ch. rec: Elizabeth, John, Zebulon, Eleazer, Gideon, James,

Nathaniel, Katherine. **Daniel**, Kit., 'yeoman (alias turner)' 1726, m. Hannah (Tidy 3) Ford(5). See Bragdon(4). **James**, turner, Kit., m. 12 Mar. 1720 Elizabeth Drown(2); in 1731 sold land at Brixam in York. **Samuel**, wit. fa.'s deed 1723. **Ichabod**, m. Deborah Spencer(6). **Eunice**, m. Richard Brawn (2). Also noted: Andrew, gunsmith, York, List 279, m. 1st by 1715 Ann Beard(3), 1st ch. Ebenezer; m. 2d int. 1 Oct. 1726 Abigail Mills. Abigail, m. Michael Brawn 1722. Benjamin, m. at York 11 Mar. 1726-7 Mary Rankin(2); one Benoni was noted ±1725. Sarah, Kit., accus. Robert Cole in 1729 (see also Ramsdell). Ebenezer, wit. for Ichabod 1730, for Peter and Judith 1732, left wid. Abigail (Benson 1) in Kit. 1748.

3 **THOMAS** (?Witham). Goods of Nicholas Frost(9 jr.) were at his ho. 1674, listed by Joseph Hammond and Tobias Lear, appraisers John Shipway, Philip Faille. See Witter.

4 **WILLIAM**(1), Kittery, Newington, plf. in ct. 1683. In 1686 his fa. deeded him half his land at Thompson's Point 'known by the name of Wm. Oliver's land,' and he got the other half by exch. with (2). Kit. Feb. 1687-8 unmar., Dover 1699, Newington in Dec. 1700 when George Brawn and w. had him bound to the peace, m. bef. June 1701 widow Mary Trickey(2) and liv. on Trickey land. In 1703 bound to the peace towards her. List 343. See also Furbush(2), Y. D. 7: 19. William, sr., and w. Mary o.c. and were bp. at Newingt. in Dec. 1723. In 1731 Portsm. paid for carrying W. W. to Newingt. Appar. his ch: **William** and **Peter**, o.c. and bp. at Newingt. 1723. One Wm. and Elizabeth Carter (see Cater 4), both of Newington, m. in 1717. See also Y. D. 13: 34. **Joseph**, taxed Portsm. 1732, bot in Newingt. 1735, w. Mercy bef. 1736.

**Woddy**, see Waddy.

**WOLCOTT**, Walcott, Wollcock, etc.

1 **ABRAHAM**, wit. an Ind. deed to Walter Phillips 1663 (Y. D. 18: 235).

2 **EDWARD** (often Wollcock), was in Boston in Dec. 1661, ±59, having shipped as mate at Barbadoes. A Kennebec wit. 1664 (Y. D. 11: 144); bondsm. for Richard Collicott 1666; Clerk of the Writs for Northampton 1667; a Kennebec wit. in 1670 and in Nov. 1672, Parsons to Parsons, and wrote this deed. At York 1673 (Y. D. 2: 193), paid for schooling Elizabeth Jackson(7) in 1676, (see also Jackson 12), apprais. Benj. Donnell's est. 1678, John Pulman's 1680, and last surely seen as a wit. with Joshua Downing 13 Sept. 1680. But one John (?Edward), mariner, was named (did not serve) as a referee with John Penwill, 28 June 1682, to fix bounds, Heard, Frost, Conley. In all

probability the 2d husb. of wid. Patience Hatch(3) who was liv. 1709.

3 **JOHN**, Newbury, in 1660 bot. 200 a., ho. and barn at Wells from Thomas Kimball, then of Hampt., who sued him for part of the purch. price in Essex ct. 1662. In Mar. 1659-60 he wit. with John Chater a Wells deed given by the Wadleighs (Y. D. 1: 126). In 1664, carpenter of Newb., contracted to build a mill for Walter Barefoot and Robert Wadleigh, a dispute betw. them being referred to three men in 1666. List 380. See also (2).

4 **WILLIAM**, a Shoals wit. 1651.

**WOLFE.**

1 **FRANCIS** (wrote Woofe), was willed John West's best kersey suit, etc., in 1663. York wit. 1667 (Y. D. 2: 34). Mary Ridgway, ±16 in 1671, said 'my master Francis Wolfe' (Midd. Files). One F. was one of Capt. Henchman's men in Aug. 1676. See also Reg. 17: 331.

2 **HENRY**. See Stevens(2).

3 **STEPHEN**, Cape Bonawagon 1672, Scarb. soldier under Scottow in Mar. 1677-8, Lists 13, 237b.

4 **WILLIAM**, cut wood on Spruce Creek by 1672 (Y. D. 2: 113).

**Wolford**, Woolford, Hans. See Walford.

**Woller**, Roger, wit. deliv. Damerils Cove Isl., Elbridge to Davison, 29 June 1658.

**WOOD.** Became 12th commonest name in N. E.

1 **ISAAC** (Woodde), around the Piscataqua, List 82.

2 **JOHN**, sr. and jr., Jonathan, List 94, certainly Woodman of Oyster River, but poss. a John Wood was at Dover Neck or Cochecho.

3 **DEACON JOHN**, Dover, d. 27 July 1773, ag. 65; see Paul Gerrish(3).

4 **JOSEPH**, weaver, Berwick, taxed 1713, bot 1714. Wife Patience (Nason 1) m. 18 Dec. 1712, o.c. and was bp. as a wid. 28 July 1728; Berw. wit. 1741. Ch: **Stephen**, **Judith**, **Margaret**, all bp. 4 Sept. 1729.

5 **RICHARD**, York, bot. Wm. Johnson's 30 a. gr. on the road to Cape Neddick 1 Mar. 1674-5, built, and with w. Dorothy sold to Joseph Preble in Apr. 1677. In 1675-6 he bot from Sampson Angier, and had 10 a. laid out by the Long Sands in 1676. Richard Place(3) was apprent. to him and w. in Oct. 1676. They disappeared the next yr. and the boy's whereabouts are unkn. until he married.

**WOODBRIDGE.** See N. E. Reg. 32: 292; 54: 401.

1 **REV. BENJAMIN**(2), minister at Kittery 1688-1689 where he had with him a

2d w. Deborah (Cushing) Tarleton, m. at Hingham 31 Aug. 1686, and liv. in half a ho. and lot at the Point built by Henry Greenland. Major John Davis gave him a deed to this in 1689 with special warr. ag. Greenland heirs and Wm. Bickham's. See also Y. D. 4: 121; 5: 1: 62; 6: 137; 7: 234-236. One of the overseers of John Bray's will. Of Portsm. 1691, he bot at Newcastle; called minister of Piscataqua in Feb. 1691-2 by Robert Hopley who asked that he preach his funeral sermon; a year's salary due at Newcastle in 1693-4; Portsm. rate abated in Sept. 1695. He sold in Newc. in 1700, being of Boston then and in 1707. Died in Medford 15 Jan. 1710, his w. surv. By 1st w. Mary Ward(3) who d. at Bristol, R. I., 11 Oct. 1685, he had **five ch.**, of whom the oldest **Elizabeth** b. at Windsor, Conn., 30 Apr. 1673, m. 1st Rev. John Clark(21), m. 2d Rev. John Odlin.

2 **REV. JOHN,** Massachusetts, had magistratical authority for N. H., which was renewed in 1679. He m. Mercy Dudley (Gov. Thomas). Ch. incl: **Benjamin**(1), **Timothy** (4) and Mr. Nathaniel Fryer's 2d w. **Dorothy.**

3 **JOHN** and Norton, York, List 279. See Norton(4).

4 **REV. TIMOTHY**(2), appar. Mr. W., 'our minister,' with whom Humphrey Churchwood, Baptist, had a long discussion on infant baptism in Jan. 1681-2. Mr. Joshua Moody's letter to Cotton Mather 14 July 1683 ment. Mr. W., who evid. was at Great Isl. See also 'Ancestry of Lydia Harmon' (W. G. Davis), p. 106, reprint of 'Lithobolia.'

**WOODBURY, Peter,** shoemaker, Wells; adm. in 1706 to Jonathan Littlefield at whose garrison he had a hut.

**WOODEN,** Woodin. See also Wotton, Wooton.

1 **JOHN,** brickmaker, Hampton 1642-1650, had w. **Mary** 12 Feb. 1644-5 (wit. for Rev. S. Batchelder), in 1648 bot land from wid. Mary Hussey (see 5) and wit. 15 Apr. 1650 Coddington to Edmund Johnson(7), who was appar. related. Lists 391b, 392, 393a. Soon at Haverhill (a landowner), Hampt., Salisb. At Portsm. working for John Cutts 1660; bot 4 a. on Long Reach 1662 (List 356h); of Portsm. 1667 when 150 a., to be laid out by Haverh. men, were gr. by Mass. on his petition: 32 yrs. an inhab., large fam. of ch., no land ever gr. him, obliged to move from place to place. Newbury 1669, Rowley 1671 (sold Hampt. land), in 1679 among those complaining they had been set off from Beverly to Wenham. Not surely seen again (see 2), but his son was

'jr.' at Bev. in 1696. An unkn. John -Woodman- (Wooden?) was k. with dau. Susanna in the Dustin massacre 15 Mar. 1696-7. Adm. on est. of one J. W., sr., of Haverh., gr. in 1721 to husb. of dau. Bethia. Kn. ch: **Mary,** b. at Haverh. 6 Mar. 1652-3, accus. with Lawrence Clinton of Ipsw. in 1677, m. him at Providence 9 Feb. 1680-1. His unnamed w. who d. at Newport in 1690, ±35, 'was nephew to John Johnson' (Reg. 69: 51). **Martha,** b. at Hampt. 12 Feb. 1654-5, wit. at Ipsw. 1674. One Martha -Wadin-, unkn. to Babson, m. Nathl. Bray at Glouc. 22 Jan. 1684. **Sarah,** b. last day of Feb. 1656-7, **John,** b. 7 Oct. 1659, both at Salisb. **Samuel,** Wenham, adm. 1685. **Ithamar,** Wells Mar. 1688-9 (tr.j.). Wife Bethia. Ch: Bethia, Samuel, Ithamar, John, bp. at Beverly 1685-1692; Nathan at Ipsw. 1693. **Hannah,** b. at Newb. 20 Oct. 1669, m. at Wells James Frost(4). **Dorcas,** b. at Rowley 10 Feb. 1671, m. at Wells Anthony Coombs(3). **Peter,** b. at Rowley 13 Mar. 1674, m. at Bev. 15 Oct. 1696 Elizabeth Mallett(1). Ch. rec: Elizabeth, Mary, Sarah, Lydia, two Bethias, at Bev. 1697-1711, and Hosea at Rochester 1713, where one Peter d. 17 May 1717 and 3 of the daus. married (see John Coombs 3).

2 **JOHN**(1), Wells, Beverly, Salem. He or fa. served in King Philip's War and had a right in Narragansett No. 1, but John who wit. ag. Gilbert Endicott at Wells in May 1683 and had a gr. there the fol. July (List 269b), seems more likely the son who was apprent. to Dep. Gov. Symonds of Ipswich. He m. bef. 25 Feb. 1690-1 Katherine (Heard 3) Littlefield(13). Of Salem 1699-1701, when they sold a Wells ho. and land (a town gr.) to Nathl. Clark, and 80 a. on Little River to Benj. Curtis. Both liv. Salem 14 June 1725. Ch: **Mary,** bp. at Beverly 6 Aug. 1696, **Daniel, Elizabeth, Hepsibah, James, Samuel,** all bp. at Salem 3 Sept. 1704, their fa. of Bev.

3 **JOHN,** mariner, Portsmouth, from London in Surrey, m. 22 May 1723 Esther Griffith (see 4) who m. 2d Thomas Greely (3 jr.). In 1744 John Griffith was app. guardian of the daus: **Hannah,** b. 18 Jan. 1724-5. **Mary,** b. 22 Mar. 1726-7.

**WOODHOUSE.**

1 **JOHN** (also Woodis), cooper, Portsmouth, bot on Great Isl. in 1668 next to Daniel Moulton; Joseph Morse wit. the deed. His fa., Richard of Boston, was gr. adm. 28 June 1670 (inv. 30 May). Two sis. also liv. in N. H., Mary with 2d husb. Joseph Morse (6), and Hannah who may have m. 1st Daniel Moulton(2), surely m. Joseph Pormort (1).

2 **PETER,** down East in 1672, ±25. List 14.

3 **PHILIP**, Portsmouth 1717. One George, ag. 70, was in Portsm. almsho. ±1781, confined to his bed for 12 yrs. past.

**WOODMAN**, a Wiltshire and Hampshire family.

1 **EDWARD**, Newbury, s. of the first Edward, bot Kennebec land from Mark Parsons and John Spencer 1687-1690, which his s. Edward (b. 20 Mar. 1669-70; Lists 189, 384a), claimed for the other children (see Hoyt's Salisb. 1: 365). No trace of the orig. Edward and w. Joanna has been found in Kittery and the John resident there (see 3) was not of their family.

2 **CAPT. *JOHN**, Oyster River, br. of (1), m. in Newbury 15 July 1656 Mary Field (1), was accepted inhab. at Dover (O. R.) 17 June 1657 and in 1660 had a 20 a. gr. on w. side of Wm. Beard's creek, n. side of Stonybrook, laid out in 1672. Here he built his garrison which withstood all attacks only to be accid. burned in 1696. Cor.j. 1657; gr.j. 1665, 1672; selectman, moderator, Dep. 1684, 1692-1696, 1699, 1703-1706, J. P., Justice Ct. Com. Pleas, and one of the outstanding men of the Province. In May 1694 Usher issued an order to Capt. John Gerrish and Capt. J. W. to discipline troops. Lists 311c, 353, 356a, 359a, 361a, 363abc, 365, 366, 367b, 368a, 49, 52, 56-60, 62-67, 94, 96. His w. Mary d. 6 July 1698 and he m. 2d 17 Oct. 1700 Sarah (Burnham 5) Huckins(2). Rev. John Pike rec. his sudden death, calling him 'an understanding man.' Will, 20 Dec. 1705—4 Feb. 1706-7; 3 ch., no wife. Ch: **Mary**, m. Edward Small(2). **Sarah**, m. John Thompson(11). **John**, d. the Sabbath bef. 10 June 1705. Lists 52, 62, 94, 96. Lt. **Jonathan**, List 94, (ag. 85 in 1750), willed all fa.'s land and mill, m. by 1699 Elizabeth Downing(5) who d. 17 Apr. 1729 wanting 5 days of threescore. Will, 2 Jan. 1749—25 Apr. 1750, names ch: Mary (the oldest, b. 1 Sept. 1699), John (the homestead and exec.), Jonathan, Joshua, Edward, Downing (the Kit. prop.) Archelaus; List 369 for all except Downing who settled in Kit. The youngest ch. Alice (b. 1710) was not named.

3 **JOHN**, Kittery, York, ferryman at Braveboat Harbor, afterw. from Kit. to Str. Bk. (sold to Nathl. Mendum 1735), ag. ±40 in Sept. 1699, ±69 in Oct. 1721, depos. in Apr. 1702 that he came a passenger from Newfoundland in the fall 13 or 14 at most yrs. ago and never was in this country bef. Pub. ho. lic. from 1693, Kit. gr. 1694, York gr. 1698 (to settle it in one yr.); infringed on Thomas Rice's ferry 1699. Portsm. 1704-1707, Kit. 1712, York 1715. In 1724 he deeded to dau. Mary and husb. for life supp., released the husb. from his bond 26 July 1740, and ack. a deed to son 29 Mar. 1743.

Ano. deed to son 25 Feb. 1744 is ment. in 1747. Lists 295-297. See also Diamond(4), Gammon(1), Lydston(2), Remick(1). A 2d w. evid. followed Mary (Raynes 1) Mendum (1) who was liv. in May -1702-, ±47, as in 1725 one McCartney called him a witch and said he had murdered two wives. The int. of one J. W. and Sarah Eggby was filed at York 7 July 1732, 'underwitten by S. E.' Ch. by w. Mary: **Anne**, b. 10 Mar. 1692-3. **John**, b. 4 May 1696, cordwainer, York, (of Exeter 1721), perh. m. Mary Hepworth in May 1723. Adm. 19 Feb. 1745-6 to Norton Woodbridge; div. 1747 to ch: Joseph, Benjamin (m. Susannah Stevens), Mary (m. George Jacobs, jr.), Anna (m. Joseph Glidden, jr.), Jonathan (he and Lois had Joseph Weare, jr., as gdn.), Elizabeth (m. Daniel Edwards), Susannah (m. Andrew Glidden), and Lois; Benj. Stone was gdn. of Elizabeth and Susannah. **Mary**, b. 1 June 1701, m. John Moore(10 jr.). Note also (4) and Pitman(1).

4 **MARY**, wit. Mary Abbott's deed to her s. Caleb Graffam in 1712. In Mar. 1713-4 ferryman(3) sold Portsm. land to Amos Fernald who m. one Mary Woodman 4 Nov. 1714.

5 **NICHOLAS**, servant to Nicholas Weeks, whose w. Judith cut his toes off and he d. 1666.

**Woodmancy**, John, List 89.

**WOODROP, Alexander**, Mr. (also Woodrop, Woldrop), app. by New York subcollector and receiver of revenues at Pemaquid and its dependencies 28 Nov. 1683 and sailed the next day as master of the barke -Elizabeth-, N. Y. to Pemaquid. Taxed there 1687. In 1738 his negro serv. Susannah, ±70, depos. ab. Mr. Thomas Giles 50 yrs. bef. Lists 16, 122, 124, 125.

**Woodsum**, Joseph, tailor, Berwick 1712, evid. first at Newcastle. List 298. See Hornabrook.

**WOODWARD**. 1 **Ezekiel**, Exeter 1694, ag. ±25. List 384a.

2 **JAMES**, bef. Piscataqua ct. 1646. His inv. filed at Dover ct. 10 Sept. 1647, with his instructions of 4 June previous. He gave to Lydia Williams cert. personal effects at Mr. Williams' ho., to Rev. Mr. Batchelder (who was a wit.), Wm. Chatterton exec. and resid. legatee. He had served Mr. Williams (32) at Saco almost a yr. John Sherburne owed him £5.

**WOODY, William**, taxed for the Mill Dam 1707, Greenland 1711-1715, Portsm. rate abated 1714. List 338a. He prob. m. Mary Leighton(4) who was a wid. 1722-1734+.

**Woollam** (or Woluen), John, ±24 in 1671, bot cider from David Campbell(2).

**Woollet, Edward** or **Edmund**, shipwright, Portsmouth. In 1718 Mr. Knight levied on his ho. See Polley.

**Woolsey,** Joel, an owner in the York patent, List 272.

**Wooton,** see Wotton.

**WORCESTER,** an English county and city.

1 **MOSES,** Kittery, s. of Rev. William of Salisbury, where b. 10 Nov. 1643. In July 1674 he bot 200 a. in Kit. from Capt. Wincoll and was there in Mar. 1674-5. Stackpole calls him a famous hunter of Ind., known as 'Old Contrary.' He m. 1st bef. 4 July 1676 Elizabeth Start(1), m. 2d 4 Apr. 1695 wid. Sarah Soper(1) and was beating her in 1697. In 1709 he and Timothy Wentworth built a mill on Worcester River. Lists 290, 296, 298. At Mr. John Hall's request he rec. £5 of the money Mr. Samuel Hall left for relief of Ind. sufferers. See also Graves(2), Hardy(8). In Nov. 1711 he deeded prop. to s. Thomas, for support if needed (Y. D. 7: 262), and gave him ano. deed in Feb. 1713-4. His w. was liv. 1714; he was in want in 1719 and in 1720-1721 gave deeds of land of his decd. s. Thomas taken on execution; in 1726 gr.s. John ord. to supp. him; in 1727 Thomas' wid. Sarah depos. that he liv. with Thomas 12 or 13 yrs. ago and she often heard him tell what Nicholas Morrell owed him for rent of his mill and land; liv. 1731 (Stackpole). Ch: **Thomas,** had Kit. gr. 1699; of Portsm., bot on the Me. side 1700-1. Lists 296-298. Adm. 1 July 1718 to wid. Sarah (not Gowell). Ch: John (List 298), Samuel, Thomas (chose his uncle Richard Gowell as gdn.). **William,** housewright, called br. of Thomas (Y. D. 8: 82), had gr. in 1703. List 291. Married at Portsm. 12 Feb. 1712-3 Mary Stephenson. See also Y. D. 11: 255. 6 or more ch. **Elizabeth,** unm. 1715 (Y. D. 8: 82).

2 **MR.** (William?). Portsmouth town rec. under date 7 Sept. 1657: 'Mr. Worster called.'

**Wormall,** ———, 1690. List 36.

**Worme.,** Court, List 334b.

**WORMSTALL, Arthur** (also Wormstead), submitted to Mass. at Wells in July 1653, but listed of Cape Porpus. In 1658-1659 in trouble with Stephen Batson over land. Removed to Saco, buying from Wm. Phillips 1661, from Thomas Williams 1662, and also bot 100 + 12 a. at Cape P. from Thomas Mercer 1666. Saco constable 1666. Worked on a day of thanksgiving in 1671, but fine remitted, as a job of necessity given him by Maj. Pendleton. Abs. from meeting 1671; sailed out of Cape P. harbor on Sunday, 1674. A refugee at Salem and took O. F. there in 1678. Of Winter Harbor or Saco, he and w. Susanna (Scadlock 2) sold three lots to John Abbott in Sept. 1681, in Nov. 1684 (w. not ment.) he deeded to s.-in-law

Daggett. At Saco in July 1686. Lists 251, 263, 244d, 245, 247, 249, 27, 33, 79; wife, 246. The surv. ch., if not the parents, ret. to Mass. in the next war. Rebecca Daggett renounc. adm. on his est. to her s. Samuel 10 May 1728; div. ordered: ⅓ to heirs of Michael and ⅔ to Rebecca who was to pay ⅓ in cash to heirs of Martha. Ch: **Rebecca,** m. William Daggett(3). **Susan,** b. 25 May 1658, and **Arthur,** b. 26 Sept. 1661 (Saco records), both d. s.p. by 1728. **Martha,** m. Robert Derby(2) who q.c. her int. to Daggetts in 1727 (Y. D. 12: 188). **Michael,** m. in Marblehead 5 July 1696 Rebecca Dimon who m. 2d 1 June 1709 Edward Hammond. 5 ch. rec. See Y. D. 11: 256; 13: 78. **John,** b. at Saco 3 Nov. 1669, d. s.p. bef. 1728.

**WORMWOOD.** Camden mentioned Wormewood. See also Small(4).

1 **JACOB**(2), Saco, Cape Porpus. Cor.j. 1661, signed a Wells pet. 30 Apr. 1668 (Doc. Hist. 4: 218), appar. m. a dau. of William Reynolds(6). Lists 244de, 259, 268b. He and Wm. Thomas wit. an unrec. deed, Cole(8) to John Barrett in Nov. 1684; Cape Porp. cor.j. 1685; lot layer and surveyor Jan. 1688-9. If alive later, he prob. found refuge in Oyster River; Bradbury says he d. bef. the resettlement at Cape Porpus. One Reynolds gr.ch. kn: **William,** with Eli Demeritt and w. Hope (sis. or cous.), all of Dover, deeded as heirs of uncle John Reynolds 14 Dec. 1725 (Y. D. 11: 249). Wife Margaret; both bp. at O. R. 29 Oct. 1721. Adm. to s. Joseph 30 Mar. 1743. Lists 368b(3), 369. 'Hist. of Durham,' 2: 399, names ch: Jacob (bot land 1727, List 369, adm. to br. Joseph 2 Feb. 1735-6), Joseph, List 369, (m. Deliverance Pomery 6), Susanna (m. John Doe 1), Martha (m. Joseph Doe 1), William, Abigail, Mary (m. Benj. York), and poss. Joanna and Alice. See also Fuller(2).

2 **WILLIAM,** Piscataqua, wit. John Lander's deed 10 Jan. 1639. List 281. In Mar. 1646-7 John Billings' wid. depos. that J. B. gave W. W. 2 acres and Lander gave him 2, evid. the 4 a. at Kit. Point, with a ho., which he sold to Crockett(6) bef. 21 Sept. 1647. Accus. of improper dealings with sailors and ord. from Star Isl. to the mainland in 1647. He succ. sued Nicholas Brown for debt in 1648 when Wm. Seeley got into trouble by taking away the bull that had been attached. A common swearer and turbulent person 1650; in Oct. that yr. he and w. allowed to sit down at Isles of Shoals, but not to sell drink. See Jones(1), Reynolds(2). In Oct. 1647 his w. was ord. to Boston to answer a charge. See also James(8). Goody W., List 75b. Ch. uncertain, but good reason to incl: **Ann,** freed from service of John Crowder(3) and w. in 1648. **Jacob. Mar-**

garet, m. (ct. 4 July 1659) Simon Bussy(3). And two who perh. could be gr.ch: John. In 1676 he, Wm. Chadbourne and John Winnock were released by the Ind. at Pemaquid (N. E. Reg. 42: 294); in 1694, one J. and Kit. men were fined for quarreling. William.

3 WILLIAM (see 2), York 4 Apr. 1679, but first at Portsm. where his rate was abated 15 Mar. 1679-80. O. A. at Y. 22 Mar. 1679-80; owned land on York River in Mar. 1683-4 (Y. D. 4: 7); gr. 1685 (firewood with James Freethy); appr. Samuel Freethy's est. 1685; bondsm. for George Norton 1685; constable 1685, 1686; gr.j. 1688. List 33. Inv. (see Bragdon 2) 14 Oct. 1690, ho. and land, carpenter's tools; adm. 3 Dec. fol. to wid. Mary, surety Wm. Young. She m. 2d John Spencer(6); liv. at Wells in July 1736, ag. ±69. Kn. ch: Mary, m. Job Low(4). Martha, m. Abraham Bowden (see Boody 1). Thomas, Wells, b. ±1684, Mr. Samuel Wheelwright's apprent., and aft. he d., served Mr. John Wheelwright 7 yrs. (see Mayer 3). He m. (ct. Oct. 1706) Jane Cole(24). Jury 1713; ±30 in July 1714; condi. gr. 1716; List 269c. He deeded to s. Benjamin in 1741 and 1744 (the homestead) for supp. of self and w. Jane; depos. in 1749 ±67 (SJC 65314), see Spencer(6); liv. 1751. Ch. appear: William, k. by Ind. 1724 (Hist. of Wells, p. 318); Thomas; Joseph; Benjamin; John, depos. in June 1772, ±50, that when 16 or 17 he and bros. Benjamin and Thomas worked lumbering on Mousam River. Daus. presum. incl: Mary, m. John Freese (see 1); Elizabeth, a Wells wit. 1731, m. Wyatt Moore(22); Abigail, m. Thomas Cousins 1742.

Worring, Richard, List 13. See Warren.

## WOTTON, Wooton.

1 EDWARD (Wooton), List 90(3). Suff. Prob. 1691 has will of one E. W., giving to his landlady Rachel Pascho and Mary Coudner. See Neighbors.

2 JOHN, Piscataqua, drunk at Saco 25 Mar. 1636 and ordered to make a pair of stocks by the last of April. Str. Bk. 1640, and deeded Muskeeto Hall, ±100 a. on Great Isl., by Francis Matthews in 1646. In 1649 he and Jonathan Coventry ack. judgm. to Mr. George Smyth, and Charles Dolson gave p/a to John Pickering to demand goods left with J. W. In 1650 he unsucc. sued George Walton for trespass, in 1655 G. W. sued him (his goods) over a cornfield, and in the Jones-Walton case it was test. that the marsh in controv. was one claimed by J. W. Lists 41, 321, 323. Ordered more to his w. 1650, 1652, 1653; in June 1653, going away, leased Muskeeto Hall to Richard Tucker, atty. for Lane(1). John Munijou wrote from Plymouth, Eng., 16 Mar. 1658-9, for wid. Ebbet W., whose husb. went to N. E. 26 or 27 yrs.

ago, and liv. at Piscataqua over 21 yrs., she staying in Plym.; ord. home to her, he came intending to take her back, but was taken in the Dutch war, lost his passage money, was put ashore in a remote place and traveled to Plym., where he d. in 5 or 6 wks.; he left Mr. Tucker and Mr. Crawley as his agents (Mass. Arch. 15 B: 258). Adm. here to Capt. B. Pendleton in Oct. 1654. In 1657 her agent here sold Muskeeto Hall to Mr. Tucker.

3 JOHN (Wotten), of Dartmouth, Eng., 1660, when Edw. Lyde(3) remitted money to him. Portsm. abated the tax of one John Wotoon (ano. rec. Notoon), smith, in Mar. 1695-6, poverty and a lame wife. See also Brown(23), Parsons(9).

WRIFORD, John, (also Wrieford), Damariscove 1672, took O. A., had tav. and liquor lic., and served on gr.j., all in 1674. Lists 13-15, 18, 189 (sr.). See also Doc. Hist. 5: 32; 6: 394. John, jr., List 189.

## WRIGHT, general in Eng. except in extreme north and south. Became 29th commonest name in N. E.

1 DANIEL, a Wells soldier from Dedham. List 267b.

2 HENRY, housewright, Kittery, York, Boston, served Mr. Roger Plaisted 10 yrs., ending some yrs. bef. his death, had Kit. gr. in 1671, was sued by Mr. Thomas Broughton in 1672 for taking away boards, but not held (see Hughes 5), and m. (ct. July 1673) Sarah Start(1). Evid. in Boston in Apr. 1681, but test. in a York case in Oct. fol., ag. ±31 (see 11). Edw. Start's gr. was laid out to him in 1699 when his w. was liv. (Y. D. 6: 110, 128). Of Boston, he sold 50 a. in Kit. to Ichabod Plaisted in 1713, List 298; depos. in July 1719, ±70, ab. York 55 yrs. bef., and again 21 July 1720, ±70, ab. Great Works. Ch. at Boston 1674-1686: Sarah, see Cooper 3 (jr.), Batten(4). Mary. Ebenezer. Ephraim. Mehitable. John. One Henry m. Hannah Wade in Boston 20 Jan. 1714.

3 CAPT. JOHN, wit. deliv. of the Vines patent 25 June 1630 (Y. D. 1: 2: 8). Note also (12).

4 JOSEPH, a York wit. 1711, Benjamin in 1724. Y. D. 8: 254; 12: 4.

5 MARGARET, 1712, when a joint warr. was issued ag. 'John Davis and Margaret Right;' Nathl. Huggins made return 'non est inventus.' See also (9).

6 NATHANIEL, Stratham, see (9). In Mar. 1699-1700 the Wm. Hilton est. owed him on a bond dated 2 May 1674. Quampscot grantee 1677, ack. judg. to Waldron in 1681, and owed pipestaves to Francis Huckins. Exeter constable 1693, 1694; adm. to Portsmouth Ch. 1696; gr.j. 1698. In 1702 his w.

was Hannah (presum. Bolles 3), wid. of Caleb Beck(1). In 1704 sued by Isaac Cole for a ho. frame built ±24 yrs. bef. betw. Thomas Reed's ho. and land of plf. Lists 52, 57, 62, 338d, 381, 384, 388, 396. Will, aged, 27 Aug. 1716 (d. 9 Sept. 1717); w. Hannah, kinsman Richard White(18). The wid. renounced adm., which was gr., c.t.a., 5 Oct. 1717 to White's wid. Sarah (Lewis).

7 **RICHARD**, 1661, Me. P. & Ct. Rec. i: 251. Of Boston?

8 **THOMAS**, Exeter, List 376a, is Wight.

9 **THOMAS**, Exeter, memb. of Portsm. No. Ch. 1699 (List 331c); see (5, 6). Appar. the cooper who wit. for Wiggins at Stratham 1707-1710, and with w. Elizabeth sold his homestead there next to the Greenland line, in 1726. List 338a. Will, of Scarboro, 1 June 1753—6 Oct. 1760, names wife Elizabeth, daus. **Elizabeth** Allen, **Margaret** McKenney, **Sarah** Warmagen; Mr. Andrew Libby, exec.

10 **THOMAS**, from London, m. Hepsibah Seavey(8). List 339. **Seven children** bp. in South Church where their mo. was rec. into full commun. 8 May 1720.

11 **WILLIAM**, York, sued by Samuel Donnell for £132 in 1680, and wit. ag. Joseph Weeden for selling liquor in 1681, when he or ano. was also called William, jr.; (2) wit. in the same case. One Wm. was the 3d husb. of Mary (Davis 41) (Dodd) Austin, but not named in her deed of Sept. 1700 (Y. D. 6: 75); she was a wid. in York in Oct. 1713 (Y. D. 9: 80).

12 ——, Mr., had owned Robert Sankey's 200 a. at Saco which were sold by Mr. Joseph Bolles to John Boaden in 1659, 'left now into the hands of the said Joseph Bolles.' See also (3).

**WYATT**, sometimes confused with White.

1 **DAVID**, mariner at Portsmouth, bound to sea in July or Aug. 1674, gave all in N. E. to Hannah Hodsdon(6). John Mains held prop. or money belonging to him.

2 **JOHN**, Portsmouth, had a deed from admrs. of John Jackson(9) in 1669, 2 a. out of the home farm, perh. indicating that his w. Salome was Jackson's dau. Inv. 5 June, adm. 28 June, 1670, to wid. Salome, who m. 2d Nathan White(18), m. 3d **Francis** Jenness(1).

3 **JOHN**, served on gr.j. (N. H.) in Mar. 1698-9, and was perh. the same man who had a first w. Elizabeth and as a last wife the widow Christian Kar (see Carr 1, Harris 19), with whom he liv. in Berwick. He was a Berw. wit. 1707, as Mr. J. W. hired land from Philip Hubbard in 1709, liv. 16 Dec. 1709. See also (4). Mrs. W. was a wit. in the Elizabeth Turbet case 1715, a wid. in Oct. 1718, and was rec. into Portsm. So. Ch. 5 June 1720; liv. at P. in Dec. 1736, ag. 80.

**Elizabeth**, dau. of John and Elizabeth, d. 15 Mar. 1713, ag. ±18 (Berw. gr.st.).

4 **LT. JOHN**, at Black Point fort when Capt. Hunnewell and his men were killed; in acct. 9 Dec. 1703 he styled himself 'late sergeant at Black Point.' See also Lucas(4). Lt. J. sold without lic. in 1706 and was ord. to appear bef. Esquires Hammond, Plaisted and Pepperell; fined for like offense 1707. This prob. identifies him as (3). One Gershom W. served under the Lieutenant.

5 **JOHN**, Newbury, m. in 1700 Mary Badger. Mr. Eben Putnam ident. him as the mariner of Arrowsic in 1718 (Y. D. 9: 94) and declared his aut. not that of Lt. John. Ch. rec. at Newb. incl: **Stephen**, m. 20 Nov. 1723 Mary Bickham(3), had a s. John bp. at Portsm. and other ch. at Newbury.

6 **JOHN**, Portsmouth 1731-1736, mate of -Charming Molly- sailing for Limerick, Ireland, in 1731, m. by 1732 Margaret (Cate 1) Gardner(2), who was a wid. 1738-1769+.

**Wyer.** See Nock(4).

**WYETH, Mr. Humphrey** (Withe, Wise), Ipswich 1635, d. soon leaving a wid. Susanna whose 2d husb. Samuel Greenfield (1) took over the prop. without authority bef. Mar. 1638-9; Essex Prob. i: 11. George Gidding and Richard Lumpkyn were named overseers for the ch. Married ch. who had their portions incl: **Abigail**, m. 1st Thomas Jones(42), m. 2d Thomas Chadwell(3 jr.), and appar. **Mary**, w. of Abraham Perkins(1). **Susanna**, not named with minor ch., m. John Bursley(4), but poss. had an earlier husb. as unlikely she m. B. by 1639. Minor ch: **Benjamin**, apprent. to Abraham Perkins for 7 yrs. from 29 Sept. 1638; Hampt. gr. 1644; List 392a. In May 1649 his step-fa. deeded Hampt. land except what already sold to Thomas Jones and B. W. **Joseph**, poss. the wit. paid fees in Apr. 1649 (Essex Q. Ct. Rec. i: 167), was claimed by Edw. Gilman in Mar. 1650, but turned over to G. Gidding who was to bind him out in Ipsw. **Em**, unmarried in Dec. 1649 (Essex Q. Ct. Rec. i: 182), poss. m. Richard Carle(1). **Sarah**, m. David Wheeler(1). **Ann**, wit. a Bursley deed as A. W. 25 Mar. 1648, m. 1st William Taylor(24), m. 2d George Pearson(2).

**YABSLEY** (also Gabsley), **John**, owed Nathan Bedford £5, ±1676. Bedford offered to forgive the debt if he would leave the country, and, after waiting 14 mos., sued him in Dover ct., John Locke of Portsm. on his bond.

**Yackham**, Thomas, Great Isl. 1690. List 319.

**Yard**, Humphrey. List 328.

**Yarington**, William, Dover 1693. Lists 94, 359b. Also Arington and Yerington.

**YEALES, Timothy,** a contracting carpenter in Boston bef. 1674 when he bot 150 a. at Ogunquit from John Barrett. Deputy marshal of Suffolk 1676, and still of Boston by various rec. until 1680. Of York 1682 and in trouble for telling the court that Christ was a carpenter. Under bond to keep the peace toward the government, 1684. York gr. 1686. Tr.j. 1680, 1686; gr.j. 1687. See Hilton(20), Langmaid(3). Sold Ogunquit lands to Nathaniel Masters 1687. Also of Isles of Shoals, 1687. His w., Naomi Frye (George of Weymouth), still his wid. in 1725. Adm. 15 Feb. 1691-2 to Capt. Francis Hooke. Ch: **Anna,** b. 25 Apr. 1673, d.y. **Mary,** b. 11 Jan. 1674, m. int. 2 Oct. 1708 James Bucklin of Rehoboth; with mo. and sis. q.c. York land to Joseph Holt, 1725; ch. James, Naomi, Timothy, Mary, Nehemiah, b. 1709-1718. **Anna,** b. 7 May 1679, (Hannah) m. Ebenezer Allen of Barrington, Bristol co. **Timothy,** Weymouth, coaster, m. Boston 30 Aug. 1716 Elizabeth Petty; gave p/a 1712 to br. Nehemiah to sell ⅔ of fa.'s land 'being only surv. ch.' (not so). **Nehemiah,** b. 17 Sept. 1689, Boston shipwright; sold fa.'s York land to Joseph Holt; adm. 1721 to wid. Hannah, who m. 2d 24 Oct. 1723 Miles Gale.

**Yeamans,** John, wit. with Elias Stileman, 1665.

**YEATON,** poss. (surely, says Mr. Libby) phonetic for Eaton.
1 **JOHN**(2), Newcastle, fisherman and husbandman, m. Elizabeth Randall(5). Taxed 1708 (List 316). Bot land near Salmon Falls (Somersworth) from br. Philip in 1730; of Somersworth in 1731 when he sold 13 a. in Rye (wit. James Randall); again of Newc. in 1735 when he bot the Jeremiah Walford est. and in 1736 when he sold the Somersw. land. Will, 8 Nov. 1756—26 Jan. 1757, names w. Elizabeth, appoints s. Richard exec. and lists ch: **John** (his heirs in will), m. by 1737 Elizabeth Wentworth (b. 1712) and was prob. that John Yeaton, joiner, on whose est. Thos. Wallingford was gr. adm. 1747. **Elizabeth** Odiorne. **Samuel.** **Mary** Odiorne. **Richard.** **Hannah** Gordon (see 2). **Philip. Joseph.** One Joseph was fishing for (1) in 1729. **Benjamin.**
2 **RICHARD,** Isles of Shoals and Newcastle, head of a fam. which, owing to complete lack of vital rec. or any indication of relative ages, is difficult to tabulate. Star Isl., 1683. Poss. his w. was Hannah, 1693-4 (List 308b). He (or a s.) taxed Newcastle 1708 (List 316). List 309 (Eaton). In 1711 John Davis(48) sold him a ho. and land on Star Isl. Adm. on est. of R. Y., sr., of the Shoals gr. to sons John and Samuel 10 Aug. 1732. Ch: **John. Samuel.** One Samuel of the Shoals

had w. Catherine and ch. bp. 1728-1741, but see (1). **Richard,** jr., of Star Isl. sold land at Newcastle to John(1) in 1729. Prob. he, not his fa., m. Margaret Crucy(1) as they would both seem to have been liv. in 1768 when the Crucy est. was divided. One Richard, adult, was bp. 27 Oct. 1728. **Philip,** Somersworth, bot land of John Drew 1714, deeded his entire est. to 'beloved friend' wid. Joanna (Pray) Roberts in 1726 and m. her, poss. his 2d w. Ch: Phebe, William, Philip, bp. Dover 1728. He prob. the Philip 'Eaton' bp. 11 Oct. 1725. Prob. **Benjamin** had dau. Elizabeth bp. 1 Oct. 1727, but see (1). No guess as to Ann and Hannah, bp. Newcastle 18 Mar. 1722.

**Yeats,** Edward, drunk while liv. on Capt. Champernowne's Isl., May 1685.

**YELLING,** Yealland, **John,** of West Allington, co. Devon, hired himself to Wm. Lange(9) of Plymouth, co. Devon, mariner, 15 Mar. 1674-5 to serve four yrs. in New Eng. The indenture was assigned to John Odiorne 20 May 1675. Fisherman, he bot at Hog Isl., Isles of Shoals, in 1683 and, with w. Tryphena, sold in 1684. Constable 1685, but sent ashore (to the mainland) for fighting that same yr. See Gould(9).

**YEO.** 1 **Allen,** seaman, Boston 1640. A. Y. & Co. had built a ho. on Edward Godfrey's land at York bef. 1647, when Yeo had died.
2 **HUGH,** sued Thomas Purchase by Abraham Shurt, attorney, 1640.
3 **LEONARD,** wit. to depos. taken in the Edward Ashley case, 1631-2.
4 **THOMAS,** Isles of Shoals, 1651', when Capt. Sampson Lane sued him for £300 on open account and he was in ct. for selling liquor to the Ind. Thomas Yeo's island, near Parker's isl., Kennebec, in 1676.

**YORK,** an English county and city.
1 **BENJAMIN**(3), ±23 in 1677-8, had fa.'s Lamprill riv. land by his will and liv. thereon. He m. Abigail Footman(2) who m. 2d after 1715 Benjamin Meakins and was again a wid. at Exeter, 1737. Lists 52, 359a, 384a. Ch: **Elizabeth,** m. Job Judkins(1). **Richard,** Exeter, prob. m. Susanna Goodwin, dau. of James(12) who in his will ment. gr. ch. John and Susanna Y. Prob. other ch., incl. Richard. Adm. to s. John 1766. **John,** m. Phaltiel Folsom(1), both adm. to Oyster Riv. Ch. 1719 and had ch. Mary, Anne, John, bp. 1717-1722, and poss. others. Lists 368b, 369. His bros. and sis. q.c. to him their int. in the Lamprill Riv. 100 a. farm. **Rachel,** m. bef. 1714 William Jones of Amesbury. **Benjamin,** Newmarket, ±81 in 1759, liv. with Capt. Richard Hilton as a boy, m. Sarah Pinder. Adm. to s. Thomas 1760, Josiah Y. (presum. ano. s.) being pd. for keeping

him and his w. for two years. Also **Abigail** (says Mr. Stackpole), m. 12 May 1729 Hezekiah Marsh, but she did not sign the family release to John.

**2 JOHN**(3), 38 in 1680, had w. Ruth. Having settled in No. Yarmouth, he sold his fa.'s farm to John Cutt 28 June 1676. Retreated to York during Philip's war, deeding N. Yar. prop. from there in 1680. Back at N. Yar. by 1683 and a trustee of the town 1684. In 1688 he pet. for confirmation of title to 300 a. on which he was liv. Lists 32, 47, 214, 357c, 359a. Taking refuge at Casco Fort in 1690 he was taken prisoner and his two eldest sons killed, when it fell 17 May. He, useless from weakness, was k. soon aft. at Norridgewock. Ch: **Richard** and **Benjamin**, ment. in gr.fa.'s will, depos. in Feb. 1687 (Mass. Arch. 128: 41-2), k. in 1690. **Ruth,** m. Henry Haskell of Gloucester, deeded int. in fa.'s N. Yar. prop. to Geo. Dennison 1735. **Joseph,** Gloucester, m. 10 Jan. 1700 Abigail Robinson who d. 13 July 1720. List 214. Only s. Joseph d. s.p., but six daus. survived: Abigail, m. 1st 23 Oct. 1718 Samuel Stevens, m. 2d Jacob Randall. Ruth, m. 27 Oct. 1720 Wm. Elwell. Mary, m. 9 Aug. 1722 Francis Sargent. Sarah, m. 24 Nov. 1725 Wm. Young. Hannah, m. 18 Mar. 1728-9 Wm. Knight (of Falmouth 1735). Rachel, m. 28 Dec. 1732 Benjamin Card(7).

**3 RICHARD,** Dover by 1635 by his own depos., had w. Elizabeth (±62 in 1680) who m. 2d bef. Oct. 1680 William Graves (6). Had ho.-lot on Dover Neck 1642, a 100 a. gr. on Lamprill Riv. in 1656 and a farm at Oyster Riv. Bot 50 a. at Littlejohn's creek from Wm. Hilton and sold it 7 Aug. 1661 to Joseph Austin. Gr.j. 1643, 1656, 1664, 1667, 1668, 1669. See Ault. Lists 47, 354abc, 355 ab, 356a, 361a, 362a, 363abc, 365, 366. Will, unsigned, 23 Apr. 1672 (inv. 27 Mar. 1674, adm. to wid. and s. John 30 June 1674) names w., ch. and gr.s. Richard and Benjamin. Four men test. in 1681 that Thos. Corbett had read the will to Wm. Graves in John York's hearing at John Partridge's ho. Div. was made in 1681. Ch: **Samuel,** b. ±1645. **Elizabeth,** m. Philip Cartee 1668. **Rachel,** m. Benjamin Hull(1). **John. Benjamin,** b. ±1655. **Grace,** under 18 in 1672, m. John Gilman(10).

**4 SAMUEL**(3), bot in partnership with James Thomas from the Ind. Jeromkin, Daniel and Robin, a tract of ±600 a. at Topsham 20 June 1670, and liv. there until Philip's war when he went to Cape Porpus. Sold out there (½ a saw-mill to John Batson and land to Isaac Cole) 1682-1684, having obtained a gr. and built a ho. at Mussel Cove (Falmouth Foreside) bef. 1680. By 1686 he had built a garrison on 100 a. at No. Yarmouth, for which he pet. for title in 1688. Lists 191, 214, 259. War drove him to Gloucester where he d. 17 Mar. 1717-8, ag. ±73. His wid. Hannah (m. bef. June 1676) d. 28 Nov. 1724. His will, 15—27 Mar. 1717-8, lists ch: **Samuel,** Ipswich, 54 in 1731 when he depos. ab. Falmouth bef. 1690, 81 in 1759 when he test. ab. the attack on the Bracketts in 1689. Taken prisoner at the fall of Casco Fort in 1690 he rem. in Canada until July 1700, having for 2 yrs. cut masts for the French navy (List 99, pp. 74, 208). He m. 1st 21 Feb. 1705-6 Mary Dutch who d. 16 Apr. 1709; m. 2d int. 27 Oct. 1711 Mary Potter; d. June 1767. His fa. had entered an East. Cl. for the Topsham land in 1715, and he obtained a gr. of 300 a. in 1721 in satisfaction thereof. He had brot ejectment suits ag. new settlers in 1720. 1 + 10 ch. **Benjamin,** 79 in 1759 when he depos. with br. Samuel, m. at Ips. 7 Dec. 1704 Mary Giddings; a miller at Cape Elizabeth (Knightville) by 1719-20. 8 ch. **Richard,** Ips., m. 17 Jan. 1710-1 Patience Hatch who m. 2d 15 Mar. 1719-20 George Harvey; d. 2 May 1718, ag. ±29. 4 ch. **Hannah,** m. 31 Oct. 1693 Edward Harraden. **Elizabeth,** m. Samuel Griffin. They q.c. to s. Samuel jr. in 1754 (Y. D. 30: 258). **Sarah,** m. Abraham Robinson. **Rachel,** m. (int. -Sarah-) Josiah Lane(5). **John,** b. Glouces. 13 Apr. 1695, d. 8 Dec. 1699. **Thomas,** d. 30 July 1699.

**5 THOMAS.** List 330a. See French(8).

**YOUNG.** Col. Banks found a Rowland Young who was twice married, in 1616 and 1618, at High Wycombe, co. Bucks.

**1 FRANCIS,** Ipswich, agent of Francis Wainwright, depos. (Me. ct.), ±24, 25 Sept. 1674.

**2 JOB**(9), York, 72 in 1736 and 1737, m. aft. Oct. 1691 wid. Sarah (Austin 5) Preble and was allowed £71 for bringing up her Preble ch. 6 Jan. 1712-3. She d. 24 May 1720. Gr.j. 1694, 1696. List 279. Deeded to s. Rowland 1715 and to sons Rowland and Job 1724. Ch: **Rowland,** prob. he who m. Hannah Preble(4), but see Rowland (Jonathan 10). 8 ch. b. York 1716-1735, their names too worn to decipher. Job, m. 7 Dec. 1727 Patience King. List 279. 12 ch. rec. York 1727-8—1750. **Lydia,** m. 1st Hopewell Weare(3), acc. Nathaniel Abbott of Andover 1724, m. 2d John Wells(6). **Sarah,** m. Joseph Favour(2).

**3 JOHN,** Exeter, gr. of 30 a. in 1670; liv. at Moses Gilman's ho. and acc. by Judith Robie(1) in 1671 but given good character by the chief citizens of Ex. He m., int. Feb. 1671-2, Sarah Wadleigh(4), 78 in 1733-4, and whose fa. gave her a marriage-portion of ⅓ his farm in 1675. Her list 376b. See also Smith(7). Paid Charles Runlett's fine, 1674. Gr.j. 1681, tavern lic. 1685, 1686. Lists 52,

62, 67, 96, 376b, 381, 383. Appeal, in his own writing, in Gilman v. Young, 1695, states that he had liv. in Ex. near 30 yrs. and 'maintaineth five persons.' Slain by Ind. and his s. wounded 10 June 1697. Adm. 28 Sept. 1697 to Peter Coffin, wid. Sarah renouncing. Ch., poss. not all: **John**, killed by Ind. when travelling between 'Pick-Pocket' and Ex. 8 Aug. 1704; adm to Peter Coffin, creditor; wid. Mary and bros. Robert and Joseph cited, James Y. a creditor. Lists 62, 96, 376b. **Robert**, wit. 1703-1709, sold to s. Jonathan in 1731 and to s. Charles in 1735; prob. also had s. James who with Charles bot back in 1726 land Robert had sold to Thos. Phipps in 1724. Lists 62, 376b, 384b. **Joseph**, Kingston, carpenter, had 40 a. gr. 1700 which he sold to br. Daniel in 1710; m. Elizabeth Sleeper (see 2) 24 Dec. 1705; d. at Kingston 2 May 1756. Lists 376b, 400. 8 ch. **Israel**, Ex. wit. 1698, wit. for Capt. Robt. Wadleigh 1701 and sold land to Robt. Wadleigh, jr. 1701-2. Lists 67, 376b. **Daniel**, bot land 1704, called neph. of Robt. Wadleigh in 1710; his mo. deeded him her 1698 gr. in 1721; in 1725 his w. was Elizabeth (Thing 2), wid. of Edward Stevens(16); both liv. 1761. Martha, w. of Thos. Dolloff was his dau. as were appar. Mary, w. of Jonathan Dolloff (m. 17 Nov. 1737) and Sarah, w. of Joseph Lawrence. **James**, a Wadleigh abuttor 1701, 1710. Lists 67, 376b.

4 **JOHN**, Falmouth 1717, Brunswick 1718, one or two men. Lists 161, 229.

5 **LT. JOSEPH**(10), York, had gr. 1696, 1713 (30 a.). List 279. He d. 6 May 1734. Will, 1 May—4 June 1734, left est. to w. Abigail for life and named her and s.-in-law John Bradbury exec. Ch: **Mary**, b. 2 Jan. 1696-7. **Abigail**, b. 22 Aug. 1699, m. Judge John Bradbury. **Phebe**, b. 25 Jan. 1701-2, m. 20 June 1728 Wymond Bradbury of Brunswick, d. 20 Apr. 1731. **Samuel**, coaster, Biddeford, b. 21 July 1704; m., int. 13 Nov. 1725, Mehitable Beane(4) who m. 2d Aquila Haines(1 jr.); d. Mar. 1730; adm. to fa. 5 Apr. 1731. Ch: Joseph, to have all lands aft. gr.mo.'s death, adm. to mo. Mehitable Haines 1752; Abigail. **Bethulah**, b. 25 Feb. 1707-8; m., int. 13 Nov. 1725, Nicholas Beale(5). **Bethia**, b. Sept. 1709, m. 30 Nov. 1731 John Stackpole.

6 **MATTHEWS**(10), York, fisherman, ±50 in 1728, m. Newbury 23 Apr. 1696 Eleanor Haines (see 1). List 279. Will, 20 Nov. 1750—1 Apr. 1751, names only surv. s. Ebenezer exec., five liv. and one decd. dau. Ch: **Susanna**, b. 3 Nov. 1696, m. 1st Ichabod Austin(6), m. 2d Magnus Redlon. **Hannah**, b. 5 Jan. 1698-9, m. John Preble(4). **Ebenezer**, b. 5 Apr. 1701; m., int. 11 Aug. 1724, Sarah Batten. List 279(2). Ch., b. 1724-1731: Susanna, Mary, Hannah, Ebenezer, Eliza-

beth. **Tabitha**, b. 6 Oct. 1705, m. Aug. 1726 William Murch. **Matthias**, b. 16 Nov. 1708, m. 19 Jan. 1733-4 Mercy Main, d. bef. 1750. **Lydia**, b. 15 Oct. 1711, m. 12 Nov. 1730 Nathan Whitney of Biddeford. **Mercy**, b. 25 Jan. 1714, m. 14 July 1736 Gershom Webber. **Eleanor**, b. 6 Jan. 1717-8, m. 18 Jan. 1739 Joseph Allen.

7 **ROBERT**(9), York, m. (ct. July 1676) Mary Sayward(1) who m. 2d by Oct. 1691 Richard Bray(6). Town gr. 1685. On 21 Aug. 1683 he escaped from a shipwreck when bound from York to Piscataqua, but when going to Kittery 22 Aug. 1690 he was k. by Ind. O. A. 1679-80; cor.j. 1685; selectman 1686; tr.j. 1689. List 96. Ch: **Mary**, m. Abraham Batten(4). **Robert**, had gr. 1712-3, sold 1717; d. s.p. at Arrowsic 2 Jan. 1717-8. **Joseph**, poss. m. 1st (ct. Jan. 1700-1) Mary Hutchins(5), surely m. by 1709 Sarah King (12). In 1717 sold land gr. to Charles Martin in 1667. Ch., rec. 1709-1728: Mary, Robert, Rowland, Joseph (m. Susanna Johnson of Andover), Bethia (m., int. 17 Jan. 1735-6 Henry Ingraham), Susanna, Joanna, Daniel, Abraham (d. 2 Apr. 1729), Nathaniel.

8 **ROBERT**. List 313f might be (7) or error for Rowland(10). List 334b might be Robert(3) or a stranger.

9 **ROWLAND**, York, fisherman, came ±1636, m. Joan Knight(16). Town gr.1653 (Bass cove). Fined for travelling to Kittery on Sunday 1666, and for drunkenness 1678. O. A. 22 Nov. 1652; j. 1650, 1655; gr.j. 1678. He and his w. deeded Knight land to s. Robert in 1680, 10 a. to s. Samuel in 1682 and the Knight homestead to s. Rowland in 1685. Lists 30, 75b, 275, 276. Ch., order unkn: **Rowland**, b. ±1648. **Richard**, Cape Porpus, m. Margery (Batson 3) Kendall, who m. 3d Robert Elliot(5). Ack. debt to Mr. Richard Cutt 1672. Gr.j. 1672. Inv. taken 18 Feb. 1672-3 by John Davis and John Batson shows ho. and 373 a. of land. John Barrett sued the wid. July 1674. **Robert**. **Samuel**. **William**, glazier, bot ho. and land 11 Feb. 1684-5 from Benj. Curtis and had town gr. 1685 as addition to ho.-lot. Bondsman for wid. Mary Wormwood 1690. Gr.j. 1691. Moved to Salem from where, as Wm. sr., glazier, he sold 50 a. in York in 1720 (Y. D. 10: 85). One Wm. Young, glazier, presum. his. s., m. Boston 26 Aug. 1708 Mary Parry, 11 ch. b. 1709-1730. **Job**, b. ±1664. **Mary**, m. Jeremiah Moulton(6). **Lydia**, m. 1st Thomas Haines(16), m. 2d Samuel Bragdon (6).

10 **ROWLAND**(9), York, fisherman, ±72 in 1720, had deed from gr.fa. Knight in 1673. He m. ±1669 Susanna Matthews(14) and liv. at Isles of Shoals until 1683 when he sold out. Susanna wit. ag. Roger Kelly 1684. Back at York 1685. In ct. 1696 for

swearing several sinful oaths, but was soon a deacon. Gr.j. 1693-4, selectman 1695. He d. 25 June 1721, ag. 72. Will, 14 Sept. 1719— 2 Jan. 1721-2, names w. and ch: **Mary**, b. ±1670, m. 1st Dependence Stover(1), m. 2d John Wells(5 jr.). **Joseph**, b. ±1672, his fa.'s exec. **Matthews**, b. ±1674. **Susanna**, ±20 in 1698 when she swore a ch. on Henry Simpson(3 jr.), m. John McIntire(1). **Elizabeth**, m. 1st Samuel Webber(10 jr.), m. 2d George Stover(2), m. 3d Hon. Samuel Came (3). **Jonathan**, m. 7 Jan. 1707-8 Margaret Stackpole. Ch. rec. 1708-1723: Miriam, m. 27 Nov. 1735 Nathaniel Chapman(4 jr.); Elizabeth, m. 5 Nov. 1734 Samuel Adams, later of Harpswell; Jerusha, m. 12 July 1739 Joseph Hatch; Rowland (there were four Rowlands in York in 1735); Abijah, m. 3 Sept. 1747 Mary MacNess of Merriconeag; John. **Benaiah**, m. Ruth Johnson(29). Ch. rec. 1715-1733: Elizabeth; Ruth; Johnson, m. 19 Jan. 1748 Betty Card; Benaiah, m. 13 July 1748 Sarah Adams; Mercy, m. 11 Nov. 1747 James Booker; Mary; Hannah, m. 8 Oct. 1753 Nicholas Booker. **Mercy**, m. Henry Simpson (see 1, 7). **Sarah**, m. Henry Brookings(3 jr.).

11 **SAMUEL**(9). In 1667 his gr.fa. Knight sued in his behalf and his fa. was sued for £42 by John Groth for 'dismembering and curing' his leg. In ct. for Sabbathbreaking at Boone Isl. in 1685. He m. Elizabeth Masterson (Nathl.) who was liv. 1712. Col. Banks states that he was k. in the Candlemas day massacre, 1691-2, and that **Rowland** Young, a boy, still in Canada 1695, was prob. his s., the other Young houses not having been attacked. The wid. prob. moved to Ipswich. Other ch: **Jonathan**, York, m. Abigail Came(3). Ch. rec. 1721-1729: Eliz-

abeth, Masterson, Sarah, Samuel, Abigail, Jonathan (d. 1 Feb. 1729). **Elizabeth**, m. Ips., int. 18 Feb. 1709-10 Joseph Greeley of Kingston (Y. D. 31: 237). **Ichabod**, Gloucester, blacksmith, m. 19 Apr. 1716 Abigail Elwell who m. 2d 29 Dec. 1724 John King; drowned at sea Oct. 1723, ag. 36. Ch. rec. 1717-1722: Samuel, d. 16 June 1717; Abigail, m. Ips. 18 Oct. 1739 Thomas Newman of Kingston; Samuel, d. 18 June 1721; Ichabod.

12 **THOMAS**, Dover, ±16 and servant of Thomas Canney, was assigned to Joseph Canney Dec. 1669. He m. Mary Roberts(12) who d. 1745 'an ancient woman.' Gr. of 30 a. 1693-4. Lists 52, 57, 62, 358d, 359ab. Constable 1700. Depos. 1717, ag. 64, ab. working for James Stackpole in 1680. Will, 18 Mar. 1726-7, left homestead to s. John and named other surv. ch: **Thomas**, in ct. for fighting 1701, d. 27 Dec. 1704 of a fever. **Jonathan**, m. 12 May 1709 Abigail Hanson(7), named in will, 1752—1756, with ch. Jonathan, Thomas, Eleazer, Isaac, James, Nathaniel, Abigail Hayes, Mary, Elizabeth and Mercy, the first eight rec. Dover 1710-1723, the last three bp. there 31 Jan. 1740. List 358d. **Nathaniel**, m. Mercy (Hanson 7) Church(2); ch. Daniel b. 4 May 1713, Mercy b. 24 May 1718. **Samuel**. One Samuel named w. Hannah and 8 ch. in will 1755—1761. **Eleazer**, Dover, m. 28 Dec. 1716 Alice Watson(5); both liv. 1736. **John**, adm. to wid. Elizabeth 29 Apr. 1741; ch. Thomas, Anne, Mary, John, all bp. 28 Mar. 1737; Mary, Hannah, Susanna, all bp. 1 Mar. 1741. **Mary**, m. Stephen Otis(2). **Lydia**, b. 29 Nov. 1694, m. John Cook(6). **Sarah**, prob. the Sarah Hicks to whom John's wid. pd. £3.

**Yousring**, John. List 307b.

**Zachery**, Daniel. See Ilsley.

# ADDITIONS AND CORRECTIONS

## LISTS

List 1. *Alter* Aslley *to* Astley.
*Alter* Gallow *to* Callow.
List 6. *Add* Peter Gresling, master's mate of the -Gift of God-.
List 18, line 9. *Add* [Dennis].
List 38, line 2. *For* Register *read* Recorder. The original document is in Mass. Arch. LXXI: 871-7, and is a copy of field notes, by an expert penman not familiar with the names.
*Alter* Deken? *to* Depen: (Dependence).
*Alter* 10 Jona. *to* Josiah.
''Mr. Penton'' presum. stands for neighborhood name Paignton.
*Alter* Cam *to* Cane [Came].
*For* Jos. Maine *read* Josiah.
*Alter* Walker's *to* Warren's.
*Alter* Hodson *to* Hodsdon.
List 41, page 8, col. 1. *Insert* 1630/1 *before* March 6.
List 52. Exeter. Charles Gredon *means* Gledon (Glidden).
List 54. *For* Haye *read* Page.
List 88. *Insert* commas *after* living *in line* 3 *and* 1676 *in line* 4. *For* misplacements *read* displacements.
List 94, page 17, line 21. *After* Urington *add* Yarington.
List 112. See Court of Asst. iii, pp. 59-63, Chamberlain Coll. E. 10. 10.
List 213. *Insert* 219 *after* vi *and* 83 *after* cxxvi.
List 224, line 8. *For* 1676 *read* 1675.
List 229. See Doc. Hist., ix, 362, 387.
List 235. Line 21, beginning Agnes Auger, should be line 17. Line 30. *Insert* 1659 *after* Oct. *After* line 22 in col. 2, *insert:* Thomas Rogers ±36 2 June 1670. Thomas Cummings ±22 2 June 1670. John Fickett ±25 2 July 1670.
List 244a. *Alter* 1653 *to* 1658.
List 249, col. 2. *Drop* Thomas Doughty *three lines.*
List 252. *For* 86 *read* 88.
List 267a. *For* Nicoles *read* Arcoles [Hercules]. *For* Tickson *read* Pickron.
List 271. The first two witnesses were for Maverick, the last two for Jeffreys.
List 273. *For* prior to 1640 *read* ab. 1642-1654.
List 276. *For* Commissions *read* Commissioners.
List 289. 1703-4. At Andrew Neal's garrison, Berwick, Capt. Brown killed 9 Indians. (Niles' Indian Wars, p. 251.)
List 298, p. 36, col. 3, line 22 from bottom. *For* Ferris *read* Fennix.
List 306c. *For* [Dari] *read* [Drew]. See Court of Asst., i: 117.

List 307b. *After* Richard Escot *add* [Westcott].
List 309. *After* Richard Easton *add* [Yeaton]. See also Doc. Hist. 1: 218.
List 311c. Transfer this list to Dover.
List 313a. *For* read Duggin? *read* means Dan O'Shaw.
List 316. The first two columns on p. 43 are a continuation of the last column on p. 42. Columns three and four are a continuation of column two of list 318a.
List 330f. *For* Almony *read* Almary.
List 339. Grantees of Barrington had paid taxes in Portsmouth 1718-1721.
List 342. *Transfer* Newington Town Book *to* List 343.
List 356L should be transferred to Portsmouth.
List 386. *Omit* About 1663.
List 399a. *For* Service *read* Services. N. H. Prov. Papers xii: 102-109.
List 399b should be added before Arrests for Rioting.

The following corrections, in part conjectural, have been suggested by Charles H. Batchelder, Esq., of Portsmouth:
List 54 (p. 527). *For* John Dame *read* John [Davis?]. *Allow* John Harrall *to stand.*
List 298. Wm. La x x *may be* Wm. Landell.
Lists 326c, 327b. *For* Samuel Cate *or* Case *read* Samuel Keais.
List 329. *For* Philip Founds *read* Philip [Siverit?].
List 332b. *Omit* Question William Keat. *Insert* Aron Moses *after* James Gerrish.
List 338a. *For* Josiah Brackett *read* Joshua Brackett.
List 355a. *For* Jan. 1655-6 *read* Dec. 1655.

## GENEALOGIES

**ABDY.** See 'Genealogy of Robert and Mary Reynolds,' 1931, pp. 41-42. Line 7. Matthew A. m. Deborah Wilson at Cambridge 10 Apr. 1688.
**ADAMS. 2 ABRAHAM.** Line 22. *Omit* Only two Mackworth ch. named in will.
**3 CHARLES.** See Rebecca (Adams) Smith (29).
**13 JONATHAN.** *Add* Widow Rebecca died 22 Dec. 1731, ±76 (Copps Hill).
**ADOVAHA, Cornelias,** had Hampton gr. of 40 a. in 1670; surmised an Indian. *(C. H. Batchelder.)*
**AGNEW.** *Add* Invent. returned 27 Nov. 1686; undated will, proved 16 Sept. 1687, gives to John Taylor (exec.) for his dau. Mary and to Peter Grant for his dau. Elizabeth.

ALCOCK. 1 JOHN. Line 13. ‡*Job.

3 JOSEPH. Line 5. *After* ver) *add* Paul(1).

ALLARD. 1 HUGH. Line 9. *Add* George Jaffrey's acct. against Richard Tucker's estate 1694 has: 'a rug for Hugh Allard.'

2 JAMES. Line 3. *Add* See Wallis(1).

ALLEN. 4 EDWARD. Line 23. *After* wife *add* See s. Edward's will, Strafford Prob. 1: 203. Line 26. *Change* Thomas *to* Joseph. Line 27. *Change* Elizabeth *to* Mary.

13 GOV. SAMUEL. *Add* In 1772 Anna Laughlin of Roxbury, widow, deeded to Samuel Laughlin of R. one-fifth of Gov. Allen's Masonian title. Samuel bought out other heirs also and evidently conducted a successful speculation about 1786. *(C. H. Batchelder.)*

15 WALTER. Line 22. *For* 1624 *read* 1724.

ALLISON. 2 RALPH. See Dixon(1), Oliver(10), Shaw(11), Watts(1).

3 RICHARD. *Add* Mr. Edward Walsh of London agreed 17 July 1661 to bring Richard Allison's wife over if she would come.

ALLY, Giles, witnessed deed Indians to Lawson, Spencer & Lake, 1653 (Y. D. 35: 51).

ALMARY. Line 8. *After* John *add* not baptized with Hannah, Bartholomew and George, 21 Jan. 1693-4.

AMAZEEN. See Messen.

AMBROSE. 3 RICHARD. See Moore(9).

AMERIDETH. See Meridaugh.

AMOS. Line 3. *Alter* 1727 *to* 1725.

ANDREWS. 3 EDWARD. Line 4. *After* patent *add* and in 1667 Mr. Gibbins was to provide for him. See also Y. D. 9: 86.

4 EDWARD. Line 9. *Read* Mary (Heard) (Hanson) Evans.

5 LIEUT. ELISHA. Line 6. *Alter* 2d *to* 3d.

6 JAMES. He was ±69 in 1694. His dau. Rebecca was b. ±1655 by gr.st. record.

7 JAMES. Line 4. *Omit* s. of Jane (Adams).

9 JOHN. Line 18. *Alter* 1653 *to* 1641-3 by depositions.

ANGIER. 2 SAMPSON. Lines 11-12. *Omit* infalic.

ARCHER. 2 RICHARD. Line 3. *Change* Elizabeth *to* Martha.

ASH. 3 THOMAS. Line 5. *Omit* Elizabeth.

ASHFIELD. See Bish in additions. Line 6. *Read* Surely Hannah named with her mother in Wm. Larrabee's will.

ASHLEY. 4 WILLIAM. He d. intestate at Providence in 1694; wife Sarah.

ATKINS. 5 THOMAS. Line 8. *Cancel sentence* One Elizabeth *etc. and read:* She m. 1st Lawrence Davis(29), m. 2d (int. 15 July 1716) Geo. Nicholson of Marblehead.

ATKINSON. 3 JOSEPH. Line 14. *Add* She m. Philip Delano, int. 26 Oct. 1695 at Newbury, where 10 ch. were recorded and also Daniel, s. of Jane Delano, b. at Portsm. 24 June 1694.

5 ‡*THEODORE. Lines 16-18. Wm. Cario engraved the names on the silver platter. *(C. H. Batchelder.)* Line 18. *Omit* List 358b.

ATWELL. 2 BENJAMIN. *Add* One young Atwell, a soldier at (?Wells) 1691, was sent to York to release another.

3 JOHN. Lines 17-18. *For* m. in Wenham, *etc., read* m. in Topsfield 19 June 1693 Margaret Maxe, both of Wenham. Line 20. *Change* Hannah *to* Lydia.

ATWOOD, Will, witn. will of Richard Seward(4) 1663.

AULT. Lines 11-12. Remembrance was ±32 in July 1682.

AUSTIN. See Donnell(5) in additions.

8 THOMAS. Line 12. *Read* m. Sarah Pinkham(1).

AVERILL. 2 JOHN. Line 9. *Change* granddau. of Nathaniel and Sarah *to* dau. of Nathaniel(4).

9 WILLIAM. *Add* Saml. Dalton owed Wm. Avery and in 1686 his heirs deeded to W. A. and w. Mary of Boston land in Hampton (Kingston). *(C. H. Batchelder.)*

AYERS. 4 JOHN. One John Ahires taxed at Strawberry Bank 1688 only.

6 NATHANIEL. He was b. 6 July 1664 (ct. record) and joined Portsm. Ch. from Boston North Ch. *Alter* List 330b *to* 330d. Line 9. *After* Nathaniel *add* bap. at Portsm. 22 Apr. 1694, s. of Nathaniel and Amy.

7 THOMAS. Lines 17-19. Mary (Jackson) Ayers d. by 1753 (N. H. deed, 41: 435); therefore ano. Mary (liv. 1754, ct. file 26370) m. Jacob Lavers, poss. the widow M. A. who accused George Massey in 1745.

8 WILLIAM. See Stevens(9).

9 ZACHARIAH. See Pitman(11).

BABB. 1 PETER. Line 20. *Alter* Sarah *to* Frances.

BAGNALL. One Walter, adult in 1569, was of Chewton, not far from Bristol and Axbridge, the home towns of Gorges and of Thomas Morton, who evidently brought our Walter over in 1624.

BAGWORTH. Widow Jane (Talbot) m. 2d 26 Nov. 1702 Wm. Haberfield of Boston. See John Endicott(2) who m. her sister.

BAKER. 13 WILLIAM. He had ch. John and Sarah, both dead by depo. of John Phillips(10 jr.) in 1749.

BALL. 7 PETER. He had w. Margaret (presum. Jackson 9) in 1685 when they had trouble with John and Richard Jackson. Line 10. *After* Jackson *add*, appar. Benjamin(2).

BALLARD. 2 JOHN. Line 3. *After* Hannah *add* See Moulton(13), Jeremiah and Joseph Jr.

BANFIELD. 2 JOHN. Lines 25-26. *For* Keziah True *read* Keziah (Hubbard) True.

BARBER. 4 JOHN. ±65 in 1736, he worked 50 yrs. ago for Robert Smart, gr.fa. of his wife Anna who was ±60 in 1736.

6 THOMAS. He m. Elizabeth Storer(1).

BARKER. 2 ENOCH. Line 4. *For* 5 ch. *read* 7 ch. bap. at Greenland.

3 ESTHER. She m. Peter Peavey (see 1).

4 NOAH. He and (2) were on Mill Dam tax list 1713.

BARNES. 1 BONAVENTURE. Boney Barnes fined in York County, 1672.

8 JOSHUA. Joshua and w. Esther (Waldron 10) deeded to Richard Waldron 27 Sept. 1698.

BARNWELL (Barnol), Richard, husband of (2), father of (1) and of Elizabeth who m. 1st John Cutts(9). See Mary Partridge(1), Gerrish(7).

BARTLETT. 2 EDWARD. Of full age, he deposed in Sloper v. Seavey, 1709.

BARTON. 1 BENJAMIN. Line 3. Witch Barton is Withbarne in Y. D. 12: 323.

5 WILLIAM. Line 9. *After* w. add Ann (Green 19). Line 26. *After* Biddeford *add* ; m. 2d John Whitney(1).

BASS. 2 PETER. Line 2. *For* Harmon *read* Johnson.

BASTON, sometimes Boston.

BATCHELDER. 4 NATHANIEL, Hampton Falls. Lines 12-14. Josiah. His death is recorded at Hampt. Falls without information that it occurred at Charlestown, N. H. His date of birth, July 1, 1695, is prob. synthetic; appears first in Pierce's Batchelder Gen., no known record. (*C. H. Batchelder.*) Lines 19-20. *Cancel* Elizabeth, b. 1694, m. Richard Sanborn. She was not named in Nathaniel's will, 1736, and appar. was the Elizabeth bap. at Hamp. 28 May 1712, no parent named. She was b. ab. 1697, from age at death. See Deborah Clifford(4) for a possibility of which there is no further evidence. (*C. H. Batchelder.*)

5 REV. STEPHEN. Statement he d. at Hackney in 1660 is a combination of trad. that he liv. to be 100, with actual death in Hackney some yrs. later of Rev. John Batchelder, who is referred to simply as 'Mr.' in a letter in Mass. Hist. Coll., and erroneously assumed to be Rev. Stephen. (*C. H. Batchelder.*)

BATSON. 1 JOHN. Line 11. See Waldron(7).

2 LT. JOHN. Lines 12-13. *After* 2d *add* 4 Oct. 1705 *and omit* bef. 15 Dec. 1705.

BATTEN. 4 JOHN. Line 10. *After* Abraham *add* son and only surviving heir 1732 (Y. D. 15: 7).

5 WILLIAM. Lines 5-7. *After* Joan *read* dau. or step-dau. of Richard Moore(15). Wm. Batten m. in Saco 12. 8 m. 1655.

BAXTER. 2 JOHN. Line 3. Wife Sarah and only ch. killed at Arundel 1726; his will names ano. w. Sarah (who was soon Sarah Hutchins) and ch.

BEALE. 2 ARTHUR. He m. Agnes or Ann Hilton(17).

BEAN. 1 DANIEL. See Fifield in additions. Line 4. Daniel. In 1727 he deeded to s. Joseph of Kingston, naming this son's uncle Joseph Sanborn of Hampton.

4 CAPT. LEWIS. Line 7. *After* 1723 *add* in 58th year.

BEARD. 3 JOSEPH. Line 13. *For* William *read* Andrew.

4 THOMAS. Line 11. *For* one Williams *read* William Williams(35).

BEARNCE, Thomas, taxed Sandy Beach 1688. Barnes?

BECK. 4 THOMAS. Line 38. *For* 30 July *read* 7 Sept. (*C. H. Batchelder.*)

BEDDEN. 1 JOHN. Bradden by orig. record. (*C. H. Batchelder.*)

BEDFORD. 1 NATHAN. Line 19. *Omit* evidently. See Gendall.

BENNETT. See Wilson(7), Y. D. 18: 91, 95.

1 ABRAHAM. Line 12. *After* Ruth *add* m. Richard Mattoon(2 jr.). Line 14. *After* Martha *add* an Exeter tailoress in 1749.

5½ HONOR. See Whitly.

BENNING, Henry, br. of Mary (Benning) Wentworth(8), had w. Elizabeth in Boston 3 Feb. 1687-8.

BERRY. 8 JOHN. Line 7. Jonathan, s. of John and Mary, b. 15 Jan. 1692/3 (*Hampton rec. from Toppan ms., supplied by C. H. Batchelder*).

13 WILLIAM. Line 5. *After* Judah *add* or Judith (Locke 3½). Line 6. *After* 2d *omit* in 1708 *and read* 10 Dec. 1716. Line 11. *For* (Thomas) *read* (see 5).

BICKFORD. 4 BENJAMIN. Line 7. *After* Greenland *add* 26 July 1711.

7 EDWARD. Line 13. *After* Hilliard *add* a semi-colon.

BICKHAM. 3 WILLIAM. Line 5. *Omit* (List 330c).

BINNS. See Bynns.

BISH. 1 JOHN. *Add* John B. and Wm. Ashfield witn. p/a given by John Moulton (9) before Jocelyn 1682. Lydia -Biss- m. Samuel Larrabee(3) and willed to s. John Bish and Wm. Beardon equally. See Morgan(8); Y. D. 11: 36.

BLACK. 3 JOSIAH. See Donnell(5) in additions.

BLACKMAN. 3 PETER. *Add* Thomas, of Boston, only son in 1726, claimed at No. Yarmouth.

BLANCHARD, Richard, Aged ±41 in Dec. 1696, he and Edw. Peavey were out-

going tenants on the Hall farm, Greenland, when Peter Babb took a lease.

**BLY. 1 JOHN.** Lines 17-18. *Omit* presum. same.

**BOADEN. 8 JOHN.** Line 3. See Simpson (5). Line 9. *Omit* m. 21 Feb. 1704-5 Mary Webber.

**BOND. 3 NICHOLAS.** He was killed in Hampton near the Salisbury line. *After* **Thomas** *add* see Mains(8), Perkins(23).

**BONYTHON. 2 JOHN.** He was ±40, 5 Apr. 1694. Lines 11-14. The Patience who wit. in 1696 must have been Patience Crucy (see 10) and 2d w. of John Bonython (2), and Patience who m. Joseph Collins their dau.

**BOOTH. 4 SIMEON.** Lines 14-15. *After* William *add* b. ab. 1664.

**BOSTON.** See Baston.

**BOUGHE, Mr.,** taxed Strawberry Bank 1690 only.

**BOULTER. 1 JOHN.** Line 4. *Cancel rest of sentence after* 1723 *and read* Grace (Lewis 9) Bly, who m. 3d Henry Dresser. Line 13. *For* 20 Jan. 1697/8 *read* 21 Dec. 1707.

**2 NATHANIEL.** Line 9. *For* 4 Mar. 1653-4 *read* 4 (1) 1653 (Norfolk rec.).

**BOUNDS, Richard.** He m. Abigail Prescott (1).

**BOWEY.** Line 2. *For* 1681 *read* 1679. He took O. A at Kittery 6 Apr. 1680.

**BOWLES. 4 JOSEPH.** Lines 7-8. *Omit* Hannah, b. about 1674, m. Joseph Hill.

**BOYNTON. 3 JOSEPH.** *Add* Oyster River wit. 1693 (N. H. Deeds 17: 115).

**BRABROOK, Seaborn** (or Bradbrook), a logger at Wells mills 1679.

**BRACKETT. 1 ANTHONY.** Lines 15-16. *For* 19 Apr. 1667 *read* 28 Dec. 1671.

**2 CAPT. ANTHONY.** Line 19. *After* 1st *add* in Roxbury 11 June 1706. *Add at end* One John B. m. Rebecca Ruggles in Roxb. 10 Apr. 1705.

**6 THOMAS.** Lines 18-20. *Omit sentence beginning* He m. 1st *and read* He m. early Mary Weeks(2) who was liv. in 1748.

**BRACY. 2 WILLIAM(1).**

**BRADBURY. 3 WYMOND.** Line 16. *For* Rowland *read* (Rowland).

**BRADDEN. 1 JAMES.** Lines 22-23. *Omit* Peter, m. 1 Jan. 1729 Elizabeth Muzeet. See Brawn(2).

**2 JOHN.** Line 20. **John.** See Bedden in additions.

**BRADFORD. 1 JOHN.** He was bur. at Portsm. 14 Feb. 1745-6 (St. John's). See Shackford (2) in additions.

**BRAGDON. 2 ARTHUR.** Line 14. *For* Lydia *read* Sarah.

**BRANSELL, Thomas,** wit. will of Richard Seward(4) and proved it before Pendleton.

**BRAWN. 2 GEORGE.** Line 5. *After* 2d *add* 1 Apr. 1700.

**3 JOHN.** Lines 2-3. *For* Wife d. of Wm. Dixon *read* Wife Anne Dixon(3).

**BREWSTER.** See Rowe(2).

**2 JOHN.** Line 18. *For* 1722 *read* 1732.

**BRIAR. 1 ELISHA.** *Add* See Mainwaring (4).

**4 CAPT. JOHN.** He d. at Portsm. 13 May 1785, aged 83.

**6 THOMAS.** Line 4. *After* 1st *read* Abigail Garland, m. at Hampton 29 May 1711; Line 10. *Add* One Judith B. m. John Moo 22 Mar. 1722 (Hampton rec., Toppan ms.).

**BROADWAY.** See Pike(11).

**BROCK. 1 ANDREW.** Lines 3-5. *After* 1711 *read* altho then dead, as his wid. Anna (Gerrish 3) m. James Jeffrey(7) bef. 1706. *Omit sentence beginning* Wid. Anna. Line 7. *Read* 1743, when he wrote from Boston to Col. Timothy Gerrish about Gerrish business matters.

**BROUGHTON. 1 CAPT. GEORGE(4).**

**4 THOMAS.** "In New England" in Visitation of Staffordshire, 1664, p. 58. See Waters's Gleanings, pp. 926, 1091; also Jordan(7).

**BROWN. 2 ANDREW.** Line 23. *After* 339. add One C. B. was a tenant of Wm. Cotton in 1718 (N. H. State Papers 32: 17).

**20 JOHN.** Line 12. *Omit* s. of Francis from Me.

**BRUCE. 1 JAMES.** *Add* Granted liberty, 23. 10. 1658, to set a house upon the Ridge so long as he shall work at his trade (shoemaker) here. (Hampton record, Toppan ms.).

**BRYANT. 2** See Barnwell in additions.

**10 ROBERT.** Taxed as Bryan(n) 1688, 1691, Braines 1690. Line 17. **Hannah,** see Samuel Morgan(7).

**BUGG, John,** worked in the Wells mills, 1679.

**BULLIS, Judith,** Portsm. wit. 1668; see Hart(2).

**BULLY. 1 JOHN.** See Spencer(9).

**BUNKER. 2 JAMES.** Line 3. List 369 belongs to James (Jr.). Line 12. *After* (6) *read* but Prov. Deed 36: 123, dated 22 Mar. 1738-9, refers to Clement and w. Rebecca. *(Mr. Edward C. Moran, Jr.)*

**3 JOHN.** Lines 11-12. *Omit sentence beginning* Adm. to son *and read* Adm. to her 26 June 1751.

**BURDIS, Ann,** same as Burgess(1).

**BURLEIGH.** Line 8. *For* (Haines) *read* (Lewis). Lines 10-11. *For* d. of Edw. and Mary (Lawrence) *read* d. of Nathaniel and —— (Lawrence).

**BURNELL. 2 TOBIAS.** He owed Clark for board, etc., 29 weeks, 3 days, from 1672, and Carter used four days' time going to Salisb. to get him buried.

BURNETT. 1 DEBORAH. She was wife of (4); she d. 17 May 1741, ag. 76 (Granary Bur. Gr.). See Rogers(14), White(14).

3 GEORGE. One George in Monhegan, List 15. See Walter(2).

BURRILL. 3 JOHN. Line 14. For 23 June 1676 read 23 Jan. 1776.

BURRINGTON. 2 THOMAS. In West India trade 1694, aged ±38. Widow Lydia liv. in Dec. 1702.

BURROUGHS. 1 REV. GEORGE. 2d col., lines 6-8. Cancel 3d marriage to Mr. John Brown, who m. Sarah dau. of Mr. Francis Burroughs of Boston; their dau. Sarah, b. 1701, m. Col. Ichabod Plaisted.

BURTON. 6 THOMAS. See Campion.

BUSHNELL. 3 JOHN. Line 1. Omit app.

BUSS. 2 JOHN. Line 11. For Bass read Buss.

BUSSY. 2 JOHN. See Hunking(9) in additions.

3 SIMON. Line 5. Read Edw. Evans(3½). William. Mary, ±12, stolen at Cape Porpus by old Doney and associates and yet detained (22 Nov. 1688), m. Renald McDonald.

4½ WILLIAM. See Stileman(2).

BUTLER. See Mercer(2).

BYNNS. See Binns.

CALL, Philip, was taxed at Portsm. 1690.

CALLEY. See Cawley.

CAME. 3 ‡*CAPT. SAMUEL(2).

CAMPBELL. 2 DAVID. See Kimball(3).

CANTE (Caute?), Philip, taxed Portsm. Dec. 1688. (C. H. Batchelder.) See Call in additions.

CAREY. 1 EDWARD. Here in Nov. 1701. 2½ JAMES (Carry) at Cape Porpus 1674 (Me. P. & Ct. Rec. ii: 287).

CARKEET. 3 WILLIAM. Line 17. After ch. add William.

CARR. 6 SAMUEL. See Kincade.

CARTER. 5 JOHN. Omit lines 7-8. 13 SAMUEL. See Wyman's Charlestown, i: 189.

CARVEATH. See Hooke(7).

CASE. 3 WILLIAM. See Haskins(6) in additions.

CASAWAH, James. Add Also, alias Essex, a negro blacksmith (List 90), liv. in James Pendleton's house 1684. See Cors and N. H. State Papers 31: 64.

CASS. 2 JOHN. Line 23. After 1663; add Ann, widow and admx. 1693; Isaac Morris and James Draper sureties and gdn. of the s. John. Likely the Ann (lines 36-37) who m. Thos. Lyons.

CATE. 1 EDWARD. Line 11. Read Margaret, m. 1st David Gardner(2), m. 2d John Wyatt. Line 14. After Edward add bap. 11 Nov. 1694.

3 JOHN. Line 4. After 1st add 27 Apr. 1692. Line 15. After m. cancel bef. 1745 and read 15 Oct. 1741. Line 23. Place Rosamond after William.

CAVERLY. 3 WILLIAM. Line 8. Moses was of Barrington when he made his will.

CAWLEY. 2 ROBERT. He was same as Robert Colley, later of Malden, whose wid. Elizabeth m. Leonard Drowne(1).

CHADBOURNE. 1 HUMPHREY. Line 27. Lucy, see Landall(1). Line 28. After Alice add b. 1663 (from age at death). Line 30. Catherine was ±62 in Apr. 1727. Line 31. Elizabeth was 71 in July 1738.

CHADWELL. 3 THOMAS. Line 11. For dau. read daus.

CHADWICK. 1 JAMES. Lines 4-5. For at Great Isl. Rachel Haskins (Wm.) read at Portsm. 6 or 7 June 1709 Rachel (Haskins) Philpott. At end add Son William (see 4).

CHANDLER. 2 JOHN. Add One Abigail C. deposed in Oct. 1682 with Thos. Abbott and Henry Fletcher about Lewis(7).

CHESLEY. 2 PHILIP. Line 17. After Esther read m. 9 Aug. 1705 John Hall (23).

CHESWELL. Line 3. Wentworth was not s. of Richard but of Hopestill (line 4). Hopestill was b. as early as 1712; his s. Wentworth was a substantial citizen and d. 8 Mar. 1817, ag. 71 (Cheswell Cem.). See articles in 'Newmarket Advertiser' 5 Oct. 1906 et seq. (C. H. Batchelder.)

CHEVALIER, two Johns. See Knight(9).

CHICK. Line 4. After 1672 add In Essex Co. 1678-9 with w. and three ch. and ord. returned to Newichawannock from Manchester in 1679.

CHILD. 1 HENRY. Add For Samuel of Piscataqua, see Hance.

CHISHOLM. 1 DANIEL. Line 19. For 10 Sept. read 19 Sept. and add m. Thos. Pennell (see 6 in additions).

CHURCH. 1 JOHN. That his two youngest ch. are rec. at Hampton, though b. 'at Cochecho,' may help identify their mo. Sarah.

CHURCHWELL. 4 JOHN. Taxed Strawberry Bk. 1690, '& farme' 1691. Line 12. After Jackson omit d. of John, mariner and read dau. of Daniel(14).

CIRCUIT. See Sercutt.

CLARK. 13 ISAAC. Line 5. For Stone read Stowe. (Mr. Clarence A. Torrey.)

14 JACOB(16).

14½ JAMES, taxed at Newcastle 1688. (C. H. Batchelder.)

15 JOHN. See Moody(1).

20 JOHN. Line 4. Omit 13 Apr. 1695. Line 5. After missing add invent. dated 18 May 1694, adm. 13 Apr. 1695, to wid. Mary.

49 SAMUEL. Line 59. *For* Sarah *read* Ann. Line 78. *For* 5 *read* 6. Line 79. *After* disclosed; *add* Josiah.

56 WILLIAM. Line 11. *For* Roberts *read* (Potts).

CLEAVES. 2 THOMAS. Line 4. *For* Davis *read* Davie.

CLEMENTS. 2 DANIEL (br. of 1?).

4 JOB. Line 7. *After* 1750 *add* ; see Wittum (1).

6 ROBERT. *For* (2) *read* (3).

CLIFFORD. 1 ISAAC. Line 3. *After* Elizabeth *add* (Pulsifer, m. at Newb. 13 Aug. 1693).

4 JOHN. Line 1. *Omit* bap. 10 May 1646. John, s. of George, was bap. in Boston on that date. Lines 13-14. *Omit* but achieved mar. 29 Dec. 1726 with Philip Welch. Line 24. *For* (Jacob) *read* (34).

CLOADE. Line 2. *For* Dill *read* Will.

CLOUDMAN. *Add* Lists 67, 358d. Line 3. *Omit* possibly born Tibbetts.

CLOYES. 1 JOHN. Lines 28-29. *After* m. *read* 1st Edward Hounsell, m. 2d.

2 JOHN. Line 16. Isaac. See Hammond(2) in additions.

5 PETER (1).

COATES. 2 ROBERT. See Y. D. 12: 256.

COBURN, Ebenezer, m. Sarah Storer(2).

COFFEE, Thomas, with consent of Geo. Elliot of Piscataqua, was apprent. in Boston for nine yrs. in 1680.

COFFIN. 1 CAPT. ELIPHALET(6). Lines 7-8. *For* Nathaniel Gilman *read* Nicholas Gilman(8).

4 PETER. Line 2. *After* Tristram *add* (5).

6 TRISTRAM. Line 6. *For* Jonathan *read* Bartholomew.

COLCORD. 1 EDWARD. Line 19. *For* Swampscot *read* Squampscot. Line 48. *For* (5) *read* (6).

2 SAMUEL. Line 18. *After* Sleeper *add* m. 2d Ebenezer Eastman of Kingston.

COLE. 34 WILLIAM. Line 9. *For* 1737-8 *read* 1637-8.

COLLANE, Matthew, Shoals, adm. 11 Mar. 1650-1 to Teage Mohonah (Me. P. & Ct. Rec. i: 159).

COLLEY. See Cawley(2), Drowne(1).

COLLINS. 8 JOHN. See Priest(5).

11 ROBERT. See the Fowler Family (1883), pp. 26-28.

CONOWAY, Robert. See Cole(24).

COOMBS. 3 ANTHONY. Line 12. *After* Rochester *add* Mass.

7 PHILIP, at the Wells mills 1679.

CORBINSON. Line 3. *After* 13. *add* Elizabeth, dau. of Samuel, formerly of Kennebec, apprent. to Nathl. Saltonstall, Esq., of Haverhill, 29 Sept. 1679. *At end add* See Purington(4).

CORS. See Casawah and additions.

CORSON. See Hobbs(3), Grace Hall(8).

CORWIN. Lines 4-5. *Omit words in parenthesis.* See Sheafe(2). R. C.'s case in 1660 was 'with a woman now dead' (Mary Poole).

COSS. 1 CHRISTOPHER. He was br. of Giles Cowes(1).

COTTON. 1 BENJAMIN(6). Line 3. *After* Golden *add* (or Gilden).

2 JOHN. Lines 2-4. *Omit* who may have m. 2d 13 Dec. 1716 Henry Nicholson of Williamsburg, Va. Line 14. *After* 2d *add* 3 Dec. 1721. Line 24. *For* George Thompson *read* Samuel Thompson(10).

5 THEOPHILUS. Line 6. *After* 2d *add* 10 Aug. 1711.

6 WILLIAM. Line 20. *For* d. bef. 27 Sept. 1706 *read* his will 6 Mar. 1689-90—30 Mar. 1691.

COUCH. 4 ROBERT. See Province Papers (N. H.) 1: 219.

COUSINS. 4 THOMAS. Line 10. 'Gr.j. 1708. Dep. Sher. 1711' belong to another if (4) was killed in 1690.

COWELL. 2 EDWARD. See Harvey(14). Line 17. Amy m. 1st 19 Oct. 1678 Joseph Sherburne (see 5) and soon m. 2d Jethro Furber. Line 19. *For* 2d *read* 3d.

4 JOHN. See (6).

6 SAMUEL. Not Samuel but a John Cowell m. Hannah Miller(9) and his are Lists 330de given under (4) John, who was a lad in 1715 and likely a son of John and Hannah.

COWES. 1 GILES. See Coss(1).

COX. 34 WILLIAM. Line 11. *Add* Son William.

CRAM. 2 JOHN. Line 21. *Add* Benjamin *before* Thomas.

CRANCH. 1 ANDREW. Lines 11-13. *After* Frances *add* by 1715; *For* bef. 1718 when *read* in 1718. See Samuel Jordan(9 jr.).

CRAWFORD. 3 MORDECAI. Line 11. *For* poss. a Maine woman *read* wid. of John Pride of Salem.

CREBER. Line 6. *For* Queries *read* Gleanings.

CRIMP. See Probate Rec. of Essex County. 1: 152.

CROCKER. 3½ JAMES, ±15, had been stolen from Wells by old Doney and band in Nov. 1688. In July 1691, servant of Samuel Hill(19), he was to be enlisted in place of young Atwell transferred.

5 JOHN. Perhaps he m. Sarah Keene. See Keene(2) and additions.

CROMWELL. 2 GILES. Line 24. *For* d. *read* b.

CROSS. 8 JOHN. Line 21. *For* Wm. Jones *read* Samuel Jones(22).

CROWLEY, Dennis, 1693. See Nelson(2).

CROWN. 2 WILLIAM. Line 19. *For* 'member' *read* non-graduate (1661).

CRUCY. 1 BARNABY. Line 4. *After* Margaret *add* (see Yeaton). Line 5. *For* Margaret *read* Patience.

6 JOHN. *Add* Patience Creasey by mark 'P' wit. Ephraim Crockett's receipt to Mr. Hooke 4 Feb. 1678 (Fogg Coll., v. 7). John C. took O. A. at Kittery 6 Apr. 1680.

10 PATIENCE. See Bonython(2) in additions.

CRUNTHER, Anne, 1648. See Moses(2). Possibly Crowder.

CUBBO, William, of Jersey, called servant in Reuben Hull's inventory.

CURRIER. 2 JEFFREY. See Ephraim Jackson(20), Lang(5).

3 RICHARD(2).

CUTLER, or Butler. See Mercer(2).

CUTTS. 9 SAMUEL. Lines 11-15. See Mary Partridge (1).

DAGGETT. 3 WILLIAM. Line 8. *After* 1727 *add* in Sutton.

DALLING. 1 JOHN. See Williams(24).

DALTON. 4 TIMOTHY. Line 28. *Omit* widower.

DAM, DAME. 3 JOHN. Line 6. *For* Sarah Hall *read* —— Hall(7). Line 10. *After* 1670 *add* servant to Capt. Joseph Lynde of Charlestown, d. of small-pox 18 Feb. 1690-1.

DAND, John, Y. D. 1: 9, 62.

DANIELS. 3 JAMES. *Add* His mortg. to Wm. Ardell Feb. 1689-90 was proved by witness 5 Mar. 1697-8.

DAVIS. 4 DAVID. Line 1. *For* John Lang *read* one Lang (see 9).

6 EMANUEL. Line 7. *For* Newton *read* New Town. Line 10. *Add* Both deposed in Boston 22 July 1714.

8 HOPKIN. See Ancestry of Charles Stinson Pillsbury and John Sargent Pillsbury, by Mrs. Mary Lovering Holman, (1938), 2: 835.

14 JAMES. Line 42. *Add* Phebe, b. 19 Apr. 1706, m. Abraham Matthews(6). Eleazer, b. 5 Oct. 1709, not in will.

18 MAJOR §‡*JOHN.

20 JOHN. Lines 3-4. *Omit* in 1680 he was com. Capt. of the Troop. Line 5. *Omit* List 50.

24 JOHN. Lines 1-2. He was appar. not an Ensign, and the juryman 1683 was his father.

29 JOHN. Line 11. *For* Harris *read* Haines (see 2).

38 JOSEPH. Line 2. *For* wid. *read* dau.

40 MOSES. Line 45. *Omit* the period betw. after *and* List.

47 ROBERT. Line 5. *Read* England; in 1658 sold lot to Thos.

58 THOMAS. Line 1. *After* Sec. *add* (N. H.).

69 Lines 15-16. *Add* Zachariah who d. unmarried in Hampt. 27 Dec. 1731 left as only heir his sis. Elizabeth, w. of Saml. Batchelder(3). They were ch. of Zachariah D. of Newbury (d. bef. Jan. 1695-6) and his w. Judith (Brown). See Essex Deeds 61: 243.

DAY. 7 WILLIAM, master of the -Primrose- 1678. See Adams(7).

DEACON, John. *Read* List 1.

DEARBORN. 1 GODFREY. Line 15. *Add at end* Another dau.

2 HENRY. Line 8. *After* 400. *read* He m. 12 July 1694. Line 18. Earliest Dearborn ms. gen. in N. E. Hist. & Gen. Soc. says H. D. m. 3d 11 June 1746 Esther Fogg, wid. of her cous. Daniel Fogg, a s. of (5).

4 JOHN. Line 1. *Transfer* ±26 in Aug. 1667 *to* 3 JOHN.

5 DEA. THOMAS(1).

DECKER. 2 JOHN. Line 12. *Change* Looe (Low?) *to* Love.

DEERING. 4 HENRY. See Benning and Wentworth(8). Line 18. *After* Ann *add* ±43 in May 1672.

DELANO. See Atkinson(3) in additions.

DELVES. Line 2. *After* Winter *add* 22 June 1700.

DEMERITT. Line 13. *Add* William, m. Abigail Pitman(9); see Clark(3). One Deborah Demerry deposed with Eli in 1702.

DENMARK. 1 JAMES. Line 17. *Add* One Abigail D. m. Ephraim Newhall in Lynn 12 Dec. 1716.

DENNEN. See Tenney(2).

DENNETT. See Wincoll(2).

2 ALEXANDER. Line 8. *For* (Mason) *read* (Manson).

DENNIS. 1 DAVIS. Poss. David Davis(4)?

6 LAWRENCE. Line 19. *Change* Mary *to* Sarah *and after* Pitman *add* (4).

DENTT. See Sanborn(4).

DERMER. *Omit* 1 EDWARD. The 1661 wit. was (3).

DIAMOND. 3 JOHN. Last line. *Add* William.

DICER. Line 1. *After* Salem *add* in May 1679 master of lighter -Endeavor- bringing shipment to the Littlefields. Line 13. *For* Joseph James *read* Wm. James(9) at Wells.

DILL. 2 DANIEL. Line 6. *After* 1699 *read* m. 1st Benjamin Hutchins(2), m. 2d Philip Carey.

DOAKS. See Phipps(5).

DOCKHAM. Line 13. *For* Sarah *read* Sarah (Nolar) Story (see Knowles 6).

DODDRIDGE. *Add* The will of one Richard Tucker of Stogumber, co. Somerset, 1646, named John D. a legatee and was wit. by three Doddridges.

DOE. 1 JOHN. Line 1. *Add* ±16 in Nov. 1685.

**3 SAMPSON.** See Stevens(9). Line 12. *For* one *read* Nicholas *and for* Smart *read* Swett(5).

**DOLBEE. 2 NICHOLAS.** See Dow's Hampton, ii: 675.

**DOLLEN. 2 JOHN.** Lines 26-27. *For* **Dau.** etc. *read* **Margaret,** m. 22 Aug. 1687 Richard Wild (Middlesex Co. record) and had a s. Richard.

**DOLLOFF.** Line 7. *For* Miriam Moulton *read* Rachel Moulton (see 16).

**DOLSON, Charles.** See Wotton(2).

**DONNELL. 1 HENRY.** Lines 26-27. *For* Jane Topp, etc., *read* See Topp and Me. P. & Ct. Rec. ii: 94.

**5 THOMAS.** Lines 17-19. *After* were *read* Johnson Harmon, Lt. Austin, Josiah Black, John Harmon, John Cole, Timothy Day, Nicholas Cane, Thos. More, also Benj. Donnell who was killed (Mass. Arch. 71: 429).

**DORE. 2 RICHARD.** Lines 13-15. *Omit* *from* and m. 2d *through* co. Glouc., Eng.

**DOW. 1 DANIEL.** Line 10. *Add* **Daniel.** See Jewett Gen. i: 84.

**DOWLING.** *Add* Taxed 1690.

**DOWNES. 4 RICHARD.** Line 32. See Thompson(8).

**9 (WILLIAM, MR.,** in Folsom, 110. Mr. Edm. must have been misread Mr. Wm.)

**DOWNING. 2 JOHN.** Line 36. *After* Nelson *add* He was 64 in 1758.

**DRAKE. 9.** *Omit entirely.*

**DRAPER. 3 NATHANIEL.** Line 7. *After* wid. *add* Esther. Line 10. *For* one Stevens *read* Wm. Stevens(24). Line 21. *After* 1736; *add* by depositions in 1791 she d. ±37 years since in 94th year.

**DREW. 4 FRANCIS** (also de Rue).

**6 JOHN.** Line 30. *Omit* 17 Jan. 1753.

**9 JOHN.** Line 6. Benj. Hanson, jr., wrote to Lt. Moses Wingate 2 July 1745: 'Your brother John Drew was killed by lightning in the month of May,' yet records show that Lt. Wingate's sis. Abigail m. Andrew Spinney(2).

**DRISCO. 5 JOHN.** Lines 5-9. *After* daus. *substitute* ch. of John and Sarah rec. at Wells: **Sarah,** b. 4 May 1683, m. Sylvanus Nock(3). **John,** b. 28 Dec. 1686. **Mercy,** b. 25 June 1688, m. Timothy Conner. By trad. (Wentworth Gen.) the bro. went away unheard from, and their mo., an Emerson, was English.

**6** *For* JOSEPH *read* JOHN(8?) m. Mary Getchell, etc. Lines 4-5. *After* Brunswick *read* Reasonably he was son of (8) and his w. the Mary Getchell in Exeter ct. 1710. See Salisb. records for 6 ch. 1710-1722, incl. **Joseph,** m. Elizabeth, etc.

**DROWNE. 1 LEONARD.** See Cawley(2) and additions.

**DUGGIN. 1 DANIEL.** *Add* Taxed 1688-1691. See Jones(21).

**DULEY.** Last line. *For* bigamy *read* incest.

**DUMMER. 2 SHUBAEL**(1).

**DURGIN. 2 WILLIAM.** Line 14. *After* verif. *add* but the Toppan ms. gives mar. of F. D. and S. M. that date.

**DURHAM. 1 HUMPHREY.** Line 9. *After* Sarah, *add* apprent. to Robt. Snell of Boston in Dec. 1679. Line 12. *After* apprent. by Boston selectm. to John Comball, Apr. 1679.

**DURRELL. 2 PHILIP.** Last line. *Omit* Dau. m. Joshua Purington. See Purington(2).

**DYER. 6 JOHN.** Line 12. *Omit* Holbrook, dau. of Samuel. See American Genealogist, 15: 50.

**7½ THOMAS** (Dier). See Moore(8).

**EARTHY.** *Add* In Salem ct. 1711, Mary and Anna E. succ. sued Philip English for poss. of land.

**EASTWICK.** Line 14. *After* **Catherine,** *add* see Randall(4).

**EBURNE 1.** Line 2. *Omit* b. ab. 1669. Her age, by depos., 67 in Dec. 1736, was understated. See Holland(7).

**EDES.** *Add* He m. at Marbleh. 21 Dec. 1691 Ann Homan (see 2, who was at his Cape Porpus house 1702).

**EDGERLY. 1 THOMAS.** Lines 1-2. *Omit* an apprent. under Capt. Isaac Johnson of Roxbury.

**EDMUNDS. 2 JOHN.** Line 2. 'Mary (his wife?)' killed by Inds., was appar. dau.-in-law of (2), wife of (5), and mo. of his 6 ch. all bap. 11 Aug. 1695. She was presum. Mary Hinkson(7); see Westbrook(1).

**3 ROBERT.** See Kelly(10).

**4 ROBERT.** See Foxwell(1), Shippen, Williams(12). Just come from Va. in 1674.

**5 THOMAS.** See John(2) in additions.

**EDWARDS. 7 MALACHI.** See Gorges(7).

**11 STEPHEN.** Line 1. *For* Robert *read* Richard.

**ELBERSON.** See Meader(4).

**ELBRIDGE. 1 GILES.** Line 9. *After* Robert *read* m. 2d Mary Hooke(3);

**ELDRIDGE.** See Y. D. 12: 312.

**ELKINS. 4 GERSHOM** m. 15 May 1667 Mary Sleeper(3).

**9 OLIVER.** See Essex Inst. Hist. Coll., Oct. 1938, p. 317.

**ELLINS. 1 ANTHONY.** Line 11. *Read* (contract 17 Oct. 1685, recorded 13 Oct. 1691).

**ELLIOT. 4 RICHARD.** Line 14. *For* 1711 *read* 1716 (by orig. rec.).

**EMERSON. 3 JOHN.** Lines 16-17. *Omit* **Margery,** m. Simeon Fernald.

**EMERY.** See Romsey records, N. E. Register 89: 376.

**EMMONS. 2 JOSEPH.** Line 16. *Add* 'Mary Emmons, old widdow' adm. Hampt. Falls Ch. 13 Apr. 1735.

**ENDICOTT. 2 JOHN.** See Bagworth in additions.

**EPPS. 1 DANIEL.** See Pierce(4).

**ERRINGTON.** *Add* From Cambridge, br. of Ann (Errington) Parker(4).

**ESTOW.** See Moulton(21).

**EVANS. 8 JOHN.** Line 26. *For* Abs. *read* Also.

**10 JOSEPH.** Lines 19-20. *After* 1717, *read* Hayes in will, prob. m. Paul Hayes, s. of John(3 jr.). **Mary**, b. 6 Mar. 1720-1, Twombly in will.

**12 ROBERT.** Line 23. *After* Esq. *add* Joseph, b. 4 June 1682.

**13 ROBERT.** Line 8. *For* Ann *read* Mary.

**16 WILLIAM.** See N. H. Hist. Soc. Col. 1: 255-257.

**FABYAN. 3 *JOHN.** Line 17. *For* one Walker *read* William Walker(5).

**FARNSEY.** See Ferniside.

**FERNISIDE.** See Farnsey.

**FIELD. 4 JOHN.** Lines 9-10. *For* Elizabeth Treworgy (Samuel) *read* Elizabeth (Treworgye 6) Parker.

**FIFIELD.** See American Genealogist, 15: 218.

**1 BENJAMIN.** Lines 11-12. *After* clerk. *read* He m. 1st one Abigail, m. 2d by 1711 Martha Andrews of Ipsw., m. 3d Mary Webster(7). 2 + 2 + 8 ch., incl. Elizabeth, b. 25 Nov. 1698, m. Hezekiah Sleeper(1) and Jonathan Webster. Line 13. *After* Dorothy *add* (Fifield). Line 16. *After* 1676 *read* was prob. Mary, and m. Daniel Bean (1). Last line. *Read* **Abigail**, m. 1715 Humphrey Holt.

**4 WILLIAM.** Line 8. *For* 8 ch. *read* 10 kn. ch. Line 11. *Read* **John**, liv. Newbury, w. Anne. Ch.

**FLETCHER. 4 JOHN.** *Add* He sold 1 a. in Portsm. to John Odiorne 14 Feb. 1675; w. Joyce ack. with him 1 Mar. 1675-6 (N. H. Deeds 3: 111a). Her Lists 331a, 335a. Not in his will. Line 12. *Omit* Wife Joane, not named in will.

**6 JOYCE.** *Omit* entirely.

**FLOOD. ½ JAMES**, with Arthur Hoddy, 5 Sept. 1687, wit. delivery of 8 small iron guns and all yards and topmasts belonging to ship -Johanna- of Portsm. (P. Severet, master) to Mr. Butler, sent by Col. Dongan to receive it. (*C. H. Batchelder.*)

**FOGG. 2 JAMES.** Line 17. *After* 1749 *read* Deborah Moulton;

**6 SETH.** Line 3. *After* 1756. *read* She was Sarah Shaw(2) acc. to Dow's Hampton, but see Reg. 26: 76. Line 13. -David- Fogg; see Dearborn(2) in additions.

**FOLGER, Dorcas** (Foulger) and Henry Moulton, wit. Nathl. Batchelder to Thos. Sleeper 1660.

**FOLSOM. 6 NATHANIEL.** Line 22. *For* Rollins *read* Norris.

**9 SAMUEL.** Line 6. *For* 1664 *read* 1663. Line 7. *After* 1664 *add* (Bell's Exeter).

**FORD. 2½ JAMES** (Forde). See Burgess.

**7 ROBERT**, here 1672 (Me. P. & Ct. Rec. ii: 247).

**FOSS. 1 JOHN.** Line 11. *After* 1700, *add* See Marden(2). Line 28. *Add* See Neale (8).

**FOWLER. 1 LUDWIG.** See Whidden(2).

**FOX. 5 THOMAS.** *Add* Still at Saco 1676, drunk.

**FOYE. 2 JAMES.** Line 29. *Omit* (Wallis).

**FREEMAN. 1 ANTHONY.** See Beverly Records and Hall(20) for 2 wives.

**FREESE. 1 JAMES.** Line 22. *After* 1725 *add* (Malden rec.).

**FRENCH. 8 THOMAS.** Line 2. *For* 1672 *read* 1686 (List 330a).

**(FRENCHMAN), Henry**, List 356j.

**FROST. 6 JOHN.** He m. at Brixham, co. Devon, 2 Dec. 1643, Rose, dau. of Leonard and Elizabeth Cruse. See Hist. of York ii: 71.

**FRYE. 1 ADRIAN.** Line 7. *For* Robert *read* John(9).

**FULLER. 1 GILES.** Line 13. *For* 1676 *read* 1673.

**FURBER. 1 JETHRO.** Lines 2-3. *Omit* sentence He m. 19 Oct. etc. and *read* He m. early Amy (Cowell 2) Sherburne (see 5).

**2 WILLIAM.** Last line. *After* 1688 *add* and July 1690. *Add* See Winslow(7).

**GARDNER. 1 CHRISTOPHER.** Line 9. *For* 1650 *read* 1640.

**7 RICHARD.** *Add* Taxed '& house,' 1714-5.

**GARLAND.** See Briar(6) in additions.

**GERMAN.** See Willey in additions.

**GERRISH. 7 RICHARD.** See Mary Partridge(1).

**GIBBONS. 1 AMBROSE.** Line 24. *For* Rebecca *read* Elizabeth.

**GILES. 6 MARK.** Line 4. *After* Sarah *add* (see Twombley 2).

**9 THOMAS.** Line 9. *For* Capt. *read* 2d Mate.

**GILMAN. 10 JOHN.** Line 27. *After* Hannah *add* (Towle 5)?

**12 JOHN.** Line 33. *For* 1823 *read* 1723.

**GLINES.** Lines 5-6. *Cancel* wife not found and *read* He m. Elizabeth, wid. of John Rand(3 jr.). *Add* **William**, 'jr.' in 1731.

**GODFREY. 5 JOSEPH.** Line 1. *For* Jos. *read* John.

**GOE.** See Gove and Gee.

**GOOCH. 5 JOHN.** Line 7. *After* (5) *add* or oldest dau. of Abraham Preble(1). Last line. *After* (6) *add* named for Nathaniel Preble?

**GOODRIDGE. 3 JEREMIAH.** Line 14. *For* were two *read* was a son. *Omit all reference to* **Philip** (lines 14-17) *and see* American Genealogist, 13: 216; 16: 44.

**5 JOSIAH.** *Add* His will, 1759-1760; ch: Benjamin, John (dec.), **Hannah** Glass, Deborah, Sarah Grant, Mary Spencer, **Elizabeth** Nason, **Christian** Seymour, Abigail Burbank, and gr.s. John Pitts.

**GOODWIN. 2 ABIEL.** Line 3. *After* Hepsibah *read* (Preble 2).

**GOSLING, Capt. Edward,** master of -Black Cock- 1676, Thos. Deverson one of the seamen. See Henderson(4).

**GOSS. 3 ROBERT.** Line 7. *Omit* one and *after* Lydia *add* Sanborn(7).

**GOTT. 2 DANIEL.** *Add* a York witn. 1707.

**GOVE. 1 EBENEZER.** Line 12. See Moulton(11) in additions. Line 13. *For* in *read* 20.

**2 EDWARD.** Line 40. *For* one *read* Lt. Moses.

**GOWELL.** Line 23. *After* **Mary** *read* Wit. the Phipps-Cutts mar. contract 1699. Lines 25-26. *After* **Sarah** *cancel rest of sentence and read* Chase by father's will, m. early Thos. Chase of Yarmouth, Mass., whose br. Capt. Jonathan C. m. Sarah Green (see 15) in Barnstable 1709. See N. E. Reg. 87: 131-2.

**GREELY. 3 THOMAS.** Lines 16-19. The wife and son given to **Thomas** belong to John.

**GREEN. 12 JOHN.** *Add* Also poss. father of (13).

**13 JOHN.** Lines 1-3. *Omit* s. of Richard Tozer's w. Judith and gr.s. of Robt. Blott of Boston. Poss. he was son of (12), altho nothing indicates the w. Julian was his mo.

**15 JOHN.** Line 12. *After* **Sarah,** *add* See Gowell in additions.

**28 WILLIAM.** *Add* Poss. m. Mary, wid. of John Libby(5).

**GREENLAND.** See Mary Pierce(8).

**GREENLEAF. 5 STEPHEN.** See Essex Deeds 33: 212. Line 11. *Cancel sentence beginning* One Stephen *and read* Stephen of York, parentage untraced, m. Mary Macress 7 Oct. 1712 in Newbury where ch. rec. 1713-1720 (first one Enoch), and four more in York. They were of Montsweag 1755 (Essex Deeds 99: 384).

**GRIFFITH. 4 HANNAH.** See Greely(3) in additions.

**GRINDAL.** See Pepperell. Line 4. *After* (1, 2). *add* Dau. **Elizabeth,** bap. at Hampton Falls 28 Aug. 1720.

**GROTH.** Line 16. *Omit all after* 5 ch. rec.

**GROVER.** See History of York (Banks), 2: 55.

**GUNNISON. 2 HUGH.** Line 30. **Sarah,** b. 1637-8, was appar. too old to m. Lewis

Tucker(16) whose w. was more reasonably an unrec. half-sis. **Sarah.**

**GWINN.** Line 10. *After* Mountfort *add* and Hatch(2) in additions.

**HAINES. 1 AQUILA.** Line 2. *For* Matthew *read* Matthews.

**HALEY. 1 ANDREW.** Line 20. *After* **Elizabeth,** *add* (called 99 in 1765; see Hoyt and additions).

**HALL. 3 ISAAC.** Line 2. *After* 1731 *add* **Susanna** and **Nathaniel Parker.** See Parker(16). Was Isaac the adopted child?

**13 JOSEPH.** Line 19. *After* March *add* (4). Line 23. *For* (9) *read* (6).

**23 RALPH.** Line 19. *After* ch. *read* Thos. Hall was named with her in 1710.

**HAM. 5 JOHN.** Line 15. *After* **Thomas** *add* (b. 3 May 1705). Line 18. *After* **Mercy** *add* (see Bond 4). Line 19. *After* **Dorcas** *add* (m. John Richards 1 Dec. 1723).

**HAMMOND. 2 JONATHAN.** Lines 27-29. **Jonathan.** In the Fogg Coll. (Maine Hist. Soc.) is a letter dated Portsm., 24 Apr. 1711, from Penhallow(2) to Col. Noyes, enclosing a letter just received from York with news that Isaac Cloyes of Wells and Jonathan H., jr., who were plowing for his fa., were killed by Ind. yesterday.

**HANCE.** Line 5. *After* Walton *add* on Great Island.

**HANSCOM. 2 THOMAS.** Line 21. **Alice.** See John Metherell.

**HARDING. 1 ANNE.** See Herdin.

**HARDY. 6 GEORGE.** *Add* Dau. **Mary,** b. Newb. 2 Feb. 1692-3 (see 7). The wid. mar. 2d Benjamin Poore.

**9 THEOPHILUS.** *Add* Will, of Exeter, cordwainer, 29 Oct.—19 Nov. 1754; w. Sarah and ch: **Biley, Dudley, Theophilus, Samuel, Mary,** w. of Richard Smith, jr.

**HARFORD. 2 NICHOLAS.** Line 15. *For* 1758 *read* to Mar. 1769 (Master Tate's Diary). Line 19. **Stephen.** See Wentworth (1).

**HARPER, William,** removed from the -Joanna- in 1687, he 'pretending he was aboard to keep poss. for Mr. Severett.' See Flood.

**HARRIS. 16 NATHANIEL,** s. of John and Bridget of Rowley. See Ancestry of Bethia Harris, (W. G. Davis), p. 14.

**19 SAMUEL.** *Add* See Hannah Harris, in will of Richard Martyn(15), 1692-3.

**HARRISON. 2 ABRAHAM.** Lines 3-4. *After* Hannah *add* (Rankin).

**HARRY.** See Morgan(7).

**HART. 10 WILLIAM.** Line 2. *For* Great Isl. *read* Gerrish's Isl.

**HARVEY. 7 MIRTH.** Mirth Harvey=Meservey?

**15 THOMAS.** Line 10. *After* £6625 *add* old tenor.

HASKINS. 6 WILLIAM. Line 40. John. By an unrec. deed, ack. bef. Thos. Giles, J. P., 18 Jan. 1687, John Hoskins, fisherman, and w. Ruth of New Harbor, sold ±1 a. of mead. at Long Cove to Wm. Case; witnesses, Nathl. Welsh, John Starkey.

HATCH. 2 JOHN. Line 26. *After* Elizabeth *add* (presum. Gwin, m. at Boston 11 July 1712). Line 30. *For* poss. *read* prob. Line 31. *After* 1713 *add* as he d. 21 Mar. 1773, ag. 60. Line 32. *After* Mary *read* (Sumner, mar. 8 Aug. 1742) was liv. 1752; he m. 2d by 1754 Alice Knight(10).

HAYES. 3 JOHN. Line 20. An adult Robert Haze '(Egrotus?)' was bp. 26 July 1724 by Rev. Caleb Cushing of Salisb.

HEALY. 2 SAMUEL. Lines 11-12. *Change* 1688-9 *to* 1687-8 *and* 1690-1 *to* 1689 (Toppan ms.).

HEARD. 3 JAMES. Line 16. Abigail. See Wittum(1).

5 JOHN. Line 38. *For* dau. *read* granddau.

HEARL. 5 WILLIAM. Line 14. *For* Landers-Turner *read* (Landers) Turner.

HELME. See The Marbury Ancestry (Colket, 1936), pp. 25-26. Priscilla Wentworth was a 2d wife and prob. not mo. of Christopher.

HENDERSON. 2 JOHN. Line 2. *For* Keel *read* Neel (orig. rec.). *(C. H. Batchelder.)*

HERDIN. See Harding(1).

HEWETT. 7 NICHOLAS. *Omit entirely and see corrections of* List 267a.

HICKS. 4 MICHAEL. Lines 2-3. W. Sarah, dau. of Thos. Walford, a case where compilers disagree. C. T. L. considers the 1699 q.c. proof that Sarah was a Walford dau. S. N. favors Sarah Peverly(2) who could speak of her mo. by her maiden name.

HILL. 9 JOHN. Lines 26-28. *For* ?Lydia *etc. read* Lydia, adm. Greenland Ch. 1728, m. 1st Michael Hicks (see 4) and in 1755 was w. of Daniel Allen of Stratham, with a dau. Elizabeth Hicks.

18 SAMUEL. Line 4. *For* fa.-in-law *read* gr.fa.-in-law (Williams 35).

HILLIARD 1. Line 2. *After* 71 *change* comma *to* period.

HILTON. 20 WILLIAM. Line 23. *Omit* sentence beginning Appar. she was Anne Parsons.

HINKSON. 1 PETER. Line 31. *Add* See Willing(2).

6 SIMON. Line 13. *Omit* (poss. sister).

7 THOMAS. Line 8. Mary. See Edmunds in additions and Westbrook(1).

HOBBS. See Mashon.

HODDY. 2 JOHN. Lines 20-22. See Plaisted(4).

HOLLAND. 7 THOMAS. One T. H. of Piscataqua, sailor, 27 July 1705, ag. 35 (Admiralty Records).

HOLLARD. See Marriner(1), Pastree, Phipps(1).

HOLLEY. See Perry(4).

HOLMAN. 2 DANIEL. See Homan(1).

HOLMES. 6 ROBERT. See Pennell(2).

HOMAN. 1 DANIEL. See Holman(2).

2 DOWNING. See Edes in additions.

HOOKELY. Printed on p. 321.

HOPKINS. 3 EDWARD. E. H., mariner, Portsm., 12 Dec. 1737, ag. 45 (N. Y. Gen. & Biog. Rec., 47: 256).

HOPLEY. See Stevens(9).

HORNABROOK, John, was a tanner, buying skins from Ind.

HORNE. 4 THOMAS. Line 5. *For* Puddling *read* Pudding.

HORNEY. See Stackpole's Durham 2: 215.

HOUNSELL, Edward, wit. a Jocelyn-Oakman deed with Wm. Clay in Aug. 1668.

HOYT. Line 25. *After* 298. *read* 'Mrs. Eliz. Hight, ag. 99, d. in Newington the first of the week beginning 24 Feb. 1765. She was m. four times, had 8 ch. and about 300 gr.ch. and great gr.ch. (N. H. Gazette.)

HUCHES? He was evid. the wit. (Huchins) to Rev. Timothy Dalton's codicil, who (Huching) released all debts to the Dalton est. in 1662.

HUCKINS. 4 ROBERT. Line 5. *For* Geo. Parkinson *read* Wm. Parkinson (Perkins 24).

HUCKTS. *For* 359c *read* 359a.

HUGGINS. 3 JOHN. Line 7. *After* Hannah *read* (Buckley by descendants, Burpee or Burkbee by Jewett's 'Early Settlers of Rowley').

HUGHES. 2 CLEMENT. Line 16. *For* liv. 1734 *read* died 1739.

HULL. 4 ISAAC. Line 1. 1665 (Banks rec.) must be error. 1685?

HUMBER. 1 EDWARD. See Hist. of Weymouth (Chamberlain), 3: 301.

HUNKING. 3 JOHN. Line 14. *For* 2d *read* last. Mr. C. H. Batchelder questions if she did not have a Foye husband bef. marrying Hunking.

9 WILLIAM. Line 15. *Omit* presum. *Add* Capt. Mark d. 11 Sept. 1782 in 83d yr.; only 3 daus. survived (newspaper rec.). Line 23. *For* Henry *read* Edward.

HUNNEWELL. 3 ISRAEL. Lines 20-22. Mr. Clarence A. Torrey, genealogist and Spofford desc., considers that there is no evid. of a 2d wife and that Mary (Spofford) was only wife and widow.

5 JOHN. Line 24. *Omit* Abial. Abial was b. bef. her mother's mar. to Hunnewell and was prob. illegit. Special provision was made for her (no surname) in will of her gr.fa. Harris, and she was appar. nameless until she m. Abel Tryon. *(Mr. Donald L. Jacobus.)*

9 ROGER. See Moore(15).

HUNTRESS. 2 GEORGE. Line 14. Merrill is Merritt in the orig. record.

HURST. 1 JOHN. One Rachel Hirst and dau. from Saybrook were warned at Boston 1717.

HUSSEY. 1 CHRISTOPHER. See Chase's Hist. of Haverhill, pp. 38, 60, 72. Line 36. *Read* Huldah *for* Hannah.

HUTCHINS. See Huches in additions.

1 DAVID. See Pettigrew.

HUTCHINSON. 3 ELIAKIM. See Phipps (7).

11 SUSANNA. Line 10. *Omit* Thomas and. Line 11. *Omit* (b. 1631 and 1635).

IRELAND. 2 PHILIP. See Randall(17).

IRISH. 2 WILLIAM. *Add* Appraised Peter Adams's est. 1672.

ISLINGTON. 1 BENJAMIN. He wit. a Pickering fam. deed in 1692.

JACKSON. 5 DR. GEORGE was bp. at Kit. 1718, 'not knowing whether he has been.'

9 JOHN. Lines 23-24. *After* daus: *read* Salome. Line 25. *After* farm); *read* Margaret.

14 JOHN, aged 59 or 60 in Jan. 1698-9. Line 26. *For* Beek *read* Beck(4), who d. 15 May 1776, ag. 82.

18 SAMUEL. Lines 13-14. *Omit* 2d mar. to Lavers(2). See Ayers(7) in additions.

JACOB. 6½ LYDIA. See Moody(3), Tucker(11).

JANDERS? Jandes? See Sanders(1).

JANVRIN. 1 JOHN. See Hurd's Hist. of Rockingham and Strafford Counties, p. 346.

JEFFREY. 1 BARNABY. Line 3. *For* may or may not have *read* evidently.

7 JAMES. He was agent unto Mr. Sampson Sheafe of Boston in N. H. for several years bef. 1683. Line 4. *For* 1719 *read* 1706. Line 6. *Omit* (?) *before* Cyprien. Line 7. *Omit* if a son. Line 20. *Add* See his Journal for 1724 in Essex Inst. Coll. 36: 331, and statement that his fa. James was b. 10 Mar. 1676 in par. of St. Agnes, co. Cornwall.

JENKINS. 11 ROWLAND. One Rowland was at Salem in Mar. 1693, ±20.

JENNER. 2 THOMAS. See N. Y. Gen. and Biog. Record 47: 114, for his will and ano. dau. Rebecca Bean.

JENNERY. Was this man Lambert Genere, Dedham, 1636?

JENNESS. 1 FRANCIS. Line 13. *For* John White *read* Nathan White(18). Line 23. *For* Hannah Mason *read* Mary Mason (see 7).

JOHNSON. 7 EDMUND. See Woodin(1).

11 FRANCIS. Line 28. *For* Madbury *read* Hanbury.

14 JAMES. Line 5. *For* ord. at Dover *read* ordinary by Dover ct.

15 JAMES. See Y. D. 15: 116.

21 JOSEPH. Line 4. *Omit* John Bly called him 'the negro.'

24 PETER. Line 6. *Omit* (John). See Moulton(16).

JONES. 8 DANIEL. See (55) below.

39 STEPHEN. Line 15. *Read* Stephen.

55 WILLIAM. See Perry(4). The deeds from Wm. Perry to Jeremiah Jones in 1753, and Daniel Jones(8) to Hugh Reed in 1710, were recorded together.

60 WILLIAM. Line 3. *For* Mason *read* Nason.

JORDAN. 1 DOMINICUS. Lines 57-59. *Omit all after* He m. *and read* 1st Dorothy Hill (Ebenezer); m. 2d, int. 13 Aug. 1753, Mary (Sawyer) Randall, wid. of Stephen (4), who d. 10 May 1796, ag. 91. 7 ch.

JOSE. 1 CHRISTOPHER. Line 14. *For* (3) *read* (4).

KEENE. 2 NATHANIEL. Line 30. *For* Proctor *read* Crocker.

KELLY. 11 ROGER. Called of Newcastle in 1709.

12 ROGER. Lines 13-17. Births of Holdridge, Mary, Esther and Roger, are rec. at Hampton, but Mary as b. 'att Exeter' and Roger's parents were 'of Exeter.'

KENNICUM. *Add* Living 1741.

KENNISTON. 5 JOHN. Line 21. *After* James *add* ±26 in Dec. 1696.

KING. 11 RICHARD. Line 2. *For* Champering *read* Clampering.

15 WILLIAM. Line 2. *For* W. H. *read* W. K.

KIRKE. 2 HENRY. Line 27. *After* 335a. *read* Admn. in N. H. to s.-in-law John Libby 30 Aug. 1728.

KNIGHT. 10 JOHN. Line 6. *After* 1766. *add* Wid. Elizabeth d. 13 May 1770, ag. 81.

14 RICHARD. See Paul(2).

19 SAMUEL. Line 1. *For* 1699 *read* 1689. Line 15. *For* Thomas *read* Samuel. (Mrs. Mary Lovering Holman.)

KNOWLTON. 2½ EZEKIEL (Nolton), List 267b.

LADD. 1 DANIEL. Line 25. *For* 1715 *read* 1815.

LAKE. 1½ JAMES, Y. D. 1: 8-9.

LAMB. 4 ROBERT. In 1690 Richard Chamberlain, R. L., Wm. Partridge and John Rawling, gent., were attorneys for John Tufton Mason.

LAMPREY. 1 BENJAMIN. Lines 21-23. Hannah. The Toppan ms. agrees with Dow as to her husband, and Dow did not use the Toppan data.

3 HENRY. He is first seen in Hampt. 20 Dec. 1660 when town ord. him notified that he would not be received as an inhabitant. The Toppan ms. has the early trad. given by Dow, and more.

LANDALL 1. See Nathaniel Pike(5).

LANE. 3 JAMES. Line 28. *For* W. Rachel *read* Wife Abigail Stevens (see 19).

LANGDON. 2 TOBIAS. Line 31. *After* Gen. *add* She was Elizabeth Butler in 1754 (her uncle Capt. Joseph's deed). Line 62. *For* W. Sarah *read* Wife Kezia True. Line 64. *After* Mary *add* (Hall). Line 65. *Omit sentence beginning* He had m.

LANGLEY. See Kent(3).

LARRABEE. 3 SAMUEL. See Bish in additions.

LARY. 2 JEREMY and 4 JOHN. By the orig. record 'Jer.' Larye of County Cork m. Hannah (Leighton) Tout.

LASH. 1 NICHOLAS. Line 8. *Omit* (presum.) *and see* Copps Hill bur. records. This Robt. wit. the will of Wm. (line 21).

LAVERS. 2 JACOB. Line 16. See Ayers (7) in additions.

LEACH. 2 JAMES. Line 21. It is suspected *(by C. H. Batchelder)* that '3d son' is misreading for 'sd son' (N. H. Probate 1: 423). Lines 21-28. See Mansfield(1, 3).

LEADER. 2 RICHARD. He was of Boston 8 Aug. 1650, ag. 41.

3 THOMAS. Line 10. *After* exec. *add* She d. at Hampt. 26 May 1657.

LEAR. 3 TOBIAS. Line 15. *Omit* there being but two ch.

LEIGHTON, Layton. Also Laighton, particularly in Portsm.

4 JOHN. Line 26. See Lary (2, 4) in additions.

8 THOMAS. Line 19. *Read* Deborah; that yr., ag. 61. Line 27. *After* Nathl. *add* Meader.

LEWIS. 8 JOHN. See Redding(1).

9 JOHN. Lines 2-3. *Omit* (Ct. June 1699).

LIBBY. 1 ANTHONY. Line 16. **Abraham.** He m. 14 Jan. 1713 Sabina Philbrick(5). Line 35. **Jacob.** He m. 29 Oct. 1719 Sarah Marston(8).

3 DAVID. Lines 30-33. *Omit rest of sentence,* 'or 6 if Elizabeth was one,' etc.

4 HENRY. Line 36. **James.** He m. 16 Mar. 1738 Abigail Larrabee.

6 JOHN. Line 62. *After* but *omit* see (3) *and read* incl. Elizabeth of Bid. who m. Abraham Townsend 17 Nov. 1743.

LIGHT. 3 JOHN. Line 18. *After* 1677-8; *add* m. Thos. Wilson(4).

LIGHTFOOT. See Whitefoot.

LITTLEFIELD. 11 FRANCIS. See Moulton(13). Line 39. *After* 1655 *read* m. Abraham Tilton(1).

15 JOHN. Line 21. *For* **Elijah** *read* **Eliab.** Line 26. *Add* **Samuel.**

LOUGEE. 1 ELLEN. See Scadlock(2).

LOUELL, Benjamin, Berwick wit. 1696 (Y. D. 5: 2: 71). Lovell?, Lowell?

LOVE. 4 JOHN. *Add* A merchant, going to N. E., 20 Dec. 1689, he was given p/a by Gov. Samuel Allen, London, merchant, to manage all his affairs in N. E.; proved by witnesses in Boston 28 June 1690.

LOVERING. See Sealy(9), Smith(41).

LUCY. 1 BENJAMIN. Line 14. *For* one *read* William.

LYDE. 2 ALLEN. Line 4. *After* Mercer. *add* Elener Loid d. 23 Apr. 1697 (Pt. of Graves).

LYFORD. 3 THOMAS. Line 14. *After* (b. 1738). *add* But see will of Edward Fifield 1765, dau. Dorothy Lyford and her ch. Thomas, Mary, Elizabeth.

LYNN. 1 EPHRAIM. Line 22. *After* 1672. *add* Called mariner, when he gave p/a. dated Portsm., 24 Dec. 1674, to trusty friend John Pickering of Piscataqua, in case pending with Mr. Francis Tucker.

LYON. 2 WILLIAM. See Cass(2) in additions.

MACE. 4 REUBEN. One Reuben Meas of Portsm. and Elizabeth Greenough of Boston pub. int. in Boston 3 Oct. 1726.

MAHON. See Matthews(4).

MALLETT. 1 HOSEA. Line 15. *For* d. *read* w.

MARCH. 4 ISRAEL. Line 15. *After* 1718; *add* and **Stephen,** 'son off Doctor Marches,' was bp. in 1720 (Hampt. Falls).

MARCHARTT. See Aldrich(1).

MARSTON. 2 EPHRAIM. Line 7. *After* (1). *add* He d. 10 Oct. 1742, ae. 90. Revoked will of June 14, 1715, is preserved. *(C. H. Batchelder.)*

3 ISAAC. He liv. in No. Hampt., also his s. Caleb and four later generations. *(C. H. Batchelder.)*

MARTIN. 12 MICHAEL. Lines 21-22. Mr. Libby, a Martyn descendant, thinks Michael, bap. 1724, was son of (18), who was unackn. son of (12) and (5) and ancestor of the mulatto fam. of Portsm.

MASHON. *Add* Poss. the John (Mashon, Mashoone, etc.) drunk in Essex Co. 1679, d. there by Sept. 1680 (inquest), who is called a Meacham and given desc. by Mr. J. W. Greene, called a single man and not a Meacham by Mrs. Mary Lovering Holman (N. Y. Gen. & Biog. Rec., vols. 65 and 69).

MASON. 14 PETER. Line 14. *Before* m. *add* Tibbetts 14.

17 ROBERT TUFTON. Line 10. *After* Robt. *add* Shadrach Walton's depo. in July 1738 sets the time as 'upwards of 40 years ago,' when he was lost on voyage from N. H. to West Indies.

MATTHEWS. 4 DENNIS. See Mahon.

11 PETER. See Sherburne(5).

MAVERICK. 2 SAMUEL. Line 12. *After* Amias *add* (Cole) Thomson(5).

McCORMICK. See O'Cormack.

MELCHER. 2 NATHANIEL. Line 31. *For* -Mons- (or Morss?) *read* Moses (orig. record).

MILLER. 1 ALEXANDER. Lines 31-32. *For* appar. d. s.p. etc. *read* d. 10 June 1697

(Copps Hill), his stone next or near that of Robt. Miller's w. Lydia who d. in 1678, ag. 32.

**MILLS. 3 HENRY.** See Miller(4).

**4 JAMES.** Line 30. *After* Patience *add* 1st m. Daniel Low(1 jr.), 2d James Worcester of Falm. and 3d Dennis Larey of Gorham.

**MITCHELL. 7 JOHN.** Line 17. *After* later. *add* Ag. 59 in Nov. 1750.

**15 THOMAS.** See Urin(2).

**MOFFATT. 1 JOHN.** Line 4. *For* mo. *read* gr.mo.

**MOODY. 3 REV. JOSHUA** (Moodey).

**6 MAJ. SAMUEL**(3) (Moodey). Lines 9-10. *Omit* At St. John's Fort, Newfoundland, bef. 1725 and. The man at St. John's was an Englishman.

**MOORE. 15 RICHARD.** *Add* For a Richard, jr., see Warren(3).

**27 WILLIAM.** See Wise(1) for 2d wife and ch.

**MORGAN. 4 JOSEPH.** See Wallis(3).

**MORSE. 3 DEBORAH.** See Wincoll(2), indicating that **Deborah** Morse(3 jr.) was dau. of (9) instead? See Sanders(13), Wall (3).

**MOSES. 1 AARON.** Line 15. He d. July 1713 by probate rec. As to the div. of the est., Mr. C. H. Batchelder makes this comment: If, as is prob., **Aaron** was the oldest son when his fa. d., he and not **James** had the double share, and on his death it passed equally to his bros. and sisters. A div. into 7 shares in 1734 therefore requires 7 surv. ch., one more than shown. The change from 8 sh. to 7 is more likely to be a correction of a misapprehension about James' having a double share than of a miscount of the ch. or of a death between 1733 and 1734.

**MOULTON. 1 BENJAMIN.** Line 10. *For* or *read* of.

**8 JOHN.** Line 10. *For* 1668 *read* 1666.

**11 JOHN.** *After* d.y. *add* (Dow's Hampton), but see Mary Moulton, w. of Edward Gove(1), b. 1 Mar. 1700 (Jonathan Swain Record).

**13 JOSEPH.** Line 36. *For* 171- *read* 1711 (orig. rec.). Line 53. *For* N. H. *read* Mass.

**MYGOOD.** *Add* Jerseyman and tavern keeper, seen 1718-1720.

**NEALE.** See Henderson(2) in additions.

**7 NATHAN** Neill (Fogg's copy of Hampton records), but misreading of Weare? See Weare(6).

**NICHOLSON. 1 HENRY.** See Cotton(2) in additions. Note also Sarah Cotton, dau. of William(2); Sarah (Cotton) Treadwell d. 16 Mar. 1770, ag. 68.

**NOBLE. 2 CHRISTOPHER.** Line 16. *For* Avlon *read* Arlon. Line 18. **Martha.** See Warren(9).

**NORMAN. 2 WILLIAM.** Line 1. *Omit* Cape Porpus.

**NORTON. 1 BONUS.** Lines 20-21. *For* 1721 *read* 1719 *in each line.*

**NOTT, Edward.** See Burgess(4).

**NOWELL.** Lines 29-31. *After* 1740-1 *read* Patience Hamilton (Gabriel), d. 1 July 1761, and she m. 2d Lt. Joseph Swett(5 jr.).

**NUDD. 1 SAMUEL.** Line 8. **James,** m. 2d Ruth (Waterhouse) Gaines.

**O'CORMACK.** See McCormick.

**ODELL.** *Add* T. O., Stratham, will 1779-1781, w. Mary, 4 ch., 1 gr.son.

**ODIORNE. 2 JOHN.** Line 21. *For* an unidentified husb. *read* Nathaniel Hazeltine. (*C. H. Batchelder.*)

**3 JOHN.** Note Katherine and Joseph Mead (2).

**7 PHILIP.** *Add* Deliverance O. and Robert Clement, jr., m. at Great Island 18 Dec. 1690 (Haverhill rec.). Clement Gen. 1: 86, calls her prob. dau. of (7).

**O'SHAW. 1 DANIEL** was constable of Great Island, 1684.

**PACKARD.** See Pickard.

**PACKER. 2 THOMAS.** Line 23. *For* ±1699 *read* 10 Oct. 1699. Lines 24-25. *For* d. in Sept. 1738 (2 sons) *read* who was bur. 20 Oct. and Rebecca, jr., 3 Nov. 1738 (2 sons surv.);

**PAINE. 5 JAMES.** *Add* In June 1738, ±66, she depos. that she was once nurse for Robert and Katherine Mason's dau.

**PALMER. 5 JOSEPH.** Line 15. *For* liv. 1717 *read* d. 16 Dec. 1717. Line 29. **Mary,** m. J. M. 22 May 1729.

**PARCHER.** See Rand(3) in additions.

**PARKER. 16 JOHN.** Line 24. *After* Spinney *add* See Hall(3) in additions.

**26 THOMAS.** Line 31. *After* Benjamin *add* ag. ±70 when bap. at North Ch., Portsm., 24 June 1750. Line 58. Grace. See Rand (3) in additions.

**PARKIS.** Or Parkhurst.

**PASTREE.** Line 10. *For* owned *read* owed.

**PEASE. 2 SAMUEL.** Line 6. *After* wid. *add* See Smith(27), Creber(2), Hist. of Martha's Vineyard 3: 386-7. Proven ch: **Samuel** whose dau. Ann m. Arthur Bennett (N. H. Deeds 37: 385). **Rebecca,** m. Nathl. Stevens by 1740. (*Mr. N. W. Davis.*)

**PENDEXTER. 1 EDWARD.** Line 2. *After* 1766 *add* ag. ±84.

**PENDLETON. 1 BRIAN.** Line 38. *After* and *add* 20 Sept. foll., with s. James, both of Stonington, sold in Newcastle, ack. bef. Pheasant Eastwick; Line 46. **Caleb.** See Snawsell.

**PENNELL 6.** *Substitute:* **THOMAS,** Gloucester, s. of Philip and Ann (Le Montais) Pinel of Isle of Jersey, m. 1st Sarah Chisemore (Chisholm 1), m. 2d her cous. Sarah Duren (Durrell 1). By 1st w. sons **Thomas**

and **Clement** who m. in Portland 1735, 1742; by 2d w. 3 ch. rec. at Glouc., incl. ano. **Thomas** of Biddeford and **Rachel** Clay of Bid. and Buxton. *(C. T. Libby.)*

**PEPPERELL.** Lines 55-56. *For* succ. his gr.fa. as 2d Baronet *read* was created Baronet.

**PERKINS. 6 GEORGE.** *Add* George P. of the Shoals in Axwell Roberts' ledger 31 July 1728. Elizabeth P. of the Shoals and Thos. Clark jr., int. at Newbury 12 July 1715.

**PERRYMAN.** See Bell's Exeter, p. 354; the first trained lawyer in Ex., b. in England 24 Dec. 1692.

**PETERS.** Read Peter or Peters. See N. Y. Gen. & Biog. Record, 48: 68, 180.

**PHILBRICK. 2 JAMES.** Line 35. *For* 1677 *read* 1697.

**10 WILLIAM.** Lines 11-12. *After* Salisbury). *read* He d. 8 July 1732 (gr.st.).

**PICKERING. 5 JOHN.** Line 11. *After* ch: *add* John, d. s.p. 1715-1720.

**PIERCE,** Peirce, Pearce.

**PIKE. 4 JOANNA.** See Williams(24).

**4¼ JOHN.** *Add* Ch. included (9).

**5 JOHN.** Line 30. *Omit* the period *after* no.

**PLAISTED. 5 ROGER.** See Sargent(3).

**POLLEY. 1 EDWARD.** Line 17. *For* Merrill *read* Merritt.

**PRATT. 4 TIMOTHY.** See Prout.

**PREBLE. 1 ABRAHAM.** Line 21. *After* d. *add* Was she Lydia, w. of John Gooch (5)?

**PRESCOTT. 1 JAMES.** Line 25. Toppan ms. calls her Temperance.

**PROUT.** See Pratt(4), Trowtte.

**PUDDINGTON.** See Purington.

**QUINT.** See Rowe(18) and additions.

**RAGG.** See Thompson's Landmarks in Ancient Dover, p. 214.

**RAND. 3 JOHN.** Line 31. *After* 1728 *add* (Reg. 24: 360), *but should read* Parcher. *(C. H. Batchelder.)*

**RANDALL. 4 JACOB.** Line 20. **Stephen.** See Jordan(1) in additions.

**6 JAMES.** Line 6. *For* (9) *read* (10).

**11 JOSEPH.** Line 4. *Omit all after* appear. (This and the two foll. corrections from *Hon. Louis S. Cox.* See his Cox Families of Holderness, 1939.)

**14 NATHANIEL**(16) *instead of* (11?). Line 5. *Omit* is prob. fraudulent.

**16 RICHARD.** *Add* **Nathaniel.** See N. H. Deeds 17: 223 Richard to s. Nathl., 30 a. gr. from Dover 1694 (deed dated 16 June and ack. 1 July 1729, recorded 2 July 1730). Also N. H. State Papers, 9: 161-167. **Elizabeth,** m. Samuel Willey(5).

**REMICK. 2 JACOB.** Line 20. *Omit* m. 2d 16 Sept. 1722 Mary Wilson. As far as appears, Elizabeth (Ham) was mo. of all the ch.

**RICKER. 1 GEORGE.** *For* (2) *read* (3).

**ROBIE. 2 ICHABOD.** Line 6. *After* will *read* 1753-1757 (d. 15 May 1757 in 93d yr.).

**3 JOHN.** Line 8. *After* Ruth(5) *add* and John Sanborn(11) whose wife's age at death fits the dau. of (3).

**5 SAMUEL.** Line 4. **Ruth.** See just above. Line 11. *For* Jonathan *read* Joshua.

**ROBINSON. 6 JOHN.** Line 7. *After* Watson. *read* In 1768 Hunking Wentworth and Margaret Landell, both over 70, depos. that they well rememb. the building of a ho. in Portsm. in 1711 for Capt. Jno. R. of sd. town, that after he was killed by Ind. his widow lived in said ho. her natural life and after her dec. her son Capt. Daniel R. lived in the same during life, etc.

**20 ——**, Shoals, had ch. bap. at Hampton Falls 20 July 1718: John, William, Peter, James, Samuel, Elizabeth.

**ROMER.** See references in vols. 2-3, N. H. State Papers.

**ROSCOE.** *Add* On 9 Sept. 1674 'Anna Risco of Paspetauk now resid. in Boston' assigned her legacy from Ruth Dalton to Mary Gee of Ipsw., dau. of 'Hezel elponi wood,' Obadiah Wood, atty. to collect it. On 6 June 1679 H. W. gave receipt for legacy to 'my sister Hannah Willix' and Francis and Susanna Jones at Great Island signed an affidavit ab. Anna Risco's maiden name.

**ROWE. 2 ANTHONY.** Lines 25-26. *After* fa. *read* ch: Anthony, Thomas, Joseph, John, James, Lazarus, Noah, Martha Noble, Mary Willey. *(C. H. Batchelder.)*

**18 THOMAS.** Line 12. *After* 1723 *add* and Jno. Quint and w. Ann o.c. and had 6 ch. bap. 26 Sept. 1736 (See Thompson's 'Landmarks in Ancient Dover,' p. 97).

**ROWELLING.** Line 2. *Add* Rollins?

**RUSSELL. 11 WILLIAM.** *Add* **Mary,** dau. of Wm., bap. at Hampt. Falls 7 June 1719.

**RYMES.** Line 10. *After* 1722 *add* Mary Clifton bur. 1 Feb. 1744-5 (St. John's, Portsm.).

**SANBORN. 1 BENJAMIN.** Line 6. *After* Tilton *add* who d. 14 Nov. 1723 (gr.st.). *After* Moulton(11) *add* and d. 10 Sept. 1757.

**SARGENT. 7 STEPHEN.** Line 8. *After* Eng. *add* Of Plymouth, ag. 36, he depos. 26 Nov. 1644 ab. this ship owned by the late Robt. Trelawney and Mr. John Winter (High Court of Admiralty Records).

**SCOTT.** See Waterhouse(2).

**SEVERETT.** See Flood and Harper in additions.

**SEWARD. 9 WILLIAM.** *Add* Ag. 70 in 1758.

**SHACKFORD. 1 JOHN.** Line 24. *Omit* one. Line 28. *Add* One Elizabeth Toome

m. Richard Currier 4 Feb. 1750 (St. John's Ch.).

**2 SAMUEL.** Line 15. **Elizabeth.** *Add* In 1758, ag. 71, she depos. ab. the will of Col. Henry Sherburne, 'her sister Bradford,' 'her son Thomas.'

**SHERBURNE. 3 HENRY.** Line 2. *For* Glebe *read* Globe. Line 22. *Before* Liv. *add* Both. Line 28. *After* 2 *read* m. 2d, 23 Jan. 1724, Mary Stacy of Marblehead, who d. 5 July 1729. Ch: Benjamin, Thomas, Mary, bp. at Marbleh. 1725-1729.

**6 JOHN.** Line 23. *For* liv. 1759 *read* who d. 10 Feb. 1762, ag. 57.

**8 SAMUEL.** Line 28. *After* (fam. rec.) *add* where Ch. rec. give his death 14 July 1769, ag. -86- and wid. Jane's 10 June 1778, ag. -70-.

**SIMPSON. 1 DANIEL.** Line 8. **Henry.** His will, 1760, naming w. Mercy, ch. and gr.ch., and br. Jonathan who was to be supported, ident. him as the husb. of Mercy (Young). The other Henry made his will 1770, naming w. Sarah, ch. and gr.ch.

**7 JOSEPH.** Line 1. *For* (2) *read* (3).

**8 THOMAS.** *Add* The s. William m. 22 Apr. 1736 Sarah Frost of Newcastle, was of Portsm. thereafter and fa. of Capt. Thos. Simpson of the -Ranger- tho Remick gives the latter a York parentage. (*C. H. Batchelder.*)

**SLOPER. 2 JOHN.** Line 10. *After* ch. *add* here, but see Timlow's Sketches of Southington, Conn., where credited with a s. Robert and desc. Lines 10-12. *C. H. Batchelder* calls John (line 10) an earlier son (prob.) and Mary (line 12) a dau. of Ambrose(3). This John is prob. the one who m. Hannah Shattuck in Boston in 1735, dropping from sight bef. a second John was bap.; and Mary m. 2d one Lucey, altho this rejects the Thos. Urann—Mary Sloper mar. (Reg. 64: 16).

**3 RICHARD.** Line 6. *After* speeches *add* At Hampton early (see Locke 3½). Line 61. *After* Sarah *add* (Salter 3). See (2) above.

**SMITH. 29 JOHN.** Line 11. *After* others, *add* drowned 1 Aug. 1692. (Toppan ms.)

**41 NICHOLAS.** Line 23. **Ann.** *Add* See Clark(23).

**STILEMAN. 2 ELIAS.** Line 5. *For* 1677 *read* 1667.

**3 RICHARD.** Line 5. *After* (1) *add* whose mar. to widow of (3) is evid. of no nearer tie.

**SUMMERS. 3 ISAAC** was Sumner, not Summers.

**SWAIN. 7 WILLIAM.** The last 4 ch. were b. as follows: **Mehitable,** 21. 6. 1683; **John,** 11. 11. 1686; **Caleb,** 13. 10. 1690; **Sarah,** 12 Nov. 1691.

**TEDD.** *Add* See Huntington, L. I., Town Records, 1: 110.

**THOMPSON. 8 ISRAEL.** *Add* **Israel,** s. of Israel Tom Beckman, Shoals, bap. 1720 (Hampt. Falls Ch. Rec.); **John,** s. of Israel Beckman Thompson, bp. 1727 (Rye).

**THRASHER.** Lines 9-10. *After* Buffum. *add* On June 13, 1774, **Deborah** Harris, widow, and **Mary** Thrasher, spinster, both of Newport, R. I., both by mark, q.c. to Nathan Winslow their share in the 1773 vote of lands to the heirs of their fa. Henry (Cumb. Deeds 8: 212). See 'Mason and Allied Families,' (1930), p. 63.

**TIBBETTS. 5 HENRY.** Line 31. *For* SJC *read* Ct. Files.

**TILTON. 3 MARY.** Mr. C. H. Batchelder suggests the poss. that she was an illegit. dau. of (4). If so, he ack. her, gave her his name (poss. her mo. d. in child-birth) and took her with him to Martha's Vineyard, yet named a legit. dau. Mary and failed to name the illegit. Mary in his will.

**TOMLIN. 3 RICHARD.** Taxed Newc. 1688-1691.

**TREEWEEK.** *Add* Taxed Strawberry Bk. 1688, 1690.

**TRIGGS.** *Add* **Thomas,** his salary overpaid 1707 (Portsm. town rec.). Lt. Wm. Cotton was suffering Triggs and Davis (Richard) to live on his land 1708. John 'Floocher' was paid for keeping 'Gimer' (Ann) Trigs in 1725.

**TRIPE.** Line 12. **Sylvanus,** b. 9 Oct. 1699 (Ipswich rec.). Line 25. **Thomas.** See Trickey(2).

**TUCKER. 26 WIDOW.** Line 3. *For* (21) *read* (19).

**URIN. 3 JOHN.** Line 25. *For* 1724-5 *read* 1734.

**VEASEY. 2 GEORGE.** Line 9. **Miriam,** m. Jonathan Fifield, br. of Edward (*Mr. Walter Lee Sheppard, jr.*).

**WALTON. 2 GEORGE.** A modern New Castle town rec. (copied from papers in the "trunk") gives births of **George** 24 Dec. 1702, **Shadrach** 1 July 1705, **John** June 1707. John d. s.p. and his br. George was deeding his property 1775-1779. Shadrach was of Barnstead 1779. (*C. H. Batchelder.*)

**WARD. 9 THOMAS.** Lines 14, 15. *After* 1655. *read* Ano. **Hannah,** under 21 in 1678, m. Lt. Joseph Swett(5).

**WATSON. 5 JONATHAN.** Line 11. *For* SJC *read* Ct. Files. Line 19. *Omit* SJC.

**WEEKS. 2 LEONARD.** Lines 52, 61, 63 and

**5 SAMUEL.** Line 12. *For* SJC *read* Ct. Files.

**WHITE. 18 NATHAN.** Line 23. *After* Sarah *add* (Lewis).

**WIBIRD. 1 JOHN** *Add* John (Vibird), s. of John and Elizabeth of the Shoals, bp. 19 June 1720 (Ipswich rec.).

**WILLETT. 6 THOMAS.** *Add* See also N. Y. Gen. & Biog. Record, 60: 7.

**WILLEY. 5 WILLIAM.** Line 15. *Omit* (German 3) *which is unproven.* Lines 16-23. *Add* But see Randall in additions.

**WILLIAMS. 7 FRANCIS.** Line 9. *For* N. H. *read* north-east.

**WILSON. 4 HUMPHREY.** Lines 15, 36. *For* SJC *read* Ct. Files.

**WINKLEY. 2 SAMUEL.** Line 33. *After* 1739 *add* Died 23 Apr. 1776, ag. 87. Lines 46-47. *For* she liv. 1762, he in 1770 *read* he liv. 1770; she d. s.p. 8 Aug. 1781.

**WISE. 1 JEREMIAH.** Line 7. *After* 1756 *add* mentions his wife.

**YEATON. 2 RICHARD.** Richard was eldest son. (*C. H. Batchelder.*)